22nd International Conference on Computational Linguistics

(COLING 2008)

AA005015

Manchester, United Kingdom
18-22 August 2008

Volume 1 of 2

ISBN: 978-1-62993-615-4

Printed from e-media with permission by:

Curran Associates, Inc.
57 Morehouse Lane
Red Hook, NY 12571

Some format issues inherent in the e-media version may also appear in this print version.

Copyright© (2008) by the Association for Computational Linguistics
All rights reserved.

Printed by Curran Associates, Inc. (2014)

For permission requests, please contact the Association for Computational Linguistics at the address below.

Association for Computational Linguistics
209 N. Eighth Street
Stroudsburg, Pennsylvania 18360

Phone: 1-570-476-8006
Fax: 1-570-476-0860

acl@aclweb.org

Additional copies of this publication are available from:

Curran Associates, Inc.
57 Morehouse Lane
Red Hook, NY 12571 USA
Phone: 845-758-0400
Fax: 845-758-2634
Email: curran@proceedings.com
Web: www.proceedings.com

Preface

COLING 2008, the 22nd International Conference on Computational Linguistics, is the first COLING conference in the UK, a country with a rich history and lively research scene in Computational Linguistics. The great response to the call for papers may have been caused by this location or it may just have been a consequence of the rapid growth of our discipline. Anyway, the 600 submissions of high average quality we received made it relatively easy for the programme committee to put together an excellent programme.

After a thorough reviewing process including a period of interactive deliberation, the programme committee selected 145 full papers and 35 poster presentations. The central criterion for the selection was scientific quality rather than geographic balance or the desirable spread across subareas. We tried to apply a multidimensional concept of quality that does not exclusively favour technically sound engineering papers but also yields some space for challenging scientific insights and first reports on novel approaches.

Looking at the distribution of the papers among subfields of CL, we made a few observations. One concerns the central theme of machine learning. Although the term machine learning only appears in the name of one single session, machine learning actually transcends nearly all represented subfields of our discipline.

After decades of hibernation, the area of machine translation has again become a central field of research. Almost all of the MT related submissions are on statistical translation but a growing number of papers describe clever combinations of methods from different paradigms. Compared with MT, the area of natural language generation is much less represented, which may partially be due to this year's International Language Generation Conference in Ohio.

The area of information extraction still keeps growing. With subareas such as opinion mining, sentiment detection and event extraction it has become rather diversified.

A special observation concerns specialized types of phrase disambiguation or classification that cannot easily be subsumed under IR or IE since the described methods could also be utilized for summarization, paraphrasing or other application types. In general it has become harder to assign method papers to just one traditional technology area. This is nicely reflected in the authors' choice of multiple keywords from different areas.

We received only few submissions on speech technologies, in our opinion even less than in earlier COLING conferences. Although this development might simply be attributed to the inevitable and ever progressing differentiation of the human language technologies, it may also be the case that the meeting market in this area is well covered by the well known speech conferences. This year's ACL conference also had just a single speech processing session.

We hope that our colleagues will forgive us for having been rather strict with double submissions. In several cases accepted submissions were finally turned down because a paper with largely overlapping contents has appeared or is scheduled to appear elsewhere. We believe that our field has to find a proper way of dealing with the increasing number of professional conferences without sacrificing the basic principles of scientific publishing.

After deciding to enrich COLING 2008 with a Best Paper Award, we received an offer to support the award from the renowned scientific publishing house Springer. This prize will first be conferred at this Conference. We are grateful to Springer for this generous donation and thank especially Olga Chiarcos for her efforts in this case.

Together with Olga Chiarcos we also thought about other ways to make COLING even more attractive and visible. Olga proposed a special book publication of extended versions of selected ground-breaking COLING papers. This is an excellent idea which we are going to implement already for this COLING conference.

Finally, we want to thank the people who were essential to this academic programme. There are the area chairs who have with great commitment and dedication steered the reviewing process to a successful end: Paul Buitelaar, Robert Dale, Mary Dalrymple, Bill Dolan, Robert Gaizauskas, Eva Hajičová, Julia Hirschberg, Chu-Ren Huang, Pierre Isabelle, Mark Johnson, Miles Osborne, Stephen Pulman, Dan Roth, Jun'ichi Tsujii. We also wish to gratefully acknowledge the successful work of our numerous reviewers who are listed on pages v-viii. Our special gratitude goes to Roger Evans and Christian Spurk. Roger has worked hard and uncompromisingly on these proceedings; he has been a very thoughtful and creative publication chair. Christian has played a central role in organizing the technical basis for the online reviewing and in the communication with authors, area chairs, reviewers and organizers.

We would also like to thank the local organizer Harold Somers for his valuable collaboration.

Less connected with this volume but essential for the overall success of the conference programme were the tutorial chair, Philipp Koehn; the workshops chair, Mark Stevenson, and all the workshop organisers; the demo chairs, Allan Ramsay and Kalina Bontcheva; the people who solicited the urgently needed sponsorships, John Tait and Anne de Roeck; as well as the colleague who recruited the student helpers, Paul Bennett.

But our greatest thanks, of course, go to the authors for their excellent contributions.

Donia Scott and Hans Uszkoreit
Programme Chairs of COLING 2008

Organizers:

Programme: Donia Scott (Open University) and Hans Uszkoreit (Universität des Saarlandes/DFKI)
Local organization: Harold Somers (University of Manchester)
Workshops: Mark Stevenson (University of Sheffield)
Tutorials: Philipp Koehn (University of Edinburgh)
Publications: Roger Evans (University of Brighton)
Demos: Allan Ramsay (University of Manchester) and Kalina Bontcheva (University of Sheffield)
Sponsorship: John Tait (IRF, Vienna) and Anne de Roeck (Open University)
Student helpers: Paul Bennett (University of Manchester)

Programme Chairs:

Donia Scott (Open University, UK)
Hans Uszkoreit (Universität des Saarlandes/DFKI, Germany)

Area Chairs:

Paul Buitelaar (DFKI, Germany)
Robert Dale (Macquarie University, Australia)
Mary Dalrymple (University of Oxford, UK)
Bill Dolan (Microsoft Research, USA)
Robert Gaizauskas (University of Sheffield, UK)
Eva Hajičová (Univerzita Karlova v Praze, Czech Republic)
Julia Hirschberg (Columbia University, USA)
Chu-Ren Huang (Academia Sinica, Taiwan)
Pierre Isabelle (NRC Institute for Information Technology, Canada)
Mark Johnson (Brown University, USA)
Miles Osborne (University of Edinburgh, UK)
Stephen Pulman (University of Oxford, UK)
Dan Roth (University of Illinois at Urbana-Champaign, USA)
Jun'ichi Tsujii (Tokyo Daigaku, Japan and University of Manchester, UK)

Invited speakers:

Dr Elizabeth Shriberg, Senior Research Psycholinguist, Speech Technology & Research Laboratory, SRI International, Menlo Park CA and International Computer Science Institute, Berkeley CA

Prof John Shawe-Taylor, Centre for Computational Statistics and Machine Learning, University College London

Programme Committee:

Eugene Agichtein
Eneko Agirre
Lars Ahrenberg
Akiko Aizawa
Manuel Alcantara
Beatrice Alex
Galen Andrew
Ash Asudeh
Bogdan Babych
Jason Baldridge
Carmen Banea
Srinivas Bangalore
Roy Bar-Haim
Marco Baroni
Regina Barzilay
Roberto Basili
Núria Bel
Linda Bell
Anja Belz
Pushpak Bhattacharyya
Dan Bikel
Alan Black
Patrick Blackburn
Phil Blunsom
Christian Boitet
Kalina Bontcheva
Johan Bos
Chris Brew
Ted Briscoe
Chris Brockett
Paul Buitelaar
Razvan Bunescu
Harry Bunt
Stephan Busemann
Miriam Butt
Bill Byrne
Janet Cahn
Chris Callison-Burch
Nicoletta Calzolari
Nicola Cancedda
Sander Canisius
Rolf Carlson
Marine Carpuat
Xavier Carreras
Justine Cassell
Eric Castelli
Jason Chang
Ming-Wei Chang
Eugene Charniak
Hsin-Hsi Chen
Keh-jiann Chen
Colin Cherry
David Chiang
Philipp Cimiano
Silvie Cinková
Stephen Clark
Kevin Cohen
Trevor Cohn
Nigel Collier
Michael Collins
Cleo Condoravdi
Michael Connor
Robin Cooper
James Curran
Ido Dagan
Robert Dale
Mary Dalrymple
Hal Daumé
Quang Xuan Do
Bill Dolan
Chris Dyer
Marc Dymetman
Markus Egg
Andreas Eisele
Jason Eisner
Mark Ellison
Micha Elsner
Alex Chenyu Fang
Christiane Fellbaum
Charles Fillmore
George Foster
Gil Francopoulo
Alex Fraser
Dayne Freitag
Atsushi Fujita
Adam Funk
Bruno Gaume
Robert Gaizauskas
Michel Galley
Aldo Gangemi
Jianfeng Gao
Zhao-Ming Gao
Claire Gardent
Eric Gaussier
Monte George
Ulrich Germann
Jonathan Ginzburg
Roxana Girju
John Goldsmith
Sharon Goldwater
Julio Gonzalo
Ralph Grishman
Claire Grover
Joakim Gustafson
Nizar Habash
Benjamin Hachey
Udo Hahn
Jan Hajič
Eva Hajičová
Keith Hall
Sanda Harabagiu
Mary Harper
Tingting He
Xiaodong He
William Headden
Mary Hearne
Marti Hearst
James Henderson
Mark Hepple
Andy Hickl
Keikichi Hirose
Julia Hirschberg
Graeme Hirst
Jerry Hobbs
Julia Hockenmaier
Merle Horne
David House
Shu-Kai Hsieh
Chu-Ren Huang

Kentaro Inui
Pierre Isabelle
David Israel
Abe Ittycheriah
Donghong Ji
Su Jian
Jing Jiang
Howard Johnson
Mark Johnson
Michael Johnston
Kristina Jokinen
Gareth Jones
Aravind Joshi
Asanee Kawtrakul
Noriko Kando
Kyoko Kanzaki
Jussi Karlgren
Junichi Kazama
Jin-Dong Kim
Tracy King
Ewan Klein
Alexandre Klementiev
Kevin Knight
Alistair Knott
Philipp Koehn
Hasida Koiti
Alexander Koller
Emiel Krahmer
Ivana Kruijff-Korbayova
Geert-Jan Kruijff
Roland Kuhn
Shankar Kumar
Sadao Kurohashi
Philippe Langlais
Stafan Larsson
Alberto Lavelli
Claudia Leacock
Matt Lease
Gary Geunbae Lee
Kiyong Lee
Lillian Lee
Gregor Leusch
Gina Levow
Hang Li
Sujian Li
Chin-Yew Lin
Ken Litkowski
Diane Litman
Bing Liu
Yang Liu
Adam Lopez
Qin Lu
Kim Teng Lua
Klaus Macherey
Wolfgang Macherey
Kikuo Maekawa
Bernardo Magnini
Inderjeet Mani
Daniel Marcu
Katja Markert
Erwin Marsi
Andrew McCallum
Diana McCarthy
David McClosky
Majorie McShane
Arul Menezes
Paola Merlo
Rada Mihalcea
Yusuke Miyao
Monica Monachini
Simonetta Montemagni
Raymond Mooney
Robert Moore
Paul Morarescu
Alessandro Moschitti
Reinhard Muskens
Tetsuya Nasukawa
Ani Nenkova
Günter Neumann
Hwee Tou Ng
Vincent Ng
Thi Minh Huyen Nguyen
Nicolas Nicolov
Joakim Nivre
Franz Och
Kemal Oflazer
Naoaki Okazaki
Manabu Okumura
Alessandro Oltramari
Miles Osborne
Martha Palmer
Shimei Pan
Bo Pang
Soo-Min Pantel
Cécile Paris
Jeff Pelletier
Gerald Penn
Marco Pennachiotti
Wim Peters
Slav Petrov
Anselmo Peñas
Manfred Pinkal
Massimo Poesio
Thierry Poibeau
Ana-Maria Popescu
Robert Porzel
Richard Power
John Prager
Ian Pratt-Hartman
Judita Preiss
Laurent Prévot
Stephen Pulman
Vasin Punyakanok
James Pustejovsky
Chris Quirk
Owen Rambow
Allan Ramsay
Ari Rappoport
Lev Ratinov
Roi Reichart
Ehud Reiter
Stefan Riezler
Ellen Riloff
Hae-Chang Rim
Brian Roark
Barbara Rosario
Mathias Rossignol
Dan Roth
Rachel Roxas
Vasile Rus
Kenji Sagae
Mark Sammons
Rajeev Sangal
Anoop Sarkar
Len Schubert
Holger Schwenk
Donia Scott
Satoshi Sekine
Stephanie Seneff
Petr Sgall
Libin Shen

Nobuyuki Shimizu
Elizabeth Shriberg
Khalil Sima'an
Michel Simard
Kevin Small
Noah Smith
Pavel Smrz
Stephen Soderland
Claudia Soria
Virach Sornlertlamvanich
Sofia Stamou
Manfred Stede
Mark Steedman
Armando Stellato
Amanda Stent
Mark Stevenson
Pavel Stranak
Tomek Strzalkowski
Le Sun
Hisami Suzuki
Jun Suzuki
Marc Swerts
Idan Szpektor
Simone Teufel
Jörg Tiedemann
Christoph Tillmann
Takenobu Tokunaga
Kentaro Torisawa
Kristina Toutanova
Isabel Trancoso
Shu-Chuan Tseng
Jun'ichi Tsujii
Dan Tufiş
Nicola Ueffing
Hans Uszkoreit
Takehito Utsuro
Kees van Deemter
Josef van Genabith
Antal van den Bosch
Walther von Hahn
Lucy Vanderwende
Sebastian Varges
Tony Veale
Paola Velardi
Ashish Venugopal
Barbora Vidová Hladká
Piek Vossen
Stephen Wan
Xinglong Wang
Taro Watanabe
Andy Way
Bonnie Webber
Davy Weissenbacher
Janyce Wiebe
Yorick Wilks
Kam-Fai Wong
Chung-Hsien Wu
Nianwen Xue
Roman Yangarber
Naoki Yoshinaga
Kun Yu
Annie Zaenen
Fabio Massimo Zanzotto
Jun Zhao
Jing Zheng
Ming Zhou
Michael Zock
Chengqing Zong
Richard Zens

TABLE OF CONTENTS

VOLUME 1

PROCEEDINGS OF THE CONFERENCE

VOLUME 2

POSTERS

DEMONSTRATION PAPERS

Two-Phased Event Relation Acquisition: Coupling the Relation-Oriented and Argument-Oriented Approaches

Shuya Abe **Kentaro Inui** **Yuji Matsumoto**
Graduate School of Information Science,
Nara Institute of Science and Technology
{shuya-a,inui,matsu}@is.naist.jp

Abstract

Addressing the task of acquiring semantic relations between events from a large corpus, we first argue the complementarity between the pattern-based relation-oriented approach and the anchor-based argument-oriented approach. We then propose a two-phased approach, which first uses lexico-syntactic patterns to acquire predicate pairs and then uses two types of anchors to identify shared arguments. The present results of our empirical evaluation on a large-scale Japanese Web corpus have shown that (a) the anchor-based filtering extensively improves the accuracy of predicate pair acquisition, (b) the two types of anchors are almost equally contributive and combining them improves recall without losing accuracy, and (c) the anchor-based method also achieves high accuracy in shared argument identification.

1 Introduction

The growing interest in practical NLP applications such as question answering, information extraction and multi-document summarization places increasing demands on the processing of relations between textual fragments such as entailment and causal relations. Such applications often need to rely on a large amount of lexical semantic knowledge. For example, a causal (and entailment) relation holds between the verb phrases *wash something* and *something is clean*, which reflects the commonsense notion that if someone has washed something, this object is clean as a result of the washing event. A crucial issue is how to obtain and maintain a potentially huge collection of such event relation instances. This paper addresses the issue of how to automatically acquire such instances of relations between events (henceforth, *event relation instances*) from a large-scale text collection.

Motivated by this issue, several research groups have reported their experiments on automatic acquisition of causal, temporal and entailment relations between event expressions (typically verbs or verb phrases) (Lin and Pantel, 2001; Inui et al., 2003; Chklovski and Pantel, 2005; Torisawa, 2006; Pekar, 2006; Zanzotto et al., 2006; Abe et al., 2008, etc.). As we explain below, however, none of these studies fully achieves the goal we pursue in this paper.

An important aspect to consider in event relation acquisition is that each event has arguments. For example, the causal relation between *wash something* and *something is clean* can be represented naturally as:

(1) $wash(\text{obj}:X) \rightarrow_{cause} is\_clean(\text{subj}:X)$,

where X is a logical variable denoting that the filler of the object slot of the *wash* event should be shared (i.e. identical) with the filler of the subject slot of the *is_clean* event.

To be more general, an instance of a given relation R can be represented as:

(2) $pred_1(\text{arg}_1:X) \rightarrow_R pred_2(\text{arg}_2:X)$,

where $pred_i$ is a natural language predicate, typically a verb or adjective, and X is a logical variable denoting which argument of one predicate and which argument of the other are shared. The goal we pursue in this paper is therefore not only (a) to find predicate pairs that are of a given relation

© 2008. Licensed under the *Creative Commons Attribution-Noncommercial-Share Alike 3.0 Unported* license (http://creativecommons.org/licenses/by-nc-sa/3.0/). Some rights reserved.

type, but also (b) to identify the arguments shared between the predicates if any. We call the former subtask *predicate pair acquisition* and the latter *shared argument identification*. As we review in the next section, however, existing state-of-the-art methods for event relation acquisition are designed to achieve only either of these two subtasks but *not both*. In this paper, we propose a two-phased method, which first uses lexico-syntactic patterns to acquire predicate pairs for a given relation type and then uses two kinds of anchors to identify shared arguments.

2 Previous work

Existing methods for event relation acquisition can be classified into two approaches, which we call the *pattern-based approach* and *anchor-based approach* in this paper.

The common idea behind the pattern-based approach is to use a small number of manually selected generic lexico-syntactic co-occurrence patterns (LSPs or simply patterns). Perhaps the simplest way of using LSPs for event relation acquisition can be seen in the method Chklovski and Pantel (2005) employ to develop their knowledge resource called *VerbOcean*. Their method uses a small number of manually selected generic LSPs such as *to* ⟨Verb-X⟩ *and then* ⟨Verb-Y⟩ [1] to obtain six types of semantic relations including *strength* (e.g. *taint* – *poison*) and *happens-before* (e.g. *marry* – *divorce*). The use of such generic patterns, however, tends to be high recall but low precision. Chklovski and Pantel (2005), for example, report that their method obtains about 29,000 verb pairs with 65.5% precision.

This low-precision problem requires an additional component for pruning extracted relations. This issue has been addressed from a variety of angles. For example, some devise heuristic statistical scores and report their impact on precision (Chklovski and Pantel, 2005; Torisawa, 2006; Zanzotto et al., 2006). Another way is to incorporate a classifier trained with supervision. Inui et al. (2003), for example, use a Japanese generic causal connective marker *tame* (because) and a supervised classifier learner to separately obtain four types of causal relations: *cause*, *precondition*, *effect* and *means*. More recently, Abe et al. (2008) propose to extend Pantel and Pennacchiotti (2006)'s Espresso algorithm, which induces specific reliable LSPs in a bootstrapping manner for entity-entity relation extraction, so that the extended algorithm can apply to event relations. Their method learns a large number of relatively specific patterns such as *cannot* ⟨find out (something)⟩ *due to the lack of* ⟨investigation⟩ in a boot-strapping fashion, which produces a remarkable improvement on precision.

The anchor-based approach, on the other hand, has emerged mainly in the context of paraphrase and entailment acquisition. This approach uses information of argument fillers (i.e. anchors) of each event expression as a useful clue for identifying event relations. A popular way of using such argument information relies on the distributional hypothesis (Harris, 1968) and identifies synonymous event expressions by seeking a set of event expressions whose argument fillers have a similar distribution. Such algorithms as DIRT (Lin and Pantel, 2001) and TE/ASE (Szpektor et al., 2004) represent this line of research.

Another way of using argument information is proposed by Pekar (2006), which identifies candidate verb pairs for the entailment relation by imposing criteria: (a) the two verbs must appear in the same local discourse-related context and (b) their arguments need to refer to the same participant, i.e. anchor. For example, if a pair of clauses *Mary bought a house.* and *The house belongs to Mary.* appear in a single local discourse-related context, two pairs of verbs, *buy*(obj:*X*) – *belong*(subj:*X*) and *buy*(subj:*X*) – *belong*(to:*X*) are identified as candidate entailment pairs.

It is by now clear that the above two approaches, which apparently have emerged somewhat independently, could play a complementary role with each other. Pattern-based methods, on the one hand, are designed to be capable of discriminating relatively fine-grained relation types. For example, the patterns used by Chklovski and Pantel (2005) identify six relation types, while Abe et al. (2008) identify two of the four causal relation types defined by Inui et al. (2003). However, these methods are severely limited for the purpose of shared argument identification because lexico-syntactic patterns are not a good indication of argument-shared structure in general. The anchor-based approach, on the other hand, works well for identifying shared arguments simply because it relies on argument information in identifying synonymous or entailment verb pairs. However, it has no direct means to discriminate more fine-grained

[1] A ⟨⟩ included in an LSP denotes, throughout this paper, a variable slot to be filled with an event expression. The filler of ⟨⟩ denotes either the lexical or syntactic constraints on the slot or an example that is to fill the slot.

specific relations such as causality and backward presupposition. To sum up, the pattern-based approach tends to be rather *relation-oriented* while the anchor-based approach tends to be *argument-oriented.*

In spite of this complementarity, however, to our best knowledge, the issue of how to benefit from both approaches has never been paid enough attention. An interesting exception could be found in Torisawa (2006)'s method of combining verb pairs extracted with a highly generic connective pattern ⟨*Verb-X*⟩ *and* ⟨*Verb-Y*⟩ together with the co-occurrence statistics between verbs and their arguments. While the reported results for inference rules with temporal ordering look promising, it is not clear yet, however, whether the method applies to other types of relations because it relies on relation-specific heuristics.

3 Two-phased event relation acquisition

3.1 The basic idea

The complementarity between the pattern-based relation-oriented approach and the anchor-based argument-oriented approach as discussed above naturally leads us to consider combining them. The method we explore in this paper is illustrated in Figure 1. The overall process has two phrases: predicate pair acquisition followed by shared argument identification. Given a relation type for acquisition, we first acquire candidate predicate pairs that are likely to be of the given relation exploiting a state-of-the-art pattern-based method. We then, in the second phase, seek anchors indicative of the shared argument for each acquired predicate pair. We consider two kinds of anchors: instance-based anchors and type-based anchors. If anchors are found, the predicate pair is verified and the associated argument pair is identified as the shared argument; otherwise, the predicate pair is discarded. As we demonstrate in the section for empirical evaluation, this verification process boosts the accuracy as well as identifying shared arguments.

3.2 Predicate pair acquisition

For predicate pair acquisition, we can choose one from a range of state-of-the-art pattern-based methods. Among others, in our experiments, we adopted Abe et al. (2008)'s method because it had an advantage in that it was capable of learning patterns as well as relation instances.

Abe et al. (2008)'s method is based on Pantel and Pennacchiotti (2006)'s *Espresso* algorithm, which is originally designed to acquire relations between entities. Espresso takes as input a small number of seed instances of a given target relation and iteratively learns co-occurrence patterns and relation instances in a bootstrapping manner. Abe et al. have made several extensions to it so that it can be applied to event relations. Since the details of this phase are not the focus of this paper, we refer the reader to (Abe et al., 2008) for further information.

3.3 Shared argument identification

For each of the predicate pairs acquired in the previous phase, in shared argument identification, we use anchors to identify which argument is shared between the predicate pair. To find anchors indicative of shared arguments, we have so far examined two methods. We detail each below.

3.3.1 Instance-based anchors

Inspired by Pekar (2006)'s way of using anchors for verb entailment acquisition, we assume that if two related predicates have a shared argument, they must tend to appear in the same local discourse-related context with the shared argument filled with the same noun phrase (i.e. anchor). As an example, let us consider discourse (2a) in Figure 1. In this local discourse context, the noun *bread* appears twice, and one *bread* fills the subject slot of *burn* while the other fills the object slot of *bake*. In such a case, we assume the two *breads* refer to the same object, namely anchor, and the subject of *burn* and the object of *bake* are shared with each other. We call such anchors *instance-based anchors* for the sake of contrast with *type-based anchors*, which we describe in 3.3.2.

We implement this assumption in the following way. Given a pair of predicates $Pred_1$ and $Pred_2$, we search a corpus for tuples ⟨$Pred_1$-Arg_1; $Pred_2$, Arg_2; *Anc*⟩ satisfying the following conditions:

(a) Anchor word *Anc* is the head of a noun phrase filling argument Arg_1 of $Pred_1$ appearing in a Web page.

(b) *Anc* also fills argument Arg_2 of $Pred_2$ appearing in the same Web page as above.

(c) *Anc* must not be any of those in the stop list.

(d) $\text{pmi}(Pred_i, Arg_i) \geq -1.0$ for $i \in \{1, 2\}$

For our experiments, we manually created the stop list, which contained 219 words including pronouns, numerals and highly generic nouns such as

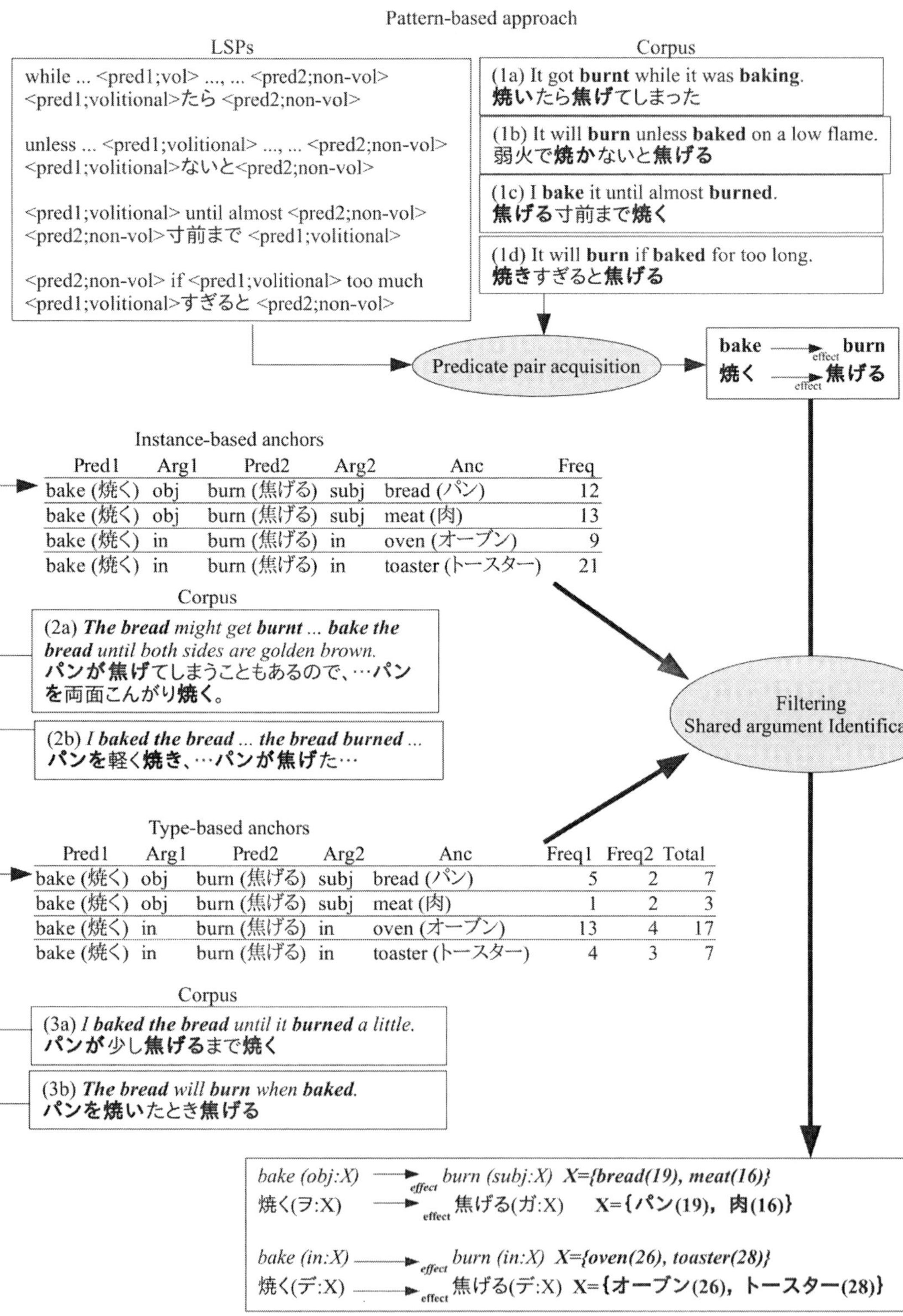

Figure 1: Two-phased event relation acquisition

"こと (thing)", "もの (thing)" and "とき (time)". pmi($Pred_i, Arg_i$) in condition (d) is the point-wise mutual information between $Pred_i$ and Arg_i. This condition is imposed for pruning wrong anchors misidentified due to parsing errors.

While Pekar carefully defines boundaries of local discourse-related context, we simply assume that every pair of predicates sharing an anchor in a Web page is somewhat related — unlike Pekar, we do not impose such constraints as paragraph boundaries. Nevertheless, as we show later in the evaluation section, our assumption works precisely enough because the looseness of our discourse boundary constraint is compensated by the constraints imposed by lexico-syntactic patterns.

We finally calculate an anchor set for each argument pair $Pred_1$-Arg_1 and $Pred_2$-Arg_2 by accumulating the obtained tuples:

$$AnchorSet(Pred_1\text{-}Arg_1, Pred_2\text{-}Arg_2) = \{Arg \mid \langle Pred_1\text{-}Arg_1; Pred_2\text{-}Arg_2; Anc\rangle\}.$$

3.3.2 Type-based anchors

Let us consider sentences (3a) and (3b) in Figure 1. These two sentences both contain predicates *bake* and *burn*. In (3a), the noun *bread* fills the object slot of *bake*, while in (3b) the same noun *bread* fills the subject slot of *burn*. In such a case, we assume the noun *bread* to be an anchor indicating that the object of *bake* and the subject of *burn* are shared with each other. We call such anchors *type-based anchors* because *bread* in (3a) and *bread* in (3b) do not refer to the same object but are identical just as type.

Given a pair of predicates $Pred_1$ and $Pred_2$, we search a corpus for sentences where $Pred_1$ and $Pred_2$ co-occur, and calculate the frequency counts of their argument fillers appearing in those sentences:

- If argument Arg_1 of $Pred_1$ is filled by noun Anc, increment the count of $\langle Pred_1\text{-}Arg_1; Pred_2; Anc\rangle$.
- If argument Arg_2 of $Pred_2$ is filled by noun Anc, increment the count of $\langle Pred_1; Pred_2\text{-}Arg_2; Anc\rangle$.

We then identify the intersection between the filler sets of $Pred_1$-Arg_1 and $Pred_2$-Arg_2 as the anchor set of that argument pair. Namely,

$$AnchSet(Pred_1\text{-}Arg_1, Pred_2\text{-}Arg_2) = S_1 \cap S_2,$$

where

$$S_1 = \{Arg \mid \langle Pred_1\text{-}Arg_1; Pred_2; Anc\rangle\},$$

$$S_2 = \{Arg \mid \langle Pred_1; Pred_2\text{-}Arg_2; Anc\rangle\}.$$

3.3.3 Application of anchor sets

We say an argument pair *covered by anchors* only if any anchor is found for it. Analogously, we say a predicate pair *covered by anchors* only if any argument pair associated with it is covered by anchors. In the phase of shared argument identification, for each given predicate pair, we carry out the following procedure:

1. Discard the predicate pair if it is not covered by anchors.
2. Choose maximally k-most frequent argument pairs associated with the predicate pair ($k = 3$ in our experiments).
3. Choose maximally l-most frequent anchors for each chosen argument pair ($l = 3$).

4 Experiments

4.1 Settings

For an empirical evaluation, we used a sample of approximately 500M sentences taken from the Web corpus collected by Kawahara and Kurohashi (2006). The sentences were dependency-parsed with CaboCha (Kudo and Matsumoto, 2002), and co-occurrence samples of event mentions were extracted. Event mentions with patterns whose frequency was less than 20 were discarded in order to reduce computational costs.

In our experiments, we considered two of Inui et al. (2003)'s four types of causal relations: *action-effect* relations (Effect in Inui et al.'s terminology) and *action-means* relations (Means). An *action-effect* relation holds between events x and y if and only if non-volitional event y is likely to happen as either a direct or indirect effect of volitional action x. For example, the action *X-ga undou-suru* (X exercises) and the event *X-ga ase-o-kaku* (X sweats) are considered to be in this type of relation. We did not require the necessity for an effect. For example, while *nomu* (drink) does not necessarily result in *futsukayoi-ni naru* (have a hangover), the assessors judged this pair correct because one can at least say that the latter *sometimes* happens *as a result of* the former. An *action-means* relation, on the other hand, holds between events x and y if and only if volitional action y is likely to be done as a part/means of volitional action x. For example, if case a event-pair is *X-ga hashiru* (X runs) is considered as a typical action that is often done as a part of the action *X-ga undou-suru* (X exercises).

For our experiments, we manually built a lexicon of over 12,000 verbs with volitionality labels, obtaining 8,968 volitional verbs, 3,597 non-volitional and 547 ambiguous. Volitional verbs include *taberu* (eat) and *kenkyu-suru* (research), while non-volitional verbs include *atatamaru* (get warm), *kowareru* (to break-*vi*) and *kanashimu* (be sad). Volitionality information was used as a feature of predicate slots in pattern-based predicate pair acquisition.

4.2 Results and discussion

4.2.1 Predicate pair acquisition

We ran the extended Espresso algorithm starting with 25 positive and 4 negative seed relation instances for the *action-effect* relation and 174 positive and 131 negative seed relations for the *action-means* relation. As a result, we obtained 9,511 patterns with 22,489 relation instances for *action-effect* and 14,119 co-occurrence patterns with 13,121 relation instances for *action-means* after 40 iterations of pattern and instance ranking/selection. The threshold parameters for selecting patterns and instances were decided in a preliminary trial. Some of the acquired instances are shown in Table 1.

We next randomly sampled 100 predicate pairs from each of four sections (1–500, 501–1500, 1501–3500 and 3500–7500) of the ranks of the acquired pairs for each relation class. Two annotators were asked to judge the correctness of each predicate pair (i.e. 800 pairs in total). They judged a predicate pair to be correct if they could produce an appropriate relation instance from that pair by adding some shared argument. For example, the pair かける (*hang/put/call*) and つながる (*connect*) was judged correct because it could constitute such a relation instance as:

(3) かける (を:X) $\rightarrow_{effect}$ つながる (が:X)
($X \in$ { 電話 })
make(obj:X) $\rightarrow_{effect}$ *go-through*(subj:X)
($X \in$ {*phone-call*})

Unfortunately, the two annotators did not agree with each other very much. out of the 400 samples, they agreed only on 294 for *action-effect* and 297 for *action-means*. However, a closer look at the results revealed that the judgements of the one annotator were considerably but very consistently more tolerant than the other. Assuming that the judgements of the latter correct, the precision and recall of those of the former would be 0.71 and 0.97 for *action-effect*, and 0.75 and 0.99 for *action-means*. These figures indicate that the two annotators agreed quite well with respect to the "goodness" of a sample, while having different criteria for strictness. For our evaluation, we decided to lean to the strict side and considered a sample correct only if it was judged correct by both annotators. The accuracy and recall achieved by the pattern-based model is shown in the column "all" under "LSPs" in Table 2.

Table 2: Accuracy and recall of relation classification

	LSPs		covered by anchors		
	all	top-N	instance	type	combined
action-effect	400	254	175	169	254
	269	185	144	143	206
(accuracy)	(0.67)	(0.72)	(0.82)	(0.84)	(0.81)
(recall)	(1.00)	(0.68)	(0.53)	(0.53)	(0.76)
action-means	400	254	178	176	254
	280	193	143	140	200
(accuracy)	(0.70)	(0.75)	(0.80)	(0.79)	(0.78)
(recall)	(1.00)	(0.68)	(0.51)	(0.50)	(0.71)

We then applied the anchor-based methods described in Section 3.3 to the above 800 sampled predicate pairs. The results are shown in the column "covered by anchors" of Table 2. Since the tendency for both relation classes is more or less the same, let us focus only on the results for *action-effect*.

As shown in the column "all" under "LSPs" in the table, the pattern-based method covered 269 out of the 400 predicate pairs sampled above. The instance-based anchors ("instance") covered 175 out of the 400 predicate pairs sampled above, and 144 of them were correct with respect to relation type. We calculate its accuracy by dividing 144 by 175 and recall by dividing 144 by 269. These figures indicate that the instance-based anchors chose correct predicate pairs at a very high accuracy while sacrificing recall. The recall, however, can be extensively improved without losing accuracy by combining the instance-based and type-based anchors, where we considered a predicate pair *covered* if it was covered by either of the instance-based and type-based anchors. The results are shown in the column "combined" under "covered by anchors" in the same table. While the type-based anchors exhibited the same tendency as the instance-based anchors (namely, high accuracy

Table 1: Examples

	Pred1	Arg1	Pred2	Arg2	Anc
action-effect	begin(開始する)	obj(ヲ)	finish(終了する)	subj(ガ)	installation(インストール), transaction(トランザクション)
action-effect	design(デザインする)	obj(ヲ)	be pretty(かわいい)	subj(ガ)	logotype(ロゴ)
action-effect	sleep(寝る)	in(デ)	be sleep(眠れる)	in(デ)	bed(ベット), futon(布団)
action-means	cure(治療する)	by(デ)	prescribe(処方する)	obj(ヲ)	medicine(薬)
action-means	cure(治療する)	obj(ヲ)	prescribe(処方する)	for(ニ)	patient(患者)
action-means	go home(帰宅する)	by(デ)	drive(運転する)	obj(デ)	car(車), car(自動車)
action-means	use(利用する)	obj(ヲ)	copy(コピーする)	obj(ヲ)	file(ファイル), data(データ)

and low recall), their coverage reasonably differed from each other, which contributed to the improvement of recall.

To summarize so far, the pattern-based method we adopted in the experiment generated a substantial number of predicate pairs with a accuracy comparative to the state of the art. The accuracy was, however, further boosted by applying both instance-based and type-based anchors. This effect is particularly important because, to our best knowledge, very few pattern-based relation acquisition models have been reported to achieve as high a accuracy as what we achieved. In the case of our pattern-based model, for reference, the 254 highly ranked pairs of the 400 samples included only 185 correct pairs, which is worse than the 206 pairs covered by anchors for both accuracy and recall (see the "top-N" column under "LSPs" in Table 2. This difference also leads us to consider incorporating our anchor-based filtering into the bootstrapping cycles of pattern-based predicate pair acquisition.

4.2.2 Shared argument identification

We next investigated the accuracy of shared argument identification. For each of the aforementioned predicate pairs covered by anchors (the 254 pairs for *action-effect* and 254 for *action-means*), we asked the same two annotators as above to judge the correctness of the shared argument information. The results of combination are shown in Table 3.

"arg-strict" shows the results of the strict judgments where the shared argument was considered to be correctly identified only when the most frequent argument pair was judged correct, while "arg-lenient" shows the results of the lenient judgments where the shared argument was considered to be correctly identified when either of the three most frequent argument pairs was judged correct. For judging the correctness of an argument pair, we had three degrees of strictness. In the most strict criterion ("anc-strict"), an argument pair was judged correct only when its maximally three anchor words were all correct, while in "anc-lenient", an argument pair was judged correct when any of the three most frequent anchor words was correct. In "anc-any", an argument pair was judged correct as far as an annotator could think of any appropriate anchor word for it. While the inter-annotator agreement was not very high, with the kappa coefficient in the "arg-strict" and "anc-any" setting 0.47 for *action-effect* and 0.42 for *action-effect*), one was again consistently more tolerant than the other. For the same reason as argued in 4.2.1, we considered an acquired relation correct only if both annotators judged it correct.

In this experiment, predicate pairs that had been judged wrong with respect to relation types were all considered wrong in all the settings. The upper bounds of accuracy, therefore, are given by those in Table 2. For "arg-$*$" with the "combined" anchors, for example, the upper bound of accuracy is 0.81. Since "arg-lenient" with "combined" and "anc-lenient" achieved 0.76 accuracy, our method turned out to be reasonably precise in identifying argument pairs and their fillers. Paying attention to "arg-strict" and "anc-strict", on the other hand, one can see a considerable drop from the lenient case, which needs to be further investigated.

5 Conclusion and future work

Motivated by the complementarity between the pattern-based relation-oriented approach and the anchor-based argument-oriented approach to event relation acquisition, we have explored a two-phased approach, which first uses patterns to acquire predicate pairs and then uses two types of anchors to identify shared arguments, reporting on the present results of our empirical evaluation. The results have shown that (a) the anchor-based filtering extensively improves the accuracy of predicate pair acquisition, (b) the instance-based and type-based anchors are almost equally contributive and combining them improves recall without los-

Table 3: Accuracy of shared argument identification

		action-effect			action-means		
		anc-strict	anc-lenient	anc-any	anc-strict	anc-lenient	anc-any
arg-strict	instance	0.64	0.71	0.71	0.61	0.66	0.66
	type	0.60	0.63	0.65	0.61	0.65	0.67
	combined	0.60	0.65	0.66	0.58	0.62	0.64
arg-lenient	instance	0.78	0.80	0.80	0.73	0.75	0.76
	type	0.68	0.71	0.72	0.67	0.69	0.71
	combined	0.74	0.76	0.77	0.71	0.73	0.74

ing accuracy, and (c) the anchor-based method also achieves high accuracy in shared argument identification.

Our future direction will be two-fold. One is evaluation. Clearly, more comprehensive evaluation needs to be done. For example, the acquired relation instances should be evaluated in some task-oriented manner. The other intriguing issue is how our anchor-based method for shared argument identification can benefit from recent advances in coreference and zero-anaphora resolution (Iida et al., 2006; Komachi et al., 2007, etc.).

References

Abe, Shuya, Kentaro Inui, and Yuji Matsumoto. 2008. Acquiring event relation knowledge by learning cooccurrence patterns and fertilizing cooccurrence samples with verbal nouns. In *Proceedings of the 3rd International Joint Conference on Natural Language Processing*, pages 497–504.

Chklovski, Timothy and Patrick Pantel. 2005. Global path-based refinement of noisy graphs applied to verb semantics. In *Proceedings of Joint Conference on Natural Language Processing*.

Harris, Zelling. 1968. Mathematical structures of language. *Interscience Tracts in Pure and Applied Mathematics*.

Iida, Ryu, Kentaro Inui, and Yuji Matsumoto. 2006. Exploiting syntactic patterns as clues in zero-anaphora resolution. In *Proceedings of the 21st International Conference on Computational Linguistics and the 44th annual meeting of the ACL*, pages 625–632. Association for Computational Linguistics.

Inui, Takashi, Kentaro Inui, and Yuji Matsumoto. 2003. What kinds and amounts of causal knowledge can be acquired from text by using connective markers as clues? In *Proceedings of the 6th International Conference on Discovery Science,*, pages 180–193.

Kawahara, Daisuke and Sadao Kurohashi. 2006. A fully-lexicalized probabilistic model for japanese syntactic and case structure analysis. In *Proceedings of the Human Language Technology Conference of the North American Chapter of the Association for Computational Linguistics*, pages 176–183.

Komachi, Mamoru, Ryu Iida, Kentaro Inui, and Yuji Matsumoto. 2007. Learning based argument structure analysis of event-nouns in japanese. In *Proceedings of the Conference of the Pacific Association for Computational Linguistics*, pages 120–128.

Kudo, Taku and Yuji Matsumoto. 2002. Japanese dependency analysis using cascaded chunking. In *Proceedings of the 6th Conference on Natural Language Learning 2002 (COLING 2002 Post-Conference Workshops)*, pages 63–69.

Lin, Dekang and Patrick Pantel. 2001. Dirt: discovery of inference rules from text. In *Proceedings of the seventh ACM SIGKDD international conference on Knowledge discovery and data mining*, pages 323–328.

Pantel, Patrick and Marco Pennacchiotti. 2006. Espresso: Leveraging generic patterns for automatically harvesting semantic relations. In *Proceedings of the 21st International Conference on Computational Linguistics and 44th Annual Meeting of the ACL*, pages 113–120.

Pekar, Viktor. 2006. Acquisition of verb entailment from text. In *Proceedings of the Human Language Technology Conference of the NAACL, Main Conference*, pages 49–56.

Szpektor, Idan, Hristo Tanev, Ido Dagan, and Bonaventura Coppola. 2004. Scaling web-based acquisition of entailment relations. In Lin, Dekang and Dekai Wu, editors, *Proceedings of EMNLP 2004*, pages 41–48, Barcelona, Spain. Association for Computational Linguistics.

Torisawa, Kentaro. 2006. Acquiring inference rules with temporal constraints by using japanese coordinated sentences and noun-verb co-occurrences. In *Proceedings of Human Language Technology Conference/North American chapter of the Association for Computational Linguistics annual meeting (HLT-NAACL06)*, pages 57–64.

Zanzotto, Fabio Massimo, Marco Pennacchiotti, and Maria Teresa Pazienza. 2006. Discovering asymmetric entailment relations between verbs using selectional preferences. In *Proceedings of the 21st International Conference on Computational Linguistics and 44th Annual Meeting of the Association for Computational Linguistics*, pages 849–856.

A Supervised Algorithm for Verb Disambiguation into VerbNet Classes

Omri Abend[1] **Roi Reichart**[2] **Ari Rappoport**[1]

[1]Institute of Computer Science , [2]ICNC
Hebrew University of Jerusalem
{omria01|roiri|arir}@cs.huji.ac.il

Abstract

VerbNet (VN) is a major large-scale English verb lexicon. Mapping verb instances to their VN classes has been proven useful for several NLP tasks. However, verbs are polysemous with respect to their VN classes. We introduce a novel supervised learning model for mapping verb instances to VN classes, using rich syntactic features and class membership constraints. We evaluate the algorithm in both in-domain and corpus adaptation scenarios. In both cases, we use the manually tagged Semlink WSJ corpus as training data. For in-domain (testing on Semlink WSJ data), we achieve 95.9% accuracy, 35.1% error reduction (ER) over a strong baseline. For adaptation, we test on the GENIA corpus and achieve 72.4% accuracy with 10.7% ER. This is the first large-scale experimentation with automatic algorithms for this task.

1 Introduction

The organization of verbs into classes whose members exhibit similar syntactic and semantic behavior has been discussed extensively in the linguistics literature (see e.g. (Levin and Rappaport Hovav, 2005; Levin, 1993)). Such an organization helps in avoiding lexicon representation redundancy and enables generalizations across similar verbs. It can also be of great practical use, e.g. in compensating NLP statistical models for data sparseness. Indeed, Levin's seminal work had motivated much research aimed at automatic discovery of verb classes (see Section 2).

VerbNet (VN) (Kipper et al., 2000; Kipper-Schuler, 2005) is a large scale, publicly available domain independent verb lexicon that builds on Levin classes and extends them with new verbs, new classes, and additional information such as semantic roles and selectional restrictions. VN classes were proven beneficial for Semantic Role Labeling (SRL) (Swier and Stevenson, 2005), Semantic Parsing (Shi and Mihalcea, 2005) and building conceptual graphs (Hensman and Dunnion, 2004). Levin-inspired classes have been used in several NLP tasks, such as Machine Translation (Dorr, 1997) and Document Classification (Klavans and Kan, 1998).

Many applications that use VN need to map verb instances onto their VN classes. However, verbs are polysemous with respect to VN classes. Semlink (Loper et al., 2007) is a dataset that maps each verb instance in the WSJ Penn Treebank to its VN class. The mapping has been created using a combination of automatic and manual methods. Yi et al. (2007) have used Semlink to improve SRL.

In this paper we present the first large-scale experimentation with a supervised machine learning classification algorithm for disambiguating verb instances to their VN classes. We use rich syntactic features extracted from a treebank-style parse tree, and utilize a learning algorithm capable of imposing class membership constraints, thus taking advantage of the nature of our task. We use Semlink as the training set.

We evaluate our algorithm in both in-domain and corpus adaptation scenarios. In the former, we test on the WSJ (using Semlink again), obtaining 95.9% accuracy with 35.1% error reduction (ER) over a strong baseline (most frequent

© 2008. Licensed under the *Creative Commons Attribution-Noncommercial-Share Alike 3.0 Unported* license (http://creativecommons.org/licenses/by-nc-sa/3.0/). Some rights reserved.

class) when using a modern statistical parser. In the corpus adaptation scenario, we disambiguate verbs in sentences taken from outside the training domain. Since the manual annotation of new corpora is costly, and since VN is designed to be a domain independent resource, adaptation results are important to the usability in NLP in practice. We manually annotated 400 sentences from GENIA (Kim et al., 2003), a medical domain corpus[1]. Testing on these, we achieved 72.4% accuracy with 10.7% ER. Our adaptation scenario is complete in the sense that the parser we use was also trained on a different corpus (WSJ). We also report experiments done using gold-standard (manually created) parses.

The most relevant previous works addressing verb instance class classification are (Lapata and Brew, 2004; Li and Brew, 2007; Girju et al., 2005). The former two do not use VerbNet and their experiments were narrower than ours, so we cannot compare to their results. The latter mapped to VN, but used a preliminary highly restricted setup where most instances were monosemous. For completeness, we compared our method to theirs[2], achieving similar results.

We review related work in Section 2, and discuss the task in Section 3. Section 4 introduces the model, Section 5 describes the experimental setup, and Section 6 presents our results.

2 Related Work

VerbNet. VN is a major electronic English verb lexicon. It is organized in a hierarchical structure of classes and sub-classes, each sub-class inheriting the full characterization of its super-class. VN is built on a refinement of the Levin classes, the intersective Levin classes (Dang et al., 1998), aimed at achieving more coherent classes both semantically and syntactically. VN was also substantially extended (Kipper et al., 2006) using the Levin classes extension proposed in (Korhonen and Briscoe, 2004). VN today contains 3626 verb *lemmas* (forms), organized in 237 main classes having 4991 verb *types* (we refer to a lemma with an ascribed class as a type). Of the 3626 lemmas, 912 are polysemous (i.e., appear in more than a single class). VN's significant coverage of the English verb lexicon is demonstrated by the 75.5% coverage of VN classes over PropBank[3] instances (Loper et al., 2007). Each class contains rich semantic information, including semantic roles of the arguments augmented with selectional restrictions, and possible subcategorization frames consisting of a syntactic description and semantic predicates with temporal information. VN thematic roles are relatively coarse, vs. the situation-specific FrameNet role system or the verb-specific PropBank role system, enabling generalizations across a wide semantic scope. Swier and Stevenson (2005) and Yi et al. (2007) used VN for SRL.

Verb type classification. Quite a few works have addressed the issue of verb type classification and in particular classification to 'Levin inspired' classes (e.g., (Schulte im Walde, 2000; Merlo and Stevenson, 2001)). Such work is not comparable to ours, as it deals with verb type (sense) rather than verb token (instance) classification.

Verb token classification. Lapata and Brew (2004) dealt with classification to Levin classes of polysemous verbs. They established a prior from the BNC in an unsupervised manner. They also showed that this prior helps in the training of a naive Bayes classifier employed to distinguish between possible verb classes of a given verb in a given frame (when the ambiguity is not solved by knowing the frame alone). Li and Brew (2007) extended this model by proposing a method to train the class disambiguator without using hand-tagged data. While these papers have good results, their experimental setup was rather narrow and used only at most 67 polysemous verbs (in 4 frames). VN includes 912 polysemous verbs, of which 695 appeared in our in-domain experiments.

Girju et al. (2005) performed the only previous work we are aware of that addresses the problem of token level verb disambiguation into VN classes. They treated the task as a supervised learning problem, proposing features based on a POS tagger, a Chunker and a named entity classifier. In order to create the data[4], they used a mapping between Propbank rolesets and VN classes, and took the instances in WSJ sections 15-18,20,21 that were annotated by Propbank and for which the roleset determines the VN class uniquely. This resulted in most instances being in fact monosemous. Their

[1]Our annotations will be made available to the community.

[2]Using the same sentences and instances, obtained from the authors.

[3]Propbank (Palmer et al., 2005) is a corpus annotation of the WSJ sections of the Penn Treebank with semantic roles of each verbal proposition.

[4]Semlink was not available then.

experiment was conducted in a WSJ in-domain scenario, and in a much narrower scope than in this paper. They had 870 (39 polysemous) unique verb lemmas, compared to 2091 (695 polysemous) in our in-domain scenario. They did not test their model in an adaptation scenario. The scope and difficulty contrast between our setup and theirs are demonstrated by the large differences in the number of instances and in the percentage of polysemous instances: 972/12431 (7.8%) in theirs, compared to 49571/84749 (58.5%) in our in-domain scenario (training+test). We compared our method to theirs for completeness and achieved similar results.

Semlink. The Semlink project (Yi et al., 2007; Loper et al., 2007) aims to create a mapping of PropBank, FrameNet (Baker et al., 1998), WordNet (henceforth WN) and VN to one another, thus allowing these resources to synergize. In addition, the project includes the most extensive token mapping of verbs to their VN classes available today. It covers all verbs in the WSJ sections of the Penn Treebank within VN coverage (out of 113K verb instances, 97K have lemmas present in VN).

3 Nature of the Task

Polysemy is a major issue in NLP. Verbs are not an exception, resulting in a single verb form (lemma) appearing in more than a single class. This polysemy is also present in the original Levin classification, where polysemous classes account for more than 48% of the BNC verb instances (Lapata and Brew, 2004).

Given a verb instance whose lemma is within the coverage of VN, given the sentence in which it appears, given a parse tree of this sentence (see below), and given the VN resource, our task is to classify the verb instance to its correct VN class. There are currently 237 possible classes[5]. Each verb has only a few possible classes (no more than 10, but only about 2.5 on the average over the polysemous verbs). Depending on the application, the parse tree for the sentence may be either a gold standard parse or a parse tree generated by a parser. We have experimented with both options.

The task can be viewed in two complementary ways: per-class and per-verb type. The per-class perspective takes into consideration the small number of classes relative to the number of types[6]. A classifier may gather valuable information for all members of a certain VN class, without seeing all of its members in the training data. From this perspective the task resembles POS tagging. In both tasks there are many dozens (or more) of possible labels, while each word has only a small subset of possible labels. Different words may receive the same label.

The per-verb perspective takes into consideration the special properties of every verb type. Even the best lexicons necessarily ignore certain idiosyncratic characteristics of the verb when assigning it to a certain class. If a verb appears many times in the corpus, it is possible to estimate its parameters to a reasonable reliability, and thus to use its specific distributional properties for disambiguation. Viewed in this manner, the task resembles a word sense disambiguation (WSD) task: each verb has a small distinct set of senses (types), and no two different verbs have the same sense.

The similarity to WSD suggests that our task might be solved by WN sense disambiguation followed by a mapping from WN to VN. However, good results are not to be expected, due to the medium quality of today's WSD algorithms and because the mapping between WN and VN is both incomplete and many-to-many[7]. Even for a perfect WN WSD algorithm, the resulting WN synset may not be mapped to VN at all or may be mapped onto multiple VN classes. We experimented with this method and obtained results below the MF baseline we used[8].

The above discussion does not rule out the possibility of obtaining reasonable results through applying a high quality WSD engine followed by a WN to VN mapping. However, there are much fewer VN classes than WN classes per verb. This may result in the WSD engine learning many distinctions that are not useful in this context, which may in turn jeopardize its performance with respect to our task. Moreover, a word sense may belong to a single verb only while a VN class contains many verbs. Consequently, the performance

[5] We ignore sub-class distinctions. This is justified since in 98.2% of the in-coverage instances in Semlink, knowing the verb and its class suffices for knowing its exact sub-class.

[6] 237 classes vs. 4991 types.

[7] In the WN to VN mapping built into VN, 14.69% of the covered WN synsets were mapped to more than a single VN class.

[8] We used the publicly available SenseLearner 2.0, the VB-Collocations model. We chose VN classes containing the lemma in random when a single mapping is not specified. We obtained 67.74% accuracy on section 00 of the WSJ, which is less than the MF baseline. See Sections 5 and 7.

on a certain lemma may benefit from training instances of other lemmas.

Note that our task is not reducible to VN frame identification (a non-trivial task given the richness of the information used to define a frame in VN). Although the categorizing criterion for Levin's classification is the subset of frames the verb may appear in (equivalently, the diathesis alternations the verbal proposition may perform), knowing only the frame in which an instance appears does not suffice, as frames are shared among classes.

4 The Learning Model

As common in supervised learning models, we encode the verb instances into feature vectors and then apply a learning algorithm to induce a classifier. We first discuss the feature set and then the learning algorithm.

Features. Our feature set heavily relies on syntactic annotation. Dorr and Jones (1996) showed that perfect knowledge of the allowable syntactic frames for a verb allows 98% accuracy in type assignment to Levin classes. This motivates the encoding of the syntactic structure of the sentence as features, since we have no access to *all* frames, only to the one appearing in the sentence.

Since some verbs may appear in the same syntactic frame in different VN classes, a model relying on the syntactic frame alone would not be able to disambiguate instances of these verbs when appearing in those frames. Hence our features include lexical context words. The parse tree enables us to use words that appear in specific syntactic slots rather than in a linear window around the verb. To this end, we use the head words of the neighboring constituents. The definition of the head of a constituent is given in (Collins, 1999).

Our feature set is comprised of two parallel sets of features. The first contains features extracted from the parse tree and the verb's lemma as a standalone feature. In the second set, each feature is a conjunction of a feature from the first set with the verb's lemma. By doing so we created a general feature space shared by all verbs, and replications of it for each and every verb. This feature selection strategy was chosen in view of the two perspectives on the task (per-class and per-verb) discussed in Section 3.

Our first set of features encodes the verb's context as inferred from the sentence's parse tree (Figure 1). We attempt to encode both the syntactic frame, by encoding the tree structure, and the argument preferences, by encoding the head words of the arguments and their POS. The restriction on the verb's parent being the head constituent of its grandparent is done in order to focus on the correct verb in verb series such as 'intend to run'.

First Feature Set
The stemmed head words, POS, parse tree labels, function tags, and ordinals of the verb's right k_r siblings (k_r is the maximum number of right siblings in the corpus. These are at most $5k_r$ different features).
The stemmed head words, POS, labels, function tags and ordinals of the verb's left k_l siblings, as above.
The stemmed head word & POS of the 'second head word' nodes on the left and right (see text for precise definition).
All of the above features employed on the siblings of the parent of the verb (only if the verb's parent is the head constituent of its grandparent)
The number of right/left siblings of the verb.
The number of right/left siblings of the verb's parent.
The parse tree label of the verb's parent.
The verb's voice (active or passive).
The verb's lemma.

Figure 1: The first set of features in our model. All of them are binary. The final feature set includes two sets: the set here, and a set obtained by its conjunction with the verb's lemma.

The 3rd cell in the table makes use of a 'second head word' node, defined as follows. Consider a left sibling (right siblings are addressed analogously) M of the verb's node. Take the node H in the subtree of M where M's head appears. H is a descendent of a node J which is a child of M. The 'second head word' node is J's sibling on the right. For example, in the sentence *We went to school* (see Figure 2) the head word of the PP 'to school' is 'to', and the 'second head word' node is 'school'. The rationale is that 'school' could be a useful feature for 'went', in addition to 'to', which is highly polysemous (note that it is also a feature for 'went', in the 1st and 2nd cells of the table). The voice feature was computed using a simple heuristic based on the verb's POS tag (past participle) and presence of auxiliary verbs to its left.

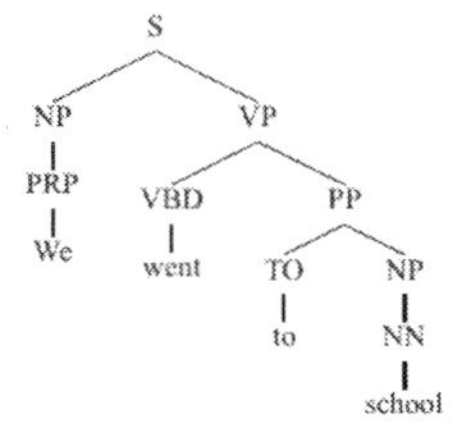

Figure 2: An example parse tree for the 'second head word' feature.

The current set of features does not detect verb particle constructions. We leave this for future research.

Learning Algorithm. Our learning task can be formulated as follows. Let x_i denote the feature vector of an instance i, and let X denote the space of all such feature vectors. The subset of possible labels for x_i is denoted by C_i, and the correct label by $c_i \in C_i$. We denote the label space by S. Let T be the training set of instances $T = \{< x_1, C_1, c_1 >, < x_2, C_2, c_2 >, ..., < x_n, C_n, c_n > \} \subseteq (X \times 2^S \times S)^n$, where n is the size of the training set. Let $< x_{n+1}, C_{n+1} > \in (X \times 2^S)$ be a new instance. Our task is to select which of the labels in C_{n+1} is its correct label c_{n+1} (x_{n+1} does not have to be a previously observed lemma, but its lemma must appear in a VN class).

The structure of the task lets us apply a learning algorithm that is especially appropriate for it. What we need is an algorithm that allows us to restrict the possible labels of each instance, both in training and in testing. The sequential model algorithm presented by Even-Zohar and Roth (2001) directly supports this requirement. We use the SNOW learning architecture for multi-class classification (Roth, 1998), which contains an implementation of that algorithm [9].

5 Experimental Setup

We used SemLink VN annotations and parse trees on sections 02-21 of the WSJ Penn Treebank for training, and section 00 as a development set, as is common in the parsing community. We performed two parallel sets of experiments, one using manually created gold standard parse trees and one using parse trees created by a state-of-the-art parser (Charniak and Johnson, 2005) (Note that this parser does not output function tags). The parser was also trained on sections 02-21 and tuned on section 00[10]. Consequently, our adaptation scenario is a full adaptation situation in which both the parser and the VerbNet training data are not in the test domain. Note that generative parser adaptation results are known to be of much lower quality than in-domain results (Lease and Charniak, 2005). The quality of the discriminative parser we used did indeed decrease in our adaptation scenario (Section 7).

The training data included 71209 VN in-scope instances (of them 41753 polysemous) and the development 3624 instances (2203 polysemous). An 'in-scope' instance is one that appears in VN and is tagged with a verb POS. The same trained model was used in both the in-domain and adaptation scenarios, which only differ in their test sets.

In-Domain. Tests were held on sections 01,22,23,24 of WSJ PTB. Test data includes all in-scope instances for which there is a SemLink annotation, yielding 13540 instances, 7798 (i.e., 57.6%) of them polysemous.

Adaptation. For the testing we annotated sentences from GENIA (Kim et al., 2003) (version 3.0.2). The GENIA corpus is composed of MEDLINE abstracts related to transcription factors in human blood cells. We annotated 400 sentences from the corpus, each including at least one in-scope verb instance. We took the first 400 sentences from the corpus that met that criterion[11]. After cleaning some GENIA POS inconsistencies, this amounts to 690 in-scope instances (380 of them polysemous). The tagging was done by two annotators with an inter-annotator agreement rate of 80.35% and Kappa 67.66%.

Baselines. We used two baselines, random and most frequent (MF). The random baseline selects uniformly and independently one of the possible classes of the verb. The most frequent (MF) baseline selects the most frequent class of the verb in the training data for verbs seen while training, and selects in random for the unseen ones. Consequently, it obtains a perfect score over the monosemous verbs. This baseline is a strong one and is common in disambiguation tasks.

We repeated all of the setup above in two sce-

[9] Experiments on development data revealed that for verbs for which almost all of the training instances are mapped to the same VN class, it is most beneficial to select that class. Thus, where more than 90% of the training instances of a verb are mapped to the same class, our algorithm mapped the instances of the verb to that class regardless of the context.

[10] For the very few sentences out of coverage for the parser, we used the MF baseline (see below).

[11] Discarding the first 120 sentences, which were used to design the annotator guidelines.

narios. In the first (*main*) scenario, in-scope instances were always mapped to VN classes, while in the second (*'other is possible'* (OIP)) scenario, in-scope instances were allowed to be tagged (during training) and classified (during test) as not belonging to any existing VN class[12]. In all cases, out-of-scope instances (verbs whose lemmas do not appear in VN) were ignored. For the OIP scenario, we used a different 'other' label for each of the lemmas, not a single label shared by them all.

6 Results

Table 1 shows our results. In addition to the overall results, we also show results for the polysemous ones alone, since the task is trivial for the monosemous ones. The results using gold standard parses effectively set an upper bound on our model's performance, while those using statistical parser output demonstrate its current usability.

In-Domain. Results are shown in the WSJ → WSJ columns of Table 1. Using gold standard parses (top), we achieve 96.42% accuracy overall. Over the polysemous verbs, the accuracy is 93.68%. This translates to an error reduction over the MF baseline of 43.35% overall and 43.22% for the polysemous verbs. In the 'other is possible' scenario (right), we obtained 36.67% error reduction. Using a state-of-the-art parser (Charniak and Johnson, 2005) (bottom), we experienced some degradation of the results (as expected), but they remained significantly above baseline. We achieve 95.9% accuracy overall and 92.77% for the polysemous verbs, which translates to about 35.13% and 35.04% error reduction respectively. In the OIP scenario, we obtained 28.95% error reduction.

The results of the random baseline for the in-domain scenario are substantially worse than the MF baseline. On the WSJ the random baseline scored 66.97% (37.51%) accuracy in the main (OIP) scenarios.

Adaptation. Here we test our model's ability to generalize across domains. Since VN is supposed to be a domain independent resource, we hope to acquire statistics that are relevant across domains as well and so to enable us to automatically map verbs in domains of various genres. The results are shown in the WSJ → GENIA columns of Table 1. When using gold standard parses, our model scored 73.16%. This translates to about 13.17% ER on GENIA. We interestingly experienced very little degradation in the results when moving to parser output, achieving 72.4% accuracy which translates to 10.71% error reduction over the MF baseline. The random baseline on GENIA was again worse than MF, obtaining 66.04% accuracy as compared to 69.09% of MF (in the OIP scenario, 39.12% compared to 46.41%).

Run-time performance. Given a parsed corpus, our main model trains and runs in no more than a few minutes for a training set of ~60K instances and a test set of ~11K instances, using a Pentium 4 CPU 2.40GHz with 1GB main memory. The bottleneck in tagging large corpora using our model is thus most likely the running time of current parsers.

7 Discussion

In this paper we introduced a new statistical model for automatically mapping verb instances into VerbNet classes, and presented the first large-scale experiments for this task, for both in-domain and corpus adaptation scenarios.

Using gold standard parse trees, we achieved 96.42% accuracy on WSJ test data, showing 43.35% error reduction over a strong baseline. For adaptation to the GENIA corpus, we showed 13.1% error reduction over the baseline. A surprising result in the context of adaptation is the little influence of using gold standard parses versus using parser output, especially given the relatively low performance of today's parsers in the adaptation task (91.4% F-score for the WSJ in-domain scenario compared to 81.24% F-score when parsing our GENIA test set). This is an interesting direction for future work.

In addition, we conducted some additional preliminary experiments in order to shed light on some aspects of the task. The experiments reported below were conducted on the development data, given gold standard parse trees.

First, motivated by the close connection between WSD and our task (see Section 3), we conducted an experiment to test the applicability of using a WSD engine. In addition to the experiments listed above, we also attempted to encode the output of a modern WSD engine (the VBCollocations Model of SenseLearner 2.0 (Mihalcea and Csomai, 2005)), both by encoding the synset (if exists) of the verb instance as a feature, and by encoding each possible mapped class of the WSD engine output synset as a feature. There are k

[12]i.e., including instances tagged by SemLink as 'none'.

		Main Scenario				'Other is Possible' (OIP) Scenario			
		WSJ→WSJ		WSJ→GENIA		WSJ→WSJ		WSJ→GENIA	
		MF	Model	MF	Model	MF	Model	MF	Model
Gold Std	Total	93.68	**96.42**	69.09	**73.16**	88.6	**92.78**	46.41	**52.46**
	ER		43.35		13.17		36.67		11.29
	Poly.	88.87	**93.68**	48.58	**55.35**	–	–	–	–
	ER		43.22		13.17		–		–
Parser	Total	93.68	**95.9**	69.09	**72.4**	88.6	**91.9**	46.41	**52.46**
	ER		35.13		10.71		28.95		11.29
	Poly.	88.87	**92.77**	48.58	**55.35**	–	–	–	–
	ER		35.04		10.72		–		–

Table 1: Accuracy and error reduction (ER) results (in percents) for our model and the MF baseline. Error reduction is computed as $\frac{MODEL-MF}{100-MF}$. Results are given for the WSJ and GENIA corpora test sets. The top table is for a model receiving gold standard parses of the test data. The bottom is for a model using (Charniak and Johnson, 2005) state-of-the-art parses of the test data. In the main scenario (left), instances were always mapped to VN classes, while in the OIP one (right) it was possible (during both training and test) to map instances as not belonging to any existing class. For the latter, no results are displayed for polysemous verbs, since each verb can be mapped both to 'other' and to at least one class.

features if there are k possible classes[13]. There was no improvement over the previous model. A possible reason for this is the performance of the WSD engine (e.g. 56.1% precision on the verbs in Senseval-3 all-words task data). Naturally, more research is needed to establish better methods of incorporating WSD information to assist in this task.

Second, we studied the relative usability of class information as opposed to verb idiosyncratic information in the VN disambiguation task. By measuring the accuracy of our model, first given the per-class features (the first set of features excluding the verb's lemma feature) and second given the per-verb features (the conjunction of the first set with the verb's lemma), we tried to address this question. We obtained 94.82% accuracy for the per-class experiment, and 95.51% for the per-verb experiment, compared to 95.95% when using both in the in-domain gold standard scenario. The MF baseline scored 92.45% on this development set. These results, which are close in the per-class experiment to those of the MF baseline, indicate that combining both approaches in the construction of the classifier is justified.

Third, we studied the importance of having a learning algorithm utilizing the task's structure (mapping into a large label space where each instance can be mapped to only a small subspace). Our choice of the algorithm in (Even-Zohar and Roth, 2001) was done in light of this requirement. We conducted an experiment in which we omitted these per-instance restrictions on the label space, effectively allowing each verb to take every label in the label space. We obtained 94.54% accuracy, which translates to 27.68% error reduction, compared to 95.95% accuracy (46.36% error reduction) when using the restrictions. These results indicate that although our feature set keeps us substantially above baseline even without the above algorithm, using it boosts our results even further. This result is different from the results obtained in (Girju et al., 2005), where the results of the unconstrained (flat) model were significantly below baseline.

As noted earlier, the field of instance level verb classification into Levin-inspired classes is far from being exhaustively explored. We intend to make our implementation of the model available to the community, to enable others to engage in further research on this task.

Acknowledgements. We would like to thank Dan Roth, Mark Sammons and Ran Luria for their help.

References

Collin F. Baker, Charles J. Fillmore and John B. Lowe, 1998. *The Berkeley FrameNet Project. Proc. of the 36th Meeting of the ACL and the 17th COLING.*

Eugene Charniak and Mark Johnson, 2005. *Coarse-*

[13]The mapping is many-to-many and partial. To overcome the first issue, given a WN sense of the verb, we encoded all possible VN classes that correspond to it. To overcome the second, we treated a verb in a certain VN class, for which the mapping to WN was available, as one that can be mapped to all WN senses of the verb.

to-fine n-best parsing and maxent discriminative reranking. Proc. of the 43rd Meeting of the ACL.

Michael Collins, 1999. *Head-driven statistical models for natural language parsing. Ph.D. thesis, University of Pennsylvania.*

Hoa Trang Dang, Karin Kipper, Martha Palmer and Joseph Rosenzweig, 1998. *Investigating regular sense extensions based on intersective Levin classes. Proc. of the 36th Meeting of the ACL and the 17th COLING.*

Bonnie J. Dorr, 1997. *Large-Scale Dictionary Construction for Foreign Language Tutoring and Interlingual Machine Translation. Machine Translation,* 12:1-55.

Bonnie J. Dorr and Douglas Jones, 1996. *Role of Word Sense Disambiguation in Lexical Acquisition: Predicting Semantics from Syntactic Cues. Proc. of the 16th COLING.*

Yair Even-Zohar and Dan Roth, 2001. *A Sequential Model for Multi-Class Classification. Proc. of the 2001 Conference on Empirical Methods in Natural Language Processing.*

Roxana Girju, Dan Roth and Mark Sammons, 2005. *Token-level Disambiguation of VerbNet classes. The Interdisciplinary Workshop on Verb Features and Verb Classes.*

Svetlana Hensman and John Dunnion, 2004. *Automatically building conceptual graphs using VerbNet and WordNet. International Symposium on Information and Communication Technologies (ISICT).*

Jin–Dong Kim, Tomoko Ohta, Yuka Teteisi and Jun'ichi Tsujii, 2003. *GENIA corpus – a semantically annotated corpus for bio-textmining. Bioinformatics, 19:i180–i182, Oxford U. Press 2003.*

Karin Kipper, Hoa Trang Dang and Martha Palmer, 2000. *Class-Based Construction of a Verb Lexicon. Proc. of the 17th National Conference on Artificial Intelligence.*

Karin Kipper-Schuler, 2005. *VerbNet: A Broad-Coverage, Comprehensive Verb Lexicon. Ph. D. thesis, University of Pennsylvania.*

Karin Kipper, Anna Korhonen, Neville Ryant and Martha Palmer, 2006. *Extending VerbNet with Novel Verb Classes. Proc. of the 5th International Conference on Language Resources and Evaluation.*

Judith Klavans and Min-Yen Kan, 1998. *Role of verbs in document analysis. Proc. of the 36th Meeting of the ACL and the 17th International Conference on Computational Linguistics.*

Anna Korhonen and Ted Briscoe, 2004. *Extended Lexical-Semantic Classification of English Verbs. Proc. of the 42nd Meeting of the ACL, Workshop on Computational Lexical Semantics.*

Mirella Lapata and Chris Brew, 2004. *Verb Class Disambiguation using Informative Priors. Computational Linguistics,* 30(1):45-73

Matthew Lease and Eugene Charniak, 2005. *Towards a Syntactic Account of Punctuation. Proc. of the 2nd International Joint Conference on Natural Language Processing.*

Beth Levin, 1993. *English Verb Classes And Alternations: A Preliminary Investigation. The University of Chicago Press.*

Beth Levin and Malka Rappaport Hovav, 2005. *Argument Realization. Cambridge University Press.*

Juanguo Li and Chris Brew, 2007. *Disambiguating Levin Verbs Using Untagged Data. Proc. of the 2007 International Conference on Recent Advances in Natural Language Processing.*

Edward Loper, Szu-ting Yi and Martha Palmer, 2007. *Combining Lexical Resources: Mapping Between PropBank and VerbNet. Proc. of the 7th International Workshop on Computational Linguistics, Tilburg, the Netherlands.*

Paola Merlo and Suzanne Stevenson. 2001. *Automatic Verb-Classification Based On Statistical Distribution Of Argument Structure. Computational Linguistics,* 27(3):373–408.

Rada Mihalcea and Andras Csomai 2005. *SenseLearner: word sense disambiguation for all words in unrestricted text. Proc. of the 43rd Meeting of the ACL , Poster Session.*

Martha Palmer, Daniel Gildea and Paul Kingsbury, 2005. *The proposition bank: A corpus annotated with semantic roles. Computational Linguistics,* 31(1).

Dan Roth, 1998. *Learning to resolve natural language ambiguities: A unified approach. Proc. of the 15th National Conference on Artificial Intelligence*

Sabine Schulte im Walde, 2000. *Clustering verbs semantically according to their alternation behavior. Proc. of the 18th COLING.*

Lei Shi and Rada Mihalcea, 2005. *Putting pieces together: Combining FrameNet, VerbNet and WordNet for robust semantic parsing. Proc. of the International Conference on Intelligent Text Processing and Computational Linguistics.*

Robert S. Swier and Suzanne Stevenson, 2005. *Exploiting a Verb Lexicon in Automatic Semantic Role Labelling. Proc. of the 2005 conference on empirical methods in natural language processing.*

Szu-ting Yi, Edward Loper and Martha Palmer, 2007. *Can Semantic Roles Generalize Across Genres? Proc. of the 2007 conference of the north american chapter of the association for computational linguistics.*

On Robustness and Domain Adaptation using SVD for Word Sense Disambiguation

Eneko Agirre and Oier Lopez de Lacalle
Informatika Fakultatea, University of the Basque Country
20018, Donostia, Basque Country
{e.agirre,oier.lopezdelacalle}@ehu.es

Abstract

In this paper we explore robustness and domain adaptation issues for Word Sense Disambiguation (WSD) using Singular Value Decomposition (SVD) and unlabeled data. We focus on the semi-supervised domain adaptation scenario, where we train on the source corpus and test on the target corpus, and try to improve results using unlabeled data. Our method yields up to 16.3% error reduction compared to state-of-the-art systems, being the first to report successful semi-supervised domain adaptation. Surprisingly the improvement comes from the use of unlabeled data from the source corpus, and not from the target corpora, meaning that we get robustness rather than domain adaptation. In addition, we study the behavior of our system on the target domain.

1 Introduction

In many Natural Language Processing (NLP) tasks we find that a large collection of manually-annotated text is used to train and test supervised machine learning models. While these models have been shown to perform very well when tested on the text collection related to the training data (what we call the **source** domain), the performance drops considerably when testing on text from other domains (called **target** domains).

In order to build models that perform well in new (target) domains we usually find two settings (Daumé III, 2007): In the **semi-supervised** setting the goal is to improve the system trained on the source domain using unlabeled data from the target domain, and the baseline is that of the system trained on the source domain. In the **supervised setting**, training data from both source and target domains are used, and the baseline is provided by the system trained on the target domain. The semi-supervised setting is the most attractive, as it would save developers the need to hand-annotate target corpora every time a new domain is to be processed.

The main goal of this paper is to use unlabeled data in order to get better domain-adaptation results for Word Sense Disambiguation (WSD) in the semi-supervised setting. Singular Value Decomposition (SVD) has been shown to find correlations between terms which are helpful to overcome the scarcity of training data in WSD (Gliozzo et al., 2005). This paper explores how this ability of SVD can be applied to the domain-adaptation of WSD systems, and we show that SVD and unlabeled data improve the results of two state-of-the-art WSD systems (k-NN and SVM). For the sake of this paper we call this set of experiments the **domain adaptation scenario**.

In addition, we also perform some related experiments on just the target domain. We use unlabeled data in order to improve the results of a system trained and tested in the target domain. These results are complementary to the domain adaptation experiments, and also provide an upperbound for semi-supervised domain adaptation. We call these experiments the **target domain scenario**. Note that both scenarios are semi-supervised, in that our focus is on the use of unlabeled data in addition to the available labeled data.

The experiments were performed on a publicly available corpus which was designed to study the effect of domain in WSD (Koeling et al., 2005). It comprises 41 nouns closely related to the SPORTS and FINANCES domains with 300 examples for each. The 300 examples were drawn from the British National Corpus (Leech, 1992) (BNC), the SPORTS section of the Reuters corpus (Leech,

© 2008. Licensed under the *Creative Commons Attribution-Noncommercial-Share Alike 3.0 Unported* license (http://creativecommons.org/licenses/by-nc-sa/3.0/). Some rights reserved.

1992), and the FINANCES section of Reuters in equal number.

The paper is structured as follows. Section 2 reviews prior work in the area. Section 3 presents the datasets used, and Section 4 the learning methods, including the application of SVD. The experimental results are presented in Section 5, for the semi-supervised domain adaptation scenario, and Section 6, for the target scenario. Section 7 presents the discussion and Section 8 the conclusions and future work.

2 Prior Work

Domain adaptation is a subject attracting more and more attention. In the semi-supervised setting, Blitzer et al. (2006) use Structural Correspondence Learning and unlabeled data to adapt a Part-of-Speech tagger. They carefully select so-called 'pivot features' to learn linear predictors, perform SVD on the weights learned by the predictor, and thus learn correspondences among features in both source and target domains. Our technique also uses SVD, but we directly apply it to all features, and thus avoid the need to define pivot features. In preliminary work we unsuccessfully tried to carry along the idea of pivot features to WSD. Zelikovitz and Hirsh (2001) use unlabeled data (so-called background knowledge) with Latent Semantic Indexing (also based on SVD) on a Text Classification task with positive results. They use related unlabeled text and include it in the term-by-document matrix to expand it and capture better the interesting properties of the data. Their approach is similar to our SMA method in Section 4.2).

In the supervised setting, a recent paper by Daumé III (2007) shows that, using a very simple feature augmentation method coupled with Support Vector Machines, he is able to effectively use both labeled target and source data to provide the best results in a number of NLP tasks. His method improves or equals over previously explored more sophisticated methods (Daumé III and Marcu, 2006; Chelba and Acero, 2004).

Regarding WSD, some initial works made basic analysis of the particular issues. Escudero et al. (2000) tested the supervised adaptation setting on the DSO corpus, which had examples from the Brown corpus and Wall Street Journal corpus. They found that the source corpus did not help when tagging the target corpus, showing that tagged corpora from each domain would suffice, and concluding that hand tagging a large general corpus would not guarantee robust broad-coverage WSD. Agirre and Martínez (2000) also used the DSO corpus in the supervised setting to show that training on a subset of the source corpora that is topically related to the target corpus does allow for some domain adaptation. Their work used the fact that the genre tags of Brown allowed to detect which parts of the corpus were related to the target corpus.

More recently, Koeling et al. (2005) presented an unsupervised system to learn the predominant senses of particular domains. Their system was based on the use of a similarity thesaurus induced from the domain corpus and WordNet. They used the same dataset as in this paper for evaluation. Chan and Ng (2007) performed supervised domain adaptation on a manually selected subset of 21 nouns from the DSO corpus. They used active learning, count-merging, and predominant sense estimation in order to save target annotation effort. They showed that adding just 30% of the target data to the source examples the same precision as the full combination of target and source data could be achieved. They also showed that using the source corpus allowed to significantly improve results when only 10%-30% of the target corpus was used for training. No data was given about the use of both tagged corpora.

Though not addressing domain adaptation, other works on WSD also used SVD and are closely related to the present paper. Gliozzo et al. (2005) used SVD to reduce the space of the term-to-document matrix, and then computed the similarity between train and test instances using a mapping to the reduced space (similar to our SMA method in Section 4.2). They combined other knowledge sources into a complex kernel using SVM. They report improved performance on a number of languages in the Senseval-3 lexical sample dataset. Our present paper differs from theirs in that we propose an additional method to use SVD (the OMT method, Section 4.2), and that we evaluate the contribution of unlabeled data and SVD in isolation, leaving combination for future work.

Ando (2006) used Alternative Structured Optimization, which is closely related to Structural Learning (cited above). He first trained one linear predictor for each target word, and then performed SVD on 7 carefully selected submatrices of the feature-to-predictor matrix of weights. The system attained small but consistent improvements (no significance data was given) on the Senseval-3 lexical sample datasets using SVD and unlabeled data.

We have previously shown (Agirre et al., 2005; Agirre and Lopez de Lacalle, 2007) that performing SVD on the feature-to-documents matrix is a simple technique that allows to improve performance with and without unlabeled data. The use of several k-NN classifiers trained on a number of reduced and original spaces was shown to rank first in the Senseval-3 dataset and second in the SemEval 2007 competition. The present work extends our own in that we present a comprehensive study on a domain adaptation dataset, producing additional insight on our method and the relation between SVD, features and unlabeled data.

3 Data sets

The dataset we use was designed for domain-related WSD experiments by Koeling et al. (2005), and is publicly available. The examples come from the BNC (Leech, 1992) and the SPORTS and FINANCES sections of the Reuters corpus (Rose et al., 2002), comprising around 300 examples (roughly 100 from each of those corpora) for each of the 41 nouns. The nouns were selected because they were salient in either the SPORTS or FINANCES domains, or because they had senses linked to those domains. The occurrences were hand-tagged with the senses from WordNet (WN) version 1.7.1 (Fellbaum, 1998).

Compared to the DSO corpus used in prior work (cf. Section 2) this corpus has been explicitly created for domain adaptation studies. DSO contains texts coming from the Brown corpus and the Wall Street Journal, but the texts are not classified according to specific domains (e.g. Sports, Finances), which make DSO less suitable to study domain adaptation.

In addition to the labeled data, we also use unlabeled data coming from the three sources used in the labeled corpus: the 'written' part of the BNC (89.7M words), the FINANCES part of Reuters (117,734 documents, 32.5M words), and the SPORTS part (35,317 documents, 9.1M words).

4 Learning features and methods

In this section, we review the learning features, the two methods to apply SVD, and the two learning algorithms used in the experiments.

4.1 Learning features

We relied on the usual features used in previous WSD work, grouped in three main sets. **Local collocations** comprise the bigrams and trigrams formed around the target word (using either lemmas, word-forms, and PoS tags[1]), those formed with the previous/posterior lemma/word-form in the sentence, and the content words in a ± 4-word window around the target. **Syntactic dependencies**[2] use the object, subject, noun-modifier, preposition, and sibling lemmas, when available. Finally, **Bag-of-words features** are the lemmas of the content words in the whole context, plus the salient bigrams in the context (Pedersen, 2001).

4.2 Features from the reduced space

Apart from the original space of features, we have the so called **SVD features**, obtained from the projection of the feature vectors into the reduced space (Deerwester et al., 1990). Basically, we set a term-by-document or feature-by-example matrix M from the corpus (see section below for more details). SVD decomposes it into three matrices, $M = U\Sigma V^T$. If the desired number of dimensions in the reduced space is p, we select p rows from Σ and V, yielding Σ_p and V_p respectively. We can map any feature vector $\vec{t}$ (which represents either a train or test example) into the p-dimensional space as follows: $\vec{t_p} = \vec{t}^T V_p \Sigma_p^{-1}$. Those mapped vectors have p dimensions, and each of the dimensions is what we call a SVD feature. We can now use the mapped vectors ($\vec{t_p}$) to train and test any learning method, as usual. We have explored two different variants in order to build the reduced matrix and obtain the SVD features, as follows.

Single Matrix for All target words (SVD-SMA). The method comprises the following steps: (i) extract bag-of-word features (terms in this case) from unlabeled corpora, (ii) build the term-by-document matrix, (iii) decompose it with SVD, and (iv) project the labeled data (train/test). This technique is very similar to previous work on SVD (Gliozzo et al., 2005; Zelikovitz and Hirsh, 2001). The dimensionality reduction is performed once, over the whole unlabeled corpus, and it is then applied to the labeled data of each word. The reduced

[1] The PoS tagging was performed with the fnTBL toolkit (Ngai and Florian, 2001)

[2] This software was kindly provided by David Yarowsky's group, from Johns Hopkins University.

space is constructed only with terms, which correspond to bag-of-words features, and thus discards the rest of the features. Given that the WSD literature has shown that all features, including local and syntactic features, are necessary for optimal performance (Pradhan et al., 2007), we propose the following alternative to construct the matrix.

One Matrix per Target word (SVD-OMT). For each word: (i) construct a corpus with its occurrences in the labeled and, if desired, unlabeled corpora, (ii) extract all features, (iii) build the feature-by-example matrix, (iv) decompose it with SVD, and (v) project all the labeled training and test data for the word. Note that this variant performs one SVD process for each target word separately, hence its name. We proposed this technique in (Agirre et al., 2005).

An important parameter when doing SVD is the number of dimensions in the reduced space (p). We tried two different values for p (25 and 200) in the BNC domain, and the results were consistent in that 25 performed better for SVD-OMT and 200 better for SVD-SMA. Those values were chosen for testing in the SPORTS and FINANCES domains, i.e. 25 for SVD-OMT and 200 for SVD-SMA.

4.3 Building Matrices

The methods in the previous section can be applied to the following matrices M:

- TRAIN: The matrix comprises features from labeled train examples alone. This matrix can only be used to obtain OMT features.
- TRAIN ∪ BNC: In addition to TRAIN, we matrix also includes unlabeled examples from the source corpus (BNC). Both OMT and SMA features can be obtained.
- TRAIN ∪ {SPORTS,FINANCES}: Like the previous, but using unlabeled examples from one of the target corpora (FINANCES or SPORTS) instead. Both OMT and SMA feature can be obtained.

Based on previous work (Agirre et al., 2005), we used 50% of the respective unlabeled corpora for OMT features, and the whole corpora for SMA.

4.4 Learning methods

We used two well known classifiers, Support Vector Machines (SVM) and k-Nearest Neighbors (k-NN). Regarding SVM we used linear kernels implemented in SVM-Light (Joachims, 1999). We estimated the soft margin (C) for each feature space and each word using a greedy process in a preliminary experiment on the source training data using cross-validation. The same C value was used in the rest of the settings.

k-NN is a memory based learning method, where the neighbors are the k most similar labeled examples to the test example. The similarity among instances is measured by the cosine of their vectors. The test instance is labeled with the sense obtaining the maximum the sum of the weighted vote of the k most similar contexts. We set k to 5 based on previous results (Agirre and Lopez de Lacalle, 2007).

5 Domain adaptation scenario

In this scenario we try to adapt a general purpose supervised WSD system trained on the source corpus (BNC) to a target corpus (either SPORTS or FINANCES) using unlabeled corpora only.

5.1 Experimental results

Table 1 shows the precision results for this scenario. Note that all methods have full coverage, i.e. they return a sense for all test examples, and therefore precision suffices to compare among systems. We have computed significance ranges for all results in this paper using bootstrap resampling (Noreen, 1989). F_1 scores outside of these intervals are assumed to be significantly different from the related F_1 score ($p < 0.05$).

The table has two main parts, each regarding to one of the target domains, SPORTS and FINANCES. The use of two target domains allows to test whether the methods behave similarly in both domains. The columns denote the classifier and SVD method used: the MFS column corresponds to the most frequent sense, k-NN-ORIG (SVM-ORIG) corresponds to performing k-NN (SVM) on the original feature space, k-NN-OMT (SVM-OMT) corresponds to k-NN (SVM) on the reduced dimensions of the OMT strategy, and k-NN-SMA (SVM-SMA) corresponds to k-NN (SVM) on the reduced dimensions of the SMA strategy (cf. Section 4.2). The rows correspond to the matrix used for SVD (cf. Section 4.3). Note that some of the cells have no result, because that combination is not applicable, e.g. using the TRAIN ∪ BNC in the original space.

In the first row (TRAIN) of Table 1 we can see that in both domains SVM on the original space outperforms k-NN with statistical signifi-

BNC → SPORTS							
matrix configuration	MFS	k-NN-ORIG	k-NN-OMT	k-NN-SMA	SVM-ORIG	SVM-OMT	SVM-SMA
TRAIN	39.0±1.3	51.7±1.3	53.0±1.6	-	53.9±1.3	47.4±1.5	-
TRAIN ∪ SPORTS	-	-	47.8±1.5	49.7±1.5	-	51.8±1.5	53.8±1.5
TRAIN ∪ BNC	-	-	**61.4**±1.4	57.1±1.5	-	57.1±1.6	57.2±1.5
BNC → FINANCES							
matrix configuration	MFS	k-NN-ORIG	k-NN-OMT	k-NN-SMA	SVM-ORIG	SVM-OMT	SVM-SMA
TRAIN	51.2±1.6	60.4±1.6	62.5±1.4	-	62.9±1.6	59.4±1.5	-
TRAIN ∪ FINANCES	-	-	57.4±1.9	60.6±1.5	-	60.4±1.4	62.7±1.4
TRAIN ∪ BNC	-	-	65.9±1.5	**68.3**±1.4	-	67.0±1.3	66.8±1.5

Table 1: Precision for the domain adaptation scenario: training on labeled source corpus, plus unlabeled corpora.

cance. Those are the baseline systems. On the same row, working on the reduced space of the TRAIN matrix with OMT allows to improve the results of k-NN, but not for SVM.

Contrary to our expectations, adding target unlabeled corpora (TRAIN ∪ SPORTS and TRAIN ∪ FINANCES rows respectively) does not improve the results over the baseline. But using the source unlabeled data (TRAIN ∪ BNC), we find that for both domains and in all four columns the results are significantly better than for the best baseline in both SPORTS and FINANCES corpora.

The best results on the TRAIN ∪ BNC row depend on the domain corpus. While k-NN-OMT obtains the best results for SPORTS, in FINANCES k-NN-SMA is best. k-NN, in principle a weaker method that SVM, is able to attain the same or superior performance than SVM on the reduced spaces.

Table 3 summarizes the main results, and also shows the error reduction figures, which range between 6.9% and 16.3%. As the most important conclusion, we want to stress that, in this scenario, we are able to build a very robust system just adding unlabeled source material, and that we fail to adapt to the domain using the target corpus. These results are relevant to improve a generic WSD system to be more robust when ported to new domains.

5.2 Controlling size

In the original experiments reported in the previous sections, the size of the unlabeled corpora was not balanced. Due to the importance of the amount of unlabeled data, we performed two control experiments for the OMT and SMA matrices on the domain adaptation scenario, focusing on the k-NN method. Regarding OMT, we used the minimum number of instances per word between BNC and each of the target domains. The system obtained 60.0 of precision using unlabeled data from BNC and 49.5 for SPORTS data (compared to 61.4 and 47.8 in table 1, respectively). We did the same in the FINANCES domain, and we obtained 65.6 of precision for BNC and 54.4 for FINANCES (compared to 65.7 and 57.4 in table 1, respectively). Although the contribution of BNC unlabeled data is slightly lower in this experiment, due to the smaller amount of data, it still outperforms the target unlabeled data by a large margin.

In the case of the SMA matrix, we used 25% of the BNC, which is comparable to the SPORTS and FINANCES sizes. The results, 56.9 of precision in SPORTS domain and 68.1 in FINANCES (compared to 57.1 and 68.3 in table 1, respectively), confirm that the size is not an important factor for SMA either.

6 Target scenario

In this second scenario we focus on the target domain. We train and test on the target domain, and use unlabeled data in order to improve the result. The goal of these experiments is to check the behavior of our method when applied to the target domain, in order to better understand the results on the domain adaptation scenario. They also provide an upperbound for semi-supervised domain adaptation.

6.1 Experimental results

The results are presented in table 2. All experiments in this section have been performed using 3-fold cross-validation. Again, we have full coverage in all cases, and the significance ranges correspond to the 95% confidence level. The table has two main parts, each regarding to one of the target domains, SPORTS and FINANCES. As in Table 1, the columns specify the classifier and SVD method used, and the rows correspond to the matrices used

SPORTS → SPORTS (*xval*)							
matrix configuration	MFS	k-NN-ORIG	k-NN-OMT	k-NN-SMA	SVM-ORIG	SVM-OMT	SVM-SMA
TRAIN	77.8±1.2	84.5±1.0	85.0±1.1	-	85.1±1.0	81.0±1.5	-
TRAIN ∪ SPORTS	-	-	**86.1**±0.9	82.7±1.1	-	85.1±1.1	80.3±1.5
TRAIN ∪ BNC	-	-	84.4±1.0	80.4±1.5	-	84.3±0.9	79.8±1.2
FINANCES → FINANCES (*xval*)							
matrix configuration	MFS	k-NN-ORIG	k-NN-OMT	k-NN-SMA	SVM-ORIG	SVM-OMT	SVM-SMA
TRAIN	82.3±1.3	87.1±1.0	87.4±1.0	-	87.0±1.0	85.5±1.1	-
TRAIN ∪ SPORTS	-	-	**87.8**±0.8	84.3±1.4	-	86.4±0.9	82.9±1.1
TRAIN ∪ BNC	-	-	87.4±1.2	83.5±1.2	-	85.7±0.9	84.3±1.1

Table 2: Precision for the target scenario: training on labeled target corpora, plus unlabeled corpora.

to obtain the features.

Table 2 shows that k-NN-OMT using the target corpus (SPORTS and FINANCES, respectively) slightly improves over the k-NN-ORIG and SVM-ORIG classifiers, with significant difference in the SPORTS domain. Contrary to the results on the previous section, the source unlabeled corpus degrades performance, but the target corpus does allow for small improvements. Note that, in this scenario, both SVM and k-NN perform similarly in the original space, but only k-NN is able to profit from the reduced space. Table 3 summarizes the best result, alongside the error reduction.

The results of these experiments allow to contrast both scenarios, and to get deeper insight about the relation between the labeled and unlabeled data when performing SVD, as we will examine in the next section.

7 Discussion

The main contribution of this paper is to show that we obtain robustness when faced with domain shifts using a semi-supervised strategy. We show that we can obtain it using a large, general, unlabeled corpus. Note that our semi-supervised method to attain robustness for domain shifts is very cost-effective, as it does not require costly hand-tagged material nor even large numbers of unlabeled data from each target domain. These results are more valuable given the lack of substantial positive results on the literature on semi-supervised or supervised domain adaptation for WSD (Escudero et al., 2000; Martínez and Agirre, 2000; Chan and Ng, 2007).

Compared to other settings, our semi-supervised results improve over the completely unsupervised system in (Koeling et al., 2005), which had 43.7% and 49.9% precision for the SPORTS and FINANCES domains respectively, but lag well behind the target domain scenario, showing that there is still room for improvement in the semi-supervised setting.

While these results are based on a lexical sample, and thus not directly generalizable to an all-words corpus, we think that they reflect the main trends for nouns, as the 41 nouns where selected among those exhibiting domain dependence (Koeling et al., 2005). We can assume, though it would be needed to be explored empirically, that other nouns exhibiting domain independence would degrade less when moving to other domains, and thus corroborate the robustness effect we have discovered.

The fact that we attain robustness rather than domain adaptation proper deserves some analysis. In the domain adaptation scenario only source unlabeled data helped, but the results on the target scenario show that it is the target unlabeled data which is helping, and not the source one. Given that SVD basically finds correlations among features, it seems that constructing the term-by-document (or feature-by-example) matrix with the training data and the unlabeled corpus related to the training data is the key factor in play here.

The reasons for this can be traced back as follows. Our source corpus is the BNC, which is a balanced corpus containing a variety of genres and domains. The 100 examples for each word that have been hand-tagged were gathered at random, and thus cover several domains. For instance, the OMT strategy for building the matrix extracts hundreds of other examples from the BNC, and when SVD collapses the features into a reduced space, it effectively captures the most important correlations in the feature-by-example matrix. When faced with examples from a new domain, the reduced matrix is able to map some of the features found in the test example to those in the train example. Such overlap is more difficult if only 100 examples from the source domain are available.

SPORTS	FINANCES	sign.	E.R (%)	method
53.9±1.3	62.9±1.6	-	-	labeled source (SVM-ORIG: baseline)
57.1±1.5	**68.3±1.4**	++	6.9/14.5	**labeled source + SVD on unlabeled source (k-NN-SMA)**
61.4±1.4	65.9±1.5	++	16.3/8.1	**labeled source + SVD on unlabeled source (k-NN-OMT)**
85.1±1.0	87.0±1.0	-	-	labeled target (SVM-ORIG: baseline)
86.1±0.9	**87.8±0.8**	+	6.7/6.1	**labeled target + SVD on unlabeled target (k-NN-OMT)**

Table 3: Summary with the most important results for the two scenarios (best results for each in bold). The significance column shows significance over baselines: ++ (significant in both target domains), + (significant in a single domain). The E.R column shows the error reduction in percentages over the baseline methods.

The unlabeled data and SVD process allow to capture correlations among the features occurring in the test data and those in the training data.

On the other hand, we are discarding all original features, as we focus on the features from the reduced space alone. The newly found correlations come at the price of possibly ignoring effective original features, causing information loss. Only when the correlations found in the reduced space outweigh this information loss do we get better performance on the reduced space than in the original space. The experiment in Section 6 is important in that it shows that the improvement is much smaller and only significant in the target domain scenario, which is in accordance with the hypothesis above. This information loss is a motivation for the combination of the features from the reduced space with the original features, which will be the focus of our future work.

Regarding the learning method and the two strategies to apply SVD, the results show that k-NN profits from the reduced spaces more than SVM, even if its baseline performance is lower than SVM. Regarding the matrix building system, in the domain adaptation scenario, k-NN-OMT obtains the best results (with statistical significance) in the SPORTS corpus, and k-NN-SMA yields the best results (with statistical significance) in the FINANCES domain. Averaging over both domains, k-NN-OMT is best. The target scenario results confirm this trend, as k-NN-OMT is superior to k-NN-SMA in both domains. These results are in accordance with our previous experience on WSD (Agirre et al., 2005), where our OMT method got better results than SMA and those of (Gliozzo et al., 2005) (who also use a method similar to SMA) on the Senseval-3 lexical sample. While OMT reduces the feature-by-example matrix of each target word, SMA reduces a single term-by-document matrix. SMA is able to find important correlations among similar terms in the corpus, but it misses the rich feature set used by WSD systems, as it focuses on bag-of-words alone. OMT on the other hand is able to find correlations between all features which are relevant to the target word only.

8 Conclusions and Future Work

In this paper we explore robustness and domain adaptation issues for Word Sense Disambiguation using SVD and unlabeled data. We focus on the semi-supervised scenario, where we train on the source corpus (BNC), test on two target corpora (SPORTS and FINANCES sections of Reuters), and improve the results using unlabeled data.

Our method yields up to 16.3% error reduction compared to SVM and k-NN on the labeled data alone, showing the first positive results on domain adaptation for WSD. In fact, we show that our results are due to the use of a large, general, unlabeled corpus, and rather than domain-adaptation proper we show robustness in face of a domain shift. This kind of robustness is even more cost-effective than semi-supervised domain adaptation, as it does not require large unlabeled corpora and repeating the computations for each new target domain.

This paper shows that the OMT technique to apply SVD that we proposed in (Agirre et al., 2005) compares favorably to SMA, which has been previously used in (Gliozzo et al., 2005), and that k-NN excels SVM on the features from the reduced space. We also show that the unlabeled data needs to be related to the training data, and that the benefits of our method are larger when faced with a domain shift (compared to test data coming from the same domain as the training data).

In the future, we plan to combine the features from the reduced space with the rest of features, either using a combination of k-NN classifiers (Agirre et al., 2005; Agirre and Lopez de Lacalle, 2007) or a complex kernel (Gliozzo et al., 2005).

A natural extension of our work would be to apply our techniques to the supervised domain adaptation scenario.

Acknowledgments

We wish to thank Diana McCarthy and Rob Koeling for kindly providing us the Reuters tagged corpora, David Martínez for helping us with the learning features, and Walter Daelemans for his advice on domain adaptation. Oier Lopez de Lacalle has a PhD grant from the Basque Government. This work is partially funded by the Education Ministry (KNOW TIN2006-15049, OpenMT TIN2006-15307-C03-02) and the Basque Country University (IT-397-07).

References

Agirre, E. and O. Lopez de Lacalle. 2007. UBC-ALM: Combining k-NN with SVD for WSD. In *Proceedings of the Fourth International Workshop on Semantic Evaluations (SemEval-2007)*. Association for Computational Linguistics.

Agirre, E., O. Lopez de Lacalle, and D. Martínez. 2005. Exploring feature spaces with svd and unlabeled data for Word Sense Disambiguation. In *Proceedings of the Conference on Recent Advances on Natural Language Processing (RANLP'05)*.

Ando, R. Kubota. 2006. Applying alternating structure optimization to word sense disambiguation. In *Proceedings of the 10th Conference on Computational Natural Language Learning (CoNLL)*.

Blitzer, J., R. McDonald, and F. Pereira. 2006. Domain adaptation with structural correspondence learning. In *Proceedings of the 2006 Conference on Empirical Methods in Natural Language Processing*.

Chan, Yee Seng and Hwee Tou Ng. 2007. Domain adaptation with active learning for word sense disambiguation. In *Proceedings of the 45th Annual Meeting of the Association of Computational Linguistics*.

Chelba, C. and A. Acero. 2004. Adaptation of maximum entropy classifier: Little data can help a lot. In *Proceedings of of th Conference on Empirical Methods in Natural Language Processing (EMNLP)*.

Daumé III, H. and D. Marcu. 2006. Domain adaptation for statistical classifiers. *Journal of Artificial Intelligence Research*, 26:101–126.

Daumé III, H. 2007. Frustratingly easy domain adaptation. In *Proceedings of the 45th Annual Meeting of the Association of Computational Linguistics*.

Deerwester, S., S. Dumais, G. Furnas, T. Landauer, and R. Harshman. 1990. Indexing by Latent Semantic Analysis. *Journal of the American Society for Information Science*.

Escudero, G., L. Márquez, and G. Rigau. 2000. An Empirical Study of the Domain Dependence of Supervised Word Sense Didanbiguation Systems. *Proceedings of the joint SIGDAT Conference on Empirical Methods in Natural Language Processing and Very Large Corpora, EMNLP/VLC*.

Fellbaum, C. 1998. *WordNet: An Electronic Lexical Database*. MIT Press.

Gliozzo, A. M., C. Giuliano, and C. Strapparava. 2005. Domain Kernels for Word Sense Disambiguation. *43nd Annual Meeting of the Association for Computational Linguistics. (ACL-05)*.

Joachims, T. 1999. Making Large–Scale SVM Learning Practical. *Advances in Kernel Methods — Support Vector Learning*, Cambridge, MA. MIT Press.

Koeling, R., D. McCarthy, and J. Carroll. 2005. Domain-specific sense distributions and predominant sense acquisition. In *Proceedings of the Human Language Technology Conference and Conference on Empirical Methods in Natural Language Processing. HLT/EMNLP*.

Leech, G. 1992. 100 million words of English: the British National Corpus. *Language Research*.

Martínez, D. and E. Agirre. 2000. One Sense per Collocation and Genre/Topic Variations. *Conference on Empirical Method in Natural Language*.

Ngai, G. and R. Florian. 2001. Transformation-Based Learning in the Fast Lane. *Proceedings of the Second Conference of the North American Chapter of the Association for Computational Linguistics*.

Noreen, E. W. 1989. *Computer-Intensive Methods for Testing Hypotheses*. John Wiley & Sons.

Pedersen, T. 2001. A Decision Tree of Bigrams is an Accurate Predictor of Word Sense. In *Proceedings of the Second Meeting of the North American Chapter of the Association for Computational Linguistics (NAACL-01)*.

Pradhan, S., E. Loper, D. Dligach, and M. Palmer. 2007. Semeval-2007 task-17: English lexical sample, srl and all words. In *Proceedings of the Fourth International Workshop on Semantic Evaluations (SemEval-2007)*.

Rose, T. G., M. Stevenson, and M. Whitehead. 2002. The reuters corpus volumen 1 from yesterday's news to tomorrow's language resources. In *Proceedings of the Third International Conference on Language Resources and Evaluation (LREC-2002)*.

Zelikovitz, S. and H. Hirsh. 2001. Using LSI for text classification in the presence of background text. In *Proceedings of CIKM-01, 10th ACM International Conference on Information and Knowledge Management*. US.

An Improved Hierarchical Bayesian Model of Language for Document Classification

Ben Allison
Department of Computer Science
University of Sheffield
UK
ben@dcs.shef.ac.uk

Abstract

This paper addresses the fundamental problem of document classification, and we focus attention on classification problems where the classes are mutually exclusive. In the course of the paper we advocate an approximate sampling distribution for word counts in documents, and demonstrate the model's capacity to outperform both the simple multinomial and more recently proposed extensions on the classification task. We also compare the classifiers to a linear SVM, and show that provided certain conditions are met, the new model allows performance which exceeds that of the SVM and attains amongst the very best published results on the Newsgroups classification task.

1 Introduction

Document classification is one of the key technologies in the emerging digital world: as the amount of textual information existing in electronic form increases exponentially, reliable automatic methods to sift through the haystack and pluck out the occasional needle are almost a necessity.

Previous comparative studies of different classifiers (for example, (Yang and Liu, 1999; Joachims, 1998; Rennie et al., 2003; Dumais et al., 1998)) have consistently shown linear Support Vector Machines to be the most appropriate method. *Generative* probabilistic classifiers, often represented by the multinomial classifier, have in these same studies performed poorly, and this empirical evidence has been bolstered by theoretical arguments (Lasserre et al., 2006).

In this paper we revisit the theme of generative classifiers for mutually exclusive classification problems, but consider classifiers employing more complex models of language; as a starting point we consider recent work (Madsen et al., 2005) which relaxes some of the multinomial assumptions. We continue and expand upon the theme of that work, but identify some weaknesses both in its theoretical motivations and practical applications. We demonstrate a new approximate model which overcomes some of these concerns, and demonstrate substantial improvements that such a model achieves on four classification tasks, three of which are standard and one of which is a newly created task. We also show the new model to be highly competitive to an SVM where the previous models are not.

§2 of the paper describes previous work which has sought a probabilistic model of language and its application to document classification. §3 describes the models we consider in this paper, and gives details of parameter estimation. §4 describes our evaluation of the models, and §5 presents the results of this evaluation. §6 explores reasons for the observed results, and finally §7 ends with some concluding remarks.

2 Related Work

The problem of finding an appropriate and tractable model for language is one which has been studied in many different areas. In many cases, the first (and often only) model is one in which counts of words are modelled as binomial– or Poisson–distributed random variables. However, the use of such distributions entails an implicit assumption

© 2008. Licensed under the *Creative Commons Attribution-Noncommercial-Share Alike 3.0 Unported* license (http://creativecommons.org/licenses/by-nc-sa/3.0/). Some rights reserved.

that the occurrence of words is the result of a fixed number of independent trials—draws from a "bag of words"—where on each trial the probability of success is constant.

Several authors, among them (Church and Gale, 1995; Katz, 1996), observe empirically such models are not always accurate predictors of actual word behaviour. This moves them to suggest distributions for word counts where the underlying probability varies between documents; thus the expected behaviour of a word in a new document is a combination of predictions for all possible probabilities. Other authors (Jansche, 2003; Eyheramendy et al., 2003; Lowe, 1999) use these same ideas to classify documents on the basis of subsets of vocabulary, in the first and third cases with encouraging results using small subsets (in the second case, the performance of the model is shown to be poor compared to the multinomial).

When one moves to consider counts of all words in some vocabulary, the proper distribution of the whole vector of word counts is multinomial. (Madsen et al., 2005) apply the same idea as for the single word (binomial) case to the multinomial, using the most convenient form of distribution to represent the way the vector of multinomial probabilities varies between documents, and report encouraging results compared to the simple multinomial. However, we show that the use of the most mathematically convenient distribution to describe the way the vector of probabilities varies entails some unwarranted and undesirable assumptions. This paper will first describe those assumptions, and then describe an approximate technique for overcoming the assumptions. We show that, combined with some alterations to estimation, the models lead to a classifier able to outperform both the multinomial classifier and a linear SVM.

3 Probabilistic Models of Language for Document Classification

In this section, we briefly describe the use of a generative model of language as applied to the problem of document classification, and also how we estimate all relevant parameters for the work which follows.

In terms of notation, we use $\tilde{c}$ to represent a random variable and c to represent an outcome. We use roman letters for observed or observable quantities and greek letters for unobservables (i.e. parameters). We write $\tilde{c} \sim \varphi(c)$ to mean that $\tilde{c}$ has probability density (discrete or continuous) $\varphi(c)$, and write $p(c)$ as shorthand for $p(\tilde{c} = c)$. Finally, we make no explicit distinction in notation between univariate and multivariate quantities; however, we use θ_j to refer to the j-th component of the vector θ.

We consider documents to be represented as vectors of count–valued random variables such that $d = \{d_1 ... d_v\}$. For classification, interest centres on the conditional distribution of the class variable, given such a document. Where documents are to be assigned to one class only (as in the case of this paper), this class is judged to be the most probable class. For generative classifiers such as those considered here, the posterior distribution of interest is modelled from the joint distribution of class and document; thus if $\tilde{c}$ is a variable representing class and $\tilde{d}$ is a vector of word counts, then:

$$p(c|d) \propto p(c) \cdot p(d|c) \qquad (1)$$

For the purposes of this work we also assume a uniform prior on $\tilde{c}$, meaning the ultimate decision is on the basis of the document alone.

Multinomial Sampling Model

A natural way to model the distribution of counts is to let $p(d|c)$ be distributed multinomially, as proposed in (Guthrie et al., 1994; McCallum and Nigam, 1998) amongst others. The multinomial model assumes that documents are the result of repeated trials, where on each trial a word is selected at random, and the probability of selecting the j-th word from class c is θ_{cj}. However, in general we will not use the subscript c – we estimate one set of parameters for each possible class.

Using multinomial sampling, the term $p(d|c)$ has distribution:

$$p_{multinomial}(d|\theta) = \frac{\left(\sum_j d_j\right)!}{\prod_j (d_j!)} \prod_j \theta_j^{d_j} \qquad (2)$$

A simple Bayes estimator for θ can be obtained by taking the prior for θ as a Dirichlet distribution, in which case the posterior is also Dirichlet. Denote the total training data for the class in question as $\mathcal{D} = \{(d_{11} ... d_{1v}) ... (d_{k1} ... d_{kv})\}$ (that is, counts of each of v words in k documents). Then if $p(\theta) \sim Dirichlet(\alpha_1 ... \alpha_v)$, the mean of $p(\theta|\mathcal{D})$ for the j-th component of θ (which is the estimate we use) is:

$$\hat{\theta}_j = \mathrm{E}[\theta_j|\mathcal{D}] = \frac{\alpha_j + n_j}{\sum_j \alpha_j + n_\bullet} \quad (3)$$

where the n_j are the sufficient statistics $\sum_i n_{ij}$, and $n_\bullet$ is $\sum_j n_j$. We follow common practice and use the standard reference Dirichlet prior, which is uniform on θ, such that $\alpha_j = 1$ for all j.

3.1 Hierarchical Sampling Models

In contrast to the model above, a hierarchical sampling model assumes that $\tilde{\theta}$ varies between documents, and has distribution which depends upon parameters η. This allows for a more realistic model, letting the probabilities of using words vary between documents subject only to some general trend.

For example, consider documents about politics: some will discuss the current British Prime Minister, Gordon Brown. In these documents, the probability of using the word *brown* (assuming case normalisation) may be relatively high. Other politics articles may discuss US politics, for example, or the UN, French elections, and so on, and these articles may have a much lower probability of using the word *brown*: perhaps just the occasional reference to the Prime Minister. A hierarchical model attempts to model the way this probability varies between documents in the politics class.

Starting with the joint distribution $p(\theta, d|\eta)$ and averaging over all possible values that θ may take in the new document gives:

$$p(d|\eta) = \int p(\theta|\eta)p(d|\theta)\, d\theta \quad (4)$$

where integration is understood to be over the entire range of possible θ. Intuitively, this allows $\tilde{\theta}$ to vary between documents subject to the restriction that $\tilde{\theta} \sim p(\theta|\eta)$, and the probability of observing a document is the average of its probability for all possible θ, weighted by $p(\theta|\eta)$. The sampling process is 1) θ is first sampled from $p(\theta|\eta)$ and then 2) d is sampled from $p(d|\theta)$, leading to the hierarchical name for such models.

Dirichlet Compound Multinomial Sampling Model

(Madsen et al., 2005) suggest a form of (4) where $p(\theta|\eta)$ is Dirichlet-distributed, leading to a *Dirichlet–Compound–Multinomial* sampling distribution. The main benefit of this assumption is that the integral of (4) can be obtained in closed form. Thus $p(d|\alpha)$ (using the standard α notation for Dirichlet parameters) has distribution:

$$p_{DCM}(d|\alpha) = \frac{\left(\sum_j d_j\right)!}{\prod_j (d_j!)} \times \frac{\Gamma\left(\sum_j \alpha_j\right)}{\Gamma\left(\sum_j d_j + \alpha_j\right)} \times \prod_j \frac{\Gamma(\alpha_j + d_j)}{\Gamma(\alpha_j)} \quad (5)$$

Maximum likelihood estimates for the α are difficult to obtain, since the likelihood for α is a function which must be maximised for all components simultaneously, leading some authors to use approximate distributions to improve the tractability of maximum likelihood estimation (Elkan, 2006). In contrast, we reparameterise the Dirichlet compound multinomial, and estimate some of the parameters in closed form.

We reparameterise the model in terms of μ and λ – μ is a vector of length v, and λ is a constant which reflects the variance of θ. Under this parametrisation, $\alpha_j = \lambda\mu_j$. The estimate we use for μ_j is simply:

$$\hat{\mu_j} = \frac{n_j}{n_\bullet} \quad (6)$$

where n_j and $n_\bullet$ are defined above. This simply matches the first moment about the mean of the distribution with the first moment about the mean of the sample. Once again letting:

$$\mathcal{D} = \{d_1 ... d_k\} = \{(d_{11} ... d_{1v}) ... (d_{k1} ... d_{kv})\}$$

denote the training data such that the d_i are individual document vectors and d_{ij} are counts of the j-th word in the i-th document, the likelihood for λ is:

$$\mathcal{L}(\lambda) = \prod_i \frac{\Gamma(\sum_j \lambda\mu_j)}{\Gamma(\sum_j d_{ij} + \lambda\mu_j)} \prod_j \frac{\Gamma(\lambda\mu_j + d_{ij})}{\Gamma(\lambda\mu_j)} \quad (7)$$

This is a one–dimensional function, and as such is much more simple to maximise using standard optimisation techniques, for example as in (Minka, 2000).

As before, however, simple maximum likelihood estimates alone are not sufficient: if a word fails to appear at all in $\mathcal{D}$, the corresponding μ_j will be zero, in which case the distribution is improper. The theoretically sound solution would be to incorporate a prior on either α or (under our parameterisation) μ; however, this would lead to high computational cost as the resulting posterior would be complicated to work with. (Madsen et al., 2005) instead set each $\hat{\alpha_j}$ as the maximum likelihood estimate plus some ϵ, in some ways echoing the estimation of θ for the multinomial model. Unfortunately, unlike a prior this strategy has the same effect regardless of the amount of training data available, whereas any true prior would have diminishing effect as the amount of training data increased. Instead, we supplement actual training data with a pseudo–document in which every word occurs once (note this is quite different to setting $\epsilon = 1$); this echoes the effect of a true prior on μ, but without the computational burden.

A Joint Beta-Binomial Sampling Model

Despite its apparent convenience and theoretical well–foundedness, the Dirichlet compound multinomial model has one serious drawback, which is emphasised by the reparameterisation. Under the Dirichlet, there is a functional dependence between the expected value of θ_j, μ_j and its variance, where the relationship is regulated by the constant λ. Thus two words whose μ_j are the same will also have the same variance in the θ_j. This is of concern since different words have different patterns of use – to use a popular turn of phrase, some words are more "bursty" than others (see (Church and Gale, 1995) for examples). In practice, we may hope to model different words as having the same expected value, but drastically different variances – unfortunately, this is not possible using the Dirichlet model.

The difficulty with switching to a different model is the evaluation of the integral in (4). The integral is in fact in many thousands of dimensions, and even if it were possible to evaluate such an integral numerically, the process would be exceptionally slow.

We overcome this problem by decomposing the term $p(d|\eta)$ into a product of independent terms of the form $p(d_j|\eta_j)$. A natural way for each of these terms to be distributed is to let the probability $p(d_j|\theta_j)$ be binomial and to let $p(\theta_j|\eta_j)$ be beta–distributed. The probability $p(d_j|\eta_j)$ (where $\eta_j = \{\alpha_j, \beta_j\}$, the parameters of the beta distribution) is then:

$$p_{bb}(d_j|\alpha_j, \beta_j) = \binom{n}{d_j} \frac{\mathrm{B}(d_j + \alpha_j, n - d_j + \beta_j)}{\mathrm{B}(\alpha_j, \beta_j)} \tag{8}$$

where $\mathrm{B}(\bullet)$ is the Beta function. The term $p(d|\eta)$ is then simply:

$$p_{beta-binomial}(d|\eta) = \prod_j p(d_j|\eta_j) \tag{9}$$

This allows means and variances for each of the θ_j to be specified separately, but this comes at a price: while the Dirichlet ensures that $\sum_j \theta_j = 1$ for all possible θ, the model above does not. Thus the model is only an approximation to a true model where components of θ have independent means and variances, and the requirements of the multinomial are fulfilled. However, given the inflexibility of the Dirichlet multinomial model, we argue that such a sacrifice is justified.

In order to estimate parameters of the Beta–Binomial model, we take a slight departure from both (Lowe, 1999) and (Jansche, 2003) who have both used a similar model previously for individual words. (Lowe, 1999) uses numerical techniques to find maximum likelihood estimates of the α_j and β_j, which was feasible in that case because of the highly restricted vocabulary and two-classes. (Jansche, 2003) argues exactly this point, and uses moment–matched estimates; our estimation is similar to that, in that we use moment–matching, but different in other regards.

Conventional parameter estimates are affected (in some way or other) by the likelihood function for a parameter, and the likelihood function is such that longer documents exert a greater influence on the overall likelihood for a parameter. That is, we note that if the true binomial parameter θ_{ij} for the j-th word in the i-th document were known, then the most sensible expected value for the distribution over θ_j would be:

$$\mathrm{E}[\theta_j] = \frac{1}{k} \times \sum_{i=1}^{k} \theta_{ij} \tag{10}$$

Whereas the expected value of conventional method–of–moments estimate is:

$$\mathrm{E}[\theta_j] = \sum_{i=1}^{k} p(\theta_{ij}) \times \hat{\theta_{ij}} \tag{11}$$

That is, a weighted mean of the maximum likelihood estimates of each of the θ_{ij}, with weights given by $p(\theta_{ij})$, i.e. the length of the i-th document. Similar effects would be observed by maximising the likelihood function numerically. This is to our minds undesireable, since we do note believe that longer documents are necessarily more representative of the population of all documents than are shorter ones (indeed, extremely long documents are likeliy to be an oddity), and in any case the goal is to capture variation in the parameters.

This leads us to suggest estimates for parameters such that the expected value of the distribution is as in 10 but with the θ_{ij} (which are unknown) replaced with their maximum likelihood estimates, $\hat{\theta}_{ij}$. We then use these estimates to specify the desired variance, leading to the simultaneous equations:

$$\frac{\alpha_j}{\alpha_j + \beta_j} = \frac{\sum_i \hat{\theta}_{ij}}{k} \tag{12}$$

$$\frac{\alpha_j \beta_j}{(\alpha_j + \beta_j)^2(\alpha_j + \beta_j + 1)} = \frac{\sum_i (\hat{\theta}_{ij} - \mathrm{E}[\theta_j])^2}{k} \tag{13}$$

As before, we supplement actual training documents with a pseudo-document in which every word occurs once to prevent any α_j being zero.

4 Evaluating the Models

This section describes evaluation of the models above on four text classification problems.

The Newsgroups task is to classify postings into one of twenty categories, and uses data originally collected in (Lang, 1995). The task involves a relatively large number of documents (approximately 20,000) with roughly even distribution of messages, giving a very low baseline of approximately 5%.

For the second task, we use a task derived from the Enron mail corpus (Klimt and Yang, 2004), described in (Allison and Guthrie, 2008). Corpus is a nine–way email authorship attribution problem, with 4071 emails (between 174 and 706 emails per author)[1]. The mean length of messages in the corpus is 75 words.

WebKB is a web–page classification task, where the goal is to determine the webpage type of the unseen document. We follow the setup of (McCallum and Nigam, 1998) and many thereafter, and use the four biggest categories, namely `student`, `faculty`, `course` and `project`. The resulting corpus consists of approximately 4,200 webpages.

The SpamAssassin corpus is made available for public use as part of the open-source Apache SpamAssassin Project[2]. It consists of email divided into three categories: `Easy Ham`, which is email unambiguously ham (i.e. not spam), `Hard Ham` which is not spam but shares many traits with spam, and finally `Spam`. The task is to apply these labels to unseen emails. We use the latest version of all datasets, and combine the easy_ham and easy_ham_2 as well as spam and spam_2 sets to form a corpus of just over 6,000 messages.

In all cases, we use 10–fold cross validation to make maximal use of the data, where folds are chosen by random assignment. We define "words" to be contiguous whitespace–delimited alpha–numeric strings, and perform no stemming or stoplisting.

For the purposes of comparison, we also present results using a linear SVM (Joachims, 1999), which we convert to multi–class problems using a one–versus–all strategy shown to be amongst the best performing strategies (Rennie and Rifkin, 2001). We normalise documents to be vectors of unit length, and resolve decision ambiguities by sole means of distance to the hyperplane. We also note that experimentation with non–linear kernels showed no consistent trends, and made very little difference to performance.

5 Results

Table 1 displays results for the three models over the four datasets. We use the simplest measure of classifier performance, accuracy, which is simply the total number of correct decisions over the ten folds, divided by the size of the corpus. In response to a growing unease over the use of significance tests (because they have a tendency to overstate significance, as well as obscure effects of sample size) we provide 95% intervals for accuracy as well as the metric itself. To calculate these, we view accuracy as an (unknown) parameter to a binomial distribution such that the number of correctly classified documents is a binomially distributed random variable. We then calculate the Bayesian interval for the parameter, as described in (Brown et al., 2001), which allows immediate quantification

[1] The corpus is available for download from www.dcs.shef.ac.uk/~ben.

[2] The corpus is available online at http://spamassassin.apache.org/publiccorpus/

of uncertainty in the true accuracy after a limited sample.

As can be seen from the performance figures, no one classifier is totally dominant, although there are obvious and substantial gains in using the Beta-Binomial model on the Newsgroups and Enron tasks when compared to all other models. The SpamAssassin corpus shows the beta–binomial model and the SVM to be considerably better than the other two models, but there is little to choose between them. The WebKB task, however, shows extremely unusual results: the SVM is head and shoulders above other methods, and of the generative approaches the multinomial is clearly superior. In all cases, the Dirichlet model actually performs worse than the multinomial model, in contrast to the observations of (Madsen et al., 2005).

In terms of comparison with other work, we note that the performance of our multinomial model agrees with that in other work, including for example (Rennie et al., 2003; Eyheramendy et al., 2003; Madsen et al., 2005; Jansche, 2003). Our Dirichlet model performs worse than that in (Madsen et al., 2005) (85% here compared to 89% in that work), which we attribute to their experimentation with alternate smoothing ϵ as described in §3.1. We note however that the Beta-Binomial model here still outperforms that work by some considerable margin. Finally, we note that our beta–binomial model outperforms that in (Jansche, 2003), which we attribute mainly to the altered estimate, but also to the partial vocabulary used in that work. In fact, (Jansche, 2003) shows there to be little to separate the beta-binomial and multinomial models for larger vocabularies, in stark contrast to the work here, and this is doubtless due to the parameter estimation.

6 Analysis

One might expect performance of a hierarchical sampling model to eclipse that of the SVM because of the nature of the decision boundary, provided certain conditions are met: the SVM estimates a linear decision boundary, and the multinomial classifier does the same. However, the decision boundaries for the hierarchical classifiers are non–linear, and can represent more complex word behaviour, provided that sufficient data exist to predict it. However, unlike generic non–linear SVMs (which made little difference compared to a linear SVM) the non–linear decision boundary here arises naturally from a model of word behaviour.

For the hierarchical models, performance rests on the ability to estimate both the rate of word occurrence θ_j and also the way that this rate varies between documents. To reliably estimate variance (and arguably rate as well) would require words to occur a sufficient number of times. However, this section will demonstrate that two of the datasets have many words which do not occur with sufficient frequency to estimate parameters, and in those two the linear SVM's performance is more comparable.

We present two quantifications of word reuse to support our conclusions. The first are frequency spectra for each of the four corpora, shown in Figure 1. The two more problematic datasets appear in the top of the figure. To generate the charts, we pool all documents from all classes in a each problem, and count the number of words that appear once, twice, and so on. The x axis is the number of times a word occurs, and the y axis the total number of words which have that count.

The WebKB corpus has the large majority of words occurring very few times (the mass of the distribution is concentrated towards the left of the chart), while the SpamAssassin corpus is more reasonable and the Newsgroups corpus has by far the most words which occur with substantial frequency (this correlates perfectly with the relative performances of the classifiers on these datasets). For the Enron corpus, it is somewhat harder to tell, since its size means no words occur with substantial frequency.

We also consider the proportion of all word pairs in a corpus in which the first word is the same as the second word. If a corpus has $n_\bullet$ words total with total counts $n_1 ... n_v$ then the statistic is:

$$r = \frac{1}{(n_\bullet(n_\bullet - 1))/2} \sum_i (n_i(n_i - 1))/2. \quad (14)$$

To measure differing tendencies to reuse words, we calculate the r statistic once for each class, and then its mean across all classes in a problem (Table 2). We note that the two corpora on which the hierarchical model dominates have much greater tendency for word reuse, meaning the extra parameters can be esimated with greater accuracy. The SpamAssassin corpus is, by this measure, a harder task, but this is somewhat mitigated by the more even frequency distribution evidenced in Figure 1; on the other hand, the WebKB corpus does

	Newsgroups	Enron Authors	WebKB	SpamAssassin
Multinomial	85.66 ± 0.5	74.55 ± 1.34	85.69 ± 1.06	95.96 ± 0.5
DCM	85.03 ± 0.51	74.43 ± 1.34	82.69 ± 1.15	91.47 ± 0.7
Beta-Bin	**91.65** $\pm 0.4^{*+}$	**83.54** $\pm 1.14^{*+}$	84.81 ± 1.08	$97.35 \pm 0.4^{*}$
SVM	$88.8 \pm 0.45^{*}$	$80 \pm 1.23^{*}$	**92.68** $\pm 0.79^{*}$	**97.65** $\pm 0.38^{*}$

Table 1: Performance of four classifiers on four tasks. Error is 95% interval for accuracy. Bold denotes best performance on a task. * denotes performance superior to multinomial which exceeds posterior uncertainty (i.e. observed performance outside 95% interval). $^+$ denotes the same for the SVM

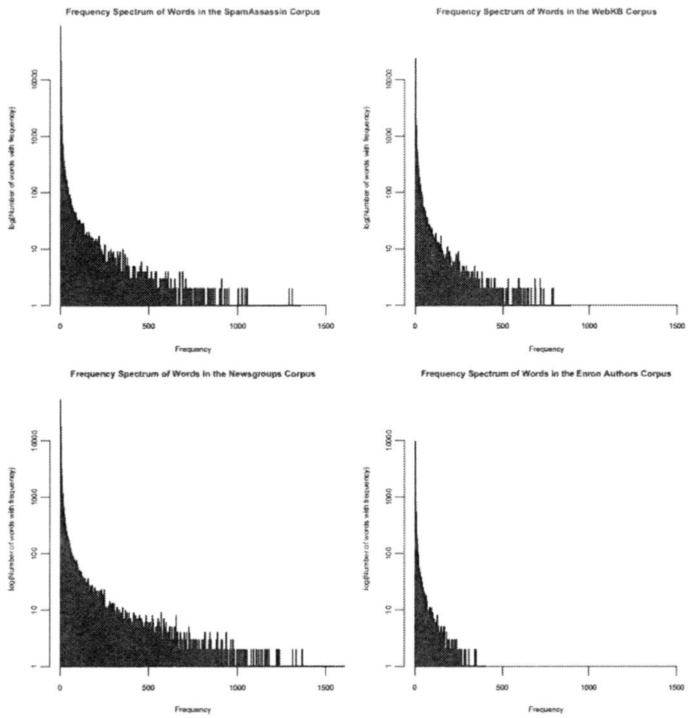

Figure 1: Frequency spectra for the four datasets. y axis is on a logarithmic scale

not look promising for the hierarchical model by either measure.

7 Conclusion

In this paper, we have advocated the use of a joint beta–binomial distribution for word counts in documents for the purposes of classification. We have shown that this model outperforms classifiers based upon both multinomial and Dirichlet Compound Multinomial distributions for word counts.

We have further made the case that, where corpora are sufficiently large as to warrant it, a generative classifier employing a hierarchical sampling model outperforms a discriminative linear SVM. We attribute this to the capacity of the proposed model to capture aspects of word behaviour beyond a simpler model. However, in cases where the data contain many infrequent words and the tendency to reuse words is relatively low, defaulting to a linear classifier (either the multinomial for a generative classifier, or preferably the linear SVM) increases performance relative to a more complex model, which cannot be fit with sufficient precision.

References

Allison, Ben and Louise Guthrie. 2008. Authorship attribution of e-mail: Comparing classifiers over a new corpus for evaluation. In *Proceedings of LREC'08.*

Brown, Lawrence D., Tony Cai, and Anirban DasGupta. 2001. Interval estimation for a binomial proportion. *Statistical Science*, 16(2):101–117, may.

	Newsgroups	Enron Authors	WebKB	SpamAssassin
Mean r	0.0090	0.0083	0.0047	0.0037

Table 2: Mean r statistic for the four problems

Church, K. and W. Gale. 1995. Poisson mixtures. *Natural Language Engineering*, 1(2):163–190.

Dumais, Susan, John Platt, David Heckerman, and Mehran Sahami. 1998. Inductive learning algorithms and representations for text categorization. In *CIKM '98*, pages 148–155.

Elkan, Charles. 2006. Clustering documents with an exponential-family approximation of the dirichlet compound multinomial distribution. In *Proceedings of the Twenty-Third International Conference on Machine Learning*.

Eyheramendy, S., D. Lewis, and D. Madigan. 2003. The naive bayes model for text categorization. *Artificial Intelligence and Statistics*.

Guthrie, Louise, Elbert Walker, and Joe Guthrie. 1994. Document classification by machine: theory and practice. In *Proceedings COLING '94*, pages 1059–1063.

Jansche, Martin. 2003. Parametric models of linguistic count data. In *ACL '03*, pages 288–295.

Joachims, Thorsten. 1998. Text categorization with support vector machines: learning with many relevant features. In Nédellec, Claire and Céline Rouveirol, editors, *Proceedings of ECML-98, 10th European Conference on Machine Learning*, pages 137–142.

Joachims, Thorsten. 1999. Making large-scale svm learning practical. *Advances in Kernel Methods - Support Vector Learning*.

Katz, Slava M. 1996. Distribution of content words and phrases in text and language modelling. *Nat. Lang. Eng.*, 2(1):15–59.

Klimt, Bryan and Yiming Yang. 2004. The enron corpus: A new dataset for email classification research. In *Proceedings of ECML 2004*, pages 217–226.

Lang, Ken. 1995. NewsWeeder: learning to filter netnews. In *Proceedings of the 12th International Conference on Machine Learning*, pages 331–339.

Lasserre, Julia A., Christopher M. Bishop, and Thomas P. Minka. 2006. Principled hybrids of generative and discriminative models. In *CVPR '06: Proceedings of the 2006 IEEE Computer Society Conference on Computer Vision and Pattern Recognition*, pages 87–94.

Lowe, S. 1999. The beta-binomial mixture model and its application to tdt tracking and detection. In *Proceedings of the DARPA Broadcast News Workshop*.

Madsen, Rasmus E., David Kauchak, and Charles Elkan. 2005. Modeling word burstiness using the Dirichlet distribution. In *ICML '05*, pages 545–552.

McCallum, A. and K. Nigam. 1998. A comparison of event models for naïve bayes text classification. In *Proceedings AAAI-98 Workshop on Learning for Text Categorization*.

Minka, Tom. 2000. Estimating a dirichlet distribution. Technical report, Microsoft Research.

Rennie, Jason D. M. and Ryan Rifkin. 2001. Improving multiclass text classification with the Support Vector Machine. Technical report, Massachusetts Insititute of Technology, Artificial Intelligence Laboratory.

Rennie, J., L. Shih, J. Teevan, and D. Karger. 2003. Tackling the poor assumptions of naive bayes text classifiers.

Yang, Y. and X. Liu. 1999. A re-examination of text categorization methods. In *22nd Annual International SIGIR*, pages 42–49, Berkley, August.

Improving Alignments for Better Confusion Networks for Combining Machine Translation Systems

Necip Fazil Ayan and **Jing Zheng** and **Wen Wang**
SRI International
Speech Technology and Research Laboratory (STAR)
333 Ravenswood Avenue
Menlo Park, CA 94025
{nfa,zj,wwang}@speech.sri.com

Abstract

The state-of-the-art system combination method for machine translation (MT) is the word-based combination using confusion networks. One of the crucial steps in confusion network decoding is the alignment of different hypotheses to each other when building a network. In this paper, we present new methods to improve alignment of hypotheses using word synonyms and a two-pass alignment strategy. We demonstrate that combination with the new alignment technique yields up to 2.9 BLEU point improvement over the best input system and up to 1.3 BLEU point improvement over a state-of-the-art combination method on two different language pairs.

1 Introduction

Combining outputs of multiple systems performing the same task has been widely explored in various fields such as speech recognition, word sense disambiguation, and word alignments, and it had been shown that the combination approaches yielded significantly better outputs than the individual systems. System combination has also been explored in the MT field, especially with the emergence of various structurally different MT systems. Various techniques include hypothesis selection from different systems using sentence-level scores, re-decoding source sentences using phrases that are used by individual systems (Rosti et al., 2007a; Huang and Papineni, 2007) and word-based combination techniques using confusion networks (Matusov et al., 2006; Sim et al., 2007; Rosti et al., 2007b). Among these, confusion network decoding of the system outputs has been shown to be more effective than the others in terms of the overall translation quality.

One of the crucial steps in confusion network decoding is the alignment of hypotheses to each other because the same meaning can be expressed with synonymous words and/or with a different word ordering in different hypotheses. Unfortunately, all the alignment algorithms used in confusion network decoding are insensitive to synonyms of words when aligning two hypotheses to each other. This paper extends the previous alignment approaches to handle word synonyms more effectively to improve alignment of different hypotheses. We also present a two-pass alignment strategy for a better alignment of hypotheses with similar words but with a different word ordering.

We evaluate our system combination approach using variants of an in-house hierarchical MT system as input systems on two different language pairs: Arabic-English and Chinese-English. Even with very similar MT systems as inputs, we show that the improved alignments yield up to an absolute 2.9 BLEU point improvement over the best input system and up to an absolute 1.3 BLEU point improvement over the old alignments in a confusion-network-based combination.

The rest of this paper is organized as follows. Section 2 presents an overview of previous system combination techniques for MT. Section 3 discusses the confusion-network-based system combination. In Section 4, we present the new hypothesis alignment techniques. Finally, Section 5 presents our experiments and results on two language pairs.

© 2008. Licensed under the *Creative Commons Attribution-Noncommercial-Share Alike 3.0 Unported* license (http://creativecommons.org/licenses/by-nc-sa/3.0/). Some rights reserved.

2 Related Work

System combination for machine translation can be done at three levels: Sentence-level, phrase-level or word-level.

Sentence-level combination is done by choosing one hypothesis among multiple MT system outputs (and possibly among n-best lists). The selection criterion can be a combination of translation model and language model scores with multiple comparison tests (Akiba et al., 2002), or statistical confidence models (Nomoto, 2004).

Phrase-level combination systems assume that the input systems provide some internal information about the system, such as phrases used by the system, and the task is to re-decode the source sentence using this additional information. The first example of this approach was the multi-engine MT system (Frederking and Nirenburg, 1994), which builds a chart using the translation units inside each input system and then uses a chart walk algorithm to find the best cover of the source sentence. Rosti et al. (2007a) collect source-to-target correspondences from the input systems, create a new translation option table using only these phrases, and re-decode the source sentence to generate better translations. In a similar work, it has been demonstrated that pruning the original phrase table according to reliable MT hypotheses and enforcing the decoder to obey the word orderings in the original system outputs improves the performance of the phrase-based combination systems (Huang and Papineni, 2007). In the absence of source-to-target phrase alignments, the sentences can be split into simple chunks using a recursive decomposition as input to MT systems (Mellebeek et al., 2006). With this approach, the final output is a combination of the best chunk translations that are selected by majority voting, system confidence scores and language model scores.

The word-level combination chooses the best translation units from different translations and combine them. The most popular method for word-based combination follows the idea behind the ROVER approach for combining speech recognition outputs (Fiscus, 1997). After reordering hypotheses and aligning to each other, the combination system builds a confusion network and chooses the path with the highest score. The following section describes confusion-network-based system combination in detail.

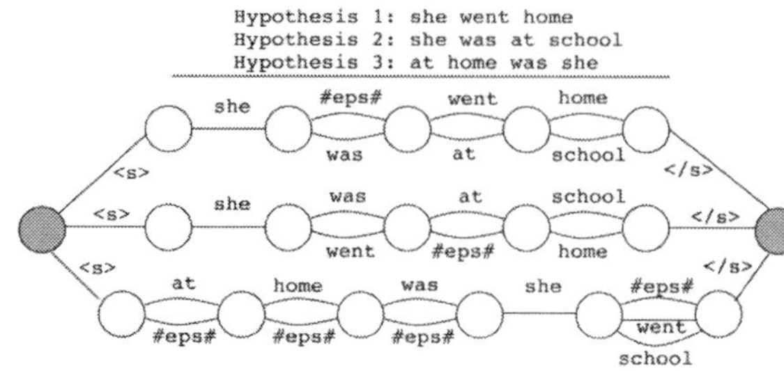

Figure 1: Alignment of three hypotheses to each other using different hypotheses as skeletons.

3 System Combination with Confusion Networks

The general architecture of a confusion-network-based system combination is as follows:

1. Extract n-best lists from MT systems.
2. Pick a skeleton translation for each segment.
3. Reorder all the other hypotheses by aligning them to the skeleton translation.
4. Build a confusion network from the reordered translations for each segment.
5. Decode the confusion network using various arc features and sentence-level scores such as LM score and word penalty.
6. Optimize feature weights on a held-out test set and re-decode.

In this framework, the success of confusion network decoding for system combination depends on two important choices: Selection of the skeleton hypothesis and alignment of other hypotheses to the skeleton.

For selecting the best skeleton, two common methods are choosing the hypothesis with the Minimum Bayes Risk with translation error rate (TER) (Snover et al., 2006) (i.e., the hypothesis with the minimum TER score when it is used as the reference against the other hypotheses) (Sim et al., 2007) or choosing the best hypotheses from each system and using each of those as a skeleton in multiple confusion networks (Rosti et al., 2007b). In this paper, we use the latter since it performs slightly better than the first method in our experiments. An example confusion network on three translations is presented in Figure 1.[1]

The major difficulty when using confusion networks for system combination for MT is aligning different hypotheses to the skeleton since the word

[1] In this paper, we use multiple confusion networks that are attached to the same start and end node. Throughout the rest of the paper, the term *confusion network* refers to one network among multiple networks used for system combination.

order might be different in different hypotheses and it is hard to align words that are shifted from one hypothesis to another. Four popular methods to align hypotheses to each other are as follows:

1. Multiple string-matching algorithm based on Levenshtein edit distance (Bangalore et al., 2001)
2. A heuristic-based matching algorithm (Jayaraman and Lavie, 2005)
3. Using GIZA++ (Och and Ney, 2000) with possibly additional training data (Matusov et al., 2006)
4. Using TER (Snover et al., 2006) between the skeleton and a given hypothesis (Sim et al., 2007; Rosti et al., 2007b)

None of these methods takes word synonyms into account during alignment of hypotheses.[2] In this work, we extend the TER-based alignment to use word stems and synonyms using the publicly available WordNet resource (Fellbaum, 1998) when aligning hypotheses to each other and show that this additional information improves the alignment and the overall translation significantly.

4 Confusion Networks with Word Synonyms and Two-pass Alignment

When building a confusion network, the goal is to put the same words on the same arcs as much as possible. Matching similar words between two hypotheses is necessary to achieve this goal.

When we align two different hypotheses using TER, it is necessary that two words have the identical spelling to be considered a match. However, in natural languages, it is possible to represent the same meaning using synonyms of words in possibly different positions. For example, in the following sentences, "*at the same time*" and "*in the meantime*", "*waiting for*" and "*expect*", and "*set*" and "*established*" correspond to each other, respectively:

Skeleton: `at the same time expect israel to abide by the deadlines set by .`

Hypothesis: `in the meantime , we are waiting for israel to abide by the established deadlines .`

Using TER, synonymous words might be aligned to each other if they appear in the same position in two hypotheses but this is less likely when two words appear in different positions. Without knowing that two words are synonyms of each other, they are considered two separate words during TER alignment.

Our goal is to create equivalence classes for each word in the given translations and modify the alignment algorithm to give priority to the matching of words that are in the same equivalence class. In this paper, the equivalence classes are generated using WordNet by extracting synonyms of each word in the translations.

To incorporate matching of word synonyms into the alignment, we followed three steps:

1. Use WordNet to extract synonyms of the words that appear in all hypotheses.
2. Augment each skeleton word with all synonymous words that appear in all the hypotheses.
3. Modify TER script to handle words with alternatives using an additional *synonym matching* operation.

In the following subsections, we describe how each of these tasks is performed.

4.1 Extracting Synonyms from WordNet

The first step is to use WordNet to extract synonyms of each word that appears in all hypotheses. This is simply done using the publicly available WordNet processing tools to extract all synonyms of the given word. To allow matching words that have the same stem or variations of the same word with different part-of-the-speech (POS) tags, we extract all synonyms of the given word regardless of their POS tag in the given translation.[3]

In the example above, it is clear that the verbs *wait* and *expect* have the same meaning but TER is unable to align these two words to each other because of different word positions. Using WordNet, we get the following two entries for the words *waiting* and *expect*, indicating that two words can be considered as synonyms of each other:

`expect`: Sense 1: *expect, anticipate* ⇒ *evaluate, pass judgment, judge*. Sense 2: *ask, require, expect* ⇒ *demand.* Sense 3: *expect, look, await,* **wait**. Sense 4: *expect* ⇒ *see, consider, reckon,*

[2] Note that the approach by Matusov et al. (2006) attempts to align synonyms and different morphological forms of words to each other but this is done implicitly, relying on the parallel text to learn word alignments.

[3] Our goal is to add as many synonyms as possible to increase the chances of a word aligning to one of its possible synonyms rather than to any other word. Therefore, we do not distinguish between the synonyms of the same word according to their confidence value or their POS tag.

```
ONE-PASS ALIGNMENT
khaddam                                     receives                  italian         house speaker
khaddam                                     receives the head of the italian chamber of    deputies
khaddam will meet with the president of the                           italian chamber of    deputies

TWO-PASS ALIGNMENT
khaddam      receives                                italian  house          speaker
khaddam      receives                  of the head italian  chamber  of the deputies
khaddam will meet      with   president of the       italian  chamber  of the deputies
```

Figure 2: Example alignment of three hypotheses with one-pass and two-pass alignment

view, regard. Sense 5: *expect* ⇒ *expect, look, await,* **wait**. Sense 6: *have a bun in the oven, bear, carry, gestate, expect* ⇒ *give birth, deliver, bear, birth, have.*

`waiting`: Sense 1: *wait.* Sense 2: *wait, hold off, hold back* ⇒ *act, move.* Sense 3: *wait,* **expect**, *look, await.* Sense 4: *wait, waitress* ⇒ *work.*

We should note that WordNet contains only *open-class words*, i.e., nouns, verbs, adjectives, and adverbs. There are no entries for determiners, prepositions, pronouns, conjunctions, and particles. For better matching of these additional POS tags, we manually created a different equivalence class for each POS tag that is not included in the WordNet so that words with the same POS tag can be considered synonymous.

4.2 Augmenting References

After extracting the synonyms of each word in the given translations, the next step is to augment each reference word with its synonyms. To avoid overgeneration of synonyms, we make the assumption that words w_i and w_j are synonyms of each other only if w_i appears in the synonym list of w_j, and w_j appears in the synonym list of w_i. To make the alignment task more efficient and faster, we restrict the synonym list to only words that appear in the given translations. In our running example, the augmented (extended) skeleton according to the second hypothesis is as follows:

Extended skeleton: `at the same time_`*`meantime`* `expect_`*`waiting`* `israel to abide by the deadlines set_`*`established`* `by .`

4.3 Modifications to TER Script

The final step is to modify TER script to favor matching of a word to its synonyms rather than to any other word. To achieve this goal, we modified the publicly available TER script, TERCOM (Snover et al., 2006), to match words in the same equivalence class at an additional *synonym cost*. In its original implementation, TERCOM builds a hash table for the n-grams that appear in both the reference and the hypothesis translation to determine possible shifts of words. To allow synonymous words to be shifted and aligned to each other, we extend the hash table for all possible synonyms of words in the skeleton. Formally, if the skeleton includes two consecutive words $w_i\_s_i$ and $w_j\_s_j$, where s_i (s_j) is a synonym of w_i (w_j), we put all four possible combinations to the hash table: w_iw_j, w_is_j, s_iw_j, and s_is_j.[4]

To give higher priority to the exact matching of words (which has zero cost during edit distance computation), we used a slightly higher cost for synonym matching, a cost of 0.1.[5] All the other operations (i.e., insertion, deletion, substitution and shifting of words) have a cost of 1.0.

4.4 Two-pass Alignment Strategy

When building a confusion network, the usual strategy is first to align each hypothesis to the skeleton separately and reorder them so that the word ordering in the given hypothesis matches the word ordering in the skeleton translation. Next a confusion network is built between all these reordered hypotheses.

One of the major problems with this process occurs when the hypotheses include additional words that do not appear in the skeleton translation, as depicted in Figure 2. Since the alignments of two different hypotheses are done independently, two hypotheses other than the skeleton may not align perfectly, especially when the additional words appear in different positions.

To overcome this issue, we employ a two-pass alignment strategy. In the first pass, we align all hypotheses to the skeleton independently and build a confusion network. Next an intermediate reference sentence is created from the confusion network generated in the first pass. To create this intermediate reference, we find the best position for each word that appears in the confusion network

[4] Note that the hash table is built in an iterative fashion. We consider adding a new n-gram only if the previous $n-1$ words appear in the hypothesis as well.

[5] Synonym matching cost was determined empirically, trying different costs from 0 to 0.5.

```
WITHOUT SYNONYM MATCHING and ONE-PASS ALIGNMENT:
at the          same time                              expect israel to abide  by
at the          same time    we                        expect israel to abide  by
at the          same time    ,   we      are waiting   for    israel to abide  by
at the          same time    we                        expect israel to abide  by
at the          same time    ,   we                    expect israel to abide  by
at the          same time    ,   waiting               for    israel to comply with
in the meantime ,     waiting                          for    israel to abide  by

WITH SYNONYM MATCHING and TWO-PASS ALIGNMENT:
at the same  time            expect       israel to abide  by
at the same  time       we   expect       israel to abide  by
at the same  time     , we   are waiting for israel to abide  by
at the same  time       we   expect       israel to abide  by
at the same  time     , we   expect       israel to abide  by
at the same  time     ,      waiting for  israel to comply with
in the       meantime ,      waiting for  israel to abide  by
```

Figure 3: Example alignment via confusion networks with and without synonym matching and two-pass alignment (using the first sentence as the skeleton)

using majority voting. The second pass uses this intermediate reference as the skeleton translation to generate the final confusion network.

When we create the intermediate reference, the number of positions for a given word is bounded by the maximum number of occurrences of the same word in any hypothesis. It is possible that two different words are mapped to the same position in the intermediate reference. If this is the case, these words are treated as synonyms when building the second confusion network, and the intermediate reference looks like the extended reference in Section 4.2.

Finally, Figure 3 presents our running example with the old alignments versus the alignments with synonym matching and two-pass alignment.

4.5 Features

Each word in the confusion network is represented by system-specific word scores. For computing scores, each hypothesis is assigned a score based on three different methods:

1. **Uniform weighting**: Each hypothesis in the n-best list has the same score of $1/n$.
2. **Rank-based weighting**: Each hypothesis is assigned a score of $1/(1+r)$, where r is the rank of the hypothesis.
3. **TM-based weighting:** Each hypothesis is weighted by the score that is assigned to the hypothesis by the translation model.

The total score of an arc with word w for a given system S is the sum of all the scores of the hypotheses in system S that contain the word w in the given position. The score for a specific arc between nodes n_i and n_j is normalized by the sum of the scores for all the arcs between n_i and n_j.

Our experiments demonstrated that rank-based weighting performs the best among all three weighting methods although the differences are small. In the rest of the paper, we report only the results with rank-based weighting.

Besides the arc scores, we employ the following features during decoding:

1. Skeleton selection features for each system,
2. NULL-word (or epsilon) insertion score,
3. Word penalty, and
4. Language model score.

Skeleton selection feature is intended to help choose the best skeleton among the input systems. NULL-word feature controls the number of epsilon arcs used in the chosen translation during the decoding and word penalty feature controls the length of the translation. For language model scores, we used a 4-gram LM that we used to train the input systems.

5 Evaluation and Results

In this section, we describe how we train the input systems and how we evaluate the proposed system combination method.

5.1 Systems and Data

To evaluate the impact of the new alignments, we tested our system combination approach using the old alignments and improved alignments on two language pairs: Arabic-English and Chinese-English. We ran the system combination on three system outputs that were generated by an in-house hierarchical phrase-based decoder, as in (Chiang, 2007). The major difference between the three systems is that they were trained on different subsets of the available training data using different word alignments.

For generating the system outputs, first a hierarchical phrase-based decoder was used to gener-

Data for Training/Tuning/Testing	Arabic-English		Chinese-English	
	# of segments	# of tokens	# of segments	# of tokens
Training Data (System1)	14.8M	170M	9.1M	207M
Training Data (System2)	618K	8.1M	13.4M	199M
Training Data (System3)	2.4M	27.5M	13.9M	208M
Tuning Set (Input Systems)	1800	51K	1800	51K
Tuning Set (System Combination)	1259	37K	1785	55K
Test Set - NIST MTEval'05	1056	32K	1082	32K
Test Set - NIST MTEval'06	1797	45K	1664	41K
Test Set - NIST MTEval'08	1360	43K	1357	34K

Table 1: Number of segments and source-side words in the training and test data.

ate three sets of unique 3000-best lists. Nine features were used in the hierarchical phrase-based systems under the log-linear model framework: a 4-gram language model (LM) score (trained on nearly 3.6 billion words using the SRILM toolkit (Stolcke, 2002)), conditional rule/phrase probabilities and lexical weights (in both directions), rule penalty, phrase penalty, and word penalty. Rules and phrases were extracted in a similar manner as described in (Chiang, 2007) from the training data with word alignments generated by GIZA++. The n-best lists were then re-scored with three additional LMs: a count-based LM built from the Google Tera word corpus, an almost parsing LM based on super-ARV tagging, and an approximated full-parser LM (Wang et al., 2007).

For Arabic-English, the first system was trained on all available training data (see Table 1 for details), with long sentences segmented into multiple segments based on IBM model 1 probabilities (Xu et al., 2005). The second system was trained on a small subset of the training data, which is mostly newswire. The third system was trained on an automatically extracted subset of the training data according to n-gram overlap in the test sets.

For Chinese-English, the first system used all the training data without any sentence segmentation. The second system used all training data after IBM-1 based sentence segmentation, with different weightings on different corpora. The third system is the same as the second system except that it used different word alignment symmetrization heuristics (grow-diag-final-and vs. grow-diag-final (Koehn et al., 2003)).

5.2 Empirical Results

All input systems were optimized on a randomly selected subset of the NIST MTEval'02, MTEval'03, and MTEval'04 test sets using minimum error rate training (MERT) (Och, 2003) to maximize BLEU score (Papineni et al., 2002). System combination was optimized on the rest of this data using MERT to maximize BLEU score. As inputs to the system combination, we used 10-best hypotheses from each of the re-ranked n-best lists. To optimize system combination, we generated unique 1000-best lists from a lattice we created from the input hypotheses, and used MERT in a similar way to MT system optimization.

System	MT'05	MT'06	MT'08
System 1	53.4	43.8	43.2
System 2	53.9	46.0	42.8
System 3	56.1	45.3	43.3
No Syns, 1-pass	56.7	47.5	44.9
w/Syns, 2-pass	57.9	48.4	46.2

Table 2: Lowercase BLEU scores (in percentages) on Arabic NIST MTEval test sets.

We evaluated system combination with improved alignments on three different NIST MTEval test sets (MTEval'05, MTEval'06 NIST portion, and MTEval'08). The final MT outputs were evaluated using lowercased BLEU scores.[6]

Tables 2 and 3 present the BLEU scores (in percentages) for the input systems and for different combination strategies on three test sets in Arabic-English and Chinese-English, respectively.

On Arabic-English, the combination with synonym matching and two-pass alignment yields absolute improvements of 1.8 to 2.9 BLEU point on three test sets over the best input system. When compared to the combination algorithm with the old alignments (i.e., 1-pass alignment with no synonym matching), the improved alignments yield an additional improvement of 0.9 to 1.3 BLEU point

[6]We used the NIST script (version 11b) for BLEU with its default settings: case-insensitive matching of up to 4-grams, and the shortest reference sentence for the brevity penalty.

System	MT'05	MT'06	MT'08
System 1	35.8	34.3	27.6
System 2	35.9	34.2	27.8
System 3	36.0	34.3	27.8
No Syns, 1-pass	38.1	36.5	27.9
w/Syns, 2-pass	38.6	37.0	28.3
No Syns, 1-pass, tuning set w/webtext			28.4
w/Syns, 2-pass, tuning set w/webtext			29.3

Table 3: Lowercase BLEU scores (in percentages) on Chinese NIST MTEval test sets.

on the three test sets.

For Chinese-English, the improvements over the previous combination algorithm are smaller. The new combination system yields up to an absolute 2.6 BLEU point improvement over the best input system and up to 0.5 BLEU point improvement over the previous combination algorithm on three different test sets. Note that for Arabic-English, the individual systems show a high variance in translation quality when compared to Chinese-English systems. This might explain why the improvements on Chinese-English are modest when compared to Arabic-English results.

We also noticed that system combination yielded much smaller improvement on Chinese MTEval'08 data when compared to other test sets, regardless of the alignment method (only 0.5 BLEU point over the best input system). We suspected that this might happen because of a mismatch between the genres of the test set and the tuning set (the amount of web text data in MTEval'08 test set is high although the tuning set does not include any web text data). To test this hypothesis, we created a new tuning set for system combination, which consists of 2000 randomly selected sentences from the previous MTEval test sets and includes web text data. Using this new tuning set, combination with the improved alignments yields a BLEU score of 29.3 on MTEval'08 data (an absolute improvement of 1.5 BLEU point over the best input system, and 0.9 BLEU point improvement over the combination with the old alignments). These new results again validate the usefulness of the improved alignments when the tuning set matches the genre of the test set.

5.3 A Comparison of the Impact of Synonym Matching and Two-pass Alignment

One last evaluation investigated the impact of each component on the overall improvement. For this purpose, we ran system combination by turning on and off each component. Table 4 presents the system combination results in terms of BLEU scores on Arabic-English test sets when each component is used on its own or when they are used together.

Synon.	2-pass	MT'05	MT'06	MT'08
No	No	56.7	47.5	44.9
Yes	No	57.3	47.8	45.2
No	Yes	57.7	48.0	45.9
Yes	Yes	57.9	48.4	46.2

Table 4: Comparison of Synonym Matching and Two-pass Alignment on Arabic-English

The results indicate that synonym matching on its own yields improvements of 0.3-0.6 BLEU points over not using synonym matching. Two-pass alignment turns out to be more useful than synonym matching, yielding an absolute improvement of up to 1 BLEU point over one-pass alignment.

6 Conclusions

We presented an extension to the previous alignment approaches to handle word synonyms more effectively in an attempt to improve the alignments between different hypotheses during confusion network decoding. We also presented a two-pass alignment strategy for a better alignment of hypotheses with similar words but with a different word ordering.

We evaluated our system combination approach on two language pairs: Arabic-English and Chinese-English. Combination with improved alignments yielded up to an absolute 2.9 BLEU point improvement over the best input system and up to an absolute 1.3 BLEU point improvement over combination with the old alignments. It is worth noting that these improvements are obtained using very similar input systems. We expect that the improvements will be higher when we use structurally different MT systems as inputs to the combiner.

Our future work includes a more effective use of existing linguistic resources to handle alignment of one word to multiple words (e.g., *al-nahayan* vs. *al nahyan*, and *threaten* vs. *pose threat*) and matching of similar (but not necessarily synonymous) words (polls vs. elections). We are also planning to extend word lattices to include phrases from the individual systems (i.e., not just the words) for more grammatical outputs.

Acknowledgments This material is based upon work supported by the Defense Advanced Research Projects Agency (DARPA) under Contract No. HR0011-06-C-0023.

References

Akiba, Yasuhiro, Taro Watanabe, and Eiichiro Sumita. 2002. Using language and translation models to select the best among outputs from multiple MT systems. In *Proc. of the 19th Intl. Conf. on Computational Linguistics (COLING'2002)*.

Bangalore, Srinivas, German Bordel, and Giuseppe Riccardi. 2001. Computing consensus translation from multiple machine translation systems. In *Proc. of IEEE Automatic Speech Recognition and Understanding Workshop (ASRU'2001)*.

Chiang, David. 2007. Hierarchical phrase-based translation. *Computational Linguistics*, 33(2):201–228.

Fellbaum, Christiane. 1998. *WordNet: An Electronic Lexical Database*. Bradford Books, March. Available at http://wordnet.princeton.edu.

Fiscus, Jonathan G. 1997. A post-processing system to yield reduced word error rates: Recognizer output voting error reduction (ROVER). In *Proc. of IEEE Automatic Speech Recognition and Understanding Workshop (ASRU'1997)*.

Frederking, Robert and Sergei Nirenburg. 1994. Three heads are better than one. In *Proc. of the 4th Conf. on Applied Natural Language Processing (ANLP'1994)*.

Huang, Fei and Kishore Papineni. 2007. Hierarchical system combination for machine translation. In *Proc. of the Conf. on Empirical Methods in Natural Language Processing (EMNLP'2007)*.

Jayaraman, Shyamsundar and Alon Lavie. 2005. Multi-engine machine translation guided by explicit word matching. In *Proc. of the 10th Annual Conf. of the European Association for Machine Translation (EAMT'2005)*.

Koehn, Philipp, Franz J. Och, and Daniel Marcu. 2003. Statistical phrase-based translation. In *Proc. of the Human Language Technology and the Meeting of the North American Chapter of the Association for Computational Linguistics Conf. (HLT/NAACL'2003)*.

Matusov, Evgeny, Nicola Ueffing, and Hermann Ney. 2006. Computing consensus translation from multiple machine translation systems using enhanced hypotheses alignment. In *Proc. of the 11th Conf. of the European Chapter of the Association for Computational Linguistics (EACL'2006)*.

Mellebeek, Bart, Karolina Owczarzak, Josef Van Genabith, and Andy Way. 2006. Multi-engine machine translation by recursive sentence decomposition. In *Proc. of the 7th Conf. of the Association for Machine Translation in the Americas (AMTA'2006)*.

Nomoto, Tadashi. 2004. Multi-engine machine translation with voted language model. In *Proc. of the 42nd Annual Meeting of the Association for Computational Linguistics (ACL'04)*.

Och, Franz J. and Hermann Ney. 2000. Improved statistical alignment models. In *Proc. of the 38th Annual Meeting of the Association for Computational Linguistics (ACL'2000)*.

Och, Franz J. 2003. Minimum error rate training in statistical machine translation. In *Proc. of the 41st Annual Meeting of the Association for Computational Linguistics (ACL'2003)*.

Papineni, Kishore, Salim Roukos, Todd Ward, and Wei-Jing Zhu. 2002. BLEU: a method for automatic evaluation of machine translation. In *Proc. of the 40th Annual Meeting of the Association for Computational Linguistics (ACL'2002)*.

Rosti, Antti-Veikko, Necip Fazil Ayan, Bing Xiang, Spyros Matsoukas, Richard Schwartz, and Bonnie Dorr. 2007a. Combining outputs from multiple machine translation systems. In *Proc. of the Human Language Technology and the Meeting of the North American Chapter of the Association for Computational Linguistics Conf. (HLT/NAACL'2007)*.

Rosti, Antti-Veikko, Spyros Matsoukas, and Richard Schwartz. 2007b. Improved word-level system combination for machine translation. In *Proc. of the 45th Annual Meeting of the Association for Computational Linguistics (ACL'2007)*.

Sim, Khe Chai, William J. Byrne, Mark J.F. Gales, Hichem Sahbi, and Phil C. Woodland. 2007. Consensus network decoding for statistical machine translation system combination. In *Proc. of the 32nd Intl. Conf. on Acoustics, Speech, and Signal Processing (ICASSP'2007)*.

Snover, Matthew, Bonnie Dorr, Rich Schwartz, Linnea Micciulla, and John Makhoul. 2006. A study of translation edit rate with targeted human annotation. In *Proc. of the 7th Conf. of the Association for Machine Translation in the Americas (AMTA'2006)*.

Stolcke, Andreas. 2002. SRILM – an extensible language modeling toolkit. In *Proc. of the Intl. Conf. on Spoken Language Processing (ICSLP'2002)*.

Wang, Wen, Andreas Stolcke, and Jing Zheng. 2007. Reranking machine translation hypotheses with structured and web-based language models. In *Proc. of the IEEE Automatic Speech Recognition and Understanding Workshop (ASRU'2007)*.

Xu, Jia, Richard Zens, and Hermann Ney. 2005. Sentence segmentation using IBM word alignment model 1. In *Proc. of the 10th Annual Conf. of the European Association for Machine Translation (EAMT'2005)*.

Verification and Implementation of Language-Based Deception Indicators in Civil and Criminal Narratives

Joan Bachenko
Deception Discovery Technologies
Oxford, NJ 07863
jbachenko@comcast.net

Eileen Fitzpatrick
Montclair State University
Montclair, NJ 07043
fitzpatricke@mail.montclair.edu

Michael Schonwetter
Deception Discovery Technologies
Minneapolis, MN 55416
mschonwetter@synchronvideo.com

Abstract

Our goal is to use natural language processing to identify deceptive and non-deceptive passages in transcribed narratives. We begin by motivating an analysis of language-based deception that relies on specific linguistic indicators to discover deceptive statements. The indicator tags are assigned to a document using a mix of automated and manual methods. Once the tags are assigned, an interpreter automatically discriminates between deceptive and truthful statements based on tag densities. The texts used in our study come entirely from "real world" sources—criminal statements, police interrogations and legal testimony. The corpus was hand-tagged for the truth value of all propositions that could be externally verified as true or false. Classification and Regression Tree techniques suggest that the approach is feasible, with the model able to identify 74.9% of the T/F propositions correctly. Implementation of an automatic tagger with a large subset of tags performed well on test data, producing an average score of 68.6% recall and 85.3% precision when compared to the performance of human taggers on the same subset.

1. Introduction

The ability to detect deceptive statements in text and speech has broad applications in law enforcement and intelligence gathering. The scientific study of deception in language dates at least from Undeutsch (1954, 1989), who hypothesized that it is "not the veracity of the reporting person but the truthfulness of the statement that matters and there are certain relatively exact, definable, descriptive criteria that form a key tool for the determination of the truthfulness of statements". Reviews by Shuy (1998), Vrij (2000), and DePaulo et al. (2003) indicate that many types of deception can be identified because the liar's verbal and non-verbal behavior varies considerably from that of the truth teller's. Even so, the literature reports that human lie detectors rarely perform at a level above chance. Vrij (2000) gives a summary of 39 studies of human ability to detect lies. The majority of the studies report accuracy rates between 45-60%, with the mean accuracy rate at 56.6%.

The goal of our research is to develop and implement a system for automatically identifying deceptive and truthful statements in narratives and transcribed interviews. We focus exclusively on verbal cues to deception for this initial experiment, ignoring at present potential prosodic cues (but see Hirschberg et al.).

© 2008. Licensed under the *Creative Commons Attribution-Noncommercial-Share Alike 3.0 Unported* license (http://creativecommons.org/licenses/by-nc-sa/3.0/). Some rights reserved.

In this paper, we describe a language-based analysis of deception that we have constructed and tested using "real world" sources—criminal narratives, police interrogations and legal testimony. Our analysis comprises two components: a set of deception indicators that are used for tagging a document and an interpreter that associates tag clusters with a deception likelihood. We tested the analysis by identifying propositions in the corpus that could be verified as true or false and then comparing the predictions of our model against this corpus of ground truth. Our analysis acheived an accuracy rate of 74.9%. In the remainder of this paper, we will present the analysis and a detailed description of our test results. Implementation of the analysis will also be discussed.

2. Studying Deception

The literature on deception comes primarily from experimental psychology where much of the concentration is on lies in social life and much of the experimentation is done in laboratory settings where subjects are prompted to lie[1]. These studies lack the element of deception under stress. Because of the difficulties of collecting and corroborating testimony in legal settings, analysis of so-called 'high stakes' data is harder to come by. To our knowledge, only two studies (Smith, 2001; Adams, 2002) correlate linguistic cues with deception using high stakes data. For our data we have relied exclusively on police department transcripts and high profile cases where the ground truth facts of the case can be established.

Previous studies correlating linguistic features with deceptive behavior (Smith, 2001; Adams, 2002; Newman et al. 2003, and studies cited in DePaulo et al. 2003) have classified narrators as truth-tellers or liars according to the presence, number and distribution of deception indicators in their narratives. Newman, et al. (2003), for example, proposes an analysis based on word likelihoods for semantically defined items such as action verbs, negative emotion words and pronouns. Narratives for their study were generated in the laboratory by student subjects. The goals of the project were to determine how well their word likelihood analysis classified the presumed author of each narrative as a liar or truth-teller and to compare their system's performance to that of human subjects. The analysis correctly achieved an overall distinction between liars and truth tellers 61% of the time.

Our research on deception detection differs from most previous work in two important ways. First, we analyze naturally occurring data, i.e. actual civil and criminal narratives instead of laboratory generated data. This gives us access to productions that cannot be replicated in laboratory experiments for ethical reasons. Second, we focus on the classification of specific statements within a narrative rather than characterizing an entire narrative or speaker as truthful or deceptive. We assume that narrators are neither always truthful nor always deceptive. Rather, every narrative consists of declarations, or assertions of fact, that retain a constant value of truth or falsehood. In this respect, we are close to Undeutsch's hypothesis in that we are not testing the veracity of the narrator but the truthfulness of the narrator's statements.

The purpose of our analysis is to assist human evaluators (e.g. legal professionals, intelligence analysts, employment interviewers) in assessing a text's contents. Hence the questions that we must answer are whether it is possible to classify specific declarations as true or deceptive using only linguistic cues and, if so, then how successfully an automated system can perform the task. Our research makes no claim as to the cause of a speaker's behavior, e.g. whether deception cues emerge as a function of emotional stress or excessive cognitive load.

3. Linguistic Markers of Deception

The literature on verbal cues to deception indicates that fabricated narrative may differ from truthful narrative at all levels from global discourse to individual word choice. Features of narrative structure and length, text coherence, factual and sensory detail, filled pauses, syntactic structure choice, verbal immediacy, negative expressions, tentative constructions, referential expressions, and particular phrasings have all been shown to differentiate truthful from deceptive statements in text (Adams, 2002; DePaulo et al., 2003; Miller and Stiff, 1993).

In the area of forensic psychology, Statement Validity Assessment is the most commonly used technique for measuring the veracity of verbal statements. SVA examines a transcribed interview for 19 criteria such as quantity of detail, embedding of the narrative in context, descriptions of interactions and reproduction of conversations (Steller & Köhnken, 1989). Tests of SVA

[1] We define deception as a deliberate attempt to mislead. We use the terms *lying* and *deceiving* interchangeably.

show that users are able to detect deception above the level of chance -- the level at which the lay person functions in identifying deception – with some criteria performing considerably better (Vrij, 2000). An SVA analysis is admissible as court evidence in Germany, the Netherlands, and Sweden.

In the criminal justice arena, another technique, Statement Analysis, or Scientific Content Analysis (SCAN), (Sapir, 1987) examines open-ended written accounts in which the writers choose where to begin and what to include in the statements. According to Sapir (1995) "when people are given the choice to give their own explanation in their own words, they would choose to be truthful . . . . it is very difficult to lie with commitment."

SCAN "claims to be able to detect instances of potential deception within the language behaviour of an individual; it does not claim to identify whether the suspect is lying" (Smith, 2001). As such, its goal is the one we have adopted: to highlight areas of a text that require clarification as part of an interview strategy.

Despite SCAN's claim that it does not aim to classify a suspect as truthful or deceptive, the validations of SCAN cues to deception to date (Smith, 2001; Adams, 2002) evaluate the technique against entire statements classified as T or F. Our approach differs in that we evaluate separately portions of the statement as true or deceptive based on the density of cues in that portion.

4. Deception Analysis for an NLP System

Our analysis is produced by two passes over the input text. In the first pass the text is tagged for deception indicators using a mix of automated and manual techniques. In the second pass the text is sent to an automated interpreter that calculates tag density using moving average and word proximity measures. The output of the interpreter is a segmentation of the text into truthful and deceptive areas.

4.1 Deception Indicators

We have selected 12 linguistic indicators of deception cited in the psychological and criminal justice literature that can be formally represented and automated in an NLP system. The indicators fall into three classes.

(1) Lack of commitment to a statement or declaration. The speaker uses linguistic devices to avoid making a direct statement of fact. Five of the indicators fit into this class: (i) linguistic hedges (described below) including non-factive verbs and nominals; (ii) qualified assertions, which leave open whether an act was performed, e.g. *I needed to get my inhaler*; (iii) unexplained lapses of time, e.g. *later that day*; (iv) overzealous expressions, e.g. *I swear to God*, and (v) rationalization of an action, e.g. *I was unfamiliar with the road.*

(2) Preference for negative expressions in word choice, syntactic structure and semantics. This class comprises three indicators: (i) negative forms, either complete words such as *never* or negative morphemes as in *inconceivable*; (ii) negative emotions, e.g. *I was a nervous wreck*; (iii) memory loss, e.g. *I forget.*

(3) Inconsistencies with respect to verb and noun forms. Four of the indicators make up this class: (i) verb tense changes (described below); (ii) thematic role changes, e.g. changing the thematic role of a NP from agent in one sentence to patient in another; (iii) noun phrase changes, where different NP forms are used for the same referent or to change the focus of a narrative; (iv) pronoun changes (described below) which are similar to noun phrase changes

To clarify our exposition, three of the indicators are described in more detail below. It is important to note with respect to these indicators of deception that deceptive passages vary considerably in the types and mix of indicators used, and the particular words used within an indicator type vary depending on factors such as race, gender, and socioeconomic status.

Verb Tense

The literature assumes that past tense narrative is the norm for truthful accounts of past events (Dulaney, 1982; Sapir, 1987; Rudacille, 1994). However, as Porter and Yuille (1996) demonstrate, it is deviations from the past tense that correlate with deception. Indeed, changes in tense are often more indicative of deception than the overall choice of tense. The most often cited example of tense change in a criminal statement is that of Susan Smith, who released the brake on her car letting her two small children inside plunge to their deaths. "I just feel hopeless," she said. "I can't do enough. My children wanted me. They needed me. And now I can't help them. I just feel like such a failure." While her statements about herself were couched in the present tense, those about her children were already in the past.

Hedges

The terms 'hedge' and 'hedging' were introduced by Lakoff (1972) to describe words "whose meaning implicitly involves fuzziness", e.g., *maybe, I guess,* and *sort of.* The use of hedges has been widely studied in logic and pragmatics, and for practical applications like translation and language teaching (for a review, see Schröder & Zimmer, 1997). In the forensic psychology literature, it has been correlated with deception (Knapp et al., 1974; Porter & Yuille, 1996; Vrij & Heaven, 1999).

Hedge types in our data include non-factive verbs like *think* and *believe*, non-factive NPs like *my understanding* and *my recollection*, epistemic adjectives and adverbs like *possible* and *approximately*, indefinite NPs like *something* and *stuff,* and miscellaneous phrases like *a glimpse* and *between 9 and 9:30.*

The particular types of hedging that appear in our data depend heavily on the socioeconomic status of the speaker and the type of crime. The 285 hedges in Jeffrey Skilling's 7562 word Enron testimony include 21 cases of *my recollection*, 9 of *my understanding*, and 7 of *to my knowledge* while the 42 hedges in the car thief's 2282 word testimony include 6 cases of *shit* (*doing a little painting, and roofing, and shit*), 6 of *just* and 4 of *probably*. Despite the differences in style, however, the deceptive behavior in both cases is similar.

Changes in Referential Expressions

Laboratory studies of deception have found that deceivers tend to use fewer self-referencing expressions (*I, my, mine*) than truth-tellers and fewer references to others (Knapp et al., 1974; Dulaney, 1982; Newman et al., 2003). In examining a specific real world narrative, however, it is impossible to tell what a narrator's truthful baseline use of referential expressions is, so the laboratory findings are hard to carry over to actual criminal narratives.

On the other hand, changes in the use of referential expressions, like changes in verb tense, have also been cited as indicative of deception (Sapir, 1987; Adams, 1996), and these changes can be captured formally. Such changes in reference often involve the distancing of an item; for example, in the narrative of Captain McDonald, he describes 'my wife' and 'my daughter' sleeping, but he reports the crime to an emergency number as follows, with his wife and daughter referred to as *some people*:

> So I told him that I needed a doctor and an ambulance and that *some people* had been stabbed.

Deceptive statements may also omit references entirely. Scott Peterson's initial police interview is characterized by a high number of omitted first person references:

> BROCCHINI: You drive straight home?
> PETERSON: To the warehouse, dropped off the boat.

4.2 Identifying a Text Passage as Deceptive or Non-deceptive

The presence or absence of a cue is not in itself sufficient to determine whether the language is deceptive or truthful. Linguistic hedges and other deception indicators often occur in normal language use. We hypothesize, however, that the distribution and density of the indicators would correlate with deceptive behavior.[2] Areas of a narrative that contain a clustering of deceptive material may consist of outright lies or they may be evasive or misleading, while areas lacking in indicator clusters are likely to be truthful.

We use a moving average (MA) program to find clusters of indicators in a text. Initially, the MA assigns each word in the text a proximity score based on its distance, measured in word count, to the nearest deception indicator. Each score is then recalculated by applying a MA window of N words. The MA sums the scores for N/2 words to the left and right of the current word and divides the result by N to obtain the revised score. Clusters of low word scores indicate deceptive areas of the text, high scoring clusters indicate truthful areas. Hence, when applied to a text, the MA allows us to segment an entire text automatically into non-overlapping regions that are identified as likely true, likely deceptive or somewhere in between.

Our approach assumes that the input text will contain sufficient language to display scoring patterns. This rules out, for example, polygraph tests where answers are confined to Yes or No as

[2] Currently the density algorithm does not take into account the possibility that some indicators may be more important than others. We plan to use the results of this initial test to determine the relative contribution of each tag type to the accuracy of the identification of deception.

well as short answer interviews that focus on simple factual statements such as names and addresses. Based on the data examined so far, we estimate the analysis requires a minimum 100 words to produce useful results.

5. Corpora and Annotation

The corpus used for developing our approach to deception detection was assembled from criminal statements, police interrogations, depositions and legal testimony; the texts describe a mix of violent and property crimes, white collar crime and civil litigation. Because of the difficulty in obtaining corpora and ground truth information, the total corpus size is small--slightly over 30,000 words.

For this experiment, we selected a corpus subset of 25,687 words. Table 1 summarizes the corpus subset:

Source	**Word Count**
Criminal statements (3)	1,527
Police interrogations (2)	3,922
Tobacco lawsuit deposition	12,762
Enron congress. testimony	7,476
Total	25,687

Table 1. Corpora Used in the Experiment

Each document in the experimental corpus was tagged for two factors: (1) linguistic deception indicators marked words and phrases associated with deception, and (2) True/False tags marked propositions that were externally verified.

5.1. Linguistic Annotation (Tagging)

A team of linguists tagged the corpus for the twelve linguistic indicators of deception described above. For each document in the corpus, two people assigned the deception tags independently. Differences in tagging were then adjudicated by the two taggers and a third linguist. Because the original tagging work was focused on research and discovery, inter-rater reliability statistics are not very revealing. However, current work on new corpora more closely resembles other tagging tasks. In this case we have found inter-rater reliability at 96%.

Tagging decisions were guided by a tagging manual that we developed. The manual provides extensive descriptions and examples of each tag type. Taggers did not have access to ground truth facts that could have influenced their tag assignments.

5.2. True/False Annotation

We then examined separate copies of each narrative for propositions that could be externally verified. The following is a single proposition that asserts, despite its length, one verifiable claim—the birthrate went down:

> *The number of births peaked in about 1955 and from there on each year there were fewer births. As a result of that each year after 1973 fewer people turned 18 so the company could no longer rely on this tremendous number of baby boomers reaching smoking age.*

Only propositions that could be verified were used. Verification came from supporting material such as police reports and court documents and from statements internal to the narrative, e.g. a confession at the end of an interview could be used to support or refute specific claims within the interview. The initial verification tagging was done by technical and legal researchers on the project. The T/F tags were later reviewed by at least one other technical researcher.

The experimental corpus contains 275 verifiable propositions. Table 2 gives examples of verified propositions in the corpus.

Example	**True**	**False**
I didn't do work specifically on teenage smoking		√
All right, man, I did it, the damage	√	
Black male wearing a coat.		√

Table 2. Examples of Verified Propositions

6. Results

The dataset contained 275 propositions, of which 164, or 59.6%, were externally verified as False and the remainder verified as True. We tested the ability of the model to predict T/F using Classification and Regression Tree (CART) analysis (Breiman, et al. 1984)[3] with 25-fold cross-validation and a misclassification cost that penalizes True misclassified as False. Table 3 shows the results of the CART analysis:

[3] We used the QUEST program described in Loh and Shih (1997) for the modeling. QUEST is available at http://www.stat.wisc.edu/~loh/quest.html.

Actual Class	Predicted Class			
		False	True	% Correct
	False	124	40	75.6
	True	29	82	73.8

Table 3. T/F Classification Based on Cue Density

We can conclude that the model identifies deceptive language at a rate significantly better than chance. Moreover, by tuning the scores to favor high recall for false propositions, it becomes possible to adapt the model to applications where low precision on true propositions is not a drawback, e.g. pre-trial interviews where investigators are looking for leads. The results in Table 4 show how we might gear the analysis to this class of applications.

Actual Class	Predicted Class			
		False	True	% Correct
	False	151	13	92.6
	True	66	45	40.5

Table 4. Penalizing F Misclassified as T

Finally, it should be noted that input to the analysis consisted of individual files with some files marked for topic changes. In preparing the data for this test, we found that, in many cases, the moving average allowed the low scores assigned to deceptive language to influence the scores of nearby truthful language. This typically occurs when the narrative contains a change in topic. For example, in the deposition excerpt below, there is a topic change from teenage smokers to the definition of psychographic studies. The hedge *so far as I know* belongs with the first topic but not the second. However, the moving average allows the low scores triggered by the hedge to improperly affect scores in the new topic:

> Q: *Do you know anybody who did have data that would allow a market penetration study of the type I've asked about to be performed.*
> A: *{So far as I know%HEDGE} only the federal government.*
> Q: *Are you familiar with the phrase psychographic study from your work at Philip Morris?*
> A: *Yes.*
> Q: *What is a psychographic study?*

To mitigate the effect of topic change, we inserted eleven topic change boundaries. The results suggest that language is "reset" when a new topic is introduced by the interviewer or interviewee.

7. A Deception Indicator Tagger

The results described in the previous section provide support for the deception indicator (DI) approach we have developed. For the implementation, we selected a subset of tags whose contextual conditions were well established by the literature and our own investigation. In these cases we were able to formalize the rules for automatic assignment of the tags. We excluded tags whose contextual conditions are still being researched, i.e., tag assignments that require human judgment.

The tagger was constructed as a rule-based system that uses a combination of context-free and context sensitive substitutions. An example of a context free substitution is "Mark all occurrences of *Oh, God* as an overzealous statement". A context sensitive substitution is the rule that interprets *something* as a hedge if it is not modified, i.e., followed by a relative clause or prepositional phrase.

In some cases the tagger refers to structure and part of speech. For example, *may* as a modal verb (*may_MD)* is a hedge. Certain verb+ infinitive complement constructions, e.g. *I attempted to open the door,* make up a qualified assertion. Syntactic structure is assigned by the CASS chunk parser (Abney, 1990). Part of speech tags are assigned by Brill's tagger (Brill, 1992). The DI tag rules apply to the output of the parser and POS tagger.

The subset of tags implemented in the tagger comprises 86% of all tags that occur in the training corpus. To see how well the DI tagger covered the subset, we first ran the tagger on the training corpus. 70% of the subset tags were correctly identified in that corpus, with 76% precision. We then tested the tagger on a test corpus of three files. Each file was also handtagged by linguistic researchers on this project. The results of the test are given in Table 5. Tag amounts refer to the number of tags belonging to the subset that was implemented.

File name	Handtags	Autotags	Correct Tags
confession	31	20	19
peterson	186	160	108
deposition	720	665	625
Total	937	845	752

Table 5. DI Tagger Results on Three Test Files

Table 6 provides a summary of the tagger's performance.

File name	Recall	Precision
confession	.61	.95
peterson	.58	.675
deposition	.868	.939
Average	.686	.853

Table 6. Summary of DI Tagger Results

These results may reflect a bias in our training data towards legal testimony—depositions are strongly represented in the corpus, police and criminal data less so. Our test corpus consists of a police interview ('peterson'), a criminal statement ('confession') and a deposition ('deposition'). The tagger's best performance is associated with the deposition.

8. Conclusion

This paper has presented new results in the study of language-based cues to deception and truthfulness; these results come entirely from "real world" sources—criminal narratives, interrogations, and legal testimony. Our goal is to provide a method of evaluating declarations within a single narrative or document rather than deeming an entire narrative (or narrator) as truthful or deceptive.

We first compared the predictions of linguistic cues that we adapted from the literature on deception against actual True/False values that were manually determined for 275 propositions in our corpus. Predictions from the linguistic indicators were determined by scoring the density of indicators in text areas that contain the propositions and using classification and regression to determine cut-off values for truth probabilities.

We then evaluated the performance of an automated tagger that implements a large subset of the linguistic indicators verified in our first experiment. The automated tagger performed well on test data, averaging 80.2% correct when compared with human performance on the same data.

The results strongly suggest that linguistic cues provide a guide to deceptive areas of a text. The predictions based on linguistic cues were correct in distinguishing False propositions over 75% of the time, and over 90% for applications where recall of False, but not True, is required. Results of the automatic tagger's performance suggest that we will eventually achieve a fully automated system for processing depositions and other documents in which veracity is an important issue.

References

Abney, S. 1990. Rapid incremental parsing with repair. In *Proceedings of the 6th New OED Conference: Electronic Text Research*, pp. 1-9. University of Waterloo, Waterloo, Ontario.

Adams, S. 1996. Statement analysis: What do suspects words really reveal? *The FBI Law Enforcement Bulletin.* 65(10). www.fbi.gov/publications/leb/1996/oct964.txt

Adams, S. 2002. *Communication under stress: indicators of veracity and deception in written narratives.* Ph.D. dissertation, Virginia Polytechnic Institute and State University

Brill, E. 1992. A simple rule-based part-of-speech tagger. In *Proceedings of the Third Conference on Applied Natural Language Processing,* pp. 152-155. Trento, Italy.

DePaulo, B. M., J.J. Lindsay, B.E. Malone, L. Muhlenbruck, K. Charlton, and H. Cooper. 2003. Cues to deception. *Psychological Bulletin,* 129(1), 74-118.

Dulaney, E.F. Jr. 1982. Changes in language behavior as a function of veracity. *Human Communication Research* 9, 75-82.

Hirschberg, J., S. Benus, J. Brenier, F. Enos, S. Friedman, S. Gilman, C. Girand, M. Graciarena, A. Kathol, L. Michaelis, B. Pellom, E. Shriberg and A. Stolcke. 2005. *INTERSPEECH 2005.* Sept. 408, Lisbon, Portugal.

Knapp, M.L., Hart, R.P., and Dennis, H.S. 1974. An exploration of deception as a communication construct. *Human Communication Research, 1,* 15-29.

Lakoff, G. 1972. Hedges: A study in meaning criteria and the logic of fuzzy concepts. In

Papers from the 8th Regional Meeting, Chicago Linguistic Society.

Loh, W.-Y. and Shih, Y.-S. 1997. Split selection methods for classification trees. *Statistica Sinica* 7:815-840.

Miller, G. R. and J. B. Stiff. 1993. *Deceptive Communication.* Sage Publications. Thousand Oaks, CA.

Newman, M. L., Pennebaker, J. W., Berry, D. S. and J. M. Richards. 2003. Lying words: predicting deception from linguistic styles. *Personality and Social Psychology Bulletin.* **29**, 665-675.

Porter, S. & Yuille, J. (1996). The language of deceit: An investigation of the verbal clues in the interrogation context. *Law & Human Behavior,* 20(4) 443-458.

Rudacille, W.C. 1994. *Identifying Lies in Disguise.* Kendall Hunt. Dubuque, IO.

Sapir, A. 1987. *Scientific Content Analysis (SCAN).* Laboratory of Scientific Interrogation. Phoenix, AZ.

Sapir, A. 1995. *The View Guidebook: Verbal Inquiry – the Effective Witness.* Laboratory of Scientific Interrogation. Phoenix, AZ.

Schröder, H. and D. Zimmer. 1997. Hedging research in pragmatics: A bibliographical research guide to hedging. In R. Markkanen and H. Schroder (eds.) *Hedging and Discourse: Approaches to the Analysis of a Pragmatic Phenomenon in Academic Text.* Walter de Gruyter, Berlin.

Shuy, R. 1998. *The Language of Confession, Interrogation and Deception.* Sage Publications, Thousand Oaks, CA.

Smith, N. 2001. Reading between the lines: An evaluation of the scientific content analysis technique (SCAN). Police Research Series. London,UK. www.homeoffice.gov.uk/rds/prgpdfs/prs135.pdf

Steller, M. and G. Kohnken. 1989. Criteria-Based Content Analysis. In D.C. Raskin (ed.) *Psychological Methods in Criminal Investigation and Evidence.* Springer-Verlag, New York, 217-245.

Undeutsch, U. 1989. The development of statement reality analysis. In J.C. Yuille (ed.) *Credibility Assessment.* Dordrecht: Kluwer, 101-121.

Undeutsch, U. (1954). Die Entwicklung der gerichtspsychologischen Gutachtertatigkeit. In A. Wellek (Ed.), Bericht uber den 19, Kongress der Deutschen Gesellschaft fur Psychologie (pp. 1132-154). Gottingen: Verlag fur Psychologie.

Vrij, A. 2000. *Detecting Lies and Deceit.* John Wiley & Sons, Chichester, UK.

Vrij, A. and Heaven, S. 1999. Vocal and verbal indicators of deception as a function of lie complexity. *Psychology, Crime, and Law 5,* 203-215.

Enhancing Multilingual Latent Semantic Analysis with Term Alignment Information

Brett W. Bader
Computer Science &
Informatics Department
Sandia National Laboratories
P. O. Box 5800, MS 1318
Albuquerque, NM 87185-1318, USA
bwbader@sandia.gov

Peter A. Chew
Cognitive Systems Research &
Applications Department
Sandia National Laboratories
P. O. Box 5800, MS 1011
Albuquerque, NM 87185-1011, USA
pchew@sandia.gov

Abstract

Latent Semantic Analysis (LSA) is based on the Singular Value Decomposition (SVD) of a term-by-document matrix for identifying relationships among terms and documents from co-occurrence patterns. Among the multiple ways of computing the SVD of a rectangular matrix X, one approach is to compute the eigenvalue decomposition (EVD) of a square 2×2 composite matrix consisting of four blocks with X and X^T in the off-diagonal blocks and zero matrices in the diagonal blocks. We point out that significant value can be added to LSA by filling in some of the values in the diagonal blocks (corresponding to explicit term-to-term or document-to-document associations) and computing a term-by-concept matrix from the EVD. For the case of multilingual LSA, we incorporate information on cross-language term alignments of the same sort used in Statistical Machine Translation (SMT). Since all elements of the proposed EVD-based approach can rely entirely on lexical statistics, hardly any price is paid for the improved empirical results. In particular, the approach, like LSA or SMT, can still be generalized to virtually any language(s); computation of the EVD takes similar resources to that of the SVD since all the blocks are sparse; and the results of EVD are just as economical as those of SVD.

© 2008. Licensed under the *Creative Commons Attribution-Noncommercial-Share Alike 3.0 Unported* license (http://creativecommons.org/licenses/by-nc-sa/3.0/). Some rights reserved.

1 Introduction

It is close to two decades now since Deerwester et al. (1990) first proposed the application of the Singular Value Decomposition (SVD) to term-by-document arrays as a statistics-based way of representing how terms and documents fit together within a semantic space. Since the approach was supposed to 'get beyond' the terms themselves to their underlying semantics, the approach became known as Latent Semantic Analysis (LSA).

Soon after this application of SVD was widely publicized, it was suggested by Berry et al. (1994) that, with a parallel corpus, the approach could be extended to pairs of languages to allow cross-language information retrieval (IR). It has since been confirmed that LSA can be applied not just to pairs of languages, but also simultaneously to *groups* of languages, again given the existence of a *multi*-parallel corpus (Chew and Abdelali 2007).

In this paper, we return to the basics of LSA by examining its relationship with SVD, and, in turn, the mathematical relationship of SVD to the eigenvalue decomposition (EVD). These details are discussed in section 2. It has previously been suggested (for example, in Hendrickson 2007) that IR results could be improved by filling in information beyond that available directly in the term-by-document matrix, and replacing SVD with the more general EVD. To our knowledge, however, these suggestions have not been publicized outside the mathematics community, nor have they been empirically tested in IR applications. With multilingual information retrieval as a use case, we consider alternatives in section 3 for implementation of this idea. One of these relies on no extraneous information beyond what is already available in the multi-parallel corpus, and is based entirely on the statistics of cross-language term alignments. 'Regular' LSA has been shown to work best when a weighting scheme such as log-entropy is applied to the elements in the term-by-document array (Dumais 1991), and in section 3 we also consider various possibilities for how the term alignments should best be weighted. Section 4 recapitulates on a framework that allows EVD with term alignments to be compared with a number of related approaches (including LSA without term alignments). This is a recapitulation, because the same testing framework has been used previously (for other linear-algebra based approaches) by Chew and Abdelali (2007) and Chew et al. (2007). The results of our comparison are presented and discussed in section 5, and we conclude upon these results and suggest further avenues for research in section 6.

2 The relationship of SVD to EVD, and its application to information retrieval

In the standard LSA framework (Deerwester et al. 1990) the (sparse) term-by-document matrix X is factorized by the singular value decomposition (SVD),

$$X = USV^T \qquad (1)$$

where U is an orthonormal matrix of left singular vectors, S is a diagonal matrix of singular values, and V is an orthonormal matrix of right singular vectors (Golub and van Loan 1996).

Typically for LSA, a *truncated* SVD is computed such that equality in (1) no longer holds and that the best rank-R least-squares approximation to matrix X is formed by keeping the R largest singular values in S and discarding the rest. This also means that the first R vectors of U and V are retained, where R indicates the number of concept dimensions in LSA. Each column vector in U maps the terms to a single arbitrary concept, such that terms which are semantically related (as determined by patterns of co-occurrence) will tend to be grouped together with large values in columns of U.

There are many ways to compute the SVD of a sparse matrix. One expedient way is to compute the eigenvalue decomposition (EVD) of either X^TX or XX^T, depending on the largest dimension of X, to obtain U or V, respectively. With U or V, one may compute the rest of the SVD by a simple matrix-matrix multiplication and renormalization.

Another way to compute the SVD is to compute the eigenvalue decomposition of the 2-by-2 block matrix

$$B = \begin{bmatrix} 0 & X \\ X^T & 0 \end{bmatrix}.$$

The eigenvalues of B are the singular values of X, replicated as both positive and negative, plus a number of zeroes if X is not square. The left and right singular vectors are contained within the eigenvectors of this composite matrix B. Assume that X is of size $m \times n$ and that $m \geq n$, with left singular vectors $U = [U_n \quad U_{m-n}]$, where U_n corresponds to the n positive singular values and U_{m-n} corresponds to the remaining m-n zero singular values. Let Q denote the orthogonal matrix of eigenvectors corresponding to the nonnegative eigenvalues of B, then the matrices of left and right singular vectors are stacked on top of each other, U on top of V, as follows:

$$Q = \frac{1}{\sqrt{2}} \begin{bmatrix} U_n & \sqrt{2} \times U_{m-n} \\ V & 0 \end{bmatrix}.$$

Hence, one may compute the truncated SVD of X by computing only the eigenvectors corresponding to the largest R eigenvalues and then extracting and rescaling the U and V matrices from Q.

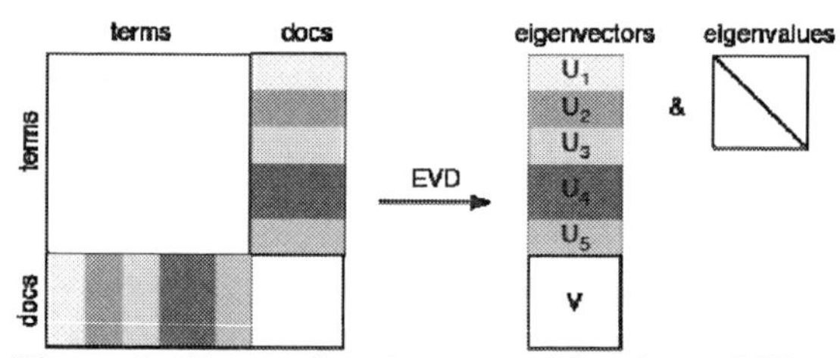

Figure 1. Eigenvalue decomposition in multilingual information retrieval

In the context of multilingual LSA using a parallel corpus, the block matrix B is depicted in Figure 1, where the terms are shaded according to each language. Each language may have a different number of terms, so the language blocks are not expected to be the same size as one another. The eigenvectors and eigenvalues of B are also shown.

We may obtain a pair of U and S matrices for each language by extracting the corresponding partition of U from the eigenvectors. We desire each language-specific U matrix to have columns of unit length, which we accomplish by computing the length of each of its columns and then rescaling the columns of U by the inverse length and multiplying the eigenvalues by these lengths for our S matrix. We call this approach 'Tucker1' because the result is identical to creating a U and S matrix for each language from the general Tucker1 model found by three-way analysis of the terms-by-documents-by-language array (Tucker 1966).

For applications in information retrieval, we usually want to compute a measure of similarity between documents. Once we have U and S, we can estimate similarities by computing the cosine of the angle between the document vectors in the smaller 'semantic space' of the R concepts found by LSA. New documents in different languages can be projected into this common semantic space by multiplying their document vectors (formed in exactly the same way as the columns for X) by the product US^{-1}, to yield a document-by-concept vector.

3 From SVD to term-alignment-based EVD

If we compute just the SVD of a term-document matrix X, then the technique we use to accomplish this (whether computing the EVD of the block matrix B or otherwise) is immaterial from a computational linguist's point of view: there is no advantage in one technique over another. However, the technique of EVD allows one to augment the LSA framework with additional information beyond just the term-document matrix. In Figure 1, the two diagonal blocks contain only zeroes, but we envision augmenting B with term alignment information such that the upper diagonal block captures any term-to-term similarities. Additional term-term alignment information serves to enhance the term-by-concept vectors in U by providing explicit, external knowledge so that LSA can learn more refined concepts. While not explored in this paper, we also envision incorporating any document-to-document similarities into the lower diagonal block.

Let D_1 and D_2 denote symmetric matrices. We augment the block matrix B and redefine it as a more general symmetric matrix,

$$B = \begin{bmatrix} D_1 & X \\ X^T & D_2 \end{bmatrix}.$$

If both D_1 and D_2 are equal to the identity matrix, then the eigenvalues of B are shifted by one, but the eigenvectors are not affected.

Since our use case here is multilingual information retrieval, imagine for the moment that an oracle provides dictionary information that matches up words in each of our language pairs (Arabic-English, Arabic-French, etc.) by meaning. Thus, for example, we might have a pairing between English *house* and French *maison*. This information may be encoded in the diagonal block D_1 by replacing zeroes in the cells for (*house, maison*) and its symmetric entry with some nonzero value indicating the strength of association for the two terms. Completing all relevant entries in D_1 in this fashion serves to strengthen the co-occurrence information in the parallel corpus that LSA normally finds via the SVD.

In the simplest approach, if the oracle indicates a match between two terms i and j, then a one could be inserted in D_1 at positions (i,j) and (j,i). If D_1 were filled with such term alignment information, the matrix B would still be sparse. Without any document-document information, then D_2 could be either the identity matrix or the zero matrix. Our experience has shown that $D_2 = 0$ works slightly better in practice. Figure 2 shows a block matrix augmented with term alignments in this fashion.

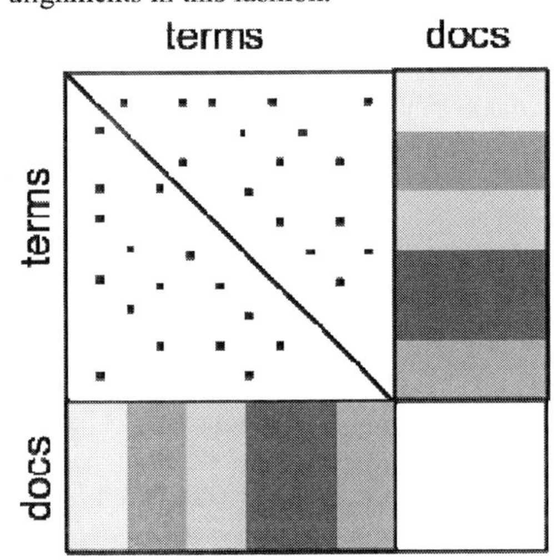

Figure 2. Augmented block matrix with term alignments

The eigenvalue decomposition of B now incorporates this extra term information provided in D_1, and the eigenvectors show stronger correspondence between those terms indicated. However, with each term aligned with one or more other terms, the row and column norms of D_1 are unequal, which means that some terms may be biased to appear more heavily in the eigenvectors. In addition, the magnitude or 'weight' of D_1 relative to X needs to be considered, otherwise the explicit alignments in D_1 and the co-occurrence information in X may be out of balance with one another. Properly normalizing and scaling D_1 may mitigate both of these risks.

There are several possibilities for normalizing the matrix D_1. Sinkhorn balancing (Sinkhorn 1964) is a popular technique for creating a doubly stochastic matrix (rows and columns all sum to 1) from a square matrix of nonnegative elements. Sinkhorn balancing is an iterative algorithm in which, at each step, the row and column sums are computed and then subsequently used to rescale the matrix. For balancing the matrix A, each iteration consists of two updates

$A \leftarrow W_R A$

$A \leftarrow A W_C$

where W_R is a diagonal matrix containing the inverse of row sums of A, and W_C is a diagonal matrix containing the inverse of column sums of A. This algorithm exhibits linear convergence, so many iterations may be needed. The algorithm may be adapted for normalizing the row and column vectors according to any norm. Our experience has shown that normalizing D_1 with respect to the Euclidean norm works well in practice.

In terms of scaling D_1 relative to X, we simply multiply D_1 by a positive scalar value, which we denote with the variable β. The optimal value of β appears to be problem dependent.

Let us return for the moment to the question of how we populate D_1 in the first place, and what each entry in that block represents. In the simple case described above, the existence of a 1 at position (i,j) indicates that an alignment exists between terms i and j, and a zero indicates that no alignment exists. But in reality, a binary encoding like this may be too simplistic. In this respect, it is instructive to consider how we populate D_1 in the light of the weighting scheme used for X, since the latter is discussed in Dumais (1991) and is by now quite well understood.

In the simplest case, an entry of 1 in X at position (i,j) can denote that term i occurs in document j, just as in our simple case with D_1. A slightly more refined alternative is to replace 1 with $f_{i,j}$, where $f_{i,j}$ denotes the raw frequency of term i within document j. But, as Dumais (1991) shows, it is significantly better in practice to use a 'log-entropy' weighting scheme. This adjusts $f_{i,j}$ first by 'dampening' high-frequency terms (using the log of the frequency), and secondly by giving a lower weight to terms which occur in many documents.[2] The former adjustment is related to an insight from Zipf's law, which is that the dampened term frequency will be in proportion to the log of the term's rank in frequency. The latter adjustment is based on information theory; a term which is scattered across many documents (such as 'and' in English) has a high entropy, and therefore lower intrinsic information content.

Suppose, therefore, that our 'dictionary' oracle could not only indicate the existence of an alignment, but also provide some numerical value for the strength of association between two aligned terms. (In practice, this is probably more than one could hope for even from the best published bilingual dictionaries.) This information could then replace the ones in D_1 prior to Sinkhorn balancing and matrix weighting.

While one cannot expect to obtain this information from published dictionaries, there is in fact a statistical approach to gathering the necessary information, which we borrow from SMT (Brown et al. 1994). All that is required is the existence of a parallel corpus, which we already have in place for multilingual LSA.

Here, an entry $f_{i,j}$ in D_1 is based on the mutual information of term I and term J, or $I(I;J)$ (capitals are used to indicate that the terms are treated here as random variables). It is an axiom that:

$$I(I;J) = H(I) + H(J) - H(I,J) \quad (2)$$

where $H(I)$ and $H(J)$ are the marginal entropies of I and J respectively, and $H(I,J)$ is the joint entropy of I and J. Properties of $H(I,J)$ include the following:

$$H(I,J) \geq H(I) \geq 0$$
$$H(I,J) \geq H(J) \geq 0$$
$$H(I,J) \leq H(I) + H(J) \quad (3)$$

Considering (2) and (3) together, it should be clear that $I(I;J)$ will range between 0 and the maximum value for $H(I)$ or $H(J)$.

For the purposes of populating D_1, we compute the entropy of a term i by considering the number of documents where i occurs, and the number of documents where i does not occur, and express these as probabilities. For the joint entropy $H(I,J)$, we need to compute four probabilities based on all the possibilities: documents where both terms occur, those where I occurs without J, those where J occurs without I, and

[2] One can also raise the global weight in the log-entropy scheme to a power (which we denote with the variable α). Selecting $\alpha \neq 1$ can, in practice, yield better results in the applications we have tested.

those where neither occur. The result of this is that a numerical value is attached to each alignment: higher values indicate that terms are strongly correlated, and lower values indicate that one term predicts little about the other. For each pair of words (*i,j*) which co-occur in any text chunk in the parallel corpus, we can say that an alignment exists if, among all the possibilities, mutual information for *i* is maximized by selecting *j*, *and* vice versa. (Since the maximization of mutual information is not necessarily reciprocal, the effect of this is to be conservative in postulating alignments.) The weight of this alignment is its mutual information (equivalent to the 'global weight' of log-entropy) multiplied by the log of one plus the number of text chunks in which that alignment appears (equivalent to the 'local weight' of log-entropy).

Some examples of English-French pairs at either end of this spectrum (where mutual information is non-zero) are given in Table 1.

I(*I;J*)	Alignment weight	*I*	*J*
0.000176	0.000176	hearing	écoutait
0.000217	0.000217	misery	misérable
…			
0.270212	2.884297	house	maison
0.321754	3.506663	king	roi
0.415702	6.025456	and	et
0.472925	5.798080	I	je

Table 1. Term alignment and mutual information

We believe that this approach, which weights alignments based on mutual information, fits very well with the log-entropy scheme used for X, since both are solidly based on the same foundation of information theory.

All together, we call this particular process LSATA, which stands for LSA with term alignments.

4 Testing framework

Since the inception of the Cross-Language Evaluation Forum (CLEF) in 2000, there has been growing interest in cross-language IR, and a number of parallel corpora have become available (for example through the Linguistic Data Consortium). Widely used examples include the Canadian Hansard parliament proceedings (in French and English). Harder to obtain are *multi*-parallel corpora – those where the same text is translated into more than two parallel languages.

One such corpus which has not yet gained wide acceptance, perhaps owing to the perception that it has less relevance to real-world applications than other parallel corpora, is the Bible. Yet the range of languages covered is unarguably unmatched elsewhere, and one might contend that its relevance is in some ways greater than, say, Hansard's, as its impact on Western culture has been broader than that of Canadian government debates. Similarly, the Quran, while not translated into as many languages as the Bible, has had a significant impact on another large segment of the world's population.

But the relevance or otherwise of the Bible and/or Quran, and the extent to which they have been accepted by the computational linguistics community at large as parallel corpora, are somewhat beside the point for us here. Our interest is in developing theory and applications which have universal applicability to as many languages as possible, regardless of the subject matter or whether the languages are ancient or modern. One might compare this approach to Chomsky's quest for Universal Grammar (Chomsky 1965), except that the theory in our case is based on lexical statistics and linear algebra rather than rule-based generative grammar.

The Bible and Quran have in fact previously been used for experiments similar to ours (e.g., Chew et al. 2007). By using these texts as parallel corpora, therefore, we facilitate direct comparison of our results with previous ones. But besides this, the Bible has some especially attractive properties for our current purposes. First, the carefulness of the translations means that we are relatively unlikely to encounter situations where cross-language term alignments are impossible because some text is missing in one of the translations. Secondly, the relatively small size of the parallel text chunks (by and large, each chunk is a verse, most of which are about a sentence in length) greatly facilitates the process of statistical term alignment. (This is based on the combinatorics: the number of possible term-to-term alignments increases approximately quadratically with the number of terms per text chunk.)

Thus, our framework is as follows. In our term-by-document matrix X, the documents are verses, and the terms are distinct wordforms in any of the five languages used in the test data in Chew et al. (2007): Arabic (AR), English (EN), French (FR), Russian (RU) and Spanish (ES). As in Chew et al. (2007), too, our test data consists of the text of the Quran in the same 5 languages. In this case, the 'documents' are the 114 parallel suras (or chapters) of the Quran. We obtained all translations of the Bible and Quran from openly-available websites such as that of Biola University (2005-2006) and http://www.kuran.gen.tr.

As already mentioned, SVD of a term-by-document matrix is equivalent to EVD of a block matrix in which two of the blocks (the non-diagonal ones) are X and X^T. As described in section 3, we fill in some of the values of D_1 with nonzeroes (from term alignments derived from the Bible). In all cases (both SVD and EVD), we performed a truncated decomposition in either 60, 240, or 300 dimensions.

SVD/EVD dimensions	Type of decomposition	Include term alignments? / weighting type	Term alignment settings		Global weight α*	Average P1	Average MP5
			Sinkhorn balanced?	β			
60	SVD	N/A			1.8	0.7116	0.5702
	Tucker1					0.7170	0.5770
	PARAFAC2					0.7420	0.6580
	LSATA	yes (binary)	no	N/A	1.8	0.7000	0.5691
			yes	4.0		0.7611	0.6474
				1.0	1.6	0.7716	0.5972
				4.0		0.7979	0.6467
		yes (log-MI)	no	N/A	1.8	0.6481	0.3804
			yes	1.0		0.7393	0.5972
				12.0		0.8088	0.6972
				1.0	1.6	0.7488	0.5789
				12.0		0.7933	0.6586
240	SVD	N/A			1.8	0.8761	0.6554
	PARAFAC2					0.8975	0.7853
300	SVD	N/A			1.8	0.8796	0.6575
	LSATA	yes (binary)	yes	4.0	1.6	**0.9421**	0.7695
		yes (log-MI)		12.0	1.8	0.8982	0.8000
					1.6	0.9182	**0.8067**

*See footnote 2.

Table 2. Results with various linear algebraic decomposition methods and weighting schemes

To evaluate the different methods against one another, we use similar measures of precision as were used with the same dataset by Chew et al. (2007): precision at 1 document (P1) (the average proportion of cases where the translation of a document ranked highest among all retrieved documents of the same language) and multilingual precision at 5 documents (MP5) (the average proportion of the top 5 ranked documents which were translations of the query document into any of the 5 languages, among all retrieved documents of *any* language). By definition, MP5 is always less than or equal to P1; MP5 measures success in multilingual clustering, while P1 measures success in retrieving documents when the source and target languages are pre-specified.

5 Results and Discussion

Table 2 above presents a summary of our results. The main point to note is that the addition of information on term alignments is clearly beneficial. An approach based on the Tucker1 decomposition algorithm, without any information on term alignments, achieves P1 of 0.7170 and MP5 of 0.5770. With scaled term alignment information, the results improve to 0.7611 and 0.6474, respectively. Using a chi-squared test, we tested the significance of the increase in P1 and found it to be highly significant ($p \approx 1.7 \times 10^{-7}$).

The results also show, however, that one needs to be careful about how the word-alignment information is added. Without some form of balancing and scaling of D_1, there is little improvement (and often significant deterioration) in the results when alignment information is included.

In addition to comparing a block EVD approach with term alignments to one without, we also compared against another decomposition method, PARAFAC2, which has been found to be more effective than SVD in cross-language IR (Chew et al. 2007). Here, the results are more equivocal. P1 is slightly higher under the LSATA approach (with binary values in D_1) than under PARAFAC2, while the reverse is true for MP5. The difference for P1 is significant at $p < 0.05$ but not at $p < 0.01$. In any case, there are risks in making a comparison between PARAFAC2 and LSATA. For one thing, PARAFAC2, as implemented here, includes no mechanism for incorporating term-alignment information. It is not clear to us yet whether such a mechanism could (mathematically or practically) be incorporated into PARAFAC2. Secondly, we are not yet confident that we have found the optimal weighting scheme for the D_1 block under the LSATA model. Our experiments with different weighting and normalization schemes for the D_1 block are still in relatively initial stages, though it can also be seen from Table 2 that by selecting certain settings under LSATA (replacing binary weighting in D_1 with mutual-information-based weighting, and applying scaling with beta = 12.0), we were able to improve upon PARAFAC2 under both measures.

Although we have not tested all settings, Table 2 also shows our best results to date with this dataset, which have come from applying EVD to the block matrix that includes D_1. The precise optimal settings for EVD appear to depend on whether the objective is to maximize P1 or MP5. For P1, our best results (0.9421) were obtained with binary weighting, global term $\alpha = 1.6$, and $\beta = 4.0$. For MP5, the best results (0.8067) were obtained with mutual-information based weighting, $\alpha = 1.8$, and $\beta = 12.0$. It appears in all cases that D_1 needs to be balanced if it contains term alignment information.

The evidence, then, appears to be strongly in favor of incorporating information beyond term-to-document associations within an IR approach based on linear algebra. It happens that LSATA offers an obvious way to do this, while other methods such as PARAFAC2 may or may not. Here, we have examined just one form of information besides term-to-document statistics: term-to-term statistics. However, there is no reason to suppose that the results might not be improved still further by incorporating information on document-to-document associations, or for that matter associations between terms or documents and other linguistic, grammatical, or contextual objects.

6 Conclusion

In this paper, we have discussed the mathematical relationship between SVD and EVD, and specifically the fact that SVD is a special case of EVD. For information retrieval, the significance of this is that SVD allows for explicit encoding of associations between terms and documents, but not between terms and terms, or between documents and documents.

By moving from the special case of SVD to the general case of EVD, however, we open up the possibility that additional information can be encoded prior to decomposition. We have examined a particular use case for SVD: multilingual information retrieval. This use case presents an interesting example of additional information which could be encoded on the term-by-term diagonal block: cross-language pairings of equivalent terms (such as *house*/*maison*). Such pairs can be obtained from bilingual dictionaries, but we can save ourselves the trouble of obtaining and using these. Multilingual LSA requires that a parallel corpus have already been obtained, and well-understood statistical term alignment procedures can be applied to obtain cross-language term-to-term associations. Moreover, if the corpus is *multi*-parallel, we can ensure that the statistical basis for alignment is the same across all language pairs.

Our results show that by including term-to-term alignment information, then performing EVD, we can improve the results of cross-language IR quite significantly.

It should be pointed out that while we have successfully used statistics-based information in the term-by-term diagonal block, there is no reason to suppose that similar or better results might not be achieved by manually filling in nonzeroes in either diagonal block. The additional information encoded by these nonzeroes could include associations known a priori between documents (e.g., they were written by the same author) or terms (e.g., they occur together in a thesaurus), or both. While in these examples the additional information required might not be available from the training corpus, and its encoding could involve moving away from an entirely statistics-based model, the additional effort could be justified depending upon the intended application.

In future work, we would like to examine in particular whether still further statistically-derivable (or readily available) data could be incorporated into the model. For example, one can conceive of a block EVD involving 'levels' beyond the 'term level' and the 'document level'. In a 3×3 block EVD, for example, one might include n-grams, terms, and documents; this approach should also be extensible to essentially all languages. Might the addition of further information lead to even higher precision? Avenues for research such as this raise their own questions, such as the type of weighting scheme which would have to be applied in a 3×3 block matrix.

In summary, however, our results give us some confidence that there can be significant benefit in making more linguistic and/or statistical information available to linear algebraic IR approaches such as EVD. Cross-language term alignments are just one example of the type of additional information which could be included; we believe that future research will uncover many more similar examples.

Acknowledgement

Sandia is a multiprogram laboratory operated by Sandia Corporation, a Lockheed Martin Company, for the United States Department of Energy's National Nuclear Security Administration under contract DE-AC04-94AL85000.

References

Michael W. Berry, Susan T. Dumais., and G. W. O'Brien. 1994. Using Linear Algebra for Intelligent Information Retrieval. *SIAM: Review* 37, 573-595.

Biola University. 2005-2006. *The Unbound Bible*. Accessed at http://www.unboundbible.org/ on Jan. 29, 2008.

Peter F. Brown, Vincent J. Della Pietra, Stephen A. Della Pietra, and Robert L. Mercer. 1994. The Mathematics of Statistical Machine Translation: Parameter Estimation. *Computational Linguistics* 19(2), 263-311.

Peter A. Chew and Ahmed Abdelali. 2007. Benefits of the 'Massively Parallel Rosetta Stone': Cross-Language Information Retrieval with over 30 Languages . *Proceedings of the 45th Annual Meeting of the Association for Computational Linguistics, ACL 2007*. Prague, Czech Republic, June 23–30, 2007. pp. 872-879.

Noam Chomsky. 1965. *Aspects of the Theory of Syntax*. Cambridge, MA: MIT Press.

S. Deerwester, S. T. Dumais, G. W. Furnas, T. K. Landauer and R. Harshman. 1990. Indexing by Latent Semantic Analysis. *Journal of the American Society for Information Science* 41:6, 391-407.

Susan Dumais. 1991. Improving the Retrieval of Information from External Sources. *Behavior Research Methods, Instruments, and Computers* 23(2):229-236.

Gene H. Golub and Charles F. van Loan. 1996. *Matrix Computations*, 3rd edition. The Johns Hopkins University Press: London.

R. A. Harshman. 1972. PARAFAC2: Mathematical and Technical Notes. *UCLA Working Papers in Phonetics* 22, 30-47.

Bruce Hendrickson. 2007. Latent Semantic Analysis and Fiedler Retrieval. *Linear Algebra and its Applications* 421 (2-3), 345-355.

P. Koehn, F. J. Och, and D. Marcu. 2003. Statistical Phrase-Based Translation. *Proceedings of the Joint Conference on Human Language Technologies and the Annual Meeting of the North American Chapter of the Association of Computational Linguistics (HLT/NAACL)*, 48-54.

P. Koehn. 2002. Europarl: a Multilingual Corpus for Evaluation of Machine Translation. Unpublished, accessed on Jan. 29, 2008 at http://www.iccs.inf.ed.ac.uk/~pkoehn/publications/europarl.pdf.

Philip Resnik, Mari Broman Olsen, and Mona Diab. 1999. The Bible as a Parallel Corpus: Annotating the "Book of 2000 Tongues". *Computers and the Humanities*, 33: 129-153.

R. Sinkhorn. 1964. A Relation between Arbitrary Positive Matrices and Doubly Stochastic Matrices. *Annals of Mathematical Statistics* 35 (2), 876-879.

Ledyard R. Tucker. 1966. Some Mathematical Notes on Three-mode Factor Analysis, *Psychometrika* 31, 279-311.

Ding Zhou, Sergey A. Orshanskiy, Hongyuan Zha, and C. Lee Giles. 2007. Co-Ranking Authors and Documents in a Heterogeneous Network. *Seventh IEEE InternationalConference on Data Mining*, 739-744.

Weakly supervised supertagging with grammar-informed initialization

Jason Baldridge
Department of Linguistics
The University of Texas at Austin
jbaldrid@mail.utexas.edu

Abstract

Much previous work has investigated weak supervision with HMMs and tag dictionaries for part-of-speech tagging, but there have been no similar investigations for the harder problem of supertagging. Here, I show that weak supervision for supertagging does work, but that it is subject to severe performance degradation when the tag dictionary is highly ambiguous. I show that lexical category complexity and information about how supertags may combine syntactically can be used to initialize the transition distributions of a first-order Hidden Markov Model for weakly supervised learning. This initialization proves more effective than starting with uniform transitions, especially when the tag dictionary is highly ambiguous.

1 Introduction

Supertagging involves assigning words lexical entries based on a lexicalized grammatical theory, such as Combinatory Categorial Grammar (CCG) (Steedman, 2000) Tree-adjoining Grammar (Joshi, 1988), or Head-driven Phrase Structure Grammar (Pollard and Sag, 1994). Supertag sets are larger than part-of-speech (POS) tag sets and their elements are generally far more articulated. For example, the English verb *join* has the POS VB and the CCG category $((S_b\backslash NP)/PP)/NP$ in CCGbank (Hockenmaier and Steedman, 2007). This category indicates that *join* requires a noun phrase to its left, another to its right, and a prepositional phrase to the right of that.

Supertags convey such detailed syntactic subcategorization information that supertag disambiguation is referred to as *almost parsing* (Bangalore and Joshi, 1999). Standard sequence prediction models are highly effective for supertagging, including Hidden Markov Models (Bangalore and Joshi, 1999; Nielsen, 2002), Maximum Entropy Markov Models (Clark, 2002; Hockenmaier et al., 2004; Clark and Curran, 2007), and Conditional Random Fields (Blunsom and Baldwin, 2006). The original motivation for supertags–parse prefiltering for lexicalized grammars–of Bangalore and Joshi (1999) has been realized to good effect: the supertagger of Clark and Curran (2007) provides staged n-best lists of multi-tags that dramatically improve parsing speed and coverage without much loss in accuracy. Espinosa et al. (2008) have shown that hypertagging (predicting the supertag associated with a logical form) can improve both speed and accuracy of wide-coverage sentence realization with CCG. Supertags have gained further relevance as they are increasingly used as features for other tasks, including machine translation (Birch et al., 2007; Hassan et al., 2007).

Supertaggers typically rely on a significant amount of carefully annotated sentences. As with many problems, there is pressing need to find strategies for reducing the amount of supervision required for producing accurate supertaggers, but as yet, no one has explored the use of weak supervision for the task. In particular, there are many dialog systems which rely on hand-crafted lexicons that both provide a starting point for bootstrapping a supertagger and which could benefit greatly from supertag pre-parse filter. For example, the dialog system used by Kruijff et al. (2007) uses a hand-

© 2008. Licensed under the *Creative Commons Attribution-Noncommercial-Share Alike 3.0 Unported* license (http://creativecommons.org/licenses/by-nc-sa/3.0/). Some rights reserved.

crafted CCG grammar for OpenCCG (White and Baldridge, 2003). It is important to stress that there are many such uses of CCG and related frameworks which do *not* rely on first annotating (even a small number of) sentences in a corpus: these define a lexicon that maps from words to categories (supertags) for a particular domain/application.

This scenario is a natural fit for learning taggers from tag dictionaries using hidden Markov models with Expectation-Maximization (EM). Here, I investigate such weakly supervised learning for supertagging and demonstrate the importance of proper initialization of the tag transition distributions of the HMM. In particular, such initialization can be done using inherent properties of the CCG formalism itself regarding how categories[1] may combine. Informed initialization should help with supertagging for two reasons. First, categories have structure–lacking in POS tags–waiting to be exploited. For example, it is far more likely *a priori* to see the category sequence (S\NP)/NP NP/N than the sequence S/S NP\NP. Given the categories for a word, this information can be used to influence our expectations about categories for adjacent words. Second, this kind of information truly matters for the task: a key aspect of supertagging that differentiates it from POS tagging is that the contextual information is much more important for the former. Lexical probabilities handle most of the ambiguity for POS tagging, but supertags are *inherently* about context and, furthermore, lexical ambiguity is much greater for supertagging, making lexical probabilities less effective.

I start by defining a distribution over lexical categories and then use this distribution as part of creating a CCG-informed transition distribution that appropriately breaks the symmetry of uniform HMM initialization. After describing how these components are included in the HMM, I describe experiments with CCGbank varying the ambiguity of the lexicon provided. I show that using knowledge about the formalism consistently improves performance, and is especially important as categorial ambiguity increases.

2 Lexical category distribution

The categories of CCG are an inductively defined set containing elements that are either atomic elements or (curried) functions specifying the canonical linear direction in which they seek their arguments. Some example entries from CCGbank are:

the := $\mathsf{NP_{nb}/N}$
of := $\mathsf{(NP\backslash NP)/NP}$
of := $\mathsf{((S\backslash NP)\backslash(S\backslash NP)/NP}$
were := $\mathsf{(S_{dcl}\backslash NP)/(S_{pss}\backslash NP)}$
buy := $\mathsf{(S_{dcl}\backslash NP)/NP}$
buy := $\mathsf{((((S_b\backslash NP)/PP)/PP)/(S_{adj}\backslash NP))/NP}$

Words can be associated with multiple categories; the distribution over these categories is typically quite skewed. For example, the first entry for *buy* occurs 33 times in CCGbank, compared with just once for the second. That the simpler category is more prevalent is unsurprising: a general strategy when creating CCG lexicons is to use simpler categories whenever possible. This points to the possibility of defining distributions over CCG lexicons based on measures of the complexity of categories. I use a simple distribution here: given a lexicon $\mathcal{L}$, the probability of a category i is inversely proportional to its complexity:

$$\Lambda_i = \frac{\frac{1}{complexity(c_i)}}{\sum_{j \in \mathcal{L}} \frac{1}{complexity(c_j)}} \qquad (1)$$

Here, a very simple complexity measure is assumed: the number of subcategories (tokens) contained in a category.[2] For example, ((S\NP)\(S\NP)/NP contains 9: S (twice), NP (thrice), S\NP (twice), (S\NP)\(S\NP), and ((S\NP)\(S\NP)/NP.

The tag transition distribution defined in the next section uses Λ to bias transitions toward simpler categories, e.g., preferring the first category for *buy* over the second. Performance when using Λ is compared to using a uniform distribution.

Other distributions could be given, e.g., one which gives more mass to adjunct categories such as (S\NP)\(S\NP) than to ones which are otherwise similar but do not display such symmetry, like (S/NP)\(NP\S). However, the most important thing for present purposes is that simpler categories are more likely than more complex ones.

This distribution imposes no internal structure on the likelihood of a lexicon. As far as Λ is concerned, lexicons can as well have the category (S\NP)\NP for transitive verbs and ((S/NP)/NP)/NP for ditransitive verbs, even though this is a highly unlikely pattern since we

[1] For the rest of the paper, I will refer to *categories* rather *supertags*, but will still refer to the task as supertagging.

[2] This worked better than using category arity or number of unique subcategory types.

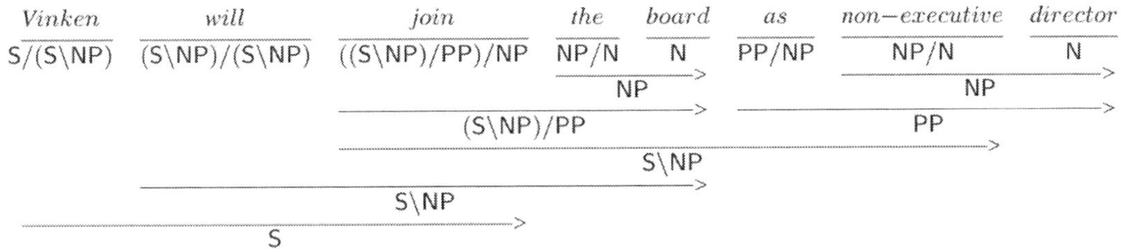

Figure 1: Normal form CCG derivation, using only application rules.

would expect both types of verbs to seek their arguments in the same direction. Languages also tend to prefer lexicons with one or the other slash direction predominating (Villavicencio, 2002). In the future, it would be interesting to consider Bayesian approaches that could encode more complex structure and assign priors over distributions over lexicons, building on these observations.

An aspect of CCGbank that relevant for Λ_i is that some categories actually are not true categories. For example, many punctuation "categories" are given as LRB, ., :, etc. In most grammars, the category of '.' is usually assumed to be S\S. The grammatical behavior of such pseudo-categories is handled via special rules in the parsers of Hockenmaier and Steedman (2007) and Clark and Curran (2007). I relabeled three of these: , to NP\NP, . to S\S and ; to (S\S)/S. A single best change was not clear for others such as LRB and :, so they were left as is.

3 Category transition distribution

CCG analyses of sentences are built up from lexical categories combining to form derived categories, until an entire sentence is reduced to a single derived category with corresponding dependencies. One of CCG's most interesting linguistic properties is it allows alternative constituents. Consider the derivations in Figures 1 and 2, which show a normal form derivation (Eisner, 1996) and fully incremental derivation, respectively. Both produce the same dependencies, guaranteed by the semantic consistency of CCG's rules (Steedman, 2000). This property of CCG of supporting multiple derivations of the same analysis has been termed *spurious ambiguity*. However, the extra constituents are anything but spurious: they are implicated in a range of CCG (along with other forms of categorial grammar) linguistic analyses, including coordination, long-distance extraction, intonation, and incremental processing.

This all boils down to associativity: just as $(1 + (4 + 2)) = ((1 + 4) + 2) = 7$, CCG ensures that *(Ed·(saw·Ted))* = *((Ed·saw)·Ted)* = S Such multiple derivations arise when adjacent categories can combine through either application or composition. Thus, we would expect that the lexical categories needed to analyze an entire sentence will more often than not be able to combine with their immediate neighbors. For example, six of seven pairs of adjacent lexical categories in the sentence in Figure 1 can combine. Only N PP/NP of *board as* cannot.[3]

This observation can be used in different ways by different models for CCG supertagging. For example, discriminative tagging models could include features that capture whether or not the current supertag can combine with the previous one and possibly via which CCG rule. Here, I show how it can be used to provide a non-uniform starting point for the transition distributions $\theta_{j|i}$ in a first-order Hidden Markov Model. This is similar to how Grenager et al. (2005) use diagonal initialization in an HMM for field segmentation to encourage the model to remain in the same state (and thus predict the same label for adjacent words). For CCG supertagging, the initialization should discourage diagonalization and establish a preference for some transitions over others.

There are many ways to define such a starting point. The simplest would be to reserve a small part of the mass spread uniformly over category pairs which cannot combine and then spread the rest of the mass uniformly over those which can. However, we can provide a more refined distribution, $\Psi_{j|i}$, by incorporating the lexical category distribution Λ_i defined in the previous section to weight these transitions according to this further information. In a similar manner to Grenager et al. (2005), I define Ψ as follows:

[3]I make the standard assumption that type-raising is performed in the lexicon, so the possibility of combining these through type-raising plus composition is not available.

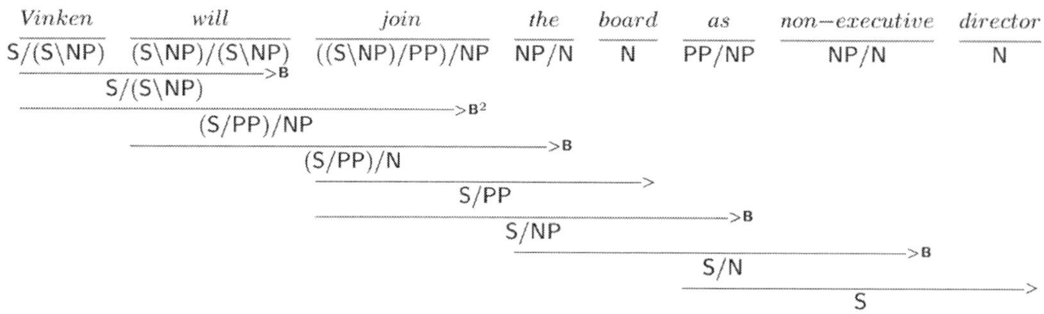

Figure 2: Incremental CCG derivation, using both application and composition (**B**) rules.

$$\Psi_{j|i} = (1-\sigma)\Lambda_j + \sigma \times \kappa(i,j) \times \frac{\Lambda_j}{\sum_{k \in \mathcal{C}|\kappa(i,k)} \Lambda_k} \quad (2)$$

where $\kappa(i,j)$ is an indicator function that returns 1 if categories c_i and c_j can combine when c_i immediately precedes c_j, σ is a global parameter that specifying the total probability of transitions that are combinable from i. Each j receives a proportion of σ according to its lexical prior probability over the sum of the lexical prior probabilities for all categories that combine with i. For the experiments in this paper, σ was set to .95. For the models referred to as ΨU and ΨU-EM in section 5, the uniform lexical probability $1/|\mathcal{C}|$ is used for Λ_i.

For $\kappa(i,j)$, I use the standard rules assumed for CCGbank parsers: forward and backward application (>, <), order-preserving composition (>**B**, <**B**), and backward crossed composition (<$\mathbf{B}_\times$) for S-rooted categories. Thus, κ(NP, S\NP)=1, κ(S/NP, NP/N)=1, κ((S\NP)/NP, (S\NP)\(S\NP))=1 and κ(S/NP, NP\NP)=0. For application, leftward and rightward arguments are handled separately by assuming that it would be possible to consume all preceding arguments of the first category and all following arguments of the second. So, κ((S/NP)\S, NP/N)=1 and κ(NP, (S\NP)/NP)=1. Unification on categories is standard (so κ(NP[nb], S\NP)=1), except that N unifies with NP only when N is the argument: κ(N, S\NP)=1, but κ(NP/N, NP)=0. This is to deal with the fact that CCGbank represents many words with N (e.g., *Mr.*|N/N *Vinken*|N *is*|(S[dcl]\NP)/NP) and assumes that a parser will include the unary type changing rule N→NP.

The HMM also has initial and final probabilities; distributions can be defined based on which categories are likely to start or end a sentence. For this, I assume only that categories which seek arguments to the left (e.g., S\NP) are less likely at the beginning of a sentence and those which seek rightward arguments are less likely at the end. The initializations for these are defined similarly to the transition distribution, substituting functions $noLeftArgs(i)$ and $noRightArgs(i)$ for $\kappa(i,j)$.

4 Model

A first-order Hidden Markov Model (bitag HMM) is used for bootstrapping a supertagger from a lexicon. See Rabiner (1989) for an extensive introduction to and discussion of HMMs. There are several reasons why this is an attractive tagging model here. First, though extra context in the form of tritag transition distributions or other techniques can improve supervised POS tagging accuracy, the accuracy of bitag HMMs is not far behind. The goal here is to investigate the *relative* gains of using CCG-based information in weakly supervised HMM learning. Second, the expectation-maximization algorithm for bitag HMMs is efficient and has been shown to be quite effective for acquiring accurate POS taggers given only a lexicon (tag dictionary) and certain favorable conditions (Banko and Moore, 2004). Third, the model's simplicity makes it straightforward to test the idea of CCG-initialization on tag transitions.

Dirichlet priors can be used to bias HMMs toward more skewed distributions (Goldwater and Griffiths, 2007; Johnson, 2007), which is especially useful in the weakly supervised setting considered here. Following Johnson (2007), I use variational Bayes EM (Beal, 2003) during the M-step for the transition distribution:

$$\theta_{j|i}^{l+1} = \frac{f(E[n_{i,j}] + \alpha_i)}{f(E[n_i] + |\mathcal{C}| \times \alpha_i)} \quad (3)$$

$$f(v) = exp(\psi(v)) \quad (4)$$

$$\psi(v) = \begin{cases} g(v - \frac{1}{2}) & \text{if } v > 7 \\ \psi(v+1) - \frac{1}{v} & \text{o.w.} \end{cases} \quad (5)$$

$$g(x) \approx log(x) + \frac{1}{24x^2} - \frac{7}{960x^4} + \frac{31}{8064x^6} - \frac{127}{30720x^8} \quad (6)$$

where $\mathcal{V}$ is the set of word types, ϕ is the *digamma* function (which is approximated by g), and α_i is the hyperparameter of the Dirichlet priors. In all experiments, the α_i parameters were set symmetrically to .005.

For experiments using the transition prior $\Psi_{j|i}$, the initial expectations of the model were set as $E[n_{i,j}] = |\mathcal{E}_i| \times \Psi_{j|i}$ and $E[n_i] = |\mathcal{E}_i|$, where $\mathcal{E}_i$ is the set of emissions for category c_i. The uniform probability $\frac{1}{|C|}$ was used in place of $\Psi_{j|i}$ for standard HMM initialization.

The emission distributions use standard EM expectations with more mass reserved for unknowns for tags with more emissions as follows:[4]

$$\phi^{l+1}_{k|i} = \frac{E[n_{i,k}] + |\mathcal{E}_i| \times \frac{1}{|\mathcal{V}|}}{E[n_i] + |\mathcal{E}_i|} \quad (7)$$

The Viterbi algorithm is used for decoding.

5 Experiments

CCGbank (Hockenmaier and Steedman, 2007) is a translation of phrase structure analyses of the Penn Treebank into CCG analyses. Here, I consider only the lexical category annotations and ignore derivations. The standard split used for weakly supervised HMM tagging experiments (Banko and Moore, 2004; Wang and Schuurmans, 2005) is used: sections 0-18 for training (*train*), 19-21 for development (*dev*), and 22-24 for testing (*test*). All parameters and models were developed using *dev*. The test set was used only once to obtain the performance figures reported here.

Counts for word types, word tokens and sentences for each data set are given in Table 1. In *train*, there are 1241 distinct categories, the ambiguity per word *type* is 1.69, and the maximum number of categories for a single word type is 126. This is much greater than for POS tags in CCGbank, for which there are 48 POS tags with an average ambiguity of 1.17 per word and a maximum of 7 tags in *train*.[5]

[4] I also experimented with a Dirichlet prior on the emissions, but it performed worse. Using a symmetric prior was actually detrimental, while performance within a percent of those achieved with the above update was achieved with Dirichlet hyperparameters set relative to $|\mathcal{E}_i|/|\mathcal{V}|$.

Dataset	Types	Tokens	Sentences
train	43063	893k	38,015
dev	14961	128k	5484
test	13898	127k	5435

Table 1: Basic statistics for the datasets.

The set of supertags was not reduced: any category found in the data used to initialize a lexicon was considered. This is one of the advantages of the HMM over using discriminative models, where typically only supertags seen at least 10 times in the training material are utilized for efficiency (Clark and Curran, 2007). Ignoring some supertags makes sense when building supervised supertaggers for pre-parse filtering, but not for learning from lexicons, where we cannot assume we have such frequencies.

For supervised training with the HMM on *train*, the performance is 87.6%. This compares to 91.4% for the C&C supertagger. The accuracy of the HMM, though quite a bit lower than that of C&C, is still quite good, indicating that it is an adequate model for the task. Note also that it uses only the words themselves and does not rely on POS tags. The performance of the C&C tagger was obtained by training the C&C POS tagger on the given dataset and tagging the evaluation material with it. Finally, the HMM trains in just a few seconds as opposed to over an hour.[6]

Five different weakly supervised scenarios are evaluated: (1) standard EM with 50 iterations (EM), (2) Ψ initialization with uniform lexical probabilities w/o EM (ΨU), (3) Ψ with Λ probabilities w/o EM ($\Psi\Lambda$), (4) Ψ with uniform lexical probabilities and 10 EM iterations, and (5) Ψ with Λ and 10 EM iterations.[7] These scenarios compare the effectiveness of standard EM with the use of grammar informed transitions; these in turn are of two varieties – one using a uniform lexical prior or one that is biased in favor of less complex categories according to Λ.

As Banko and Moore (2004) discovered when

[5] Note that the POS tag information is not used in these experiments, except for by the C&C tagger.

[6] It should be stressed that the goal of this paper is **not** to compete on supervised performance with C&C; instead, this comparison shows that the HMM supervised performance is reasonable and is thus relevant for bootstrapping.

[7] The number of iterations for standard and grammar informed iteration were determined by performance on *dev*.

reimplementing several previous HMMs for POS tagging, the lexicons had been limited to contain only tags occurring above a particular frequency. For POS tagging, this keeps a cleaner lexicon that avoids errors in annotated data (such as *the* tagged as VB) and rare tags (such as *a* tagged as SYM). When learning from a lexicon alone, such elements receive the same weight as their other (correct or more fundamental) tags in initializing the HMM. The problem of rare tags turns out to be very important for weakly supervised CCG supertagging.[8]

To consider the effect of the CCG-based initialization for lexicons with differing ambiguity, I use tag cutoffs that remove any lexical entry containing a category that appears with a particular word less than X% of the time (Banko and Moore, 2004), as well as using no cutoffs at all. Recall that the goal of these experiments is to investigate the relative difference in performance between using the grammar-based initialization or not, given some (possibly hand-crafted) lexicon. Lexicon cutoffs actually constitute a strong source of supervision because they use tag frequencies (which would not be known for a hand-crafted lexicon), so it should be stressed that they are used here only so that this relative performance can be measured for different ambiguity levels.

Table 2 provides accuracy for **ambiguous** words (and not including punctuation) for the five scenarios, varying the cutoff to measure the effect of progressively allowing more lexical ambiguity (and much rarer categories). The number of ambiguous, non-punctuation tokens is 101,167.

The first thing to note is performance given only the lexicon and the ΨU or $\Psi\Lambda$ initialization of the transitions. These correspond to taggers which have only been given the lexicon and have not utilized any data to improve their estimates of the transition and emission probabilities. Interestingly, both do quite well with a clean lexicon: see the columns under ΨU and $\Psi\Lambda$. These indicate that initializing the transitions based on whether categories can combine does indeed appropriately capture key aspects of category transitions. Furthermore, using the lexical category distribution ($\Psi\Lambda$) to create the transition initialization provides a better starting point than the uniform one (ΨU), especially as lexical ambiguity increases.

Cutoff	EM	ΨU	$\Psi\Lambda$	ΨU-EM	$\Psi\Lambda$-EM
.1	77.4	73.1	74.7	80.0	79.6
.05	69.1	70.6	72.5	79.2	79.2
.01	60.2	62.2	65.0	75.4	76.7
.005	52.2	57.8	59.0	72.5	73.8
.001	41.3	45.5	48.2	63.0	67.6
None	33.0	33.9	37.8	52.9	56.1

Table 2: Performance on *ambiguous* word types of the HMM with standard EM (uniform starting transitions), just the initial Ψ transitions (ΨU and $\Psi\Lambda$), and EM initialized with ΨU and $\Psi\Lambda$, for lexicons with varied cutoffs. Note also that these scores do not include punctuation.

Next, note that both ΨU-EM and $\Psi\Lambda$-EM beat the randomly initialized EM for all cutoff levels. For the 10% tag cutoff (the first row), there is an absolute difference of over 2% for both.[9] As the ambiguity increases, the grammar-informed initialization has a much stronger effect. In the extreme case of using no cutoff at all (the *None* row of Table 2), ΨU-EM and $\Psi\Lambda$-EM beat EM by 19.9% and 23.1%, respectively. Finally, using the lexical category distribution Λ instead of a uniform one is much more effective when there is more lexical ambiguity (e.g., compare the .01 through None rows of the ΨU-EM and $\Psi\Lambda$-EM columns), but has a negligible effect with less ambiguity (rows .05 and .01). This demonstrates that the grammar-based initialization can be effectively exploited – it is in fact crucial for improving performance when we are given much more ambiguous lexicons.

The majority of errors with $\Psi\Lambda$-EM involve marking adjectives (N/N) as nouns (N) or vice versa, and assigning the wrong prepositional category (usually the simpler noun phrase post-modifier (NP\NP)/NP instead of the verb phrase modifier ((S\NP)\(S\NP))/NP. Both of these kinds of errors, and others, could potentially be corrected if the categories proposed by the tagger were further filtered by an attempt to parse each sentence with the categories.

6 Related work

The idea of using knowledge from the formalism for constraining supertagging originates with Ban-

[8] CCGbank actually corrects many errors in the Penn Treebank, and does not suffer as much from mistagged examples. However, there were two instances of an ill-formed category ((S[b]\NP)/NP)/ in wsj_0595 for the words *own* and *keep*. These were corrected to (S[b]\NP)/NP.

[9] For comparison with the performance of 87.6% for the fully supervised HMM on **all** tokens, Ψ-EM achieves 82.1% and 58.9% using a cutoff of .1 or no cutoff, respectively.

galore and Joshi (1999). They used constraints based on how elementary trees of Tree-Adjoining Grammar could or could not combine as filters to block out tags that do not fit in certain locations in the string. My approach is different is several ways. First, they dealt with fully supervised supertagging; here I show that using this knowledge is important for weakly supervised supertagging where we are given only a tag dictionary (lexicon). Second, my approach encodes grammar-based cues only as an initial bias, so categories are never explicitly filtered. Finally, I use CCG rather than TAG, which makes it possible to exploit a much higher degree of associativity in derivations. This in turn makes it easier to utilize prior knowledge about adjacent contexts – precisely what is needed for using the grammar to influence the transition probabilities of a bigram HMM.

On the other hand, Bangalore and Joshi (1999) use constraints that act at greater distances than I have considered here. For example, if one wishes to provide a word with the category ((S\NP)/PP)/NP, then there should be a word with a category which results in a PP two or more words to its right – this is something which the bigram transitions considered here cannot capture. An interesting way to extend the present approach would be to enforce such patterns as posterior constraints during EM (Graca et al., 2007).

Recent work considers a damaged tag dictionary by assuming that tags are known only for words that occur more than once or twice (Toutanova and Johnson, 2007). A very interesting aspect of this work is that they explicitly model ambiguity classes to exploit commonality in the lexicon between different word forms, which could be even more useful for supertagging.

In a grammar development context, it is often the case that only some of the categories for a word have been assigned. This is the scenario considered by Haghighi and Klein (2006) for POS tagging: how to construct an accurate tagger given a set of tags and a few example words for each of those tags. They use distributional similarity of words to define features for tagging that effectively allow such prototype words to stand in for others. This idea could be used with my approach as well; the most obvious way would be to use prototype words to suggest extra categories (beyond the tag dictionary) for known words and a reduced set of categories for unknown words.

Other work aims to do truly unsupervised learning of taggers, such as Goldwater and Griffiths (2007) and Johnson (2007). No tag dictionaries are assumed, and the models are parametrized with Dirichlet priors. The states of these models implicitly represent tags; however, it actually is not clear what the states in such models truly represent: they are (probably interesting) clusters that may or may not correspond to what we normally think of as parts-of-speech. POS tags are relatively inert, passive elements in a grammar, whereas CCG categories are the very drivers of grammatical analysis. That is, syntax is *projected*, quite locally, by lexical categories. It would thus be interesting to consider the induction of categories with grammar-based priors with such models.

7 Conclusion

I have shown that weakly supervised learning can indeed be used to induce supertaggers from a lexicon mapping words to their possible categories, but that the extra ambiguity in the supertagging task over that of POS tagging makes performance much more sensitive to rare categories that occur in larger, more ambiguous lexicons. However, I have also shown that the CCG formalism itself can provide the basis for useful distributions over lexical categories and tag transitions in a bitag HMM. By using these distributions to initialize the HMM, it is possible to improve performance regardless of the underlying ambiguity. This is especially important for reducing error when the lexicon used for bootstrapping is highly ambiguous and contains very rare categories.

Acknowledgments

Thanks to the UT Austin Natural Language Learning group and three anonymous reviewers for useful comments and feedback. This work was supported by NSF grant BCS-0651988 and a Faculty Research Assignment from UT Austin.

References

Bangalore, Srinivas and Aravind K. Joshi. 1999. Supertagging: an approach to almost parsing. *Computational Linguistics*, 25(2):237–265.

Banko, Michele and Robert C. Moore. 2004. Part-of-speech tagging in context. In *Proceedings of COLING*.

Beal, Matthew. 2003. *Variational Algorithms for Approximate Inference*. Ph.D. thesis, University of Cambridge.

Birch, Alexandra, Miles Osborne, and Philipp Koehn. 2007. CCG supertags in factored statistical machine translation. In *Proceedings of the 2nd Workshop on Statistical Machine Translation*.

Blunsom, Phil and Timothy Baldwin. 2006. Multilingual deep lexical acquisition for HPSGs via supertagging. In *Proceedings of EMNLP 06*, pages 164–171.

Clark, Stephen and James Curran. 2007. Wide-coverage efficient statistical parsing with CCG and log-linear models. *Computational Linguistics*, 33(4).

Clark, Stephen. 2002. Supertagging for combinatory categorial grammar. In *Proceedings of TAG+6*, pages 19–24, Venice, Italy.

Eisner, Jason. 1996. Efficient normal-form parsing for combinatory categorial grammars. In *Proceedings of the 35th ACL*.

Espinosa, Dominic, Michael White, and Dennis Mehay. 2008. Hypertagging: Supertagging for surface realization with CCG. In *Proceedings of ACL-08: HLT*, pages 183–191, Columbus, Ohio, June.

Goldwater, Sharon and Tom Griffiths. 2007. A fully Bayesian approach to unsupervised part-of-speech tagging. In *Proceedings of the 45th ACL*.

Graca, Joao, Kuzman Ganchev, and Ben Taskar. 2007. Expectation maximization, posterior constraints, and statistical alignment. In *Proceedings of NIPS07*.

Grenager, Trond, Dan Klein, and Christopher D. Manning. 2005. Unsupervised learning of field segmentation models for information extraction. In *Proceedings of the 43rd ACL*, pages 371–378.

Haghighi, Aria and Dan Klein. 2006. Prototype-driven learning for sequence models. In *Proceedings of HLT-NAACL 2006*.

Hassan, Hany, Khalil Sima'an, and Andy Way. 2007. Supertagged phrase-based statistical machine translation. In *Proceedings of the 45th ACL*.

Hockenmaier, Julia and Mark Steedman. 2007. CCGbank: A corpus of CCG derivations and dependency structures extracted from the Penn Treebank. *Computational Linguistics*, 33(3):355–396.

Hockenmaier, Julia, Gann Bierner, and Jason Baldridge. 2004. Extending the coverage of a CCG system. *Research in Language and Computation*, 2:165–208.

Johnson, Mark. 2007. Why doesn't EM find good HMM POS-taggers? In *Proceedings of the EMNLP-CoNLL 2007*.

Joshi, Aravind. 1988. Tree Adjoining Grammars. In Dowty, David, Lauri Karttunen, and Arnold Zwicky, editors, *Natural Language Parsing*, pages 206–250. Cambridge University Press, Cambridge.

Kruijff, Geert-Jan M., Hendrik Zender, Patric Jensfelt, and Henrik I. Christensen. 2007. Situated dialogue and spacial organization: What, where,...and why? *International Journal of Advanced Robotic Systems*, 4(1):125–138.

Nielsen, Leif. 2002. Supertagging with combinatory categorial grammar. In *Proceedings of the Seventh ESSLLI Student Session*, pages 209–220.

Pollard, Carl and Ivan Sag. 1994. *Head Driven Phrase Structure Grammar*. CSLI/Chicago University Press, Chicago.

Rabiner, Lawrence. 1989. A tutorial on Hidden Markov Models and selected applications in speech recognition. *Proceedings of the IEEE*, 77(2):257–286.

Steedman, Mark. 2000. *The Syntactic Process*. The MIT Press, Cambridge Mass.

Toutanova, Kristina and Mark Johnson. 2007. A Bayesian LDA-based model for semi-supervised part-of-speech tagging. In *Proceedings of NIPS 20*.

Villavicencio, Aline. 2002. *The Acquisition of a Unification-Based Generalised Categorial Grammar*. Ph.D. thesis, University of Cambridge.

Wang, Qin Iris and Dal Schuurmans. 2005. Improved estimation for unsupervised part-of-speech tagging. In *EEE International Conference on Natural Language Processing and Knowledge Engineering*.

White, Michael and Jason Baldridge. 2003. Adapting chart realization to CCG. In *Proceedings of ENLG*.

Good Neighbors Make Good Senses: Exploiting Distributional Similarity for Unsupervised WSD

Samuel Brody
School of Informatics
University of Edinburgh
s.brody@sms.ed.ac.uk

Mirella Lapata
School of Informatics
University of Edinburgh
mlap@inf.ed.ac.uk

Abstract

We present an automatic method for sense-labeling of text in an unsupervised manner. The method makes use of distributionally similar words to derive an automatically labeled training set, which is then used to train a standard supervised classifier for distinguishing word senses. Experimental results on the Senseval-2 and Senseval-3 datasets show that our approach yields significant improvements over state-of-the-art unsupervised methods, and is competitive with supervised ones, while eliminating the annotation cost.

1 Introduction

Word sense disambiguation (WSD), the task of identifying the intended meaning (sense) of words in context, is a long-standing problem in Natural Language Processing. Sense disambiguation is often characterized as an intermediate task, which is not an end in itself, but has the potential to improve many applications. Examples include summarization (Barzilay and Elhadad, 1997), question answering (Ramakrishnan et al., 2003) and machine translation (Chan and Ng, 2007).

WSD is commonly treated as a supervised classification task. Assuming we have access to data that has been hand-labeled with correct word senses, we can train a classifier to assign senses to unseen words in context. While this approach often achieves high accuracy, adequately large sense labeled data sets are unfortunately difficult to obtain. For many words, domains, languages, and sense inventories they are unavailable, and in most cases it is unreasonable to expect to acquire them. Ng (1997) estimates that a high accuracy domain-independent system for WSD would probably need a corpus of about 3.2 million sense tagged words. At a throughput of one word per minute (Edmonds, 2000), this would require about 27 person-years of human annotation effort.

SemCor (Fellbaum, 1998) is one of the few corpora that have been manually annotated for all words — it contains sense labels for 23,346 lemmas. In spite of being widely used, SemCor contains too few tagged instances for the majority of polysemous words (typically fewer than 10 each). Supervised methods require much larger data sets than this to perform adequately.

The problem of obtaining sufficient labeled data, often referred to as the *data acquisition bottleneck*, creates a significant barrier to the use of supervised WSD methods in real world applications. In this work we wish to take advantage of the high accuracy and strong capabilities of supervised methods, while eliminating the need for human annotation of training data. Our approach exploits a sense inventory such as WordNet (Fellbaum, 1998) and corpus data to *automatically* create a collection of sense labeled instances which can subsequently serve to train any supervised classifier. The key premise of our work is that a word's senses can be broadly described by semantically related words. So, rather than laboriously annotating all instances of a polysemous word with its senses, we collect instances of its related words and treat them as sense labels for the target word. The method is inexpensive, language-independent, and can be used to create large sense-labeled data without human intervention. Our results demonstrate significant improvements over state-of-the-art unsupervised methods that do not make use of hand-labeled annotations.

In the following section we provide an overview

©2008. Licensed under the *Creative Commons Attribution-Noncommercial-Share Alike 3.0 Unported* license (http://creativecommons.org/licenses/by-nc-sa/3.0/). Some rights reserved.

of existing work on unsupervised WSD. Section 3 introduces our method for automatically creating sense annotations. We present our evaluation framework in Section 4 and results in Section 5.

2 Related Work

The data requirements for supervised WSD and the current paucity of suitably annotated corpora for many languages and text genres, has sparked considerable interest in unsupervised methods. These typically come in two flavors: (1) developing algorithms that assign word senses without relying on a sense-labeled corpus (Lesk, 1986; Galley and McKeown, 2003) and (2) making use of pseudo-labels, i.e., labelled data that has not been specifically annotated for sense disambiguation purposes but contains some form of sense distinctions (Gale et al., 1992; Leacock et al., 1998). We briefly discuss representative examples of both approaches, with a bias to those closely related to our own work.

Unsupervised Algorithms One of the first approaches to unsupervised WSD, and the foundation of many algorithms to come, was originally introduced by Lesk (1986). The method assigns a sense to a target ambiguous word by comparing the dictionary definitions of each of its senses with the words in the surrounding context. The sense whose definition has the highest overlap (i.e., words in common) with the context is assumed to be the correct one. Despite its simplicity, the algorithm provides a good baseline for comparison. Coverage can be increased by augmenting the dictionary definition (gloss) of each sense with the glosses of related words and senses (Banerjee and Pedersen, 2003).

Although most algorithms disambiguate word senses in context, McCarthy et al. (2004) propose a method that does not rely on contextual cues. Their algorithm capitalizes on the fact that the distribution of word senses is highly skewed. A large number of frequent words is often associated with one dominant sense. Indeed, current supervised methods rarely outperform the simple heuristic of choosing the most common sense in the training data (henceforth "the first sense heuristic"), despite taking local context into account. Rather than obtaining the first sense via annotating word senses manually, McCarthy et al. propose to acquire first senses automatically and use them for disambiguation. Thus, by design, their algorithm assigns the same sense to all instances of a polysemous word.

Their approach is based on the observation that distributionally similar neighbors often provide cues about a word's senses. Assuming that a set of neighbors is available, the algorithm quantifies the degree of similarity between the neighbors and the sense descriptions of the polysemous word. The sense with the highest overall similarity is the first sense. Specifically, the approach makes use of two similarity measures which complement each other and provide a large amount of data regarding the word senses. Distributional similarity indicates the similarity between words in the distributional feature space, whereas WordNet similarity in the 'semantic' space, is used to discover which sense of the ambiguous word is used in the corpus, and causing the distributional similarity.

Pseudo-labels as Training Instances Gale et al. (1992) pioneered the use of parallel corpora as a source of sense-tagged data. Their key insight is that different translations of an ambiguous word can serve to distinguish its senses. Ng et al. (2003) extend this approach further and demonstrate that it is feasible for large scale WSD. They gather examples from English-Chinese parallel corpora and use automatic word alignment as a means of obtaining a translation dictionary. Translations are next assigned to senses of English ambiguous words. English instances corresponding to these translations serve as training data.

It has become common to use related words from a dictionary to learn contextual cues for WSD (Mihalcea, 2002). Perhaps the first incarnation of this idea is found in Leacock et al. (1998), who describe a system for acquiring topical contexts that can be used to distinguish between senses. For each sense, related monosemous words are extracted from WordNet using the various relationship connections between sense entries (e.g., hyponymy, hypernymy). Their system then queries the Web with these related words. The contexts surrounding the relatives of a specific sense are presumed to be indicators of that sense, and used for disambiguation. A similar idea, proposed by Yarowsky (1992), is to use a thesaurus and acquire informative contexts from words in the same category as the target.

Our own work uses insights gained from unsupervised methods with the aim of creating large datasets of sense-labeled instances without explicit manual coding. Unlike Ng et al. (2003) our algorithm works on monolingual corpora, which are much more abundant than parallel ones, and is fully automatic. In their approach translations and their English senses must be associated manually. Similarly to McCarthy et al. (2004), we assume that words related to the target word are useful indicators of its senses. Importantly, our method disambiguates words in context and is able to assign additional senses, besides the first one.

3 Method

As discussed earlier, our aim is to alleviate the need for manual annotation by creating a large dataset labeled with word senses without human intervention. This dataset can be subsequently used by any supervised machine learning algorithm. We assume here that we have access to a corpus and a sense inventory. We first obtain a list of words that are semantically related to our target word. In the remainder of this paper we use the term "neighbors" to refer to these words. Next, we separate the neighbors into sense-specific groups. Finally, we replace the occurrences of each neighbor in our corpus with an instance of the target word, labeled with the matching sense for that neighbor. The procedure has two important steps: (1) acquiring neighbors and (2) associating them with appropriate senses. We describe our implementation of each stage in more detail below.

Neighbor Acquisition Considerable latitude is allowed in specifying appropriate neighbors for the target word. Broadly speaking, the neighbors can be extracted from a corpus or from a semantic resource, for example the dictionary providing the sense inventory. A wealth of algorithms have been proposed in the literature for acquiring distributional neighbors from a corpus (see Weeds (2003) for an overview). They differ as to which features they consider and how they use the distributional statistics to calculate similarity.

Lin's (1998) information-theoretic similarity measure is commonly used in lexicon acquisition tasks and has demonstrated good performance in unsupervised WSD (McCarthy et al., 2004). It operates over dependency relations. A word w is described by a set $T(w)$ of co-occurrence triplets $< w, r, w' >$, which can be viewed as a sparsely represented feature vector, where r represents the type of relation (e.g., *object-of*, *subject-of*, *modified-by*) between w and its dependent w'. The similarity between w_1 and w_2 is then defined as:

$$\frac{\sum_{(r,w)\in T(w_1)\cap T(w_2)} I(w_1,r,w)+I(w_2,r,w)}{\sum_{(r,w)\in T(w_1)} I(w_1,r,w)+\sum_{(r,w)\in T(w_2)} I(w_2,r,w)}$$

where $I(w,r,w')$ is the *information value* of w with regard to (r,w'), defined as:

$$I(w,r,w') = \log \frac{count(w,r,w')\cdot count(r)}{count(*,r,w')\cdot count(w,r,*)}$$

The measure is used to estimate the pairwise similarity between the target word and all other words in the corpus (with the same part of speech); the k words most similar to the target are selected as its neighbors.

A potential caveat with Lin's (1998) distributional similarity measure is its reliance on syntactic information for obtaining dependency relations. Parsing resources may not be available for all languages or domains. An alternative is to use a measure of distributional similarity which considers word collocation statistics and therefore does not require a syntactic parser (see Weeds (2003)).

As mentioned earlier, it is also possible to obtain neighbors simply by consulting a semantic dictionary. In WordNet, for example, we can assume that WordNet relations, (e.g., hypernymy, hyponymy, synonymy) indicate words which are semantic neighbors. An advantage of using distributional neighbors is that they reflect the characteristics of the corpus we wish to disambiguate and are potentially better suited for capturing sense differences across genres and domains, whereas dictionary-based neighbors are corpus-invariant.

Associating Neighbors with Senses If the neighbors are extracted from WordNet, it is not necessary to associate them with their senses as they are already assigned a specific sense. Distributional similarity methods, however, do not provide a way to distinguish which neighbors pertain to each sense of the target. For that purpose, we adapt a method proposed by McCarthy et al. (2004). Specifically, for each acquired neighbor, we choose the sense of the target which gives the highest semantic similarity score to *any* sense of the neighbor. There are a large number of semantic similarity measures to choose from (see Budanitsky and Hirst (2001) for an overview). We use Lesk's measure as modified by Banerjee and Pedersen (2003) for two reasons. First, it has been shown to perform well in the related task of predominant sense detection (McCarthy et al., 2004). Second, it has the advantage of relying only upon the sense definitions, rather than the complex graph structure which is unique to WordNet. This makes the method more suitable for use with other sense inventories.

Note that unlike McCarthy et al. (2004), we are associating neighbors with senses, rather than merely trying to detect the predominant sense, and therefore we require more precision in our selection. When it is unclear which sense of the target word is most similar to a given neighbor (when the scores of two or more senses are close together), that neighbor is discarded.

As an example, consider the word *sense*, which has four meanings[1] in WordNet: (1) a general conscious **awareness** (e.g., *a sense of security*), (2) the **meaning** of a word (e.g., *the dictionary gave several senses for the word*), (3) sound practical **judgment** (e.g., *I can't see the sense in doing it now*), and (4) a natural appreciation or **ability** (e.g., *keen musical sense*). On the British National Corpus (BNC), using Lin's (1998) similarity method, we retrieve the following neighbors for the first and second sense, respectively:

1. awareness, feeling, instinct, enthusiasm, sensation, vision, tradition, consciousness, anger, panic, loyalty
2. emotion, belief, meaning, manner, necessity, tension, motivation

No neighbors are associated with the last two senses, indicating that they are not prevalent enough in the BNC to be detected by this method.

Once sense-specific neighbors are acquired, the next stage is to replace all instances of the neighbors in the corpus with the target ambiguous word labeled with the appropriate sense. For example, when encountering the sentence "... *attempt to state the **meaning** of a word*", our method would automatically transform this to "... *attempt to state the **sense** (s#2) of a word.*" These *pseudo-labeled* instances comprise the training instances we provide to our machine learning algorithms.

4 Experimental Setup

We evaluated the performance of our approach on benchmark datasets. In this section we give details regarding our training and test data, and describe the features and machine learners we employed. Finally, we discuss the methods to which we compare our approach.

4.1 Data

Our experiments use a subset of the data provided for the English lexical sample task in the Senseval 2 (Preiss and Yarowsky, 2001) and Senseval 3 (Mihalcea and Edmonds, 2004) evaluation exercises. Since our method does not require hand tagged training data, we merged the provided training and test data into a single test set.

As a proof of concept we focus on the disambiguation of nouns, since they constitute the largest portion of content words (50% in the BNC). In addition, WordNet, which is our semantic resource and point of comparison, has a wide coverage of nouns. Also, for many tasks and applications (e.g., web queries) nouns are the most frequently encountered part-of-speech (Jansen et al., 2000). We made use of the coarse-grained sense groupings provided for both Senseval datasets. For many applications (e.g., information retrieval) coarsely defined senses are more useful (see Snow et al. (2007) for discussion).

Our training data was created from the BNC using different ways of obtaining the neighbors of the target word. As described in Section 3 we retrieved neighbors using Lin's (1998) similarity measure on a RASP parsed (Briscoe and Carroll, 2002) version of the BNC. We used subject and object dependencies, as well as adjective and noun modifier dependencies. We also created training data sets using collocational neighbors. Specifically, using the InfoMap toolkit[2], we constructed vector-based representations for individual words from the BNC using a term-document matrix and the cosine similarity measure. Vectors were initially constructed with 1,000 dimensions, the most frequent content words. The space was reduced to 100 dimensions with singular value decomposition. Finally, we also extracted neighbors from WordNet using first-order and sibling relations (i.e., hyponyms of the same hypernym). A problem often encountered when using dictionary-based neighbors is that they are themselves polysemous, and the related sense is often not the most prominent one in the corpus, which leads to noisy data. We therefore experimented with using *all* neighbors for a given word

[1] We are using the coarse-grained representation according to Senseval 2 annotators. The sense definitions are simplified for the sake of brevity.

[2] http://infomap.stanford.edu/

"The philosophical explanation of authority is not an attempt to state the **sense** of a word."	
Contextual features	
±10 words	explanation, of, authority, be, ...
±5 words	an, attempt, to, state, of, a, ...
Collocational features	
-2/+0 *n*-gram	_state_the_X
-1/+1 *n*-gram	_the_X_of
-0/+2 *n*-gram	_X_of_a
-2/+0 POS *n*-gram	_Verb_Det_X
-1/+1 POS *n*-gram	_Det_X_Prep
-0/+2 POS *n*-gram	_X_Prep_Det
Syntactic features	
Object of Verb	obj_of_state

Table 1: Example sentence and extracted features for the word *sense*; X denotes the target word.

or only those which are *monosemous* and hopefully less noisy. In all cases we used 50 neighbors, the most similar nouns to the target.

4.2 Features

We used a rich feature space based on lemmas, part-of-speech (POS) tags and a variety of positional and syntactic relationships of the target word capturing both immediate local context and wider context. These feature types have been widely used in WSD algorithms (see Lee and Ng (2002) for an evaluation of their effectiveness). Their use is illustrated on a sample English sentence for the target word *sense* in Table 1.

4.3 Supervised Classifiers

One of our evaluation goals was to examine the effect of our training-data creation procedure on different types of classifiers and determine which ones are most suited for use with our method. We therefore chose three supervised classifiers (support vector machines, maximum entropy, and label propagation) which are based on different learning paradigms and have shown competitive performance in WSD (Niu et al., 2005; Preiss and Yarowsky, 2001; Mihalcea and Edmonds, 2004). We summarize below their main characteristics and differences.

Support Vector Machines SVMs model classification as the problem of finding a separating hyperplane in a high dimensional vector space. They focus on differentiating between the most problematic cases — instances which are close to each other in the high dimensional space, but have different labels. They are discriminative, rather than generative, and do not explicitly model the classes. SVMs have been applied successfully in many NLP tasks. We used the multi-class bound-constrained support vector classification (SVC) version of SVM described in Hsu and Lin (2001) and implemented in the BSVM package[3]. All parameters were set to their default values with the exception of the misclassification penalty, which was set to a high value (1,000) to penalize labeling all instances with the most frequent sense.

Maximum Entropy Model Maximum entropy-based classifiers are a common alternative to other probabilistic classifiers, such as Naive Bayes, and have received much interest in various NLP tasks ranging from part-of-speech tagging to parsing and text classification. They represent a probabilistic, global constrained approach. They assume a uniform, zero-knowledge model, under the constraints of the training dataset. The classifier finds the (unique) maximal entropy model which conforms to the expected feature distribution of the training data. In our experiments, we used Megam[4] a publicly available maximum entropy classifier (Daumé III, 2004) with the default parameters.

Label Propagation The basic Label Propagation algorithm (Zhu and Ghahramani, 2002) represents labeled and unlabeled instances as nodes in an undirected graph with weighted edges. Initially only the known data nodes are labeled. The goal is to propagate labels from labeled to unlabeled points along the weighted edges. The weights are based on distance in a high-dimensional space. At each iteration, only the original labels are fixed, whereas the propagated labels are "soft", and may change in subsequent iterations. This property allows the final labeling to be affected by more distant labels, that have propagated further, and gives the algorithm a global aspect. We used SemiL[5], a publicly available implementation of label propagation (all parameters were set to default values).

4.4 Comparison with State-of-the-art

As an upper bound, we considered the accuracy of our classifiers when trained on the manually-labeled Senseval data (using the same experimental settings and 5-fold crossvalidation). This can be used to estimate the expected decrease in accuracy caused solely by the use of our automatic sense labeling method. We also compared our approach to other unsupervised ones. These include McCarthy

[3]http://www.csie.ntu.edu.tw/~cjlin/bsvm/
[4]http://www.isi.edu/~hdaume/megam/index.html
[5]http://www.engineers.auckland.ac.nz/~vkec001

et al.'s (2004) method for inferring the predominant sense and Lesk's (1986) algorithm. We modified the latter slightly so as to increase its coverage and used McCarthy et al.'s first sense heuristic to disambiguate unknown instances where no overlap was found. For McCarthy et al. we used parameters they report as optimal.

5 Results

The evaluation of our method was motivated by three questions: (1) How do different choices in constructing the pseudo-labeled training data affect WSD performance? Here, we would like to assess whether the origin of the target word neighbors (e.g., from a corpus or dictionary) matters. (2) What is the degree of noise and subsequent loss in accuracy incurred by our method? (3) How does the proposed approach compare against other unsupervised methods? In particular, we are interested to find out whether we outperform McCarthy et al.'s (2004) related method for predominant sense detection.

5.1 The Choice of Neighbors

Our results are summarized in Table 2. We report accuracy (rather than F-score) since all algorithms labeled all instances. The three center columns present our results with the automatically constructed training sets.

The best accuracies are observed when the labels are created from distributionally similar words using Lin's (1998) dependency-based similarity measure (Depend). We observe a small decrease in performance (within the range of 2%–4%) when using collocational neighbors without any syntactic information.[6] Using the neighbors provided by WordNet leads to worse results than using distributional neighbors. The differences in performance are significant[7] ($p < 0.01$) on both Senseval datasets for all classifiers and for both WordNet configurations, i.e., using all neighbors (AllWN) vs. monosemous ones (MonoWN).

This result may seem counterintuitive since neighbors provided by a semantic resource are based on expert knowledge and are often more accurate than those obtained automatically. However, semantic resources like WordNet are designed to be as general as possible without a specific corpus or domain in mind. They will therefore provide related words for all senses, even rare ones, which may not appear in our chosen corpus. Distributional methods, on the other hand, are anchored in the corpus. The extracted neighbors are usually relevant and representative of the corpus. Another drawback of resource-based neighbors is that they often do not share local behavior, i.e., they do not appear in the same immediate local context and do not share the same syntax. For this reason, the useful information that can be extracted from their contexts tends to be topical (e.g., words that are indicative of the domain), rather than local (e.g., grammatical dependencies). Topical information is mostly useful when the difference between senses can be attributed to a specific domain. However, for many words and senses, this is not the case (Leacock et al., 1998).

5.2 Comparison against Manual Labels

The rightmost column of Table 2 shows the accuracy of our classifiers when these are trained on the manually annotated Senseval datasets. In general, all algorithms exhibit a similar level of performance when trained on hand-coded data, with slightly lower scores for Senseval 3. On Senseval 2, the SVM is significantly better than the other two classifiers ($p < 0.01$). On Senseval 3, label propagation is significantly worse than the others ($p < 0.01$). The results shown here do not represent the highest achievable performance in a supervised setting, but rather those obtained without extensive parameter tuning. The best performing systems on coarse-grained nouns in Senseval 2 and 3 (Preiss and Yarowsky, 2001; Mihalcea and Edmonds, 2004) achieved approximately 76% and 80%, respectively. Besides being more finely tuned, these systems employed more sophisticated learning paradigms (e.g., ensemble learning).

When we compare the results from the manually labeled data to those achieved with the distributional neighbors, we can see that use of our pseudo-labels results in accuracies that are approximately 8–10% lower. Since the results were achieved using the same feature set and classifier settings, the comparison provides an estimate of the expected decrease in accuracy due only to our unsupervised tagging method. With more detailed feature engineering and more sophisticated machine learning methods, we could probably improve our classifiers' performance on the automatically labeled dataset. Also note that improvements in supervised methods can be expected to automatically translate to improvements in unsupervised

[6] We omit these results from the table for brevity.

[7] Throughout, we report significance using a χ^2 test.

Senseval 2	AllWN	MonoWN	Depend	Manual
SVM	48.12	53.29	64.38	72.52
MaxEnt	40.93	52.11	62.32	71.91
LP	42.67	49.54	63.32	69.28
McCarthy	59.98			
Lesk	48.12			

Senseval 3	AllWN	MonoWN	Depend	Manual
SVM	53.16	46.32	57.47	71.22
MaxEnt	49.67	44.85	57.35	71.75
LP	47.41	43.60	60.60	67.57
McCarthy	57.14			
Lesk	48.66			

Table 2: Accuracy (%) on Senseval 2 and 3 lexical samples. Support vector machines (SVM), maximum entropy (MaxEnt) and label propagation (LP) are trained on automatically and manually labeled data sets

WSD using our method.

Interestingly, label propagation performed relatively poorly on the manually labeled data. However, it ranks highly when using the automatic labels. This may be due to the fact that LP is the only algorithm that does not separate the training and test set (it is principally a semi-supervised method), allowing the properties of both to influence the structure of the resulting graph. Since the instances in the training data are not actual occurrences of the target word, it is important to learn which instances in the training set are closest to a given instance in the test set. The two other algorithms only attempt to distinguish between classes in the training set.

5.3 Other Unsupervised Methods

As shown in Table 2 our classifiers are significantly better than Lesk on both Senseval datasets ($p < 0.01$). They also significantly outperform the automatically acquired predominant sense (McCarthy) on Senseval 2 (for the Maximum Entropy classifier, the difference is significant at $p < 0.05$). On Senseval 3, all classifiers quantitatively outperform the first sense heuristic, but the difference is statistically significant only for label propagation ($p < 0.01$). The differences in performance on the two datasets can be explained by analyzing their sense distributions. Senseval 3 has a higher level of ambiguity (4.35 senses per word, on average, compared to 3.28 for Senseval 2), and is therefore a more difficult dataset. Although Senseval 3 has a slightly lower percentage of first sense instances, the higher ambiguity means that the skew is, in fact, much higher than in Senseval 2. A high skew towards the predominant sense means there are less instances from which we can learn about the rarer senses, and that we run a higher risk when labeling an instance as one of the rarer senses (instead of defaulting to the predominant one).

Senseval 2	Depend		Manual	
SVM	14.3	(60.1)	16.9	(60.4)
MaxEnt	6.3	(66.9)	17.1	(56.7)
LP	8.9	(63.3)	14.8	(49.4)

Senseval 3	Depend		Manual	
SVM	17.6	(45.0)	23.3	(60.0)
MaxEnt	8.5	(55.0)	23.7	(60.9)
LP	5.6	(60.9)	17.8	(53.5)

Table 3: Percentage of non-first instances in automatically and manually labeled training data; numbers in parentheses show the classifiers' accuracy on these instances.

Our method shares some of the principles of McCarthy et al.'s (2004) unsupervised algorithm. However, instead of focusing on detecting a single predominant sense throughout the corpus, we build a dataset that will allow us to learn about and identify all existing (prevalent) senses. Despite the fact that the first-sense heuristic is a strong baseline, and fall-back option in case of limited local information, it is not a true context-specific WSD algorithm. Any approach that ignores local context, and labels all instances with a single sense has limited effectiveness when WSD is needed in an application. Context-indifferent methods run the risk of completely mistaking the predominant sense, thereby mis-labeling most of the instances, whereas approaches that consider local context are less prone to such large-scope errors.

We further analyzed the performance of our method by examining instances labeled with senses other than the most frequent one. Table 3 shows the percentage of such instances depending on the machine learner and type of training data (automatic versus manual) being employed. It also presents the classifiers' accuracy (figures in parentheses) with regard to only the non-first senses. When trained on the automatically labeled data, our classifiers tend to be more conservative in assigning non-first senses. Interestingly, we obtain similar accuracies with the classifiers trained on the manually labeled data, even though the latter assign more non-first senses. It is worth noting that the SVM labels two to three times as many instances with non-first-sense labels, yet achieves similar levels of overall accuracy to the other classifiers (compare Tables 2 and 3) and only slightly lower accuracy on the non-first senses. This would make it a better choice when it is important to have more data on rarer senses.

6 Conclusions and Future Work

We have presented an unsupervised approach to WSD which retains many of the advantages of supervised methods, while being free of the costly requirement for human annotation. We demonstrate that classifiers trained using our method can out-perform state-of-the-art unsupervised methods, and approach the accuracy of fully-supervised methods trained on manually-labeled data.

In the future we plan to scale our system to the all-words task. There is nothing inherent in our method that restricts us to the lexical sample, which we chose primarily to assess the feasibility of our ideas. Another interesting direction concerns the use of our method in a semi-supervised setting. For example, we could automatically acquire labeled instances for words whose senses are rare in a manually tagged dataset. Finally, we could potentially improve accuracy, at the expense of coverage, by estimating confidence scores on the classifiers' predictions, and assigning labels only to instances with high confidence.

Acknowledgments

The authors acknowledge the support of EPSRC (grant EP/C538447/1) and would like to thank David Talbot for his insightful suggestions.

References

S. Banerjee, T. Pedersen. 2003. Extended gloss overlaps as a measure of semantic relatedness. In *Proc. of the 18th IJCAI*, 805–810, Acapulco.

R. Barzilay, M. Elhadad. 1997. Using lexical chains for text summarization. In *Proc. of the Intelligent Scalable Text Summarization Workshop*, Madrid, Spain.

T. Briscoe, J. Carroll. 2002. Robust accurate statistical annotation of general text. In *Proc. of the 3rd LREC*, 1499–1504, Las Palmas, Gran Canaria.

A. Budanitsky, G. Hirst. 2001. Semantic distance in WordNet: An experimental, application-oriented evaluation of five measures. In *Proc. of the ACL Worskhop on WordNet and Other Lexical Resources*, Pittsburgh, PA.

Y. S. Chan, H. T. Ng. 2007. Word sense disambiguation improves statistical machine translation. In *Proc. of the 45th ACL*, 33–40, Prague, Czech Republic.

H. Daumé III. 2004. Notes on CG and LM-BFGS optimization of logistic regression.

P. Edmonds. 2000. Designing a task for SENSEVAL-2, 2000. Technical note.

C. Fellbaum, ed. 1998. *WordNet: An Electronic Database*. MIT Press, Cambridge, MA.

W. Gale, K. Church, D. Yarowsky. 1992. A method for disambiguating word senses in a large corpus. *Computers and the Humanities*, 26(2):415–439.

M. Galley, K. McKeown. 2003. Improving word sense disambiguation in lexical chaining. In *Proc. of the 18th IJCAI*, 1486–1488, Acapulco.

C. Hsu, C. Lin. 2001. A comparison of methods for multiclass support vector machines, 2001. Technical report, Department of Computer Science and Information Engineering, National Taiwan University, Taipei, Taiwan.

B. J. Jansen, A. Spink, A. Pfaff. 2000. Linguistic aspects of web queries, 2000. American Society of Information Science, Chicago.

C. Leacock, M. Chodorow, G. A. Miller. 1998. Using corpus statistics and wordnet relations for sense identification. *Computational Linguistics*, 24(1):147–165.

Y. K. Lee, H. T. Ng. 2002. An empirical evaluation of knowledge sources and learning algorithms for word sense disambiguation. In *Proc. of the EMNLP*, 41–48, NJ.

M. Lesk. 1986. Automatic sense disambiguation using machine readable dictionaries: How to tell a pine cone from an ice cream cone. In *Proc. of the 5th SIGDOC*, 24–26, New York, NY.

D. Lin. 1998. Automatic retrieval and clustering of similar words. In *Proc. of the ACL/COLING*, 768–774, Montreal.

D. McCarthy, R. Koeling, J. Weeds, J. Carroll. 2004. Finding predominant senses in untagged text. In *Proc. of the 42th ACL*, 280–287, Barcelona, Spain.

R. F. Mihalcea, P. Edmonds, eds. 2004. *Proc. of the SENSEVAL-3*, Barcelona, 2004.

R. F. Mihalcea. 2002. Word sense disambiguation with pattern learning and automatic feature selection. *Natural Language Engineering*, 8(4):343–358.

H. T. Ng, B. Wang, Y. S. Chan. 2003. Exploiting parallel texts for word sense disambiguation: an empirical study. In *Proc. of the 41st ACL*, 455–462, Sapporo, Japan.

H. T. Ng. 1997. Getting serious about word sense disambiguation. In *Proc. of the ACL SIGLEX Workshop on Tagging Text with Lexical Semantics: Why, What, and How?*, 1–7, Washington, DC.

Z. Y. Niu, D. H. Ji, C. L. Tan. 2005. Word sense disambiguation using label propagation based semi-supervised learning. In *Proc. of the 43rd ACL*, 395–402, Ann Arbor.

J. Preiss, D. Yarowsky, eds. 2001. *Proc. of the 2nd International Workshop on Evaluating Word Sense Disambiguation Systems*, Toulouse, France, 2001.

G. Ramakrishnan, A. Jadhav, A. Joshi, S. Chakrabarti, P. Bhattacharyya. 2003. Question answering via Bayesian inference on lexical relations. In *Proc. of the ACL 2003 workshop on Multilingual summarization and QA*, 1–10.

R. Snow, S. Prakash, D. Jurafsky, A. Y. Ng. 2007. Learning to merge word senses. In *Proc. of the EMNLP/CoNLL*, 1005–1014, Prague, Czech Republic.

J. Weeds. 2003. *Measures and Applications of Lexical Distributional Similarity*. Ph.D. thesis, University of Sussex.

D. Yarowsky. 1992. Word-sense disambiguation using statistical models of Roget's categories trained on large corpora. In *Proc. of the 14th COLING*, 454–460, Nantes, France.

X. Zhu, Z. Ghahramani. 2002. Learning from labeled and unlabeled data with label propagation. Technical report, CMU-CALD-02, 2002.

A Classification of Dialogue Actions in Tutorial Dialogue

Mark Buckley and **Magdalena Wolska**
Dept. of Computational Linguistics
Saarland University
66041 Saarbrücken, Germany
{buckley|magda}@coli.uni-sb.de

Abstract

In this paper we present a taxonomy of dialogue moves which describe the actions that students and tutors perform in tutorial dialogue. We are motivated by the need for a categorisation of such actions in order to develop computational models for tutorial dialogue. As such, we build both on existing work on dialogue move categorisation for tutorial dialogue as well as dialogue taxonomies for general dialogue. Our taxonomy has been prepared by analysing a corpus of tutorial dialogues on mathematical theorem proving. We also detail an annotation experiment in which we apply the taxonomy and discuss idiosyncrasies in the data which influence the decisions in the dialogue move classification.

1 Introduction

The field of Intelligent Tutoring Systems has seen recent developments moving towards adding natural language capabilities to computer-based tutoring (Graesser et al., 1999; Zinn, 2004; Litman and Silliman, 2004), motivated by empirical investigations which point to the effectiveness of human tutors (Bloom, 1984; Moore, 1993; Graesser et al., 1995). However, to be able to interact with a student through the medium of natural language dialogue, the system must have a model of how such tutorial dialogues can progress and what utterances are licenced. In order to develop such a model of dialogue, we need to understand and describe the "actions" performed with words, i.e. speech acts (Austin, 1955) or *dialogue moves*. This involves identifying and categorising the functions that utterances may have in dialogue and their relationships to each other.

Researchers in conversation and dialogue theory have proposed various general categorisations of dialogue moves. DIT++ (Bunt, 2000) is an example of a comprehensive multidimensional taxonomy of dialogue acts for information dialogues based on DAMSL (Allen and Core, 1997), a general-purpose extensible taxonomy proposed as a standard for dialogue annotation. The DAMSL dialogue act taxonomy characterises utterances along four dimensions which correspond to four levels of functions utterances may have. The forward looking function describes the utterance's effect on the following interaction, the backward looking function, its relation to previous dialogue, the communicative status describes the comprehensibility or interpretability of the utterance, and the information level characterises the content of the utterance.

Tsovaltzi and Karagjosova (2004) proposed an extension of the DAMSL classification based on an analysis of tutorial dialogue corpora. The proposed taxonomy adds a **Task** dimension which concentrates on tutor actions in the dialogue.[1] Building on this work, we propose a further extension to this taxonomy inspired by our analysis from the point of view of task-related goals. The classification we present (i) includes modifications of the DAMSL categorisation motivated by tutorial dialogue, (ii) accounts for student's actions, and (iii) introduces a **Task progress** dimension whose purpose is to characterise the completion status of a generally viewed "task", instantiated for the purpose of tutorial dialogue. We validated our dialogue act categorisation in a small-scale annotation experiment whose results we present.

This paper is organised as follows: In Section 2 we introduce our data and taxonomy development

© 2008. Licensed under the *Creative Commons Attribution-Noncommercial-Share Alike 3.0 Unported* license (http://creativecommons.org/licenses/by-nc-sa/3.0/). Some rights reserved.

[1] This classification has not been, to our knowledge, quantitatively evaluated.

methodology. In Section 3 we present the taxonomy. The results of the annotation experiment and their discussion are presented in Section 4. Section 5 presents related work and Section 6 concludes the paper.

2 The Data and Analysis Methodology

Our work is based on an analysis of two corpora of tutorial dialogues on mathematical theorem proving. We use the data to (i) verify the general dialogue dimensions of the DAMSL taxonomy in the context of tutorial dialogues, and (ii) extend the taxonomy by developing the task dimension. While the specific task-level moves are instantiated for the mathematics tutoring domain, our aim is to maintain generality that would allow us to model task-level moves in other tutoring domains as well as task-oriented dialogues in general. Below we briefly introduce the corpora and outline our methodology.

Corpora We analysed two corpora of tutorial dialogues in the domain of mathematical theorem proving collected in Wizard-of-Oz experiments in which a human tutor (wizard) simulated the system's behaviour (Benzmüller et al., 2003; Benzmüller et al., 2006a). The domains of mathematics in the first (Corpus-I) and second (Corpus-II) corpora are naive set theory and binary relations respectively (Wolska et al., 2004; Benzmüller et al., 2006b).

In both experiments the dialogues were conducted in German using the keyboard and a graphical user interface. The tutoring in the experiment described in (Benzmüller et al., 2003) was performed under three experimental conditions. The control group (8 subjects) were tutored according to the *minimal feedback* strategy in which the tutor's reactions were limited to informing the student as to the correctness and completeness of their contributions. In the *didactic* group (7 subjects) and *socratic* group (7 subjects) the tutor's strategy focused on disclosing partial solutions to the student in case of lack of progress and leading toward the solution (hinting) respectively. Given the tutoring strategy the verbosity of the *minimal feedback* tutors was limited, while in both other conditions as well as in the other experiment, the subjects and the tutors were unconstrained in terms of the linguistic realisation of their turns. Table 1 shows the overview of the size of the corpora in terms of the number of turns.

	Corpus-I	Corpus-II
no. subjects	22	37
no. turns	775	1917
no. student turns	332	937
no. tutor turns	443	980

Table 1: Overview of the corpora

Methodology In developing the taxonomy we pursued the following iterative methodology:

First, in order to build the initial taxonomy, we analysed 18 dialogues from Corpus-I containing 299 utterances (the development set). The purpose of this analysis was to (i) verify the general suitability of the DAMSL scheme in the tutoring domain,[2] (ii) identify features of dialogues moves relevant in tutoring that were not present in the original taxonomy (see the discussion in Section 4), (iii) identify an initial set of task-level moves. We descriptively defined the move types and wrote draft annotation guidelines.

Second, we applied the initial taxonomy to 4 dialogues (108 utterances) taken from the two corpora in an annotation task performed independently by the authors of this paper (a preliminary test set), after which we extended the taxonomy and refined the existing category definitions. Finally, we randomly[3] selected an 64-utterance subset taken from both corpora (validation set) to test the coverage of the final taxonomy.

3 A Dialogue Move Taxonomy

Our goal in the analysis of the development set and preliminary test set of the corpus was to determine a categorisation of the actions that can be performed by students and tutors in tutorial dialogues. The taxonomy which we have created from this categorisation contains the dialogue moves which realise these actions. Now the utterances performed by students and tutors realise actions which may or may not address or have an effect on the current task. We thus speak of the task-level function of an utterance in addition to a general dialogue level function which all utterances have. Task-level vs. general dialogue level function is therefore the basic split in our taxonomy.

[2]We expected this to be suitable because DAMSL is a taxonomy with general applicability.

[3]We avoided dialogues in which the student's utterances contained formulas only.

The full definition of the taxonomy is presented in Table 2. For each dialogue move we give a short explanation of what function it is intended to capture as well as a short example. In the following sections we discuss some of our design decisions.

3.1 The Forward and Backward Dimensions

At the general dialogue level we follow the DAMSL taxonomy and categorise the functions of utterances according to their relationship with the previous dialogue and their effect on the dialogue to follow. For these functions we use a **Forward** dimension and a **Backward** dimension, respectively. In general, we try to accommodate the DAMSL categories in order to build as much as possible on existing generally accepted work on dialogue moves. The forward dimension captures utterances which are either assertions, requests or commands. The backward dimension captures utterances which agree or disagree with previous utterances, address questions, signal the understanding status of previous utterances, or stand in some information relation to previous utterances. The main differences between DAMSL and our categorisation within these two dimensions are the following: (i) we combine DAMSL's Assert and Re-assert in a single category Assert which may be optionally marked as repeating information, (ii) we combine DAMSL's Action-directive and Info-request in a higher-level category of Requests, (iii) in place of DAMSL's Answer, we introduce a more general Address category in the backward dimension with subcategories Answer, Deflect, and Neutral, where Deflect accounts for avoiding answering and Neutral refers to those utterances which simply address a previous information request without answering it or a previous action directive without acceding to it. The remaining DAMSL categories were left unchanged; they are also not presented in Table 2.

3.2 The Task and Task Progress Dimensions

At the task level we have utterances which address the task at hand. These can mean altering the state of the task solution, for instance by performing a step in the solution, or talking about the task solution without altering it, for instance making statements about previously performed steps. We divide the task related actions in those which address the task directly and those which address the solution construction process, and capture these in the task and task progress dimensions respectively.

The **Task** dimension contains most of the task related dialogue moves. We follow Tsovaltzi and Karagjosova (2004) by splitting the task dimension into two subdivisions which relate to the parallel tasks being carried out and the roles of the dialogue participants. Since the roles of student and tutor restrict what actions can be performed by the speakers, we split the task dimension into actions which contribute to the solving task and those which contribute to the teaching task. Actions in the solving task are typically performed by the student, actions in the teaching task are typically performed by the tutor and are pedagogically motivated. This is important for example to differentiate between requests for task level information — requests coming from the student are of an information seeking nature, those that come from the tutor contribute to diagnostic or pedagogical goals.

Within the solving task, changes or additions to the solution are captured by Solution-step, which may be a new step or an extension of an existing step, and Solution-strategy. Solution-strategy is divided into stating a strategy which will be followed and stating a solution step which will be performed in the future. The difference between these is that the statement of a future step refers to a single step in the solution which the student is committing to perform, whereas a strategy is a more abstract concept. A strategy is more like a solution approach which may consist of a number of steps, however which actual steps are to be performed is left open. In the domain of mathematical theorem proving a strategy may refer to a particular proving technique, for instance a proof by induction or by contradiction, which may be realised by an utterance such as "I will now do a proof by induction". Exactly what constitutes a step and a strategy is a matter of how the domain is modelled.

Request-assistance covers actions which ask for help with the task. Within the teaching task, Solution-step-evaluation refers to utterances that convey the correctness or otherwise of steps. Domain relevant requests ask for domain related information such as definitions. Hint covers direct hints about how to continue the task, for instance by giving away a concept which should be used by the student. The hint category will need to cover many different kinds of actions depending on the tutorial strategy which tutors follow — we have not subdivided this category and refer to Tsovaltzi et al. (2004) where this is further elaborated.

The **Task Progress** dimension equates in part to the task management dimension in DAMSL. Here the dialogue moves related to the current task are those which start, finish, restart or abandon it. The student can indicate the status of the solution construction process to be on-track or finished or signal that he is lost.

In summary, we have prepared our taxonomy of dialogue moves for tutoring by adding a **Task** and **Task Progress** dimensions to the original DAMSL taxonomy. We have tried to keep as close to the DAMSL specification as possible with regard to the general dialogue level function of dialogue moves, while at the same time adapting it to capture the phenomena of tutorial dialogue. Although some moves will typically by performed by either the student or the tutor (for example, only the tutor will realistically give hints) we do not introduce any constraints which restrict this.

4 Validating the Taxonomy

We used the taxonomy to perform a small-scale annotation experiment on a validation set taken from the two corpora introduced in Section 2. The data had previously been segmented into utterances. The goal of this experiment was to see whether our categorisation can be reliably applied to data and to validate the coverage of the taxonomy. The annotation was carried out by two annotators (the authors of this paper), following the definitions of the dialogue moves informally presented above. We did not consider the category information-relation because no definition is given by the original DAMSL taxonomy, however we will return to the question of information relation later in the discussion.

Results Inter-annotator agreement was calculated using Cohen's kappa (Cohen, 1960) and the results of the experiment are given in the following table.

Dimension	κ value
Forward	0.87
Backward	0.47
Task	0.75
Task Progress	0.91

These results can be considered very good for the **Forward** and **Task Progress** dimensions, good for the **Task** dimension, and low for the **Backward** dimension. Among the categories with the lowest agreement were Neutral at 0.11 and Step-augmentation at 0.37. In this preliminary evaluation our strategy was not to use an category "other" for utterances which did not appear to belong to any existing category, but rather to try to fit the annotation to the categories as they are. We marked possibly problematic utterances for further discussion.

Example We give examples of two fully annotated dialogue excerpts in Figure 1. The examples illustrate some of the types of problematic utterances which the corpora contain. For instance both utterances "Really?" and "Yes?" are questions and could appear to be information requests, but in fact act more like prompts to continue, for which we had no category. Similarly the functions of the questions in sequence in the second example are difficult to abstract. We have tagged these as Neutral, since they discharge the obligations introduced by the questions before them, but the link between consecutive interrogative utterances is elusive.

Discussion We will now briefly discuss the results and findings of our annotation experiment and allude to some of the possible causes of the difficulties we encountered.

The nature of tutorial dialogue is an underlying factor which makes it difficult to annotate categories reliably. Students tend to be very concise, which makes it difficult to determine how the student intended to relate the latest input to the previous discourse. This is reflected in our agreement score for the backward dimension, which at 0.47 is much lower than the other dimensions, as well as in the agreement score of 0.37 for the Solution-step augmentation category, which is heavily dependent on previous context. This result may even point to a general characteristic of tutorial dialogue which makes computational modelling challenging. In particular the Neutral category resulted in conflicting annotations because it is often unclear, as in the examples shown above, whether Requests are being answered or merely addressed.

We have found that tutors typically perform utterances which contribute to many different goals — for instance they can simultaneously reject proposed solution steps while giving hints on how to continue in the task. The purpose of multidimensional dialogue move taxonomies is to handle this very multifunctionality, and while this is success-

Utterance	Forward	Backward	Task
S: It holds that $P(C \cup (A \cap B)) \subseteq P(C) \cup \ldots$	assert		solution-step:new
T: Really?	info-request	reject	signal-incorrect
S: no it's not,		answer	
S: the other way around	assert		solution-step:new
T: that's right at last	assert	accept	signal-correct
S: $R \circ S := \{(x,y) \mid \exists z(z \in M \wedge (x,z) \in R \wedge \ldots$	assert		solution-step:new
T: That's right!	assert	accept	signal-correct
S: now i want the inverse of that	assert		state-future-step
T: yes?		neutral	hint
S: $(R \circ S)^{-1}$	assert	neutral	solution-step:new
T: = ?	info-request	request-clar	request-explanation
S: How will the system answer?	info-request	neutral	
T: What's the question?	info-request	neutral	
S: Can the system conclude $(R \circ S)^{-1}$ from $R \circ S$	info-request	neutral	
T: yes	assert	answer	
T: But try it yourself!	action-dir		hint

Figure 1: Annotated example from the corpus

ful to a point, conflicts in the annotation experiment have highlighted some dual functions within the same category. For instance, utterances simultaneously rejecting steps and requesting explanations of the errors in the steps were found a number of times.

We have found at least three categories that may need to be added to the current taxonomy to make it cover tutorial dialogue more completely. As discussed above, a prompt type in the forward dimension seems necessary. In addition, we would foresee a backward category which corrects a previous utterance, a category in the solving task which requests the next step in the solution, and a category in the task progress dimension to check if the current task is being restarted. Similar categories are proposed by Tsovaltzi and Karagjosova (2004), and may be taken up.

We can draw attention to the fact that there are many interrelations between the dimensions which are not captured by our presentation of the taxonomy, and which may for instance be accounted for by introducing constraints on label combinations. We observe that many utterances stand in some information relation (a DAMSL category) to the previous discourse, although we have not further specified what this relation might be. Such utterances are typically step augmentations, and could be described for instance (in RST terms) as elaborations.

Finally we have adopted Tsovaltzi and Karagjosova's top-level structure, with **Task** as a dimension. However, we observe that it would be equally valid and more in keeping with the original DAMSL categorisation of utterance functions to make use of the existing Task sub-category of the **Info-level** dimension. Similarly, our **Task progress** corresponds to **Info-level**'s sub-category Task management. This is a straightforward structural change which will not affect the annotation results within these categories.

5 Related Work

The original DAMSL taxonomy was applied to and evaluated on the TRAINS corpus of problem solving dialogues (Core and Allen, 1997). In this annotation a single label **Task** was used to mark all task-related utterances. In the Verbmobil project, a set of dialogue moves specific to negotiation was proposed (Alexandersson et al., 1997). These moves capture only the task-specific functions of the utterances. Similarly, the HCRC Map Task coding scheme concentrates on the task functions of utterances, here specific to instruction-giving dialogues. This classification is based on conversational games approach to dialogue semantics (Houghton, 1986).

The DIT++ taxonomy of dialogue acts (Bunt, 2006) provides a more fine grained categorisation of general dialogue actions, however there is no one category or dimension dedicated to task specific functions. The category closest to (a subset of) our **Task** dimension would be Activity-Specific Functions, which however is defined in terms of performative verbs or graphical actions. In the tutoring domain not all task-related actions are realised by performatives.

There are a number of categorisations of dialogue actions specific to tutoring and motivated by the development of tutorial dialogue systems. Closely related to our work is a recent study by

Porayska-Pomsta et al. (2008), who categorise task related student actions and tutor feedback in a investigation of student affect. (Dzikovska et al., 2006) propose a flat coding scheme for tutorial dialogues on mathematics and relate it to a model of collaborative problem solving dialogue. A simpler taxonomy is presented by Marineau et al. (2000) which differs from our approach in that it was developed with the goal of automatic classification in an intelligent tutoring system. In a pedagogically motivated analysis of a corpus of tutorial dialogues on computer literacy, Graesser et al. (1999) categorise tutors' actions in order to propose a model of tutorial dialogue structure.

6 Conclusions and Future Work

In this paper we have presented a taxonomy of dialogue moves which captures the actions performed in by students and tutors in a corpus of tutorial dialogues. We then detailed an annotation experiment which applied the taxonomy to a validation data set and achieved good inter-annotator agreement. This preliminary study showed that we are able to cover the data well. We did however find a number of problematic phenomena in the data, such as that of relating task level actions to the previous discourse, which are of particular importance for classifying tutorial dialogue actions.

In our future work we plan a larger scale annotation of a further test set of our corpus, which we believe will confirm the tendencies found so far. We also intend to apply our taxonomy in an annotation of tutorial dialogue dealing with different task domains, for example, tutorial dialogue corpora in domains other than mathematics and general problem-solving dialogues (e.g. TRAINS). One of the goals of our work is to inform the development of models for tutorial dialogue, and so with a view towards operationalisation of the dialogue moves in our taxonomy, we will work on an axiomatic formalisation of the dialogue moves. This can form important input into developing a plan-based model for tutorial dialogue.

References

Alexandersson, Jan, Bianka Buschbeck-Wolf, Tsutomu Fujinami, Elisabeth Maier, Norbert Reithinger, Birte Schmitz, and Melanie Siegel. 1997. Dialogue acts in verbmobil-2. Technical report, DFKI.

Allen, James and Mark Core. 1997. Draft of DAMSL: Dialogue act markup in several layers. *DRI: Discourse Research Initiative*, University of Pennsylvania. `http://www.cs.rochester.edu/research/cisd/resources/damsl/RevisedManual/`.

Austin, John L. 1955. *How to do things with Words*. 2005, second edition. William James Lectures.

Benzmüller, Christoph, Armin Fiedler, Malte Gabsdil, Helmut Horacek, Ivana Kruijff-Korbayová, Manfred Pinkal, Jörg Siekmann, Dimitra Tsovaltzi, Bao Quoc Vo, and Magdalena Wolska. 2003. A Wizard-of-Oz experiment for tutorial dialogues in mathematics. In Aleven, Vincent, Ulrich Hoppe, Judy Kay, Riichiro Mizoguchi, Helen Pain, Felisa Verdejo, and Kalina Yacef, editors, *AIED2003 Supplementary Proceedings*, volume VIII: Advanced Technologies for Mathematics Education, pages 471–481, Sydney, Australia. School of Information Technologies, University of Sydney.

Benzmüller, Christoph, Helmut Horacek, Ivana Kruijff-Korbayová, Henri Lesourd, Marvin Schiller, and Magdalena Wolska. 2006a. DiaWozII – A Tool for Wizard-of-Oz Experiments in Mathematics. In *Proceedings of the 29th Annual German Conference on Artificial Intelligence (KI-06), Lecture Notes in Computer Science*, number 4314, pages 159–173, Bremen, Germany. Springer-Verlag.

Benzmüller, Christoph, Helmut Horacek, Henri Lesourd, Ivana Kruijff-Korbayová, Marvin Schiller, and Magdalena Wolska. 2006b. A corpus of tutorial dialogs on theorem proving; the influence of the presentation of the study-material. In *Proceedings of the 5th International Conference on Language Resources and Evaluation (LREC-06)*, pages 1766–1769, Genoa, Italy. ELDA.

Bloom, B. 1984. The 2 Sigma Problem: The Search for Methods of Group Instruction as Effective as One-to-One Tutoring. *Educational Researcher*, 13(6):4–16.

Bunt, Harry. 2000. Dialogue pragmatics and context specification. In Bunt, Harry and William Black, editors, *Abduction, Belief and Context in Dialogue. Studies in Computational Pragmatics*, volume 1, pages 81–150. Benjamins.

Bunt, Harry. 2006. Dimensions in Dialogue Act Annotation. In *Proceedings of the 5th International Conference on Language Resources and Evaluation (LREC-06)*, pages 919–924, Genova, Italy.

Cohen, Jacob. 1960. A coefficient of agreement for nominal scales. *Educational and Psychological Measurement*, 20(1):37–46.

Core, Mark G. and James F. Allen. 1997. Coding dialogues with the DAMSL annotation scheme. In Traum, David, editor, *Working Notes: AAAI Fall Symposium on Communicative Action in Humans and Machines*, pages 28–35. AAAI, Menlo Park, CA, USA.

Dzikovska, Myroslava O., Charles B. Callaway, Matthew Stone, and Johanna D. Moore. 2006. Understanding student input for tutorial dialogue in procedural domains. In Schlangen, David and Raquel Fernandez, editors, *Proceedings of Brandial, the 10th Workshop on the Semantics and Pragmatics of Dialogue*, pages 10–17.

Graesser, A. C., N. K. Person, and J. P. Magliano. 1995. Collaborative dialogue patterns in naturalistic one-on-one tutoring. *Applied Cognitive Psychology*, 9:495–522.

Graesser, Arthur C., Katja Wiemer-Hastings, Peter Wiemer-Hastings, and Roger Kreuz. 1999. Autotutor: A simulation of a human tutor. *Cognitive Systems Research*, 1:35–51.

Houghton, G. 1986. *The Production of Language in Dialogue: A Computational Model*. Ph.D. thesis, University of Sussex.

Litman, Diane J. and Scott Silliman. 2004. ITSPOKE: An Intelligent Tutoring Spoken Dialogue System. In *Proceedings of the Human Language Technology Conference: 4th Meeting of the North American Chapter of the Association for Computational Linguistics (HLT/NAACL) (Companion Proceedings)*, Boston, MA.

Marineau, Johanna, Peter Wiemer-Hastings, Derek Harter, Brent Olde, Patrick Chipman, Ashish Karnavat, Victoria Pomeroy, Sonya Rajan, and Art Graesser. 2000. Classification of speech acts in tutorial dialogue. In *Proceedings of the Workshop on Modeling Human Teaching Tactics and Strategies, ITS 2000*, pages 65–71.

Moore, Johanna. 1993. What makes human explanations effective? In *Proceedings of the 15th Meeting of the Cognitive Science Society*, pages 131–136, Hillsdale, NJ.

Porayska-Pomsta, Kaśka, Manolis Mavrikis, and Helen Pain. 2008. Diagnosing and acting on student affect: the tutor's perspective. *User Modeling and User-Adapted Interaction*, 18(1-2):125–173.

Tsovaltzi, Dimitra and Elena Karagjosova. 2004. A View on Dialogue Move Taxonomies for Tutorial Dialogues. In Strube, Michael and Candy Sidner, editors, *Proceedings of 5th SIGdial Workshop on Discourse and Dialogue*, pages 35–38, Cambridge, Massachusetts, USA. Association for Computational Linguistics.

Tsovaltzi, Dimitra, Armin Fiedler, and Helmut Horacek. 2004. A multi-dimensional taxonomy for automating hinting. In Lester, James C., Rosa Maria Vicari, and Fábio Paraguaçu, editors, *Intelligent Tutoring Systems — 7th International Conference (ITS-04)*, number 3220 in LNCS, pages 772–781. Springer.

Wolska, M., B. Q. Vo, D. Tsovaltzi, I. Kruijff-Korbayova, E. Karagjosova, H. Horacek, M. Gabsdil, A. Fiedler, and C. Benzmüller. 2004. An annotated corpus of tutorial dialogs on mathematical theorem proving. In *Proceedings of the Fourth International Conference on Language Resources and Evaluation (LREC-04)*, pages 1007–1010, Lisbon.

Zinn, Claus. 2004. Flexible dialogue management in natural-language enhanced tutoring. In *Konvens 2004 Workshop on Advanced Topics in Modeling Natural Language Dialog*, pages 28–35, Vienna, Austria.

Label	Explanation	Example
Forward Dimension		
Assert	Makes a claim about the world	"It holds that P"
Request	Introduces an obligation on the hearer to answer	
Action-directive	The obligation is that an action is performed	"Please show the following "
Info-request	Request for a piece of information	"What is the definition of...?"
Open-option	Suggestion of future action without obligation	"You could do a proof by induction"
Backward Dimension		
Agreement	Acceptance or rejection of plans or propositions	
Accept	Accepts a proposal	"Ok"
Reject	Rejects a proposal	"That's incorrect"
Address	Responses to requests	
Answer	Answers a previously posed info-request	"Yes"/"No"
Deflect	Shows inability or unwillingness to answer	"I can't answer that"
Neutral	Addresses without answering or deflecting	"Why do you ask?"
Information relation	Relation to an antecedent utterance	
Understanding related	Refers to problems understanding the speaker	
Request clarification	Asks to clarify a previous utterance	"What do you mean by X?"
Request rephrase	Asks for a repeat/rephrase of an utterance	"Could you repeat that?"
Signal non-understanding	Catch-all for signalling understanding problems	
Task Dimension: Solving Task		
Solution-step	Refers to a step to the current solution	
Step augmentation	Adds to an existing step	"Concluded using Rule X"
New	Contributes a new step	"Rewrite formula A to B"
Solution-strategy	Refers to a solution strategy	
State strategy	States a solution strategy which will be used	"I now do a case split"
state future step	State a step that will be executed later	"I will use DeMorgan2"
Request assistance	Ask for help with the task	
Request concept explanation	Ask to explain a domain concept	"What does P mean?"
Request worked example	Ask for an example to be presented	"Could you give me an example?"
Request solution strategy	Ask what strategy to proceed with	"How should i do this task?"
Task Dimension: Teaching Task		
Solution-step-evaluation	References to evaluations of soln steps	
Signal correct	Indicates the step was correct	"Correct!"
Signal incorrect	Indicates the step was incorrect	"Wrong!"
Hint	Give a hint towards solving the task	
Give-away-concept	Give away a concept to help with the task	"You should use rule X"
Request domain relevant	Requests which refer to domain concepts	
Explain	Ask for an explanation to be given	"T: What is the defn of powerset?"
Identify	Ask for a concept to be identified	"T: What does $\subseteq$ denote?"
Define	Ask for a definition	"What is the definition of...?"
Task Progress		
Start task	Starts the solution construction process	"Please prove $P = Q$"
Finish task	Indicates end of the solution construction process	"I'm done", "Q.E.D"
Restart task	Indicates solution being started again	"Start again"
Give-up task	Abandons the current solution attempt	"I give up"
Task solution status	References to solution progress	
On-track	Solution construction is on track	"Am i ok?", "You're doing fine"
Lost	Indicates speaker is lost in current solution	"I'm lost"

Table 2: The full taxonomy. Each type is given along with an explanation and an example

A Concept-Centered Approach to Noun-Compound Interpretation

Cristina Butnariu
School of Computer Science and Informatics
University College Dublin
Belfield, Dublin 4
Ioana.Butnariu@ucd.ie

Tony Veale
School of Computer Science and Informatics
University College Dublin
Belfield, Dublin 4
Tony.Veale@ucd.ie

Abstract

A noun-compound is a compressed proposition that requires an audience to recover the implicit relationship between two concepts that are expressed as nouns. Listeners recover this relationship by considering the most typical relations afforded by each concept. These relational possibilities are evident at a linguistic level in the syntagmatic patterns that connect nouns to the verbal actions that act upon, or are facilitated by, these nouns. We present a model of noun-compound interpretation that first learns the relational possibilities for individual nouns from corpora, and which then uses these to hypothesize about the most likely relationship that underpins a noun compound.

1 Introduction

Noun compounds hide a remarkable depth of conceptual machinery behind a simple syntactic form, *Noun-Noun*, and thus pose a considerable problem for the computational processing of language (Johnston and Busa, 1996). It is not just that compounds are commonplace in language, or that their interpretation requires a synthesis of lexical, semantic, and pragmatic information sources (Finin, 1980); compounds provide a highly compressed picture of the workings of concept combination, so there are as many ways of interpreting a noun compound as there are ways of combining the underlying concepts (Gagné, 2002). Linguists have thus attempted to understand noun-compounds as full propositions in which a phrase with two nouns connected by an explicit relation – usually expressed as a verb and a preposition – is compressed into a pair of nouns (Levi, 1978). Since these noun-pairs must allow an audience to reconstruct the decompressed proposition, there must be some systematic means by which the missing relation can easily be inferred.

This framing of the problem as a search for a missing relation suggests two broad strategies for the interpretation of compounds. In the first, the top-down strategy, we assume that there are only so many ways of combining two concepts; by enumerating these ways, we can view the problem of interpretation as a problem of classification, in which compounds are placed into separate classes that each correspond to a single manner of concept connection (Kim and Baldwin, 2006), (Nastase and Szpakowicz, 2003). This strategy explicitly shaped the SemEval task on classifying semantic relations between nominals (Girju *et al.*, 2007) and so is employed by all of the systems that participated in that task. In the second, the bottom-up strategy, we assume that it is futile to try and enumerate the many ways in which concepts can relationally combine, but look instead to large corpora to discover the ways in which different word combinations are explicitly framed by language (Nakov, 2006), (Turney, 2006a).

In this paper we describe an approach that employs the bottom-up strategy with an open- rather than closed-inventory of inter-concept relations. These relations are acquired from the analysis of large corpora, such as the Web IT corpus of Google n-grams (Brants and Franz, 2006). We argue that an understanding of noun-compounds requires an understanding of lexicalized concept combination, which in turn requires an understanding of how lexical concepts can be used and connected to others. As such, we do not use corpora as a means of

© 2008. Licensed under the *Creative Commons Attribution-Noncommercial-Share Alike 3.0 Unported* license (http://creativecommons.org/licenses/by-nc-sa/3.0/). Some rights reserved.

characterizing noun-compounds themselves, but as a means of characterizing the action possibilities of the individual nouns that can participate in a compound. In other words, we attempt to characterize those properties of different concepts denoted by nouns to help predict how those nouns will combine with others, and through which relations. For instance, "diamonds" can be used to cover and encrust jewelry or to provide a sharp tip for various tools; we see the former usage in "diamond bracelet" and the latter in "diamond saw". Likewise, "cheese" is a solid substance which can be cut, as in "cheese knife", an edible substance that can used as a filling, as in "cheese sandwich", and a substance that can be melted as a topping, as in "cheese pizza". It follows that a sandwich can be filled, a pizza can be topped, knives can cut and a bracelet can have a covering of gems. We use relational possibilities as a general term for what are sometimes called the qualia of a word (Pustejovsky, 1995), and learn the linguistic relational possibilities of nouns by seeking out specific textual patterns in corpora.

In section 2 we consider the most currently relevant elements of the substantial body of past work in this area. In section 3 we describe how corpus analysis is used to identify the most common lexico-semantic relational possibilities of nouns, while in section 4 we describe how these relations are used, in conjunction with web-based validation, to interpret specific noun-compounds. We present an evaluation of this approach in section 5 and conclude the paper with some final remarks in section 6.

2 Related Work

Machine-learning and example-based approaches to noun-compounds generally favor the top-down strategy for defining relations, since it allows training data and exemplars/cases to be labeled using a fixed inventory of relational classes. As noted earlier, this strategy is characteristic of the systems that participated in the SemEval task on classifying semantic relations between nominals (Girju *et al.*, 2007), such as Butnariu and Veale (2007). Though the inventory is fixed in size, it can be defined using varying levels of abstraction; for instance, Nastase and Szpakowicz (2003) use an inventory of 35 relations, 5 of which are top level relations with the remaining 30 at the lower level. The top-down strategy pre-dates these computational approaches, and is a key aspect of the foundational work of Levi (1978) and of subsequent work by Gagné and Shoben (1997), both of whom posit a small set of semantic relations as underpinning all noun compounds. More recently, Kim and Baldwin (2005) use a fixed inventory of semantic relations to annotate a case-base of examples; new compounds are understood by determining their lexical similarity to the closest annotated compounds in the case-base. Kim and Baldwin (2006) link their relations to specific seed verbs that linguistically convey these relations, and then train a classifier to recognize which semantic relation is implied by a pair of nouns connected by a given intervening verb. This approach appears to be sensitive to the number of seed verbs; on a test involving 453 noun compounds, an accuracy of 52.6% is achieved with 84 seed verbs, but just 46.6% with 57 seed verbs.

Verbs understandably play a key role in the interpretation of compounds, since some kind of predicate must be recovered to link both nouns. For instance, Levi (1978) uses verbs to make explicit the implicit relation between the nouns of a compound, while Finin (1980) characterizes the relation in a noun-noun compound using an inventory of all the possible verbs that can link both nouns; thus, e.g. *salt water* is interpreted using a relation like *dissolved_in*. Nakov (2006) takes a similar approach, and uses verb-centred paraphrases to express the semantic relations between the nouns of a compound. He argues that the meaning of a compound is best expressed via a collection of appropriate verbs rather than via the abstract relations (such as **Cause, Location**) that are used in more traditional approaches, such as those of Levi (1978) and Gagné (2002).

Nakov (2006) pursues a bottom-up strategy in which an open-ended inventory of relations is discovered using linguistic evidence. Turney (2006a, 2006b) similarly pursues a bottom-up, data-driven approach, in which semantic relations are expressed via representative lexico-syntactic patterns that are mined from large text corpora. Turney (2006a) sorts these relational patterns by *pertinence*, a measure that reflects the similarity of the noun pairs in the corpus in which each pattern is observed to occur. Patterns which are relatively unambiguous and which serve to cluster noun pairs with similar meanings have higher pertinence than those that do not.

The approach described here is similarly corpus-based and verb-centric, but it is also noun-centric rather than pair-centric, which is to say, we use corpus analysis to learn about the relational behavior of individual nouns rather than pairs of nouns. Like many other authors, from Finin (1980) to Nakov (2006), we see the problem of compound interpretation as a problem of paraphrase generation, in which a suitable verb (with an optional preposition) is used to linguistically re-frame the compound as a complete proposition. This linguistic frame is a relational possibilities of one of the nouns that is apt for the other. Following Gagné and Shoben (1997), this relational possibilities is frequently suggested by the modifier noun, but as we now describe, it may also be suggested by the head.

3 Acquisition of Relational Possibilities

The meaning of a noun compound can be paraphrased in a variety of ways. For instance, consider the compound "headache pill", which might be paraphrased as follows:

```
P1:  headache-inducing pill
P2:  headache prevention pill
P3:  pill for treating headaches
P4:  pill that causes headaches
P5:  pill that is prescribed for
     headaches
P6:  pill that prevents headaches
```

Some paraphrases are syntactic variants of others (e.g., P2 and P6), others employ lexical variation (e.g., P1 and P4) and others are co-descriptions of the same event (e.g., P3 and P5 or P5 and P6). It thus seems unreasonable to try and reduce these meanings to a single semantic relation, since the compound can be used to mean several of P1 … P6 simultaneously. Rather than try to construct an inventory of logical relations, closed or otherwise, we shall instead treat linguistic frames like "for treating X", "that prevents X". etc. as proxies for the relations themselves, while retaining the capacity to treat syntactic variants as proxies for the same relation. Moreover, these linguistic frames are relational possibilities of specific words, so that "-inducing X" is a relational possibility of "headache" while "for treating X" is a relational possibility of "pill". Thus, a compound of the form "headache X" might be re-framed as "headache-inducing X" and a compound of the form "X pill" might be re-framed as "pill that prevents X", "pill that causes X" or "pill for treating X".

The relational possibilities of individual words can be acquired from a large n-gram corpus like that of Brants and Franz (2006), as derived from Google's web index. Table 1 summarizes the linguistic relational possibilities that can be derived from specific n-gram patterns.

Google n-gram pattern	*Relational possibilities*	*Logical Form*
X – Verb+ing	X Verb+ing Y	verb(X, Y)
X – Verb+ed	X Verb+ed Y	verb(X, Y)
Verb+ed prep X	Y Verb+ed prep X	verb_prep(Y, X)
X Verb+ed	X Verb+ed prep Y	verb_prep(X, Y)
for Verb+ing X	Y for Verb+ing X	verb(Y, X)
X for Verb+ing	X for Verb+ing Y	verb(X, Y)
that Verb+s X	Y that Verb+s X	verb(Y, X)
X that Verb+s	X that Verb+s Y	verb(X, Y)

Table 1. *For an anchor noun X, the n-gram (left) suggests relational possibilities (middle) to link to a generic noun Y; different linguistic relational possibilities can have the same logical form (right).*

For example, we extract the following linguistic relational possibilities for the noun "diamond", where Google frequencies are given in parentheses:

```
accented_with_diamonds(4224),
encrusted_with_diamonds(3990),
decorated_with_diamonds(2616),
based_on_diamond(2148),
covered_with_diamonds(2018),
filled_with_diamonds(1942),
adorned_with_diamonds(1462),
coated_with_diamond(1150),
for_buying_diamonds(618),
for_grading_diamonds(342),
for_cutting_diamonds(430),
dusted_in_diamond(168),
bedecked_with_diamonds(140),
tipped_with_diamond(108),
crowned_with_diamonds(98),
for_exporting_diamonds(98),
embossed_with_diamond(90),
edged_with_diamonds(82),
drilled_with_diamond(86),
that_sells_diamonds(44)...
```

A hat may be *crowned* with diamonds, a watch *decorated* with diamonds, a bracelet *covered* with diamonds, a throne encrusted with diamonds and a king *bedecked* with diamonds – each is an elaboration of a basic *covering* relation, but each adds nuances of its own that we do not want to lose in an interpretation that is maximally specific to the nouns concerned. We therefore take the view that relations should be as open-ended and nuanced as the linguistic evidence suggests; if one needs to see two different relations as broadly equivalent, resources like WordNet (Fellbaum, 1998) can be used to make the generalization.

4 Interpreting Noun Compounds

We see interpretation of a compound M-H as a two-stage process of divergent generation followed by convergent validation. The generation process simply considers the relational possibilities associated either with the modifier M or the head H and generates a paraphrase from each. Consider the compound "yeast bread" where M = "yeast" and H = "bread"; the relational possibilities for "yeast" and "bread" and used to generate a set of potential paraphrases as shown in Table 2. For clarity, "M" and "H" denote the parts of each paraphrase frame that will be filled with the modifier and head respectively.

Relational possibilities for M	Paraphrases for M-H
H Verb+ed prep M *e.g., H derived from yeast*	H Verb+ed prep M *e.g., bread derived from yeast*
H that Verb+s M *e.g., H that contains yeast*	H that Verb+s M *e.g., bread that contains yeast*
Relational possibilities for H	**Paraphrase for M-H**
H Verb+ed prep M *e.g., bread prepared with M*	H Verb+ed prep M *e.g., bread prepared with yeast*
H that Verb+s M *e.g., bread that has M*	H that Verb+s M *e.g., bread that has yeast*

Table 2. *Relational possibilities of the head (H) and modifier (M) nouns used for paraphrasing.*

The relational possibilities for the head noun "bread" yield the following paraphrases, where numbers in parentheses are Google frequencies for the original n-grams on which each paraphrase is based:

```
"bread made from yeast" (6335),
"bread topped with yeast"
(6043), "bread made with yeast"
(4726), "bread stuffed with
yeast" (3871), "bread baked in
yeast" (3341), bread made of
yeast" (3064), "bread served
with yeast" (3012), "bread
soaked in yeast" (2975), "bread
dipped in yeast" (2873), "bread
filled with yeast" (2783), ...
```

Similarly, the relational possibilities for the modifier noun "yeast" yield the following paraphrases:

```
"bread expressed in yeast"
(14058), "bread leavened with
yeast" (10816), "bread derived
from yeast" (2562), "bread
based on yeast" (1200), "bread
fermented with yeast" (842),
"bread raised with yeast"
(736), "bread induced in yeast"
(342) , "bread infected with
yeast" (262), "bread filled
with yeast" (120), …
```

While these two sets of relational possibilities capture the most salient activities in which "yeast" and "bread" participate, many of the paraphrases listed here are inappropriate for "yeast bread". Candidate paraphrases for a noun compound are useful only when one has a means of determining the degree to which paraphrases are meaningful and apt and of rejecting those which are not. This process typically assumes that a meaningful paraphrase is one for which evidence of prior usage can be found in a large corpus (like the web); the greater this evidence, the more favored a given paraphrase should be. This assumption is central to Nakov (2006), who uses templates to find paraphrases for a noun compound on the web. These templates use the Google wildcard * to indicate the position of a verb so that the specific verbs at the heart of a paraphrase can be mined from the snippets that are returned. Nakov (2007) uses the schematic patterns "N1 that * N2", "N2 that * N1", "N1 * N2" and "N2 * N1", where the wildcard can stand for as many a eight contiguous words.

Relational possibilities allow us, in the first divergent stage of interpretation, to generate fully-formed paraphrases that do not require wildcards, so the second convergent stage of interpretation simply needs to validate these paraphrases by finding one or more instances of each on the web. Indeed, an especially compelling paraphrase may be found in the Google n-grams themselves, without recourse to the web. For instance, the paraphrase "bread leavened with yeast" has a frequency of 56 in the database of Google 4-grams, while the paraphrase "bread based on yeast" has such a low web frequency of 2 hits that it can be validated only by going to the web.

But web-based validation has its limitations: it cannot account for novel and creative compounds, nor can it account for conventional compounds whose meaning is not echoed in an expanded paraphrase-form on the web. Thus, we also consider an alternate validation procedure for those paraphrases that can be generated both from a modifier noun relational possibility *and* from a head noun relational possibility. For example, "bread filled with yeast" can be derived from the head relational possibility "bread filled with X" which has a frequency of 2783, and from the modifier relational possibility "X filled with yeast" which has a frequency of just 120. This dual basis for generation provides evidence that the paraphrase is meaningful without the need to actually find the paraphrase on the web. We refer to the validation of paraphrases in this way as validation by *matching relational possibilities* of the modifier and head nouns.

This *matching relational possibilities* procedure does not require web validation, and so does not produce a web frequency for each paraphrase. We thus need to assign a score to a paraphrase based on the web frequencies of the matching relational possibilities that give rise to it. For simplicity, we add the web frequency of the head relational possibility (e.g., 2783 from "bread filled with X") to the frequency of the modifier relational possibility (e.g., 120 from "X filled with yeast") to obtain an invented frequency for the generated paraphrase (e.g., 2903 for "bread filled with yeast").

The third and more restricted validation procedure we employ is a hybrid one, based on the intersection of the two procedures above: we require web-validation of paraphrases that are already validated by virtue of arising from matching head and modifier relational possibilities. In this case, we rank the paraphrases by their actual web frequency. The set of paraphrases validated by the hybrid approach will be a subset of the paraphrases validated by the other two validation methods; the size of this subset will be informative about the relative utility of each procedure.

5 Empirical Evaluation

To evaluate the relational possibility approach to noun-noun interpretation, we perform two experiments: one to consider how well the set of validated paraphrases can be mapped to the abstract relations used by (Nastase and Szpakowicz, 2003) to annotate their noun-noun compounds, and one to consider how well these paraphrases match the paraphrases offered by humans for the same noun compounds. To understand the role of different validation strategies, we use three variants of the model that correspond to the three means of validating paraphrases: model-1 uses the presence of the relational possibility on the web as the mark of a valid paraphrase; model-2 uses the matching relational possibilities procedure to validate a paraphrase (i.e., the paraphrase must arise from both an relational possibility of the modifier *and* of the head); a third model, model-3 intersects both validation procedures. In each case, validated paraphrases are ranked by their frequency scores, as found explicitly on the web in the case of model-1 and model-3, or as invented in model-2.

5.1 Mapping compounds to abstract relations

In the first experiment, we test the relational possibility model on a set of noun-noun compounds from Nastase and Szpakowicz (2003), whose data is pre-classified into abstract classes of semantic relations (i.e., **Agent**, **Instrument**, **Location**). We perform a manual analysis on the paraphrases that are generated and validated for each noun pair, to measure how accurately each paraphrase matches the pre-classified abstract semantic relation. The Nastase and Szpakowicz (2003) dataset comprises 600 word pairs of the form adj-noun, adv-noun and noun-noun; for this experiment we use only the 329 noun-noun pairs, which are each pre-labeled with one of 28 different semantic relations.

We consider and quantify two eventualities here: those situations in which the relational possibility model generates and validates a paraphrase that closely corresponds to the semantic relation assigned by Nastase and Szpakowicz (2003); and those situations in which the relational possibility model generates and validates an interpretation that a human judge considers a plausible and sensible interpretation of a compound regardless of Nastase and Szpakowicz (2003)'s interpretation. Table 3 presents validated relational possibilities for the compound "olive oil", where those that match the pre-classified relation are in bold, and those that are otherwise plausible are italicized.

Paraphrases generated by web-based validation	*Paraphrases generated by matching relational possibilities*	*Paraphrases generated by Nakov (2007)*
extracted from (189), **obtained from** (132), *mixed with* (87), **made from** (75), **produced from** (38), **pressed from** (35), *colored* (25), *infused* (20), *enriched with* (16), **made of** (14), *flavored* (13), **made with** (12), **derived** (10), **based** (10), produced by (9), *blended with* (8), *coloured* (7), **based on** (7), *combined with* (6), **found in** (6), dissolved in (6), served with (6), **contained in** (5), replaced by (4), *flavoured* (3), **come from** (3)...	used in (25839), **obtained from** (15352), **extracted from** (14561), **made from** (11627), **found in** (11524), used for (9919), *mixed with* (9781), **produced from** (7794), produced by (6776), **made with** (5423), used as (4880), **are in** (4577), **contained in** (4551), **come from** (4241), **based on** (4135), *combined with* (4029), added to (3848), made in (3608) ...	**come from** (13), **be obtained from** (11), **be extracted from** (10), **be made from** (9), **be produced from** (7), **be released from** (4), *taste like* (4), **be beaten from** (3), **be produced with** (3) , **emerge from** (3)

Table 3. *Validated paraphrases for "olive oil"; matches with Nastase and Szpakowicz are in bold; other sensible interpretations are italicized.*

We also consider the rank of the paraphrases that match the relations assigned by Nastase and Szpakowicz (2003) to this data set. Figure 1 graphs the F-measure for the relational possibilities approach when this relation is the top-ranked validated paraphrase, when it is in the top two validated paraphrases, and more generally, when it is in the top n validated paraphrases, n <= 20. Model-1 (web-based validation) out-performs Model-2 (matching relational possibilities, with no web validation) when we consider just a small window of top ranked paraphrases, but this situation reverses as the window (whose size is given on the x-axis) is enlarged.

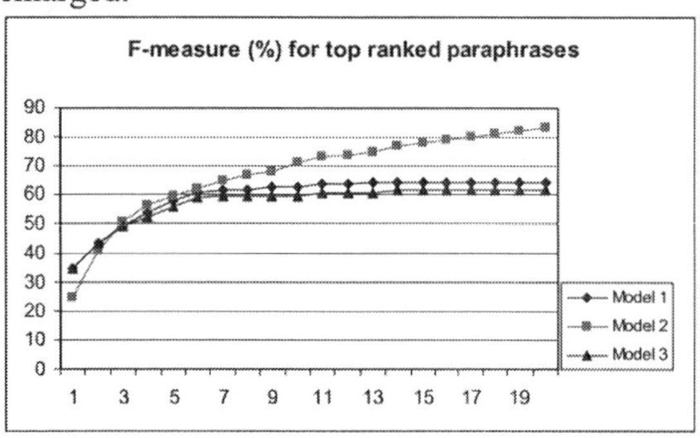

Figure 1. *F-measure for target semantic relations of top n ranked paraphrases generated with Model-1, Model-2 and Model-3.*

Model 3 (which requires both matching relational possibilities *and* web validation) shows similar results to Model 2 (web validation only), which suggests that the matching relational possibilities criterion is strongly predictive of web-validation. This further suggests that matching relational possibilities alone can reliably validate a paraphrase even when web evidence is lacking, as will be the case in creative noun compounds.

During this evaluation process, we observe a tendency for specific paraphrases to co-occur when conveying a certain relation. For instance, *Y obtained from X* typically co-occurs with *Y produced from X* to indicate Nastase and Szpakowicz's **Source** relation, while *Y caused by X* co-occurs with *Y induced by X* to convey their **Effect** relation, and *Y owned by X* co-occur with *Y held by X* to indicate their **Possessor** relation. This observation is similar to that of Nakov (2007), who performs a manual analysis of paraphrases obtains from web-mining. The results he reports are similar to those obtained using the relational possibilities approach, as shown in Table 3.

5.2 Comparing human-generated paraphrases

In the second experiment, we compared the paraphrases validated by the relational possibilities approach to human-generated paraphrases reported by Nakov (2007) and to the paraphrases generated by Nakov's own web-mining approach to this task. Nakov (2007) collected human paraphrases for each noun-compound in his data-set (250 noun compounds listed in the appendix of Levi, 1978) by asking subjects to rephrase a noun-compound using a relative-clause centred around a single verb with an optional preposition. This rephrasing elicited human-generated paraphrases like the following:

```
'neck vein is a vein that comes
            from the neck'
'neck vein is a vein that drains
            the neck'
```

Nakov then extracted normalized verbs and prepositions from these paraphrases to obtain a reduced verb-based form for each, e.g., to obtain the reduced forms *come from* and *drain* from the above examples. He used 174 subjects for this task, to generate around 17,000 reduced forms, or 71 forms per compound.

For each of his 250 noun pairs we constructed three vectors *h*, *w*, and *a*, using human-generated paraphrase verbs and their frequencies (h), Nakov's web-extracted verbs and their frequencies (w) and the verbs of the paraphrases obtained using the relational possibilities approach and their frequencies (a). Following Nakov (2007), we then calculated the cosine correlation between two frequency vectors using the formula:

$$sim_{cos}(h,w) = \sum h_i w_i / \sqrt{\sum h_i^2} \sqrt{\sum w_i^2}$$

For ease of comparison, the *a* vector is populated with verbs and frequencies from just two patterns, *Y Verb+ed Prep X* and *Y that Verb+s X*. In Table 4 we report the average cosine correlation across the vectors for all 250 noun pairs, to compare for the three validation models the relational possibilities-based and Nakov's web-generated paraphrases and the relational possibilities -based and human-elicited paraphrases. Also shown, in the last row, is the average cosine correlation between Nakov's web-mined paraphrases and human-elicited paraphrases, as reported in Nakov (2007).

Model 1 (web-validation)	
correlation to humans	26.8 %
correlation to web-mined approach	27.1 %
Model 2 (matching relational possibilities)	
correlation to humans	17 %
correlation to web-mined approach	14.25 %
Model 3 (intersection of Model-1 and Model-2)	
correlation to humans	27.9 %
correlation to web-mined approach	28 %
Web-mining (Nakov, 2007)	
correlation to humans	31.8%

Table 4. *Average correlation between web-mined paraphrases and relational possibilities-based paraphrases with human elicitations.*

The results show the difference in quality of the paraphrases validated by each of our models. The matching-relational possibilities model (Model 2) yields the largest number of paraphrases. In the first experiment we showed that this model outperforms the other two when we consider just top-ranked paraphrases, but here it appears that this wider range of potentially creative interpretations diminishes the cosine correlation with human-elicited interpretations. But the most plausible paraphrases come to the fore in the hybrid model (Model 3), whose paraphrases are a subset of those of Models 1 and 2. This hybrid approach also outperforms Model 1 and compares well with the results obtained by web mining.

The difference in cosine correlation between human-elicited and relational possibitlies-based paraphrases in Model-3 (27.9%) and Nakov's web-mined and human-elicited paraphrases (31.8%) can be justified both by the type of patterns used in the comparison, and by the type of patterns used to validate paraphrases. For one, we consider paraphrases generated using just two forms of relational possibilities, *Y Verb+ed Prep X* and *Y that Verb+s X*, since these can be directly compared to the type of relative-clause paraphrases used in this experiment. Furthermore, relational possibilities are derived from Google n-grams where $n < 6$, we allow up to four words to intervene between the modifier and the head in a paraphrase, while the web-mining paraphrases benefit from a larger window of intervening words (up to 8). Nonetheless, in 88 out of the 250 pairs, the correlation between relational possibilities-based and human-elicited paraphrases is larger than that observed for the web-mining approach.

6 Conclusions

Since the meaning of noun compounds arises from a combination of individual noun meanings, it follows that the key input to the process of compound interpretation is detailed linguistic knowledge about how these nouns are conventionally used in language. This point may seem obvious, but a model of compounding can place so much emphasis on the behavior of noun-pairs that the linguistic behavior of nouns in isolation is easily over-looked.

We have presented a model of noun-compounding that places nouns and their specific linguistic relational possibilities at the centre of processing. When one considers that linguistic relational possibilities capture aspects of noun meaning such as purpose, constitution and agency, their realization here can be viewed as a generalized and lexicalized aspect of qualia structure in the sense of Pustejovsky (1995) and Johnston and Busa (1996). Indeed, the n-gram patterns used to extract these relational possibilities from corpora are not unlike the patterns used by Cimiano and Wenderoth (2007) to harvest qualia structures from the web.

We conclude from the empirical observation that the hybrid model outperforms the web-based model (albeit slimly) in experiment 2 while both perform equally well in experiment 1, is that the modifier and head are of comparable performance when paraphrasing the interpretations of noun compounds. Recall that the web-validation approach (Model-1) generates interpretations from either the modifier or the head, while the matching-relational possibilities and hybrid models require both to contribute equally.

Necessary extensions to the approach include the acquisition of more relational possibilities of greater linguistic complexity, the ability to organize relational possibilities hierarchically according to their underlying semantic meanings, and the ability to recognize an implication structure among different but related relational possibilities.

Acknowledgement

We would like to thank Preslav Nakov for providing us the data used in the second experiment.

References

Brants, T., and Franz, A. 2006. *Web 1t 5-gram version 1*, Linguistic Data Consortium.

Butnariu, C., and Veale T. 2007. A hybrid model for detecting semantic relations between noun pairs in text. *In Proc. of the Fourth International Workshop on Semantic Evaluations (SemEval-2007),* Prague,. Association for Computational Linguistics.

Cimiano, P., and Wenderoth, J. 2007. Automatic Acquisition of Ranked Qualia Structures from the Web. *In Proc. of the 45th Annual Meeting of the ACL*, pp 888-895.

Fellbaum, C. 1998. *WordNet, an electronic lexical database.* Cambridge: MIT Press.

Finin, T. 1980. *The semantic interpretation of compound nominals*. Urbana, Illinois: University of Illinois dissertation.

Gagné, C. L., and Shoben, E. J. 1997. Influence of thematic relations on the comprehension of modifier-noun combinations. *Journal of Experimental Psychology: Learning, Memory, and Cognition*, 23, 71–87

Gagné, C. L. 2002. Lexical and Relational Influences on the Processing of Novel Compounds. *Brain and Language* 81(1-3), pp 723-735.

Girju, R., Nakov, P. Nastase, V., Szpakowicz, S., Turney, P., and Yuret, D. 2007. Semeval-2007 task 04: Classification of semantic relations between nominals. *In Proc. of the Fourth International Workshop on Semantic Evaluations (SemEval-2007),* 13–18, Prague, Czech Republic. ACL.

Johnston, M., and Busa, F. 1996. Qualia structure and the compositional interpretation of compounds. *In Proc. of the ACL SIGLEX workshop on breadth and depth of semantic lexicons*, Santa Cruz, CA.

Kim, S. N., and Baldwin, T. 2006. Interpreting semantic relations in noun compounds via verb semantics. *In Proc. of the 21st International Conference on Computational Linguistics and the 44th annual meeting of the ACL,* pp 491–498, NJ, USA.

Kim, S. N., and Baldwin, T. 2005. Automatic interpretation of noun compounds using WordNet similarity. *In Proc. of the 2nd International Joint Conference On Natural Language Processing*, pp 945–956, Cheju, Korea.

Levi, J. 1978. *The syntax and semantics of complex nominals*. NY: Academic Press.

Nakov, P., and Hearst, M. A. 2006. Using verbs to characterize noun-noun relations. In *AIMSA, Jerome Euzenat and John Domingue (eds.), vol. 4183 of Lecture Notes in Computer Science*, pp 233–244. Springer.

Nakov, P. 2007. *Using the Web as an Implicit Training Set: Application to Noun Compound Syntax and Semantics.* Ph.D. Dissertation, University of California at Berkeley.

Nastase, V., and Szpakowicz, S. 2003. Exploring noun-modifier semantic relations. *In Proc. of the 5th International Workshop on Computational Semantics (IWCS-5)*, pp 285–301, Tilburg, The Netherlands.

Pustejovsky, J. 1995. *The Generative Lexicon.* The MIT Press, Cambridge, MA.

Turney, P. 2006a. Expressing implicit semantic relations without supervision. In *Proc. of the 21st International Conference on Computational Linguistics and the 44th annual meeting of the ACL*, pp 313–320, NJ, USA.

Turney, P. D. 2006b. Similarity of semantic relations. *Computational Linguistics,* 32, pp 379–416.

Are Morpho-Syntactic Features More Predictive for the Resolution of Noun Phrase Coordination Ambiguity than Lexico-Semantic Similarity Scores?

Ekaterina Buyko and **Udo Hahn**
Jena University
Language & Information Engineering (JULIE) Lab
Fürstengraben 30, 07743 Jena, Germany
ekaterina.buyko|udo.hahn@uni-jena.de

Abstract

Coordinations in noun phrases often pose the problem that elliptified parts have to be reconstructed for proper semantic interpretation. Unfortunately, the detection of coordinated heads and identification of elliptified elements notoriously lead to ambiguous reconstruction alternatives. While linguistic intuition suggests that semantic criteria might play an important, if not superior, role in disambiguating resolution alternatives, our experiments on the re-annotated WSJ part of the Penn Treebank indicate that solely morpho-syntactic criteria are more predictive than solely lexico-semantic ones. We also found that the combination of both criteria does not yield any substantial improvement.

1 Introduction

Looking at noun phrases such as

'cat and dog owner'

'novels and travel books'

their proper coordination reading (and asymmetric distribution of coordinated heads) as

'cat owner' AND *'dog owner'*

'novels' AND *'travel books'*

seems to be licensed by the striking semantic similarity between *'cat'* and *'dog'*, and *'novels'* and *'books'*, respectively. If this were a general rule, then automatic procedures for the resolution of coordination ambiguities had to rely on the *a priori* provision of potentially large amounts of semantic background knowledge to make this similarity explicit. Furthermore, any changes in languages or domains where such resources were missing (or, were incomplete) would severely hamper coordination analysis.

Indeed, previous research has gathered lot of evidence that conjoined elements tend to be semantically similar. The important role of semantic similarity criteria for properly sorting out conjuncts was first tested by Resnik (1999). He introduced an information-content-based similarity measure that uses WORDNET (Fellbaum, 1998) as a lexico-semantic resource and came up with the claim that semantic similarity is helpful to achieve higher coverage in coordination resolution for coordinated noun phrases of the form *'noun1* and *noun2 noun3'* than similarity measures based on morphological information only.

In a similar vein, Hogan (2007b) inspected WORDNET similarity and relatedness measures and investigated their role in conjunct identification. Her data reveals that several measures of semantic word similarity can indeed detect conjunct similarity. For the majority of these similarity measures, the differences between the mean similarity of coordinated elements and non-coordinated ones were statistically significant. However, it also became evident that these were only slight differences, and not all coordinated heads were semantically related as evidenced, e.g., by *'work'/'harmony'* in *'hard work and harmony'*. The significance tests did also not reveal particularly useful measures for conjunct identification.

Rus et al. (2002) in an earlier study presented an alternative heuristics-based approach to conjunct identification for coordinations of the form *'noun1* and *noun2 noun3'*. They exploit, e.g., look-ups in WORDNET for a compound noun as a con-

© 2008. Licensed under the *Creative Commons Attribution-Noncommercial-Share Alike 3.0 Unported* license (http://creativecommons.org/licenses/by-nc-sa/3.0/). Some rights reserved.

cept, and for the sibling relation between nouns in the coordination and report bracketing precision of 87.4% on 525 candidate coordinations. Although the authors demonstrated that WORDNET was really helpful in coordination resolution, the evaluation was only conducted on compound nouns extracted from WORDNET's noun hierachy and, furthermore, the senses of nouns were manually tagged in advance for the experiments.

Despite this preference for semantic criteria, one might still raise the question how far non-semantic criteria might guide the resolution of noun phrase coordination ambiguities, e.g., by means of the distribution of resolution alternatives in a large corpus or plain lexical or morpho-syntactic criteria. This idea has already been explored before by various researchers from different methodological angles including distribution-based statistical approaches (e.g., Chantree et al. (2005), Nakov and Hearst (2005)), similarity-based approaches incorporating orthographical, morpho-syntactic, and syntactic similarity criteria (e.g., Agarwal and Boggess (1992), Okumura and Muraki (1994)), as well as a combination of distribution information and syntactic criteria (Hogan, 2007a).

Statistical approaches enumerate all candidate conjuncts and calculate the respective likelihood according to a distribution estimated on a corpus. For the coordination *'movie and television industry'* the distributional similarity of *'movie'* and *'industry'* and the collocation frequencies of the pairs [*'movie'* - *'industry'*] and [*'television'* - *'industry'*] would be compared against each other. However, for such an approach only an F-measure under 50% was reported (Chantree et al., 2005). Unsupervised Web-distribution-based algorithms (Nakov and Hearst, 2005) achieved 80% on the disambiguation of coordinations of the fixed form *'noun1 and noun2 noun3'*. Hogan (2007a) presented a method for the disambiguation of noun phrase coordination by modelling two sources of information, *viz.* distribution-based similarity between conjuncts and the dependency between conjunct heads. This method was incorporated in Bikel's parsing model (Bikel, 2004) and achieved an increase in NP coordination dependency F-score from 69.9% to 73.8%.

Similarity-based approaches consider those elements of a coordination as conjuncts which are most 'similar' under syntactic, morphological, or even semantic aspects. Agarwal and Boggess (1992) include in their NP coordination analysis syntactic and some semantic information about candidate conjuncts and achieve an accuracy boost up to 82%. Okumura and Muraki (1994) estimate the similarity of candidate conjuncts by means of a similarity function which incorporates syntactic, orthographical, and semantic information about the conjuncts. The model provides about 75% accuracy.

The resolution of coordination ambiguity can also be tried at parsing time. Charniak and Johnson (2005), e.g., supply a discriminative reranker that uses e.g., features to capture syntactic parallelism across conjuncts. The reranker achieves an F-score of 91%.

Recently, discriminative learning-based approaches were proposed, which exploit only lexical, morpho-syntactic features and the symmetry of conjuncts. Shimbo and Hara (2007) incorporate morpho-syntactic and symmetry features in a discriminative learning model and end up with 57% F-measure on the GENIA corpus (Ohta et al., 2002). Buyko et al. (2007) employ Conditional Random Fields (Lafferty et al., 2001) and successfully tested this technique in the biomedical domain for the identification and resolution of elliptified conjuncts. They evaluate on the GENIA corpus and report an F-score of 93% for the reconstruction of the elliptical conjuncts employing lexical and morpho-syntactic criteria only. At least two questions remain — whether the latter approach can achieve similar results in the newswire language domain (and is thus portable), and whether the incorporation of additional semantic criteria in this approach might boost the resolution rate, or not (and is thus possibly more parsimonious). The latter question is the main problem we deal with in this paper.

2 Data Sets for the Experiments

2.1 Coordination Annotation in the PENN TREEBANK

For our experiments, we used the WSJ part of the PENN TREEBANK (Marcus et al., 1993). Some researchers (e.g., Hogan (2007a)) had recently found several inconsistencies in its annotation of the bracketing of coordinations in NPs. These bugs were shown to pose problems for training and testing of coordination resolution and parsing tools. Fortunately, a re-annotated version has been provided by Vadas and Curran (2007), with a focus on the internal structure of NPs. They added additional bracketing annotation for each noun phrase in the WSJ section of the PENN TREEBANK assuming a right-bracketing structure in NPs. In addition, they introduced tags, e.g., 'NML' for explicitly marking any left-branching constituents as in

(NP (NML (JJ *industrial*) (CC *and*) (NN *food*)) (NNS *goods*))

where *'industrial'* and *'food'* are conjuncts. In the example

(NP (DT *some*) (NN *food*) (CC *and*) (NN *household*) (NNS *goods*))

the structure of the noun phrase is already correct and should not be annotated further, since *'household goods'* is already right-most and is coordinated with *'food'*. Still, in the original PENN TREEBANK annotation, we find annotations of noun phrases such as

(NP (NN *royalty*) (CC *and*) (NP (NN *rock*) (NNS *stars*)))

that remain unchanged after the re-annotation process.

2.2 Coordination Corpus

We, first, extracted a set of 3,333 non-nested NP coordinations involving noun compounds and one conjunction, with a maximal number of nine nouns (no prepositional phrases were considered). We focused on two patterns in the re-annotated WSJ portion:

(1) Noun phrases containing at least two nouns and a conjunction as sister nodes as in

(NP (NML (NN *movie*) (CC *and*) (NN *book*)) (NNS *pirates*))

or in

(NP (DT *some*) (NN *food*) (CC *and*) (NN *household*) (NNS *goods*))

(2) Noun phrases containing at least two noun phrases and a conjunction as sister nodes (as they remained unchanged from the original PENN TREEBANK version). Thereby, the second noun phrase contains at least two nouns as sister nodes as in

(NP (NP (NNP *France*)) (CC *and*) (NP (NNP *Hong*) (NNP *Kong*)))

We removed from this original set NPs which could not be reduced to the following pattern:[1]

$(W)\ N_1$ and $(W)\ N_2\ N_3$,

where (W) is a sequence of i tokens with $i \geq 0$ as in *'street lamps$_{N_1}$ and ficus$_{N_2}$ trees$_{N_3}$'*.

The remaining major data set (A) then contained 2,687 NP coordinations. A second data set (B) was formed, which is a proper subset of A and contained only those coordination structures that match the following pattern:

$(X)\ N_1$ and $(W)\ N_2\ N_3$,

where (X) is defined as a sequence of i tokens $(i \geq 0)$ with all part-of-speech (POS) tags except nouns and (W) defined as above; e.g., *'a happy cat$_{N_1}$ and dog$_{N_2}$ owner$_{N_3}$'*. Test set B contains, in our opinion, a selection of less 'hard' coordinations from the set A, and includes 1,560 items.

All these patterns focus on three forms of *conjunctions*, namely *'and'*, *'or'*, and *'but not'*, which connect two *conjuncts* (the extension of which varies in our data from one up to maximally eight tokens as in *'London's "Big Bang" 1986 deregulation and Toronto's "Little Bang" the same year'*.

The remainders from the conjunctions and the two conjuncts in a coordinated NP are called *shared elements* (e.g., *'owner'* and *'a happy'* in the above example). It is evident that the correct recognition of conjunct boundaries allows for the proper identification of the shared elements.

Set A contains 1,455 coordinations where N_1 and N_3 are coordinated (e.g, *'food and household goods'*) and 1,232 coordinations where N_1 and N_2 are coordinated (e.g., *'cotton and acetate fibers'*). Set B consists of 643 coordinations where N_1 and N_3 are coordinated and 917 coordinations where N_1 and N_2 are coordinated.

The extracted data sets were converted into an IO representation of tokens labeled as *'C'* for conjunct, *'CC'* for conjunction, and *'S'* for the shared element(s). The noun phrase *'cotton and acetate fibers'*, e.g., is represented as a sequence '*C CC C S*', while *'food and household goods'* is represented as a sequence '*C CC C C*'.

3 Methods

We here compare three different approaches to the resolution of noun phrase coordination ambiguity, *viz.* ones relying solely on morpho-syntactic information, solely on lexico-semantic information, and a cumulative combination of both. As far as semantic information is concerned we make use of various WORDNET similarity measures.

[1] These are typically coordinations of the form '$(W)N_1$ and N_2', e.g., *'government sources and lobbyists'*, where W is a sequence of i tokens $(i \geq 0)$. 646 coordinations of this type occurred in the WSJ portion of the PTB.

3.1 Baselines

We used three baselines for resolving noun phrase coordination ambiguities — one incorporating only lexico-semantic information, the *WordNet Similarity* baseline, and two alternative ones incorporating only morpho-syntactic and syntactic parse information, the *Number Agreement* and the *Bikel Parser* baseline, respectively.

3.1.1 WORDNET Similarity (WN) Baseline

Our lexico-semantic baseline comes with WORDNET semantic similarity scores of putatively coordinated nouns. For our experiments, we used the implementation of WORDNET similarity and relatedness measures provided by Ted Pedersen.[2] The following similarity measures were considered: two measures based on path lenghts between concepts (*path* and *lch* (Leacock et al., 1998)), three measures based on information content, i.e., corpus-based measures of the specificity of a concept (*res* (Resnik, 1999), *lin* (Lin, 1998), and *jcn* (Jiang and Conrath, 1997)). Furthermore, we used two relatedness measures, namely, *lesk* (Banerjee and Pedersen, 2003) and *vector* (Patwardhan et al., 2003), which score the similarity of the glosses of both concepts. We applied these similarity measures to any pair of putatively coordinated nouns in the noun phrases from our data sets, *A* and *B*. To determine potential conjuncts we calculate two similarity scores relative to the structures discussed in Section 2.2:

$s_1 = sim(N_1, N_2)$ and $s_2 = sim(N_1, N_3)$

Our final score is the maximum over both scores which is then the semantic indicator for the most plausible resolution of the coordination.

3.1.2 Number Agreement (NA) Baseline

We compared here the number agreement between selected nouns (see Resnik (1999)). Accordingly, N_1 and N_2 are coordinated, if $number(N_1) = number(N_2)$ AND $number(N_1) \neq number(N_3)$, while N_1 and N_3 are coordinated, if $number(N_1) = number(N_3)$ AND $number(N_1) \neq number(N_2)$.

3.1.3 Post-Processing Heuristics

In the *WN* and *NA* baselines, after the detection of coordinated elements we used simple heuristics to tag the remaining part of the noun phrase. If N_1 and N_2 were hypothesized to be coordinated, then all tokens preceding N_1 were tagged as shared elements, N_3 was tagged as shared element as well, while all tokens between the conjunction and N_2 were tagged as conjuncts. For example, in *'a happy dog$_{N_1}$ and cat$_{N_2}$ owner$_{N_3}$'* we identify *'dog'* and *'cat'* as coordinated elements and tag *'a happy'* and *'owner'* as shared elements. The final resolution looks like *'S S C CC C S'*. If N_1 and N_3 were hypothesized to be coordinated, then all other elements except conjunctions were tagged as parts of conjuncts, as well.

3.1.4 Bikel Parser (BP) Baseline

We used the well-known Bikel Parser (Bikel, 2004) in its original version and the one used by Collins (2003). We trained both of them only with NPs extracted from the re-annotated version of WSJ (see Section 2) and converted the bracketing output of the parsers to the IO representation for NP coordinations for further evaluations.

3.2 Chunking of Conjuncts with CRFs

The approach to conjunct identification presented by Buyko et al. (2007) employs Conditional Random Fields (CRF) (Lafferty et al., 2001),[3] which assign a label to each token of coordinated NPs according to its function in the coordination: *'C'* for conjuncts, *'CC'* for conjunctions, and *'S'* for shared elements. Since non-nested conjuncts can be assumed to be in a sequential order, sequential learning approaches (instead of single position classification approaches) seem appropriate here.

Buyko et al. (2007) report an F-measure of 93% on conjunct identification in the GENIA corpus. They use a feature set including lexical (words), and morpho-syntactic features (POS tags, morpho-syntactic similarity of putative conjuncts), but exclude any semantic criteria. The morpho-syntactic similarity features were generated from a rule-based approach to conjunct identification using the maximal symmetry of conjuncts as constituted by their respective POS annotation.

We here intend to apply this approach for resolving coordination ambiguities involving noun compounds in the newswire language such as *'president and chief executive'*. This restricts the spectrum of considered coordinations in noun phrases to more complicated cases than those considered by Buyko et al. (2007). We will thus test the various resolution models under harder test conditions,

[2] `http://www.d.umn.edu/~tpederse/`

[3] They employ the linear-chain CRF implementation from the MALLET toolsuite available at `http://mallet.cs.umass.edu/index.php/Main_Page`

Feature Class	Description
default feature	prior probability distribution over the possible argument labels
lexical	word
morpho-syntactic	the token's POS tag; output labels of the morpho-syntactic similarity (*'C'*, *'CC'* and *'S'*) (see Buyko et al. (2007)); output labels of the number agreement baseline (*'C'*, *'CC'* and *'S'*)
semantic *WN*	output labels of the WORDNET similarity baseline (*'C'*, *'CC'* and *'S'*)
contextual	conjunctions of all features of neighboring tokens (two tokens to the left and one token to the right)

Table 1: Feature Classes Used for Conjunct Identification

since Buyko et al. consider, e.g., adjective coordinations in noun phrases such as *'positive and negative IL-2 regulator'* that are predominant in the biomedical language domain.

We also propose in this work an extension of the feature space in terms of lexico-semantic features (see Table 1), information that originates from similarity computations on WORDNET data. Furthermore, we do not use orthographical features of the original approach as they are well suited only for the biomedical language domain.

4 Results and Error Analysis

To evaluate the different approaches to conjunct identification, we used recall and precision scores since they are well suited for the evaluation of segmentation tasks. Two types of decisions were evaluated – the assignment of *'C'* labels denoting conjuncts in terms of the F-measure, and (given the tagged conjuncts) the *accuracy* of the complete coordination resolution. A coordination is resolved properly only, if all tokens of both conjuncts are correctly identified.

We carried out a ten-fold cross-validation of all ML-based methods (Bikel parser (Bikel, 2004) and CRF-based conjunct identification (Buyko et al., 2007)). For the evaluation of the *NA* and *WN* baselines, we tested their performance on the complete data sets, *A* and *B* (see Section 2).

As Table 2 depicts the *NA* baseline achieved an accuracy of 28.4% on *A* (36.6% on *B*), the Bikel parser reached 77.2% on *A* (73.4% in *B*), while the *WN* baseline got in its best run (*vector* measure) an accuracy of 41.7% on *A* (49.6% on *B*). These results already reveal that parsing almost dramatically outperforms the coordination resolution based on the *NA* similarity by up to 35.5% points. The results of the *WN* baseline indicate that the best similarity measure for conjunct identification is the *vector* similarity (Patwardhan et al., 2003) that scores the similarity between the glosses of the concepts.

Our error analysis of the *WN* baseline on the test set *A* reveals that its low accuracy has various reasons. First, about 37% of the coordinations could not be resolved due to the absence of at least one noun involved in the coordination from the WORDNET. These coordinations usually include named entities such as person and organization names (e.g., *'brothers Francis and Gilbert Gros'*). These coverage gaps have clearly a negative effect on the resolution results for all WORDNET similarity measures.

To find out errors which are specific for the considered similarity measures, we have chosen the *res* measure and inspected the analysis results on all noun phrases where nouns are covered by WORDNET. The remaining set of coordinations contains 1,740 noun phrases. 1,022 coordinations (59%) of this set were completely resolved by the *WN* baseline, while 1,117 coordinations (64% of the remaining part, 41.5% of the test set *A*) could be at least partly resolved. Obviously, the coordinated heads are properly detected by the *res* measure but our heuristics for tagging the remaining modifiers (see Subsection 3.1.3) fail to provide the correct conjunct boundaries.

623 coordinations (36%) were mis-classified by the *res* measure. A closer look at this data reveals two types of errors. The first and minor type is the misleading selection of putatively coordinated heads N_1, N_2, and N_3. We presuppose in the *WN* baseline that the heads appear right-most in the noun phrase, although that is not always the case as illustrated by the phrase *'Northern California earthquake and Hurricane Hugo'*. The *res* measure detected correctly a higher similarity between *'earthquake'* (N_1) and *'hurricane'* (N_2), but *'Hugo'* (N_3) is a modifier of *'hurricane'*. Although the *res* measure works fine, the coordination cannot be properly resolved due to syntactic reasons. In some cases, N_2 is wrongly selected as in *'life and health insurance operation'* where the *WN* baseline selects *'insurance'* as right-most noun (except the last noun *'operation'*) and not *'health'*.[4]

[4] *'turbine$_{N_2}$'* is, however, correctly selected in *'steam turbine and gas turbine plants'*.

	Set A		Set B	
	Recall/Precision/F-Score	Accuracy	Recall/Precision/F-Score	Accuracy
NA	32.7 / 75.9 / 45.7	28.4	41.6 / 83.9 / 55.6	36.6
Bikel	85.6 / 85.4 / 85.5	77.2	83.8 / 83.6 / 83.7	73.4
Bikel (Collins)	85.9 / 85.7 / 85.8	77.5	83.6 83.4 / 83.5	72.9
WN jcn	45.6 / 69.3 / 55.0	36.2	54.7 / 72.1 / 62.2	41.2
WN lch	48.7 / 70.8 / 57.7	39.2	57.8 / 74.1 / 65.0	44.4
WN lesk	49.2 / 66.2 / 56.5	38.1	59.3 / 70.3 / 64.3	43.3
WN lin	44.7 / 69.9 / 54.6	35.5	53.5 / 72.6 / 61.6	40.5
WN res	45.9 / 71.8 / 56.0	37.4	55.7 / 75.8 / 64.2	43.8
WN path	48.7 / 70.8 / 57.7	39.2	57.8 / 74.1 / 65.0	44.4
WN **vector**	51.2 / 68.9 / 58.8	**41.7**	62.8 / 74.5 / 68.1	**49.6**
CRF (default), contextual	75.2 / 72.4 / 73.8	60.3	77.9 / 75.1 / 76.5	63.1
+ Lexical, morpho-syntactic	87.1 / 87.2 / 87.1	**77.9**	88.1/ 88.0 / 88.0	**78.8**
+ WN (lesk)	87.2 / 87.2 / 87.2	**78.0**	88.2/ 88.2 / 88.2	**79.1**
CRF (default), contextual + only WN (lesk)	79.3 / 78.4 / 78.9	64.8	81.2 / 80.6 / 80.9	66.9
CRF (default), contextual + only morpho-syntactic	86.2 / 86.3 / 86.3	76.6	87.6 / 87.6 / 87.6	78.1

Table 2: F-measure of Conjunct Identification and Accuracy of Coordination Resolution on the WSJ Section of the PENN TREEBANK Corpus

The second type of error comes as erroneous classifications of the *res* measure such as in *'hospitals and blood banks'* where *'hospitals'* and *'blood'* have a higher similarity than *'hospitals'* and *'banks'* although they are, in fact, coordinated here. *'hotels and large restaurant chains'*, *'records and music publishing'*, *'chemicals and textiles company'* are other examples for the observation that the coordinated elements have a lower similarity as non-coordinated ones.

We also carried out a ten-fold cross-validation of the CRF-based approach for the conjunct identification. First of all, the CRF-based approach (with and without *WN* similarity) achieved the highest accuracy score – up to 78.0% on set *A*, and 79.1% on *B* – compared with all other approaches we scrutinized on. We also tested the performance of the original semantics-free approach and the additional effects of the WORDNET similarity measures (see Table 2). Although the integration of semantic information leads to a mild gain compared with the original approach (up to 0.3% points, with the *lesk* measure), the results indicate that no substantial benefit can be traced to semantic features.

We ran several tests with solely morpho-syntactic features (as enumerated in Table 1) and solely *WN* features, too. They reveal that solely morpho-syntactic features are up to 11.8% points more predictive than *WN* features. The best results were still achieved using the gloss-oriented *lesk* measure (see Table 3).

The inspection of the errors types from the various runs is not fully conclusive though. After adding *WN* features to both sets, we detected some improvements for conjunct tagging with high *WN* similarity. Some conjunct boundaries could be corrected as in *'record and movie producer'* where, in the first run, *'producer'* was tagged as a conjunct and was corrected as being shared by integrating *WN* features. But we also detected a degrading tagging behavior of conjuncts with *WN* features where the *WN* similarity was not helpful at all as in *'chairman and chief designer'* where *'chairman'* and *'chief'* under the influence of *WN* features were judged to be conjuncts. We found out that the addition of *WN* features positively influences the classification of coordinations where N_1 and N_2 are coordinated, while it increased errors in the classification of coordinations where N_1 and N_3 are coordinated.

In addition, we calculated intersections between the set *A* error data (unique) of the *res WN* baseline (1400 phrases) and the error data of the CRF approach without *WN* features (391), and the error data of the CRF approach with *WN* features (385), respectively. These error data sets contain noun phrases where coordinated heads could not be properly detected. The set of the *res WN* baseline and the set of the CRF approach without *WN* features have an intersection of 230 instances, where 138 instances could not be found in the WORDNET. That means that for about 161 instances (59%) in the mis-classified data of the CRF approach the additional *WN* features would not be helpful. The intersection remains similar (226 instances) between the set of the *res WN* base-

Default, Context, Lexical, Morpho-Syntactic Feats.	WN Sim	Recall Precision / F-Score	Accuracy
√		88.1/ 88.0 / 88.0	78.8
√	*jcn*	87.9/ 87.8 / 87.9	78.3
√	*lch*	87.9 / 87.9 / 87.9	78.5
√	***lesk***	88.2/ 88.2 / 88.2	**79.1**
√	*lin*	88.0 / 88.0 / 88.0	78.8
√	*res*	88.2 / 88.2 / 88.2	79.0
√	*path*	87.9 / 87.9 / 87.9	78.5
√	*vector*	87.8 / 87.7 / 87.7	78.2

Table 3: Conjunct Identification — Cross-validation on the WSJ section of the PENN TREEBANK Corpus on Test Set *B*

line and the set of the CRF approach enriched with *WN* features. The intersection between the errror sets of the both CRF approaches includes 352 instances. The integration of the *WN* features was not helful for almost the complete error data from the original CRF approach. We have previously shown that the *res WN* baseline features correlate with the correct label sequence for only 1,117 coordinations (41.5%) of the complete evaluation set *A* and the features thus do not seem to be effective in our approach.

Furthermore, we evaluated the results of the CRF approach only for the correct detection of coordinated heads (see above for the *res* measure and intersection counts) and disregarded the modifier classification. The results — 85.3% on set *A* and 85.4% on set *B* — reveal that the classification of modifiers is a major source of classification errors. In both configurations the problematic noun phrases are the ones with (e.g., adjectival) modifiers. The boundaries of conjuncts are not properly recognized in such noun phrases, as for example in *'American comic book and television series'* where the correct label sequence is *'S C C CC C S'*, since *'American'* is the shared modifier of *'book'* and *'television'*, while *'comic'* just modifies *'book'*.

As most adjectives appearing at the beginning of the noun phrase as in *'medical products and services company'* tend to be used as shared modifiers of coordinations in our data, this, erroneously, leads to false taggings, e.g., *'personal'* in *'personal computer and software design'* as a shared element. To cope adequately with modifiers we need to integrate more appropriate features such as collocation frequencies of modifiers and coordinated heads. The detection of a higher collocation frequency of *'personal computer'* in comparison to *'personal software'* (e.g., using the procedures proposed by Wermter and Hahn (2004)) would help tagging the conjunct boundaries.

5 Conclusions and Future Work

We investigated the problem of noun phrase coordination resolution as a segmentation problem among conjuncts involved in the coordination. While resolving coordination ellipsis is often considered as a semantically constrained problem, we wanted to assess a less 'costly' solution strategy, namely relying on 'cheaper' to get syntactic criteria as much as possible, though not sacrificing the accurary of resolutions.

We, first looked at morpho-syntactic criteria only and lexico-semantic criteria only, and then at the combination of both approaches. The evaluation results from a variety of experiments reveal that the major part of ambiguous coordinations can be resolved using solely morpho-syntactic features. Surprising as it might be, the semantic information as derived from the WORDNET similarity measures does not yield any further substantial improvement for our approach. This is somehow counter-intuitive, but our findings, unlike those from earlier studies which emphasized the role of semantic criteria, are based on extensive corpus data – the PENN TREEBANK.

Results from our error analysis will guide future work to further boost results. Particular emphasis will be laid on the integration of named entity recognizers, collocation frequencies and distributional similarity data as also advocated by Chantree et al. (2005).

The presented sequential labeling-based approach to coordination resolution was here applied to the resolution of a special type of ambiguous noun phrases. In general, this approach can easily be applied to the resolution of other types of coordinative structures in noun phrases as already presented in Buyko et al. (2007). As far as other phrasal types (e.g., verbal phrases) are concerned, long-distance coordinations play a much more prominent role. The token-based labeling approach may be thus substituted by a chunk-based approach operating on sentences.

Acknowledgements

This research was partly funded by the German Ministry of Education and Research within the STEMNET project (01DS001A-C) and by the EC within the BOOTSTREP project (FP6-028099).

References

Agarwal, R. and L. Boggess. 1992. A simple but useful approach to conjunct identification. In *Proceedings of the 30th Annual Meeting of the Association for Computational Linguistics*, pages 15–21. Newark, DE, USA, 28 June - 2 July 1992.

Banerjee, S. and T. Pedersen. 2003. Extended gloss overlaps as a measure of semantic relatedness. In *IJCAI'03 – Proceedings of the 18th International Joint Conference on Artificial Intelligence*, pages 805–810. Acapulco, Mexico, August 9-15, 2003.

Bikel, D. 2004. Intricacies of Collins' parsing model. *Computational Linguistics*, 30(4):479–511.

Buyko, E., K. Tomanek, and U. Hahn. 2007. Resolution of coordination ellipses in biological named entities using Conditional Random Fields. In *PACLING 2007 - Proceedings of the 10th Conference of the Pacific Association for Computational Linguistics*, pages 163–171. Melbourne, Australia, September 19-21, 2007.

Chantree, F. A. Kilgarriff, A. de Roeck, and A. Willis. 2005. Disambiguating coordinations using word distribution information. In *RANLP 2005 – Proceedings of the Intl. Conference on 'Recent Advances in Natural Language Processing'*, pages 144–151. Borovets, Bulgaria, 21-23 September, 2005.

Charniak, E. and M. Johnson. 2005. Coarse-to-fine *n*-best parsing and MaxEnt discriminative reranking. In *ACL'05 – Proceedings of the 43rd Annual Meeting of the Association for Computational Linguistics*, pages 173–180. Ann Arbor, MI, 25-30 June 2005.

Collins, M. 2003. Head-driven statistical models for natural language parsing. *Computational Linguistics*, 29(4):589–637.

Fellbaum, C., editor. 1998. WORDNET*: An Electronic Lexical Database*. MIT Press.

Hogan, D. 2007a. Coordinate noun phrase disambiguation in a generative parsing model. In *ACL'07 – Proceedings of the 45th Annual Meeting of the Association of Computational Linguistics*, pages 680–687. Prague, Czech Republic, June 28-29, 2007.

Hogan, D. 2007b. Empirical measurements of lexical similarity in noun phrase conjuncts. In *Proceedings of the 45th Annual Meeting of the Association of Computational Linguistics. Demo and Poster Sessions*, pages 149–152. Prague, Czech Republic, June 28-29, 2007.

Jiang, J. and D. Conrath. 1997. Semantic similarity based on corpus statistics and lexical taxonomy. In *ROCLING-X – Proceedings of the 1997 International Conference on Research in Computational Linguistics*. Taipei, Taiwan, August 22-24, 1997.

Lafferty, J., A. McCallum, and F. Pereira. 2001. Conditional Random Fields: Probabilistic models for segmenting and labeling sequence data. In *ICML-2001 – Proceedings of the 18th International Conference on Machine Learning*, pages 282–289. Williams College, MA, USA, June 28 - July 1, 2001.

Leacock, C., M. Chodorow, and G. Miller. 1998. Using corpus statistics and WORDNET relations for sense identification. *Computational Linguistics*, 24(1):147–165.

Lin, D. 1998. An information-theoretic definition of similarity. In *Proceedings of the 15th International Conference on Machine Learning*, pages 296–304. Madison, WI, USA, July 24-27, 1998.

Marcus, M., B. Santorini, and M.-A. Marcinkiewicz. 1993. Building a large annotated corpus of English: The PENN TREEBANK. *Computational Linguistics*, 19(2):313–330.

Nakov, P. and M. Hearst. 2005. Using the Web as an implicit training set: Application to structural ambiguity resolution. In *HLT-EMNLP'05 – Proceedings of the 5th Human Language Technology Conference and 2005 Conference on Empirical Methods in Natural Language Processing*, pages 835–842. Vancouver, B.C., Canada, October 6-8, 2005.

Ohta, T., Y. Tateisi, and J.-D. Kim. 2002. The GENIA corpus: An annotated research abstract corpus in molecular biology domain. In *HLT 2002 – Proceedings of the 2nd International Conference on Human Language Technology Research*, pages 82–86. San Diego, CA, USA, March 24-27, 2002.

Okumura, A. and K. Muraki. 1994. Symmetric pattern matching analysis for English coordinate structures. In *ANLP 1994 – Proceedings of the 4th Conference on Applied Natural Language Processing*, pages 41–46. Stuttgart, Germany, 13-15 October 1994.

Patwardhan, S., S. Banerjee, and T. Pedersen. 2003. Using measures of semantic relatedness for word sense disambiguation. In *CICLing 2003 – Proceedings 4th Intl. Conference on Computational Linguistics and Intelligent Text Processing*, pages 241–257. Mexico City, Mexico, February 16-22, 2003.

Resnik, P. 1999. Semantic similarity in a taxonomy: An information-based measure and its application to problems of ambiguity in natural language. *Journal of Artificial Intelligence Research*, 11:95–130.

Rus, V., D. Moldovan, and O. Bolohan. 2002. Bracketing compound nouns for logic form derivation. In *FLAIRS 2002 – Proceedings of the 15th International Florida Artificial Intelligence Research Society Conference*, pages 198–202. Pensacola Beach, FL, USA, May 14-16, 2002.

Shimbo, M. and K. Hara. 2007. A discriminative learning model for coordinate conjunctions. In *EMNLP-CoNLL 2007 – Proceedings of the 2007 Joint Conference on Empirical Methods in Natural Language Processing and Computational Natural Language Learning*, pages 610–619. Prague,Czech Republic, June 28-29, 2007.

Vadas, D. and J. Curran. 2007. Adding noun phrase structure to the PENN TREEBANK. In *ACL'07 – Proceedings of the 45th Annual Meeting of the Association of Computational Linguistics*, pages 240–247. Prague, Czech Republic, June 28-29, 2007.

Wermter, J. and U. Hahn. 2004. Collocation extraction based on modifiability statistics. In *COLING 2004 – Proceedings of the 20th International Conference on Computational Linguistics*, pages 980–986. Geneva, Switzerland, August 23-27, 2004.

ParaMetric: An Automatic Evaluation Metric for Paraphrasing

Chris Callison-Burch
Center for Speech and Language Processing
Johns Hopkins University
3400 N. Charles St.
Baltimore, MD 21218

Trevor Cohn **Mirella Lapata**
School of Informatics
University of Edinburgh
2 Buccleuch Place
Edinburgh, EH8 9LW

Abstract

We present ParaMetric, an automatic evaluation metric for data-driven approaches to paraphrasing. ParaMetric provides an objective measure of quality using a collection of multiple translations whose paraphrases have been manually annotated. ParaMetric calculates precision and recall scores by comparing the paraphrases discovered by automatic paraphrasing techniques against gold standard alignments of words and phrases within equivalent sentences. We report scores for several established paraphrasing techniques.

1 Introduction

Paraphrasing is useful in a variety of natural language processing applications including natural language generation, question answering, multi-document summarization and machine translation evaluation. These applications require paraphrases for a wide variety of domains and language usage. Therefore building hand-crafted lexical resources such as WordNet (Miller, 1990) would be far too laborious. As such, a number of data-driven approaches to paraphrasing have been developed (Lin and Pantel, 2001; Barzilay and McKeown, 2001; Barzilay and Lee, 2003; Pang et al., 2003; Quirk et al., 2004; Bannard and Callison-Burch, 2005). Despite this spate of research, no objective evaluation metric has been proposed.

In absence of a repeatable automatic evaluation, the quality of these paraphrasing techniques was gauged using subjective manual evaluations. Section 2 gives a survey of the various evaluation methodologies used in previous research. It has not been possible to directly compare paraphrasing techniques, because each one was evaluated using its own idiosyncratic experimental design. Moreover, because these evaluations were performed manually, they are difficult to replicate.

We introduce an automatic evaluation metric, called ParaMetric, which uses paraphrasing techniques to be compared and enables an evaluation to be easily repeated in subsequent research. ParaMetric utilizes data sets which have been annotated with paraphrases. ParaMetric compares automatic paraphrases against reference paraphrases.

In this paper we:

- Present a novel automatic evaluation metric for data-driven paraphrasing methods;
- Describe how manual alignments are created by annotating correspondences between words in multiple translations;
- Show how phrase extraction heuristics from statistical machine translation can be used to enumerate paraphrases from the alignments;
- Report ParaMetric scores for a number of existing paraphrasing methods.

2 Related Work

No consensus has been reached with respect to the proper methodology to use when evaluating paraphrase quality. This section reviews past methods for paraphrase evaluation.

Researchers usually present the quality of their automatic paraphrasing technique in terms of a subjective manual evaluation. These have used a variety of criteria. For example, Barzilay and McKeown (2001) evaluated their paraphrases by asking judges whether paraphrases were "approximately conceptually equivalent." Ibrahim et al. (2003) asked judges whether their paraphrases were "roughly interchangeable given the genre." Bannard and Callison-Burch (2005) replaced phrases with paraphrases in a number of

©2008. Licensed under the *Creative Commons Attribution-Noncommercial-Share Alike 3.0 Unported* license (http://creativecommons.org/licenses/by-nc-sa/3.0/). Some rights reserved.

sentences and asked judges whether the substitutions "preserved meaning and remained grammatical." These subjective evaluations are rather vaguely defined and not easy to reproduce.

Others evaluate paraphrases in terms of whether they improve performance on particular tasks. Callison-Burch et al. (2006b) measure improvements in translation quality in terms of Bleu score (Papineni et al., 2002) and in terms of subjective human evaluation when paraphrases are integrated into a statistical machine translation system. Lin and Pantel (2001) manually judge whether a paraphrase might be used to answer questions from the TREC question-answering track. To date, no one has used task-based evaluation to compare different paraphrasing methods. Even if such an evaluation were performed, it is unclear whether the results would hold for a different task. Because of this, we strive for a general evaluation rather than a task-specific one.

Dolan et al. (2004) create a set of manual word alignments between pairs of English sentences. We create a similar type of data, as described in Section 4. Dolan et al. use heuristics to draw pairs of English sentences from a comparable corpus of newswire articles, and treat these as potential paraphrases. In some cases these sentence pairs are good examples of paraphrases, and in some cases they are not. Our data differs because it is drawn from multiple translations of the same foreign sentences. Barzilay (2003) suggested that multiple translations of the same foreign source text were a perfect source for "naturally occurring paraphrases" because they are samples of text which convey the same meaning but are produced by different writers. That being said, it may be possible to use Dolan et al's data toward a similar end. Cohn et al. (to appear) compares the use of the multiple translation corpus with the MSR corpus for this task.

The work described here is similar to work in summarization evaluation. For example, in the Pyramid Method (Nenkova et al., 2007) content units that are similar across human-generated summaries are hand-aligned. These can have alternative wordings, and are manually grouped. The idea of capturing these and building a resource for evaluating summaries is in the same spirit as our methodology.

3 Challenges for Evaluating Paraphrases Automatically

There are several problems inherent to automatically evaluating paraphrases. First and foremost, developing an exhaustive list of paraphrases for any given phrase is difficult. Lin and Pantel (2001) illustrate the difficulties that people have generating a complete list of paraphrases, reporting that they missed many examples generated by a system that were subsequently judged to be correct. If a list of reference paraphrases is incomplete, then using it to calculate precision will give inaccurate numbers. Precision will be falsely low if the system produces correct paraphrases which are not in the reference list. Additionally, recall is indeterminable because there is no way of knowing how many correct paraphrases exist.

There are further impediments to automatically evaluating paraphrases. Even if we were able to come up with a reasonably exhaustive list of paraphrases for a phrase, the acceptability of each paraphrase would vary depending on the context of the original phrase (Szpektor et al., 2007). While lexical and phrasal paraphrases can be evaluated by comparing them against a list of known paraphrases (perhaps customized for particular contexts), this cannot be naturally done for structural paraphrases which may transform whole sentences.

We attempt to resolve these problems by having annotators indicate correspondences in pairs of equivalent sentences. Rather than having people enumerate paraphrases, we asked that they perform the simper task of aligning paraphrases. After developing these manual "gold standard alignments" we can gauge how well different automatic paraphrases are at *aligning* paraphrases within equivalent sentences. By evaluating the performance of paraphrasing techniques at alignment, rather than at matching a list of reference paraphrases, we obviate the need to have a complete set of paraphrases.

We describe how sets of reference paraphrases can be extracted from the gold standard alignments. While these sets will obviously be fragmentary, we attempt to make them more complete by aligning *groups* of equivalent sentences rather than only pairs. The paraphrase sets that we extract are appropriate for the particular contexts. Moreover they may potentially be used to study structural paraphrases, although we do not examine that

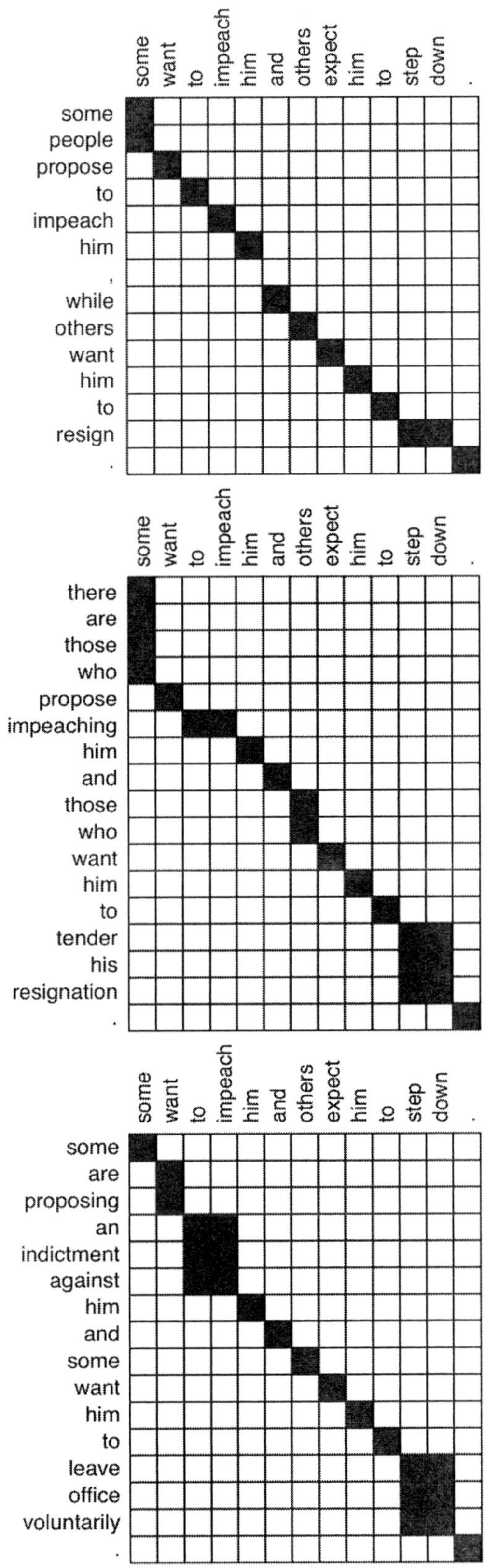

Figure 1: Pairs of English sentences were aligned by hand. Black squares indicate paraphrase correspondences.

in this paper.

4 Manually Aligning Paraphrases

We asked monolingual English speakers to align corresponding words and phrases across pairs of equivalent English sentences. The English sentences were equivalent because they were translations of the same foreign language text created by different human translators. Our annotators were instructed to align parts of the sentences which had the same meaning. Annotators were asked to prefer smaller one-to-one word alignments, but were allowed to create one-to-many and many-to-many alignments where appropriate. They were given a set of annotation guidelines covering special cases such as repetition, pronouns, genitives, phrasal verbs and omissions (Callison-Burch et al., 2006a). The manual correspondences are treated as *gold standard alignments*.

We use a corpus that contains eleven English translations of Chinese newswire documents, which were commissioned from different translation agencies by the Linguistics Data Consortium[1]. The data was created for the Bleu machine translation evaluation metric (Papineni et al., 2002), which uses multiple translations as a way of capturing allowable variation in translation. Whereas the Bleu metric requires no further information, our method requires a one-off annotation to explicitly show which parts of the multiple translations constitute paraphrases.

The rationale behind using a corpus with eleven translations was that a greater number of translations would likely result in a greater number of paraphrases for each phrase. Figure 1 shows the alignments that were created between one sentence and three of its ten corresponding translations. Table 1 gives a list of non-identical words and phrases that can be paired by way of the word alignments. These are the *basic paraphrases* contained within the three sentence pairs. Each phrase has up to three paraphrases. The maximum number of paraphrases for a given span in each sentence is bounded by the number of equivalent sentences that it is paired with.

In addition to these basic paraphrases, longer paraphrases can also be obtained using the heuristic presented in Och and Ney (2004) for extracting phrase pairs (PP) from word alignments A, between a foreign sentence f_1^J and an English sen-

[1] See LDC catalog number 2002T01.

some	some people, there are those who
want	propose, are proposing
to impeach	an indictment against, impeaching
and	while
others	some, those who
expect	want
step down	resign, leave office voluntarily, tender his resignation

Table 1: Non-identical words and phrases which are identified as being in correspondence by the alignments in Figure 1.

tence e_1^I:

$$PP(f_1^J, e_1^I, A) = \{(f_j^{j+m}, e_i^{i+n}):$$
$$\forall (i', j') \in A : j \leq j' \leq j+m \leftrightarrow i \leq i' \leq i+n$$
$$\wedge \exists (i', j') \in A : j \leq j' \leq j+m \wedge \leftrightarrow i \leq i' \leq i+n\}$$

When we apply the phrase extraction heuristic to aligned English sentences, we add the constraint $f_j^{j+m} \neq e_i^{i+n}$ to exclude phrases that are identical. This heuristic would allow "*some people propose to impeach him,*" "*some are proposing an indictment against him,*" and "*there are those who propose impeaching him*" to be extracted as paraphrases of "*some want to impeach him.*" The heuristic extracts a total of 142 non-identical phrase pairs from the three sentences given in Figure 1.

For the results reported in this paper, annotators aligned *50 groups* of 10 pairs of equivalent sentences, for a total of *500 sentence pairs*. These were assembled by pairing the first of the LDC translations with the other ten (i.e. 1-2, 1-3, 1-4, ..., 1-11). The choice of pairing one sentence with the others instead of doing all pairwise combinations was made simply because the latter would not seem to add much information. However, the choice of using the first translator as the key was arbitrary.

Annotators corrected a set of automatic word alignments that were created using Giza++ (Och and Ney, 2003), which was trained on a total of 109,230 sentence pairs created from all pairwise combinations of the eleven translations of 993 Chinese sentences.

The average amount of time spent on each of the sentence pairs was 77 seconds, with just over eleven hours spent to annotate all 500 sentence pairs. Although each sentence pair in our data set was annotated by a single annotator, Cohn et al. (to appear) analyzed the inter-annotator agreement for randomly selected phrase pairs from the same corpus, and found inter-annotator agreement of $\hat{C} = 0.85$ over the aligned words and $\hat{C} = 0.63$ over the alignments between basic phrase pairs, where $\hat{C}$ is measure of inter-rater agreement in the style of Kupper and Hafner (1989).

5 ParaMetric Scores

We can exploit the manually aligned data to compute scores in two different fashions. First, we can calculate how well an automatic paraphrasing technique is able *to align* the paraphrases in a sentence pair. Second, we can calculate the *lower-bound on precision* for a paraphrasing technique and its *relative recall* by enumerating the paraphrases from each of the sentence groups. The first of these score types does not require groups of sentences, only pairs.

We calculate alignment accuracy by comparing the manual alignments for the sentence pairs in the test corpus with the alignments that the automatic paraphrasing techniques produce for the same sentence pairs. We enumerate all non-identical phrase pairs within the manually word-aligned sentence pairs and within the automatically word aligned sentence pairs using PP. We calculate the precision and recall of the alignments by taking the intersection of the paraphrases extracted from the manual alignments M, and the paraphrases extracted from a system's alignments S:

$$Align_{Prec} = \frac{\sum_{<e_1,e_2>\in C} |PP(e_1, e_2, S) \cap PP(e_1, e_2, M)|}{\sum_{<e_1,e_2>\in C} |PP(e_1, e_2, S)|}$$

$$Align_{Recall} = \frac{\sum_{<e_1,e_2>\in C} |PP(e_1, e_2, S) \cap PP(e_1, e_2, M)|}{\sum_{<e_1,e_2>\in C} |PP(e_1, e_2, M)|}$$

Where e_1, e_2 are pairs of English sentence from the test corpus.

Measuring a paraphrasing method's performance on the task of *aligning* the paraphrases is somewhat different than what most paraphrasing methods do. Most methods produce a list of paraphrases for a given input phrase, drawing from a large set of rules or a corpus larger than our small test set. We therefore also attempt to measure precision and recall by comparing the set of paraphrases that method M produces for phrase p that occurs in sentence s. We denote this set as $para_M(p, s)$, where s is an optional argument for methods that constrain their paraphrases based on context.

Our reference sets of paraphrases are generated in a per group fashion. We enumerate the reference paraphrases for phrase p in sentence s in group G as

$$para_{REF}(p_1, s_1, G) =$$
$$\{p_2 : \forall(p_1, p_2) \in \sum_{<s_1,s_2,A>\in G} PP(s_1, s_2, A)\}$$

The maximum size of this set is the number of sentence pairs in G. Because this set of reference paraphrases is incomplete, we can only calculate a lower bound on the precision of a paraphrasing method and its recall relative to the reference paraphrases. We call these *LB-Precision* and *Rel-Recall* and calculate them as follows:

LB-Precision =

$$\sum_{<s,G>\in C} \sum_{p\in s} \frac{|para_M(p, s) \cap para_{REF}(p_1, s, G)|}{|para_M(p, s)|}$$

Rel-Recall =

$$\sum_{<s,G>\in C} \sum_{p\in s} \frac{|para_M(p, s) \cap para_{REF}(p_1, s, G)|}{|para_{REF}(p_1, s, G)|}$$

For these metrics we require the test corpus C to be a held-out set and restrict the automatic paraphrasing techniques from drawing paraphrases from it. The idea is instead to see how well these techniques are able to draw paraphrases from the other sources of data which they would normally use.

6 Paraphrasing Techniques

There are a number of established methods for extracting paraphrases from data. We describe the following methods in this section and evaluate them in the next:

- Pang et al. (2003) used *syntactic alignment* to merge parse trees of multiple translations,
- Quirk et al. (2004) treated paraphrasing as *monolingual statistical machine translation*,
- Bannard and Callison-Burch (2005) used *bilingual parallel corpora* to extract paraphrases.

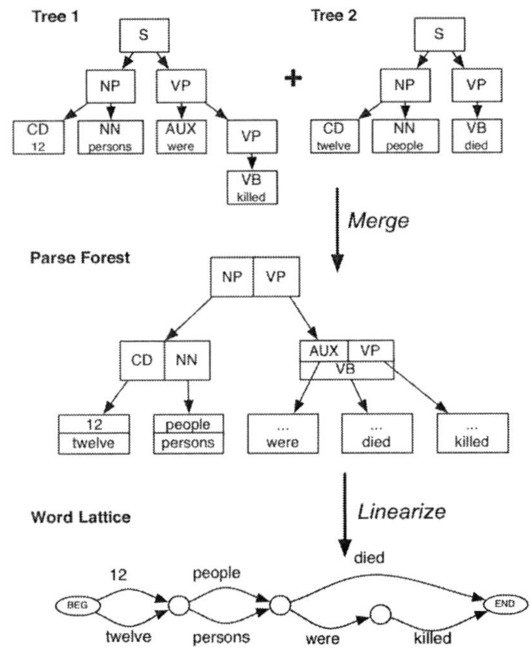

Figure 2: Pang et al. (2003) created word graphs by merging parse trees. Paths with the same start and end nodes are treated as paraphrases.

Pang et al. (2003) use multiple translations to learn paraphrases using a syntax-based alignment algorithm, illustrated in Figure 2. Parse trees were merged into forests by grouping constituents of the same type (for example, the two NPs and two VPs are grouped). Parse forests were mapped onto finite state word graphs by creating alternative paths for every group of merged nodes. Different paths within the resulting word lattice are treated as paraphrases of each other. For example, in the word lattice in Figure 2, *people were killed*, *persons died*, *persons were killed*, and *people died* are all possible paraphrases of each other.

Quirk et al. (2004) treated paraphrasing as "monolingual statistical machine translation." They created a "parallel corpus" containing pairs of English sentences by drawing sentences with a low edit distance from news articles that were written about the same topic on the same date, but published by different newspapers. They formulated the problem of paraphrasing in probabilistic terms in the same way it had been defined in the statistical machine translation literature:

$$\begin{aligned} \hat{e}_2 &= \arg\max_{e_2} p(e_2|e_1) \\ &= \arg\max_{e_2} p(e_1|e_2)p(e_2) \end{aligned}$$

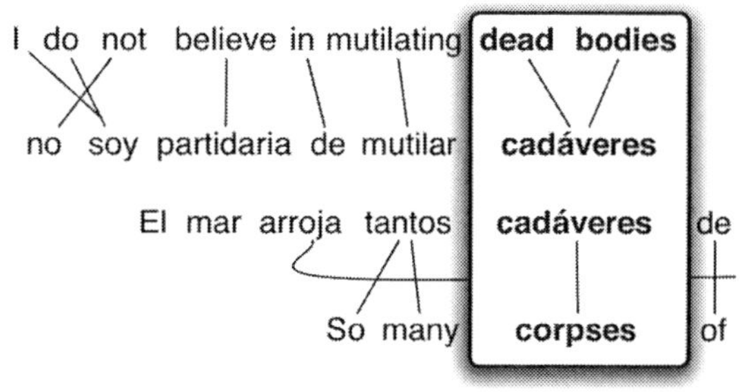

Figure 3: Bannard and Callison-Burch (2005) extracted paraphrases by equating English phrases that share a common translation.

	Parallel Corpora	Syntactic Alignment	Monolingual SMT
$Align_{Prec}$	.62	.65	.73
$Align_{Recall}$	.11	.10	.46
LB-Precision	.14	.33	.68
Rel-Recall	.07	.03	.01

Table 2: Summary results for scoring the different paraphrasing techniques using our proposed automatic evaluations.

Where $p(e_1|e_2)$ is estimated by training word alignment models over the "parallel corpus" as in the IBM Models (Brown et al., 1993), and phrase translations are extracted from word alignments as in the Alignment Template Model (Och, 2002).

Bannard and Callison-Burch (2005) also used techniques from statistical machine translation to identify paraphrases. Rather than drawing pairs of English sentences from a comparable corpus, Bannard and Callison-Burch (2005) used bilingual parallel corpora. They identified English paraphrases by pivoting through phrases in another language. They located foreign language translations of an English phrase, and treated the other English translations of those foreign phrases as potential paraphrases. Figure 3 illustrates how a Spanish phrase can be used as a point of identification for English paraphrases in this way. Bannard and Callison-Burch (2005) defined a paraphrase probability $p(e_2|e_1)$ in terms of the translation model probabilities $p(f|e_1)$ and $p(e_2|f)$. Since e_1 can translate as multiple foreign language phrases, they sum over f, and since multiple parallel corpora can be used they summed over each parallel corpus C:

$$\begin{aligned}\hat{e_2} &= \arg\max_{e_2 \neq e_1} p(e_2|e_1) \\ &\approx \arg\max_{e_2 \neq e_1} \sum_{C} \sum_{f\ in\ C} p(f|e_1)p(e_2|f)\end{aligned}$$

7 Comparing Paraphrasing Techniques with ParaMetric

7.1 Training data for word alignments

In order to calculate $Align_{Prec}$ and $Align_{Recall}$ for the different paraphrasing techniques, we had them automatically align the 500 manually aligned sentence pairs in our test sets.

Bo Pang provided syntactic alignments for the 500 sentence pairs. The word lattices combine the groups of sentences. When measuring alignment quality, we took pains to try to limit the extracted phrase pairs to those which occurred in each sentence pair, but we acknowledge that our methodology may be flawed.

We created training data for the monolingual statistical machine translation method using all pairwise combination of eleven English translations in LDC2002T01. All combinations of the eleven translations of the 993 sentences in that corpus resulted in 109,230 sentence pairs with 3,266,769 words on each side. We used this data to train an alignment model, and applied it to the 500 sentence pairs in our test set.

We used the parallel corpus method to align each pair of English sentences by creating intermediate alignments through their Chinese source sentences. The bilingual word alignment model was trained on a Chinese-English parallel corpus from the NIST MT Evaluation consisting of 40 million words. This was used to align the 550 Chinese-English sentence pairs constructed from the test set.

7.2 Training data for precision and recall

Each of the paraphrasing methods generated paraphrases for *LB-Precision* and *Rel-Recall* using larger training sets of data than for the alignments. For the syntax-based alignment method, we excluded the 50 word lattices corresponding to the test set. We used the remaining 849 lattices for the LDC multiple translation corpus. For the monolingual statistical machine translation method, we downloaded the Microsoft Research Paraphrase Phrase Table, which contained paraphrases for nearly 9 million phrases, generated from the method described in Quirk et al. (2004). For the parallel corpus method, we derived paraphrases from the entire Europarl corpus, which contains parallel corpora between English and 10 other languages, with approximately 30 million words per language. We limited both the Quirk et al. (2004) and the Bannard and Callison-Burch (2005) paraphrases to those with a probability greater than or equal to 1%.

7.3 Results

Table 2 gives a summary of how each of the paraphrasing techniques scored using the four different automatic metrics. The precision of their alignments was in the same ballpark, with each paraphrasing method reaching above 60%. The monolingual SMT method vastly outstripped the others in terms of recall and therefore seems to be the best on the simplified task of aligning paraphrases within pairs of equivalent sentences.

For the task of generating paraphrases from unrestricted resources, the monolingual SMT method again had the highest precision, although time time its recall was quite low. The 500 manually aligned sentence pairs contained 14,078 unique paraphrases for phrases of 5 words or less. The monolingual SMT method only posited 230 paraphrases with 156 of them being correct. By contrast, the syntactic alignment method posited 1,213 with 399 correct, and the parallel corpus method posited 6,914 with 998 correct. Since the reference lists are incomplete by their very nature, the *LB-Precision* score gives a lower-bound on the precision, and the *Rel-Recall* gives recall only with respect to the partial list of paraphrases.

Table 3 gives the performance of the different paraphrasing techniques for different phrase lengths.

8 Conclusions

In this paper we defined a number of automatic scores for data-driven approaches to paraphrasing, which we collectively dub "ParaMetric". We discussed the inherent difficulties in automatically assessing paraphrase quality. These are due primarily to the fact that it is exceedingly difficult to create an exhaustive list of paraphrases. To address this problem, we introduce an artificial task of aligning paraphrases within pairs of equivalent English sentences, which guarantees accurate precision and recall numbers. In order to measure alignment quality, we create a set of gold standard alignments. While the creation of this data does require some effort, it seems to be a manageable amount, and the inter-annotator agreement seems reasonable.

Since alignment is not perfectly matched with what we would like automatic paraphrasing techniques to do, we also use the gold standard alignment data to measure a lower bound on the precision of a method's paraphrases, as well as its recall relative to the limited set of paraphrases. Future studies should examine how well these scores rank different paraphrasing methods when compared to human judgments. Follow up work should investigate the number of equivalent English sentences that are required for reasonably complete lists of paraphrases. In this work we aligned sets of eleven different English sentences, but we acknowledge that such a data set is rare and might make it difficult to port this method to other domains or languages.

The goal of this work is to develop a set of scores that both allows different paraphrasing techniques to be compared objectively and provides an easily repeatable method for automatically evaluating paraphrases. This has hitherto not been possible. The availability of an objective, automatic evaluation metric for paraphrasing has the potential to impact research in the area in a number of ways. It not only allows for the comparison of different approaches to paraphrasing, as shown in this paper, but also provides a way to tune the parameters of a single system in order to optimize its quality.

Acknowledgments

The authors are grateful to Bo Pang for providing the word lattices from her method, to Stefan Riezler for his comments on an early draft of this paper, and to Michelle Bland for proofreading. This work was supported by the National Science Foundation under Grant No. 0713448. The views and findings are the authors' alone.

References

Bannard, Colin and Chris Callison-Burch. 2005. Paraphrasing with bilingual parallel corpora. In *Proceedings of the 43rd Annual Meeting of the Association for Computational Linguistics (ACL-2005)*, Ann Arbor, Michigan.

Barzilay, Regina and Lillian Lee. 2003. Learning to paraphrase: An unsupervised approach us-

	$Align_{Prec}$			$Align_{Recall}$			*LB-Precision*			*Rel-Recall*		
	Parallel Corpora	Syntactic Alignment	Monolingual SMT	Parallel Corpora	Syntactic Alignment	Monolingual SMT	Parallel Corpora	Syntactic Alignment	Monolingual SMT	Parallel Corpora	Syntactic Alignment	Monolingual SMT
Length = 1	.54	.48	.64	.24	.18	.56	.15	.25	.59	.20	.16	.02
Length $\leq$ 2	.56	.56	.69	.19	.13	.52	.15	.31	.66	.18	.10	.03
Length $\leq$ 3	.59	.60	.71	.14	.12	.49	.15	.32	.66	.13	.06	.02
Length $\leq$ 4	.60	.63	.72	.12	.11	.48	.14	.33	.68	.09	.04	.01
Length $\leq$ 5	.62	.65	.73	.11	.10	.46	.14	.33	.68	.07	.03	.01

Table 3: Results for paraphrases of continuous subphrases of various lengths.

ing multiple-sequence alignment. In *Proceedings of HLT/NAACL-2003*, Edmonton, Alberta.

Barzilay, Regina and Kathleen McKeown. 2001. Extracting paraphrases from a parallel corpus. In *Proceedings of the 39th Annual Meeting of the Association for Computational Linguistics (ACL-2001)*.

Barzilay, Regina. 2003. *Information Fusion for Mutlidocument Summarization: Paraphrasing and Generation*. Ph.D. thesis, Columbia University, New York.

Brown, Peter, Stephen Della Pietra, Vincent Della Pietra, and Robert Mercer. 1993. The mathematics of machine translation: Parameter estimation. *Computational Linguistics*, 19(2):263–311, June.

Callison-Burch, Chris, Trevor Cohn, and Mirella Lapata. 2006a. Annotation guidelines for paraphrase alignment. Tech report, University of Edinburgh.

Callison-Burch, Chris, Philipp Koehn, and Miles Osborne. 2006b. Improved statistical machine translation using paraphrases. In *Proceedings of HLT/NAACL-2006*, New York, New York.

Cohn, Trevor, Chris Callison-Burch, and Mirella Lapata. to appear. Constructing corpora for the development and evaluation of paraphrase systems. *Computational Linguistics*.

Dolan, Bill, Chris Quirk, and Chris Brockett. 2004. Unsupervised construction of large paraphrase corpora: Exploiting massively parallel news sources. In *Proceedings of the 20th International Conference on Computational Linguistics*.

Ibrahim, Ali, Boris Katz, and Jimmy Lin. 2003. Extracting structural paraphrases from aligned monolingual corpora. In *Proceedings of the Second International Workshop on Paraphrasing (ACL 2003)*.

Kupper, Lawrence L. and Kerry B. Hafner. 1989. On assessing interrater agreement for multiple attribute responses. *Biometrics*, 45(3):957–967.

Lin, Dekang and Patrick Pantel. 2001. Discovery of inference rules from text. *Natural Language Engineering*, 7(3):343–360.

Miller, George A. 1990. Wordnet: An on-line lexical database. *Special Issue of the International Journal of Lexicography*, 3(4).

Nenkova, Ani, Rebecca Passonneau, and Kathleen McKeown. 2007. The pyramid method: incorporating human content selection variation in summarization evaluation. *ACM Transactions on Speech and Language Processing*, 4(2).

Och, Franz Josef and Hermann Ney. 2003. A systematic comparison of various statistical alignment models. *Computational Linguistics*, 29(1):19–51.

Och, Franz Josef and Hermann Ney. 2004. The alignment template approach to statistical machine translation. *Computational Linguistics*, 30(4):417–449.

Och, Franz Josef. 2002. *Statistical Machine Translation: From Single-Word Models to Alignment Templates*. Ph.D. thesis, RWTH Aachen Department of Computer Science, Aachen, Germany.

Pang, Bo, Kevin Knight, and Daniel Marcu. 2003. Syntax-based alignment of multiple translations: Extracting paraphrases and generating new sentences. In *Proceedings of HLT/NAACL-2003*, Edmonton, Alberta.

Papineni, Kishore, Salim Roukos, Todd Ward, and Wei-Jing Zhu. 2002. Bleu: A method for automatic evaluation of machine translation. In *Proceedings of the 40th Annual Meeting of the Association for Computational Linguistics (ACL-2002)*, Philadelphia, Pennsylvania.

Quirk, Chris, Chris Brockett, and William Dolan. 2004. Monolingual machine translation for paraphrase generation. In *Proceedings of the 2004 Conference on Empirical Methods in Natural Language Processing (EMNLP-2004)*, Barcelona, Spain.

Szpektor, Idan, Eyal Shnarch, and Ido Dagan. 2007. Instance-based evaluation of entailment rule acquisition. In *Proceedings of the 45th Annual Meeting of the Association for Computational Linguistics (ACL-2007)*, Prague, Czech Republic.

Regenerating Hypotheses for Statistical Machine Translation

Boxing Chen, Min Zhang, Aiti Aw and **Haizhou Li**
Department of Human Language Technology
Institute for Infocomm Research
21 Heng Mui Keng Terrace, 119613, Singapore
{bxchen, mzhang, aaiti, hli}@i2r.a-star.edu.sg

Abstract

This paper studies three techniques that improve the quality of N-best hypotheses through additional regeneration process. Unlike the multi-system consensus approach where multiple translation systems are used, our improvement is achieved through the expansion of the N-best hypotheses from a single system. We explore three different methods to implement the regeneration process: re-decoding, n-gram expansion, and confusion network-based regeneration. Experiments on Chinese-to-English NIST and IWSLT tasks show that all three methods obtain consistent improvements. Moreover, the combination of the three strategies achieves further improvements and outperforms the baseline by 0.81 BLEU-score on IWSLT'06, 0.57 on NIST'03, 0.61 on NIST'05 test set respectively.

1 Introduction

State-of-the-art Statistical Machine Translation (SMT) systems usually adopt a two-pass search strategy (Och, 2003; Koehn, et al., 2003) as shown in Figure 1. In the first pass, a decoding algorithm is applied to generate an N-best list of translation hypotheses, while in the second pass, the final translation is selected by rescoring and re-ranking the N-best translations through additional feature functions. The fundamental assumption behind using a second pass is that the generated N-best list may contain better translations than the best choice found by the decoder. Therefore, the performance of a two-pass SMT system can be improved from two aspects, i.e. scoring models and the quality of the N-best hypotheses.

Rescoring pass improves the performance of machine translation by enhancing the scoring models with more global sophisticated and discriminative feature functions. The idea for applying two passes instead of one is that some global feature functions cannot be easily decomposed into local scores and computed during decoding. Furthermore, rescoring allows some feature functions, such as word and n-gram posterior probabilities, to be estimated on the N-best list (Ueffing, 2003; Chen et al., 2005; Zens and Ney, 2006).

In this two-pass method, translation performance hinges on the N-best hypotheses that are generated in the first pass (since rescoring occurs on these), so adding the translation candidates generated by other MT systems to these hypotheses could potentially improve the performance. This technique is called system combination (Bangalore et al., 2001; Matusov et al., 2006; Sim et al., 2007; Rosti et al., 2007a; Rosti et al., 2007b).

We have instead chosen to regenerate new hypotheses from the original N-best list, a technique which we call *regeneration*. Regeneration is an intermediate pass between decoding and rescoring as depicted in Figure 2. Given the original N-best list (N-best1) generated by the decoder, this regeneration pass creates new translation hypotheses from this list to form another N-best list (N-best2). These two N-best lists are then combined and given to the rescoring pass to derive the best translation.

We implement three methods to regenerate new hypotheses: re-decoding, n-gram expansion and confusion network. Re-decoding (Rosti et al., 2007a) based regeneration re-decodes the source sentence using original LM as well as new trans-

© 2008. Licensed under the *Creative Commons Attribution-Noncommercial-Share Alike 3.0 Unported* license (http://creativecommons.org/licenses/by-nc-sa/3.0/). Some rights reserved.

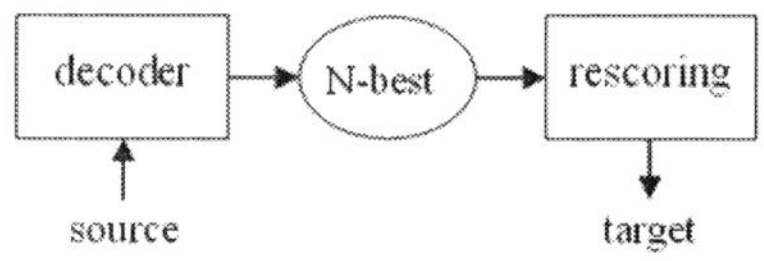

Figure 1: Structure of a typical two-pass machine translation system. N-best translations are generated by the decoder and the 1-best translation is returned after rescored with additional feature functions.

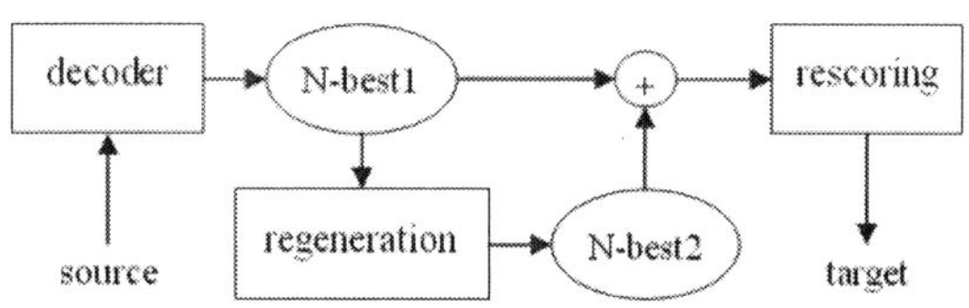

Figure 2: Structure of a three-pass machine translation system with the new regeneration pass. The original N-best translations list (N-best1) is expanded to generate a new N-best translations list (N-best2) before the rescoring pass.

lation and reordering models that are trained on the source-to-target N-best translations generated in the first pass. N-gram expansion (Chen et al., 2007) regenerates more hypotheses by continuously expanding the partial hypotheses through an n-gram language model trained on the original N-best translations. And confusion network generates new hypotheses based on confusion network decoding (Matusov et al., 2006), where the confusion network is built on the original N-best translations.

Confusion network and re-decoding have been well studied in the combination of different MT systems (Bangalore et al., 2001; Matusov et al., 2006; Sim et al., 2007; Rosti et al., 2007a; Rosti et al., 2007b). Researchers have used confusion network to compute consensus translations from the outputs of different MT systems and improve the performance over each single systems. (Rosti et al., 2007a) also used re-decoding to do system combination by extracting sentence-specific phrase translation tables from the outputs of different MT systems and running a phrase-based decoding with this new translation table. Finally, N-gram expansion method (Chen et al., 2007) collects sub-strings occurring in the N-best list to produce alternative translations.

This work demonstrates that a state-of-the-art MT system can be further improved by means of *regeneration* which expands its own N-best translations other than taking the translation candidates from the other MT systems.

2 SMT Process

Phrase-based statistical machine translation systems are usually modeled through a log-linear framework (Och and Ney, 2002). By introducing the hidden word alignment variable a (Brown et al., 1993), the optimal translation can be searched for based on the following criterion:

$$\tilde{e}^* = \arg\max_{e,a}\left(\sum_{m=1}^{M} \lambda_m h_m(\tilde{e}, \tilde{f}, a)\right) \qquad (1)$$

where $\tilde{e}$ is a string of phrases in the target language, $\tilde{f}$ is the source language string of phrases, $h_m(\tilde{e}, \tilde{f}, a)$ are feature functions, weights λ_m are typically optimized to maximize the scoring function (Och, 2003).

Our MT baseline system is based on Moses decoder (Koehn et al., 2007) with word alignment obtained from GIZA++ (Och et al., 2003). The translation model (TM), lexicalized word reordering model (RM) are trained using the tools provided in the open source Moses package. Language model (LM) is trained with SRILM toolkit (Stolcke, 2002) with modified Kneser-Ney smoothing method (Chen and Goodman, 1998).

3 Regeneration Methods

Given the original N-best translations, regeneration pass is to generate M new target translations which are not seen in the original N-best choices.

3.1 Regeneration with Re-decoding

One way of regeneration is by running the decoding again to obtain new hypotheses through a re-decoding process (Rosti et al., 2007a). In this work, the same decoder (Moses) is used to produce the new M-best translations using a new translation model and reordering model trained over the word-aligned source input and original N-best target hypotheses. Although the target-to-source phrase alignments are available in the original N-best hypotheses, to enlarge the difference between the new M-best translations and the original N-best translations, we re-align the words using GIZA++.

Weights of the decoder are re-optimized by the tool in the Moses package over the development set. The process of such a re-decoding is summarized as follows:

1. Run GIZA++ to align the words between the source input and target N-best translations;
2. Train translation and reordering model;
3. Optimize the weights of the decoder with the new models;
4. Decode the source input by using new models and new weights to generate N+M distinct translations ("distinct" here refers to the target language string only, not considering the phrase segmentation, etc.);
5. Output M-best translations which are not seen in the original N-best translations.

Re-decoding on test set follows the same steps, but without the tuning step, step 3.

3.2 Regeneration with N-gram Expansion

N-gram expansion (Chen et al., 2007) combines the sub-strings occurred in the original N-best translations to generate new hypotheses. Firstly, all n-grams from the original N-best translations are collected. Then the partial hypotheses are continuously expanded by appending a word through the n-grams collected in the first step. We explain this method in more detail using the following example.

Suppose we have four original hypotheses shown in Figure 3. Firstly, we collect all the 3-grams from the original hypotheses. The first n-grams of all original entries in the N-best list are set as the initial partial hypotheses. They are: *it's 5 minutes, it is 5, it's about 5* and *i walk 5*. Then the expansion of a partial hypothesis starts by computing the set of n-grams matching its last n-1 words. As shown in Figure 4, the n-gram *5 minutes on* matches the last two words of the partial hypothesis *it's about 5 minutes*. So the hypothesis is expanded to *it's about 5 minutes on*. The expansion continues until the partial hypothesis ends with a special end-of-sentence symbol that occurs at the end of all N-best strings.

Figure 5 shows some new hypotheses that are generated from the example in Figure 3. This is an example excerpted from our development data. One reference is also given in Figure 5; the first new generated hypothesis is equal to this reference. But unfortunately, there is no such hypothesis in the original N-best translations.

During the new hypotheses generation, the translation outputs of a given source sentence are computed through a beam-search algorithm with a log-linear combination of the feature functions. In addition to n-gram frequency and n-gram posterior probability which have been used in (Chen et al., 2007), we also used language model, direct/inverse IBM model 1, and word penalty in this work. The size of the beam is set to N+M, to ensure more than M new hypotheses are generated.

Original hypotheses	1. it's 5 minutes on foot . 2. it is 5 minutes on foot . 3. it's about 5 minutes' to walk . 4. i walk 5 minutes .
n-grams	it's 5 minutes, 5 minutes on, ... on foot ., about 5 minutes ...... 5 minutes .

Figure 3: Example of original hypotheses and 3-grams collected from them.

partial hyp.	it's	about	5	minutes	
n-gram	+		5	minutes	on
new partial hyp.	it's	about	5	minutes	on

Figure 4: Expanding a partial hypothesis via a matching n-gram.

New hypotheses	it's about 5 minutes on foot . it's 5 minutes . i walk 5 minutes on foot . ...
Reference	it's about five minutes on foot .

Figure 5: New generated hypotheses through n-gram expansion and one reference.

3.3 Regeneration with Confusion Network

Confusion network based regeneration builds a confusion network over the original N-best hypotheses, and then extracts M-best hypotheses from it. The word order in the N-best translations could be very different, so we need to choose a hypothesis with the "most correct" word order as the confusion network skeleton (alignment reference), then align and reorder other hypotheses in this word order.

Some previous work compute the consensus translation under MT system combination, which differ from ours in the way of choosing the skeleton and aligning the words. Matusov et al. (2006) let every hypothesis play the role of the skeleton once and used GIZA++ to get word alignment. Bangalore et al. (2001), Sim et al. (2007), Rosti et al. (2007a), and Rosti et al. (2007b) chose the hypothesis that best agrees with other hypotheses on average as the skeleton. Bangalore et al. (2001) used a WER based alignment and Sim et al. (2007), Rosti et al. (2007a), and Rosti et al. (2007b) used minimum Translation Error Rate

(TER) based alignment to build the confusion network.

Choosing alignment reference: Since the N-best translations are ranked, choosing the first best hypothesis as the skeleton is straightforward in our work.

Aligning words: As a confusion network can be easily built from a one-to-one alignment, we develop our algorithm based on the one-to-one assumption and use competitive linking algorithm (Melamed, 2000) for our word alignment. Firstly, an association score is computed for every possible word pair from the skeleton and sentence to be aligned. Then a greedy algorithm is applied to select the best word-alignment. In this paper, we use a linear combination of multiple association scores, as suggested in (Kraif and Chen, 2004). As the two sentences to be aligned are in the same language, the association scores are computed on the following four clues. They are cognate (S_1), word class (S_2), synonyms (S_3), and position difference (S_4). The four scores are linearly combined with empirically determined weights as shown is Equation 2.

$$S(f_j, e_i) = \sum_{k=1}^{4} \lambda_k \times S_k \qquad (2)$$

Reordering words: After word alignment, the words in all other hypotheses are reordered to match the word order of the skeleton. The aligned words are reordered according to their alignment indices. The unaligned words are reordered in two strategies: moved with its previous word or next word. In this work, additional experiments suggested that moving the unaligned word with its previous word achieve better performance. In the case that the first word is unaligned, it will be moved with its next word. Each word is assigned a score based on a simple voting scheme. Figure 6 shows an example of creating a confusion network.

Extracting M-best translations: New translations are extracted from the confusion network. We again use beam-search algorithm to derive new hypotheses. The same feature functions proposed in Section 3.2 are used to score the partial hypotheses. Moreover, we also use position based word probability (i.e. in Figure 6, the words in position 5, "on" scored a probability of 0.5, and "ε" scored a probability of 0.25) as a feature function. Figure 6 shows some examples of new hypotheses generated through confusion network regeneration.

Original hypotheses	**1. it's 5 minutes on foot .** 2. it is 5 minutes on foot . 3. it's about 5 minutes' to walk . 4. i walk 5 minutes .
Alignments	**it's 5 minutes on foot . ε** it 5 minutes on foot . is it's 5 minutes' to walk . about i 5 minutes ε walk .
Confusion network	**it's ε 5 minutes on foot .** it is 5 minutes on foot . it's about 5 minutes' to walk . i ε 5 minutes ε walk .
New hypotheses	1. it's about five minutes on foot . 2. it about five minutes on foot . 3. it's about five minutes on walk . 4. i about 5 minutes to work .

Figure 6: Example of creating a confusion network from the word alignments, and new hypotheses generated through the confusion network. The sentence in bold is the alignment reference.

4 Rescoring model

Since the final N+M-best hypotheses are produced either from different methods or same decoder with different models, local feature functions of each hypothesis are not directly comparable, and thus inadequate for rescoring. We hence exploit rich global feature functions in the rescoring models to compensate the loss of local feature functions. We apply the following 10 feature functions and optimize the weight of each feature function using the tool in Moses package.

- direct and inverse IBM model 1 and 3
- association score, i.e. hyper-geometric distribution probabilities and mutual information
- lexicalized word/block reordering rules (Chen et al., 2006)
- 6-gram target LM
- 8-gram target word-class based LM, word-classes are clustered by GIZA++
- length ratio between source and target sentence
- question feature (Chen et al., 2005)
- linear sum of n-grams relative frequencies within N-best translations (Chen et al., 2005)
- n-gram posterior probabilities within the N-best translations (Zens and Ney, 2006)
- sentence length posterior probabilities (Zens and Ney, 2006)

5 Experiments

5.1 Tasks

We carried out two sets of experiments on two different datasets. One is in spoken language domain while the other is on newswire corpus. Both experiments are on Chinese-to-English translation.

Experiments on spoken language domain were carried out on the *Basic Traveling Expression Corpus* (BTEC) (Takezawa et al., 2002) Chinese- to-English data augmented with *HIT-corpus*[1]. BTEC is a multilingual speech corpus which contains sentences spoken by tourists. 40K sentence-pairs are used in our experiment. *HIT-corpus* is a balanced corpus and has 500K sentence-pairs in total. We selected 360K sentence-pairs that are more similar to BTEC data according to its sub-topic. Additionally, the English sentences of *Tanaka* corpus[2] were also used to train our LM. We ran experiments on an IWSLT[3] *challenge track* which uses IWSLT-2006[4] DEV clean text set as development set and IWSLT-2006 TEST clean text as test set. Table 1 summarizes the statistics of the training, dev and test data for IWSLT task.

Experiments on newswire domain were carried out on the FBIS[5] corpus. We used NIST[6] 2002 MT evaluation test set as our development set, and the NIST 2003, 2005 test sets as our test sets. Table 2 summarizes the statistics of the training, dev and test data for NIST task.

data		Chinese	English
Train	Sentences	406,122	
	Words	4,443K	4,591K
	Vocabulary	69,989	61,087
Dev.	Sentences	489	489×7
	Words	5,896	45,449
Test	Sentences	500	500×7
	Words	6,296	51,227
Additional target data	Sentences	-	155K
	Words	-	1.7M

Table 1: Statistics of training, development and test data for IWSLT task.

[1] http://mitlab.hit.edu.cn/

[2] http://www.csse.monash.edu.au/~jwb/tanakacorpus.html

[3] International Workshop for Spoken Language Translation

[4] http:// www.slc.atr.jp/IWSLT2006/

[5] LDC2003E14

[6] http://www.nist.gov/speech/tests/mt/

data		Chinese	English
Train	Sentences	238,761	
	Words	7.0M	8.9M
	Vocabulary	56,223	63,941
NIST 02 (dev)	Sentences	878	878×4
	Words	23,248	108,616
NIST 03 (test)	Sentences	919	919×4
	Words	25,820	116,547
NIST 05 (test)	Sentences	1,082	1,082×4
	Words	30,544	141,915
Additional target data	Sentences	-	2.2M
	Words	-	61.5M

Table 2: Statistics of training, development and test data for NIST task.

		Dev set		Test set	
System	#hypo	BLEU	NIST	BLEU	NIST
1-best	-	29.98	7.468	29.10	7.103
RESC1	1,200	31.60	7.657	30.42	7.165
RD	1,200	32.46	7.664	30.95	7.175
NE	1,200	32.58	7.660	31.02	7.178
CN	1,200	32.33	7.671	30.82	7.200
RESC2	2,000	31.72	7.659	30.55	7.166
COMB	2,000	**32.98**	**7.673**	**31.36**	**7.202**

Table 3: Translation performances (BLEU% and NIST scores) of IWSLT task: decoder (1-best), rescoring on original 1,200 N-best (RESC1) and 2,000 N-best hypotheses (RESC2), re-decoding (RD), n-gram expansion (NE), confusion network (CN) and combination of all hypotheses (COMB).

5.2 Results

We set N = 800 and M = 400 for IWSLT task, i.e. 800 distinct translations for each source input are extracted from the decoder and used for regeneration; and 400 new hypotheses are generated for each regeneration system: re-decoding (RD), n-gram expansion (NE) and confusion network (CN). System COMB combines the original N-best and the three regenerated M-best hypotheses lists (totally, 2,000 distinct hypotheses: 800 + 3×400). Then each system computes the 1-best translation through rescoring and re-ranking its hypotheses list. For comparison purpose, the performance of rescoring on two sets of original N-best translations are also computed and they are applied based on 1,200 (RESC1) and 2,000 (RESC2) distinct hypotheses extracted from the decoder. For NIST task, we set N = 1,600, and M = 800, thus, RESC2 and COMB compute 1-

System	#hypo	NIST'02 (dev)		NIST'03 (test)		NIST'05 (test)	
		BLEU	NIST	BLEU	NIST	BLEU	NIST
1-best	1	27.67	8.498	26.68	8.271	24.82	7.856
RESC1	2,400	28.13	8.519	27.09	8.312	25.29	7.868
RD	2,400	28.46	8.518	27.34	8.320	25.54	7.897
NE	2,400	28.52	8.539	27.47	8.329	25.65	7.907
CN	2,400	28.40	8.545	27.30	8.332	25.54	7.913
RESC2	4,000	28.27	8.522	27.21	8.320	25.43	7.875
COMB	4,000	**28.92**	**8.602**	**27.78**	**8.401**	**26.04**	**7.994**

Table 4: Translation performances (BLEU% and NIST scores) of NIST task: decoder (1-best), rescoring on original 2,400 N-best (RESC1) and 4,000 N-best hypotheses (RESC2), re-decoding (RD), n-gram expansion (NE), confusion network (CN) and combination of all hypotheses (COMB).

1	Reference	No tax is needed for this item . Thank you .
	RESC2	you don't have to do not need to pay duty on this . thank you .
	COMB (RD)	not need to pay duty on this . thank you .
2	Reference	Certainly . The fitting room is over there . Please come with me .
	RESC2	the fitting room is over there . can you come with me .
	COMB (NE)	yes , you can . the fitting room is over there . please come with me .
3	Reference	OK . I will bring it to you in five minutes .
	RESC2	a good five minutes , we will give you .
	COMB (CN)	ok . after five minutes , i will give it to you .

Table 5: Translations output by system RESC2 and COMB on IWSLT task (case-insensitive).

best from 4,000 (1,600 + 3×800) distinct hypotheses.

Our evaluation metrics are BLEU (Papineni et al., 2002) and NIST, which are to perform case-insensitive matching of n-grams up to $n = 4$. The translation performance of IWSLT task and NIST task is reported in Tables 3 and 4 respectively. The row "1-best" reports the scores of the translations produced by the decoder. The column "#hypo" means the size of the N-best hypotheses involved in rescoring. Note that on top of the same global feature functions as mentioned in Section 4, the local feature functions used during decoding were also involved in rescoring RESC1 and RESC2.

First of all, we note that both BLEU and NIST scores of the first decoding step were improved through rescoring. If rescoring was applied after regeneration on the N+M best lists, additional improvements were gained for all the development and test sets on all three regeneration systems. Absolute improvement on BLEU score of 0.4-0.6 on IWSLT'06 test set and 0.25-0.35 on NIST test sets were obtained when compared with system RESC1. Comparing the performance of three regeneration methods, we can see that re-decoding and confusion network based method achieved very similar improvement; while n-gram expansion based regeneration obtained slightly better improvement than the other two methods. Combining all regenerated hypotheses with the original hypotheses further increased the scores on both tasks. Compared with RESC2, system COMB obtained absolute improvement of 0.81 (31.36 – 30.55) BLEU score on IWSLT'06 test set, 0.57 (27.28 – 27.21) BLEU score on NIST'03 and 0.61 (26.04 – 25.43) BLEU score on NIST'05 respectively.

We further illustrate the effectiveness of the regeneration mechanism using some translation examples obtained from system RESC2 and COMB as shown in Table 5.

6 Discussion

To better interpret the performance improvement; first let us check if the regeneration pass has produced better hypotheses. We computed the oracle scores on all four 1,200-best lists in IWSLT task. The oracle chooses the translation with the lowest word error rate (WER) with respect to the references in all cases. The results are reported in Table 6. It is worth noticing that the first 800-best (original N-best) hypotheses are the same in all four lists, with differences found only in the remaining 400 hypotheses (M-best). The consistent improvement of oracle scores shows that the translation candidates have been really improved.

From another viewpoint, Table 7 shows the number of translations generated by each method in the final translation output (translations of COMB). After re-ranking N+3M entries, it is observed that more than 25% (e.g. for IWSLT'06 test set, (50+74+39)/500=32.6%; NIST'03 test set, (77+85+68)/919=25.1%; NIST'05 test set, (95+110+82)/1082=26.5%) of best scored outputs were generated by the regeneration pass, showing that new generated translations are quite often the rescoring winner. This also proved that the new-generated hypotheses contain better ones than the original ones.

List		BLEU	NIST	WER	PER
Dev.	Moses	46.10	8.765	36.29	30.94
	RD	46.91	8.764	35.29	30.62
	NE	46.95	8.811	36.05	30.72
	CN	46.85	8.769	36.17	30.83
Test	Moses	45.09	8.403	37.07	32.04
	RD	45.67	8.418	36.50	31.82
	NE	45.82	8.481	36.44	31.70
	CN	45.68	8.471	36.55	31.81

Table 6: Oracle scores (BLEU%, NIST, WER% and PER%) on IWSLT task 1,200-best lists of four systems: decoder (Moses), re-decoding (RD), n-gram expansion (NE) and confusion network (CN).

		# sentence				
	Set	Tot.	Orig.	RD	NE	CN
IWSLT	Dev	489	325	52	76	36
	Test	500	337	50	74	39
NIST	NIST 02	878	613	92	100	73
	NIST 03	919	689	77	85	68
	NIST 05	1082	795	95	110	82

Table 7: Number of translations generated by each method in the final translation output of system COMB: decoder (Orig.), re-decoding (RD), n-gram expansion (NE) and confusion network (CN). "Tot." is the size of the dev/test set.

Then, let us consider each single regeneration method to understand why regeneration can produce better hypotheses. Re-decoding may introduce new and better phrase-pairs which are extracted from the N-best hypotheses to the translation model thus generate better hypotheses. N-gram expansion can (almost) fully exploit the search space of target strings, which can be generated by an n-gram LM. As a result, it can produce alternative translations which contain word re-orderings and phrase structures not considered by the search algorithm of the decoder (Chen, et al., 2007). Confusion network based regeneration reinforces the word choice by considering the posterior probabilities of words occur in the N-best translations.

7 Conclusions

In this paper, we proposed a novel three-pass SMT framework against the typical two-pass system. This framework enhanced the quality of the translation candidates generated by our proposed regeneration pass and improved the final translation performance. Three regeneration methods were introduced, namely, re-decoding, word-based n-gram expansion, and confusion network based regeneration.

Experiments were based on the state-of-the-art phrase-based decoder and carried out on the IWSLT and NIST Chinese-to-English task. We showed that all three methods improved the performance with the n-gram expansion method achieving the greatest improvement. Moreover, the combination of the three methods further improves the performance.

We conclude that translation performance can be improved by increasing the potential of translation candidates to contain better translations. We have presented an alternative solution to ameliorate the quality of translation candidates in a way that differs from system combination which takes translations from other MT systems. We demonstrated that the translation performance could be self-boosted by expanding the N-best list through hypotheses regeneration.

References

S. Bangalore, G. Bordel, and G. Riccardi. 2001. Computing consensus translation from multiple machine translation systems. In *Proceeding of IEEE workshop on Automatic Speech Recognition and Understanding*, pages 351–354. Madonna di Campiglio, Italy.

P. F. Brown, V. J. Della Pietra, S. A. Della Pietra & R. L. Mercer. 1993. The Mathematics of Statistical Machine Translation: Parameter Estimation. *Computational Linguistics*, 19(2) 263-312.

B. Chen, R. Cattoni, N. Bertoldi, M. Cettolo and M. Federico. 2005. The ITC-irst SMT System for

IWSLT-2005. In *Proceeding of IWSLT-2005*, pp.98-104, Pittsburgh, USA, October.

B. Chen, M. Cettolo and M. Federico. 2006. Reordering Rules for Phrase-based Statistical Machine Translation. In *Proceeding of IWSLT-2006*, Kyoto, Japan.

B. Chen, M. Federico and M. Cettolo. 2007. Better N-best Translations through Generative n-gram Language Models. In *Proceeding of MT Summit XI*. Copenhagen, Denmark.

S. F. Chen and J. T. Goodman. 1998. An Empirical Study of Smoothing Techniques for Language Modeling. *Technical Report TR-10-98*, Computer Science Group, Harvard University.

P. Koehn, F. J. Och and D. Marcu. 2003. Statistical Phrase-based Translation. In *Proceedings of HLT/NAACL*, pp 127-133, Edmonton, Canada.

P. Koehn, H. Hoang, A. Birch, C. Callison-Burch, M. Federico, N. Bertoldi, B. Cowan, W. Shen, C. Moran, R. Zens, C. Dyer, O. Bojar, A. Constantin and E. Herbst. 2007. Moses: Open Source Toolkit for Statistical Machine Translation. In *Proceeding of ACL-2007*, pp. 177-180, Prague, Czech Republic.

O. Kraif, B. Chen. 2004. Combining clues for lexical level aligning using the Null hypothesis approach. In *Proceeding of COLING-2004*, Geneva, pp. 1261-1264.

E. Matusov, N. Ueffing, and H. Ney. 2006. Computing consensus translation from multiple machine translation systems using enhanced hypotheses alignment. In *Proceeding of EACL-2006*, Trento, Italy.

I. D. Melamed. 2000. Models of translational equivalence among words. *Computational Linguistics*, 26(2), pp. 221-249.

F. J. Och. 2003. Minimum error rate training in statistical machine translation. In *Proceedings of ACL-2003*. Sapporo, Japan.

F. J. Och and H. Ney. 2003. A Systematic Comparison of Various Statistical Alignment Models. *Computational Linguistics*, 29(1), pp. 19-51.

K. Papineni, S. Roukos, T. Ward, and W.J. Zhu. 2002. BLEU: a method for automatic evaluation of machine translation. In *Proceeding of ACL-2002*.

A. Rosti, N. F. Ayan, B. Xiang, S. Matsoukas, R. Schwartz and B. Dorr. 2007a. Combining Outputs from Multiple Machine Translation Systems. In *Proceeding of NAACL-HLT-2007*, pp. 228-235. Rochester, NY.

A. Rosti, S. Matsoukas and R. Schwartz. 2007b. Improved Word-Level System Combination for Machine Translation. In *Proceeding of ACL-2007*, Prague.

K. C. Sim, W. J. Byrne, M. J.F. Gales, H. Sahbi, and P. C. Woodland. 2007. Consensus network decoding for statistical machine translation system combination. In *Proceeding of ICASSP-2007*.

A. Stolcke. 2002. SRILM - an extensible language modelling toolkit. In *Proceeding of ICSLP-2002*. 901-904.

T. Takezawa, E. Sumita, F. Sugaya, H. Yamamoto, and S. Yamamoto. 2002. Toward a broad-coverage bilingual corpus for speech translation of travel conversations in the real world. In *Proceeding of LREC-2002*, Las Palmas de Gran Canaria, Spain.

R. Zens and H. Ney. 2006. N-gram Posterior Probabilities for Statistical Machine Translation. In *Proceeding of HLT-NAACL Workshop on SMT*, pp. 72-77, NY.

Learning Reliable Information for Dependency Parsing Adaptation

Wenliang Chen†, Youzheng Wu‡, Hitoshi Isahara*
†Language Infrastructure Group
‡Spoken Language Communication Group, ATR
*Machine Translation Group
National Institute of Information and Communications Technology
3-5 Hikari-dai, Seika-cho, Soraku-gun, Kyoto, Japan, 619-0289
{chenwl, youzheng.wu, isahara}@nict.go.jp

Abstract

In this paper, we focus on the adaptation problem that has a large labeled data in the source domain and a large but unlabeled data in the target domain. Our aim is to learn reliable information from unlabeled target domain data for dependency parsing adaptation. Current state-of-the-art statistical parsers perform much better for shorter dependencies than for longer ones. Thus we propose an adaptation approach by learning reliable information on shorter dependencies in an unlabeled target data to help parse longer distance words. The unlabeled data is parsed by a dependency parser trained on labeled source domain data. The experimental results indicate that our proposed approach outperforms the baseline system, and is better than current state-of-the-art adaptation techniques.

1 Introduction

Dependency parsing aims to build the dependency relations between words in a sentence. There are many supervised learning methods for training high-performance dependency parsers(Nivre et al., 2007), if given sufficient labeled data. However, the performance of parsers declines when we are in the situation that a parser is trained in one "source" domain but is to parse the sentences in a second "target" domain. There are two tasks(Daumé III, 2007) for the domain adaptation problem. The first one is that we have a large labeled data in the source domain and a small labeled data in target domain. The second is similar, but instead of having a small labeled target data, we have a large but unlabeled target data. In this paper, we focus on the latter one.

©2008. Licensed under the *Creative Commons Attribution-Noncommercial-Share Alike 3.0 Unported* license (http://creativecommons.org/licenses/by-nc-sa/3.0/). Some rights reserved.

Current statistical dependency parsers perform worse while the distance of two words is becoming longer for domain adaptation. An important characteristic of parsing adaptation is that the parsers perform much better for shorter dependencies than for longer ones (the score at length l is much higher than the scores at length> l).

In this paper, we propose an approach by using the information on shorter dependencies in auto-parsed target data to help parse longer distance words for adapting a parser. Compared with the adaptation methods of Sagae and Tsujii (2007) and Reichart and Rappoport (2007), our approach uses the information on word pairs in auto-parsed data instead of using the whole sentences as newly labeled data for training new parsers. It is difficult to detect reliable parsed sentences, but we can find relative reliable parsed word pairs according to dependency length. The experimental results show that our approach significantly outperforms baseline system and current state of the art techniques.

2 Motivation and prior work

In dependency parsing, we assign head-dependent relations between words in a sentence. A simple example is shown in Figure 1, where the arc between *a* and *hat* indicates that *hat* is the head of *a*.

Current statistical dependency parsers perform better if the dependency lengthes are shorter (McDonald and Nivre, 2007). Here the length of the dependency from word w_i to word w_j is simply equal to $|i - j|$. Figure 2 shows the results (F_1

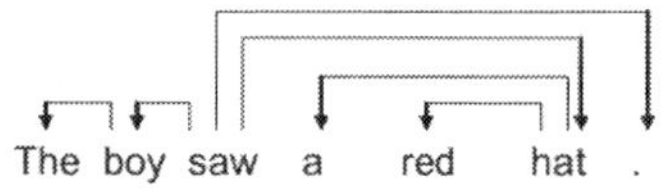

Figure 1: An example for dependency relations.

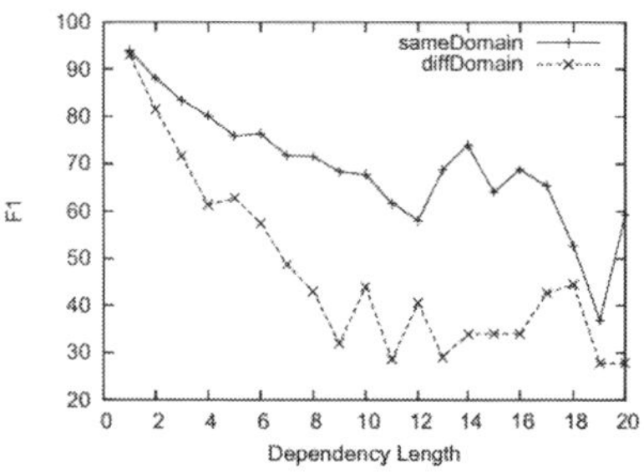

Figure 2: The scores relative to dependency length. "SameDomain" refers to training and testing in the same domain, and "diffDomain" refers to training and testing in two domains (domain adaptation).

score)[1] on our testing data, provided by a deterministic parser, which is trained on labeled source data. Comparing two curves at the figure, we find that the scores of diffDomain decreases much more sharply than the scores of sameDomain, when dependency length increases. The score decreases from about 92% at length 1 to 50% at 7. When lengthes are larger than 7, the scores are below 50%. We also find that the score at length l is much higher (around 10%) than the score at length $l+1$ from length 1 to 7. There is only one exception that the score at length 4 is a little less than the score at length 5. But this does not change so much and the scores at length 4 and 5 are much higher than the one at length 6.

Two words (word w_i and word w_j) having a dependency relation in one sentence can be adjacent words (word distance = 1), neighboring words (word distance = 2), or the words with distance > 2 in other sentences. Here the distance of word pair (word w_i and word w_j) is equal to $|i-j|$. For example, "a" and "hat" has dependency relation in the sentence at Figure 1. They can also be adjacent words in the sentence "The boy saw a hat." and the words with distance = 3 in "I see a red beautiful hat.". This makes it possible for the word pairs with different distances to share the information.

According to the above observations, we present an idea that *the information on shorter dependencies in auto-parsed target data is reliable for parsing the words with longer distance* for domain adaptation. Here, "shorter" is not exactly short. That is to say, the information on dependency length l in auto-parsed data can be used to help parse the words whose distances are longer than l when testing, where l can be any number. We do not use the dependencies whose lengthes are too long because the accuracies of long dependencies are very low.

In the following content, we demonstrate our idea with an example. The example shows how to use the information on length 1 to help parse two words whose distance is longer than 1. Similarly, the information on length l can also be used to help parse the words whose distance is longer than l.

Figure 2 shows that the dependency parser performs best at tagging the relations between adjacent words. Thus, we expect that dependencies of adjacent words in auto-parsed target data can provide useful information for parsing words whose distances are longer than 1. We suppose that our task is Chinese dependency parsing adaptation.

Here, we have two words "大型JJ(large-scale)" and "展览NN(exhibition)". Figure 3 shows the examples in which word distances of these two words are different. For the sentences in the bottom part, there is a ambiguity of "JJ + NN1 + NN2" at "大型JJ(large-scale)/艺术NN(art)/展览NN(exhibition)", "大型JJ(large-scale)/文化NN(culture)/艺术NN(art)/展览NN(exhibition)" and "大型JJ(large-scale)/中国NR(China)/文化NN(culture)/艺术NN(art)/展览NN(exhibition)". Both NN1 and NN2 could be the head of JJ. In the examples in the upper part, "大型JJ(large-scale)" and "展览NN(exhibition)" are adjacent words, for which current parsers can work well. We use a parser to parse the sentences in the upper part. "展览(exhibition)" is assigned as the head of "大型(large-scale)". Then we expect the information from the upper part can help parse the sentences in the bottom part. Now, we consider what a learning model could do to assign the appropriate relation between "大型(large-scale)" and "展览(exhibition)" in the bottom part. We provide additional information that "展览(exhibition)" is the possible head of "大型(large-scale)" in the auto-parsed data (the upper part). In this way, the learning model may use this information to make correct decision.

[1] $F_1 = 2 \times precision \times recall/(precision + recall)$ where precision is the percentage of predicted arcs of length d that are correct and recall is the percentage of gold standard arcs of length d that are correctly predicted.

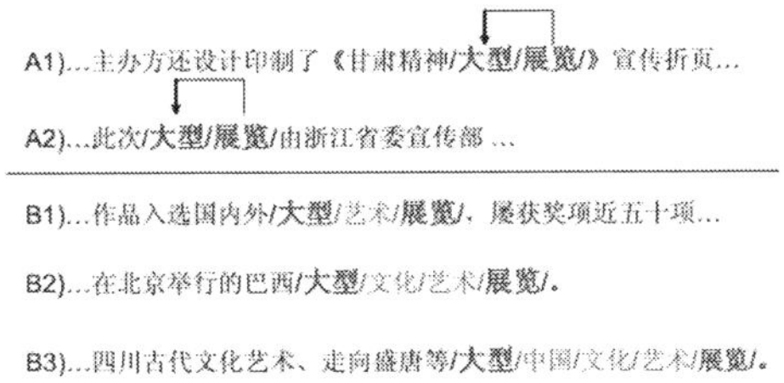

Figure 3: Examples for "大型(large-scale)" and "展览(exhibition)". The upper part (A) refers to the sentences from unlabeled data and the bottom part (B) refers to the sentences waiting for parsing.

Up to now, we demonstrate how to use the information on length 1. Similarly, we can use the information on length 2, 3, ... By this way, we propose an approach by exploiting the information from a large-scale unlabeled target data for dependency parsing adaptation.

In this paper, our approach is to use unlabeled data for parsing adaptation. There are several studies relevant to ours as described below.

CoNLL 2007(Nivre et al., 2007) organized a shared task for domain adaptation without annotated data in new domain. The labeled data was from the Wall Street Journal, the development data was from biomedical abstracts, and the testing data was from chemical abstracts and parent-child dialogues. Additionally, a large unlabeled corpus was provided. The systems by Sagae and Tsujii (2007), Attardi et al. (2007), and Dredze et al. (2007) performed top three in the shared task.

Sagae and Tsujii (2007) presented a procedure similar to a single iteration of co-training. Firstly, they trained two parsers on labeled source data. Then the two parsers were used to parse the sentences in unlabeled data. They selected only identical parsing results produced by the two parsers. Finally, they retrained a parser on newly parsed sentences and the original labeled data. They performed the highest scores for this track. Attardi et al. (2007) presented a procedure with correcting errors by a revision techniques. Dredze et al. (2007) submitted parsing results without adaptation. They declared that it was difficult to significantly improve performance on any test domain beyond that of a state-of-the-art parser. Their error analysis suggested that the primary cause of loss from adaptation is because of differences in the annotation guidelines. Without specific knowledge of the target domain's annotation standards, significant improvement can not be made.

Reichart and Rappoport (2007) studied self-training method for domain adaptation (The WSJ data and the Brown data) of phrase-based parsers. McClosky et al. (2006) presented a successful instance of parsing with self-training by using a reranker. Both of them used the whole sentences as newly labeled data for adapting the parsers, while our approach uses the information on word pairs.

Chen et al. (2008) presented an approach by using the information of adjacent words for in-domain parsing. As Figure 2 shows, the score curves of sameDomain (in-domain) parsing and diffDomain (out-domain) parsing are quite different. Our work focuses on parsing adaptation and is based on the fact that current parsers perform much better for shorter dependencies than for longer ones. This causes that our work differs in that we use the information on shorter dependencies in auto-parsed target data to help parse the words with longer distance for parsing adaptation. In this paper, "shorter" and "longer" are relative. Length l is relatively shorter than length $l+1$, where l can be any number.

3 The parsing approach

In this paper, we choose the model described by Nivre (2003) as our parsing model. It is a deterministic parser and works quite well in the shared-task of CoNLL2006(Nivre et al., 2006).

3.1 The parsing model

The Nivre (2003) model is a shift-reduce type algorithm, which uses a stack to store processed tokens and a queue to store remaining input tokens. It can perform dependency parsing in O(n) time. The dependency parsing tree is built from atomic actions in a left-to-right pass over the input. The parsing actions are defined by four operations: Shift, Reduce, Left-Arc, and Right-Arc, for the stack and the queue. TOP is the token on top of the stack and NEXT is next token in the queue. The Left-Arc and Right-Arc operations mean that there is a dependency relation between TOP and NEXT.

The model uses a classifier to produce a sequence of actions for a sentence. In this paper, we use the SVM model. And LIBSVM(Chang and Lin, 2001) is used in our experiments.

Note that the approach (see section 4)we present in this paper can also be applied to other parsers, such as the parser by Yamada and Matsumoto (2003), or the one by McDonald et al. (2006).

3.2 Parsing with basic features

The parser is a history-based parsing model, which relies on features of the parsed tokens to predict next parsing action. We represent basic features based on words and part-of-speech (POS) tags. The basic features are listed as follows:

- Lexical Features on TOP: the word of TOP, the word of the head of TOP, and the words of leftmost and rightmost dependent of TOP.
- Lexical Features on NEXT: the word of NEXT and the word of the token immediately after NEXT in the original input string.
- POS features on TOP: the POS of TOP, the POS of the token immediately below TOP, and the POS of leftmost and rightmost dependent of TOP.
- POS features on NEXT: the POS of NEXT, the POS of next three tokens after NEXT, and the POS of the token immediately before NEXT in original input string.

Based on the above parsing model and basic features, we train a basic parser on annotated source data. In the following content, we call this parser Basic Parser.

4 Domain adaptation with shorter dependency

This section presents our adaptation approach by using the information based on relative shorter dependencies in auto-parsed data to help parse the words whose distances are longer. Firstly, we use the Basic Parser to parse all the sentences in unlabeled target data. Then we explore reliable information based on dependency relations in auto-parsed data. Finally, we incorporate the features based on reliable information into the parser to improve performance.

4.1 Extracting word pairs from auto-parsed data

In this section, we collect word pairs from the auto-parsed data. At first, we collect the word pairs with length 1. In a parsed sentence, if two words have dependency relation and their word distance is 1, we will add this word pair into the list L_{dep} and count its frequency. We also consider the direction, LA for left arc and RA for right arc. For example, "大型(large-scale)" and "展览(exhibition)" are adjacent words in the sentence "我们(We)/举办(held)/大型(large-scale)/展览(exhibition)/。" and have a left dependency arc assigned by the Basic Parser. The word pair "大型(large-scale)-展览(exhibition)" with "LA" is added into L_{dep}.

Similarly, we collect the pairs whose word distances are longer than 1. In L_{dep}, with length l and direction dr(LA or RA), the pair p_u has $freq_l(p_u : dr)$. For example, $freq_2(p_u : LA) = 3$ refers to the word pair p_u with left arc(LA) occurs 3 times in the auto-parsed data when two words' distance is 2. Because figure 2 shows that the accuracies of long dependencies are low, we only collect the pairs whose distances are not larger than a predefined length l_{max}.

4.2 The adaptation approach

The word pair p_t is the pair $< w_i, w_j >$.

4.2.1 The information on shorter distances

If the distance of p_t is d, we will use the pairs whose lengthes are less than d. It results in the words with different distances using different set of word pairs in L_{dep}. For example, if d is 5, we can use the pairs with dependency lengthes from 1 to 4 in L_{dep}. The information is represented by the equation as follows:

$$I_d(p_t : dr) = \begin{cases} 0 & p_t \notin L_{dep} \\ freq_1(p_t : dr) & d = 1 \\ \sum_{l=1}^{d-1} freq_l(p_t : dr) & d > 1 \end{cases} \tag{1}$$

4.2.2 Classifying into buckets

According to $I_d(p_t : dr)$, word pairs are grouped into different buckets as follows:

$$Bucket_d(p_t : dr) = \begin{cases} B_0 & I_d(p_t : dr) = 0 \\ B_1 & 0 < I_d(p_t : dr) \le f_1 \\ \ldots & \\ B_n & f_{n-1} < I_d(p_t : dr) \le f_n \\ B_a & f_n < I_d(p_t : dr) \end{cases} \tag{2}$$

where, $f_1, f_2, ..., f_n$ are the thresholds. For example, I_3(大型-展览:LA) is 20, $f_3 = 15$ and $f_4 = 25$. Then it is grouped into the bucket B_4. We set $f_1 = 2$, $f_2 = 8$, and $f_3 = 15$ in the experiments.

4.2.3 Parsing with the adapting Features

Based on the buckets of word pairs, we represent new features on labeled source data for the parser. We call these new features adapting features. According to different word distances between TOP and NEXT, the features are listed at Table 1. So we have 8 types of the adapting features, including 2 types for distance=1, 3 types for distance=2, and 3 types for distance≥3. Each feature is formatted as "DistanceType:FeatureType:Bucket", where DistanceType is D1, D2, or D3 corresponding to three distances, FeatureType is FB0, FB1, or FB_1 corresponding to three positions. Here, if a word pair has two dependency directions in L_{dep}, we will choose the direction having higher frequency.

Then using the parsing model of Nivre (2003), we train a new parser based on the adapting features and basic features.

distance	FB_1	FB0	FB1
=1		+	+
=2	+	+	+
≥3	+	+	+

Table 1: Adapting features. FB0 refers to the bucket of the word pair of TOP and NEXT, FB1 refers to the bucket of the word pair of TOP and next token after NEXT, and FB_1 refers to the bucket of the word pair of TOP and the token immediately before NEXT. "+" refers to this item having this type of feature.

4.2.4 An example

We show an example for representing the adapting features. For example, we have the string "大型JJ(large-scale)/文化NN(culture)/艺术NN(art)/展览NN(exhibition)/。". And "大型(large-scale)" is TOP and "展览(exhibition)" is NEXT. Because the distance of TOP and NEXT is 3, we have three features. We suppose that (FB0) the bucket of the word pair ("大型-展览") of TOP and NEXT is bucket B_4, (FB1) the bucket of the word pair ("大型-。") of TOP and next token after NEXT is bucket B_0, and (FB_1) the bucket of the word pair ("大型-艺术")of TOP and the token immediately before NEXT is bucket B_1. Then, we have the features: "D3:FB0:B_4", "D3:FB1:B_0", and "D3:FB_1:B_1".

4.3 Adaptation for unknown word[2]

The unknown word problem is an important issue for domain adaptation(Dredze et al., 2007). Our approach can work for improving performance of parsing unknown word pairs in which there is at least one unknown word. We collect word pairs including unknown word pairs at Section 4.1. Then unknown word pairs in testing data are also mapped into one of the buckets via Equation (2). So known word pairs can share the features with unknown word pairs.

[2]An unknown word is a word that is not included in training data.

5 Experimental setup

CoNLL 2007(Nivre et al., 2007) organized the domain adaptation task and provided a data set in English. However, the data set had differences between the annotation guidelines in source and target domains. Without specific knowledge of the target domain's annotation standards, significant improvement can not be made(Dredze et al., 2007). In this paper, we discussed the situation that the data of source and target domains were annotated under the same annotation guideline. So we used a data set converted from Penn Chinese Treebank (CTB)[3].

Labeled data: the CTB(V5.0) was used in our experiments. The data set was converted by the same rules for conversion as Chen et al. (2008) did. We used files 1-270, 400-554, and 600-931 as source domain training data (STrain), files 271-300 as source domain testing data (STest) and files 590-596 as target domain testing data (TTest). We used the gold standard segmentation and POS tags in the CTB. The target domain data was from Sinorama magazine, Taiwan and the source domain data was mainly from Xinhua newswire, mainland of China. The genres of these two parts were quite different. Table 2 shows the statistical information of the data sets. Given the words of the STrain data, TTest included 30.79% unknown words. We also checked the distribution of POS tags. The difference was large, too.

Unlabeled data: three data sets were used in our experiments, including the PFR data (5.44M words), the CKIP data (5.44M words), and the SINO data (25K words). The PFR corpus[4] included the documents from People's Daily at 1998 and we used about 1/3 of all sentences. The CKIP[5] corpus was used for SIGHAN word segmentation bakeoff 2005. To simplify, we used their segmentation. The SINO data was the files 1001-1151 of CTB, also from Sinorama magazine, the same as our testing target data. We removed the annotation tags from the SINO data. Among the three unlabeled data, the SINO data was closest to testing target data because they came from the same resource. Table 2 lists the information of data sets. From the table, we found that the PFR data was

[3]More detailed information can be found at http://www.cis.upenn.edu/~chinese/.

[4]More detailed information can be found at http://www.icl.pku.edu.

[5]More detailed information can be found at http://rocling.iis.sinica.edu.tw/CKIP/index.htm

	Num Of Words	Unknown Word Rate
STrain	17983	-
STest	1829	9.73
TTest	1783	30.79
CKIP	140k	-
STest	1829	11.42
TTest	1783	8.63
PFR	123k	-
STest	1829	8.58
TTest	1783	15.64

Table 2: The information of the data sets

closer to source domain and the CKIP data was closer to target domain.

To assign POS tags for the unlabeled data, we used the package TNT (Brants, 2000) to train a POS tagger on training data. Because the PFR data and the CTB used different POS standards, we did not use the POS tags in the PFR data.

We measured the quality of the parser by the unlabeled attachment score (UAS), i.e., the percentage of tokens with correct head. We also reported the accuracy of ROOT.

6 Results

In the following content, OURS refers to our proposed approach. The baseline system refers to the Basic Parser.

6.1 Basic experiments

In this section, we examined the performance of baseline systems and our proposed approach with different unlabeled data sets.

Table 3 shows the experimental results, where "OURS with SINO(GOLD)" refers to the parser using gold standard POS tags, and "OURS with SINO(AUTO)" refers to the parser using auto-assigned POS tags. From the two results of baseline, we found that the parser performed very differently in two domains by 8.24%.

With the help of SINO(AUTO), OURS provided 1.11% improvement for UAS and 6.16% for ROOT. If we used gold standard POS tags, the score was 78.40% for UAS (1.34% improvement), and 65.40% for ROOT (6.64% improvement). By using the SINO data, our approach achieved significant improvements over baseline system. It was surprised that OURS with CKIP achieved 78.30% score, just a little lower than the one with SINO(GOLD). The reason may be that the size of the CKIP data was much bigger than the SINO data. So we can obtain more word pairs from the CKIP data. The parser achieved 0.30% improvement with PFR. Even though the size of the SINO data was smaller, the parser performed well with its help.

Data	UAS	ROOT
baseline(STest)	85.30	88.21
baseline(TTest)	77.06	58.76
OURS with SINO(GOLD)	78.40(+1.34)	65.40
OURS with SINO(AUTO)	78.17(+1.11)	64.92
OURS with CKIP	78.30(+1.24)	65.87
OURS with PFR	77.36(+0.30)	63.03

Table 3: Basic results

l_{max}	SINO(GOLD)	SINO(AUTO)
1	77.84	77.80
3	78.03	77.95
5	78.22	**78.17**
7	**78.40**	78.11
9	78.38	78.13
∞	78.35	78.09

Table 4: The effect of different l_{max}

These results indicated that we should collect the unlabeled data that is closer to target domain or larger. The improvements of OURS with CKIP and OURS with SINO were significant in one-tail paired t-test ($p < 10^{-5}$).

6.2 The effect of different l_{max}

Table 4 shows the experimental results, where l_{max} is described at Section 4.1. With SINO(GOLD), our parser performed best at $l_{max} = 7$. And with SINO(AUTO), it performed best at $l_{max} = 5$. These indicated that our approach can incorporate pairs with different lengthes to improve performance. We also found that the long dependencies were not reliable, as the curve (diffDomain) of Figure 2 showed that the scores were less than 50% when lengthes were larger than 8.

6.3 Comparison of other systems

In this section, we turned to compare our approach with other methods. We implemented two systems: SelfTrain and CoTrain. The SelfTrain system was following to the method described by Reichart and Rappoport (2007) and randomly selected new auto-parsed sentences. The CoTrain system was similar to the learning scheme described by Sagae and Tsujii (2007). However, we did not use the same parsing algorithms as the ones used by Sagae and Tsujii (2007). Firstly, we

Method	UAS	ROOT
baseline	77.06	58.76
SelfTrain	77.44	60.18
CoTrain	77.57	60.81
OURS	78.30	65.87

Table 5: The results of several adaptation methods with CKIP

trained a forward parser (same as our baseline system) and a backward parser. Then the identical parsed sentences by the two parsers were selected as newly labeled data. Finally, we retrained a forward parser with new training data. We selected the sentences having about 200k words from the CKIP data as newly labeled data for the SelfTrain and CoTrain systems.

Table 5 shows the experimental results. Both systems provided about 0.4%-0.5% improvement over baseline system. Our approach performed best among all systems. Another problem was that the time for training the SelfTrain and CoTrain systems became much longer because they almost used double size of training data.

7 Analysis

In this section, we try to understand the benefit in our proposed adaptation methods. Here, we compare OURS's results with baseline's.

7.1 Improvement relative to dependency length

We presented an idea that using the information on shorter dependencies in auto-parsed target data to help parse the words with longer distance for domain adaptation. In this section, we investigated how our approach performed for parsing longer distance words. Figure 4 shows the improvement relative to dependency length. From the figure, we found that our approach always performed better than baseline when dependency lengthes were 1-7. Especially, our approach achieved improvements by 2.58% at length 3, 5.38% at 6, and 3.67% at 7. For longer ones, the improvement was not stable. One reason may be that the numbers of longer ones were small. Another reason was that parsing long distance words was very difficult. However, we still found that our approach did improve the performance for longer ones, by performing better at 8 points and worse at 5 points when length was not less than 8.

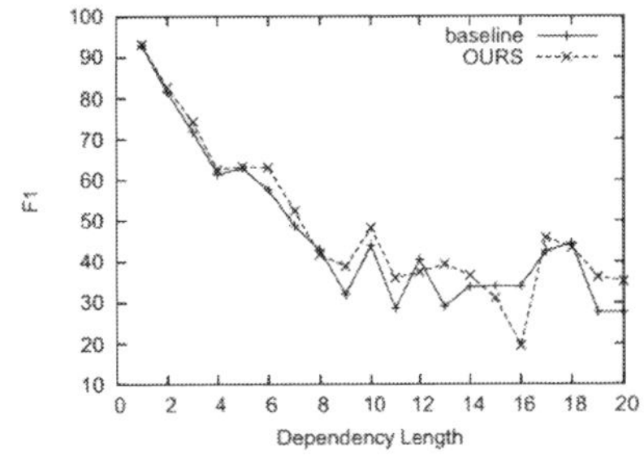

Figure 4: Performance as a function of dependency length

7.2 Improvement relative to unknown words

The unknown word problem is an important issue for adaptation. Our approach can partially release the unknown word problem. We listed the data of the numbers of unknown words from 0 to 8 because the number of sentences was very small for others. We grouped each sentence into one of three classes: (Better) those where our approach's score increased relative to the baseline's score, (NoChange) those where the score remained the same, and (Worse) those where the score had a relative decrease. We added another class (NoWorse) by merging Better and NoChange.

Figure 5 shows the experimental results, where x axis refers to the number of unknown words in one sentence and y axis refers to how many percent the class has. For example, for the sentences having 5 unknown words, about 45.45% improved, 22.73% became worse, 31.82% kept unchanged, and 77.27% did not become worse. The NoWorse curve showed that regardless of the number of unknown words in a sentence, there was more than 60% chance that our approach did not harm the result. The Better curve and Worse curve showed that our approach always provided better results. Our approach achieved most improvement for the middle ones. The reason was that parsing the sentence having too many unknown words was very difficult.

7.3 Improvement relative to POS pairs

In this section, we listed the improvements relative to POS tags of paired words having a dependency relation. Table 6 shows the accuracies of baseline and OURS on TOP 20 POS pairs (ordered by the frequencies of their occurrences in testing data), where "A1" refers to the accuracy of baseline, "A2" refers to the accuracy of OURS, and "Pairs" is the POS pairs of dependent-head.

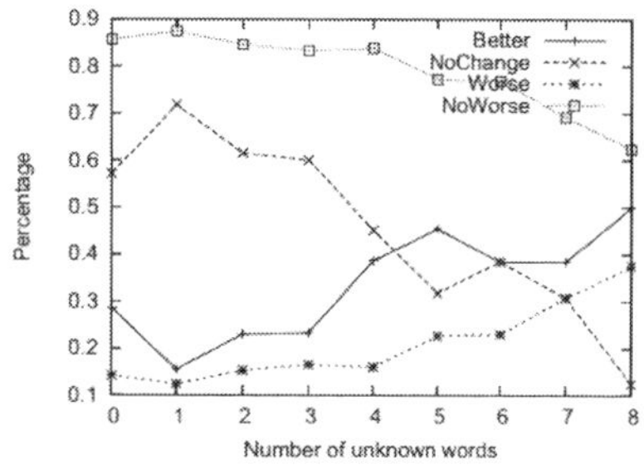

Figure 5: Performance as a function of number of unknown words

Pairs	A1	A2(A2-A1)	Pairs	A1	A2(A2-A1)
NN-VV	79.61	81.90(+2.29)	DEG-NN	94.74	94.74(=)
VV-VV	50.00	50.40(+0.40)	CD-M	96.77	97.85(+1.08)
NN-NN	86.08	87.26(+1.18)	NN-P	76.92	76.92(=)
AD-VV	91.01	91.01(=)	JJ-NN	92.11	94.74(+2.63)
P-VV	68.60	70.25(+1.65)	AD-VA	98.55	98.55(=)
DEC-NN	97.48	98.32(+0.84)	NN-VA	78.95	84.21(+5.26)
NR-VV	81.98	81.98(=)	NN-DEG	96.43	94.64(-1.79)
VV-DEC	74.07	73.15(-0.92)	VV-VC	40.82	46.94(+6.12)
NR-NN	87.85	87.85(=)	AD-VC	95.92	93.88(-2.04)
NN-VC	90.91	91.92(+1.01)	VA-VV	60.87	67.39(+6.52)

Table 6: Improvement relative to POS pairs

For example, "NN-VV" means that "NN" is the POS of the dependent and "VV" is the POS of the head. And baseline yielded 79.61% accuracy and OURS yielded 81.90% (2.29% higher) on "NN-VV". From the table, we found that our approach worked well for most POS pairs (better for eleven pairs, no change for six, and worse for three).

8 Conclusion

This paper presents a simple but effective approach to adapt dependency parser by using unlabeled target data. We extract the information on shorter dependencies in an unlabeled data parsed by a basic parser to help parse longer distance words. The experimental results show that our approach significantly outperforms baseline system and current state of the art adaptation techniques.

There are a lot of ways in which this research could be continued. First, we can apply our approach to other languages because our approach is independent on language. Second, we can enlarge the unlabeled data set to obtain more word pairs to provide more information for the parsers.

References

Attardi, Giuseppe, Felice Dell'Orletta, Maria Simi, Atanas Chanev, and Massimiliano Ciaramita. 2007. Multilingual dependency parsing and domain adaptation using DeSR. In *Proceedings of the CoNLL Shared Task Session of EMNLP-CoNLL 2007*, pages 1112–1118.

Brants, T. 2000. TnT–a statistical part-of-speech tagger. *Proceedings of the 6th Conference on Applied Natural Language Processing*, pages 224–231.

Chang, C.C. and C.J. Lin. 2001. LIBSVM: a library for support vector machines. *Software available at http://www. csie. ntu. edu. tw/cjlin/libsvm.*

Chen, W., D. Kawahara, K. Uchimoto, Y. Zhang, and H. Isahara. 2008. Dependency parsing with short dependency relations in unlabeled data. In *Proceedings of IJCNLP 2008.*

Daumé III, Hal. 2007. Frustratingly easy domain adaptation. In *Proceedings of ACL 2007*, Prague, Czech Republic.

Dredze, Mark, John Blitzer, Partha Pratim Talukdar, Kuzman Ganchev, João Graca, and Fernando Pereira. 2007. Frustratingly hard domain adaptation for dependency parsing. In *Proceedings of the CoNLL Shared Task Session of EMNLP-CoNLL 2007*, pages 1051–1055.

McClosky, D., E. Charniak, and M. Johnson. 2006. Reranking and self-training for parser adaptation. In *Proceedings of Coling-ACL*, pages 337–344.

McDonald, Ryan and Joakim Nivre. 2007. Characterizing the errors of data-driven dependency parsing models. In *Proceedings of EMNLP-CoNLL*, pages 122–131.

McDonald, Ryan, Kevin Lerman, and Fernando Pereira. 2006. Multilingual dependency analysis with a two-stage discriminative parser. In *Proceedings of CoNLL-X*, New York City, June.

Nivre, J., J. Hall, J. Nilsson, G. Eryigit, and S Marinov. 2006. Labeled pseudo-projective dependency parsing with support vector machines. In *CoNLL-X*.

Nivre, Joakim, Johan Hall, Sandra Kübler, Ryan McDonald, Jens Nilsson, Sebastian Riedel, and Deniz Yuret. 2007. The CoNLL 2007 shared task on dependency parsing. In *Proceedings of the CoNLL Shared Task Session of EMNLP-CoNLL 2007*, pages 915–932.

Nivre, J. 2003. An efficient algorithm for projective dependency parsing. In *Proceedings of IWPT2003*, pages 149–160.

Reichart, Roi and Ari Rappoport. 2007. Self-training for enhancement and domain adaptation of statistical parsers trained on small datasets. In *Proceedings of ACL*, Prague, Czech Republic, June.

Sagae, Kenji and Jun'ichi Tsujii. 2007. Dependency parsing and domain adaptation with LR models and parser ensembles. In *Proceedings of the CoNLL Shared Task Session of EMNLP-CoNLL 2007*, pages 1044–1050.

Yamada, H. and Y. Matsumoto. 2003. Statistical dependency analysis with support vector machines. In *Proceedings of IWPT2003*, pages 195–206.

Other-Anaphora Resolution in Biomedical Texts with Automatically Mined Patterns

Chen Bin[#], Yang Xiaofeng[$], Su Jian[^] and Tan Chew Lim[*]
[#*]School of Computing, National University of Singapore
[$^]Institute for Infocomm Research, A-STAR, Singapore
{[#]chenbin, [*]tancl}@comp.nus.edu.sg
{[$]xiaofengy, [^]sujian}@i2r.a-star.edu.sg

Abstract

This paper proposes an *other*-anaphora resolution approach in bio-medical texts. It utilizes automatically mined patterns to discover the semantic relation between an anaphor and a candidate antecedent. The knowledge from lexical patterns is incorporated in a machine learning framework to perform anaphora resolution. The experiments show that machine learning approach combined with the auto-mined knowledge is effective for *other*-anaphora resolution in the biomedical domain. Our system with auto-mined patterns gives an accuracy of 56.5%., yielding 16.2% improvement against the baseline system without pattern features, and 9% improvement against the system using manually designed patterns.

1 Introduction

The last decade has seen an explosive growth in the amount of textual information in biomedicine. There is a need for an effective and efficient text-mining system to gather and utilize the knowledge encoded in the biomedical literature.

For a correct discourse analysis, a text-mining system should have the capability of understanding the reference relations among different expressions in texts. Hence, anaphor resolution, the task of resolving a given text expression to its referred expression in prior texts, is important for an intelligent text processing system.

In linguistics, an expression that points back to a previously mentioned expression is called an anaphor, and the expression being referred to by the anaphor is called its antecedent. Most previous work on anaphora resolution aims at *identity*-anaphora in which both an anaphor and its antecedent are mentions of the same entity.

In this paper, we focus on a special type of anaphora resolution, namely, *other*-anaphora resolution, in which an anaphor to be resolved has a prefix modifier "other" or "another". The antecedent of an *other*-anaphor is a complement expression to the anaphor in a super set. In other words, an *other*-anaphor is a set of elements excluding the element(s) specified by the antecedent. If the modifier "other" or "another" is removed, an anaphor becomes the super set including the antecedent. Thus, *other*-anaphora in fact represents a "part-whole" relation. Consider the following text

"IL-10 inhibits nuclear stimulation of nuclear factor kappa B (NF kappa B).
Several other transcription factors including NF-IL-6, AP-1, AP-2, GR, CREB, Oct-1, and Sp-1 are not affected by IL-10."

Here, the expression "*other transcription factors*" is an *other*-anaphor, while the "*NF kappa B*" is its antecedent. The anaphor refers to any transcription factors except the antecedent. By removing the lexical modifier "other", we can get a supper set "*transcription factors*" that includes the antecedent. The anaphor and antecedent thus have a "part-whole" relation[1].

Other-anaphora resolution is an important sub-task in information extraction for biomedical

© 2008. Licensed under the *Creative Commons Attribution-Noncommercial-Share Alike 3.0 Unported* license (http://creativecommons.org/licenses/by-nc-sa/3.0/). Some rights reserved.

[1] Other-anaphora could be also held between expressions that have subset-set or member-collection relations. In this paper, we treat them in a uniform way by using the patterned-based method.

domain. It also contributes to biomedical ontology building as it targeted at a "part-whole" relation which is in the same hierarchical orders as in ontology. Furthermore, *other*-anaphora resolution is a first-step exploration in the resolution of bridging anaphora. Furthermore, other-anaphora resolution is a first-step exploration in the resolution of bridging, a special anaphora phenomenon in which the semantic relation between an anaphor and its antecedent is more complex (e.g. part-whole) than co-reference.

Previous work on *other*-anaphora resolution relies on knowledge resources, for example, ontology like WordNet to determine the "part-whole" relation. However, in the biomedical domain, a document is full of technical terms which are usually missing in a general-purpose ontology. To deal with this problem, pattern-based approaches have been widely employed, in which a pattern that represents the "part-whole" relation is designed. Two expressions are connected with the specific pattern and form a query. The query is searched in a large corpus for the occurrence frequency which would indicate how likely the two given expressions have the part-whole relation. The solution can avoid the efforts of constructing the ontology knowledge for the "part-whole" relation. However, the pattern is designed in an ad-hoc method, usually from linguistic intuition and its effectiveness for *other*-anaphora resolution is not guaranteed.

In this paper, we propose a method to automatically mine effective patterns for *other*-anaphora resolution in biomedical texts. Our method runs on a small collection of seed word pairs. It searches a large corpus (e.g., PubMed abstracts as in our system) for the texts where the seed pairs co-occur, and collects the surrounding words as the surface patterns. The automatically found patterns will be used in a machine learning framework for *other*-anaphora resolution. To our knowledge, our work is the first effort of applying the pattern-base technique to *other*-anaphora resolution in biomedical texts.

The rest of this paper is organized as follows. Section 2 introduces previous related work. Section 3 describes the machine learning framework for *other*-anaphora resolution. Section 4 presents in detail our method for automatically pattern mining. Section 5 gives experiment results and has some discussions. Finally, Section 6 concludes the paper and shows some future work.

2 Related Work

Previous work on *other*-anaphora resolution commonly depends on human engineered knowledge and/or deep semantic knowledge for the "part-whole" relation, and mostly works only in the news domain.

Markert *et al.*, (2003) presented a pattern-based algorithm for *other*-anaphor resolution. They used a manually designed pattern "ANTECEDENT *and/or other* ANAPHOR ". Given two expression to be resolved, a query is formed by instantiating the pattern with the two given expressions. The query is searched in the Web. The higher the hit number returned, the more likely that the anaphor and the antecedent candidate have the "part-whole" relation. The anaphor is resolved to the candidate with the highest hit number. Their work was tested on 120 *other*-anaphora cases extracted from Wall Street Journal. The final accuracy was 52.5%.

Modjeska *et al.*, (2003) also presented a similar pattern-based method for *other*-anaphora resolution, using the same pattern "ANTECEDENT *and/or other* ANAPHOR". The hit number returned from the Web is used as a feature for a Naïve Bayesian Classifier to resolve *other*-anaphors. Other features include surface words, substring matching, distance, gender/number agreement, and semantic tag of the NP. They evaluated their method with 500 *other*-anaphor cases extracted from Wall Street Journal, and reported a result of 60.8% precision and 53.4% recall.

Markert and Nissim (2005) compared three systems for *other*-anaphora resolution, using the same data set as in (Modjeska *et al.*, 2003).

The first system consults WordNet for the part-whole relation. The WordNet provides information on meronym/holonym (part-of relation) and hypernym/ hyponym (type-of relation). Their system achieves a performance of 56.8% for precision and 37.0% for recall.

The second and third systems employ the pattern based approach, employing the same manual pattern "ANTECEDENT *and/or other* ANAPHOR". The second system did search in British Nation Corpus, giving 62.6% precision and 26.2% recall. The third system did search in the Web as in (Markert *et al.*, 2003), giving 53.8% precision and 51.7% recall.

3 Anaphora Resolution System

3.1 Corpus

In our study, we used the GENIA corpus[2] for our *other*-anaphora resolution in biomedical texts. The corpus consists of 2000 MEDLINE abstracts (around 440,000 words). From the GENIA corpus, we extracted 598 *other*-anaphora cases. The 598 cases do not contain compound prepositions or idiomatic uses of "other", like "on the other hand" and "other than". And all these anaphors have their antecedents found in the current and previous two sentences of the *other*-anaphor. On average, there are 15.33 candidate antecedents for each anaphor to be resolved.

To conduct *other*-anaphora resolution, an input document is preprocessed through a pipeline of NLP components, including tokenization, sentence boundary detection, part-of-speech (POS) tagging, noun phrase (NP) chunking, and named-entity recognition (NER). These preprocessing modules are aimed to determine the boundaries of each NP in a text, and to provide necessary information of an NP for subsequent processing. In our system, we employed the tool-kits built by our group for these components. The POS tagger was trained and tested on the GENIA corpus (version 2.1) and achieved an accuracy of 97.4%. The NP-chunking module, evaluated on UPEN WSJ TreeBank, produced 94% F-measure. The NER module, trained on GENIA corpus (version 3.0), achieved 71.2% F-measure covering 22 entity types (e.g., Virus, Protein, Cell, DNA, etc).

3.2 Learning Framework

Our *other*-anaphora resolution system adopts the common learning-based model for *identity*-anaphora resolution, as employed by (Soon *et al.*, 2001) and (Ng and Cardie, 2002).

In the learning framework, a training or testing instance has the form of $fv(candi_j, ana)$ where $candi_j$ is the jth candidates of the antecedent of anaphor ana. An instance is labelled as positive if $candi_j$ is the antecedent of ana, or negative if $candi_j$ is not the antecedent of ana. An instance is associated with a feature vector which records different properties and relations between ana and $candi_j$. The features used in our system will be discussed later in the paper.

During training, for each *other*-anaphor, we consider as the candidate antecedents the preceding NPs in its current and previous two sentences. A positive instance is formed by pairing the anaphor and the correct antecedent. And a set of negative instances is formed by pairing the anaphor and each of the other candidates.

Based on these generated training instances, we can train a binary classifier using any discriminative learning algorithm. In our work, we employed support vector machine (SVM) due to its good performance in high dimensional feature vector spaces.

During the resolution process, for each *other*-anaphor encountered, all of the preceding NPs in a three-sentence window are considered. A test instance is created for each of the candidate antecedents. The feature vector is presented to the trained classifier to determine the *other*-anaphoric relation. The candidate with highest SVM outcome value is selected as the antecedent.

3.3 Baseline Features

Knowledge is usually represented as features for machine learning. In our system, we used the following groups of features for *other*-anaphora resolution

- **Word Distance Indicator**

This feature measures the word distance between an anaphor and a candidate antecedent, with the assumption that the candidate closer to the anaphor has a higher preference to be the antecedent.

- **Same Sentence Indicator**

This feature is either 0 or 1 indicating whether an anaphor and a candidate antecedent are in the same sentence. Here, the assumption is that the candidate in the same sentence as the anaphor is preferred for the antecedent.

- **Semantic Group Indicators**

A named-entity can be classified to a semantic category such as "DNA", "RNA", "Protein" and so on[3]. Thus we use a set of features to record the category pair of an anaphor and a candidate antecedent. For example, "DNA-DNA" is generated for the case when both anaphor and candidate are DNAs. And "DNA-Protein" is generated if an anaphor is a DNA and a candidate is a protein. These features indicate whether a semantic group can refer to another.

Note that an anaphor and its antecedent may possibly belong to different semantic categories. For example, in the GENIA corpus we found that

---

[2] http://www-tsujii.is.s.u-tokyo.ac.jp/~genia/topics/Corpus/

[3] In our study, we followed the semantic categories defined in the annotation scheme of the GENIA corpus.

in some cases an expression of a protein name actually denotes the gene that encodes the protein. Thus for a given anaphor and a candidate under consideration, it is necessary to record the pair-wise semantic groups, instead of using a single feature indicating whether two expressions are of the same group.

The semantic group for a named entity is given by our preprocessing NER. For the common NPs produced from the NP chunker, we classify the semantic group by looking for the words inside NPs. For example, an NP ending with "cells" is classified to "Cell" group while an NP ending with "gene" or "allele" is classified to "DNA" group.

- **Lexical Pattern Indicators**

In some cases, the surrounding words of an anaphor and a candidate antecedent strongly indicate the "part-whole" relation. For example, in "*...asthma and other hypereosinophilic diseases*", the reference between "*other hypereosinophilic diseases*" and "*asthma*" is clear if the in-between words "*and other*" are taken into consideration. Another example of such a hint pattern is "*one... the other ...*" The feature is 1 if the specific patterns are present for the current anaphor and candidate pair. A candidate with such a feature is preferred to be the antecedent.

- **Hierarchical Name Indicator**

This feature indicates whether an antecedent candidate is a substring of an anaphor or vice versa. This feature is used to capture cases like "*Jun*" and "*JunB*" ("*Jun*" is a family of protein while "*JunB*" is a member of this family). In many cases, an expression that is a super set comes with certain postfix words, for example, "family members" in

"*Fludarabine caused a specific depletion of* ***STAT1 protein*** *(and mRNA) but not of* ***other STAT family members***."

This kind of phenomenon is more common in bio-medical texts than in news articles.

3.4 SVM Training and Classification

In our system, we utilized the open-source software SVM-Light[4] for the classifier training and testing. SVM is a robust statistical model which has been applied to many NLP tasks. SVM tries to learn a separating line to separate the positive instances from negative instances. Kernel transformations are applied for non-linear separable cases (Vapnik, 1995). In our study, we just used the default learning parameters provided by SVM-Light with the linear kernel. A more sophisticated kernel may further improve the performance.

4 Using Auto-mined Pattern Features

The baseline features listed in Section 3.3 only rely on shallow lexical, position and semantic information about an anaphor and a candidate antecedent. It could not, nevertheless, disclose the "part-whole" relation between two given expressions. In section 2, we have shown some existing pattern-based solutions that mine the "part-whole" relation in a large corpus with some patterns that can represent the relation. However, these manually designed patterns are usually selected by heuristics, which may not necessarily lead to a high coverage with a good accuracy in different domains. To overcome this shortcoming, we would like to use an automatic method to mine effective patterns from a large data set. First, we create a set of seed pairs of the "part-whole" relation. And then, we use the seed pairs to discover the patterns that encode the "part-whole" relation from a large data set (PubMed as in our system). Such a solution is supposed to improve the coverage of lexical patterns, while still retain the desired "part-whole" relation for *other*-anaphora resolution.

The overview of our system with the automatic mined patterns is illustrated in figure 1.

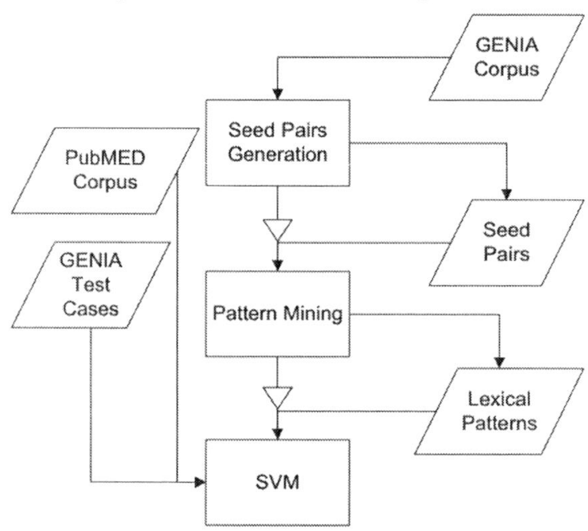

Figure 1: System Overview

There are three major parts in our system, namely, seed-pairs generation, pattern mining and SVM learning and classification. In the subsequent subsections, we will discuss each of the three parts in details.

[4] http://svmlight.joachims.org/

4.1 Seed Pairs Preparation

A seed pair is a pair of phrases/words following "part-whole" order, for example,

"*integrin alpha*" - "*adhesion molecules*"

where "*integrin alpha*" is a kind of "*adhesion molecules*".

We extracted the seed pairs automatically from the GENIA corpus. The auto-extracting procedure makes uses of some lexical clues like "A, *such as* B, C *and* D", "A *(e.g.* B *and* C)", "A *including B*" and etc. The capital letter A, B, C and D refer to a noun phrase such as "*integrin alpha*" and "*adhesion molecules*". For each occurrence of "A *such as* B, C *and* D", the program will generate seed pairs "B-A", "C-A" and "D-A".

Consider the following example,

"Mouse thymoma line EL-4 cells produce cytokines ***such as*** *interleukin (IL) -2, IL-3, IL-4, IL-10, and granulocyte-macrophage colony-stimulating factor in response to phorbol 12-myristate 13-acetate (PMA)."*

We can extract the following seed pairs,

"interleukin (IL) -2" – "cytokines"
"IL -3" – "cytokines"
"IL -4" – "cytokines"
"IL -10" – "cytokines"
"granulocyte-macrophage colony-stimulating factor" – "cytokines"

A similar action is taken for other lexical clues. Totally, we got 909 distinct seed pairs extracted from the GENIA corpus.

After the seed pairs have been extracted, an automatic verification of the seed pairs is performed. The first purpose of the verification is to correct chunking errors. For example, "*HLA Class II Gene*" may likely be wrongly split into "*HLA Class*" and "*II Gene*". This kind of errors is repaired by several simple syntactic rules. The second purpose of the verification is to remove the inappropriate seed pairs. In our system, we abandoned the seed pairs containing pronouns like "those", "they", or nouns like "element", "member" and "agent". Such seed pairs may either find no patterns, or lead to meaningless patterns because "those" or "*elements*" have no specific semantics and could refer to anything.

4.2 Pattern Mining

Having obtained the set of seed pairs, we will use them to mine patterns for the "part-whole" relation. For each seed pair "*antecedent - anaphor*" (*anaphor* represents the NP for the "whole", while *antecedent* represents the NP for the "part"), our system will search in a large data set for two queries: "*antecedent * anaphor*" and "*anaphor * antecedent*" where the "*" denotes any sequence of words or symbols. For a returned search results, the text in between "*antecedent*" and "*anaphora*" is extracted as a pattern.

In our study, we used PubMed 2007 data set for the pattern mining. The data set contains about 52,000 abstracts with around 9,400,000 words, and is an ideal large-scale resource for pattern mining.

Consider, as an example, a seed pair "*NK kappa B* " – "*transcription factor*". Suppose that a returned sentence for the query "*NK kappa B * transcription factor*" is

"*...NK kappa B* ***family*** *transcription factors...*"

And a returned sentence for the query "*transcription factor * NK kappa B*" is

"*...transcription factors,* ***including*** *NF kappa B...*"

We can extract a pattern,

"ANTECEDENT *family* ANAPHOR" from the first sentence and a pattern

"ANAPHOR, *including* ANTECEDENT" from the second sentence.

We restrict the patterns so that no pattern span across two or more sentences. In other words, the pattern shall not contain the symbol ".". The violated patterns will be removed.

The count that a pattern occurs in the PubMed for a seed pair is recorded. As a pattern could be reduced by different seed pairs, we define the occurrence frequency of a pattern as the sum of the counts of the pattern for all the seed pairs, using following formula:

$$C_{pat_i} = \sum_{s_i \in S} Occ(pat_i, s_j) \qquad Eq(1)$$

where C_{pat_i} is the frequency of pattern pat_i; s_j is a seed pair; S is the set of all seed pairs. $Occ(pat_i, s_j)$ is the count of the pattern pat_i for s_j.

All the mined patterns are sorted according to its frequency as defined in $Eq(1)$.

4.3 Pattern Application

For classifier training and testing, the patterns with high frequency are used as features. In our system, we used the top 40 patterns, while we also examined the influence the number of the patterns on the performance. (See Section 5.2)

Given an instance $fv(candi_j, ana)$ and a pattern feature pat_i , a query is constructed by instantiating with $candi_j$ *and* ana. For example, for an instance $fv("NF\ Kappa\ B", "transcription\ factors")$ and a pattern feature "ANAPHOR, ***including*** ANTECEDENT", we can get a query "*transcription factors,* ***including*** *NF kappa B*". The query is searched in the PubMed data set. The count of the query is recorded. The value of the pattern feature of a candidate is calculated by normalizing the occurrence frequency among all the candidates of the anaphor.

For demonstration, suppose we have an anaphor "*other transcription factors*" with two antecedent candidates "*IL-10*" and "*NF kappa B*". Given a pattern feature "ANAPHOR, ***including*** ANTECEDENT", the count of the query "*transcription factors,* ***including*** *IL-10*" is 100 while that for "*transcription factors,* ***including*** *NF-Kappa B*" is 300. Then the values of the pattern feature for "*IL-10*" and "*NF kappa B*" are 0.25 ($\frac{100}{100+300}$) and 0.75 ($\frac{300}{100+300}$), respectively.

The value of a pattern feature can be interpreted as a degree of belief that an anaphor and a candidate antecedent have the "part-whole" relation, with regard to the specific pattern. Since the value of a pattern feature is normalized among all the candidates, it could indicate the preference of a candidate against other competing candidates.

5 Experiment Results

5.1 Experiments Setup

In our experiments, we conducted a 3-fold cross validation to evaluate the performances. The total 598 *other*-anaphora cases were divided into 3 sets of size 200, 199 and 199 respectively. For each experiment, two sets were used for training while the other set was used for testing.

For evaluation, we used the accuracy as the performance metric, which is defined as the correctly resolved *other*-anaphors divided by all the testing *other*-anaphors, that is,

$$accuracy = \frac{\#\ \text{of correctly resolved anaphors}}{\#\ \text{of total anaphors}}$$

5.2 Experiments Results

Table 1 shows the performance of different *other*-anaphora resolution systems. The first line is for the baseline system with only the normal features as described in Section 3.3. From the table, we can find that the baseline system only achieves around 40% accuracy. A performance is lower than a similar system in news domain by Modjeska *et al.*, (2003) where they reported 51.6 % precision with 40.6% recall. This difference is probably because they utilized more semantic knowledge such as hypernymy and meronymy acquired from WordNet. Such knowledge, nevertheless, is not easily available in the biomedical domain.

Sys	Fold-1	Fold-2	Fold-3	Overall
Baseline No Pattern	42.0 % 84/200	38.2 % 76/199	40.7 % 81/199	40.3 % 241/598
Manual Pattern	49.0 % 98/200	45.7 % 91/199	47.7 % 95/199	47.5 % 284/598
Auto-mined Pattern	**59.0 % 118/200**	**53.8 % 107/199**	**56.8 % 113/199**	**56.5 % 338/598**

Table 1: Performance Comparisons

In our experiments, we tested the system with manually designed pattern features. We tried 10 patterns that can represent the "part-whole" relation. Table 2 summaries the patterns used in the system. Among them, the pattern "Anaphor *such as* Antecedent" and "Antecedent *and other* Anaphor" are commonly used in previous pattern based approaches (Markert *et al.,* 2003; Modjeska *et al.,* 2003).

Pattern
ANTECEDENT *is a kind of* ANAPHOR
ANTECEDENT *is a type of* ANAPHOR
ANTECEDENT *is a member of* ANAPHOR
ANTECEDENT *is a part of* ANAPHOR
ANAPHOR *such as* ANTECEDENT
ANTECEDENT *and other* ANAPHOR
ANTECEDENT *within* ANAPHOR
ANTECEDENT *is a component of* ANAPHOR
ANTECEDENT *is a sort of* ANAPHOR
ANTECEDENT *belongs to* ANAPHOR

Table 2: Manually Selected Patterns

The second line of Table 1 shows the results of the system with the manual pattern features. We can find that adding these pattern features produces an overall accuracy of 47%, yielding an increase of 7% accuracy against the baseline system without the pattern features.

The improvement in accuracy is consistent with previous work using the pattern-based approaches in the news domain (Modjeska *et al.*, 2003). However, we found the performance in the biomedical domain is worse than that in the news domain. For example, Modjeska *et al.* (2003) reported a precision around 53%. This difference of performance suggests that the manually designed patterns may not necessarily work equally well in different domains.

The last system we examined in the experiment is the one with the automatically mined pattern features. Table 3 summarizes the top mined patterns ranked based on their occurrence frequency. Some of the patterns are intuitively good representation of the "part-whole" relation. For example, "ANAPHOR, *including* ANTECEDENT". "ANAPHOR, *such as* ANTECEDENT" and "ANAPHOR *and other* ANTECEDENT" which are in the manually designed pattern list, are generated.

The last line of Table 1 lists the result of the system with automatically mined pattern features. It outperforms the baseline system (up to 16% accuracy), and the system with manually selected patterns (9% accuracy). These results prove that our pattern features are effective for the *other*-anaphora resolution.

Pattern	Freq
ANAPHOR, *including* ANTECEDENT	1213
ANAPHOR *including* ANTECEDENT	726
ANTECEDENT *family* ANAPHOR	583
ANAPHOR *such as* ANTECEDENT	542
ANTECEDENT *transcription* ANAPHOR	439
ANAPHOR, *such as* ANTECEDENT	295
ANTECEDENT *and other* ANAPHOR	270
ANAPHOR *and* ANTECEDENT	250
ANTECEDENT, *dendritic* ANAPHOR	246
ANTECEDENT *and* ANAPHOR	238
ANTECEDENT *human* ANAPHOR	223
ANAPHOR *(e.g.,* ANTECEDENT	213
ANTECEDENT/*rel* ANAPHOR	188
ANTECEDENT-*like* ANAPHOR	188
ANAPHOR *against* ANTECEDENT	163

Table 3: Auto-Mined Patterns

To further compare the manually designed patterns and the automatically discovered patterns. We examined the coverage rate of the two pattern sets. The coverage rate measures the capability that a set of patterns could lead to positive anaphor-antecedent pairs. An *other*-anaphor is said to be **covered** by a pattern set, if the anaphor and its antecedent could be hit (i.e., the corresponding query has a non-zero hit number) by at least one pattern in the list. Thus the coverage rate could be defined as

$$Coverage(P) = \frac{\text{\#anaphors covered by the pattern set P}}{\text{\# total anaphors}}$$

The coverage rates of the two pattern sets are tabulated in table 4. It is apparent that the auto-mined patterns have a significantly higher coverage (more than twice) than the manually designed patterns.

Patterns	Coverage Rate
Manually Designed	36.0 %
Auto-Mined	92.1 %

Table 4: Coverage Comparison

In our experiments we were also concerned about the usefulness of each individual pattern. For this purpose, we examined the loss of the accuracy when withdrawing a pattern feature from the feature list. The top 10 patterns with the largest accuracy loss are summarized in table 5.

Pattern	Acc Loss
ANAPHOR, *including* ANTECEDENT	4.18%
ANAPHOR *including* ANTECEDENT	3.18%
ANAPHOR *such as* ANTECEDENT	2.84%
ANTECEDENT *transcription* ANAPHOR	2.17%
ANTECEDENT *and other* ANAPHOR	2.01%
ANAPHOR, *such as* ANTECEDENT	1.84%
ANTECEDENT *family* ANAPHOR	1.84%
ANAPHOR *(e.g.,* ANTECEDENT	1.51%
ANTECEDENT-*like* ANAPHOR	1.17%
ANTECEDENT/*rel* ANAPHOR	1.17%

Table 5: Usefulness of Each Pattern

The process of automatic pattern mining would generate numerous surface patterns. It is not reasonable to use all the patterns as features. As mentioned in section 4.3, we rank the pattern based on their occurrence frequency and select the top ones as the features. It would be interesting to see how the number of patterns influences the performance of anaphora resolution. In figure 2, we plot the accuracy under different number top pattern features. We can find by using more patterns, the coverage keeps increasing. The accuracy also increases, but it reaches the peak with around 40 patterns. With more patterns, the accuracy remains at the same level. This is because the low frequency patterns usually are not that indicative of the "part-whole" relation. Including these pattern features would bring noises but not help the performance. The flat curve after the peak point suggests that the machine learning algorithm can effectively identify the importance of the pattern features for the resolution decision, and therefore including non-indicative patterns would not damage the performance.

In our experiment, we also interested to compare the utility of PubMed with other general data sets. Thus, we tested pattern mining by using the Google-5-grams corpus[5] which lists the hit number of all the queries of five words or less in the Web. Unfortunately, we found that the performance is worse than using PubMed. The patterns mined from the Web corpus only gives an accuracy of around 41%, almost the same as the baseline system without using any pattern features. The bad performance is due to the fact that most of bio-medical names are quite long (2~4 words) and occur infrequently in the non-technique data set. Consequently, a query formed by a biomedical seed pair usually cannot be found in the Web corpus (We found the coverage of the auto-mined patterns mined from the corpus is only about 20%).

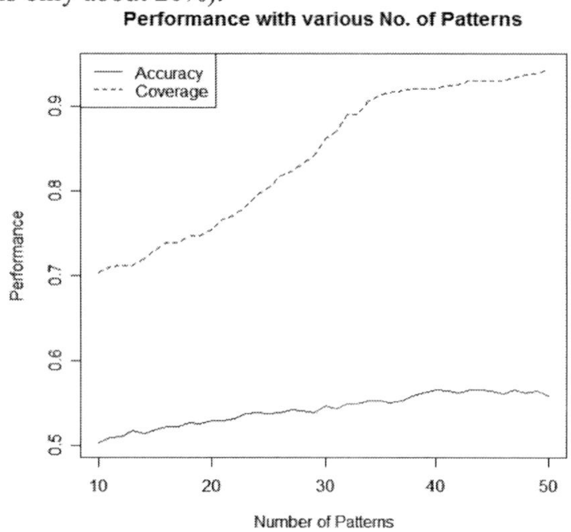

Figure 2: Performance of Various No. of Patterns

6 Conclusion & Future Works

In this paper, we have presented how to automatically mined pattern features for learning-based *other*-anaphora resolution in bio-medical texts. The patterns that represent the "part-whole" relations are automatically mined from a large data set. They are used as features for a SVM-based classifier learning and testing. The results of our experiments show a reasonably good performance with 56.5% accuracy). It outperforms (16% in accuracy) the baseline system without the pattern features, and also beats (9%) the system with manually designed pattern features.

There are several directions for future work. We would like to employ a pattern pruning process to remove those less indicative patterns such as "ANAPHOR, ANTECEDENT". And we also plan to perform pattern normalization which integrates two similar or literally identical patterns into a single one. By doing so, the useful patterns may come to the top of the pattern list. Also we would like to explore ontology resources like MESH and Genes Ontology, which can provide enriched hierarchies of bio-medical terms and thus would benefit other-anaphora resolution.

Acknowledgements

This study on co-reference resolution is partially supported by a Specific Targeted Research Project (STREP) of the European Union's 6th Framework Programme within IST call 4, Bootstrapping of Ontologies and Terminologies STrategic REsearch Project (BOOTStrep).

References

Castano J, Zhang J and Pustejovsky J. Anaphora Resolution in Biomedical Literature. Submitted to *International Symposium on Reference Resolution* 2002, Alicante, Spain

Clark H. Bridging. *In Thinking. Readings in Cognitive Science.* Johnson-Laird and Wason edition. Cambridge. Cambridge University Press; 1977.411–420

Gasperin C and Vieira R. Using Word Similarity Lists for Resolving Indirect Anaphora. In *Proceedings of ACL Workshop on Reference Resolution and Its Application. 30 June 2004; Barcelona.* 2004.40-46

Girju R, Badulescu A and Moldovan D. Automatic Discovery of Part-Whole Relations. *Computational Linguistics,* 2006, 32(2):83-135

Bernauer J.. Analysis of Part-Whole Relation and Subsumption in Medical Domain. *Data Knowledge Enginnering* 1996, 20:405-415

Markert K. and Nissim M. Comparing Knowledge Sources for Nominal Anaphora Resolution. *Computational Linguistics*, 2005, 31(3):367-402

Markert K, Modjeska N and Nissim M. Using the Web for Nominal Anaphora Resolution. In *Proceedings of EACL Workshop on the Computational Treatment of Anaphora. 14 April 2003; Budapest.* 2003.39-46

Mitokov R. Anaphor Resolution. The State of The Art. Working Paper, University of Wolverhampton, UK, 1999

Modjeska N, Markert K and Nissim M. Using the Web in Machine Learning for Other-anaphor Resolution. In *Proceedings of the 2003 Conference on Empirical Methods in Natural Language Processing. July2003,Sapporo.*176-183

Soon WM, Ng HT and Lim CY. A Machine Learning Approach to Coreference Resolution of Noun Phrases. *Computational Linguistics,* 2001, 27(4).521-544

Vapnik, V. Chapter 5 Methods of Pattern Recognition. In *The Nature of Statistical Learning Theory.* New York. Springer-Verlag, 1995.123-167

Varzi C. Parts, Wholes, and Part-whole Relation. The Prospects of the Mereotopology. *Data & Knowledge Engineering,* 1996, 20.259-286

Vieira R, Bick E, Coelho J, Muller V, Collovini S, Souza J and Rino L. Semantic Tagging for Resolution of Indirect Anaphora. In *Proceedings of 7th SIGdial Workshop on Discourse and Dialogue. July 2006; Sydney.*76-79

Burges C. A Tutorial on Supporting Vector Machines for Pattern Recognition. *Data Mining and Knowledge Discovery* 1998, 2:121-167

Ng V. and Cardie C. Improving machine learning approaches to coreference resolution. In *Proceedings of Annual Conference for Association of Computational Linguistics 2002*, Philadelphia.104-111

[5] http://www.ldc.upenn.edu/Catalog/CatalogEntry.jsp?catalogId=LDC2006T13

Latent Morpho-Semantic Analysis: Multilingual Information Retrieval with Character N-Grams and Mutual Information

Peter A. Chew, Brett W. Bader
Sandia National Laboratories
P. O. Box 5800
Albuquerque, NM 87185, USA
{pchew,bwbader}@sandia.gov

Ahmed Abdelali
New Mexico State University
P.O. Box 30002, Mail Stop 3CRL
Las Cruces, NM 88003-8001, USA
ahmed@crl.nmsu.edu

Abstract

We describe an entirely statistics-based, unsupervised, and language-independent approach to multilingual information retrieval, which we call Latent Morpho-Semantic Analysis (LMSA). LMSA overcomes some of the shortcomings of related previous approaches such as Latent Semantic Analysis (LSA). LMSA has an important theoretical advantage over LSA: it combines well-known techniques in a novel way to break the terms of LSA down into units which correspond more closely to morphemes. Thus, it has a particular appeal for use with morphologically complex languages such as Arabic. We show through empirical results that the theoretical advantages of LMSA can translate into significant gains in precision in multilingual information retrieval tests. These gains are not matched either when a standard stemmer is used with LSA, or when terms are indiscriminately broken down into n-grams.

1 Introduction

As the linguistic diversity of textual resources increases, and need for access to those resources grows, there is also greater demand for efficient information retrieval (IR) methods which are truly language-independent. In the ideal but possibly unattainable case, an IR algorithm would produce equally reliable results for any language pair: for example, a query in English would retrieve equally good results in Arabic as in French.

A number of developments in recent years have brought that goal more within reach. One of the factors that severely hampered early attempts at machine translation, for example, was the lack of available computing power. However, Moore's Law, the driving force of change in computing since then, has opened the way for recent progress in the field, such as Statistical Machine Translation (SMT) (Koehn et al. 2003). Even more closely related to the topic of the present paper, implementations of the Singular Value Decomposition (SVD) (which is at the heart of LSA), and related algorithms such as PARAFAC2 (Harshman 1972), have become both more widely available and more powerful. SVD, for example, is available in both commercial off-the-shelf packages and at least one open-source implementation designed to run on a parallel cluster (Heroux et al. 2005).

Despite these advances, there are (as yet) not fully surmounted obstacles to working with certain language pairs, particularly when the languages are not closely related. This is demonstrated in Chew and Abdelali (2008). At least in part, this has to do with the lexical statistics of the languages concerned. For example, because Arabic has a much richer morphological structure than English and French (meaning is varied through the addition of prefixes and suffixes rather than separate terms such as particles), it has a considerably higher type-to-token

© 2008. Licensed under the *Creative Commons Attribution-Noncommercial-Share Alike 3.0 Unported* license (http://creativecommons.org/licenses/by-nc-sa/3.0/). Some rights reserved.

ratio. Exactly this type of language-specific statistical variation seems to lead to difficulties for statistics-based techniques such as LSA, as evidenced by lower cross-language information retrieval (CLIR) precision for Arabic/English than for French/English (Chew and Abdelali 2008).

In this paper, we present a strategy for overcoming these difficulties. In section 2, we outline the basic problem and the thinking behind our approach: that breaking words down into morphemes, or at least morphologically significant subconstituents, should enable greater inter-language comparability. This in turn should in theory lead to improved CLIR results. Several alternatives for achieving this are considered in section 3. One of these, a novel combination of mutual-information-based morphological tokenization (a step beyond simple n-gram tokenization) and SVD, is what we call LMSA. Section 4 discusses the framework for testing our intuitions, and the results of these tests are presented and discussed in section 5. Finally, we draw some conclusions and outline possible directions for future research in section 6.

2 The problem

In many approaches to IR, the underlying method is to represent a corpus as a term-by-document matrix in which each row corresponds to a unique term[2], and each column to a document in the corpus. The standard LSA framework (Deerwester et al. 1990) is no different, except that the (sparse) term-by-document matrix X is subjected to SVD,

$$X = USV^T \quad (1)$$

where U is a smaller but dense term-by-concept matrix, S is a diagonal matrix of singular values, and V is a dense document-by-concept matrix for the documents used in training. Effectively, U and V respectively map the terms and documents to a single set of arbitrary concepts, such that semantically related terms or documents (as determined by patterns of co-occurrence) will tend to be similar; similarity is usually measured by taking the cosine between two (term or document) vectors. New documents can also be projected into the LSA 'semantic space' by multiplying their document vectors (formed in exactly the same way as the columns for X) by the product US^{-1}, to yield document-by-concept vectors. LSA is a completely unsupervised approach to IR in that associations between terms simply fall out when SVD is applied to the data.

With cross-language or multilingual LSA, the approach differs little from that just outlined. The only required modification is in the training data: the term-by-document matrix must be formed from a parallel corpus, in which each document is the *combination* of text from the parallel languages (as described in Berry et al. 1994). Clearly, this IR model cannot be deployed to any languages not in the parallel corpus used for training SVD. However, recent work (Chew et al. 2007) shows not only that there is no limit (at least up to a certain point) to the number of languages that can be processed in parallel, but that precision actually increases for given language pairs as more other languages are included. In practice, the factors which limit the addition of parallel languages are likely to be computational power and the availability of parallel aligned text. As noted in section 1, the first of these is less and less of an issue; and regarding the second, parallel corpora (which are the mainstay of many current approaches to computational linguistics and IR, particularly in real-world applications) are becoming increasingly available. Substantially all of the Bible, in particular, is already electronically available in at least 40-50 languages from diverse language families (Biola University 2005-2006).

Yet, there are clearly variations in how well CLIR works. In previous results (Chew et al. 2007, Chew and Abdelali 2008) it is noticeable in particular that the results for Arabic and Russian (the two most morphologically complex languages for which they present results) are consistently poorer than they are for other languages. To our knowledge, no solution for this has been proposed and validated. Ideally, a solution would both make sense theoretically (or linguistically) and be statistics-based rather than rule-based, consistent with the general framework of LSA and other recent developments in the field, such as SMT, and avoiding the need to build a separate grammar for every new language – an expensive undertaking.

Translation	Types	Tokens	Ratio
English (KJV)	12,335	789,744	1.56%
French (Darby)	20,428	812,947	2.51%
Spanish (RV 1909)	28,456	704,004	4.04%
Russian (Syn 1876)	47,226	560,524	8.43%
Arabic (S. Van Dyke)	55,300	440,435	12.56%

Table 1. Lexical statistics in a parallel corpus

[2] Pragmatically, terms can be defined very straightforwardly in the regular expressions language as sequences of characters delimited by non-word characters.

To begin to assess the problem, one can compare the lexical statistics for the Bible from Chew et al. (2007), which should be directly comparable since they are from a parallel corpus. These are arranged in Table 1 in order of type-to-token ratio.

This ordering also corresponds to the ordering of languages on a scale from 'analytic' to 'synthetic': meaning is shaped in the former by the use of particles and word order, and in the latter by inflection and suffixation. Some examples illustrating differences between Russian and English in this respect are given in Table 2.

English	I read	you read	they read
Russian	читаю	читаешь	читают

Table 2. Analytic versus synthetic languages

The element in Russian, of course, which corresponds to 'read' is the stem 'чита', but this is embedded within a larger term. Hence, in all three examples, Russian takes one term to express what in English takes two terms. The same occurs (although to a lesser extent) in English, in which 'read' and 'reads' are treated as distinct terms. Without any further context (such as sentences in which these terms are instantiated), the similarity in meaning between 'read' and 'reads' will be readily apparent to any linguist, simply because of the shared orthography and morphology. But for an approach like standard LSA in which terms are defined simply as distinct entities delimited by non-word characters, the morphology is considered immaterial – it is invisible. The only way a standard term-based approach can detect any similarity between 'read' and 'reads' is through the associations of terms in documents. Clearly, then, such an approach operates under a handicap.

Two unfortunate consequences will inevitably result from this. First, some terms will be treated as out-of-vocabulary even when at least some of the semantics could perhaps have been derived from a part of the term. For example, if the training corpus contains 'read' and 'reads' but not 'reading', valuable information is lost every time 'reading' is encountered in a new document to which LSA might be deployed. Secondly, associations that should be made between *in-vocabulary* terms will also be missed. Perhaps a reason that more attention has not been devoted to this is that the problem can largely be disregarded in highly analytic languages like English. But, as previous results such as Chew and Abdelali's (2008) show, for a language like Arabic, the adverse consequences of a morphology-blind approach are more severe. The question then is: how can information which is clearly available in the training corpus be more fully leveraged without sacrificing efficiency?

3 Possible solutions

3.1 Replacing terms with n-grams

At first glance, one might think that stemming would be an answer. Stemming has been shown to improve IR, in particular for morphologically complex languages (recent examples, including with Arabic, are Lavie et al. 2004 and Abdou et al. 2005). We are not aware, however, of any previous results that show unequivocally that stemming is beneficial specifically in CLIR. Chew and Abdelali (2008) examine the use of a light stemmer for Arabic (Darwish 2002), and while this does result in a small overall increase in overall precision, there is paradoxically no increase for Arabic. The problem may be that the approach for Arabic needs to be matched by a similar approach for other languages in the parallel corpus. However, since stemmers are usually tailored to particular languages – and may even be unavailable for some languages – use of existing stemmers may not always be an option.

Another more obviously language-independent approach is to replace terms with character n-grams[3]. This is feasible for more or less any language, regardless of script. Moreover, implementation of a similar idea is described in McNamee and Mayfield (2004) and applied specifically to CLIR. However, McNamee and Mayfield's CLIR results are solely for European languages written in the Roman script. This is why they are able to obtain, in their words, 'surprisingly good results… without translation [of the query]', and without using LSA in any form. With related languages in the same script, and particularly when n-grams are used in place of terms, the existence of cognates means that many translations can easily be identified, since they probably share many of the same n-grams (e.g. French 'parisien' versus English 'Parisian'). When languages do not all share the same script or come from the same language family, however, the task can be considerably harder.

Since the approach of n-gram tokenization has the advantages of being entirely statistically-

[3] Hereafter, we use the term 'n-grams' to refer specifically to character (not word) n-grams.

based and language-independent, however, we examined whether it could be combined with LSA to allow CLIR (including cross-script retrieval), and whether this would lead to any advantage over term-based LSA. Our intuition was that some (although not all) n-grams would correspond to morphologically significant subconstituents of terms, such as 'read' from 'reading', and therefore associations at the morpheme level might be facilitated. The steps for this approach are listed in Table 3.

1	Form a term-by-document array from the parallel corpus as described above
2	For each term, list all (overlapping) n-grams[4]
3	Replace terms in the term-by-document array with n-grams, to form an n-gram-by-document array
4	Subject the n-gram-by-document array to SVD to produce an n-gram-by-concept U matrix, singular values (the diagonal S matrix), and document-by-concept V matrix
5	Project new documents into the semantic space by multiplying their vectors by US^{-1}

Table 3. Steps for n-gram-based LSA

Under all approaches, we selected the same log-entropy term weighting scheme that we used for standard LSA. Thus, whether a term t stands for a wordform or an n-gram, its weighted frequency W in a particular document k is given by:

$$W = \log_2 (F + 1) \times (1 + H_t / \log_2 (N))^{\alpha} \quad (2)$$

where F is the raw frequency of t in k, H_t is the entropy of the term or n-gram across all documents, N is the number of documents in the corpus, and α is some arbitrary constant (a power to which the global weight is raised). We have found that an $\alpha > 1$ improves precision by changing the relative distribution of weighted frequencies. Common terms with high entropy become much less influential in the SVD.

It should be noted that step (2) in Table 3 is similar to McNamee and Mayfield's approach, except that we did not include word-spanning n-grams, owing to computational constraints. We also tried two variants of step (2), one in which all n-grams were of the same length (as per McNamee and Mayfield 2004), and one in which n-grams of different lengths were mixed. Under the second of these, the number of rows in both the term-by-document and U matrices is of course considerably larger. For example, Table 4 shows that the number of rows in the n-gram-by-document matrix for English (EN) under the first variant (with n = 6) is 19,801, while under the second (with n ≤ 6) it is 58,907. Comparable statistics are given for Arabic (AR), Spanish (ES), French (FR) and Russian (RU).

n=	AR	EN	ES	FR	RU
1	35	27	41	41	47
2	939	516	728	708	827
3	11,127	4,267	5,563	5,067	7,808
4	40,835	13,927	19,686	15,948	30,702
5	53,671	20,369	35,526	25,253	54,647
6	39,822	19,801	42,408	28,274	65,308
Total	146,429	58,907	103,952	75,291	159,339

Table 4. Number of distinct n-grams by language and length, up to length 6, based on Bible text

3.2 Replacing terms with morphemes: LMSA

We also attempted a related approach with *non-overlapping* n-grams. This set of experiments was guided by the intuition that not all n-grams are morphologically significant. Before we discuss the details of this approach, consider the English example 'comingle'. Here, 'co' + 'mingle' are likely to be more significant to the overall meaning than 'coming' + 'le' – in fact, the presence of the n-gram 'coming' could be misleading in this case. One way to model this would be to change the weighting scheme. The problem with this is that the weighting for one token has to be contingent on the weighting for another in the same term. Otherwise, in this example, the n-gram 'coming' would presumably receive a high weighting based on its frequency elsewhere in the corpus.

An alternative is to select the tokenization which maximizes mutual information (MI). Brown et al. (1992) describe one application of MI to identify word collocations; Kashioka et al. (1998) describe another, based on MI of character n-grams, for morphological analysis of Japanese. The pointwise MI of a pair s_1 and s_2 as adjacent symbols is

$$MI = \log P(s_1 s_2) - \log P(s_1) - \log P(s_2) \quad (3)$$

If s_1 follows s_2 less often than expected on the basis of their independent frequencies, then MI is negative; otherwise, it is positive.

In our application, we want to consider all candidate tokenizations, sum MI for each candidate, and rule out all but one candidate. A to-

[4] As an example, for 'cat', the complete list of overlapping n-grams would be 'c', 'a', 't', 'ca', 'at', and 'cat'.

kenization is a candidate if it exhaustively parses the entire string and has no overlapping tokens. Thus, for 'comingle', co+mingle, coming+le, comingle, c+o+m+i+n+g+l+e, etc., are some of the candidates, but comi+ngl and com+mingle are not. To obtain MI, we need to compute the log probability (logp) of every n-gram in the corpus. If S_k (k = 1, …, K) denotes the set of all n-grams of length k, and s_n is a particular n-gram of length n, then we compute logp for s_n as:

$$\text{logp} = \log F(s_n) - \log \Sigma\,(F(S_n)) \qquad (4)$$

where $F(s_n)$ is the frequency of s_n in the corpus, and $\Sigma\,(F(S_n))$ is the sum of the frequencies of all S_n in the corpus.[5] In all cases, logp is negative, and MI is maximized when the magnitude of the sum of logp for all elements in the tokenization (also negative) is minimized, i.e. closest to zero. Tokenizations consisting of one, two or more elements (respective examples are comingle, co+mingle, and co+ming+le) will all receive a score, although those with fewer elements will tend to be favored.

We considered some minor variants in the settings for this approach in which word-initial and word-final n-grams were indexed separately from word-medial n-grams. Guided by McNamee and Mayfield's (2004) finding that there is an optimal (language-dependent) value of k for S_k, we also varied the maximum length of n-grams allowed in tokenizations. Under all settings, we followed steps 3-5 from Table 3 (including SVD) from here on.

This approach (which we call latent *morpho*-semantic analysis), then, is like LSA, except that the types and tokens are statistically-derived morphemes rather than terms. Whatever LMSA variant is used, the underlying approach to morphological tokenization is completely language-independent. Example output is shown in Table 5 for wordforms from the Russian lemma пресмыкаться 'to crawl', where the common stem (or at least an approximation thereof) is correctly identified.

Wordform	Tokenization	
пресмыкающемуся	пресмыкаю	щемуся
пресмыкающимися	пресмыкаю	щимися
пресмыкающимся	пресмыкаю	щимся
пресмыкающихся	пресмыкаю	щихся

Table 5. Examples of MI-based tokenization

[5] Note that (4) is closely related to the 'weighted mutual information' measure used in Goldsmith (2001: 172).

We do not directly test the accuracy of these tokenizations. Rather, measures of CLIR precision (described in section 4) indirectly validate our morphological tokenizations.

4 Testing framework

To assess our results on a basis comparable with previous work, we used the same training and test data as used in Chew et al. (2007) and Chew and Abdelali (2008). The training data consists of the text of the Bible in 31,226 parallel chunks, corresponding generally to verses, in Arabic, English, French, Russian and Spanish. The test data is the text of the Quran in the same 5 languages, in 114 parallel chunks corresponding to suras (chapters).

Questions are sometimes raised as to how representative the Bible and/or Quran are of modern language. However, there is little question that the number and diversity of parallel languages covered by the Bible[6] is not matched elsewhere (Resnik et al. 1999), even by more mainstream parallel corpora such as Europarl (Koehn 2002)[7]. The diversity of languages covered is a particularly important criterion for our purposes, since we would like to look at methods which enhance retrieval for languages across the analytic-synthetic spectrum. The Bible also has the advantage of being readily available in electronic form: we downloaded all our data in a tab-delimited, verse-indexed format from the 'Unbound Bible' website mentioned above (Biola University, 2005-2006).

In accordance with previous work, we split the test set into each of the 10 possible language-pair combinations: AR-EN, AR-FR, EN-FR, and so on. For each language pair and test, 228 distinct 'queries' were submitted – each query consisting of one of the 228 sura 'documents'. To assess the aggregate performance of the framework, we used average precision at 1 document, hereafter 'P1' (1 if the translation of the document ranked highest, zero otherwise – thus, a fairly strict measure of precision). We also measured precision on a basis not used by Chew et al. (2007) or Chew and Abdelali (2008): multilingual precision at 5 documents (hereafter 'MP5'). For this,

[6] At December 31, 2006, complete translations existed in 429 languages, and partial translations in 2,426 languages (Bible Society 2007).

[7] Since the Europarl text is extracted from the proceedings of the European Parliament, the languages represented are generally closely-related to one another (most being Germanic or Romance).

each of the 570 documents (114 suras, each in 5 languages) is submitted as a query. The results are drawn from the pool of all five languages, so MP5 represents the percentage, on average, of the top 5 documents which are translations of the query. This measure is still stricter than P1 (this is a mathematical necessity) because the retrieval task is harder. Essentially, MP5 measures how well similar documents cluster across languages, while P1 measures how reliably document translations are retrieved when the target language is known.

5 Results and Discussion

The following tables show the results of our tests. First, we present in Table 6 the results using standard LSA, in which terms are sequences of characters delimited by non-word characters. Here, in essence, we reperformed an experiment in Chew and Abdelali (2008).

P1 (overall average: 0.8796)					
	AR	EN	ES	FR	RU
AR	1.0000	0.7544	0.7193	0.7368	0.7544
EN	0.7719	1.0000	0.9123	0.9386	0.9474
ES	0.6316	0.9298	1.0000	0.9298	0.8947
FR	0.7719	0.9035	0.9298	1.0000	0.9386
RU	0.7719	0.9298	0.9035	0.9211	1.0000
MP5: AR 0.4456, EN 0.7211, ES 0.6649, FR 0.7614, RU 0.6947; **overall average: 0.6575**					

Table 6. Results with standard LSA

Our results differ from Chew and Abdelali's (2008) – our precision is higher – because we use a different value of α in equation (2) above (here, 1.8 rather than 1). Generally, we selected α so as to maximize MP5; discussion of this is beyond the scope of this paper, and not strictly relevant in any case, since we present like-for-like comparisons throughout this section. However, Table 6 shows clearly that our results replicate those previously published, in that precision for Arabic (the most 'synthetic' of the five languages) is consistently lower than for the other four.

The next set of results (in Table 7) is for LSA with SVD of an array in which the rows correspond to all overlapping, but not word-spanning, n-grams of fixed length. The best results here, for n=4, are essentially no better on average than those obtained with standard LSA. However, averaging across languages obscures the fact that results for Arabic have significantly improved (for example, where Arabic documents are used as queries, MP5 is now 0.6205 instead of 0.4456). Still, the fact that average MP5 is essentially unchanged means that this is at the expense of results for other languages.

n =	Average P1	Average MP5
3	0.8340	0.4951
4	0.8779	0.6761
5	0.8232	0.6365
6	0.6957	0.5197
7	0.5321	0.3986

Table 7. Results with LSA / overlapping n-grams of fixed length

Now we present results in Table 8 where SVD is performed on an array in which the rows correspond to all overlapping, but not word-spanning, n-grams of *any* length (varying maximum length).

n ≤	Average P1	Average MP5
3	0.8235	0.3909
4	0.9039	0.6256
5	0.9095	0.6839
6	0.8863	0.6716
7	0.8635	0.6470

Table 8. Results with LSA / overlapping n-grams of variable length

Here, the best results (with n<=5) more clearly improve upon LSA: the increases in both P1 and MP5, though each only about 0.03 in absolute terms, are highly significant ($p < 0.005$). Very likely this is related to the fact that when n-grams are used in place of words, the out-of-vocabulary problem is alleviated. But there is quite a high computational cost, which will become apparent in Table 10 and the discussion accompanying it.

A practical advantage of the 'morpheme'-by-document array of LMSA, on the other hand, is that this cost is substantially reduced. This is because, as already mentioned, the vast majority of n-grams are eliminated from consideration. However, does taking this step significantly hurt performance? The results for LMSA presented in Table 9 provide an answer to this.

For P1, the results are comparable to standard LSA when we select settings of $n \leq 7$ (maximum permitted morpheme length) or above. But under the stricter MP5 measure, LMSA not only significantly outperforms standard LSA ($p < 0.001$, at $n \leq 9$); the results are also superior to those obtained under any other method we tested. The improvement in MP5 is comparable to that for P1 – 0.677 to 0.707 – when Chew and Abdelali (2008) use the Darwish Arabic light stemmer to provide input to LSA; our approach, however, has the advantage that it is fully unsupervised.

n ≤	Average P1	Average MP5
4	0.6947	0.4411
5	0.8151	0.6102
6	0.8614	0.6793
7	0.8709	0.6912
8	0.8663	0.6856
9	0.8765	0.6909
10	0.8772	0.6740

Table 9. Results with LMSA[8]

As when n-grams are used without MI, fewer types are out-of-vocabulary: for example, with certain settings for LMSA, we found that the percentage of out-of-vocabulary types dropped from 65% under LSA to 29% under LMSA, and the effect was even more marked for Arabic taken individually (78.5% to 34.4%). This is despite the fact mentioned above that LMSA arrays are more economical than LSA arrays: in fact, as Table 10 shows, 22% more economical (the size of the U matrix output by SVD, used to create vectors for new documents, is determined solely by the number of rows, or types). Note also that both LSA and LMSA are significantly more economical than SVD with overlapping n-grams.

Technique	**Rows**	**Nonzeros**
LSA	163,745	2,684,938
LSA with overlapping n-grams (where n ≤ 5)	527,506	45,878,062
LMSA	127,722	3,215,078

Table 10. Comparative matrix sizes

Even the results in Table 9 can still be improved upon. Following McNamee and Mayfield's insight that different length n-grams may be optimal for different languages, we attempted to improve precision further by varying *n* independently by language. For all languages but Arabic, n ≤ 9 seems to work well (either increasing or decreasing maximum n resulted in a drop in precision), but by setting n ≤ 6 for Arabic, P1 increased to 0.8874 and MP5 to 0.7368. As comparison of Table 11 with Table 6 shows, some of the most significant individual increases were for Arabic. It should however be noted that the optimal value for n may be dataset-dependent.

Since n is a *maximum* length (unlike in McNamee and Mayfield's experiments), one might expect that increasing n should never result in a drop in precision. We believe the benefit to limiting the size of n is connected to Brown et al.'s (1992: 470) observation that 'as *n* increases, the accuracy of an n-gram model increases, but the reliability of our parameter estimates, drawn as they must be from a limited training text, decreases'. Effectively, the probabilities used in MI are unrepresentatively high for longer n-grams (this becomes clear if one considers the extreme example of an n-gram the same length as the training corpus).

P1 (overall average: 0.8874)					
	AR	EN	ES	FR	RU
AR	1.0000	0.7895	0.7719	0.7281	0.7807
EN	0.8158	1.0000	0.9298	0.9298	0.9123
ES	0.7807	0.9474	1.0000	0.9123	0.8684
FR	0.7632	0.9035	0.9474	1.0000	0.8947
RU	0.7456	0.9298	0.9298	0.9035	1.0000
MP5: AR 0.5140, EN 0.8035, ES 0.8228, FR 0.8035, RU 0.7404; **overall average: 0.7368**					

Table 11. Best results with LMSA

If setting a maximum value for n makes sense in general, the idea of a lower maximum for Arabic in particular also seems reasonable since Arabic words, generally written as they are without vowels, contain on average fewer characters than the other four languages, and contain roots which are usually three or fewer characters long.

6 Conclusion

In this paper, we have demonstrated LMSA, a linguistically (specifically, morphologically) more sophisticated alternative to LSA. By computing mutual information of character n-grams of non-fixed length, we are able to obtain an approximation to a morpheme-by-document matrix which can substitute for the commonly-used term-by-document matrix. At the same time, because mutual information is based entirely on statistics, rather than grammar rules, all the advantages of LSA (language-independence, speed of implementation and fast run-time processing) are retained. In fact, some of these advantages may be increased since the number of index items is often lower.

Although from a linguist's point of view the theoretical advantages of LMSA may be intrinsically satisfying, the benefit is not confined to the theoretical realm. Our empirical results show that LMSA also brings practical benefits, particularly when performing IR with morphologically complex languages like Arabic. Principally, this seems to be due to two factors: alleviation of the

[8] These results are with the stipulation that word-initial and word-final n-grams are distinguished from word-medial n-grams. We also ran experiments in which this distinction was not made. Detailed results are not presented here; suffice it to say that when word-medial and other morphemes were not distinguished, precision was hurt somewhat (lowering it often by several percentage points).

out-of-vocabulary problem and improvement in the associations made by SVD.

We believe that the results we have presented may point the way towards still more sophisticated types of analysis, particularly for multilingual text. We would like to explore, for example, whether it is possible to use tensor decomposition methods like PARAFAC2 to leverage associations between n-grams, words, documents and languages to still better advantage.

Finally, it is worth pointing out that our approach offers an indirect way to test our statistics-based approach to morphological analysis. The better our 'morphemes' correspond to minimal semantic units (as theory dictates they should), the more coherently our system should work overall. In this case, our final arbiter of the system's overall performance is CLIR precision.

In short, our initial attempts appear to show that statistics-based morphological analysis can be integrated into a larger information retrieval architecture with some success.

Acknowledgement

Sandia is a multiprogram laboratory operated by Sandia Corporation, a Lockheed Martin Company, for the United States Department of Energy's National Nuclear Security Administration under contract DE-AC04-94AL85000.

References

S. Abdou, P. Ruck, and J. Savoy. 2005. Evaluation of Stemming, Query Expansion and Manual Indexing Approaches for the Genomic Task. *Proceedings of TREC 2005*.

M. W. Berry, S. T. Dumais., and G. W. O'Brien. 1994. Using Linear Algebra for Intelligent Information Retrieval. *SIAM: Review* 37, 573-595.

Bible Society. 2006. *A Statistical Summary of Languages with the Scriptures*. Accessed Jan 5 2007 at http://www.biblesociety.org/latestnews/latest341-slr2005stats.html.

Biola University. 2005-2006. *The Unbound Bible*. Accessed Jan 29 2008 at http://www.unboundbible.org/.

P. F. Brown, P. V. deSouza, R. L. Mercer, V. J. Della Pietra, and J. C. Lai. 1992. Class-Based *n*-gram Models of Natural Language. *Computational Linguistics* 18(4), 467-479.

P. Chew and A. Abdelali. 2007. Benefits of the 'Massively Parallel Rosetta Stone': Cross-Language Information Retrieval with over 30 Languages. *Proceedings of the Association for Computational Linguistics*, 872-879.

P. Chew and A. Abdelali. 2008. The Effects of Language Relatedness on Multilingual Information Retrieval: A Case Study With Indo-European and Semitic Languages. *Proceedings of the Workshop on Cross-Language Information Access*.

K. Darwish. 2002. Building a shallow Arabic morphological analyzer in one day. *Proceedings of the Association for Computational Linguistics*, 47-54.

S. Deerwester, S. T. Dumais, G. W. Furnas, T. K. Landauer and R. Harshman. 1990. Indexing by Latent Semantic Analysis. *Journal of the American Society for Information Science* 41:6, 391-407.

J. Goldsmith. 2001. Unsupervised Learning of the Morphology of a Natural Language. *Computational Linguistics* 27(2), 153-198.

R. A. Harshman. 1972. PARAFAC2: Mathematical and Technical Notes. *UCLA Working Papers in Phonetics* 22, 30-47.

M. Heroux, R. Bartlett, V. Howle, R. Hoekstra, J. Hu, T. Kolda, R. Lehoucq, K. Long, R. Pawlowski, E. Phipps, A. Salinger, H. Thornquist, R. Tuminaro, J. Willenbring, A. Williams, and K. Stanley. 2005. An Overview of the Trilinos Project. *ACM Transactions on Mathematical Software* 31:3, 397-423.

H. Kashioka, Y. Kawata, Y. Kinjo, A. Finch and E. W. Black. 1998. Use of Mutual Information Based Character Clusters in Dictionary-less Morphological Analysis of Japanese. *Proceedings of the 17th International Conference on Computational Linguistics Vol. 1*: 658-662.

P. Koehn, F. J. Och, and D. Marcu. 2003. Statistical Phrase-Based Translation. *Proceedings of the Joint Conference on Human Language Technologies and NAACL*, 48-54.

P. Koehn. 2002. Europarl: a Multilingual Corpus for Evaluation of Machine Translation. Unpublished. Accessed Jan 29 2008 at http://www.iccs.inf.ed.ac.uk /~pkoehn/publications/europarl.pdf.

A. Lavie, E. Peterson, K. Probst, S. Wintner, and Y. Eytani. 2004. Rapid Prototyping of a Transfer-Based Hebrew-to-English Machine Translation System. *Proceedings of the TMI-04*.

P. McNamee and J. Mayfield. 2004. Character *N*-Gram Tokenization for European Language Text Retrieval. *Information Retrieval* 7, 73-97.

P. Resnik, M. Broman Olsen, and M. Diab. 1999. The Bible as a Parallel Corpus: Annotating the "Book of 2000 Tongues". *Computers and the Humanities* 33: 129-153.

Sentence Compression Beyond Word Deletion

Trevor Cohn and **Mirella Lapata**
School of Informatics
University of Edinburgh
{tcohn,mlap}@inf.ed.ac.uk

Abstract

In this paper we generalise the sentence compression task. Rather than simply shorten a sentence by deleting words or constituents, as in previous work, we rewrite it using additional operations such as substitution, reordering, and insertion. We present a new corpus that is suited to our task and a discriminative tree-to-tree transduction model that can naturally account for structural and lexical mismatches. The model incorporates a novel grammar extraction method, uses a language model for coherent output, and can be easily tuned to a wide range of compression specific loss functions.

1 Introduction

Automatic sentence compression can be broadly described as the task of creating a grammatical summary of a single sentence with minimal information loss. It has recently attracted much attention, in part because of its relevance to applications. Examples include the generation of subtitles from spoken transcripts (Vandeghinste and Pan, 2004), the display of text on small screens such as mobile phones or PDAs (Corston-Oliver, 2001), and, notably, summarisation (Jing, 2000; Lin, 2003).

Most prior work has focused on a specific instantiation of sentence compression, namely word deletion. Given an input sentence of words, $w_1, w_2 \ldots w_n$, a compression is formed by dropping any subset of these words (Knight and Marcu, 2002). The simplification renders the task computationally feasible, allowing efficient decoding using a dynamic program (Knight and Marcu, 2002; Turner and Charniak, 2005; McDonald, 2006). Furthermore, constraining the problem to word deletion affords substantial modeling flexibility. Indeed, a variety of models have been successfully developed for this task ranging from instantiations of the noisy-channel model (Knight and Marcu, 2002; Galley and McKeown, 2007; Turner and Charniak, 2005), to large-margin learning (McDonald, 2006; Cohn and Lapata, 2007), and Integer Linear Programming (Clarke, 2008). However, the simplification also renders the task somewhat artificial. There are many rewrite operations that could compress a sentence, besides deletion, including reordering, substitution, and insertion. In fact, professional abstractors tend to use these operations to transform selected sentences from an article into the corresponding summary sentences (Jing, 2000).

Therefore, in this paper we consider sentence compression from a more general perspective and generate *abstracts* rather than *extracts*. In this framework, the goal is to find a summary of the original sentence which is grammatical and conveys the most important information without necessarily using the same words in the same order. Our task is related to, but different from, paraphrase extraction (Barzilay, 2003). We must not only have access to paraphrases (i.e., rewrite rules), but also be able to combine them in order to generate new text, while attempting to produce a shorter resulting string. Quirk et al. (2004) present an end-to-end paraphrasing system inspired by phrase-based machine translation that can both acquire paraphrases and use them to generate new strings. However, their model is limited to lexical substitution — no reordering takes place — and is

© 2008. Licensed under the *Creative Commons Attribution-Noncommercial-Share Alike 3.0 Unported* license (http://creativecommons.org/licenses/by-nc-sa/3.0/). Some rights reserved.

lacking the compression objective.

Once we move away from extractive compression we are faced with two problems. First, we must find an appropriate training set for our abstractive task. Compression corpora are not naturally available and existing paraphrase corpora do not normally contain compressions. Our second problem concerns the modeling task itself. Ideally, our learning framework should handle structural mismatches and complex rewriting operations.

In what follows, we first present a new corpus for abstractive compression which we created by having annotators compress sentences while rewriting them. Besides obtaining useful data for modeling purposes, we also demonstrate that abstractive compression is a meaningful task. We then present a tree-to-tree transducer capable of transforming an input parse tree into a compressed parse tree. Our approach is based on synchronous tree substitution grammar (STSG, Eisner (2003)), a formalism that can account for structural mismatches, and is trained discriminatively. Specifically, we generalise the model of Cohn and Lapata (2007) to our abstractive task. We present a novel tree-to-tree grammar extraction method which acquires paraphrases from bilingual corpora and ensure coherent output by including a ngram language model as a feature. We also develop a number of loss functions suited to the abstractive compression task. We hope that some of the work described here might be of relevance to other generation tasks such as machine translation (Eisner, 2003), multi-document summarisation (Barzilay, 2003), and text simplification (Carroll et al., 1999).

2 Abstractive Compression Corpus

A stumbling block to studying abstractive sentence compression is the lack of widely available corpora for training and testing. Previous work has been conducted almost exclusively on Ziff-Davis, a corpus derived automatically from document abstract pairs (Knight and Marcu, 2002), or on human-authored corpora (Clarke, 2008). Unfortunately, none of these data sources are suited to our problem since they have been produced with a single rewriting operation, namely word deletion. Although there is a greater supply of paraphrasing corpora, such as the Multiple-Translation Chinese (MTC) corpus[1] and the Microsoft Research (MSR) Paraphrase Corpus (Quirk et al., 2004), they are also not ideal, since they have not been created with compression in mind. They contain ample rewriting operations, however they do not explicitly target information loss.

For the reasons just described, we created our own corpus. We collected 30 newspaper articles (575 sentences) from the British National Corpus (BNC) and the American News Text corpus, for which we obtained manual compressions. In order to confirm that the task was feasible, five of these documents were initially compressed by two annotators (not the authors). The annotators were given instructions that explained the task and defined sentence compression with the aid of examples. They were asked to paraphrase while preserving the most important information and ensuring the compressed sentences remained grammatical. They were encouraged to use any rewriting operations that seemed appropriate, e.g., to delete words, add new words, substitute them or reorder them.

Assessing inter-annotator agreement is notoriously difficult for paraphrasing tasks (Barzilay, 2003) since there can be many valid outputs for a given input. Also our task is doubly subjective in deciding which information to remove from the sentence and how to rewrite it. In default of an agreement measure that is well suited to the task and takes both decisions into account, we assessed them separately. We first examined whether the annotators compressed at a similar level. The compression rate was 56% for one annotator and 54% for the other.[2] We also assessed whether they agreed in their rewrites by measuring BLEU (Papineni et al., 2002). The inter-annotator BLEU score was 23.79%, compared with the source agreement BLEU of only 13.22%. Both the compression rate and BLEU score indicate that the task is well-defined and the compressions valid. The remaining 25 documents were compressed by a single annotator to ensure consistency. All our experiments used the data from this annotator.[3]

Table 1 illustrates some examples from our corpus. As can be seen, some sentences contain a single rewrite operation. For instance, a PP is paraphrased with a genitive (see (1)), a subordinate clause with a present participle (see (2)), a passive sentence with an active one (see (3)). However, in most cases many rewrite decisions take place all at once. Consider sentence (4). Here, the conjunction *high winds and snowfalls* is abbreviated to

[1]Available by the LDC, Catalog Number LDC2002T01, ISBN 1-58563-217-1.

[2]The term "compression rate" refers to the percentage of words retained in the compression.

[3]Available from http://homepages.inf.ed.ac.uk/tcohn/paraphrase.

1a.	The future of the nation is in your hands.
1b.	The nation's future is in your hands.
2a.	As he entered a polling booth in Katutura, he said.
2b.	Entering a polling booth in Katutura, he said.
3a.	Mr Usta was examined by Dr Raymond Crockett, a Harley Street physician specialising in kidney disease.
3b.	Dr Raymond Crockett, a Harley Street physician, examined Mr Usta.
4a.	High winds and snowfalls have, however, grounded at a lower level the powerful US Navy Sea Stallion helicopters used to transport the slabs.
4b.	Bad weather, however, has grounded the helicopters transporting the slabs.
5a.	To experts in international law and relations, the US action demonstrates a breach by a major power of international conventions.
5b.	Experts say the US are in breach of international conventions.

Table 1: Compression examples from our corpus; (a) sentences are the source, (b) sentences the target.

bad weather and the infinitive clause *to transport* to the present participle *transporting*. Note that the prenominal modifiers *US Navy Sea Stallion* and the verb *used* have been removed. In sentence (5), the verb *say* is added and the NP *a breach by a major power of international conventions* is paraphrased by the sentence *the US are in breach of international conventions*.

3 Basic Model

Our work builds on the model developed by Cohn and Lapata (2007). They formulate sentence compression as a tree-to-tree rewriting task. A synchronous tree substitution grammar (STSG, Eisner (2003)) licenses the space of all possible rewrites. Each grammar rule is assigned a weight, and these weights are learnt in discriminative training. For prediction, a specialised generation algorithm finds the best scoring compression using the grammar rules. Cohn and Lapata apply this model to extractive compression with state-of-the-art results.

This model is appealing for our task for several reasons. Firstly, the synchronous grammar provides expressive power to model consistent syntactic effects such as reordering, changes in nonterminal categories and lexical substitution. Secondly, it is discriminatively trained, which allows for the incorporation of all manner of powerful features. Thirdly, the learning framework can be tailored to the task by choosing an appropriate loss function. In the following we describe their model in more detail with emphasis on the synchronous grammar, the model structure, and the prediction and training algorithms. Section 4 presents our extensions and modifications.

Grammar The grammar defines a space of tree pairs over uncompressed and compressed sentences, which we refer to henceforth as the *source* and *target*. We use the grammar to find the set of sister target sentences for a given source sentence. Figure 1 shows a toy grammar and the set of possible target (output) trees for the given source (input) tree. Each output tree is created by applying a series of grammar rules, where each rule matches a fragment of the source and creates a fragment of the target tree. A rule in the grammar consists of a pair of elementary trees and a mapping between the variables (frontier non-terminals) in both trees. A *derivation* is a sequence of rules yielding a target tree with no remaining variables.

Grammar rules:
⟨S, S⟩ → ⟨NP$\boxed{1}$ VBD$\boxed{2}$ NP$\boxed{3}$, NP$\boxed{1}$ VBD$\boxed{2}$ NP$\boxed{3}$⟩
⟨S, S⟩ → ⟨NP$\boxed{1}$ VBD$\boxed{2}$ NP$\boxed{3}$, NP$\boxed{3}$ was VBN$\boxed{2}$ by NP$\boxed{1}$⟩
⟨NP, NP⟩ → ⟨he, him⟩
⟨NP, NP⟩ → ⟨he, he⟩
⟨NP, NP⟩ → ⟨he, Peter⟩
⟨VBD, VBN⟩ → ⟨sang, sung⟩
⟨NP, NP⟩ → ⟨a song, a song⟩

Input tree:
[S [NP He$_{NP}$ [VP sang$_{VBD}$ [NP a$_{DT}$ song$_{NN}$]]]

Output trees:
[S [NP He] [VP sang [NP a song]]]
[S [NP Him] [VP sang [NP a song]]]
[S [NP Peter] [VP sang [NP a song]]]
[S [NP A song] [VP was [VP sung [PP by he]]]]
[S [NP A song] [VP was [VP sung [PP by him]]]]
[S [NP A song] [VP was [VP sung [PP by Peter]]]]

Figure 1: Example grammar and the output trees it licences for an input tree. The numbered boxes in the rules denote linked variables. Pre-terminal categories are not shown for the output trees for the sake of brevity.

Cohn and Lapata (2007) extract a STSG from a parsed, word-aligned corpus of source and target sentences. Specifically, they extract the *minimal set* of synchronous rules which can describe each tree pair. These rules are minimal in the sense that they cannot be made smaller (e.g., by replacing a subtree with a variable) while still honouring the word-alignment.

Decoding The grammar allows us to search for all sister trees for a given tree. The decoder maximises over this space:

$$\mathbf{y}^* = \arg\max_{\mathbf{y}:S(\mathbf{y})=\mathbf{x}} \Psi(\mathbf{y}) \qquad (1)$$

$$\text{where} \quad \Psi(\mathbf{y}) = \sum_{r \in \mathbf{y}} \langle \phi(r, S(\mathbf{y})), \lambda \rangle \qquad (2)$$

Here $\mathbf{x}$ is the source (uncompressed) tree, $\mathbf{y}$ is a derivation which produces the source tree, $S(\mathbf{y}) = \mathbf{x}$, and a target tree, $T(\mathbf{y})$,[4] and r is a grammar rule. The Ψ function scores the derivation and

[4]Equation 1 optimises over derivations rather than target trees to allow tractable inference.

is defined in (2) as a linear function over the rules used. Each rule's score is an inner product between its feature vector, $\phi(r, \mathbf{y}_S)$, and the model parameters, λ. The feature functions are set by hand, while the model parameters are learned in training.

The maximisation problem in (1) can be solved efficiently using a dynamic program. Derivations will have common sub-structures whenever they transduce the same source sub-tree into a target sub-tree. This is captured in a chart, leading to an efficient bottom-up algorithm. The asymptotic time complexity of this search is $O(SR)$ where S is the number of source nodes and R is the number of rules matching a given node.

Training The model is trained using SVM^{struct}, a large margin method for structured output problems (Joachims, 2005; Tsochantaridis et al., 2005). This training method allows the use of a configurable loss function, $\Delta(\mathbf{y}^*, \mathbf{y})$, which measures the extent to which the model's prediction, $\mathbf{y}$, differs from the reference, $\mathbf{y}^*$. Central to training is the search for a derivation which is both high scoring and has high loss compared to the gold standard.[5] This requires finding the maximiser of $H(\mathbf{y})$ in one of:

$$\begin{aligned} H_s &= (1 - \langle \Psi(\mathbf{y}^*) - \Psi(\mathbf{y}), \lambda \rangle)\Delta(\mathbf{y}^*, \mathbf{y}) \\ H_m &= \Delta(\mathbf{y}^*, \mathbf{y}) - \langle \Psi(\mathbf{y}^*) - \Psi(\mathbf{y}), \lambda \rangle \end{aligned} \quad (3)$$

where the subscripts s and m denote *slack* and *margin* rescaling, which are different formulations of the training problem (see Tsochantaridis et al. (2005) and Taskar et al. (2003) for details).

The search for the maximiser of $H(\mathbf{y})$ in (3) requires the tracking of the loss value. This can be achieved by extending the decoding algorithm such that the chart cells also store the loss parameters (e.g., for precision, the number of true and false positives (Joachims, 2005)). Consequently, this extension leads to a considerably higher time and space complexity compared to decoding. For example, with precision loss the time complexity is $O(S^3R)$ as each step must consider $O(S^2)$ possible loss parameter values.

4 Extensions

In this section we present our extensions of Cohn and Lapata's (2007) model. The latter was designed with the simpler extractive compression in mind and cannot be readily applied to our task.

[5]Spurious ambiguity in the grammar means that there are often many derivations linking the source and target. We follow Cohn and Lapata (2007) by choosing the derivation with the most rules, which should provide good generalisation.

Grammar It is relatively straightforward to extract a grammar from our corpus. This grammar will contain many rules encoding deletions and structural transformations but there will be many unobserved paraphrases, no matter how good the extraction method (recall that our corpus consists solely of 565 sentences). For this reason, we extract a grammar from our abstractive corpus in the manner of Cohn and Lapata (2007) (see Section 5 for details) and augment it with a larger grammar obtained from a parallel bilingual corpus. Crucially, our second grammar will not contain compression rules, just paraphrasing ones. We leave it to the model to learn which rules serve the compression objective.

Our paraphrase grammar extraction method uses bilingual pivoting to learn paraphrases over syntax tree fragments, i.e., STSG rules. Pivoting treats the paraphrasing problem as a two-stage translation process. Some English text is translated to a foreign language, and then translated back into English (Bannard and Callison-Burch, 2005):

$$p(e'|e) = \sum_f p(e'|f)p(f|e) \quad (4)$$

where $p(f|e)$ is the probability of translating an English string e into a foreign string f and $p(e'|f)$ the probability of translating the same foreign string into some other English string e'. We thus obtain English-English translation probabilities $p(e'|e)$ by marginalizing out the foreign text.

Instead of using strings (Bannard and Callison-Burch, 2005), we use elementary trees on the English side, resulting in a monolingual STSG. We obtain the elementary trees and foreign strings using the GKHM algorithm (Galley et al., 2004). This takes as input a bilingual word-aligned corpus with trees on one side, and finds the minimal set of tree fragments and their corresponding strings which is consistent with the word alignment. This process is illustrated in Figure 2 where the aligned pair on the left gives rise to the rules shown on the right. Note that the English rules and foreign strings shown include variable indices where they have been generalised. We estimate $p(f|e)$ and $p(e'|f)$ from the set of tree-to-string rules and then then pivot each tree fragment to produce STSG rules. Figure 3 illustrates the process for the [VP does not VP] fragment.

Modeling and Decoding Our grammar is much larger and noisier than a grammar extracted solely for deletion-based compression. So, in order to encourage coherence and inform lexical se-

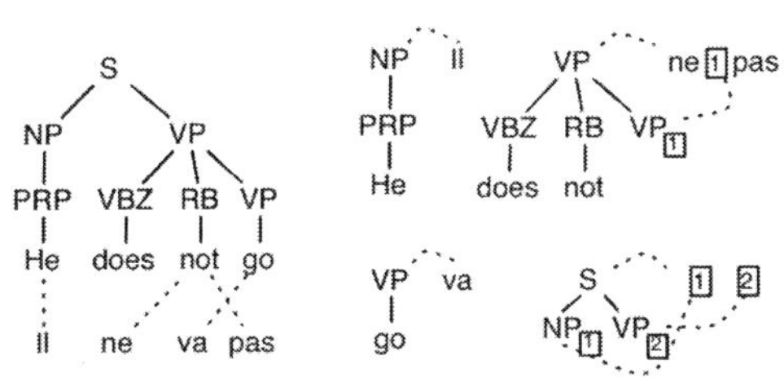

Figure 2: Tree-to-string grammar extraction using the GHKM algorithm, showing the aligned sentence pair and the resulting rules as tree fragments and their matching strings. The boxed numbers denote variables.

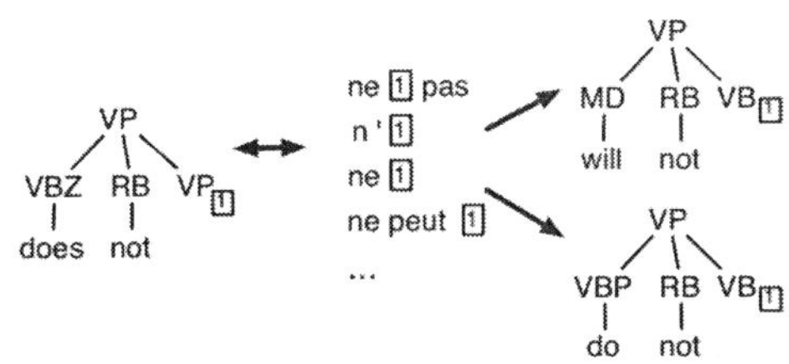

Figure 3: Pivoting the [VP does not VP] fragment.

lection we incorporate a ngram language model (LM) as a feature. This requires adapting the scoring function, Ψ, in (2) to allow features over target ngrams:

$$\Psi(\mathbf{y}) = \sum_{r \in \mathbf{y}} \langle \phi(r, S(\mathbf{y})), \lambda \rangle + \sum_{m \in T(\mathbf{y})} \langle \psi(m, S(\mathbf{y})), \lambda \rangle \quad (5)$$

where m are the ngrams and ψ is a new feature function over these ngrams (we use only one ngram feature: the trigram log-probability). Sadly, the scoring function in (5) renders the chart-based search used for training and decoding intractable. In order to provide sufficient context to the chart-based algorithm, we must also store in each chart cell the $n-1$ target tokens at the left and right edges of its yield. This is equivalent to using as our grammar the intersection between the original grammar and the ngram LM (Chiang, 2007), and increases the decoding complexity to an infeasible $O(SRL^{2(n-1)V})$ where L is the size of the lexicon. We adopt a popular approach in syntax-inspired machine translation to address this problem (Chiang, 2007). The idea is to use a beam-search over the intersection grammar coupled with the cube-pruning heuristic. The beam limits the number of items in a given chart cell to a fixed constant, regardless of the number of possible LM contexts and non-terminal categories. Cube-pruning further limits the number of items considered for inclusion in the beam, reducing the time complexity to a more manageable $O(SRBV)$ where B is the beam size. We refer the interested reader to Chiang (2007) for details.

Training The extensions to the model in (5) also necessitate changes in the training procedure. Recall that training the basic model of Cohn and Lapata (2007) requires finding the maximiser of $H(\mathbf{y})$ in (3). Their model uses a chart-based algorithm for this purpose. As in decoding we also use a beam search for training, thereby avoiding the exponential time complexity of exact search. The beam search requires an estimate of the quality for incomplete derivations. We use the margin rescaling objective, H_m in (3), and approximate the loss using the current (incomplete) loss parameter values in each chart cell. We use a wide beam of 200 unique items or 500 items in total to reduce the impact of the approximation.

Our loss functions are tailored to the task and draw inspiration from metrics developed for extractive compression but also for summarisation and machine translation. They are based on the Hamming distance over unordered bags of items. This measures the number of predicted items that did not appear in the reference, along with a penalty for short output:

$$\Delta_{hamming}(\mathbf{y}^*, \mathbf{y}) = f + \max(l - (t+f), 0) \quad (6)$$

where t and f are the number of true and false positives, respectively, when comparing the predicted target, $\mathbf{y}$, with the reference, $\mathbf{y}^*$, and l is the length of the reference. The second term penalises short output, as predicting very little or nothing would otherwise be unpenalised. We have three Hamming loss functions over: 1) tokens, 2) ngrams ($n \leq 3$), or 3) CFG productions. These losses all operate on unordered bags and therefore might reward erroneous predictions. For example, a permutation of the reference tokens has zero token-loss. The CFG and ngram losses have overlapping items which encode a partial order, and therefore are less affected.

In addition, we developed a fourth loss function to measure the edit distance between the model's prediction and the reference, both as bags-of-tokens. This measures the number of insertions and deletions. In contrast to the previous loss functions, this requires the true positive counts to be clipped to the number of occurrences of each type in the reference. The edit distance is given by:

$$\Delta_{edit}(\mathbf{y}^*, \mathbf{y}) = p + q - 2\sum_i \min(p_i, q_i) \quad (7)$$

where p and q denote the number of target tokens in the predicted and reference derivation, respectively, and p_i and q_i are the counts for type i.

$\langle$ADJP,NP$\rangle$	$\rightarrow$ $\langle$subject [PP to NP$_{\boxed{1}}$], part [PP of NP$_{\boxed{1}}$]$\rangle$	(T)
$\langle$ADVP,RB$\rangle$	$\rightarrow$ $\langle$as well, also$\rangle$	(T)
$\langle$ADJP,JJ$\rangle$	$\rightarrow$ $\langle$too little, insufficient$\rangle$	(P)
$\langle$S,S$\rangle$	$\rightarrow$ $\langle$S$_{\boxed{1}}$ and S$_{\boxed{2}}$, S$_{\boxed{2}}$ and S$_{\boxed{1}}$$\rangle$	(P)
$\langle$NP,NP$\rangle$	$\rightarrow$ $\langle$DT$_{\boxed{1}}$ NN$_{\boxed{2}}$, DT$_{\boxed{1}}$ NN$_{\boxed{2}}$$\rangle$	(S)
$\langle$NP,NP$\rangle$	$\rightarrow$ $\langle$DT$_{\boxed{1}}$ NN$_{\boxed{2}}$, NN$_{\boxed{2}}$$\rangle$	(S)

Table 2: Sample grammar rules extracted from the training set (T), pivoted set (P) or generated from the source (S).

5 Experimental Design

In this section we present our experimental set-up for assessing the performance of our model. We give details on the corpora and grammars we used, model parameters and features,[6] the baseline used for comparison with our approach, and explain how our system output was evaluated.

Grammar Extraction Our grammar used rules extracted directly from our compression corpus (the training partition, 480 sentences) and a bilingual corpus (see Table 2 for examples). The former corpus was word-aligned using the Berkeley aligner (Liang et al., 2006) initialised with a lexicon of word identity mappings, and parsed with Bikel's (2002) parser. From this we extracted grammar rules following the technique described in Cohn and Lapata (2007). For the pivot grammar we use the French-English Europarl v2 which contains approximately 688K sentences. Again, the corpus was aligned using the Berkeley aligner and the English side was parsed with Bikel's parser. We extracted tree-to-string rules using our implementation of the GHKM method. To ameliorate the effects of poor alignments on the grammar, we removed singleton rules before pivoting.

In addition to the two grammars described, we scanned the source trees in the compression corpus and included STSG rules to copy each CFG production or delete up to two of its children. This is illustrated in Table 2 where the last two rules are derived from the CFG production NP$\rightarrow$DT NN in the source tree. All trees are rooted with a distinguished TOP non-terminal which allows the explicit modelling of sentence spanning sub-trees. These grammars each had 44,199 (pivot), 7,813 (train) and 22,555 (copy) rules. We took their union, resulting in 58,281 unique rules and 13,619 unique source elementary trees.

Model Parameters Our model was trained on 480 sentences, 36 sentences were used for development and 59 for testing. We used a variety of syntax-based, lexical and compression-specific features (196,419 in total). These are summarised in Table 3. We also use a trigram language model trained on the BNC (100 million words) using the SRI Language Modeling toolkit (Stolcke, 2002), with modified Kneser-Ney smoothing.

For every rule:
origin of rule
for each origin, o: $\log p_o(s,t)$, $\log p_o(s\|t)$, $\log p_o(t\|s)$
$s_R, t_R, s_R \vee t_R$
$s, t, s \vee t, s = t$
both s and t are pre-terminals and $s = t$ or $s \neq t$
number of terminals/variables/dropped variables
ordering of variables as numbers/non-terminals
non-terminal sequence of vars identical after reordering
pre-terminal or terminal sequences are identical
number/identity of common/inserted/dropped terminals
source is shorter/longer than target
target is a compression of the source using deletes
For every ngram :
$\log p(w_i \| \mathbf{w}_{i-(n-1)}^{i-1})$

Table 3: The feature set. Rules were drawn from the training set, bilingual pivoting and directly from the source trees. s and t are the source and target elementary trees in a rule, the subscript $_R$ references the root non-terminal, $\mathbf{w}$ are the terminals in the target tree.

An important parameter in our modeling framework is the choice of loss function. We evaluated the loss functions presented in Section 4 on the development set. We ran our system for each of the four loss functions and asked two human judges to rate the output on a scale of 1 to 5. The Hamming loss over tokens performed best with a mean rating of 3.18, closely followed by the edit distance (3.17). We chose the former over the latter as it is less coarsely approximated during search.

Baseline There are no existing models that can be readily trained on our abstractive compression data. Instead, we use Cohn and Lapata's (2007) extractive model as a baseline. The latter was trained on an extractive compression corpus drawn from the BNC (Clarke, 2008) and tuned to provide a similar compression rate to our system. Note that their model is a strong baseline: it performed significantly better than competitive approaches (McDonald, 2006) across a variety of compression corpora.

Evaluation Methodology Sentence compression output is commonly evaluated by eliciting human judgments. Following Knight and Marcu (2002), we asked participants to rate the grammaticality of the target compressions and how well they preserved the most important information from the source. In both cases they used a five point rating scale where a high number indicates better performance. We randomly selected 30 sentences from the test portion of our corpus. These

[6] The software and corpus can be downloaded from `http://homepages.inf.ed.ac.uk/tcohn/paraphrase`.

Models	Grammaticality	Importance	CompR
Extract	3.10*	2.43*	82.5
Abstract	3.38*	2.85*†	79.2
Gold	4.51	4.02	58.4

Table 4: Mean ratings on compression output elicited by humans; *: significantly different from the gold standard; †: significantly different from the baseline.

sentences were compressed automatically by our model and the baseline. We also included gold standard compressions. Our materials thus consisted of 90 (30 × 3) source-target sentences. We collected ratings from 22 unpaid volunteers, all self reported native English speakers. Both studies were conducted over the Internet using a custom built web interface.

6 Results

Our results are summarised in Table 4, where we show the mean ratings for our system (Abstract), the baseline (Extract), and the gold standard. We first performed an Analysis of Variance (ANOVA) to examine the effect of different system compressions. The ANOVA revealed a reliable effect on both grammaticality and importance (significant over both subjects and items ($p < 0.01$)).

We next examined in more detail between-system differences. Post-hoc Tukey tests revealed that our abstractive model received significantly higher ratings than the baseline in terms of importance ($\alpha < 0.01$). We conjecture that this is due to the synchronous grammar we employ which is larger and more expressive than the baseline. In the extractive case, a word sequence is either deleted or retained. We may, however, want to retain the meaning of the sequence while rendering the sentence shorter, and this is precisely what our model can achieve, e.g., by allowing substitutions. As far as grammaticality is concerned, our abstractive model is numerically better than the extractive baseline but the difference is not statistically significant. Note that our model has to work a lot harder than the baseline to preserve grammaticality since we allow arbitrary rewrites which may lead to agreement or tense mismatches, and selectional preference violations. The scope for errors is greatly reduced when performing solely deletions.

Finally, both the abstractive and extractive outputs are perceived as significantly worse than the gold standard both in terms of grammaticality and importance ($\alpha < 0.01$). This is not surprising: human-authored compressions are more fluent and tend to omit genuinely superfluous information. This is also mirrored in the compression rates shown in Table 4. When compressing, humans employ not only linguistic but also world knowledge which is not accessible to our model. Although the system can be forced to match the human compression rate, the grammaticality and information content both suffer. More sophisticated features could allow the system to narrow this gap.

O: Kurtz came from Missouri, and at the age of 14, hitch-hiked to Los Angeles seeking top diving coaches. E: Kurtz came from Missouri, and at 14, hitch-hiked to Los Angeles seeking top diving coaches. A: Kurtz hitch-hiked to Los Angeles seeking top diving coaches. G: Kurtz came from Missouri, and at 14, hitch-hiked to Los Angeles seeking diving coaches.
O: The scheme was intended for people of poor or moderate means. E: The scheme was intended for people of poor means. A: The scheme was planned for poor people. G: The scheme was intended for the poor.
O: He died last Thursday at his home from complications following a fall, said his wife author Margo Kurtz. E: He died last at his home from complications following a fall, said wife, author Margo Kurtz. A: His wife author Margo Kurtz died from complications after a decline. G: He died from complications following a fall.
O: But a month ago, she returned to Britain, taking the children with her. E: She returned to Britain, taking the children. A: But she took the children with him. G: But she returned to Britain with the children.

Table 5: Compression examples including human and system output (O: original sentence, E: Extractive model, A: Abstractive model, G: gold standard)

We next examined the output of our system in more detail by recording the number of substitutions, deletions and insertions it performed on the test data. Deletions accounted for 67% of rewrite operations, substitutions for 27%, and insertions for 6%. Interestingly, we observe a similar ratio in the human compressions. Here, deletions are also the most common rewrite operation (69%) followed by substitutions (24%), and insertions (7%). The ability to perform substitutions and insertions increases the compression potential of our system, but can also result in drastic meaning changes. In most cases (63%) the compressions produced by our system did not distort the meaning of the original. Humans are clearly better at this, 96.5% of their compressions were meaning preserving.

We illustrate example output of our system in Table 5. For comparison we also present the gold standard compressions and baseline output. In the first sentence the system rendered *Kurtz* the subject of *hitch-hiked*. At the same time it deleted the verb and its adjunct from the first conjunct (*came from Missouri*) as well as the temporal modifier *at the age of 14* from the second conjunct. The second sentence shows some paraphrasing: the verb *intended* is substituted with *planned* and *poor* is now modifying *people* rather than *means*. In the third example, our system applies multiple rewrites. It deletes *last Thursday at his home*, moves *wife author Margo Kurtz* to the subject position, and substitutes *fall* with *decline*. Unfortunately, the compressed sentence expresses a rather different meaning from the original. It is not Margo Kurtz who died but her husband. Finally, our last sentence illustrates a counter-intuitive substitution, the pronoun *her* is rewritten as *him*. This is because they share the French translation *lui* and thus pivoting learns to replace the less common word (in legal corpora) *her* with *him*. This problem could be addressed by pivoting over multiple bitexts with different foreign languages.

Possible extensions and improvements to the current model are many and varied. Firstly, as hinted at above, the model would benefit from extensive feature engineering, including source conditioned features and ngram features besides the LM. A richer grammar would also boost performance. This could be found by pivoting over more bitexts in many foreign languages or making use of existing or paraphrase corpora. Finally, we plan to apply the model to other paraphrasing tasks including fully abstractive document summarisation (Daumé III and Marcu, 2002).

Acknowledgements

The authors acknowledge the support of EPSRC (grants GR/T04540/01 and GR/T04557/01). Special thanks to Phil Blunsom, James Clarke and Miles Osborne for their insightful suggestions.

References

C. Bannard, C. Callison-Burch. 2005. Paraphrasing with bilingual parallel corpora. In *Proceedings of the 43rd ACL*, 255–262, Ann Arbor, MI.

R. Barzilay. 2003. *Information Fusion for Multi-Document Summarization: Praphrasing and Generation*. Ph.D. thesis, Columbia University.

D. Bikel. 2002. Design of a multi-lingual, parallel-processing statistical parsing engine. In *Proceedings of the HLT*, 24–27, San Diego, CA.

J. Carroll, G. Minnen, D. Pearce, Y. Canning, S. Devlin, J. Tait. 1999. Simplifying text for language impaired readers. In *Proceedings of the 9th EACL*, 269–270, Bergen, Norway.

D. Chiang. 2007. Hierarchical phrase-based translation. *Computational Linguistics*, 33(2):201–228.

J. Clarke. 2008. *Global Inference for Sentence Compression: An Integer Linear Programming Approach*. Ph.D. thesis, University of Edinburgh.

T. Cohn, M. Lapata. 2007. Large margin synchronous generation and its application to sentence compression. In *Proceedings of the EMNLP/CoNLL*, 73–82, Prague, Czech Republic.

S. Corston-Oliver. 2001. Text Compaction for Display on Very Small Screens. In *Proceedings of the NAACL Workshop on Automatic Summarization*, 89–98, Pittsburgh, PA.

H. Daumé III, D. Marcu. 2002. A noisy-channel model for document compression. In *Proceedings of the 40th ACL*, 449–456, Philadelphia, PA.

J. Eisner. 2003. Learning non-isomorphic tree mappings for machine translation. In *Proceedings of the ACL Interactive Poster/Demonstration Sessions*, 205–208, Sapporo, Japan.

M. Galley, K. McKeown. 2007. Lexicalized Markov grammars for sentence compression. In *Proceedings of the NAACL/HLT*, 180–187, Rochester, NY.

M. Galley, M. Hopkins, K. Knight, D. Marcu. 2004. What's in a translation rule? In *Proceedings of the HLT/NAACL*, 273–280, Boston, MA.

H. Jing. 2000. Sentence reduction for automatic text summarization. In *Proceedings of the ANLP*, 310–315, Seattle, WA.

T. Joachims. 2005. A support vector method for multivariate performance measures. In *Proceedings of the 22nd ICML*, 377–384, Bonn, Germany.

K. Knight, D. Marcu. 2002. Summarization beyond sentence extraction: a probabilistic approach to sentence compression. *Artificial Intelligence*, 139(1):91–107.

P. Liang, B. Taskar, D. Klein. 2006. Alignment by agreement. In *Proceedings of the HLT/NAACL*, 104–111, New York, NY.

C.-Y. Lin. 2003. Improving summarization performance by sentence compression — a pilot study. In *Proceedings of the 6th International Workshop on Information Retrieval with Asian Languages*, 1–8, Sapporo, Japan.

R. McDonald. 2006. Discriminative sentence compression with soft syntactic constraints. In *Proceedings of the 11th EACL*, 297–304, Trento, Italy.

K. Papineni, S. Roukos, T. Ward, W.-J. Zhu. 2002. BLEU: a method for automatic evaluation of machine translation. In *Proceedings of the 40th ACL*, 311–318, Philadelphia, PA.

C. Quirk, C. Brockett, W. Dolan. 2004. Monolingual machine translation for paraphrase generation. In *Proceedings of the EMNLP*, 142–149, Barcelona, Spain.

A. Stolcke. 2002. SRILM – an extensible language modeling toolkit. In *Proceedings of the ICSLP*, Denver, CO.

B. Taskar, C. Guestrin, D. Koller. 2003. Max margin Markov networks. In *Proceedings of NIPS 16*.

I. Tsochantaridis, T. Joachims, T. Hofmann, Y. Altun. 2005. Large margin methods for structured and interdependent output variables. *Journal of Machine Learning Research*, 6:1453–1484.

J. Turner, E. Charniak. 2005. Supervised and unsupervised learning for sentence compression. In *Proceedings of 43rd ACL*, 290–297, Ann Arbor, MI.

V. Vandeghinste, Y. Pan. 2004. Sentence compression for automated subtitling: A hybrid approach. In *Proceedings of the ACL Workshop on Text Summarization*, 89–95, Barcelona, Spain.

Mind the Gap: Dangers of Divorcing Evaluations of Summary Content from Linguistic Quality

John M. Conroy
IDA/Center for Computing Sciences
Bowie, Maryland, USA
conroy@super.org

Hoa Trang Dang
Information Access Division
National Institute of Standards and Technology
Gaithersburg, Maryland, USA
hoa.dang@nist.gov

Abstract

In this paper, we analyze the state of current human and automatic evaluation of topic-focused summarization in the Document Understanding Conference main task for 2005-2007. The analyses show that while ROUGE has very strong correlation with responsiveness for both human and automatic summaries, there is a significant gap in responsiveness between humans and systems which is not accounted for by the ROUGE metrics. In addition to teasing out gaps in the current automatic evaluation, we propose a method to maximize the strength of current automatic evaluations by using the method of canonical correlation. We apply this new evaluation method, which we call ROSE (ROUGE Optimal Summarization Evaluation), to find the optimal linear combination of ROUGE scores to maximize correlation with human responsiveness.

1 Introduction

ROUGE (Lin, 2004) and its linguistically-motivated descendent, Basic Elements (BE) (Hovy et al., 2005), evaluate a summary by computing its overlap with a set of model (human) summaries; ROUGE considers lexical n-grams as the unit for comparing the overlap between summaries, while Basic Elements uses larger units of comparison based on the output of syntactic parsers. The ROUGE/BE toolkit has become the standard automatic method for evaluating the content of machine-generated summaries, but the correlation of these automatic scores with human evaluation metrics has not always been consistent.

In this paper, we analyze the state of current human and automatic evaluation of topic-focused summarization. Using the results of the Document Understanding Conference main task for 2005-2007 we explore the correlation between variants of ROUGE and the human metrics of responsiveness and linguistic quality. The analyses expose a number of challenges and several surprising results. In particular, while ROUGE has very strong correlation with responsiveness for both human and system summaries, there is a significant gap in responsiveness between humans and systems which is not accounted for by the ROUGE metrics. One cause of the gap is that many automatic summarizers truncate the last sentence of their summary, which shows significant reduction in the responsiveness score but does not result in a statistically significant drop in ROUGE scores. In addition to teasing out gaps in the current automatic evaluation, we propose a method to maximize the strength of current automatic evaluations by using the method of canonical correlation. We apply this new evaluation method, which we call ROSE (ROUGE Optimal Summarization Evaluation), to find the optimal linear combination of ROUGE metrics to maximize correlation with human responsiveness.

2 DUC 2005-2007 Task and Evaluation

The main task for DUC 2005-2007 was a complex question-focused summarization task that required summarizers to piece together information from multiple documents to answer a question or set of questions as posed in a DUC topic statement. The topic statement was a request for infor-

© 2008. Licensed under the *Creative Commons Attribution-Noncommercial-Share Alike 3.0 Unported* license (http://creativecommons.org/licenses/by-nc-sa/3.0/). Some rights reserved.

mation that could not be met by just stating a name, date, quantity, etc. The summarization task was the same for both human and automatic summarizers: Given a topic statement and a set of 25-50 relevant newswire documents, the summarization task was to create from the documents a brief, well-organized, fluent summary that answered the need for information expressed in the topic statement. The summary could be no longer than 250 words. Summaries over the size limit were truncated, and no bonus was given for creating a shorter summary.

NIST Assessors developed the DUC topics used as test data. There were 50 DUC topics each year in 2005-2006, and 45 topics in DUC 2007. Each year, 10 NIST assessors produced a total of 4 human summaries for each of the topics. The assessor who developed a particular topic always wrote one of the 4 summaries for that topic.

NIST manually assessed each summary for both content and readability. Readability was assessed using a set of linguistic quality questions; summary content was assessed using the pseudo-extrinsic measure of *content responsiveness*.

All summaries for a given topic were judged by a single assessor who was usually the same as the topic developer. In all cases, the assessor was one of the summarizers for the topic. Assessors first judged each summary for a topic for *readability*, assigning a separate score for each of 5 linguistic qualities; each summary for the topic was then judged for *content responsiveness*. Each of these manual evaluations was based on a five-point scale (1=very poor, 5=very good), resulting in 6 scores for each summary.

2.1 Evaluation of Readability

The readability of the summaries was assessed using five linguistic quality questions which measured qualities of the summary that *did not* involve comparison with a reference summary or DUC topic. The linguistic qualities measured were *Q1: Grammaticality, Q2: Non-redundancy, Q3: Referential clarity, Q4: Focus, and Q5: Structure and coherence*.

2.2 Evaluation of Content

NIST performed manual pseudo-extrinsic evaluation of peer summaries in the form of assessment of responsiveness. Responsiveness differs from other measures of summary content such as SEE coverage (Lin and Hovy, 2002) and Pyramid scores (Nenkova and Passonneau, 2004) in that it does not compare a peer summary against a set of known human summaries. Rather, the assessor is given a list of randomly ordered, unlabeled summaries (both human and system-generated) for a topic, and must assign a responsiveness score to each summary (after having read all the summaries first).

In DUC 2005-2007, NIST assessors assigned a *content* responsiveness score to each summary; content responsiveness indicated the amount of information in the summary that helped to satisfy the information need expressed in the topic statement. For content responsiveness, the linguistic quality of the summary was to play a role in the assessment only insofar as it interfered with the expression of information and reduced the amount of information that was conveyed.

In DUC 2006, assessors assigned an additional *overall* responsiveness score, which was based on both information content and readability. Assessors judged overall responsiveness only *after* judging all their topics for readability and content responsiveness; however, they were not given direct access to these previously assigned scores, but were told to give their "gut" reaction to the overall responsiveness of each summary.

The content responsiveness score provides a coarse manual measure of information coverage; overall responsiveness reflects a combination of readability and content. Content responsiveness was largely responsible for determining how assessors perceived the overall quality of a summary, but readability also played an important role. While poor readability could downgrade the overall responsiveness of a summary that had very good content responsiveness, very good readability could sometimes bolster the overall responsiveness score of a less information-laden summary (Dang, 2006). Attempts at greater readability in 2006 paid off among the peers with the best overall responsiveness scores. However, the automatic peers generally had poor readability, and the average overall responsiveness for each peer was generally much lower than its average content responsiveness.

In addition to the human assessment of responsiveness, NIST computed three "official" automatic scores using ROUGE and Basic Elements: ROUGE-2, ROUGE-SU4, and ROUGE-BE recall. For the BE evaluation, summaries were parsed with Minipar (Lin, 2005), and BE-F were extracted and matched using the Head-Modifier criterion. Jackknifing was used for each $[peer, topic]$ pair so that human and automatic peers could be compared.

3 An Analysis of the Metrics

Figure 1 shows the average scores for each summarizer for DUC 2005, 2006, and 2007. For each year we report the Pearson correlation coefficient for ROUGE-2, ROUGE-SU4, and ROUGE-BE (denoted ρ_{R2}, ρ_{SU4} and ρ_{BE}), against content responsiveness. This correlation is computed including just the systems as the human summarizers are clearly distributed differently.[1] To highlight the trend in the correlation we fit the systems data using robust linear regression. This line could be used to extrapolate the system performance if ROUGE scores were to increase.

As seen in Figure 1, while both the manual and the automatic ROUGE scores of the human summarizers remained relatively constant over the years, the systems made significant progress in their automatic scores, with the top systems performing within statistical confidence of the human summarizers in the ROUGE metrics as reported by Conroy et al. (2007). While the content responsiveness scores of the systems also increased as a group over the years, all systems performed significantly worse than humans in content responsiveness as measured by Tukey's honestly significant difference criterion (Conroy et al., 2007). Thus, there is not only a gap in performance between humans and systems on this task as measured manually by content responsiveness, but there is also a "metric gap" in using any single variant of ROUGE to predict content responsiveness. This metric gap becomes more pronounced as system performance improves to the point where ROUGE is unable to distinguish between systems and humans.

We turn next to an analysis of sources of the performance gap and "metric gap". Responsiveness is a subjective measure, and because NIST uses the same humans both to generate abstracts and to evaluate the abstracts, there is the possibility that humans may give high scores to their own abstract

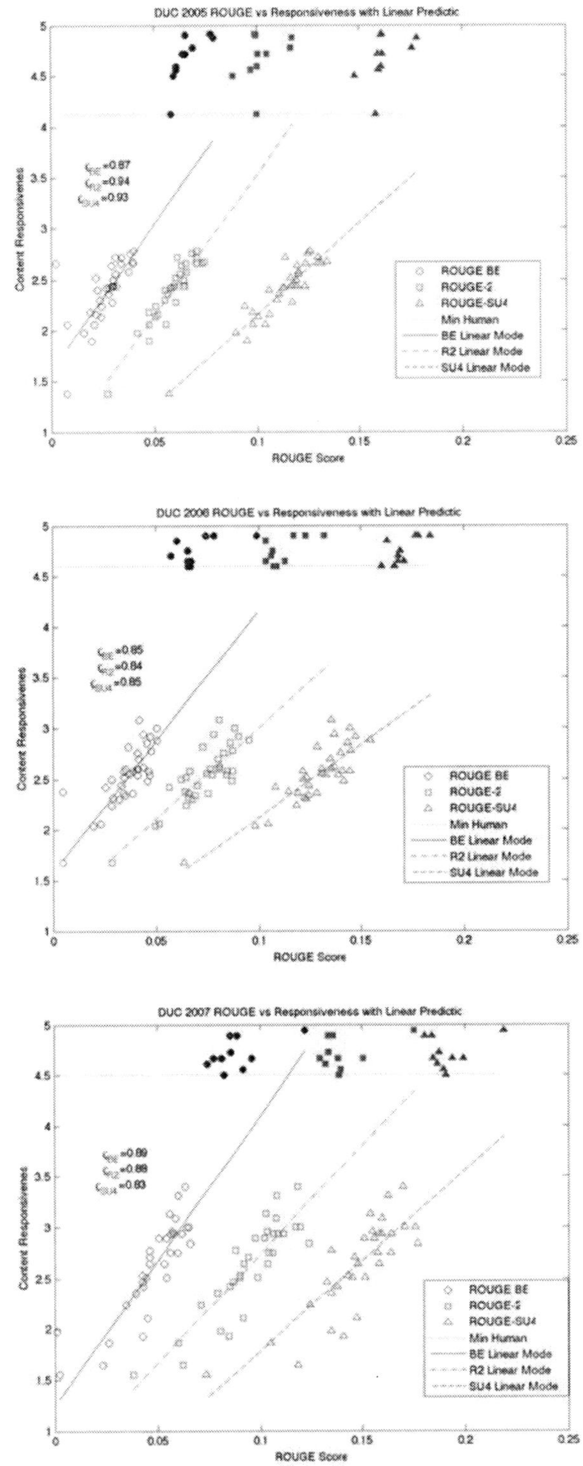

Figure 1: Scatter plot of average manual content responsiveness vs. automatic ROUGE scores (ROUGE-BE, ROUGE-2, and ROUGE-SU4) for humans (filled points) and systems (unfilled points), for DUC 2005-2007.

[1] One system each year in 2005-2007 had formatting problems in their summaries which resulted in abnormally low ROUGE-BE scores. While these systems are included in the scatter plot, they are not included in the correlation coefficient computation.

just because it not surprisingly "says what they would say." To test this hypothesis we performed one-side Student $T-$test, testing if the group of "Self-Assessed" abstracts had significantly higher responsiveness for DUC 2005-2007. Indeed, as Table 1 shows in each year and for both content and overall responsiveness, humans gave significantly higher scores to their own abstracts than the other human abstracts. This bias adds to the gap in content responsiveness between the human and automatic summarizers. Fortunately, this effect is dampened by the fact that NIST used 10 assessors and on average a human got to assess their own abstract only 25% of the time. It is noteworthy to add that at the Multi-lingual Summarization Evaluation of 2006, the human assessors were not the abstractors. This and other factors, notably an easier task, lead to there being no gap in performance between the human and the top scoring system (Schlesinger et al., 2008).

Table 1: Mean responsiveness assessment by humans for their own (Self) vs. Other abstracts.

Data	Self	Other	Signif
DUC 2005 Content	4.88	4.61	0.00277
DUC 2006 Content	4.96	4.68	0.00052
DUC 2006 Overall	4.94	4.67	0.00326
DUC 2007 Content	4.87	4.65	0.01931

We next examine the correlation between responsiveness and each of the five (manual) metrics for linguistic quality. We divide the correlation into three groups: Human (the group of 10 human summarizers), Systems (the automatic systems entered into DUC), and Combined (the union of these two groups). Table 2 gives the Pearson correlation coefficient and the $p-$value of statistical significance between content responsiveness and each of the five linguistic quality questions for DUC 2005-2007. For DUC 2005 there is no significant correlation between the average score of a human or automatic summarizer on linguistic questions and the content responsiveness score. The fact that there is a significant correlation in the "Combined" case is primarily due to the fact that the human summarizers scored higher as a group than the systems in the content metric as well as the linguistic metrics.

In DUC 2006 and 2007, the linguistic question which rewards summaries for not having redundancy (Q2) has a significant *negative* correlation with content responsiveness in the group of systems. This negative correlation is due largely to the fact that a number of low scoring systems (including the baseline) have no significant redundancy. Rarely does any system have sentences which are near duplicates. However, many systems, even those with relatively high responsiveness scores, still suffer from clause level redundancy, much of it in the form of noun phrases for which a human summarizer would employ pronouns.

Table 3 gives additional correlations between *overall* responsiveness and the linguistic questions for DUC 2006. We contrast the correlations for DUC 2006 in Table 2 vs. those in Table 3. Not surprisingly, overall responsiveness, which intentionally penalizes summaries for linguistic problems, does correlate more strongly with the linguistic questions than content responsiveness. Also, we note that the DUC 2007 correlations for *content* responsiveness appear more like those for DUC 2006 *overall* responsiveness than the corresponding correlations for DUC 2006 content responsiveness. NIST did not have sufficient time in 2007 to perform an overall responsiveness evaluation. We hypothesize that the assessors, many of whom worked on DUC 2006, may have inadvertently taken linguistic quality into account more in 2007 than in 2006 for the content responsiveness, since only one measure was done in 2007.

Finally, it was hypothesized at the DUC 2006 workshop[2] that the human assessors penalize systems in content responsiveness which end with a sentence fragment, more than could be accounted for by the missing content of the sentence fragment. We tested the hypothesis by comparing the average grammaticality (Q1), content responsiveness, and ROUGE scores of the 15 systems in DUC 2007 that ended their summaries with a complete sentence, against the 17 systems whose summaries ended with a sentence fragment. Table 4 gives a summary of the results. As measured by a Student $T-$test, systems that ended their summaries with a complete sentence had significantly higher content responsiveness scores than those that did not; however, there was no significant difference in ROUGE scores. The table lists ROUGE-2 as an example; these results are consistent with both ROUGE-BE and ROUGE-SU4.

Because linguistic quality clearly influences content responsiveness, automatic methods of evaluating summary content that try to maximize

[2]Lucy Vanderwende, personal communication

Table 2: Correlation and p-values between Content Responsiveness and Linguistic Quality Questions, DUC 2005-2007

Year	Group	Q1 Grammar	Q2 Non-redund.	Q3 Refer. Clarity	Q4 Focus	Q5 Structure/Coherence
2005	Humans	-0.10(0.78)	0.03(0.94)	0.06(0.87)	0.23(0.53)	0.31(0.39)
2005	Systems	-0.05(0.79)	0.15(0.42)	0.19(0.29)	0.30(0.10)	0.08(0.66)
2005	Combined	0.72(0.00)	0.75(0.00)	0.87(0.00)	0.90(0.00)	0.91(0.00)
2006	Humans	0.26(0.47)	0.15(0.69)	0.04(0.91)	0.64(0.05)	0.40(0.26)
2006	Systems	0.33(0.05)	-0.38(0.03)	0.27(0.11)	0.41(0.01)	0.16(0.35)
2006	Combined	0.74(0.00)	0.68(0.00)	0.86(0.00)	0.87(0.00)	0.89(0.00)
2007	Humans	0.80(0.01)	0.73(0.02)	0.24(0.51)	0.57(0.09)	0.47(0.17)
2007	Systems	0.60(0.00)	-0.43(0.01)	0.59(0.00)	0.71(0.00)	0.49(0.00)
2007	Combined	0.77(0.00)	0.72(0.00)	0.85(0.00)	0.92(0.00)	0.90(0.00)

Table 3: Correlation and p-values between Overall Responsiveness and Linguistic Quality Questions, DUC 2006

Group	Q1 Grammar	Q2 Non-redund.	Q3 Refer. Clarity	Q4 Focus	Q5 Structure/Coherence
Humans	0.60(0.06)	0.27(0.45)	0.39(0.26)	0.74(0.01)	0.82(0.00)
Systems	0.49(0.00)	-0.23(0.19)	0.55(0.00)	0.64(0.00)	0.49(0.00)
Combined	0.77(0.00)	0.72(0.00)	0.89(0.00)	0.89(0.00)	0.93(0.00)

Table 4: Average scores of DUC 2007 systems ending with a complete sentence vs. those ending with a fragment.

Metric	Sentence	Fragment	Signif
Grammaticality	3.88	3.24	0.011
Content Resp.	2.79	2.46	0.021
ROUGE-2	0.098	0.092	0.408

correlation with content responsiveness should attempt to include some measures of linguistic quality. We hypothesize that different variants of ROUGE may capture different qualities of a summary; for example, ROUGE-1 may be a good indicator of the relevance of summary content, but ROUGE variants that take into account larger contexts may capture linguistic qualities of the summary. Hence, a combination of scores (including measures of linguistic quality) would be a better predictor of "content" responsiveness.[3] In the next section, we present a new evaluation metric that finds a linear combination of ROUGE metrics which, in general, has stronger correlation with content responsiveness than any of the current ROUGE metrics.

[3]An additional weakness in the automatic metrics, which we do not attempt to address in our current work, is their inability to adequately handle the generalizations that are often made in model summaries (Dang, 2006), which are abstractive as opposed to the extractive summaries of most systems.

4 ROSE: Un Melange de ROUGEs

We developed an automatic content evaluation model which combines multiple ROUGE scores using canonical correlation (Hotelling, 1935). Canonical correlation finds the linear combination of ROUGE scores that has maximum correlation with human responsiveness on a given data set. As this family of models is a "blend" of ROUGE scores we call this metric ROSE, for ROUGE Optimal Summarization Evaluation. We first apply canonical correlation for each year of DUC using a Monte Carlo method. We then report on preliminary experiments that use ROSE models from one year to predict content responsiveness in subsequent years.

4.1 Blending ROUGE Scoring with a Canonical Correlation Model

Suppose we are given a set of ROUGE scores and the corresponding content responsiveness scores.

We let a_{ij}, for $i = 1, ..., m$ and $j = 1, .., n$, be the ROUGE score of type j for the summarizer i, and b_i the human content evaluation metric. Canonical correlation finds an $n-$long vector x such that

$$x = \text{argmax } \rho(\sum_{j=1}^{n} a_{ij}x_j, b_i), \quad (1)$$

where $\rho(x, y)$ is the Pearson correlation between x and y. A similar approach has been used by Liu and Gildea (2007) in the application of machine translation metrics, where they use a gradient optimization method to solve the maximization problem.

Canonical correlation actually solves a more general correlation optimization problem, where the goal is to find two linear combinations of variables to maximize the correlation between two sub-spaces. In the application of document summarization, we may wish to consider a matrix B of human evaluation metrics where b_{ij} is the $j-$th human evaluation for the $i-$th summarizer. We could include, for example, content and overall responsiveness or linguistic questions. Here we solve for (x, y) in the equation below:

$$(x, y) = \text{argmax } \rho(\sum_{j=1}^{n} a_{ij}x_j, \sum_{j=1}^{k} b_{ij}y_j). \quad (2)$$

This maximization procedure can be solved via a generalized eigenvalue problem, which we computed in Matlab using a routine distributed by Borga (2000). For the case studied here, as given in Equation (1), the generalized eigenvalue reduces to a linear least squares problem.

To find strong canonical correlations we decided to explore a large space of metrics. To this end, we included in our optimization 7 ROUGE automatic metrics: ROUGE-1,2,3,4,L,SU4, and BE to predict content responsiveness and (for DUC 2006) overall responsiveness. As our analyses of the previous section indicated for DUC 2006 and 2007 there was a significant correlation between the linguistic questions and content responsiveness. We add questions 1 and 4 to our canonical correlation model to see to what extent these questions could improve the correlation with content responsiveness. While the linguistic questions evaluation scores are manually generated we combine them with the automatic methods of ROUGE in an attempt see to what extent these non-content scores can better model both content and overall responsiveness. Thus, in all we consider 9 variables to predict responsiveness. In order to perform an evaluation that would avoid over-fitting the data we used a Monte Carlo method of resampling to evaluate which of the $2^9 - 1 = 511$ combinations of variables (canonical variates) to include in the model. [4]

In each experiment of the Monte Carlo method we randomly held back 1/4 of the data (human and system summarizers) for testing and used 3/4 of the data to build a canonical variate model. We found 4000 random samples sufficient to achieve accuracy within at least 2 digits. For each of the canonical variate models, 4000 trials are performed and then the computed model is applied to the held-back portion of the data and its Pearson correlation and p-value is reported. These 4000 correlations (and p-values) are then used to estimate the median correlation for a canonical variate. The median is computed from the subset of 4000 experiments with statistically significant correlations on the testing data (95% confidence, a p-value less then 0.05). The canonical variate with the highest estimated median correlation is then compared with the best performing ROUGE method. We compare the best of 504=511-7 canonical variates with the best of the 7 ROUGE variants by using the Mann-Whitney U-test, which tests for equal medians.

The procedure is then repeated using only the systems to find the ROSE model that gives the best prediction for just machine summarizers.

Table 5 gives the results of the Monte Carlo experiments. In each case the best canonical variate and the estimated median correlation are reported over the set of ROUGE scores and the ROUGE scores in union with the linguistic questions. As these results are based on 4000 trials they are more reliable than the simple correlation analysis done using the three official DUC automatic metrics, ROUGE-2, SU4, and BE. We note, in particular, that occasionally ROUGE-1 and ROUGE-L were found to be the best predictor even when linguistic questions were allowed in the model. Not surprisingly, the human evaluation of overall responsiveness was harder to predict and the optimal variants included both linguistic questions 1 and 4.

The ROSE models give the best combinations

[4] We also removed one system each year that had a poor ROUGE-BE score due to formatting problems.

Table 5: Monte Carlo Results for Canonical Correlation Model. A * by a variant indicates that it differs significantly from the best single ROUGE correlation with a p-value of 10^{-7} or less as measured by a Mann Whitney U-test.

Year Metric	Summarizer	Best ROUGE	Corr.	ROSE_{ROUGE}	Corr.	$\text{ROSE}_{(ROUGE,Q)}$	Corr.
2005 Content	All	BE	0.976	R1,R2,R4,SU4,BE*	0.981	R1,R2,R3,RL,SU4,BE,Q4*	0.986
2005 Content	Systems	R2	0.939	R1,R2,RL	0.940	R2,RL,SU4,Q4	0.941
2006 Content	All	RL	0.928	R1,R2,R3,R4*	0.942	RL,Q1*	0.960
2006 Content	Systems	R1	0.900	R1	0.900	R1	0.900
2007 Content	All	BE	0.937	R1,R4,RL,BE	0.940	BE,Q4*	0.966
2007 Content	Systems	R3	0.906	RL,BE*	0.915	R1,RL,BE,Q1*	0.929
2006 Overall	All	BE	0.893	R1,R2,R3,R4*	0.913	R3,R4,Q1,Q4*	0.946
2006 Overall	Systems	RL	0.854	RL	0.854	R1,R3,SU4,Q1,Q4*	0.894

of ROUGE scores to give maximum correlation with the human judgement of content or overall responsiveness. The ROSE models based on just ROUGE for the automatic summarizers are an appropriate method to use to compare systems that did not compete in DUC with those that did.

4.2 Applying ROSE across the Years

To further evaluate the generality of the ROSE model we apply DUC 2005 canonical correlation models to DUC 2006 and DUC 2007, and similarly apply the DUC 2006 model to the DUC 2007 data. In these experiments we measure the stability of a ROSE model from one year to the next. (Note, we have also computed a model based on the combined data of DUC 2005 and DUC 2006 for use with DUC 2007 and these results are comparable to those presented.) Here, for simplicity, we restrict the ROSE model to use only the "official" ROUGE metrics to build a model based on a given year and then evaluate that model on a subsequent year. Table 6 gives results for ROSE models constructed from only ROUGE-2, ROUGE-SU4, ROUGE-BE, and content responsiveness to create the ROSE model for each year; results are also given for ROSE models ($\text{ROSE}_{+Q1,4}$) which also includes the linguistic questions on grammaticality (Q1) and focus (Q4).

The ROSE models built from only ROUGE scores had mixed results, sometimes performing worse than a single ROUGE score (e.g., the ROSE model trained on DUC 2005 and evaluated on DUC 2006), but in other cases performing as well as or better than single ROUGE scores. These preliminary results with ROSE illustrate the difficulty in finding a single canonical variate that can be used from year to year to build ROSE models based on previous years' data. We hypothesize that the task is made more difficult due to humans changing their criteria for judging content responsiveness over the years.

On the other hand, $\text{ROSE}_{+Q1,4}$ models that included the linguistic questions Q1 and Q4 always yielded the best correlation with content responsiveness both for the systems and for the group of combined systems and human summarizers.

5 Conclusions

We analyzed the results of the topic-focused summarization task using the data from DUC 2005-2007. Our main concern was to expose causes of the gap that currently exists between automatic and human evaluation of summary content. As the automatic ROUGE scores of system summaries approaches that of human summaries, the disparity between automatic and manual measures of summary content becomes a more important concern. We find that there is a slight bias in the human evaluation: humans give their own summaries significantly higher scores. Furthermore, the responsiveness metric appears to be time varying, i.e., the humans changed their standards for judging responsiveness over the years, making it difficult to use automatic scores from one year to predict responsiveness in another year.

Assessors naturally tend toward taking linguistic quality into account when assessing summaries. The instructions for assessing content responsiveness implicitly acknowledges this; what is surprising is the extent to which linguistic quality does influence content responsiveness. In particular, we demonstrated that content responsiveness in DUC 2006 and 2007 correlated with the linguistic quality questions of grammar (Q1) and focus (Q4), and that systems were significantly penalized in content responsiveness when their summary ended

Table 6: Correlation and p-values between content responsiveness and various metrics for each "Test" year of DUC. ROSE models were constructed using DUC data from "Train" year and evaluated on data from "Test" year.

Train/Test	Summarizer	R2	SU4	BE	Q1	Q4	ROSE	ROSE$_{+Q1,4}$
2005/2006	Humans	0.64(0.05)	0.69(0.03)	0.57(0.09)	0.26(0.47)	0.64(0.05)	0.59 (0.07)	0.61(0.06)
2005/2006	Systems	0.83(0.00)	0.85(0.00)	0.85(0.00)	0.33(0.06)	0.41(0.02)	0.83 (0.00)	0.85(0.00)
2005/2006	All	0.90(0.00)	0.88(0.00)	0.90(0.00)	0.74(0.00)	0.87(0.00)	0.90 (0.00)	0.93(0.00)
2005/2007	Humans	0.41(0.24)	0.26(0.47)	0.55(0.10)	0.80(0.01)	0.57(0.09)	0.53 (0.12)	0.57(0.09)
2005/2007	Systems	0.88(0.00)	0.84(0.00)	0.89(0.00)	0.56(0.00)	0.68(0.00)	0.90 (0.00)	0.92(0.00)
2005/2007	All	0.91(0.00)	0.88(0.00)	0.92(0.00)	0.77(0.00)	0.92(0.00)	0.92 (0.00)	0.94(0.00)
2006/2007	Humans	0.41(0.24)	0.26(0.47)	0.55(0.10)	0.80(0.01)	0.57(0.09)	0.52(0.12)	0.67(0.03)
2006/2007	Systems	0.88(0.00)	0.84(0.00)	0.89(0.00)	0.56(0.00)	0.68(0.00)	0.89 (0.00)	0.90(0.00)
2006/2007	All	0.91(0.00)	0.88(0.00)	0.92(0.00)	0.77(0.00)	0.92(0.00)	0.92(0.00)	0.96(0.00)

with a sentence fragment even though the automatic content measures did not show a statistically significant difference. The influence of linguistic quality on "content" responsiveness contributes to the evaluation gap that we see between ROUGE/BE and this coarse human measure of summary content.

Automatic methods of evaluating summary content that try to maximize correlation with content responsiveness should therefore attempt to include some measures of linguistic quality. We found that a blending of ROUGE scores using canonical correlation gave higher correlations with content and overall responsiveness. When the linguistic questions Q1 and Q4 were added to the ROSE model, correlations of up to 0.96 were observed. This result leads to a natural question: What automatic methods could be used to approximate the linguistic questions? The work of Barzilay and Lapata (2005) on local coherence might be a possible candidate for estimating focus (Q4), while an automatic parser could be run on the summaries and the induced score could be used as a surrogate for grammaticality (Q1).

References

Barzilay, Regina and Mirella Lapata. 2005. Modeling local coherence: An entity-based approach. In *Proceedings of the 43rd Annual Meeting of the Association for Computational Linguistics (ACL'05)*, pages 141–148, Ann Arbor, Michigan, June. Association for Computational Linguistics.

Borga, Magnus. 2000. Matlab function cca().

Conroy, John M., Judith D. Schlesinger, and Dianne P. O'Leary. 2007. CLASSY 2007 at DUC 2007. In *Proceedings of the Seventh Document Understanding Conference (DUC)*, Rochester, New York.

Dang, Hoa Trang. 2006. Overview of DUC 2006. In *Proceedings of the Sixth Document Understanding Conference (DUC)*, New York City, New York.

Hotelling, H. 1935. The most predictable criterion. *Journal of Educational Psychology*, 26:139–142.

Hovy, Eduard, Chin-Yew Lin, and Liang Zhou. 2005. Evaluating duc 2005 using Basic Elements. In *Proceedings of the Fifth Document Understanding Conference (DUC)*, Vancouver, Canada.

Lin, Chin-Yew and Eduard Hovy. 2002. Manual and automatic evaluation of summaries. In *Proceedings of the ACL-02 Workshop on Automatic Summarization*, Philadelphia, PA.

Lin, Chin-Yew. 2004. ROUGE: A package for automatic evaluation of summaries. In *Proceedings of the ACL-04 Workshop: Text Summarization Branches Out*, pages 74–81, Barcelona, Spain.

Lin, Dekang. 2005. A dependency-base method for evaluating broad-coverage parsers. In *Proceedings of the Nineteenth International Joint Conference on Artificial Intelligence (IJCAI)*, Edinburgh, Scotland.

Liu, Ding and Daniel Gildea. 2007. Source-language features and maximum correlation training for machine translation evaluation. In *Proceedings of the 2007 Meeting of the North American chapter of the Association for Computational Linguistics (NAACL-07)*.

Nenkova, Ani and Rebecca Passonneau. 2004. Evaluating content selection in summarization: The pyramid method. In *Proceedings of the Human Language Technology Conference of the North American Chapter of the Association for Computational Linguistics*, pages 145–152, Boston, MA.

Schlesinger, Judith D., Dianne P. O'Leary, and John M. Conroy. 2008. Arabic/English multi-document summarization with CLASSY—the past and the future. In *Conference on Intelligent Text Processing and Computational Linguistics 2008*. Lecture Notes in Computer Science, Springer-Verlag. to appear.

Hybrid processing for grammar and style checking

Berthold Crysmann♣, Nuria Bertomeu♠, Peter Adolphs♡, Dan Flickinger◇, Tina Klüwer♣♡

♣ Universität Bonn, Poppeldorfer Allee 47, D-53115 Bonn, {bcr,tkl}@ifk.uni-bonn.de
♠ Zentrum für Allgemeine Sprachwissenschaft, Berlin, nuria.bertomeu@dfki.de
♡ DFKI GmbH, Berlin, {peter.adolphs,kluewer}@dfki.de
◇ CSLI, Stanford University, danf@csli.stanford.edu

Abstract

This paper presents an implemented hybrid approach to grammar and style checking, combining an industrial pattern-based grammar and style checker with bidirectional, large-scale HPSG grammars for German and English. Under this approach, deep processing is applied selectively based on the error hypotheses of a shallow system. We have conducted a comparative evaluation of the two components, supporting an integration scenario where the shallow system is best used for error detection, whereas the HPSG grammars add error correction for both grammar and controlled language style errors.

1 Introduction

With the enormous amount of multilingual technical documentation produced by companies nowadays grammar and controlled language checking (henceforth: style checking) is becoming an application highly in demand. It is not only a helpful tool for authors, but also facilitates the translation of documents into foreign languages. Through the use of controlled language by the authors, documents can be automatically translated more successfully than with the use of free language. Style checking should make authors aware of the constructions which should not be used, as well as aiding in reformulating them. This can save a lot of translation costs for companies producing large amounts of mulitilingual documentation. Another application of grammar and style checking is the development of tutorial systems for learning a foreign language, as well as any kind of authoring system for non-native speakers.

Previous approaches to grammar and style checking can be divided into those based on finite state methods and those based on linguistically motivated grammars. To the former group belong e.g. the systems FLAG (Bredenkamp et al., 2000a; Bredenkamp et al., 2000b) and MultiLint (Haller, 1996; Schmidt-Wigger, 1998). The basic approach taken by such systems is the description of error patterns through finite state automata. The automata access the textual input enriched with annotations from shallow linguistic analysis components, such as part-of-speech tagging, morphology and chunking. In FLAG, for instance, the annotation delivered by the shallow components is integrated into a complex feature structure. Rules are defined as finite state automata over feature structures. The great advantages of such systems are their robustness and efficient processing, which make them highly suitable for real-life grammar and style checking applications. However, since shallow modules usually cannot provide a full syntactic analysis, the coverage of these systems is limited to error types not requiring a broader (non-local) syntactic context for their detection. Therefore their precision in the recognition of non-local errors is not satisfactory.

Another short-coming of most shallow approaches to grammar checking is that they typically do not provide error correction: owing to the absence of an integrated target grammar, generation of repairs cannot take the syntactic context into account: as a result, some of the repairs suggested by shallow systems are not globally well-formed.

Grammar-based error checking constitutes the other main strand in language checking technology. These systems are typically equipped with a model of target well-formedness. The main problem, when applied to the task of error checking is that the sentences that are the focus of a grammar checker are ideally outside the scope of the grammar. To address this problem, grammar-based checkers typically employ robustness techniques (Ravin, 1988; Jensen et al., 1993; Douglas, 1995; Menzel, 1998; Heinecke et al., 1998). The addition of robustness features, while inevitable for a grammar-based approach, has the disadvantage of considerably slowing down runtime performance. Another issue with purely grammar-based checking is related to the scarce distribution of actual errors: thus, most effort is spent on the processing of perfectly impeccable utterances. Finally, since coverage of real-world grammars is never perfect, these system also have difficulty to distinguish be-

© 2008. Licensed under the *Creative Commons Attribution-Noncommercial-Share Alike 3.0 Unported* license (http://creativecommons.org/licenses/by-nc-sa/3.0/). Some rights reserved.

tween extragrammatical and truly ungrammatical sentences. Conversely, since grammars often overgenerate, a successful parse does not guarantee wellformedness either.

One of the two major robustness techniques used in the context of grammar-based language checking are constraint relaxation (see e.g. (Douglas, 1995; Menzel, 1998; Heinecke et al., 1998)), which is typically realised by means of modifications to the parser (e.g. relaxation levels, robust unification). An alternative approach is error anticipation where errors are explicitly modelled by means of grammar rules, so-called MAL-rules (McCoy et al., 1996). This approach has already been investigated with an HPSG grammar, the ERG (Copestake and Flickinger, 2000), in the scenario of a tutorial system for language learning by (Bender et al., 2004). We will follow this approach in the part of our hybrid system based on deep processing.

Finite state methods and linguistically motivated grammars are not only compatible, but also complementary. Shallow methods are robust and efficient, while deep processing based on grammars provides high precision and detail. With the focussed application of deep analysis in finite state based grammar and style checking systems, both coverage and precision can be improved, while the performance remains acceptable for real-world applications. The combination of shallow and deep components, hybrid processing, has already been investigated in several modular architectures, such as GATE (Gaizauskas et al., 1996), Whiteboard (Crysmann et al., 2002) and Heart-of-Gold (Callmeier et al., 2004). Moreover, the improvement in efficiency and robustness in deep processing together with methods for its efficient application makes the employment of deep processing in real-world applications quite feasible. Hybrid processing has been used for applications such as information extraction and question answering. But to the best of our knowledge, the application of hybrid processing to grammar and style checking has not been previously investigated.

In this paper, we present an implemented prototype of a hybrid grammar and style checking system for German and English, called Checkpoint. As the baseline shallow system we have taken an industrial strength grammar and controlled language style checker, which is based on the FLAG technology. The deep processing platform used in the project is the PET parser (Callmeier, 2000) operating on wide-coverage English and German HPSG grammars, the English Resource Grammar (ERG) (Copestake and Flickinger, 2000) and the German Grammar (GG) (Müller and Kasper, 2000; Crysmann, 2005; Crysmann, 2007), respectively. The ERG and the GG have been developed for over 15 years and have already been used as deep processing engines in the Heart-of-Gold hybrid processing platform. We have developed an approach for the selective application of deep processing based on the error hypotheses of the shallow system. Error detection in the deep system follows a MAL-rule approach. In order to compare the benefits of the selective application of deep processing with its nonselective application, we have developed two scenarios: one parallel and one integrated. While the parallel (nonselective) scenario enables improvement in both recall and precision, the integrated (selective) scenario only enables improvement in precision. However, the performance of the integrated approach is much better. We have also investigated several possibilities of integrating deep processing in the selective scenario. Since the HPSG grammars are suitable both for parsing and generation, the system can successfully provide both error corrections and paraphrases of stylistic errors. For the purpose of investigation, evaluation and statistical parse ranking, we have collected and annotated several corpora of texts from technical manuals. Finally, the approach has been evaluated regarding error detection and performance.

2 The approach

Checkpoint has two main goals: (a) improving the precision and recall of existing pattern-based grammar and style checking systems for error types whose detection requires considering more than the strictly local syntactic context; and (b) generating error corrections for both grammar and style errors. Accordingly, we have chosen to focus on certain error types based on the difficulties of the pattern-based system.

2.1 Anticipation of grammar errors

Grammar errors are detected by means of error anticipation rules, or MAL-rules. MAL-rules exactly model errors, so that erroneous sentences can be parsed by the grammar. For this purpose we enlarged two HPSG grammars for German, the GG, and English, the ERG, with MAL-rules for error types that were problematic for the pattern-based shallow system. For German the following phenomena have been handled: subject verb agreement (*subject_verb_agreement*), NP internal agreement (*NP_internal_agreement*), confusion of the complementiser "dass" with the homophonous pronoun or determiner "das" (*dass_das*), as well as editing errors, such as local and non local repetition of words (*repetitions*). Here follow some examples (taken from the FLAG error corpus (Becker et al., 2000), and *die tageszeitung 'taz'*, a German newspaper):

(1) Auch in AOL gibt es Newsgroups, die dieses Thema *diskutiert* [=diskutieren]. (FLAG)
Also in AOL are there newgroups, which (Pl) this topic *discuss* (Sg).
'There are also newsgroups in AOL which discuss this topic.'

(2) Ich habe dem *ganze* [=ganzen] Geschehen von meinem Sofa aus zugesehen. (FLAG)
I have the *whole* (wrong adj. form) events from my couch out watched.
'I have watched the whole events from my couch.'

(3) Vor allem im Süden ... *führten* [=haben] die Liberalen der MR einen heftigen Wahlkampf gegen die PS *geführt*. (taz, June 2007)
Above all in the south ... *led* (past tense) the liberals of the MR a hard election campaign against the PS *led* (past participle).
'Particularly in the south, the liberals of the MR led a hard election campaign against the PS.'

For English, MAL-rules for errors concerning subject verb agreement and missing determiners were implemented.

2.2 Detection of stylistic errors

Stylistic errors are grammatical constructions that are dispreferred in a particular register or type of document. Sometimes certain constructions are not desirable because machine translation systems have problems dealing with them or because they prevent easy understanding. In such cases a controlled language approach is taken, where the problematic constructions are paraphrased into equivalent less problematic constructions. Since these constructions are grammatical they can be parsed and, thus, detected. A generation of a paraphrase is possible based on the semantic representation obtained through parsing. For German the following phenomena were handled: passive, future and implicit conditional sentences, as in the following example:

(4) Wartet man zulange, kriegt man keine Karten.
Waits one too long, gets one no tickets.
'If one waits too long one gets no tickets.'

Correct: Wenn man zulange wartet, kriegt man keine Karten.

For English we focussed on the following phenomena: passive (*avoid_passive*), future (*avoid_future*), modal verbs (*avoid_modal_verbs*), subjunctive (*avoid_subjunctive*), stand-alone deictic pronouns (*use_this_that_these_those_with_noun*) and clause order in conditional sentences (*condition_must_precede_action*).

2.3 Integrated vs. parallel scenarios

We have developed two integration scenarios: an integrated one and a parallel one. In the parallel scenario the pattern-based shallow system and the deep processing parser run independently of each other, that is, all sentences are parsed independent of whether the shallow system has found an error in them. In the integrated scenario the deep parser is only called for those sentences where the shallow system has detected some error of the type of those which Checkpoint is able to process (enumerated in subsection 2.1). The parallel scenario allows improvement in the recall of the shallow system, since Checkpoint can find errors that the shallow system has not found. In the integrated scenario, on the contrary, only the precision of the shallow system can be improved, since Checkpoint departs from the hypotheses of the shallow system. The integrated scenario, however, promises to perform better in time than the parallel scenario, since only a fraction of the whole text has to be scanned for errors. Moreover, the performance of the integrated system can also be improved with the selective activation of the MAL-rules that model the specific errors found by the shallow system. This greatly reduces the enormous search space of the parsing algorithms and the processing time resulting from the simultaneous processing of several MAL-rules.

The integration of the shallow system and the deep parser has been achieved through an extension of the PET parser that allows it to receive any kind of input information and integrate this into the chart. This preprocessing information can be, for example, part-of-speech tagging, morphology and lemmatisation, and already guides the parsing process. It allows, for instance, recognition of unknown words or identification of the correct lexical entry in cases where there is ambiguity. An input format in terms of feature structures, the "Feature Structure Chart" (FSC) format, has been developed for this purpose (Adolphs et al., 2008). The shallow system, thus, produces a feature structure chart, based on the information delivered by the various shallow modules, and this information is given as input to the PET deep parser, which reads it and integrates it into the chart.

Error hypotheses from the shallow system are passed to the deep parser by means of specific features in the input feature structure (MAL-features) of every input token in the FSC, permitting selective activation of MAL-rules. To this end, the original FSC generated by the shallow system, which contains information on the part-of-speech, the lemma and morphological features such as number, gender and case, will be extended with MAL-features. These MAL-features correspond to the class of some MAL-rule in the grammar and have boolean values. Signs in the grammar are specified for these MAL-features. MAL-rules are defined such that they can only take as their daughters edges with a positive value for the corresponding MAL-feature. All information in the FSC input tokens is passed to the tokens in the chart through a feature called TOKEN in lexical items. Thus, error hypotheses are passed from the input tokens to the lexical items in the chart by stating that the values of the MAL-features in the lexical items are equal to the values of the MAL-features in the corresponding input tokens in the FSC.

The values of the MAL-features are obtained by checking the error report delivered by the shallow system. For certain errors detected by the shallow system there is a mapping to MAL-features. The value of a MAL-feature will be set to "+" if the shallow system has found the corresponding error. The rest of the MAL-features can be set to "bool" if we want to allow other MAL-rules to fire (which can improve recall, but increases ambiguity and, consequently, has a negative effect on performance). The values of the rest of the MAL-features can also be set to "-", if we want to prevent other MAL-rules from firing (which allows improvement only in precision, but limits ambiguity and, consequently, results in better performance). There is also the possibility of activating the relevant MAL-features only for those tokens which are, according to the shallow system, within the error span, instead of activating the MAL-features for all tokens in the erroneous sentence.

2.4 Generation of corrections and paraphrases

One of the advantages of using deep processing in grammar and style checking is the possibility of generating corrections and paraphrases which obey the constraints imposed by the syntactic context. Since the HPSG grammars that we are using are suitable both for parsing and generation, this is straightforward. Robust parsing delivers as output a semantic representation in the Minimal Recursion Semantics formalism (MRS) (Copestake et al., 2006) of the sentence which can be used for generation with the LKB (Carroll et al., 1999).

The MAL-rules directly assign well-formed semantic representations from which a correct surface string can be generated. In the case of stylistic errors, transfer rules are used to generate the desired paraphrase, using MRS-to-MRS mapping rules modelled on the semantic transfer-based machine translation approach of (Lœnning et al., 2004).

We identified two areas where generation of repairs will actually provide a considerable added value to a grammar checking system: first, for non-native speakers, simple highlighting of the error location is often insufficient, since the user may not be familiar with the rules of the language. Second, some areas, in particular stylistic ones may involve considerable rearrangement of the entire sentence. In these cases, generation of repairs and paraphrases can reduce editing cost and also minimise the issue of editing errors associated with non-local phenomena.

The generator and HPSG grammars we use are able to provide a range of realisations for a given semantic input. As a result, realisation ranking is of utmost importance. In order to select repairs which are both smooth and maximally faithful to the input, modulo the error site, of course, we combined two methods: a discriminative PCFG-model trained on a generation treebank, enhanced by an n-gram language model, cf. (Velldal and Oepen, 2005), and an alignment approach that chooses the most conservative edit from a set of input realisations. As our similarity measure, we employed a variant of BLEU score (NEVA), suggested in (Forsbom, 2003). The probabilistic ranking models we trained achieve an exact match accuracy of 73% for both English (Velldal and Oepen, 2005) and German (as evaluated on the subset of TiGer the error corpus was based on).

3 Error corpora

In order to learn more about the frequencies of the different error types, to induce statistical models that allow us to obtain the best parse in the domain of technical manuals and to evaluate our implemented approach to grammar and style checking, we collected and manually annotated corpora from the domain of technical documentation.

Since errors in pre-edited text tend to be very scarcely distributed, manual annotation is quite costly. As a result, instance of certain well-known error types cannot be tested in a greater variety of linguistic environments. To overcome this problem, we semi-automatically derived an additional error corpus from a treebank of German.

English For purposes of evaluation in a real world scenario, we constructed a corpus for English, consisting of 12241 sentences (169459 words) from technical manuals. The corpus was semi-automatically annotated with several types of grammar and style errors. For this purpose annotation guidelines were developed, which contained the description of the errors together with examples of each and their possible corrections. The annotation took place in two phases. First, we wanted to find out about the precision of the shallow system, so we ran the shallow system over the data. This resulted in an annotation for each error found consisting of the erroneous sentence, the error span and the type of error. The annotators, who were native speakers, then decided whether the errors had been correctly detected. In the second phase, we aimed to create a gold standard, so as to be able to evaluate both the shallow system and Checkpoint regarding recall and precision. For this purpose, we extracted the errors that had been annotated as correctly detected in the previous phase and the annotators only had to find the non-detected errors in the rest of the corpus. For the latter, they also marked the span and identified the error type.

Subsets of these two datasets were treebanked with the corresponding HPSG grammars. We employed the treebanking methodology developed for Redwoods (Oepen et al., 2002), which involved first parsing a corpus and recording for each item the alternative analyses (the parse forest) assigned by the grammar, then manually identifying the correct analysis (if available) within that parse forest. This approach provides both a gold standard syntactic/semantic analysis for each parsed item, and positive and negative training data for building an accurate statistical model for automatic parse selection.

German For German, we pursued a complementary approach towards corpus construction. Here the focus lay on creating a test and evaluation corpus that provided instances of common error types in a variety of linguistic contexts. Since manual error annotation is highly costly, owing to scarce error distributions in pre-edited text, we chose to automatically derive an error corpus from an existing treebank resource. As for the error types, we focussed on those errors which are arguably performance errors, as e.g. missing final consonants in inflectional endings, the confusion of homophonous complementiser and relative pronoun, or else, editing errors, such as local and non-local duplicates.

We introduced instances of errors in a subcorpus of the German TiGer treebank (Brants et al., 2002), nicknamed TiG-ERR, consisting of 77275 words (5652 sentences) from newspaper texts. All the sentences in this subcorpus were parsable, so that an evaluation of Checkpoint in the ideal situation of 100% coverage could be carried out. The artificially introduced errors were of the following types: *subject_verb_agreement*, *NP_internal_agreement*, *dass/das*, and *repetitions*, all of them already illustrated with examples in section 2.1.

Additionally, we annotated a corpus of technical documents for these error types to estimate the distribution of these error types in pre-edited text.

4 Error models

In order to construct a statistical parse-ranking model which could determine the intended use of a MAL-rule in the analysis of a sentence where the grammar produced analyses both with and without MAL-rules, the English treebank was constructed using the version of the ERG which included the MAL-rules. 4000 sentences from the English corpus were presented to the parser, of which 86.8% could be parsed with the ERG, and of these, the annotators found an intended analysis for 2500 sentences, including some which correctly used MAL-rules. From these annotations, a customised parse selection model was computed and then used in parsing all of the corpus, this time recording only the one analysis determined to be most likely according to this model. We also compared accuracy of error detection based on this new model with the accuracy of a pre-existing parse-selection model trained on tourism data for LOGON, and confirmed that the new model indeed improved over the old one.

For German, we have not created a specific statistical model yet, but, instead, we have used an existing parse selection model (Crysmann, 2008) and combined it with some heuristics which enable us to select the best error hypothesis. The heuristics check for each parsed sentence whether there is an analysis containing no MAL-rule. If there is one and this is not ranked as the best parse, it is moved to the first position in the parse list. As a result, we can eliminate a high percentage of false alarms.

5 Evaluation results

We have evaluated the English and the German versions of Checkpoint against the corpora described in section 3.

German For German we have taken as a test corpus standard the TiG-ERR subcorpus containing the automatically introduced errors, and have parsed all its sentences. The following table shows the frequencies of the different types of handled errors in the corpus of technical manuals, the FLAG error corpus (Becker et al., 2000), and in the TiG-ERR corpus. The electronic version of the FLAG corpus consists of 14,492 sentences, containing 1,547 grammar or style errors.

ERROR TYPE	MANUALS	FLAG	TiG-ERR
NP_internal_agr	119	180	2258
subject_verb_agr	17	63	748
dass/das	1	152	75
repetitions	19	n/a	2571

Table 1: Frequencies of the error types for German

The following charts show the values for recall and precision for the shallow system and Checkpoint. As you can see, Checkpoint improves the recall for the error types *subject_verb_agreement* and *NP_internal_agreement*, whereas the precision remains more or less the same. For the error type *dass/das* Checkpoint improves both recall and precision. For the error type *repetitions*, which is only partially handled by the spell checker in the shallow system, Checkpoint reaches considerable recall and precision values.

Deep processing on average improves the recall of the shallow system by 21% and the precision remains equal at 0.83. According to the error frequencies in the corpus of technical manuals, deep processing would improve the recall of the shallow system by only 1.7%, since the error types *subject_verb_agreement*, *NP_internal_agreement* and *dass/das* only make up 6.57% of the total amount of annotated errors. However, as we found out later, the corpora of technical manuals consist of texts that have already undergone correction, so the errors are very sparse.

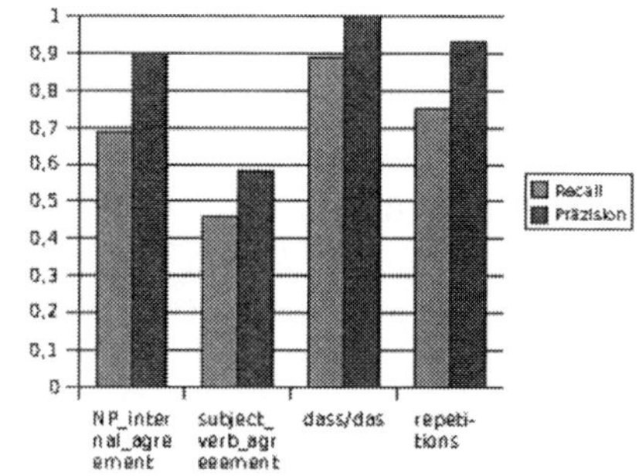

Figure 1: Checkpoint values for recall and precision for German

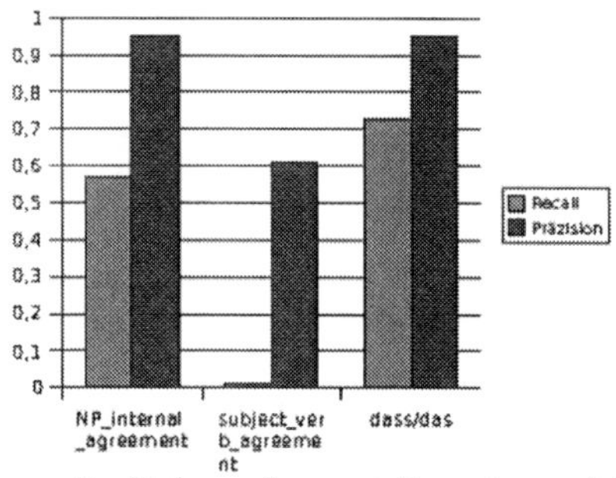

Figure 2: Values for recall and precision for the shallow system for German

Through the MAL-rules the coverage of the GG on the TiG-ERR corpus increased to 85% - 95%, whereas without the MAL-rules the coverage was 10%. This 10% coverage included overgeneration by the grammar, as well as sentences that, after the automatic insertion of errors, still remained grammatical, although they didn't express the intended meaning any more.

The performance of the parallel and integrated scenarios was compared. The ambiguity of the MAL-rules, that is, the possibility of applying several MAL-rules to a unique error, considerably deteriorates the performance when processing sentences containing several errors. In a subcorpus containing *NP_internal_agreement* errors, the average processing time per sentence increases from 8.3 seconds with the selective activation of MAL-rules to 31.4 seconds with the activation of all MAL-rules. Particularly the MAL-rules modeling the error *subject_verb_agreement* are a source of ambiguity. If these MAL-rules are only selectively activated the average processing time per sentence decreases to 14.9 seconds.

Finally, we have evaluated the performance of the German grammar in the task of error correction, using non-local duplicates and adjectival agreement errors as a test bed. For these error types, the German HPSG grammar generated repairs for 85.4% of the detected non-local duplicates and 90% of the detected agreement errors.

English For English we have only implemented and evaluated the parallel scenario. The focus for English evaluation was the recognition of those stylistic errors whose correction requires a restructuring of the sentence, and the generation of the corresponding paraphrases. The recognition of such error types is not based on MAL-rules, but on certain already existing rules in the grammar. The approach was evaluated taking the manually annotated English corpus of technical manuals as a gold standard. The following table shows the frequencies of the error types handled by Checkpoint.

ERROR TYPE	OCCURRENCES
avoid_future	404
avoid_modal_verbs	657
avoid_passive	213

Table 2: Frequencies of the error types for English

The PET parser with the ERG reached 86.1% coverage on the full corpus. The following charts show the values for recall and precision for Checkpoint and the shallow system.

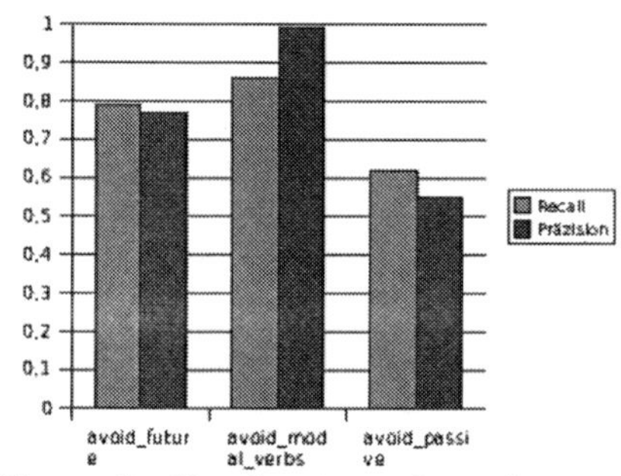

Figure 3: Checkpoint values for recall and precision for English

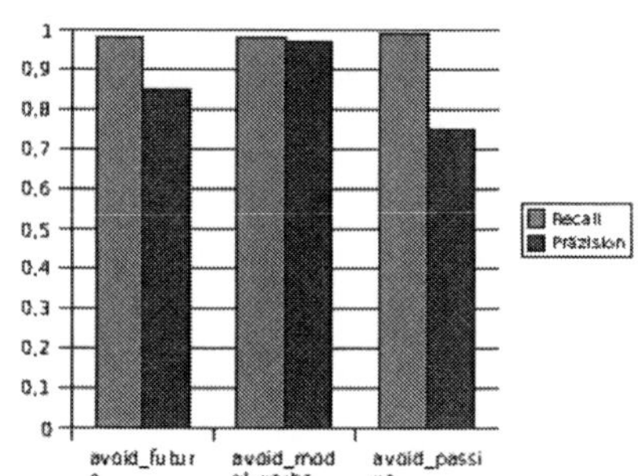

Figure 4: Values for recall and precision for the shallow system for English

As one can see, for the stylistic errors *avoid_future* and *avoid_modal_verbs*, Checkpoint reaches values which, although relatively high, are lower than the shallow system. In most cases a paraphrase for these errors can be constructed, so the improvement Checkpoint provides here is the generation of corrections. For the error type *avoid_passive* the precision is not so high, which is due in part to mistakes in the manual annotation. The passive sentences found by Checkpoint are actually passive sentences. However, these were not annotated as passives, because the annotators were told to annotate only those stylistic errors for which a paraphrase was possible. The same happens for stylistic errors like *avoid_subjunctive*, *use_this_that_these_those_with_noun* and *condition_must_precede_action*. In principle, Checkpoint is very good at finding these types of errors, but we cannot yet present a reliable evaluation here, since only those errors were annotated for which a paraphrase was possible. This approach is reasonable, since no error alarm should be produced when there is no other possibility of expressing the same. However, since we have not yet developed a method which allows us to automatically distinguish those cases for which a paraphrase is possible from those for which none is, we would need to annotate all occurrences of a phenomenon in the corpus, and introduce a further annotation tag for the paraphrase potential of the sentence.

Nevertheless, even if the grammar-based research prototype cannot beat the industrial pattern-based system in terms of f-measures, we still believe that the results are highly valuable in the context of our integrated hybrid scenario: Since the full reversibility of the ERG has already been established independently by (Velldal and Oepen, 2005), the combined system is able to generate error correction for a great proportion of the errors detected by the shallow component. This includes 80% and above for *avoid_future* and *avoid_modal_verbs*.

6 Summary and conclusions

In this paper we have presented an implemented approach to grammar and style checking based on hybrid processing. The hybrid system has two components: a shallow grammar and style checking system based on the FLAG technology, and the PET deep parser operating on linguistically motivated grammars for German and English. The German version of the hybrid system improves the recall and in certain cases the precision of the shallow system and generates error corrections. For English, the hybrid system in most cases successfully generates paraphrases of sentences containing stylistic errors. Although we only have explored some of the possibilities of integrating deep and shallow processing for the grammar and style checking application, these results speak for the feasibility of using hybrid processing in this task.

We have developed an integrated strategy which forwards the output of the shallow system, including both the output from several pre-processing linguistic modules and the error hypotheses, as input to the deep parser. This procedure not only improves the robustness of the deep parser with the recognition of unknown words and reduces ambiguity by instantiating only those lexical items consistent with the hypotheses of the POS tagger or the morphology; but it also allows the selective application of grammar rules, which considerably reduces the search space for parsing and, consequently, improves performance. Based on the error hypotheses of the shallow system, the selective application of grammar rules is achieved by positing features in the Feature Structure Chart whose particular values are a pre-condition for MAL-rules to apply. The improvement in performance suggests that this strategy can be extensible to parsing in general based on pre-processing components. Given the output of a chunker, for example, certain syntactic configurations can already be excluded. Having features whose values allow one to switch off certain rules not compatible with these configurations would considerably reduce the search space.

On the other hand, we have run the two modules independently from each other to find out how the recall of the shallow system can be improved by deep processing. The fact that for several error types, such as *subject_verb_agreement* and *NP_internal_agreement*, recall can be considerably improved suggests that, in order not to parse all sentences, the shallow system should send an error hypothesis to the deep system when finding particular syntactic configurations which may indicate the occurrence of such errors. In this way, such error hypotheses, although not reliably detectable by the shallow system alone, could be confirmed or discarded with a focussed application of deep processing, which would not be as resource consuming as parsing every sentence.

One of the results of the experiment has been an on-line demonstration system. The running system shows that the different modules can be easily combined with each other. Our hybrid approach, however, is generic and portable. Although implemented for our specific baseline system, it can in principle be used with other shallow systems.

Acknowledgements

The research reported in this paper has been carried out as part of the DFKI project Checkpoint, running from February until November 2007. The project was funded by the ProFIT program of the Federal State of Berlin and the EFRE program of the European Union.

References

Adolphs P., S. Oepen, U. Callmeier, B. Crysmann, and B. Kiefer. 2008. Some Fine Points of Hybrid Natural Language Parsing. Proceedings LREC-2008, Marrakech, Morocco.

Becker M., A. Bredenkamp, B. Crysmann, and J. Klein. 2003. Annotation of error types for a German newsgroup corpus. In A. Abeillé, editor, *Treebanks. Building and Using Parsed Corpora*, number 20 in Text, Speech And Language Technology. Kluwer, Dordrecht.

Bender, E. M., D. Flickinger, S. Oepen, A. Walsh, and T. Baldwin. 2004. Arboretum: Using a precision grammar for grammar checking in call. In *InSTIL/ICALL symposium 2004. NLP and speech technologies in advanced language learning systems.* Venice, Italy.

Brants, T., S. Dipper, S. Hansen, W. Lezius, and G. Smith. 2002. The TIGER Treebank. In *Proceedings of the Workshop on Treebanks and Linguistic Theories.* Sozopol.

Bredenkamp, A., B. Crysmann and M. Petrea. 2000. Looking for errors: A declarative formalism for resource-adaptive language checking. In *Proceedings LREC-2000.* Athens, Greece.

Bredenkamp, A., B. Crysmann and M. Petrea. 2000. Building multilingual controlled language performance checkers. In *Proceedings of the CLAW 2000.* Seattle, WA.

Callmeier, U., A. Eisele, U. Schäfer, and M. Siegel. 2004. The Deepthought core architecture framework. In *Proceedings of LREC-2004*, 1205–1208, Lisbon, Portugal.

Callmeier, Ulrich. 2000. PET — a platform for experimentation with efficient HPSG processing techniques. *Natural Language Engineering* 6(1):99–108.

Carroll, John and Ann Copestake and Dan Flickinger and Victor Poznanski. 1999. An efficient chart generator for semi-lexicalist grammars. *Proceedings of ENLG*, pp. 86–95.

Copestake, A., and D. Flickinger. 2000. An open-source grammar development environment and broad-coverage english grammar using HPSG. In *Proceedings LREC-2000.* Athens, Greece.

Copestake, A., D. Flickinger, C. Pollard, and I. Sag. 2006. Minimal recursion semantics: an introduction. *Research on Language and Computation* 3(4):281–332.

Crysmann, B., A. Frank, B. Kiefer, S. Müller, G. Neumann, J. Piskorski, U. Schäfer, M. Siegel, H. Uszkoreit, F. Xu, M. Becker, and H.-U. Krieger. An integrated architecture for shallow and deep processing. In *Proceedings of ACL 2002*, University of Pennsylvania, Philadelphia, 2002.

Crysmann B. 2005. Relative clause extraposition in German: An efficient and portable implementation. *Research on Language and Computation*, 3(1):61–82.

Crysmann B. 2007 Local ambiguity packing and discontinuity in German. In T. Baldwin, M. Dras, J. Hockenmaier, T. H. King, and G. van Noord, editors, *Proceedings of the ACL 2007 Workshop on Deep Linguistic Processing*, pages 144–151, Prague, Czech Republic.

Crysmann B. 2008. Parse Selection with a German HPSG Grammar. In S. Kübler and G. Penn, editors, *Proceedings of the ACL 2008 Workshop on Parsing German (PaGe)*, pages 9–15, Columbus, Ohio, USA.

Douglas, S. 1995. Robust PATR for error detection and correction. In A. Schoeter and C. Vogel (Eds.)*Nonclassical feature systems*, Vol. 10, pp. 139-156. Centre for Cognitive Science, University of Edinburgh.

Forsbom, E. 2003. Training a Super Model Look-Alike. *Proceedings of the MT Summit IX Workshop "Towards Systemizing MT Evaluation", pp. 29-36.*

Gaizauskas, R., H. Cunningham, Y. Wilks, P. Rodgers and K. Humphreys. 1996. GATE: An environment to support research and development in natural language engineering. In *Proceedings of the 8th IEEE international conference on tools with artificial intelligence.* Toulouse, France.

Jensen, K., G. E., Heidorn and S. D. Richardson (Eds.). 1993. Natural language processing: The PLNLP approach. Boston - Dordrecht - London.

Haller, J. 1996. MULTILINT: A technical documentation system with multilingual intelligence. In *Translating and the computer 18.* London.

Heinecke, J., J. Kunze, W. Menzel, and I. Schroeder. 1998. Eliminative parsing with graded constraints. In *Proceedings ACL/Coling 1998*, Vol. I, pp. 526-530. Universite de Montreal, Montreal, Quebec, Canada.

Lœnning J. T. , S. Oepen, D. Beermann, L. Hellan, J. Carroll, H. Dyvik, D. Flickinger, J. B. Johannessen, P. Meurer, T. Nordgård, V. Rosén and E. Velldal. 2004. LOGON. A Norwegian MT effort. In *Proceedings of the Workshop in Recent Advances in Scandinavian Machine Translation.* Uppsala, Sweden.

McCoy, K. F., C. A. Pennington, and L. Z. Suri. 1996. English error correction: A syntactic user model based on principled "mal-rule" scoring. In *Proceedings of UM-96, the Fifth International Conference on User Modeling*, pp. 59-66. Kona, Hawaii.

Menzel, W. 1998. Constraint satisfaction for robust parsing of natural language. In *Theoretical and Experimental Artificial Intelligence*, 10 (1), 77-89.

Müller, S., and W. Kasper. 2000. HPSG analysis of German. In W. Walster (Ed.), *Verbmobil: Foundations of Speech-to-Speech Translation*, 238–253 Springer, Berlin.

Oepen, S., K. Toutanova, S. Shieber, C. Manning, D. Flickinger and T Brants. 2002. The LinGO Redwoods Treebank. Motivation and Preliminary Applications. In *Proceedings of COLING 2002.* Taipei, Taiwan.

Ravin, Y. 1998. Grammar errors and style weaknesses in a text-critiquing system. In *IEEE Transactions on Communication*, 31 (3)

Schmidt-Wigger, A. 1998. Grammar and style checking for German. In *Proceedings of CLAW 98.* Pittsburgh, PA.

Velldal, E. and S. Oepen. 2005. Maximum entropy models for realization ranking. In *Proceedings of the 10th MT-Summit (X), Phuket, Thailand.*

KnowNet: Building a Large Net of Knowledge from the Web

Montse Cuadros
TALP Research Center, UPC
Barcelona, Spain
cuadros@lsi.upc.edu

German Rigau
IXA NLP Group, UPV/EHU
Donostia, Spain
german.rigau@ehu.es

Abstract

This paper presents a new fully automatic method for building highly dense and accurate knowledge bases from existing semantic resources. Basically, the method uses a wide-coverage and accurate knowledge-based Word Sense Disambiguation algorithm to assign the most appropriate senses to large sets of topically related words acquired from the web. KnowNet, the resulting knowledge-base which connects large sets of semantically-related concepts is a major step towards the autonomous acquisition of knowledge from raw corpora. In fact, KnowNet is several times larger than any available knowledge resource encoding relations between synsets, and the knowledge KnowNet contains outperform any other resource when is empirically evaluated in a common framework.

1 Introduction

Using large-scale knowledge bases, such as WordNet (Fellbaum, 1998), has become a usual, often necessary, practice for most current Natural Language Processing (NLP) systems. Even now, building large and rich enough knowledge bases for broad–coverage semantic processing takes a great deal of expensive manual effort involving large research groups during long periods of development. In fact, hundreds of person-years have been invested in the development of wordnets for various languages (Vossen, 1998). For example, in more than ten years of manual construction (from 1995 to 2006, that is from version 1.5 to 3.0), WordNet grew from 103,445 to 235,402 semantic relations[1]. But this data does not seem to be rich enough to support advanced concept-based NLP applications directly. It seems that applications will not scale up to work in open domains without more detailed and rich general-purpose (and also domain-specific) semantic knowledge built by automatic means. Obviously, this fact has severely hampered the state-of-the-art of advanced NLP applications.

However, the Princeton WordNet (WN) is by far the most widely-used knowledge base (Fellbaum, 1998). In fact, WordNet is being used world-wide for anchoring different types of semantic knowledge including wordnets for languages other than English (Atserias et al., 2004), domain knowledge (Magnini and Cavaglià, 2000) or ontologies like SUMO (Niles and Pease, 2001) or the EuroWordNet Top Concept Ontology (Álvez et al., 2008). It contains manually coded information about English nouns, verbs, adjectives and adverbs and is organized around the notion of a *synset*. A synset is a set of words with the same part-of-speech that can be interchanged in a certain context. For example, <*party, political_party*> form a synset because they can be used to refer to the same concept. A synset is often further described by a gloss, in this case: "an organization to gain political power" and by explicit semantic relations to other synsets.

Fortunately, during the last years the research community has devised a large set of innovative methods and tools for large-scale automatic acquisition of lexical knowledge from structured and unstructured corpora. Among others we can men-

© 2008. Licensed under the *Creative Commons Attribution-Noncommercial-Share Alike 3.0 Unported* license (http://creativecommons.org/licenses/by-nc-sa/3.0/). Some rights reserved.

[1] Symmetric relations are counted only once.

tion eXtended WordNet (Mihalcea and Moldovan, 2001), large collections of semantic preferences acquired from SemCor (Agirre and Martinez, 2001; Agirre and Martinez, 2002) or acquired from British National Corpus (BNC) (McCarthy, 2001), large-scale Topic Signatures for each synset acquired from the web (Agirre and de Lacalle, 2004) or knowledge about individuals from Wikipedia (Suchanek et al., 2007). Obviously, all these semantic resources have been acquired using a very different methods, tools and corpora. As expected, each semantic resource has different volume and accuracy figures when evaluated in a common and controlled framework (Cuadros and Rigau, 2006).

However, not all these large-scale resources encode semantic relations between synsets. In some cases, only relations between synsets and words have been acquired. This is the case of the Topic Signatures acquired from the web (Agirre and de Lacalle, 2004). This is one of the largest semantic resources ever built with around one hundred million relations between synsets and semantically related words [2].

A knowledge net or KnowNet (KN), is an extensible, large and accurate knowledge base, which has been derived by semantically disambiguating small portions of the Topic Signatures acquired from the web. Basically, the method uses a robust and accurate knowledge-based Word Sense Disambiguation algorithm to assign the most appropriate senses to the topic words associated to a particular synset. The resulting knowledge-base which connects large sets of topically-related concepts is a major step towards the autonomous acquisition of knowledge from raw text.

Table 1 compares the different volumes of semantic relations between synset pairs of available knowledge bases and the newly created KnowNets[3].

Varying from five to twenty the number of processed words from each Topic Signature, we created automatically four different KnowNet versions with millions of new semantic relations between synsets. In fact, KnowNet is several times larger than WordNet, and when evaluated empirically in a common framework, the knowledge it contains outperforms any other semantic resource.

After this introduction, section 2 describes the Topic Signatures acquired from the web. Section

[2]Available at http://ixa.si.ehu.es/Ixa/resources/sensecorpus

[3]These KnowNet versions are available at http://adimen.si.ehu.es

Source	#relations
Princeton WN3.0	235,402
Selectional Preferences from SemCor	203,546
eXtended WN	550,922
Co-occurring relations from SemCor	932,008
New KnowNet-5	231,163
New KnowNet-10	689,610
New KnowNet-15	1,378,286
New KnowNet-20	2,358,927

Table 1: Number of synset relations

3 presents the approach we followed for building highly dense and accurate knowledge bases from the Topic Signatures. In section 4, we present the evaluation framework used in this study. Section 5 describes the results when evaluating different versions of KnowNet and finally, section 6 presents some concluding remarks and future work.

2 Topic Signatures

Topic Signatures (TS) are word vectors related to a particular topic (Lin and Hovy, 2000). Topic Signatures are built by retrieving context words of a target topic from a large corpora. This study considers word senses as topics. Basically, the acquisition of TS consists of:

- acquiring the best possible corpus examples for a particular word sense (usually characterizing each word sense as a query and performing a search on the corpus for those examples that best match the queries)
- building the TS by selecting the context words that best represent the word sense from the selected corpora.

The Topic Signatures acquired from the web (hereinafter TSWEB) constitutes one of the largest semantic resource available with around 100 million relations (between synsets and words) (Agirre and de Lacalle, 2004). Inspired by the work of (Leacock et al., 1998), TSWEB was constructed using monosemous relatives from WN (synonyms, hypernyms, direct and indirect hyponyms, and siblings), querying Google and retrieving up to one thousand snippets per query (that is, a word sense), extracting the salient words with distinctive frequency using TFIDF. Thus, TSWEB consist of large ordered lists of words with weights associated to the polysemous nouns of WN1.6. The number of constructed topic signatures is 35,250 with an average size per signature of 6,877 words.

tammany#n	0.0319
federalist#n	0.0315
whig#n	0.0300
missionary#j	0.0229
Democratic#n	0.0218
nazi#j	0.0202
republican#n	0.0189
constitutional#n	0.0186
conservative#j	0.0148
socialist#n	0.0140

Table 2: TS of party#n#1 (first 10 out of 12,890 total words)

When evaluating TSWEB, we used at maximum the first 700 words while for building KnowNet we used at maximum the first 20 words.

For example, table 2 presents the first words (lemmas and part-of-speech) and weights of the Topic Signature acquired for party#n#1[4].

3 Building highly connected and dense knowledge bases

We acquired by fully automatic means highly connected and dense knowledge bases by disambiguating small portions of the Topic Signatures obtained from the web, increasing the total number of semantic relations from less than one million (the current number of available relations) to millions of new and accurate semantic relations between synsets. We applied a knowledge–based all–words Word Sense Disambiguation algorithm to the Topic Signatures for deriving a sense vector from each word vector.

3.1 SSI-Dijkstra

We have implemented a version of the Structural Semantic Interconnections algorithm (SSI), a knowledge-based iterative approach to Word Sense Disambiguation (Navigli and Velardi, 2005). The SSI algorithm is very simple and consists of an initialization step and a set of iterative steps (see algorithm 1).

Given W, an ordered list of words to be disambiguated, the SSI algorithm performs as follows. During the initialization step, all monosemous words are included into the set I of already interpreted words, and the polysemous words are included in P (all of them pending to be disambiguated). At each step, the set I is used to disambiguate one word of P, selecting the word sense which is closer to the set I of already disambiguated words. Once a sense is selected, the word sense is removed from P and included into I. The algorithm finishes when no more pending words remain in P.

Algorithm 1 SSI-Dijkstra Algorithm

```
SSI (T: list of terms)
for each {t ∈ T} do
  I[t] = ∅
  if t is monosemous then
    I[t] := the only sense of t
  else
    P := P ∪ {t}
  end if
end for
repeat
  P' := P
  for each {t ∈ P} do
    BestSense := ∅
    MaxValue := 0
    for each {sense s of t} do
      W[s] := 0
      N[s] := 0
      for each {sense s' ∈ I} do
        w := DijsktraShortestPath(s, s')
        if w > 0 then
          W[s] := W[s] + (1/w)
          N[s] := N[s] + 1
        end if
      end for
      if N[s] > 0 then
        NewValue := W[s]/N[s]
        if NewValue > MaxValue then
          MaxValue := NewValue
          BestSense := s
        end if
      end if
    end for
    if MaxValue > 0 then
      I[t] := BestSense
      P := P \ {t}
    end if
  end for
until P ≠ P'
return (I, P);
```

Initially, the list I of interpreted words should include the senses of the monosemous words in W, or a fixed set of word senses[5]. However, when dis-

[4]This format stands for word#pos#sense.

[5]If no monosemous words are found or if no initial senses are provided, the algorithm could make an initial guess based on the most probable sense of the less ambiguous word of W.

ambiguating a TS of a word sense *s* (for instance party#n#1), the list I already includes *s*.

In order to measure the proximity of one synset to the rest of synsets of I, we use part of the knowledge already available to build a very large connected graph with 99,635 nodes (synsets) and 636,077 edges. This graph includes the set of direct relations between synsets gathered from WordNet and eXtended WordNet. On that graph, we used a very efficient graph library, BoostGraph[6] to compute the Dijkstra algorithm. The Dijkstra algorithm is a greedy algorithm for computing the shortest path distance between one node an the rest of nodes of a graph. In that way, we can compute very efficiently the shortest distance between any two given nodes of a graph. We call this version of the SSI algorithm, SSI-Dijkstra.

SSI-Dijkstra has very interesting properties. For instance, it always provides the minimum distance between two synsets. That is, the algorithm always provides an answer being the minimum distance close or far. In contrast, the original SSI algorithm not always provides a path distance because it depends on a predefined grammar of semantic relations. In fact, the SSI-Dijkstra algorithm compares the distances between the synsets of a word and all the synsets already interpreted in I. At each step, the SSI-Dijkstra algorithm selects the synset which is closer to I (the set of already interpreted words).

Furthermore, this approach is completely language independent. The same graph can be used for any language having words connected to WordNet.

3.2 Building KnowNet

We developed KnowNet (KN), a large-scale and extensible knowledge base, by applying SSI-Dijkstra to each topic signature from TSWEB.

We have generated four different versions of KnowNet applying SSI-Dijkstra to only the first 5, 10, 15 and 20 words for each TS. SSI-Dijkstra used only the knowledge present in WordNet and eXtended WordNet which consist of a very large connected graph with 99,635 nodes (synsets) and 636,077 edges (semantic relations).

We generated each KnowNet by applying the SSI-Dijkstra algorithm to the whole TSWEB (processing the first words of each of the 35,250 topic signatures). For each TS, we obtained the direct relations from the topic (a word sense) to the disambiguated word senses of the TS (for instance, party#n#1->federalist#n#1), but also the indirect relations between disambiguated words from the TS (for instance, federalist#n#1->republican#n#1). Finally, we removed symmetric and repeated relations.

[6]http://www.boost.org

KB	WN+XWN	#relations	#synsets
KN-5	3,1%	231,163	39,864
KN-10	5,0%	689,610	45,817
KN-15	6,9%	1,378,286	48,521
KN-20	8,5%	2,358,927	50,789

Table 3: Size and percentage of overlapping relations between KnowNet versions and WN+XWN

Table 3 shows the overlaping percentage between each KnowNet and the knowledge contained into WordNet and eXtended WordNet, and the total number of relations and synsets of each resource. For instance, only 8,5% of the total direct relations included into WN+XWN are also present in KnowNet-20. This means that the rest of relations from KnowNet-20 are new. As expected, each KnowNet is very large, ranging from hundreds of thousands to millions of new semantic relations between synsets among increasing sets of synsets.

4 Evaluation framework

In order to empirically establish the relative quality of these new semantic resources, we used the evaluation framework of task 16 of SemEval-2007: Evaluation of wide coverage knowledge resources (Cuadros and Rigau, 2007).

In this framework all knowledge resources are evaluated on a common WSD task. In particular, we used the noun-sets of the English Lexical Sample task of Senseval-3 and SemEval-2007 exercises which consists of 20 and 35 nouns respectively. All performances are evaluated on the test data using the fine-grained scoring system provided by the organizers.

Furthermore, trying to be as neutral as possible with respect to the resources studied, we applied systematically the same disambiguation method to all of them. Recall that our main goal is to establish a fair comparison of the knowledge resources rather than providing the best disambiguation technique for a particular knowledge base. All knowledge bases are evaluated as topic signatures. That is, word vectors with weights associated to a particular synset which are obtained by collecting those word senses appearing in the synsets directly related to the topics. This simple representation tries to be as neutral as possible with respect to the resources used.

A common WSD method has been applied to all knowledge resources. A simple word overlapping counting is performed between the topic signature representing a word sense and the test example[7]. The synset having higher overlapping word counts is selected. In fact, this is a very simple WSD method which only considers the topical information around the word to be disambiguated. Finally, we should remark that the results are not skewed (for instance, for resolving ties) by the most frequent sense in WN or any other statistically predicted knowledge.

4.1 Baselines

We have designed a number of baselines in order to establish a complete evaluation framework for comparing the performance of each semantic resource on the English WSD tasks.

RANDOM: For each target word, this method selects a random sense. This baseline can be considered as a lower-bound.

SEMCOR-MFS: This baseline selects the most frequent sense of the target word in SemCor.

WN-MFS: This baseline is obtained by selecting the most frequent sense (the first sense in WN1.6) of the target word. WordNet word-senses were ranked using SemCor and other sense-annotated corpora. Thus, WN-MFS and SemCor-MFS are similar, but not equal.

TRAIN-MFS: This baseline selects the most frequent sense in the training corpus of the target word.

TRAIN: This baseline uses the training corpus to directly build a Topic Signature using TFIDF measure for each word sense and selecting at maximum the first 450 words. Note that in WSD evaluation frameworks, this is a very basic baseline. However, in our evaluation framework, this "WSD baseline" could be considered as an upper-bound. We do not expect to obtain better topic signatures for a particular sense than from its own annotated corpus.

4.2 Other Large-scale Knowledge Resources

In order to measure the relative quality of the new resources, we include in the evaluation a wide range of large-scale knowledge resources connected to WordNet.

WN (Fellbaum, 1998): This resource uses the different direct relations encoded in WN1.6 and WN2.0. We also tested WN^2 using relations at distance 1 and 2, WN^3 using relations at distances 1 to 3 and WN^4 using relations at distances 1 to 4.

XWN (Mihalcea and Moldovan, 2001): This resource uses the direct relations encoded in eXtended WN.

spBNC (McCarthy, 2001): This resource contains 707,618 selectional preferences acquired for subjects and objects from BNC.

spSemCor (Agirre and Martinez, 2002): This resource contains the selectional preferences acquired for subjects and objects from SemCor.

MCR (Atserias et al., 2004): This resource integrates the direct relations of WN, XWN and spSemCor.

TSSEM (Cuadros et al., 2007): These Topic Signatures have been constructed using SemCor.For each word-sense appearing in SemCor, we gather all sentences for that word sense, building a TS using TFIDF for all word-senses co-occurring in those sentences.

4.3 Integrated Knowledge Resources

We also evaluated the performance of the integration (removing duplicated relations) of some of these resources.

WN+XWN: This resource integrates the direct relations of WN and XWN. We also tested $(WN+XWN)^2$ (using either WN or XWN relations at distances 1 and 2).

MCR (Atserias et al., 2004): This resource integrates the direct relations of WN, XWN and spSemCor.

WN+XWN+KN-20: This resource integrates the direct relations of WN, XWN and KnowNet-20.

5 KnowNet Evaluation

We evaluated KnowNet using the same framework explained in section 4. That is, the noun part of the test set from the English Senseval-3 and SemEval-2007 English lexical sample tasks.

5.1 Senseval-3 evaluation

Table 4 presents ordered by F1 measure, the performance in terms of precision (P), recall (R) and

[7]We also consider those multiword terms appearing in WN.

KB	P	R	F1	Av. Size
TRAIN	*65.1*	*65.1*	*65.1*	450
TRAIN-MFS	*54.5*	*54.5*	*54.5*	
WN-MFS	*53.0*	*53.0*	*53.0*	
TSSEM	52.5	52.4	52.4	103
SEMCOR-MFS	*49.0*	*49.1*	*49.0*	
MCR^2	45.1	45.1	45.1	26,429
WN+XWN+KN-20	44.8	44.8	44.8	671
MCR	45.3	43.7	44.5	129
KnowNet-20	44.1	44.1	44.1	610
KnowNet-15	43.9	43.9	43.9	339
spSemCor	43.1	38.7	40.8	56
KnowNet-10	40.1	40.0	40.0	154
$(WN+XWN)^2$	38.5	38.0	38.3	5,730
WN+XWN	40.0	34.2	36.8	74
TSWEB	36.1	35.9	36.0	1,721
XWN	38.8	32.5	35.4	69
KnowNet-5	35.0	35.0	35.0	44
WN^3	35.0	34.7	34.8	503
WN^4	33.2	33.1	33.2	2,346
WN^2	33.1	27.5	30.0	105
spBNC	36.3	25.4	29.9	128
WN	44.9	18.4	26.1	14
RANDOM	*19.1*	*19.1*	*19.1*	

Table 4: P, R and F1 fine-grained results for the resources evaluated at Senseval-3, English Lexical Sample Task.

F1 measure (F1, harmonic mean of recall and precision) of each knowledge resource on Senseval-3 and the average size of the TS per word-sense. The different KnowNet versions appear marked in bold and the baselines appear in italics.

As expected, RANDOM obtains the poorest result. The most frequent senses obtained from SemCor (SEMCOR-MFS) and WN (WN-MFS) are both below the most frequent sense of the training corpus (TRAIN-MFS). However, all of them are far below to the Topic Signatures acquired using the training corpus (TRAIN).

The best results are obtained by TSSEM (with F1 of 52.4). The lowest result is obtained by the knowledge directly gathered from WN mainly because of its poor coverage (R of 18.4 and F1 of 26.1). Interestingly, the knowledge integrated in the MCR although partly derived by automatic means performs much better in terms of precision, recall and F1 measures than using them separately (F1 with 18.4 points higher than WN, 9.1 than XWN and 3.7 than spSemCor).

Despite its small size, the resources derived from SemCor obtain better results than its counterparts using much larger corpora (TSSEM vs. TSWEB and spSemCor vs. spBNC).

Regarding the baselines, all knowledge resources surpass RANDOM, but none achieves neither WN-MFS, TRAIN-MFS nor TRAIN. Only TSSEM obtains better results than SEMCOR-MFS and is very close to the most frequent sense of WN (WN-MFS) and the training (TRAIN-MFS).

Regarding the expansions and combinations, the performance of WN is improved using words at distances up to 2, and up to 3, but it decreases using distances up to 4. Interestingly, none of these WN expansions achieve the results of XWN. Finally, $(WN+XWN)^2$ performs better than WN+XWN and MCR^2 slightly better than MCR[8].

The different versions of KnowNet consistently obtain better performances as they increase the window size of processed words of TSWEB. As expected, KnowNet-5 obtain the lower results. However, it performs better than WN (and all its extensions) and spBNC. Interestingly, from KnowNet-10, all KnowNet versions surpass the knowledge resources used for their construction (WN, XWN, TSWEB and WN+XWN). In fact, KnowNet-10 also outperforms $(WN+XWN)^2$ with much more relations per sense. Also interesting is that KnowNet-10 and KnowNet-20 obtain better performance than spSemCor which was derived from annotated corpora. However, KnowNet-20 only performs slightly better than KnowNet-15 while almost doubling the number of relations.

These initial results seem to be very promising. If we do not consider the resources derived from manually sense annotated data (spSemCor, MCR, TSSEM, etc.), KnowNet-10 performs better that any knowledge resource derived by manual or automatic means. In fact, KnowNet-15 and KnowNet-20 outperforms spSemCor which was derived from manually annotated corpora. This is a very interesting result since these KnowNet versions have been derived only with the knowledge coming from WN and the web (that is, TSWEB), and WN and XWN as a knowledge source for SSI-Dijkstra[9].

Regarding the integration of resources, WN+XWN+KN-20 performs better than MCR and similarly to MCR^2 (having less than 50 times its size). Also interesting is that WN+XWN+KN-20 have better performance than their individual resources, indicating a complementary knowledge. In fact, WN+XWN+KN-20 performs much better than the resources from which it derives (WN, XWN and TSWEB).

[8] No further distances have been tested

[9] eXtended WordNet only has 17,185 manually labeled senses.

KB	P	R	F1	Av. Size
TRAIN	87.6	87.6	87.6	450
TRAIN-MFS	81.2	79.6	80.4	
WN-MFS	66.2	59.9	62.9	
WN+XWN+KN-20	53.0	53.0	53.0	627
$(\text{WN+XWN})^2$	54.9	51.1	52.9	5,153
TSWEB	54.8	47.8	51.0	700
KnowNet-20	49.5	46.1	47.7	561
KnowNet-15	47.0	43.5	45.2	308
XWN	50.1	39.8	44.4	96
KnowNet-10	44.0	39.8	41.8	139
WN+XWN	45.4	36.8	40.7	101
SEMCOR-MFS	42.4	38.4	40.3	
MCR	40.2	35.5	37.7	149
TSSEM	35.1	32.7	33.9	428
KnowNet-5	35.5	26.5	30.3	41
MCR^2	32.4	29.5	30.9	24,896
WN^3	29.3	26.3	27.7	584
RANDOM	27.4	27.4	27.4	
WN^2	25.9	27.4	26.6	72
spSemCor	31.4	23.0	26.5	51.0
WN^4	26.1	23.9	24.9	2,710
WN	36.8	16.1	22.4	13
spBNC	24.4	18.1	20.8	290

Table 5: P, R and F1 fine-grained results for the resources evaluated at SemEval-2007, English Lexical Sample Task.

5.2 SemEval-2007 evaluation

Table 5 presents ordered by F1 measure, the performance in terms of precision (P), recall (R) and F1 measure (F1) of each knowledge resource on SemEval-2007 and its average size of the TS per word-sense[10]. Again, the different KnowNet versions appear marked in bold and the baselines appear in italics.

As in the previous evaluation, RANDOM obtains the poorest result. The most frequent senses obtained from SemCor (SEMCOR-MFS) and WN (WN-MFS) are both far below the most frequent sense of the training corpus (TRAIN-MFS), and all of them are below the Topic Signatures acquired using the training corpus (TRAIN).

Interestingly, on SemEval-2007, all the knowledge resources behave differently. Now, the best individual results are obtained by TSWEB, while in this case TSSEM obtains very modest results. The lowest result is obtained by the knowledge encoded in spBNC.

Regarding the baselines, spBNC, WN (and also WN^2 and WN^4) and spSemCor do not surpass RANDOM, and none achieves neither WN-MFS, TRAIN-MFS nor TRAIN. Now, WN+XWN, XWN, TSWEB and $(\text{WN+XWN})^2$ obtain better results than SEMCOR-MFS but far below the most frequent sense of WN (WN-MFS) and the training (TRAIN-MFS).

Regarding other expansions and combinations, the performance of WN is improved using words at distances up to 2, and up to 3, but it decreases using distances up to 4. Again, none of these WN expansions achieve the results of XWN. Finally, $(\text{WN+XWN})^2$ performs better than WN+XWN and MCR^2 slightly better than MCR[11].

On SemEval-2007, the different versions of KnowNet consistently obtain better performances as they incease the window size of processed words of TSWEB. As expected, KnowNet-5 obtain the lower results. However, it performs better than spBNC, WN (and all its extensions), spSemCor and MCR^2. This time, all KnowNet versions perform worse than TSWEB. However, as in the previous evaluation, KnowNet-10 outperforms WN+XWN, and this time, also TSSEM and the MCR, with much more relations per sense. Also interesting is that from KnowNet-10, all KnowNet versions perform better than the resources derived from manually sense annotated corpora (spSemCor, MCR, TSSEM, etc.).

Regarding the integration of resources, WN+XWN+KN-20 performs better than any knowledge resource derived by manual or automatic means. Again, it is interesting to note that WN+XWN+KN-20 have better performance than their individual resources, indicating a complementary knowledge. In fact, WN+XWN+KN-20 performs much better than the resources from which it derives (WN, XWN and TSWEB).

5.3 Discussion

When comparing the ranking of the different knowledge resources, the different versions of KnowNet seem to be more robust and stable across corpora changes. For instance, in both evaluation frameworks (Senseval-3 and SemEval-2007), KnowNet-20 ranks 5th and 4th, respectively ($(\text{WN+XWN})^2$ ranks 8th and 2nd, TSSEM ranks 1st and 10th, MCR ranks 4th and 9th, TSWEB ranks 11th and 3rd, etc.). In fact, WN+XWN+KN-20 ranks 3rd and 1st, respectively.

[10]The average size is different with respect Senseval-3 because the words selected for this task are different

[11]No further distances have been tested

6 Conclusions and future research

It is our belief, that accurate semantic processing (such as WSD) would rely not only on sophisticated algorithms but on knowledge intensive approaches. The results presented in this paper suggests that much more research on acquiring and using large-scale semantic resources should be addressed.

The knowledge acquisition bottleneck problem is particularly acute for open domain (and also domain specific) semantic processing. The initial results obtained for the different versions of KnowNet seem to be a major step towards the autonomous acquisition of knowledge from raw corpora, since they are several times larger than the available knowledge resources which encode relations between synsets, and the knowledge they contain outperform any other resource when is empirically evaluated in a common framework.

It remains for future research the evaluation of these KnowNet versions in combination with other large-scale semantic resources or in a cross-lingual setting.

Acknowledgments

We want to thank Aitor Soroa for his technical support and the anonymous reviewers for their comments. This work has been supported by KNOW (TIN2006-15049-C03-01) and KYOTO (ICT-2007-211423).

References

Agirre, E. and O. Lopez de Lacalle. 2004. Publicly available topic signatures for all wordnet nominal senses. In *Proceedings of LREC*, Lisbon, Portugal.

Agirre, E. and D. Martinez. 2001. Learning class-to-class selectional preferences. In *Proceedings of CoNLL*, Toulouse, France.

Agirre, E. and D. Martinez. 2002. Integrating selectional preferences in wordnet. In *Proceedings of GWC*, Mysore, India.

Álvez, J., J. Atserias, J. Carrera, S. Climent, A. Oliver, and G. Rigau. 2008. Consistent annotation of eurowordnet with the top concept ontology. In *Proceedings of Fourth International WordNet Conference (GWC'08)*.

Atserias, J., L. Villarejo, G. Rigau, E. Agirre, J. Carroll, B. Magnini, and Piek Vossen. 2004. The meaning multilingual central repository. In *Proceedings of GWC*, Brno, Czech Republic.

Cuadros, M. and G. Rigau. 2006. Quality assessment of large scale knowledge resources. In *Proceedings of the EMNLP*.

Cuadros, M. and G. Rigau. 2007. Semeval-2007 task 16: Evaluation of wide coverage knowledge resources. In *Proceedings of the Fourth International Workshop on Semantic Evaluations (SemEval-2007)*.

Cuadros, M., G. Rigau, and M. Castillo. 2007. Evaluating large-scale knowledge resources across languages. In *Proceedings of RANLP*.

Fellbaum, C., editor. 1998. *WordNet. An Electronic Lexical Database*. The MIT Press.

Leacock, C., M. Chodorow, and G. Miller. 1998. Using Corpus Statistics and WordNet Relations for Sense Identification. *Computational Linguistics*, 24(1):147–166.

Lin, C. and E. Hovy. 2000. The automated acquisition of topic signatures for text summarization. In *Proceedings of COLING*. Strasbourg, France.

Magnini, B. and G. Cavaglià. 2000. Integrating subject field codes into wordnet. In *Proceedings of LREC*, Athens. Greece.

McCarthy, D. 2001. *Lexical Acquisition at the Syntax-Semantics Interface: Diathesis Aternations, Subcategorization Frames and Selectional Preferences*. Ph.D. thesis, University of Sussex.

Mihalcea, R. and D. Moldovan. 2001. extended wordnet: Progress report. In *Proceedings of NAACL Workshop on WordNet and Other Lexical Resources*, Pittsburgh, PA.

Navigli, R. and P. Velardi. 2005. Structural semantic interconnections: a knowledge-based approach to word sense disambiguation. *IEEE Transactions on Pattern Analysis and Machine Intelligence (PAMI)*, 27(7):1063–1074.

Niles, I. and A. Pease. 2001. Towards a standard upper ontology. In *Proceedings of the 2nd International Conference on Formal Ontology in Information Systems (FOIS-2001)*, pages 17–19. Chris Welty and Barry Smith, eds.

Suchanek, Fabian M., Gjergji Kasneci, and Gerhard Weikum. 2007. Yago: A Core of Semantic Knowledge. In *16th international World Wide Web conference (WWW 2007)*, New York, NY, USA. ACM Press.

Vossen, P., editor. 1998. *EuroWordNet: A Multilingual Database with Lexical Semantic Networks* . Kluwer Academic Publishers .

A classifier-based approach to preposition and determiner error correction in L2 English

Rachele De Felice and Stephen G. Pulman
Oxford University Computing Laboratory
Wolfson Building, Parks Road, Oxford OX1 3QD, UK
{rachele.defelice|stephen.pulman}@comlab.ox.ac.uk

Abstract

In this paper, we present an approach to the automatic identification and correction of preposition and determiner errors in non-native (L2) English writing. We show that models of use for these parts of speech can be learned with an accuracy of 70.06% and 92.15% respectively on L1 text, and present first results in an error detection task for L2 writing.

1 Introduction

The field of research in natural language processing (NLP) applications for L2 language is constantly growing. This is largely driven by the expanding population of L2 English speakers, whose varying levels of ability may require different types of NLP tools from those designed primarily for native speakers of the language. These include applications for use by the individual and within instructional contexts. Among the key tools are error-checking applications, focusing particularly on areas which learners find the most challenging. Prepositions and determiners are known to be one of the most frequent sources of error for L2 English speakers, a finding supported by our analysis of a small error-tagged corpus we created (determiners 17% of errors, prepositions 12%). Therefore, in developing a system for automatic error detection in L2 writing, it seems desirable to focus on these problematic, and very common, parts of speech (POS).

This paper gives a brief overview of the problems posed by these POS and of related work. We then present our proposed approach on both L1 and L2 data and discuss the results obtained so far.

© 2008. Licensed under the *Creative Commons Attribution-Noncommercial-Share Alike 3.0 Unported* license (http://creativecommons.org/licenses/by-nc-sa/3.0/). Some rights reserved.

2 The problem

2.1 Prepositions

Prepositions are challenging for learners because they can appear to have an idiosyncratic behaviour which does not follow any predictable pattern even across nearly identical contexts. For example, we say *I study* ***in*** *Boston* but *I study* ***at*** *MIT*; or *He is independent* ***of*** *his parents*, but *dependent* ***on*** *his son*. As it is hard even for L1 speakers to articulate the reasons for these differences, it is not surprising that learners find it difficult to master prepositions.

2.2 Determiners

Determiners pose a somewhat different problem from prepositions as, unlike them, their choice is more dependent on the wider discourse context than on individual lexical items. The relation between a noun and a determiner is less strict than that between a verb or noun and a preposition, the main factor in determiner choice being the specific properties of the noun's context. For example, we can say *boys like sport* or ***the*** *boys like sport*, depending on whether we are making a general statement about all boys or referring to a specific group. Equally, both *she ate* ***an*** *apple* and *she ate* ***the*** *apple* are grammatically well-formed sentences, but only one may be appropriate in a given context, depending on whether the apple has been mentioned previously. Therefore, here, too, it is very hard to come up with clear-cut rules predicting every possible kind of occurrence.

3 Related work

Although in the past there has been some research on determiner choice in L1 for applications such as generation and machine translation output, work to date on automatic error detection in L2 writing has been fairly limited. Izumi et al. (2004) train a maximum entropy classifier to recognise various errors using contextual features. They report results for different error types (e.g. omission - precision 75.7%, recall 45.67%; replacement - P 31.17%, R 8%), but there is no break-down of results by individual POS. Han et al. (2006) use a maximum entropy classifier to detect determiner errors, achieving 83% accuracy. Chodorow et al. (2007) present an approach to preposition error detection which also uses a model based on a maximum entropy classifier trained on a set of contextual features, together with a rule-based filter. They report 80% precision and 30% recall. Finally, Gamon et al. (2008) use a complex system including a decision tree and a language model for both preposition and determiner errors, while Yi et al. (2008) propose a web count-based system to correct determiner errors (P 62%, R 41%).

The work presented here displays some similarities to the papers mentioned above in its use of a maximum entropy classifier and a set of features. However, our feature set is more linguistically sophisticated in that it relies on a full syntactic analysis of the data. It includes some semantic components which we believe play a role in correct class assignment.

4 Contextual models for prepositions and determiners

4.1 Feature set

The approach proposed in this paper is based on the belief that although it is difficult to formulate hard and fast rules for correct preposition and determiner usage, there is enough underlying regularity of characteristic syntactic and semantic contexts to be able to predict usage to an acceptable degree of accuracy. We use a corpus of grammatically correct English to train a maximum entropy classifier on examples of correct usage. The classifier can therefore learn to associate a given preposition or determiner to particular contexts, and reliably predict a class when presented with a novel instance of a context for one or the other.

The L1 source we use is the British National Corpus (BNC) as we believe this offers a representative sample of different text types. We represent training and testing items as vectors of values for linguistically motivated contextual features. Our feature vectors include 18 feature categories for determiners and 13 for prepositions; the main ones are illustrated in Table 1 and Table 2 respectively. Further determiner features note whether the noun is modified by a predeterminer, possessive, numeral, and/or a relative clause, and whether it is part of a 'there is...' phrase. Additional preposition features refer to the grade of any adjectives or adverbs modified (base, comparative, superlative) and to whether the items modified are modified by more than one PP[1].

Head noun	'apple'
Number	singular
Noun type	count
Named entity?	no
WordNet category	food, plant
Prep modification?	yes, 'on'
Object of Prep?	no
Adj modification?	yes, 'juicy'
Adj grade	superlative
POS ±3	VV, DT, JJS, IN, DT, NN

Table 1: Determiner feature set for *Pick **the** juiciest apple on the tree.*

POS modified	verb
Lexical item modified	'drive'
WordNet Category	motion
Subcat frame	pp_to
POS of object	noun
Object lexical item	'London'
Named entity?	yes, type = location
POS ±3	NNP, VBD, NNP
Grammatical relation	iobj

Table 2: Preposition feature set for *John drove **to** London.*

In De Felice and Pulman (2007), we described some of the preprocessing required and offered some motivation for this approach. As for our choice of features, we aim to capture all the elements of a sentence which we believe to have an effect on preposition and determiner choice, and which can be easily extracted automatically - this is a key consideration as all the features derived rely on automatic processing of the text. Grammatical relations refer to RASP-style grammatical relations between heads and complements in which the preposition occurs (see e.g. (Briscoe et al.,

[1]A full discussion of each feature, including motivation for its inclusion and an assessment of its contribution to the model, is found in De Felice (forthcoming).

Author	Accuracy
Baseline	26.94%
Gamon et al. 08	64.93%
Chodorow et al. 07	69.00%
Our model	**70.06%**

Table 3: Classifier performance on L1 prepositions

2006)). Semantic word type information is taken from WordNet lexicographer classes, 40 broad semantic categories which all nouns and verbs in WordNet belong to[2] (e.g. 'verb of motion', 'noun denoting food'), while the POStags are from the Penn Treebank tagset - we note the POS of three words either side of the target word[3]. For each occurrence of a preposition or determiner in the corpus, we obtain a feature vector consisting of the preposition or determiner and its context, described in terms of the features noted above.

5 Acquiring the models

5.1 Prepositions

At the moment, we restrict our analysis to the nine most frequent prepositions in the data: ***at, by, for, from, in, of, on, to,*** and ***with***, to ensure a sufficient amount of data for training. This gives a training dataset comprising 8,898,359 instances. We use a standard maximum entropy classifier [4] and do not omit any features, although we plan to experiment with different feature combinations to determine if, and how, this would impact the classifier's performance. Before testing our model on learner data, it is important to ascertain that it can correctly associate prepositions to a given context in grammatical, well-edited data. We therefore tested the model on a section of the BNC not used in training, section J. Our best result to date is **70.06%** accuracy (test set size: 536,193). Table 3 relates our results to others reported in the literature on comparable tasks. The baseline refers to always choosing the most frequent option, namely ***of***.

We can see that our model's performance compares favourably to the best results in the literature, although direct comparisons are hard to draw since different groups train and test on different preposition sets and on different types of data (British vs. American English, BNC vs. news reports, and so on). Furthermore, it should be noted that Gamon et al. report more than one figure in their results, as there are two components to their model: one determining whether a preposition is needed, and the other deciding what the preposition should be. The figure reported here refers to the latter task, as it is the most similar to the one we are evaluating. Additionally, Chodorow et al. also discuss some modifications to their model which can increase accuracy; the result noted here is the one more directly comparable to our own approach.

	Proportion of training data	Precision	Recall
of	27.83% (2,501,327)	74.28%	90.47%
to	20.64% (1,855,304)	85.99%	81.73%
in	17.68% (1,589,718)	60.15%	67.60%
for	8.01% (720,369)	55.47%	43.78%
on	6.54% (587,871)	58.52%	45.81%
with	6.03% (541,696)	58.13%	46.33%
at	4.72% (424,539)	57.44%	52.12%
by	4.69% (421,430)	63.83%	56.51%
from	3.86% (347,105)	59.20%	32.07%

Table 4: L1 results - individual prepositions

5.1.1 Further discussion

To fully assess the model's performance on the L1 data, it is important to consider factors such as performance on individual prepositions, the relationship between training dataset size and accuracy, and the kinds of errors made by the model.

Table 4 shows the classifier's performance on individual prepositions together with the size of their training datasets. At first glance, a clear correlation appears between the amount of data seen in training and precision and recall, as evidenced for example by ***of*** or ***to***, for which the classifier achieves a very high score. In other cases, however, the correlation is not so clear-cut. For example ***by*** has one of the smallest data sets in training but higher scores than many of the other prepositions, while ***for*** is notable for the opposite reason, namely having a large dataset but some of the lowest scores.

The absence of a definite relation between dataset size and performance suggests that there might be a cline of 'learnability' for these prepositions: different prepositions' contexts may be more or less uniquely identifiable, or they may have more or fewer senses, leading to less confusion for the classifier. One simple way of verifying the latter case is by looking at the number of senses assigned to the prepositions by a resource

[2]No word sense disambiguation was performed at this stage.

[3]In NPs with a null determiner, the target is the head noun.

[4]Developed by James Curran.

Target prep	*Confused with*								
	at	**by**	**for**	**from**	**in**	**of**	**on**	**to**	**with**
at	xx	4.65%	10.82%	2.95%	36.83%	19.46%	9.17%	10.28%	5.85%
by	6.54%	xx	8.50%	2.58%	41.38%	19.44%	5.41%	10.04%	6.10%
for	8.19%	3.93%	xx	1.91%	25.67%	36.12%	5.60%	11.29%	7.28%
from	6.19%	4.14%	6.72%	xx	26.98%	26.74%	7.70%	16.45%	5.07%
in	7.16%	9.28%	10.68%	3.01%	xx	43.40%	10.92%	8.96%	6.59%
of	3.95%	2.00%	18.81%	3.36%	40.21%	xx	9.46%	14.77%	7.43%
on	5.49%	3.85%	8.66%	2.29%	32.88%	27.92%	xx	12.20%	6.71%
to	9.77%	3.82%	11.49%	3.71%	24.86%	27.95%	9.43%	xx	8.95%
with	3.66%	4.43%	12.06%	2.24%	28.08%	26.63%	6.81%	16.10%	xx

Table 5: Confusion matrix for L1 data - prepositions

such as the Oxford English Dictionary. However, we find no good correlation between the two as the preposition with the most senses is ***of*** (16), and that with the fewest is ***from*** (1), thus negating the idea that fewer senses make a preposition easier to learn. The reason may therefore be found elsewhere, e.g. in the lexical properties of the contexts.

A good picture of the model's errors can be had by looking at the confusion matrix in Table 5, which reports, for each preposition, what the classifier's incorrect decision was. Analysis of these errors may establish whether they are related to the dataset size issue noted above, or have a more linguistically grounded explanation.

From the table, the frequency effect appears evident: in almost every case, the three most frequent wrong choices are the three most frequent prepositions, ***to***, ***of***, and ***in***, although interestingly not in that order, ***in*** usually being the first choice. Conversely, the less frequent prepositions are less often suggested as the classifier's choice. This effect precludes the possibility at the moment of drawing any linguistic conclusions. These may only be gleaned by looking at the errors for the three more frequent prepositions. We see for example that there seems to be a strong relation between ***of*** and ***for***, the cause of which is not immediately clear: perhaps they both often occur within noun phrases (e.g. *book of recipes*, *book for recipes*). More predictable is the confusion between ***to*** and ***from***, and between locative prepositions such as ***to*** and ***at***, although the effect is less strong for other potentially confusable pairs such as ***in*** and ***at*** or ***on***.

Table 6 gives some examples of instances where the classifier's chosen preposition differs from that found in the original text. In most cases, the classifier's suggestion is also grammatically correct,

Classifier choice	Correct phrase
demands **of** the sector	demands **for**...
condition **for** development	condition **of**...
travel **to** speed	travel **at**...
look **at** the USA	look **to**...

Table 6: Examples of classifier errors on preposition L1 task

Author	Accuracy
Baseline	59.83%
Han et al. 06	83.00%
Gamon et al. 08	86.07%
Turner and Charniak 07	86.74%
Our model	**92.15%**

Table 7: Classifier performance - L1 determiners

but the overall meaning of the phrases changes somewhat. For example, while the *demands* ***of*** *the sector* are usually made by the sector itself, the *demands* ***for*** *the sector* suggest that someone else may be making them. These are subtle differences which it may be impossible to capture without a more sophisticated understanding of the wider context.

The example with *travel*, on the other hand, yields an ungrammatical result. We assume that the classifier has acquired a very strong link between the lexical item *travel* and the preposition ***to*** that directs it towards this choice (cf. also the example of *look at/to*). This suggests that individual lexical items play an important role in preposition choice along with other more general syntactic and semantic properties of the context.

	% of training data	Prec.	Recall
a	9.61% (388,476)	70.52%	53.50%
the	29.19% (1,180,435)	85.17%	91.51%
null	61.20% (2,475,014)	98.63%	98.79%

Table 8: L1 results - individual determiners

Target det	*Confused with*		
	a	**the**	**null**
a	xx	92.92%	7.08%
the	80.66%	xx	19.34%
null	14.51%	85.49%	xx

Table 9: Confusion matrix for L1 determiners

5.2 Determiners

For the determiner task, we also consider only the three most frequent cases (***a, the, null***), which gives us a training dataset consisting of 4,043,925 instances. We achieve accuracy of 92.15% on the L1 data (test set size: 305,264), as shown in Table 7. Again, the baseline refers to the most frequent class, ***null***.

The best reported results to date on determiner selection are those in Turner and Charniak (2007). Our model outperforms their n-gram language model approach by over 5%. Since the two approaches are not tested on the same data this comparison is not conclusive, but we are optimistic that there is a real difference in accuracy since the type of texts used are not dissimilar. As in the case of the prepositions, it is interesting to see whether this high performance is equally distributed across the three classes; this information is reported in Table 8. Here we can see that there is a very strong correlation between amount of data seen in training and precision and recall. The indefinite article's lower 'learnability', and its lower frequency appears not to be peculiar to our data, as it is also found by Gamon et al. among others.

The disparity in training is a reflection of the distribution of determiners in the English language. Perhaps if this imbalance were addressed, the model would more confidently learn contexts of use for ***a***, too, which would be desirable in view of using this information for error correction. On the other hand, this would create a distorted representation of the composition of English, which may not be what we want in a statistical model of language. We plan to experiment with smaller scale, more similar datasets to ascertain whether the issue is one of training size or of inherent difficulty in learning about the indefinite article's occurrence.

In looking at the confusion matrix for determiners (Table 9), it is interesting to note that for the classifier's mistakes involving ***a*** or ***the***, the erroneous choice is in the almost always the other determiner rather than the null case. This suggests that the frequency effect is not so strong as to override any true linguistic information the model has acquired, otherwise the predominant choice would always be the null case. On the contrary, these results show that the model is indeed capable of distinguishing between contexts which require a determiner and those which do not, but requires further fine tuning to perform better in knowing which of the two determiner options to choose. Perhaps the introduction of a discourse dimension might assist in this respect. We plan to experiment with some simple heuristics: for example, given a sequence 'Determiner Noun', has the noun appeared in the preceding few sentences? If so, we might expect ***the*** to be the correct choice rather than ***a***.

6 Testing the model

6.1 Working with L2 text

To evaluate the model's performance on learner data, we use a subsection of the Cambridge Learner Corpus (CLC)[5]. We envisage our model to eventually be of assistance to learners in analysing their writing and identifying instances of preposition or determiner usage which do not correspond to what it has been trained to expect; the more probable instance would be suggested as a more appropriate alternative. In using NLP tools and techniques which have been developed with and for L1 language, a loss of performance on L2 data is to be expected. These methods usually expect grammatically well-formed input; learner text is often ungrammatical, misspelled, and different in content and structure from typical L1 resources such as the WSJ and the BNC.

6.2 Prepositions

For the preposition task, we extract 2523 instances of preposition use from the CLC (1282 correct, 1241 incorrect) and ask the classifier to mark them

[5]The CLC is a computerised database of contemporary written learner English (currently over 25m words). It was developed jointly by Cambridge ESOL and Cambridge University Press. The Cambridge Error Coding System has been developed and applied manually to the data by Cambridge University Press.

Instance type	Accuracy
Correct	66.7%
Incorrect	70%

Table 10: Accuracy on L2 data - prepositions. Accuracy on incorrect instances refers to the classifier successfully identifying the preposition in the text as not appropriate for that context.

as correct or incorrect. The results from this task are presented in Table 10. These first results suggest that the model is fairly robust: the accuracy rate on the correct data, for example, is not much lower than that on the L1 data. In an application designed to assist learners, it is important to aim to reduce the rate of false alarms - cases where the original is correct, but the model flags an error - to a minimum, so it is positive that this result is comparatively high. Accuracy on error identification is at first glance even more encouraging. However, if we look at the suggestions the model makes to replace the erroneous preposition, we find that these are correct only 51.5% of the time, greatly reducing its usefulness.

6.2.1 Further discussion

A first analysis of the classifier's decisions and its errors points to various factors which could be impairing its performance. Spelling mistakes in the input are one of the most immediate ones. For example, in the sentence *I'm Franch, responsable* ***on*** *the computer services*, the classifier is not able to suggest a correct alternative to the erroneous ***on***: since it does not recognise the adjective as a misspelling of *responsible*, it loses the information associated with this lexical feature, which could potentially determine the preposition choice.

A more complex problem arises when poor grammar in the input misleads the parser so that the information it gives for a sentence is incorrect, especially as regards PP attachment. In this example, *I wold like following equipment* ***to*** *my speech: computer, modem socket and microphone*, the missing *the* leads the parser to treat *following* as a verb, and believes it to be the verb to which the preposition is attached. It therefore suggests ***from*** as a correction, which is a reasonable choice given the frequency of phrases such as *to follow from*. However, this was not what the PP was meant to modify: impaired performance from the parser could be a significant negative factor in the model's performance. It would be interesting to test the model on texts written by students of different levels of proficiency, as their grammar may be more error-free and more likely to be parsed correctly. Alternatively, we could modify the parser so as to skip cases where it requires several attempts before producing a parse, as these more challenging cases could be indicative of very poorly structured sentences in which misused prepositions are dependent on more complex errors.

A different kind of problem impacting our accuracy scores derives from those instances where the classifier selects a preposition which can be correct in the given context, but is not the correct one in that particular case. In the example *I received a beautiful present* ***at*** *my birthday*, the classifier identifies the presence of the error, and suggests the grammatically and pragmatically appropriate correction ***for***. The corpus annotators, however, indicate ***on*** as the correct choice. Since we use their annotations as the benchmark against which to evaluate the model, this instance is counted as the classifier being wrong because it disagrees with the annotators. A better indication of the model's performance may be to independently judge its decisions, to avoid being subject to the annotators' bias. Finally, we are beginning to look at the relations between preposition errors and other types of error such as verb choice, and how these are annotated in the data.

An overview of the classifier's error patterns for the data in this task shows that they are largely similar to those observed in the L1 data. This suggests that the gap in performance between L1 and L2 is due more to the challenges posed by learner text than by inherent shortcomings in the model, and therefore that the key to better performance is likely to lie in overcoming these problems. In future work we plan to use L2 data where some of the spelling errors and non-preposition or determiner errors have been corrected so that we can see which of the other errors are worth focussing on first.

6.3 Determiners

Our work on determiner error correction is still in the early stages. We follow a similar procedure to the prepositions task, selecting a number of both correct and incorrect instances. On the former (set size 2000) accuracy is comparable to that on L1 data: **92.2%**. The danger of false alarms, then, appears not to be as significant as for the prepositions task. On the incorrect instances (set size ca. 1200), however, accuracy is less than 10%.

Preliminary error analysis shows that the model is successful at identifying cases of misused determiner, e.g. ***a*** for ***the*** or vice versa, doing so in over two-thirds of cases. However, by far the most frequent error type for determiners is not confusion between indefinite and definite article, but omitting an article where one is needed. At the moment, the model detects very few of these errors, no doubt influenced by the preponderance of ***null*** cases seen in training. Furthermore, some of the issues raised earlier in discussing the application of NLP tools to L2 language hold for this task, too.

In addition to those, though, in this task more than for prepositions we believe that differences in text type between the training texts - the BNC - and the testing material - learner essays - has a significant negative effect on the model. In this task, the lexical items play a crucial role in class assignment. If the noun in question has not been seen in training, the classifier may be unable to make an informed choice. Although the BNC comprises a wide variety of texts, there may not be a sufficient number covering topics typical of learner essays, such as 'business letters' or 'postcards to penpals'. Also, the BNC was created with material from almost 20 years ago, and learners writing in contemporary English may use lexical items which are not very frequently seen in the BNC. A clear example of this discrepancy is the noun *internet*, which requires the definite article in English, but not in several other languages, leading to countless sentences such as *I saw it in internet*, *I booked it on internet*, and so on. This is one of the errors the model never detects: a fact which is not surprising when we consider that this noun occurs only four times in the whole of the training data. It may be therefore necessary to consider using alternative sources of training data to overcome this problem and improve the classifier's performance.

7 Comparison to human learners

In developing this model, our first aim was not to create something which learns like a human, but something that works in the best and most efficient possible way. However, it is interesting to see whether human learners and classifiers display similar patterns of errors in preposition choice. This information has twofold value: as well as being of pedagogical assistance to instructors of English L2, were the classifier to display student-like error patterns, insights into 'error triggers' could be derived from the L2 pedagogical literature to improve the classifier. The analysis of the types of errors made by human learners yields some insights which might be worthy of further investigation. A clear one is the confusion between the three locative and temporal prepositions ***at***, ***in***, and ***on*** (typical sentence: *The training programme will start **at** the 1st August*). This type of error is made often by both learners and the model on both types of data, suggesting that perhaps further attention to features might be necessary to improve discrimination between these three prepositions.

There are also interesting divergences. For example, a common source of confusion in learners is between ***by*** and ***from***, as in *I like it because it's **from** my favourite band.* However, this confusion is not very frequent in the model, a difference which could be explained either by the fact that, as noted above, performance on ***from*** is very low and so the classifier is unlikely to suggest it, or that in training the contexts seen for ***by*** are sufficiently distinctive that the classifier is not misled like the learners.

Finally, a surprising difference comes from looking at what ***to*** is confused with. The model often suggests ***at*** where ***to*** would be correct. This is perhaps not entirely unusual as both can occur with locative complements (one can *go to a place* or *be at a place*) and this similarity could be confusing the classifier. Learners, however, although they do make this kind of mistake, are much more hampered by the confusion between ***for*** and ***to***, as in *She was helpful **for** me* or *This is interesting **for** you.* In other words, for learners it seems that the abstract use of this preposition, its benefactive sense, is much more problematic than the spatial sense. We can hypothesise that the classifier is less distracted by these cases because the effect of the lexical features is stronger.

A more detailed discussion of the issues arising from the comparison of confusion pairs cannot be had here. However, in noting both divergences and similarities between the two learners, human and machine, we may be able to derive useful insights into the way the learning processes operate, and what factors could be more or less important for them.

8 Conclusions and future directions

This paper discussed a contextual feature based approach to the automatic acquisition of models of use for prepositions and determiners, which achieve an accuracy of 70.06% and 92.15% respectively, and showed how it can be applied to an error correction task for L2 writing, with promising early results. There are several directions that can be pursued to improve accuracy on both types of data. The classifier can be further fine-tuned to acquire more reliable models of use for the two POS. We can also experiment with its confidence thresholds, for example allowing it to make another suggestion when its confidence in its first choice is low. Furthermore, issues relating to the use of NLP tools with L2 data must be addressed, such as factoring out spelling or other errors in the data, and perhaps training on text types which are more similar to the CLC. In the longer term, we also envisage mining the information implicit in our training data to create a lexical resource describing the statistical tendencies observed.

Acknowledgements

We wish to thank Stephen Clark and Laura Rimell for stimulating discussions and the anonymous reviewers for their helpful comments. We acknowledge Cambridge University Press's assistance in accessing the Cambridge Learner Corpus data. Rachele De Felice was supported by an AHRC scholarship for the duration of her studies.

References

Briscoe, Ted, John Carroll, and Rebecca Watson. 2006. The second release of the RASP system. In *COLING-ACL 06 Demo Session*.

Chodorow, Martin, Joel Tetreault, and Na-Rae Han. 2007. Detection of grammatical errors involving prepositions. In *Proceedings of the 4th ACL-SIGSEM Workshop on Prepositions*.

De Felice, Rachele and Stephen Pulman. 2007. Automatically acquiring models of preposition use. In *Proceedings of the 4th ACL-SIGSEM Workshop on Prepositions*.

De Felice, Rachele. forthcoming. *Recognising preposition and determiner errors in learner English*. Ph.D. thesis, Oxford University Computing Laboratory.

Gamon, M., J. Gao, C. Brockett, A. Klementiev, W. Dolan, D. Belenko, and L. Vanderwende. 2008. Using contextual speller techniques and language modeling for ESL error correction. In *Proceedings of IJCNLP*.

Han, Na-Rae, Martin Chodorow, and Claudia Leacock. 2006. Detecting errors in English article usage by non-native speakers. *Natural Language Engineering*, 12(1):115–129.

Izumi, Emi, Kiyotaka Uchimoto, and Hitoshi Isahara. 2004. SST speech corpus of Japanese learners' English and automatic detection of learners' errors. *ICAME*, 28:31–48.

Turner, Jenine and Eugen Charniak. 2007. Language modeling for determiner selection. In *NAACL-HLT Companion volume*.

Yi, Xing, Jianfeng Gao, and William Dolan. 2008. A web-based English proofing system for ESL users. In *Proceedings of IJCNLP*.

Pedagogically Useful Extractive Summaries for Science Education

Sebastian de la Chica, Faisal Ahmad, James H. Martin, Tamara Sumner
Institute of Cognitive Science
Department of Computer Science
University of Colorado at Boulder
sebastian.delachica, faisal.ahmad, james.martin,
tamara.sumner@colorado.edu

Abstract

This paper describes the design and evaluation of an extractive summarizer for educational science content called COGENT. COGENT extends MEAD based on strategies elicited from an empirical study with science domain and instructional design experts. COGENT identifies sentences containing pedagogically relevant concepts for a specific science domain. The algorithms pursue a hybrid approach integrating both domain independent bottom-up sentence scoring features and domain-aware top-down features. Evaluation results indicate that COGENT outperforms existing summarizers and generates summaries that closely resemble those generated by human experts. COGENT concept inventories appear to also support the computational identification of student misconceptions about earthquakes and plate tectonics.

1 Introduction

Multidocument summarization (MDS) research efforts have resulted in significant advancements in algorithm and system design (Mani, 2001). Many of these efforts have focused on summarizing news articles, but not significantly explored the research issues arising from processing educational content to support pedagogical applications. This paper describes our research into the application of MDS techniques to educational science content to generate pedagogically useful summaries.

Knowledge maps are graphical representations of domain information laid out as networks of nodes containing rich concept descriptions interconnected using a fixed set of relationship types (Holley and Dansereau, 1984). Knowledge maps are a variant of the concept maps used to capture, assess, and track student knowledge in education research (Novak and Gowin, 1984). Learning research indicates that knowledge maps may be useful cognitive scaffolds, helping users lacking domain expertise to understand the macro-level structure of an information space (O'Donnell et al., 2002). Knowledge maps have emerged as an effective representation to generate conceptual browsers that help students navigate educational digital libraries, such as the Digital Library for Earth System Education (DLESE.org) (Butcher et al., 2006). In addition, knowledge maps have proven useful for domain and instructional experts to capture domain knowledge from digital library resources and to analyze student understanding for the purposes of providing formative assessments (Ahmad et al., 2007).

Knowledge maps have proven useful both as representations of knowledge for assessment purposes and as learning resources for presentation to students. However, domain knowledge map construction by experts is an expensive knowledge engineering activity. In this paper, we describe our progress towards the automated generation of pedagogically useful extractive summaries from educational texts about a science domain. In the context of automated knowledge map generation, summary sentences correspond to concepts. While the detection of relationships between concepts is also part of our overall research agenda, this paper focuses solely on concept identification using MDS techniques. The remainder of this paper is organized as fol-

© 2008. Licensed under the *Creative Commons Attribution-Noncommercial-Share Alike 3.0 Unported* license (http://creativecommons.org/licenses/by-nc-sa/3.0/). Some rights reserved.

lows. First, we review related work in the areas of automated concept extraction from texts and extractive summarization. We then describe the empirical study we have conducted to understand how domain and instructional design experts identify pedagogically important science concepts in educational digital library resources. Next, we provide a detailed description of the algorithms we have designed based on expert strategies elicited from our empirical study. We then present and discuss our evaluation results using automated summarization metrics and human judgments. Finally, we present our conclusions and future work in this area.

2 Related Work

Our work is informed by efforts to automate the acquisition of ontology concepts from text. OntoLearn (Navigli and Velardi, 2004) extracts domain terminology from a collection of texts using a syntactic parse to identify candidate terms that are filtered based on domain relevance and connected using a semantic interpretation based on word sense disambiguation. The newly identified concepts and relationships are used to update an existing ontology. Knowledge Puzzle focuses on n-grams to produce candidate terms filtered based on term frequency in the input documents and on the number of relationships associated with a given term (Zouaq et al., 2007). This approach leverages pattern extraction techniques to identify concepts and relationships. While these approaches produce ontologies useful for computational purposes, the identified concepts are of a very fine granularity and therefore may yield graphs not suitable for identifying student misconceptions or for presentation back to the student. Clustering by committee has also been used to discover concepts from a text by grouping terms into conceptually related clusters (Lin and Pantel, 2002). The resulting clusters appear to be tightly related, but operate at a very fine level of granularity. Our approach focuses on sentences as units of knowledge to produce concise representations that may be useful both as computational objects and as learning resources to present back to the student. Therefore, extractive summarization research also informs our work.

Topic representation and topic themes have been used to explore promising MDS techniques (Harabagiu and Lacatusu, 2005). Recent efforts in graph-based MDS have integrated sentence affinity, information richness and diversity penalties to produce very promising results (Wan and Yang, 2006). Finally, MEAD is a widely used multi-document summarization and evaluation platform (Radev et al., 2000). MEAD research efforts have resulted in significant contributions to support the development of summarization applications (Radev et al., 2000). While all these systems have produced promising results in automated evaluations, none have directly targeted educational content as input or the generation of pedagogically useful summaries. We are directly building upon MEAD due its focus on sentence extraction and its high degree of modularization.

3 Empirical Study

We have conducted a study to capture how human experts construct and use knowledge maps. In this 10-month study, we examined how experts created knowledge maps from educational digital libraries and how they used the maps to assess student work and provide personalized feedback.

In this paper, we are focusing on the knowledge map construction aspects of the study. Four geology and instructional design experts collaboratively selected 20 resources from DLESE to construct a domain knowledge map on earthquakes and plates tectonics for high school age learners. The experts independently created knowledge maps of individual resources which they collaboratively merged into the final domain knowledge map in a one-day workshop. The resulting domain knowledge map consisted of 564 nodes containing domain concepts and 578 relationships. The concepts consist of 7,846 words, or 5% of the total number of words in the original resources. Figure 1 shows a fragment of the domain knowledge map created by our experts.

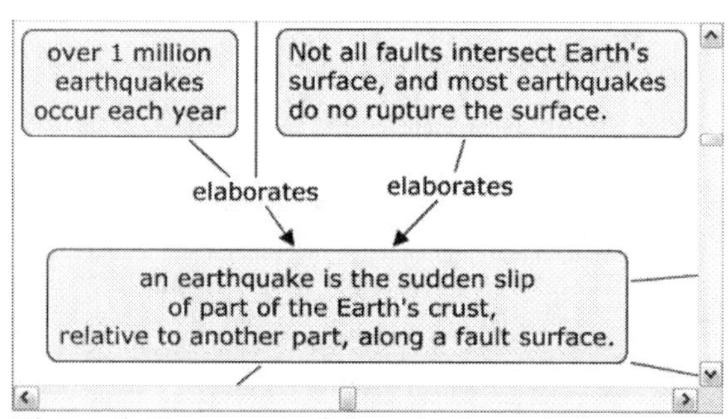

Figure 1. Fragment of domain knowledge map created by domain and instructional experts

Experts created nodes containing concepts of varying granularity, including nouns, noun phrases, partial sentences, single sentences, and multiple sentences. Our analysis of this domain knowledge map indicates that experts relied on copying-and-pasting (58%) and paraphrasing (37%) to create most domain concepts. Only 5% of the nodes could not be traced directly to the original resources.

Experts used relationship types in a Zipf-like distribution with the top 10 relationship types accounting for 64% of all relationships. The top 2 relationship types each accounted for more than 10% of all relationships: elaborations (19% or 110 links) and examples (14% or 78 links).

We have established the completeness of this domain knowledge map by asking a domain expert to assess its content coverage of nationally-recognized educational goals on earthquakes and plate tectonics for high school age learners using the American Association for the Advancement of Science (AAAS) Benchmarks (Project 2061, 1993). The results indicate adequate content coverage of the relevant *AAAS Benchmarks* achieved through 82 of the concepts (15%) with the remaining 482 concepts (85%) providing very detailed elaborations of the associated learning goals.

Qualitative analysis of the verbal protocols captured during the study indicates that all experts used external sources to construct the domain knowledge map. Experts made references to their own knowledge (e.g., "I know that…"), to content learned or taught in geology courses, to other resources used in the study, and to the National Science Education Standards (NSES), a comprehensive collection of nationally-recognized science learning goals for K-12 students (National Research Council, 1996).

We have examined sentence extraction agreement between experts using a kappa measure that accounts for prevalence of judgments and conflicting biases amongst experts, called PABA-kappa (Byrt et al., 1993). The average PABA-kappa value of 0.62 indicates that our experts substantially agree on sentence extraction from digital library resources. While this study was not designed as an annotation project to support summarization evaluation, this level of agreement indicates that the concepts selected by the experts may serve as the reference summary to evaluate the performance of our summarizer.

4 Summarizer for Science Education

Creating a knowledge map from a collection of input texts involves identifying sentences containing important domain concepts, linking concepts, and labeling those links. This paper focuses solely on identifying and extracting pedagogically relevant sentences as domain concepts. We have designed and implemented an extractive summarizer for educational science content, called COGENT, based on MEAD version 3.11 (Radev et al., 2000). COGENT processes a collection of educational digital library resources by first preprocessing each resource using Tidy (tidy.sourceforge.net) to fix improperly formatted HTML code. COGENT then merges multiple web pages into a single HTML document and extracts the contents of each resource into a plain text file. We have extended MEAD with sentence scoring features based on domain content, document structure, and sentence length.

4.1 Domain Content

We have designed two sentence-scoring features that aim to capture the domain content relevance of each sentence: the educational standards feature and the gazetteer feature.

We have developed a feature that models how human experts used external sources to identify and extract concepts. The *educational standards* feature uses the textual description of the relevant AAAS Benchmarks on earthquakes and plate tectonics for high-school age learners and the associated NSES. Each sentence receives a score based on its similarity to the text contents of the learning goals and educational standards computed using a TFIDF (Term Frequency-Inverse Document Frequency) approach (Salton and Buckley, 1988). We have used KinoSearch, a Perl implementation of the Lucene search engine (lucene.apache.org), to create an index that includes the AAAS Benchmarks learning goal description (boosted by 2), subject (boosted by 8), and keywords (boosted by 2), plus the text of the associated national standards (not boosted). Sentence scores are based on the similarity scores generated by KinoSearch in response to a query consisting of the sentence text.

To account for the large number of examples used by the experts in the domain knowledge map (14% of all links), we have developed a feature that reflects the number and relevance of the geographical names in each sentence. Earth science examples often refer to names of geographical places, including geological formations on the planet. The *gazetteer* feature leverages the Alexandria Digital Library (ADL) Gazetteer service (Hill, 2000) to check whether named entities identified in each sentence match entries in the ADL Gazetteer. A gazetteer is a georeferencing resource containing information about locations and place-names, including latitude and longitude as well as type information about the corresponding geographical feature. Each sentence receives a score based on a TFIDF approach where the TF is the number of times a particular location name appears in the sentence and the IDF is the inverse of the count of gazetteer entries matching the location name. If the ADL Gazetteer returns a large number of results for a given place-name, it means there are many geographical locations identified by that name. Our assumption is that unique names may be more pedagogically relevant. For example, Ohio receives an IDF score of 0.0625 because the ADL Gazetteer contains 16 entries so named, while the Mid-Atlantic Ridge, the distinctive underwater mountain range dividing the Atlantic Ocean, receives a score of 1.0 as it appears only once.

4.2 Document Structure

Based on the intuition that the HTML structure of a web site reflects content relevancy, we have developed the hypertext feature. The *hypertext* feature assigns a higher score to sentences contained under higher level HTML headings.

Heading	Bonus
H1	1/1 = 1.00
H2	1/2 = 0.50
H3	1/3 = 0.33
H4	1/4 = 0.25
H5	1/5 = 0.20
H6	1/6 = 0.17

Table 1. Hypertext feature heading bonus

Within a given heading level, the hypertext feature assigns a higher score to sentences that appear earlier within that level based on both relative paragraph order within the heading and relative sentence position within each paragraph. The equation used to compute the hypertext score for a sentence is

$$hypertext\_score = heading\_bonus * \sqrt[4]{1/par\_no} * \sqrt[4]{1/sent\_no}$$

where *heading_bonus* is obtained from Table 1, *par_no* is the paragraph number within the heading, and *sent_no* is the sentence number within the paragraph. We use the $\sqrt[4]{1/x}$ function to attenuate the contributions to the feature score of later paragraphs and sentences. Initially, we used the same function MEAD uses to modulate its position feature ($\sqrt[2]{1/x}$), but initial experimentation indicated this function decayed too rapidly, resulting in later sentences being over-penalized.

4.3 Sentence Length

To promote the extraction of sentences containing scientific concepts, we have developed the *content word density* feature. This feature makes a cut-off decision based on the ratio of content words to function words in a sentence. The content word density feature uses a pre-populated list of function words (a stopword list) to calculate the ratio of content to function words within each sentence, keeping sentences that meet or exceed the ratio of 50%. This cut-off value implies that the extracted sentences contain relatively more content words than function words.

4.4 Sentence Scoring and Selection

We compute the final score of each sentence by adding the scores obtained for the MEAD default configuration features (centroid and position) to the scores for the COGENT features (educational standards, gazetteer, and hypertext). After the sentences have been sorted according to their cumulative scores, we keep sentences that pass the cut-off constraints, including the MEAD length feature equal or greater than 9 and COGENT content word density equal or greater than 50%. We use the MEAD cosine re-ranker to eliminate redundant sentences based on a cutoff similarity value of 0.7. Since human experts used only 5% of the total word count in the resources, we have configured MEAD to use a 5% word compression rate.

5 Evaluation

We have evaluated COGENT by processing the 20 digital library resources used in the empirical study and comparing its output against the concepts identified by the experts.

5.1 Quality

To assess the quality of the generated summaries, we have examined three configurations: *Random*, *Default*, and *COGENT*. The *Random* configuration extracts a random collection of sentences from the input texts. The *Default* configuration uses the MEAD default centroid, position and length (cut-off value of 9) sentence scoring features. Finally, the *COGENT* configuration includes the MEAD default features and the COGENT features. The Default and COGENT configurations use the MEAD cosine function with a threshold of 0.7 to eliminate redundant sentences. All three configurations use a word compression factor of 5% resulting in summaries of very similar length.

For this evaluation, we leverage ROUGE (Lin and Hovy, 2003) to address the relative quality of the generated summaries based on common n-gram counts and longest common subsequence (LCS). We report on ROUGE-1 (unigrams), ROUGE-2 (bigrams), ROUGE W-1.2 (weighted LCS), and ROUGE-S* (skip bigrams) as they appear to correlate well with human judgments for longer multi-document summaries, particularly ROUGE-1 (Lin, 2004). Table 2 shows the results of this ROUGE-based evaluation including recall (R), precision (P), and balanced f-measure (F).

		Random	Default	COGENT
R-1	R	0.4855	0.4976	0.6073
	P	0.5026	0.5688	0.6034
	F	0.4939	0.5308	0.6054
R-2	R	0.0972	0.1321	0.1907
	P	0.1006	0.1510	0.1895
	F	0.0989	0.1409	0.1901
R-W-1.2	R	0.0929	0.0951	0.1185
	P	0.1533	0.1733	0.1877
	F	0.1157	0.1228	0.1453
R-S*	R	0.2481	0.2620	0.3820
	P	0.2657	0.3424	0.3772
	F	0.2566	0.2969	0.3796

Table 2. Quality evaluation results (5% word compression)

COGENT consistently outperforms the Random and Default baselines based on all four reported ROUGE measures. Given that much of the original research efforts on MEAD have centered on news articles, this result is not surprising. Pedagogical content, such as the educational digital library resources used in our work, differs in rhetorical intent, structure and terminology from the news articles leveraged by the MEAD researchers. However, the COGENT features described here are complementary to the default MEAD configuration. COGENT can best be characterized as a hybrid MDS, integrating bottom-up (centroid, position, length, hypertext, and content word density) and top-down (educational standards and gazetteer) sentence scoring features. This hybrid approach reflects our findings from observing expert behaviors for identifying concepts from educational digital library resources. We believe the overall improvement in quality scores may be due to the COGENT features targeting different dimensions of what constitutes a pedagogically effective summary than the default MEAD features.

To characterize the COGENT summary contents, one of our research team members manually generated a summary corresponding to the best case for an extractive summarizer. This *Best Case* summary comprises the sentences from the digital library resources that align to the concepts selected by the human experts in our empirical study. Since the experts created concepts of varying granularity, this alignment produces the list of sentences that the experts would have produced if they had only selected single sentences to create concepts for their domain knowledge map. This summary comprises 621 sentences consisting of 13,116 words, or about a 9% word compression.

For this aspect of the evaluation, we have used ROUGE-L, an LCS metric computed using ROUGE. The ROUGE-L computation examines the union LCS between each reference sentence and all the sentences in the candidate summary. We believe this metric may be well-suited to reflect the degree of linguistic surface structure similarity between summaries. We postulate that ROUGE-L may be able to account for the explicitly copy-pasted concepts and to detect the more subtle similarities with paraphrased concepts in the expert-generated domain knowledge map. We have also used the content-based evaluation capabilities of MEAD to report on a cosine measure to capture similarity between the candidate summaries and the reference. Table 3 shows the results of this aspect of the evaluation including recall (R), precision (P), and balanced f-measure (F).

		Random (5%)	Default (5%)	COGENT (5%)	Best Case (9%)
R-L	R	0.4814	0.4919	0.6021	0.9669
	P	0.4982	0.5623	0.5982	0.6256
	F	0.4897	0.5248	0.6001	0.7597
Cosine		0.5382	0.6748	0.8325	0.9323

Table 3. Content-based evaluation results (word compression in parentheses)

COGENT consistently outperforms the Random and Default baselines on both the ROUGE-L and cosine measures. Given the cosine value of 0.8325, it appears COGENT extracts sentences containing similar terms in very similar frequency distribution as the experts.

The ROUGE-L scores also consistently indicate that the COGENT summary may be closer to the reference summary in relative word ordering than either the Random or Default configurations. However, the scores for the Best Case summary reveal two interesting points. First, the ROUGE-L recall score for COGENT (R=0. 6021) is lower than that obtained by the Best Case summary (R=0.9669), meaning our summarizer appears to be extracting different sentences than those selected by the experts. Given the high cosine similarity with the reference summary (0.8325), we hypothesize that COGENT may be selecting sentences that cover very similar concepts to those selected by the experts only expressed differently. Second, we would have expected the ROUGE-L precision score for the Best Case configuration to be closer to 1.0. Instead, the Best Case precision score is 0.6256, only a minor improvement over COGENT (P=0.5982). Since the sentences in the Best Case summary come directly from the digital library resources, we hypothesize that experts may have used extensive linguistic transformations for paraphrased concepts, resulting in structures that ROUGE-L could not identify as similar.

Given the difference in word compression for the Best Case summary, we have performed an incremental analysis using the ROUGE-L measure shown in Figure 2.

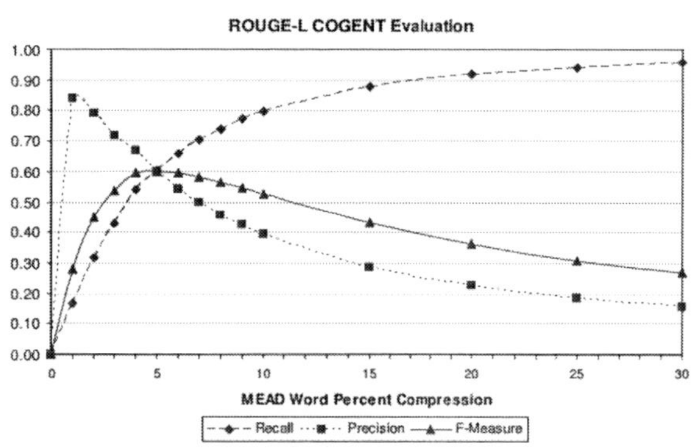

Figure 2. COGENT ROUGE-L results at different word compression rates

This graph shows improved COGENT performance in ROUGE-L recall as the length of the summary increases, while both precision and f-measure degrade. COGENT can match the recall scores of the Best Case summary (R=0.9669) by making the generated summary longer (30% word compression rate or 32,619 words), but the precision would suffer a sizeable decay (P=0.1558). For educational applications, more comprehensive concept inventories (longer summaries) may be better suited for computational purposes, such as pedagogical reasoning about student understanding, while more succinct inventories (shorter summaries) may be more appropriate for display to the student.

5.2 Pedagogical Utility

We have evaluated COGENT's pedagogical utility in the context of computationally identifying student scientific misconceptions. We have developed algorithms that reliably detect incorrect statements in student essays by comparing an expert-created domain knowledge map to an expert-created knowledge map of an essay. These algorithms use textual entailment techniques based on a shallow linguistic analysis of knowledge map concepts to identify sentences that contradict concepts in the domain knowledge map. Initial evaluation results indicate that these algorithms identify incorrect statements nearly as adeptly as human experts.

	Manual Expert Agreement	Expert Knowledge Maps	COGENT Concept Inventory
Recall	0.69	0.87	0.93
Precision	0.69	0.57	0.57
F-Measure	0.69	0.68	0.69

Table 4. Incorrect statement identification evaluation results

As shown in Table 4, the algorithms detect 87% of all incorrect statements identified by experts and 57% of the reported incorrect statements agree with human judgments on the same task. By comparison, experts show 69% overlap on average along both dimensions. Introducing the COGENT concept inventory in place of the expert-created domain knowledge map improves recall performance, as the algorithms return 93% of all incorrect statements reported by the experts, while preserving 57% precision. These results indicate that the generated summary covers the necessary pedagogical concepts to computationally identify student scientific misconceptions.

Informal sampling of the sentences selected by COGENT shows the following three important science concepts receiving the highest scores:

1. Earthquakes are the result of forces deep within the Earth's interior that continuously affect the surface of the Earth.
2. Scientists believed that the movement of the Earth's plates bends and squeezes the rocks at the edges of the plates.
3. In particular, four major scientific developments spurred the formulation of the plate-

tectonics theory: (1) demonstration of the ruggedness and youth of the ocean floor; (2) confirmation of repeated reversals of the Earth magnetic field in the geologic past; (3) emergence of the seafloor-spreading hypothesis and associated recycling of oceanic crust; and (4) precise documentation that the world's earthquake and volcanic activity is concentrated along oceanic trenches and submarine mountain ranges.

For a more rigorous analysis of the pedagogical utility of the COGENT concepts, we asked an instructional expert with domain expertise in geology to evaluate the 326 sentences returned by COGENT. The expert used a 5-point Likert scale to judge whether each concept would be pedagogically useful in the context of a concept inventory on earthquakes and plate tectonics knowledge for high school age learners. The expert agreed or strongly agreed that 60% of the sentences would be pedagogically useful, with 30% of the sentences being potentially useful and only 10% of the sentences being judged as not useful. These results indicate that COGENT appears to perform quite well at identifying sentences that contain information relevant for learning about the domain.

We have also completed an ablation study to identify the relative contribution of the COGENT features to the quality of the summary. We have focused on the cosine metric to capture the overall similarity between the COGENT concept inventory and the concepts from the expert-created knowledge map.

Features	Cosine
All Features	0.8325
(Gazetteer)	0.5545
(Hypertext)	0.5575
(Educational Standards)	0.8083
(Content Word Density)	0.8271

Table 5. Feature ablation evaluation results for COGENT

Table 5 shows the cosine similarity between the concept inventory generated after taking the feature shown in parentheses out of the summarizer. The results are ordered from low-to-high such that the feature contributing the most to the all-features cosine score appears at the top of the table. Removing either the gazetteer or the hypertext feature causes the largest drops in similarity indicating the importance of the use of examples and the relevance of document structure for the quality of the COGENT-generated summary. Meanwhile both the educational standards and content word density appear to provide modest but useful improvements to the quality of the COGENT summary.

Given that our algorithms have only been evaluated on the topic of earthquakes and plate tectonics for high school age learners, COGENT may be limited in its ability to transcend domains due to its reliance on two domain-aware sentence scoring features: educational standards and gazetteer. However, the educational standards feature may be applicable across other science topics because the *AAAS Benchmarks* and NSES provide very thorough and detailed coverage of a wide range of topics for the Science, Technology, Engineering, and Math disciplines for grades K-12. Only the gazetteer feature would need to be replaced, especially given its significant contribution to the quality of the generated summary as indicated by the results of the ablation study. We believe these results highlight the need to generalize our approach, perhaps using a classifier for identifying examples in educational texts without resorting to overly domain-specific language resources, such as the ADL Gazetteer. Overall, the evaluation results indicate that our approach holds promise for effectively identifying concepts for inclusion in the construction of a pedagogically useful domain knowledge map from educational science content.

6 Conclusions and Future Work

In this paper, we have presented a multi-document summarization system, COGENT, that integrates bottom-up and top-down sentence scoring features to identify pedagogically relevant concepts from educational digital library resources. Our results indicate that COGENT generates concept inventories that resemble those identified by experts and outperforms existing multi-document summarization systems. We have also used the COGENT concept inventory as input to our misconception identification algorithms and the evaluation results indicate the algorithms perform as well as when using an expert-created domain knowledge map. In the context of generating domain knowledge maps, our next step is to explore how machine learning techniques may be employed to connect concepts with links.

Automating the process of creating inventories of important pedagogical concepts represents an important step towards creating scalable intelligent learning and tutoring systems. We hope our progress in this direction may contribute to increase the interest within the computational linguistics research community in novel educational technology research.

Acknowledgments

This research is funded in part by the National Science Foundation under NSF IIS/ALT Award 0537194. Any opinions, findings, and conclusions or recommendations expressed in this material are those of the author(s) and do not necessarily reflect the views of the NSF.

References

Ahmad, F., de la Chica, S., Butcher, K., Sumner, T. and Martin, J.H. (2007, June 17-23). Towards automatic conceptual personalization tools. In Proceedings of the 7th ACM/IEEE-CS Joint Conference on Digital Libraries, (Vancouver, British Columbia, Canada, 2007), pages 452 - 461.

Butcher, K.R., Bhushan, S. and Sumner, T. (2006). Multimedia displays for conceptual discovery: information seeking with strand maps. ACM Multimedia Systems, 11 (3), pages 236-248.

Byrt, T., Bishop, J. and Carlin, J.B. (1993). Bias, prevalence, and kappa. Journal of Clinical Epidemiology, 46 (5), pages 423-429.

Harabagiu, S. and Lacatusu, F. (2005, August 15-19). Topic themes for multi-document summarization. In Proceedings of the 28th Annual International ACM SIGIR Conference on Research and Development in Information Retrieval, (Salvador, Brazil, 2005), pages 202-209.

Hardy, H., Shimizu, N., Strzalkowski, T., Ting, L., Wise, G.B. and Zhang, X. (2002). Summarizing large document sets using concept-based clustering. In Proceedings of the Human Language Technology Conference 2002, (San Diego, California, United States, 2002), pages 222-227.

Hill, L.L. (2000, September 18-20). Core elements of digital gazetteers: placenames, categories, and footprints. In Proceedings of the 4th European Conference on Digital Libraries, (Lisbon, Portugal, 2000), pages 280-290.

Holley, C.D. and Dansereau, D.F. (1984). Spatial learning strategies: Techniques, applications, and related issues. Academic Press, Orlando, Florida.

Lin, C.Y. (2004). ROUGE: A package for automatic evaluation of summaries. In Proceedings of the Workshop on Text Summarization Branches Out, (Barcelona, Spain, 2004).

Lin, C.Y. and Hovy, E. (2003, May-June). Automatic evaluation of summaries using n-gram co-occurrence statistics. In Proceedings of the Human Language Technology Conference of the North American Chapter of the Association for Computational Linguistics, HLT-NAACL, (Edmonton, Canada, 2003), pages 71-78.

Lin, D. and Pantel, P. (2002, August 24-September 1). Concept discovery from text. In Proceedings of the 19th International Conference on Computational Linguistics, (Taipei, Taiwan, 2002), pages 1-7.

Mani, I. (2001). Automatic Summarization. Mitkov, R. (Ed.) John Benjamins B.V., Amsterdam, The Netherlands.

National Research Council. (1996). National Science Education Standards. National Academy Press, Washington, DC.

Navigli, R. and Velardi, P. (2004). Learning domain ontologies from document warehouses and dedicated websites. Computational Linguistics, 30 (2), pages 151-179.

Novak, J.D. and Gowin, D.B. (1984). Learning how to learn. Cambridge University Press, New York, New York.

O'Donnell, A.M., Dansereau, D.F. and Hall, R.H. (2002). Knowledge maps as scaffolds for cognitive processing. Educational Psychology Review, 14 (1), pages 71-86.

Project 2061. (1993). Benchmarks for science literacy. Oxford University Press, New York, New York, United States.

Radev, D.R., Jing, H. and Budzikowska, M. (2000). Centroid-based summarization of multiple documents: sentence extraction, utility-based evaluation, and user studies. In Proceedings of the ANLP/NAACL 2000 Workshop on Summarization, (2000), pages 21-30.

Salton, G. and Buckley, C. (1988). Term-weighting approaches in automatic text retrieval. Information Processing and Management, 24 (5), pages 513-523.

Wan, X. and Yang, J. (2006, June 5th-7th). Improved affinity graph based multi-document summarization. In Proceedings of the Human Language Technology Conference of the North American Chapter of the Association for Computational Linguistics, (New York City, New York, 2006), pages 181-184.

Zouaq, A., Nkambou, R. and Frasson, C. (2007, July 9-13). Learning a domain ontology in the Knowledge Puzzle project. In Proceedings of the Fifth International Workshop on Ontologies and Semantic Web for E-Learning, (Marina del Rey, California, 2007).

Looking for Trouble

Stijn De Saeger **Kentaro Torisawa**
Language Infrastructure Group
National Institute of Information
and Communications Technology
{stijn,torisawa}@nict.go.jp

Jun'ichi Kazama
School of Information Science
Japan Advanced Institute
of Science and Technology
kazama@jaist.ac.jp

Abstract

This paper presents a method for mining potential *troubles* or *obstacles* related to the use of a given *object*. Some example instances of this relation are ⟨*medicine, side effect*⟩ and ⟨*amusement park, height restriction*⟩. Our acquisition method consists of three steps. First, we use an unsupervised method to collect training samples from Web documents. Second, a set of expressions generally referring to troubles is acquired by a supervised learning method. Finally, the acquired troubles are associated with objects so that each of the resulting pairs consists of an object and a trouble or obstacle in *using* that object. To show the effectiveness of our method we conducted experiments using a large collection of Japanese Web documents for acquisition. Experimental results show an 85.5% precision for the top 10,000 acquired troubles, and a 74% precision for the top 10% of over 60,000 acquired object-trouble pairs.

1 Introduction

The Stanford Encyclopedia of Philosophy defines an artifact as "*...an object that has been intentionally made or produced for a certain purpose*". Because of this purpose-orientedness, most human actions relating to an object or artifact fall into two broad categories — actions relating to its intended use (e.g. *reading a book*), and the preparations necessary therefore (like *buying the book*). Information concerning potential obstacles, harmful effects or troubles that interfere with this intended use is therefore highly relevant to the user. While some such troubles are self-evident, others represent a genuine obstacle whose existence was thusfar unknown to the user. For example, in early 2008 a food poisoning case caused a big media stir in Japan when dozens of people fell ill after eating Chinese-imported frozen food products containing residual traces of toxic pesticides. While supposedly the presence of toxic chemicals in imported frozen foods had already been established on several occasions before, until the recent incidents public awareness of these facts remained low. In retrospect, a publicly available system suggesting "residual agrichemicals" as a potential danger with the consumption of "frozen foods" based on information mined from a large collection of Web documents might have led to earlier detection of this crisis. From the viewpoint of manufacturers as well, regularly monitoring the Internet for product names and associated troubles may allow them to find out about perceived flaws in their products sooner and avoid large scale recalls and damage to their brand.

For a less dramatic example, searching for *"Tokyo Disneyland"* on the Internet typically yields many commercial sites offering travel deals, but little or no information about potential obstacles such as "height restrictions" (constraints on who can enjoy a given attraction[1]) and "traffic jams" (a necessary preparation for enjoying a theme park is actually getting there in time). Ofter users have no way of finding out about this until they actually go there.

These examples demonstrate the importance of a highly accurate automatic method for acquiring what we will call "object-trouble" relations — pairs $\langle e_o, e_t \rangle$ in which the thing referred to by e_t constitutes an (actual or potential) trouble, obstacle or risk in the *context of use* of an object e_o.

©2008. Licensed under the *Creative Commons Attribution-Noncommercial-Share Alike 3.0 Unported* license (http://creativecommons.org/licenses/by-nc-sa/3.0/). Some rights reserved.

[1] For example, one has to be over 3 ft. tall to get on the Splash Mountain.

Large scale acquisition of this type of contextual knowledge has not been thoroughly studied so far. In this paper, we propose a method for automatically acquiring Japanese noun phrases referring to troubles, (henceforth referred to as *trouble expressions*), and associating them with expressions denoting artifacts, objects or facilities.

Our acquisition method consists of three steps. As a first step, we use an unsupervised method for efficiently collecting training data from a Web corpus. Then, a set of expressions denoting troubles is acquired by a supervised learning method — Support Vector Machines (Vapnik, 1998) — trained on this data. Finally, the acquired trouble expressions are paired with noun phrases referring to objects, using a combination of pairwise mutual information and a verb-noun dependency filter based on statistics in a Web corpus.

A broad focus on noun-verb dependencies — and in particular the distinction between dependency relations with *negated* versus *non-negated* verbs – is the main characteristic of our method. While this distinction did not prove useful for improving the supervised classifier's performance in step 2, it forms the basis underlying the unsupervised method for training sample selection in the first step, and the final filtering mechanism in the third step.

The rest of this paper is organized as follows. Section 2 points out related work. Section 3 examines the notion of trouble expressions and their evidences. Section 4 describes our method, whose experimental results are discussed in Section 5.

2 Related Work

Our goal of automatically acquiring object-trouble pairs from Web documents is perhaps best viewed as a problem of semantic relation extraction. Recently the Automatic Content Extraction (ACE) program (Doddington et al., 2004) is a well-known benchmark task concerned with the automatic recognition of semantic relations from unstructured text. Typical target relations include "Reaction" and "Production" (Pantel and Pennacchiootti, 2006), "person-affiliation" and "organization-location" (Zelenko et al., 2002), "part-whole" (Berland and Charniak, 1999; Girju et al., 2006) and temporal precedence relations between events (Chklovski and Pantel, 2004; Torisawa, 2006). Our current task of acquiring "object-trouble" relations is new and object-trouble relations are inherently more abstract and indirect than relations like "person-affiliation" — they crucially depend on additional knowledge about *whether* and *how* a given object's use might be hampered by a specific trouble.

Another line of research closely related to our work is the recognition of semantic orientation and sentiment analysis (Turney, 2002; Takamura et al., 2006; Kaji and Kitsuregawa, 2006). Clearly troubles should be associated with a negative orientation of an expression, but studies on the acquisition of semantic orientation traditionally do not bother with the context of evaluation. While recent work on sentiment analysis has started to associate sentiment-related attribute-evaluation pairs to objects (Kobayashi et al., 2007), these attributes usually concern *intrinsic* properties of the objects, such as a digital camera's colors — they do not extend to sentiment-related factors *external* to the object like "traffic jams" for theme parks. The acquisition method proposed in this work addresses both these matters.

Finally, our task of acquiring trouble expressions can be regarded as hyponymy acquisition, where target expressions are hyponyms of the word "trouble". Although we used the classical lexico-syntactic patterns for hyponymy acquisition (Hearst, 1992; Imasumi, 2001; Ando et al., 2003) to reflect this intuition, our experiments show we were unable to attain satisfactory performance using lexico-syntactic patterns alone. Thus, we also use verb-noun dependencies as evidence in learning (Pantel and Ravichandran, 2004; Shinzato and Torisawa, 2004). We treat the evidences uniformly as elements in a feature vector given to a supervised learning method, which allowed us to extract a considerably larger number of trouble expressions than could be acquired by sparse lexico-syntactic patterns alone, while still keeping decent precision. What kind of hyponymy relations can be acquired by noun-verb dependencies is still an open question in NLP. In this work we show that at least trouble expressions can successfully be acquired based on noun-verb dependency information alone.

3 Trouble Expressions and Features for Their Acquisition

In section 1 we have characterized trouble expressions as a kind of "trouble" that occurs in the specific context of using some object, in other words:

1. *hyponym* ni nita *hypernym* (*hyponym* similar to *hypernym*)
2. *hyponym* to yobareru *hypernym* (*hypernym* called *hyponym*)
3. *hyponym* igai no *hypernym* (*hypernym* other than *hyponym*)
4. *hyponym* no youna *hypernym* (*hypernym* like *hyponym*)
5. *hyponym* to iu *hypernym* (*hypernym* called *hyponym*)
6. *hyponym* nado(no|,) *hypernym* (*hypernym* such as *hyponym*)

Table 1: Japanese lexico-syntactic patterns for hyponymy relations

as hyponyms of "trouble". Hence one source of evidence for acquisition are hyponymy relations with "trouble" or its synonyms. Another characterization of trouble expressions is to think of them as obstacles in a broad sense: things that prevent certain actions from being undertaken properly. In this sense *traffic jams* and *sickness* are troubles since they prevent people from going places and doing things. This assumption underlies a second important class of evidences for learning.

More precisely, the evidence used for learning is classified into three categories: (i) lexico-syntactic patterns for hyponymy relations, (ii) dependency relations between expressions and negated verbs, and (iii) dependency relations between expressions and non-negated verbs. The first two categories are assumed to contain positive evidence of trouble expressions, while we assumed the third to function mostly as negative evidence. Our experiments show that (i) turns out to be less useful than expected, while the combination of (ii) and (iii) alone already gave quite reasonable precision in acquiring trouble expressions. Each category of evidence is described further below.

3.1 Lexico-syntactic patterns for hyponymy

Since trouble expressions are hyponyms of "trouble", one obvious way of acquiring trouble expressions is to use classical lexico-syntactic patterns for hyponymy acquisition (Hearst, 1992). Table 1 lists some of the patterns proposed in studies on hyponymy acquisition for Japanese (Ando et al., 2003; Imasumi, 2001) that are utilized in this work.

In actual acquisition, we instantiated the *hypernym* positions in the patterns by Japanese translations of "trouble" and its synonyms, namely toraburu (troubles), sainan (accidents), saigai (disasters) and shougai (obstacles or handicaps), and used the instantiated patterns as evidence. Hereafter, we call these patterns **LSPHs** (Lexico-Syntactic Patterns for Hyponymy).

3.2 Dependency relations with Verbs

We expect expressions that frequently refer to troubles to have a distinct *dependency profile*, by which we mean a specific set of dependency relations with verbs (i.e. occurrences in specific *argument positions*). If T is a trouble expression, then given a sufficiently large corpus one would expect to find a reasonable number of instantiations of patterns like the following:

- T kept X from doing Y.
- X didn't enjoy Y because of T.

Similarly, "X enjoyed T" would present negative evidence for T being a trouble expression. Rather than single out a set of particular dependency relations suspected to be indicative of trouble expressions, we let a supervised classifier learn an appropriate weight for each feature in a large vector of dependency relations. Two classes of dependency relations proved to be especially beneficial in determining trouble candidates in an unsupervised manner, so we discuss them in more detail below.

Dependency relations with negated verbs Following our characterization of troubles as things that *prevent* specific actions from taking place, we expect a good deal of trouble expressions to appear in patterns like the following.

- X cannot go to Y *because of* T.
- X did not enjoy Y *because of* T.

The important points in the above are (i) the negated verbs and (ii) the mention of T as the reason for not verb-ing. The following are Japanese translations of the above patterns. Here P denotes postpositions (Japanese case markers), V stands for verbs and the phrase "because of" is translated as the postposition de.

- T de Y ni ikenai.
  (de: P, ni: P, ikenai: V (cannot go))
- T de X ga tanoshikunakatta.
  (de: P, ga: P, tanoshikunakatta: V (did not enjoy))

We refer to the following dependency relations between expressions marked with the postposition de and negated verbs in these patterns as **DNVs** (Dependencies to Negated Verbs).

$$T \text{ de} \rightarrow \text{negated verb} \quad (1)$$

We allow any verb to be the negated verb, expecting that inappropriate verbs will be less weighted by machine learning techniques. For instance, the dependency relations to negated verbs with an originally negative orientation such as "suffer" and "die" will not work as positive examples for trouble expressions.

Unfortunately, these patterns still present only *weak* evidence for trouble expressions. The precision of the trouble expressions collected using DNV patterns is extremely low — around 6.5%. This is due to the postposition de's ambiguity — besides "because of" relations it also functions as a marker for location, time and instrument relations, among others. As a result, non-trouble expressions such as "by car" (instrument) and "in Tokyo" (location) are marked by the postposition de as well.

We consider a second class of dependency relations, acting mostly as a counter to the noisy expressions introduced by the ambiguity of the postposition de.

Dependency relations with non-negated verbs The final type of evidence is formulated as the following dependency relation.

$$T \text{ de} \rightarrow \text{non-negated verb}$$

We call this type of relation **DAVs** (Dependencies to Affirmative Verbs). The use of these patterns is motivated by the intuition that noisy expressions found with DNVs, such as expressions about locations or instruments, will also frequently appear with non-negated verbs. That is, if you observe "cannot go to Y (by / because of) X" and X is not a trouble expression, then you can expect to find "can go to Y (by / because of) X" as well.

Our initial expectation was that the DNV and DAV evidences observed with the postposition de alone would contain sufficient information to obtain an accurate classifier, but this expectation was not borne out by our early experiments. As it turns out, using dependency relations to verbs in *all* argument positions as features to the SVM resulted roughly in a 10$\sim$15% increase in precision. Therefore in our final experiments we let the DNV and DAV evidence consist of dependencies with four additional postpositions (ha, ga, wo and ni), which are used to indicate topicalization, subject, object and indirect object. We found that the SVM was quite successful in learning a dependency profile for trouble expressions based on this information.

Nonetheless, the DNV/DAV patterns proved to be useful besides as evidence for supervised learning, for instance in gathering sufficient trouble candidates and sample selection when preparing training data [2].

4 Method

As mentioned, our method for finding troubles in using some objects consists of three steps, described in more detail below.

Step 1 Gather training data with a sufficient amount of positive samples using an unsupervised method to reduce the workload of manual annotation.

Step 2 Collect expressions commonly perceived as troubles by using the evidences described in the previous section.

Step 3 Identify pairs of trouble expressions and objects such that the trouble expressions represent an obstacle in using the objects.

4.1 Step 1: Gathering Training Data

We considered noun phrases observed with the LSPH and DNV evidences as candidate trouble expressions. However, we still found only 7% of the samples observed with these evidences to be real troubles. Because of the diversity of our evidences (dependencies with verbs) we need a reasonable amount of positive samples in order to obtain an accurate classifier. Without some sample selection scheme, we would have to manually annotate about 8000 samples in order to obtain only 560 positive samples in the training data. For this reason we used the following scoring function as an unsupervised method for sample selection.

$$Score(e) = \frac{f_{\text{LSPH}}(e) + f_{\text{DNV}}(e)}{f_{\text{LSPH}}(e) + f_{\text{DNV}}(e) + f_{\text{DAV}}(e)} \quad (2)$$

Here, $f_{\text{LSPH}}(e)$, $f_{\text{DNV}}(e)$ and $f_{\text{DAV}}(e)$ are the frequencies that expression e appears with the respective evidences. Intuitively, this function gives

[2] We will discuss yet another use of the DNV evidence in step 2 of our acquisition method.

a large score to expressions that occur frequently with the positive evidences for trouble expressions (LSPHs and DNVs), or those that appear rarely with the negative evidences (DAVs). In preparing training data we ranked all candidates according to the above score, and annotated N elements from the top and bottom of the ranking as training data. In our experiments, the top elements included a reasonable number of positive samples (25.8%) while there were almost none in the worst elements.

4.2 Step 2: Finding Trouble Expressions

In this step our aim is to acquire expressions often associated with troubles. We use a supervised classifier, namely Support Vector Machines (SVMs) (Vapnik, 1998) for distinguishing troubles from non-troubles, based on the evidences described above. Each dimension of the feature vector presented to the SVM corresponds to the observation of a particular evidence (i.e., these are binary features). We tried using frequencies instead of binary feature values but could not find any significant improvement in performance. After learning we sort the candidate trouble expressions according to their distance to the hyperplane learned by the SVM, and consider the top N expressions in the sorted list as true trouble expressions.

4.3 Step 2: Identifying Object-Trouble Pairs

In this third stage we rank possible combinations of objects and trouble expressions acquired in the previous step according to their degree of association and apply a filter using negated verbs to the top pairs in the ranking. The final output of our method is the top N pairs that survived the filtering. We describe each step below.

Generating Object-Trouble Pairs To generate and rank object-trouble pairs we use a variant of pairwise mutual information that scores an object-trouble pair $\langle e_o, e_t \rangle$ based on the observed frequency of the following pattern.

$$\underset{}{e_o} \quad \underset{\text{P}}{\texttt{no}} \quad \underset{}{e_t} \tag{3}$$

The postposition no is a genitive case marker, and the whole pattern can be translated as "e_t of / in e_o". We assume that appearance of expression e_t in this pattern refers to a trouble in using the object e_o.

More precisely, we generate all possible combinations of trouble expression and objects and rank them according to the following score.

$$I(e_o, e_t) = \frac{f(\text{“}e_o \texttt{ no } e_t\text{”})}{f(\text{“}e_o\text{”})f(\text{“}e_t\text{”})} \tag{4}$$

where $f(e)$ denotes an expression e's frequency. This score is large when the pattern "e_o no e_t" is observed more frequently than can be expected from e_o and e_t's individual frequencies. Frequency data for all noun phrases was precomputed for the whole Web corpus.

Filtering Object-Trouble Pairs The filtering in the second step is based on the following assumption.

Assumption If a trouble expression e_t refers to a trouble in using an object e_o, there is a verb v such that v frequently co-occurs with e_o and v has the following dependency relation with e_t.

$$e_t \;\; \texttt{de} \rightarrow \text{negated } v$$

The intuition behind this assumption can be explained as follows. First, if e_o denotes an object or artifact then its frequently co-occurring verbs are likely to be related to a use of e_o. Second, if e_t is a trouble in using e_o, there is some action associated with e_o that e_t prevents or hinders, implying that e_t should be observed with its negation. For instance, if "traffic jam" is a trouble in using an amusement park, then we can expect the following pattern to appear also in a corpus.

juutai	de	yuuenchi	ni	ikenai.
traffic jam	P	*theme park*	P	V (cannot go)

  cannot go to a theme park because of a traffic jam

The verb "to go" co-occurs often with the noun "theme park" and the above pattern contains the dependency relation "traffic jam de → cannot go". Substituting v in the hypothesis for "to go", the assumption becomes valid. Because of data sparseness the above pattern may not actually appear in the corpus, but even so the dependency relation "traffic jam de → cannot go" may be observed with other facilities, and thus making the assumption hold anyway.

As a final filtering procedure, we gathered K verbs most frequently co-occurring with each object and checked if the trouble expression in the pair has dependency relations with the K verbs in negated form and the postposition de. If none of the K verbs has such a dependency with the trouble expression, the pair is discarded. Otherwise, it is produced as the final output of our method.

5 Experimental Results

5.1 Finding Trouble Expressions

We extracted noun phrases observed in LSPH, DNV and DAV patterns from 6×10^9 sentences in about 10^8 crawled Japanese Web documents, and used the LSPH and DNV data [3] as candidate trouble expressions. After restricting the noun phrases to those observed more than 10 times in the evidences, we had 136,212 noun phrases. We denote this set as D. Extracting 200 random samples from D we found the ratio of troubles to non-troubles was around 7% and thus expected to find about 10,000 real trouble expressions in D. [4]

Using the sample selection method described in Section 4.2 we prepared 6,500 annotated samples taken from D as training data. The top 3,500 samples included 912 positive samples and the worst 3,000 had just 9 positives, thereby confirming the effectiveness of the scoring function for selecting a reasonable amount of positive samples. Our final training data thus contained 14% positives.

For the feature vectors we included dependencies with all verbs occurring more than 30 times in our Web corpus. Besides the LSPH, DNV and DAV evidences discussed previously, we also included 10 additional binary features indicating for each of the five postpositions whether the expression was observed with DNV or DAV evidence *at all*, and found that including this information improved performance.

We trained a classifier with a polynomial kernel of degree 1 on these evidences using the software TinySVM[5], and evaluated the results obtained by the supervised acquisition method by asking three human raters whether a randomly selected sample expression denotes a kind of "trouble" in general situations. More specifically, we asked whether the expression is a kind of toraburu (trouble), sainan (accident), saigai (disaster) or shougai (obstacle or handicap).[6] For various

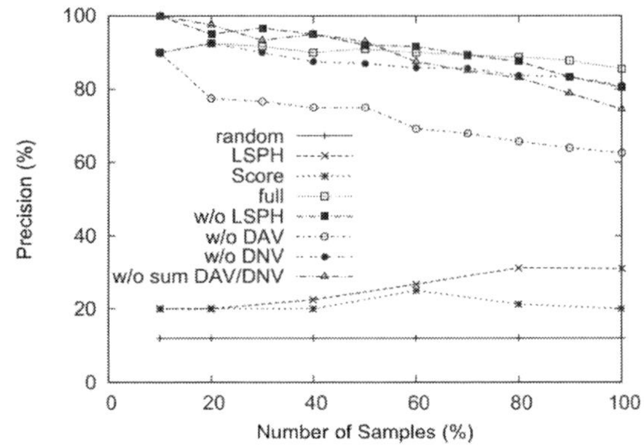

Figure 1: Performance of trouble expression acquisition (all 3 raters)

combinations of evidences (described below), we presented 200 randomly sampled expressions from the top 10,000 expressions ranked according to the distance to the hyperplane learned by the SVM. Samples of all the compared methods are merged and shuffled before evaluation. The kappa statistic for assessing the inter-rater agreement was 0.78, indicating substantial agreement according to Landis and Koch, 1977.[7] We made no effort to remove samples used in training from the experiment, and found that the samples scored by the raters (1281 in total, after removal of duplicates) contained 67 training samples. The 200 samples from the "full" classifier contained 12 of these.

Fig. 1 shows the precision of the acquired trouble expressions compared to the samples labeled as troubles by all three raters. We sorted the samples according to their distance to the SVM hyperplane and plotted the precision of the top N samples. The best overall precision (85.5%) was obtained by a classifier trained on the full combination of evidences (labeled "full" in Fig. 1), maintaining over 90% precision for the top 70% of the 200 samples.

The remaining results show the relative contributions of the evidences. They were obtained by retraining the "full" classifier with a particular set of evidences removed, respectively LSPH evidences (labeled "w/o LSPH"), DNV evidences ("w/o DNV"), DAV evidences ("w/o DAV") and the 10 features indicating the observation of

[3] We restricted noun phrases from the DNV data to those found with the postposition de, as these are most likely to refer to troubles.

[4] Thus, in the experiments we evaluated the top 10,000 samples output by our method.

[5] http://chasen.org/~taku/software/TinySVM/

[6] Actually one of the raters is a co-author of this paper, but he had no knowledge of the experimental setting nor had seen the acquired data prior to the experiment.

[7] This kappa value was calculated over the sum total of samples presented to the raters for scoring (duplicates removed).

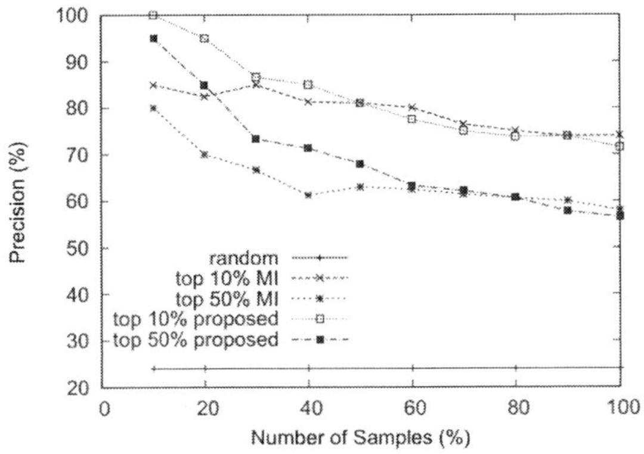

Figure 2: Performance of object-trouble pair acquisition (3 raters)

rank /raters	object	trouble expressions
1/3	kousoku douro (highway)	sakeyoi unten (drunk driving)
7/3	kouseibushitsu (antibiotics)	ranyou (abuse)
8/3	suidousui (tap water)	suiatsu teika (drop in water pressure)
21/3	nouyaku (agrichemicals)	zanryuubushitsu (residue)
98/2	kikai (machine)	gohandan (judgement error)
136/3	zaisan (estate)	souzoku funsou (succession dispute)

Figure 3: Examples of acquired object-trouble pairs

DAV/DNV evidence per postposition ("w/o sum DAV/DNV").

As Fig. 1 shows, leaving out DNV and even LSPH evidences did not affect performance as much as we expected, while leaving out the DAV dependencies gave more than 20% worse results. Of further interest is the importance of the binary features for DAV/DNV presence per postposition ("w/o sum DAV/DNV"). The absence of these 10 binary features accounts for a 10% precision loss compared to the full feature set (75%).

We also compared it with a baseline method using only lexico-syntactic patterns. We extracted 100 random noun phrases from the LSPH evidence in D for evaluation ("LSPH" in Fig. 1). The precision for this method was 31%, confirming that lexico-syntactic patterns for hyponymy constitute fairly weak evidence for predicting trouble expressions when used alone. "Score" shows the precision of the top 100 samples output by our *Score* function from section 4. Finally, "random" (drawn as a straight line) denotes 100 random samples from D and roughly corresponds to our estimate of 7% true positives.

5.2 Identifying Object-Trouble Pairs

For the second step, we assumed the top 10,000 expressions obtained by our best-scoring supervised learning method ("full" in the previous experiments) to be trouble expressions, and proceeded to combine them with terms denoting artifacts or facilities.

We randomly picked 2,500 words that appeared as direct objects of the verbs `kau` ("to buy"), `tsukau` ("to use"), `tsukuru` ("to make"), `taberu` ("to eat") and `tanoshimu` ("to enjoy") more than 500 times in our Web corpus, assuming that this would yield a representative set of noun phrases denoting objects or artifacts.[8] Combining this set of objects with the acquired trouble expressions gave a list of 61,873 object-trouble pairs (all pairs $\langle e_o, e_t \rangle$ with at least one occurrence of the pattern "e_o `no` e_t"). Of this list, 58,570 pairs survived the DNV filtering step and form the final output of our method. For the DNV filtering, we used the top 30 verbs most frequently co-occurring with the object.

We again evaluated the resulting object-trouble pairs by asking three human raters whether the presented pairs consist of an object and an expression referring to an actual or potential trouble *in using* the object. The kappa statistic was 0.60, indicating *moderate* inter-rater agreement.

Fig. 2 shows the precision of the acquired pairs when comparing with what are considered true object-trouble relations by all three raters. Some examples of the pairs obtained by our method are listed in table 3 along with their ranking and the number of raters who judged the pair to be correct.

The precision for our proposed method when considering the top 10% of pairs ranked by the I score and filtered by the method described in section 4.3 is 71.5% ("top 10% proposed" in Fig. 2), which is actually worse than the results obtained *without* the final DNV filtering ("top 10% MI", 74%). For the first half of all samples however, we do observe some performance increase by the filtering, though both methods appear to converge in the second half of the graph. This tendency is mirrored closely when considering the results for the top 50% of all pairs (respectively "top 50% proposed" and "top 50% MI" in Fig. 2). The 15% decrease in precision compared to top 10% results

[8] We manually removed pronouns from this set.

indicates that performance drops gradually when moving to the lower ranked pairs.

6 Concluding Remarks and Future Work

We have presented an automatic method for finding potential troubles in using objects, mainly artifacts and facilities. Our method acquired 10,000 trouble expressions with 85.5% precision, and over 6000 pairs of objects and trouble expressions with 74% precision.

Currently, we are developing an Internet search engine frontend that issues warnings about potential troubles related to search keywords. Although we were able to acquire object-trouble pairs with reasonable precision, we plan to make a large-scale highly precise list of troubles by manually checking the output of our method. We expect such a list to lead to even more acurate object-trouble pair acquisition.

References

Ando, M., S. Sekine, and S. Ishizaki. 2003. Automatic extraction of hyponyms from newspaper using lexicosyntactic patterns. In *IPSJ SIG Technical Report 2003-NL-157*, pages 77–82. in Japanese.

Berland, M. and E. Charniak. 1999. Finding parts in very large corpora. In *Proc. of ACL-1999*, pages 57–64.

Chklovski, T. and P. Pantel. 2004. Verbocean: Mining the web for fine-grained semantic verb relations. In *Proc. of EMNLP-04*.

Doddington, G., A. Mitchell, M. Przybocki, L. Ramshaw, S. Strassel, and R. Weischedel. 2004. The Automatic Content Extraction (ACE) Program–Tasks, Data, and Evaluation. *Proceedings of LREC 2004*, pages 837–840.

Girju, R., A. Badulescu, and D. Moldvan. 2006. Automatic discovery of part-whole relations. *Computational Linguistics*, 32(1):83–135.

Hearst, M. 1992. Automatic acquisition of hyponyms from large text corpora. In *Proc. of COLING'92*, pages 539–545.

Imasumi, K. 2001. Automatic acqusition of hyponymy relations from coordinated noun phrases and appositions. Master's thesis, Kyushu Institute of Technology.

Kaji, N. and M. Kitsuregawa. 2006. Automatic construction of polarity-tagged corpus from html documents. In *Proc. of COLING/ACL 2006*, pages 452–459. (poster session).

Kobayashi, N., K. Inui, and Y. Matsumoto. 2007. Extracting aspect-evaluation and aspect-of relations in opinion mining. In *Proc. of EMNLP-CoNLL 2007*, pages 1065–1074.

Pantel, P. and M. Pennacchiootti. 2006. Espresso: Leveranging generic patterns for automatically harvesting semantic relations. In *Proc. of COLING/ACL-06*, pages 113–120.

Pantel, P. and D. Ravichandran. 2004. Automatically labelling semantic classes. In *Proc. of HLT/NAACL-04*, pages 321–328.

Shinzato, K. and K. Torisawa. 2004. Acquiring hyponymy relations from web documents. In *HLT/NAACL-04*, pages 73–80.

Takamura, H., T. Inui, and M. Okumura. 2006. Latent variable models for semantic orientation of phrases. In *Proc. of EACL 2006*, pages 201–208.

Torisawa, K. 2006. Acquiring inference rules with temporal constraints by using japanese coordinated sentences and noun-verb co-occurrences. In Moore, R.C., J.A. Bilmes, J. Chu-Carroll, and M. Sanderson, editors, *HLT-NAACL*. The Association for Computational Linguistics.

Turney, P. 2002. Thumbs up or thumbs down? semantic orientation applied to unsupervised classification of reviews. In *Proc. of ACL'02*, pages 417–424.

Vapnik, Vladimir N. 1998. *Statistical Learning Theory*. Wiley-Interscience.

Zelenko, D., C. Aone, and A. Richardella. 2002. Kernel methods for relation extraction. In *EMNLP '02: Proceedings of the ACL-02 conference on Empirical methods in natural language processing*, pages 71–78, Morristown, NJ, USA. Association for Computational Linguistics.

Re-estimation of Lexical Parameters for Treebank PCFGs

Tejaswini Deoskar
Department of Linguistics
Cornell University
td72@cornell.edu

Abstract

We present procedures which pool lexical information estimated from unlabeled data via the Inside-Outside algorithm, with lexical information from a treebank PCFG. The procedures produce substantial improvements (up to 31.6% error reduction) on the task of determining subcategorization frames of novel verbs, relative to a smoothed Penn Treebank-trained PCFG. Even with relatively small quantities of unlabeled training data, the re-estimated models show promising improvements in labeled bracketing *f*-scores on Wall Street Journal parsing, and substantial benefit in acquiring the subcategorization preferences of low-frequency verbs.

1 Introduction

In order to obtain the meaning of a sentence automatically, it is necessary to have access to its syntactic analysis at some level of complexity. Many NLP applications like translation, question-answering, etc. might benefit from the availability of syntactic parses. Probabilistic parsers trained over labeled data have high accuracy on in-domain data: lexicalized parsers get an *f*-score of up to 90.0% on Wall Street Journal data (Charniak and Johnson (2005)'s re-ranking parser), while recently, unlexicalized PCFGs have also been shown to perform much better than previously believed (Klein and Manning, 2003). However, the limited size of annotated training data results in many parameters of a PCFG being badly estimated when trained on annotated data. The Zipfian nature of a text corpus results in PCFG parameters related to the properties of specific words being especially badly estimated. For instance, about 38% of verbs in the training sections of the Penn Treebank (PTB) (Marcus et al., 1993) occur only once – the lexical properties of these verbs (such as their most common subcategorization frames) cannot be represented accurately in a model trained exclusively on the Penn Treebank.

The research reported here addresses this issue. We start with an unlexicalized PCFG trained on the PTB. We then re-estimate the parameters of this PCFG from raw text using an unsupervised estimation method based on the Inside-Outside algorithm (Lari and Young, 1990), an instance of the Expectation Maximization algorithm (Dempster et al., 1977) for PCFG induction. The re-estimation improves *f*-score on the standard test section of the PTB significantly. Our focus is on learning lexical parameters i.e. those parameters related to the lexico-syntactic properties of open-class words. Examples of such properties are: subcategorization frames of verbs and nouns, attachment preference of adverbs to sentential, verbal or nominal nodes, attachment preference of PPs to a verbal or nominal node, etc.

The current research is related to semi-supervised training paradigms like self-training – these methods are currently being explored to improve the performance of existing PCFG models by utilizing unlabeled data. For example, McCloskey et al. (2006) achieve a 1.1% improvement in labeled bracketing *f*-score by the use of unlabeled data to self-train the parser-reranker system from Charniak and Johnson (2005). Earlier research on inside-outside estimation of PCFG models has reported some positive results as well

© 2008. Licensed under the *Creative Commons Attribution-Noncommercial-Share Alike 3.0 Unported* license (http://creativecommons.org/licenses/by-nc-sa/3.0/). Some rights reserved.

(Pereira and Schabes, 1992; Carroll and Rooth, 1998; Beil et al., 1999; imWalde, 2002). In some of these cases, an initial model is derived by other means – inside-outside is used to *re-estimate* the initial model. However, many questions still remain open about its efficacy for PCFG re-estimation. Grammars used previously have not been treebank grammars (for e.g., Carroll and Rooth (1998) and Beil et al. (1999) used hand-crafted grammars), hence these models could not be evaluated according to standardized evaluations in the parsing literature. In the current work, we use a Penn Treebank based grammar; hence all re-estimated grammars can be evaluated using standardized criteria.

The rest of the paper is organized as follows: First, we describe in brief the construction of an unlexicalized PCFG from the PTB. We then describe a procedure based on the inside-outside algorithm to re-estimate the lexical parameters of this PCFG from unlabeled Wall Street Journal data. Finally, we present evaluations of the re-estimated models, based on labeled bracketing measures and on the detection of subcategorization frames of verbs: there is a 31.6% reduction in error for novel verbs and up to 8.97% reduction in overall subcategorization error.

2 Unlexicalized treebank PCFG

We build an unlexicalized PCFG from the standard training sections of the PTB. As is common (Collins, 1997; Johnson, 1998; Klein and Manning, 2003; Schmid, 2006), the treebank is first transformed in various ways, in order to give an accurate PCFG. In our framework, treebank trees are augmented with extra features; the methodology involves constructing a feature-constraint grammar from a context-free treebank backbone grammar. The detailed methodology is described in Deoskar and Rooth (2008)[1]. A PCFG is trained on the transformed treebank, with these added features incorporated into the PCFG's non-terminal categories. The framework affords us the flexibility to stipulate the features to be incorporated in the PCFG categories, as parameters of the PCFG.

Our features are largely designed to have a linguistically relevant interpretation[2]. For example, there is a feature on verbs which denotes the subcategorization frame of the verb (with values like intransitive, transitive, etc.). Similarly, there are features which denote the type of clause (finite, infinite, small clause, etc.), the subject type of clausal nodes, the attachment of adverbs, valence of nouns, etc. Unlike most existing treebank PCFGs, all PTB function tags are retained, as are all empty categories.

	this paper	Schmid	K&M
Recall	86.5	86.3	85.1
Precision	86.7	86.9	86.3
F-score	86.6	86.6	85.7

Table 1: Labeled bracketing scores, PTB sec. 23.

As a measure of the quality of the transformed-PTB based PCFG, Table 1 gives the labeled bracketing scores on the standard test section 23 of the PTB, comparing them to unlexicalized PCFG scores in (Schmid, 2006) and (Klein and Manning, 2003) (K&M). The current PCFG *f*-score is comparable to the state-of-the-art in unlexicalized PCFGs ((Schmid, 2006), to our knowledge). We stopped grammar development when the *f*-score reached state-of-the-art since our goal was to use this grammar as the initial model and baseline for the unsupervised re-estimation procedure, described in the next section.

3 Inside-Outside Re-estimation

As a basic unsupervised estimation method, we use standard inside-outside estimation of PCFGs, which realizes EM estimation (Lari and Young, 1990; Pereira and Schabes, 1992). We use the notation $I(C, e)$ to designate the new frequency model, computed via inside-outside from the corpus C by using a probability model based on the frequency model e[3]. The iterative inside-outside re-estimation procedure has the following simple form (Eq.1), where each successive frequency model e_{i+1} is estimated from the corpus C using a probability model determined by the previous frequency model e_i. Our notation always refers to fre-

[1] The reason for using this framework (as opposed to using available unlexicalized PCFGs) is that it allows us flexibility in designing features of interest, and can also be used for languages other than English with existing treebanks.

[2] In addition we also have some features that do not have a linguistic interpretation, but result in a good PCFG, such as a *parent* feature on some categories, following Johnson (1998).

[3] The inside-outside algorithm uses an existing grammar model and a raw text corpus (incomplete data) to obtain corresponding complete data (a set of analyses/parses for the corpus sentences). A new grammar model is then estimated from this complete data. See (Prescher, 2003) for an explanation using the standard EM notions of incomplete/complete data.

quency models such as e_i, rather than the relative-frequency probability models they determine[4].

$$\begin{aligned} e_1 &= I(C, e_0) \\ &\dots \\ e_{i+1} &= I(C, e_i) \end{aligned} \tag{1}$$

3.1 Interleaved Inside-Outside

It is well-known that while lexicalization is useful, lexical parameters determined from the treebank are poorly estimated because of the sparseness of treebank data for particular words (e.g. Hindle and Rooth (1993)). Gildea (2001) and Bikel (2004) show that removing bilexical dependencies hardly hurts the performance of the Collins Model2 parser, although there is the benefit of lexicalization in the form of lexico-syntactic dependencies – structures being conditioned on words. On the other hand, structural parameters are comparatively well-estimated from treebanks since they are not keyed to particular words. Thus, it might be beneficial to use a combination of supervised and unsupervised estimation for lexical parameters, while obtaining syntactic (structural) parameters solely by supervised estimation (i.e. from a treebank). The experiments in this paper are based on this idea. In an unlexicalised PCFG like the one described in §2, it is easy to make the distinction between structural parameters (non-terminal rules) and lexical parameters (preterminal to terminal rules).

To this end, we define a modified inside-outside procedure in which a frequency transformation $T(c, t)$ is interleaved between the iterations of the standard inside-outside procedure. The form of this interleaved procedure is shown in Eq. 2. In Eq. 2, t designates a smoothed treebank model (the smoothing procedure is described later in §3.1.1). This smoothed treebank model is used as the prior model for the inside-outside re-estimation procedure. For each iteration i, c_i represent models obtained by inside-outside estimation. d_i represent *derived* models obtained by performing a transformation T on c_i. The transformation T combines the re-estimated model c_i and the smoothed treebank model t (hence represented as $T(c_i, t)$).

$$\begin{aligned} d_0 &= t && \textit{smoothed treebank model} \\ c_1 &= I(C, d_0) && \textit{estimation step} \\ d_1 &= T(c_1, t) && \textit{transformation step} \\ &\dots \\ c_{i+1} &= I(C, d_i) && \textit{estimation step} \\ d_{i+1} &= T(c_{i+1}, t) && \textit{transformation step} \end{aligned} \tag{2}$$

The lexical parameters for the treebank model t or the re-estimated models c_i are represented as $t(w, \tau, \iota)$ or $c_i(w, \tau, \iota)$, where w is the terminal word, τ is the PTB-style PoS tag, and ι is the sequence of additional features incorporated into the PoS tag (the entries in our lexicon have the form $w.\tau.\iota$ with an associated frequency). The transformation T preserves the marginal frequencies seen in the treebank model. A marginal tag-incorporation frequency is defined by summation:

$$f(\tau, \iota) = \sum_w f(w, \tau, \iota). \tag{3}$$

The transformation T is used to obtain the derived models d_i and consists of two parts, corresponding to the syntactic and the lexical parameters of d_i:

- The syntactic parameters of d_i are copied from t.
- To obtain the lexical parameters of d_i, lexical parameters from the treebank model t and lexical parameters from the re-estimated model are linearly combined, shown in Eq. 4.

$$d_i(w, \tau, \iota) = (1 - \lambda_{\tau,\iota}) t(w, \tau, \iota) + \lambda_{\tau,\iota} \bar{c}_i(w, \tau, \iota) \tag{4}$$

where $\lambda_{\tau,\iota}$ is a parameter with $0 < \lambda_{\tau,\iota} < 1$ which may depend on the tag and incorporation. The term $\bar{c}_i(w, \tau, \iota)$ in Eq. 4 is obtained by scaling the frequencies in $c_i(w, \tau, \iota)$, as shown in Eq. 5.

$$\bar{c}_i(w, \tau, \iota) = \frac{t(\tau, \iota)}{c_i(\tau, \iota)} c_i(w, \tau, \iota). \tag{5}$$

In terms of probability models determined from the frequency models, the effect of T is to allocate a fixed proportion of the probability mass for each τ, ι to the corpus, and share it out among words w in proportion to relative frequencies $\frac{c_i(w,\tau,\iota)}{c_i(\tau,\iota)}$ in the inside-outside estimate c_i. Eqs. 6 and 7 verify that marginals are preserved in the derived model d.

$$\begin{aligned} \bar{c}(\tau, \iota) &= \textstyle\sum_w \bar{c}(w, \tau, \iota) = \sum_w \frac{t(\tau,\iota)}{c(\tau,\iota)} c(w, \tau, \iota) \\ &= \frac{t(\tau,\iota)}{c(\tau,\iota)} \textstyle\sum_w c(w, \tau, \iota) \\ &= \frac{t(\tau,\iota)}{c(\tau,i)} c(\tau, \iota) = t(\tau, \iota). \end{aligned} \tag{6}$$

[4] We use a frequency-based notation because we use out-of-the-box software Bitpar (Schmid, 2004) which implements inside-outside estimation – Bitpar reads in frequency models and converts them to relative frequency models. We justify the use of the frequency-based notation by ensuring that all marginal frequencies in the treebank model are always preserved in all other models.

$$
\begin{aligned}
d(\tau,\iota) &= \textstyle\sum_w d(w,\tau,\iota) \\
&= \textstyle\sum_w (1-\lambda_{\tau,\iota}) t(w,\tau,\iota) + \lambda_{\tau,\iota}\bar{c}(w,\tau,\iota) \\
&= (1-\lambda_{\tau,\iota}) \textstyle\sum_w t(w,\tau,\iota) \\
&+ \lambda_{\tau,\iota} \textstyle\sum_w \bar{c}(w,\tau,\iota) \\
&= (1-\lambda_{\tau,\iota}) t(\tau,\iota) + \lambda_{\tau,\iota}\bar{c}(\tau,\iota) \\
&= (1-\lambda_{\tau,\iota}) t(\tau,\iota) + \lambda_{\tau,\iota} t(\tau,\iota) \\
&= t(\tau,\iota).
\end{aligned} \tag{7}
$$

3.1.1 Smoothing the treebank model

To initialize the iterative procedures, a smoothing scheme is required which allocates frequency to combinations of words w and PoS tags τ which are not present in the treebank model but are present in the corpus, and also to all possible incorporations of a PoS tag. Otherwise, if the unsmoothed treebank model (t_0) has zero frequency for some lexical parameter, the inside-outside estimate $I(C, t_0)$ for that parameter would also be zero, and new lexical entries would never be induced.

The smoothed treebank model t is obtained from the unsmoothed model t_0 as follows. First a PoS tagger (Treetagger, (Schmid, 1994)) is run on the unsupervised corpus C, which assigns PTB-style PoS tags to the corpus. Tokens of words and PoS tags are tabulated to obtain a frequency table $g(w, \tau)$. Each frequency $g(w, \tau)$ is split among possible incorporations ι in proportion to a ratio of marginal frequencies in t_0:

$$
g(w,\tau,\iota) = \frac{t_0(\tau,\iota)}{t_0(\tau)} g(w,\tau) \tag{8}
$$

The smoothed model t is defined as an interpolation of g and t_0 for lexical parameters as shown in 9, with syntactic parameters copied from t_0.

$$
t(w,\tau,\iota) = (1-\lambda_{\tau,\iota}) t_0(w,\tau,\iota) + \lambda_{\tau,\iota} g(w,\tau,\iota) \tag{9}
$$

3.2 Experimental setup

The treebank grammar is trained over sections 0-22 of the transformed PTB (minus about 7000 sentences held out for testing). Testset I contains 1331 sentences and is constructed as follows: First, we select 117 verbs whose frequency in PTB sections 0-22 is between 10-20 (mid-frequency verbs). All sentences containing occurrences of these verbs are held out from the training data to form Testset I. The effect of holding out these sentences is to make these 117 verbs *novel* (i.e. unseen in training). This testset is used to evaluate the learning of subcategorization frames of novel verbs. We also construct another testset (Testset II) by holding out every 10th sentence in PTB sections 0-22 (4310 sentences).

The corpus used for re-estimation is about 4 million words of unannotated Wall Street Journal text (year 1997) (sentence length<25 words). The re-estimation was carried out using Bitpar (Schmid, 2004) for inside-outside estimation. The parameter λ in Eq. 4 was set to 0.5 for all τ and ι, giving equal weight to the treebank and the re-estimated lexicons. Starting from a smoothed treebank grammar t, we separately ran 6 iterations of the interleaved estimation procedure defined in Eq. 2, and 4 iterations of standard inside-outside estimation. This gave us two series of models corresponding to the two procedures.

4 Labeled Bracketing Results

As a basic evaluation of the re-estimated grammars, we report the labeled bracketing scores on the standard test section 23 of the PTB (Table 2). Using the re-estimated models, maximum probability (viterbi) parses were obtained for all sentences in sec. 23, after stripping away the treebank annotation, including the pre-terminal tag. The baseline is the treebank model t_{0t}[5]. The scores for re-estimated grammars from successive iterations are under columns It 1, It 2, etc. All models obtained using the interleaved procedure show an improvement over the baseline. The best model is obtained after 2 iterations, after which the score reduces a little. Statistically significant improvements are marked with *, with p<0.005 for recall and p<0.0001 for precision for the best model. Table 2 also shows scores for grammars estimated using the standard inside-outside procedure. The first re-estimated model is better than any model obtained from either procedure. Notice however, the disparity in precision and recall – precision is much lower than recall. This is not surprising; inside-outside is known to converge to incorrect solutions for PCFGs (Lari and Young, 1990; de Marcken, 1995). This causes the *f*-score to deteriorate in successive iterations.

[5]This baseline is slightly lower than that reported in Table 1 due to holding out an additional 7000 sentences from the treebank training set. In order to accommodate unknown words from the test data (sec 23), the treebank model t_0 is smoothed in a manner similar to that shown in Eq. 9, with the test words (tagged using Treetagger) forming $g(w, \tau)$ and $\lambda = 0.1$. A testset is always merged with a given model in this manner before parsing, to account for unknown words.

		t_{0t}	It 1	It 2	It 3	It 4	It 5	It 6
Interleaved	Recall	86.48	86.72	***86.79**	*86.79	*86.78	86.81	86.72
Procedure	Precision	86.61	86.95	***87.07**	*87.06	*87.07	87.04	87.01
	f-score	86.55	86.83	***86.93**	*86.92	*86.92	86.92	86.86
Standard	Recall	86.48	87.95	87.11	86.42	85.55		
Procedure	Precision	86.61	85.99	84.79	83.37	82.06		
	f-score	86.5	86.96	85.93	84.87	83.77		

Table 2: Labeled Bracketing scores for various models, on PTB section 23.

The improvement in labeled bracketing *f*-score for the interleaved procedure is small, but is an encouraging result. The benefit to the re-estimated models comes only from better estimates of lexical parameters. We expect that re-estimation will benefit parameters associated with low frequency words - lexical parameters for high frequency words are bound to be estimated accurately from the treebank. We did not expect a large impact on labeled bracketing scores, given that low frequency words have correspondingly few occurrences in this test dataset. It is possible that the impact on *f*-score will be higher for a test set from a different domain. Note also that the size of our unlabeled training corpus (~4M words) is relatively small – only about 4 times the PTB.

5 Verbal Subcategorization

We focus on learning verbal subcategorization, as a typical case of lexico-syntactic information. The subcategorization frame (SF) of verbs is a parameter of our PCFG - verbal tags in the PCFG are followed by an incorporation sequence that denotes the SF for that verb. We evaluate the re-estimated models on the task of detecting correct SFs of verbs in maximum-probability (viterbi) parses obtained using the models. All tokens of verbs and their preterminal symbols (consisting of a PoS tag and an incorporation sequence encoding the SF) are extracted from the viterbi parses of sentences in a testset. This tag-SF sequence is compared to a gold standard, and is scored correct if the two match exactly. PoS errors are scored as incorrect, even if the SF is correct. The gold standard is obtained from the transformed PTB trees.

The incorporation sequence corresponding to the SF consists of 3 features: The first one denotes basic categories of subcategorization such as transitive, intransitive, ditransitive, NP-PP, S, etc. The second feature denotes, for clausal complements, the type of clause (finite, infinite, small clause,

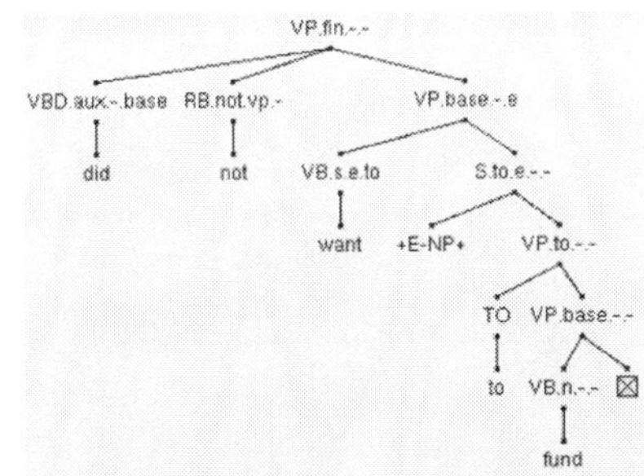

Figure 1: A subcat. frame for control verb *want*.

etc.). The third feature encodes the nature of the subject of the clausal complements (empty category or non-empty). For example, the verb *considered* in the treebank sentence *They are officially considered strategic* gets a preterminal sequence of VBD.s.e.sc. This sequence indicates a past tense verb (VBD) with a clausal complement (s) which has an empty subject (e) since the sentence is passive and is of the type *small clause* (sc). A control verb (with an infinitival complement) in the sentence fragment *..did not want to fund X..* gets the frame s.e.to (see Fig. 1 for an example of a verb with its complement, as parsed by our PCFG). We have a total of 81 categories of SFs (without counting specific prepositions for prepositional frames), making fairly fine-grained distinctions of verbal categories.

5.1 Learning Subcat Frames of Novel Verbs

We measure the error rate in the detection of the subcategorization frame of 1360 tokens of 117 verbs in Testset I. Recall from §3.2 that these verbs are novel verbs with respect to the treebank model. Table 3 shows this error rate (i.e. the fraction of test items which receive incorrect tag-incorporations in viterbi parses) for various models obtained using the interleaved and standard re-estimation procedures. t_{0t1} is the treebank model t_0 with the test data from Testset I merged in (to

Iteration i	Interleaved Procedure	Standard Procedure
t_{0t1}	33.36	33.36
1	*24.40	28.69
2	*23.45	25.56
3	*23.05	27.86
4	*22.89	28.41
5	***22.81**	-
6	*22.83	-

Table 3: Subcat. error for novel verbs (Testset I).

account for unknown words) using the smoothing scheme given in Eq. 9. This model has no verb specific information for the test verbs. For each test verb, it has a smoothed SF distribution proportional to the SF distribution for all verbs of that tag. The baseline error is 33.36%. This means that there is enough information in the average distribution of all verbs to correctly assign the subcategorization frame to novel verbs in 66.64% cases. For the models obtained using the interleaved re-estimation, the error rate falls to the lowest value of 22.81% for the model obtained in the 5th iteration: an absolute reduction of 10.55 points, and a percentage error-reduction of 31.6%. The error reduction is statistically significant for all iterations compared to the baseline, with the 5th iteration being also significantly better than the 1st. The models obtained using standard re-estimation do not perform as well. Even for the model from the first iteration, whose labeled bracketing score was highest, the SF error is higher than the corresponding model from the interleaved procedure (possibly due to the low precision of this model). The error rate for the standard procedure starts to increase after the 2nd iteration in contrast to the interleaved procedure.

5.2 Analysis of subcategorization learning

While the re-estimation clearly results in gains in SF detection for novel verbs, we also perform an evaluation for all verbs (novel and non-novel) in a given testset (Testset II as described in §3.2). The overall error reduction using the interleaved procedure is 8.97% (in Iteration 1). In order to better understand the relative efficacy of the supervised and unsupervised estimation for lexical items of different frequencies, we break up the set of test verbs into subsets based on their frequency of occurrence in the PTB training data, and evaluate them separately. Table 4 shows the error rates for verbs divided into these sets. We present error rates only for Iteration 1 in Table 4, since most of the error reduction takes place with the 1st iteration. Statistically significant reductions are marked with * (confidence>99.9) and ** (>95). The second row shows error rates for verbs which have zero frequency in the treebank training data (i.e. novel verbs): Note that this error reduction is much less than the 31.6% in Testset I. These verbs are truly rare and hence have much fewer occurrences in the unlabeled corpus than Testset I verbs, which were artificially made novel (but are really mid-frequency verbs). This might indicate that error rates will decrease further if the size of the unlabeled corpus is increased. There is substantial error reduction for low-frequency verbs (<21 PTB occurrences). This is not hard to understand: the PTB does not provide enough data to have good parameter estimates for these verbs. For mid-to-high frequency verbs (from 21 to 500), the benefit of the unsupervised procedure reduces, though error reduction is still positive. Surprisingly, the error reduction for very high frequency verbs (more than 500 occurrences in the treebank) is also fairly high: we expected that parameters for high frequency words would benefit the least from the unsupervised estimation, given that they are already common enough in the PTB to be accurately estimated from it. The high frequency verbs (>500

TB Freq	t_{0t2}	It 1	Abs.Reduc	%Reduc
all	18.5	16.84	1.66	*8.97
0	41.26	33.01	8.25	*19.99
1	32.69	24.52	8.17	*24.99
2	36.55	22.76	13.79	*37.73
3	26.59	19.08	7.51	*28.24
4	22.38	20.28	2.1	9.38
5	24.63	19.40	5.23	*21.23
6-10	22.24	19.59	2.65	**11.92
11-20	21.54	18.02	3.52	*16.34
21-50	19.41	19.11	0.3	1.55
51-100	19.44	19.09	0.35	1.80
101-200	18.71	18.57	0.14	0.75
201-500	23.06	22.31	0.75	3.25
501-1K	18.07	16.82	1.25	6.92
1K-2K	12.38	12.25	0.13	1.05
2K-5K	9.42	7.62	1.8	*19.11
>5K	10.54	10.13	0.41	3.89

Table 4: Subcat. error breakup (Testset II)

occurrences) consist of very few types– mainly auxiliaries, some light verbs (*make*, *do*) and a few others (*rose*, *say*). It is possible that re-estimation from large data is beneficial for light verbs since they have a larger number of frames. The frequency range $2K$-$5K$ consists solely of auxiliary verbs. Examination of viterbi parses shows that improved results are largely due to better detection of predicative frames in re-estimated models.

To measure the impact of more unlabeled training data, we ran the interleaved procedure with 8M words of WSJ text. The SF error for novel verbs reduces to 22.06% in the 2nd iteration (significantly different from the best error of 22.81% in the 5th iteration for 4M words of training data)). We also get an improved overall error reduction of 9.9% on Testset II for the larger training data, as compared to 8.97% previously.

5.3 Previous Work

While there has been substantial previous work on the task of SF acquisition from corpora (Brent (1991); Manning (1993); Briscoe and Carroll (1997); Korhonen (2002), amongst others), we find that relatively few parsing-based evaluations are reported. Since their goal is to build probabilistic SF dictionaries, these systems are evaluated either against existing dictionaries, or on distributional similarity measures. Most are evaluated on testsets of *high*-frequency verbs (unlike the present work), in order to gauge the effectiveness of the acquisition strategy. Briscoe and Carroll (1997) report a token-based evaluation for seven verb types– their system gets an average recall accuracy of 80.9% for these verbs (which appear to be high-frequency verbs). This is slightly lower than the present system, which has an overall accuracy of 83.16% (on Testset II (It 1), as shown in Table 4). However, for low frequency verbs (exemplars $<$10) they report that their results are around chance. A parsing evaluation of their lexicon using an unlexicalized grammar as baseline, on 250 sentences from the Suzanne treebank gave a small (but not statistically significant) improvement in *f*-score (from 71.49 to 72.14%). Korhonen (2002) reports a parsing-based evaluation on 500 test sentences. She found a small increase in *f*-score (of grammatical relations markup) from 76.03 to 76.76. In general PARSEVAL measures are not very sensitive to subcategorization (Carroll et al., 1998); they therefore use a dependency-based evaluation. In the present research as well, we obtain statistically significant but quite small improvements in *f*-score (§4). Since we are interested in acquisition of PCFG lexicons, we focus our evaluations on verbal subcategorization of token occurrences of verbs in viterbi parses.

6 Conclusions

We have presented a methodology for incorporating additional lexical information from unlabeled data into an unlexicalized treebank PCFG. We obtain a large error reduction (31.6%) in SF detection for novel verbs as compared to a treebank baseline. The interleaved re-estimation scheme gives a significant increase in labeled bracketing scores from a relatively small unlabeled corpus. The interleaved scheme has an advantage over standard inside-outside PCFG estimation, as measured both by labeled bracketing scores and on the task of detecting SFs of novel verbs. Since our re-estimated models are treebank models, all evaluations are against treebank standards.

The grammar we worked with has very few incorporated features compared to the grammar used by, say Klein and Manning (2003). It would make sense to experiment with grammars with much richer sets of incorporated features. Features related to structure-selection by categories other than verbs – nouns, adverbs and adjectives – might be beneficial. These features should be incorporated as PCFG parameters, similar to verbal subcategorization. Experiments with 8 million words of training data gave significantly better results than with 4 million words, indicating that larger training sets will be beneficial as well. It would also be useful to make the transformation T of lexical parameters sensitive to treebank frequency of words. For instance, more weight should be given to the treebank model rather than the corpus model for mid-to-high frequency words, by making the parameter λ in T sensitive to frequency.

This methodology is relevant to the task of *domain-adaption*. Hara et al. (2007) find that retraining a model of HPSG lexical entry assignments is more critical for domain adaptation than re-training a structural model alone. Our PCFG captures many of the important dependencies captured in a framework like HPSG; in addition, we can use unlabeled data from a new domain in an unsupervised fashion for re-estimating lexical parameters, an important consideration in domain-adaption. Preliminary experiments on this task using New York Times unlabeled data with the PTB-trained PCFG show promising results.

Acknowledgments

I am grateful to Mats Rooth for extensive comments and guidance during the course of this research. The inside-outside re-estimation was conducted using the resources of the Cornell University Center for Advanced Computing.

References

F. Beil, G. Carroll, D. Prescher, S. Riezler, and M. Rooth. 1999. Inside-outside estimation of a lexicalized PCFG for German. In *Proceedings of the 37th meeting of ACL.*

Dan Bikel. 2004. Intricacies of Collins' Parser. *Computational Linguistics*, 30(4):479–511.

M. Brent. 1991. Automatic acquisition of subcategorization frames from untagged text. In *Proceedings of the 29th meeting of ACL.*

Ted Briscoe and John Carroll. 1997. Automatic Extraction of Subcategorization from Corpora. In *Proceedings of the 5th ACL Conference on Applied NLP.*

G. Carroll and M. Rooth. 1998. Valence induction with a head-lexicalized PCFG. In *Proceedings of EMNLP 1998.*

J. Carroll, G. Minnen, and E. Briscoe. 1998. Can subcategorization probabilities help parsing. In *Proceedings of 6th ACL/SIGDAT Workshop on Very Large Corpora.*

Eugene Charniak and Mark Johnson. 2005. Coarse-to-fine n-best parsing and MaxEnt discriminative reranking. In *Proceedings of 43rd meeting of ACL.*

Michael Collins. 1997. Three generative, lexicalised models for statistical parsing. In *Proceedings of the 35th meeting of ACL.*

Carl de Marcken. 1995. On the unsupervised induction of Phrase Structure grammars. In *3rd Workshop on Very Large Corpora.*

A. P. Dempster, N. M. Laird, and D. B. Rubin. 1977. Maximum likelihood estimation from incomplete data via the EM algorithm. *J. Royal Statistical Society*, 39(B):1–38.

Tejaswini Deoskar and Mats Rooth. 2008. Induction of Treebank-Aligned Lexical Resources. In *Proceedings of 6th LREC.*

Daniel Gildea. 2001. Corpus Variation and Parser Performance. In *Proceedings of EMNLP 2001.*

T. Hara, Y. Miyao, and J. Tsujii. 2007. Evaluating Impact of Re-training a Lexical Disambiguation Model on Domain Adaptation of an HPSG Parser. In *Proceedings of the 10th International Conference on Parsing Technologies.*

Donald Hindle and Mats Rooth. 1993. Structural ambiguity and lexical relations. *Computational Linguistics*, 18(2):103–120.

Sabine Schulte imWalde. 2002. A Subcategorisation Lexicon for German Verbs induced from a Lexicalised PCFG. In *Proceedings of LREC 2002.*

Mark Johnson. 1998. PCFG models of linguistic tree representations. *Computational Linguistics*, 24(4).

D. Klein and C. Manning. 2003. Accurate unlexicalized parsing. In *Proceedings of the 41st ACL.*

Anna Korhonen. 2002. *Subcategorization Acquisition.* Ph.D. thesis, Univ. of Cambridge.

K. Lari and S. J. Young. 1990. The estimation of stochastic context-free grammars using the Inside-Outside algorithm. *Computer Speech and Language*, 4:35–56.

C. Manning. 1993. Automatic acquisition of a large subcategorization dictionary from corpora. In *Proceedings of the 31st meeting of ACL.*

M. P. Marcus, B. Santorini, and M. A. Marcinkiewicz. 1993. Building a Large Annotated Corpus of English: The Penn Treebank. *Computational Linguistics*, 19(2):313–330.

D. McCloskey, E. Charniak, and M. Johnson. 2006. Effective Self-Training for Parsing. In *Proceedings of HLT-NAACL 2006.*

Pereira and Schabes. 1992. Inside-Outside re-estimation from partially bracketed corpora. In *Proceedings of the 30th meeting of ACL.*

Detlef Prescher. 2003. A Tutorial on the Expectation-Maximization Algorithm Including Maximum-Likelihood Estimation and EM Training of Probabilistic Context-Free Grammars. ESSLLI 2003.

Helmut Schmid. 1994. Probabilistic Part-of-Speech Tagging Using Decision Trees. In *Proceedings of International Conference on New Methods in Language Processing.*

Helmut Schmid. 2004. Efficient Parsing of Highly Ambiguous Context-Free Grammars with Bit Vectors. In *Proceedings of the 20th COLING.*

Helmut Schmid. 2006. Trace Prediction and Recovery with Unlexicalised PCFGs and Slash Features. In *Proceedings of the 21st Conference on Computational Linguistics (COLING).*

Representations for category disambiguation

Markus Dickinson
Indiana University
Bloomington, IN 47405
md7@indiana.edu

Abstract

As it serves as a basis for POS tagging, category induction, and human category acquisition, we investigate the information needed to disambiguate a word in a local context, when using corpus categories. Specifically, we increase the recall of an error detection method by abstracting the word to be disambiguated to a representation containing information about some of its inherent properties, namely the set of categories it can potentially have. This work thus provides insights into the relation of corpus categories to categories derived from local contexts.

1 Introduction and Motivation

Category induction techniques generally rely on local contexts, i.e., surrounding words, to cluster word types together (e.g., Clark, 2003; Schütze, 1995), using information of a kind also found in human category acquisition tasks (e.g., Mintz, 2002, 2003). Such information is also at the core of standard part-of-speech (POS) tagging, or disambiguation, methods (see, e.g., Manning and Schütze, 1999, ch. 10), with the contexts generally abstracted to POS tags. The contextual information is similar in both tasks because induction is founded in part upon the notion that local contexts are useful for disambiguation: one morphosyntactically clusters words which should have the same category in the same contexts. But which contexts count as being the "same"? And to what extent do categories based on context distributions resemble corpus annotation categories? Since disambiguation is in some sense more primary, to begin to answer these questions we investigate which representations are effective for category disambiguation.

Disambiguating a word's category in context has of course been explored in other situations, especially POS tagging. Rarely, however, has it been shown as to which information is the most accurate at disambiguation and which information is absolutely necessary, without mixing these issues with other tagging issues, such as smoothing and unknown word tagging. We need techniques which isolate disambiguation, placing less emphasis on generalizing contexts to new data. To determine the essential information needed for accurate disambiguation, we start with a precise model and generalize it. Changing the model in small ways and evaluating the resulting precision will indicate how particular aspects of the representation are contributing to successful disambiguation.

The central question of this paper is: which representation (of a word and its context) indicates that two situations should be categorized the same? In this context, POS annotation error detection provides an ideal setting to explore representations for disambiguation. Error detection relies on the assumption that words should be annotated consistently—in other words, contexts are grouped which accurately identify the category of a word as being consistent—and it does this with an emphasis on high precision. In essence, error detection already investigates where disambiguation can be done, often using local contexts (e.g., Dickinson, 2005). With an emphasis on high precision, however, many corpus instances are essentially uncategorized and are thus in need of generalization.

To get at the central question of an appropriate

©2008. Licensed under the *Creative Commons Attribution-Noncommercial-Share Alike 3.0 Unported* license (http://creativecommons.org/licenses/by-nc-sa/3.0/). Some rights reserved.

representation for disambiguation, then, our task is to generalize error detection and increase the recall of errors found in a corpus by exploiting more general properties of a corpus. Given that annotation errors can have a profound impact on the quality of training and testing on such data (see Dickinson, 2005, ch. 1), this task also serves an immense practical need in its own right.

In exploring error detection recall, we can connect the task to another with much of the same emphasis. Human category acquisition experiments have also focused on precision: instead of asking how every word is categorized, they examine how some words are categorized, from which others can be bootstrapped. As outlined in sections 2 and 3, we can use such studies as a starting point for generalizing error detection.

2 Background

2.1 The variation n-gram method

The error detection method we build from is the variation n-gram method (Dickinson and Meurers, 2003; Dickinson, 2005). The approach detects items which occur multiple times in the corpus with varying annotation, the so-called *variation nuclei*. A nucleus with its repeated surrounding context is referred to as a *variation n-gram*. Every detected variation in the annotation of a nucleus is classified as an error or a genuine ambiguity using a basic heuristic requiring at least one word of context on each side of the nucleus.

For example, in the WSJ corpus, part of the Penn Treebank 3 release (Marcus et al., 1993), the string in (1) is a variation 12-gram since *off* is a variation nucleus that is tagged preposition (IN) in one corpus occurrence and particle (RP) in another.[1] Dickinson (2005) shows that examining those cases with identical local context—in this case, looking at *ward off a*—results in an estimated error detection precision of 92.5%.

(1) to ward off a hostile takeover attempt by two European shipping concerns

This method can be applied to syntactic annotation, and for this annotation, one can increase the recall of errors found by abstracting the nuclei to POS tags (Boyd et al., 2007). Clearly, this is not a feasible abstraction here, given that we are attempting to detect errors in POS annotation.

[1]To distinguish variation nuclei, we shade them in gray and underline the immediately surrounding context.

2.2 Frames for language acquisition

Research on language acquisition has addressed the question of how humans discover and learn categories of words, using virtually the same contexts as in the variation n-gram method. Mintz (2002) shows that local context, in the form of a *frame* of two words surrounding a target word, leads to categorization in adults of the target, and Mintz (2003) shows that frequent frames supply category information, consistent across child language corpora. A frame is defined as "two jointly occurring words with one word intervening" (Mintz, 2003), e.g., *you __ it*. The frame is not decomposed into its left side and right side (cf., e.g., Redington et al., 1998; Clark, 2003) , but instead is taken as the occurrence of both sides. The *target word* is the intervening word, but it is not included in the frame (unlike variation nuclei).

For category acquisition, only *frequent frames* are used, those with a frequency above a certain threshold. Frequent frames predict category membership: the set of words appearing in a given frame should represent a single category. The frequent frame *you __ it*, for example, largely identifies verbs, as shown in (2), taken from the CHILDES database of child-directed speech (MacWhinney, 2000). Analyzing the frequent frames in six subcorpora of CHILDES, Mintz (2003) obtains both high type and high token accuracy in grouping words into the same categories.

(2) a. you put it
    b. you see it

To take this work as a basis for investigating disambiguation, some points are in order about the results. First, accuracies slightly degrade when moving from the "Standard Labeling" category set[2] to the more fine-grained "Expanded Labeling" category set,[3] i.e., a .98 to .91 drop in token accuracy and .93 to .91 drop in type accuracy. It is not clear what happens with even more fine-grained corpus tagsets. Secondly, Mintz (2003) assumes that, at least for his experiments, each word has only one class (see also Redington et al., 1998, p. 439-440). The tasks of category induction and category disambiguation are thus conflated into a single step. We do not know for sure whether frames induce

[2]Categories = noun, verb, adjective, preposition, adverb, determiner, *wh*-word, *not*, conjunction, and interjection.

[3]Nouns split into nouns and pronouns; verbs split into verbs, auxiliaries, and copula

coherent sets of words or whether they accurately disambiguate a word, or both. In other words, can frames be used to group the target words (induction) or to group the contexts (disambiguation)?

While we investigate using frames for disambiguation in English (and somewhat in German), the concept of a frame has been shown to be cross-linguistically viable (Chemla et al., in press), and in principle could extend to languages encoding relations through morphology instead of linear order (see the discussion in Mintz, 2003).

3 Generalizing error detection via frames

Both strands of research employ local contexts for identifying categories, but the variation n-gram method relies on identical words to serve as variation nuclei, or target words to be disambiguated. To increase the recall of the method in a way relating to acquisition, the nucleus should be abstracted to something more general than a word. As a (frequent) frame does not include the target, predicting that the category within that context is always the same, a first step in abstracting the nucleus is to require no similarity between nuclei.

We thus search for all identical nuclei with frame context—or what we will call *framed variation nuclei*—such that there is variation in labeling for the nucleus, but we require no identity of the nucleus. We investigate the WSJ portion of the Penn Treebank, and, to provide more robust evaluation, also compare the TIGER corpus of German, version 2 (Brants et al., 2002) where appropriate. Given that punctuation is less informative for determining a category, we remove from consideration frames containing punctuation as one of the context words, and obtain 48,717 variations in the WSJ and 22,613 in TIGER.

Although basic hand-examination reveals some errors, a majority of cases contain acceptable variations. As one example, in the WSJ the frame *the __ of* occurs as the most frequent frame with variation in labeling for the target (5737 instances). This is a nominal position, and thus we find variation between a variety of correct nominal tags: cardinal number (CD), adjective (JJ, JJR, JJS), common noun (NN, NNS), and proper noun (NNP, NNPS), in addition to the erroneous verbal tags VBD (past tense verb) and VBG (verb, *-ing* form). Restricting our attention to the frequent frames, as in Mintz (2003), is not helpful: the problem occurs irrespective of frequency. Indeed, there is an average of 2.56 categories per variation, with one variation (*and __ in*) having 21 categories. This is consistent in TIGER, which has 2.57 categories per variation and 22 categories for *und __ in*.

While more context could help, the real issue is the definition of a nucleus. In the example above, which nominal tag is used depends upon inherent properties of the word involved. Consider the frame *that __ the*. Among the 18 possible tags, there is variation between NN (common noun) for words like *afternoon* and VBZ (present tense verb, 3rd person singular) for words like *says*. Both are legitimate, and the primary way to tell is by examining information about the target word. In generalizing the nucleus, instead of abstracting it to nothing, we need to abstract it to something indicating broad characteristics of the word.

4 An appropriate level of abstraction

On the one hand, the variation n-gram method has high precision; on the other, using frames results in high recall, but too low a precision to sort through. Both methods rely on the same identical contexts; the issue is in finding which words are comparable. Consider the frame *n't __ that*. Some words are inherently similar and should have the same tags: the correct *n't help/VB that* and the erroneous *n't matter/NN that*, for instance, are comparable. Other cases are not: *one/CD* and *shown/VBN* can never have the same category. We need to find classes of words that, within the same context, should not vary in their annotation, and it makes sense to compare words in context if they have the same category possibilities.

4.1 Complete ambiguity classes

Ambiguity classes capture the relevant property we are interested in: words with the same category possibilities are grouped together.[4] And ambiguity classes have been shown to be successfully employed, in a variety of ways, to improve POS tagging (e.g., Cutting et al., 1992; Daelemans et al., 1996; Dickinson, 2007; Goldberg et al., 2008; Tseng et al., 2005). Only certain words can take one of two (or more) tags, and these should be disambiguated in the same way in context. As an example of how using ambiguity classes as variation nuclei can increase recall, consider the frame *being __ by* in example (3). There are at least 27

[4]One could group affixes by ambiguity class for languages like Chinese (cf. CTBMorph features in Tseng et al., 2005).

different VBN (past participle) verbs appearing between *being* and *by* (3a), but none of these verbs ever appear as VBD here, even though all of them could be VBD. Two other VBD/VBN verbs, *rejected* (3b) and *played* (3c), erroneously appear as VBD here, but never as VBN. With the nucleus VBD/VBN, we can find this erroneous variation.

(3) a. being { raised/VBN , infringed/VBN , supported/VBN , ... } by

b. as probable as being rejected/VBD by the Book-of-the-Month Club

c. the ... role in takeover financing being played/VBD by Japanese banks

Thus, to define *complete ambiguity class* variation nuclei, we make a first pass through the corpus to calculate every word's ambiguity class. On a second pass, the ambiguity class serves as the (framed) variation nucleus, e.g., *being VBD/VBN by*. Ambiguity class nuclei with more than one tag in a frame context are flagged as a potential error.

4.2 Pairwise ambiguity classes

While abstracting to a word's possible classes can increase the number of errors found, potentially erroneous classes prevent further increased recall. For example, the class for *plans* is erroneously classified as NNS/VBP/VBZ, even though its one instance of VBP (present tense verb, non-3rd person singular) in the corpus is erroneous. Without that case, we would have NNS/VBZ and more directly comparable words.

As a second experiment, then, we define *pairwise ambiguity class* variation nuclei, using subsets of ambiguity classes to define a nucleus. If the variation is only between NNS and VBZ, we need to allow all words with NNS/VBZ variation to count as comparable nuclei. As above, we calculated a word's ambiguity class during a first pass. In the second pass through the corpus, we break the ambiguity class down into its pairs, and each relevant pair is stored as a variation nucleus. The relevant pairs of tags are those which contain the tag at that position since classes without that tag can never have meaningful variation. Taking the example of *company plans to*, with the ambiguity class NNS/VBP/VBZ for *plans*, if the current corpus position marks *plans* as NNS, then we store the two trigrams in (4).

(4) a. company NNS/VBZ to

b. company NNS/VBP to

Looking over the whole corpus, we find variation between NNS and VBZ, but none between NNS and VBP. In principle, this instance of *plans/NNS* could be in both an NNS/VBZ and an NNS/VBP variation; this is necessary since we do not a priori know which variations will be problematic.

5 Results and Insights

5.1 Complete ambiguity classes

Using complete ambiguity class variation nuclei, we find 4131 framed variation nuclei in the WSJ. Almost all variations involve only two or three tags, with 2.03 tags per variation. TIGER has 626 framed variation nuclei, with 2.01 tags per variation.

From the 4131 variations, we randomly sampled 100 cases and hand-evaluated whether they contain an error, and whether its detection is attributable to the generalization to complete ambiguity classes. Of the 100, 79 of the cases contain at least one error, and 15 of these cases are new examples, i.e., cases without identical words. With a point estimate of .79, we estimate 3263 errors and obtain a 95% confidence interval of (0.7102, 0.8698), meaning that we predict between 2933 and 3593 of the 4131 cases contain errors. The 79 erroneous cases point to 134 token errors, of which 23 are new.

In addition to increasing the recall of the method, the cases are arguably more thoroughly grouped than before. For instance, we see in (5) that both *pretax* and *third-quarter* vary between JJ and NN in the variation *said JJ/NN profit*, with *first-half* additionally appearing only as JJ. Since JJ is the correct tag for all instances, the two NN errors are detected with word nuclei, but here all the relevant examples are together. This provides evidence for the claim that an ambiguity class is a level of abstraction supporting identical disambiguation in the same context.

(5) said { first-half/JJ , third-quarter/JJ , pretax/JJ , third-quarter/NN , pretax/NN } profit

The recall has increased, but 79% is below the 92.5% precision previously obtained for the variation n-gram method with word nuclei (Dickinson, 2005). However, that result used *distinct* variation nuclei, meaning that the longest contexts were examined before working down to shorter contexts. Furthermore, it is not clear how well the original word nuclei method scales up to larger corpora. Some of the new false positives we observe would likely be false positives for word nuclei, given more data. For example, the new method turns up *generally VBD/VBN the* as a false positive, as in (6), because of the non-local tagset distinction and short context. With more data, we are more likely to see an acceptable use of, e.g., *generally favored/VBD the*, a false positive for word nuclei. In some sense, then, this 79% precision might be a more general indication of the method's precision for this tagset and genre.

(6) a. TV news coverage has generally favored/VBN the government

b. Members ... generally received/VBD the regional officials

Finally, of the 21 false positives (20 of which are new), five of them stem from an error in the ambiguity class, corresponding to five token errors. For example, there is variation for JJ/NN words in the frame *of __ pills*, as in (7). However, *poison* should never be JJ: its ambiguity class should be NN, not the incorrect JJ/NN. For error detection, this means 84 of the 100 samples lead to some kind of POS error; for investigating disambiguation contexts, this means that 83% (79/95) of the cases support complete disambiguation. Thus, when abstracting to ambiguity class nuclei, local context generally provides sufficient information for disambiguation (see also section 6).

(7) of { birth-control/JJ , poison/NN } pills

One limitation of the variation n-gram method is the fact that some distinctions often need non-local information (cf. (6)). A bigger problem for grouping words by ambiguity classes is the fact that annotation can be semantically-based. For example, the variation *of JJ/NN bank* is a legitimate ambiguity because the distinction between JJ and NN is semantic. Compare *a sort of merchant/NN bank* with *an extension of senior/JJ bank debt*: both nuclei are clearly in a noun modifier position, but the tags are different based on what they denote. This shows the limitations of local distributional information without lexical information, for making these tagset distinctions.

5.2 Pairwise ambiguity classes

With pairwise ambiguity classes serving as variation nuclei, we find 6235 variation frames in the WSJ and 874 in TIGER, significant increases over using complete ambiguity class nuclei. To evaluate the method, we want to know: a) how many total errors we detect, b) how many of these were detected by using either complete or pairwise ambiguity classes, and c) how many were detected specifically with pairwise ambiguity classes.

A sample of 100 of the WSJ cases reveals (a) 59 total errors, (b) 18 of which involve ambiguity class nuclei that would not have been found with word nuclei. Of these 18, (c) 8 cases can only be found by extending the method to pairwise classes. For the point estimate of .59, we estimate approximately 3679 variations to be errors (95% CI: 3078 to 4280 errors). The 59 erroneous variations point to a total of (a) 134 token errors, (b) 30 of which were detected by ambiguity classes; (c) 17 of these were detected by pairwise ambiguity classes. Clearly, using pairwise ambiguity classes increases the number of errors found.

As an example, consider (8), centering on the frame *came __ for*. The original variation n-gram method turns up no variation here, but neither does the complete ambiguity class extension: *in* has the ambiguity class FW/IN/NN/RB/RBR/RP, and *out* the class IN/JJ/NN/RB/RP. Since the only relevant variation is between IN and RP, the pairwise nuclei method turns up such cases with the variation *came IN/RP for*, pointing to an error in the two cases of *out*.

(8) a. accounts came in/RP for some blocks

b. numbers came out/IN for September

c. he again came out/IN for an amendment

But what of the 41 false positives, 22 of which are due to the pairwise classes? We have increased recall, but there is also a 20% absolute drop in precision. Is this tradeoff worth it? To answer this, it is important to note that 15 of the false positives are due to faulty ambiguity classes, as discussed above, and 10 of those 15 are from pairwise classes. For error detection, this means 74 of the 100 samples lead to some POS error; for investigating disambiguation contexts, this means 69% (59/85) of the cases support disambiguation.

Additionally, the 15 cases point to 53 token errors, much more than in the previous experiment, due to 44 token errors from the new pairwise ambiguity classes. For example, in the variation frame *as DT/JJ sales*, the words which vary are *a* (tagged DT (determiner), with a complete ambiguity class of DT/FW/IN/JJ/LS/NNP/SYM) and *many* (tagged JJ, with an ambiguity class of DT/JJ/NNS/PDT/RB/VB). Unsurprisingly, *a* should never have been tagged JJ in the corpus, i.e., its ambiguity class is wrong.

In addition to the issue of erroneous tags in an ambiguity class, atypical tags also pose a problem. Consider the frame *that JJ/RB in*, as illustrated in (9), with acceptable variation. It might appear that *sometime* has a problem with its ambiguity class, but the use of JJ is actually correct, as shown in (10), where *sometime* is atypically modifying a noun. To counter atypical uses, one could use only "typical" ambiguity classes (cf. Dickinson, 2007) or define ambiguity classes according to order of frequency (cf. Daelemans et al., 1996), e.g., JJ/RB vs. RB/JJ.

(9) a. a departure from the past that many/JJ in the industry ...

b. hope that sometime/RB in the near future

(10) real estate magnate and sometime/JJ raider Donald Trump

This illustrates that the selection of an abstracted class for a nucleus definition is non-trivial, and ambiguity classes are simply an approximation.

POS contexts One problem for our method is that word contexts are not always truly comparable; identical context words can be used differently. For instance, with the variation *that NN/VBP along* in (11), the uses of *that* are clearly distinct and are marked as such by their tags.

(11) a. gifts that/WDT go/VBP along with purchases

b. We are considering that/DT offer/NN along with all other alternatives

But do tagset categories actually aid in local disambiguation? To quickly gauge this, we take the previous sample of 100 variations and recover the POS information for the context. Isolating those cases with non-identical POS tags for the same word contexts, we find 10 examples and hypothesize that these will more likely be acceptable variations. Interestingly, however, of those ten, six successfully identified errors; it turns out that the POS of the word is often irrelevant for disambiguation. For the variation *paid JJR/RBR than* in (12), for example, the tag of the context word *paid* is different in these cases, but that does not matter for the tag of *more*, which should be consistent.

(12) a. they paid/VBD more/JJR than $ 1 million

b. he has paid/VBN more/RBR than $ 70,000

More problematically, four of the erroneous variation nuclei also contained POS errors in the context, as in example (13). The variation *all CC/RB disappeared* points to an error in the word *but*, yet there is also a noticeable inconsistency in the word *all*.

(13) a. have all/DT but/CC disappeared

b. have all/RB but/RB disappeared

In other words, it is often the case that we should ignore the POS of the context words, due to the fact that erroneous contexts exist and, more importantly, that not all categories aid in disambiguation. Exploring which contextual categories aid in target category disambiguation (cf., e.g., Brants, 1997) could aid in developing better disambiguation models, and perhaps also a better sense of what categories are useful to induce (e.g., a broader category *Verb* in (12) for *paid*).

6 Representations for disambiguation

We have shown that local lexical context provides a generally unambiguous context for corpus tags, given sufficient information about the word to be disambiguated. The information need not be very abstract, either: frames using ambiguity class nuclei only require a word's category possibilities. Even for many unsupervised situations, this is available from a lexicon (e.g., Banko and Moore, 2004; Goldberg et al., 2008).

We have only looked at cases with variation in tagging; fully gauging the accuracy of such a data representation for disambiguation requires more of the framed nuclei from the corpus, including those without variation. For this, we could take all framed nuclei from a corpus and compare the level of ambiguity for differing abstractions. However, most framed nuclei occur only once, and it is not clear how meaningful it is to say that these are unambiguous. Thus, we examine framed nuclei which occur at least twice and report in table 1 for the WSJ how unambiguous a particular level of nucleus abstraction is.[5]

Abstraction	Unamb.	Total	Accuracy
Word	84,784	87,390	97.02%
Complete AC	90,341	94,472	95.63%
No info.	51,945	100,662	51.60%

Table 1: Disambiguation accuracy for the WSJ

While abstracting to the case where the nucleus contains no information (*No info.*) creates more cases which are classifiable—over 100,000—the accuracy of disambiguation drops from the upper 90% range to 52%. Note, however, that the abstraction to complete ambiguity class (AC) nuclei has minimal degradation in accuracy, yet increases the number of accurately classified cases. When we recall that approximately 79% of of the 4131 variation frames should have a single tag, i.e., 3263 cases, this means that the overall disambiguation accuracy is estimated to be 99.08% (93,604/94,472).

In addition to the disambiguation accuracy of frames, we can look at the accuracy of word tokens identified by frames. To gauge this, we identify the most likely tag of each framed variation nucleus and assign it to all instances of the nucleus. In the case of ties, one tag is randomly selected; since we are only calculating overall word token accuracy, the exact tag selected is unimportant. The results of comparing to the benchmark tags are given in table 2. Even though the abstraction to no information identifies more word tokens, the ambiguity class abstraction correctly categorizes nearly as many words.

Abstraction	Correct	Total	Accuracy
Word	340,860	345,139	98.76%
Complete AC	441,603	448,402	98.74%
No info.	444,635	582,601	76.32%

Table 2: Word token accuracy for the WSJ

With the smaller and likely more accurately tagged TIGER corpus, we find exactly the same trends, as shown in table 3. This supports the claim across corpora that local context is often sufficient to disambiguate a word, if some information from the word—here, the category possibilities—is present in the nucleus.

[5]As pairwise ambiguity classes involve more than one nucleus per corpus position, we use complete ambiguity classes.

Abstraction	Unamb.	Total	Accuracy
Word	37,038	37,324	99.23%
Complete AC	47,832	48,458	98.71%
No info.	33,881	56,494	59.97%

Table 3: Disambiguation accuracy for TIGER

The poor accuracy for framed nuclei with no information indicates that methods which intend to match corpus annotation categories could face difficulties in obtaining a single category without using more information. There is still much space to explore, however, between using ambiguity class nuclei and no information, in order to further increase the number of comparable cases without losing accuracy and in order to be more knowledge-free.

7 Summary and Outlook

Motivated by work on category acquisition, we have shown that local contexts—i.e., immediately surrounding words, or frames—can delineate corpus categories when the level of abstraction for the word to be disambiguated indicates some inherent properties of the word, namely the categories it can have. By abstracting away from lexical items to broader classes of words, we have been able to increase the recall of an error detection method without much drop in its precision.

Having successfully defined a representation for disambiguation, the next step is to make the representation more general, in order to include more comparable instances. As what we have done is essentially a form of nearest neighbor classification, one could in the future explore more sophisticated techniques to cluster contexts.

At the same time, we wish to use as little annotated knowledge as possible. Thus, an orthogonal line of research can involve inducing classes for words which are more general than single categories, i.e., something akin to ambiguity classes (see, e.g., the discussion of ambiguity class guessers in Goldberg et al., 2008). This could make error detection completely independent of the annotation and, more importantly, lead to an improved understanding of the best knowledge-free representation for disambiguation.

Since induction is founded to some extent upon disambiguating contexts, this work has some bearing on the evaluation of induced categories with corpus annotation; not only is there more than one tagset in existence (see discussion in Clark, 2003), but annotation schemes make distinctions that morphosyntactic contexts cannot readily capture. For example, there is an implicit notion of inherency in the distinction between JJ and NN in the Penn Treebank (Santorini, 1990, p. 12-13). Fully outlining these inherent properties could provide insights into induction and its evaluation.

Acknowledgments

Thanks to the three anonymous reviewers for their useful comments and to Charles Jochim for helpful discussion. This material is based upon work supported by the National Science Foundation under Grant No. IIS-0623837.

References

Banko, Michele and Robert C. Moore (2004). Part-of-Speech Tagging in Context. In *Proceedings of COLING 2004*. Geneva, Switzerland, pp. 556–561.

Boyd, Adriane, Markus Dickinson and Detmar Meurers (2007). Increasing the Recall of Corpus Annotation Error Detection. In *Proceedings of TLT 2007*. Bergen, Norway, pp. 19–30.

Brants, Sabine, Stefanie Dipper, Silvia Hansen, Wolfgang Lezius and George Smith (2002). The TIGER Treebank. In *Proceedings of TLT-02*. Sozopol, Bulgaria.

Brants, Thorsten (1997). Internal and External Tagsets in Part-of-Speech Tagging. In *Proceedings of Eurospeech*. Rhodes, Greece.

Chemla, E., T. H. Mintz, S. Bernal and A. Christophe (in press). Categorizing words using 'Frequent Frames': What cross-linguisic analyses reveal about core principles. *Developmental Science* .

Clark, Alexander (2003). Combining Distributional and Morphological Information for Part of Speech Induction. In *Proceedings of EACL-03*. Budapest, pp. 59–66.

Cutting, Doug, Julian Kupiec, Jan Pedersen and Penelope Sibun (1992). A Practical part-of-speech tagger. In *Proceedings of the ANLP-92*. Trento, Italy, pp. 133–140.

Daelemans, Walter, Jakub Zavrel, Peter Berck and Steven Gillis (1996). MBT: A Memory-Based Part of Speech Tagger-Generator. In *Proceedings of the Fourth Workshop on Very Large Corpora (VLC)*. Copenhagen, pp. 14–27.

Dickinson, Markus (2005). Error detection and correction in annotated corpora. Ph.D. thesis, The Ohio State University.

Dickinson, Markus (2007). Determining Ambiguity Classes for Part-of-Speech Tagging. In *Proceedings of RANLP-07*. Borovets, Bulgaria.

Dickinson, Markus and W. Detmar Meurers (2003). Detecting Errors in Part-of-Speech Annotation. In *Proceedings of EACL-03*. Budapest, pp. 107–114.

Goldberg, Yoav, Meni Adler and Michael Elhadad (2008). EM Can Find Pretty Good HMM POS-Taggers (When Given a Good Start). In *Proceedings of ACL-08*. Columbus, OH, pp. 746–754.

MacWhinney, Brian (2000). *The CHILDES project: Tools for analyzing talk*. Mahwah, NJ: Lawrence Erlbaum Associates, third edn.

Manning, Christopher D. and Hinrich Schütze (1999). *Foundations of Statistical Natural Language Processing*. Cambridge, MA: The MIT Press.

Marcus, M., Beatrice Santorini and M. A. Marcinkiewicz (1993). Building a large annotated corpus of English: The Penn Treebank. *Computational Linguistics* 19(2), 313–330.

Mintz, Toben H. (2002). Category induction from distributional cues in an artificial language. *Memory & Cognition* 30, 678–686.

Mintz, Toben H. (2003). Frequent frames as a cue for grammatical categories in child directed speech. *Cognition* 90, 91–117.

Redington, Martin, Nick Chater and Steven Finch (1998). Distributional Information: A Powerful Cue for Acquiring Syntactic Categories. *Cognitive Science* 22(4), 425–469.

Santorini, Beatrice (1990). *Part-Of-Speech Tagging Guidelines for the Penn Treebank Project (3rd Revision, 2nd printing)*. Tech. Rep. MS-CIS-90-47, The University of Pennsylvania, Philadelphia, PA.

Schütze, Hinrich (1995). Distributional Part-of-Speech Tagging. In *Proceedings of EACL-95*. Dublin, Ireland, pp. 141–148.

Tseng, Huihsin, Daniel Jurafsky and Christopher Manning (2005). Morphological features help POS tagging of unknown words across language varieties. In *Proceedings of the Fourth SIGHAN Workshop on Chinese Language Processing*.

Syntactic Reordering Integrated with Phrase-based SMT

Jakob Elming
Computational Linguistics
Copenhagen Business School
jel.isv@cbs.dk

Abstract

We present a novel approach to word reordering which successfully integrates syntactic structural knowledge with phrase-based SMT. This is done by constructing a lattice of alternatives based on automatically learned probabilistic syntactic rules. In decoding, the alternatives are scored based on the output word order, not the order of the input. Unlike previous approaches, this makes it possible to successfully integrate syntactic reordering with phrase-based SMT. On an English-Danish task, we achieve an absolute improvement in translation quality of 1.1 % BLEU. Manual evaluation supports the claim that the present approach is significantly superior to previous approaches.

1 Introduction

The emergence of phrase-based statistical machine translation (PSMT) (Koehn et al., 2003) has been one of the major developments in statistical approaches to translation. Allowing translation of word sequences (phrases) instead of single words provides SMT with a robustness in word selection and local word reordering.

PSMT has two means of reordering the words. Either a phrase pair has been learned where the target word order differs from the source (phrase internal reordering), or distance penalized orderings of target phrases are attempted in decoding (phrase external reordering). The first solution is strong, the second is weak.

The second solution is necessary for reorderings within a previously unseen sequence or over distances greater than the maximal phrase length. In this case, the system in essence relies on the target side language model to get the correct word order. The choice is made without knowing what the source is. Basically, it is a bias against phrase external reordering.

It seems clear that reordering often depends on higher level linguistic information, which is absent from PSMT. In recent work, there has been some progress towards integrating syntactic information with the statistical approach to reordering. In works such as (Xia and McCord, 2004; Collins et al., 2005; Wang et al., 2007; Habash, 2007), reordering decisions are done "deterministically", thus placing these decisions outside the actual PSMT system by learning to translate from a reordered source language. (Crego and Mariño, 2007; Zhang et al., 2007; Li et al., 2007) are more in the spirit of PSMT, in that multiple reorderings are presented to the PSMT system as (possibly weighted) options.

Still, there remains a basic conflict between the syntactic reordering rules and the PSMT system: one that is most likely due to the discrepancy between the translation units (phrases) and units of the linguistic rules, as (Zhang et al., 2007) point out.

In this paper, we proceed in the spirit of the non-deterministic approaches by providing the decoder with multiple source reorderings. But instead of scoring the input word order, we score the order of the output. By doing this, we avoid the integration problems of previous approaches.

It should be noted that even though the experi-

© 2008. Licensed under the *Creative Commons Attribution-Noncommercial-Share Alike 3.0 Unported* license (http://creativecommons.org/licenses/by-nc-sa/3.0/). Some rights reserved.

ments are conducted within a source reordering approach, this scoring is also compatible with other approach. We will, however, not look further into this possiblity in the present paper.

In addition, we automatically learn reordering rules based on several levels of linguistic information from word form to subordination and syntactic structure to produce reordering rules that are not restricted to operations on syntactic tree structure nodes.

In the next section, we discuss and contrast related work. Section 3 describes aspects of English and Danish structure that are relevant to reordering. Section 4 describes the automatic induction of reordering rules and its integration in PSMT. In section 5, we describe the SMT system used in the experiments. Section 6 evaluates and discusses the present approach.

2 Related Work

While several recent authors have achieved positive results, it has been difficult to integrate syntactic information while retaining the strengths of the statistical approach.

Several approaches do deterministic reordering. These do not integrate the reordering in the PSMT system; instead they place it outside the system by first reordering the source language, and then having a PSMT system translate from reordered source language to target language. (Collins et al., 2005; Wang et al., 2007) do this using manually created rules, and (Xia and McCord, 2004) and (Habash, 2007) use automatically extracted rules. All use rules extracted from syntactic parses.

As mentioned by (Al-Onaizan and Papineni, 2006), it can be problematic that these deterministic choices are beyond the scope of optimization and cannot be undone by the decoder. That is, there is no way to make up for bad information in later translation steps.

Another approach is non-deterministic. This provides the decoder with both the original and the reordered source sentence. (Crego and Mariño, 2007) operate within Ngram-based SMT. They make use of syntactic structure to reorder the input into a word lattice. Since the paths are not weighted, the lattice merely narrows down the size of the search space. The decoder is not given reason to trust one path (reordering) over another.

(Zhang et al., 2007) assign weights to the paths of their input word lattice. Instead of hierarchical linguistic structure, they use reordering rules based on POS and syntactic chunks, and train the system with both original and reordered source word order on a restricted data set (<500K words). Their system does not out-perform a standard PSMT system. As they themselves point out, a reason for this might be that their reordering approach is not fully integrated with PSMT. This is one of the main problems addressed in the present work.

(Li et al., 2007) use weighted n-best lists as input for the decoder. They use rules based on a syntactic parse, allowing children of a tree node to swap place. This is excessively restrictive. For example, a common reordering in English-Danish translation has the subject change place with the finite verb. Since the verb is often embedded in a VP containing additional words that should not be moved, such rules cannot be captured by local reordering on tree nodes.

In many cases, the exact same word order that is obtained through a source sentence reordering, is also accessible through a phrase internal reordering. A negative consequence of source order (SO) scoring as done by (Zhang et al., 2007) and (Li et al., 2007) is that they bias against the valuable phrase internal reorderings by only promoting the source sentence reordering. As described in section 4.3, we solve this problem by reordering the input string, but scoring the output string, thus allowing the strengths of PSMT to co-exist with rule-based reordering.

3 Language comparison

The two languages examined in this investigation, English and Danish, are very similar from a structural point of view. A word alignment will most often display an almost one-to-one correlation. In the hand-aligned data, only 39% of the sentences contain reorderings (following the notion of reordering as defined in 4.1). On average, a sentence contains 0.66 reorderings.

One of the main differences between English and Danish word order is that Danish is a verb-second language: the finite verb of a declarative main clause must always be the second constituent. Since this is not the case for English, a reordering rule should move the subject of an English sentence to the right of the finite verb, if the first position is filled by something other than the subject. This is exemplified by (1) (examples are annotated with English gloss and translation), where 'they'

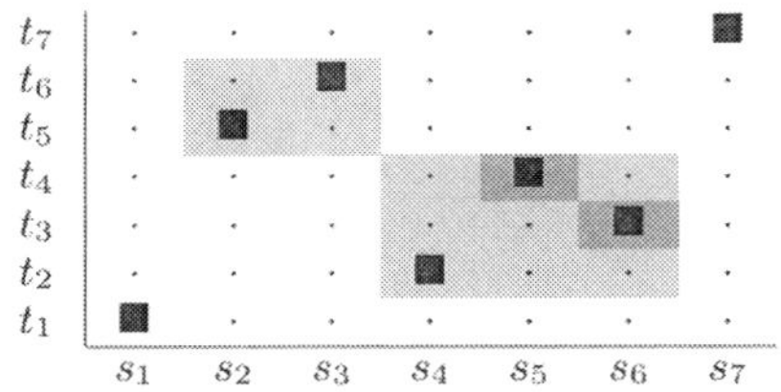

Table 1: Reordering example

should move to the right of 'come' to get the Danish word order as seen in the gloss.

(1) nu kommer de
[now come **they**]
*'here **they** come'*

Another difference is that Danish sentence adverbials in a subordinate clause move to the left of the finite verb. This is illustrated in example (2). This example also shows the difficulty for a PSMT system. Since the trigram 'han kan ikke' is frequent in Danish main clauses, and 'han ikke kan' is frequent in subordinate clauses, we need information on subordination to get the correct word order. This information can be obtained from the conjunction 'that'. A trigram PSMT system would not be able to handle the reordering in (2), since 'that' is beyond the scope of 'not'.

(2) han siger at han ikke kan se
[he says that he **not** can see]
*'he says that he can **not** see'*

In the main clause, on the other hand, Danish prefers the sentence adverbial to appear to the right of the finite verb. Therefore, if the English adverbial appears to the left of the finite verb in a main clause, it should move right as in example (3).

(3) hun så aldrig skibet
[she saw **never** the ship]
*'she **never** saw the ship'*

4 Reordering rules

4.1 Definition of reordering

In this experiment, reordering is defined as two word sequences exchanging positions. These two sequences are restricted by the following conditions:

- **Parallel consecutive:** They have to make up consecutive sequences of words, and each has to align to a consecutive sequence of words.
- **Maximal:** They have to be the longest possible consecutive sequences changing place.
- **Adjacent:** They have to appear next to each other on both source and target side.

The sequences are not restricted in length, making both short and long distance reordering possible. Furthermore, they need not be phrases in the sense that they appear as an entry in the phrase table.

Table 1 illustrates reordering in a word alignment matrix. The table contains reorderings between the light grey sequences (s_2^3 and s_4^6)[1] and the dark grey sequences (s_5^5 and s_6^6). On the other hand, the sequences s_3^3 and s_4^5 are e.g. not considered reordered, since neither are maximal, and s_4^5 is not consecutive on the target side.

4.2 Rule induction

In section 3, we pointed out that subordination is very important for word order differences between English and Danish. In addition, the sentence position of constituents plays a role. All this information is present in a syntactic sentence parse. A subordinate clause is defined as inside an SBAR constituent; otherwise it is a main clause. The constituent position can be extracted from the sentence start tag and the following syntactic phrases. POS and word form are also included to allow for more specific/lexicalized rules.

Besides including this information for the candidate reordering sequences (left sequence (LS) and right sequence (RS)), we also include it for the set of possible left (LC) and right (RC) contexts of these. The span of the contexts varies from a single word to all the way to the sentence border. Table 2 contains an example of the information available to the learning algorithm. In the example, LS and RS should change place, since the first position is occupied by something other than the subject in a main clause.

In order to minimize the training data, word and POS sequences are limited to 4 words, and phrase structure (PS) sequences are limited to 3 constituents. In addition, an entry is only used if at least one of these three levels is not too long for

[1]Notation: s_x^y means the consecutive source sequence covering words x to y.

<table>
<tr><th>Level</th><th>LC</th><th>LS</th><th>RS</th><th>RC</th></tr>
<tr><td>WORD</td><td><s> today , || today , || ,</td><td>he</td><td>was driving</td><td>home || home . || home . < /s></td></tr>
<tr><td>POS</td><td><S> NN , || NN , || ,</td><td>PRP</td><td>AUX VBG</td><td>NN || NN . || NN . < /S></td></tr>
<tr><td>PS</td><td><S> NP , || NP , || ,</td><td>NP</td><td>AUX VBG</td><td>ADVP || ADVP . || ADVP . < /S></td></tr>
<tr><td>SUBORD</td><td>main</td><td>main</td><td>main</td><td>main</td></tr>
</table>

Table 2: Example of experience for learning. Possible contexts separated by ||.

both LS and RS, and too long contexts are not included in the set. This does not constrain the possible length of a reordering, since a PS sequence of length 1 can cover an entire sentence.

In order to extract rules from the annotated data, we use a rule-based classifier, Ripper (Cohen, 1996). The motivation for using Ripper is that it allows features to be sets of strings, which fits well with our representation of the context, and it produces easily readable rules that allow better understanding of the decisions being made. In section 6.2, extracted rules are exemplified and analyzed.

The probabilities of the rules are estimated using Maximum Likelihood Estimation based on the information supplied by Ripper on the performance of the individual rules on the training data. These logarithmic probabilities are easily integratable in the log-linear PSMT model as an additional parameter by simple addition.

The rules are extracted from the hand-aligned, Copenhagen Danish-English Dependency Treebank (Buch-Kromann et al., 2007). 5478 sentences from the news paper domain containing 111,805 English words and 100,185 Danish words. The English side is parsed using a state-of-the-art statistical English parser (Charniak, 2000).

4.3 Integrating rule-based reordering in PSMT

The integration of the rule-based reordering in our PSMT system is carried out in two separate stages:

1. Reorder the source sentence to assimilate the word order of the target language.

2. Score the target word order according to the relevant rules.

Stage 1) is done in a non-deterministic fashion by generating a word lattice as input in the spirit of e.g. (Zens et al., 2002; Crego and Mariño, 2007; Zhang et al., 2007). This way, the system has both the original word order, and the reorderings predicted by the rule set. The different paths of the word lattice are merely given as equal suggestions to the decoder. They are in no way individually weighted.

Separating stage 2) from stage 1) is motivated by the fact that reordering can have two distinct origins. They can occur because of stage 1), i.e. the lattice reordering of the original English word order (phrase *external* reordering), and they can occur inside a single phrase (phrase *internal* reordering). We are, however, interested in doing *phrase-independent*, word reordering. We want to promote rule-predicted reorderings, regardless of whether they owe their existence to a syntactic rule or a phrase table entry.

This is accomplished by letting the actual scoring of the reordering focus on the target string. The decoder is informed of where a rule has predicted a reordering, how much it costs to do the reordering, and how much it costs to avoid it. This is then checked for each hypothezised target string by keeping track of what *source position target order* (SPTO) it corresponds to.

The SPTO is a representation of which source position the word in each target position originates from. Putting it differently, the hypotheses contain two parallel strings; a target word string and its SPTO string. In order to access this information, each phrase table entry is annotated with its internal word alignment, which is available as an intermediate product from phrase table creation. If a phrase pair has multiple word alignments, the most frequent is chosen.

Table 3 exemplifies the SPTO scoring. The source sentence is *'today he was late'*, and a rule has predicted that word 3 and 4 should change place. When the decoder has covered the first four input words, two of the hypotheses might be H1 and H2. At this point, it becomes apparent that H2 contains the desired SPTO (namely '4 3'), and it get assigned the reordering cost. H1 does not contain the rule-suggested SPTO (in stead, the words are in the order '3 4'), and it gets the violation cost. Both these scorings are performed in a phrase-

Source sentence:	$today_1\ ,_2\ he_3\ was_4\ late_5$	
Rule:	$3\ 4 \rightarrow 4\ 3$	
Hypothesis	Target string	SPTO
H1	idag han var	1 3 4
H2	idag var han	1 4 3

Table 3: Example of SPTO scoring during decoding at source word 4.

independent manner. The decoder assigns the reordering cost to H2 without knowing whether the reordering is internal (due to a phrase table entry) or external (due to a syntactic rule).

Phrase internal reorderings at other points of the sentence, i.e. points that are not covered by a rule, are not judged by the reordering model. Our rule extraction does not learn every possible reordering between the two languages, but only the most general ones. If no rule has an opinion at a certain point in a sentence, the decoder is free to chose the translation it prefers without reordering cost.

Separating the scoring from the source language reordering also has the advantage that the SPTO scoring in essence is compatible with other approaches such as a traditional PSMT system. We will, however, not examine this possibility further in the present paper.

5 The PSMT system

The baseline is the PSMT system used for the 2006 NAACL SMT workshop (Koehn and Monz, 2006) with phrase length 3 and a trigram language model (Stolcke, 2002). The system was trained on the English and Danish part of the Europarl corpus version 3 (Koehn, 2005). Fourth quarter of 2000 was removed in order to use *the common test set* of 11369 sentences (330,082 English words and 309,942 Danish words with one reference) for testing. In addition, fourth quarter of 2001 was removed for development purposes. Of these, 10194 were used for various analysis purposes, thereby keeping the test data perfectly unseen. 500 sentences were taken from the development set for tuning the decoder parameters. This was done using the Downhill Simplex algorithm. In total, 1,137,088 sentences containing 31,376,034 English words and 29,571,518 Danish words were left for training the phrase table and language model.

The decoder used for the baseline system is Pharaoh (Koehn, 2004) with its distance-penalizing reordering model. For the experiments, we use our own decoder which — except for the reordering model — uses the same knowledge sources as Pharaoh, i.e. bidirectional phrase translation model and lexical weighting model, phrase and word penalty, and target language model. Its behavior is comparable to Pharaoh when doing monotone decoding.

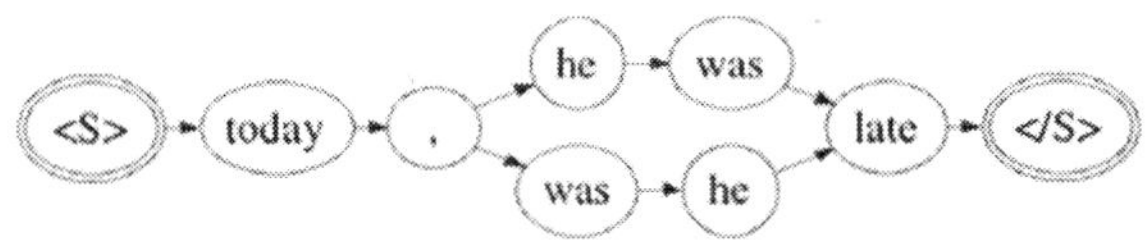

Figure 1: Example word lattice.

System	Dev	Test	Swap Subset
Baseline	0.262	0.252	0.234
no scoring	0.267	0.256	0.241
SO scoring	0.268	0.258	0.244
SPTO scoring	0.268	0.258	0.245

Table 4: BLEU scores for different scoring methods.

The search algorithm of our decoder is similar to the RG graph decoder of (Zens et al., 2002). It expects a word lattice as input. Figure 1 shows the word lattice for the example in table 3.

Since the input format defines all possible word orders, a simple monotone search is sufficient. Using a language model of order n, for each hypothezised target string ending in the same n-1-gram, we only have to extend the highest scoring hypothesis. None of the others can possibly outperform this one later on. This is because the maximal context evaluating a phrase extending this hypothesis, is the history (n-1-gram) of the first word of that phrase. The decoder is not able to look any further back at the preceeding string.

6 Evaluation

6.1 Results and discussion

The SPTO reordering approach is evaluated on the 11369 sentences of *the common test set*. Results are listed in table 4 along with results on the development set. We also report on the *swap subset*. These are the 3853 sentences where the approach actually motivated reorderings in the test set, internal or external. The remaining 7516 sentences were not influenced by the SPTO reordering approach.

System	BLEU	Avr. Human rating
Baseline	0.234	3.00 (2.56)
no scoring	0.240	3.00 (2.74)
SO scoring	0.239	3.00 (2.62)
SPTO scoring	0.244	2.00 (2.08)

Table 5: Evaluation on the set where SO and SPTO produce different translations. Average human ratings are medians with means in parenthesis, lower scores are better, 1 is the best score.

Decoder choice	SO	SPTO
Phrase internal reordering	401	1538
Phrase external reordering	3846	2849
Reject reordering	1468	1328

Table 6: The choices made based on the SO and SPTO scoring for the 5715 reorderings proposed by the rules for the test data.

We report on 1) the baseline PSMT system, 2) a system provided with a rule reordered word lattice but no scoring, 3) the same system but with an SO scoring in the spirit of (Zhang et al., 2007; Li et al., 2007), and finally 4) the same system but with the SPTO scoring.

The SPTO approach gets an increase over the baseline PSMT system of 0.6 % BLEU. The swap subset, however, shows that the extracted rules are somewhat restricted, only resulting in swap in $\frac{1}{3}$ of the sentences. The relevant set, i.e. the set where the present approach actually differs from the baseline, is therefore the swap subset. This way, we concentrate on the actual focus of the paper, namely the syntactically motivated SPTO reordering. Here we achieve an increase in performance of 1.1 % BLEU.

Comparing to the other scoring approaches does not show much improvement. A possible explanation is that the rules do not apply very often, in combination with the fact that the SO and SPTO scoring mechanisms most often behave alike. The difference in SO and SPTO scoring only leads to a difference in translation in 10% of the sentences where reordering is done. This set is interesting, since it provides a focus on the difference between the SO and the SPTO approaches. In table 5, we evaluate on this set.

The BLEU scores on the entire set indicate that SPTO is a superior scoring method. To back this observation, the 100 first sentences are manually evaluated by two native speakers of Danish. (Callison-Burch et al., 2007) show that ranking sentences gives higher inter-annotator agreement than scoring adequacy and fluency. We therefore employ this evaluation method, asking the evaluators to rank sentences from the four systems given the input sentence. Ties are allowed. The annotators had reasonable inter-annotator agreement ($\kappa = 0.523$, $P(A) = 0.69$, $P(E) = 0.35$). Table 5 shows the average ratings of the systems. This clearly shows the SPTO scoring to be significantly superior to the other methods ($p < 0.05$).

Most of the cases (55) where SPTO outperforms SO are cases where SPTO knows that a phrase pair contains the desired reordering, but SO does not. Therefore, SO has to use an external reordering which brings poorer translation than the internal reordering, because the words are translated individually rather than by a single phrase (37 cases), or it has to reject the desired reordering (18 cases), which also hurts translation, since it does not get the correct word order.

Table 6 shows the effect of SO and SPTO scoring in decoding. Most noticeable is that the SO scoring is strongly biased against phrase internal reorderings; SPTO uses nearly four times as many phrase internal reorderings as SO. In addition, SPTO is a little less likely to reject a rule proposed reordering.

6.2 Rule analysis

The rule induction resulted in a rule set containing 27 rules. Of these, 22 concerned different ways of identifying contexts where a reordering should occur due to the verb second nature of Danish. 4 rules had to do with adverbials in main and in subordinate clauses, and the remaining rule expressed that currency is written after the amount in Danish, while it is the other way around in English. Since the training data however only includes Danish Crowns, the rule was lexicalized to 'DKK'.

Table 7 shows a few of the most frequently used rules. The first three rules deal with the verb second phenomenon. The only difference among these is the left context. Either it is a prepositional phrase, a subordinate clause or an adverbial. These are three ways that the algorithm has learned to identify the verb second phenomenon conditions. Rule 3 is interesting in that it is lexicalized. In the learning data, the Danish correspondent to 'however' is most often not topicalized, and the subject

No	LC	LS	RS	RC
1	PS: <S> PP ,	PS: NP	POS: FV	
2	PS: SBAR ,	PS: NP	POS: FV	
3	PS: ADVP , ! WORD: however ,	PS: NP	POS: FV	
4		PS: FV	POS: RB	PS: VP SUB: sub
5	PS: <S> NP SUB: main	PS: ADVP	POS: FV	

Table 7: Example rules and their application statistics.

is therefore not forced from the initial position. As a consequence, the rule states that it should only apply, if 'however' is not included in the left context of the reordering.

Rule 4 handles the placement of adverbials in a subordinate clause. Since the right context is subordinate and a verb phrase, the current sequences must also be subordinate. In contrast, the fifth rule deals with adverbials in a main clause, since the left context noun phrase is in a main clause.

A problem with the hand-aligned data used for rule-induction is that it is out of domain compared to the Europarl data used to train the SMT system. The hand-aligned data is news paper texts, and Europarl is transcribed spoken language from the European Parliament. Due to its spoken nature, Europarl contains frequent sentence-initial forms of address. That is, left adjacent elements that are not integrated parts of the sentence as in example (4).

This is not straightforward, because on the surface these look a lot like topicalized constructions, as in example (5). In topicalized constructions, it is an integrated part of the sentence that is moved to the front in order to affect the flow of discourse information. This difference is crucial for the reordering rules, since 'i' and 'have' should reorder in (5), but not in (4), in order to get Danish word order.

(4) mr president , i have three points .

(5) as president , i have three points .

When translating the development set, it became clear that many constructions like (4) were reordered. Since these constructions were not present in the hand-aligned data, the learning algorithm did not have the data to learn this difference.

We therefore included a manual, lexicalized rule stating that if the left context contained one of a set of titles (mr, mrs, ms, madam, gentlemen), the reordering should not take place. Since the learning includes word form information, this is a rule that the learning algorithm is able to learn. To a great extent, the rule eliminates the problem.

The above examples also illustrate that local reordering (in this case as local as two neighboring words) can be a problem for PSMT, since even though the reordering is local, the information about whether to reorder or not is not necessarily local.

6.3 Reordering analysis

In this section, we will show and discuss a few examples of the reorderings made by the SPTO approach. Table 8 contain two translations taken from the test set.

In translation 1), the subject (bold) is correctly moved to the right of the finite verb (italics), which the baseline system fails to do. Moving the finite verb away from the infinite verb 'feature', however, leads to incorrect agreement between these. While the baseline correctly retains the infinite form ('stå'), the language model forces another finite form (the past tense 'stod') in the SPTO reordering approach.

Translation 2) illustrates the handling of adverbials. The first reordering is in a main clause, therefore, the adverbial is moved to the right of the finite verb. The second reordering occurs in a subordinate clause, and the adverbial is moved to the left of the finite verb. Neither of these are handled successfully by the baseline system.

In this case, the reordering leads to better word selection. The English 'aims to' corresponds to the Danish 'sigter mod', which the SPTO approach gets correct. However, the baseline system translates 'to' to its much more common translation 'at', because 'to' is separated from 'aims' by the adverbial 'principally'.

7 Conclusion and Future Plans

We have described a novel approach to word reordering in SMT, which successfully integrates syntactically motivated reordering in phrase-based SMT. This is achieved by reordering the input string, but scoring on the output string. As opposed to previous approaches, this neither biases against phrase internal nor external reorderings. We achieve an absolute improvement in translation quality of 1.1 % BLEU. A result that is supported by manual evaluation, which shows that the SPTO

1	S	based on this viewpoint , **every small port and every ferry port which handles a great deal of tourist traffic** *should* feature on the european list .
	B	baseret på dette synspunkt , **ethvert lille havn og alle færgehavnen som håndterer en stor turist trafik** *skal* stå på den europæiske liste .
	P	baseret på dette synspunkt , *skal* **alle de små havne , og alle færgehavnen som behandler mange af turister trafik** stod på den europæiske liste .
2	S	the rapporteur **generally** *welcomes* the proposals in the commission white paper on this subject but is apprehensive of the possible implications of the reform , which *aims* **principally** to decentralise the implementation of competition rules .
	B	ordføreren **generelt** *bifalder* forslagene i kommissionens hvidbog om dette emne , men er bekymret for de mulige konsekvenser af den reform , som *sigter* **hovedsagelig** at decentralisere gennemførelsen af konkurrencereglerne .
	P	ordføreren *bifalder* **generelt** forslagene i kommissionens hvidbog om dette emne , men er bekymret for de mulige konsekvenser af den reform , som **især** *sigter* mod at decentralisere gennemførelsen af konkurrencereglerne .

Table 8: Examples of reorderings. S is source, B is baseline, and P is the SPTO approach. The elements that have been reordered in the P sentence are marked alike in all sentences. The text in bold has changed place with the text in italics.

approach is significantly superior to previous approaches.

In the future, we plan to apply this approach to English-Arabic translation. We expect greater gains, due to the higher need for reordering between these less-related languages. We also want to examine the relation between word alignment method and the extracted rules and the relationship between reordering and word selection. Finally, a limitation of the current experiments is that they only allow rule-based external reorderings. Since the SPTO scoring is not tied to a source reordering approach, we want to examine the effect of simply adding it as an additional parameter to the baseline PSMT system. This way, all external reorderings are made possible, but only the rule-supported ones get promoted.

References

Al-Onaizan, Y. and K. Papineni. 2006. Distortion models for statistical machine translation. In *Proceedings of 44th ACL*.

Buch-Kromann, M., J. Wedekind, and J. Elming. 2007. The Copenhagen Danish-English Dependency Treebank v. 2.0. http://www.isv.cbs.dk/~mbk/cdt2.0.

Callison-Burch, C., C. Fordyce, P. Koehn, C. Monz, and J. Schroeder. 2007. (Meta-) evaluation of machine translation. In *Proceedings of ACL-2007 Workshop on Statistical Machine Translation*.

Charniak, E. 2000. A maximum-entropy-inspired parser. In *Proceedings of the 1st NAACL*.

Cohen, W. 1996. Learning trees and rules with set-valued features. In *Proceedings of the 14th AAAI*.

Collins, M., P. Koehn, and I. Kucerova. 2005. Clause restructuring for statistical machine translation. In *Proceedings of the 43rd ACL*.

Crego, J. M. and J. B. Mariño. 2007. Syntax-enhanced n-gram-based smt. In *Proceedings of the 11th MT Summit*.

Habash, N. 2007. Syntactic preprocessing for statistical machine translation. In *Proceedings of the 11th MT Summit*.

Koehn, P. and C. Monz. 2006. Manual and automatic evaluation of machine translation between european languages. In *Proceedings on the WSMT*.

Koehn, P., F. J. Och, and D. Marcu. 2003. Statistical phrase-based translation. In *Proceedings of NAACL*.

Koehn, P. 2004. Pharaoh: a beam search decoder for phrase-based statistical machine translation models. In *Proceedings of AMTA*.

Koehn, P. 2005. Europarl: A parallel corpus for statistical machine translation. In *Proceedings of MT Summit*.

Li, C., M. Li, D. Zhang, M. Li, M. Zhou, and Y. Guan. 2007. A probabilistic approach to syntax-based reordering for statistical machine translation. In *Proceedings of the 45th ACL*.

Stolcke, A. 2002. Srilm – an extensible language modeling toolkit. In *Proceedings of the International Conference on Spoken Language Processing*.

Wang, C., M. Collins, and P. Koehn. 2007. Chinese syntactic reordering for statistical machine translation. In *Proceedings of EMNLP-CoNLL*.

Xia, F. and M. McCord. 2004. Improving a statistical mt system with automatically learned rewrite patterns. In *Proceedings of Coling*.

Zens, R., F. J. Och, and H. Ney. 2002. Phrase-based statistical machine translation. In Jarke, M., J. Koehler, and G. Lakemeyer, editors, *KI - 2002: Advances in Artificial Intelligence. 25. Annual German Conference on AI*. Springer Verlag.

Zhang, Y., R. Zens, and H. Ney. 2007. Improved chunk-level reordering for statistical machine translation. In *Proceedings of the IWSLT*.

Efficient Parsing with the Product-Free Lambek Calculus

Timothy A. D. Fowler
Department of Computer Science
University of Toronto
10 King's College Road, Toronto, ON, M5S 3G4, Canada
tfowler@cs.toronto.edu

Abstract

This paper provides a parsing algorithm for the Lambek calculus which is polynomial time for a more general fragment of the Lambek calculus than any previously known algorithm. The algorithm runs in worst-case time $O(n^5)$ when restricted to a certain fragment of the Lambek calculus which is motivated by empirical analysis. In addition, a set of parameterized inputs are given, showing why the algorithm has exponential worst-case running time for the Lambek calculus in general.

1 Introduction

A wide variety of grammar formalisms have been explored in the past for parsing natural language sentences. The most prominent of these formalisms has been context free grammars (CFGs) but a collection of formalisms known as categorial grammar (CG) (Ajdukiewicz, 1935; Dowty et al., 1981; Steedman, 2000) has received interest because of some significant advantages over CFGs.

First, CG is inherently lexicalized due to the fact that all of the variation between grammars is captured by the lexicon. This is a result of the rich categories which CG uses in its lexicon to specify the functor-argument relationships between lexical items. A distinct advantage of this lexicalization is that the processing of sentences depends upon only those categories contained in the string and not some global set of rules. Second, CG has the advantage that it centrally adopts the principle of compositionality, as outlined in Montague grammar (Montague, 1974), allowing the semantic derivation to exactly parallel the syntactic derivation. This leads to a semantical form which is easily extractable from the syntactic parse.

A large number of CG formalisms have been introduced including, among others, the Lambek calculus (Lambek, 1958) and Combinatory Categorial Grammar (CCG) (Steedman, 2000). Of these, CCG has received the most zealous computational attention. Impressive results have been achieved culminating in the state-of-the-art parser of Clark and Curran (2004) which has been used as the parser for the Pascal Rich Textual Entailment Challenge entry of Bos and Markert (2005). The appeal of CCG can be attributed to the existence of efficient parsing algorithms for it and the fact that it recognizes a mildly context-sensitive language class (Joshi et al., 1989), a language class more powerful than the context free languages (CFLs) that has been argued to be necessary for natural language syntax. The Lambek calculus provides an ideal contrast between CCG and CFGs by being a CG formalism like CCG but by recognizing the CFLs like CFGs (Pentus, 1997).

The primary goal of this paper is to provide an algorithm for parsing with the Lambek calculus and to sketch its correctness. Furthermore, a time bound of $O(n^5)$ will be shown for this algorithm when restricted to product-free categories of bounded order (see section 2 for a definition). The restriction to bounded order is not a significant restriction, due to the fact that categories in CCGbank[1] (Hockenmaier, 2003), a CCG corpus, have a maximum order of 5 and an average order of 0.78 by token. In addition to the presentation of the algorithm, we will provide a parameterized set of in-

©2008. Licensed under the *Creative Commons Attribution-Noncommercial-Share Alike 3.0 Unported* license (http://creativecommons.org/licenses/by-nc-sa/3.0/). Some rights reserved.

[1] Although CCGbank was built for CCG, we believe that transforming it into a Lambek calculus bank is feasible.

puts (of unbounded order) on which the algorithm has exponential running time.

The variant of the Lambek calculus considered here is the product-free Lambek calculus chosen for three reasons. First, it is the foundation of all other non-associative variants of the Lambek calculus including the original Lambek calculus (Lambek, 1958) and the multi-modal Lambek calculus (Moortgat, 1996). Second, the calculus with product is NP-complete (Pentus, 2006), while the sequent derivability in the product-free fragment is still unknown. Finally, the only connectives included are / and \, which are the same connectives as in CCG, providing a corpus for future work such as building a probabilistic Lambek calculus parser.

2 Problem specification

Parsing with the Lambek calculus is treated as a logical derivation problem. First, the words of a sentence are assigned *categories* which are built from *basic categories* (e.g. NP and S) and the connectives \ and /. For example, the category for transitive verbs is $(NP\backslash S)/NP$ and the category for adverbs is $(S/NP)\backslash(S/NP)$[2]. Intuitively, the \ and / operators specify the arguments of a word and the direction in which those arguments need to be found. Next, the *sequent* is built by combining the sequence of the categories for the words with the $\vdash$ symbol and the sentence category (e.g. S).

Strictly speaking, this paper only considers the parsing of categories without considering multiple lexical entries per word. However, using techniques such as supertagging, the results presented here yield an efficient method for the broader problem of parsing sentences. Therefore, we can take the size of the input n to be the number of *basic* categories in the sequent.

A parse tree for the sentence corresponds to a proof of its sequent and is restricted to rules following the templates in figure 1. In figure 1, lowercase Greek letters represent categories and uppercase Greek letters represent sequences of categories. A proof for the sentence "Who loves him?" is given in figure 2.

The version of the Lambek calculus presented above is known as the product-free Lambek calculus allowing empty premises and will be denoted by L. In addition, we will consider the fragment L^k, obtained by restricting L to categories of order bounded by k. The *order* of a category, which can be viewed as the depth of the nesting of argument implications, is defined as:

$$\frac{}{\alpha \vdash \alpha}$$

$$\frac{\Gamma \vdash \alpha \qquad \Delta\beta\Theta \vdash \gamma}{\Delta\Gamma\alpha\backslash\beta\Theta \vdash \gamma} \qquad \frac{\alpha\Gamma \vdash \beta}{\Gamma \vdash \alpha\backslash\beta}$$

$$\frac{\Gamma \vdash \alpha \qquad \Delta\beta\Theta \vdash \gamma}{\Delta\beta/\alpha\Gamma\Theta \vdash \gamma} \qquad \frac{\Gamma\alpha \vdash \beta}{\Gamma \vdash \beta/\alpha}$$

Figure 1: The sequent presentation of L.

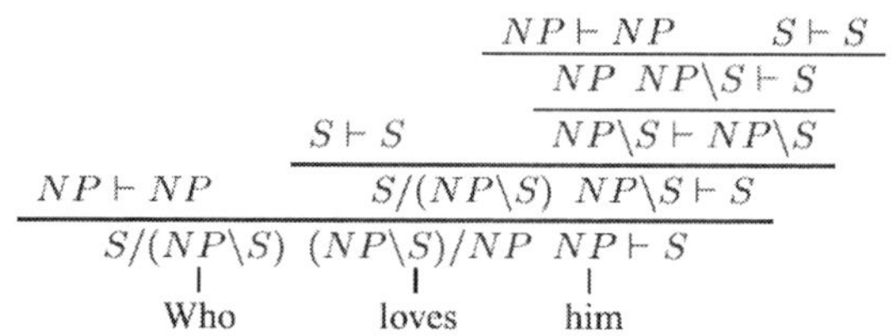

Figure 2: A derivation for "Who loves him?".

$$o(\alpha) = 0 \text{ for } \alpha \text{ a basic category}$$
$$o(\alpha/\beta) = o(\beta\backslash\alpha) = \max(o(\alpha), o(\beta) + 1)$$

For example, $o((NP\backslash S)/NP) = 1$ and $o((S/NP)\backslash(S/NP)) = 2$.

3 Related work

Two other papers have provided algorithms similar to the one presented here.

Carpenter and Morrill (2005) provided a graph representation and a dynamic programming algorithm for parsing in the Lambek calculus with product. However, due to there use of the Lambek calculus with product and to their choice of correctness conditions, they did not obtain a polynomial time algorithm for any significant fragment of the calculus.

Aarts (1994) provided an algorithm for L^2 which is not correct for L. Ours is polynomial time for L^k, for any constant k, and is correct for L, albeit in exponential running time.

A number of authors have provided polynomial time algorithms for parsing with CCG which gives some insight into how good our bound of $O(n^5)$ is. In particular, Vijay-Shanker and Weir (1994) provided a chart parsing algorithm for CCG with a time bound of $O(n^6)$.

4 An algorithm for parsing with L

This section presents a chart parsing algorithm similar to CYK where entries in the chart are arcs annotated with graphs. The graphs will be referred

[2] We use Ajdukiewicz notation, not Steedman notation.

to as abstract term graphs (ATGs) since they are graph representations of abstractions over semantic terms. ATGs will be presented in this section by construction. See section 5 for their connection to the proof structures of Roorda (1991).

The algorithm consists of two steps. First, the base case is computed by building the *base ATG* B and determining the set of *surface variables* by using the proof frames of Roorda (1991). Second, the chart is filled in iteratively according to the algorithms specified in the appendix. The details for these two steps can be found in sections 4.1 and 4.2, respectively. Section 4.3 introduces a procedure for culling extraneous ATGs which is necessary for the polynomial time proof and section 4.4 discusses recovery of proofs from the packed chart. An example of the algorithm is given in figure 3.

For parsing with L, the input is a sequent and for parsing with L^k, the input is a sequent with categories whose order is bounded by k. Upon completion, the algorithm outputs "YES" if there is an arc from 0 to $n-1$ and "NO" otherwise.

4.1 Computing the base case

Computing the base case consists of building the proof frame and then translating it into a graph, the base ATG B.

4.1.1 Building the proof frame

Proof frames are the part of the theory of proof nets which we need to build the base ATG. The proof frame for a sequent is a structure built on top of the categories of the sentence. To build the proof frame, all categories in the sequent are assigned a polarity and labelled by a fresh variable. Categories to the left of $\vdash$ are assigned negative polarity and the category to the right of $\vdash$ is assigned positive polarity. Then, the four decomposition rules shown in table 1 are used to build a tree-like structure (see figure 3). The decomposition rules are read from bottom to top and show how to decompose a category based on its main connective and polarity. In table 1, d is the label of the category being decomposed, f, g and h are fresh variables and order of premises is important.

The bottom of the proof frame consists of the original sequent's categories with labels and polarities. These are called *terminal formulae*. The top of the proof frame consists of basic categories with labels and polarities. These are called the *axiomatic formulae*. In addition, we will distinguish

$$\frac{\alpha \overset{+}{:} f \qquad \beta \overset{-}{:} df}{\alpha\backslash\beta \overset{-}{:} d} \qquad \frac{\beta \overset{+}{:} h \qquad \alpha \overset{-}{:} g}{\alpha\backslash\beta \overset{+}{:} d}$$

$$\frac{\alpha \overset{-}{:} df \qquad \beta \overset{+}{:} f}{\alpha/\beta \overset{-}{:} d} \qquad \frac{\beta \overset{-}{:} g \qquad \alpha \overset{+}{:} h}{\alpha/\beta \overset{+}{:} d}$$

Table 1: The proof frame decomposition rules.

the leftmost variable in the label of each axiomatic formula as its *surface variable*. See figure 3 for an example.

4.1.2 Building the Base ATG

The base ATG B is built from the proof frame in the following way. The vertices of the base ATG are the surface variables plus a new special vertex τ. The edges of ATGs come in two forms: Labelled and unlabeled, specified as $\langle s, d, l\rangle$ and $\langle s, d\rangle$, respectively, where s is the source, d is the destination and l, where present, is the label.

To define the edge set of B, we need the following:

Definition. For a variable u that labels a positive category in a proof frame, the *axiomatic reflection*, $\rho(u)$, is the unique surface variable v such that on the upward path from u and v in the proof frame, there is no formula of negative polarity. For example, in figure 3, $\rho(b) = c$.

The edgeset E of the base ATG is as follows:

1. $\langle m, \rho(p_i)\rangle \in E$ for $1 \leq i \leq k$ where $mp_1 \ldots p_k$ appears as the label of some negative axiomatic formula

2. $\langle \tau, \rho(t)\rangle \in E$ where t is the label of the positive terminal formula

3. For each rule with a positive conclusion, negative premise labelled by g and positive premise labelled by h, $\langle \rho(h), g, g\rangle \in E$

A labeled edge in an ATG specifies that its source must eventually connect to its destination to complete a path corresponding to its label. For example, G_1 contains the edge $\langle c, e, d\rangle$ which indicates that to complete the path from c to d, we must connect c to e. In contrast, an unlabeled edge in an ATG specifies that its source is already connected to its destination. For example, in figure 3, G_3 contains the edge $\langle a, f\rangle$ which indicates that there is some path, over previously deleted nodes, which connects a to f.

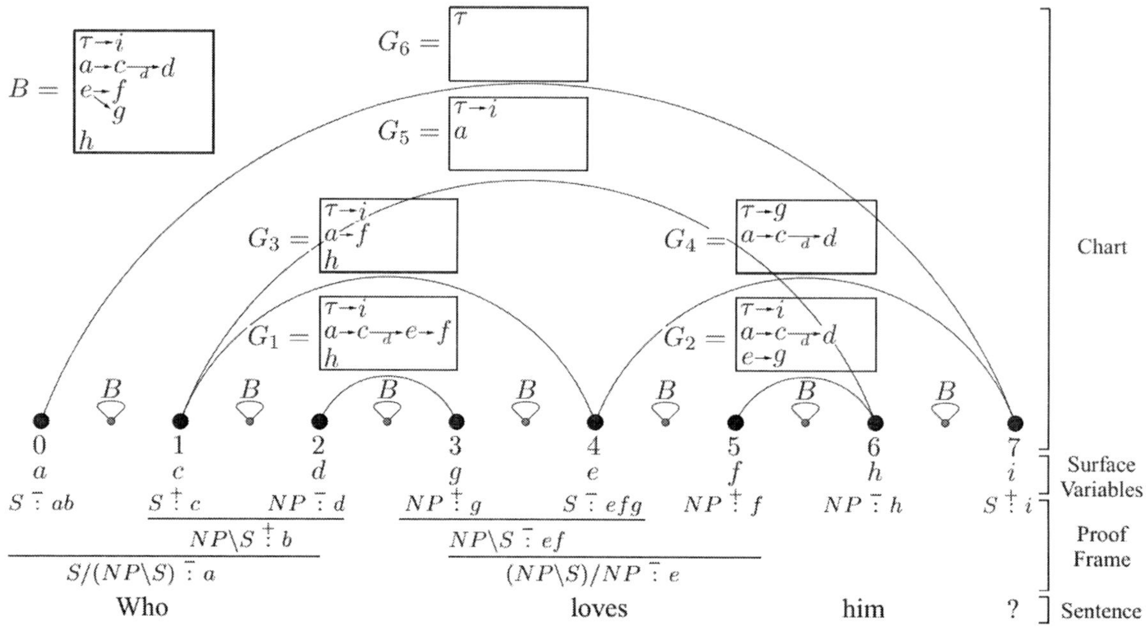

Figure 3: The algorithm's final state on the sequent $S/(NP\backslash S)\ (NP\backslash S)/NP\ NP \vdash S$.

Note that all nodes in an ATG have unlabeled in-degree of either 0 or 1 and that the vertices of an ATG are the surface variables found outside its arc.

4.2 Filling in the chart

Once the base ATG and the sequence of surface variables is determined, we can begin filling in the chart. The term *entry* refers to the collection of arcs beginning and ending at the same nodes of the chart. An arc's *length* is the difference between its beginning and end points, which is always odd. Note that each entry in the example in figure 3 contains only one arc. We will iterate across the entries of the chart and at each entry, we will attempt a *Bracketing* and a number of *Adjoinings*. If an attempt results in a *violation*, no new ATG is inserted into the chart. Otherwise, a new ATG is computed and inserted at an appropriate entry.

Bracketing is an operation on a single ATG where we attempt to extend its arc by connecting two nodes with the same basic category and opposite polarity. For example, G_3 is the result of bracketing G_1. Adjoining, on the other hand, is an operation on two adjacent ATGs where we attempt to unify their ATGs into one larger ATG. For example, G_5 is the result of adjoining G_3 and G_2.

The chart filling process is described by algorithm 1 in the appendix. The chart in figure 3 is filled by the graphs $G_1, \ldots, G_6$, in that order. A walk through of the example is given in the remainder of this section. Arcs of length 1 are treated specially, since they are derived directly from the base ATG. To show this, the base ATG is shown at pseudo-nodes, labeled by Bs.

4.2.1 Inserting arcs of length 1

This section corresponds to lines 1-2 of algorithm 1 in the appendix. For each arc from i to $i+1$, we will attempt to bracket the base ATG from axiomatic formula i to axiomatic formula $i+1$.

To follow our example, the first step is to consider inserting an arc from 0 to 1 by bracketing B. Bracketing causes a positive surface variable to be connected to a negative surface variable and in this case, a cycle from a to c and back to a is formed resulting in the violation on line 12 of algorithm 2. Therefore, no arc is inserted.

Then, the second step considers inserting an arc from 1 to 2. However, axiomatic formula 1 has category S and axiomatic formula 2 has category NP which results in the violation on line 3 of algorithm 2 since they are not the same.

Next, we attempt to insert an arc from 2 to 3. In this case, no violations occur meaning that we can insert the arc. The intuition is that the ATG for this arc is obtained by connecting g to d in the base ATG. Since c must eventually connect to d ($c \rightarrow_d d$), and now g connects to d, the in-degree constraint on ATG nodes requires that the path connecting c to d pass through g. Further-

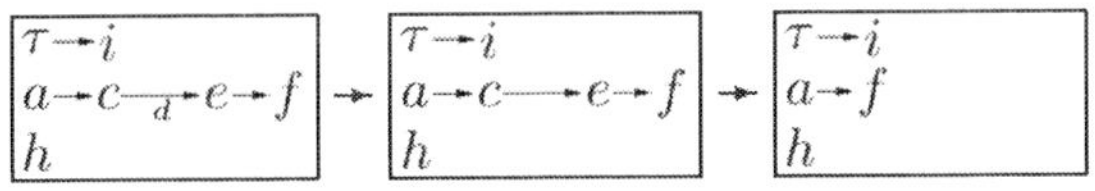

Figure 4: The intuition for bracketing from c to e.

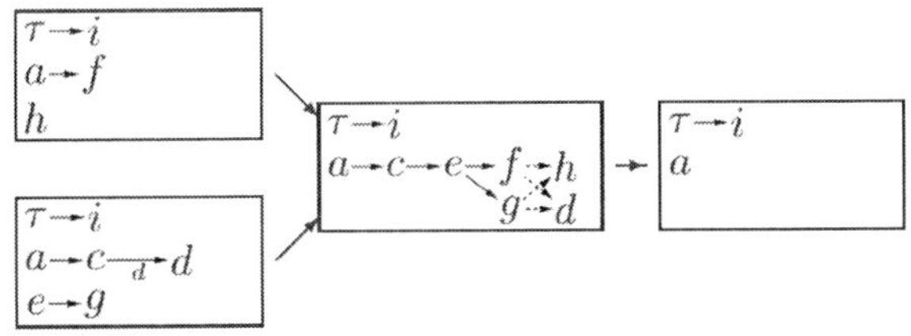

Figure 5: The intuition for adjoining two ATGs.

more, the only way to connect c to g is through e. So $c \rightarrow_d e$. Then, we delete d and g.

This procedure continues until we have considered all possible arcs of length 1.

4.2.2 Inserting arcs of length 3 and greater

Next, we iterate across graphs in the chart and for each, consider whether its ATG can be bracketed with the axiomatic formulae on either side of it and whether it can be adjoined with any of the other graphs in the chart. This process closely resembles CYK parsing as described on lines 3-10 of algorithm 1. The choice of shortest to longest is important because part of the invariant of our dynamic program is that all derivable ATGs on shorter arcs have already been added.

Following our example, the first graph to be considered is G_1. First, we attempt to bracket it from axiomatic formulae 1 to 4. As before, this intuitively involves connecting c to e in the ATG for this arc. This is allowed because no cycles are formed and no labelled edges are prohibited from eventually being connected. Then, as before, we delete the vertices c and e and as a result connect a to f, resulting in G_3. The bracketing process is illustrated in figure 4.

Next, we consider all graphs to which G_1 could adjoin and there are none, since such graphs would need to annotate arcs which either end at 1 or begin at 4. After processing G_1, we process G_2, which has a successful bracketing resulting in G_4 and no successful adjoinings.

Next, we process G_3. Bracketing it is prohibited, as it would result in a cycle from a to f and back to a. However, it is possible to adjoin G_3 with G_2, since they are adjacent.

The adjoining of two graphs can be viewed as a kind of intersection of the two ATGs, in the sense that we are combining the information in both graphs to yield a single more concise graph. Attempting an adjoining involves traversing the two graphs being adjoined and the base ATG in both a forward and a backward direction as specified in algorithms 4 and 5 in the appendix.

The intuition behind these traversals is to generate a picture of what the combination of the two graphs must look like as illustrated in figure 5. In general, we can only reconstruct those parts of the graph which are necessary for determining the resultant ATG and no more. The dotted edges indicate uncertainty about the edges present at this stage of the algorithm. Adjoining G_2 and G_3 does not fail and the resultant graph is G_5.

Note that this example does not contain any instances of two identical ATGs being inserted multiple times into the chart which occurs often in large examples yielding significant savings of computation.

4.3 Culling of extraneous ATGs

It often happens that an entry in the chart contains two ATGs such that if one of them is extendable to a complete proof then the other necessarily is as well. In this case, the former can be discarded. We will outline such a method here that is important for the polynomial time proof.

Definition. ATGs G_1 and G_2 are *equivalent* if some surjection of edge labels to edge labels applied to the those of G_1 yields those of G_2.

Then, if two ATGs in a chart are equivalent, one can be discarded.

4.4 Recovering proofs from a packed chart

The algorithm as described above is a method for answering the decision problem for sequent derivability in the Lambek calculus. However, we can annotate the ATGs with the ATGs they are derived from so that a complete set of Roorda-style proof nets, and thus the proofs themselves, can be recovered.

5 Correctness

Correctness of the algorithm is obtained by using structural induction to prove the equivalence of the constructive definition of ATGs outlined in section 4 and a definition based on semantic terms given in this section:

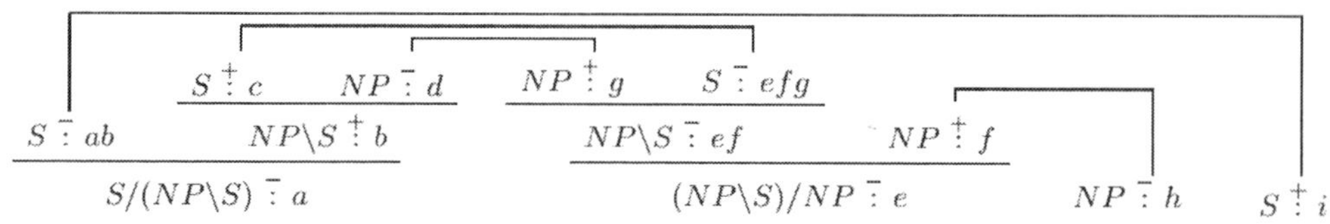

Figure 6: A proof structure for "Who loves him?".

Definition. A *partial proof structure* is a proof frame together with a matching of the axiomatic formulae. A *proof structure* is a partial proof structure whose matching is complete.

An example is given in figure 6. Proof structures correspond to proofs under certain conditions and our conditions will be based on the semantic term of the proof given to us by the Curry-Howard isomorphism for the Lambek calculus (Roorda, 1991). To do this, we interpret left rules as functional application and right rules as functional abstraction of lambda terms. Under this interpretation, the semantic term obtained from the proof structure in figure 6 is $a\lambda d.ehd$.

As in Roorda (1991), proof structures correspond to a proof if the semantic term assigned to the sentence category is a well formed lambda term which includes all the terms assigned to the words of the sentence. Then, ATGs are graph representations of abstractions of the undetermined portion of semantic terms of partial proof structures. Unlabeled edges correspond to functional applications whose arguments must still be determined and labelled edges correspond to functional abstractions whose body does not yet contain an instance of the abstracted variable. The violations which occur during the execution of the algorithm correspond to the various ways in which a lambda term can be ill formed.

6 Asymptotic Running Time Complexity

In this section we provide proof sketches for the runtime of the algorithm. Let $f(n)$ be a bound on the number of arcs occurring in an entry in the chart where n is the number of axiomatic formulae. Then, observe that the number of edges within an ATG is $O(n^2)$ and the number of edges adjacent to a vertex is $O(n)$, due to basic properties of ATGs.

Then, it is not hard to prove that the worst case running time of Bracketing is $O(n^2)$, which is dominated by the for loops of lines 20-23 of algorithm 2.

Next, with some effort, we can see that the worst case running time of Adjoining is dominated by the execution of the procedures Fore and Back. But, since there are at most a linear number of labels l and for each label l we need to visit each vertex in G_1 and G_2 at most a constant number of times, the worst case running time is $O(n^2)$.

Then, for each ATG, we attempt at most one bracketing and adjoinings with at most $2n+1$ other entries for which there can be $(2n+1)f(n)$ ATGs. Therefore, each entry can be processed in worst case time $O(n^3 f(n)^2)$.

Finally, there are $O(n^2)$ entries in the chart, which means that the entire algorithm takes time $O(n^5 f(n)^2)$ in the worst case. Sections 6.1 and 6.2 discuss the function $f(n)$.

6.1 Runtime for L^k

By structural induction on the proof frame decomposition rules and the base ATG building algorithm, it can be proven that in L^k the length of the longest path in the base ATG is bounded by k.

Next, consider a partition of the surface variables into a pair of sets such that the axiomatic formulae corresponding to the surface variables within each set are contiguous. For the example in figure 3, one such pair of sets is $S_1 = \{a, c, d, g\}$ and $S_2 = \{e, f, h, i\}$. Then, given such a partition, it can be proven that there is at least one maximal path P in the base ATG such that all vertices in one set that are adjacent to a vertex in the other set are either in P or adjacent to some vertex in P. For example, a maximal path for S_1 and S_2 is $P = e \rightarrow g$.

An entry in the chart induces two such partitions, one at the left edge of the entry and one at the right edge. Therefore, we obtain two such maximal paths and for any ATG G in this entry and any vertex v not in or adjacent to one of these paths, either v is not in G or v has the same neighbourhood in G as it has in the base ATG. Then, the number of vertices adjacent to vertices in these paths can be as many as n. However, if we put these vertices into sets such that vertices in a set have identical neighbourhoods, the number of sets is dependant only on k.

In the worst case, the out-neighbourhood of one of these sets can be any set of these sets. So, we get a bound for $f(n)$ to be $O(k^2 4^k)$. Therefore, because k is constant in L^k, $f(n)$ is constant and the running time of the algorithm for L^k is $O(n^5)$ in the worst case.

6.2 Runtime for L

Despite the results of section 6.1, this algorithm has an exponential running time for L. We demonstrate this with the following set of parameterized sequents:

$$\begin{aligned} F(1) &= ((A/A)\backslash A)\backslash A \\ F(i) &= ((A/(A/F_{i-1}))\backslash A)\backslash A \text{ for } i > 1 \\ U(n) &= F_n \ F_n \vdash A\backslash A \end{aligned}$$

Theorem. *There are* $\frac{(2n-1)!}{n!(n-1)!} \in \Theta(4^n)$ *distinct arcs in the entry from* n *to* $3n-1$ *in the chart for* $U(n)$.

Proof. By induction and a mapping from the possible matchings to the possible permutations of a sequence of length $2n-1$ such that two subsequences of length n and $n-1$ are in order. □

7 Conclusions and Future Work

We have presented a novel algorithm for parsing in the Lambek calculus, sketched its correctness and shown that it is polynomial time in the bounded-order case. Furthermore, we presented a set of parameterized sequents proving that the algorithm is exponential time in the general case, which aids future research in finding either a polynomial time algorithm or an NP-completeness proof for L.

In addition, this algorithm provides another step toward evaluating the Lambek calculus against both CFGs (to evaluate the importance of Categorial Grammar) and CCG (to evaluate the importance of the mildly context-sensitive languages).

In the future, we plan on determining the running time of this algorithm on an actual corpus, such as a modified version of CCGbank, and then to empirically evaluate the Lambek calculus for natural language processing. In addition, we would like to investigate extending this algorithm to more complex variants of the Lambek calculus such as the multi-modal calculus using the proof nets of Moot and Puite (2002).

Acknowledgments

Many thanks to Gerald Penn, for his insightful comments and for guiding this research.

References

Aarts, Erik. 1994. Proving Theorems of the Second Order Lambek Calculus in Polynomial Time. *Studia Logica*, 53:373–387.

Ajdukiewicz, Kazimierz. 1935. Die syntaktische Konnexitat. *Studia Philosophica*, 1(1-27).

Bos, Johan and Katja Markert. 2005. Recognising textual entailment with logical inference. *Proceedings of HLT and EMNLP*, pages 628–635.

Carpenter, Bob and Glyn Morrill. 2005. Switch Graphs for Parsing Type Logical Grammars. *Proceedings of IWPT '05, Vancouver*.

Clark, Steven and James R. Curran. 2004. Parsing the WSJ using CCG and log-linear models. *Proceedings of ACL '04*, pages 104–111.

Dowty, David R., Robert E. Wall, and Stanley Peters. 1981. *Introduction to Montague Semantics*. Reidel.

Hockenmaier, Julia. 2003. *Data and Models for Statistical Parsing with Combinatory Categorial Grammar*. Ph.D. thesis, University of Edinburgh.

Joshi, Aravind K., K. Vijay-Shanker, and David J. Weir. 1989. *The Convergence of Mildly Context-sensitive Grammar Formalisms*. University of Pennsylvania.

Lambek, Joachim. 1958. The mathematics of sentence structure. *American Mathematical Monthly*, 65:154–170.

Montague, Richard. 1974. *Formal philosophy: selected papers of Richard Montague*. Yale University Press New Haven.

Moortgat, Michael. 1996. Multimodal linguistic inference. *Journal of Logic, Language and Information*, 5(3):349–385.

Moot, Richard and Quintijn Puite. 2002. Proof Nets for the Multimodal Lambek Calculus. *Studia Logica*, 71(3):415–442.

Pentus, Mati. 1997. Product-Free Lambek Calculus and Context-Free Grammars. *The Journal of Symbolic Logic*, 62(2):648–660.

Pentus, Mati. 2006. Lambek calculus is NP-complete. *Theoretical Computer Science*, 357(1-3):186–201.

Roorda, Dirk. 1991. *Resource Logics: Proof-theoretical Investigations*. Ph.D. thesis, Universiteit van Amsterdam.

Steedman, Mark. 2000. *The Syntactic Process*. Bradford Books.

Vijay-Shanker, K. and David J. Weir. 1994. Parsing Some Constrained Grammar Formalisms. *Computational Linguistics*, 19(4):591–636.

Appendix. Algorithm Pseudocode

The term *source set* refers to the out-neighbourhood of τ. The term *minus variable* refers to surface variables obtained from negative axiomatic formulae plus τ. X_i refers to the ith axiomatic formula.

Algorithm 1 Chart Iteration

for $i = 0$ to $n-1$ **do**
  Bracketing(B, X_i, X_{i+1})
for $l = 1, 3, 5, \ldots$ to $n-1$ **do**
  for $e = 0$ to $n-l-1$ **do**
    for each arc from e to $e+l$ with ATG G **do**
      Bracketing(G, X_{e-1} to X_{e+l+1})
      Adjoin G to ATGs from $e-l-1$ to $e-1$
      for $al = 1, 3, ..., l-2$ **do**
        Adjoin G to ATGs from $e-al-1$ to $e-1$
        Adjoin G to ATGs from $e{+}l{+}1$ to $e{+}l{+}al{+}1$

Algorithm 2 Bracketing(G, X_i, X_j)

$C_i \overset{p_i}{:} l_i = X_i$ and $C_j \overset{p_j}{:} l_j = X_j$
if $C_i \neq C_j$ **then**
  $Violation$: Mismatched Basic Categories
if $p_i = p_j$ **then**
  $Violation$: Mismatched Polarities
Let $m, p \in \{i, j\}$ such that p_m is negative and p_p is positive
if G is not from 1 to $n-1$ and the source set of G is the singleton l_p and l_m has out-degree 0 in G **then**
  $Violation$: Empty Source Set
if the edge $\langle l_m, l_p\rangle \in G$ **then**
  $Violation$: Cycle Exists
if l_p is in the source set of G and there exists an in-edge of m with label l such that no edge from p to m has label l and no edge from a vertex other than p to a vertex other than m has label l **then**
  $Violation$: Path Completion Impossible
if m has out-degree 0 and and there exists an out-edge of p with label l such that no edge from p to m has label l and no edge from a vertex other than p to a vertex other than m has label l **then**
  $Violation$: Path Completion Impossible
Copy G to yield H
for each edge $\langle l_p, l_m, l\rangle \in G$ **do**
  Delete all edges from H with label l
Delete l_m, l_p and all their incident edges from H
Let in_p be the in-neighbour of l_p in G
for each q in the out-neighbourhood of l_m in G **do**
  Insert $\langle in_p, q\rangle$ into H
  for each edge $\langle p, d, l\rangle$ in G **do**
    Insert $\langle q, d, l\rangle$ into H
for each edge $\langle q, m, l\rangle$ in G **do**
  Insert $\langle q, in_p, l\rangle$ into H
if H contains a cycle **then**
  $Violation$: Future Cycle Required
return H

Algorithm 3 Adjoining(G_1, G_2)

Let V_H be the intersection of the vertices in G_1 and G_2
if $V_H \neq \tau$ and $Fore(\tau, G_1, G_2) \cap V_H = \emptyset$ **then**
  $Violation$: Empty Source Set
for each l such that l labels an edge in G_1 and G_2 **do**
  Let $\langle p, m, l\rangle$ be the unique edge labelled l in B
  if $Fore(p, G_1, G_2, l) \cap Back(m, G_1, G_2) = \emptyset$ **then**
    if $Fore(p) \cap V_H = \emptyset$ **then**
      $Violation$: Path Completion Impossible
    if $Back(m) \cap V_H = \tau$ **then**
      $Violation$: Path Completion Impossible
Let H be the graph with vertex set V_H and no edges
for each minus variable $m \in V_H$ **do**
  for each $p \in Fore(m, G_1, G_2, \emptyset)$ **do**
    Insert $\langle m, p\rangle$ into H
for each l such that l labels an edge in G_1 and G_2 **do**
  Let $\langle p, m, l\rangle$ be the unique edge labelled l in B
  if $Fore(p, G_1, G_2, l) \cap Back(m, G_1, G_2) = \emptyset$ **then**
    for each $q \in Fore(p, G_1, G_2, l) \cap V_H$ **do**
      Insert $\langle q, Back(m, G_1, G_2) \cap V_H, l\rangle$ into H
return H

Algorithm 4 Fore(v, G_1, G_2, l)

if $v \in G_1$ and $v \in G_2$ **then**
  return $\{v\}$
else
  if v is a minus vertex **then**
    S = $\cup_{i \in \{1,2\}}$Out-neighbourhood$_{G_i}$ v
  else if v is a plus vertex **then**
    Let j be such that $v \in G_j$
    S = $\cup_{e \in \text{Edges labelled by} l}$Source of e
  F = S
  while S is not empty **do**
    Remove any element u from S
    Let m be the in-neighbour of u in B
    if u does not appear in one of G_1, G_2 and m does not appear in the other **then**
      Let i be such that $m \in G_i$
      Let O be the out-neighbourhood of m in G_i
      $S = S \cup O$
      $F = F \cup O$
    $F = F \cup \{m\}$
  return F

Algorithm 5 Back(m, G_1, G_2)

if $m \in G_1$ and $m \in G_2$ **then**
  return $\{m\}$
else
  Let $i, j \in \{1, 2\}$ be such that $m \in G_i$ and $m \notin G_j$
  Let m' be the destination of the edges labelled by m in G_j
  $M = \{m, m'\}$
  while $m' \notin G_1$ and $m' \notin G_2$ **do**
    Let $i', j' \in \{1, 2\}$ be such that $m' \in G_{i'}$ and $m' \notin G_{j'}$
    Let $p \in G_{j'}$ be an out-neighbour of m' in B
    Let m'' be the in-neighbour of p in $G_{j'}$
    $m' = m''$
    $M = M \cup \{m''\}$
  return M

A Probabilistic Model for Measuring Grammaticality and Similarity of Automatically Generated Paraphrases of Predicate Phrases

Atsushi Fujita **Satoshi Sato**
Graduate School of Engineering, Nagoya University
{fujita,ssato}@nuee.nagoya-u.ac.jp

Abstract

The most critical issue in generating and recognizing paraphrases is development of wide-coverage paraphrase knowledge. Previous work on paraphrase acquisition has collected lexicalized pairs of expressions; however, the results do not ensure full coverage of the various paraphrase phenomena. This paper focuses on productive paraphrases realized by general transformation patterns, and addresses the issues in generating instances of phrasal paraphrases with those patterns. Our probabilistic model computes how two phrases are likely to be correct paraphrases. The model consists of two components: (i) a structured N-gram language model that ensures grammaticality and (ii) a distributional similarity measure for estimating semantic equivalence and substitutability.

1 Introduction

In many languages, a concept can be expressed with several different linguistic expressions. Handling such synonymous expressions in a given language, i.e., paraphrases, is one of the key issues in a broad range of natural language processing tasks. For example, the technology for identifying paraphrases would play an important role in aggregating the wealth of uninhibited opinions about products and services that are available on the Web, from both the consumers and producers viewpoint. On the other hand, whenever we draw up a document, we always seek the most appropriate expression for conveying our ideas. In such a situation, a system that generates and proposes alternative expressions would be extremely beneficial.

© Atsushi Fujita and Satoshi Sato, 2008. Licensed under the *Creative Commons Attribution-Noncommercial-Share Alike 3.0 Unported* license. Some rights reserved. http://creativecommons.org/licenses/by-nc-sa/3.0/

Most of previous work on generating and recognizing paraphrases has been dedicated to developing context-free paraphrase knowledge. It is typically represented with pairs of fragmentary expressions that satisfy the following conditions:

Condition 1. Semantically equivalent
Condition 2. Substitutable in some context

The most critical issue in developing such knowledge is ensuring the coverage of the paraphrase phenomena. To attain this coverage, we have proposed a strategy for dividing paraphrase phenomena into the following two classes (Fujita et al., 2007):

(1) **Non-productive (idiosyncratic) paraphrases**
  a. burst into tears ⇔ cried
  b. comfort ⇔ console
(Barzilay and McKeown, 2001)

(2) **Productive paraphrases**
  a. be in our favor ⇔ be favorable to us
  b. show a sharp decrease ⇔ decrease sharply
(Fujita et al., 2007)

Typical examples of **non-productive paraphrases** are lexical paraphrases such as those shown in (1) and idiomatic paraphrases of literal phrases (e.g., "kick the bucket" ⇔ "die"). Knowledge of this class of paraphrases should be stored statically, because they cannot be represented with abstract patterns. On the other hand, a **productive paraphrase** is one having a degree of regularity, as exhibited by the examples in (2). It is therefore reasonable to represent them with a set of general patterns such as those shown in (3). This attains a higher coverage, while keeping the knowledge manageable.

(3) a. N_1 V N_2 ⇔ N_1's V-*ing* of N_2
  b. N_1 V N_2 ⇔ N_2 be V-*en* by N_1
(Harris, 1957)

Various methods have been proposed to acquire paraphrase knowledge (these are reviewed in Section 2.1) where pairs of **existing expres-**

sions are collected from the given corpus, taking the above two conditions into account. On the other hand, another issue arises when **paraphrase knowledge is generated** from the patterns for productive paraphrases such as shown in (3) by instantiating variables with specific words, namely,

Condition 3. Both expressions are grammatical

This paper proposes a probabilistic model for computing how likely a given pair of expressions satisfy the aforementioned three conditions. In particular, we focus on the post-generation assessment of automatically generated productive paraphrases of predicate phrases in Japanese.

In the next section, we review previous approaches and models. The proposed probabilistic model is then presented in Section 3, where the grammaticality factor and similarity factor are derived from a conditional probability. In Section 4, the settings for and results of an empirical experiment are detailed. Finally, Section 5 summarizes this paper.

2 Previous work

2.1 Acquiring paraphrase knowledge

The task of automatically acquiring paraphrase knowledge is drawing the attention of an increasing number of researchers. They are tackling the problem of how precisely paraphrase knowledge can be acquired, although they have tended to notice that it is hard to acquire paraphrase knowledge that ensures full coverage of the various paraphrase phenomena from existing text corpora alone. To date, two streams of research have evolved: one acquires paraphrase knowledge from parallel/comparable corpora, while the other uses the regular corpus.

Several alignment techniques have been proposed to acquire paraphrase knowledge from parallel/comparable corpora, imitating the techniques devised for machine translation. Multiple translations of the same text (Barzilay and McKeown, 2001), corresponding articles from multiple news sources (Barzilay and Lee, 2003; Quirk et al., 2004; Dolan et al., 2004), and bilingual corpus (Bannard and Callison-Burch, 2005) have been utilized. Unfortunately, this approach produces only a low coverage because the size of the parallel/comparable corpora is limited.

In the second stream, i.e., paraphrase acquisition from the regular corpus, the distributional hypothesis (Harris, 1968) has been adopted. The similarity of two expressions, computed from this hypothesis, is called distributional similarity. The essence of this measure is summarized as follows:

Feature representation: to compute the similarity, given expressions are first mapped to certain feature representations. Expressions that co-occur with the given expression, such as adjacent words (Barzilay and McKeown, 2001; Lin and Pantel, 2001), and modifiers/modifiees (Yamamoto, 2002; Weeds et al., 2005), have so far been examined.

Feature weighting: to precisely compute the similarity, the weight for each feature is adjusted. Point-wise mutual information (Lin, 1998) and Relative Feature Focus (Geffet and Dagan, 2004) are well-known examples.

Feature comparison measures: to convert two feature sets into a scalar value, several measures have been proposed, such as cosine, Lin's measure (Lin, 1998), Kullback-Leibler (KL) divergence and its variants.

While most researchers extract fully-lexicalized pairs of words or word sequences only, two algorithms collect template-like knowledge using dependency parsers. DIRT (Lin and Pantel, 2001) collects pairs of paths in dependency parses that connect two nominal entities. TEASE (Szpektor et al., 2004) discovers dependency sub-parses from the Web, based on sets of representative entities for a given lexical item. The output of these systems contains the variable slots as shown in (4).

(4) a. X wrote $Y \Leftrightarrow X$ is the author of Y
b. X solves $Y \Leftrightarrow X$ deals with Y
(Lin and Pantel, 2001)

The knowledge in (4) falls between that in (1), which is fully lexicalized, and that in (3), which is almost fully abstracted. As a way of enriching such a template-like knowledge, Pantel et al. (2007) proposed the notion of inferential selectional preference and collected expressions that would fill those slots.

As mentioned in Section 1, the aim of the studies reviewed here is to collect paraphrase knowledge. Thus, they need not to take the grammaticality of expressions into account.

2.2 Generating paraphrase instances

Representing productive paraphrases with a set of general patterns makes them maintainable and attains a higher coverage of the paraphrase phenomena. From the transformation grammar (Harris, 1957), this approach has been adopted by many researchers (Mel'čuk and Polguère, 1987; Jacquemin, 1999; Fujita et al., 2007). An important issue arises when such a pattern is used to generate instances of paraphrases by replacing its variables with specific words. This involves assessing the grammaticality of two expressions in addition to their semantic equivalence and substitutability.

As a post-generation assessment of automatically generated productive paraphrases, we have applied distributional similarity measures (Fujita and Sato, 2008). Our findings from a series of empirical experiments are summarized as follows:

- Search engines are useful for retrieving the contextual features of predicate phrases despite some limitations (Kilgarriff, 2007).
- Distributional similarity measures produce a tolerable level of performance.

The grammaticality of a phrase, however, is merely assessed by issuing the phrase as a query to a commercial search engine. Although a more frequent expression is more grammatical, the length bias should also be considered in the assessment.

Quirk et al. (2004) built a paraphrase generation model from a monolingual comparable corpus based on a statistical machine translation framework, where the language model assesses the grammaticality of the translations, i.e., generated expressions. The translation model, however, is not suitable for generating productive paraphrases, because it learns word alignments at the surface level. To cover all of the productive paraphrases, we require an non-real comparable corpus in which all instances of productive paraphrases have a chance of being aligned. Furthermore, as the translation model optimizes the word alignment at the sentence level, the substitutability of the aligned word sequences cannot be explicitly guaranteed.

2.3 Existing measures for paraphrases

To date, no model has been established that takes into account all of the three aforementioned conditions. With the ultimate aim of building an ideal model, this section overviews the characteristics and drawbacks of the four existing measures.

Lin's measure

Lin (1998) proposed a symmetrical measure:

$$Par_{Lin}(s \Leftrightarrow t) = \frac{\sum_{f \in F_s \cap F_t} (w(s,f) + w(t,f))}{\sum_{f \in F_s} w(s,f) + \sum_{f \in F_t} w(t,f)},$$

where F_s and F_t denote sets of features with positive weights for words s and t, respectively.

Although this measure has been widely cited and has so far exhibited good performance, its symmetry seems unnatural. Moreover, it may not work well for dealing with general predicate phrases because it is hard to enumerate all phrases to determine the weights of features $w(\cdot, f)$. We thus simply adopted the co-occurrence frequency of the phrase and the feature as in (Fujita and Sato, 2008).

Skew divergence

The skew divergence, a variant of KL divergence, was proposed in (Lee, 1999) based on an insight: the substitutability of one word for another need not be symmetrical. The divergence is given by the following formula:

$$d_{skew}(t,s) = D\left(P_s \| \alpha P_t + (1-\alpha) P_s\right),$$

where P_s and P_t are the probability distributions of features for the given original and substituted words s and t, respectively. $0 \leq \alpha \leq 1$ is a parameter for approximating KL divergence D. The score can be recast into a similarity score via, for example, the following function (Fujita and Sato, 2008):

$$Par_{skew}(s \Rightarrow t) = \exp\left(-d_{skew}(t,s)\right).$$

This measure offers an advantage: the weight for each feature is determined theoretically. However, the optimization of α is difficult because it varies according to the task and even the data size (confidence of probability distributions).

Translation-based conditional probability

Bannard and Callison-Burch (2005) proposed a probabilistic model for acquiring phrasal paraphrases[1]. The likelihood of t as a paraphrase of the given phrase s is defined as follows:

$$P(t|s) = \sum_{f \in tr(s) \cap tr(t)} P(t|f) P(f|s),$$

where $tr(e)$ stands for a set of foreign language phrases that are aligned with e in the given parallel corpus. Parameters $P(t|f)$ and $P(f|s)$ are also estimated using the given parallel corpus. A large-scale parallel corpus may enable us to precisely acquire a large amount of paraphrase knowledge. It

[1] In their definition, the term "phrase" is a sequence of words, while in this paper it designates the subtrees governed by predicates (Fujita et al., 2007).

is not feasible, however, to build (or obtain) a parallel corpus in which all the instances of productive paraphrases are translated to the same expression in the other side of language.

3 Proposed probabilistic model

3.1 Formulation with conditional probability

Recall that our aim is to establish a measure that computes the likelihood of a given pair of automatically generated predicate phrases satisfying the following three conditions:

Condition 1. Semantically equivalent
Condition 2. Substitutable in some context
Condition 3. Both expressions are grammatical

Based on the characteristics of the existing measures reviewed in Section 2.3, we propose a probabilistic model. Let s and t be the source and target predicate phrase, respectively. Assuming that s is grammatical, the degree to which the above conditions are satisfied is formalized as a conditional probability $P(t|s)$, as in (Bannard and Callison-Burch, 2005). Then, assuming that s and t are paradigmatic (i.e., paraphrases) and thus do not co-occur, the proposed model is derived as follows:

$$\begin{aligned} P(t|s) &= \sum_{f \in F} P(t|f)P(f|s) \\ &= \sum_{f \in F} \frac{P(f|t)P(t)}{P(f)} P(f|s) \\ &= P(t) \sum_{f \in F} \frac{P(f|t)P(f|s)}{P(f)}, \end{aligned}$$

where F denotes a set of features. The first factor $P(t)$ is called the **grammaticality factor** because it quantifies the degree to which condition 3 is satisfied, except that we assume that the given s is grammatical. The second factor $\sum_{f \in F} \frac{P(f|t)P(f|s)}{P(f)}$ ($Sim(s,t)$, hereafter), on the other hand, is called the **similarity factor** because it approximates the degree to which conditions 1 and 2 are satisfied by summing up the overlap of the features of two expressions s and t.

The characteristics and advantages of the proposed model are summarized as follows:

1) Asymmetric.
2) Grammaticality is assessed by $P(t)$.
3) No heuristic is introduced. As the skew divergence, the weight of the features can be simply estimated as conditional probabilities $P(f|t)$ and $P(f|s)$ and marginal probability $P(f)$.
4) There is no need to enumerate all the phrases. s and t are merely the given conditions.

The following subsections describe each factor.

3.2 Grammaticality factor

The factor $P(t)$ quantifies how the phrase t is grammatical using statistical language model.

Unlike English, in Japanese, predicates such as verbs and adjectives do not necessarily determine the order of their arguments, although they have some preference. For example, both of the two sentences in (5) are grammatical.

(5) a. *kare-wa* ***pasuta-o*** ***hashi-de*** *taberu.*
he-TOP pasta-ACC chopsticks-IMP to eat
He eats pasta with chopsticks.

b. *kare-wa* ***hashi-de*** ***pasuta-o*** *taberu.*
he-TOP chopsticks-IMP pasta-ACC to eat
He eats pasta with chopsticks.

This motivates us to use structured N-gram language models (Habash, 2004). Given a phrase t, its grammaticality $P(t)$ is formulated as follows, assuming a ($N-$ 1)-th order Markov process for generating its dependency structure $T(t)$:

$$P(t) = \left[\prod_{i=1...|T(t)|} P_d(c_i|d_i^1, d_i^2, \ldots, d_i^{N-1}) \right]^{1/|T(t)|},$$

where $|T(t)|$ stands for the number of nodes in $T(t)$. To ignore the length bias of the target phrase, a normalization factor $1/|T(t)|$ is introduced. d_i^j denotes the direct ancestor node of the i-th node c_i, where j is the distance from c_i; for example, d_i^1 and d_i^2 are the parent and grandparent nodes of c_i, respectively.

Then, a concrete definition of the nodes in the dependency structure is given. Widely-used Japanese dependency parsers such as CaboCha[2] and KNP[3] consider a sequence of words as a node called a "*bunsetsu*" that consists of at least one content word followed by a sequence of function words if any. The hyphenated word sequences in (6) exemplify those nodes.

(6) *kitto* *kare-ha* *kyou-no*
surely he-TOP today-GEN
kaigi-ni-ha *ko-nai-daro-u.*
meeting-DAT-TOP to come-NEG-must
He will surely not come to today's meeting.

As *bunsetsu* can be quite long, involving more than ten words, regarding it as a node makes the model complex. Therefore, we compare the

[2]http://chasen.org/~taku/software/cabocha/
[3]http://nlp.kuee.kyoto-u.ac.jp/nl-resource/knp.html

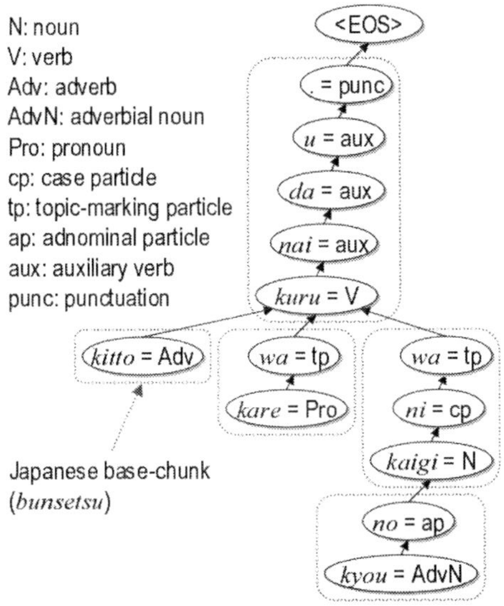

Figure 1: MDS of sentence (6).

following two versions of dependency structures whose nodes are smaller than *bunsetsu*.

MDS: Morpheme-based dependency structure (Takahashi et al., 2001) regards a morpheme as a node. MDS of sentence (6) is shown in Figure 1.

CFDS: The node of a content-function-based dependency structure is either a sequence of content words or of function words. CFDS of sentence (6) is shown Figure 2.

Structured N-gram language models were created from 15 years of Mainichi newspaper articles[4] using a dependency parser Cabocha, with N being varied from 1 to 3. Then, the 3-gram conditional probability $P_d(c_i|d_i^1, d_i^2)$ is given by the linear interpolation of those three models as follows:

$$\begin{aligned} P_d(c_i|d_i^1, d_i^2) &= \lambda_3 P_{ML}(c_i|d_i^1, d_i^2) \\ &\quad + \lambda_2 P_{ML}(c_i|d_i^1) \\ &\quad + \lambda_1 P_{ML}(c_i), \\ \text{s.t.} \quad \sum_j \lambda_j &= 1, \end{aligned}$$

where mixture weights λ_j are selected via an EM algorithm using development data[5] that has not been used for estimating P_{ML}.

3.3 Similarity factor

The similarity factor $Sim(s, t)$ quantifies how two phrases s and t are similar by comparing two sets of contextual features $f \in F$ for s and t.

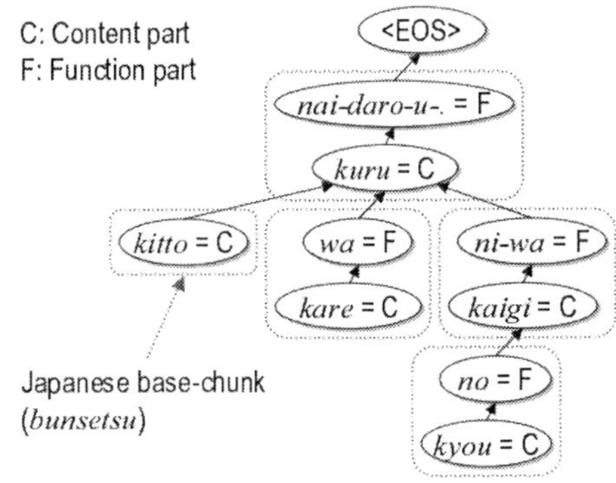

Figure 2: CFDS of sentence (6).

We employ the following two types of feature sets, which we have examined in our previous work (Fujita and Sato, 2008), where a feature f consists of an expression e and a relation r:

BOW: A pair of phrases is likely to be semantically similar, if the distributions of the words surrounding the phrases is similar. The relation set R_{BOW} contains only "co-occur_in_the_same_sentence".

MOD: A pair of phrases is likely to be substitutable with each other, provided they share a number of instances of modifiers and modifiees: the set of the relation R_{MOD} consists of two relations "modifier" and "modifiee".

Conditional probability distributions $P(f|s)$ and $P(f|t)$ are estimated using a Web search engine as in (Fujita and Sato, 2008). Given a phrase p, snippets of Web pages are firstly obtained via Yahoo API[6] by issuing p as a query. The maximum number of snippets is set to 1,000. Then, the features of the phrase are retrieved from those snippets using a morphological analyzer ChaSen[7] and CaboCha. Finally, the conditional probability distribution $P(f|p)$ is estimated as follows:

$$\begin{aligned} P(f|p) &= P(\langle r, e\rangle|p) \\ &= \frac{freq_{sni}(p, r, e)}{\sum_{r' \in R} \sum_{e'} freq_{sni}(p, r', e')}, \end{aligned}$$

where $freq_{sni}(p, r, e)$ stands for the frequency of the expression e appealing with the phrase p in relation r within the snippets for p.

The weight for features $P(f)$ is estimated using a static corpus based on the following equation:

$$\begin{aligned} P(f) &= P(\langle r, e\rangle) \\ &= \frac{freq_{cp}(r, e)}{\sum_{r' \in R} \sum_{e'} freq_{cp}(r', e')}, \end{aligned}$$

[4] Mainichi 1991-2005 (1.5GB, 21M sentences).

[5] Yomiuri 2005 (350MB, 4.7M sentences) and Asahi 2005 (180MB, 2.7M sentences).

[6] http://developer.yahoo.co.jp/search/

[7] http://chasen.naist.jp/hiki/ChaSen/

where $freq_{cp}(r, e)$ indicates the frequency of the expression e appearing with something in relation r within the given corpus. Two different sorts of corpora are separately used to build two variations of $P(f)$. The one is Mainichi, which is used for building structured N-gram language models in Section 3.2, while the other is a huge corpus consisting of 470M sentences collected from the Web (Kawahara and Kurohashi, 2006).

4 Experiments

4.1 Data

We conducted an empirical experiment to evaluate the proposed model using the test suite developed in (Fujita and Sato, 2008). The test suite consists of 176,541 pairs of paraphrase candidates that are automatically generated using a pattern-based paraphrase generation system (Fujita et al., 2007) for 4,002 relatively high-frequency phrases sampled from a newspaper corpus[8].

To evaluate the system from a generation viewpoint, i.e., how well a system can rank a correct candidate first, we extracted paraphrase candidates for 200 randomly sampled source phrases from the test suite. Table 1 shows the statistics of the test data. The "All-Yield" column shows that the number of candidates for a source phrase varies considerably, which implies that the data contains cases that have various difficulties. While the average number of candidates for each source phrase was 48.3 (the maximum was 186), it was dramatically reduced through extracting features for each source and candidate paraphrase from Web snippets: to 5.2 with BOW and to 4.8 with MOD. This suggests that a large number of spurious phrases were generated but discarded by going to the Web, and the task was significantly simplified.

4.2 Questions

Through this experiment, we evaluated several versions of the proposed model to answer the following questions:

Q1. Is the proposed model superior to existing measures in practice? Par_{Lin} and Par_{skew} are regarded as being the baseline.

Q2. Which language model performs better at estimating $P(t)$? MDS and CFDS are compared.

Q3. Which corpus performs better at estimating $P(f)$? The advantage of Kawahara's huge corpus (WebCP) over Mainichi is evaluated.

Q4. Which set of features performs better? In addition to BOW and MOD, the harmonic mean of the scores derived from BOW and MOD is examined (referred to as HAR).

Q5. Can the quality of $P(f|s)$ and $P(f|t)$ be improved by using a larger number of snippets? As the maximum number of snippets (N_S), we compared 500 and 1,000.

[8] The grammaticality of the source phrases are guaranteed.

Table 1: Statistics of test data ("Ph.": # of phrases).

Phrase type	Source Ph.	All Ph.	All Yield	BOW Ph.	BOW Yield	MOD Ph.	MOD Yield
N:C:V	18	57	3.2	54	3.0	54	3.0
N_1:N_2:C:V	57	4,596	80.6	594	10.4	551	9.7
N:C:V_1:V_2	54	4,767	88.3	255	4.7	232	4.3
N:C:Adv:V	16	51	3.2	39	2.4	38	2.4
Adj:N:C:V	2	8	4.0	5	2.5	5	2.5
N:C:Adj	53	173	3.3	86	1.6	83	1.6
Total	200	9,652	48.3	1,033	5.2	963	4.8

4.3 Results

Two assessors were asked to judge paraphrase candidates that are ranked first by either of the above models if each candidate satisfies each of the three conditions. The results for all the above options are summarized in Table 2, where the strict precision is calculated based on those cases that gain two positive judgements, while the lenient precision is for at least one positive judgement.

A1: Our greatest concern is the actual performance of our probabilistic model. However, no variation of the proposed model could outperform the existing models (Par_{Lin} and Par_{skew}) that only assess similarity. Furthermore, McNemer's test with $p < 0.05$ revealed that the precisions of all the models, except the combination of CFDS for $P(t)$ and Mainichi for $P(f)$, were significantly worse than those of the best models.

To clarify the cause of these disappointing results, we investigated the performance of each factor. Table 3 shows how well the grammaticality factors select a grammatical phrase, while Table 4 illustrates how well the similarity factors rank a correct paraphrase first. As shown in these tables, neither factor performed the task well, although combinations produced a slight improvement in performance. A detailed discussion is given below in A2 for the grammaticality factors, and in A3-A5 for the similarity factors.

A2: Comparisons between MDS and CFDS revealed that CFDS always produced better results than MDS not only when used for measuring grammaticality (Table 3), but also when used as a

Table 2: Precision for 200 test cases.

$N_S = 500$	Strict			Lenient		
Model	BOW	MOD	HAR	BOW	MOD	HAR
Par_{Lin}	78 (39%)	**88** (44%)	87 (44%)	116 (58%)	**128** (64%)	127 (64%)
Par_{skew}	81 (41%)	**88** (44%)	**88** (44%)	120 (60%)	127 (64%)	**128** (64%)
MDS, Mainichi	72 (36%)	73 (37%)	76 (38%)	109 (55%)	112 (56%)	114 (57%)
MDS, WebCP	71 (36%)	73 (37%)	72 (36%)	108 (54%)	110 (55%)	113 (57%)
CFDS, Mainichi	79 (40%)	78 (39%)	**83** (42%)	120 (60%)	119 (60%)	**123** (62%)
CFDS, WebCP	79 (40%)	77 (39%)	80 (40%)	118 (59%)	116 (58%)	118 (59%)
$N_S = 1{,}000$	Strict			Lenient		
Model	BOW	MOD	HAR	BOW	MOD	HAR
Par_{Lin}	79 (40%)	88 (44%)	88 (44%)	116 (58%)	128 (64%)	**129** (65%)
Par_{skew}	84 (42%)	**89** (45%)	**89** (45%)	121 (61%)	128 (64%)	128 (64%)
MDS, Mainichi	72 (36%)	75 (38%)	76 (38%)	109 (55%)	114 (57%)	114 (57%)
MDS, WebCP	71 (36%)	74 (37%)	72 (36%)	109 (55%)	111 (56%)	113 (57%)
CFDS, Mainichi	79 (40%)	82 (41%)	**83** (42%)	121 (61%)	121 (61%)	**122** (61%)
CFDS, WebCP	79 (40%)	78 (39%)	79 (40%)	119 (60%)	116 (58%)	119 (60%)

Table 3: Precision of measuring grammaticality.

Model	Strict	Lenient
MDS	104 (52%)	141 (71%)
CFDS	**108** (54%)	**142** (71%)

Table 4: Precision of similarity factors.

		Strict			Lenient		
N_S	Corpus	BOW	MOD	HAR	BOW	MOD	HAR
500	Mainichi	60 (30%)	68 (34%)	**74** (37%)	98 (49%)	109 (55%)	114 (57%)
500	WebCP	57 (28%)	61 (31%)	**74** (37%)	94 (47%)	99 (50%)	**120** (60%)
1,000	Mainichi	57 (28%)	70 (35%)	**74** (37%)	92 (46%)	113 (57%)	116 (58%)
1,000	WebCP	57 (28%)	60 (30%)	72 (36%)	93 (47%)	96 (48%)	116 (58%)

component of the entire model (Table 2). This result is quite natural because MDS cannot verify the collocation between content words in those cases where a number of function words appear between them. On the other hand, CFDS with $N = 3$ could verify this as a result of treating the sequence of function words as a single node.

As mentioned in A1, however, a more sophisticated language model must enhance the proposed model. One way of obtaining a suitable granularity of nodes is to introduce latent classes, such as the Semi-Markov class model (Okanohara and Tsujii, 2007). The existence of many orthographic variants of both the content and function words may prevent us from accurately estimating the grammaticality. We plan to normalize these variations by using several existing resources such as the Japanese functional expression dictionary (Matsuyoshi, 2008).

A3: Contrary to our expectations, the huge Web corpus did not offer any advantage over the newspaper corpus: Mainichi always produced better results than WebCP when it was combined with the grammaticality factor or when MOD was used.

We can speculate that morphological and dependency parsers produce errors when features are extracted, because they are tuned to newspaper articles. Likewise, $P(f|s)$ and $P(f|t)$ may involve noise even though they are estimated using relatively clean parts of Web text that are retrieved by querying phrase candidates.

A4: For Par_{Lin} and Par_{skew}, different sets of features led to consistent results with our previous experiments in (Fujita and Sato, 2008), i.e., BOW $<$ MOD $\simeq$ HAR. On the other hand, for the proposed models, MOD and HAR led to only small or sometimes negative effects. When the similarity factor was used alone, however, these features beat BOW. Furthermore, the impact of combining BOW and MOD into HAR was significant.

Given this tendency, it is expected that the grammaticality factor might be excessively emphasized. Our probability model was derived straightforwardly from the conditional probability $P(t|s)$; however, the combination of the two factors should be tuned according to their implementation.

A5: Finally, the influence of the number of Web snippets was analyzed; no significant difference was observed.

This is because we could retrieve more than 500 snippets for only 172 pairs of expressions among our test samples. As it is time-consuming to obtain a large number of Web snippets, the trade-off between the number of Web snippets and the performance should be investigated further, although the quality of the Web snippets and what appears at the top of the search results will vary according to several factors other than linguistic ones.

5 Conclusion

A pair of expressions qualifies as paraphrases iff they are semantically equivalent, substitutable in some context, and grammatical. In cases where paraphrase knowledge is represented with abstract patterns to attain a high coverage of the paraphrase phenomena, we should assess not only the first and second conditions, but also the third condition.

In this paper, we proposed a probabilistic model for computing how two phrases are likely to be paraphrases. The proposed model consists of two components: (i) a structured N-gram language model that ensures grammaticality and (ii) a distributional similarity measure for estimating semantic equivalence and substitutability between two phrases. Through an experiment, we empirically evaluated the performance of the proposed model and analyzed the characteristics.

Future work includes building a more sophisticated structured language model to improve the performance of the proposed model and conducting an experiment on template-like paraphrase knowledge for other than productive paraphrases.

References

Bannard, Colin and Chris Callison-Burch. 2005. Paraphrasing with bilingual parallel corpora. In *Proceedings of the 43rd Annual Meeting of the Association for Computational Linguistics (ACL)*, pages 597–604.

Barzilay, Regina and Kathleen R. McKeown. 2001. Extracting paraphrases from a parallel corpus. In *Proceedings of the 39th Annual Meeting of the Association for Computational Linguistics (ACL)*, pages 50–57.

Barzilay, Regina and Lillian Lee. 2003. Learning to paraphrase: an unsupervised approach using multiple-sequence alignment. In *Proceedings of the 2003 Human Language Technology Conference and the North American Chapter of the Association for Computational Linguistics (HLT-NAACL)*, pages 16–23.

Dolan, Bill, Chris Quirk, and Chris Brockett. 2004. Unsupervised construction of large paraphrase corpora: exploiting massively parallel news sources. In *Proceedings of the 20th International Conference on Computational Linguistics (COLING)*, pages 350–356.

Fujita, Atsushi, Shuhei Kato, Naoki Kato, and Satoshi Sato. 2007. A compositional approach toward dynamic phrasal thesaurus. In *Proceedings of the ACL-PASCAL Workshop on Textual Entailment and Paraphrasing (WTEP)*, pages 151–158.

Fujita, Atsushi and Satoshi Sato. 2008. Computing paraphrasability of syntactic variants using Web snippets. In *Proceedings of the 3rd International Joint Conference on Natural Language Processing (IJCNLP)*, pages 537–544.

Geffet, Maayan and Ido Dagan. 2004. Feature vector quality and distributional similarity. In *Proceedings of the 20th International Conference on Computational Linguistics (COLING)*, pages 247–253.

Habash, Nizar. 2004. The use of a structural N-gram language model in generation-heavy hybrid machine translation. In *Proceedings of the 3rd International Natural Language Generation Conference (INLG)*, pages 61–69.

Harris, Zellig. 1957. Co-occurrence and transformation in linguistic structure. *Language*, 33(3):283–340.

Harris, Zellig. 1968. *Mathematical structures of language*. John Wiley & Sons.

Jacquemin, Christian. 1999. Syntagmatic and paradigmatic representations of term variation. In *Proceedings of the 37th Annual Meeting of the Association for Computational Linguistics (ACL)*, pages 341–348.

Kawahara, Daisuke and Sadao Kurohashi. 2006. Case frame compilation from the Web using high-performance computing. In *Proceedings of the 5th International Conference on Language Resources and Evaluation (LREC)*.

Kilgarriff, Adam. 2007. Googleology is bad science. *Computational Linguistics*, 33(1):147–151.

Lee, Lillian. 1999. Measures of distributional similarity. In *Proceedings of the 37th Annual Meeting of the Association for Computational Linguistics (ACL)*, pages 25–32.

Lin, Dekang. 1998. Automatic retrieval and clustering of similar words. In *Proceedings of the 36th Annual Meeting of the Association for Computational Linguistics and the 17th International Conference on Computational Linguistics (COLING-ACL)*, pages 768–774.

Lin, Dekang and Patrick Pantel. 2001. Discovery of inference rules for question answering. *Natural Language Engineering*, 7(4):343–360.

Matsuyoshi, Suguru. 2008. *Hierarchically organized dictionary of Japanese functional expressions: design, compilation and application*. Ph.D. thesis, Graduate School of Informatics, Kyoto University.

Mel'čuk, Igor and Alain Polguère. 1987. A formal lexicon in meaning-text theory (or how to do lexica with words). *Computational Linguistics*, 13(3-4):261–275.

Okanohara, Daisuke and Jun'ichi Tsujii. 2007. A discriminative language model with pseudo-negative samples. In *Proceedings of the 45th Annual Meeting of the Association for Computational Linguistics (ACL)*, pages 73–80.

Pantel, Patrick, Rahul Bhagat, Bonaventura Coppola, Timothy Chklovski, and Eduard Hovy. 2007. ISP: Learning inferential selectional preferences. In *Proceedings of Human Language Technologies 2007: The Conference of the North American Chapter of the Association for Computational Linguistics (NAACL-HLT)*, pages 564–571.

Quirk, Chris, Chris Brockett, and William Dolan. 2004. Monolingual machine translation for paraphrase generation. In *Proceedings of the 2004 Conference on Empirical Methods in Natural Language Processing (EMNLP)*, pages 142–149.

Szpektor, Idan, Hristo Tanev, Ido Dagan, and Bonaventura Coppola. 2004. Scaling Web-based acquisition of entailment relations. In *Proceedings of the 2004 Conference on Empirical Methods in Natural Language Processing (EMNLP)*, pages 41–48.

Takahashi, Tetsuro, Tomoya Iwakura, Ryu Iida, Atsushi Fujita, and Kentaro Inui. 2001. KURA: a transfer-based lexico-structural paraphrasing engine. In *Proceedings of the 6th Natural Language Processing Pacific Rim Symposium (NLPRS) Workshop on Automatic Paraphrasing: Theories and Applications*, pages 37–46.

Weeds, Julie, David Weir, and Bill Keller. 2005. The distributional similarity of sub-parses. In *Proceedings of the ACL Workshop on Empirical Modeling of Semantic Equivalence and Entailment*, pages 7–12.

Yamamoto, Kazuhide. 2002. Acquisition of lexical paraphrases from texts. In *Proceedings of the 2nd International Workshop on Computational Terminology (CompuTerm)*, pages 22–28.

Retrieving Bilingual Verb–noun Collocations by Integrating Cross-Language Category Hierarchies

Fumiyo Fukumoto **Yoshimi Suzuki** **Kazuyuki Yamashita***
Interdisciplinary Graduate School of Medicine and Engineering
Univ. of Yamanashi
{fukumoto, ysuzuki}@yamanashi.ac.jp

*The Center for Educational Research
Faculty of Education and Human Sciences
Univ. of Yamanashi
kazuyuki@yamanashi.ac.jp

Abstract

This paper presents a method of retrieving bilingual collocations of a verb and its objective noun from cross-lingual documents with similar contents. Relevant documents are obtained by integrating cross-language hierarchies. The results showed a 15.1% improvement over the baseline non-hierarchy model, and a 6.0% improvement over use of relevant documents retrieved from a single hierarchy. Moreover, we found that some of the retrieved collocations were domain-specific.

1 Introduction

A bilingual lexicon is important for cross-lingual NLP applications, such as CLIR, and multilingual topic tracking. Much of the previous work on finding bilingual lexicons has made use of comparable corpora, which exhibit various degrees of parallelism. Fung *et al.* (2004) described corpora ranging from noisy parallel, to comparable, and finally to very non-parallel. Obviously, the latter are easy to collect because very non-parallel corpora consist of sets of documents in two different languages from the same period of dates. However, a good solution is required to produce a higher quality of lexicon retrieval.

In this paper, we focus on English and Japanese bilingual verb–objective noun collocations which we call **verb–noun collocations** and retrieve them using very non-parallel corpora. The method first finds cross-lingual relevant document pairs with similar contents from non-parallel corpora, and then we estimate bilingual verb–noun collocations within these relevant documents. Relevant documents are defined here as pairs of English and Japanese documents that report identical or closely related contents, *e.g.*, a pair of documents describing an aircraft crash and the ensuing investigation to compensate the victims' families or any safety measures proposed as a result of the crash. In the task of retrieving cross-lingual relevant documents, it is crucial to identify an *event* as something occurs at some specific place and time associated with some specific action. One solution is to use a *topic*, *i.e.*, category in the hierarchical structure, such as Internet directories. Although a topic is not an event, it can be a broader class of event. Therefore, it is helpful for retrieving relevant documents, and thus bilingual verb–noun collocations. Consider the Reuters'96 and Mainichi newspaper documents shown in Figure 1. The documents report on the same event, "Russian space station collides with cargo craft," were published within two days of each other, and have overlapping content. Moreover, as indicated by the double-headed arrows in the figure, there are a number of bilingual collocations. However, as shown in Figure 1, the Reuters document is classified into "Science and Technology," while the Mainichi document is classified into "Space Navigation". This is natural because categories in the hierarchical structures are defined by different human experts. Therefore, a hierarchy tends to have some bias in both defining hierarchical structure and classifying documents, and as a result some hierarchies written in one language are coarse-grained, while others written in other languages are fine-grained. Our attempt using the results of integrating different hierarchies for retrieving relevant documents was postulated to be able to solve this defect of the differences in

©2008. Licensed under the *Creative Commons Attribution-Noncommercial-Share Alike 3.0 Unported* license (http://creativecommons.org/licenses/by-nc-sa/3.0/). Some rights reserved.

Date=970625 Category = Science and Technology
RUSSIA: Russian space station collides with cargo craft.

Russia's Mir space station collided on Wed. with a cargo craft during a manual docking exercise, raising fresh doubts about the safety of the poorly financed Russian space programme.

Russian space officials described the collision as ``the most serious accident in recent times''; involving the ageing vessel but said there was no immediate danger to a U.S. astronaut and two Russian cosmonauts on board.

. . . .

The unmanned, Russian-owned Progress cargo craft collided at 1.20p.m. (0920 GMT) with the Spectra scientific module attached to the main section of Mir, causing a partial loss of air pressure.

A spokesman for the U.S. space agency NASA said earlier on Wed. that the crew had been able to seal off the damaged compartment after the collision.

Date=970626325 Category = Space Navigation
衝突事故…ミール「深刻」 太陽電池システムに穴、電力不足の可能性

【モスクワ25日石郷岡建】ロシアの宇宙ステーション管制センターは25日、宇宙ステーション「ミール」と無人宇宙貨物船「プログレス34」の衝突事故について、「最近にない深刻な事故」と発表、特に太陽電池システムの一部破損による、電力不足の可能性を示唆した。

. . . .

事故の詳細は不明だが、宇宙貨物船「プログレス35」の打ち上げ(今月27日予定)・到着を前に、同船のドッキング場所を用意するため、すでに「ミール」にドッキングしていた「プログレス34」の移動をしていたところ、25日午後、「プログレス34」がステーションの「スペクトル科学モジュール」と呼ばれる部分に激突。同ジュール部分の一部が破損し、船内の空気が外に流れ出した。
「ミール」の宇宙飛行士たちは、事故後直ちに、本体とモジュール部分を遮断。

Figure 1: Relevant document pairs

hierarchies, and to improve the efficiency and efficacy of retrieving collocations.

2 System Description

The method consists of three steps: integrating category hierarchies, retrieving cross-lingual relevant documents, and retrieving collocations from relevant documents.

2.1 Integrating Hierarchies

The method for integrating different category hierarchies does not simply merge two different hierarchies into a large hierarchy, but instead retrieves pairs of categories, where each category is relevant to each other.[1] The procedure consists of two substeps: Cross-language text classification (CLTC) and estimating category correspondences.

2.1.1 Cross-language text classification

The corpora we used are the Reuters'96 and the RWCP of the Mainichi Japanese newspapers. In the CLTC task, we used English and Japanese data to train the Reuters'96 categorical hierarchy and the Mainichi UDC code hierarchy (Mainichi hierarchy), respectively. In the Reuters'96 hierarchy, the system was trained using labeled English documents, and classified translated labeled Japanese documents. Similarly, for Mainichi hierarchy, the system was trained using labeled Japanese documents, and classified translated labeled English documents. We used Japanese-English and English-Japanese MT software.

[1]The reason for retrieving pairs of categories is that each categorical hierarchy is defined by individual human experts, and different linguists often identify different numbers of categories for the same concepts. Therefore, it is impossible to handle *full* integration of hierarchies.

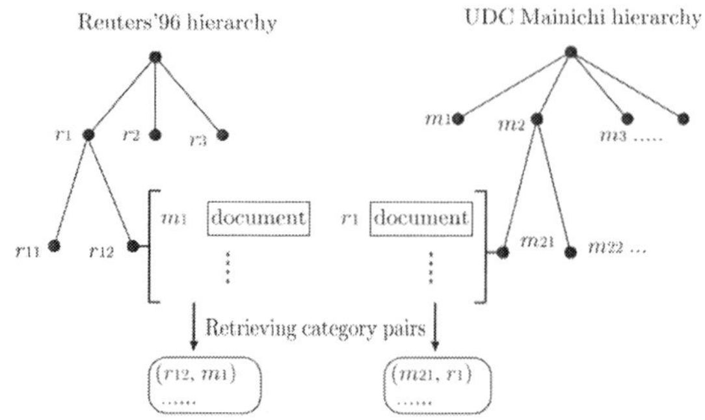

Figure 2: Cross-language text classification

We used a learning model, Support Vector Machines (SVMs) (Vapnik, 1995), to classify documents, as SVMs have been shown to be effective for text classification. We used the "One-against-the-Rest" version of the SVMs at each level of a hierarchy. We classify test documents using a hierarchy by learning separate classifiers at each internal node of the hierarchy. We used a Boolean function $b(L_1)\&\&\cdots\&\&b(L_m)$, where $b(L_i)$ is a decision threshold value of the i-th hierarchical level. The process is repeated by greedily selecting subbranches until a leaf is reached.

We classified translated Mainichi documents with Mainichi category m into Reuters categories using SVMs classifiers. Similarly, each translated Reuters document with category r was classified into Mainichi categories. Figure 2 illustrates the classification of Reuters and Mainichi documents. A document with Mainichi category "$m1$" is classified into Reuters category "$r12$", and a document with Reuters category "$r1$" is classified into Mainichi category "$m21$". As a result, we obtained category pairs, *e.g.*, ($r12$, $m1$), and ($m21$, $r1$), from the documents assigned to the categories in each hierarchy.

2.1.2 Estimating category correspondences

The assumption of category correspondences is that semantically similar categories, such as "Equity markets" and "Bond markets" exhibit similar statistical properties than dissimilar categories, such as "Equity markets" and "Sports". We applied χ^2 statistics to the results of CLTC. Let us take a look at the Reuters'96 hierarchy. Suppose that the translated Mainichi document with Mainichi category $m \in M$ (where M is a set of Mainichi categories) is assigned to Reuters category $r \in R$ (R is a set of Reuters'96 categories). We can retrieve Reuters and Mainichi category pairs, and estimate category correspondences according to the χ^2 statistics shown in Eq. (1).

$$\chi^2(r,m) = \frac{f(r,m) - E(r,m)}{E(r,m)} \quad (1)$$

$$\text{where} \quad E(r,m) = S_r \times \frac{S_m}{S_R},$$

$$S_r = \sum_{k \in M} f(r,k), \quad S_R = \sum_{r \in R} S_r.$$

Here, the co-occurrence frequency of r and m, $f(r,m)$ is equal to the number of category m documents assigned to r. Similar to the Reuters hierarchy, we can estimate category correspondences from Mainichi hierarchy, and extract a pair (r, m) according to the χ^2 value. We note that the similarity obtained by each hierarchy does not have a fixed range. Thus, we apply the normalization strategy shown in Eq. (2) to the results obtained by each hierarchy to bring the similarity value into the range [0,1].

$$\chi^2_{new}(r,m) = \frac{\chi^2_{old}(r,m) - \chi^2_{min}(r,m)}{\chi^2_{max}(r,m) - \chi^2_{min}(r,m)}. \quad (2)$$

Let SP_r and SP_m are a set of pairs obtained by Reuters hierarchy and Mainichi hierarchy, respectively. We construct the set of r and m category pairs, $SP_{(r,m)} = \{(r,m) \mid (r,m) \in SP_r \cap SP_m\}$, where each pair is sorted in descending order of χ^2 value. For each pair of $SP_{(r,m)}$, if the value of χ^2 is higher than a lower bound L_{χ^2}, two categories, r and m, are regarded as similar.[2]

2.2 Retrieval of Relevant Documents

We used the results of category correspondences from the Reuters and Mainichi hierarchies to retrieve relevant documents. Recall that we used English and Japanese documents with quite different hierarchical structures. The task thus consists of two criteria: retrieving relevant documents based on English (we call this Int_hi & Eng) and in Japanese (Int_hi & Jap). Let d_i^r $(1 \le i \le s)$ be a Reuters document that is classified into the Reuters category r. Let d_j^m $(1 \le j \le t)$ be a Mainichi

[2] We set χ^2 value of each element of $SP_{(r,m)}$ to a higher value of either $(r,m) \in SP_r$ or $(r,m) \in SP_m$.

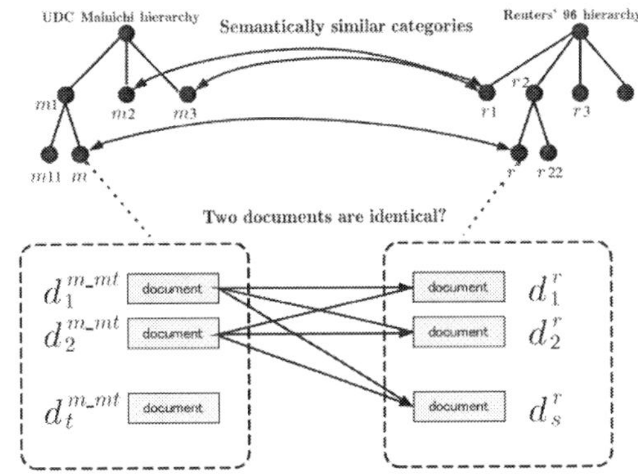

Figure 3: Retrieving relevant documents

document that belongs to the Mainichi category m. Here, s and t are the number of documents classified into r and m, respectively. Each Reuters document d_i^r is translated into a Japanese document $d_i^{r\_mt}$ by an MT system. Each Mainichi document d_j^m is translated into an English document $d_j^{m\_mt}$.

Retrieving relevant documents itself is quite simple. As illustrated in Figure 3, in "Int_hi & Eng" with a set of similar categories consisting of r and m, for each Reuters and translated Mainichi document, we calculate BM25 similarities between them.

$$\text{BM25}(d_i^r, d_j^{m\_mt}) = \sum_{w \in d_j^{m\_mt}} w^{(1)} \frac{(k_1+1)tf}{K+tf} \frac{(k_3+1)qtf}{k_3+qtf}, \quad (3)$$

where w is a word within $d_j^{m\_mt}$, and $w^{(1)}$ is the weight of w, $w^{(1)} = \log \frac{(N-n+0.5)}{(n+0.5)}$. N is the number of Reuters documents within the same category r, and n is the number of documents which contains w. K refers to $k_1((1-b) + b\frac{dl}{avdl})$. k_1, b, and k_3 are parameters and set to 1, 1, and 1,000, respectively. dl is the document length of d_i^r and $avdl$ is the average document length in words. tf and qtf are the frequency of occurrence of w in d_i^r, and $d_j^{m\_mt}$, respectively. If the similarity value between them is higher than a lower bound L_θ, we regarded these as relevant documents. The procedure is applied to all documents belonging to the sets of similar categories. "Int_hi & Jap" is the same as "Int_hi & Eng" except for the use of $d_i^{r\_mt}$ and d_j^m for comparison. We compared the performance of these tasks, and found that "Int_hi & Eng" was better than "Int_hi & Jap". In section 3, we show results with "Int_hi & Eng" due to lack of space.

2.3 Acquisition of Bilingual Collocations

The final step is to estimate bilingual correspondences from relevant documents. All Japanese documents were parsed using the syntactic analyzer CaboCha (Kudo and Matsumoto, 2003). English documents were parsed with the syntactic analyzer (Lin, 1993). In both English and Japanese, we extracted all the dependency triplets(obj, n, v). Here, n refers to a noun which is an $object(obj)$ of a verb v in a sentence.[3] Hereafter, we describe the Reuters English dependency triplet as vn_r, and that of Mainichi as vn_m. The method to retrieve bilingual correspondences consists of two sub-steps: document-based retrieval and sentence-based retrieval.

2.3.1 Document-based retrieval

We extract vn_r and vn_m pairs from the results of relevant documents:

$$\{vn_r, vn_m\} \ s.t.\ {}^{\exists}d_i^r \ni vn_r,\ {}^{\exists}d_j^m \ni vn_m \quad \text{BM25}(d_i^r, d_j^{m\text{-}mt}) \geq L_\theta \,. \tag{4}$$

Next, we estimate the bilingual correspondences according to the $\chi^2(vn_r, vn_m)$ statistics shown in Eq. (1). In Eq. (1), we replace r by vn_r and m by vn_m. $f(r, m)$ is replaced by $f(vn_r, vn_m)$, *i.e.*, the co-occurrence frequency of vn_r and vn_m.

2.3.2 Sentence-based retrieval

We note that bilingual correspondences obtained by document-based retrieval are not reliable. This is because many verb–noun collocations appear in a pair of relevant documents, as can be seen from Figure 1. Therefore, we applied sentence-based retrieval to the results obtained by document-based retrieval. First, we extract vn_r and vn_m pairs the χ^2 values of which are higher than 0. Next, for each vn_r and vn_m pair, we assign sentence-based similarity:

$$S\_sim(vn_r, vn_m) = \max_{S\_vn_r \in Set_r, S\_vn_m \in Set_m} sim(S\_vn_r, S\_vn_m) \,. \tag{5}$$

Here, Set_r and Set_m are a set of sentences that include vn_r and vn_m, respectively. The similarity between S_vn_r and S_vn_m is shown in Eq. (6).

[3]We used the particle "wo" as an object relationship in Japanese.

$$sim(S\_vn_r, S\_vn_m) = \frac{co(S\_vn_r \cap S^{mt}\_vn_m)}{|\, S\_vn_r \,| + |\, S^{mt}\_vn_m \,| - 2co(S\_vn_r \cap S^{mt}\_vn_m) + 2} \,, \tag{6}$$

where $|X|$ is the number of content words in a sentence X, and $co(S\_vn_r \cap S^{mt}\_vn_m)$ refers to the number of content words that appear in both S_vn_r and $S^{mt}\_vn_m$. $S^{mt}\_vn_m$ is a translation result of S_vm_m. We retrieved vn_r and vn_m as a bilingual lexicon that satisfies:

$$\{vn_r, vn_m\} = \operatorname*{argmax}_{\{vn_{r'} \in BP(vn_m),\ vn_m\}} S\_sim(vn_{r'}, vn_m) \,, \tag{7}$$

where $BP(vn_m)$ is a set of bilingual verb–noun pairs, each of which includes vn_m on the Japanese side.

3 Experiments

3.1 Integrating hierarchies

3.1.1 Experimental setup

We used Reuters'96 and UDC code hierarchies. The Reuters'96 corpus from 20th Aug. 1996 to 19th Aug. 1997 consists of 806,791 documents organized into coarse-grained categories, *i.e.*, 126 categories with a four-level hierarchy. The RWCP corpus labeled with UDC codes selected from 1994 Mainichi newspaper consists of 27,755 documents organized into a fine-grained categories, *i.e.*, 9,951 categories with a seven-level hierarchy (RWCP., 1998). We used Japanese-English and English-Japanese MT software (Internet Honyaku-no-Ousama for Linux, Ver.5, IBM Corp.) for CLTC. We divided both Reuters'96 (from 20th Aug. 1996 to 19th May 1997) and RWCP corpora into two equal sets: a training set to train SVM classifiers, and a test set for TC to generate pairs of similar categories. We divided the test set into two parts: the first was used to estimate thresholds, *i.e.*, a decision threshold b used in CLTC, and lower bound L_{χ^2}; and the second was used to generate pairs of similar categories using the threshold. We chose $b = 0$ for each level of a hierarchy. The lower bound L_{χ^2} was .003.

We selected 109 categories from Reuters and 4,739 categories from Mainichi, which have at least five documents in each set. We used content words for both English and Japanese documents. We compared the results obtained by hierarchical approach to those obtained by the flat

Table 1: Performance of category correspondences

	Hierarchy			Flat		
	Prec	Rec	F1	Prec	Rec	F1
Mai & Reu	.503	.463	**.482**	.462	.389	**.422**
Reu	.342	.329	.335	.240	.296	.265
Mai	.157	.293	.204	.149	.277	.194

non-hierarchical approach. Moreover, in the hierarchical approach, we applied a Boolean function to each test document.

For evaluation of category correspondences, we used F1-score (F1) which is a measure that balances precision (Prec) and recall (Rec). Let Cor be a set of correct category pairs.[4] The precise definitions of the precision and recall of the task are given below:

$$\text{Prec} = \frac{|\{(r,m) \mid (r,m) \in Cor, \chi^2(r,m) \geq L_{\chi^2}\}|}{|\{(r,m) \mid \chi^2(r,m) \geq L_{\chi^2}\}|}$$

$$\text{Rec} = \frac{|\{(r,m) \mid (r,m) \in Cor, \chi^2(r,m) \geq L_{\chi^2}\}|}{|\{(r,m) \mid (r,m) \in Cor\}|}$$

3.1.2 Results

Table 1 shows F1 of category correspondences with L_{χ^2} = .003. "Mai & Reu" shows the results obtained by our method. "Mai" and "Reu" show the results using only one hierarchy. For example, "Mai" shows the results in which both Mainichi and translated Reuters documents are classified into categories with Mainichi hierarchy, and estimated category correspondences.

Integrating hierarchies is more effective than only a single hierarchy. Moreover, we found advantages in the F1 for the hierarchical approach ("Hierarchy" in Table 1) in comparison with a baseline flat approach ("Flat"). We note that the result of "Mai" was worse than that of "Reu" in both approaches. One reason is that the accuracy of TC. The micro-average F1 of TC for Reuters hierarchy was .815, while that of Mainichi was .673, as Mainichi hierarchy consists of many categories, and the number of training data for each category were smaller than those of Reuters. The results obtained by our method depend on the performance of TC. Therefore, it will be necessary to examine some semi-supervised learning techniques to improve classification accuracy.

[4]The classification was determined to be correct if the two human judges agreed on the evaluation.

Table 2: Data for retrieving documents

Jap → Eng(± 3)	Total # of doc.		Total # of relevant doc.
	Jap	Eng	
26/06/97	391	15,482	513

3.2 Relevant document retrieval

3.2.1 Experimental setup

The training data for choosing the lower bound L_θ used in the relevant document retrieval is Reuters and RWCP from 13th to 21st Jun. 1997. The difference in dates between them is less than ± 3 days. For example, when the date of the RWCP document is 18th Jun., the corresponding Reuters date is from 15th to 21st Jun. We chose L_θ that maximized the average F1 among them. Table 2 shows the test data, *i.e.*, the total number of collected documents and the number of related documents collected manually for the evaluation.[5] We implemented the following approaches including related work, and compared these results with those obtained by our methods, Int_hi & Eng.

1. **No_hierarchy**: Categories with each hierarchy are not used in the approach. The approach is the same as the method reported by Collier *et al.* (1998) except for term weights and similarities. We calculate similarities between Reuters and translated Mainichi documents, where the difference in dates is less than ± 3 days. (**No_hi & Eng**).

2. **Hierarchy**: The approach uses only Reuters hierarchy (we call this **Reu Hierarchy**). Reuters documents and translated Mainichi documents are classified into categories with Reuters hierarchy. We calculate BM25 between Reuters and Mainichi documents within the same category. The procedure is applied for all categories of the hierarchies.

The judgment of relevant documents was the same as our method: if the value of similarity between two documents is higher than a lower bound L_θ, we regarded them as relevant documents.

3.2.2 Results

The retrieval results are shown in Table 3 and Figure 4. Table 3 shows best performance of each method against L_θ. As can be seen clearly from Table 3 and Figure 4, the results with integrating hierarchies improved overall performance.

[5]The classification was determined by two human.

Table 3: Retrieval performance

	Prec	Rec	F1-score	L_θ
No_hi & Eng	.417	.322	.363	40
Reu Hierarchy	.356	**.544**	.430	20
Int_hi & Eng	.839	**.585**	.689	20

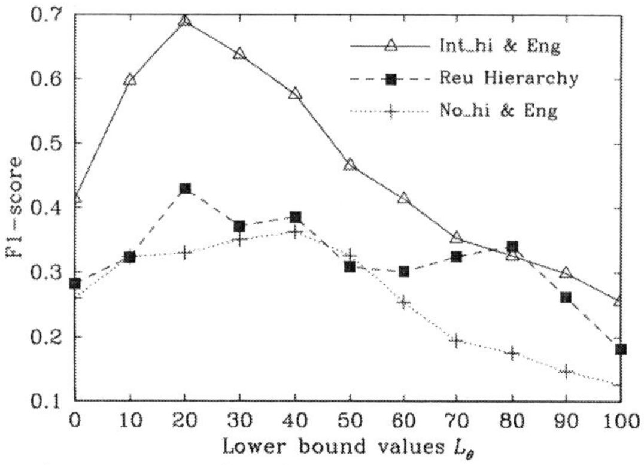

Figure 4: F1 of retrieving relevant documents

Table 4 shows the total number of document pairs (P), Reuters (E), and Mainichi documents (J), which satisfied the similarity lower bound L_θ. As shown in Table 4, the number of retrieved pairs by non-hierarchy approach was much greater than that of "Int_hi & Eng" at all L_θ values. This is because pairs are retrieved by using only the BM25. Therefore, many of the document pairs retrieved do not have closely related contents, even if L_θ is set to a higher value.

The results of a single hierarchy showed recall of .544, while that of the integrating hierarchies was .585 at the same L_θ value (20), as shown in Table 3. This is because in the single hierarchy method, there are some translated Mainichi documents that are not correctly classified into categories with the Reuters hierarchy. For example, "Hashimoto remarks on fx rates" in Mainichi documents should be classified into Reuters category "Forex markets," but it was classified into "Government". As a result, "U.S. Treasury has no comment on Hashimoto fx remarks" in Reuters category "Forex markets" and the document "Hashimoto" are not retrieved by a single hierarchy approach. In contrast, in the integrating method, these two documents are classified correctly into a pair of similar categories, *i.e.*, the "U.S Treasury" is classified into Reuters category "Forex markets", and the "Hashimoto" is classified into Mainichi category "Money and banking". These observations show that our method contributes to the retrieval of relevant documents.

Table 4: # of documents vs L_θ

Approach		Lower Bound L_θ				
		100	80	60	40	20
No_hi & Eng	p	188	319	630	1,229	3,000
	E	150	272	543	987	2,053
	J	13	16	19	22	25
Reu Hierarchy	p	12	17	25	47	186
	E	8	12	19	36	142
	J	8	10	12	18	25
Int_hi & Eng	p	46	61	83	135	218
	E	32	43	60	99	158
	J	4	4	5	7	9

Table 5: # of J/E document pairs with L_θ

Approach & (L_θ)	pairs	Eng	Jap
No_hi & Eng (40)	3,042,166	428,042	70,080
Reu Hierarchy (20)	27,181,243	43,0181	99,452
Int_hi & Eng (20)	81,904,243	45,965	654,787

3.3 Bilingual Verb–noun Collocations

Finally, we report the results of bilingual verb–noun collocations.

3.3.1 Experimental setup

The data for relevant document retrieval was the Reuters and Mainichi corpora from the same period, *i.e.*, 20th Aug. 1996 to 19th Aug. 1997. The total number of Reuters documents was 806,791, and that of Mainichi was 119,822. As the number of Reuters documents was far greater than that of Mainichi documents, we estimated collocations from the results of cross-lingually retrieving relevant English documents with Japanese query documents. The difference in dates between them was less than $\pm$ 3 days. Table 5 shows retrieved relevant documents that showed best performance of each method against L_θ. From these data, we extracted bilingual verb-noun collocations.

3.3.2 Results

Table 6 shows the numbers of English and Japanese monolingual verb–noun collocations, those of candidate collocations against which bilingual correspondences were estimated, and those of correct collocations. "D & S" of candidate collocations indicates the number of collocations when we applied both document- and sentence-based retrieval. "Doc" indicates the number of collocations when we applied only document-based retrieval. "D & S" and "Doc" of correct collocations show the number of correct collocations in the topmost 1,000 according to sentence similarity and the χ^2 statistics, respectively. As shown in

Table 6, the results obtained by integrating hierarchies showed a 15.1% (32.8 - 17.7) improvement over the baseline non-hierarchy model, and a 6.0% (32.8 - 26.8) improvement over use of a single hierarchy. We manually compared those 328 bilingual collocations with an existing bilingual lexicon where 78 of them (23.8%) were not included in it.[6] Moreover, 168 of 328 (51.2%) were not correctly translated by Japanese-English MT software.[7] These observations clearly support the usefulness of the method.

It is very important to compare the column "rate" for the numbers of candidate collocations with that for the numbers of correct collocations. In all approaches, sentence-based retrieval was effective in removing useless collocations, especially in our method, about 1.5% of the size obtained by "Doc" was retrieved, while about 4.6(328/72) times the number of correct collocations were obtained in the topmost 1,000 collocations. These observations showed that sentence-based retrieval contributes to a marked reduction in the number of useless collocations without a decrease in accuracy.

The last column in Table 6 shows the results using Inverse Rank Score (IRS), which is a measure of system performance by considering the rank of correct bilingual collocations within the candidate collocations. It is the sum of the inverse rank of each matching collocations, *e.g.*, correct collocations by manual evaluation matches at ranks 2 and 4 give an IRS of $\frac{1}{2} + \frac{1}{4} = 0.75$. With at most 1,000 collocations, the maximum IRS score is 7.485, and the higher the IRS value, the better the system performance. As shown in Table 6, the performance by integrating hierarchies was much better than that of the non-hierarchical approach, and slightly better than those obtained by a single hierarchy. However, correct retrieved collocations were different from each other. Table 7 lists examples of bilingual collocations obtained by a single hierarchy and integrating hierarchies. The category is "Sport".[8] (x,y) of category pair in Table 7 refer to Reuters and Mainichi category correspondences. Examples in Table 7 denote only English verb–noun collocations.

It is interesting to note that 12 of 154 collocations, such as "earn medal" and "block shot" obtained by integrating hierarchies were also obtained by a single hierarchy approach. However, other collocations such as "get strikeout" and "make birdie" which were obtained in a particular category (Sport, Baseball) and (Sport, Golf), did not appear in either of the results using a single hierarchy or a non hierarchical approach. These observations again clearly support the usefulness of our method.

4 Previous Work

Much of the previous work on finding bilingual lexicons used comparable corpora. One attempt involved directly retrieving bilingual lexicons from corpora. One approach focused on extracting word translations (Gaussier et al., 2004). The techniques were based on the idea that semantically similar words appear in similar contexts. Unlike parallel corpora, the position of a word in a document is useless for translation into the other language. In these techniques, the frequency of words in the monolingual document is calculated and their contextual similarity is measured across languages. Another approach focused on sentence extraction (Fung and Cheung, 2004). One limitation of all these methods is that they need to control the experimental evaluation to avoid estimation of every bilingual lexicon appearing in comparable corpora.

The alternative consists of two steps: first, cross-lingual relevant documents are retrieved from comparable corpora, then bilingual term correspondences within these relevant documents are estimated. Thus, the accuracy depends on the performance of relevant documents retrieval. Much of the previous work in finding relevant documents used MT systems or existing bilingual lexicons to translate one language into another. Document pairs are then retrieved using some measure of document similarity. Another approach to retrieving relevant documents involves the collection of relevant document URLs from the WWW (Resnik and Smith, 2003). Utsuro *et al.* (2003) proposed a method for acquiring bilingual lexicons that involved retrieval of relevant English and Japanese documents from news sites on the WWW. Our work is also applicable to retrieval of relevant documents on the web because it estimates every bilingual lexicon only appearing in

[6] We used an existing bilingual lexicon, Eijiro on the Web, 1.91 million words, (http://www.alc.co.jp) for evaluation. If collocations were not included, the estimation was determined by two human judges.

[7] The number of words in the Japanese-English dictionary (Internet Honyaku-no-Ousama for Linux, Ver.5, IBM Corp.) was about 250,000.

[8] We obtained 98 category pairs in the Sport category.

Table 6: Numbers of monolingual and bilingual verb–noun collocations

Approach & (L_θ)	# of Monolingual patterns		Candidate collocations			# of Correct collocations (top 1,000)			Inverse rank score (top 1,000)	
			# of collocations		rate (D & S/ Doc)	# of collocations		rate (D & S/ Doc)		
	Jap	Eng	D & S	Doc		D & S	Doc		D & S	Doc
No_hi & Eng (40)	25,163	44,762	25,163	6,976,214	.361	**177**	62	2.9	1.35	0.71
Reu Hierarchy (20)	10,576	37,022	10,576	1,272,102	.831	**268**	64	4.2	2.24	1.41
Int_hi & Eng (20)	8,347	21,524	8,347	560,472	1.489	**328**	72	4.6	2.33	1.46

Table 7: Examples of bilingual verb–noun collocations

Approach & (L_θ)	Category or category pair	# of collocations		# of correct collocations(%)	Examples (English)
		D & S	Doc		
Reu_Hierarchy (20)	Sport	262	19,391	36(13.7)	create chance, **earn medal**, feel pressure **block shot**, establish record, take chance
Int_hi & Eng (20)	(Sport, Baseball)	110	8,838	24(21.8)	**get strikeout**, leave base, throw pitch
	(Sport, Relay)	177	3,418	18(10.2)	lead ranking, run km, win athletic
	(Sport, Tennis)	115	2,656	32(27.8)	lose prize_money, play exhibition_game
	(Sport, Golf)	131	2,654	28(21.4)	**make birdie**, have birdie, hole putt, miss putt
	(Sport, Soccer)	86	1,317	34(39.5)	**block shot**, score defender, give free kick
	(Sport, Sumo)	75	773	2(2.7)	lead sumo, set championship
	(Sport, Ski_jump)	68	661	10(14.7)	postpone downhill, **earn medal**
	(Sport, Football)	37	461	6(16.2)	play football, lease football_stadium

a set of smaller documents belonging to pairs of similar categories. Munteanu and Marcu (2006) proposed a method for extracting parallel subsentential fragments from very non-parallel bilingual corpora. The method is based on the fact that very non-parallel corpora has none or few good sentence pairs, while existing methods for exploiting comparable corpora look for parallel data at the sentence level. Their methodology is the first aimed at detecting sub-sentential correspondences, while they have not reported that the method is also applicable for large amount of data with good performance, especially in the case of large-scale evaluation such as that presented in this paper.

5 Conclusion

We have developed an approach to bilingual verb–noun collocations from non-parallel corpora. The results showed the effectiveness of the method. Future work will include: (i) applying the method to retrieve other types of collocations (Smadja, 1993), and (ii) evaluating the method using Internet directories.

References

Collier, N., H. Hirakawa, and A. Kumano. 1998. Machine Translation vs. Dictionary Term Translation - a Comparison for English-Japanese News Article Alignment. In *Proc. of 36th ACL and 17th COLING.*, pages 263–267.

Fung, P. and P. Cheung. 2004. Mining Very Non-Parallel Corpora: Parallel Sentence and Lexicon Extraction vie Bootstrapping and EM. In *Proc. of EMNLP2004.*, pages 57–63.

Gaussier, E., H-M. Renders, I. Matveeva, C. Goutte, and H. Déjean. 2004. A Geometric View on Bilingual Lexicon Extraction from Comparable Corpora. In *Proc. of 42nd ACL*, pages 527–534.

Kudo, T. and Y. Matsumoto. 2003. Fast Methods for Kernel-based Text Analysis. In *Proc. of 41th ACL*, pages 24–31.

Lin, D. 1993. Principle-based Parsing without Overgeneration. In *Proc. of 31st ACL*, pages 112–120.

Munteanu, D. S. and D. Marcu. 2006. Extracting Parallel Sub-Sentential Fragments from Non-Parallel Corpora. In *Proc. of 21st COLING and 44th ACL.*, pages 81–88.

Resnik, P. and N. A. Smith. 2003. The Web as a Parallel Corpus. *Computational Linguistics.*, 29(3):349–380.

RWCP. 1998. Rwc Text Database. In *Real World Computing Partnership.*

Smadja, F. 1993. Retrieving Collocations from Text: Xtract. *Computational Linguistics.*, 19(1):243–178.

Utsuro, T., T. Horiuchi, T. Hamamoto, K. Hino, and T. Nakayama. 2003. Effect of Cross-Language IR in Bilingual Lexicon Acquisition from Comparable Corpora. In *Proc. of 10th EACL.*, pages 355–362.

Vapnik, V. 1995. *The Nature of Statistical Learning Theory.* Springer.

Mining Opinions in Comparative Sentences

Murthy Ganapathibhotla
Department of Computer Science
University of Illinois at Chicago
851 South Morgan Street
Chicago, IL 60607-7053
sganapat@cs.uic.edu

Bing Liu
Department of Computer Science
University of Illinois at Chicago
851 South Morgan Street
Chicago, IL 60607-7053
liub@cs.uic.edu

Abstract

This paper studies sentiment analysis from the user-generated content on the Web. In particular, it focuses on mining opinions from comparative sentences, i.e., to determine which entities in a comparison are preferred by its author. A typical comparative sentence compares two or more entities. For example, the sentence, "*the picture quality of Camera X is better than that of Camera Y*", compares two entities "*Camera X*" and "*Camera Y*" with regard to their picture quality. Clearly, "*Camera X*" is the preferred entity. Existing research has studied the problem of extracting some key elements in a comparative sentence. However, there is still no study of mining opinions from comparative sentences, i.e., identifying preferred entities of the author. This paper studies this problem, and proposes a technique to solve the problem. Our experiments using comparative sentences from product reviews and forum posts show that the approach is effective.

1 Introduction

In the past few years, there was a growing interest in mining opinions in the user-generated content (UGC) on the Web, e.g., customer reviews, forum posts, and blogs. One major focus is sentiment classification and opinion mining (e.g., Pang et al 2002; Turney 2002; Hu and Liu 2004; Wilson et al 2004; Kim and Hovy 2004; Popescu and Etzioni 2005)

© 2008. Licensed under the *Creative Commons Attribution-Noncommercial-Share Alike 3.0 Unported* license (http://creativecommons.org/licenses/by-nc-sa/3.0/). Some rights reserved.

However, these studies mainly center on *direct opinions* or *sentiments* expressed on entities. Little study has been done on comparisons, which represent another type of opinion-bearing text. Comparisons are related to but are also quite different from direct opinions. For example, a typical direct opinion sentence is "*the picture quality of Camera X is great*", while a typical comparative sentence is "*the picture quality of Camera X is better than that of Camera Y.*" We can see that comparisons use different language constructs from direct opinions. A comparison typically expresses a comparative opinion on two or more entities with regard to their shared features or attributes, e.g., "*picture quality*". Although direct opinions are most common in UGC, comparisons are also widely used (about 10% of the sentences), especially in forum discussions where users often ask questions such as "X vs. Y" (X and Y are competing products). Discussions are then centered on comparisons.

Jindal and Liu (2006) proposed a technique to identify comparative sentences from reviews and forum posts, and to extract entities, comparative words, and entity features that are being compared. For example, in the sentence, "*Camera X has longer battery life than Camera Y*", the technique extracts "*Camera X*" and "*Camera Y*" as entities, and "*longer*" as the comparative word and "*battery life*" as the attribute of the cameras being compared. However, the technique does not find which entity is preferred by the author. For this example, clearly "*Camera Y*" is the preferred camera with respect to the "*battery life*" of the cameras. This paper aims to solve this problem, which is useful in many applications because the preferred entity is the key piece of information in a comparative opinion. For example, a potential customer clearly wants to buy the product that is better or preferred.

In this work, we treat a sentence as the basic

information unit. Our objective is thus to identify the preferred entity in each comparative sentence. A useful observation about comparative sentences is that in each such sentence there is usually a comparative word (e.g., "*better*", "*worse*" and *–er* word) or a superlative word (e.g., "*best*", "*worst*" and *–est* word). The entities being compared often appear on the two sides of the comparative word. A superlative sentence may only have one entity, e.g., "*Camera X is the best*". For simplicity, we use comparative words (sentences) to mean both *comparative words* (*sentences*) and *superlative words* (*sentences*).

Clearly, the preferred entity in a comparative sentence is mainly determined by the comparative word in the sentence. Some comparative words explicitly indicate user preferences, e.g., "*better*", "*worse*", and "*best*". We call such words *opinionated comparative words*. For example, in the sentence, "*the picture quality of Camera X is better than that of Camera Y*", *Camera X* is preferred due to the opinionated comparative word "*better*".

However, many comparative words are not opinionated, or their opinion orientations (i.e., positive or negative) depend on the context and/or the application domain. For instance, the word "*longer*" is not opinionated as it is normally used to express that the length of some feature of an entity is greater than the length of the same feature of another entity. However, in a particular context, it can express a desired (or *positive*) or undesired (or *negative*) state. For example, in the sentence, "*the battery life of Camera X is longer than Camera Y*", "*longer*" clearly expresses a desired state for "*battery life*" (although this is an objective sentence with no explicit opinion). "*Camera X*" is thus preferred with regard to "*battery life*" of the cameras. The opinion in this sentence is called an *implicit opinion*. We also say that "*longer*" is positive in this context. We know this because of our existing domain knowledge. However, "*longer*" may also be used to express an undesirable state in a different context, e.g., "*Program X's execution time is longer than Program Y*". *longer*" is clearly negative here. "*Program Y*" is thus preferred. We call comparative words such as "*longer*" and "*smaller*" *context-dependent opinion comparatives*.

Sentences with opinionated words (e.g., "*better*", and "*worse*") are usually easy to handle. Then the key to solve our problem is to identify the opinion orientations (positive or negative) of context-dependent comparative words. To this end, two questions need to be answered: (1) what is a context and (2) how to use the context to help determine the opinion orientation of a comparative word?

The simple answer to question (1) is the whole sentence. However, a whole sentence as context is too complex because it may contain too much irrelevant information, which can confuse the system. Intuitively, we want to use the smallest context that can determine the orientation of the comparative word. Obviously, the comparative word itself must be involved. We thus conjecture that the context should consist of the *entity feature* being compared and the *comparative word*. Our experimental results show that this context definition works quite well.

To answer the second question, we need external information or knowledge because there is no way that a computer program can solve the problem by analyzing the sentence itself. In this paper, we propose to use the external information in customer reviews on the Web to help solve the problem. There are a large number of such reviews on almost any product or service. These reviews can be readily downloaded from many sites. In our work, we use reviews from epinions.com. Each review in epinions.com has separate Pros and Cons (which is also the case in most other review sites). Thus, positive and negative opinions are known as they are separated by reviewers. However, they cannot be used directly because Pros and Cons seldom contain comparative words. We need to deal with this problem. Essentially, the proposed method computes whether the comparative word and the feature are more associated in Pros or in Cons. If they are more associated in Pros (or Cons) than Cons (or Pros), then the comparative word is likely to be positive (or negative) for the feature. A new association measure is also proposed to suit our purpose. Our experiment results show that it can achieve high precision and recall.

2 Related Work

Sentiment analysis has been studied by many researchers recently. Two main directions are sentiment classification at the document and sentence levels, and feature-based opinion mining. Sentiment classification at the document level investigates ways to classify each evaluative document (e.g., product review) as positive or negative (Pang et al 2002; Turney 2002). Sentiment classification at the sentence-level has also been studied (e.g., Riloff and Wiebe 2003; Kim and Hovy 2004; Wilson et al 2004; Gamon et al

2005; Stoyanov and Cardie 2006). These works are different from ours as we study comparatives.

The works in (Hu and Liu 2004; Liu et al 2005; Popescu and Etzioni 2005; Mei et al 2007) perform opinion mining at the feature level. The task involves (1) extracting entity features (e.g., "*picture quality*" and "*battery life*" in a camera review) and (2) finding orientations (positive, negative or neutral) of opinions expressed on the features by reviewers. Again, our work is different because we deal with comparisons.

Discovering orientations of context dependent opinion comparative words is related to identifying domain opinion words (Hatzivassiloglou and McKeown 1997; Kanayama and Nasukawa 2006). Both works use *conjunction rules* to find such words from large domain corpora. One conjunction rule states that when two opinion words are linked by "and", their opinions are the same. Our method is different in three aspects. First, we argue that finding domain opinion words is problematic because in the same domain the same word may indicate different opinions depending on what features it is applied to. For example, in the camera domain, "*long*" is positive in "*the battery life is very long*" but negative in "*it takes a long time to focus*". Thus, we should consider both the feature and the opinion word rather than only the opinion word. Second, we focus on studying opinionated comparative words. Third, our technique is quite different as we utilize readily available external opinion sources.

As discussed in the introduction, a closely related work to ours is (Jindal and Liu 2006). However, it does not find which entities are preferred by authors. Bos and Nissim (2006) proposes a method to extract some useful items from superlative sentences. Fiszman et al (2007) studied the problem of identifying which entity has more of certain features in comparative sentences. It does not find which entity is preferred.

3 Problem Statement

Definition (entity and feature): An *entity* is the name of a person, a product, a company, a location, etc, under comparison in a comparative sentence. A *feature* is a part or attribute of the entity that is being compared.

For example, in the sentence, "*Camera X's battery life is longer than that of Camera Y*", "*Camera X*" and "*Camera Y*" are entities and "*battery life*" is the camera feature.

Types of Comparatives

1) *Non-equal gradable*: Relations of the type *greater* or *less than* that express a total ordering of some entities with regard to their shared features. For example, the sentence, "*Camera X's battery life is longer than that of Camera Y*", orders "*Camera X*" and "*Camera Y*" based on their shared feature "*battery life*".
2) *Equative*: Relations of the type *equal to* that state two objects as equal with respect to some features, e.g., "*Camera X and Camera Y are about the same size*".
3) *Superlative*: Relations of the type *greater* or *less than all others* that rank one object over all others, "*Camera X's battery life is the longest*".
4) *Non-gradable:* Sentences which compare features of two or more entities, but do not explicitly grade them, e.g., "*Camera X and Camera Y have different features*"

The first three types are called *gradable* comparatives. This paper focuses on the first and the third types as they express ordering relationships of entities. Equative and non-gradable sentences usually do not express preferences.

Definition (comparative relation): A *comparative relation* is the following:

<ComparativeWord, Features, EntityS1, EntityS2, Type>

ComparativeWord is the keyword used to express a comparative relation in the sentence. *Features* is a set of features being compared. *Entity*S1 and *Entity*S2 are sets of entities being compared. Entities in EntityS1 appear on the left of the comparative word and entities in EntityS2 appear on the right. *Type* is *non-equal gradable, equative* or *superlative*. Let us see an example. For the sentence *"Camera X has longer battery life than Camera Y,"* the extracted relation is:

<longer, {battery life}, {Camera X}, {Camera Y}, non-equal gradable>.

We assume that the work in (Jindal and Liu 2006) has extracted the above relation from a comparative sentence. In this work, we aim to identify the preferred entity of the author, which is not studied in (Jindal and Liu 2006).

Our objective: Given the extracted comparative relation from a comparative sentence, we want to identify whether the entities in EntityS1 or in EntityS2 are preferred by the author.

4 Proposed Technique

We now present the proposed technique. As discussed above, the primary determining factors of the preferred entity in a comparative sentence are the feature being compared and the comparative word, which we conjecture, form the context for opinions (or preferred entities). We develop our ideas from here.

4.1 Comparatives and superlatives

In English, comparatives and superlatives are special forms of adjectives and adverbs. In general, comparatives are formed by adding the suffix "*-er*" and superlatives are formed by adding the suffix "*–est*" to the *base adjectives* and *adverbs*. We call this type of comparatives and superlatives *Type 1 comparatives* and *superlatives*. For simplicity, we will use Type 1 comparatives to represent both from now on.

Adjectives and adverbs with two syllables or more and not ending in *y* do not form comparatives or superlatives by adding "*–er*" or "*–est*". Instead, "*more*", "*most*", "*less*" and "*least*" are used before such words, e.g., "*more beautiful*". We call this type of comparatives and superlatives *Type 2 comparatives* and *Type 2 superlatives*. These two types are called *regular comparatives* and *superlatives* respectively.

In English, there are also some *irregular comparatives* and *superlatives*, which do not follow the above rules, i.e., "*more*", "*most*", "*less*", "*least*", "*better*", "*best*", "*worse*", "*worst*", "*further/farther*" and "*furthest/farthest*". They behave similarly to Type 1 comparatives and superlatives and thus are grouped under Type 1.

Apart from these comparatives and superlatives, there are *non-standard words* that express gradable comparisons, e.g., "*prefer*", and "*superior*". For example, the sentence, "*in term of battery life, Camera X is superior to Camera Y*", says that "*Camera X*" is preferred. We obtained a list of 27 such words from (Jindal and Liu 2006) (which used more words, but most of them are not used to express gradable comparisons). Since these words behave similarly to Type 1 comparatives, they are thus grouped under Type 1.

Further analysis also shows that we can group comparatives into two categories according to whether they express increased or decreased values:

Increasing comparatives: Such a comparative expresses an increased value of a quantity, e.g., "*more*", and "*longer*".

Decreasing comparatives: Such a comparative expresses a decreased value of a quantity, e.g., "*less*", and "*fewer*".

As we will see later, this categorization is very useful in identifying the preferred entity.

Since comparatives originate from adjectives and adverbs, they may carry positive or negative sentiments/opinions. Along this dimension, we can divide them into two categories.

1. *Opinionated comparatives*: For Type 1 comparatives, this category contains words such as "*better*", "*worse*", etc, which has explicit opinions. In sentences involving such words, it is normally easy to determine which entity is the preferred one of the sentence author.

   In the case of Type 2 comparatives, formed by adding "*more*", "*less*", "*most*", and "*least*" before adjectives or adverbs, the opinion (or preferred entity) is determined by both words. The following rules apply:

   "increasing comparative" Negative → Negative Opinion
   "increasing comparative" Positive → Positive Opinion
   "decreasing comparative" Negative → Positive Opinion
   "decreasing comparative" Positive → Negative Opinion

   The first rule says that the combination of an increasing comparative word (e.g., "*more*") and a negative opinion adjective/adverb (e.g., "*awful*") implies a negative Type 2 comparative. The other rules are similar. These rules are intuitive and will not be discussed further.

2. *Comparatives with context-dependent opinions*: These comparatives are used to compare gradable quantities of entities. In the case of Type 1 comparatives, such words include "*higher*", "*lower*", etc. Although they do not explicitly describe the opinion of the author, they often carry *implicit sentiments* or *preferences* based on contexts. For example, in "*Car X has higher mileage per gallon than Car Y*", it is hard to know whether "*higher*" is positive or negative without domain knowledge. It is only when the two words, "*higher*" and "*mileage*", are combined we know that "*higher*" is desirable for "*mileage*" from our domain knowledge.

   In the case of Type 2 comparatives, the situation is similar. However, the comparative word ("*more*", "*most*", "*less*" or "*least*"), the adjective/adverb and the feature are all important in determining the opinion or the preference. If we know whether the comparative word is increasing or decreasing (which is easy since there are only four such words), then the opinion can be determined by applying the four rules above in (1).

For this work, we used the *opinion word* list from (Hu and Liu 2004), which was compiled using a bootstrapping approach based on WordNet. For opinionated comparatives, due to the observation below we simply convert the opinion adjectives/adverbs to their comparative forms, which is done automatically based on grammar (comparative formation) rules described above and WordNet.

Observation: If a word is positive (or negative), then its comparative or superlative form is also positive (or negative), e.g., "*good*", "*better*" and "*best*".

After the conversion, these words are manually categorized into increasing and decreasing comparatives. Although this consumes some time, it is only a one-time effort.

4.2 Contexts

To deal with comparatives with context dependent opinions, we need contexts. It is conjectured that the comparative and the feature in the sentence form the context. This works very well. For a Type 2 comparative, we only need the feature and the adjective/adverb to form a context. For example, in the sentence, "*Program X runs more quickly than Program Y*", the context is the pair, ("*run*", "*quickly*"), where "*run*" is a verb feature. If we find out that ("*run*", "*quickly*") is positive based on some external information, we can conclude that "*Program X*" is preferred using one of the four rules above since "*more*" is an increasing comparative.

We will use such contexts to find opinion orientations of comparatives with regard to some features from the external information, i.e., Pros and Cons in online reviews.

4.3 Pros and Cons in Reviews

Figure 1 shows a popular review format. The reviewer first describes Pros and Cons briefly, and then writes a full review.

Pros and Cons are used in our work for two main reasons. First, the brief information in Pros and Cons contains the essential information related to opinions. Each phrase or sentence segment usually contains an entity feature and an opinion word. Second, depending on whether it is in Pros or in Cons, the user opinion on the product feature is clear.

To use the Pros and Cons phrases, we separate them use punctuations and words, i.e., *','*, *'.'*, *'and'*, *and* *'but'*. Pros in Figure 1 can be separated into 5 phrases or segments,

great photos	<photo>
easy to use	<use>
good manual	<manual>
many options	<option>
takes videos	<video>

We can see that each segment describes an entity feature on which the reviewer has expressed an opinion. The entity feature for each segment is listed within <>.

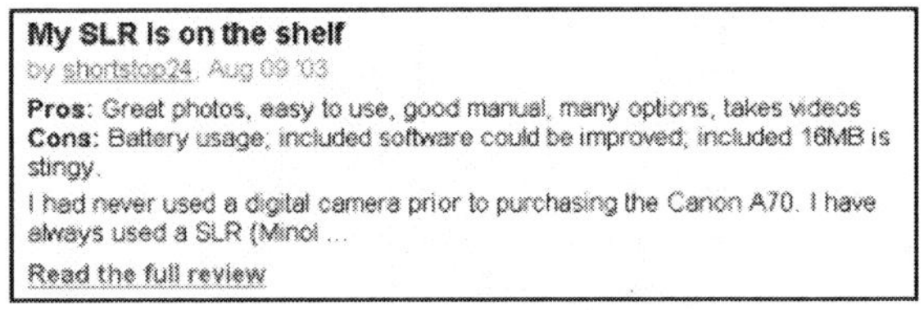

Figure 1: An example review

4.4 Identifying Preferred Entities: The Algorithm

Since we use Pros and Cons as the external information source to help determine whether the combination of a comparative and an entity feature is positive or negative, we need to find comparative and entity features words in Pros and Cons. However, in Pros and Cons, comparatives are seldom used (entity features are always there). Thus we need to first convert comparatives to their base forms. This can be done automatically using WordNet and grammar rules described in Section 4.1. We will not discuss the process here as it is fairly straightforward.

We now put everything together to identify the preferred entity in a comparative sentence. For easy reference, we denote the comparative word as *C* and the feature being compared as *F*. After obtaining the base forms of *C*, we work on two main cases for the two types of comparatives:

Case 1. Type 1 Comparative or Superlative: There are four sub-cases.

1.A. *C is opinionated*: If the comparative or superlative *C* has a positive orientation (e.g., "*better*"), EntityS1 (which appears before *C* in the sentence) is temporarily assigned as the preferred entity. Otherwise, EntityS2 is assigned as the preferred entity. The reason for the temporary assignment is that the sentence may contain negations, e.g., "*not*", which is discussed below.

1.B. *C is not opinionated but F is opinionated*: An example is, "*Car X generates more noise than Car Y*", which has the feature *F* "*noise*", a negative noun. If the orientation of *F* is positive and *C* is an increasing comparative word, we assign EntityS1 as the preferred entity. Otherwise, we assign EntityS2 as the preferred entity. The possibilities are listed as four rules below, which are derived from the 4 rules earlier:

"increasing *C*" + Positive → EntityS1 preferred
"decreasing *C*" + Positive → EntityS2 preferred

"increasing C" + Negative → EntityS2 preferred
"decreasing C" + Negative → EntityS1 preferred

"Positive" and "Negative" stand for the orientation of feature F being positive and negative respectively.

1.C. *Both* C and F *are not opinionated*: In this case, we need external information to identify the preferred entity. We use phrases in Pros and Cons from reviews.

In this case, we look for the feature F and comparative word C, (i.e., the context) in the list of phrases in Pros and Cons. In order to find whether the combination of C and F indicates a positive or negative opinion, we compute their associations in Pros and in Cons. If they are more associated in Pros than in Cons, we conclude that the combination indicates a positive sentiment, and otherwise a negative sentiment. The result decides the preferred entity. Point-wise mutual information (PMI) is commonly used for computing the association of two terms (e.g., Turney 2002), which is defined as:

$$PMI(F, C) = log\frac{Pr(F, C)}{Pr(F)Pr(C)}.$$

However, we argue that PMI is not a suitable measure for our purpose. The reason is that PMI is symmetric in the sense that $PMI(F, C)$ is the same as $PMI(C, F)$. However, in our case, the feature F and comparative word C association is not symmetric because although a feature is usually modified by a particular adjective word, the adjective word can modify many other features. For example, "*long*" can be used in "*long lag*", but it can also be used in "*long battery life*", "*long execution time*" and many others. Thus, this association is asymmetric. We are more interested in the conditional probability of C (including its synonyms) given F, which is essentially the confidence measure in traditional data mining. However, confidence does not handle well the situation where C occurs frequently but F appears rarely. In such cases a high conditional probability $Pr(C|F)$ may just represent some pure chance, and consequently the resulting association may be spurious. We propose the following measure, which we call *one-side association* (*OSA*), and it works quite well:

$$OSA(F, C) = log\frac{Pr(F, C)Pr(C|F)}{Pr(F)Pr(C)}$$

The difference between OSA and PMI is the conditional probability $Pr(C|F)$ used in OSA, which biases the mutual association of F and C to one side.

Given the comparative word C and the feature F, we first compute an OSA value for positive, denoted by $OSA_P(F, C)$, and then compute an OSA value for negative, denoted by $OSA_N(F, C)$. The decision rule is simply the following:

If $OSA_P(F, C) - OSA_N(F, C) \geq 0$ then
EntityS1 is preferred
Otherwise, EntityS2 is preferred

Computing $\boldsymbol{OSA_P(F, C)}$: We need to compute $Pr_P(F, C)$, for which we need to count the number of times that comparative word C and the feature F co-occur. Instead of using C alone, we also use its base forms and synonyms and antonyms. Similarly, for F, we also use its synonyms. If C (or a synonym of C) and F (or a synonym) co-occur in a Pros phrase, we count 1. If an antonym of C and F (or a synonym) co-occur in a Cons phrase, we also count 1. Thus, although we only evaluate for positive, we actually use both Pros and Cons. This is important because it allows us to find more occurrences to produce more reliable results. Synonyms and antonyms are obtained from WordNet. Currently, synonyms and antonyms are only found for single word features.

We then count the number of occurrences of the comparative word C and the feature F separately in both Pros and Cons to compute $Pr_P(F)$ and $Pr_P(C)$. In counting the number of occurrences of C, we consider both its synonyms in Pros and antonyms in Cons. In counting the number of occurrences of F, we consider its synonyms in both Pros and Cons.

Computing $\boldsymbol{OSA_N(F, C)}$: To compute $Pr_N(F, C)$, we use a similar strategy as for computing $Pr_P(F, C)$. In this case, we start with Cons.

1.D. C *is a feature indicator*: An example sentence is "*Camera X is smaller than Camera Y*", where "*smaller*" is the *feature indicator* for feature "*size*". In this case, we simply count the number of times (denoted by $n+$) that C appears in Pros and the number of times (denoted by $n-$) that C appears in Cons. If $n+ \geq n-$, we temporarily assign EntityS1 as the preferred entity. Otherwise, we assign EntityS2 as the preferred entity. Note that in some sentences, the entity features do not appear explicitly in the sentences but are implied. The words that imply the features are called *feature indicators*.

Case 2: Type 2 Comparative or Superlative: There are two sub-cases:

2.A. *Adjective/adverb in the comparison is opinionated*: In this case, the feature *F* is not important. An example sentence is:

"*Car X has more beautiful interior than Car Y*",

"*more*" is an increasing comparative, and "*beautiful*" is the adjective with a positive orientation (the feature *F* is "*interior*"). "*Car X*" is clearly preferred in this case.

Another example is: "*Car X is more beautiful than Car Y*". In this case, "*beautiful*" is a feature indicator for the feature "*appearance*". Again, "*Car X*" is preferred. This sub-case can be handled similarly as case 1.B.

2.B. *adjective/adverb in the comparison is not opinionated*: If the adjective/adverb in comparison is a feature indicator, we can use the method in 1.D. Otherwise, we form a context using the feature and adjective/adverb, and apply the method in 1.C. We then combine the result with the comparative word before the adjective/adverb to decide based on the rules in 1.B.

Negations: The steps above temporarily determine which entity is the preferred entity. However, a comparative sentence may contain a negation word or phrase (we have compiled 26 of them), e.g., "*Camera X's battery life is not longer than that of Camera Y.*" Without considering "*not*", "*Camera X*" is preferred. After considering "*not*", we assign the preferred entity to "*Camera Y*". This decision may be problematic because "*not longer*" does not mean "*shorter*" (thus it can also be seen to have no preference).

5 Evaluation

A system, called PCS (*P*referred entities in *C*omparative *S*entences), has been implemented based the proposed method. Since there is no existing system that can perform the task, we could not compare with an existing approach. Below, we first describe the evaluation datasets and then present the results.

5.1 Evaluation Datasets

Our comparative sentence dataset consists of two subsets. The first subset is from (Jindal and Liu 2006), which are product review and forum discussion sentences on *digital cameras, DVD players, MP3 players, Intel vs AMD, Coke vs Pepsi,* and *Microsoft vs Google*. The original dataset used in (Jindal and Liu 2006) also contains many non-gradable comparative sentences, which are not used here as most such sentences do not express any preferences.

To make the data more diverse, we collected more forum discussion data about mobile phones from http://www.howardforums.com/, and reviews from amazon.com and cnet.com on products such as *laptops*, *cameras* and *mobile phones*. Table 1 gives the number of sentences from these two sources. Although we only have 837 comparative sentences, they were collected from thousands of sentences in reviews and forums. About 10% of the sentences from them are comparative sentences.

Skewed Distribution: An interesting observation about comparative sentences is that a large proportion (based on our data) of them (84%) has EntityS1 as the preferred entity. This means that when people make comparisons, they tend to put the preferred entities first.

Pros and Cons corpus: The Pros and Cons corpus was crawled from reviews of epinions.com. It has 15162 Pros and 15162 Cons extracted from 15162 reviews of three types of products, i.e., digital cameras (8479), and printers (5778), and Strollers (905).

Table 1. Sentences from different sources

Data Sources	**No. of Comparative Sentences**
(Jindal and Liu 2006)	418
Reviews and forum posts	419
Total	837

5.2 Results

The results on the whole dataset are given in Table 2. Note that 84% of the sentences have EntityS1 as the preferred entity. If a system does nothing but simply announces that EntityS1 is preferred, we will have the accuracy of 84%. However, PCS using the OSA measure achieves the accuracy of 94.4%, which is much better than the baseline of taking the majority. Since in skewed datasets accuracy does not reflect the prediction well, we will mainly use precision (Prec.), recall (Rec.) and F-score (F) in evaluation. For the case that EntityS1 is preferred, the algorithm does extremely well. For the case that EntityS2 is preferred, the algorithm also does well although not as well as for the EntityS1 case. Based on our observation, we found that in such cases, the sentences are usually more complex.

Next, we compare with the case that the system does not use Pros and Cons (then OSA or PMI is not needed) (row 2). When a sentence requires context dependency handling, the system simply takes the majority as the default, i.e., assigning EntityS1 as the preferred entity. From the results in Table 2, we can see that F-scores are all worse. In the case that EntityS1 is the preferred entity, taking defaults is not so bad, which is not surprising because of the skewed data distribution. Even in this case, the precision improvement of PCS(OSA) is statistically significant at the 95% confidence level. The recall is slight less but their difference is not statistically significant. When EntityS2 is the preferred entity, its F-score (row 2) is much worse, which shows that our technique is effective. The recall improvement of PCS (OSA) is dramatic (statistically significant at the 95% confidence level). The two precisions are not statistically different. For OSA vs. PMI, see below.

Table 2: Preferred entity identification: whole data

	EntityS1 Preferred			**EntityS2 Preferred**		
	Prec.	*Rec.*	*F*	*Prec.*	*Rec.*	*F*
PCS (OSA)	0.967	0.966	0.966	0.822	0.828	0.825
PCS: No Pros & Cons	0.925	0.980	0.952	0.848	0.582	0.690
PCS (PMI)	0.967	0.961	0.964	0.804	0.828	0.816

Now let us look at only the 187 sentences that need context dependency handling. The data is still skewed. 72.2% of the sentences have EntityS1 as the preferred entities. Table 3 shows the results of PCS with and without using Pros and Cons. The results of PCS without Pros and Cons (OSA or PMI is not needed) are based on assigning EntityS1 as preferred for every sentence (taking the majority). Again, we can see that using external Pros and Cons (PCS(OSA)) helps dramatically. Not surprisingly, the improvements are statistically significant except the recall when EntityS1 is preferred.

Table 3: Preferred entity identification with 187 sentences that need context dependency handling

	EntityS1 Preferred			**EntityS2 Preferred**		
	Prec.	*Rec.*	*F*	*Prec.*	*Rec.*	*F*
PCS (OSA)	0.896	0.877	0.886	0.696	0.736	0.716
PCS: No Pros & Cons	0.722	1.000	0.839	0.000	0.000	0.000
PCS (PMI)	0.894	0.855	0.874	0.661	0.736	0.696

OSA vs. PMI: Comparing PCS(OSA) with PCS (PMI) (Table 3), OSA is better in F-score when EntityS1 is preferred by 1.2%, and better in F-score when EntityS2 is preferred by 2%. Although OSA's improvements over PMI are not large, we believe that in principle OSA is a more suitable measure. Comparing with PMI when the whole dataset is used (Table 2), OSA's gains are less because the number of sentences requiring context dependency handling is small (22%).

6 Conclusions

This paper studied sentiments expressed in comparative sentences. To our knowledge, no work has been reported on this topic. This paper proposed an effective method to solve the problem, which also deals with context based sentiments by exploiting external information available on the Web. To use the external information, we needed a measure of association of the comparative word and the entity feature. A new measure, called *one-side association* (OSA), was then proposed. Experimental results show that the technique produces accurate results.

References

Bos, J. and Nissim, M. An Empirical Approach to the Interpretation of Superlatives. *EMNLP-06, 2006.*

Esuli, A and Sebastiani, F. Determining Term Subjectivity and Term Orientation for Opinion Mining, *EACL'06*, 2006.

Fiszman, M., Demner-Fushman, D., Lang, F., Goetz, P., and Rindflesch, T. Interpreting Comparative Constructions in Biomedical Text. BioNLP, 2007.

Gamon, M., Aue, A., Corston-Oliver, S. and Ringger, E.K. Pulse: Mining customer opinions from free text. IDA'2005.

Hatzivassiloglou, V. and McKeown, K. Predicting the Semantic Orientation of Adjectives. *ACL-EACL'97.*

Hu, M and Liu, B. Mining and summarizing customer reviews. *KDD'04*, 2004.

Jindal, N. and Liu, B. Mining Comparative Sentences and Relations. *AAAI'06*, 2006.

Kanayama, H and Nasukawa, T. Fully automatic lexicon expansion for domain-oriented sentiment analysis. *EMNLP'06.*

Kim, S. and Hovy, E. Determining the Sentiment of Opinions. *COLING'04*, 2004.

Liu, B, Hu, M. and Cheng, J. Opinion Observer: Analyzing and Comparing Opinions on the Web. *WWW'05*, 2005.

Mei, Q., Ling, X., Wondra, W., Su, H. and Zhai, C. Topic Sentiment Mixture: Modeling Facets and Opinions in Weblogs. *WWW'07*, 2007.

Pang, B., Lee, L. and Vaithyanathan, S. Thumbs up? Sentiment Classification Using Machine Learning Techniques. EMNLP'02, 2002.

Popescu, A.-M. and Etzioni, O. Extracting Product Features and Opinions from Reviews. EMNLP'05.

Riloff, E & Wiebe, J. Learning extraction patterns for subjective expressions. EMNLP'03, 2003.

Stoyanov, V. and Cardie, C. Toward opinion summarization: Linking the sources. In Proc. of the Workshop on Sentiment and Subjectivity in Text, 2006.

Turney, P. Thumbs Up or Thumbs Down? Semantic Orientation Applied to Unsupervised Classification of Reviews.ACL-2002.

Wiebe, J. and Mihalcea, R. Word Sense and Subjectivity. ACL'06, 2006.

Wilson, T., Wiebe, J. and Hwa, R. Just how mad are you? Finding strong and weak opinion clauses. AAAI'04, 2004.

Integrating a unification-based semantics in a large scale Lexicalised Tree Adjoining Grammar for French

Claire Gardent
CNRS / LORIA
Equipe Talaris, Bat. B
615, rue du jardin botanique
54600 Villers les Nancy
France
claire.gardent@loria.fr

Abstract

In contrast to LFG and HPSG, there is to date no large scale Tree Adjoining Grammar (TAG) equiped with a compositional semantics. In this paper, we report on the integration of a unification-based semantics into a Feature-Based Lexicalised TAG for French consisting of around 6 000 trees. We focus on verb semantics and show how factorisation can be used to support a compact and principled encoding of the semantic information that needs to be associated with each of the verbal elementary trees. The factorisation is made possible by the use of XMG, a high-level linguistic formalism designed to specify and compile computational grammars and in particular, grammars based on non-local trees or tree descriptions.

1 Introduction

Whilst there exists large scale LFGs (Lexical Functional Grammar) and HPSGs (Head-Driven Phrase Structure Grammar) equipped with a compositional semantics (Copestake et al., 2001; Frank and van Genabith, 2001), available Tree Adjoining Grammars remain largely syntactic.

One reason for this is that there has been, up to recently, much debate about how best to combine TAG with a compositional semantics. Should it be based on the derived or the derivation tree ? Should Feature-Based LTAG be used or should synchronous TAG? Many proposals have been put forward but only recently did sufficient consensus emerge to support the specification of a TAG based compositional semantics. In a nutshell, it can be achieved either by using a synchronous TAG (Nesson and Shieber, 2006) (in this case, the grammar explicitely describes and synchronises syntax and semantics structures) or by using Feature-Based LTAG (in which case, the synchronisation between syntax and semantics is mediated by the unification of semantic indices associated with the FTAG elementary trees).

Another more practical reason for the absence of large scale TAGs integrating a compositional semantics is the lack of available computational frameworks. Up to recently, there has been no available grammar writing environment and parser that would support the integration of compositional semantics into a TAG. One step in that direction is provided by the development of XMG(Duchier et al., 2004), a formalism which supports the specification of Feature-Based LTAGs equipped with a compositional semantics à la (Gardent and Kallmeyer, 2003).

In this paper, we report on the integration of a unification-based semantics into a Feature-Based LTAG for French which consists of around 6 000 trees. This integration is specified using XMG and we show how this formalism can be used to support a compact and principled encoding of the semantic information that needs to be associated with each of the 6 000 elementary trees.

The article is structured as follows. We start (section 2) by presenting XMG and showing how it supports the specification of Feature-Based LTAGs equipped with a compositional semantics. We then present SEMFRAG, the FTAG grammar for French that we developed (section 3). In section 4, we show how XMG can be used to minimise the development cost involved in enriching such

© 2008. Licensed under the *Creative Commons Attribution-Noncommercial-Share Alike 3.0 Unported* license (http://creativecommons.org/licenses/by-nc-sa/3.0/). Some rights reserved.

a grammar with a compositional semantics. Section 5 compares the approach with related work and concludes with pointers for further research.

2 The XMG formalism

The XMG formalism was designed to support the development and factorisation of computational grammars for Natural Language. Like PATR II it is theory neutral in that its use is not restricted to a single grammatical theory. Unlike PATR II however, the language provided by XMG allows the linguist to talk about the basic building blocks not only of rule based computational linguistic theories such as as HPSG (Head Driven Phrase Structure Grammar) and LFG (Lexical Functional Grammar) but also of tree based theories such as TAG (Tree Adjoining Grammar). As we shall see, this involves allowing for sophisticated node naming and identification mechanisms. Other differences between PATR II and XMG include a more general use of disjunction, the use of colours to control tree construction and a more natural encoding of trees and of semantic representation than is permitted by PATR II. A detailed definition of the XMG formalism is given in (Duchier et al., 2004). In what follows, we give an intuitive presentation of XMG emphasising the points that support a strongly factorised specification of grammars and in particular, of SEMFRAG. We start by presenting the basic building blocks XMG allows the linguist to talk about (2.1). We then go on to discuss the factorising mechanisms it supports (2.2). Finally, we introduce the several node naming and identification mechanisms it provides (2.3).

2.1 The basic building blocks

In XMG, the basic building blocks are CLASSES which may be specified along three dimensions : a syntactic dimension (SYN) which consists of a tree description whose node variables can be decorated with feature structures; a semantic dimension (SEM) consisting of a flat semantic formula; and a syntax/semantic interface (INTERFACE) for synchronising semantic formulae and tree descriptions .

SYN. The syntactic dimension in XMG allows the linguist to specify tree descriptions i.e., trees that can be underspecified with respect to both dominance and precedence. The trees described may be either local or extended and their nodes may be decorated with either one or two feature structures (two for TAG TOP and BOTTOM feature structures).

SEM. Using the semantic dimension, the linguist can specify unification based flat semantic formulae in the sense of (Copestake et al., 2001) i.e., non recursive formulae describing first order formulae with lambda binders replaced by unification variables and where scope may be underspecified. Semantic schemas can also be specified in which predicates are replaced by unification variables that will be instantiated during lexical lookup. For instance, the SEM dimension may include the following semantic formula and schema[1]:

(1) a. Every: $l_0 : \forall(X, h_1, h_2), h_1 \geq L_1, h_2 \geq L_2$

b. Binary Relation Schema: $l_1 : P(E), l_1 : Theta_1(E, X), l_1 : Theta_2(E, Y)$

In (1a), the flat semantic formula associated with *every* underspecifies scope by stating that the scope handle h_2 scopes, directly or indirectly ($\geq$), over (the label L_2 associated with) the scopal argument.In (1b) on the other hand, underspecification bears on the predicate P and the theta roles $Theta_1, Theta_2$ which are unification variables whose value will be provided by the lexicon. In this way, this binary relation schema can be used to represent the semantics of all verbs denoting a binary relation. The lexicon will then specify for each verb the relevant relation and theta roles.

INTERFACE. The third XMG dimension permits synchronising syntax and semantics. In essence, features that are used in SYN or in SEM can be assigned global names in the INTERFACE dimension and synchronised using variable sharing. For instance, given a feature-value pair F = X occuring in the SYN dimension and a semantic parameter Y occuring in the SEM dimension, the following interface constraint permits both unifying ("synchronising") X and Y and assigning them the global names IDX and ARG respectively :

(2) IDX = $\boxed{1} X$, ARG = $\boxed{1} Y$

As we shall see in section 4.2.2, the interface allows for a natural and highly factorised means of stating syntax/semantics linking constraints (e.g., the subject constituent provides the semantic index for the first semantic argument).

[1]Here and in what follows, we adopt the convention that identifiers starting with an upper case letter are unification variables.

2.2 Factorising mechanisms

An important feature of a linguistic formalism is that it supports a high level of factorisation thus facilitating grammar development, debugging and maintenance. In XMG, factorising can be achieved using disjunctions, conjunctions and inheritance of classes. As argued in (Crabbé, 2005), classes disjunction supports the description of alternatives, for instance, to describe the alternative possible realisations of a subject (see below). As usual, conjunction and inheritance of classes permits combining the content of two classes[2].

2.3 Node naming and identification mechanisms

In combining tree descriptions, the linguist often wants to identify nodes across descriptions. One distinguishing feature of XMG it that it supports a sophisticated treatment of node naming and node identification (Gardent and Parmentier, 2006).

Node naming. In XMG, node names are by default local to a class. However explicit IMPORT and EXPORT declarations can be used to make names "visible" to children classes. An EXPORT declaration makes the exported name(s) visible to all children classes. Conversely restrictive IMPORT declarations can be used either to block or to rename exported variables that are visible through inheritance.

Node identification. As we have just seen, IMPORT and EXPORT declarations can be used to make names "visible" to children classes and thereby idendify nodes from different classes. For instance, if class C_1 inherits from class C_2, C_1 refers to a node variable X and C_2 exports X, then X denotes the same node in both C_1 and C_2.

However, this mechanism only works within a single branch of the inheritance hierarchy. Indeed in case of multiple inheritance (two classes C_1 and C_2 export the same variable X to a third class inheriting from both C_1 and C_2), identification will fail (X will not be interpreted as denoting the same node in both C_1 and C_2). To remedy this shortcoming, XMG allows for explicit node identifications. Thus in the above case, X can be identified using the constraint $C_1.X = C_2.X$.

[2]The distinction between conjunction and inheritance has to do with some intricate issues concerning node identifications which we will not address here. See (Gardent and Parmentier, 2006) for a detailed discussion on this.

This concludes our informal presentation of XMG. For a more precise definition of its syntax, semantic and compilation process, we refer the reader to (Duchier et al., 2004).

3 SemFraG

To illustrate the expressive power of XMG, we now show how it can be used to specify SEMFRAG, a TAG for French which integrates a unification based compositional semantics. We start by presenting the grammar produced by the XMG specification.

SEMFRAG is a unification based version of LTAG namely, Feature-based TAG. A Feature-based TAG (FTAG, (Vijay-Shanker and Joshi, 1988)) consists of a set of (auxiliary or initial) elementary trees and of two tree composition operations: substitution and adjunction. Initial trees are trees whose leaves are labelled with substitution nodes (marked with a downarrow) or terminal categories. Auxiliary trees are distinguished by a foot node (marked with a star) whose category must be the same as that of the root node. Substitution inserts a tree onto a substitution node of some other tree while adjunction inserts an auxiliary tree into a tree. In an FTAG, the tree nodes are furthermore decorated with two feature structures (called TOP and BOTTOM) which are unified during derivation as follows. On substitution, the top of the substitution node is unified with the top of the root node of the tree being substituted in. On adjunction, the top of the root of the auxiliary tree is unified with the top of the node where adjunction takes place; and the bottom features of the foot node are unified with the bottom features of this node. At the end of a derivation, the top and bottom of all nodes in the derived tree are unified.

To associate semantic representations with natural language expressions, the FTAG is modified as proposed in (Gardent and Kallmeyer, 2003). Each

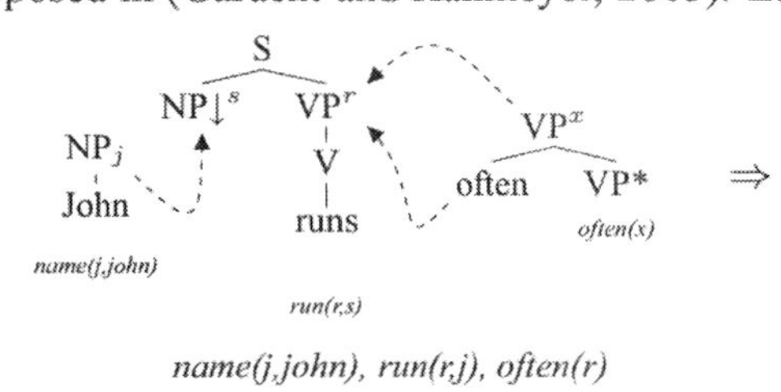

Figure 1: Flat Semantics for "John often runs"

elementary tree is associated with a flat semantic

representation. For instance, in Figure 1,[3] the trees for *John, runs* and *often* are associated with the semantics *name(j,john), run(r,s)* and *often(x)* respectively.

The arguments of a semantic functor are represented by unification variables which occur both in the semantic representation of this functor and on some nodes of the associated syntactic tree. For instance in Figure 1, the semantic index s occurring in the semantic representation of *runs* also occurs on the subject substitution node of the associated elementary tree.

The value of semantic arguments is then determined by the unifications taking place during derivation. For instance, the semantic index s in the tree for *runs* is unified during substitution with the semantic indices labelling the root nodes of the tree for *John*. As a result, the semantics of *John often runs* is

(3) {`name(j,john),run(r,j),often(r)`}

SEMFRAG describes a core fragment of French and contains around 6 000 elementary trees. It covers some 35 basic verbal subcategorisation frames and for each of these frames, the set of argument redistributions (active, passive, middle, neuter, reflexivisation, impersonal, passive impersonal) and of argument realisations (cliticisation, extraction, omission, permutations, etc.) possible for this frame. Predicative (adjectival, nominal and prepositional) and light verb constructions are also covered as well as subcategorising nouns and adjectives. Basic descriptions are provided for the remaining constructions i.e., adverbs, determiners and prepositions.

4 Implementing SEMFRAG using XMG

We now illustrate the power of XMG by showing how it can be used to produce a highly factorised specification of SEMFRAG, an FTAG of 6 000 trees enriched with a unification based compositional semantics. Given the space constraints, we concentrate on the verbal trees (trees anchored by verbs). We start (4.1) by summarising the specification of SEMFRAG verbal syntactic trees given in (Crabbé, 2005). We then (4.2) show how this specification of the syntax of verbal trees can be enriched with a unification based compositional semantics. We show in particular that this enrichment can be performed using only a limited set of general principles.

4.1 Syntax

The syntactic dimension of SEMFRAG was specified in (Crabbé, 2005). For the verbal trees, it can be summarised as follows.

First, tree families are specified as disjunctions of diatheses. For instance, the N0VN1 family[4] is defined as :

$$\begin{array}{lll} nOVn1 & \rightarrow & (\ \ dianOVn1Active \\ & & \vee\ \ dianOVn1Passive \\ & & \vee\ \ dianOVn1dePassive \\ & & \vee\ \ dianOVn1ShortPassive \\ & & \vee\ \ dianOVn1ImpersonalPassive \\ & & \vee\ \ dianOVn1middle \\ & & \vee\ \ dianOVn1Reflexive\ \ ) \end{array} \quad (1)$$

Second, diatheses are defined as conjunctions of classes. For instance, *dian0Vn1Active* is defined as:

$$\begin{array}{lll} dian0Vn1Active & \rightarrow & (\ \ Subject \\ & & \wedge\ \ ActiveVerbForm \\ & & \wedge\ \ Object\ \ ) \end{array} \quad (2)$$

Third, each grammatical function appearing in the definition of a diathesis is defined as a disjunction of classes, each class representing a possible realisation of that function. For instance, the *Subject* class is:

$$\begin{array}{lll} Subject & \rightarrow & (\ \ CanonicalSubject \\ & & \vee\ \ RelativisedSubject \\ & & \vee\ \ WhSubject \\ & & \vee\ \ CleftSubject \\ & & \vee\ \ CliticSubject\ \ ) \end{array} \quad (3)$$

Fourth, each class describing a possible grammatical function realisation specifies the adequate tree description. For instance, the fragments for *CanonicalSubject, ActiveVerbForm* and *CanonicalObject* are sketched in Figure 2[5].

In sum, the XMG specification relies on a fairly intuitive use of classes disjunctions and conjunctions. Moreover, the basic leaf classes (i.e., the most deeply embedded disjuncts and conjuncts in the grammar specification) are defined by inheritance, the inheritance hierarchy encoding the sharing of tree description fragments and/or feature

[3] C^x/C_x abbreviate a node with category C and a top/bottom feature structure including the feature-value pair { **index** : x}.

[4] In TAG, a tree family gathers all the elementary trees associated with verbs of a given syntactic type. Thus, the N0VN1 family contains all the trees describing the syntactic contexts in which a verb taking two nominal arguments (i.e., a transitive verb) can occur.

[5] Due to space constraints, these fragments are simplified in that features are omitted.

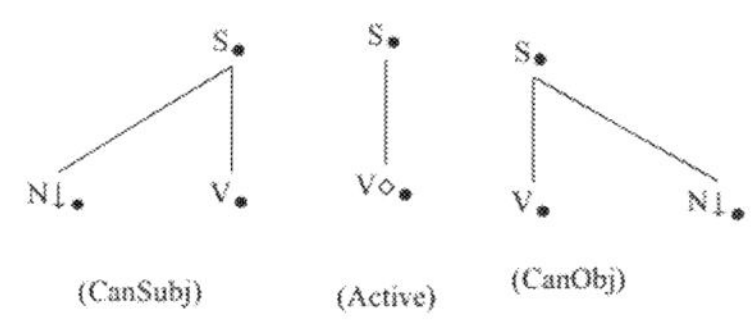

Figure 2: Tree fragments

structures between leaf classes. As a result, several thousand trees are specified using only a few hundred classes.

4.2 Semantics

Just like grammar engineering is a complex issue, enriching a computational grammar with a compositional semantics is potentially time consuming and error prone. We now show that XMG permits this enrichment by means of a few general semantic principles thus minimising both work and the risk of errors. To enrich a purely syntactic FTAG with the type of unification based semantics described in section 3, three main changes need to be carried out.

First, trees must be labelled with appropriate semantic indices and labels. For instance, the subject node of a verbal tree must be labelled with a semantic index.

Second, trees must be associated with appropriate semantic schemas. For instance, the trees of the *n0Vn1* family must be associated with a semantic schema representing a binary relation.

Third, variable sharing between semantic schemas and syntactic trees must be enforced. For instance, the semantic index of the subject node of an active verb should be identified with the first semantic argument of the associated semantic schema.

We now provide an XMG encoding of this information. As for the syntax, we proceed top-down from the verb families down to argument realisation and node labelling.

4.2.1 Associating trees with semantic formulae.

As indicated in the previous section, trees in TAG are grouped into tree families. We use this feature to associate in one fell swoop all the trees of a given family with the appropriate semantic schema. For instance, to associate transitive verbs with a binary relation schema, the syntactic specification given in (1) is modified to:

$$\begin{array}{lll} \textit{n0Vn1} & \rightarrow & \textit{binaryRel} \ \wedge \\ & & (\ \textit{dian0Vn1Active} \\ & & \vee\ \textit{dian0Vn1Passive} \\ & & \vee\ \textit{dian0Vn1dePassive} \\ & & \vee\ \textit{dian0Vn1ShortPassive} \\ & & \vee\ \textit{dian0Vn1ImpersonalPassive} \\ & & \vee\ \textit{dian0Vn1middle} \\ & & \vee\ \textit{dian0Vn1Reflexive}\ ) \end{array} \tag{4}$$

4.2.2 Linking constraints

Next the correct syntax/semantic interface constraints must be specified for each diathesis. That is, the correct mapping between syntactic and semantic arguments must be enforced. This is done in two steps.

First, we define a set of INTERFACE constraints of the form

$$index_F = V, arg_i = V$$

which are meant to enforce the identification of the semantic index ($index_F$) labelling a given tree node with grammatical function F (e.g., F = subject) with the index (arg_i) representing the i-th argument in a semantic schema. For instance, when combined with a class C containing a variable X named[6] arg_1 and a variable Y named $index_{subject}$, the *SubjArg1* linking constraint

$$index_{subject} = V, arg_1 = V$$

ensures that X and Y are identified. Assuming further that arg_1 is used to name the first semantic argument and $index_{subject}$ to name the value of the index feature labelling a subject node[7], this constraint ensures a subject/arg_1 mapping.

Given such interface constraints, we then refine the diathesis definitions so as to ensure the correct bindings. For instance, the specification in (2) is modified to :

$$\begin{array}{lll} \textit{dian0Vn1Active} & \rightarrow & (\ SubjArg1 \\ & & \wedge\ ObjArg2 \\ & & \wedge\ Subject \\ & & \wedge\ ActiveVerbForm \\ & & \wedge\ Object\ ) \end{array} \tag{5}$$

whilst the passive diathesis is specified as:

$$\begin{array}{lll} \textit{dian0Vn1Passive} & \rightarrow & (\ SubjArg2 \\ & & \wedge\ CagentArg1 \\ & & \wedge\ Subject \\ & & \wedge\ PassiveVerbForm \\ & & \wedge\ Cagent\ ) \end{array} \tag{6}$$

[6] As explained in section 2, interface constraints can be used to assign global names to values inside a class.

[7] We will see in the next section how to ensure the appropriate naming of syntactic indices and semantic arguments.

4.2.3 Labelling trees with semantic indices.

The above scheme relies on the assumption that tree nodes are appropriately labelled with semantic indices (e.g., the subject node must be labelled with a semantic index) and that these indices are appropriately named (arg_1 must denote the parameter representing the first argument of a binary relation and $index_{subject}$ the value of the index feature on a subject node). As suggested in (Gardent, 2007), a complete semantic labelling of a TAG with the semantic features necessary to enrich this TAG with the unification based compositional semantics sketched in section 3 can be obtained by applying the following *labelling principles*[8]:

Argument labelling: In trees associated with semantic functors, each argument node is labelled with a semantic index[9] named after the grammatical function of the argument node (e.g., $index_{subject}$ for a subject node).

Anchor projection: The anchor node projects its label up to its maximal projection.

Foot projection: A foot node projects its label up to the root[10]

Controller/Controllee: In trees associated with control verbs, the semantic index of the controller is identified with the value of the controlled index occuring on the sentential argument node.

As we shall now see, XMG permits a fairly direct encoding of these principles.

Argument labelling. In the tree associated with a syntactic functor (e.g., a verb), each tree node representing a syntactic argument (e.g., the subject node) should be labelled with a semantic index named after the grammatical function of that node (e.g., $index_{subject}$).

To label argument nodes with an appropriately named semantic index, we first define a set of classes encapsulating a node with an index and a name. We then identify this node with the appropriate tree nodes.

More specifically, we define for each grammatical function $Function \in \{subject, object, cagent, iobject, \ldots\}$, a semantic class $FunctionSem$ which associates with an (exported) node called $xFunction$ the feature value pair *index* = *I* and an interface constraint of the form $index_{Function} = I$. For instance, the class $SubjectSem$ associates the node $xSubject$ with the feature value pair *index* = *I* and the interface constraint $index_{subject} = I$.

$$subjectSem \longrightarrow \begin{array}{l}[syn] : xSubject[index = I] \\ [interface] : [index_{subject} = I]\end{array} \quad (7)$$

When specifying the tree fragments describing the possible realisations of the grammatical functions, the (exported) argument node is systematically named $xArg$.

Finally, we modify the specification of the grammatical functions realisations to import the appropriate semantic class and identify $xArg$ and $xFunction$ nodes. For instance, 3 above is changed to:

$$Subject \longrightarrow \begin{array}{l} SubjectSem \ \wedge \\ xArg = xSubject \ \wedge \\ (\ CanonicalSubject \\ \vee \ RelativisedSubject \\ \vee \ WhSubject \\ \vee \ CleftSubject \\ \vee \ CliticSubject \ ) \end{array} \quad (8)$$

As a result, all $xArg$ nodes in the tree descriptions associated with a subject realisation are labelled with an index *I* feature whose global name is $index_{subject}$.

Controller/Controllee. Value sharing between the semantic index of the controller (e.g., the subject of the control verb) and that of the controllee (e.g., the empty subject of the infinitival complement) is enforced using linking constraints between the semantic index labelling the controller node and that labelling the sentential argument node of the control verb. Control verb definitions then import the appropriate (object or subject control) linking constraint.

Anchor and foot projection. The anchor (foot) projection principle stipulate the projection of semantic indices from the anchor (foot) node up to the maximal projection (root). To enforce these principles, we define a set of anchor projection classes as illustrated in Figure 3. We then "glue" these projection skeletons onto the relevant syntactic trees by importing them in their definition and explicitely identifying the anchor node of the semantic projection classes with the anchor or foot node of these trees. Since the solutions must be trees, the nodes dominating the anchor node of the

[8]Because of space constraints, the principles required to handle quantification are omitted.

[9]For simplicity, we only talk about indices here. However, to be complete, labels are also need to be taken into account.

[10]The foot projection principle only applies to foot nodes that are not argument nodes i.e., to modifiee nodes.

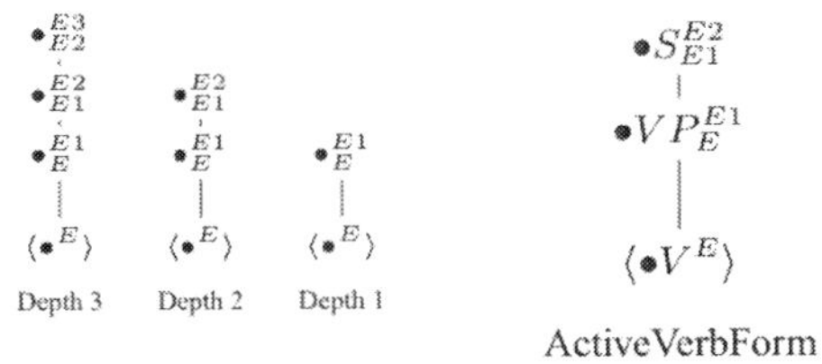

Figure 3: Anchor/Foot projection

projection class will deterministically be unified with those dominating the anchor or foot node of the trees being combined with. For instance, for verbs, the class specifying the verbal spine (e.g., *ActiveVerbForm*, cf. 2) will import a projection class and equate the anchor node of the verbal spine with that of the projection skeleton. As a result, the verb projects its index up to the root (modulo the renaming made necessary by the possibility of an adjunction) as illustrated on the right inside of Figure 3.

4.3 Discussion

Arguably, the XMG encoding we provided to enrich an FTAG with a unification based compositional semantics, is compact and principled.

It is principled in that it provides a direct and transparent formulation of the main principles underlying the integration in a TAG of the unification based semantics sketched in Section 3.

It is compact in that the number of modifications needed to enrich syntax with semantics is relatively small: 76 class definitions and 498 class calls are sufficient to associate the required semantic information (semantic schemas, semantic indices and index projections) with roughly 6000 trees. Crucially, this means that the time involved in integrating the semantics in the grammar is small (roughly a week linguist work) and further that the maintenance, extension and debugging of the semantic component is greatly facilitated.

Both these points rely on the expressivity of XMG. More in particular, the encoding heavily relies on two specific features of XMG namely, *generalised classes disjunctions* and the possibility to use *global names* not only for tree nodes but also for feature values and semantic parameters.

Generalised classes disjunctions are used to associate large sets of trees with semantic schema (section 4.2.1) and to label sets of tree fragments with the appropriately named index (section 4.2.3). Intuitively, generalised classes disjunction and conjunction permit factoring out the common operand of an enumeration (e.g., instead of enumerating $(a \wedge b) \vee (a \wedge c) \vee (a \wedge d) \vee \ldots$, we can specify $a \wedge (b \vee c \vee d)$). In practice, this means that the number of statements necessary to specify the grammar can be greatly reduced. For instance, the association of several thousands of verb trees with a semantic schema is enforced by a total of 176 statements. In contrast, standard linguistic formalisms such as PATR IIor the LKB only allow disjunctions over atomic feature values.

Global names in turn, were used to support a direct encoding of linking constraints (section 4.2.2). 37 linking constraints definitions and 255 linking constraints calls are sufficient to ensure the appropriate mapping between syntactic and semantic arguments in verb trees as well as adjectival and nominal predicative trees. More generally, the possibility to introduce global names not only for tree nodes as in e.g., (Vijay-Shanker and Schabes, 1992) but also for feature values and semantic parameters allows for a simple and direct encoding of constraints applying to identifiers occuring "far apart" in a given tree (for instance, between the index of the subject node in a controlverb tree and that of a PRO index of its infinitival argument).

5 Conclusion

Whilst the development of standard unification-based grammars is well supported by the design of formalisms such as PATR II, the XLE and the LKB, formalisms for developing Tree-Based Grammars have received less attention. XMG aims to remedy this shortcoming by providing a formalism that supports talking about trees, tree sharing and tree labelling.

Trees of arbitrary (finite) depth can be described using underspecified tree descriptions. Additionally, trees can be combined with further linguistic dimensions such as semantic representations and a syntax/semantic interface to form more complex linguistic units.

Tree sharing is supported by the inheritance, the conjunction and the disjunction of tree descriptions together with a sophisticated identifier handling mechanism : identifiers are by default local but can be made global or semi-global, on demand. Furthermore, identifiers can be identified either explicitely (using either the interface or explicit identification constraints) or implicitely (through inheritance or through the use of colours, a mechanism not discussed here).

Finally, tree labelling can be expressed by associating tree nodes with one or two (for TAG) feature structures. Importantly, feature values can be assigned global names thereby allowing for the specification of constraints on features that are "far apart from each other" within a tree.

In this paper, we have argued that these features of XMG are effective in supporting an encoding of an FTAG with a unification based compositional semantics which is principled, transparent and compact. These features also markedly distinguish XMG from existing formalisms used to encode tree based grammars such as the non-monotonic encoding of TAG proposed in (Evans et al., 1995) (in contrast, XMG is fully monotonic) and the tree descriptions based approaches proposed in (Candito, 1996; Xia et al., 1998) where in particular, tree descriptions can only be conjoined (not disjoined) and where identification across tree fragments is restricted to nodes.

More in general, we believe that expressive formalisms are necessary to allow not only for the quick development of symbolic tree based grammars but also for their comparison and for the factoring of several grammars be they different wrt to the language they handle (as for instance in the HPSG Delphin or in the LFG Pargram project) or in the semantics they integrate e.g., a glue semantics as proposed in (Frank and van Genabith, 2001), a lambda-based semantics as proposed in (Gardent, 2007) or as shown here, a unification based flat semantics.

References

M.H. Candito. 1996. A principle-based hierarchical representation of LTAGs. In *Proc. of COLING'96, Kopenhagen.*

A. Copestake, A. Lascarides, and D. Flickinger. 2001. An algebra for semantic construction in constraint-based grammars. In *Proc. of ACL*, Toulouse, France.

B. Crabbé. 2005. *Représentation informatique de grammaires fortement lexicalisées.* Ph.D. thesis, Université Henri Poincaré, Nancy.

D. Duchier, J. Le Roux, and Y. Parmentier. 2004. The metagrammar compiler. In *2nde confrence internationale Oz/Mozart (MOZ'2004)*, Charleroi.

R. Evans, G. Gazdar, and D. Weir. 1995. Encoding lexicalized tree adjoining grammars with a nonmonotonic inheritance hierarchy. In *Proc. of ACL.*

A. Frank and J. van Genabith. 2001. Ll-based semantics for ltag - and what it teaches us about lfg and ltag. In *Proc. of the LFG'01 Conference*, Hong Kong. CSLI Online Publications.

C. Gardent and L. Kallmeyer. 2003. Semantic construction in ftag. In *Proc. of EACL*, Budapest, Hungary.

C. Gardent and Y. Parmentier. 2006. Coreference handling in xmg. In *Proc. of COLING (Poster)*, Sydney, Australia.

C. Gardent. 2007. Tree adjoining grammar, semantic calculi and labelling invariant. In *Proc. of IWCS.*

Rebecca Nesson and Stuart M. Shieber. 2006. Simpler TAG semantics through synchronization. In *Proceedings of the 11th Conference on Formal Grammar*, Malaga, Spain, 29–30 July.

K. Vijay-Shanker and A. K. Joshi. 1988. Feature structures based tree adjoining grammar. In *Proc. of COLING*, pages 714–719, Budapest.

K. Vijay-Shanker and Y. Schabes. 1992. Structure sharing in lexicalised tree adjoining grammar. In *Proc. of COLING 92*, pages 205–211.

F. Xia, M. Palmer, K. Vijay-Shanker, and J. Rosenzweig. 1998. Consistent grammar development using partial-tree descriptions for lexicalized tree adjoining grammar. *Proc. of TAG+4.*

Statistical anaphora resolution in biomedical texts

Caroline Gasperin **Ted Briscoe**
Computer Laboratory
University of Cambridge
Cambridge, UK
{cvg20,ejb}@cl.cam.ac.uk

Abstract

This paper presents a probabilistic model for resolution of non-pronominal anaphora in biomedical texts. The model seeks to find the antecedents of anaphoric expressions, both coreferent and associative ones, and also to identify discourse-new expressions. We consider only the noun phrases referring to biomedical entities. The model reaches state-of-the art performance: 56-69% precision and 54-67% recall on coreferent cases, and reasonable performance on different classes of associative cases.

1 Introduction

Inspired by Ge et al. (1998) probabilistic model for pronoun resolution, we have developed a model for resolution of non-pronominal anaphora in biomedical texts.

The probabilistic model results from a simple decomposition process applied to a conditional probability equation that involves several parameters (features). The decomposition makes use of Bayes' theorem and independence assumptions, and aims to decrease the impact of data sparseness on the model, so that even small training corpora can be viable. The decomposed model can be understood as a more sophisticated version of the naive-Bayes algorithm, since we consider the dependence among some of the features instead of full independence as in naive Bayes. Probabilistic models can return a confidence measure (probability) for each decision they make, while decision trees, for example, cannot. Another advantage of this type of model is the fact that they consider the prior probability of each class, while other machine-learning techniques such as SVMs and neural networks do not.

Our model seeks to classify the relation between an anaphoric expression and an antecedent candidate as coreferent, associative or neither. It computes the probability of each pair of anaphor and candidate for each class. The candidate with the highest overall probability for each class is selected as the antecedent for that class, or no antecedent is selected if the probability of no relation overcomes the positive probabilities; in this case, the expression is considered to be new to the discourse.

Coreferent cases are the ones in which the anaphoric expression and its antecedent refer to the same entity in the real world, as below:

(1) "The expression of **reaper** has been shown ... **the gene** encodes ..."

Associative cases are the ones in which the anaphoric expression and its antecedent refer to different entities, but where the antecedent plays a role in defining the meaning of the anaphoric expression, as in Example 2:

(2) "**Drosophila gene Bok** interacts with ... expression of **Bok protein** promotes apoptosis ..."

Discourse new cases usually consist of the first mention of an entity in the text, so no antecedent can be found for it.

We have focused on the biomedical domain for two reasons. Firstly, there is a vast demand from the biomedical field for information extraction efforts (which require NLP processing, including

©2008. Licensed under the *Creative Commons Attribution-Noncommercial-Share Alike 3.0 Unported* license (http://creativecommons.org/licenses/by-nc-sa/3.0/). Some rights reserved.

anaphora resolution), in order to process the exponentially increasing number of journal publications, which are the major source of novel knowledge to be extracted and condensed into domain databases for easy access. Secondly, anaphora resolution can benefit from the several sources of refined semantic knowledge that are not commonly available for other domains, such as biomedical databases, ontologies, and terminologies.

In the next section, we describe the anaphoric relations that we found in biomedical texts, which we are considering for the resolution process. In Section 3 we describe our probabilistic model, and in Section 4 the corpus created for training it. In Section 5 we present and discuss the results achieved by the model, and compare it with a baseline system and a decision-tree-based system.

2 Anaphora cases in biomedical text

Biomedical texts differ from other genres of text (e.g. newswire, fiction) in several points. Different types of NPs have a particular distribution in biomedical articles. For example, pronouns are very rare, accounting for a very small percentage of the noun phrases[1]; on the other hand, proper names occur very often, given the frequent mention of gene and protein names and the names of other biomedical entities. A system for anaphora resolution in the biomedical domain can benefit from focusing on the most common types of noun phrases, that is, non-pronominal ones.

In biomedical articles, the reader needs background knowledge to understand the underlying relation between the entities mentioned in the text in order to understand the text. For instance, in Example 2 the reader is expected to know that a gene encodes a protein (which usually carries its name), so that he/she can capture the anaphoric relation and understand the sentence. This aspect emphasises the need for semantic information as part of the anaphora resolution process.

Another aspect affecting the anaphoric relations in biomedical texts are the writing conventions adopted in the biomedical domain to distinguish between the mention of a gene name and the mention of the protein encoded by that gene. The most usual convention is writing gene names with lowercase italicised letters and protein names with non-italicised uppercase letters. The existence of such conventions allows for constructions where the reader keeps the conventions in mind to understand the text, as below.

(3) "Drosophila has recently been shown also to have a CED-4/Apaf-1 homolog, named **Dark/HAC-1/Dapaf-1**. ... Loss of function mutations in ***dark/hac-1/dapaf-1*** result in ..."

Among the associative cases present in biomedical text, we were able to distinguish two main types of relations. The first, which we call "biotype" relations, are associative relations between biomedical entities with different semantic types, which we call biotypes (e.g. gene, gene product, part of gene). This is the case of Example 2 and 3[2]. If we take into account the specific biotype of the entities that are involved in a biotype relation, it is possible to determine a WordNet-like semantic relation behind the anaphora relation. For example, a biotype relation between a 'gene' and a 'variant' of gene can be considered an hyponymy relation, the relation between a 'gene' and a transcript (part of gene) can be seen as a meronymy relation.

The second type of associative relation is more common to other domains as well, we call it "set-member" relation. It consists of cases where the anaphor refers to a set that contains the antecedent, or vice-versa, as in Examples 4 and 5.

(4) ... **ced-4** and **ced-9** ... **the genes** ...

(5) ... **the mammalian anti-apoptotic protein Bcl-2** ... **Bcl-2 family** ...

3 The resolution model

Our probabilistic model aims to find the closest coreferent and/or associative antecedent for all non-pronominal NPs that refer to biomedical entities. Among non-pronominal NPs we distinguish proper names, definite NPs (e.g. "the gene"), demonstrative NPs (e.g. "this gene"), indefinite NPs (e.g. "a gene"), quantified NPs (e.g. "four genes", "some genes") and other NPs.

We consider the three classes of anaphoric relations mentioned above: coreferent, associative biotype, and associative set-member.

We have chosen 11 features to describe the anaphoric relations between two noun phrases. The features are presented in Table 1. Most features are domain-independent, while one, *gp*, is

[1]About 3% of the noun phrases according to the corpus presented in Section 4.

[2]Associative relations between proper names are not known to happen in other domains, and are made possible in the biomedical domain given the existence of naming conventions.

specific for the biomedical domain. Our feature set covers the basic aspects that influence anaphoric relations: the form of the anaphor's NP, string matching, semantic class matching, number agreement, and distance.

Given these features, for each antecedent candidate a of an anaphor A, we compute the probability P of an specific class of anaphoric relation C between a and A. P is defined as follows:

$$P(C = \text{`class'} | f_A, f_a, hm_{a,A}, hmm_{a,A}, mm_{a,A}, num_{a,A}, sr_a, bm_{a,A}, gp_{a,A}, d_{a,A}, dm_{a,A})$$

For each pair of a given anaphor and an antecedent candidate we compute P for C='coreferent', C='biotype', and C='set-member'. We also compute C='none', that represents the probability of no relation between the NPs.

We decompose the probability P and assume independence among some of the features in order to handle the sparseness of the training data. In the following equations, we omit the subscripted indexes of the relational features for clarity.

$$P(C|f_A, f_a, hm, hmm, mm, num, sr, bm, gp, d, dm) = \frac{P(C)P(f_A, f_a, hm, hmm, mm, num, sr, bm, gp, d, dm|C)}{P(f_A, f_a, hm, hmm, mm, num, sr, bm, gp, d, dm)} \quad (1)$$

Equation 1 is obtained by applying Bayes' theorem to the initial equation. $P(C)$ is the prior probability of each class, it will encode the distribution of the classes in the training data. As the denominator contains feature values that change according to the candidate being considered, we cannot eliminate it in the usual fashion, so we keep it in order to normalise P across all candidates. From this equation, we then selectively apply the chain rule to both numerator and denominator until we get to the following equation:

$$= \frac{\begin{array}{c} P(C)\ P(f_A|C)\ P(f_a|C, f_A)\ P(d, dm|C, f_A, f_a) \\ P(sr|C, f_A, f_a, d, dm)\ P(bm, gp|C, f_A, f_a, d, dm, sr) \\ P(num|C, f_A, f_a, d, dm, sr, bm, gp) \\ P(hm, hmm, mm|C, f_A, f_a, d, dm, sr, bm, gp, num) \end{array}}{\begin{array}{c} P(f_A)\ P(f_a|f_A)\ P(d, dm|f_A, f_a) \\ P(sr|f_A, f_a, d, dm)\ P(bm, gp|f_A, f_a, d, dm, sr) \\ P(num|f_A, f_a, d, dm, sr, bm, gp) \\ P(hm, hmm, mm|f_A, f_a, d, dm, sr, bm, gp, num) \end{array}} \quad (2)$$

Following the decomposition, we eliminate some of the dependencies among the features that we consider unnecessary[3]. We consider that the lexical features hm, hmm, and mm are not dependent on distance d or dm, nor on sr, gp or num, so:

$$P(hm, hmm, mm|C, f_A, f_a, d, dm, sr, bm, gp, num) \propto P(hm, hmm, mm|C, f_A, f_a, bm)$$

We model num as independent from d, dm, sr, bm, and gp, so:

$$P(num|C, f_A, f_a, d, dm, sr, bm, gp) \propto P(num|C, f_A, f_a)$$

We also assume the semantic features bm, and gp as independent from all features but C:

$$P(bm, gp|C, f_A, f_a, d, dm, sr) \propto P(bm, gp|C)$$

We also assume sr to be independent of f_A and f_a:

$$P(sr|C, f_A, f_a, d, dm) \propto P(sr|C, d, dm)$$

The final equation then becomes:

$$P(C|f_A, f_a, hm, hmm, mm, num, sr, bm, gp, d, dm) = \frac{\begin{array}{c} P(C)\ P(f_A|C)\ P(f_a|C, f_A)\ P(d, dm|C, f_A, f_a) \\ P(sr|C, d, dm)\ P(bm, gp|C)\ P(num|C, f_A, f_a) \\ P(hm, hmm, mm|C, f_A, f_a, bm) \end{array}}{\begin{array}{c} P(f_A)\ P(f_a|f_A)\ P(d, dm|f_A, f_a) \\ P(sr|d, dm)\ P(bm, gp)\ P(num|f_A, f_a) \\ P(hm, hmm, mm|f_A, f_a, bm) \end{array}} \quad (3)$$

4 Training

There are very few biomedical corpora annotated with anaphora information, and all of them are built from paper abstracts (Cohen et al., 2005), instead of full papers. As anaphora is a phenomenon that develops through a text, we believe that short abstracts are not the best source to work with and decided to concentrate on full papers.

In order to collect the statistics to train our model, we have manually annotated anaphoric relations between biomedical entities in 5 full-text articles (approx. 33,300 words)[4], which are part of the Drosophila molecular biology literature. The corpus and annotation process are described in (Gasperin et al., 2007). To the best of our knowledge, this corpus is the first corpus of biomedical full-text articles to be annotated with anaphora information.

[3]For brevity, we only show this process for the numerator, although the same is assumed for the denominator.

[4]Corpus available via the FlySlip project website http://www.wiki.cl.cam.ac.uk/rowiki/NaturalLanguage/FlySlip

Feature	Possible values
f_A	Form of noun phrase of the anaphor A: 'pn', 'defnp', 'demnp', 'indefnp', 'quantnp', or 'np'.
f_a	Form of noun phrase of the antecedent candidate a: same values as for f_A.
$hm_{a,A}$	Head-noun matching: 'yes' if the anaphor's and the candidate's head nouns match, 'no' otherwise.
$hmm_{a,A}$	Head-modifier matching: 'yes' if the anaphor's head noun matches any of the candidate's pre-modifiers, or vice-versa, 'no' otherwise.
$mm_{a,A}$	Modifier matching: 'yes' if anaphor and candidate have at least one head modifier in common, 'no' otherwise.
$num_{a,A}$	Number agreement: 'yes' if anaphor and candidate agree in number, 'no' otherwise.
$sr_{a,A}$	Syntactic relation between anaphor and candidate: 'none', 'apposition', 'subj-obj', 'pp', and few others.
$bm_{a,A}$	Biotype matching: 'yes' if anaphor's and candidate's biotype (semantic class) match, 'no' otherwise.
$gp_{a,A}$	is biotype *gene* or *product*? 'yes' if the anaphor biotype or candidate biotype is *gene* or *product*, 'no' otherwise. This feature is mainly to distinguish which pairs can hold biotype relations.
$d_{a,A}$	Distance in sentences between the anaphor and the candidate.
$dm_{a,A}$	Distance in number of entities (markables) between the anaphor and the candidate.

Table 1: Feature set

Before annotating anaphora, we have preprocessed the articles in order to (1) tag gene names, (2) identify all NPs, and (3) classify the NPs according to their domain type, which we call biotype. To tag all gene names in the corpus, we have applied the gene name recogniser developed by Vlachos et al. (2006). To identify all NPs, their subconstituents (head, modifiers, determiner) and broader pre- and post-modification patterns, we have used the RASP parser (Briscoe et al., 2006). To classify the NPs according to their type in biomedical terms, we have adopted the Sequence Ontology (SO)[5] (Eilbeck and Lewis, 2004). SO is a fine-grained ontology, which contains the names of practically all entities that participate in genomic sequences, besides the relations among these entities (e.g. is-a, part-of, derived-from relations). We derived from SO seven biotypes to be used to classify the entities in the text, namely: "gene", "gene product", "part of gene", "part of product", "gene variant", "gene subtype", and "gene supertype". We also created the biotype "other-bio" to be associated with noun phrases that contain a gene name (identified by the gene name recogniser) but whose head noun does not fit any of the other biotypes. All NPs were tagged with their biotypes, and NPs for which no biotypes were found were excluded.

The gene-name tags, NP boundaries and biotypes resulting from the preprocessing phase were revised and corrected by hand before the anaphoric relations were annotated.

For each biotyped NP we annotated its closest coreferent antecedent (if found) and its closest associative antecedent (if found), from one of the associative classes. From our annotation, we can infer coreference chains by merging the coreferent links between mentions of a same entity.

The annotated relations, and the features derived from them, are used as training data for the probabilistic model above. We have also considered negative training samples, which result from the absence of an anaphoric relation between a NP that precedes an anaphoric expression and was not marked as its antecedent (nor marked as part of the same coreference chain of its antecedent). The negative samples outnumber considerably the number of positive samples (annotated cases). Table 2 presents the distribution of the cases among the classes of anaphora relations.

We note that around 80% of the definite NPs are anaphoric in our corpus, instead of the 50% presented in (Vieira and Poesio, 2000) for newspaper texts. Nearly all demonstrative NPs (93%) are anaphoric. More than 70% of the proper names take part in coreference relations, as they inherently refer to a specific named entity, but nevertheless 5% of them take part in associative biotype relations, due to the fact that a gene and the protein it synthesizes usually share the same name. 44% of quantified NPs take part in set-member relations, as they usually refer to more than one entity. Finally 51% of indefinite NPs are discourse new.

To balance the ratio between positive and negative training samples, we have clustered the negative samples and kept only a portion of each cluster, proportional to its size. All negative samples that have the same values for all features are grouped together (consequently, a cluster is formed by a set of identical samples) and only $\frac{1}{10}$ of each cluster members is kept, resulting in 85,314 negative samples. This way, small clusters (with less than 10 members), which

[5]http://www.sequenceontology.org/

Class/NPs	pn	defnp	demnp	indefnp	quantnp	other np	Total
coreferent	689	429	70	40	54	396	1678
biotype	43	102	3	8	4	114	274
set-member	151	126	26	14	68	158	543
discourse new	63	107	0	72	38	156	436
none	873,731						

Table 2: Training instances, according to anaphoric class and to NP form

are likely to represent noisy samples (similar to positive ones), are eliminated, and bigger clusters are shrunk; however the shape of the distribution of the negative samples is preserved. For example, our biggest cluster (feature values are: f_A='pn', f_a='pn', hm='no', hmm='no', mm='no', bm='yes', gp='yes', num='yes', sr='none', d='16<', dm='50<') with 33,998 instances is reduced to 3,399 – still considerably more numerous than any positive sample.

Other works have used a different strategy to reduce the imbalance between positive and negative samples (Soon et al., 2001; Ng and Cardie, 2002; Strube et al., 2002), where only samples composed by a negative antecedent that is closer than the annotated one are considered. We compare the performance of both strategies in Section 5.1 and show that ours is more effective. The higher the number of negative samples, the higher the precision of the resolution, but the lower the recall.

5 Results

Given the small size of our corpus, we did not hold out a test set. Instead, we have measured the average performance achieved by the model in a 10-fold cross-validation setting, using the whole of the annotated corpus.

We consider as antecedent candidates all noun phrases that precede the anaphor. For a given anaphor, we first select as antecedent according to each anaphora class the candidate with the highest value for P for that class. We also compute $P(C=\text{'none'})$ for all candidates. If $P(C=\text{'coreferent'}) > P(C=\text{'none'})$ for the selected coreferent antecedent, it is kept as the resulting antecedent. The same is tested for the selected associative antecedent with the highest probability, independent of the type of associative class. For set-member cases, where an anaphor can have multiple antecedents, if more than one candidate has an equally high probability, all these candidates are kept. When no coreferent or associative antecedent is found (or when $P(C=\text{'none'})$ is higher on both cases) the anaphor is classified as discourse new.

Table 3 presents the performance scores we achieved for each anaphora class. The first column, 'perfect', shows the result of a strict evaluation, where we consider as correct all pairs that match exactly an antecedent-anaphor pair in the annotated data. On the other hand, column 'relaxed' treats as correct also the pairs where the assigned antecedent is not the exact match in the annotated data but is coreferent with it.

It is clear that the results for coreferent cases are much better than for associative cases, but the latter are known to be more challenging. On top of that, the 'relaxed' column shows considerable improvements in comparison to 'perfect'. That means that several anaphors are being linked to the correct coreference chain, despite not being linked to the closest antecedent. This happens mainly in cases where there is no string matching between the closest antecedent and the anaphor, causing an earlier mention of the same entity with matching head and/or modifiers to get higher probability. We believe we can approximate 'perfect' to 'relaxed' results if we extend the string matching features to represent the whole coreference chain, that is, consider a positive matching when the anaphor match any of the elements in a chain, similarly to the idea presented in (Yang et al., 2004).

We believe that the lower overall performance for associative cases is due to the difficulty of selecting features that capture all aspects involved in associative relations. Our set of features is clearly failing to cover some of these aspects, and a deeper feature study should be the best way to boost the scores. However, despite lower, these performance

Class	Perfect			Relaxed		
	P	R	F	P	R	F
coreferent	56.3	54.7	55.5	69.4	67.4	68.3
biotype	28.5	35.0	31.4	31.2	37.9	34.2
set-member	35.4	38.2	36.7	38.5	41.5	40.0
discourse new	44.3	53.4	48.4	44.3	53.4	48.4

Table 3: Performance of the probabilistic model

scores are higher that the ones from previous approaches for newspaper texts, which used for instance the WordNet (Poesio et al., 1997) or the Internet (Bunescu, 2003) as source of semantic knowledge.

We have analysed our features and observed that the string matching features hm, hmm, and mm, the number agreement feature num, biotype matching bm, and distance in markables dm are the core features and achieve reasonable performance. However, f_A and f_a play an important role, they increase the precision of coreferent cases and boost considerably the performance of the associative ones. This is due to the different distribution of NP types across the relations as shown is Table 2. The remaining features focused on specific cases: gp improved biotype recall, by boosting the probability of a biotype relation when anaphor or candidate had specific biotypes; and sr improved precision and recall of coreferent cases.

Table 4 shows the 'perfect' performance scores according to each class of NP. The resolution of proper names achieves the highest scores among all types of NPs for most classes. That is due to their limited structure, since proper names usually do not have elaborated pre-modification or modification at all, so our string matching features carried simpler patterns for these NPs. Indefinite and quantified NPs achieved the lowest scores for coreferent cases, since the highest percentage of training instances for these NPs are not coreferent (as seen in Table 2). Indefinite NPs, as expected, have the best scores for discourse new cases.

5.1 Comparing to other approaches

We have tried training our probabilistic model using a different strategy than the one described in Section 4 for selecting negative samples. This strategy consists of selecting only the negative samples that occur between the anaphor and its coreferent antecedent, not considering candidates that are further away than the antecedent. This strategy was first used for anaphora resolution by Soon et al. (2001). Column 'prob+closest' on Table 5 shows the performance scores. In our dataset, this strategy was able to reduce the number of negative samples to about $\frac{1}{3}$ of its size, while our strategy reduces it to $\frac{1}{10}$. The larger number of negative samples increases the precision scores and reduces the recall scores for all positive classes, while the opposite happens for the negative class, which defines the discourse new scores. We reckon that the considerable drop on recall numbers for the associative cases would make the system less viable, while the low precision for discourse new cases shows that many anaphoric cases are left unresolved. We view our strategy, based on the clustering of negative samples and consecutive cluster size reduction, to be more effective at proportionally eliminating negative samples that are less frequent and that are more likely to be noisy.

We compare our model to a rule-based baseline system that we have previously developed. The baseline system (Gasperin, 2006) for each anaphoric expression: 1) selects as coreferent antecedent the closest preceding NP that has the same head noun, same biotype and agrees in number with the anaphor, and 2) selects as associative antecedent the closest preceding NP that has the same head noun, same biotype but disagrees in number with the anaphor, or that has the same head noun or a modifier matching the anaphor head (or vice-versa) or matching modifiers, agrees in number but has different biotypes. The baseline system does not distinguish between different types of associative cases, although it aims to cover biotype and set-member cases. If no antecedent that matches these criteria is found, the anaphor is considered discourse new. Column 'baseline' on Table 5 shows the performance scores for the baseline system. The scores for coreferent cases are reasonable, despite being below our probabilistic model, while the scores for associative cases, especially recall, are considerably lower. The baseline system relies on some sort of string matching between anaphor and antecedent, and is not able to infer a relation between expressions when the matching does not happen. That is one of the main aspects that the probabilistic system tries to overcome by weighting the contribution of all features.

We also compared our model to a system based on decision trees, since this approach has been taken by several corpus-based anaphora resolution systems (Soon et al., 2001; Ng and Cardie, 2002; Strube et al., 2002). We have induced a decision tree using the C4.5 algorithm implemented in the Weka tool (Witten and Frank, 2005); we have used the same features used for our probabilistic model. We selected as the antecedent the candidate which is the closest one to the anaphor for which a class other then 'none' is assigned by the decision tree. The 'perfect' and 'relaxed' scores for C4.5 are pre-

Class	coreferent			biotype			set-member			discourse new		
	P	R	F	P	R	F	P	R	F	P	R	F
pn	77.5	71.9	74.6	26.8	25.5	26.1	53.7	65.7	59.1	35.1	59.3	44.1
defnp	48.0	47.3	47.6	26.3	28.1	27.2	29.2	26.1	27.6	38.8	51.8	44.4
demnp	57.8	48.5	52.8	-	-	-	71.4	57.6	63.8	-	-	-
indefnp	27.0	34.2	30.2	14.2	12.5	13.3	21.0	28.5	24.2	63.4	54.7	58.8
quantnp	11.2	12.9	12.0	-	-	-	28.5	37.6	32.5	37.1	34.2	35.6
other np	41.3	41.4	41.4	30.9	48.2	37.7	19.3	19.4	19.4	49.7	56.0	52.6

Table 4: Performance of the probabilistic model ('perfect') per NP form

sented in the last two columns of Table 5. We note that the difference between 'perfect' and 'relaxed' scores is not as large as for our probabilistic model; that shows that decision trees are more often getting even the coreference chain wrong, not just the closest antecedent. We assume this is due to the lack of ranking among the candidates, since we adopt the default strategy of selecting the closest candidate that gets a positive class according to the tree.

The main disadvantage of both the baseline and decision tree systems when compared to the probabilistic model, besides the lower performance, is that they do not provide a probability assigned to each decision they make, which makes it impossible to know how confident the model is for different cases and to take advantage of that information to improve the system. This aspect also makes it difficult to develop a consistent strategy for returning multiple antecedents for set-member cases, since there is no obvious way to do it.

6 Related work

We are not aware of any learning-based system which has dealt with coreferent as well as associative cases of anaphora.

Viera and Poesio (2000) have developed a heuristic-based system for coreferent and associative anaphora resolution of definite NPs in newspaper texts, and have reached 62% recall and 83% precision for direct anaphora (coreferent cases with same head noun), but poor performance for bridging cases (associative cases + coreferent cases with different head nouns) using WordNet as souce of semantic knowledge.

Ng and Cardie (2002), extending the work of Soon et al. (2001), have developed a machine-learning system just for coreference resolution of all types of NPs, also on newspaper texts. Their best results were 64.2% recall and 78.0% precision.

The best-known system to resolve anaphora in the biomedical domain is the work of Castaño et al. (2002), who developed a salience-based system for resolution of coreferent cases. It seeks to resolve pronouns and nominal (which they call sortal) anaphora. As a source of semantic knowledge, they have used the UMLS Semantic Network types[6], which they report to be too coarse grained, and assume that a finer-grained typing strategy would help to increase the precision of the resolution system. They achieved 74% precision and 75% recall on a very small test set.

Yang et al. (2004) implemented a machine-learning approach to coreference resolution similar to Ng and Cardie's, and evaluated it on a portion of the GENIA corpus, which is tagged with semantic information based on the GENIA Ontology[7]. They achieved recall of 80.2% and precision of 77.4%.

Both the Castaño et al. and Yang et al. systems have been developed based on abstracts of biomedical articles, instead of full-text articles, which involve only restricted use of anaphora.

7 Conclusion and future work

We have presented a probabilistic model for resolving anaphoric NPs in biomedical texts. We are not aware of previous works which have dealt with coreferent and associative anaphora in the biomedical domain. Our model, despite being simple and being trained on a very small corpus, coped well with its task of finding antecedents for coreferent and associative cases of anaphora, and was able to achieve state-of-the-art performance. It has outperformed our baseline system and a decision-tree-based system using the same set of features.

Our model returns a probability for each classification it makes, and this can be used as a confidence measure that can be exploited to improve the system itself or by external applications.

Due to our small corpus, we had to limit the

[6]http://www.nlm.nih.gov/research/umls/

[7]http://www-tsujii.is.s.u-tokyo.ac.jp/GENIA/

Class	Prob+Closest			Baseline			C4.5			C4.5 relaxed		
	P	R	F	P	R	F	P	R	F	P	R	F
coreferent	66.2	50.0	56.9	47.0	57.6	51.8	49.6	58.1	53.5	52.7	61.6	56.8
biotype	31.1	10.1	15.2	28.6	10.7	15.6	21.7	28.5	24.6	22.9	29.9	26.0
set-member	46.3	17.5	25.4				28.5	31.3	29.8	30.4	33.3	31.8
discourse new	31.3	88.1	46.2	37.3	30.2	33.4	48.5	32.5	38.9	48.5	32.5	38.9

Table 5: Performance of other models

number and the complexity of the features we use, since the more features, the more sparse the data, and the more training data needed. However, we aim to expand the feature set with more fine-grained features.

Our current work involves using the probabilistic model presented here as part of an active learning framework. The confidence of the model for each decision (probability) is used to selectively gather more samples from unlabelled data and iteratively improve the performance of the system.

The probabilistic model is intended to replace the baseline system in a tool designed to help biology researchers to curate scientific papers (Karamanis et al., 2008).

Acknowledgements

This work is part of the BBSRC-funded FlySlip project. Caroline Gasperin is funded by a CAPES award from the Brazilian government.

References

Briscoe, Edward J., John Carroll, and Rebecca Watson. 2006. The second release of the RASP system. In *Proceedings of ACL-COLING 06*, Sydney, Australia.

Bunescu, Razvan. 2003. Associative anaphora resolution: A web-based approach. In *Proceedings of EACL 2003 - Workshop on The Computational Treatment of Anaphora*, Budapest.

Castaño, José, Jason Zhang, and James Pustejovsky. 2002. Anaphora resolution in biomedical literature. In *Proceedings of International Symposium on Reference Resolution for NLP 2002*, Alicante, Spain.

Cohen, K. Bretonnel, Lynne Fox, Philip Ogren, and Lawrence Hunter. 2005. Corpus design for biomedical natural language processsing. In *Proceedings of the ACL-ISMB Workshop on Linking Biological Literature, Ontologies and Databases*, Detroit.

Eilbeck, Karen and Suzanna E. Lewis. 2004. Sequence ontology annotation guide. *Comparative and Functional Genomics*, 5:642–647.

Gasperin, Caroline, Nikiforos Karamanis, and Ruth Seal. 2007. Annotation of anaphoric relations in biomedical full-text articles using a domain-relevant scheme. In *Proceedings of DAARC 2007*, Lagos, Portugal.

Gasperin, Caroline. 2006. Semi-supervised anaphora resolution in biomedical texts. In *Proceedings of BioNLP'06*, New York.

Ge, Niyu, John Hale, and Eugene Charniak. 1998. A statistical approach to anaphora resolution. In *Proceedings of the Sixth Workshop on Very Large Corpora - COLING-ACL'98*, Montreal, Canada.

Karamanis, Nikiforos, Ruth Seal, Ian Lewin, Peter McQuilton, Andreas Vlachos, Caroline Gasperin, Rachel Drysdale, and Ted Briscoe. 2008. Natural language processing in aid of flybase curators. *BMC Bioinformatics*, 9(193).

Ng, Vincent and Claire Cardie. 2002. Improving machine learning approaches to coreference resolution. In *Proceedings of ACL 2002*, Philadelphia.

Poesio, Massimo, Renata Vieira, and Simone Teufel. 1997. Resolving bridging descriptions in unrestricted texts. In *Proceedings of the Workshop on Operational Factors In Practical, Robust Anaphora Resolution for Unrestricted Texts*, Madrid.

Soon, Wee Meng, Hwee Tou Ng, and Daniel Chung Yong Lim. 2001. A machine learning approach to coreference resolution of noun phrases. *Computational Linguistics*, 27(4):521–544.

Strube, Michael, Stefan Rapp, and Christoph Müller. 2002. The influence of minimum edit distance on reference resolution. In *Proceedings of the EMNLP 2002*, Philadelphia.

Vieira, Renata and Massimo Poesio. 2000. An empirically-based system for processing definite descriptions. *Computational Linguistics*, 26(4):525–579.

Vlachos, Andreas and Caroline Gasperin. 2006. Bootstrapping and evaluating named entity recognition in the biomedical domain. In *Proceedings of BioNLP at HLT-NAACL 2006*, pages 138–145, New York.

Witten, Ian H. and Eibe Frank. 2005. *Data Mining: Practical machine learning tools and techniques, 2nd Edition*. Morgan Kaufmann, San Francisco.

Yang, X., J. Su, G. Zhou, and C. L. Tan. 2004. An NP-cluster based approach to coreference resolution. In *Proceedings of COLING 2004*, Geneva, Switzerland.

Instance-Based Ontology Population Exploiting Named-Entity Substitution

Claudio Giuliano
Fondazione Bruno Kessler
Trento, Italy
giuliano@fbk.eu

Alfio Gliozzo
Laboratory for Applied Ontology
Italian National Research Council
Rome, Italy
alfio.gliozzo@cnr.istc.it

Abstract

We present an approach to ontology population based on a lexical substitution technique. It consists in estimating the plausibility of sentences where the named entity to be classified is substituted with the ones contained in the training data, in our case, a partially populated ontology. Plausibility is estimated by using Web data, while the classification algorithm is instance-based. We evaluated our method on two different ontology population tasks. Experiments show that our solution is effective, outperforming existing methods, and it can be applied to practical ontology population problems.

1 Introduction

Semantic Web and knowledge management applications require to populate the concepts of their domain ontologies with individuals and find their relationships from various data sources, including databases and natural language texts. As the extensional part of an ontology (the ABox) is often manually populated, this activity can be very time-consuming, requiring considerable human effort. The development of automatic techniques for ontology population is then a crucial research area. Natural language processing techniques are natural candidates to solve this problem as most of the data contained in the Web and in the companies' intranets is free text. Information extraction (IE) is commonly employed to (semi-) automate such a task.

Current state-of-the-art IE systems are mostly based on general purpose supervised machine learning techniques (e.g., kernel methods). However, supervised systems achieve acceptable accuracy only if they are supplied with a sufficiently large amount of training data, usually consisting of manually annotated texts. Consequently, they can be only used to populate top-level concepts of ontologies (e.g., people, locations, organizations). In fact, when the number of subclasses increases the number of annotated documents required to find sufficient positive examples for all subclasses becomes too large to be practical. As domain ontologies usually contain hundreds of concepts arranged in deep class/subclass hierarchies, alternative techniques have to be found to recognize fine-grained distinctions (e.g., to categorize people as scientists and scientists as physicists, mathematicians, biologists, etc.).

In this paper, we present an approach to the classification of named entities into fine-grained ontological categories based on a method successfully employed in lexical substitution.[1] In particular, we predict the fine-grained category of a named entity, previously recognized, by simply estimating the plausibility of sentences where the entity to be classified is substituted with the ones contained in the training data, in our case, a partially populated ontology.

In most of the cases, ontologies are partially populated during the development phase and after that the annotation cost is practically negligible, making this method highly attractive in many applicative domains. This allows us to define an instance-based learning approach for fine-grained

© 2008. Licensed under the *Creative Commons Attribution-Noncommercial-Share Alike 3.0 Unported* license (http://creativecommons.org/licenses/by-nc-sa/3.0/). Some rights reserved.

[1] Lexical substitution consists in identifying the most likely alternatives (substitutes) of a target word given its context (McCarthy, 2002).

entity categorization that exploits the Web to collect evidence of the new entities and does not require any labeled text for supervision, only a partially populated ontology. Therefore, it can be used in different domains and languages to enrich an existing ontology with new entities extracted from texts by a named-entity recognition system and/or databases.

We evaluated our method on the benchmark proposed by Tanev and Magnini (2006) to provide a fair comparison with other approaches, and on a general purpose ontology of people derived from WordNet (Fellbaum, 1998) to perform a more extensive evaluation. Specifically, the experiments were designed to investigate the effectiveness of our approach at different levels of generality and with different amounts of training data. The results show that it significantly outperforms the baseline methods and, where a comparison is possible, other approaches and achieves a good performance with a small number of examples per category. Error analysis shows that most of the misclassification errors are due to the finer-grained distinctions between instances of the same super-class.

2 Lexical Substitutability and Ontology Population

Our approach is based on the assumption that entities that occur in similar contexts belong to the same concept(s). This can be seen as a special case of the distributional hypothesis, that is, terms that occur in the same contexts tend to have similar meanings (Harris, 1954).

If our assumption is correct, then given an instance in different contexts one can substitute it with another of the same ontological type (i.e., of the same category) and probably generate true statements. In fact, most of the predicates that can be asserted for an instance of a particular category can also be asserted for other instances of the same category. For instance, the sentence "Ayrton Senna is a F1 Legend" preserves its truthfulness when Ayrton Senna is replaced with Michael Schumacher, while it is false when Ayrton Senna is replaced with the MotoGP champion Valentino Rossi.

For our purposes, the Web provides a simple and effective solution to the problem of determining whether a statement is true or false. Due to the high redundancy of the Web, the high frequency of a statement generated by a substitution usually provides sufficient evidence for its truth, allowing us to easily implement an automatic method for fine-grained entity classification. Following this intuition, we developed an ontology population technique adopting pre-classified entities as training data (i.e., a partially populated ontology) to classify new ones.

When a new instance has to be classified, we first collect snippets containing it from the Web. Then, for each snippet, we substitute the new instance with each of the training instances. The snippets play a crucial role in our approach because we expect that they provide the features that characterize the category to which the entity belongs. Thus, it is important to collect a sufficiently large number of snippets to capture the features that allow a fine-grained classification.

To estimate the correctness of each substitution, we calculate a plausibility score using a modified version of the lexical substitution algorithm introduced in Giuliano et al. (2007), that assigns higher scores to the substitutions that generate highly frequent sentences on the Web. In particular, this technique ranks a given list of synonyms according to a similarity metric based on the occurrences in the Web 1T 5-gram corpus,[2] which specify n-grams frequencies in a large Web sample. This technique achieved the state-of-the-art performance on the English Lexical Substitution task at SemEval 2007 (McCarthy and Navigli, 2007).

Finally, on the basis of these plausibility scores, the algorithm assigns the new instance to the category whose individuals show a closer linguistic behavior (i.e., they can be substituted generating plausible statements).

3 The IBOP algorithm

In this section, we describe the algorithmic and mathematical details of our approach. The instance-based ontology population (IBOP) algorithm is an instance-based supervised machine learning approach.[3] The proposed algorithm is summarized as follows:

Step 1 For each candidate instance i, we collect the first N snippets containing i from the Web. For instance, 3 snippets for the candidate instance Ayrton Senna are "The death of Ayrton Senna at

[2] `http://www.ldc.upenn.edu/Catalog/CatalogEntry.jsp?catalogId=LDC2006T13`.

[3] An analogy between instance-based learning methods and our approach is left to future work.

the 1994 San Marino GP", "triple world champion Ayrton Senna", and "about F1 legend Ayrton Senna".

Step 2 Then, for each retrieved snippet q_k ($1 \leqslant k \leqslant N$), we derive a list of hypothesis phrases by replacing i with each training instance j from the given ontology. For instance, from the snippet "about F1 legend Ayrton Senna", we derive "about F1 legend Michael Schumacher" and "about F1 legend Valentino Rossi", assuming to have the former classified as F1 driver and the latter as MotoGP driver.

Step 3 For each hypothesis phrase h_j, we calculate the plausibility score s_j using a variant of the scoring procedure defined in Giuliano et al. (2007). In our case, s_j is given by the sum of the pointwise mutual information (PMI) of all the n-grams ($1 < n \leqslant 5$) that contain j divided by the self-information of the right and left contexts.[4] Dividing by the self-information allows us to penalize the hypotheses that have contexts with a low information content, such as sequences of stop words. The frequency of the n-grams is estimated from the Web 1T 5-gram corpus. For instance, from the hypothesis phrase "about F1 legend Michael Schumacher", we generate and score the following n-grams: "legend Michael Schumacher", "F1 legend Michael Schumacher", and "about F1 legend Michael Schumacher".

Step 4 To obtain an overall score s_c for the category c, we sum the scores obtained from each training instance of category c for all snippets, as defined in Equation 1.

$$s_c = \sum_{k=1}^{N} \sum_{l=1}^{M} s_l, \tag{1}$$

where M is the number of training instances for the category c.[5]

Step 5 Finally, the instance i is categorized with that concept having the maximum score:

$$c^* = \begin{cases} \operatorname{argmax}_c s_c & \text{if } s_c \geqslant \theta; \\ \emptyset & \text{otherwise.} \end{cases} \tag{2}$$

[4]The pointwise mutual information is defined as the log of the deviation between the observed frequency of a n-gram and the probability of that n-gram if it were independent and the self-information is a measure of the information content of a n-gram ($-\log p$, where p is the probability of the n-gram).

[5]Experiments using the sum of average or argmax score yield worst results.

Where a higher value of the parameter θ increases precision but degrades recall.

4 Benchmarks

For evaluating the proposed algorithm and comparing it with other algorithms, we adopted the two benchmarks described below.

4.1 Tanev and Magnini Benchmark

Tanev and Magnini (2006) proposed a benchmark ontology that consists of two high-level named entity categories (i.e., person and location) both having five fine-grained subclasses (i.e., mountain, lake, river, city, and country as subtypes of location; statesman, writer, athlete, actor, and inventor are subtypes of person). WordNet and Wikipedia were used as primary data sources for populating the evaluation ontology. In total, the ontology is populated with 280 instances which were not ambiguous (with respect to the ontology). We extracted the training set from WordNet, collecting 20 examples per sub-category, of course, not already contained in the test set.

4.2 People Ontology

The benchmark described in the previous section is clearly a toy problem, and it does not allow us to evaluate the effectiveness of our method, in particular the ability to perform fine-grained classifications. To address this problem, we developed a larger ontology of people (called People Ontology), characterized by a complex taxonomy having multiple layers and containing thousands of instances. This ontology has been extracted from WordNet, that we adapted to our purpose after a re-engineering phase. In fact, we need a formal specification of the conceptualizations that are expressed by means of WordNet's synsets, and, in particular, we need a clear distinction between individuals and categories, as well as a robust categorization mechanism to assign individuals to general concepts.

This result can be achieved by following the directives defined by Gangemi et al. (2003) for OntoWordNet, in which the informal WordNet semantics is re-engineered in terms of a description logic. We follow an analogous approach. Firstly, any possible instance in WordNet 1.7.1 has been identified by looking for all those synsets containing at least one word starting with a capital letter. The result is a set of instances I. All the remaining

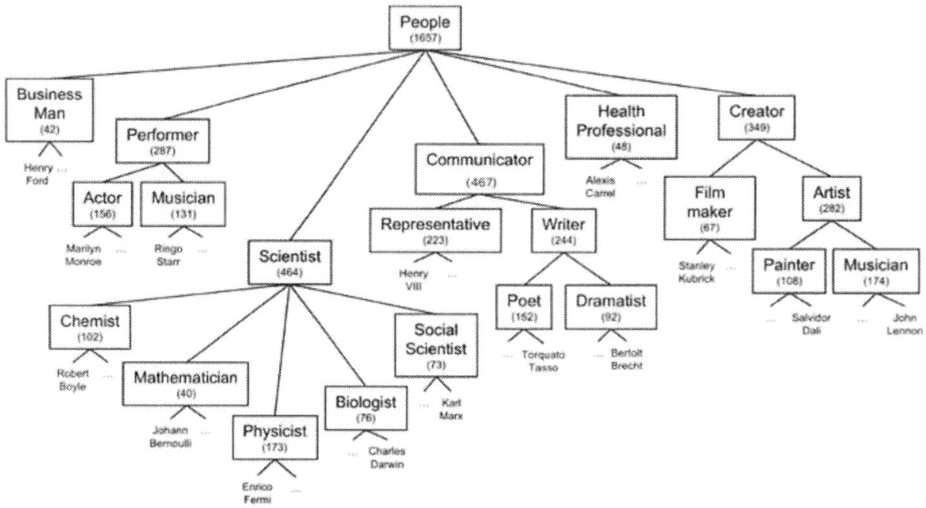

Figure 1: The taxonomy of the People Ontology extracted from WordNet 1.7.1. Numbers in brackets are the total numbers of individuals per category. Concepts that have less than 40 instances were removed.

synsets are then regarded as concepts, collected in the set C. Then, is_a relations between synsets are converted into one of the following standard OWL-DL constructs:

X subclass_of Y if X is_a Y and $X \in C$ and $Y \in C$

X instance_of Y if X is_a Y and $X \in I$ and $Y \in C$

The formal semantics of both $subclass\_of$ and $instance\_of$ is formally defined in OWL-DL. $subclass\_of$ is a transitive relation (i.e., $X subclass\_of Y$ and $Y subclass\_of Z$ implies $X subclass\_of Z$) and the $instance\_of$ relation has the following property: $X instance\_of Y$ and $Y subclass\_of Z$ implies $X instance\_of Z$.

To define the People Ontology, we selected the sub-hierarchy of WordNet representing people, identifying the corresponding top-level synset X = {*person, individual, someone, somebody, mortal, soul*}, and collecting all the classes Y such that Y is a subclass of X and all the instances I such that I is an instance of Y. We discovered that many concepts in the derived hierarchy were empty or scarcely populated. As we need a sufficient amount data to obtain statistically significant results, we eliminated the classes that contain less than 40 instances from the ontology. The derived ontology contains 1627 instances structured in 21 sub-categories (Figure 1). Finally, we randomly split its individuals into two equally sized subsets. The results reported in the following section were evaluated using two-fold cross-validation on these two subsets.

5 Evaluation

In this section, we present the performance of the IBOP algorithm on the evaluation benchmarks described in the previous section.

5.1 Experimental Setting

For each individual, we collected 100 entity mentions in their context by querying Google^{TM}. As most of them are names of celebrities, the Web provided sufficient data.[6]

We approached the population task as a standard categorization problem, trying to assign new instances to the most specific category. We measured standard precision/recall figures. In addition, we evaluated the classifier accuracy at the most abstract level, by inheriting the predictions from sub-concepts to super-concepts. For example, when an instance is assigned to a specific category (e.g., Musician), it is also (implicitly) assigned to all its super-classes (e.g., Artist and Creator). This operation is performed according to the extensional semantics of the description logic, as described in the previous section. Following this approach, we are able to evaluate the effectiveness of our algorithm at any level of generality. The micro- and macro-averaged F_1 have been evaluated by taking into account both specific and generic classes at the same time. In this way, we tend to penalize the

[6] A study of how the number of snippets N would impact the performance of the IBOP algorithm has been deferred to future work.

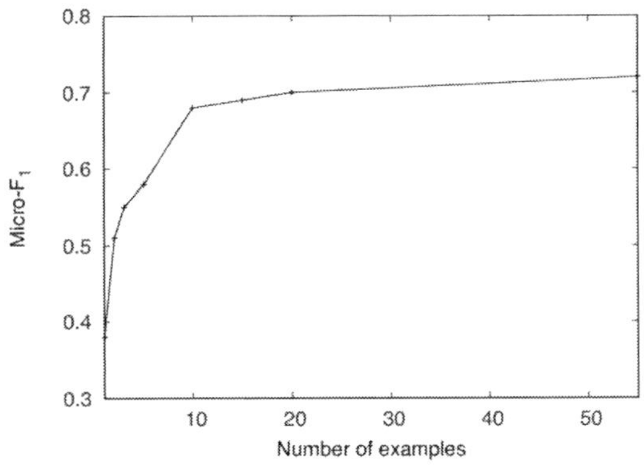

Figure 2: Learning curve on the People Ontology.

gross misclassification errors (e.g., Biologist vs. Poet), while minor errors (e.g., Poet vs. Dramatist) are less relevant. This approach is similar to the one proposed by Melamed and Resnik (2000) for a similar hierarchical categorization task.

5.2 Accuracy

Table 1 shows micro- and macro-averaged results of the proposed method obtained on the Tanev and Magnini (2006) benchmark and compares them with the class-example (Tanev and Magnini, 2006), IBLE (Giuliano and Gliozzo, 2007), and class-word (Cimiano and Völker, 2005) methods, respectively. Table 2 shows micro- and macro-averaged results of the proposed method obtained on the People Ontology and compares them with the random and most frequent baseline methods.[7] In both experiments, the IBOP algorithm was trained on 20 examples per category and setting the parameter $\theta = 0$ in Equation 2.

For the People Ontology, we performed a disaggregated evaluation, whose results are shown in Table 3, while Figure 2 shows the learning curve. The experiment was conducted setting the parameter $\theta = 0$.

System	Micro-F_1	Macro-F_1
IBOP	73	71
Class-Example	68	62
IBLE	57	47
Class-Word	42	33

Table 1: Comparison of different ontology population techniques on the Tanev and Magnini (2006) benchmark.

[7] The most frequent category has been estimated on the training data.

System	Micro-F_1	Macro-F_1
IBOP	70.1	62.3
Random	15.4	15.5
Most Frequent	20.7	3.3

Table 2: Comparison between the IBOP algorithm and the baseline methods on the People Ontology.

Class	Prec	Recall	F_1
Scientist	84.4	73.3	78.4
Physicist	63.0	39.3	48.4
Mathematician	25.0	67.5	36.5
Chemist	44.2	52.0	47.7
Biologist	62.5	13.2	21.7
Social scientist	43.1	30.1	35.5
Performer	76.5	66.9	71.4
Actor	67.5	67.9	67.7
Musician	68.1	48.9	56.9
Creator	70.6	84.5	76.9
Film Maker	52.9	68.7	59.7
Artist	72.8	85.5	78.6
Painter	74.4	86.1	79.8
Musician	68.9	81.6	74.7
Comunicator	76.4	83.1	79.6
Writer	78.6	76.6	77.6
Poet	67.4	61.2	64.1
Dramatist	65.0	70.7	67.7
Representative	84.8	76.7	80.6
Business man	47.2	40.5	43.6
Health professional	29.3	25.0	27.0
micro	69.6	70.7	70.1
macro	62.3	70.7	62.3

Table 3: Results for each category of the People Ontology.

5.3 Confusion Matrix

Table 4 shows the confusion matrix for the People Ontology task, in which the rows are ground truth classes and the columns are predictions. The experiment was conducted using 20 training examples per category and setting the parameter $\theta = 0$. The matrix has been calculated for the finer-grained categories and, then, grouped according to their top-level concepts.

5.4 Precision/Recall Tradeoff

Figure 3 shows the precision/recall curve for the People Ontology task obtained varying the parameter θ in Equation 2. The experiment was conducted using 20 training examples per category.

5.5 Discussion

The results obtained are undoubtedly satisfactory. Table 1 shows that our approach outperforms the other three methods on the Tanev and Magnini (2006) benchmark. Note that the Class-Example approach has been trained on 1194 named enti-

	Scientist					Performer		Creator			Communicator			Business	Health
	Phy	Mat	Che	Bio	Soc	Act	Mus	Fil	Pai	Mus	Poe	Dra	Rep	man	prof
Phy	68	40	25	3	11	2	0	0	3	1	7	1	7	2	3
Mat	3	27	1	0	0	0	0	1	0	0	4	0	2	1	1
Che	12	10	53	2	7	3	1	2	2	0	1	0	4	4	1
Bio	4	12	13	10	3	3	0	1	5	2	4	1	11	2	5
Soc	6	3	4	1	22	4	0	2	2	3	4	1	12	0	9
Act	3	1	2	0	0	106	6	20	0	3	2	4	7	1	1
Mus	1	1	2	0	0	16	64	5	2	28	2	2	7	0	1
Fil	0	0	0	0	0	7	0	46	0	4	1	1	4	3	1
Pai	2	1	0	0	1	1	1	2	93	3	1	0	2	1	0
Mus	1	0	0	0	0	1	16	2	3	142	1	3	2	1	2
Poe	1	2	1	0	1	2	3	3	6	12	93	20	6	1	1
Dra	0	2	1	0	0	3	0	2	2	3	9	65	1	2	2
Rep	0	6	7	0	3	6	1	0	3	2	5	0	189	1	0
Bus	3	3	6	0	0	0	1	1	0	1	2	0	6	17	2
Hea	4	0	5	0	3	3	1	0	4	2	2	2	10	0	12

Table 4: Confusion matrix for the finer-grained categories grouped according to their top-level concepts of the People Ontology.

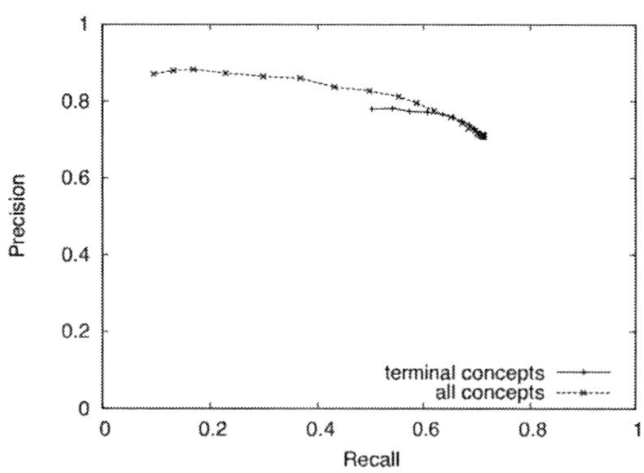

Figure 3: Precision/recall curve on the People Ontology.

ties, almost 60 examples per category, whereas we achieved the same result with around 10 examples per category. On the other hand, as Table 2 shows, the IBOP algorithm is effective in populating a more complex ontology and significantly outperforms the random and most frequent baselines.

An important characteristic of the algorithm is the small number of examples required per category. This affects both the prediction accuracy and the computation time (this is generally a common property of instance-based algorithms). Therefore, finding an optimal tradeoff between the training size and the performance is crucial. The learning curve (Figure 2) shows that the algorithm outperforms the baselines with only 1 example per category and achieves a good accuracy ($F_1 \approx 67\%$) with only 10 examples per category, while it reaches a plateau around 20 examples ($F_1 \approx 70\%$), but leaving a little room for improvement.

Table 4 shows that misclassification errors are largely distributed among categories belonging to the same super-class (i.e., the blocks on the main diagonal are more densely populated than others). As expected, the algorithm is much more accurate for the top-level concepts (i.e., Scientist, Communicator, etc.), where the category distinctions are clearer, while a further fine-grained classification, in some cases, is even difficult for human annotators. In particular, results are higher for fine-grained categories densely populated and with a small number of sibling categories (i.e., Painter and Musician). We have observed that the results on sparse categories can be made more precise by increasing the training size, generally at the expense of a lower recall.

We tried to maximize precision by varying the parameter θ in Equation 2, that is, avoiding all assignments where the plausibility score is lower than a given threshold. Figure 3 shows that the precision can be significantly enhanced ($\sim 90\%$) at the expense of poor recall ($\sim 20\%$), while the algorithm achieves 80% precision at around 50% recall.

Finally, we performed some preliminary error analysis, investigating the misclassifications in the categories Scientists and Musicians. Several errors are due to lack of information in WordNet, For example, Leonhard Euler was a mathematician and physicist, however, in WordNet, he is classified as physicist, and our system classifies him as mathematician. On the other hand, for simplicity, the algorithm returns a single category per instance, however, the test set contains many entities that are classified in more than one category. For instance, Bertolt Brecht is both poet and dramatist and the system classified him as dramatist. Another interesting case is the presence of two categories Musician, one is subclass of Performer and the other of Artist, in which, for instance, Ringo Starr is a performer while John Lennon is an artist, while the system classified both as performers.

6 Related work

Brin (1998) defined a methodology to extract information from the Web starting from a small set of seed examples, then alternately learning extraction patterns from seeds, and further seeds from patterns. Despite the fact that the evaluation was on relation extraction the method is general and might be applied to entity extraction and categorization. The approach was further extended by Agichtein and Gravano (2000). Our approach differs from theirs in that we do not learn patterns. Thus, we do not require ad hoc strategies for generating patterns and estimating their reliability, a crucial issue in these approaches as "bad" patterns may extract wrong seeds instances that in turn may generate even more inaccurate patterns in the following iteration.

Fleischman and Hovy (2002) approached the ontology population problem as a supervised classification task. They compare different machine learning algorithms, providing instances in their context as training examples as well as more global semantic information derived from topic signature and WordNet.

Alfonseca and Manandhar (2002) and Cimiano and Völker (2005) present similar approaches relying on the Harris' distributional hypothesis and the vector-space model. They assign a particular instance represented by a certain context vector to the concept corresponding to the most similar vector. Contexts are represented using lexical-syntactic features.

KnowItAll (Etzioni et al., 2005) uses a search engine and semantic patterns (similar to those defined by Hearst (1992)) to classify named entities on the Web. The approach uses simple techniques from the ontology learning field to perform extraction and then annotation. It also is able to perform very simple pattern induction, consisting of looking at n words before and n words after the occurrence of an example in the document. With pattern learning, KnowItAll becomes a bootstrapped learning system, where rules are used to learn new seeds, which in turn are used to learn new rules. A similar approach is used in C-PANKOW (Cimiano et al., 2005). Compared to KnowItAll and C-PANKOW, our approach does not need handcrafted patterns as input. They are implicitly found by substituting the training instances in the contexts of the input entities. Another key difference is that concepts in the ontology do not need to be lexicalized.

Tanev and Magnini (2006) proposed a weakly-supervised method that requires as training data a list of terms without context for each category under consideration. Given a generic syntactically parsed corpus containing at least each training entity twice, the algorithm learns, for each category, a feature vector describing the contexts where those entities occur. Then, it compares the new (unknown) entity with the so obtained feature vectors, assigning it to the most similar category. Even though we used a significantly smaller number of training instances, we obtained better results on their benchmark.

More recently, Giuliano and Gliozzo (2007) proposed an unsupervised approach based on lexical entailment, consisting in assigning an entity to the category whose lexicalization can be replaced with its occurrences in a corpus preserving the meaning. A disadvantage is that the concepts in the ontology have to be lexicalized, as they are used as training examples. Our approach is based on a similar idea, but with the main difference that an instance is substituted with other instances rather than with their category names. Considering that, in most of the cases, ontologies are partially populated during the development phase, and hence the annotation cost is marginal, our approach is a realistic alternative for practical ontology population problems.

7 Conclusions and Future Work

We have described an instance-based algorithm for automatic fine-grained categorization of named entities, previously identified by an entity recognition system or already present in a database. This method is meant to provide an effective solution to the ontology population problem. It exploits the Web or a domain corpus to collect evidence of the new instances and does not require labeled texts for supervision, but a partially populated ontology.

The experimental results show that, where a comparison is possible, our method outperforms previous methods and it can be applied to different domains and languages to (semi-) automatically enrich an existing ontology.

Future work will address the definition of a hierarchical categorization strategy where instances are classified in a top-down manner, in order to efficiently populate very large ontologies, since we plan to apply this method to extract structured information from Wikipedia. Furthermore, we will investigate how co-reference resolution might well benefit from our ontology classification. Finally, we plan to exploit the IBOP algorithm for ontology mapping and multilingual alignment of lexical resources.

Acknowledgments

Claudio Giuliano is supported by the X-Media project (`http://www.x-media-project.org`), sponsored by the European Commission as part of the Information Society Technologies (IST) program under EC grant number IST-FP6-026978.

References

Agichtein, Eugene and Luis Gravano. 2000. Snowball: extracting relations from large plain-text collections. In *DL '00: Proceedings of the fifth ACM conference on Digital libraries*, pages 85–94, New York, NY, USA. ACM.

Alfonseca, Enrique and Suresh Manandhar. 2002. Extending a lexical ontology by a combination of distributional semantics signatures. In *EKAW '02: Proceedings of the 13th International Conference on Knowledge Engineering and Knowledge Management. Ontologies and the Semantic Web*, pages 1–7, London, UK. Springer-Verlag.

Brin, Sergey. 1998. Extracting patterns and relations from the world wide web. In *WebDB Workshop at 6th International Conference on Extending Database Technology, EDBT'98.*

Cimiano, Philipp and Johanna Völker. 2005. Towards large-scale, open-domain and ontology-based named entity classification. In *Proceedings of RANLP'05*, pages 66– 166–172, Borovets, Bulgaria.

Cimiano, Philipp, Günter Ladwig, and Steffen Staab. 2005. Gimme the context: Context-driven automatic semantic annotation with C-PANKOW. In Ellis, Allan and Tatsuya Hagino, editors, *Proceedings of the 14th World Wide Web Conference*, pages 332 – 341, Chiba, Japan, MAY. ACM Press.

Etzioni, Oren, Michael Cafarella, Doug Downey, Ana M. Popescu, Tal Shaked, Stephen Soderland, Daniel S. Weld, and Alexander Yates. 2005. Unsupervised named-entity extraction from the web: An experimental study. *Artificial Intelligence*, 165(1):191–134.

Fellbaum, Christiane. 1998. *WordNet. An Electronic Lexical Database*. MIT Press, Cambridge, MA.

Fleischman, Michael and Eduard Hovy. 2002. Fine grained classification of named entities. In *Proceedings of the 19th International Conference on Computational Linguistics*, Taipei, Taiwan.

Gangemi, Aldo, Roberto Navigli, and Paola Velardi. 2003. Axiomatizing WordNet glosses in the OntoWordNet project. In *Proocedings of the Workshop on Human Language Technology for the Semantic Web and Web Services at ISWC 2003*, Sanibel Island, Florida.

Giuliano, Claudio and Alfio Gliozzo. 2007. Instance based lexical entailment for ontology population. In *Proceedings of the 2007 Joint Conference on Empirical Methods in Natural Language Processing and Computational Natural Language Learning (EMNLP-CoNLL)*, pages 248–256.

Giuliano, Claudio, Alfio Gliozzo, and Carlo Strapparava. 2007. Fbk-irst: Lexical substitution task exploiting domain and syntagmatic coherence. In *Proceedings of the Fourth International Workshop on Semantic Evaluations (SemEval-2007)*, pages 145–148, Prague, Czech Republic, June.

Harris, Zellig. 1954. Distributional structure. *WORD*, 10:146–162.

Hearst, Marti A. 1992. Automatic acquisition of hyponyms from large text corpora. In *Proceedings of the Fourteenth International Conference on Computational Linguistics*, Nantes, France, July.

McCarthy, Diana and Roberto Navigli. 2007. Semeval-2007 task 10: English lexical substitution task. In *Proceedings of the Fourth International Workshop on Semantic Evaluations (SemEval-2007)*, pages 48–53, Prague, Czech Republic, June.

McCarthy, Diana. 2002. Lexical substitution as a task for WSD evaluation. In *Proceedings of the ACL-02 workshop on Word Sense Disambiguation*, pages 109–115, Morristown, NJ, USA.

Melamed, I. Dan and Philip Resnik. 2000. Tagger evaluation given hierarchical tag sets. *Computers and the Humanities*, pages 79–84.

Tanev, Hristo and Bernardo Magnini. 2006. Weakly supervised approaches for ontology population. In *Proceedings of the Eleventh Conference of the European Chapter of the Association for Computational Linguistics (EACL-2006)*, Trento, Italy.

Measuring Topic Homogeneity and its Application to Dictionary-based Word Sense Disambiguation

Ann Gledson and John Keane
School of Computer Science, University of Manchester
Oxford Road, Manchester, UK M13 9PL
{ann.gledson,john.keane}@manchester.ac.uk

Abstract

The use of topical features is abundant in Natural Language Processing (NLP), a major example being in dictionary-based Word Sense Disambiguation (WSD). Yet previous research does not attempt to measure the level of topic cohesion in documents, despite assertions of its effects. This paper introduces a quantitative measure of *Topic Homogeneity* using a range of NLP resources and not requiring prior knowledge of correct senses. Evaluation is performed firstly by using the WordNet::Domains package to create word-sets with varying levels of homogeneity and comparing our results with those expected. Additionally, to evaluate each measure's potential value, the homogeneity results are correlated against those of 3 co-occurrence/dictionary-based WSD techniques, tested on 1040 Semcor and SENSEVAL sub-documents. Many low-moderate correlations are found to exist with several in the moderate range (above .40). These correlations surpass polysemy and sense-entropy, the 2 most cited factors affecting WSD. Finally, a combined homogeneity measure achieves correlations of up to .52.

1 Introduction

Topical features in NLP consist of unordered bags of words, often the context of a target word or phrase. In WSD for example, the word *bank* in the sentence: 'If you're OK being tied to one *bank*, you can get all your *financial* products there.' might be assigned its monetary sense, based on the occurrence of the term *financial*. Often referred to as 'topical features', these are an important part of many NLP methods, such as WSD (Yarowsky 1995) and Topic Area Detection (TAD) (Hearst 1997). Furthermore, in the SENSEVAL WSD competitions they are included in the highest performing systems.

We assert that the effectiveness of topical features in NLP depends upon the level of topic homogeneity in the text. To illustrate two extremes: the disambiguation of the word *bank* might be more difficult if occurring in i) a work of fiction describing a series of activities which includes the phrases: 'stroll along the river' and 'pick up her cheque book'; than in ii) a news report on a bank in financial difficulty (a topically homogeneous text).

This paper contributes a set of unsupervised Topic Homogeneity measures requiring no knowledge of correct senses. A variety of NLP resources are utilized and a set of evaluation methods devised, providing useful results. The paper is structured as follows: Section 2 outlines related work; Section 3 describes the experiments focusing on the resources used and their associated homogeneity measures; in Section 4 three evaluation methods are described, including a WSD task-based evaluation; Conclusions and future work are presented in Section 5.

2 Related Work

TAD research (Hearst 1997) has revealed that word patterns within texts can be used to locate topic areas. Salton and Allan (1994) distinguish between homogenous texts, where the topic of the text might be ascertained from a small number of paragraphs, and heterogeneous texts, where topic areas change considerably. Unfortunately, this research only detects topic homogeneity at inter-paragraph level. We assert that

© 2008. Licensed under the *Creative Commons Attribution-Noncommercial-Share Alike 3.0 Unported* license (http://creativecommons.org/licenses/by-nc-sa/3.0/). Some rights reserved.

the strength of relationships between the *words* of a text can vary from one text to another and that this is likely to affect the usefulness of topic features in NLP tasks. Caracciolo et-al (2004) also indicate that documents can vary in topical structure, mentioning text homogeneity as an important feature but they do not evaluate these findings explicitly.

Lexical cohesion (Halliday and Hasan 1976) is the analysis of the way the phrases and sentences of a text adhere to form a unified, comprehensible whole. Morris and Hirst (1991) describe a set of relationships between word-pairs, which include their likelihood to co-occur. These are used to create Lexical chains, which are sequences of related words in a document. The 2 main reasons for creating these chains are that they are 'an aid in the resolution of ambiguity' and they determine 'coherence and discourse structure'. We propose the use of lexical chains, alongside other methods, to measure document homogeneity.

Measuring the semantic relatedness between words is an important area in NLP, and has been used in areas such as WSD, Lexical Chaining and Malapropism Detection. Budanitsky & Hirst (2006) evaluate 5 such measures, based on lexically assigned similarities, and conclude that an area of future research should be the capture of 'non-classical' relationships not found in dictionaries, such as distributional similarity. Weeds and Weir (2006) evaluate distributional similarities using document retrieval from the BNC. Chen et-al (2006) and Bollegala et-al (2007) use web search-engine results. All of the reported similarity measures are between two words (or texts) only. We extend these to calculate the topic homogeneity of groups containing up to 10 words.

A small number of unsupervised WSD methods exist which take topic areas and/or document types into account (eg Gliozzo et-al 2004, McCarthy et-al 2007), but these work at corpus level and do not measure the level of topical homogeneity in each text. An exception is the WSD work by Navigli and Velardi (2005) who report differing results for 3 types of text: *unfocussed*, *mid-technical* (eg finance articles) and *overly technical* (eg computer networks).

3 Experiments

We propose the creation of a quantifiable measure of text homogeneity in order to predict the effectiveness of using co-occurrence features in WSD. In this initial set of experiments, documents are divided into simple ~50 content-word blocks, regardless of topic boundaries, to maximize the range of homogeneity levels in the texts and to nullify the effects of text length. The long-term objective is for documents to be divided into topic areas at the pre-processing stage, using a TAD algorithm. We also propose to take a single homogeneity measure of each entire sub-text, as opposed to using a sliding window approach, as the latter would be over-complex and comparable with a similarity-based WSD process.

3.1 Input Texts

The documents of Semcor[2] and SENSEVAL (2 & 3) are used in the experiments. Each text is divided into sub-documents of approximately 50 content-words[3]. All documents are converted into Semcor 2.1 format.

From the resulting sub-documents, 1040 random Semcor texts and the entire set of 73 SENSEVAL 2 and 3 texts are used in the experiments.

3.2 Text Pre-Processing

Non-topic words are found to have a negative effect on NLP methods using topic features, such as WSD (eg Yarowsky 1993, Leacock et-al 1998), and are therefore excluded from our topic homogeneity experiments. Unfortunately, no precise definition of non-topic words exists. Under ideal conditions, where correct senses are known, we define non-topic words as word-senses appearing in over 25% of all Semcor texts and/or being marked as *factotum* in the WordNet Domains 3.2 package (Magnini and Cavaglia 2000).

As the experiments described in this work assume no such prior knowledge, an approximation of the criteria used above is made. A J48 (pruned) decision tree is used to decide whether each word is non-topical. The input attributes were the PoS, sense-count, Semcor distribution (*SenseEntropy*) of its possible senses, whether all of the word's senses are factotum, and the percent of Semcor documents containing that word. The training and test data was the entire set of Semcor and SENSEVAL 2 and 3 English all-word task data and the minimum node size was set to 4000 instances to minimize the tree size and prevent over-training. Using a 10-fold cross-validation test mode the tree obtains 83% accura-

---

[2] Using the Brown-1 and Brown-2 documents only

[3] Splits are made as near as possible to the 50 content-word length whilst keeping sentences intact.

cy. The learned filter for selecting non-topical nouns and verbs is:

(All-Senses = Factotum) || (Corpus-Hit-Percent >25.0%) || ((Sense_Count > 1) && (PoS = v)) || ((Sense_Count > 3) && (*SenseEntropy* > 0.5668))

Upon entry into the system, each sub-document has all such words labeled as non-topical. The remaining words are labeled as topic-content. The confusion matrix output is shown in Table 1.

Classified As →	**OTHER**	**NON-TOPIC**
OTHER	15017	5768
NON-TOPIC	4278	34292

Table 1: J48 Confusion Matrix

In addition, only nouns and verbs are considered in the experiments as these word types are considered most likely to contain topical information.

3.3 Homogeneity Measures

Five homogeneity measures have been created that cover a broad range of techniques for embodying topic-area information in natural language texts. This is to facilitate comparisons between different techniques and if such a variety of aspects is captured, it improves the likelihood of a successful combination of the methods to produce an optimised measure. Each takes a full pre-processed sub-document as input and outputs a single score.

Word Entropy

It is possible to capture topic homogeneity by using simple measures that require minimal reliance on external resources. Word entropy is considered as having the potential to reflect topical cohesion.

To measure *WordEntropy*, the frequency of each topic-content lemma of an input document *d* is obtained, and *Entropy(d)* is measured using this set of frequencies, as follows:

$$- \sum_{i=1..n} p(x_i) \log_2 p(x_i) \qquad [1]$$

Where n is the number of different topic content lemmas in d, and $p(x_i)$ is calculated as

$$\text{frequency}(\text{lemma}_i)/\sum_{j=1..n}\text{frequency}(\text{lemma}_j) \qquad [2]$$

As *Entropy(d)* is affected by n and n varies from one document to another, *Entropy(d)* is normalised by dividing it by the maximum possible Entropy calculation for d, that is if all lemmas had equal frequencies.

WordNet Similarities

WordNet::Similarities 1.04 (Pedersen et-al 2004) is publicly available software which uses aspects of WordNet to 'measure the semantic similarity and relatedness between a pair of concepts'. The package can measure similarities between lemma pairs, where no knowledge of the correct sense or PoS is required. These similarities can be easily adapted to assist with the measurement of document homogeneity, by comparing similarities between sets of word-PoS pairs in the document.

Three WordNet Similarities homogeneity measures ($AvgSim_{Measure}$) are calculated for each document as follows: **Step 1**: Order the topic-content lemmas of the input text firstly in descending order of frequency, and then by first appearance in the text. **Step 2**: Take the first n lemmas from this list (where n is all lemmas up to a maximum of 10) and add to *FreqLemmas*. **Step 3**: Calculate the mean of all of the similarity measures between each pair of lemmas in *FreqLemmas*. *AvgSim* can be defined as:

$$\text{Mean}(\sum_{i=1..n} \sum_{j=i+1..n} Sim_{Measure}(\text{lemma}_i, \text{lemma}_j)) \qquad [3]$$

Where $Sim_{Measure}(\text{lemma}_i, \text{lemma}_j)$ is the WordNet::Similarity calculation between lemma_i and lemma_j, where all allowable PoS combinations for the two lemmas when using the selected similarity measure are included.

The WordNet Similarity measures selected for use are Lesk, JCN[4], and Lch (see Pedersen et-al (2004) and Patwardhan et-al (2003) for details), as each measure represents one of the 3 main algorithm types available: WordNet Gloss overlaps, information content of the least common subsumer and path lengths respectively.

Yahoo Internet Searches

The web as a corpus has been successfully used for many areas in NLP such as WSD (Mihalcea and Moldovan 1999), obtaining frequencies for bigrams (Keller and Lapata 2003) and measuring word similarity (Bollegala et-al 2007). Such reliance on Web search-engine results does come with caveats, the most important in this context being that reported hit counts are not always reliable, mostly due to the counting of duplicate documents. (Kilgarriff 2007).

Using web-searches as part of the homogeneity measure is considered important to our experiments, as it provides up-to-date information on word co-occurrence frequencies in the largest available collection of English language docu-

[4] TheBNC information-content file is loaded.

ments. In addition, it is a measure that does not rely on WordNet. It is therefore necessary to produce a web-based homogeneity measure that limits the effects of inaccurate hit counts.

The *SearchYahoo* homogeneity measure is calculated for each document *d* as follows:

Steps 1 and 2: Perform steps 1 and 2 described above (WordNet Similarities). **Step 3**: Using an internet search-engine, obtain the hit counts of each member of *Freqlemmas*. **Step 4**: Order the *resulting Frequlemmas* list of *n* lemma/hit-counts combinations in descending order of hit-counts and save this list to *IndivHitsDesc*. **Step 5**: For each lemma of *IndivHitsDesc*, save to *CombiHitsDesc* preserving the ordering. **Step 6**: For each member of *CombiHitsDesc*: $CombiHitsDesc_i$, obtain the hit counts of the associated lemma, along with the concatenated lemmas of all preceding list members of *CombiHitsDesc* ($CombiHitsDesc_0$ to $CombiHitsDesc_{[i-1]}$). This list of lemmas are concatenated together using ' AND ' as the delimiter. **Step 7**: Calculate the gradients of the best-fit lines for the hit-counts of *IndivHitsDesc* and *CombiHitsDesc*: creating *gradIndiv* and *gradCombi* respectively. **Step 8**: *SearchYahoo* is calculated for *d* as *gradIndiv* minus *gradCombi*.

As *SearchYahoo* is taken as the difference between the two descending gradients, the measure is more likely to reveal the effects of the probability of the set of lemmas co-occurring in the same documents, rather than by influences such as duplicate documents. If the decline in hit-counts from $IndivHitsDesc_{[i-1]}$ to $IndivHitsDesc_{[i]}$ is high, then the decline in the number of hits from $CombiHitsDesc_{[i-1]}$ to $CombiHitsDesc_{[i]}$ is also expected to be higher, and the converse for lower drops is also expected. Deviations from these expectations are reflected in the final homogeneity measure and are assumed to be caused by the likelihood of lemmas co-occurring together in internet texts.

A web-service enabled search-engine was required to create a fully automated process. The Google search-engine hit-counts were less suitable, as they did not always decline as the number of query terms increased. This is perhaps because of the way in which Google combines the results of several search-engine hubs. The Yahoo web-services were therefore selected, as these produced the necessary declines for the measure to work.

Further evaluation of the Yahoo Internet searching homogeneity measure is presented in Gledson and Keane (2008), along with comparisons with similar methods using the Google and Windows LiveSearch web-services.

WordNet Domains

Magnini et-al (2002) describe the WordNet Domains[5] (Magnini and Cavaglia 2000) package as:

> 'an extension of WordNet in which synsets have been annotated with one or more domain labels, selected from a hierarchically organized set of about two hundred labels'.
> (Magnini et-al 2002 p.361)

They describe a domain (eg 'Politics') as 'a set of words between which there are strong semantic relations'. This resource is useful for measuring topic homogeneity, as it stores topic area information for word-senses directly, and complements the other measures, thus contributing to a diverse set of measures.

Two WordNet Domains homogeneity measures are calculated: *DomEntropy* and *DomTop3Percent*. These are calculated for each input document *d* as follows:

Step 1: Add each topic-content lemma of *d* to the list *TopicContents*. **Step 2**: for each WordNet sense of each topic-content lemma in *TopicContents*, find all associated domains using the Domains package, and add these to a *DomainCounts* list. This list contains each distinct domain *dom* present in the document, each with its associated count of the number of times it occurs in *TopicContents*: $freq(dom_i)$. **Step 3**: Calculate *DomEntropy* using the equation [1] above, where *n* is the number of items in *DomainCounts*, and

$$p(x_i) = \text{freq}(\text{dom}_i) \,/\, \textstyle\sum_{j=1..n} \text{freq}(\text{dom}_j) \qquad [4]$$

Step 4: Calculate *DomTop3Percent* as follows:

$$100\,(\textstyle\sum_{i=1..3} \text{freq}(\text{dom}_i) \,/\, \sum_{j=1..n} \text{freq}(\text{dom}_j)) \qquad [5]$$

Lexical Chaining

'Lexical chains are defined as clusters of semantically related words' (Doran et-al 2004). These words are usually related by electronic dictionaries such as WordNet or Roget's Thesaurus, and chains are created using a natural language text as input.

The lexical chaining method used in our experiments is a greedy version of the algorithm described in Ecran and Cicekli (2007). Their method uses the WordNet dictionary and calculates all possible chains in the text. We adopt a greedy approach to chaining, as it is only necessary to get an overall estimate of the levels of topic homogeneity within the text, rather than producing

[5] We use version 3.2 released Feb 2007

lists of keywords or document summaries. The *LexChain* homogeneity measure is calculated for the input document *d* as follows:

Step 1: Add each topic-content noun occurrence in d to the list *UnusedNouns*. **Step 2**: For each item in *UnusedNouns*, find all other items in *UnusedNouns* that it is related to and add them to its corresponding *RelatedNouns* list. Each item of *RelatedNouns* is mapped to a score (*relScore*) using the following system (Ercan and Cicekli 2007): 10 points are awarded if the word-senses have identical lemmas or belong to the same WordNet 2.1 synset. 7 points are awarded if it is a hyponymy relationship and 4 points are awarded if it is a holonymy relationship. **Step 3**: Create chains: Iterate through *UnusedNouns* recursively, adding all related senses to the first chain, until no further linked nouns can be found. As each new node (*UnusedNouns* item) is added to the chain, remove it from *UnusedNouns*. Continue creating further chains, until no more related nouns can be found. **Step 4**: Calculate the *chainScore* of each chain by adding together all of the *relScores* contained for each sense, at each node. **Step 5**: Set *LexChain* as the *ChainScore* of the highest scoring chain.

3.4 Adjusting for Polysemy and Skew

Each of the homogeneity measures (except *WordEntropy*) has the potential to be affected by the average polysemy and sense skews of the document. The effects are measured statistically using linear regression and the resulting line of best fit equation is used to reverse them.

To calculate the adjustments for each measure, the effects of polysemy and skew must be approximated. This is achieved by applying linear regression[6] over the entire result set. The homogeneity measure is entered as the dependant variable and the appropriate[7] average polysemy and skew measures (per doc) are input as independent variables. If the homogeneity measure is affected by either (or both) of the independent variables and the effect is statistically significant, a line of best fit equation is output representing the gradient of the effect caused by those variable(s). The appropriate homogeneity measure for each input document is adjusted by subtracting the co-efficient of the gradient multiplied by the appropriate variable(s): polysemy and/or skew.

[6] Using SPSS 13.0 statistical software package.

[7] Avg. document polysemy/skews are only calculated for lemmas incl. in homogeneity measures.

4 Evaluation and Discussion

It is anticipated that the main users of a set of topic homogeneity measures are other NLP techniques. They are, therefore, best measured in terms of the actual results of the processes they are intended to improve. Human judgments can be subjective (Doran et-al 2004) and are therefore deemed inappropriate for the evaluation of this task.

Three methods are used to evaluate the homogeneity measures. Firstly, each measure is compared with its equivalent where only correct senses are used. Secondly, the WordNet::Domains (version 3.2) hierarchy (Magnini and Cavaglia 2000) is used to generate sets of words with varying levels of topic homogeneity. Each set is then tested using the proposed measures, and the results compared with those expected. Finally, the usefulness of each measure is tested by evaluating their ability to indicate the likely outcome of several co-occurrence/dictionary-based WSD measures. In the WSD literature, the main non-topic related variables reported as affecting WSD results are polysemy and skew, so these two measures will be used as the baselines.

4.1 All Senses vs. Correct Senses

Table 2 show the set of measures correlated against their correct-sense complements, where only correct senses are utilized. Most of the results are in the moderate range (.40-.60) with $AvgSim_{LESK}$ and *LexChains* achieving correlations in the high and very-high ranges. Only the SENSEVAL *DomEntropy* result falls below the moderate level, indicating that homogeneity information is, in general, not negated by incorrect-sense noise.

Measure	**Correlation (Pearson's R)**	
	Semcor	SENSEVAL
$AvgSim_{LESK}$	0.814**	0.834**
$AvgSim_{JCN}$	0.491**	0.610**
$AvgSim_{LCH}$	0.569**	0.474**
DomEntropy	0.575**	0.371**
DomTop3%	0.535**	0.444**
LexChain	0.659**	0.967**

**Significant at the .01 level (2-tailed)

Table 2: Correlation with correct-sense equivalents.

4.2 WordNet::Domains

The WordNet Domains package (Magnini and Cavaglia 2000) assigns domains to each sense of the WordNet electronic dictionary. Therefore, for each domain a relevant list of words can be extracted. The domains are arranged hierarchically, allowing sets of words with a varied degree of topic homogeneity to be selected. For example, for a highly heterogeneous set, 10 words can be selected from any domain, including factotum (level-0: the non-topic related category). For a slightly less heterogeneous set, words might be selected randomly from a level-1 category (eg 'Applied_Science'), and any of the categories it subsumes (eg Agriculture, Architecture, Buildings etc). The levels range from level-0 (factotum) to level-4; we merge levels 3 and 4 as level-4 domains are relatively few and are viewed as similar to level-3. This combined set is henceforth known as level-3.

For our experiments, we have collected 2 random samples of 10 words for every WordNet domain (167 domains) and then increased the number of sets from level-0 to level-2 domains, to make the number of sets from each level more similar. The final level counts are: levels 0 to 2 have 100 word-sets each and level 3 has 192 word-sets. The sets contain 10 words each. We then assign an expected score to each set, equal to its domain level.

Measure	Correlation (Pearson's R)	
	All	Extreme
SearchYahoo	0.46**	0.80**
$AvgSim_{LESK}$	0.23**	0.15*
$AvgSim_{JCN}$	0.47**	0.45**
$AvgSim_{LCH}$	0.35**	0.25**
DomEntropy	0.70**	0.75**
DomTop3%	0.75**	0.83**
LexChain	0.42**	0.40**

**Significant at the .01 level (2-tailed)
*Significant at the .05 level (2-tailed)

Table 3: Correlation with expected scores for *WordNet::Domains* selected sets

The first column of results on Table 3 represents the correlations with expected results for all 492 word-sets. The high WordNet::Domains results (*DomEntropy* and *DomTop3%*) probably reflect the fact that they are produced using the same resource as the creation of the test sets. On the other hand, knowledge of correct senses is not required for the homogeneity measures and these scores indicate that they are capable nonetheless of capturing topic homogeneity. The *SearchYahoo*, $AvgSims_{JCN}$ and *LexChain* methods all produce promising results with correlations in the moderate range (0.40 to 0.59) and again indicate that they can capture topic homogeneity.

To indicate whether the measures are more capable of distinguishing between extreme levels of homogeneity, we repeated the above tests, but included only those sets of level-0 and level-3. The results displayed in the final column of Table 3 and provide evidence that this might be the case for the WordNet::Domains measures and *SearchYahoo*, as the correlations are significantly higher for these more extreme test sets.

4.3 Dictionary-based WSD

The three WSD algorithms selected for evaluation are the technique described in Mihalcea and Moldovan (2000) and two WordNet Similarities measures: Lesk and JCN, adapted for WSD as described in Patwardhan et-al (2004), in which they are found to achieve the best performances. Each WSD technique uses the entire document as the context for each target word. The method of Mihalcea and Moldovan (2000) is included as it incorporates several techniques, all complementary to our overall set of evaluation methods. For our experiments it is split into three: *Mih-ALL:* covering all 8 procedures, including one that relies on co-location information; *Mih-4*: utilising 'procedure-4', which involves the use of noun co-occurrence and WordNet hyponymy data; and *Mih-5-8*: using procedures 5 to 8, which involves synonymy and hyponymy. The results are adjusted to remove the effects of polysemy and *SenseEntropy* (section 3.4).

In Table 4, the fine-grained WSD accuracy results (for topic-content words) are compared to those of the homogeneity measures, (including the correct-sense measures which set the high-standard benchmark). As a baseline, non-adjusted WSD accuracies are compared with the average *polysemy* and average *Sense Entropy* of each document.

All of the 'all-senses' results, except *DomainEntropy,* are statistically significant and achieve at least low-moderate correlations with one or more of the WSD measures. All of the measures outperform the baseline correlations for most of the WSD algorithms displayed.

A *COMBINED* measure is calculated for the all-sense and the correct-sense sets of measures respectively. The measures included (based on their individual performances and maintaining maximum diversity) are $AvgSims_{JCN}$, *WordEntropy*, *DomTop3Percent*, *LexChain* and *SearchYahoo*. Each of these result sets are ordered by homogeneity score (most homogeneous

		SENSEVAL 2 & 3					SEMCOR				
		Mih ALL	Mih 4	Mih 5-8	LESK	JCN	Mih ALL	Mih 4	Mih 5-8	LESK	JCN
ALL Senses	*Word Entropy*				**-.325**	**-.301**	**-.419**	**-.442**	**-.206**		**-.286**
	$AvgSim_{LESK}$				**.500**		**.138**	**.132**	**.211**	**.121**	**.097**
	$AvgSim_{JCN}$	.286	.276	**.357**	.233		**.255**	**.231**	**.284**		**.081**
	$AvgSim_{LCH}$	.271	*.211*	*.224*	*.202*		**.254**	**.248**	**.285**		**.104**
	DomEntropy	*-.193*	*-.205*				**-.163**	**-.157**			**-.091**
	DomTop3%	**.308**	.281				**.224**	**.215**	**.145**		**.108**
	LexChain				**.344**		**.328**	**.345**	**.296**		**.095**
	SearchYahoo	-.232	**-.290**	**-.317**	**-.295**		**-.105**	**-.116**		**-.085**	**-.089**
	COMBINED	**.382**	**.421**	.270	*.243*	*.171*	**.521**	**.517**	**.256**		**.350**
CORRECT Senses	$AvgSim_{LESK}$	**.461**	**.467**		**.630**	*.189*	**.186**	**.174**	**.237**	**.171**	**.115**
	$AvgSim_{JCN}$	.257		.272	**.357**	**.325**	**.218**	**.162**	**.234**		**.210**
	$AvgSim_{LCH}$	**.310**		**.483**	*.187*		**.198**	**.181**	**.247**		**.122**
	DomEntropy	**-.340**	-.295				**-.334**	**-.335**	**-.106**		**-.270**
	DomTop3%	**.376**	**.353**			*.214*	**.398**	**.393**	**.144**		**.316**
	LexChain				**.372**	**.297**	**.426**	**.440**	**.164**	**.112**	**.364**
	COMBINED	**.398**	**.363**		**.398**	**.379**	**.519**	**.494**	**.294**		**.434**
Baseline	*AvgPolysemy*	*-.100*	*-.030*	-.234	(.252)	*(.113)*	**(.146)**	**(.169)**	*-.004*	*.032*	**-.144**
	AvgSenseEntropy	*.031*	*-.044*	*.143*	**-.307**	*-.019*	-.073	-.064	-.083	*.041*	**-.141**

Results in bold: significant at the 0.01 level (2-tailed); Results in non-bold: significant at the 0.05 level (2-tailed)
Italicised results: not significant at the 0.05 level but considered to be of interest
Bracketed results: inverse to expectations
All WSD results are adjusted for polysemy / *SenseEntropy*, with the exception of where compared with baselines.

Table 4: Topic-content word WSD accuracy vs. Homogeneity: Correlations

first) and banded into 5 groups making 4 cut-points at equal percentiles and numbering them from 5 down to 1 respectively. The combined measure for each document is the sum of all such scores. These measures often outperform all of the individual methods and achieve correlations of up to .52 in Semcor, the largest of the datasets.

5 Conclusions and Further Work

This paper presents a first attempt to measure *Topic Homogeneity* using a variety of NLP resources. A set of 5 unsupervised homogeneity measures are presented that require no prior knowledge of correct senses and which exhibit moderate to high degrees of correlation with their correct-sense-only equivalents. When used to measure word-sets created using the WordNet::Domains package and which have varying levels of homogeneity, they are found to correlate well with expected results, further supporting our conjecture that they represent topical homogeneity information. Finally, when compared with WSD topic-content word accuracies, the effect of topic homogeneity is shown to surpass that of polysemy and sense-entropy, which have been recognized previously as having an influence on such results. By combining these measures, correlations are improved further, often outperforming the individual methods and achieving up to .52 for over 1000 random Semcor sub-documents, again indicating their potential importance. Correlations in SENSEVAL are often higher, but due to the lower number of documents, it is more difficult to obtain statistically significant results.

Our results provide evidence that improvements could be made to WSD and other NLP methods which utilise topic features, by adapting the algorithms used depending on the level of topic cohesion of the input text. For example, window-sizes for obtaining contextual data might be expanded or reduced, based on the homogeneity level of the target text. Furthermore, non-topical features such as collocation and grammatical cues might be given more emphasis when disambiguating heterogeneous documents.

Further work includes testing the measures on other NLP tasks. A machine learning approach might also be used to further optimize the combination of homogeneity measures. Finally, it is intended that our approach should eventually be combined with a TAD method to improve WSD results.

References

Bollegala, Danushka, Yutaka Matuo and Mitsuru Ishizuka, 2007. Measuring Semantic Similarity between Words Using Web Search Engines. *In Procs World Wide Web Conference*, Banff, Alberta.

Caracciolo, Caterina, Willem van Hage and Maarten de Rijke, 2004. Towards Topic Driven Access to Full Text Documents, in *Research and Advanced*

Technology for Digital Libraries, LNCS, 3232, pp 495-500

Chen, Hsin-Hsi, Ming-Shun Lin and Yu-Chuan Wei, 2006. Novel Association Measures Using Web Search with Double Checking. In *Proc.s 21st Intl. Conference on Computational Linguistics and 44th Annual Meeting of the ACL*, pp. 1009-1016

Doran, William, Nicola Stokes, Joe Carthy and John Dunnion, 2004. Assessing the Impact of Lexical Chain Scoring Methods and Sentence Extraction Schemes on Summarization, *LNCS 2945*, pp 627-635, CICLing 2004

Ercan, Gonenc and Ilyas Cicekli, 2007. Using Lexical Chains for Keyword extraction, *Information Processing and Management*, 43(2007), pp 1705-1714.

Gledson, Ann and John Keane, 2008. Using web-search results to measure word-group similarity. *In Procs 22nd Intl Conference on Computational Linguistics (COLING)*, Manchester. (To Appear)

Gliozzo, Alfio, Carlo Strapparava and Ido Dagan, 2004. Unsupervised and Supervised Exploitation of Semantic Domains in Lexical Disambiguation, *Computer Speech and Language*

Halliday, Michael and Ruqaiya Hasan, 1976. Cohesion in English, *Longman Group*

Hearst , Marti, 1997. Text Tiling: segmenting text into multi-paragraph subtopic passages, *Computational Linguistics*, 23(1), pp 33-64

Keller, Frank and Mirella Lapata, 2003. Using the Web to Obtain Frequencies for Unseen Bigrams, *Computational Linguistics*, 29(3)

Kilgarriff, Adam, 2007. Googleology is bad science, *Computational Linguistics*, 33(1), pp 147-151

Leacock, Claudia, Martin Choderow and George A. Miller, 1998. Using Corpus Statistics and Wordnet Relations for Sense Identification, *Computational Linguistics*, 24(1), pp 147-165

McCarthy, Diana, Rob Koeling, Julie Weeds and John Carroll, 2007. Unsupervised Acquisition of Predominant Word Senses, *Computational Linguistics*, 33(4), pp. 553-590.

Magnini, Bernardo and Gabriela Cavaglià, 2000. Integrating Subject Field Codes into WordNet. In Procs *LREC-2000,* Athens, Greece, 2000, pp 1413-1418.

Magnini, Bernardo, Carlo Strapparava, Giovanni Pezzulo and Alfio Gliozzo, 2002. The Role of Domain Information in Word Sense Disambiguation. *Natural Language Engineering*, 8(4), pp 359-373

Mihalcea, Rada and Dan Moldovan, 1999. A method for word sense disambiguation of unrestricted txt. *In Procs. 37th Meeting of ACL*, pp 152-158

Mihalcea, Rada and Dan Moldovan, 2000. An Iterative Approach to Word Sense Disambiguation, *In Proc. FLAIRS 2000*, pp. 219-223, Orlando

Morris, Jane and Graeme Hirst, 1991. Lexical Cohesion Computed by Thesaural Relations as an Indicator of the Structure of Text, *Computational Linguistics*, 17(1), pp. 21-48.

Navigli, Roberto, Paola Velardi, 2005. Structural Semantic Interconnections: A Knowledge-Based Approach to Word Sense Disambiguation, *IEEE Transactions on Pattern Analysis and Machine Intelligence*, 27(7), pp. 1075-1086, July.

Patwardhan, Siddharth, Satanjeev Banerjee and Ted Pedersen, 2003. Using Measures of Semantic Relatedness for Word Sense Disambiguation, *LNCS 2588*, pp 241-257, CICLing 2003

Pedersen, Ted, Siddharth Patwardhan and Jason Michelizzi, 2004. WordNet::Similarity – Measuring the Relatedness of Concepts, *In Procs 19th National Conference on Artificial Intelligence.*

Salton, Gerard and James Allan, 1994. Automatic text decomposition and structuring, *In Procs. RIAO International Conference*, New York.

Weeds, Julie and, David Weir, 2006, Co-occurrence Retreival: A Flexible Framework for Lexical Distributional Similarity. *Computational Linguistics*, 31(4), pp 433-475.

Yarowsky, David, (1995), Unsupervised word sense disambiguation rivaling supervised methods. *In Procs 33rd Annual Meeting of the Association for Computational Linguistics (ACL) 1995*, pp 189-196

Using Web-Search Results to Measure Word-Group Similarity

Ann Gledson and John Keane
School of Computer Science,
University of Manchester
Oxford Road, Manchester, UK M13 9PL
{ann.gledson,john.keane}@manchester.ac.uk

Abstract

Semantic relatedness between words is important to many NLP tasks, and numerous measures exist which use a variety of resources. Thus far, such work is confined to measuring similarity between two words (or two texts), and only a handful utilize the web as a corpus. This paper introduces a distributional similarity measure which uses internet search counts and also extends to calculating the similarity within word-groups. The evaluation results are encouraging: for word-pairs, the correlations with human judgments are comparable with state-of-the-art web-search page-count heuristics. When used to measure similarities within sets of 10 words, the results correlate highly (up to 0.8) with those expected. Relatively little comparison has been made between the results of different search-engines. Here, we compare experimental results from Google, Windows Live Search and Yahoo and find noticeable differences.

1 Introduction

The propensity of words to appear together in texts, also known as their distributional similarity is an important part of Natural Language Processing (NLP):

> 'The need to determine semantic relatedness... between two lexically expressed concepts is a problem that pervades much of [NLP].' (Budanitsky and Hirst 2006)

Such requirements are evident in word sense disambiguation (WSD) (Patwardhan et-al 2003), spelling correction (Budanitsky and Hirst 2006) and Lexical Chaining (Morris and Hirst 1991).

As well as measuring the co-occurrence of word-pairs, it is also considered useful to extend these measures to calculate the likelihood of sets of words to appear together. For example, Caracciolo et-al (2004) evaluate two established topic area detection (TAD) algorithms and indicate text homogeneity as a document feature affecting the results. Furthermore, Gliozzo et-al (2004) and McCarthy et-al (2007) highlight the importance of topic features for WSD and Navigli and Velardi (2005) report differing WSD results for 3 types of text: unfocussed, mid-technical (eg finance articles) and overly technical (eg interoperability and computer networks). Measures of word-group similarity can be used to calculate the level of topic cohesion in texts, and the potential for this to be used to benefit NLP areas such as WSD and TAD has been indicated in Gledson and Keane (2008).

We consider web-searching an important part of measuring similarity, as it provides up-to-date information on word co-occurrence frequencies in the largest available collection of English language documents. We propose a simple measure that uses internet search counts by measuring the decline in the number of hits as more words (from the word-set to be measured) are appended to a query string using the 'AND' operator. To offset against the effect of individual word hit-counts, the above gradient is compared to that of the individual word hit counts – arranged in descending order of hits returned.

The paper is structured as follows: in Section 2 we describe related work in the areas of word similarity and the use of search-engine counts in NLP. Section 3 outlines the algorithm to be used for our similarity measure which can utilise any search-engine that is web-service enabled. Sec-

© 2008. Licensed under the *Creative Commons Attribution-Noncommercial-Share Alike 3.0 Unported* license (http://creativecommons.org/licenses/by-nc-sa/3.0/). Some rights reserved.

tion 4 describes and discusses the results of the evaluation techniques used, one for evaluating word-pair similarities, which compares with previous work and human judgements, and three for evaluating word-group similarities. Section 5 outlines the conclusions drawn from these experiments and Section 6 discusses further work.

2 Related Work

The most commonly used similarity measures are based on the WordNet lexical database (eg Budanitsky and Hirst 2006, Hughes and Ramage 2007) and a number of such measures have been made publicly available (Pedersen et-al 2004). The problem with such methods is that they are confined to measuring words in terms of the lexical connections manually assigned to them. Language is evolving continuously and the continual maintenance and updating of such databases is highly labour intensive, therefore, such lexical resources can never be fully up-to-date. In addition, the lexical connections made between words and concepts do not cover all possible relations between words. An important relationship between words is distributional similarity and Budanitsky and Hirst (2006) conclude that the capture of these 'non-classical' relationships is an important area of future research.

Weeds and Weir (2006) use a 'co-occurrence retrieval method to compute word relatedness, which is described as analogous to the precision and recall metrics of document retrieval. They observe the 'plausibility' of substituting word-1 for word-2 within verb/object-noun grammatical relationships. This method is restricted to document retrieval from the BNC corpus, due to the pre-requisite that words are part-of-speech tagged and that some grammatical parsing is performed. The similarity measure that we have developed is simpler and does not rely on pre-processing of texts. This distributional similarity measure calculates the propensity of words to appear together, regardless of part-of-speech or grammatical functions.

We assert that the world-wide-web can be used to capture distributional similarity, and is less likely to suffer from problems of coverage, found in smaller corpora. The web as a corpus has been successfully used for many areas in NLP (Kilgarriff and Grefenstette 2003) such as WSD (Mihalcea and Moldovan 1999), obtaining frequencies for bigrams (Keller and Lapata 2003) and noun compound bracketing (Nakov and Hearst 2005). Such reliance on web search-engine results does come with caveats, the most important (in this context) being that the reported hit counts may not be entirely trustworthy (Kilgarriff 2007).

Strube and Ponzetto's (2006) use the Wikipedia database, which includes a taxonomy of categories, and they adapt 'well established semantic relatedness measures originally developed for WordNet'. They achieve a correlation coefficient of 0.48 with human judgments, which is stated as being higher than a Google-only and WordNet-only based measure for the largest of their test datasets (the 353 word-pairs of 353-TC)

Chen et-al (2006) use the snippet's returned from web-searches, in order to perform word similarity measurement that captures 'new usages' of ever evolving, 'live' languages. A double checking model is utilized which combines the number of occurrences of the first word in the snippets of the second word, and vice-versa. This work achieves a correlation coefficient of 0.85 with the Miller and Charles (1998) dataset of 28 word-pairs, but to achieve the best results, 600-700 snippets are required for each word-pair, requiring extra text-processing and searching.

The work most similar to ours is the set of page-counting techniques of Bollegala et-al (2007). They combine the use of web-search page-counts with the analysis of the returned text snippets and achieve impressive correlations with human judgment (0.834 with the Miller and Charles dataset). The text-snippet analysis is more complex than that of Chen et-al (2006), as the optimal number of snippets is over 1000, and their process involves complex pattern matching, which may not scale well to measuring word-groups similarity. Their page counting heuristics utilize 4 popular co-occurrence methods: Jaccard, Overlap (Simpson), Dice and PMI (Point-wise mutual information) but again, these techniques are not designed to scale up to larger numbers of input words.

Mihalcea et-al (2006) and Gabrilovich and Markovitch (2007) achieve good results when comparing texts, the former utilizing the inverse-document frequency heuristic and the latter indexing the entire Wikipedia database and comparing vector representations of the two inputs.

None of the above work is adapted to be used on single groups of words as a measure of topic cohesion. They could be adapted by combining similarity results between many pairs, but this might similarly have a high computational cost. In addition, no comparisons of different web-search engines are made when using web-counts.

As the use of web-counts is precarious (Kigarriff 2007), these types of comparisons are of high practical value.

3 Similarity Measure

The proposed measure can be used with any web-service enabled search-engine and in our experiments we compare three such search-engines: Yahoo *[Yahoo]*, Windows Live Search *[Live-Search]* and Google *[Google]*. The similarity measure $WebSim_{[search\text{-}engine]}$ is calculated for each document d as follows:

Step 1: Add the required set of *n* lemmas to the *Lemmas* list.

Step 2: Using an internet *search-engine*, obtain the hit counts of each member of *Lemmas*.

Step 3: Order the resulting list of n lemma/hit-counts combinations in descending order of hit-counts and save lemma/hit combinations to *IndivHitsDesc*.

Step 4: For each lemma of *IndivHitsDesc*, save to *CombiHitsDesc* preserving the ordering.

Step 5: For each member of *CombiHitsDesc*: *CombiHitsDesci*, obtain the hit counts of the associated lemma, along with the concatenated lemmas of all preceding list members of *CombiHitsDesc* (*CombiHitsDesc*[0] to *CombiHitsDesc*[i-1]). This list of lemmas are concatenated together using ' AND ' as the delimiter.

Step 6: Calculate the gradients of the best-fit lines for the hit-counts of *IndivHitsDesc* and *CombiHitsDesc*: creating *gradIndiv* and *gradCombi* respectively.

Step 7: $WebSim_{[search\text{-}engine]}$ is calculated for d as *gradIndiv* minus *gradCombi*.

As $WebSim_{[search\text{-}engine]}$ is taken as the difference between the two descending gradients, the measure is more likely to reveal the affects of the probability of the set of lemmas co-occurring in the same documents, rather than by influences such as duplicate documents. If the decline in hit-counts from *IndivHitsDesc*[i-1] to *IndivHitsDesc*[i] is high, then the decline in the number of hits from *CombiHitsDesc*[i-1] to *CombiHitsDesc*[i] is also expected to be higher, and the converse, for lower drops is also expected. Deviations from these expectations are reflected in the final homogeneity measure and are assumed to be caused by the likelihood of lemmas co-occurring together in internet texts.

Search-engines are required that publish a set of web-services for a fully automated process. The Google, Yahoo and Windows Live Search search-engines have been selected and the results of each measure are compared. In response to important problems highlighted by Kilgarriff (2007) relating to the use of web counts in NLP experiments: firstly, a measure is proposed between words that does not require the pre-annotation of part-of-speech information and does not rely on query syntax / meta-language. Secondly, our measure relies on the use of web-search *page* counts (as opposed to word instance counts) as we are measuring the likelihood of co-occurrence in the same text. Finally, measures are taken to try to avoid the problem of arbitrary search-engine counts. For example, each measure is the result of a comparison between the decline rates of 2 sets of hit counts and the full set of queries for each input text are taken within a 20 second interval (for groups of 10 words). In addition, for the Google and Yahoo measures the web-service request parameter includes options to avoid the return of the same web-page (Google: 'filter_alike_results'; Yahoo: 'AllowSimilar').

4 Evaluation

Four methods of evaluation are used to verify that the similarity measure is capable of measuring similarity between words. These methods are selected to be as varied as possible, to provide a fuller understanding of the usefulness of our technique and to verify that it is working as expected.

4.1 Word-pairs

The results of Rubenstein and Goodenough (1965) (65 word-pairs), Miller and Charles (1998) (30 word-pair subset of Rubenstein and Goodenough 1965) and Finkelstein et-al (2002) (353 word-pairs) are used to evaluate the ability of the proposed method to calculate the similarity between word-pairs. These results sets list the similarity scores of the word-pairs as assigned by humans. Although this does provide a useful benchmark, extremely high, or perfect correlations are unrealistic, as those involved in the experiments were asked to think about the words association in terms of lexical relations such as synonymy as opposed to the broader idea of distributional similarity. Nevertheless, in conjunction with other evaluation techniques, these comparisons can still be useful, as some correlation would be expected if our measure was functioning as required.

In addition, our results are compared with the page-count based similarity scores of Bollegala

Measure	Correlation (Pearson's R)
WebSim$_{[YAHOO]}$	-0.57**
WebSim$_{[LIVE-SEARCH]}$	**-0.60****
WebSim$_{[GOOGLE]}$	-0.43**
Google-Jaccard (Strube & Ponzetto 2006)	*0.41*
pl (path-lengths) (Strube & Ponzetto 2006)	*0.56*
wup (Strube & Ponzetto 2006)	*0.52*
lch (Strube & Ponzetto 2006)	*0.54*

** Significant at the 0.01 level (2-tailed)

Italics: Statistical significance not specified in Strube and Ponzetto (2006)

Table 1: Correlation with Human Ratings on Rubenstein-Goodenough dataset

Measure	Correlation (Pearson's R)
WebSim$_{[YAHOO]}$	**-0.55****
WebSim$_{[LIVE-SEARCH]}$	-0.53**
WebSim$_{[GOOGLE]}$	-0.39*
Jaccard (Bollegala et-al 2007)	*0.26*
Dice (Bollegala et-al 2007)	*0.27*
Overlap (Bollegala et-al 2007)	*0.38*
PMI (Bollegala et-al 2007)	***0.55***
pl (Strube & Ponzetto 2006)	*0.49*

** Significant at the 0.01 level (2-tailed)

* Significant at the 0.05 level (2-tailed)

Italics: Statistical significance not specified in Bollegala et-al (2007) or Strube and Ponzetto (2006)

Table 2: Correlation with Human Ratings on Miller-Charles' dataset

Measure	Correlation (Pearson's R)
WebSim$_{[YAHOO]}$	-0.37**
WebSim$_{[LIVE-SEARCH]}$	-0.40**
WebSim$_{[GOOGLE]}$	-0.119*
Google-Jaccard (Strube & Ponzetto 2006)	*0.18*
wup (Strube & Ponzetto 2006)	***0.48***
lch (Strube & Ponzetto 2006)	***0.48***

** Significant at the 0.01 level (2-tailed)

* Significant at the 0.05 level (2-tailed)

Italics: Statistical significance not specified in Strube and Ponzetto (2006)

Table 3: Correlation with Human Ratings on 353-TC dataset

et-al (2007) and the best performing Wikipedia-based measures of Strube and Ponzetto (2006). The former gauge similarity using a number of popular co-occurrence measures adapted for web-search page-counts and their method is considered closest to our approach. The individual results for each word-pair are shown in Tables 1, 2 and 3. They indicate that moderate correlations exists, particularly in the Rubenstein and Goodenough set. *WebSim*$_{[YAHOO]}$ and *WebSim*$_{[LIVE SEARCH]}$ significantly outperform the *WebSim*$_{[GOOGLE]}$ method. This may be due to Google's results being more erratic. Google's returned counts were sometimes found to increase as extra 'AND' clauses were added to the query string. This is perhaps because of the way in which Google combines the results of several search-engine hubs. (This was accommodated to a degree by setting any negative scores to zero.) All three of the methods were comparable with the results of Bollegala et-al (2007), with the *WebSim*$_{[LIVE SEARCH]}$ measure performing at the highest levels and *WebSim*$_{[YAHOO]}$ producing the highest of all measures on the Miller and Charles (1998) dataset. (Unfortunately, Bollegala et-al (2007) do not compare their results with the Rubenstein-Goodenough and 353-TC dataset.) In the largest (353-TC) dataset, the *WebSim*$_{[YAHOO]}$ and *WebSim*$_{[LIVE SEARCH]}$ results were found to be, lower, but comparable with the best of Strube and Ponzetto's (2006) Wikipedia-based results and significantly higher than their Jaccard measure, adapted to use Google web-search page-counts.

Set	Words
A	law, crime, perpetrator, prison, sentence, judge, jury, police, justice, criminal
B	astrology, “star sign", Libra, Gemini, Sagittarius, zodiac, constellation, Leo, Scorpio, birthday
C	ocean, "hydrothermal vent", fauna, botanical, biogeography, tube-worm, Atlantic, species, biology, habitat
D	economy, credit, bank, inflation, "interest rate", finance, capital, expenditure, market, profit
E	health, diet, swimming, fitness, exercise, "heart disease", stroke, fruit, jogging, work
F	football, stadium, striker, trophy, match, referee, pitch, crowd, manager, kick
G	education, exam, teacher, timetable, classroom, pupils, homework, results, parents, teenager
H	country, election, president, vote, leader, population, opposition, party, government, count
J	computer, "hard drive", keyboard, connection, monitor, RAM, speaker, "mother board", CPU, internet
K	"film star", drugs, money, millionaire, fame, music, actor, debut, beauty, paparazzi
M	"house prices", monthly, mortgage, home, borrowing, "buy-to-let", figures, homeowners, lending, trend
N	inmates, overcrowding, prisoners, custody, release, warden, cell, bars, violence, detention

Table 4: Manually selected test sets

4.2 Word-groups

In order to indicate whether the proposed measure is capable of measuring similarity amongst a set of words, a broad range of evaluation methods is required. No human evaluations exist, and to produce such a data-set would be difficult due to the larger quantity of data to evaluate. The following three methods are used:

Manual Selection of Word-groups

The manual selection of word-groups, for testing the proposed measure is an important part of its evaluation as it is possible to construct word-sets of varying similarity, so that expected results can be predicted and then compared with actual results. In addition, the datasets created can be easily manipulated to range from highly homogenous / similar sets of words to extremely heterogeneous – where words are highly unlikely to appear together. The latter is achieved by systematically merging the groups together, until a complete mixture of words from different word-sets is produced.

The method used to compile the words groups is as follows: firstly, groups of words with a known propensity to appear together were selected by browsing popular internet web-sites (see Table 4 for the words contained in each set). Secondly for each of these original sets, a series of 5 measures is taken, the first with all words from the original set (to illustrate, this might be represented as AAAAAAAAAA – where each letter represent a word from the set shown), this therefore is the most homogeneous group. Then two words from this set are replaced with two from a new set (eg B) (AAAAAAAABB). Then a further two words (again originally from set A) are replaced with two more words from another new set (eg from Set C) (AAAAAABBCC), and so on, until the final set of 10 words to be measured consists of 5 pairs of words, each from 5 different sets (AABBCCDDEE). These steps were first performed for sets A, B, C, D and E and then for sets F, G, H, J and K respectively. The results were compared (using Pearson's correlation) against the expected results. For example: AAAAAAAAAA = 10 points, AAAAAAAABB = 8 points, AAAAAABBCC = 6 points, AAAABBCCDD = 4 points and AABBCCDDEE = 2 points.

On the whole, the word-groups contained in each of these two sets of sets are considered to be heterogeneous (eg A is dissimilar to B, C, D and E etc). To introduce more 'blurring' of these categories, a third set of sets was measured, consisting of the word-sets A, D, H, M and N. It was considered more conceivable that the words in these sets could be found in the same documents. The expected results for this set of measures were modified slightly to become: AAAAAAAAAA = 8 points, AAAAAAAABB = 7 points, AAAAAABBCC = 6 points, AAAABBCCDD = 5 points and AABBCCDDEE = 4 points. This was done to reflect the fact that the differences between the highest and lowest were expected to be less.

Measure	Correlation (Pearson's R) Heteroge-neous Sets only: ABCDE FGHJK	 Homogenous Sets Included: ABCDE FGHJK +ADHMN
$WebSim_{[YAHOO]}$	**-.80****	**-.68****
$WebSim_{[LIVE\text{-}SEARCH]}$	-.65**	-.57**
$WebSim_{[GOOGLE]}$	-.70**	-.64**

**Significant at the .01 level (2-tailed)

Table 5: Correlation with expected scores for *manually* selected sets

As illustrated in Table 5, the 'Heterogeneous Sets' group similarity scores were found to correlate very highly with those expected, with the *WebSim*[YAHOO] measure achieving .80. The *WebSim*[GOOGLE] measure was also found to improve when tested on groups of words.

The measures were found to perform less well when the third set of word-sets, containing more closely related members, was introduced (Table 5, final column). This indicates that the measures are better at distinguishing between highly homogeneous and highly heterogeneous word-sets, but appear less proficient at distinguishing between word-sets with moderate levels of topic homogeneity.

WordNet::Domains Selection of Word-groups

The WordNet Domains package[2] (Magnini and Cavaglia 2000) assigns domains to each sense of the WordNet electronic dictionary. Therefore, for each domain a relevant list of words can be extracted. The domains are arranged hierarchically, allowing sets of words with a varied degree of topic homogeneity to be selected. For example, for a highly heterogeneous set, 10 words can be selected from any domain, including factotum (level-0: the non-topic related category). For a slightly less heterogeneous set, words might be selected randomly from a level-1 category (eg 'Applied_Science'), and any of the categories it subsumes (eg Agriculture, Architecture, Buildings etc). The levels range from level-0 (factotum) to level-4; we merge levels 3 and 4 as level-4 domains are relatively few and are viewed as similar to level-3. This combined set is henceforth known as level-3.

Measure	Correlation (Pearson's R)	
	All	Extreme Only
WebSim[YAHOO]	**-0.46****	**-0.80****
WebSim[LIVE-SEARCH]	-0.06	-0.23**
WebSim[GOOGLE]	-0.42**	-0.71**

**Significant at the .01 level (2-tailed)

Table 6: Correlation with expected scores for *WordNet::Domains* selected sets

For our experiments, we collected 2 random samples of 10 words for every WordNet domain (167 domains) and then increased the number of sets from level-0 to level-2 domains, to make the number of sets from each level more similar. The final level counts are: levels 0 to 2 have 100 word-sets each and level 3 has 192 word-sets. The word-sets contain 10 words each. We then assign an expected score to each set, equal to its domain level.

Table 6 displays the resulting correlation between the *WebSim* scores and the expected scores (column: 'All'). In the previous section, we observed that the measures are less competent at distinguishing between moderate levels of homogeneity, and the WordNet::Domain test sets contain many sets which could be described as having moderate homogeneity. To further test this, we repeated the above WordNet::Domain tests, but included only those sets of level-0 and level-3. The results displayed in the final column of Table 6 and provide further evidence that this might be the case, as the correlations are significantly higher for these more extreme test sets.

SENSEVAL 2 & 3 Data

The selection of the most frequent words from natural language documents is another important part of our evaluation, as it is representative of real-world data-sets. As it is anticipated that our results could be of use for WSD, we opted to measure the topic homogeneity of a publicly available set of documents from a well established WSD competition. The documents of the SENSEVAL 2 & 3[3] English all-words WSD task were divided into 73 sub-documents, each containing approximately 50 content-words. The stop-words and non-topical[4] content words of each sub-document were then removed and the remaining words lemmatised and aggregated by lemma. This list of lemmas was then arranged in descending order of the number of occurrences in the sub-document. The top-10 most frequent lemmas were selected as input to the similarity measure. The results for each set along with descriptions of the documents used are displayed in Table 7.

The scientific documents (d01) could be viewed as the most homogeneous, with the earthquake accounts (d002) and the work of fiction (d000) being considered the most heterogeneous. With this in mind, it is evident in Table 7 that the *WebSim*[MSN] measure performed the least well and other two methods performed as expected, and with identical rankings.

Further analysis is required to compare these results with the WSD results for the same

[2] We use version 3.2 released Feb 2007

[3] See http://www.senseval.org/

[4] Non-topical words are those that are found in over 25% of Semcor documents or have their correct sense(s) belonging to the 'Factotum' category in the WordNet Domains package by Magnini and Cavaglia (2000).

Text	Description	Average *WebSim* [YAHOO]	Average *WebSim* [GOOGLE]	Average *WebSim* [MSN]
d00	**Change-Ringing**: – History of Campanology, Churches, Social History Typical set = {bell, church, tower, "change ringing", English, peculiarity, rest, stone, faithful, evensong}	1.52 (4)	1.10 (4)	1.11 (5)
d01	**Cancer Cell Research**: Typical Set = {cancer, gene, parent, protein, cell, growth, "suppressor gene", individual, scientist, beneficiary}	*1.19 (1)*	*.93 (1)*	.89 (2)
d02	**Education**: Typical Set = {child, belief, nature, parent, education, medium, politician, "elementary school", creativity}	1.36 (3)	1.05 (3)	1.03 (3)
d000	**Fiction**: Typical set = {stranger, drinking, occasion, street, "moving van", intersection, brake, guy, mouth, truck}	1.55 (5)	1.18 (5)	1.03 (3)
d001	**US Presidential Elections**: Typical set = {district, candidate, half-century, election, percentage, president, vote, hopeful, reminder, ticket}	1.29 (2)	.96 (2)	*.85 (1)*
d002	**California Earthquake** – First hand accounts / stories Typical Set = {computer, quake, subscriber, earthquake, resident, solace, "personal computer", hundred, "check in", "bulletin board"}	**1.63 (6)**	**1.32 (6)**	**1.13 (6)**

Rankings for each measure are shown in brackets

Table 7: Average group similarity measures of the SENSEVAL 2 and 3 datasets

documents, as performed by Gledson and Keane (2008), and this is highlighted as part of the further work.

5 Conclusions

We proposed a simple web-based similarity measure which relies on page-counts only, can be utilized to measure the similarity of entire sets of words in addition to word-pairs and can use any web-service enabled search engine. When used to measure similarities between two words, our technique is comparable with other state-of-the art web-search page-counting techniques (and outperforms most). The measure is found to correlate to a moderate level (the highest being .60 correlation) with human judgments. When used to measure similarities between sets of 10 words, the results are similarly encouraging and show the expected variations for word-groups with different levels of homogeneity. Where word-groups are manually created, with known expectations of the similarities between each word-set, correlations with these expected results are as high as .80. Noticeable differences between the performances of each of the 3 search-engines, for each evaluation method, are evident. Google performs poorly for the word-pair similarity measures and Yahoo and Live Search both perform substantially better. For the word-set comparisons, Google performance improves (perhaps as the erratic single counts are stabilised as larger sets of words are used), but Yahoo is again superior and MSN performs much less well. Overall, our results indicate that the Yahoo measure is the most consistent and reliable.

6 Further Work

The group similarity measure calculates the propensity of words to co-occur with one-another, which can be described as a measure of the topic homogeneity of the set of input words. Gledson and Keane (2008) propose the use of further measures of topic homogeneity using a variety of available resources. These measures are compared with the results of WSD approaches reliant on topic features and low to moderate correlations are found to exist. It is also proposed that useful correlations with other NLP techniques utilising topical features (such as TAD and Malapropism Detection) might also exist.

The word-group similarity measures performed better for extreme levels of topic homogeneity. The measures must be improved to enable them to distinguish between moderate homogeneity levels. This may be achieved by combining our simple measure with other word similarity/relatedness techniques such as the use of WordNet Domains, or Lexical Chaining.

It is expected that polysemy counts of words influence the outcome of these experiments, especially for the word-pairs which have less data and are more susceptible to erratic counts. Results might be improved by measuring and offsetting these effects.

In addition, an upper limit of word-set cardinality should be determined, which is the maximum number of input words that can be measured. Further testing is necessary using a range of set cardinalities, to obtain optimal values.

References

Bollegala, D., Matsuo, Y., Ishizuka, M., 2007. Measuring Semantic Similarity between Words Using Web Search Engines. In Proceedings of World-Wide-Web Conference 2007 (Track: Semantic Web), Banff, Alberta, Canada. pp. 757-766.

Budanitsky, A. and Hirst, G. 2006. Evaluating WordNet-based Measures of Lexical Semantic Relatedness. *Computational Linguistics* , 32(1), pp. 13--47.

Caracciolo, C., Willem van Hage and Maarten de Rijke, 2004. Towards Topic Driven Access to Full Text Documents, in *Research and Advanced Technology for Digital Libraries, LNCS*, 3232, pp 495-500

Chen, Hsin-Hsi, Ming-Shun Lin and Yu-Chuan Wei, 2006. Novel Association Measures Using Web Search with Double Checking. In *Proc.s 21st Intl. Conference on Computational Linguistics and 44th Annual Meeting of the ACL*, pp. 1009-1016

Finkelstein, Lev, Evgeniy Gabrilovich, Yossi Matias, Ehud Rivlin, Zach Solan, Gadi Wolfman, and Eytan Ruppin, 2002. Placing Search in Context: The Concept Revisited, *ACM Transactions on Information Systems*, 20(1), pp. 116-131, January

Gabrilovich, Evgeniy and Shaul Markovitch, 2007. Computing Semantic Relatedness using Wikipedia-based Explicit Semantic Analysis. *In Proc.s Intl. Joint Conference on Artificial Intelligence 2007*, Hyderabad, India.

Gledson, Ann and John Keane. 2008. Measuring topic homogeneity and its application to word sense disambiguation. *In Procs 22nd Intl Conference on Computational Linguistics (COLING)*, Manchester. (To Appear)

Gliozzo, Alfio, Carlo Strapparava and Ido Dagan, 2004. Unsupervised and Supervised Exploitation of Semantic Domains in Lexical Disambiguation, *Computer Speech and Language*

Hughes, T. and D. Ramage, 2007. Lexical Semantic Relatedness with Random Graph Walks, *In Proc.s of the 2007 Joint Conference on Empirical Methods in Natural Language Processing and Computational Natural Language Learning*, pp. 581-589, Prague.

Keller, F. and Lapata, M., 2003. Using the Web to Obtain Frequencies for Unseen Bigrams, *Computational Linguistics*, 29(3)

Kilgarriff, Adam, 2007. Googleology is Bad Science. Computational Linguistics, 33(1), pp. 147—151.

Kilgarriff, A and Grefenstette, G., 2003. Web as Corpus, In Introduction to the special issue on the web as corpus, *Computational Linguistics*, 29(3), pp. 333--347

Magnini, B. and Cavaglià, Gabriela. 2000. Integrating Subject Field Codes into WordNet. *In Proceedings of LREC-2000,* Athens, Greece, 2000, pp 1413-1418.

McCarthy, Diana, Rob Koeling, Julie Weeds and John Carroll, 2007. Unsupervised Acquisition of Predominant Word Senses, *Computational Linguistics*, 33(4), pp. 553-590.

Mihalcea, R and Moldovan, D., 1999. A method for word sense disambiguation of unrestricted txt. *In Proceedings of the 37th Meeting of ACL*, pp 152-158

Mihalcea, Rada, Courtney Corley and Carlo Strapparava, 2006. Corpus-based and Knowledge-based Measures of Text Semantic Similarity, *In Proc.s of American Association for Artificial Intelligence 2006*

Miller, G. and Charles, W., 1998. Contextual correlates of semantic similarity. *Language and Cognitive Processes*, 6(1), pp. 1--28.

Morris, J. and Hirst, G., 1991. Lexical Cohesion Computed by Thesaural Relations as an Indicator of the Structure of Text, *Computational Linguistics*, 17(1), pp. 21-48

Nakov, P. and Hearst, M. 2005. Search Engine Statistics Beyond the n-gram: Application to Noun Compound Bracketing, *In Proceedings of the 9th Conference on CoNLL*, pp. 17--24, Ann Arbor, June

Navigli, Roberto, Paola Velardi, 2005. Structural Semantic Interconnections: A Knowledge-Based Approach to Word Sense Disambiguation, *IEEE Transactions on Pattern Analysis and Machine Intelligence*, 27(7), pp. 1075-1086, July.

Patwardhan, S., Banerjee, S. and Pedersen, T., (2003). Using Measures of Semantic Relatedness for Word Sense Disambiguation, *LNCS 2588 - CICLing 2003*, pp. 241--257.

Pedersen, Ted, Siddharth Patwardhan and Jason Michelizzi, 2004. WordNet::Similarity – Measuring the Relatedness of Concepts, *In Proc.s 19th National Conference on Artificial Intelligence.*

Rubenstein, H. and Goodenough, J., 1965. Contextual correlates of synonymy. Communications of the ACM, 8, pp. 627--633.

Strube, Michael and Paolo Ponzetto, 2006. WikiRelate! Computing Semantic Relatedness Using Wikipedia, *In Proc.s of American Association for Artificial Intelligence 2006*

Weeds, Julie and, David Weir, 2006. Co-occurrence Retrieval: A Flexible Framework for Lexical Distributional Similarity. *Computational Linguistics*, 31(4), pp 433-475.

An Algorithm for Adverbial Aspect Shift

Sabine Gründer
Department of Computer Science, University of Leipzig
Johannisgasse 26, 04103 Leipzig, Germany
gruender@uni-leipzig.de

Abstract

The paper offers a new type of approach to the semantic phenomenon of adverbial aspect shift within the framework of finite-state temporal semantics. The heart of the proposal is a supervaluational concept of underspecification, and the idea of treating the meanings of temporal prepositions as dynamic presuppositions. The simple shifting algorithm used in the present approach derives the correct set of possible readings on the basis of lexical semantic input only, and, furthermore, may claim cognitive plausibility.

1 Introduction

The referents of temporally determined sentences are usually talked of as *situations*. The traditional ontological classification schema (Vendler, 1957) divides up the respective situational types into at least four abstract subclasses: *states, activities, accomplishments* and *achievements*. This aspectual taxonomy takes into account the internal temporal structure of the situations, and is based on a small number of features, such as: *telic, dynamic, durative*.

Situations are referred to by verbal phrases. Differences in truth conditions, presuppositions and entailments of the respective sentences, as well as effects on temporal sequencing in discourse are plausibly built on the aforementioned structural differences. That the assumed ontological aspectual classification is reflected on linguistic level is (at least partly) borne out by a number of language internal testing procedures, such as grammaticality effects in connection with imperative, progressive, pseudo cleft and adverbial constructions.

The aspectual character of a verbal phrase is not solely fixed on the basis of verbal lexical information but can change during the process of semantic composition under the influence of nominal arguments and prepositional phrases, tense and aspectual markers, aspectual auxiliaries, or temporal adverbials. Accordingly, the aim of a theory of aspect is to determine the aspectual characteristics of complex verbal phrases on the basis of semantic information associated with certain of its parts.

In the last thirty years, considerable progress has been made in formally describing the aspectual contribution of nominal and prepositional arguments. However as far as the aspectual behavior of temporal adverbials is concerned, some puzzling sets of data still await proper explanation and appropriate formalization. The observation that problems arise right at that point gets particularly worrying given that the very same types of examples are standardly used as linguistic test cases to differentiate telic from atelic verbal phrases. Therefore, if we could find significant problems with the theory just here, the whole idea of a language internal criterion for the division of verbal expressions according to the aspectual situational schema would suddenly become vague and ungrounded.

The troublesome examples under discussion test for compatibility of a verbal phrase with "for" and "in"-adverbials. According to observational facts - so the traditional story goes - atelic states and activities admit modification by a "for"-adverbial, but give rise to ungrammaticality when combined with an "in"-adverbial. For telic achievements and accomplishments things are precisely the other

© 2008. Licensed under the *Creative Commons Attribution-Noncommercial-Share Alike 3.0 Unported* license (http://creativecommons.org/licenses/by-nc-sa/3.0/). Some rights reserved.

way around. The data under (1) and (2) shortly repeat this well-known pattern.

(1) *be quiet for an hour / *in an hour*
*swim for an hour / *in an hour*

(2) *arrive *for an hour / in an hour*
*build a tower *for an hour / in an hour*

However, after closer inspection, these claimed test cases do not seem to be as simple and clear cut as one would like, given their fundamental theoretical status. The marked phrases, far from being ungrammatical, quite naturally display several kinds of meanings. The focus of the "in"-temporal adverbial under (1) can be read as being shifted from the situation itself towards its *pre-phase*, which is to lead up to the swimming process or to the state of being quiet only an hour later than the present. In cases where an *implicit boundary* for the activity is given by context (e. g., a triathlon competition) the process itself can be also modified by the adverbial. For the telic examples in (2), an *iterative* interpretation appears to be available, with the "for"-adverbial giving the duration of the whole complex situation rather than just of one of the included basic events. Another interpretational possibility here is to let the adverbial fix the duration of the *preparatory phase*, i. e., when the change is under development, which precedes the culmination of the situation. Finally, the "for"-adverbial is also able to modify the *result state* following the culmination of the event.

These phenomena in connection with the application of temporal adverbials to situations that are - under the perspective of traditional aspectual theory - not suitable for them have proven to be notoriously difficult to treat in every kind of available framework. At the same time, the observed cases do not have the status of real exceptions, but appear cross-linguistical and spread over the whole verbal lexicon. Therefore, no theory of aspect can be seen as fully adequate as long as it is not able to account for this flexibility in adverbial semantics. The aim of this paper is to work out a semantic analysis of the cases in question which allows to derive the correct set of possible readings in a simple and fully compositional manner. Additionally, the proposal will aim at explaining the underlying semantic mechanism in terms of a more general cognitive principle.

2 The State of the Art

Before turning to my own proposal for an analysis of aspectual meaning shifts in connection with the interpretation of temporal adverbial modifiers, let me briefly discuss the idea figuring prominently in virtually all recent approaches, e. g., (Pulman, 1997), (deSwart, 1998). I am going to argue that by following this general line of thought too strictly, linguistic research so far failed to answer the question about the source of the semantic flexibility of temporal adverbials (compare (Gruender, 2008)). The claim to be made in this section is that the problems one can point out come about inevitably and for principle reasons. And that they should be seen as the result of an attempt to take a good metaphor too literally.

Moens and Steedman (1988) conceived temporal adverbials as "*functions which 'coerce' their inputs to the appropriate type, by a loose* [sic!] *analogy with type-coercion in programming languages*". Under this perspective, aspectual shift is triggered by a conflict between the aspectual type of the situation to be modified and the aspectual constraint set by the temporal preposition heading the modifier.[1] Coercion operators, then, are thought to adapt the verbal input on the level of model-theoretical interpretation by mapping one sort of situation onto another. The underlying model is commonly supposed to include situations as first-order objects of the four basic types previously mentioned, i. e., *states, activities, accomplishments* and *achievements*.

A first problem is immediately evident with this approach. Since the temporal prepositions constrain the aspectual type of the situation only as far as telicity is concerned, the relation established by coercion cannot be *functional*. With there being no types *telic* and *atelic* but just two more specified primitive types for each case, which are fulfilling the respective aspectual requirement equally well, application of coercion inevitably leaves one with several possible outputs. Since, on the other hand, in examples of real type-coercion, as applied in programming languages, the introduced relation is always functional, a first clear, formal difference

[1] Accordingly, the approach is not going to treat examples (i. e. "hiccup all day") where aspectual shifts appear to follow solely from conceptual background knowledge concerning default durations of certain sorts of events, rather than being triggered by a formal semantic conflict in aspectual type requirements. Likewise, I will disregard the possibility of generic interpretations.

between the operations in the two domains has to be noted. A simple mapping between two primitive situations cannot be what is formally going on in cases of meaning shifts triggered by temporal adverbials, as the relevant formal criterion is too general as to effectively constrain the output type.

This problem becomes even more serious when we take into account the variety of aspectual shifts that actually occur according to the previously given examples. There it becomes clear that even if confined to one of the assumed primitive ontological sorts, the output value of the operation would still remain underspecified. So, for instance, after applying a "for"-adverbial to an accomplishment, the iterative and the result state interpretation count as stative alike. According to the type-coercion paradigm, however, in order to remedy ungrammaticality just one such type-adapted output value would have been sufficient. The fact of there being this exact number and kinds of readings therefore becomes a miracle, which the theory is unable to explain and formally account for.

On the one hand, when the telicity/atelicity constraint is associated with the temporal adverbial in the known way, it generally seems to be too loose with respect to the observed transitions, at the same time it appears to be too restrictive. In the boundary reading, the adverbial is successfully applied to a situational concept carrying the wrong telicity feature without any visible aspectual shifts occuring. At this point the type-coercion paradigm obviously is as close as it could be to being led into contradiction.

How do these very general problems present themselves within the known theoretical approaches? In the course of semantic composition coercion operations get introduced as some kind of metavariables. These variables are instantiated by a variety of concrete operations which relate the input situation to an output situation in all the ways possible. The answer to the decisive question of which functions actually are the ones possible here, however, is just read off the data. From theory alone nothing beyond the telicity/atelicity requirement for the output value would follow, and even this prediction is not strictly borne out, as was argued in the previous paragraph. Therefore, the solution has just been given by empirical observation rather than derived through any theoretical systematization. Here, semantic formalization has become a mere record of the data without further explanatory power.

Furthermore, by having set theoretical focus on the ontological level when implementing aspectual shifts, linguistic research has taken up a perspective entirely extrinsic to language and the adaptive powers of meanings themselves. In result of following the type-coercion metaphor, language comprehension is seen as proceeding via an implicit series of program clashes, only to be repaired by simply not obeying to compositional rules for combining lexical semantic information any longer. However, according to a linguistically inspired, *representational* view, the manipulations at work in case of aspectual shifting would take place within the realm of *Fregean sense*, rather than that of *reference*. The denotation of a situational expression so would constantly get re-computed, as semantic composition proceeds, via the systematic modification of its meaning. By not only involving ontological type information but also semantic information proper, such transition process should effectively determine the denotation of the respective output situational concept in the end, and therefore deliver the theoretical derivation of the aspectual shifting operations that we are after.

Summarizing the result of this section, I claim that the analogy between aspect shift as triggered by temporal adverbials and type-coercion as known in the programming language domain is not as close as generally assumed, and surely does not recommend itself for direct implementation. Applying the formal mechanism used in the latter case too strictly to the former, inevitably leads to the interrelated problems mentioned, and seems by now to obstruct a deeper understanding of what is actually going on when senses change and adapt of their own accord.

3 The Framework

In this section, I will shortly introduce a decompositional approach to event semantics within the framework of finite-state temporal semantics developed by Fernando (2003), (2004). The decision to apply this kind of formalism in the present context was motivated by the intuition that what was needed to appropriately handle aspectual semantic phenomena was the concept of a situation as a complex but logically coherent, dynamic unit. That means, if aspectual features are defined with respect to some internal, temporal structure of a situation, and if aspectual transitions proceed via shifting focus of an adverbial along the time line from one part of that structure to another, this very structure must be represented by the formalism, and has to be made easily accessible by the formal operations. Obviously, the traditional Davidsonean event semantics, where events are seen as indivisible *atoms*, and modifiers as just indifferently predicating over such atoms, is not a convenient formal tool in this respect.

In Fernando's approach a situational concept, is characterized as a *regular language*, accepted by a finite-state automata, that may amount to a finite Kripke model with partial valuations. Each string of such language is viewed as a temporal sequence of observations or a *comic stripe*. The symbols in the alphabet of the language are the still-pictures or snapshots to be strung together in chronological order. Given a finite set Φ of formulas, or fluents, a symbol consists of a consistent subset of Φ, which non-exhaustively enumerates what holds true at some single point in time. Therefore, a situation is represented not just as an atom, but all its internal states are taken into account as well.

A suitable compositional device for stepwise construction of complex situational concepts is available in form of a regular operation *superposition* (&) over two languages (L and L′). Superposition performs componentwise alignment of strings of equal length and is realized model-theoretically as conjunction.

$$L \,\&\, L' = \bigcup_{k \geq 1} \{(\sigma_1 \cup \sigma'_1)\ldots(\sigma_k \cup \sigma'_k) \mid \sigma_1 \ldots \sigma_k \in L, \sigma'_1 \ldots \sigma'_k \in L'\}$$

A simple example (by Fernando), deriving the representation for the phrase "rain from dawn to dusk", should make clear the general idea ($\square$ stands for $\emptyset$-as-a-symbol, boxes replacing braces).

$$\boxed{\text{rain}}^{+} \,\&\, \boxed{\text{dawn}}\,\square^{+} \,\&\, \square^{+}\,\boxed{\text{dusk}} = \boxed{\begin{matrix}\text{rain,}\\ \text{dawn}\end{matrix}}\,\boxed{\text{rain}}^{*}\,\boxed{\begin{matrix}\text{rain,}\\ \text{dusk}\end{matrix}}$$

Negation of symbols is defined in De Morgan style by:

$$\neg\square = \Phi;\ \neg\,\boxed{\phi_1,\ldots,\phi_n} = \boxed{\neg\phi_1} + \ldots + \boxed{\neg\phi_n}$$

(writing + for non-deterministic choice).

Fernando's central idea for a definition of aspectual features is to formally base it on the symbols α and ω that start and finish a given language, respectively. This serves to enable a nice formal encoding of the idea of a situational type being initially or finally *bounded* or *unbounded*. If the condition α is immediately switched after the first stage an initial boundary is marked; if α is preserved the concept is initially unbounded. In the same way ω can be used to mark a final boundary. Aspectual features then just enumerate all the possibilities for a corresponding concept to be bounded or unbounded in that sense.

$$\begin{aligned} \textit{telic}\ (\mathrm{L}) &= \neg\omega(\mathrm{L})^{+}\,\square \\ \textit{iter}\ (\mathrm{L}) &= \square\,\omega(\mathrm{L})^{+} \\ \textit{prog}\ (\mathrm{L}) &= \square\,\neg\alpha(\mathrm{L})^{+} \\ \textit{reten}\ (\mathrm{L}) &= \alpha(\mathrm{L})^{+}\,\square \end{aligned}$$

Notably, on this perspective, the four classical aspectual classes are derivable as the set of logically possible cross-combinations of the four aspectual features as defined above. The corresponding properties of being initially or finally bounded, are marked by using a short binary code, with the first digit referring to the beginning, the second to the ending, and 1 and 0 indicating the presence or absence of a boundary, respectively. If we let *a* and *o* refer to the two boundary marking propositions inside the symbols α and ω we get the abstract characterizations on the very right.

state:	reten, iter	(0 0)	$\boxed{a, o}^{+}$
activity:	prog, iter	(1 0)	$\boxed{a, \neg o}\,\boxed{\neg a, o}^{+}$
achievem.:	reten, telic	(0 1)	$\boxed{a, \neg o}^{+}\,\boxed{\neg a, o}$
accompl.:	prog, telic	(1 1)	$\boxed{a, \neg o}\,\boxed{\neg a, \neg o}^{+}\,\boxed{\neg a, o}$

The following translations, which give formalizations within the framework of two of the initial examples, "swim" and "build a tower", may serve as a concrete illustration.[2]

(3) $\boxed{\neg\exists x \neq \emptyset\ (\mathrm{swim}(x))}\,\boxed{\exists x \neq \emptyset\ (\mathrm{swim}(x))}^{+}$

(4) $\boxed{\neg\exists x \leq t\ (\mathrm{build}(x))}\,\boxed{\exists x \leq t\ (\mathrm{build}(x)), \neg\mathrm{build}(t)}^{+}\,\boxed{\mathrm{build}(t)}$

4 The Proposal

Within the formalism introduced so far, the commonly assumed constraint on the interpretability of temporal adverbials reads as follows (where *V* represents a verbal phrase, and *I* an expression denoting a temporal interval):

$$\Lambda(\mathrm{V}\ \textit{in}\ \mathrm{I}) = \{\Lambda(\mathrm{V}) \,\&\, \Lambda(\mathrm{I}) \text{ if } \Lambda(\mathrm{V}) \text{ is telic; } \emptyset \text{ otherwise}\}$$
$$\Lambda(\mathrm{V}\ \textit{for}\ \mathrm{I}) = \{\Lambda(\mathrm{V}) \,\&\, \Lambda(\mathrm{I}) \text{ if } \Lambda(\mathrm{V}) \text{ is iter; else } \emptyset \text{ otherwise}\}.$$

[2]For the sake of abbreviation, here and in all that follows obvious entailment relations are taken into account. So, for instance, $\neg a$ is suppressed in presence of o here.

The aim of this section is to improve on that by giving room, within the semantic framework itself, for those kinds of adapted interpretations that actually occur, as shown by the initial examples. The approach will set the representational view (section 2) at work here, as it makes use of the possibility to introduce the concept of *underspecification*.

The logical heart of the proposal to be made is *Supervaluation Theory*, developed by van Fraassen (1969) as a formal tool for handling *presupposition failure*. The more general theoretical aim of van Fraassen was to account for the "third possibility" beside the classical valuations *Truth* and *False* in a way that preserves as much as possible from the classical framework. So, notably, while the supervaluationist denies the metalogical *Principle of Bivalence*, he still accepts the logical *Law of Excluded Middle* together with all other classical tautologies. This decisive difference to the several three-valued logical systems known is due to the idea of using *truth-value gaps* rather than a proper third value. Ordinary partial valuations are extended to supervaluations by considering the possible completions of a given model, that is the set of classical valuations such that all missing values get filled up in one way or the other.

Take metavariable M to stand for partial models, M′ to range over all possible completions of M, and M* to be the *supermodel* of M, comprising M together with all its M′.

> A *supervaluation* based on M is a function that assigns *Truth* with respect to M* to a proposition ϕ just in case ϕ is classically true in all M′, *False* just in case it is false in all M′, and # (*gap*) otherwise.

That means, if a proposition ϕ has received supervalue # there are underlying, more precise models such that ϕ is true in some of them and false in others.

With this additional technical equipment available, let me now turn back to the problem of giving an appropriately flexible, but non-ambiguous formal characterization of the semantic contribution of temporal adverbials. The main task obviously consists in offering a proper semantics for the prepositions "in" and "for" that accords with the overall aspectual semantic formalism rather than just stipulating ungrammaticality. In order to keep the idea of a language internal criterion for the aspectual characteristics of a situation intact while allowing for the observed interpretational flexibility, those semantic characterizations should effectively constrain the basic applications of the adverbials in the way commonly assumed, but at the same time allowing and triggering compositional adaptions of sense via meaning shifts. The algorithm I am going to introduce is proceeding in three steps, illustrated here firstly by means of a telic example, and afterwards an atelic one. The general lead-in will be the idea of formally treating aspectually sensitive temporal prepositions as some kind of *dynamic, structural presuppositions*.

As the *starting point*, I assume the representations of the meanings of the two temporal prepositions "in" and "for" under (5) and (6). These formalizations take into account the known preferences with respect to the aspectual type of the situational concept to be modified by encoding the properties *telic* and *iter* according to the formal definitions given in the previous section.

(5) $\Lambda(\mathit{in}) = \boxed{\neg o}^{+}\,\square$ (6) $\Lambda(\mathit{for}) = \square\,\boxed{o}^{+}$

In the first, preparatory step of composition, the prepositions get combined via superposition with the nominal phrase "an hour", as done below.

(7) $\Lambda(\mathit{for\ an\ hour}) = \square\,\boxed{\mathrm{o}}^{+} \;\&\; \boxed{\mathrm{time(m)}}\,\square^{+}\,\boxed{\mathrm{time(n),\ hour(m,n)}}$

$= \boxed{\mathrm{time(m)}}\,\boxed{\mathrm{O}}^{+}\,\boxed{\mathrm{O,\ time(n),\ hour(m,n)}}$

(8) $\Lambda(\mathit{in\ an\ hour}) = \boxed{\neg\mathrm{o}}^{+}\,\square \;\&\; \boxed{\mathrm{time(m)}}\,\square^{+}\,\boxed{\mathrm{time(n),\ hour(m,n)}}$

$= \boxed{\neg\mathrm{o},\ \mathrm{time(m)}}\,\boxed{\neg\mathrm{o}}^{+}\,\boxed{\mathrm{time(n),\ hour(m,n)}}$

Now, the adverbials are ready for modifying the situational concepts, whose abstract aspectual characterizations are given once more in (9) and (10).[3] The explanation will proceed with respect to the telic example first.

(9) $\Lambda(\mathrm{V}^{\mathrm{iter}}) = \boxed{a,\neg o}\,\boxed{\neg a, o}^{+}$

(10) $\Lambda(\mathrm{V}^{\mathrm{tel}}) = \boxed{a,\neg o}\,\boxed{\neg a,\neg o}^{+}\,\boxed{\neg a, o}$

In its *first*, obligatory phase, the algorithm combines the representation of the temporal adverbial with the abstract characterization of the situational concept by means of *superposition*. If the aspectual type of the situational concept agrees with the structural condition set by the preposition, the

[3]Here, an activity is chosen as the atelic example, an accomplishment as the telic one. For states and achievements, though, the respective procedures would work out in exact parallel.

incorporation of prepositional meaning does not have any visible effect. The semantic material just combines normally via superposition, as can be seen in (11), and the algorithm finishes here.

(11) $\Lambda(\mathrm{V}^{\mathrm{tel}}$ *in an hour*$) =$

$$\boxed{a, \neg o, \mathrm{time(m)}}\ \boxed{\neg a, \neg o}^{+}\ \boxed{\neg a, o, \mathrm{time(n)}, \mathrm{hour(m,n)}}$$

However, in case of an aspectual clash between preposition and event description, combining the concepts leads to a contradiction at some predetermined position inside the complex situational type, as happens in (12). This formal accident can be traced back to the preposition and the situational type contributing different claims with respect to the truth-value of the proposition o, encoding the telicity feature.

(12) $\Lambda(\mathrm{V}^{\mathrm{tel}}$ **for an hour*$) =$

$$\boxed{a, \neg o, \mathrm{time(m)}}\ \boxed{\neg a, \underline{\neg o, o}}^{+}\ \boxed{\neg a, o, \mathrm{time(n)}, \mathrm{hour(m,n)}}$$

As these are the cases where interesting aspectual shifts turn up, the real action starts here. In its *second* phase, the algorithm applies a *repairing* mechanism by assigning a truth-value gap (#) to the proposition that previously had received contradictory valuations. The rationale behind this may be thought of as not passing judgement in the face of equally probable but opposing evidences.

(13) $\Lambda(\mathrm{V}^{\mathrm{tel}}$ *#for an hour*$) =$

$$\boxed{a, \neg o, \mathit{time(m)}}\ \boxed{\neg a, \underline{\#o}}^{+}\ \boxed{\neg a, o, \mathit{time(n)}, \mathit{hour(m,n)}}$$

The general formal rule applied here is right the one standardly assumed for other cases of presupposition failure. That means, the meaning of a temporal preposition is thought of as some kind of dynamic, structural presupposition with respect to the development of the truth value of a certain proposition. Its semantic contribution is empty in case the verbal concept it combines with shows the right internal structure, but it causes the introduction of a truth-value gap at a particular position inside the situational string whenever its structural constraint is not satisfied. In the latter case, the result of this semantic operation is a situational concept which is *underspecified* with respect to the *aspectual feature* telic (*#telic*).

As stated above, lacking a truth-value in the sense of supervaluationism, consists in the capacity in principle to make precise in more than one way. That means, for the proposition o having been marked # in a supermodel M*, there are underlying models in M′ such that o is true in one of them but false in the other. This *determination* of previously underspecified information in all possible directions, by grounding the freshly introduced supervalue # in the underlying classical models, is just what the algorithm is supposed to do in its *third*, last step. Intuitively, instead of loosing any information previously received, the ideal language user is developing different hypothetical interpretations separately. This might be taken as a strategy to save monotonicity of the interpretation process by allowing reciprocal adaptions between preposition and situation. The two obvious outputs with respect to the telic example are spelled out below.

(14) $\Lambda^{1}(\mathrm{V}^{\mathrm{tel}}$ *for an hour*$) =$

$$\boxed{a, \neg o, \mathrm{time(m)}}\ \boxed{\neg a, \underline{o}}^{+}\ \boxed{\neg a, o, \mathrm{time(n)}, \mathrm{hour(m,n)}}$$

(15) $\Lambda^{2}(\mathrm{V}^{\mathrm{tel}}$ *for an hour*$) =$

$$\boxed{a, \neg o, \mathrm{time(m)}}\ \boxed{\neg a, \underline{\neg o}}^{+}\ \boxed{\neg a, o, \mathrm{time(n)}, \mathrm{hour(m,n)}}$$

This reintroduction of truth-values after a forced gap gives rise to a specific set of new regular languages. What situational concepts do those rebuilt structures encode? In (14) the result state description appears to have spread over the entire internal part of the expression. Under this perspective the preparatory phase got abstracted away, and the event culminates immediately after start. In consequence, the adverbial now gets interpreted as indicating the duration of the *result state* of the situation. Obviously, this is one of the readings we had found in connection with the modification of telic situational concepts by "for"-adverbials at the very beginning. Under (16) this point gets further illustrated with the help of the familiar example ("build a tower for an hour").

(16) $\boxed{\begin{array}{l}\neg\exists x \leq t\ (\mathrm{build}(x)),\\ \mathrm{time(m)}\end{array}}\ \boxed{\begin{array}{l}\exists x \leq t\ (\mathrm{build}(x)),\\ \mathrm{build}(t)\end{array}}^{+}\ \boxed{\begin{array}{l}\mathrm{build}(t),\\ \mathrm{time(n)}, \mathrm{hour(m,n)}\end{array}}$

In contrast, the second way to make precise the aspectually underspecified concept in (13) leads up to the description under (15). Here, the preparatory phase is making up the whole inner part of the regular expression. Consequently, applying the temporal adverbial gives the description of an event that takes an hour to culminate. What we have here clearly amounts to the *preparatory phase* reading of the "for "-adverbial. Again, (17) offers concrete illustration.

(17) $\boxed{\begin{array}{l}\neg\exists x \leq t\ (\mathrm{build}(x)),\\ \mathrm{time(m)}\end{array}}\ \boxed{\begin{array}{l}\exists x \leq t\ (\mathrm{build}(x)),\\ \neg\mathrm{build}(t)\end{array}}^{+}\ \boxed{\begin{array}{l}\mathrm{build}(t),\\ \mathrm{time(n)}, \mathrm{hour(m,n)}\end{array}}$

Notice that the formal mechanism does in principal not serve to get rid of the factivity entailment for the result state here. While this seems plausible for examples like "grow old for many years", it is certainly not so for "read a book for a few minutes". I take this ambivalence as indicating that this question is not a matter of aspectual logical form, causing "hard" semantic inferences, but that it depends on background knowledge concerning default durations of certain kinds of events. With respect to the above example, this would mean that in order to eventually strip off the result state, a second, pragmatic principle would have to get applied to the intermediate, semantic output gained here.

So far so good. But what about the *iterative* reading we found as the third possibility when looking at this kind of example at the very beginning? To get this interpretation derived, let us take one out of the several different-sized strings encoded by the regular expression in (13), which, for instance, may look like this.

(18) $\Lambda'(V^{tel}\ {}^{\#}\textit{for an hour}) =$

$$\boxed{a, \neg o, time(m)}\ \boxed{\neg a, \underline{\#o}}\ \boxed{\neg a, \underline{\#o}}\ \boxed{\neg a, \underline{\#o}}\ \boxed{\neg a, \underline{\#o}}\ \boxed{\neg a, o, time(n), hour(m,n)}$$

Now, obviously, different classical valuations can be chosen for different states, leading, for instance, to the pattern under (19).

(19) $\Lambda^3(V^{tel}\ {}^{\#}\textit{for an hour}) =$

$$\boxed{a, \neg o, time(m)}\ \boxed{\neg a, \underline{o}}\ \boxed{\neg a, \underline{\neg o}}\ \boxed{\neg a, \underline{o}}\ \boxed{\neg a, \underline{\neg o}}\ \boxed{\neg a, o, time(n), hour(m,n)}$$

That means, preparatory phases freely alternate with result states, thereby forming a situational description which can only be interpreted as referring to a situation comprising several iterations of the original event. This complex situation as a whole becomes the attaching point of the temporal information carried by the adverbial. Under (20) this move is spelled out with respect to the concrete example.

(20) $$\boxed{\neg\exists x \leq t\,(build(x)), time(m)}\ \boxed{build(t)}\ \boxed{\exists x \leq t\,(build(x)), \neg build(t)}\ \boxed{build(t)}\ \ldots$$
$$\boxed{\exists x \leq t\,(build(x)), \neg build(t)}\ \boxed{build(t), time(n), hour(m,n)}$$

After having derived all possible interpretations of a "for"-adverbial when applied to a telic concept, the task of accounting for adapted readings of an "in"-adverbial modifying an atelic situational description is still at stake. A *preparatory phase* and a *boundary* reading is what we would wish the semantic mechanism to deliver here. The following formulas are the result of trying out the three steps of the shifting algorithm - superposition, reparation, determination - for the atelic case.

(21) $\Lambda(V^{iter}\ {}^{*}\textit{in an hour}) =$

$$\boxed{a, \neg o, time(m)}\ \boxed{\neg a, \underline{o, \neg o}}^{+}\ \boxed{\neg a, o, time(n), hour(m,n)}$$

As before, in order to escape contradiction the algorithm proceeds by underspecifying the critical telicity structural information. The side effect of the truth-value gap spreading over from o to a in the atelic example in (22) is due to the fact of the both proposition generally being negation variants of each other here (compare (3)).

(22) $\Lambda(V^{iter}\ {}^{\#}\textit{in an hour}) =$

$$\boxed{a, \neg o, time(m)}\ \boxed{\#a, \underline{\#o}}^{+}\ \boxed{\neg a, o, time(n), hour(m,n)}$$

Then, fulfilling the third, determination step with respect to the above underspecified concept, leads to the following two regular languages.

(23) $\Lambda^1(V^{iter}\ \textit{in an hour}) =$

$$\boxed{a, \neg o, time(m)}\ \boxed{a, \underline{\neg o}}^{+}\ \boxed{\neg a, o, time(n), hour(m,n)}$$

(24) $\Lambda^2(V^{iter}\ \textit{in an hour}) =$

$$\boxed{a, \neg o, time(m)}\ \boxed{\neg a, \underline{o}}^{+}\ \boxed{\neg a, o, time(n), hour(m,n)}$$

In (23) the start of the phase of activity is postponed to the very last symbol. On that basis, the temporal adverbial gets interpreted as specifying the duration of the respective pre-phase. In (24), on the other hand, the activity phase of the situation got spread over the entire real suffix of the regular expression. Therefore, the adverbial adds information concerning the temporal boundaries of the whole situation. So, both known interpretational possibilities can be accounted for by the proposed formalism.[4] Again, the concrete example ("swim in an hour") may ease understanding.

(25) $$\boxed{\neg\exists x \neq \emptyset\,(swim(x)), time(m)}\ \boxed{\neg\exists x \neq \emptyset\,(swim(x))}^{+}\ \boxed{\exists x \neq \emptyset\,(swim(x)), time(n), hour(m,n)}$$

(26) $$\boxed{\neg\exists x \neq \emptyset\,(swim(x)), time(m)}\ \boxed{\exists x \neq \emptyset\,(swim(x))}^{+}\ \boxed{\exists x \neq \emptyset\,(swim(x)), time(n), hour(m,n)}$$

The aim of the semantic interpretation process has been achieved at this point. It was to make provision for the set of possible readings found in the cases under consideration in a fully composi-

[4] The formally possible third variant, parallel to the iterative interpretation gained for the telic example, is not very prominent here and usually not discussed in the literature. But there are certainly special contexts in which this description may nevertheless apply (imagine some sort of interval training session, for instance). So, there is no over-generation here.

tional manner, i. e., only using lexical semantic entries and general rules for combining them. Further methods will have to apply in order to filter out the best actual candidate with the help of more contextual information and world knowledge.

5 Conclusion

The aim of this paper was to show how the meaning potential of temporal adverbials can be formally accounted for, and to give room, within the compositional semantic framework itself, for an efficient derivation and systematic explanation of the exact number and kinds of possible readings.

According to the proposal made here, aspectual shifts consist in restructuring a situational concept from inside rather than in simple mappings from one atomic event onto another. Aspectual transitions thus happen with respect to linguistic representations rather than ontological entities and are made on a finer, subatomic semantic level.

The heart of the proposal is the concept of aspectual underspecification and the idea of formally treating the meaning of temporal prepositions as some kind of dynamic, structural presuppositions. Thus, the whole process is triggered by some kind of type conflict, as traditionally assumed, but gets now controlled by the introduction and consequent filling in of a truth-value gap. Literally, the meaning of a verbal phrase including an aspectual clash between temporal adverbial modifier and situational concept to be modified is an aspectually underspecified situational concept. The possible aspectually shifted readings then appear as the different ways of specifying it.

As opposed to what is the case in traditional theories of aspect shift, those possible ways of specifying are compositionally determined, i. e. by exclusive recurrence of semantic material already present in the enriched representation, and via application of the standardly assumed rule for cases of presupposition failure. Therefore, the semantic process in question is analysed here as entirely language internal.

Another interesting feature of the proposed algorithm when compared to the traditional approach seems to be that it is not the one-sided compliance of letting the verbal phrase possibly be type-changed by the adverbial, but rather the idea of allowing reciprocal adaptations that finally leaves us with the right set of predictions. Hereby, monotonicity of the overall interpretation process is preserved.

Last but not least, the procedure of systematically introducing underspecification as some kind of claimed ignorance in the presence of conflicting evidence, and of subsequently trying out all possible specifications separately, seems to be a plausible hypothesis about the rational strategies we really may use when adapting sense.

References

de Swart, Henriette. 1998. Aspectual Shift and Coercion. *Natural Language and Linguistic Theory*, 16:347–385.

Fernando, Tim. 2003. Finite-state descriptions for temporal semantics. *Computing Meaning*, volume 3. Kluwer, Tilburg.

Fernando, Tim. 2004. A finite-state Approach to Events in Natural Language Semantics. *Journal of Logic and Computation*, 14(1):79–92.

Gründer, Sabine. 2008. Aspectual Shift as Supervaluation. (*to appear*), Available under: *http://www.asv.informatik.uni-leipzig.de/opencms/opencms/asv/de/Mitarbeiter/Sabine_Gruender.html*

Moens, Marc and Steedman, Mark. 1988. Temporal Ontology and Temporal Reference. *Computational Linguistics*, 14(2):15–28.

Pulman, Stephen, G. 1997. Aspectual Shift as Type Coercion. *Transactions of the Philological Society*, 95(2):279–317.

Vendler, Zeno. 1957. Verbs and Times. *Philosophical Review*, 66:143–160.

van Fraassen, Bas. 1969. Presuppositions, supervaluations and free logic. in K. Lambert (ed) *The Logical Way of Doing Things*, 67–91. Yale University Press, New Haven.

Dependency-Based N-Gram Models for General Purpose Sentence Realisation

Yuqing Guo
NCLT, School of Computing
Dublin City University
Dublin 9, Ireland
yguo@computing.dcu.ie

Josef van Genabith
NCLT, School of Computing
Dublin City University
IBM CAS, Dublin, Ireland
josef@computing.dcu.ie

Haifeng Wang
Toshiba (China)
Research & Development Center
Beijing, 100738, China
wanghaifeng@rdc.toshiba.com.cn

Abstract

We present dependency-based n-gram models for general-purpose, wide-coverage, probabilistic sentence realisation. Our method linearises unordered dependencies in input representations *directly* rather than via the application of grammar rules, as in traditional chart-based generators. The method is simple, efficient, and achieves competitive accuracy and complete coverage on standard English (Penn-II, 0.7440 BLEU, 0.05 sec/sent) and Chinese (CTB6, 0.7123 BLEU, 0.14 sec/sent) test data.

1 Introduction

Sentence generation,[1] or surface realisation can be described as the problem of producing syntactically, morphologically, and orthographically correct sentences from a given semantic or syntactic representation.

Most general-purpose realisation systems developed to date transform the input into surface form via the application of a set of grammar rules based on particular linguistic theories, e.g. Lexical Functional Grammar (LFG), Head-Driven Phrase Structure Grammar (HPSG), Combinatory Categorial Grammar (CCG), Tree Adjoining Grammar (TAG) etc. These grammar rules are either carefully handcrafted, as those used in FUF/SURGE (Elhadad, 1991), LKB (Carroll et al., 1999), OpenCCG (White, 2004) and XLE (Crouch et al., 2007), or created semi-automatically (Belz, 2007), or fully automatically extracted from annotated corpora, like the HPSG (Nakanishi et al., 2005), LFG (Cahill and van Genabith, 2006; Hogan et al., 2007) and CCG (White et al., 2007) resources derived from the Penn-II Treebank (PTB) (Marcus et al., 1993).

Over the last decade, probabilistic models have become widely used in the field of natural language generation (NLG), often in the form of a realisation ranker in a two-stage generation architecture. The two-stage methodology is characterised by a separation between generation and selection, in which rule-based methods are used to generate a space of possible paraphrases, and statistical methods are used to select the most likely realisation from the space. By and large, two statistical models are used in the rankers to choose output strings:

- N-gram language models over different units, such as word-level bigram/trigram models (Bangalore and Rambow, 2000; Langkilde, 2000), or factored language models integrated with syntactic tags (White et al., 2007).
- Log-linear models with different syntactic and semantic features (Velldal and Oepen, 2005; Nakanishi et al., 2005; Cahill et al., 2007).

To date, however, probabilistic models learning *direct* mappings from generation input to surface strings, without the effort to construct a grammar, have rarely been explored. An exception is Ratnaparkhi (2000), who presents maximum entropy models to learn attribute ordering and lexical choice for sentence generation from a semantic representation of attribute-value pairs, restricted to an air travel domain.

© 2008. Licensed under the *Creative Commons Attribution-Noncommercial-Share Alike 3.0 Unported* license (http://creativecommons.org/licenses/by-nc-sa/3.0/). Some rights reserved.

[1] In this paper, the term "generation" is used generally for what is more strictly referred to by the term "tactical generation" or "surface realisation".

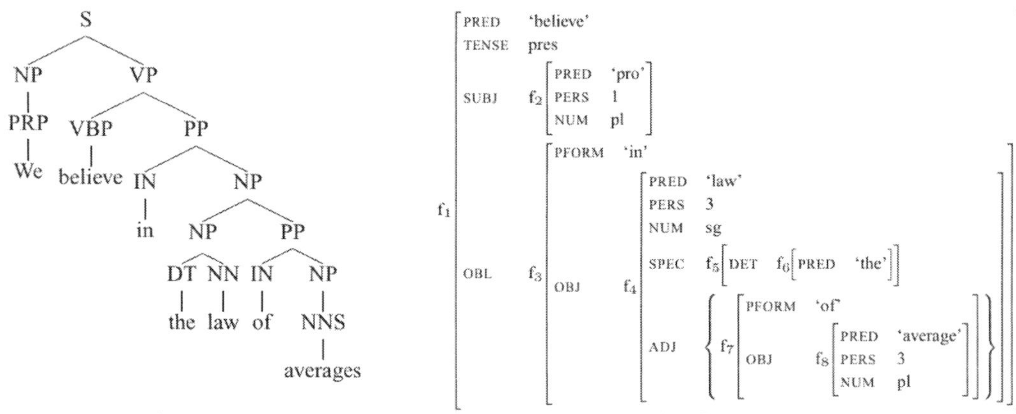

(a.) c-structure (b.) f-structure

string position	We 1	believe 2	in 3	the 4	law 5	of 6	averages 7
f_1	SUBJ	PRED	OBL				
f_3			PFORM		OBJ		
f_4				SPEC	PRED	ADJ	
f_7						PFORM	OBJ

(c.) linearised grammatical functions / bilexical dependencies

Figure 1: C- and f-structures for the sentence *We believe in the law of averages.*

In this paper, we develop an efficient, wide-coverage generator based on simple n-gram models to directly linearise dependency relations from the input representations. Our work is aimed at general-purpose sentence generation but couched in the framework of Lexical Functional Grammar. We give an overview of LFG and the dependency representations we use in Section 2. We describe the general idea of our dependency-based generation in Section 3 and give details of the n-gram generation models in Section 4. Section 5 explains the experiments and provides results for both English and Chinese data. Section 6 compares the results with previous work and between languages. Finally we conclude with a summary and outline future work.

2 LFG-Based Generation

2.1 Lexical Functional Grammar

Lexical Functional Grammar (Kaplan and Bresnan, 1982) is a constraint-based grammar formalism which postulates (minimally) two levels of representation: c(onstituent)-structure and f(unctional)-structure. As illustrated in Figure 1, a c-structure is a conventional phrase structure tree and captures surface grammatical configurations. The f-structure encodes more abstract functional relations like SUBJ(ect), OBJ(ect) and ADJ(unct). F-structures are hierarchical attribute-value matrix representations of bilexical labelled dependencies, approximating to basic predicate-argument/adjunct structures.[2] Attributes in f-structure come in two different types:

- Grammatical Functions (GFs) indicate the relationship between the predicate and dependents. GFs can be divided into:
  - arguments are subcategorised for by the predicate, such as SUBJ(ect), OBJ(ect), and thus can only occur once in each local f-structure.
  - modifiers like ADJ(unct), COORD(inate) are not subcategorised for by the predicate, and can occur any number of times in a local f-structure.
- Atomic-valued features describe linguistic properties of the predicate, such as TENSE, ASPECT, MOOD, PERS, NUM, CASE etc.

2.2 Generation from F-Structures

Work on generation in LFG generally assumes that the generation task is to determine the set of strings of the language that corresponds to a specified f-structure, given a particular grammar (Kaplan and Wedekind, 2000). Previous work on generation

[2] F-structures can be also interpreted as quasi-logical forms (van Genabith and Crouch, 1996), which more closely resemble inputs used by some other generators.

within LFG includes the XLE,[3] Cahill and van Genabith (2006), Hogan et al. (2007) and Cahill et al. (2007). The XLE generates sentences from f-structures according to parallel handcrafted grammars for English, French, German, Norwegian, Japanese, and Urdu. Based on the German XLE resources, Cahill et al. (2007) describe a two-stage, log-linear generation model. Cahill and van Genabith (2006) and Hogan et al. (2007) present a chart generator using wide-coverage PCFG-based LFG approximations automatically acquired from treebanks (Cahill et al., 2004).

3 Dependency-Based Generation: the Basic Idea

Traditional LFG generation models can be regarded as the reverse process of parsing, and use bi-directional f-structure-annotated CFG rules. In a sense, the generation process is driven by an input dependency (or f-structure) representation, but proceeds through the "detour" of using dependency-annotated CFG (or PCFG) grammars and chart-based generators. In this paper, we develop a simple n-gram and dependency-based, wide-coverage, robust, probabilistic generation model, which cuts out the middle-man from previous approaches: the CFG-component.

Our approach is data-driven: following the methodology in (Cahill et al., 2004; Guo et al., 2007), we automatically convert the English Penn-II treebank and the Chinese Penn Treebank (Xue et al., 2005) into f-structure banks. F-structures such as Figure 1(b.) are unordered, i.e. they do *not* carry information on to the relative surface order of local GFs. In order to generate a string from an f-structure, we need to linearise the GFs (at each level of embedding) in the f-structure (and map lemmas and features to surface forms). We do this in terms of n-gram models over GFs. In order to build the n-gram models, we linearise the f-structures automatically produced from treebanks by associating the numerical string position (word offset from start of the sentence) with the predicate in each local f-structure, producing GF sequences as in Figure 1(c.).

Even though the n-gram models are exemplified using LFG f-structures, they are general-purpose models and thus suitable for any bilexical labelled dependency (Nivre, 2006) or predicate-argument type representations, such as the labelled feature-value structures used in HALogen and the functional descriptions in the FUF/SURGE system.

4 N-Gram Models for Dependency-Based Generation

4.1 Basic N-Gram Model

The primary task of a sentence generator is to determine the linear order of constituents and words, represented as lemmas in predicates in f-structures. At a particular local f-structure, the task of generating a string covered by the local f-structure is equivalent to linearising all the GFs present at that local f-structure. E.g. in f_4 in Figure 1, the unordered set of local GFs {SPEC, PRED, ADJ} generates the surface sequence "the law of averages". We linearise the GFs in the set by computing n-gram models, similar to traditional word-based language models, except using the names of GFs (including PRED) instead of words. Given a (sub-) f-structure F containing m GFs, the n-gram model searches for the best surface sequence $S_1^m = s_1 ... s_m$ generated by the GF linearisation $GF_1^m = GF_1 ... GF_m$, which maximises the probability $P(GF_1^m)$. Using n-gram models, $P(GF_1^m)$ is calculated according to Eq.(1).

$$\begin{aligned} P(GF_1^m) &= P(GF_1 ... GF_m) \\ &= \prod_{k=1}^{m} P(GF_k | GF_{k-n+1}^{k-1}) \end{aligned} \quad (1)$$

4.2 Factored N-Gram Models

In addition to the basic n-gram model over bare GFs, we integrate contextual and fine-grained lexical information into several factored models. Eq.(2) additionally conditions the probability of the n-gram on the parent GF label of the current local f-structure f_i, Eq.(3) on the instantiated PRED of the local f-structure f_i, and Eq.(4) lexicalises the model, where each GF is augmented with its own predicate lemma.

$$P^g(GF_1^m) = \prod_{k=1}^{m} P(GF_k | GF_{k-n+1}^{k-1}, GF_i) \quad (2)$$

$$P^p(GF_1^m) = \prod_{k=1}^{m} P(GF_k | GF_{k-n+1}^{k-1}, Pred_i) \quad (3)$$

$$P^l(GF_1^m) = \prod_{k=1}^{m} P(Lex_k | Lex_{k-n+1}^{k-1}) \quad (4)$$

[3] http://www2.parc.com/isl/groups/nltt/xle/

To avoid data sparseness, the factored n-gram models P^f are smoothed by linearly interpolating the basic n-gram model P, as in Eq.(5).

$$\hat{P}^f(GF_1^m) = \lambda P^f(GF_1^m) + (1-\lambda)P(GF_1^m) \quad (5)$$

Additionally, the lexicalised n-gram models P^l are combined with the other two models conditioned on the additional parent GF P^g and PRED P^p, as shown in Eqs. (6) & (7), respectively.

$$\hat{P}^{lg}(GF_1^m) = \lambda_1 P^l(GF_1^m) + \lambda_2 P^g(GF_1^m) + \lambda_3 P(GF_1^m) \quad (6)$$

$$\hat{P}^{lp}(GF_1^m) = \lambda_1 P^l(GF_1^m) + \lambda_2 P^p(GF_1^m) + \lambda_3 P(GF_1^m) \quad (7)$$

$$where \ \sum \lambda_i = 1$$

Table 1 exemplifies the different n-gram models for the local f-structure f_4 in Figure 1.

Model	N-grams			Cond.
basic (P)	SPEC	PRED	ADJ	
gf (P^g)	SPEC	PRED	ADJ	OBL
pred (P^p)	SPEC	PRED	ADJ	'law'
lex (P^l)	SPEC	PRED['law']	ADJ['of']	

Table 1: Examples of n-grams for f_4 in Figure 1

Besides grammatical functions, we also make use of atomic-valued features like TENSE, PERS, NUM (etc.) to aid linearisation. The attributes and values of these features are integrated into the GF n-grams for disambiguation (see Section 5.2).

4.3 Generation Algorithm

Our basic n-gram based generation model implements the simplifying assumption that linearisation at one sub-f-structure is independent of linearisation at any other sub-f-structures. This assumption is feasible for projective dependencies. In most cases (at least in English and Chinese), non-projective dependencies are only used to account for Long-Distance Dependencies (LDDs). Consider sentence (1) discussed in Carroll et al. (1999) and its corresponding f-structure in Figure 2. In LFG f-structures, LDDs are represented via reentrancies between "dislocated" TOPIC, TOPIC_REL, FOCUS (etc.) GFs and "source" GFs subcategorised for by local predicates, but only the dislocated GFs are instantiated in generation. Therefore traces of the source GFs in input f-structures are removed before generation, and non-projective dependencies are transformed into simple projective dependencies.

(1) How quickly did the newspapers say the athlete ran?

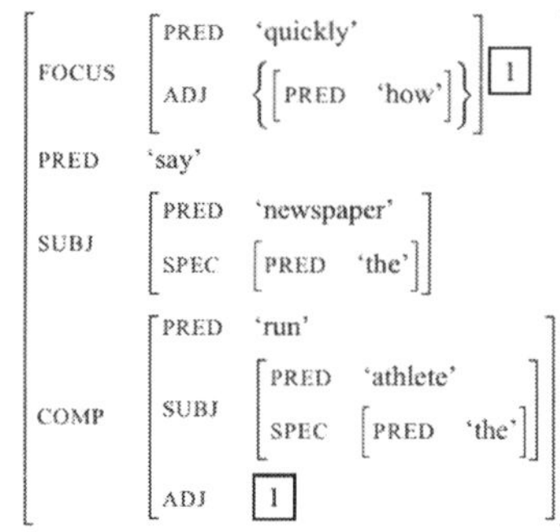

Figure 2: schematic f-structure for *How quickly did the newspapers say the athlete ran?*

In summary, given an input f-structure f, the core algorithm of the generator recursively traverses f and at each sub-f-structure f_i:

1. instantiates the local predicate at f_i and performs inflections/declensions if necessary
2. calculates the GF linearisations present at f_i by n-gram models
3. finds the most probable GF sequence among all possibilities by Viterbi search
4. generates the string covered by f_i according to the linearised GFs

5 Experiments and Evaluation

To test the performance and coverage of our n-gram-based generation models, experiments are carried out for both English and Chinese, two languages with distinct properties.

5.1 Experiment Design

Experiments on English data are carried out on the WSJ portion of the PTB, using standard training/test/development splits, viz 39,832 sentences from sections 02-21 are used for training, 2,416 sentences from section 23 for testing, while 1,700 sentences from section 22 are held out for development. The latest version of the Penn Chinese Treebank 6.0 (CTB6), excluding the portion of ACE broadcast news, is used for experiments on Chinese data.[4] We follow the recommended splits (in the list-of-file of CTB6) to divide the data into test set, development set and training set. The training set includes 756 files with a total of 15,663 sentences. The test set includes 84 files with 1,708

[4]Sentences labelled as fragment are not included in our development and test set.

sentences. The development set includes 50 files with 1,116 sentences. Table 2 shows some of the characteristics of the English and Chinese data obtained from the development sets.

Development Set	English	Chinese
num of sent	1,700	1,116
max length of sent (#words)	110	145
ave length of sent (#words)	23	31
num of local fstr	23,289	15,847
num of local fstr per sent	13.70	14.20
max length of local fstr (#gfs)	12	16
ave length of local fstr (#gfs)	2.56	2.90

Table 2: Comparison English and Chinese data

The n-gram models are created using the SRILM toolkit (Stolcke, 2002) with Good-Turning smoothing for both the Chinese and English data. For morphological realisation of English, a set of lexical macros is automatically extracted from the training data. This is not required for Chinese surface realisation as Chinese has very little morphology. Lexical macro examples are listed in Table 3.

lexical macro	surface word
pred=law, num=sg, pers=3	law
pred=average, num=pl, pers=3	averages
pred=believe, num=pl, tense=pres	believe

Table 3: Examples of lexical macros

The input to our generator are unordered f-structures automatically derived from the development and test set trees of our treebanks, which do *not* contain any string position information. But, due to the particulars of the automatic f-structure annotation algorithm, the order of sub-f-structures in set-valued GFs, such as ADJ, COORD, happens to correspond to their surface order. To avoid unfairly inflating evaluation results, we lexically re-order the GFs in each sub-f-structure of the development and test input before the generation process. This resembles the "permute, no dir" type experiment in (Langkilde, 2002).

5.2 Experimental Results

Following (Langkilde, 2002) and other work on general-purpose generators, BLEU score (Papineni et al., 2002), average NIST simple string accuracy (SSA) and percentage of exactly matched sentences are adopted as evaluation metrics. As our system guarantees that all input f-structures can generate a complete sentence, special coverage-dependent evaluation (as has been adopted in most grammar-based generation systems) is not necessary in our experiments.

Experiments are carried out on an Intel Pentium 4 server, with a 3.80GHz CPU and 3GB memory. It takes less than 2 minutes to generate all 2,416 sentences (with average sentence length of 21 words) of WSJ section 23 (average 0.05 sec per sentence), and approximately 4 minutes to generate 1,708 sentences (with average sentence length of 30 words) of CTB test data (average 0.14 sec per sentence), using 4-gram models in all experiments. Our evaluation results for English and Chinese data are shown in Tables 4 and 5, respectively.

Different n-gram models perform nearly consistently in all the experiments on both English and Chinese data. The results show that factored n-gram models outperform the basic n-gram models, and in turn the combined n-gram models outperform single n-gram models. The combined model interpolating n-grams over lexicalised GFs with n-grams conditioned on PRED achieves the best results in both experiments on English (with feature names) and Chinese (with feature names & values), with BLEU scores of 0.7440 and 0.7123 respectively, and full coverage.

Lexicalisation plays an important role in both English and Chinese, boosting the BLEU score without features from 0.5074 to 0.6741 for English, and from 0.5752 to 0.6639 for Chinese.

Atomic-valued features play an important role in English, and boost the BLEU score from 0.5074 in the baseline model to 0.6842 when feature names are integrated into the n-gram models. However, feature names in Chinese only increase the BLEU score from 0.5752 to 0.6160. This is likely to be the case as English has a richer morphology than Chinese, and important function words such as 'if', 'to', 'that' are encoded in atomic-valued features in English f-structures, which helps to determine string order. However, combined feature names and values work better on Chinese data, but turn out to hurt the n-gram model performance for English data. This may suggest that the feature names in English already include enough information, while the value of morphological features, such as TENSE, NUM does not provide any new information to help determine word order, but aggravate data sparseness instead.

WSJ Sec23	Without Features			Feature Names			Feature Names & Values		
Model	ExMatch	BLEU	SSA	ExMatch	BLEU	SSA	ExMatch	BLEU	SSA
baseline	5.30%	0.5074	57.29%	15.27%	0.6842	69.48%	15.15%	0.6829	69.15%
gf	6.62%	0.5318	60.06%	16.76%	0.6969	71.51%	16.68%	0.6977	71.55%
pred	8.03%	0.5697	60.73%	16.72%	0.7035	70.12%	16.76%	0.7042	71.08%
lex	12.87%	0.6741	69.43%	19.41%	0.7384	74.76%	18.96%	0.7375	74.12%
lex+gf	12.62%	0.6611	69.41%	19.70%	0.7388	74.98%	19.74%	0.7405	75.08%
lex+pred	12.25%	0.6569	68.04%	**19.83%**	**0.7440**	**75.34%**	19.58%	0.7422	75.04%

Table 4: Results for English Penn-II WSJ section 23

Test	Without Features			Feature Names			Feature Names & Values		
Model	ExMatch	BLEU	SSA	ExMatch	BLEU	SSA	ExMatch	BLEU	SSA
baseline	8.96%	0.5752	51.92%	11.77%	0.6160	54.64%	12.30%	0.6239	55.20%
gf	9.54%	0.6009	53.02%	12.53%	0.6391	55.78%	13.47%	0.6486	56.60%
pred	10.07%	0.6180	53.80%	13.35%	0.6608	56.72%	14.46%	0.6720	57.67%
lex	13.93%	0.6639	59.61%	15.16%	0.6770	60.44%	15.98%	0.6804	60.20%
lex+gf	14.81%	0.6773	59.92%	15.52%	0.6911	60.97%	16.80%	0.6957	61.07%
lex+pred	16.04%	0.6952	60.82%	16.22%	0.7060	61.45%	**17.51%**	**0.7123**	**61.54%**

Table 5: Results for Chinese CTB6 test data

WSJ Sec23	Sentence length $\leq$ 20 words				All sentences			
	Coverage	ExMatch	BLEU	SSA	Coverage	ExMatch	BLEU	SSA
Langkilde(2002)					82.7%	28.2%	**0.757**	69.6%
Callaway(2003)					98.7%	**49.0%**		**88.84%**
Nakanishi(2005)	90.75%		**0.7733**		83.6%		0.705	
Cahill(2006)	98.65%		0.7077	73.73%	98.05%		0.6651	68.08%
Hogan(2007)	100%		0.7139		99.96%		0.6882	70.92%
White(2007)					94.3%	6.9%	0.5768	
this paper	**100%**	35.40%	0.7625	81.09%	**100%**	19.83%	0.7440	75.34%

Table 6: Cross system comparison of results for English WSJ section 23

6 Discussion

6.1 Comparison to Previous Work

It is very difficult to compare sentence generators since the information contained in the input representation varies greatly between systems. The most direct comparison is between our system and those presented in Cahill and van Genabith (2006) and Hogan et al. (2007), as they also use treebank-based automatically generated f-structures as the generator inputs. The labelled feature-value structures used in HALogen (Langkilde, 2002) and functional descriptions in FUF/SURGE (Callaway, 2003) also bear some broad similarities to our f-structures. A number of systems using different input but adopting the same evaluation metrics and testing on the same data are listed in Table 6.

Surprisingly (or not), the best results are achieved by a purely symbolic generation system—FUF/SURGE (Callaway, 2003). However the approach uses handcrafted grammars which are very time-consuming to produce and adapt to different languages and domains. Langkilde (2002) reports results for experiments with varying levels of linguistic detail in the input given to the generator. The type "permute, no dir" is most comparable to the level of information contained in our f-structure in that the modifiers (adjuncts, coordinates etc.) in the input are not ordered. However her labelled feature-value structure is more specific than our f-structure as it also includes syntactic properties such as part-of-speech, which might contribute to the higher BLEU score of HALogen. And moreover, in HALogen nearly 20% of the sentences are only partially generated (or not at all). Nakanishi et al. (2005) carry out experiments on sentences up to 20 words, with BLEU scores slightly higher than ours. However their results without sentence length limitation (listed in the right column), for 500 sentences randomly selected from WSJ Sec22 are lower than ours, even at a lower coverage. Overall our system is competitive, with best results for coverage (100%), second best for BLEU and SSA scores, and third best overall on exact match. However, we admit that automatic metrics such as BLEU are not fully reliable to compare different systems, and results vary widely depending on the coverage of the systems and the specificity of the generation input.

6.2 Error Analysis and Differences Between the Languages

Though our dependency-based n-gram models perform well in both the English and Chinese experiments, we are surprised that experiments on English data produce better results than those for Chinese. It is widely accepted that English generation is more difficult than Chinese, due to morphological inflections and the somewhat less predictable word order of English compared to Chinese. This is reflected by the results of the baseline models. Chinese has a BLEU score of 0.5752 and 8.96% exact match, both are higher than those of English. However with feature augmentation and lexicalisation, the results for English data exceed Chinese. This is probably because of the following reasons:

Data size of the English training set is more than twice that of Chinese.

Grammatical functions are more fine-grained in English f-structures than those in Chinese. There are 32 GFs defined for English compared to 20 for Chinese in our input f-structures.

Properties of the languages and data sets are different. For example, due to lack of inflection and case markers, many sequences of VPs in Chinese have to be treated as coordinates, whereas their counterparts in English act as different grammatical functions, e.g. (2).

(2) 投资 百万 兴建 这个 工程
invest million build this construction
'invest million yuan *to* build the construction'

This results in a total of 7,377 coordinates (4.32 per sentence) in the Chinese development data, compared to 2,699 (1.12 per sentence) in the English data. The most extreme case in the Chinese data features 14 coordinates of country names in a local f-structure. This may account for the low SSA score for the Chinese experiments, as many coordinates are tied in the n-gram scoring method and can not be ordered correctly. Examining the development data shows different types of coordination errors:

- syntactic coordinates, but not semantic coordinates, as in sentence (2).
- syntactic and semantic coordinates, but usually expressed in a fixed order, e.g. (3).

  (3) 改革 开放
  reform opening-up
  'reform and opening up'

- syntactic and semantic coordinates, which can freely swap positions, e.g. (4).

  (4) 充沛的 精力 和 敏捷的 思维
  plentiful energy and quick thinking
  'energetic and agile'

At the current stage, our n-gram generation model only keeps the most likely realisation for each local f-structure. We believe that packing all equivalent elements, like coordinates in a local f-structure into equivalent classes, and outputing n-best candidate realisations will greatly increase the SSA score and may also further benefit the efficiency of the algorithm.

7 Conclusions and Further Work

We have described a number of increasingly sophisticated n-gram models for sentence generation from labelled bilexical dependencies, in the form of LFG f-structures. The models include additional conditioning on parent GFs and different degrees of lexicalisation. Our method is simple, highly efficient, broad coverage and accurate in practice. We present experiments on English and Chinese, showing that the method generalises well to different languages and data sets. We are currently exploring further combinations of conditioning context and lexicalisation, application to different languages and to dependency representations used to train state-of-the-art dependency parsers (Nivre, 2006).

Acknowledgments

This research is funded by Science Foundation Ireland grant 04/IN/I527. We thank Aoife Cahill for providing the treebank-based LFG resources for the English data. We gratefully acknowledge the feedback provided by our anonymous reviewers.

References

Bangalore, Srinivas and Rambow, Owen. 2000. Exploiting a Probabilistic Hierarchical Model for Generation. *Proceedings of the 18th International Conference on Computational Linguistics*, 42–48. Saarbrücken, Germany.

Belz, Anja. 2007. Probabilistic Generation of Weather Forecast Texts. *Proceedings of the Conference of the North American Chapter of the Association for Computational Linguistics*, 164–171. New York.

Cahill, Aoife, Burke, Michael, O'Donovan, Ruth, van Genabith, Josef and Way, Andy. 2004. Long-Distance Dependency Resolution in Automatically

Acquired Wide-Coverage PCFG-Based LFG Approximations. In *Proceedings of the 42nd Annual Meeting of the Association for Computational Linguistics*, 320-327. Barcelona, Spain.

Cahill, Aoife and van Genabith, Josef. 2006. Robust PCFG-Based Generation Using Automatically Acquired LFG Approximations. *Proceedings of the 21st International Conference on Computational Linguistics and 44th Annual Meeting of the Association for Computational Linguistics*, 1033–1040. Sydney, Australia.

Cahill, Aoife, Forst, Martin and Rohrer, Christian. 2007. Stochastic Realisation Ranking for a Free Word Order Language. *Proceedings of the 11th European Workshop on Natural Language Generation*, 17–24. Schloss Dagstuhl, Germany.

Callaway, Charles B.. 2003. Evaluating Coverage for Large Symbolic NLG Grammars. *Proceedings of the Eighteenth International Joint Conference on Artificial Intelligence*, 811–817. Acapulco, Mexico.

Carroll, John, Copestake, Ann, Flickinger, Dan and Poznanski, Victor. 1999. An efficient chart generator for (semi-)lexicalist grammars. *Proceedings of the 7th European Workshop on Natural Language Generation*, 86–95. Toulouse, France.

Crouch, Dick, Dalrymple, Mary, Kaplan, Ron, King, Tracy, Maxwell, John and Newman, Paula. 2007. XLE Documentation. Palo Alto Research Center, CA.

Elhadad, Michael. 1991. FUF: The universal unifier user manual version 5.0. Technical Report CUCS-038-91. Dept. of Computer Science, Columbia University.

Guo, Yuqing and van Genabith, Josef and Wang, Haifeng. 2007. Treebank-based Acquisition of LFG Resources for Chinese. *Proceedings of LFG07 Conference*, 214–232. Stanford, CA, USA.

Hogan, Deirdre Cafferkey, Conor Cahill, Aoife and van Genabith, Josef. 2007. Exploiting Multi-Word Units in History-Based Probabilistic Generation. *Proceedings of the 2007 Joint Conference on Empirical Methods in Natural Language Processing and CoNLL*, 267–276. Prague, Czech Republic.

Kaplan, Ronald and Bresnan, Joan. 1982. Lexical Functional Grammar: a Formal System for Grammatical Representation. *The Mental Representation of Grammatical Relations*, 173–282. MIT Press, Cambridge.

Kaplan, Ronald and Wedekind, Jurgen. 2000. LFG Generation Produces Context-free Languages. *Proceedings of the 18th International Conference on Computational Linguistics*, 425–431. Saarbrücken, Germany.

Langkilde, Irene. 2000. Forest-Based Statistical Sentence Generation. *Proceedings of 1st Meeting of the North American Chapter of the Association for Computational Linguistics*, 170–177. Seattle, WA.

Langkilde, Irene. 2002. An Empirical Verification of Coverage and Correctness for a General-Purpose Sentence Generator. *Proceedings of the Second International Conference on Natural Language Generation*, 17–24. New York, USA.

Marcus, Mitchell P., Santorini, Beatrice and Marcinkiewicz, Mary Ann. 1993. Building a large annotated corpus of English: The Penn Treebank. *Computational Linguistics*, 19(2).

Nakanishi, Hiroko and Nakanishi, Yusuke and Tsujii, Jun'ichi. 2005. Probabilistic Models for Disambiguation of an HPSG-Based Chart Generator. *Proceedings of the 9th International Workshop on Parsing Technology*, 93–102. Vancouver, British Columbia.

Nivre, Joakim. 2006. Inductive Dependency Parsing. Springer.

Papineni, Kishore, Roukos, Salim, Ward, Todd and Zhu, Wei-Jing. 2002. Bleu: a Method for Automatic Evaluation of Machine Translation. *Proceedings of the 40th Annual Meeting of the Association for Computational Linguistics*, 311-318. Philadelphia, USA.

Ratnaparkhi, Adwait. 2000. Trainable methods for natural language generation. *Proceedings of NAACL 2000*, 194–201. Seattle, WA.

Stolcke, Andreas. 2002. SRILM-An Extensible Language Modeling Toolkit. *Proceedings of International Conference of Spoken Language Processing*. Denver, Colorado.

van Genabith, Josef and Crouch, Dick. 1996. Direct and underspecified interpretations of LFG f-structures. *Proceedings of the 16th conference on Computational linguistics*, 262–267. Copenhagen, Denmark

Velldal, Erik and Oepen, Stephan. 2005. Maximum entropy models for realization ranking. *Proceedings of the MTSummit '05*.

White, Michael. 2004. Reining in CCG Chart Realization. *Proceedings of the third International Natural Language Generation Conference*. Hampshire, UK.

White, Michael, Rajkumar, Rajakrishnan and Martin, Scott. 2007. Towards Broad Coverage Surface Realization with CCG. *Proceedings of the MT Summit XI Workshop*, 22–30. Copenhagen, Danmark.

Xue, Nianwen, Xia, Fei, Chiou, Fu dong and Palmer, Martha. 2005. The Penn Chinese TreeBank: Phrase Structure Annotation of a Large Corpus. *Natural Language Engineering*, 11(2): 207–238.

Homotopy-based Semi-Supervised Hidden Markov Models for Sequence Labeling*

Gholamreza Haffari and **Anoop Sarkar**
School of Computing Science
Simon Fraser University
Burnaby, BC, Canada
{ghaffar1,anoop}@cs.sfu.ca

Abstract

This paper explores the use of the homotopy method for training a semi-supervised Hidden Markov Model (HMM) used for sequence labeling. We provide a novel polynomial-time algorithm to trace the local maximum of the likelihood function for HMMs from full weight on the labeled data to full weight on the unlabeled data. We present an experimental analysis of different techniques for choosing the best balance between labeled and unlabeled data based on the characteristics observed along this path. Furthermore, experimental results on the field segmentation task in information extraction show that the Homotopy-based method significantly outperforms EM-based semi-supervised learning, and provides a more accurate alternative to the use of held-out data to pick the best balance for combining labeled and unlabeled data.

1 Introduction

In semi-supervised learning, given a sample containing both labeled data L and unlabeled data U, the maximum likelihood estimator Θ^{mle} maximizes:

$$\mathcal{L}(\Theta) := \sum_{(\mathbf{x},\mathbf{y})\in L} \log P(\mathbf{x},\mathbf{y}|\Theta) + \sum_{\mathbf{x}\in U} \log P(\mathbf{x}|\Theta) \quad (1)$$

where $\mathbf{y}$ is a structured output label, e.g. a sequence of tags in the part-of-speech tagging task, or parse trees in the statistical parsing task. When the number of labeled instances is very small compared to the unlabeled instances, i.e. $|L| \ll |U|$, the likelihood of labeled data is dominated by that of unlabeled data, and the valuable information in the labeled data is almost completely ignored.

Several studies in the natural language processing (NLP) literature have shown that as the size of unlabeled data increases, the performance of the model with Θ^{mle} may deteriorate, most notably in (Merialdo, 1993; Nigam et al., 2000). One strategy commonly used to alleviate this problem is to explicitly weigh the contribution of labeled and unlabeled data in (1) by $\lambda \in [0,1]$. This new parameter controls the influence of unlabeled data but is estimated either by (a) an ad-hoc setting, where labeled data is given more weight than unlabeled data, or (b) by using the EM algorithm or (c) by using a held-out set. But each of these alternatives is problematic: the ad-hoc strategy does not work well in general; the EM algorithm ignores the labeled data almost entirely; and using held-out data involves finding a good step size for the search, but small changes in λ may cause drastic changes in the estimated parameters and the performance of the resulting model. Moreover, if labeled data is scarce, which is usually the case, using a held-out set wastes a valuable resource[1].

In this paper, we use continuation techniques (Corduneanu and Jaakkola, 2002) for determining λ for structured prediction tasks involving HMMs, and more broadly, the product of multinomials (PoM) model. We provide a polynomial-time algorithm for HMMs to trace the local maxima of the likelihood function from full weight on the labeled data to full weight on the unlabeled data. In doing so, we introduce dynamic programming algorithms for HMMs that enable the efficient computation over unlabeled data of the covariance between pairs of state transition counts and pairs of state-state and state-observation counts. We present a detailed experimental analysis of different techniques for choosing the best balance be-

* We would like to thank Shihao Ji and the anonymous reviewers for their comments. This research was supported in part by NSERC, Canada.

* © 2008. Licensed under the *Creative Commons Attribution-Noncommercial-Share Alike 3.0 Unported* license (http://creativecommons.org/licenses/by-nc-sa/3.0/). Some rights reserved.

[1] Apart from these reasons, we also provide an experimental comparision between the homotopy based approach, the EM algorithm, and the use of a held out set.

tween labeled and unlabeled data based on the characteristics observed along this path. Furthermore, experimental results on the field segmentation task in information extraction show that the Homotopy-based method significantly outperforms EM-based semi-supervised learning, and provides a more accurate alternative to the use of held-out data to pick the best balance for combining labeled and unlabeled data. We argue this approach is a *best bet* method which is robust to different settings and types of labeled and unlabeled data combinations.

2 Homotopy Continuation

A continuation method embeds a given hard root finding problem $G(\Theta) = 0$ into a family of problems $H(\Theta(\lambda), \lambda) = 0$ parameterized by λ such that $H(\Theta(1), 1) = 0$ is the original given problem, and $H(\Theta(0), 0) = 0$ is an easy problem $F(\Theta) = 0$ (Richter and DeCarlo, 1983). We start from a solution Θ_0 for $F(\Theta) = 0$, and deform it to a solution Θ_1 for $G(\Theta) = 0$ while keeping track of the solutions of the intermediate problems[2]. A simple deformation or homotopy function is:

$$H(\Theta, \lambda) = (1 - \lambda)F(\Theta) + \lambda G(\Theta) \qquad (2)$$

There are many ways to define a homotopy map, but it is not trivial to always guarantee the existence of a path of solutions for the intermediate problems. Fortunately for the homotopy map we will consider in this paper, the path of solutions which starts from $\lambda = 0$ to $\lambda = 1$ exists and is unique.

In order to find the path numerically, we seek a curve $\Theta(\lambda)$ which satisfies $H(\Theta(\lambda), \lambda) = 0$. This is found by differentiating with respect to λ and solving the resulting differential equation. To handle singularities along the path and to be able to follow the path beyond them, we introduce a new variable s (which in our case is the unit path length) and solve the following differential equation for $(\Theta(s), \lambda(s))$:

$$\frac{\partial H(\Theta, \lambda)}{\partial \Theta} \frac{d\Theta}{ds} + \frac{\partial H(\Theta, \lambda)}{\partial \lambda} \frac{d\lambda}{ds} = 0 \qquad (3)$$

subject to $||(\frac{d\Theta}{ds}, \frac{d\lambda}{ds})||_2 = 1$ and the initial condition $(\Theta(0), \lambda(0)) = (\Theta_0, 0)$. We use the Euler method (see Algorithm 1) to solve (3) but higher order methods such as Runge-Kutta of order 2 or 3 can also be used.

3 Homotopy-based Parameter Estimation

One way to control the contribution of the labeled and unlabeled data is to parameterize the log likelihood function as $\mathcal{L}_\lambda(\Theta)$ defined by

$$\frac{1-\lambda}{|L|} \sum_{(x,y)\in L} \log P(x, y|\Theta) + \frac{\lambda}{|U|} \sum_{x \in U} \log P(x|\Theta)$$

How do we choose the best λ? An operator called $EM_\lambda$is used with the property that its fixed points (locally) maximize $\mathcal{L}_\lambda(\Theta)$. Starting from a fixed point of EM_λ when λ is zero[3], the path of fixed point of this operator is *followed* for $\lambda > 0$ by continuation techniques. Finally the best value for λ is chosen based on the characteristics observed along the path. One option is to choose an allocation value where the first critical[4] point occurs had we followed the path based on λ, i.e. without introducing s (see Sec. 2). Beyond the first critical point, the fixed points may not have their roots in the starting point which has all the information from labeled data (Corduneanu and Jaakkola, 2002). Alternatively, an allocation may be chosen which corresponds to the model that gives the maximum entropy for label distributions of unlabeled instances (Ji et al., 2007). In our experiments, we compare all of these methods for determining the choice of λ.

3.1 Product of Multinomials Model

Product of Multinomials (PoM) model is an important class of probabilistic models especially for NLP which includes HMMs and PCFGs among others (Collins, 2005). In the PoM model, the probability of a pair $(\mathbf{x}, \mathbf{y})$ is

$$P(\mathbf{x}, \mathbf{y}|\Theta) = \prod_{m=1}^{M} \prod_{\omega \in \Omega_m} \Theta_m(\omega)^{Count(\mathbf{x},\mathbf{y},\omega)} \qquad (4)$$

where $Count(\mathbf{x}, \mathbf{y}, \omega)$ shows how many times an outcome $\omega \in \Omega_m$ has been seen in the input-output pair $(\mathbf{x}, \mathbf{y})$, and M is the total number of multinomials. A multinomial distribution parameterized

[2]This deformation gives us a solution *path* $(\Theta(\lambda), \lambda)$ in $\mathbb{R}^{d+1}$ for $\lambda \in [0, 1]$, where each component of the d-dimensional solution vector $\Theta(\lambda) = (\theta_1(\lambda), .., \theta_d(\lambda))$ is a function of λ.

[3]In general, EM_0 can have multiple local maxima, but in our case, EM_0 has only one global maximum, found analytically using relative frequency estimation.

[4]A critical point is where a discontinuity or bifurcation occurs. In our setting, almost all of the critical points correspond to discontinuities (Corduneanu, 2002).

by Θ_m is put on each discrete space Ω_m where the probability of an outcome ω is denoted by $\Theta_m(\omega)$. So for each space Ω_m, we have $\sum_{\omega \in \Omega_m} \Theta_m(\omega) = 1$.

Consider an HMM with K states. There are three types of parameters: (i) initial state probabilities $P(s)$ which is a multinomial over states $\Theta_0(s)$, (ii) state transition probabilities $P(s'|s)$ which are K multinomials over states $\Theta_s(s')$, and (iii) emission probabilities $P(a|s)$ which are K multinomials over observation alphabet $\Theta_{s+K}(a)$. To compute the probability of a pair $(\mathbf{x}, \mathbf{y})$, normally we go through the sequence and multiply the probability of the seen state-state and state-observation events:

$$P(\mathbf{x}, \mathbf{y}|\Theta) = \Theta_0(y_0)\Theta_{y_1+K}(x_1) \prod_{t=2}^{|y|} \Theta_{y_{t-1}}(y_t)\Theta_{y_t+K}(x_t)$$

which is in the form of (4) if it is written in terms of the multinomials involved.

3.2 EM_λ Operator for the PoM Model

Usually EM is used to maximize $\mathcal{L}(\Theta)$ and estimate the model parameters in the situation where some parts of the training data are hidden. EM has an intuitive description for the PoM model: starting from an arbitrary value for parameters, iteratively update the probability mass of each event proportional to its count in labeled data plus its *expected* count in the unlabeled data, until convergence.

By changing the EM's update rule, we get an algorithm for maximizing $\mathcal{L}_\lambda(\Theta)$:

$$\tilde{\Theta}_m(\omega) = \frac{1-\lambda}{|L|} \sum_{(\mathbf{x},\mathbf{y}) \in L} Count(\mathbf{x}, \mathbf{y}, \omega) +$$

$$\frac{\lambda}{|U|} \sum_{\mathbf{x} \in U} \sum_{\mathbf{y} \in \mathcal{Y}_\mathbf{x}} Count(\mathbf{x}, \mathbf{y}, \omega) P(\mathbf{y}|\mathbf{x}, \Theta^{old}) \quad (5)$$

where $\tilde{\Theta}_m$ is the unnormalized parameter vector, i.e. $\Theta_m(\omega) = \frac{\tilde{\Theta}_m(\omega)}{\sum_{\omega \in \Omega_m} \tilde{\Theta}_m(\omega)}$. The expected counts can be computed efficiently based on the forward-backward recurrence for HMMs (Rabiner, 1989) and inside-outside recurrence for PCFGs (Lari and Young, 1990). The right hand side of (5) is an operator we call EM_λ which transforms the old parameter values to their new (unnormalized) values. EM_0 and EM_1 correspond respectively to purely supervised and unsupervised parameter estimation settings, and:

$$EM_\lambda(\Theta) = (1-\lambda)EM_0(\Theta) + \lambda EM_1(\Theta) \quad (6)$$

3.3 Homotopy for the PoM Model

The iterative maximization algorithm, described in the previous section, proceeds until it reaches a fixed point $EM_\lambda(\Theta) = \tilde{\Theta}$, where based on (6):

$$(1-\lambda)\underbrace{(\tilde{\Theta} - EM_0(\Theta))}_{F(\Theta)} + \lambda\underbrace{(\tilde{\Theta} - EM_1(\Theta))}_{G(\Theta)} = 0 \quad (7)$$

The above condition governs the (local) maxima of EM_λ. Comparing to (2) we can see that (7) can be viewed as a homotopy map.

We can generalize (7) by replacing $(1-\lambda)$ with a function $g_1(\lambda)$ and λ with $g_2(\lambda)$[5]. This corresponds to other ways of balancing labeled and unlabeled data log-likelihoods in (1). Moreover, we may partition the parameter set and use the homotopy method to just estimate the parameters in one partition while keeping the rest of parameters fixed (to inject some domain knowledge to the estimation procedure), or repeat it through partitions. We will see this in Sec. 5.2 where the transition matrix of an HMM is frozen and the emission probabilities are learned with the continuation method.

Algorithm 1 describes how to use continuation techniques used for homotopy maps in order to trace the path of fixed points for the EM_λ operator. The algorithm uses the Euler method to solve the following differential equation governing the fixed points of EM_λ:

$$\begin{bmatrix} \lambda \nabla_{\tilde{\Theta}} EM_1(\Theta) - I & EM_1(\Theta) - EM_0 \end{bmatrix} \begin{bmatrix} \frac{d\tilde{\Theta}}{d\lambda} \end{bmatrix} = 0$$

For PoM models $\nabla_{\tilde{\Theta}} EM_1(\Theta)$ can be written compactly as follows[6]:

$$\frac{1}{|U|} \sum_{x \in U} COV_{P(\mathbf{y}|\mathbf{x},\Theta)}\Big[Count(\mathbf{x}, \mathbf{y})\Big] \cdot \mathbf{H} \quad (8)$$

where $COV_{P(\mathbf{y}|\mathbf{x},\Theta)}[Count(\mathbf{x}, \mathbf{y})]$ is the conditional covariance matrix of *all* features $Count(\mathbf{x}, \mathbf{y}, \omega)$ given an unlabeled instance $\mathbf{x}$. We denote the entry corresponding to events ω_1 and ω_2 of this matrix by $COV_{P(\mathbf{y}|\mathbf{x},\Theta)}(\omega_1, \omega_2)$; $\mathbf{H}$ is a block diagonal matrix built from $\mathbf{H}_{\Omega_i}$ where

$$\mathbf{H}_{\Omega_i} = (\tilde{\Theta}_i(\alpha_1), .., \tilde{\Theta}_i(\alpha_{|\Omega_i|})) \cdot \mathbf{I} - \frac{\mathbf{1}_{|\Omega_i| \times |\Omega_i|}}{\sum_{\alpha \in \Omega_i} \tilde{\Theta}_i(\alpha)}$$

[5] However the following two conditions must be satisfied: (i) the deformation map is reduced to $(\tilde{\Theta} - EM_0(\Theta))$ at $\lambda = 0$ and $(\tilde{\Theta} - EM_1(\Theta))$ at $\lambda = 1$, and (ii) the path of solutions exists for Eqn. (2).

[6] A full derivation is provided in (Haffari and Sarkar, 2008)

Algorithm 1 Homotopy Continuation for EM_λ

Input: Labeled data set L
Input: Unlabeled data set U
Input: Step size δ
Initialize $[\tilde{\Theta} \quad \lambda] = [EM_0 \quad 0]$ based on L
$\eta^{old} \leftarrow [\mathbf{0} \quad 1]$
repeat
  Compute $\nabla_{\tilde{\Theta}} EM_1(\Theta)$ and $EM_1(\Theta)$ based on unlabeled data U
  Compute $\eta = [d\tilde{\Theta} \quad d\lambda]$ as the kernel of $[\lambda \nabla_{\tilde{\Theta}} EM_1(\Theta) - I \quad EM_1(\Theta) - EM_0]$
  if $\eta \cdot \eta^{old} < 0$ **then**
    $\eta \leftarrow -\eta$
  end if
  $[\tilde{\Theta} \quad \lambda] \leftarrow [\tilde{\Theta} \quad \lambda] + \delta \frac{\eta}{||\eta||_2}$
  $\eta^{old} \leftarrow \eta$
until $\lambda \geq 1$

Computing the covariance matrix in (8) is a challenging problem because it consists of summing quantities over all possible structures $\mathcal{Y}_{\mathbf{x}}$ associated with each unlabeled instance $\mathbf{x}$, which is exponential in the size of the input for HMMs.

4 Efficient Computation of the Covariance Matrix

The entry $COV_{P(\mathbf{y}|\mathbf{x},\Theta)}(\omega_1, \omega_2)$ of the features covariance matrix is

$$\mathbf{E}[Count(\mathbf{x}, \mathbf{y}, \omega_1)Count(\mathbf{x}, \mathbf{y}, \omega_2)] - \mathbf{E}[Count(\mathbf{x}, \mathbf{y}, \omega_1)]\mathbf{E}[Count(\mathbf{x}, \mathbf{y}, \omega_2)]$$

where the expectations are taken under $P(\mathbf{y}|\mathbf{x}, \Theta)$. To efficiently calculate the covariance, we need to be able to efficiently compute the expectations. The *linear* count expectations can be computed efficiently by the forward-backward recurrence for HMMs. However, we have to design new algorithms for *quadratic* count expectations which will be done in the rest of this section.

We add a special **begin** symbol to the sequences and replace the initial probabilities with $P(s|\mathbf{begin})$. Based on the terminology used in (4), the outcomes belong to two categories: $\omega = (s, s')$ where state s' follows state s, and $\omega = (s, a)$ where symbol a is emitted from state s. Define the feature function $f_\omega(\mathbf{x}, \mathbf{y}, t)$ to be 1 if the outcome ω happens at time step t, and 0 otherwise. Based on the fact that $Count(\mathbf{x}, \mathbf{y}, \omega) = \sum_{t=1}^{|\mathbf{x}|} f_\omega(\mathbf{x}, \mathbf{y}, t)$, we have

$$\mathbf{E}[Count(\mathbf{x}, \mathbf{y}, \omega_1)Count(\mathbf{x}, \mathbf{y}, \omega_2)] = \sum_{t_1}\sum_{t_2}\sum_{\mathbf{y}\in\mathcal{Y}_x} f_{\omega_1}(\mathbf{x}, \mathbf{y}, t_1) f_{\omega_2}(\mathbf{x}, \mathbf{y}, t_2) P(\mathbf{y}|\mathbf{x}, \Theta)$$

which is the summation of $|\mathbf{x}|^2$ different expectations. Fixing two positions t_1 and t_2, each expectation is the probability (over all possible labels) of observing ω_1 and ω_2 at these two positions respectively, which can be efficiently computed using the following data structure. Prepare an auxiliary table $Z^{\mathbf{x}}$ containing $P(x_{[i+1,j]}, s_i, s_j)$, for every pair of states s_i and s_j for all positions i, j $(i \leq j)$:

$$Z^{\mathbf{x}}_{i,j}(s_i, s_j) = \sum_{s_{i+1},\ldots,s_{j-1}} \prod_{k=i}^{j-1} P(s_{k+1}|s_k)P(x_{k+1}|s_{k+1})$$

Let matrix $M^{\mathbf{x}}_k = [M^{\mathbf{x}}_k(s, s')]$ where $M^{\mathbf{x}}_k(s, s') = P(s'|s)P(x_k|s')$; then $Z^{\mathbf{x}}_{i,j} = \prod_{k=i}^{j-1} M^{\mathbf{x}}_k$. Forward and backward probabilities can also be computed from $Z^{\mathbf{x}}$, so building this table helps to compute both linear and quadratic count expectations.

With this table, computing the quadratic counts is straightforward. When both events are of type state-observation, i.e. $\omega = (s, a)$ and $\omega' = (s', a')$, their expected quadratic count can be computed as

$$\sum_{t_1}\sum_{t_2} \delta_{x_{t_1},a}\delta_{x_{t_2},a'} \Big[\sum_k P(k|\mathbf{begin}) Z^{\mathbf{x}}_{1,t_1}(k, s). Z^{\mathbf{x}}_{t_1,t_2}(s, s'). \sum_k Z^{\mathbf{x}}_{t_2,n}(s', k) P(\mathbf{end}|k)\Big]$$

where $\delta_{x_t,a}$ is 1 if x_t is equal to a and 0 otherwise. Likewise we can compute the expected quadratic counts for other combination of events: (i) both are of type state-state, (ii) one is of type state-state and the other state-observation.

There are $\frac{L(L+1)}{2}$ tables needed for a sequence of length L, and the time complexity of building each of them is $\mathcal{O}(K^3)$ where K is the number of states in the HMM. When computing the covariance matrix, the observations are fixed and there is no need to consider all possible combinations of observations and states. The most expensive part of the computation is the situation where the two events are of type state-state which amounts to $\mathcal{O}(L^2K^4)$ matrix updates. Noting that a single entry needs $\mathcal{O}(K)$ for its updating, the time complexity of computing expected quadratic counts for a single sequence is $\mathcal{O}(L^2K^5)$. The space needed to store the auxiliary tables is $\mathcal{O}(L^2K^2)$ and the space needed for covariance matrix is $\mathcal{O}((K^2 + NK)^2)$ where N is the alphabet size.

5 Experimental Results

In the field segmentation task, a document is considered to be a sequence of fields. The goal is

[*EDITOR* A. Elmagarmid, editor.] [*TITLE* Transaction Models for Advanced Database Applications] [*PUBLISHER* Morgan-Kaufmann,] [*DATE* 1992.]

Figure 1: A field segmentation example for Citations dataset.

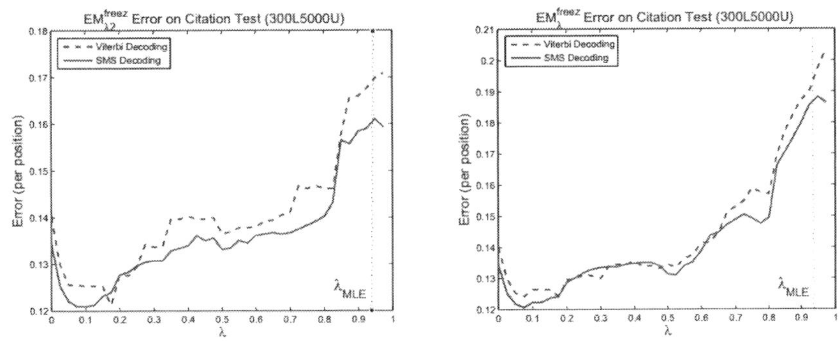

(a) (b)

Figure 2: EM_λ error rates while increasing the allocation from 0 to 1 by the step size 0.025.

to segment the document into fields, and to label each field. In our experiments we use the bibliographic citation dataset described in (Peng and McCallum, 2004) (see Fig. 1 for an example of the input and expected label output for this task). This dataset has 500 annotated citations with 13 fields; 5000 unannotated citations were added to it later by (Grenager et al., 2005). The annotated data is split into a 300-document training set, a 100-document development (dev) set, and a 100-document test set[7].

We use a first order HMM with the size of hidden states equal to the number of fields (equal to 13). We freeze the transition probabilities to what has been observed in the labeled data and only learn the emission probabilities. The transition probabilities are kept frozen due to the nature of this task in which the transition information can be learned with very little labeled data, e.g. first start with 'author' then move to 'title' and so on. However, the challenging aspect of this dataset is to find the segment spans for each field, which depends on learning the emission probabilities, based on the fixed transition probabilities.

At test time, we use both Viterbi (most probable sequence of states) decoding and sequence of most probable states decoding methods, and abbreviate them by Viterbi and SMS respectively. We report results in terms of precision, recall and F-measure for finding the citation fields, as well as accuracy calculated per position, i.e. the ratio of the words labeled correctly for sequences to all of the words. The segment-based precision and recall scores are, of course, lower than the accuracy computed on the per-token basis. However, both these numbers need to be taken into account in order to understand performance in the field segmentation task. Each input word sequence in this task is very long (with an average length of 36.7) but the number of fields to be recovered is a small number comparatively (on average there are 5.4 field segments in a sentence where the average length of a segment is 6.8). Even a few one-word mistakes in finding the full segment span leads to a drastic fall in precision and recall. The situation is quite different from part-of-speech tagging, or even noun-phrase chunking using sequence learning methods. Thus, for this task both the per-token accuracy as well as the segment precision and recall are equally important in gauging performance.

Smoothing to remove zero components in the starting point is crucial otherwise these features do not generalize well and yet we know that they have been observed in the unlabeled data. We use a simple add-ϵ smoothing, where ϵ is .2 for transition table entries and .05 for the emission table entries. In all experiments, we deal with unknown words in test data by replacing words seen less than 5 times in training by the unknown word token.

5.1 Problems with MLE

MLE chooses to set $\lambda = \frac{|U|}{|L|+|U|}$ which almost ignores labeled data information and puts all the weight on the unlabeled data[8]. To see this empirically, we show the per position error rates at dif-

[7]From http://www.stanford.edu/grenager/data/unsupie.tgz

[8]One anonymous reviewer suggests using $\lambda = \frac{|L|}{|L|+|U|}$ but the "best bet" for different tasks that we mention in the Introduction may not necessarily be a small λ value.

ferent source allocation for HMMs trained on 300 labeled and 5000 unlabeled sequences for the Citation dataset in Fig. 2(a). For each allocation we have run EM_λ algorithm, initialized to smoothed counts from labeled data, until convergence. As the plots show, initially the error decreases as λ increases; however, it starts to increase after λ passes a certain value. MLE has higher error rates compared to complete data estimate, and its performance is far from the best way of combining labeled and unlabeled data.

In Fig. 2(b), we have done similar experiment with the difference that for each value of λ, the starting point of the EM_λ is the final solution found in the previous value of λ. As seen in the plot, the intermediate local optima have better performance compared to the previous experiment, but still the imbalance between labeled and unlabeled data negatively affects the quality of the solutions compared to the purely supervised solution.

The likelihood surface is non-convex and has many local maxima. Here EM performs hill climbing on the likelihood surface, and arguably the resulting (locally optimal) model may not reflect the quality of the globally optimal MLE. But we conjecture that even the MLE model(s) which globally maximize the likelihood may suffer from the problem of the size imbalance between labeled and unlabeled data, since what matters is the influence of unlabeled data on the likelihood. (Chang et. al., 2007) also report on using hard-EM on these datasets[9] in which the performance degrades compared to the purely supervised model.

5.2 Choosing λ in Homotopy-based HMM

We analyze different criteria in picking the best value of λ based on inspection of the continuation path. The following criteria are considered:

- **monotone:** The first iteration in which the monotonicity of the path is changed, or equivalently the first iteration in which the determinant of $\lambda\nabla_{\bar{\Theta}}EM_1(\Theta) - I$ in Algorithm 1 becomes zero (Corduneanu and Jaakkola, 2002).
- **minEig:** Instead of looking into the determinant of the above matrix, consider its minimum eigenvalue. Across all iterations, choose the one for which this minimum eigenvalue is the lowest.
- **maxEnt:** Choose the iteration whose model puts the maximum entropy on the labeling distribution for unlabeled data (Ji et al., 2007).

[9]In Hard-EM, the probability mass is fully assigned to the most probable label, instead of all possible labels.

The second criterion is new, and experimentally has shown a good performance; it indicates the amount of singularity of a matrix.

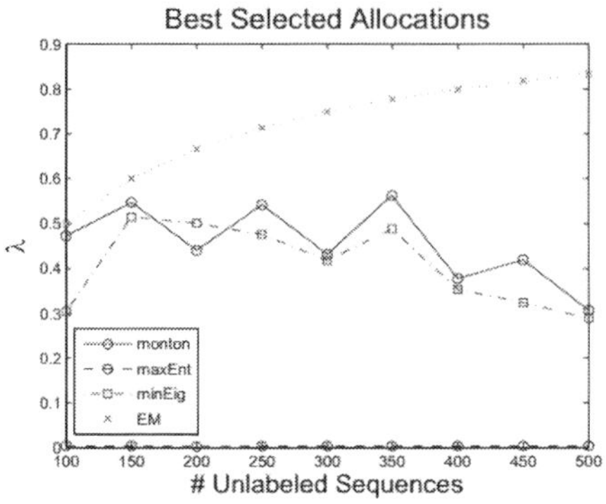

Figure 3: λ values picked by different methods. The size of the labeled data is fixed to 100, and results are averaged over 4 runs. The λ values picked by MaxEnt method for 500 unlabeled examples was .008.

We fix 100 labeled sequences and vary the number of unlabeled sequences from 100 to 500 by a step of 50. All of the experiments are repeated four times with different randomly chosen unlabeled datasets, and the results are the average over four runs. The chosen allocations based on the described criteria are plotted in Figure 3, and their associated performance measures can be seen in Figure 4.

Figure 3 shows that as the unlabeled data set grows, the reliance of 'minEig' and 'monotone' methods on unlabeled data decreases whereas in EM it increases. The 'minEig' method is more conservative than 'monotone' in that it usually chooses smaller λ values. The plots in Figure 4 show that homotopy-based HMM always outperforms EM-based HMM. Moreover, 'maxEnt' method outperforms other ways of picking λ. However, as the size of the unlabeled data increases, the three methods tend to have similar performances.

5.3 Homotopy v.s. other methods

In the second set of experiments, we compare the performance of the homotopy based method against the competitive methods for picking the value of λ.

We use all of the labeled sequences (size is 300) and vary the number of unlabeled sequences from 300 to 1000 by the step size of 100. For the first competitive method, 100 labeled sequences are put in a held out set and used to select the best value

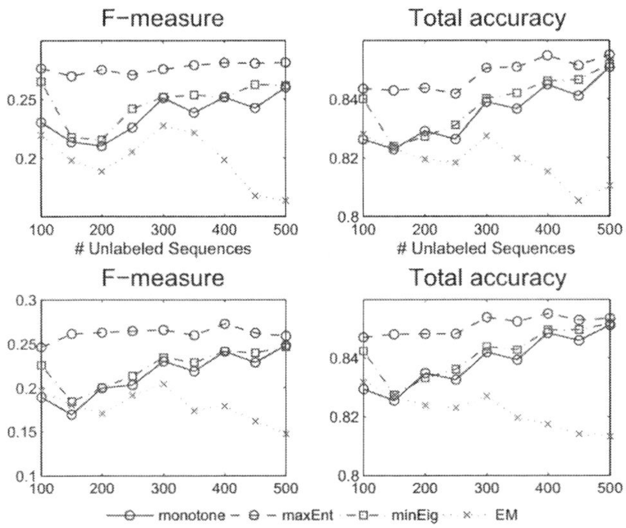

Figure 4: The comparison of different techniques for choosing the best allocation based on datasets with 100 labeled sequences and varying number of unlabeled sequences. Each figure shows the average over 4 runs. F-measure is calculated based on the *segments*, and total accuracy is calculated based on tokens in individual positions. The two plots in the top represent Viterbi decoding, and the two plots in the bottom represent SMS decoding.

of λ based on brute-force search using a fixed step size; afterwards, this value is used to train HMM (based on 200 remaining labeled sequences and unlabeled data). The second competitive method, which we call 'Oracle', is similar to the previous method except we use the test set as the held out set and all of the 300 labeled sequences as the training set. In a sense, the resulting model is the best we can expect from cross validation based on the knowledge of true labels for the test set. Despite the name 'Oracle', in this setting the λ value is selected based on the log-likelihood criterion, so it is possible that the 'Oracle' method is outperformed by another method in terms of precision/recall/f-score. Finally, EM is considered as the third baseline.

The results are summarized in Table 1. When decoding based on SMS, the homotopy-based HMM outperforms the 'Held-out' method for all of performance measures, and generally behaves better than the 'Oracle' method. When decoding based on Viterbi, the accuracy of the homotopy-based HMM is better than 'Held-out' and is in the same range as the 'Oracle'; the three methods have roughly the same f-score. The λ value found by Homotopy gives a small weight to unlabeled data, and so it might seem that it is ignoring the unlabeled data. This is not the case, even with a small weight the unlabeled data has an impact, as can be seen in the comparison with the purely Supervised baseline in Table 1 where the Homotopy method outperforms the Supervised baseline by more than 3.5 points of f-score with SMS-decoding. Homotopy-based HMM with SMS-decoding outperforms all of the other methods.

We noticed that accuracy was better for 700 unlabeled examples in this dataset, and so we include those results as well in Table 1. We observed some noise in unlabeled sequences; so as the size of the unlabeled data set grows, this noise increases as well. In addition to finding the right balance between labeled and unlabeled data, this is another factor in semi-supervised learning. For each particular unlabeled dataset size (we experimented using 300 to 1000 unlabeled data with a step size of 100) the Homotopy method outperforms the other alternatives.

6 Related Previous Work

Homotopy based parameter estimation was originally proposed in (Corduneanu and Jaakkola, 2002) for Naïve Bayes models and mixture of Gaussians, and (Ji et al., 2007) used it for HMM-based sequence *classification* which means that an input sequence $\mathbf{x}$ is classified into a class label $y \in \{1, \ldots, k\}$ (the class label is not structured, i.e. not a sequence of tags). The classification is done using a collection of k HMMs by computing $\Pr(\mathbf{x}, y \mid \Theta^y)$ which sums over all states in each HMM Θ^y for input $\mathbf{x}$. The algorithms in (Ji et al., 2007) could be adapted to the task of sequence labeling, but we argue that our algorithms provide a straightforward and direct solution.

There have been some studies using the Citation dataset, but it is not easy to directly compare their results due to differences in preprocessing, the amount of the previous knowledge and rich features used by the models, and the training data which were used. (Chang et. al., 2007) used a first order HMM in order to investigate injecting prior domain knowledge to self-training style bootstrapping by encoding human knowledge into declarative constraints. (Grenager et al., 2005) used a first order HMM which has a diagonal transition matrix and a specialized boundary model. In both works, the number of *randomly* selected labeled and unlabeled training data is varied, which makes a di-

	size of unlab data	λ	Viterbi decoding		SMS decoding	
			p, r, f-score	accuracy	p, r, f-score	accuracy
Homotopy	700	.004	.292, .290, .290	87.1%	.321, .332, **.326**	**89%**
	1000	.004	.292, .291, .291	87.9%	.296, .298, .296	88.6%
Held-out	700	.220	.311, .291, .297	87.1%	.295, .288, .289	87.2%
	1000	.320	.300, .276, .283	86.9%	.308, .281, .287	87.2%
Oracle	700	.150	.284, .293, .287	87.8%	.295, .313, .303	88%
	1000	.200	.285, .294, .289	87.9%	.277, .292, .284	88.7%
EM	700	.700	.213, .211, .211	84.8%	.213, .220, .216	85.2%
	1000	.770	.199, .198, .198	83.7%	.187, .198, .192	83.6%
Supervised	0	0	.281, .278, .279	87%	.298, .280, .288	88.4%

Table 1: Results using entire labeled data with segment precision/recall/f-score and token based accuracy.

rect numerical comparison impossible. (Peng and McCallum, 2004) used only labeled data to train conditional random fields and HMMs with second order state transitions where they allow observation in each position to depend on the current state as well as observation of the previous position.

7 Conclusion

In many NLP tasks, the addition of unlabeled data to labeled data can *decrease* the performance on that task. This is often because the unlabeled data can overwhelm the information obtained from the labeled data. In this paper, we have described a methodology and provided efficient algorithms for an approach that attempts to ensure that unlabeled data does not hurt performance. The experimental results show that homotopy-based training performs better than other commonly used competitive methods. We plan to explore faster ways for computing the (approximate) covariance matrix, e.g., label sequences can be sampled from $P(\mathbf{y}|\mathbf{x}, \Theta)$ and an approximation of the covariance matrix can be computed based on these samples. Also, it is possible to compute the covariance matrix in polynomial-time for labels which have richer interdependencies such as those generated by a context free grammars (Haffari and Sarkar, 2008). Finally, in Algorithm 1 we used a fixed step size; the number of iterations in the homotopy path following can be reduced greatly with adaptive step size methods (Allgower and Georg, 1993).

References

E. L. Allgower, K. Georg 1993. Continuation and Path Following, *Acta Numerica*, 2:1-64.

M. Chang and L. Ratinov and D. Roth. 2007. Guiding Semi-Supervision with Constraint-Driven Learning, ACL 2007.

M. Collins 2005. Notes on the EM Algorithm, NLP course notes, MIT.

A. Corduneanu. 2002. Stable Mixing of Complete and Incomplete Information, Masters Thesis, MIT.

A. Corduneanu and T. Jaakkola. 2002. Continuation Methods for Mixing Heterogeneous Sources, UAI 2002.

T. Grenager, D. Klein, and C. Manning. 2005. Unsupervised Learning of Field Segmentation Models for Information Extraction, ACL 2005.

G. Haffari and A. Sarkar. 2008. A Continuation Method for Semi-supervised Learning in Product of Multinomials Models, Technical Report. Simon Fraser University. School of Computing Science.

K. Lari, and S. Young. 1990. The estimation of stochastic context-free grammars using the inside-outside algorithm, *Computer Speech and Language* (4).

S. Ji, L. Watson and L. Carin. 2007. Semi-Supervised Learning of Hidden Markov Models via a Homotopy Method, manuscript.

B. Merialdo. 1993. Tagging English text with a probabilistic model, *Computational Linguistics*

K. Nigam, A. McCallum, S. Thrun and T. Mitchell. 2000. Text Classification from Labeled and Unlabeled Documents using EM, *Machine Learning*, 39. p. 103-134.

F. Peng and A. McCallum. 2004. Accurate Information Extraction from Research Papers using Conditional Random Fields, HLT-NAACL 2004.

L. Rabiner. 1989. A Tutorial on Hidden Markov Models and Selected Applications in Speech Recognition, *Proc. of the IEEE*, 77(2).

S. Richter, and R. DeCarlo. 1983. Continuation methods: Theory and applications, *IEEE Trans. on Automatic Control*, Vol 26, issue 6.

Tracking the Dynamic Evolution of Participant Salience in a Discussion

Ahmed Hassan
University of Michigan
hassanam@umich.edu

Anthony Fader
University of Michigan
afader@umich.edu

Michael H. Crespin
University of Georgia
crespin@uga.edu

Kevin M. Quinn
Harvard University
kquinn@fsa.harvard.edu

Burt L. Monroe
Pennsylvania State University
burtmonroe@psu.edu

Michael Colaresi
Michigan State University
colaresi@msu.edu

Dragomir R. Radev
University of Michigan
radev@umich.edu

Abstract

We introduce a technique for analyzing the temporal evolution of the salience of participants in a discussion. Our method can dynamically track how the relative importance of speakers evolve over time using graph based techniques. Speaker salience is computed based on the eigenvector centrality in a graph representation of participants in a discussion. Two participants in a discussion are linked with an edge if they use similar rhetoric. The method is dynamic in the sense that the graph evolves over time to capture the evolution inherent to the participants salience. We used our method to track the salience of members of the US Senate using data from the US Congressional Record. Our analysis investigated how the salience of speakers changes over time. Our results show that the scores can capture speaker centrality in topics as well as events that result in change of salience or influence among different participants.

1 Introduction

There are several sources of data that record speeches or participations in debates or discussions among a group of speakers or participants. Those include parliamentary records, blogs, and news groups. This data represents a very important and unexploited source of information that contains several trends and ideas. In any debate or discussion, there are certain types of persons who influence other people and pass information or advice to them. Those persons are often regarded as experts in the field or simply influential people and they tend to affect the ideas and rhetoric of other participants. This effect can be tracked down by tracking the similarity between different speeches. We can then imagine a debate with many people arguing about many different things as a network of speeches or participations interacting with each other. We can then try to identify the most salient or important participants by identifying the most central speeches in this network and associating them with their speakers. When we have a large dataset of debates and conversations that expand over a long period of time, the salience of participants becomes a dynamic property that changes over time. To capture this dynamic nature of the process, the graph of speeches must evolve over time such that we have a different graph at each instance of time that reflects the interaction of speeches at this instant.

We apply our method to the *US Congressional Record*. The *US Congressional Record* documents everything said and done in the US Congress House and Senate. The speeches in this data set are made by a large number of people over a long period of time. Using political speeches as test data for the proposed method adds an extra layer of meaning onto the measure of speakers salience. Speaker salience of the Congress members can reflect the importance or influence in the US legislative process. The way salience scores evolve over time can answer several interesting issues like how the influence of the speakers vary with majority status and change of party control. It can also study the dynamics of the relative distribution of attention to each topic area in different time periods.

© 2008. Licensed under the *Creative Commons Attribution-Noncommercial-Share Alike 3.0 Unported* license (http://creativecommons.org/licenses/by-nc-sa/3.0/). Some rights reserved.

The rest of this paper will proceed as follows. Section 2 reviews some related work. In Section 3, we describe how the data can be clustered into different topic clusters. In Section 4, we describe our method for computing the salience of different participant in a discussion, we also describe how to the network of speakers varies over time. Section 5 describes the experimental setup. Finally, we present the conclusions in Section 6.

2 Related Work

Several methods have been proposed for identifying the most central nodes in a network. Degree centrality, closeness, and betweenness (Newman, 2003) are among the most known methods for measuring centrality of nodes in a network. Eigenvector centrality is another powerful method that that has been applied to several types of networks. For example it has been used to measure centrality in hyperlinked web pages networks (Brin and Page, 1998; Kleinberg, 1998), lexical networks (Erkan and Radev, 2004; Mihalcea and Tarau, 2004; Kurland and Lee, 2005; Kurland and Lee, 2006), and semantic networks (Mihalcea et al., 2004).

The interest of applying natural language processing techniques in the area of political science has been recently increasing.

(Quinn et al., 2006) introduce a multinomial mixture model to cluster political speeches into topics or related categories. In (Porter et al., 2005), a network analysis of the members and committees of the US House of Representatives is performed. The authors prove that there are connections linking some political positions to certain committees. This suggests that there are factors affecting committee membership and that they are not determined at random. In (Thomas et al., 2006), the authors try to automatically classify speeches, from the US Congress debates, as supporting or opposing a given topic by taking advantage of the voting records of the speakers. (Fader et al., 2007) introduce MavenRank , which is a method based on lexical centrality that identifies the most influential members of the US Senate. It computes a single salience score for each speaker that is constant over time.

In this paper, we introduce a new method for tracking the evolution of the salience of participants in a discussion over time. Our method is based on the ones described in (Erkan and Radev, 2004; Mihalcea and Tarau, 2004; Fader et al., 2007), The objective of this paper is to dynamically rank speakers or participants in a discussion. The proposed method is dynamic in the sense that the computed importance varies over time.

3 Topic Clusters

Before applying the proposed method to a data set with speeches in multiple topics, we first need to divide the speech documents into topic clusters. We used the model described in (Quinn et al., 2006) for this purpose. The model presented in this paper assumes that the probabilities of a document belonging to a certain topic varies smoothly over time and the words within a given document have exactly the same probability of being drawn from a particular topic (Quinn et al., 2006). These two properties make the model different than standard mixture models (McLachlan and Peel, 2000) and the latent Dirichlet allocation model of (Blei et al., 2003). The model of (Quinn et al., 2006) is most closely related to the model of (Blei and Lafferty, 2006), who present a generalization of the model used by (Quinn et al., 2006).

The output from the topic model is a $D \times K$ matrix $\mathbf{Z}$ where D is the number of speeches , K is the number of topics and the element z_{dk} represents the probability of the dth speech being generated by topic k. We then assign each speech d to the kth cluster where $k = \arg\max_j z_{dj}$. If the maximum value is not unique, one of the clusters having the maximum value is arbitrary selected.

4 Speaker Centrality

In this section we describe how to build a network of speeches and use it to identify speaker centrality. We also describe how to generate different projections of the network at different times, and how to use those projection to get dynamic salience scores.

4.1 Computing Speaker Salience

The method we used is similar to the methods described in (Erkan and Radev, 2004; Mihalcea and Tarau, 2004; Kurland and Lee, 2005), which were originally used for ranking sentences and documents in extractive summarization and information retrieval systems.

A collection of speeches can be represented as a network where similar speeches are linked to each other. The proposed method is based on the premise that important speeches tend to be lexically similar to other important speeches, and important speeches tend to belong to important speakers. Hence given a collection of speeches and a similarity measure, we can build a network and define the centrality score of a speech recursively in terms of the scores of other similar speeches. Later, we can compute the salience of a speaker as the sum of the centrality measure of all his speeches.

To measure the similarity between two speeches, we use the bag-of-words model to represent each sentence as an N-dimensional vector of tf-idf scores, where N is the number of all possible words in the target language. The similarity between two speeches is then computed using the cosine similarity between the two vectors.

A vector of term frequencies is used to represent each speech. Those term frequencies are weighted according to the relative importance of the given term in the cluster.

The vectors representing speeches contain term frequencies (or *tf*), which are weighted according to their inverse document frequencies to account for the relative importance of the given term in the cluster. The inverse document frequency of a term w is given by (Sparck-Jones, 1972)

$$\mathrm{idf}(w) = \log\left(\frac{N}{n_w}\right) \quad (1)$$

where n_w is the number of speeches in the cluster containing the term w, and N is the number of documents in the cluster. We calculated idf values specific to each topic, rather than to all speeches. We preferred to use *topic-specific* idf values because the relative importance of words may vary from one topic to the other.

The tf-idf cosine similarity measure is computed as the cosine of the angle between the tf-idf vectors. It is defined as follows:

$$\frac{\sum_{w \in u,v} \mathrm{tf}_u(w)\,\mathrm{tf}_v(w)\,\mathrm{idf}(w)^2}{\sqrt{\sum_{w \in u}(\mathrm{tf}_u(w)\,\mathrm{idf}(w))^2}\sqrt{\sum_{w \in v}(\mathrm{tf}_v(w)\,\mathrm{idf}(w))^2}}, \quad (2)$$

The choice of tf-idf scores to measure speech similarity is an arbitrary choice. Some other possible similarity measures are edit distance, language models (Kurland and Lee, 2005), or generation probabilities (Erkan, 2006).

The recursive definition of the score of any speech s in the speeches network is given by

$$p(s) = \sum_{t \in adj[s]} \frac{p(t)}{deg(t)} \quad (3)$$

where $deg(t)$ is the degree of node t, and $adj[s]$ is the set of all speeches adjacent to s in the network. This can be rewritten in matrix notation as:

$$\mathbf{p} = \mathbf{pB} \quad (4)$$

where $\mathbf{p} = (p(s_1), p(s_2), \ldots, p(s_N))$ and the matrix $\mathbf{B}$ is the row normalized similarity matrix of the graph

$$\mathbf{B}(i,j) = \frac{\mathbf{S}(i,j)}{\sum_k \mathbf{S}(i,k)} \quad (5)$$

where $\mathbf{S}(i,j) = \mathrm{sim}(s_i, s_j)$. Equation (4) shows that the vector of salience scores $\mathbf{p}$ is the left eigenvector of $\mathbf{B}$ with eigenvalue 1.

The matrix $\mathbf{B}$ can be thought of as a stochastic matrix that acts as transition matrix of a Markov chain. An element $\mathbf{X(i,j)}$ of a stochastic matrix specifies the transition probability from state i to state j in the corresponding Markov chain. And the whole process can be seen as a Markovian random walk on the speeches graph. To help the random walker escape from periodic or disconnected components, (Brin and Page, 1998) suggests reserving a small escape probability at each node that represents a chance of jumping to any node in the graph, making the Markov chain irreducible and aperiodic, which guarantees the existence of the eigenvector.

Equation (4) can then be rewritten, assuming a uniform escape probability, as:

$$\mathbf{p} = \mathbf{p}[d\mathbf{U} + (1-d)\mathbf{B}] \quad (6)$$

where N is the total number of nodes, $\mathbf{U}$ is a square matrix with $\mathbf{U}(i,j) = 1/N$ for all i, j, and d is the escape probability chosen in the interval $[0.1, 0.2]$ (Brin and Page, 1998).

4.2 Dynamic Salience Scores

We use the time stamps associated with the data to compute dynamic salience scores $p_T(u)$ that identify central speakers at some time T. To do this, we create a speech graph that evolves over time.

Let T be the current date and let u and v be two speech documents that occur on days t_u and t_v. Our goal is to discount the lexical similarity of u and v based on how far apart they are. One way to do this is by defining a new similarity measure $s(u, v; T)$ as:

$$s(u,v;T) = \text{tf-idf-cosine}(u,v) \cdot f(u,v;T) \quad (7)$$

where $f(u, v; T)$ is a function taking values in $[0, 1]$.

If $f(u, v; T) = 1$ for all u, v, and T, then time is ignored when calculating similarity and $p_T(u) = p(u)$. On the other hand, suppose we let

$$f(u, v; T) = \begin{cases} 1 & \text{if } t_u = t_v = T, \\ 0 & \text{else.} \end{cases} \quad (8)$$

This removes all edges that link a speech, occurring at some time T, to all other speeches occurring at some time other than T and the ranking algorithm will be run on what is essentially the subgraph of documents restricted to time T (although the isolated speech documents will receive small non-zero scores because of the escape probability from Section 4.1). These two cases act as the extreme boundaries of possible functions f: in the first case time difference has no effect on document similarity, while in the second case two documents must occur on the same day to be similar.

We use the following time weight functions in our experiments. In each case, we assume that the speeches represented by speech documents u and v have already occurred, that is, $t_u, t_v \leq T$. We will use the convention that $f(u, v; T) = 0$ if $t_u > T$ or $t_v > T$ for all time weight functions, which captures the idea that speeches that have not yet occurred have no influence on the graph at time T. Also define

$$\text{age}(u, v; T) = T - \min\{t_u, t_v\} \quad (9)$$

which gives the age of the oldest speech document from the pair u, v at time T.

- *Exponential:* Given a parameter $a > 0$, define

  $$f_{\text{exp},a}(u, v; T) = e^{-a\,\text{age}(u,v;T)}. \quad (10)$$

  This function will decrease the impact of similarity as time increases in an exponential fashion. a is a parameter that controls how fast this happens, where a larger value of a makes earlier speeches have a small impact on current scores and a smaller value of a means that earlier speeches will have a larger impact on current scores.

- *Linear:* Given $b > 0$, define

  $$f_{\text{lin},d}(u, v; T) = \begin{cases} 1 - \frac{1}{b}\,\text{age}(u, v; T) \\ \quad \text{if age}(u, v; T) \leq b \\ 0 \quad \text{if age}(u, v; T) > b \end{cases} \quad (11)$$

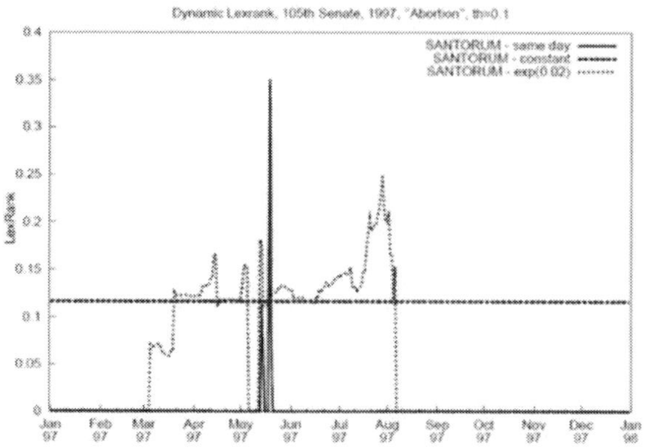

Figure 1: The Dynamic boundary cases for Senator Santorum.

  This function gives speech documents that occur at time T full weight and then decreases their weight linearly towards time $T + b$, where it becomes 0.

- *Boundary:* Given $d \geq 0$, define

  $$f_{\text{bnd},d}(u, v; T) = \begin{cases} 1 & \text{if age}(u, v; T) \leq d \\ 0 & \text{if age}(u, v; T) > d \end{cases} \quad (12)$$

  This function gives speech documents occurring within d days of T the regular tf-idf similarity score, but sets the similarity of speech documents occurring outside of d days to 0. The case when $d = 0$ is one of the boundary cases explained above.

Figure 1 gives an example of different time weighting functions for Senator Rick Santorum (R - Pennsylvania) on topic 22 (Abortion) during 1997, the first session of the 105th Congress. The dashed line shows the case when time has no effect on similarity (his score is constant over time), while the solid line shows the case where only speeches on the current day are considered similar (his score spikes only on days where he speaks and is near zero otherwise). The dotted line shows the case when the influence of older speeches decreases exponentially, which is more dynamic than the first case but smoother than the second case.

5 Experiments and Results

5.1 Data

We used the United States Congressional Speech corpus (Monroe et al., 2006) in our experiment.

This corpus is in XML formatted version of the electronic *United States Congressional Record* from the Library of Congress[1]. The *Congressional Record* is a verbatim transcript of the speeches made in the US House of Representatives and Senate and includes tens of thousands of speeches per year (Monroe et al., 2006). The data we used cover the period from January 2001 to January 2003.

5.2 Experimental Setup

We used results from (Quinn et al., 2006) to get topic clusters from the data, as described in Section 3. The total number of topics was 42. The average sized topic cluster had several hundred speech documents (Quinn et al., 2006).

We set up a pipeline using a Perl implementation of the proposed method We ran it on the topic clusters and ranked the speakers based on the centrality scores of their speeches. The graph nodes were speech documents. A speaker's score was determined by the average of the scores of the speeches given by that speaker. After comparing the different time weighting function as shown in Figure 1, we decided to use the exponential time weight function for all the experiments discussed below. Exponential time weighting function decreases the impact of similarity as time increases in an exponential fashion. It also allows us to control the rate of decay using the parameter a.

5.3 Baseline

We compare the performance of our system to a simple baseline that calculates the salience of a speaker as a weighted count of the number of times he has spoken. The baseline gives high weight to recent speeches . The weight decreases as the speeches gets older. The salience score of a speaker is calculate as follows:

$$BS(i) = \sum_{d} \gamma^{d_0 - d} * S_d^i \tag{13}$$

Where $BS(i)$ is the baseline score of speaker i, γ is the discounting factor, d_0 is the current date, and S_d^i is the number of speeches made by speaker i at date d. We used $\gamma = 0.9$ for all our experiments.

5.4 Results

One way to evaluate the dynamic salience scores, is to look at changes when party control of the chamber switches. Similar to (Hartog and Monroe, 2004), we exploit the party switch made by Senator Jim Jeffords of Vermont and the resulting change in majority control of the Senate during the 107th Congress as a quasi-experimental design. In short, Jeffords announced his switch on May 24, 2001 from Republican to Independent status, effective June 6, 2001. Jeffords stated that he would vote with the Democrats to organize the Senate, giving the Democrats a one-seat advantage and change control of the Senate from the Republicans back to the Democrats. This change of majority status during the 107th Congress allows us to ignore many of the factors that could potentially influence dynamic salience scores at the start of a new congress.

On average, we expect committee chairs or a member of the majority party to be the most important speaker on each topic followed by ranking members or a member of the minority party. If our measure is capturing dynamics in the centrality of Senators, we expect Republicans to be more central before the Jeffords switch and Democrats becoming central soon afterwards, assuming the topic is being discussed on the Senate floor. We show that the proposed technique captures several interesting events in the data and also show that the baseline explained above fails to capture the same set of events.

Figure 2(a) shows the dynamic salience scores over time for Senator John McCain (R - Arizona) and Senator Carl Levin (D - Michigan) on topic 5 (Armed Forces 2) for the 107th Senate. McCain was the most salient speaker for this topic until June 2001. Soon after the change in majority status a switch happened and Levin, the new chair of Senate Armed Services, replaced McCain as the most salient speaker. On the other hand, Figure 2(b) shows the baseline scores for the same topic and same speakers. We notice here that the baseline failed to capture the switch of salience near June 2001.

We can also observe similar behavior in Figure 3(a). This figure shows how Senate Majority Leader Trent Lott (R - Mississippi) was the most salient speaker on topic 35 (Procedural Legislation) until July 2001. Topic 35 does not map to a specific committee but rather is related to maneuvering bills through the legislative process on the floor, a job generally delegated to members in the Senate leadership. Just after his party gained

[1] http://thomas.loc.gov

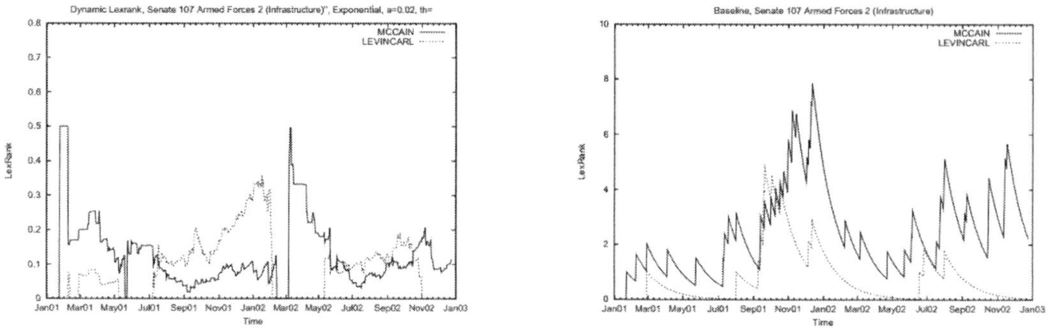

(a) Dynamic Lexrank

(b) Baseline

Figure 2: The Switch of Speakers Salience near Jun 2001 for Topic 5(Armed Forces 2).

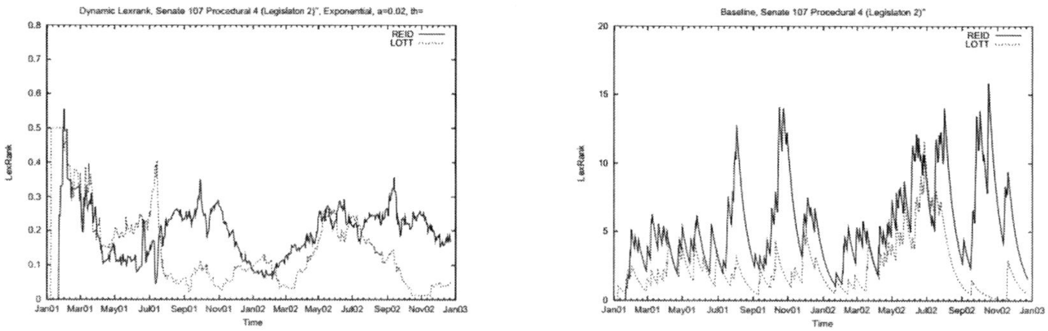

(a) Dynamic Lexrank

(b) Baseline

Figure 3: The Switch of Speakers Salience near Jun 2001 for Topic 35(Procedural Legislation).

majority status, Senator Harry Reid (D - Nevada) became the most salient speaker for this topic. This is consistent with Reid's switch from Assistant minority Leader to Assistant majority Leader. Again the baseline scores for the same topic and speakers in Figure 3(b) fails to capture the switch.

An even more interesting test would be to check whether the Democrats in general become more central than Republicans after the Jeffords switch. Figure 4(a) shows the normalized sum of the scores of all the Democrats and all the Republicans on topic 5 (Armed Forces 2) for the 107th Senate. The figure shows how the Republicans were most salient until soon after the Jeffords switch when the Democrats regained the majority and became more salient. We even discovered similar behavior when we studied how the average salience of Democrats and Republicans change across all topics. This is shown in Figure 5(a) where we can see that the Republicans were more salient on average for all topics until June 2001. Soon after the change in majority status, Democrats became more central. Figures 4(b) and 5(b) show the same results using the baseline system. We notice that the number of speeches made by the Democrats and the Republicans is very similar in most of the times. Even when one of the parties has more speeches than the other, it does not quite reflect the salience of the speakers or the parties in general.

An alternative approach to evaluate the dynamic scores is to exploit the cyclical nature of the legislative process as some bills are re-authorized on a fairly regular time schedule. For example, the farm bill comes due about every five years. As a new topic is coming up for debate, we expect the saliency scores for relevant legislators to increase.

Figure 6 shows the dynamic scores of Senator Thomas Harkin (D - Iowa), and Senator Richard

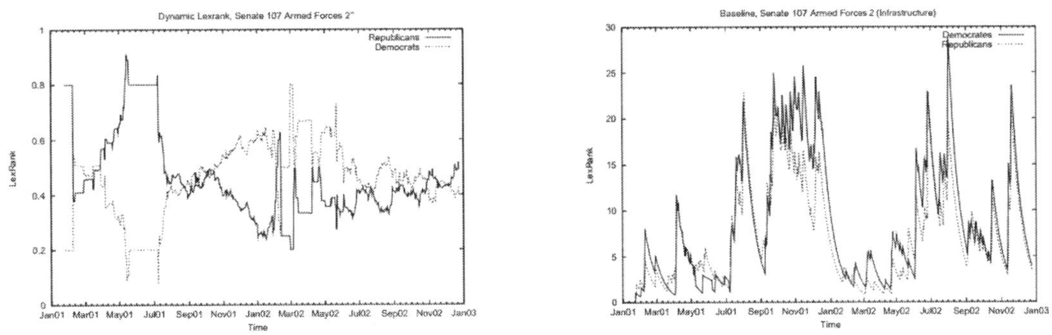

(a) Dynamic Lexrank (b) Baseline

Figure 4: The Switch of Speakers Salience near Jun 2001 for Topic 5(Armed Forces 2), Republicans vs Democrats.

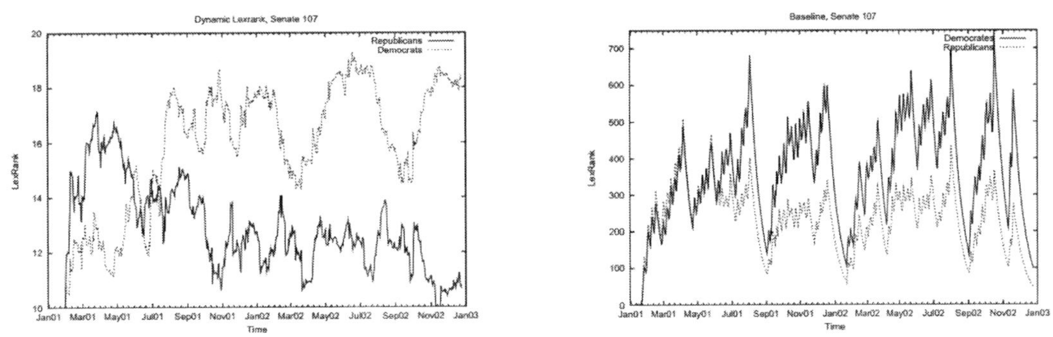

(a) Dynamic Lexrank (b) Baseline

Figure 5: The Switch of Speakers Salience near Jun 2001 for All Topics, Republicans vs Democrats.

Lugar (R - Indiana) during the 107th senate on topic 24 (Agriculture). The two senators were identified, by the proposed method, as the most salient speakers for this topic, as expected, since they both served as chairmen of the Senate Committee on Agriculture, Nutrition, and Forestry when their party was in the majority during the 107th Senate. This committee was in charge of shepherding the Farm Bill through the Senate. The scores of both senators on the agriculture topic significantly increased starting late 2001 until June 2002. The debate began on the bill starting in September of 2001 and it was not passed until May 2002.

6 Conclusion

We presented a graph based method for analyzing the temporal evolution of the salience of participants in a discussion. We used this method to track the evolution of salience of speakers in the *US Congressional Record*. We showed that the way salience scores evolve over time can answer several interesting issues. We tracked how the influence of the speakers vary with majority status and change of party control. We also show how a baseline system that depends on the number of speeches fails to capture the interesting events captured by the proposed system. We also studied the dynamics of the relative distribution of attention to each topic area in different time periods and captured the cyclical nature of the legislative process as some bills are re-authorized on a fairly regular time schedule.

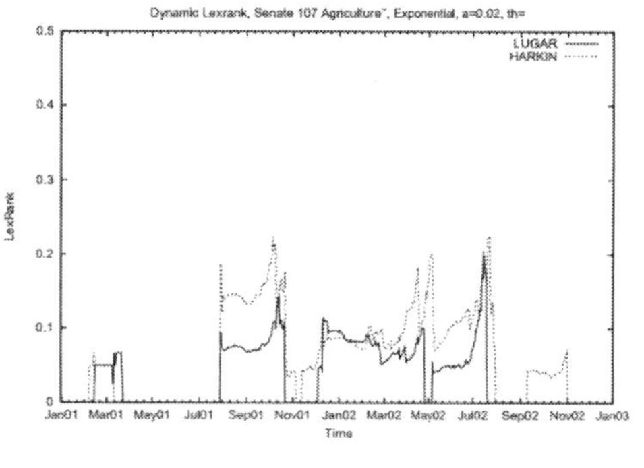

Figure 6: The Farm Bill Discussions on the Relative Distribution of Attention to Topic 24 (Agriculture).

Acknowledgments

This paper is based upon work supported by the National Science Foundation under Grant No. 0527513, "DHB: The dynamics of Political Representation and Political Rhetoric". Any opinions, findings, and conclusions or recommendations expressed in this paper are those of the authors and do not necessarily reflect the views of the National Science Foundation.

References

Blei, David and John Lafferty. 2006. Dynamic topic models. In *ICML 2006*.

Blei, David, Andrew Ng, and Michael Jordan. 2003. Latent dirichlet allocation. *Journal of Machine Learning Research*, 3:993–1022.

Brin, Sergey and Lawrence Page. 1998. The anatomy of a large-scale hypertextual Web search engine. *CNIS*, 30(1–7):107–117.

Erkan, Güneş and Dragomir Radev. 2004. Lexrank: Graph-based centrality as salience in text summarization. *Journal of Artificial Intelligence Research (JAIR)*.

Erkan, Gunes. 2006. Language model-based document clustering using random walks. In *HLT/NAACL 2006*, pages 479–486. Association for Computational Linguistics.

Fader, Anthony, Dragomir Radev, Michael Crespin, Burt Monroe, Kevin Quinn, and Michael Colaresi. 2007. Mavenrank: Identifying influential members of the us senate using lexical centrality. In *EMNLP 2007*.

Hartog, Chris Den and Nathan Monroe. 2004. The value of majority status: The effect of jeffords's switch on asset prices of republican and democratic firms. *Legislative Studies Quarterly*, 33:63–84.

Kleinberg, Jon. 1998. Authoritative sources in a hyperlinked environment. In *the ACM-SIAM Symposium on Discrete Algorithms*, pages 668–677.

Kurland, Oren and Lillian Lee. 2005. PageRank without hyperlinks: Structural re-ranking using links induced by language models. In *SIGIR 2005*, pages 306–313.

Kurland, Oren and Lillian Lee. 2006. Respect my authority! HITS without hyperlinks, utilizing cluster-based language models. In *SIGIR 2006*, pages 83–90.

McLachlan, Geoffrey and David Peel. 2000. *Finite Mixture Models*. New York: Wiley.

Mihalcea, Rada and Paul Tarau. 2004. TextRank: Bringing order into texts. In *EMNLP 2004*.

Mihalcea, Rada, Paul Tarau, and Elizabeth Figa. 2004. Pagerank on semantic networks, with application to word sense disambiguation. In *COLING 2004*, pages 1126–1132.

Monroe, Burt, Cheryl Monroe, Kevin Quinn, Dragomir Radev, Michael Crespin, Michael Colaresi, Anthony Fader, Jacob Balazer, and Steven Abney. 2006. United states congressional speech corpus. Department of Political Science, The Pennsylvania State University.

Newman, Mark. 2003. A measure of betweenness centrality based on random walks. Technical Report cond-mat/0309045, Arxiv.org.

Porter, Mason, Peter Mucha, Miark Newman, and Casey Warmbrand. 2005. A network analysis of committees in the U.S. House of Representatives. *PNAS*, 102(20).

Quinn, Kevin, Burt Monroe, Michael Colaresi, Michael Crespin, and Dragomir Radev. 2006. An automated method of topic-coding legislative speech over time with application to the 105th-108th U.S. senate. In *Midwest Political Science Association Meeting*.

Sparck-Jones, Karen. 1972. A statistical interpretation of term specificity and its application in retrieval. *Journal of Documentation*, 28(1):11–20.

Thomas, Matt, Bo Pang, and Lillian Lee. 2006. Get out the vote: Determining support or opposition from Congressional floor-debate transcripts. In *EMNLP 2006*, pages 327–335.

Improving Statistical Machine Translation using Lexicalized Rule Selection

Zhongjun He[1,2] and **Qun Liu**[1] and **Shouxun Lin**[1]
[1]Key Laboratory of Intelligent Information Processing
Institute of Computing Technology
Chinese Academy of Sciences
Beijing, 100190, China
[2]Graduate University of Chinese Academy of Sciences
Beijing, 100049, China
{zjhe,liuqun,sxlin}@ict.ac.cn

Abstract

This paper proposes a novel lexicalized approach for rule selection for syntax-based statistical machine translation (SMT). We build maximum entropy (MaxEnt) models which combine rich context information for selecting translation rules during decoding. We successfully integrate the MaxEnt-based rule selection models into the state-of-the-art syntax-based SMT model. Experiments show that our lexicalized approach for rule selection achieves statistically significant improvements over the state-of-the-art SMT system.

1 Introduction

The syntax-based statistical machine translation (SMT) models (Chiang, 2005; Liu et al., 2006; Galley et al., 2006; Huang et al., 2006) use rules with hierarchical structures as translation knowledge, which can capture long-distance reorderings. Generally, a translation rule consists of a left-hand-side (LHS) [1]and a right-hand-side (RHS). The LHS and RHS can be words, phrases, or even syntactic trees, depending on SMT models. Translation rules can be learned automatically from parallel corpus. Usually, an LHS may correspond to multiple RHS's in multiple rules. Therefore, in statistical machine translation, the rule selection task is to select the correct RHS for an LHS during decoding.

The conventional approach for rule selection is to use precomputed translation probabilities which are estimated from the training corpus, as well as a n-gram language model which is trained on the target language. The limitation of this method is that it ignores context information (especially on the source-side) during decoding. Take the hierarchical model (Chiang, 2005) as an example. Consider the following rules for Chinese-to-English translation [2]:

(1) $X \rightarrow \langle$ 在 $X_{\boxed{1}}$ 的 $X_{\boxed{2}}$, $X_{\boxed{2}}$ in $X_{\boxed{1}}$ $\rangle$

(2) $X \rightarrow \langle$ 在 $X_{\boxed{1}}$ 的 $X_{\boxed{2}}$, at $X_{\boxed{1}}$'s $X_{\boxed{2}}$ $\rangle$

(3) $X \rightarrow \langle$ 在 $X_{\boxed{1}}$ 的 $X_{\boxed{2}}$, with $X_{\boxed{2}}$ of $X_{\boxed{1}}$ $\rangle$

These rules have the same source-side, and all of them can pattern-match all the following source phrases:

(a) 在 [经济 领域]$_1$ 的 [合作]$_2$
in economic field 's cooperation

[cooperation]$_2$ in [the economic field]$_1$

(b) 在 [今天]$_1$ 的 [会议 上]$_2$
at today 's meeting on

at [today]$_1$'s [meeting]$_2$

(c) 在 [人民]$_1$ 的 [支持 下]$_2$
with people 's support under

with [the support]$_2$ of [the people]$_1$

Given a source phrase, how does the decoder know which rule is suitable? In fact, rule (1) and rule (2) have different syntactic structures (the left two trees of Figure 1). Thus rule (1) can be used for translating noun phrase (a), and rule (2) can be applied to prepositional phrase (b). The weakness

© 2008. Licensed under the *Creative Commons Attribution-Noncommercial-Share Alike 3.0 Unported* license (http://creativecommons.org/licenses/by-nc-sa/3.0/). Some rights reserved.

[1]In this paper, we use LHS and source-side interchangeably (so are RHS and target-side).

[2]In this paper, we use Chinese and English as the source and target language, respectively.

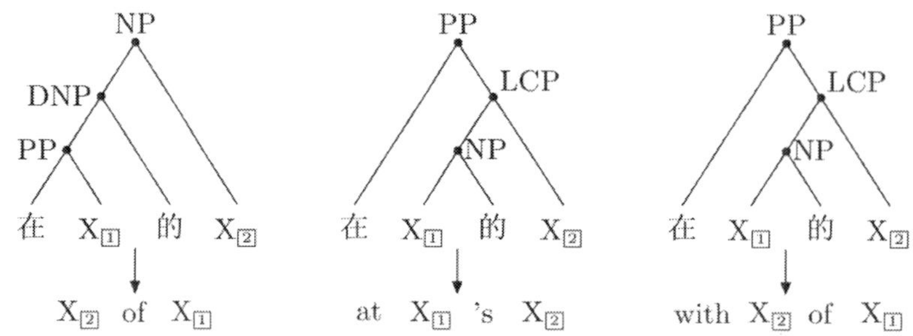

Figure 1: Syntactic structures of the same source-side in different rules.

of Chiang's hierarchical model is that it cannot distinguish different structures on the source-side. The linguistically syntax-based models (Liu et al., 2006; Huang et al., 2006) can distinguish syntactic structures by parsing source sentence. However, as an LHS tree may correspond to different RHS strings in different rules (the right two rules of Figure 1), these models also face the rule selection problem during decoding.

In this paper, we propose a lexicalized approach for rule selection for syntax-based statistical machine translation. We use the maximum entropy approach to combine various context features, e.g., context words of rules, boundary words of phrases, parts-of-speech (POS) information. Therefore, the decoder can use rich context information to perform context-dependent rule selection. We build a maximum entropy based rule selection (MaxEnt RS) model for each *ambiguous hierarchical LHS*, the LHS which contains nonterminals and corresponds to multiple RHS's in multiple rules. We integrate the MaxEnt RS models into the state-of-the-art hierarchical SMT system (Chiang, 2005). Experiments show that the lexicalized rule selection approach improves translation quality of the state-of-the-art SMT system, and the improvements are statistically significant.

2 Previous Work

2.1 The Selection Problem in SMT

Statistical machine translation systems usually face the selection problem because of the one-to-many correspondence between the source and target language. Recent researches showed that rich context information can help SMT systems perform selection and improves translation quality.

The discriminative phrasal reordering models (Xiong et al., 2006; Zens and Ney, 2006) provided a lexicalized method for phrase reordering. In these models, LHS and RHS can be considered as phrases and reordering types, respectively. Therefore the selection task is to select a reordering type for phrases. They use a MaxEnt model to combine context features and distinguished two kinds of reorderings between two adjacent phrases: monotone or swap. However, our method is more generic, we perform lexicalized rule selection for syntax-based SMT models. In these models, the rules with hierarchical structures can handle reorderings of non-adjacent phrases. Furthermore, the rule selection can be considered as a multi-class classification task, while the phrase reordering between two adjacent phrases is a two-class classification task.

Recently, word sense disambiguation (WSD) techniques improved the performance of SMT systems by helping the decoder perform lexical selection. Carpuat and Wu (2007b) integrated a WSD system into a phrase-based SMT system, Pharaoh (Koehn, 2004a). Furthermore, they extended WSD to phrase sense disambiguation (PSD) (Carpuat and Wu, 2007a). Either the WSD or PSD system combines rich context information to solve the ambiguity problem for words or phrases. Their experiments showed stable improvements of translation quality. These are different from our work. On one hand, they focus on solving the lexical ambiguity problem, and use a WSD or PSD system to predict translations for phrases which only consist of words. However, we put emphasis on rule selection, and predict translations for hierarchical LHS's which consist of both words and nonterminals. On the other hand, they incorporated a WSD or PSD system into a phrase-based SMT system with a weak distortion model for phrase reordering. While we incorporate MaxEnt RS models into the state-of-the-art syntax-based SMT system, which captures phrase reordering by using a hierarchical model.

Chan et al. (2007) incorporated a WSD system into the hierarchical SMT system, Hiero (Chiang, 2005), and reported statistically significant improvement. But they only focused on solving ambiguity for terminals of translation rules, and limited the length of terminals up to 2. Different from their work, we consider a translation rule as a whole, which contains both terminals and nonterminals. Moreover, they explored features for the WSD system only on the source-side. While we define context features for the MaxEnt RS models on both the source-side and target-side.

2.2 The Hierarchical Model

The hierarchical model (Chiang, 2005; Chiang, 2007) is built on a weighted synchronous context-free grammar (SCFG) . A SCFG rule has the following form:

(4) $$X \rightarrow \langle \alpha, \gamma, \sim \rangle$$

where X is a nonterminal, α is an LHS string consists of terminals and nonterminals, γ is the translation of α, $\sim$ defines a one-one correspondence between nonterminals in α and γ. For example,

(5) X → ⟨ 经济 发展, economic development⟩

(6) X → ⟨ $X_{\boxed{1}}$ 的 $X_{\boxed{2}}$, the $X_{\boxed{2}}$ of $X_{\boxed{1}}$⟩

Rule (5) contains only terminals, which is similar to phrase-to-phrase translation in phrase-based SMT models. Rule (6) contains both terminals and nonterminals, which causes a reordering of phrases. The hierarchical model uses the maximum likelihood method to estimate translation probabilities for a phrase pair $\langle \alpha, \gamma \rangle$, independent of any other context information.

To perform translation, Chiang uses a log-linear model (Och and Ney, 2002) to combine various features. The weight of a derivation D is computed by:

(7) $$w(D) = \prod_i \phi_i(D)^{\lambda_i}$$

where $\phi_i(D)$ is a feature function and λ_i is the feature weight of $\phi_i(D)$. During decoding, the decoder searches the best derivation with the lowest cost by applying SCFG rules. However, the rule selections are independent of context information, except the left neighboring $n-1$ target words for computing n-gram language model.

3 Lexicalized Rule Selection

The rule selection task can be considered as a multi-class classification task. For a source-side, each corresponding target-side is a label. The maximum entropy approach (Berger et al., 1996) is known to be well suited to solve the classification problem. Therefore, we build a maximum entropy based rule selection (MaxEnt RS) model for each ambiguous hierarchical LHS. In this section, we will describe how to build the MaxEnt RS models and how to integrate them into the hierarchical SMT model.

3.1 The MaxEnt RS Model

Following (Chiang, 2005), we use $\langle \alpha, \gamma \rangle$ to represent a SCFG rule extracted from the training corpus, where α and γ are source and target strings, respectively. The nonterminals in α and γ are represented by X_k, where k is an index indicating one-one correspondence between nonterminals in source and target sides. Let us use $f(X_k)$ to represent the source text covered by X_k, and $e(X_k)$ to represent the translation of $f(X_k)$. Let $C(\alpha)$ be the context information of source text matched by α, and $C(\gamma)$ be the context information of target text matched by γ. Under the MaxEnt model, we have:

(8) $$P_{rs}(\gamma|\alpha, f(X_k), e(X_k)) = \frac{\exp[\sum_i \lambda_i h_i(C(\gamma), C(\alpha), f(X_k), e(X_k))]}{\sum_{\gamma'} \exp[\sum_i \lambda_i h_i(C(\gamma'), C(\alpha), f(X_k), e(X_k))]}$$

where h_i is a binary feature function, λ_i is the feature weight of h_i. The MaxEnt RS model combines rich context information of grammar rules, as well as information of the subphrases which will be reduced to nonterminal X during decoding. However, these information is ignored by Chiang's hierarchical model.

We design three kinds of features for a rule $\langle \alpha, \gamma \rangle$:

- Lexical features, which are the words immediately to the left and right of α, and boundary words of subphrase $f(X_k)$ and $e(X_k)$;

- Parts-of-speech (POS) features, which are POS tags of the source words defined in lexical features.

- Length features, which are the length of subphrases $f(X_k)$ and $e(X_k)$.

Side	Type	Name	Description
Source-side	Lexical Features	$W\alpha_{-1}$	The source word immediately to the left of α
		$W\alpha_{+1}$	The source word immediately to the right of α
		$WL_{f(X_k)}$	The first word of $f(X_k)$
		$WR_{f(X_k)}$	The last word of $f(X_k)$
	POS Features	$P\alpha_{-1}$	POS of $W\alpha_{-1}$
		$P\alpha_{+1}$	POS of $W\alpha_{+1}$
		$PL_{f(X_k)}$	POS of $WL_{f(X_k)}$
		$PR_{f(X_k)}$	POS of $WR_{f(X_k)}$
	Length Feature	$LEN_{f(X_k)}$	Length of source subphrase $f(X_k)$
Target-side	Lexical Features	$WL_{e(X_k)}$	The first word of $e(X_k)$
		$WR_{e(X_k)}$	The last word of $e(X_k)$
	Length Feature	$LEN_{e(X_k)}$	Length of target subphrase $e(X_k)$

Table 1: Feature categories of the MaxEnt RS model.

Type	Feature
Lexical Features	$W\alpha_{-1}$=加强 $W\alpha_{+1}$=。
	$WL_{f(X_1)}$=经济 $WR_{f(X_1)}$=领域 $WL_{f(X_2)}$=合作 $WR_{f(X_1)}$=合作
	$WL_{e(X_1)}$=economic $WR_{e(X_1)}$=field $WL_{e(X_2)}$=cooperation $WR_{f(X_1)}$=cooperation
POS Features	$P\alpha_{-1}$=v $W\alpha_{+1}$=wj
	$PL_{f(X_1)}$=n $PR_{f(X_1)}$=n $PL_{f(X_2)}$=vn $PR_{f(X_2)}$=vn
Length Feature	$LEN_{f(X_1)}$=2 $LEN_{f(X_2)}$=1 $LEN_{e(X_1)}$=2 $LEN_{e(X_2)}$=1

Table 2: Features of rule $X \rightarrow \langle$ 在 $X_{\boxed{1}}$ 的 $X_{\boxed{2}}$, $X_{\boxed{2}}$ in the $X_{\boxed{1}}$ $\rangle$.

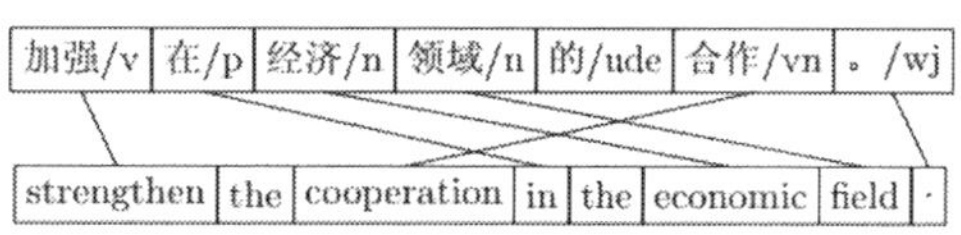

Figure 2: An training example for rule extraction.

Table 1 shows these features in detail.

These features can be easily gathered according to Chinag's rule extraction method (Chiang, 2005). We use an example for illustration. Figure 2 is a word-aligned training example with POS tags on the source side. We can obtain a SCFG rule:

(9) $X \rightarrow \langle$ 在 $X_{\boxed{1}}$ 的 $X_{\boxed{2}}$, $X_{\boxed{2}}$ in the $X_{\boxed{1}}$ $\rangle$

Where the source phrases covered by $X_{\boxed{1}}$ and $X_{\boxed{2}}$ are "经济 领域" and "合作", respectively. Table 2 shows features of this rule. Note that following (Chiang, 2005), we limit the number of nonterminals of a rule up to 2. Thus a rule may have 20 features at most.

After extracting features from the training corpus, we use the toolkit implemented by Zhang (2004) to train a MaxEnt RS model for each ambiguous hierarchical LHS. We set iteration number to 100 and Gaussian prior to 1.

3.2 Integrating the MaxEnt RS Models into the SMT Model

We integrate the MaxEnt RS models into the SMT model during the translation of each source sentence. Thus the MaxEnt RS models can help the decoder perform context-dependent rule selection during decoding.

In (Chiang, 2005), the log-linear model combines 8 features: the translation probabilities $P(\gamma|\alpha)$ and $P(\alpha|\gamma)$, the lexical weights $P_w(\gamma|\alpha)$ and $P_w(\alpha|\gamma)$, the language model, the word penalty, the phrase penalty, and the glue rule penalty. For integration, we add two new features:

- $P_{rs}(\gamma|\alpha, f(X_k), e(X_k))$. This feature is computed by the MaxEnt RS model, which gives a probability that the model selecting a target-side γ given an ambiguous source-side α, considering context information.

- $P_{rsn} = exp(1)$. This feature is similar to phrase penalty feature. In our experiments, we find that some source-sides are not ambiguous, and correspond to only one target-side. However, if a source-side α' is not ambiguous, the first feature P_{rs} will be set to 1.0. In fact, these rules are not reliable since they usually occur only once in the training corpus. Therefore, we use this feature to reward the ambiguous source-side. During decoding, if an LHS has multiple translations, this feature is set to $exp(1)$, otherwise it is set to $exp(0)$.

The advantage of our integration is that we need not change the main decoding algorithm of a SMT system. Furthermore, the weights of the new features can be trained together with other features of the translation model.

Chiang (2007) uses the CKY algorithm with a cube pruning method for decoding. This method can significantly reduce the search space by efficiently computing the top-n items rather than all possible items at a node, using the k-best Algorithms of Huang and Chiang (2005) to speed up the computation. In cube pruning, the translation model is treated as the monotonic backbone of the search space, while the language model score is a non-monotonic cost that distorts the search space (see (Huang and Chiang, 2005) for definition of monotonicity). Similarly, in the MaxEnt RS model, source-side features form a monotonic score while target-side features constitute a non-monotonic cost that can be seen as part of the language model.

For translating a source sentence F_I^J, the decoder adopts a bottom-up strategy. All derivations are stored in a *chart* structure. Each cell $c[i, j]$ of the chart contains all partial derivations which correspond to the source phrase f_i^j. For translating a source-side span $[i, j]$, we first select all possible rules from the rule table. Meanwhile, we can obtain features of the MaxEnt RS models which are defined on the source-side since they are fixed before decoding. During decoding, for a source phrase f_i^j, suppose the rule

$$\text{(10)} \qquad X \rightarrow \langle f_i^k X_{\boxed{1}} f_t^j, e_{i'}^{k'} X_{\boxed{1}} e_{t'}^{j'} \rangle$$

is selected by the decoder, where $i \leq k < t \leq j$ and $k+1 < t$, then we can gather features which are defined on the target-side of the subphrase $X_{\boxed{1}}$ from the ancestor chart cell $c[k+1, t-1]$ since the span $[k+1, t-1]$ has already been covered. Then the new feature scores P_{rs} and P_{rsn} can be computed. Therefore, the cost of the derivation can be obtained. Finally, the decoding is completed when the whole sentence is covered, and the best derivation of the source sentence F_I^J is the item with the lowest cost in cell $c[I, J]$.

4 Experiments

4.1 Corpus

We carry out experiments on two translation tasks with different sizes and domains of the training corpus.

- IWSLT-05: We use about 40,000 sentence pairs from the BTEC corpus with 354k Chinese words and 378k English words as our training data. The English part is used to train a trigram language model. We use IWSLT-04 test set as the development set and IWSLT-05 test set as the test set.
- NIST-03: We use the FBIS corpus as the training corpus, which contains 239k sentence pairs with 6.9M Chinese words and 8.9M English words. For this task, we train two trigram language models on the English part of the training corpus and the Xinhua portion of the Gigaword corpus, respectively. NIST-02 test set is used as the development set and NIST-03 test set is used as the test set.

4.2 Training

To train the translation model, we first run GIZA++ (Och and Ney, 2000) to obtain word alignment in both translation directions. Then the word alignment is refined by performing "grow-diag-final" method (Koehn et al., 2003). We use the same method suggested in (Chiang, 2005) to extract SCFG grammar rules. Meanwhile, we gather context features for training the MaxEnt RS models. The maximum initial phrase length is set to 10 and the maximum rule length of the source-side is set to 5.

We use SRI Language Modeling Toolkit (Stolcke, 2002) to train language models for both tasks. We use minimum error rate training (Och, 2003) to tune the feature weights for the log-linear model.

The translation quality is evaluated by BLEU metric (Papineni et al., 2002), as calculated by mteval-v11b.pl with case-insensitive matching of n-grams, where $n = 4$.

4.3 Baseline

We reimplement the decoder of Hiero (Chiang, 2007) in C++, which is the state-of-the-art SMT

System	IWSLT-05	NIST-03
Baseline	56.20	28.05
+ MaxEnt RS		
SLex	56.51	28.26
PF	56.95	28.78
SLex+PF	56.99	28.89
SLex+PF+SLen	57.10	28.96
SLex+PF +SLen+TF	57.20	29.02

Table 3: BLEU-4 scores (case-insensitive) on IWSLT-05 task and NIST MT-03 task. SLex = Source-side Lexical Features, PF = POS Features, SLen = Source-side Length Feature, TF = Target-side features.

system. During decoding, we set $b = 100$ to prune grammar rules, $\beta = 10$, $b = 30$ to prune X cells, and $\beta = 10$, $b = 15$ to prune S cells. For cube pruning, we set the threshold $\epsilon = 1.0$. See (Chiang, 2007) for meanings of these pruning parameters.

The baseline system uses precomputed phrase translation probabilities and two trigram language models to perform rule selection, independent of any other context information. The results are shown in the row *Baseline* of Table 3. For IWSLT-05 task, the baseline system achieves a BLEU-4 score of 56.20. For NIST MT-03 task, the BLEU-4 score is 28.05 .

4.4 Baseline + MaxEnt RS

As described in Section 3.2, we add two new features to integrate the MaxEnt RS models into the hierarchical model. To run the decoder, we share the same pruning settings with the baseline system. Table 3 shows the results.

Using all features defined in Section 3.1 to train the MaxEnt RS models, for IWSLT-05 task, the BLEU-4 score is 57.20, which achieves an absolute improvement of 1.0 over the baseline. For NIST-03 task, our system obtains a BLEU-4 score of 29.02, with an absolute improvement of 0.97 over the baseline. Using Zhang's significance tester (Zhang et al., 2004) to perform paired bootstrap sampling (Koehn, 2004b), both improvements on the two tasks are statistically significant at $p < 0.05$.

In order to explore the utility of the context features, we train the MaxEnt RS models on different feature sets. We find that POS features are the most useful features since they can generalize over all training examples. Moreover, length feature also yields improvement. However, these features are never used in the baseline.

	NO. of LHS	NO. of H-LHS	NO. of AH-LHS
NIST MT-03	163,097	148,671	95,424
Baseline	12,069	7,164	5,745
+MaxEnt RS (All features)	12,655	10,306	9,259

Table 4: Number of possible source-sides of SCFG rules for NIST-03 task and number of source-sides of the best translation. H-LHS = Hierarchical LHS, AH-LHS = Ambiguous hierarchical LHS.

5 Analysis

Table 4 shows the number of source-sides of the SCFG rules for NIST-03 task. After extracting grammar rules from the training corpus, there are 163,097 source-sides match the test corpus, 91.15% are hierarchical LHS's (H-LHS, the LHS which contains nonterminals). For the hierarchical LHS's, 64.18% are ambiguous (AH-LHS, the H-LHS which has multiple translations). This indicates that the decoder will face serious rule selection problem during decoding. We also note the number of the source-sides of the best translation for the test corpus. For the baseline system, the number of H-LHS only account for 59.36% of total LHS's. However, by incorporating MaxEnt RS models, that proportion increases to 81.44%, since the number of AH-LHS increases. The reason is that, we use the feature P_{rsn} to reward ambiguous hierarchical LHS's. This has some advantages. On one hand, H-LHS can capture phrase reorderings. On the other hand, AH-LHS is more reliable than non-ambiguous LHS, since most non-ambiguous LHS's occur only once in the training corpus.

In order to know how the MaxEnt RS models improve the performance of the SMT system, we study the best translation of Baseline and Baseline+MaxEnt RS. We find that the MaxEnt RS models improve translation quality in 2 ways.

5.1 Better Phrase reordering

Since the SCFG rules which contain nonterminals can capture reordering of phrases, better rule selection will produce better phrase reordering. For example, the source sentence "... [联合国 安全 理事会]$_1$ 的 [五 个 常任 理事国]$_2$ ... " is translated as follows:

- Reference: ... *the five permanent members of the UN Security Council ...*
- Baseline: ... *the [United Nations Security Council]$_1$ [five permanent members]$_2$ ...*
- +MaxEnt RS: ... *[the five permanent members]$_2$ of [the UN Security Council]$_1$ ...*

The source sentence is translated incorrectly by the baseline system, which selects the rule

(11) $X \rightarrow \langle X_{\boxed{1}}$ 的 $X_{\boxed{2}}$, the $X_{\boxed{1}} X_{\boxed{2}} \rangle$

and produces a monotone translation. In contrast, by considering information of the subphrases $X_{\boxed{1}}$ and $X_{\boxed{2}}$, the MaxEnt RS model chooses the rule

(12) $X \rightarrow \langle X_{\boxed{1}}$ 的 $X_{\boxed{2}}$, $X_{\boxed{2}}$ of $X_{\boxed{1}} \rangle$

and obtains a correct translation by swapping $X_{\boxed{1}}$ and $X_{\boxed{2}}$ on the target-side.

5.2 Better Lexical Translation

The MaxEnt RS models can also help the decoder perform better lexical translation than the baseline. This is because the SCFG rules contain terminals. When the decoder selects a rule for a source-side, it also determines the translations of the source terminals. For example, the translations of the source sentence "恐怕 这 趟 航班 已经 订 满 了 。" are as follows:

- Reference *I'm afraid this flight is full.*
- Baseline: *I'm afraid already booked for this flight.*
- +MaxEnt RS: *I'm afraid this flight is full.*

Here, the baseline translates the Chinese phrase "订 满" into "booked" by using the rule:

(13) $X \rightarrow \langle X_{\boxed{1}}$ 订 满, $X_{\boxed{1}}$ booked$\rangle$

The meaning is not fully expressed since the Chinese word "满" is not translated. However, the MaxEnt RS model obtains a correct translation by using the rule:

(14) $X \rightarrow \langle X_{\boxed{1}}$ 订 满, $X_{\boxed{1}}$ full $\rangle$

However, we also find that some results produced by the MaxEnt RS models seem to decrease the BLEU score. An interesting example is the translation of the source sentence "这 条 街 叫 什么 ? ":

- Reference1: *What is the name of this street?*
- Reference2: *What is this street called?*
- Baseline: *What is the name of this street?*
- +MaxEnt RS: *What's this street called?*

In fact, both translations are correct. But the translation of the baseline fully matches *Reference1*. Although the translation produced by the MaxEnt RS model is almost the same as *Reference2*, as the BLEU metric is based on n-gram matching, the translation "What's" cannot match "What is" in *Reference2*. Therefore, the MaxEnt RS model achieves a lower BLEU score.

6 Conclusion

In this paper, we propose a generic lexicalized approach for rule selection. We build maximum entropy based rule selection models for each ambiguous hierarchical source-side of translation rules. The MaxEnt RS models combine rich context information, which can help the decoder perform context-dependent rule selection during decoding. We integrate the MaxEnt RS models into the hierarchical SMT model by adding two new features. Experiments show that the lexicalized approach for rule selection achieves statistically significant improvements over the state-of-the-art syntax-based SMT system.

Furthermore, our approach not only can be used for the formally syntax-based SMT systems, but also can be applied to the linguistically syntax-based SMT systems. For future work, we will explore more sophisticated features for the MaxEnt RS models and integrate the models into the linguistically syntax-based SMT systems.

Acknowledgements

We would like to show our special thanks to Hwee Tou Ng, Liang Huang, Yajuan Lv and Yang Liu for their valuable suggestions. We also appreciate the anonymous reviewers for their detailed comments and recommendations. This work was supported by the National Natural Science Foundation of China (NO. 60573188 and 60736014), and the High Technology Research and Development Program of China (NO. 2006AA010108).

References

Berger, A. L., S. A. Della Pietra, and V. J. Della. 1996. A maximum entropy approach to natural language processing. *Computational Linguistics*, page 22(1):39 - 72.

Carpuat, Marine and Dekai Wu. 2007a. How phrase sense disambiguation outperforms word sense disambiguation for statistical machine translation. In *11th Conference on Theoretical and Methodological Issues in Machine Translation*, pages 43–52.

Carpuat, Marine and Dekai Wu. 2007b. Improving statistical machine translation using word sense disambiguation. In *Proceedings of EMNLP-CoNLL 2007*, pages 61–72.

Chan, Yee Seng, Hwee Tou Ng, and David Chiang. 2007. Word sense disambiguation improves statistical machine translation. In *Proceedings of the 45th Annual Meeting of the Association for Computational Linguistics*, pages 33–40.

Chiang, David. 2005. A hierarchical phrase-based model for statistical machine translation. In *Proceedings of the 43rd Annual Meeting of the Association for Computational Linguistics*, pages 263–270.

Chiang, David. 2007. Hierarchical phrase-based translation. *Computational Linguistics*, pages 33(2):201–228.

Galley, Michel, Jonathan Graehl, Kevin Knight, Daniel Marcu, Steve DeNeefe, Wei Wang, and Ignacio Thayer. 2006. Scalable inference and training of context-rich syntactic translation models. In *Proceedings of COLING-ACL 2006*, pages 961–968.

Huang, Liang and David Chiang. 2005. Better k-best parsing. In *Proceedings of the 9th International Workshop on Parsing Technologies.*

Huang, Liang, Kevin Knight, and Aravind Joshi. 2006. Statistical syntax-directed translation with extended domain of locality. In *Proceedings of the 7th Biennial Conference of the Association for Machine Translation in the Americas.*

Koehn, Philipp, Franz J. Och, and Daniel Marcu. 2003. Statistical phrase-based translation. In *Proceedings of HLT-NAACL 2003*, pages 127–133.

Koehn, Philipp. 2004a. Pharaoh: a beam search decoder for phrase-based statistical machine translation models. In *Proceedings of the Sixth Conference of the Association for Machine Translation in the Americas*, pages 115–124.

Koehn, Philipp. 2004b. Statistical significance tests for machine translation evaluation. In *Proceedings of the 2004 Conference on Empirical Methods in Natural Language Processing (EMNLP)*, pages 388–395.

Liu, Yang, Qun Liu, and Shouxun Lin. 2006. Tree-to-string alignment template for statistical machine translation. In *Proceedings of the 44th Annual Meeting of the Association for Computational Linguistics*, pages 609–616.

Och, Franz Josef and Hermann Ney. 2000. Improved statistical alignment models. In *Proceedings of the 38th Annual Meeting of the Association for Computational Linguistics*, pages 440–447.

Och, Franz Josef and Hermann Ney. 2002. Discriminative training and maximum entropy models for statistical machine translation. In *Proceedings of the 40th Annual Meeting of the Association for Computational Linguistics*, pages 295–302.

Och, Franz Josef. 2003. Minimum error rate training in statistical machine translation. In *Proceedings of the 41st Annual Meeting of the Association for Computational Linguistics*, pages 160–167.

Papineni, K., S. Roukos, T. Ward, and W.-J. Zhu. 2002. Bleu: a method for automatic evaluation of machine translation. In *Proceedings of the 40th Annual Meeting of the Association for Computational Linguistics*, pages 311–318.

Stolcke, Andreas. 2002. Srilm – an extensible language modeling toolkit. In *Proceedings of the International Conference on Spoken language Processing*, volume 2, pages 901–904.

Xiong, Deyi, Qun Liu, and Shouxun Lin. 2006. Maximum entropy based phrase reordering model for statistical machine translation. In *Proceedings of the 44th Annual Meeting of the Association for Computational Linguistics*, pages 521–528.

Zens, Richard and Hermann Ney. 2006. Discriminative reordering models for statistical machine translation. In *Proceedings of the Workshop on Statistical Machine Translation*, pages 55–63.

Zhang, Ying, Stephan Vogel, and Alex Waibel. 2004. Interpreting bleu/nist scores: How much improvement do we need to have a better system? In *Proceedings of the Fourth International Conference on Language Resources and Evaluation*, pages 2051–2054.

Zhang, Le. 2004. Maximum entropy modeling toolkit for python and c++. available at http://homepages.inf.ed.ac.uk/s0450736/maxent_toolkit.html.

Evaluating Unsupervised Part-of-Speech Tagging for Grammar Induction

William P. Headden III, David McClosky, Eugene Charniak
Brown Laboratory for Linguistic Information Processing (BLLIP)
Brown University
Providence, RI 02912
{headdenw,dmcc,ec}@cs.brown.edu

Abstract

This paper explores the relationship between various measures of unsupervised part-of-speech tag induction and the performance of both supervised and unsupervised parsing models trained on induced tags. We find that no standard tagging metrics correlate well with unsupervised parsing performance, and several metrics grounded in information theory have no strong relationship with even supervised parsing performance.

1 Introduction

There has been a great deal of recent interest in the unsupervised discovery of syntactic structure from text, both parts-of-speech (Johnson, 2007; Goldwater and Griffiths, 2007; Biemann, 2006; Dasgupta and Ng, 2007) and deeper grammatical structure like constituency and dependency trees (Klein and Manning, 2004; Smith, 2006; Bod, 2006; Seginer, 2007; Van Zaanen, 2001). While some grammar induction systems operate on raw text, many of the most successful ones presume prior part-of-speech tagging. Meanwhile, most recent work in part-of-speech induction focuses on increasing the degree to which their tags match hand-annotated ones such as those in the Penn Treebank.

In this work our goal is to evaluate how improvements in part-of-speech tag induction affects grammar induction. Using several different unsupervised taggers, we induce tags and train three grammar induction systems on the results.

©2008. Licensed under the *Creative Commons Attribution-Noncommercial-Share Alike 3.0 Unported* license (http://creativecommons.org/licenses/by-nc-sa/3.0/). Some rights reserved.

We then explore the relationship between the performance on common unsupervised tagging metrics and the performance of resulting grammar induction systems. Disconcertingly we find that they bear little to no relationship.

This paper is organized as follows. In Section 2 we discuss unsupervised part-of-speech induction systems and common methods of evaluation. In Section 3, we describe grammar induction in general and discuss the systems with which we evaluate taggings. We present our experiments in Section 4, and finally conclude in Section 5.

2 Part-of-speech Tag Induction

Part-of-speech tag induction can be thought of as a clustering problem where, given a corpus of words, we aim to group word tokens into syntactic classes.

Two tasks are commonly labeled unsupervised part-of-speech induction. In the first, tag induction systems are allowed the use of a tagging dictionary, which specifies for each word a set of possible parts-of-speech (Merialdo, 1994; Smith and Eisner, 2005; Goldwater and Griffiths, 2007). In the second, only the word tokens and sentence boundaries are given. In this work we focus on this latter task to explore grammar induction in a maximally unsupervised context.

Tag induction systems typically focus on two sorts of features: distributional and morphological. Distributional refers to what sorts of words appear in close proximity to the word in question, while morphological refers to modeling the internal structure of a word. All the systems below make use of distributional information, whereas only two use morphological features.

We primarily focus on the metrics used to evaluate induced taggings. The catalogue of recent part-of-speech systems is large, and we can only test the tagging metrics using a few systems. Recent work that we do not explore explicitly includes (Biemann, 2006; Dasgupta and Ng, 2007; Freitag, 2004; Smith and Eisner, 2005). We have selected a few systems, described below, that represent a broad range of features and techniques to make our evaluation of the metrics as broad as possible.

2.1 Clustering using SVD and K-means

Schütze (1995) presents a series of part-of-speech inducers based on distributional clustering. We implement the baseline system, which Klein and Manning (2002) use for their grammar induction experiments with induced part-of-speech tags. For each word type w in the vocabulary V, the system forms a feature row vector consisting of the number of times each of the F most frequent words occur to the left of w and to the right of w. It normalizes these row vectors and assembles them into a $|V| \times 2F$ matrix. It then performs a Singular Value Decomposition on the matrix and rank reduces it to decrease its dimensionality to d principle components ($d < 2F$). This results in a representation of each word as a point in a d dimensional space. We follow Klein and Manning (2002) in using K-means to cluster the d dimensional word vectors into parts-of-speech. We use the $F = 500$ most frequent words as left and right context features, and reduce to a dimensionality of $d = 50$. We refer to this system as SVD in our experiments.

The other systems described in Schütze (1995) make use of more complicated feature models. We chose the baseline system primarily to match previous evaluations of grammar induction using induced tags (Klein and Manning, 2002).

2.2 Hidden Markov Models

One simple family of models for part-of-speech induction are the Hidden Markov Models (HMMs), in which there is a sequence of hidden state variables $t_1 ... t_n$ (for us, the part-of-speech tags). Each state t_i is conditioned on the previous $n-1$ states $t_{i-1} ... t_{i-n+1}$, and every t_i emits an observed word w_i conditioned on t_i. There is a single start state that emits nothing, as well as a single stop state, which emits an end-of-sentence marker with probability 1 and does not transition further. In our experiments we use the bitag HMM, in which each state t_i depends only on state t_{i-1}.

The classic method of training HMMs for part-of-speech induction is the Baum-Welch (Baum, 1972) variant of the Expectation-Maximization (EM) algorithm, which searches for a local maximum in the likelihood of the observed words.

Other methods approach the problem from a Bayesian perspective. These methods place Dirichlet priors over the parameters of each transition and emission multinomial. For an HMM with a set of states T and a set of output symbols V:

$$\forall t \in T \quad \theta_t \sim Dir(\alpha_1, ... \alpha_{|T|}) \quad (1)$$

$$\forall t \in T \quad \eta_t \sim Dir(\beta_1, ... \beta_{|V|}) \quad (2)$$

$$t_i | t_{i-1}, \theta_{t_i-1} \sim Multi(\theta_{t_{i-1}}) \quad (3)$$

$$w_i | t_i, \eta_{t_i} \sim Multi(\eta_{t_i}) \quad (4)$$

One advantage of the Bayesian approach is that the prior allows us to bias learning toward sparser structures, by setting the Dirichlet hyperparameters α, β to a value less than one (Johnson, 2007; Goldwater and Griffiths, 2007). This increases the probability of multinomial distributions which put most of their mass on a few events, instead of distributing them broadly across many events. There is evidence that this leads to better performance on some part-of-speech induction metrics (Johnson, 2007; Goldwater and Griffiths, 2007).

There are both MCMC and variational approaches to estimating HMMs with sparse Dirichlet priors; we chose the latter (Variational Bayes or VB) due to its simple implementation as a minor modification to Baum-Welch. Johnson (2007) evaluates both estimation techniques on the Bayesian bitag model; Goldwater and Griffiths (2007) emphasize the advantage in the MCMC approach of integrating out the HMM parameters in a tritag model, yielding a tagging supported by many different parameter settings.

Following the setup in Johnson (2007), we initialize the transition and emission distributions to be uniform with a small amount of noise, and run EM and VB for 1000 iterations. We label these systems as HMM-EM and HMM-VB respectively in our experiments. In our VB experiments we set $\alpha_i = \beta_j = 0.1, \forall i \in \{1, ..., |T|\}, j \in \{1, ..., |V|\}$, which yielded the best performance on most reported metrics in Johnson (2007). We use maximum marginal decoding, which Johnson (2007) reports performs better than Viterbi decoding.

2.3 Systems with Morphology

Clark (2003) presents several part-of-speech induction systems which incorporate morphological as well as distributional information. We use the implementation found on his website.[1]

2.3.1 Ney-Essen with Morphology

The simplest model is based on work by (Ney et al., 1994). It uses a bitag HMM, with the restriction that each word type in the vocabulary can only be generated by a single part-of-speech. Thus the tag induction task here reduces to finding a multiway partition of the vocabulary. The learning algorithm greedily reassigns each word type to the part-of-speech that results in the greatest increase in likelihood.

In order to incorporate morphology, Clark (2003) associates with each part-of-speech a HMM with letter emissions. The vocabulary is generated by generating a series of word types from the letter HMM of each part-of-speech. These can model very basic concatenative morphology. The parameters of the HMMs are estimated by running a single iteration of Forward-Backward after each round of reassigning words to tags. In our experiments we evaluate both the model without morphology (NE in our experiments), and the morphological model, trying both 5 and 10 states in the letter HMM (NEMorph5, NEMorph10 respectively).

2.3.2 Two-Level HMM

The final part-of-speech inducer we try from Clark (2003) is a two-level HMM. This is similar to the previous model, except it lifts the restriction that a word appear under only one part-of-speech. Alternatively, one could think of this model as a standard HMM, whose emission distributions incorporate a mixture of a letter HMM and a standard multinomial. Training uses a simple variation of Forward-Backward. In the experiments in this paper, we initialize the mixture parameters to .5, and try 5 states in the letter HMM. We refer to this model as 2HMM.

2.4 Tag Evaluation

Objective evaluation in any clustering task is always difficult, since there are many ways to define good clusters. Typically it involves a mixture of subjective evaluation and a comparison of the clusters to those found by human annotators. In the realm of part-of-speech induction, there are several common ways of doing the latter. These split into two groups: accuracy and information-theoretic criteria.

[1] http://www.cs.rhul.ac.uk/home/alexc/pos.tar.gz

Accuracy, given some mapping between the set of induced classes and the gold standard labels, is the number of words in the corpus that have been marked with the correct gold label divided by the total number of word tokens. The main challenge facing these metrics is deciding how to to map each induced part-of-speech class to a gold tag. One option is what Johnson (2007) calls "many-to-one" (M-to-1) accuracy, in which each induced tag is labeled with its most frequent gold tag. Although this results in a situation where multiple induced tags may share a single gold tag, it does not punish a system for providing tags of a finer granularity than the gold standard.

In contrast, "one-to-one" (1-to-1) accuracy restricts each gold tag to having a single induced tag. The mapping typically is made to try to give the most favorable mapping in terms of accuracy, typically using a greedy assignment (Haghighi and Klein, 2006). In cases where the number of gold tags is different than the number of induced tags, some must necessarily remain unassigned (Johnson, 2007).

In addition to accuracy, there are several information theoretic criteria presented in the literature. These escape the problem of trying to find an appropriate mapping between induced and gold tags, at the expense of perhaps being less intuitive.

Let T_I be the tag assignments to the words in the corpus created by an unsupervised tagger, and let T_G be the gold standard tag assignments. Clark (2003) uses Shannon's conditional entropy of the gold tagging given the induced tagging $H(T_G|T_I)$. Lower entropy indicates less uncertainty in the gold tagging if we already know the induced tagging. Freitag (2004) uses the similar "cluster-conditional tag perplexity" which is merely $exp(H(T_G|T_I))^2$. Since cluster-conditional tag perplexity is a monotonic function of $H(T_G|T_I)$, we only report the latter.

Goldwater and Griffiths (2007) propose using the Variation of Information of Meilă (2003):

$$VI(T_G;T_I) = H(T_G|T_I) + H(T_I|T_G)$$

VI represents the change in information when going from one clustering to another. It holds the nice properties of being nonnegative, symmetric, as well as fulfilling the triangle inequality.

[2] Freitag (2004) measures entropy in nats, while we use bits. The difference is a constant factor.

3 Grammar Induction

In addition to parts-of-speech, we also want to discover deeper syntactic relationships. Grammar induction is the problem of determining these relationships in an unsupervised fashion. This can be thought of more concretely as an unsupervised parsing task. As there are many languages and domains with few treebank resources, systems that can learn syntactic structure from unlabeled data would be valuable. Most work on this problem has focused on either dependency induction, which we discuss in Section 3.2, or on constituent induction, which we examine in the next section.

The Grammar Induction systems we use to evaluate the above taggers are the Constituent-Context Model (CCM), the Dependency Model with Valence (DMV), and a model which combines the two (CCM+DMV) outlined in (Klein and Manning, 2002; Klein and Manning, 2004).

3.1 Constituent Grammar Induction

Klein and Manning (2002) present a generative model for inducing constituent boundaries from part-of-speech tagged text. The model first generates a bracketing $B = \{B_{ij}\}_{1 \leq i \leq j \leq n}$, which specifies whether each span (i, j) in the sentence is a constituent or a distituent. Next, given the constituency or distituency of the span B_{ij}, the model generates the part-of-speech yield of the span $t_i ... t_j$, and the one-tag context window of the span t_{i-1}, t_{j+1}. $P(t_i ... t_j | B_{ij})$ and $P(t_{i-1}, t_{j+1} | B_{ij})$ are multinomial distributions. The model is trained using EM.

We evaluate induced constituency trees against those of the Penn Treebank using the versions of unlabeled precision, recall, and F-score used by Klein and Manning (2002). These ignore trivial brackets and multiple constituents spanning the same bracket. They evaluate their CCM system on the Penn Treebank WSJ sentences of length 10 or less, using part-of-speech tags induced by the baseline system of Schütze (1995). They report that switching to induced tags decreases the overall bracketing F-score from 71.1 to 63.2, although the recall of VP and S constituents actually improves. Additionally, they find that NP and PP recall decreases substantially with induced tags. They attribute this to the fact that nouns end up in many induced tags.

There has been quite a bit of other work on constituency induction. Smith and Eisner (2004) present an alternative estimation technique for CCM which uses annealing to try to escape local maxima. Bod (2006) describes an unsupervised system within the Data-Oriented-Parsing framework. Several approaches try to learn structure directly from raw text. Seginer (2007) has an incremental parsing approach using a novel representation called common-cover-links, which can be converted to constituent brackets. Van Zaanen (2001)'s ABL attempts to align sentences to determine what sequences of words are substitutable.

The work closest in spirit to this paper is Cramer (2007), who evaluates several grammar induction systems on the Eindhoven corpus (Dutch). One of his experiments compares the grammar induction performance of these systems starting with tags induced using the system described by Biemann (2006), to the performance of the systems on manually-marked tags. However he does not evaluate to what degree better tagging performance leads to improvement in these systems.

3.2 Dependency Grammar Induction

A dependency tree is a directed graph whose nodes are words in the sentence. A directed edge exists between two words if the target word (argument) is a dependent of the source word (head). Each word token may be the argument of only one head, but a head may have several arguments. One word is the head of the sentence, and is often thought of as the argument of a virtual "Root" node.

Klein and Manning (2004) present their Dependency Model with Valence (DMV) for the unsupervised induction of dependencies. Like the constituency model, DMV works from parts-of-speech. Under this model, for a given head, h, they first generate the parts-of-speech of the arguments to the right of h, and then those to the left. Generating the arguments in a particular direction breaks down into two parts: deciding whether to stop generating in this direction, and if not, what part-of-speech to generate as the argument. The argument decision conditions on h and the direction. The stopping decision conditions on this and also on whether h has already generated an argument in this direction, thereby capturing the limited notion of valence from which the model takes its name. It is worth noting that this model can only represent projective dependency trees, i.e. those without crossing edges.

Dependencies are typically evaluated using di-

Tagger	No. Tags	Tagging Metrics				Grammar Induction Metrics					
						CCM	CCM+DMV			DMV	
		1-to-1	$H(T_G\|T_I)$	M-to-1	VI	UF1	DA	UA	UF1	DA	UA
Gold		1.00	0.00	1.00	0.00	71.50	52.90	67.60	56.50	45.40	63.80
HMM-EM	10	0.39	2.67	0.41	4.39	**58.89**	40.12	**59.26**	**59.43**	**36.77**	**57.37**
HMM-EM	20	**0.43**	2.28	0.48	4.54	**57.31**	**51.16**	**64.66**	**61.33**	**38.65**	**58.57**
HMM-EM	50	0.36	1.83	0.58	4.92	**56.56**	**48.03**	**63.84**	**58.02**	**39.30**	**58.84**
HMM-VB	10	0.40	2.75	0.41	4.42	39.05	27.72	52.84	**58.64**	23.94	51.64
HMM-VB	20	0.40	2.63	0.43	4.65	37.60	33.77	55.97	40.30	30.36	51.53
HMM-VB	50	0.38	2.70	0.42	5.01	34.68	37.29	57.72	39.82	29.03	50.50
NE	10	0.34	2.74	0.40	4.32	28.80	20.70	50.60	32.70	26.20	48.90
NE	20	**0.48**	2.02	0.55	**3.76**	32.50	36.00	**59.30**	40.60	32.80	54.00
NEMorph10	10	**0.44**	2.46	0.47	**3.74**	29.03	25.99	53.80	34.58	26.98	48.72
NEMorph10	20	**0.48**	1.94	0.56	**3.65**	31.95	35.85	57.93	38.22	30.45	50.72
NEMorph10	50	**0.47**	1.24	**0.72**	**3.60**	31.07	36.29	57.76	39.28	31.50	52.83
NEMorph5	10	**0.45**	2.50	0.47	**3.76**	29.04	22.72	51.58	32.67	23.62	47.89
NEMorph5	20	**0.44**	2.02	0.56	**3.80**	31.94	24.17	52.43	32.90	22.41	47.17
NEMorph5	50	**0.47**	**1.27**	**0.72**	**3.64**	31.39	38.63	**59.44**	40.23	34.26	**54.63**
2HMM	10	0.38	2.78	0.41	4.55	31.63	36.35	**58.87**	44.97	28.43	49.32
2HMM	20	0.41	2.35	0.48	4.71	42.39	43.91	**60.74**	50.85	29.32	50.69
2HMM	50	0.37	1.92	0.58	5.11	41.18	**49.94**	**64.87**	**57.84**	**39.24**	**59.14**
SVD	10	0.31	3.07	0.34	4.99	37.77	27.64	49.56	36.46	20.74	45.52
SVD	20	0.33	2.73	0.40	4.99	37.17	30.14	51.66	37.66	22.24	46.25
SVD	50	0.34	2.37	0.47	5.18	36.87	37.66	56.49	52.83	22.50	46.52
SVD	100	0.34	2.03	0.53	5.37	45.46	41.68	**58.83**	**64.20**	20.81	44.36
SVD	200	0.32	1.72	0.59	5.59	**61.90**	34.79	52.25	**59.93**	22.66	42.30

Table 1: The performance of the taggers regarding both tag and grammar induction metrics on WSJ sections 0-10, averaged over 10 runs. Bold indicates the result was within 10 percent of the best-scoring induced system for a given metric.

rected and undirected accuracy. These are the total number of proposed edges that appear in the gold tree divided by the total number of edges (the number of words in the sentence). Directed accuracy gives credit to a proposed edge if it is in the gold tree and is in the correct direction, while undirected accuracy ignores the direction.

Klein and Manning (2004) also present a model which combines CCM and DMV into a single model, which we show as CCM+DMV. In their experiments, this model performed better on both the constituency and dependency induction tasks. As with CCM, Klein and Manning (2004) similarly evaluate the combined CCM+DMV system using tags induced with the same method. Again they find that overall bracketing F-score decreases from 77.6 to 72.9 and directed dependency accuracy measures decreases from 47.5 to 42.3 when switching to induced tags from gold. However for each metric, the systems still do quite well with induced tags.

As in the constituency case, Smith (2006) presents several alternative estimation procedures for DMV, which try to minimize the local maximum problems inherent in EM. It is thus possible these methods might yield better performance for the models when run off of induced tags.

4 Experiments

We induce tags with each system on the Penn Treebank Wall Street Journal (Marcus et al., 1994), sections 0-10, which contain 20,260 sentences. We vary the number of tags (10, 20, 50) and run each system 10 times for a given setting. The result of each run is used as the input to the CCM, DMV, and CCM+DMV systems. While the tags are induced from all sentences in the section, following the practice in (Klein and Manning, 2002; Klein and Manning, 2004), we remove punctuation, and consider only sentences of length not greater than 10 in our grammar induction experiments. Taggings are evaluated after punctuation is removed, but before filtering for length.

To explore the relationship between tagging metrics and the resulting performance of grammar induction systems, we examine each pair of tagging and grammar induction metrics. Consider the following two examples: DMV directed accuracy vs. $H(T_G|T_I)$ (Figure 1), and CCM f-score vs. variation of information (Figure 2). These were selected because they have relatively high magnitude τs. From these plots it is clear that although there may be a slight correspondence, the relationships are weak at best.

Each tagging and grammar induction metric gives us a ranking over the set of taggings of the data generated over the course of our experiments. These are ordered from best to worst according to the metric, so for instance $H(T_G|T_I)$ would give highest rank to its lowest value. We can compare the two rankings using Kendall's τ (see Lapata (2006) for an overview), a nonparametric measure of correspondence for rankings. τ measures the difference between the number of concordant pairs (items the two rankings place in the same order) and discordant pairs (those the rankings place in opposite order), divided by the total number of pairs. A value of 1 indicates the rankings have perfect correspondence, -1 indicates they are in the opposite order, and 0 indicates they are independent. The τ values are shown in Table 2. The scatter-plot in Figure 1 shows the τ with the greatest magnitude. However, we can see that even these rankings have barely any relationship.

An objection one might raise is that the lack of correspondence reflects poorly not on these metrics, but upon the grammar induction systems we use to evaluate them. There might be something about these models in particular which yields these low correlations. For instance these grammar inducers all estimate their models using EM, which can get caught easily in a local maximum.

To this possibility, we respond by pointing to performance on gold tags, which is consistently high for all grammar induction metrics. There is clearly some property of the gold tags which is exploited by the grammar induction systems even in the absence of better estimation procedures. This property is not reflected in the tagging metrics.

The scores for each system for tagging and grammar induction, averaged over the 10 runs, are shown in Table 1. Additionally, we included runs of the SVD-tagger for 100 and 200 tags, since running this system is still practical with these numbers of tags. The Ney-Essen with Morphology taggers perform at or near the top on the various tagging metrics, but not well on the grammar induction tasks on average. HMM-EM seems to perform on average quite well on all the grammar induction tasks, while the SVD-based systems yield the top bracketing F-scores, making use of larger numbers of tags.

Tagging Metrics	Grammar Induction Metrics					
	CCM	CCM+DMV			DMV	
	UF1	DA	UA	UF1	DA	UA
1-to-1	-0.22	-0.04	0.05	-0.13	0.13	0.12
M-to-1	-0.09	0.17	0.24	0.03	0.26	0.25
$H(T_G\|T_I)$	0.01	0.21	0.27	0.07	0.29	0.28
VI	-0.25	-0.17	-0.06	-0.20	0.07	0.07

Table 2: Kendall's τ, between tag and grammar induction criteria.

4.1 Supervised Experiments

One question we might ask is whether these tagging metrics capture information relevant to any parsing task. We explored this by experimenting with a supervised parser, training off trees where the gold parts-of-speech have been removed and replaced with induced tags. Our expectation was that the brackets, the head propagation paths, and the phrasal categories in the training trees would be sufficient to overcome any loss in information that the gold tags might provide. Additionally it was possible the induced tags would ignore rare parts-of-speech such as FW, and make better use of the available tags, perhaps using new distributional clues not in the original tags.

To this end we modified the Charniak Parser (Charniak, 2000) to train off induced parts-of-speech. The Charniak parser is a lexicalized PCFG parser for which the part-of-speech of a head word is a key aspect of its model. During training, the head-paths from the gold part-of-speech tags are retained, but we replace the tags themselves.

We ran experiments using the bitag HMM from Section 2.2 trained using EM, as well as with the Schütze SVD tagger from Section 2.1. The parser was trained on sections 2-21 of the Penn Treebank for training and section 24 was used for evaluation.

As before we calculated τ scores between each tagging metric and supervised f-score. Unlike the unsupervised evaluation where we used the metric UF1, we use the standard EVALB calculation of unlabeled f-score. The results are shown in Table 3.

The contrast with the unsupervised case is vast, with very high τs for both accuracy metrics. Consider f-score vs. many-to-one, plotted in Figure 3. The correspondence here is very clear: taggings with high accuracy do actually reflect on better parser performance. Note, however, that the correspondence between the information theoretic measures and parsing performance is still rather weak.

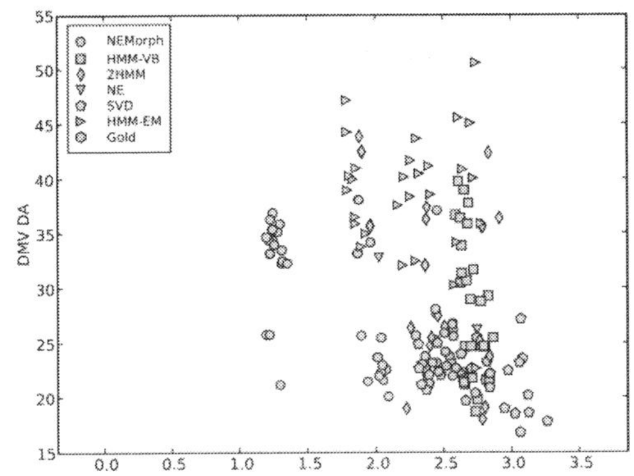

Figure 1: DMV Directed Accuracy vs. $H(T_G|T_I)$

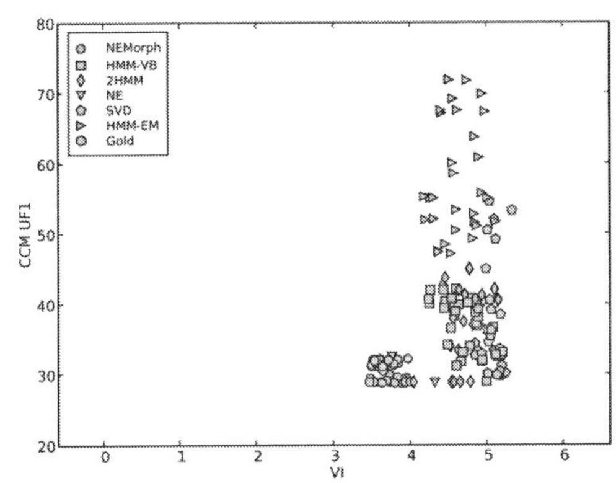

Figure 2: CCM fscore vs. tagging variation of information.

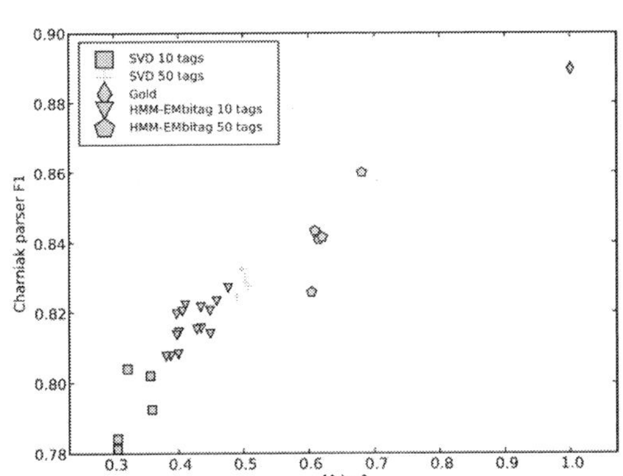

Figure 3: Supervised parsing f-score vs. tagging many-to-one accuracy.

Tagging Metric	Supervised F1
1-to-1	0.62
M-to-1	0.83
$H(T_G\|T_I)$	-0.19
VI	0.25

Table 3: Kendall's τ, between tag induction criteria and supervised parsing unlabeled bracketing F-score.

Interestingly, parsing performance and speed does degrade considerably when training off induced tags. We are not sure what causes this. One possibility is in the lexicalized stage of the parser, where the probability of a head word is smoothed primarily by its part-of-speech tag. This requires that the tag be a good proxy for the syntactic role of the head. In any case this warrants further investigation.

5 Conclusion and Future Work

In this work, we found that none of the most common part-of-speech tagging metrics bear a strong relationship to good grammar induction performance. Although our experiments only involve English, the poor correspondence we find between the various tagging metrics and grammar induction performance raises concerns about their relationship more broadly. We additionally found that while tagging accuracy measures do correlate with better supervised parsing, common information theoretic ones do not strongly predict better performance on either task. Furthermore, the supervised experiments indicate that informative part-of-speech tags are important for good parsing.

The next step is to explore better tagging metrics that correspond more strongly to better grammar induction performance. A good metric should use all the information we have, including the gold trees, to evaluate. Finally, we should explore grammar induction schemes that do not rely on prior parts-of-speech, instead learning them from raw text at the same time as deeper structure.

Acknowledgments

We thank Dan Klein for his grammar induction code, as well as Matt Lease and other members of BLLIP for their feedback. This work was partially supported by DARPA GALE contract HR0011-06-2-0001 and NSF award 0631667.

References

Baum, L.E. 1972. An inequality and associated maximization techniques in statistical estimation of probabilistic functions of Markov processes. *Inequalities*, 3:1–8.

Biemann, Chris. 2006. Unsupervised part-of-speech tagging employing efficient graph clustering. In *Proceedings of the COLING/ACL 2006 Student Research Workshop*, pages 7–12, Sydney, Australia.

Bod, Rens. 2006. An all-subtrees approach to unsupervised parsing. In *Proceedings of Coling/ACL 2006*, pages 865–872.

Charniak, Eugene. 2000. A maximum-entropy-inspired parser. In *Proceedings of the North American Chapter of the ACL 2000*, pages 132–139.

Clark, Alexander. 2003. Combining distributional and morphological information for part of speech induction. In *Proceedings of EACL 2003*, pages 59–66, Budapest, Hungary.

Cramer, Bart. 2007. Limitations of current grammar induction algorithms. In *Proceedings of the ACL 2007 Student Research Workshop*, pages 43–48.

Dasgupta, Sajib and Vincent Ng. 2007. Unsupervised part-of-speech acquisition for resource-scarce languages. In *Proceedings of the EMNLP/CoNLL 2007*, pages 218–227.

Freitag, Dayne. 2004. Toward unsupervised whole-corpus tagging. In *Proceedings of Coling 2004*, pages 357–363, Aug 23–Aug 27.

Goldwater, Sharon and Tom Griffiths. 2007. A fully bayesian approach to unsupervised part-of-speech tagging. In *Proceedings of the ACL 2007*, pages 744–751.

Haghighi, Aria and Dan Klein. 2006. Prototype-driven learning for sequence models. In *Proceedings of HLT/NAACL 2006*, pages 320-327, New York, USA.

Johnson, Mark. 2007. Why doesn't EM find good HMM POS-taggers? In *Proceedings of the EMNLP/CoNLL 2007*, pages 296–305.

Klein, Dan and Christopher Manning. 2002. A generative constituent-context model for improved grammar induction. In *Proceedings of ACL 2002*.

Klein, Dan and Christopher Manning. 2004. Corpus-based induction of syntactic structure: Models of dependency and constituency. In *Proceedings of ACL 2004*, pages 478–485, Barcelona, Spain, July.

Lapata, Mirella. 2006. Automatic evaluation of information ordering: Kendall's tau. *Computational Linguistics*, 32(4):1–14.

Marcus, Mitchell, Grace Kim, Mary Ann Marcinkiewicz, Robert MacIntyre, Ann Bies, Mark Ferguson, Karen Katz, and Britta Schasberger. 1994. The Penn Treebank: Annotating Predicate Argument Structure. In *Proceedings of the 1994 ARPA Human Language Technology Workshop*.

Meilă, Marina. 2003. Comparing clusterings. *Proceedings of the Conference on Computational Learning Theory (COLT)*.

Merialdo, Bernard. 1994. Tagging english text with a probabilistic model. *Computational Linguistics*, 20(2):154–172.

Ney, Herman, Ute Essen, and Renhard Knesser. 1994. On structuring probabilistic dependencies in stochastic language modelling. *Computer Speech and Language*, 8:1–38.

Schütze, Hinrich. 1995. Distributional part-of-speech tagging. In *Proceedings of the 7th conference of the EACL*, pages 141–148.

Seginer, Yoav. 2007. Fast unsupervised incremental parsing. In *Proceedings of the 45th Annual Meeting of the Association of Computational Linguistics*, pages 384–391, Prague, Czech Republic.

Smith, Noah A. and Jason Eisner. 2004. Annealing techniques for unsupervised statistical language learning. In *Proceedings of ACL 2004*, pages 487–494, Barcelona, Spain.

Smith, Noah A. and Jason Eisner. 2005. Contrastive estimation: Training log-linear models on unlabeled data. In *Proceedings of ACL 2005*, pages 354–362, Ann Arbor, Michigan.

Smith, Noah A. 2006. *Novel Estimation Methods for Unsupervised Discovery of Latent Structure in Natural Language Text*. Ph.D. thesis, Department of Computer Science, Johns Hopkins University, October.

Van Zaanen, Menno M. 2001. *Bootstrapping Structure into Language: Alignment-Based Learning*. Ph.D. thesis, University of Leeds, September.

Using Discourse Commitments to Recognize Textual Entailment

Andrew Hickl
Language Computer Corporation
1701 North Collins Boulevard Suite 2000
Richardson, Texas 75080 USA
andy@languagecomputer.com

Abstract

In this paper, we introduce a new framework for recognizing textual entailment (RTE) which depends on extraction of the set of publicly-held beliefs – known as *discourse commitments* – that can be ascribed to the author of a text (*t*) or a hypothesis (*h*). We show that once a set of commitments have been extracted from a *t-h* pair, the task of recognizing textual entailment is reduced to the identification of the commitments from a *t* which support the inference of the *h*. Our system correctly identified entailment relationships in more than 80% of *t-h* pairs taken from all three of the previous PASCAL RTE Challenges, without the need for additional sources of training data.

1 Introduction

Systems participating in the PASCAL Recognizing Textual Entailment (RTE) Challenges (Dagan et al., 2005) have successfully employed a variety of "shallow" techniques in order to recognize instances of textual entailment, including methods based on: (1) sets of heuristics (Vanderwende et al., 2006), (2) measures of term overlap (Jijkoun and de Rijke, 2005) (or other measures of semantic "relatedness" (Glickman et al., 2005), (3) the alignment of graphs created from syntactic or semantic dependencies (Haghighi et al., 2005), or (4) statistical classifiers which leverage a wide range of features, including the output of paraphrase generation (Hickl et al., 2006), inference rule generation (Szpektor et al., 2007), or model building systems (Bos and Markert, 2006).

While these relatively "shallow" approaches have shown much promise in RTE for entailment pairs where the text and hypothesis remain short, we expect that performance of these types of systems will ultimately degrade as longer and more syntactically complex entailment pairs are considered. For example, given a "short" *t-h* pair (as in (1)), we might expect that a feature-based comparison of the *t* and the *h* would be sufficient to identify that the *t* textually entailed the *h*.

(1) Short *t-h* Pair
  a. **Text:** Mack Sennett was involved in the production of "The Extra Girl".
  b. **Hypothesis:** "The Extra Girl" was produced by Sennett.

The additional information included in a longer *t* (like the one in (2)) can make for a much more challenging entailment computation. While the evidence supporting the *h* is included in the *t*, systems must be able to establish that (1) *Mack Sennett* was involved in producing a *Mabel Normand vehicle* and (2) that *"The Extra Girl"* and the *Mabel Normand vehicle* refer to the same film.

(2) Long *t-h* Pair
  a. **Text:** "The Extra Girl" (1923) is the story of a small-town girl, Sue Graham (played by Mabel Normand) who comes to Hollywood to be in the pictures. This Mabel Normand vehicle, produced by Mack Sennett, followed earlier films about the film industry and also paved the way for later films about Hollywood, such as King Vidor's "Show People" (1928).
  b. **Hypothesis:** "The Extra Girl" was produced by Sennett.

In order to remain effective as texts get longer, we believe that RTE systems will need to employ techniques that will enable them to enumerate the

©2008. Licensed under the *Creative Commons Attribution-Noncommercial-Share Alike 3.0 Unported* license (http://creativecommons.org/licenses/by-nc-sa/3.0/). Some rights reserved.

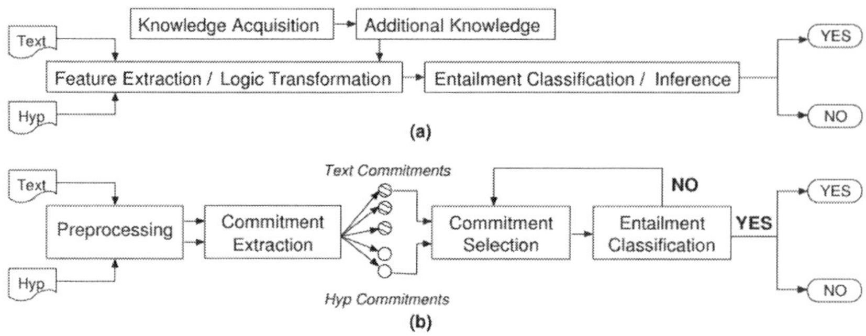

Figure 1: Two Architectures of RTE Systems.

set of propositions which are inferable from a text-hypothesis pair.

We introduce a new framework for recognizing textual entailment which depends on extraction of a subset of the publicly-held beliefs – or *discourse commitments* – available from the linguistic meaning of a text or hypothesis. We show that once even a small set of discourse commitments have been extracted from a text-hypothesis pair, the task of RTE can be reduced to the identification of the one (or more) commitments from the t which are most likely to support the inference of each commitment extracted from the h.

We have found that a commitment-based approach to RTE provides state-of-the-art results on the PASCAL RTE task even when large external knowledge resources are not available. While our approach does depend on a set of specially-tailored heuristics which makes it possible to enumerate some of the commitments from a *t-h* pair, we show that reasonably high levels of performance are possible (as much as 84.9% accuracy), given even a small number of extractors.

The rest of this paper is organized in the following way. Section 2 describes the organization of most current statistical systems for RTE, while Sections 3, 4, and 5 describe details of the algorithms we have developed for the RTE system we discuss in this paper. Section 6 presents our experimental results, and Section 7 presents our conclusions.

2 Recognizing Textual Entailment

Recognizing whether the information expressed in a h can be inferred from the information expressed in a t can be cast either as (1) a classification problem or (2) a formal textual inference problem, performed either by theorem proving or model checking. While these approaches apply radically different solutions to the same problem, both methods involve the translation of natural language into some sort of suitable meaning representation, such as real-valued features (in the case of classification), or axioms or models (in the case of formal methods). We argue that performing this translation necessarily requires systems to acquire forms of (linguistic and/or real-world) knowledge which may not be derivable from the surface form of a t or h. (See Figure 1a for an illustration of the architecture of a prototypical RTE system.)

In order to acquire forms of linguistic knowledge for RTE, we have developed a novel framework which depends on the extraction of *discourse commitments* from a text-hypothesis pair. Following (Gunlogson, 2001; Stalnaker, 1979), we assume discourse commitments represent the set of propositions which can necessarily be inferred to be true given a conventional reading of a text. (Figure 2 lists the set of commitments that were extracted from a *t-h* pair included in the PASCAL RTE-3 Test Set.[1])

Formally, we assume that given a commitment set $\{c_t\}$ consisting of the set of discourse commitments inferable from a text t and a hypothesis h, we define the task of RTE as a search for the commitment $c \in \{c_t\}$ which maximizes the likelihood that c textually entails h.

In our architecture (illustrated in Figure 1b), discourse commitments are first extracted from both the t and the h using the approach described in Section 3. Once commitment sets have been extracted for the t and the h, we then use a *commitment selection* module (described in Section 4) in order to perform a term-based alignment of each commitment extracted from the t against each commitment extracted from the h. The top-ranked pair of commitments (c_{t_i}, c_{h_i}) is then sent to an

[1]Under our approach, commitments are extracted from both the t and the h. Our system failed to extract any commitments from the h used in this example, however.

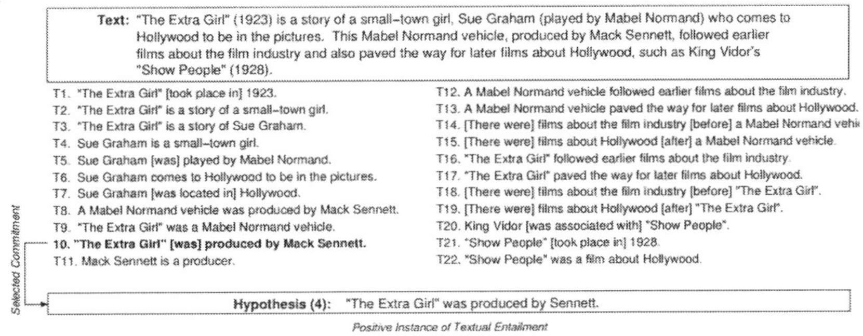

Figure 2: Text Commitments Extracted from Example 4 (RTE-3).

entailment computation module (described in Section 5), which estimates the likelihood that the selected c_{t_i} textually entails the c_{h_i} (and by extension, the likelihood that t textually entails h). Commitment pairs are considered in ranked order until a positive judgment is returned, or until no more commitments above a threshold remain.

3 Extracting Discourse Commitments from Natural Language Texts

Work in *semantic parsing* (Wong and Mooney, 2007; Zettlemoyer and Collins, 2005) has used statistical and symbolic techniques to convert natural language texts into a logical meaning representation (MR) which can be leveraged by formal reasoning systems. While this work has explored how output from syntactic parsers can be used to represent the meaning of a text independent of its actual surface form, these approaches have focused on the propositional semantics explicitly encoded by predicates and have not addressed other phenomena (such as conversational implicature or linguistic presupposition) – which are not encoded overtly in the syntax.

Our work focuses on how an approach based on lightweight extraction rules can be used to enumerating a subset of the discourse commitments that are inferable from a *t*-*h* pair. While heuristically "unpacking" all of commitments of a t or h may be (nearly) impossible, we believe that our work represents an important first step towards determining the relative value of these additional commitments for textual inference applications, such as RTE. Our commitment extraction algorithm is presented in Algorithm 1.

Commitments are extracted from each t and h using an implementation of the probabilistic finite-state transducer (FST)-based extraction framework described in (Eisner, 2002; Eisner, 2003). Given a

Algorithm 1 Extracting Discourse Commitments

Input: A set S of sentences from the t or h
Output: A set of discourse commitments
loop
  Pre-process the decompositions to identify lexical, syntactic, semantic, and discourse information
  Produce syntactic decompositions of the sentences in S
  Produce commitments of propositional content
  Produce commitments for supplemental expressions
  Extract predefined set of relations
  Perform coreference resolution for each commitment
  Generate paraphrases of each commitment
  Generate a natural-language string for each commitment
  if any of the generated strings is not in S **then**
    Add the generated strings to S
  else
    return S
  end if
end loop

syntactically and semantically-parsed input string, our system returns a series of output representations which can be mapped (given a set of generation heuristics) to natural language sentences which represent each of the individual commitments which can be extracted from that string. Commitments were extracted using a series of weighted regular expressions (which we present in the form of rules for convenience); weights were learned for each regular expression $r \in R$ using our implementation of (Eisner, 2002). After each candidate commitment was processed by the FST, the natural language form of each returned commitment was then resubmitted to the FST for additional round(s) of extraction until no additional commitments could be extracted from the input string.

Text-hypothesis pairs are initially submitted to a *preprocessing* module which performed (1) part-of-speech tagging, (2) named entity recognition, (3) syntactic dependency parsing, (4) semantic dependency parsing, (5) normalized temporal expressions, and (6) coreference resolution.[2]

Pairs are then submitted to a *sentence decomposition* module, which uses a set of heuristics in order to transform complex sentences containing subordination, relative clauses, lists, and coordination into sets of well-formed simple sentences.

Propositional Content: In order to capture assertions encoded by predicates and predicate nominals, we used semantic dependency information output by a predicate-based semantic parser to generate "simplified" commitments for each possible combination of their optional and obligatory arguments. (Here, arguments assigned a PropBank-style role label of ARG_m – or ARG_2 or higher – were considered to be optional arguments.)

Supplemental Expressions: Recent work by (Potts, 2005; Huddleston and Pullum, 2002) has demonstrated that the class of supplemental expressions – including appositives, *as*-clauses, parentheticals, parenthetical adverbs, non-restrictive relative clauses, and epithets – trigger conventional implicatures (CI) whose truth is necessarily presupposed, even if the truth conditions of a sentence are not satisfied. Rules to extract supplemental expressions were implemented in our weighted FST framework; generation heuristics were then used to create new sentences which specify the CI conveyed by the expression.

(3) "The Extra Girl" (1923) is a story of a small-town girl, Sue Graham (played by Mabel Normand) who comes to Hollywood to be in the pictures.
   a. "The Extra Girl" [took place in] 1923.
   b. "The Extra Girl" is the story of a small-town girl.
   c. Sue Graham is a small-town girl.
   d. Sue Graham [was] played by Mabel Normand.
   e. Sue Graham [came] to Hollywood to be in the pictures.

Relation Extraction: We used an in-house, heuristic-based relation extraction system to recognize six types[3] of semantic relations between named entities, including: (1) *artifact* (e.g. OWNER-OF), (2) *general affiliation* (e.g. LOCATION-OF), (3) *organization affiliation* (e.g. EMPLOYEE-OF), (4) *part-whole*, (5) *social affiliation* (e.g. RELATED-TO), and (6) *physical location* (e.g. LOCATED-NEAR) relations.

(4) Sue Graham [came] to Hollywood to be in the pictures.
   a. **location-of:** Sue Graham [was located in] Hollywood.
   b. **location-of:** The pictures [were located in] Hollywood.

Coreference Resolution: We use our own implementation of (Ng, 2005) to resolve instances of pronominal and nominal coreference in order to expand the number of commitments available to the system. After a set of co-referential entity mentions were detected (e.g. *"The Extra Girl", this Mabel Normand vehicle*), new commitments were generated from the existing set of commitments which incorporated each co-referential mention.

(5) **Coreference:** ("The Extra Girl",this Mabel Normand vehicle)
   a. ["The Extra Girl"] [was] produced by Mack Sennett.
   b. ["The Extra Girl"] followed earlier films about the film industry.
   c. ["The Extra Girl"] also paved the way for later films about Hollywood.

Paraphrasing: We used a lightweight, knowledge-lean paraphrasing approach in order to expand the set of commitments considered by our system.

In order to identify other possible linguistic encodings for each commitment – without generating a large number of spurious paraphrases which could introduce errorful knowledge into a commitment set – we focused only on generating paraphrases of two-place predicates (i.e. predicates which encode a semantic dependency between two arguments).

The algorithm we use is presented in Algorithm 2. Under this method, a semantic parser (trained on the semantic dependencies in PropBank and NomBank) was used to identify pairs of arguments ($\langle a_i, a_j \rangle$) (where $i, j \in \{a_0, a_1, a_2, a_m\}$) from each c; each pair of arguments identified in c are then used to generate paraphrases from sets of sentences containing both a_0 and a_i.[4] The top 1000 sentences containing each pair of arguments were then retrieved from

[2] We used publicly-available software when possible to facilitate comparison with other researchers' work in this area. We used the *C&C Tools* (Curran et al., 2007) to perform part-of-speech tagging and parsing and a version of the alias-i *LingPipe* named entity recognizer in conjunction with Language Computer Corporation's own systems for syntactic and semantic dependency parsing, named entity recognition (*CiceroLite*), temporal normalization, and coreference resolution.

[3] These six types were selected because they performed at better than than 70% F-Measure on a sample of *t-h* pairs selected from the PASCAL RTE datasets. Other relation types with lesser performance were not used in our experiments.

[4] Arguments in PropBank and NomBank are assigned an index corresponding to their semantic role.

the WWW; sentences containing both arguments were then filtered and clustered into sets that were presumed to be likely paraphrases.

Algorithm 2 Paraphrase Clustering

```
Input: Pairs of arguments, ⟨a_i, a_j⟩, where i, j ∈ {a_0, a_1, a_2, a_m}
Output: Sets of paraphrased sentences, {s_{cl_i...cl_n}}
for all pairs ⟨a_i, a_j⟩ do
    Retrieve 1000 s containing ⟨a_i, a_j⟩ from WWW
    Compute token distance between a_0,a_i (span(a_i, a_j))
    Filter each s with 2 ≤ span(a_i, a_j) ≤ 8
    Complete-link cluster {s} into clusters {cl}
    Filter cl with size (size(cl)) ≤ 10
    return All sentences {s_{cl_i...cl_n}}
    Add all sentences {s_{cl_i...cl_n}} to commitment set C
end for
```

Parameters were computed using maximum likelihood estimation (and normalized to sum to 1), based on a linear interpolation of three measures of the "goodness" of p (as compared to the original input sentence, s).

$$para(p|s) = \lambda_{wn} para(p|s) + \lambda_{freq} para(p|s) + \lambda_{dist} para(p|s) \quad (1)$$

Each candidate paraphrase was then assigned a *paraphrase score* as in (Glickman and Dagan, 2005). The likelihood that a word w_p from a paraphrase was a valid paraphrase of a word from an original commitment w_c was computed as in (2), where $p(w_p)$ and $p(w_o)$ computed from the relative frequency of the occurrence of w_p and w_o in the set of clusters generated for c, and $p(k)$ was computed from the frequency of each "overlapping" term found in the paraphrase and the original c. The top 5 paraphrases generated for each c were then used to generate new versions of each commitment.

$$p_{para}(w_p|w_o) = p(w_p)p(w_o) \prod_{i=1}{}^{n} p(k_i) \quad (2)$$

4 Commitment Selection

Following Commitment Extraction, we used a lexical alignment technique first introduced in (Taskar et al., 2005b) in order to select the commitment extracted from t (henceforth, c_t) which represents the best alignment for each of the individual commitments extracted from h (henceforth, c_h).

We assume that the alignment of two discourse commitments can be cast as a maximum weighted matching problem in which each pair of words (t_i,h_j) in an commitment pair (c_t,c_h) is assigned a score $s_{ij}(t, h)$ corresponding to the likelihood that t_i is aligned to h_j.[5] As with (Taskar et al., 2005b), we use the large-margin structured prediction model introduced in (Taskar et al., 2005a) in order to compute a set of parameters w (computed with respect to a set of features f) which maximize the number of correct alignment predictions ($\bar{y}_i$) made given a set of training examples (x_i), as in Equation (3).

$$y_i = \arg\max_{\bar{y}_i \in Y} w^\top f(x_i, \bar{y}_i), \forall i \quad (3)$$

We used three sets of features in our model: (1) string features (including Levenshtein edit distance, string equality, and stemmed string equality), (2) lexico-semantic features (including WordNet Similarity (Pedersen et al., 2004)), and (3) word association features (computed using the Dice coefficient (Dice, 1945)[6]). Training data came from hand-annotated token alignments for each of the 800 entailment pairs included in the RTE-3 Development Set

Following alignment, we used the sum of the edge scores ($\sum_{i,j=1}{}^{n} s_{ij}(t_i, h_j)$) computed for each of the possible (c_t, c_h) pairs in order to search for the c_t which represented the *reciprocal best hit* (Mushegian and Koonin, 1996) of each c_h extracted from the hypothesis. This was performed by selecting a commitment pair (c_t, c_h) where c_t was the top-scoring alignment candidate for c_h and c_h was the top-scoring alignment candidate for c_t. If no reciprocal best-hit could be found for any of the commitments extracted from the h, the system automatically returned a TE judgment of NO.

5 Entailment Classification

We used a decision tree to estimate the likelihood that a commitment pair represented a valid instance of textual entailment. Confidence values associated with each leaf node (i.e. YES or NO) were normalized and used to rank examples for the official submission. Features were selected manually by performing ten-fold cross validation on the combined development sets from the three previous PASCAL RTE Challenges (2400 examples).

[5] In order to ensure that content from the h is reflected in the t, we assume that each word from the h is aligned to exactly one or zero words from the t.

[6] The Dice coefficient was computed as $Dice(i) = \frac{2C_{th}(i)}{C_t(i)C_h(i)}$, where C_{th} is equal to the number of times a word i was found in both the t and an h of a single entailment pair, while C_t and C_h were equal to the number of times a word was found in any t or h, respectively. A hand-crafted corpus of 100,000 entailment pairs was used to compute values for C_t, C_h, and C_{th}.

Features used in our classifier were selected from a number of sources, including (Hickl et al., 2006; Zanzotto et al., 2006; Glickman and Dagan, 2005).

A partial list of the features used in the Entailment Classifier used in our system is provided in Figure 3.

ALIGNMENT FEATURES: Derived from the results of the alignment of each pair of commitments performed during Commitment Selection.
◇1◇ LONGEST COMMON STRING: This feature represents the longest contiguous string common to both texts.
◇2◇ UNALIGNED CHUNK: This feature represents the number of chunks in one text that are not aligned with a chunk from the other
◇3◇ LEXICAL ENTAILMENT PROBABILITY: Defined as in (Glickman and Dagan, 2005).

DEPENDENCY FEATURES: Computed from the semantic dependencies identified by the PropBank- and NomBank-based semantic parsers.
◇1◇ ENTITY-ARG MATCH: This is a boolean feature which fires when aligned entities were assigned the same argument role label.
◇2◇ ENTITY-NEAR-ARG MATCH: This feature is collapsing the arguments Arg_1 and Arg_2 (as well as the Arg_M subtypes) into single categories for the purpose of counting matches.
◇3◇ PREDICATE-ARG MATCH: This boolean feature is flagged when at least two aligned arguments have the same role.
◇4◇ PREDICATE-NEAR-ARG MATCH: This feature is collapsing the arguments Arg_1 and Arg_2 (as well as the Arg_M subtypes) into single categories for the purpose of counting matches.

SEMANTIC/PRAGMATIC FEATURES: Extracted during preprocessing.
◇1◇ NAMED ENTITY CLASS: This feature has a different value for each of the 150 named entity classes.
◇2◇ TEMPORAL NORMALIZATION: This boolean feature is flagged when the temporal expressions are normalized to the same ISO 8601 equivalents.
◇3◇ MODALITY MARKER: This boolean feature is flagged when the two texts use the same modal verbs.
◇4◇ SPEECH-ACT: This boolean feature is flagged when the lexicons indicate the same speech act in both texts.
◇5◇ FACTIVITY MARKER: This boolean feature is flagged when the factivity markers indicate either TRUE or FALSE in both texts simultaneously.
◇6◇ BELIEF MARKER: This boolean feature is set when the belief markers indicate either TRUE or FALSE in both texts simultaneously.

Figure 3: Features used in the Entailment Classifier

6 Experiments and Results

We evaluated the performance of our commitment-based system for RTE against the 1600 examples found in the PASCAL RTE-2 and RTE-3 datasets.[7] Table 1 presents results from our system when trained on the 1600 examples taken from the RTE-2 and RTE-3 Test Sets.

Accuracy varied significantly (p <0.05) across each of the four tasks. Performance (in terms of accuracy and average precision) was highest on the QA set (88.9% accuracy) and lowest on the IE set (76.9%). The length of the *text* (either "short" or "long") did not significantly impact performance, however; in fact, as can be seen in Table 1, average accuracy was nearly the same for examples featuring "short" or "long" *texts*.

Task	Length	IE	IR	QA	SUM	Total
RTE-2	Short	0.753	0.883	0.863	0.855	0.8385
RTE-3	Short	0.784	0.911	0.909	0.869	0.8331
RTE-3	Long	0.789	0.778	0.943	0.778	0.8290
Total	–	0.7690	0.8790	0.8890	0.8600	0.8493

Table 1: Performance of Commitment-based RTE.

In order to quantify the impact that additional sources of training data could have on the performance an RTE system (and to facilitate comparisons with top systems like (Hickl et al., 2006), which were trained on tens of thousands of entailment pairs), we used the techniques described in (Bensley and Hickl, 2008) to generate a large training set of 100,000 text-hypothesis pairs in order to train our entailment classifier. Table 2 summarizes the performance of our RTE system on the RTE-2 and RTE-3 Test Sets when trained on increasing amounts of training data.[8]

Training Corpus	Accuracy	Average Precision
800 pairs (RTE-2 Dev)	0.8493	0.8611
10,000 pairs	0.8550	0.8742
25,000 pairs	0.8489	0.8322
50,000 pairs	0.8575	0.8505
100,000 pairs	0.8850	0.8785

Table 2: Impact of Training Corpus Size.

Unlike (Hickl et al., 2006), we experienced only a small increase (3%) in overall accuracy when training on increasingly larger corpora of examples. While large training corpora may provide an important source of knowledge for RTE, these results suggest that our commitment extraction-based approach may nullify the gains in performance seen by pure classification-based approaches. We believe that by training an entailment classification model based on the output of a commitment extraction module, we can reduce the number of deleterious features included in the model – and thereby, reduce the overall number of training examples needed to achieve the same level of performance.

In a second experiment, we investigated the performance gains that could be attributed to the choice of weighting function used to select commitments from a commitment set. In order to

[7]Data created for the PASCAL RTE-2 and RTE-3 challenges was organized into four datasets which sought to approximate the kinds of inference required by four different NLP applications: information extraction (IE), information retrieval (IR), question-answering (QA), and summarization (SUM). The RTE-3 Test Sets includes 683 "short" examples and 117 "long" examples; the RTE-2 Test Set includes 800 "short" examples.

[8]In the RTE evaluations, *accuracy* is defined as the percentage of entailment judgments correctly identified by the system. Average precision is defined as "the average of the system's precision values at all points in the ranked list in which recall increases".

Approach	Without Paraphrasing	With Paraphrasing	Δ
Term overlap (Zanzotto et al., 2006)	0.5950	0.6750	+0.0800
Approximate Tree Edit Distance (Schilder and McInnes, 2006)	0.6550	0.5933	-0.0617
LEP (Glickman et al., 2005)	0.6000	0.6800	+0.0800
Lexical Similarity (Adams, 2006)	0.6200	0.6788	+0.0588
Graph Matching (MacCartney et al., 2006)	0.6433	0.6533	+0.0100
Classification-Based Alignment (Hickl et al., 2006)	0.7650	0.7700	+ 0.0050
Structured Prediction-Based Alignment (Taskar et al., 2005a)	0.7900	0.8493	+ 0.0593

Table 3: Impact of Commitment Selection Learning.

perform this comparison, we implemented a total of 7 different functions previously investigated by teams participating in the previous PASCAL RTE Challenges, including (1) a simple term-overlap measure introduced as a baseline in (Zanzotto et al., 2006), (2) the approximate tree edit distance metric used by (Schilder and McInnes, 2006), (3) (Glickman et al., 2005)'s measure of lexical entailment probability (LEP), (4) the lexical similarity measure described in (Adams, 2006), (5) our interpretation of the semantic graph-matching approach described in (MacCartney et al., 2006), (6) the classification-based term alignment approach described in (Hickl et al., 2006), and (7) the structured prediction-based alignment approach introduced in this paper. Results from this 7-way comparison are presented in Table 3.

While we found that the choice of mechanism used to weight commitments did significantly impact RTE performance ($p < 0.05$), the inclusion of generated paraphrases appeared to only have a slight positive impact on overall performance, boosting RTE accuracy by an average of 3.1% (across the 7 methods), and by a total of 5.9% in the approach we describe in this paper. While paraphrasing can be used to enhance the performance of some current RTE systems (see performance of the Tree Edit Distance-based RTE system for a case where paraphrasing negatively impacted performance), realized gains are still relatively modest across most approaches.

In a third experiment, we found that RTE performance depended on both the type – and the number – of commitments extracted from a *t-h* pair, regardless of the learning algorithm used in commitment selection. Table 4 presents results from experiments when (1) no commitment extraction was conducted, (2) extraction strategies were run in isolation[9], (3) combinations of extraction strategies were considered, or (4) all of possible extraction strategies (listed in Section 3) were considered. The best-performing condition for each RTE strategy is presented in **bold**.

Increasing the amount of linguistic knowledge available from a commitment set did significantly ($p < 0.05$) impact the performance of RTE, regardless of the actual learning algorithm used to compute the likelihood of an entailment relationship. Combining all four extraction strategies proved best for four RTE approaches (Term Overlap, Lexical Entailment Probability, Graph Matching, and Structured Prediction-based Alignment). Including coreference-based commitments reduced the accuracy of two RTE strategies (Lexical Similarity and Classification-based Alignment). This is most likely due to the fact that coreference-based commitments reincorporate the antecedent of pronouns and other referring expressions into the generated commitments, thereby adding additional lexical information to the sets of features used in computing entailment.

[9]Four strategies were considered: (1) syntactic decomposition (*SD*), (2) supplemental expression (*SE*) extraction, (3) coreference resolution (*Coref*), (4) and paraphrasing (*Para*).

7 Conclusions

This paper introduced a new framework for recognizing textual entailment which depends on the extraction of the discourse commitments that can be inferred from a conventional interpretation of a text passage. By explicitly enumerating the set of inferences that can be drawn from a t or h, our approach is able to reduce the task of RTE to the identification of the set of commitments that support the inference of each corresponding commitment extracted from a hypothesis. This approach correctly classified more than 80% of examples from the PASCAL RTE Test Sets, without the need for additional sources of training data.

Acknowledgments

This material is based upon work funded in whole or in part by the U.S. Government and any opinions, findings, conclusions, or recommendations expressed in this material are those of the authors and do not necessarily reflect the views of the U.S. Government.

References

Adams, Rod. 2006. Textual entailment through extended lexical overlap. In *Proceedings of the Second PASCAL Recognising Textual Entailment Challenge (RTE-2)*.

	None	Individual Strategies				Strategy Combinations			All
		SD	SE	Coref	Para	SD+SE	SD,SE,Coref	SD,SE,Para	
Term Overlap	0.5708	0.5750	0.5850	0.5758	0.5925	0.5950	0.5925	0.6500	**0.6750**
Approximate Tree Edit Distance	0.5117	0.6158	0.6175	0.5142	0.5158	**0.6592**	0.6583	0.6108	0.5930
Lexical Entailment Probability	0.6067	0.6300	0.5950	0.5942	0.6475	0.6292	0.6000	0.6658	**0.6800**
Lexical Similarity	0.5833	0.5875	0.5817	0.5850	0.5975	0.6100	0.6200	**0.6825**	0.6800
Graph Matching	0.5850	0.6667	0.6450	0.6483	0.6017	0.6317	0.6430	0.6208	**0.6530**
Classification-Based Alignment	0.6692	0.6825	0.6700	0.6758	0.6842	0.7508	0.7492	**0.7992**	0.7700
Structured Prediction-Based Alignment	0.6750	0.7083	0.6875	0.6675	0.6742	0.7492	0.7900	0.7842	**0.8493**

Table 4: Impact of Commitment Availability.

Bensley, Jeremy and Andrew Hickl. 2008. Unsupervised Resource Creation for Textual Inference Applications. In *LREC 2008*, Marrakech.

Bos, Johan and Katya Markert. 2006. When logical inference helps in determining textual entailment (and when it doesn't). In *Proceedings of the Second PASCAL Recognizing Textual Entailment Conference*, Venice, Italy.

Curran, James, Stephen Clark, and Johan Bos. 2007. Linguistically Motivated Large-Scale NLP with C-and-C and Boxer. In *ACL 2007 (Demonstration Session)*, Prague.

Dagan, Ido, Oren Glickman, and Bernardo Magnini. 2005. The PASCAL Recognizing Textual Entailment Challenge. In *Proceedings of the PASCAL Challenges Workshop*.

Dice, L.R. 1945. Measures of the Amount of Ecologic Association Between Species. In *Journal of Ecology*, volume 26, pages 297–302.

Glickman, Oren and Ido Dagan. 2005. A Probabilistic Setting and Lexical Co-occurrence Model for Textual Entailment. In *Proceedings of the ACL Workshop on Empirical Modeling of Semantic Equivalence and Entailment*, Ann Arbor, USA.

Glickman, Oren, Ido Dagan, and Moshe Koppel. 2005. Web based textual entailment. In *Proceedings of the First PASCAL Recognizing Textual Entailment Work-shop*.

Gunlogson, Christine. 2001. *True to Form: Rising and Falling Declaratives as Questions in English*. Ph.D. thesis, University of California, Santa Cruz.

Haghighi, Aria, Andrew Ng, and Christopher Manning. 2005. Robust textual inference via graph matching. In *Proceedings of Human Language Technology Conference and Conference on Empirical Methods in Natural Language Processing*, pages 387–394.

Hickl, Andrew, John Williams, Jeremy Bensley, Kirk Roberts, Bryan Rink, and Ying Shi. 2006. Recognizing Textual Entailment with LCC's Groundhog System. In *Proceedings of the Second PASCAL Challenges Workshop*.

Huddleston, Rodney and Geoffrey Pullum, editors, 2002. *The Cambridge Grammar of the English Language*. CambridgeUniversity Press.

Jijkoun, V. and M. de Rijke. 2005. Recognizing Textual Entailment Using Lexical Similarity. In *Proceedings of the First PASCAL Challenges Workshop*.

MacCartney, Bill, Trond Grenager, Marie-Catherine de Marneffe, Daniel Cer, and Christopher D. Manning. 2006. Learning to recognize features of valid textual entailments. In *Proceedings of the Human Language Technology Conference of the NAACL, Main Conference*, pages 41–48, New York City, USA, June. Association for Computational Linguistics.

Mushegian, Arcady and Eugene Koonin. 1996. A minimal gene set for cellular life derived by compraison of complete bacterial genomes. In *Proceedings of the National Academies of Science*, volume 93, pages 10268–10273.

Pedersen, T., S. Patwardhan, and J. Michelizzi. 2004. WordNet::Similarity - Measuring the Relatedness of Concepts. In *Proceedings of the Nineteenth National Conference on Artificial Intelligence (AAAI-04)*, San Jose, CA.

Potts, Christopher, editor, 2005. *The Logic of Conventional Implicatures*. Oxford University Press.

Schilder, F. and B. Thomson McInnes. 2006. TLR at DUC 2006: Approximate Tree Similarity and a New Evaluation Regime. In *Proceedings of HLT-NAACL Document Understanding Workshop (DUC 2006)*.

Stalnaker, Robert, 1979. *Assertion*, volume 9, pages 315–332.

Szpektor, Idan, Eyal Shnarch, and Ido Dagan. 2007. Instance-based evaluation of entailment rule acquisition. In *Proceedings of the 45th Annual Meeting of the Association of Computational Linguistics*, pages 456–463, Prague, Czech Republic, June. Association for Computational Linguistics.

Taskar, Ben, Simone Lacoste-Julien, and Michael Jordan. 2005a. Structured prediction via the extragradient method. In *Proceedings of Neural Information Processing Systems*.

Taskar, Ben, Simone Lacoste-Julien, and Dan Klein. 2005b. A discriminative matching approach to word alignment. In *Proceedings of Human Language Technology Conference and Empirical Methods in Natural Language Processing (HLT/EMNLP 2005)*.

Vanderwende, Lucy, Arul Menezes, and Rion Snow. 2006. Microsoft Research at RTE-2: Syntactic Contributions in the Entailment Task: an implementation. In *Proceedings of the Second PASCAL Challenges Workshop*.

Wong, Yuk Wah and Raymond Mooney. 2007. Learning synchronous grammars for semantic parsing with lambda calculus. In *Proceedings of the 45th Annual Meeting of the Association of Computational Linguistics*, pages 960–967, Prague, Czech Republic, June. Association for Computational Linguistics.

Zanzotto, F., A. Moschitti, M. Pennacchiotti, and M. Pazienza. 2006. Learning textual entailment from examples. In *Proceedings of the Second PASCAL Challenges Workshop*.

Zettlemoyer, L. S. and M. Collins. 2005. Learning to map sentences to logical form: Structured classification with probabilistic categorial grammars. In *Proceedings of UAI-05*.

Modeling Chinese Documents with Topical Word-Character Models

Wei Hu[1] **Nobuyuki Shimizu**[2]
[1]Department of Computer Science
Shanghai Jiao Tong University
Shanghai, China 200240
{no_bit,hysheng}
@sjtu.edu.cn

Hiroshi Nakagawa[2] **Huanye Sheng**[1]
[2]Information Technology Center
The University of Tokyo
Tokyo, Japan 113-0033
{shimizu, nakagawa}
@r.dl.itc.u-tokyo.ac.jp

Abstract

As Chinese text is written without word boundaries, effectively recognizing Chinese words is like recognizing collocations in English, substituting characters for words and words for collocations. However, existing topical models that involve collocations have a common limitation. Instead of directly assigning a topic to a collocation, they take the topic of a word within the collocation as the topic of the whole collocation. This is unsatisfactory for topical modeling of Chinese documents. Thus, we propose a topical word-character model (TWC), which allows two distinct types of topics: *word topic* and *character topic*. We evaluated TWC both qualitatively and quantitatively to show that it is a powerful and a promising topic model.

1 Introduction

Topic models (Blei et al., 2003; Griffiths & Steyvers 2004, 2007) are a class of statistical models in which documents are expressed as mixtures of topics, where a topic is a probability distribution over words. A topic model is a generative model for documents: it specifies a probabilistic procedure for generating documents. To make a new document, we choose a distribution over topics. Then, for each word in this document, we randomly select a topic from the distribution, and draw a word from the topic. Once we have a topic model, we can invert the generating process, inferring the set of topics that was responsible for generating a collection of documents.

Although most topic models treat a document as a bag-of-words, the assumption has obvious shortcomings. Suppose there are many documents about art and musicals in New York. Then, we find a topic represented by words such as "art", "musical", and "New", instead of getting "New York". The bag-of-words assumption makes the topic model split a collocation—a phrase with meaning beyond the individual words—into individual words that have a different meaning. One example of a collocation is the phrase "white house". In politics, it carries a special meaning beyond a house that is white, whereas "yellow house" does not.

While it is reasonable for English, the equivalent bag-of-characters assumption is especially troublesome for modeling Chinese documents, where almost all basic vocabularies are the equivalents of English collocations. In Chinese, some of the most commonly used couple-of-thousand characters are combined to make up a word, and no word boundary is given in the text. Effectively, Chinese words are like collocations in English. The difficulty is that there are overwhelmingly more of them, enough to render a bag-of-character assumption unreasonable for Chinese. Therefore, a topical model for Chinese should be capable of detecting the boundary between two words, as well as assigning a topic to each word.

While topic models for Chinese documents bear some similarity to collocation models in English, existing topical collocation discovery models, such as the LDA (latent Dirichelt allocation) Collocation model (LDACOL) (Griffiths et al., 2007) and the topical N-gram model (TNG) (Wang et al., 2007), do not directly assign a topic to a collocation. These models find the boundaries of phrases and assign a topic to each word. The problem is in the next step—the topic of the collocation is exactly the same as one of the words. This is like saying that the topic of "white

© 2008. Licensed under the *Creative Commons Attribution-Noncommercial-Share Alike 3.0 Unported* license (http://creativecommons.org/licenses/by-nc-sa/3.0/). Some rights reserved.

house" is the same as either that of "white" or "house". We propose a new topical model, the topical word-character model (TWC), which aims to overcome these limitations.

We evaluated the model both quantitatively and qualitatively. For the quantitative analysis, we compared the performance of TWC and TNG using a standard measure *perplexity*. For the qualitative analysis, we evaluated TWC's ability to discover Chinese words and assign topics in comparison with TNG.

The rest of the paper is organized as follows. Section 2 reviews topic models that aim to include collocations explicitly in the model and analyzes their limitations. Section 3 presents our new model TWC. Section 4 gives details of our consideration on inference for TWC. Section 5 presents our qualitative and quantitative experiments. Section 6 concludes with a summary and briefly mentions future work.

2 Topic Models for Collocation Discovery

Since Chinese word discovery is similar to English collocation discovery, we first review some related topic models for collocation discovery.

Although collocation discovery has long been studied, most methods are based on frequency or variance. LDACOL is an attempt to model collocations in a topical scheme. Starting from the LDA topic model, LDACOL introduces special random variables $\vec{x}$. Variable $x_i = 1$ implies that the corresponding word w_i and previous word w_{i-1} belong to the same phrase, while $x_i = 0$ implies otherwise. Thus, LDACOL can decide the length of a phrase dynamically.

TNG is a powerful generalization of LDACOL. Its graphical model is shown in Figure 1.

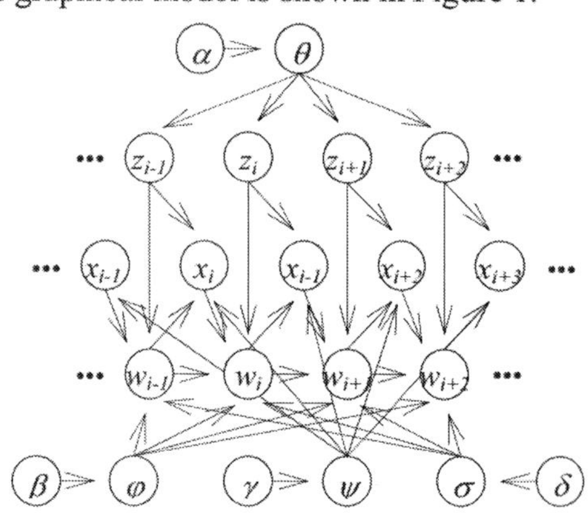

Figure 1: Topical n-gram model.

The model is defined in terms of three sets of variables: a sequence of words $\vec{w}$, a sequence of topics $\vec{z}$, and a sequence of indicators $\vec{x}$. TNG assumes the following generative process for documents.

1. For each document d, draw $\theta_d \sim$ Dirichlet(α).
2. For each topic z, draw $\varphi_z \sim$ Dirichlet(β).
3. For each topic z and each word w, draw σ_{zw} ~ Dirichlet(δ).
4. For each topic z and each word w, draw ψ_{zw} ~ Beta(γ).
5. For each word $w_{d,i}$ in document d:
   (a) draw $x_{d,i} \sim$ Bernoulli($\psi_{z_{d,i-1}, w_{d,i-1}}$),
   (b) draw $z_{d,i} \sim$ Discrete(θ_d),
   (c) draw $w_{d,i} \sim$ Discrete($\varphi_{z_{d,i}}$) if $x_{d,i}=0$,
   draw $w_{d,i} \sim$ Discrete($\sigma_{z_{d,i}, w_{d,i-1}}$) if $x_{d,i}=1$,

where α, β, δ are Dirichlet priors and γ is a Beta prior, $z_{d,i}$ denotes the ith topic assignment in document d, $w_{d,i}$ denotes the ith word in document d, and $x_{d,i}$ denotes the indicator between $w_{d,i-1}$ and $w_{d,i}$. Note that the variable $x_{d,i} = 1$ implies that word $w_{d,i-1}$ and its neighbor $w_{d,i}$ belong to the same phrase, while $x_{d,i} = 0$ implies otherwise. However, the topics assigned to them ($z_{d,i-1}$ and $z_{d,i}$) are not required to be identical to each other. To decide the topic of a phrase, we can simply take the first (or last) word's topic or the most common topic in the phrase. The authors of TNG prefer to choose the last word's topic as the phrase topic because the last noun in a collocation is usually the "head noun" in English.

However, this simple strategy may be ineffective when we apply TNG to Chinese documents. The topics of "比赛" (game) and "锦标赛" (tournament) should be represented by their last characters while those of "农民" (farmer) and "农业" (agriculture) should be represented by their first characters. And occasionally, the topic of a Chinese word is not identical to any topic of its component characters. For example "蓝牙" (Bluetooth) is neither a color nor a tooth.

To overcome the limitation of TNG, we must discard its underlying assumption: that the topic of a whole word is the same as the topic of at least one of its components.

3 Modeling Word Topic and Character Topic

This section describes our topical word-character model (TWC), which models two distinct types of topics: *word topic* and *character topic*.

3.1 Word topic and character topic

To solve the problem associated with the "蓝牙" (Bluetooth) example, we need to distinguish between the topics of characters and words. Therefore, we introduce a new type of topic for words in addition to the topics assigned to characters. When generating a Chinese character, we first draw a word topic and then choose a character topic. A schematic description of this model is shown in Figure 2.

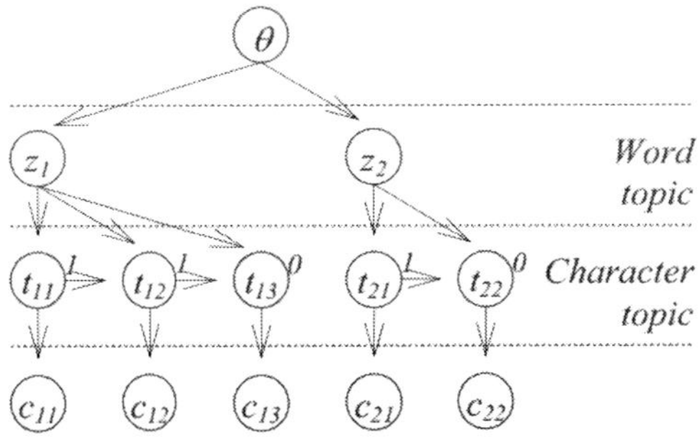

Figure 2: Schematic description of modeling Chinese documents with character and word topics.

Here, we use random variables $\vec{z}$ and $\vec{t}$ to denote word and character topics, respectively. Note that the *word topic* and *character topics* have a hierarchical tree-like structure (upper layer in Figure 2), whereas *character topics* and *characters* form a hidden Markov model (HMM) (lower layer in Figure 2).

3.2 Topical word-character model (TWC)

There are some indicators in the upper-right corner of each character topic in Figure 2. They help us to tell whether the current character belongs to the same word as the previous one. Now the question left is how to probabilistically draw these indicators, i.e., how to determine the length of the Markov chain.

There are two ways to set the values of the indicators. One is similar to that applied in the hidden semi-Markov model (HSMM), which generates the duration of a segment from the state. Accordingly, we could first choose the length of a word from the distribution associated with the word topic and then assign *0* or *1* to each indicator. The other method is to directly draw indicators from the distribution associated with the previous character and topic, just as LDACOL and TNG do. The difference between these two methods is that the former determines the length of a word in advance while the latter increases the length dynamically.

We prefer the second choice because it takes into consideration a lot of context information. In fact, our experimental results indicate that it has better performance.

The formal definition of our model with word and character topics is as follows.

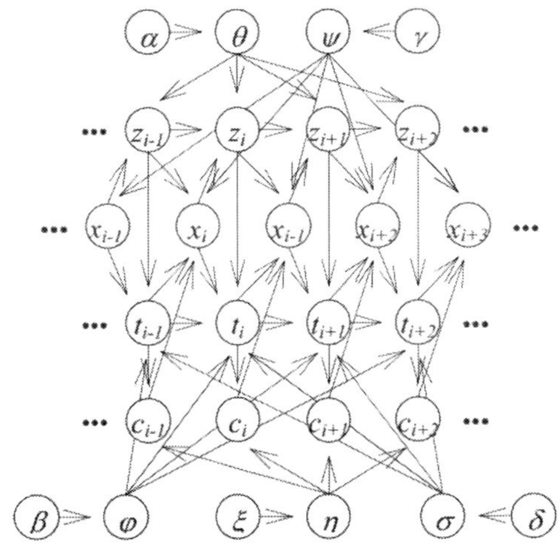

Figure 3: Topical word-character model.

TWC has four sets of variables: a sequence of characters $\vec{c}$, a sequence of character topics $\vec{t}$, a sequence of word topics $\vec{z}$, and a sequence of indicators $\vec{x}$. A document is generated via the following procedure.

1. For each document d, draw $\theta_d \sim$ Dirichlet(α);
2. For each word topic z, draw $\varphi_z \sim$ Dirichlet(β);
3. For each word topic z and each character topic t, draw $\sigma_{zt} \sim$ Dirichlet(δ);
4. For each word topic z, each character topic t and each character c, draw $\psi_{ztc} \sim$ Beta(γ);
5. For each character topic t, draw $\eta_t \sim$ Dirichlet(ξ);
6. For each character $c_{d,i}$ in document d:
   (a) draw $x_{d,i} \sim$ Bernoulli($\psi_{z_{d,i-1}, t_{d,i-1}, c_{d,i-1}}$);
   (b) draw $z_{d,i} \sim$ Discrete (θ_d) if $x_{d,i}=0$;
   $z_{d,i} = z_{d,i-1}$ if $x_{d,i}=1$;
   (c) draw $t_{d,i} \sim$ Discrete($\varphi_{z_{d,i}}$) if $x_{d,i}=0$;
   draw $t_{d,i} \sim$ Discrete($\sigma_{z_{d,i}, t_{d,i-1}}$) if $x_{d,i}=1$;
   (d) draw $c_{d,i} \sim$ Discrete($\eta_{t_{d,i}}$).

Here, α, β, δ, η are Dirichlet priors and γ is a Beta prior, $z_{d,i}$ denotes the ith word topic assignment in document d, $t_{d,i}$ denotes the ith character topic assignment in document d, $c_{d,i}$ denotes the ith character in document d, and $x_{d,i}$ denotes the indicator between $c_{d,i-1}$ and $c_{d,i}$.

Note that compared with the schematic model in Figure 2, each character has its corresponding word topic in the TWC model. This is because we cannot decide how many words there will be in a document and how many characters there will be in a certain word in advance. In other words, the structure of the ideal model is not fixed. Therefore, we duplicate word topic variables for each character.

4 Inference with TWC

Many approximate inference techniques such as variational methods, expectation propagation, and Gibbs sampling can be applied to graphical models. We use Gibbs sampling to perform our Bayesian inference in TWC.

Gibbs sampling is a simple and widely applicable Markov chain Monte Carlo (MCMC) algorithm. In a traditional procedure, variables are sequentially sampled from their distributions conditioned on all other variables in the model.

An extension of the basic approach is to choose blocks of variables first and then sample jointly from the variables in each block in turn, conditioned on the remaining variables; this is called blocking Gibbs sampling.

When sampling for TWC, we separate variables into three types of blocks in the following manner (as shown in Figure 4).

1. character variables t_i
2. indicators x_i, whose value is 1 after n iterations
3. word topics z_i, z_{i+1}, …, z_{i+l-1} and indicator x_i, satisfying $x_i = x_{i+l} = 1$ and $x_j = 0$ (j from i to $i+l-1$) after n iterations

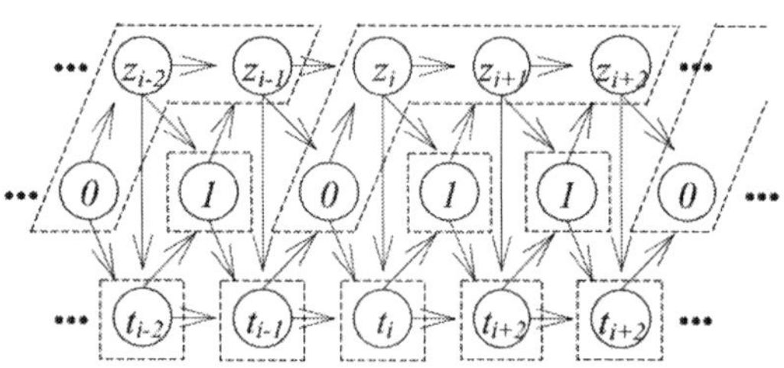

Figure 4: Illustration of partition in a certain iteration.

Note that variables $\vec{\theta}, \vec{\varphi}, \vec{\sigma}, \vec{\psi}$ and $\vec{\eta}$ are not sampled. This is because we can integrate them out according to their conjugate priors. We only need to sample variables $\vec{z}$, $\vec{x}$, and $\vec{t}$.

Before discussing the inference of conditional probabilities, let us analyze our partition strategy in detail. We will explain the reasons for (1) sampling z_i, z_{i+1}, …, z_{i+l-1} together and (2) sampling $\vec{z}$ and x_i together

1. Why do we sample z_i, z_{i+1}, …, z_{i+l-1} together?

Assume that we draw z_i, z_{i+1}, …, z_{i+l-1} one by one, and it is now time to sample z_{i+1} according to the conditional probability

$$P(z_{i+1} = j \mid \vec{z}_{-(i+1)}, \vec{x}, \vec{t}, \vec{c}, \alpha, \beta, \delta, \gamma, \xi),$$

where $\vec{z}_{-(i+1)}$ denotes a word topic except z_{i+1}.

Recall step 6-b in the generative TWC model: it says "If $x_{d,i} = 1$, then $z_{d,i} = z_{d,i-1}$", which implies

$$P(z_{i+1} \mid z_i, x_{i+1} = 1) = I(z_{i+1} = z_i).$$

As this probability is a factorial of the target probability, it follows that

$$P(z_{i+1} = j \mid \vec{z}_{-(i+1)}, \vec{x}, \vec{t}, \vec{c}, \alpha, \beta, \delta, \gamma, \xi) = 0$$

for all $j \neq z_i$. In other words, z_{i+1} should be equal to z_i and not change during sampling.

It seems that step 6-b in the generative model causes the problem. But supposing that we do not set z_{i+1} to z_i; it is still more reasonable to sample $\vec{z}$ together. According to our partition principle, x_i, x_{i+1}, …, x_{i+l-1}, x_{i+l} is a continuous indicator sequence whose head and tail are both 0 and the rest are 1, which implies that character string c_i, c_{i+1}, …, c_{i+l-1} forms a word and has the same word topic. Recall the schematic model in Figure 2: the *word topic* and *character topics* have a tree-like structure and each word has only one word topic node. We add some auxiliary duplicates just because the ideal model is not fixed. Therefore, it is natural to sample the word topic together with its duplicates.

2. Why do we sample $\vec{z}$ and x_i together?

Let us consider the probability of converting x_i from 0 to 1 in the current sampling iteration. Assume that the number of word topics is 3, $z_{i-1} = 2$, and

$$P(z_i = \ldots = z_{i+l-1} = j \mid x_i = 0) = 1/3 \quad (1 \leq j \leq 3),$$

$$P(x_i = k \mid z_i = \ldots = z_{i+l-1} = 2) = 1/2 \quad (0 \leq k \leq 1),$$

where other variables and priors are omitted. If we first sample $\vec{z}$ and next sample x_i, then the probability of drawing 1 for x_i is $1/6$, according to the multiplication principle. If we sample $\vec{z}$ and x_i together, the probability of drawing 1 for x_i is $P(z_i = \ldots = z_{i+l-1} = 2, x_i = 1)$.

Since

$$1 = \sum_{k=0}^{1} \sum_{j=1}^{3} P(z_i = \ldots = z_{i+l-1} = j, x_i = k)$$

$$= \sum_{j=1}^{3} P(z_i = \ldots = z_{i+l-1} = j, x_i = 0)$$

$$+ (z_i = \ldots = z_{i+l-1} = 2, x_i = 1) \quad (z_{i-1} = 2)$$

and

$$P(z_i = \ldots = z_{i+l-1} = 2, x_i = 1)$$

$$= P(z_i = ... = z_{i+l-1} = 2, x_i = 0)$$
$$= P(z_i = ... = z_{i+l-1} = j, x_i = 0) \quad (1 \le j \le 3)'$$

we get

$$P(z_i = ... = z_{i+l-1} = 2, x_i = 1) = 1/4 > 1/6 .$$

In conclusion, the model is more likely to form long words, if we sample $\vec{z}$ and x_i together. This is preferred because both TNG and TWC tend to produce shorter words than we would like.

For each type of block, we need to work out the corresponding conditional probability.

$$P(t_{d,i} = s \mid \vec{z}, \vec{x}, \vec{t}_{d,-i}, \vec{c}, \alpha, \beta, \delta, \gamma, \xi)$$
$$P(x_{d,i} = k \mid \vec{z}, \vec{x}_{d,-i}, \vec{t}, \vec{c}, \alpha, \beta, \delta, \gamma, \xi)$$
$$P(z_{d,i} = z_{d,i+1} = \cdots = z_{d,i+l-1} = j, x_{d,i} = k \mid \vec{z}_{d,-(i:i+l-1)}, \vec{x}_{d,-i}, \vec{t}, \vec{c}, \alpha, \beta, \delta, \gamma, \xi)$$

where $\vec{t}_{d,-i}$ denotes the character topic assignments except $t_{d,i}$, $\vec{x}_{d,-i}$ denotes the indicators except $x_{d,i}$, and $\vec{z}_{d,-(i:i+l-1)}$ denotes the word topic assignments except $\vec{z}_{d,j}$ (j from i to $i+l-1$). Details of the derivation of these conditional probabilities are provided in Appendix A.1.

5 Experiments

In this section, we discuss our evaluation of TWC in Chinese document modeling and Chinese word and topic discovery.

5.1 Modeling documents

To evaluate the generalization performance of our model, we trained both TWC and TNG on a Chinese corpus and computed the perplexity of the held-out test set. Perplexity, which indicates the uncertainty in predicting a single character, is a standard measure of performance for statistical models of natural language. A lower perplexity score indicates better generalization performance.

Formally, the perplexities for TWC and TNG are defined as follows.

$$perplexity_{TWC}(D_{test}) = \exp\{-\frac{\sum_{d=1}^{D} \log p(\vec{c}_d \mid \hat{\theta}, \hat{\varphi}, \hat{\sigma}, \hat{\psi}, \hat{\eta})}{\sum_{d=1}^{D} N_d}\},$$

where D_{test} is the testing data, D is the number of documents in D_{test}, N_d is the number of characters in document d, $\hat{\theta}_{d,z}$ is simply set to $1/Z$ (Z is number of word topics), and $\hat{\varphi}, \hat{\sigma}, \hat{\psi}, \hat{\eta}$ are posterior estimates provided by applying TWC to training data. Details of the parameter estimation for TWC are provided in Appendix A.2.

$$perplexity_{TNG}(D_{test}) = \exp\{-\frac{\sum_{d=1}^{D} \log p(\vec{c}_d \mid \hat{\theta}, \hat{\varphi}, \hat{\sigma}, \hat{\psi})}{\sum_{d=1}^{D} N_d}\},$$

where D_{test}, D, and N_d are the same as defined for the TWC perplexity, $\hat{\theta}_{d,z}$ is simply set to $1/T$ (T is number of topics), and $\hat{\varphi}, \hat{\sigma}, \hat{\psi}$ are posterior estimates provided by applying TNG to training data.

Now, the remaining question is how to work out the likelihood function in the definition of perplexity. The likelihood function can be obtained by marginalizing latent variables, but the time complexity is exponential. Therefore, we propose an efficient method of computing the likelihood that is similar to the *forward* algorithm for an HMM. Details of the *forward* approach to computing likelihood for TWC and TNG are provided in Appendix B.

In our experiments, we used a subset of Chinese corpus LDC2005T14. The dataset contains 6000 documents with 4476 unique characters and 2,454,616 characters. We evaluated both TWC and TNG using 10-fold cross validation. In each experiment, both models ran for 500 iterations on 90% of the data and computed the complexity for the remaining 10% of the data.

TWC used fixed Dirichlet (Beta) priors $\alpha=1$, $\beta=1$, $\delta=1$, $\gamma=0.1$ and $\xi=0.01$ while TNG used $\alpha=1$, $\beta=0.01$, $\delta=0.01$, and $\gamma=0.1$.

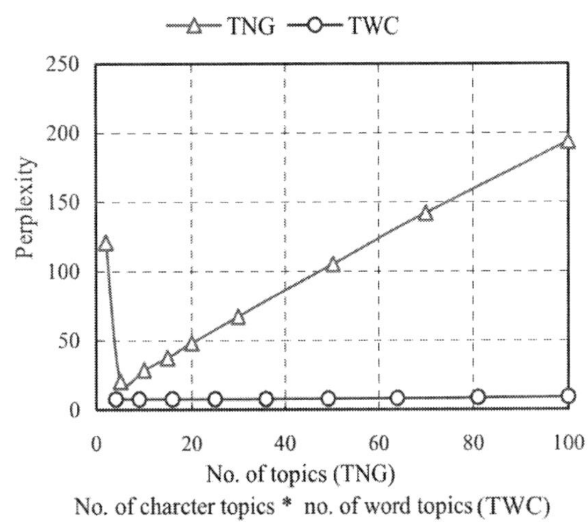

Figure 5: Perplexity results with LDC2005T14 corpora for TNG and TWC.

The results of these computations are shown in Figure 5. Note that the abscissa for TWC is the number of word topics (Z) multiplied by the number of character topics (T), while the abscissa for TNG is the number of topics (T). They both represent the number of partitions into which the model classifies characters.

Chance performance results in a perplexity equal to the number of unique characters, which was 4476 in our experiments. Therefore, both TWC and TNG are competitive models. And the lower curve shows that TWC is much better than TNG.

We also found that both perplexity curves increased with the number of partitions. In other words, both models suffer from overfitting issues. This is because the documents in a test set are very likely to contain words that do not appear in any of the documents in the training set. Such words will have a very low probability, which is inversely proportional to the number of partitions. Therefore, the perplexity of TWC increased from 7.3513 ($Z*T=2*2$) to 8.9953 ($Z*T=10*10$), while that of TNG increased from 20.3789 ($T=5$) to 193.6065 ($T=100$).

5.2 Chinese word and topic discovery

As shown in the previous subsection, TWC is a competitive method for topically modeling Chinese documents. Next, we show its ability to extract Chinese words and topics in comparison with TNG.

In our qualitative experiments, the task of Chinese word and topic discovery was addressed as a supervised learning problem, where a set of words with their topical assignments was given as a seed set. Each seed can be viewed as some constraints imposed on the TWC and TNG models. For example, suppose that "教师" (teacher) together with its assignment "education" is a seed. This assumption implies that the indicator between characters "教" and "师" is 1 and that the (word) topic for each character is "education".

We make use of such constraints in a simple but effective way. In each sampling iteration, we first sample all variables as usual and then reset observed variables according to the constraints.

We used 8000 Chinese documents in the Chinese Gigaword corpus (LDC2005T14) provided by the Linguistic Data Consortium for our experiments. The dataset contains 4651 unique characters and 3,295,810 characters.

The number of word topics in TWC, the number of character topics in TWC, and the number of topics in TNG were all set to 15. Furthermore, 16 seeds scattered in 4 distinct topics were given, as listed in Table 1 column "seed". Dirichlet (Beta) priors were set to the same values as described in the previous subsection.

Word and topic assignments were extracted after running 300 Gibbs sampling iterations on the training corpus together with the seed set. For the TNG model, we took the first character's topic as the topic of the word. We omitted one-character words and ranked the extracted words using the following formula

$$\frac{occ_i(W)}{\sum_{i=1}^{15} occ_i(W)},$$

where $occ_i(W)$ represents how many words were assigned to (word) topic i. The top-50 extracted words are presented in Table 1.

We find found that both TWC and TNG could assemble many common words used in corresponding topics. And the TWC model had advantages over the TNG model in the following three respects.

First, TNG drew more words related to the seeds. In Table 1, highly related words are marked in pink (underline) and partly related words are marked in blue (italic). It is clear that the TWC column is more colorful than the TNG column.

Secondly, we found that many words extracted by TNG had the same prefix. For example, consider the topic "agriculture": there are 14 words marked with superscript 1 in Table 1. They all have the prefix "农". This is because we took the first character's topic as the topic of the word. Although this strategy is beneficial in some cases, such as for words with prefix "农", it is detrimental in other cases. For example, "甘蔗" (sugar cane) and "甘肃" (Gansu) have the same prefix and topic assignment, but the latter is a name of a province in China and is not related to agriculture. Similarly, even though the character string "伊外" does not form a Chinese word, this string "伊外" and "伊朗" (Iran) are classified in the same cluster. Compared with TNG, TWC can also extract words whose topics are identical to the topic of any character. For example, the topics "自由泳" (freestyle swimming), "混合泳" (medley swimming), and "蝶泳" (butterfly stroke) depend on their suffixes.

Thirdly, although TNG stands for "topical n-gram model", it infrequently draws words containing more than two characters. On the other hand, the TWC model extracts many n-character words, such as "美国总统布什" (president of United States, George Bush), "个人混合泳" (individual medley), and "百分之四" (four per-

Seeds	TNG	TWC
足球(football) 球员(player) 比赛(match) 冠军 (championship)	撑竿, 乒乓, 比赛, 球员, 足球, 冠军, 选手, 摔跤, 世兵, 淘汰, 训练, 纪录, 选拔, 世界, 宇宙, 选择, 分钟, 朝鲜, 今晚, 威廉, 分别, 邀请, 分之, 世纪, 分裂, 辽宁, 分歧, 姑娘, 纪念, 香港, 今天, 结果, 公斤, 结束, 今年, 北京, 公里, 分析, 威胁, 毛腿, 分配, 开幕, 沈阳, 分子, 开始, 记者, 负责, 蒙古, 今后, 保持	蝶泳, 标赛 ^{2}, 上届, 自由泳, 混合泳, 比分, 总分, 冠军, 接力, 单打, 蛙泳, 比赛, 赵剑, 大师, 女子, 第一名, 速滑, 本届, 选手, 苏联队, 冰球, 亚军, 游泳, 国队 ^{2}, 决赛, 第三名, 两枚, 第七届, 国选手 ^{2}, 个人混合泳, 全能, 金牌, 男子, 战胜, 谢军, 夺得, 银牌, 两项, 名列, 公斤级, 冬运会, 训练, 苏联, 美分, 领先, 获得, 成绩, 目的, 运动员, 第三
粮食 (foodstuff) 农村 (country) 农民 (farmer) 水稻 (paddies)	粮食, 农贸 ^{1}, 水稻, 农林 ^{1}, 橄榄, 农副 ^{1}, 农药 ^{1}, 农户 ^{1}, 蘑菇, 农膜 ^{1}, 农村 ^{1}, 灌溉, 农牧 ^{1}, 农闲 ^{1}, 蔬菜, 潍坊, 农业 ^{1}, 农机, 农奴 ^{1}, 玫瑰, 农民 ^{1}, 农垦 ^{1}, 柑桔, 农田 ^{1}, 挂钩, 鞠躬, 甘蔗, 甘薯, 覆盖, 甘肃, 笼罩, 帐篷, 土壤, 偏僻, 灿烂, 左右, 拉玛, 拉萨, 公斤, 帮助, 丝绸, 公路, 群众, 公顷, 公里, 百姓, 沙漠, 蒙古, 积累, 培育	农村, 推广, 农民, 粮食, 水稻, 苜蓿, 秸秆, 流通, 农户, 农产, 乡镇, 社会化, 土地, 丰收, 灌溉, 妇女, 农业, 增产, 责任制, 基层, 万只 ^{2}, 全省, 亿公斤 ^{2}, 试验, 百分之八, 多万 ^{2}, 反映, 科技, 各地, 当地, 多公斤 ^{2}, 集体, 服务, 承包, 公斤, 负担, 配套, 万公斤 ^{2}, 生产, 投入, 全县, 亿亩 ^{2}, 万户 ^{2}, 生活, 百分之四, 生育, 销售, 总产, 人均, 年产
学校 (school) 教师 (teacher) 学生 (student) 教育 (education)	叮嘱, 学生, 教训, 教徒, 遐迩, 孤寡, 学校, 骆驹, 腼腆, 教界, 喇叭, 教材, 学雷锋, 荟萃, 教授, 学儒, 慷慨, 教师, 教练, 蜘蛛, 钥匙, 凛冽, 骄傲, 教育, 歹徒, 巾帼, 瞻仰, 残疾, 雷锋, 学谦, 雷洁, 裕禄, 烹饪, 姑娘, 残废, 舞蹈, 兄弟, 旗帜, 儿童, 精彩, 学习, 遗址, 兢兢, 呼唤, 纪念, 李瑞, 群岛, 记载, 精锐, 精神	学校, 学生, 教育, 教师, 国防, 民族, 宣传, 毕业, 学习, 经费, 培养, 职工, 纪律, 知识, 家庭, 重视, 实施, 教材, 事业, 培训, 社会主义, 文化, 进一步, 工作, 只有, 保证, 继续, 活动, 任务, 推动, 小标题, 帮助, 通过, 通讯, 思想, 加强, 研究, 记者, 考试, 开始, 要求, 先后, 期间, 开展, 方面, 问题, 精神, 技术, 地区, 成绩
战争 (war) 士兵 (solider) 将军 (general) 武器 (weapon)	伊外, 伊朗, 朝圣, 伊斯, 朝柱, 巴勒, 士兵, 拉维, 巴基, 威尔, 拉曼, 摧毁, 伊始, 伊利, 朝觐, 巴嫩, 摧残, 伊奇, 轰炸, 巴塞, 伊格, 海盗, 海夫, 巴格, 巴黎, 巴乔, 轰鸣, 巴西, 袭击, 武器, 伊沙, 拉彻, 避难, 拉法, 葡萄, 将军, 战壕, 伊拉, 威者, 战舰, 战双, 拉脱, 伊军, 战飞, 拉姆, 伊拉克, 拉瓜, 战争, 拉底, 伊拉姆	战争, 将军, 武器, 士兵, 钱其琛, 轰炸, 导弹, 撤军, 美军, 美国总统布什, 伊军, 讨论海湾, 今天进入第 ^{2}, 对海湾 ^{2}, 科威特, 综合报道, 海湾, 危机, 多国部队, 爆发, 新闻分析, 死亡, 地面, 结束后, 之一, 摧毁, 综述, 结束, 爆发以来, 战舰, 伊拉克, 号决议 ^{2}, 表示, 万桶, 提供, 造成, 宣布, 美国, 包括, 问题, 目前, 同时, 今年, 公里, 去年, 其中, 美元, 亿元, 万元, 万吨

Table 1: Top-50 words extracted by TWC and TNG.

cent). This is partly due to our sampling strategy, discussed in subsection 4.1, which increases the probability of forming long words.

We also found that some extracted character strings were very close to real Chinese words. For instance, "标赛" is a substring of "锦标赛" (tournament); "国选手" is a suffix of "中国选手" (Chinese player), "美国选手" (American player), and "法国选手" (French player); and "万公斤" is a substring of "十万公斤" (100 thousand kilograms) and "五万公斤" (50 thousand kilograms). (Such substrings are marked with superscript 2 in Table 1.) We believe that this result occurred because the training corpus was not large enough and that TWC will achieve better performance with a large dataset.

6 Conclusion and Future Work

In this paper, we presented a topical word-character (TWC) model, which models two distinct types of topics: *word topic* and *character topic*. The experimental results show that TWC is a powerful approach to modeling Chinese documents according to the standard evaluation measure of *perplexity*. We also demonstrated TWC's ability to detect words and assign topics.

Since TWC is a straightforward improvement that removes the limitations of existing topical collocation models, we expect that its application to English collocation will also result in higher performance.

Appendix A.1 Gibbs Sampling Derivation for TWC

Symbols used here are defined as follows.

C is the number of unique characters, T is the number of character topics, and Z is the number of word topics.

N_d denotes the number of characters in a document d.

$I(\cdot)$ is an indicator function, taking the value 1 when its argument is true, and 0 otherwise.

$q_{d,z,0}$ represents how words are assigned to topic z in document d; $p_{z,t,c,k}$ represents how many times an indicator is k given the previous character c, the previous character topic t, and the previous word topic z; $n_{z,t,0}$ represents how many times a character topic is t given a word topic z and the corresponding indicator 0; $m_{z,v,t,1}$ represents how many times a character topic is t given a word topic z, the previous character topic v, and the corresponding indicator 1; and $r_{t,c}$ represents how many times character c is assigned to character topic t.

$$P(t_{d,i}=s\mid \vec{z},\vec{x},\vec{t}_{d,-i},\vec{c},\alpha,\beta,\delta,\gamma,\xi)$$

$$\propto \int\prod_{d'=1}^{D}P(\vec{\theta}_{d'}\mid\alpha)\cdot\prod_{d'=1}^{D}\prod_{i'=1}^{N_{d'}}P(z_{d',i'}\mid x_{d',i'},z_{d',i'-1},\vec{\theta}_{d'})\cdot d\vec{\theta}\times$$

$$\int\prod_{z'=1}^{Z}\prod_{t'=1}^{T}\prod_{c'=1}^{C}P(\vec{\psi}_{z',t',c'}\mid\gamma)\cdot\prod_{d'=1}^{D}\prod_{i'=1}^{N_{d'}}P(x_{d',i'}\mid\vec{\psi}_{z_{d',i'-1},t_{d',i'-1},c_{d',i'-1}})\cdot d\vec{\psi}$$

$$\times\iint\prod_{z'=1}^{Z}P(\vec{\varphi}_{z'}\mid\beta)\cdot\prod_{z'=1}^{Z}\prod_{t'=1}^{T}P(\vec{\sigma}_{z',t'}\mid\delta)\cdot\prod_{d'=1}^{D}\prod_{i'=1}^{N_{d'}}P(t_{d',i'}\mid x_{d',i'},\vec{\varphi}_{z_{d',i'}},$$

$$\vec{\sigma}_{z_{d',i'},t_{d',i'-1}}) \cdot d\vec{\varphi} \cdot d\vec{\sigma} \times \int \prod_{t'=1}^{T} P(\vec{\eta}_{t'} \mid \xi) \cdot \prod_{d'=1}^{D} \prod_{i'=1}^{N_{d'}} P(c_{d',i'} \mid \vec{\eta}_{t_{d',i'}}) \cdot d\vec{\eta}$$

$$\propto \int \prod_{z'=1}^{Z} \prod_{t'=1}^{T} \prod_{c'=1}^{C} \frac{\Gamma(2\gamma)}{\Gamma(\gamma)^2} \cdot \prod_{x'=1}^{2} (\psi^{x'}_{z',t',c'})^{\gamma-1} \cdot \prod_{x'=1}^{2} (\psi^{x'}_{z',t',c'})^{p_{z',t',c',x'}} \cdot$$

$$\psi^{x_{d,i+1}}_{z_{d,i},s,c_{d,i}} \cdot d\vec{\psi} \times \int \prod_{t'=1}^{T} \frac{\Gamma(C\xi)}{\Gamma(\xi)^C} \cdot \prod_{c'=1}^{C} (\eta^{c'}_{t'})^{\xi-1} \prod_{c'=1}^{C} (\eta^{c'}_{t'})^{r_{t',c'}} \cdot \eta^{c_{d,i}}_{s} d\vec{\eta} \times$$

$$\iint \prod_{z'=1}^{Z} \frac{\Gamma(T\beta)}{\Gamma(\beta)^T} \cdot \prod_{t'=1}^{T} (\varphi^{t'}_{z'})^{\beta-1} \cdot \prod_{t'=1}^{T} (\varphi^{t'}_{z'})^{n_{z',t',0}} \cdot \prod_{z'=1}^{Z} \prod_{t'=1}^{T} \frac{\Gamma(T\delta)}{\Gamma(\delta)^T} \cdot$$

$$\prod_{v'=1}^{T} (\sigma^{v'}_{z',t'})^{\delta-1} \cdot \prod_{v'=1}^{T} (\sigma^{v'}_{z',t'})^{m_{z',t',v',1}} \cdot \begin{cases} \varphi^{s}_{z_{d,i}} & x_{d,i}=0 \\ \sigma^{s}_{z_{d,i},t_{d,i-1}} & x_{d,i}=1 \end{cases} \cdot d\vec{\varphi} \cdot d\vec{\sigma}$$

$$\propto \frac{p_{z_{d,i},s,c_{d,i},x_{d,i}} + \gamma}{p_{z_{d,i},s,c_{d,i},*} + 2\gamma} \times \frac{r_{s,c_{d,i}} + \xi}{r_{s,*} + C\xi} \times \begin{cases} \dfrac{n_{z_{d,i},s,0} + \beta}{n_{z_{d,i},*,0} + T\beta} & x_{d,i} = 0 \\ \dfrac{m_{z_{d,i},t_{d,i-1},s,1} + \delta}{m_{z_{d,i},t_{d,i-1},*,1} + T\delta} & x_{d,i} = 1 \end{cases}$$

Similarly,

$$P(x_{d,i} = k \mid \vec{z}, \vec{x}_{d,-i}, \vec{t}, \vec{c}, \alpha, \beta, \delta, \gamma, \xi)$$

$$\propto \begin{cases} \dfrac{q_{d,z_{d,i},0} + \alpha}{q_{d,*,0} + Z\alpha} & k=0 \\ I(z_{d,i} = z_{d,i-1}) & k=1 \end{cases} \times \frac{p_{z_{d,i-1},t_{d,i-1},c_{d,i-1},k} + \gamma}{p_{z_{d,i-1},t_{d,i-1},c_{d,i-1},*} + 2\gamma} \times$$

$$\begin{cases} \dfrac{n_{z_{d,i},t_{d,i},0} + \beta}{n_{z_{d,i},*,0} + T\beta} & k=0 \\ \dfrac{m_{z_{d,i},t_{d,i-1},t_{d,i},1} + \delta}{m_{z_{d,i},t_{d,i-1},*,1} + T\delta} & k=1 \end{cases}$$

$$P(z_{d,i} = z_{d,i+1} = \cdots = z_{d,i+l-1} = j, x_{d,i} = k \mid \vec{z}_{d,-(i:i+l-1)}, \vec{x}_{d,-i}, \vec{t},$$
$$\vec{c}, \alpha, \beta, \delta, \gamma, \xi)$$

$$\propto \begin{cases} \dfrac{q_{d,j,0} + \alpha}{q_{d,*,0} + Z\alpha} & k=0 \\ I(z_{d,i-1} = j) & k=1 \end{cases} \times \frac{p_{z_{d,i-1},t_{d,i-1},c_{d,i-1},k} + \gamma}{p_{z_{d,i-1},t_{d,i-1},c_{d,i-1},*} + 2\gamma} \cdot$$

$$\prod_{u=2}^{l+1} \frac{p_{j,t_{d,i+u-2},c_{d,i+u-2},x_{d,i+u-1}} + \gamma}{p_{j,t_{d,i+u-2},c_{d,i+u-2},*} + 2\gamma} \times \prod_{u=2}^{l} \left(\frac{m_{j,t_{d,i+u-2},t_{d,i+u-1},1} + \delta}{m_{j,t_{d,i+u-2},*,1} + T\delta}\right) \cdot$$

$$\begin{cases} \dfrac{n_{j,t_{d,i},0} + \beta}{n_{j,*,0} + T\beta} & k=0 \\ \dfrac{m_{j,t_{d,i-1},t_{d,i},1} + \delta}{m_{j,t_{d,i-1},*,1} + T\delta} & k=1 \end{cases}$$

Appendix A.2 Parameter estimation for TWC

After each Gibbs sampling iteration, we obtain posterior estimates $\hat{\hat{\theta}}, \hat{\hat{\varphi}}, \hat{\hat{\sigma}}, \hat{\hat{\psi}}$ and r by

$$\hat{\theta}_{d,z} = \frac{q_{d,z,0} + \alpha}{q_{d,*,0} + Z\alpha} \qquad \hat{\psi}_{z,t,c,k} = \frac{p_{z,t,c,k} + \gamma}{p_{z,t,c,*} + 2\gamma}$$

$$\hat{\sigma}_{z,v,t} = \frac{m_{z,v,t,1} + \delta}{m_{z,v,*,1} + T\delta} \qquad \hat{\varphi}_{z,t} = \frac{n_{z,t,0} + \beta}{n_{z,*,0} + T\beta} \quad ,$$

$$\hat{\eta}_{t,c} = \frac{r_{t,c} + \xi}{r_{t,*} + C\xi}$$

where the symbols are the same as those defined in Appendix A.1. These values correspond to the predictive distribution over new word topics, new indicators, new character topics, and new characters.

Appendix B. Likelihood Function Derivation for TWC and TNG

To compute the likelihood function for TWC, a quaternion function g_i is defined as follows: (formula has a broken character)

$$g_i(r,s,u,v) \triangleq P(c_{d,1}, c_{d,2}, \ldots, c_{d,i}, z_{d,i} = r, x_{d,i} = s,$$
$$t_{d,i-1} = u, t_{d,i} = v \mid \hat{\hat{\theta}}, \hat{\hat{\varphi}}, \hat{\hat{\sigma}}, \hat{\hat{\psi}}, \hat{\hat{\eta}})$$

Then, it is clear that

$$P(\vec{c}_d \mid \hat{\hat{\theta}}, \hat{\hat{\varphi}}, \hat{\hat{\sigma}}, \hat{\hat{\psi}}, \hat{\eta}) = \sum_{r=1}^{Z} \sum_{s=0}^{1} \sum_{u=1}^{T} \sum_{v=1}^{T} g_{N_d}(r,s,u,v) \, ,$$

where Z is the number of word topics and T is the number of character topics. The function g_i can be rewritten in a recursive manner.

$$g_1(r,1,u,v) = 0$$

$$g_1(r,0,u,v) = \hat{\theta}^r_d \times \frac{1}{T} \times \varphi^v_r \times \eta^{c_{d,1}}_v$$

$$g_{i+1}(r,s,u,v) = \sum_{j=1}^{Z} \sum_{k=0}^{1} \sum_{l=1}^{T} g_i(j,k,l,u) \times \hat{\psi}^s_{j,u,c_{d,i}} \times \hat{\eta}^{c_{d,i+1}}_v$$
$$\times \begin{cases} \hat{\theta}^r_d \\ I(r=j) \end{cases} \times \begin{matrix} \hat{\varphi}^v_r & s=0 \\ \hat{\sigma}^v_{r,u} & s=1 \end{matrix}$$

Similarly we can define function h_i to help compute the likelihood for TNG. (formula has a broken character)

$$h_i(r,s) \triangleq P(c_{d,1}, \ldots, c_{d,i}, z_i = r, x_i = s \mid \hat{\hat{\theta}}, \hat{\hat{\varphi}}, \hat{\hat{\sigma}}, \hat{\hat{\psi}})$$

$$P(\vec{c}_d \mid \hat{\hat{\theta}}, \hat{\hat{\varphi}}, \hat{\hat{\sigma}}, \hat{\hat{\psi}}) = \sum_{r=1}^{Z} \sum_{s=0}^{1} h_{N_d}(r,s)$$

$$h_1(r,1) = 0$$

$$h_1(r,0) = \hat{\theta}^r_d \times \hat{\varphi}^{c_{d,1}}_r$$

$$h_{i+1}(r,s) = \sum_{j=1}^{Z} \sum_{k=0}^{1} h_i(j,k) \times \hat{\psi}^s_{j,c_{d,i}} \times \hat{\theta}^r_d \times \begin{cases} \hat{\varphi}^{c_{d,i+1}}_r & s=0 \\ \hat{\sigma}^{c_{d,i+1}}_{r,c_{d,i}} & s=1 \end{cases}$$

References

Blei, D. M., Ng, A. Y., and Jordan, M. J. 2003. Latent Dirichlet allocation. *Journal of Machine Learning Research*, 3:993–1022.

Griffiths, T. L. and Steyvers, M. 2004. Finding Scientific Topics. *Proceedings of the National Academy of Sciences, 101 (suppl. 1)*, 5228-5235.

Steyvers, M. and Griffiths, T. L. 2007. Probabilistic topic models. *Latent Semantic Analysis: A Road to Meaning.* Laurence Erlbaum.

Griffiths, T. L., Steyvers, M., and Tenenbaum, J. B. T. 2007. Topics in Semantic Representation *Psychological Review*, 114(2), 211-244.

Wang, X., McCallum, A., and Wei, X. 2007. Topical N-grams: Phrase and Topic Discovery, with an Application to Information Retrieval. *Proceedings of the 7th IEEE International Conference on Data Mining* (ICDM 2007).

Non-Compositional Language Model and Pattern Dictionary Development for Japanese Compound and Complex Sentences

Satoru Ikehara, Masato Tokuhisa, Jin'ichi Murakami
Tottori University,
Koyama-Minami Tottori, 680-8552, Japan
{ikehara, tokuhisa, murakami}@ike.tottori-u.ac.jp

Abstract

To realize high quality machine translation, we proposed a *Non-Compositional Language Model*, and developed a sentence pattern dictionary of 226,800 pattern pairs for Japanese compound and complex sentences consisting of 2 or 3 clauses. In pattern generation from a parallel corpus, *Compositional Constituents* that could be generalized were 74% of independent words, 24% of phrases and only 15% of clauses. This means that in Japanese-to-English MT, most of the translation results as shown in the parallel corpus could not be obtained by methods based on *Compositional Semantics*. This dictionary achieved a *syntactic coverage* of 98% and a *semantic coverage* of 78%. It will substantially improve translation quality.

1 Introduction

A wide variety of machine translation (MT) methods are being studied(Nagao, 1996; Brown et al., 1990; Vogel et al., 2003), but to obtain high-quality translations between languages belonging to different families that are alien each other is difficult. Most practical systems still employ a transfer method based on *compositional semantics*. A problem with this method is that it produces translations by separating the syntactic structure from meaning, and is thus liable to lose the meaning of the source text.

© 2008. Licensed under the *Creative Commons Attribution-Noncommercial-Share Alike 3.0 Unported* license (http://creativecommons.org/licenses/by-nc-sa/3.0/). Some rights reserved.

Better translation quality can be expected from *pattern-based MT* and *example-based MT* where the syntactic structure and semantics are handled together. However, *pattern-based MT* require immense pattern dictionaries that are difficult to develop(Jung et al., 1999; Uchino et al., 2001).

Meanwhile, *example-based MT*(Nagao, 1984; Sato, 1992; Brown, 1999) obtains translation results by substituting semantically similar elements in structurally matching translation examples, so a pre-prepared pattern dictionary is not needed. However, the capability to substitute a constituent in an example changes from one example to the next, and to automate this judgement is impossible. This problem could be addressed by manually tagging each example beforehand to specify which constituents can be substituted, but the resulting method would be just another *pattern-based* translation method.

Attention has been focused on the use of *cognitive grammar*(Langacker, 1987) and *construction grammar*(Fillmore, 1988) in the search to find methods that might help to resolve this problem. However, the standards for determining the structural meaning units and the granularity needed for meaning analysis have not been clarified.

As a method in which the syntactic structure and meaning are dealt with as an integral whole, a sentence pattern (SP)-dictionary called *A-Japanese Lexicon* has already been developed for Japanese simple sentences(Ikehara et al., 1997). This dictionary includes 14,800 valency patterns. The translation quality of Japanese simple sentences into English was 90% and this could be improved up to 97% by additional pattern pairs(Kanadechi et al., 2003).

Therefore in this study we developed an SP-dictionary for translating compound and complex sentences. First we proposed a *Non-compositional Language model* (*NL-model*) and a method for creating sentence patterns. Based on these, we built a large scale SP-dictionary from a parallel corpus through the generalization of compositional constituents.

2 Language Model

Conventional MT methods are based on the concept of *compositional semantics*. However, real languages have many expressions to which this concept cannot be applied. Solving this problem requires finding a mechanism acquiring the meaning of entire expressions before their constituents are analyzed.

2.1 Expressions and Constituents

Arita(1987) has pointed out that humans employ a framework of expressions (*semantic structure*) in their mother tongue in the process of conceptualizing objects. In the semantic structure that come to mind during the process when a speaker is forming a concept, two types of constituents to be considered those that cause the overall meaning to be lost when other constituents are substituted for them, and those that do not cause the overall meaning to be lost when an alternative constituent is substituted for them. Based on this idea, we derived the following definitions.

Definition 1: Types of constituents:

A compositional constituent (*C-constituent*) is defined as the constituent for which there are one or more alternative constituents and for which *the meaning of a semantic structure* does not change when this constituent is substituted. Any other constituent is defined as non-compositional constituent (*N-constituent*).

Definition 2: Types of expressions:

A compositional expression (*C-expression*) is defined as an expression that consists entirely of C-constituents, and a non-compositional expression (*N-expression*) is defined as an expression that has one or more N-constituents.

Before we applying these definitions to actual linguistic expressions, we need to clarify what we mean by "*the meaning of a semantic structure*." This is very important problem for semantic analysis, because the guranularity needed for semantic analysis is determined by the way of the meaning defiition.

In this study, considering applications to Japanese-to-English MT, the meaning of Japanese semantic structures defined in terms of English semantic structures.[1]

Figure 1 shows an example. The source text is a Japanese expression expressing a relationship between two events: "*directly after some event happened, somebody performed some action,*" and this meaning is defined by the English expression. For individual constituents such as "she" and "college," there are domains of substitutable constituents with which they can be substituted without changing the English semantic structure, so these constituents are classified into C-constituents.

2.2 Characteristics of C-constituents

From the above definitions, we can see that a C-constituent possesses the following characteristics. From these characteristics, possible guidelines for pattern-forming can be obtained.

- #1: The number and the scope of C-constituents depends on the language used for defining the meanings of expressions.
- #2: C-constituents need to be independent of each other.
- #3: The domain of alternatives for a C-constituent is syntactically and semantically limited.
- #4: Whether a constituent is compositional depends on the way it is articulated.
- #5: C-constituents are defined in relation to the entire expression. Many times these expressions consist of plural words, and some of them are N-expressions.

2.3 Non-compositional Language Model

According to definition 1, any linguistic expression consists of zero or more C-constituents and one or more N-constituents. The scope of these constituents can be arbitrarily selected. Then, we assume that C-constituents are extracted from expressions with a meaningful range (e.g., a word, phrase or clause). The C-constituent extracted in

[1] In this way, when the meaning of a linguistic expression is defi ned in another natural language, semantic ambiguity occurs in the language used in the defi nition. However, in the case of MT, the meaning of the translation results is understood by a speaker of the target language, so it is not thought to constitute a problem.

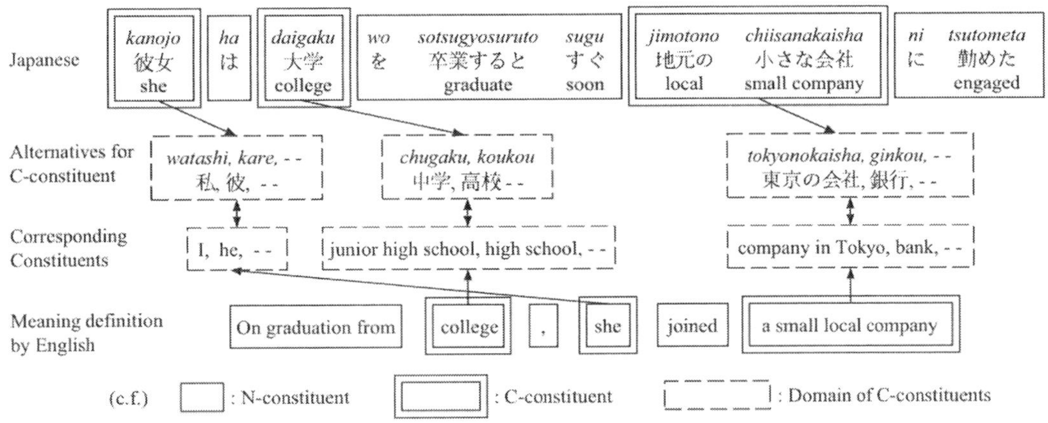

Figure 1: Corresponding Relationships of C-constituents between Japanese and English

this way may itself also be a N-expression according to characteristic #5, so a linguistic expression can generally be expressed with the language model designated as the *NL-model* in Figure 2.

As this figure shows, when C-constituents are repeatedly extracted from an N-expression, the end result is an N-expression that contains no C-constituent. Although the resulting N-expression may just be a single word, it could also be an idiomatic phrase that has no substitutable constituents. Thus, in *NL-model*, linguistic expressions can finally be articulated into N-constituents and N-expressions.

The difference from conventional *Compositional Language model* (*CL-model*) is in that *NL-model* does not assumes that all of expressions can be articulated into only C-constituents[2].

3 Pattern Forming

3.1 Principles of Pattern-forming

Not only words but also meaningful expression units such as phrases and sentences represent concepts, and the semantic structures of these expressions represent higher order concepts(Ikehara, 2003). Then, if we develop a pattern dictionary of semantic structures for expressions, higher order concept can be taken out of each expression by pattern matching.

An important aspect of the *NL-model* is that the N-expressions that appear at each stage of the decomposition are meaningful expression units. In this process, loss of the original meaning can be avoided by using a semantic dictionary for N-expressions at each stage. For example, if linguistic expressions are classified into sentences, clauses and phrases, and pattern dictionaries are prepared for N-expressions at each of these levels, then this would provide a mechanism for scooping up the meaning of entire sentences.

We think that patterns are a suitable framework for expressing the structure of N-expressions, because:

(a) N-constituents cannot be replaced by any other constituent, so a literal description is appropriate,

(b) the order of constituents is not flexible and often fixed.

Therefore, in this study we use a pattern- forming approach for N-expressions.

The Japanese-to-English parallel corpus is a typical example in which the meaning of Japanese expressions is defined by English expressions. Pattern pairs were therefore produced for N-expressions in the parallel corpus by extracting C-constituents and generalizing them.

When a parallel corpus is used, the following two types of constituents need to be considered as C-constituents:

(1) the constituent to which there is a semantically corresponding constituent in the English expression,

(2) the constituent to which there is no corresponding constituent in English, but deleting

[2]Translations by matching larger text unit are used in conventional MT including recent phrase-based SMT. But it is only that they regard phrases as C-constituents. The fact remains that entire expression is regarded as C-expression.

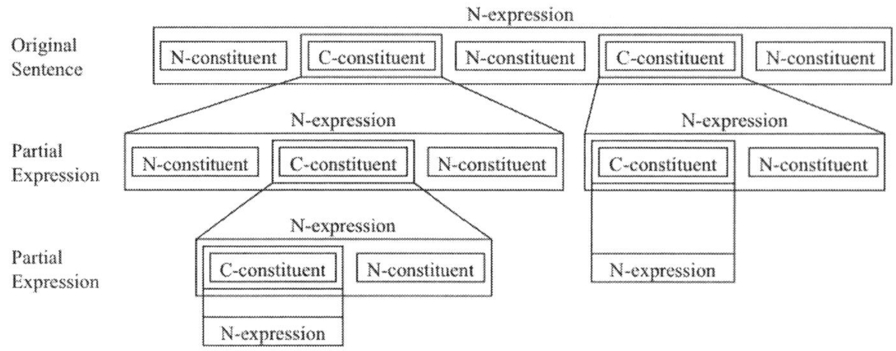

Figure 2: Non-compositional Language Model (*NL-model*)

this constituent from the Japanese expression does not cause any change in the corresponding English expression.

3.2 Pattern Description Language

A pattern description language was designed to achieve the following aims:

a) patterns can be semi-automatically generated from the result of morphological analysis of a parallel corpus, and

b) patterns can be defined according to the degree of generalization.

Here, a) is important in that it allows the development of large-scale SP-dictionaries. This condition also means that there is no need for syntactic or semantic analysis when comparing the input text with the SP-dictionary. If these analyses were required, problems would occur due to vagueness of interpretation, and the significance of the pattern method would be halved.

The descriptors used in this language are shown in Table 1. They are divided into four classes: *literals*, *variables*, *functions*, and *symbols*. As a rule, C-constituents are declared using *variables*(independent constituents), *functions*(subordinate constituents), and *symbols*(structural constituents), while N-constituents are declared by using the *literal* of words.

Constituents of a pattern are classified as either essential or optional. An essential constituent is one without which it would be impossible to define a corresponding relationship with the English pattern. An optional constituent is one that allows a corresponding English pattern to be defined even when it is omitted.

Optional constituents are further classified into two types. One type contains constituents that can be omitted from both the English and Japanese expression. The other contains constituents that do not appear in either the English or the Japanese expression, but these constituents can be inserted into those expressions.

3.3 Generalization of C-constituents

(1) Generalization by Variables

According to the characteristics of #3, when generalizing C-constituents by *variables*, the domain of a *variable* needs to be specified by syntactic attributes and semantic attributes. A syntactic attribute is represented by a variable name and a semantic attribute is represented by an argument attached to the variable. Attentions need to be paid to the following points in this generalization.

(a) A C-constituent may itself be an N-expression.

(b) Corresponding English constituents do not necessarily have the same syntactic attributes.

(2) Generalization by Functions

Conjugated forms of words that have been converted into *variables* are specified by *a word form function* when necessary. Also, particles and subordinate words such as auxiliary verbs are specified using *a Tense aspect modality function* when necessary.

(3) Generalization by Symbols

Fluctuations in expressions are also C-constituents. These are declared using *symbols*.

Symbols are also used to specify omitted subjects and objects when necessary. The optional constituents mentioned in section 3.2(2) are also C-constituents and word order that do not change

Table 1: Descriptors of Pattern Description Language

#	Classification	Types (The number of descriptors)
1	*Literal*	Japanese Character, English Character
2	*Variable*(17)	*Word variable*(11), *Phrase variable*(5), *Clause variable*(1)
3	*Function*(151)	*Word form function*(33), *Tense aspect modality function*(56), *Part of speech transfer function*(8), *Macro function*(20), *Group function*(9), *Extraction function*(2), *Literal function*(2), others
4	Symbol(10)	*Insertion mark, Optional mark, Permutation mark, Changeable position mark, Supplementation mark*, Others

c.f. For futher details, look at pattern pair examples shown in Table 2.

Table 2: Examples of Generated SPs

		Word-level SP
Example sentence	J	*ukkarishite* うっかりして by mistate / *teikikenwo* 定期券を season ticket / *ieni* 家に at home / *wasuretekita* 忘れてきた。 left
	E	I was so careless as to leave my season ticket at home.
Sentence Pattern	J	(*ha*, *te*, *wo*, *ni*) #1[N1(4)は]/V2(3003)て/N3(932)を/N4(447)に/V5(1809).tekita。
	E	I was so AJ(V2) as to V5 #1[N1_poss] N3 at N4.
	c.f.	(a) N1, N3, N4: *Noun Variables*, (b) V2, V5: *Verb Variables*, (c) (4), (3003): Semantic attribute numbers specifying semantic constratints on a variable, (d) #1[...]: Omissible constituents (*Optional mark*) (e) /: constituents that is able to appear in the input sentence (*Insertion mark*), (f) .tekita: Function for specifying a predicate suffix (*Tense aspect modality function*), (g) AJ(V2): Adjective form of the value of *verb variable* V2 (*Part of speech transfer function*), (h) N1_poss: Value of N1 transformed into possessive case (*Word form function*)
		Phrase-level SP
Example sentence	J	*sonoketsuronha* その結論は the conclusion / *ayamattazenteini* 誤った前提に false premise / *motoduiteiru* 基づいている based on / *nodakara* のだから because / *ayamaridearu* 誤りである。 be wrong
	E	The conclusion is wrong in that it is based on a false premise.
Sentence Pattern	J	(*ha*, *ni*, *nodakara*) NP1(1022)は/V2(1513).ta/N3(2449)に/V4(9100).teiruのだから/N5(1453).dantei。
	E	NP1 is AJ(N5) in that it V4 on AJ(V2) N3.
	c.f.	(a) NP1: *Noun phrase variable*
		Clause-level SP
Example sentence	J	*soreha* それは that / *kiwameteyuudokudearu* 極めて有毒である extreamely harmfull / *node* ので because / *siyouni* 使用に use / *atatteha* 当たっては upon / *junibunni* 十二分に fully / *chuuisi* 注意し pay attention / *nakutehanaranai* なくてはならない。 must
	E	It is significantly toxic so that great caution must be taken with its use.
Sentence Pattern	J	(*node*, *niatatteha*) CL1(2492).tearuので、N2(2005)に当たっては/VP3(3901).gimu。
	E	so+that(CL1, VP3.must.passive with subj(CL1)_poss N2)
	c.f.	(a) CL1: *Clause variable*, (b) so+that(..., ...): *Macro function* that generates a "so that" sentence structure, (c) subj(CL): An *extraction function* that extracts the subject from the value of a clause variable

the entire meaning are also considered as structural C-constituents, and are declared with a *symbol.*

(4) Higher-level Generalization

Fine-grained generalization is performed by, for example, using *equal-value group functions* and *corresponding group functions* whereby multiple functions are grouped together, or by using *literal functions* to apply fine constraints to the domains of *variables*. The declaration of English patterns is also simplified by using *macro functions* to synthesize a wide variety of English constructions such as *so-that* constructions.

4 Development of SP-dictionary

(1) Pattern Generation Process

A parallel corpus for basic compound and complex sentences with two or three clauses was prepared, and this corpus was generalized to produce a SP-dictionary as follows.

Step 1: Creation of parallel corpus:

A parallel corpus consisting of 1 million sentence pairs was created from about 30 types of documents.

Step 2: Extraction of translation examples:

From the results of morphological analysis of this corpus, we extracted 150,000 target example sentences. Analytical errors were corrected manually.

Step 3: Pattern generation:

Using resources such as Japanese-English word dictionaries, semantically corresponding relationships were found and converted into *variables*, *functions*, and *symbols* in the following three steps:

(a) *Word-level* generalization:
Compositional independent words are converted into *word variables*.

(b) *Phrase-level* generalization:
Compositional phrases are converted into *phrase variables*.

(c) *Clause-level* generalization:
Compositional clauses are converted into *clause variables*.

For C-constituents that can be automatically recognized, the generalization is performed automatically, while cases that cannot be judged automatically are entrusted to a language analyst. Example of patterns produced in this way are shown in Table 2.

(2) Number of Generated Patterns

Table 3 shows the number of different patterns in

Table 3: Number of Generated SPs

Type of SPs	*Word Level*	*Phrase Level*	*Clause Level*	Total
Compound	61,171	39,243	18,173	118,587
Complex	48,123	32,049	5,778	85,950
Mixed Type	12,510	8,146	1,524	22,280
Total	121,904	79,438	25,475	226,817

Table 4: Ratio of C-constituents

Constituents	No. of constituents	No. of variables	Ratio of C-constituent
Words*	734,528	542,925	73.9 %
Phrases	463,636	111,359	24.0 %
Clauses	267,601	39,718	14.8 %

* : Independent words such as nouns and verbs.

the resulting SP-dictionary. The number of patterns was largest for *word-level* patterns, followed by *phrase-level* and *clause-level* patterns. The number of patterns created at the *clause level* was particularly small.

(3) Ratio of C-constituents

Table 4 shows the number of constituents converted into *variables* at each level of generalization. The ratio of generalized C-constituents was 74% at the *word level* and 24% at the *phrase level*, but just 15% at the *clause level*. This means that most of the clauses in the parallel corpus are N-constituents, which are impossible to generalize.

Acoodingly a semantically suitable translation as found in a parallel corpus cannot be obtained when N-constituents are extracted, translated, and incorporated into an original sentence.

5 Coverage of SP-dictionary

In the Pattern method based on NL-model, it is very important to know whether a pattern dictionary that cover most of the semantic structures can be developed.

(1) Experimental Conditions

We produced a program (pattern parser) to compare input sentences against the SP-dictionary, and used it for evaluations.

Ten thousand sentences that we randomly selected from the example sentences were used for creating the patterns and used in experiments. Since the input sentences will always match the patterns from which they were created, experiments were conducted in the manner of *cross-validation*.

Normally more than one pattern matches to an input sentence, and not all of them are necessarily

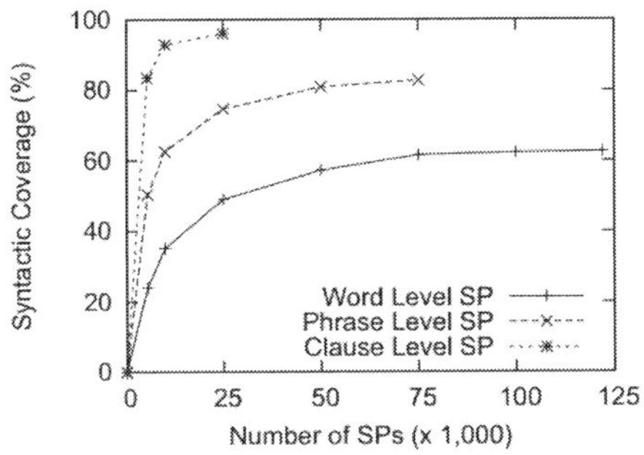

Figure 3: Saturation of Syntactic Coverage

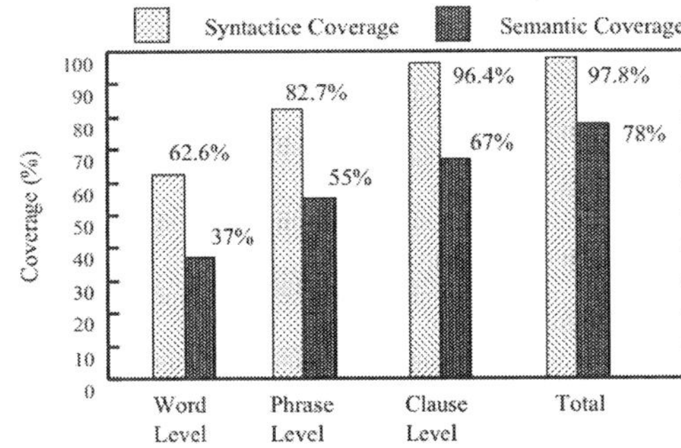

Figure 4: Syntactic and Semantic Coverage

correct in semantics. Therefore, the coverage was evaluated according to the following two parameters:

- **Syntactic coverage:** The ratio of input sentences that are matched to at least one pattern.
- **Semantic coverage:** The ratio of input sentences for which there is one or more semantically correct pattern.

(2) Saturation of Syntactic Coverage
Figure 3 shows the relationship between the number of patterns and the *syntactic coverage* at the *word, phrase,* and *clause levels*. As the number of patterns increases, *syntactic coverage* saturates rapidly.

In the case of simple sentences, it was reported that the number of valency patterns required to cover all of them more or less completely was estimated to be 25 thousands(Shirai et al., 1995).

When the patterns are rearranged in order of their frequency of matching, the saturation speed in Figure 3 becomes about five times faster. Then, we would expect the number of required patterns for compound and complex sentences to be somewhere in the tens of thousands or thereabouts as is the case of simple sentences.

(3) Evaluation of Coverage
Figure 4 shows the results of our evaluation of the coverage of the SP-dictionary. The results show that the whole dictionary covered almost all input sentences. However, many cases of matches to semantically inappropriate patterns occurred, and the *semantic coverage* decreased to 78% when these were eliminated.

(4) Semantic Coverage
The applicable range of the patterns is *level* smaller in the order of *word, phrase* and *clause level*. Accordingly, for an input sentence that matches pat-

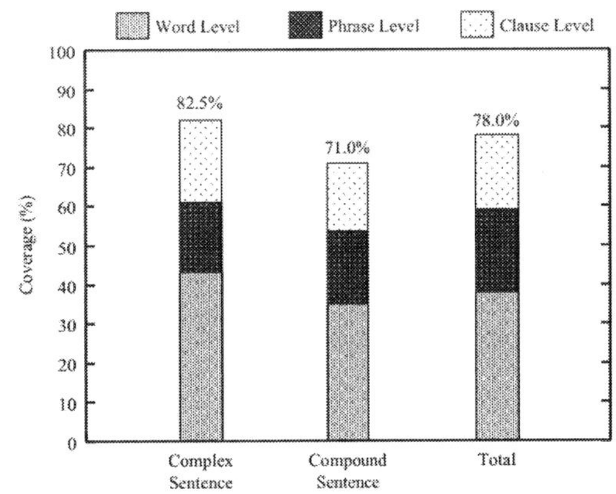

Figure 5: *Semantic Coverage* by 3 Level Patterns

terns on multiple levels, to select and use the most semantically appropriate pattern based on this sequence is probably preferable.

Figure 5 shows the ratio of patterns that are used when they are selected based on this sequence. As this figure shows, overall *semantic coverage* is considered to be high enough for practical use. The achievement of such a large-scale SP-dictionary is unprecedented in the world.

6 Summary

We proposed a *NL-model* and a pattern forming method based on the model. We also developed an SP-dictionary of basic Japanese compounds and complex sentences that contains 227,000 pattern pairs.

The important aspects of NL-model is in that this model provides the standards for determining the structural meaning units and granularity needed for meaning analysis.

According to our evaluation, the ratios of C-constituents that could be generalized by variables were 74% for independent words and 24% for phrases, while that for clauses was only 15%. This means that in Japanese to English MT, high quality translations for compound and complex sentences as found in a parallel corpus cannot be obtained with methods based on *Compositional Semantics*. We also found that the *syntactic coverage* of the SP-dictionary was 98%, and the *semantic coverage* was 78%. These coverages are considered to be high enough for practical use.

The SP-dictionary is aimed at the translation of N-expressions. For C-expressions, conventional MT methods can be applied, so we expect that translation quality will be substantially improved by incorporating this dictionary into conventional MT systems

The patterns can be used as a mesh for scooping up the entire meaning of expressions. We also expect that they will be used for semantic analysis in a wide range of applications other than MT.

Acknowledgements

This study was performed with the support of the Core Research for Evolutional Science and Technology (CREST) program of the Japan Science and Technology Agency (JST). Our sincere thanks go out to everyone concerned and to all the research group members who cooperated with this study.

References

Arita, Jun. 1987. *Lecture on German Language*, volume II. Nankodo Publisher.

Brown, P. F., R. John, S. D. Pietra, F. Jelinek, J. D. Lfferty, R. L Mercar, and P. S. Roossin. 1990. A statistical approach to machine translation. *Computational Linguistics*, 16(2):79–85.

Brown, R. D. 1999. Adding linguistic knowledge to a lexical example-based translation system. In *TMI 99*:22–32.

Fillmore, C. 1988. The mechanics of construction grammar. *Berkeley Linguistics Society*, 14:35–55.

Ikehara, Satoru, Masahiro Miyazaki, Satoshi Shirai, Akio Yokoo, Hiromi Nakaiwa, Kentaro Ogura, Yoshifumi Ooyama, and Yoshihiko Hayashi. 1997. *A-Japanese-Lexicon*. Iwanami Book Store.

Ikehara, Satoru. 2003. Concepts represented by linguistic expressions and translation. *IEICE-SIG-TL*, TL2003-25:7–12.

Jung, H., S. Yuh, T. Kim, and S. Park. 1999. A pattern-based approach using compound unit recognition and its hybridization with rule-based translation. *Computational Intelligence*, 15(2):114–127.

Kanadechi, Masato, Masato Tokuhisa, Junichi Murakami, and Satoru Ikehara. 2003. Translation quality evaluations of verbs and nouns by valency pattern dictionary. *ISPGJ-SIG-NL*, 2003-NL-153:119–124.

Langacker, R. W. 1987. *Foundation of Cognitive Grammar*. Stanford University Press.

Nagao, Makoto. 1984. A framework of a mechanical translation between japanese and english by analogy principle. In Eithorn, A. and R. Barneji, editors, *Artifi cial and Human Intelligence*:173–180. North-Holland.

Nagao, Makoto. 1996. *Natural Language Processing*. Iwanami Book Store.

Sato, Satoshi. 1992. An example based translation and system. In *COLING-91*:1259–1263.

Shirai, Satoshi, Satoru Ikehara, Akio Yokoo, and Hiroko Inoue. 1995. The quantity of valency pattern pairs required for Japanese to English MT and their compilation. In *NLPRS'95*, volume 1:443–448.

Uchino, Hajime, Satoshi Shirai, Akio Yokoo, Yoshifumi Ooyama, and Osamu Furuse. 2001. Japanese to english machine translation system for news flash - alt-flash. *IEICE Transaction*, J84-D-II(6):1168–117.

Vogel, S., Y. Zhang, F. Huang, A. Tribble, A. Venugopal, B. Zhao, and A. Waibel. 2003. The cmu statistical machine translation system. In *MT Summit IX*:402–409.

Japanese Dependency Parsing Using a Tournament Model

Masakazu Iwatate and **Masayuki Asahara** and **Yuji Matsumoto**
Nara Institute of Science and Technology, Japan
8916-5, Takayama, Ikoma, Nara, Japan, 630-0192
{masakazu-i, masayu-a, matsu}@is.naist.jp

Abstract

In Japanese dependency parsing, Kudo's relative preference-based method (Kudo and Matsumoto, 2005) outperforms both deterministic and probabilistic CKY-based parsing methods. In Kudo's method, for each dependent word (or chunk) a log-linear model estimates relative preference of all other candidate words (or chunks) for being as its head. This cannot be considered in the deterministic parsing methods. We propose an algorithm based on a tournament model, in which the relative preferences are directly modeled by one-on-one games in a step-ladder tournament. In an evaluation experiment with *Kyoto Text Corpus Version 4.0*, the proposed method outperforms previous approaches, including the relative preference-based method.

1 Introduction

The shared tasks of multi-lingual dependency parsing took place at CoNLL-2006 (Buchholz and Marsi, 2006) and CoNLL-2007 (Nivre et al., 2007). Many language-independent parsing algorithms were proposed there. The algorithms need to adapt to various dependency structure constraints according to target languages: projective vs. non-projective, head-initial vs. head-final, and single-rooted vs. multi-rooted. Eisner (1996) proposed a CKY-like $O(n^3)$ algorithm. Yamada and Matsumoto (2003) proposed a shift-reduce-like $O(n^2)$ deterministic algorithm. Nivre et al. (2003; 2004) also proposed a shift-reduce-like

©2008. Licensed under the *Creative Commons Attribution-Noncommercial-Share Alike 3.0 Unported* license (http://creativecommons.org/licenses/by-nc-sa/3.0/). Some rights reserved.

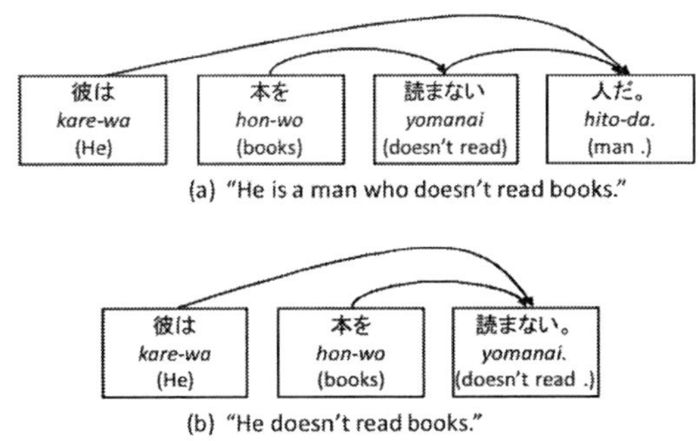

Figure 1: Examples of Japanese sentences.

$O(n)$ deterministic algorithm for projective languages. The model is enhanced for non-projective languages by Nivre and Nilsson (2005). McDonald et al. (2005) proposed a method based on search of maximum spanning trees employing the Chu-Liu-Edmonds algorithm (hereafter "**CLE algorithm**") (Chu and Liu, 1965; Edmonds, 1967). Most Japanese dependency parsers are based on *bunsetsu units*, which are similar concept to English base phrases. The constraints in Japanese dependency structure are stronger than those in other languages. Japanese dependency structures have the following constraints: head-final, single-head, single-rooted, connected, acyclic and projective. Figure 1 shows examples of Japanese sentences and their dependency structures. Each box represents a *bunsetsu*. A dependency relation is represented by an edge from a dependent to its head. Though sentence (a) is similar to sentence (b), the syntactic structures of these two are different, especially because "*kare-wa*" directly depends on "*yomanai*" in (b) but not in (a).

In dependency parsing of Japanese, deterministic algorithms outperform probabilistic CKY methods. Kudo and Matsumoto (2002) applied the cascaded chunking algorithm (hereafter "**CC algorithm**") to Japanese dependency parsing. Yamada's method (Yamada and Matsumoto, 2003) employed a similar algorithm. Sassano (2004) proposed a linear-order shift-reduce-like algorithm (hereafter "**SR algorithm**"), which is similar to Nivre's algorithm (Nivre, 2003). These deterministic algorithms are biased to select nearer candidate heads since they examine the candidates sequentially, and once they find a plausible one they never consider further candidates.

We experimented the CLE algorithm with Japanese dependency parsing, and found that the CLE algorithm is comparable to or in some cases poorer than the deterministic algorithms in our experiments. Actually, the CLE algorithm is not suitable for some of the constraints in Japanese dependency structures: head-final and projective. First, head-final means that dependency relation always goes from left to right. Second, since the CLE algorithm may produce non-projective dependency trees, we need to conduct projectivity check in the algorithm.

Kudo and Matsumoto (2005) proposed a relative preference-based method (hereafter "**relative preference method**"). They defined the parsing algorithm as series of selection steps of the most likely head for each *bunsetsu* out of all candidates. The method has so far achieved the highest accuracy in the experiments with *Kyoto Text Corpus Version 3.0* data [1], since other deterministic methods do not consider relative preference among candidate heads but solely consider whether the focused-on pair of *bunsetsu's* is in a dependency relation or not.

We propose a model that takes a *bunsetsu* and two candidate heads into consideration and selects the better candidate head out of those two. This step is repeated in a step ladder tournament to get the best candidate head (hereafter we call this model as a "**tournament model**"). The tournament model was first introduced by Iida et al. (2003) for coreference resolution. We applied this model to selecting the most plausible candidate head for each *bunsetsu* except for the sentence final one.

Section 2 describes the tournament model comparing with previous research. Section 3 describes how the tournament model is applied to Japanese dependency parsing. Section 4 shows the results of evaluation experiments. Section 5 shows our current and future work, and Section 6 gives conclusions of this research.

[1]Note: Sassano's SR algorithm is the highest by experiment with the smaller data *Kyoto Text Corpus Version 2.0* Relative preference method and SR algorithm are not compared directly with the same data.

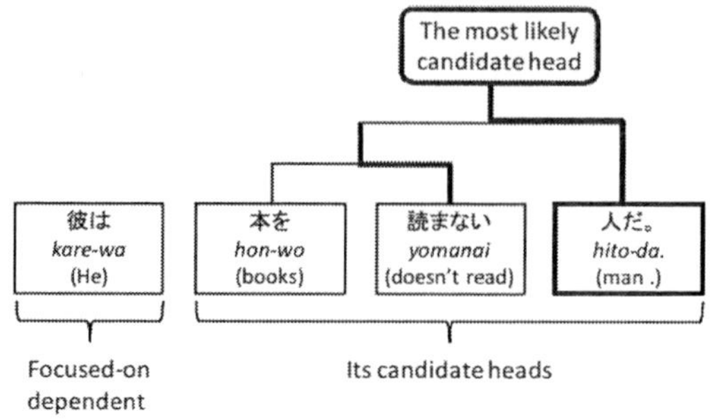

Figure 2: Example of a tournament.

2 Tournament Model

The tournament model was first introduced by Iida et al. (2003) for coreference resolution. The model chooses the most likely candidate in a step-ladder tournament, that is a sequence of one-on-one games between candidate referents for a given anaphoric expression. In each game, the winner is chosen by a binary classifier such as SVMs.

We applied the tournament model to Japanese dependency parsing taking into consideration Japanese constraints. The projective constraint is easily met. When selecting candidate heads for the focused-on dependent, we only consider those candidates that introduce no crossing dependency.

Figure 2 illustrates a tournament. The focused-on dependent *bunsetsu* is "*kare-wa*", and the candidate heads are the three *bunsetsu's* on the right-hand side: "*hon-wo*", "*yomanai*" and "*hito-da*". The first game is "*hon-wo*" vs. "*yomanai*". Then the next game is the winner of the first game vs. "*hito-da*". The winner of the second game (i.e., "*hito-da*") is chosen as the most likely candidate of the dependent, "*kare-wa*".

In the tournament model, the most likely head of a given bunsetsu is determined by a series of one-on-one games in a tournament. Below, we present the advantages of the tournament model by comparison with the previous methods.

2.1 Scope of Feature Views

The CC algorithm and SR algorithm consider only a pair of *bunsetsu's* – a dependent and its candidate head – in the parsing action determination (hereafter "**2-tuple model**"). The same 2-tuple may or may not have a dependency relation when they appear in different context. For example, both (a) and (b) in Figure 1 include the two *bunsetsu's*, "*kare-wa*" and "*yomanai*"; in (b) they have a dependency relation, but not in (a). The 2-tuple models and relative preference method cannot discriminate between these two patterns without considering contextual features [2]. The tournament model can be regarded as a "**3-tuple model**," which considers three *bunsetsu's* – a dependent and two candidate heads. The discriminative performance of the 3-tuple model is greater than the 2-tuple models, since it directly compares two candidate heads and selects the one that is more plausible than the other candidate. Consider Figure 1 again. In (a), "*kare-wa*" does not depend on "*yomanai*" because there is another *bunsetsu* "*hito-da*" which is a more plausible head. 2-tuple models may use this information as a contextual feature, but the effect is indirect. On the other hand, the tournament model directly compares these candidates and always selects the better one. The situation becomes crucial when the true head appears outside of the context window of the current candidate. 2-tuple models have to select the head without consulting such information. The advantage of the tournament model is its capability of deferring the decision by always keeping the current best candidate head. On the other hand, a disadvantage of the tournament model is its space and time complexity. The size of features is larger since they come from three *bunsetsu's*. The size of training instances is also larger.

2.2 Relative Position in a Sentence

We name the two candidate heads in the 3-tuple model as "the nearer candidate head" and "the farther candidate head." The dependent, the nearer candidate head and the farther candidate head appear in this order in Japanese sentences. The order defines the relative position of the contextual features. The distance between the dependent and a candidate head is another feature to represent the relative position. In previous research, the distance has been represented by feature buckets, such as 1, 2-5, or 6+. While for some dependents and their heads whether the distance is 1 or not is important, absolute distance is not so important since Japanese is a free-order language. Relative positions are more informative since some dependents tend to appear closer to other dependents, such as objects that tend to appear closer to predicates compared with other complements. The tournament model represents both the distance and relative position as features.

The deterministic algorithms are biased to select nearer candidate heads. As most dependent and head pairs appear within a close window, this tendency does not cause many errors; deterministic algorithms are weak at finding correct heads that appear in a long distance as pointed out in Kudo and Matsumoto (2005).

2.3 Relative Preferences

What the dependency parsers try to learn is relative preference of *bunsetsu* dependency, i.e., how a dependent selects its head among others. The relative preference method (Kudo and Matsumoto, 2005) learns the relative preferences among the candidate heads by a discriminative framework. The relative preferences are learned with the log-linear model so as to give larger probability to the correct dependent-head pair over any other candidates. McDonald's method (2005) with the CLE algorithm learns the relative preferences by a perceptron algorithm – MIRA (Crammer and Singer, 2003), so that the correct dependent-head link receives a higher score. The tournament model learns which candidate is more likely to be the head between two candidates in a one-on-one game in a tournament. Therefore, all of those parsing algorithms try to learn the way to give the highest preference to the correct dependent-head pair among all possibilities though in different settings.

While the relative preference method and McDonald's method consider all candidate heads independently in a discriminative model, the tournament model evaluates which candidate is more likely to be the head between the latest winner and the new candidate. The latest winner has already defeated all of the preceding candidates. If the new candidate beats the latest winner, it becomes the new winner, meaning that it is the most preferred candidate among others so far considered. Through this way of comparison with the runner-up candidates, the tournament model uses richer information in learning relative preferences than the models in which all candidates are independently considered.

[2] Contextual features are features neither in the dependent nor in the candidate head(s).

```
// N: # of bunsetsu's in input sentence
// true_head[j]: bunsetsu j's head at
//                    training data
// gen(j,i1,i2,LEFT): generate
//   an example where bunsetsu j is
//   dependent of i1
// gen(j,i1,i2,RIGHT): generate
//   an example where bunsetsu j is
//   dependent of i2

for j = 1 to N-1 do
  h = true_head[j];
  for i = j+1 to h-1 do
            gen(j,i,h,RIGHT);
  for i = h+1 to N do
            gen(j,h,i,LEFT);
end-for;
```

Figure 3: Pseudo code of training example generation procedure.

```
// N: # of bunsetsu's in
//        input sentence
// head[]: (analyzed-) head of bunsetsu
// classify(j,i1,i2): ask SVM
//   which candidate  (i1 or i2) is
//   more likely for head of j.
//   return LEFT if i1 wins.
//   return RIGHT if i2 wins.

head[] = {2,3,...,N-1,N,EOS};
for j = N-1 downto 1 do
  h = j+1;
  i = head[h];
  while i != EOS do
    if classify(j,h,i)==RIGHT
         then h = i;
    i = head[i];
  end-while;
  head[j] = h;
end-for;
```

Figure 4: Pseudo code of parsing algorithm.

3 Proposed Algorithm

3.1 Training Example Generation Algorithm

As shown in Figure 3, for each dependent, we generate pairs of the correct head and all other candidate heads. On the example generation, the procedure does not take into account the projective constraint; all *bunsetsu's* on the right-hand side of the focused-on dependent are candidate heads.

Table 1 shows all examples generated from two sentences shown in Figure 1. 2-tuple models generate training examples formed as (dependent, candidate). So, from the sentences of Figure 1, it generates opposite classes to the pair (*kare-wa*, *hito-da*). On the other hand, the examples generated by the tournament model do not contain such inconsistency.

3.2 Parsing Algorithm

The tournament model has quite wide freeness in the parsing steps. We introduce one of the tournament algorithms, in which the dependents are picked from right to left; and the games of the tournament are performed from left to right. This parsing algorithm takes into account the projective and head-final constraints.

This algorithm is shown in Figure 4. The overall parsing process moves from right to left. On selecting the head for a dependent all of the *bunsetsu*'s to the right of the dependent have already been decided. In Figure 4, the array "head" stores the parsed results and ensures that only non-crossing candidate heads are taken into consideration.

Note that the structure of the tournament has little effect on the results (< 0.1) in our preliminary experiments. We tried 2×2 options: the dependents are picked from right to left or from left to right; and the games of the tournament are performed from right to left or from left to right. We choose the most natural combination for Japanese dependency parsing, which is easy to implement.

4 Experiment

4.1 Settings

We implemented the tournament model, the CC algorithm (Kudo and Matsumoto, 2002), SR algorithm (Sassano, 2004) and CLE algorithm (McDonald et al., 2005) with SVM classifiers. We evaluated dependency accuracy and sentence accuracy using *Kyoto Text Corpus Version 4.0*, which is composed by newspaper articles. Dependency accuracy is the percentage of correct dependencies out of all dependency relations. Sentence accuracy is the percentage of sentences in which all dependencies are determined correctly. Dependency accuracy is calculated excluding the rightmost *bunsetsu* of each sentence. [3] Sentences that consist of one *bunsetsu* are not used in our experiments.

We use January 1st to 8th (7,587 sentences) for the training data. We use January 9th (1,213 sentences), 10th (1,479 sentences) and 15th (1,179 sentences) for the test data. We use TinySVM [4] as a binary classifier. Cubic polynomial kernel is

[3] Most research such as Kudo's (2005) uses this criteria.

[4] http://chasen.org/~taku/software/TinySVM/

Sentence	Focused-on dependent	Left(Nearer) candidate	Right(Farther) candidate	Class label
(a)	*kare-wa*	*hon-wo*	*hito-da.*	RIGHT
(a)	*kare-wa*	*yomanai*	*hito-da.*	RIGHT
(a)	*hon-wo*	*yomanai*	*hito-da.*	LEFT
(b)	*kare-wa*	*hon-wo*	*yomanai.*	RIGHT

Table 1: Generated examples from sentences in Figure 1.

used for the kernel function. Cost of constraint violation is 1.0. These SVM settings are the same as previous research (Kudo and Matsumoto, 2002; Sassano, 2004). All experiments were performed on Dual Core Xeon 3GHz x 2 Linux machines.

4.2 Features

Here we describe features used in our experiments. Note that for the tournament model, features corresponding to candidates are created for each of the nearer and farther candidates. We define the *information* of a word as the following features: lexical forms, coarse-grained POS tags, full POS tags and inflected forms. We also define the *information* of a *bunsetsu* as word *information* for each of *syuji* and *gokei*. *Syuji* is the head content word of the *bunsetsu*, defined as the rightmost content word. *Gokei* is the representative function word of the *bunsetsu*, defined as the rightmost functional word.

Existence of punctuations or brackets, whether the *bunsetsu* is the first bunsetsu in the sentence, and whether it is the final bunsetsu in the sentence are also members of *information* of a *bunsetsu*.

Standard features are the following: *Information* of the dependent and the candidate heads, distance between the dependent and the candidate heads (1, 2-5 or 6+ *bunsetsu's*), all punctuations, brackets and all particles between the dependent and the candidate heads.

Additional features are the following: All case particles in the dependent and the candidate heads, *information* of the leftmost word in the candidate heads, and the lexical form of the neighboring *bunsetsu* to the right of the candidate heads.

Case particle features are the following: All case particles appearing in the candidates' dependent. These features are intended to take into consideration the correlation between the case particles in the dependent of a head. When the head is a verb, it has a similar effect of learning case frame information.

Standard and additional features are introduced by Sassano (2004). The case particle feature is newly introduced in this paper. Features corresponding to the already-determined dependency relation are called *dynamic* features, and the other contextual features are called *static* features. Standard and additional features are static features, and case particle features are dynamic features. Whether a dynamic feature is available for a parsing algorithm depends on the parsing order of the algorithm.

4.3 Parsing Accuracy

The parsing accuracies of our model and previous models are summarized in Table 2. Note that, since the CLE algorithm is non-deterministic and dynamic features are not available for this algorithm, we use only a *standard and additional* feature set instead of an *all* feature set. By McNemar test ($p < 0.01$) on the dependency accuracy, the tournament model significantly outperforms most of other methods except for the SR algorithm on January 10th data with all features ($p = 0.083$) and the CC algorithm on January 10th data with all features ($p = 0.099$). The difference between the tournament models with all features and with the standard feature only is significant except for on January 9th data ($p = 0.25$).

The highest dependency accuracy reported for January 9th of *Kyoto Text Corpus Version 2.0* is 89.56% by Sassano(2004)'s SR algorithm. [5]

Since we don't have the outputs of Sassano's experiments, we cannot do a McNemar test between the tournament model and Sassano's results. Our model outperforms Sassano's results by the dependency accuracy, but the difference between these two is not significant by prop test ($p = 0.097$).

When we add the additional and case particle features, the improvement of our model is less than that of other algorithms. This is interpreted that our model can consider richer contextual informa-

[5]This accuracy in Sassano (2004) is not for *Kyoto Text Corpus Version 4.0* but *Version 2.0* The feature set of Sassano's experiment is also different from our experiment.

Method	Features	Jan. 9th	Jan.10th	Jan. 15th
Tournament	Standard feature only	89.89/49.63	89.63/48.34	89.40/49.70
	All features	**90.09/49.71**	**90.11/49.02**	**90.35/52.59**
SR algorithm	Standard feature only	88.18/45.92	88.80/44.76	88.03/47.24
(Sassano, 2004)	All features	89.22/47.90	89.79/47.87	89.55/49.79
CC algorithm	Standard feature only	88.17/45.92	88.80/44.76	88.00/47.24
(Kudo and Matsumoto, 2002)	All features	89.22/47.90	89.80/47.94	89.53/49.79
CLE algorithm	Standard feature only	88.64/45.34	88.16/43.14	88.07/45.21
(McDonald et al., 2005)	Standard and Additional	89.21/46.83	89.05/45.03	88.90/48.43

Table 2: Dependency and sentence accuracy [%] using 7,587 sentences as training data.

tion within the algorithm itself than other models.

This result also shows that the accuracies of the SR algorithm and CC algorithm are comparable when using the same features. However, this does not mean that their substantial power is comparable because the parsing order limits the available dynamic features.

4.4 Parsing Speed

Parsing time and the size of the training examples are shown in Table 3. All features were used. The column "# Step" represents the number of SVM classification steps in parsing all the test data. Time complexity of the tournament model and CC algorithm are $O(n^2)$ and that of the SR algorithm is $O(n)$. The tournament model needs 1.7 times more SVM classification steps and is 4 times slower than the SR algorithm. The reason for this difference in steps (x1.7) and time (x4) is the number of training examples and features in the SVM classification.

4.5 Comparison to Relative Preference Method

We performed another experiment under the same settings as Kudo's (2005) to compare the tournament model and relative preference method. The corpus is *Kyoto Text Corpus Version 3.0* since Kudo and Matsumoto (2005) used this corpus. Training data is articles from January 1st to 11th and editorials from January to August (24,263 sentences). Test data is articles from January 14th to 17th and editorials from October to December (9,287 sentences). We did not perform parameter engineering by development data, although Kudo and Matsumoto (2005) performed it. The criteria for dependency accuracy are the same as the experiments above. However, the criteria for sentence accuracy in this section include all sentences, even if the length is one as Kudo and Matsumoto (2005) did.

The results are shown in Table 4. Note that Kudo and Matsumoto (2005) and our feature sets are different. Only the CC Algorithm is tested with both feature sets. Our feature set looks better than Kudo's. By McNemar test ($p < 0.01$) on the dependency accuracy, the tournament model outperforms both the SR and CC algorithms significantly. Since we don't have the outputs of relative preference methods, we cannot do a McNemar test between the tournament model and the relative preference methods. By prop test ($p < 0.01$) on the dependency accuracy, our model significantly outperforms the relative preference method of Kudo and Matsumoto (2005). Though our model outperforms the "combination" model of Kudo and Matsumoto (2005) by the dependency accuracy, the difference between these two is not significant by prop test ($p = 0.014$). [6]

Note that, a log-linear model is used in Kudo's experiment. The log-linear model has shorter training time than SVM. The log-linear model requires feature combination engineering by hand, while SVMs automatically consider the feature combination by the use of polynomial kernels.

5 Discussion and Future Work

In our error analysis, many errors are observed in coordination structures. Sassano (2004) reported that introduction of features of coordinated *bun-*

[6] The "combination" model is the combination of the CC algorithm and relative preference method. In Kudo's experiment, whereas the relative preference method outperforms the CC algorithm for long-distance relations, it is reversed for short-distance relations. They determined the optimal combination (the threshold set at *bunsetsu* length 3) using the development set. In our experiment, the tournament model outperforms the CC and SR algorithms for relations of all lengths. Therefore, the tournament model doesn't need such ad hoc combination.

Method	# Step	Time[s]	# Example	# Feature
Tournament	26396	371	374579	56165
SR algorithm (Sassano, 2004)	15641	80	94669	37183
CC algorithm (Kudo and Matsumoto, 2002)	18922	99	112759	37183

Table 3: Parsing time and the size of the training examples.

Method	Features	Dep. Acc.	Sentence Acc.
Tournament	All	**91.96**	**57.44**
SR algorithm (Sassano, 2004)	All	91.48	55.67
CC algorithm (Kudo and Matsumoto, 2002)	All	91.47	55.65
Combination – CC and Relative preference	Kudo's (2005)	91.66	56.30
Relative preference (Kudo and Matsumoto, 2005)	Kudo's (2005)	91.37	56.00
CC algorithm (Kudo and Matsumoto, 2002)	Kudo's (2005)	91.23	55.59

Table 4: Dependency and sentence accuracy [%] using 24,263 sentences as training data with all features: comparison with Kudo(2005)'s experiments.

setsu improves accuracy. In *Kyoto Text Corpus Version 4.0*, coordination and apposition are annotated with different types of dependency relation. We did not use this information in parsing. A simple extension is to include those dependency types. Another extension is to employ a coordination analyzer as a separate process as proposed by Shimbo and Hara (2007).

Incorporating co-occurrence information will also improve the parsing accuracy. One usage of such information is verb-noun co-occurrence information that would represent selectional preference for case-frame information. Abekawa and Okumura (2006) proposed a reranking method of k-best dependency analyzer outputs using co-occurrence information. We have already developed a method to output k-best dependency trees. One of our future works is to test the reranking method using co-occurrence information on the k-best dependency trees.

Multilingual parsing is another goal. Japanese is a strict head-final language. However, most languages do not have such constraint. A different parsing algorithm should be employed for other less constrained languages so as to relax this constraint. A simple solution is to introduce a discrimination model according to whether the head is on the left-hand-side or on the right-hand-side of a dependent. Existence of projective constraint does not matter for the tournament model. The tournament model can be extended to relax the projective constraint. The preliminary results for English are shown in our CoNLL Shared Task 2008 report (Watanabe et al., 2008). The unlabeled syntactic dependency accuracy of 90.73% for WSJ data shows that the model is also effective in other (not strictly head final, non-projective) languages. In parsing word sequences, $O(n^2)$ time complexity becomes a serious problem compared to parsing *bunsetsu* sequences. Since a *bunsetsu* is a base phrase in Japanese, the number of *bunsetsu's* is much less than the number of words. One solution is to perform base phrase chunking in advance and to apply dependency parsing on the base phrase sequences.

A reviewer pointed out similarities between our model and RankSVM. RankSVM compares pairs of elements to find out relative ordering between elements. Our tournament model is a special case where two elements are compared, but with a specific viewpoint of a focused dependent.

6 Conclusions

We proposed a Japanese dependency parsing algorithm using the tournament model. The tournament model is a 3-tuple *bunsetsu* model and improves discriminative performance of selecting correct head compared with the conventional 2-tuple models. The most likely candidate head is selected by one-on-one games in the step-ladder tournament. The proposed model considers the relative position between the nearer and farther candidates. The model also considers all candidate heads, which are not considered in deterministic parsing algorithms. The tournament model is robust for the free-order language. The accuracy of our model significantly outperforms that of the previous methods in most experiment settings. Even though the problem of parsing speed remains, our research showed that considering two or more candidate heads simultaneously can achieve more accurate parsing.

References

Abekawa, Takeshi and Manabu Okumura. 2006. Japanese Dependency Parsing Using Co-occurrence Information and a Combination of Case Elements. In *Proceedings of the 21st International Conference on Computational Linguistics and 44th Annual Meeting of the Association for Computational Linguistics (COLING-ACL 2006)*, pages 833–840.

Buchholz, Sabine and Erwin Marsi. 2006. CoNLL-X Shared Task on Multilingual Dependency Parsing. In *CoNLL-2006: Proceedings of the Tenth Conference on Computational Natural Language Learning*, pages 149–164.

Chu, Yoeng-Jin and Tseng-Hong Liu. 1965. On the shortest arborescence of a directed graph. *Science Sinica*, 14:1396–1400.

Crammer, Koby and Yoram Singer. 2003. Ultraconservative Online Algorithms for Multiclass Problems. *Journal of Machine Learning Research*, 3:951–991.

Edmonds, Jack. 1967. Optimum branchings. *Journal of Research of the Natural Bureau of Standards*, 71B:233–240.

Eisner, Jason M. 1996. Three New Probabilistic Models for Dependency Parsing: An Exploration. In *COLING-96: Proceedings of the 16th Conference on Computational Linguistics - Volume 1*, pages 340–345.

Iida, Ryu, Kentaro Inui, Hiroya Takamura, and Yuji Matsumoto. 2003. Incorporating Contextual Cues in Trainable Models for Coreference Resolution. In *EACL Workshop 'The Computational Treatment of Anaphora'*.

Kudo, Taku and Yuji Matsumoto. 2002. Japanese Dependency Analysis Using Cascaded Chunking. In *CoNLL-2002: Proceedings of the Sixth Conference on Computational Language Learning*, pages 1–7.

Kudo, Taku and Yuji Matsumoto. 2005. Japanese Dependency Parsing Using Relative Preference of Dependency (in Japanese). *Information Processing Society of Japan, Journal*, 46(4):1082–1092.

McDonald, Ryan, Koby Crammer, and Fernando Pereira. 2005. Online Large-Margin Training of Dependency Parsers. In *ACL-2005: Proceedings of 43rd Annual Meeting of the Association for Computational Linguistics*, pages 523–530.

Nivre, Joakim and Jens Nilsson. 2005. Psuedo-Projective Dependency Parsing. In *ACL-2005: Proceedings of 43rd Annual Meeting of the Association for Computational Linguistics*, pages 99–106.

Nivre, Joakim and Mario Scholz. 2004. Deterministic Dependency Parsing of English Text. In *COLING-2004: Proceedings of the 20th International Conference on Computational Linguistics*, pages 64–70.

Nivre, Joakim, Johan Hall, Sandra Kübler, Ryan McDonald, Jens Nilsson, Sebastian Riedel, and Deniz Yuret. 2007. The CoNLL 2007 Shared Task on Dependency Parsing. In *CoNLL-2007: Proceedings of the CoNLL Shared Task Session of EMNLP-CoNLL-2007*, pages 915–932.

Nivre, Joakim. 2003. An Efficient Algorithm for Projective Dependency Parsing. In *IWPT-2003: 8th International Workshop on Parsing Technology*, pages 149–160.

Sassano, Manabu. 2004. Linear-Time Dependency Analysis for Japanese. In *COLING-2004: Proceedings of the 20th International Conference on Computational Linguistics*, pages 8–14.

Shimbo, Masashi and Kazuo Hara. 2007. A Discriminative Learning Model for Coordinate Conjunctions. In *Proceedings of the 2007 Joint Conference on Empirical Methods in Natural Language Processing and Computational Natural Language Learning (EMNLP-CoNLL)*, pages 610–619.

Watanabe, Yotaro, Masakazu Iwatate, Masayuki Asahara, and Yuji Matsumoto. 2008. A Pipeline Approach for Syntactic and Semantic Dependency Parsing. In *Proceedings of the Twelfth Conference on Computational Natural Language Learning (To Appear)*.

Yamada, Hiroyasu and Yuji Matsumoto. 2003. Statistical Dependency Analysis with Support Vector Machines. In *IWPT-2003: 8th International Workshop on Parsing Technology*, pages 195–206.

Contents Modelling of Neo-Sumerian Ur III Economic Text Corpus

Wojciech Jaworski
Institute of Informatics
Warsaw University
Banacha 2, 02-097 Warsaw, Poland
wjaworski@mimuw.edu.pl

Abstract

This paper describes a system for processing economic documents written in the ancient Sumerian language. The system is application-oriented and takes advantage of the simplicity of ancient economy. We have developed an ontology for a selected branch of economic activities. We translate the documents into a meaning representation language by means of a semantic grammar. The meaning representation language is constructed in a way that allows us to handle massive ambiguity caused by: the specifics of the Sumerian writing system (signs' polyvalence, lack of mid-word signs), our incomplete knowledge of the Sumerian language and frequent damages of documents. The system is augmented with the capability of processing documents whose parts describe concepts not included in the ontology and grammar. As an effect we obtain a structural description of the documents contents in the meaning representation language, ready to use in historical research.

1 Introduction

Sumerians lived from prehistoric times until late 3rd millennium BC in lower Mesopotamia (modern Iraq). Sumer was the first highly developed urban civilisation, which used cuneiform script. During the period of the 3rd dynasty of Ur (2100 BC-2000 BC), whose power extended as far as present Iraq and western Iran, the state introduced a centrally planned economy with an extensive bureaucratic apparatus.

Civil servants reported on clay tablets agriculture and factory production, lists of worker salaries, summaries of executed work, distribution of commodities, goods, animals etc., lists of sacrificed animals, travel diets and other economical information.

Archaeologists dug out about 100000 of tablets from that period (known also as the Neo-Sumerian period). The corpus of 44365 tablets (as of March 26, 2008) is available in electronic version in the database of Cuneiform Digital Library Initiative (CDLI, 2006), run by the University of California in Los Angeles and Max Planck Institute for the History of Science. Tablets are stored in the form of Latin transliteration, often accompanied by photographs or drawings (which are irrelevant for us).

Economic documents are an essential source of information about ancient Sumer. The corpus contains crucial information about economic, social and political history of the state, as well as its political system and administration structure. The sources of this type provide the most complete information about the daily life of those days. For more information about the economy of the Ur III kingdom see for example (Stepien, 1996; Sharlach, 2004; Steinkeller, 1987).

As more and more Neo-Sumerian economic documents were published, the problem arose of searching for documents relevant to the investigated topic, and the problem of representing the content of a large number of documents in a concise way.

As a solution to these problems we propose a knowledge base, that would assist in prosopographic (identification of Sumerian officials), his-

©2008. Licensed under the *Creative Commons Attribution-Noncommercial-Share Alike 3.0 Unported* license (http://creativecommons.org/licenses/by-nc-sa/3.0/). Some rights reserved.

Figure 1: An example of a transliterated cuneiform tablet from Ur III

`&P123831 = OIP 121, 101`	
`tablet`	
`obverse`	
`1. 1(disz) sila4 ur-mes ensi2`	*1 lamb Urmes governor*
`2. 1(disz)# sila4 da-da dumu lugal`	*1 lamb Dada son of king*
`3. 1(disz)# sila4 id-da-a`	*1 lamb Idda*
`reverse`	
`1. u4 2(u) 3(asz@t)-kam`	*Day 23*
`$ 1 line blank`	
`3. mu-DU`	*delivery*
`4. ab-ba-sa6-ga i3-dab5`	*Abbasaga received*
`5. iti sze-KIN-ku5`	*month sze-kin-ku5*
`6. mu en {d}inanna ba-hun`	*Year when high priest of goddess Innana was elevated to office*
`left`	
`1. 3(disz)`	*3*

torical and philological research. For our studies, we selected a subcorpus of 11891 documents concerning distribution of domestic animals.

The design of our system was determined by two factors: the characteristics of the underlying corpus and and the functionality needed by historians who are end-users of the system.

We developed an ontology for the selected subcorpus. It determins the structure of the knowledge base. It also defines the components of the meaning representation language, which we use for storing data in the knowledge base.

We translate the documents into the meaning representation language by means of a semantic grammar. The grammar has the strength equal to a regular language. Grammar symbols are equipped with semantic values that carry information included in the texts. Semantic values are generated during the parsing process by means of semantic attachments to grammar symbols.

The meaning representation language is constructed in a way that allows it to handle ambiguities caused by: the inherent ambiguity of the Sumerian writing system (signs' polyvalence, lack of mid-word signs), our incomplete knowledge of the Sumerian language and frequent damages of tablets.

The system is augmented with the capability of processing documents whose parts describe concepts not included in the ontology and grammar. We keep the ontology itself small (circa 30 concepts) because we include in it only concepts that are commonly found in documents. This approach is determined by the needs of the intended users: historians need a structural representation for typical information contained in the documents, which would provide insight into the structure and activity of Sumerian administration and analyse it by means of statistical methods; rare, untypical phrases are thoroughly examined and interpreted manually.

The paper is organised as follows: In Section 2 we describe the Neo-Sumerian Ur III Economic Text Corpus. In Section 3 we present the ontology for documents. In Sections 4, 5, 6 we define accordingly: the meaning representation language, grammar, representation semantic values of grammar symbols and semantic attachments. In Section 8 we show how to extract transaction descriptions from the documents. In Section 9 we present applications of the system. Section 10 draws conclusions.

2 Ur III text corpus

Sumerian writing system was like a rebus, without punctuation signs, also with large amount of polyvalential signs. According to the rule of polyvalence one sign could, depending on the context, be read differently. For example the `DU` sign meaning — a leg, could have also other translations like: `gin` — to go, `gub` — to stand straight, `tum2` — to bring, etc.

Phonetical values of signs are most often single syllables. Simple words are written by single ideograms equipped with phonetically written affixes. More complicated terms can be represented by combinations of multiple signs. Due to lack of mid-word signs and agglutinative character of the Sumerian language, it is hard to identify if we read a word or a phrase, and define its borders in the text. For more information about the Sumerian language see (Labat and Malbran-Labat, 1988).

The fact that administrative documents are written in bureaucratic language which is full of nota-

Figure 2: Ontology of Sumerian economic text corpus

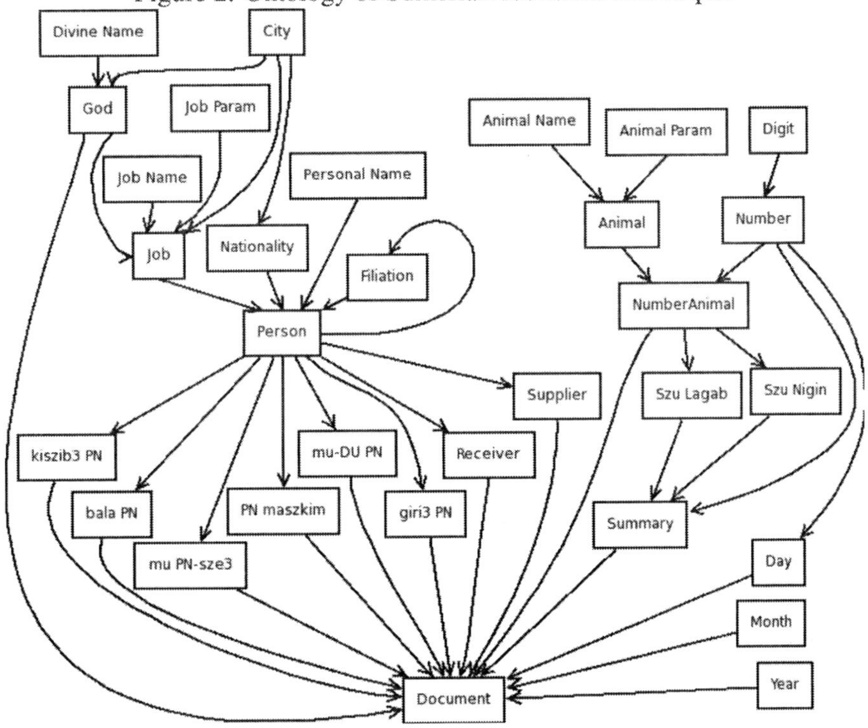

tion abbreviations, lacks most of grammatical affixes and does not have uniformed spelling for non-Sumerian words, makes the situation even more complicated.

Texts are often physically damaged. Damages can concern one or many following signs. Sometimes many following lines are illegible. In the transliterations damages are marked by special symbols or descriptions in English, German, French, etc., depending on translator's nationality.

Fig. 1 presents the contents of a typical Sumerian document. This documents reports the transfers of lambs from 3 people to `ab-ba-sa6-ga`, an official of the Ur III state. They took place in the 23th day of the month `sze-kin-ku5` in the year when the high priest of goddess Innana was elevated to office.

3 Ontology

As we mentioned above, we examine the subcorpus of documents concerning distribution of breeding animals. The distribution was organised in the form of transactions. During each transaction one **Person**, called **Supplier**, transfers a **Number** of animals to another Person, called **Receiver**. **Animal** description consists of information like: species, age, gender, fodder, etc. Person is described by means of his/her **Name**, **Filiation**, **Job** and/or **Nationality**. Apart from the Supplier and Receiver, other Persons might have assisted in the transaction:

giri3 PN Middleman between Supplier and and Receiver

mu-DU PN Person on whose account the transaction took place, Receiver is probably Mu Du's representative

mu PN-sze3 Person in whose name the Receiver or Supplier acted.

kiszib3 PN Person who sealed the document

PN maszkim Overseer of the transaction

bala PN Person who provides goods as royal tax.

The roles are named after the Sumerian phrases used to introduce them **PN** states for **Personal Name**), their meaning is still studied by sumerologists. One of applications of our research is to provide more facts on their meaning.

There are a few kinds of **Summaries** of various animal types in the documents, denoted by concepts: **Szu Lagab**, **Szu Nigin** as well as single **Number**. Dates of transactions are also provided.

Figure 3: The semantics of text. Observe the use of domain knowledge and the representation of ambiguous semantics for year name.

$$\begin{array}{l}
\texttt{Number}(q_1, 1) \wedge \texttt{Animal}(a_1, \texttt{sila4}) \wedge \texttt{Name}(n_1, \texttt{ur-mes}) \wedge \texttt{Job}(j_1, \texttt{ensi2}) \wedge \\
\quad \wedge \texttt{Person}(m_1, n_1, j_1) \wedge \texttt{Supplier}(s_1, m_1) \wedge \texttt{NumberAnimalName}(nam_1, q_1, a_1, s_1) \wedge \\
\wedge \texttt{Number}(q_2, 1) \wedge \texttt{Animal}(a_2, \texttt{sila4}) \wedge \texttt{Name}(n_2, \texttt{da-da}) \wedge \texttt{Job}(j_2, \texttt{lugal}) \wedge \\
\quad \wedge \texttt{Person}(m_2, j_2) \wedge \texttt{Filiation}(f_1, \texttt{dumu}, m_2) \wedge \texttt{Person}(m_3, n_2, f_1) \wedge \texttt{Supplier}(s_2, m_3) \wedge \texttt{NumberAnimalName}(nam_2, q_2, a_2, s_2) \wedge \\
\wedge \texttt{Number}(q_3, 1) \wedge \texttt{Animal}(a_3, \texttt{sila4}) \wedge \texttt{Name}(n_3, \text{id-da-a}) \wedge \texttt{Person}(m_4, n_3) \wedge \texttt{Supplier}(s_3, m_4) \wedge \texttt{NumberAnimalName}(nam_3, q_3, a_3, s_3) \wedge \\
\wedge \texttt{NumberAnimalNamelist}(l_1, nam_1, nam_2, nam_3) \wedge \\
\wedge \texttt{Day}(d_1, 23) \wedge \\
\wedge \texttt{Delivery}(del_1) \wedge \\
\wedge \texttt{Name}(n_4, \texttt{ab-ba-sa6-ga}) \wedge \texttt{Person}(m_5, n_4) \wedge \texttt{Receiver}(r_1, m_5) \wedge \\
\wedge \texttt{Month}(month_1, 12) \wedge \\
\wedge \big(\texttt{Year}(y_1, \texttt{AS5}) \vee \texttt{Year}(y_1, \texttt{IS4})\big) \wedge \\
\wedge \texttt{Number}(q_4, 3) \wedge \texttt{Summary}(s_1, q_4) \wedge \\
\wedge \texttt{Document}(t_1, l_1, d_1, del_1, r_1, m_1, y_1)
\end{array}$$

The dependencies between concepts have meronymical nature. They witness the fact that one object is a part, property, attribute or description of another one. Fig. 2 presents the diagram of dependencies between concepts.

Animals, roles and dates are transaction attributes. Yet, often one document describes many transactions and their common attribute values are written only once in the document. As a result, transactions are entangled and the individual transaction do not appear explicitly until the very last phase of processing.

4 Meaning representation language

The meaning representation language represents concepts included in the data and dependencies between them. Syntax of the language is defined as follows: We have a set of constants and a set of predicate names. Constants play the role of labels for entities described in the data. Predicates consist of lists of one or more arguments. Number of arguments for a given predicate is not fixed. Predicates represent relations on finite sequences of entities. Names of most predicates are identical to the names of the related ontological concepts. The first argument of a predicate is an object which belongs to the ontological concept denoted by predicate name.

Predicates are atomic formulas. Compound formulas are composed of one or more atomic formulae connected by conjunctions and/or disjunctions. We do not use quantifiers, functions and negation.

Fig. 3 we provide our example tablet written in formal language. `Number`, `Animal`, `Name`, `Person`, `Receiver`, `Year`, `Document`, etc. denote corresponding ontological categories. $q_1, q_2, a_1, m_1, del_1$, etc. represent objects described in the text.

For example:

- $\texttt{Day}(d_1, 23)$ means that d_1 is a **Day** and its number is 23.
- $\texttt{Name}(n_1, \texttt{ur-mes})$ means that n_1 is a **Name** written as `ur-mes`.
- $\texttt{Job}(j_1, \texttt{ensi2})$ means that j_1 is a **Job** called `ensi2`.
- $\texttt{Name}(n_1, \texttt{ur-mes}) \wedge \texttt{Job}(j_1, \texttt{ensi2}) \wedge \texttt{Person}(m_1, n_1, j_1)$ means that n_1 is a **Name** written as `ur-mes` and j_1 is a **Job** called `ensi2` and m_1 is a **Person** described by n_1 and j_1.
- $\texttt{NumberAnimalName}(nam_1, q_1, a_1, s_1)$ refers to the triple of **Number**, **Animal** and **Supplier** referenced by q_1, a_1, s_1 and represented by nam_1.
- $\texttt{Year}(y_1, \texttt{AS5}) \vee \texttt{Year}(y_1, \texttt{IS4})$ means that y_1 is 5th **Year** of reign of king Amar-Sin or 4th **Year** of reign of king Ibbi-Sin.

5 Syntax analysis

From the linguistic point of view, an economic document is a single sentence, whose length may vary from below 50 up to more than 5000 signs. The documents from the subcorpus are in general words of a regular language. Connections between words and phrases are determined by their positions in text. Taking this into account we decided to perform the syntax analysis by means of a grammar that generates a regular language.

We use semantic categories (such as divine names, personal names, job names, year names etc.) to describe dependencies between words. Apart from describing word connections, grammar plays the role of a lexicon and is used for determining word borders.

Morphological analysis is not needed, due to the agglutinative character of Sumerian and absence of most grammatical suffixes in economic documents.

We define the grammar as follows:

$$G = (\Sigma, N, X_I, R, +, \prec)$$

where

- Σ is a finite set of terminal symbols,
- N is a finite set of non-terminal symbols.
- $X_I \in N$ is the start-symbol of G.
- R is a finite set of production rules. Each production has the form $A \rightarrow \alpha$ or $A \rightarrow \beta+$, where A is a non-terminal and α is a sequence of terminals and non-terminals and $\beta \in \Sigma \cup N$. $A \rightarrow \beta+$ is a shortcut for an infinite set of rules: $A \rightarrow \beta, A \rightarrow \beta\beta, A \rightarrow \beta\beta\beta, \ldots$. We call such rules *accumulation rules*.
- $\prec$ is binary relation on $\Sigma \cup N$ such that $A \prec B$ if and only if there is a rule $A \rightarrow \alpha$ in R such that B belongs to α or there is a rule $A \rightarrow B+$.
- $\prec$ is an irreflexive and transitive partial order. This guarantees that G is recursion-free and generates a regular language.

We will call every subsequence parsed to a grammar symbol a *phrase*.

Proposition 1 *Language L can be generated by a grammar of the form defined above if and only if L is regular.*

Names of the symbols in the grammar reflect the concept names. Example rules:

Head		Body
Name	::=	ur mes
Person	::=	Name Job
Person	::=	Name
Person	::=	Job
NumberAnimal	::=	Number Animal
NumberAnimalList	::=	Animal +

We represent all the possible derivation trees for a given text and grammar by means of a directed acyclic graph whose edges are labelled by grammar symbols. We call it *a chart*.

The text is a sequence of signs. We represent this sequence as an oriented graph which is a list with signs as edges. Vertices of this graph are numbers pointing to the position in text. Then for each rule we find all paths in the graph with sequences of edge labels that match the body of the rule, and add to the graph new edges from the beginnings to the ends of those paths, and label them with the rule head. We will denote an edge labelled α from vertex i to vertex j by $\alpha_{i,j}$.

6 Semantic analysis

In case of an ambiguous grammar (as in our case), the number of possible syntax derivation trees may be exponential in the sequence length. The concept of chart is intended to be their common, compact representation. The number of possible semantic values of the sequence is equal to the number of syntax derivation trees. That is why we cannot represent them directly. Instead, we distribute the semantic values across the chart. Our method resembles to the approach known in the literature as Minimal Recursion Semantics (Copestake et al., 1999)

The formulas of the meaning representation language are spread across the chart. Consider the edge $\alpha_{i,j}$ of chart. This edge was created as the result of parsing a phrase. The phrase describes an entity. We represent this entity by means of a constant $a_{\alpha,i,j}$. We describe its properties derived from the phrase by the formula of meaning representation language. Such a formula is composed out of constants which represent entities and predicates that describe syntactic structure connecting them. We name this formula the *semantic value of the grammar symbol* and denote it as $[\![\alpha]\!]_{i,j}$.

The formula $[\![\alpha]\!]_{i,j}$ has the following structure:

$$\bigvee_{k=1}^{n} p_k(a_{\alpha,i,j}, a_{\alpha_1^k,i_1^k,j_1^k}, \ldots$$

$$\ldots, a_{\alpha_{m_k}^k,i_{m_k}^k,j_{m_k}^k}) \wedge \bigwedge_{l=1}^{m_k} [\![\alpha_l^k]\!]_{i_l^k,j_l^k},$$

where α_l^k are labels corresponding to the symbols in the body of the rule used to create the edge $\alpha_{i,j}$. Each $[\![\alpha_l^k]\!]_{i_l^k,j_l^k}$ is assigned to the edge $\alpha^k_{l\,i_l^k,j_l^k}$, so only the set of atomic formulae

$$\{p_1(a_{\alpha,i,j}, a_{\alpha_1^1,i_1^1,j_1^1}, \ldots, a_{\alpha_{m_k}^1,i_{m_k}^1,j_{m_k}^1}), \ldots$$

$$\ldots, p_n(a_{\alpha,i,j}, a_{\alpha_1^n,i_1^n,j_1^n}, \ldots, a_{\alpha_{m_k}^n,i_{m_k}^n,j_{m_k}^n})\}$$

must by associated with graph edge on the implementation level. Semantics for a terminal symbol $\alpha_{i,j}$ is a one-argument predicate whose name is α and whose argument is variable $a_{\alpha,i,j}$.

Figure 4: Chart

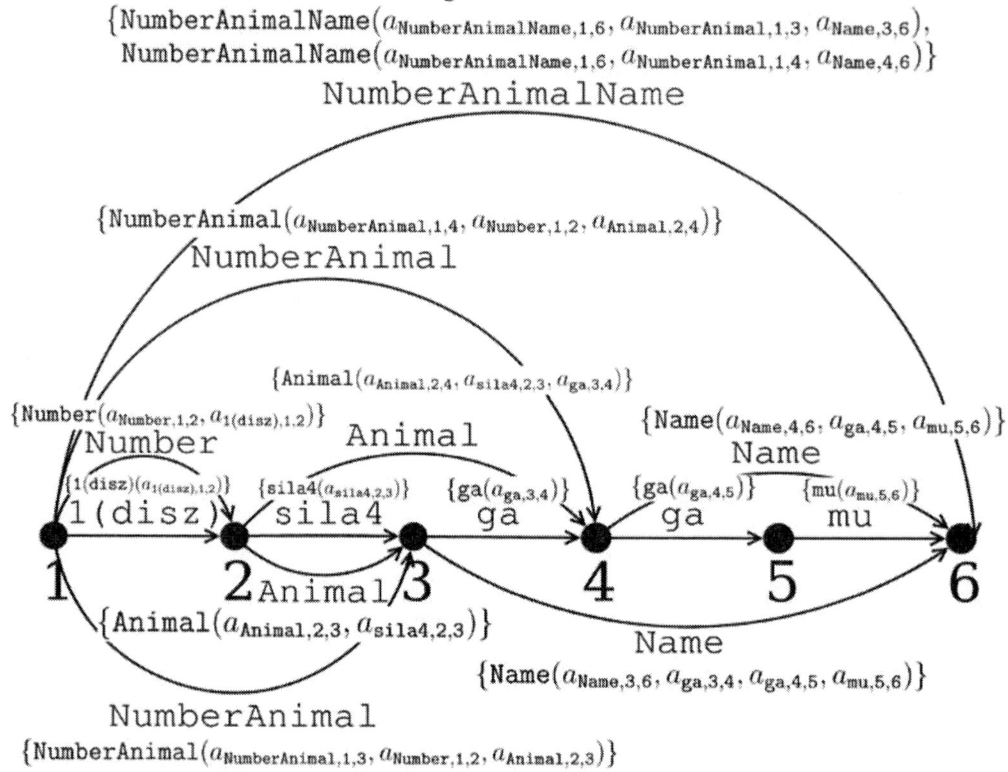

Figure 5: Semantic values of grammar symbols

$$[\![\texttt{Name}]\!]_{4,6} = \texttt{Name}(a_{\texttt{Name},4,6}, a_{\texttt{ga},4,5}, a_{\texttt{mu},5,6}) \wedge [\![\texttt{ga}]\!]_{4,5} \wedge [\![\texttt{mu}]\!]_{5,6} =$$

$$= \texttt{Name}(a_{\texttt{Name},4,6}, a_{\texttt{ga},4,5}, a_{\texttt{mu},5,6}) \wedge \texttt{ga}(a_{\texttt{ga},4,5}) \wedge \texttt{mu}(a_{\texttt{mu},5,6})$$

$$[\![\texttt{NumberAnimalName}]\!]_{1,6} =$$

$$(\texttt{NumberAnimalName}(a_{\texttt{NumberAnimalName},1,6}, a_{\texttt{NumberAnimal},1,3}, a_{\texttt{Name},3,6}) \wedge [\![\texttt{NumberAnimal}]\!]_{1,3} \wedge [\![\texttt{Name}]\!]_{3,6}) \vee$$

$$\vee\ (\texttt{NumberAnimalName}(a_{\texttt{NumberAnimalName},1,6}, a_{\texttt{NumberAnimal},1,4}, a_{\texttt{Name},4,6}) \wedge [\![\texttt{NumberAnimal}]\!]_{1,4} \wedge [\![\texttt{Name}]\!]_{4,6})$$

On Fig. 4 we present an example a chart. The names of predicates associated with the grammar symbols are usually identical to their names. The first argument of each predicate is a constant that represents an entity described by the phrase. Indices of this constant identify the edge into which this phrase was parsed.

On Fig. 5 we show semantic values for some of the edges for chart on Fig. 4. For example the semantic value of the edge $\texttt{Name}_{4,6}$ (denoted as $[\![\texttt{Name}]\!]_{4,6}$) is calculated to be the formula $\texttt{Name}(a_{\texttt{Name},4,6}, a_{\texttt{ga},4,5}, a_{\texttt{mu},5,6})$, because the constant $a_{\texttt{ga},4,5}$ refers to the edge $\texttt{ga}_{4,5}$ and $a_{\texttt{mu},5,6}$ to $\texttt{mu}_{5,6}$.

Ambiguous phrases may be parsed to a number of predicates. Each predicate generated for a given subsequence is a possible description of an entity. That is why we point that entity by the same constant in each predicate (consider for example semantic value of an edge $[\![\texttt{NumberAnimalName}]\!]_{1,6}$).

We connect different possible subsequence interpretations using disjunction. Domain knowledge provides constraints on relations. These constraints may, for example, make the disjunction mutually exclusive.

We represent the semantic value of a symbol generated by an accumulation rule as a graph, whose vertices are constants that are arguments of the predicate. Each path from the first to the last vertex in such a graph represents a list of predicate arguments. The predicates are connected by disjunction.

Semantic values of grammar symbols are constructed using semantic attachments of grammar rules. Semantic attachments are functions that compose semantics of greater objects out of the semantics of smaller ones. Predicate sets associated with edges of chart are arguments and values for these functions.

Upon the end of the parsing process we obtain an edge labelled by the start symbol of the grammar. Its semantic value is a formula which contains every possible translation of the entire text into the meaning representation language.

There are three types of rules that occur during the corpus processing:

- Rules that make up the lexicon
  `Name ::= ur mes`
  $\mathtt{Name}(var_{\mathtt{Name}}, var_{\mathtt{ur}}, var_{\mathtt{mes}})$

- Rules that describe the document structure
  `Person ::= Name Job`
  $\mathtt{Person}(var_{\mathtt{Person}}, var_{\mathtt{Name}}, var_{\mathtt{Job}})$
  `Person ::= Name`
  $\mathtt{Person}(var_{\mathtt{Person}}, var_{\mathtt{Name}})$
  `Person ::= Job`
  $\mathtt{Person}(var_{\mathtt{Person}}, var_{\mathtt{Job}})$

- Rules that introduce domain knowledge (numbers, year names etc)
  `YearGod ::= d inanna`
  $\{\mathtt{AS04}(var_{\mathtt{YearGod}}), \mathtt{AS05}(var_{\mathtt{YearGod}}))\}$
  `Year ::= mu en YearGod Verb`
  $\{p(var_{\mathtt{Year}}) : p \in val_{\mathtt{YearGod}} \cap val_{\mathtt{Verb}}\}$

$var_{\mathtt{Name}}$ is a variable, whose index is an edge labelled by the symbol `Name`. $val_{\mathtt{YearGod}}$ is a set of predicate names connected with the symbol `YearGod`.

7 Incomplete ontology and damaged documents

In every corpus, there is a number of phrases that cannot be expressed using concepts typical for that corpus. These phrases are rare, irregular and devoid of characteristic contexts.

In order to obtain completely parsed documents we must develop a semantic representation for documents we partially do not understand. We close the ontology with the **Other Information** concept, which is treated as a transaction attribute and refers to information not included in the rest of concepts.

Parser recognises phrases it does not understand using the following heuristics: Boundaries of transaction attributes are correlated with verse boundaries. If the parser does not recognise the content of a verse it decides that this verse contains **Other Information**.

Apart from being not understood the texts are often damaged. There are several types of damages in documents.

When a single sign is illegible, it is denoted in the document as `x`. The parser considers the `x` symbol as a wildcard that may be matched with any terminal symbol.

When a part of a verse is broken, it is denoted in the document by `[...]`. We estimate the number of signs in the broken verse counting the number of signs in the other verses in the document. Then we replace the `[...]` symbol by a sequence of `x` symbols.

We do not estimate precise contents of broken phrases, we only determine their role in the document and ontological category. This allows us to avoid combinatorial explosion while parsing damaged documents.

When a whole verse or a number of verses is broken we assume that they have syntactic structure of a typical verse or contain **Other Information**.

8 Transaction Extraction

After performing the semantic analysis we know the concepts used in the document, its topic and structure. Now, we extract transactions from the documents.

Transactions extracted from our example document (Fig. 1) are presented on Fig. 6. Extracted transactions are are represented as edges of chart and they compose a formula of meaning representation language. For unequivocal tablets this formula is a simple conjunction of transaction predicates, whilst ambiguous documents provide transactions which are connected by conjunction and disjunction as well.

While extracting transactions, we analyse document summaries: we correlate the number of animals with their quantity written down in the document summary. This allows us to reduce the number of ambiguities generated by document damages and specifics of writing system.

We extracted 68619 transactions from the selected subcorpus with precision 86% and recall 90%.

Figure 6: Transactions described in the text (already with resolved **Year** ambiguities).

Date	Number	Animal	Supplier	Receiver
`23-11-AS05`	`1`	`sila4`	`ur-mes ensi2`	`ab-ba-sa6-ga`
`23-11-AS05`	`1`	`sila4`	`da-da dumu lugal`	`ab-ba-sa6-ga`
`23-11-AS05`	`1`	`sila4`	`id-da-a`	`ab-ba-sa6-ga`

9 Applications

Our methodology proved its usefulness in several applications.

The first, simple, but powerful and needed application is document retrieval. The system allows us to retrieve documents that satisfy queries concerning concepts and structure of the texts.

It is worth mentioning that due to the script polyvalence, text damages and editor records mixed with Sumerian text, matching a sequence of signs in a document is not a trivial task.

Using the transaction based knowledge representation we found pairs of documents that contain information about the same transaction. This task is important due to the fact that this is the way to follow the distribution process and administration activity.

The system provides help also in the tasks of: identification o Sumerian officials (prosopography); determining relations between Sumerian officials in terms of number of commodities that are transferred between them; classification of types of documents generated by Sumerian administration; research on Sumerian language itself.

10 Conclusions

We presented an ontology driven methodology for processing Sumerian economic documents. We applied it with a success to sumerological research problems.

We plan to extend the ontology, grammar and lexicon so that the system could process the whole corpus of Neo-Sumerian economic documents. It will allow us to construction of the model of Sumerian economics. We will estimate the contents of unavailable documents be means of statistic based approximation and machine learning methods.

Language characteristics have little influence on the system construction, so nothing prevents the system form being applied to narrow subject matter corpora written in other languages. Especially the problems of incomplete ontologies and partial data (caused for example by damages done to documents) are independent from the language characteristics.

Acknowledgements

I would like to thank Jerzy Tyszkiewicz for the inspiration in my work. I would also like to thank Marek Stępień for the support with his knowledge of Sumerian language.

The research has been supported by the grant N-N206-400234 from Ministry of Science and Higher Education of the Republic of Poland.

References

Copestake, A., D. Flickinger and A. Sag. 1999. *Minimal recursion semantics: An introduction*. CSLI, Stanford University.

Cuneiform Digital Library Initiative, The. 2006. `http://cdli.ucla.edu`.

Jaworski, W. 2006. Learning Compound Decision Functions for Sequential Data in Dialog with Experts. In: S. Greco et al. (Eds.) *Proc. RSCTC 2006*, LNAI 4259, Springer, pp. 627-636.

Jurafsky, D., J. H. Martin. 2000. *Speech and Language Processing: An Introduction to Natural Language Processing, Computational Linguistics, and Speech Recognition*. Prentice-Hall.

Labat, R., F. Malbran-Labat. 1988. *Manuel d'epigraphie akkadienne Signes, Syllabaire, ideogrammes*, 6th edition. Geuthner (Librarie Orientaliste Paul Geuthner S.A.).

Sharlach, T.M. 2004. *Provincial Taxation and the Ur III State*. Leiden-Boston.

Steinkeller, P. 1987. The Administrative and Economic Organization of the Ur III State: The Core and the Periphery. In: R.D. Biggs, Mc.G. Gibson (Eds.) *The Organization of Power: Aspect of Bureaucracy in the Ancient Near East*. SAOC 46, Chicago, s.19-41

Stępień, M. 1996. *Animal Husbandry in the Ancient Near East: A Prosopographic Study of Third-Millennium Umma*. Bethesda, Md. : CDL Press.

Generating Chinese Couplets using a Statistical MT Approach

Long Jiang
Microsoft Research Asia
Sigma Center, No. 49, Zhichun Road
Haidian District, Beijing 100190, PRC
longj@microsoft.com

Ming Zhou
Microsoft Research Asia
Sigma Center, No. 49, Zhichun Road
Haidian District, Beijing 100190, PRC
mingzhou@microsoft.com

Abstract

Part of the unique cultural heritage of China is the game of Chinese couplets (duìlián). One person challenges the other person with a sentence (first sentence). The other person then replies with a sentence (second sentence) equal in length and word segmentation, in a way that corresponding words in the two sentences match each other by obeying certain constraints on semantic, syntactic, and lexical relatedness. This task is viewed as a difficult problem in AI and has not been explored in the research community.

In this paper, we regard this task as a kind of machine translation process. We present a phrase-based SMT approach to generate the second sentence. First, the system takes as input the first sentence, and generates as output an N-best list of proposed second sentences, using a phrase-based SMT decoder. Then, a set of filters is used to remove candidates violating linguistic constraints. Finally, a Ranking SVM is applied to rerank the candidates. A comprehensive evaluation, using both human judgments and BLEU scores, has been conducted, and the results demonstrate that this approach is very successful.

1 Introduction

Chinese antithetical couplets, called "duìlián", form a special type of poetry composed of two sentences. They use condensed language, but have deep and sometimes ambivalent meanings. The two sentences making up the couplet are called the "first sentence" (FS) and the "second sentence" (SS) respectively.

Chinese couplets are considered an important cultural heritage. A couplet is often written in calligraphy on vertical red banners, and typically placed on either side of a door or in a large hall during special occasions such as wedding ceremonies and the Chinese New Year. People also use couplets to celebrate birthdays, mark the openings of a business, and commemorate historical events. Chinese couplets have also been used effectively in teaching Chinese in China.

An example of a Chinese couplet is "海 阔 凭 鱼 跃; 天 高 任 鸟 飞", where the FS is "海 阔 凭 鱼 跃" and the SS is "天 高 任 鸟 飞". It says that the sea is wide enough so that fish can jump at their pleasure, and the sky is high enough so that bird can fly unrestrictedly. The correspondence between individual words of the FS and SS is shown here:

海 sea	阔 wide	凭 allow	鱼 fish	跃 jump
|	|	|	|	|
天 sky	高 high	任 permit	鸟 bird	飞 fly

Figure 1. An Example of a Chinese Couplet.

Generating the SS of a Chinese couplet given the FS can be viewed as a big challenge in AI. As far as we know, there is no previous work to tackle this problem.

The general process of generating a SS given a FS is like this: for each word in the FS, find some words that can be used as the counterparts in the SS; then from the word lattice, select one word at each position in the SS so that the se-

© 2008. Licensed under the *Creative Commons Attribution-Noncommercial-Share Alike 3.0 Unported* license (http://creativecommons.org/licenses/by-nc-sa/3.0/). Some rights reserved.

lected words form a fluent sentence satisfying the constraints of Chinese couplets. This process is similar to translating a source language sentence into a target language sentence without word insertion, deletion and reordering, but the target sentence should satisfy some linguistic constraints. Based on this observation, we propose a multi-phase statistical machine translation approach to generate the SS. First, a phrase-based SMT model is applied to generate an N-best list of SS candidates. Then, a set of filters based on linguistic constraints for Chinese couplets is used to remove low quality candidates. Finally, a Ranking SVM is applied to rerank the candidates.

We implemented a web service based on our approach (anonymous URL). A user can input a FS, and our software outputs its top 10 best-scoring SS candidates. Tens of thousands of people use our service every day.

The rest of the paper is organized as follows. In Section 2, we explain the motivation of our work. Then Sections 3 and 4 detail our multi-phase SMT approach for the SS generation. The experimental results and evaluation are reported in Section 5 and related work on computer poetry is summarized in Section 6. In Section 7, we conclude our study and point out the future work.

2 Motivation

Chinese couplets vary widely in length. A short couplet could consist of two sentences each containing only one or two characters while a longer couplet may reach several hundred characters. However, the length of sentences in most Chinese couplets is between 5 and 10 characters. There are also diverse forms of writing couplets. For instance, in one form, the FS and SS are similar in meaning, while in another, they have to oppose in meaning.

However, no matter which form a couplet follows, it generally must conform to the following constraints:

Constraint 1: The two sentences of a couplet agree in length and word segmentation. For example, if a FS contains 7 characters and the first two characters form a word, then the qualified SS should also contain 7 characters with the first two forming a word.

Constraint 2: Tones are generally "coinciding and harmonious": In Chinese, every character is pronounced either "Ping" (平) or "Ze" (仄). In a Chinese couplet, the character at the end of the FS should be "Ze" (pronounced in a sharp downward tone); the character at the end of the SS should be "Ping" (pronounced in a level tone).

Constraint 3: Corresponding words in the two sentences should agree in their part of speech and characteristics. For instance, a noun in the SS should correspond to a noun at the same position in the FS. A named entity should correspond to a named entity.

Constraint 4: The contents of the two sentences should be related, but not duplicated.

Constraint 5: The two sentences should be identical in their writing styles. For instance, if there is a repetition of words, characters, or pronunciations in the FS, the SS should contain an identical repetition. And if there is a character decomposition in the FS, i.e., the FS contains a character and its "component characters", the SS should contain a character decomposition at the corresponding positions.

Character decomposition is an interesting language phenomenon in Chinese: some Chinese characters can be decomposed into other characters. For example, "好" (good) can be decomposed into "女" (daughter) and "子" (son). As illustrated in Figure 2, the left part of "好" is "女" and the right part is "子". "女" and "子" are called the "component characters" of "好".

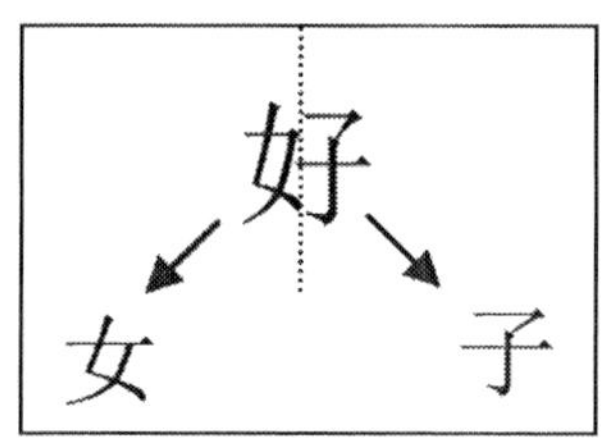

Figure 2. Character Decomposition.

Compared to western couplets, which also consist of two sentences that usually rhyme and have the same number of syllables, Chinese couplets have much stronger constraints. Because in Chinese each character has one and only one syllable, the same number of syllables means the same number of characters. Moreover, the constraints of the FS and SS on consistency of part of speech sequence and writing style make Chinese couplets have more regular form.

Given the FS, writing a good SS to match it is a difficult task because the SS must conform to constraints on syntax, rhyme and semantics, as described above. It also requires the writer to innovatively use extensive knowledge in different disciplines. Some of the difficulties can be seen from the following example:

有	女	有	子	方	称	好
have	daughter	have	son	so	call	good
|	|	|	|	|	|	|
缺	鱼	缺	羊	敢	叫	鲜
lack	fish	lack	mutton	dare	call	delicious

Figure 3. An Example of a Complicated Couplet.

Figure 3 shows a complicated couplet of "有女有子方称好; 缺鱼缺羊敢叫鲜" (Once one has a daughter and son, one's life is complete; who would dare call a meal without fish and mutton delicious? In China, there is an old saying that courses made of fish and mutton are most delicious). The FS contains a repeated character "有" (have), and a character decomposition: "好" (good) and its "component characters" "女" (daughter) and "子" (son). So it requires that the qualified FS should contain identical character repletion and character decomposition. A perfect SS worked out after multiple attempts by many people for this FS is "缺鱼缺羊敢叫鲜", which equally contains a repeated character "缺" (lack), and a character decomposition: "鲜" (fresh) and its "component characters" "鱼" (fish) and "羊" (mutton) at the corresponding positions. And the meanings of the two sentences are also parallel: they tell us what is important in life and what is important in cuisine, respectively.

3 Couplet Generation Model

In this paper, a multi-phase SMT approach is designed, where an SMT system generates an N-best list of candidates and then a ranking model is used to determine the new ranking of the N-best results using additional features. This approach is similar to recent reranking approaches of SMT (Och and Ney, 2004). In the SMT system, a phrase-based log-linear model is applied where two phrase translation models, two lexical weights and a language model are used to score the output sentences, and a monotone phrase-based decoder is employed to get the N-best results. Then a set of filters based on linguistic constraints of Chinese couplets are used to remove candidates of low quality. Finally a Ranking SVM model is used to rerank the candidates using additional features like word associations, etc.

3.1 Phrase-based SMT Model

Given a FS denoted as $F=\{f_1, f_2, ..., f_n\}$, our objective is to seek a SS denoted as $S=\{s_1, s_2, ..., s_n\}$, where f_i and s_i are Chinese characters, so that $p(S|F)$ is maximized. Following Och and Ney (2002), we depart from the traditional noisy-channel approach and use a more general log-linear model. Then the S^* that maximizes $p(S|F)$ can be expressed as follows:

$$S^* = \arg\max_S p(S \mid F) = \arg\max_S \sum_{i=1}^{M} \lambda_i \log h_i(S, F) \quad (1)$$

where the $h_i(S,F)$ are feature functions and M is the number of feature functions. In our design, characters are used instead of words as translation units to form phrases. This is because Chinese couplets use dense language like traditional Chinese and most of words contain only one character. If we try to incorporate Chinese word segmentation, it may bring in unexpected errors. However, we will still report the comparison to the word-based method in Subsection 5.3.

Among features commonly used in phrase-based SMT, five features, listed in Table 1, were selected for our model. To apply phrase-based features, S and F are segmented into phrases $\bar{s}_1 ... \bar{s}_I$ and $\bar{f}_1 ... \bar{f}_I$, respectively. We assume a uniform distribution over all possible segmentations.

$h_1(S,F)=\prod_{i=1}^{I} p(\bar{f}_i \mid \bar{s}_i)$	Phrase translation model
$h_2(S,F)=\prod_{i=1}^{I} p(\bar{s}_i \mid \bar{f}_i)$	Inverted phrase translation model
$h_3(S,F)=\prod_{i=1}^{I} p_w(\bar{f}_i \mid \bar{s}_i)$	Lexical weight
$h_4(S,F)=\prod_{i=1}^{I} p_w(\bar{s}_i \mid \bar{f}_i)$	Inverted lexical weight
$h_5(S,F)=p(S)$	Language model

Table 1. Features in our SMT Model.

Phrase translation model (PTM)

In a phrase-based SMT model, phrases can be any substring that may not necessarily be linguistically motivated. In our implementation, we extract phrases of up to 4-character-grams.

In a Chinese couplet, there is generally a direct one-to-one mapping between corresponding words in the FS and SS, respectively. As a result, the ith character/phrase in F is exactly "translated" into the ith character/phrase in S. Based on this rule, the phrase translation probability $p(\bar{f}_i \mid \bar{s}_i)$ can be estimated by relative frequency on a training corpus:

$$p(\overline{f_i} \mid \overline{s_i}) = \frac{count(\overline{f_i}, \overline{s_i})}{\sum_{r=1}^{m} count(\overline{f_r}, \overline{s_i})} \quad (2)$$

where m is the number of distinct phrases that can be mapped to the phrase $\overline{s_i}$ and $count(\overline{f_i}, \overline{s_i})$ is the number of occurrences that $\overline{f_i}$ and $\overline{s_i}$ appear at the corresponding positions in a couplet.

The inverted phrase translation model $p(\overline{s_i} \mid \overline{f_i})$ has been proven useful in previous SMT research work (Och and Ney, 2002); so we also include it in our phrase-based SMT model.

Lexical weight (LW)

Previous research work on phrase-based SMT has found that it is important to validate the quality of a phrase translation pair (Koehn et al., 2003). A good way to do this is to check its lexical weight $p_w(\overline{f_i} \mid \overline{s_i})$, which indicates how well its words translate to each other:

$$p_w(\overline{f_i} \mid \overline{s_i}) = \prod_{j=1}^{Ni} p(f_j \mid s_j) \quad (3)$$

where Ni is the number of characters in $\overline{f_i}$ or $\overline{s_i}$, f_j and s_j are characters in $\overline{f_i}$ and $\overline{s_i}$ respectively, and $p(f_j \mid s_j)$ is the character translation probability of s_j into f_j. Like in phrase translation probability estimation, $p(f_j \mid s_j)$ can be computed by relative frequency:

$$p(f_j \mid s_j) = \frac{count(f_j, s_j)}{\sum_{r=1}^{m} count(f_r, s_j)} \quad (4)$$

where m is the number of distinct characters that can be mapped to the character s_j and $count(f_j, s_j)$ is the number of occurrences that s_j and f_j appear at the corresponding positions in a couplet.

Like for the phrase translation model, we also use an inverted lexical weight $p_w(\overline{s_i} \mid \overline{f_i})$ in addition to the conventional lexical weight $p_w(\overline{f_i} \mid \overline{s_i})$ in our phrase-based SMT model.

Language model (LM)

A character-based trigram language model with Katz back-off is constructed from the training data to estimate the language model $p(S)$ using Maximum Likelihood Estimation.

3.2 Model Training

A Chinese couplet corpus is necessary for estimating the phrase and character translation probabilities. Currently, there is, however, no large-sized Chinese couplet collection available. Based on our observation, there are many pages on the web containing classic Chinese couplets collectively. So we used the method proposed by (Fan et al., 2007) to recursively mine those couplets with the help of some seed couplets. The method can automatically learn patterns in a page which contains collectively Chinese couplets and then apply the learned pattern to extract more Chinese couplets. There are also some online forums where Chinese couplet fans meet. When some people post FSs on the forums, many other people submit their SSs in response. Such data seems useful for our model training. So we crawled all posted FSs with all their replied SSs. Then from the crawled data, FSs having over 20 unique SSs are selected as development or testing set (see Subsection 5.1), and others are used for model training. Finally, with web mining approach, we collected 670,000 couplets.

To enhance the couplet database crawled from the web, we also mined pairs of sentences of poetry which satisfied the constraints of couplets although they were not originally intended as couplets. For instance, in eight-sentence Tang poetry, the third and fourth sentences and the fifth and sixth sentences form pairs basically satisfying the constraints of Chinese couplets. Therefore, these sentence pairs can be used as couplets in our training algorithm. In that way we get additional 300,000 sentence pairs yielding a total of 970,000 sentence pairs of training data.

Because the relationships between words and phrases in the FS and SS are usually reversible, to alleviate the data sparseness, we reverse the FS and SS in the training couplets and merge them with original training data for estimating translation probabilities.

For the language people use in Chinese couplets is same as that in Chinese poetry, for the purpose of smoothing the language model we add about 1,600,000 sentences from ancient Chinese poetry to train language model, which are not necessarily couplets.

To estimate the weights λ_i in formula (1), we use Minimum Error Rate Training (MERT) algorithm, which is widely used for phrase-based SMT model training (Och, 2003). The training data and criteria (BLEU) for MERT will be explained in Subsection 5.1.

4 Couplet Generation

In this section, we will detail each step of the generation of the second sentence.

4.1 Decoding for N-best Candidates

First, we use a phrase-based decoder similar to the one by (Koehn et al., 2003) to generate an N-best list of SS candidates. Because there is no word reordering operation in the SS generation, our decoder is a monotonic decoder. In addition, the input FS is often shorter than ordinary MT input sentence, so our decoder is more efficient.

4.2 Linguistic Filters

A set of filters is used to remove candidates that violate linguistic constraints that well-formed Chinese couplets should obey.

Repetition filter

This filter removes candidates based on various rules related to word or character repetition. One such rule requires that if there are characters that are identical in the FS, then the corresponding characters in the SS should be identical too. For example, in a FS "有 女 有 子 方 称 好" (have daughter have son so call good), the word "有" is repeating. The legal SS should also contain corresponding repeating words. For instance, a qualified second sentence "缺 鱼 缺 羊 敢 叫 鲜" (lack fish lack mutton dare call delicious) would be legal because "缺" corresponds to "有" and is repeating in the same way. Conversely, if there are no identical words in the FS, then the SS should have no identical words.

Pronunciation repetition filter

This filter works similarly to the repetition filter above except it checks the pronunciation of characters not the character surfaces. The pronunciation of a character can be looked up from a Chinese character pronunciation dictionary. For simplicity, we only use the first pronunciation in the dictionary for polyphones.

Character decomposition filter

We compiled a Chinese character decomposition table from which one can look up what characters a Chinese character can be decomposed into. The decomposition information can be derived from the strokes of each character in a dictionary and then verified by human. Based on this table, we can easily filter out those SS candidates which contain different character decompositions at the corresponding positions from the FS.

Phonetic harmony filter

We filter out the SSs with improper tones at the end character position according to the Chinese character pronunciation dictionary.

4.3 Reranking Based on Multiple Features

In many cases, long-distance constraints are very helpful in selecting good SSs, however, it is difficult to incorporate them in the framework of dynamic programming decoding algorithm. To solve this issue, we designed an SVM-based reranking model incorporating long-distance features to select better candidates.

As shown in formula (5), $\vec{x}$ is the feature vector of a SS candidate, and $\vec{w}$ is the vector of weights. $\langle \cdot,\cdot \rangle$ stands for an inner product. f is the decision function with which we rank the candidates.

$$f_{\vec{w}}(\vec{x}) = \langle \vec{w}, \vec{x} \rangle \qquad (5)$$

Besides the five features used in the phrase-based SMT model, additional features for reranking are as follows:

1. Mutual information (MI) score:

This feature is designed to measure the semantic consistency of words in a SS candidate. For example, the two candidates "天 高 任 鸟 飞" (sky high permit bird fly) and "天 高 任 狗 叫" (sky high permit dog bark) have similar PTM, LW and LM scores. However, human beings recognize the former as a better phrase, because "天 高" (sky high) and "狗 叫" (dog bark) in the latter sentence do not make any sense together. MI can capture the associations between words, whether they are adjacent or not.

Specifically, given a SS candidate $S = \{s_1, s_2, ..., s_n\}$, we use the following formula to compute the MI score:

$$MI(S) = \sum_{i=1}^{n-1} \sum_{j=i+1}^{n} I(s_i, s_j) = \sum_{i=1}^{n-1} \sum_{j=i+1}^{n} \log \frac{p(s_i, s_j)}{p(s_i)p(s_j)} \qquad (6)$$

The parameters $p(s_i,s_j)$, $p(s_i)$ and $p(s_j)$ are estimated using Maximum Likelihood Estimation on the same training data as for training PTM.

2. MI-based structural similarity (MISS) score:

In a Chinese couplet, if two words in the FS are strongly associated, their corresponding words in the SS should also be strongly associated, and vice versa. For example, in the couplet "海 阔 凭 鱼 跃; 天 高 任 鸟 飞" (sea wide allow fish jump; sky high permit bird fly), the word pairs "海"

(sea) and "阔" (wide), "海" (sea) and "鱼" (fish), "鱼" (fish) and "跃" (jump) in the FS are all strongly associated. Similarly, the corresponding word pairs "天" (sky) and "高" (high), "天" (sky) and "鸟" (bird), "鸟" (bird) and "飞" (fly) in the SS are all strongly associated. To measure this kind of structural similarity, we develop a measure function called MI-based structural similarity score. Specifically, given the FS $F=\{f_1, f_2, ..., f_n\}$, we first build its vector $V_f=\{v_{12}, v_{13}, .., v_{1n}, v_{23}, , v_{n-1n}\}$, where v_{ij} is the mutual information of f_i and f_j (i.e., $I(f_i, f_j)$ in formula (6)). Then we build a vector V_s for each SS candidate in the same way. We use a cosine function to compute the similarity between the two vectors as the MISS score:

$$MISS(F,S) = \cos(V_f, V_s) = \frac{V_f \bullet V_s}{|V_f| \times |V_s|} \tag{7}$$

To estimate the parameter vector in the Ranking SVM model, we used an existing training tool, SVM Light[2], and a labeled training corpus. We selected 200 FSs with a length of 7 or 8 characters. For each of them, 50 SS candidates are generated using the N-best SMT decoder. Two operators are asked to label each SS candidate as positive if the candidate is acceptable and as negative if not. After removing 10 FSs and their SS candidates as they had no corresponding positive SS, we got 190 FSs with 9,500 labeled SS candidates (negative: 6,728; positive: 2,772) to train the Ranking SVM model.

5 Experimental Results

5.1 Evaluation Method

Automatic evaluation is very important for parameter estimation and system tuning. An automatic evaluation needs a standard answer data set and a metric to show for a given input sentence the closeness of the system output to the standard answers. Since generating the SS given the FS can be viewed as a kind of machine translation process, the widely accepted automatic SMT evaluation methods may be applied to evaluate the generated SSs.

BLEU (Papineni, et al, 2002) is widely used for automatic evaluation of machine translation systems. It measures the similarity between the MT system output and human-made reference translations. The BLEU metric ranges from 0 to 1 and a higher BLEU score stands for better translation quality.

$$BLEU = BP \bullet \exp\left(\sum_{n=1}^{N} w_n \log p_n\right) \tag{8}$$

Some adaptation is necessary to use BLEU for evaluation of our couplet generator. First, p_n, the n-gram precision, should be position-sensitive in the evaluation of SSs. Second, BP, the brevity penalty, should be removed, because all system outputs have the same length and it has no effect in evaluating SSs. Moreover, because the couplet sentences usually have less than 10 characters, we set n to 3 for the evaluation of SSs, while in MT evaluation n is often set to 4.

It is important to note that the more reference translations we have for a testing sentence, the more reasonable the evaluation score is. From couplet forums mentioned in Subsection 3.2, we collected 1,051 FSs with diverse styles and each of them has over 20 unique SS references. After removing some noisy references by human, each of them has 24.3 references on average. The minimum and maximum number of references is 20 and 40. Out of these data, 600 were selected for MERT training and the remaining 451 for testing.

5.2 BLEU vs. Human Evaluation

To justify whether BLEU is suitable for evaluating generated SSs, we compare BLEU with human evaluation. Figure 4 shows a linear regression of the human evaluation scores as a function of the BLEU score for our 6 systems which generate SSs given FSs. Among the 6 systems, three are implemented using a word-based SMT model with 100K, 400K, and 970K couplets for training, respectively, while the other three are implemented using a phrase-based SMT model with 100K, 400K, and 970K couplets for training, respectively. The word-based SMT model contains only two features: word translation model and language model. The word translation model is trained on the corpus segmented by a Chinese word breaker implemented by (Gao et al., 2003). We selected 100 FSs from the testing data set; for each of them, the best SS candidate was generated using each system. Then we computed the BLEU score and the human score of each system.

The human score is the average score of all SS candidates. Each candidate is scored 1 if it is acceptable, and 0 if not. The correlation of 0.92 indicates that BLEU tracks human judgment well.

[2] http://svmlight.joachims.org/

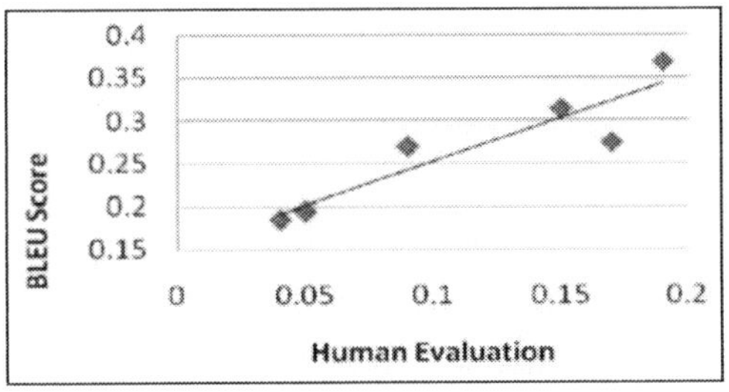

Figure 4: BLEU Predicts Human Judgments.

5.3 Translation Unit Setting

We conducted some experiments to compare the system performances with different translation unit settings: character-based, word-based and phrase-based. In each setting, we only use translation probability and language model as features. And after SMT decoder, we use the same filtering but no reranking. We use all 451 testing data and the results are listed below:

Translation Unit setting	BLEU
character-based	0.236
word-based	0.261
phrase-based	0.276

Table 2. Different Translation Unit Setting.

As shown in Table 2, the word-based translation model achieves 0.025 higher of BLEU score than the character-based model. And the phrase-based model gets the highest score. The improvement shows that phrase-based model works better than word-based and character-based model in our task of SS generation.

5.4 Feature Evaluation

We also conducted some experiments incrementally to evaluate the features used in our phrase-based SMT model and reranking model. All testing data are used. The results are listed below.

	Features	BLEU
Phrase-based SMT Model	Phrase TM(PTM) + LM	0.276
	+ Inverted PTM	0.282
	+ Lexical Weight (LW)	0.315
	+ Inverted LW	0.348
Ranking SVM	+ Mutual information (MI)	0.356
	+ MI-based structural similarity	0.361

Table 3. Feature Evaluation.

As shown in Table 3, with two features: the phrase translation model and the language model, the phrase-based SMT model can achieve a 0.276 of BLEU score. When we add more features incrementally, the BLEU score is improved consistently. Furthermore, with the Ranking SVM model, the score is improved by 0.13 percent, from 0.348 to 0.361. This means our reranking model is helpful.

5.5 Overall Performance Evaluation

In addition to the BLEU evaluation, we also carried out human evaluation. We select 100 FSs from the log data of our couplet web service mentioned in Section 1. For each FS, 10 best SS candidates are generated using our best system. Then each SS candidate is labeled by human as acceptable or not. The evaluation is carried out using top-1 and top-10 results based on top-n inclusion rate. Top-n inclusion rate is defined as the percentage of the test sentences whose top-n outputs contain at least one acceptable SS. The results are listed below:

	Top-1	Top-10
Top-n inclusion rate	0.21	0.73

Table 4. Overall Performance Evaluation.

As shown in Table 4, our system can get a 0.21 of top-1 inclusion rate and 0.73 of top-10 inclusion rate. The numbers seem a little low, but remember that generating a SS given a FS is a quite difficult job, and even humans cannot do it well in limit time, for example, 5 minute per FS. However, what is more important is that our system can provide users diversified SSs and many unacceptable SSs generated by our system can be easily refined by users to become acceptable.

We also made careful analysis on the 27 FSs whose top-10 outputs contain no acceptable SS. As shown in Table 5, the errors mainly come from three aspects: unidentified named entity, complicated character decomposition and repetition. An example of complicated repetition is "近世 进士 尽是 近视" (modern /scholar/all/myopic, modern scholars are all myopic). In this sentence, the pronunciations of the four words are identical (jìnshì), a qualified SS must be meaningful and posses same repetitions, which poses a big challenge to the system.

Mistake types	# of FS
Mistakes with named entities	6
Complicated character decomposition	5
Complicated repetition	4
Mistakes of miscellaneous types	12

Table 5. Error Analysis.

6 Related Work

To the best of our knowledge, no research has been published on generating the SS given the FS of a Chinese couplet. However, because our task can be viewed as generating the second line of a special type of poetry given the first line, we consider automatic poetry generation to be the most closely related existing research area.

As to computer-assisted Chinese poetry generation, Luo has developed a tool[3] which provides the rhyme templates of forms of classical Chinese poetry and a dictionary in which one can look up the tone of a Chinese character. Both the rhyme templates and the dictionary were compiled by human efforts.

For other languages, approaches to creating poetry with computers began in 1959 when Theo Lutz created the first examples of "Computer Poetry" in Germany (Hartman, 1996). Masterman finished a haiku producer (Manurung et al., 2000). Other systems include RACTER and PROSE (Hartman, 1996). Approaches to poetry generation can roughly be classified into template-based, evolutionary, and case-based reasoning. Typically, for the template-based approach, the generation process randomly chooses words from a hand-crafted lexicon and then fills in the gaps provided by a template-based grammar. In computer poetry systems, the starting point is a given message, or communicative goal, and the aim is to produce a string of text that conveys that message according to the linguistic resources available.

There is a big difference between our task and poetry generation. When generating the SS of a Chinese couplet, the FS is given. The task of generating the SS to match the FS is more well-defined than generating all sentences of a poem. Furthermore, the constraints on Chinese couplets mentioned above will enable us to do a more objective evaluation of the generated SSs.

7 Conclusions and Future Work

This paper presents a novel approach to solve the problem of generating Chinese couplets. An SMT approach is proposed to generate the SSs for a FS of a Chinese couplet. The system is comprised of a phrase-based SMT model for the generation of an N-best list of SS candidates, a set of linguistic filters to remove unqualified candidates to meet the special constraints of Chinese couplets, and a discriminative reranking model incorporating multi-dimensional features to get better results. The experimental results show that this approach is very promising.

As a future work, it would be interesting to investigate how this approach can be used in poetry generation.

[3] http://cls.hs.yzu.edu.tw

References

P. F. Brown, S. A. Della Pietra, V. J. Della Pietra and R. L. Mercer. 1993. The mathematics of statistical machine translation: parameter estimation. Computational Linguistics, 19:2, 263-311.

David Chiang. 2005. A Hierarchical Phrase-Based Model for Statistical Machine Translation. In Proc. of the 43rd Meeting of the Association for Computational Linguistics, pages 263-270.

B. Díaz-Agudo, P. Gervás and P. González-Calero. 2002. Poetry generation in COLIBRI. In Proc. of the 6th European Conference on Case Based Reasoning, Aberdeen, Scotland.

C. Fan, L. Jiang, M. Zhou, S.-L. Wang. 2007. Mining Collective Pair Data from the Web. In Proc. of the International Conference on Machine Learning and Cybernetics 2007, pages 3997-4002.

Jianfeng Gao, Mu Li and Changning Huang. 2003. Improved source-channel models for Chinese word segmentation. In Proc. of the 41st Meeting of the Association for Computational Linguistics.

Charles O. Hartman. 1996. Virtual Muse: Experiments in Computer Poetry. Wesleyan University Press.

P. Koehn, F. J. Och and D. Marcu. 2003. Statistical phrase-based translation, In HLT-NAACL 2003, pages 48-54.

H. Manurung, G. Ritchie and H. Thompson. 2001. Towards a computational model of poetry generation. In Proc. of the AISB-00 Symposium on Creative and Cultural Aspects of AI, 2001.

F. J. Och. 2003. Minimum error rate training in statistical machine translation. In Proc. of the 41st Meeting of the Association for Computational Linguistics.

F. J. Och and H. Ney. 2002. Discriminative training and maximum entropy models for statistical machine translation. In Proc. of the 40th Meeting of the Association for Computational Linguistics.

F. J. Och and H. Ney. 2004. The Alignment Template Approach to Statistical Machine Translation. Computational Linguistics, 30:417-449.

K. Papineni, S. Roukos, T. Ward and W.-J. Zhu. 2002. BLEU: a Method for automatic evaluation of machine translation. In Proc. of the 40th Meeting of the Association for Computational Linguistics.

Word Lattice Reranking for Chinese Word Segmentation and Part-of-Speech Tagging

Wenbin Jiang [† ‡] **Haitao Mi** [† ‡] **Qun Liu** [†]

[†]Key Lab. of Intelligent Information Processing
Institute of Computing Technology
Chinese Academy of Sciences
P.O. Box 2704, Beijing 100190, China
[‡]Graduate University of Chinese Academy of Sciences
Beijing, 100049, China
{jiangwenbin,htmi,liuqun}@ict.ac.cn

Abstract

In this paper, we describe a new reranking strategy named word lattice reranking, for the task of joint Chinese word segmentation and part-of-speech (POS) tagging. As a derivation of the forest reranking for parsing (Huang, 2008), this strategy reranks on the pruned word lattice, which potentially contains much more candidates while using less storage, compared with the traditional n-best list reranking. With a perceptron classifier trained with local features as the baseline, word lattice reranking performs reranking with non-local features that can't be easily incorporated into the perceptron baseline. Experimental results show that, this strategy achieves improvement on both segmentation and POS tagging, above the perceptron baseline and the n-best list reranking.

1 Introduction

Recent work for Chinese word segmentation and POS tagging pays much attention to discriminative methods, such as Maximum Entropy Model (ME) (Ratnaparkhi and Adwait, 1996), Conditional Random Fields (CRFs) (Lafferty et al., 2001), perceptron training algorithm (Collins, 2002), etc. Compared to generative ones such as Hidden Markov Model (HMM) (Rabiner, 1989; Fine et al., 1998), discriminative models have the advantage of flexibility in representing features, and usually obtains almost perfect accuracy in two tasks.

Originated by Xue and Shen (2003), the typical approach of discriminative models conducts segmentation in a classification style, by assigning each character a positional tag indicating its relative position in the word. If we extend these positional tags to include POS information, segmentation and POS tagging can be performed by a single pass under a unify classification framework (Ng and Low, 2004). In the rest of the paper, we call this operation mode Joint S&T. Experiments of Ng and Low (2004) shown that, compared with performing segmentation and POS tagging one at a time, Joint S&T can achieve higher accuracy not only on segmentation but also on POS tagging.

Besides the usual local features such as the character-based ones (Xue and Shen, 2003; Ng and Low, 2004), many non-local features related to POSs or words can also be employed to improve performance. However, as such features are generated dynamically during the decoding procedure, incorporating these features directly into the classifier results in problems. First, the classifier's feature space will grow much rapidly, which is apt to overfit on training corpus. Second, the variance of non-local features caused by the model evolution during the training procedure will hurt the parameter tuning. Last but not the lest, since the current predication relies on the results of prior predications, exact inference by dynamic programming can't be obtained, and then we have to maintain a n-best candidate list at each considering position, which also evokes the potential risk of depressing the parameter tuning procedure. As a result, many theoretically useful features such as higher-order word- or POS- grams can not be utilized efficiently.

A widely used approach of using non-local features is the well-known reranking technique, which has been proved effective in many NLP tasks, for instance, syntactic parsing and machine

© 2008. Licensed to the Coling 2008 Organizing Committee for publication in Coling 2008 and for re-publishing in any form or medium.

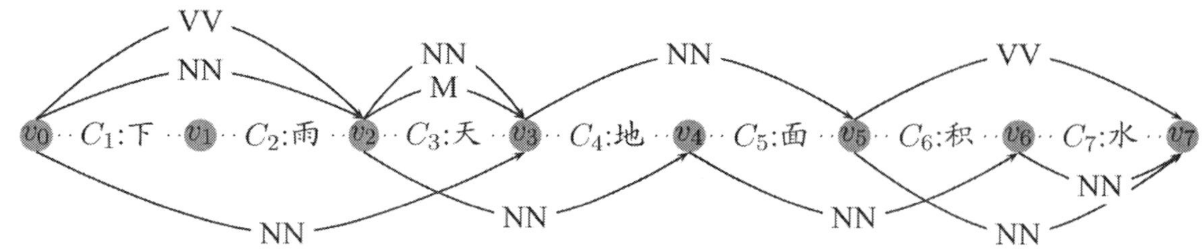

Figure 1: Pruned word lattice as directed graph. The character sequence we choose is "下-雨-天-地-面-积-水". For clarity, we represent each subsequence-POS pair as a single edge, while ignore the corresponding scores of the edges.

translation (Collins, 2000; Huang, 2008), etc. Especially, Huang (2008) reranked the packed forest, which contains exponentially many parses. Inspired by his work, we propose word lattice reranking, a strategy that reranks the pruned word lattice outputted by a baseline classifier, rather than only a n-best list. Word lattice, a directed graph as shown in Figure 1, is a packed structure that can represent many possibilities of segmentation and POS tagging. Our experiments on the Penn Chinese Treebank 5.0 show that, reranking on word lattice gains obvious improvement over the baseline classifier and the reranking on n-best list. Compared against the baseline, we obtain an error reduction of 11.9% on segmentation, and 16.3% on Joint S&T.

2 Word Lattice

Formally, a word lattice L is a directed graph $\langle V, E\rangle$, where V is the node set, and E is the edge set. Suppose the word lattice is for sentence $C_{1:n} = C_1..C_n$, node $v_i \in V$ $(i = 1..n-1)$ denotes the position between C_i and C_{i+1}, while v_0 before C_1 is the source node, and v_n after C_n is the sink node. An edge $e \in E$ departs from v_b and arrives at v_e $(0 \le b < e \le n)$, it covers a subsequence of $C_{1:n}$, which is recognized as a possible word. Considering Joint S&T, we label each edge a POS tag to represent a word-POS pair. A series of adjoining edges forms a path, and a path connecting the source node and the sink node is called diameter, which indicates a specific pattern of segmentation and POS tagging. For a diameter d, $|d|$ denotes the length of d, which is the count of edges contained in this diameter. In Figure 1, the path $p' = \widehat{v_0\,v_3} \rightarrow \widehat{v_3\,v_5} \rightarrow \widehat{v_5\,v_7}$ is a diameter, and $|p'|$ is 3.

2.1 Oracle Diameter in Lattice

Given a sentence s, its reference r and pruned word lattice L generated by the baseline classifier, the oracle diameter d^* of L is define as the diameter most similar to r. With F-measure as the scoring function, we can identify d^* using the algorithm depicted in Algorithm 1, which is adapted to lexical analysis from the forest oracle computation of Huang (2008).

Before describe this algorithm in detail, we depict the key point for finding the oracle diameter. Given the system's output y and the reference y^*, using $|y|$ and $|y^*|$ to denote word counts of them respectively, and $|y \cap y^*|$ to denote matched word count of $|y|$ and $|y^*|$, F-measure can be computed by:

$$F(y, y^*) = \frac{2PR}{P+R} = \frac{2|y \cap y^*|}{|y| + |y^*|} \quad (1)$$

Here, $P = \frac{|y \cap y^*|}{|y|}$ is precision, and $R = \frac{|y \cap y^*|}{|y^*|}$ is recall. Notice that $F(y, y^*)$ isn't a linear function, we need access the largest $|y \cap y^*|$ for each possible $|y|$ in order to determine the diameter with maximum F, or another word, we should know the maximum matched word count for each possible diameter length.

The algorithm shown in Algorithm 1 works in a dynamic programming manner. A table node $T[i, j]$ is defined for sequence span $[i, j]$, and it has a structure S to remember the best $|y_{i:j} \cap y^*_{i:j}|$ for each $|y_{i:j}|$, as well as the back pointer for this best choice. The for-loop in line $2-14$ processes for each node $T[i, j]$ in a shorter-span-first order. Line $3-7$ initialize $T[i, j]$ according to the reference r and the word lattice's edge set $L \cdot E$. If there exists an edge e in $L \cdot E$ covering the span $[i, j]$, then we

Algorithm 1 Oracle Diameter, à la Huang (2008, Sec. 4.1).

1: **Input**: sentence s, reference r and lattice L
2: **for** $[i,j] \subseteq [1,|s|]$ in topological order **do**
3:   **if** $\exists e \in L \cdot E$ s.t. e spans from i to j **then**
4:     **if** $e \cdot label$ exists in r **then**
5:       $T[i,j] \cdot S[1] \leftarrow 1$
6:     **else**
7:       $T[i,j] \cdot S[1] \leftarrow 0$
8:   **for** k s.t. $T[i,k-1]$ and $T[k,j]$ defined **do**
9:     **for** p s.t. $T[i,k-1] \cdot S[p]$ defined **do**
10:       **for** q s.t. $T[k,j] \cdot S[q]$ defined **do**
11:         $n \leftarrow T[i,k-1] \cdot S[p] + T[k,j] \cdot S[q]$
12:         **if** $n > T[i,j] \cdot S[p+q]$ **then**
13:           $T[i,j] \cdot S[p+q] \leftarrow n$
14:           $T[i,j] \cdot S[p+q] \cdot bp \leftarrow \langle k,p,q \rangle$
15: $t \leftarrow argmax_t \frac{2 \times T[1,|s|] \cdot S[t]}{t+|r|}$
16: $d^* \leftarrow Tr(T[1,|s|] \cdot S[t].bp)$
17: **Output:** oracle diameter: d^*

define $T[i,j]$, otherwise we leave this node undefined. In the first situation, we initialize this node's S structure according to whether the word-POS pair of e is in the reference (line $4-7$). Line $8-14$ update $T[i,j]$'s S structure using the S structures from all possible child-node pair, $T[i,k-1]$ and $T[k,j]$. Especially, line $9-10$ enumerate all combinations of p and q, where p and q each represent a kind of diameter length in $T[i,k-1]$ and $T[k,j]$. Line $12-14$ refreshes the structure S of node $T[i,j]$ when necessary, and meanwhile, a back pointer $\langle k,p,q \rangle$ is also recorded. When the dynamic programming procedure ends, we select the diameter length t of the top node $T[1,|s|]$, which maximizes the F-measure formula in line 15, then we use function Tr to find the oracle diameter d^* by tracing the back pointer *bp*.

2.2 Generation of the Word Lattice

We can generate the pruned word lattice using the baseline classifier, with a slight modification. The classifier conducts decoding by considering each character in a left-to-right fashion. At each considering position i, the classifier enumerates all candidate results for subsequence $C_{1:i}$, by attaching each current candidate word-POS pair p to the tail of each candidate result at p's prior position, as the endmost of the new generated candidate. We give each p a score, which is the highest, among all $C_{1:i}$'s candidates that have p as their endmost. Then we select N word-POS pairs with the highest scores, and insert them to the lattice's edge set. This approach of selecting edges implies that, for the lattice's node set, we generate a node v_i at each position i. Because N is the limitation on the count

Algorithm 2 Lattice generation algorithm.

1: **Input**: character sequence $C_{1:n}$
2: $E \leftarrow \emptyset$
3: **for** $i \leftarrow 1 .. n$ **do**
4:   $cands \leftarrow \emptyset$
5:   **for** $l \leftarrow 1 ..$ min(i, K) **do**
6:     $w \leftarrow C_{i-l+1:i}$
7:     **for** $t \in POS$ **do**
8:       $p \leftarrow \langle w, t \rangle$
9:       $p \cdot score \leftarrow Eval(p)$
10:       $s \leftarrow p \cdot score + Best[i-l]$
11:       $Best[i] \leftarrow max(s, Best[i])$
12:       insert $\langle s, p \rangle$ into $cands$
13:   sort $cands$ according to s
14:   $E \leftarrow E \cup cands[1..N] \cdot p$
15: **Output:** edge set of lattice: E

of edges that point to the node at position i, we call this pruning strategy *in-degree pruning*. The generation algorithm is shown in Algorithm 2.

Line $3-14$ consider each character C_i in sequence, $cands$ is used to keep the edges closing at position i. Line 5 enumerates the candidate words ending with C_i and no longer than K, where K is 20 in our experiments. Line 5 enumerates all POS tags for the current candidate word w, where POS denotes the POS tag set. Function $Eval$ in line 9 returns the score for word-POS pair p from the baseline classifier. The array $Best$ preserve the score for sequence $C_{1:i}$'s best labelling results. After all possible word-POS pairs (or edges) considered, line $13-14$ select the N edges we want, and add them to edge set E.

Though this pruning strategy seems relative rough — simple pruning for edge set while no pruning for node set, we still achieve a promising improvement by reranking on such lattices. We believe more elaborate pruning strategy will results in more valuable pruned lattice.

3 Reranking

A unified framework can be applied to describing reranking for both n-best list and pruned word lattices (Collins, 2000; Huang, 2008). Given the candidate set $cand(s)$ for sentence s, the reranker selects the best item $\hat{y}$ from $cand(s)$:

$$\hat{y} = \underset{y \in cand(s)}{\text{argmax}} \, \mathbf{w} \cdot \mathbf{f}(y) \qquad (2)$$

For reranking n-best list, $cand(s)$ is simply the set of n best results from the baseline classifier. While for reranking word lattice, $cand(s)$ is the set of all diameters that are impliedly built in the lattice. $\mathbf{w} \cdot \mathbf{f}(y)$ is the dot product between a feature vector $\mathbf{f}$ and a weight vector w, its value is used to

Algorithm 3 Perceptron training for reranking

Input: Training examples$\{cand(s_i), y_i^*\}_{i=1}^N$
$\mathbf{w} \leftarrow \mathbf{0}$
for $t \leftarrow 1 .. T$ **do**
  for $i \leftarrow 1 .. N$ **do**
    $\hat{y} \leftarrow \arg max_{y \in cand(s_i)} \mathbf{w} \cdot \mathbf{f}(y)$
    if $\hat{y} \neq y_i^*$ **then**
      $\mathbf{w} \leftarrow \mathbf{w} + \mathbf{f}(y_i^*) - \mathbf{f}(\hat{y})$
Output: Parameters: $\mathbf{w}$

Non-local Template	Comment
W_0T_0	current word-POS pair
W_{-1}	word 1-gram before W_0T_0
T_{-1}	POS 1-gram before W_0T_0
$T_{-2}T_{-1}$	POS 2-gram before W_0T_0
$T_{-3}T_{-2}T_{-1}$	POS 3-gram before W_0T_0

Table 1: Non-local feature templates used for reranking

rerank $cand(s)$. Following usual practice in parsing, the first feature $f_1(y)$ is specified as the score outputted by the baseline classifier, and its value is a real number. The other features are non-local ones such as word- and POS- n-grams extracted from candidates in n-best list (for n-best reranking) or diameters (for word lattice reranking), and they are $0-1$ valued.

3.1 Training of the Reranker

We adopt the perceptron algorithm (Collins, 2002) to train the reranker. as shown in Algorithm 3. We use a simple refinement strategy of "averaged parameters" of Collins (2002) to alleviate overfitting on the training corpus and obtain more stable performance.

For every training example $\{cand(s_i), y_i^*\}$, y_i^* denotes the best candidate in $cand(s_i)$. For n-best reranking, the best candidate is easy to find, whereas for word lattice reranking, we should use the algorithm in Algorithm 1 to determine the oracle diameter, which represents the best candidate result.

3.2 Non-local Feature Templates

The non-local feature templates we use to train the reranker are listed in Table 1. Notice that all features generated from these templates don't contain "future" words or POS tags, it means that we only use current or history word- or POS- n-grams to evaluate the current considering word-POS pair. Although it is possible to use "future" information in n-best list reranking, it's not the same when we rerank the pruned word lattice. As we have to traverse the lattice topologically, we face difficulty in utilizing the information ahead of the current considering node.

Algorithm 4 Cube pruning for non-local features.

1: **function** CUBE(L)
2:   **for** $v \in L \cdot V$ in topological order **do**
3:     NBEST(v)
4:   **return** $\mathbf{D_{v_{sink}}}[1]$
5: **procedure** NBEST(v)
6:   $heap \leftarrow \emptyset$
7:   **for** v' topologically before v **do**
8:     $\mathbf{\Delta} \leftarrow$ all edges from v' to v
9:     $p \leftarrow \langle \mathbf{D_{v'}}, \mathbf{\Delta} \rangle$
10:     $\langle p, \mathbf{1} \rangle \cdot score \leftarrow Eval(p, \mathbf{1})$
11:     PUSH($\langle p, \mathbf{1} \rangle, heap$)
12:   HEAPIFY($heap$)
13:   $buf \leftarrow \emptyset$
14:   **while** $|heap| > 0$ and $|buf| < N$ **do**
15:     $item \leftarrow$ POP-MAX($heap$)
16:     append $item$ to buf
17:     PUSHSUCC($item, heap$)
18:   sort buf to $\mathbf{D_v}$
19: **procedure** PUSHSUCC($\langle p, \mathbf{j} \rangle, heap$)
20:   p is $\langle \mathbf{vec_1}, \mathbf{vec_2} \rangle$
21:   **for** $i \leftarrow 1..2$ **do**
22:     $\mathbf{j}' \leftarrow \mathbf{j} + \mathbf{b^i}$
23:     **if** $|\mathbf{vec_i}| \geq j_i'$ **then**
24:       $\langle p, \mathbf{j}' \rangle \cdot score \leftarrow Eval(p, \mathbf{j}')$
25:       PUSH($\langle p, \mathbf{j}' \rangle, heap$)

3.3 Reranking by Cube Pruning

Because of the non-local features such as word- and POS- n-grams, the reranking procedure is similar to machine translation decoding with intergrated language models, and should maintain a list of N best candidates at each node of the lattice. To speed up the procedure of obtaining the N best candidates, following Huang (2008, Sec. 3.3), we adapt the cube pruning method from machine translation (Chiang, 2007; Huang and Chiang 2007) which is based on efficient k-best parsing algorithms (Huang and Chiang, 2005).

As shown in Algorithm 4, cube pruning works topologically in the pruned word lattice, and maintains a list of N best derivations at each node. When deducing a new derivation by attaching a current word-POS pair to the tail of a antecedent derivation, a function $Eval$ is used to compute the new derivation's score (line 10 and 24). We use a max-heap $heap$ to hold the candidates for the next-best derivation. Line $7-11$ initialize $heap$ to the set of top derivations along each deducing source, the vector pair $\langle \mathbf{D_{v_{head}}}, \mathbf{\Delta} \rangle$.Here, $\mathbf{\Delta}$ denotes the vector of current word-POS pairs, while $\mathbf{D_{v_{head}}}$ denotes the vector of N best derivations at $\mathbf{\Delta}$'s antecedent node. Then at each iteration,

Non-lexical-target	Instances
$C_n\ (n=-2..2)$	C_{-2}=下, C_{-1}=雨, C_0=天, C_1=地, C_2=面
$C_nC_{n+1}\ (n=-2..1)$	$C_{-2}C_{-1}$=下雨, $C_{-1}C_0$=雨天, C_0C_1=天地, C_1C_2=地面
$C_{-1}C_1$	$C_{-1}C_1$=雨地
Lexical-target	**Instances**
$C_0C_n\ (n=-2..2)$	C_0C_{-2}=天下, C_0C_{-1}=天雨, C_0C_0=天天, C_0C_1=天地, C_0C_2=天面
$C_0C_nC_{n+1}\ (n=-2..1)$	$C_0C_{-2}C_{-1}$=天下雨, $C_0C_{-1}C_0$=天雨天, $C_0C_0C_1$=天天地, $C_0C_1C_2$=天地面
$C_0C_{-1}C_1$	$C_0C_{-1}C_1$ = 天雨地

Table 2: Feature templates and instances. Suppose we consider the third character "天" in the sequence "下雨天地面".

we pop the best derivation from $heap$ (line 15), and push its successors into $heap$ (line 17), until we get N derivations or $heap$ is empty. In line 22 of function PUSHSUCC, **j** is a vector composed of two index numbers, indicating the two candidates' indexes in the two vectors of the deducing source p, where the two candidates are selected to deduce a new derivation. $\mathbf{j}'$ is a increment vector, whose ith dimension is 1, while others are 0. As non-local features (word- and POS- n-grams) are used by function $Eval$ to compute derivation's score, the derivations extracted from $heap$ may be out of order. So we use a buffer buf to keep extracted derivations (line 16), then sort buf and put its first N items to $\mathbf{D_v}$ (line 18).

4 Baseline Perceptron Classifier

4.1 Joint S&T as Classification

Following Jiang et al. (2008), we describe segmentation and Joint S&T as below:

For a given Chinese sentence appearing as a character sequence:

$$C_{1:n} = C_1\ C_2\ ..\ C_n$$

the goal of segmentation is splitting the sequence into several subsequences:

$$C_{1:e_1}\ C_{e_1+1:e_2}\ ..\ C_{e_{m-1}+1:e_m}$$

While in Joint S&T, each of these subsequences is labelled a POS tag:

$$C_{1:e_1}/t_1\ C_{e_1+1:e_2}/t_2\ ..\ C_{e_{m-1}+1:e_m}/t_m$$

Where $C_i(i=1..n)$ denotes a character, $C_{l:r}(l \leq r)$ denotes the subsequence ranging from C_l to C_r, and $t_i(i=1..m, m \leq n)$ denotes the POS tag of $C_{e_{i-1}+1:e_i}$.

If we label each character a positional tag indicating its relative position in an expected subsequence, we can obtain the segmentation result accordingly. As described in Ng and Low (2004) and Jiang et al. (2008), we use s indicating a *single-*character word, while b, m and e indicating the *begin*, *middle* and *end* of a word respectively. With these positional tags, the segmentation transforms to a classification problem. For Joint S&T, we expand positional tags by attaching POS to their tails as postfix. As each tag now contains both positional- and POS- information, Joint S&T can also be resolved in a classification style framework. It means that, a subsequence is a word with POS t, only if the positional part of the tag sequence conforms to s or bm^*e pattern, and each element in the POS part equals to t. For example, a tag sequence $b\_NN\ m\_NN\ e\_NN$ represents a three-character word with POS tag NN.

4.2 Feature Templates

The features we use to build the classifier are generated from the templates of Ng and Low (2004). For convenience of comparing with other, they didn't adopt the ones containing external knowledge, such as punctuation information. All their templates are shown in Table 2. C denotes a character, while its subscript indicates its position relative to the current considering character(it has the subscript 0).

The table's upper column lists the templates that immediately from Ng and Low (2004). they named these templates *non-lexical-target* because predications derived from them can predicate without considering the current character C_0. Templates called *lexical-target* in the column below are introduced by Jiang et al. (2008). They are generated by adding an additional field C_0 to each *non-lexical-target* template, so they can carry out predication not only according to the context, but also according to the current character itself.

Notice that features derived from the templates in Table 2 are all local features, which means all features are determined only by the training instances, and they can be generated before the training procedure.

Algorithm 5 Perceptron training algorithm.

```
Input: Training examples (x_i, y_i)
α ← 0
for t ← 1 .. T do
    for i ← 1 .. N do
        z_i ← arg max_{z∈GEN(x_i)} Φ(x_i, z) · α
        if z_i ≠ y_i then
            α ← α + Φ(x_i, y_i) − Φ(x_i, z_i)
Output: Parameters: α
```

4.3 Training of the Classifier

Collins (2002)'s perceptron training algorithm were adopted again, to learn a discriminative classifier, mapping from inputs $x \in X$ to outputs $y \in Y$. Here x is a character sequence, and y is the sequence of classification result of each character in x. For segmentation, the classification result is a positional tag, while for Joint S&T, it is an extended tag with POS information. X denotes the set of character sequence, while Y denotes the corresponding set of tag sequence.

According to Collins (2002), the function $\mathbf{GEN}(x)$ generates all candidate tag sequences for the character sequence x , the representation $\mathbf{\Phi}$ maps each training example $(x, y) \in X \times Y$ to a feature vector $\mathbf{\Phi}(x, y) \in R^d$, and the parameter vector $\alpha \in R^d$ is the weight vector corresponding to the expected perceptron model's feature space. For a given input character sequence x, the mission of the classifier is to find the tag sequence $F(x)$ satisfying:

$$F(x) = \underset{y \in \mathbf{GEN}(x)}{\operatorname{argmax}} \ \mathbf{\Phi}(x, y) \cdot \alpha \quad (3)$$

The inner product $\mathbf{\Phi}(x, y) \cdot \alpha$ is the score of the result y given x, it represents how much plausibly we can label character sequence x as tag sequence y. The training algorithm is depicted in Algorithm 5. We also use the "averaged parameters" strategy to alleviate overfitting.

5 Experiments

Our experiments are conducted on the Penn Chinese Treebank 5.0 (CTB 5.0). Following usual practice of Chinese parsing, we choose chapters $1-260$ (18074 sentences) as the training set, chapters $301 - 325$ (350 sentences) as the development set, and chapters $271 - 300$ (348 sentences) as the final test set. We report the performance of the baseline classifier, and then compare the performance of the word lattice reranking against the

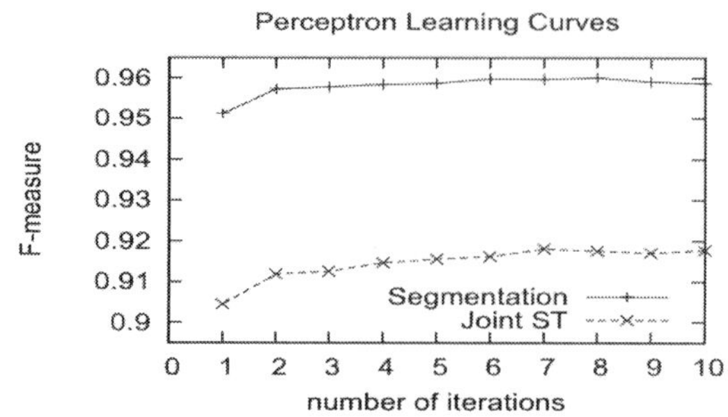

Figure 2: Baseline averaged perceptron learning curves for segmentation and Joint S&T.

n-best reranking, based on this baseline classifier. For each experiment, we give accuracies on segmentation and Joint S&T. Analogous to the situation in parsing, the accuracy of Joint S&T means that, a word-POS is recognized only if both the positional- and POS- tags are correctly labelled for each character in the word's span.

5.1 Baseline Perceptron Classifier

The perceptron classifier are trained on the training set using features generated from the templates in Table 2, and the development set is used to determine the best parameter vector. Figure 2 shows the learning curves for segmentation and Joint S&T on the development set. We choose the averaged parameter vector after 7 iterations for the final test, this parameter vector achieves an F-measure of 0.973 on segmentation, and 0.925 on Joint S&T. Although the accuracy on segmentation is quite high, it is obviously lower on Joint S&T. Experiments of Ng and Low (2004) on CTB 3.0 also shown the similar trend, where they obtained F-measure 0.952 on segmentation, and 0.919 on Joint S&T.

5.2 Preparation for Reranking

For n-best reranking, we can easily generate n best results for every training instance, by a modification for the baseline classifier to hold n best candidates at each considering point. For word lattice reranking, we use the algorithm in Algorithm 2 to generate the pruned word lattice. Given a training instance s_i, its n best result list or pruned word lattice is used as a reranking instance $cand(s_i)$, the best candidate result (of the n best list) or oracle diameter (of the pruned word lattice) is the reranking target y_i^*. We find the best result of the n best results simply by computing each result's

F-measure, and we determine the oracle diameter of the pruned word lattice using the algorithm depicted in Algorithm 1. All pairs of $cand(s_i)$ and y_i^* deduced from the baseline model's training instances comprise the training set for reranking. The development set and test set for reranking are obtained in the same way. For the reranking training set $\{cand(s_i), y_i^*\}_{i=1}^N$, $\{y_i^*\}_{i=1}^N$ is called oracle set, and the F-measure of $\{y_i^*\}_{i=1}^N$ against the reference set is called oracle F-measure. We use the oracle F-measure indicating the utmost improvement that an reranking algorithm can achieve.

5.3 Results and Analysis

The flows of the n-best list reranking and the pruned word lattice reranking are similar to the training procedure for the baseline classifier. The training set for reranking is used to tune the parameter vector of the reranker, while the development set for reranking is used to determine the optimal number of iterations for the reranker's training procedure.

We compare the performance of the word lattice reranking against the n-best list reranking. Table 3 shows the experimental results. The upper four rows are the experimental results for n-best list reranking, while the four rows below are for word lattice reranking. In n-best list reranking, with list size 20, the oracle F-measure on Joint S&T is 0.9455, and the reranked F-measure is 0.9280. When list size grows up to 50, the oracle F-measure on Joint S&T jumps to 0.9552, while the reranked F-measure becomes 0.9302. However, when n grows to 100, it brings tiny improvement over the situation of $n = 50$. In word lattice reranking, there is a trend similar to that in n-best reranking, the performance difference between $in\_degree = 2$ and $in\_degree = 5$ is obvious, whereas the setting $in\_degree = 10$ does not obtain a notable improvement over the performance of $in\_degree = 5$. We also notice that even with a relative small in_degree limitation, such as $in\_degree = 5$, the oracle F-measures for segmentation and Joint S&T both reach a quite high level. This indicates the pruned word lattice contains much more possibilities of segmentation and tagging, compared to n-best list.

With the setting $in\_degree = 5$, the oracle F-measure on Joint S&T reaches 0.9774, and the reranked F-measure climbs to 0.9336. It achieves an error reduction of 16.3% on Joint S&T, and an error reduction of 11.9% on segmentation, over the

n-best	Ora Seg	Tst Seg	Ora S&T	Tst S&T
20	0.9827	0.9749	0.9455	0.9280
50	0.9903	0.9754	0.9552	0.9302
100	0.9907	0.9755	0.9558	0.9305
Degree	**Ora Seg**	**Rnk Seg**	**Ora S&T**	**Rnk S&T**
2	0.9898	0.9753	0.9549	0.9296
5	0.9927	0.9774	0.9768	0.9336
10	0.9934	0.9774	0.9779	0.9337

Table 3: Performance of n-best list reranking and word lattice reranking. n-best: the size of the n-best list for n-best list reranking; Degree: the in degree limitation for word lattice reranking; Ora Seg: oracle F-measure on segmentation of n-best lists or word lattices; Ora S&T: oracle F-measure on Joint S&T of n-best lists or word lattices; Rnk Seg: F-measure on segmentation of reranked result; Rnk S&T: F-measure on Joint S&T of reranked result

baseline classifier. While for n-best reranking with setting $n = 50$, the Joint S&T's error reduction is 6.9% , and the segmentation's error reduction is 8.9%. We can see that reranking on pruned word lattice is a practical method for segmentation and POS tagging. Even with a much small data representation, it obtains obvious advantage over the n-best list reranking.

Comparing between the baseline and the two reranking techniques, We find the non-local information such as word- or POS- grams do improve accuracy of segmentation and POS tagging, and we also find the reranking technique is effective to utilize these kinds of information. As even a small scale n-best list or pruned word lattice can achieve a rather high oracle F-measure, reranking technique, especially the word lattice reranking would be a promising refining strategy for segmentation and POS tagging. This is based on this viewpoint: On the one hand, compared with the initial input character sequence, the pruned word lattice has a quite smaller search space while with a high oracle F-measure, which enables us to conduct more precise reranking over this search space to find the best result. On the other hand, as the structure of the search space is approximately outlined by the topological directed architecture of pruned word lattice, we have a much wider choice for feature selection, which means that we would be able to utilize not only features topologically before the current considering position, just like those depicted in Table 2 in section 4, but also information topologically after it, for example the next word W_1 or the next POS tag T_1. We believe the pruned word lattice reranking technique will obtain higher improvement, if we develop more precise reranking algorithm and more appropriate features.

6 Conclusion

This paper describes a reranking strategy called word lattice reranking. As a derivation of the forest reranking of Huang (2008), it performs reranking on pruned word lattice, instead of on n-best list. Using word- and POS- gram information, this reranking technique achieves an error reduction of 16.3% on Joint S&T, and 11.9% on segmentation, over the baseline classifier, and it also outperforms reranking on n-best list. It confirms that word lattice reranking can effectively use non-local information to select the best candidate result, from a relative small representation structure while with a quite high oracle F-measure. However, our reranking implementation is relative coarse, and it must have many chances for improvement. In future work, we will develop more precise pruning algorithm for word lattice generation, to further cut down the search space while maintaining the oracle F-measure. We will also investigate the feature selection strategy under the word lattice architecture, for effective use of non-local information.

Acknowledgement

This work was supported by National Natural Science Foundation of China, Contracts 60736014 and 60573188, and 863 State Key Project No. 2006AA010108. We show our special thanks to Liang Huang for his valuable suggestions.

References

Collins, Michael. 2000. Discriminative reranking for natural language parsing. In *Proceedings of the 17th International Conference on Machine Learning*, pages 175–182.

Collins, Michael. 2002. Discriminative training methods for hidden markov models: Theory and experiments with perceptron algorithms. In *Proceedings of the Empirical Methods in Natural Language Processing Conference*, pages 1–8, Philadelphia, USA.

Fine, Shai, Yoram Singer, and Naftali Tishby. 1998. The hierarchical hidden markov model: Analysis and applications. In *Machine Learning*, pages 32–41.

Huang, Liang. 2008. Forest reranking: Discriminative parsing with non-local features. In *Proceedings of the 46th Annual Meeting of the Association for Computational Linguistics*.

Jiang, Wenbin, Liang Huang, Yajuan Lv, and Qun Liu. 2008. A cascaded linear model for joint chinese word segmentation and part-of-speech tagging. In *Proceedings of the 46th Annual Meeting of the Association for Computational Linguistics*.

Lafferty, John, Andrew McCallum, and Fernando Pereira. 2001. Conditional random fields: Probabilistic models for segmenting and labeling sequence data. In *Proceedings of the 23rd International Conference on Machine Learning*, pages 282–289, Massachusetts, USA.

Ng, Hwee Tou and Jin Kiat Low. 2004. Chinese part-of-speech tagging: One-at-a-time or all-at-once? word-based or character-based? In *Proceedings of the Empirical Methods in Natural Language Processing Conference*.

Rabiner, Lawrence. R. 1989. A tutorial on hidden markov models and selected applications in speech recognition. In *Proceedings of IEEE*, pages 257–286.

Ratnaparkhi and Adwait. 1996. A maximum entropy part-of-speech tagger. In *Proceedings of the Empirical Methods in Natural Language Processing Conference*.

Xue, Nianwen and Libin Shen. 2003. Chinese word segmentation as lmr tagging. In *Proceedings of SIGHAN Workshop*.

The Effect of Syntactic Representation on Semantic Role Labeling

Richard Johansson and **Pierre Nugues**
Lund University, Sweden
{richard, pierre}@cs.lth.se

Abstract

Almost all automatic semantic role labeling (SRL) systems rely on a preliminary parsing step that derives a syntactic structure from the sentence being analyzed. This makes the choice of syntactic representation an essential design decision. In this paper, we study the influence of syntactic representation on the performance of SRL systems. Specifically, we compare constituent-based and dependency-based representations for SRL of English in the FrameNet paradigm.

Contrary to previous claims, our results demonstrate that the systems based on dependencies perform roughly as well as those based on constituents: For the argument classification task, dependency-based systems perform slightly higher on average, while the opposite holds for the argument identification task. This is remarkable because dependency parsers are still in their infancy while constituent parsing is more mature. Furthermore, the results show that dependency-based semantic role classifiers rely less on lexicalized features, which makes them more robust to domain changes and makes them learn more efficiently with respect to the amount of training data.

1 Introduction

The role-semantic paradigm has a long and rich history in linguistics, and the NLP community has recently devoted much attention to developing accurate and robust methods for performing role-semantic analysis automatically (Gildea and Jurafsky, 2002; Litkowski, 2004; Carreras and Màrquez, 2005; Baker et al., 2007). It is widely conjectured that an increased SRL accuracy will lead to improvements in certain NLP applications, especially template-filling systems. SRL has also been used in prototypes of more advanced semantics-based applications such as textual entailment recognition.

It has previously been shown that SRL systems need a syntactic structure as input (Gildea and Palmer, 2002; Punyakanok et al., 2008). An important consideration is then what information this input should represent. By habit, most systems for automatic role-semantic analysis have used Penn-style constituents (Marcus et al., 1993) produced by Collins' (1997) or Charniak's (2000) parsers. The influence of the syntactic formalism on SRL has only been considered in a few previous articles. For instance, Gildea and Hockenmaier (2003) reported that a CCG-based parser gives improved results over the Collins parser.

Dependency syntax has only received little attention for the SRL task, despite a surge of interest in dependency parsing during the last few years (Buchholz and Marsi, 2006). Early examples of dependency-based SRL systems, which used gold-standard dependency treebanks, include Žabokrtský et al. (2002) and Hacioglu (2004). Two studies that compared the respective performances of constituent-based and dependency-based SRL systems (Pradhan et al., 2005; Swanson and Gordon, 2006), both using automatic parsers, reported that the constituent-based systems outperformed the dependency-based ones by a very wide margin. However, the figures reported in these studies can be misleading since the comparison involved a 10-year-old rule-based dependency parser versus a state-of-the-art statistical constituent parser. The recent progress in statistical dependency parsing gives grounds for a new evaluation.

© 2008. Licensed under the *Creative Commons Attribution-Noncommercial-Share Alike 3.0 Unported* license (http://creativecommons.org/licenses/by-nc-sa/3.0/). Some rights reserved.

In addition, there are a number of linguistic motivations why dependency syntax could be beneficial in an SRL context. First, complex linguistic phenomena such as *wh*-word extraction and topicalization can be transparently represented by allowing nonprojective dependency links. These links also justify why dependency syntax is often considered superior for free-word-order languages; it is even very questionable whether the traditional constituent-based SRL strategies are viable for such languages. Second, *grammatical function* such as subject and object is an integral concept in dependency syntax. This concept is intuitive when reasoning about the link between syntax and semantics, and it has been used earlier in semantic interpreters such as Absity (Hirst, 1983). However, except from a few tentative experiments (Toutanova et al., 2005), grammatical function is not explicitly used by current automatic SRL systems, but instead emulated from constituent trees by features like the constituent position and the governing category. More generally, these linguistic reasons have made a number of linguists argue that dependency structures are more suitable for explaining the syntax-semantics interface (Mel'čuk, 1988; Hudson, 1984).

In this work, we provide a new evaluation of the influence of the syntactic representation on semantic role labeling in English. Contrary to previously reported results, we show that dependency-based systems are on a par with constituent-based systems or perform nearly as well. Furthermore, we show that semantic role classifiers using a dependency parser learn faster than their constituent-based counterparts and therefore need less training data to achieve similar performances. Finally, dependency-based role classifiers are more robust to vocabulary change and outperform constituent-based systems when using out-of-domain test sets.

2 Statistical Dependency Parsing for English

Except for small-scale efforts, there is no dependency treebank of significant size for English. Statistical dependency parsers of English must therefore rely on dependency structures automatically converted from a constituent corpus such as the Penn Treebank (Marcus et al., 1993).

Typical approaches to conversion of constituent structures into dependencies are based on hand-constructed head percolation rules, an idea that has its roots in lexicalized constituent parsing (Magerman, 1994; Collins, 1997). The head rules created by Yamada and Matsumoto (2003) have been used in almost all recent work on statistical dependency parsing of English (Nivre and Scholz, 2004; McDonald et al., 2005).

Recently, Johansson and Nugues (2007) extended the head percolation strategy to incorporate long-distance links such as *wh*-movement and topicalization, and used the full set of grammatical function tags from Penn in addition to a number of inferred tags (in total 57 function tags). A dependency parser based on this syntax was used in the best-performing system in the SemEval-2007 task on Frame-semantic Structure Extraction (Baker et al., 2007), and the conversion method (in two different forms) was used for the English data in the CoNLL Shared Tasks of 2007 and 2008.

3 Automatic Semantic Role Labeling with Constituents and Dependencies

To study the influence of syntactic representation on SRL performance, we developed a framework that could be easily parametrized to process either constituent or dependency input[1]. This section describes its implementation. As the role-semantic paradigm, we used FrameNet (Baker et al., 1998).

3.1 Systems

We built SRL systems based on six different parsers. All parsers were trained on the Penn Treebank, either directly for the constituent parsers or through the LTH constituent-to-dependency converter (Johansson and Nugues, 2007). Our systems are identified as follows:

LTH. A dependency-based system using the LTH parser (Johansson and Nugues, 2008).

Malt. A dependency-based system using MaltParser (Nivre et al., 2007).

MST. A dependency-based system using MSTParser (McDonald et al., 2005).

C&J. A constituent-based system using the reranking parser (the May 2006 version) by Charniak and Johnson (2005).

Charniak. A constituent-based system using Charniak's parser (Charniak, 2000).

Collins. A constituent-based system using Collins' parser (Collins, 1997).

[1]Our implementation is available for download at `http://nlp.cs.lth.se/fnlabeler`.

MaltParser is an incremental greedy classifier-based parser based on SVMs, while the LTH parser and MSTParser use exact edge-factored search with a linear model trained using online margin-based structure learning. MaltParser and MSTParser have achieved state-of-the-art results for a wide range of languages in the 2006 and 2007 CoNLL Shared Tasks on dependency parsing, and the LTH parser obtained the best result in the 2008 CoNLL Shared Task on joint syntactic and semantic parsing. Charniak's and Collins' parsers are widely used constituent parsers for English, and the C&J parser is the best-performing freely available constituent parser at the time of writing according to published figures. Charniak's parser and the C&J parser come with a built-in part-of-speech tagger; all other systems used the Stanford tagger (Toutanova et al., 2003).

Following Gildea and Jurafsky (2002), the SRL problem is traditionally divided into two subtasks: identifying the arguments and labeling them with semantic roles. Although state-of-the-art SRL systems use sophisticated statistical models to perform these two tasks jointly (e.g. Toutanova et al., 2005, Johansson and Nugues, 2008), we implemented them as two independent support vector classifiers to be able to analyze the impact of syntactic representation on each task separately. The features used by the classifiers are traditional, although the features for the dependency-based classifiers needed some adaptation. Table 1 enumerates the features, which are described in more detail in Appendix A. The differences in the feature sets reflect the structural differences between constituent and dependency trees: The constituent-only features are based on phrase tags and the dependency-only features on grammatical functions labels.

Features	Argument identification	Argument classification
TARGETLEMMA	C,D	C,D
FEs	C,D	C,D
TARGETPOS	C,D	C,D
VOICE	C,D	C,D
POSITION	C,D	C,D
ARGWORD/POS	C,D	C,D
LEFTWORD/POS	C,D	C,D
RIGHTWORD/POS	C,D	C,D
PARENTWORD/POS	C,D	
C-SUBCAT	C	C
C-PATH	C	C
PHRASETYPE	C	C
GOVCAT	C	C
D-SUBCAT	D	D
D-PATH	D	D
CHILDDEPSET	D	D
PARENTHASOBJ	D	
RELTOPARENT	D	
FUNCTION		D

Table 1: Classifier features. The features used by the constituent-based and the dependency-based systems are marked C and D, respectively.

3.2 Dependency-based Argument Identification

The argument identification step consists of finding the arguments for a given predicate. For constituent-based SRL, this problem is formulated as selecting a subset of the constituents in a parse tree. This is then implemented in practice as a binary classifier that determines whether or not a given constituent is an argument. We approached the problem similarly in the dependency framework, applying the classifier on dependency nodes rather than constituents. In both cases, the identification step was preceded by a pruning stage that heuristically removes parse tree nodes unlikely to represent arguments (Xue and Palmer, 2004).

To score the performance of the argument identifier, traditional evaluation procedures treat the identification as a *bracketing problem*, meaning that the entities scored by the evaluation procedure are labeled snippets of text; however, it is questionable whether this is the proper way to evaluate a task whose purpose is to find *semantic relations* between logical entities. We believe that the same criticisms that have been leveled at the PARSEVAL metric for constituent structures are equally valid for the bracket-based evaluation of SRL systems. The inappropriateness of the traditional metric has led to a number of alternative metrics (Litkowski, 2004; Baker et al., 2007).

We have stuck to the traditional bracket-based scoring metric for compatibility with previous results, but since it represents the arguments as labeled spans, a conversion step is needed when using dependencies. Algorithm 1 shows how the spans are constructed from the argument dependency nodes. For each argument node, the algorithm computes the yield Y, the set of dependency nodes to include in the bracketing. This set is then partitioned into contiguous parts, which are then converted into spans. In most cases, the yield is just the subtree dominated by the argument node. However, if the argument dominates the predicate, then the branch containing the predicate is removed. Also, FrameNet allows arguments to coincide with the predicate; in this case, the yield is just the predicate node.

Algorithm 1 Span creation from argument dependency nodes.

input Predicate node p, argument node a
if a does not dominate p
  $Y \leftarrow \{n; a \text{ dominates } n\}$
else if $p = a$
  $Y \leftarrow \{p\}$
else
  $c \leftarrow$ the child of a that dominates p
  $Y \leftarrow \{n; a \text{ dominates } n\} \setminus \{n; c \text{ dominates } n\}$
end if
$S \leftarrow$ partition of Y into contiguous subsets
return $\{(\text{min-index } s, \text{max-index } s); s \in S\}$

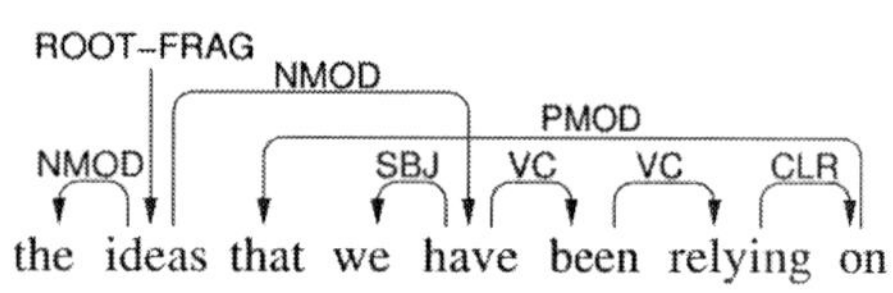

Figure 1: Example of a dependency tree containing a predicate *relying* with three arguments: *the ideas*, *we*, and *on ... that*.

To illustrate Algorithm 1, consider Figure 1. In this sentence, the predicate *relying* has three arguments: *the ideas*, *we*, and *on ... that*. The simplest of them is *we*, which does not dominate its predicate and which is not discontinuous. A more complex case is the discontinuous argument headed by *on*, where the yield $\{on, that\}$ is partitioned into two subsets that result in two separate spans. Finally, the dependency node *ideas* dominates the predicate. In this case, the algorithm removes the subtree headed by *have*, so the remaining yield is $\{the, ideas\}$.

4 Experiments

We carried out a number of experiments to compare the influence of the syntactic representation on different aspects of SRL performance. We used the FrameNet example corpus and running-text corpus, from which we randomly sampled a training and test set. The training set consisted of 134,697 predicates and 271,560 arguments, and the test set of 14,952 predicates and 30,173 arguments. This does not include null-instantiated arguments, which were removed from the training and test sets.

4.1 Argument Identification

Before evaluating the full automatic argument identification systems, we studied the effect of the span creation from dependency nodes (Algorithm 1). To do this, we measured the upper-bound recall of argument identification using the conventional span-based evaluation metric. We compared the quality of *pruned* spans (Algorithm 1) to *unpruned* spans (a baseline method that brackets the full subtree). Table 2 shows the results of this experiment. The figures show that proper span creation is essential when the traditional metrics are used: For all dependency-based systems, the upper-bound recall increases significantly. However, the dependency-based systems generally have lower figures for the upper-bound recall than constituent-based ones.

System	Pruned	Unpruned
LTH	83.9	82.1
Malt	82.1	78.3
MST	80.4	77.1
C&J	85.3	
Charniak	83.4	
Collins	81.8	

Table 2: Upper-bound recall for argument identification.

Our first experiment investigated how the syntactic representation influenced the performance of the argument identification step. Table 3 shows the result of this evaluation. As can be seen, the constituent-based systems outperform the dependency-based systems on average. However, the picture is not clear enough to draw any firm conclusion about a fundamental structural difference. There are also a number of reasons to be cautious: First, the dependency parsers were trained on a treebanks that had been automatically created from a constituent treebank, which probably results in a slight decrease in annotation quality. Second, dependency parsing is still a developing field, while constituent parsing is more mature. The best constituent parser (C&J) is a reranking parser utilizing global features, while the dependency parsers use local features only; we believe that a reranker could be used to improve the dependency parsers as well.

System	P	R	F1
LTH	79.7	77.3	78.5
Malt	77.4	73.8	75.6
MST	73.9	71.9	72.9
C&J	81.4	77.3	79.2
Charniak	79.8	75.0	77.3
Collins	78.4	72.9	75.6

Table 3: Argument identification performance.

Differences between parsers using the same syntactic formalism are also considerable, which suggests that the attachment accuracy is probably the most important parameter when choosing a parser for this task.

4.2 Argument Classification

To evaluate the argument classification accuracies, we provided the systems with gold-standard arguments, which were then automatically classified. Table 4 shows the results.

System	Accuracy
LTH	89.6
Malt	88.5
MST	88.1
C&J	88.9
Charniak	88.5
Collins	88.3

Table 4: Semantic role classification accuracy.

Here, the situation is different: the best dependency-based system make 6.3% fewer errors than the best constituent-based one, a statistically significant difference at the 99.9% level according to a McNemar test. Again, there are no clear differences that can be attributed to syntactic formalism. However, this result is positive, because it shows clearly that SRL can be used in situations where only dependency parsers are available.

On the other hand, it may seem paradoxical that the rich set of grammatical functions used by the dependency-based systems did not lead to a clearer difference between the groups, despite the linguistic intuition that this feature should be useful for argument classification. Especially for for the second- and third-best systems (Malt and MST versus Charniak and Collins), the performance figures are almost identical. However, all systems use lexical features of the argument, and given enough training data, one may say that the grammatical function is implicitly encoded in these features. This suggests that lexical features are more important for constituent-based systems than for dependency-based ones.

4.3 Robustness of SRL Classifiers

In this section, we test the hypothesis that the SRL systems based on dependency syntax rely less heavily on lexical features. We also investigate two parameters that are influenced by lexicalization: domain sensitivity and the amount of training data required by classifiers.

Tests of Unlexicalized Models

To test the hypothesis about the reliance on lexicalization, we carried out a series of experiments where we set aside the lexical features of the argument. Table 5 shows the results.

As expected, there is a sharp drop in performance for all systems, but the results are very clear: When no argument lexical features are available, the dependency-based systems have a superior performance. The difference between MST and C&J constitutes an error reduction of 6.9% and is statistically significant at the 99.9% level.

System	Accuracy
LTH	83.0
Malt	81.9
MST	81.7
C&J	80.3
Charniak	80.0
Collins	79.8

Table 5: Accuracy for unlexicalized role classifiers. Dependency-based systems make at least 6.9% fewer errors.

Training Set Size

Since the dependency-based systems rely less on lexicalization, we can expect them to have a steeper learning curve. To investigate this, we trained semantic role classifiers using training sets of varying sizes and compared the average classification accuracies of the two groups. Figure 2 shows the reduction in classification error of the dependency-based group compared to the constituent-based group (again, all systems were lexicalized). For small training sets, the differences are large; the largest observed error reduction was 5.4% with a training set of 25,000 instances. When the training set size increases, the difference between the groups decreases. The plot is consistent with our hypothesis that the grammatical function features used by the dependency-based systems make generalization easier for statistical classifiers. We interpret the flatter learning curves for constituent-based systems as a consequence of lexicalization – these systems need more training data to use lexical information to capture grammatical function information implicitly.

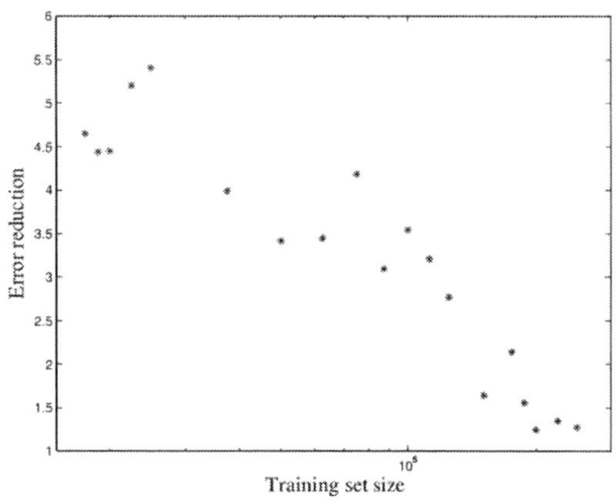

Figure 2: Error reduction of average dependency-based systems as a function of training set size.

Out-of-domain Test Sets

We finally conducted an evaluation of the semantic role classification accuracies on an out-of-domain test set: the FrameNet-annotated Nuclear Threat Initiative texts from SemEval task (Baker et al., 2007). Table 6 shows the results. This corpus contained 9,039 predicates and 15,343 arguments. The writing style is very different from the FrameNet training data, and the annotated data contain several instances of predicates and frames unseen in the training set. We thus see that all systems suffer severely from domain sensitivity, but we also see that the dependency-based systems are more resilient – the difference between MST and C&J is statistically significant at the 97.5% level and corresponds to an error reduction of 2%. The experiment reconfirms previous results (Carreras and Màrquez, 2005) that the argument classification part of SRL systems is sensitive to domain changes, and Pradhan et al. (2008) argued that an important reason for this is that the lexical features are heavily domain-dependent. Our results are consistent with this hypothesis, and suggest that the inclusion of grammatical function features is an effective way to mitigate this sensitivity.

System	Accuracy
LTH	71.1
Malt	70.1
MST	70.1
C&J	69.5
Charniak	69.3
Collins	69.3

Table 6: Classification accuracy on the NTI texts. Dependency-based systems make 2% fewer errors.

5 Discussion

We have described a set of experiments that investigate the relation between syntactic representation and semantic role labeling performance, specifically focusing on a comparison between constituent- and dependency-based SRL systems.

A first conclusion is that our dependency-based systems perform more or less as well as the more mature constituent-based systems: For the argument classification task, dependency-based systems are slightly better on average, while the constituent-based systems perform slightly higher in argument identification.

This result contrasts with previously published comparisons, which used less accurate dependency parsers, and shows that semantic analyzers can be implemented for languages where constituent parsers are not available. While traditional constituent-based SRL techniques have so far been applied to languages characterized by simple morphology and rigid word order, such as English and Chinese, we think that dependency-based SRL can be particularly useful for languages with a free word order.

For dependency-based systems, the conversion from parse tree nodes to argument spans, which are needed to use the traditional span-based evaluation method, is less trivial than in the constituent case. To make a comparison feasible, we implemented an algorithm for span creation from argument nodes. However, the fundamental problem lies in evaluation – the field needs to design new evaluation procedures that use some sort of link-based scoring method. The evaluation metrics used in the SemEval task on Frame-semantic

Structure Extraction and the 2008 CoNLL Shared Task are examples of steps in the right direction.

Our second main result is that for argument classification, dependency-based systems rely less heavily on lexicalization, and we suggest that this is because they use features based on grammatical function labels. These features make the learning curve steeper when training the classifier, and improve robustness to domain changes.

A Features Used by the Classifiers

The following subsections itemize the features used by the systems. All examples are given with respect to the sentence *she gave the horse an apple*. The constituent and dependency trees are shown in Figure 3. For this sentence, the predicate is *gave*, which has the FrameNet frame GIVING. It has three arguments: *she*, which has the DONOR role; *the horse*, the RECIPIENT; and *an apple*, the THEME.

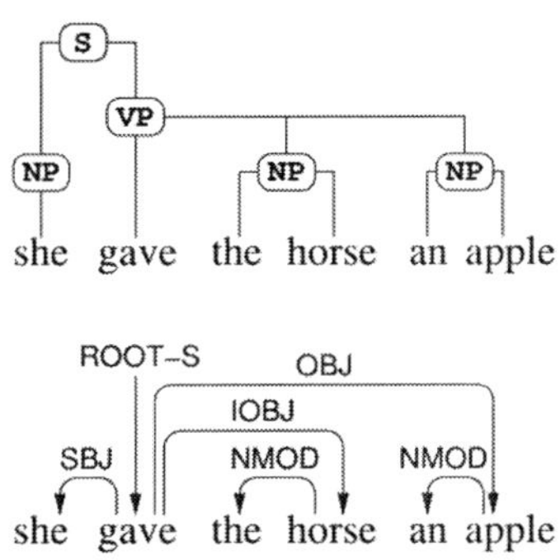

Figure 3: Examples of parse trees.

A.1 Common Features

The following features are used by both the constituent-based and the dependency-based semantic analyzers. Head-finding rules (Johansson and Nugues, 2007) were applied when heads of constituents were needed.

TARGETLEMMA. The lemma of the target word itself, e.g. *give*.

FES. For a given frame, the set of available frame elements listed in FrameNet. For instance, for *give* in the GIVING frame, we have 12 frame elements: DONOR, RECIPIENT, THEME, ...

TARGETPOS. Part-of-speech tag for the target word.

VOICE. For verbs, this feature is Active or Passive. For other types of words, it is not defined.

POSITION. Position of the head word of the argument with respect to the target word: Before, After, or On.

ARGWORD and ARGPOS. Lexical form and part-of-speech tag of the head word of the argument.

LEFTWORD and LEFTPOS. Form and part-of-speech tag of the leftmost dependent of the argument head.

RIGHTWORD and RIGHTPOS. Form and part-of-speech tag of the rightmost dependent of the argument head.

PARENTWORD and PARENTPOS. Form and part-of-speech tag of the parent node of the target.

A.2 Features Used by the Constituent-based Analyzer Only

C-SUBCAT. Subcategorization frame: corresponds to the phrase-structure rule used to expand the phrase around the target. For *give* in the example, this feature is `VP→VB NP NP`.

C-PATH. A string representation of the path through the constituent tree from the target word to the argument constituent. For instance, the path from *gave* to *she* is `↑VP-↑S-↓NP`.

PHRASETYPE. Phrase type of the argument constituent, e.g. `NP` for *she*.

GOVCAT. Governing category: this feature is either `S` or `VP`, and is found by starting at the argument constituent and moving upwards until either a `VP` or a sentence node (`S`, `SINV`, or `SQ`) is found. For instance, for *she*, this feature is `S`, while for *the horse*, it is `VP`. This can be thought of as a very primitive way of distinguishing subjects and objects.

A.3 Features Used by the Dependency-based Analyzer Only

D-SUBCAT. Subcategorization frame: the grammatical functions of the dependents concatenated. For *gave*, this feature is `SBJ+IOBJ+OBJ`.

D-PATH. A string representation of the path through the dependency tree from the target node to the argument node. Moving upwards through verb chains is not counted in this path string. In the example, the path from *gave* to *she* is `↓SBJ`.

CHILDDEPSET. The set of grammatical functions of the direct dependents of the target node. For instance, for *give*, this is { SBJ, IOBJ, OBJ }.

PARENTHASOBJ. Binary feature that is set to true if the parent of the target has an object.

RELTOPARENT. Dependency relation between the target node and its parent.

FUNCTION. The grammatical function of the argument node. For direct dependents of the target, this feature is identical to the D-PATH.

References

Baker, Collin F., Charles J. Fillmore, and John B. Lowe. 1998. The Berkeley FrameNet Project. In *Proceedings of COLING/ACL-1998.*

Baker, Collin, Michael Ellsworth, and Katrin Erk. 2007. SemEval task 19: Frame semantic structure extraction. In *Proceedings of SemEval-2007.*

Buchholz, Sabine and Erwin Marsi. 2006. CoNLL-X shared task on multilingual dependency parsing. In *Proceedings of the CoNLL-X.*

Carreras, Xavier and Lluís Màrquez. 2005. Introduction to the CoNLL-2005 shared task: Semantic role labeling. In *Proceedings of CoNLL-2005.*

Charniak, Eugene and Mark Johnson. 2005. Coarse-to-fine n-best parsing and MaxEnt discriminative reranking. In *Proceedings of ACL.*

Charniak, Eugene. 2000. A maximum-entropy-inspired parser. In *Proceedings of NAACL-2000.*

Collins, Michael. 1997. Three generative, lexicalised models for statistical parsing. In *Proceedings of ACL/EACL-1997.*

Gildea, Daniel and Julia Hockenmaier. 2003. Identifying semantic roles using combinatory categorial grammar. In *Proceedings of EMNLP-2003.*

Gildea, Daniel and Daniel Jurafsky. 2002. Automatic labeling of semantic roles. *Computational Linguistics*, 28(3):245–288.

Gildea, Daniel and Martha Palmer. 2002. The necessity of syntactic parsing for predicate argument recognition. In *Proceedings of the ACL-2002.*

Hacioglu, Kadri. 2004. Semantic role labeling using dependency trees. In *Proceedings of COLING-2004.*

Hirst, Graeme. 1983. A foundation for semantic interpretation. In *Proceedings of the ACL-1983.*

Hudson, Richard. 1984. *Word Grammar.* Blackwell.

Johansson, Richard and Pierre Nugues. 2007. Extended constituent-to-dependency conversion for English. In *Proceedings of NODALIDA 2007.*

Johansson, Richard and Pierre Nugues. 2008. Dependency-based syntactic–semantic analysis with PropBank and NomBank. In *Proceedings of CoNLL–2008.*

Litkowski, Ken. 2004. Senseval-3 task: Automatic labeling of semantic roles. In *Proceedings of Senseval-3.*

Magerman, David M. 1994. Natural language parsing as statistical pattern recognition. Ph.D. thesis, Stanford University.

Marcus, Mitchell P., Beatrice Santorini, and Mary Ann Marcinkiewicz. 1993. Building a large annotated corpus of English: the Penn Treebank. *Computational Linguistics*, 19(2):313–330.

McDonald, Ryan, Koby Crammer, and Fernando Pereira. 2005. Online large-margin training of dependency parsers. In *Proceedings of ACL-2005.*

Mel'čuk, Igor A. 1988. *Dependency Syntax: Theory and Practice.* State University Press of New York.

Nivre, Joakim and Mario Scholz. 2004. Deterministic dependency parsing of English text. In *Proceedings of COLING-2004.*

Nivre, Joakim, Johan Hall, Jens Nilsson, Atanas Chanev, Gülşen Eryiğit, Sandra Kübler, Svetoslav Marinov, and Erwin Marsi. 2007. MaltParser: A language-independent system for data-driven dependency parsing. *Natural Language Engineering*, 13(2):95–135.

Pradhan, Sameer, Wayne Ward, Kadri Hacioglu, James Martin, and Daniel Jurafsky. 2005. Semantic role labeling using different syntactic views. In *Proceedings of ACL-2005.*

Pradhan, Sameer, Wayne Ward, and James H. Martin. 2008. Towards robust semantic role labeling. *Computational Linguistics*, 34(2):289–310.

Punyakanok, Vasin, Dan Roth, and Wen-tau Yih. 2008. The importance of syntactic parsing and inference in semantic role labeling. *Computational Linguistics*, 34(2):257–287.

Swanson, Reid and Andrew S. Gordon. 2006. A comparison of alternative parse tree paths for labeling semantic roles. In *Proceedings of COLING/ACL-2006.*

Toutanova, Kristina, Dan Klein, Christopher Manning, and Yoram Singer. 2003. Feature-rich part-of-speech tagging with a cyclic dependency network. In *Proceedings of HLT-NAACL-2003.*

Toutanova, Kristina, Aria Haghighi, and Christopher D. Manning. 2005. Joint learning improves semantic role labeling. In *Proceedings of ACL-2005.*

Žabokrtský, Zdeněk, Petr Sgall, and Sašo Džeroski. 2002. A machine learning approach to automatic functor assignment in the Prague dependency treebank. In *Proceedings of LREC-2002.*

Xue, Nianwen and Martha Palmer. 2004. Calibrating features for semantic role labeling. In *Proceedings of EMNLP-2004.*

Yamada, Hiroyasu and Yuji Matsumoto. 2003. Statistical dependency analysis with support vector machines. In *Proceedings of IWPT-2003.*

Using Hidden Markov Random Fields to Combine Distributional and Pattern-based Word Clustering

Nobuhiro Kaji and **Masaru Kitsuregawa**
Institute of Industrial Science, University of Tokyo
4-6-1 Komaba, Meguro-ku, Tokyo 153-8505 Japan
{kaji,kitsure}@tkl.iis.u-tokyo.ac.jp

Abstract

Word clustering is a conventional and important NLP task, and the literature has suggested two kinds of approaches to this problem. One is based on the distributional similarity and the other relies on the co-occurrence of two words in lexico-syntactic patterns. Although the two methods have been discussed separately, it is promising to combine them since they are complementary with each other. This paper proposes to integrate them using hidden Markov random fields and demonstrates its effectiveness through experiments.

1 Introduction

Word clustering is a technique of grouping similar words together, and it is important for various NLP systems. Applications of word clustering include language modeling (Brown et al., 1992), text classification (Baker and McCallum, 1998), thesaurus construction (Lin, 1998) and so on. Furthermore, recent studies revealed that word clustering is useful for semi-supervised learning in NLP (Miller et al., 2004; Li and McCallum, 2005; Kazama and Torisawa, 2008; Koo et al., 2008).

A well-known approach to grouping similar words is to use distribution of contexts in which target words appear. It is founded on the hypothesis that similar words tend to appear in similar contexts (Harris, 1968). Based on this idea, some studies proposed probabilistic models for word clustering (Pereira et al., 1993; Li and Abe, 1998; Rooth et al., 1999; Torisawa, 2002). Others proposed distributional similarity measures between words (Hindle, 1990; Lin, 1998; Lee, 1999; Weeds et al., 2004). Once such similarity is defined, it is trivial to perform clustering.

On the other hand, some researchers utilized co-occurrence for word clustering. The idea behind it is that similar words tend to co-occur in certain patterns. Considerable efforts have been devoted to measure word similarity based on co-occurrence frequency of two words in a window (Church and Hanks, 1989; Turney, 2001; Terra and Clarke, 2003; Matsuo et al., 2006). In addition to the classical window-based technique, some studies investigated the use of lexico-syntactic patterns (e.g., X or Y) to get more accurate co-occurrence statistics (Chilovski and Pantel, 2004; Bollegala et al., 2007).

These two approaches are complementary with each other, because they are founded on different hypotheses and utilize different corpus statistics. Consider to cluster a set of words based on the distributional similarity. It is likely that some words are difficult to cluster due to the data sparseness or some other problems, while we can still expect that those words are correctly classified using patterns.

This consideration leads us to combine distributional and pattern-based word clustering. In this paper we propose to combine them using mixture models based on hidden Markov random fields. This model was originally proposed by (Basu et al., 2004) for semi-supervised clustering. In semi-supervised clustering, the system is provided with supervision in the form of pair-wise constraints specifying data points that are likely to belong to the same cluster. These constraints are directly incorporated into the clustering process as a prior knowledge. Our idea is to view the co-occurrence

© 2008. Licensed under the *Creative Commons Attribution-Noncommercial-Share Alike 3.0 Unported* license (http://creativecommons.org/licenses/by-nc-sa/3.0/). Some rights reserved.

of two words in lexico-syntactic patterns as constraints, and incorporate them into distributional word clustering.

In summary, this paper discusses the problem of integrating multiple approaches for word clustering. We consider that the clustering results are improved if multiple approaches are successfully combined and if they are complementary with each other. Our contribution is to provide a probabilistic framework for this problem. Although our proposal aims at combining the distributional and pattern-based approaches, it is also applicable to combine other approaches like (Lin et al., 2003), as we will discuss in Section 5.4.

2 Distributional Clustering

This and next section describe distributional and pattern-based word clustering respectively. Section 4 will explain how to combine them.

2.1 Probabilistic model

In distributional word clustering, similarity between words (= nouns) is measured by the distribution of contexts in which they appear. As a context, verbs that appear in certain grammatical relations with the target nouns are typically used. Using the distribution of such verbs, we can express a noun n by a feature vector $\phi(n)$:

$$\phi(n) = (f_{nv_1}, f_{nv_2}, \ldots f_{nv_V})$$

where f_{nv_i} denotes the frequency of noun-verb pair (n, v_i), and V denotes the number of distinct verbs. The basic idea of using the distribution for clustering is to group n and n' together if $\phi(n)$ and $\phi(n')$ are similar.

Let us consider a soft clustering model. We hypothesize that $\phi(n)$ is a mixture of multinomial, and the probability of n is defined by[1]

$$\begin{aligned} p(n) &= \sum_{z=1}^{Z} p(z)p(\phi(n)|z) \\ &= \sum_{z=1}^{Z} \pi_z \frac{f_n!}{\prod_v f_{nv}!} \prod_v \mu_{vz}^{f_{nv}} \end{aligned}$$

where Z is the number of mixture components, π_z is the mixing coefficient ($\sum_z \pi_z = 1$), $f_n = \sum_v f_{nv}$ is the total number of occurrence of n, and μ_{vz} is the parameter of the multinomial distribution ($\sum_v \mu_{vz} = 1$). In this model the hidden variables can be interpreted as semantic class of nouns.

Now consider a set of nouns $\mathbf{n} = \{n_i\}_{i=1}^N$. Let $\mathbf{z} = \{z_i\}_{i=1}^N$ be a set of hidden variables corresponding to $\mathbf{n}$. Assuming that the hidden variables are independent and n_i is also independent of other nouns given the hidden variables, the probability of $\mathbf{n}$ is defined by

$$p(\mathbf{n}) = \sum_{\mathbf{z}} p(\mathbf{z})p(\mathbf{n}|\mathbf{z})$$

where

$$\begin{aligned} p(\mathbf{z}) &= \prod_{i=1}^{N} p(z_i) \\ p(\mathbf{n}|\mathbf{z}) &= \prod_{i=1}^{N} p(n_i|z_i). \end{aligned}$$

Hereafter, we use $p(n|z)$ instead of $p(\phi(n)|z)$ to keep the notation simple. $p(\mathbf{n}|\mathbf{z})$ is the conditional distribution on all nouns given all the hidden variables, and $p(\mathbf{z})$ is the prior distribution on the hidden variables. Computing the log-likelihood of the complete data $(\mathbf{n}, \mathbf{z})$, we found

$$\log p(\mathbf{n}, \mathbf{z}) = \sum_{i=1}^{N} \log p(z_i)p(n_i|z_i). \quad (1)$$

2.2 Parameter estimation

The parameters can be estimated by the EM algorithm. In the E-step, $p(z_i|n_i)$ is computed based on current parameters. It is computed by

$$\begin{aligned} p(z_i = k|n_i) &= \frac{p(z_i = k)p(n_i|z_i = k)}{\sum_z p(z)p(n_i|z)} \\ &= \frac{\pi_k \prod_v \mu_{vk}^{f_{n_iv}}}{\sum_z \pi_z \prod_v \mu_{vz}^{f_{n_iv}}}. \end{aligned}$$

In the M-step, the parameters are re-estimated by using the result of the E-step:

$$\begin{aligned} \mu_{\gamma k} &= \frac{\alpha + \sum_i f_{n_i\gamma} p(z_i = k|n_i)}{\alpha V + \sum_v \sum_i f_{n_iv} p(z_i = k|n_i)} \\ \pi_k &= \frac{\alpha + \sum_i p(z_i = k|n_i)}{\alpha Z + \sum_z \sum_i p(z_i = z|n_i)} \end{aligned}$$

where α is a smoothing factor.[2] Both steps are repeated until a convergence criteria is satisfied. The important point to note is that the E-step can be computed using the above equation because the hidden variables are independent.

[1] We ignored $p(f_n)$ by assuming that it is independent of hidden variables. See (McCallum and Nigam, 1998) for detail discussion.

[2] α=1.0 in our experiment.

X *ya* Y	X *mo* Y *mo*	X *to* Y *to*	X, Y *nado*
(X or Y)	(X and Y)	(X and Y)	(X, Y etc.)

Table 1: Four lexico-syntactic patterns, where X and Y are extracted as co-occurring words. Note that *ya*, *mo*, and *to* are Japanese postpositions, and they correspond to *or* or *and* in English.

3 Pattern-based Clustering

A graph-based algorithm was employed in order to cluster words using patterns.

3.1 Graph Construction

We first construct the graph in which vertices and edges correspond to words and their co-occurrences in patterns respectively (Figure 1). We employed four lexico-syntactic patterns (Table 1) to extract co-occurrence of two words from corpus. Note that we target Japanese in this paper although our proposal is independent of languages. The edges are weighted by the strength of co-occurrence that is computed by the Point-wise Mutual Information (PMI):

$$\mathrm{PMI}(n_i, n_j) = \log \frac{f(n_i, n_j) f(*, *)}{f(n_i, *) f(*, n_j)}$$

where $f(n_i, n_j)$ is the co-occurrence frequency of two nouns, and '$*$' means summation over all nouns. If PMI is less than zero, the edge is removed.

3.2 Graph Partitioning

Assuming that similar words tend to co-occur in the lexico-syntactic patterns, it is reasonable to consider that a dense subgraph is a good cluster (Figure 1). Following (Matsuo et al., 2006), we exploit the Newman clustering (Newman, 2004) to partition the graph into such dense subgraphs.

We start by describing Newman's algorithm for unweighted graphs and we will generalize it to weighted graphs later. The Newman clustering is an algorithm that divides a graph into subgraphs based on connectivity. Roughly speaking, it divides a graph such that there are a lot of edges between vertices in the same cluster. In the algorithm goodness of clustering is measured by score Q:

$$Q = \sum_i \left(e_{ii} - a_i^2 \right)$$

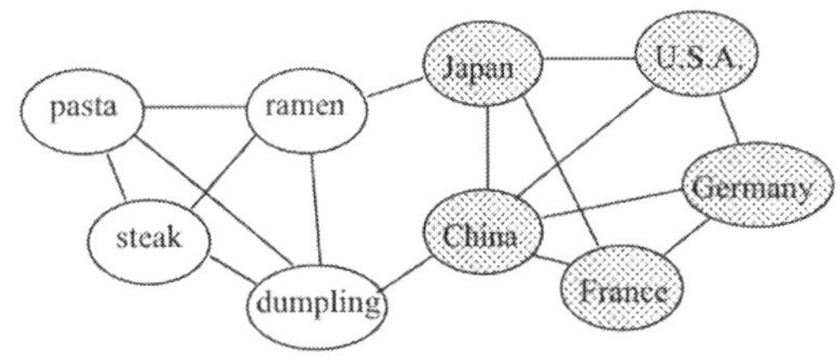

Figure 1: An example of the graph consisting of two dense subgraphs.

where

$$e_{ij} = \frac{\text{\# of edges between two vertices in cluster } i \text{ and } j}{\text{\# of all edges}}$$

$$a_i = \sum_k e_{ik}.$$

The term e_{ij} is the fraction of edges between cluster i and j. a_i is the sum of e_{ik} over all clusters, and a_i^2 represents the expected number of fraction of edges within the cluster i when edges are given at random. See (Newman, 2004) for the detail.

The Newman clustering optimizes Q in an agglomerative fashion. At the beginning of the algorithm every vertex forms a singleton cluster, and we repeatedly merge two clusters so that the join results in the largest increase in Q. The change in Q when cluster i and j are merged is given by

$$\Delta Q = e_{ij} + e_{ji} - 2a_i a_j = 2(e_{ij} - a_i a_j).$$

The above procedure is repeated until Q reaches local maximum.

The algorithm can be easily generalized to weighted graphs by substituting "sum of weights of edges" for "# of edges" in the definition of e_{ij}. The other part of the algorithm remains the same.

4 Integration based on Hidden Markov Random Fields

This section represents how to integrate the distribution and pattern for word clustering.

4.1 Background and idea

Clustering has long been discussed as an unsupervised learning problem. In some applications, however, it is possible to provide some form of supervision by hand in order to improve the clustering result. This motivated researchers to investigate semi-supervised clustering, which uses not only unlabeled data but supervision in the form of pair-wise constraints (Basu et al., 2004). In this framework, the clustering system is provided with a set of pair-wise constraints specifying data points that are likely to belong to the same cluster. These constraints are directly incorporated into the clustering process as a prior knowledge.

Our idea is to view the co-occurrence of two words in lexico-syntactic patterns as constraints, and incorporate them into the distributional clustering. The rest of this section describes how to extend the distributional clustering so as to incorporate the constraints, and how to generate the constraints using the patterns.

4.2 Probabilistic model

Let $\mathbb{C}$ be a set of pair-wise constraints, and consider to incorporate the constraints into the distributional clustering (Section 2). In what follows we assume each constraint $\langle i, j \rangle \in \mathbb{C}$ represents that z_i and z_j are likely to have the same value, and it is associated with a weight $w_{ij} (> 0)$ corresponding to a penalty for constraint violation.

It is easy to extend the distributional clustering algorithm so as to incorporate the constraints. This is done by just changing the prior distribution on hidden variables $p(\mathbf{z})$. Following (Basu et al., 2004), we construct the Markov random field on the hidden variables so as to incorporate the constraints. The new prior distribution is defined as

$$p(\mathbf{z}) = \prod_{i=1}^{N} p(z_i) \times \frac{1}{G} \exp\{-\sum_{\langle i,j \rangle \in \mathbb{C}} \delta(z_i \neq z_j) w_{ij}\}$$

where $\delta(\cdot)$ is the delta function. $\delta(z_i \neq z_j)$ takes one if the constraint $\langle i, j \rangle$ is violated and otherwise zero. G is the normalization factor of the Markov random field (the second term).

By examining the log-likelihood of the complete data, we can see how violation of constraints is penalized. Using the new prior distribution, we get

$$\begin{aligned} \log p(\mathbf{n}, \mathbf{z}) &= \sum_{i=1}^{N} \log p(z_i) p(n_i | z_i) \\ &- \sum_{\langle i,j \rangle \in \mathbb{C}} \delta(z_i \neq z_j) w_{ij} \\ &- \log G. \end{aligned}$$

The first term in the right-hand side is equal to the log-likelihood of the multinomial mixture, namely equation (1). The second term can be interpreted as the penalty for constraint violation. The last term is a constant.

It is worth pointing out that the resulting algorithm makes a soft assignment and polysemous words can belong to more than one clusters.

4.3 Parameter estimation

The parameters are estimated by the EM algorithm. The M-step is exactly the same as discussed in Section 2.2. The problem is that the hidden variables are no longer independent and the E-step requires the calculation of

$$\begin{aligned} p(z_i | \mathbf{n}) &= \sum_{\mathbf{z}_{\neg i}} p(\mathbf{z}_{\neg i}, z_i | \mathbf{n}) \\ &\propto \sum_{\mathbf{z}_{\neg i}} p(\mathbf{z}_{\neg i}, z_i) p(\mathbf{n} | \mathbf{z}_{\neg i}, z_i) \end{aligned}$$

where $\mathbf{z}_{\neg i}$ means all hidden variables but z_i. The computation of the above equation is intractable because the summation in it requires $O(Z^{N-1})$ operations.

Instead of exactly computing $p(z_i | \mathbf{n})$, we approximate it by using the mean field approximation (Lange et al., 2005). In the mean field approximation, $p(\mathbf{z}|\mathbf{n})$ is approximated by a factorized distribution $q(\mathbf{z})$, in which all hidden variables are independent:

$$q(\mathbf{z}) = \prod_{i=1}^{N} q_i(z_i). \tag{2}$$

Using $q(\mathbf{z})$ instead of $p(\mathbf{z}|\mathbf{n})$, computation of the E-step can be written as follows:

$$p(z_i | \mathbf{n}) \simeq \sum_{\mathbf{z}_{\neg i}} q(\mathbf{z}_{\neg i}, z_i) = q_i(z_i). \tag{3}$$

The parameters of $q(\mathbf{z})$ are determined such that the KL divergence between $q(\mathbf{z})$ and $p(\mathbf{z}|\mathbf{n})$ is minimized. In other words, the approximate distribution $q(\mathbf{z})$ is determined by minimizing

$$\sum_{\mathbf{z}} q(\mathbf{z}) \log \frac{q(\mathbf{z})}{p(\mathbf{z}|\mathbf{n})} \tag{4}$$

under the condition that $\sum_k q_i(z_i = k) = 1$ for all i. This optimization problem can be resolved by introducing Lagrange multipliers. Because we cannot get the solution in closed form, an iterative method is employed. Taking the derivative of equation (4) with respect to a parameter $q_{ik} = q_i(z_i = k)$ and setting it to zero, we get the following updating formula:

$$q_{ik}^{(t+1)} \propto p(n_i, k) \exp\{-\sum_{j \in \mathbb{N}_i} (1 - q_{jk}^{(t)}) w_{ij}\} \tag{5}$$

where $\mathbb{N}_i = \{j | \langle i,j \rangle \in \mathbb{C}\}$ and $q_{ik}^{(t)}$ is the value of q_{ik} at t-th iteration. The derivation of this formula is found in Appendix.

4.4 Generation of constraints

It is often pointed out that even small amounts of misspecified constraints significantly decrease the performance of semi-supervised clustering. This is because the error of misspecified constraints is propagated to the entire transitive neighborhoods of the constrained data (Nelson and Cohen, 2007). As an example, consider that we have two constraints $\langle i,j \rangle$ and $\langle j,k \rangle$. If the former is misspecified one, the error propagate to k through j.

To tackle this problem, we propose a technique to put an upper bound θ on the size of the transitive neighborhoods. Our constraint generation process is as follows. To begin with, we modified the Newman clustering so that the maximum cluster size does not exceed θ. This can be done by prohibiting such merge that results in larger cluster than θ. Given the result of the modified Newman clustering, it is straightforward to generate constraints. Constraints are generated between two nouns in the same cluster if they co-occur in the lexico-syntactic patterns at least one time. The penalty for constraint violation w_{ij} was set to PMI(n_i, n_j). This procedure obviously ensures that the size of the transitive neighborhoods is less than θ.

5 Experiments

5.1 Data sets

We parsed 15 years of news articles by KNP[3] so as to obtain data sets for the distributional and pattern-based word clustering (Table 2). The number of distinct nouns in total was 297,719. Note that, due to the computational efficiency, we removed such nouns that appeared less than 10 times with verbs and did not appear at all in the patterns.

A test set was created using manually tailored Japanese thesaurus (Ikehara et al., 1997). We randomly selected 500 unambiguous nouns from 25 categories (20 words for each category).

5.2 Baselines

For comparison we implemented the following baseline systems.

- The multinomial mixture (Section 2).
- The Newman clustering (Newman, 2004).

[3]http://nlp.kuee.kyoto-u.ac.jp/nl-resource/

nouns	208,934
verbs	64,954
noun-verb pairs	4,804,715
nouns	245,465
noun-noun pairs	633,302

Table 2: Data sets statistics. The first and second row shows the number of distinct words (and word pairs) used for the distributional and pattern-based word clustering respectively.

- Three K-means algorithms using different distributional similarity or dissimilarity measures: cosine, α-skew divergence (Lee, 1999)[4], and Lin's similarity (Lin, 1998).
- The CBC algorithm (Lin and Pantel, 2002; Pantel and Lin, 2002).

5.3 Evaluation procedure

All the nouns in the data set were clustered by the proposed and baseline systems.[5] For the mixture models and K-means, the number of clusters was set to 1,000. The parameter θ was set to 100.

The result was assessed by precision and recall using the test data. The precision and recall were computed by the B-CUBED algorithm as follows (Bagga and Baldwin, 1998). For each noun n_i in the test data, precision$_i$ and recall$_i$ are defined as

$$\text{precision}_i = \frac{|S_i \cap T_i|}{|S_i|}$$

$$\text{recall}_i = \frac{|S_i \cap T_i|}{|T_i|}$$

where S_i is the system generated cluster containing n_i and T_i is the goldstandard cluster containing n_i. The precision and recall are defined as an average of precision$_i$ and recall$_i$ for all the nouns in the test data respectively. The result of soft clustering models cannot be directly evaluated by the precision and recall. In such cases, each noun is assigned to the cluster that maximizes $p(z|n)$.

5.4 The result and discussion

Table 3 shows the experimental results. The best results for each statistic are shown in bold. For the mixture models and K-means, the precision and recall are an average of 10 trials.

Table 3 demonstrates the impact of combining distribution and pattern. Our method outperformed

[4]$\alpha = 0.99$ in our experiment.

[5]Our implementation is available from http://www.tkl.iis.u-tokyo.ac.jp/~kaji/clustering.

	P	R	F_1
proposed	.383	**.437**	**.408**
multinomial mixture	.360	.374	.367
Newman (2004)	.318	.353	.334
cosine	.603	.114	.192
α-skew divergence (Lee, 1999)	.730	.155	.255
Lin's similarity (Lin, 1998)	.691	.096	.169
CBC (Lin and Pantel, 2002)	**.981**	.060	.114

Table 3: Precision, recall, and F-measure.

all the baseline systems. It was statistically significantly better than the multinomial mixture ($P < 0.01$, Mann-Whitney U-test). Note that it is possible to improve some baseline systems, especially CBC, by tuning the parameters. For CBC we simply used the same parameter values as reported in (Lin and Pantel, 2002).

Compared with the multinomial mixture, one advantage of our method is that it has broad coverage. Our method can successfully handle *unknown words*, which do not appear with verbs at all (i.e., $f_n = 0$ and $\phi(n)$ is zero vector), if they co-occur with other words in the lexico-syntactic patterns. For unknown words, the hidden variables are determined based only on $p(\mathbf{z})$ because $p(n|z)$ takes the same value for all hidden variables. This means that our method clusters unknown words using pair-wise constraints. On the other hand, the multinomial mixture assigns all the unknown words to the cluster that maximizes $p(z)$.

The test set included 51 unknown words.[6] We split the test set into two parts: $f_n = 0$ and $f_n \neq 0$, and calculated precision and recall for each subset (Table 4). Although the improvement is especially significant for the unknown words, we can clearly confirm the improvement for both subsets. For the Newman clustering we can discuss similar things (Table 5). Different from the Newman clustering, our method can handle nouns that do not co-occur with other nouns if $0 < f_n$. In this case the test set included 64 unknown words.

It is interesting to point out that our framework can further incorporate lexico-syntactic patterns for dissimilar words (Lin et al., 2003). Namely, we can use patterns so as to prevent distributionally similar but semantically different words (e.g., ally and supporter (Lin et al., 2003)) from being assigned to the same cluster. This can be achieved by using cannot-link constraints, which specify data points that are likely to belong to different clusters (Basu et al., 2004). The remaining problem is which patterns to use so as to extract dissimilar words. Although this problem has already been discussed by (Lin et al., 2003), they mainly addressed antonyms. We believe that a more exhaustive investigation is required. In addition, it is still unclear whether dissimilar words are really useful to improve clustering results.

One problem that we did not examine is how to determine optimal number of clusters. In the experiment, the number was decided with trial-and-error through our initial experiment. We leave it as our future work to test methods of automatically determining the cluster number (Pedersen and Kulkarni, 2006; Blei and Jordan, 2006).

[6]The baseline systems assigned the unknown words to a default cluster as the multinomial mixture does.

	$f_n = 0$			$f_n \neq 0$		
	P	R	F_1	P	R	F_1
proposed	**.320**	.632	**.435**	**.412**	**.450**	**.430**
multi.	.099	**1.000**	.181	.402	.394	.398

Table 4: Detail comparison with the multinomial mixture.

	$f(n_i, *) = 0$			$f(n_i, *) \neq 0$		
	P	R	F_1	P	R	F_1
proposed	**.600**	.456	**.518**	**.380**	**.479**	**.424**
Newman	.071	**1.000**	.133	.354	.412	.381

Table 5: Detail comparison with the Newman clustering.

6 Related work

As far as we know, the distributional and pattern-based word clustering have been discussed independently (e.g., (Pazienza et al., 2006)). One of the most relevant work is (Bollegala et al., 2007), which proposed to integrate various patterns in order to measure semantic similarity between words. Although they extensively discussed the use of patterns, they did not address the distributional approach.

Mirkin (2006) pointed out the importance of integrating distributional similarity and lexico-syntactic patterns, and showed how to combine the two approaches for textual entailment acquisition. Although their work inspired our research, we discussed word clustering, which is related to but different from entailment acquisition.

Lin (2003) also proposed to use both distributional similarity and lexico-syntactic patterns for finding synonyms. However, they present an opposite viewpoint from our research. Their proposal is to exploit patterns in order to filter dissimilar words. As we have already discussed, the integration of such patterns can also be formalized using similar probabilistic model to ours.

A variety of studies discussed determining polarity of words. Because this problem is ternary (positive, negative, and neutral) classification of words, it can be seen as one kind of word clustering. The literature suggested two methods of determining polarity, and they are analogous to the distributional and co-occurrence-based approaches in word clustering (Takamura et al., 2005; Higashiyama et al., 2008). We consider it is also promising to integrate them for polarity determination.

7 Conclusion

The distributional and pattern-based word clustering have long been discussed separately despite the potentiality for their integration. In this paper, we provided a probabilistic framework for combining the two approaches, and demonstrated that the clustering result is significantly improved.

Our important future work is to extend current framework so as to incorporate patterns for dissimilar words using cannot-link constraints. We consider such patterns further improve the clustering result.

Combining distribution and pattern is important for other NLP problems as well (e.g., entailment acquisition, polarity determination). Although this paper examined word clustering, we consider a part of our idea can be applied to other problems.

Acknowledgement

This work was supported by the *Comprehensive Development of e-Society Foundation Software* program of the Ministry of Education, Culture, Sports, Science and Technology, Japan.

References

Bagga, Amit and Breck Baldwin. 1998. Entity-based cross-document coreferencing using the vector space model. In *Proceedings of ACL*, pages 79–85.

Baker, L. Douglas and Andrew Kachites McCallum. 1998. Distributional clustering of words for text classification. In *Proceedings of SIGIR*, pages 96–103.

Basu, Sugato, Mikhail Bilenko, and Raymond J. Mooney. 2004. A probabilistic framework for semi-supervised clustering. In *Proceedings of SIGKDD*, pages 59–68.

Blei, David M. and Michael I. Jordan. 2006. Variational inference for Dirichlet process mixtures. *Bayesian Analysis*, 1(1):121–144.

Bollegala, Danushka, Yutaka Matsuo, and Mitsuru Ishizuka. 2007. An integrated approach to measuring semantic similarity between words using information available on the web. In *Proceedings of NAACL*, pages 340–347.

Brown, Peter F., Vincent J. Della Pietra, Peter V. deSouza, Jenifer C. Lai, and Rober L. Mercer. 1992. Class-based n-gram models of natural language. *Computational Linguistics*, 18(4):467–479.

Chilovski, Timothy and Patrick Pantel. 2004. VERBOCEAN: Mining the web for fine-grained semantic verb relations. In *Proceedings of EMNLP*, pages 33–40.

Church, Kenneth Ward and Patrick Hanks. 1989. Word association norms, mutual information, and lexicography. In *Proceedings of ACL*, pages 76–83.

Harris, Zellig. 1968. *Mathematical Structure of Language*. New York: Wiley.

Higashiyama, Masahiko, Kentaro Inui, and Yuji Matsumoto. 2008. Learning polarity of nouns by selectional preferences of predicates (in Japanese). In *Proceedings of the Association for NLP*, pages 584–587.

Hindle, Donald. 1990. Noun classification from predicate-argument structure. In *Proceedings of ACL*, pages 268–275.

Ikehara, Satoru, Masahiro Miyazaki, Satoshi Shirai, Akio Yokoo, Hiromi Nakaiwa, Kentarou Ogura, and Yoshifumi Oyama Yoshihiko Hayashi, editors. 1997. *Japanese Lexicon*. Iwanami Publishing.

Kazama, Jun'ichi and Kentaro Torisawa. 2008. Inducing gazetteers for named entity recognition by large-scale clustering of dependency relations. In *Proceedings of ACL*, pages 407–415.

Koo, Terry, Xavier Carreras, and Michael Collins. 2008. Simple semi-supervised dependency parsing. In *Proceedings of ACL*, pages 595–603.

Lange, Tilman, Martin H.C. Law, Anil K. Jain, and Joachim M. Buhmann. 2005. Learning with constrained and unlabelled data. In *Proceedings of CVPR*, pages 731–738.

Lee, Lillian. 1999. Measures of distributional similarity. In *Proceedings of ACL*, pages 25–32.

Li, Hang and Naoki Abe. 1998. Word clustering and disambiguation based on co-occurrence. In *Proceedings of ACL-COLING*, pages 749–755.

Li, Wei and Andrew McCallum. 2005. Semi-supervised sequence modeling with syntactic topic models. In *Proceedings of AAAI*, pages 813–818.

Lin, Dekang and Patrick Pantel. 2002. Concept discovery from text. In *Proceeodings of COLING*, pages 577–583.

Lin, Dekang, Shaojun Zhao, Lijuan Qin, and Ming Zhou. 2003. Identifying synonyms among distributionally similar words. In *Proceedings of IJCAI*, pages 1492–1493.

Lin, Dekang. 1998. Automatic retrieval and clustering of similar words. In *Proceedings of ACL-COLING*, pages 768–774.

Matsuo, Yutaka, Takeshi Sakaki, Koki Uchiyama, and Mitsuru Ishizuka. 2006. Graph-based word clustering using a web search engine. In *Proceedings of EMNLP*, pages 542–550.

McCallum, Andrew and Kamal Nigam. 1998. A comparison of event models for naive Bayes text classification. In *Proceedings of AAAI Workshop on Learning for Text Categorization*, pages 41–48.

Miller, Scott, Jethran Guinness, and Alex Zamanian. 2004. Name tagging with word clusters and discriminative training. In *Proceedings of NAACL*, pages 579–586.

Mirkin, Shachar, Ido Dagan, and Maayan Geffet. 2006. Integrating pattern-based and distributional similarity methods for lexical entailment acquisition. In *Proceedings of COLING-ACL Poster Sessions*, pages 579–586.

Nelson, Blaine and Ira Cohen. 2007. Revisiting probabilistic models for clustering with pair-wise constraints. In *Proceedings of ICML*, pages 673–680.

Newman, Mark. 2004. Fast algorithm for detecting community structure in networks. In *Phys. Rev. E 69*.

Pantel, Patrick and Dekang Lin. 2002. Discovering word senses from text. In *Proceedings of SIGKDD*, pages 613–619.

Pazienza, Maria Teresa, Marco Pennacchiotti, and Fabio Massimo Zanzotto. 2006. Discovering verb relations in corpora: Distributional versus non-distributional approaches. In *Proceedings of IEA/AIE*, pages 1042–1052.

Pedersen, Ted and Anagha Kulkarni. 2006. Automatic cluster stopping with criterion functions and the gap statistic. In *Proceedings of HLT/NAACL, Companion Volume*, pages 276–279.

Pereira, Fernando, Naftali Tishby, and Lillian Lee. 1993. Distributional clustering of english words. In *Proceedings of ACL*, pages 183–190.

Rooth, Mats, Stefan Riezler, Detlef Prescher, Glenn Garrroll, and Franz Beil. 1999. Inducing a semantically annotated lexicon via EM-based clustering. In *Proceedings of ACL*, pages 104–111.

Takamura, Hiroya, Takashi Inui, and Manabu Okumura. 2005. Extracting semantic orientations of words using spin model. In *Proceedings of ACL*, pages 133–140.

Terra, Egidio and C.L.A. Clarke. 2003. Frequency estimates for statistical word similarity measures. In *Proceedings of NAACL*, pages 165–172.

Torisawa, Kentaro. 2002. An unsupervised learning method for associative relationships between verb phrases. In *Proceedings of COLING*, pages 1009–1015.

Turney, Peter. 2001. Mining the web for synonyms: PMI-IR versus LSA on TOEFL. In *Proceedings of ECML*, pages 491–502.

Weeds, Julie, David Weir, and Diana McCarthy. 2004. Characterising measures of lexical distributional similarity. In *Proceedings of COLING*, pages 1015–1021.

Appendix. Derivation of the updating formula

We can rewrite equation (4) as follows:

$$
\begin{aligned}
(4) &= \sum_{\mathbf{z}} q(\mathbf{z}) \log q(\mathbf{z}) && (6)\\
&- \sum_{\mathbf{z}} q(\mathbf{z}) \sum_{i=1}^{N} \log p(n_i, z_i) && (7)\\
&+ \sum_{\mathbf{z}} q(\mathbf{z}) \sum_{\langle i,j\rangle \in \mathbb{C}} \delta(z_i \neq z_j) w_{ij} && (8)\\
&+ \text{const} && (9)
\end{aligned}
$$

where we made use of the fact that $\log p(\mathbf{z}|\mathbf{n}) = \log p(\mathbf{n}|\mathbf{z})p(\mathbf{z}) + \text{const}$. Taking the derivative of equation (6), (7), and (8) with respect to q_{ik}, we found

$$
\begin{aligned}
\frac{\partial(6)}{\partial q_{ik}} &= \log q_{ik} + \text{const}\\
\frac{\partial(7)}{\partial q_{ik}} &= -\log p(n_i, k) + \text{const}\\
\frac{\partial(8)}{\partial q_{ik}} &= \sum_{\mathbf{z}_{\neg i}} q(\mathbf{z}_{\neg i}) \sum_{j \in \mathbb{N}_i} \delta(z_j \neq k) w_{ij} + \text{const}\\
&= \sum_{j \in \mathbb{N}_i} \sum_{\mathbf{z}_{\neg i}} q(\mathbf{z}_{\neg i}) \delta(z_j \neq k) w_{ij} + \text{const}\\
&= \sum_{j \in \mathbb{N}_i} (1 - q_{jk}) w_{ij} + \text{const}
\end{aligned}
$$

where const denotes terms independent of k. Making use of these results, the updating formula can be derived by taking the derivative of equation (4) with respect to q_{ik} and setting it to zero.

Textual Demand Analysis: Detection of Users' Wants and Needs from Opinions

Hiroshi Kanayama **Tetsuya Nasukawa**
Tokyo Research Laboratory, IBM Japan, Ltd.
1623-14 Shimotsuruma, Yamato-shi, Kanagawa-ken, 242-8502 Japan
{hkana,nasukawa}@jp.ibm.com

Abstract

This paper tackles *textual demand analysis*, the task of capturing what people want or need, rather than identifying what they like or dislike, on which much conventional work has focused. It exploits syntactic patterns as clues to detect previously unknown demands, and requires domain-dependent knowledge to get high recall. To build such patterns we created an unsupervised pattern induction method relying on the hypothesis that there are commonly desired aspects throughout a domain corpus. Experimental results show that the proposed method detects twice to four times as many demand expressions in Japanese discussion forums compared to a baseline method.

1 Introduction

Increasingly we can access many opinions towards products, services, or companies through electronic documents including questionnaires, call logs, and other consumer-generated media (CGM) such as Internet discussion forums and blogs. It is very important for companies to get insights from their customers' opinions by analyzing such documents in large numbers.

The most popular way to utilize such data has involved *sentiment analysis* (SA) (Nasukawa and Yi, 2003; Yi et al., 2003), which is the task of recognizing the writers' feelings as expressed in positive or negative comments. Typically, a SA system focuses on expressions to identify the strong or weak points of the subjects as in (1) or in the writers' evaluations as in (2).

(1) I think the pictures are beautiful.
(2) I don't like this camera very much.

Here we call them *polar expressions* because they convey positive or negative polarities. By counting the polar expressions related to products or services, one can quantitatively compare the goodness of competing services, find the drawbacks of specific products, and so on.

In addition to polar expressions, there are other types of expressions that provide valuable information, especially for the supplier side rather than the consumer side. Examples (3) and (4) express the demands of the writers.

(3) I'd be happy if it is equipped with a crisp LCD.
(4) I'm waiting for a single-lens reflex less than 30,000 yen to come on the market.

We call such expressions "*demand expressions*", and the underlined phrases "*demand targets*."

While sentiment analysis reveals evaluations of existing products or services, the task proposed here, textual demand analysis[1], gives more direct suggestions to companies: things they should do to attract customers. For example, by investigating demand targets, companies can add new functions to products on the market or plan new services to satisfy customers. These activities should lead to positive evaluations in the future.

Interestingly, demand expressions may be noise in sentiment analysis, because the demand expressions do not actually convey positive or neg-

© 2008. Licensed under the *Creative Commons Attribution-Noncommercial-Share Alike 3.0 Unported* license (http://creativecommons.org/licenses/by-nc-sa/3.0/). Some rights reserved.

[1] Note that textual demand analysis is different from the demand analysis in the field of marketing or software engineering.

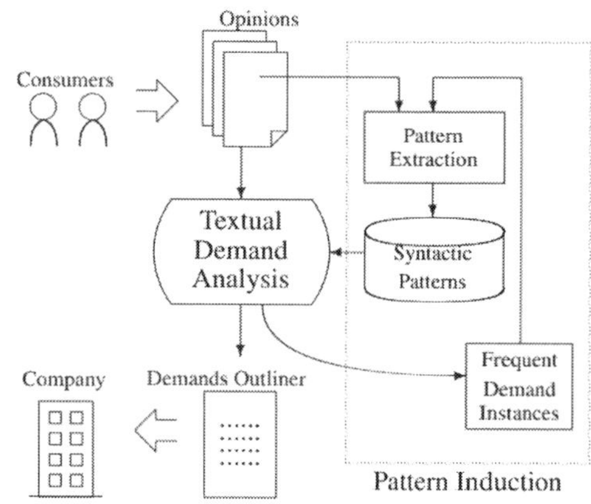

Figure 1: A demand analysis system and the flow of the pattern induction method.

ative evaluations of existing products or services, even though these demand expressions often contain positive or negative words, as in Example (3) which contains the positive expressions 'happy' and 'crisp LCD'.

The detection of novel demand targets requires deep syntactic information because such demand targets themselves can not be predefined. For example, to regard the underlined parts of (3) and (4) as demand targets, the non-underlined parts of these sentences have to be properly interpreted as triggers. This is a major difference from sentiment analysis where the polar expressions can be defined in the lexicon.

The left parts of Figure 1 illustrate the concepts of a system that visualizes the users' demands described in the input opinion data, where the main analysis component processes the documents and extracts the demand targets. The output of the system is created by a demand outliner, which the company uses to grasp the trends of consumers' demands.

The syntactic patterns that can be used as clues to demand expressions depend on the topic domain or the writing style. To organize this linguistic knowledge we propose an unsupervised induction method for syntactic patterns. The right part of Figure 1 shows the flow of pattern induction.

In the next section, we review related work, and Section 3 defines our task more formally. In Section 4 we describe a naive approach to the task and Section 5 shows a form of unsupervised pattern induction used to cover more demand expressions. Section 6 gives the experimental results and we conclude in Section 7.

2 Related Work

Sentiment analysis (SA) and related topics have been extensively studied in recent years. The textual demand analysis proposed in this paper shares some properties with phrase-level SA, the detection of sentiments and evaluations expressed in phrases, rather than document-level SA, the classification of documents in terms of goodness of reputation. Yi et al. (2003) pointed out that the multiple sentiment aspects in a document should be extracted, and Nasukawa and Yi (2003) clarified the need for deep syntactic analysis for the phrase-level SA.

The acquisition of clues is a key technology in these research efforts, as seen in learning methods for document-level SA (Hatzivassiloglou and McKeown, 1997; Turney, 2002) and for phrase-level SA (Wilson et al., 2005; Kanayama and Nasukawa, 2006).

As well as the sentiment expressions leading to evaluations, there are many semantic aspects to be extracted from documents which contain writers' opinions, such as subjectivity (Wiebe and Mihalcea, 2006), comparative sentences (Jindal and Liu, 2006), or predictive expressions (Kim and Hovy, 2007). However, the extraction of the contents of writers' demands which this paper handles is less studied while this type of information is very valuable for commercial applications.

For the tasks of information extraction and relation extraction, bootstrapping approaches have been proven successful (Yangarber, 2003; Pantel and Pennacchiotti, 2006). The pattern induction method in this paper exploits their ideas, but their application to the demand detection is not trivial, because some instances of demands are previously unknown and do not appear frequently, so they have to be abstracted effectively.

The work by Inui et al. (2003) handles semantics of a type similar to ours. They aimed to detect the requests in the responses to open-ended questionnaires, seeking *direct requests* such as "... てほしい" ('[I] would like you to ...') and other forms which can be paraphrased as direct requests. They classified sentences into requests or non-requests, where their source documents were responses to questionnaires, and where more than 60% of the utterances could be regarded as requests of some sort. In contrast, our method detects the content of the demands in the form of noun phrases, and handles more general target documents including

CGM documents that contain much more diverse utterances.

3 Task Definition

As shown in Section 1, our goal is to create a system to enumerate in an easily understandable way the demand targets in the input text. This section describes the definition of a demand target and its representation format.

3.1 Demand targets

Demands or requests written in opinion texts can be represented by verb phrases as in *e.g.* 'I want to V.' and 'I want you to V.', or noun phrases as in 'I want N.'[2] In this paper we focus on the last type, *i.e.* noun phrases which represent desired objects, because they are easier to aggregate and grasp than verb phrases. Another reason is that some demands represented with a verb phrase only describe the objects that are desired. For example, 'I want to buy N' and 'I want you to provide N' can be simply interpreted as meaning that N is what the writer wants. We call such a noun phrase a *demand target*, and these are the outputs of our system.

For applications, the demand targets to be detected by the system depend on the type of input documents. For example, from a consumers' forum on digital cameras, the underlined parts in Examples (3) and (4) from Section 1 apparently describe the writer's demands, so they are valuable information for such users of demand analysis such as the makers of digital camera. However, the request in Example (5) does not express the author's demands about any digital camera, but rather it is written for other participants in the forum. This type should be excluded from the output.

(5) Please give me a good advice.

In contrast, when the responses to a questionnaire about the activities of an organization are processed, statements such as Example (5) should be regarded as a demand target, since the writer wrote it as a request to the sponsor of the questionnaire and the 'advice' is indeed a thing that can be provided by the sponsoring organization.

3.2 Representation of demand targets

A demand target tends to be expressed by a noun phrase with modifiers, as seen in Examples (3) and

[2] 'V' and 'N' indicate a verb phrase and a noun phrase, respectively.

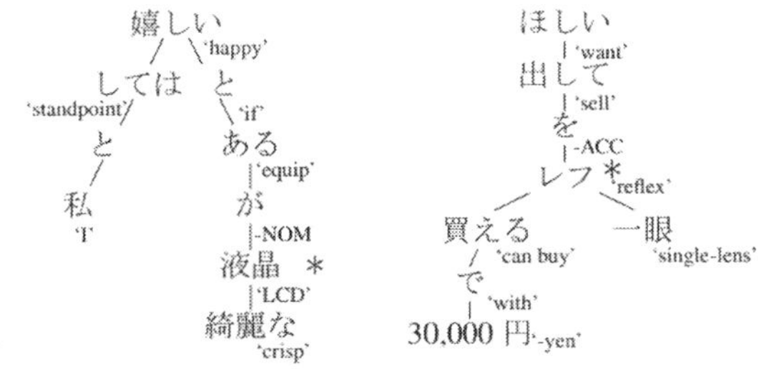

Figure 2: Syntactic trees for the sentences (6) and (7). '*' indicates the headword of the demand targets.

(4), rather than by a single noun. The headwords of such phrases (*e.g.* 'LCD' in (3) and 'reflex' in (4)) represent the main categories of the demanded objects, but they are not distinctive enough to recognize as knowledge of the authors' demands.

Therefore the key task of this research was to find ways to markup the headword of a noun phrase that represents the content of a demand in the syntactic parse tree. Examples (6) and (7) are the original Japanese sentences corresponding to Examples (3) and (4).

(6) 私としては綺麗な液晶があると嬉しい。
'I'd be happy if it is equipped with a crisp LCD.'

(7) ３万円で買える一眼レフを出してほしい。
'[I'm] waiting for a single-lens reflex less than 30,000 yen to come on the market.'

Figure 2 represents the parse trees corresponding to sentences (6) and (7), where the demand targets are identified by the mark '*'.

This simple representation is advantageous for both the collection of and the deeper investigation of the demand targets. One can easily grasp the content of a demand if the application shows the whole surface structure of the subtree under '*' in the tree, *e.g.* the underlined parts of Examples (6) and (7). At the same time the tree structure supports the further analysis of the trends of the demands by picking up the headwords or modifiers prominent in the subtrees that were detected as demand targets.

4 Baseline Method of Textual Demand Analysis

This section describes an algorithm to extract demand targets with high precision and describes a preliminary experiment to measure the performance.

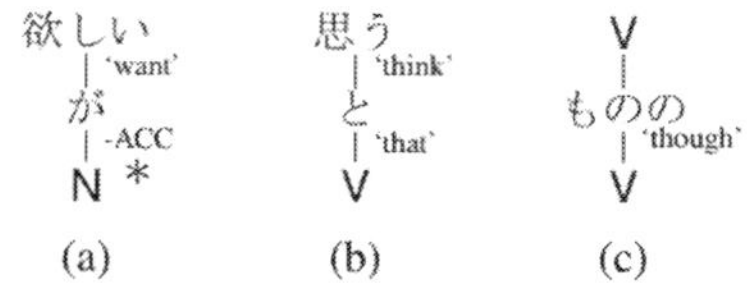

Figure 3: (a) is a demand pattern which indicates that the noun in N^* is detected as a demand target. (b) and (c) are auxiliary patterns, where V indicates the node matches any verb.

4.1 Syntactic patterns and top-down matching

A major purpose of textual demand analysis is to discover novel demands embedded in the text, thus the triggers of their detection should not be a predefined set of demand targets but should be their surrounding syntactic information. We use two types of syntactic patterns shown in Figure 3. Those patterns are compared with the syntactic tree as the parsing result of the input sentence.

The pattern (a) in Figure 3 is a *demand pattern*, which is used to search for demand targets. The node with the '∗' mark indicates the corresponding node will be the headword of a demand target. Hence we write the pattern (a) as "N*-が-欲しい" for simplicity. The patterns are applied in a top-down manner, that is, initially the top node of the input tree is examined to see whether or not the node and its combination of children nodes match with one of the patterns in the pattern repository. This method supports higher precision in the detection than the surface pattern matching. For example, the expression "不良品が欲しい人はいない" ('There is no one who wants low quality goods') should not be misunderstood to express a demand.

The patterns (b) and (c) in Figure 3 are *auxiliary patterns*. These are used to apply the demand patterns to nodes other than the root of the syntactic tree. For example, by applying the patterns (b) and (c), the pattern (a) can then be applied to the expressions "N が欲しいと思っています" ('I think that I want N') and "N が欲しいものの、お金が足りない" ('Though I want N, I don't have enough money'), respectively, even though "N*-が-欲しい" doesn't appear at the top of the trees. In other words, the auxiliary patterns contribute to generate variations of the demand patterns.

In addition, simple rules can be applied to filter out certain meaningless outputs. When a noun phrase that matched to the '∗' part of the demand pattern was a pronoun or very common noun (*e.g.* 'camera' in the camera domain) without any modifier, it is not output as a demand target.

Table 1: The result on the small gold standard with DP_1. PM signifies surface pattern matching, TM signifies tree matching. '+AP' means that auxiliary patterns are used.

Method	Precision		Recall	
PM	39%	(14/36)	25%	(14/56)
TM	92%	(11/12)	20%	(11/56)
TM+AP	94%	(17/18)	30%	(17/56)

4.2 Preliminary experiment

We conducted a preliminary experiment to assess the feasibility of our approach.

We prepared a small gold-standard dataset which consists of 1,152 sentences from a discussion forum on digital cameras, for which two human annotators attached marks to the demand targets. There were 56 demand targets that at least one of the annotators detected, and the sentence-level agreement value[3] was $\kappa = 0.73$, which is regarded as a good level of agreement. There was no sentence in which the two annotators attached marks to different nouns.

First, we made a minimum set of demand patterns DP_1, which contained only one basic pattern "N*-が-欲しい[4]" ('I want N*').

To see the effect of the top-down matching and the auxiliary patterns described in Section 4.1, demand targets in the gold-standard corpus were automatically detected using three methods: pattern matching with surface strings like "が欲しい" (PM), tree matching without the auxiliary patterns (TM), and tree matching with the auxiliary patterns[5] (TM+AP).

Table 1 shows the results. The top-down matching on the syntactic tree resulted in much higher precision than the surface pattern matching, and the auxiliary patterns improved the recall. The only misdetection in the tree matching method was due to an error in the sentence segmentation.

However, all of them show low recall values,

[3]The agreement on whether or not the sentence has a demand target.

[4]Apparent character variations like '欲しい' and 'ほしい', and alternative forms of particles were aggregated in the parsing process.

[5]A total of 95 auxiliary patterns which Kanayama et al. (2004) used for the sentiment analysis.

Table 2: The list of augmented demand patterns DP_q.

N*-が-欲しい (I want N*), N*-を-望む (I hope N*), N*-を-お願い-する (Please [give] N*), N*-を-願う (I wish N*), N*-を-して-下さい (Please do N*), N*-を-頼む (I ask [you] N*), N*-が-ある-べきだ (N* should be), N*-を-して-頂きたい (Please do N*)

Table 3: The result with the minimum set of demand patterns DP_1 and the larger set DP_q.

Patterns	Precision		Recall	
DP_1	94%	(17/18)	30%	(17/56)
DP_q	78%	(18/22)	32%	(18/56)

since only one demand pattern was used. To make the recall higher, we created another set of demand patterns DP_q listed in Table 2, which are generally used as clues for the request expressions in the analysis of responses to open-ended questionnaires. They are derived from the previous work on request classification (Yamamoto et al., 2007).

The result in Table 3 shows that the patterns newly added in DP_q do not perform well. This is because these patterns appear in responses to questionnaires but are not suitable for the writing styles used in discussion forums, as mentioned in Section 3.1.

Therefore we used the TM+AP method with the minimum pattern set DP_1 as the baseline in this paper rather than the pattern set DP_q.

5 Automatic Pattern Induction

The preliminary experiment in Section 4.2 showed that high precision can be obtained by the top-down matching method, and at the same time, revealed the difficulty in building demand patterns to achieve high recall. To overcome this problem, we devised an automatic pattern induction algorithm.

5.1 Frequent fragments of demand targets

Here we make an assumption that there are commonly desired aspects or things throughout a domain corpus. Based on this assumption, we extract the syntactic fragments which appear relatively frequently as the elements of demand targets from the training corpus in a specific domain.

First we obtain demand targets from the domain corpus, in this case from the discussion forum on digital cameras, by using the baseline method with

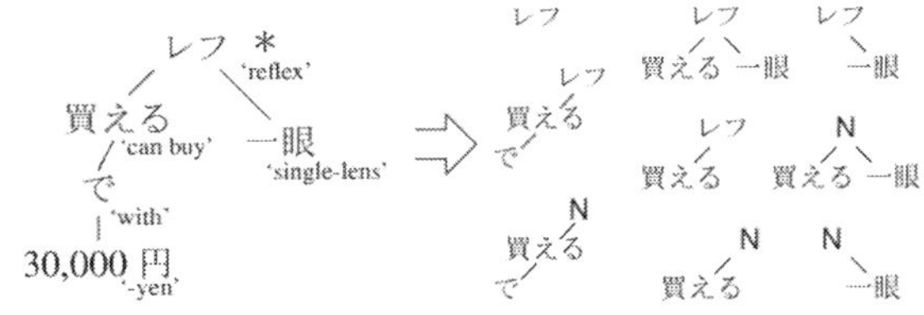

Figure 4: Sample extraction of demand instances from a demand target detected by the system. 'N' denotes the wildcard for any nouns.

the pattern set DP_1. Next, *demand instances* are extracted from each demand target. A demand instance is a one-to-three-node subtree of a demand target, and shares the root node with the demand target. The root node that is modified by one or more nodes can be replaced with a wildcard. Figure 4 shows a sample extraction of demand instances from a demand target "3万円で買える一眼レフ" ('single-lens reflex less than 30,000 yen'), where nine demand instances are extracted, and four of them have a wildcard at the root node.

The demand instances which appear more than θ_f times in the corpus are selected as *frequent demand instances* (FDIs), and each FDI is assigned the following reliability value r_i:

$$r_i = \frac{\text{freq}_{DT}(i)}{\text{freq}(i)} \tag{8}$$

where 'freq(i)' denotes the frequency of the instance subtree in the whole corpus and 'freq$_{DT}(i)$' means the i's frequency in the demand targets. The notion of an instance's reliability is inspired by the method of relation extraction (Pantel and Pennacchiotti, 2006), but our usage is different from theirs. Here we use the reliability value only for the relative comparison among demand instances, so normalization of the values is not needed. The intrinsic difference from the instance of relation extraction is that the demand instances are not the final outputs of the extraction, but are just triggers for new demand patterns.

When θ_f was set to 5, a total of 42 FDIs which had reliabilities above 0.01 were picked from 150,000 postings in the discussion forum on digital cameras. Table 4 shows examples of FDIs.

5.2 Frequent patterns as the clue

The FDIs with high reliability correspond to aspects which are likely to be demanded, therefore the syntactic structures which often govern such

Table 4: Examples of frequent demand instances (FDIs) with $r_i > 0.01$ in the digital camera domain. '-' denotes the split of nodes.

れる-デジカメ ('digital camera - which can')
mm-レンズ ('mm - lens'), 後継機 ('newer model'),
良い-もの ('good - thing'), 明るい-レンズ ('sharp lens'),
綺麗な-N ('beautiful - N'), マクロ-N ('macro - N'), ···

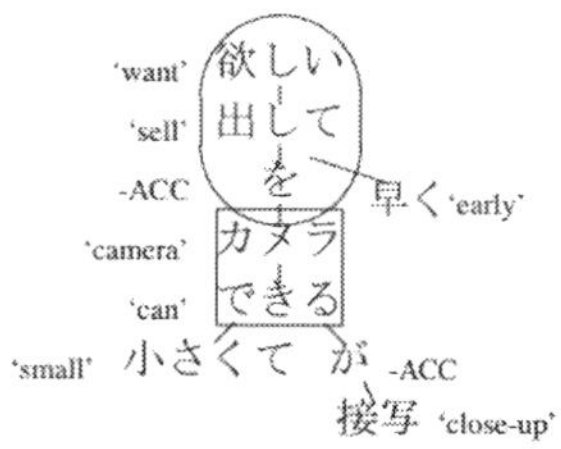

Figure 5: An example of extraction of a candidate demand pattern. From the sentence "小さくて接写ができるカメラ を早く出して欲しい。" ('I want a small camera with the close-up function sold earlier'), the CDP "N* -を-出して-欲しい" (the oval) is extracted, triggered by the FDI "できる-カメラ" (the square).

Table 5: The extracted candidate demand patterns (CDPs) sorted by their reliability.

Candidate Demand Pattern	Reliability
N*-が-あれば-良い (be good if it includes N*)	1.70×10^{-2}
N*-を-買って-下さい (please buy N*)	1.48×10^{-2}
N*-が-あると-良い (be good if it includes N*)	1.12×10^{-2}
N*-が-あると-便利だ (be convenient if it includes N*)	4.81×10^{-3}
N*-を-買おうと-思って-いる ([I'm] going to buy N*)	3.32×10^{-3}
N*-が-あれば-便利だ (be convenient if it includes N*)	3.00×10^{-3}
N*-を-出して-欲しい ([I] want N* to be sold)	1.88×10^{-3}
N*-が-希望-だ (N* is longed for)	1.34×10^{-3}
N*-を-薦める ([I] recommend N*)	1.06×10^{-3}
N*-の-購入-を-検討して-いる ([I'm] thinking about buying N*)	8.92×10^{-4}
N*-が-不足する (N* is lacking)	3.53×10^{-4}
⋮	⋮
N*-を-使う (to use N*)	5.28×10^{-5}
N*-を-購入する (to purchase N*)	4.31×10^{-5}
N*-で-撮る (to take [pictures] with N*)	6.06×10^{-6}
⋮	⋮

FDIs are expected to be clues for detecting additional demands.

Following this expectation, the *candidate demand patterns* (hence CDPs) are extracted. A CDP is a subtree that connects the head of an FDI and the root of the syntactic tree, or auxiliary patterns which cover the root of the tree. A CDP forms a node sequence without a branch, and corresponds to a sentence-final expression in Japanese that usually conveys modality information. Figure 5 illustrates the extraction of a CDP from a syntactic tree triggered by an FDI.

For each CDP extracted in this way, the reliability is determined by Equation (9):

$$r_p = \sum_{i \in FDI} \frac{\text{freq}(i, p) \cdot r_i}{\text{freq}(p)} \quad (9)$$

where freq(i, p) denotes the frequency of the collocation of the instance i and the pattern p, and freq(p) is the frequency of p in the entire corpus. These ratios are summed up over all of the FDIs, weighted by the reliability of the instance. Also r_p is used only for the relative comparison among CDPs, so it is not normalized to be in the range [0,1].

Table 5 shows the CDPs which appeared 10 times or more and their reliability values. Some of them apparently reflect the writing style of the discussion forum and the digital camera domain. The effect of these patterns will be verified in Section 6.

6 Evaluation

We conducted experiments to assess the contributions of the candidate demand patterns acquired in Section 5.

6.1 Experimental setup

In Section 4.2 we created a gold-standard dataset with human annotations, however, the number of annotation is not enough to fairly compare the several methods due to the sparseness of the demand targets in the original corpus, and it would be very laborious to prepare a larger annotated dataset.

Therefore we used an unannotated corpus for the evaluation in this section. A total of 50,000 postings in the digital camera forum[6] were processed by each method, and 100 demand targets were randomly selected from the system output for each trial and a human evaluator decided for each demand target whether or not it referred to any demanded object related to the domain.

[6]They are separate from the 150,000 postings used for the training.

Table 6: The evaluations when CDPs with reliability more than θ were used.

θ	Precision	Recall	F1
∞	93%	30%	0.45
10^{-2}	91%	31%	0.46
10^{-3}	87%	37%	0.52
10^{-4}	68%	59%	**0.63**
10^{-5}	33%	57%	0.42

In this way, the precision can be computed directly, and the recall can be estimated as follows:

$$\text{Rec}(T) \simeq \frac{\text{Num}(T)\text{Prec}(T)\text{Rec}(B)}{\text{Num}(B)\text{Prec}(B)} \quad (10)$$

where Rec(), Prec(), and Num() denote the recall, the precision, and the number of demand targets detected by the system in the entire test corpus, respectively, and T and B denote the tested method and the baseline method, respectively. Prec(B) is assumed to be 30% as observed in the preliminary experiment.

6.2 Effect of new demand patterns

The CDFs for the digital camera domain that were acquired with the method in Section 5 are tested by varying the threshold θ. The CDFs which have reliability value more than θ were added to the demand pattern set. Table 6 shows the results. The baseline method was without any newly acquired demand patterns (*i.e.* $\theta = \infty$), thus it is the same condition as the DP_1 in the preliminary experiment in Section 4.2.

When θ was set to 10^{-3}, the recall increased drastically with little harm to the precision. The value of $\theta = 10^{-5}$ did not work well because the precision was very low and the increase of the recall was limited. The value $\theta = 10^{-4}$ performed best in terms of the F1 value.

We observed the demand targets derived from the new demand patterns. In most cases desirable functions and features of the digital cameras were successfully obtained from conditional positive expressions such as "N*-が-あると-便利だ" ('be convenient if it includes N*'). Also, preferred machines were clarified by the expression "N*-を-買って-下さい" ('please buy N*') which is in a postings to recommend something to other users. On the other hand, the expression "N*-が-不足する" ('N* is lacking') tend to result in noisy demand targets.

Table 7: The extracted CDPs and their reliability for the domain of company's questionnaire.

Candidate Demand Pattern	Reliability
N*-を-望む ([I] hope N*)	3.10×10^{-2}
N*-を-願い-たい ([I] want to ask for N*)	1.37×10^{-2}
N*-を-願う ([I] wish N*)	4.92×10^{-3}
N*-が-望ま-れる (N* is hoped for)	1.45×10^{-3}
N*-を-提供して-欲しい ([I] want N* to be provided)	1.04×10^{-3}
N*-が-必要-と-考える ([I] think N* is necessary)	6.72×10^{-4}
⋮	⋮
N*-が-不足して-いる (N* is lacking)	1.02×10^{-4}
N*-が-悪い (N* is bad)	7.22×10^{-5}
⋮	⋮

We also tried the iterative acquisition using the newly acquired patterns, but the useful patterns were rarely acquired in the second step. This is because FDIs cannot be definitive triggers, and the first seed pattern "N*-が-欲しい" ('I want N*') was a prominently reliable pattern compared with the other demand patterns.

6.3 Applicability to other demand targets

The pattern induction method was expected to have advantage that domain-dependent patterns can be acquired, and indeed some of the patterns were specific for the digital camera domain as shown in Table 5. To see the applicability of our algorithm to other domains or other types of text, the pattern induction was tested on another corpus.

The responses to a questionnaire about collaboration process in a company were used as the corpus. Unlike the discussion forum on digital cameras, the writing style of direct request such as 'Please provide N*' was observed frequently, and the demand targets are much more dense in the corpus. Table 7 shows the CDPs acquired in this domain, and Table 8 shows the evaluation where 25,000 and 5,000 sentences were used for the training and the test, respectively.

As a result, higher precision was achieved in this domain than in the digital camera domain, because the demands are stated more explicitly in the responses to the questionnaires. Unlike in the digital camera domain, the pattern "N*-が-不足-している" ('N* is lacking') worked well because in many cases of this domain what are lacking equal to what are needed. For example, "効率の良い話し合いが不足している" ('effective discussion is lack-

Table 8: The evaluations for the company questionnaire domain. The initial recall was estimated as 15%. DC10^{-4} means that the CDPs for the digital camera domain ($\theta = 10^4$) were used.

θ	Precision	Recall	F1
∞	98%	15%	0.26
10^{-2}	96%	24%	0.39
10^{-3}	92%	30%	0.45
10^{-4}	85%	71%	**0.77**
10^{-5}	41%	73%	0.53
DC10^{-4}	72%	40%	0.51

ing') implies that the effective discussion is a demand.

When the demand patterns acquired in the digital camera domain (DC10^{-4}) were used, the increase of the recall was limited. These results support the value of the unsupervised pattern induction method which works for any domain when only a raw domain corpus is provided.

7 Conclusion

We formalized the task *textual demand analysis* and proposed a pattern induction method to increase the coverage of the automatic detection of demand targets. The pattern induction proposed here allows for the discovery of novel demands that can be represented by various forms of noun phrases, though they were triggered by frequently appeared syntactic fragments. Beyond sentiment analysis, textual demand analysis provides valuable knowledge for industries, clarifying not only the favorable aspects in the current products, but also the essential features in the future.

References

Hatzivassiloglou, Vasileios and Kathleen R. McKeown. 1997. Predicting the semantic orientation of adjectives. In *Proceedings of the 35th ACL and the 8th EACL*, pages 174–181.

Inui, Hiroko, Masao Utiyama, and Hitoshi Isahara. 2003. Criterion for judging request intention in response texts of open-ended questionnaires. In *Proceedings of the second international workshop on Paraphrasing*, pages 49–56.

Jindal, Nitin and Bing Liu. 2006. Mining comparative sentences and relations. In *Proceedings of the 21st National Conference on Artificial Intelligence (AAAI2006)*.

Kanayama, Hiroshi and Tetsuya Nasukawa. 2006. Fully automatic lexicon extraction for domain-oriented sentiment analysis. In *Proceedings of the 2006 Conference on Empirical Methods in Natural Language Processing (EMNLP)*, pages 355–363.

Kanayama, Hiroshi, Tetsuya Nasukawa, and Hideo Watanabe. 2004. Deeper sentiment analysis using machine translation technology. In *Proceedings of 20th International Conference on Computational Linguistics (COLING)*, pages 494–500.

Kim, Soo-Min and Eduard Hovy. 2007. Crystal: Analyzing predictive opinions on the Web. In *Proceedings of the 2007 Joint Conference on Empirical Methods in Natural Language Processing and Computational Natural Language Learning (EMNLP-CoNLL)*, pages 1056–1064.

Nasukawa, Tetsuya and Jeonghee Yi. 2003. Sentiment analysis: Capturing favorability using natural language processing. In *Proceedings of the Second International Conferences on Knowledge Capture*, pages 70–77.

Pantel, Patrick and Marco Pennacchiotti. 2006. Espresso: leveraging generic patterns for automatically harvesting semantic relations. In *ACL '06: Proceedings of the 21st International Conference on Computational Linguistics and the 44th annual meeting of the ACL*, pages 113–120.

Turney, Peter D. 2002. Thumbs up or thumbs down? Semantic orientation applied to unsupervised classification of reviews. In *Proc. of the 40th ACL Conf.*, pages 417–424.

Wiebe, Janyce and Rada Mihalcea. 2006. Word sense and subjectivity. In *ACL '06: Proceedings of the 21st International Conference on Computational Linguistics and the 44th annual meeting of the ACL*, pages 1065–1072.

Wilson, Theresa, Janyce Wiebe, and Paul Hoffmann. 2005. Recognizing contextual polarity in phrase-level sentiment analysis. In *Proceedings of HLT Conference and Conference on EMNLP*, pages 347–354, October.

Yamamoto, Mizuki, Takashi Inui, Hiroya Takamura, Satoko Marumoto, Hiroko Otsuka, and Manabu Okumura. 2007. Extracting demands and their reasons in answers to open-ended questionnaires. In *The 13th Annual Meeting of The Association for Natural Language Processing*. (in Japanese).

Yangarber, Roman. 2003. Counter-training in the discovery of semantic patterns. In *Proceedings of the 41st annual meeting of the ACL*, pages 343–350.

Yi, Jeonghee, Tetsuya Nasukawa, Razvan Bunescu, and Wayne Niblack. 2003. Sentiment analyzer: Extracting sentiments about a given topic using natural language processing techniques. In *Proceedings of the Third IEEE International Conference on Data Mining*, pages 427–434.

A Local Alignment Kernel in the Context of NLP

Sophia Katrenko
Informatics Institute
University of Amsterdam
the Netherlands
katrenko@science.uva.nl

Pieter Adriaans
Informatics Institute
University of Amsterdam
the Netherlands
pietera@science.uva.nl

Abstract

This paper discusses local alignment kernels in the context of the relation extraction task. We define a local alignment kernel based on the Smith-Waterman measure as a sequence similarity metric and proceed with a range of possibilities for computing a similarity between elements of sequences. We propose to use distributional similarity measures on elements and by doing so we are able to incorporate extra information from the unlabeled data into a learning task. Our experiments suggest that a LA kernel provides promising results on some biomedical corpora largely outperforming a baseline.

1 Introduction

Relation extraction is one of the tasks in the natural language processing which is constantly revisited. To date, there are many methods which have been proposed to tackle it. Such approaches often benefit from using syntactic information (Bunescu and Mooney, 2006) and background knowledge (Sekimizu et al., 1998). However, it would be interesting to employ additional information not necessarily contained in the training set. This paper presents a contribution to the work on relation extraction by combining statistical information with string distance measures. In particular, we propose to use a local alignment kernel to detect relations.

The paper is organized as follows. We start with the definition of a local alignment kernel and show how it is defined on the Smith-Waterman measure. We proceed by discussing how a substitution matrix can be constructed in the context of natural language processing tasks. Once a method is described, we turn to the task of relation extraction and present an experimental part. We conclude by mentioning possible future directions.

2 A Local Aligment Kernel

Kernel methods are widely used for a variety of natural language processing task, starting from PoS tagging to information extraction. Many of the approaches employ the idea of combining kernels together which leads to a convolution kernel (Haussler, 1999). The examples of convolution methods being successfully used in NLP are kernels based on dependency trees and shallow parsing (Moschitti, 2006; Zelenko et al., 2003). Local alignment (LA) kernels also belong to the family of convolution kernels but have not yet been applied to NLP problems.

Although the approaches listed above proved to be accurate, they only use kernels which are designed by computing inner products between vectors of sequences. Intuitively, methods using more elaborate measures of similarity could provide better results but kernels defined on such measures are not necessarily positive semi-definite. Recent work in the biomedical field shows that it is possible to design valid kernels based on a similarity measure by solving the diagonal dominance problem to ensure the semi-definiteness (Saigo et al., 2006). To illustrate it, Saigo et al. (2004) consider the Smith-Waterman (SW) similarity measure (Smith and Waterman, 1981) which has often been used to compare two sequences of amino acids. The original Smith-Waterman score is calculated to achieve the best local alignment allow-

© 2008. Licensed under the *Creative Commons Attribution-Noncommercial-Share Alike 3.0 Unported* license (http://creativecommons.org/licenses/by-nc-sa/3.0/). Some rights reserved.

ing gaps.

The Smith-Waterman measure belongs to the string distance metrics which can be divided into term-based, edit-distance and HMM based metrics (Cohen et al., 2003). Term-based distances such as metrics based on TF-IDF score, consider a pair of word sequences as two sets of words neglecting their order. In contrast, edit string distances treat the entire sequences and, by comparing them, calculate the minimal number of the transformation operations converting a sequence x into a sequence y. Examples of string edit distances are Levenshtein, Needleman-Wunsch and Smith-Waterman metrics. Levenshtein distance has been used in natural language processing field as a component in the variety of tasks, including semantic role labeling (Tjong Kim Sang et al., 2005), construction of the paraphrase corpora (Dolan et al., 2004), evaluation of machine translation output (Leusch et al., 2003), and others. Smith-Waterman distance is mostly used in the biological domain, there are, however, some applications of a modified Smith-Waterman distance to the text data as well (Monge and Elkan, 1996), (Cohen et al., 2003). HMM based measures present probabilistic extensions of edit distances.

According to the definition of a LA kernel, two strings (sequences) are considered similar if they have many local alignments with high scores (Saigo et al., 2006). Given two sequences $x = x_1 x_2 \ldots x_n$ and $y = y_1 y_2 \ldots y_m$ of length n and m respectively, Smith-Waterman distance is defined as the local alignment score of their best alignment:

$$SW(x,y) = \max_{\pi \in A(x,y)} s(x,y,\pi) \quad (1)$$

In the equation above, $s(x,y,\pi)$ is a score of a local alignment π of sequence x and y and A denotes the set of all possible alignments. This definition can be rewritten by means of dynamic programming as follows:

$$SW(i,j) = max \begin{cases} 0 \\ SW(i-1,j-1) + d(x_i,y_j) \\ SW(i-1,j) - G \\ SW(i,j-1) - G \end{cases} \quad (2)$$

In Equation 2, $d(x_i, y_j)$ denotes a substitution score between two elements x_i and y_j and G stands for a gap penalty.

Unfortunately, the direct application of the Smith-Waterman score will not result in the valid kernel. A valid kernel based on the Smith-Waterman distance can be defined by summing up the contribution of all possible alignments as follows (Saigo et al., 2004):

$$K_{LA} = \sum_{\pi \in A(x,y)} e^{\beta \cdot s(x,y,\pi)} \quad (3)$$

It is shown that in the limit a LA kernel approaches the Smith-Waterman score:

$$\lim_{\beta \to \infty} ln\Big(\frac{1}{\beta} K_{LA}(x,y)\Big) = SW(x,y) \quad (4)$$

The results in the biological domain suggest that kernels based on the Smith-Waterman distance are more relevant for the comparison of amino acids than string kernels. It is not clear whether this holds when applied to natural language processing tasks. In our view, it depends on the parameters which are used, such as a substitution matrix and the penalty gaps. It has been shown by Saigo (2006) that given a substitution matrix which is equal to the identity matrix and no penalty gap, the Smith-Waterman score is a string kernel.

2.1 How to define a substitution matrix $d(\cdot,\cdot)$?

In order to use Smith-Waterman distance for our purposes, it is necessary to define a substitution matrix. Unlike a matrix in the original Smith-Waterman measure defined by the similarity of amino acids or a substitution matrix in (Monge and Elkan, 1996) based on the exact and approximate match of two characters (for instance, m and n), we introduce a matrix based on the distributional similarity measures. In our view, they are the most natural measures for the text data. In other words, if we are to compare any two words given two sequences of words, the elements sharing the same contexts should be more similar to each other than those that do not. In the context of the LA kernel, such metrics can be especially useful. Consider, for instance, the labeled sequences of words which are used as input for a machine learning method. To compare the sequences, we have to be able to compare their elements, i.e. words. Now, if there are some words in the test data that do not occur in the training set, it is still possible to carry out a comparison if additional evidence is present. Such evidence can be provided by the distributional similarity metrics.

There are a number of measures proposed over the years, including such metrics as cosine, dice coefficient, and Jaccard distance. Distributional similarity measures have been extensively studied in (Lee, 1999; Weeds et al., 2004).

We have chosen the following metrics: *dice*, *cosine* and *l2 (euclidean)* whose definitions are given in Table 1. Here, x_i and y_j denote two words and c stands for a context. Similarly to (Lee, 1999), we use unsmoothed relative frequencies to derive probability estimates P. In the definition of the *dice* coefficient, $F(x_i) = \{c : P(c|x_i) > 0\}$. We are mainly interested in the symmetric measures ($d(x_i, y_j) = d(y_j, x_i)$) because of a symmetric positive semi-definite matrix required by kernel methods. Consequently, such measures as the skew divergence were excluded from the consideration (Lee, 1999).

The Euclidean measure as defined in Table 1 does not necessarily vary from 0 to 1. It was therefore normalized by dividing an *l2* score in Table 1 by a maximum score and retracting it from 1.

Measure	Formula
cosine	$d(x_i, y_j) = \frac{\sum_c P(c\|x_i) \cdot P(c\|y_j)}{\sqrt{\sum_c P(c\|x_i)^2 \sum_c P(c\|y_j)^2}}$
dice	$d(x_i, y_j) = \frac{2 \cdot F(x_i) \cap F(y_j)}{F(x_i) \cup F(y_j)}$
l2	$d(x_i, y_j) = \sqrt{\sum_c (P(c\|x_i) - P(c\|y_j))^2}$

Table 1: Distributional similarity measures.

3 A relation extraction task

Many approaches to relation extraction consider syntactic information. In this paper we focus on dependency parsing. The experiments in the past have already shown syntactic analysis to be useful for relation learning. Like other work we extract a path between two nodes which correspond to the arguments of a binary relation. We also assume that each analysis results in a tree and since it is an acyclic graph, there exists only one path between each pair of nodes. We do not consider, however, the other structures that might be derived from the full syntactic analysis as in, for example, subtree kernels (Moschitti, 2006).

Consider, for instance, an example of interaction among proteins (5) whose syntactic analysis is given in Fig. 1. Here, there is a relation between *Cbf3* and three proteins, *Cbf3a*, *Cbf3b* and *Cbf3c* expressed by a verb *contain*. We believe that this partial information extracted from the dependency trees should be sufficient for relation learning and can be used as a representation for the learning method.

(5) Cbf3 contains three proteins, Cbf3a, Cbf3b and Cbf3c.

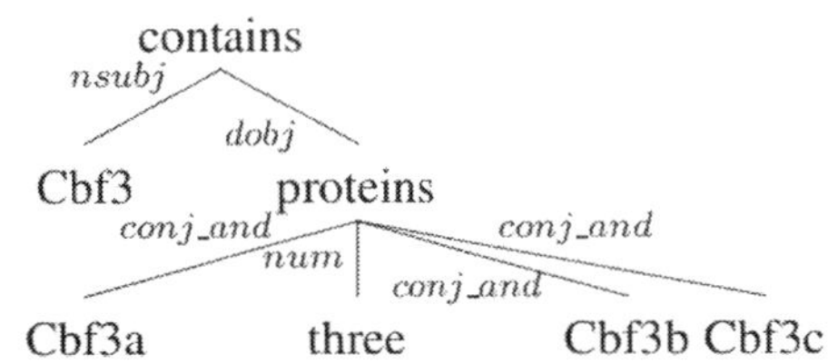

Figure 1: Stanford parser output

Representation: dependency paths
Cfb3 $\xrightarrow{nsubj}$ contains $\xleftarrow{dobj}$ proteins $\xleftarrow{conj\_and}$ Cbf3a
Cfb3 $\xrightarrow{nsubj}$ contains $\xleftarrow{dobj}$ proteins $\xleftarrow{conj\_and}$ Cbf3b
Cfb3 $\xrightarrow{nsubj}$ contains $\xleftarrow{dobj}$ proteins $\xleftarrow{conj\_and}$ Cbf3c

4 Experiments

4.1 Set-up

Data We use two corpora which both come from the biomedical field and contain annotations of either interacting proteins `BC-PPI` (1,000 sentences)[1] or the interactions among proteins and genes `LLL`[2] (77 sentences in the training set and 87 in the test set) (Nédellec, 2005). The `BC-PPI` corpus was created by sampling sentences from the BioCreAtive challenge, the `LLL` corpus was composed by querying Medline with the term *Bacillus subtilis*. The difference between the two corpora lies in the directionality of interactions. The former corpus contains both symmetric and asymmetric interactions while in the latter they are strictly asymmetric. We analyzed the `BC` corpus with the Stanford parser. [3] The `LLL` corpus has already been preprocessed by the Link parser.

To estimate distributional similarity, we use `TREC 2006 Genomics` collection (Hersch, 2006) which contains 162,259 documents from

[1]available from `http://www2.informatik.hu-berlin.de/~hakenber/`

[2]available from `http://genome.jouy.inra.fr/texte/LLLchallenge/`

[3]available from `http://nlp.stanford.edu/software/lex-parser.shtml\#Download`

49 journals. All documents have been preprocessed by removing HTML-tags, citations in the text and reference sections and stemmed by the Porter stemmer (van Rijsbergen et al., 1980). Furthermore, the query-likelihood approach with Dirichlet smoothing (Chen, 1996) is used to retrieve document passages given a query. All words occurring in the set of input sequences are fed as queries. Immediate context surrounding each pair of words is used as features to calculate distributional similarity of these words. We set the context window to ± 2 (2 tokens to the right and 2 tokens to the left of a word in focus) and do not perform any kind of further preprocessing such as PoS tagging.

Recall that in Section 2.1 we defined a substitution matrix solely based on the words. However, the representation we employ also contains information on syntactic functions and directions (Fig. 1). To take this into account, we revise the definition of $d(\cdot,\cdot)$. We assume sequences $x = x_1 x_2 \ldots x_n$ and $y = y_1 y_2 \ldots y_m$ to contain words ($x_i \in W$) and syntactic functions accompanied by direction ($x_i \notin W$). Then,

$$d'(x_i, y_j) = \begin{cases} d(x_i, y_j) & x_i, y_j \in W \\ 1 & x_i, y_j \notin W \ \& \ x_i = y_j \\ 0 & x_i, y_j \notin W \ \& \ x_i \neq y_j \\ 0 & x_i \in W \ \& \ y_j \notin W \\ 0 & x_i \notin W \ \& \ y_j \in W \end{cases} \quad (6)$$

Baseline To test how well local alignment kernels perform compared to the kernels proposed in the past, we implemented a method described in (Bunescu and Mooney, 2005) as a baseline. Here, similarly to our approach, the shortest path between relation arguments is extracted and a kernel between two sequences (paths) x and y is computed as follows:

$$K(x, y) = \begin{cases} 0 & m \neq n \\ \prod_{i=1}^{n} f(x_i, y_i) & m = n \end{cases} \quad (7)$$

In Eq. 7, $f(x_i, y_i)$ is the number of common features shared by x_i and y_i. Bunescu and Mooney (2005) use several features such as word ($protesters$), part of speech tag (NNS), generalized part of speech tag ($Noun$), and entity type (e.g., $PERSON$) if applicable. In addition, a direction feature ($\rightarrow$ or $\leftarrow$) is employed. In our experiments we also use lemma, part of speech tag and direction but we do not consider an entity type or negative polarity of items.

Kernels that we compute are used together with LibSVM (Chang and Lin, 2001) to detect hyperplanes separating positive examples from the negative ones. Before plugging all kernel matrices into LibSVM, they were normalized as in Eq. 8.

$$K(x', y') = \frac{K(x, y)}{\sqrt{K(x, x) K(y, y)}} + 1 \quad (8)$$

To compute LA matrices we use the distributed ASCI supercomputer 3 (DAS-3) [4] which allows us to speed up the process of sequence comparison. In particular, because of symmetricity of the resulting matrices for n sequences we need to carry out $n(n-1)/2$ comparisons to build a matrix. Computations are done in parallel by reserving a number of nodes of DAS-3 and concatenating the outputs later on.

4.2 Experiment I: Distributional measures and their impact on the final performance

Distributional similarity measures have been used for various tasks in the past. For instance, (Lee, 1999) employs them to detect similar nouns based on the verb-object cooccurrence pairs. The results suggest the *Jaccard's* coefficient to be one of the best performing measures followed by some others including *cosine*. *Euclidean* distance fell into the group with the largest error rates. It is of considerable interest to test whether these metrics have an impact on the performance of a LA kernel. We do not employ *Jaccard's* measure but the *dice* coefficient is monotonic in it.

While computing a distributional similarity, it may happen that a given word x does not occur in the corpus. To handle such cases, we always set $d(x, x) = 1$. To estimate distributional similarity, a number of hits returned by querying the TREC collection is set to 500. Gaps are defined through the gaps opening and extension costs. In our experiments, the gap opening cost is set to 1.2, the extension cost to 0.2 and the scaling parameter β to 1.

The 10-fold cross-validation results on the `BC-PPI` corpus are presented in Table 2 and on the `LLL` training data set in Table 3. The LA kernel

[4] `http://www.cs.vu.nl/das3`

based on the distributional similarity measures performs significantly better than the baseline. In contrast to the baseline, it is able to handle sequences of different lengths including gaps. According to the Eq. 7, a comparison of any two sequences of different lengths results in the 0-score. Nevertheless it still yields high recall while precision is much lower. Interestingly, the results of the shortest path approach on the ACE corpus (Bunescu and Mooney, 2005) were reversed by boosting precision while decreasing recall.

Method	Pr,%	R,%	F_1,%
LAK-dice	75.56	79.72	77.56
LAK-cosine	76.4	**80.66**	78.13
LAK-l2	**77.56**	79.31	**78.42**
Baseline	32.04	75.63	45.00

Table 2: Results on the BC-PPI data set

At first glance, the LA kernel based on the distributional similarity measures that we selected provides similar performance. We can notice that the $l2$ metric seems to be the best performing measure. On the BC-PPI data, the method based on the $l2$ measure outperforms the methods based on $dice$ and on $cosine$ but the differences are not significant.

On the LLL data set, the LA method using distributional similarity measures significantly outperforms both baselines and also yields better results than an approach based on shallow linguistic information (Giuliano et al., 2006). Giuliano et al. (2006) use no syntactic information. Recent work reported in (Fundel, 2007) also uses dependency information but in contrast to our method, it serves as representation on which extraction rules are defined.

The choice of the distributional measure does not seem to affect the overall performance very much. But in contrast to the BC-PPI data set, the kernels which use $dice$ and $cosine$ measures significantly outperform the one based on $l2$ (paired t-test, $\alpha = 0.01$).

Method	Pr,%	R,%	F_1,%
LAK-dice	**74.25**	87.94	**80.51**
LAK-cosine	73.99	**88.23**	80.48
LAK-l2	69.28	87.6	77.37
(Fundel, 2007)	68	83	75
(Giuliano et al., 2006)	62.10	61.30	61.70
Baseline	39.02	100.00	56.13

Table 3: Results on the LLL data set

coreferences	Pr,%	R,%	F_1,%
with (LAK-dice)	**60.00**	31.00	**40.90**
w/o (LAK-dice)	**71.00**	50.00	58.60
with (Giuliano et al., 2006)	29.00	31.00	30.00
w/o (Giuliano et al., 2006)	54.80	**62.90**	58.60

Table 4: Results on the LLL test data set

We also verified how well our method performs on the LLL test data. Surpisingly, precision is still high (for both subsets, with co-references and without them) while recall suffers. We hypothesize that it is due to the fact that for some sentences only incomplete parses are provided and, consequently, no dependency paths between the entities are found. For 91 out of 567 possible interaction pairs generated on the test data, there is no dependency path extracted. In contrast, work reported in (Giuliano et al., 2006) does not make use of syntactic information which on the data without coreferences yields higher recall.

4.2.1 Experiment Ia: Impact of distributional measures estimation

We believe that accuracy of LA kernel crucially depends on the substitution matrix, i.e. an accurate estimate of distributional similarity. In most cases, to obtain accurate estimates it is needed to use a large corpus. However, it is unclear whether differences in the estimates derived from corpora of different sizes would affect the overall performance of the LA kernel. To investigate it, we conducted several experiments by varying a number of retrieved passages.

Table 5 contains the most similar words to *adhere*, *expression* and *sigF* detected by the $dice$ measure in descending order (by varying the number of passages retrieved per query). While the order of the most similar words for *sigF* does not change very much from one setting to another, estimates for *adhere* and *expression* depend more on the number of passages retrieved. Moreover, not only the actual ordering changes, but also the number of similar words does. For instance, while there are only four words similar to *adhere* found when 100 passages per each query are used, already 12 similar words to *adhere* are detected when the count of extracted documents is set to 1,000 passages per query.

We also notice that the most similar words to

	adhere	expression	sigF
dice@100	contribute, belong, bind, map	processing, overlap, production, localization, sequestration	cotC, tagA, rocG, tagF, whiG
dice@500	contribute, belong, bind, occur, result	end, localization, presence, processing, absence	sigE, comK, cotC, sigG, tagA
dice@1,000	contribute, bind, convert, occur, belong	presence, assembly, localization, processing, activation	sigE, comK, cotC, sigG, tagA
dice@1,500	bind, contribute, convert, correspond, belong	localization, assembly, presence, activation, processing	sigE, comK, cotC, sigG, tagA

Table 5: Top 5 similar words (LLL data set)

sigF are all named entities. Even though *sigF* does not occur in the training data, we can still hypothesize that it is likely to be a target of the relation because of *sigE*, *cotC* and *tagA*. These three genes can be found in the training set and they are usually targets (second argument) of the interaction relation.

Table 6 shows results on the LLL data set by varying the size of the data used for estimation of distributional similarity (*dice* measure). We observe the decrease in precision and in recall when increasing the number of hits to 1,500. Changing the number of hits from 500 to 1,000 results in a subtle increase in recall.

Size	Pr,%	R,%	F_1,%
dice@500	74.25	87.94	80.51
dice@1,000	74.38	**88.02**	80.62
dice@1,500	69.87	86.85	77.43

Table 6: Estimation settings for the LLL data set

Size	Pr,%	R,%	F_1,%
dice@100	75.56	79.72	77.58
dice@500	76.72	**81.01**	78.8
dice@1,000	76.56	80.78	78.61

Table 7: Estimation settings for the BC-PPI data set

The results on the BC-PPI data set show a similar tendency. However the observed differences are not statistically significant in the latter case. These subtle changes in recall and precision can be attributed to the relatively low absolute values of the similarity scores. For instance, even though an order of similar words in Table 5 changes while increasing the data used for estimation, a difference between the absolute values can be quite small.

4.2.2 Experiment Ib: Impact of the scaling parameter β

Saigo et al. (2004) have already shown that the parameter β has the significant impact on the results accuracy. We have also carried out some preliminary experiments by setting the opening gap to 12, the extension gap to 2 and by varying the parameter β. The kernel matrices were normalized as in Eq. 8. The results on the BC-PPI data set (dice500) are given in Table 8.

β	Pr,%	R,%	F_1,%
0.5	17.72	94.87	29.85
1	38.84	89.42	54.14
10	67.72	76.67	71.90

Table 8: Impact of β on the performance on the BC-PPI data set

The results indicate that decreasing β leads to the decrease in the overall performance. However, if the values of gap penalties are lower and β is set to 1, the results are better. This suggests that the final performance of the LA kernel is influenced by a combination of parameters and their choice is crucial for obtaining the good performance.

5 Related Work

We have already mentioned some relevant work on relation extraction while introducing the local alignment kernel. Most work done for relation extraction considers binary relations in sentential context (McDonald, 2005). Current techniques for relation extraction include hand-written patterns (Sekimizu et al., 1998), kernel methods (Zelenko et al., 2003), pattern induction methods (Snow et al., 2005), and finite-state automata (Pustejovsky et al., 2002).

Kernel methods have become very popular in natural language processing in general and for learning relations, in particular (Culotta and Sorensen, 2004). There are many kernels defined for the text data. For instance, string kernels are special kernels which consider inner products of all subsequences from the given sequences of elements (Lodhi et al., 2002). They can be further extended to syllable kernels which proved to perform well for text categorization (Saunders et al., 2002).

For relation learning, Zelenko et al.(2003) use shallow parsing in conjunction with contiguous and non-contiguous kernels to learn relations. Bunescu et al.(2006) define several kernels to accomplish the same task. First, they introduce the sequential kernels and show that such method out-performs the longest match approach. Next, Bunescu et al. (2006) propose kernels for the paths in dependency trees (which is referred to as a shortest path between two arguments of a given relation). In this paper we used their method based on dependency parsing as one of the baselines. Giuliano (2006) takes this approach further by defining several kernels using local context and sentential context. An advantage of Giuliano's method (2006) lies in the simpler representation which does not use syntactic structure. In this case, even if parsing fails on certain sentences, it is still possible to handle them.

6 Conclusions

We presented a novel approach to relation extraction which is based on the local alignments of sequences. To compare two sequences, additional information is used which is not necessarily contained in the training data. By employing distributional measures we obtain a considerable improvement over two baselines and work reported before.

The choice of a distributional similarity measure does not seem to affect the overall performance very much. Based on the experiments we have conducted, we conclude that the LA kernel using *dice* and *cosine* measures perform similarly on the `LLL` data set and the `BC-PPI` corpus. On the `LLL` corpus, the LA kernel employing *l2* shows a significant decrease in performance. But concerning statistical significance, the method using *dice* significantly outperforms the one based *l2* measure only on `LLL` corpus while there is no significant improvement on the `BC-PPI` data set noticed.

We use contextual information to measure distributional similarity. In this setting any two words can be compared no matter which parts of speech they belong to. As dependency paths contain various words along with nouns and verbs, other methods often mentioned in the literature would be more difficult to use. However, in the future we are going to extend this approach by using syntactically analyzed corpora and by estimating distributional similarity from it. It would allow us to use more accurate estimates and to discriminate between lexically ambiguous words. Similarity measures on the words that belong to other parts of speech can be still estimated using the local context only.

Acknowledgments

The authors thank Vera Hollink, Victor de Boer and anonymous reviewers for their valuable comments. This work was carried out in the context of the Virtual Laboratory for e-Science project (`www.vl-e.nl`). This project is supported by a BSIK grant from the Dutch Ministry of Education, Culture and Science (OC&W) and is part of the ICT innovation program of the Ministry of Economic Affairs (EZ).

References

Yevgeny (Eugene) Agichtein. 2005. Extracting Relations from Large Text Collections. *Ph.D. Thesis, Columbia University.*

Razvan C. Bunescu and Raymond J.Mooney. 2006. Extracting Relations from Text. From Word Sequences to Dependency Paths. *In book "Text Mining and Natural Language Processing", Anne Kao and Steve Poteet (Eds).*

Razvan C. Bunescu and Raymond J.Mooney. 2005. A Shortest Path Dependency Kernel for Relation Extraction. *In Proceedings of the Joint Conference on Human Language Technology / Empirical Methods in Natural Language Processing (HLT/EMNLP), Vancouver, BC.*

Chih-Chung Chang and Chih-Jen Lin. 2001. LIBSVM: a library for support vector machines. *Software available at* `http://www.csie.ntu.edu.tw/~cjlin/libsvm`

Stanley F. Chen and Joshua Goodman. 1996. An Empirical Study of Smoothing Techniques for Language Modeling. *In ACL'96.*

William W. Cohen, Pradeep Ravikumar and Stephen Fienberg. 2003. A Comparison of String Distance Metrics for Name-Matching Tasks. *In IIWeb 2003, pages 73-78.*

Aron Culotta and Jeffrey Sorensen. 2003. Dependency Tree Kernels for Relation Extraction. *In ACL 2003.*

William B. Dolan, Chris Quirk and Chris Brockett. 2004. Unsupervised Construction of Large Paraphrase Corpora: Exploiting Massively Parallel News Sources. *In Proceedings of COLING 2004, Geneva, Switzerland.*

Katrin Fundel, Robert Küffner, and Ralf Zimmer. 2007. RelEx - Relation Extraction using dependency parse trees. *In Bioinformatics, vol. 23, no. 3.*

Claudio Giuliano, Alberto Lavelli, and Lorenza Romano. 2006. Exploiting Shallow Linguistic Information for Relation Extraction from Biomedical Literature. *In EACL 2006.*

David Haussler. 1999. Convolution Kernels on Discrete Structures. *UC Santa Cruz Technical Report UCS-CRL-99-10.*

William Hersch, Aaron M. Cohen, Phoebe Roberts and Hari K. Rakapalli. 2006. TREC 2006 Genomics Track Overview. *In Proceedings of the 15th Text Retrieval Conference.*

Lillian Lee. 1999. Measures of distributional similarity. *In Proceedings of the 37th annual meeting of the Association for Computational Linguistics on Computational Linguistics, pages 25-32.*

G. Leusch, N. Ueffing and H. Ney. 2003. A Novel String-to-String Distance Measure with Applications to Machine Translation Evaluation. *In Machine Translation Summit IX, New Orleans, LO, pages 240-247.*

Huma Lodhi, Craig Saunders, John Shawe-Taylor, Nello Christianini, and Chris Watkins. 2002. Text Classification using String Kernels. *In Journal of Machine Learning Research, 2, pages 419-444.*

Ryan McDonald. 2005. Extracting Relations from Unstructured Text. *Technical Report: MS-CIS-05-06.*

Alvaro E. Monge and Charles Elkan. 1996. The Field Matching Problem: Algorithms and Applications. *In KDD 1996, pages 267-270.*

Alessandro Moschitti. Efficient Convolution Kernels for Dependency and Constituent Syntactic Trees. *In ECML 2006, pages 318-329.*

Cl. Nédellec. 2005. Learning Language in Logic - Genic Interaction Extraction Challenge. *In Proceedings of the Learning Language in Logic workshop.*

J. Pustejovsky, J. Castano, J. Zhang, B. Cochran, M. Kotecki. 2002. Robust Relational Parsing over Biomedical Literature: Extracting Inhibit Relations. *Pacific Symposium on Biocomputing.*

Fabio Rinaldi, Gerold Schneider, Kaarel Kaljurand, James Dowdall, Christos Andronis, Andreas Persidis, and Ourania Konstanti. 2004. Mining relations in the GENIA corpus. *In "Second European Workshop on Data Mining and Text Mining for Bioinformatics", in conjunction with ECML/PKDD 2004, September.*

Hiroto Saigo, Jean-Philippe Vert, Nobuhisa Ueda and Tatsuya Akutsu. 2004. Protein homology detection using string alignment kernels. *In "Bioinformatics", vol. 20 no. 11, pages 1682-1689.*

Hiroto Saigo, Jean-Philippe Vert, and Tatsuya Akutsu. 2006. Optimizing amino acid substitution matrices with a local alignment kernel. *In "BMC Bioinformatics", 7:246.*

C. Saunders, H. Tschach, and J. Shawe-Taylor. 2002. Syllables and other String Kernel Extensions. *In Proceesings of the Nineteenth International Conference on Machine Learning (ICML'02).*

T. Sekimizu, H. Park, and J. Tsujii. 1998. Identifying the interaction between genes and gene products based on frequently seen verbs in medline abstracts. *In Genome Informatics.*

T. F. Smith and M. S. Waterman. 1987. Identification of Common Molecular Subsequences. *In J. Mol. Biol. 147, 195–197.*

Rion Snow, Daniel Jurafsky, and Andrew Y. Ng. 2005. Learning syntactic patterns for automatic hypernym discovery. *NIPS 17.*

Erik Tjong Kim Sang, Sander Canisius, Antal van den Bosch and Toine Bogers. 2005. Applying spelling error correction techniques for improving semantic role labeling. *In Proceedings of the Ninth Conference on Natural Language Learning, CoNLL-2005, June 29-30, 2005, Ann Arbor, MI.*

Lonneke van der Plas and Jörg Tiedemann. 2006. Finding Synonyms Using Automatic Word Alignment and Measures of Distributional Similarity. *In Proceedings of ACL/Coling.*

C. J. van Rijsbergen, S. E. Robertson and M. F. Porter. 1980. New models in probabilistic information retrieval. *London: British Library. (British Library Research and Development Report, no. 5587).*

Julie Weeds, David Weir and Diana McCarthy. 2004. Characterising measures of lexical distributional similarity. *In Proceedings of CoLing 2004.*

Dmitry Zelenko, Ch. Aone, and A. Richardella. 2003. Kernel Methods for Relation Extraction. *Journal of Machine Learning Research 3 (2003), 1083-1106.*

Coordination Disambiguation without Any Similarities

Daisuke Kawahara
National Institute of Information and Communications Technology,
3-5 Hikaridai Seika-cho, Soraku-gun,
Kyoto, 619-0289, Japan
dk@nict.go.jp

Sadao Kurohashi
Graduate School of Informatics,
Kyoto University,
Yoshida-Honmachi, Sakyo-ku,
Kyoto, 606-8501, Japan
kuro@i.kyoto-u.ac.jp

Abstract

The use of similarities has been one of the main approaches to resolve the ambiguities of coordinate structures. In this paper, we present an alternative method for coordination disambiguation, which does not use similarities. Our hypothesis is that coordinate structures are supported by surrounding dependency relations, and that such dependency relations rather yield similarity between conjuncts, which humans feel. Based on this hypothesis, we built a Japanese fully-lexicalized generative parser that includes coordination disambiguation. Experimental results on web sentences indicated the effectiveness of our approach, and endorsed our hypothesis.

1 Introduction

The interpretation of coordinate structures directly affects the meaning of the text. Addressing coordination ambiguities is fundamental to natural language understanding. Previous studies on coordination disambiguation suggested that conjuncts in coordinate structures have syntactic or semantic similarities, and dealt with coordination ambiguities using (sub-)string matching, part-of-speech matching, semantic similarities, and so forth (Agarwal and Boggess, 1992). Semantic similarities are acquired from thesauri (Kurohashi and Nagao, 1994; Resnik, 1999) or distributional similarity (Chantree et al., 2005).

© 2008. Licensed under the *Creative Commons Attribution-Noncommercial-Share Alike 3.0 Unported* license (http://creativecommons.org/licenses/by-nc-sa/3.0/). Some rights reserved.

For instance, consider the following example:

(1) eat Caesar salad and Italian pasta

The above methods detect the similarity between *salad* and *pasta* using a thesaurus or distributional similarity, and identify the coordinate structure that conjoins *salad* and *pasta*. They do not use the information of the word *eat*.

On the other hand, this coordinate structure can be analyzed by using selectional preference of *eat*. Since *eat* is likely to have *salad* and *pasta* as its objects, it is plausible that *salad* and *pasta* are coordinated. Such selectional preferences are thought to support the construction of coordinate structures and to yield similarity between conjuncts on the contrary.

We present a method of coordination disambiguation without using similarities. Coordinate structures are supported by their surrounding dependency relations that provide selectional preferences. These relations implicitly work as similarities, and thus it is not necessary to use similarities explicitly.

In this paper, we focus on Japanese. Coordination disambiguation is integrated in a fully-lexicalized generative dependency parser (Kawahara and Kurohashi, 2007). For the selectional preferences, we use lexical knowledge, such as case frames, which is extracted from a large raw corpus.

The remainder of this paper is organized as follows. Section 2 summarizes previous work related to coordination disambiguation and its integration into parsing. Section 3 briefly describes the background of this study. Section 4 overviews our idea, and section 5 describes our model in detail. Section 6 is devoted to our experiments. Finally, section 7 gives the conclusions.

2 Related Work

Previous work on coordination disambiguation has focused mainly on finding the scope of coordinate structures.

There are several methods that use similarities between the heads of conjuncts. Similarities are obtained from manually assigned semantic tags (Agarwal and Boggess, 1992), a thesaurus (Resnik, 1999) and a distributional thesaurus (Chantree et al., 2005). Other approaches used cooccurrence statistics. To determine the attachments of ambiguous coordinate noun phrases, Goldberg (1999) applied a cooccurrence-based probabilistic model, and Nakov and Hearst (2005) used web-based frequencies. The performance of these methods ranges from 50% to 80%.

Of the above approaches, Resnik (1999) and Nakov and Hearst (2005) considered the statistics of noun-noun modification. For example, the coordinate structure "((mail and securities) fraud)" is guided by the estimation that *mail fraud* is a salient compound nominal phrase. On the other hand, the coordinate structure "(corn and (peanut butter))" is led because *corn butter* is not a familiar concept. They did not use the selectional preferences of the predicates that the conjuncts depend on. Therefore, this idea is subsumed into ours.

The previously described methods focused on coordination disambiguation. Some research has been undertaken that integrated coordination disambiguation into parsing.

Several techniques have considered the characteristics of coordinate structures in a generative or reranking parser. Dubey et al. (2006) proposed an unlexicalized PCFG parser that modified PCFG probabilities to condition the existence of syntactic parallelism. Hogan (2007) improved a generative lexicalized parser by considering the symmetry between words in each conjunct. As for a reranking parser, Charniak and Johnson (2005) incorporated some features of syntactic parallelism in coordinate structures into their MaxEnt reranking parser.

Nilsson et al. tried to transform the tree representation of a treebank into a more suitable representation for data-driven dependency parsers (Nilsson et al., 2006; Nilsson et al., 2007). One of their targets is the representation of coordinate structures. They succeeded in improving a deterministic parser, but failed for a globally optimized discriminative parser.

Kurohashi and Nagao proposed a Japanese parsing method that included coordinate structure detection (Kurohashi and Nagao, 1994). Their method first detects coordinate structures in a sentence, and then determines the dependency structure of the sentence under the constraints of the detected coordinate structures. Their method correctly analyzed 97 out of 150 Japanese sentences. Kawahara and Kurohashi (2007) integrated this method into a generative parsing model. Shimbo and Hara (2007) considered many features for coordination disambiguation and automatically optimized their weights, which were heuristically determined in Kurohashi and Nagao (1994), using a discriminative learning model.

A number of machine learning-based approaches to Japanese parsing have been developed. Among them, the best parsers are the SVM-based dependency analyzers (Kudo and Matsumoto, 2002; Sassano, 2004). In particular, Sassano added some features to improve his parser by enabling it to detect coordinate structures (Sassano, 2004). However, the added features did not contribute to improving the parsing accuracy. Tamura et al. (2007) learned not only standard modifier-head relations but also ancestor-descendant relations. With this treatment, their method can indirectly improve the handling of coordinate structures in limited cases.

3 Background

3.1 Japanese Grammar

Let us first briefly introduce Japanese grammar. The structure of a Japanese sentence can be described well by the dependency relation between *bunsetsus*. A *bunsetsu* is a basic unit of dependency, consisting of one or more content words and the following zero or more function words. A *bunsetsu* corresponds to a base phrase in English and *eojeol* in Korean. The Japanese language is head-final, that is, a *bunsetsu* depends on another *bunsetsu* to its right (but not necessarily the adjacent *bunsetsu*).

For example, consider the following sentence[1]:

(2) *ane-to* *gakkou-ni* *itta*
sister-CMI school-ALL went

(went to school with (my) sister)

[1] In this paper, we use the following abbreviations: NOM (nominative), ACC (accusative), ABL (ablative), ALL (allative), CMI (comitative), CNJ (conjunction) and TM (topic marker).

This sentence consists of three *bunsetsus*. The final *bunsetsu*, *itta*, is a predicate, and the other *bunsetsus*, *ane-to* and *gakkou-ni*, are its arguments. Their endings, *to* and *ni*, are postpositions that function as case markers.

3.2 Treebank

To evaluate our method, we use a web corpus that is manually annotated using the criteria of the Kyoto Text Corpus (Kurohashi and Nagao, 1998). The Kyoto Text Corpus is syntactically annotated in dependency formalism, and consists of 40K Japanese newspaper sentences. The web corpus, which is used in our evaluation, consists of 759 sentences extracted from the web.

Under the annotation criteria of the Kyoto Text Corpus, the last *bunsetsu* in a pre-conjunct depends on the last *bunsetsu* in a post-conjunct, as shown in the dependency trees of Figure 1.

4 Our Idea of Addressing Coordination Ambiguities

The target of our approach is nominal coordinate structures. Consider, for example, the following sentence, which contains a nominal coordinate structure.

(3) *jinkou-no* *zouka-**to*** *taiki-no*
population-GEN increase-CNJ air-GEN

osen-ga *sokushin-sareta*
pollution-NOM stimulated

(increase of population and pollution of air were stimulated)

In this sentence, the postposition *to* is a coordinate conjunction[2]. In Japanese, a coordinate conjunction is attached to a verb or noun, forming a *bunsetsu*, like case-marking postpositions. We call a *bunsetsu* that contains a coordinate conjunction *coordination key bunsetsu*.

The coordinate structure in example (3) has four possible scopes as depicted in Figure 1. In this figure, our parser generates the constituent words according to the arrows in the reverse direction. Note that the words that have "1/2" marks are generated from multiple words, because they depend on a coordinate structure. In this case, their generative probabilities, which are described later, are averaged.

The scope patterns in Figure 1 can be written in English as follows:

a. (population increase) and (air pollution)

b. population (increase and (air pollution))

c. ((population increase) and air) pollution

d. population (increase and air) pollution

In (a) and (b), two arguments, *zouka* (increase) and *osen* (pollution), are generated from the verb *sokushin-sareta* (stimulated), and are eligible for the *ga* (NOM) words of the verb *sokushin-sareta* (stimulated). However, (b) is not appropriate, because we cannot say the nominal compound "*jinkou-no osen*" (pollution of population). In (c) and (d), the heads of conjuncts, *zouka* (increase) and *taiki* (air), are generated from *osen* (pollution). These cases are also inappropriate, because we cannot say the nominal compound "*zouka-no osen*" (pollution of increase). Accordingly, in this case, the correct scope, (a), is derived based on the selectional preferences of predicates and nouns.

In this framework, we require selectional preferences. We use case frames for predicates (Kawahara and Kurohashi, 2006) and occurrences of noun-noun modifications for nouns. Both of them are extracted from a large amount of raw text.

5 Our Model of Coordination Disambiguation

This section describes an integrated model of coordination disambiguation in a generative parsing framework. First, we describe resources for selectional preferences, and then illustrate our model of coordination disambiguation.

5.1 Resources for Selectional Preferences

As the resources of selectional preferences to support coordinate structures, we use automatically constructed case frames and cooccurrences of noun-noun modifications.

5.1.1 Automatically Constructed Case Frames

We employ automatically constructed case frames (Kawahara and Kurohashi, 2006). This section outlines the method for constructing the case frames.

[2]Note that the postposition *to* can be used as a coordinate conjunction and also a comitative case marker as in example (2). The detection of coordinate conjunctions is a task of coordination disambiguation as well as the identification of coordination scopes. Both of these tasks are simultaneously handled in our method.

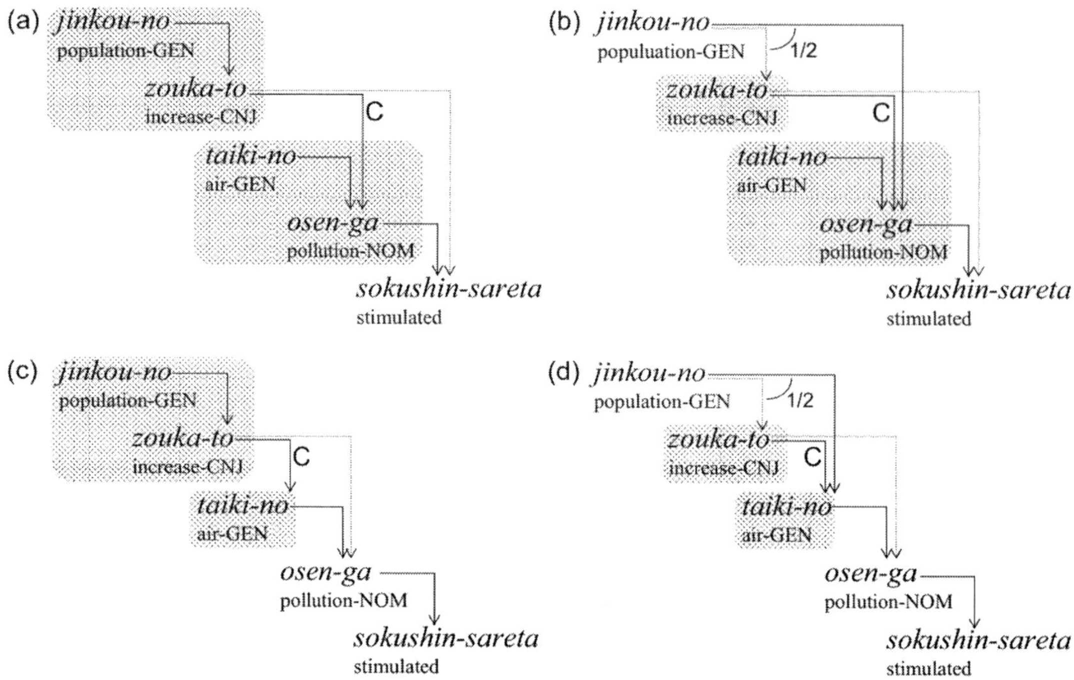

Figure 1: Four possible coordination scopes for example (3). Rounded rectangles represent conjuncts. The solid arrows represent dependency trees. The dotted arrows represent the additional processes of generation for coordinate structures. Note that the arrows with coordinate relation ("C" mark) do not participate in generation instead.

Table 1: Acquired case frames of *yaku*. Example words are expressed only in English due to space limitation. The number following each word denotes its frequency.

	CS	examples
yaku (1) (bake)	*ga*	I:18, person:15, craftsman:10, ···
	wo	bread:2484, meat:1521, cake:1283, ···
	de	oven:1630, frying pan:1311, ···
yaku (2) (have difficulty)	*ga*	teacher:3, government:3, person:3, ···
	wo	fingers:2950
	ni	attack:18, action:15, son:15, ···
yaku (3) (burn)	*ga*	maker:1, distributor:1
	wo	data:178, file:107, copy:9, ···
	ni	R:1583, CD:664, CDR:3, ···
⋮	⋮	⋮

A large corpus is automatically parsed, and case frames are constructed from modifier-head examples in the resulting parses. The problems of automatic case frame construction are syntactic and semantic ambiguities. That is to say, the parsing results inevitably contain errors, and verb senses are intrinsically ambiguous. To cope with these problems, case frames are gradually constructed from reliable modifier-head examples.

First, modifier-head examples that have no syntactic ambiguity are extracted, and they are disambiguated by a pair consisting of a verb and its closest case component. Such pairs are explicitly expressed on the surface of text, and are thought to play an important role in sentence meanings. For instance, examples are distinguished not by verbs (e.g., "*yaku*" (bake/broil/have difficulty)), but by pairs (e.g., "*pan-wo yaku*" (bake bread), "*niku-wo yaku*" (broil meat), and "*te-wo yaku*" (have difficulty)). Modifier-head examples are aggregated in this way, and yield basic case frames.

Thereafter, the basic case frames are clustered to merge similar case frames. For example, since "*pan-wo yaku*" (bake bread) and "*niku-wo yaku*" (broil meat) are similar, they are clustered. The similarity is measured using a thesaurus (The National Institute for Japanese Language, 2004).

Using this gradual procedure, we constructed case frames from a web corpus (Kawahara and Kurohashi, 2006). The case frames were obtained from approximately 500M sentences extracted from the web corpus. They consisted of 90,000 verbs, and the average number of case frames for a verb was 34.3.

In Table 1, some examples of the resulting case frames of the verb *yaku* are listed. In this table, 'CS' indicates a case slot.

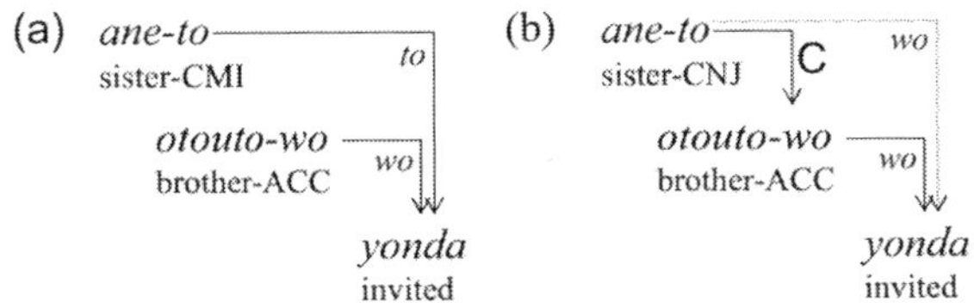

Figure 2: Dependency trees and generation processes for example (4). This example sentence has two possible dependency structures according to the interpretation of *to*: comitative in (a) and coordinate conjunction in (b).

5.1.2 Cooccurrences of Noun-noun Modifications

Adnominal nouns have selectional preferences to nouns, and thus this characteristic is useful for coordination disambiguation (Resnik, 1999). We collect dependency relations between nouns from automatic parses of the web corpus. As a result, 10.7M unique dependency relations were obtained.

5.2 Our Model

We employ a probabilistic generative dependency parser (Kawahara and Kurohashi, 2007) as a base model. This base model measures similarities between conjuncts in the same way as (Kurohashi and Nagao, 1994), and calculates probabilities of generating these similarities. Our proposed model, however, does not do both of them. Our model purely depends on selectional preferences provided by automatically acquired lexical knowledge.

Our model gives probabilities to all the possible dependency structures for an input sentence, and selects the structure that has the highest probability. For example, consider the following sentence:

(4) *ane-**to*** *otouto-wo* *yonda*
sister-CNJ brother-ACC invited

(invited (my) sister and brother)

For this sentence, our model assesses the two dependency structures (a) and (b) in Figure 2. In our model, both of the pre-conjunct and post-conjunct are generated from the predicate. That is, in (b), both *ane* (sister) and *otouto* (brother) with *wo* (ACC) are generated from *yonda* (invited). To identify the correct structure, (b), it is essential that both *ane* (sister) and *otouto* (brother) are eligible for the accusative words of *yonda* (invited). Therefore, selectional preferences play an important role in coordination disambiguation. On the other hand, in (a), *ane* (sister) with *to* (CMI) is generated from *yonda* (invited), and also *otouto* (brother) with *wo* (ACC) is generated from *yonda*. However, *yonda* is not likely to have the *to* case slot, so the probability of (a) is lower than that of (b). Our model can finally select the correct structure, (b), which has the highest probability. This kind of assessment is also performed to resolve the scope ambiguities of coordinate structures as shown in Figure 1.

This model gives a probability to each possible dependency structure, T, and case structure, L, of the input sentence, S, and outputs the dependency and case structure that have the highest probability. That is to say, the model selects the dependency structure, T_{best}, and the case structure, L_{best}, that maximize the probability, $P(T, L|S)$:

$$\begin{aligned}(T_{best}, L_{best}) &= \text{argmax}_{(T,L)} P(T, L|S) \\ &= \text{argmax}_{(T,L)} \frac{P(T, L, S)}{P(S)} \\ &= \text{argmax}_{(T,L)} P(T, L, S) \quad (1)\end{aligned}$$

The last equation is derived because $P(S)$ is constant.

The model considers a clause as a generation unit and generates the input sentence from the end of the sentence in turn. The probability $P(T, L, S)$ is defined as the product of probabilities for generating clause C_i as follows:

$$P(T, L, S) = \prod_{C_i \in S} P(C_i, rel_{ih_i}|C_{h_i}) \quad (2)$$

C_{h_i} is C_i's modifying clause, and rel_{ih_i} is the dependency relation between C_i and C_{h_i}. The main clause, C_n, at the end of a sentence does not have a modifying head, but a virtual clause C_{h_n} = EOS (End Of Sentence) is added. Dependency relation rel_{ih_i} is classified into two types, C (coordinate) and D (normal dependency).

Clause C_i is decomposed into its clause type, f_i, (including the predicate's inflection and function words) and its remaining content part C_i'. Clause C_{h_i} is also decomposed into its content part, C_{h_i}', and its clause type, f_{h_i}.

$$\begin{aligned}P(C_i, rel_{ih_i}|C_{h_i}) &= P(C_i', f_i, rel_{ih_i}|C_{h_i}', f_{h_i}) \\ &\approx P(C_i', rel_{ih_i}|f_i, C_{h_i}') \times P(f_i|f_{h_i}) \\ &\approx P(C_i'|rel_{ih_i}, f_i, C_{h_i}') \times P(rel_{ih_i}|f_i) \\ &\quad \times P(f_i|f_{h_i}) \quad (3)\end{aligned}$$

Equation (3) is derived using appropriate approximations described in Kawahara and Kurohashi (2007).

We call $P(C_i'|rel_{ih_i}, f_i, C_{h_i}')$ *generative probability of a content part*, and $P(rel_{ih_i}|f_i)$ *generative probability of a dependency relation*. The following two subsections describe these probabilities.

5.2.1 Generative Probability of Dependency Relation

The most important feature to determine whether two clauses are coordinate is a coordination key. Therefore, we consider a coordination key, k_i, as clause type f_i. The generative probability of a dependency relation, $P(rel_{ih_i}|f_i)$, is defined as follows:

$$P(rel_{ih_i}|f_i) = P(rel_{ih_i}|k_i) \quad (4)$$

We classified coordination keys into 52 classes according to the classification described in (Kurohashi and Nagao, 1994). If type f_i does not contain a coordination key, the relation is always D (normal dependency), that is, $P(rel_{ih_i}|f_i) = P(D|\phi) = 1$.

The generative probability of a dependency relation was estimated from the Kyoto Text Corpus using maximum likelihood.

5.2.2 Generative Probability of Content Part

The generative probability of a content part changes according to the class of a content part, C_i'. We classify C_i' into two classes: predicate clause and nominal phrase.

If C_i' is a predicate clause, C_i' represents a case structure. We consider that a case structure consists of a predicate, v_i, a case frame, CF_l, and a case assignment, CA_k. Case assignment CA_k represents correspondences between the input case components and the case slots shown in Figure 3. Thus, the generative probability of a content part is decomposed as follows:

$$\begin{aligned} & P_v(C_i'|rel_{ih_i}, f_i, C_{h_i}') \\ & = P(v_i, CF_l, CA_k|rel_{ih_i}, f_i, C_{h_i}') \\ & \approx P(v_i|rel_{ih_i}, f_i, w_{h_i}) \\ & \quad \times P(CF_l|v_i) \\ & \quad \times P(CA_k|CF_l, f_i) \end{aligned} \quad (5)$$

These generative probabilities are estimated from case frames themselves and parsing results of a large web corpus.

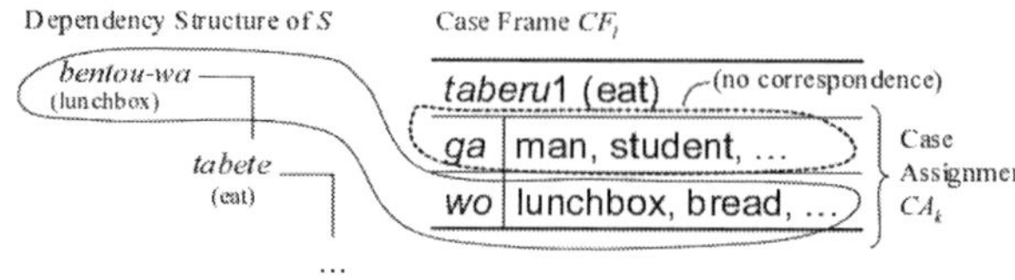

Figure 3: Example of case assignment.

If C_i' is a nominal phrase and consists of a noun n_i, we consider the following probability instead of equation (5):

$$P_n(C_i'|rel_{ih_i}, f_i, C_{h_i}') \approx P(n_i|rel_{ih_i}, f_i, w_{h_i})$$

This is because a noun does not have a case frame or any case components in the current framework. Since we do not use cooccurrences of coordinate phrases as used in the base model, rel_{ih_i} is always D (normal dependency). This probability is estimated from the cooccurrences of noun-noun modifications using maximum likelihood.

6 Experiments

We evaluated the dependency structures that were output by our model. The case frames used in this paper were automatically constructed from 500M Japanese sentences obtained from the web.

In this work, the parameters related to unlexical types were calculated from the Kyoto Text Corpus, which is a small tagged corpus of newspaper articles, and lexical parameters were obtained from a huge web corpus. To evaluate the effectiveness of our model, our experiments were conducted using web sentences. As the test corpus, we used 759 web sentences [3], which are described in section 3.2. We also used the Kyoto Text Corpus as a development corpus to optimize the smoothing parameters. The system input was automatically tagged using the JUMAN morphological analyzer [4].

We used two baseline systems for comparative purposes: a rule-based dependency parser (Kurohashi and Nagao, 1994) and the probabilistic generative model of dependency, coordinate and case structure analysis (Kawahara and Kurohashi, 2007)[5].

6.1 Evaluation of Dependency Structures

We evaluated the dependency structures that were analyzed by the proposed model. Evaluating the

[3]The test set was not used to construct case frames or estimate probabilities.

[4]http://nlp.kuee.kyoto-u.ac.jp/nl-resource/juman-e.html

[5]http://nlp.kuee.kyoto-u.ac.jp/nl-resource/knp-e.html

Table 2: Experimental results of dependency structures. "all" represents the accuracy of all the dependencies, and "coordination key" represents the accuracy of only the coordination key *bunsetsus*.

	rule-coord-w/sim	prob-coord-w/sim	prob-coord-wo/sim
all	3,821/4,389 (87.1%)	3,852/4,389 (87.8%)	3,877/4,389 (88.3%)
coordination key	878/1,106 (79.4%)	881/1,106 (79.7%)	897/1,106 (81.1%)

scope ambiguity of coordinate structures is subsumed within this dependency evaluation. The dependency structures obtained were evaluated with regard to dependency accuracy — the proportion of correct dependencies out of all dependencies except for the last one in the sentence end [6]. Table 2 lists the dependency accuracy. In this table, "rule-coord-w/sim" represents a rule-based dependency parser; "prob-coord-w/sim" represents the probabilistic parser of dependency, coordinate and case structure (Kawahara and Kurohashi, 2007); and "prob-coord-wo/sim" represents our proposed model. "all" represents the overall accuracy, and "coordination key" represents the accuracy of only the coordination key *bunsetsus*. The proposed model, "prob-coord-wo/sim", significantly outperformed both "rule-coord-w/sim" and "prob-coord-w/sim" (McNemar's test; $p < 0.05$) for "all".

Figure 4 shows some analyses that are correctly analyzed by the proposed method. For example, in sentence (1), our model can recognize the correct coordinate structure that conjoins "*densya-no hassyaaizu*" (departure signals of trains) and "*keitaidenwa-no tyakushinon*" (ring tones of cell phones). This is because the case frame of "*ongaku-ni naru*" (become music) is likely to generate "*hassyaaizu*" (departure signal) and "*tyakushinon*" (ring tone).

To compare our results with a state-of-the-art discriminative dependency parser, we input the same test corpus into an SVM-based Japanese dependency parser, CaboCha[7](Kudo and Matsumoto, 2002). Its dependency accuracy was 86.7% (3,807/4,389), which is close to that of "rule-coord-w/sim". This low accuracy is attributed to the lack of the consideration of coordinate structures. Though dependency structures are closely related to coordinate structures, the CaboCha parser failed to incorporate coordination features. Another cause of the low accuracy is the out-of-domain training corpus. That is, the parser is trained on a newspaper corpus, whereas the test corpus is obtained from the web, because of the non-availability of a tagged web corpus that is large enough to train a supervised parser.

6.2 Discussion

We presented a method for coordination disambiguation without using similarities, and this method achieved better performance than the conventional approaches based on similarities. Though we do not use similarities, we implicitly consider similarities between conjuncts. This is because the heads of pre- and post-conjuncts share a case marker and a predicate, and thus they are essentially similar. Our idea is related to the notion of distributional similarity. Chantree et al. (2005) applied the distributional similarity proposed by Lin (1998) to coordination disambiguation. Lin extracted from a corpus dependency triples of two words and the grammatical relationship between them, and considered that similar words are likely to have similar dependency relations. The difference between Chantree et al. (2005) and ours is that their method does not use the information of verbs in the sentence under consideration, but use only the cooccurrence information extracted from a corpus.

On the other hand, the disadvantage of our model is that it cannot consider the parallelism of conjuncts, which still seems to exist in especially strong coordinate structures. Handling of such parallelism is an open question of our model.

The generation process adopted in this work is similar to the design of dependency structure described in Hudson (1990), which lets the conjuncts have a dependency relation to the predicate. Nilsson et al. (2006) mentioned this notion, but did not consider this idea in their experiments of tree transformations for data-driven dependency parsers. In addition, it is not necessary for our method to transform dependency trees in pre- and post-processes, because we just changed the process of generation in the generative parser.

7 Conclusion

In this paper, we first came up with a hypothesis that coordinate structures are supported by

[6]Since Japanese is head-final, the second to last *bunsetsu* unambiguously depends on the last *bunsetsu*, and the last *bunsetsu* has no dependency.

[7]http://chasen.org/~taku/software/cabocha/

(1)	*densya-no*	*hassyaaizu-ya,*	*keitaidenwa-no*	*tyakushinon-madega*	*ongaku-ni*	*naru-hodoni,*	...	
	train-GEN	departure signal	cell phone-GEN	ring tone-also	music-ACC	become		

(departure signals of trains and ring tones of cell phones become music, ...)

(2)	*nabe-ni*	*dashijiru*	*3 kappu-to,*	*nokori-no*	*syouyu,*	*mirin,*	*sake-wo*	*irete,*	...
	pot-DAT	stock	three cups-and	remainder-GEN	soy	mirin	sake-ACC	pour	

(pour three cups of stock and remaining soy, mirin and sake to the pot, ...)

Figure 4: Examples of correct analyses. The dotted lines represent the analysis by the baseline, "prob-coord-w/sim", and the solid lines represent the analysis by the proposed method, "prob-coord-wo/sim".

surrounding dependency relations. Based on this hypothesis, we built an integrated probabilistic model for coordination disambiguation and dependency/case structure analysis. This model does not make use of similarities to analyze coordinate structures, but takes advantage of selectional preferences from a huge raw corpus and large-scale case frames. The experimental results indicate the effectiveness of our model, and thus support our hypothesis. Our future work involves incorporating ellipsis resolution to develop an integrated model for syntactic, case, and ellipsis analysis.

References

Agarwal, Rajeev and Lois Boggess. 1992. A simple but useful approach to conjunct identification. In *Proceedings of ACL1992*, pages 15–21.

Chantree, Francis, Adam Kilgarriff, Anne de Roeck, and Alistair Wills. 2005. Disambiguating coordinations using word distribution information. In *Proceedings of RANLP2005*.

Charniak, Eugene and Mark Johnson. 2005. Coarse-to-fine n-best parsing and maxent discriminative reranking. In *Proceedings of ACL2005*, pages 173–180.

Dubey, Amit, Frank Keller, and Patrick Sturt. 2006. Integrating syntactic priming into an incremental probabilistic parser, with an application to psycholinguistic modeling. In *Proceedings of COLING-ACL2006*, pages 417–424.

Goldberg, Miriam. 1999. An unsupervised model for statistically determining coordinate phrase attachment. In *Proceedings of ACL1999*, pages 610–614.

Hogan, Deirdre. 2007. Coordinate noun phrase disambiguation in a generative parsing model. In *Proceedings of ACL2007*, pages 680–687.

Hudson, Richard. 1990. *English Word Grammar*. Blackwell.

Kawahara, Daisuke and Sadao Kurohashi. 2006. Case frame compilation from the web using high-performance computing. In *Proceedings of LREC2006*.

Kawahara, Daisuke and Sadao Kurohashi. 2007. Probabilistic coordination disambiguation in a fully-lexicalized Japanese parser. In *Proceedings of EMNLP-CoNLL2007*, pages 306–314.

Kudo, Taku and Yuji Matsumoto. 2002. Japanese dependency analysis using cascaded chunking. In *Proceedings of CoNLL2002*, pages 29–35.

Kurohashi, Sadao and Makoto Nagao. 1994. A syntactic analysis method of long Japanese sentences based on the detection of conjunctive structures. *Computational Linguistics*, 20(4):507–534.

Kurohashi, Sadao and Makoto Nagao. 1998. Building a Japanese parsed corpus while improving the parsing system. In *Proceedings of LREC1998*, pages 719–724.

Lin, Dekang. 1998. Automatic retrieval and clustering of similar words. In *Proceedings of COLING-ACL98*, pages 768–774.

Nakov, Preslav and Marti Hearst. 2005. Using the web as an implicit training set: Application to structural ambiguity resolution. In *Proceedings of HLT-EMNLP2005*, pages 835–842.

Nilsson, Jens, Joakim Nivre, and Johan Hall. 2006. Graph transformations in data-driven dependency parsing. In *Proceedings of COLING-ACL2006*, pages 257–264.

Nilsson, Jens, Joakim Nivre, and Johan Hall. 2007. Generalizing tree transformations for inductive dependency parsing. In *Proceedings of ACL2007*, pages 968–975.

Resnik, Philip. 1999. Semantic similarity in a taxonomy: An information-based measure and its application to problems of ambiguity in natural language. *Journal of Artificial Intelligence Research*, 11:95–130.

Sassano, Manabu. 2004. Linear-time dependency analysis for Japanese. In *Proceedings of COLING2004*, pages 8–14.

Shimbo, Masashi and Kazuo Hara. 2007. A discriminative learning model for coordinate conjunctions. In *Proceedings of EMNLP-CoNLL2007*, pages 610–619.

Tamura, Akihiro, Hiroya Takamura, and Manabu Okumura. 2007. Japanese dependency analysis using the ancestor-descendant relation. In *Proceedings of EMNLP-CoNLL2007*, pages 600–609.

The National Institute for Japanese Language. 2004. *Bunruigoihyo*. Dainippon Tosho, (In Japanese).

Generation of Referring Expressions: Managing Structural Ambiguities *

Imtiaz Hussain Khan and **Kees van Deemter** and **Graeme Ritchie**
Department of Computing Science
University of Aberdeen
Aberdeen AB24 3UE, U.K.
{i.h.khan,k.vdeemter,g.ritchie}@abdn.ac.uk

Abstract

Existing algorithms for the Generation of Referring Expressions tend to generate distinguishing descriptions at the semantic level, disregarding the ways in which surface issues can affect their quality. This paper considers how these algorithms should deal with surface ambiguity, focussing on structural ambiguity. We propose that not all ambiguity is worth avoiding, and suggest some ways forward that attempt to avoid unwanted interpretations. We sketch the design of an algorithm motivated by our experimental findings.

1 Introduction

A Noun Phrase (NP) is a referring expression if its communicative purpose is to identify an object to a hearer. The Generation of Referring Expressions (GRE) is an integral part of most Natural Language Generation (NLG) systems (Reiter and Dale, 2000). The GRE task can informally be stated as follows. Given an intended referent (i.e., the object to be identified) and a set of distractors (i.e., other objects that can be confused with the referent), find a description that allows a hearer to identify its referent uniquely (Dale, 1992). Such a description is called a **Distinguishing Description** (DD). In practice, however, most GRE algorithms build sets of semantic properties available in a Knowledge Base (KB), rather than descriptions in natural language; surface issues are often ignored (exceptions are: (Stone and Webber, 1998; Krahmer and Theune, 2002; Siddharthan and Copestake, 2004)). This is an important limitation, for example because *ambiguities* can be introduced in the step from properties to language descriptions. Such "surface ambiguities" take centerstage in this paper. More specifically, we shall be investigating situations where they lead to referential ambiguity, that is, unclarity as to what the intended referent of a referring expression is.

Example 1: Consider a scenario in which there are sheep and goats along with other animals, grazing in a meadow; some of the sheep and goats are black while others are either brown or yellow. Suppose our task is to single out the black sheep and black goats from the rest of the animals. Suppose an algorithm has generated the logical form[1] (Black ∩ Sheep) ∪ (Black ∩ Goats), which could be realised as either *the black sheep and the black goats* or, more briefly, as *the black sheep and goats*. The latter NP expresses two non-equivalent logical formulae: (i) (Black ∩ Sheep) ∪ Goats, and (ii) (Black ∩ Sheep) ∪ (Black ∩ Goats). Since both formulae correspond with a set of animals in the domain, referential ambiguity can result. On the other hand, *the black sheep and goats* is shorter and possibly more fluent. This example highlights the possible tension between brevity and lack of ambiguity. The question facing us in this paper is how to balance them.

This paper examines how GRE should deal with structural ambiguity, focussing on ambiguity of the form *the Adj Noun1 and Noun2*, also known as coordination ambiguity. We call referring expressions of this form **scopally ambiguous**, as the scope of *Adj* is unclear between wide scope (*Adj* applies to both nouns) and narrow scope (*Adj* applies only to *Noun1*).

* This work is supported by a University of Aberdeen Sixth Century Studentship, and EPSRC grant EP/E011764/1.

*© 2008. Licensed under the Creative Commons Attribution-Noncommercial-Share Alike 3.0 Unported. Some rights reserved.

[1] In this paper, we use set-theoretic operators instead of logical connectives to represent logical forms.

2 Approach

A cursory view of corpora such as the British National Corpus (BNC) reveals that there are many instances of coordination ambiguity:

1. *the black cats and dogs*
2. *the bearded men and women*
3. *the old men and women in the hats*

Psycholinguistic evidence suggests that, in many cases, these ambiguities could cause confusion for a hearer (Tanenhaus and Trueswell, 1995). Hence, it seems justifiable to have GRE avoid such kind of ambiguities. However, it also seems plausible that some readings may be very unlikely. For example, in (2) a wide-scope reading is, arguably, very unlikely. Abney and others have argued that every sentence is potentially ambiguous between many parses, even though we may not even notice this ambiguity (Abney, 1996; Wasow et al., 2005). This suggests that, in GRE as well, it might not be feasible to avoid all referential ambiguities all the time, and that the choice of referring expression should sometimes involve a balancing act in which *degree* of ambiguity is balanced against other properties of the generated expression, such as its length or fluency.

Building on earlier work by Inui et al. (Inui et al., 1992), Neumann (Neumann, 1994) suggested a general generate-parse-revise model for NLG, based on a reversible grammar. His generator generates a string which is then parsed to detect any structural ambiguities. If a string is found to be ambiguous then revision is used to produce an alternative, non-ambiguous string instead (if such a string exists). The likelihood of the different interpretations is not taken into account, however.

Our approach to the problem is to find out the likelihood of each interpretation of an NP, and to tailor GRE to avoid all **distractor interpretations** (i.e., interpretations that can be confused with the intended one) as suggested in (van Deemter, 2004). An interpretation can be confused with the intended one if it is more likely or almost as likely as the intended one. The problem is, how to determine the likelihood of different interpretations.

3 Getting likelihood from the BNC

In scopally ambiguous referring expressions, there is a tension between wide- and narrow-scope interpretations. This can be viewed in terms of two competing forces: a *Coordination Force*, whereby *Noun1* and *Noun2* attract each other to form a syntactic unit, and a *Modification Force*, whereby *Adj* and *Noun1* attract each other to form a syntactic unit. Computational linguists have proposed using language corpora to estimate the likelihood of an interpretation (Wu and Furugori, 1998; Chantree et al., 2006). Chantree et al. used information from the Sketch Engine database (Kilgarriff, 2003) operating on the BNC to resolve coordination ambiguity. The Sketch Engine contains grammatical triples in the form of Word Sketches for each word, with each triple accompanied by a salience value indicating the likelihood of occurrence of the word with its argument in a grammatical relation. Word Sketches summarise the words' grammatical and collocational behavior.

Chantree et al. gathered a dataset of ambiguous phrases from a corpus of requirements specifications, and collected human judgements about their interpretations. They then used machine learning techniques combined with various heuristics to determine the most likely interpretation of a coordination. They identified two heuristics as particularly useful. One was the Coordination-Matches Heuristic: *if a coordination between two head nouns occurs (at all) within the corpus, then a wide-scope reading is likely.* The other was the Collocation-Frequency Heuristic: *if a modifier is collocated more frequently with the nearest head word than with the head word further away, then a narrow-scope reading is likely.* The best performance was achieved by combining the two heuristics: wide-scope reading is likely if Coordination-Matches heuristic gives a positive result and Collocation-Frequency heuristic gives a negative result. We decided to modify Chantree et al.'s approach in two ways and apply the modified approach to NLG.

Firstly, it seemed unlikely to us in the general case that the deciding factor is always whether two words co-occur *at all*. We therefore decided to separate cooccurence percentages into ones that are very high and ones that are very low. Secondly, we observed that Chantree et al. take Coordination Force into account when they predict wide scope, but *not* when they predict narrow scope. It would be more systematic – and more useful to an NLG system, which has to cope with all possible inputs – to consider all four combinations, of strong and weak, coordination and modification force. We define that there will be a Strong Coordination Force (SCF) if the collocational frequency between the two nouns is *high*, and a Weak Coordination Force (WCF) otherwise. Similarly, we define that there will be a Strong Modification Force (SMF) if the collocational frequency of *Adj* is *high* with *Noun1* and *low* with *Noun2*, and a Weak Modification Force (WMF) otherwise.

After a preliminary investigation of the data, we decided to operationalise high collocational frequency between two words as meaning that either of the two words appears among the top 30% collocates of the other word in a grammatical relation (of interest); low collocational frequency means that neither of the two words appears among the top 70% collocates of the other word in a grammatical relation. The hypotheses resulting from the above changes are investigated in the following section.

4 Empirical Studies

We conducted three experiments. The first two experiments ask what interpretation of a scopally ambiguous NP is the most plausible, thereby testing our generalisation of Chantree's hypotheses. Knowing how an NP is interpreted is useful for an NLG system but not sufficient, because ambiguity needs to be traded off against other factors. For this reason, our third experiment asks which of several NPs are *preferred* by a reader.

4.1 Interpreting NPs

We use all four possible combinations of coordination and modification forces to predict an interpretation of a scopally ambiguous referring expression (see Table-1). An SMF would make a wide-scope reading highly unlikely (cf. (Wu and Furugori, 1998)). For instance, in *the bearded men and women* there is an SCF and an SMF, but in fact this phrase would be interpreted as a narrow-scope reading because of the scarcity of bearded women. On the other hand, a WMF could be in favor of a wide-scope reading. We expect that human readers would opt for wide- and narrow-scope readings according to Table 1.

Table 1: Predicting an interpretation

Hypothesis 1:	SCF	$\wedge$ SMF	$\Rightarrow$	NS
Hypothesis 2:	SCF	$\wedge$ WMF	$\Rightarrow$	WS
Hypothesis 3:	WCF	$\wedge$ SMF	$\Rightarrow$	NS
Hypothesis 4:	WCF	$\wedge$ WMF	$\Rightarrow$	WS

WS: Wide scope; NS: Narrow scope

To test these hypotheses, we conducted two interpretation experiments, and rather than asking expert linguists to annotate the strings, we examined how ordinary readers interpret structurally ambiguous strings. In these experiments, given a referential domain and an English NP which attempts to identify a subset of objects in the domain, participants were asked to find the referent set of the NP.

4.1.1 Experiment 1

In this experiment, referential domains were constructed using real photographs of animals with some of the features printed alongside each photograph. Features were printed because 1) in a pilot study, we observed that some participants had difficulty in discerning some features in some of the photographs, and 2) we attribute some unusual features to some objects, e.g., we attributed cats with the feature BARKING although cats don't bark in reality. Two pairs of nouns were used: one with SCF, and the other with WCF. For each pair of nouns, four different adjectives were used: two with SMF, and two with WMF. A trial in this experiment consists of a set of 9 pictures (placed in a 3 x 3 grid), and an English NP underneath these pictures. A sample trial is shown in Figure 1. Participants' task was to remove the pictures (by mouse clicks on the pictures) that were referred to by the NP. A removed picture was immediately replaced by a blank rectangle (of the same size).

In each trial, we made sure that both wide- and narrow-scope readings are applicable. For example, for the instruction *Please, remove the red lions and horses*, in the domain there were 2 red lions, 2 red horses, and some (at least one) non-red horses. If a participant removes 2 red lions and 2 red horses, we count it as a wide-scope reading. However, if (s)he removes *all* the horses we count it as a narrow-scope reading. We also used 8 fillers, which do not

Figure 1: Interpreting an NP (using pictures)

contain a coordination in the NP (e.g., *the dogs on the left*). 60 self-reported native or fluent speakers of English, students from various UK universities, did the experiment on the web.[2]

Results and Discussion: Results were analysed according to whether a participant opted for a wide- or narrow-scope reading. The participants' responses are shown in Table 2. A two-tailed sign binomial test was used to calculate statistical significance. The data indicate that word distribution information can reliably predict a wide-scope reading. However, our predictions for a narrow-scope reading are not confirmed. This may have been because of an intrinsic bias in favour of wide-scope interpretations. Another potential problem with the experiment is that some of the NPs shown to participants were rather unusual, involving bearded women, etc. Although the printed features underneath the pictures forced participants to take these unusual cases seriously, the clash between the picture (of a woman) and the printed feature ('BEARDED') that arose in such cases may have made participants' responses unreliable. To avoid this problem we now turn to an experimental setup where we use Euler diagrams instead of iconic pictures.

4.1.2 Experiment 2

This experiment mirrors experiment 1, but we used Euler diagrams instead of pictures

[2]Here and in the other experiments reported in this paper, we ascertained that no important differences existed between the two groups of subjects. Focussing on Experiment 1, for example, no significant difference in the percentages of wide scope interpretations was found between native speakers and subjects who were merely fluent in English.

Table 2: Response proportions: Experiment 1

Force		PR	PJ	p-value
SCF	SMF	NS	NS (25/60)	0.52
SCF	WMF	WS	WS (57/60)	< 0.001
WCF	SMF	NS	NS (26/60)	0.12
WCF	WMF	WS	WS (53/60)	< 0.001

PR: Predicted Reading; PJ: Participants' Judgement

to represent domain entities. Participants received a mini-tutorial on our version of Euler diagrams, where shaded areas denote the sets to which an NP might refer. The purpose of this tutorial was to make sure that the participants understand the semantics of these diagrams. A sample trial is shown in Figure 2 (where we expect that participants would remove the diagram on the right, which is counted as a wide-scope response). 60 self-reported native or fluent speakers of English, students from various UK universities, took part in this web-based experiment.

Figure 2: Interpreting an NP (Euler diagrams)

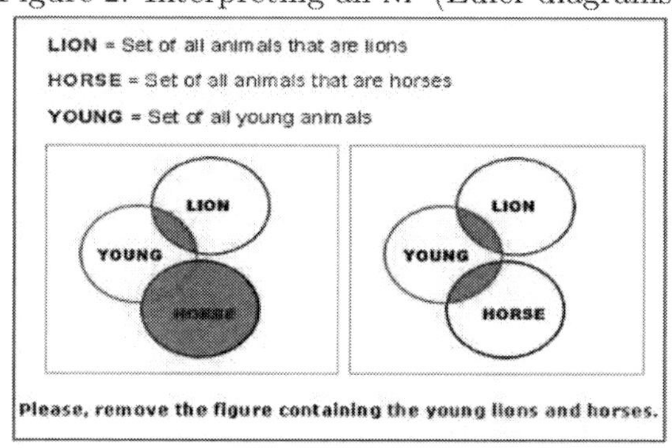

Results and Discussion: Results were recorded according to whether a participant opted for a wide- or narrow-scope reading. The participants' responses are shown in Table 3. A two-tailed sign binomial test was used to calculate statistical significance of the results. This time, all four hypotheses are confirmed. We also observed, however, that in scopally ambiguous expressions, a narrow-scope reading tends to be particularly frequent in the *extreme* case where *Adj* has a zero co-occurrence with *Noun2* (in the BNC). We note that these results are in line with Chantree et al.

A critic might argue that the problem that was noted in connection with Experiment 1 applies to Experiment 2 as well, because it shows diagrams involving a "problematic" in-

Table 3: Response proportions: Experiment 2

Force		PR	PJ	p-value
SCF	SMF	NS	NS (51/60)	< 0.001
SCF	WMF	WS	WS (55/60)	< 0.001
WCF	SMF	NS	NS (46/60)	< 0.001
WCF	WMF	WS	WS (54/60)	< 0.001

tersection between, for example, BEARDED and WOMEN. The fact that women (arguably) cannot be bearded could cause subjects to reject these diagrams (choosing the other diagram instead, as in the diagram included in Fig. 3, which does not involve such an intersection). We would argue, however, that this does not cause an unwanted bias. The scarcity of bearded women is a legitimate reason for subjects to believe that a diagram that asserts their existence cannot be a proper interpretation of "bearded men and women"; it is just one of the many things that the corpus-based approach captures indirectly, without representing it explicitly. It is equally applicable to expressions like "handsome men and women", where the corpus tells us that 'handsome' and 'women' do not go together well (even though one probably would not say they do not exist).

We have seen that Word Sketches can make reasonable predictions concerning the likelihood of the different interpretations of the NPs. But an NP that is *clear* (i.e., not likely to be misunderstood) may have other disadvantages. For example, it may lack fluency or it may be perceived as unnecessarily lengthy. For this reason, we also conducted an additional experiment in which we tested readers' preferences.

4.2 Choosing the best NP

The question of how to choose between different NPs could be approached in a number of different ways: asking hearers which of several descriptions they prefer, asking hearers to rate several descriptions, measuring interpretation effort (time), measuring hearers' errors etc.. We conducted a readers' preference experiment where participants were asked to compare pairs of natural language descriptions of one and the same target set, selecting the one they found more appropriate. Brief descriptions took the form *the Adj Noun1 and Noun2*. Non-brief descriptions took the forms *the Adj Noun1 and the Noun2* (for NS) and *the Adj Noun1 and the Adj Noun2* (for WS). A description is said to be clear if its predicted reading is the same as the intended one. By definition a non-brief description is always clear. Each description could either be brief or not ($\pm b$) and also clear or not ($\pm c$) (but not ($-b$, $-c$), as this combination is not applicable in the present setting). We expected to find that:

Hypothesis 5: ($+c, +b$) descriptions are preferred over ones that are ($+c, -b$).
Hypothesis 6: ($+c, -b$) descriptions are preferred over ones that are ($-c, +b$).

4.2.1 Experiment 3

In this experiment, referential domains were represented using Euler diagrams. In each trial, participants were shown an Euler diagram, with some of its area filled to indicate the target referent. They were also shown two English NPs, which attempted to identify the filled area. A sample trial, where the intended reading is narrow scope, is shown in Figure 3. Each hypothesis was tested under two conditions: 1) where the intended reading (IR) was WS; and 2) where the IR was NS. The 4 comparisons thus corresponded to 4 conditions (where PR stands for predicted reading):

Figure 3: Sample Trial: Choosing the best NP

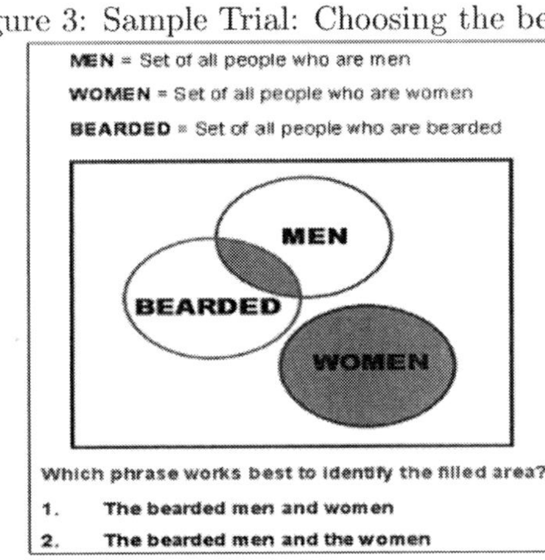

C1. IR = WS & PR = WS
($+c, +b$) vs. ($+c, -b$)
C2. IR = NS & PR = NS
($+c, +b$) vs. ($+c, -b$)
C3. IR = WS & PR = NS
($-c, +b$) vs. ($+c, -b$)
C4. IR = NS & PR = WS
($-c, +b$) vs. ($+c, -b$)

46 self-reported native or fluent speakers of En-

glish, students from various UK universities, did the experiment on the web.

Results and Discussion: Results were coded according to whether a participant's choice was $\pm b$ and/or $\pm c$. Table 4 displays response proportions. A two-tailed sign binomial test was used to calculate statistical significance of the results. The results confirm our hypotheses in all conditions, being highly statistically significant ($p < 0.001$).

Table 4: Response proportions: Experiment 3

	C1	C2	C3	C4
+b	91.3%	67.9%	26.1	14.5
+c	-	-	73.9%	88.5%

4.3 Summary of the Empirical Data

As hypothesised, Kilgarriff's Word Sketches can be used to predict the most likely reading of a scopally ambiguous expression. It is also important to note that it is the Modification Force which is the deciding factor for a particular reading. Moreover, other things being equal, brief descriptions are preferred over longer ones. Since Experiment 2 (and, to an extent, Experiment 1) confirmed our hypotheses, we could have based our algorithm on these. As was noted in section 4.1.2, however, our data also suggest a slight modification of Hypotheses 1 and 3, because a preference for narrow scope existed mainly when the Adjective and the second Noun co-occurred very rarely. Therefore, we shall use a modified version of Strong Modification Force (SMF): SMF$'$ will mean that Adj and Noun2 have *zero* (rather than below 30%) cooccurrence in the BNC.

5 Applying results to GRE

In this section, we show how the results of the previous sections can be exploited in GRE. The patterns explored in the above correspond to *disjunctive* plural references. Disjunction is required whenever there is no conjunction of atomic properties that sets the elements of a set of referents apart from all the other objects in the domain. Recall example 1 (from §1), where the aim is to single out the black sheep and black goats from the rest of the animals. This task cannot be performed by a simple conjunction (i.e., of the form 'the X', where X contains adjectives and nouns only), so disjunctions become unavoidable.

Various proposals have been made for allowing GRE algorithms to produce referring expressions of this kind (Stone, 2000; van Deemter, 2002; Gardent, 2002; Horacek, 2004). Here we take as our starting point the approach of (Gatt, 2007) (henceforth Gatt's Algorithm with Partitioning or GAP). GAP is the only algorithm that produces a DD in Disjunctive Normal Form (DNF) while also guaranteeing that every "part" of the partition contains a noun. The DNF takes the form: $S_1 \cup S_2 ... \cup S_n$, where each S_i itself expresses a conjunction of atomic properties. (For example, S_1 might be Sheep $\cap$ Black, while S_2 is Goat $\cap$ Black.) We sketch two extensions of this approach: the first, purely formal extension ensures that a *set* of such logical formulae is generated, rather than just one formula; all of these formulae are unambiguous, and logically equivalent with each other; but they all map to different strings of words. This is because we assume a very direct Linguistic Realisation strategy in which, for example, ((Black $\cap$ Sheep) $\cup$ Goats) is worded as *the black sheep and goats*; syntactic ambiguity results from the lack of brackets in the English NP. The second, empirically based extension is to choose the "best" element of the set (of formulae) by making use of our experimental outcomes so as to balance clarity and brevity.

Since our predictions are based on words, we propose a model that constructs descriptions from words and in which the description building process is driven by words. We compute the *extension* (where the extension of a word w consists of all objects to which w applies) of a potentially ambiguous word by unifying the extensions of all its interpretations. Let $p_1, p_2, ..., p_n$ be the properties that a word w can express. Then the extension of w is:

$$[\![w]\!] = \bigcup_{i=1}^{i=n} [\![p_i]\!] \qquad (1)$$

In what follows, a domain consists of a set $\mathbb{D}$ of objects, and a set $\mathbb{P}$ of properties applicable to objects in $\mathbb{D}$. Given a set of target referents $\mathbb{R} \subseteq \mathbb{D}$, the proposed algorithm will:

- lexicalise each $p \in \mathbb{P}$ into words; Lexicalisation takes a property as input and returns the set of possible realisations of that property. For example, a property, say, AGED will be realised as (a set of) words $\{old, aged, senior\}$.

- build a DD in DNF using words, where the extension of a word is computed as indicated in equation 1. Each S_i must contain a head noun. For example, in the scenario presented in Example 1 under §1, it would produce a DD like: $(black \cap sheep) \cup (black \cap goats)$.
- apply transformation rules on the DD to construct a set of DDs that are logically equivalent to the DD. (See below.)
- realise each description in the set as English NPs using appropriate syntax. Each description is realised as one and only one NP, using the above realisation strategy.
- determine the most likely reading of each NP, by making use of Word Sketches.
- select the NP that is optimal given our empirical findings. (See below.)

Transformation Rules: In connection with reference to sets, it has been proposed to use the Q-M algorithm (McCluskey,) to find the *shortest* formula equivalent to a given input formula (van Deemter, 2002). In the present setting, the shortest formula might lead to a confusing NP after linguistic realisation. For example, the formula Black ∩ (Cats ∪ Dogs) might be realised as *the black cats and dogs*, which could easily be misunderstood as (Black ∩ Cats) ∪ Dogs. For this purpose, we propose to use a set of transformation rules that allow us to find a set of formulae logically equivalent to the original formula; the aim is to make the set large enough that all the relevant expressive choices (as investigated in this paper) are represented. In particular, we need the following rules that operate on DNFs (where A is an adjective; B_1 and B_2 are nouns; X and Y are combinations of adjectives and nouns).

1. $((A \cap B_1) \cup (A \cap B_2)) \Rightarrow (A \cap (B_1 \cup B_2))$
2. $(X \cup Y) \Rightarrow (Y \cup X)$

After application of these transformation rules, the original description φ (i.e., the formula produced by an algorithm such as GAP) is replaced by a *set* of formulae $\mathbb{F}$ all of whose elements are logically equivalent to φ. The elements of $\mathbb{F}$ are then realised as NPs. The *clarity* of each NP is determined as follows (where PR and IR stand for predicted reading and intended reading, respectively).

```
If SMF' then PR is NS
Else If WMF then PR is WS
Else PR is {NS, WS}
EndIf
If (PR = IR) then NP is clear
Else NP is unclear
EndIf
```

If, after transformations, several of the resulting descriptions are clear then the choice between them needs to be taken on other grounds. To do this, we give preference to the shortest of all descriptions that are clear (measured in terms of number of words in the NP). If ties still arise then we suggest that fluency is taken into account, for example by preferring NP whose structure is most frequent in the BNC. This procedure will often result in NPs that are 'clear' even though they are syntactically ambiguous.

Example 2: Let the domain be represented as: $\{$MAN(e_1, e_2, e_6), WOMAN(e_3, e_4, e_5), YOUNG(e_5, e_6), OLD$(e_1, e_2, e_3, e_4)\}$. Our task is to single out $\{e_1, e_2, e_3, e_4\}$ from rest of the entities. First, properties are lexicalised into words. Suppose the relevant words are the ones in the list $\mathbb{Q} = \langle man,\ woman,\ old,\ young\rangle$. Then, the algorithm takes each word $w \in \mathbb{Q}$ in turn and constructs a DD: $(old \cap man) \cup (old \cap woman)$. The transformation rules then produce $\{old \cap (man \cup woman), old \cap (woman \cup man), (old \cap man) \cup (old \cap woman), (old \cap woman) \cup (old \cap man)\}$. These formulae are realised as: (1) *the old men and women*, (2) *the old women and men*, (3) *the old men and the old women* and (4) *the old women and the old men*. The NPs (1) and (2) are structurally ambiguous, but the Word Sketches rule out the unintended reading of both NPs (with narrow scope for the adjective), so they are both clear. The NPs (3) and (4) are structurally unambiguous. All NPs are therefore clear, but (1) and (2) are preferred because they are shorter than (3) and (4). Corpus frequency suggests that the tie between (1) and (2) is resolved by opting for the more frequent pattern (1).

6 Conclusions and future work

We highlighted that structural ambiguity, which is often ignored in the GRE could cause confusion for a hearer and, therefore, should be dealt with. Based on psycholinguistic evidence that avoidance of all ambiguity is hard, we suggested an approach that avoids referring expressions that have distractor interpretations. We did: (1) interpretation experiments and found that Word Sketches can be used to make distractor interpretation precise; and (2) an experiment with human readers that trades-off clarity and brevity. A GRE algorithm is sketched that balances these factors based on our experimental findings.

We aim to extend this work in two directions. First, we hypothesise that our approach can help NLG systems handle other surface ambiguities, for instance involving PP-attachment. Second, we realise that contextual factors are likely to affect people's interpretive and generative inclinations. Therefore, in light of the work reported in this paper, it would be interesting to explore the effect of co-occurrences in a given text upon the interpretation of NPs occurring later *in that same text*, since the effect of such earlier occurrences on readers' interpretation could conceivably 'drown out' the generic likelihoods based on Word Sketches that have formed the main subject matter of this paper.

References

Abney, S. 1996. Statistical methods and linguistics. In Klavans, Judith and Philip Resnik, editors, *The Balancing Act: Combining Symbolic and Statistical Approaches to Language*, pages 1–26. The MIT Press, Cambridge, Massachusetts.

Chantree, F., B. Nuseibeh, A. de Roeck, and A. Willis. 2006. Identifying nocuous ambiguities in requirements specifications. In *Proceedings of 14th IEEE International Requirements Engineering conference*, Minnesota, U.S.A.

Dale, R. 1992. *Generating Referring Expressions: Building Descriptions in a Domain of Objects and Processes.* MIT Press.

Gardent, C. 2002. Generating minimal definite descriptions. In *Proceedings of the 40th Annual Meeting of the ACL*, Philadelphia, USA.

Gatt, A. 2007. *Generating Coherent References to Multiple Entities.* Ph.D. thesis, University of Aberdeen, Aberdeen, Scotland.

Horacek, H. 2004. On referring to sets of objects naturally. In *Proceedings of the 3rd International Conference on NLG*, pages 70–79, UK.

Inui, K., T. Tokunaga, and H. Tanaka. 1992. Text revision: A model and its implementation. In *Proceedings of the 6th International Workshop on NLG*, pages 215–230, Berlin, Heidelberg.

Kilgarriff, A. 2003. Thesauruses for natural language processing. In *Proceedings of NLP-KE*, pages 5–13, Beijing, China.

Krahmer, E. and M. Theune. 2002. Efficient context-sensitive generation of referring expressions. In van Deemter, K. and R. Kibble, editors, *Information Sharing: Reference and Presupposition in Language Generation and Interpretation, CSLI Publications*, pages 223–264.

McCluskey, E. J. *Introduction to the Theory of Switching Circuits.* McGraw-Hill Book Co.

Neumann, G. 1994. *A Uniform Computational Model for Natural Language Parsing and Generation.* Ph.D. thesis, University of the Saarland.

Reiter, E. and R. Dale. 2000. *Building Natural Language Generation Systems.* Cambridge University Press.

Siddharthan, A. and A. Copestake. 2004. Generating referring expressions in open domains. In *Proceedings of the 42nd Annual Meeting of the ACL*, Barcelona, Spain.

Stone, M. and B. Webber. 1998. Textual economy through close coupling of syntax and semantics. In *Proceedings of the 9th International Workshop on NLG*, pages 178–187, New Brunswick, New Jersey.

Stone, M. 2000. On identifying sets. In *Proceedings of the 1st INLG Conference*, pages 116–123, Mitzpe Ramon.

Tanenhaus, M.K. and J.C. Trueswell. 1995. Sentence comprehension. In Miller, J. and P. Eimas, editors, *Handbook of Perception and Cognition, Vol. 11: Speech, Language and Communication*, pages 217–262. New York: Academic Press.

van Deemter, K. 2002. Generating referring expressions: Boolean extensions of the incremental algorithm. *Comp. Linguistics*, 28(1):37–52.

van Deemter, K. 2004. Towards a probabilistic version of bidirectional OT syntax and semantics. *Journal of Semantics*, 21(3):251–281.

Wasow, T., A. Perfors, and D. Beaver. 2005. The puzzle of ambiguity. In Orgun, O. and P. Sells, editors, *Morphology and The Web of Grammar: Essays in Memory of Steven G. Lapointe.* CSLI Publications.

Wu, H. and T. Furugori. 1998. A computational method for resolving ambiguities in coordinate structures. In *Proceedings of PACLIC-12*, pages 263–270, National University of Singapore.

Normalizing SMS: are two metaphors better than one ?

Catherine Kobus
Orange Labs
2, avenue Pierre Marzin
F-22300 Lannion

François Yvon
Univ Paris-Sud 11 & LIMSI/CNRS
BP 133
F-91403 Orsay Cedex

Géraldine Damnati
Orange Labs
2, avenue Pierre Marzin
F-22300 Lannion

{catherine.kobus,geraldine.damnati}@orange-ftgroup.com, yvon@limsi.fr

Abstract

Electronic written texts used in computer-mediated interactions (e-mails, blogs, chats, etc) present major deviations from the norm of the language. This paper presents an comparative study of systems aiming at normalizing the orthography of French SMS messages: after discussing the linguistic peculiarities of these messages, and possible approaches to their automatic normalization, we present, evaluate and contrast two systems, one drawing inspiration from the Machine Translation task; the other using techniques that are commonly used in automatic speech recognition devices. Combining both approaches, our best normalization system achieves about 11% Word Error Rate on a test set of about 3000 unseen messages.

1 Introduction

The rapid dissemination of electronic communication devices (e-mails, Short Messaging Systems (SMS), chatrooms, instant messaging programs, blogs, etc) has triggered the emergence of new forms of written texts (see eg. (Crystal, 2001; Véronis and Guimier de Neef, 2006)). Addressed to relatives or peers, written on the spur of the moment, using interfaces, each with its specific constraints (computer keyboards, PDAs, mobile phones keypads), these electronic messages are characterised by massive and systematic deviations from the orthographic norm, as well as by a non conventional use of alphabetical symbols. In fact, letter and punctuation marks are not only used to conventionally encode a phonetic content, but also to introduce meta-discourse, and to signal emotions, verbal effects (eg. laughters), or attitudes (humor, derision, emphasis etc). If each media enforces its own set of constraints and promotes idiosyncratic forms of writings, these new types of texts nonetheless share a lot of commonalities. To effectively process these messages, it is thus necessary to develop robust language processing tools, capable of bearing with the extreme form of "noise" they contain. In this study, we focus more specifically on SMS, which, due to the paucity of their input interface (mobile phone keypads) seem to constitute the most challenging type of data. To a large extent, the techniques we present in this paper are also applicable to other types of electronic messages.

The "SMS language" (or "texting language") has been the subject of several linguistic studies (notably, for French, (Anis, 2001; Fairon et al., 2006)), which have emphasized its main characteristics, amongst which the extraordinary orthographic variability of lexical forms. In brief, this variability results partly from the mixing of several encoding systems: in SMS, the usual alphabetic system competes with a more "phonetic" type of writing (e.g. *rite* for *right*[1]), as well as with traces of a "consonantic" spelling (vowels are deleted, as in *wrk* for *work* or *cn* for *can*), and with non-conventional use of letters or numbers, sometimes used to encode the phonetic value of their

©2008. Licensed under the *Creative Commons Attribution-Noncommercial-Share Alike 3.0 Unported* license (http://creativecommons.org/licenses/by-nc-sa/3.0/). Some rights reserved.

[1] We will illustrate this general presentation of the SMS language using examples taken from English messages, even though our systems deal with French messages. As far as we can see, the same types of deviations from the orthographic norm are observed in both languages, albeit in different proportions. A more thorough comparison of both languages certainly remains to be carried out.

spelling, as in *ani1* for *anyone*. These spelling systems can also be mixed as in *Rtst* (for *artist*) or *bcum* (for *become*). This variability is also the result of an informal style of communication, which licenses many deviations from the orthographic (simplification of repeated consonants, use of nonconventional abreviations) and grammatical (absence of case distinction, erratic use of punctuation marks, non-respect of agreement or tense markers, etc) prescriptions, notwithstanding truly unintentional typos. Finally, practitioners of the texting language excel in devising acronyms which condense, sometimes in a radical way, multi-word units: this is for instance the case with *afair*, which stands for *as far as I recall*. As a result, from a natural language processing (NLP) point of view, these messages contain an abnormally high rate of out-of-vocabulary forms, and the ambiguity of existing word forms is aggravated, two factors that contribute to degrade the performance of natural language processing tools. Recovering a normalized orthography seems thus to be a necessary preprocessing step for many real-world NLP applications, such as text-to-speech, translation, or text mining applications (filtering, routing, information retrieval, etc).

These short messages have so far received relatively little attention from the NLP community[2]: see, for English, (Aw et al., 2006; Choudhury et al., 2007), which both address the problem with statistical learning techniques, and, for French, (Guimier de Neef et al., 2007), which details a complete pipe-line of hand-crafted, symbolic, modules. In fact, the problem of normalizing SMS shares a lot of commonalities with other NLP applications, and can be addressed from several viewpoints. The first, maybe the most natural angle, is to make an analogy with the spelling correction problem. This problem has been extensively studied in the past and a variety of statistical approaches are readily available, most notably the "noisy channel" approach (see eg. (Church and Gale, 1991; Brill and Moore, 2000; Toutanova and Moore, 2002)). An alternative metaphor is the translation metaphor: under this view, the normalization task is accomplished by taking the SMS language as a foreign language, and using standard (statistical) translation techniques. Both views have their own merit, and their limitations, which we shall review shortly. In this paper, we propose yet another metaphor, which stems from the similarities between the SMS language and speech, and notably from the fact that in SMS, word separators are much less reliable than in conventional writings. As a result, it seems necessary to implement techniques, which are, as in speech recognition, capable of recovering the correct word segmentation.

The main contribution of this work is to present, evaluate and contrast two approaches to the SMS normalization problem. We demonstrate that both approaches have different advantages and pitfalls, and show their combination yields significant improvements wrt. to both single systems.

This paper is organized as follows: in section 2, we discuss these three metaphors; then go on to describe our own implementation of two different systems for normalizing SMS in 3. A comparative evaluation of these systems is conducted in section 4, where we emphasize the complementarity of both approaches, and assess the performance of a combined systems. Section 5 presents a summary of the main findings and future prospects.

2 Three metaphors for SMS normalization systems

In this section, we set the general problem of SMS normalization, and discuss, based on the analysis of SMS examples, the relevance of various NLP approaches to this task.

2.1 The "spell checking" metaphor

A first approach to the problem considers each input token as "noisy" version of the correct word form: normalization is thus viewed as a spell checking task. The spell-checking problem has received considerable attention in the past, and a variety of correction techniques have been proposed: in this context, noisy channel models (Church and Gale, 1991; Brill and Moore, 2000; Toutanova and Moore, 2002), to quote just a few, constitute one of the predominant and most successfull approaches. Under this paradigm, correction is performed on a word-per-word basis, and concerns primarily out-of-vocabulary tokens: the general assumptions are that most words are correctly spelled, and that in-vocabulary words should preferably be left un-

[2] A couple of on-line SMS-to-English translation systems are accessible on the Internet, see notably `http://www.transl8it.com/` and `http://www.lingo2word.com/`; "Netspeak" dictionaries, again for English, also abound. The situation is more or less comparable for French, see eg `http://www.traducteur-sms.com/`.

touched. In this context, the best correction(s) w of an erroneous word v is retrieved from the dictionary by combining the individual context independant probability of w with an error model probability, which computes the probability of mistyping v for w, based on the surface similarity between both forms. The key component here is the error model, which should not only capture orthographic similarities (Brill and Moore, 2000), but also phonetic similarities (Toutanova and Moore, 2002).

This framework easily extends to the case where several words should simultaneously be corrected: it is simply a matter of exploring the lattice of all possible corrections, which can be re-ranked using conventional tools such as statistical language models. This is basically the idea behind the reac system (Michel Simard, 2001),which recovers the correct accentuation of unaccented French texts using an error model, complemented with a statistical language model.

As far as SMS are concerned, this approach is essentially the one followed by (Choudhury et al., 2007), which models the joint probability of observing the word w represented by the character sequence $c_1 ... c_l$ by a Hidden Markov Model (HMM) whose topology takes into account both "graphemic" variants (typos, omissions of repeated letters, etc) and "phonemic" variants (i.e spellings that resemble the word's pronunciation). This HMM is initialized by considering the word's received orthography and phonology, with additional transitions to account for the possibility of inserting, substituting or deleting symbols. For the most frequent words in the corpus, the various parameters associated with these transitions are estimated on a training corpus; various heuristic are then used to plug these values in the HMMs that model the less frequent dictionary items.

2.2 The "translation" metaphor

A second approach to the problem consists in adopting the translation metaphor: using this analogy, the SMS language is just another foreign language and the normalization can be viewed as a "pure" machine translation (MT) task.

Using machine translation tools might be regarded as "an overkill" (Choudhury et al., 2007), considering the close relationships between source and target languages. Furthermore, learning the kinds of many-to-many correspondences between source and target sentences that make up for the high translation accuracy of phrase-based systems might be seen as introducing an unnecessary complexity, as SMS tend to be shorter, in terms of words, than their normalized counterparts. This suggests that looking for many (on the normalized side) to one (on the SMS side) might be good enough to capture most pairings. Finally, statistical machine translation tools incorporate mechanisms to model the possible mismatch in word order between source and target, which are virtually non-existing when it comes to translating SMS.

This metaphor is, nonetheless, the one resorted to in (Aw et al., 2006), which uses a statistical phrase-based machine translation tool to convert English SMS texts into standardized English. This system incorporates some of the peculiarities of this translation task, which both simplifies the construction of the phrase-table and the decoding search algorithm. Using this system, (Aw et al., 2006) reports a 0.81 BLEU (Papineni et al., 2001) score on a set of 5,000 English SMS.

Normalization as translation is certainly a natural, and simple to implement, idea. Using phrase-based systems, it becomes possible to model (context-dependant) one-to-many relationships that are out-of-reach of the spell checking approach. We feel that it still overlooks some aspects of the task, notably the fact that the lexical creativity attested in SMS messages can hardly be captured in a static phrase table, where correspondences between SMS phrases and normalized phrases are learned by rote, rather than modeled.

2.3 The "speech recognition" metaphor

The SMS language has on occasions been described, sometimes abusively, as being closer to oral productions than to regular written texts. If we do not subscribe to this view, we nonetheless feel that a third metaphor is worth considering, that we call the "automatic speech recognition" (ASR) metaphor. This analogy stems from the fact that, for a significant fraction of tokens, the spelling of SMS forms tends to be a closer approximation of the phonemic representation of a word than of is its normative spelling.

In the speech recognition metaphor, an SMS message is thus primarily viewed as an alphabetic/syllabic approximation of a phonetic form. Given a suitable mechanism for converting the SMS stream into a phone lattice, the problem of SMS normalization becomes very similar to that of speech recognition, that is, the decoding of a word sequence in a (weighted) phone lattice. It actually becomes a much simpler problem, as (i) the acoustic ambiguity of speech input is typically much higher than the phonemic indeterminacy of SMS messages, (ii) some segmentation information is already available in the SMS text, which is in sharp contrast with (continuous) speech recognition, where word boundaries have to be uncovered.

Based on this general principle, we devised an ASR-like normalization system, which has three additional benefits: using a phonemic approximation provides the system with the ability to correct some (unintentional) typos; adopting an ASR-like architecture provides us with a "natural" framework for resegmenting agglutinated word forms; finally, in the larger context of SMS-to-speech applications, which is one of our targeted applications, the computation of a phonemic representation of the message can prove extremely valuable.

3 Two normalization systems

3.1 The MT-like system

Our first normalization system is entirely based on open-source, public domain packages for statistical machine translation. Giza++ (Och and Ney, 2003) is used to induce, based on statistical principles (Brown et al., 1990), an automatic word alignment of SMS tokens with their normalized counterparts; Moses (Koehn et al., 2007) is used to learn the various parameters of the phrase-based model, to optimize the weight combination and to perform the translation using a multi-stack search algorithm; the SRI language model toolkit (Stolcke, 2002) is finally used to estimate statistical language models. For this system, the training set has been split in a learning set[3] (approximately 25000 messages) and a development set (about 11700 messages), which is used to tune parameters.

As suggested in the previous sections, we have constrained both systems to consider only "monotonic" alignments between the source and the target languages.

3.2 The ASR-like system

In a nutshell, our second normalization system mimics the behavior of speech recognition system and decodes SMS message through a non-deterministic phonemic transduction; based on preliminary experiments, this simple architecture was augmented by an additional mechanism which specifically deals with out-of-vocabulary tokens.

In the following, we denote Λ the set of alphabetic symbols, Π the set of phonemic symbols, and Ω the set of lexical items. Using these notations, our architecture can be described as a pipe-line of the following components:

- the first processing step consists in a dictionary-based grapheme-to-phoneme conversion of some highly idiosyncratic forms, which deals with tokens[4] whose spelling in SMS does not reflect the phonemic content of the corresponding lexical item(s). This is, for instance, the case for common abbreviations (eg. *btw* for *by the way*) and for instances of "consonantic" spellings. The dictionnary used in the experiments reported above contains about 4,200 entries.

  This module is implemented as a finite-state transducer E which transduces letter sequences in Λ^* into mixed grapheme and phoneme sequences (in $(\Lambda \cup \Pi)^*$).

- the second module converts the graphemic portions of the input message into a phonemic string using a set of manually encoded *non-deterministic* letter-to-phone rules; these rules notably encode the possibility for each symbol to encode its spelling (eg. *u* for /ju/ or *R* for /ər/). Our system currently comprises about 150 letter-to-phone rules. The output of this module is a phone lattice, which represents all the possible pronunciations of the complete input stream.

  This module is also implemented as a finite-state transducer P representing a rational relation between $(\Lambda \cup \Pi)^*$ and Π^*: each grapheme-to-phoneme rule is compiled into a finite-state transducer; these individual rules are then, once properly ordered, combined through the composition operator. The resulting finite-state machine is denoted P.

- this phone lattice is then turned into a word based lattice, using an inverted pronunciation dictionary, which registers the known associations between phone sequences and words. This inverted dictionary contains approximately 21K words, which are the most

[3]See section 4 for a description of the corpora.

[4]At this stage, we take advantage of usual word separators to identify tokens in the message.

frequent words in our reference training corpus. This module is also implemented as a finite-state transducer D, which maps sequences in Π^* to sequences in Ω^*.

A key aspect of this module is its ability to alter the original tokenization, by freely inserting word separators whenever a phonetic word is recognized, no matter whether it corresponds to a complete input token or not. This mechanism is illustrated on Figure 1. As a result, this system can bear with agglutinations (i.e. absence of one or several word separators) in the input sequence.

- the final processing step consists in searching the word lattice for the most probable word sequence, as computed by a statistical language model (here, a smoothed n-gram language model estimated on the training corpus). Here again, the entire process is computed through finite state operations: the output language of the previous steps is intersected with the stochastic language model S (a weighted finite-state acceptor), and the most likely path is computed through dynamic programming.

As mentioned earlier, each module is implemented as a finite state acceptor or transducer; these modules are built and combined using tools from the FSM (Mohri et al., 1998) and the GRM (Allauzen et al., 2005) toolkit. As a result, the entire normalization process is computed by a weighted transducer ($E \circ P \circ D \circ S$), which can be optimized off-line as is commonly done in finite-state speech recognition systems (Mohri and Riley, 1998).

In addition to these four main modules, the preprocessing module of the ASR-like system contains a number of small enhancements that improve the normalization of dates and hours. We furthermore had to modify the processing of out-of-vocabulary words: in the architecture sketched above, any word that does not belong to the vocabulary has to be decomposed into smaller, known, words, causing systematic errors. Our final ASR-like system allows these forms to be either decomposed phonetically or copied verbatim in the output. A complete description of this system is given in (Kobus et al., 2008).

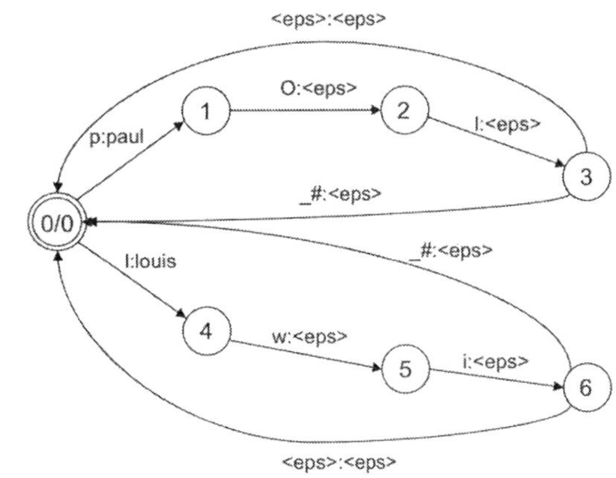

Figure 1: Transducing phone sequences into word sequences with a dictionary

This simplistic inverted dictionary recognizes two phonemic sequences: /lwi/ (for Louis) and /pOl/ (for Paul). Upon recognition of any such sequence, two transitions loop back to the initial state: one carries the input symbol '#', which is used whenever a word separator is encountered; the other is an ε transition, which allows to re-segment the input stream.

4 Experiments

4.1 Experimental protocol

The experiments reported below use two corpora. The first one has been collected at the University of Aix-en-Provence (Hocq, 2006); it contains approximately 9700 messages. The second corpus has been gathered in Belgium by the Catholic University of Louvain, and totals about 30000 messages (Fairon and Paumier, 2006). Both corpora contain, for each message, a reference normalization which has been produced and validated by human annotators. Both corpora were merged, lowercased, stripped from punctuation signs and standardized (in particular with respect to the anonymization conventions). This database was split in a training set (about 36700 messages) and a distinct test set of about 3000 messages. The training set was used both to train and tune the MT-like system and to estimate a 3-gram language model required in both approaches, using standard back-off procedures. Some relevant statistics regarding the sub-corpora that were used for training are given in Table 4.1.

For the evaluation, contrarily to (Aw et al., 2006; Guimier de Neef et al., 2007), who by analogy

	Aix	Louvain	Total
# messages	8,700	28,000	36,700
Original messages			
avg. length	14.3	21.6	19.9
# tokens	124 700	606 100	730 800
# types	13 600	37 900	43 600
% unknown	43.7 %	30.4 %	32.7 %
Normalized messages			
avg. length	15.4	23.2	21.3
# tokens	133 800	650 100	783 900
# types	8 200	20 800	23 300

Table 1: Statistics of the training corpora

Statistics on the original messages are computed after preprocessing (punctuation removal, etc.); the length of a message is the number of tokens; % unknown is the percentage of tokens that do not occur in the normalized message.

	Sub	Ins	Del	WER	SER
initial	33.23	0.42	8.54	42.18	91.39
ASR-like	11.94	2.21	2.36	16.51	76.05
MT-like	7.34	0.71	4.22	12.26	63.41

Table 2: Evaluation of the baseline systems

Columns 'Sub', 'Ins', and 'Del' report respectively the number of substitution, insertion and deletion errors at the word level.

with the machine translation task, assess their system with the BLEU metric (Papineni et al., 2001), we decided to measure the performance of our normalization tool with the Word Error Rate (WER) and Sentence Error Rate (SER) metrics. This choice is motivated by the fact that the outcome of the normalization process is _ notwithstanding a couple of arbitrary normalization decisions _ almost deterministic, and does not warrant the use of BLEU, which is more appropriate to evaluate tasks with multiple references. Additionally, we feel that error rates are easier to interprete than BLEU values; for the sake of comparisons, some BLEU scores will nonetheless be reported.

4.2 Baseline results

In a first series of experiments, we evaluate our two systems and analyze their respective strengths and weakness. Table 4.2 reports the results of these experiments; the line 'initial' gives the corresponding numbers for the original messages, which gives a rough idea of the number of words that must be modified. As these results demonstrate, the MT-like system proves to be much more accurate than the ASR-like system.

Looking at the errors, the main problem with the latter system stems from the loss of the original spelling and tokenization information incurred during the grapheme-to-phoneme conversion step: as a consequence, many words that were correctly spelled in the input message are erroneously resegmented and decoded. This is evidenced by the high number of substitutions and insertions produced by this system, a large number of which concern function words. This phenomena is accentuated by the excessive liberality of grapheme-to-phoneme rules. For instance, to account for the erratic use of accentuated letters in SMS, the most general pronunciation rule for letter *e* (incidentally, *e* is the most frequent letter in French) predicts five pronunciations: /ə/, /e/, /ɛ/, /œ/, /ø/, plus the possibility of being deleted. As a result, first group verbal forms such as *aime* ('I or he/he love(s)') yield (at least) six different pronunciations, which result in many more combinations after resegmentation, such as *aime* ('(I, you, he/she) love(s)'), *aimé* ('loved'), *aimer* ('to love'), *aime et* ('I love and), *aime est* (I love is) etc. The same occurs with *de* ('of (the)', 'some-SING') and *le* ('the-SING'), which, through the phonemic encoding/decoding, become systematically ambiguous with their corresponding plural *des* and *les*. Sorting out the correct combination seems to be too hard a task for the statistical language model, since all these hypotheses include very high frequency tokens.

The MT-like system is significantly less error-prone: an error analysis reveals that the most common errors concern the insertion or deletion of function words, which can be attributed to noisy alignments in the phrase table. Another frequent source of error stems from agglutinated forms, notably combinations of clitic(s)+verb (e.g. *jtombrai* for *je tomberai* ('I will fall'), *jrentr* for *je rentre* ('I am coming back')) or (preposition and/or article)+noun or verbs (e.g. *cours 2droit* for *cours de droit* ('law class'), *dsortir* for *de sortir* ('to go out')...): whenever these forms are met in the training corpus, they can be correctly decoded; however, many novel forms only occur in the test set, owing to the fact that these types of agglutinations are "productive" (in the appropriate context). Contrarily to the findings of (Choudhury et al., 2007), which considered English messages, our corpus study reveals that this phenomena is far from marginal, and is a systematic source of errors for the MT system. It is noteworthy that about 17% of the tokens in the test SMS corpus do not occur in the training set, when the "true" out-of-vocabulary rate (computed on the reference messages) is only about 2.1 %.

Both systems are finally at pain to correctly recover the right number/gender/tense agreement, which is a general problem with n-gram language models in French, aggravated here by some irreducible indeterminacy: should '*désolé*' (masc.) in '*je suis désolé*' be corrected as '*désolée*' (fem) ? ultimately, this depends on the sex of the sender, which may be deduced from some other, potentially long distant, part of the message; the same indeterminacy occurs with the normalization of '*1*', which can be mapped to '*un*' (masc.) or '*une*' (fem); with '*aurai*' ('I will have'), which can be mapped with '*aurai*' or '*aurais*' ('I would have'), etc.

4.3 System combination

The analysis of normalization errors reveals that both systems have different strengths and weaknesses, suggesting that they could be used in combination. Indeed, oracle selection of the best output on a per message basis would yield an overall 9,63 WER, about 2.5 points absolute below the performance of the MT-like system.

Various ways to combine both approaches have been considered: we eventually decided to use the MT-like system for producing a first normalization; out-of-vocabulary tokens in the original SMS appear untouched in this output. For each of these, we use the ASR-like system to produce a series of "local" hypothesis, which are combined in a word lattice. This lattice is rescored with the statistical language model to yield the final output. This simple combination proved to yield significant improvements, decreasing the word-error rate from 12.26 to 10.82. The corresponding BLEU score is close to 0,8, in line with the findings of (Aw et al., 2006) for English, and comparing favorably with the 0.68 score reported in (Guimier de Neef et al., 2007) (for French, using a different test bed). Preliminary experiments suggest that using n-best list outputs from Moses instead of just the one best could buy us an small additional WER decrease.

The typical improvements brought by the combined system are illustrated by the following example, where two cases of agglutinated word forms are corrected, resulting in a correct output:

SMS	*oublié2tdir: tom a pomé c foto dlui en string*
MT-like	*oublié2tdir tom a paumé ses photos dlui en string*
Combined	*oublié de te dire tom a paumé ses photos de lui en string*
	(I) forgot to tell you (that) tom lost photos of himself in a thong

5 Conclusion and Perspectives

In this paper, we studied various ways to address the problem of normalization of SMS, by drawing analogy with related NLP problems, and accordingly reusing as much as possible existing tools or modules. Following (Aw et al., 2006), we found that using off-the-shell statistical MT systems allows to achieve very satisfactory WER; combining this system with a system based on an analogy with the speech recognition problem yields an additional 1.5 absolute improvement in WER. As it stands, our statistical normalization system seems to be sufficiently efficient to be used for text mining purposes; it also provides a useful tool to quantitatively analyze the various mechanisms involved in SMS spelling. The problem nonetheless remains far from being solved: our best system still makes at least one error on about 60% of the test messages.

There are a number of obvious improvements we might consider, such as using more accurate grapheme-to-phoneme rules, or plugging in a larger statistical language model, but we feel these would buy us only small increase in performance. As a first step to improve our normalization system, we would rather like to combine the existing approaches with a spell-checking approach. The most natural way to proceed would be to devise an alternative letter-to-word finite-state transducer C, aimed at converting space separated sequences of alphabetic symbols to the corresponding sequence of words, allowing for usual spelling errors (deletion/insertion of a letter, substitution, etc). Using the notations of section 3.2, the normalization system would thus be computed by the following finite state machine: $([E \circ P \circ D] \cup C) \circ S$.

Another natural extension would be to make this finite-state transducer stochastic: again, this would be a rather simple matter to train this transducer using the forward-backward algorithm (see (Jansche, 2003)) on the available training data.

6 acknowledgments

The authors wish to thank E. Guimier de Neef for providing us with one of the databases and other useful resources. Many thanks to our anonymous reviewers for helpful comments.

References

Allauzen, Cyril, Mehryar Mohri, and Brian Roark. 2005. The design principles and algorithms of a weighted grammar library. *International Journal of Foundations of Computer Science*, 16(3):403–421.

Anis, Jacques. 2001. *Parlez-vous texto ? Guide des nouveaux langages du réseau*. Éditions du Cherche Midi.

Aw, Aiti, Min Zhang, Juan Xiao, and Jian Su. 2006. A phrase-based statistical model for SMS text normalization. In *Proceedings of COLING/ACL*, pages 33–40.

Brill, Eric and Robert C. Moore. 2000. An improved error model for noisy channel spelling correction. In *Proceedings of the 38th Annual Meeting of the Association for Computational Linguistics*, pages 286–293, Hong Kong.

Brown, Peter F., John Cocke, Stephen Della Pietra, Vincent J. Della Pietra, Frederick Jelinek, John D. Lafferty, Robert L. Mercer, and Paul S. Roossin. 1990. A statistical approach to machine translation. *Journal of Natural Language Engineering*, 16(2):79–85.

Choudhury, Monojit, Rahul Saraf, Vijit Jain, Sudeshna Sarkar, and Anupam Basu. 2007. Investigation and modeling of the structure of texting language. In *Proceedings of the IJCAI Workshop on "Analytics for Noisy Unstructured Text Data"*, pages 63–70, Hyderabad, India.

Church, Kenneth W. and William Gale. 1991. Probability scoring for spelling correction. *Statistics and Computing*, 1:91–103.

Crystal, David. 2001. *Language and the Internet*. Cambridge University Press.

Fairon, Cédrick and Sébastien Paumier. 2006. A translated corpus of 30,000 French SMS. In *Proceedings of LREC 2006*, Genoa, Italy.

Fairon, Cédrick, Jean René Klein, and Sébastien Paumier. 2006. *Le langage SMS*. UCL Presses Universitaires de Louvain.

Guimier de Neef, Émilie, Arnaud Debeurme, and Jungyeul Park. 2007. TILT correcteur de SMS : évaluation et bilan quantitatif. In *Actes de TALN*, pages 123–132, Toulouse, France.

Hocq, S. 2006. étude des sms en français : constitution et exploitation d'un corpus aligné sms-langue standard. Technical report, Université Aix-Marseille.

Jansche, Martin. 2003. *Inference of string mappings for language technology*. Ph.D. thesis, Ohio State University.

Kobus, Catherine, François Yvon, and Géraldine Damnati. 2008. Transcrire les SMS comme on reconnaît la parole. In *Actes de la Conférence sur le Traitement Automatique des Langues (TALN'08)*, pages 128–138, Avignon, France.

Koehn, Philipp, Hieu Hoang, Alexandra Birch, Chris Callison-Burch, Marcello Federico, Nicola Bertoldi, Brooke Cowan, Wade Shen, Christine Moran, Richard Zens, Chris Dyer, Ondrej Bojar, Alexandra Constantin, and Evan Herbst. 2007. Moses: Open source toolkit for statistical machine translation. In *Proc. Annual Meeting of the Association for Computational Linguistics (ACL), demonstration session*, Prague, Czech Republic.

Michel Simard, Alexandre Deslauriers. 2001. Real-time automatic insertion of accents in French text. *Natural Language Engineering*, 7(2):143–165.

Mohri, Mehryar and Michael Riley. 1998. Network optimisation for large vocabulary speech recognition. *Speech Communication*, 25(3):1–12.

Mohri, Mehryar, Fernando Pereira, and Michael Riley. 1998. A rational design for a weighted finite-state transducer library. *Lecture Notes in Computer Science*, (1438).

Och, Franz Josef and Hermann Ney. 2003. A systematic comparison of various statistical alignment models. *Computational Linguistics*, 29(1):19–51.

Papineni, Kishore, Salim Roukos, Todd Ward, and Wei-Jing Zhu. 2001. Bleu: a method for automatic evaluation of machine translation. Technical Report RC22176 (W0109-022), IBM Research Division, Thomas J. Watson Research Center.

Stolcke, Andreas. 2002. Srilm – an extensible language modeling toolkit. In *Proceedings of the International Conference on Spoken Langage Processing (ICSLP)*, volume 2, pages 901–904, Denver, CO.

Toutanova, Kristina and Robert Moore. 2002. Pronunciation modeling for improved spelling correction. In *Proceedings of the 40th Annual Meeting of the Association for Computational Linguistics*, pages 144–151, Philadelphia, PA.

Véronis, Jean and Émilie Guimier de Neef. 2006. Le traitement des nouvelles formes de communication écrite. In Sabah, Gérard, editor, *Compréhension automatique des langues et interaction*, pages 227–248. Paris: Hermès Science.

The Choice of Features for Classification of Verbs in Biomedical Texts

Anna Korhonen
University of Cambridge
Computer Laboratory
15 JJ Thomson Avenue
Cambridge CB3 0FD, UK
alk23@cl.cam.ac.uk

Yuval Krymolowski
Dept. of Computer Science
Haifa University
Israel
yuvalkry@gmail.com

Nigel Collier
National Institute of Informatics
Hitotsubashi 2-1-2
Chiyoda-ku, Tokyo 101-8430
Japan
collier@nii.ac.jp

Abstract

We conduct large-scale experiments to investigate optimal features for classification of verbs in biomedical texts. We introduce a range of feature sets and associated extraction techniques, and evaluate them thoroughly using a robust method new to the task: cost-based framework for pairwise clustering. Our best results compare favourably with earlier ones. Interestingly, they are obtained with sophisticated feature sets which include lexical and semantic information about selectional preferences of verbs. The latter are acquired automatically from corpus data using a fully unsupervised method.

1 Introduction

Recent years have seen a massive growth in the scientific literature in the domain of biomedicine. Because future research in the biomedical sciences depends on making use of all this existing knowledge, there is a strong need for the development of natural language processing (NLP) tools which can be used to automatically locate, organize and manage facts related to published experimental results.

Major progress has been made on information retrieval and on the extraction of specific relations (e.g. between proteins and cell types) from biomedical texts (Ananiadou et al., 2006). Other tasks, such as the extraction of factual information, remain a bigger challenge.

Researchers have recently begun to use deeper NLP techniques (e.g. statistical parsing) for im-

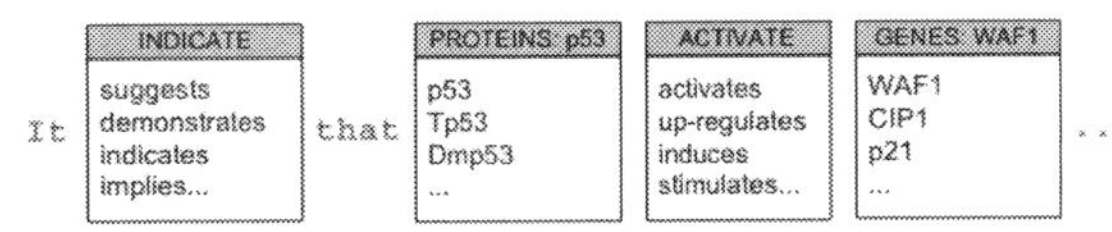

Figure 1: Sample lexical classes

proved processing of the challenging linguistic structures (e.g. complex nominals, modal subordination, anaphoric links) in biomedical texts. For optimal performance, many of these techniques require richer syntactic and semantic information than is provided by existing domain lexicons (e.g. UMLS metathesaurus and lexicon[1]). This particularly applies to verbs, which are central to the structure and meaning of sentences.

Where the information is absent, *lexical classification* can compensate for it, or aid in obtaining it. Lexical classes which capture the close relation between the syntax and semantics of verbs provide generalizations about a range of linguistic properties (Levin, 1993). For example, consider the INDICATE and ACTIVATE verb classes in Figure 1. Their members have similar subcategorization frames SCFs (e.g. *activate / up-regulate / induce / stimulate* NP) and selectional preferences (e.g. *activate / up-regulate / induce / stimulate* GENES:WAF1), and they can be used to make similar statements describing similar events (e.g. PROTEINS:P53 ACTIVATE GENES:WAF1).

Lexical classes can be used to abstract away from individual words, or to build a lexical organization which predicts much of the behaviour of a new word by associating it with an appropriate class. They have proved useful for various NLP application tasks, e.g. parsing, word sense dis-

©2008. Licensed under the *Creative Commons Attribution-Noncommercial-Share Alike 3.0 Unported* license (http://creativecommons.org/licenses/by-nc-sa/3.0/). Some rights reserved.

[1] http://www.nlm.nih.gov/research/umls

ambiguation, semantic role labeling, information extraction, question-answering, machine translation (Dorr, 1997; Prescher et al., 2000; Swier and Stevenson, 2004; Dang, 2004; Shi and Mihalcea, 2005). A large-scale classification specific to the biomedical data could support key BIO-NLP tasks such as anaphora resolution, predicate-argument identification, event extraction and the identification of biomedical (e.g. interaction) relations. However, no such classification is available.

Recent research shows that it is possible to automatically induce lexical classes from corpora with promising accuracy (Schulte im Walde, 2006; Joanis et al., 2007; Sun et al., 2008). A number of machine learning (ML) methods have been applied to classify mainly syntactic features (e.g. subcategorization frames (SCFs)) extracted from cross-domain corpora using e.g. part-of-speech tagging or robust statistical parsing techniques. Korhonen et al. (2006) have recently applied such an approach to biomedical texts. Their preliminary experiment shows encouraging results but further work is required before such an approach can be used to benefit practical BIO-NLP.

We conduct a large-scale investigation to find optimal features for biomedical verb classification. We introduce a range of theoretically-motivated feature sets and evaluate them thoroughly using a robust method new to the task: a cost-based framework for pairwise clustering. Our best results compare favourably with earlier ones. Interestingly, they are obtained using feature sets which have proved challenging in general language verb classification: ones which incorporate information about selectional preferences of verbs. Unlike in earlier work, we acquire the latter from corpus data using a fully unsupervised method.

We present our lexical classification approach in section 2 and data in section 3. Experimental evaluation is reported in section 4. Section 5 provides discussion and section 6 concludes.

2 Approach

Our lexical classification approach involves (i) extracting features from corpus data and (ii) clustering them. These steps are described in the following two sections, respectively.

2.1 Features

Lexical classifications are based on diathesis alternations which manifest in alternating sets of syntactic frames (Levin, 1993). Most verb classification approaches have therefore employed shallow syntactic slots or SCFs as basic features. Some have supplemented them with further information about verb tense, voice, and/or semantic selectional preferences on argument heads.[2]

The preliminary experiment on biomedical verb classification (Korhonen et al., 2006) employed basic syntactic features only: SCFs extracted from corpus data using the system of Briscoe and Carroll (1997) which operates on the output of a domain-independent robust statistical parser (RASP) (Briscoe and Carroll, 2002). Because such deep syntactic features seem ideally suited for challenging biomedical data, we adopted the same basic approach, but we designed and extracted a range of novel feature sets which include additional syntactic and semantic information.

The SCF extraction system assigns each occurrence of a verb in the parsed data as a member of one of the 163 verbal SCFs, builds a lexical entry for each verb (type) and SCF combination, and filters noisy entries out of the lexicon. We do not employ the filter in our work because its primary aim is to filter out SCFs containing adjuncts (as opposed to arguments). Adjuncts have been shown to be beneficial for general language verb classification (Sun et al., 2008; Joanis et al., 2007) and particularly meaningful in biomedical texts (Cohen and Hunter, 2006).

The lexical entries provide various information useful for verb classification, including e.g. the frequency of the entry in the data, the part-of-speech (POS) tags of verb tokens, the argument heads in argument positions, the prepositions in PP frames, and the number of verbal occurrences in active and passive. Making use of this information we designed ten feature sets for experimentation.

The first three feature sets F1-F3 include basic SCF frequency information for each verb:

F1: SCFs and their relative frequencies. The SCFs abstract over lexically governed particles and prepositions.

F2: F1 with two high frequency PP frames parameterized for prepositions: the simple PP and NP-PP frames refined according to the prepositions provided in the lexical entries (e.g. PP_*at*, PP_*on*, PP_*in*).

[2]See section 5 for discussion on previous work.

F3: F2 with 13 additional high frequency PP frames parameterized for prepositions.

Although prepositions are an important part of the syntactic description of lexical classes and therefore F3 should be the most informative feature set, we controlled the number of PP frames parameterized for prepositions to examine the effect of sparse data in automatic classification.

F4-F7 build on the most refined SCF-based feature set F3, supplementing it with information about verb tense (F4-F5) and voice (F6-F7):

F4: The frequencies of POS tags (e.g. VVD for *activated*) calculated over all the SCFs of the verb.

F5: The frequencies of POS tags calculated specific to each SCF of the verb.

F6: The frequency of the active and passive occurrences of the verb (calculated over all the SCFs of the verb).

F7: The frequency of the active and passive occurrences of the verb (calculated specific to each SCF of the verb).

Also F8-F10 build on feature set F3. They supplement it with information about lexical or semantic selectional preferences (SPs) of the verbs in the following slots: subject, direct object, second object, and the NP within the PP complement. The SPs are acquired using argument head data in the ten most frequent SCFs. We use two baseline methods (F8 and F9) which employ raw data and one method based on clustering (F10):

F8: The raw argument head types are considered as SP classes.

F9: Only those raw argument head types which occur with four or more verbs with frequency of ≥ 3 are considered as SP classes.

F10: SPs are acquired by clustering those argument heads which occur with ten or more verbs with frequency of ≥ 3. We used the PC clustering method described below in section 2. The number of clusters K_{np} was set to 10, 20, and 50 to produce SP classes. We call the feature sets corresponding to these different values of K_{np} F10A, F10B and F10C, respectively. Since the clustering algorithms have an element of randomness, clustering was ran 100 times. The output is a result of voting among the outputs of the runs.

F3-F10 are entirely novel feature sets in biomedical verb classification. Variations of some of them have been used in earlier work on general language classification (see section 5 for details).

2.2 Classification

The clustering method which proved the best in the preliminary experiment on biomedical verb classification was Information Bottleneck (IB) (Tishby et al., 1999). We compare this method against a probabilistic method: a cost-based framework for pairwise clustering (PC) (Puzicha et al., 2000).

2.2.1 Information Bottleneck

IB is an information-theoretic method which controls the balance between: (i) the *loss* of information by representing verbs as clusters ($I(Clusters; Verbs)$), which has to be minimal, and (ii) the *relevance* of the output clusters for representing the SCF distribution ($I(Clusters; \text{SCFs})$) which has to be maximal. The balance between these two quantities ensures optimal compression of data through clusters. The trade-off between the two constraints is realized through minimising the cost function:

$$\mathcal{L}_{\text{IB}} = I(Clusters; Verbs) - \beta I(Clusters; \text{SCFs}),$$

where β is a parameter that balances the constraints. IB takes three inputs: (i) SCF-verb -based distributions, (ii) the desired number of clusters $\mathcal{K}$, and (iii) the initial value of β. It then looks for the minimal β that decreases $\mathcal{L}_{\text{IB}}$ compared to its value with the initial β, using the given $\mathcal{K}$. IB delivers as output the probabilities $p(K|V)$.

2.2.2 Pairwise Clustering

PC is a method where a cost criterion guides the search for a suitable clustering configuration. This criterion is realized through a cost function $H(S, M)$ where

(i) $S = \{\text{sim}(a, b)\}$, $a, b \in A$: a collection of pairwise similarity values, each of which pertains to a pair of data elements $a, b \in A$.

(ii) $M = (A_1, \ldots, A_k)$: a candidate clustering configuration, specifying assignments of all elements into the disjoint clusters (that is $\cup A_j = A$ and $A_j \cap A_{j'} = \phi$ for every $1 \leq j < j' \leq k$).

1 Have an effect on activity (BIO/29)	9 Report (GEN/30)
1.1 Activate / Inactivate	**9.1 Investigate**
1.1.1 Change activity: *activate, inhibit*	9.1.1 Examine: *evaluate, analyze*
1.1.2 Suppress: *suppress, repres s*	9.1.2 Establish: *test, investigate*
1.1.3 Stimulate: *stimulate*	9.1.3 Confirm: *verify, determine*
1.1.4 Inactivate: *delay, diminish*	**9.2 Suggest**
1.2 Affect	9.2.1 Presentational:
1.2.1 Modulate: *stabilize, modulate*	*hypothesize, conclude*
1.2.2 Regulate: *control, support*	9.2.2 Cognitive:
1.3 Increase / decrease: *increase, decrease*	*consider, believe*
1.4 Modify: *modify, catalyze*	**9.3 Indicate:** *demonstrate, imply*

Table 1: Sample classes from the gold standard

Journal	Years	Words
Genes & Development	2003-5	4.7M
Journal of Biological Chemistry	2004 (Vol.1-9)	5.2M
The Journal of Cell Biology	2003-5	5.6M
Cancer Research	2005	6.5M
Carcinogenesis	2003-5	3.4M
Nature Immunology	2003-5	2.3M
Drug Metabolism and Disposition	2003-5	2.3M
Toxicological Sciences	2003-5	3.1M
Total:		33.1M

Table 2: Data from MEDLINE

The cost function is defined as follows:

$$H = -\sum n_j \cdot \text{Avgsim}_j\,,$$
$$\text{Avgsim}_j = \frac{1}{n_j \cdot (n_j - 1)} \sum_{\{a,b \in A_j\}} \text{sim}(a, b)$$

where n_j is the size of the jth cluster and Avgsim_j is the average similarity between cluster members. We used the Jensen-Shannon divergence (JS) as the similarity measure.

3 Data

3.1 Test Verbs and Gold Standard

We employed in our experiments the same gold standard as earlier employed by Korhonen et al. (2006). This three level gold standard was created by a team of human experts: 4 domain experts and 2 linguists. It includes 192 test verbs (typically frequent verbs in biomedical journal articles) classified into 16, 34 and 50 classes, respectively. The classes created by domain experts are labeled as BIO and those created by linguists as GEN. BIO classes include 116 verbs whose analysis required domain knowledge (e.g. *activate, solubilize, harvest*). GEN classes include 76 general or scientific text verbs (e.g. *demonstrate, hypothesize, appear*). Each class is associated with 1-30 member verbs. Table 1 illustrates two of the gold standard classes with 1-2 example verbs per (sub-)class.

3.2 Test Data

We downloaded the data from the MEDLINE database, from eight journals covering various areas of biomedicine. The first column in table 2 lists each journal, the second shows the years from which the articles were downloaded, and the third indicates the size of the data. We experimented with two test sets: 1) The 15.5M word sub-set shown in the first three rows of the table (this was used for creating the gold standard). 2) All the data: this new larger data was necessary for experiments with new feature sets as the most refined ones do not appear in 1) with sufficient frequency.

SCF	F1	98	39
	F2	247	64
	F3	486	75
F3 + tense	F4	490	79
	F5	920	176
F3 + voice	F6	488	77
	F7	682	153
F3 + SP	F8	150407	2112
	F9	13352	344
	F10A	110280	2091
	F10B	115208	2091
	F10C	114793	2091

Table 3: (i) The total number of features and (ii) the average per verb for all the feature sets

4 Experimental Evaluation

4.1 Processing the Data

The data was first processed using the feature extraction module. Table 3 shows (i) the total number of features in each feature set and (ii) the average per verb in the resulting lexicon. The classification module was then applied. We requested $\mathcal{K} = 2$ to 60 clusters from both clustering methods. We did not want to enforce the actual number of classes but preferred to let the class hierarchy emerge from the clustering results. In order to find the values of $\mathcal{K}$ where the clustering output might correspond to a level in the class hierarchy we used the relevance criterion. For each method (clustering method and feature set combination) we choose as informative $\mathcal{K}$'s the values for which the relevance information $I(Clusters; \text{SCF}s)$) increases more sharply between $\mathcal{K}-1$ and $\mathcal{K}$ clusters than between $\mathcal{K}$ and $\mathcal{K}+1$. We then chose for evaluation the outputs corresponding only to informative values of $\mathcal{K}$. The clustering was run 50 times for each method. The output is a result of voting among the outputs of the runs.

4.2 Measures

The clusters were evaluated against the gold standard using four methods. The first measure, the *adjusted pairwise precision*, evaluates clusters in terms of verb pairs:

$$\text{APP} = \frac{1}{\mathcal{K}} \sum_{i=1}^{\mathcal{K}} \frac{\text{num. of correct pairs in } k_i}{\text{num. of pairs in } k_i} \cdot \frac{|k_i|-1}{|k_i|+1}$$

APP is the average proportion of all within-cluster pairs that are correctly co-assigned. Multiplied by a factor that increases with cluster size it compensates for a bias towards small clusters.

The second measure is *modified purity*, a global measure which evaluates the mean precision of clusters. Each cluster is associated with its prevalent class. The number of verbs in a cluster K that take this class is denoted by $n_{\text{prevalent}}(K)$. Verbs that do not take it are considered as errors. Clusters where $n_{\text{prevalent}}(K) = 1$ are disregarded as not to introduce a bias towards singletons:

$$m\text{PUR} = \frac{\sum_{n_{\text{prevalent}}(k_i) \geq 2} n_{\text{prevalent}}(k_i)}{\text{number of verbs}}$$

The third measure is the *weighted class accuracy*, the proportion of members of dominant clusters DOM-CLUST_i within all classes c_i.

$$\text{ACC} = \frac{\sum_{i=1}^{C} \text{verbs in } \text{DOM-CLUST}_i}{\text{number of verbs}}$$

mPUR can be seen to measure the precision of clusters and ACC the recall. We define an F measure as the harmonic mean of mPUR and ACC:

$$F = \frac{2 \cdot m\text{PUR} \cdot \text{ACC}}{m\text{PUR} + \text{ACC}}$$

The experiments were run 50 times on each input to get the distribution of performance due to the randomness in the initial clustering. We calculated the average performance and standard deviation from the results of these runs.

4.3 Results for Test Set 1

We first compared IB and PC on the smaller test set 1 using feature set F2. We chose for evaluation the outputs corresponding to the most informative values of $\mathcal{K}$: 20, 33, 53 for IB, and 19, 26, 51 for PC. In the results included in table 4 IB shows slightly better performance than PC, but the difference is not significant for K=34 and 50. We decided to use PC for larger experiments because it has two advantages over IB: 1) It can cluster the large test set 2 with $\mathcal{K} = 10 - 60$ in minutes, while IB requires a day for this. 2) It can deal with (and combine) different feature sets, while IB runs into numerical problems. Due to its speed and flexibility PC is thus more suitable for larger-scale experiments involving comparison of complex feature sets.

4.4 Results for Test Set 2

Tables 5 and 6 include the PC results on the larger test set 2. Table 5 shows the results for each individual feature set (indicated in the second column). It shows also the standard deviations (σ_{avg}) of the four performance measures averaged across all the runs. These are very similar for 16, 34, and 50 classes and hence only included in one of the columns. In addition, σ_{diff} is indicated. This is $\sqrt{2} \cdot \sigma_{\text{avg}}$ and used for calculating the significance of the performance differences. In the following discussion we consider a difference of more than $2\sigma_{\text{diff}}$ ($p > 97.7\%$) as significant.

The first feature sets F1-F3 include basic SCF (frequency) information for each verb, F2-F3 refined with prepositions. F2 shows clearly better results than F1 (over 10 F-measure) at all the levels of gold standard. This demonstrates the usefulness of prepositions for the task. When moving to F3 the performance decreases for 34 and 50 classes, while improving for 16 classes, but these differences are not statistically significant.

Feature sets F4-F10 build on F3. F4-F5 include information about verb tense. This information proves quite useful for verb classification, particularly when specific to individual SCFs. When compared against the baseline featureset F3, F5 is clearly better - particularly at 50 classes where the difference is 3.9 in F-measure ($2\sigma_{\text{diff}}$). Verb voice information is not equally helpful: F6-F7 are not better than F3. In some comparisons they are worse, e.g. F7 vs. F3 at 16 classes.

F8-F10 supplement F3 with information about SPs. Surprisingly, these lexical and semantic features prove the most useful for our task. At the level of 34 and 50 classes, the best SP features are even better than the best tense features (the difference is statistically significant), and they yield notable improvement over the baseline features (e.g. 6.8 difference in F-measure between F9 and F3). The performance is not equally good at 16 classes. This makes perfect sense because class members are unlikely to have similar SPs at such a coarse level of semantic classification.

When comparing the five sets of SPs features against each other, F9 and F10C produce the best results at 34 and 50 classes. F9 uses raw (filtered) argument head data for SP acquisition while F10C uses clustering. It is interesting that the difference between these two very different methods is not statistically significant. Whether one employs

	16 Classes				34 Classes				50 Classes			
	APP	mPUR	ACC	F	APP	mPUR	ACC	F	APP	mPUR	ACC	F
IB	74	77	66	71	69	75	81	77	54	72	79	75
PC	71	78	58	67	64	71	81	75	63	71	73	72
±	1.1	1.0	1.0	0.8	1.8	1.6	1.3	1.4	2.1	1.5	1.6	1.1

Table 4: Performance on test set 1

		16 Classes				34 Classes				50 Classes			
		APP	mPUR	ACC	F	APP	mPUR	ACC	F	APP	mPUR	ACC	F
SCF	F1	62.7	68.2	54.6	60.6	50.4	58.4	53.4	55.8	41.5	50.3	55.7	52.9
	F2	68.7	76.4	66.4	71.1	61.9	65.5	65.8	65.6	53.9	61.2	65.4	63.2
	F3	69.3	77.7	67.6	72.3	61.6	66.0	64.0	65.0	53.7	60.2	65.9	62.9
F3 + tense	F4	70.1	77.5	65.5	71.0	62.0	70.3	69.4	69.8	53.3	60.6	68.0	64.1
	F5	68.5	75.4	71.7	73.5	61.9	67.8	68.2	68.0	58.2	62.7	71.7	66.8
F3 + voice	F6	70.6	78.1	64.0	70.4	61.2	66.0	65.8	65.9	54.3	59.6	70.1	64.4
	F7	74.0	79.5	59.7	68.2	62.6	65.4	65.1	65.2	55.1	60.9	69.2	64.7
F3 + SP	F8	77.1	78.2	61.6	68.9	69.6	69.3	71.2	70.2	61.3	62.7	71.1	66.6
	F9	72.4	77.1	64.0	69.9	72.2	72.0	71.6	71.8	62.3	65.6	72.4	68.8
	F10A	75.6	80.0	63.2	70.6	66.1	69.2	70.6	69.9	59.4	63.5	69.0	66.2
	F10B	68.8	77.1	69.2	72.9	65.3	67.2	69.8	68.5	59.9	61.9	70.5	65.9
	F10C	74.1	78.9	65.7	71.7	68.8	71.7	69.7	70.7	59.8	63.4	71.1	67.0
	σ_{avg}	2.2	1.5	1.8	1.4								
	σ_{diff}	3.1	2.1	2.5	2.0								

Table 5: Performance on test set 2: PC clustering results for individual feature sets at the three levels of gold standard. σ_{avg} and σ_{diff} were calculated across all the three classification levels.

16 CL.	F5+F9	F4+ F10C	F5	F5+ F8
APP	72.3	68.2	68.5	72.2
mPUR	76.4	77.0	75.4	76.5
ACC	73.6	70.9	71.7	69.9
F	75.0	73.8	73.5	73.0
34 CL.	F5+ F9	F5+ F8	F9	F4+ F10A
APP	68.7	71.0	72.2	62.9
mPUR	70.1	71.0	72.0	68.4
ACC	74.8	73.4	71.6	75.0
F	72.4	72.2	71.8	71.5
50 CL.	F9	F5+ F9	F5+ F8	F4+ F9
APP	62.3	59.8	62.8	59.7
mPUR	65.6	63.8	64.1	63.1
ACC	72.4	72.7	71.0	71.8
F	68.8	68.0	67.4	67.1

Table 6: Results for the top four feature set combinations. All the feature sets build on F3.

fine grained clusters (F10C) or coarse-grained ones (F10A) as SPs does not make much difference.

We next combined various feature sets. Table 6 shows the performance for the top four combinations. Comparing these results against the ones in Table 5, (see the σ_{diff} values in Table 5) we can see that combining feature sets does not result in better performance[3]. The only exception is the difference in APP and mPUR between F9 and F4 + F10A at N=34. However, these results show similar tendencies as the earlier ones: at 16 classes the most useful features are based on verb tense, while at 34 and 50 classes they are based on SPs.

5 Discussion

The results presented in the previous section are in interesting contrast with those reported in earlier work. In previous work on general language verb classification, syntactic features (slots or SCFs) have proved generally the most helpful features, e.g. (Schulte im Walde, 2006; Joanis et al., 2007). The preliminary experiment on biomedical verb classification (Korhonen et al., 2006) experimented only with them. In our experiments, SCFs proved useful baseline features. When we refined them further, we faced sparse data problems: considerable improvement was obtained when moving from F1 to F2, but not when moving to F3. Although many verb classes are sensitive to preposition types, many of the types are low in frequency. Future work could address this problem by employing smoothing techniques, or backing off to preposition classes.

Joanis et al. (2007) experimented with tense and voice -based features in general English verb classification. They offered no significant improvement over basic syntactic features. Also in our experiments, we obtained little improvement with voice features. This could be due to the

[3]Recall that all F4-F10 are actually already 'combined' with F3 - we do not refer to this combination here.

un-distinctiveness of passive in biomedical texts where it is used typically with high frequency. However, tense-based features clearly improved the baseline performance in our experiments. This could be partly because we 'parameterize' POS information for SCFs, and partly because semantically similar verbs in biomedical language tend to behave similarly also in terms of tense (Friedman et al., 2002).

Joanis (2002) and Schulte im Walde (2006) used SP-based features in general English and German verb classifications, respectively. The former acquired them from WordNet (Miller, 1990) and the latter from GermaNet (Kunze, 2000). Joanis (2002) obtained no improvement over syntactic features while Schulte im Walde (2006) obtained, but the improvement was not significant. In our experiments, SP features gave the best results and the clearest improvement over the baseline features at the finer-grained levels of classification where class members are indeed likely to be the most uniform in terms of their SPs.

We obtained this improvement despite using a fully unsupervised approach to SP acquisition. We did not exploit lexical resources like Joanis (2002) and Schulte im Walde (2006) because it would have required combining general resources (e.g. WordNet) with domain specific ones (e.g. UMLS). We opted for a simpler approach in this initial work – using raw argument heads and clustering – and obtained surprisingly good results. In our experiments filtering of raw argument heads and clustering with N=50 produced equivalent results, suggesting that relatively fine-grained clusters are optimal. Future work will require qualitative analysis of noun clusters and comparison of these against classes in lexical resources to determine an optimal method for SP acquisition.

Does the fact that we obtain good results with features which have not proved helpful in general language classification indicate a need for domain-specific feature engineering? We do not believe so. The feature sets we experimented with are theoretically well-motivated and should, in principle, also aid general language verb classification. We believe they proved helpful in our experiments because being domain-specific, biomedical language is conventionalised and therefore less varied in terms of verb sense and usage than general language. For example, verbs have stronger SPs for their argument heads when many of their corpus occurrences are of similar sense. This renders SP-based features more useful for classification.

Due to differences in the data, methods, and experimental setup, direct comparison of our performance figures with previously published ones is difficult. The closest comparison point with general language is (Korhonen et al., 2003) which reported 59% mPUR using IB to assign 110 polysemous English verbs into 34 classes. Our best results are substantially better (72-80% mPUR). It is encouraging that we obtained such good results despite focusing on a linguistically challenging domain.

In addition to the points mentioned earlier, our future plans include seeding automatic classification with more sophisticated information acquired automatically from domain-specific texts (e.g. using named entity recognition and anaphoric linking (Vlachos et al., 2006)). We will also explore semi-automatic ML technology and active learning in aiding the classification. Finally, we plan to conduct a bigger experiment with a larger number of verbs, make the resulting classification publicly available, and demonstrate its usefulness for practical BIO-NLP application tasks.

6 Conclusion

We reported large-scale experiments to investigate the optimal characteristics of features required for biomedical verb classification. A range of feature sets and associated extraction methods were introduced for this work, along with a robust clustering method capable of dealing with large data and complex feature sets. A number of experiments were reported. The best performing feature sets proved to be the ones which include information about SCFs supplemented with information about verb tense and SPs in particular. The latter were acquired automatically from corpus data using an unsupervised method. Similar feature sets have not proved equally useful in earlier work in general language verb classification. We discussed reasons for this and highlighted several areas for future work.

Acknowledgement

Work on this paper was funded by the Royal Society, EPSRC ('ACLEX' project, GR/T19919/01) and MRC ('CRAB' project, G0601766), UK.

References

Ananiadou, S., B. D. Kell, and J. Tsujii. 2006. Text mining and its potential applications in systems biology. *Trends in Biotechnology*, 24(12):571–579.

Briscoe, E. J. and J. Carroll. 1997. Automatic extraction of subcategorization from corpora. In 5th *ACL Conference on Applied Natural Language Processing*, pages 356–363, Washington DC.

Briscoe, E. J. and J. Carroll. 2002. Robust accurate statistical annotation of general text. In 3rd *International Conference on Language Resources and Evaluation*, pages 1499–1504, Las Palmas, Gran Canaria.

Cohen, K. B. and L. Hunter. 2006. A critical review of PASBio's argument structures for biomedical verbs. *BMC Bioinformatics*, 7(3).

Dang, H. T. 2004. *Investigations into the Role of Lexical Semantics in Word Sense Disambiguation*. Ph.D. thesis, CIS, University of Pennsylvania.

Dorr, B. J. 1997. Large-scale dictionary construction for foreign language tutoring and interlingual machine translation. *Machine Translation*, 12(4):271–322.

Friedman, C., P. Kra, and A. Rzhetsky. 2002. Two biomedical sublanguages: a description based on the theories of zellig harris. *Journal of Biomedical Informatics*, 35(4):222–235.

Joanis, E., S. Stevenson, and D. James. 2007. A general feature space for automatic verb classification. *Natural Language Engineering*.

Joanis, E. 2002. Automatic verb classification using a general feature space. Master's thesis, University of Toronto.

Korhonen, A., Y. Krymolowski, and N. Collier. 2006. Automatic classification of verbs in biomedical texts. In *ACL-COLING*, Sydney, Australia.

Kunze, C. 2000. Extension and use of germanet, a lexical-semantic database. In *2nd International Conference on Language Resources and Evaluation*, Athens, Greece.

Levin, B. 1993. *English Verb Classes and Alternations*. Chicago University Press, Chicago.

Miller, G. A. 1990. WordNet: An on-line lexical database. *International Journal of Lexicography*, 3(4):235–312.

Prescher, D., S. Riezler, and M. Rooth. 2000. Using a probabilistic class-based lexicon for lexical ambiguity resolution. In *18th International Conference on Computational Linguistics*, pages 649–655, Saarbrücken, Germany.

Puzicha, J., T. Hofmann, and J. M. Buhmann. 2000. A theory of proximity-based clustering: structure detection by optimization. *Pattern Recognition*, 33(4):617–634.

Schulte im Walde, S. 2006. Experiments on the automatic induction of german semantic verb classes. *Computational Linguistics*, 32(2):159–194.

Shi, L. and R. Mihalcea. 2005. Putting pieces together: Combining FrameNet, VerbNet and WordNet for robust semantic parsing. In *Proceedings of the Sixth International Conference on Intelligent Text Processing and Computational Linguistics*, Mexico City, Mexico.

Sun, L., A. Korhonen, and Y. Krymolowski. 2008. Verb class discovery from rich syntactic data. In *9th International Conference on Intelligent Text Processing and Computational Linguistics*, Haifa, Israel.

Swier, R. and S. Stevenson. 2004. Unsupervised semantic role labelling. In *Proceedings of the 2004 Conference on Empirical Methods in Natural Language Processing*, pages 95–102, Barcelona, Spain, August.

Tishby, N., F. C. Pereira, and W. Bialek. 1999. The information bottleneck method. In *Proc. of the* 37th *Annual Allerton Conference on Communication, Control and Computing*, pages 368–377.

Vlachos, A., C. Gasperin, I. Lewin, and E. J. Briscoe. 2006. Bootstrapping the recognition and anaphoric linking of named entitites in drosophila articles. In *Pacific Symposium in Biocomputing*, Maui, Hawaii.

Extending a Thesaurus with Words from Pan-Chinese Sources

Oi Yee Kwong[†‡] **and Benjamin K. Tsou**[‡]
[†]Department of Chinese, Translation and Linguistics
[‡]Language Information Sciences Research Centre
City University of Hong Kong
Tat Chee Avenue, Kowloon, Hong Kong
{rlolivia, rlbtsou}@cityu.edu.hk

Abstract

In this paper, we work on extending a Chinese thesaurus with words distinctly used in various Chinese communities. The acquisition and classification of such region-specific lexical items is an important step toward the larger goal of constructing a Pan-Chinese lexical resource. In particular, we extend a previous study in three respects: (1) to improve automatic classification by removing duplicated words from the thesaurus, (2) to experiment with classifying words at the subclass level and semantic head level, and (3) to further investigate the possible effects of data heterogeneity between the region-specific words and words in the thesaurus on classification performance. Automatic classification was based on the similarity between a target word and individual categories of words in the thesaurus, measured by the cosine function. Experiments were done on 120 target words from four regions. The automatic classification results were evaluated against a gold standard obtained from human judgements. In general accuracy reached 80% or more with the top 10 (out of 80+) and top 100 (out of 1,300+) candidates considered at the subclass level and semantic head level respectively, provided that the appropriate data sources were used.

1 Introduction

A unique problem in Chinese language processing arises from the extensive lexical variations among major Chinese speech communities. Although different communities (e.g. Beijing, Hong Kong, Taipei and Singapore) often share a large core lexicon, lexical variations could occur in at least two ways. On the one hand, even the same word forms shared by various communities could be used with different meanings. For instance, the word 居屋 (*ju1wu1*)[1] refers to general housing in Mainland China but specifically to housing under the Home Ownership Scheme in Hong Kong. On the other hand, there are substantially different lexical items used for lexicalizing common or region-specific concepts. For example, while the word 住房 (*zhu4fang2*) is similarly used as 居屋 to mean general housing in Mainland China, it is rarely seen in the Hong Kong context; and 下崗 (*xia4gang3*) is specific, if not exclusive, to Mainland China for referring to a special concept of unemployment.

Existing Chinese lexical resources are often based on language use in one particular region and are therefore not comprehensive enough to capture the substantial *regional variation* as an important part of the lexical knowledge, which will be useful and critical for many NLP applications, including natural language understanding, information retrieval, and machine translation.

Tsou and Kwong (2006) proposed a comprehensive Pan-Chinese lexical resource, using a large and unique synchronous Chinese corpus as an authentic source of lexical variation among various Chinese speech communities. They also studied the feasibility of taking an existing Chinese thesaurus as leverage and classifying new words from various Chinese communities with respect to the classificatory structure therein (Kwong and Tsou, 2007). They used the catego-

© 2008. Licensed under the *Creative Commons Attribution-Noncommercial-Share Alike 3.0 Unported* license (http://creativecommons.org/licenses/by-nc-sa/3.0/). Some rights reserved.

[1] The transcriptions in brackets are based on Hanyu Pinyin.

ries at the subclass level of the *Tongyici Cilin* (同義詞詞林, abbreviated as Cilin hereafter) for the task. The classification was done by comparing the similarity of a target word (i.e. the word to be classified) and individual categories of words in the thesaurus based on a feature vector of co-occurring words in a corpus. Since words in the thesaurus are mostly based on lexical items used in Mainland China, and the target words come from various Chinese communities, a major issue in the classification task is thus the heterogeneity of the data sources. It was hypothesized that the datasets from which the features were extracted (for the target words and words in the thesaurus respectively) may affect the performance of automatic classification. The experimental results supported the hypothesis in part, and the actual effect varied with datasets from individual regions. Moreover, there is room to improve the overall accuracy for the method to be useful in practice, and it appears that the duplicated words in the thesaurus might have skewed the similarity measurement to a certain extent.

The current study thus attempts to extend this previous study in three respects: (1) to improve automatic classification by removing duplicated words from the thesaurus, (2) to experiment with classifying words at the subclass level and semantic head level (a finer level), and (3) to further investigate the possible effects of data heterogeneity between the region-specific words and words in the thesaurus on classification performance.

In Section 2, we will briefly review related work and the background of the current study. In Sections 3 and 4, we will describe the materials used and the experimental setup respectively. Results will be presented in Section 5 and discussed in Section 6, followed by a conclusion in Section 7.

2 Related Work

To build a semantic lexicon, one has to identify the relation between words within a semantic hierarchy, and to group similar words together into a class. Previous work on automatic methods for building semantic lexicons could be divided into two main groups. One is automatic thesaurus acquisition, that is, to identify synonyms or topically related words from corpora based on various measures of similarity (e.g. Riloff and Shepherd, 1997; Lin, 1998; Caraballo, 1999; Thelen and Riloff, 2002; You and Chen, 2006).

Another line of research, which is more closely related to the current study, is to extend existing thesauri by classifying new words with respect to their given structures (e.g. Tokunaga *et al.*, 1997; Pekar, 2004). An early effort along this line is Hearst (1992), who attempted to identify hyponyms from large text corpora, based on a set of lexico-syntactic patterns, to augment and critique the content of WordNet. Ciaramita (2002) compared several models in classifying nouns with respect to a simplified version of WordNet and signified the gain in performance with morphological features. For Chinese, Tseng (2003) proposed a method based on morphological similarity to assign a Cilin category to unknown words from the Sinica corpus which were not in the Chinese Electronic Dictionary and Cilin; but somehow the test data were taken from Cilin, and therefore could not really demonstrate the effectiveness with unknown words found in the Sinica corpus.

Kwong and Tsou (2007) attempted to classify words distinctly used in Beijing, Hong Kong, Singapore, and Taiwan, with respect to the Cilin classificatory structure. They brought up the issue of data heterogeneity in the task. In general, automatic classification of words via similarity measurement between two words, or between a word and a class of words, was often done on words from a similar data source, with the assumption that the feature vectors under comparison are directly comparable. In the Pan-Chinese context, however, the words to be classified come from corpora collected from various Chinese speech communities, but the words in the thesaurus are often based on usages found in a particular community, such as Mainland China in the case of Cilin. It is thus questionable whether the words in Cilin would appear in comparable contexts in texts from other places, thus affecting the similarity measurement. In view of this heterogeneous nature of the data, they experimented with extracting feature vectors for the Cilin words from different datasets and found that the classification of words from Taipei was most affected in this regard.

In general, up to 85% accuracy was reached with the top 15 candidates for classification at the Cilin subclass level. This performance, however, should be improved for the method to be useful in practice. It is observed that Cilin, as most other thesauri, does not have a mutually exclusive classification. Many words appear in more than one category (at various levels). Such duplication may affect the similarity comparison between a target word and words in a category. The current study thus attempts to avoid this confounding factor by removing duplicated words from Cilin for the comparison of similarity, and to extend the classification to a finer level.

3 Materials

3.1 The Tongyici Cilin

The *Tongyici Cilin* (同義詞詞林) (Mei *et al.*, 1984) is a Chinese synonym dictionary, or more often known as a Chinese thesaurus in the tradition of the Roget's Thesaurus for English. The Roget's Thesaurus has about 1,000 numbered semantic heads, more generally grouped under higher level semantic classes and subclasses, and more specifically differentiated into paragraphs and semicolon-separated word groups. Similarly, some 70,000 Chinese lexical items are organized into a hierarchy of broad conceptual categories in Cilin. Its classification consists of 12 top-level semantic classes, 94 subclasses, 1,428 semantic heads and 3,925 paragraphs. It was first published in the 1980s and was based on lexical usages mostly of post-1949 Mainland China. In the current study, we will focus on the subclass level and semantic head level. Some example subclasses and semantic heads are shown in Table 1.

We classify words with respect to the subclass level and semantic head level (that is, second and third levels in the Cilin organisation). Moreover, we skip class K and class L as the former contains mostly function words and the latter longer expressions. We are thus considering 88 subclasses and 1,356 semantic heads in this study.

Within classes A to J, there are 7,517 words which were found to appear in more than one category. Upon removing these entries, 44,588 words were used in the similarity comparison for the current study.

Class	Subclasses	Semantic Heads
A 人 (Human)	Aa … Ae 職業 (Occupation) Af 身份 (Identity) … An	Aa01 … Ae10 軍官 將士 軍人 士兵 (commander, soldier) … An07
B 物 (Things)	Ba … Bb 擬狀物 (Shape) … Bi 動物 (Animal)… Bm 材料 (Material)…Bq 衣物 (Clothing) … Br	Ba01 … Bm08 煤 炭 (coal, carbon) … Bn03 房間 (room) … Br14
C 時間與空間 (Time and Space)	Ca 時間 (Time) Cb 空間 (Space)	Ca01 … Ca18 年 (year) … Cb28 場所 (location) … Cb30
D 抽象事物 (Abstract entities)	Da 事情 情況 (Condition) … Df 意識 (Ideology) … Di 社會 政法 (Society) Dj 經濟 (Economics) … Dm 機構 (Organization) Dn 數量 單位 (Quantity)	Da01 … Di10 團體 派別 (group, party) … Dj04 資本 利潤 利息 債務 (capital, interest) Dj05 貨幣 票據 (currency, invoice) … Dm01 政府 (government) … Dn10
E 特徵 (Characteristics)	Ea … Ed 性質 (Property)… Ef	Ea01 … Ed03 好 壞 (goodness, badness) … Ef14
F 動作 (Action)	Fa … Fd 全身動作 (Body action)	Fa01 … Fb01 走 跑 (run) … Fd09
G 心理活動 (Psychological activities)	Ga … Gb 心理活動 (Psychological activities)… Gc	Ga01 … Gb01 想像 思考 斟酌 著想 (imagine, think) … Gc04
H 活動 (Activities)	Ha … He 經濟活動 (Economic activities) … Hd 生產 (Production) … Hf 交通 運輸 (Transportation) Hg 教衛科研 (Scientific research)… Hi 社交 (Social contact) Hj 生活 (Livelihood)	Ha01 … Hc09 主持 指揮 統率 執掌 管轄 (in charge, administer, lead) … He03 買 賣 (buy, sell) … Hg01 教育 傳授 示範 (teach, demo) … Hj12 做 施展 合作 嘗試 (do, cooperate, try) … Hn13
I 現象與狀態 (Phenomenon and state)	Ia … If 境遇 (Circumstance) Ig 始末 (Process)… Ih	Ia01 … Ig01 開始 結束 (begin, end) … Ih05 增多 添補 減少 (increase, decrease) … Ih13
J 關聯 (Association)	Ja 聯繫 (Liaison) Jb 異同 (Similarity and Difference) Jc 配合 (Matching) … Je	Ja01 … Jc01 適應 相配 符合 (adapt, match) … Je14

Table 1 Some Examples of Cilin Subclasses and Semantic Heads

3.2 The LIVAC Synchronous Corpus

LIVAC (http://www.livac.org) stands for Linguistic Variation in Chinese Speech Communities. It is a synchronous corpus developed and dynamically maintained by the Language Information Sciences Research Centre of the City University of Hong Kong since 1995 (Tsou and Lai, 2003). The corpus consists of newspaper articles collected regularly and synchronously from six Chinese speech communities, namely Hong Kong, Beijing, Taipei, Singapore, Shanghai, and Macau. Texts collected cover a variety of domains, including front page news stories, local news, international news, editorials, sports news, entertainment news, and financial news. Up to December 2007, the corpus has already accumulated over 250 million character tokens which, upon automatic word segmentation and manual verification, yielded about 1.2 million word types.

For the present study, we made use of subcorpora consisting of the *financial news* sections collected over the 9-year period 1995-2004 from Beijing (BJ), Hong Kong (HK), Singapore (SG), and Taipei (TW). Table 2 shows the sizes of the subcorpora.

Region	Size of Financial Subcorpus (rounded to nearest 1K)	
	Word Token	**Word Type**
BJ	232K	20K
HK	970K	38K
SG	621K	28K
TW	254K	22K

Table 2 Sizes of Individual Subcorpora

3.3 Test Data

Kwong and Tsou (2006) observed that among the unique lexical items found from the individual subcorpora, only about 30-40% are covered by Cilin, but not necessarily in the expected senses. In other words, Cilin could in fact be enriched with over 60% of the unique items from various regions.

In the current study, we sampled the most frequent 30 words distinctly and predominantly used in each of the BJ, HK, SG, and TW subcorpus. Classification was based on their similarity with each of the Cilin subclasses and semantic heads, compared by the cosine measure, as discussed in Section 4.2.

4 Experiments

4.1 Setting the Gold Standard

Three linguistics undergraduate students and one research student on computational linguistics from the City University of Hong Kong were asked to assign what they would consider to be the most appropriate Cilin category (at the subclass and semantic head level) to each of the 120 target words.

All human judges reported difficulties in various degrees in assigning Cilin categories to the target words. The major problem came from the regional specificity and thus the unfamiliarity of the judges with the respective lexical items and contexts. For example, all judges reported problem with the term 自撮 (*zi4cuo1*), one of the target words from Singapore referring to 自撮股市 (*zi4cuo1gu3shi4*, CLOB in the Singaporean stock market), which is specific to Singapore.

Notwithstanding the difficulty, the inter-annotator agreement, as measured by *Kappa*, was found to be 0.6870 at the subclass level and 0.5971 at the semantic head level.

We took a "loose" approach to form the gold standard, which includes all categories (at the subclass level and semantic head level respectively) assigned by one or more judges. Automatic classification will be considered "correct" if any of these categories is matched.

4.2 Automatic Classification

Each target word was compared to all Cilin categories and automatically classified to the category which is most similar to it. The Cilin data was first pre-processed to remove duplicated words.

We compute the similarity by the cosine between the two corresponding feature vectors containing *all co-occurring content words* in a corpus within a window of ±5 words (excluding many general adjectives and adverbs, and numbers and proper names were all ignored). The feature vector of a Cilin category is based on the union of the features from all individual members in the category.

The cosine of two feature vectors $\vec{v}$ and $\vec{w}$ is computed as

$$\cos(\vec{v},\vec{w}) = \frac{\vec{v}\cdot\vec{w}}{|\vec{v}||\vec{w}|}$$

The feature vector of a given target word is extracted from the respective subcorpus from which the target word was found (called the target subcorpus hereafter). To study the data heterogeneity effect, we experimented with two conditions for the extraction of feature vectors for Cilin words: from the target subcorpus or from the BJ subcorpus which is assumed to be representative of usages in Mainland China.

All automatic classification results were evaluated against the gold standard based on human judgements as discussed in Section 4.1. Classification performance is measured based on the correctness of the top *N* candidates.

4.3 Baseline

A simple baseline measure was obtained by ranking the subclasses in descending order of the number of words they cover. It was assumed that the bigger the subclass size, the more likely it covers a new term. The top *N* candidates in this ranking were checked against the gold standard as above.

5 Results

In the following discussion, we will use labels in the form of *<Cat>-<Target>-<CilinFeatSource>* to refer to the various testing conditions, where *Cat* refers to the category type, *Target* to the originating source of the target words, and *CilinFeatSource* to the source from which the feature vectors for the Cilin words were extracted. Thus the label Sub-hk-hk means classification of HK target words at the Cilin subclass level, with feature vectors for target words and Cilin words extracted from the HK subcorpus; and the label Head-tw-bj means classification of TW target words at the Cilin semantic head level, with feature vectors for the target words extracted from the TW subcorpus and those for the Cilin words extracted from the BJ subcorpus.

5.1 Pre-processing of Cilin

Figure 1 shows the comparison of classification accuracy for words from the four regions at the subclass level before and after duplicates in Cilin were removed. All feature vectors were extracted from the respective target corpora.

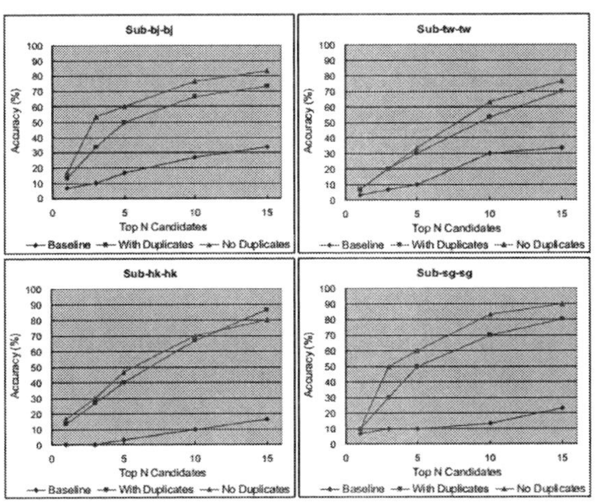

Figure 1 Effect of Pre-processing Cilin

It can be seen from Figure 1 that removing duplicated words in Cilin could improve the classification of words from all regions at the subclass level.

5.2 Data Heterogeneity Effect

As explained earlier, since the words to be classified come from various Chinese speech communities, but the words in Cilin are mostly based on usages found in Mainland China, it is uncertain whether the words in Cilin would appear in comparable contexts in texts from other places, for the similarity measurement to be effective. Hence, we experimented with two conditions for extracting feature vectors for the Cilin words. While the features for a target word to be classified are extracted from the respective target subcorpus, the features for the Cilin words are extracted either from the target subcorpus or from the BJ subcorpus. Figure 2 shows the data heterogeneity effect on the classification of target words from various regions at the subclass level.

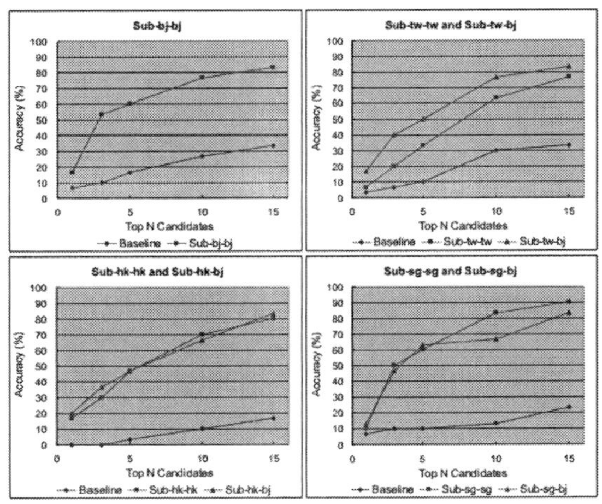

Figure 2 Data Heterogeneity Effect

The data heterogeneity effect is most noticeable for the TW words. Extracting features for the Cilin words from the BJ subcorpus always gives better classification results for the TW words, than if the features were extracted from the TW subcorpus. The difference between Sub-hk-hk and Sub-hk-bj, and that between Sub-sg-sg and Sub-sg-bj, however, is not as great. This suggests that the lexical difference is particularly significant between BJ and TW.

5.3 Fine-grainedness of Classification

The semantic head level is more fine-grained than the subclass level, and is expected to be more difficult for classification. Figure 3 shows the results of classification at the semantic head level, with the effect of data heterogeneity.

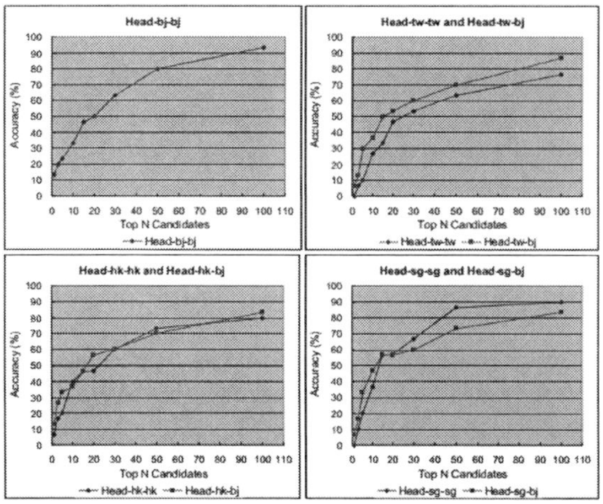

Figure 3 Semantic Head Level Classification

It is observed from Figures 2 and 3 that data heterogeneity affects the classification of TW words at both the subclass and semantic head level. In both cases, features for Cilin words extracted from BJ subcorpus work better than those from TW subcorpus. A somewhat opposite effect was observed for SG target words, especially beyond the top 5 to 10 candidates. There is not much difference for the HK target words.

The classification at the semantic head level is expectedly less precise than that at the subclass level. At the subclass level, 80% or more accuracy could be reached with the top 10 candidates considered, whereas the top 50 candidates or more would be needed to reach a similar level of accuracy at the semantic head level. This is nevertheless encouraging in view of the total number of categories at the semantic head level.

6 Discussions

6.1 Overall Classification Accuracy

From the results reported in the last section, it can be seen that removing the duplicated words in Cilin could help improve the classification accuracy at all conditions. This is because some words, which appear in more than one category at the subclass or semantic head level, might skew the similarity measured between a target word and a given category. An example will be discussed in Section 6.3.

In general, the top 10 candidates could lead to over 80% accuracy at the subclass level (much improved from previous results before removing duplicates in Cilin, where it usually took the top 15 candidates to reach about 80% accuracy). At the semantic head level, the top 50 candidates could lead to over 70% accuracy for HK and TW words and to 80% or more for BJ and SG words. The accuracy, nevertheless, is also dependent on the datasets from which features were extracted, as shown in Sections 5.2 and 5.3 above and further discussed below.

6.2 Regional Variation

The various Chinese speech communities might differ not only in the lexical items they use, but also in the way they use the lexical items in common. The demand on cross-cultural knowledge thus poses a challenge for building a Pan-Chinese lexical resource manually. Cilin, for instance, is quite biased in language use in Mainland China, and it requires experts with knowledge of a wide variety of Chinese terms to be able to manually classify lexical items specific to other Chinese speech communities. It is therefore even more important to devise robust ways for automatic classification of words from various regions.

The data heterogeneity effect is quite different for the classification of SG words and TW words, but apparently not very significant for HK words. Beyond the top 5 to 10 candidates, features extracted from the SG subcorpus for Cilin words seem to have an advantage. This suggests that although the SG subcorpus shares those words in Cilin, the context in which they are used might be slightly different from their use in Mainland China. Thus extracting their contextual features from the SG subcorpus might better reflect their usage and make them more comparable with the target words from SG. For the TW words, on the contrary, features for Cilin words extracted from the BJ subcorpus always have an advantage over those extracted from the TW subcorpus. As Kwong and Tsou (2006) observed, Beijing and Taipei data share the least number of lexical items among the four regions under investigation. Words in Cilin therefore might not have the appropriate contextual feature vectors extracted from the TW subcorpus.

6.3 Analysis for Individual Words

In order to study the actual effect of various experimental conditions on the classification of individual target words, we also worked out the change in the ranking (Δr) of the correct category for each target word. A negative Δr thus corresponds to an improvement in the classification as the new ranking of the correct category is smaller (earlier) than the old one. Table 3 shows some examples with improvement in this regard. The Rank column refers to the rank of the correct category in Sub-{bj,hk,tw,sg}-bj, $\Delta r(D)$ is the change after duplicates were removed from Cilin, and $\Delta r(H)$ is the change from Sub-*x*-*x* conditions.

No.	Word (Region)	Rank	$\Delta r(D)$	$\Delta r(H)$
1	信息化 (BJ)	1	-6	-
2	再就業 (BJ)	3	-15	-
3	下崗 (BJ)	1	-1	-
4	抗旱 (BJ)	1	-2	-
5	質檢 (BJ)	3	-2	-
6	大市 (HK)	4	-4	-6
7	入市 (HK)	2	-3	-6
8	國企股 (HK)	1	-6	-1
9	息口 (HK)	1	-8	-5
10	沽售 (HK)	2	-4	-5
11	新元 (SG)	1	-3	-4
12	馬股 (SG)	1	-12	-1
13	閉市價 (SG)	1	-3	-1
14	附加股 (SG)	2	-2	-4
15	容積率 (SG)	2	-7	1
16	投信 (TW)	3	-1	-13
17	成長率 (TW)	2	-3	-7
18	金控 (TW)	1	0	-3
19	買超 (TW)	6	-3	-20
20	行庫 (TW)	3	-6	-5

Table 3 Ranking Change for Individual Words[2]

Take the example of the BJ target word 信息化 (*xin4xi1hua4*, informationize). Before duplicated words were removed from Cilin, the most appropriate subclass (Ih:Change) ranked 7th in the automatic classification. Upon the removal of duplicated words, subclass Ih ranked first in the results. The words shared by other top ranking subclasses (e.g. Je:influence, Da:condition, etc.) such as 加 (*jia1*, increase), 推 (*tui1*, push), 提高 (*ti2gao1*, raise), etc., may have skewed the similarity comparison by introducing many common co-occurring words which are not particularly characteristic of any subclass.

For the TW target word 投信 (*tou2xin4*, investment trust), the appropriate subclass (Dm:organization) soared from the 16th to the 3rd when features were extracted for the Cilin words from the BJ subcorpus instead of the TW subcorpus. It was observed that both vectors have a large part in common, but the one extracted from TW subcorpus contained many more spurious features which might not be characteristic of the subclass, thus affecting the similarity score.

It is also apparent that region-specific but common concepts like 寫字樓 (*xie3zi4lou2*, office), 組屋 (*zu3wu1*, apartment), and 私宅 (*si1zhai2*, private residence), etc., are more adversely affected when features for Cilin words were extracted from the BJ subcorpus instead of the respective target subcorpora, while other more core financial concepts could often take advantage of the former. Thus it appears that the domain and concept specificity could also affect the effectiveness of the method.

6.4 Future Directions

There is room to improve the results at both the subclass and semantic head level. More qualitative analysis is needed for the data heterogeneity effect. The category size, and as pointed out above, the domain and concept specificity are also worth further investigation. The latter will thus involve the classification of words from other special domains like sports, as well as those from the general domain.

One problem we need to address in the next step is the class imbalance problem as Cilin categories could differ considerably in size, which will affect the number of features and subsequent classification. For this we plan to try the *k nearest neighbours* approach. In addition, the features might need to be constrained, as simple co-occurrence might be too coarse for distinguishing the subtle characteristics among Cilin categories.

7 Conclusion

We have worked on extending a Chinese thesaurus with words distinctly used in various Chinese communities. Classification results have improved as duplicated words in Cilin were removed. In view of the demand on cross-cultural knowledge for building a Pan-Chinese lexical resource manually, it is particularly important to devise robust ways for automatic acquisition of such a resource. Automatic classification of words with respect to an existing classificatory structure with proper datasets for feature extraction should be a prominent direction in this re-

[2] English gloss: 1-informationize, 2-re-employed, 3-unemployed, 4-resist drought, 5-quality check, 6-general trend of stock market, 7-buy in stocks, 8-H stock, 9-interest rate, 10-sell (stocks), 11-Singaporean dollar, 12-Malaysian stocks, 13-closing price, 14-rights issue, 15-holding space rate, 16-investment trust, 17-growth rate, 18-financial holdings, 19-over-bought, 20-bank.

gard. Further investigation is needed to better understand the interaction among data heterogeneity, category size, feature selection, and the domain and concept specificity of the words.

Acknowledgements

The work described in this paper was supported by a grant from the Research Grants Council of the Hong Kong Special Administrative Region, China (Project No. CityU 1317/03H). The authors would like to thank Jingbo Zhu for useful discussions on an earlier draft of this paper, and the anonymous reviewers for their comments on the submission.

References

Caraballo, S.A. (1999) Automatic construction of a hypernym-labeled noun hierarchy from text. In *Proceedings of the 37th Annual Meeting of the Association for Computational Linguistics (ACL'99)*, Maryland, USA, pp.120-126.

Ciaramita, M. (2002) Boosting automatic lexical acquisition with morphological information. In *Proceedings of the ACL'02 Workshop on Unsupervised Lexical Acquisition*, Philadelphia, USA, pp.17-25.

Hearst, M. (1992) Automatic Acquisition of Hyponyms from Large Text Corpora. In *Proceedings of the 14th International Conference on Computational Linguistics (COLING-92)*, Nantes, France, pp.539-545.

Kwong, O.Y. and Tsou, B.K. (2006) Feasibility of Enriching a Chinese Synonym Dictionary with a Synchronous Chinese Corpus. In T. Salakoski, F. Ginter, S. Pyysalo and T. Pahikkala (Eds.), *Advances in Natural Language Processing: Proceedings of FinTAL 2006.* Lecture Notes in Artificial Intelligence, Vol.4139, pp.322-332, Springer-Verlag.

Kwong, O.Y. and Tsou, B.K. (2007) Extending a Thesaurus in the Pan-Chinese Context. In *Proceedings of the 2007 Joint Conference on Empirical Methods in Natural Language Processing and Computational Natural Language Learning (EMNLP-CoNLL-2007)*, Prague, pp.325-333.

Lin, D. (1998) Automatic Retrieval and Clustering of Similar Words. In *Proceedings of the 36th Annual Meeting of the Association for Computational Linguistics and 17th International Conference on Computational Linguistics (COLING-ACL'98)*, Montreal, Canada, pp.768-774.

Mei *et al.* 梅家駒、竺一鳴、高蘊琦、殷鴻翔 (1984) 《同義詞詞林》 (*Tongyici Cilin*). 商務印書館 (Commercial Press) / 上海辭書出版社.

Pekar, V. (2004) Linguistic Preprocessing for Distributional Classification of Words. In *Proceedings of the COLING2004 Workshop on Enhancing and Using Electronic Dictionaries*, Geneva.

Riloff, E. and Shepherd, J. (1997) A corpus-based approach for building semantic lexicons. In *Proceedings of the Second Conference on Empirical Methods in Natural Language Processing*, Providence, Rhode Island, pp.117-124.

Thelen, M. and Riloff, E. (2002) A Bootstrapping Method for Learning Semantic Lexicons using Extraction Pattern Contexts. In *Proceedings of the 2002 Conference on Empirical Methods in Natural Language Processing (EMNLP 2002)*, Philadelphia, USA.

Tokunaga, T., Fujii, A., Iwayama, M., Sakurai, N. and Tanaka, H. (1997) Extending a thesaurus by classifying words. In *Proceedings of the ACL Workshop on Automatic Information Extraction and Building of Lexical Semantic Resources for NLP Applications*, Madrid, pp.16-21.

Tseng, H. (2003) Semantic Classification of Chinese Unknown Words. In the *Proceedings of the ACL-2003 Student Research Workshop, Companion Volume to the Proceedings of the 41st Annual Meeting of the Association for Computational Linguistics*, Sapporo, Japan.

Tsou, B.K. and Kwong, O.Y. (2006) Toward a Pan-Chinese Thesaurus. In *Proceedings of the Fifth International Conference on Language Resources and Evaluation (LREC 2006)*, Genoa, Italy.

Tsou, B.K. and Lai, T.B.Y. 鄒嘉彥、黎邦洋 (2003) 漢語共時語料庫與信息開發. In B. Xu, M. Sun and G. Jin 徐波、孫茂松、靳光瑾 (Eds.), 《中文信息處理若干重要問題》 (*Issues in Chinese Language Processing*). 北京：科學出版社, pp.147-165

You, J-M. and Chen, K-J. (2006) Improving Context Vector Models by Feature Clustering for Automatic Thesaurus Construction. In *Proceedings of the Fifth SIGHAN Workshop on Chinese Language Processing*, COLING-ACL 2006, Sydney, Australia, pp.1-8.

Stopping Criteria for Active Learning of Named Entity Recognition

Florian Laws
Institute for NLP
Universität Stuttgart
fl@ifnlp.org

Hinrich Schütze
Institute for NLP
Universität Stuttgart
hs999@ifnlp.org

Abstract

Active learning is a proven method for reducing the cost of creating the training sets that are necessary for statistical NLP. However, there has been little work on stopping criteria for active learning. An operational stopping criterion is necessary to be able to use active learning in NLP applications. We investigate three different stopping criteria for active learning of named entity recognition (NER) and show that one of them, *gradient-based stopping*, (i) reliably stops active learning, (ii) achieves near-optimal NER performance, (iii) and needs only about 20% as much training data as exhaustive labeling.

1 Introduction

Supervised statistical learning methods are important and widely successful tools for natural language processing. These methods learn by estimating a statistical model on labeled training data. Often, these models require a large amount of training data that needs to be hand-annotated by human experts. This is time-consuming and expensive. Active learning (AL) reduces this annotation effort by selecting unlabeled examples that are maximally informative for the statistical learning method and handing them to a human annotator for labeling. The statistical model is then updated with the newly gathered information. In this paper, we adopt the uncertainty sampling approach to AL (Lewis and Gale, 1994). Uncertainty sampling selects those examples in the pool as most informative for which the statistical classifier is least certain in its classification decision.

©2008. Licensed under the *Creative Commons Attribution-Noncommercial-Share Alike 3.0 Unported* license (http://creativecommons.org/licenses/by-nc-sa/3.0/). Some rights reserved.

While AL is an active area of research in NLP, the issue of determining when to stop the AL process has only recently come into focus (Zhu and Hovy, 2007; Vlachos, 2008). This is somewhat surprising because the main purpose of active learning is to save on annotation effort; deciding on the point when enough data is annotated is crucial to fulfilling this goal.

We investigate three different stopping criteria in this paper. First, a user of a classification system may want to set a *minimum absolute performance* for the system to be deployed. The standard way of assessing classifier performance uses a held-out labeled test set. However, labeling a test set of sufficient size is contrary to the goal of minimizing annotation effort and impractical in most real-world settings. We will show that the classifier can estimate its own performance using only an unlabeled reference set and propose to stop active learning if estimated performance reaches the threshold set by the user. The estimation is somewhat inaccurate, however, and we investigate possible reasons for estimation error.

An alternative criterion is based on *maximum possible performance*. We will show that our performance estimation method supports stopping AL at a point where performance is almost optimal.

The third and last criterion is *convergence*. The basic idea here is to stop active learning when more examples from the pool do not contribute more information, indicated either by the fact that the classifier has reached maximum performance or by the fact that the "uncertainty" of the classifier cannot be decreased further. We determine the point where the pool has become uninformative by computing the gradient of either performance or uncertainty.

This paper is organized as follows. Section 2 shows that three uncertainty measures achieve near-optimal performance for NER at a fraction of the labeling cost of exhaustive labeling of the training set. In Section 3, we introduce a new method for estimating the performance of an actively learned classifier in support of stopping active learning when a certain level of performance has been reached. Section 4 shows that the stopping criterion of reaching peak confidence is not applicable to NER with multiclass logistic regression. Section 5 presents stopping criteria based on convergence. Sections 6 and 7 discuss related work and present our conclusions.

2 Selection Functions

For measuring the uncertainty of a classification decision in uncertainty sampling there exist diverse measures appropriate for different basic classifiers (e.g. margin-based measures for SVMs, and measures based on class probability for classification). Choosing such an uncertainty measure is relatively straightforward for a binary classification problem, but for multiclass problems we need different measures, and it is not obvious which will perform best.

Following Schein (2005), but in the context of NER, we compare several measures of uncertainty for multiclass logistic regression. For a given measure $M_{i,X}$, we select in each iteration the unlabeled example(s) in the pool that have the *smallest* value for $M_{i,X}$ (corresponding to the *maximum* uncertainty).

1-Entropy.

$$M_{i,\mathit{1\text{-}Entropy}} = 1 - H(\hat{p}(.|x_i)) = 1 + \sum_j \hat{p}(c_j|x_i) \log \hat{p}(c_j|x_i)$$

where $\hat{p}(c_j|x_i)$ is the current estimate of the probability of class c_j given the example x_i.[1] *1-Entropy* favors examples where the classifier assigns similar probabilities to all classes.

Margin. If c and c' are the two most likely classes, the margin is defined as follows:

$$M_{i,\mathit{Margin}} = |\hat{p}(c|x_i) - \hat{p}(c'|x_i)|$$

Margin picks examples where the distinction between two likely classes is hard.

[1] We use *1-Entropy* instead of entropy, so all three measures will have lower values for less certain instances.

MinMax.

$$M_{i,\mathit{MinMax}} = \max_j(\hat{p}(c_j|x_i))$$

The rationale here is that a low probability of the selected class indicates uncertainty. We propose *MinMax* as a measure that is more directly based on the classifier's decision for a particular example. The other two measures also take into account the classifier's assessment of classes that were *not* chosen for the unlabeled example.

2.1 Experiments

We used the newswire section of the ACE 2005 Multilingual Training Corpus (128 documents, 66,015 tokens) for our experiments. A subset of the documents was randomly sampled into an evaluation set that consists of 6301 tokens. We used 30.000 of the remaining tokens as the uncertainty sampling pool. The rest was left aside for future experiments. We use the BBR package (Genkin et al., 2007) for binary logistic regression as our base classifier, with default values for all of BBR's parameters. As our main focus is on AL, we only use basic features like capitalization, puctuation as well as word identity, prefixes and suffixes, each for the classified word itself and for left and right contexts.

We train separate classifiers for each named entity (NE) class and another one for the class "not an NE" (0). For each token we normalize the output probability of the individual classifiers so they sum to 1 and then select for each token the class with the highest probability. Evaluation is performed by comparing individual tokens to the gold standard.[2]

Using all labeled training data as our fully supervised baseline results in a performance of 78.7% F_1 (henceforth: F) and 96.6% accuracy. This is comparable to the accuracy of 96.29% reported by (Daume III, 2007) on the newswire domain. Daumé's work is the only study known to us that uses the ACE dataset, but not the proprietary ACE value score. In the rest of this paper, we report F scores, because we believe that F is a more informative measure for NER than accuracy.

We use AL based on uncertainty sampling. We start with a seed set of ten consecutive tokens randomly selected from the training pool and label it. In each round of AL we select the ten tokens with the smallest value of $M_{i,X}$ (where

[2] Chunk-based NER results are not directly comparable with this token-based evaluation.

Selection	Baseline		Peak perf.	
1-Entropy	78.7	2139 (7.1%)	80.8	3460 (11.5%)
MinMax	78.7	2108 (7.0%)	80.8	3650 (12.1%)
Margin	78.7	2019 (6.7%)	81.2	3694 (12.3%)

Table 1: Percentage of data needed by AL to reach baseline or peak performance.

$X \in \{1\text{-}Entropy, Margin, MinMax\}$) from the remaining pool, including tokens with the label 0. We then label these tokens and add them to the labeled training set. The classifiers are retrained with the new training set and the AL loop repeats. We performed 20 runs of the experiments, each with the same sampling pool, but a different seed set, randomly selected as described above.

Table 1 shows that AL is quite successful for NER. Only 7% of the training data is needed to achieve the same performance as the supervised baseline.

Furthermore we find that after the baseline performance is reached the increase in performance quickly levels off to a point where using more training data does not yield performance improvements anymore. In fact, our experiments show that there is a peak in performance reached at about 12% of the training data and performance decreases again after this point (see Figure 1). The peak is more prominent if the pool is large. On a pool of 30,000 tokens, peak performance is about 2.5% F-Score better than the baseline; on a 6000 token pool, the difference is only about 1.7%. Therefore, once the peak is reached, the AL process should stop, even if the annotation budget is not yet used up.

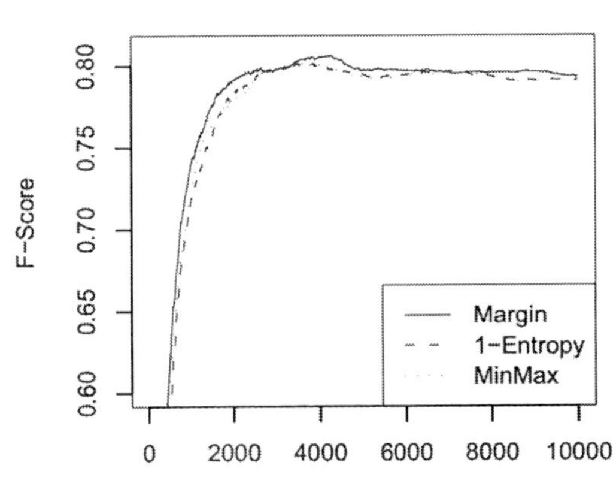

Figure 1: Performance as a function of number of labeled training examples used

Comparing the different selection functions, we found little difference between their performance. *Margin* performs significantly better (Student's t-test, $\alpha = 0.05$), but the difference is small ($< 1\%$ F-Score). If we compare two AL processes (say *Margin* and *1-Entropy*) that were started with the same pool and seed set and stop both processes when they each reach their respective peak performances, *Margin* has a better peak performance of 0.3% F-Score on average (significant at $\alpha = 0.05$).

The differences between *1-Entropy* and *MinMax* are not statistically significant, except for a short start-up phase (see Figure 1).

3 Performance Estimation

In practical applications, classifiers can only be reliably deployed when they attain a predefined *minimum absolute performance* level. Thus, we would like to determine if this level has been reached and then stop the annotation process. However, this is not a simple task, because in these settings there is no labeled test set available to evaluate performance. Creating this test set would mean a substantial annotation effort, which is what we want to avoid by using AL in the first place. Therefore, we will try to estimate the classifier's performance on unlabeled data.

Following Lewis (1995), we estimate the F-Score based on the current estimates of the class probabilities. Based on the F measure's definition as the harmonic mean of precision (P) and recall (R), we can write F as a function of true positives (TP), false positives (TP) and false negatives (FN):

$$F = \frac{2 \cdot P \cdot R}{P + R} = \frac{2\text{TP}}{2\text{TP} + \text{FP} + \text{FN}}$$

Similar to Lewis, we estimate $\hat{\text{TP}}$, $\hat{\text{FP}}$, $\hat{\text{FN}}$, but we need to extend their work from binary classification to 1-vs-all multiclass classification:

$$\hat{\text{TP}} = \sum_i^n \sum_j^E \hat{p}(c_j|x_i) d_{i,j} \quad (1)$$

$$\hat{\text{FP}} = \sum_i^n \sum_j^E (1 - \hat{p}(c_j|x_i)) d_{i,j} \quad (2)$$

$$\hat{\text{FN}} = \sum_i^n \sum_j^E \hat{p}(c_j|x_i)(1 - d_{i,j}) \quad (3)$$

where n is the number of examples, E is the number of named entity classes, excluding the "not an NE" class. $\hat{p}(c_j|x_i)$ is the estimated probability that example x_i has class c_j. The flag $d_{i,j}$ indicates "is winning class": $d_{i,j} = 1$ if $j = \text{argmax}_j \hat{p}(c_j|x_i)$ and $d_{i,j} = 0$ else.

Like standard NER evaluation schemes, e.g. (Tjong Kim Sang and De Meulder, 2003), we consider only those decisions to be TPs where (i) the reference class matches the selected class and (ii) this class is not "not an NE". When estimating TP, we assume that the probability of a match equals the probability of the selected class (which is $\hat{p}(c_j|x_i) \cdot d_{i,j}$). The probability of making an FP error is just the remaining probability mass. For FN, we can calculate the estimated probability by summing up the class probabilities of the non-selected named entity classes.

3.1 Evaluation of Performance Estimation

To evaluate the performance estimation method, we ran it on an *unlabeled reference set*. The reference set is a set of unlabeled data distinct from the sampling pool. In our experiments, we use the tokens in the test set from 2.1, but with the labels stripped off.

We compare the true performance on the test set (reported as "True" in Table 2) with the estimate (reported as "Lewis"). The Δ columns report the difference of the named method to "True". We also tested leave-one-out (LOO) estimation of F, P and R using the data of the selected training set.

	True	Lewis	Δ Lewis	LOO	Δ LOO
F	79	92	+13	85	+6
P	81	92	+11	86	+5
R	77	92	+15	84	+7

Table 2: Performance estimation. LOO and Lewis overestimate true F by 6% and 13%, respectively.

We find that both methods overestimate precision and recall by a large margin. We also note that the peak in performance at about 4200 training examples that we found when evaluating on held-out data (see Figure 1) does not occur when evaluating performance using the Lewis method. Instead, the estimate of F grows monotonically. This means that we cannot use a peak of estimated F as a criterion for stopping. When setting an absolute threshold of $F = 80\%$ for stopping, active learning stops at about 1000 iterations, yielding a true performance of only $F = 73\%$ (selection by *Margin*, 20 trials). This indicates that we cannot directly use Lewis estimates for stopping.

3.2 Error Analysis

The reason for the overestimation is that the logistic regression classifier is too confident in its own decision. For positive decisions, the class probability very often is close to 1, for negative decisions, it is close to 0. As a result, the estimator gives very little score for FN (Equation 3) or FP (Equation 2) in most instances, which leads to the high overestimation of performance.

To verify this, we grouped the empirical probability of a selected class being the correct class in bins according to the estimated probability of the logistic classifier. Table 3 shows this empirical probability given a class and its estimate. The table is split into two halves, such that the empirical probabilities for positive decisions (the class got chosen as the best class) and negative decisions are shown separately. The top value in each cell ("emp") shows the empirical probability as opposed to the estimated probability, which is the value below ("est"). The product of the difference of these two probabilities and the number of instances that were counted into this bin ("cnt"), gives an estimate of how much the probability estimates in the bin contribute to the error (absolute value) of the performance estimation.

The table shows that class probabilities are in fact estimated too optimistically. For many of the entries in the positives table, the estimated probabilities are greater than the empirical probabilities. In the negatives table, the estimated probabilities are smaller. In both cases, the estimates are closer to the respective extreme values 1 or 0, which means they are overconfident. Note that for positive decisions, the estimation error of the values in a single bin contributes to the overall estimation error in two ways: overestimating TPs and underestimating FPs. For example, the estimation error for the cell in bold is 29.2, contributing -29.2 for FP (underestimation) and $+29.2$ for TP (overestimation). Also note that due to the high number of non-NE tokens in the text, there is a large number of negative decisions for each entity-class classifier; thus, small differences in the probabilities make large contributions to error.

We ran a separate experiment in which we trained a classifier on the entire labeled pool. The Lewis estimator overestimated F by 12% in this case. This indicates that the estimation error does not primarily come from the biased selection of training examples inherent in the selective sam-

		negative decisions			positive decisions			
		0-.2	.2-.4	.4-.6	.2-.4	.4-.6	.6-.8	.8-1
O	emp	0.0643	0.269	0.25	0.0	0.25	0.233	0.991
	est	0.00825	0.295	0.438	0.394	0.537	0.714	0.999
	cnt	607	26	12	1	16	30	5609
	err	34	-0.67	-2.25	0.394(tn)	4.6 (tn)	14.4 (tn)	45.4 (tn)
GPE	emp	0.00384	0.391	0.5	0.0	0.333	0.571	**0.875**
	est	0.000812	0.296	0.435	0.357	0.535	0.687	**0.989**
	cnt	5985	23	6	1	9	21	**256**
	err	18.1 (fn)	2.19 (fn)	0.388 (fn)	0.357 (fp)	1.82 (fp)	2.42 (fp)	**29.2 (fp)**
ORG	emp	0.00853	0.393	0.667		0.5	0.615	0.828
	est	0.000847	0.283	0.441		0.545	0.71	0.968
	cnt	6093	28	12		14	26	128
	err	46.8 (fn)	3.06 (fn)	2.7 (fn)		0.631 (fp)	2.46 (fp)	17.9 (fp)
PER	emp	0.0041	0.455	0.5		0.273	0.5	0.93
	est	0.000748	0.283	0.48		0.563	0.718	0.98
	cnt	6102	22	6		11	18	142
	err	20.4 (fn)	3.78 (fn)	0.121 (fn)		3.2 (fp)	3.93 (fp)	7.19 (fp)

Table 3: Empirical probabilities and contribution to estimation errors. (We omit small classes and empty columns.) Example (cell in bold): 256 tokens were estimated to be a GPE by the classifier with estimated probabilities between 0.8 and 1.0. The average estimate was 0.989. In reality, only 224 of these tokens (87.5%) were GPEs. The contribution of this cell to the overall FP count is $(0.989 - 0.875) \cdot 256 \approx 29.2$.

pling method, but from bias inherent in either the whole pool of training data or the base classifier.

3.3 Towards a Better Estimate

Over-optimistic estimates for precision and recall stem from the classifier's over-optimistic probability estimates. We try to correct the estimates by replacing the predicted class probabilities with the appropriate value in an empirical probability table like the one shown in Table 3. However, since in practice we do not have labels for the test set, we cannot compute the empirical probabilities directly. Instead, we use leave-one-out estimation to bootstrap the adjustment table from the selected training data. The adjusted estimation shows a marked increase in the estimates for FP and FN, leading to a quite accurate estimate for precision ($+5$ absolute error), but the now pessimistic estimate for recall (-16) leads to underestimation of F-Score overall (-8) (see Table 4).

	True	Lewis	adj. Lewis	Δ adj. Lewis
F	78	91	70	-8
P	81	93	86	+5
R	76	89	60	-16
TP	520	596	555	+35
FP	125	48	90	-35
FN	163	70	379	+216

Table 4: Lewis estimation with adjusted probabilities

As we see, the adjustment overshoots for recall, indicating that the new estimated probabilities are still off. There could be several reasons for this. The first reason is that the bin width is quite coarse, as there are only five bins for the entire probability interval, each bin covering a range of 0.2. However, using finer bin widths can lead to data sparsity problems.

Another reason might be the estimation errors within individual bins that compound to a quite large overall error especially in the negative case. Finally, differences in the distributions of training set and reference set could cause unreliable estimates. The empirical probabilities for the adjustment table are estimated with leave-one-out on the training set. However, since the training set is created by selective sampling, it will be biased.

4 Confidence-based Stopping

We have found that performance estimation is not yet reliable enough to stop when a desired performance level is reached. However, since there is a maximum performance that can be reached on any given sampling pool, the annotation process still should stop at this point regardless of whether a target performance level has been reached or not. We therefore seek a stopping criterion that finds the *maximum possible performance* when the classifier is iteratively trained on a given sampling pool. Again, in practice we do not have a labeled test set to evaluate against, so we have to try to find the stopping point from either the remaining pool, or the separate unlabeled reference set.

Vlachos (2008) proposes to calculate the *confidence* of the classifier by using the *average uncer-*

tainty on the unlabeled reference set. For multiclass problems, he uses SVM classifiers with the SVM margin size as the uncertainty measure. Using this measure, Vlachos reports finding, albeit distorted by fluctuations, a peak pattern in this confidence measure that coincides with reaching maximal performance in his experiments. He then suggests to use this *peak confidence* as the stopping criterion.

However, in our experiments with multiclass logistic regression, we could not find this peak pattern when calculating the confidence using the three uncertainty measures introduced above: *1-Entropy*, *Margin* and *MinMax*.

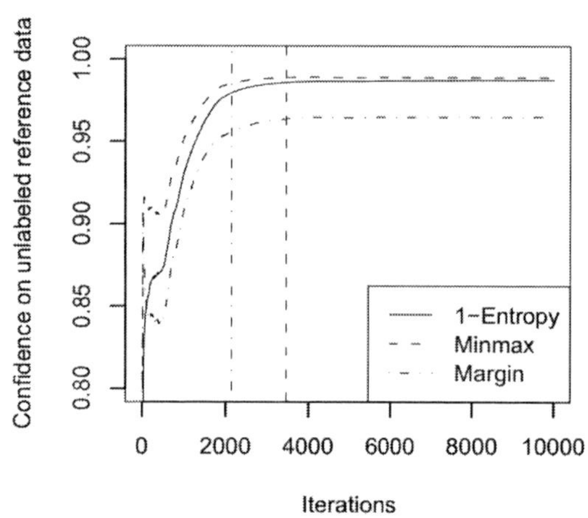

Figure 2: Confidence on unlabeled reference set (selection: *1-Entropy*). The vertical lines indicate when baseline and optimal performance are reached. There is no peak pattern in the curves, so reaching peak confidence cannot be used as a stopping criterion.

In Figure 2, we show the three measures, averaged over 20 trials as described in section 2.1. Due to instability of AL during start-up, there are some fluctuations in the first 100 iterations. After 500 iterations the confidence curves stabilize and at about 4000 iterations approach asymptotes, without exhibiting peak patterns. Thus, the proposed criterion of *peak confidence* based on average reference uncertainty does not seem applicable for controlling AL with multiclass logistic regression.

5 Gradient-based Stopping

Since we cannot use peaks for stopping, we propose to stop when a base measurement character-

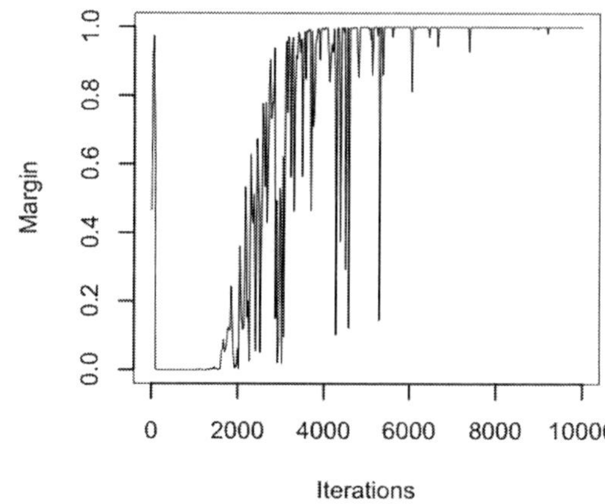

Figure 3: *Margin* uncertainty of selected instance (single run). The graph demonstrates that without smoothing this criterion is too noisy.

izing the progress of active learning has converged. We identify the point of convergence by computing gradients. We find that the rise of the performance estimation slows to an almost horizontal slope at about the time when the true performance reaches its peak. We therefore propose the following new stopping criterion: Estimate the gradient of the curve and stop when it approaches 0. Since we do not need an accurate estimation of absolute performance here, we can use the unadjusted Lewis estimate for this method. We call this stopping criterion (estimated) *performance convergence*.

In a similar way, we can use the gradient of the uncertainty of the last selected instance. The instance that was selected last is always the one with maximum uncertainty, and thus the most informative for training. When the uncertainty measure comes close to the extreme value of 1, we decide that there are no informative examples left in the pool and we stop the AL process. (Unfortunately, 1 is minimum uncertainty and 0 is maximum uncertainty according to our definitions of the three measures.) The gradient of the uncertainty measure approaches 0 at this point (see Figure 3), so we can again use a gradient criterion for implementing this idea. We call this stopping criterion *uncertainty convergence*.

In Figure 3, which shows a graph of the *Margin* uncertainty of the selected instance, we can also see that it is quite noisy. The value drops sharply when some examples are encountered but quickly returns to the previous level after a few iterations. The performance estimation measure is slightly noisy as well, so we need a robust way of computing the gradient. We achieve this with a moving median approach. At each step, we compute the median of $w_2 = \{a_{n-k}, \ldots, a_n\}$ (the last n values) and of $w_1 = \{a_{n-k-1}, \ldots, a_{n-1}\}$ (the previous last n values). Each value a_i is the performance at iteration i (for the performance gradient) or the uncertainty of the instance selected in iteration i (for the uncertainty gradient).

We then estimate the gradient using the medians of the two windows:

$$g = (\text{median}(w_2) - \text{median}(w_1))/1 \quad (4)$$

For the performance estimate, which is less noisy, we can also use the arithmetic mean instead of the median. In this case, we simply replace "median" with "mean" in Equation 4.

We found that a window of size $k = 100$ yields good results in mitigating the noise while still reacting fast enough to the changes in the gradient. We combine this criterion with a maximum criterion and only stop if the last value a_n is a new maximum. We stop the AL process when (i) the current certainty or estimated performance is a new maximum and (ii) the newly calculated gradient g is positive and (iii) g falls below a predefined level ϵ.

5.1 Evaluation

We show the results of gradient stopping applied to each of the three uncertainty measures and the Lewis estimate. For comparison, we also include results with a threshold-based criterion, where AL stops when the uncertainty measure of the selected instance reaches a threshold of $1-\epsilon$. This is similar to (Zhu and Hovy, 2007), but extended by us to all three uncertainty measures.

Table 5 shows results for each criterion. The "Stop" value indicates number of tokens at which the stopping criterion stopped AL. "ΔBl" indicates the difference between baseline performance and performance at the stopping point, "ΔPk" the difference to peak performance. The "sd" columns show the respective standard deviations.

We find that all stopping criteria stop before 20% of the pool is used, providing a large reduction in annotation effort. While the point of peak performance can not be precisely found by the criteria, all criteria reliably stop at a performance level that surpasses the fully supervised baseline. The threshold criteria seem to be a bit better in finding a stopping point closer to optimal performance. Not unsurprisingly, the stopping function that matches the selection function performs best. The gradient methods, however, seem to be providing better-than-baseline performance more consistently (less variation) and might require less tuning of the threshold parameter when other factors (e.g., the batch size) change. If lower noise allows it, as for the Lewis estimate, moving averages should be used in place of moving medians.

6 Related Work

Schütze et al. (2006) studied a Lewis-based performance estimation method in a binary text classification setting. They attribute difficulties in estimating recall to a "missed cluster effect", meaning that the active sampling procedure is failing to select some clusters of relevant training examples in the pool that are too dissimilar to the relevant examples already known. Diversity measures as proposed by (Shen et al., 2004) might help in mitigating this effect, but our experiments show that there are fundamental differences between text classification and NER. Since missed clusters of relevant examples in the training data would eventually be used as we exhaustively label the entire pool, we should see improvements in recall when the missed clusters get used. Instead, we observed in section 2.1, that there are no further performance gains after a certain portion of the pool is labeled. Thus, all examples that the classifier can make use of must have been taken into account, and there appear to be no missed clusters.

Tomanek et al. (2007) present a stopping criterion for query-by-committee-based AL that is based on the rate of disagreement of the classifiers in the committee. While our uncertainty convergence criterion can only be applied to uncertainty sampling, the performance convergence criterion can be used in a committee-based setting.

Li and Sethi (2006) estimate the conditional error as a measure of uncertainty in selection (instead of using it for stopping as we do), using a variable-bin histogram for improving the error estimates. They do not evaluate the quality of the probability estimates. As with our stopping criterion, we expect this selection criterion to be the more effective the more accurate the probability estimates are. We therefore believe that our method of improving probability estimates based on LOO bins could improve their selection criterion.

Stop crit.	ϵ	Peak	Stop		Δ Bl	sd	Δ Pk	sd
1-Entropy threshold	0.01	80.8	3645	12.0%	1.44	0.7	−0.68	0.4
MinMax threshold	0.01	80.8	3133	10.3%	0.11	1.0	−2.0	0.8
Margin threshold	0.01	80.8	3158	10.4%	1.1	0.8	−1.0	0.8
1-Entropy gradient	0.00005	80.8	4572	15.0%	0.97	0.4	−1.1	0.5
MinMax gradient	0.00005	80.8	4397	14.5%	1.02	0.4	−1.1	0.5
Margin gradient	0.00005	80.8	5292	17.5%	0.81	0.3	−1.32	0.4
Lewis grd. (Median)	0.00005	80.8	2791	9.2%	0.8	1.4	−1.3	1.4
Lewis grd. (Mean)	0.00005	80.8	3999	13.1%	1.1	0.8	−0.95	0.6

Table 5: Performance at stopping points (baseline perf. 78.7, Selection: *1-Entropy*)

7 Conclusion and Future Work

In this paper, we presented several criteria to stop the AL process. For stopping the training at a user-defined performance level, we proposed a method for estimating classifier performance in a multiclass classification setting. While we could achieve acceptable accuracy in estimation of precision, we find that recall estimation is hard. Estimation is not accurate enough to assist in making a reliable decision if the performance of the classifier is acceptable for practical use. In the future, we plan to improve on performance estimation quality, e.g., by using the variable-bin approach suggested by Li and Sethi (2006).

Nevertheless, we showed that the gradient of the performance estimate can successfully be used as a stopping criterion relative to the optimal performance that is attainable on a given pool. We also describe stopping criteria based on the gradient of the uncertainty measure of the instances selected for training. The criteria reliably determine stopping points that result in a performance that is better than the supervised baseline and close to the optimal performance. We believe that these criteria can be applied to any AL setting based on uncertainty sampling, not just NER.

If it turns out that the maximum possible performance does not meet a user's expectations, the user needs to acquire fresh data and refill the pool. This might lead to an approach to reduce the computational cost of AL we want to evaluate in future work: Subdivide a large sampling pool into smaller sub-pools, run AL sequentially on the sub-pools. When the stopping criterion is reached, switch to the next sub-pool.

We also found that uncertainty curves of the selected examples are quite noisy. We would like to investigate which properties of the training examples cause these drops in the uncertainty curve.

References

Daume III, Hal. 2007. Frustratingly easy domain adaptation. In *ACL-07*, pages 256–263.

Genkin, A., D.D. Lewis, and D. Madigan. 2007. Large-scale bayesian logistic regression for text categorization. *Technometrics*, 49(3):291–304.

Lewis, D.D. and W.A. Gale. 1994. A sequential algorithm for training text classifiers. *ACM SIGIR*.

Lewis, D.D. 1995. Evaluating and optimizing autonomous text classification systems. *ACM SIGIR*.

Li, M. and I.K. Sethi. 2006. Confidence-Based Active Learning. *IEEE Transactions on Pattern Analysis and Machine Intelligence*, 28(8):1251–1261.

Schein, Andrew I. 2005. *Active Learning for Logistic Regression*. Ph.D. thesis, University of Pennsylvania.

Schütze, H., E. Velipasaoglu, and J.O. Pedersen. 2006. Performance thresholding in practical text classification. In *CIKM*, pages 662–671.

Shen, Dan, Jie Zhang, Jian Su, Guodong Zhou, and Chew-Lim Tan. 2004. Multi-criteria-based active learning for named entity recognition. In *ACL '04*.

Tjong Kim Sang, Erik F. and Fien De Meulder. 2003. Introduction to the conll-2003 shared task: Language-independent named entity recognition. In *Proceedings of CoNLL-2003*, pages 142–147.

Tomanek, Katrin, Joachim Wermter, and Udo Hahn. 2007. An approach to text corpus construction which cuts annotation costs and maintains reusability of annotated data. In *EMNLP-CoNLL*.

Vlachos, Andreas. 2008. A stopping criterion for active learning. *Computer Speech and Language*, 22(3):295–312.

Zhu, J. and E. Hovy. 2007. Active learning for word sense disambiguation with methods for addressing the class imbalance problem. In *EMNLP-CoNLL*.

Reading the Markets:
Forecasting Public Opinion of Political Candidates by News Analysis

Kevin Lerman
Dept. of Computer Science
Columbia University
New York, NY USA
klerman@cs.columbia.edu

Ari Gilder and **Mark Dredze**
Dept. of CIS
University of Pennsylvania
Philadelphia, PA USA
agilder@alumni.upenn.edu
mdredze@cis.upenn.edu

Fernando Pereira
Google, Inc.
1600 Amphitheatre Parkway
Mountain View, CA USA
pereira@google.com

Abstract

Media reporting shapes public opinion which can in turn influence events, particularly in political elections, in which candidates both respond to and shape public perception of their campaigns. We use computational linguistics to automatically predict the impact of news on public perception of political candidates. Our system uses daily newspaper articles to predict shifts in public opinion as reflected in prediction markets. We discuss various types of features designed for this problem. The news system improves market prediction over baseline market systems.

1 Introduction

The mass media can affect world events by swaying public opinion, officials and decision makers. Financial investors who evaluate the economic performance of a company can be swayed by positive and negative perceptions about the company in the media, directly impacting its economic position. The same is true of politics, where a candidate's performance is impacted by media influenced public perception. Computational linguistics can discover such signals in the news. For example, Devitt and Ahmad (2007) gave a computable metric of polarity in financial news text consistent with human judgments. Koppel and Shtrimberg (2004) used a daily news analysis to predict financial market performance, though predictions could not be used for future investment decisions. Recently, a study conducted of the 2007 French presidential election showed a correlation between the frequency of a candidate's name in the news and electoral success (Véronis, 2007).

This work forecasts day-to-day changes in public perception of political candidates from daily news. Measuring daily public perception with polls is problematic since they are conducted by a variety of organizations at different intervals and are not easily comparable. Instead, we rely on daily measurements from prediction markets.

We present a computational system that uses both external linguistic information and internal market indicators to forecast public opinion measured by prediction markets. We use features from syntactic dependency parses of the news and a user-defined set of market entities. Successive news days are compared to determine the novel component of each day's news resulting in features for a machine learning system. A combination system uses this information as well as predictions from internal market forces to model prediction markets better than several baselines. Results show that news articles can be mined to predict changes in public opinion.

Opinion *forecasting* differs from that of opinion *analysis*, such as extracting opinions, evaluating sentiment, and extracting predictions (Kim and Hovy, 2007). Contrary to these tasks, our system receives objective news, not subjective opinions, and learns what events will impact public opinion. For example, "oil prices rose" is a fact but will likely shape opinions. This work analyzes news (cause) to predict future opinions (effect). This affects the structure of our task: we consider a time-series setting since we must use past data to predict future opinions, rather than analyzing opinions in batch across the whole dataset.

© 2008. Licensed under the *Creative Commons Attribution-Noncommercial-Share Alike 3.0 Unported* license (http://creativecommons.org/licenses/by-nc-sa/3.0/). Some rights reserved.

We begin with an introduction to prediction markets. Several methods for new feature extraction are explored as well as market history baselines. Systems are evaluated on prediction markets from the 2004 US Presidential election. We close with a discussion of related and future work.

2 Prediction Markets

Prediction markets, such as TradeSports and the Iowa Electronic Markets[1], provide a setting similar to financial markets wherein shares represent not companies or commodities, but an outcome of a sporting, financial or political event. For example, during the 2004 US Presidential election, one could purchase a share of "George W. Bush to win the 2004 US Presidential election" or "John Kerry to win the 2004 US Presidential election." A pay-out of $1 is awarded to winning shareholders at market's end, e.g. Bush wins the election. In the interim, price fluctuations driven by supply and demand indicate the perception of the event's likelihood, which indicates public opinion of an event. Several studies show the accuracy of prediction markets in predicting future events (Wolfers and Zitzewitz, 2004; Servan-Schreiber et al., 2004; Pennock et al., 2000), such as the success of upcoming movies (Jank and Foutz, 2007), political stock markets (Forsythe et al., 1999) and sports betting markets (Williams, 1999).

Market investors rely on daily news reports to dictate investment actions. If something positive happens for Bush (e.g. Saddam Hussein is captured), Bush will appear more likely to win, so demand increases for "Bush to win" shares, and the price rises. Likewise, if something negative for Bush occurs (e.g. casualties in Iraq increase), people will think he is less likely to win, sell their shares, and the price drops. Therefore, prediction markets can be seen as rapid response indicators of public mood concerning political candidates. Market-internal factors, such as general investor mood and market history, also affect price. For instance, a positive news story for a candidate may have less impact if investors dislike the candidate. Explaining market behavior requires modeling news information external to the market and internal trends to the market.

This work uses the 2004 US Presidential election markets from Iowa Electronic Markets. Each market provides a daily average price, which indicates the overall market sentiment for a candidate on a given day. The goal of the prediction system is to predict the price direction for the next day (up or down) given all available information up to the current day: previous days' market pricing/volume information and the morning news. Market history represents information internal to the market: if an investor has no knowledge of external events, what is the most likely direction for the market? This information can capture general trends and volatility of the market. The daily news is the external information that influences the market. This provides information, independent of any internal market effects to which investors will respond. A learning system for each information source is developed and combined to explain market behavior. The following sections describe these systems.

[1] www.tradesports.com, www.biz.uiowa.edu/iem/

3 External Information: News

Changes in market price are likely responses to current events reported in the news. Investors read the morning paper and act based on perceptions of events. Can a system with access to this same information make good investment decisions?

Our system operates in an iterative (online) fashion. On each day (round) the news for that day is used to construct a new instance. A logistic regression classifier is trained on all previous days and the resulting classifier predicts the price movement of the new instance. The system either profits or loses money according to this prediction. It then receives the actual price movement and labels the instance accordingly (up or down). This setting is straightforward; the difficulty is in choosing a good feature representation for the classifier. We now explore several representation techniques.

3.1 Bag-of-Words Features

The prediction task can be treated as a document classification problem, where the document is the day's news and the label is the direction of the market. Document classification systems typically rely on bag-of-words features, where each feature indicates the number of occurrences of a word in the document. The news for a given day is represented by a normalized unit length vector of counts, excluding common stop words and features that occur fewer than 20 times in our corpus.

3.2 News Focus Features

Simple bag-of-words features may not capture relevant news information. Public opinion is influenced by new events – a change in focus. The day after a debate, most papers may declare Bush the winner, yielding a rise in the price of a "Bush to win" share. However, while the debate may be discussed for several days after the event, public opinion of Bush will probably not continue to rise on old news. Changes in public opinion should reflect changes in daily news coverage. Instead of constructing features for a single day, they can represent differences between two days of news coverage, i.e. the novelty of the coverage. Given the counts of feature i on day t as c_i^t, where feature i may be the unigram "scandal," and the set of features on day t as $\mathbf{C}^t$, the fraction of news focus for each feature is $f_i^t = \frac{c_i^t}{|\mathbf{C}^t|}$. The news focus change (Δ) for feature i on day t is defined as,

$$\Delta f_i^t = \log\left(\frac{f_i^t}{\frac{1}{3}(f_i^{t-1} + f_i^{t-2} + f_i^{t-3})}\right), \quad (1)$$

where the numerator is the focus of news on feature i today and the denominator is the average focus over the previous three days. The resulting value captures the change in focus on day t, where a value greater than 0 means increased focus and a value less than 0 decreased focus. Feature counts were smoothed by adding a constant (10).

3.3 Entity Features

As shown by Wiebe et al. (2005), it is important to know not only what is being said but about whom it is said. The term "victorious" by itself is meaningless when discussing an election – meaning comes from the subject. Similarly, the word "scandal" is bad for a candidate but good for the opponent. Subjects can often be determined by proximity. If the word "scandal" and Bush are mentioned in the same sentence, this is likely to be bad for Bush. A small set of entities relevant to a market can be defined a priori to give context to features. For example, the entities "Bush," "Kerry" and "Iraq" were known to be relevant before the general election. Kim and Hovy (2007) make a similar assumption.

News is filtered for sentences that mention exactly one of these entities. Such sentences are likely about that entity, and the extracted features are conjunctions of the word and the entity. For example, the sentence "Bush is facing another scandal" produces the feature "bush-scandal" instead of just "scandal." [2] Context disambiguation comes at a high cost: about 70% of all sentences do not contain any predefined entities and about 7% contain more than one entity. These likely relevant sentences are unfortunately discarded, although future work could reduce the number of discarded sentences using coreference resolution.

3.4 Dependency Features

While entity features are helpful they cannot process multiple entity sentences, nearly a quarter of the entity sentences. These sentences may be the most helpful since they indicate entity interactions. Consider the following three example sentences:

- Bush defeated Kerry in the debate.
- Kerry defeated Bush in the debate.
- Kerry, a senator from Massachusetts, defeated President Bush in last night's debate.

Obviously, the first two sentences have very different meanings for each candidate's campaign. However, representations considered so far do not differentiate between these sentences, nor would any heuristic using proximity to an entity. [3] Effective features rely on the proper identification of the subject and object of "defeated." Longer n-grams, which would be very sparse, would succeed for the first two sentences but not the third.

To capture these interactions, features were extracted from dependency parses of the news articles. Sentences were part of speech tagged (Toutanova et al., 2003), parsed with a dependency parser and labeled with grammatical function labels (McDonald et al., 2006). The resulting parses encode dependencies for each sentence, where word relationships are expressed as parent-child links. The parse for the third sentence above indicates that "Kerry" is the subject of "defeated," and "Bush" is the object. Features are extracted from parse trees containing the pre-defined entities (section 3.3), using the parent, grandparent, aunts, nieces, children, and siblings of any instances of the pre-defined entities we observe. Features are conjoined indicators of the node's lexical entry, part of speech tag and dependency relation

[2] Other methods can identify the subject of sentiment expressions, but our text is objective news. Therefore, we employ this approximate method.

[3] Several failed heuristics were tried, such as associating each word to an entity within a fixed window in the sentence or the closer entity if two were in the window.

Feature	*Good For*
Kerry ← plan → the	Kerry
poll → showed → Bush	Bush
won → Kerry[4]	Kerry
agenda → 's → Bush	Kerry
Kerry ← spokesperson → campaign	Bush

Table 1: Simplified examples of features from the general election market. Arrows point from parent to child. Features also include the word's dependency relation labels and parts of speech.

label. For aunts, nieces, and children, the common ancestor is used, and in the case of grandparent, the intervening parent is included. Each of these conjunctions includes the discovered entity and back-off features are included by removing some of the other information. Note that besides extracting more precise information from the news text, this handles sentences with multiple entities, since it associates parts of a sentence with different entities. In practice, we use this in conjunction with News Focus. Useful features from the general election market are in table 1. Note that they capture events and not opinions. For example, the last feature indicates that a statement by the Kerry campaign was good for Bush, possibly because Kerry was reacting to criticism.

4 Internal Information: Market History

News cannot explain all market trends. Momentum in the market, market inefficiencies, and slow news days can affect share price. A candidate who does well will likely continue to do well unless new events occur. Learning general market behavior can help explain these price movements.

For each day t, we create an instance using features for the price and volume at day $t-1$ and the price and volume change between days $t-1$ and $t-2$. We train using a ridge regression [5] on all previous days (labeled with their actual price movements) to forecast the movement for day t, which we convert into a binary value: up or down.

[4]This feature matches phrases like "Kerry won [the debate]" and "[something] won Kerry [support]"

[5]This outperformed more sophisticated algorithms, including the logistic regression used earlier. This may be due to the fact that many market history features (e.g. previous price movements) are very similar in nature to the future price movements being predicted.

5 Combined System

Since both news and internal market information are important for modeling market behavior, each one cannot be evaluated in isolation. For example, a successful news system may learn to spot important events for a candidate, but cannot explain the price movements of a slow news day. A combination of the market history system and news features is needed to model the markets.

Expert algorithms for combining prediction systems have been well studied. However, experiments with the popular weighted majority algorithm (Littlestone and Warmuth, 1989) yielded poor performance since it attempts to learn the optimal balance between systems while our setting has rapidly shifting quality between few experts with little data for learning. Instead, a simple heuristic was used to select the best performing predictor on each day. We compare the 3-day prediction accuracy (measured in total earnings) for each system (news and market history) to determine the current best system. The use of a small window allows rapid change in systems. When neither system has a better 3-day accuracy the combined system will only predict if the two systems agree and abstain otherwise. This strategy measures how accurately a news system can account for price movements when non-news movements are accounted for by market history. The combined system improved over individual evaluations of each system on every market [6].

6 Evaluation

Daily pricing information was obtained from the Iowa Electronic Markets for the 2004 US Presidential election for six Democratic primary contenders (Clark, Clinton, Dean, Gephardt, Kerry and Lieberman) and two general election candidates (Bush and Kerry). Market length varied as some candidates entered the race later than others: the DNC markets for Clinton, Gephardt, Kerry, and Lieberman were each 332 days long, while Dean's was 130 days and Clark's 106. The general election market for Bush was 153 days long, while Kerry's was 142. [7] The price delta for each day was taken as the difference between the average

[6]This outperformed a single model built over all features, perhaps due to the differing natures of the feature types we used.

[7]The first 11 days of the Kerry general election market were removed due to strange price fluctuations in the data.

price between the previous and current day. Market data also included the daily volume that was used as a market history feature. Entities selected for each market were the names of all candidates involved in the election and "Iraq."

News articles covering the election were obtained from Factiva[8], an online news archive run by Dow Jones. Since the system must make a prediction at the beginning of each day, only articles from daily newspapers released early in the morning were included. The corpus contained approximately 50 articles per day over a span of 3 months to almost a year, depending on the market. [9]

While most classification systems are evaluated by measuring their accuracy on cross-validation experiments, both the method and the metric are unsuitable to our task. A decision for a given day must be made with knowledge of only the previous days, ruling out cross validation. In fact, we observed improved results when the system was allowed access to future articles through cross-validation. Further, raw prediction accuracy is not a suitable metric for evaluation because it ignores the magnitude in price shifts each day. A system should be rewarded proportional to the significance of the day's market change.

To address these issues we used a chronological evaluation where systems were rewarded for correct predictions in proportion to the magnitude of that day's shift, i.e. the ability to profit from the market. This metric is analogous to weighted accuracy. On each day, the system is provided with all available morning news and market history from which an instance is created using one of the feature schemes described above. We then predict whether the market price will rise or fall and the system either earns or loses the price change for that day if it was right or wrong respectively. The system then learns the correct price movement and the process is repeated for the next day.[10] Systems that correctly forecast public opinions from the news will make more money. In economic terms, this is equivalent to buying or short-selling a single share of the market and then selling or covering the short at the end of the day.[11] Scores were normalized for comparison across markets using the maximum profit obtainable by an omniscient system that always predicts correctly.

Market		*History*	*Baseline*
DNC	Clark	20	13
	Clinton	38	-8
	Dean	23	24
	Gephardt	8	1
	Kerry	-6	6
	Lieberman	3	2
General	Kerry	2	15
	Bush	21	20
Average (% omniscience)		13.6	9.1

Table 2: Results using history features for prediction compared with a baseline system that invests according to the previous day's result.

Baseline systems for both news and market history are included. The news baseline follows the spirit of a study of the French presidential election (Véronis, 2007), which showed that candidate mentions correlate to electoral success. Attempts to follow this method directly – predicting market movement based on raw candidate mentions – did very poorly. Instead, we trained our learning system with features representing daily mention counts of each entity. For a market history baseline, we make a simple assumption about market behavior: the current market trend will continue, predict today's behavior for tomorrow.

There were too many features to learn in the short duration of the markets so only features that appeared at least 20 times were included, reducing bag-of-words features from 88.8k to 28.3k and parsing features from 1150k to 15.9k. A real world system could use online feature selection.

6.1 Results

First, we establish performance without news information by testing the market history system alone. Table 2 shows the profit of the history prediction and baseline systems. While learning beats the rule based system on average, both earn impressive profits considering that random trading would break even. These results corroborate the inefficient market observation of Pennock et al. (2000). Additionally, the general election markets sometimes both increased or decreased, an impossible result in an efficient zero-sum market.

[8]`http://www.factiva.com/`

[9]While 50 articles may not seem like much, humans read far less text before making investment decisions.

[10]This scheme is called "online learning" for which a whole class of algorithms apply. We used batch algorithms since training happens only once per day.

[11]More complex investment schemes are possible than what has been described here. We choose a simple scheme to make the evaluation more transparent.

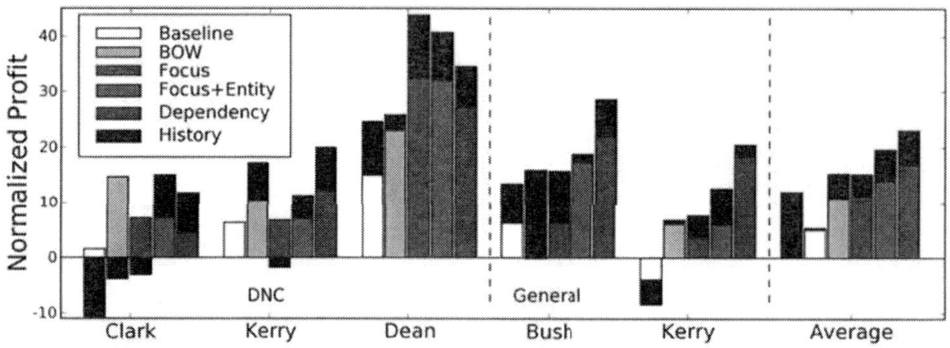

Figure 1: Results for the different news features and combined system across five markets. Bottom bars can be compared to evaluate news components and combined with the stacked black bars (history system) give combined performance. The average performance (far right) shows improved performance from each news system over the market history system.

During initial news evaluations with the combined system, the primary election markets did either very poorly or quite well. The news prediction component lost money for Clinton, Gephardt, and Lieberman while Clark, Dean and Kerry all made money. Readers familiar with the 2004 election will immediately see the difference between the groups. The first three candidates were minor contenders for the nomination and were not newsmakers. Hillary Clinton never even declared her candidacy. The average number of mentions per day for these candidates in our data was 20. In contrast, the second group were all major contenders for the nomination and an average mention of 94 in our data. Clearly, the news system can only do well when it observes news that effects the market. The system does well on both general election markets where the average candidate mention per day was 503. Since the Clinton, Gephardt and Lieberman campaigns were not newsworthy, they are omitted from the results.

Results for news based prediction systems are shown in figure 1. The figure shows the profit made from both news features (bottom bars) and market history (top black bars) when evaluated as a combined system. Bottom bars can be compared to evaluate news systems and each is combined with its top bar to indicate total performance. Negative bars indicate negative earnings (i.e. weighted accuracy below 50%). Averages across all markets for the news systems and the market history system are shown on the right. In each market, the baseline news system makes a small profit, but the overall performance of the combined system is worse than the market history system alone, showing that the news baseline is ineffective. However, all news features improve over the market history system; news information helps to explain market behaviors. Additionally, each more advanced set of news features improves, with dependency features yielding the best system in a majority of markets. The dependency system was able to learn more complex interactions between words in news articles. As an example, the system learns that when Kerry is the subject of "accused" his price increases but decreased when he is the object. Similarly, when "Bush" is the subject of "plans" (i.e. Bush is making plans), his price increased. But when he appears as a modifier of the plural noun "plans" (comments about Bush policies), his price falls. Earning profit indicates that our systems were able to correctly forecast changes in public opinion from objective news text.

The combined system proved an effective way of modeling the market with both information sources. Figure 2 shows the profits of the dependency news system, the market history system, and the combined system's profits and decision on two segments from the Kerry DNC market. In the first segment, the history system predicts a downward trend in the market (increasing profit) and the second segment shows the final days of the market, where Kerry was winning primaries and the news system correctly predicted a market increase.

Véronis (2007) observed a connection between electoral success and candidate mentions in news media. The average daily mentions in the general election was 520 for Bush (election winner) and

485 for Kerry. However, for the three major DNC candidates, Dean had 183, Clark 56 and Kerry (election winner) had the least at 43. Most Kerry articles occurred towards the end of the race when it was clear he would win, while early articles focused on the early leader Dean. Also, news activity did not indicate market movement direction; median candidate mentions for a positive market day was 210 and 192 for a negative day.

Dependency news system accuracy was correlated with news activity. On days when the news component was correct – although not always chosen – there were 226 median candidate mentions compared to 156 for incorrect days. Additionally, the system was more successful at predicting negative days. While days for which it was incorrect the market moved up or down equally, when it was correct and selected it predicted buy 42% of the time and sell 58%, indicating that the system better tracked negative news impacts.

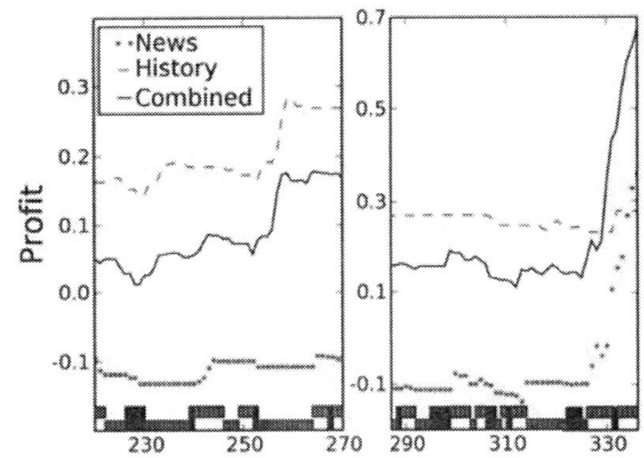

Figure 2: Two selections from the Kerry DNC market showing profits over time (days) for dependency news, history and combined systems. Each day's chosen system is indicated by the bottom stripe as red (upper) for news, blue (lower) for history, and black for ties.

7 Related Work

Many studies have examined the effects of news on financial markets. Koppel and Shtrimberg (2004) found a low correlation between news and the stock market, likely because of the extreme efficiency of the stock market (Gidófalvi, 2001). Two studies reported success but worked with a very small time granularity (10 minutes) (Lavrenko et al., 2000; Mittermayer and Knolmayer, 2006). It appears that neither system accounts for the time-series nature of news during learning, instead using cross-validation experiments which is unsuitable for evaluation of time-series data. Our own preliminary cross-validation experiments yielded much better results than chronological evaluation since the system trains using future information, and with much more training data than is actually available for most days. Recent work has examined prediction market behavior and underlying principles (Serrano-Padial, 2007). [12] Pennock et al. (2000) found that prediction markets are somewhat efficient and some have theorized that news could predict these markets, which we have confirmed (Debnath et al., 2003; Pennock et al., 2001; Servan-Schreiber et al., 2004).

Others have explored the concurrent modeling of text corpora and time series, such as using stock market data and language modeling to identify influential news stories (Lavrenko et al., 2000). Hurst and Nigam (2004) combined syntactic and semantic information for text polarity extraction.

Our task is related to but distinct from sentiment analysis, which focuses on judgments in opinions and, recently, predictions given by opinions. Specifically, Kim and Hovy (2007) identify which political candidate is predicted to win by an opinion posted on a message board and aggregate opinions to correctly predict an election result. While the domain and some techniques are similar to our own, we deal with fundamentally different problems. We do not consider opinions but instead analyze objective news to learn events that will impact opinions. Opinions express subjective statements about elections whereas news reports events. We use public opinion as a measure of an events impact. Additionally, they use generalized features similar to our own identification of entities by replacing (a larger set of) known entities with generalized terms. In contrast, we use syntactic structures to create generalized ngram features. Note that our features (table 1) do not indicate opinions in contrast to the Kim and Hovy features. Finally, Kim and Hovy had a batch setting to predict election winners while we have a time-series setting that tracked daily public opinion of candidates.

8 Conclusion and Future Work

We have presented a system for forecasting public opinion about political candidates using news me-

[12] For a sample of the literature on prediction markets, see the proceedings of the recent Prediction Market workshops (http://betforgood.com/events/pm2007/index.html).

dia. Our results indicate that computational systems can process media reports and learn which events impact political candidates. Additionally, the system does better when the candidate appears more frequently and for negative events. A news source analysis could reveal which outlets most influence public opinion. A feature analysis could reveal which events trigger public reactions. While these results and analyses have significance for political analysis they could extend to other genres, such as financial markets. We have shown that feature extraction using syntactic parses can generalize typical bag-of-word features and improve performance, a non-trivial result as dependency parses contain significant errors and can limit the selection of words. Also, combining the internal market baseline with a news system improved performance, suggesting that forecasting future public opinions requires a combination of new information and continuing trends, neither of which can be captured by the other.

References

Debnath, S., D. M. Pennock, C. L. Giles, and S. Lawrence. 2003. Information incorporation in online in-game sports betting markets. In *Electronic Commerce*.

Devitt, Ann and Khurshid Ahmad. 2007. Sentiment polarity identification in financial news: A cohesion-based approach. In *Association for Computational Linguistics (ACL)*.

Forsythe, R., T.A. Rietz, , and T.W. Ross. 1999. Wishes, expectations, and actions: A survey on price formation in election stock markets. *Journal of Economic Behavior and Organization*, 39:83–110.

Gidófalvi, G. 2001. Using news articles to predict stock price movements. Technical report, Univ. of California San Diego, San Diego.

Hurst, Matthew and Kamal Nigam. 2004. Retrieving topical sentiments from online document collections. In *Document Recognition and Retrieval XI*.

Jank, Wolfgang and Natasha Foutz. 2007. Using virtual stock exchanges to forecast box-office revenue via functional shape analysis. In *The Prediction Markets Workshop at Electronic Commerce*.

Kim, Soo-Min and Eduard Hovy. 2007. Crystal: Analyzing predictive opinions on the web. In *Empirical Methods in Natural Language Processing (EMNLP)*.

Koppel, M. and I. Shtrimberg. 2004. Good news or bad news? let the market decide. In *AAAI Spring Symposium on Exploring Attitude and Affect in Text: Theories and Applications*.

Lavrenko, V., M. Schmill, D. Lawrie, P. Ogilvie, D. Jensen, and J. Allan. 2000. Mining of concurrent text and time series. In *KDD*.

Littlestone, Nick and Manfred K. Warmuth. 1989. The weighted majority algorithm. In *IEEE Symposium on Foundations of Computer Science*.

McDonald, R., K. Lerman, and F. Pereira. 2006. Multilingual dependency parsing with a two-stage discriminative parser. In *Conference on Natural Language Learning (CoNLL)*.

Mittermayer, M. and G. Knolmayer. 2006. NewsCATS: A news categorization and trading system. In *International Conference in Data Mining*.

Pennock, D. M., S. Lawrence, C. L. Giles, and F. A. Nielsen. 2000. The power of play: Efficiency and forecast accuracy in web market games. Technical Report 2000-168, NEC Research Institute.

Pennock, D. M., S. Lawrence, F. A. Nielsen, and C. L. Giles. 2001. Extracting collective probabilistic forecasts from web games. In *KDD*.

Serrano-Padial, Ricardo. 2007. Strategic foundations of prediction markets and the efficient markets hypothesis. In *The Prediction Markets Workshop at Electronic Commerce*.

Servan-Schreiber, E., J. Wolfers, D. M. Pennock, and B. Galebach. 2004. Prediction markets: Does money matter? *Electronic Markets*, 14.

Toutanova, K., D. Klein, C. Manning, and Y. Singer. 2003. Feature-rich part-of-speech tagging with a cyclic dependency network. In *HLT-NAACL*.

Véronis, Jean. 2007. La presse a fait mieux que les sondeurs. http://aixtal.blogspot.com/2007/04/2007-la-presse-fait-mieux-que-les.html.

Wiebe, Janyce, Theresa Wilson, and Claire Cardie. 2005. Annotating expressions of opinions and emotions in language. *LREC*, 39:165–210.

Williams, L.V. 1999. Information efficiency in betting markets: A survey. *Bulletin of Economic Research*, 51:1–30.

Wolfers, J. and E. Zitzewitz. 2004. Prediction markets. *Journal of Economic Perspectives*, 18(2):107–126.

Classifying *What-type* Questions by *Head Noun* Tagging

Fangtao Li, Xian Zhang, Jinhui Yuan, Xiaoyan Zhu
State Key Laboratory on Intelligent Technology and Systems
Tsinghua National Laboratory for Information Science and Technology
Department of Computer Sci. and Tech., Tsinghua University, Beijing 100084, China
zxy-dcs@tsinghua.edu.cn

Abstract

Classifying *what-type* questions into proper semantic categories is found more challenging than classifying other types in question answering systems. In this paper, we propose to classify *what-type* questions by *head noun* tagging. The approach highlights the role of *head nouns* as the category discriminator of *what-type* questions. To reduce the semantic ambiguities of *head noun*, we integrate local syntactic feature, semantic feature and category dependency among adjacent nouns with Conditional Random Fields (CRFs). Experiments on standard question classification data set show that the approach achieves state-of-the-art performances.

1 Introduction

Question classification is a crucial component of modern question answering system. It classifies questions into several semantic categories which indicate the expected semantic type of answers to the questions. The semantic category helps to filter out irrelevant answer candidates, and determine the answer selection strategies.

The widely used question category criteria is a two-layered taxonomy developed by Li and Roth (2002) from UIUC. The hierarchy contains 6 coarse classes and 50 fine classes as shown in Table 1. In this paper, we focus on fine-category classification. Each fine category will be denoted as "Coarse:fine", such as "HUM:individual".

A *what-type* question is defined as the one whose question word is "what", "which", "name" or "list". It is a dominant type in question answering system. Li and Roth (2006) find that the distribution of *what-type* questions over the semantic classes is quite diverse, and they are more difficult to be classified than other types. Table 2 shows the classification accuracies of each question word in UIUC data set using Support Vector Machine (SVM) with unigram features. *What-type* questions account for more than 70 percent in the data set, but the classification accuracy of this type only achieves 75.50%. In this experiment, 90.53% (86 over 95) of the errors are generated by *what-type* questions. Due to its challenge, this paper focuses on *what-type* question classification.

Coarse	Fine
ABBR	abbreviation, expression
DESC	definition, description, manner, reason
ENTY	animal, body, color, creation, currency, disease/medicine, event, food, instrument, language, letter, other, plant, product, religion, sport, substance, symbol, technique, term, vehicle, word
HUM	description, group, individual, title
LOC	city, country, mountain, other, state
NUM	code, count, date, distance, money, order, other, percent, period, speed, temperature, size, weight

Table 1. Question Ontology

	Total	Wrong	Accuracy
What-type	351	86	75.50%
Where	26	2	92.31%
When	26	0	100.0%
Who	47	3	93.62%
How	46	4	91.30%
Why	4	0	100.0%
Total	500	95	81.00%

Table 2. Classification performance for each question words with unigram

Head noun has been presented to play an important role in classifying *what-type* questions (Metzler and Croft, 2005). It refers to the noun reflecting the focus of a question, such as "flower" in the question "What is Hawaii's state

© 2008. Licensed under the *Creative Commons Attribution-Noncommercial-Share Alike 3.0 Unported* license (http://creativecommons.org/licenses/by-nc-sa/3.0/). Some rights reserved.

flower?". These nouns can effectively reduce the noise generated by other words. If the *head noun* "length" is identified from the question "What is the length of the coastline of the state of Alaska?", this question can be easily classified into "NUM:distance". However, the above SVM misclassified this question into "LOC:-state", as the words "state" and "Alaska" confused the classifier. Considering another two questions expressed in (Zhang and Lee, 2002), "Which university did the president graduate from?" and "Which president is a graduate of the Harvard University", although they contain similar words, it is not difficult to distinguish them with the *head nouns* "university" and "president" respectively.

Nevertheless, a *head noun* may correspond to several semantic categories. In this situation, we need to incorporate the *head noun* context for disambiguation. The potentially useful context features include local syntactic features, semantic features and neighbor's semantic category. Take the noun "money" as an example, it possibly corresponds to two categories: "NUM:money" and "ENTY:currency". If there is an adjacent word falling into "Loc:country" category, the "money" tends to belong to "ENTY:currency". Otherwise, if the "ENTY:product" or "HUM:individual" surrounds it, the word "money" may refer to "NUM:money".

Based on the above notions, we propose a new strategy to classify *what-type* questions by word tagging, and the selected *head noun* determines question category. The question classification task is formulated into word sequence tagging problem. All the question words are divided into semantic words and non-semantic words. The semantic word expresses certain semantic category, such as "dog" corresponding to category "ENTITY:animal", while "have" corresponding to no category. The label for semantic words is one of the question categories, and "O" is for non-semantic word. Here, we just consider the nouns as semantic words, others as non-semantic words. Each word in a question will be tagged as a label using Conditional Random Fields model, and the *head noun*'s label is chosen as the question category.

In conclusion, the CRFs based approach has two main steps: the first step is to tag all the words in questions using CRFs, and the second step is choosing the *head noun*'s label as the question category. It can use the *head noun* to eliminate the noisy words, and take advantages of CRFs model to integrate not only the syntactic and semantic features, but also the adjacent categories to tag *head noun*.

The rest of this paper is organized as follows: Section 2 discusses related work. Section 3 introduces the Condition Random Fields(CRFs) and the defined Long-Dependency CRFs (LDCRFs). Section 4 describes the features used in the LDCRFs. The *head noun* extraction method is presented in Section 5. We evaluate the proposed approach in Section 6. Section 7 concludes this paper and discusses future work.

2 Related works

Question Answering Track was first introduced in the Text REtrieval Conference (TREC) in 1999. Since then, question classification has been a popular topic in the research community of text mining. Simple question classification approaches usually employ hand-crafted rules (such as Prager et. al, 1999), which are effective for specific question taxonomy. However, laborious human effort is required to create these rules.

Some other systems employed machine learning approaches to classify questions. Li and Roth (2002) presented a hierarchical classifier based on the Sparse Network of Winnows (Snow) architecture. Tow classifiers were involved in this work: the first one classified questions into the coarse categories; and the other classified questions into fine categories. Several syntactic and semantic features, including semi-automatically constructed class-specific relational features, were extracted and compared in their experiments. The results showed that the hierarchical classifier was effective for question classification task.

Metzler and Croft (2005) used prior knowledge about correlations between question words and types to train word-specific question classifiers. They identified the question words firstly, and trained separate classifier for each question word. WordNet was used as semantic features to boost the classification performance. In this paper, according to question word, all the questions are classifie into two categories: *what-type* ones and non-*what-type* one.

Recent question classification methods have paid more attention on the syntactic structure of sentence. They used a parser to get the syntactic tree, and then took advantage of the structure information. Zhang and Lee (2002) proposed a tree kernel Support Vector Machine classifier and experiment results showed that syntactic information and tree kernel could solve this problem. Nguyen et al. (2007) proposed a subtree mining method for question classification. They formulated question classification as tree category determination, and maximum entropy and boosting model with subtree features were used. The experiment results showed that the subtree mining method can achieve a higher accuracy in question classification task.

In this paper, we formulate the *what-type* question classification as word sequence tagging problem. The tagged label is either one of the question categories for nouns s or "O" for other words. Since *head noun* can be the discriminator for a question, its tag is extracted as the question category in our work. A long-dependency Conditional Random Fields Classifier is defined to tag question words with the features which not only include the syntactic and semantic features, but also the semantic categories' transition features.

3 Conditional Random Fields

Conditional Random Fields (CRFs) are a type of discriminative probabilistic model proposed for labeling sequential data (Lafferty et al. 2001). Its definition is as follows:

Definition: Let $G=(V,E)$ *be a graph such that* $\mathbf{Y}=(Y_v)_{v\in V}$ *, so that* $\mathbf{Y}$ *is indexed by the vertices of* G *. Then* $(\mathbf{X},\mathbf{Y})$ *is a conditional random field in case, when conditioned on* $\mathbf{X}$ *, the random variables* Y_v *obey the Markov property with respect to the graph:* $p(Y_v \mid \mathbf{X}, Y_w, w\neq v) = p(Y_v \mid \mathbf{X}, Y_w, w\sim v)$ *, where* $w\sim v$ *means that* w *and* v *are neighbors in* G *.*

The joint distribution over the label sequence $\mathbf{Y}$ given $\mathbf{X}$ has the form

$$p(\mathbf{Y}\mid\mathbf{X})=\frac{1}{Z(\mathbf{X})}\exp\left(\sum_{e\in E,i}\lambda_i t_i(e,\mathbf{Y}\mid e,\mathbf{X})+\sum_{v\in V,i}\mu_i s_i(v,\mathbf{Y}\mid v,\mathbf{X})\right),$$

where $Z(\mathbf{X})$ is a normalization factor, s_i is a *state* feature function and t_i is a *transition* feature function, λ_i and μ_i are the corresponding weights.

Here we assume the features are given, then the parameter estimation problem is to determine the parameters $\theta=(\lambda_1,\lambda_2,\ldots,\mu_1,\mu_2,\ldots)$ from training data. The inference problem is to find the most probable label sequence $\hat{\mathbf{y}}$ for input sequence $\mathbf{x}$.

In the training set, we label all the noun words with semantic question categories, and other words will be labeled by "O". We suppose that only adjacent noun words connect with each other, and there is no edge between noun and non-noun words, i.e., noun word and non-noun words may share neighbor's state features, but they are not connected by an edge. A labeled example is shown as "What/O was/O Queen/HUM:individual Victria/HUM:individual 's/O title/HUM:title regarding/O India/LOC:-country". In this labeled sentence, only three edges connect four noun words: Queen, Victria, title and India.

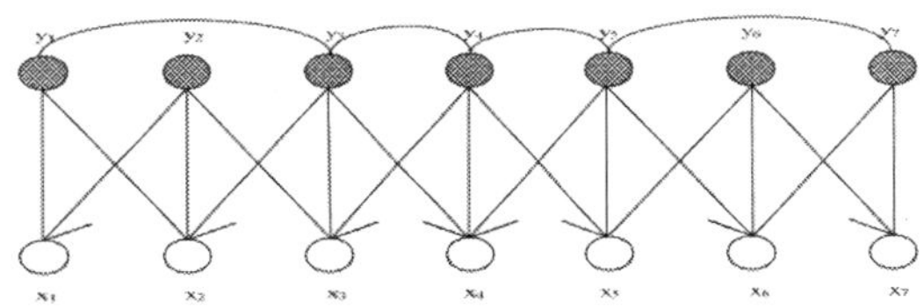

Figure 1. Long-Dependency CRFs, the dotted lines summarize many outgoing edges

With this assumption, we define a Long-Dependency Conditional Random Fields (LDCRFs) model (see Figure 1). The long dependency means that the target words may have no edge with its neighbors, but connect with other words at a long distance. It can be considered as a type of linear- chain CRFs. Its parameter estimation problem and inference problem can be solved by the algorithm for chain-structure CRFs (Sutton and McCallum, 2007).

4 Feature Sets

One of the most attractive advantages of CRFs is that they can integrate rich features, including not only state features, but also transition features. In this section, we will introduce the syntactic, semantic and transition features used in our sequence tagging approach.

4.1 Syntactic Features

The questions, which have similar syntactic style, intend to belong to the same category. Besides words, part-of-speech, chunker, parser information and question length are used as syntactic features.

All the words are lemmatized to root forms, and a window size (here is 4) is set to utilize the surrounding words.

The part-of-speech (POS) tagging is completed by SS Tagger (Tsuruoka and Tsujii, 2005), with our own improvement.

The noun phrase chunking (NP chunking) module uses the basic NP chunker software from

(Ramshaw and Marcus, 1995) to recognize the noun phrases in the question.

The importance of question syntactic structure is reported in (Zhang and Lee, 2002; Nguyen et al. 2007). They used complex machine learning method to capture the tree architecture. The LDCRFs based approach just selects parent node, relation with parent and governor for each target word generated from Minipar(Lin, 1999).

The length of question is another important syntactic feature. In our experiment, a threshold is set to denote the length as "high" or "low".

4.2 Semantic Features

Semantic features concern what words mean and how these meanings combine in sentence to form sentence meanings. Named Entity is a predefined semantic category for noun word. WordNet (Fellbaum, 1998) is a public semantic lexicon for English language, and it is used to get hypernym for noun word and synset for head verb which is the first notional verb in the sentence.

Named Entity: Named entity recognizer assigns a semantic category to the noun phrase. It is widely used to provide semantic information in text mining. In this paper, Stanford Named Entity Recognizer (Finkel et al. 2005) is used to classify noun phrases into four semantic categories: PERSON, LOCATION, ORGANIZARION and MISC.

Noun Hypernym: Hypernyms can be considered as semantic abstractions. It helps to narrow the gap between training set and testing set. For example, "What is Maryland's state bird?", if we recursively find the bird's hypernym "animal", which appeared in training set, this question can be easily classified.

In training set, we try to select appropriate hypernyms for each category. An correct WordNet sense is first assigned for each polysemous noun, and then all its hypernyms are recursively extracted. The sense determination step is processed with the algorithm in (Pedersen et al. 2005). They disambiguate word sense by assigning a target word the sense, which is most related to the senses of its neighboring words.

Since the word sense disambiguation method has low performance, with F1-measure below 50% reported in (Pedersen et al. 2005), a feature selection method is used to extract the most discriminative hypernyms. The hypernyms selection method is processed as follows: we first remove the low frequency hypernyms, and select the hypernyms using a chi-square method. The chi-square value measures the lack of independence between a hypernym h and category c_j. It is defined as:

$$\chi^2(h, c_j) = \frac{(A+B+C+D)\times(AD-CB)^2}{(A+C)\times(B+D)\times(A+B)\times(C+D)}$$

where A is the number of hypernym h, which belongs to category c_j; B is the number of h out of c_j; C is the number of other hypernyms in c_j; D is the number of other hypernyms out of c_j.

We set a threshold to select the most discriminative hypernym set. Extracted examples are shown in Figure 2.

ENTITY:animal:
animal, carnivore, chordate, equine, horse, living_thing, vertebrate, mammal, odd-toed_ungulate, organism, placental

ENTITY:food:
alcohol, beer, beverage, brew, cereal, condiment, crop, drink, drug_of_abuse, flavorer, food, foodstuff, helping, indefinite_quantity, ingredient, liquid, output, produce, small_indefinite_quantity, production, solid, substance, vegetable

Figure 2. Examples of extracted hypernym

It can be seen that these hypernyms are appropriate to describe the semantic meaning of the category. They are expected to work as the class-specific relational features which are semi-constructed by (Li and Roth, 2002). In our approach, we just use the noun's minimum upper hypernym, existing in training set, as the feature.

Head Verb Synset: To avoid losing question verb information, we extract head verb, which is the first notional verb in a question, and expand it using WordNet synset as feature. The head verb extraction is based on the following simple rules:

If the first word is "name" or "list", the head verb will be denoted as this word. If the first verb following question word is "do" or other auxiliary verb, the next verb is extracted as head verb. Otherwise the head verb is extracted as the first verb after question word.

4.3 Transition Features

State transition feature captures the contextual constraints among labels. We define it as

$$t_{y',y}(e=<i,i+1>, \mathbf{Y} \mid e, \mathbf{X}) = \delta(\mathbf{Y} \mid e=<y',y>).$$

Where *e* represents the edge between adjacent nouns. It captures adjacent categories as features to tag the target noun. Note that, for simplicity, the value of above feature is independent of the observations X.

5 Head Noun Extraction

After tagging all the words in a question, we will extract *head noun* and assign its tagged label to the question as the final question classification result.

The *head noun* extraction is a simple heuristic method inspired by (Metzler and Croft, 2005). We first run a POS tagger on each question, and post-process them to make sure that each sentence has at least one noun word. Next, the first NP chunk after the question word is extracted by shallow parsing. The *head noun* is determined by the following heuristic rules:

1. If the NP chunker is before the first verb, or the NP chunk is after the first verb but there is no possessive case after the NP chunker, we mark the rightmost word in the chunker as *head noun*.
2. Otherwise, extract the next NP chunker and recursively process the above rules.

Although this method may depend on the performance of POS tagger and shallow parser, it achieves the accuracy of over 95% on the UIUC data set in our implementation.

6 Experiments

6.1 Experiment Settings

Data Set:

We evaluate the proposed approach on the UIUC data set (Li and Roth, 2002). 5500 questions are selected for training, and 500 questions are selected for testing. The classification categories have been introduced as question ontology in section 1. This paper only focuses on 50 fine classes.

To train the LDCRFs, we manually labeled all the noun words with one of 50 fine categories. Other words are labeled with "O". One of the labeled examples is "What/O was/O Queen/HUM:individual Victria/HUM:individual 's/O title/HUM:title regarding/O India/LOC:country". Ten people labeled 3407 *what-type* questions as training set. Each question was independently annotated by two people and reviewed by the third. For words which have more than one category, the annotators selected the most salient one according to the context. For testing set, 351 *what-type* questions were selected for experiments evaluation.

Evaluation metric:

Accuracy performance is widely used to evaluate question classification methods [Li and Roth, 2002; Zhang and Lee, 2003, Melter and Croft, 2004; Nguyen et al. 2007].

6.2 Approach Performance Evaluation

	# Wrong	Accuracy
SVM	86	75.50%
LDCRFs-based	80	77.20%

Table 3. LDCRFS-based Approach V.S. SVM

Table 3 shows the compared results between the proposed LDCRFs based approach and SVM with unigram feature. The LDCRFs based approach achieves accuracy of 77.20%, compared with 75.50% of SVM. Observing the detailed classification results, we conclude two advantages of LDCRFs over SVMs. First LDCRFs based approach focuses on *head noun* to reduce the noise generated by other words. The question "What is the length of the coastline of the state of Alaska?" is misclassified as "LOC:state" by SVM, whereas it is correctly classified by our approach. Second, LDCRFs based approach can utilize rich features, including not only state features, but also transition features. With the new features involved, LDCRFs is expected to improve classification performance. This unigram result is used as our baseline. The following experiments are conducted to test the new feature contribution.

Syntactic Features:

In addition to words, four types of features, including part-of-speech (POS), chunker, parser information (Parser), and question length (Length), are extracted as syntactic features.

	Accuracy
Unigram (U)	77.20%
U+POS	78.35%
U+Chunker	77.20%
U+Parser	79.20%
U+Length	77.49%
Total Syn	80.06%

Table 4. Syntactic Feature Performance

From the syntactic feature results in Table 4, we can draw the following conclusions:

(a). Among four types of syntactic features, pars-

er information contributes mostly. (Metzler and Croft, 2005) once claimed that it didn't make improvement by just incorporating these information as explicit feature, and they should be used implicitly via a tree structure. Without using the complex tree mining and representing technique, our LDCRFs-based approach just incorporates the word parent, relation with parent and word governor from Minipar as features. The experiments show that the parser information feature is able to capture the syntactic structure information, and it makes much improvement in this sequence tagging approach.
(b) Question length makes small improvement. However, the chunker features make no improvement, consistent with the observation reported by (Li and Roth, 2006).
© The best accuracy (80.06%) is achieved by integrating all the syntactic features.

Semantic Features:

	Accuracy
Unigram(U)	77.20%
U+NE	77.20%
U+HVSyn	78.63%
U+NHype	78.35%
Total Sem	80.06%

Table 5. Semantic Feature Performance

The semantic features include Named Entity (NE), Noun Hypernym (NHype) and Head Verb Synset (HVSyn).
From Table 5 we can draw the following conclusions:
(a) NE makes no improvement in classification task. The reason is that the named entity recognizer contains only four semantic categories. It is too coarse to distinguish 50 fined-categories.
(b) The LDCRFs-based approach just considers the noun words as semantic words. The head verb synsets (HVSyn) are imported as one of semantic features. The experiment results show that it is effective to incorporate the head verb as features, which achieves the best individual accuracy among semantic features.
(c) Noun hypernyms (NHype) are the most important semantic features. They narrow the semantic gap between training set and testing set. From Section 4.2, we can see that the selected noun hypernyms are appropriate for each category. While, the experiment with NHype features doesn't make considerable improvement as we previously thought. The reason may come from the fact that the word sense disambiguation method has low performance. A hypernym selection method is used in training set, but we didn't tackle the error in testing set. Once the word sense disambiguation is wrong, it will not make improvement, but generate noise (see the discussion examples in next section).
(d) It is an interesting result that using all the semantic features can achieve the same accuracy as the syntactic features (80.06%).

Feature Combination:

In this section, we carry out experiments to examine whether the performance can be boosted by integrating syntactic features and semantic features. Several results are shown in Table 6. The experiments show that:
(a) Parser Information and Head Verb Synset are both the most contributive features for syntactic set and semantic feature set. While the performance with these two features can't beat the performance by combining Parser Information and Noun Hypernyms.

	Accuracy
U+POS+NE+HVSyn	80.91%
U+Parser+NHype	81.77%
U+Parser+HVSyn	80.91%
U+POS+Length+NHype	80.63%
Total	82.05%

Table 6. Combined Feature Performance

(b) The best result for classifying *what-type* questions with our approach is achieved by integrating all the features. The accuracy is 82.05%, which is 18.7 percent error reduction (from 22.08% to 17.95%) over unigram feature set. It shows that the features we extract are effectively used in our CRFs based approach.

Transition Feature:

Transition feature can capture the information between adjacent categories. It offers another semantic feature for LDCRFs-based approach.

	No transition features	With transition features
Syn	79.20%	80.06%
Sem	79.49%	80.06%
Total	81.48%	82.05%

Table 7. Transition Feature Performance

The performances of all these three experiment decline without the transition features. It shows that the dependency between adjacent semantic categories contributes to the classifier performance.

6.3 System Performance Comparison and Discussion

In this section, the *what-type* questions and non-*what-type* questions are combined to show the final result. Non-*what-type* questions are classified using SVM with unigrams as reported in Section 1, and *what-type* questions are classified by the LDCRFs based approach. The combined results are used to compare with the current question classification methods.

Classifier	Accuracy
Li's Hierarchical method	84.20%
Nguyen's tree method	83.60%
Metzler's U+ WordNet method	82.20%
LDCRFs-based with U+Parser	83.60%
LDCRFs-based with U+NHype	83.00%
LDCRFs-based with total features	85.60%

Table 8. Comparison with related work

Table 8 shows the accuracies of the LDCRFs based question classification approach with different feature sets, in comparison with the tree method (Nguyen et al. 2007), the WordNet Method (Metzler and Croft, 2005) and the hierarchical method (Li and Roth, 2002). We can see the LDCRFs-based approach is effective:

(a) Without formulating the syntactic structure as a tree, the LDCRFs-based approach still achieves accuracy 83.60% with unigram and parser information, which is the same as Nguyen's tree classifier.

(b) Although the LDCRFs-based approach with unigrams and Noun Hypernyms generates noise as described in Section 6.2, it still outperforms the Metzler's method using WordNet and unigram features (83.00% v.s. 82.20%).

(c) The experiment with total features achieves the accuracy of 85.60%. It outperforms Li's Hierarchical classifier, even they use semi-automatic constructed features.

6.3.1 Analysis and Discussion

Even the sequence tagging model achieves high accuracy performance, there still exists many problems. We use the matrix defined in Li and Roth (2002) to show the performance errors. The metric is defined as follows:

$$D_{ij} = Err_{ij} * 2/(N_i + N_j)$$

Where Err_{ij} is the number of questions in class i that are misclassified as belong to class j, Ni and Nj are the numbers of questions in class i and j respectively.

From the matrix in Figure 3, we can see two major mistake pairs are "ENTY:substance" and "ENTY:other", "ENTY:currency" and "NUM:money". They really have similar meanings, which confuses even human beings.

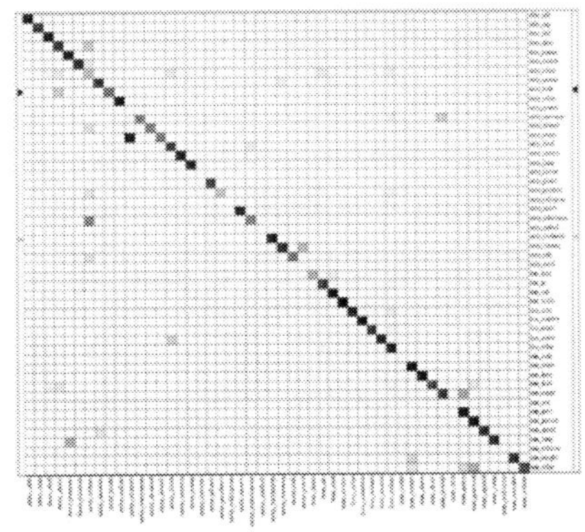

Figure 3. The gray-scale map of Matrix D[n,n]. The gray scale of the small box in position [i,j] denotes *D[i,j]*. The larger *Dij* is, the darker the color is.

Several factors influence the performance:

(a) *Head noun* extraction error: This error is mainly caused by errors of POS tagger and shallow parser. For the wrong POS example "what/WP hemisphere/EX is/VBZ the/DT Philippines/NNPS in/IN ?/.", "Philippines" is extracted as head word. The result is misclassified into "LOC:country". For the shallow parser error example "what/WP/B-NP is/VBZ/B-VP the/D T/BNP speed/NN/I-NP humminbirds/NNS /I-NP fly/V- BP/B-VP ?/./O", "hummingbirds" is extract as head word, rather than "speed". The question is misclassified into "ENTY:animal".

(b) WordNet sense disambiguation errors: In question "What is the highest dam in the U.S. ?" The real sense for dam is dam#1: a barrier constructed to contain the flow of water or to keep out the sea; while the disambiguation method determine the second sense as dam#2: a metric unit of length equal to ten meters.

(c) Lack of *head nouns*: the CRFs based approach is sensitive to the *Head Noun*. If the question doesn't contain the *head noun*, it is difficult to produce the correct result, such as the question "What is done with worn or outdated flags?" In the future work, we will focus on the *head noun* absence problem.

7 Conclusion

In this paper, we propose a novel approach with Conditional Random Fields to classify *what-type* questions. We first use the CRFs model to label all the words in a question, and then choose the label of *head noun* as the question category. As far as we know, this is the first trial to formulate question classification into word sequence tagging problem. We believe that the model has two distinguished advantages:

1. Extracting *head noun* can eliminate the noise generated by the non-head words
2. The Conditional Random Fields model can integrate rich features, including not only the syntactic and semantic features, but also the transition features between labels.

Experiments show that the LDCRFs-based approach can achieve comparable performance to those of the state-of-the-art question answering systems. With the addition of more features, the performance of the LDCRFs based approach can be expected to be further improved.

Acknowledgement

This work is supported by National Natural Science Foundation of China (60572084, 60621062), Hi-tech Research and Development Program of China (2006AA02Z321), National Basic Research Program of China (2007CB311003). Thank Shuang Lin and Jiao Li for revising this paper. Thanks for the reviewers' comments.

References

Christiane Fellbaum. 1998. *WordNet: an Electronic Lexical Database.* MIT Press.

Prager, J., D. Radev, E. Brown, A. Coden, and V. Samn. 1999. *'The use of predictive annotation for question answering in TREC'.* In: Proceedings of the 8th Text Retrieval Conference (TREC-8).

John Lafferty, Andrew McCallum, Fernando Pereira. 2001. *Conditional Random Fields: Probabilistic Models for Segmenting and Labeling Sequence Data.* In *Proceedings of* ICML-2001.

Li, X. and D. Roth. 2002. *Learning question classifiers.* In Proceedings of the 19th International Conference on Compuatational Linguistics (COLING), pages 556–562.

Zhang, D. and W. Lee. 2003. *Question classification using support vector machines.* In Proceedings of the 26th Annual International ACM SIGIR conference, pages 26–32

Donald Metzler and W. Bruce Croft. 2004. *Analysis of Statistical Question Classfication for Fact-based Questions.* In Journal of Information Retrieval.

Ted Pedersen, Satanjeev Banerjee, and Siddharth Patwardhan . 2005. *Maximizing Semantic Relatedness to Perform Word Sense Disambiguation.* University of Minnesota Supercomputing Institute Research Report UMSI 2005/25, March.

Xin Li, Dan Roth. 2006. *Learning Question Classifiers: The Role of Semantic Information.* In Natural Language Engineering, 12(3):229-249

Minh Le Nguyen, Thanh Tri Nguyen and Akira Shimazu. 2007. *Subtree Mining for Question Classification Problem.* In Proceedings of the 20th International Conference on Artificial Intelligence. Pages 1695-1700.

C. Sutton and A. McCallum. 2007. *An introduction to conditional random fields for relational learning.* In L. Getoor and B. Taskar (Eds.). Introduction to statistical relational learning. MIT Press.

Y. Tsuruoka and J. Tsujii,. 2005. *Bidirectional inference with the easiest-first strategy for tagging sequence data.* In Proc. HLT/EMNLP'05, Vancouver, October, pp. 467-474.

L. Ramshaw and M. Marcus. 1995. *Text chunking using transformation-based learning*, Proc. 3rd Workshop on Very Large Corpora, pp. 82–94.

J.R. Finkel, T. Grenager and C. Manning. 2005. *Incorporating non-local information into information extraction systems by Gibbs sampling.* Proc. 43rd Annual Meeting of ACL, pp. 363–370.

D. Lin. 1999. *MINIPAR: a minimalist parser. In Maryland Linguistics Colloquium*, University of Maryland, College Park.

PNR²: Ranking Sentences with Positive and Negative Reinforcement for Query-Oriented Update Summarization

Li Wenjie[1], Wei Furu[1,2], Lu Qin[1], He Yanxiang[2]

[1]Department of Computing
The Hong Kong Polytechnic University, HK
{csfwei, cswjli, csluqin}
@comp.polyu.edu.hk

[2]Department of Computer Science
and Technology, Wuhan University, China
{frwei, yxhe@whu.edu.cn}

Abstract

Query-oriented update summarization is an emerging summarization task very recently. It brings new challenges to the sentence ranking algorithms that require not only to locate the important and query-relevant information, but also to capture the new information when document collections evolve. In this paper, we propose a novel graph based sentence ranking algorithm, namely PNR², for update summarization. Inspired by the intuition that "a sentence receives a *positive* influence from the sentences that correlate to it in the same collection, whereas a sentence receives a *negative* influence from the sentences that correlates to it in the different (perhaps previously read) collection", PNR² models both the positive and the negative mutual reinforcement in the ranking process. Automatic evaluation on the DUC 2007 data set pilot task demonstrates the effectiveness of the algorithm.

1 Introduction

The explosion of the WWW has brought with it a vast board of information. It has become virtually impossible for anyone to read and understand large numbers of individual documents that are abundantly available. Automatic document summarization provides an effective means to manage such an exponentially increased collection of information and to support information seeking and condensing goals.

The main evaluation forum that provides benchmarks for researchers working on document summarization to exchange their ideas and experiences is the Document Understanding Conferences (DUC). The goals of the DUC evaluations are to enable researchers to participate in large-scale experiments upon the standard benchmark and to increase the availability of appropriate evaluation techniques. Over the past years, the DUC evaluations have evolved gradually from single-document summarization to multi-document summarization and from generic summarization to query-oriented summarization. Query-oriented multi-document summarization initiated in 2005 aims to produce a short and concise summary for a collection of topic relevant documents according to a given query that describes a user's particular interests.

Previous summarization tasks are all targeted on a single document or a static collection of documents on a given topic. However, the document collections can change (actually grow) dynamically when the topic evolves over time. New documents are continuously added into the topic during the whole lifecycle of the topic and normally they bring the new information into the topic. To cater for the need of summarizing a dynamic collection of documents, the DUC evaluations piloted update summarization in 2007. The task of update summarization differs from previous summarization tasks in that the latter aims to dig out the salient information in a topic while the former cares the information not only salient but also novel.

Up to the present, the predominant approaches in document summarization regardless of the nature and the goals of the tasks have still been built upon the sentence extraction framework.

© 2008. Licensed under the *Creative Commons Attribution-Noncommercial-Share Alike 3.0 Unported* license (http://creativecommons.org/licenses/by-nc-sa/3.0/). Some rights reserved.

Under this framework, sentence ranking is the issue of most concern. In general, two kinds of sentences need to be evaluated in update summarization, i.e. the sentences in an early (old) document collection A (denoted by S^A) and the sentences in a late (new) document collection B (denoted by S^B). Given the changes from S^A to S^B, an update summarization approach may be concerned about four ranking issues: (1) rank S^A independently; (2) re-rank S^A after S^B comes; (3) rank S^B independently; and (4) rank S^B given that S^A is provided. Among them, (4) is of most concern. It should be noting that both (2) and (4) need to consider the influence from the sentences in the same and different collections.

In this study, we made an attempt to capture the intuition that

> "A sentence receives a *positive* influence from the sentences that correlate to it in the same collection, whereas a sentence receives a *negative* influence from the sentences that correlates to it in the different collection."

We represent the sentences in A or B as a text graph constructed using the same approach as was used in Erkan and Radev (2004a, 2004b). Different from the existing PageRank-like algorithms adopted in document summarization, we propose a novel sentence ranking algorithm, called PNR^2 (Ranking with Positive and Negative Reinforcement). While PageRank models the positive mutual reinforcement among the sentences in the graph, PNR^2 is capable of modeling both positive and negative reinforcement in the ranking process.

The remainder of this paper is organized as follows. Section 2 introduces the background of the work presented in this paper, including existing graph-based summarization models, descriptions of update summarization and time-based ranking solutions with web graph and text graph. Section 3 then proposes PNR^2, a sentence ranking algorithm based on positive and negative reinforcement and presents a query-oriented update summarization model. Next, Section 4 reports experiments and evaluation results. Finally, Section 5 concludes the paper.

2 Background and Related Work

2.1 Previous Work in Graph-based Document Summarization

Graph-based ranking algorithms such as Google's PageRank (Brin and Page, 1998) and Kleinberg's HITS (Kleinberg, 1999) have been successfully used in the analysis of the link structure of the WWW. Now they are springing up in the community of document summarization. The major concerns in graph-based summarization researches include how to model the documents using text graph and how to transform existing web page ranking algorithms to their variations that could accommodate various summarization requirements.

Erkan and Radev (2004a and 2004b) represented the documents as a weighted undirected graph by taking sentences as vertices and cosine similarity between sentences as the edge weight function. An algorithm called LexRank, adapted from PageRank, was applied to calculate sentence significance, which was then used as the criterion to rank and select summary sentences. Meanwhile, Mihalcea and Tarau (2004) presented their PageRank variation, called TextRank, in the same year. Besides, they reported experimental comparison of three different graph-based sentence ranking algorithms obtained from Positional Power Function, HITS and PageRank (Mihalcea and Tarau, 2005). Both HITS and PageRank performed excellently.

Likewise, the use of PageRank family was also very popular in event-based summarization approaches (Leskovec et al., 2004; Vanderwende et al., 2004; Yoshioka and Haraguchi, 2004; Li et al., 2006). In contrast to conventional sentence-based approaches, newly emerged event-based approaches took event terms, such as verbs and action nouns and their associated named entities as graph nodes, and connected nodes according to their co-occurrence information or semantic dependency relations. They were able to provide finer text representation and thus could be in favor of sentence compression which was targeted to include more informative contents in a fixed-length summary. Nevertheless, these advantages lied on appropriately defining and selecting event terms.

All above-mentioned representative work was concerned with generic summarization. Later on, graph-based ranking algorithms were introduced in query-oriented summarization too when this new challenge became a hot research topic recently. For example, a topic-sensitive version of PageRank was proposed in (OtterBacher et al., 2005). The same algorithm was followed by Wan et al. (2006) and Lin et al. (2007) who further investigated on its application in query-oriented update summarization.

2.2 The DUC 2007 Update Summarization Task Description

The DUC 2007 update summarization pilot task is to create short (100 words) multi-document summaries under the assumption that the reader has already read some number of previous documents. Each of 10 topics contains 25 documents. For each topic, the documents are sorted in chronological order and then partitioned into three collections, "A", "B" and "C". The participants are then required to generate (1) a summary for "A"; (2) an update summary for "B" assuming documents in "A" have already been read; and (3) an update summary for "C" assuming documents in "A" and "B" have already been read. Growing out of the DUC 2007, the Text Analysis Conference (TAC) 2008 planed to keep only the DUC 2007 task (1) and (2).

Each topic collection in the DUC 2007 (will also in the TAC 2008) is accompanied with a query that describes a user's interests and focuses. System-generated summaries should include as many responses relevant to the given query as possible. Here is a query example from the DUC 2007 document collection "D0703A".

<topic>
<num> D0703A *</num>*
<title> Steps toward introduction of the Euro. *</title>*
<narr> Describe steps taken and worldwide reaction prior to introduction of the Euro on January 1, 1999. Include predictions and expectations reported in the press. *</narr>*
</topic> [D0703A]

Update summarization is definitely a time-related task. An appropriate ranking algorithm must be the one capable of coping with the change or the time issues.

2.3 Time-based Ranking Solutions with Web Graph and Text Graph

Graph based models in document summarization are inspired by the idea behind web graph models which have been successfully used by current search engines. As a matter of fact, adding time dimension into the web graph has been extensively studied in recent literature.

Basically, the evolution in the web graph stems from (1) adding new edges between two existing nodes; (2) adding new nodes in the existing graph (consequently adding new edges between the existing nodes and the new nodes or among the new nodes); and (3) deleting existing edges or nodes. Berberich et al. (2004 and 2005) developed two link analysis methods, i.e. T-Rank Light and T-Rank, by taking into account two temporal aspects, i.e. freshness (i.e. timestamp of most recent update) and activity (i.e. update rates) of the pages and the links. They modeled the web as an evolving graph in which each nodes and edges (i.e. web pages and hyperlinks) were annotated with time information. The time information in the graph indicated different kinds of events in the lifespan of the nodes and edges, such as creation, deletion and modifications. Then they derived a subgraph of the evolving graph with respect to the user's temporal interest. Finally, the time information of the nodes and the edges were used to modify the random walk model as was used in PageRank. Specifically, they used it to modify the random jump probabilities (in both T-Rank Light and T-Rank) and the transition probabilities (in T-Rank only).

Meanwhile, Yu et al. (2004 and 2005) introduced a time-weighted PageRank, called TimedPageRank, for ranking in a network of scientific publications. In their approach, citations were weighted based on their ages. Then a post-processing step decayed the authority of a publication based on the publication's age. Later, Yang et al. (2007) proposed TemporalRank, based on which they computed the page importance from two perspectives: the importance from the current web graph snapshot and the accumulated historical importance from previous web graph snapshot. They used a kinetic model to interpret TemporalRank and showed it could be regarded as a solution to an ordinary differential equation.

In conclusion, Yu et al. tried to cope with the problem that PageRank favors over old pages whose in-degrees are greater than those of new pages. They worked on a static single snapshot of the web graph, and their algorithm could work well on all pages in the web graph. Yang et al., on the other hand, worked on a series of web graphs at different snapshots. Their algorithm was able to provide more robust ranking of the web pages, but could not alleviate the problem carried by time dimension at each web graph snapshot. This is because they directly applied the original PageRank to rank the pages. In other words, the old pages still obtained higher scores while the newly coming pages still got lower scores. Berberich et al. focused their efforts on the evolution of nodes and edges in the web graph. However, their algorithms did not work when the temporal interest of the user (or query) was not available.

As for graph based update summarization, Wan (2007) presented the TimedTextRank algorithm by following the same idea presented in the work of Yu et al. Given three collections of chronologically ordered documents, Lin et al. (2007) proposed to construct the TimeStamped graph (TSG) graph by incrementally adding the sentences to the graph. They modified the construction of the text graph, but the ranking algorithm was the same as the one proposed by OtterBacher et al.

Nevertheless, the text graph is different from the web graph. The evolution in the text graph is limited to the type (2) in the web graph. The nodes and edges can not be deleted or modified once they are inserted. In other words, we are only interested in the changes caused when new sentences are introduced into the existing text graph. As a result, the ideas from Berberich et al. cannot be adopted directly in the text graph. Similarly, the problem in web graph as stated in the work of Yu et al. (i.e. "new pages, which may be of high quality, have few or no in-links and are left behind.") does not exist in the text graph at all. More precisely, the new coming sentences are equally treated as the existing sentences, and the degree (in or out) of the new sentences are also equally accumulated as the old sentences. Directly applying the ideas from the work of Yu et al. does not always make sense in the text graph. Recall that the main task for sentence ranking in update summarization is to rank S^B given S^A. So the idea from Yang et al. is also not applicable.

In fact, the key points include not only maximizing the importance in the current new document collection but also minimizing the redundancy to the old document collection when ranking the sentences for update summarization. Time dimension does contribute here, but it is not the only way to consider the changes. Unlike the web graph, the easily-captured content information in a text graph can provide additional means to analyze the influence of the changes.

To conclude the previous discussions, adding temporal information to the text graph is different from it in the web graph. Capturing operations (such as addition, deletion, modification of web pages and hyperlinks) is most concerned in the web graph; however, prohibiting redundant information from the old documents is the most critical issue in the text graph.

3 Positive and Negative Reinforcement Ranking for Update Summarization

Existing document summarization approaches basically follow the same processes: (1) first calculate the significance of the sentences with reference to the given query with/without using some sorts of sentence relations; (2) then rank the sentences according to certain criteria and measures; (3) finally extract the top-ranked but non-redundant sentences from the original documents to create a summary. Under this extractive framework, undoubtedly the two critical processes involved are sentence ranking and sentence selection. In the following sections, we will first introduce the sentence ranking algorithm based on ranking with positive and negative reinforcement, and then we present the sentence selection strategy.

3.1 Ranking with Positive and Negative Reinforcement (PNR^2)

Previous graph-based sentence ranking algorithms is capable to model the fact that a sentence is important if it correlates to (many) other important sentences. We call this positive mutual reinforcement. In this paper, we study two kinds of reinforcement, namely positive and negative reinforcement, among two document collections, as illustrated in Figure 1.

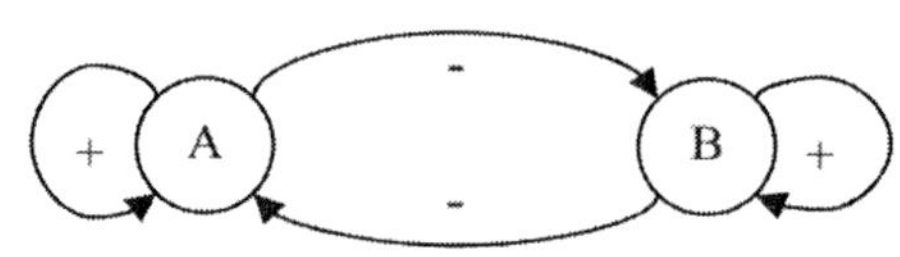

Figure 1 Positive and Negative Reinforcement

In Figure 1, "A" and "B" denote two document collections about the same topics ("A" is the old document collection, "B" is the new document collection), S^A and S^B denote the sentences in "A" and "B". We assume:

1. S^A performs positive reinforcement on its own internally;
2. S^A performs negative reinforcement on S^B externally;
3. S^B performs negative reinforcement on S^A externally;
4. S^B performs positive reinforcement on its own internally.

Positive reinforcement captures the intuition that a sentence is more important if it associates to the other important sentences in the same collection. Negative reinforcement, on the other hand, reflects the fact that a sentence is less important if it associates to the important sentences in the other collection, since such a sentence might repeat the same or very similar information which is supposed to be included in the summary generated for the other collection.

Let R_A and R_B denote the ranking of the sentences in A and B, the reinforcement can be formally described as

$$\begin{cases} R_A^{(k+1)} = \alpha_1 \cdot M_{AA} \cdot R_A^{(k)} + \beta_1 \cdot M_{AB} \cdot R_B^{(k)} + \gamma_1 \cdot \vec{p}_A \\ R_B^{(k+1)} = \beta_2 \cdot M_{BA} \cdot R_A^{(k)} + \alpha_2 \cdot M_{BB} \cdot R_B^{(k)} + \gamma_2 \cdot \vec{p}_B \end{cases} \quad (1)$$

where the four matrices M_{AA}, M_{BB}, M_{AB} and M_{BA} are the affinity matrices of the sentences in S^A, in S^B, from S^A to S^B and from S^B to S^A. $W = \begin{bmatrix} \alpha_1 & \beta_1 \\ \beta_2 & \alpha_2 \end{bmatrix}$ is a weight matrix to balance the reinforcement among different sentences. Notice that $\beta_1, \beta_2 < 0$ such that they perform negative reinforcement. $\vec{p}_A$ and $\vec{p}_B$ are two bias vectors, with $0 < \gamma_1, \gamma_2 < 1$ as the damping factors. $\vec{p}_A = \left[\frac{1}{n}\right]_{n\times 1}$, where n is the order of M_{AA}. $\vec{p}_B$ is defined in the same way. We will further define the affinity matrices in section 3.2 later. With the above reinforcement ranking equation, it is also true that

1. A sentence in S^B correlates to many new sentences in S^B is supposed to receive a high ranking from R_B, and
2. A sentence in S^B correlates to many old sentences in S^A is supposed to receive a low ranking from R_B.

Let $R = [R_A \ R_B]^T$ and $\vec{p} = [\gamma_1 \cdot \vec{p}_A \ \gamma_2 \cdot \vec{p}_B]^T$, then the above iterative equation (1) corresponds to the linear system,

$$(I - M) \cdot R = \vec{p} \quad (2)$$

where, $M = \begin{bmatrix} \alpha_1 M_{AA} & \beta_1 M_{AB} \\ \beta_2 M_{BA} & \alpha_2 M_{BB} \end{bmatrix}$.

Up to now, the PNR^2 is still query-independent. That means only the content of the sentences is considered. However, for the tasks of query-oriented summarization, the reinforcement should obviously bias to the user's query. In this work, we integrate query information into PNR^2 by defining the vector $\vec{p}$ as $\vec{p}_i = rel(s_i \mid q)$, where $rel(s_i \mid q)$ denotes the relevance of the sentence s_i to the query q.

To guarantee the solution of the linear system Equation (2), we make the following two transformations on M. First M is normalized by columns. If all the elements in a column are zero, we replace zero elements with $1/n$ (n is the total number of the elements in that column). Second, M is multiplied by a decay factor θ ($0<\theta<1$), such that each element in M is scaled down but the meaning of M will not be changed.

Finally, Equation (2) is rewritten as,

$$(I - \theta \cdot M) \cdot R = \vec{p} \quad (3)$$

The matrix $(I - \theta \cdot M)$ is a strictly diagonally dominant matrix now, and the solution of the linear system Equation (3) exists.

3.2 Sentence Ranking based on PNR^2

We use the above mentioned PNR^2 framework to rank the sentences in both S^A and S^B simultaneously. Section 3.2 defines the affinity matrices and presents the ranking algorithm.

The affinity (i.e. similarity) between two sentences is measured by the cosine similarity of the corresponding two word vectors, i.e.

$$M[i, j] = sim(s_i, s_j) \quad (4)$$

where $sim(s_i, s_j) = \frac{\vec{s}_i \bullet \vec{s}_j}{\|\vec{s}_i\| \cdot \|\vec{s}_j\|}$. However, when calculating the affinity matrices M_{AA} and M_{BB}, the similarity of a sentence to itself is defined as 0, i.e.

$$M[i, j] = \begin{cases} sim(s_i, s_j) & i \neq j \\ 0 & i = j \end{cases} \quad (5)$$

Furthermore, the relevance of a sentence to the query q is defined as

$$rel(s_i, q) = \frac{\vec{s}_i \bullet \vec{q}}{\|\vec{s}_i\| * \|\vec{q}\|} \quad (6)$$

Algorithm 1. RankSentence(S^A, S^B, q)
Input: The old sentence set S^A, the new sentence set S^B, and the query q.
Output: The ranking vectors R of S^A and S^B.
1: Construct the affinity matrices, and set the weight matrix W;
2: Construct the matrix $A = (I - \theta \cdot M)$.
3: Choose (randomly) the initial non-negative vectors $R^{(0)} = [1 \cdots 1]^T$;
4: $k \leftarrow 0$, $\nabla \leftarrow 0$;
5: **Repeat**
6: $R_i^{(k+1)} = \frac{1}{a_{ij}} \left(\vec{p}_i - \sum_{j<i} a_{ij} R_j^{(k+1)} - \sum_{j>i} a_{ij} R_j^{(k)}\right)$;
7: $\nabla \leftarrow \max\left(\left\|R^{(k+1)} - R^{(k)}\right\|\right)$;
8: $R^{(k+1)}$ is normalized such that the maximal element in $R^{(k+1)}$ is 1.

```
    k ← k + 1;
Until ∇ < ζ[1];
R ← R^(k);
Return.
```

Now, we are ready to adopt the Gauss-Seidel method to solve the linear system Equation (3), and an iterative algorithm is developed to rank the sentences in S^A and S^B.

After sentence ranking, the sentences in S^B with higher ranking will be considered to be included in the final summary.

3.3 Sentence Selection by Removing Redundancy

When multiple documents are summarized, the problem of information redundancy is more severe than it is in single document summarization. Redundancy removal is a must. Since our focus is designing effective sentence ranking approach, we apply the following simple sentence selection algorithm.

Algorithm 2. GenerateSummary(S, length)

Input: sentence collection S (ranked in descending order of significance) and *length* (the given summary length limitation)
Output: The generated summary Π

$\Pi \leftarrow \{\}$;
$l \leftarrow length$;
For $i \leftarrow 0$ to $|S|$ **do**
  $threshold \leftarrow \max(sim(s_i, s) \mid s \in \Pi)$;
  If $threshold <= 0.9$[2] **do**
    $\Pi \leftarrow \Pi \cup s_i$;
    $l \leftarrow l - len(s_i)$;
    If ($l <= 0$) **break**;
  End
End
Return Π.

4 Experimental Studies

4.1 Data Set and Evaluation Metrics

The experiments are set up on the DUC 2007 update pilot task data set. Each collection of documents is accompanied with a query description representing a user's information need. We simply focus on generating a summary for the document collection "B" given that the user has read the document collection "A", which is a typical update summarization task.

Table 1 below shows the basic statistics of the DUC 2007 update data set. Stop-words in both documents and queries are removed[3] and the remaining words are stemmed by Porter Stemmer[4]. According to the task definition, system-generated summaries are strictly limited to 100 English words in length. We incrementally add into a summary the highest ranked sentence of concern if it doesn't significantly repeat the information already included in the summary until the word limitation is reached.

	A	B
Average number of documents	10	10
Average number of sentences	237.6	177.3

Table 1. Basic Statistics of DUC2007 Update Data Set

As for the evaluation metric, it is difficult to come up with a universally accepted method that can measure the quality of machine-generated summaries accurately and effectively. Many literatures have addressed different methods for automatic evaluations other than human judges. Among them, ROUGE[5] (Lin and Hovy, 2003) is supposed to produce the most reliable scores in correspondence with human evaluations. Given the fact that judgments by humans are time-consuming and labor-intensive, and more important, ROUGE has been officially adopted for the DUC evaluations since 2005, like the other researchers, we also choose it as the evaluation criteria.

In the following experiments, the sentences and the queries are all represented as the vectors of words. The relevance of a sentence to the query is calculated by cosine similarity. Notice that the word weights are normally measured by the document-level TF*IDF scheme in conventional vector space models. However, we believe that it is more reasonable to use the sentence-level inverse sentence frequency (ISF) rather than document-level IDF when dealing with sentence-level text processing. This has been verified in our early study.

4.2 Comparison of Positive and Negative Reinforcement Ranking Strategy

The aim of the following experiments is to investigate the different reinforcement ranking strategies. Three algorithms (i.e. PR(B),

[1] ζ is a pre-defined small real number as the convergence threshold.
[2] In fact, this is a tunable parameter in the algorithm. We use the value of 0.9 by our intuition.

[3] A list of 199 words is used to filter stop-words.
[4] http://www.tartarus.org/~martin/PorterStemmer.
[5] ROUGE version 1.5.5 is used.

PR(A+B), PR(A+B/A)) are implemented as reference. These algorithms are all based on the query-sensitive LexRank (OtterBacher et al., 2005). The differences are two-fold: (1) the document collection(s) used to build the text graph are different; and (2) after ranking, the sentence selection strategies are different. In particular, PR(B) only uses the sentences in "B" to build the graph, and the other two consider the sentences in both "A" and in "B". Only the sentences in "B" are considered to be selected in PR(B) and PR(A+B/A), but all the sentences in "A" and "B" have the same chance to be selected in PR(A+B). Only the sentences from B are considered to be selected in the final summaries in PNR^2 as well. In the following experiments, the damping factor is set to 0.85 in the first three algorithms as the same in PageRank. The weight matrix W is set to $\begin{bmatrix} 1 & -0.5 \\ -0.5 & 1 \end{bmatrix}$ in the proposed algorithm (i.e. PNR^2) and $\gamma_1 = \gamma_2 = 0.5$. We have obtained reasonable good results with the decay factor θ between 0.3 and 0.8. So we set it to 0.5 in this paper.

Notice that the three PageRank-like graph-based ranking algorithms can be viewed as only the positive reinforcement among the sentences is considered, while both positive and negative reinforcement are considered in PNR^2 as mentioned before. Table 2 below shows the results of recall scores of ROUGE-1, ROUGE-2 and ROUGE-SU4 along with their 95% confidential internals within square brackets.

	ROUGE -1	ROUGE -2	ROUGE-SU4
PR(B)	0.3323 [0.3164,0.3501]	0.0814 [0.0670,0.0959]	0.1165 0.1053,0.1286]
PR(A+B)	0.3059 [0.2841,0.3256]	0.0746 [0.0613,0.0893]	0.1064 [0.0938,0.1186]
PR(A+B/A)	0.3376 [0.3186,0.3572]	0.0865 [0.0724,0.1007]	0.1222 [0.1104,0.1304]
PNR^2	**0.3616** [0.3464,0.3756]	**0.0895** [0.0810,0.0987]	**0.1291** [0.1208,0.1384]

Table 2. Experiment Results

We come to the following three conclusions. First, it is not surprising that PR(B) and PR(A+B/A) outperform PR(A+B), because the update task obviously prefers the sentences from the new documents (i.e. "B"). Second, PR(A+B/A) outperforms PR(B) because the sentences in "A" can provide useful information in ranking the sentences in "B", although we do not select the sentences ranked high in "A". Third, PNR^2 achieves the best performance. PNR^2 is above PR(A+B/A) by 7.11% of ROUGE-1, 3.47% of ROUGE-2, and 5.65% of ROUGE-SU4. This result confirms the idea and algorithm proposed in this work.

4.3 Comparison with DUC 2007 Systems

Twenty-four systems have been submitted to the DUC for evaluation in the 2007 update task. Table 3 compares our PNR^2 with them. For reference, we present the following representative ROUGE results of (1) the best and worst participating system performance, and (2) the average ROUGE scores (i.e. AVG). We can then easily locate the positions of the proposed models among them.

	PNR^2	**Mean**	**Best / Worst**
ROUGE-1	**0.3616**	0.3262	0.3768/0.2621
ROUGE2	**0.0895**	0.0745	0.1117/0.0365
ROUGE-SU4	**0.1291**	0.1128	0.1430/0.0745

Table 3. System Comparison

4.4 Discussion

In this work, we use the sentences in the same sentence set for positive reinforcement and sentences in the different set for negative reinforcement. Precisely, the old sentences perform negative reinforcement over the new sentences while the new sentences perform positive reinforcement over each other. This is reasonable although we may have a more comprehensive alternation. Old sentences may express old topics, but they may also express emerging new topics. Similarly, new sentences are supposed to express new topics, but they may also express the continuation of old topics. As a result, it will be more comprehensive to classify the whole sentences (both new sentences and old sentences together) into two categories, i.e. old topics oriented sentences and new topic oriented sentences, and then to apply these two sentence sets in the PNR^2 framework. This will be further studied in our future work.

Moreover, in the update summarization task, the summary length is restricted to about 100 words. In this situation, we find that sentence simplification is even more important in our investigations. We will also work on this issue in our forthcoming studies.

5 Conclusion

In this paper, we propose a novel sentence ranking algorithm, namely PNR^2, for update summarization. As our pilot study, we simply assume to receive two chronologically ordered document collections and evaluate the summaries generated for the collection given later. With PNR^2, sentences from the new (i.e. late) document collection perform positive reinforcement among each other but they receive negative reinforcement from the sentences in the old (i.e. early) document collection. Positive and negative reinforcement are concerned simultaneously in the ranking process. As a result, PNR^2 favors the sentences biased to the sentences that are important in the new collection and meanwhile novel to the sentences in the old collection. As a matter of fact, this positive and negative ranking scheme is general enough and can be used in many other situations, such as social network analysis etc.

Acknowledgements

The research work presented in this paper was partially supported by the grants from RGC of HKSAR (Project No: PolyU5217/07E), NSF of China (Project No: 60703008) and the Hong Kong Polytechnic University (Project No: A-PA6L).

References

Klaus Berberich, Michalis Vazirgiannis, and Gerhard Weikum. 2004. G.T-Rank: Time-Aware Authority Ranking. In Algorithms and Models for the Web-Graph: Third International Workshop, WAW, pp 131-141.

Klaus Berberich, Michalis Vazirgiannis, and Gerhard Weikum. 2005. Time-Aware Authority Ranking. Journal of Internet Mathematics, 2(3): 301-332.

Klaus Lorenz Berberich. 2004. Time-aware and Trend-based Authority Ranking. Master Thesis, Saarlandes University, Germany.

Sergey Brin and Lawrence Page. 1998. The Anatomy of a Large-scale Hypertextual Web Search Engine. Computer Networks and ISDN Systems, 30(1-7):107-117.

Gunes Erkan and Dragomir R. Radev. 2004a. LexPageRank: Prestige in Multi-Document Text Summarization, in Proceedings of EMNLP, pp365-371.

Gunes Erkan and Dragomir R. Radev. 2004b. LexRank: Graph-based Centrality as Salience in Text Summarization, Journal of Artificial Intelligence Research 22:457-479.

Jon M. Kleinberg. 1999. Authoritative Sources in Hyperlinked Environment, Journal of the ACM, 46(5):604-632.

Jure Leskovec, Marko Grobelnik and Natasa Milic-Frayling. 2004. Learning Sub-structures of Document Semantic Graphs for Document Summarization, in Proceedings of LinkKDD Workshop, pp133-138.

Wenjie Li, Mingli Wu, Qin Lu, Wei Xu and Chunfa Yuan. 2006. Extractive Summarization using Intra- and Inter-Event Relevance, in Proceedings of ACL/COLING, pp369-376.

Chin-Yew Lin and Eduard Hovy. 2003. Automatic Evaluation of Summaries Using N-gram Co-occurrence Statistics, in Proceedings of HLT-NAACL, pp71-78.

Ziheng Lin, Tat-Seng Chua, Min-Yen Kan, Wee Sun Lee, Long Qiu, and Shiren Ye. 2007. NUS at DUC 2007: Using Evolutionary Models for Text. In Proceedings of Document Understanding Conference (DUC) 2007.

Rada Mihalcea and Paul Tarau. 2004. TextRank - Bringing Order into Text, in Proceedings of EMNLP, pp404-411.

Rada Mihalcea. 2004. Graph-based Ranking Algorithms for Sentence Extraction, Applied to Text Summarization, in Proceedings of ACL (Companion Volume).

Jahna OtterBacher, Gunes Erkan, Dragomir R. Radev. 2005. Using Random Walks for Question-focused Sentence Retrieval, in Proceedings of HLT/EMNLP, pp915-922.

Lucy Vanderwende, Michele Banko and Arul Menezes. 2004. Event-Centric Summary Generation, in Working Notes of DUC 2004.

Xiaojun Wan, Jianwu Yang and Jianguo Xiao. 2006. Using Cross-Document Random Walks for Topic-Focused Multi-Document Summarization, in Proceedings of the 2006 IEEE/WIC/ACM International Conference on Web Intelligence, pp1012-1018.

Xiaojun Wan. 2007. TimedTextRank: Adding the Temporal Dimension to Multi-document Summarization. In Proceedings of 30th ACM SIGIR, pp 867-868.

Lei Yang, Lei Qi, Yan-Ping Zhao, Bin Gao, and Tie-Yan Liu. 2007. Link Analysis using Time Series of Web Graphs. In Proceedings of CIKM'07.

Masaharu Yoshioka and Makoto Haraguchi. 2004. Multiple News Articles Summarization based on Event Reference Information, in Working Notes of NTCIR-4.

Philip S. Yu, Xin Li, and Bing Liu. 2004. On the Temporal Dimension of Search. In Proceedings of the 13th International World Wide Web Conference on Alternate Track Papers and Posters, pp 448-449.

Philip S. Yu, Xin Li, and Bing Liu. 2005. Adding the Temporal Dimension to Search – A Case Study in Publication Search. In Proceedings of the 2005 IEEE/WIC/ACM International Conference on Web Intelligence.

Understanding and Summarizing Answers in Community-Based Question Answering Services

Yuanjie Liu[1], Shasha Li[2], Yunbo Cao[1,3], Chin-Yew Lin[3], Dingyi Han[1], Yong Yu[1]

[1]Shanghai Jiao Tong University, Shanghai, China, 200240 {lyjgeorge,handy,yyu}@apex.sjtu.edu.cn

[2]National University of Defense Technology, Changsha, China, 410074 Shashali@nudt.edu.cn

[3]Microsoft Research Asia, Beijing, China, 100080 {yunbo.cao,cyl}@microsoft.com

Abstract

Community-based question answering (cQA) services have accumulated millions of questions and their answers over time. In the process of accumulation, cQA services assume that questions always have unique *best answers*. However, with an in-depth analysis of questions and answers on cQA services, we find that the assumption cannot be true. According to the analysis, at least 78% of the cQA best answers are reusable when similar questions are asked again, but no more than 48% of them are indeed the unique *best answers*. We conduct the analysis by *proposing taxonomies for cQA questions and answers*. To better reuse the cQA content, we also *propose applying automatic summarization techniques to summarize answers*. Our results show that question-type oriented summarization techniques can improve cQA answer quality significantly.

1 Introduction

Community-based question and answering (cQA) service is becoming a popular type of search related activity. Major search engines around the world have rolled out their own versions of cQA service. Yahoo! Answers, Baidu Zhidao, and Naver Ji-Sik-In[1] are some examples.

In general, a cQA service has the following workflow. First, a question is posted by the asker in a cQA service and then people in the community can answer the question. After enough number of answers are collected, a best answer can be chosen by the asker or voted by the community. The resulting question and answer archives are large knowledge repositories and can be used to complement online search. For example, Naver's Ji-Sik-In (Knowledge iN) has accumulated about 70 million entries[2].

In an ideal scenario, a search engine can serve similar questions or use best answers as search result snippets when similar queries are submitted. To support such applications, we have to assume the best answers from cQA services are good and relevant answers for their pairing questions. However, the assumption might not be true as exemplified by the following examples.

Question Title	Which actress has the most seductive voice?..could range from a giggly goldie hawn..to a sultry anne bancroft?
Question Description	or any other type of voice that you find alluring. ..
Best Answer (Polls & Surveys)	Fenella Fielding, wow!!!!
Best Answer (Movies)	i think joanna lumlley has a really sexy voice

Table 1. Same Question / Different Best Answers

Question Title	Does anyone know of any birthdays coming up soon?
Question Description	Celerities, people you know, you? Anyway I need the name and the date. If you want to know it is for my site, http://www.jessicaparke2.piczo.com... and that is not site advertising.
Answer	Novembers Are: Paul Dickov nov 1st Nelly (not furtado) nov 2nd ...
Best Answer	Check imdb.com, they have this celebrity birthdays listed.

Table 2. Question with Alternative Answers

Table 1 presents a question asking community opinions about "*who is the actress has the most seductive voice*". The asker posted the same question twice at different Yahoo! Answers categories: one in *Polls & Surveys* and one in *Movies*.

© 2008. Licensed under the *Creative Commons Attribution- Noncommercial-Share Alike 3.0 Unported* license (http://creativecommons.org/licenses/by-nc-sa/3.0/). Some rights reserved.

[1] Yahoo! Answers: answers.yahoo.com; Baidu Zhidao: zhidao.baidu.com; Naver Ji-Sik-In: kin.naver.com

[2]www.iht.com/articles/2007/07/04/technology/naver.php

Two different best answers were chosen by the same asker due to non-overlapping of answers. Table 2 shows another example, it asks about "*the coming birthdays of stars*". The best answer chosen by the asker is very good because it provides useful URL information where the asker can find her answers. However, other answers listed a variety of birthdays of stars that also answered the question. These two examples indicate that the conventional cQA policy of allowing askers or voters to choose best answers might be working fine with the purpose of cQA but it might not be a good one if we want to reuse these *best answers* without any post-processing.

To find out what might be the alternatives to the *best answers*, we first carried out an in-depth analysis of cQA data by *developing taxonomies for questions and answers*. Then we propose summarizing answers in a consideration of *question type*, as the alternative to the *best answers*. For example, for the '*actress voice*' question, a summary of different people's opinions ranked by popularity might be a better way for expressing the question's answers. Similar to the '*actress voice*' question, the '*celebrity birthday*' question does not have a fix set of answers but is different from the '*actress voice*' question that its answers are facts not opinions. For fact-based open ended questions, combining different answers will be useful for reuse of those answers.

The rest of this paper is arranged as follows. We review related work in Section 2. We develop a framework for answer type taxonomy in Section 3 and a cQA question taxonomy in Section 4. Section 5 presents methods to summarize cQA answers. Finally, we conclude this paper and discuss future work in Section 6.

2 Related Work

Previous research on cQA (community-based Question and Answering) domain focused on three major areas: (1) how to find similar questions given a new question (Jeon et al. 2005a; Jeon et al., 2005b), (2) how to find experts given a community network(Liu et al., 2005; Jurczyk & Agichtein, 2007), and (3) how to measure answer quality and its effect on question retrieval. The third area of focus is the most relevant to our research. Jeon et al. (2006)'s work on assessing cQA answer quality is one typical example. They found that about 1/3 of the answers among the 1,700 Q&A pairs from Naver.com cQA data have quality problems and approximately 1/10 of them have bad answers[3]. They used 13 non-textual features and trained a maximum entropy model to predict answer quality. They showed that retrieval relevance was significantly improved when answer quality measure was integrated in a log likelihood retrieval model.

As mentioned in Section 1, cQA services provide an alternative way for users to find information online. Questions posted on cQA sites should reflect users' needs as queries submitted to search engines do. Broder (2002) proposed that search queries can be classified into three categories, i.e. *navigational, informational,* and *transactional*. Ross and Levinson (2004) suggested a more elaborated taxonomy with five more subcategories for informational queries and four more subcategories for resource (transactional) queries. In open-domain question answering research that automatic systems are required to extract exact answers from a text database given a set of factoid questions (Voorhees and M. Ellen, 2003), all top performing systems had incorporated question taxonomies (Hovy et al., 2001; Moldovan et al., 2000; Lytinen et al., 2002; Jijkoun et al., 2005). Based on the past experiences from the annual NIST TREC Question and Answering Track[4] (TREC QA Track), an international forum dedicating to evaluate and compare different open-domain question answering systems, we conjecture that a cQA question taxonomy would help us determine what type of best answer is expected given a question type.

Automatic summarization of cQA answers is one of the main focuses of this paper. We propose that summarization techniques (Hovy and Lin, 1999; Lin and Hovy, 2002) can be used to create cQA answer summaries for different question types. Creating an answer summary given a question and its answers can be seen as a multi-document summarization task. We simply replace documents with answers and apply these techniques to generate the answer summary. The task has been one of the main tasks the Document Understanding Conference[5] since 2004.

3 A Framework for Answer Type

To study how to exploit the best answers of cQA, we need to first analyze cQA answers. We would like to know whether the existing best answer of a specific question is good for reuse. If not, we

[3] Answers in Jeon el al.'s work were rated in three levels: good, medium, and bad.
[4] http://trec.nist.gov/data/qamain.html
[5] http://duc.nist.gov

want to understand why and what the alternatives are. We will refer to the 'best answers' selected by cQA askers or voters as BA henceforth to differentiate it with best answers annotated or automatically generated in our experiments.

We made use of questions from Yahoo! Answers for developing and testing our framework for answer type. There are over 1,000 hierarchical categories in Yahoo! Answers. By manually examining 400 randomly selected questions from the 4 most popular top Yahoo! Answers categories (100 questions from each category) – *Entertainment & Music (E&M)*, *Society & Culture (S&C)*, *Health*, and *Computers & Internet (C&I)*, we developed a cQA answer type taxonomy based on *the principle of BA reusability* that determines a BA's answer type based on "*if the BA can be reused or not when a question that is similar to the BA's question is asked again*".

One of the authors carried out this manual exercise and developed the initial answer taxonomy. The taxonomy was then modified through discussions among the authors. We asked three annotators to do the annotation. We assigned the category label that was agreed by at least two annotators. If none of the three annotators agreed on a single category label, one of the authors made the final decision. The answer type taxonomy is described in this section and we discuss the question type and the relation with answer taxonomy in next section.

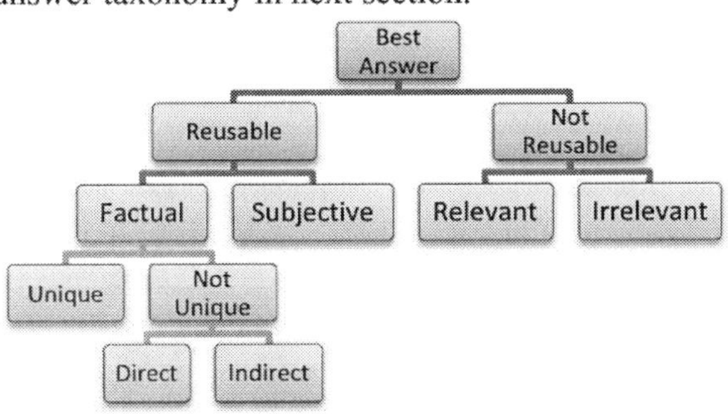

Figure 1. cQA Services BA Type Taxonomy.

Figure 1 shows the resulting answer type taxonomy. It first divides BA into two categories: *Reusable* and *Not Reusable*. A *Reusable* BA means that it can be reused as the best answer if a similar question to its question is asked again; while a *Not Reusable* BA means it cannot be reused. The *Reusable* BA is further divided into *Factual* and *Subjective*. A *Factual* BA is a fact that can be used as the best answer; while a *Subjective* BA is one of the opinions that can be used as the best answer.

The *Factual* BA type has two subtypes: *Unique* and *Not Unique*. A *Unique* BA has only a unique best answer to its question and no other answer add more information; while a *Not Unique* BA has other alternative best answers. The *Not Unique* BA type is divided into two subtypes: *Direct* and *Indirect*. A *Direct* BA answers its question directly; while an *Indirect* BA answers its question through inference. For example, the question mentioned in section 1 has the *Indirect* BA which gives a website reference, while there is also a *Direct* answer just gives the birthday lists.

A *Subjective* BA answers questions that look for opinions or recommendations. For example, a question asked "Which is the best sci-fi movie?" Each answerer would have his own idea.

The *Not Reusable* BA has two subtypes: *Relevant* and *Irrelevant*. A *Relevant* BA could not be used as a best answer to its question but it is relevant to its question, for example, a question asked "*Why was "I Can't Hate You Anymore" by Nick Lachey so shortlived?*" A *Relevant* BA said "*I'm not sure where you live, but in NJ, especially South Jersey, that song was played out...*", this answer is relevant but without knowing the asker's location which does not really answer the question; an *Irrelevant* BA could not be used as a best answer to its question and it is irrelevant to its question. The BA "*It appears that the question period has expired. If an answer has been given that meets your needs, please pick a 'best answer'.*" of the question "*how to forward an email without showing the email addresses in the To box*" is in this case.

Answer Type	C&I	E&M	Health	S&C
Unique	47%	28%	48%	13%
Direct	28%	7%	30%	18%
Indirect	9%	3%	5%	2%
Factual Total	**84%**	**38%**	**83%**	**33%**
Subjective	4%	40%	7%	50%
Reusable Total	**88%**	**78%**	**90%**	**83%**
Relevant	3%	1%	1%	0%
Irrelevant	9%	21%	9%	17%
Not Reusable Total	**12%**	**22%**	**10%**	**17%**

Table 3. Distribution of Answer Type

Table 3 shows the distribution of Answer types on four categories. Unique answers are no more than 48%. The C&I and the Health categories tend to have more factual BAs than other two categories.

Among the four categories, S&C answers are mostly not unique and have a high percentage (50%) of subjective answers. This indicates that the one BA per cQA question chosen by its asker or voters is not good enough for reuse as the best answer. However, we might be able to apply automatic summarization techniques to create summarized answers for at least half of reusable (but not unique) answers. We provide some possible solutions in Section 5.

Category	Percentage
Computer & Internet	18%
Entertainment & Music	17%
Health	21%
Society & Culture	20%

Table 4. Disagreement on Answer Type

Table 4 shows the percentage of questions over which none of the three annotators agreed on a single category label. The results show that the question taxonomy developed above is pretty stable (over at least 79% questions).

4 A CQA Question Taxonomy

As we were developing our answer type taxonomy, we often could not solely rely on answers themselves and had to consider their questions as well. As we discussed in Section 2, the type of question would help us determine the expected best answer types.

Rose and Levinson's (2004) taxonomy of search engine queries has similar goal to ours though their taxonomy was developed to classify search engine queries. Instead of starting from scratch, we followed the basic hierarchy of R&L's taxonomy and made some modifications to accommodate the particular of cQA services.

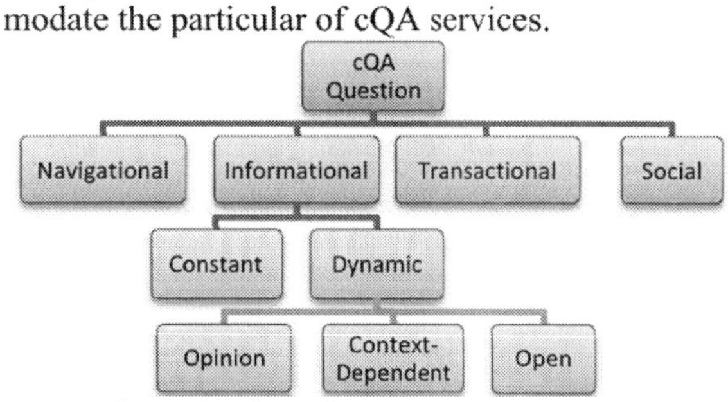

Figure 2. Question Type Taxonomy

Figure 2 shows the resulting question taxonomy. We retain Broder's taxonomy at top levels and propose a new *Social* category. *Navigational*, *Informational* and *Transactional* are defined similar as in Broder's taxonomy while *Social* category consists of questions that do not intend to get an answer but just were used to elicit interaction with people in cQA services.

Navigational category contains questions seeking URLs of specific websites that the asker would like to visit, for example, "*Does anybody know the fan sites of Hannah Montana?*"

Transactional category contains questions tend to get resources. A typical one is "*Is there a computer program that lets you create a planet?*"

For *Information* category, we first divide it into two subcategories: *Constant* and *Dynamic*. *Constant* questions have a fixed or stable set of answers while *dynamic* questions do not. This dichotomy of informational category is to support our intention to establish intuitive mapping between the question taxonomy and the answer taxonomy. *Constant* question type is similar to R&L's closed query type. An example constant question is "*Which country has the largest population?*" but "*What is the population of China?*" would be a dynamic question.

For *Dynamic* category, we define three subcategories: *Opinion*, *Context-Dependent* and *Open*. *Opinion* questions are those asking for opinions. Questions in this category seek opinions from people in cQA communities about what they think of some people, some events, or some objects. "*Is Microsoft Vista worth it?*" is an example. *Context-dependent* questions are those questions having different answers according to the different context. For example, the question "*What is the population of China?*" should have different answers according to the different date. *Open* category contains questions asking for some facts or methods. The questions usually have a variety of answers or their answer themselves may have unconstrained depth. The question "*Can you list some birthdays of stars in the coming week?*" is an example. This essentially follows R&L's open query category. It also includes what is not covered by the opinion and context-dependent categories.

The new *Social* category is specific to cQA services. Questions in this category do not intend to get an answer. These questions include telling jokes and expressing askers' own ideas. Essentially, askers treat cQA service as chatting rooms or online forums. The question "*Why do so many lazy people come on here simply just to ask...?*" together with the question description "*how to become a hacker? It really isn't that hard to do a google search...hopefully some of the people that will continue to ask, will click the link below so they can give up faster...* " actually is expressing a negative sentiment towards a number of people who asked how to become a hacker.

Table 5 shows the distribution of different question types on 4 different Yahoo! Answers categories. We observe that constant questions only occupy 11% ~ 20% while navigational questions are even fewer such that they do not occur in the sample questions. This is reasonable since people very likely would be able to use search engines to discover answers of navigational and constant questions. They do not have to ask these types of question on community-based question answering services. On the contrary, open and opinion questions are frequently asked, it ranges from 56%~83%.

Question Type	C&I	E&M	Health	S&C
Navigational Total	**0%**	**0%**	**0%**	**0%**
Constant	15%	20%	15%	11%
Opinion	8%	37%	16%	60%
Context Dependent	0%	1%	1%	0%
Open	59%	19%	67%	18%
Dynamic Total	**67%**	**57%**	**84%**	**78%**
Informational Total	**82%**	**77%**	**99%**	**89%**
Transactional Total	**14%**	**8%**	**0%**	**1%**
Social Total	**4%**	**15%**	**1%**	**10%**

Table 5 Distribution of Question Type

Intersection Number	UNI	DIR	IND	SUB	REL	IRR
Navigational	0	0	0	0	0	0
Constant	**48**	9	3	0	1	0
Open	**51**	**62**	13	15	5	17
Context-dep	0	0	1	0	0	1
Opinion	15	13	1	**84**	0	8
Transactional	**10**	7	4	1	0	1
Social	0	0	0	1	0	**29**

Table 6. Question Answer Correlation

Table 6 (UNI: *unique*, DIR: *direct*, IND: *indirect*, SUB: *subjective*, REL: *relevant*, IRR: *irrelevant*) gives the correlation statistics of question type vs. answer type. There exists a strong correlation between question type and answer type. Every question type tends to be associated with only one or two answer types (bold numbers in Table 6).

5 Question-Type Oriented Answer Summarization

Since the BAs for at least half of questions do not cover all useful information of other answers, it is better to adopt post-processing techniques such as answer summarization for better reuse of the BAs. As observed in the previous sections, answer types can be basically predicted by question type. Thus, in this section, we propose to use multi-document summarization (MDS) techniques for summarizing answers according to question type. Here we assume that question type can be determined automatically. In the following sub-sections, we will focus on the summarization of answers to *open* or *opinion* questions as they occupy more than half of the cQA questions.

5.1 Open Questions

Algorithm: For *open* questions, we follow typical MDS procedure: topic identification, interpretation & fusion, and then summary generation (Hovy and Lin, 1999; Lin and Hovy, 2002). Table 7 describes the algorithm.

1. Employ the clustering algorithm on answers
2. Extract the noun phrases in each cluster, using a shallow parser.[6]
3. For each cluster and each label (or noun phrase), calculate the score by using the Relevance Scoring Function:

$$\sum_{w} p(w|\theta)PMI(w, l|C) - D(\theta|C)$$

Where θ is the cluster, w is the word, l is the label or noun phrase, C is the background context which is composed of 5,000 questions in the same category, $p(\cdot)$ is conditional probability, $PMI(\cdot)$ is pointwise mutual information, and $D(\cdot)$ is KL-divergence

4. Extract the key answer which contains the noun phrase that has the highest score in each cluster
5. Rank these key answers by cluster size and present the results.

Table 7. Summarization Algorithm(Open-Type)

In the first step, we use a bottom-up approach for clustering answers to do topic identification. Initially, each answer forms a cluster. Then we combine the most similar two clusters as a new cluster if their similarity is higher than a threshold. This process is repeated until no new clusters can be formed. For computing similarities, we regard the highest cosine similarity of two sentences from two different clusters as the similarity of the two clusters. Then we extract salient noun phrases, i.e. cluster labels, from each cluster using the first-order relevance scoring function proposed by Mei et al. (2007), (step 2,3 in Table 7). In the fusion phase (step 4), these phrases are then used to rank answers within their cluster. Finally in the generation phase (step 5), we present the summarized answer by extracting the most important answer in every cluster and sort them according to the cluster size where they come from.

Case Example: Table 8 presents an example of summarization results of open-type questions. The question asks how to change Windows XP desktop to Mac style. There are many softwares providing such functionalities. The BA only lists one choice – the StarDock products, while other answers suggest Flyakite and LiteStep. The automatic summarized answer (ASA) contains a variety of for turning Windows XP desktop into Mac style with their names highlighted as cluster labels. Compared with manually-summarized answer (MSA), ASA contains most information of MSA while retains similar length with BA and MSA.

5.2 Opinion Questions

Algorithm: For *opinion* questions, a comprehensive investigation of this topic would be beyond the scope of this paper since this is still a field

[6] http://opennlp.sourceforge.net

Question
(http://answers.yahoo.com/question/?qid=1005120801427)
What is the best way to make XP look like Mac osX?
Best Answer Chosen
I found the best way to do this is to use WindowsBlinds. A program that, if you use the total StarDock, package will allow you to add the ObjectBar in addition to changed the toolbars to be OS X stylized. If you want added functionality you can download programs off the internet that will mimic the Expose feature which will show you a tiled set of all open windows. Programs that will do this include: WinPlosion, Windows Exposer, and Top Desk
Auto-summarized Answer
LiteStep: An additional option is LiteStep - a "Shell Replacement" for Windows that has a variety of themes you can install. Undoubtedly there are various Mac OSX themes avaialable for LiteStep. I have included a source to a max osx theme for Litestep at customize.org. **Flyakite:**Flyakite is a transformation pack and the most comprehensive in terms of converting an XP system's look to that of an OS X system, google it up and you should find it, v3 seems to be in development and should be out soon. **Window Blinds:**http://www.stardock.com/products/windowb...
Manually-summarized Answer
One way is to use WindowsBlinds. The package will allow you to add the ObjectBar for changing to the OSX theme. You can also make added functionality of Expose feature by downloading the programs like WinPlosion, Windows Exposer and Top Desk. The URL of it is http://www.stardock.com/products/windowblinds/. Another option is to use Flyakite which is a transformation pack. The third Option is the LiteStep, it is a "Shell Replacement" for windows that has a variety of Mac OSX tehmes you can install. The url is http://litestep.net and I have included a source of Mac OS theme for Litestep at http://www.customize.org/details/33409.

Table 8. Summary of Open-Question

under active development (Wiebe et al., 2003; Kim and Hovy, 2004). We build a simple yet novel opinion-focused answer summarizer which provides a global view of all answers. We divide opinion questions into two subcategories. One is *sentiment*-oriented question that asks the sentiment about something, for example, "*what do you think of ...*". The other is *list*-oriented question that intends to get a list of answers and see what item is the most popular.

For sentiment-oriented questions, askers care about how many people support or against something. We use an opinion word dictionary[7], a cue phrase list, a simple voting strategy, and some heuristic rules to classify the sentences into *Support*, *Neutral*, or *Against* category and use the overall attitude with key sentences to build summarization. For list-oriented questions, a simple counting algorithm that tallies different answers of questions together with their supporting votes would be good answer summaries. Details of the algorithm are shown in Table 9, 10.

Case Example: Table 11 presents the summarization result of an sentiment-oriented question, it asks "whether it is strange for a 16-year child to talk to a teddy bear?", the BA is a negative response. However, if we consider all answers, we find that half of the answers agree but another half of them disagree. The distribution of different sentiments is similar as MSA. Table 12 shows the summarization result of a list-oriented question, the question asks "*what is the best sci-fi movie?*" The BA just gives one choice "Independence day" while the summarized answer gives a list of best sci-fi movies with the number of supporting vote. Though it is not complete compared with MSA, it contains most of the options which has highest votes among all answers.

1. Employ the same cluster procedure of Open-Type question.
2. If an answer begins with negative cue phrase (e.g. "*No, it isn't*" etc.), it is annotated as *Against*. If a response begins with positive cue phrase (e.g. "*Yes, it is*" etc.), it is annotated as *Support*.
3. For a clause, if number of positive sentiment word is larger than negative sentiment word, the sentiment of the clause is *Positive*. Otherwise, the sentiment of the clause is *Negative*.
4. If there are negative indicators such as "*don't/never/...*" in front of the clause, the sentiment should be reversed.
5. If number of negative clauses is larger than number of positive clauses, the sentiment of the answer is *Negative*. Otherwise, the sentiment of the answer is *Positive*.
6. Denote the sentiment value of question as s(q), the sentiment value of an answer as s(a), and then the final sentiment of the answer is logical AND of s(q) and s(a)
7. Present key sentiments with attitude label

Table 9. Summarization Algorithm (Sentiment-Opinion)

1. Segment the answers into sentences
2. Cluster sentences by using similar process in open-type
3. For each cluster, choose the key sentence based on mutual information between itself and other sentences within the cluster
4. Rank the key sentences by the cluster size and present them ogether with votes

Table 10. Summarization Algorithm (List-Opinion)

Question (http://answers.yahoo.com/question/?qid=1006050125145)
I am 16 and i stil talk to my erm..teddy bear..am i wierd???
Best Answer Chosen
not at all i'm 14 and i too do that
Auto-summarized Answer
Support **A:** It's might be a little uncommon for a 16 year old to talk to a teddy bear but there would be a serious problem if you told me that your teddy bear answered back as you talked to him!!:) **A:** I slept with my teddy bear until I graduated. Can't say that I ever had a conversation with him, but if I had I'm sure he would've been a very good listener. **Against** **A:** i talk to a seed im growing .. its not weird .... :) **A:** No, you're not weird.....you're Pratheek! :D **A:** no, i like to hold on to my old memories too. i do it sometimes too. **A:** It will get weird when he starts to answer back! **A:** not really. it depends how you talk i mean not if you talk to it like its a little kid like my brother does. Overall Attitude: **Support 5 / Neutral 1 / Against 5**
Manually-summarized Answer
support (vote 4) **neutral** (vote 2) **against** (vote 5) reasons: i like to hold on to my old memories too. (vote 1) I slept with my teddy bear until I graduated. (vote 1) i'm 14 and i too do that (vote 1)

Table 11. Summary of Sentiment-Opinion Question

[7] Inquirer dictionary http://www.wjh.harvard.edu/~inquirer.

Question (http://answers.yahoo.com/question/?qid=20060718083151AACYQJn)
What is the best sci-fi movie u ever saw?
Best Answer Chosen
Independance Day
Auto-summarized Answer
star wars (5) Blade Runner (3) fi movie has to be Night of the Lepus (2) But the best "B" sci (2) I liked Stargate it didn't scare me and I thought they did a great job recreating Egypt (3) Independance Day (3)
Manually-summarized Answer
Star Wars (vote 6); The Matrix (vote 3); Independence Day (vote 2); Blade Runner (vote 2); Starship Troopers (vote 2); Alien (vote 2); Alien v.s Predator (vote 1); MST3K (vote 1);

Table 12. Summary of List-Opinion Question

5.3 Experiments

Information Content: To evaluate the effectiveness of automatic summarization, we use the information content criterion for comparing ASA with BA. It focuses on whether ASA or BA contains more useful information to the question. Information point is used in the evaluation. Usually, one kind of solution for *open* questions or one kind of reason for *opinion* questions can contribute one information point. By summing all information points in both ASA and BA, we then can compare which one contains more information. Intuitively, longer texts would contain more information. Thus, when comparing the information content, we limit the length of ASA with several levels to do the evaluation. Take question in Table 8 as an example, the BA just gives one software, which contributes one information point while the ASA lists three kinds of software which contributes three information points. Thus, ASA is considered better than BA.

For each question, we generate 100%, 150%, and 200% BA word-length ASAs. Three annotators are asked to determine whether an ASA is better than, equal to, or worse than its corresponding BA in terms of information content. Voting strategy is used to determine the final label. If three labels are all different, it is labeled as Unknown. We extract 163 *open* questions and 121 *opinion* questions from all four categories by using final question category labels mentioned in Section 4. To make meaningful comparison, questions having unique answers or having only one answer are excluded. After the removal, there are 104 *open* questions and 99 *opinion* questions left for comparison. The results are shown in Table 13.

We are encouraged by the evaluation results that our automatic summarization methods generate better coverage of contents in most of the cases at every answer summary length. We observe a big difference between 100% and 150% answer summaries. It should not be a surprise since a 150% answer summary contains 50% more content than its corresponding BA. While at the 100% length, we still have about 30% ASAs better than BA. Questions which have better ASA than BA usually have a long BA but with little information. Table 14 provides the example. By using summarization, answers that are compact and direct to the question can be included. The results indicate that summary compression technique might be helpful to pack more information in short answers.

Open	ASA Better	BA Better	Equal	Unknown
100%	30%	12%	45%	13%
150%	55%	7%	28%	10%
200%	63%	4%	24%	9%
Opinion	**ASA Better**	**BA Better**	**Equal**	**Unknown**
100%	37%	20%	32%	11%
150%	44%	16%	30%	10%
200%	54%	16%	23%	7%

Table 13. Evaluation by Information Content

Q	Why wont japanese characters burn onto the DVD?
BA	man, the answers here are too stupid for hteir own.You are creating a DVD on Western Platform. I take it, you are using an OS that is in English?In order to "view" japanese as part of your filenames, you need your operating system to accept Japanese coding (characters).If you are using Windows, then you will need ot isntall the Japanese character Set for your operating system If you are using MacOS . i have no idea.
100% ASA	**The dvd writer** Probably because your burner, the DVD writer, doesn't support double bytes code, such as Japanese, Korean, and Chinese. Check the supporting language of your software. Or change all the file name in single byte code, like alphabets. man, the answers here are too stupid for hteir own. You are creating a DVD on Western Platform. I take it, you are using an OS that is in English?

Table 14. Examples of 100% ASA

Readability: Besides the information content, we would also like to study the readability of automatic summarized answers. 10 questions (each from *open* and *opinion* category) are extracted and we make both manual summarized answer (MSA) and automatic summarized answer (ASA) for comparison with BA. We used the information content (INFO) and readability (READ) criteria for evaluation. The readability is judged basically by the time for understanding. We make two kinds of comparison: ASA vs. BA and MSA vs. BA. The first one is used to judge whether the current summarization method is better than current cQA scenario. The second one is used as an expectation for how much the summarization methods can be better than BA.

For ASA vs. BA, the results in Table 15 show that all the annotators agree ASAs providing more information content but not being with satisfying readability. For MSA vs. BA, better results in readability can be achieved as Table 16. This suggests that the proposed approach can succeed as more sophisticated summarization techniques are developed.

Open	Annotator 1		Annotator 2		Annotator 3	
ASA	INFO	READ	INFO	READ	INFO	READ
Better	40%	10%	90%	10%	80%	0%
Equal	60%	60%	10%	80%	20%	60%
Worse	0%	30%	0%	10%	0%	40%
Opinion	**Annotator 1**		**Annotator 2**		**Annotator 3**	
ASA	INFO	READ	INFO	READ	INFO	READ
Better	90%	10%	90%	10%	70%	40%
Equal	10%	60%	10%	60%	10%	20%
Worse	0%	30%	0%	30%	20%	40%

Table 15. ASA vs. BA Evaluation

Open	Annotator 1		Annotator 2		Annotator 3	
MSA	INFO	READ	INFO	READ	INFO	READ
Better	100%	30%	100%	90%	100%	90%
Equal	0%	50%	0%	0%	0%	0%
Worse	0%	20%	0%	10%	0%	10%
Opinion	**Annotator 1**		**Annotator 2**		**Annotator 3**	
MSA	INFO	READ	INFO	READ	INFO	READ
Better	90%	20%	60%	70%	100%	100%
Equal	10%	80%	40%	30%	0%	0%
Worse	0%	0%	0%	0%	0%	0%

Table 16. MSA vs. BA Evaluation

6 Conclusion and Future Work

In this paper, we have carried out a comprehensive analysis of the question types in community-based question answering (cQA) services and have developed taxonomies for questions and answers. We find that questions do not always have unique best answers. *Open* and *opinion* questions usually have multiple good answers. They occupied about 56%~83% and most of their best answers can be improved. By using question type as a guide, we propose applying automatic summarization techniques to summarization answers or improving cQA best answers through answer editing. Our results show that customized question-type focused summarization techniques can improve cQA answer quality significantly.

Looking into the future, we are to develop automatic question type identification methods to fully automate answer summarization. Furthermore, we would also like to utilize more sophisticated summarization techniques to improve content compaction and readability.

Acknowledgements

We thank the anonymous reviewers for their valuable suggestions and comments to this paper.

References

Broder A. A taxonomy of web search. 2002. SIGIR Forum Vol.36, No. 2, 3-10.

Hovy Edward, Laurie Gerber, Ulf Hermjakob, Chin-Yew Lin, Deepak Ravichandran. 2001. Toward Semantics-Based Answer Pinpointing. In *Proc. of HLT'01*.

Hovy E., C. Lin. 1999. Automated Text Summarization and the SUMMARIST System. In Advances in Automated Text Summarization

Jeon J., W. B. Croft, and J. Lee. 2005a. Finding semantically similar questions based on their answers. In *Proc. of SIGIR'05*.

Jeon J., W. B. Croft, and J. Lee. 2005b. Finding similar questions in large question and answer archives. In *Proc. of CIKM'05*.

Jurczyk P., E. Agichtein. 2007. Hits on question answer portals: exploration of link analysis for author ranking. In *Proc. of SIGIR '07*.

Jeon J. , W.B. Croft, J. Lee, S. Park. 2006. A Framework to predict the quality of answers with non-textual features. In *Proc. of SIGIR '06*.

Jijkoun V., M. R. 2005. Retrieving Answers from Frequently Asked Questions Pages on the Web. In *Proc. of CIKM'05*.

Kleinberg J. 1999. Authoritative sources in a hyper-linked environment. Journal of the ACM, vol. 46,

Kim S., E. Hovy. 2004. Determining the Sentiment of Opinions. In *Proc. of COLING'04*.

Liu X., W.B. Croft, M. Koll. 2005. Finding experts in community-based question-answering services. In *Proc. of CIKM '05*.

Lin C.Y., E. Hovy. 2002. From single to multi-document summarization: a prototype system and its evaluation. In *Proc. of ACL'02*.

Lytinen S., N. Tomuro. 2002. The Use of Question Types to Match Questions in FAQFinder. In *Proc. of AAAI'02*.

Moldovan D., S. Harabagiu, et al. 2000. The Structure and an Open-Domain Question Answering System. In *Proc. of ACL'00*.

Mei Q., X. Shen, C. Zhai. 2007. Automatic labeling of multinomial topic models. In *Proc. of KDD'07*.

Rose D. E., D. Levinson. 2004. Understanding user goals in web search. In *Proc. of WWW '04*.

Voorhees, M. Ellen. 2003. Overview of the TREC 2003 Question Answering Track. In *Proc. of TREC'03*.

Wiebe J., E. Breck, et al. 2003. Recognizing and Organizing Opinions Expressed in the World Press

Tera-Scale Translation Models via Pattern Matching

Adam Lopez
School of Informatics, University of Edinburgh
10 Crichton Street, Edinburgh EH8 9AB, United Kingdom
alopez@inf.ed.ac.uk

Abstract

Translation model size is growing at a pace that outstrips improvements in computing power, and this hinders research on many interesting models. We show how an algorithmic scaling technique can be used to easily handle very large models. Using this technique, we explore several large model variants and show an improvement 1.4 BLEU on the NIST 2006 Chinese-English task. This opens the door for work on a variety of models that are much less constrained by computational limitations.

1 Introduction

Translation model size is growing quickly due to the use of larger training corpora and more complex models. As an example of the growth in available training data, consider the curated Europarl corpus (Koehn, 2005), which more than doubled in size from 20 to 44 million words between 2003 and 2007.[1] As an example of model complexity, consider the popular hierarchical phrase-based model of Chiang (2007), which can translate discontiguous phrases. Under the loosest interpretation of this capability, any subset of words in a sentence can be a phrase. Therefore, the number of rules that the model can learn is exponential in sentence length unless strict heuristics are used, which may limit the model's effectiveness. Many other models translate discontiguous phrases, and the size of their extracted rulesets is such a pervasive problem that it is a recurring topic in the literature (Chiang, 2007; DeNeefe et al., 2007; Simard et al., 2005).

Most decoder implementations assume that all model rules and parameters are known in advance. With very large models, computing all rules and parameters can be very slow. This is a bottleneck in experimental settings where we wish to explore many model variants, and therefore presents a real impediment to full exploration of their potential. We present a solution to this problem.

To fully motivate the discussion, we give a concrete example of a very large model, which we generate using simple techniques that are known to improve translation accuracy. The model takes 77 CPU days to compute and consumes nearly a terabyte of external storage (§2). We show how to solve the problem with a previously developed algorithmic scaling technique that we call **translation by pattern matching** (§3). The key idea behind this technique is that rules and parameters are computed only as needed. Using this technique, we explore a series of large models, giving experimental results along a variety of scaling axes (§4). Our results extend previous findings on the use of long phrases in translation, shed light on the source of improved performance in hierarchical phrase-based models, and show that our tera-scale translation model outperforms a strong baseline.

2 A Tera-Scale Translation Model

We will focus on the hierarchical phrase-based model of Chiang (2007). It compares favorably

This research was conducted while I was at the University of Maryland. I thank David Chiang, Bonnie Dorr, Doug Oard, Philip Resnik, and the anonymous reviewers for comments, and especially Chris Dyer for many helpful discussions and for running the Moses experiments. This research was supported by the GALE program of the Defense Advanced Research Projects Agency, Contract No. HR0011-06-2-001 and by the EuroMatrix project funded by the European Commission (6th Framework Programme).

© 2008. Licensed under the *Creative Commons Attribution-Noncommercial-Share Alike 3.0 Unported* license (http://creativecommons.org/licenses/by-nc-sa/3.0/). Some rights reserved.

[1] Statistics from http://www.statmt.org/europarl.

with conventional phrase-based translation (Koehn et al., 2003) on Chinese-English news translation (Chiang, 2007). We found that a baseline system trained on 27 million words of news data is already quite strong, but we suspect that it would be possible to improve it using some simple techniques.

Add additional training data. Our baseline already uses much of the available curated news data, but there is at least three times as much curated data available in the United Nations proceedings. Adding the UN data gives us a training corpus of 107 million words per language.

Change the word alignments. Our baseline uses Giza++ alignments (Och and Ney, 2003) symmetrized with the grow-diag-final-and heuristic (Koehn et al., 2003). We replace these with the maximum entropy aligments of Ayan and Dorr (2006b). They reported improvements of 1.6 BLEU in Chinese-English translation, though with much less training data.

Change the bilingual phrase extraction heuristic. Our baseline uses a **tight** heuristic, requiring aligned words at phrase edges. However, Ayan and Dorr (2006a) showed that a **loose** heuristic, allowing unaligned words at the phrase edges, improved accuracy by 3.7 BLEU with some alignments, again with much less training data.

Quadrupling the amount of training data predictably increases model size. The interaction of the alignment and phrase extraction heuristic increases the model size much more. This is because the maximum entropy alignments are sparse—fewer than 70% of the words are aligned. Consider a contiguous phrase chosen at random from a training sentence. With our sparse alignments, the chance that both of its edge words are aligned is less than half. The tight heuristic discards many possible phrases on this basis alone. The situation worsens with discontiguous phrases. However, with the loose heuristic, we see the opposite effect. Not only is a randomly chosen source phrase with unaligned edge words legal, but it may have many translations, since its minimal alignment in the target is likely to have one or more adjacent unaligned words, and any combination of these can be part of a valid target phrase.

To make matters concrete, we estimated the size of the translation model that would be produced using these modifications. We did not actually compute the full model, for reasons that will become apparent. Instead, we modified Chiang's extractor to simply report the number of rules that it would normally extract. We then computed the ratio of extracted rules to that of the baseline system. Under the rough assumption that the number of unique rules and representation size grows linearly in the number of extracted rules, we were then able to estimate the size of the large model. The results show that it would be impractical to compute the model (Table 1). Merely counting all of the rule occurrences took nearly 5 days on our 17-node research cluster. This does not even include the time required for sorting and scoring the rules, which we did not attempt. The resulting model would be nearly two orders of magnitude larger than the largest one we could find in the literature (Table 2).

3 Translation by Pattern Matching

Clearly, substantial experimentation with models this large is impossible unless we have considerable resources at our disposal. To get around this problem, we use an algorithmic scaling technique that we call translation by pattern matching. In this approach, the training text and its word alignment reside in memory. We then translate as follows.

```
for each input sentence do
  for each possible phrase in the sentence do
    Find its occurrences in the source text
    for each occurrence do
      Extract its aligned target phrase (if any)
    for each extracted phrase pair do
      Score using maximum likelihood
  Decode as usual using the scored rules
```

A similar method is used in example-based translation (Brown, 2004). It was applied to phrase-based translation by Callison-Burch et al. (2005) and Zhang and Vogel (2005). The key point is that the complete translation model is never actually computed—rules and associated parameters are computed only as needed. Obviously, the on-demand computation must be very fast. If we can achieve this, then the model can in principle be arbitrarily large. Callison-Burch et al. (2005) and Zhang and Vogel (2005) give very similar recipes for application to phrase-based models.

Fast lookup using pattern matching algorithms. The complexity of the naïve algorithm to find all occurrences of a source phrase in a training text T is linear in the length of the text, $O(|T|)$. This is much too slow for large texts. They solve this using an index data structure called a suffix

	Baseline	Large
Rules extracted (millions)	195	19,300
Extract time (CPU hours)	10.8	1,840
Unique rules (millions)	67	6,600*
Extract file size (GB)	9.3	917*
Model size (GB)	6.1	604*

Table 1: Extraction time and model sizes. The model size reported is the size of the files containing an external prefix tree representation (Zens and Ney, 2007). *Denotes estimated quantities.

Citation	Millions of rules
Simard et al. (2005)	(filtered) 4
Chiang (2007)	(filtered) 6
DeNeefe et al. (2007)	57
Zens and Ney (2007)	225
this paper	6,600

Table 2: Model sizes in the literature.

array (Manber and Myers, 1993). Its size is $4|T|$ bytes and it enables lookup of any length-m substring of T in $O(m + \log |T|)$ time.

Fast extraction using sampling. The complexity of extracting target phrases is linear in the number of source phrase occurrences. For very frequent source phrases, this is expensive. They solve this problem by extracting only from a sample of the found source phrases, capping the sample size at 100. For less frequent source phrases, all possible targets are extracted.

Fast scoring using maximum likelihood. Scoring the phrase pairs is linear in the number of pairs if we use the maximum likelihood estimate $p(e|f)$ for source phrase f and target phrase e. Since each source phrase only has small number of targets (up to the sample limit), this step is fast. However, notice that we cannot easily compute the target-to-source probability $p(f|e)$ as is commonly done. We address this in §4.1.

Callison-Burch et al. (2005) and Zhang and Vogel (2005) found that these steps added only tenths of a second to per-sentence decoding time, which we independently confirmed (Lopez, 2008, Chapter 3). Their techniques also apply to discontiguous phrases, except for the pattern matching algorithm, which only works for contiguous phrases. Since our model (and many others) uses discontiguous phrases, we must use a different algorithm. The most straightforward way to accomplish this is to use the fast suffix array lookup for the contiguous subphrases of a discontiguous phrase, and then to combine the results. Suppose that we have substrings u and v, and a gap character X which can match any arbitrary sequence of words. Then to look up the phrase uXv, we first find all occurrences of u, and all occurrences of v. We can then compute all cases where an occurrence of u precedes and occurrence of v in the same sentence.

The complexity of this last step is linear in the number of occurrences of u and v. If either u or v is very frequent, this is too slow. Lopez (2007; 2008) solves this with a series of empirically fast exact algorithms. We briefly sketch the solution here; for details see Lopez (2008, Chapter 4).

Lossless pruning. For each phrase, we only search if we have already successfully found both its longest suffix and longest prefix. For example, if a, b, c, and d are all words, then we only search for phrase $abXcd$ if we have already found occurrences of phrases $abXc$ and $bXcd$.

Precomputation of expensive searches. For phrases containing multiple very frequent subphrases, we precompute the list of occurrences into an inverted index. That is, if both u and v are frequent, we simply precompute all locations of uXv and vXu.

Fast merge algorithm. For phrases pairing a frequent subphrase with infrequent subphrases, we use a merge algorithm whose upper bound complexity is logarithmic in the number of occurrences of the frequent subphrase. That is, if $count(u)$ is small, and $count(v)$ is big, then we can find uXv in at most $O(count(u) \cdot \log(count(v)))$ time.

Our implementation is a fast extension to the Hiero decoder (Chiang, 2007), written in Pyrex.[2] It is an order of magnitude faster than the Python implementation of Lopez (2007). Pattern matching, extraction, and scoring steps add approximately 2 seconds to per-sentence decoding time, slowing decoding by about 50% compared with a conventional exact model representation using external prefix trees (Zens and Ney, 2007). See Lopez (2008, Chapter 4) for analysis.

4 Experiments

Although the algorithmic issues of translation by pattern matching are largely solved, none of the previous work has reported any improvements in

[2]Pyrex combines Python and C code for performance. http://www.cosc.canterbury.ac.nz/greg.ewing/python/Pyrex/

state of the art with very large models.[3] In the remainder of this work, we scratch the surface of possible uses.

We experimented on Chinese-English newswire translation. Except where noted, each system was trained on 27 million words of newswire data, aligned with GIZA++ (Och and Ney, 2003) and symmetrized with the grow-diag-final-and heuristic (Koehn et al., 2003). In all experiments that follow, each system configuration was independently optimized on the NIST 2003 Chinese-English test set (919 sentences) using minimum error rate training (Och, 2003) and tested on the NIST 2005 Chinese-English task (1082 sentences). Optimization and measurement were done with the NIST implementation of case-insensitive BLEU 4n4r (Papineni et al., 2002).[4]

4.1 Baseline

We compared translation by pattern matching with a conventional exact model representation using external prefix trees (Zens and Ney, 2007). To make model computation efficient for the latter case, we followed the heuristic limits on phrase extraction used by Chiang (2007).

- Phrases were restricted to five words. Each gap character counts as a single word regardless of how many actual words it spans. Thus phrase aXb consisting of words a and b separated by a gap is three words.
- Phrases were restricted to a span of ten words in the training data.
- Phrases were restricted to two gaps.
- Gaps were required to span at least two words in the training data.
- Phrases were extracted using a tight heuristic.

Chiang (2007) uses eight features, so we incorporate these into the conventional baseline. However, as discussed previously in §3, the pattern matching architecture makes it difficult to compute the target-to-source translation probability, so this feature is not included in the pattern matching system. This may not be a problem—Och and Ney (2002) observed that this feature could be replaced by the source-to-target probability without loss of accuracy. Preliminary experiments suggested that two other features in Chiang's model based on rule counts were not informative, so we considered a model containing only five features.

1. Sum of logarithms of source-to-target phrase translation probabilities.
2. Sum of logarithms of source-to-target lexical weighting (Koehn et al., 2003).
3. Sum of logarithms of target-to-source lexical weighting.
4. Sum of logarithms of a trigram language model.
5. A word count feature.

The sample size (see §3) for the pattern matching system was 300.[5] Results show that both translation by pattern matching and reduced feature set are harmless to translation accuracy (Table 3).

4.2 Rapid Prototyping via Pattern Matching

Even in this limited experiment, translation by pattern matching improved experimental turnaround. For the conventional system, it took 10.8 hours to compute the full model, which required 6.1GB of space. For the pattern matching system, it took only 8 minutes to compute all data structures and indexes. These required only 852MB of space.

There are two tradeoffs. First, memory use is higher in the pattern matching system, since the conventional representation resides on disk. Second, per-sentence decoding time with the pattern matching system is slower by about 2 seconds due to the expense of computing rules and parameters on demand. Even so, the experimental turnaround time with the pattern matching system was still faster. We would need to decode nearly 20,000 sentences with it to equal the computation time of conventional model construction. We might need to decode this many times during MERT, but only because it decodes the same test set many times. However, it is straightforward to extract all rules for the development set using pattern matching, and use them in a conventional system for MERT.

[3] Zhang and Vogel (2005) report improvements, but all of their results are far below state of the art for the reported task. This may be because their system was not tuned using minimum error rate training (Och, 2003).

[4] ftp://jaguar.ncsl.nist.gov/mt/resources/mteval-v11b.pl

[5] We use deterministic sampling, which is useful for reproducibility and for minimum error rate training (Och, 2003). See Lopez (2008, Chapter 3) for details.

System	BLEU
Conventional (eight features)	30.7
Conventional (five features)	30.6
Pattern matching (five features)	30.9

Table 3: Baseline system results.

Taking our five-feature pattern matching system as a starting point, we next considered several ways in which we might scale up the translation model. Here the benefits of prototyping become more apparent. If we were to run the following experiments in a conventional system, we would need to compute a new model for each condition. With translation by pattern matching, nearly every variant uses the same underlying representation, so it was rarely even necessary to recompute data structures and indexes.

4.3 Relaxing Length Restrictions

Increasing the maximum phrase length in standard phrase-based translation does not improve BLEU (Koehn et al., 2003; Zens and Ney, 2007). However, this effect has not yet been evaluated in hierarchical phrase-based translation.

We experimented with two analogues to the maximum phrase length. First, we varied the limit on source phrase length (counting each gap as a single word), the closest direct analogue. Chiang (2007) used a limit of five. We found that accuracy plateaus at this baseline setting (Figure 1). Second, we varied the limit on the span of phrases extracted from the training text. Suppose we are interested in a source phrase uXv. If u and v are collocated in a training sentence, but within a span longer than the limit, then the model is prevented from learning a rule that translates this discontiguous phrase as a single unit. Chiang (2007) fixes this limit at ten. Again, accuracy plateaus near the baseline setting (Figure 2).

Our results are similar to those for conventional phrase-based models (Koehn et al., 2003; Zens and Ney, 2007). Though scaling along these axes is unhelpful, there is still a large space for exploration.

4.4 Interlude: Hierarchical Phrase-Based Translation versus Lexical Reordering

In a related line of inquiry, we considered the effect of increasing the number of gaps in phrases. Chiang (2007) limits them to two. Although we consider more than this, we also considered fewer,

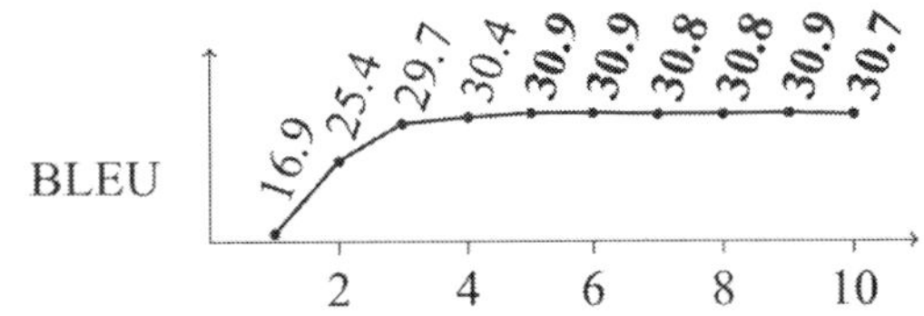

Figure 1: Effect of the maximum phrase length.

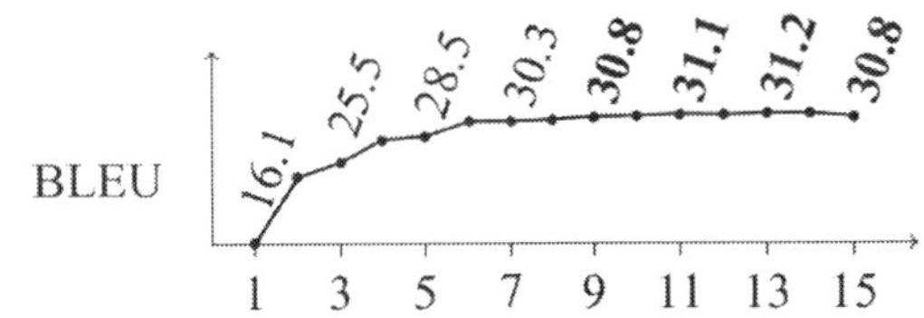

Figure 2: Effect of the maximum phrase span.

to gain insight into the hierarchical model.

Hierarchical phrase-based translation is often reported to be better than conventional phrase-based translation, but the actual reason for this is unknown. It is often argued that the ability to translate discontiguous phrases is important to modeling translation (Chiang, 2007; Simard et al., 2005; Quirk and Menezes, 2006), and it may be that this explains the results. However, there is another hypothesis. The model can also translate phrases in the form uX or Xu (a single contiguous unit and a gap). If it learns that uX often translates as Xu', then in addition to learning that u translates as u', it has also learned that u switches places with a neighboring phrase during translation. This is similar to **lexicalized reordering** in conventional phrase-based models (Tillman, 2004; Al-Onaizan and Papineni, 2006).[6] If this is the real benefit of the hierarchical model, then the ability to translate discontiguous phrases may be irrelevant.

To tease apart these claims, we make the following distinction. Rules in which both source and target phrases contain a single contiguous element—that is, in the form u, Xu, uX, or XuX—encode lexicalized reordering in hierarchical form. Rules representing the translation of discontiguous units—minimally uXv—encode translation knowledge that is strictly outside the purview of lexical reordering.

We ran experiments varying both the number of contiguous subphrases and the number of gaps (Ta-

[6]This hypothesis was suggested independently in personal communications with several researchers, including Chris Callison-Burch, Chris Dyer, Alex Fraser, and Franz Och.

ble 4). For comparison, we also include results of the phrase-based system Moses (Koehn et al., 2007) with and without lexicalized reordering.

Our results are consistent with those found elsewhere in the literature. The strictest setting allowing no gaps replicates a result in Chiang (2007, Table 7), with significantly worse accuracy than all others. The most striking result is that the accuracy of Moses with lexicalized reordering is indistinguishable from the accuracy of the full hierarchical system. Both improve over non-lexicalized Moses by about 1.4 BLEU. The hierarchical emulation owes its performance only partially to lexicalized reordering. Additional improvement is seen when we add discontiguous phrases. That the effect of lexicalized reordering is weaker in the hierarchical model is unsurprising, since its parameterization is much simpler than the one used by the Moses, which includes several specialized features for this purpose. This suggests that the hierarchical model could be improved through better parameterization, and still benefit from the translation of discontiguous phrases.

Finally, we observe that using more gaps does not improve the hierarchical model.

Subphrases	Gaps	Example	BLEU
1	0	u	26.3
1	1	uX, Xu	30.2*
1	2	XuX	30.0*
2	1	uXv	30.5
2	2	$uXvX, XuXv$	**30.8**
3	2	$uXvXw$	**30.9**
4	3	$uXvXwXy$	**30.9**
5	4	$uXvXwXyXz$	**30.8**
Moses without lexicalized reordering			29.4
Moses with lexicalized reordering			**30.7**

Table 4: Comparison with Moses and effect of the maximum number of subphrases and gaps. *Denotes emulation of lexicalized reordering.

4.5 The Tera-Scale Model

These are interesting scientific findings, but we have so far failed to show an improvement over the baseline. For this, we return to the tera-scale model of §2. Recall that in this model, we modify the baseline by adding 80 million words of UN data and using sparse maximum entropy alignments with a loose phrase extraction heuristic.

To avoid conflating rules learned from in-domain newswire and out-of-domain UN data, we treat each corpus independently. We sample from up to 300 source phrase occurrences from each, and compute lexical weighting and the source-to-target phrase translation probabilities separately for both samples. For the UN corpus, the resulting probabilities are incorporated into three new features. These features receive a value of zero for any rule computed from the newswire data. Likewise, the baseline source-to-target phrase translation probability and lexical weighting features receive a value of zero for rules computed from the UN data.

We make one more modification to the model that is quite easy with pattern matching. We notice that it is not always possible to extract a translation for a source phrase occurrence, even under the loose heuristic. This is because there may be no consistently aligned target phrase according to the alignment. If a phrase occurs frequently but we can only rarely extract a translation for it, then our confidence that it represents a natural unit of translation should diminish. Conversely, if we usually extract a translation, then the phrase is probably a good unit of translation. We call this property **coherence**. Conventional offline extraction methods usually ignore coherence. If a phrase occurs many times but we can only extract a translation for it a few times, then those translations tend to receive very high probabilities, even though they might simply be the result of noisy alignments.

We can incorporate the notion of coherence directly into the phrase translation probability. In the baseline model, the denominator of this probability is the sum of the number of rule occurrences containing the source phrase, following Koehn et al. (2003).[7] We replace this with the number of attempted extractions. This parameterization may interact nicely with the loose extraction heuristic, reducing the probability of many greedily extracted but otherwise noisy phrases.

We compared the baseline with our tera-scale model. Since we had already performed substantial experimentation with the NIST 2005 set, we also included the NIST 2006 task as a new held-out test set. Results including variants produced by ablating a single modification on the development set are given in Table 5.

We also compared our modified system with an augmented baseline using a 5-gram language

[7] Or the sample size, whichever is less.

System	NIST 2005 BLEU	NIST 2005 loss	NIST 2006 BLEU
Tera-Scale Model (all modifications)	32.6	–	28.4
with grow-diag-final-and instead of maximum entropy alignment	32.1	-0.5	
with tight extraction heuristic instead of loose	31.6	-1.0	
without UN data	31.6	-1.0	
without separate UN features	32.2	-0.4	
with standard $p(f\|e)$ instead of coherent $p(f\|e)$	31.7	-0.9	
Baseline (conventional)	30.7	-1.9	
Baseline (pattern matching)	30.9	-1.7	27.0

Table 5: Results of scaling modifications and ablation experiments.

model and rule-based number translation. The objective of this experiment is to ensure that our improvements are complementary to better language modeling, which often subsumes other improvements. The new baseline achieves a score of 31.9 on the NIST 2005 set, making it nearly the same as the state-of-the-art results reported by Chiang (2007). Our modifications increase this to 34.5, a substantial improvement of 2.6 BLEU.

5 Related Work and Open Problems

There are several other useful approaches to scaling translation models. Zens and Ney (2007) remove constraints imposed by the size of main memory by using an external data structure. Johnson et al. (2007) substantially reduce model size with a filtering method. However, neither of these approaches addresses the preprocessing bottleneck. To our knowledge, the strand of research initiated by Callison-Burch et al. (2005) and Zhang and Vogel (2005) and extended here is the first to do so. Dyer et al. (2008) address this bottleneck with a promising approach based on parallel processing, showing reductions in real time that are linear in the number of CPUs. However, they do not reduce the overall CPU time. Our techniques also benefit from parallel processing, but they reduce overall CPU time, thus comparing favorably even in this scenario.[8] Moreover, our method works even with limited parallel processing.

Although we saw success with this approach, there are some interesting open problems. As discussed in §4.2, there are tradeoffs in the form of slower decoding and increased memory usage. Decoding speed might be partially addressed using a mixture of online and offline computation as in Zhang and Vogel (2005), but faster algorithms are still needed. Memory use is important in non-distributed systems since our data structures will compete with the language model for memory. It may be possible to address this problem with a novel data structure known as a compressed self-index (Navarro and Mäkinen, 2007), which supports fast pattern matching on a representation that is close in size to the information-theoretic minimum required by the data.

Our approach is currently limited by the requirement for very fast parameter estimation. As we saw, this appears to prevent us from computing the target-to-source probabilities. It would also appear to limit our ability to use discriminative training methods, since these tend to be much slower than the analytical maximum likelihood estimate. Discriminative methods are desirable for feature-rich models that we would like to explore with pattern matching. For example, Chan et al. (2007) and Carpuat and Wu (2007) improve translation accuracy using discriminatively trained models with contextual features of source phrases. Their features are easy to obtain at runtime using our approach, which finds source phrases in context. However, to make their experiments tractable, they trained their discriminative models offline only for the specific phrases of the test set. Combining discriminative learning with our approach is an open problem.

6 Conclusion

We showed that very large translation models present an interesting engineering challenge, and illustrated a solution to this challenge using pattern matching algorithms. This enables practical, rapid exploration of vastly larger models than those currently in use. We believe that many other improvements are possible when the size of our models is

[8] All of our reported decoding runs were done in parallel.

unconstrained by resource limitations.

References

Yaser Al-Onaizan and Kishore Papineni. 2006. Distortion models for statistical machine translation. In *Proc. of ACL-COLING*, pages 529–536, Jul.

Necip Fazil Ayan and Bonnie Dorr. 2006a. Going beyond AER: An extensive analysis of word alignments and their impact on MT. In *Proc. of ACL-COLING*, pages 9–16, Jul.

Necip Fazil Ayan and Bonnie J. Dorr. 2006b. A maximum entropy approach to combining word alignments. In *Proc. of HLT-NAACL*, pages 96–103, Jun.

Ralf D. Brown. 2004. A modified Burrows-Wheeler transform for highly-scalable example-based translation. In *Proc. of AMTA*, number 3265 in LNCS, pages 27–36. Springer, Sep.

Chris Callison-Burch, Colin Bannard, and Josh Schroeder. 2005. Scaling phrase-based statistical machine translation to larger corpora and longer phrases. In *Proc. of ACL*, pages 255–262, Jun.

Marine Carpuat and Dekai Wu. 2007. Improving statistical machine translation using word sense disambiguation. In *Proc. of ACL*, pages 61–72, Jun.

Yee Seng Chan, Hwee Tou Ng, and David Chiang. 2007. Word sense disambiguation improves statistical machine translation. In *Proc. of ACL*, pages 33–40, Jun.

David Chiang. 2007. Hierarchical phrase-based translation. *Computational Linguistics*, 33(2):201–228.

Steve DeNeefe, Kevin Knight, Wei Wang, and Daniel Marcu. 2007. What can syntax-based MT learn from phrase-based MT? In *Proc. of EMNLP-CoNLL*, pages 755–763, Jun.

Chris Dyer, Aaron Cordova, Alex Mont, and Jimmy Lin. 2008. Fast, easy, and cheap: Construction of statistical machine translation models with mapreduce. In *Proc. of the Workshop on Statistical Machine Translation*, pages 199–207, Jun.

Howard Johnson, Joel Martin, George Foster, and Roland Kuhn. 2007. Improving translation quality by discarding most of the phrasetable. In *Proc. of EMNLP-CoNLL*, pages 967–975, Jun.

Philipp Koehn, Franz Josef Och, and Daniel Marcu. 2003. Statistical phrase-based translation. In *Proc. of HLT-NAACL*, pages 127–133, May.

Philipp Koehn, Hieu Hoang, Alexandra Birch, Chris Callison-Burch, Marcello Federico, Nicola Bertoldi, Brooke Cowan, Wade Shen, Christine Moran, Richard Zens, Chris Dyer, Ondrej Bojar, Alexandra Constantin, and Evan Herbst. 2007. Moses: Open source toolkit for statistical machine translation. In *Proc. of ACL Demo and Poster Sessions*, pages 177–180, Jun.

Philipp Koehn. 2005. Europarl: A parallel corpus for statistical machine translation. In *Proc. of MT Summit*.

Adam Lopez. 2007. Hierarchical phrase-based translation with suffix arrays. In *Proc. of EMNLP-CoNLL*, pages 976–985, Jun.

Adam Lopez. 2008. *Machine Translation by Pattern Matching*. Ph.D. thesis, University of Maryland, Mar.

Udi Manber and Gene Myers. 1993. Suffix arrays: A new method for on-line string searches. *SIAM Journal of Computing*, 22(5):935–948.

Gonzalo Navarro and Veli Mäkinen. 2007. Compressed full-text indexes. *ACM Computing Surveys*, 39(1), Apr.

Franz Josef Och and Hermann Ney. 2002. Discriminative training and maximum entropy models for machine translation. In *Proc. of ACL*, pages 156–163, Jul.

Franz Josef Och and Hermann Ney. 2003. A systematic comparison of various statistical alignment models. *Computational Linguistics*, 29(1):19–51, Mar.

Franz Josef Och. 2003. Minimum error rate training in statistical machine translation. In *Proc. of ACL*, Jul.

Kishore Papineni, Salim Roukos, Todd Ward, and Wei-Jing Zhu. 2002. BLEU: a method for automatic evaluation of machine translation. In *Proc. of ACL*, pages 311–318, Jul.

Chris Quirk and Arul Menezes. 2006. Do we need phrases? Challenging the conventional wisdom in statistical machine translation. In *Proc. of HLT-NAACL*, pages 8–16, Jun.

Michel Simard, Nicola Cancedda, Bruno Cavestro, Marc Dymetman, Eric Gaussier, Cyril Goutte, Kenji Yamada, Philippe Langlais, and Arne Mauser. 2005. Translating with non-contiguous phrases. In *Proc. of HLT-EMNLP*, pages 755–762, Oct.

Christoph Tillman. 2004. A unigram orientation model for statistical machine translation. In *Proc. of HLT-NAACL: Short Papers*, pages 101–104, May.

Richard Zens and Hermann Ney. 2007. Efficient phrase-table representation for machine translation with applications to online MT and speech translation. In *Proc. of HLT-NAACL*.

Ying Zhang and Stephan Vogel. 2005. An efficient phrase-to-phrase alignment model for arbitrarily long phrase and large corpora. In *Proc. of EAMT*, May.

Authorship Attribution and Verification with Many Authors and Limited Data

Kim Luyckx and **Walter Daelemans**
CNTS Language Technology Group
University of Antwerp
Prinsstraat 13, 2000 Antwerp, Belgium
{kim.luyckx,walter.daelemans}@ua.ac.be

Abstract

Most studies in statistical or machine learning based authorship attribution focus on two or a few authors. This leads to an overestimation of the importance of the features extracted from the training data and found to be discriminating for these small sets of authors. Most studies also use sizes of training data that are unrealistic for situations in which stylometry is applied (e.g., forensics), and thereby overestimate the accuracy of their approach in these situations. A more realistic interpretation of the task is as an *authorship verification* problem that we approximate by pooling data from many different authors as negative examples. In this paper, we show, on the basis of a new corpus with 145 authors, what the effect is of many authors on feature selection and learning, and show robustness of a memory-based learning approach in doing authorship attribution and verification with many authors and limited training data when compared to eager learning methods such as SVMs and maximum entropy learning.

1 Introduction

In traditional studies on authorship attribution, the focus is on small sets of authors. Trying to classify an unseen text as being written by one of two or of a few authors is a relatively simple task, which in most cases can be solved with high reliability and accuracies over 95%. An early statistical study by Mosteller and Wallace (1964) adopted distributions of function words as a discriminating feature to settle the disputed authorship of the Federalist Papers between three candidate authors (Alexander Hamilton, James Madison, and John Jay). The advantage of distributions of function words and syntactic features is that they are not under the author's conscious control, and therefore provide good clues for authorship (Holmes, 1994). Frequencies of rewrite rules (Baayen et al., 1996), n-grams of syntactic labels from partial parsing (Hirst and Feiguina, 2007), n-grams of parts-of-speech (Diederich et al., 2000), function words (Miranda García and Calle Martín, 2007), and functional lexical features (Argamon et al., 2007) have all been claimed to be reliable markers of style. There is of course a difference between claims about types of features and claims about individual features of that type. E.g., it may be correct to claim that distributions of function words are important markers of author identity, but the distribution of a particular function word, while useful to distinguish between one particular pair of authors, may be irrelevant when comparing another pair of authors.

The field of authorship attribution is however dominated by studies potentially overestimating the importance of these specific predictive features in experiments discriminating between only two or a few authors. Taking into account a larger set of authors allows the computation of the degree of variability encountered in text on a single topic of different (types of) features. Recently, research has started to focus on authorship attribution on larger sets of authors: 8 (Van Halteren, 2005), 20 (Argamon et al., 2003), 114 (Madigan et al., 2005), or up

© Kim Luyckx & Walter Daelemans, 2008. Licensed under the *Creative Commons Attribution-Noncommercial-Share Alike 3.0 Unported* license (http://creativecommons.org/licenses/by-nc-sa/3.0/). Some rights reserved.

to thousands of authors (Koppel et al., 2006) (see Section 5).

A second problem in traditional studies are the unrealistic sizes of training data, which also makes the task considerably easier. Researchers tend to use over 10,000 words per author (Argamon et al., 2007; Burrows, 2007; Gamon, 2004; Hirst and Feiguina, 2007; Madigan et al., 2005; Stamatatos, 2007), which is regarded to be 'a reliable minimum for an authorial set' (Burrows, 2007). When no long texts are available, for example in poems (Coyotl-Morales et al., 2006) or student essays (Van Halteren, 2005), a large number of short texts is selected for training for each author. One of the few studies focusing on small texts is Feiguina and Hirst (2007), but they select hundreds of these short texts (here 100, 200 or 500 words). The accuracy of any of these studies with unrealistic sizes of training data is overestimated when compared to realistic situations. When only limited data is available for a specific author, the author attribution task becomes much more difficult. In forensics, where often only one small text per candidate author is available, traditional approaches are less reliable than expected from reported results.

In this paper, we present a more realistic interpretation of the authorship attribution task, viz. as a problem of *authorship verification*. This is a much more natural task, since the group of potential authors for a document is essentially *unknown*. Forensic experts not only want to identify the author given a small set of suspects, they also want to make sure the author is not someone else not under investigation. They often deal with short e-mails or letters and have only limited data available. The central question in authorship verification is *Did candidate author x write the document?* Of the three basic approaches to authorship verification - also including a one-class learning approach (Koppel et al., 2007) - we selected a *one vs. all* approach. This approach is similar to the one investigated by Argamon et al. (2003), which allows for a better comparison of results. With only few positive instances and a large number of negative instances to learn from, we are dealing with highly skewed class distributions.

We show, on the basis of a new corpus with 145 authors, what the effect is of many authors on feature selection and learning, and show robustness of a memory-based learning approach in doing authorship attribution and verification with many authors and limited training data when compared to eager learning methods such as SVMs and maximum entropy learning. As far as feature selection is concerned, we find that similar *types* of features tend to work well for small and large sets of authors, but that no generalisations can be made about *individual* features. Classification accuracy is clearly overestimated in authorship attribution with few authors. Experiments in authorship verification with a *one vs. all* approach reveal that machine learning methods are able to correctly classify up to 56% of the positive instances in test data.

For our experiments, we use the *Personae* corpus, a collection of student essays by 145 authors (see Section 2). Most studies in stylometry focus on English, whereas our focus is on Dutch written language. Nevertheless, the techniques used are transferable to other languages.

2 Corpus

The 200,000-word *Personae* corpus[1] used in this study consists of 145 student (BA level) essays of about 1400 words about a documentary on Artificial Life, thereby keeping markers of genre, register, topic, age, and education level relatively constant. These essays contain a factual description of the documentary and the students' opinion about it. The task was voluntary and students producing an essay were rewarded with two cinema tickets. The students also took an online Myers-Briggs Type Indicator (MBTI) (Briggs Myers and Myers, 1980) test and submitted their profile, the text and some user information via a website. All students released the copyright of their text and explicitly allowed the use of their text and associated personality profile for research, which makes it possible to distribute the corpus. The corpus cannot only be used for authorship attribution and verification experiments, but also for personality prediction. More information about the motivation behind the corpus and results from exploratory experiments in personality prediction can be found in Luyckx & Daelemans (2008).

3 Methodology

We approach authorship attribution and verification as automatic text categorization tasks that label documents according to a set of predefined categories (Sebastiani, 2002, 3). Like in most text cat-

[1]The *Personae* corpus can be downloaded from http://www.cnts.ua.ac.be/~kim/Personae.html

egorization systems, we take a two-step approach in which our system (i) achieves automatic selection of features that have high predictive value for the categories to be learned (see Section 3.1), and (ii) uses machine learning algorithms to learn to categorize new documents by using the features selected in the first step (see Section 3.2).

3.1 Feature Extraction

Syntactic features have been proposed as more reliable style markers than for example token-level features since they are not under the conscious control of the author (Baayen et al., 1996; Argamon et al., 2007). To allow the selection of linguistic features rather than (n-grams of) terms, robust and accurate text analysis tools such as lemmatizers, part of speech taggers, chunkers etc., are needed. We use the Memory-Based Shallow Parser (MBSP) (Daelemans and van den Bosch, 2005), which gives an incomplete parse of the input text, to extract reliable syntactic features. MBSP tokenizes the input, performs a part-of-speech analysis, looks for noun phrase, verb phrase and other phrase chunks and detects subject and object of the sentence and a number of other grammatical relations.

Word or part-of-speech (n-grams) occurring more often than expected with either of the categories are extracted automatically for every document. We use the χ^2 metric (see Figure 1), which calculates the expected and observed frequency for every item in every category, to identify features that are able to discriminate between the categories under investigation.

$$\chi^2 = \sum_{i=1}^{k} \frac{(\chi_i - \mu_i)^2}{\sigma_i}$$

Figure 1: Chi-square formula

Distributions of n-grams of lexical features (*lex*) are represented numerically in the feature vectors, as well as of n-grams of both fine-grained (*pos*) and coarse-grained parts-of-speech (*cgp*). The most predictive function words are present in the *fwd* feature set. For all of these features, the χ^2 value is calculated.

An implementation of the Flesch-Kincaid metric indicating the readability of a text, along with its components (viz., mean word and sentence length) and the type-token ratio (which indicates vocabulary richness) are also represented (*tok*).

3.2 Experimental Set-Up

This paper focuses on three topics, each with their own experimental set-up:

(a) the effect of many authors on feature selection and learning;

(b) the effect of limited data in authorship attribution;

(c) the results of authorship verification using many authors and limited data on learning.

For (a), we perform experiments in authorship attribution while gradually increasing the number of authors. First, we select a hundred random samples of 2, 5 and 10 authors in order to minimize the effect of chance, then select one random sample of 20, 50, 100 authors and finally experiment with all 145 authors (Section 5.1).

We investigate (b) by performing authorship attribution on 2 and 145 authors while gradually increasing the amount of training data, keeping test set size constant at 20% of the entire corpus. The resulting learning curve will be used to compare performance of eager and lazy learners (see Section 5.1).

The authorship verification task (c) - which is closer to a realistic situation in e.g. forensics - using limited data and many authors is approximated as a skewed binary classification task (*one vs. all*). For each of the 145 authors, we have 80% of the text in training and 20% in test. The negative class contains 80% of each of the other 144 author's training data in training and 20% in test (see Section 5.2).

All experiments for (a), (b) and (c) are performed using 5-fold cross-validation. This allows us to get a reliable indication of how well the learner will do when it is asked to make new predictions on the held-out test set. The data set is divided into five subsets containing two fragments of equal size per author. Five times one of the subsets is used as test set and the other subsets as training set.

The feature vectors that are fed into the machine learning algorithm contain the top-n features (n=50) with highest χ^2 value. Every text fragment is split into ten equal parts, each part being represented by means of a feature vector, resulting in 1450 vectors per fold (divided over training and test).

For classification, we experimented with both lazy and eager supervised learning methods. As an implementation of the lazy learning approach we used TiMBL (Tilburg Memory-Based Learner) (Daelemans et al., 2007), a supervised inductive algorithm for learning classification tasks based on the *k-nn* algorithm with various extensions for dealing with nominal features and feature relevance weighting. Memory-based learning stores feature representations of training instances in memory without abstraction and classifies new instances by matching their feature representation to all instances in memory. From these 'nearest neighbors', the class of the test item is extrapolated.

As eager learners, we selected SMO, an implementation of Support-Vector Machines (SVM) using Sequential Minimal Optimization (Platt, 1998), and Maxent, an implementation of Maximum Entropy learning (Le, 2006). SMO is embedded in the WEKA (Waikato Environment for Knowledge Analysis) software package (Witten and Frank, 1999).

Our expectation is that eager learners will tend to overgeneralize for this task when dealing with limited training data, while lazy learners, by delaying generalization over training data until the test phase, will be at an advantage when dealing with limited data. Unlike eager learners, they will not ignore - i.e. not abstract away from - the frequently occurring infrequent or untypical patterns in the training data, that will nevertheless be useful in generalization.

4 Results and Discussion

In this section, we present results of experiments concerning the three main issues of this paper (see Section 3.2 for the experimental set-up):

(a) the effect of many authors on feature selection and learning;

(b) the effect of limited data in authorship attribution;

(c) the results of authorship verification using many authors and limited data on learning.

4.1 Authorship Attribution

(a) Figure 2 shows the effect of many authors in authorship attribution experiments using memory-based learning (TiMBL) (k=1) and separate feature sets. Most authorship attribution studies focus on a small set of authors and report good results, but systematically increasing the amount of authors under investigation leads to a significant decrease in performance. In the 2-author task (100 experiments with random samples of 2 authors), we achieve an average accuracy of 96.90%, which is in line with results reported in other studies on small sets of authors. The 5-, 10- (both in 100 experiments with random samples) and 20-author tasks show a gradual decrease in performance with results up to 88%, 82% and 76% accuracy, respectively. A significant fall in accuracy comes with the 50- and 100-author attribution task, where accuracy drops below 52% for the best performing feature sets. Experiments with all 145 authors from the corpus (as a multiclass problem) show an accuracy up to 34%. Studies reporting on accuracies over 95% are clearly overestimating their performance on a small set of authors.

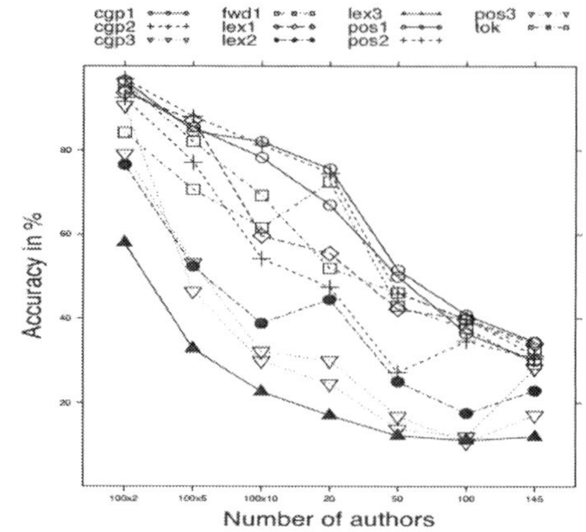

Figure 2: The effect of many authors using single feature sets

Incremental combinations of feature sets performing well in authorship attribution lead to an accuracy of almost 50% in the 145-author case, as is shown in Figure 3. This indicates that providing a more heterogeneous set of features improves the system significantly. Memory-based learning shows robustness for a large set of authors in authorship attribution.

As far as feature selection is concerned, we find that similar *types* of features tend to work well for small and large sets of authors in our corpus, but that no generalisations can be made about *individual* features towards other corpora or studies, since this is highly dependent of the specific authors selected.

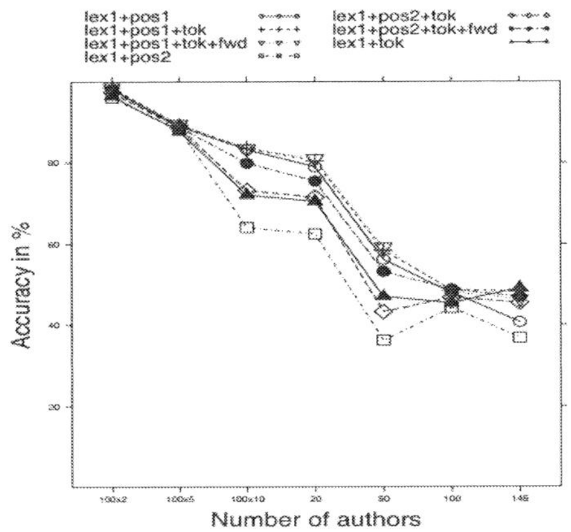

Figure 3: The effect of many authors using combinations of feature sets

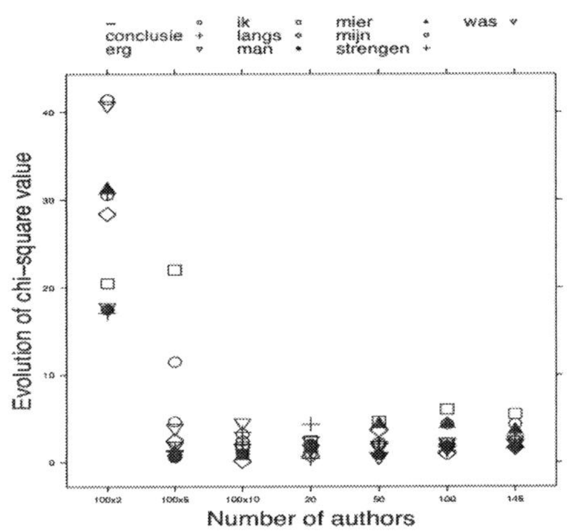

Figure 4: The effect of many authors on χ^2 value for 2-author discriminating features

Figure 4 shows the top-ten features with highest χ^2 value in one of the randomly selected 2-author samples. In 5-author cases, we see that some of these features have some discriminating power, but with the increase of the number of authors comes a decrease in importance.

(b) The effect of limited data is demonstrated by means of a learning curve. The performance of lazy learner TiMBL is compared to that of eager learners Maxent (Maximum Entropy Learning) and SMO (Support-Vector Machines) when comparing different training set sizes. Figure 5 shows the evolution of learning in authorship attribution using the *lex1* feature set. Although memory-based learning does show robustness when dealing with limited data, we cannot show a clear superiority on this aspect to the eager learning methods in this experiment. However, results are good enough to

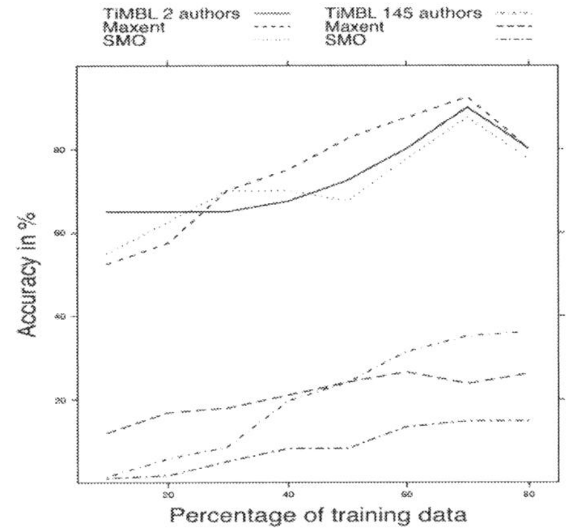

Figure 5: The effect of limited data in authorship attribution on *lex1*

warrant continuing the experiments on authorship verification with this method.

4.2 Authorship Verification

(c) We now focus on a more realistic interpretation of the authorship attribution task, viz. as a authorship *verification* problem. Forensic experts want to answer both questions of authorship attribution (*Which of the n candidate authors wrote the document?*) and verification (*Did candidate author x write the document?*). They often deal with limited data like short e-mails or letters, and the amount of candidate authors is essentially unknown. With only few positive instances (of 1 author) and a large amount of negative instances (of 144 authors in our corpus), we are dealing with highly skewed class distributions.

We approximate the author verification problem by defining a binary classification task with the author fragments as positive training data, and the fragments of all the other authors as negative training data. A more elegant formulation would be as a one-class problem (providing only positive training data), but in exploratory experiments, these one-class learning approaches did not yield useful results.

We evaluate authorship verification experiments by referring to precision and recall of the positive class. Recall represents the proportional number of times an instance of the positive class has correctly been classified as positive. Precision shows the proportion of test instances predicted by the system to be positive that was correctly classified as such.

Feature set	Precision	Recall	F-score
tok	20.66%	15.93%	17.99%
fwd	37.89%	8.41%	13.76%
lex1	**56.04%**	7.03%	12.49%
lex2	47.95%	5.66%	10.12%
lex3	34.05%	8.73%	13.90%
cgp1	25.70%	24.55%	25.11%
cgp2	36.35%	18.28%	24.33%
cgp3	33.13%	3.79%	6.80%
pos1	42.42%	0.97%	1.90%
pos2	42.66%	4.21%	7.66%
pos3	38.75%	2.14%	4.06%

Table 1: Results of *one vs. all* Authorship Verification experiments using MBL

Table 1 shows the results for the positive class of *one vs. all* authorship verification using memory-based learning. We see that memory-based learning on the authorship verification task is able to correctly classify up to 56% of the positive class which is highly underrepresented in both training and test data. Despite the very skewed class distributions, memory-based learning scores reasonably well on this approximation of authorship verification with limited data. The most important lesson is that in a realistic set-up of the task of authorship verification, the accuracy to be expected is much lower than what in general can be found in the published literature.

5 Related Research

As mentioned earlier, most research in authorship attribution starts from unrealistic assumptions about numbers of authors and amount of training data available. We list here the exceptions to this general rule. These studies partially agree with our own results. Argamon et al. (2003) report on results in authorship attribution on twenty authors in a corpus of Usenet newsgroups on a variety of topics. Depending on the topic, results vary from 25% (books, computer theory) to 45% accuracy (computer language) for the 20-author task. Linguistic profiling, a technique presented by Van Halteren (2005), takes large numbers of linguistic features to compare separate authors to average profiles. In a set of eight authors, a linguistic profiling system correctly classifies 97% of the test documents. Madigan et al. (2005) use a collection of data released by Reuters consisting of 114 authors, each represented by a minimum of 200 texts. Results of Bayesian multinomial logistic regression on this corpus show error rates between 97% and 20%, depending on the type of features applied. This is only partially comparable to the authorship attribution results on 145 authors presented in this paper because of the large amount of data in the Madigan et al. (2005) study, while our system works on limited data. In a study of weblog corpora, Koppel et al. (2006) show that authorship attribution with thousands of candidate authors is reasonably reliable, since the system gave an answer in 31.3% of the cases, while the answer is correct in almost 90% of the cases. Whereas these cases show similar results as ours, we believe this study is the first to study the effect of training set size and number of authors involved systematically.

When applied to author verification on eight authors, the linguistic profiling system (Van Halteren, 2005) has a False Reject Rate (FRR) of 0% and a False Accept Rate (FAR) of 8.1%. Argamon et al. (2003) also report on *one vs. all* learning in a set of twenty authors. Results vary from 19% (books, computer theory) to 43% (computer language) accuracy, depending on the topics. Madigan et al. (2005) also did authorship verification experiments on their corpus of 114 authors we described above. They vary the number of target, decoy, and test authors to find that the ideal split is 10-50-54, which produces an error rate of 24%. Koppel et al. (2007) also report on results in *one vs. all* experiments. Using a corpus of 21 books by 10 authors in different genres (including essays, plays, and novels), their system scores a precision of 22.30% and recall of 95%. Our system performs better in precision and worse in recall. Their corpus nevertheless consists of 21 books (each represented by more than forty 500-word chunks) by 10 authors, which makes the task considerably less difficult.

6 Conclusions and Further Research

A lot of the research in authorship attribution is performed on a small set of authors and unrealistic sizes of data, which is an artificial situation. Most of these studies not only overestimate the performance of their system, but also the importance of linguistic features in experiments discriminating between only two or a small number of authors. In this paper, we have shown the effect of many authors and limited data in authorship attribution and verification. When systematically increasing the number of authors in authorship attribution, we see that performance drops significantly. Similar types of features work well for different amounts of authors in our corpus, but generalizations about individual features are not useful.

Memory-based learning shows robustness when dealing with limited data, which is essential in e.g. forensics. Results from experiments in authorship attribution on 145 authors indicate that in almost 50% of the cases, a text from one of the 145 authors is classified correctly. Using combinations of good working lexical and syntactic features leads to significant improvements. The authorship verification task is a much more difficult task, which, in our approximation of it, leads to a correct classification in 56% of the test cases. It is clear that studies reporting over 95% accuracy on a 2-author study are overestimating their performance and the importance of the features selected.

Further research with the 145-author corpus will involve a study of handling with imbalanced data and experimenting with other machine learning algorithms for authorship attribution and verification and a more systematic study of the behavior of different types of learning methods (including feature selection and other optimization issues) on this problem.

Acknowledgements

This study has been carried out in the framework of the 'Computational Techniques for Stylometry for Dutch' project, funded by the National Fund for Scientific Research (FWO) in Belgium. We would like to thank the reviewers for their comments which helped improve this paper.

References

Argamon, Shlomo, Marin Saric, and Sterling S. Stein. 2003. Style mining of electronic messages for multiple authorship discrimination: First results. In *Proceedings of the 2003 Association for Computing Machinery Conference on Knowledge Discovery and Data Mining (ACM SIGKDD)*, pages 475–480.

Argamon, Shlomo, Casey Whitelaw, Paul Chase, Sushant Dawhle, Sobhan R. Hota, Navendu Carg, and Shlomo Levitan. 2007. Stylistic text classification using functional lexical features. *Journal of the American Society of Information Science and Technology*, 58(6):802–822.

Baayen, Harald R., Hans Van Halteren, and Fiona Tweedie. 1996. Outside the cave of shadows: Using syntactic annotation to enhance authorship attribution. *Literary and Linguistic Computing*, 11(3):121–131.

Briggs Myers, Isabel and Peter B. Myers. 1980. *Gifts differing: Understanding personality type.* Mountain View, CA: Davies-Black Publishing.

Burrows, John. 2007. All the way through: Testing for authorship in different frequency data. *Literary and Linguistic Computing*, 22(1):27–47.

Coyotl-Morales, Rosa M., Luis Villaseñor Pineda, Manuel Montes-y Gómez, and Paolo Rosso. 2006. Authorship attribution using word sequences. In *Proceedings of the Iberoamerican Congress on Pattern Recognition (CIARP)*, pages 844–853.

Daelemans, Walter and Antal van den Bosch. 2005. *Memory-Based Language Processing.* Studies in Natural Language Processing. Cambridge, UK: Cambridge University Press.

Daelemans, Walter, Jakub Zavrel, Ko van der Sloot, and Antal van den Bosch. 2007. TiMBL: Tilburg Memory Based Learner, version 6.1, Reference Guide. Technical Report ILK Research Group Technical Report Series no. 07-07, ILK Research Group, University of Tilburg.

Diederich, Joachim, Jörg. Kindermann, Edda Leopold, and Gerhard Paass. 2000. Authorship attribution with Support Vector Machines. *Applied Intelligence*, 19(1-2):109–123.

Feiguina, Ol'ga and Graeme Hirst. 2007. Authorship attribution for small texts: literary and forensic experiments. In *Proceedings of the 30th International Conference of the Special Interest Group on Information Retrieval: Workshop on Plagiarism Analysis, Authorship Identification, and Near-Duplicate Detection (SIGIR)*.

Gamon, Michael. 2004. Linguistic correlates of style: Authorship classification with deep linguistic analysis features. In *Proceedings of the 2004 International Conference on Computational Linguistics (COLING)*, pages 611–617.

Hirst, Graeme and Ol'ga Feiguina. 2007. Bigrams of syntactic labels for authorship discrimination of short texts. *Literary and Linguistic Computing*, 22(4):405–417.

Holmes, D. 1994. Authorship Attribution. *Computers and the Humanities*, 28(2):87–106.

Koppel, Moshe, Jonathan Schler, Shlomo Argamon, and Eran Messeri. 2006. Authorship attribution with thousands of candidate authors. In *Proceedings of the 29th International Conference of the Special Interest Group on Information Retrieval (SIGIR)*, pages 659–660.

Koppel, Moshe, Jonathan Schler, and Elisheva Bonchek-Dokow. 2007. Measuring differentiability: Unmasking pseudonymous authors. *Journal of Machine Learning Research*, 8:1261–1276.

Le, Zhang. 2006. Maximum Entropy Modeling Toolkit for Python and C++. Version 20061005.

Luyckx, Kim and Walter Daelemans. 2008. Personae: a corpus for author and personality prediction from text. In *Proceedings of the 6th International Conference on Language Resources and Evaluation (LREC)*.

Madigan, David, Alexander Genkin, David D. Lewis, Shlomo Argamon, Dmitriy Fradkin, and Li Ye. 2005. Author identification on the large scale. In *Proceedings of the 2005 Meeting of the Classification Society of North America (CSNA)*.

Miranda García, Antonio and Javier Calle Martín. 2007. Function words in authorship attribution studies. *Literary and Linguistic Computing*, 22(1):49–66.

Mosteller, F. and D. Wallace. 1964. Inference and disputed authorship: the Federalist. *Series in Behavioral Science: Quantitative Methods Edition*.

Platt, John, 1998. *Advances in Kernel Methods - Support Vector Learning*, chapter Fast training of Support Vector Machines using Sequential Minimal Optimization, pages 185–208.

Sebastiani, Fabrizio. 2002. Machine learning in automated text categorization. *Association for Computing Machinery (ACM) Computing Surveys*, 34(1):1–47.

Stamatatos, Efstathios. 2007. Author identification using imbalanced and limited training texts. In *Proceedings of the 18th International Conference on Database and Expert Systems Applications (DEXA)*, pages 237–241.

Van Halteren, Hans. 2005. Linguistic profiling for author recognition and verification. In *Proceedings of the 2005 Meeting of the Association for Computational Linguistics (ACL)*.

Witten, Ian and Eibe Frank. 1999. *Data Mining: Practical Machine Learning Tools with Java Implementations*. San Fransisco: Morgan Kaufmann.

Modeling Semantic Containment and Exclusion in Natural Language Inference

Bill MacCartney
Stanford University
wcmac@cs.stanford.edu

Christopher D. Manning
Stanford University
manning@cs.stanford.edu

Abstract

We propose an approach to natural language inference based on a model of *natural logic*, which identifies valid inferences by their lexical and syntactic features, without full semantic interpretation. We greatly extend past work in natural logic, which has focused solely on semantic containment and monotonicity, to incorporate both semantic exclusion and implicativity. Our system decomposes an inference problem into a sequence of atomic edits linking premise to hypothesis; predicts a lexical entailment relation for each edit using a statistical classifier; propagates these relations upward through a syntax tree according to semantic properties of intermediate nodes; and composes the resulting entailment relations across the edit sequence. We evaluate our system on the FraCaS test suite, and achieve a 27% reduction in error from previous work. We also show that hybridizing an existing RTE system with our natural logic system yields significant gains on the RTE3 test suite.

1 Introduction

A necessary (if not sufficient) condition for true natural language understanding is a mastery of open-domain *natural language inference* (NLI): the task of determining whether a natural-language hypothesis can be inferred from a given premise. Indeed, NLI can enable more immediate applications, such as semantic search and question answering (Harabagiu and Hickl, 2006). In recent years a spectrum of approaches to robust, open-domain NLI have been explored within the context of the Recognizing Textual Entailment challenge (Dagan et al., 2005). Up to now, the most successful approaches have used fairly shallow semantic representations, relying on measures of lexical or semantic overlap (Jijkoun and de Rijke, 2005), pattern-based relation extraction (Romano et al., 2006), or approximate matching of predicate-argument structure (Hickl et al., 2006). Such methods, while robust and often effective, are at best partial solutions, unable to explain even simple forms of logical inference. For example, most shallow approaches would fail to license the introduction of *large* in the following example:

(1) Every firm saw costs grow more than expected, even after adjusting for inflation.
―――――――――――――――
Every *large* firm saw costs grow.

At the other extreme, some researchers have approached NLI as logical deduction, building on work in theoretical semantics to translate sentences into first-order logic (FOL), and then applying a theorem prover or model builder (Akhmatova, 2005; Fowler et al., 2005). Regrettably, such approaches tend to founder on the myriad complexities of full semantic interpretation, including tense, aspect, causality, intensionality, modality, vagueness, idioms, indexicals, ellipsis, and many other issues. (What is the right FOL representation of (1), for example?) FOL-based systems that have attained high precision (Bos and Markert, 2006) have done so at the cost of very poor recall.

This work explores a middle way, by developing a computational model of what Lakoff (1970) called *natural logic*, which characterizes valid patterns of inference in terms of syntactic forms re-

© 2008. Licensed under the *Creative Commons Attribution-Noncommercial-Share Alike 3.0 Unported* license (http://creativecommons.org/licenses/by-nc-sa/3.0/). Some rights reserved.

sembling natural language as much as possible.[1] For example, natural logic might sanction (1) by observing that: in ordinary (*upward monotone*) contexts, deleting modifiers preserves truth; in *downward monotone* contexts, inserting modifiers preserves truth; and *every* is downward monotone in its restrictor NP. A natural logic system can thus achieve the expressivity and precision needed to handle a great variety of simple logical inferences, while sidestepping the difficulties of full semantic interpretation.

2 A theory of natural logic

The natural logic approach originated in traditional logic (e.g., Aristotle's syllogisms), and was revived in a formal form by van Benthem (1986) and Sánchez Valencia (1991), who proposed a natural logic based on categorial grammar to handle inferences involving containment relations and upward and downward monotonicity, such as (1). Their *monotonicity calculus* explains inferences involving even nested inversions of monotonicity, but because it lacks any representation of exclusion (as opposed to containment), it cannot explain simple inferences such as (38) and (205) in table 2, below.

Another model which arguably follows the natural logic tradition (though not presented as such) was developed by Nairn et al. (2006) to explain inversions and nestings of implicative (and factive) predicates, as in *Ed did not forget to force Dave to leave* $\models$ *Dave left.* Their *implication projection algorithm* bears some resemblance to the monotonicity calculus, but does not incorporate containment relations or explain interactions between implicatives and monotonicity, and thus fails to license *John refused to dance* $\models$ *John didn't tango.*

We propose a new model of natural logic which generalizes the monotonicity calculus to cover inferences involving exclusion, and (partly) unifies it with Nairn et al.'s model of implicatives. We (1) augment the set of entailment relations used in monotonicity calculus to include representations of exclusion; (2) generalize the concept of monotonicity to one of *projectivity*, which describes how the entailments of a compound expression depend on the entailments of its parts; and (3) describe a weak proof procedure based on composing entailment relations across chains of atomic edits.

[1] Natural logic should not be confused with *natural deduction*, a proof system for first-order logic.

Entailment relations. We employ an inventory of seven mutually exclusive *basic entailment relations*, defined by analogy with set relations: equivalence (*couch* $=$ *sofa*); forward entailment (*crow* $\sqsubset$ *bird*) and its converse (*European* $\sqsupset$ *French*); negation, or exhaustive exclusion (*human* $\hat{}$ *nonhuman*); alternation, or non-exhaustive exclusion (*cat* $|$ *dog*); cover, or non-exclusive exhaustion (*animal* $\smile$ *nonhuman*); and independence (*hungry* $\#$ *hippo*), which covers all other cases. As in the monotonicity calculus, we define these relations for expressions of every semantic type: sentences, common and proper nouns, transitive and intransitive verbs, adjectives, and so on. For example, among generalized quantifiers, we find that *all* $=$ *every*, *every* $\sqsubset$ *some*, *some* $\hat{}$ *no*, *no* $|$ *every*, *at least four* $\smile$ *at most six*, and *most* $\#$ *ten or more*.[2]

Projectivity. In order to explain the entailments of a compound expression as a function of the entailments of its parts, we categorize semantic functions according to their *projectivity class*, a concept which generalizes both Sánchez Valencia's monotonicity classes (upward, downward, and non-monotone) and the nine implication signatures of Nairn et al. The projectivity class of a function f describes how the entailment relation between $f(x)$ and $f(y)$ depends on the entailment relation between x and y. Consider simple negation (*not*). Like most functions, it projects $=$ and $\#$ without change (*not happy* $=$ *not glad* and *isn't swimming* $\#$ *isn't hungry*). As a downward monotone function, it swaps $\sqsubset$ and $\sqsupset$ (*didn't kiss* $\sqsupset$ *didn't touch*). But we can also establish that it projects $\hat{}$ without change (*not human* $\hat{}$ *not nonhuman*) and swaps $|$ and $\smile$ (*not French* $\smile$ *not German*, *not more than 4* $|$ *not less than 6*). By contrast, an implicative like *refuse*, though it also swaps $\sqsubset$ and $\sqsupset$ (*refuse to tango* $\sqsupset$ *refuse to dance*), projects $\hat{}$ as $|$ (*refuse to stay* $|$ *refuse to go*) and projects both $|$ and $\smile$ as $\#$ (*refuse to tango* $\#$ *refuse to waltz*).

Projectivity thus allows us to determine the entailments of a compound expression recursively, by propagating entailments upward through a semantic composition tree according to the projectivity class of each node on the path to the root. For example, the semantics of *Nobody can enter with-*

[2] Some of these assertions assume *existential import*, i.e., that the predicates to which the quantifiers are applied have non-empty denotations. This assumption, standard in traditional logic, seems justifiable in the context of informal natural language inference (Böttner, 1988).

out a shirt might be represented by the tree (*nobody* (*can* ((*without* (*a shirt*)) *enter*))). Since *shirt* ⊏ *clothes*, and since *without* is downward monotone, we have *without shirt* ⊐ *without clothes*. Since *nobody* is also downward monotone, it follows that *Nobody can enter without a shirt* ⊏ *Nobody can enter without clothes*.

Inference. Let $x' = e(x)$ be the result of applying an *atomic edit* e (the insertion, deletion, or substitution of a subexpression) to a compound expression x. The entailment relation between x and x' is found by projecting the entailment relation generated by e upward through x's semantic composition tree. Substitutions generate relations according to the meanings of the substituends. Most deletions generate the ⊏ relation (*red socks* ⊏ *socks*). (Insertions are symmetric: they typically generate ⊐.) However, some items have special behavior. For example, deleting (or inserting) *not* generates ^ (*not hungry* ^ *hungry*).

If two expressions are connected by a chain of atomic edits, we can determine the entailment relation between them by composing (as in Tarskian relation algebra) the entailment relations generated by each edit. The result may be a basic entailment relation, or may be a union of such relations, with larger unions conveying less information about entailment. This possibility, coupled with the need to find a chain of atomic edits which preserves relevant entailment relations, limits the power of the proof procedure described.

Implicatives. The account of implicatives and factives given by Nairn et al. hinges on a classification of implicative and factive operators into nine *implication signatures*, according to their implications—positive (+), negative (–), or null (∘)—in both positive and negative contexts. Thus *refuse* has implication signature –/∘, because it carries a negative implication in a positive context (*refused to dance* implies *didn't dance*), and no implication in a negative context (*didn't refuse to dance* implies neither *danced* nor *didn't dance*).

Most of the phenomena observed by Nairn et al. can be explained within our framework by specifying, for each signature, the relation generated when an operator of that signature is deleted from a compound expression. For example, deleting signature –/∘ generates | (*Jim refused to dance* | *Jim danced*); under negation, this is projected as ‿ (*Jim didn't refuse to dance* ‿ *Jim didn't dance*). By contrast, deleting signature ∘/– generates ⊐ (*Jim attempted to dance* ⊐ *Jim danced*); under negation, this is projected as ⊏ (*Jim didn't attempt to dance* ⊏ *Jim didn't dance*).[3]

We can also account for monotonicity effects of implicative and factive operators by describing the projectivity properties of each implication signature: signatures +/–, +/∘, and ∘/– are upward monotone (*attempt to tango* ⊏ *attempt to dance*); signatures –/+, –/∘, and ∘/+ are downward monotone (*refuse to dance* ⊏ *refuse to tango*); and signatures +/+, –/–, and ∘/∘ are non-monotone (*think dancing is fun* # *think tangoing is fun*).

3 The NatLog system

Our implementation of natural logic, the *NatLog* system, uses a multi-stage architecture like those of (Marsi and Krahmer, 2005; MacCartney et al., 2006), comprising (1) linguistic analysis, (2) alignment, (3) lexical entailment classification, (4) entailment projection, and (5) entailment composition. We'll use the following inference as a running example:

(2) Jimmy Dean refused to move without blue jeans.
James Dean didn't dance without pants.

The example is admittedly contrived, but it compactly exhibits containment, exclusion, and implicativity. How the NatLog system handles this example is depicted in table 1.

Linguistic analysis. Relative to other NLI systems, the NatLog system does comparatively little linguistic pre-processing. We rely on the Stanford parser (Klein and Manning, 2003), a Penn Treebank-trained statistical parser, for tokenization, lemmatization, part-of-speech tagging, and phrase-structure parsing.

By far the most important analysis performed at this stage, however, is *projectivity marking*, in which we compute the effective projectivity for each token span in each input sentence. In the premise of (2), for example, we want to determine that the effective projectivity is upward monotone

[3] Factives, however, do not fit as neatly as implicatives: For example, deleting signature +/+ generates ⊏ (*Jim forgot that dancing is fun* ⊏ *dancing is fun*); yet under negation, this is projected not as ⊐, but as | (*Jim didn't forget that dancing is fun* | *dancing isn't fun*). The problem arises because the implication carried by a factive is not an entailment, but a presupposition. As is well known, the projection behavior of presuppositions differs from that of entailments (van der Sandt, 1992). In the current work, we set presuppositions aside.

premise	Jimmy Dean	refused to			move	without	blue	jeans
hypothesis	James Dean		did	n't	dance	without		pants
edit index	1	2	3	4	5	6	7	8
edit type	SUB	DEL	INS	INS	SUB	MAT	DEL	SUB
lex features	str_sim=0.67	implic:+/○	cat:aux	cat:neg	hyponym			hypernym
lex entrel	=	$\mid$	=	^	⊐	=	⊏	⊏
projectivity	↑	↑	↑	↑	↓	↓	↑	↑
atomic entrel	=	$\mid$	=	^	⊏	=	⊏	⊏
composition	=	$\mid$	$\mid$	⊏	⊏	⊏	⊏	⊏

Table 1: An example of the operation of the NatLog model.

unary operator: *without*
  pattern: `IN < /^[Ww]ithout$/`
  argument 1: projectivity ↓ on dominating PP
    pattern: `__ > PP=proj`

binary operator: *most*
  pattern: `JJS < /^[Mm]ost$/ !> QP`
  argument 1: projectivity $\not\updownarrow$ on dominating NP
    pattern: `__ >+(NP) (NP=proj !> NP)`
  argument 2: projectivity ↑ on dominating S
    pattern: `__ >> (S=proj !> S)`

Figure 1: Some projectivity operator definitions.

for *Jimmy Dean* and *refused to*, downward monotone for *move* and *without*, and upward monotone for *blue* and *jeans*. Our choice of a Treebank-trained parser (driven by the goal of broad coverage) complicates this effort, because the nesting of constituents in phrase-structure parses does not always correspond to the structure of idealized semantic composition trees. Our solution is imperfect but effective. We define a list of operator types affecting projectivity (e.g., implicatives like *refuse to*, prepositions like *without*), and for each type we specify its arity and a Tregex tree pattern (Levy and Andrew, 2006) which permits us to identify its occurrences in our Treebank parses. We also specify, for each argument position of each type, both the projectivity class and another Tregex pattern which helps us to determine the sentence span over which the operator's effect is projected. (Figure 1 shows some example definitions.) The marking process computes these projections, performs projectivity composition where needed, and marks each token span with its final effective projectivity.

Alignment. Next, we establish an *alignment* between the premise P and hypothesis H, represented by a sequence of *atomic edits* over spans of word tokens. This alignment representation is symmetric and many-to-many, and is general enough to include various other alignment representations as special cases. We define four edit types: *deletion* (DEL) of a span from P, *insertion* (INS) of a span into H, *substitution* (SUB) of an H span for a P span, and *match* (MAT) of an H span to a P span. Each edit is parameterized by the token indices at which it operates, and edit indices may "cross", permitting representation of movement. The first four lines of table 1 depict a possible alignment for our example problem.

An alignment decomposes an inference problem into a sequence of atomic inference problems, one for each atomic edit. Note that edits are ordered, and that this ordering defines a path from P to H through intermediate forms. (Edit order need not correspond to sentence order, though it does in our example.) The relative ordering of certain kinds of edits (e.g., the insertion of *not*) may influence the effective projectivity applicable for other edits; consequently, the NatLog system can reorder edits to maximize the benefit of the projectivity marking performed during linguistic analysis.

This paper does not present new algorithms for alignment; we focus instead on identifying entailment relations between aligned sentence pairs. The experiments described in sections 4 and 5 use alignments from other sources.

Lexical entailment classification. Much of the heavy lifting in the NatLog system is done by the *lexical entailment model*, which uses a classifier to predict an entailment relation for each atomic edit based solely on features of the lexical items involved, independent of context. (For example, this model should assign the entailment relation ⊐ to the edit SUB(*move*, *dance*), regardless of whether the effective projectivity at the locus of the edit is upward monotone, downward monotone, or something else.) In the case of a SUB edit, the features include:

- WordNet-derived measures of synonymy, hyponymy, and antonymy between sub-

stituends;
- other features indicating semantic relatedness: the WordNet-based Jiang-Conrath measure (Jiang and Conrath, 1997) and a feature based on NomBank (Meyers et al., 2004);
- string similarity features based on Levenshtein string-edit distance between lemmas;
- lexical category features, indicating whether the substituends are prepositions, possessives, articles, auxiliaries, pronouns, proper nouns, operator adjectives, punctuation, etc.;
- quantifier category features, which identify classes of quantifiers with similar properties;
- a feature for unequal numeric expressions

For DEL edits, we use only the lexical category features and a feature based on a custom-built resource which maps implicatives and factives to their implication signatures. (As noted in section 2, however, most DEL edits just have $\sqsubset$ as the target lexical entailment relation.) INS edits are treated symmetrically.

The model uses a decision tree classifier trained on 2,449 hand-annotated training examples (1,525 SUB edits and 924 DEL/INS edits). The decision tree is minimally pruned, and contains about 180 leaves. When tested on the training data, the classifier achieves >99% accuracy, indicating that our feature representation successfully captures nearly all relevant distinctions between examples.

Lexical features and lexical entailment relations for our example appear on lines 5 and 6 of table 1.

Entailment projection. The lexical entailment relations generated by each atomic edit can now be projected upward to determine the corresponding atomic entailment relations, that is, the entailment relations between successive intermediate forms on the path from P to H, as defined by the alignment. Strictly speaking, the effective projectivity for a particular edit should be computed based on the intermediate form upon which the edit operates, since the projectivity properties of this form can depend on preceding edits. However, the NatLog system minimizes the need to compute projectivity in intermediate forms by reordering the edits in an alignment in such a way that effective projectivity can, in most cases, simply be taken from the projectivity marking of P and H performed during the linguistic analysis stage.

The effective projectivity and resulting atomic entailment relation for each edit in our running example are depicted in lines 7 and 8 of table 1. For all (non-MAT) edits but one, the effective projectivity is upward monotone, so that the atomic entailment relation is identical with the lexical entailment relation. However, the SUB(*move*, *dance*) edit occurs in a downward monotone context, so that the lexical relation $\sqsupset$ is converted to $\sqsubset$ at the atomic level.

Entailment composition. Finally, the atomic entailment relations predicted for each edit are combined, via relation composition, to produce an overall prediction for the inference problem. Relation composition is deterministic, and for the most part follows intuitive rules: $\sqsubset$ composed with $\sqsubset$ yields $\sqsubset$; $\sqsupset$ composed with $\sqsupset$ yields $\sqsupset$; $\#$ composed with any relation yields $\#$; $=$ composed with any relation yields that relation, and so on. Composition tends to "degenerate" towards $\#$, in the sense that the composition of a chain of randomly-selected relations tends toward $\#$ as the chain grows longer. This chaining of entailments across edits can be compared to the method presented in (Harmeling, 2007); however, that approach assigns to each edit merely a probability of preserving truth, not an entailment relation.

The last line of table 1 shows the cumulative composition of the atomic entailment relations in the line above. Particular noteworthy is the fact that $|$ and $^\wedge$ compose to yield $\sqsubset$. (To illustrate: if A excludes B (*fish* $|$ *human*) and B is the negation of C (*human* $^\wedge$ *nonhuman*), then A entails C (*fish* $\sqsubset$ *nonhuman*).) The final entailment relation in this line, $\sqsubset$, is NatLog's final (and correct) answer for our example problem.

4 Evaluating on FraCaS problems

The FraCaS test suite (Cooper et al., 1996) contains 346 NLI problems, divided into nine sections, each focused on a specific category of semantic phenomena (listed in table 3). Each problem consists of one or more premise sentences, a question sentence, and one of three answers: *yes* (the union of $\sqsubset$ and $=$), *no* (the union of $|$ and $^\wedge$), or *unknown* (the union of $\sqsupset$, $\smile$, and $\#$). Table 2 shows some example problems.

To facilitate comparison with previous work, we have evaluated our system using a version of the FraCas data prepared by (MacCartney and Manning, 2007), in which multiple-premise problems (44% of the total) and problems lacking a hypothesis or a well-defined answer (3% of the total) are excluded; question sentences have been converted

§	ID	Premise	Hypothesis	Ans
1	38	No delegate finished the report.	Some delegate finished the report on time.	*no*
1	48	At most ten commissioners spend time at home.	At most ten c...s spend a lot of time at home.	*yes*
2	83	Either Smith, Jones or Anderson signed the contract.	Jones signed the contract.	*unk*
5	205	Dumbo is a large animal.	Dumbo is a small animal.	*no*
6	233	ITEL won more orders than APCOM.	ITEL won some orders.	*yes*
9	335	Smith believed that ITEL had won the contract in 1992.	ITEL won the contract in 1992.	*unk*

Table 2: Illustrative examples from the FraCaS test suite

System	#	P %	R %	Acc %
most common class	183	55.74	100.00	55.74
MacCartney07	183	68.89	60.78	59.56
NatLog	183	89.33	65.69	**70.49**

§	Section	#	P %	R %	Acc %
1	Quantifiers	44	95.24	100.00	**97.73**
2	Plurals	24	90.00	64.29	75.00
3	Anaphora	6	100.00	60.00	50.00
4	Ellipsis	25	100.00	5.26	24.00
5	Adjectives	15	71.43	83.33	80.00
6	Comparatives	16	88.89	88.89	81.25
7	Temporal	36	85.71	70.59	58.33
8	Verbs	8	80.00	66.67	62.50
9	Attitudes	9	100.00	83.33	88.89
1, 2, 5, 6, 9		108	90.38	85.45	**87.04**

Table 3: Performance on FraCaS problems (three-way classification). The columns show the number of problems, precision and recall for the *yes* class, and accuracy. Results for NatLog are broken out by section.

		guess			
		yes	*no*	*unk*	total
answer	*yes*	67	4	31	102
	no	1	16	4	21
	unk	7	7	46	60
	total	75	27	81	183

Table 4: Confusions on FraCaS data (all sections)

to declarative hypotheses; and alignments between premise and hypothesis have been automatically generated and manually corrected.

Results are shown in table 3. We achieve overall accuracy of 70.49%, representing a 27% error reduction from (MacCartney and Manning, 2007). In the section concerning quantifiers, which is both the largest and the most amenable to natural logic, all problems but one are answered correctly.[4] We also answer all but one problems correctly in the (admittedly small) section on attitudes, which involves implicatives and factives. Unsurprisingly, performance is mediocre in four sections concerning semantic phenomena (e.g., ellipsis) not relevant to natural logic and not modeled by the system. But in the other five sections (about 60% of the problems), we achieve accuracy of 87.04%, an error reduction of 61% from (MacCartney and Manning, 2007). What's more, precision is high in nearly every section: even outside its areas of expertise, the system rarely predicts entailment when none exists.

Since the NatLog system was developed with FraCaS problems in mind, these results do not constitute a proper evaluation on unseen test data. On the other hand, the system does no training on FraCaS data, and has had no opportunity to learn its biases. (Otherwise, accuracy on §4 could not fall so far below the baseline.) The system not only answers most problems correctly, but usually does so for valid reasons, particular within its areas of expertise. All in all, the results fulfill our main goal in testing on FraCaS: to demonstrate the representational and inferential adequacy of our model of natural logic.

The confusion matrix shown in table 4 reveals an interesting property of the NatLog system. The commonest confusions are those where the answer is *yes* but we guess *unknown*. This reflects both the bias toward *yes* in the FraCaS data, and the system's tendency to predict *unknown* (entailment relation $\#$) when confused: given the composition rules for entailment relations, the system can predict *yes* only if all atomic-level predictions are either $\sqsubset$ or $=$.

5 Evaluating on RTE problems

NLI problems from the PASCAL RTE Challenge (Dagan et al., 2005) differ from FraCaS problems in several important ways. (See table 5 for examples.) Instead of textbook examples of seman-

[4] In fact, the sole exception is disputable, since it hinges on whether *many* refers to proportion (apparently, the view held by the FraCaS authors) or absolute quantity.

ID	Premise	Hypothesis	Answer
71	As leaders gather in Argentina ahead of this weekends regional talks, Hugo Chávez, Venezuela's populist president is using an energy windfall to win friends and promote his vision of 21st-century socialism.	Hugo Chávez acts as Venezuela's president.	*yes*
788	Democrat members of the Ways and Means Committee, where tax bills are written and advanced, do not have strong small business voting records.	Democrat members had strong small business voting records.	*no*

Table 5: Illustrative examples from the RTE3 development set

tic phenomena, RTE problems are more natural-seeming, with premises collected "in the wild" from newswire. The premises are much longer, averaging 35 words (vs. 11 words for FraCaS). Also, RTE aims at binary classification: the RTE *no* combines the *no* and *unk* answers in FraCaS.

Due to the character of RTE problems, we do not expect NatLog to be a good general-purpose solution to solving all RTE problems. First, most RTE problems depend on forms of inference, such as paraphrase, temporal reasoning, or relation extraction, which NatLog is not designed to address. Second, in most RTE problems, the edit distance between premise and hypothesis is relatively large. More atomic edits means a greater chance that errors made in lexical entailment classification or projection will propagate, via entailment composition, to the system's final output. Rather, in applying NatLog to RTE, we hope to make reliable predictions on a subset of RTE problems, trading recall for precision. If we succeed, then we may be able to hybridize with a broad-coverage RTE system to obtain better results than either system individually—the same strategy that was adopted by (Bos and Markert, 2006) for their FOL-based system. For this purpose, we have chosen to use the Stanford RTE system described in (de Marneffe et al., 2006). We also use the Stanford system to generate alignments when evaluating NatLog on RTE problems.

Table 6 shows the performance of NatLog on RTE3 data. Relative to the Stanford system, NatLog achieves high precision on its *yes* predictions—above 70%—suggesting that hybridizing may be effective. For comparison, the FOL-based system reported in (Bos and Markert, 2006) attained a similarly high precision of 76% on RTE2 problems, but was able to make a positive prediction in only about 4% of cases. NatLog makes positive predictions far more often—in about 25% of cases.

The Stanford system makes *yes/no* predictions by thresholding a real-valued *inference score*. To construct a hybrid system, we adjust the Stanford inference scores by $+\Delta$ or $-\Delta$, depending on whether or not NatLog predicts *yes*. We choose Δ by optimizing development set accuracy, while adjusting the threshold to generate balanced predictions (that is, equal numbers of *yes* and *no* predictions). As an additional experiment, we fix Δ at this value and then adjust the threshold to optimize development set accuracy, resulting in an excess of *yes* predictions. (Since this optimization is based solely on development data, its use on test data is fully legitimate.) Results for these two cases are shown in table 6. The parameters tuned on development data gave good results on test data. The optimized hybrid system attained an absolute accuracy gain of 4% over the Stanford system, corresponding to an extra 32 problems answered correctly. This result is statistically significant ($p < 0.05$, McNemar's test, 2-tailed).

System	Data	% Yes	P %	R %	Acc %
Stanford	dev	50.25	68.66	66.99	67.25
	test	50.00	61.75	60.24	60.50
NatLog	dev	22.50	**73.89**	32.38	59.25
	test	26.38	**70.14**	36.10	59.38
Hybrid, bal.	dev	50.00	70.25	68.20	68.75
	test	50.00	65.50	63.90	64.25
Hybrid, opt.	dev	56.00	69.20	75.24	**70.00**
	test	54.50	64.45	68.54	**64.50**

Table 6: Performance of various systems on RTE3 (two-way classification). The columns show the data set used (800 problems each), the proportion of *yes* predictions, precision and recall for the *yes* class, and accuracy.

The gains attributable to NatLog are exemplified by problem 788 (table 5). NatLog sanctions the deletion of a restrictive modifier and an appositive from the premise, and recognizes that deleting a negation generates a contradiction; thus it correctly answers *no*. On the other hand, there are many RTE problems where NatLog's precision works against it. For example, NatLog answers *no* to problem 71 because it cannot account for the insertion of *acts as* in the hypothesis. Fortunately, both the Stanford system and the hybrid system answer this problem correctly.

6 Conclusion

We do not claim natural logic to be a universal solution for NLI. Many important types of inference are not amenable to natural logic, including paraphrase (*Eve was let go* $\models$ *Eve lost her job*), verb alternation (*he drained the oil* $\models$ *the oil drained*), relation extraction (*Aho, a trader at UBS, ...* $\models$ *Aho works for UBS*), common-sense reasoning (*the sink overflowed* $\models$ *the floor got wet*), and so on.

Moreover, because natural logic has a weaker proof theory than FOL, some inferences lie beyond its deductive power. For example, it cannot explain inferences involving De Morgan's laws for quantifiers, as in *Not all birds fly* = *Some birds don't fly*.

However, by incorporating semantic containment, semantic exclusion, and implicativity, the model of natural logic developed in this paper succeeds in explaining a great variety of everyday patterns of inference. Ultimately, open-domain NLI is likely to require combining disparate reasoners, and a facility for natural logic inference is a good candidate to be a component of such a solution.

Acknowledgements The authors wish to thank the anonymous reviewers for their helpful comments. This work was supported in part by ARDA's Advanced Question Answering for Intelligence (AQUAINT) Program.

References

Akhmatova, Elena. 2005. Textual entailment resolution via atomic propositions. In *Proceedings of the PASCAL Challenges Workshop on Recognising Textual Entailment*.

Bos, Johan and Katja Markert. 2006. When logical inference helps determining textual entailment (and when it doesn't). In *Proceedings of the Second PASCAL Challenges Workshop on Recognizing Textual Entailment*.

Böttner, Michael. 1988. A note on existential import. *Studia Logica*, 47(1):35–40.

Dagan, Ido, Oren Glickman, and Bernardo Magnini. 2005. The PASCAL Recognising Textual Entailment Challenge. In *Proceedings of the PASCAL Challenges Workshop on Recognising Textual Entailment*.

de Marneffe, Marie-Catherine, Bill MacCartney, Trond Grenager, Daniel Cer, Anna Rafferty, and Christopher D. Manning. 2006. Learning to distinguish valid textual entailments. In *Proceedings of the Second PASCAL Challenges Workshop on Recognizing Textual Entailment*.

Fowler, Abraham, Bob Hauser, Daniel Hodges, Ian Niles, Adrian Novischi, and Jens Stephan. 2005. Applying COGEX to recognize textual entailment. In *Proceedings of the PASCAL Challenges Workshop on Recognising Textual Entailment*.

Harabagiu, Sanda and Andrew Hickl. 2006. Using scenario knowledge in automatic question answering. In *Proceedings of the Workshop on Task-Focused Summarization and Question Answering*, pages 32–39, Sydney.

Harmeling, Stefan. 2007. An extensible probabilistic transformation-based approach to the Third Recognizing Textual Entailment Challenge. In *ACL-07 Workshop on Textual Entailment and Paraphrasing*, Prague.

Hickl, Andrew, John Williams, Jeremy Bensley, Kirk Roberts, Bryan Rink, and Ying Shi. 2006. Recognizing textual entailment with LCC's GROUNDHOG system. In *Proceedings of the Second PASCAL Challenges Workshop on Recognizing Textual Entailment*.

Jiang, Jay J. and David W. Conrath. 1997. Semantic similarity based on corpus statistics and lexical taxonomy. In *Proceedings of the International Conference on Research in Computational Linguistics*.

Jijkoun, Valentin and Maarten de Rijke. 2005. Recognizing textual entailment using lexical similarity. In *Proceedings of the PASCAL Challenges Workshop on Recognizing Textual Entailment*, pages 73–76.

Klein, Dan and Christopher D. Manning. 2003. Accurate unlexicalized parsing. In *Proceedings of ACL-03*, Sapporo.

Lakoff, George. 1970. Linguistics and natural logic. *Synthese*, 22:151–271.

Levy, Roger and Galen Andrew. 2006. Tregex and Tsurgeon: tools for querying and manipulating tree data structures. In *Proceedings of LREC-06*, Genoa.

MacCartney, Bill and Christopher D. Manning. 2007. Natural logic for textual inference. In *ACL-07 Workshop on Textual Entailment and Paraphrasing*, Prague.

MacCartney, Bill, Trond Grenager, Marie-Catherine de Marneffe, Daniel Cer, and Christopher D. Manning. 2006. Learning to recognize features of valid textual entailments. In *Proceedings of NAACL-06*, New York.

Marsi, Erwin and Emiel Krahmer. 2005. Classification of semantic relations by humans and machines. In *ACL-05 Workshop on Empirical Modeling of Semantic Equivalence and Entailment*, Ann Arbor.

Nairn, Rowan, Cleo Condoravdi, and Lauri Karttunen. 2006. Computing relative polarity for textual inference. In *Proceedings of ICoS-5 (Inference in Computational Semantics)*, Buxton, UK.

Romano, Lorenza, Milen Kouylekov, Idan Szpektor, Ido Dagan, and Alberto Lavelli. 2006. Investigating a generic paraphrase-based approach for relation extraction. In *Proceedings of EACL 2006*.

Sánchez Valencia, Victor. 1991. *Studies on Natural Logic and Categorial Grammar*. Ph.D. thesis, University of Amsterdam.

van Benthem, Johan. 1986. *Essays in logical semantics*. Reidel, Dordrecht.

van der Sandt, Rob A. 1992. Presupposition projection as anaphora resolution. *Journal of Semantics*, 9(4):333–377.

Linguistically-based sub-sentential alignment for terminology extraction from a bilingual automotive corpus

Lieve Macken and **Els Lefever** and **Veronique Hoste**
Language and Translation Technology Team
Ghent University College
Belgium
{Lieve.Macken, Els.Lefever, Veronique.Hoste}@hogent.be

Abstract

We present a sub-sentential alignment system that links linguistically motivated phrases in parallel texts based on lexical correspondences and syntactic similarity. We compare the performance of our sub-sentential alignment system with different symmetrization heuristics that combine the GIZA++ alignments of both translation directions. We demonstrate that the aligned linguistically motivated phrases are a useful means to extract bilingual terminology and more specifically complex multiword terms.

1 Introduction

This research has been carried out in the framework of a customer project for PSA Peugeot Citroën. The final goal of the project is a reduction and terminological unification process of PSA's database, which contains all text strings that are used for compiling user manuals. French being the source language, all French entries have been translated to some extent into the twenty different languages that are part of the customer's portfolio. Two sub-projects have been defined:

1. automatic terminology extraction for all languages taking French as the pivot language
2. improved consistency of the database entries, e.g. through the automatic replacement of synonyms by the preferred term (decided in (1))

©2008. Licensed under the *Creative Commons Attribution-Noncommercial-Share Alike 3.0 Unported* license (http://creativecommons.org/licenses/by-nc-sa/3.0/). Some rights reserved.

This paper presents a novel terminology extraction method applied to the French-English part of the database.

There is a long tradition of research into bilingual terminology extraction (Kupiec, 1993), (Gaussier, 1998). In most systems, candidate terms are first identified in the source language based on predefined PoS patterns – for French, *N N*, *N Prep N*, and *N Adj* are typical patterns. In a second step, the translation candidates are extracted from the bilingual corpus based on word alignments. In recent work, Itagaki et al. (2007) use the phrase table derived from the GIZA++ alignments to identify the translations.

We use a different and more flexible approach. We developed a sub-sentential alignment system that links linguistically motivated phrases in parallel texts based on lexical correspondences and syntactic similarity. Rather than predefining terms as sequences of PoS patterns, we first generate candidate terms starting from the aligned phrases. In a second step, we use a general purpose corpus and the n-gram frequency of the automotive corpus to determine the specificity of the terms.

The remainder of this paper is organized as follows: Section 2 describes the corpus. In Section 3, we present our linguistically-based sub-sentential alignment system and in Section 4 we describe how we use the aligned phrases for terminology extraction.

2 Automotive corpus

For developing our terminology extraction module, we have used the French-English sentence-aligned database that contains 363,651 entries. These entries can be full sentences, parts of sentences, as well as isolated words and are aligned across languages by means of a unique ID. The

	PoS tagging error rate	Lemmatisation error rate	PoS after update	Lemmas after update
French	4.50 %	2.29 %	1.92 %	1.22 %
English	5.16 %	3.13 %	2.66 %	3.03 %

Table 1: Part-of-Speech tagging and lemmatisation error rate on the test sentences

average sentence length of a database entry is 9 words.

2.1 Linguistic annotation

In order to ensure consistent processing of the languages in the corpus (e.g. Italian, Spanish, German), we have used the freely availabe TreeTagger tool (Schmid, 1994) for performing tokenisation, part-of-speech tagging and lemmatisation of the corpus. In order to evaluate the domain-adaptability of the tagger, we have manually validated the quality of the TreeTagger output for a training set of 12,200 tokens (about 1,200 sentences). We have used this validated set to derive a list of hard coded PoS tags (e.g. the French word *vis* can be a noun or verb, but is always a noun in our corpus) as well as post-processing rules for remediating erroneous PoS tags. We additionally annotated 350 test sentences (about 3,500 tokens). Table 1 shows the error rate figures for PoS-tagging and lemmatisation before and after updating the default output of the TreeTagger tool.

We further enriched the corpora with chunk information. During text chunking, syntactically related words are combined into non-overlapping chunks based on PoS information. We developed rule-based chunkers for English and French. The rule-based chunkers contain distituency rules, i.e. the rules add a chunk boundary when two part-of-speech codes cannot occur in the same constituent. The following example shows a French-English sentence pair divided in non-overlapping chunks:

> Fr: valable | uniquement | pour la ceinture | de sécurité avant latérale | du côté passager
> En: applies | only | to the outer seat belt | on the passenger side

We manually indicated chunk boundaries in the 350-sentences test corpus and evaluated the rule-based chunkers by running the CoNLL-evalscript (Tjong Kim Sang and Buchholz, 2000). We obtained precision scores of 89% and 87% and recall scores of 91% and 91% for French and English respectively.

	# Words	# Sentence pairs
Short (< 8 words)	4,496	404
Medium (8-19 words)	4,493	212
Long (> 19 words)	4,498	97
Total	13,487	713
Development corpus	4,423	231

Table 2: Number of words and sentence pairs in the three test corpora and the development corpus

2.2 Test corpora

As we expect that sentence length has an impact on the alignment performance, we created three test corpora with varying sentence length. We distinguished short sentences (2-7 words), medium-length sentences (8-19 words) and long sentences (> 19 words). Each test corpus contains approximately 4,500 words.

We also compiled a development corpus containing sentences of varying sentence length to debug the system and to determine the value of the thresholds used in the system. The formal characteristics of the test corpora and the training corpus are given in Table 2.

3 Sub-sentential alignment

Sub-sentential alignments – and the underlying word alignments – are used in the context of Machine Translation to create phrase tables for phrase-based statistical machine translation systems (Koehn et al., 2007). A stand-alone sub-sentential alignment module however, is also useful for human translators if incorporated in CAT-tools, e.g. sophisticated bilingual concordance systems, or in sub-sentential translation memory systems (Gotti et al., 2005). A quite obvious application of a sub-sentential alignment system is the creation of bilingual dictionaries and terminology extraction from bilingual corpora (Melamed, 2000), (Itagaki et al., 2007).

In the context of statistical machine translation, GIZA++ is one of the most widely used word alignment toolkits. GIZA++ implements the IBM models and is used in Moses (Koehn et al., 2007) to generate the initial source-to-target and target-to-source word alignments after which some symmetrization heuristics combine the alignments of both translation directions.

We present an alternative – linguistically-based – approach, that starts from a lexical probabilistic bilingual dictionary generated by IBM Model One.

3.1 Architecture

The basic idea behind our approach is that – at least for European languages – translations conveying the same meaning use to a certain extent the same building blocks from which this meaning is composed: i.e. we assume that to a large extent noun and prepositional phrases, verb phrases and adverbial phrases in one language directly map to similar constituents in the other language[1]. The extent to which our basic assumption holds depends on the translation strategy that was used. Text types that are typically translated in a more literal way (e.g. user manuals) will contain more direct correspondences.

We conceive our sub-sentential aligner as a cascade model consisting of two phases. The objective of the first phase is to link *anchor chunks*, i.e. chunks that can be linked with a very high precision. Those anchor chunks are linked based on lexical clues and syntactic similarity. In the second phase, we will try to model the more complex translational correspondences based on observed translation shift patterns. The anchor chunks of the first phase will be used to limit the search space in the second phase.

As the application at hand is terminology extraction, we are interested in alignments with very high precision. As the automotive corpus contains rather literal translations, we expect that a high percentage of anchor chunks can be retrieved using only the first phase of our approach.

The sub-sentential alignment system takes as input sentence-aligned texts, together with additional linguistic annotations (part-of-speech codes and lemmas) for the source and the target text.

In the first step of the process, the source and target sentences are divided into chunks based on PoS information, and lexical correspondences are retrieved from a bilingual dictionary. During anchor chunk alignment, the sub-sentential aligner links chunks based on lexical correspondences and chunk similarity.

3.2 Bilingual Dictionary

We used the Perl implementation of IBM Model One that is part of the Microsoft Bilingual Sentence Aligner (Moore, 2002) to derive a bilingual dictionary from a parallel corpus. IBM Model One is a purely *lexical* model: it only takes into account word frequencies of source and target sentences[2].

The IBM models allow only 1:n word mappings, and are therefore asymmetric. To overcome this problem, we ran the model in two directions: from French to English and from English to French. To get high-accuracy links, only the words pairs occurring in both the French-English and English-French word lists were retained, and the probabilities were averaged. To get rid of the noise produced by the translation model, only the entries with an averaged value of at least 0.1 were retained. This value was set experimentally[3].

The resulting bilingual dictionary contains 28,990 English-French word pairs. The bilingual dictionary is used to create the lexical link matrix for each sentence pair.

3.3 Lexical Link Matrix

For each source and target word in each sentence pair, all translations for the word form and the lemma are retrieved from the bilingual dictionary.

In the process of building the lexical link matrix, function words are neglected. Given the frequency of function words in a sentence, linking function words based on lexical information alone, often results in erroneous alignments. For that reason no lexical links are created for the following word classes: determiners, prepositions, coordinating conjunctions, possessive pronouns and punctuation symbols.

For all content words, if a source word occurs in the set of possible translations of a target word, or if a target word occurs in the set of possible translations of the source words, a lexical link is created. Identical strings in source and target language are also linked.

3.4 Anchor chunks

Anchor chunk alignment comprises two steps. In a first step, we select candidate anchor chunks; in a second step we test the syntactic similarity of the candidate anchor chunks.

3.4.1 Selecting candidate anchor chunks

The candidate anchor chunks are selected based on the information available in the lexical link matrix.

[1] The more syntax-aware SMT systems assume that to a certain extent syntactic relationships in one language directly map to syntactic relationships in the other, which Hwa (2002) calls the *Direct Correspondence Assumption*.

[2] The higher numbered IBM Models build on IBM Model One and take into account word order (distortion) and model the probability that a source word aligns to n target words (fertility).

[3] Lowering this threshold significantly decreased precision scores of the sub-sentential alignment system.

For each source chunk a candidate target chunk is constructed. The candidate target chunk is built by concatenating all target chunks from a *begin index* until an *end index*. The begin index points to the first target chunk with a lexical link to the source chunk under consideration. The end index points to the last target chunk with a lexical link to the source chunk under consideration. In this way, 1:1 and 1:n candidate target chunks are built.

The process of selecting candidate chunks as described above, is performed a second time starting from the target sentence. In this way additional n:1 candidates are constructed.

3.4.2 Testing chunk similarity

For each selected candidate pair, a *similarity test* is performed. Chunks are considered to be similar if at least a certain percentage of words of source and target chunk(s) are either linked by means of a lexical link or can be linked on the basis of corresponding part-of-speech codes. All word classes can be linked based on PoS codes.

In addition to linking words based on PoS codes, a small set of predefined language-dependent rules were implemented to handle function words. For example:

- Extra function words (determiners and prepositions) in source or target language are linked together with their noun to the noun's translation.

- In French, the preposition *de* is contracted with the definitive articles *le* and *les* to *du* and *des* respectively. The contracted determiners are linked to an English preposition and determiner.

The percentage of words that have to be linked was empirically set at 85%.

3.5 Remaining chunks

In a second step, chunks consisting of one function word – mostly punctuation marks and conjunctions – are linked based on corresponding part-of-speech codes if its left or right neighbour on the diagonal is an anchor chunk. Corresponding final punctuation marks are also linked.

In a final step, additional candidates are constructed by selecting non-anchor chunks in the source and target sentence that have corresponding left and right anchor chunks as neigbours. The anchor chunks of the first step are used as contextual information to link n:m chunks or chunks for which no lexical link was found in the lexical link matrix.

In Figure 1, the chunks [Fr: gradient] – [En: gradient] and the final punctuation mark have been retrieved in the first step as anchor chunk. In the last step, the n:m chunk [Fr: de remontée pédale d' embrayage] – [En: of rising of the clutch pedal] is selected as candidate anchor chunk because it is enclosed within anchor chunks.

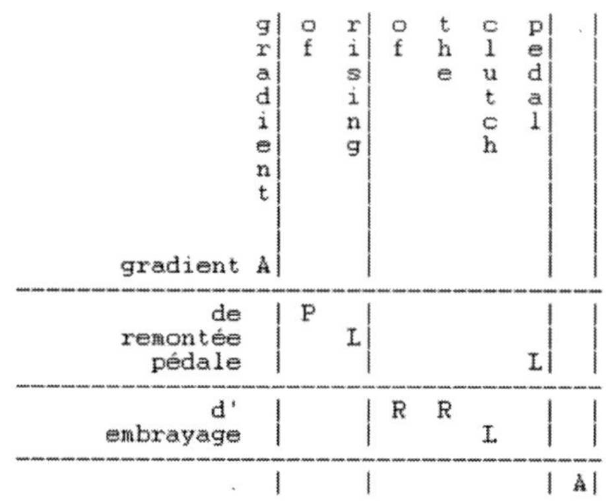

Figure 1: n:m candidate chunk: 'A' stands for anchor chunks, 'L' for lexical links, 'P' for words linked on the basis of corresponding PoS codes and 'R' for words linked by language-dependent rules.

As the contextual clues (the left and right neigbours of the additional candidate chunks are anchor chunks) provide some extra indication that the chunks can be linked, the similarity test for the final candidates was somewhat relaxed: the percentage of words that have to be linked was lowered to 0.80 and a more relaxed PoS matching function was used:

- Verbs and nouns can be linked
  Fr: pour permettre de **vidanger** proprement le circuit
  En: to permit clean **draining** of the system

- Adjectives and nouns can be linked
  Fr: l' **entrée** d' air
  En: **incoming** air

- Past participles can be linked to past tense[4]

3.6 Evaluation

All translational correspondences were manually indicated in the three test corpora (see section 2.2).

[4]The English PoS tagger often tags a past participle erroneously as a past tense.

We adapted the annotation guidelines of Macken (2007) to the French-English language pair, and used three different types of links: *regular* links for straightforward correspondences, *fuzzy* links for translation-specific shifts of various kinds, and *null* links for words for which no correspondence could be indicated. Figure 2 shows an example.

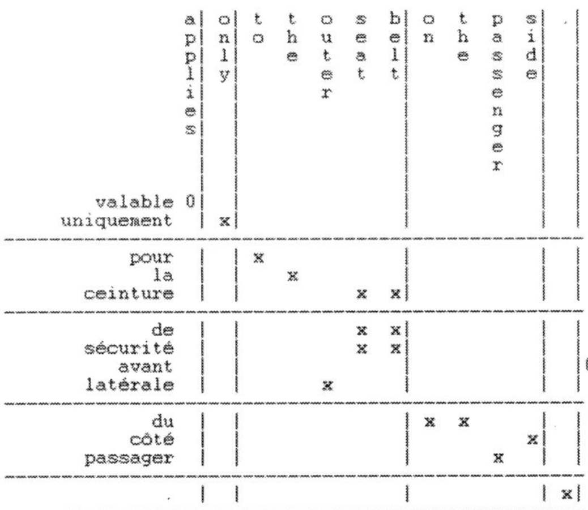

Figure 2: Manual reference: regular links are indicated by x's, fuzzy links and null links by 0's

To evaluate the system's performance, we used the evaluation methodology of Och and Ney (2003). Och and Ney distinguished *sure* alignments (S) and *possible* alignments (P) and introduced the following redefined precision and recall measures:

$$precision = \frac{|A \cap P|}{|A|}, recall = \frac{|A \cap S|}{|S|} \quad (1)$$

and the alignment error rate (AER):

$$AER(S, P; A) = 1 - \frac{|A \cap P| + |A \cap S|}{|A| + |S|} \quad (2)$$

We consider all regular links of the manual reference as *sure* alignments and all fuzzy and null links as *possible* alignments to compare the output of our system with the manual reference.

We trained statistical translation models using Moses. Moses uses the GIZA++ toolkit (IBM Model 1-4) in both translation directions (source to target, target to source) and allows for different symmetrization heuristics to combine the alignments of both translation directions. We used three different heuristics: *grow-diag-final* (default), *intersection* and *union*.

	SHORT			MEDIUM			LONG		
	p	r	e	p	r	e	p	r	e
∩	.99	.83	.10	.98	.73	.16	.99	.77	.13
∪	.95	.92	.07	.91	.86	.11	.91	.89	.10
Gdf	.95	.91	.07	.93	.85	.11	.94	.88	**.09**
Ling.	.96	.93	**.06**	.94	.88	**.09**	.92	.87	.10

Table 3: Precision (p), recall (r) and alignment error rate (e) for three symmetrization heuristics based on the GIZA++ alignments (intersection(∩), union (∪), Grow-diag-final (Gdf)) vs the linguistically-based system (Ling.) for the three test corpora

Table 3 compares the alignment quality of our linguistically-based system with the purely statistical approaches. Overall, the results confirm our assumption that shorter sentences are easier to align than longer sentences. As expected, the *intersection* heuristic aligns words with a very high precision (98-99%). We further observe that the alignment error rate of the linguistically-based system is the lowest for the short and medium-length sentences, but that on the long sentences the default symmetrization heuristic yields the best results. Manual inspection of the alignments revealed that in some long sentences, the linguistically-based system misaligns repeated terms in long sentences, a phenomenon that occured frequently in the long sentence corpus. As expected, the linguistically-based system scores better on function words.

Overall, on this data set, the linguistically-based system yields results that are comparable to the results obtained by the complex and computationally expensive chain of IBM models.

4 Terminology extraction

As described in Section 1, we generate candidate terms starting from the aligned anchor chunks. In a second step, we use a general purpose corpus and the n-gram frequency of the automotive corpus to determine the specificity of the terms.

4.1 Generating candidate terms

English and French use a different compounding strategy. In English, the most frequently used compounding strategy is the concatenation of nouns, while in French prepositional phrases are concatenated. The following example illustrates the different compounding strategy:

Fr: une procédure d' initialisation du calculateur
de boîte de vitesses automatique

En: an automatic gearbox ECU initialisation procedure

We start from the anchor chunks as they are the minimal chunks that could be linked together. We implemented two heuristics to generate additional French candidate terms: a first heuristic strips off adjectives and a second heuristic considers each N + PP pattern as candidate term.

For each French candidate term, the English translation is constructed on the basis of the word alignments. The following candidate terms are generated for our example:

1	procédure d' initialisation du calculateur de boîte de vitesses automatique	automatic gearbox ECU initialisation procedure
2	procédure d' initialisation du calculateur de boîte de vitesses	gearbox ECU initialisation procedure
3	procédure d' initialisation	initialisation procedure
4	initialisation du calculateur	ECU initialisation
5	calculateur de boîte de vitesses	gearbox ECU
6	boîte de vitesses automatique	automatic gearbox
7	boîte de vitesses	gearbox
8	procédure	procedure
9	initialisation	initialisation
10	calculateur	ECU
11	automatique	automatic

4.2 Filtering of candidate terms

As our terminology extraction module is meant to generate a bilingual automotive lexicon, every entry in our lexicon should refer to a concept or action that is relevant in an automotive context. This also means we want to include the minimal semantical units (e.g. seat belt) as well as the larger semantical units (e.g. outer front seat belt) of a parent-child term relationship. In order to decide on which terms should be kept in our lexicon, we have combined two algorithms: Log-Likelihood for single word entries and Mutual Expectation Measure for multiword entries.

4.2.1 Log-Likelihood Measure

In order to detect single word terms that are *distinctive* enough to be kept in our bilingual lexicon, we have applied the Log-Likelihood measure (LL). This metric considers frequencies of words weighted over two different corpora (in our case a technical automotive corpus and the more general purpose corpus "Le Monde"), in order to assign high LL-values to words having much higher or lower frequencies than expected. Daille (1995) has determined empirically that LL is an accurate measure for finding the most *surprisingly* frequent words in a corpus. Low LL values on the other hand allow to retrieve common vocabulary with high frequencies in both corpora. We have created a frequency list for both corpora and calculated the Log-Likelihood values for each word in this frequency list. In the formula below, N corresponds to the number of words in the corpus, whereas the *observed values* O correspond to the real frequencies of a word in the corpus. The formula for calculating both the expected values (E) and the Log-Likelihood have been described in detail by (Rayson and Garside, 2000).

$$E_i = \frac{N_i \sum_i O_i}{\sum_i N_i} \tag{3}$$

We used the resulting Expected values for calculating the Log-Likelihood:

$$-2ln\lambda = 2\sum_i O_i ln(\frac{O_i}{E_i}) \tag{4}$$

Manual inspection of the Log-Likelihood figures confirmed our hypothesis that more domain-specific terms in our corpus got high LL-values. As we are mainly interested in finding distinctive terms in the automotive corpus, we have only kept those terms showing positive Expected Values in our domain-specific corpus combined with user-defined Log-Likelihood values. Examples of French-English translation pairs that are filtered out using the LL values are:

Fr: tout – En: entire
Fr: propre – En: clean
Fr: interdits – En: prohibited
Fr: nombre – En: number

4.2.2 Mutual Expectation Measure

Dias and Kaalep (2003) have developed the Mutual Expectation measure for evaluating the degree of cohesiveness between words in a text. We have applied this metric on our list of multiword terms, to exclude multiword terms which components do not occur together more often than expected by chance. In a first step, we have calculated all n-gram frequencies (up to 8-grams) for our English and French sentences. We use these frequencies to derive the Normalised Expectation (NE) values for all multiword entries, as specified by the formula of Dias and Kaalep:

$$NE = \frac{prob(n-gram)}{\frac{1}{n}\sum prob(n-1-grams)} \quad (5)$$

The Normalised Expectation value expresses the cost, in terms of cohesiveness, of the possible loss of one word in an n-gram. The higher the frequency of the n-1-grams, the smaller the NE, and the smaller the chance that it is a valid multiword expression. As simple n-gram frequency also seems to be a valid criterion for multiword term identification (Daille, 1995), the NE values are multiplied by the n-gram frequency to obtain the final Mutual Expectation (ME) value.

We have calculated Mutual Expectation values for all French and English multiword terms and filtered out incomplete or erroneous terms having very low ME values. The following example has been filtered out:

Fr: permettant d'alimenter le circuit d'eau arrière
En: to supply the rear water circuit
Incomplete term:
eau arrière - rear water (should be Fr: circuit d'eau arrière - En: rear water circuit)

4.3 Evaluation of the Terminology Extraction Module

To evaluate the terminology extraction module, we used all sentences of the three test corpora (see Section 2.2). We compared the performance of our algorithm with the output of a commercial state-of-the-art terminology extraction program SDL MultiTerm Extract[5]. MultiTerm first extracts source language terms and identifies in a separate step the term translations. MultiTerm makes use of basic vocubulary lists to exclude general vocabulary words from the candidate term list. We ran MultiTerm Extract with the default settings on 70,000 aligned sentences[6] of the automotive corpus. The extracted terms of our system have been filtered by applying Log-Likelihood thresholds (for single word terms) and Mutual Expectation thresholds (for multiword terms). Tabel 4 shows the number of terms after each reduction phase.

The output of both systems has been manually labeled taking into account the following guidelines:

[5]www.translationzone.com/en/products/sdlmultitermextract

[6]70,000 sentences was the maximum size of the corpus that could be processed within MultiTerm Extract.

	# extracted entries	# entries after ME filtering	# entries after LL filtering
Anchor chunk approach	2778	2688	2549
Multiterm Extract	1337	N/A	N/A

Table 4: Figures after Log-Likelihood and Mutual Expectation reduction

Anchor chunk approach	Correct	Not correct	Maybe correct
Multiwords	78.5%	19%	2.5%
Single words	89.5%	9.5%	1%
All terms	83%	15%	2%
Multiterm Extract	Correct	Not correct	Maybe correct
Multiwords	51%	48.5%	0.5%
Single words	83%	16%	1%
All terms	66%	33.5%	0.5%

Table 5: Results Term Extraction Module

- judge the quality of the bilingual entry as a whole, meaning that the French and English terms should express the same concept
- each entry should form a semantic unit and refer to an existing concept or action in the automotive context

During manual validation, the following three labels have been used: *OK* (valid entry), *NOK* (not a valid entry) and *MAYBE* (when the annotator was not sure about the correct label). Table 5 lists the results of both our system and MultiTerm Extract and illustrates that our linguistically based alignment approach works particularly well for the extraction of more complex multiword expressions.

Error analysis on the errors made by the anchor chunk approach revealed the following error types:

1. compounds that are only partially retrieved in one of the two languages:

ceinture (valable uniquement pour la **ceinture de sécurité** avant latérale)	outer seat belt (applies only to the outer **seat belt**)

2. fuzzy word links (different grammatical and syntactical structures, paraphrases etc) that result in bad lexicon entries:

fusibles (montage avec vide-poches inférieur fixe **sans rangement des fusibles**)	no fuse (fitting with fixed lower storage compartment with **no fuse storage**)

3. translation errors in the parallel corpus:

automatique (tableau de commande climatisation **automatique**)	additional (**additional** air conditioning unit control panel)

4. ambiguous words that cause PoS and chunking errors (in the corpus *avant* is usually used as an adjective, but in the example it has a prepositional function as *avant de*):

câbles avant	cables
(repérer la position des câbles **avant de** les déclipper)	(mark the position of the cables **before** unclipping them)

5 Conclusions and future work

We presented a sub-sentential alignment system that links linguistically motivated phrases in parallel texts based on lexical correspondences and syntactic similarity. Overall, the obtained alignment scores are comparable to the scores of the state-of-the-art statistical approach that is used in Moses.

The results show that the aligned linguistically motivated phrases are a useful means to extract bilingual terminology for French-English. In the short term, we will test our methodology on other language pairs, i.e. French-Dutch, French-Spanish and French-Swedish. We will also compare our work with other bilingual term extraction programs.

6 Acknowledgement

We would like to thank PSA Peugeot Citroën for funding this project.

References

Daille, B. 1995. Study and implementation of combined techniques for automatic extraction of terminology. In Klavans, J. and P. Resnik, editors, *The Balancing Act: Combining Symbolic and Statistical Approaches to Language*, pages 49–66. MIT Press, Cambridge, Massachusetts; London, England.

Dias, G. and H. Kaalep. 2003. Automatic Extraction of Multiword Units for Estonian: Phrasal Verbs. *Languages in Development*, 41:81–91.

Gaussier, E. 1998. Flow Network Models for Word Alignment and Terminology Extraction from Bilingual Corpora . In *36th Annual Meeting of the Association for Computational Linguistics and 17th International Conference on Computational Linguistics (Proceedings of COLING-ACL '98)*, pages 444–450, Université de Montréal, Montreal, Quebec, Canada.

Gotti, F., P. Langlais, E. Macklovitch, D. Bourigault, B. Robichaud, and C. Coulombe. 2005. 3GTM: a third-generation translation memory. In *Proceedings of the 3rd Computational Linguistics in the North-East (CLiNE) Workshop*, Gatineau, Québec.

Hwa, R., P. Resnik, A. Weinberg, and O. Kolak. 2002. Evaluating translational correspondence using annotation projection. In *Proceedings of the 40th Annual Meeting of the Association for Computational Linguistics (ACL)*, pages 392–399, Philadelphia, PA, USA.

Itagaki, M., T. Aikawa, and X. He. 2007. Automatic Validation of Terminology Consistency with Statistical Method. In Maegaard, Bente, editor, *Machine Translation Summit XI*, pages 269–274, Copenhagen, Denmark. European Associaton for Machine Translation.

Koehn, P., H. Hoang, A. Birch, C. Callison-Burch, M. Federico, N. Bertoldi, B. Cowan, W. Shen, C. Moran, R. Zens, C. Dyer, O. Bojar, A. Constantin, and E. Herbst. 2007. Moses: Open Source Toolkit for Statistical Machine Translation. In *Proceedings of the ACL 2007 Demo and Poster Sessions*, pages 177–180, Prague, Czech Republic.

Kupiec, J. 1993. An algorithm for finding noun phrase correspondences in bilingual corpora. In *Proceedings of the 31st Annual Meeting of the Association for Computational Linguistics*.

Macken, L. 2007. Analysis of translational correspondence in view of sub-sentential alignment. In *Proceedings of the METIS-II Workshop on New Approaches to Machine Translation*, pages 97–105, Leuven, Belgium.

Melamed, I. Dan. 2000. Models of translational equivalence among words. *Computational Linguistics*, 26(2):221–249.

Moore, R. C. 2002. Fast and accurate sentence alignment of bilingual corpora. In *Proceedings of the 5th Conference of the Association for Machine Translation in the Americas*, Machine Translation: from research to real users, pages 135–244, Tiburon, California.

Och, F. J. and H. Ney. 2003. A systematic comparison of various statistical alignment models. *Computational Linguistics*, 29(1):19–51.

Rayson, P. and R. Garside. 2000. Comparing corpora using frequency profiling. In *Proceedings of the workshop on Comparing Corpora, 38th annual meeting of the Association for Computational Linguistics (ACL 2000)*, pages 1–6.

Schmid, H. 1994. Probabilistic part-of-speech tagging using decision trees. In *International Conference on New Methods in Language Processing*, Manchester, UK.

Tjong Kim Sang, Erik F. and Sabine Buchholz. 2000. Introduction to the CoNLL-2000 Shared Task: Chunking. In *CoNLL-2000 and LLL-2000*, pages 127–132, Lisbon, Portugal.

Hindi Urdu Machine Transliteration using Finite-state Transducers

M G Abbas Malik **Christian Boitet**
GTALP, Laboratoire d'Informatique Grenoble
Université Joseph Fourier, France
abbas.malik@imag.fr,
Christian.Boitet@imag.fr

Pushpak Bhattacharyya
Dept. of Computer Science and Engineering,
IIT Bombay, India
pb@cse.iitb.ac.in

Abstract

Finite-state Transducers (FST) can be very efficient to implement inter-dialectal transliteration. We illustrate this on the Hindi and Urdu language pair. FSTs can also be used for translation between surface-close languages. We introduce UIT (universal intermediate transcription) for the same pair on the basis of their common phonetic repository in such a way that it can be extended to other languages like Arabic, Chinese, English, French, *etc.* We describe a transliteration model based on FST and UIT, and evaluate it on Hindi and Urdu corpora.

1 Introduction

Transliteration is mainly used to transcribe a word written in one language in the writing system of the other language, thereby keeping an approximate phonetic equivalence. It is useful for MT (to create possible equivalents of unknown words) (Knight and Stall, 1998; Paola and Sanjeev, 2003), cross-lingual information retrieval (Pirkola et al, 2003), the development of multilingual resources (Yan et al, 2003) and multilingual text and speech processing. Inter-dialectal translation without lexical changes is quite useful and sometimes even necessary when the dialects in question use different scripts; it can be achieved by transliteration alone. That is the case of HUMT (Hindi-Urdu Machine Transliteration) where each word has to be transliterated from Hindi to Urdu and *vice versa*, irrespective of its type (noun, verb, *etc.* and not only proper noun or unknown word).

"One man's Hindi is another man's Urdu" (Rai, 2000). The major difference between Hindi and Urdu is that the former is written in Devanagari script with a more Sanskritized vocabulary and the latter is written in Urdu script (derivation of Persio-Arabic script) with more vocabulary borrowed from Persian and Arabic. In contrast to the transcriptional difference, Hindi and Urdu share grammar, morphology, a huge vocabulary, history, classical literature, cultural heritage, *etc.* Hindi is the National language of India with 366 million native speakers. Urdu is the National and one of the state languages of Pakistan and India respectively with 60 million native speakers (Rahman, 2004). Table 1 gives an idea about the size of Hindi and Urdu.

	Native Speakers	2nd Language Speakers	Total
Hindi	366,000,000	487,000,000	853,000,000
Urdu	60,290,000	104,000,000	164,290,000
Total	426,290,000	591,000,000	**1,017,000,000**

Table 1: Hindi and Urdu speakers

Hindi and Urdu, being varieties of the same language, cover a huge proportion of world's population. People from Hindi and Urdu communities can understand the verbal expressions of each other but not the written expressions. HUMT is an effort to bridge this scriptural divide between India and Pakistan.

Hindi and Urdu scripts are briefly introduced in section 2. Universal Intermediate Transcription (UIT) is described in section 3, and UIT mappings for Hindi and Urdu are given in section 4. Contextual HUMT rules are presented and discussed in section 5. An HUMT system implementation and its evaluation are provided in section 6 and 7. Section 8 is on future work and conclusion.

© 2008. Licensed under the *Creative Commons Attribution-Noncommercial-Share Alike 3.0 Unported* license (http://creativecommons.org/licenses/by-nc-sa/3.0/). Some rights reserved.

2 HUMT

There exist three languages at the border between India and Pakistan: Kashmiri, Punjabi and Sindhi. All of them are mainly written in two scripts, one being a derivation of the Persio-Arabic script and the other being Devanagari script. A person using the Persio-Arabic script cannot understand the Devanagari script and *vice versa*. The same is true for Hindi and Urdu which are varieties or dialects of the same language, called *Hindustani* by Platts (1909).

PMT (Punjabi Machine Transliteration) (Malik, 2006) was a first effort to bridge this scriptural divide between the two scripts of Punjabi namely Shahmukhi (a derivation of Perio-Arabic script) and Gurmukhi (a derivation of Landa, Shardha and Takri, old Indian scripts). HUMT is a logical extension of PMT. Our HUMT system is generic and flexible such that it will be extendable to handle similar cases like Kashmiri, Punjabi, Sindhi, *etc.* HUMT is also a special type of machine transliteration like PMT.

A brief account of Hindi and Urdu is first given for unacquainted readers.

2.1 Hindi

The Devanagari (literally "godly urban") script, a simplified version of the alphabet used for Sanskrit, is a left-to-right script. Each consonant symbol inherits by default the vowel sound [ə]. Two or more consonants may be combined together to form a cluster called Conjunct that marks the absence of the inherited vowel [ə] between two consonants (Kellogg, 1872; Montaut, 2004). A sentence illustrating Devanagari is given below:

हिन्दी हिन्दुस्तान की क़ौमी ज़ुबान है.

[hɪnd̪i hɪnd̪ustɑn ki qɔmi zubɑn hæ]

(Hindi is the national language of India)

2.2 Urdu

Urdu is written in an alphabet derived from the Persio-Arabic alphabet. It is a right-to-left script and the shape assumed by a character in a word is context-sensitive, *i.e.* the shape of a character is different depending on whether its position is at the beginning, in the middle or at the end of a word (Zia, 1999). A sentence illustrating Urdu is given below:

اردو پاکستان کی قومی زبان ہے۔

[ʊrd̪u pɑkɪstɑn ki qɔmi zubɑn hæ]

(Urdu is the National Language of Pakistan.)

3 Universal Intermediate Transcription

UIT (Universal Intermediate Transcription) is a scheme to transcribe texts in Hindi, Urdu, Punjabi, *etc.* in an unambiguous way encoded in ASCII range 32 – 126, since a text in this range is portable across computers and operating systems (James 1993; Wells, 1995). SAMPA (Speech Assessment Methods Phonetic Alphabet) is a widely accepted scheme for encoding the IPA (International Phonetic Alphabet) into ASCII. It was first developed for Danish, Dutch, French, German and Italian, and since then it has been extended to many languages like Arabic, Czech, English, Greek, Hebrew, Portuguese, Russian, Spanish, Swedish, Thai, Turkish, *etc.*

We define UIT as a logical extension of SAMPA. The UIT encoding for Hindi and Urdu is developed on the basis of rules and principles of SAMPA and X-SAMPA (Wells, 1995), that cover all symbols on the IPA chart. Phonemes are the most appropriate invariants to mediate between the scripts of Hindi, Punjabi, Urdu, *etc.*, so that the encoding choice is logical and suitable.

4 Analysis of Scripts and UIT Mappings

For the analysis and comparison, scripts of Hindi and Urdu are divided into different groups on the basis of character types.

4.1 Consonants

These are grouped into two categories:

Aspirated Consonants: Hindi and Urdu both have 15 aspirated consonants. In Hindi, 11 aspirated consonants are represented by separate characters *e.g.* ख [k^h], भ [b^h], *etc.* The remaining 4 consonants are represented by combining a simple consonant to be aspirated and the conjunct form of HA ह[h], *e.g.* ल [l] + ् + ह [h] = ल्ह [l^h].

In Urdu, all aspirated consonants are represented by a combination of a simple consonant to be aspirated and Heh Doachashmee (ھ) [h], *e.g.* ک [k] + ھ [h] = کھ [k^h], ب [b] + ھ [h] = بھ [b^h], ل [l] + ھ [h] = لھ [l^h], *etc.*

The UIT mapping for aspirated consonants is given in Table 2.

Hindi	Urdu	UIT	Hindi	Urdu	UIT
भ	بھ [b^h]	b_h	र्ह	رھ [r^h]	r_h
फ	پھ [p^h]	p_h	ढ़	ڑھ [ɽ^h]	r`_h
थ	تھ [t̪^{h}]	t_d_h	ख	کھ [k^h]	k_h
ठ	ٹھ [ʈ^h]	t`_h	घ	گھ [g^h]	g_h
झ	جھ [ʤ^h]	d_Z_h	ल्ह	لھ [l^h]	l_h

छ	چھ [ʧʰ]	t_S_h	म्ह	مھ [mʰ]	m_h
ध	دھ [d̪ʰ]	d_d_h	न्ह	نھ [nʰ]	n_h
ढ	ڈھ [ɖʰ]	d`_h			

Table 2: Hindi Urdu aspirated consonants

Non-aspirated Consonants: Hindi has 29 non-aspirated consonant symbols representing 28 consonant sounds as both SHA (श) and SSA (ष) represent the same sound [ʃ]. Similarly Urdu has 35 consonant symbols representing 27 sounds as multiple characters are used to represent the same sound *e.g.* Heh (ح) and Heh-Goal (ہ) represent the sound [h] and Theh (ث), Seen (س) and Sad (ص) represent the sound [s], *etc.*

UIT mapping for non-aspirated consonants is given in Table 3.

Hindi	Urdu	UIT	Hindi	Urdu	UIT
ब	ب [b]	b	स	ص [s]	s2
प	پ [p]	p	ज़	ض [z]	z2
त	ت [t̪]	t_d	त	ط [t̪]	t_d1
ट	ٹ [ʈ]	t`	ज़	ظ [z]	z3
स	ث [s]	s1	-	ع [ʔ]	?
ज	ج [ʤ]	d_Z	ग़	غ [ɣ]	X
च	چ [ʧ]	t_S	फ़	ف [f]	f
ह	ح [h]	h1	क़	ق [q]	q
ख़	خ [x]	x	क	ک [k]	k
द	د [d̪]	d_d	ग	گ [g]	g
ड	ڈ [ɖ]	d`	ल	ل [l]	l
ज़	ذ [z]	z1	म	م [m]	m
र	ر [r]	r	न	ن [n]	n
ड़	ڑ [ɽ]	r`	व	و [v]	v
ज़	ز [z]	z	ह	ہ [h]	h
ज़	ژ [ʒ]	Z	य	ی [j]	j
स	س [s]	s	त	ۃ [t̪]	t_d2
श	ش [ʃ]	S	ण	- [ɳ]	n`
ष	ش [ʃ]	S1	ं	ں [ŋ]	~

Table 3: Hindi Urdu non-aspirated consonants

4.2 Vowels

Hindi has 11 vowels and 10 of them have nasalized forms. They are represented by 11 independent vowel symbols *e.g.* आ [ɑ], ऊ [u], औ [ɔ], *etc.* and 10 dependent vowel symbols *e.g.* ा [ɑ], ू [u], ौ [ɔ], *etc.* called *maatraas*. When a vowel comes at the start of a word or a syllable, the independent form is used; otherwise the dependent form is used (Kellogg, 1872; Montaut, 2004).

Urdu contains 10 vowels and 7 of them have nasalized forms (Hussain, 2004; Khan, 1997). Urdu vowels are represented using four long vowels (Alef Madda (آ), Alef (ا), Vav (و) and Choti Yeh (ی)) and three short vowels (Arabic Fatha – Zabar َ, Arabic Damma – Pesh ُ and Arabic Kasra – Zer ِ). Vowel representation is context-sensitive in Urdu. Vav (و) and Choti Yeh (ی) are also used as consonants.

Hamza (ء) is a place holder between two successive vowel sounds, *e.g.* in کمائی [kəmɑi] (earning), Hamza (ء) separates the two vowel sounds Alef (ا) [ɑ] and Choti Yeh (ی) [i]. Noonghunna (ں) is used as nasalization marker. Analysis and mapping of Hindi Urdu vowels is given in Table 5.

4.3 Diacritical Marks

Urdu contains 15 diacritical marks. They represent vowel sounds, except Hamza-e-Izafat ٔ and Kasr-e-Izafat ِ that are used to build compound words, *e.g.* اِدارۂ سائنس [ɪd̪ɑrəhɪsɑɪns] (Institute of Science), تارِیخِ پیدائش [tɑrixɪpedɑɪʃ] (date of birth), *etc.* Shadda ّ is used to geminate a consonant *e.g.* ربّ [rəbb] (God), اچّھا [əʧʧʰɑ] (good), *etc.* Jazm ْ is used to mark the absence of a vowel after the base consonant (Platts, 1909). In Hindi, the conjunct form is used to geminate a consonant. Urdu diacritical marks mapping is given in Table 4.

Hindi	Urdu	UIT	Hindi	Urdu	UIT
-	◌َ [ə]	@	ा	◌ٰ [ɑ]	A
ि	◌ِ [ɪ]	I	न	◌ً [ən]	@n
ु	◌ُ [ʊ]	U	ुन	◌ٌ [ʊn]	Un
ू	◌ٗ [u]	u	िन	◌ٍ [ɪn]	In
ी	◌ٖ [i]	i			

Table 4: Diacritical Marks of Urdu

Diacritical marks are present in Urdu but sparingly used by people. They are very important for the correct pronunciation and understanding the meanings of a word. For example,

یہ سڑک بہت چوڑی ہے۔

[je səɽək bʊhət̪ ʧɔɽi hæ] (This is a wide road.)

میری چوڑی سرخ ہے۔

[meri ʧuɽi surəx hæ] (My bangle is red.)

In the first sentence, the word چوڑی is pronounced as [ʧɔɽi] (wide) and in the second, it is pronounced as [ʧuɽi] (bangle). There should be Zabar (َ◌) and Pesh (ُ◌) after Cheh (چ) in above words and correct transcriptions are چَوڑی (wide) and چُوڑی (bangle). Thus diacritical marks are essential for removing ambiguities, natural language processing and speech synthesis.

Vowel	Urdu	Hindi (UIT)
ə	It is represented by Alef (ا) + Zabar َ- at the start of a word *e.g.* اب [əb] (now) and by Zabar َ- in the middle of a word respectively *e.g.* رَب [rəbb] (God). It never comes at the end of a word.	अ (@)
ɑ	It is represented by Alef Madda (آ) at the start of a word *e.g.* آدمی [ɑd̪mi] (man) and by Alef (ا) or Alef Madda (آ) in the middle of a word *e.g.* جانا [ʤɑnɑ] (go), بلآخر [bɪlɑxər] (at last). At the end of a word, it is represented by Alef (ا). In some Arabic loan words, it is represented by Choti Yeh (ی) + Khari Zabar ٰ- at the end of a word *e.g.* اعلیٰ [əʔlɑ] (Superior) and by Khari Zabar ٰ- in the middle of a word *e.g.* الٰہی [ɪlɑhi] (God).	आ or ा (A)
e	It is represented by Alef (ا) + Choti Yeh (ی) at the start of a word *e.g.* ایثار [esɑr] (sacrifice), ایک [ek] (one), *etc.* and by Choti Yeh (ی) or Baree Yeh (ے) in the middle of a word *e.g.* میرا [merɑ] (mine), اندھیرا [ənd̪ʰerɑ] (darkness), بےگھر [begʰər] (homeless) *etc.* At the end of a word, It is represented by Baree Yeh (ے) *e.g.* سارے [sɑre] (all).	ए or े (e)
æ	It is represented by Alef (ا) + Zabar َ- + Choti Yeh (ی) at the start of a word *e.g.* ایہہ [æh] (this) and by Zabar َ- + Choti Yeh (ی) in the middle of a word *e.g.* مَیل [mæl] (dirt). At the end of a word, it is represented by Zabar َ- + Baree Yeh (ے) *e.g.* ہَے [hæ] (is).	ऐ or ै ({)
ɪ	It is represented by Alef (ا) + Zer ِ- at the start of a word *e.g.* اِس [ɪs] (this) and by Zer ِ- in the middle of a word *e.g.* بارِش [bɑrɪʃ] (rain). It never comes at the end of a word. At the end of a word, it is used as Kasr-e-Izafat to build compound words.	इ or ि (I)
i	It is represented by Alef (ا) + Zer ِ- + Choti Yeh (ی) at the start of a word *e.g.* اِیمان [imɑn] (belief) and by Zer ِ- + Choti Yeh (ی) in the middle or at the end of a word *e.g.* امیری [ɑmiri] (richness), قریب [qərib] (near), *etc.*	ई or ी (i)
ʊ	It is represented by Alef (ا) + Pesh ُ- at the start of a word *e.g.* اُدَھر [ʊd̪d̪ʰər] (there) and by Pesh ُ- in the middle of a word *e.g.* مُل [mʊll] (price). It never comes at the end of a word.	उ or ु (U)
u	It is represented by Alef (ا) + Pesh ُ- + Vav (و) at the start of a word *e.g.* اونگھتا [ũgʰət̪ɑ] (dozzing) and by Pesh ُ- + Vav (و) in the middle or at the end of a word *e.g.* صُورت [surət̪] (face), ترازُو [t̪ərɑzu] (physical balance), *etc.*	ऊ or ू (u)
o	It is represented by Alef (ا) + Vav (و) at the start of a word *e.g.* اوچھا [oʧʰɑ] (nasty) and by Vav (و) in the middle or at the end of a word *e.g.* ہولی [holi] (slowly), کہو [kəho] (say), *etc.*	ओ or ो (o)
ɔ	It is represented by Alef (ا) + Zabar َ- + Vav (و) at the start of a word *e.g.* اوٹ [ɔʈ] (hindrance) and by Zabar َ- + Vav (و) in the middle or at the end of a word *e.g.* مَوت [mɔt̪] (death).	औ or ौ (O)
r̥	It is represented by a consonant symbol Reh (ر) [r] as this vowel is only present in Sanskrit loan words. It is almost not used in modern standard Hindi. It is not present in Urdu as it is used only in Sanskrit loan words.	ऋ or ृ (r1)
Note: In Hindi, Nasalization of a vowel is done by adding Anunasik (ँ) or Anusavar (ं) after the vowel. Anusavar (ं) is used when the vowel graph goes over the upper line; otherwise Anunasik (ँ) is used (Kellogg, 1872; Montaut, 2004). In UIT, ~ is added at end of UIT encoding for nasalization of all above vowels except the last one that do not have a nasalized form.		

Table 5: Analysis and Mapping of Hindi Urdu Vowels

5 HUMT Rules

In this section, UIT mappings of Hindi Urdu alphabets and contextual rules that are necessary for Hindi-Urdu transliteration are discussed.

5.1 UIT Mappings

UIT mappings for Hindi and Urdu alphabets and their vowels are given in Table 2 – 5. In Hindi, SHA (श) and SSA (ष) both represent the sound [ʃ] and have one equivalent symbol in Urdu, *i.e.* Sheen (ش). To make distinction between SHA (श) and SSA (ष) in UIT, they are mapped on S and S1 respectively. Similarly in Urdu, Seh (ث), Seen (س) and Sad (ص) represent the sound [s] and have one equivalent symbol in Hindi, *i.e.* SA (स). To make distinction among them in UIT, they are mapped on s1, s and s2 respectively. All similar cases are shown in Table 6.

IPA	Urdu (UIT)	Hindi (UIT)
t̪	ت (t_d), ط (t_d1), ۃ (t_d2)	त (t_d)
s	ث (s1), س (s), ص (s2)	स (s)
H	ح (h1), ہ (h)	ह (h)

z	ذ (z1), ز (z), ژ (Z), ض (z2), ظ (z3)	ज़ (z)
ʃ	ش (S)	श (S), ष (S1)
r	ر (r)	र (r), ऋ (r1)

Table 6: Multiple Characters for one IPA

Multi-equivalences are problematic for Hindi-Urdu transliteration.

UIT is extendable to other languages like English, French, Kashmiri, Punjabi, Sindhi, *etc.* For example, Punjabi has one extra character than Urdu *i.e.* Rnoon [ɳ] (ݨ), it is mapped on 'n`' in UIT. Similarly, UIT, a phonetic encoding scheme, can be extended to other languages.

All these mappings can be implemented by simple finite-state transducers using XEROX's XFST (Beesley and Karttunen, 2003) language. A sample XFST code is given in Figure 1.

```
read regex [ب -> b, پ -> p, ج -> [d "_" Z] ];
read regex [[ج ھ] -> [d "_" Z "_" h]];
read regex [و -> v, ی -> j || .#. _ ];
read regex [و -> v, ی -> j || _ [آ | ا]];
read regex [ی -> e || CONSONANTS _ ];
read regex [ ی -> i || _ [ں | .#.]];
...
read regex [ब -> b, प -> p, ज़ -> z, झ -> [d "_" Z "_" h]];
read regex [अ -> "@", आ -> A, ई -> i || .#. _ ]
...
```

Figure 1: Sample XFST code

Finite-state transducers are robust and time and space efficient (Mohri, 1997). They are a logical choice for Hindi-Urdu transliteration via UIT as this problem could also be seen as string matching and producing an analysis string as an output like finite-state morphological analysis.

5.2 Contextual HUMT Rules

UIT mappings need to be accompanied by necessary contextual HUMT rules for correct Hindi to Urdu transliteration and *vice versa.*

For example, Vav (و) and Choti Yeh (ی) are used to represent vowels like [o], [ɔ], [i], [e], *etc.* but they are also used as consonants. Vav (و) and Choti Yeh (ی) are consonants when they come at the beginning of a word or when they are followed by Alef mada (آ) or Alef (ا). Also, Choti Yeh (ی) represents the vowel [e] when it is preceded by a consonant but when it comes at the end of a word and is preceded by a consonant then it represents the vowel [i]. These rules are shown in red colour in Figure 1.

Thus HUMT contextual rules are necessary for Hindi-Urdu transliteration and they can also be implemented as finite-state transducer using XFST. All these rules can't be given here due to shortage of space.

6 HUMT System

The HUMT system exploits the simplicity, robustness, power and time and space efficiency of finite-state transducers. Exactly the same transducer that encodes a Hindi or Urdu text into UIT can be used in the reverse direction to generate Hindi or Urdu text from the UIT encoded text. This two-way power of the finite-state transducer (Mohri, 1997) has significantly reduced the amount of efforts to build the HUMT system. Another very important and powerful strength of finite-state transducers, they can be composed together to build a single transducer that can perform the same task that could be done with help of two or more transducers when applied sequentially (Mohri, 1997), not only allows us to build a direct Hindi ↔ Urdu transducer, but also helps to divide difficult and complex problems into simple ones, and has indeed simplified the process of building the HUMT system. A direct Hindi ↔ Urdu transducer can be used in applications where UIT encoding is not necessary like Hindi-Urdu MT system.

The HUMT system can be extended to perform transliteration between two or more different scripts used for the same languages like Kashmiri, Kazakh, Malay, Punjabi, Sindhi, *etc.* or between language pairs like English–Hindi, English–Urdu, English–French, *etc.* by just introducing the respective transducers in the `Finite-state Transducer Manager` of the HUMT system to build a *multilingual machine transliteration system.*

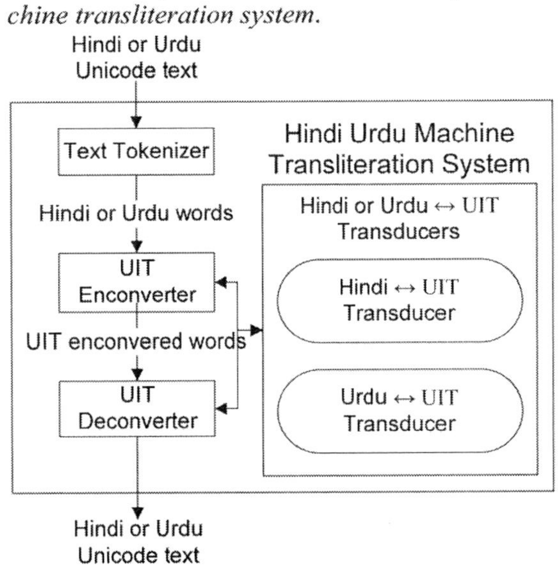

Figure 2: HUMT System

In the HUMT system, `Text Tokenizer` takes the input Hindi or Urdu Unicode text, tokenizes it into Hindi or Urdu words and passes them to `UIT Enconverter`. The enconverter enconverts Hindi or Urdu words into UIT words using the appropriate transducer from `Finite-state Transducers Manager`, *e.g.* for Hindi words, it uses the Hindi ↔ UIT transducer. It passes these UIT encoded words to `UIT Deconverter`, which deconverts them into Hindi or Urdu words using the appropriate transducer from `Finite-state Transducers Manager` in reverse and generates the target Hindi or Urdu text.

6.1 Enconversion of Hindi-Urdu to UIT

Hindi ↔ UIT transducer is a composition of the mapping rules transducers and the contextual rules transducers. This is clearly shown in figure 3 with a sample XFST code.

```
clear stack
set char-encoding UTF-8
define CONSONANTS [क | ख | ग | घ | ङ | छ | ज];
read regex [ ् -> J, ः -> h, ़ -> 0];
read regex [क -> k, ख -> [k "_" h], ग -> g, घ -> [g "_"
h], ङ -> [n "@" g], च -> [t "_" S], छ -> [t "_" S "_" h]];
read regex [[क ् क] -> [k k], [क ् ख] -> [k k "_" h],
[ग ् ग] -> [g g], [ग ् घ] -> [g g "_" h]];
...
read regex [[क ि] -> [k h], [न] -> [n A], [य े] -> [j h],
[व े] -> [v h] || .#. _ .#.];
compose net
```

Figure 3: Sample code for Hindi ↔ UIT Transducer

How the HUMT system works is shown with the help of an example. Take the Hindi sentence:

फ़ाख़्ता मुहब्बत और अमन का निशान है

[fɑxət̪ɑ mʊhəbət̪ ɔr əmən kɑ nɪʃɑn hæ]

(Dove is symbol of love and peace)

This sentence is received by the `Text Tokenizer` and is tokenized into Hindi words, which are enconverted into UIT words using the mapping and the contextual rules of Hindi ↔ UIT transducer by the `UIT Enconverter`. The Hindi Words and the UIT enconversions are given in Table 7.

Hindi Words	UIT
फ़ाख़्ता [fɑxət̪ɑ]	fAx@t_dA
मुहब्बत [mʊhəbət̪]	mUh@b@t_d
और [ɔr]	Or
अमन [əmən]	@m@n
का [kɑ]	kA
निशान [nɪʃɑn]	nISAn
है [hæ]	H{

Table 7: Hindi Words with UIT

6.2 Deconversion of UIT to Hindi-Urdu

For the deconversion, Hindi ↔ UIT or Urdu ↔ UIT transducer is applied in reverse on the UIT enconverted words to generate Hindi or Urdu words. To continue with the example in the previous section, the UIT words are deconverted into the Urdu words by the `UIT Deconverter` using Urdu ↔ UIT transducer in reverse. The Urdu words are given in table 8 with the Hindi and the UIT words.

Hindi	UIT	Urdu
फ़ाख़्ता [fɑxət̪ɑ]	fAx@t_dA	فاختا
मुहब्बत [mʊhəbət̪]	mUh@b@t_d	مُحبت
और [ɔr]	Or	اور
अमन [əmən]	@m@n	امن
का [kɑ]	kA	کا
निशान [nɪʃɑn]	nISAn	نِشان
है [hæ]	H{	ہَے

Table 8: Hindi, UIT and Urdu Words

Finally, the following Urdu sentence is generated from Urdu words.

فاختا مُحبت اور امن کا نِشان ہَے

Here the word फ़ाख़्ता [fɑxət̪ɑ] (Dove) is transliterated wrongly into 'فاختا' because the vowel [ɑ] at the end of some Urdu words (borrowed from Persian language) is transcribed with help of Heh-gol [h] (ہ). This phenomenon is a problem for Hindi to Urdu transliteration but not for Urdu to Hindi transliteration.

7 Evaluation Experiments and Results

For evaluation purpose, we used a Hindi corpus, containing 374,150 words, and an Urdu corpus with 38,099 words. The Hindi corpus is extracted from the Hindi WordNet[2] developed by the Resource Center for Indian Language Technology Solutions, CSE Department, Indian Institute of Technology (IIT) Bombay, India and from the project CIFLI (GETALP-LIG[3], University Joseph Fourier), a project for building resources and tools for network-based "linguistic survival" communication between French, English and Indian languages like Hindi, Tamil, etc. The Urdu corpus was developed manually from a book titled "ظلمت کدہ" [zʊlmət̪ kədɑ]. The Hindi-Urdu corpus contains in total 412,249 words.

The HUMT system is an initial step to build Urdu resources and add Urdu to the languages of

[2] http://www.cfilt.iitb.ac.in

[3] http://www.liglab.fr

SurviTra-CIFLI (Survival Translation) (Boitet et al, 2007), a multilingual digital phrase-book to help tourists for communication and enquiries like restaurant, hotel reservation, flight enquiry, etc.

To reduce evaluation and testing efforts, unique words are extracted from the Hindi-Urdu corpus and are transliterated using the HUMT system. These unique words and their transliterations are checked for accuracy with the help of dictionaries (Platts, 1911; Feroz).

7.1 Urdu → Hindi Transliteration Results

While transliterating Urdu into Hindi, multiple problems occur like multi-equivalences, no equivalence, missing diacritical marks in Urdu text. For example, Sheen [ʃ] (ش) can be transliterated in Hindi into SHA [ʃ] (श) or SSA [ʃ] (ष) that are present in 7,917 and 6,399 corpus words respectively. Sheen [ʃ] (ش) is transliterated into SHA [ʃ] (श) by default. Thus, 6,399 words containing SSA [ʃ] (ष) are wrongly transliterated into Hindi using HUMT. Urdu to Hindi multi-equivalences cases are given in Table 9 with their frequencies.

Urdu	Hindi (corpus Frequency)
ش [ʃ]	श (7917), ष (6399)
ر [r]	र (79,345), ऋ (199)

Table 9: Urdu → Hindi Multi-equivalences

Some Hindi characters do not have equivalent characters in Urdu, *e.g.* NNA [ɳ] (ण), retroflexed version of [n], has approximately mapped onto Noon [n] (ن). This creates a problem when a word actually containing NNA [ɳ] (ण) is transliterated from Urdu to Hindi. No-equivalence cases are given in Table 10.

Urdu	Hindi (corpus Frequency)
-	ण (4744)
-	ङ (0)
-	ञ (532)

Table 10: Urdu → Hindi No-equivalences

Missing diacritical marks is the major problem when transliterating Urdu into Hindi. The importance of diacritical marks has already been explained in section 4.3. This work assumed that all necessary diacritical marks are present in Urdu text because they play a vital role in Urdu to Hindi transliterations. Results of Urdu to Hindi transliteration are given in Table 11.

	Error Words	Accuracy
Corpus	11,874	97.12%
Unique Words	123	98.54%

Table 11: Urdu → Hindi Transliteration Results

7.2 Hindi → Urdu Transliteration Results

Hindi → Urdu transliteration also have multi-equivalences and no-equivalence problems that are given in Table 12.

Hindi	Urdu (corpus Frequency)
त	ت (41,751), ط (1312)
स	س (53,289), ص (751), ث (86)
ह	ہ (72,850), ح (1800)
ज़	ز (2551), ض (1489), ذ (228), ظ (215), ژ (2)
-	ع (2857)

Table 12: Hindi → Urdu Multi & No equivalences

Results of Hindi to Urdu transliteration are given in Table 13.

	Error Words	Accuracy
Corpus	8,740	97.88%
Unique Words	1400	83.41%

Table 13: Hindi → Urdu Transliteration Results

Interestingly, Hindi to Urdu conversion is 14.47% less accurate on the unique words as compared to its result on the corpus data that is a contrasting fact for the reverse conversion.

The HUMT system gives 97.12% accuracy for Urdu to Hindi and 97.88% accuracy for Hindi to Urdu. Thus, the HUMT system works with 97.50% accuracy.

8 Future Implications

Hindi-Urdu transliteration is one of the cases where one language is written in two or more mutually incomprehensible scripts like Kazakh, Kashmiri, Malay, Punjabi, Sindhi, *etc.* The HUMT system can be enhanced by extending UIT and introducing the respective finite-state transducers. It can similarly be enhanced to transliterate between language pairs, *e.g.* English-Arabic, English-Hindi, English-Urdu, French-Hindi, *etc.* Thus, it can be enhanced to build a *multilingual machine transliteration system* that can be used for *cross-scriptural transliteration* and MT.

We are intended to resolve the problems of multi-equivalences, no-equivalences and the most importantly the restoration of diacritical marks in Urdu text that are observed but left unattended in the current work. Restoration of diacritical marks in Urdu, Sindhi, Punjabi, Kashmiri, *etc.* texts is essential for word sense disambiguation, natural language processing and speech synthesis of the said languages.

The HUMT system will also provide a basis for the development of *Inter-dialectal* translation system and MT system for *surface-close* languages like Indonesian-Malay, Japanese-Korean,

Hindi-Marathi, Hindi-Urdu, *etc.* Translation of the *surface-close* languages or *inter-dialectal* translation can be performed by using mainly transliteration and some lexical translations. Thus HUMT will also provide basis for *Cross-Scriptural Transliteration, Cross-scriptural Information Retrieval, Cross-scriptural Application Development, inter-dialectal translation* and *translation of surface-close languages*.

9 Conclusion

Finite-state transducers are very efficient, robust, and simple to use. Their simplicity and powerful features are exploited in the HUMT model to perform Hindi-Urdu transliteration using UIT that is a generic and flexible encoding scheme to uniquely encode natural languages into ASCII. The HUMT system gives 97.50% accuracy when it is applied on the Hindi-Urdu corpora containing 412,249 words in total. It is an endeavor to bridge the scriptural, ethnical, cultural and geographical division between 1,017 millions people around the globe.

Acknowledgement

This study is partially supported by the project CIFLI funded under ARCUS-INDIA program by *Ministry of Foreign Affairs* and *Rhône-Alpes* region.

References

Beesley, Kenneth R. and Karttunen, Lauri. 2003. *Finite State Morphology*. CSLI Publications, USA.

Boitet, Christian. Bhattacharayya, Pushpak. Blanc, Etienne. Meena, Sanjay. Boudhh, Sangharsh. Fafiotte, Georges. Falaise, Achille. Vacchani, Vishal. 2007. *Building Hindi-French-English-UNL Resources for SurviTra-CIFLI, a linguistic survival system under construction*. Proceedings of the Seventh Symposium on NLP, 13 – 15 December, Chonburi, Thailand.

Feroz ul Din. فیروزاللغات اردو Feroz Sons Publishers, Lahore, Pakistan.

Hussain, Sarmad. 2004. *Letter to Sound Rules for Urdu Text to Speech System*. Proceedings of Workshop on Computational Approaches to Arabic Script-based Languages, COLING 2004, Geneva, Switzerland.

James, L. Hieronymus. 1993. *ASCII Phonetic Symbols for the World's Languages: Worldbet*. AT&T Bell Laboratories, Murray Hill, NJ 07974, USA.

Kellogg, Rev. S. H. 1872. *A Grammar of Hindi Language*. Delhi, Oriental Book Reprints.

Khan, Mehboob Alam. 1997. اردو کا صوتی نظام (Sound System in Urdu) National Language Authority, Pakistan.

Knight, K. and Graehl, J. 1998. *Machine Transliteration*. Computational Linguistics, 24(4).

Knight, K. and Stall, B G. 1998. *Translating Names and Technical Terms in Arabic Tex*. Proceedings of the COLING/ACL Workshop on Computational Approaches to Semitic Languages.

Malik, M. G. Abbas. 2006. *Punjabi Machine Transliteration*. Proceedings of the 21st International Conference on Computational Linguistics and 44th Annual Meeting of the ACL, July 2006, Sydney.

Mohri, Mehryar. 1997. *Finite-state Transducers in Language and Speech Processing*. Computational Linguistics, 23(2).

Montaut A. 2004. *A Linguistic Grammar of Hindi*. Studies in Indo-European Linguistics Series, München, Lincom Europa.

Paola, V. and Sanjeev, K. 2003. *Transliteration of proper names in cross-language applications*. Proceedings of the 26th annual International ACM SIGIR conference on research and development in information retrieval.

Pirkola, A. Toivonen, J. Keskustalo, H. Visala, K. and Järvelin, K. 2003. *Fuzzy translation of cross-lingual spelling variants*. Proceedings of the 26th Annual international ACM SIGIR Conference on Research and Development in informaion Retrieval, Toronto, Canada.

Platts, John T. 1909. *A Grammar of the Hindustani or Urdu Language*. Crosby Lockwood and Son, 7 Stationers Hall Court, Ludgate hill, London. E.C.

Platts, John T. 1911. *A Dictionary of Urdu, Classical Hindi and English*. Crosby Lockwood and Son, 7 Stationers Hall Court, Ludgate hill, London, E.C.

Rahman, Tariq. 2004. *Language Policy and Localization in Pakistan: Proposal for a Paradigmatic Shift*. Crossing the Digital Divide, SCALLA Conference on Computational Linguistics.

Rai, Alok. 2000. *Hindi Nationalism*. Orient Longman Private Limited, New Delhi.

Wells, J C. 1995. *Computer-coding the IPA: A Proposed Extension of SAMPA*. University College London. http://www.phon.ucl.ac.uk/home/sampa/ipasam-x.pdf.

Yan Qu, Gregory Grefenstette, David A. Evans. 2003. *Automatic transliteration for Japanese-to-English text retrieval*. Proceedings of the 26th annual interntional ACM SIGIR conference on Research and development in information retrieval.

Zia, Khaver. 1999a. *Standard Code Table for Urdu*. Proceedings of 4th Symposium on Multilingual Information Processing (MLIT-4), Yangon, Myanmar, CICC, Japan.

Comparative Parser Performance Analysis across Grammar Frameworks through Automatic Tree Conversion using Synchronous Grammars

Takuya Matsuzaki [1] **Jun'ichi Tsujii** [1,2,3]

1. Department of Computer Science, University of Tokyo, Japan
2. School of Computer Science, University of Manchester, UK
3. National Center for Text Mining, UK

{matuzaki, tsujii}@is.s.u-tokyo.ac.jp

Abstract

This paper presents a methodology for the comparative performance analysis of the parsers developed for different grammar frameworks. For such a comparison, we need a common representation format of the parsing results since the representation of the parsing results depends on the grammar frameworks; hence they are not directly comparable to each other. We first convert the parsing result to a shallow CFG analysis by using an automatic tree converter based on synchronous grammars. The use of such a shallow representation as a common format has the advantage of reduced noise introduced by the conversion in comparison with the noise produced by the conversion to deeper representations. We compared an HPSG parser with several CFG parsers in our experiment and found that meaningful differences among the parsers' performance can still be observed by such a shallow representation.

1 Introduction

Recently, there have been advancement made in the parsing techniques for large-scale lexicalized grammars (Clark and Curran, 2004; Ninomiya et al., 2005; Ninomiya et al., 2007), and it have presumably been accelerated by the development of the semi-automatic acquisition techniques of large-scale lexicalized grammars from parsed corpora (Hockenmaier and Steedman, 2007; Miyao et al., 2005). In many of the studies on lexicalized grammar parsing, the accuracy of the parsing results is evaluated in terms of the accuracy of the semantic representations output by the parsers. Since the formalisms for the semantic representation are different across the grammar frameworks, it has been difficult to directly compare the performance of the parsers developed for different grammar frameworks.

Several researchers in the field of lexicalized grammar parsing have recently started to seek a common representation of parsing results across different grammar frameworks (Clark and Curran, 2007; Miyao et al., 2007). For example, Clark and Curran (2007) developed a set of mapping rules from the output of a Combinatorial Categorial grammar parser to the Grammatical Relations (GR) (Carroll et al., 1998). They found that the manual development of such mapping rules is not a trivial task; their mapping rules covered only 85% of the GRs in a GR-annotated corpus; i.e., 15% of the GRs in the corpus could not be covered by the mapping from the gold-standard CCG analyses of those sentences.

We propose another method for the cross-framework performance analysis of the parsers wherein the output of parsers are first converted to a CFG tree. Specifically, we use CFG trees of the style used in the Penn Treebank (PTB) (Marcus et al., 1994), in which the non-terminal labels are simple phrasal categories (i.e., we do not use function-tags, empty nodes, and co-indexing). We hereafter name such CFG trees, 'PTB-CFG trees.' We use an automatic tree converter based on a stochastic synchronous grammar in order to make the PTB-CFG trees from the analyses based on a lexicalized grammar.

In such a shallow representation, some infor-

©2008. Licensed under the *Creative Commons Attribution-Noncommercial-Share Alike 3.0 Unported* license (http://creativecommons.org/licenses/by-nc-sa/3.0/). Some rights reserved.

mation given by the lexicalized parsers is lost. For instance, long-distance dependency and control/raising distinction cannot be directly represented in the PTB-CFG tree. From the viewpoint of NLP-application developer, the parser evaluation based on such a shallow representation may be not very informative because performance metrics based on the shallow representation, e.g., labeled bracketing accuracy, do not serve as a direct indicator of the usefulness of the parser in their applications. Nevertheless, we consider the parser performance analysis based on the shallow representation is still very useful from the viewpoint of *parser developers* because the accuracy of the structure of the CFG-trees is, though not an ideal one, a good indicator of the parsers' structural disambiguation performance.

In addition, there are at least two advantages in using the CFG-trees as the common representation for the evaluation. The first advantage is that the conversion from the parser's output to the CFG-trees can be achieved with much higher accuracy than to deeper representations like GRs; we obtained a conversion accuracy of around 98% in our experiments using an HPSG grammar. The accuracy of the conversion is critical in the quantitative comparison of parsers that have similar performances because the difference in the parsers' ability would soon be masked by the errors introduced in the conversion process. The second advantage is that we can compare the converted output directly against the outputs of the well-studied CFG-parsers derived from PTB.

In the experiments, we applied the conversion to an HPSG parser, and compared the results against several CFG parsers. We found that the parsing accuracy of the HPSG parser is a few points lower than state-of-the-art CFG parsers in terms of the labeled bracketing accuracy. By further investigating the parsing results, we have identified a portion of the reason for the discrepancy, which comes from the difference in the architecture of the parsers.

2 Background

In this section, we first give a brief overview of the semi-automatic acquisition framework of lexicalized grammars. Although our methodology is also applicable to manually developed grammars, in this paper, we concentrate on the evaluation of the parsers developed for lexicalized grammars derived from a CFG treebank. Next, we introduce a specific instance of the treebank-derived lexicalized grammars used in our experiment: the Enju English HPSG grammar. Using the Enju grammar as a concrete example, we present the motivations for our tree conversion method based on a stochastic synchronous grammar. We also provide a summary of the basic concepts and terminologies of the stochastic synchronous grammar.

2.1 Semi-automatic Acquisition of Lexicalized Grammars

A lexicalized grammar generally has two components: a small set of grammar rules and a large set of lexical items. The grammar rules represent generic grammatical constraints while the lexical items represent word-specific characteristics. An analysis of a sentence is created by iteratively combining lexical items assigned to to the words in the sentence by applying the grammar rules.

Several researchers have suggested to extract the lexicon; i.e., the set of lexical items, from a treebank such as PTB. Most of the lexicon acquisition methods proceed as follows:

1. Fix the the grammar rules and the basic design of the lexical items.
2. Re-analyse the sentences in terms of the target grammar framework, exploiting the analysis given in the source treebank. A re-analysis is generally represented as a derivation of the sentence; i.e., a history of rule applications.
3. Find a lexical item for each word in the sentences so that it matches the re-analysis of the sentence, and extract it.

We used the pairs of the original trees and the re-analyses of the same sentence as a parallel treebank, from which we extract a synchronous grammar.

2.2 The Enju HPSG Grammar

We used the Enju English HPSG grammar (Miyao et al., 2005) [1] in the experiments. The design of the grammar basically follows the definition in the text by Pollard and Sag (1994). A program called Mayz is distributed with the grammar, which was

[1] Version 2.2., publicly available from http://www-tsujii.is.s.u-tokyo.ac.jp/enju

used to make the HPSG treebank (i.e., a set of re-analyses based on the HPSG grammar) from PTB; the lexicon was extracted from the HPSG treebank. We reproduced the HPSG treebank using the program.

An analysis of a sentence in the HPSG formalism is represented by a phrasal tree, in which each node is assigned a data structure called typed feature structure (TFS). The TFS represents syntactic/semantic structures of the corresponding phrase. To convert an HPSG analysis to a corresponding PTB-CFG trees, we first map the TFSs to atomic symbols like PP, NP, NX, etc. (33 symbols in total). We hereafter name such HPSG trees after the TFS-to-symbol mapping, 'simplified HPSG trees.' Similarly to the PTB-CFG trees, the simplified HPSG trees do not include empty categories, co-indexing, and function-tags. However, we cannot attain a PTB-CFG tree by simply mapping those atomic symbols to the corresponding PTB non-terminal symbols, because the analyses by the PTB-CFG and the HPSG yield different tree structures for the same sentence.

The conversion of the tree structure from HPSG trees to PTB-CFG trees can be regarded as the inverse-mapping of the transformation from PTB trees to HPSG trees implemented in the Mayz program. A most notable transformation is the binarization of the PTB trees; all the branches in the HPSG treebank are unary or binary. The binarization scheme used in Mayz is similar to the head-centered binarization, which is often used for the extraction of 'Markovised' PCFGs from the treebank. Mayz identifies the head daughters by using a modified version of Collins' head finding rules (Collins, 1999). It is also notable that the PTB-to-HPSG transformation by Mayz often makes a bracketing in the HPSG analyses that crosses with the original bracketing in the PTB. Such a transformation is used, for instance, to change the attachment level of an article to a noun phrase with a post-modifier (Figure 1).

The tree transformation by Mayz is achieved by sequentially applying many tree transformation rules to an input PTB tree. Although each of the rules operates on a relatively small region of the tree, the net result can be a very complex transformation. It is thus very difficult, if not impossible, to invert the transformation programmatically.

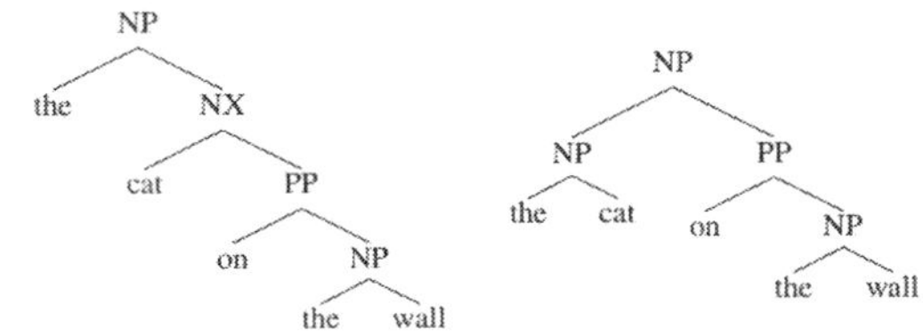

Figure 1: Different attachment level of the articles: HPSG analysis (left) and PTB-CFG analysis (right).

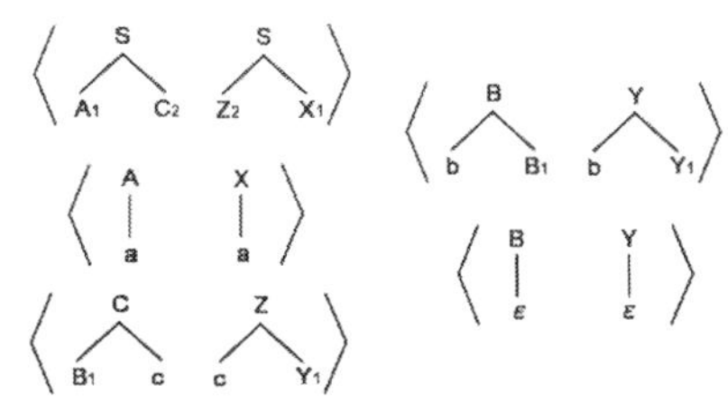

Figure 2: An example of synchronous CFG

2.3 Stochastic Synchronous Tree-Substitution Grammar for Tree Conversion

For the purpose of the inverted transformation of simplified HPSG trees to PTB-CFG trees, we use a statistical approach based on the stochastic synchronous grammars. Stochastic synchronous grammars are a family of probabilistic models that generate a pair of trees by recursively applying *synchronous productions*, starting with a pair of initial symbols. See e.g., Eisner (2003) for a more formal definition. Figure 2 shows an example of synchronous CFG, which generates the pairs of strings of the form $(\mathbf{ab}^m\mathbf{c}, \mathbf{cb}^m\mathbf{a})$. Each non-terminal symbol on the yields of the synchronous production is linked to a non-terminal symbol on the other rule's yield. In the figure, the links are represented by subscripts. A linked pair of the non-terminal symbols is simultaneously expanded by another synchronous production.

The probability of a derivation D of a tree pair $\langle S, T\rangle$ is defined as the product of the probability of the pair of initial symbols (i.e., the root nodes of S and T), and the probabilities of the synchronous productions used in the derivation:

$$P(D) = P\left(\left\langle R^1, R^2\right\rangle\right) \prod_{\langle t_i^1, t_i^2\rangle \in D} P\left(\left\langle t_i^1, t_i^2\right\rangle\right),$$

where $\langle R^1, R^2\rangle$ is the pair of the symbols of the root nodes of S and T, and $\langle t_i^1, t_i^2\rangle$ is a synchronous production.

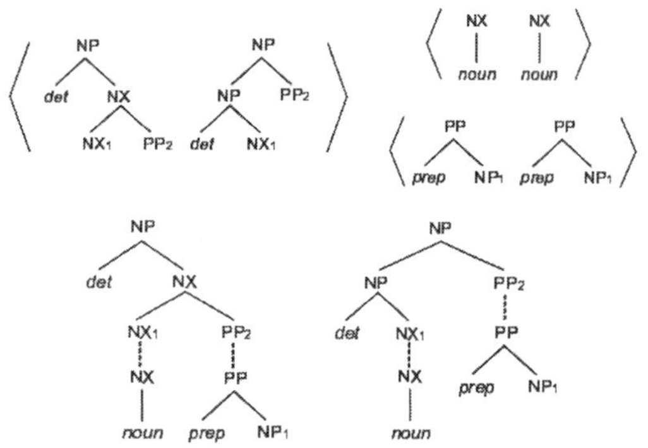

Figure 3: An example of synchronous TSG: synchronous productions (top) and a synchronous derivation (bottom).

Stochastic synchronous grammars have been used in several machine-translation systems to serve as a model of tree-to-tree translation (e.g., (Eisner, 2003; Chiang, 2007)). Our objective of automatic conversion between syntactic analyses is similar to the tree-to-tree machine translation. An important difference is that, for our purpose, the generated tree pair should have the same yields since they are two analyses of the same sentence. We also want the synchronous grammar to be able to generate a pair of trees wherein some constituents in one tree cross with the constituents in the other tree; for example, such a tree-transformation is necessary to change the article-attachment levels.

We show below that, by means of a simple algorithm, we can obtain a synchronous tree-substitution grammar (STSG) that meets the above two requirements. Synchronous productions in STSGs may include a local tree of depth greater than one. Figure 3 shows a tiny STSG that generates two different analyses for PP-modified NPs. Furthermore, a part of the derivation of the two analyses is presented; the dotted-lines indicate applications of the synchronous productions.

3 Tree Transformation Based on a Stochastic Synchronous Grammar

3.1 Extraction of Synchronous Grammars

We created an STSG from a parallel treebank, in which a sentence is assigned with a PTB-CFG tree and a simplified HPSG tree. The synchronous productions were obtained by splitting the tree pairs at several pairs of non-terminal nodes. Specifically, for a tree pair (T_1, T_2) for a sentence s,

1. we select a set of 'common-span node pairs' $\{(N_i^1, N_i^2) | N_i^1 \in T_1, N_i^2 \in T_2, i = 1, \ldots k\}$, which is a set of pairs of non-terminal nodes that dominate the same span of s, and then
2. split (T_1, T_2) at each (N_i^1, N_i^2) for $i = 1, \ldots, k$.

For tree pairs that do not include unary productions, the above procedure uniquely determines a collection of pairs of tree-fragments (t_i^1, t_i^2) by splitting the tree pair at all the common-span node pairs. For tree pairs including unary productions, we chose the split points $\{(N_i^1, N_i^2)\}$ so that they yield a pair of the longest unary chains as a tree-fragment pair when both T_1 and T_2 include one or more unary production dominating a common span. When only T_1 (or T_2) includes one or more unary productions on a common span, we selected the upper-most node of the chain of the unary productions in T_1, and the corresponding node in T_2 as the split points.

A node on the yields of the resulting tree-fragments is either a terminal node or a node in a common-span node pair that is selected as a split node. We make the synchronous productions by placing links between the common-span node pairs on the yields of the tree-fragment pairs. We can show that the grammar obtained as above only generates pairs of identical sentences by noting that the terminal symbols on the yields of two local trees in a synchronous production, if any, are always identical.

By regarding the division of tree-pairs into the tree-fragment pairs as a synchronous derivation, we get the maximum-likelihood estimates of the probabilities of the synchronous productions:

$$P(\langle t_1, t_2 \rangle) = \frac{\text{Count}(\langle t_1, t_2 \rangle)}{\text{Count}(\langle \text{root\_of}(t_1), \text{root\_of}(t_2) \rangle)},$$

where Count(·) represents the number of the synchronous productions or the pair of their root symbols observed in the derivations.

As is clear from the construction, certain types of conversions can not be handled properly by the STSG. For instance, the apparent conversion rule between the right-branching analysis of the listing: (*rats*, (*cows*, (*tigers*, ... (*and pigs*))...) and left-branching analysis: (...((*rats*, *cows*,) *tigers*,) ... *and pigs*) can not be represented in its full generality by the STSG. We however expect that most of such cases could be handled by combining the STSG-based conversion with a programmatic conversion.

3.2 Tree Conversion Algorithm

We can define a conversion function $f(S)$, which takes a tree S and returns the converted tree T, as:

$$f(S) = \operatorname*{argmax}_T P(T|S) = \operatorname*{argmax}_T P(S,T),$$

where $P(S,T)$ is the marginal probability of the tree pair $\langle S,T\rangle$. The marginal probability is the sum of the probabilities of all the derivations that generate the tree pair $\langle S,T\rangle$. Since the synchronous productions in a STSG may include a local tree of any depth, there are exponentially many derivations that generate the same tree pair. To our knowledge, no polynomial time algorithm is known for the above optimization problem.

We have instead searched the max-probability synchronous derivation of the tree pair of the form $\langle S,\cdot\rangle$ and taken the opponent tree as the conversion result of the input tree S:

$$f(S) = \operatorname*{argmax}_T \operatorname*{argmax}_{D:\text{deriv.of}\langle S,T\rangle} P(D).$$

We used Eisner's decoding algorithm (Eisner, 2003), which is similar to the Viterbi algorithm for HMMs, to obtain the max-probability derivation.

3.3 A Back-off Mechanism for the Conversion

In our preliminary experiment, a certain number of source trees were not covered by the synchronous grammar. For the trees that are not covered by the synchronous grammar, we used a set of "back-off rules," which are synchronous productions consisting of two 1-level local trees:

$$\{\langle X \rightarrow \alpha, Y \rightarrow \beta\rangle \mid \quad X \in N_1, \alpha \in (N_1 \cup \Sigma)^*, \\ Y \in N_2, \beta \in (N_2 \cup \Sigma)^*\},$$

where N_1 and N_2 are the sets of non-terminal symbols used in the two treebanks, and Σ is the set of terminal symbols. We assign small scores to the back-off rules as:

$$\text{score}_{\langle X\rightarrow\alpha, Y\rightarrow\beta\rangle} = \epsilon P(X \rightarrow \alpha) \prod P(B_i|A_i),$$

where ϵ is a small constant, $P(X \rightarrow \alpha)$ is the maximum-likelihood estimate of the PCFG rule probability of $X \rightarrow \alpha$ in the source treebank, and $\prod P(B_i|A_i)$ is the product of 're-labeling probabilities' for the pairs of linked non-terminal symbols in α and β, defined as:

$$P(B|A) = \frac{\text{Count}(\langle A,B\rangle)}{\sum_{B'} \text{Count}(\langle A,B'\rangle)},$$

where Count($\cdot$) represents the number of common-span node pairs used as the split points.

When a source tree is not covered by the original synchronous productions, we add the back-off rules to the synchronous productions, and search for the highest-scored derivation. The score of a derivation including the back-off rules is defined as the product of the probabilities of the original synchronous productions, and the scores of the back-off rules. We set the value of ϵ to be sufficiently small so that the highest-scored derivation includes a minimum number of back-off rules.

4 Experiments

4.1 Experiment Setting

We compared the performance of an HPSG parser with several CFG parsers. The HPSG parser is the Enju parser (Ninomiya et al., 2007), which has been developed for parsing with the Enju HPSG grammar. A disambiguation module based on a discriminative maximum-entropy model is used in the Enju parser. We compared the Enju parser with four CFG parsers: Stanford's lexicalized parser (Klein and Manning, 2003), Collins' parser (Collins, 1999), Charniak's parser (Charniak, 2000), and Charniak and Johnson's reranking parser (Charniak and Johnson, 2005). The first three parsers are based on treebank PCFGs derived from PTB. The last parser is a combination of Charniak's parser and a reranking module based on a maximum-entropy model. The Enju parser and Collins' parser require POS-tagged sentences as the input. A POS tagger distributed with the Enju parser was used for the POS-tagging.

We used a standard split of PTB for the training/development/test data: sections 02-21 for the extraction of the synchronous grammar, section 22 for the development, and section 23 for the evaluation of the parsers. Some of the trees in PTB are missing in the HPSG treebank because the Enju grammar does not cover all sentences in PTB. Section 23 of the HPSG treebank, which was used as the gold-standard of the HPSG analyses in the experiments, thus contains fewer sentences (2,278 sentences) than the original PTB section 23 (2,416 sentences). We use a notation, "section 23*," to indicate the portion of PTB section 23 covered by the Enju grammar.

Each parser's output was evaluated in the following three representations:

- PTB-CFG trees: We converted the Enju

parser's output to PTB-CFG trees by using a synchronous grammar. For the CFG parsers, we used their output as is.

- Simplified HPSG trees: We converted the CFG parsers' output to simplified HPSG trees by using another synchronous grammar. The Enju parser's output was mapped to simplified HPSG trees. This was achieved by simply mapping the TFSs assigned to the non-terminal nodes to atomic symbols.
- Unlabeled word-word dependency: We extracted head-modifier dependencies from the PTB-CFG trees by using Collins' head finding rules.

The evaluation in the unlabeled word-word dependency is motivated by the expectation that, by converting PTB-CFG trees to an even simpler representation, we can reduce the effect of the noise introduced in the conversion of the Enju parser's output to the PTB-CFG trees.

4.2 Extraction of Synchronous grammars

The stochastic synchronous grammars used for the tree-to-tree conversion were extracted from a parallel treebank consisting of the PTB-CFG trees in sections 02-21 of PTB and the simplified HPSG trees mapped from the HPSG treebank created by the Mayz. We treated the POS tags, which are common to the PTB-CFG grammar and the Enju HPSG grammar, as the terminal symbols.

Although we can use a single synchronous grammar for the conversion of both directions (i.e., from PTB-CFG trees to simplified HPSG trees, and the opposite), we used two different synchronous grammars to achieve better conversion accuracies. The two synchronous grammars were created by applying different pre-processing to the parallel treebank. Specifically, for the HPSG→PTB-CFG direction, 1) the PTB-CFG trees in the parallel treebank were binarized in such a way that maximized the number of common-span node pairs;[2] 2) commas in the PTB-CFG trees were raised as high as possible, approximating the change of the position of commas by the Mayz program; 3) the POS tags for 'not' are changed from 'RB' to 'RB-not,' because in PTB, 'not' is treated differently from other adverbs; 4) base NPs in PTB-CFG trees are marked as 'NP-B.' The PTB-CFG trees converted from the Enju parser's output were post-processed so that the effect of the pre-processing was removed; i.e., artificially created non-terminal nodes like '$A*$' were removed, 'RB-not' was changed to 'RB', and 'NP-B' was changed to 'NP.'[3]

For the PTB-CFG→HPSG direction, 1) PTB-CFG trees in the parallel treebank are head-centered-binarized by using Collins' head finding rules; 2) the same pre-processing as for the comma-raising, 'not' adverbs, and base NPs was applied to the PTB-CFG trees. The same pre-processing was applied to the CFG parsers' output before the conversion to simplified HPSG trees.

4.3 Accuracy of the Tree Conversion

To evaluate the accuracy of the tree conversion, we converted the trees in section 23* of the HPSG/PTB treebank into the other format (target format) and compared the conversion results against the corresponding trees in the gold-standard treebank of the target format. Table 1 presents the result of the evaluation. With the exception of the last column, the columns list the PARSEVAL metrics of the converted trees. The last column headed 'back-off%' shows the percentages of the trees for which the back-off mechanism described in Section 3 were used. The accuracy of the word-word dependencies extracted from the PTB-CFG trees converted from the HPSG treebank was 98.76%.[4]

On average, a tree in section 23* of the HPSG treebank includes 0.89 brackets that cross with the brackets in the corresponding tree in the PTB-CFG treebank, and a tree in the PTB-CFG treebank includes 0.78 brackets that cross with the brackets in the corresponding tree in the HPSG treebank. The figures in the column headed CBs (average number of crossing brackets) show that most of such crossing brackets are 'corrected' by the conversion.

4.4 Comparative Parser Evaluation using Common Representations

We measured the labeled bracketing accuracy of the parsers' output in the PTB-CFG tree representation (on section 23), and in the simplified HPSG

[2]The non-terminal nodes artificially introduced in the binarization process were labeled as '$A*$', where 'A' is the label of the nearest 'non-artificial' ancestor node.

[3]The positions of commas were left unchanged, because we ignored commas in the evaluation, just as in the standard way of evaluating CFG parsers based on the PARSEVAL metrics.

[4]Dependency relations involving a punctuation mark as the modifier were not counted in the evaluation.

Conversion direction	LP	LR	F_1	CBs	0 CBs	$\leq$ 2 CBs	back-off%
HPSG → PTB-CFG	98.41	98.08	98.24	0.01	99.34	100.00	2.59
PTB-CFG → HPSG	97.54	97.45	97.49	0.13	93.99	98.33	10.80

Table 1: Accuracy of the tree conversion

Parser	LP	LR	F_1
Charniak and Johnson	91.79	90.88	91.33
Charniak	89.49	88.78	89.13
Collins (model 3)	88.62	88.28	88.45
Collins (model 2)	88.48	88.15	88.31
Collins (model 1)	87.94	87.51	87.72
Stanford lexicalized	86.36	86.47	86.41
Enju + tree conv.	87.18	86.47	86.82

Table 2: PTB-CFG tree evaluation

Parser (+ tree conv.)	LP	LR	F_1
Charniak and Johnson	91.44	91.31	91.37
Charniak	90.07	89.97	90.02
Collins (model 3)	88.79	88.38	88.58
Collins (model 2)	88.74	88.33	88.53
Collins (model 1)	88.62	88.48	88.54
Stanford lexicalized	88.04	88.12	88.08
Enju	90.79	90.30	90.54

Table 3: Simplified HPSG tree Evaluation

Parser	accuracy
Charniak and Johnson	93.66
Charniak	92.50
Collins (model 3)	91.15
Collins (model 2)	91.12
Collins (model 1)	90.66
Stanford lexicalized	90.91
Enju + tree conv.	90.77

Table 4: Unlabeled dependency evaluation

Modifier	Head		Enju	Charinak	p-value
t_m	t_c	t_w	X (Z)	Y (W)	
VB	ROOT	NN	20 (20)	1 (1)	8.57e-5
NN	VB	NN	69 (94)	30 (55)	1.34e-4
NN	VB	ROOT	14 (14)	0 (0)	5.12e-4
CD	CD	IN	0 (0)	11 (11)	2.57e-3
CD	NN	CD	12 (12)	1 (2)	5.55e-3
VB	VB	NN	17 (26)	4 (9)	8.83e-3
DT	NN	VB	10 (15)	1 (4)	1.59e-2
DT	NN	JJ	7 (10)	0 (3)	2.33e-2
VB	VB	MD	7 (9)	0 (1)	2.33e-2
TO	VB	NN	24 (31)	10 (19)	2.58e-2

Table 5: Error types with smallest p-values

tree representation (on section 23*). The results are shown in Table 2 and Table 3. The accuracy of word-word dependencies extracted from the PTB-CFG representation is shown in Table 4. As shown in the previous section, approximately 2% of the brackets are wrong and approximately 1% of the word-word dependencies are wrong after the conversion in both direction even if a parser gives 100% correct output. Taking this into consideration, we might conclude, utilizing the results shown in the three tables, that the performance of the Enju parser is roughly the same level as Collins' parser and Stanford's lexicalized parser. Another notable fact depicted in the tables is that Charniak and Johnson's reranking parser outperforms the Enju parser even in the simplified HPSG tree representation.

4.5 Comparative Error Analysis

To closely examine the difference in the parsers' performances, we conducted a comparative error analysis using the word-word dependency representation of the parsing results. Specifically, we tested the difference in the ability of resolving specific types of syntactic ambiguities between two parsers by using McNemar's test. To make the samples for the McNemar's test, we identified a subset of tokens of type t_m in the test set that have a true head of type t_c and another word of type t_w that is confusable as the head. For example, a subset of tokens where (t_m, t_c, t_w) = (preposition, noun, verb) can be used to test the difference in the parsers' ability to resolve PP-attachment ambiguities, by extracting the pairs of the predicted head words for the prepositions from two parsers' output, and using them as the sample set for the McNemar's test. When comparing two parsers A and B, we approximated such a subset of tokens by collecting the tokens of type t_m, which have true head of type t_c, and for which either A or B predicted a wrong head of type t_w.

We show the results of the comparison between the Enju parser and the Charinak's parser in Table 5. We used section 22 of PTB for this experiment. The table lists the type of the ambiguities (t_m, t_c, t_w) for which the accuracies by the two parsers differ with the smallest p-values. Note that the POS types t_m, t_c, and t_w are determined from the gold-standard POS tags, not the POS tags given by parsers or the POS tagger. In the table, X is the number of the tokens of type (t_m, t_c, t_w) for which only the Enju parser outputs wrong heads; Z is the total number of wrong predictions of that type made by the Enju parser; Y and W are defined similarly for the Charinak's parser.

The results indicate, for example, that there is a significant difference between the two parsers in the ability to identify the root of a sentence (the first and third row). Investigation of the Enju parser's output including the root identification errors revealed that almost all of the errors of this type were caused by POS-tagging error; for example, when the matrix verb of a sentence, like 'costs,' is mistakenly tagged as a noun, the matrix verb is not identified as the root (as in the case with the first row), and the subject is often mistakenly identified as the root (as in the case with the third row). This weak-point of the Enju parser is a consequence of the architecture of the parser, wherein the POS-tagging phase is completely separated from the parsing phase. Although this weak-point has already been pointed out (Yoshida et al., 2007), we expect that we can identify other reasons for the difference in the parsers' performances by investigating the other types of errors with small p-values as well.

5 Conclusion

We have proposed the use of shallow CFG analyses as the common representation for the comparative performance analysis of parsers based on different grammar frameworks. We have presented a method to convert the parsers' output to the shallow CFG analyses that is based on synchronous grammars. The experimental results showed that our method gave a conversion accuracy of around 98% in terms of the labeled bracketing accuracy, which was sufficiently high for extracting a meaningful conclusion from a quantitative comparison of the parsers' performance. Furthermore, we conducted a comparative analysis of the parsing results represented in word-word dependencies extracted from the shallow CFG analyses. As a result, we could identified a weak-point of the HPSG parser that comes from the parser's architecture.

Acknowledgements

This work was partially supported by Grant-in-Aid for Specially Promoted Research (MEXT, Japan).

References

Carroll, J., T. Briscoe, and A. Sanlippo. 1998. Parser evaluation : A survey and a new proposal. In *In Proceedings First Conference on Linguistic Resources*, pages 447–455.

Charniak, E. and M. Johnson. 2005. Coarse-to-fine n-best parsing and maxent discriminative reranking. In *Proc. ACL*, pages 173–180.

Charniak, E. 2000. A maximum-entropy-inspired parser. In *Proc. NAACL*, pages 132–139.

Chiang, D. 2007. Hierarchical phrase-based translation. *Comput. Linguist.*, 33(2):201–228.

Clark, S. and J. R. Curran. 2004. The importance of supertagging for wide-coverage ccg parsing. In *Proc. COLING*, pages 282–288.

Clark, S. and J. Curran. 2007. Formalism-independent parser evaluation with ccg and depbank. In *Proc. ACL*, pages 248–255.

Collins, M. 1999. *Head-driven statistical models for natural language parsing*. Ph.D. thesis, University of Pennsylvania.

Eisner, J. 2003. Learning non-isomorphic tree mappings for machine translation. In *Proc. ACL, Companion Volume*, pages 205–208.

Hockenmaier, J. and M. Steedman. 2007. Ccgbank: A corpus of ccg derivations and dependency structures extracted from the penn treebank. *Computational Linguistics*, 33(3):355–396.

Klein, D. and C. D. Manning. 2003. A parsing: fast exact viterbi parse selection. In *Proc. NAACL*, pages 40–47.

Marcus, M. P., B. Santorini, and M. A. Marcinkiewicz. 1994. Building a large annotated corpus of english: The Penn Treebank. *Computational Linguistics*, 19(2):313–330.

Miyao, Y., T. Ninomiya, and J. Tsujii. 2005. Corpus-oriented grammar development for acquiring a Head-driven Phrase Structure Grammar from the Penn Treebank. In *Natural Language Processing - IJCNLP 2004*, volume 3248 of *LNAI*, pages 684–693. Springer-Verlag.

Miyao, Y., K. Sagae, and J. Tsujii. 2007. Towards framework-independent evaluation of deep linguistic parsers. In *Proc. GEAF*, pages 238–258.

Ninomiya, T., Y. Tsuruoka, Y. Miyao, and J. Tsujii. 2005. Efficacy of beam thresholding, unification filtering and hybrid parsing in probabilistic hpsg parsing. In *Proc. IWPT*, pages 103–114.

Ninomiya, T., T. Matsuzaki, Y. Miyao, and J. Tsujii. 2007. A log-linear model with an n-gram reference distribution for accurate hpsg parsing. In *Proc. IWPT*, pages 60–68.

Pollard, C. and I. A. Sag. 1994. *Head-Driven Phrase Structure Grammar*. University of Chicago Press.

Yoshida, K., Y. Tsuruoka, Y. Miyao, and J. Tsujii. 2007. Ambiguous part-of-speech tagging for improving accuracy and domain portability of syntactic parsers. In *Proc. IJCAI*, pages 1783–1788.

What's the Date?
High Accuracy Interpretation of Weekday Names

Paweł Mazur[1,2]

[1]Institute of Applied Informatics,
Wrocław University of Technology
Wyb. Wyspiańskiego 27,
50-370 Wrocław, Poland
Pawel.Mazur@pwr.wroc.pl

Robert Dale[2]

[2]Centre for Language Technology,
Macquarie University,
NSW 2109, Sydney, Australia
{mpawel,rdale}@ics.mq.edu.au

Abstract

In this paper we present a study on the interpretation of weekday names in texts. Our algorithm for assigning a date to a weekday name achieves 95.91% accuracy on a test data set based on the ACE 2005 Training Corpus, outperforming previously reported techniques run against this same data. We also provide the first detailed comparison of various approaches to the problem using this test data set, employing re-implementations of key techniques from the literature and a range of additional heuristic-based approaches.

1 Introduction

Many temporal expressions in text are underspecified, requiring contextually-sourced information in order to determine their correct interpretation. In some cases, it is sufficient to determine what is sometimes called the **temporal focus**, so that the precise location of a relative temporal expression on a timeline can be determined with respect to this 'time of speaking'. Consider, for example, expressions like the following:

(1) three days ago
(2) last Monday
(3) in two weeks time

Once we know the temporal focus, calculation of the temporal location referred to in each of these cases is straightforward, since the temporal expressions themselves explicitly indicate what we will call **the direction of offset** (here, respectively, past, past and future). However, in other cases there is no explicit indication of the direction of offset from the temporal focus. This is most obviously the case when bare expressions based on calendar cycles—i.e., weekday names and month names—are used, as in the following example:

(4) Jones met with Defense Minister Paulo Portas on *Tuesday* and will meet Foreign Minister Antonio Martins da Cruz before leaving Portugal *Wednesday*.

Here, the proper interpretation of the references to *Tuesday* and *Wednesday* requires at the least a correct syntactic analysis of the sentence, in order to locate the **controlling verb** for each weekday name. The tense of this verb can then be used to determine the direction—either in the past or in the future—in which we need to look to establish the fully specified date referred to. In the case of example (4), this means determining that *Tuesday* is in the scope of the verb *met*, and that *Wednesday* is in the scope of the verb group *will meet*. As we note below, it turns out that there are cases where even the controlling verb does not provide sufficient information to determine the direction of offset. But even in those cases where the tense of the verb *does* provide the relevant information, there are two problems. First, especially when the sentences considered are complex, there is a non-negligible likelihood that the analysis returned by a parser may not be correct, and this is especially the case when the sentences in question contain structures such as prepositional phrases: the attachment of these is notoriously a source of ambiguity, and they just happen to often be the hosts to temporal expressions. Second, even if a parser provides the correct analysis, parsing technology is still compu-

© 2008. Licensed under the *Creative Commons Attribution-Noncommercial-Share Alike 3.0 Unported* license (http://creativecommons.org/licenses/by-nc-sa/3.0/). Some rights reserved.

tationally expensive to use when processing very large bodies of text; if we are interested in time-stamping events described in significant volumes of data, we would prefer to have a faster, more heuristic-based approach.

In this paper, we explore the development of a fast and high accuracy algorithm for the interpretation of weekday names, in particular with regard to determining the direction of offset to be used in the temporal interpretation of these expressions: in essence, how can we determine whether the day referred to is in the past or in the future?

The rest of the paper is structured as follows. In Section 2 we present some general observations on the interpretation of weekday names in text. Section 3 provides a review of related work. In Section 4 we describe the corpus used for evaluation, and in Section 5 we describe in detail the various algorithms we evaluated. Section 6 compares the results of the various algorithms when applied to the corpus, and Section 7 provides an error analysis. Finally, in Section 8 we draw some conclusions and point to future work.

2 The Problem

The interpretation of relative temporal expressions[1] can be seen as a two step process: (1) first we have to determine a reference point for the interpretation of the expression;[2] (2) then we have to calculate the actual position of the referred-to time on the timeline.

Once we have the reference point determined, the interpretation of the offset from this reference point requires us to determine the magnitude and direction of offset. As noted above, in some cases the tense of the controlling verb will indicate the direction of offset; but prepositional attachment ambiguity can easily damage the reliability of such an approach, as demonstrated by the following minimal pair:

(5) We can show you some pictures on *Monday*.
(6) We can show you some pictures from *Monday*.

In example (5), the correct PP attachment is required in order to determine that *Monday* is in the scope of the verb group *can show*, allowing us to infer that the Monday in question is in the future. Example (6), on the other hand, is quite ambiguous and requires world knowledge in order to determine the correct attachment.

We are interested, therefore, in determining whether some heuristic method might provide good results. In the rest of this paper, we focus on the determination of the direction of offset. We will not explicitly address the question of determining the temporal focus: although this is clearly a key ingredient, we have found that using the document creation date performs well for the kinds of documents (typically newswire stories and similar document types) we are working with. More sophisticated strategies for temporal focus tracking would likely be required in other genres.

3 Related Work

The literature contains a number of approaches to the interpretation of weekday names, although we are not aware of any pre-existing direct comparison of these approaches.[3]

Filatova and Hovy (2001) assign time stamps to clauses in which an event is mentioned. As part of the overall process, they use a heuristic for the interpretation of weekday names: if the day name in a clause is the same as that of the temporal focus, then the temporal focus is used;[4] otherwise, they look for any 'signal words' or check the tense of the verb in the clause. An analogous approach is taken for the interpretation of month names.

Negri and Marseglia (2005), in their rule-based system for temporal expression recognition and normalisation, use what they call 'context words', such as *following* or *later*, to decide on the interpretation of a weekday name. Consider the following example:

(7) He started studying on March 30 2004, and passed the exam the following *Friday*.

Here, having identified the date *March 30 2004* (which happens to be a Tuesday), they then recognise the structure '*following* + trigger' and reason that the *Friday* is three days later.

[1]In the literature, a variety of different terms are used: (Schilder and Habel, 2001) call these expressions **indexicals**, and (Han et al., 2006b) uses the term **relative** for what we call **anaphoric** references: in our terminology, both deictic and anaphorical expressions are relative.

[2]This reference point is often referred to as the **temporal focus** or **temporal anchor**.

[3]Although Ahn et al. (2007) compared their results with those presented by Mani and Wilson (2000), they went on to point out that, for a variety of reasons, the numbers they provided were not really comparable.

[4]Filatova and Hovy use the term **reference point** for what we call the temporal focus.

There have also been machine-learning approaches to the interpretation of temporal expressions. Ahn et al. (2005) describes a system developed and tested on the ACE 2004 TERN test corpus. Using lexical features, such as the occurrence of *last* or *earlier* in a context window of three words, their maximum entropy classifier picked the correct direction ('backward', 'same', or 'forward') with an accuracy of 59%; the addition of features encoding information about tense increased the result to 61%.

Ahn et al. (2007) go on to describe a system using a classifier based on support vector machines and an extended set of features over a larger subset of the data. This algorithm was used to determine the direction of all relative temporal expressions, not just the names of weekdays. They used three sets of features:

1. Character type patterns, lexical features such as weekday name and numeric year, a context window of two words to the left, and several parse-based features: the phrase type, the phrase head and initial word (and POS tag), and the dependency parent (and corresponding relation) of the head.

2. The tense of the closest verb (w.r.t. dependency path), the POS tag of the verb, and the POS tags of any verbal elements directly related to this verb.

3. Features comparing year, month name and day name of a temporal expression to those of the document creation date.

Their experiments demonstrated that the third set was the most useful.

Han et al. (2006a) report on the development of the Time Calculus for Natural Language (TCNL), a compact formalism designed to capture the meaning of temporal expressions in natural language, which is built on top of their constraint-based calendar model (see (Han and Lavie, 2004)). In this formalism each temporal expression is converted to a formula in TCNL, which then can be processed to calculate the value of a temporal expression. Interpretation of weekday names uses the tense of the nearest verb chunk and the presence of lexical items such as *next*. Their temporal focus tracking mechanism allows correct interpretation of cases like 'I am free *next week*. How about *Friday*?', where the TCNL formula for *Friday*, being +{fri}, reflects the occurrence of *next* in the preceding sentence.

Table 1: ACE 2005 Training Corpus

Domain	#Docs	#Words	# TIMEX2
BC	60	40415	626
BN	226	55967	1455
CTS	39	39845	409
NW	106	48399	1235
UN	49	37366	741
WL	119	37897	1003
Total	599	259889	5469

Table 2: Weekdays in ACE 2005 Training Corpus

Domain	#Docs	# TIMEX2	# per doc
BC	4	7 (1.91%)	1.75
BN	25	31 (8.47%)	1.24
CTS	2	2 (0.54%)	1.00
NW	102	292 (79.56%)	2.86
UN	3	3 (0.81%)	1.00
WL	19	32 (8.72%)	1.68
Total	155	367 (100%)	2.37

Most closely relevant to the work described in the present paper are the approaches described in (Baldwin, 2002), (Jang et al., 2004) and (Mani and Wilson, 2000). Since we have re-implemented versions of these algorithms for the present paper, we leave description of these to Section 5.

4 Corpus and Experimental Setup

For this work we used the ACE 2005 Training Corpus, which is publicly available and distributed by the Linguistic Data Consortium (LDC).[5] It has already become the gold standard in the information extraction community, especially for the temporal expression recognition and normalisation (TERN) task, and currently it provides the largest available corpus of annotated temporal expressions. Table 1 presents some relevant statistics, and Table 2 shows the distribution of bare weekday names (as TIMEX2 counts) in the corpus across the various genres represented.[6]

For the work described here, we used only those documents in the corpus that contained at least one weekday name; all subsequent analysis makes use only of the gold standard annotations of the bare weekday names in these documents, thus significantly reducing corpus processing time. This results in a total of 367 instances, once errors (of which there are quite a few) in the gold standard

[5] The corpus's catalogue number is LDC2006T06.

[6] BC = Broadcast Conversations; BN = Broadcast News; CTS = Conversational Telephone Speech; NW = Newswire; UN = Usenet Newsgroups; and WL = Weblogs.

annotations have been repaired. We made the following changes to the gold standard data:

- One day name had been missed by the annotators; we added this.
- Some 40 values were corrected from the format YYYY-Wnn-m to YYYY-MM-DD: although both are correct in some sense, the ACE guidelines indicate that the second is the preferred form.
- Eight cases where the incorrect value had been provided by the annotators were corrected.

Specific details of these corrections, and the complete data set used, are available on the web.[7]

5 Evaluated Approaches

We implemented and evaluated a number of both simple and more complex approaches to determining what date is meant in a text when a bare weekday name is used. These methods, described below, can be divided into two main classes: (a) 7-day window based, and (b) tense analysis based. Our new algorithm is a hybrid solution that incorporates ideas from both of these approaches.

5.1 Baselines

Our baselines are motivated by the observation that days referred to by bare weekday names are typically temporally close to the temporal focus.[8] **Past 7-day Window (inclusive)**: This baseline looks for the specified day in a 7-day window whose last day is the temporal focus. In other words, day names are always assumed to refer to days in the last week, including the 'day of speaking'.

Past 7-day window (exclusive): This is the same as the approach just described, except that we look for the referred-to day in the week leading up to but not including the 'day of speaking'.

Future 7-day window (inclusive): This is the future-oriented version of the first approach described above: we look for the specified day in a 7-day window whose first day is the temporal focus. This assumes that all day name references are to the present or future.[9]

[7] Visit `http://TimexPortal.info`.

[8] Recall that in the present work we take the temporal focus to be the document creation date.

[9] An informal check of email data drove Han et al. (2005) to use the simple strategy of always assuming that weekday names refer to days in the future.

Future 7-day window (exclusive): In this case the 7-day window starts on the day following the 'day of speaking'.

5.2 Algorithms

5.2.1 Baldwin's 7-Day Window

This algorithm was presented in (Baldwin, 2002; Jang et al., 2004). It is similar to our window-based baselines, but in this case the temporal focus is the middle day of the 7-day window. This approach was used in their research after observing that 96.97% of weekday name expressions in their English corpus referred to dates within such a window. Suppose we have the following sentence in a document with creation date 2003-06-16 (a Monday):

(8) Police arrested her in Abilene, Texas, *Saturday* where she had moved with a friend June 2.

The 7-day window then spans from Friday (June 13) to Thursday (June 19). The reference to *Saturday* is assigned (correctly) the value of the second day in the window, i.e. 2003-06-14. Note that this method will deliver the wrong result when the referred-to day actually falls further than three days either side of the temporal focus. Suppose, for example, we have the following sentence in a document written on 2005-01-01 (a Saturday):

(9) We got into Heathrow on *Monday* morning.

Here the 7-day window spans from Wednesday to Tuesday, and so the reference to *Monday* will be assigned the incorrect interpretation 2005-01-03.

5.2.2 Mani and Wilson's Tense Estimation

In the system presented in (Mani and Wilson, 2000), weekday name interpretation is implemented as part of a sequence of interpretation rules for temporal expression interpretation more generally. This algorithm attempts to establish the tense of what we have called the controlling verb in the following way. First, it looks backwards from the temporal expression in question to any previous temporal expression in the sentence, or if there is none, to the beginning of the sentence. If no verb is found here, then it looks between the temporal expression and the end of the sentence; and if a verb is still not found, then it looks in front of any preceding temporal expression found back to the beginning of the sentence. If the verb found is in past tense, the direction of offset is assumed to be

Table 3: Interpretation rules

Tense	Example	Direction
Present Continuous	I am flying to New York on Monday.	Future
Past Simple	I wrote a paper on Monday.	Past
Future Simple	I will write a paper on Monday.	Future
Present Perfect	I have been writing a paper since Monday.	Past
Bare Past Participle	The draft written on Monday was useless.	Past
Modal Verb	I should finish the paper on Monday.	Future
Modal Verb + *have*	I should have submitted the paper on Monday.	Past

backwards; if the tense is future, then the forward direction is used. If the verb found is in present tense, then the temporal expression is passed to a further set of interpretation rules, which check for things like the occurrence of lexical markers such as *since* or *until*.[10] For example, in example (4), repeated below, the algorithm would correctly pick *met* for *Tuesday* and *will meet* for *Wednesday*, interpreting Tuesday as a day in a past and Wednesday as a day in future.

(4) Jones met with Defense Minister Paulo Portas on *Tuesday* and will meet Foreign Minister Antonio Martins da Cruz before leaving Portugal *Wednesday*.

However, this approach will not correctly interpret example (10):

(10) Still a decision has to made on what, if any, punishment he will face in the wake of that incident *Tuesday* night.

In this case, the wrong verb will be identified, and the direction of offset will be incorrect.

5.2.3 Simple Tense Estimation

As an alternative to Mani and Wilson's approach, we also implemented a much simpler tense estimation heuristic. This checks whether the sentence contains any tokens with the VBD (i.e., past tense) part of speech tag;[11] if one is found, then the direction of offset is assumed to be backwards, and if not, then we use the forward direction. In the case of example (4), this will assign the correct value to *Tuesday*, but the wrong value to *Wednesday*.

[10] We have reimplemented this algorithm based on the description given in the cited paper, but some details are unclear, so we acknowledge that the original implementation might produce slightly different results.

[11] Where POS tags are required in our algorithms, we used Mark Hepple's part of speech tagger, an implementation of which is available as a plugin for the GATE platform (`http://gate.ac.uk`).

5.2.4 Dependency-based Tense Determination

The two previous algorithms attempt to determine the controlling verb using very simple heuristics. Of course, a more reliable way of determining the controlling verb is to use a parser. We used the Stanford parser's dependency information output (see (de Marneffe et al., 2006)) to find the controlling verb of a weekday name in a sentence. This algorithm does this by traversing the resulting dependency tree from the node containing the weekday name to its root until a verb is found, and then following further dependencies to identify the whole verbal sequence.

5.2.5 A Hybrid Algorithm

Heuristic methods for determining tense are risky, especially as the distance between the controlling verb and the temporal expression increases. We therefore propose a hybrid approach that attempts to leverage both tense estimation approaches like Mani and Wilson's, and Baldwin's window-based approach. This algorithm was developed on the basis of an error analysis of the results of using Baldwin's algorithm. It embodies a two-step approach, where we first look only in the very local environment for clues as to the tense of the controlling verb, then fall back on Baldwin's algorithm if no such evidence is found close by. First, we check if the temporal preposition *since* appears immediately in front of a weekday name; if so, the direction of offset is assumed to be backwards; otherwise, the algorithm looks for any verbs in a window of three tokens before and three tokens after the temporal expression. If a verb is found, then its tense is used to determine the direction (using the same rules as in Mani and Wilson's approach). If no verb is found, then a 7-day window with the temporal focus as the middle day is used, just as in Baldwin's algorithm.

Table 4: Results

Algorithm	Errors	Correct
Past 7-day Window (Inclusive)	51	316 (86.10%)
Past 7-day Window (Exclusive)	240	127 (34.60%)
Future 7-day Window (Inclus.)	129	238 (64.85%)
Future 7-day Window (Exclus.)	316	51 (13.90%)
Sentence Tense Estimation	38	329 (89.65%)
Dependency-Based	29	338 (92.10%)
Mani and Wilson's	27	340 (92.64%)
Baldwin's 7-day Window	21	346 (94.28%)
Voting	16	351 (95.64%)
Hybrid	15	352 (95.91%)

Table 5: Processing times

Algorithm	Time [seconds]
Past 7-day Window (inclusive)	79.9
Past 7-day Window (exclusive)	79.7
Future 7-day Window (inclus.)	79.2
Future 7-day Window (exclus.)	79.4
Sentence Tense Estimation	80.6
Dependency-Based	616.5
Mani and Wilson's	80.9
Baldwin's 7-day Window	79.4
Voting	636.1
Hybrid	80.2

5.2.6 Voting

This algorithm uses a voting mechanism over the output of Baldwin's, Mani and Wilson's, and the Dependency-based Tense Determination algorithms. If all values are different (no majority) then Baldwin's result is used.

5.3 Tense Interpretation Rules

Once the verb group is found by any particular algorithm, it needs to be analysed to determine what its tense is; this information is then used to determine the direction of offset. The interpretation rules are summarized in Table 3.

6 Results

Table 4 presents the results achieved with each of the algorithms.

The 51% difference between the inclusive and exclusive baselines is indicative of the fact that, in this data, in over 50% of cases the correct date was in fact the document creation date. This phenomenon is due to the large proportion of newswire data in the corpus; in this genre, it is common to use the weekday name even when reporting on events that happen on the same day as the reporting takes place. Also of note is that the best performing baseline, 'Past 7-day window (inclusive)', achieves 86.10% accuracy despite its being an extremely naive approach.

All the algorithms tested here performed better than the baselines. The best performing algorithm was the Hybrid method, which made 15 errors, resulting in an accuracy of 95.91%; the Voting method came second with 16 errors. Baldwin's 7-day window algorithm correctly interpreted 94.28% of weekday names. The big advantage of this algorithm, along with all the baselines, is their complete resource independence: they do not use any parsers or POS taggers.

Perhaps surprisingly, Mani and Wilson's tense estimation heuristic was more effective than tense determination based on a dependency parse tree; this reinforces our earlier point about the risks of using parsers. It is also important to note that there are huge differences in execution time for parser-based approaches. Table 5 presents times for processing the entire corpus for temporal expression recognition and interpretation; the parser-based algorithm required 616 seconds, in contrast to around 80 seconds for each of the other algorithms.[12]

There were 296 cases (80.65%) that were correctly interpreted by all of the following algorithms: Sentence Tense Estimation, Mani and Wilson's, Dependency-based Tense Determination, Baldwin's 7-day Window, and Hybrid. There are also three cases where all these algorithms provided an incorrect value:[13]

(11) reporter: *friday night* in the gaza strip and a journalist is about to lose his life.

(12) president bush head to the g-8 summit in france on *friday* with victory over saddam hussein and in his pocket and a soaring approval rating by the american public, but do europeans share the same enthusiasm for the president?

(13) I will return this piece of shit on Friday, only to rent another vehicle *Monday morning* while we take the wife's car to the shop to get her 1400 bucks worth of damage repaired.

[12]Note that the parser was only called for those sentences that contained bare weekday names, and not for other sentences in these documents.

[13]We present these examples with their original spelling and casing.

In example (11), the algorithms interpreted *Friday night* as a day in future. However, this text is a case of what is sometimes called the **historical present**, where for rhetorical effect the author speaks in present tense from a past point in time; it is not obvious how any algorithm would determine the correct answer here. Example (12) is ungrammatical as a consequence of a missing 's' in *head*; consequently, the POS tagger did not annotate this word as a verb, and the algorithms identified *do* or *bush* as a verb, leading to the decision that the referred-to *friday* is in the future; however, the gold standard interpretation puts this in the past (note that, even with the correct verb form of *heads*, all the algorithms would still get the wrong date). It so happens the correct date here is also outside the 7-day window. In example (13), because the weekday name used is the same as the day name of the document creation date, all the algorithms assigned the document creation date instead of a date seven days later.

7 Error Analysis

The Hybrid Algorithm achieved the best accuracy of 95.91%, which corresponds to 15 error cases. These were as follows:

- Eight cases where there was no verb found in the three-token neighbourhood of the temporal expression; in these cases the 7-day window method was used, but this did not find the correct value.
- Three cases where the algorithm identified a verb that was not the controlling verb; for example, it picked *will meet* instead of *met* to interpret *Tuesday* in the sentence given in example (4).
- Two cases where the document creation date was very misleading (see below).
- Two cases where past tense was used to talk about plans for the future which were subsequently cancelled, as in *discussions were scheduled to end Friday, when Kelly was to fly....*

In 204 cases the algorithm interpreted the weekday name based on a verb found in the three-token neighbourhood; and in 163 cases it used the fallback 7-day window strategy. Since the Hybrid Algorithm was built as an extension of Baldwin's method, it is worth knowing whether there were any cases where the original 7-day window method got the correct value and the Hybrid Algorithm got it wrong. There were six such cases:

- Two of them occurred for documents with a misleading document creation date. In a typical example, a document with the timestamp 17-04-2004 (a Thursday) contained the sentence 'Malaysia's Appeal Court *Friday* refused to overturn the conviction ...'. As the document timestamp was used as the temporal focus, *Friday* was interpreted as a day in the past, when in fact it was the day after the timestamp.
- The other two cases demonstrate a weakness in our approach, exemplified by the sentence given in example (4): here the algorithm incorrectly uses the verb group *will meet* when interpreting *Tuesday*.
- The remaining two cases were cases where the verb groups *were scheduled to end* and *scheduled to begin* were used to talk about future events.

In these last cases, the controlling verb is an infinitive, and there is no way, in the absence of either world knowledge or a much more sophisticated analysis of the text, of determining whether the scheduled event is in the past or the future. Sentences like these are a particular problem for Mani and Wilson's algorithm, where a significant number of misinterpretations involve sentences in which the past tense is used to talk about subsequently-changed plans for future, as in the following:

(14) A summit between Sharon and his Palestinian counterpart, Mahmoud Abbas, had been planned for *Wednesday* but was postponed ...

Here, this utterance could be legitimately produced both before and after the Wednesday in question, so no simple algorithm will be able to determine the direction of offset.

8 Conclusions and Future Work

We have investigated the problem of the interpretation of bare weekday names in texts, and presented a new heuristic which extends Baldwin's (2002) approach. Our evaluations on a widely-available data set show that our Hybrid Algorithm was the best performing algorithm, achieving an accuracy of 95.91% with 15 errors out of 367 instances. The algorithm is implemented within our DANTE system for temporal expression interpretation (Dale and Mazur, 2006; Mazur and Dale, 2007).

It seems quite possible that our heuristics take advantage of phenomena that are specific to newswire texts and other similar types of reportage. Although these are precisely the kinds of texts where, in our own work, we need to provide fast processing of large volumes of text, it remains to be seen how these heuristics fare when faced with a broader range of text types. In particular, other text types are likely to require more sophisticated approaches to temporal focus tracking than we have used here.

Also, we have not attempted to replicate here the machine learning approaches described in (Ahn et al., 2005) and (Ahn et al., 2007), nor Han's use of constraint satisfaction problem methods (see (Han et al., 2006a)). The comparative evaluation of these is left for future work.

References

Ahn, D., S. F. Adafre, and M. de Rijke. 2005. Recognizing and interpreting temporal expressions in open domain texts. In *We Will Show Them: Essays in Honour of Dov Gabbay, Vol 1*, pages 31–50.

Ahn, D., Joris van Rantwijk, and Maarten de Rijke. 2007. A Cascaded Machine Learning Approach to Interpreting Temporal Expressions. In *Proc. of HLT: The Annual Conference of the North American Chapter of the ACL (NAACL-HLT 2007)*.

Baldwin, J. 2002. Learning Temporal Annotation of French News. Master's thesis, Dept. of Linguistics, Georgetown University, April.

Dale, R. and P. Mazur. 2006. Local Semantics in the Interpretation of Temporal Expressions. In *Proceedings of the Workshop on Annotating and Reasoning about Time and Events*, pages 9–16, Sydney, Australia, July.

de Marneffe, M.-C., B. MacCartney, and Ch. D. Manning. 2006. Generating Typed Dependency Parses from Phrase Structure Parses. In *Proceedings of the IEEE / ACL 2006 Workshop on Spoken Language Technology*.

Filatova, E. and E. Hovy. 2001. Assigning Time-Stamps to Event-Clauses. In Harper, L., I. Mani, and B. Sundheim, editors, *Proceedings of the Workshop on Temporal and Spatial Information Processing*, pages 1–8, Morristown, NJ, USA.

Han, B. and A. Lavie. 2004. A Framework for Resolution of Time in Natural Language. *ACM Transactions on Asian Language Information Processing (TALIP)*, 3(1):11–32.

Han, B., D. Gates, and L. Levin. 2005. Anchoring Temporal Expressions in Scheduling-related Emails. In Katz, Graham, James Pustejovsky, and Frank Schilder, editors, *Annotating, Extracting and Reasoning about Time and Events*, Dagstuhl Seminar Proceedings.

Han, B., D. Gates, and L. Levin. 2006a. From Language to Time: A Temporal Expression Anchorer. In *Proceedings of the Thirteenth International Symposium on Temporal Representation and Reasoning*, pages 196–203.

Han, B., D. Gates, and L. Levin. 2006b. Understanding Temporal Expressions in Emails. In *Proceedings of the Human Language Technology Conference of the North American Chapter of the Association of Computational Linguistics*, pages 136–143, Morristown, NJ, USA.

Jang, S. B., J. Baldwin, and I. Mani. 2004. Automatic TIMEX2 Tagging of Korean News. *ACM Transactions on Asian Language Information Processing (TALIP)*, 3(1):51–65.

Mani, I. and G. Wilson. 2000. Robust Temporal Processing of News. In *Proceedings of the 38th Annual Meeting of the Association for Computational Linguistics*, pages 69–76, Morristown, NJ, USA.

Mazur, P. and R. Dale. 2007. The DANTE Temporal Expression Tagger. In Vetulani, Zygmunt, editor, *Proceedings of the 3rd Language & Technology Conference (LTC)*.

Negri, M. and L. Marseglia. 2005. Recognition and Normalization of Time Expressions: ITC-IRST at TERN 2004. Technical Report WP3.7, Information Society Technologies, February.

Schilder, F. and Ch. Habel. 2001. From Temporal Expressions to Temporal Information: Semantic Tagging of News Messages. In Harper, L., I. Mani, and B. Sundheim, editors, *Proc. of the Workshop on Temporal and Spatial Information Processing*, pages 1–8, Morristown, NJ, USA.

When is Self-Training Effective for Parsing?

David McClosky, Eugene Charniak, and Mark Johnson
Brown Laboratory for Linguistic Information Processing (BLLIP)
Brown University
Providence, RI 02912
{dmcc|ec|mj}@cs.brown.edu

Abstract

Self-training has been shown capable of improving on state-of-the-art parser performance (McClosky et al., 2006) despite the conventional wisdom on the matter and several studies to the contrary (Charniak, 1997; Steedman et al., 2003). However, it has remained unclear when and why self-training is helpful. In this paper, we test four hypotheses (namely, presence of a phase transition, impact of search errors, value of non-generative reranker features, and effects of unknown words). From these experiments, we gain a better understanding of why self-training works for parsing. Since improvements from self-training are correlated with unknown bigrams and biheads but not unknown words, the benefit of self-training appears most influenced by seeing known words in new combinations.

1 Introduction

Supervised statistical parsers attempt to capture patterns of syntactic structure from a labeled set of examples for the purpose of annotating new sentences with their structure (Bod, 2003; Charniak and Johnson, 2005; Collins and Koo, 2005; Petrov et al., 2006; Titov and Henderson, 2007). These annotations can be used by various higher-level applications such as semantic role labeling (Pradhan et al., 2007) and machine translation (Yamada and Knight, 2001).

©2008. Licensed under the *Creative Commons Attribution-Noncommercial-Share Alike 3.0 Unported* license (http://creativecommons.org/licenses/by-nc-sa/3.0/). Some rights reserved.

However, labeled training data is expensive to annotate. Given the large amount of unlabeled text available for many domains and languages, techniques which allow us to use both labeled and unlabeled text to train our models are desirable. These methods are called semi-supervised. Self-training is a specific type of semi-supervised learning. In self-training, first we train a model on the labeled data and use that model to label the unlabeled data. From the combination of our original labeled data and the newly labeled data, we train a second model – our self-trained model. The process can be iterated, where the self-trained model is used to label new data in the next iteration. One can think of self-training as a simple case of co-training (Blum and Mitchell, 1998) using a single learner instead of several. Alternatively, one can think of it as one step of the Viterbi EM algorithm.

Studies prior to McClosky et al. (2006) failed to show a benefit to parsing from self-training (Charniak, 1997; Steedman et al., 2003). While the recent success of self-training has demonstrated its merit, it remains unclear why self-training helps in some cases but not others. Our goal is to better understand when and why self-training is beneficial.

In Section 2, we discuss the previous applications of self-training to parsing. Section 3 describes our experimental setup. We present and test four hypotheses of why self-training helps in Section 4 and conclude with discussion and future work in Section 5.

2 Previous Work

To our knowledge, the first reported uses of self-training for parsing are by Charniak (1997). He used his parser trained on the Wall Street Journal (WSJ, Mitch Marcus et al. (1993)) to parse 30 million words of unparsed WSJ text. He then trained a self-trained model from the combination of the newly parsed text with WSJ training data. However, the self-trained model did not improve on the original model.

Self-training and co-training were subsequently investigated in the 2002 CLSP Summer Workshop at Johns Hopkins University (Steedman et al., 2003). They considered several different parameter settings, but in all cases, the number of sentences parsed per iteration of self-training was relatively small (30 sentences). They performed many iterations of self-training. The largest seed size (amount of labeled training data) they used was 10,000 sentences from WSJ, though many experiments used only 500 or 1,000 sentences. They found that under these parameters, self-training did not yield a significant gain.

Reichart and Rappoport (2007) showed that one can self-train with only a generative parser if the seed size is small. The conditions are similar to Steedman et al. (2003), but only one iteration of self-training is performed (i.e. all unlabeled data is labeled at once).[1] In this scenario, unknown words (words seen in the unlabeled data but not in training) were a useful predictor of when self-training improves performance.

McClosky et al. (2006) showed that self-training improves parsing accuracy when the two-stage Charniak and Johnson (2005) reranking parser is used. Using both stages (a generative parser and discriminative reranker) to label the unlabeled data set is necessary to improve performance. Only retraining the first stage had a positive effect. However, after retraining the first stage, both stages produced better parses. Unlike Steedman et al. (2003), the training seed size is large and only one iteration of self-training is performed. Error analysis revealed that most improvement comes from sentences with lengths between 20 and 40 words. Surprisingly, improvements were also correlated with the number of conjunctions but not with the number of unknown words in the sentence.

To summarize, several factors have been identified as good predictors of when self-training improves performance, but a full explanation of why self-training works is lacking. Previous work establishes that parsing all unlabeled sentences at once (rather than over many iterations) is important for successful self-training. The full effect of seed size and the reranker on self-training is not well understood.

[1]Performing multiple iterations presumably fails because the parsing models become increasingly biased. However, this remains untested in the large seed case.

3 Experimental Setup

We use the Charniak and Johnson reranking parser (outlined below), though we expect many of these results to generalize to other generative parsers and discriminative rerankers. Our corpora consist of WSJ for labeled data and NANC (North American News Text Corpus, Graff (1995)) for unlabeled data. We use the standard WSJ division for parsing: sections 2-21 for training (39,382 sentences) and section 24 for development (1,346 sentences). Given self-training's varied performance in the past, many of our experiments use the concatenation of sections 1, 22, and 24 (5,039 sentences) rather than the standard development set for more robust testing.

A full description of the reranking parser can be found in Charniak and Johnson (2005). Briefly put, the reranking parser consists of two stages: A generative lexicalized PCFG parser which proposes a list of the n most probable parses (n-best list) followed by a discriminative reranker which reorders the n-best list. The reranker uses about 1.3 million features to help score the trees, the most important of which is the first stage parser's probability. In Section 4.3, we mention two classes of reranker features in more depth. Since some of experiments rely on details of the first stage parser, we present a summary of the parsing model.

3.1 The Parsing Model

The parsing model assigns a probability to a parse π by a top-down process of considering each constituent c in π and, for each c, first guessing the preterminal of c, $t(c)$ then the lexical head of c, $h(c)$, and then the expansion of c into further constituents $e(c)$. Thus the probability of a parse is given by the equation

$$\begin{aligned} p(\pi) &= \prod_{c \in \pi} p(t(c) \mid l(c), \mathcal{R}(c)) \\ &\quad \cdot p(h(c) \mid t(c), l(c), \mathcal{R}(c)) \\ &\quad \cdot p(e(c) \mid l(c), t(c), h(c), \mathcal{R}(c)) \end{aligned}$$

where $l(c)$ is the label of c (e.g., whether it is a noun phrase (np), verb phrase, etc.) and $\mathcal{R}(c)$ is the relevant history of c — information outside c that the probability model deems important in determining the probability in question.

For each expansion $e(c)$ we distinguish one of the children as the "middle" child $M(c)$. $M(c)$ is the constituent from which the head lexical item h is obtained according to deterministic rules that pick the head of a constituent from among the heads of its children. To the left of M is a sequence of one or more left labels $L_i(c)$ including the special termination symbol $\triangle$ and similarly for the labels to the right, $R_i(c)$. Thus an expansion $e(c)$ looks like:

$$l \rightarrow \triangle L_m...L_1 M R_1...R_n \triangle. \quad (1)$$

The expansion is generated by guessing first M, then in order L_1 through L_{m+1} (= $\triangle$), and similarly for R_1 through R_{n+1}.

So the parser assigns a probability to the parse based upon five probability distributions, T (the part of speech of the head), H (the head), M (the child constituent which includes the head), L (children to the left of M), and R (children to the right of M).

4 Testing the Four Hypotheses

The question of why self-training helps in some cases (McClosky et al., 2006; Reichart and Rappoport, 2007) but not others (Charniak, 1997; Steedman et al., 2003) has inspired various theories. We investigate four of these to better understand when and why self-training helps. At a high level, the hypotheses are (1) self-training helps after a phase transition, (2) self-training reduces search errors, (3) specific classes of reranker features are needed for self-training, and (4) self-training improves because we see new combinations of words.

4.1 Phase Transition

The phase transition hypothesis is that once a parser has achieved a certain threshold of performance, it can label data sufficiently accurately. Once this happens, the labels will be "good enough" for self-training.

To test the phase transition hypothesis, we use the same parser as McClosky et al. (2006) but train on only a fraction of WSJ to see if self-training is still helpful. This is similar to some of the experiments by Reichart and Rappoport (2007) but with the use of a reranker and slightly larger seed sizes. The self-training protocol is the same as in (Charniak, 1997; McClosky et al., 2006; Reichart and Rappoport, 2007): we parse the entire unlabeled corpus in one iteration. We start by taking a random subset of the WSJ training sections (2-21), accepting each sentence with 10% probability. With the sampled training section and the standard development data, we train a parser and a reranker. In Table 1, we show the performance of the parser with and without the reranker. For reference, we show the performance when using the complete training division as well. Unsurprisingly, both metrics drop as we decrease the amount of training data. These scores represent our baselines for this experiment.

Using this parser model, we parse one million sentences from NANC, both with and without the reranker. We combine these one million sentences with the sampled subsets of WSJ training and train new parser models from them.[2]

Finally, we evaluate these self-trained models (Table 2). The numbers in parentheses indicate the change from the corresponding non-self-trained model. As in Reichart and Rappoport (2007), we see large improvements when self-training on a small seed size (10%) without using the reranker. However, using the reranker to parse the self-training and/or evaluation sentences further improves results. From McClosky et al. (2006), we know that when 100% of the training data is used, self-training does not improve performance without a reranker.

From this we conclude that there is no such threshold phase transition in this case. High performance is not a requirement to successfully use self-training for parsing, since there are lower performing parsers which can self-train and higher performing parsers which cannot. The higher performing Charniak and Johnson (2005) parser without reranker achieves an f-score of 89.0 on section 24 when trained on all of WSJ. This parser does not benefit from self-training unless paired with a reranker. Contrast this with the same parser trained on only 10% of WSJ, where it gets an f-score of 85.8 (Table 2) or the small seed models of Reichart and Rappoport (2007). Both of these lower performing parsers can successfully self-train. Additionally, we now know that while a reranker is not required for self-training when the seed size is small, it still helps performance considerably (f-score improves from 87.7 to 89.0 in the 10% case).

[2] We do not weight the original WSJ data, though our expectation is that performance would improve if WSJ were given a higher relative weight. This is left as future work.

% WSJ	# sentences	Parser f-score	Reranking parser f-score
10	3,995	85.8	87.0
100	39,832	89.9	91.5

Table 1: Parser and reranking parser performance on sentences $\leq$ 100 words in sections 1, 22, and 24 when trained on different amounts of training data. % WSJ is the percentage of WSJ training data trained on (sampled randomly). Note that the full amount of development data is still used as held out data.

Parsed NANC with reranker?	Parser f-score	Reranking parser f-score
No	87.7 (+1.9)	88.7 (+1.7)
Yes	88.4 (+2.6)	89.0 (+2.0)

Table 2: Effect of self-training using only 10% of WSJ as labeled data. The parser model is trained from one million parsed sentences from NANC + WSJ training. The first column indicates whether the million NANC sentences were parsed by the parser or reranking parser. The second and third columns differ in whether the reranker is used to parse the *test* sentences (WSJ sections 1, 22, and 24, sentences 100 words and shorter). Numbers in parentheses are the improvements over the corresponding non-self-trained parser.

4.2 Search Errors

Another possible explanation of self-training's improvements is that seeing newly labeled data results in fewer search errors (Daniel Marcu, personal communication). A search error would indicate that the parsing model could have produced better (more probable) parses if not for heuristics in the search procedure. The additional parse trees may help produce sharper distributions and reduce data sparsity, making the search process easier. To test this, first we present some statistics on the n-best lists ($n = 50$) from the baseline WSJ trained parser and self-trained model[3] from McClosky et al. (2006). We use each model to parse sentences from held-out data (sections 1, 22, and 24) and examine the n-best lists.

We compute statistics of the WSJ and self-trained n-best lists with the goal of understanding how much they intersect and whether there are search errors. On average, the n-best lists overlap by 66.0%. Put another way, this means that about a third of the parses from each model are unique, so the parsers do find a fair number of different parses in their search. The next question is where the differences in the n-best lists lie — if all the differences were near the bottom, this would be less meaningful. Let W and S represent the n-best lists from the baseline WSJ and self-trained parsers, respectively. The $top_m(\ell)$ function returns the highest scoring parse in the n-best list ℓ according to the reranker and parser model m.[4] Almost 40% of the time, the top parse in the self-trained model is not in the WSJ model's n-best list, ($top_s(S) \notin W$) though the two models agree on the top parse roughly 42.4% of the time ($top_s(S) = top_w(W)$). Search errors can be formulated as $top_s(S) \notin W \wedge top_s(S) = top_w(W \cup S)$. This captures sentences where the parse that the reranker chose in the self-trained model is not present in the WSJ model's n-best list, but if the parse were added to the WSJ model's list, the parse's probability in the WSJ model and other reranker features would have caused it to be chosen. These search errors occur in only 2.5% of the n-best lists. At first glance, one might think that this could be enough to account for the differences, since the self-trained model is only several tenths better in f-score. However, we know from McClosky et al. (2006) that on average, parses do not change between the WSJ and self-trained models and when they do, they only improve slightly more than half the time. For this reason, we run a second test more focused on performance.

For our second test we help the WSJ trained model find the parses that the self-trained model found. For each sentence, we start with the n-best list ($n = 500$ here) from the WSJ trained parser, W. We then consider parses in the self-trained parser's n-best list, S, that are not present in W ($S - W$). For each of these parses, we determine its probability under the WSJ trained parsing

[3] `http://bllip.cs.brown.edu/selftraining/`

[4] Recall that the parser's probability is a reranker feature so the parsing model influences the ranking.

Model	f-score
WSJ	91.5
WSJ & search help	91.7
Self-trained	92.0

Table 3: Test of whether "search help" from the self-trained model impacts the WSJ trained model. WSJ + search help is made by adding self-trained parses not proposed by the WSJ trained parser but to which the parser assigns a positive probability. The WSJ reranker is used in all cases to select the best parse for sections 1, 22, and 24.

model. If the probability is non-zero, we add the parse to the n-best list W, otherwise we ignore the parse. In other words, we find parses that the WSJ trained model could have produced but didn't due to search heuristics. In Table 3, we show the performance of the WSJ trained model, the model with "search help" as described above, and the self-trained model on WSJ sections 1, 22, and 24. The WSJ reranker is used to pick the best parse from each n-best list. WSJ with search help performs slightly better than WSJ alone but does not reach the level of the self-trained model. From these experiments, we conclude that reduced search errors can only explain a small amount of self-training's improvements.

4.3 Non-generative reranker features

We examine the role of specific reranker features by training rerankers using only subsets of the features. Our goal is to determine whether some classes of reranker features benefit self-training more than others. We hypothesize that features which are not easily captured by the generative first-stage parser are the most beneficial for self-training. If we treat the parser and reranking parser as different (but clearly dependent) views, this is a bit like co-training. If the reranker uses features which are captured by the first-stage, the views may be too similar for there to be an improvement.

We consider two classes of features (GEN and EDGE) and their complements (NON-GEN and NON-EDGE).[5] GEN consists of features that are roughly captured by the first-stage generative parser: rule rewrites, head-child dependencies, etc. EDGE features describe items across constituent boundaries. This includes the words and parts of speech of the tokens on the edges between constituents and the labels of these constituents. This represents a specific class of features not captured by the first-stage. These subsets and their sizes are shown in Table 4. For comparison, we also include the results of experiments using the full feature set, as in McClosky et al. (2006), labeled ALL. The GEN features are roughly one third the size of the full feature set.

[5]A small number of features overlap hence these sizes do not add up.

Feature set	# features	f-score
GEN	448,349	90.4
NON-GEN	885,492	91.1
EDGE	601,578	91.0
NON-EDGE	732,263	91.1
ALL	1,333,519	91.3

Table 4: Sizes and performance of reranker feature subsets. Reranking parser f-scores are on all sentences in section 24.

We evaluate the effect of these new reranker models on self-training (Table 4). For each feature set, we do the following: We parse one million NANC sentences with the reranking parser. Combining the parses with WSJ training data, we train a new first-stage model. Using this new first-stage model and the reranker subset, we evaluate on section 24 of WSJ. GEN's performance is weaker while the other three subsets achieve almost the same score as the full feature set. This confirms our hypothesis that when the reranker helps in self-training it is due to features which are not captured by the generative first-stage model.

4.4 Unknown Words

Given the large size of the parsed self-training corpus, it contains an immense number of parsing events which never occur in the training corpus. The most obvious of these events is words — the vocabulary grows from 39,548 to 265,926 words as we transition from the WSJ trained model to the self-trained model. Slightly less obvious is bigrams. There are roughly 330,000 bigrams in WSJ training data and approximately 4.8 million new bigrams in the self-training corpus.

One hypothesis (Mitch Marcus, personal communication) is that the parser is able to learn a lot of new bilexical head-to-head dependencies (biheads) from self-training. The reasoning is as follows: Assume the self-training corpus is parsed in a mostly correct manner. If there are not too many new pairs of words in a sentence, there is a decent chance that we can tag these words correctly and bracket them in a reasonable fashion from context. Thus, using these parses as part of the training data improves parsing because should we see these pairs of words together in the future, we will be more likely to connect them together properly.

We test this hypothesis in two ways. First, we perform an extension of the factor analysis similar to that in McClosky et al. (2006). This is done via a generalized linear regression model intended to determine which features of parse trees can predict when the self-training model will perform better. We consider many of the same features (e.g. bucketed sentence length, number of conjunctions, and number of unknown words) but also consider two new features: unknown bigrams and unknown biheads. Unknown items (words, bigrams, biheads) are calculated by counting the number of items which have never been seen in WSJ training but have been seen in the parsed NANC data. Given these features, we take the f-scores for each sentence when parsed by the WSJ and self-trained models and look at the differences. Our goal is to find out which features, if any, can predict these f-score differences. Specifically, we ask the question of whether seeing more unknown items indicates whether we are more likely to see improvements when self-training.

The effect of unknown items on self-training's relative performance is summarized in Figure 1. For each item, we show the total number of incorrect parse nodes in sentences that contain the item. We also show the change in the number of correct parse nodes in these sentences between the WSJ and self-trained models. A positive change means that performance improved under self-training. In other words, looking at Figure 1a, the greatest performance improvement occurs, perhaps surprisingly, when we have seen no unknown words. As we see more unknown words, the improvement from self-training decreases. This is a pretty clear indication that unknown words are not a good predictor of when self-training improves performance.

A possible objection that one might raise is that using unknown biheads as a regression feature will bias our results if they are counted from gold trees instead of parsed trees. Seeing a bihead in training will cause the otherwise sparse biheads distribution to be extremely peaked around that bihead. If we see the same pair of words in testing, we are likely to connect them in the same fashion. Thus, if we count unknown biheads from gold trees, this feature may explain away other improvements: When gold trees contain a bihead found in our self-training data, we will almost always see an improvement. However, given the similar trends in Figures 1b and 1c, we propose that unknown bigrams can be thought of as a rough approximation of unknown biheads.

f-score		Model
89.8	$*$	WSJ (baseline)
89.8	$*$	WSJ+NANC M
89.9	$*$	WSJ+NANC T
89.9	$*$	WSJ+NANC L
90.0	$*$	WSJ+NANC R
90.0		WSJ+NANC MT
90.1		WSJ+NANC H
90.2		WSJ+NANC LR
90.3		WSJ+NANC LRT
90.4		WSJ+NANC LMRT
90.4		WSJ+NANC LMR
90.5		WSJ+NANC LRH
90.7	$\circledast$	WSJ+NANC LMRH
90.8	$\circledast$	WSJ+NANC (fully self-trained)

Table 5: Performance of the first-stage parser on various combinations of distributions WSJ and WSJ+NANC (self-trained) models on sections 1, 22, and 24. Distributions are L (left expansion), R (right expansion), H (head word), M (head phrasal category), and T (head POS tag). $*$ and $\circledast$ indicate the model is not significantly different from baseline and self-trained model, respectively.

The regression analysis reveals that unknown bigrams and unknown biheads are good predictors of f-score improvements. The significant predictors from McClosky et al. (2006) such as the number of conjunctions or sentence length continue to be helpful whereas unknown words are a weak predictor at best. These results are apparent in Figure 1: as stated before, seeing more unknown words does not correlate with improvements. However, seeing more unknown bigrams and biheads does predict these changes fairly well. When we have seen zero or one new bigrams or biheads, self-training negatively impacts performance. After seeing two or more, we see positive effects until about six to ten after which improvements taper off.

To see the effect of biheads on performance more directly, we also experiment by interpolating between the WSJ and self-trained models on a distribution level. To do this, we take specific distributions (see Section 3.1) from the self-trained model and have them override the corresponding distributions in a compatible WSJ trained model. From this we hope to show which distributions self-training boosts. According to the biheads hypothesis, the H distribution (which captures information about head-to-head dependencies) should account for most of the improvement.

The results of moving these distributions is shown in Table 5. For each new model, we show whether the model's performance is not significantly different than the baseline model (indicated by $*$) or not significantly different than the self-trained model ($\circledast$). H (biheads) is the strongest single feature and the only one to be significantly better than the baseline. Nevertheless, it is only 0.3% higher, accounting for 30% of the full self-training improvement. In general, the performance improvements from distributions are additive ($+/-$ 0.1%). Self-training improves all distributions, so biheads are not the full picture. Nevertheless, they remain the strongest single feature.

5 Discussion

The experiments in this paper have clarified many details about the nature of self-training for parsing. We have ruled out the phase transition hypothesis entirely. Reduced search errors are responsible for some, but not all, of the improvements in self-training. We have confirmed that non-generative reranker features are more beneficial than generative reranker features since they make the reranking parser more different from the base parser. Finally, we have found that while unknown bigrams and biheads are a significant source of improvement, they are not the sole source of it. Since unknown words do not correlate well with self-training improvements, there must be something about the unknown bigrams and biheads which are aid the parser. Our belief is that new combinations of words we have already seen guides the parser in the right direction. Additionally, these new combinations result in more peaked distributions which decreases the number of search errors.

However, while these experiments and others get us closer to understanding self-training, we still lack a complete explanation. Naturally, the hy-

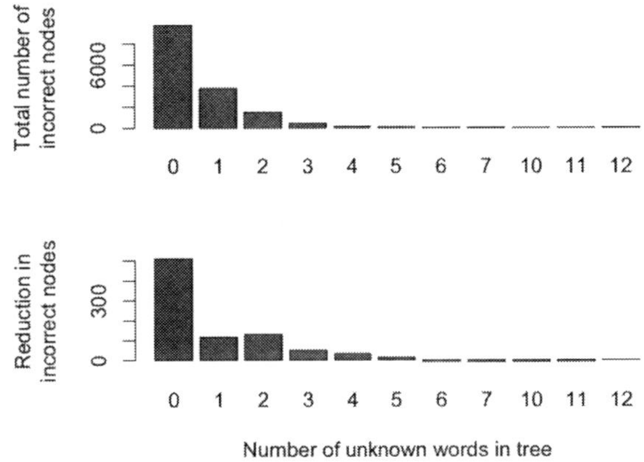

(a) Effect of unknown words on performance

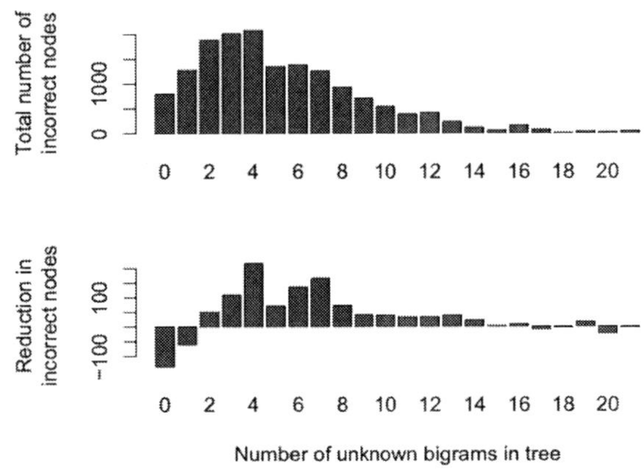

(b) Effect of unknown bigrams on performance

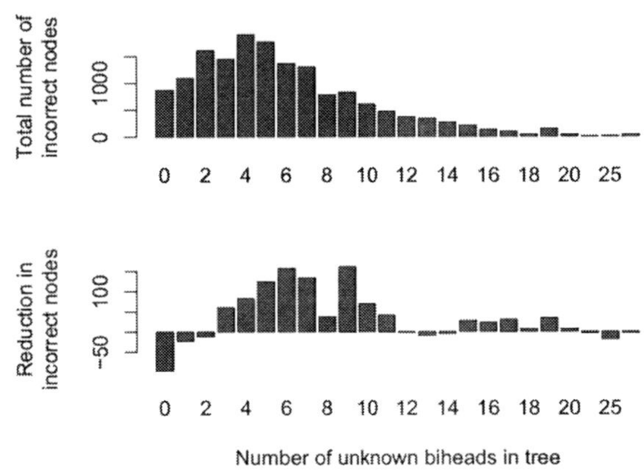

(c) Effect of unknown biheads on performance

Figure 1: Change in the number of incorrect parse tree nodes between WSJ and self-trained models as a function of number of unknown items. Seeing any number of unknown words results in fewer errors on average whereas seeing zero or one unknown bigrams or biheads is likely to hurt performance.

potheses tested are by no means exhaustive. Additionally, we have only considered generative constituency parsers here and a good direction for future research would be to see if self-training generalizes to a broader class of parsers. We suspect that using a generative parser/discriminative reranker paradigm should allow self-training to extend to other parsing formalisms.

Recall that in Reichart and Rappoport (2007) where only a small amount of labeled data was used, the number of unknown words in a sentence was a strong predictor of self-training benefits. When a large amount of labeled data is available, unknown words are no longer correlated with these gains, but unknown bigrams and biheads are. When using a small amount of training data, unknown words are useful since we have not seen very many words yet. As the amount of training data increases, we see fewer new words but the number of new bigrams and biheads remains high. We postulate that this difference may help explain the shift from unknown words to unknown bigrams and biheads. We hope to further investigate the role of these unknown items by seeing how our analyses change under different amounts of labeled data relative to unknown item rates.

Acknowledgments

This work was supported by DARPA GALE contract HR0011-06-2-0001. We would like to thank Matt Lease, the rest of the BLLIP team, and our anonymous reviewers for their comments. Any opinions, findings, and conclusions or recommendations expressed in this paper are those of the authors and do not necessarily reflect the views of DARPA.

References

Blum, Avrim and Tom Mitchell. 1998. Combining labeled and unlabeled data with co-training. In *Proceedings of the 11th Annual Conference on Computational Learning Theory (COLT-98)*.

Bod, Rens. 2003. An efficient implementation of a new DOP model. In *10th Conference of the European Chapter of the Association for Computational Linguistics*, Budapest, Hungary.

Charniak, Eugene and Mark Johnson. 2005. Coarse-to-fine *n*-best parsing and MaxEnt discriminative reranking. In *Proc. of the 2005 Meeting of the Assoc. for Computational Linguistics (ACL)*, pages 173–180.

Charniak, Eugene. 1997. Statistical parsing with a context-free grammar and word statistics. In *Proc. AAAI*, pages 598–603.

Collins, Michael and Terry Koo. 2005. Discriminative Reranking for Natural Language Parsing. *Computational Linguistics*, 31(1):25–69.

Graff, David. 1995. *North American News Text Corpus*. Linguistic Data Consortium. LDC95T21.

McClosky, David, Eugene Charniak, and Mark Johnson. 2006. Effective self-training for parsing. In *Proceedings of the Human Language Technology Conference of the NAACL, Main Conference*, pages 152–159.

Mitch Marcus et al. 1993. Building a large annotated corpus of English: The Penn Treebank. *Comp. Linguistics*, 19(2):313–330.

Petrov, Slav, Leon Barrett, Romain Thibaux, and Dan Klein. 2006. Learning accurate, compact, and interpretable tree annotation. In *Proceedings of the 21st International Conference on Computational Linguistics and 44th Annual Meeting of the Association for Computational Linguistics*, pages 433–440, Sydney, Australia, July. Association for Computational Linguistics.

Pradhan, Sameer, Wayne Ward, and James Martin. 2007. Towards robust semantic role labeling. In *Human Language Technologies 2007: The Conference of the North American Chapter of the Association for Computational Linguistics; Proceedings of the Main Conference*, pages 556–563, Rochester, New York, April. Association for Computational Linguistics.

Reichart, Roi and Ari Rappoport. 2007. Self-training for enhancement and domain adaptation of statistical parsers trained on small datasets. *Proceedings of the 45th Annual Meeting of the Association of Computational Linguistics*, pages 616–623.

Steedman, Mark, Steven Baker, Jeremiah Crim, Stephen Clark, Julia Hockenmaier, Rebecca Hwa, Miles Osborne, Paul Ruhlen, and Anoop Sarkar. 2003. CLSP WS-02 Final Report: Semi-Supervised Training for Statistical Parsing. Technical report, Johns Hopkins University.

Titov, Ivan and James Henderson. 2007. Constituent parsing with incremental sigmoid belief networks. In *Proceedings of the 45th Annual Meeting of the Association of Computational Linguistics*, pages 632–639, Prague, Czech Republic, June. Association for Computational Linguistics.

Yamada, Kenji and Kevin Knight. 2001. A syntax-based statistical translation model. In *Proceedings of the 39th Annual Meeting of the Association for Computational Linguistics*, pages 523–529.

A Syntactic Time-Series Model for Parsing Fluent and Disfluent Speech *

Tim Miller
Department of Computer Science
and Engineering
University of Minnesota
tmill@cs.umn.edu

William Schuler
Department of Computer Science
and Engineering
University of Minnesota
schuler@cs.umn.edu

Abstract

This paper describes an incremental approach to parsing transcribed spontaneous speech containing disfluencies with a Hierarchical Hidden Markov Model (HHMM). This model makes use of the right-corner transform, which has been shown to increase non-incremental parsing accuracy on transcribed spontaneous speech (Miller and Schuler, 2008), using trees transformed in this manner to train the HHMM parser. Not only do the representations used in this model align with structure in speech repairs, but as an HMM-like time-series model, it can be directly integrated into conventional speech recognition systems run on continuous streams of audio. A system implementing this model is evaluated on the standard task of parsing the Switchboard corpus, and achieves an improvement over the standard baseline probabilistic CYK parser.

1 Introduction

Disfluency is one obstacle preventing speech recognition systems from being able to recognize spontaneous speech. Perhaps the most challenging aspect of disfluency recognition is the phenomenon of speech repair, which involves a speaker realizing a mistake, cutting off the flow of speech, and then continuing on, possibly retracing and replacing part of the utterance to that point. This paper will describe a system which applies a syntactic model of speech repair to a time-series parsing model, and evaluate that system on the standard Switchboard corpus parsing task.

The speech repair terminology used here follows that of Shriberg (1994). A speech repair consists of a *reparandum*, an *interruption point*, and the *alteration*. The reparandum contains the words that the speaker means to replace, including both words that are in error and words that will be retraced. The interruption point is the point in time where the stream of speech is actually stopped, and the repairing of the mistake can begin. The alteration contains the words that are meant to replace the words in the reparandum.

2 Background

Historically, research in speech repair has focused on acoustic cues such as pauses and prosodic contours for detecting repairs, which could then be excised from the text for improved transcription. Recent work has also looked at the possible contribution of higher-level cues, including syntactic structure, in the detection of speech repair. Some of this work is inspired by Levelt's (1983) investigation of the syntactic and semantic variables in speech repairs, particularly his well-formedness rule, which states that the reparandum and alteration of a repair typically have the same consitituent label, similar to coordination.

Hale et al. (2006) use Levelt's well-formedness rule to justify an annotation scheme where unfinished categories (marked X-UNF) have the UNF label appended to all ancestral category labels all the way up to the top-most constituent beneath an EDITED label (EDITED labels denoting a reparandum). They reason that this should prevent grammar rules of finished constituents in the corpus from corrupting the grammar of unfinished constituents. While this annotation proves helpful, it also leads to the unfortunate result that a large reparandum requires several special repair rules to be applied, even though the actual error is only

* The authors would like to thank the anonymous reviewers for their input. This research was supported by National Science Foundation CAREER/PECASE award 0447685. The views expressed are not necessarily endorsed by the sponsors.
© 2008. Licensed under the *Creative Commons Attribution-Noncommercial-Share Alike 3.0 Unported* license (http://creativecommons.org/licenses/by-nc-sa/3.0/). Some rights reserved.

happening at one point.

Intuitively, though, it seems that an error is only occurring at the end of the reparandum, and that until that point only fluent grammar rules are being applied by the speaker. This intuition has also been confirmed by empirical studies (Nakatani and Hirschberg, 1994), which show that there is no obvious error signal in speech up until the moment of interruption. Although speakers may retrace much of the reparandum for clarity or other reasons, ideally the reparandum contains nothing but standard grammatical rules until the speech is interrupted.[1]

Another recent approach to this problem (Johnson and Charniak, 2004) uses a tree-adjoining grammar (TAG) approach to define a mapping between a source sentence possibly containing a repair, and a target, fluent sentence. The use of the TAG channel model is justified by the putative crossing dependencies seen in repairs like *... a flight to Boston, uh, I mean, to Denver...* where there is repetition from the reparandum to the repair. Essentially, this model is building up the reparandum and alteration in tandem, based on these crossing dependencies. While this is an interesting model, it focuses on detection and removal of EDITED sections, and subsequent parsing of cleaned up speech. As such, it introduces challenges for integrating the system into a real-time speech recognizer.

Recent work by Miller and Schuler (2008) showed how a probabilistic grammar trained on trees modified by use of the *right-corner transform* can improve parsing accuracy over an unmodified grammar when tested on the Switchboard corpus. The approach described here builds on that work in using right-corner transformed trees, and extends it by mapping them to a time-series model to do parsing directly in a model of the sort used in speech recognition. This system is shown to be more accurate than a baseline CYK parser when used to parse the Switchboard corpus. The remainder of this section will review the right-corner transform, followed by Section 3, which will step through an extended example giving details about the transform process and its applicability to the problem of processing speech repairs.

[1]One objection to this claim is the case of multiple nested repairs. In this case, though, we presume that all reparanda were originally intended by the speaker to be fluent at the time of generation.

2.1 Right-corner transform

The right-corner transform rewrites syntax trees, turning all right branching structure into left branching structure, and leaving left branching structure as is. As a result, constituent structure can be explicitly built from the bottom up during incremental recognition. This arrangement is well-suited to recognition of speech with errors, because it allows constituent structure to be built up using fluent speech rules until the moment of interruption, at which point a special repair rule may be applied.

Before transforming the trees in the grammar into right-corner trees, trees are binarized in the same manner as Johnson (1998b) and Klein and Manning (2003).[2] Binarized trees are then transformed into right-corner trees using transform rules similar to those described by Johnson (1998a). In this transform, all right branching sequences in each tree are transformed into left branching sequences of symbols of the form A_1/A_2, denoting an incomplete instance of category A_1 lacking an instance of category A_2 to the right.[3]

Rewrite rules for the right-corner transform are shown below, first flattening right-branching structure:

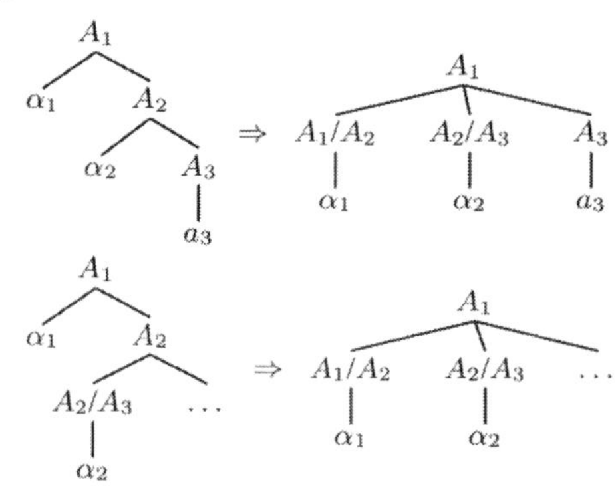

then replacing it with left-branching structure:

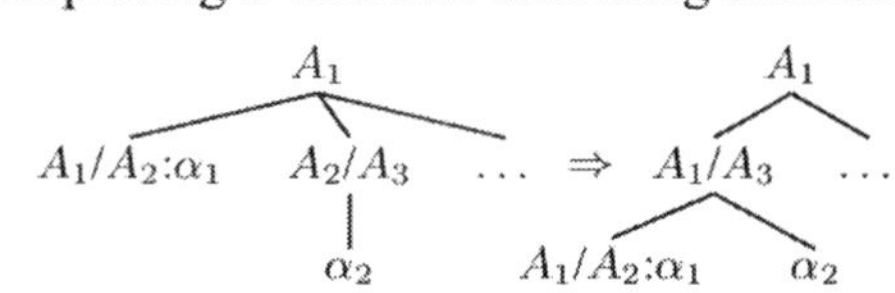

Here, the first two rewrite rules are applied iteratively (bottom-up on the tree) to flatten all right branching structure, using incomplete constituents

[2]For the details of the particular binarization process used here, see Miller and Schuler (2008).

[3]Here, all A_i denote nonterminal symbols, and all α_i denote subtrees; the notation $A_1{:}\alpha_1$ indicates a subtree α_1 with label A_1; and all rewrites are applied recursively, from leaves to root.

to record the original nonterminal ordering. The third rule is then applied to generate left branching structure, preserving this ordering.

Because this process turns right expansion into left expansion (leaving center expansion as the only stack consumer), right-corner transformed trees also require less stack memory than ordinary phrase structure trees. This key property of the right-corner transform is exploited in the mapping of transformed training trees to a time-series model. This property will be examined further in Section 5.

3 Speech Repair Example

A substantial example of a speech repair from the Switchboard corpus can be seen in Figures 1 and 2, in which the same repair and surrounding context is shown after the preliminary binarization process, and after the right-corner transform. Figure 1 also shows, in brackets, the augmented annotation described above from Hale et al. (2006). This scheme consisted of adding -X to an EDITED label which produced a category X (daughter annotation), as well as propagating the -UNF label at the right corner of the tree up through every parent below the EDITED root.

3.1 Re-annotation of speech repair

Before applying the right-corner transform, some corpus pre-processing steps are applied — Figure 1 shows an example tree after these changes. These steps aim to improve on the default annotation of repair in the Switchboard corpus by making the representation more in line with linguistic as well as processing desiderata.

The standard annotation practice of having the EDITED label as the category at the root of a reparandum does not represent any proposed linguistic phenomenon, and it conflates speech repairs of different categories. As a result, the parser is unable to make use of information about which syntactic category the reparandum was originally intended to be. This information would be useful in the example discussed here, since an unfinished NP is followed by a completed NP. The daughter annotation used by Hale et al. fixes this annotation to allow the parser to have access to this information. The annotation scheme in this paper also makes use of the daughter annotation.

In addition, trees are modified to reduce the arity of speech repair rules, and to change the model of how repairs occur. The default Switchboard has, e.g. an NP reparandum (headed by EDITED) and the NP alteration represented as siblings in the syntax tree. This annotation seems to implicitly model all repairs as stopping the process of producing the current constituent, then starting a new one. In contrast, the representation here models repairs of this type as a speaker generating a partial noun phrase, realizing an error, and then continuing to generate *the same noun phrase*. This representation scheme thus represents the beginning of an effort to distinguish between repairs that are changing the direction of the utterance and those that are just fixing a local mistake.

3.2 Right-corner transform model of speech repair

The right corner transform is then applied to this example in Figure 2. The resulting tree representation is especially valuable because it models human production of speech repairs well, by not applying any special rule until the moment of interruption.

In the example in Figure 1, there is an unfinished constituent (PP-UNF) at the end of the reparandum. This standard annotation is deficient because even if an unfinished consituent like PP-UNF is correctly recognized, and the speaker is essentially in an error state, there may be several partially completed constituents above — in Figure 1, the NP, PP, and NP above the PP-UNF. These constituents need to be completed, but using the standard annotation there is only one chance to make use of the information about the error that has occurred — the 'NP $\rightarrow$ NP PP-UNF' rule. Thus, by the time the error section is completed, there is no information by which a parsing algorithm could choose to reduce the topmost NP to EDITED (or EDITED-NP) other than independent rule probabilities.

The approach used by Hale et al. (2006) works because the information about the transition to an "error state" is propagated up the tree, in the form of the -UNF tags. As the parsing chart is filled in from the bottom up, each rule applied is essentially coming out of a special repair rule set, and so at the top of the tree the EDITED hypothesis is much more likely. However, this requires that several fluent speech rules from the data set be modified for use in a special repair grammar, which not only reduces the amount of available training data,

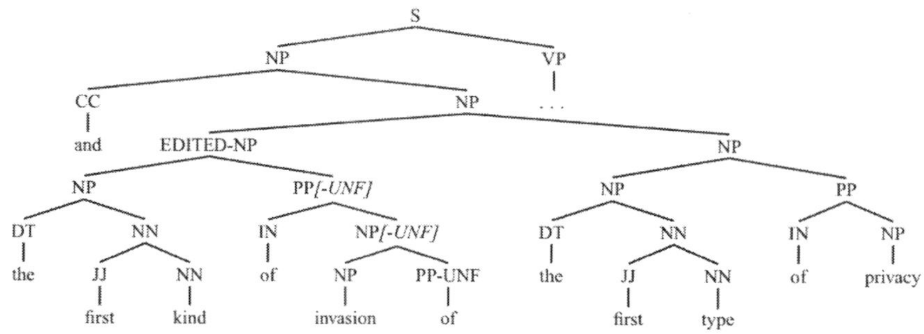

Figure 1: Binarized tree repair structure, with the -UNF propagation as in Hale et al. (2006) shown in brackets.

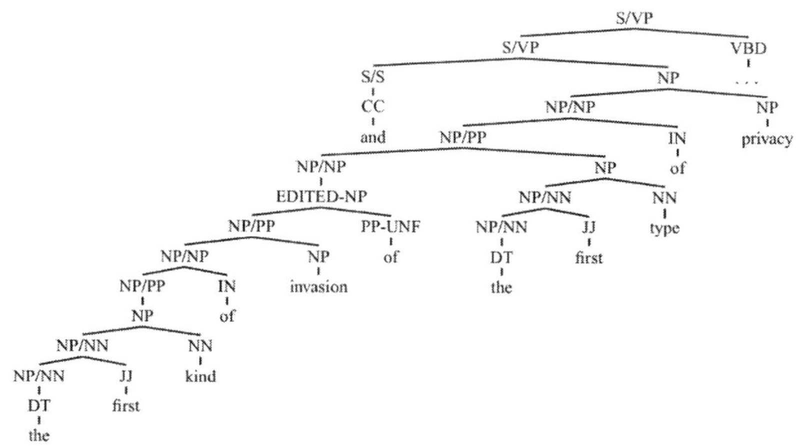

Figure 2: Right-corner transformed tree with repair structure

but violates our intuition that reparanda are usually fluent up until the actual edit occurs.

The right corner transform works in a different way, by building up constituent structure from left to right. In Figure 2, the same repair is shown as it appears in the training data for this system. With this representation, the problem noticed by Hale and colleagues has been solved in a different way, by incrementally building up *left-branching* rather than right-branching structure, so that only a single special error rule is required at the end of the constituent. As seen in the figure, all of the structure beneath the EDITED-NP label is built using rules from the fluent grammar. It is only at one point, when the PP-UNF is found, that a repair rule is applied and the EDITED-NP section is found. The next step in the process is that the NP essentially restarts (the NP/NP label), and the subsequent words start to build up what will be the NP alteration in a fluent manner.

To summarize, while the -UNF propagation scheme often requires the entire reparandum to be generated from a speech repair rule set, this scheme only requires one special rule, where the moment of interruption actually occurred. This reduces the number of special speech repair rules that need to be learned and saves more potential examples of fluent speech rules, and therefore potentially makes better use of limited data.

4 Mapping to an HHMM

This section describes how a corpus of trees transformed as above can be mapped to a time-series model called a Hierarchical Hidden Markov Model (HHMM) in order to incorporate parsing into speech decoding. This suggests that this approach can be used in applications using streaming speech input, unlike other parsing approaches which are cubic time on input length at best, and require input to be pre-segmented.

This section will begin by showing how HHMMs can model linguistic structure by extending standard Hidden Markov Models (HMMs) used in speech recognition, and will follow with a description of how right-corner transformed trees can be mapped to this model topology.

4.1 Hierarchical HMMs

In general, the hidden state in an HMM can be as simple or complex as necessary. This can include factorizing the hidden state into any number of interdependent random variables modeling the substates of the complex hidden state. A Hierarchical Hidden Markov Model is essentially an HMM with a specific factorization that is useful in many domains — the hidden state at each time step is factored into d random variables which function as a stack, and d additional boolean random variables which regulate the operations of the stack through time. The boolean random variables are typically marginalized out when performing inference on a sequence.

While the vertical direction of the hidden substates (at a fixed t) represents a stack at a single point in time, the horizontal direction of the hidden sub-states (at a fixed d) can be viewed as simple HMMs at depth d, taking direction from the HMM above them and controlling those below them. This interpretation will be useful when formally defining the transitions between the stack elements at different time steps below.

Formally, HMMs characterize speech or text as a sequence of hidden states q_t (which may consist of speech sounds, words, and/or other hypothesized syntactic or semantic information), and observed states o_t at corresponding time steps t (typically short, overlapping frames of an audio signal, or words or characters in a text processing application). A most likely sequence of hidden states $\hat{q}_{1..T}$ can then be hypothesized given any sequence of observed states $o_{1..T}$, using Bayes' Law (Equation 2) and Markov independence assumptions (Equation 3) to define a full $\mathsf{P}(q_{1..T} \mid o_{1..T})$ probability as the product of a *Language Model* *(Θ_{L})* prior probability and an *Observation Model* *(Θ_{O})* likelihood probability:

$$\hat{q}_{1..T} = \operatorname*{argmax}_{q_{1..T}} \mathsf{P}(q_{1..T} \mid o_{1..T}) \quad (1)$$

$$= \operatorname*{argmax}_{q_{1..T}} \mathsf{P}(q_{1..T}) \cdot \mathsf{P}(o_{1..T} \mid q_{1..T}) \quad (2)$$

$$\stackrel{\mathrm{def}}{=} \operatorname*{argmax}_{q_{1..T}} \prod_{t=1}^{T} \mathsf{P}_{\Theta_{\mathrm{L}}}(q_t \mid q_{t\text{-}1}) \cdot \mathsf{P}_{\Theta_{\mathrm{O}}}(o_t \mid q_t) \quad (3)$$

Language model transitions $\mathsf{P}_{\Theta_{\mathrm{L}}}(q_t \mid q_{t-1})$ over complex hidden states q_t can be modeled using synchronized levels of stacked-up component HMMs in a Hierarchic Hidden Markov Model (HHMM) (Murphy and Paskin, 2001). HHMM transition probabilities are calculated in two phases: a 'reduce' phase (resulting in an intermediate, marginalized state f_t), in which component HMMs may terminate; and a 'shift' phase (resulting in a modeled state q_t), in which unterminated HMMs transition, and terminated HMMs are re-initialized from their parent HMMs. Variables over intermediate f_t and modeled q_t states are factored into sequences of depth-specific variables — one for each of D levels in the HMM hierarchy:

$$f_t = \langle f_t^1 \dots f_t^D \rangle \quad (4)$$

$$q_t = \langle q_t^1 \dots q_t^D \rangle \quad (5)$$

Transition probabilities are then calculated as a product of transition probabilities at each level, using level-specific 'reduce' Θ_{F} and 'shift' Θ_{Q} models:

$$\mathsf{P}_{\Theta_{\mathrm{L}}}(q_t | q_{t\text{-}1}) = \sum_{f_t} \mathsf{P}(f_t | q_{t\text{-}1}) \cdot \mathsf{P}(q_t | f_t\, q_{t\text{-}1}) \quad (6)$$

$$\stackrel{\mathrm{def}}{=} \sum_{f_t^{1..D}} \prod_{d=1}^{D} \mathsf{P}_{\Theta_{\mathrm{F}}}(f_t^d \mid f_t^{d\text{+}1}\, q_{t\text{-}1}^d\, q_{t\text{-}1}^{d\text{-}1}) \cdot \mathsf{P}_{\Theta_{\mathrm{Q}}}(q_t^d \mid f_t^{d\text{+}1}\, f_t^d\;\, q_{t\text{-}1}^d\, q_t^{d\text{-}1}) \quad (7)$$

with f_t^{D+1} and q_t^0 defined as constants.

Shift and reduce probabilities are now defined in terms of finitely recursive FSAs with probability distributions over transition, recursive expansion, and final-state status of states at each hierarchy level. In simple HHMMs, each intermediate state variable is a boolean switching variable $f_t^d \in \{\mathbf{0}, \mathbf{1}\}$ and each modeled state variable is a syntactic, lexical, or phonetic state q_t^d. The intermediate variable f_t^d is true (equal to $\mathbf{1}$) with probability 1 if there is a transition at the level immediately below d and the stack element q_{t-1}^d is a final state, and false (equal to $\mathbf{0}$) with probability 1 otherwise:[4]

$$\mathsf{P}_{\Theta_{\mathrm{F}}}(f_t^d \mid f_t^{d+1}\, q_{t-1}^d\, q_{t-1}^{d-1}) \stackrel{\mathrm{def}}{=} \begin{cases} \text{if } f_t^{d+1} = \mathbf{0} : [f_t^d = \mathbf{0}] \\ \text{if } f_t^{d+1} = \mathbf{1} : \mathsf{P}_{\Theta_{\text{F-Reduce}}}(f_t^d \mid q_{t-1}^d, q_{t-1}^{d-1}) \end{cases} \quad (8)$$

where $f^{D+1} = \mathbf{1}$ and $q_t^0 = \mathbf{ROOT}$.

Shift probabilities at each level are defined using level-specific transition $\Theta_{\text{Q-Trans}}$ and expan-

[4]Here $[\cdot]$ is an indicator function: $[\phi] = 1$ if ϕ is true, 0 otherwise.

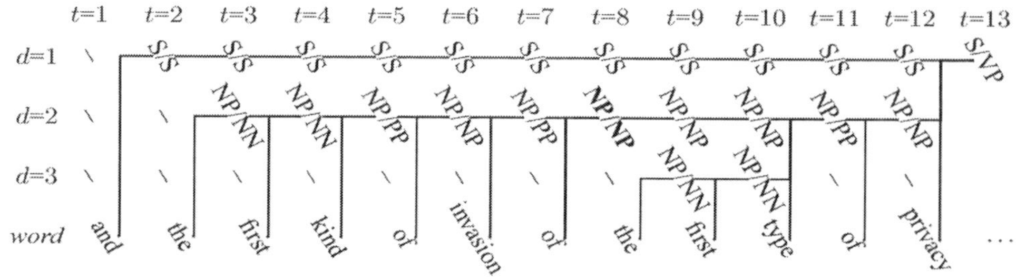

Figure 3: Sample tree from Figure 2 mapped to q_t^d variable positions of an HHMM at each stack depth d (vertical) and time step t (horizontal). Values for final-state variables f_t^d are not shown. Note that some nonterminal labels have been omitted; labels for these nodes can be reconstructed from their children. This includes the EDITED-NP nonterminal that occurs as a child of the NP/NP at t=8, d=2, indicated in boldface.

sion $\Theta_{\text{Q-Expand}}$ models:

$$
\mathsf{P}_{\Theta_{\text{Q}}}(q_t^d \mid f_t^{d+1} f_t^d \, q_{t-1}^d q_t^{d-1}) \stackrel{\text{def}}{=}
\begin{cases}
\text{if } f_t^{d+1}{=}\mathbf{0},\ f_t^d{=}\mathbf{0} : [q_t^d{=}q_{t-1}^d] \\
\text{if } f_t^{d+1}{=}\mathbf{1},\ f_t^d{=}\mathbf{0} : \mathsf{P}_{\Theta_{\text{Q-Trans}}}(q_t^d \mid q_{t-1}^d q_t^{d-1}) \\
\text{if } f_t^{d+1}{=}\mathbf{1},\ f_t^d{=}\mathbf{1} : \mathsf{P}_{\Theta_{\text{Q-Expand}}}(q_t^d \mid q_t^{d-1})
\end{cases}
\quad (9)
$$

where $f^{D+1} = \mathbf{1}$ and $q_t^0 = \mathbf{ROOT}$. This model is conditioned on final-state switching variables at and immediately below the current HHMM level. If there is no final state immediately below the current level (the first case above), it deterministically copies the current HHMM state forward to the next time step. If there is a final state immediately below the current level (the second case above), it transitions the HHMM state at the current level, according to the distribution $\Theta_{\text{Q-Trans}}$. And if the state at the current level is final (the third case above), it re-initializes this state given the state at the level above, according to the distribution $\Theta_{\text{Q-Expand}}$. The overall effect is that higher-level HMMs are allowed to transition only when lower-level HMMs terminate. An HHMM therefore behaves like a probabilistic implementation of a pushdown automaton (or 'shift-reduce' parser) with a finite stack, where the maximum stack depth is equal to the number of levels in the HHMM hierarchy.

4.2 Mapping trees to HHMM derivations

Any tree can now be mapped to an HHMM derivation by aligning the nonterminals with q_t^d categories. First, it is necessary to define rightward depth d, right index position t, and final (right) child status f, for every nonterminal node A in a tree, where:

- d is defined to be the number of right branches between node A and the root,
- t is defined to be the number of words beneath or to the left of node A, and
- f is defined to be $\mathbf{0}$ if node A is a left (or unary) child, $\mathbf{1}$ otherwise.

Any binary-branching tree can then be annotated with these values and rewritten to define labels and final-state values for every combination of d and t covered by the tree. This process simply copies stacked up constituents over multiple time steps, while other constituents are being recognized. Coordinates $d, t \leq D, T$ that are not covered by the tree are assigned label '$-$', and $f = \mathbf{1}$. The resulting label and final-state values at each node now define a value of q_t^d and f_{t+1}^d for each depth d and time step t of the HHMM (see Figure 3). Probabilities for HHMM models $\Theta_{\text{Q-Expand}}$, $\Theta_{\text{Q-Trans}}$, and $\Theta_{\text{F-Reduce}}$ can then be estimated from these values directly. Like the right-corner transform, this mapping is reversible, so q and f values can be taken from a hypothesized most likely sequence and mapped back to trees (which can then undergo the reverse of the right-corner transform to become ordinary phrase structure trees).

5 HHMM Application to Speech Repair

While the HHMM parser described above can produce the same output as a standard probablistic CYK parser (the most likely parse tree), the different parsing strategy of an HHMM parser and the close connection of this system with a probabilistic model of semantics present potential benefits to the recognition of disfluent speech.

First, by using a depth-limited stack, this model better adheres to psycholinguistically observed short term memory limits that the human parser and generator are likely to obey (Cowan, 2001; Miller, 1956). The use of a depth-limited stack is enabled by the right-corner transform's property of transforming right expansions to left expansions, which minimizes stack usage. Corpus studies (Schuler et al., 2008) suggest that broad coverage parsing can be achieved via this transform using only four stack elements. In practical terms this means that the model is less likely than a standard CYK parser to spend time and probability mass on analyses that conflict with the memory limits humans appear to be constrained by when generating and understanding speech.

Second, this model is part of a more general framework that incorporates a model of referential semantics into the parsing model of the HHMM (Schuler et al., in press). While the framework evaluated in this paper models only the syntactic contribution to speech repair, there are some cases where syntactic cues are not sufficient to distinguish disfluent from fluent utterances. In many of these cases, semantic information is the only way to tell that an utterance contains a repair.[5] A recognition system that incorporates referential semantics with syntax should improve the accuracy of speech repair recognition as it has been shown to increase recognition of entities in fluent speech recognition.

Finally, the semantic model just described, as well as the mechanics of the HHMM parser on a right-corner transformed grammar, combine to form a model that accounts for two previously distant aspects of speech processing: referential semantics and speech repair. From the generative view of language processing, the model starts with a desired referent, and based on that referent selects the appropriate syntactic structures, and within those it selects the appropriate lexical items to unambiguously describe the referent. In the semantic sense, then, the model is operating in a top-down fashion, with the referent being the driving force for the generation of syntax and words. However, since the model is also working in a left-to-right fashion on a highly left-branching grammar, there is also a bottom-up composition of constituents, which models the phenomenon of speech repair naturally and accurately.

6 Evaluation

The evaluation of this system was performed on the Switchboard corpus of transcribed conversational speech, using the *mrg* annotations in directories 2 and 3 for training, and the files sw4004.mrg to sw4153.mrg in directory 4 for evaluation, following Johnson and Charniak (2004). In addition to testing the HHMM parser on the Switchboard corpus, the experiment testing a CYK parser from Miller and Schuler (2008) was replicated, with slightly better results due to a change in the evaluation script[6] and small changes in the binarization process (both of these changes affect the baseline and test systems).

The input to the system consists of the terminal symbols from the trees in the corpus section mentioned above. The terminal symbol strings are first pre-processed by stripping punctuation and empty categories, which could not be expected from the output of a speech recognizer. In addition, any information about repair is stripped from the input, including partial words, repair symbols,[7] and interruption point information. While an integrated system for processing and parsing speech may use both acoustic and syntactic information to find repairs, and thus may have access to some of this information about where interruptions occur, this testing paradigm is intended to evaluate the use of the right-corner transform in a time-series model on parsing speech repair. To make a fair comparison to the CYK baseline of Hale et al. (2006), the recognizer was given correct part-of-speech tags as input along with words.

The results presented here use two standard metrics for assessing accuracy of transcribed speech with repairs. The first metric, Parseval F-measure, takes into account precision and recall of all non-terminal (and non pre-terminal) constituents in a hypothesized tree relative to the gold standard. The second metric, EDIT-finding F, measures precision and recall of the words tagged as EDITED in the hypothesized tree relative to those tagged EDITED

[5] For example, the sentence "The red... uh... blue box" is more likely to be considered a repair in a context with single colored boxes, whereas the sentence "The big... uh... blue box" is less likely to be considered a repair in the same context, although the two sentences have the same syntactic structure.

[6] Specifically, we switched to using the evalb tool created by Sekine and Collins (1997).

[7] The Switchboard corpus has special terminal symbols indicating e.g. the start and end of the reparandum.

in the gold standard. F score is defined as usual, $2pr/(p+r)$ for precision p and recall r.

Table 1 below shows the results of experiments using the model of speech repair described in this paper. The 'Baseline' result shows the accuracy of the binarized grammar at parsing the Switchboard test set. The 'RCT' result shows the accuracy of parsing when the right-corner transform is performed on the trees in the training set prior to training. Finally, the 'HHMM+RCT' results shows the accuracy of the HHMM parser system described in this paper, trained on right-corner trees mapped to the random variables at each time step. 'CYK' and 'TAG' lines show relevant results from related work.

System	Parseval F	EDIT F
Baseline	**63.43**	**41.82**
CYK (H06)	71.16	41.7
RCT	**73.21**	**61.03**
HHMM+RCT	**77.15**	**68.03**
TAG-based model (JC04)	–	79.7

Table 1: Summary of results.

These results show an improvement over the standard CYK parsing algorithm, in both overall parsing accuracy and EDIT-finding accuracy. This shows that the HHMM parser, which is more applicable to speech input due to its asymptotic linear time complexity, does not need to sacrifice any accuracy to do so, and indeed improves on accuracy for both metrics under consideration.

7 Conclusion

The work described here has extended previous work for recognizing disfluent speech to an incremental model, moving in a direction that holds promise for eventual direct implementation in a speech recognizer.

Extending this model to actual speech adds some complexity, since disfluency phenomena are difficult to detect in an audio signal. However, there are also advantages in this extension, since the extra phonological variables and acoustic observations contain information that can be useful in the recognition of disfluency phenomena.

References

Cowan, Nelson. 2001. The magical number 4 in short-term memory: A reconsideration of mental storage capacity. *Behavioral and Brain Sciences*, 24:87–185.

Hale, John, Izhak Shafran, Lisa Yung, Bonnie Dorr, Mary Harper, Anna Krasnyanskaya, Matthew Lease, Yang Liu, Brian Roark, Matthew Snover, and Robin Stewart. 2006. PCFGs with syntactic and prosodic indicators of speech repairs. In *Proceedings of the 45th Annual Conference of the Association for Computational Linguistics (COLING-ACL)*.

Johnson, Mark and Eugene Charniak. 2004. A tag-based noisy channel model of speech repairs. In *Proceedings of the 42nd Annual Meeting of the Association for Computational Linguistics (ACL '04)*, pages 33–39, Barcelona, Spain.

Johnson, Mark. 1998a. Finite state approximation of constraint-based grammars using left-corner grammar transforms. In *Proceedings of COLING/ACL*, pages 619–623.

Johnson, Mark. 1998b. PCFG models of linguistic tree representation. *Computational Linguistics*, 24:613–632.

Klein, Dan and Christopher D. Manning. 2003. Accurate unlexicalized parsing. In *Proceedings of the 41st Annual Meeting of the Association for Computational Linguistics*, pages 423–430.

Levelt, William J.M. 1983. Monitoring and self-repair in speech. *Cognition*, 14:41–104.

Miller, Tim and William Schuler. 2008. A unified syntactic model for parsing fluent and disfluent speech. In *Proceedings of the 46th Annual Meeting of the Association for Computational Linguistics (ACL '08)*.

Miller, George A. 1956. The magical number seven, plus or minus two: Some limits on our capacity for processing information. *Psychological Review*, 63:81–97.

Murphy, Kevin P. and Mark A. Paskin. 2001. Linear time inference in hierarchical HMMs. In *Proc. NIPS*, pages 833–840.

Nakatani, C. and J. Hirschberg. 1994. A corpus-based study of repair cues in spontaneous speech. *The Journal of the Acoustic Society of America*, 95:1603–1616.

Schuler, William, Samir AbdelRahman, Tim Miller, and Lane Schwartz. 2008. Toward a psycholinguistically-motivated model of language. In *Proceedings of COLING*, Manchester, UK.

Schuler, William, Stephen Wu, and Lane Schwartz. in press. A framework for fast incremental interpretation during speech decoding. *Computational Linguistics*.

Sekine, Satoshi and Michael Collins. 1997. Evalb bracket scoring program.

Shriberg, Elizabeth. 1994. *Preliminaries to a Theory of Speech Disfluencies*. Ph.D. thesis, University of California at Berkeley.

Applying Discourse Analysis and Data Mining Methods to Spoken OSCE Assessments

Meladel Mistica, Timothy Baldwin
The University of Melbourne
CSSE
{mmistica,tim}
@csse.unimelb.edu.au

Marisa Cordella, Simon Musgrave
Monash University
School of Languages, Cultures and Linguistics
{marisa.cordella,simon.musgrave}
@arts.monash.edu.au

Abstract

This paper looks at the transcribed data of patient-doctor consultations in an examination setting. The doctors are internationally qualified and enrolled in a bridging course as preparation for their Australian Medical Council examination. In this study, we attempt to ascertain if there are measurable linguistic features of the consultations, and to investigate whether there is any relevant information about the communicative styles of the qualifying doctors that may predict satisfactory or non-satisfactory examination outcomes. We have taken a discourse analysis approach in this study, where the core unit of analysis is a 'turn'. We approach this problem as a binary classification task and employ data mining methods to see whether the application of which to richly annotated dialogues can produce a system with an adequate predictive capacity.

1 Introduction

This paper describes our experimentation with applying data mining methods to transcribed doctor–patient consultations. It is in essence a discovery project: we apply methods to a field and task that is not ordinarily associated with such approaches in order to ascertain whether this could make for a tractable learning task.

The task involves the extraction of discourse features from doctor–patient consultations performed by international medical graduates (IMGs), and what is known as 'simulated patients' (Vu et al., 1994), respectively. The IMGs are enrolled in a bridging course in Melbourne as preparation for their Australian Medical Council (AMC) examination, the successful completion of which is one of the pre-requisites to becoming a fully accredited practitioner in Australia. This partially replicates the AMC examination by studying in detail how IMGs perform two objective structured clinical examinations (OSCEs). See Section 2 for full details of the examination environment and participants involved.

The main questions raised when initiating this study were:

- How objective is the testing?
- What is the importance placed on language skills in OSCE environments?
- What makes for a successful OSCE?

In this research, we aim to build classifiers that make reasonable predictions of the data being tested, and possibly point us in the right direction with respect to the questions above. From the classifiers we build, we also hope to ascertain which of our features best predict a successful examination.

We organise the paper as follows. In Section 2, we briefly describe the examination environment and process, the marking scheme, and the participants involved in the testing of the IMGs. We also outline some of the issues that have arisen with regard to the current methods of IMG testing. In Section 3, we present details of the data used. Section 4 describes the features we develop for the task and discusses the reasoning behind the selection of features from a discourse analysis perspective. Section 5 discusses the results of the experiments, with further examination of the data. The

©2008. Licensed under the *Creative Commons Attribution-Noncommercial-Share Alike 3.0 Unported* license (http://creativecommons.org/licenses/by-nc-sa/3.0/). Some rights reserved.

last two sections, Sections 6 and 7, comprise a discussion of the results and concluding remarks.

2 Background

With Western nations becoming increasingly reliant on medical professionals trained overseas, there is, in turn, a growing need to develop a reliable means of objectively assessing IMGs. The shortage of medical doctors is a worldwide phenomenon currently affecting many Western societies such as the UK, Canada, US and New Zealand, which compete for the best medical practitioners available around the world. Australia is not immune to this global phenomenon, and in the last two decades the shortage of local medical practitioners in Australia has worsened (Birrell et al., 2004). Challenges to the healthcare system in the country are particularly evident in the areas of providing medical care for a growing elderly population and of servicing rural areas, where locally trained doctors do not feel particularly attracted to practise medicine (Han et al., 2006). Currently 35% of the rural medical workforce and 20% of the total national medical workforce consist of IMGs (Flynn, 2006). These figures may increase even further in some regions (Spike, 2006), as preparation of fully educated and trained local medical graduates takes up to thirteen years to complete.

There is considerable disparity among IMGs in their background training, clinical skills, understanding of the health system and communication skills (McGrath, 2004). In order to be registered to practice in Australia, IMGs must successfully complete the Australian Medical Council examinations and a period of supervised training. The medical knowledge of IMGs is assessed in two ways: by multiple choice examinations and by clinical examinations. This second form of examination consists of a series of simulated medical consultations in which a role-player takes the part of the patient, and the IMG's professional knowledge, lay-cultural knowledge, socio-cultural assumptions, institutional norms, and values and personal experiences are all in full display during the unfolding of the medical event (Roberts et al., 2003). Whenever cultural factors are not shared with their patients, the interpretative schema and therefore the comprehension of speech are affected by this lack of commonality in the participants' inferences and contextual cues (Gumperz, 1999). Such effects are likely to cause miscommunication in medical visits and have a potential negative effect on patients' satisfaction in the consultation. Identification of the communication difficulties faced by IMGs can therefore inform modifications to the training provided to IMGs when they prepare for the Australian Medical Council examinations, as well as suggesting more nuanced and targeted procedures for assessing communicative skills within those examinations, all with the goal of working toward a better equipped medical workforce for the future. The use of automated analytic procedures to try to establish objective criteria for communicative success is an important step in this process.

Assessing language knowledge and competence quantitatively is not a novel concept in second language learning assessment. However, the application of data mining methods to automatically assess language proficiency in a discourse setting is novel. Levow et al. (1999) propose an architecture to automatically assess language proficiency. In their paper, they propose an architecture that employs data mining methods, but do not build classifiers over their spoken data to test this proposal. A closely related line of research is on the automatic classification of discourse elements to assess the quality of a written genre (Burstein et al., 2001). Like this work, it focuses on extracting features from the discourse as a whole. But unlike this study, the authors extract high level features, such as rhetorical structure, of written discourse. The study we present in this paper is rather unique in its approach to language assessment.

3 Data

The data is taken from transcribed recordings of examinations from students enrolled in a bridging course at Box Hill Hospital in Melbourne, Australia. Each candidate was video-recorded enacting medical consultation scenarios with what is known as a standardised or simulated patient (SP). This method of testing is known as an objective structured clinical examination (OSCE), which is an emulation of a doctor–patient consultation, much like a role-play setting.

In this study, the role of the patient (SP) is enacted by a qualified doctor who follows a script, and has well-defined ailment(s) and accompanying concerns. Even though the SP assumes the same ailment and disposition with all the candidates, the interaction between the candidate and the SP is uncued and free-form. They simply present the information in a standardised manner across all candidates and perform the role of the patient as felicitously as possible.

For this set of examinations there are 2 types of OSCE stations referred to as STD (sexually transmitted disease – genital herpes) and BC (bowel cancer). The SP for the STD station is played by a female doctor. The patient she plays has genital herpes and is concerned about how this will affect her chances of falling pregnant, and how this condition may also affect her baby. The SP for the BC station is played by an older male. A tumour is discovered in his bowel lining and he is reluctant to undergo any treatment because one of his good friends suffered a similar condition and his quality of life was severely diminished.

Even though the consultation is free to be negotiated between doctor (candidate) and patient (simulated patient), each of the OSCEs cannot exceed 8 minutes, and is terminated by the examiner if it does so.

3.1 Transcription

The recordings are transcribed in ELAN, a multimedia annotation tool developed at the Max Planck Institute, to help encode low-level linguistic features such as overlapping and timing information. The information and features extracted from the discourse are largely based on a 'turn'.

Here we consider a turn as being normally dominated by one speaker. It can be made up of multiple intonation units. When there is backchannelling, overlapping, or any interruption by the other participant, then the turn is encoded as ending at the end of the interrupted intonation unit. Otherwise, transition pauses commonly signal turn changes, unless latching occurs.

Given that the OSCE setting aims to emulate as close as possible a real medical consultation, this interaction, like all uncued spoken dialogues, also has evidence of complicated turn-taking negotiations, disfluent and unintelligible speech, interrupted speech, challenges for the floor, and the like, all of which must be encoded and noted in ELAN. Transcribing such data is not a trivial matter. In addition, transcribing the data in order to extract these features is also a demanding task in itself, which makes creating data for such tasks an involved process.

Disfluencies and repairs are encoded in a limited way, only by way of marking up truncated or unfinished words. We also do not take a fine-grained approach in encoding delaying strategies (Clark et al., 2002), that is we do not differentiate whether the *uh* or *ah* encoded represents lexical search, a wish to hold the floor, a wish to give up the floor or buying time to construct what to say next.

3.2 OSCE scoring

In an OSCE setting, candidates are given an overall pass or fail rating for each station by an OSCE examiner observing the interaction. This overall evaluation can be based on a number of performance criteria which tests the candidates medical, clinical and communication skills (Grand'Maison et al., 1992). The OSCE marking scheme used for this study consists of 5 assessable categories, as follows:

APPROACH: the ability of the candidate to communicate with the patient;

HISTORY: the ability of the candidate to collect medical history;

INTERPRETATION: how well does the candidate interpret his or her investigation in order to formulate an appropriate diagnosis;

MANAGEMENT: how well does the candidate formulate a management plan for the diagnosis;

COUNSELLING: is the candidate able to give appropriate counselling to the patient.

The first category tests language knowledge and competency both at the lexical and discourse level, while the remaining four categories test medical knowledge and clinical competency.

4 Feature Engineering

We extracted a total of 38 features from the transcribed data. Some of these features are based on what is marked up according to the transcription scheme, while others are based on timing information or lexical information as encoded in ELAN. These include features such as signals for delaying speaking or hesitation (Clark et al., 2002), features of conversational dominance (Itakura, 2000), the manner in which turn-taking is negotiated (Sacks et al., 1974), temporal features such as pausing (ten Bosch et al., 2005), as well as our own features, which include 'lexical introduction', and 'lexical repeat'.

In encoding features of conversational dominance, we focus on *participatory dominance* (Itakura, 2000), which looks at which speaker contributes most to the dialogue in terms of content.

Lexical introduction refers to a non-stop word that is introduced by the doctor (IMG) or the patient (SP), while *lexical repeat* encodes how many times a word introduced by the other interlocutor is repeated by the speaker.

Almost all of the features developed are continuous, based on timing information or word counts. The only binary feature used encodes whether the doctor initiates the consultation or not.

As mentioned in the previous section, the features developed were largely based on turns. This is to capture, along with other features such as overlapping and pauses, the interactional aspect of the communication. For example, conversational cooperation and speaker reassurance can be captured with these features. Another aspect to the development of these features, particularly for the lexical-based features, is whether the IMG has a suitable vocabularly and if they employ it appropriately in the interaction.

We arrive at 11 feature sets from which we build our classifiers, as described in Table 1.

Not all features are exclusive to any one feature set, that is, it is possible for a single feature to belong to a number of feature sets.

The sets were designed to isolate possible characteristics of not only the discourse as a whole, but how the participants negotiated their interaction. These features sets were developed from observing each of the consultations with the expectation that these were salient and determining features of a successful examination.

Feature set	Example features
all	- all 38 features
cooperation	- overall word count - length of interaction - number of turns
hesitation	- number of *uh* and *ah* - number of unfinished words
overlap	- number of overlapping words - length of overlap (time)
pause	- transition pauses - within turn pauses
timeBased	- all time-based features
turns	- all turn-based features - number of turns - longest turn - single word responses
uniqNrepeat	- number of introduced content words by each speaker - number of times speaker uses word introduced by other
wordBased	- number of words in dialogue - longest number of words in a turn
patient	- all SP-based features
doctor	- all IMG-based features

Table 1: The 11 feature sets developed

5 Experiments

There was a total of 11 OSCE candidates, all of whom performed an STD and a BC station, giving us in total 22 instances for this binary classification task to predict a pass or fail examination result. Of the 22 instances, we had 5 failures and 17 passes. Given the small number of instances, we maximised our dataset by employing 10-fold stratified cross-validation, as well as leave-one-out cross-validation which uses all but one instance in training and the held-out instance for testing.

The baseline system we use for comparison is zero-R, or majority vote. For our supervised classifier, we employ a lazy learner in the form of the IB1 algorithm implemented in WEKA.

5.1 Results for Feature Sets

Our initial classifiers held some promise. The classifier built from all of the features was equivalent to the baseline system, and the combination of the word-based features surpassed the baseline's results, as shown in Table 2.

To evaluate our system, we employ simple classification accuracy, in addition to precision, recall and F-score. Classification accuracy is the proportion of correct predictions by the classifier, irrespective of class. Precision gauges how successful the pass predictions of a given classifier are, while recall gives us an indication of how successful a given classifier is at identifying the candidates who actually passed. Finally, F-score is a composite of precision and recall, and gives us an overall performance rating relative to passed candidates.

The least successful classifier was built on the

	10-fold cross validation				Leave-one-out cross validation			
Feature set	Accuracy	Precision	Recall	F-score	Accuracy	Precision	Recall	F-score
baseline	.773	.773	1.00	.872	.773	.773	1.00	.872
all	**.773**	**.773**	**1.00**	**.872**	**.773**	**.773**	**1.00**	**.872**
cooperation	.682	**.789**	.824	.806	.682	**.778**	.824	.800
hesitation	.636	.737	.824	.778	.636	.737	.824	.778
overlap	**.773**	**.833**	.882	.857	**.773**	**.833**	.882	.857
pause	.682	**.778**	.824	.800	.727	**.789**	.882	.833
timeBased	.500	.647	.688	.667	.545	.706	.706	.706
turns	.727	**.789**	.882	.833	.727	**.789**	.882	.833
uniqNrepeat	.636	.765	.765	.765	.682	**.778**	.824	.800
wordBased	**.864**	**.850**	**1.00**	**.919**	**.864**	**.850**	**1.00**	**.919**
patient	.727	**.867**	.765	.813	.727	**.867**	.765	.813
doctor	.733	**.800**	.941	.865	.727	**.789**	.882	.833

Table 2: Classification results for STD and BC

feature set based on timing, which contains information such as the overall length of the dialogue, the overall length of transition pauses, in-turn pauses and other time-based features. This was most surprising because as a general observation, candidates who allowed extended pauses and uncomfortable silences were those who seemed to perform poorly, and those who did not leave too many silences, and could maintain the flow of the dialogue, seemed to perform well.

Given the small number of training instances each classifier is based on, these first results were somewhat encouraging. With respect to the baseline, the overall performance of two of the systems equalled or surpassed the baseline in terms of F-score. Most of the classifiers performed well in terms of precision but less well in terms of recall, i.e. when the classifiers predicted a pass they were generally correct, but there were significant numbers of candidates who were predicted to have failed but passed in practice.

5.2 Data Introspection Retrospectively

Although the results show promise, it was expected that more of the feature sets would return more favourable results. The possible reasons why the time-based features, and many of the other feature sets developed, did not perform as well as expected may have been because the features used in building the classifiers could have been combined in a better way, or because the data itself had too many anomalies or was too disparate. We would expect that extra data could iron out such anomalies, but developing additional data is expensive and more recordings are not always available. The advantage of having a small dataset is that we are able to do fine-grained annotation of the data, but the obvious disadvantage is that we cannot easily generate extra amounts of training data.

One very noticeable feature of the OSCE stations was that the STD SP had a very different communicative style to that of the the BC SP. Based on this observation we conducted tests given the hypothesis that the possible bias in the data could have stemmed from having two very different testing approaches from the two SPs. In general, the BC SP was more leading and in a sense more forgiving with the candidates. In contrast to this, the STD SP tended to be more felicitous in her role as a patient, allowing awkward silences and not prompting the candidates for further exploration.

We conduct the Mann-Whitney test, a rank sum test, over the data in order to diagnose whether the poor results were due to the distribution of the data or whether the classifiers built with the selected features were simply poor predictors. The Mann-Whitney test ascertains whether there is a difference in the population mean of the two samples given, without making any assumptions about the distribution of the data.

We sub-sample the data in two ways in examining its homogeneity: (a) FAIL juxtaposed with PASS candidates; and (b) BC juxtaposed with STD stations. Test (a) essentially tests which examinable category contributes the most to a pass or fail outcome, whilst test (b) examines whether there is an inherent difference in the way the test-

Category	OVERALL	APPROACH	HISTORY	INTERPRETATION	MANAGEMENT	COUNSELLING
z-score	1.84	1.21	-0.03	2.53	0.85	1.64

Table 3: Mann-Whitney z-score for BC and STD samples (OVERALL is the cumulative total of all 5 categories)

Category	OVERALL	APPROACH	HISTORY	INTERPRETATION	MANAGEMENT	COUNSELLING
z-score	-3.29	-3.13	-2.43	-2.31	-2.31	-1.57

Table 4: Mann-Whitney z-score for failed and passed samples

ing was conducted between the BC and STD stations.

BC vs. STD

We use the ranking from the 5 assessable categories outlined in Section 3 and obtain the Mann-Whitney z-score for each category. The z-score gives us an indication of how disparate the two separated datasets, BC and STD, are. The further away from 0 the z-score is, the greater the evidence that BC and STD data are not from the same population, and should be treated as such. The results of this test, as seen in Table 3, show that these two groups differ quite markedly: the candidates were consistently marked differently for all assessable categories except HISTORY. This is a striking peculiarity because each candidate was tested in both the STD and BC stations.

Based on the above, we can posit that the distinct testing styles of the STD and BC SPs were the reason for our original lacklustre results, and that the two data samples need to be treated separately for the classifiers to perform consistently.

FAIL vs. PASS

In addition to the BC vs. STD test, we also test how the failing candidates differ from the passing candidates across the evaluation criteria.

The main idea behind this test is to see which of the assessable categories contributed the most in the overall outcome of the examination. For this test, we would not expect the absolute z-score of any of the assessment components to exceed the absolute z-score of the OVERALL category given that it is the cumulative scores of all categories.

The results in Table 4 suggest that APPROACH correlates most highly with the pass/fail divide in the OSCE assessments, followed by HISTORY, then INTERPRETATION and MANAGEMENT, and finally COUNSELLING. Recall that APPROACH is the component that assesses language and communication skills. In particular, it assesses the style and appropriateness of the way candidates convey information, from lexical choice to displaying empathy through communication style. Given that APPROACH correlates most strongly with the assessment result, the decision to focus our feature engineering efforts on linguistic aspects of the doctor–patient interaction would appear justified.

5.3 Results for STD & BC Data

Given the results from the Mann-Whitney tests reported in the previous section, we separate the data into two lots: those from the STD station, and those from the BC station.

Even though there were very few instances in the original dataset, we aim to see in these experiments whether this separation improves the performance of the classifiers. We build classifiers over each dataset using the same features as before.

The results of the tests performed over the separated datasets, as shown in Table 5, show a big improvement over the baseline for STD, while the BC dataset is more problematic.

In the STD group, we see that four feature sets, *all*, *turns*, *wordBased* and *patient* equal or surpass the baseline F-score.

In contrast to this, upon examination of the performance of the classifiers built over the BC dataset, we do not observe any improvements over the baseline and the results are markedly worse than those for the combined dataset. Having said this, when we combine the outputs of the two component classifiers, the F-score for *all* features is 0.882, an improvement over the original combined system.

6 Discussion

The OSCE assessment does not merely examine the language skills of the candidates, but it also as-

	BC				STD			
Feature Set	Accuracy	Precision	Recall	F-score	Accuracy	Precision	Recall	F-score
baseline	.818	.818	1.00	.900	.727	.727	1.00	.842
all	.727	**.875**	.778	.824	**.909**	**.889**	**1.00**	**.941**
cooperation	.727	.800	.889	.842	.364	.571	.500	.533
hesitation	.636	.778	.778	.778	.636	.700	.875	.778
overlap	.727	.800	.889	.842	.636	.700	.875	.778
pause	**.818**	**.889**	.889	.889	.545	.667	.750	.706
timeBased	.636	**.857**	.667	.750	.545	.667	.750	.706
turns	.636	.778	.778	.778	**.818**	**.800**	**1.00**	**.889**
uniqNrepeat	.727	.800	.889	.842	**.727**	**.778**	.875	.824
wordBased	.636	.778	.778	.778	**.909**	**.889**	**1.00**	**.941**
patient	.727	**.875**	.778	.824	**.818**	**.875**	.875	**.875**
doctor	**.818**	**.818**	**1.00**	**.900**	.455	.625	.625	.625

Table 5: Results for separated BC and STD datasets (leave-one-out)

sesses the efficacy of their communication skills in conveying correct and accurate medical information within a clinical setting. It can be seen from Table 4 that there is a high correlation between the overall pass or fail and the assessable category APPROACH.

The examiners' subjectivity of overall performance is minimised by the highly structured examination setup and well-defined assessment criteria. However, as shown in Table 3, the communicative style of the SP is a contributing factor to the perception of successful clinical and communication skills. The Mann-Whitney tests suggest that an SP's approach and their apparent satisfaction during the clinical encounter can affect the judgement of the examiner.

Additional inspection of the data revealed that the assessment criteria which focused on language and communication skills correlated highly with an overall pass grade, moreso than the other criteria. This seems to suggest that more emphasis should be placed on language skills and communication style in the assessment of the candidates.

Assessing language competency is no trivial matter, and capturing the linguistic features of dialogues in an attempt to define competence, as we have done here, is a demanding task in itself. Although many of our features were focused on turn-taking, speaker response and interaction, we did not develop features that encompass the information structure of the communicative event.

It is assumed that miscommunication between non-native and native speakers of a language is due to a lack of language knowledge pertaining to syntax, morphology or lexical semantics. However many of these communication difficulties arise not because of this lack of grammatical knowledge, but through a difference in discourse styles or information structure as governed by different cultures (Wiberg, 2003; Li, 1999).

Given that the word-based feature sets were the most successful predictors of an OSCE outcome, future work of this kind could make use of medical-based lexicons to gauge whether technical or non-technical word usage in such environments is judged favourably. In addition, further work should be done to test the hypothesis that information structure or rhetorical structure does impact on overall perception of a successful communication, such as a variation on the methods employed by Burstein et al. (2001).

One obvious improvement to this study would be to reduce the expense in producing the annotated data. Future work could also be done in automatically extracting features from non-transcribed data, such as timing information based on pause length and the turn length of each speaker.

7 Conclusions

In this research, we have built classifiers over transcribed doctor–patient consultations in an attempt to predict OSCE outcomes. We achieved encouraging results based on a range of lexical and discourse-oriented features.

In our first experiments, we combined the data from two discrete stations in an attempt to maximise training data, and achieved modest results. Subsequent analysis with the Mann-Whitney test indicated both that success in the APPROACH category correlates strongly with an overall successful OSCE, and that the data for the two stations is markedly different in nature. Based on this finding, we conduct tests over the data for the individual stations with noticeable improvements to the results.

The results of this exploratory study have been quite encouraging, given the novel domain and limited data. We have shown that a data mining approach to OSCE assessment is feasible, which we hope will open the way to increased interest in automated medical assessment based on linguistic analysis.

References

Birrell, Bob, Lesleyanne Hawthorne. 2004. Medicare Plus and overseas trained doctors. *People and Place*, 12(2):83–99.

ten Bosch, Louis, Nelleke Oostdijk, Lou Boves. 2005. On temporal aspects of turn taking in conversational dialogues. *Speech Communication*, 47(2005):80–86.

Burstein, Jill, Daniel Marcu, Slava Andreyev, Martin Chodorow. 2001. Towards Automatic Classification of Discourse Elements in Essays. *ACL*, 90-97.

Clark, Herber H., Jean E. Fox Tree. 2002. Using *uh* and *um* in spontaneous speaking. *Cognition*, 84(2002):73–111.

Flynn, Joanna. 2006. Medical Release. *Australian Medical Council*, 17(August 2006).

Grand'Maison, Paul, Joëlle Lescop, Paul Rainsberry, Carlos A. Brailovsky. 1992. Large-scale use of an objective, structured clinical examination for licensing family physicians. *Canadian Medical Association*, 146(10):1735–1740.

Gumperz, John. 1999. On Interactional Sociolinguistic Method. In *Talk, Work and Institutional Order. Discourse in Medical, Mediation and Management Settings* S. Sarangi and C. Robers (*eds*), 453–471.

Han, Gil-Soo, John .S Humphreys. 2006. Integratoin and retention of international medical graduates in rural communities. A typological analysis. *The Australian Sociological Association*, 42(2):189–207.

Itakura, Hiroko. 2000. Describing conversational dominance. *Journal of Pragmatics*, 33(2001):1859–1880.

Levow, Gina-Anne, Mari Broman Olsen. 1999. Modeling the language assessment process and result: Proposed architecture for an automatic oral proficiency assessment. *Workshop On Computer Mediated Language Assessment And Evaluation In Natural Language Processing*.

Li, Han Zao. 1999. Comunication Information in Conversations: A Cross-cultural Comparison. *International Journal of Intercultural Relations*, 23(3):387–409.

McGrath, Barry. 2004. Overseas-trained doctors. Integration of overseas-trained doctors in the Australian medical workforce. *The Medical Journal of Australia*, 181(11/12):640–642.

Roberts, Celia, Val Wass, Roger Jones, Srikant Sarangi, Annie Gillett. 2003. A discourse analysis study of 'good' and 'poor' communication in an OSCE: a proposed new framework for teaching students. *Medical Education*, 50:192–201.

Sacks, Harvey, Emanuel A. Schegloff, Gail Jefferson. 1974. A Simplest Systematics for the Organization of Turn-Taking for Conversation. *Language*, 50(4):696–735.

Spike, Neil. 2006. International Medical Graduates: The Australian perspective. *Acad Med*, 81):842–846.

Vu, Nu Viet, Howard S. Barrows. 1994. Use of Standardized Patients in Clinical Assessments: Recents Developments and Measurement Findings. *Educational Researcher*, 23(3):23–30.

Wiberg, Eva. 2003. Interactional context in L2 dialogues. *Journal of Pragmatics*, 35(2003):389–407.

Random Restarts in Minimum Error Rate Training for Statistical Machine Translation

Robert C. Moore and **Chris Quirk**
Microsoft Research
Redmond, WA 98052, USA
bobmoore@microsoft.com, chrisq@microsoft.com

Abstract

Och's (2003) minimum error rate training (MERT) procedure is the most commonly used method for training feature weights in statistical machine translation (SMT) models. The use of multiple randomized starting points in MERT is a well-established practice, although there seems to be no published systematic study of its benefits. We compare several ways of performing random restarts with MERT. We find that all of our random restart methods outperform MERT without random restarts, and we develop some refinements of random restarts that are superior to the most common approach with regard to resulting model quality and training time.

1 Introduction

Och (2003) introduced minimum error rate training (MERT) for optimizing feature weights in statistical machine translation (SMT) models, and demonstrated that it produced higher translation quality scores than maximizing the conditional likelihood of a maximum entropy model using the same features. Och's method performs a series of one-dimensional optimizations of the feature weight vector, using an innovative line search that takes advantage of special properties of the mapping from sets of feature weights to the resulting translation quality measurement. Och's line search is guaranteed to find a global optimum, whereas more general line search methods are guaranteed only to find a local optimum.

©2008. Licensed under the *Creative Commons Attribution-Noncommercial-Share Alike 3.0 Unported* license (http://creativecommons.org/licenses/by-nc-sa/3.0/). Some rights reserved.

Global optimization along one dimension at a time, however, does not insure global optimization in all dimensions. Hence, as Och briefly mentions, "to avoid finding a poor local optimum," MERT can be augmented by trying multiple random starting points for each optimization search within the overall algorithm. However, we are not aware of any published study of the effects of random restarts in the MERT optimization search.

We first compare a variant of Och's method with and without multiple starting points for the optimization search, selecting initial starting points randomly according to a uniform distribution. We find that using multiple random restarts can substantially improve the resulting model in terms of translation quality as measured by the BLEU metric, but that training time also increases substantially. We next try selecting starting points by a random walk from the last local optimum reached, rather than by sampling from a uniform distribution. We find this provides a slight additional improvement in BLEU score, and is significantly faster, although still slower than training without random restarts.

Finally we look at two methods for speeding up training by pruning the set of hypotheses considered. We find that, under some circumstances, this can speed up training so that it takes very little additional time compared to the original method without restarts, with no significant reduction in BLEU score compared to the best training methods in our experiments.

2 Och's MERT procedure

While minimum error rate training for SMT is theoretically possible by directly applying general numerical optimization techniques, such as the downhill simplex method or Powell's method

(Press, 2002), naive use of these techniques would involve repeated translation of the training sentences using hundreds or thousands of combinations of feature weights, which is clearly impractical given the speed of most SMT decoders.

Och's optimization method saves expensive SMT decoding time by generating lists of n-best translation hypotheses, and their feature values according to the SMT model, and then optimizing feature weights just with respect to those hypotheses. In this way, as many different feature weight settings as necessary can be explored without re-running the decoder. The translation quality measurement for the training corpus can be estimated for a given point in feature weight space by finding the highest scoring translation hypothesis, out of the current set of hypotheses, for each sentence in the training set. This is typically orders of magnitude faster than re-running the decoder for each combination of feature weights.

Since the resulting feature weights are optimized only for one particular set of translation hypotheses, the decoder may actually produce different results when run with those weights. Therefore Och iterates the process, re-running the decoder with the optimized feature weights to produce new sets of n-best translation hypotheses, merging these with the previous sets of hypotheses, and re-optimizing the feature weights relative to the expanded hypothesis sets. This process is repeated until no more new hypotheses are obtained for any sentence in the training set.

Another innovation by Och is a method of numerical optimization that takes advantage of the fact that, while translation quality metrics may have continous values, they are always applied to the discrete outputs of a translation decoder. This means that any measure of translation quality can change with variation in feature weights only at discrete points where the decoder output changes.

Och takes advantage of this through an efficient procedure for finding all the points along a one-dimensional line in feature weight space at which the highest scoring translation hypothesis changes, given the current set of hypotheses for a particular sentence. By merging the lists of such points for all sentences in the training set, he finds all the points at which the highest scoring hypothesis changes for any training sentence.

Finding the optimal value of the feature weights along the line being optimized then requires simply evaluating the translation quality metric for each range of values for the feature weights between two such consecutive points. This can be done efficiently by tracking incremental changes in the sufficient statistics for the translation quality metric as we iterate through the points where things change. Och uses this procedure as a line search method in an iterative optimization procedure, until no additional improvement in the translation quality metric is obtained, given the current sets of translation hypotheses.

3 Optimization with Random Restarts

Although Och's line search is globally optimal, this is not sufficient to guarantee that a series of line searches will find the globally optimal combination of all feature weights. To avoid getting stuck at an inferior local optimum during MERT, it is usual to perform multiple optimization searches over each expanded set of translation hypotheses starting from different initial points. Typically, one of these points is the best point found while optimizing over the previous set of translation hypotheses.[1] Additional starting points are then selected by independently choosing initial values for each feature weight according to a uniform distribution over a fixed interval, say -1.0 to $+1.0$. The best point reached, starting from either the previous optimum or one of the random restart points, is selected as the optimum for the current set of hypotheses. This widely-used procedure is described by Koehn et al. (2007, p. 50).

3.1 Preliminary evaluation

In our first experiments, we compared a variant of Och's MERT procedure with and without random restarts as described above. For our training and test data we used the English-French subset of the Europarl corpus provided for the shared task (Koehn and Monz, 2006) at the Statistical Machine Translation workshop held in conjunction with the 2006 HLT-NAACL conference. We built a standard baseline phrasal SMT system, as described by Koehn et al. (2003), for translating from English to French (E-to-F), using the word alignments and French target language model provided by the workshop organizers.

We trained a model with the standard eight features: E-to-F and F-to-E phrase translation log

[1]Since additional hypotheses have been added, initiating an optimization search from this point on the new set of hypotheses will often lead to a higher local optimum.

probabilities, E-to-F and F-to-E phrase translation lexical scores, French language model log probabilities, phrase pair count, French word count, and distortion score. Feature weight optimization was performed on the designated 2000-sentence-pair development set, and the resulting feature weights were evaluated on the designated 2000-sentence-pair development test set, using the BLEU-4 metric with one reference translation per sentence.

At each decoding iteration we generated the 100-best translation hypotheses found by our phrasal SMT decoder. To generate the initial 100-best list, we applied the policy of setting the weights for features we expected to be positively correlated with BLEU to 1, the weights for features we expected to be negatively correlated with BLEU to -1, and the remaining weights to 0. In this case, we set the initial distortion score weight to -1, the phrase count weight to 0, and all other feature weights to 1.

We made a common modification of the MERT procedure described by Och, by replacing Powell's method (Press, 2002) for selecting the directions in which to search the feature weight space, with simple co-ordinate ascent—following Koehn et al. (2007)—repeatedly optimizing one feature weight at a time while holding the others fixed, until all feature weights are at optimum values, given the values of the other feature weights. Powell's method is not designed to reach a better local optimum than co-ordinate ascent, but does have convergence guarantees under certain idealized conditions. However, we have observed informally that, in MERT, co-ordinate ascent always seems to converge relatively quickly, with Powell's method offering no clear advantage.

We also modified Och's termination test slightly. As noted above, Och suggests terminating the overall procedure when n-best decoding fails to produce any hypotheses that have not already been seen. Without random restarts, this will guarantee convergence because the last set of feature weights selected will still be a local optimum.[2] However, if we go through the coordinate ascent procedure without finding a better set of feature weights, then we do not have to perform the last iteration of n-best decoding, because it will necessarily produce the same n-best lists as the previous iteration, as long as the decoder is deterministic. Thus we can terminate the overall procedure if either we either fail to generate any new hypotheses in n-best decoding, or the optimium set of feature weights does not change in the coordinate ascent phase of training. In fact, we relax the termination test a bit more than this, and terminate if no feature weight changes by more than 1.0%.

Without random restarts, we found that MERT converged in 8 decoding iterations, with the resulting model producing a BLEU score of 31.12 on the development test set. For the experiment with random restarts, after each iteration of 100-best decoding, we searched from 20 initial points, 19 points selected by uniform sampling over the interval $[-1, 1]$ for each feature weight, plus the optimum point found for the previous set of hypotheses. This procedure converged in 10 decoding iterations, with a BLEU score of 32.02 on the development test set, an improvement of 0.90 BLEU, compared to MERT without random restarts.

While the difference in BLEU score with and without random restarts was substantial, training with random restarts took much longer. With our phrasal decoder and our MERT implementation, optimizing feature weights took 3894 seconds without random restarts and 12690 seconds with random restarts.[3] We therefore asked the question whether there was some other way to invest extra time in training feature weights that might be just as effective as performing random restarts. The obvious thing to try is using larger n-best lists, so we re-ran the training without random restarts, using n-best lists of 200 and 300.

Using n-best lists of 200 produced a noticeable improvement in training without restarts, converging in 9 decoding iterations taking 7877 seconds, and producing a BLEU score of 31.83 on the development test set. Using n-best lists of 300 converged in 8 decoding iterations taking 8973 seconds, but the BLEU score on the development test set fell back to 31.16. Thus, simply increasing the size of the n-best list does not seem to be a reliable method for improving the results obtained by MERT without random restarts.

4 Random Walk Restarts

In the procedure described above, the initial values for each feature weight are independently sampled

[2]With random restarts, there can be no guarantee of convergence, unless we have a true global optimization method, or we enumerate all possible hypotheses permitted by the model.

[3]Timings are for single-threaded execution using a desktop PC with 3.60 GHz Intel Xeon processors.

from a uniform distribution over the range $[-1, 1]$. We have observed anecdotally, however, that if the selected starting point itself produces a BLEU score much below the best we have seen so far, coordinate ascent search is very unlikely to take us to a point that is better than the current best. In order to bias the selection of restarting points towards better scores, we select starting points by random walk from the ending point of the last coordinate ascent search.

The idea is to perform a series of cautious steps in feature weight space guided by training set BLEU. We begin the walk at the ending point of the last coordinate ascent search; let us call this point $\vec{w}^{(0)}$. Each step updates the feature weights in a manner inspired by Metropolis-Hastings sampling (Hastings, 1970). Starting from the current feature weight vector $\vec{w}^{(i)}$, we sample a small update from a multivariate Gaussian distribution with mean of 0 and diagonal covariance matrix $\sigma^2 I$. This update is added to the current value to produce a new potential feature weight vector. The BLEU scores for the old and the new feature weight vector are compared. The new feature weight vector is always accepted if the BLEU score on the training set is improved; however if the BLEU score drops, the new vector is accepted with a probability that depends on how close the new BLEU score is to the previous one. After a fixed number of steps, the walk is terminated, and we produce a value to use as the initial point for the next round of coordinate ascent.

There are several wrinkles, however. First, we prefer that the scores not fall substantially during the random walk. Therefore we establish a baseline value of $m = \text{BLEU}(\vec{w}^{(0)}) - 0.005$ (i.e., 1/2 BLEU point below the initial value) and do not allow a step to go below this baseline value. To ensure this, each step progresses as follows:

$$\begin{aligned} \vec{d}^{(i)} &\sim \text{GAUSSIAN}(0, \sigma^2 I) \\ \vec{v}^{(i)} &= \vec{w}^{(i)} + \vec{d}^{(i)} \\ u^{(i)} &\sim \text{UNIFORM}(0, 1) \\ \vec{w}^{(i+1)} &= \begin{cases} \vec{v}^{(i)} & \text{if } \frac{\text{BLEU}(\vec{v}^{(i)}) - m}{\text{BLEU}(\vec{w}^{(i)}) - m} \geq u^{(i)} \\ \vec{w}^{(i)} & \text{otherwise.} \end{cases} \end{aligned}$$

With this update rule, we know that $\vec{w}^{(i+1)}$ will never go below m, since the initial value is not below m, and any step moving below m will result in a negative ratio and therefore not be accepted.

So far, σ^2 is left as a free parameter. An initial value of 0.001 performs well in our experience, though in general it may result in steps that are consistently too small (so that only a very local neighborhood is explored) or too large (so that the vast majority of steps are rejected). Therefore we devote the first half of the steps to "burn-in"; that is, tuning the variance parameter so that approximately 60% of the steps are accepted. During burn-in, we compute the acceptance rate after each step. If it is less than 60%, we multiply σ^2 by 0.99; if greater, we multiply by 1.01.

The final twist is in selection of the point used for the next iteration of coordinate ascent. Rather than using the final point of the random walk $\vec{w}^{(n)}$, we return the feature weight vector that achieved the highest BLEU score after burn-in: $\vec{w}^\star = \arg\max_{\vec{w}^{(i)}, n/2 < i \leq n} \text{BLEU}(\vec{w})$. This ensures that the new feature weight vector has a relatively high objective function value yet is likely very different from the initial point.

4.1 Preliminary evaluation

To evaluate the random walk selection procedure, we used a similar experimental set-up to the previous one, testing on the 2006 English-French Europarl corpus, using n-best lists of 100, and 20 starting points for each coordinate ascent search—one being the best point found for the previous hypothesis set, and the other 19 selected by our random walk procedure. We set the number of steps to be used in each random walk to 500. This procedure converged in 6 decoding iterations taking 8458 seconds, with a BLEU score of 32.13 on the development test set. This is an improvement of 0.11 BLEU over the uniform random restart method, and it also took only 67% as much time. The speed up was due to the fact that random walk method converged in 2 fewer decoding iterations, although the average time per iteration was greater (1410 seconds vs. 1269 seconds) because of the extra time needed for the random walk.

5 Hypothesis Set Pruning

MERT with random walk restarts seems to produce better models than either MERT with uniform random restarts or with no restarts, but it is still slower than MERT with no restarts by more than a factor of 2. The difference between 3894 seconds (1.08 hours) and 8458 seconds (2.35 hours) to optimize feature weights may not seem important, given how long the rest of the process of building and training an SMT system takes; however, to truly optimize an SMT system would actually require performing feature weight training many times to find optimum values of hyper-parameters such as maximum phrase size and distortion limit. This kind of optimization is rarely done for every small model change, because of how long feature weight optimization takes; so it seems well worth the effort to speed up the optimization process as much as possible.

To try to speed up the feature weight optimization process, we have tried pruning the set of hypotheses that MERT is applied to. The time taken by the random walk and coordinate ascent phases of MERT with random walk restarts is roughly linear in the number of translation hypotheses examined. In the experiment described in Section 4.1, after the first 100-best decoding iteration there were 196,319 hypotheses in the n-best lists, and MERT took 347 seconds. After merging all hypotheses from 6 iterations of 100-best decoding there were 800,580 hypotheses, and MERT took 1380 seconds.

We conjectured that a large proportion of these hypotheses are both low scoring according to most submodels and low in measured translation quality, so that omitting them would make little difference to the feature weight optimization optimization process.[4] We attempt to identify such hypotheses by extracting some additional information from Och's line search procedure.

Och's line search procedure takes note of every hypothesis that is the highest scoring hypothesis for a particular sentence for some value of the feature weight being optimized by the line search. The hypotheses that are never the highest scoring hypothesis for any combination of feature values explored effectively play no role in the MERT procedure. We conjectured that hypotheses that are never selected as potentially highest scoring in a particular round of MERT could be pruned from the hypothesis set without adversely affecting the quality of the feature weights eventually produced.

We tested two implementations of this type of hypothesis pruning. In the more conservative implementation, after each decoding iteration, we note all the hypotheses that are ever "touched" (i.e., ever the highest scoring) during the coordinate ascent search either from the initial starting point or from one of the random restarts. Any hypothesis that is never touched is pruned from the sets of hypotheses that are merged with the results of subsequent n-best decoding iterations. We refer to this as "post-restart" pruning.

In the more aggressive implementation, after each decoding iteration, we note all the hypotheses that are touched during the coordinate ascent search from the initial starting point. The hypotheses that are not touched are pruned from the hypothesis set before any random restarts. We refer to this as "pre-restart" pruning.

5.1 Preliminary evaluation

We evaluated both post- and pre-restart pruning with random walk restarts, under the same conditions used to evaluate random walk restarts without pruning. With post-restart pruning, feature weight training converged in 8 decoding iterations taking 7790 seconds, with a BLEU score of 32.14 on the development test set. The last set of restarts of MERT had 276,134 hypotheses to consider, a reduction of more than 65% compared to no pruning. With pre-restart pruning, feature weight training converged in 7 decoding iterations taking 4556 seconds, with a BLEU score of 32.17 on the development test set. The last set of restarts of MERT had only 64,346 hypotheses to consider, a reduction of 92% compared to no pruning.

Neither method of pruning degraded translation quality as measured by BLEU; in fact, BLEU scores increased by a trivial amount with pruning. Post-restart pruning speeded up training only slightly, primarily because it took more decoding iterations to converge. Time per decoding iteration was reduced from 1409 seconds to 974 seconds. Pre-restart pruning was substantially faster overall, as well as in terms of time per decoding iteration, which was 650 seconds.

Additional insight into the differences between feature weight optimization methods can be gained by evaluating the feature weight sets produced after each decoding iteration. Figure 1 plots the BLEU score obtained on the development test set as a function of the cumulative time taken to produce the corresponding feature weights, for each of the training runs we have described so far.

We observe a clear gap between the results obtained from random walk restarts and those from either uniform random restarts or no restarts. Note in particular that, although the uniform ran-

[4]Hypotheses that are of low translation quality, but high scoring according to some submodels, need to be retained so that the feature weights are tuned to avoid selecting them.

Restart Method	Pruning Method	Num Starts	Num N-best	Decoding Iterations	Total Seconds	MERT Seconds	Dev-test BLEU	Conf Level
none	none	1	100	8	3894	276	31.12	> 0.999
none	none	1	300	8	8973	1173	31.17	> 0.999
none	none	1	200	9	7877	717	31.83	0.999
uniform rand	none	5	100	7	4294	917	31.95	0.993
uniform rand	none	30	100	11	19345	13306	31.98	0.995
uniform rand	none	20	100	10	12690	7613	32.02	0.984
uniform rand	none	10	100	10	9059	3898	32.02	0.984
random walk	pre-restart	30	100	12	9963	3016	32.04	0.999
random walk	pre-restart	5	100	11	7696	619	32.10	0.962
random walk	none	30	100	7	14055	10887	32.10	0.959
random walk	pre-restart	10	100	14	8581	1254	32.10	0.986
random walk	post-restart	10	100	9	6985	2236	32.11	0.938
random walk	none	20	100	6	8458	5766	32.13	0.909
random walk	post-restart	20	100	8	7790	3965	32.14	0.857
random walk	none	10	100	8	8338	4280	32.15	0.840
random walk	pre-restart	20	100	7	4556	1179	32.17	0.712
random walk	post-restart	5	100	10	6103	1114	32.18	0.794
random walk	post-restart	30	100	8	9811	6218	32.20	0.554
random walk	none	5	100	10	7741	3047	32.21	0.000

Table 1: Extended Evaluation Results.

dom restart method eventually comes within 0.15 BLEU points of the best result using random walk restarts, it takes far longer to get there. The uniform restart run produces noticably inferior BLEU scores until just before convergence, while with the random walk method, the BLEU score increases quite quickly and then stays essentially flat for several iterations before convergence.

We also note that there appears to be less real difference among our three variations on random walk restarts than there might seem to be from their times to convergence. Although pre-restart pruning was much faster to convergence than either of the other variants, all three reached approximately the same BLEU score in the same amount of time, if intermediate points are considered. This suggests that our convergence test, while more liberal than Och's, still may be more conservative than necessary when using random walk restarts.

6 Extended Evaluation

We now extend the previous evaluations in two ways. First, we repeat all the experiments on optimization with 20 starting points, using 5, 10, and 30 starting points, to see whether we can trade off training time for translation quality by changing that parameter setting, and if so, whether any settings seem clearly better than others.

Second, we note that different optimization methods lead to convergence at different numbers of decoding iterations. This means that which method produces the shortest total training time will depend on the relative time taken by n-best decoding and the MERT procedure itself (including the random walk selection procedure, if that is used). By co-incidence, these times happened to be roughly comparable in our experiments.[5] In a situation where decoding is much slower than MERT, however, the main determinant of overall training time would be how many decoding iterations are needed. On the other hand, if decoding was made much faster, say, through algorithmic improvements or by using a compute cluster, total training time would be dominated by MERT proper. We therefore report number of decoding iterations to convergence and pure MERT time (excluding decoding and hypothesis set merging) for each of our experiments, in addition to total feature weight training time.

Table 1 reports these three measures of com-

[5] In our complete set of training experiments encompassing 187 decoding iterations, decoding averaged 521 seconds per iteration, and MERT (excluding decoding and hypothesis set merging) averaged 421 seconds per (decoding) iteration.

putational effort, plus BLEU score on the development test set, sorted by ascending BLEU score, for 19 variations on MERT: 3 n-best list sizes for MERT without restarts, and 4 different numbers of restarts for 4 different versions of MERT with restarts (uniform random selection, random walk selection without pruning, random walk selection with post-restart pruning, and random walk selection with pre-restart pruning).

The final column of Table 1 is a confidence score reflecting the estimated probability that the translation model produced (at convergence) by the MERT variant for that row of the table is *not* as good in terms of BLEU score as the variant that yielded the highest BLEU score (at convergence) that we observed in these experiments. These probabilities were estimated by Koehn's (2004) paired bootstrap resampling method, run for at least 100,000 samples per comparison.

The 11 models obtaining a BLEU score of 31.10 or less are all estimated to be at least 95% likely to have worse translation quality than the best scoring model. We therefore dismiss these models from further consideration,[6] including all models trained without random restarts, as well as all models trained with uniform random restarts, leaving only models trained with random walk restarts.

With random walk restarts, post-restart pruning remains under consideration at all numbers of restarts tried. For random walk restarts without pruning, only the model produced by 30 starting points has been eliminated, and for pre-restart pruning, only the model produced by 20 starts remains under consideration. This suggests that pre-restart pruning may be too aggressive and, thus, overly sensitive to the number of restarts.

To get a better picture of the remaining 8 models, see Figures 2–4. Despite convergence times ranging from 4456 to 9811 seconds, in Figure 2 we observe that, if feature weights after each decoding iteration are considered, the relationships between training time and BLEU score are remarkably similar. In Figure 3, BLEU score varies considerably up to 3 decoding iterations, but above that, BLEU scores are very close, and almost flat. In fact, we see almost no benefit from more than 7 decoding iterations for any model.

Finally, Figure 4 shows some noticeable differences between random walk variants in respect to MERT time proper. Thus, while the choice of random walk variant chosen may matter little if decoding is slow, it seems that it can have an important impact if decoding is fast. If we combine the results shown here with the observation from Figure 3 that there seems to be no benefit to trying more than 7 decoding iterations, it appears that perhaps the best trade-off between translation quality and training time would be obtained by using post-restart pruning, with 5 starting points per decoding iteration, cutting off training after 7 iterations. This took a total of 4009 seconds to train, compared to 7741 seconds for the highest scoring model on the development test set considered in Table 1 (produced by random walk restarts with no pruning, 5 starting points per decoding iteration, at convergence after 10 iterations).

To validate the proposal to use the suggested faster training procedure, we compared the two models under discussion on the 2000 in-domain sentence pairs for the designated final test set for our corpus. The model produced by the suggested training procedure resulted in a BLEU score of 31.92, with the model that scored highest on the development test set scoring an insignificantly worse 31.89. In contast, the highest scoring model of the three trained with no restarts produced a BLEU score of 31.55 on the final test set, which was worse than either of the random walk methods evaluated on the final test set, at confidence levels exceeding 0.996 according to the paired bootstrap resampling test.

7 Conclusions

We believe that our results show very convincingly that using random restarts in MERT improves the BLEU scores produced by the resulting models. They also seem to show that starting point selection by random walk is slightly superior to uniform random selection. Finally, our experiments suggest that time to carry out MERT can be significantly reduced by using as few as 5 starting points per decoding iteration, performing post-restart pruning of hypothesis sets, and cutting off training after a fixed number of decoding iterations (perhaps 7) rather than waiting for convergence.

References

Hastings, W. Keith. 1970. Monte Carlo sampling methods using Markov chains and their applications. *Biometrika* 57: 97–109.

[6]We estimate the joint probability that these 11 models are all worse than our best scoring model to be 0.882, by multiplying the confidence scores for all these models.

Koehn, Philipp, and Christof Monz. 2006. Manual and automatic evaluation of machine translation between European languages. In *Proceedings of the Workshop on Statistical Machine Translation*, New York City, USA, 102–121.

Koehn, Philipp, Franz Josep Och, and Daniel Marcu. 2003. Statistical Phrase-Based Translation. In *Proceedings of Human Language Technology Conference of the North American Chapter of the Association for Computational Linguistics*, Edmondton, Alberta, Canada, 127–133.

Koehn, Philipp. 2004. Statistical significance tests for machine translation evaluation. In *Proceedings of the 2004 Conference on Empirical Methods in Natural Language Processing*, Barcelona, Spain, 388–395.

Koehn, Philipp, et al. 2007. *Open Source Toolkit for Statistical Machine Translation: Factored Translation Models and Confusion Network Decoding*. Final Report of the 2006 Language Engineering Workshop, Johns Hopkins University, Center for Speech and Language Processing.

Och, Franz Josef. 2003. Minimum error rate training in statistical machine translation. In *Proceedings of the 41st Annual Meeting of the Association for Computational Linguistics*, Sapporo, Japan, 160–167.

Press, William H., et al. 2002. *Numerical Recipes in C++*. Cambridge University Press, Cambridge, UK.

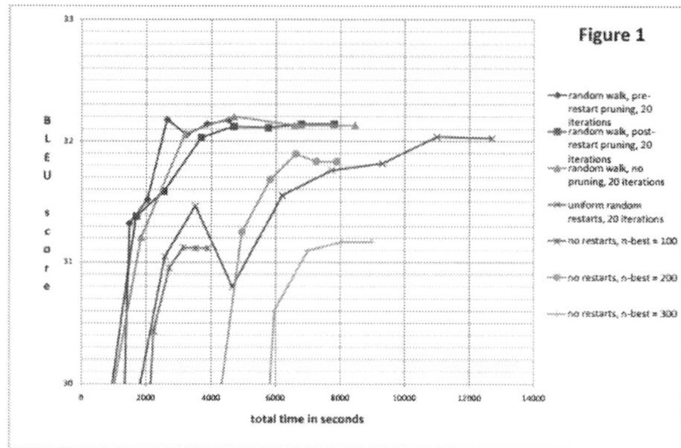

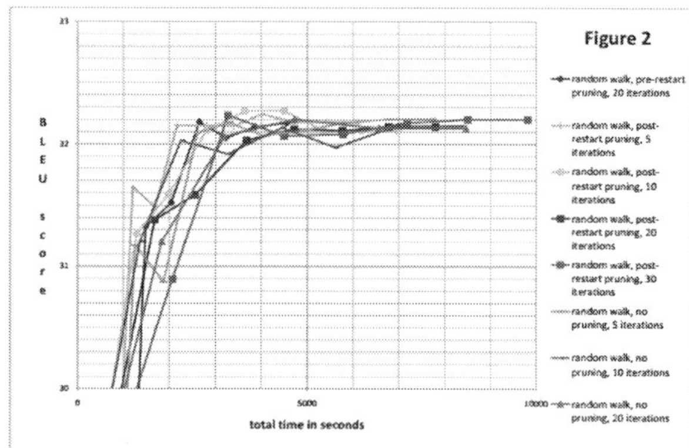

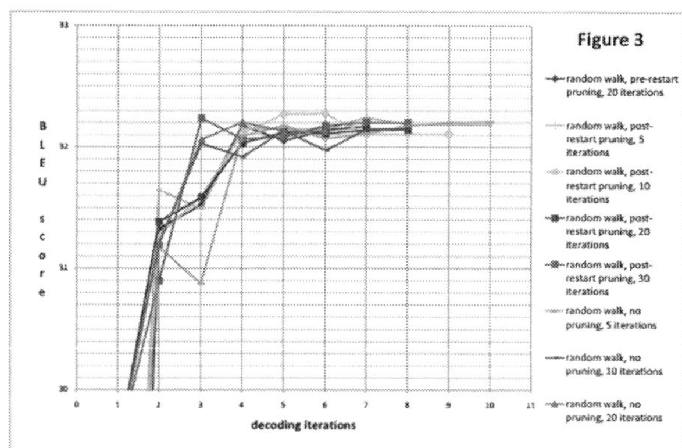

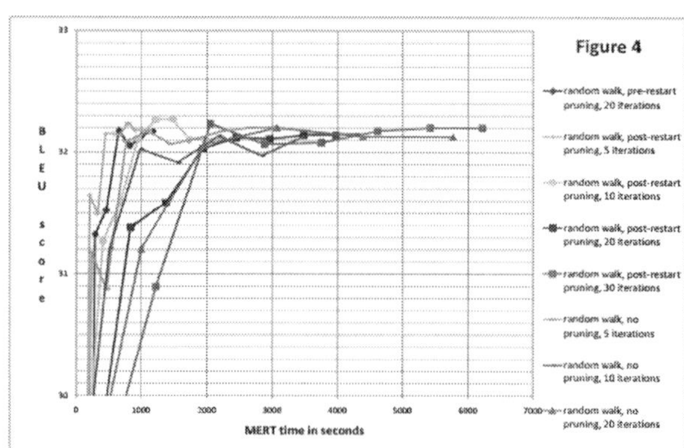

Robust Similarity Measures for Named Entities Matching

Erwan Moreau[1]
Institut Télécom ParisTech
& LTCI CNRS
erwan.moreau@enst.fr

François Yvon
Univ. Paris Sud
& LIMSI CNRS
yvon@limsi.fr

Olivier Cappé
Institut Télécom ParisTech
& LTCI CNRS
cappe@enst.fr

Abstract

Matching coreferent named entities without prior knowledge requires good similarity measures. Soft-TFIDF is a fine-grained measure which performs well in this task. We propose to enhance this kind of metrics, through a generic model in which measures may be mixed, and show experimentally the relevance of this approach.

1 Introduction

In this paper, we study the problem of matching coreferent named entities (NE in short) in text collections, focusing primarily on orthographic variations in nominal groups (we do not handle the case of pronominal references). Identifying textual variations in entities is useful in many text mining and/or information retrieval tasks (see for example (Pouliquen et al., 2006)). As described in the literature (e.g. (Christen, 2006)), textual differences between entities are due to various reasons: typographical errors, names written in different ways (with/without first name/title, etc.), abbreviations, lack of precision in organization names, transliterations, etc. For example, one wants *"Mr. Rumyantsev"* to match with *"Alexander Rumyanstev"* but not with *"Mr. Ryabev"*. Here we do not address the related problem of disambiguation[2] (e.g. knowing whether a given occurrence of *"George Bush"* refers to the 41st or 43rd president of the USA), because it is technically very different from the matching problem.

There are different ways to tackle the problem of NE matching: the first and certainly most reliable one consists in studying the specific features of the data, and then use any available tool to design a specialized method for the matching task. This approach will generally take advantage of language-specific (e.g. in (Freeman et al., 2006)) and domain-specific knowledge, of any external resources (e.g. database, names dictionaries, etc.), and of any information about the entities to process, e.g. their type (person name, organization, etc.), or internal structure (e.g. in (Prager et al., 2007)). In such an in-depth approach, supervised learning is helpful: it has been used for example in a database context[3] in (Bilenko et al., 2003), but this approach requires labeled data which is usually costly. All those data specific appproaches would necessitate some sort of human expertise.

The second approach is the *robust* one: we propose here to try to match any kind of NE, extracted from "real world" (potentially noisy) sources, without any kind of prior knowledge[4]. One looks for coreferent NE, whatever their type, source, language[5] or quality[6]. Such robust similarity methods may be useful for a lot of generic tasks, in which maximum accuracy is not the main criterion, or simply where the required resources are not available.

The literature on string comparison metrics is abundant, containing both general techniques and

© 2008. Licensed under the *Creative Commons Attribution-Noncommercial-Share Alike 3.0 Unported* license (http://creativecommons.org/licenses/by-nc-sa/3.0/). Some rights reserved.

[1]Now at LIPN - Univ. Paris 13 & UMR CNRS 7030.

[2]Which is essential in the Web People Search task.

[3]The matching task is quite different in this framework, because one observes records (structured information).

[4]In this kind of knowledge are included the need for hand-tuning parameters or defining specific thresholds.

[5]Actually we have only studied English and French (our approach is neither "multilingual", in the sense that it is not specific to multilingual documents).

[6]In particular, this task clearly depends on the NE recognition step, which may introduce errors.

more linguistically motivated measures, see e.g. (Cohen et al., 2003) for a review. From a bird's eye view, these measures can be sorted in two classes: "Sequential character-based methods" and "Bag-of-words methods"[7]. Both classes show relevant results, but do not capture the same kind of similarity. In a robust approach for NE matching, one needs a more fine-grained method, which performs at least as well as bag-of-words methods, without ignoring coreferent pairs that such methods miss.

A first attempt in this direction was introduced in (Cohen et al., 2003), in the form of a measure called *Soft-TFIDF*. We will show that this measure has theoretical pitfalls and a few practical drawbacks. Nevertheless, Soft-TFIDF outperforms the better standard string similarity measures in the NE matching task. That is why we propose to generalize and improve its principle, and show experimentally that this approach is relevant.

In section 2 we introduce standard similarity measures and enhance the definition of Soft-TFIDF. Then we define a generic model in which similarity measures may be combined (section 3). Finally, section 4 shows that experiments with two different corpora validate our approach.

2 Approximate matching methods

We present below some of the main string similarity measures used to match named entities (Christen, 2006; Cohen et al., 2003; Bilenko et al., 2003).

2.1 Classical metrics

2.1.1 Sequential character based methods

Levenshtein edit distance. This well-known distance metric d represents the minimum number of insertions, deletions or substitutions needed to transform a string x into another string y. For example, $d(kitten, sitting) = 3$ ($k \mapsto s$, $e \mapsto i$, $\varepsilon \mapsto g$). The corresponding normalized similarity measure is defined as $s = 1 - d/max(|x|, |y|)$. A lot of variants and/or improvements exist (Navarro, 2001), among which:

- *Damerau.* One basic edit operation is added: a *transposition* consists in swapping two characters;
- *Needleman-Wunch.* Basic edit operation costs are parameterized: G is the cost of a gap (insertion or deletion), and there is a function $cost(c, c')$ which gives the cost of substituting c with c' for any pair of characters (c, c').

Jaro metric (Winkler, 1999). This measure is based on the number and the order of common characters. Given two strings $x = a_1 \dots a_n$ and $y = b_1 \dots b_m$, let $H = \min(n, m)/2$: a_i is *in common* with y if there exists b_j in y such that $a_i = b_j$ and $i - H \leq j \leq i + H$. Let $x' = a'_1 \dots a'_{n'}$ (resp. $y' = b'_1 \dots b'_{m'}$) be the sequence of characters from x (resp. y) in common with y (resp. x), in the order they appear in x (resp. y). Any position i such that $a'_i \neq b'_i$ is called a *transposition*. Let T be the number of transpositions between x' and y' divided by 2:

$$Jaro(x, y) = \frac{1}{3} \times \left(\frac{|x'|}{|x|} + \frac{|y'|}{|y|} + \frac{|y'| - T}{|y'|} \right)$$

2.1.2 Bag-of-words methods

With these methods, each NE is represented as a set of *features* (generally words or characters n-grams[8]). Let $X = \{x_i\}_{1 \leq i \leq n}$ and $Y = \{y_i\}_{1 \leq i \leq m}$ be the sets representing the entities x, y. Simplest measures only count the number of elements in common[9], e.g:

$$Overlap(x, y) = \frac{|X \cap Y|}{min(|X|, |Y|)}$$

Some more subtle techniques are based on a vector representation of entities x and y, which may take into account parameters that are are not included in the sets themselves. Let $A = (a_1, \dots, a_{|\Sigma|})$ and $B = (b_1, \dots, b_{|\Sigma|})$ be such vectors[10], the widely used cosine similarity is:

$$cos(A, B) = \frac{\sum_{i=1}^{|\Sigma|} a_i b_i}{\sqrt{\sum_{i=1}^{|\Sigma|} a_i^2} \sqrt{\sum_{i=1}^{|\Sigma|} b_i^2}}$$

Traditionally, TF-IDF weights are used in vectors (*Term Frequency-Inverse Document Frequency*). In the NE case, this value represents the importance each feature w (e.g. word) has for an entity x belonging to the set E of entities:

$$\mathrm{tf}(w, x) = \frac{n_{w,x}}{\sum_{w' \in \Sigma} n_{w',x}}, \mathrm{idf}(w) = \log \frac{|E|}{|\{x \in E | w \in x\}|},$$

$$\mathrm{tfidf}(w, x) = \mathrm{tf}(w, x) \times \mathrm{idf}(w).$$

with $n_{w,x}$ the number of times w appears in x. Thus the similarity score is $\mathrm{CosTFIDF}(x, y) = Cos(A, B)$, where each a_i (resp. b_i) in A (resp. in B) is $\mathrm{tfidf}(w_i, x)$ (resp. $\mathrm{tfidf}(w_i, y)$).

[7] We omit measures based on phonetic similarity such as Soundex, because they are language-specific and/or type-specific (person names).

[8] In the remaining the term *n-grams* is always used for *characters n-grams*.

[9] $|E|$ denotes the number of elements in E.

[10] Σ is the vocabulary, containing all possible features.

2.2 Special measures for NE matching

Experiments show that sequential character-based measures catch mainly coreferent pairs of long NE that differ only by a few characters. Bag-of-words methods suit better to the NE matching problem, since they are more flexible about word order and position. But a lot of coreferent pairs can not be identified by such measures, because of small differences between words: for example, *"Director ElBaradei"* and *"Director-General ElBareidi"* is out of reach for such methods. That is why "second level" measures are relevant: their principle is to apply a sub-measure sim' to all pairs of words between the two NE and to compute a final score based on these values. This approach is possible because NE generally contain only a few words.

Monge-Elkan measure belongs to this category: it simply computes the average of the better pairs of words according to the sub-measure:

$$sim(x, y) = \frac{1}{n} \sum_{i=1}^{n} \max_{j=1}^{m}(sim'(x_i, y_j)).$$

But experiments show that Monge-Elkan does not perform well. Actually, its very simple behavior favors too much short entities, because averaging penalizes a lot every non-matching word.

A more elaborated measure is proposed in (Cohen et al., 2003): *Soft-TFIDF* is intended precisely to take advantage of the good results obtained with Cosine/TFIDF, without automatically discarding words which are not strictly identical. The original definition is the following: let CLOSE(θ, X, Y) be the set of words $w \in X$ such that there exists a word $v \in Y$ such that $sim'(w, v) > \theta$. Let $N(w, Y) = \max(\{sim'(w, v) | v \in Y\})$. For any $w \in$ CLOSE(θ, X, Y), let

$S_{w,X,Y} = weight(w, X) \cdot weight(w, Y) \cdot N(w, Y)$, where $weight(w, Z) = \dfrac{\text{tfidf}(w, Z)}{\sqrt{\sum_{w \in Z} \text{tfidf}(w, Z)^2}}$.

Finally,

$$\text{SoftTFIDF}(X, Y) = \sum_{w \in \text{CLOSE}(\theta, X, Y)} S_{w,X,Y}.$$

This definition is not entirely correct, because $weight(w, Y) = 0$ if $w \notin Y$ (in other words, w must appear in both X and Y, thus SoftTFIDF(X, Y) would always be equal to CosTFIDF(X, Y)). We propose instead the following corrected definition, which corresponds to the implementation the authors provided in the package SecondString[11]:

Let CLOSEST$(\theta, w, Z) = \{v \in Z \mid \forall v' \in Z : sim'(w, v) \geq sim'(w, v') \wedge sim'(w, v) > \theta\}$.

$$\text{SoftTFIDF}(X, Y) = \sum_{w \in X} weight(w, X) \cdot \alpha_{w,Y},$$

where $\alpha_{w,Z} = 0$ if CLOSEST$(\theta, w, Z) = \emptyset$, and $\alpha_{w,Z} = weight(w', Z) \cdot sim'(w, w')$ otherwise, with[12] $w' \in$ CLOSEST(θ, w, Z).

As one may see, SoftTFIDF relies on the same principle than Monge-Elkan: for each word x_i in the first entity, find a word y_j in the second one that maximizes $sim'(x_i, y_j)$. Therefore, these measures have both the drawback not to be symmetric. Furthermore, there is another theoretical pitfall with SoftTFIDF: in Monge-Elkan, the final score is simply normalized in $[0, 1]$ using the average among words of the first entity. According to the principle of the Cosine angle of TF-IDF-weighted vectors, SoftTFIDF uses both vectors norms. However the way words are "approximately matched" does not forbid the matching of a given word in the second entity twice: in this case, normalization is wrong because this word is counted only once in the norm of the second vector. Consequently there is a potential overflow: actually it is not hard to find simple examples where the final score is greater than 1, even if this case is unlikely with real NE and a high threshold θ.

3 Generalizing Soft-TFIDF

3.1 A unifying framework for similarity measures

We propose to formalize similarity measures in the generic model below. This model is intended to define, compare and possibly mix different kinds of measures. The underlying idea is simply that most measures may be viewed as a process following different steps: representation as a sequence of features[13] (e.g. tokenization), alignment and a way to compute the final score. We propose to define a similarity measure sim through these three steps, each of them is modeled as a function[14]:

Representation. Given a set F of *features*, let features$(e) = \langle a_1, \ldots, a_n \rangle$ be a function that as-

[11] http://secondstring.sourceforge.net

[12] If $|$CLOSEST$(\theta, w, Z)| > 1$, pick any such w' in the set. In the case of matching words between NE, this should almost never happen.

[13] We use the word *feature* for the sake of generality.

[14] Of course, alternative definitions may be relevant. In particular one may wish to allow the alignment function to return a set of graphs instead of only one. In the same way, one may wish to add a special vertex ε to the graph, in order to represent the fact that a feature is not matched by adding an edge between this feature and ε.

signs an (ordered) sequence of features to any entity e ($a_i \in F$ for any i). Features may be of any kind (e.g. characters, words, n-grams, or even contextual elements of the entity) ;

Alignment. Given a function $sim^F : F^2 \mapsto \mathbb{R}$ which defines similarity between any pair of features, let $align(\langle a_1, \dots, a_n \rangle, \langle a'_1, \dots, a'_{n'} \rangle) = G$ be a function which assigns a graph G to any pair of features sequences. $G = (V, E)$ is a bipartite weighted graph where:

- The set of vertices is $V = A \cup A'$, where A and A' are the partitions defined as $A = \{v_1, \dots, v_n\}$ and $A' = \{v'_1, \dots, v'_{n'}\}$. Each v_i (resp. v'_i) represents (the position of) the corresponding feature a_i (resp. a'_i) ;
- The set of weighted edges is $E = \{(v_{i_j}, v'_{i'_j}, s_j)\}_{1 \le j \le |E|}$, where $v_{i_j} \in A$, $v'_{i'_j} \in A'$. Weights s_j generally depend on $sim^F(a_{i_j}, a'_{i'_j})$.

Scoring. Finally $sim = score(G)$, where $score$ assigns a real value (possibly normalized in $[0, 1]$) to the alignment G.

The representation step is not particularly original, since different kinds of representation have already been used both with sequential methods and "bag-of-features" methods. However our model also entails an alignment step, which does not exist with bag-of-features methods. Actually, the alignment is implicit with such methods, and we will show that making it visible is essential in the case of NE matching.

In the remaining of this paper we will only consider normalized metrics (scores belong to $[0, 1]$).

3.2 Revisiting classical similarity measures

Measures presented in section 2 may be defined within the model presented above. This modelization is only intended to provide a theoretical viewpoint on the measures: for all practical purposes, standard implementations are clearly more efficient. Below we do not detail the representation step, because there is no difficulty with it, and also because it is interesting to consider that any measure may be used with different kinds of features, as we will show in the next section. Let $S = \langle a_1, \dots, a_n \rangle = \text{features}(e)$ and $S' = \langle a'_1, \dots, a'_{n'} \rangle = \text{features}(e')$ for any pair of entities (e, e').

3.2.1 Levenshtein-like similarity

The function $align_{lev}(S, S')$ is defined in the following way: let $\mathcal{G}_{lev}$ be the set of all graphs $G = (V, E)$ such that any pair of edges $(v_{i_j}, v'_{i'_j}, s_j), (v_{i_k}, v'_{i'_k}, s_k) \in E$ satisfies $(i_j < i_k \wedge i'_j < i'_k) \vee (i_j > i_k \wedge i'_j > i'_k)$. This constraint ensures that the sequential order of features is respected[15], and that no feature may be matched twice. In the simplest form of Levenshtein[16], $sim^F(a, b) = 1$ if $a = b$ and 0 otherwise: for any $(v_{i_j}, v'_{i'_j}, s_j) \in E$, $s_j = sim^F(a_{i_j}, a'_{i'_j})$. Let

$$sim(G) = M - n_g \cdot cost_g - |E| + \sum_{(v_{i_j}, v'_{i'_j}, s_j) \in E} s_j,$$

where $M = \max(n, n')$ and n_g is the number of vertices that are not connected (i.e. the number of inserted or deleted words). $cost_g = 1$ in the simple Levenshtein form, but may be a parameter in the Needleman-Wunch variant (gap cost). In brief, the principle in this definition is to count the positions where no edit operation is needed: thus maximizing $sim(G)$ is equivalent to minimizing the cost of an alignment:

$align_{lev}(S, S') = G$, where G is any graph such that $sim(G) = \max(\{sim(G') | G' \in \mathcal{G}_{lev}\})$.

Finally, the function $score_{lev}$ is simply defined as $score_{lev}(G) = sim(G) / \max(n, n')$. It is not hard to see that this definition is equivalent to the usual one (see section 2): basically, the graph represents the concept called *trace* in (Wagner and Fischer, 1974), except that the cost function is "reversed" to become a similarity function.

Figure 1: Example of Levenshtein alignment

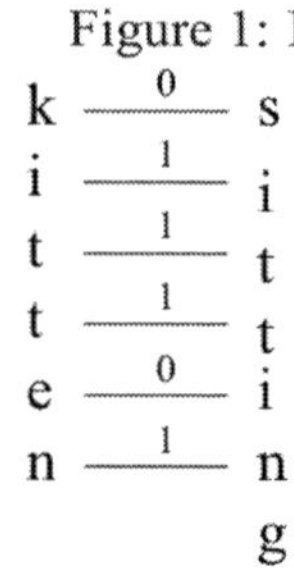

Suppose $cost_g = 1$:

$sim(G) = M - n_g - |E| + \sum_{e_j \in E} s_j$

$sim(G) = 7 - 1 - 6 + 4$

$sim(G) = 4$

$score_{lev}(G) = 4/7$.

3.2.2 Bag of features

For all simple measures using only sets of features, the function $align_{bag}(S, S')$ is defined in the following way: let $\mathcal{G}$ be the set of all graphs

[15] Constraints are a bit more complex for Damerau.

[16] In the Needleman-Wunch variant, sim^F should depend on the cost function, e.g.: $sim^F(a, b) = 1 - cost(a, b)$.

$G = (V, E)$ such that if $(v_{i_j}, v'_{i'_j}, s_j) \in E$ then $a_{i_j} = a'_{i'_j}$ (equivalently $sim^F(a_{i_j}, a'_{i'_j}) = 1$). Now let $once(\mathcal{G})$ be the set of all $G \in \mathcal{G}$ such that any pair of edges $(v_{i_j}, v'_{i'_j}, s_j), (v_{i_k}, v'_{i'_k}, s_k) \in E$ satisfies $i_j \neq i_k \wedge i'_j \neq i'_k$ (at most one match for each feature), and $a_{i_j} \neq a_{i_k}$ (a feature occurring several times is matched only once). Let $sim(G) = \sum_{(v_{i_j}, v'_{i'_j}, s_j) \in E} s_j$ for any $G = (V, E)$. $align_{bag}(S, S') = G$, where G is any graph such that $sim(G) = \max(\{sim(G') \mid G' \in once(\mathcal{G})\})$.

Since all weights are equal to 1, one may show that $sim(G) = |S \cap S'|$ for any $G \in once(\mathcal{G})$. Thus the $score$ function is simply used for normalization, depending on the given measure: for example, $score_{overlap}(G) = \dfrac{sim(G)}{\min(n, n')}$.

3.2.3 Soft-TFIDF

The case of Cosine measure with TFIDF weighted vectors is a bit different. Here we define the SoftTFIDF version: let $align_{soft}(S, S')$ be the graph $G = (V, E)$ defined as[17] $(v_{i_j}, v'_{i'_j}, s_j) \in E$ if and only if $a'_{i'_j} = select(\text{CLOSEST}(\theta, a_{i_j}, S'))$, where CLOSEST is the function defined in section 2 and $select(E)$ is a function returning the first element in E if $|E| > 0$, and is undefined otherwise[18]. For any such edge, the weight s_j is

$$s_j = sim^F(a_{i_j}, a'_{i'_j}) \cdot \frac{\text{idf}(a_{i_j})}{n} \cdot \frac{\text{idf}(a'_{i'_j})}{n'}.$$

Once again, let $sim(G) = \sum_{(v_{i_j}, v'_{i'_j}, s_j) \in E} s_j$.

$score_{soft}(G) = sim(G) / (\|S\| \cdot \|S'\|)$, where

$$\|\langle a_1, \ldots, a_n \rangle\| = \sqrt{\sum_{i=1}^{n} \left(\frac{\text{idf}(a_i)}{n} \right)^2}.$$

Although it is not explicitly used in this definition, term frequency is taken into account through the number of edges: suppose a given term t appears m times in S and m' times in S', all m vertices corresponding to t in A (the partition representing S) will be connected to all m' vertices corresponding to t in A'. Thus there will be $m \times m'$ edges, which is exactly the unnormalized product of term frequencies $\text{tf}(t, S) \cdot \text{tf}(t, S') \cdot n \cdot n'$. Thus summing $m \times m'$ times $\text{idf}(t)/n \cdot \text{idf}(t)/n'$ in $sim(G)$ is equal to $\text{tfidf}(t, S) \cdot \text{tfidf}(t, S')$ (normalization is computed in the same way).

[17] In the simple case of CosTFIDF, the condition would be: $(v_{i_j}, v'_{i'_j}, s_j) \in E$ if and only if $a_{i_j} = a'_{i'_j}$. In other words, all identical features (and only they) are connected.

[18] "the first element" means that $select(E)$ may return any $e \in E$, provided the same element is always returned for the same set.

3.3 Meta-Levenshtein: Soft-TFIDF with Levenshtein alignment

We have shown in part 2.2 that there are some pitfalls in Soft-TFIDF, especially in the way the alignment is computed: no symmetry, possible score overflow. But experiments show that taking words IDF into account increases performance, and that Soft-TFIDF, i.e. the possible matching of words that are not strictly identical, increases performance (see section 4). That is why improving this kind of measure is interesting. Following the model we proposed above, we propose to mix the cosine-like similarity used in Soft-TFIDF with a Levenshtein-like alignment. The following measure, called *Meta-Levenshtein* (ML for short), takes IDFs into account but is not a bag-of-features metrics.

Let us define $align_{ML}$ in the following way: let $\mathcal{G}_{ML}$ be defined exactly as the set of graphs $\mathcal{G}_{lev}$ (see part 3.2.1), except that weights are defined as in the case of Soft-TFIDF: for any $G = (V, E) \in \mathcal{G}_{lev}$ and for any edge $(v_{i_j}, v'_{i'_j}, s_j) \in E$, let

$$s_j = sim^F(a_{i_j}, a'_{i'_j}) \cdot \frac{\text{idf}(a_{i_j})}{n} \cdot \frac{\text{idf}(a'_{i'_j})}{n'}.$$

Let $sim(G) = \sum_{(v_{i_j}, v'_{i'_j}, s_j) \in E} s_j$, and

$align_{ML}(S, S') = G$, where G is such that $sim(G) = \max(\{sim(G') \mid G' \in \mathcal{G}_{ML}\})$. Finally, $score_{ML}(G) = sim(G) / (\|S\| \cdot \|S'\|)$.

Compared to Soft-TFIDF, ML solves the problem of symmetry ($ML(S, S') = ML(S', S)$), and also the potential overflow, because no feature may be matched twice (see fig. 2). Of course, the alignment is less flexible in ML, since it must satisfy the sequential order of features. Practically, this measure may be efficiently implemented in the same way as Levenshtein similarity, including optionally the Damerau extension for transpositions. We have also tested a simple variant with possible extended transpositions, i.e. cases like ABC compared to CA, where both C and A are matched.

3.4 Recursive combinations for NE matching

One of the points we want to emphasize through the generic framework presented above is the mod-

Figure 2: Soft-TFIDF vs. ML alignment

With $sim(A, D) \geq \theta$, and $sim(C, E) \geq sim(B, E) \geq \theta$:

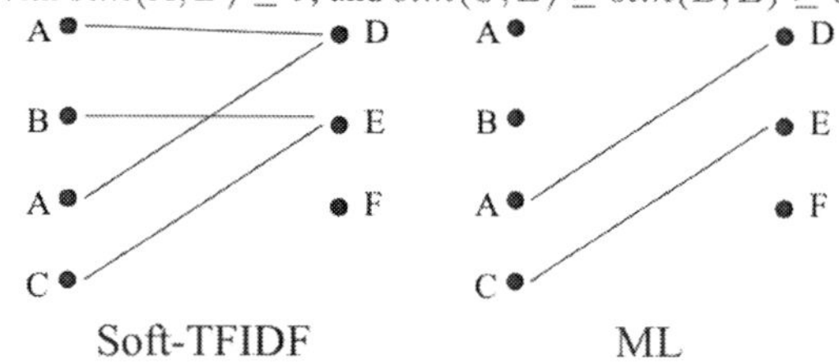

ularity of similarity measures. Our viewpoint is that traditional measures may be seen not only in their original context, but also as modular parameterized functions. The first application of such a definition is already in use in the form of measures like Monge-Elkan or Soft-TFIDF, which rely on some sub-measure to compare words inside NEs. But we will show that modularity is also useful at a lower level: measures concerning words may rely on similarity between (for example) n-grams, and even at this restricted level numerous possible kinds of similarity may be used.

Moreover, from the viewpoint of applications it is not very costly to compute similarities between n-grams and even between words. The number of n-grams is clearly bounded, and the number of words is not so high because there are only about 2 words by entity in average, and overall some words appear very often in entities[19].

4 Experiments

4.1 Data

Two corpora were used. Both contain mainly news and press articles, collected from various international sources. The first one, called "Iran Nuclear Threat" (INT in short), is in English and was extracted from the NTI (*Nuclear Threat Initiative*) web site[20]. It is 236,000 words long. Our second corpus, called "French Speaking Medias" (FSM in short), is 856,000 words long. It was extracted from a regular crawling of a set of French-speaking international newspapers web sites during a short time-frame (in July 2007). GATE[21] was used as the named entities recognizer for INT, whereas Arisem[22] performed the tagging of NEs for FSM. Recognition errors[23] appear in both corpora, but significantly less in FSM. We restricted the sets of NEs to those recognized as locations, organizations and persons, and decided to work only on entities appearing at least twice. Finally for INT (resp. FSM) we obtain 1,588 distinct NE (resp. 3,278) accounting altogether for 33,147 (resp. 23,725) occurrences.

Of course, it would be too costly to manually label as match (positive) or non-match (negative) the whole set containing $n \times (n-1)/2$ pairs, for the observed values of n. The approach consisting in labeling only a randomly chosen subset of pairs is ineffective, because of the disproportion between the number of negative and positive pairs (less than 0.1%). Therefore we tried to find all positive pairs, assuming the remaining lot are negative. Practically, the labeling step was based only on the best pairs as identified by a large set of measures[24]. The guidelines we used for labeling are the following: any incomplete, over-tagged or simply wrongly recognized NE is discarded. Then remaining pairs are classified as positive (coreferent), negative (non-coreferent), or "don't know"[25].

Corpus	Discarded	Pos.	Neg.	Don't know
INT	416 / 1,588	764	2,821	302
FSM	745 / 3,278	741	32,348	419

According to our initial hypotheses, all non-tagged pairs are considered as negative in the experiments below. "Don't know" pairs are ignored. As a further note, about 20% of the pairs are not orthographically similar (e.g. acronyms and their expansion): these pairs are out of reach of our techniques, and would require additional knowledge.

4.2 Observations

4.2.1 Taking IDF into account

To evaluate the contribution of IDF[26] in scoring the coreference degree between NE, let us ob-

[19]In the corpora we studied, 1172 NE (resp. 2533) contain 1107 distinct words (resp. 2785).

[20]`http://www.nti.org`

[21]`http://gate.ac.uk`

[22]`http://www.arisem.com`

[23]Mainly truncated entities, over-tagged entities, and common nouns beginning with a capital letter.

[24]This is a potential methodological bias, but we hope to have kept its effect as low as possible: the measures we used are quite diverse and do not assign good scores to the same pairs; therefore, for each measure, we expect that the potential misses (false negatives) will be matched by some other measure, thus allowing a fair evaluation of its performance. A few positive pairs are manually added (mainly acronyms).

[25]All ambiguous cases, mainly due to some missing precision (e.g. *"Ministry of Foreign Affairs"* and *"Russian Ministry of Foreign Affairs"*), and more rarely homonymy (e.g. *"Lebedev"* and *"[Valery|Oleg] Lebedev"*)

[26]It may be noticed that the Term Frequency in TFIDF is rarely important, since a given word appear almost always only once in a NE.

serve the differences among best scored pairs for measures Bag-of-words Cosine and Cosine over TFIDF weighted vectors. For example, the former will assign 0.5 to pair *"Prime Minister Tony Blair"/"Blair"* (from corpus INT), whereas the latter gives 0.61. As expected, IDF weights lighten the effect of non-informative words and strengthen important words. In both corpora, The F1-measure for TFIDF Cosine is about 10 points (in average) better than for Bag-of-words Cosine (see fig. 3).

4.2.2 Soft-TFIDF problems: normalization, threshold and sub-measure

As we have explained in section 2.2, the Soft-TFIDF measure (Cohen et al., 2003) may suffer from normalization problems. This is probably the reason why the authors seem to use it parsimoniously, i.e. only in the case words are very close (which is verified using a high threshold θ). Indeed, problems occur when the sub-measure and/or the threshold are not carefully chosen, causing performances drop: using Jaro measure with a very low threshold (0.2 here), performances are even worst than Bag-of-words cosine (see fig. 3). This is due to the *double matching* problem: for example, pair *"Tehran Times (Tehran)"/"Inter Press Service"* (from INT) is scored more than 1.0 because *"Tehran"* matches *"Inter"* twice: even with a low score as a coefficient, *"Inter"* has a high IDF compared to *"Press"* and *"Service"*, so counting it twice makes normalization wrong.

However, this problem may be solved by choosing a more adequate sub-measure: experiments show that using the CosTFIDF measure with bigrams or trigrams outperforms standard CosTFIDF. Of course, there are some positive pairs that are found "later" by Soft-TFIDF, since it may only increase score. But the "soft" comparison brings back to the top ranked pairs a lot of positive ones. In both corpora, the best sub-measure found is CosTFIDF with trigrams. *"Mohamed ElBaradei"/"Director Mohammad ElBaradei"* (INT) or *"Chine"/"China"* (FSM) are typical positive pairs found by this measure but not by standard CosTFIDF. Here no threshold is needed anymore because the sub-measure has been chosen with care, depending on the data, in order to avoid the normalization problem. This is clearly a drawback for Soft-TFIDF: it may perform well, but only with hand-tuning sub-measure and/or threshold.

4.2.3 Beyond Soft-TFIDF: (recursive) ML

In the FSM corpus, replacing Soft-TFIDF with (simple) Meta-Levenshtein at the word level does not decrease performance, even though the alignment is more constrained in the latter case. Using the same sub-measure to compare words (trigrams CosTFIDF), it does neither increase performance. A few positive pairs are missed in the INT corpus, due to the more flexible word order in English: *"U.S. State Department"/"US Department of State"* is such an example (12 among 764 are concerned). This problem is easily solved with the ML variant with extended transposition (see part 3.3): in both corpora, there are no positive pairs requiring more than a gap of one word in the alignment. Thus this measure is not only performant but also robust, since it does not need any hand-tuning.

As a second step, we want to improve results by selecting a more fine-grained sub-measure. We have tried several ideas, such as using different kinds of n-grams similarity inside the words similarity measure. Firstly, trigrams performed better than bigrams or simple characters. Secondly, the best trigrams similarity method found is actually very simple: it consists in using CosTFIDF computed on the *trigrams contexts*, i.e. the set of closest[27] trigrams of all occurrences of the given trigram. Unsurprisingly, good scores are generally obtained for pairs of trigrams that have common characters. But it seems that this approach also enhances robustness, because it finds similarities between "close characters": in the French corpus, one observes quite good scores between trigrams containing an accentuated version and the non accentuated version of the same character. Furthermore, some character encoding errors are somehow corrected this way[28]. This is possibly the reason why the improvement of results is better in FSM than in INT (see table 1).

Finally, using also ML to compute similarity *between* words[29] yields the best results. This means that compared to the simple CosTFIDF sub-measure, one does not compare bags of trigrams but ordered sequences of trigrams[30].

[27]We have tried different window sizes for such contexts, from 2 to 10 trigrams long: performances were approximately the same. We only consider trigrams found in the entities.

[28]For example, the *ï* in the name *"Lugovoï"* appears also in FSM as *i*, as *y*, as *ä*, and is sometimes deleted.

[29]i.e. not only between sequences of words: in this case ML is run between trigrams at the word level, and then another time between words at the NE level.

[30]It is hard to tell whether it is the sequential alignment or

Figure 3: F1-Measures for FSM (percentages)

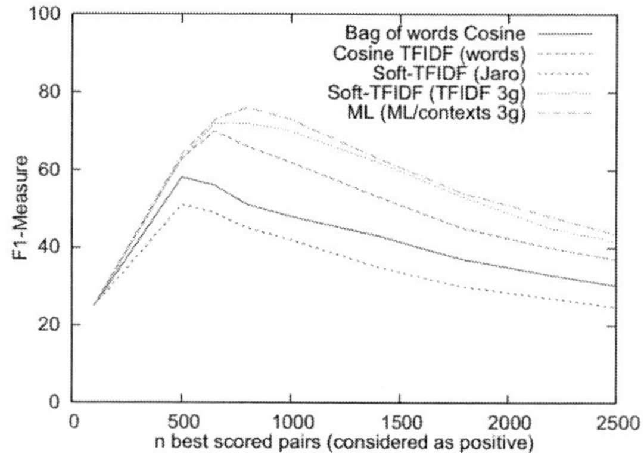

Example: for Cosine TFIDF with words, if the threshold is set in such a way that (only) the 1000 top ranked pairs are classified as positive, then the F1-measure is around 60%.

Table 1: Best F1-measures (percentages)

	INT			FSM		
Measure	F1	P	R	F1	P	R
Cosine	51.6	63.2	43.6	59.5	76.2	48.7
CosTFIDF	62.6	71.7	55.6	69.9	84.2	59.8
Soft TFIDF/3g	68.6	74.2	63.9	73.1	79.8	67.6
ML/ML-context	70.6	72.6	68.7	77.0	82.5	72.2

P/R: Corresponding Precision/Recall.

4.3 Global results

Results are synthesized in table 1, which is based on the maximum F1-measure for each measure. One observes that F1-measure is 3 to 6 points better for Soft-TFIDF than for standard TF-IDF, and that our measure still increases F1-measure by 2 (INT) to 4 points (FSM). Results show that its contribution consists mainly in improving the recall, which means that our measure is able to catch more positive pairs than Soft-TFIDF: for example, the pair *"Fatah Al Islam"/ "Fateh el-Islam"* (FSM) is scored 0.54 by SoftTFIDF and 0.70 by ML. Our measure remains the best for all values of n in fig. 3, and results are similar for F0.5-measure and F2-measure: thus, irrespective of specific application needs which may favor precision or recall, ML seems preferable.

5 Conclusion

In conclusion, we have proposed a generic model to show that similarity measures may be combined in numerous ways. We have tested such a combination, based on Soft-TFIDF, which performs better than all existing similarity metrics on two corpora. Our measure is robust, since it does not rely on any kind of prior knowledge. Thus it may be easily used, in particular in applications where NE matching is useful but is not the essential task.

the "right" use of the trigrams sub-measure which is responsible for the improvement, since the only possible comparison at this level is Soft-TFIDF.

Acknowledgements

This work has been funded by the National Project Cap Digital - Infom@gic. We thank Loïs Rigouste (Pertimm) and Nicolas Dessaigne and Aurélie Migeotte (Arisem) for providing us with the annotated French corpus.

References

Bilenko, Mikhail, Raymond J. Mooney, William W. Cohen, Pradeep Ravikumar, and Stephen E. Fienberg. 2003. Adaptive name matching in information integration. *IEEE Intelligent Systems*, 18(5):16–23.

Christen, Peter. 2006. A comparison of personal name matching: Techniques and practical issues. Technical Report TR-CS-06-02, Department of Computer Science, The Australian National University, Canberra 0200 ACT, Australia, September.

Cohen, William W., Pradeep Ravikumar, and Stephen E. Fienberg. 2003. A comparison of string distance metrics for name-matching tasks. In Kambhampati, Subbarao and Craig A. Knoblock, editors, *Proceedings of IJCAI-03 Workshop on Information Integration on the Web (IIWeb-03), August 9-10, 2003, Acapulco, Mexico*, pages 73–78.

Freeman, Andrew, Sherri L. Condon, and Christopher Ackerman. 2006. Cross linguistic name matching in English and Arabic. In Moore, Robert C., Jeff A. Bilmes, Jennifer Chu-Carroll, and Mark Sanderson, editors, *Proc. HLT-NAACL*.

Navarro, Gonzalo. 2001. A guided tour to approximate string matching. *ACM Comput. Surv.*, 33(1):31–88.

Pouliquen, Bruno, Ralf Steinberger, Camelia Ignat, Irina Temnikova, Anna Widiger, Wajdi Zaghouani, and Jan Zizka. 2006. Multilingual person name recognition and transliteration. *CORELA - Cognition, Representation, Langage*.

Prager, John, Sarah Luger, and Jennifer Chu-Carroll. 2007. Type nanotheories: a framework for term comparison. In *Proceedings of CIKM '07*, pages 701–710, New York, NY, USA. ACM.

Wagner, R. and M. Fischer. 1974. The string-to-string correction problem. *JACM*, 21(1):168–173.

Winkler, W. E. 1999. The state of record linkage and current research problems. Technical Report RR99/04, US Bureau of the Census.

Modeling the Structure and Dynamics of the Consonant Inventories: A Complex Network Approach

Animesh Mukherjee[1], **Monojit Choudhury**[2], **Anupam Basu**[1], **Niloy Ganguly**[1]
[1]Department of Computer Science and Engineering,
Indian Institute of Technology, Kharagpur, India – 721302
[2]Microsoft Research India, Bangalore, India – 560080
{animeshm,anupam,niloy}@cse.iitkgp.ernet.in,
monojitc@microsoft.com

Abstract

We study the self-organization of the consonant inventories through a complex network approach. We observe that the distribution of occurrence as well as co-occurrence of the consonants across languages follow a power-law behavior. The co-occurrence network of consonants exhibits a high clustering coefficient. We propose four novel synthesis models for these networks (each of which is a refinement of the earlier) so as to successively match with higher accuracy (a) the above mentioned topological properties as well as (b) the linguistic property of *feature economy* exhibited by the consonant inventories. We conclude by arguing that a possible interpretation of this mechanism of network growth is the process of child language acquisition. Such models essentially increase our understanding of the structure of languages that is influenced by their evolutionary dynamics and this, in turn, can be extremely useful for building future NLP applications.

1 Introduction

A large number of regular patterns are observed across the sound inventories of human languages. These regularities are arguably a consequence of the self-organization that is instrumental in the emergence of these inventories (de Boer, 2000). Many attempts have been made by functional phonologists for explaining this self-organizing behavior through certain general principles such as *maximal perceptual contrast* (Liljencrants and Lindblom, 1972), *ease of articulation* (Lindblom and Maddieson, 1988; de Boer, 2000), and *ease of learnability* (de Boer, 2000). In fact, there are a lot of studies that attempt to explain the emergence of the vowel inventories through the application of one or more of the above principles (Liljencrants and Lindblom, 1972; de Boer, 2000). Some studies have also been carried out in the area of linguistics that seek to reason the observed patterns in the consonant inventories (Trubetzkoy, 1939; Lindblom and Maddieson, 1988; Boersma, 1998; Clements, 2008). Nevertheless, most of these works are confined to certain individual principles rather than formulating a general theory describing the emergence of these regular patterns across the consonant inventories.

The self-organization of the consonant inventories emerges due to an interaction of different forces acting upon them. In order to identify the nature of these interactions one has to understand the growth dynamics of these inventories. The theories of *complex networks* provide a number of growth models that have proved to be extremely successful in explaining the evolutionary dynamics of various social (Newman, 2001; Ramasco et al., 2004), biological (Jeong et al., 2000) and other natural systems. The basic framework for the current study develops around two such complex networks namely, the **Pho**neme-**La**nguage **Net**work or **PlaNet** (Choudhury et al., 2006) and its one-mode projection, the **Pho**neme-Phoneme **Net**work or **PhoNet** (Mukherjee et al.2007a). We begin by analyzing some of the structural properties (Sec. 2) of the networks and observe that the consonant nodes in both PlaNet and PhoNet follow a power-law-like degree distribution. Moreover, PhoNet

© 2008. Licensed under the *Creative Commons Attribution-Noncommercial-Share Alike 3.0 Unported* license (http://creativecommons.org/licenses/by-nc-sa/3.0/). Some rights reserved.

is characterized by a high clustering coefficient, a property that has been found to be prevalent in many other social networks (Newman, 2001; Ramasco et al., 2004).

We propose four synthesis models for PlaNet (Sec. 3), each of which employ a variant of a *preferential attachment* (Barabási and Albert, 1999) based growth kernel[1]. While the first two models are independent of the characteristic properties of the (consonant) nodes, the following two use them. These models are successively refined not only to reproduce the topological properties of PlaNet and PhoNet, but also to match the linguistic property of *feature economy* (Boersma, 1998; Clements, 2008) that is observed across the consonant inventories. The underlying growth rules for each of these individual models helps us to interpret the cause of the emergence of at least one (or more) of the aforementioned properties. We conclude (Sec. 4) by providing a possible interpretation of the proposed mathematical model that we finally develop in terms of child language acquisition.

There are three major contributions of this work. Firstly, it provides a fascinating account of the structure and the evolution of the human speech sound systems. Furthermore, the introduction of the node property based synthesis model is a significant contribution to the field of complex networks. On a broader perspective, this work shows how statistical mechanics can be applied in understanding the structure of a linguistic system, which in turn can be extremely useful in developing future NLP applications.

2 Properties of the Consonant Inventories

In this section, we briefly recapitulate the definitions of PlaNet and PhoNet, the data source, construction procedure for the networks and some of their important structural properties. We also revisit the concept of feature economy and the method used for its quantification.

2.1 Structural Properties of the Consonant Networks

PlaNet is a bipartite graph $G = \langle V_L, V_C, E_{pl} \rangle$ consisting of two sets of nodes namely, V_L (labeled by the languages) and V_C (labeled by the consonants);

[1]The word kernel here refers to the function or mathematical formula that drives the growth of the network.

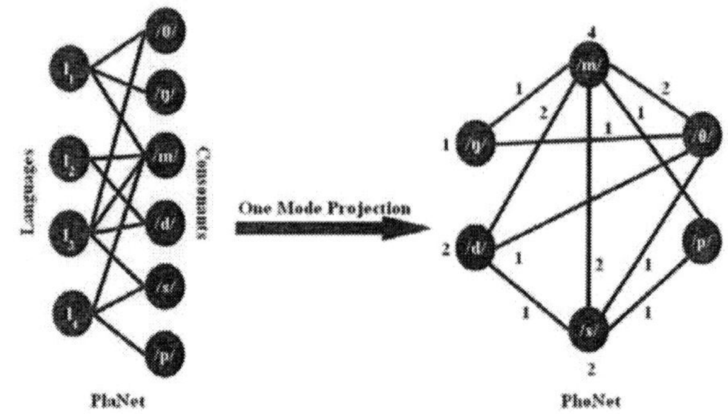

Figure 1: Illustration of the nodes and edges of PlaNet and PhoNet.

E_{pl} is the set of edges running between V_L and V_C. There is an edge $e \in E_{pl}$ from a node $v_l \in V_L$ to a node $v_c \in V_C$ iff the consonant c is present in the inventory of language l.

PhoNet is the one-mode projection of PlaNet onto the consonant nodes i.e., a network of consonants in which two nodes are linked by an edge with weight as many times as they co-occur across languages. Hence, it can be represented by a graph $G = \langle V_C, E_{ph} \rangle$, where V_C is the set of consonant nodes and E_{ph} is the set of edges connecting these nodes in G. There is an edge $e \in E_{ph}$ if the two nodes (read consonants) that are connected by e co-occur in at least one language and the number of languages they co-occur in defines the weight of the edge e. Figure 1 shows the nodes and the edges of PlaNet and PhoNet.

Data Source and Network Construction: Like many other earlier studies (Liljencrants and Lindblom, 1972; Lindblom and Maddieson, 1988; de Boer, 2000; Hinskens and Weijer, 2003), we use the UCLA Phonological Segment Inventory Database (UPSID) (Maddieson, 1984) as the source of our data. There are 317 languages in the database with a total of 541 consonants found across them. Each consonant is characterized by a set of phonological features (Trubetzkoy, 1931), which distinguishes it from others. UPSID uses articulatory features to describe the consonants, which can be broadly categorized into three different types namely the *manner of articulation*, the *place of articulation* and *phonation*. Manner of articulation specifies how the flow of air takes place in the vocal tract during articulation of a consonant, whereas place of articulation specifies the active speech organ and also the place where it acts. Phonation describes the vibration of the vo-

Manner of Articulation	Place of Articulation	Phonation
tap	velar	voiced
flap	uvular	voiceless
trill	dental	
click	palatal	
nasal	glottal	
plosive	bilabial	
r-sound	alveolar	
fricative	retroflex	
affricate	pharyngeal	
implosive	labial-velar	
approximant	labio-dental	
ejective stop	labial-palatal	
affricated click	dental-palatal	
ejective affricate	dental-alveolar	
ejective fricative	palato-alveolar	
lateral approximant		

Table 1: The table shows some of the important features listed in UPSID. Over 99% of the UPSID languages have bilabial, dental-alveolar and velar plosives. Furthermore, voiceless plosives outnumber the voiced ones (92% vs. 67%). 93% of the languages have at least one fricative, 97% have at least one nasal and 96% have at least one liquid. Approximants occur in fewer than 95% of the languages.

cal cords during the articulation of a consonant. Apart from these three major classes there are also some secondary articulatory features found in certain languages. There are around 52 features listed in UPSID; the important ones are noted in Table 1. Note that in UPSID the features are assumed to be binary-valued and therefore, each consonant can be represented by a binary vector.

We have used UPSID in order to construct PlaNet and PhoNet. Consequently, $|V_L| = 317$ (in PlaNet) and $|V_C| = 541$. The number of edges in PlaNet and PhoNet are 7022 and 30412 respectively.

Degree Distributions of PlaNet and PhoNet: The degree distribution is the fraction of nodes, denoted by P_k, which have a degree[2] greater than or equal to k (Newman, 2003). The degree distribution of the consonant nodes in PlaNet and PhoNet are shown in Figure 2 in the log-log scale. Both the plots show a power-law behavior ($P_k \propto k^{-\alpha}$) with exponential cut-offs towards the ends. The value of α is 0.71 for PlaNet and 0.89 for PhoNet.

Clustering Coefficient of PhoNet: The clustering coefficient for a node i is the proportion of links between the nodes that are the neighbors of i divided by the number of links that could possibly exist between them (Newman, 2003). Since PhoNet is a weighted graph the above definition is suitably modified by the one presented in (Barrat et al., 2004). According to this definition, the clustering coefficient for a node i is,

$$c_i = \frac{1}{\left(\sum_{\forall j} w_{ij}\right)(k_i - 1)} \sum_{\forall j,l} \frac{(w_{ij} + w_{il})}{2} a_{ij} a_{il} a_{jl} \quad (1)$$

where j and l are neighbors of i; k_i represents the plain degree of the node i; w_{ij}, w_{jl} and w_{il} denote the weights of the edges connecting nodes i and j, j and l, and i and l respectively; a_{ij}, a_{il}, a_{jl} are boolean variables, which are true iff there is an edge between the nodes i and j, i and l, and j and l respectively. The clustering coefficient of the network (c_{av}) is equal to the average clustering coefficient of the nodes. The value of c_{av} for PhoNet is 0.89, which is significantly higher than that of a random graph with the same number of nodes and edges (0.08).

2.2 Linguistic Properties: Feature Economy and its Quantification

The principle of feature economy states that languages tend to use a small number of *distinctive* features and maximize their combinatorial possibilities to generate a large number of consonants (Boersma, 1998; Clements, 2008). Stated differently, a given consonant will have a higher than expected chance of occurrence in inventories in which all of its features have already distinctively occurred in the other consonants. This principle immediately implies that the consonants chosen by a language should share a considerable number of features among them. The quantification process, which is a refinement of the idea presented in (Mukherjee et al.2007b), is as follows.

Feature Entropy: For an inventory of size N, let there be p_f consonants for which a particular feature f (recall that we assume f to be binary-valued) is present and q_f other consonants for which the same is absent. Therefore, the probability that a consonant (chosen uniformly at random from this inventory) contains the feature f is $\frac{p_f}{N}$ and the probability that it does not contain the feature is $\frac{q_f}{N}$ (=1$-\frac{p_f}{N}$). One can think of f as an independent random variable, which can take values 1 and 0, and $\frac{p_f}{N}$ and $\frac{q_f}{N}$ define the probability distribution of f. Therefore, for any given inventory, we can define the binary entropy H_f (Shannon and Weaver, 1949) for the feature f as

$$H_f = -\frac{p_f}{N}\log_2\frac{p_f}{N} - \frac{q_f}{N}\log_2\frac{q_f}{N} \quad (2)$$

[2] For a weighted graph like PhoNet, the degree of a node i is the sum of weights on the edges that are incident on i.

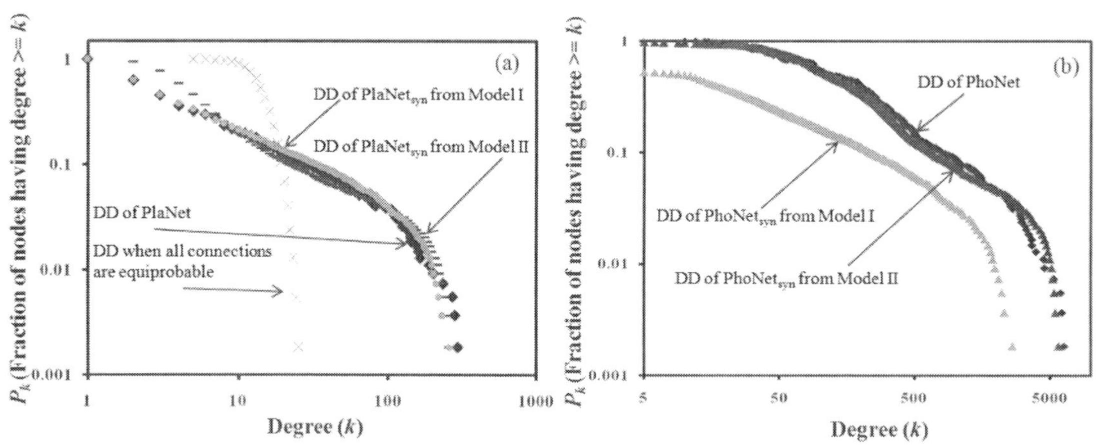

Figure 2: Degree distribution (DD) of PlaNet along with that of PlaNet$_{syn}$ obtained from Model I and II respectively; (b) DD of PhoNet along with that of PhoNet$_{syn}$ obtained from Model I and II respectively. Both the plots are in log-log scale.

If F is the set of all features present in the consonants forming the inventory, then *feature entropy* F_E is the sum of the binary entropies with respect to all the features, that is

$$F_E = \sum_{f \in F} H_f = \sum_{f \in F} \left(-\frac{p_f}{N}\log_2\frac{p_f}{N} - \frac{q_f}{N}\log_2\frac{q_f}{N}\right) \quad (3)$$

Since we have assumed that f is an independent random variable, F_E is the joint entropy of the system. In other words, F_E provides an estimate of the number of discriminative features present in the consonants of an inventory that a speaker (e.g., parent) has to communicate to a learner (e.g., child) during language transmission. The lower the value of F_E the higher is the feature economy. The curve marked as (R) in Figure 3 shows the average feature entropy of the consonant inventories of a particular size[3] (y-axis) versus the inventory size (x-axis).

3 Synthesis Models

In this section, we describe four synthesis models that incrementally attempt to explain the emergence of the structural properties of PlaNet and PhoNet as well as the feature entropy exhibited by the consonant inventories. In all these models, we assume that the distribution of the consonant inventory size, i.e., the degrees of the language nodes in PlaNet, are known *a priori*.

[3]Let there be n inventories of a particular size k. The average feature entropy of the inventories of size k is $\frac{1}{n}\sum_{i=1}^{n} F_{E_i}$, where F_{E_i} signifies the feature entropy of the ith inventory of size k.

3.1 Model I: Preferential Attachment Kernel

This model employs a modified version of the kernel described in (Choudhury et al., 2006), which is the only work in literature that attempts to explain the emergence of the consonant inventories in the framework of complex networks.

Let us assume that a language node $L_i \in V_L$ has a degree k_i. The consonant nodes in V_C are assumed to be unlabeled, i.e, they are not marked by the distinctive features that characterize them. We first sort the nodes L_1 through L_{317} in the ascending order of their degrees. At each time step a node L_j, chosen in order, preferentially attaches itself with k_j *distinct* nodes (call each such node C_i) of the set V_C. The probability $Pr(C_i)$ with which the node L_j attaches itself to the node C_i is given by,

$$Pr(C_i) = \frac{d_i^{\alpha} + \epsilon}{\sum_{i' \in V_C'} (d_{i'}^{\alpha} + \epsilon)} \quad (4)$$

where, d_i is the current degree of the node C_i, V_C' is the set of nodes in V_C that are not already connected to L_j, ϵ is the smoothing parameter that facilitates random attachments and α indicates whether the attachment kernel is sub-linear ($\alpha < 1$), linear ($\alpha = 1$) or super-linear ($\alpha > 1$). Note that the modification from the earlier kernel (Choudhury et al., 2006) is brought about by the introduction of α. The above process is repeated until all the language nodes $L_j \in V_L$ get connected to k_j consonant nodes (refer to Figure. 6 of (Choudhury et al., 2006) for an illustration of the steps of the synthesis process). Thus, we have the synthesized version of PlaNet, which we shall call PlaNet_{syn} henceforth.

The Simulation Results: We simulate the above model to obtain PlaNet_{syn} for 100 different runs and average the results over all of them. We find that the degree distributions that emerge fit the empirical data well for $\alpha \in [1.4,1.5]$ and $\epsilon \in [0.4,0.6]$, the best being at $\alpha = 1.44$ and $\epsilon = 0.5$ (shown in Figure 2). In fact, the mean error[4] between the real and the synthesized distributions for the best choice of parameters is as small as 0.01. Note that this error in case of the model presented in (Choudhury et al., 2006) was 0.03. Furthermore, as we shall see shortly, a super-linear kernel can explain various other topological properties more accurately than a linear kernel.

In absence of preferential attachment i.e., when all the connections to the consonant nodes are equiprobable, the mean error rises to 0.35.

A possible reason behind the success of this model is the fact that language is a constantly changing system and preferential attachment plays a significant role in this change. For instance, during the change those consonants that belong to languages that are more prevalent among the speakers of a generation have higher chances of being transmitted to the speakers of the subsequent generations (Blevins, 2004). This heterogeneity in the choice of the consonants manifests itself as preferential attachment. We conjecture that the value of α is a function of the societal structure and the cognitive capabilities of human beings. The exact nature of this function is currently not known and a topic for future research. The parameter ϵ in this case may be thought of as modeling the randomness of the system.

Nevertheless, the degree distribution of PhoNet_{syn}, which is the one-mode projection of PlaNet_{syn}, does not match the real data well (see Figure 2). The mean error between the two distributions is 0.45. Furthermore, the clustering coefficient of PhoNet_{syn} is 0.55 and differs largely from that of PhoNet. The primary reason for this deviation in the results is that PhoNet exhibits strong patterns of co-occurrences (Mukherjee et al.2007a) and this fact is not taken into account by Model I. In order to circumvent the above problem, we introduce the concept of *triad* (i.e., fully connected triplet) formation and thereby refine the model in the following section.

[4]Mean error is defined as the average difference between the ordinate pairs (say y and y') where the abscissas are equal. In other words, if there are N such ordinate pairs then the mean error can be expressed as $\frac{\sum |y-y'|}{N}$.

3.2 Model II: Kernel based on Triad Formation

The triad model (Peltomäki and Alava, 2006) builds up on the concept of *neighborhood* formation. Two consonant nodes C_1 and C_2 become neighbors if a language node at any step of the synthesis process attaches itself to both C_1 and C_2. Let the probability of triad formation be denoted by p_t. At each time step a language node L_j (chosen from the set of language nodes sorted in ascending order of their degrees) makes the first connection preferentially to a consonant node $C_i \in V_C$ to which L_j is not already connected following the distribution $Pr(C_i)$. For the rest of the (k_j-1) connections L_j attaches itself preferentially to only the neighbors of C_i to which L_j is not yet connected with a probability p_t. Consequently, L_j connects itself preferentially to the non-neighbors of C_i to which L_j is not yet connected with a probability $(1 - p_t)$. The neighbor set of C_i gets updated accordingly. Note that every time the node C_i and its neighbors are chosen they together impose a clique on the one-mode projection. This phenomenon leads to the formation of a large number of triangles in the one-mode projection thereby increasing the clustering coefficient of the resultant network.

The Simulation Results: We carry out 100 different simulation runs of the above model for a particular set of parameter values to obtain PlaNet_{syn} and average the results over all of them. We explore several parameter settings in the range as follows: $\alpha \in [1,1.5]$ (in steps of 0.1), $\epsilon \in [0.2,0.4]$ (in steps of 0.1) and $p_t \in [0.70,0.95]$ (in steps of 0.05). We also observe that if we traverse any further along one or more of the dimensions of the parameter space then the results get worse. The best result emerges for $\alpha = 1.3$, $\epsilon = 0.3$ and $p_t = 0.8$.

Figure 2 shows the degree distribution of the consonant nodes of PlaNet_{syn} and PlaNet. The mean error between the two distributions is 0.04 approximately and is therefore worse than the result obtained from Model I. Nevertheless, the average clustering coefficient of PhoNet_{syn} in this case is 0.85, which is within 4.5% of that of PhoNet. Moreover, in this process the mean error between the degree distribution of PhoNet_{syn} and PhoNet (as illustrated in Figure 2) has got reduced drastically from 0.45 to 0.03.

One can again find a possible association of this model with the phenomena of language change. If a group of consonants largely co-occur in the languages of a generation of speakers then it is very likely that all of them get transmitted together in the subsequent generations (Blevins, 2004). The triad formation probability ensures that if a pair of consonant nodes become neighbors of each other in a particular step of the synthesis process then the choice of such a pair should be highly preferred in the subsequent steps of the process. This is coherent with the aforementioned phenomenon of transmission of consonants in groups over linguistic generations. Since the value of p_t that we obtain is quite high, it may be argued that such transmissions are largely prevalent in nature.

Although Model II reproduces the structural properties of PlaNet and PhoNet quite accurately, as we shall see shortly, it fails to generate inventories that closely match the real ones in terms of feature entropy. However, at this point, recall that Model II assumes that the consonant nodes are unlabeled; therefore, the inventories that are produced as a result of the synthesis are composed of consonants, which unlike the real inventories, are not marked by their distinctive features. In order to label them we perform the following,

The Labeling Scheme:

1. Sort the consonants of UPSID in the decreasing order of their frequency of occurrence and call this list of consonants $ListC[1 \cdots 541]$,
2. Sort the V_C nodes of PlaNet$_{syn}$ in decreasing order of their degree and call this list of nodes $ListN[1 \cdots 541]$,
3. $\forall_{1 \leq i \leq 541}\ ListN[i] \longleftarrow ListC[i]$

The Figure 3 indicates that the curve for the real inventories (R) and those obtained from Model II (M2) are significantly different from each other. This difference arises due to the fact that in Model II, the choice of a consonant from the set of neighbors is solely degree-dependent, where the relationships between the features are not taken into consideration. Therefore, in order to eliminate this problem, we introduce the model using the feature-based kernel in the next section.

3.3 Model III: Feature-based Kernel

In this model, we assume that each of the consonant nodes are labeled, that is each of them are

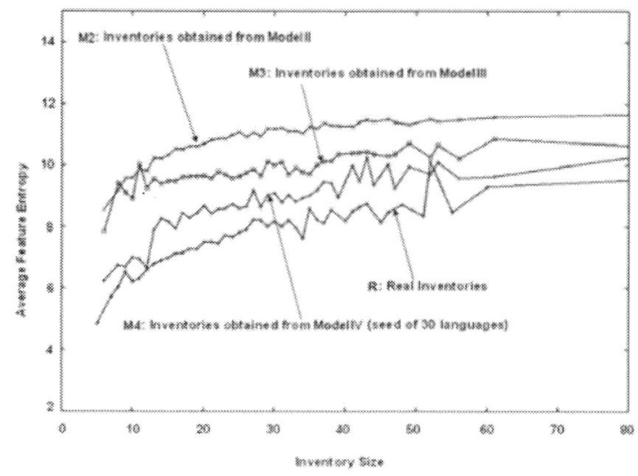

Figure 3: Average feature entropy of the inventories of a particular size (y-axis) versus the inventory size (x-axis).

marked by a set of distinctive features. The attachment kernel in this case has two components one of which is preferential while the other favors the choice of those consonants that are at a low feature distance (the number of feature positions they differ at) from the already chosen ones. Let us denote the feature distance between two consonants C_i and $C_i^{'}$ by $D(C_i, C_i^{'})$. We define the *affinity*, $A(C_i, C_i^{'})$, between C_i and $C_i^{'}$ as

$$A(C_i, C_i^{'}) = \frac{1}{D(C_i, C_i^{'})} \qquad (5)$$

Therefore, the lower the feature distance between C_i and $C_i^{'}$ the higher is the affinity between them.

At each time step a language node establishes the first connection with a consonant node (say C_i) preferentially following the distribution $Pr(C_i)$ like the previous models. The rest of the connections to any arbitrary consonant node $C_i^{'}$ (not yet connected to the language node) are made following the distribution $(1 - w)Pr(C_i^{'}) + wPr_{aff}(C_i, C_i^{'})$, where

$$Pr_{aff}(C_i, C_i^{'}) = \frac{A(C_i, C_i^{'})}{\sum_{\forall C_i^{'}} A(C_i, C_i^{'})} \qquad (6)$$

and $0 < w < 1$.

Simulation Results: We perform 100 different simulation runs of the above model for a particular set of parameter values to obtain PlaNet$_{syn}$ and average the results over all of them. We explore different parameter settings in the range as follows: $\alpha \in$ [1,2] (in steps of 0.1), $\epsilon \in$ [0.1,1] (in steps of 0.1) and $w \in$ [0.1,0.5] (in steps of 0.05). The best result in terms of the structural properties of PlaNet and PhoNet emerges for $\alpha = 1.6$, $\epsilon = 0.3$ and $w = 0.2$.

In this case, the mean error between the degree distribution curves for PlaNet_{syn} and PlaNet is 0.05 and that between of PhoNet_{syn} and PhoNet is 0.02. Furthermore, the clustering coefficient of PhoNet_{syn} in this case is 0.84, which is within 5.6% of that of PhoNet. The above results show that the structural properties of the synthesized networks in this case are quite similar to those obtained through the triad model. Nevertheless, the average feature entropy of the inventories produced (see curve M3 in Figure 3) are more close to that of the real ones now (for quantitative comparison see Table 2).

Therefore, it turns out that the groups of consonants that largely co-occur in the languages of a linguistic generation are actually driven by the principle of feature economy (see (Clements, 2008; Mukherjee et al.2007a) for details).

However, note that even for Model III the nodes that are chosen for attachment in the initial stages of the synthesis process are arbitrary and consequently, the labels of the nodes of PlaNet_{syn} do not have a one-to-one correspondence with that of PlaNet, which is the main reason behind the difference in the result between them. In order to overcome this problem we can make use of a small set of real inventories to bootstrap the model.

3.4 Model IV: Feature-based Kernel and Bootstrapping

In order to create a bias towards the labeling scheme prevalent in PlaNet, we use 30 (around 10% of the) real languages as a seed (chosen randomly) for Model III; i.e., they are used by the model for bootstrapping. The idea is summarized below.

1. Select 30 real inventories at random and construct a PlaNet from them. Call this network the initial PlaNet_{syn}.
2. The rest of the language nodes are incrementally added to this initial PlaNet_{syn} using Model III.

Simulation Results: The best fit now emerges at $\alpha = 1.35$, $\epsilon = 0.3$ and $w = 0.15$. The mean error between the degree distribution of PlaNet and PlaNet_{syn} is 0.05 and that between PhoNet and PhoNet_{syn} is 0.02. The clustering coefficient of PhoNet_{syn} is 0.83 in this case (within 6.7% of that of PhoNet).

Results	Model I	Model II	Model III	Model IV
ME: DD of PlaNet & PlaNet_{syn}	0.01	0.04	0.05	0.05
ME: DD of PhoNet & PhoNet_{syn}	0.45	0.03	0.02	0.02
% Err: Clustering Coefficient	38.2	04.5	05.6	06.7
ME: Avg. F_E of Real & Synth. Inv.	3.40	3.00	2.10	0.93
α	1.44	1.30	1.60	1.35
ϵ	0.5	0.3	0.3	0.3
p_t	–	0.8	–	–
w	–	–	0.20	0.15

Table 2: Important results obtained from each of the models. ME: Mean Error, DD: Degree Distribution.

The inventories that are produced as a result of the bootstrapping have an average feature entropy closer to the real inventories (see curve M4 in Figure 3) than the earlier models. Hence, we find that this improved labeling strategy brings about a global betterment in our results unlike in the previous cases. The larger the number of languages used for the purpose of bootstrapping the better are the results mainly in terms of the match in the feature entropy curves.

4 Conclusion

We dedicated the preceding sections of this article to analyze and synthesize the consonant inventories of the world's languages in the framework of a complex network. Table 2 summarizes the results obtained from the four models so that the reader can easily compare them. Some of our important observations are

- The distribution of occurrence and co-occurrence of consonants across languages roughly follow a power law,
- The co-occurrence network of consonants has a large clustering coefficient,
- Groups of consonants that largely co-occur across languages are driven by feature economy (which can be expressed through feature entropy),
- Each of the above properties emerges due to different reasons, which are successively unfurled by our models.

So far, we have tried to explain the physical significance of our models in terms of the process of language change. Language change is a collective phenomenon that functions at the level of a population of speakers (Steels, 2000). Nevertheless, it is also possible to explain the significance of the models at the level of an individual, primarily in terms of the process of language acquisition, which largely governs the course of language change. In the initial years of language development every child passes through a stage called *babbling* during which he/she learns to produce non-meaningful sequences of consonants and vowels, some of which are not even used in the language to which they are exposed (Jakobson, 1968; Locke, 1983). Clear preferences can be observed for learning certain sounds such as plosives and nasals, whereas fricatives and liquids are avoided. In fact, this hierarchy of preference during the babbling stage follows the cross-linguistic frequency distribution of the consonants. This innate frequency dependent preference towards certain phonemes might be because of phonetic reasons (i.e., for articulatory/perceptual benefits). In all our models, this innate preference gets captured through the process of preferential attachment. However, at the same time, in the context of learning a particular inventory the ease of learning the individual consonants also plays an important role. The lower the number of new feature distinctions to be learnt, the higher the ease of learning the consonant. Therefore, there are two orthogonal preferences: (a) the occurrence frequency dependent preference (that is innate), and (b) the feature-dependent preference (that increases the ease of learning), which are instrumental in the acquisition of the inventories. The feature-based kernel is essentially a linear combination of these two mutually orthogonal factors.

References

A.-L. Barabási and R. Albert. 1999. Emergence of scaling in random networks. *Science* **286**, 509-512.

A. Barrat, M. Barthélemy, R. Pastor-Satorras and A. Vespignani. 2004. The architecture of complex weighted networks. *PNAS* **101**, 3747–3752.

J. Blevins. 2004. *Evolutionary Phonology: The Emergence of Sound Patterns*, Cambridge University Press, Cambridge.

B. de Boer. 2000. Self-organisation in vowel systems. *Journal of Phonetics* **28**(4), 441–465.

P. Boersma. 1998. *Functional Phonology*, The Hague: Holland Academic Graphics.

M. Choudhury, A. Mukherjee, A. Basu and N. Ganguly. 2006. Analysis and synthesis of the distribution of consonants over languages: A complex network approach. *Proceedings of COLING-ACL06*, 128–135.

G. N. Clements. 2008. The role of features in speech sound inventories. In Eric Raimy & Charles Cairns, eds.,*Contemporary Views on Architecture and Representations in Phonological Theory*, Cambridge, MA: MIT Press.

F. Hinskens and J. Weijer. 2003. Patterns of segmental modification in consonant inventories: A cross-linguistic study. *Linguistics* **41**(6), 1041–1084.

R. Jakobson. 1968. *Child Language, Aphasia and Phonological Universals*. The Hague: Mouton.

H. Jeong, B. Tombor, R. Albert, Z. N. Oltvai and A. L. Barabási. 2000. The large-scale organization of metabolic networks. *Nature* **406** 651-654.

J. Liljencrants and B. Lindblom. 1972. Numerical simulation of vowel quality systems: the role of perceptual contrast. *Language* **48**, 839–862.

B. Lindblom and I. Maddieson. 1988. Phonetic universals in consonant systems. *Language, Speech, and Mind*, 62–78, Routledge, London.

J. L. Locke. 1983. *Phonological Acquisition and Change*. Academic Press New York.

I. Maddieson. 1984. *Patterns of Sounds*, Cambridge University Press, Cambridge.

A. Mukherjee, M. Choudhury, A. Basu and N. Ganguly. 2007a. Modeling the co-occurrence principles of the consonant inventories: A complex network approach. *Int. Jour. of Mod. Phys. C* **18**(2), 281–295.

A. Mukherjee, M. Choudhury, A. Basu and N. Ganguly. 2007b. Redundancy ratio: An invariant property of the consonant inventories of the world's languages *Proceedings of ACL07*, 104–111.

M. E. J. Newman. 2001. Scientific collaboration networks. *Physical Review E* **64**, 016131.

M. E. J. Newman. 2003. The structure and function of complex networks. *SIAM Review* **45**, 167–256.

M. Peltomäki and M. Alava. 2006. Correlations in bipartite collaboration networks. *Journal of Statistical Mechanics: Theory and Experiment*, P01010.

J. J. Ramasco, S. N. Dorogovtsev and R. Pastor-Satorras. 2004. Self-organization of collaboration networks. *Physical Review E* **70**, 036106.

C. E. Shannon and W. Weaver. 1949. *The Mathematical Theory of Information*. University of Illinois Press, Urbana.

L. Steels. 2000. Language as a complex adaptive system. In: Schoenauer, M., editor, *Proceedings of PPSN VI, LNCS*, 17–26.

N. Trubetzkoy. 1931. Die phonologischen systeme. *TCLP* **4**, 96–116.

N. Trubetzkoy. 1969. *Principles of Phonology*. English translation of *Grundzüge der Phonologie, 1939*, University of California Press, Berkeley.

Detecting multiple facets of an event using graph-based unsupervised methods

Pradeep Muthukrishnan
Dept of EECS
University of Michigan
mpradeep@umich.edu

Joshua Gerrish
School of Information
University of Michigan
jgerrish@umich.edu

Dragomir R. Radev
Dept of EECS &
School of Information,
University of Michigan
radev@umich.edu

Abstract

We propose a new unsupervised method for topic detection that automatically identifies the different facets of an event. We use pointwise Kullback-Leibler divergence along with the Jaccard coefficient to build a topic graph which represents the community structure of the different facets. The problem is formulated as a weighted set cover problem with dynamically varying weights. The algorithm is domain-independent and generates a representative set of informative and discriminative phrases that cover the entire event. We evaluate this algorithm on a large collection of blog postings about different news events and report promising results.

1 Introduction

Finding a list of topics that a collection of documents cover is an important problem in information retrieval. Topics can be used to describe or summarize the collection, or they can be used to cluster the collection. Topics provide a short and informative description of the documents that can be used for quickly browsing and finding related documents.

Inside a given corpus, there may be multiple topics. Individual documents can also contain multiple topics.

Traditionally, information retrieval systems return a ranked list of query results based on the similarity between the user's query and the documents. Unfortunately, the results returned will often be redundant. Users may need to reformulate their search to find the specific topic they are interested in. This active searching process leads to inefficiencies, especially in cases where queries or information needs are ambiguous.For example, a user wants to get an overview of the Virginia tech shootings, then the first query he/she might try is "Virginia tech shooting". Most of the results returned would be posts just mentioning the shootings and the death toll. But the user might want a more detailed overview of the shootings. Thus this leads to continuously reformulating the search query to discover all the facets of the event.

© 2008. Licensed under the *Creative Commons Attribution-Noncommercial-Share Alike 3.0 Unported* license (http://creativecommons.org/licenses/by-nc-sa/3.0/). Some rights reserved.

2 Related Work

Topic detection and tracking was studied extensively on newswire and broadcast collections by the NIST TDT research program (Allan et al.,). The large number of people blogging on the web provides a new source of information for topic detection and tracking.

The TDT task defines topics as "an event or activity, along with all directly related events and activities." In this paper we will stay with this definition of topic.

Zhai et al. proposed several methods for dealing with a related task, which they called *subtopic retrieval* (Zhai et al., 2003). This is an information retrieval task where the goal is to retrieve and return documents that cover the different subtopics of a given query. As they point out, the utility of each document is dependent on the other documents in the ranking, which violates the independent relevance assumption traditionally used in IR.

Blei et al. (Blei et al., 2003) proposed Latent Dirichlet Allocation (LDA), a generative model that allows sets of documents to be explained by unobserved groups of documents, each based on a single topic. The LDA model assumes the bag-of-words model and posits that each document is composed of different topics. Specifically, each word's existence is attributed to one of the document's topic. This algorithm outputs a set of n-grams for each topic whereas our algorithm models each subtopic using a single n-gram. Due to limitations of time we were not able to compare this approach with ours. We plan to have this comparison in our future work.

To reduce the complexity of this task, a candidate set of subtopics needs to be generated that cover the document collection. We choose to use a keyphrase detection algorithm to generate topic labels. Several keyphrase extraction algorithms have been discussed in the literature, including ones based on machine learning methods (Turney, 2000), (Hulth, 2003) and tf-idf ((Frank et al., 1999)). Our method uses language models and pointwise mutual information expressed as the Kullback-Leibler divergence.

Kullback-Leibler divergence has been found to be an effective method of finding keyphrases in text collections. But identification of keyphrases is not enough to find topics in document. The keyphrases identified may describe the entire collection, or aspects of the collection. We wish to summarize subtopics within these collections.

The problem of subtopic detection is also related to novelty detection in (Allan et al.,). In this problem, given a set of previously seen documents, the task is to determine whether a new document contains new or novel content. The TREC 2002 novelty track, the task was to discard sentences that did not contain new material. This is similar to our goal of reducing redundancy in the list of returned subtopics.

In most cases, novelty detection is implemented as an online algorithm. The system has a set of existing documents they have seen up until a certain point. The task is to determine whether a new document is novel based on the previous documents. Once a decision has been made, the status of that document is fixed. The subtopic detection task differs from this because it is an offline task. The algorithm typically has access to the entire document set. Our method differs from this novelty detection task in that it has access to the entire document collection.

2.1 Existing redundancy measures

Zhang et al. examine five different redundancy measures for adaptive information filtering (Zhang et al.,). Information filtering systems return relevant documents in a document stream to a user. Examples of information filtering systems include traditional information retrieval systems that return relevant documents depending on the user's query.

The redundancy measures Zhang et al. examine are based on online analysis of documents. They identify two methods of measuring redundancy:

- Given n documents, they are considered one by one, and suppose we have processed i documents and we have k clusters. Now we need to process the $i+1^{th}$ document. We compute the distance of the $i+1^{th}$ document with the k clusters and add the document to the closest cluster if the distance is above a certain threshold, else we create a new cluster with only the $i+1^{th}$ document.
- Measure distance between the new document and each previously seen document.

They evaluate several measures like set difference, geometric distance, Distributional similarity and mixture models. Evaluating the five systems, they found that cosine similarity was the most effective measure, followed by the new mixture model measure.

3 Data

We choose several news events that occurred in 2007 and 2008 based on the popularity in the blogosphere. We were looking for events that were widely discussed and commented on. The events in our collection are the top-level events that we have gathered. Table 1 lists the events that were chosen for analysis:

To help illustrate our subtopic detection method, we will use the Virginia Tech tragedy as an example throughout the rest of this paper. People throughout the blogosphere posted responses expressing support and condolences for the people involved, along with their own opinions on what caused it.

Figures 1 and 2 show two different responses to the event. The quote in figure 1 shows an example post from LiveJournal, a popular blogging community. In this post, the user is discussing his view on gun control, a hotly debated topic in the aftermath of the shooting. Figure 2 expresses another person's emotional response to this event. Both posts show different aspects of the same story. Our subtopic detection system seeks to automatically

Event	Description	Posts	Dates
iPhone	iPhone release hype	48810	June 20 , 2007 - July 7, 2007
petfoodrecall	Melamine tainted petfood recall	4285	March 10, 2007 - May 10, 2007
spitzer	Eliot Spitzer prostitution scandal	10379	March 6, 2008 - March 23, 2008
vtech	Virginia Tech shooting	12256	April 16, 2007 - April 30, 2007

Table 1: Major events summarized

identify these and other distinct discussions that occur around an event.

> After the Virginia Tech murders, there's the usual outcry for something to be done, and in particular, for more gun control. As usual, I am not persuaded. The Virginia Tech campus had gun control, which meant that Cho Seung-Hui was in violation of the law even before he started shooting, and also that no law-abiding citizens were able to draw.

Figure 1: Example blog post from LiveJournal discussing gun control (Rosen, 2007)

> ... Predictably, there have been rumblings in the media that video games contributed to Cho Seung-Hui's massacre at Virginia Tech. Jack Thompson has come out screaming, referring to gamers as "knuckleheads" and calling video games "mental masturbation" all the while referring to himself as an "educator" and "pioneer" out to "right" society. ...

Figure 2: Example blog post discussing video games (hoopdog, 2007)

Figure 3 shows a generalized Venn diagram (Kestler et al., 2005) of the cluster overlap between different keyphrases from the Virginia Tech event.

3.1 Preprocessing

Data was collected from the Blogocenter bloglines database. The Blogocenter group at UCLA has been retrieving RSS feeds from the Bloglines, Blogspot, Microsoft Live Spaces, and syndic8 aggregators for the past several years. They currently have over 192 million blog posts collected.

For each news item, relevant posts were retrieved, based on keyword searching and date of blog post. Posts from the date of occurrence of the item to two weeks after the event occurred

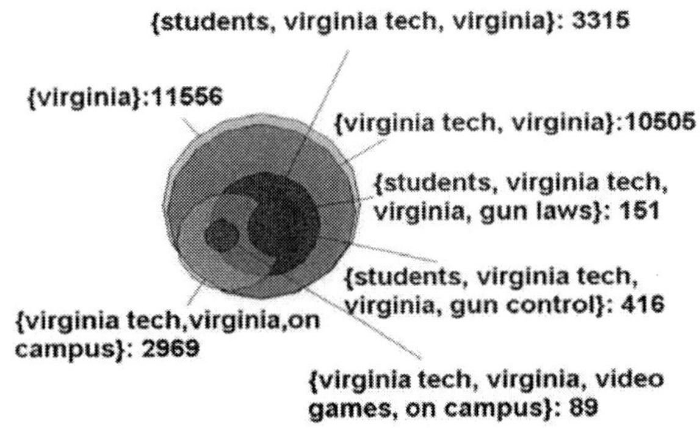

Figure 3: Generalized Venn diagram of topic overlap in the Virginia Tech collection

were gathered, regardless of the actual length of the event.

Since many RSS feeds indexed by Bloglines are from commercial news organizations or commercial sites, we had to clean up the retrieved data. Table 1 lists the event we analyzed along with basic statistics.

4 Method

Our algorithm should find discriminative labels for the different topics that exist in a collection of documents. Taken together, these labels should satisfy the following conditions:

- Describe a large portion of the collection
- The overlap between the topics should be minimal

This task is similar to Minimum Set Cover, which is NP-complete (Garey and Johnson, 1990). Therefore, trying to find the optimal solution by enumerating all possible phrases in the corpus would be impossible, instead we propose a two-step method for subtopic detection.

The first step is to generate a list of candidate phrases. These phrases should be informative and representative of all of the different subtopics. The second step should select from these phrases consistent with the two conditions stated above.

4.1 Generating Candidate Phrases

We want to generate a list of phrases that have a high probability of covering the document space. There are many methods that could be used to find informative keyphrases. One such method is using the standard information retrieval TF-IDF model (Salton and McGill, 1986).

Witten et al.(Witten et al., 1999) proposed KEA, an algorithm which generates a list of candidate keyphrases using lexical features. They keyphrases are then selected from these candidates using a supervised machine learning algorithm. This approach is not plausible for our purposes because of the following two reasons.

1. The algorithm is domain-dependent and needs a training set of documents with annotated keyphrases. But our data sets come from various domains and it is not a very viable option to create a training set for each domain.
2. The algorithm generates keyphrases for a single document, but for our purposes we need keyphrases for a corpus.

Another method is using Kullback-Leibler divergence to find informative keyphrases. We found that KL divergence generated good candidate topics.

Tomokiyo and Hurst (2003) developed a method of extracting keyphrases using statistical language models. They considered keyphrases as consisting of two features, *phraseness* and *informativeness*. Phraseness is described by them as the "degree to which a given word sequence is considered to be a phrase." For example, collocations could be considered sequences with a high phraseness. Informativeness is the extent to which a phrase captures the key idea or main topic in a set of documents.

To find keyphrases, they compared two language models, the target document set and a background corpus. Pointwise KL divergence was chosen as the method of finding the difference between two language models.

The KL divergence $D(p||q)$ between two probability mass functions $p(x)$ and $q(x)$ with alphabet χ is given in equation 1.

$$D(p||q) = \sum_{x \in \chi} p(x) log \frac{p(x)}{q(x)} \quad (1)$$

KL divergence is an asymmetric function. $D(p||q)$ may not equal $D(q||p)$.

Pointwise KL divergence is the individual contribution of x to the loss of the entire distribution. The pointwise KL divergence of a single phrase w is $\delta_w(p||q)$:

$$\delta_w(p||q) = p(w) log \frac{p(w)}{q(w)} \quad (2)$$

The phraseness of a phrase can be found by comparing the foreground n-gram language model against the background unigram model. For example, if we were judging the phraseness of "gun control", we would find the pointwise KL divergence of "gun control" between the foreground bigram language model and the foreground unigram language model.

$$\varphi_p = \delta_w(LM_{fg}{}^N || LM_{fg}{}^1) \quad (3)$$

The informativeness of a phrase can be found by finding the pointwise KL divergence of the foreground model against the background model.

$$\varphi_i = \delta_w(LM_{fg}{}^N || LM_{bg}{}^N) \quad (4)$$

A unified score can be formed by adding the phraseness and informative score: $\varphi = \varphi_p + \varphi_i$

4.2 Selecting Topic Labels

Once keyphrases have been extracted from the document set, they are sorted based on their combined score. We select the top n-ranked keyphrases as candidate phrases. This step will hereafter be referred to as "KL divergence module".

Based on our chosen task conditions regarding coverage of the documents and minimized overlap between topics, we need an undirected mapping between phrases and documents. A natural representation for this is a bipartite graph where the two sets of nodes are phrases and documents. Let the graph be: $G = (W, D, E)$ where W is the set of candidate phrases generated by the first step and D is the entire set of documents. E is the set of edges between W and D where there is an edge between a phrase and a document if the document contains the phrase.

We formulate the task as a variation of Weighted Set Cover problem in theoretical computer science. In normal Set Cover we are given a collection of sets S over a universe U, and the goal is to select a minimal subset of S such that the whole universe, U is covered. Unfortunately this problem is NP-complete (Garey and Johnson, 1990), so we must

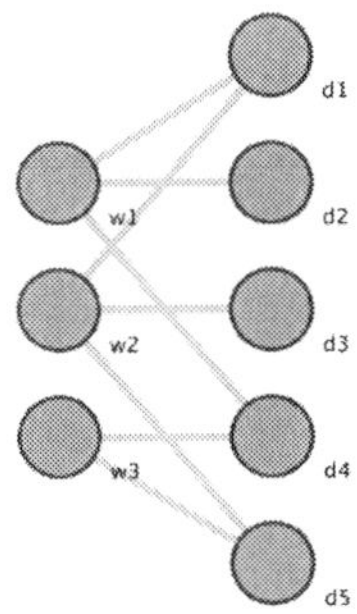

Figure 4: Bipartite graph representation of topic document coverage, where the d_i's are the documents and the w_i's are the n-grams

settle for an approximate solution. But fortunately there exist very good α-approximation algorithms for this problem (Cui, 2007).

The difference in Weighted Set Cover is that each set has an associated real-valued weight or cost and the goal is to find the minimal or maximal cost subset which covers the universe U.

In our problem, each phrase can be thought of as a set of the documents which contain it. The universe is the set of all documents.

4.3 Greedy Algorithm

To solve the above problem, we propose a greedy algorithm. This algorithm computes a cost for each node iteratively and selects the node with the lowest cost at every iteration. The cost of a keyphrase should be such that we do not choose a phrase with very high coverage, like "Virginia" and at the same time not choose words with very low document frequency since a very small collection of documents can not be judged a topic.

Based on these two conditions we have come up with a linear combination of two cost components, similar to Maximal Marginal Relevance (MMR) (Carbonell and Goldstein, 1998).

1. Relative Document Size:

$$f_1(w_i) = \frac{|adj(w_i)|}{N} \tag{5}$$

   where $|adj(w_i)|$ is the document frequency of the word.

   This factor takes into account that we do not want to choose words which cover the whole document collection. For example, phrases such as "Virginia" or "Virginia tech" are bad subtopics, because they cover most of the document set.

2. Redundancy Penalty:

   We want to choose elements that do not have a lot of overlap with other elements. One measure of set overlap is the Jaccard similarity coefficient:

$$J(A, B) = \frac{|A \cap B|}{|A \cup B|} \tag{6}$$

$$f_2(w_i) = 1 - \frac{\sum_{w_j \in W - w_i} J(w_i, w_j)}{|W| - 1} \tag{7}$$

   This component is essentially $1-$ average Jaccard similarity.

   We calculate the pairwise Jaccard coefficient between the target keyphrase and every other keyphrase. The pairwise coefficient vector provides information on how much overlap there is between a keyphrase and every other keyphrase. Phrases with a high average Jaccard coefficient are general facets that cover the entire collection. Phrases with a low Jaccard coefficient are facets that cover specific topics with little overlap.

3. Subtopic Redundancy Memory Effect

   Once a keyphrase has been chosen we also want to penalize other keyphrases that cover the same content or documents. Equation 8 represents a redundancy "memory" for each keyphrase or subtopic. This memory is updated for every step in the greedy algorithm.

$$R(w_i) = R(w_i) + J(w_i, w_j) \tag{8}$$

   where w_j is the newly selected phrase.

A general cost function can be formed from a linear combination of the three cost components. We provide two parameters, α and β to represent the trade-off between coverage, cohesiveness and intersection. For our experiments, we found that an α value of 0.7 and a β value of 0.2 performed well.

$$\begin{aligned} cost(w_i) &= \alpha \times f_1(w_i) \\ &+\beta \times f_2(w_i) \\ &+(1-(\alpha+\beta)) \times R(w_i) \end{aligned} \tag{9}$$

The pseudocode for the greedy algorithm is given in Figure 5. It should be noted that the algorithm requires the costs to be recomputed after every iteration. This is because the cost of a keyphrase may change due to a change in any of the three components. This is because after selecting a keyphrase, it might make another keyphrase redundant, that is, covering the same content. This makes the whole problem a dynamic weighted set cover problem. Hence, the performance guarantees associated with the greedy algorithm for the Weighted Set Cover problem do not hold true for the dynamic version.

Algorithm *Greedy algorithm for weighted set-cover*
Input: Graph $G = (W, D, E)$

```
N: number of documents to cover

Output: Set of discriminative phrases for the different topics
W = {w_1, w_2, ..., w_n}
W_chosen = ∅
num_docs_covered = 0
while num_docs_covered < N
    do for w_i ∈ W
            do cost(w_i) = α × f_1(w_i)
                +β × f_2(w_i)
                +(1 − (α + β)) × R(w_i)
        w_selected = argmax_w cost(w_i)
        for w_i ∈ W
            do R(w_i) = R(w_i) + J(w_selected, w_i)
        num_docs_covered = num_docs_covered +
        |adj(w_selected)|
        W_chosen = W_chosen ∪ {w_selected}
        W = W − {w_selected}
        D = D − adj(selected)
return W_chosen
```

Figure 5: A greedy set-cover algorithm for detecting sub-topics

5 Experiments

As a baseline measure, we extracted the top k phrases from the word distribution as the topic labels. As a gold standard, we manually annotated the four different collections of blog posts. Each annotator generated a list of subtopics.

6 Evaluation

In evaluating topic detection, there exist two categories of methods, *intrinsic* and *extrinsic* (Liddy, 2001). Extrinsic methods evaluate the labels against a particular task whereas intrinsic methods measure the quality of the labels directly. We provide intrinsic and extrinsic evaluations of our algorithm.

To evaluate our facet detection algorithm, we created a gold standard list of facets for each data set. A list of the top 300 keyphrases generated by the KL divergence module was given to two evaluators. The evaluators were the first and second author of this paper. The evaluators labeled each keyphrase as a positive example of a subtopic or a negative example of a subtopic. The positive examples taken together form the gold standard. For this evaluation process we defined a positive subtopic as a cohesive collection of documents discussing the same topic.

Cohen's Kappa coefficient (Cohen, 1960) was calculated for the gold standard. Table 6 lists the κ value for the four data sets.

iPhone	petfoodrecall	spitzer	vtech
0.62	0.86	0.77	0.88

Table 2: Kappa scores for the gold standard

The kappa scores for the *petfoodrecall* and *vtech* datasets showed good agreement among the raters, while the spitzer data set had only fair agreement. For the *iPhone* data set, both evaluators had a large amount of disagreement on what they considered subtopics.

A separate group of two evaluators was given the output from our graph-based algorithm, a list of the top KL divergence keyphrases of the same length, and the gold standard for all four data sets. Evaluators were asked to rate the keyphrases on a scale from one to five, with one indicating a poor subtopic, and five indicating a good subtopic. The number k of subtopics for the algorithm was cutoff where the f-score is maximized. The same number of phrases was chosen for KL divergence as well. Table 3 lists the cutoffs for the four data sets.

iPhone	*Petfood recall*	*Spitzer*	*Vtech*
25	30	24	18

Table 3: Number of generated subtopics for each collection.

In addition, the precision, F-score, coverage and average pairwise Jaccard coefficient were calculated for the four data sets. Precision, recall and the F-score are given in table 4. The precision, recall and F-score for the gold standards is one. The others are shown in table 5. Average pairwise Jaccard coefficient is calculated by finding the Jaccard coefficient for every pair of subtopics in the output and averaging this value. This value is a measure of the redundancy. The average relevance is a normalized version of the combined "phraseness" and "informativeness" score calculated by the keyphrase detection module. This value is normalized by dividing by the KL divergence for the entire 300 phrase list. This provides a relevancy score for the output.

Data set	Precision	Recall	F-score
iphone			
KL-Divergence	0.08	0.10	0.09
Graph-based method	0.52	0.60	0.56
petfoodrecall			
KL-Divergence	0.37	0.39	0.38
Graph-based method	0.61	0.57	0.59
spitzer			
KL-Divergence	0.10	0.08	0.09
Graph-based method	0.79	0.59	0.68
vtech			
KL-Divergence	0.05	0.06	0.05
Graph-based method	0.72	0.76	0.74

Table 4: Precision, recall and F-score for the baseline and graph-based algorithm.

Data set	Coverage	Average pairwise JC	Normalized KL divergence	Human rating
iphone				
KL-Divergence	40168	0.08	18.19	1.92
Gold standard	12977	0.02	2.81	3.13
Graph-based	9850	0.01	1.98	2.82
petfoodrecall				
KL-Divergence	4280	0.18	19.53	1.82
Gold standard	2659	0.05	4.30	3.43
Graph-based	2055	0.01	1.75	2.81
spitzer				
KL-Divergence	9291	0.19	22.90	1.33
Gold standard	4036	0.03	2.29	3.31
Graph-based	2468	0.01	1.60	2.88
vtech				
KL-Divergence	12215	0.29	24.61	1.61
Gold standard	5058	0.03	2.79	3.76
Graph-based	4342	0.01	1.66	3.28

Table 5: Coverage, overlap and relevance and evaluation scores for the gold standard, baseline and graph-based method.

7 Results

Table 6 shows some of the different subtopics chosen by our algorithm for the different data sets. There is no manual involvement required in the algorithm except for the intial preprocessing to remove commercial news feeds and spam posts. Our graph-based method performs very well and almost achieves the gold standard's rating. The F-score for the *iPhone* data set was only 0.56, but we believe part of this may be because this data set did not have clearly defined subtopics, as shown by the low agreement (0.62) among human evaluators.

Spitzer	*Petfood recall*
Ashley Alexandra Dupre	Under Wal-Mart
Oberweis	Xuzhou Anying
Emperor's club	People who buy
Governor of New	Cuts and Gravy
Spitzer's resignation	Cat and Dog
Dr Laura	Cats and Dogs
Mayflower hotel	Food and Drug
Sex workers	Cyanuric acid
former New york	recent pet
High priced prostitution	industrial chemical
McGreevey	massive pet food
Geraldine Ferraro	Royal canin
High priced call	Iams and Eukanuba
legally blind	Dry food
money laundering	
Virginia Tech shooting	*iPhone*
Korean American	Photo sent from
Gun Ownership	Waiting in line
Holocaust survivor	About the iPhone
Mentally ill	Unlimited data
Shooting spree	From my iPhone
Don Imus	cell phones
Video Games	Multi-touch
Gun free zone	Guided tour
West Ambler Johnston	iPhone launch
Columbine High school	Walt Mossberg
Self defense	Apple Inc
Two hours later	Windows Mobile
Gun violence	June 29th
Seung Hui Cho	Web browser
Second Amendment	Activation
South Korean	

Table 6: Different topics chosen by the graph-based algorithm for the different data sets

Figure 6 shows the trade off between coverage and redundancy. This graph clearly shows that the overlap between the subtopics increases very slowly as compared to the number of documents covered. The slope of the curves increases slowly when the number of documents to be covered is small and later increases rapidly. This means that initially there are a lot of small focused subtopics and once we have selected all the focused ones the algorithm is forced to pick the bigger topics and hence the average pairwise intersection increases.

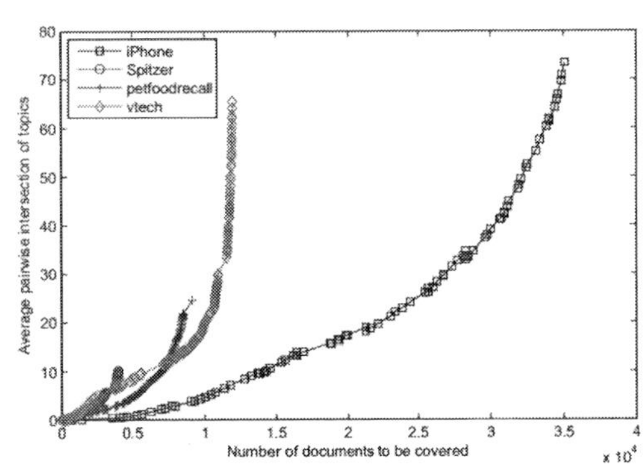

Figure 6: Subtopic redundancy vs. coverage

8 Conclusion

We have presented a new algorithm based on weighted set cover for finding subtopics in a corpus of selected blog postings. The algorithm performs very well in practice compared to the baseline standard, which outputs the top keyphrases according to the Kullback-Leibler divergence method. While the baseline standard outputs keyphrases which are redundant, in the sense, they cover the same documents, the graph-based method outputs keyphrases which have very little intersection. We provide a new method of ranking keyphrases that can help users find different facets of an event.

The identification of facets has many applications to natural language processing. Once facets have been identified in a collection, documents can be clustered based on these facets. These clusters can be used to generate document summaries or for visualization of the event space.

The keyphrases themselves provide a succinct summary of the different subtopics. In future work, we intend to investigate summarization of documents based on subtopic clustering using this method.

9 Acknowledgments

This work was supported by NSF grants IIS 0534323 "Collaborative Research: BlogoCenter - Infrastructure for Collecting, Mining and Accessing Blogs" awarded to The University of Michigan and "iOPENER: A Flexible Framework to Support Rapid Learning in Unfamiliar Research Domains", jointly awarded to U. of Michigan and U. of Maryland as IIS 0705832." Also we would like to thank Vahed Qazvinian and Arzucan Özgür for helping with the evaluation and their valuable suggestions. Any opinions, findings, and conclusions or recommendations expressed in this material are those of the authors and do not necessarily reflect the views of the National Science Foundation.

References

Allan, James, Courtney Wade, and Alvaro Bolivar. Retrieval and novelty detection at the sentence level. *SIGIR 2003*, pages 314–321.

Blei, D., A. Ng, and M. Jordan. 2003. Latent dirichlet allocation. *Journal of Machine Learning Research*, 3:993–1022, January.

Carbonell, Jaime G. and Jade Goldstein. 1998. The use of MMR, diversity-based reranking for reordering documents and producing summaries. *SIGIR 1998*, pages 335–336.

Cohen, J. 1960. A coefficient of agreement for nominal scales. *Educational and Psychological Measurement*, 20:37.

Cui, Peng. 2007. A tighter analysis of set cover greedy algorithm for test set. In *ESCAPE*, pages 24–35.

Frank, Eibe, Gordon W. Paynter, Ian H. Witten, Carl Gutwin, and Craig G. Nevill-Manning. 1999. Domain-specific keyphrase extraction. *Sixteenth International Joint Conference on Artificial Intelligence*, pages 668–673.

Garey, Michael R. and David S. Johnson. 1990. *Computers and Intractability; A Guide to the Theory of NP-Completeness*. W. H. Freeman.

hoopdog. 2007. Follow-up: Blame game. http://hoopdogg.livejournal.com/39060.html.

Hulth, Anette. 2003. Improved automatic keyword extraction given more linguistic knowledge. *EMNLP 2003*, pages 216–223.

Kestler, Hans A., Andre Muller, Thomas M. Gress, and Malte Buchholz. 2005. Generalized venn diagrams: a new method of visualizing complex genetic set relations. *Bioinformatics*, 21:1592–1595, April.

Liddy, Elizabeth. 2001. Advances in automatic text summarization. *Information Retrieval*, 4:82–83.

Rosen, Nicholas D. 2007. Gun control and mental health. http://ndrosen.livejournal.com/128715.html.

Salton, G. and M. J. McGill. 1986. *Introduction to Modern Information Retrieval*. McGraw-Hill, Inc. New York, NY, USA.

Tomokiyo, Takashi and Matthew Hurst. 2003. A language model approach to keyphrase extraction. *ACL 2003 workshop on Multiword expressions: analysis, acquisition and treatment - Volume 18*, pages 33–40.

Turney, Peter D. 2000. Learning algorithms for keyphrase extraction. *Information Retrieval*, 2:303–336.

Witten, Ian H., Gordon W. Paynter, Eibe Frank, Carl Gutwin, and Craig G. Nevill-Manning. 1999. KEA: Practical automatic keyphrase extraction. In *1st ACM/IEEE-CS joint conference on Digital libraries*, pages 254–255.

Zhai, Chengxiang, William W. Cohen, and John Lafferty. 2003. Beyond independent relevance: methods and evaluation metrics for subtopic retrieval. *SIGIR 2003*, pages 10–17.

Zhang, Yi, James P. Callan, and Thomas P. Minka. Novelty and redundancy detection in adaptive filtering. In *SIGIR 2002*, pages 81–88.

Investigating Statistical Techniques for Sentence-Level Event Classification

Martina Naughton
School of Computer Science,
University College Dublin,
Belfield, Dublin 4, Ireland

Nicola Stokes
NICTA Victoria Laboratory,
University of Melbourne,
Victoria, Australia

Joe Carthy
School of Computer Science
University College Dublin
Belfield, Dublin 4, Ireland

Abstract

The ability to correctly classify sentences that describe events is an important task for many natural language applications such as Question Answering (QA) and Summarisation. In this paper, we treat event detection as a sentence level text classification problem. We compare the performance of two approaches to this task: a Support Vector Machine (SVM) classifier and a Language Modeling (LM) approach. We also investigate a rule based method that uses hand crafted lists of terms derived from WordNet. These terms are strongly associated with a given event type, and can be used to identify sentences describing instances of that type. We use two datasets in our experiments, and evaluate each technique on six distinct event types. Our results indicate that the SVM consistently outperform the LM technique for this task. More interestingly, we discover that the manual rule based classification system is a very powerful baseline that outperforms the SVM on three of the six event types.

1 Introduction

Event detection is a core Natural Language Processing (NLP) task that focuses on the automatic identification and classification of various event types in text. This task has applications in automatic Text Summararisation and Question Answering (QA). For example, event recognition is a core task in QA since the majority of web user questions have been found to relate to events and situations in the world (Saurí et al., 2005). For complex questions such as *How many people were killed in Baghdad in March?*, QA systems often rely on event detection systems to identify all relevant events in a set of documents before formulating an answer. More recently, much research in summarisation has focused on the use of phrasal concepts such as events to represent sentences in extractive summarisation systems. Specifically, (Filatova and Hatzivassiloglou, 2004) use event-based features to represent sentences and shows that this approach improves the quality of the final summaries when compared with a baseline bag-of-words approach.

In this paper, we investigate the use of statistical methods for identifying the sentences in a document that describe one or more instances of a specified event type. We treat this task as a text classification problem where each sentence in a given document is either classified as containing an instance of the target event or not. We view this task as a filtering step in a larger pipeline NLP architecture (e.g. a QA system) which helps speed up subsequent processing by removing irrelevant, non-event sentences.

Two event detection approaches are explored in this paper. More specifically, we train a Support Vector Machine (SVM) using a variety of term, lexical and additional event based features to encode each train/test instance. We also adopt a probabilistic language modeling approach that captures how text within sentences that describe event instances is likely to be generated. We estimate a series of models using three well-known smoothing approaches, including LaPlace, Jelinek-Mercer and Absolute Discounting Smoothing. Their overall behavior on classification performance is ex-

©2008. Licensed under the *Creative Commons Attribution-Noncommercial-Share Alike 3.0 Unported* license (http://creativecommons.org/licenses/by-nc-sa/3.0/). Some rights reserved.

amined. One advantage of language modeling for text classification is that instead of explicitly pre-computing features and selecting a subset based on arbitrary decisions (as is often the case with standard classification learning approaches such as an SVM), the language modeling approach simply considers all terms occurring in the text as candidate features, and implicitly considers the contribution of every feature in the final model. Thus, language modeling approaches avoids a potentially error-prone feature selection process.

Event classification at a sentence level is a challenging task. For example, if the target event is "Die", we want our system to extract sentences like *"5 people were killed in the explosion."* and *"A young boy and his mother were found dead on Wednesday evening."*. However, it also needs to detect complex cases like: *"An ambulance rushed the soldier to hospital, but efforts to save him failed."* and reject instances like *"Fragmentation mines have a killing range of 100 feet."*. It seems intuitive that a naïve system that selects only sentences that contain terms with senses connected with death like "kill", "die" or "execute" as positive instances would catch many positive cases. However, there are instances where this approach would fail. In this work we evaluate the effectiveness of such a shallow NLP approach, by developing a manual rule based system that finds sentences connected to a target event type using a hand crafted list of terms created with senses found in WordNet.

We use two datasets in our experiments. The first is the ACE 2005 Multilingual Training Corpus (Walker et al., 2006) that was annotated for 33 different event types. However, within the ACE data the number of instances referring to each event type is somewhat limited. For this reason, we select the six types with the highest frequency in the data. These include "Die", "Attack", "Transport", "Meet", "Injure" and "Charge-indict" types. The second corpus is a collection of articles from the Iraq Body Count (IBC) database[1] annotated for the "Die" event. This dataset arose from a larger humanitarian project that focuses on the collection of fatalities statistics from unstructured news data. We use this additional corpus to augment the amount of data used for training and testing the "Die" event type, and to investigate the use of extra training data on overall classification performance.

Overall, our results demonstrate that the trained SVM proves to be more effective than the LM based approach for this task across all event types. We also show that our baseline system, a hand crafted rule-based system, performs surprisingly well. The remainder of this paper is organised as follows. Section 2 covers related work. We continue with details of the datasets used in the experiments in Section 3. Section 4 describes our event classification approaches while Section 5 presents their results. We conclude with a discussion of experimental observations and opportunities for future work in Section 6.

2 Background and Related Work

Event detection, in the context of news stories, has been an active area of research for the best part of ten years. For example, the NIST sponsored Topic Detection and Tracking (TDT) project, which began in 1998 investigated the development of technologies that could detect novel events in segmented or unsegmented news streams, and track the progression of these event over time (Allan et al., 1998). Although this project ended in 2004, event detection is still investigated by more recently established projects such as the Automatic Content Extraction (ACE) program, and in domains outside of news text such as Biomedical Text Processing (Murff et al., 2003).

The aim of the TDT First Story Detection (FSD) or New Event Detection (NED) task was to flag documents that discuss breaking news stories as they arrive on a news stream. Dragon Systems adopted a LM approach to this task (Allan et al., 1998; Yamron et al., 2002) building discriminator topic models from the collection and representing documents using unigram term frequencies. Then they used a single-pass clustering algorithm to determine the documents that describe new events. The overall goal of the TDT Event Tracking task was to track the development of specific events over time. However, these TDT tasks were somewhat restrictive in the sense that detection is carried out at document level. Our work differs from TDT research since event detection is performed at a sentence level where the amount of data to build discriminate models for recognising event instances is far more limited.

The goal of the ACE Event Detection and Recognition task is to identify all event instances (as well as the attributes and participants of each

[1] `http://www.iraqbodycount.org/`

Table 1: ACE Corpus Statistics

	Die	Injure	Attack	Meet	Transport	Charge-Indict
Number of Documents	154	50	235	84	181	43
Avg. document length	29.19	29.74	29.62	31.41	32.78	14.81
Avg. event instances per document	2.31	1.64	3.55	1.55	2.55	1.72
Avg. event instances per sentence	1.13	1.11	1.12	1.02	1.08	1.03

Table 2: IBC Corpus Statistics

	IBC Corpus
Number of Documents	332
Number of Sources	77
Avg. document length	25.98
Avg. events per document	4.6
Avg. events per sentence	1.14

instance) of a pre-specified set of event types. An ACE event is defined as a specific occurence involving zero or more ACE entities[2], values and time expressions. Two spans of text are used to identify each event: the event *trigger* and the event *mention*. An event *trigger* or *anchor* is the word that most clearly expresses its occurrence. In many cases, this will be the main verb in the event mention. It can also appear as a noun ("The **meeting** lasted 5 hours.") or an adjective ("the **dead** men ..."). The event *mention* is the sentence that describes the event. Even though the task of identifying event mentions is not directly evaluated in ACE, systems still need to identify them so that the various attributes and participants within the mention can be extracted. The algorithms evaluated in this paper can also be applied to the detection of event mentions that contain the ACE events. Overall five sites participated in this task in 2005. The most similar work to that describe in this paper is detailed in (Ahn, 2006), who treats the task of finding all event triggers (used to identify each event) as a word classification task where the task is to classify every term in a document with a label defined by 34 classes. Features used included various lexical, WordNet, dependency and related entity features.

3 Corpora

The ACE 2005 Multilingual Corpus was annotated for Entities, Relations and Events. It consists of articles originating from six difference sources including Newswire (20%), Broadcast News (20%), Broadcast Conversation (15%), Weblog (15%), Usenet Newsgroups (15%) and Conversational Telephone Speech (15%). Statistics on the documents in this collection are presented in Table 1. We evaluate our methods on the following event types which have a high number of instances in the collection: "Die", "Attack", "Transport", "Meet", "Injure" and "Charge-indict".

The data we use from the IBC database consists of Newswire articles gathered from 77 different news sources. Statistics describing this dataset are contained in Table 2. To obtain a gold standard set of annotations for articles in the IBC corpus, we asked ten volunteers to mark up all the "Die" event instances. To maintain consistency across both datasets, events in the IBC corpus were identified in a manner that conforms to the ACE annotation guidelines. In order to approximate the level of inter-annotation agreement achieved for the IBC corpus, two annotators were asked to annotate a disjoint set of 250 documents. Inter-rater agreements were calculated using the kappa statistic that was first proposed by (Cohen, 1960). Using the annotated data, a kappa score of 0.67 was obtained, indicating that while the task is difficult for humans the data is still useful for our training and test purposes. Discrepancies were adjudicated and resolved by an independent volunteer.

4 Event Detection as Classification

We treat the task of determining whether a given sentence describes an instance of the target event as a binary text classification task where it is assigned one of the following classes:

- **On-Event Sentence:** a sentence that contains one or more instances of the target event type.
- **Off-Event Sentence:** a sentence that does not contain any instances of the target event type.

4.1 A Machine Learning Approach

In an attempt to develop a gold standard approach for this task we use Support Vector Machines (SVM) to automatically classify each instance as either an "on-event" or "off-event" sentence. SVMs have been shown to be robust in

[2]An ACE Entity is an entity identified using guidelines outlined by ACE Entity Detection and Recognition task.

classification tasks involving text where the dimensionality is high (Joachims, 1998). Each sentence forms a train/test instance for our classifier and is encoded using the following set of features.

Terms: Stemmed terms with a frequency in the training data greater than 2 were used as a term feature. Stopwords were not used as term features.

Noun Chunks: All noun chunks (e.g. "american soldier") with a frequency greater than 2 in the training data were also used as a feature.

Lexical Information: The presence or absence of each part of speech (POS) tag and chunk tag was used as a feature. We use the Maximum Entropy POS tagger and Chunker that are available with the C&C Toolkit (Curran et al., 2007). The POS Tagger uses the standard set of grammatical categories from the Penn Treebank and the chunker recognises the standard set of grammatical chunk tags: NP, VP, PP, ADJP, ADVP and so on.

Additional Features: We added the following additional features to the feature vector: sentence length, sentence position, presence/absence of negative terms (e.g. no, not, didn't, don't, isn't, hasn't), presence/absence of a modal terms (e.g. may, might, shall, should, must, will), a lookahead feature that indicates whether the next sentence is an event sentence, a look-back feature indicating whether or not the previous sentence is an event sentence and the presence/absence of a time-stamp. Time-stamps were identified using inhouse software developed by the Language Technology Group at the University of Melbourne[3].

In the past, feature selection methods have been found to have a positive effect on classification accuracy of text classification tasks. To examine the effects of such techniques on this task, we use Information Gain (IG) to reduce the number of features used by the classifier by a factor of 2.

4.2 Language Modeling Approaches

The Language modeling approach presented here is based on Bayesian decision theory. Consider the situation where we wish to classify a sentence s_k into a category $c \in C = \{C_1 \ldots\ldots C_{|C|}\}$. One approach is to choose the category that has the largest posterior probability given the training text:

$$c^* = \arg\max_{c \in C} \{Pr(c|s_k)\} \quad (1)$$

Specifically, we construct a language model $LM(c_i)$ for each class c_i. All models built are unigram models that use a maximum likelihood estimator to approximate term probabilities. According to this model (built from sentences $\{s_1 \ldots s_m\}$ belonging to class c_i in the training data) we can calculate the probability that term w was generated from class c_i as:

$$P(w|LM(c_i)) = \frac{tf(w, c_i)}{|c_i|} \quad (2)$$

where $tf(w, c_i)$ is the term frequency of term w in c_i (that is, $\{s_1 \ldots s_m\}$) and $|c_i|$ is the total number of terms in class c_i. We make the usual assumptions that word co-occurences are independent. As a result, the probability of a sentence is the product of the probabilities of its terms. We calculate the probability that a given test sentence s_k belongs to class c_i as follows:

$$P(s_k|LM(c_i)) = \prod_{w \in s_k} P(w|LM(c_i)) \quad (3)$$

However, this model will generally underestimate the probability of any unseen word in the sentence, that is terms that do not appear in the training data used to build the language model. To combat this, smoothing techniques are used to assign a non-zero probability to the unseen words, which improves the accuracy of the overall term probability estimation. Many smoothing methods have been proposed over the years, and in general, they work by discounting the probabilities of seen terms and assign this extra probability mass to unseen words. In IR, it has been found that the choice of smoothing method significantly affects retrieval performance (Zhai and Lafferty, 2001; Kraaij and Spitters, 2003). For this reason, we experiment with the Laplace, Jelinek-Mercer and Absolute Discounting Smoothing methods, and compare their effects on classification performance in Section 5.

For this classification task, we normalise all numeric references, locations, person names and organisations to "DIGIT", "LOC", "PER", and "ORG" respectively. This helps to reduce the dimensionality of our models, and improve their classification accuracy, particular in cases where unseen instances of these entities occur in the test data.

4.3 Baseline Measures

We compare the performance our ML and LM approaches to the following plausible baseline systems: **Random** assigns each instance (sentence)

[3]http://www.cs.mu.oz.au/research/lt/

randomly to one of the possible classes. While **Majority Class Baseline** assigns each instance to the class that is most frequent in the training data. In our case, this is the "off-event" class.

According to the ACE annotation guidelines[4] event instances are identified in the text by finding event triggers that explicitly mark the occurrence of the event. As a result, each event instance tagged in our datasets have a corresponding trigger that the annotators used to identify it. For example, terms like "killing", "death" and "murder" are common triggers used to identify the "Die" event type. Therefore, we expect that a system that selects sentences containing one or more candidate trigger terms as positive "on-event" sentences for a given event type, would be a suitable baseline for this task. To investigate this further we add the following baseline system:

Manual Trigger-Based Classification: For each event type, we use WordNet to manually create a list of terms that are synonyms or hyponyms (is a type of) of the event type. For example, in the case of the "Meet" and "Die" events common trigger terms include {"*encounter*", "*visit*", "*reunite*"} and {"*die*", "*suicide*", "*assassination*"} respectively. We classify each sentence for a given event type as follows: if a sentence contains one or more terms in the trigger list for that event type then it is assigned to the "on-event" class for that type. Otherwise it is assigned to the "off-event" class. Table 3 contains the number of trigger terms used for each event[5].

Table 3: Trigger term lists for the six event types used in the experiments.

Event Type	Number of triggers terms
Die	29
Transport	14
Meet	12
Injure	10
Charge-Indict	8
Attack	8

5 Evaluation Methodology & Results

A standard measure for classification performance is classification accuracy. However for corpora where the class distribution is skewed (as is the case in our datasets where approx. 90% of the instances belong to the "off-event" class) this measure can be misleading. So instead we have used precision, recall and F1 to evaluate each technique. If a is the number of sentences correctly classified by a system to class i, b is the total number of sentences classified to class i by a system, and c is the total number of human-annotated sentences in class i. Then the precision and recall for class i can be defined as follows: $Prec_i = \frac{a}{b}$, $Recall_i = \frac{a}{c}$. Finally, F1 (the harmonic mean between precision and recall) for class i is defined as $F1_i = \frac{2 \times Prec_i \times Recall_i}{Prec_i + Recall_i}$. In the results presented in this section we present the precision recall and F1 for each class as well as the overall accuracy score.

Results: In our experiments we use a relatively efficient implementation of an SVM called the Sequential Minimal Optimisation (SMO) algorithm (Platt, 1999) which is provided by the Weka framework (Witten and Frank, 2000). Results presented in this section are divided into two parts. In the first part, all results were obtained using the IBC dataset where the target event type is "Die". We provide a more detailed comparison of the performance of each algorithm using this type as more data was available for it. In the second section, we examine the effectiveness of each approach for all six event types (listed in Section 3) using the ACE data. All reported scores were generated using 50:50 randomly selected train/test splits averaged over 5 runs.

As part of the first set of results Table 4 shows the precision, recall and F1 achieved for the "on-event" and "off-event" classes as well as the overall classification accuracy obtained by each approach. Two variations of the SVM were built. The first version (denoted in the table by SVM(All Features IG)) was built using all terms, nouns chunks, lexical and additional features to encode each train/test instance where the features were reduced using IG. In the second version, the same features were used but no feature reduction was carried out (denoted in the table by SVM(All Features)). LangModel(JM), LangModel(DS) and LangModel(LP) represent language models smoothed using Jelinek-Mercer, Discount Smoothing and LaPlace techniques respectively. Overall these results suggest that the SVM using IG for feature selection is the most effective method for correctly classifying both "on-event" and "off-event" sentences. Specifically, it achieves 90.23% and 96.70% F1 score for these

[4]Available at `http://projects.ldc.upenn.edu/ace/annotation/`

[5]The lists of the trigger terms used for each event type are available at `http://inismor.ucd.ie/~martina/`

Table 4: % Precision, Recall and F1 for both classes as well as the classification accuracy achieved by all algorithms using a 50:50 train/test split where the target event type is "Die".

Algorithm	On-Event Class			Off-Event Class			Accuracy
	Precision	Recall	F1	Precision	Recall	F1	
SVM(All Features IG)	**90.61**	**89.87**	**90.23**	**96.15**	**97.26**	**96.70**	**94.60**
SVM(All Features)	89.63	88.52	89.06	96.08	96.49	96.28	94.45
Trigger-Based Classification	83.10	93.34	87.92	97.25	93.24	95.20	93.09
LangModel(DS)	63.11	82.4	71.46	93.13	83.16	87.86	82.98
LangModel(JM)	59.46	86.01	70.31	94.22	79.53	86.25	81.22
LangModel(LP)	59.22	79.56	67.89	91.89	80.88	86.03	80.54
Majority Class ("off-event")	0.0	0.0	0.0	74.50	100.00	85.38	74.17
Random	26.57	51.73	35.10	75.58	50.0	60.18	50.34

Table 5: % F1 for both classes achieved by the SVM using different combinations of features.

Features	F1(On-Event)	F1(Off-Event)
terms	89.52	96.43
terms + nc	89.58	96.31
terms + nc + lex	89.62	96.44
All Features	**90.23**	**96.70**

classes respectively. When IG is not used we see a marginal decrease of approx. 1% in these scores. The fact that both versions of the SVM obtain approx. 90% F1 scores for the "on-event" class is extremely encouraging when you consider the large skew in class distribution that is present here (i.e., the majority of training instances belong to the"off-event" class).

To examine the effects of the various features on overall performance, we evaluated the SVM using different feature combinations. These results are shown in Table 5 where "terms", "nc", and "lex" denote the terms, noun chunks and lexical feature sets respectively. "All Features" includes these features and the "Additional Features" described in Section 4.1. One obvious conclusion from this table is that terms alone prove to be the most valuable features for this task. Only a little increase in performance is achieved by adding the other feature sets.

The graphs in Figure 1 shows the % F1 of both classes achieved by all methods using varying levels of training data. From these graphs we see that the SVM obtains over 80% F1 for the "on-event" class and over 90% F1 for the "off-event" class when only 10% of the training data is used. These results increase gradually when the amount of training data increases. For levels of training data greater than 30% the SVM consistency achieves higher F1 scores for both classes than all other methods for this task.

In general, the language modeling based techniques are not as effective as the SVM approach for this classification task. However, from Table 4 we see that all language models achieve approx. 70% F1 for the "on-event" class and approx. 86% F1 for the "off-event" class when only 50% of the IBC data is used to build the models. This is encouraging since they require little or no feature engineering and less time to train. Models smoothed with the Laplace method tend to have the least impact out of the three model variations. This is due to the fact that this method assigns the same probability to all unseen terms. Thus, a term like "professor" that may only occur once in the dataset has the same likelihood of occurring in an "on-event" sentence as a term like "kill" that has a very high frequency in the dataset. In contrast, the Jelinek-Mercer and Absolute Discounting smoothing methods estimate the probability of unseen terms according to a background model built using the entire collection. Therefore, the probabilities assigned to unseen words is proportional to their global distribution in the entire corpus. Consequently, the probabilities assigned to unseen terms tend to be more reliable approximations of true term probabilities.

Overall, the trigger-based classification baseline approach performs very well achieving similar scores to the SVM. This suggests that selecting sentences with terms associated with the target event is an effective way of solving this problem. That said, it still makes mistakes that the SVM and language models have the ability to correct. For example, many sentences that contain terms like "*suicide*" and "*killing*" as part of a noun phase (e.g. "*suicide driver*" or "*killing range*") do not report a death. The trigger classification baseline will classify these as an "on-event" instances whereas the SVM correctly places them in the "off-event" category. More interesting are the cases missed by the trigger classification baseline and SVM that are

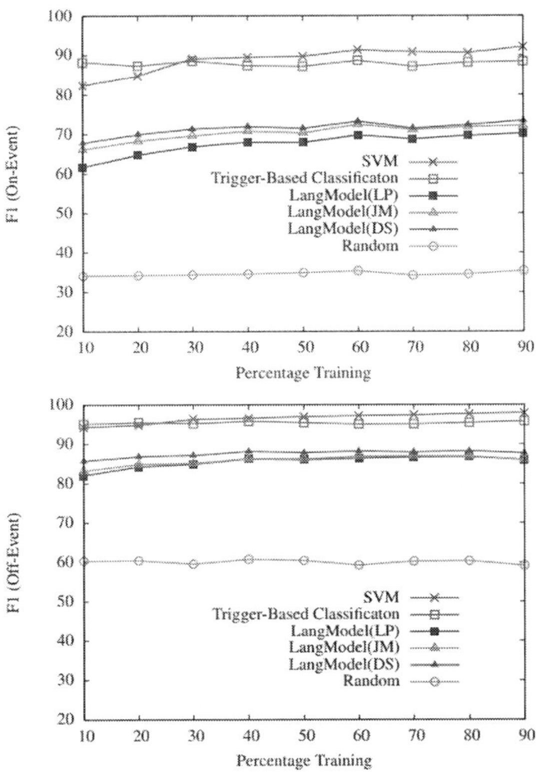

Figure 1: % F1 for the on-event (top) and off-event (bottom) classes for all methods using varying levels of training data where the target event is "Die".

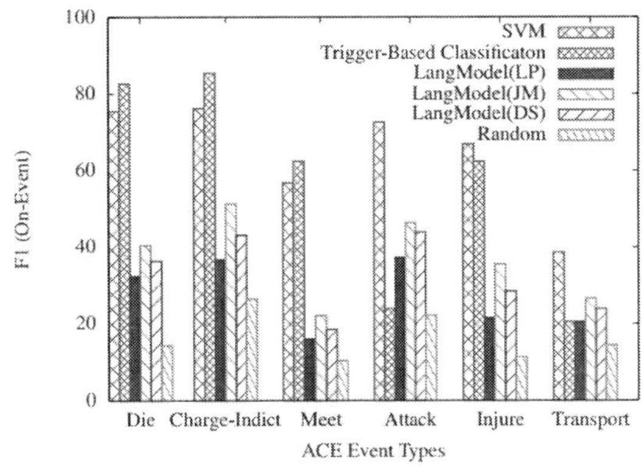

Figure 2: % F1 of the "on-event" class achieved by all methods for the six ACE event types.

corrected by the language models. These include sentences like "*Three bodies were found yesterday in central Baghdad.*" and "*If the Americans have killed them, then why dont they show the tape.*". In fact, it turns out that over 50% of the errors produced by the SVM and manual trigger-based approach when the target event is "Die" are classified correctly by the language models. Although this is encouraging, the overall error rate of the language modeling approach is too high to rely on it alone. However, this evidence suggests that it may prove useful in the future to somehow combine the predictions of all three approaches in a way that improves overall classification performance.

We now move on to the second part of the experiments. Here, we present the results for six event types (as listed in Section 3) using only data from ACE corpus. Figure 2 shows the % F1 of the "on-event" class achieved by all approaches for each event type. We have omitted the % F1 scores for the "off-event" class as they do not vary significantly across event types and are similar to those reported in Table 4. The SVM, language models, trigger-based and random baselines achieve approx. 96%, 95%, 86% and 60% "off-event" F1 scores respectively across all event types.

On the other hand, Figure 2 demonstrates that the performance of each approach for the "on-event" class varies considerably across the event types. For instance, the trigger-based classification baseline out-performs all other approaches achieving over 60% F1 score for the "Meet", "Die" and "Charge-Indict" types. However for events like "Attack" and "Transport" this baselines F1 score drops to approx. 20% thus achieving scores that are only marginally above the random baseline. Interestingly, we notice that although it performs better for events like "Meet" and "Charge-Indict", the number of trigger terms used to detect these types is much smaller than the number used for the "Attack" and "Transport" types (see Table 3). This indicates that event types where this simple baseline performs well are those where the vocabulary used to describe them is small. Event types where it achieves poor results are broader types like "Transport" and "Attack" that cover a larger spectrum of event instances from heterogeneous contexts and situations. However, we see from Figure 2 that the SVM performs well on such event types and as a result out-performs the trigger-based selection process by approximately a factor of 4 for the "Attack" event and a factor of 2 for the "Transport" event.

When we compare both datasets we find that the ACE data is made up of newswire articles, Broadcast news, broadcast conversational texts, weblogs, usenet newsgroup texts and conversational telephone speech that has been transcribed, whereas the IBC corpus consists mainly of newswire articles reporting fatalities during the Iraqi War. As a result, event instances in the ACE data describing the "Die" event type are likely to report fatalities not only from Iraq but also from more diverse contexts and situations. To investigate how performance differs for the "Die" event type across these datasets, we compare the IBC results in Table 4 with the ACE results in Figure 2. We find that the F1 scores of the "off-event" class are not affected much. However, the F1 scores for the "on-event" class for the SVM and trigger-based baseline are reduced by margins of approx. 12% and 5% respectively. We also notice that the performance of the unigram language models are reduced significantly by a factor of 2 indicating that they struggle to approximate accurate term probabilities when the vocabulary is more diverse and the amount of training data is limited.

6 Discussion

Sentence level event classification is an important first step for many NLP applications such as QA and summarisation systems. For each event type used in our experiments we treated this as a binary classification task and compared a variety of approaches for identifying sentences that described instances of that type. The results showed that the trained SVM was more effective than the language modeling approaches across all event types. Another interesting contribution of this paper is that the trigger-based classification baseline performed better than expected. Specifically, for three of the six event types it out-performed the trained SVM. This suggests that although there are cases where such terms appear in sentences that do not describe instances of a given type (for instance, "*The boy was nearly killed.*"), these cases are in the minority. However, the success of this baseline is somewhat dependent on the nature of the event in question. For broader events like "Transport" and "Attack" where the trigger terms can be harder to predict, it performs quiet poorly. Therefore, as part of future work, we hope to investigate ways of automating the creation of these term lists for a specified event type as this proved to be an effective approach to this task.

Acknowledgements. This research was supported by the Irish Research Council for Science, Engineering & Technology (IRCSET) and IBM under grant RS/2004/IBM/1. The authors also wishes to thank the members of the Language Technology Research Group at the University of Melbourne and NICTA for their helpful discussions regarding this research.

References

Ahn, David. 2006. The stages of event extraction. In *Proceedings of the ACL Workshop on Annotating and Reasoning about Time and Events*, pages 1–8, Sydney, Australia, July.

Allan, James, Jaime Carbonell, George Doddington, Jonathon Yamron, and Yiming Yang. 1998. Topic detection and tracking pilot study. final report.

Cohen, Jacob. 1960. A coeficient of agreement for nominal scales. *Educational and Psychological Measurement*, 20(1):37–46.

Curran, James, Stephen Clark, and Johan Bos. 2007. Linguistically motivated large-scale nlp with c & c and boxer. In *Proceedings of the ACL 2007 Demonstrations Session (ACL-07 demo)*, pages 29–32.

Filatova, Elena and Vasileios Hatzivassiloglou. 2004. Event-based extractive summarization. In *In Proceedings of ACL Workshop on Summarization*, pages 104 – 111.

Joachims, Thorsten. 1998. Text categorization with support vector machines: learning with many relevant features. In Nédellec, Claire and Céline Rouveirol, editors, *Proceedings of the 10th ECML*, pages 137–142, Chemnitz, DE. Springer Verlag, Heidelberg, DE.

Kraaij, Wessel and Martijn Spitters. 2003. Language models for topic tracking. In Croft, Bruce and John Lafferty, editors, *Language Models for Information Retrieval*. Kluwer Academic Publishers.

Murff, Harvey, Vimla Patel, George Hripcsak, and David Bates. 2003. Detecting adverse events for patient safety research: a review of current methodologies. *Journal of Biomedical Informatics*, 36(1/2):131–143.

Platt, John. 1999. Fast training of support vector machines using sequential minimal optimization. *Advances in kernel methods: support vector learning*, pages 185–208.

Saurí, Roser, Robert Knippen, Marc Verhagen, and James Pustejovsky. 2005. Evita: a robust event recognizer for qa systems. In *HLT*, pages 700–707.

Walker, Christopher., Stephanie. Strassel, Julie Medero, and Linguistic Data Consortium. 2006. *ACE 2005 Multilingual Training Corpus*. Linguistic Data Consortium, University of Pennsylvania.

Witten, Ian and Eibe Frank. 2000. *Data mining: practical machine learning tools and techniques with Java implementations*. Morgan Kaufmann Publishers Inc.

Yamron, JP, L. Gillick, P. van Mulbregt, and S. Knecht. 2002. Statistical models of topical content. *The Kluwer International Series on Information Retrieval*, pages 115–134.

Zhai, Chengxiang and John Lafferty. 2001. A study of smoothing methods for language models applied to ad hoc information retrieval. In *Research and Development in Information Retrieval*, pages 334–342.

Exploring Domain Differences for the Design of Pronoun Resolution Systems for Biomedical Text

Ngan L.T. Nguyen **Jin-Dong Kim**
Department of Computer Science, University of Tokyo, Hongo 7-3-1, Tokyo, Japan
{nltngan, jdkim}@is.s.u-tokyo.ac.jp

Abstract

Much effort in the research community has been spent on solving the anaphora resolution or pronoun resolution problem, and in particular for news texts. In order to selectively inherit the previous works and solve the same problem for a new domain, we carried out a comparative study with three different corpora: MUC, ACE for the news texts, and GENIA for bio-medical papers. Our corpus analysis and experimental results show the significant differences in the use of pronouns in the two domains, thus by properly considering the characteristics of a domain, we can improve the performance of pronoun resolution for that domain.

1 Introduction

Pronoun resolution is the task of determining the **antecedent** of an **anaphoric** pronoun, or a pronoun pointing back to some previously mentioned item in a text. For example, in the sentence, *"**The IL-2 gene** displays both T cell specific and inducible expression: **it** is only expressed in CD4+ T cells after antigenic or mitogenic stimulation,"* the pronoun *"it"* should be resolved to refer to *"the IL-2 gene,"* and thus, we have an **anaphora link**.

Pronoun resolution is an important task in the family of reference resolution tasks, including anaphora resolution and co-reference resolution, which are known as significant parts of text understanding systems. Recently the need to have more powerful information extraction systems for biomedical technical papers has motivated researchers to solve the same task for the biomedical domain. Castano (Castano et al., 2002) resolved the sortal and pronominal anaphora, by using a salience measure, which is the sum of all feature scores. Kim and Park (Kim and C.Park, 2004) introduced BioAR, a biomedical anaphora resolution system that relates entity mentions in text with their corresponding Swiss-Prot entries. This system resolves anaphoric pronouns by using heuristic rules and seven patterns for parallelism. However, the sizes of the data sets used in their experiments were small. In the former system, 46 and 54 MEDLINE abstracts were used for the development set, and the test set respectively, and the test set in the latter work contained only sixteen anaphoric pronouns. Contrary to their work, in this work we made use of GENIA, a large co-reference annotated corpus for the bio domain, containing 1999 MEDLINE abstracts.

While there are quite a few works on this task for the bio-medical domain, for other domains, and especially for the news domain, a myriad of works on pronoun resolution has been carried out by the NLP researchers (Mitkov, 2002). Since Soon (Soon et al., 2001) started the trend of using the machine learning approach by using a binary classifier in a pairwise manner for solving co-reference resolution problem, many machine learning-based systems have been built, using both supervised and, unsupervised learning methods (Haghighi and Klein, 2007). Such methods were claimed to be comparable with traditional methods. However, the problems caused by domain differences, which strongly affect a deep-semantics related task like pronoun resolution, have not yet been studied well enough.

In order to recognize the important factors in

© 2008. Licensed under the *Creative Commons Attribution-Noncommercial-Share Alike 3.0 Unported* license (http://creativecommons.org/licenses/by-nc-sa/3.0/). Some rights reserved.

building an effective machine learning-based pronoun resolution system, and in particular for the bio-domain, we have built a machine learning-based pronoun resolver and observed the contributions of different features in the pronoun resolution process. In our experiments for the news domain, we used the MUC-7 and ACE corpora, and for the biomedical domain, we employed the GENIA co-reference corpus.

Section 2 describes the noticeable issues related to the corpora, and their preprocessing. Section 3 describes the implementation of our pronoun resolution system, including the resolution model and the features used. Our experiment settings, evaluation scheme, and experimental results are presented in Section 4. Finally, we conclude our paper in Section 5.

2 Corpora

In this section, we briefly introduce three corpora used in our experiments: MUC-7, ACE, and GENIA, and discuss the differences in their annotation schemes. Afterwards, we analyzed the major differences in the distributions of anaphoric pronouns in these data sets, which provide important information for the design of features used in the pronoun resolution process.

The MUC-7 co-reference corpus is a collection of news wire articles from the source for North American News Text Corpora. It contains the *training*, *dry run* test, and *formal run* test sets. The dry run and formal run have different domains; the dry run (and training) consists of aircrash scenarios, while the formal run consists of missile launch scenarios. The ACE (phase 2) corpus for named entity detection contains three data sets: news wire (NWIRE), broadcast news (BNEWS), and newspaper (NPAPER). Each data set is divided into 2 parts for training (*train*), and for development testing (*devtest*). For the bio-domain, we use the GENIA co-reference corpus, containing 1999 abstracts selected from MEDLINE: a huge source of bio-domain scientific papers.

These three corpora are all manually annotated with co-reference information; i.e., the information where mentions refer to the same entities. However, since the annotation schemes used are not the same, these corpora contain some significant differences, which may affect our reference resolution systems.

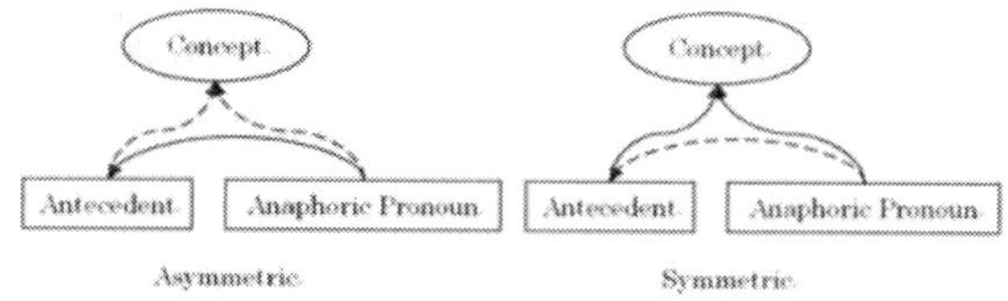

Figure 1: The symmetric and asymmetric annotation schemes. The dotted lines represent implicit links between the elements.

2.1 Variations in co-reference annotation schemes

We started by introducing some important terminologies together with some noticeable issues related to the common co-reference annotation scheme. Later, we mention the differences among the annotation schemes of the three corpora used in our experiments.

There are three main elements in the co-reference corpus annotation: the anaphoric expressions, which are anaphoric pronouns in the case of the pronominal anaphora, their antecedents, and the referred concepts. Depending on either the *asymmetric scheme* employed in MUC (Lynette, 1997) and GENIA (Hong, 2004) or the *symmetric scheme* in ACE (NIST, 2003), the annotation task is defined as either an anaphor-antecedent linking, or mention-concept linking task, correspondingly (See Figure 1). Moreover, each annotation scheme provides its own guidelines for recognizing and annotating these three elements, causing the variations across different co-reference annotated corpora.

In the annotation schemes, mentions which may join in the co-reference relationship are called *markable*. All of the three annotation schemes record both a maximal and a minimal boundary of markables, in concerning the evaluation schemes. However, the types of markables to be annotated, and the ways to decide their maximal boundary, are not the same in every annotation scheme.

Table 1 shows the concepts annotated for each corpora according to the annotation schemes. While the number of concepts in the ACE corpus is limited to only 5 entity types, the GENIA and MUC annotation schemes do not clearly specify the concept types. This means that every possible concept in the text domains can join the anaphora relations; i.e., can be annotated as markables. This in turn makes the resolution task become more difficult.

Table 1: Possible concepts according to the annotation schemes

GENIA	ACE	MUC
(Not specified explicitly) -Bio entities	5 types of entities -Person -Organization -Facility -Location -GPE(Geo-political Entity)	(Not specified explicitly) -Person -Organization -Location -Date -Time -Money -Percent

Table 2: Possible types of anaphor according to the annotation schemes (O: allowed, X: not allowed, U: unspecified)

TYPE	GENIA	ACE	MUC
Personal pronoun	O	O	O
Demonstrative pronoun	O	O	O
Possessive pronoun	O	O	O
Reflexive pronoun	O	O	U
Indefinite pronoun (e.g., *both*)	O	U	U
Pleonastic pronoun *it*	X	U	U
Bound anaphor	X	U	O
Mention with empty head (e.g., *five* of)	X	U	U
here, there	U	O	U

The possible types of annotated anaphoric pronouns are given in Table 2. **O** denotes the type of pronoun, which may be annotated as markable, in contrast to **X**, which denotes the type of pronoun, which is not allowed to be annotated as markable. The notation **U** represents the annotation scheme that does not state how a type should be treated because that type is not popular in the domain, or the scheme does not allow the annotation of such a type implicitly.

Using the similar notations as in Table 2, Table 3 shows the possible syntactic structures of antecedents according to the annotation schemes, which are also the structures of markables in real annotations. In practice, such structural variations may cause troubles for automatically markable recognition, so in the experiments with pronoun resolution, gold markables are often used to eliminate error-prone problems.

2.2 Corpus preprocessing

Our objective anaphoric pronouns are limited to the following types: personal pronouns (all cases), possessive pronouns, and demonstrative pronouns, which have a nominal antecedent. In addition to these types of pronouns, the annotated corpora contain other types of pronominal anaphora, including "both," "one," numeric mentions (GENIA), and bound anaphora (ACE). However, analysis statistics show that such pronouns occupy less than 5% of the total pronouns in the GENIA corpus, thus we have ignored them.

Table 3: Possible types of antecedent according to the annotation schemes (O: allowed, X: not allowed, U: unspecified)

TYPE	GENIA	ACE	MUC
Pronominal	X	O	O
Noun used as a modifier (embedded in NP)	X	O	O
Name, named entity (embedded in NP)	X	O	O
Gerund	U	U	X
NP with a head noun (definite and indefinite)	O	O	O
Conjoint NP (with more than one head)	O	X	O
Coordinated NP	O	O	O
Predicate nominal	X	O	O
NP with a restrictive appositive phrase	X	O	O
NP with a non-restrictive appositive phrase	X	O	O
NP with a restrictive prepositional phrase	O	O	O
NP with a non-restrictive prepositional phrase	X	O	O
NP with a restrictive relative clause	O	O	O
NP with a non-restrictive relative clause	O	O	O
Infinitive clause	O	U	U
Date, Currency expressions, and percentages	U	U	O
Proper adjective (e.g.,*French*)	U	O	U
here, there	X	O	U

In the preprocessing step, for each corpus, we extract the gold pronominal anaphora links, which link the anaphoric pronouns with their antecedents. Although MUC and GENIA used the same asymmetric annotation schemes, picking one gold antecedent in a set of co-referenced mentions is not straightforward, since pronouns in GENIA are not allowed to be linked with a pronomial antecedent, while in the MUC corpus, this kind of link is allowed. In order to achieve the fairest comparative experimental results, we uniformly choose the nearest item in the co-reference chain of a pronoun, and make a gold anaphora link. This policy is best suited for ACE, thanks to the symmetric scheme used.

Table 4: Sizes of the data sets (number of anaphoric pronoun)

	GENIA	ACE	MUC
Training set	1442	2427	371
Test set	357	633	240

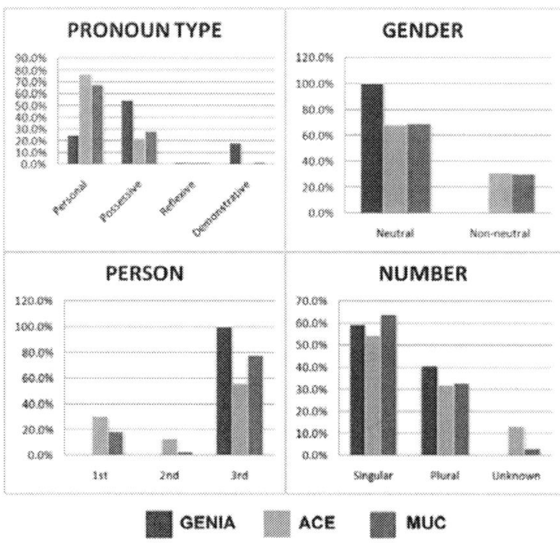

Figure 2: Analysis of anaphoric pronoun in different data sets

2.3 Statistics

In the following step, we analyze the extracted anaphora links for the three corpora. The analysis statistics in Figure 2 show the differences of the distributions of pronoun types and pronoun properties in three data sets: MUC-7, GENIA, and BNEWS from ACE. Note that only four major types out of the nine types of anaphoric pronouns mentioned in the previous section are counted. In particular, the chosen types correspond to those rows in Table 2 that contain at least two **O**.

We can see that all of the anaphoric pronouns in GENIA are neutral-gender and third-person pronouns. Another difference is that the number of demonstrative pronouns in GENIA comes to about 20%, which is much more than in other data sets.

As each type of pronoun has its own referential characteristics, such differences in the distributions of pronouns can significantly affect the pronoun resolution. This will be shown in our experiments, and analysis of the experimental results will be given in the following section.

3 Implementation

3.1 Pronoun resolution model

We built a machine learning based pronoun resolution engine using a Maximum Entropy ranker model (Berger et al., 1996), similar with Denis and Baldridge's model (Denis and Baldridge, 2007). For every anaphoric pronoun π, the ranker selects the most likely antecedent candidate α, from a set of k candidate markables.

$$P_r(\alpha_j|\pi) = \frac{\exp\left(\sum_{i=1}^{n} \lambda_i f_i(\pi, \alpha_j)\right)}{\sum_k \exp\left(\sum_{i=1}^{n} \lambda_i f_i(\pi, \alpha_k)\right)} \quad (1)$$

We constructed the training examples in the following way: for each gold anaphora link in the training corpus, we created a positive instance, and negative training instances are created by pairing the pronoun with all of the other markables appearing in a window of w preceding sentences. In all the experiments on ACE and MUC, we set w to 10 sentences, while for GENIA, w is set to 5. This setting is based on our corpus analysis showing that many of the gold antecedents in the bio-domain texts are in at most three sentences from their anaphors. In the resolution phase, the same method for collecting instances was also applied.

3.2 Features

Table 5 shows the *primitive features* used in our system, which are grouped into *feature groups* according to the type of information that they carry. Note that the actual features used by the ranker are distance features (*sdist*, and *tdist*), and not only the primitive features themselves, but also the combinations of these primitive features. The pronoun resolution model makes use of the discriminative power of these combinatory features. For example, the combination of *P_num* and *C_num* tests the *agreement* in number between the anaphoric pronoun and its candidate. Such agreements in number and gender are one of the constraints in the anaphora phenomenon, and have been exploited in almost all machine learning-based pronoun resolution frameworks (Soon et al., 2001).

Each primitive feature is from a layer of text analysis (see *Layer*), which can be morphological (*mor.*), syntactic (*syn.*), or semantic (*sem.*). The second column represents the feature sets that are used in our experiments. The *explanation* column in the table shows the way we extract feature values from texts, with the exception of the primitive feature *P_semw*, reflecting the context information of the anaphoric pronoun. This feature value is determined in the following way. If the pronoun is a subject, then *P_semw* is its governing head verb, and if it is a possessive adjective, then *P_semw* is the head noun of the noun phrase containing that pronoun. A default value is used if the pronoun belongs to neither of the above cases.

The last column of this table shows an example of the feature characterization for the anaphora link *PMA-its* in this discourse: *"By comparison, **PMA** is a very inefficient inducer of the jun gene family in Jurkat cells. Similar to **its** effect on the induction of AP1 by okadaic acid, PMA inhibits the induction of c-jun mRNA by okadaic acid."*

We divided the feature groups into 3 feature sets: *fundamental*, *baseline* and *additional*. The *fundamental* feature set contains the indispensable features for solving pronoun resolution. The *baseline* feature set mostly includes morphological features, reflecting the properties of text mentions, and in particular the pronoun properties such as *gender*, *number*, etc. The features in the *additional* feature set are used to exploit higher levels of knowledge through more semantic and syntactic features. We also include in this feature set the features that have been used in some previous work in order to clarify their contributions in our system.

4 Experiments

4.1 Experiment setting and evaluation scoring

For each corpus, we trained our resolver on the training set, and then applied it to the development test set. For the case of the ACE corpus, we only used the *train* part of the BNEWS data set for training, and applied on the corresponding *devtest* data set. We randomly splitted the GENIA corpus it into 2 parts: the *train*, and the *heldout* data sets, which contain 1599 and 400 abstracts, respectively. For the MUC corpus, we used the *dryrun* part for training, and the *formal* part for testing.

Similar to previous works, all of the experimental results in this paper are reported in *success rate* (Mitkov, 2002), calculated using the following formula.

$$\textit{Success rate} = \frac{\textit{Number of successfully resolved anaphors}}{\textit{Number of all anaphors}} \quad (2)$$

The input of our resolver are the gold mentions annotated in the corpora. The output anaphora links of a pronoun resolution system are evaluated following two criteria. In criterion 1, the recognized antecedent of an anaphoric pronoun is considered correct only when it matches the antecedent in the gold anaphora link of that pronoun. Criterion 2 is a bit looser when the recognized antecedent just needs to match one of the antecedents of a pronoun in its co-reference chain. This criterion has been used by most of the previous works, including Denis and Baldridge's system (Denis and Baldridge, 2007).

4.2 Baseline resolver

In this experiment, we use the baseline feature set presented in section 3.2. One of the reasons in choosing these features for the baseline system, is that they are basic features that have been used by most of the previous reference resolution systems. Moreover, we wanted to see how these features contribute to the resolution process for different corpora, presented in the next section.

Our baseline system achieved a 71.41% success rate on the BNEWS data set (Table 6, criterion 2), which is comparable to the result of Denis and Baldridge's system on the same data set (Denis and Baldridge, 2007). Moreover, we can see that the differences caused by the two criteria are not the same for every data set. For the news domain data sets, the differences vary from 4.17% (MUC) to 6.8% (ACE), which is high in comparison with the percentages of GENIA, which were less than two percent. This can be explained by the fact that pronouns in news texts are used more repeatedly than those in bio-medical texts. Because bio-entities are neutral-gender mentions, and are referred by the neutral gender and third person pronouns, the repeated use of pronouns may increase the ambiguity of the text, and confuse the readers.

To prevent the confusion of the readers, we chose just one data set BNEWS to represent the ACE corpus and present our further analysis experiments on these three data sets: GENIA, ACE (BNEWS), and MUC (MUC-7).

4.3 Contributions of the features in the baseline resolver

In order to observe the effects of the features in the baseline pronoun resolver, we omitted each feature group from the whole feature set, retrained our resolution models with the new feature set, and applied them to the three data sets: GENIA,

Table 5: Features used in the pronoun resolver

Layer	Feature set	Group	Primitive Feature	Explanation	Example
mor.	fundamental	mention type	P_type	pronoun type	possessive pronoun
			C_type	candidate mention type	proper name
	baseline	sdist	CP_sdis	distance in sentence	1
		tdist	CP_tdis	normalized distance in token	17
		numb	P_numb	number of p	singular
			C_numb	number of c	unknown
		pers	P_pers	person of p	third person
			C_pers	person of c	third person
		gend	P_gend	gender of p	neutral
			C_gend	gender of c	neutral
		pfam	P_pfam	family of p	it
			C_pfam	family of c	null
		string	P_word	pronoun string	*its*
			C_head	candidate head string	*PMA*
syn.	additional	pos	P_lpos	POS of the left word of p	TO
			P_rpos	POS of the right word of p	NN
			C_lpos	POS of the left word of c	COMMA
			C_rpos	POS of the right word of c	VBZ (*is*)
		parg	P_parg	argument role of p	null
			C_parg	argument role of c	arg1
sem.		netype	C_netype	entity type of c	null
mor.		last3c	C_last3c	the last 3 characters of c	*pma*
syn.		comb	P_semw	*see Section 3.2*	*effect*
other			C_1stnp	first NP in a sentence or not	false

Table 6: Baseline system evalutation (C1: criterion 1, C2: criterion 2, D: difference between criterion 1 and 2)

	GENIA	ACE	MUC
C1	70.31	64.61	57.08
C2	71.43	71.41	61.25
Diff	1.12	6.80	4.17

BNEWS, and MUC. Pronoun type and mention type are the most significant features, and thus, are not omitted in this experiment.

Table 7 shows the experimental results: the first column is the feature group name, and the following three columns show the resolution accuracy of the three corpora. The figures in the parentheses show the degradation, when we exclude the corresponding group from the baseline feature set. Our data analysis show some noticeable issues:

Number features (*numb*) :

The number-combination features are the most significant features in bio-texts while they are not so effective on ACE, and even perform negatively on MUC. One of the reasons behind this, is that in the bio-texts, all of the anaphoric pronouns have a deterministic number; i.e., either singular or plural (Section 2.3), while the news texts contain first- and second-person pronouns whose numbers are unspecified. Another reason emerges from the non-pronominal types of mentions, which play a role as antecedents. The number property of these mentions is characterized in the markable detection phase based on the part-of-speech tag, the head noun, and the phrase structure of those mentions. In particular, the MUC corpus contains many coordinated-structured mentions (Section 2.1), which are difficult for markable characterization.

Person features and pronoun family (*pers* and *pfam*) :

The absence of the *pers* features caused the biggest loss for the resolution success rate on the ACE corpus, because the co-reference chains in this corpus contain a lot of pronouns, and it is easier for the pronoun resolver to determine a pronominal antecedent than to determine a non-pronominal antecedent. The same phenomena can be observed with *pfam* features. The bio-text only contains third-person anaphoric pronouns (Section 2.3), so the person features do not have any profits.

Distance features (*sdist* and *tdist*) :

Our baseline resolver again confirmed that the sentence distance is an indispensable feature in pronoun resolution. However, the token-based distance did not show any improvements on the MUC corpus. Analyzing the MUC anaphora links, we found that these *tdist* features resulted in 10 correct anaphora links, but also mis-recognized 10 antecedents.

Table 7: Feature contributions in the baseline system (evaluation criterion 1)

Excluded	GENIA	ACE	MUC
none	70.31	64.61	57.08
-sdist	67.23(−3.08)	63.51(−1.10)	51.67(−5.41)
-tdist	70.03(−0.28)	59.56(−5.05)	57.08(+0.00)
-numb	65.83(−4.48)	61.77(−2.84)	58.33(+1.25)
-pers	70.31(+0.00)	57.19(−7.42)	55.42(−1.66)
-gend	69.75(−0.56)	64.45(−0.16)	56.67(−0.41)
-pfam	71.15(+0.84)	63.51(−1.10)	57.92(+0.84)
-string	68.07(−2.24)	61.93(−2.68)	55.83(−1.25)

4.4 Contributions of additional features to the baseline feature set

In addition to the baseline feature set, we enhanced our resolver with more features. Among them, there are two noticeable features: the grammatical role of pronouns or antecedent candidates, and the named entity type of the candidates. The other feature groups are used in Denis and Baldridge's system, which we also want to test in our system.

Table 8 shows the resolution results and the increase when adding the corresponding feature group. With the exception of the *last3c* features, the others significantly improved the resolution success rate on bio-texts, although they did not have clear contributions to the news domain data sets. The following is our further analysis to see the way that these features can contribute to the pronoun resolution process.

Semantic features (*netype*)

The first feature we would like to observe is the combination of *C_netype* and *P_semw* features, which contributed to the increase by 3.64 points. We further conducted a small test by excluding this combination from the *netype* feature group, but the success rate remained unchanged from the baseline result. This signifies that this combination contributed the most to the above increase.

The combination of *C_netype* and *P_semw* features exploits the co-ocurrence of the semantic type of the candidate antecedent and the *context word*, which appears in some relationship with the pronoun. This combination feature uses the information similar to the semantic compatibility features proposed by Yang (Yang et al., 2005) and Bergsma (Bergsma and Lin, 2006). Depending on the pronoun type, the feature extractor decides which relationship is used. For example, the resolver successfully recognizes the antecedent of the pronoun *its* in this discourse: *"**HSF3** is constitutively expressed in the erythroblast cell line HD6 , the lymphoblast cell line MSB , and embryo fibroblasts , and yet **its** DNA-binding activity is induced only upon exposure of HD6 cells to heat shock ,"* because *HSF3* was detected as a Protein entity, which has a strong association with the governing head noun *activity* of the pronoun.

Another example is the correct anaphora link between *"it"* and *"the viral protein"* in the following sentence, which the other features failed to detect. *"Tax , **the viral protein** , is thought to be crucial in the development of the disease , since **it** transforms healthy T cells in vitro and induces tumors in transgenic animals."* The correct antecedent was recognized due to the bias given to the association of the Protein entity type, and the governing verb, *"transform"* of the pronoun. The experimental results show the contribution of the domain knowledge to the pronoun resolution, and the potential combination use of such knowledge with the syntactic features.

Parse features (*parg*)

The combinations of the primitive features of grammatical roles significantly improved the performance of our resolver. The following examples show the correct anaphora links resulting from using the parse features:

- *"By comparison, **PMA** is a very inefficient inducer of the jun gene family in Jurkat cells. Similar to **its** effect on the induction of AP1 by okadaic acid, PMA inhibits the induction of c-jun mRNA by okadaic acid."*

In this example, the possessive pronoun *"its"* in the second sentence corefers to *"PMA"*, the subject of the preceding sentence.

Among the combination features in this group, one noticeable feature is the combination of *C_parg*, *Sdist*, and *P_type* which contains the association of the grammatical role of the candidate, the sentence-based distance, and the pronoun type. The idea of adding this combination is based on the Centering theory (Walker et al., 1998), a theory of discourse successfully used in pronoun resolution. This simple feature shows the potential of encoding centering theory in the machine learning features, based on the parse information.

Feature integration

Finally, we integrated all of the positive feature groups for each data set in the above experiments, and tested this combining feature set. Table

Table 8: Additional features and their contributions (evaluation criterion 1)

Added	GENIA	ACE	MUC
none	70.31	64.61	57.08
+pos	75.63(+5.32)	62.88(−1.73)	57.50(+0.42)
+parg	73.67(+3.36)	63.82(−0.79)	58.75(+1.67)
+netype	73.95(+3.64)	64.30(−0.31)	58.33(+1.25)
+last3c	67.51(−2.80)	62.09(−2.52)	56.67(−0.41)
+comb	72.83(+2.52)	63.82(−0.79)	56.25(−0.83)

Table 9: Feature integration

	GENIA	ACE	MUC
C1	79.55 (+9.24)	64.61 (+0.00)	60.42 (+3.34)
C2	**80.95** (+9.52)	**71.41** (+0.00)	**66.25** (+5.00)

9 shows a significant increase in the performance of the resolver on GENIA and MUC.

5 Conclusion and future work

Through the differences in the corpus annotation schemes, in the corpora themselves, and in contributions of resolution factors to the pronoun resolution process, we can see that adapting pronoun resolution for a different domain is not an easy task. A good study on the types of anaphoric pronouns and entity mention structures beforehand can help design a better feature set for our machine learning-based pronoun resolution system and thus, can save much time and labor.

As shown in this paper, for the news domain, the properties of anaphoric pronouns contain rich information about their antecedents, which is very useful in the resolution process. While in biomedical text, it is more important to capture the information to connect a pronoun and its antecedent from their surrounding context, because the anaphoric pronouns themselves contain almost no information of their antecedents with the exception of the *numbers*.

As a future work, it would be interesting to see how the system performs in other domains. More experiments should be designed to make the influences of annotation schemes on the pronoun resolution process clearer.

References

Berger, Adam L., Vincent J. Della Pietra, and Stephen A. Della Pietra. 1996. A maximum entropy approach to natural language processing. *Computational Linguistics*, 22(1):39–71.

Bergsma, Shane and Dekang Lin. 2006. Bootstrapping path-based pronoun resolution. In *Proceedings of the 21st International Conference on Computational Linguistics and the 44th annual meeting of the ACL*, pages 33–40.

Castano, Jose, Jason Zhang, and James Pusterjovsky. 2002. Anaphora resolution in biomedical literature. In *Int'l Symposium Reference Resolution in NLP*.

Denis, Pascal and J. Baldridge. 2007. A ranking approach to pronoun resolution. In *Proceedings of the 20th International Joint Conference on Artificial Intelligence (IJCAI07)*.

Haghighi, Aria and Dan Klein. 2007. Unsupervised coreference resolution in a nonparametric bayesian model. In *Proceedings of the 45th Annual Meeting of the Association of Computational Linguistics*, pages 848–855.

Hong, Huaqing. 2004. Coreference annotation scheme for medco corpus.

Kim, Jung-Jae and Jong C.Park. 2004. Bioar: Anaphora resolution for relating protein names to proteome database entries. In *Proceedings of the ACL 2004: Workshop on Reference Resolution and its Applications*, pages 79–86.

Lynette, Hirschman. 1997. Muc-7 coreference task definition.

Mitkov, Ruslan. 2002. *Anaphora resolution*. Pearson Education, London, Great Britain.

NIST. 2003. Entity detection and tracking - phrase 1 edt and metonymy annotation guidelines version 2.5.1 20030502.

Soon, W., H. Ng, and D. Lim. 2001. A machine learning approach to coreference resolution of noun phrases. *Computational Linguistics*, 27(4):521–544.

Walker, Marilyn A., Aravind K. Joshi, and Ellen F. Prince. 1998. *Centering Theory in Discourse*. Clarendon Press, Oxford.

Yang, Xiaofeng, Jian Su, and Chew-Lim Tan. 2005. Improving pronoun resolution using statistics-based semantic compatibility information. In *Proceedings of the 43rd Annual meeting of the Association for Computational Linguistics (ACL05)*, pages 427–434.

Computer aided correction and extension of a syntactic wide-coverage lexicon

Lionel NICOLAS◇, Benoît SAGOT♣, Miguel A. MOLINERO♠,
Jacques FARRÉ◇, Éric DE LA CLERGERIE♣

◇Team RL, Laboratory I3S - UNSA + CNRS, 06903 Sophia Antipolis, France
{lnicolas, jf}@i3s.unice.fr
♣Project ALPAGE, INRIA Rocquencourt + Paris 7, 78153 Le Chesnay, France
{benoit.sagot, Eric.De_La_Clergerie}@inria.fr
♠Grupo LYS, Univ. de A Coruña, 15001 A Coruña, España
mmolinero@udc.es

Abstract

The effectiveness of parsers based on manually created resources, namely a grammar and a lexicon, rely mostly on the quality of these resources. Thus, increasing the parser coverage and precision usually implies improving these two resources. Their manual improvement is a time consuming and complex task : identifying which resource is the true culprit for a given mistake is not always obvious, as well as finding the mistake and correcting it.

Some techniques, like van Noord (2004) or Sagot and Villemonte de La Clergerie (2006), bring a convenient way to automatically identify forms having potentially erroneous entries in a lexicon. We have integrated and extended such techniques in a wider process which, thanks to the grammar ability to tell how these forms could be used as part of correct parses, is able to propose lexical corrections for the identified entries.

We present in this paper an implementation of this process and discuss the main results we have obtained on a syntactic wide-coverage French lexicon.

1 Introduction

Increasing the coverage and precision of non-trained parsers based on manually created grammar and lexicon, relies mostly on the improvement of these two resources.

The manual improvement of wide coverage linguistic resources is a labour-extensive, complex and error prone task, requiring an important human expert work.

In order to minimize human intervention, simplify the process and increase its relevance, automatic or semi-automatic tools can be used. We present one such tool, using raw inputs, which detects shortcomings of a lexicon and helps correct them by proposing relevant corrections.

Detecting forms erroneously or incompletely described in the lexicon is achieved by applying two techniques which exhibit *suspicious forms* and associate them with a set of non parsable sentences.

Proposing relevant corrections relies on the following assumption: when studying the expectations of a grammar for a suspicious form in various non-parsable sentences, we can observe expected use patterns for this form. Those patterns can be regarded as possible corrections for the lexicon. In a metaphorical way, we believe the problem to be due to the lexicon[1], and we ask the grammar to express possible corrections for the lexicon.

The set of techniques we present here is fully system and language independent: it can be easily applied to most existing lexica and unification-grammar based parsers. The only condition is to provide lexically and grammatically valid inputs, such as law texts or newspapers, in order to ensure that the rejection of a sentence is only due to errors

© 2008. Licensed under the *Creative Commons Attribution-Noncommercial-Share Alike 3.0 Unported* license (http://creativecommons.org/licenses/by-nc-sa/3.0/). Some rights reserved.

[1] We will discuss later lexical forms incorrectly suspected because of errors in other components of the parsing system, notably the grammar.

in some components on which the parser relies on.

This paper is organized as follows. We start by giving a global view of the whole process (Sect. 2) that we later detail step by step (Sect. 3, 4, 5, 6 and 7). We then compare our work with previously publicated ones (Sect. 8) right before exposing the practical context and the results obtained (Sect. 9). Finally, we outline the planned improvements (Sect. 10) and conclude (Sect. 11).

2 Global view

A lexical form is generally described in a lexicon with one or more entries including different kinds of information: the POS (part of speech), morphologic features, syntactic features and sometimes semantic features.

A form will cause a parsing failure if its description in the lexicon leads to a conflict with the grammar expectations for this form, i.e., if grammar and lexicon do not agree on a particular instance of the form in a given sentence.

For practical reasons, we make a difference between conflicts concerning the POS, that we now call **POS defect**, and conflicts concerning the features, that we now call **overspecification**. POS defect generally happen with homonyms, i.e., with forms related to frequent lemmas while a seldom used one is missing in the lexicon. Overspecification is usually caused by the difficulty of describing exhaustively all the subcategorization frames of a lemma (optional arguments, polysemy, etc.). Therefore, if for a given lemma the most restrictive frames are also the most frequent, some entries can be overspecified and induce such conflicts.

We generate lexical corrections according to the following process.

1. We first detect suspicious forms and associate them with a set of non-parsable sentences in which the form is suspected to be responsible of the sentences' parsing failures.

2. We get as close as possible to the set of parses that the grammar would have allowed with an error-free lexicon. We achieve this goal by underspecifying the suspicious form, i.e., we increase the set of its possible POS (that is, by virtually adding new entries to the lexicon) and/or underspecify the morphological and syntactic informations of a given existing entry. A full underspecification can be simulated in the following way: during the parsing process, each time a lexical information is checked about the suspicious form, the lexicon is bypassed and all the constraints are considered as satisfied. We actually achieved this operation by replacing the suspicious form in the associated sentences with special forms called **wildcards**.

3. If the suspicious form has been correctly detected, such underspecification increases the parsing rate (except for sentences for which the form was not the only problem). In the newly successful parses, the form became whatever the grammar wanted it to be, i.e., it has matched any morphological, syntactic or semantic pattern required. Those patterns are the data we use to generate the corrections. We thus extract the instances of the wildcard in the newly producted parses, and after ranking, we propose them as corrections.

4. Finally, we manually validate and apply the corrections.

We will now explain with details how each step is achieved, starting with the detection of suspicious forms.

3 Detection of suspicious forms

In order to detect erroneous entries in a lexicon, we have developed and implemented two techniques : a shallow technique to identify POS defects and an extended version of an existing parser-based technique to (mostly) identify overspecification. Both provide for the form a suspicion rate and a set of associated non-parsable sentences.

3.1 Tagger-based detection of POS defects

This technique is based on a stochastic tagger. The underlying idea is to generate new POS for forms in the input corpus by using an especially configured stochastic tagger (Molinero et al., 2007). Such a tagger considers every form belonging to open POS (adjectives, common nouns, adverbs, verbs and proper nouns) as unknown. Candidate POS for unknown forms are then proposed by the tagger's guesser and the most likely to be correct are selected by the tagging process itself. Thus, new POS arise for some forms present in the input.

To obtain such a tagger, we have used two training sets. One is a training corpus composed of manually tagged sentences (330k words) extracted from the French Paris 7 Treebank (Abeillé, 2003), and the other one is composed of a small list of lemmas belonging to closed POS (prepositions, determiners, pronouns and punctuation marks). The tagger was modified so that only lemmas present in the second set are considered as known.

After applying the tagger on the input corpus, we extracted the produced pairs of form/POS and checked their presence in the lexicon. Every non present pair has been proposed as POS defect candidate. The emergence of false positives has been smoothed by sorting the POS defect candidates according to the following measure:

$$(n_{wt}/n_w) * log(n_{wt}),$$

where n_{wt} is the number of occurrences of the form w tagged as t and n_w is the total number of occurrences of the form w.

3.2 Parsing-based suspicious forms detection

The technique described hereafter extends the ideas exposed in (Sagot and Villemonte de La Clergerie, 2006), in which suspicious forms are detected through a statistical analysis of the parsing success and errors produced by a parser.

This error mining technique relies on the following idea.

- When the parsing of a sentence known to be lexically and grammatically correct fails, there is no automatic and unquestionable way to decide if this rejection is caused by an error in the lexicon or by a flaw in another component of the parsing system (grammar, etc.).
- Given the parsing results of a large corpus of reliable sentences, the more often a lexical form appears in non-parsable sentences and not in parsable ones, the more likely it is that its lexical entries are erroneous. This suspicion is reinforced if it appears in non-parsable sentences together with forms that appear mostly in parsable ones.

The statistical computation establishes a relevant list of lexical forms that are likely to be incorrectly or incompletely described in the lexicon.

As such, the main drawback of this approach is the dependence to the quality of the grammar used. Indeed, if a specific form is naturally tied with some syntactic construction non-handled by the grammar, this form will always be found in rejected sentences and will thus be unfairly suspected. Nevertheless, we limited this drawback by applying two extensions.

The first, already described in (Sagot and Villemonte de La Clergerie, 2006), mixes the detection results obtained from various parsers with different grammars, hence with different shortcomings.

The second extension detects short-range representative syntactic patterns non-handled by the grammar and filters the non-parsable sentences where they appear. To do so, we reduce every sentence to a single POS sequence through the use of a tagger and train a maximum entropy classifier (Daumé III, 2004) with the different possible trigrams and the corresponding parse failure or success. Even if non-perfect (the tagger or the maximum entropy classifier might be mistaken at some point), this pre-filtering has proved to noticeably increase the quality of the suspicious forms provided.

We will now explain how we manage to permit the parsing process of the associated non-parsable sentences in order to extract afterwise the corrections hypotheses.

4 Parsing originally non-parsable sentences with wildcards

As explained in Sect. 2, in order to generate lexical corrections, we first need to get as close as possible to the set of parses that the grammar would have allowed with an error-free lexicon. We achieve this goal by replacing in the associated sentences every suspicious forms with special underspecified forms called **wildcards**.

The simplest way would be to use totally underspecified wildcards. Indeed, this would have the benefit to cover all kinds of conflicts and thus, it would notably increase the parsing coverage. However, as observed by (Fouvry, 2003), it introduces an unnecessary ambiguity which usually leads to a severe overgeneration of parses or to no parses at all because of time or memory shortage. In a metaphorical way, we said that we wanted the grammar to tell us what lexical information it would have accepted for the suspicious form. Well, by introducing a totally underspecified wildcard, either the grammar has so many things to say that it is hard to know what to listen to, or it has so many things to think about that it stutters and does not say anything at all.

Therefore, we refined the wildcard by introducing some data. For technical, linguistic and readability reasons, we added POS information.

When facing a **POS defect**, we need the parser to explore other grammar rules than those already visited during the failed parses. We thus generate wildcards with different POS than those already present in the lexicon for the suspicious form.

When facing an **overspecification**, we need the parser to explore the same grammar rules without being stopped by unification failures. We thus generate wildcards with the same POS than those already present in the lexicon, but with no feature-level constraints.

When suspicious forms were correctly detected, such exchanges usually increases the parsing rate of the associated sentences. Those parses place the wildcards in grammatical contexts/patterns which clearly express what lexical informations the grammar would have accepted for the suspicious forms.

We will now explain how we extract the correction hypotheses from the newly obtained parses and how we rank them.

5 Extracting corrections hypotheses

The extraction directly depends on how one planes to use the correction hypotheses. In a previous work (Nicolas et al., 2007), we extracted the corrections proposals in the parser's output format. Such a way to process had three important drawbacks :

- one needed to understand the parser's output format before being able to study the corrections;
- merging results produced by various parsers was difficult, although it is an efficient solution to tackle most limitations of the process (see Sect. 6.2);
- some parts of the correction proposals were using representations that are not easy to relate with the format used by the lexicon (specific tagsets, under- or overspecified information w.r.t. the lexicon, etc.).

We therefore developed for each of the parsers used a conversion module in order to extract from a given parse the instantiated lexical entry of each wildcard in the format used by the lexicon.

6 Ranking corrections hypotheses

Natural languages are ambiguous, and so need to be the grammars that model them. For example, in many romance languages, an adjective can be used as a noun and a noun as an adjective.

Consequently, an inadequate wildcard may perfectly lead to new parses and provide irrelevant corrections. We thus separate the correction hypotheses according to their corresponding wildcard before ranking them. Afterwards, the parsing rate induced by each type of wildcard and the associated parsed sentences allows to easily identify which wildcard is the correct one.

When only one parser is used to generate correction hypotheses, ranking correction hypotheses proves straightforward, but, as we will explain, the results heavily depend on the quality of the grammar. We thus put together correction hypotheses obtained thanks to different parsers in order to rank them in a more sophisticated way.

6.1 Baseline ranking: single parser mode

The correction hypotheses obtained after introducing a wildcard are generally irrelevant, i.e., most of them are parasitic hypotheses resulting from the ambiguity brought by the wildcards. Nevertheless, among all these hypotheses, some are valid, or at least close to valid. In the scope of only one sentence, there is no reliable way to determine which corrections are the valid ones. But, if we consider simultaneously various sentences that contain the same suspicious form embedded in different syntactic structures, we usually observe a strong variability of the noisy correction hypotheses. On the opposite, if some stable correction hypothesis is proposed for various sentences, it is likely to be valid, i.e, to represent the correct sense of the form according to the grammar. We thus simply rank correction hypotheses according to the number of sentences that have produced them.

6.2 Reducing grammar influence: multi-parser mode

Using various parsers not only improves the suspicious forms detection (Sect. 3.2), it also allows to merge correction hypotheses in order to minimize the influence of the shortcomings of the grammars. When some form is naturally related to syntactic constructions that are not correctly handled by the grammar, this form is always found in rejected sentences, and therefore is always suspected. Replacing it by wildcards will only produce incorrect corrections or no correction at all because the problem is not related to the lexicon.

Having various sets of non-parsable sentences for a given suspicious form f, and various sets of correction hypotheses for f, one can discard (or consider less relevant) correction hypotheses according to the following three statements:

- If any form in a sentence is actually incorrectly described in the lexicon, then this sentence should be non-parsable for both parsers. Correction hypotheses produced from sentences that are non-parsable for only one parser should be discarded.
- For the same reason, correction hypotheses produced with sentences in which only one parser made f identified as a suspicious form should be avoided.
- Finally, correction hypotheses proposed by only one of both parsers (or proposed much more often by one parser than by the other one) might just be the consequence of the ambiguity of one grammar. Afterall, both grammar describe the same language, they should find an agreement about the uses of a form.

In our experiments, we decided to apply the following ranking scheme: for a given suspicious form, we only keep the corrections hypotheses that are obtained from sentences that were originally non-parsable and parsable after a wildcard introduction for both parsers. Afterwards, we separately rank the correction hypotheses for each parser and merge the results.

We will now explain how we manually validate the ranked correction hypotheses.

7 Manual validation of the corrections

When studying the ranked corrections for a given wildcard, there might be three cases:

1. There are no corrections at all: the form was unfairly suspected or the generation of wildcards was inadequate. It also happens when the erroneous entries of the suspicious form are not the only reasons for all the parsing failures.
2. There are relevant corrections: the form was correctly detected, the generation of wildcards was adequate and the form was the only reason for various parsing failures.
3. There are irrelevant corrections: the ambiguity introduced by the relevant or irrelevant wildcards opened the path to irrelevant parses providing irrelevant corrections.

It is truly important to note that an incorrectly suspected form may perfectly lead to irrelevant corrections brought by the ambiguity introduced. Consequently, unless the grammar used, the detection of suspicious form and the generation of wildcards are perfect, such a correcting process should always be semi-automatic (manually validated) and not automatic.

Now that the whole system has been explained with details, we will expose the similarities and differences of our methods with previously publicated ones.

8 Related works

Since efficient and linguistically relevant lexical and grammatical formalisms have been developed, the acquisition/extension/correction of linguistic ressources has been an active research field, especially during the last decade.

The idea to infer lexical data from the grammatical context first appeared in 1990 (Erbach, 1990). The combination with error mining/detection technique, such as van Noord (2004), begun in 2006 (van de Cruys, 2006; Yi and Kordoni, 2006). Except in our previous work (2007), nobody has combined it with the technique described in Sagot and Villemonte de La Clergerie (2006). The idea of prefiltering the sentences (Sec. 3.2) to improve the error mining performance has never been applied so far.

The wildcards generation started to be refined with Barg and Walther (1998). Since then, the wildcards are partially underspecified and restrained to open class POS. In Yi and Kordoni (2006), the authors use an elegant technique based on an entropy classifier to select the most adequate wildcards.

The way to rank the corrections is usually based on a trained tool (van de Cruys, 2006; Yi and Kordoni, 2006), such as an entropy classifier. Surprisingly, the evaluation of hypotheses on various sentences for a same suspicious form in order to discriminate the irrelevant ones has never been considered so far.

Finally, all the previous works were achieved with HPSG parsers and no results has been exposed until 2005. van de Cruys (2006) expose its results for each POS and one can clearly observe, for complex lemmas like verbs, the impossibility to apply such set of techniques in an automatic way without harming the quality of the lexicon. The results would be even worse if applied to corpus with sentences non-covered by the grammar because no relevant corrections could be generated but irrelevant ones might perfectly be.

9 Results

We now expose the results of our experiments by describing the practical context, giving some correction examples and discussing the effectiveness of the correction process through the parsing rate increases we have obtained.

9.1 Practical context

The lexicon we are improving is called the *Lefff*.[2] This wide-coverage morphological and syntactic French lexicon has been built partly automatically (Sagot et al., 2006) and is under constant development. At the time these lines are written, it contains more than 520 000 entries. The less data an entry has, the more specified it is.

We used two parsers based on two different grammars in order to improve the quality of our corrections.

- The FRMG (***French Meta-Grammar***) grammar is generated in an hybrid TAG/TIG form from a more abstract meta-grammar with highly factorized trees (Thomasset and Villemonte de La Clergerie, 2005).
- The SxLFG-Fr grammar (Boullier and Sagot, 2006), is an efficient deep non-probabilistic LFG grammar.

The corpus used is extracted from the French politics newspaper *Le monde diplomatique*. This corpora is composed with around 280 000 sentences of 25 or less elements and 4,3 million of words in total.

9.2 Examples of corrections

9.2.1 POS corrections

Most of the POS corrections performed were about missing forms or about adjectives that could be used as noun and vice versa. Here are some examples :

- israélien (*israeli*) as an adjective,
- portugais (*portuguese*) as an adjective,
- politiques (*politic*) as a common noun,
- parabolique (*parabolic*) as an adjective,
- pittoresque (*picturesque*) as an adjective,
- minutieux (*meticulous*) as an adjective.

9.2.2 Features corrections

As one can expect, most of the features corrections performed were about lemmas with complex subcategorization frames / features, i.e., essentially verbs.

- "revenir" (*to come back*) did not handle constructions like *to come back from* or *to come back in*
- "se partager" (*to share*) did not handle constructions like *to share something between*.
- "aimer" (*to love*) was described as always expecting a direct object and an attribute.
- "livrer" (*to deliver*) did not handle constructions like *to deliver to somebody*.

9.3 Correction process relevance

As explained earlier (Sect. 7), this process might generate erroneous corrections, especially if general corpora with sentences non-covered by the grammar are used and various correction sessions are made. Globally, the accuracy of the corrections goes decreasing after each session. Indeed, there are less and less lexical mistakes to correct after each session. Anyway, we are more interested in improving efficiently our lexicon. We thus prove the relevance of the whole process by showing the gains of parsing rate obtained during our experiments. One must keep in mind that the corrections are manually validated, i.e, the noticeable increases of parsing coverage (Figure 1) are mostly due to the improvement of the quality of the lexicon.

Table 1 lists the number of lexical forms updated at each session.

Except for the second session, all correction sessions have been achieved with the error mining and the hypothesis generation modules. The second session has been achieved with the POS defect mining module only (Sect. 3.1). We planned to

[2]Lexique des formes fléchies du français/Lexicon of inflected forms of French.

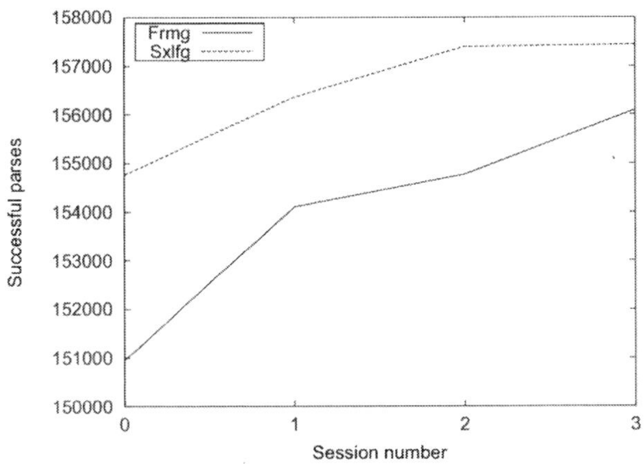

Figure 1: Number of sentences successfully parsed after each session.

Session	1	2	3	total
nc	30	99	1	130
adj	66	694	27	787
verbs	1183	0	385	1568
adv	1	7	0	8
total	1280	800	413	2493

Table 1: Lexical forms updated at each session

interface it with the hypothesis generation module but we could not finish it on time. Nevertheless, the suspicious form list provided was good and simple enough (mostly proper nouns, adjectives and common nouns) to be reviewed without the help of the hypothesis generation module.

As expected, we were quickly limited by the quality of the grammars and by the corpus used. Indeed, the lexicon and the grammars have been developed together for the last few years, using this same corpus for test. Thus, the error mining technique came, after few corrections sessions, to provide us irrelevant suspicious forms. The tagger-based detection of POS defects can only be used once on each corpus. Further correction and extension sessions make sense only after grammar improvements or obtention of new corpora.

Nevertheless, we have already detected and corrected 254 lemmas corresponding to 2493 forms. The coverage rate (percentage of sentences for which a full parse is found) has undergone an absolute increase of 3,41% (5141 sentences) for the FRMG parser and 1,73% (2677 sentences) for the SXLFG parser. Thoses results were achieved in only few hours of manual work on the lexicon !

9.4 Discussion

This set of techniques has two major qualities.

The first one, as one can observe through our results, it allows to improve significantly a lexicon in a short amount of time.

The second one is related to the main drawback of our approach: the dependence to the grammars used. If in a non-parsable sentence, none of the suspicious forms is a true culprit (there are no relevant correction), then this sentence can be considered as lexically correct w.r.t. the current state of the grammar. It thus exhibits shortcomings of the grammar and can be used to improve it.

A cycling process which alternatively and incrementally improves both the lexicon and the grammar can then be elaborated. This data is even more important considering the fact that nowadays, large scale French TreeBank are rare.

10 Future developments

The whole system has globally proved to be mature. Nevertheless, we are planning the following improvements to continue our investigation.

- We need to interface the POS defect mining module with the hypothesis generation one.
- The tagger-based detection of POS defects is still young and can be improved.
- We will refine the wildcard generation in a similar way as done in (Yi and Kordoni, 2006).
- In order to pursue the corrections of the lexicon, we will improve our grammars according to the corpus of failed sentences. It is now globally representative of shortcomings of the grammars, thus we are thinking about developing some detection techniques in order to emphasize cases of error for the grammar. The entropy model built by the maximum entropy classifier should be a good starting point.

11 Conclusion

The path taken, highlighted by the dependence on the grammar, seems to be a promising one. It will allow to develop a cycling process which alternatively and incrementally improves both the lexicon and the grammar.

The correction process of lexicon presented here is now globally mature and has proved to be relevant and effective in practice. Indeed, noticeable improvements of the lexicon could be achieved in a few amount of manual work.

The time spend to validate the corrections generated has also confirmed our doubts about evolving such process to an automatic one.

We will definitively continue the correction sessions after upgrading some components.

Acknowledgement We thank the COLE team (University of Vigo, Spain) for granting us access to their computers.

We would like to thanks Sylvain Schmitz and the reviewers for their valuable comments.

The POS mining technique could be achieved partially thanks to the support of Ministerio de Educación y Ciencia of Spain (HUM2007-66607-C04-02) and the Xunta de Galicia ("Galician Network for Language Processing and Information Retrieval" 2006-2009).

References

Abeillé, Anne. 2003. Annotation morpho-syntaxique. Paper available at http://www.llf.cnrs.fr/Gens/Abeille/guide-morpho-synt.02.pdf, January.

Barg, Petra and Markus Walther. 1998. Processing unkonwn words in hpsg. In *Proceedings of the 36th Conference of the ACL and the 17th International Conference on Computational Linguistics.*

Boullier, Pierre and Benoît Sagot. 2006. Efficient parsing of large corpora with a deep LFG parser. In *Proceedings of LREC'06.*

Daumé III, Hal. 2004. Notes on CG and LM-BFGS optimization of logistic regression. Paper available at http://pub.hal3.name/daume04cg-bfgs, implementation available at http://hal3.name/megam/, August.

Erbach, Gregor. 1990. Syntactic processing of unknown words. In *IWBS Report 131.*

Fouvry, Frederik. 2003. Lexicon acquisition with a large coverage unification-based grammar. In *Companion to the 10th of EACL.*

Molinero, Miguel A., Fco. Mario Barcala, Juan Otero, and Jorge Graña. 2007. Practical application of one-pass viterbi algorithm in tokenization and pos tagging. *Recent Advances in Natural Language Processing (RANLP). Proceedings, pp. 35-40.*

Nicolas, Lionel, Jacques Farré, and Éric Villemonte de La Clergerie. 2007. Correction mining in parsing results. In *Proceedings of LTC'07.*

Sagot, Benoît and Éric Villemonte de La Clergerie. 2006. Error mining in parsing results. In *Proceedings of ACL/COLING'06*, pages 329–336. Association for Computational Linguistics.

Sagot, Benoît, Lionel Clément, Éric Villemonte de La Clergerie, and Pierre Boullier. 2006. The Lefff 2 syntactic lexicon for french: architecture, acquisition, use. In *Proceedings of LREC'06.*

Thomasset, François and Éric Villemonte de La Clergerie. 2005. Comment obtenir plus des méta-grammaires. In *Proceedings of TALN'05.*

van de Cruys, Tim. 2006. Automatically extending the lexicon for parsing. In *Proceedings of the eleventh ESSLLI student session.*

van Noord, Gertjan. 2004. Error mining for wide-coverage grammar engineering. In *Proceedings of ACL 2004.*

Yi, Zhang and Valia Kordoni. 2006. Automated deep lexical acquisition for robust open texts processing. In *Proceedings of LREC-2006.*

Parsing the SynTagRus Treebank of Russian

Joakim Nivre
Växjö University and
Uppsala University
joakim.nivre@vxu.se

Igor M. Boguslavsky
Universidad Politécnica
de Madrid
Departamento de
Inteligencia Artificial
igor@opera.dia.fi.upm.es

Leonid L. Iomdin
Russian Academy
of Sciences
Institute for Information
Transmission Problems
iomdin@iitp.ru

Abstract

We present the first results on parsing the SynTagRus treebank of Russian with a data-driven dependency parser, achieving a labeled attachment score of over 82% and an unlabeled attachment score of 89%. A feature analysis shows that high parsing accuracy is crucially dependent on the use of both lexical and morphological features. We conjecture that the latter result can be generalized to richly inflected languages in general, provided that sufficient amounts of training data are available.

1 Introduction

Dependency-based syntactic parsing has become increasingly popular in computational linguistics in recent years. One of the reasons for the growing interest is apparently the belief that dependency-based representations should be more suitable for languages that exhibit free or flexible word order and where most of the clues to syntactic structure are found in lexical and morphological features, rather than in syntactic categories and word order configurations. Some support for this view can be found in the results from the CoNLL shared tasks on dependency parsing in 2006 and 2007, where a variety of data-driven methods for dependency parsing have been applied with encouraging results to languages of great typological diversity (Buchholz and Marsi, 2006; Nivre et al., 2007a).

However, there are still important differences in parsing accuracy for different language types. For example, Nivre et al. (2007a) observe that the languages included in the 2007 CoNLL shared task can be divided into three distinct groups with respect to top accuracy scores, with relatively low accuracy for richly inflected languages like Arabic and Basque, medium accuracy for agglutinating languages like Hungarian and Turkish, and high accuracy for more configurational languages like English and Chinese. A complicating factor in this kind of comparison is the fact that the syntactic annotation in treebanks varies across languages, in such a way that it is very difficult to tease apart the impact on parsing accuracy of linguistic structure, on the one hand, and linguistic annotation, on the other. It is also worth noting that the majority of the data sets used in the CoNLL shared tasks are not derived from treebanks with genuine dependency annotation, but have been obtained through conversion from other kinds of annotation. And the data sets that do come with original dependency annotation are generally fairly small, with less than 100,000 words available for training, the notable exception of course being the Prague Dependency Treebank of Czech (Hajič et al., 2001), which is one of the largest and most widely used treebanks in the field.

This paper contributes to the growing literature on dependency parsing for typologically diverse languages by presenting the first results on parsing the Russian treebank SynTagRus (Boguslavsky et al., 2000; Boguslavsky et al., 2002). There are several factors that make this treebank an interesting resource in this context. First of all, it contains a genuine dependency annotation, theoretically grounded in the long tradition of dependency grammar for Slavic languages, represented by the work of Tesnière (1959) and Mel'čuk (1988), among others. Secondly, with close to

© Joakim Nivre, Igor M. Boguslavsky, and Leonid L. Iomdin, 2008. Licensed under the *Creative Commons Attribution-Noncommercial-Share Alike 3.0 Unported* license (http://creativecommons.org/licenses/by-nc-sa/3.0/). Some rights reserved.

500,000 tokens, the treebank is larger than most other available dependency treebanks and provides a good basis for experimental investigations using data-driven methods. Thirdly, the Russian language, which has not been included in previous experimental evaluations such as the CoNLL shared tasks, is a richly inflected language with free word order and thus representative of the class of languages that tend to pose problems for the currently available parsing models. Taken together, these factors imply that experiments using the SYNTAGRUS treebank may be able to shed further light on the complex interplay between language type, annotation scheme, and training set size, as determinants of parsing accuracy for data-driven dependency parsers.

The experimental parsing results presented in this paper have been obtained using MaltParser, a freely available system for data-driven dependency parsing with state-of-the-art accuracy for most languages in previous evaluations (Buchholz and Marsi, 2006; Nivre et al., 2007a; Nivre et al., 2007b). Besides establishing a first benchmark for the SYNTAGRUS treebank, we analyze the influence of different kinds of features on parsing accuracy, showing conclusively that both lexical and morphological features are crucial for obtaining good parsing accuracy. All results are based on input with gold standard annotations, which means that the results can be seen to establish an upper bound on what can be achieved when parsing raw text. However, this also means that results are comparable to those from the CoNLL shared tasks, which have been obtained under the same conditions.

The rest of the paper is structured as follows. Section 2 introduces the SYNTAGRUS treebank, section 3 describes the MaltParser system used in the experiments, and section 4 presents experimental results and analysis. Section 5 contains conclusions and future work.

2 The SYNTAGRUS Treebank

The Russian dependency treebank, SYNTAGRUS, is being developed by the Computational Linguistics Laboratory, Institute of Information Transmission Problems, Russian Academy of Sciences. Currently the treebank contains over 32,000 sentences (roughly 460,000 words) belonging to texts from a variety of genres (contemporary fiction, popular science, newspaper and journal articles dated between 1960 and 2008, texts of online news, etc.) and it is growing steadily. It is an integral but fully autonomous part of the Russian National Corpus developed in a nationwide research project and can be freely consulted on the Web (http://www.ruscorpora.ru/).

Since Russian is a language with relatively free word order, SYNTAGRUS adopted a dependency-based annotation scheme, in a way parallel to the Prague Dependency Treebank (Hajič et al., 2001). The treebank is so far the only corpus of Russian supplied with comprehensive morphological annotation and syntactic annotation in the form of a complete dependency tree provided for every sentence.

Figure 1 shows the dependency tree for the sentence Наибольшее возмущение участников митинга вызвал продолжающийся рост цен на бензин, устанавливаемых нефтяными компаниями (It was the continuing growth of petrol prices set by oil companies that caused the greatest indignation of the participants of the meeting). In the dependency tree, nodes represent words (lemmas), annotated with parts of speech and morphological features, while arcs are labeled with syntactic dependency types. There are over 65 distinct dependency labels in the treebank, half of which are taken from Mel'čuk's Meaning⇔Text Theory (Mel'čuk, 1988). Dependency types that are used in figure 1 include:

1. предик (predicative), which, prototypically, represents the relation between the verbal predicate as head and its subject as dependent;
2. 1-компл (first complement), which denotes the relation between a predicate word as head and its direct complement as dependent;
3. агент (agentive), which introduces the relation between a predicate word (verbal noun or verb in the passive voice) as head and its agent in the instrumental case as dependent;
4. квазиагент (quasi-agentive), which relates any predicate noun as head with its first syntactic actant as dependent, if the latter is not eligible for being qualified as the noun's agent;
5. опред (modifier), which connects a noun head with an adjective/participle dependent if the latter serves as an adjectival modifier to the noun;

Figure 1: A syntactically annotated sentence from the SYNTAGRUS treebank.

6. предл (prepositional), which accounts for the relation between a preposition as head and a noun as dependent.

Dependency trees in SYNTAGRUS may contain non-projective dependencies. Normally, one token corresponds to one node in the dependency tree. There are however a noticeable number of exceptions, the most important of which are the following:

1. compound words like пятидесятиэтажный (fifty-storied), where one token corresponds to two or more nodes;
2. so-called phantom nodes for the representation of hard cases of ellipsis, which do not correspond to any particular token in the sentence; for example, Я купил рубашку, а он галстук (I bought a shirt and he a tie), which is expanded into Я купил рубашку, а он купил$_{\text{PHANTOM}}$ галстук (I bought a shirt and he bought$_{\text{PHANTOM}}$ a tie);
3. multiword expressions like по крайней мере (at least), where several tokens correspond to one node.

Syntactic annotation is performed semi-automatically: sentences are first processed by the rule-based Russian parser of an advanced NLP system, ETAP-3 (Apresian et al., 2003) and then edited manually by linguists who handle errors of the parser as well as cases of ambiguity that cannot be reliably resolved without extra-linguistic knowledge. The parser processes raw sentences without prior part-of-speech tagging.

Morphological annotation in SYNTAGRUS is based on a comprehensive morphological dictionary of Russian that counts about 130,000 entries (over 4 million word forms). The ETAP-3 morphological analyzer uses the dictionary to produce morphological annotation of words belonging to the corpus, including lemma, part-of-speech tag and additional morphological features dependent on the part of speech: animacy, gender, number, case, degree of comparison, short form (of adjectives and participles), representation (of verbs), aspect, tense, mood, person, voice, composite form, and attenuation.

Statistics for the version of SYNTAGRUS used for the experiments described in this paper are as follows:

- 32,242 sentences, belonging to the fiction genre (9.8%), texts of online news (12.4%), newspaper and journal articles (77.8%);
- 461,297 tokens, including expressions with non-alphabetical symbols (e.g., 10, 1.200, \$333, +70C, #) but excluding punctuation;
- 31,683 distinct word types, of which 635 with a frequency greater than 100, 5041 greater than 10, and 18231 greater than 1;
- 3,414 sentences (10.3%) with non-projective

	POS	DEP	MOR	LEM	LEX
TOP	+	+	+	+	+
TOP−1	+				
HEAD(TOP)				+	+
LDEP(TOP)		+			
RDEP(TOP)		+			
NEXT	+		+	+	+
NEXT+1	+		+	+	+
NEXT+2	+				
NEXT+3	+				
LDEP(NEXT)		+			

Table 1: History-based features (TOP = token on top of stack; NEXT = next token in input buffer; HEAD(w) = head of w; LDEP(w) = leftmost dependent of w; RDEP(w) = leftmost dependent of w).

dependencies and 3,934 non-projective dependency arcs in total;

- 478 sentences (1.5%) containing phantom nodes and 631 phantom nodes in total.

3 MaltParser

MaltParser (Nivre et al., 2007b) is a language-independent system for data-driven dependency parsing, based on a transition-based parsing model (McDonald and Nivre, 2007). More precisely, the approach is based on four essential components:

- A transition-based deterministic algorithm for building labeled projective dependency graphs in linear time (Nivre, 2003).
- History-based feature models for predicting the next parser action (Black et al., 1992; Magerman, 1995; Ratnaparkhi, 1997).
- Discriminative classifiers for mapping histories to parser actions (Kudo and Matsumoto, 2002; Yamada and Matsumoto, 2003).
- Pseudo-projective parsing for recovering non-projective structures (Nivre and Nilsson, 2005).

In the following subsections, we briefly describe each of these four components in turn.

3.1 Parsing Algorithm

The parser uses the deterministic algorithm for labeled dependency parsing first proposed by Nivre (2003). The algorithm builds a labeled dependency graph in one left-to-right pass over the input, using a stack to store partially processed tokens and adding arcs using four elementary actions (where TOP is the token on top of the stack and NEXT is the next token):

- **Shift**: Push NEXT onto the stack.
- **Reduce**: Pop the stack.
- **Right-Arc**(r): Add an arc labeled r from TOP to NEXT; push NEXT onto the stack.
- **Left-Arc**(r): Add an arc labeled r from NEXT to TOP; pop the stack.

Parser actions are predicted using a history-based feature model (section 3.2) and SVM classifiers (section 3.3). Although the parser only derives projective graphs, the fact that these graphs are labeled allows non-projective dependencies to be captured using the pseudo-projective approach of Nivre and Nilsson (2005) (section 3.4).

3.2 History-Based Feature Models

History-based parsing models rely on features of the derivation history to predict the next parser action (Black et al., 1992). The features used are all symbolic and defined in terms of five different node attributes:

- POS = part of speech (atomic)
- DEP = dependency type
- MOR = morphological features (set)
- LEM = lemma
- LEX = word form

Features of the type DEP have a special status in that they are extracted during parsing from the partially built dependency graph and are updated dynamically during parsing. The other four feature types (LEX, LEM, POS, and MOR) are given as part of the input to the parser and remain static during the processing of a sentence. Of these four feature types, all except LEX presupposes that the input has been preprocessed by a lemmatizer, tagger and morphological analyzer, respectively, but for the experiments reported below we use gold standard annotation from the treebank.

In order to study the influence of different features, we have experimented with different combinations of the five feature types, where the baseline model contains only POS and DEP features, while more complex models add MOR, LEM, and LEX features in different combinations. The exact features included for each feature type are shown in table 1, where rows denote tokens in a parser configuration (defined relative to the stack, the remaining input, and the partially built dependency graph), and where columns correspond to feature types. The selection of features in each group was tuned on a development set as described in section 4.

3.3 Discriminative Classifiers

We use support vector machines (Vapnik, 1995) to predict the next parser action from a feature vector representing the history. More specifically, we use LIBSVM (Chang and Lin, 2001) with a quadratic kernel $K(x_i, x_j) = (\gamma x_i^T x_j + r)^2$ and the built-in one-versus-all strategy for multi-class classification. Symbolic features are converted to numerical features using the standard technique of binarization, and we split the set values of MOR features into their atomic components. In order to speed up training, we also divide the training data into smaller bins according to the feature POS of NEXT, and train separate classifiers on each bin.

3.4 Pseudo-Projective Parsing

Pseudo-projective parsing was proposed by Nivre and Nilsson (2005) as a way of dealing with non-projective structures in a projective data-driven parser. We projectivize training data by a minimal transformation, lifting non-projective arcs one step at a time, and extending the arc label of lifted arcs using the encoding scheme called HEAD by Nivre and Nilsson (2005), which means that a lifted arc is assigned the label $r\uparrow h$, where r is the original label and h is the label of the original head in the non-projective dependency graph.

Non-projective dependencies can be recovered by an inverse transformation applied to the dependency graph output by the parser, using a left-to-right, top-down, breadth-first search, guided by the extended arc labels $r\uparrow h$ assigned by the parser.

4 Experiments

In this section we describe the first experiments on parsing the SYNTAGRUS treebank using a data-driven parser. The experimental setup is described in section 4.1, while the experimental results are presented and discussed in section 4.2.

4.1 Experimental Setup

All experiments have been performed on the version of SYNTAGRUS described in section 2, converted to the CoNLL data format (Buchholz and Marsi, 2006).[1] The available data were divided into 80% for training, 10% for development, and 10% for final testing, using a pseudo-randomized split. The development set was used for tuning parameters of the parsing algorithm and pseudo-projective parsing technique, and for feature selection within the feature groups not included in the baseline model (i.e., MOR, LEM, and LEX). The test set was used for evaluating the finally selected models once.

The evaluation metrics used are *labeled attachment score* (LAS) – the percentage of tokens that are assigned the correct head and dependency type – and *unlabeled attachment score* (UAS) – the percentage of tokens that are assigned the correct head (regardless of dependency type). In addition, we present precision and recall for non-projective dependencies. Punctuation tokens are excluded in all scores, but phantom tokens are included. We use McNemar's test for statistical significance.

Model	Count	LAS	UAS
Base = POS + DEP	46506	60.2	76.0
B1 = Base + MOR	46506	73.0	84.5
B2 = Base + LEM	46506	75.5	84.6
B3 = Base + LEX	46506	74.5	84.6
BM1 = B1 + LEM	46506	82.3	89.0
BM2 = B1 + LEX	46506	81.0	88.8
All = B1 + LEM + LEX	46506	82.3	89.1

Table 2: Parsing accuracy for different feature models on the final test set (Count = Number of tokens in the test set, LAS = Labeled attachment score, UAS = Unlabeled attachment score).

4.2 Results and Discussion

Table 2 gives the parsing accuracy for different feature models on the held-out test set, measured as labeled attachment score (LAS) and unlabeled attachment score (UAS). With respect to LAS, there are statistically significant differences between all models except BM1 and All ($p < 0.01$). With respect to UAS, there are statistically significant differences between four groups, such that $\{\text{Base}\} < \{\text{B1, B2, B3}\} < \{\text{BM2}\} < \{\text{BM1, All}\}$, but there

[1] Since SYNTAGRUS only distinguishes ten different parts of speech (not counting morphological features), the fields CPOSTAG and POSTAG in the CoNLL format – for coarse-grained and fine-grained parts of speech – were given the same content.

are no differences within these groups.[2]

Looking at the results for different models, we see that while the baseline model (Base) achieves a modest 60.2% LAS and 76.0% UAS, the addition of only one additional feature group (B1–B3) boosts unlabeled accuracy by close to ten percentage points and labeled accuracy by up to fifteen percentage points. Somewhat surprisingly, the differences between models B1–B3 are very small, and only differences with respect to LAS are statistically significant, which may be taken to suggest that morphological and lexical features capture the same type of information. However, this hypothesis is clearly refuted by the results for models BM1 and BM2, where the addition of lexical features on top of morphological features gives a further gain in LAS of eight to ten percentage points (and over four percentage points for UAS).

Comparing the use of raw word forms (LEX) and lemmas (LEM) as lexical features, we see a slight advantage for the latter, at least for labeled accuracy. However, it must be remembered that the experiments are based on gold standard input annotation, which probably leads to an overestimation of the value of LEM features. Finally, it is worth noting that including both LEX and LEM features does not result in a significant improvement over the model with only LEM features, which may be a sign of saturation, although this may again change in the presence of noisy LEM features.

The experimental results show conclusively that both morphological and lexical features are crucial for achieving high parsing accuracy. It may seem that they are most important for labeled accuracy, where the gain in absolute percentage points is the greatest with respect to the baseline, but it must be remembered that the unlabeled scores start at a higher level, thus leaving less room for improvement. In fact, the total error reduction from Base to All is over 50% for both LAS and UAS.

Table 3 gives a more detailed picture of parsing performance for the best model (All), by breaking down both LAS and UAS by the part-of-speech tag of the dependent. We note that accuracy is higher than average for nouns (S), adjectives (A), particles (PART), and reasonably good for verbs (V). For prepositions (PR), conjunctions (CONJ), and adverbs (ADV), accuracy is considerably lower, which may be attributed to attachment ambiguities. It is also worth noting that both prepositions and adverbs have considerably higher UAS than LAS (almost twenty percentage points for prepositions), which shows that even when they are attached correctly they are are often mislabeled. The remaining parts of speech are too infrequent to warrant any conclusions.

Part of Speech	Count	LAS	UAS
S (noun)	7303	86.7	93.3
A (adjective)	7024	92.8	94.2
V (verb)	6946	81.9	85.8
PR (preposition)	5302	60.0	79.0
CONJ (conjunction)	2998	76.1	80.7
ADV (adverb)	2855	72.3	83.3
PART (particle)	1833	88.1	89.6
NUM (numeral)	807	88.7	93.6
NID (foreign word)	142	76.5	91.5
COM (compound)	32	93.8	96.9
P (proposition word)	7	57.1	85.7
INTJ (interjection)	5	0.0	20.0

Table 3: Accuracy by part of speech on the final test set for All features (Count = Number of tokens in the test set, LAS = Labeled attachment score, UAS = Unlabeled attachment score).

Looking specifically at non-projective dependencies, we find that the best model has a labeled precision of 68.8 and a labeled recall of 31.4. The corresponding unlabeled figures are 73.3 and 33.4.[3] This confirms the results of previous studies showing that the pseudo-projective parsing technique used by MaltParser tends to give high precision – given that non-projective dependencies are among the most difficult to parse correctly – but rather low recall (McDonald and Nivre, 2007). It is also worth mentioning that phantom tokens, i.e., empty tokens inserted for the analysis of certain elliptical constructions (see section 2), have a labeled precision of 82.4 and a labeled recall of 82.8 (89.2 and 89.6 unlabeled), which is very close to the average accuracy, despite being very infrequent. However, it must be remembered that these tokens were given as part of the input in these experiments. In order to correctly analyse these tokens and their dependencies when parsing raw text, they would have to be recovered in a pre-processing phase along the lines of Dienes

[2]For the difference BM2 < BM1, $0.01 < p < 0.05$; for all other differences, $p < 0.01$.

[3]The precision is the percentage of non-projective dependencies predicted by the parser that were correct, while the recall is the percentage of true non-projective dependencies that were correctly predicted by the parser.

and Dubey (2003).

Summing up, the main result of the experimental evaluation is that both morphological and lexical features are crucial for attaining high accuracy when training and evaluating on the representations found in the SYNTAGRUS treebank of Russian. With regard to morphological features this is in line with a number of recent studies showing the importance of morphology for parsing languages with less rigid word order, including work on Spanish (Cowan and Collins, 2005), Hebrew (Tsarfaty, 2006; Tsarfaty and Sima'an, 2007), Turkish (Eryigit et al., 2006), and Swedish (Øvrelid and Nivre, 2007).

With regard to lexical features, the situation is more complex in that there are a number of studies questioning the usefulness of lexical features in statistical parsing and arguing that equivalent or better results can be achieved with unlexicalized models provided that linguistic categories can be split flexibly into more fine-grained categories, either using hand-crafted splits, as in the seminal work of Klein and Manning (2003), or using hidden variables and unsupervised learning, as in the more recent work by Petrov et al. (2006), among others. There are even studies showing that lexicalization can be harmful when parsing richly inflected languages like German (Dubey and Keller, 2003) and Turkish (Eryiğit and Oflazer, 2006).

However, it is worth noting that most of these results have been obtained either for models of constituency-based parsing or for models of dependency parsing suffering from sparse data.[4] In the experiments presented here, we have used a transition-based model for dependency parsing that has much fewer parameters than state-of-the-art probabilistic models for constituency parsing. Moreover, we have been able to use a relatively large training set, thereby minimizing the effect of sparseness for lexical features. We therefore conjecture that the beneficial effect of lexical features on parsing accuracy will generalize to other richly inflected languages when similar conditions hold.

As far as we know, these are the first results for a large-scale data-driven parser for Russian. There do exist several rule-based parsers for Russian, such as the ETAP-3 parser (Apresian et al., 2003) and a Link Grammar parser,[5] as well as a prototype of a hybrid system based on the ETAP-3 parser enriched with statistics extracted from SYNTAGRUS (Boguslavsky et al., 2003; Chardin, 2004), but differences in both input format and output representations make it difficult to compare the performance directly.

[4] The latter case applies to the probabilistic model of dependency parsing explored by Eryiğit and Oflazer (2006).

[5] http://sz.ru/parser/

5 Conclusion

We have presented the first results on parsing the SYNTAGRUS treebank of Russian using a data-driven dependency parser. Besides establishing a first benchmark for the SYNTAGRUS treebank, we have analyzed the influence of different kinds of features on parsing accuracy, showing conclusively that both lexical and morphological features are crucial for obtaining good parsing accuracy. We hypothesize that this result can be generalized to other richly inflected languages, provided that sufficient amounts of data are available.

Future work includes a deeper analysis of the influence of individual features, both morphological and lexical, as well as an evaluation of the parser under more realistic conditions without gold standard annotation in the input. This will require not only automatic morphological analysis and disambiguation but also a mechanism for inserting so-called phantom tokens in elliptical constructions.

Acknowledgments

We want to thank Ivan Chardin for initiating this collaboration and Jens Nilsson for converting the SYNTAGRUS data to the CoNLL format. We are grateful to the Russian Foundation of Basic Research for partial support of this research (grant no. 07-06-00339).

References

Apresian, Ju., I. Boguslavsky, L. Iomdin, A. Lazursky, V. Sannikov, V. Sizov, and L. Tsinman. 2003. ETAP-3 linguistic processor: A full-fledged NLP implementation of the MTT. In *Proceedings of the First International Conference on Meaning-Text Theory*, 279–288.

Black, E., F. Jelinek, J. D. Lafferty, D. M. Magerman, R. L. Mercer, and S. Roukos. 1992. Towards history-based grammars: Using richer models for probabilistic parsing. In *Proceedings of the 5th DARPA Speech and Natural Language Workshop*, 31–37.

Boguslavsky, I., S. Grigorieva, N. Grigoriev, L. Kreidlin, and N. Frid. 2000. Dependency treebank for Russian: Concept, tools, types of information. In *Proceedings of COLING*, 987–991.

Boguslavsky, I., I. Chardin, S. Grigorieva, N. Grigoriev, L. Iomdin, L. Kreidlin, and N. Frid. 2002. Development of a dependency treebank for Russian and its possible applications in NLP. In *Proceedings of LREC*, page 852856.

Boguslavsky, I. M., L. L. Iomdin, V. S. Sizov, and I. Chardin. 2003. Parsing with a treebank. In *Proceedings of the Conference on Cognitive Modeling in Linguistics* [In Russian].

Buchholz, S. and E. Marsi. 2006. CoNLL-X shared task on multilingual dependency parsing. In *Proceedings of CoNLL*, 149–164.

Chang, C.-C. and C.-J. Lin, 2001. *LIBSVM: A Library for Support Vector Machines*. Software available at http://www.csie.ntu.edu.tw/~cjlin/libsvm.

Chardin, Ivan. 2004. *Dependency Treebanks and Their Use in Parsing*. Ph.D. thesis, Russian Academy of Science [In Russian].

Cowan, B. and M. Collins. 2005. Morphology and reranking for the statistical parsing of spanish. In *Proceedings of HLT/EMNLP*, 795–802.

Dienes, P. and A. Dubey. 2003. Deep syntactic processing by combining shallow methods. In *Proceedings of ACL*, 431–438.

Dubey, A. and F. Keller. 2003. Probabilistic parsing for German using sister-head dependencies. In *Proceedings of ACL*, 96–103.

Eryiğit, G. and K. Oflazer. 2006. Statistical dependency parsing of Turkish. In *Proceedings of EACL*, 89–96.

Eryigit, G., J. Nivre, and K. Oflazer. 2006. The incremental use of morphological information and lexicalization in data-driven dependency parsing. In *Proceedings of the 21st International Conference on the Computer Processing of Oriental Languages*, 498–507.

Hajič, J., B. Vidova Hladka, J. Panevová, E. Hajičová, P. Sgall, and P. Pajas. 2001. Prague Dependency Treebank 1.0. LDC, 2001T10.

Klein, D. and C. D. Manning. 2003. Accurate unlexicalized parsing. In *Proceedings of ACL*, 423–430.

Kudo, T. and Y. Matsumoto. 2002. Japanese dependency analysis using cascaded chunking. In *Proceedings of CoNLL*, 63–69.

Magerman, D. M. 1995. Statistical decision-tree models for parsing. In *Proceedings of ACL*, 276–283.

McDonald, R. and J. Nivre. 2007. Characterizing the errors of data-driven dependency parsing models. In *Proceedings of EMNLP-CoNLL*, 122–131.

Mel'čuk, I. 1988. *Dependency Syntax: Theory and Practice*. State University of New York Press.

Nivre, J. and J. Nilsson. 2005. Pseudo-projective dependency parsing. In *Proceedings of ACL*, 99–106.

Nivre, J., J. Hall, S. Kübler, R. McDonald, J. Nilsson, S. Riedel, and D. Yuret. 2007a. The CoNLL 2007 shared task on dependency parsing. In *Proceedings of the CoNLL Shared Task of EMNLP-CoNLL 2007*, 915–932.

Nivre, J., J. Hall, J. Nilsson, A. Chanev, G. Eryiğit, S. Kübler, S. Marinov, and E. Marsi. 2007b. MaltParser: A language-independent system for data-driven dependency parsing. *Natural Language Engineering*, 13:95–135.

Nivre, J. 2003. An efficient algorithm for projective dependency parsing. In *Proceedings of IWPT*, 149–160.

Øvrelid, L. and J. Nivre. 2007. When word order and part-of-speech tags are not enough – swedish dependency parsing with rich linguistic features. In *Proceedings of RANLP*, 447–451.

Petrov, S., L. Barrett, R. Thibaux, and D. Klein. 2006. Learning accurate, compact, and interpretable tree annotation. In *Proceedings of COLING/ACL*, 433–440.

Ratnaparkhi, A. 1997. A linear observed time statistical parser based on maximum entropy models. In *Proceedings of EMNLP*, 1–10.

Tesnière, L. 1959. *Éléments de syntaxe structurale*. Editions Klincksieck.

Tsarfaty, R. and K. Sima'an. 2007. Three-dimensional parametrization for parsing morphologically rich languages. In *Proceedings of IWPT*, 156–167.

Tsarfaty, R. 2006. Integrated morphological and syntactic disambiguation for modern hebrew. In *Proceedings of the COLING/ACL 2006 Student Research Workshop*, 49–54.

Vapnik, V. N. 1995. *The Nature of Statistical Learning Theory*. Springer.

Yamada, H. and Y. Matsumoto. 2003. Statistical dependency analysis with support vector machines. In *Proceedings of IWPT*, 195–206.

Semantic Classification with Distributional Kernels

Diarmuid Ó Séaghdha
Computer Laboratory
University of Cambridge
15 JJ Thomson Avenue
Cambridge CB3 0FD
United Kingdom
do242@cl.cam.ac.uk

Ann Copestake
Computer Laboratory
University of Cambridge
15 JJ Thomson Avenue
Cambridge CB3 0FD
United Kingdom
aac10@cl.cam.ac.uk

Abstract

Distributional measures of lexical similarity and kernel methods for classification are well-known tools in Natural Language Processing. We bring these two methods together by introducing *distributional kernels* that compare co-occurrence probability distributions. We demonstrate the effectiveness of these kernels by presenting state-of-the-art results on datasets for three semantic classification: compound noun interpretation, identification of semantic relations between nominals and semantic classification of verbs. Finally, we consider explanations for the impressive performance of distributional kernels and sketch some promising generalisations.

1 Introduction

This paper draws a connection between two well-known topics in statistical Natural Language Processing: distributional measures of lexical similarity and kernel methods for classification. Distributional similarity measures quantify the similarity between pairs of words through their observed co-occurrences with other words in corpus data. The kernel functions used in support vector machine classifiers also allow an interpretation as similarity measures; however, not all similarity measures can be used as kernels. In particular, kernel functions must satisfy the mathematical property of *positive semi-definiteness*. In Section 2 we consider kernel functions suitable for comparing co-occurrence probability distributions and show that these kernels are closely related to measures known from the distributional similarity literature. We apply these *distributional kernels* to three semantic classification tasks: compound noun interpretation, identification of semantic relations between nominals and semantic classification of verbs. In all cases, the distributional kernels outperform the linear and Gaussian kernels standardly used for SVM classification and furthermore achieve state-of-the-art results. In Section 4 we provide a concrete explanation for the superior performance of distributional kernels, and in Section 5 we outline some promising directions for future research.

© 2008. Licensed under the *Creative Commons Attribution-Noncommercial-Share Alike 3.0 Unported* license (http://creativecommons.org/licenses/by-nc-sa/3.0/). Some rights reserved.

2 Theory

2.1 Distributional Similarity Measures

Distributional approaches to lexical similarity assume that words appearing in similar contexts are likely to have similar or related meanings. To measure distributional similarity, we use a representation of words based on observation of their relations with other words. Specifically, a target word w is represented in terms of a set C of admissible co-occurrence types $c = (r, w')$, where the word w' belongs to a co-occurrence vocabulary V_c and r is a relation that holds between w and w'. Co-occurrence relations may be syntactic (e.g., verb-argument, conjunct-conjunct) or may simply be one of proximity in text. Counts $f(w, c)$ of a target word w's co-occurrences can be estimated from language corpora, and these counts can be weighted in a variety of ways to reflect prior knowledge or to reduce statistical noise. A simple weighting method is to represent each word w as a vector of co-occurrence probabilities $(P(c_1|w), \ldots, P(c_{|C|}|w))$. This vector defines the parameters of a categorical or multinomial probability distribution, giving a useful probabilistic interpretation of the distributional model. As the vector for each target word must sum to 1, the marginal distributions of target words have little effect on the resulting similarity estimates. Many similarity measures and weighting functions have been proposed for distributional vectors; comparative studies include Lee (1999), Curran (2003) and Weeds and Weir (2005).

2.2 Kernel Methods for Computing Similarity and Distance

In this section we describe two classes of functions, positive semi-definite and negative semi-definite kernels, and state some relationships between these classes. The mathematical treatment follows Berg et al. (1984). A good general introduction to kernels and support vector machines is the book by Cristianini and Shawe-Taylor (2000).

Let $\mathcal{X}$ be a set of items and let $k : \mathcal{X} \times \mathcal{X} \rightarrow \mathbb{R}$ be a symmetric real-valued function on pairs of items in $\mathcal{X}$. Then k is a *positive semi-definite (psd) kernel* if for all finite n-element sets $X \subseteq \mathcal{X}$, the $n \times n$ *Gram matrix* K defined by $K_{ij} = k(x_i, x_j)$ satisfies the property

$$v'Kv \geq 0,\ \forall v \in \mathbb{R}^n \tag{1}$$

This is equivalent to requiring that k define an inner product in a Hilbert space $\mathcal{F}$ which may be the same as $\mathcal{X}$ or may differ in dimensionality or in type ($\mathcal{F}$ is by definition a vector space, but $\mathcal{X}$ need not be). An intuitive interpretation of psd kernels is that they provide a similarity measure on members of $\mathcal{X}$ based on an embedding ϕ from input space $\mathcal{X}$ into feature space $\mathcal{F}$. It can be shown that a function is psd if and only if all Gram matrices K have no negative eigenvalues.

Kernel functions have received significant attention in recent years through their applications in machine learning, most notably support vector machines (SVMs, Cortes and Vapnik (1995)). SVM classifiers learn a decision boundary between two data classes that maximises the minimum distance or *margin* from the training points in each class to the boundary. The notion of distance used and the feature space in which the boundary is set are determined by the choice of kernel function. So long as the kernel satisfies (1), the SVM optimisation algorithm is guaranteed to converge to a global optimum that affords the geometric interpretation of margin maximisation. Besides these desirable optimisation properties, kernel methods have the advantage that the choice of kernel can be based on prior knowledge about the problem and on the nature of the data.

A *negative semi-definite (nsd) kernel* is a symmetric function $\tilde{k} : \mathcal{X} \times \mathcal{X} \rightarrow \mathbb{R}$ such that for all finite n-element sets $X \subseteq \mathcal{X}$ and for all vectors $v = (v_1, \ldots, v_n) \in \mathbb{R}^n$ with $\sum_i v_i = 0$

$$v'\tilde{K}v \leq 0 \tag{2}$$

Whereas positive semi-definite kernels correspond to inner products in a Hilbert space $\mathcal{F}$, negative semi-definite kernels correspond to squared distances. In particular, if $\tilde{k}(x, y) = 0$ only when $x = y$ then $\sqrt{\tilde{k}}$ is a metric. If a function k is psd, then $-k$ is always nsd, but the converse does not hold.[1] However, Berg et al. (1984) describe two simple methods for inducing a positive semi-definite function k from negative semi-definite $\tilde{k}$:

$$k(x,y) = \tilde{k}(x, x_0) + \tilde{k}(y, x_0) - \tilde{k}(x, y) - \tilde{k}(x_0, x_0),\ \forall x_0 \in \mathcal{X} \tag{3a}$$

$$k(x,y) = \exp(-\alpha\tilde{k}(x,y)),\ \forall \alpha > 0 \tag{3b}$$

The point x_0 in (3a) can be viewed as providing an origin in $\mathcal{F}$ that is the image of some point in the input space $\mathcal{X}$; the choice of x_0 does not have an effect on SVM classification. A familiar example of these transformations arises if we take $\tilde{k}$ to be the squared Euclidean L_2 distance $\|x - y\|^2 = \sum_i (x_i - y_i)^2$. Applying (3a) and setting x_0 to be the zero vector, we obtain a quantity that is twice the linear kernel $k(x, y) = \sum_i x_i y_i$. Applying (3b) we derive the Gaussian kernel $k(x, y) = \exp(-\alpha\|x - y\|^2)$. In the next section we consider kernels obtained by plugging alternative squared metrics into equations (3a) and (3b).

2.3 Distributional Kernels

Given the effectiveness of distributional similarity measures for numerous tasks in NLP and the interpretation of kernels as similarity functions, it seems natural to consider the use of kernels tailored for co-occurrence distributions when performing semantic classification. As shown in Section 2.2 the standardly used linear and Gaussian kernels derive from the L_2 distance, yet Lee (1999) has shown that this distance measure is relatively poor at comparing co-occurrence distributions. Information theory provides a number of alternative distance functions on probability measures, of which the L_1 distance (also called *variational distance*), Kullback-Leibler divergence and Jensen-Shannon divergence are well-known in NLP and

[1]Negated nsd functions are sometimes called *conditionally psd*; they constitute a superset of the psd functions.

Distance	Definition	Derived linear kernel
$(L_2 \text{ distance})^2$	$\sum_c (P(c\|w_1) - P(c\|w_2))^2$	$\sum_c P(c\|w_1)P(c\|w_2)$
L_1 distance	$\sum_c \|P(c\|w_1) - P(c\|w_2)\|$	$\sum_c \min(P(c\|w_1), P(c\|w_2))$
Jensen-Shannon divergence	$\sum_c P(c\|w_1)\log_2(\frac{2P(c\|w_1)}{P(c\|w_1)+P(c\|w_2)}) + P(c\|w_2)\log_2(\frac{2P(c\|w_2)}{P(c\|w_1)+P(c\|w_2)})$	$-\sum_c P(c\|w_1)\log_2(\frac{P(c\|w_1)}{P(c\|w_1)+P(c\|w_2)}) + P(c\|w_2)\log_2(\frac{P(c\|w_2)}{P(c\|w_1)+P(c\|w_2)})$
Hellinger distance	$\sum_c(\sqrt{P(c\|w_1)} - \sqrt{P(c\|w_2)})^2$	$\sum_c \sqrt{P(c\|w_1)P(c\|w_2)}$

Table 1: Squared metric distances on co-occurrence distributions and corresponding linear kernels

were shown by Lee to give better similarity estimates than the L_2 distance.

In Section 2.2 we have seen how to derive psd kernels (similarities) from nsd kernels (distances). It seems likely that distance measures that are known to work well for comparing co-occurrence distributions will also give us suitable psd similarity measures. Negative semi-definite kernels are by definition symmetric, which rules the Kullback-Leibler divergence and Lee's (1999) α-skew divergence out of consideration. The nsd condition (2) is met if the distance function is a squared metric in a Hilbert space. In this paper we use a parametric family of squared Hilbertian metrics on probability distributions that has been discussed by Hein and Bousquet (2005). This family contains many familiar distances including the L_1 distance, Jensen-Shannon divergence (*JSD*) and the Hellinger distance used in statistics, though not the squared L_2 distance. Positive semi-definite *distributional kernels* can be derived from these distances through equations (3a) and (3b). We interpret the distributional kernels produced by (3a) and (3b) as analogues of the linear and Gaussian kernels respectively, given by a different norm or concept of distance in the feature space $\mathcal{F}$. Hence the *linear* distributional kernels produced by (3a) correspond to inner products in the input space $\mathcal{X}$, and the *rbf* distributional kernels produced by (3b) are radial basis functions corresponding to inner products in a high-dimensional Hilbert space of Gaussian-like functions. In this paper we use the unmodified term "linear kernel" in the standard sense of the linear kernel derived from the L_2 distance and make explicit the related distance when referring to other linear kernels, e.g., the "JSD linear kernel". Likewise, we use the standard term "Gaussian" to refer to the L_2 rbf kernel, and denote other rbf kernels as, for example, the "JSD rbf kernel".

Table 1 lists relevant squared metric distances and their derived linear kernels. The linear kernel derived from the L_1 distance is the same as the *difference-weighted token-based similarity* measure of Weeds and Weir (2005). The JSD linear kernel can be rewritten as (2 - *JSD*), where JSD is the value of the Jensen-Shannon divergence. This formulation is used as a similarity measure by Lin (1999). Dagan et al. (1999) use a similarity measure $10^{-\alpha JSD}$, though they acknowledge that this transformation is heuristically motivated. The rbf kernel $\exp(-\alpha JSD)$ provides a theoretically sound alternative when the psd property is required. It follows from the above discussion that these previously known distributional similarity measures are valid kernel functions and can be used directly for SVM classification.

Finally, we consider the status of other popular distributional measures. The familiar cosine similarity measure is provably a valid psd kernel, as it is the L_2 linear kernel calculated between L_2-normalised vectors. Distributional vectors are by definition L_1-normalised (they sum to 1), but there is evidence that L_2 normalisation is optimal when using L_2 kernels for tasks such as text categorisation (Leopold and Kindermann, 2002). Indeed, in the experiments described below L_2-normalised feature vectors are used with the L_2 kernels, and the L_2 linear kernel function then becomes identical to the cosine similarity. Other similarity measures, such as that of Lin (1998), can be shown to be non-psd by calculating similarity matrices from real or artificial data and showing that their nonzero eigenvalues are not all positive, as is required by psd functions.

3 Practice

3.1 General Methodology

All experiments were performed using the LIBSVM Support Vector Machine library (Chang and Lin, 2001), modified to implement one-against-all classification. The members of the distributional kernel family all performed similarly but the Jensen-Shannon divergence kernels gave the most consistently impressive results, and we restrict discussion to these kernels due to considerations of space and clarity. In each experiment we compare the standard linear and Gaussian kernels with the linear and JSD rbf kernels. As a preprocessing step for the L_2 kernels, each feature vector was normalised to have unit L_2 norm. For the Jensen-Shannon kernels, the feature vectors were normalised to have unit L_1 norm, i.e., to define a probability distribution. For all datasets and all training-test splits the SVM cost parameter C was optimised in the range $(2^{-6}, 2^{-4}, \ldots, 2^{12})$ through cross-validation on the training set. In addition, the width parameter α was optimised in the same way for the rbf kernels. The number of optimisation folds differed according to the size of the dataset and the number of training-test splits to be evaluated: we used 10 folds for the compound task, leave-one-out cross-validation for SemEval Task 4 and 25 folds for the verb classification task.

3.2 Compound Noun Interpretation

The task of interpreting the semantics of noun compounds is one which has recently received considerable attention (Lauer, 1995; Girju et al., 2005; Turney, 2006). For a given noun-noun compound, the problem is to identify the semantic relation between the compound's constituents – that a *kitchen knife* is a *knife used in a kitchen* but a *steel knife* is a *knife made of steel*.[2] The difficulty of the task is due to the fact that the knowledge required to interpret compounds is not made explicit in the contexts where they appear, and hence standard context-based methods for classifying semantic relations in text cannot be applied. Most previous work making use of lexical similarity has been based on WordNet measures (Kim and Baldwin, 2005; Girju et al., 2005). Ó Séaghdha and Copestake (2007) were to our knowledge the first to apply a distributional model. Here we build on their methodology by introducing a probabilistic feature weighting scheme and applying the new distributional kernels.

For our experiments we used the dataset of Ó Séaghdha and Copestake (2007), which consists of 1443 noun compounds annotated with six semantic relations: *BE*, *HAVE*, *IN*, *AGENT*, *INSTRUMENT* and *ABOUT*.[3] The classification baseline associated with always choosing the most frequent relation (*IN*) is 21.3%. For each compound (N_1, N_2) in the dataset, we associate the co-occurrence probability vector $(P(c_1|N_1), \ldots, P(c_{|C|}|N_1))$ with N_1 and the vector $(P(c_1|N_2), \ldots, P(c_{|C|}|N_2))$ with N_2. The probability vector for the compound is created by appending the two constituent vectors, each scaled by 0.5 to weight both constituents equally and ensure that the new vector sums to 1. These probability vectors are used to compute the Jensen-Shannon kernel values. The preprocessing step for the L_2 kernels is analogous, except that the co-occurrence *frequency* vector $(f(c_1, N_i), \ldots, f(c_{|C|}, N_i))$ for each constituent N_i is normalised to have unit L_2 norm (instead of unit L_1 norm); the combined feature vector for each data item is also L_2-normalised.[4]

The co-occurrence relation we counted to estimate the probability vectors was the conjunction relation. This relation gives sparse but high-quality information, and was shown to be effective by Ó Séaghdha and Copestake. We extracted two feature sets from two very different corpora. The first is the 90 million word written component of the British National Corpus (Burnard, 1995). This corpus was parsed with the RASP parser (Briscoe et al., 2006) and all instances of the `conj` grammatical relation were counted. The co-occurrence vocabulary V_c was set to the 10,000 words most frequently entering into a `conj` relation across the corpus. The second corpus we used was the Web 1T 5-Gram Corpus (Brants and Franz, 2006), which contains frequency counts for n-grams up to length 5 extracted from Google's index of approximately 1 trillion words of Web text. As the nature of this corpus precludes parsing, we used a simple pattern-based technique to extract conjunctions. An n-gram was judged to contain a conjunction co-occurrence between N_i and N_j if it con-

[2] In the classification scheme considered here, *kitchen knife* would have the label *IN* and *steel knife* would be labelled *BE*.

[3] This dataset is available from `http://www.cl.cam.ac.uk/~do242/resources.html`.

[4] The importance of performing both normalisation steps was suggested to us by an anonymous reviewer's comments.

	BNC		5-Gram	
Kernel	Acc	F	Acc	F
Linear	57.9	55.8	55.0	52.5
Gaussian	58.0	56.2	53.5	50.8
JSD (linear)	**59.9**	57.8	60.2	58.1
JSD (rbf)	59.8	**57.9**	**61.0**	**58.8**

Table 2: Results for compound interpretation

	BNC		5-Gram	
Kernel	Acc	F	Acc	F
Linear	67.6	57.1	65.4	63.3
Gaussian	66.8	60.7	65.6	62.9
JSD (linear)	**71.4**	**68.8**	69.6	65.8
JSD (rbf)	69.9	66.7	**70.7**	**67.5**

Table 3: Results for SemEval Task 4

tained the pattern N_i *and* $(\neg N)^*$ N_j $(\neg N)^*$. A noun dictionary automatically constructed from WordNet and an electronic version of Webster's 1913 Unabridged Dictionary determined the sets of admissible nouns {N} and non-nouns {¬N}.[5] The vocabulary V_c was again set to the 10,000 most frequent conjuncts, and the probability estimates $P(c|w)$ were based on the n-gram frequencies for each n-gram matching the extraction pattern. A third feature set extracted from the 5-Gram Corpus by using a larger set of joining terms was also studied but the results were not significantly different from the sparser conjunction feature sets and are not presented here.

Performance was measured by splitting the data into five folds and performing cross-validation. Results for the two feature sets and four kernels are presented in Table 2. The kernels derived from the Jensen-Shannon divergence clearly outperform the L_2 distance-based linear and Gaussian kernels in both accuracy and macro-averaged F-score. The best performing kernel-feature combination is the Jensen-Shannon rbf kernel with the 5-Gram features, which attains 61.0% accuracy and 58.8% F-score. This surpasses the best previous result of 57.1% accuracy, 55.3% F-score that was reported by Ó Séaghdha and Copestake (2007) for this dataset. That result was obtained by combining a distributional model with a relational similarity model based on string kernels; incorporating relational similarity into the system described here improves performance even further (Ó Séaghdha, 2008).

3.3 SemEval Task 4

Task 4 at the 2007 SemEval competition (Girju et al., 2007) focused on the identification of semantic relations among nominals in text. Identification of each of seven relations was designed as a binary classification task with 140 training sentences and around 70 test sentences.[6] To ensure that the task be a challenging one, the negative test examples were all "near misses" in that they were plausible candidates for the relation to hold but failed to meet one of the criteria for that relation. This was achieved by selecting both positive and negative examples from the results of the same targeted Google queries. The majority-class baseline for this task gives Accuracy = 57.0%, F-score = 30.8%, while the all-true baseline (label every test sentence positive) gives Accuracy = 48.5%, F-score = 64.8%.

We used the same feature sets and kernels as in Section 3.2. The results are presented in Table 3. Again, the JSD kernels outperform the standard L_2 kernels by a considerable margin. The best performing feature-kernel combination achieves 71.4% Accuracy and 68.8% F-score, higher than the best performance attained in the SemEval competition without using WordNet similarity measures (Accuracy = 67.0%, F-score = 65.1%; Nakov and Hearst (2007)). This is also higher than the performance of all but three of the 14 SemEval entries which did use WordNet. Davidov and Rappoport (2008) have recently described a WordNet-free method that attains slightly lower accuracy (70.1%) and slightly higher F-score (70.6%) than our method. Taken together, Davidov and Rappoport's results and ours define the current state of the art on this task.

3.4 Verb Classification

To investigate the effectiveness of distributional kernels on a different kind of semantic classification task, we tested our methods on the verb class data of Sun et al. (2008). This dataset consists of 204 verbs assigned to 17 of Levin's (1993) verb classes. Each verb is represented by a set of features corresponding to the distribution of its instances across subcategorisation frames (SCFs).

[5]The electronic version of Webster's is available from `http://msowww.anu.edu.au/~ralph/OPTED/`.

[6]The relations are *Cause-Effect*, *Instrument-Agency*, *Product-Producer*, *Origin-Entity*, *Theme-Tool*, *Part-Whole* and *Content-Container*.

	FS3		FS5	
Kernel	Acc	F	Acc	F
Linear	67.1	65.5	67.6	65.9
Gaussian	60.8	58.6	62.7	60.2
JSD (linear)	**70.6**	**67.3**	69.6	66.4
JSD (rbf)	68.6	65.1	**70.1**	**67.2**
Sun et al. (SVM)	57.8	58.2	57.3	57.4
Sun et al. (GS)	59.3	57.1	64.2	62.5

Table 4: Results for leave-one-out verb classification and comparison with Sun et al.'s (2008) SVM and Gaussian fitting methods

These frames include information about syntactic constituents (*NP*, *NP_NP*, *NP_SCOMP*, ...) and some lexical information about subcategorised prepositions (*NP_with*, *out*, ...). The feature values are counts of SCFs extracted from a large corpus. As the feature vector for each verb naturally defines a probability distribution over SCFs, it seems intuitive to apply distributional kernels to the problem of predicting Levin classes for verbs.

Sun et al. use multiple feature sets of varying sparsity and noisiness. We report results on the two feature sets for which they reported best performance; for continuity we keep the names *FS3* and *FS5* for these feature sets. These were derived from the least filtered and hence least sparse subcategorisation lexicon (which they call VALEX 1) and differ in the granularity of prepositional SCFs. The SCF representation in FS5 is richer and hence potentially more discriminative, but it is also sparser. Using an SVM with a Gaussian kernel, Sun et al. achieved their best results on FS3. Perhaps surprisingly, their best results overall were attained with FS5 by a simple method based on fitting multivariate Gaussian distributions to each class in the training data and assigning the maximum likelihood class to test points.

Following Sun et al., we use a leave-one-out measure of verb classification performance. As the examples are distributed equally across the 17 classes, the random baseline accuracy is 5.9%. Table 4 presents our results with L_2 and JSD kernels, as well as those of Sun et al. The best overall performance is attained by the JSD linear kernel, which scores higher than the L_2-derived kernels on both feature sets. The L_2 linear kernel also performs quite well and with consistency. The JSD rbf kernel was less consistent over cross-validation runs, seemingly due to uncertainty in selecting the optimal α parameter value; it clearly outperforms the L_2 linear kernel on one feature set (FS5) but on the other (FS3) it attains a slightly lower F-score while maintaining a higher accuracy. The Gaussian kernel seems particularly ill-suited to this dataset, performing significantly worse than the other kernels. The difference between Sun et al.'s results with the Gaussian kernel and ours with the same kernel may be due to the use of one-against-all classification here instead of one-against-one, or it may be due to differences in preprocessing or parameter optimisation.

4 The effect of marginal distributions

It is natural to ask why distributional kernels perform better than the standard linear and Gaussian kernels. One answer might be that just as information theory provides the "correct" notion of information for many purposes, it also provides the "correct" notion of distance between probability distributions. Hein and Bousquet (2005) show that their family of distributional kernels are invariant to bijective transformations of the event space C and suggest that this property is a valuable one for image histogram classification where data may be represented in a range of equivalent colour spaces. However, it is not clear that this confers an advantage when comparing lexical co-occurrence distributions; when transformations are performed on the space of co-occurrence types, they are generally not information-conserving, for example lemmatisation or stemming.

A more practical explanation is that the distributional kernels and distances are less sensitive than the (squared) L_2 distance and its derived kernels to the marginal frequencies of co-occurrence types. When a type c has high frequency we expect that it will have higher variance, i.e., the differences $|P(c|w_1) - P(c|w_2)|$ will tend to be greater even if c is not a more important signifier of similarity.[7] These differences contribute quadratically to the L_2 distance and hence also to the associated rbf kernel, i.e., the Gaussian kernel. It is also easy to see that types c for which $P(c|w_i)$ tends to be large will dominate the value of the linear kernel. This explanation is also plausibly a factor in the relatively poor performance of L_2 distance as a lexical dissimilarity measure, as demon-

[7] Chapelle et al. (1999) give a similar explanation for the performance of a related family of kernels on a histogram classification task.

strated by Lee (1999). In contrast, the differences $|P(c|w_1) - P(c|w_2)|$ are not squared in the L_1 distance formula, and the minimum function in the L_1 linear kernel dampens the effect of high-variance co-occurrence types. The Jensen-Shannon formula is more difficult to interpret, as the difference terms do not directly appear. While co-occurrence types with large $P(c|w_1)$ and $P(c|w_2)$ do contribute more to the distance and kernel values, it is the proportional size of the difference that appears in the log term rather than its magnitude. Finally, the Hellinger distance and kernels squash the variance associated with c through the square root function.

5 Discussion and Future Directions

Kernels on probability measures have been discussed in the machine learning literature (Kondor and Jebara, 2003; Cuturi et al., 2005; Hein and Bousquet, 2005), but they have previously been applied only to standard image and text classification benchmark tasks. We seem to be the first to use distributional kernels for semantic classification and to note their connection with familiar lexical similarity measures. Indeed, the only research we are aware of on kernels tailored for lexical similarity is the small body of work on WordNet kernels, e.g., Basili et al. (2006). In contrast, Support Vector Machines have been widely adopted for computational semantic tasks, from word sense disambiguation (Gliozzo et al., 2005) to semantic role labelling (Pradhan et al., 2004). The standard feature sets for semantic role labelling and many other tasks are collections of heterogeneous features that do not correspond to probability distributions. So long as the features are restricted to positive values, distributional kernels can be applied; it will be interesting (and informative) to see whether they retain their superiority in this setting.

One advantage of kernel methods is that kernels can be defined for non-vectorial data structures such as strings, trees, graphs and sets. A promising topic of future research is the design of distributional kernels for comparing structured objects, based on the feature space embedding associated with convolution kernels (Haussler, 1999). These kernels map structures in $\mathcal{X}$ into a space whose dimensions correspond to substructures of the elements of $\mathcal{X}$. Thus strings are mapped onto vectors of substring counts, and trees are mapped onto vectors of subtree counts. We adopt the perspective that this mapping represents structures $x_i \in \mathcal{X}$ as measures over substructures $\bar{x}_1, \dots, \bar{x}_d$. Properly normalised, this gives a distributional probability vector $(P(\bar{x}_1), \dots, P(\bar{x}_d))$ similar to those used for computing lexical similarity. This perspective motivates the use of distributional inner products instead of the dot products implicitly used in standard convolution kernels. Several authors have suggested applying distributional similarity measures to sentences and phrases for tasks such as question answering (Lin and Pantel, 2001; Weeds et al., 2005). Distributional kernels on strings and trees should provide a flexible implementation of these suggestions that is compatible with SVM classification and does not require manual feature engineering. Furthermore, there is a ready generalisation to kernels on sets of structures; if a set is represented as the normalised sum of its member embeddings in feature space $\mathcal{F}$, distributional methods can be applied directly.

6 Conclusion

In this paper we have introduced distributional kernels for classification with co-occurrence probability distributions. The suitability of distributional kernels for semantic classification is intuitive, given their relation to proven distributional methods for computing semantic similarity, and in practice they work very well. As these kernels give state-of-the-art results on the three datasets we have tested, we expect that they will prove useful for a wide range of semantic classification problems in future.

Acknowledgements

We are grateful to Andreas Vlachos and three anonymous reviewers for their useful comments, and to Anna Korhonen for providing the verb classification dataset. This work was supported in part by EPSRC Grant EP/C010035/1.

References

Basili, Roberto, Marco Cammisa, and Alessandro Moschitti. 2006. A semantic kernel to classify texts with very few training examples. *Informatica*, 30(2):163–172.

Berg, Christian, Jens P. R. Christensen, and Paul Ressel. 1984. *Harmonic Analysis on Semigroups: Theory of Positive Definite and Related Functions*. Springer, Berlin.

Brants, Thorsten and Alex Franz, 2006. *Web 1T 5-gram Corpus Version 1.1*. Linguistic Data Consortium.

Briscoe, Ted, John Carroll, and Rebecca Watson. 2006. The second release of the RASP system. In *Proceedings of the ACL Interactive Presentation Sessions*.

Burnard, Lou, 1995. *Users' Guide for the British National Corpus*. British National Corpus Consortium, Oxford University Computing Service.

Chang, Chih-Chung and Chih-Jen Lin, 2001. *LIBSVM: a library for support vector machines*. Software available at `http://www.csie.ntu.edu.tw/~cjlin/libsvm`.

Chapelle, Olivier, Patrick Haffner, and Vladimir N. Vapnik. 1999. Support vector machines for histogram-based image classification. *IEEE Transactions on Neural Networks*, 10(5):1055–1064.

Cortes, Corinna and Vladimir Vapnik. 1995. Support vector networks. *Machine Learning*, 20(3):273–297.

Cristianini, Nello and John Shawe-Taylor. 2000. *An Introduction to Support Vector Machines*. Cambridge University Press, Cambridge.

Curran, James. 2003. *From Distributional to Semantic Similarity*. Ph.D. thesis, University of Edinburgh.

Cuturi, Marco, Kenji Fukumizu, and Jean-Philippe Vert. 2005. Semigroup kernels on measures. *Journal of Machine Learning Research*, 6:1169–1198.

Dagan, Ido, Lillian Lee, and Fernando Pereira. 1999. Similarity-based models of word cooccurrence probabilities. *Machine Learning*, 34(1–4):43–69.

Davidov, Dmitry and Ari Rappoport. 2008. Classification of semantic relationships between nominals using pattern clusters. In *Proceedings of the 46th Annual Meeting of the Association for Computational Linguistics*.

Girju, Roxana, Dan Moldovan, Marta Tatu, and Daniel Antohe. 2005. On the semantics of noun compounds. *Computer Speech and Language*, 19(4):479–496.

Girju, Roxana, Preslav Nakov, Vivi Nastase, Stan Szpakowicz, Peter Turney, and Deniz Yuret. 2007. SemEval-2007 Task 04: Classification of semantic relations between nominals. In *Proceedings of the 4th International Workshop on Semantic Evaluations*.

Gliozzo, Alfio, Claudio Giuliano, and Carlo Strapparava. 2005. Domain kernels for word sense disambiguation. In *Proceedings of the 43rd Annual Meeting of the Association for Computational Linguistics*.

Haussler, David. 1999. Convolution kernels on discrete structures. Technical Report UCSC-CRL-99-10, Computer Science Department, University of California at Santa Cruz.

Hein, Matthias and Olivier Bousquet. 2005. Hilbertian metrics and positive definite kernels on probability measures. In *Proceedings of the 10th International Workshop on Artificial Intelligence and Statistics*.

Kim, Su Nam and Timothy Baldwin. 2005. Automatic interpretation of noun compounds using WordNet similarity. In *Proceedings of the 2nd International Joint Conference on Natural Language Processing*.

Kondor, Risi and Tony Jebara. 2003. A kernel between sets of vectors. In *Proceedings of the 20th International Conference on Machine Learning*.

Lauer, Mark. 1995. *Designing Statistical Language Learners: Experiments on Compound Nouns*. Ph.D. thesis, Macquarie University.

Lee, Lillian. 1999. Measures of distributional similarity. In *Proceedings of the 37th Annual Meeting of the Association for Computational Linguistics*.

Leopold, Edda and Jörg Kindermann. 2002. Text categorization with support vector machines. how to represent texts in input space? *Machine Learning*, 46(1–3):423–444.

Levin, Beth. 1993. *English Verb Classes and Alternations: A Preliminary Investigation*. University of Chicago Press, Chicago.

Lin, Dekang and Patrick Pantel. 2001. Discovery of inference rules for question answering. *Natural Language Engineering*, 7(4):343–360.

Lin, Dekang. 1998. An information-theoretic definition of similarity. In *Proceedings of the 15th International Conference on Machine Learning*.

Nakov, Preslav I. and Marti A. Hearst. 2007. UCB: System description for SemEval Task #4. In *Proceedings of the 4th International Workshop on Semantic Evaluations*.

Ó Séaghdha, Diarmuid and Ann Copestake. 2007. Co-occurrence contexts for noun compound interpretation. In *Proceedings of the ACL Workshop on a Broader Perspective on Multiword Expressions*.

Ó Séaghdha, Diarmuid. 2008. *Learning Compound Noun Semantics*. Ph.D. thesis, Computer Laboratory, University of Cambridge. In preparation.

Pradhan, Sameer, Kadri Hacioglu, Valerie Krugler, Wayne Ward, James H. Martin, and Daniel Jurafsky. 2004. Support vector learning for semantic argument classification. *Machine Learning*, 60(1):11–39.

Sun, Lin, Anna Korhonen, and Yuval Krymolowski. 2008. Verb class discovery from rich syntactic data. In *Proceedings of the 9th International Conference on Intelligent Text Processing and Computational Linguistics*.

Turney, Peter D. 2006. Similarity of semantic relations. *Computational Linguistics*, 32(3):379–416.

Weeds, Julie and David Weir. 2005. Co-occurrence retrieval: A flexible framework for lexical distributional similarity. *Computational Linguistics*, 31(4):439–476.

Weeds, Julie, David Weir, and Bill Keller. 2005. The distributional similarity of sub-parses. In *Proceedings of the ACL Workshop on Empirical Modeling of Semantic Equivalence and Entailment*.

A Discriminative Alignment Model for Abbreviation Recognition

Naoaki Okazaki†
okazaki@is.s.u-tokyo.ac.jp

Sophia Ananiadou‡
sophia.ananiadou@manchester.ac.uk

Jun'ichi Tsujii†‡
tsujii@is.s.u-tokyo.ac.jp

†Graduate School of Information Science and Technology
University of Tokyo
7-3-1 Hongo, Bunkyo-ku
Tokyo 113-8656, Japan

‡School of Computer Science,
University of Manchester
National Centre for Text Mining (NaCTeM)
Manchester Interdisciplinary Biocentre
131 Princess Street, Manchester M1 7DN, UK

Abstract

This paper presents a discriminative alignment model for extracting abbreviations and their full forms appearing in actual text. The task of abbreviation recognition is formalized as a *sequential alignment problem*, which finds the optimal alignment (origins of abbreviation letters) between two strings (abbreviation and full form). We design a large amount of fine-grained features that directly express the events where letters produce or do not produce abbreviations. We obtain the optimal combination of features on an *aligned* abbreviation corpus by using the maximum entropy framework. The experimental results show the usefulness of the alignment model and corpus for improving abbreviation recognition.

1 Introduction

Abbreviations present two major challenges in natural language processing: *term variation* and *ambiguity*. Abbreviations substitute for expanded terms (e.g., *dynamic programming*) through the use of shortened term-forms (e.g., *DP*). At the same time, the abbreviation *DP* appearing alone in text is ambiguous, in that it may refer to different concepts, e.g., *data processing*, *dirichlet process*, *differential probability*. Associating abbreviations and their full forms is useful for various applications including named entity recognition, information retrieval, and question answering.

©2008. Licensed under the *Creative Commons Attribution-Noncommercial-Share Alike 3.0 Unported* license (http://creativecommons.org/licenses/by-nc-sa/3.0/). Some rights reserved.

The task of *abbreviation recognition*, in which abbreviations and their expanded forms appearing in actual text are extracted, addresses the term variation problem caused by the increase in the number of abbreviations (Chang and Schütze, 2006). Furthermore, abbreviation recognition is also crucial for disambiguating abbreviations (Pakhomov, 2002; Gaudan et al., 2005; Yu et al., 2006), providing sense inventories (lists of abbreviation definitions), training corpora (context information of full forms), and local definitions of abbreviations. Hence, abbreviation recognition plays a key role in abbreviation management.

Numerous researchers have proposed a variety of heuristics for recognizing abbreviation definitions, e.g., the use of initials, capitalizations, syllable boundaries, stop words, lengths of abbreviations, and co-occurrence statistics (Park and Byrd, 2001; Wren and Garner, 2002; Liu and Friedman, 2003; Okazaki and Ananiadou, 2006; Zhou et al., 2006; Jain et al., 2007). Schwartz and Hearst (2003) implemented a simple algorithm that finds the shortest expression containing all alphanumerical letters of an abbreviation. Adar (2004) presented four scoring rules to choose the most likely expanded form in multiple candidates. Ao and Takagi (2005) designed more detailed conditions for accepting or discarding candidates of abbreviation definitions.

However, these studies have limitations in discovering an optimal combination of heuristic rules from manual observations of a corpus. For example, when expressions *transcription factor 1* and *thyroid transcription factor 1* are full-form candidates for the abbreviation *TTF-1*[1], an algorithm should choose the latter expression over the shorter

[1]In this paper, we use straight and wavy underlines to represent correct and incorrect origins of abbreviation letters.

expression (former). Previous studies hardly handle abbreviation definitions where full forms (e.g., *water activity*) shuffle their abbreviation letters (e.g., *AW*). It is also difficult to reject 'negative' definitions in a text; for example, an algorithm should not extract an abbreviation definition from the text, "the replicon encodes a large replication protein (RepA)," since *RepA* provides a description of the protein rather than an abbreviation.

In order to acquire the optimal rules from the corpora, several researchers applied machine learning methods. Chang and Schütze (2006) applied logistic regression to combine nine features. Nadeau and Turney (2005) also designed seventeen features to classify candidates of abbreviation definitions into positive or negative instances by using the Support Vector Machine (SVM). Notwithstanding, contrary to our expectations, the machine-learning approach could not report better results than those with hand-crafted rules.

We identify the major problem in the previous machine-learning approach: these studies did not model associations between abbreviation letters and their origins, but focused only on indirect features such as *the number of abbreviation letters that appear at the head of a full form*. This was probably because the training corpus did not include annotations on the exact origins of abbreviation letters but only pairs of abbreviations and full forms. It was thus difficult to design effective features for abbreviation recognition and to reuse the knowledge obtained from the training processes.

In this paper, we formalize the task of abbreviation recognition as a *sequential alignment problem*, which finds the optimal alignment (origins of abbreviation letters) between two strings (abbreviation and full form). We design a large amount of features that directly express the events where letters produce or do not produce abbreviations. Preparing an *aligned* abbreviation corpus, we obtain the optimal combination of the features by using the maximum entropy framework (Berger et al., 1996). We report the remarkable improvements and conclude this paper.

2 Proposed method

2.1 Abbreviation alignment model

We express a sentence x as a sequence of letters $(x_1, ..., x_L)$, and an abbreviation candidate $\boldsymbol{y}$ in the sentence as a sequence of letters $(y_1, ..., y_M)$. We define a *letter mapping* $a = (i, j)$ to indicate that the abbreviation letter y_j is produced by the letter in the full form x_i. A null mapping $a = (i, 0)$ indicates that the letter in the sentence x_i is unused to form the abbreviation. Similarly, a null mapping $a = (0, j)$ indicates that the abbreviation letter y_j does not originate from any letter in $\boldsymbol{x}$. We define $a_{(x)}$ and $a_{(y)}$ in order to represent the first and second elements of the letter mapping a. In other words, $a_{(x)}$ and $a_{(y)}$ are equal to i and j respectively, when $a = (i, j)$. Finally, an abbreviation alignment $\boldsymbol{a}$ is defined as a sequence of letter mappings, $\boldsymbol{a} = (a_1, ..., a_T)$, where T represents the number of mappings in the alignment.

Let us consider the following example sentence:

> *We investigate the effect of thyroid transcription factor 1 (TTF-1).*

This sentence contains an abbreviation candidate *TTF-1* in parentheses[2]. Figure 1 illustrates the correct alignment $\boldsymbol{a}$ (bottom line) and its two-dimensional representation for the example sentence[3]; the abbreviation letters 't,' 't,' 'f,' '-,' and '1' originate from x_{30}, x_{38}, x_{52}, nowhere (null mapping), and x_{59} respectively.

We directly model the conditional probability of the alignment $\boldsymbol{a}$, given $\boldsymbol{x}$ and $\boldsymbol{y}$, using the maximum entropy framework (Berger et al., 1996),

$$P(\boldsymbol{a}|\boldsymbol{x},\boldsymbol{y}) = \frac{\exp\{\boldsymbol{\Lambda}\cdot\boldsymbol{F}(\boldsymbol{a},\boldsymbol{x},\boldsymbol{y})\}}{\sum\limits_{\boldsymbol{a}\in C(\boldsymbol{x},\boldsymbol{y})}\exp\{\boldsymbol{\Lambda}\cdot\boldsymbol{F}(\boldsymbol{a},\boldsymbol{x},\boldsymbol{y})\}}. \quad (1)$$

In Formula 1, $\boldsymbol{F} = \{f_1, ..., f_K\}$ is a global feature vector whose elements present K feature functions, $\boldsymbol{\Lambda} = \{\lambda_1, ..., \lambda_K\}$ denotes a weight vector for the feature functions, and $C(\boldsymbol{x},\boldsymbol{y})$ yields a set of possible alignments for the given $\boldsymbol{x}$ and $\boldsymbol{y}$. We obtain the following decision rule to choose the most probable alignment $\hat{\boldsymbol{a}}$ for given $\boldsymbol{x}$ and $\boldsymbol{y}$,

$$\hat{\boldsymbol{a}} = \underset{\boldsymbol{a}\in C(\boldsymbol{x},\boldsymbol{y})}{\operatorname{argmax}} P(\boldsymbol{a}|\boldsymbol{x},\boldsymbol{y}). \quad (2)$$

Note that a set of possible alignments $C(\boldsymbol{x},\boldsymbol{y})$ always includes a *negative alignment* whose elements are filled with null-mappings (refer to Section 2.3 for further detail). This allows the formula to withdraw the abbreviation candidate $\boldsymbol{y}$ when any expression in $\boldsymbol{x}$ is unlikely to be a definition.

[2] Refer to Section 3.1 for text makers for abbreviations.
[3] We ignore non-alphabetical letters in abbreviations.

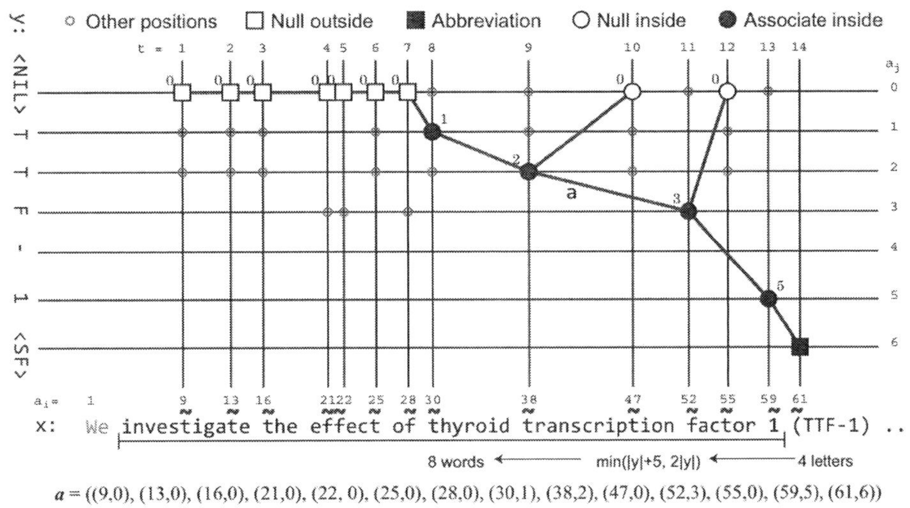

Figure 1: The correct alignment for the example sentence and its two dimensional representation.

2.2 Features

The main advantage of the discriminative alignment model is its ability to incorporate a wide range of non-independent features. Inspired by feature engineering for Conditional Random Fields (CRFs) (Lafferty et al., 2001), we design two kinds of features: *unigram* (state) features defined on each letter mapping, and *bigram* (transition) features defined on each pair of adjacent letter mappings. Given a triplet, $\boldsymbol{a}$, $\boldsymbol{x}$, and $\boldsymbol{y}$, a global feature function $f_k(\boldsymbol{a}, \boldsymbol{x}, \boldsymbol{y}) \in \boldsymbol{F}$ sums up the boolean values (0 or 1) of the corresponding local feature $g_k(\boldsymbol{a}, \boldsymbol{x}, \boldsymbol{y}, t)$ at $t \in \{1, ..., T\}$,

$$f_k(\boldsymbol{a}, \boldsymbol{x}, \boldsymbol{y}) = \sum_{t=1}^{T} g_k(\boldsymbol{a}, \boldsymbol{x}, \boldsymbol{y}, t). \quad (3)$$

In other words, $f_k(\boldsymbol{a}, \boldsymbol{x}, \boldsymbol{y})$ counts the number of times the local feature is fired in the alignment $\boldsymbol{a}$.

A unigram feature corresponds to the observation at x_i and y_j associated by a mapping $a_t = (i, j)$. A unigram feature encodes the condition where the letter in the full form x_i is chosen or unchosen for producing the abbreviation letter y_j. For example, we may infer from the letter mapping at $a_8 = (30, 1)$ in Figure 1, that x_{30} is mapped to y_1 because: x_{30} is at the head of the word, y_1 is a capital letter, and both x_{30} and y_1 are at the head of the word and abbreviation.

Bigram features, combining two observations at a_s and a_t ($1 \leq s < t \leq T$), are useful in capturing the common characteristics shared by an abbreviation definition. For instance, we may presume in Figure 1 that the head letters in the full form might be selectively used for producing the abbreviation, based on the observations at $a_8 = (30, 1)$ and $a_9 = (38, 2)$. In order to focus on the conditions for consecutive non-null mappings, we choose the previous position s for the given t.

$$s = \begin{cases} t-1 & (a_{t(y)} = 0 \vee \forall u : a_{u(y)} = 0) \\ \max\limits_{1 \leq u < t} \{u \mid a_{u(y)} \neq 0\} & \text{(otherwise)} \end{cases} \quad (4)$$

Formula 4 prefers the non-null mapping that is the most adjacent to t over the previous mapping ($t - 1$). In Figure 1, transitions a_9—a_{11} and a_{11}—a_{13} exist for this reason.

In this study, we express unigram and bigram features with atomic functions (Table 1) that encode observation events of $x_{a_{t(x)}}$, $y_{a_{t(y)}}$, a_t, $x_{a_{s(x)}}$—$x_{a_{t(x)}}$, and $y_{a_{s(y)}}$—$y_{a_{t(y)}}$. Atomic functions x_ctype, y_ctype, x_position, and y_position present common heuristics used by previous studies. The function x_word examines the existence of stop words (e.g., *the*, *of*, *in*) to prevent them from producing abbreviation letters. We also include x_pos (part-of-speech of the word) since a number of full forms are noun phrases.

Functions x_diff, x_diff_wd, and y_diff are designed specifically for bigram features, receiving two positions s and t in their arguments. The function x_diff mainly deals with abbreviation definitions that include consecutive letters of their full forms, e.g., *amplifier (AMP)*. The function

Function	Return value
$\text{x\_ctype}_\delta(\boldsymbol{a}, \boldsymbol{x}, t)$	$x_{a_{t(x)}+\delta}$ is {U (uppercase), L (lowercase), D (digit), W (whitespace), S (symbol) } letter
$\text{x\_position}_\delta(\boldsymbol{a}, \boldsymbol{x}, t)$	$x_{a_{t(x)}+\delta}$ is at the {H (head), T (tail), S (syllable head), I (inner), W (whitespace) } of the word
$\text{x\_char}_\delta(\boldsymbol{a}, \boldsymbol{x}, t)$	The lower-cased letter of $x_{a_{t(x)}+\delta}$
$\text{x\_word}_\delta(\boldsymbol{a}, \boldsymbol{x}, t)$	The lower-cased word (offset position δ) containing the letter $x_{a_{t(x)}}$
$\text{x\_pos}_\delta(\boldsymbol{a}, \boldsymbol{x}, t)$	The part-of-speech code of the word (offset position δ) containing the letter $x_{a_{t(x)}}$
$\text{y\_ctype}(\boldsymbol{a}, \boldsymbol{y}, t)$	$y_{a_{t(y)}}$ is {N (NIL) U (uppercase), L (lowercase), D (digit), S (symbol) } letter
$\text{y\_position}(\boldsymbol{a}, \boldsymbol{y}, t)$	$y_{a_{t(y)}}$ is at the {N (NIL) H (head), T (tail), I (inner)} of the word
$\text{y\_char}(\boldsymbol{a}, \boldsymbol{y}, t)$	The lower-cased letter of $y_{a_{t(y)}}$
$\text{a\_state}(\boldsymbol{a}, \boldsymbol{y}, t)$	$\{\texttt{SKIP}\ (a_{t(y)} = 0), \texttt{MATCH}\ (1 \leq a_{t(y)} \leq \lvert\boldsymbol{y}\rvert), \texttt{ABBR}\ (a_{t(y)} = \lvert\boldsymbol{y}\rvert + 1)\}$
$\text{x\_diff}(\boldsymbol{a}, \boldsymbol{x}, s, t)$	$(a_{t(x)} - a_{s(x)})$ if letters $x_{a_{t(x)}}$ and $x_{a_{s(x)}}$ are in the same word, NONE otherwise
$\text{x\_diff\_wd}(\boldsymbol{a}, \boldsymbol{x}, s, t)$	The number of words between $x_{a_{t(x)}}$ and $x_{a_{s(x)}}$
$\text{y\_diff}(\boldsymbol{a}, \boldsymbol{y}, s, t)$	$(a_{t(y)} - a_{s(y)})$

Table 1: Atomic functions to encode observation events in $\boldsymbol{x}$ and $\boldsymbol{y}$

Combination	Rules
unigram(t)	$\text{xy\_unigram}(t) \otimes \{\text{a\_state}(t)\}$
xy_unigram(t)	$\text{x\_unigram}(t) \oplus \text{y\_unigram}(t) \oplus (\text{x\_unigram}(t) \otimes \text{y\_unigram}(t))$
x_unigram(t)	$\text{x\_state}_0(\text{t}) \oplus \text{x\_state}_{-1}(\text{t}) \oplus \text{x\_state}_1(\text{t})$
	$\oplus(\text{x\_state}_{-1}(\text{t}) \otimes \text{x\_state}_0(\text{t})) \oplus (\text{x\_state}_0(\text{t}) \otimes \text{x\_state}_1(\text{t}))$
y_unigram(t)	$\{\text{y\_ctype}(t), \text{y\_position}(t), \text{y\_ctype}(t)\text{y\_position}(t)\}$
$\text{x\_state}_\delta(\text{t})$	$\{\text{x\_ctype}_\delta(t), \text{x\_position}_\delta(t), \text{x\_char}_\delta(t), \text{x\_word}_\delta(t), \text{x\_pos}_\delta(t), \text{x\_ctype}_\delta(t)\text{x\_position}_\delta(t),$
	$\text{x\_position}_\delta(t)\text{x\_pos}_\delta(t), \text{x\_pos}_\delta(t)\text{x\_ctype}_\delta(t), \text{x\_ctype}_\delta(t)\text{x\_position}_\delta(t)\text{x\_pos}_\delta(t)\}$
bigram(s, t)	$\text{xy\_bigram}(s, t) \otimes \{\text{a\_state}(s)\text{a\_state}(t)\}$
xy_bigram(s, t)	$(\text{x\_state}_0(s) \otimes \text{x\_state}_0(t) \otimes \text{trans(s, t)}) \oplus (\text{y\_unigram}(s) \otimes \text{y\_unigram}(t) \otimes \text{trans(s, t)})$
	$\oplus(\text{x\_state}_0(s) \otimes \text{y\_unigram}(s) \otimes \text{x\_state}_0(t) \otimes \text{y\_unigram}(t) \otimes \text{trans(s, t)})$
trans(s, t)	$\{\text{x\_diff}(s, t), \text{x\_diff\_wd}(s, t), \text{y\_diff}(s, t)\}$

Table 2: Generation rules for unigram and bigram features.

x_diff_wd measures the distance of two words. The function y_diff models the ordering of abbreviation letters; this function always returns non-negative values if the abbreviation contains letters in the same order as in its full form.

We express unigram and bigram features with the atomic functions. For example, Formula 5 defines a unigram feature for the event where the capital letter in a full-form word $x_{a_{t(x)}}$ produces the identical abbreviation letter $y_{a_{t(y)}}$.

$$g_k(\boldsymbol{a}, \boldsymbol{x}, \boldsymbol{y}, t) = \begin{cases} 1 & \text{x\_ctype}_0(\boldsymbol{a}, \boldsymbol{x}, t) = \text{U} \\ & \wedge\ \text{y\_ctype}(\boldsymbol{a}, \boldsymbol{y}, t) = \text{U} \\ & \wedge\ \text{a\_state}(\boldsymbol{a}, \boldsymbol{y}, t) = \texttt{MATCH} \\ 0 & \text{(otherwise)} \end{cases} \tag{5}$$

For notation simplicity, we rewrite this boolean function as (arguments $\boldsymbol{a}$, $\boldsymbol{x}$, and $\boldsymbol{y}$ are omitted),

$$\mathbf{1}_{\{\text{x\_ctype}_0(t)\text{y\_ctype}(t)\text{a\_state}(t)=\text{U;U;MATCH}\}}. \tag{6}$$

In this formula, $\mathbf{1}_{\{v=\tilde{v}\}}$ is an indicator function that equals 1 when $v = \tilde{v}$ and 0 otherwise. The term v presents a *generation rule* for a feature, i.e., a combination rule of atomic functions.

Table 2 displays the complete list of generation rules for unigram and bigram features[4], unigram(t) and bigram(s, t). For each generation rule in unigram(t) and bigram(s, t), we define boolean functions that test the possible values yielded by the corresponding atomic function(s).

2.3 Alignment candidates

Formula 1 requires a sum over the possible alignments, which amounts to 2^{LM} for a sentence (L letters) with an abbreviation (M letters). It is unrealistic to compute the partition factor of the formula directly; therefore, the factor has been computed by dynamic programing (McCallum et al., 2005; Blunsom and Cohn, 2006; Shimbo and Hara, 2007) or approximated by the n-best list of highly probable alignments (Och and Ney, 2002; Liu et al., 2005). Fortunately, we can prune alignments that are unlikely to present full forms, by introducing the natural assumptions for abbreviation definitions:

[4] In Table 2, a set of curly brackets $\{\}$ denotes a list (array) rather than a mathematical set. Operators $\oplus$ and $\otimes$ present concatenation and Cartesian product of lists. For instance, when $A = \{a, b\}$ and $B = \{c, d\}$, $A \oplus B = \{a, b, c, d\}$ and $A \otimes B = \{ac, ad, bc, bd\}$.

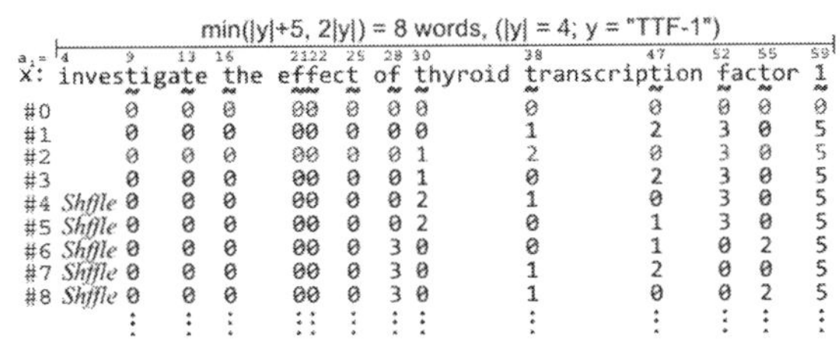

Figure 2: A part of the possible alignments for the abbreviation *TTF-1* in the example sentence.

1. A full form may appear $\min(m + 5, 2m)$ words before its abbreviation in the same sentence, where m is the number of alphanumeric letters in the abbreviation (Park and Byrd, 2001).

2. Every alphanumeric letter in an abbreviation must be associated with the identical (case-insensitive) letter in its full form.

3. An abbreviation letter must not originate from multiple letters in its full form; a full-form letter must not produce multiple letters.

4. Words in a full form may be *shuffled* at most d times, so that all alphanumeric letters in the corresponding abbreviation appear in the rearranged full form in the same order. We define a shuffle operation as removing a series of word(s) from a full form, and inserting the removed word(s) to another position.

5. A full form does not necessarily exist in the text span defined by assumption 1.

Due to the space limitation, we do not describe the algorithm for obtaining possible alignments that are compatible with these assumptions. Alternatively, Figure 2 illustrates a part of possible alignments $C(\boldsymbol{x}, \boldsymbol{y})$ for the example sentence. The alignment #2 represents the correct definition for the abbreviation *TTF-1*. We always include the *negative alignment* (e.g., #0) where no abbreviation letters are associated with any letters in $\boldsymbol{x}$.

The alignments #4–8 interpret the generation process of the abbreviation by shuffling the words in $\boldsymbol{x}$. For example, the alignment #6 moves the word 'of' to the position between 'factor' and '1'. Shuffled alignments cover abbreviation definitions such as *receptor of estrogen (ER)* and *water activity (AW)*. We call the parameter d, *distortion parameter*, which controls the acceptable level of reordering (distortion) for the abbreviation letters.

2.4 Parameter estimation

Parameter estimation for the abbreviation alignment model is essentially the same as for general maximum entropy models. Given a training set that consists of N instances, $((\boldsymbol{a}^{(1)}, \boldsymbol{x}^{(1)}, \boldsymbol{y}^{(1)}), ..., (\boldsymbol{a}^{(N)}, \boldsymbol{x}^{(N)}, \boldsymbol{y}^{(N)}))$, we maximize the log-likelihood of the conditional probability distribution by using the maximum a posterior (MAP) estimation. In order to avoid overfitting, we regularize the log-likelihood with either the L_1 or L_2 norm of the weight vector $\boldsymbol{\Lambda}$,

$$\mathcal{L}_1 = \sum_{n=1}^{N} \log P(\boldsymbol{a}^{(n)} | \boldsymbol{x}^{(n)}, \boldsymbol{y}^{(n)}) - \frac{||\boldsymbol{\Lambda}||_1}{\sigma_1}, \quad (7)$$

$$\mathcal{L}_2 = \sum_{n=1}^{N} \log P(\boldsymbol{a}^{(n)} | \boldsymbol{x}^{(n)}, \boldsymbol{y}^{(n)}) - \frac{||\boldsymbol{\Lambda}||_2^2}{2\sigma_2^2}. \quad (8)$$

In these formulas, σ_1 and σ_2 are regularization parameters for the L_1 and L_2 norms. Formulas 7 and 8 are maximized by the Orthant-Wise Limited-memory Quasi-Newton (OW-LQN) method (Andrew and Gao, 2007) and the Limited-memory BFGS (L-BFGS) method (Nocedal, 1980)[5].

3 Experiments

3.1 Aligned abbreviation corpus

The Medstract Gold Standard Corpus (Pustejovsky et al., 2002) was widely used for evaluating abbreviation recognition methods (Schwartz and Hearst, 2003; Adar, 2004). However, we cannot use this corpus for training the abbreviation alignment model, since it lacks annotations on the origins of abbreviation letters. In addition, the size of the corpus is insufficient for a supervised machine-learning method.

Therefore, we built our training corpus with 1,000 scientific abstracts that were randomly chosen from the MEDLINE database. Although the alignment model is independent of linguistic patterns for abbreviation definitions, in the corpus we found only three abbreviation definitions that were described without parentheses. Hence, we employed parenthetical expressions, *full-form* '(' *abbreviation* ')', to locate possible abbreviation definitions (Wren and Garner, 2002). In order to exclude parentheses inserting clauses into passages,

[5]We used *Classias* for parameter estimation: http://www.chokkan.org/software/classias/

we consider the inner expression of parentheses as an abbreviation candidate, only if the expression consists of two words at most, the length of the expression is between two to ten characters, the expression contains at least an alphabetic letter, and the first character is alphanumeric.

We asked a human annotator to assign reference abbreviation alignments for 1,420 parenthetical expressions (instances) in the corpus. If a parenthetical expression did not introduce an abbreviation, e.g., "... received treatment at 24 months (RRMS)," the corresponding instance would have a negative alignment (as #0 in Figure 2). Eventually, our aligned corpus consisted of 864 (60.8%) abbreviation definitions (with positive alignments) and 556 (39.2%) other usages of parentheses (with negative alignments). Note that the log-likelihood in Formula 7 or 8 increases only if the probabilistic model predicts the reference alignments, regardless of whether they are positive or negative.

3.2 Baseline systems

We prepared five state-of-the-art systems of abbreviation recognition as baselines: Schwartz and Hearst's method (SH) (Schwartz and Hearst, 2003), SaRAD (Adar, 2004), ALICE (Ao and Takagi, 2005), Chang and Schütze's method (CS) (Chang and Schütze, 2006), and Nadeau and Turney's method (NT) (Nadeau and Turney, 2005). We utilized the implementations available on the Web for SH[6], CS[7][8], and ALICE[9], and we reproduced SaRAD and NT, based on their papers.

Our implementation of NT consists of a classifier that discriminates between positive (true) and negative (false) full forms, using all of the feature functions presented in the original paper. Although the original paper presented heuristics for generating full-form candidates, we replaced the candidate generator with the function $C(\boldsymbol{x}, \boldsymbol{y})$, so that the classifier and our alignment model can receive the same set of full-form candidates. The classifier of the NT system was modeled by the LIBSVM implementation[10] with Radial Basis Function (RBF) kernel[11]. If multiple full-form candidates for an abbreviation are classified as positives, we choose the candidate that yields the highest probability estimate.

System	P	R	F1
Schwartz & Hearst (SH)	**.978**	.940	.959
SaRAD	.891	.919	.905
ALICE	.961	.920	.940
Chang & Schütze (CS)	.942	.900	.921
Nadeau & Turney (NT)	.954	.871	.910
Proposed ($d = 0$; L_1)	.973	.969	**.971**
Proposed ($d = 0$; L_2)	.964	.968	.966
Proposed ($d = 1$; L_1)	.960	**.981**	**.971**
Proposed ($d = 1$; L_2)	.957	.976	.967

Table 3: Performance on our corpus.

3.3 Results

We trained and evaluated the proposed method on our corpus by performing 10-fold cross validation[12]. Our corpus includes 13 out of 864 (1.5%) abbreviation definitions in which the abbreviation letters are shuffled. Thus, we have examined two different distortion parameters, $d = 0, 1$ in this experiment. The average numbers of candidates produced by the candidate generator $C(\boldsymbol{x}, \boldsymbol{y})$ per instance were 8.46 ($d = 0$) and 69.1 ($d = 1$), respectively. The alignment model was trained in a reasonable execution time[13], ca. 5 minutes ($d = 0$) and 1.5 hours ($d = 1$).

Table 3 reports the precision (P), recall (R), and F1 score (F1) on the basis of the number of correct abbreviation definitions recognized by each system. The proposed method achieved the best F1 score (0.971) of all systems. The inclusion of distorted abbreviations ($d = 1$) gained the highest recall (0.981 with L_1 regularization). Baseline systems with refined heuristics (SaRAD and ALICE) could not outperform the simplest system (SH). The previous approaches with machine learning (CS and NT) were roughly comparable to rule-based methods.

We also evaluated the alignment model on the Medstract Gold Standard development corpus to examine the adaptability of the alignment model trained with our corpus (Table 4). Since the origi-

[6] Abbreviation Definition Recognition Software: http://biotext.berkeley.edu/software.html

[7] Biomedical Abbreviation Server: http://abbreviation.stanford.edu/

[8] We applied a score cutoff of 0.14.

[9] Abbreviation LIfter using Corpus-based Extraction: http://uvdb3.hgc.jp/ALICE/ALICE_index.html

[10] LIBSVM – A Library for Support Vector Machines: http://www.csie.ntu.edu.tw/~cjlin/libsvm/

[11] We tuned kernel parameters $C = 128$ and $\gamma = 2.0$ by using the grid-search tool in the LIBSVM distribution.

[12] We determined the regularization parameters as $\sigma_1 = 3$ and $\sigma_2 = 3$ after testing $\{0.1, 0.2, 0.3, 0.5, 1, 2, 3, 5, 10\}$ for the regularization parameters. The difference between the highest and lowest F1 scores was 1.8%.

[13] On Intel Dual-Core Xeon 5160/3GHz CPU, excluding time for feature generation and data input/output.

System	P	R	F1
Schwartz & Hearst (SH)	.942	.891	.916
SaRAD	.909	.859	.884
ALICE	.960	**.945**	.953
Chang & Schütze (CS)	.858	.852	.855
Nadeau & Turney (NT)	.889	.875	.882
Proposed ($d = 1$; L_1)	**.976**	**.945**	**.960**

Table 4: Performance on Medstract corpus.

#	Atomic function(s)	F1
(1)	x_position + x_ctype	.905
(2)	(1) + x_char + y_char	.885
(3)	(1) + x_word + x_pos	.941
(4)	(1) + x_diff + x_diff_wd + y_diff	.959
(5)	(1) + y_position + y_ctype	.964
(6)	All atomic functions	.966

Table 5: Effect of atomic functions ($d = 0$; L_2).

nal version of the Medstract corpus includes annotation errors, we used the version revised by Ao and Takagi (2005). For this reason, the performance of ALICE might be over-estimated in this evaluation; ALICE delivered much better results than Schwartz & Hearst's method on this corpus.

The abbreviation alignment model trained with our corpus ($d = 1$; L_1) outperformed the baseline systems for all evaluation metrics. It is notable that the model could recognize abbreviation definitions with shuffled letters, e.g., *transfer of single embryo (SET)* and *inorganic phosphate (PI)*, without any manual tuning for this corpus. In some false cases, the alignment model yielded incorrect probability estimates. For example, the probabilities of the alignments *prepubertal bipolarity*, *bipolarity*, and non-definition (negative) for the abbreviation *BP* were computed as 3.4%, 89.6%, and 6.7%, respectively; but the first expression *prepubertal bipolarity* is the correct definition for the abbreviation.

Table 5 shows F1 scores of the proposed method trained with different sets of atomic functions. The baseline setting (1), which built features only with x_position and x_ctype functions, gained a 0.905 F1 score; further, adding more atomic functions generally improves the score. However, the x_char and y_char functions decreased the performance since the alignment model was prone to overfit to the training data, relying on the existence of specific letters in the training instances. Interestingly, the model was flexible enough to achieve a high performance with four atomic functions (5).

Table 6 demonstrates the ability for our approach to obtain effective features; the table shows the top 10 (out of 850,009) features with high

#	Feature	λ
1	U: x_position$_0$=H;y_ctype$_0$=U;y_position$_0$=H/M	1.7370
2	B: y_position$_0$=I/y_position$_0$=I/x_diff=1/M-M	1.3470
3	U: x_ctype$_{-1}$=L;x_ctype$_0$=L/S	0.96342
4	B: x_ctype$_0$=L/x_ctype$_0$=L/x_diff_wd=0/M-M	0.94009
5	U: x_position$_0$=I;x_char$_1$='t'/S	0.91645
6	U: x_position$_0$=H;x_pos$_0$=NN;y_ctype$_0$=U/M	0.86786
7	U: x_ctype$_{-1}$=S;x$_c$type$_0$=L;M	0.86474
8	B: x_char$_0$='o'/x_ctype$_0$=L/y_diff=0/M-S	0.71262
9	U: x_char$_{-1}$='o';x_ctype$_0$=L/M	0.69764
10	B: x_position$_0$=H/x_ctype$_0$=U/y_diff=1/M-M	0.66418

Table 6: Top ten features with high weights.

weights assigned by the MAP estimation with L_1 regularization. A unigram and bigram features have prefixes "U:" and "B:" respectively; a feature expresses conditions at s (bigram features only), conditions at t, and mapping status (match or skip) separated by '/' symbols. For example, the #1 feature associates a letter at the head of a full-form word with the uppercase letter at the head of its abbreviation. The #4 feature is difficult to obtain from manual observations, i.e., the bigram feature suggests the production of two abbreviation letters from two lowercase letters in the same word.

4 Conclusion

We have presented a novel approach for recognizing abbreviation definitions. The task of abbreviation recognition was successfully formalized as a sequential alignment problem. We developed an aligned abbreviation corpus, and obtained fine-grained features that express the events wherein a full forum produces an abbreviation letter. The experimental results showed remarkable improvements and usefulness of the alignment approach for abbreviation recognition. We expect the usefullness of the discriminative model for building an comprehensible abbreviation dictionary.

Future work would be to model cases in which a full form yields non-identical letters (e.g., *'one'* $\rightarrow$ *'1'* and *'deficient'* $\rightarrow$ '-'), and to demonstrate this approach with more generic linguistic patterns (e.g., *aka*, *abbreviated as*, etc.). We also plan to explore a method for training a model with an unaligned abbreviation corpus, estimating the alignments simultaneously from the corpus.

Acknowledgments

This work was partially supported by Grant-in-Aid for Scientific Research on Priority Areas (MEXT, Japan), and Solution-Oriented Research for Science and Technology (JST, Japan).

References

Adar, Eytan. 2004. SaRAD: A simple and robust abbreviation dictionary. *Bioinformatics*, 20(4):527–533.

Andrew, Galen and Jianfeng Gao. 2007. Scalable training of L_1-regularized log-linear models. In *Proceedings of the 24th International Conference on Machine Learning (ICML 2007)*, pages 33–40.

Ao, Hiroko and Toshihisa Takagi. 2005. ALICE: An algorithm to extract abbreviations from MEDLINE. *Journal of the American Medical Informatics Association*, 12(5):576–586.

Berger, Adam L., Vincent J. Della Pietra, and Stephen A. Della Pietra. 1996. A maximum entropy approach to natural language processing. *Computational Linguistics*, 22(1):39–71.

Blunsom, Phil and Trevor Cohn. 2006. Discriminative word alignment with conditional random fields. In *Proceedings of the 21st International Conference on Computational Linguistics and the 44th annual meeting of the Association for Computational Linguistics (Coling-ACL 2006)*, pages 65–72.

Chang, Jeffrey T. and Hinrich Schütze. 2006. Abbreviations in biomedical text. In Ananiadou, Sophia and John McNaught, editors, *Text Mining for Biology and Biomedicine*, pages 99–119. Artech House, Inc.

Gaudan, Sylvain, Harald Kirsch, and Dietrich Rebholz-Schuhmann. 2005. Resolving abbreviations to their senses in Medline. *Bioinformatics*, 21(18):3658–3664.

Jain, Alpa, Silviu Cucerzan, and Saliha Azzam. 2007. Acronym-expansion recognition and ranking on the web. In *Proceedings of the IEEE International Conference on Information Reuse and Integration (IRI 2007)*, pages 209–214.

Lafferty, John, Andrew McCallum, and Fernando Pereira. 2001. Conditional random fields: Probabilistic models for segmenting and labeling sequence data. In *Proceedings of the 18th International Conference on Machine Learning (ICML 2001)*, pages 282–289.

Liu, Hongfang and Carol Friedman. 2003. Mining terminological knowledge in large biomedical corpora. In *the 8th Pacific Symposium on Biocomputing (PSB 2003)*, pages 415–426.

Liu, Yang, Qun Liu, and Shouxun Lin. 2005. Log-linear models for word alignment. In *Proceedings of the 43rd Annual Meeting on Association for Computational Linguistics (ACL 2005)*, pages 459–466.

McCallum, Andrew, Kedar Bellare, and Fernando Pereira. 2005. A conditional random field for discriminatively-trained finite-state string edit distance. In *Proceedings of the 21st Conference on Uncertainty in Artificial Intelligence (UAI 2005)*, pages 388–395.

Nadeau, David and Peter D. Turney. 2005. A supervised learning approach to acronym identification. In *the 8th Canadian Conference on Artificial Intelligence (AI'2005) (LNAI 3501)*, page 10 pages.

Nocedal, Jorge. 1980. Updating quasi-newton matrices with limited storage. *Mathematics of Computation*, 35(151):773–782.

Och, Franz Josef and Hermann Ney. 2002. Discriminative training and maximum entropy models for statistical machine translation. In *Proceedings of the 40th Annual Meeting on Association for Computational Linguistics (ACL 2002)*, pages 295–302.

Okazaki, Naoaki and Sophia Ananiadou. 2006. Building an abbreviation dictionary using a term recognition approach. *Bioinformatics*, 22(24):3089–3095.

Pakhomov, Serguei. 2002. Semi-supervised maximum entropy based approach to acronym and abbreviation normalization in medical texts. In *Proceedings of the 40th Annual Meeting on Association for Computational Linguistics (ACL 2002)*, pages 160–167.

Park, Youngja and Roy J. Byrd. 2001. Hybrid text mining for finding abbreviations and their definitions. In *Proceedings of the 2001 Conference on Empirical Methods in Natural Language Processing (EMNLP 2001)*, pages 126–133.

Pustejovsky, James, José Castaño, Roser Saurí, Anna Rumshinsky, Jason Zhang, and Wei Luo. 2002. Medstract: creating large-scale information servers for biomedical libraries. In *Proceedings of the ACL-02 workshop on Natural language processing in the biomedical domain*, pages 85–92.

Schwartz, Ariel S. and Marti A. Hearst. 2003. A simple algorithm for identifying abbreviation definitions in biomedical text. In *the 8th Pacific Symposium on Biocomputing (PSB 2003)*, pages 451–462.

Shimbo, Masashi and Kazuo Hara. 2007. A discriminative learning model for coordinate conjunctions. In *Proceedings of the 2007 Joint Conference on Empirical Methods in Natural Language Processing and Computational Natural Language Learning (EMNLP-CoNLL 2007)*, pages 610–619.

Wren, Jonathan D. and Harold R. Garner. 2002. Heuristics for identification of acronym-definition patterns within text: towards an automated construction of comprehensive acronym-definition dictionaries. *Methods of Information in Medicine*, 41(5):426–434.

Yu, Hong, Won Kim, Vasileios Hatzivassiloglou, and John Wilbur. 2006. A large scale, corpus-based approach for automatically disambiguating biomedical abbreviations. *ACM Transactions on Information Systems (TOIS)*, 24(3):380–404.

Zhou, Wei, Vetle I. Torvik, and Neil R. Smalheiser. 2006. ADAM: another database of abbreviations in MEDLINE. *Bioinformatics*, 22(22):2813–2818.

Semantic role assignment for event nominalisations by leveraging verbal data

Sebastian Padó
Department of Linguistics
Stanford University
450 Serra Mall
Stanford CA 94305, USA
pado@stanford.edu

Marco Pennacchiotti and **Caroline Sporleder**
Computational Linguistics
Saarland University
Postfach 15 11 50
66041 Saarbrücken, Germany
{pennacchiotti|csporled}@coli.uni-sb.de

Abstract

This paper presents a novel approach to the task of semantic role labelling for event nominalisations, which make up a considerable fraction of predicates in running text, but are underrepresented in terms of training data and difficult to model. We propose to address this situation by *data expansion*. We construct a model for nominal role labelling solely from verbal training data. The best quality results from salvaging grammatical features where applicable, and generalising over lexical heads otherwise.

1 Introduction

The last years have seen a large body of work on modelling the semantic properties of individual words, both in the form of hand-built resources like WordNet and data-driven methods like semantic space models. It is still much less clear how the combined meaning of phrases can be described. *Semantic roles* describe an important aspect of phrasal meaning by characterising the relationship between predicates and their arguments on a semantic level (e.g., agent, patient). They generalise over surface categories (such as subject, object) and variations (such as diathesis alternations). Two frameworks for semantic roles have found wide use in the community, PropBank (Palmer et al., 2005) and FrameNet (Fillmore et al., 2003). Their corpora are used to train supervised models for semantic role labelling (SRL) of new text (Gildea and Jurafsky, 2002; Carreras and Màrquez, 2005). The resulting analysis can benefit a number of applications, such as Information Extraction (Moschitti et al., 2003) or Question Answering (Frank et al., 2007).

A commonly encountered criticism of semantic roles, and arguably a major obstacle to their adoption in NLP, is their *limited coverage*. Since manual semantic role tagging is costly, it is hardly conceivable that gold standard annotation will ultimately be available for every predicate of English. In addition, the *lexically specific* nature of the mapping between surface syntax and semantic roles makes it difficult to generalise from seen predicates to unseen predicates for which no training data is available. Techniques for extending the coverage of SRL therefore address an important need.

Unfortunately, pioneering work in unsupervised SRL (Swier and Stevenson, 2004; Grenager and Manning, 2006) currently either relies on a small number of semantic roles, or cannot identify equivalent roles across predicates. A promising alternative direction is *automatic data expansion*, i.e., leveraging existing annotations to classify unseen, but similar, predicates. The feasibility of this approach was demonstrated by Gordon and Swanson (2007) for syntactically similar verbs. However, their approach requires at least one annotated instance of each new predicate, limiting its practicability.

In this paper, we present a pilot study on the application of automatic data expansion to *event nominalisations* of verbs, such as *agreement* for *agree* or *destruction* for *destroy*. While event nominalisations often afford the same semantic roles as verbs, and often replace them in written language (Gurevich et al., 2006), they have played a largely marginal role in annotation. PropBank has only annotated verbs.[1] FrameNet annotates nouns, but covers far fewer nouns than verbs. The same

© 2008. Licensed under the *Creative Commons Attribution-Noncommercial-Share Alike 3.0 Unported* license (http://creativecommons.org/licenses/by-nc-sa/3.0/). Some rights reserved.

[1] A follow-up project, NomBank (Meyers et al., 2004), has since provided annotations for nominal instances, too.

situation holds in other languages (Erk et al., 2003).

Our fundamental intuition is that it is possible to increase the annotation coverage of event nominalisations by data expansion from verbal instances, since the verbal and nominal predicates share a large part of the underlying argument structure. We assume that annotation is available for verbal instances. Then, for a given instance of a nominalisation and its arguments, the aim is to assign semantic role labels to these arguments. We solve this task by constructing *mappings* between the arguments of the noun and the semantic roles realised by the verb's arguments. Crucially, unlike previous work (Liu and Ng, 2007), we do not employ a classical supervised approach, and thus do not require any nominal annotations.

Structure of the paper. Sec. 2 provides background on nominalisations and SRL. Sec. 3 provides concrete details on our expansion-based approach to SRL for nominalisations. The second part of the paper (Sec. 4–6) provides a first evaluation of different mapping strategies based on syntactic, semantic, and hybrid information. Sec. 8 concludes.

2 Nominalisations

Nominalisations (or *deverbal nouns*) are commonly defined as nouns morphologically derived from verbs, usually by suffixation (Quirk et al., 1985). They have been classified into at least three categories in the linguistic literature, *event, result,* and *agent/patient* nominalisations (Grimshaw, 1990).

Event and *result* nominalisations account for the bulk of deverbal nouns. The first class refers to an event/activity/process, with the nominal expressing this action (e.g. *killing, destruction*). Nouns in the second class describe the result or goal of an action (e.g. *agreement*). Many nominals have both an event and a result reading (e.g., *selection* can mean the process of selecting or the selected object). Choosing a single reading for an instance is often difficult; see Nunes (1993); Grimshaw (1990).

A smaller class is *agent/patient* nominalisations. Agent nominals are usually identified by suffixes such as *-er, -or, -ant* (e.g. *speaker, applicant*), while patient nominalisations end with *-ee, -ed* (e.g. *employee*). While these nominalisations can be analysed as events (*the baker's bread* implies that baking has taken place), they more naturally refer to participants. In consequence, agent/patient nominals tend to realise fewer arguments – the average in FrameNet is 1.46 arguments, compared to 1.74

PropBank	
Verbs (Carreras and Màrquez, 2005)	80%
Nouns (Liu and Ng, 2007)	73%
FrameNet	
Verbs (Mihalcea and Edmonds, 2005)	72%
Nouns (Pradhan et al., 2004)	64%

Table 1: F-Scores for supervised SRL (end-to-end)

for events/results. As our goal is nominal SRL, we concentrate on the event/results class.

SRL for nominalisations. Compared to the wealth of studies on verbal SRL (e.g., Gildea and Jurafsky (2002); Fleischman and Hovy (2003)), there is relatively little work that specifically addresses nominal SRL. Nouns are generally treated like verbs: the task is split into two classification steps, argument recognition (telling arguments from non-arguments) and argument labelling (labelling recognised arguments with a role). Nominal SRL also typically draws on feature sets that are similar to those for verbs, i.e., comprising mainly syntactic and lexical-semantic information (Liu and Ng, 2007; Jiang and Ng, 2006).

On the other hand, there is converging evidence that nominal SRL is somewhat more difficult than verbal SRL. Table 1 shows some results for both verbal and nominal SRL from the literature. For both PropBank and for FrameNet, we find a difference of 7–8% F-Score. Note, however, that these studies use different datasets and are thus not directly comparable.

In order to confirm the difference between nouns and verbs, we modelled a controlled dataset (described in detail in Sec. 4) of verbs and corresponding event nominalisations. We used Shalmaneser (Erk and Padó, 2006), to our knowledge the only freely available SRL system that handles nouns. SRL models were trained on verbs and nouns separately, using the same settings and features. Table 2 shows the results, averaged over 10 cross-validation (CV) folds. Accuracy was about equal in the recognition step, and 5% higher for verbs in the labelling step. We analysed these results by fitting a *logit mixed model*. These models determine which *fixed factors* are responsible for differences in a response variable (here: SRL performance) while correcting for imbalances introduced by *random factors* (see Jaeger (2008)). We modelled the training and test set sizes and the predicates' parts of speech as fixed effects, and frames and CV folds as random factors.

For both argument recognition and labelling, the

Step	Verbs	Nouns
Arg recognition (F_1, class FE)	0.59	0.60
Arg labelling (Accuracy)	0.70	0.65

Table 2: FrameNet SRL on verbs and nouns

amount of training data turned out to be a significant factor, i.e., more data leads to higher results. While the part of speech was not systematically linked to performance for argument recognition, it was a highly significant predictor of accuracy in the labelling step: Even when training set size was taken into account, verbal arguments were still significantly easier to label ($z=4.5$, $p<0.001$).

In sum, these results lend empirical support to claims that nominal arguments are less tightly coupled to syntactic realisation than verbal ones (Carlson, 1984); their interpretation is harder to capture with shallow cues.

3 Data Expansion for Nominal SRL

The previous section has established two observations. First, the argument structures of verbs and their event nominalisations correspond largely. Second, nominal SRL is a difficult task, even given nominal training data, which is hard to obtain.

Our proposal in this paper is to take advantage of the first observation to address the second. We do so by modelling SRL for event nominalisations as a *data expansion* task — i.e., using existing *verbal* annotations to carry out SRL for novel *nominal* instances. In this manner, we do away completely with the need for manual annotation of nominal instances that is required for previous supervised approaches (cf. Sec. 2). Consider the following examples, given in format [constituent]$_{\textbf{grammatical function/}\text{SEMANTIC ROLE}}$:

(1) a. [Peter]$_{\textbf{Subj/}\text{COGNIZER}}$ *laughs* [about the joke]$_{\textbf{PP-about/}\text{STIMULUS}}$

b. [Peter]$_{\textbf{Subj/}\text{COGNIZER}}$ *laughs* [at him]$_{\textbf{PP-at/}\text{STIMULUS}}$

(2) [Peter's]$_{\textbf{Prenom-Gen/?}}$ [hearty]$_{\textbf{Prenom-Mod/?}}$ *laughter* [about the event]$_{\textbf{PP-about/?}}$

The sentences with the verbal predicate *laugh* in (1) are labelled with semantic roles, while the NP containing the event nominalisation *laughter* in (2) is not. The question we face are what information from (1) can be re-used to perform argument recognition and labelling on (2), and how.

In this respect, there is a fundamental difference between lexical-semantic and syntactic information. *Lexical-semantic* features, such as the head word, are basically independent of the predicate's part of speech. Thus, the information from (1) that *Peter* is a COGNIZER can be used directly for the analysis of the occurrence of *Peter* in (2). Unfortunately, pure lexical features tend to be sparse: the head word of the last role, *event*, is unseen in (1), and due to its abstract nature, also difficult to classify through semantic similarity. Therefore, it is necessary to consider *syntactic* features as well. However, these vary substantially between verbs and nouns. When they are applicable to both parts of speech, some mileage can be apparently gained: the phrase in (2) headed by *event* can be classified as STIMULUS because it is an *about*-PP like (1a). In contrast, no direct inferences can be drawn about prenominal genitives or modifiers which do not exist for verbs.

In the remainder of this paper, we will present experiments on different ways of combining syntactic and lexical-semantic information to balance precision and recall in data expansion. We address argument recognition and labelling separately, since the two tasks require different kinds of information. We assume that the frame has been determined beforehand with word sense disambiguation methods.

4 Data

The dataset for our study consists of the annotated FrameNet 1.3 examples. We obtained pairs of verbs and corresponding event/result nominalisations by intersecting the FrameNet predicate list with a list of nominalisations obtained from Celex (Baayen et al., 1995) and Nomlex (Macleod et al., 1998). We found 306 nominalisations with corresponding verbs in the same frame, but excluded some pairs where either the nominalisation was not of the event/result type, or no annotated FrameNet examples were available for either verb or noun. The final dataset, consisting of 265 pairs exemplifying 117 frames, served for both the analysis in Section 2 and the evaluations in subsequent sections. For the evaluations, we used the 26,479 verbal role instances (2,066 distinct role types) as training data and the 6,502 nominal role instances (993 distinct role types) as test data. The specification of the dataset can be downloaded from `http://www.coli.uni-sb.de/~pado/nom_data.html`.

5 Argument Recognition

Argument recognition is usually modelled as a supervised machine learning task. Unfortunately, ar-

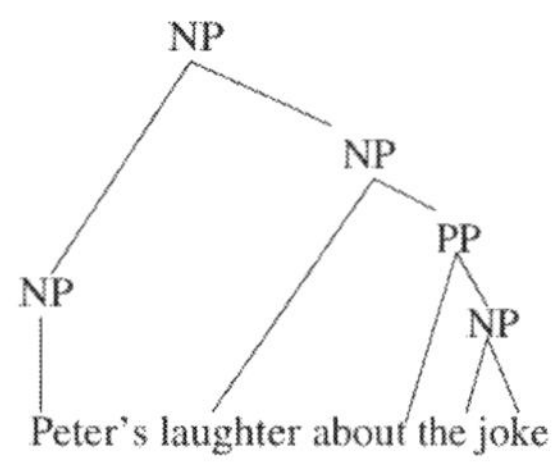

Figure 1: Parse tree for example sentence

gument recognition – at least within predicates – relies heavily on syntactic features, with the grammatical function (or alternatively syntactic path) feature as the single most important predictor (Gildea and Jurafsky, 2002). Since we are bootstrapping from verbal instances to nominal ones, and since there is typically considerable variation between nominal and verbal subcategorisation patterns, we cannot model argument recognition as a supervised task. Instead, we follow up on an idea developed by Xue and Palmer (2004) for verbal SRL, who characterise the set of grammatical functions that could fill a semantic role in the first place. In our appplication, we simply extract all syntactic arguments of the nominalisation, including any premodifiers. We make no attempt to distinguish between adjuncts and compulsory arguments. Fig. 1 shows an example: in the NP *Peter's laughter about the joke*, the noun *laughter* has two syntactic arguments: the PP *about the joke* and the premodifying NP *Peter's*. Both are extracted as (potential) arguments.

This method cannot identify roles that are syntactically *non-local*, i.e., those that are not in the maximal projection of the frame evoking noun. Such roles are more common for nouns than for verbs. Example 3 shows that an "external" NP like *Bill* can be analysed as filling the HELPER role of the noun *help*. However, the overall proportion of non-local roles is still fairly small in our data (around 10%).

(3) [Bill]$_{\text{HELPER}}$ offered *help* in case of need.

Table 3 gives the argument recognition results for our rule-based system on all roles in the gold standard and on the local roles alone. This simple approach is surprisingly effective, achieving an overall F-Measure of 76.89% on all roles, while on local roles the F-Measure increases to 82.83% due to the higher recall. Precision is 82.01%, as not all syntactic arguments do fill a role. For example, modal modifiers such as *hearty* in (2) rarely fill a (core) role in FrameNet. False-negative errors, which affect recall, are partly due to parser errors and partly

Roles	*Precision*	*Recall*	*F-Measure*
all roles	82.01	72.37	76.89
local roles	82.01	83.66	82.83

Table 3: Argument recognition (local / all roles).

to role fillers that do not correspond to constituents or that are embedded in syntactic arguments. For instance, in (4) the PP *in this country*, which fills the PLACE role of *cause*, is embedded in the PP *of suffering in this country*, which fills the role EFFECT. We extract only the larger PP.

(4) the *causes* [of suffering [in this country]$_{\textbf{PP-in}}$]$_{\textbf{PP-of}}$

6 Argument Labelling

Argument labelling presents a different picture from argument recognition. Here, both syntactic and lexical-semantic information contribute to success in the task. We present three model families for nominal argument labelling that take different stances with respect to this observation.

The first (*naive-semantic*) and the second (*naive-syntactic*) model families represent extreme positions that attempt to re-use verbal information as directly as possible. Models from the third family, *distributional* models infer the role of a noun's arguments by computing the semantic similarity between nominal arguments and semantic representations of the verb roles given by the role fillers' semantic heads.[2] In the *lexical-level* instantiation, the mapping is established between individual noun arguments and roles. In the *function-level* instantiation, complete nominal grammatical functions are mapped onto roles.[3]

6.1 Naive semantic model

The naive semantic model (*naive sem*) implements the assumption that lexical-semantic features provide the same predictive evidence for verbal and nominal arguments (cf. Sec. 3). It can be thought of as constructing the trivial *identity mapping* between the values of nominal and verbal semantic features. To test the usefulness of this model, we train the Shalmaneser SRL system (Erk and Padó, 2006) on the verbal instances of the dataset described

[2]Usually, the semantic head of a phrase is its syntactic head. Exceptions occur e.g. for PPs, where the semantic head is the syntactic head of the embedded NP.

[3]We compute grammatical functions as phrase types plus relative position; for PPs, we add the preposition.

in Sec. 4, using only the lexical-semantic features (head word, first word, last word). We then apply the resulting models directly to the corresponding nominal instances.

6.2 Naive syntactic model

The intuition of this model (*naive syn*) is that grammatical functions shared between verbs and nouns are likely to express the same semantic roles. It maps all grammatical functions of a verb g_v onto the identical functions of the corresponding noun g_n and then assigns the most frequent role realised by g_v to all arguments with grammatical function g_n. For example, if PPs headed by *about* for the verb *laugh* typically realise the STIMULUS role, all arguments of the noun *laughter* which are realised as *PP-about* are also assigned the STIMULUS role.

We predict that this strategy has a "high precision–low recall" profile: It produces reliable mappings for those grammatical functions that are preserved across verb and noun, in particular prepositional phrases; however, it fails for grammatical functions that only occur for one part of speech.

This problem becomes particular pertinent for two prominent role types, namely AGENT-style roles (deep subjects) and PATIENT-style roles (deep objects). These roles are usually expressed via different and ambiguous noun and verb functions (Gurevich et al., 2006). For verbs, the AGENT is typically expressed by the *Subject*, while for nouns it is expressed by a *Pre-Modifier*. The PATIENT is commonly realised as the *Object* for verbs, and either as a *Pre-Modifier* or as a *PP-of* for nouns. As the noun's *Pre-Modifier* is highly ambiguous, it is also ineffective to apply a *non-identity* mapping such as $(subject_v, Pre\text{-}Modifier_n)$ or $(object_v, Pre\text{-}Modifier_n)$.[4]

A final variation of this model is the *generalised naive syntactic model* (*naive sem-gen*), where we assign the role most frequently realised by a given function across *all* verbs in the frame. This method alleviates data sparseness stemming from functions never seen with particular verbs and is fairly safe, since mapping within frames tends to be uniform.

6.3 Distributional models

The distributional models construct mappings between verbal and nominal semantic heads. In contrast to the naive semantic model, they make use of some measure of semantic similarity to find mappings, and optionally use syntactic constraints to guide generalisation. In this manner, distributional models can deal with unseen feature values more effectively. In sentences (1) and (2), for example, an ideal distributional model would find the head word *event* in (2) to be more semantically similar to the head *joke* in (1a) than to head *him* in (1b). The resulting mapping $(joke, event)$ leads to the assignment of the role STIMULUS to *event*.

Semantic Similarity. *Semantic similarity measures* are commonly used to compute similarity between two lexemes. There are two main types of similarity: *Ontology-based*, computed through the closeness of two lexemes in a lexical database (e.g., WordNet); and *distributional*, given by some measure of the distance between the lexemes' vector representations in a semantic co-occurrence space. We chose the latter approach because it tends to have a higher coverage and it is knowledge-lean, requiring just an unannotated corpus.

We compute distributional-similarity with a semantic space model based on lexical co-occurrences backed by syntactic relations (Padó and Lapata, 2007).[5] The model is constructed from the British National Corpus (BNC), using the 2.000 most pairs of words and grammatical functions as dimensions. As similarity measure, we use cosine distance on log-likelihood transformed counts.

Lexical level model. The lexical level model (*dist-lex*) assigns to each nominal argument the verb role that it is semantically most similar to. Each role is represented by the semantic heads of its fillers. For example, suppose that the role STIMULUS of the verb *laugh* has been realised by the heads *story, scene, joke,* and *tale*. Then, in *"Peter's laughter about the event"*, we analyse *event* as STIMULUS, since *event* is similar to these heads.

Formally, each argument head l is represented by a co-occurrence vector $\vec{l}$. A verb role $r_v \in R_v$ is modelled by the centroid $\vec{r_v}$ of its instances' heads:

$$\vec{r_v} = \frac{1}{|L_{r_v}|} \sum_{l \in L_{r_v}} \vec{l}$$

Roles are assigned to nominal argument heads $l_n \in L_n$ by finding the semantically most similar role r

[4] Lapata (2002) has shown that the mapping can be disambiguated for individual nominalisations. Her model, using lexical-semantic, contextual and pragmatic information, is outside the scope of the present paper.

[5] We also experimented with bag-of-words based vector spaces, which showed worse performance throughout.

while the grammatical function g_n is ignored:

$$r(l_n, g_n) = argmax_{r_v \in R_v} sim_{cos}(\vec{l_n}, \vec{r_v})$$

Function level model. The syntactic level model (*dist-fun*) generalises the lexical level model by exploiting the intuition that, within nouns, most semantic roles tend to be consistently realised by one specific grammatical function. This function can be identified as the one most semantically similar to the role's representation. Following the example above, suppose that the grammatical function *PP-about* of *laughter* has as semantic heads the lexemes: *event, story, news*. Then, it is likely to express the role STIMULUS, as its heads are semantically similar to those of the verbal fillers of this role: *story, scene, sentence, tale*. For each nominalisation, this model constructs mappings (r_v, g_n) between a verbal semantic role r_v and a nominal grammatical function g_n. The representations for roles are computed as described above. We compute the semantic representations for grammatical functions, in parallel to the roles' definition above, as the centroid of their fillers' representations L_{g_n}:

$$\vec{g_n} = \frac{1}{|L_{g_n}|} \sum_{l \in L_{g_n}} \vec{l}$$

The assignment of a role to a nominal arguments is now determined by the argument's grammatical function g_n; its lemma l_n only enters indirectly, via the similarity computation:

$$r(l_n, g_n) = argmax_{r_v \in R_v} sim_{cos}(\vec{r_v}, \vec{g_n})$$

This strategy guarantees that each nominal grammatical function is mapped to exactly one role. In the inverse direction, roles can be left unmapped or mapped to more than one function.[6]

6.4 Hybrid models

Our last class combines the naive and distributional models with a back-off approach. We first attempt to harness the reliable naive syntactic approach whenever a mapping for the argument's grammatical function is available. If this fails, it backs off to a distributional model. This strategy helps to recover the frequent AGENT- and PATIENT-style roles that cannot be recovered on syntactic grounds.

[6]We also experimented with a global optimisation strategy where we maximised the overall similarity between roles and functions subject to different constraints (e.g., perfect matching). Unfortunately, this strategy did not improve results.

	System		*Accuracy*
BL	baseline	random	17.09
BL	baseline	most common	42.97
Naive	naive syn		15.29
Naive	naive syn-gen		21.56
Naive	naive sem		24.00
Dist	dist-lex		44.57
Dist	dist-fun		52.00
Hybrid	naive syn	+ dist-lex	48.22
Hybrid	naive syn-gen	+ dist-lex	50.54
Hybrid	naive syn	+ dist-fun	54.39
Hybrid	**naive syn-gen**	**+ dist-fun**	**56.42**

Table 4: Results for nominal argument labelling

In (2), a hybrid model would assign the role STIMULUS to the argument headed by *event*, using the naive syntactic mapping $(PP\text{-}about_v, PP\text{-}about_n)$ derived from (1a). For the prenominal modifier, no syntactic mapping is available; thus, it backs off to lexical-semantic evidence from (1a-b) to analyse *Peter* as COGNIZER.

We experiment with two hybrid models: naive syntactic plus lexical level distributional (*naive syn + dist-lex*), and naive syntactic plus functional level distributional (*naive syn + dist-fun*).

7 Experimental results

The results of our experiments are reported in Table 4. The models are compared against two baselines: A *random baseline* which randomly chooses one of the verb roles for each of the arguments of the corresponding noun; a *most common baseline* which assigns to each nominal argument the most frequent role of the corresponding verb – i.e. the role which has most fillers. All models with the exception of *naive syn* significantly outperform the random baseline, but only *dist-fun* and all hybrid models outperform the *most common* baseline.

In general, the best performing methods are the hybrid ones, with best accuracy achieved by *naive syn-gen + dist-fun*. Non-hybrid approaches always have lower accuracy. This validates our main hypothesis in this paper, namely that the combination of syntactic information with distributional semantics is a promising strategy.

Matching our predictions, the low accuracy of the naive syntactic model is mainly due to a lack of *coverage*. In fact, the model leaves 5,010 of the 6,502 gold standard noun fillers unassigned since they realise syntactic roles that are unseen for the verbs in question. A large part of these are *PreModifier* and *PP-of* functions, which are central for nouns, but mostly ungrammatical for verbs. On the 1,492 fillers for which a role was assigned, the model obtains an accuracy of 67%, indicating a reasonably high, but not perfect, accuracy for shared grammatical functions. The remaining errors stem from two sources. First, many grammatical functions are ambiguous, causing wrong assignments by a "syntax-only" model. For example, *PP-in* can indicate both TIME and PLACE for many nominalisations.Second, a certain number of grammatical functions do not preserve their role between verb to noun (Hull and Gomez, 1996). For example, *PP-to* realises the MESSAGE role of the verb *require* but the ADDRESSEE role of the noun *request*.

Distributional models show in general better performance than the naive syntactic approach (approx. +25% accuracy). They do not suffer from the coverage problem, since they assign a role to each filler. Yet, the accuracy over *assigned* roles is lower than for the syntactic approach (52% for dist-fun).

We conclude that in the limited cases where a pure syntactic mapping is applicable, it is far more reliable than methods which are mainly based on lexical-semantic information. The major limitation of the latter is that lexical-semantics tend to fail when roles are semantically very similar. For example, for the noun *announcement*, the syntactic-level distributional model wrongly builds the mapping (ADDRESSEE, *PP-by*) instead of (SPEAKER, *PP-by*), because the two roles are very similar semantically (the computed similarities of the *PP-by* arguments to ADDRESSEE and SPEAKER in the semantic space are 0.94 and 0.92, respectively).

The syntactic-level distributional model outperforms the lexical-level, suggesting that generalising the mapping at the argument level offers more stable statistical evidence to find the correct role, i.e. a *set* of noun arguments better defines the semantics of the mapping than a *single* argument. This is mostly the case when the context vector of the argument is not a good representation because the semantic head is ambiguous, infrequent or atypical. Consider, for example, the following sentence for the noun *violation*:

(5) Sterne's Tristram Shandy consists of a series of *violations* [of literary conventions]$_{\text{PP-OF/NORM}}$

The syntactic-level model builds the correct mapping (NORM, *PP-of*), as the role fillers of the verb *violate* (e.g. *principle, right, treaty, law*) are very similar to the noun's category fillers (e.g. *convention, rule, agreement, treaty, norm*), causing the centroids of NORM and *PP-of* to be close in the space. The lexical-level model, however, builds the incorrect mapping (PROTAGONIST, *convention*). This happens because *convention* is ambiguous, and one of its senses (*"a large formal assembly"*) is compatible with the PROTAGONIST role, and happens to have a large influence on the position of the vector for *convention*. Unfortunately, this is not the sense in which the word is used in this sentence.

8 Conclusions

We have presented a data expansion approach to SRL for event nominalisations. Instead of relying on manually annotated nominal training data, we harness annotated data for verbs to bootstrap a semantic role labeller for nouns. For argument recognition, we use a simple rule-based approach. For argument labelling, we profit from the fact that the argument structures of event nominalisations and the corresponding verbs are typically similar. This allows us to learn a mapping between verbal roles and nominal arguments, using syntactic features, lexical-semantic similarity, or both.

We found that our rule-based approach for argument recognition works fairly well. For argument labelling, our approach does not yet attain the performance of supervised models, but has the crucial advantage of not requiring any labelled data for nominal predicates.

We achieved the highest accuracy with a hybrid syntactic-semantic model, which indicates that both types of information need to be combined for optimal results. A purely syntactic approach results in a high precision, but low coverage because frequent grammatical functions in particular cannot be trivially mapped. Backing off to semantic similarity provides additional coverage. However, semantic similarity has to be considered on the level of complete functions rather than individual instances to promote "uniformity" in the mappings.

In this paper, we have only considered nominal SRL by *data expansion*, i.e. we only applied our approach to those nominalisations for which we have annotated data for the corresponding verbs. However, even if no data is available for the corresponding *verb*, it might still be possible to bootstrap from other verbs in the same *frame* (assuming that the frame is known for the nominalisation) and we plan to pursue this idea in furture research. We also intend to investigate whether a joint optimisation of the mapping constrained by additional syntactic information such as subcategorisation frames leads to better results. Finally, we will verify that our methods, which we have evaluated on English FrameNet data, carry over to other corpora and languages.

Acknowledgments. Our work was partly funded by the German Research Foundation DFG (grant PI 154/9-3).

References

Baayen, R., R. Piepenbrock, and L. Gulikers, 1995. *The CELEX Lexical Database (Release 2)*. LDC.

Carlson, G. 1984. Thematic roles and their role in semantic interpretation. *Linguistics*, 22:259–279.

Carreras, X. and L. Màrquez, editors. 2005. *Proceedings of the CoNLL shared task: Semantic role labelling*, Ann Arbor, MI.

Erk, K. and S. Padó. 2006. Shalmaneser – a flexible toolbox for semantic role assignment. In *Proceedings of LREC*, Genoa, Italy.

Erk, K., A. Kowalski, S. Padó, and M. Pinkal. 2003. Towards a resource for lexical semantics: A large German corpus with extensive semantic annotation. In *Proceedings of ACL*, pages 537–544, Sapporo, Japan.

Fillmore, C., C. Johnson, and M. Petruck. 2003. Background to FrameNet. *International Journal of Lexicography*, 16:235–250.

Fleischman, M. and E. Hovy. 2003. Maximum entropy models for FrameNet classification. In *Proceedings of EMNLP*, pages 49–56, Sapporo, Japan.

Frank, A., H.-U. Krieger, F. Xu, H. Uszkoreit, B. Crysmann, B. Jörg, and U. Schäfer. 2007. Question answering from structured knowledge sources. *Journal of Applied Logic*, 5(1):20–48.

Gildea, D. and D. Jurafsky. 2002. Automatic labeling of semantic roles. *Computational Linguistics*, 28(3):245–288.

Gordon, A. and R. Swanson. 2007. Generalizing semantic role annotations across syntactically similar verbs. In *Proceedings of ACL*, pages 192–199, Prague, Czechia.

Grenager, T. and C. Manning. 2006. Unsupervised discovery of a statistical verb lexicon. In *Proceedings of EMNLP*, pages 1–8, Sydney, Australia.

Grimshaw, J. 1990. *Argument Structure*. MIT Press.

Gurevich, O., R. Crouch, T. King, and V. de Paiva. 2006. Deverbal nouns in knowledge representation. In *Proceedings of FLAIRS*, pages 670–675, Melbourne Beach, FL.

Hull, R. and F. Gomez. 1996. Semantic interpretation of nominalizations. In *Proceedings of AAAI*, pages 1062–1068, Portland, OR.

Jaeger, T. 2008. Categorical data analysis: Away from ANOVAs and toward Logit Mixed Models. *Journal of Memory and Language*. To appear.

Jiang, Zheng Ping and Hwee Tou Ng. 2006. Semantic role labeling of NomBank: A maximum entropy approach. In *Proceedings of EMNLP*, pages 138–145, Sydney, Australia.

Lapata, M. 2002. The disambiguation of nominalisations. *Computational Linguistics*, 28(3):357–388.

Liu, C. and H. Ng. 2007. Learning predictive structures for semantic role labeling of NomBank. In *Proceedings of ACL*, pages 208–215, Prague, Czechia.

Macleod, C., R. Grishman, A. Meyers, L. Barrett, and R. Reeves. 1998. Nomlex: A lexicon of nominalizations. In *Proceedings of EURALEX*, Liège, Belgium.

Meyers, A., R. Reeves, C. Macleod, R. Szekely, V. Zielinska, B. Young, and R. Grishman. 2004. Annotating Noun Argument Structure for NomBank. In *Proceedings of LREC*, Lisbon, Portugal.

Mihalcea, Rada and Phil Edmonds, editors. 2005. *Proceedings of Senseval-3: The Third International Workshop on the Evaluation of Systems for the Semantic Analysis of Text*, Barcelona, Spain.

Moschitti, A., P. Morarescu, and S. Harabagiu. 2003. Open-domain information extraction via automatic semantic labeling. In *Proceedings of FLAIRS*, pages 397–401, St. Augustine, FL.

Nunes, M. 1993. Argument linking in English derived nominals. In Valin, Robert D. Van, editor, *Advances in Role and Reference Grammar*, pages 372–432. John Benjamins.

Padó, S. and M. Lapata. 2007. Dependency-based construction of semantic space models. *Computational Linguistics*, 33(2):161–199.

Palmer, M., D. Gildea, and P. Kingsbury. 2005. The Proposition Bank: An annotated corpus of semantic roles. *Computational Linguistics*, 31(1):71–106.

Pradhan, S., H. Sun, W. Ward, J. Martin, and D. Jurafsky. 2004. Parsing arguments of nominalizations in English and Chinese. In *Proceedings of HLT/NAACL*, pages 141–144, Boston, MA.

Quirk, R., S. Greenbaum, G. Leech, and J. Svartvik. 1985. *A Comprehensive Grammar of the English Language*. Longman.

Swier, R. and S. Stevenson. 2004. Unsupervised semantic role labelling. In *Proceedings of EMNLP*, pages 95–102.

Xue, N. and M. Palmer. 2004. Calibrating features for semantic role labeling. In *Proceedings of EMNLP*, pages 88–94, Barcelona, Spain.

Recent Advances in a Feature-rich Framework for Treebank Annotation

Petr Pajas
Charles Univ. in Prague, MFF ÚFAL
Malostranské nám. 25
118 00 Prague 1 – Czech Rep.
pajas@ufal.ms.mff.cuni.cz

Jan Štěpánek
Charles Univ. in Prague, MFF ÚFAL
Malostranské nám. 25
118 00 Prague 1 – Czech Rep.
stepanek@ufal.ms.mff.cuni.cz

Abstract

This paper presents recent advances in an established treebank annotation framework comprising of an abstract XML-based data format, fully customizable editor of tree-based annotations, a toolkit for all kinds of automated data processing with support for cluster computing, and a work-in-progress database-driven search engine with a graphical user interface built into the tree editor.

1 Introduction

Constructing a treebank is a complicated process. Among other things it requires a good choice of tools, varying from elementary data conversion scripts over annotation tools and tools for consistency checking, to tools used for semi-automatic treebank building (POS taggers, syntactic parsers). If no existing tool fits the needs, a new one has to be developed (or some existing tool adapted or extended, which, however, seldom happens in practice). The variety of tools that exist and emerged from various treebanking projects shows that there is no simple solution that would fit all. It is sometimes a small missing feature or an incompatible data format that disqualifies certain otherwise well-established tools in the eyes of those who decide which tools to use for their annotation project.

This paper presents an annotation framework that was from its very beginning designed to be extensible and independent of any particular annotation schema. While reflecting the feedback from several treebanking projects, it evolved into a set of generic tools that is open to all kinds of annotations that involve tree structures. By this paper we would like not only to promote this framework, but also show that due to its open nature, it may be easily extended to fit new requirements. The first three sections describe base components of the framework, an abstract data format, a versatile annotation tool for tree-oriented annotations, and a framework for automatic annotation processing; some of these components have been mentioned in earlier publications, but the framework has neither been published in its integrity nor described in much detail. The last section describes a query engine that is a newest addition to the framework, first presented by this paper.

2 Data format

The base data format selected for the present annotation framework, both for data exchange and as a memory-model reference, is PML (Pajas and Štěpánek, 2006). PML is an abstract XML-based format intended to be generally applicable to all types of annotation purposes, and especially suitable for multi-layered treebank annotations following the stand-of principles. A notable feature that distinguishes PML from other encoding schemes, like Tiger-XML (Mengel and Lezius, 2000), XCES (Ide and Romary, 2003), or maybe even SynAF by ISO TC37/SC4 (Declerck, 2006), is its generic and open nature. Rather than being targeted to one particular annotation schema or being a set of specifically targeted encoding conventions, PML is an open system, where a new type of annotation can be introduced easily by creating a simple XML file called PML schema, which describes the annotation by means of declaring the relevant data types and possibly assigning certain roles to these data types. The roles in the con-

©2008. Licensed under the *Creative Commons Attribution-Noncommercial-Share Alike 3.0 Unported* license (http://creativecommons.org/licenses/by-nc-sa/3.0/). Some rights reserved.

text of PML are just labels from a pre-defined set that can be used to mark the declarations according to their purpose. For instance, the roles indicate which data structures represent the nodes of the trees, how the node data structures are nested to form a tree, which field in a data structure carries its unique ID (if any), or which field carries a link to the annotated data or other layers of annotation, and so on. PML schema can define all kinds of annotations varying from linear annotations through constituency or dependency trees, to complex graph-oriented annotation systems. The PML schema provides information for validating the annotation data as well as for creating a relevant data model for their in-memory representation.

To give an example, the annotation of the Prague Dependency Treebank 2.0 (PDT) (Hajič and others, 2006), which was published in the PML format, consists of four annotation layers, each defined by its own PML schema: a lowest word-form layer consisting of tokenized text segmented just into documents and paragraphs; a morphological layer segmenting the token stream of the previous layer to sentences and attaching morphological form, lemma, and tag to each token; an analytical layer building a morpho-syntactic dependency tree from the words of each sentence (morphologically analyzed on the previous layer); and a tectogrammatical layer consisting of deep-syntactic dependency trees interlinked in a $N{:}M$ manner with the analytical layer and a valency lexicon and carrying further relational annotation, such as coreference and quotation sets. All these features are formally described by the respective PML schemas.

The fundamental toolkit for PML comprises of a validator (based on compiling PML schemas to RelaxNG grammars accompanied by Schematron rules), and API, consisting of a Perl library (basic interfaces for Java and C++ are planned). The input/output functions of the library are modular and can work with local files as well as with remote resources accessible via HTTP, FTP or SSH protocols (with pluggable support for other protocols). Additionally, the library supports on-the-fly XSLT-based format conversions that can be easily plugged in via a simple configuration file. Consequently, the API can transparently handle even non-PML data formats. Currently there are about a dozen input/output conversion filters available, covering various existing data formats including the TigerXML format, the formats of the Penn Treebank (Marcus et al., 1994), the CoNLL-X shared task format (Buchholz and Marsi, 2006), and the formats of the Latin Dependency (Bamman and Crane, 2006), Sinica (Chu-Ren et al., 2000), Slovene Dependency (Džeroski et al., 2006) (SDT), and Alpino (van der Beek et al., 2002) treebanks. Support for XCES formats is planned as soon as a final release of XCES is available.

This basic toolkit is further supplemented by various auxiliary tools, such as `pmlcopy` which allows one to copy, move, rename, or GZip sets of interconnected PML data files without breaking the internal URL-based references.

3 Tree Editor

The heart of the annotation framework is a multiplatform graphical tree editor called TrEd, (Hajič et al., 2001).

TrEd was from the beginning designed to be annotation-schema independent, extensible and configurable. TrEd can work with any PML data format whose PML schema correctly defines (via roles) at least one sequence of trees. Beside PML format, TrEd can work with many other data formats, either by means of the modular input/output interface of the PML library or using its own input/output backends.

The basic editing capabilities of TrEd allow the user to easily modify the tree structure with drag-and-drop operations and to easily edit the associated data. Although this is sufficient for most annotation tasks, the annotation process can be greatly accelerated by a set of custom extension functions, called macros, written in Perl. Macros are usually created to simplify the most common tasks done by the annotators. They can be called either from menu or by keyboard shortcuts.

Although TrEd ensures that the result of the annotation is in accord with the related PML schema, there is still a chance that an annotator errs in some other aspect of the annotation. For this reason TrEd offers the possibility to write macros that incorporate custom consistency tests into the built-in editing commands of TrEd. Such tests can prevent the user from making accidental mistakes (like assigning a case to a verb or subordinating a Subject to a particle). Macros can also completely disable some dangerous editing commands (for example, the PDT annotation modes in TrEd disable the possibility to add or delete tokens or trees).

While macros provide means to extend, accelerate and control the annotation capabilities of TrEd, the concept of style-sheets gives users control over the visual presentation of the annotated data. Style-sheets, among other, offer the possibility to: visually differentiate nodes and edges by color, shape, size or line style according to arbitrary criteria; assemble the data associated with nodes and edges to node and edge labels; alter node positioning and padding; visualize additional edges and cross-structure relations by means of arrows or other types of connections; control the content and styling of the text (usually the annotated sentence) displayed in a box above the tree. TrEd can also balance trees, visualize disconnected groups of nodes, zoom the tree view arbitrarily, and display trees in a vertical mode, see Fig. 1.

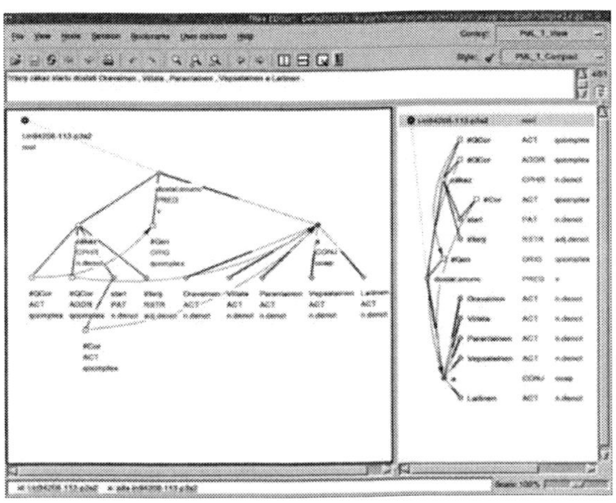

Figure 1: The same tree displayed using horizontal and vertical display mode in TrEd

Due to model/view separation, TrEd provides means for controlling which nodes are actually displayed (it is thus possible to write modes that collapse subtrees, hide auxiliary nodes, completely skip some levels of the tree, display multiple trees at once (Fig. 2), or even display additional "virtual" nodes and edges that are not actually present in the underlying data structures).

So far, TrEd has been selected as annotation tool for PDT and several similarly structured treebanking projects like Slovene (Džeroski et al., 2006), Croatian (Tadić, 2007), or Greek Dependency Treebanks (Prokopidis et al., 2005), but also for Penn-style Alpino Treebank (van der Beek et al., 2002), the semantic annotation in the Dutch

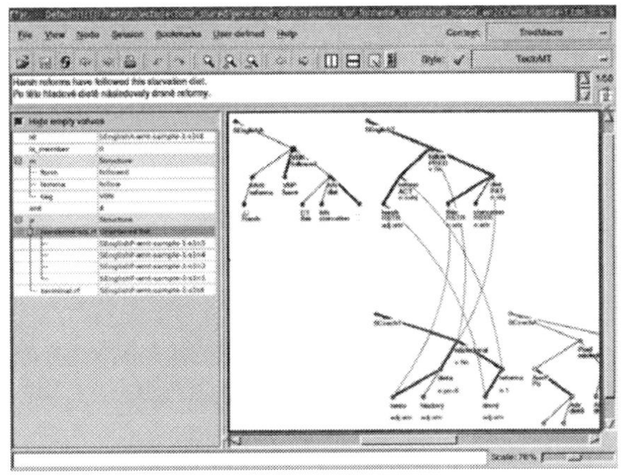

Figure 2: The main window visualizing node-to-node alignment of trees in the TectoMT project (Žabokrtský et al., 2008); side-bar shows data associated with the selected node.

language Corpus Initiative project (Trapman and Monachesi, 2006), as well as for annotation of morphology using so-called MorphoTrees (Smrž and Pajas, 2004) in the Prague Arabic Dependency Treebank (where it was also used for annotation of the dependency trees in the PDT style). While most other projects use off-line conversion

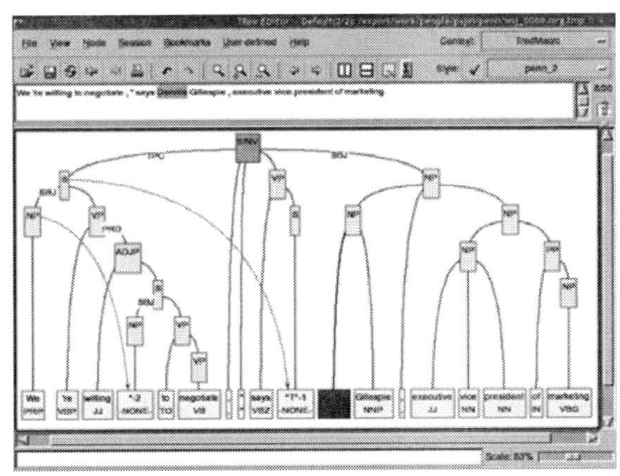

Figure 3: One possible way of displaying Penn Treebank data in TrEd

to some format directly supported by TrEd, for Alpino Treebank a better approach has been selected: the PML library has been configured to convert between Alpino XML format and PML transparently on-the-fly using two simple XSLT stylesheets created for this purpose.

Like some other annotation tools, for example DepAnn (Kakkonen, 2006), TrEd provides means for comparing two (or more) annotations and visually marking the differences. This functionality is currently provided by macros tailored especially for the PDT annotations. Modifying these macros for specific needs of other tree-based annotations should be easy.

4 Automated processing

The same code-base that runs TrEd (except for the GUI) is used in a command-line tool for automated processing of the annotated data called BTrEd. This tool allows one to search, transform or modify the data by means of small programs written in Perl known from TrEd as macros. Given a list of files, the tool opens the files one after another and applies a given macro on each of them (or, if one chooses, to each tree or each node). With the powerful API of TrEd and the expressiveness of the Perl programming language at hand, one can very easy prepare scripts that gather information, create reports, or automate some parts of the annotation process; in some cases the script can be as short to fit on the command-line.

It is often the case that one has to process a large amount of data repeatedly with one or more scripts. To avoid the need of reading the data into memory upon each execution, BTrEd is augmented by a client-server interface and a client tool called NTrEd. NTrEd, given a list of computer hostnames or IP addresses and a list of files, starts remotely on each of the computers a server-mode instance of BTrEd and distributes the supplied data among these servers (either equally or according to CPU load). Since only file-names are transferred in the communication, some form of shared data storage is assumed. The BTrEd servers read their respective share of the treebank, keep it in their RAM and await client connections. Once the servers are started in this way, one can pass a script to NTrEd as one would do with BTrEd; the tool forwards the script to the servers and collecting the results, outputs them in the same way as a stand-alone BTrEd would. If the script modifies the data, the user can send a request to the servers to either save the changed files or reload them, discarding all modifications. Security of NTrEd is achieved by means of SHA-based authentication (completely transparent to the user) and, optionally, by SSH tunneling.

Since one machine can run multiple instances of BTrEd server, each user of a computer cluster can run its own set of BTrEd servers without interfering with other users. Concurrent work of several users on the same data is supported by TrEd and BTrEd by a simple system of file locks, similar to that of GNU Emacs.

This kind of processing was exploited heavily during the post-annotation checking phases of PDT 2.0 production (Štěpánek, 2006). Employing a cluster consisting from about ten computers, a typical consistency-checking script processed the whole amount of PDT 2.0 (1.5 million analytical nodes and 700 thousand tectogrammatical nodes) in just a few seconds. This was particularly helpful for rapid prototyping or testing hypotheses and it accelerated the whole process enormously.

The NTrEd system, keeping the data in RAM of the servers, is sufficient for small to medium-sized corpora. For huge corpora in scale of terabytes it may not be the case. For processing such huge amounts of data, another tool called JTrEd was recently added to the framework. JTrEd is a wrapper script that simplifies distribution of BTrEd tasks over a computer cluster controlled by the Sun Grid Engine (SGE).

The BTrEd machinery is not intended just for small scripts. A project building a full MT engine on top of this framework is in progress (Žabokrtský et al., 2008).

5 Data-base driven query engine

One of the reasons for which tree-banks are created is that they cover and capture a representative number of syntactic constructions of the particular language. However, to be able to identify them effectively, one has to employ some querying system, consisting of a sufficiently expressive query language and an engine that can search the treebank and present the user with all occurrences matching the constraints of the query.

While for complex queries the tools described in the previous section serve well to users with basic programming skills,'every-day' querying by linguistic public requires a more accessible user-interface. In this section we describe a working prototype of a new query engine and its user interface, based on the data representation and tools described in the preceding sections. First, however, we briefly review some existing solutions.

For searching over PDT a tool called Net-Graph (Mírovský, 2006) is traditionally used. This tool's graphical interface allows the users to formulate their queries in a very natural way, namely as trees whose structures correspond to the structures of the desired search results (although one may specify, for example, that an edge in the query tree should actually match a path in the result tree). Each node in the query tree can carry a set of attributes that match or otherwise constrain the attributes of the corresponding node in the result tree. The query can further put some cardinality constraints on the matching nodes; these are formulated using a special set of labels on the query tree. A great advantage of NetGraph is its web-enabled user interface (Java applet). The underlying query engine is written in C, and although relatively simplistic (i.e. no indexing or planning techniques are used), for PDT-sized corpus it offers reasonable speed for the interactive use. Certain disadvantages of the NetGraph system in our view are: lack of support for querying relations between two or more trees; no support for multi-layered annotations; limited means of expressing attribute constraints and their boolean combinations; restriction to a limited legacy data format.

Probably the best-known query languages for tree structures nowadays are XPath and XQuery, promoted by (and in case of the latter bound to) the XML technology. The advantage of these query languages is that there are several implementations to choose from. Beside searching, some tools (e.g. XSH2 (Pajas, 2005)) provide means for XPath-based data modification. For these reasons, XPath searches over XML-encoded treebank data are promoted (Bouma and Kloosterman, 2002). The disadvantage is, however, that being restricted to the XML data model, users of such tools have to query over a particular XML encoding of the data which often in some way or other obscures the actual annotation schema and relations the annotation represents. Besides, it can be argued that XPath alone does not provide sufficient expressiveness for typical linguistic queries.

As a remedy for the last deficiency, Steven Bird et al. (Bird et al., 2006) proposed a concise query language named LPath, which, while extending core XPath, was designed with the needs of linguistic queries in mind. Their query system is powered by a relational database in which the queries are translated from LPath to SQL. To enable efficient evaluation of constraints on horizontal and vertical relationships between two nodes of a tree by the relational database, the database representation of the trees uses a simple labeling scheme which labels each node with several integers so that the relationship constraints translate in SQL to simple comparisons of the respective integer labels.

It has been shown (Lai and Bird, 2005) that further extension to the LPath language, known as LPath+, is already 1st-order complete. It should, however, be noted that 1st-order completeness has little to do with the practical expressiveness of the language; certain queries, easily expressed in 1st-order logic, only translate to LPath+ at the cost of combinatorial explosion in the size of the query. For example, like XPath, the only way LPath+ offers to match two non-identical sibling nodes is to reach one by the child axis and the other using the following-sibling or preceding-sibling axes from the first one; thus for a query with n sibling nodes whose constraints do not necessarily imply inequality and which can appear in the tree in arbitrary order, the LPath+ query must, in general, enumerate a disjunction of all the $n!$ possible permutations. This may not be a problem when querying over English treebanks, but is a serious handicap for querying over treebanks for languages with free word-order.

There are several other tools for querying over treebanks, we are aware at least of TIGERSearch (Lezius, 2002) for annotations in the TigerXML format, and TGrep2 (Rohde, 2001) for Penn Treebank and similar, which we shall not describe here in detail as they are well known.

For the PML-based annotation system presented in this paper, we have developed a prototype of a new querying system, referred to, just for the purposes of this paper, as PML Tree Query (PML-TQ). The new system attempts to equal the qualities of the above mentioned systems and additionally provide

- a query language with sufficient expressiveness yet without complex formalisms
- unified treatment of structural and non-structural, inter- and cross-layer relationships
- basic reporting capabilities (computing number or distribution of occurrences, etc.)
- a graphical query editor built into TrEd
- a scriptable and extensible interface

At the current stage, PML-TQ provides a prototype query language supporting arbitrary logical conditions on attributes of nodes and their inter- and cross-layer relations, optional nodes, and basic cardinality constraints. A result of an evaluation of a PML-TQ can be either a set of matches, each match being a set of nodes in the treebank corresponding to the nodes in the query, or a report with some information computed from these node sets. The reporting capabilities of PML-TQ allow one to perform various aggregations on the result node sets and compute statistics over the aggregated groups. Thus, one may easily formulate queries such as *"what is the maximum, minimum, and average depth of a tree in the treebank"*, *"what preposition forms correspond on the surface layer to tectogrammatical nodes with the functor* `DIR3` *and what is their distribution"*, *"what is the most common functor for a child node of a node with functor* `PRED`*"*, *"what is the joint distribution of functors for nodes in the parent-child relation"*, etc.

In the graphical representation of PML-TQ, relations between nodes are represented by arrows. Each PML-TQ query forms a tree or forest whose edges represent basic relations between nodes and possibly nesting of subqueries and whose nodes can be interconnected by additional arrows representing further relations.

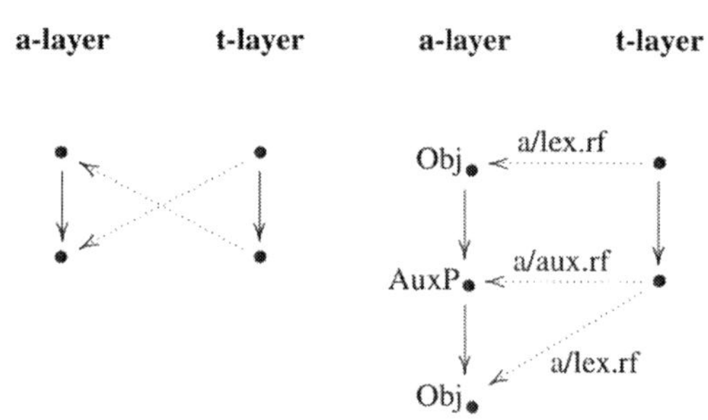

Figure 4: Examples of cross-layer queries in PML-TQ. Query on the left finds dependency that got reversed on the PDT tectogrammatical layer compared to the analytical layer; the query on the right finds tectogrammatical nodes corresponding to an analytical object governing a prepositional object.

Apart from the graphical representation, PML-TQ queries can be formulated in a textual form with syntax resembling XPath (but substantially more expressive). A query is parsed from this syntax into a syntactic tree encoded in PML; in this representation the queries can be stored, visualized, and graphically manipulated in TrEd.

There are presently two engines that can evaluate PML-TQ queries. To utilize the modern RDBMS technology for performance and scalability, we have created a translator of PML-TQ to SQL. One can thus query over a static treebank stored in a database (for encoding tree-structures into database tables, we have adopted a labeling system similar to that described in (Bird et al., 2006)). For querying over data that change (e.g. a file currently open in TrEd or a bunch of files with annotation in progress), we have implemented a simple, yet still relatively fast, evaluator in Perl with a basic planner that can perform PML-TQ searches over PML data sequentially in either TrEd, BTrEd, NTrEd, or JTrEd.

Having two engines behind our query interface in TrEd has several benefits. The annotators will be able to perform identical queries over a corpus stored in a remote SQL database as well as to search in their own locally stored data. The developers of scripts for BTrEd will be able to formulate parts of their scripts briefly as PML-TQ queries whose correctness they will be able to verify independently on a treebank using the SQL backend using an interactive environment.

The SQL-based execution system has currently two database backends for feature and performance comparison: Oracle Express 10g and Postgres SQL. We use Perl DBI modules to interconnect these backends with the TrEd toolkit.

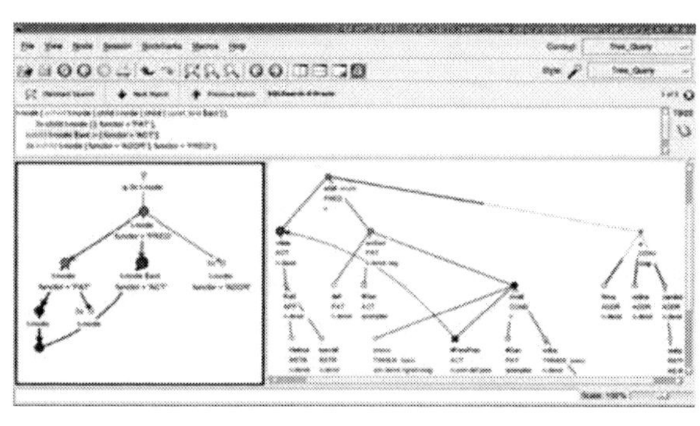

Figure 5: PML-TQ interface in TrEd. Top: the query as text, bottom left the query tree, bottom right a matching tree from PDT 2.0.

The search results can be presented in TrEd in one of several ways. Results of queries that make use of the report-generating facilities of PML-TQ are displayed simply as tables in a text window. Most PML-TQ queries, however, return matching nodes or trees. To display them, TrEd retrieves corresponding URLs and node positions from the database and reads the actual data from the PML files that must currently be accessible locally or remotely via HTTP, FTP or SSH. Since there are situations when the original data cannot be accessed in this way, we are working on a solution that would allow TrEd to fetch and reconstruct the trees directly from the database.

For populating the database system with treebanks, we have developed a tool that can transfer arbitrary PML-encoded data into a set of database tables suitable for PML-TQ querying. The information about available inter-layer and cross-layer relations is automatically extracted from the PML schema and can be further adjusted by a few command-line parameters.

We have evaluated our database search engine using queries obtained by several means. We had the luck that the developer of NetGraph kindly provided us with all queries collected from real NetGraph users over the past few years in the server logs. We thus obtained almost 9000 queries for the analytical layer and about 5000 queries for the tectogrammatical layer of PDT 2.0. By translating them to PML-TQ with a simple Perl script, we obtained a large collection for testing the basic functionality and performance of our system. To that we added a set of queries that test more advanced PML-TQ features and, for comparison, several queries analogous to the LPath query examples given in (Bird et al., 2006).

When we first run our complete query collection on the Oracle database with 1.5 million nodes and about 88 thousand trees from the analytical layer of PDT, we were surprised to see that out of 8188 queries, 8102 computes in a fraction of second, further 33 in less then 2 seconds, further 36 in less than 10 seconds, 14 in less than 20 seconds and only 5 in more than one minute. Four of these, however, took extremely long time to compute (from hours to days). We observed that all these time-consuming queries were rather similar: they imposed either no or too week constraints on the nodes and sometimes the query tree had a rather large number of auto-morphisms (there was a query consisting of a node with six identical child-nodes none of which carried any constraints). We then found a tree in our data set that contained a node with 85 children. This gives roughly 10^{12} solutions to the query with six siblings on this tree alone.

In some cases the queries can be rewritten using cardinality constraints ("find all nodes with at least 6 children"), which avoids the combinatorial explosion. Since we felt this may not always be possible, we also tried to remove from our data set all trees with more than 20 siblings (44 trees from 70K) that turned out to be mostly TV listings anyway. After that, the performance for the four of the problematic queries improved dramatically: first 100 matches were found in a few seconds and fist 10^6 matches in less than 10 minutes.

Although we have modified the query compiler to suggest cardinality constraints were it seems appropriate and to automatically eliminate some types of automorphisms on the query tree by imposing a strict ordering on the permutable query nodes, we think it is neither possible to completely secure the query system against time-exhaustive queries nor to reliably detect such queries automatically. The querying interface therefore gives the users the option to select a reasonable maximum number of results and allows them to cancel the query evaluation at any time.

6 Conclusion

Over last few years our annotation framework made a considerable leap, from a simple annotation tool to a feature-rich system with several interoperating components. The complete framework is publicly available, either under the General Public License License (GPL), the Perl Artistic License or other GPL-compatible free license. A public release of the tree query interface described in the previous section is scheduled for mid to end of 2008.

7 Acknowledgment

This paper as well as the development of the framework is supported by the grant Information Society of GA AV ČR under contract 1ET101120503.

References

Bamman, David and Gregory Crane. 2006. The design and use of a Latin dependency treebank. In *Proceedings of the Fifth International Workshop on Treebanks and Linguistic Theories (TLT 2006)*, pages 67–78, Prague.

Bird, Steven, Yi Chen, Susan B. Davidson, Haejoong Lee, and Yifeng Zheng. 2006. Designing and evaluating an XPath dialect for linguistic queries. In

ICDE '06: Proceedings of the 22nd International Conference on Data Engineering, page 52, Washington, DC, USA. IEEE Computer Society.

Bouma, Gosse and Geert Kloosterman. 2002. Querying dependency treebanks in XML. In *Proceedings of the Third international conference on Language Resources and Evaluation (LREC)*, Gran Canaria.

Buchholz, Sabine and Erwin Marsi. 2006. CoNLL-X shared task on multilingual dependency parsing. In *Proceedings CoNLL-X*.

Chu-Ren, Huang, Keh-Jiann Chen, Feng-Yi Chen, Keh-Jiann Chen, Zhao-Ming Gao, and Kuang-Yu Chen. 2000. Sinica treebank: Design criteria, annotation guidelines, and on-line interface. In *Proceedings of 2nd Chinese Language Processing Workshop (Held in conjunction with ACL-2000)*, pages 29–37, Hong Kong, October 7.

Declerck, Thierry. 2006. Synaf: Towards a standard for syntactic annotation. In *Proceedings of the 5th International Conference on Language Resources and Evaluation (LREC 2006)*, pages 209–232.

Džeroski, Sašo, Tomaž Erjavec, Nina Ledinek, Petr Pajas, Zdeněk Žabokrtský, and Andreja Žele. 2006. Towards a slovene dependency treebank. In *Proceedings of the 5th International Conference on Language Resources and Evaluation (LREC 2006)*, pages 1388–1391.

Hajič, Jan, Barbora Vidová-Hladká, and Petr Pajas. 2001. The Prague Dependency Treebank: Annotation Structure and Support. In *Proceedings of the IRCS Workshop on Linguistic Databases*, pages 105–114, Philadelphia, USA. University of Pennsylvania.

Hajič, Jan et al. 2006. The Prague Dependency Treebank 2.0. CD-ROM. CAT: LDC2006T01.

Ide, Nancy and R. Romary. 2003. Encoding syntactic annotation. In Abillé, A., editor, *Building and Using Parsed Corpora*. Kluwer, Dordrecht.

Kakkonen, Tuomo. 2006. Depann - an annotation tool for dependency treebanks. In *Proceedings of the 11th ESSLLI Student Session at the 18th European Summer School in Logic, Language and Information*, pages 214–225, Malaga, Spain.

Lai, Catherine and Steven Bird. 2005. LPath+: A first-order complete language for linguistic tree query. In *Proceedings of the 19th Pacific Asia Conference on Language (PACLIC)*, Information and Computation, pages 1–12, Taipei, Taiwan. Academia Sinica.

Lezius, Wolfgang. 2002. *Ein Suchwerkzeug für syntaktisch annotierte Textkorpora*. Ph.D. thesis, IMS, University of Stuttgart, December. Arbeitspapiere des Instituts für Maschinelle Sprachverarbeitung (AIMS), volume 8, number 4.

Marcus, Mitchell P., Grace Kim, Mary Ann Marcinkiewicz, Robert MacIntyre, Ann Bies, Mark Ferguson, Karen Katz, and Britta Schasberger. 1994. The penn treebank: Annotating predicate argument structure. In *HLT*. Morgan Kaufmann.

Mengel, A. and W. Lezius. 2000. An XML-based representation format for syntactically annotated corpora.

Mírovský, Jiří. 2006. Netgraph: A tool for searching in prague dependency treebank 2.0. In Hajič, Jan and Joakim Nivre, editors, *Proceedings of the Fifth Workshop on Treebanks and Linguistic Theories (TLT)*, pages 211–222, Prague, Czech Republic.

Pajas, Petr and Jan Štěpánek. 2006. XML-based representation of multi-layered annotation in the PDT 2.0. In *Proceedings of the LREC Workshop on Merging and Layering Linguistic Information (LREC 2006)*, pages 40–47.

Pajas, Petr. 2005. XSH - XML Editing Shell (an introduction). In *Proceedings of XMLPrague conference on XML 2005*, pages 69–78, Prague.

Prokopidis, P, E Desypri, M Koutsombogera, H Papageorgiou, and S Piperidis. 2005. Theoretical and practical issues in the construction of a greek dependency treebank. In *In Proc. of the 4th Workshop on Treebanks and Linguistic Theories (TLT*, pages 149–160.

Rohde, D. 2001. TGrep2 the next-generation search engine for parse trees. http://tedlab.mit.edu/ dr/-Tgrep2/.

Smrž, Otakar and Petr Pajas. 2004. MorphoTrees of Arabic and Their Annotation in the TrEd Environment. In Nikkhou, Mahtab, editor, *Proceedings of the NEMLAR International Conference on Arabic Language Resources and Tools*, pages 38—41, Cairo. ELDA.

Štěpánek, Jan. 2006. Post-annotation checking of prague dependency treebank 2.0 data. In *Proceedings of the 9th International Conference, TSD 2006*, number 4188 in Lecture Notes In Computer Science, pages 277–284. Springer-Verlag Berlin Heidelberg.

Tadić, Marko. 2007. Building the croatian dependency treebank: the initial stages. In *Contemporary Linguistics*, volume 63, pages 85–92.

Trapman, Jantine and Paola Monachesi. 2006. Manual for the. annotation of semantic roles in D-Coi. Technical report, University of Utrecht.

van der Beek, Leonoor, Gosse Bouma, Robert Malouf, and Gertjan van Noord. 2002. The alpino dependency treebank. In *Computational Linguistics in the Netherlands CLIN 2001*, Rodopi.

Žabokrtský, Zdeněk, Jan Ptáček, and Petr Pajas. 2008. TectoMT: Highly modular hybrid MT system with tectogramatics used as transfer layer. (To appear).

A Joint Information Model for *n*-best Ranking

Patrick Pantel
Yahoo! Inc.
Santa Clara, CA 95054
me@patrickpantel.com

Vishnu Vyas
USC Information Sciences Institute
Marina del Rey, CA
vishnu@isi.edu

Abstract

In this paper, we present a method for modeling joint information when generating *n*-best lists. We apply the method to a novel task of *characterizing the similarity of a group of terms* where only a small set of many possible semantic properties may be displayed to a user. We demonstrate that considering the results jointly, by accounting for the information overlap between results, generates better *n*-best lists than considering them independently. We propose an information theoretic objective function for modeling the joint information in an *n*-best list and show empirical evidence that humans prefer the result sets produced by our joint model. Our results show with 95% confidence that the *n*-best lists generated by our joint ranking model are significantly different from a baseline independent model 50.0% ± 3.1% of the time, out of which they are preferred 76.6% ± 5.2% of the time.

1 Introduction

Ranking result sets is a pervasive problem in the NLP and IR communities, exemplified by keyword search engines such as Google (Brin and Page 1998), machine translation systems (Zhang et al. 2006), and recommender systems (Shardanand and Maes 1995; Resnick and Varian 1997).

Consider the lexical semantics task of *explaining why a set of terms are similar*: given a set of terms and a large set of possible explanations for their similarity, one must choose only the best *n* explanations to display to a user. There are many ways to explain why terms are similar[2]; one way is to list the semantic properties that are shared by the terms. For example, consider the following set of terms corresponding to *fruit names*:

```
{apple, ume, pawpaw, quince}
```

Example semantic properties that could be used to explain their similarity include: *they are products*, *they can be eaten*, *they are solid* (but not *they are companies*, for example). The list of such semantic properties can be very large and some are much more informative than others. For example, the property *can-be-eaten* is much more informative of the similarity of {*apple*, *ume*, *pawpaw*, *quince*} than the property *is-solid*. Using a simple measure of association between properties and queries, explained in detail later in this paper, one can rank each property and obtain the following three highest scoring properties for explaining the similarity of these terms:

```
{they are products, they can be
imported, they can be exported}
```

Even though *can be imported* and *can be exported* are highly ranked explanations, taken jointly, once we know one the other does not offer much more information since most things that can be imported can also be exported. In other words, there is a large overlap in information between the two properties. A more informative set of explanations could be obtained by replacing one of these two properties with a property that scored lower but had less information overlap with the others, for example:

© 2008. Licensed under the *Creative Commons Attribution-Noncommercial-Share Alike 3.0 Unported* license (http://creativecommons.org/licenses/by-nc-sa/3.0/). Some rights reserved.

[2] In (Vyas and Pantel 2008), we explore the task of explaining the similarity between terms in detail. In this paper, we focus on the task of choosing the best set of explanations given a set of candidates.

```
{they are products, they can be
imported, they can be eaten}
```

Even though, taken alone, the property *can be eaten* may not be as informative as *can be exported*, it does indeed add more information to the explanation set when considered jointly with the other explanations.

In this paper, we propose an information theoretic objective function for modeling the joint information in an *n*-best list. Derived using conditional self-information, we measure the amount of information that each property contributes to a query. Intuitively, when adding a new property to a result set, we should prefer a property that contributes the maximum amount of information to the existing set. In our experiments, we show empirical evidence that humans prefer our joint model's result sets on the task of explaining why a set of terms are similar.

The remainder of this paper is organized as follows. In the next section, we review related literature and position our contribution within that landscape. Section 3 presents the task of explaining the similarity of a set of terms and describes a method for generating candidate explanations from which we will apply our ranking model. In Section 4, we formally define our ranking task and present our Joint Information Ranking model. Experimental results are presented in Section 5 and finally, we conclude with a discussion and future work.

2 Related Work

There are a vast number of applications of ranking and its importance to the commercial success at companies such as Google and Yahoo have fueled a great deal of research in recent years. In this paper, we investigate one particular aspect of ranking, the importance of considering the results in an *n*-best list jointly because of the information overlap issues described in the introduction, and one particular application, namely explaining why a set of terms are similar.

Considering results jointly is not a new idea and is very similar to the concept of diversity-based ranking introduced in the IR community by Carbonell and Goldstein (1998). In short, selecting an *n*-best list is a balancing act between maximizing the relevance of the list and the information novelty of its results. One commonly used approach is to define a measure of novelty/semantic similarity between documents and to apply heuristics to reduce the relevance score of a result item (a hit) by a function of the similarity of this item to other results in the list (Carbonell and Goldstein 1998; Zhu et al. 2007). Another common approach is to cluster result documents according to their semantic similarity and present clusters to users instead of individual documents (Hearst and Pedersen 1996; Leuski 2001; Liu and Croft 2004). In this paper, we argue that the balance between relevance and novelty can be captured by a formal model that maximizes the joint information content of a result set. Instead of ranking documents in an IR setting, we focus in this paper on a new task of selecting the best semantic properties that describe the similarity of a set of query terms.

By no means an exhaustive list, the most commonly cited ranking and scoring algorithms are HITS (Kleinberg 1998) and PageRank (Page et al. 1998), which rank hyperlinked documents using the concepts of hubs and authorities. The most well-known keyword scoring methods within the IR community are the *tf-idf* (Salton and McGill 1983) and pointwise mutual information (Church and Hanks 1989) measures, which put more importance on matching keywords that occur frequently in a document relative to the total number of documents that contain the keyword (by normalizing term frequencies with inverse document frequencies). Various methods including *tf-idf* have been comparatively evaluated by Salton and Buckley (1987). Creating *n*-best lists using the above algorithms produce result sets where each result is considered independently. In this paper, we investigate the utility of considering the result sets jointly and compare our joint method to a pointwise mutual information model.

Within the NLP community, *n*-best list ranking has been looked at carefully in parsing, extractive summarization (Barzilay et al. 1999; Hovy and Lin 1998), and machine translation (Zhang et al. 2006), to name a few. The problem of learning to rank a set of objects by combining a given collection of ranking functions using boosting techniques is investigated in (Freund et al. 2003). This rank boosting technique has been used in re-ranking parsers (Collins and Koo 2000; Charniak and Johnson 2005). Such re-ranking approaches usually improve the likelihood of candidate results using extraneous features and, for example in parsing, the properties of the trees. In this paper, we focus on a difference task: the lexical semantics task of selecting the best semantic properties that help explain why a set of query terms are similar. Unlike in parsing and machine translation, we are not ultimately looking for the best single result, but instead the n-best.

Looking at commercial applications, there are many examples showcasing the importance of ranking, for example Internet search engines like Google and Yahoo (Brin and Page 1998). Another application is online recommendation systems where suggestions must be ranked before being presented to a user (Shardanand and Maes 1995). Also, in online social networks such as Facebook and LinkedIn, new connections or communities are suggested to users by leveraging their social connections (Spretus, et al. 2005).

3 Explaining Similarity

Several applications, such as IR engines, return the n-best ranked results to a query. Although we expect our joint information model, presented in Section 4.2, to generalize to many ranking tasks, our focus in this paper is on the task of choosing the n-best explanations that describe the similarity of a set of terms. That is, given a set of terms, one must choose the best set of characterizations of why the terms are similar, chosen from a large set of possible explanations.

Analyzing the different ways in which one can explain/characterize the similarity between terms is beyond the scope of this paper[3]. The types of explanations that we consider in this paper are semantic properties that are shared by the terms. For example, consider the query terms {*apple, ume, pawpaw, quince*} presented in Section 1. An example set of properties that explains the similarity of these words might include {*they are products, they can be imported, they can be exported, they are tasty, they grow*}.

The range of possible semantic properties is large. For the above example, we may have offered many other properties like {*they are entities, they can be eaten, they have skin, they are words, they can be roasted, they can be shipped*, etc.} Choosing a high quality concise set of properties is the goal of this paper.

Our hypothesis is that considering items in a result set jointly for ranking produces better result sets than considering them independently. An important question then is: what is a utility function for measuring a *better* result? We propose that a result set is considered better than another if a person could more easily reconstruct the original query from it. Or, in other words, a result set is considered better than another if it reduces more the uncertainty of what the original query was. Here, reducing the uncertainty means making it easier for a human to understand the original question (i.e., a good explanation should clarify the query).

Formally, we define our ranking task as:

Task Definition: Given a query $Q = \{q_1, q_2, ..., q_m\}$ and a set of candidate properties $R = \{r_1, r_2, ..., r_k\}$, where q is a term and r is a property, find the set of properties $R' = \{r_1, r_2, ..., r_n\}$ that most reduces the uncertainty of Q, where $n << k$.

Recall from Section 1 the example Q = {*apple, ume, pawpaw, quince*}. The set of properties:

```
{they are products, they can be
imported, they can be eaten}
```

is preferred over the set

```
{they are products, they can be
imported, they can be exported}
```

since it reduces more the uncertainty of what the original query is. That is, if we hid the query {*apple, ume, pawpaw, quince*} from a person, the first set of properties would help more that person guess the query elements than the second properties.

In Section 4, we describe two models for measuring this uncertainty reduction and in Section 5.1, we describe an evaluation methodology for quantifying this reduction in uncertainty using human judgments.

3.1 Source of Properties

What is the source of the semantic properties to be used as explanations? Following Lin (1998), we use syntactic dependencies between words to model their semantic properties. The assumption here is that some grammatical relations, such as *subject* and *object* can often yield semantic properties of terms. For example, given enough corpus occurrences of a phrase like "*students eat many apples*", then we can infer the properties *can-be-eaten* for *apples* and *can-eat* for *students*. Unfortunately, many grammatical relations do not specify semantic properties, such as most *conjunction* relations for example. In this paper, we use a combination of corpus statistics and manual filters of grammatical relations (such as omitting conjunction relations) to uncover candidate semantic properties, as described in the next section. With this method, we unfortunately uncover some non-semantic properties and fail to uncover some correct semantic properties.

[3] This topic is the focus of (Vyas and Pantel 2008).

Improving the candidate lists of semantic properties is grounds for further investigation.

3.2 Extracting Properties

Given a set of similar terms, we look at the overlapping syntactic dependencies between the words in the set to form candidate semantic properties. Example properties extracted by our system (described below) for a random sample of two instances from a cluster of food, {*apple*, *beef*}, include[4]:

```
shredded, sliced, lean, sour, de-
licious, cooked, import, export,
eat, cook, dice, taste, market,
consume, slice, ...
```

We obtain candidate properties by parsing a large textual corpus with the Minipar parser (Lin 1993)[5]. For each word in the corpus, we extract all of its dependency links, forming a feature vector of syntactic dependencies. For example, below is a sample of the feature vector for the word *apple*:

```
adj-mod:gala, adj-mod:shredded,
object-of:caramelize, object-of:eat,
object-of:import, ...
```

Intersecting *apple*'s feature vector with *beef*'s, we are left with the following candidate properties:

```
adj-mod:shredded, object-of:eat,
object-of:import, ...
```

In this paper, we omit the relation name of the syntactic dependencies, and instead write:

```
shredded, eat, import, ...
```

This list of syntactic dependencies forms the candidate properties for our ranking task defined in Section 3.

In Section 4, we use corpus statistics over these syntactic dependencies to find the most informative properties that explain the similarity of a set of terms. Some syntactic dependencies are not reliably descriptive of the similarity of words such as conjunctions and determiners. We omit these dependency links from our model.

4 Ranking Models

In this section, we present our ranking models for choosing the *n*-best results to a query according to our task definition from Section 3. The models are expected to generalize to many ranking tasks, however in this paper we focus solely on the problem of choosing the best semantic properties that describe the similarity of a set of terms.

In the next section, we outline our baseline independent model, which is based on a commonly used ranking metric in lexical semantics for selecting the most informative properties of a term. Then in Section 4.2, we propose our new model for considering the properties jointly.

4.1 EIIR: Expected Independent Information Ranking Model (Baseline Model)

Recall the task definition from Section 3. Finding a property r that most reduces the uncertainty in a query set Q can be modeled by measuring the strength of association between r and Q. Following Pantel and Lin (2002), we use pointwise mutual information (*pmi*) to measure the association strength between two events q and r, where q is a term in Q and r is syntactic dependency, as follows (Church and Hanks 1989):

$$pmi(q,r) = \log \frac{\frac{c(q,r)}{N}}{\frac{\sum_{w \in W} c(w,r)}{N} \times \frac{\sum_{f \in F} c(q,f)}{N}} \qquad (4.1)$$

where $c(q,r)$ is the frequency of r in the feature vector of q (as defined in Section 3.2), W is the set of all words in our corpus, F is the set of all syntactic dependencies in our corpus, and $N = \sum_{w \in W} \sum_{f \in F} c(w,f)$ is the total frequency count of all features of all words.

We estimate the association strength between a property r and a set of terms Q by taking the expected *pmi* between r and each term in Q as:

$$pmi(Q,r) = \sum_{q \in Q} P(q)\, pmi(q,r) \qquad (4.2)$$

where $P(q)$ is the probability of q in the corpus.

Finally, the EIIR model chooses an *n*-best list by selecting the n properties from R that have highest $pmi(Q, r)$.

4.2 JIR: Joint Information Ranking Model

The hypothesis of this paper is that considering items in an *n*-best result set jointly for ranking produces better result sets than considering them independently, an example of which is shown in Section 1.

Recall our task definition from Section 3: to select an *n*-best list R' from R such that it most reduces the uncertainty of Q. Recall that for explaining the similarity of terms, Q is the set of

[4] We omit the syntactic relations for readability.

[5] Section 5.1 describes the specific corpus and method that was used to obtain our reported results.

query words to be explained and R is the set of all properties shared by words in Q. The above task of finding R' can be captured by the following objective function:

$$R' = \underset{R' \subset R}{\arg\min}\, I(Q \mid R') \tag{4.3}$$

where $I(Q|R')$ is the amount of information in Q given R':[6]

$$I(Q \mid R') = \sum_{q \in Q} P(q) \times I(q \mid R') \tag{4.4}$$

where $P(q)$ is the probability of term q in our corpus (defined in the Section 4.1) and $I(q|R')$ is the amount of information in q given R', which is defined as the conditional self-information between q and R' (Merhav and Feder 1998):

$$\begin{aligned} I(q \mid R') &= I(q \mid r_1, r_2, \ldots, r_n) \\ &= -\log P(q \mid r_1, r_2, \ldots, r_n) \\ &= -\log \frac{c(q, R')}{c(*, R')} \end{aligned} \tag{4.5}$$

where $c(q,R')$ is the frequency of all properties in R' occurring with word q and $*$ represents all possible terms in the corpus[7]. We have:

$$c(q, R') = \sum_{r \in R'} c(q, r) \text{ and } c(*, R') = \sum_{r \in R'} \sum_{q \in Q'} c(q, r)$$

where $c(q,r)$ is defined as in Section 4.1 and Q' is the set of all words that have all the properties in R'. Computing $c(*,R')$ efficiently can be done using a reverse index from properties to terms.

The *Joint Information Ranking* model (JIR) is the objective function in Eq. 4.3. We find a suboptimal solution to Eq. 4.3 using a greedy algorithm by starting with an empty set R' and iteratively adding one property r at a time into R' such that:

$$r = \underset{r \in R - R'}{\arg\min} \sum_{q \in Q} P(q) \times I(q \mid R' \cup r) \tag{4.6}$$

The intuition behind this algorithm is as follows: when choosing a property r to add to a partial result set, we should choose the r that contributes the maximum amount of information to the existing set (where all properties are considered jointly).

[6] Note that finding the set R' that minimizes the amount of information in Q given R' equates to finding the R' that reduces most the uncertainty in Q.

[7] Note that each property in R' is shared by q because of the way the candidate properties in R were constructed (see Section 3.2).

A brute force optimal solution to Eq. 4.3 involves computing $I(Q|R')$ for all subsets R' of size n of R. In future work, we will investigate heuristic search algorithms for finding better solutions to Eq. 4.3, but our experimental results discussed in Section 5 show that our greedy solution to Eq. 4.3 already yields significantly better n-best lists than the baseline EIIR model.

5 Experimental Results

In this section, we show empirical evidence that considering items in an n-best result set jointly for ranking produces better result sets than considering them independently. We validate this claim by testing whether or not human judges prefer the set of explanations generated by our joint model (JIR) over the independent model (EIIR).

5.1 Experimental Setup

We trained the probabilities described in Section 4 using corpus statistics extracted from the TREC-9 and TREC-2002 Aquaint collections consisting of approximately 600 million words. We used the Minipar parser (Lin 1993) to analyze each sentence and we collected the frequency counts of the grammatical contexts output by Minipar and used them to compute the probability and pointwise mutual information values from Sections 4.1 and 4.2. Given any set of words Q from the corpus, our joint and independent models generate a ranked list of n-best explanations (i.e., properties) for the similarity of the words.

Recall the example set Q = {*apple*, *beef*} from Section 3.2. Following Section 3.2, all grammatical contexts output by Minipar that both words share form a candidate explanation set R for their similarity. For {*apple*, *beef*}, our systems found 312 candidate explanations. Applying the independent ranking model, EIIR, we obtain the following top-5 best explanations, R':

```
product, import of, export, ban
on, industry
```

Using the joint model, JIR, we obtain:

```
export, product, eat, ban on,
from menu
```

5.2 Comparing Ranking Models

In order to obtain a representative set of similar terms as queries to our systems, we randomly chose 100 concepts from the CBC collection (Pantel and Lin 2002) consisting of 1628 clusters of nouns. For each of these concepts, we randomly chose a set of cluster instances (nouns),

Table 1. Confusion matrix between the two judges on the annotation task over all explanation set sizes ($n = 1 \ldots 5$).

	JIR	*EIIR*	*EQUAL*
JIR	**153**	2	48
EIIR	11	**33**	19
EQUAL	29	7	**198**

Table 2. Inter-annotator agreement statistics over varying explanation set sizes *n*.

n	*AGREEMENT (%)*	*KAPPA (κ)*
1	75.0	0.47
2	70.0	0.50
3	77.0	0.62
4	78.0	0.63
5	84.0	0.73

where the size of each set was randomly chosen to consist of two or three noun (chosen to reduce the runtime of our algorithm). For example, three of our randomly sampled concepts were *Music*, *Flowers*, and *Alcohol* and below are the random instances selected from these concepts:

- {*concerto*, *quartet*, *Fifth Symphony*}
- {*daffodil*, *lily*}
- {*gin*, *alcohol*, *rum*}

Each of these three samples forms a query. Applying both our *EIIR* and *JIR* models, we generated the top-5 explanations for each of the 100 samples. For example, below are the explanations returned for {*daffodil*, *lily*}:

- **EIIR**: *bulb, bouquet of, yellow, pink, hybrid*
- **JIR**: *flowering, bulb, bouquet of, hybrid, yellow*

Two judges then independently annotated 500 test cases using the following scheme. For each of the 100 samples, a judge is presented with the sample along with the top-1 explanation of both systems, randomly ordered for each sample such that the judge can never know which system generated which explanation. The judge then must make one of the following three choices:

- **Explanation 1**: The judge prefers the first explanation to the second.
- **Explanation 2**: The judge prefers the second explanation to the first.
- **Equal**: The judge cannot determine that one explanation is better than the other.

The judge is then presented with the top-2 explanations from each system, then the top-3, top-4, and finally the top-5 explanations, making the above annotation decision each time. Once the judge has seen the top-5 explanations for the sample, the judge moves on to the next sample and repeats this process until all 100 samples are annotated. Allowing the judges to see the top-1, top-2, up to top-5 explanations allows us to later inspect how our ranking algorithms perform on different sizes of explanation sets.

The above annotation task was performed independently by two judges and the resulting agreement between the judges, using the Kappa statistic (Siegel and Castellan Jr. 1988), was $\kappa = 0.60$. Table 1 lists the full confusion matrix on the annotation task. On just the annotations of the top-5 explanations, the agreement was $\kappa = 0.73$. Table 2 lists the Kappas for the different sizes of explanation sets. It is more difficult for judges to determine the quality of smaller explanation sets.

For the above top-5 explanations for the query {*daffodil*, *lily*}, both judges preferred the JIR properties since *flowering* was deemed more informative than *pink* given that we also know the property *yellow*.

5.2.1 Evaluation Results

Table 3 shows sample *n*-best lists generated by our system and Table 4 presents the results of the experiment described in the previous section. Table 4 lists the preferences of the judges for the *n*-best lists generated by the independent and joint models, in terms of the percentage of samples preferred by each judge on each model. We report our results on both all 500 annotations and on the 100 annotations for the explanation sets of size $n = 5$. Instead of using an adjudicator for resolving the two judges' disagreements, we weighted each judge's decision by 0.5. We used bootstrap resampling to obtain the 95% confidence intervals.

The judges significantly preferred the joint model over the independent model. Looking at all annotated explanation sets (varying *n* from 1 to 5), the *n*-best lists from *JIR* were preferred 39.7% of the time. On the 50.0% ± 3.1% test cases where one list was preferred over another, the JIR lists were preferred overall 76.6% ± 5.2% of the time, with 95% confidence. Caution should be taken when interpreting the results for $n < 3$ since the annotator agreement for these was very low. However, as shown in Figure 1, human preference for the *JIR* model was higher at $n \geq 3$.

Table 3. Five example *n*-best lists, drawn from our random sample described in Section 5.1, using the joint *JIR* model and the independent *EIIR* model (for *n*=5).

Query (Q)	*JIR n-best (R')*	*EIIR n-best (R')*
{gin, alcohol, rum}	*drink, spike with, sell, use, consume*	*sell, drink, use, consume, buy*
{Temple University, Michigan State}	*political science at, professor at, director at, student at, attend*	*professor at, professor, director at, student at, student*
{concerto, quartet, Fifth Symphony}	*Beethoven, his, play, write, performance*	*his, play, write, performance, perform*
{ranch house, loft}	*offer, brick, sprawling, rambling, turn-of-the-century*	*his, live, her, buy, small*
{dysentery, tuberculosis}	*morbidity, die of, case, patient, suffer from*	*die of, case, patient, case of, have*

Table 4. Percentage of test cases where the judges preferred *JIR* vs. *EIIR* vs. they had no preference, computed over all explanation set sizes ($n = 1 \ldots 5$) vs. only the explanation sets of size $n = 5$.

SYSTEM	ALL (95% CONF†)	N=5 (95% CONF†)
JIR	39.7% ± 3.0%	43.7% ± 6.9%
EIIR	10.4% ± 1.3%	10.1% ± 4.2%
Equal	50.0% ± 3.1%	45.2% ± 6.9%

†95% confidence intervals estimated using bootstrap resampling.

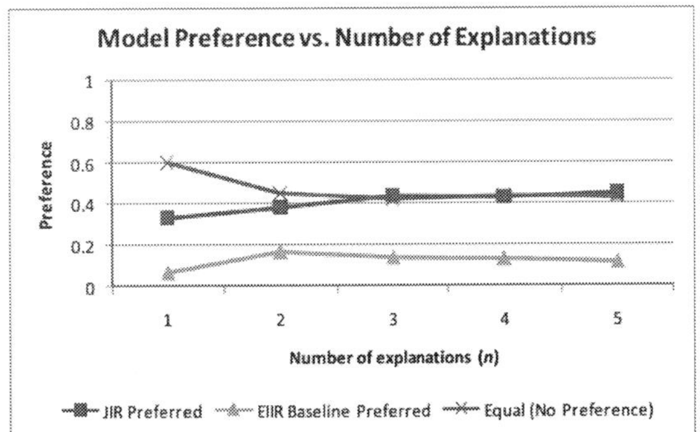

Figure 1. Percentage of human preference for each model with varying sizes of explanation sets (*n*).

5.2.2 Discussion and Error Analysis

Figure 1 illustrates the annotated preferences over varying sizes of explanation sets, for $n \in [1 .. 5]$. Except in the case where only one explanation is returned, we see consistent preferences between the judges. Manual inspection of the size 1 explanation sets showed that often one property is not enough to understand the similarity of the query words. For example, consider the following two explanation sets: *{sell}* and *{drink}*. If you did not know the original query *Q*, one list would not be much better than the other in determining what the query was. But, by adding one more property, we get: *{sell, drink}* and *{drink, spike with}*. The second explanation list reduces much more the uncertainty that the query consists of *alcoholic beverages*, as you probably guessed (the first list also reduces the uncertainty, but not as much as the second). The above example is taken from our random sample list for the query words *{gin, alcohol, rum}* – the explanation *{drink, spike with}* was generated using the JIR model.

We manually inspected some of the sample queries where both judges preferred the EIIR *n*-best list. One such sample query was: *{Jerry Falwell, Jim Bakker, Pat Robertson}*. The *n*-best lists returned by the JIR and EIIR models respectively were *{televangelist, evangelist, Rev., television, founder}* and *{evangelist, television, Rev., founder, religious}*. Both judges preferred the EIIR list because of the overlap in information between *televangelist* and *evangelist*. The problem here in JIR was that the word *televangelist* was very rare in the corpus and thus few terms had both the feature *televangelist* and *evangelist*. We would expect in a larger corpus to see a larger overlap with the two features, in which case *evangelist* would not be chosen by the JIR model.

As discussed in Section 2, considering results jointly is not a new idea and is very similar to the concept of diversity-based ranking introduced in the IR community by Carbonell and Goldstein (1998). Their proposed technique, called maximal marginal relevance (MMR), forms the basis of most schemes used today and works as follows. Initially, each result item is scored independently of the others. Then, the *n*-best list is selected by iteratively choosing the highest scoring result and then discounting each remaining candidate's score by some function of the similarity (or information gain) between that candidate and the currently selected members of the *n*-best list. In practice, these heuristic-based algorithms are fast to compute and are used heavily by commercial IR engines. The purpose of this paper is to investigate a principled definition of diversity using the concept of maximal joint information. The objective function proposed in Eq. 4.3 provides a basis for understanding diversity through the lens of information theory. Although this paper focuses on the task of explaining the similarity of terms, we plan in future work to apply our method to an IR task in order to compare and contrast our method with MMR.

6 Conclusion

This paper investigates the problem of *n*-best ranking on the lexical semantics task of explaining/characterizing the similarity of a group of terms where only a small set of many possible semantic properties may be displayed to a user. We propose that considering the results jointly, by accounting for the information overlap between results, helps generate better *n*-best lists. We presented an information theoretic objective function, called *Joint Information Ranking*, for modeling the joint information in an *n*-best list. On our lexical semantics task, empirical evidence shows that humans significantly prefer JIR *n*-best lists over a baseline model that considers the explanations independently. Our results show that the *n*-best lists generated by the joint model are judged to be significantly different from those generated by the independent model 50.0% ± 3.1% of the time, out of which they are preferred 76.6% ± 5.2% of the time, with 95% confidence.

In future work, we plan to investigate other joint models using latent semantic analysis techniques, and to investigate heuristic algorithms to both optimize search efficiency and to better approximate our *JIR* objective function. Although applied only to the task of characterizing the similarity of terms, it is our hope that the JIR model will generalize well to many ranking tasks, from keyword search ranking, to recommendation systems, to advertisement placements.

References

Barzilay, R.; McKeown, K.; and Elhadad, M. 1999. Information Fusion in the Context of Multi-Document Summarization. In *Proceedings of ACL-1999*. pp. 550-557. College Park, MD.

Brin, S. and Page, L. 1998. The Anatomy of a Large-Scale Hypertextual Web Search Engine. *Computer Networks and ISDN Systems*, 30:107-117.

Carbonell, J. G. and Goldstein, J. 1998. The Use of MMR, Diversity-Based Reranking for Reordering Documents and Producing Summaries. In *Proceedings of SIGIR-1998*. pp. 335-336.

Charniak, E. and Johnson, M. 2005. Coarse-to-fine n-best parsing and MaxEnt disciriminative reranking. In *Proceedings of ACL-2005*. pp. 173-180. Ann Arbor, MI.

Church, K. and Hanks, P. 1989. Word association norms, mutual information, and lexicography. In *Proceedings of ACL-89*. pp. 76-83. Vancouver, Canada.

Collins, M. and Koo, T. 2000. Discriminative Reranking for Natural Laguage Parsing. In *Proceedings ICML-2000*. pp. 175-182. Palo Alto, CA

Freund, Y.; Iyer, R.; Schapier, E.R and Singer, Y. 2003. An efficient boosting algorithm for combining preferences. The Journal of Machine Learning Research, 4:933-969.

Harris, Z. 1985. Distributional structure. In: Katz, J. J. (ed.) *The Philosophy of Linguistics*. New York: Oxford University Press. pp. 26-47.

Hearst, M. A. and Pedersen, J. O. 1996. Reexamining the cluster hypothesis: Scatter/gather on retrieval results. In *Proceedings of SIGIR-1996*. pp. 76-84. Zurich, Switzerland.

Hovy, E.H. and Lin, C.-Y. 1998. Automated Text Summarization in SUMMARIST. In M. Maybury and I. Mani (eds), *Advances in Automatic Text Summarization. Cambridge*, MIT Press.

Kleinberg, J. 1998. Authoritative sources in a hyperlinked environment. In *Proceedings of the Ninth Annual ACM-SIAM Symposium on Discrete Algorithms*. Pp. 668-677. New York, NY.

Leuski, A. 2001. Evaluating document clustering for interactive information retrieval. In *Proceedings of CIKM-2001*. pp. 33-40. Atlanta, GA.

Lin, D. 1998. Automatic retrieval and clustering of similar words. In *Proceedings of COLING/ACL-98*. pp. 768-774. Montreal, Canada.

Lin, D. 1993. Parsing Without OverGeneration. In *Proceedings of ACL-93*. pp. 112-120. Columbus, OH.

Liu, X. and Croft, W. B. 2004. Cluster-based retrieval using language models. In *Proceedings of SIGIR-2004*. pp. 186-193. Sheffield, UK.

Merhav, N. and Feder, M. 1998. Universal Prediction. *IEEE Transactions on Information Theory*, 44(6):2124-2147.

Page, L.; Brin, S.; Motwani R.; Winograd, T. 1998. *The PageRank Citation Ranking: Bringing Order to the Web*. Stanford Digital Library Technologies Project.

Pantel, P. and Lin, D. 2002. Discovering Word Senses from Text. In *Proceedings of KDD-02*. pp. 613-619. Edmonton, Canada.

Resnick, P. and Varian, H. R. 1997. Recommender Systems. *Communications of the ACM*, 40(3):56-58.

Salton, G. and Buckley, C. 1987. Term Weighting Approaches in Automatic Text Retrieval. *Technical Report:TR81-887*, Ithaca, NY.

Salton, G. and McGill, M. J. 1983. *Introduction to Modern Information Retrieval*. McGraw Hill.

Shardanand, U. and Maes, P. 1995. Social Information Filtering: Algorithms for Automating "Word of Mouth". In *Proceedings of ACM CHI-1995*. pp. 210-217. New York.

Siegel, S. and Castellan Jr., N. J. 1988. Nonparametric Statistics for the Behavioral Sciences. McGraw-Hill.

Spretus, E.; Sahami, M.; and Buyukkokten, O. 2005. Evaluating Similarity Measures: A Large-Scale Study in the Orkut Social Network. In *Proceedings of SIGKDD-2005*. pp. 678-684. Chicago, IL.

Vyas, V. and Pantel, P. 2008. Explaining Similarity of Terms. In *Proceedings of COLING-2008*. Manchester, England.

Zhu, X.; Goldberg, A.; Van Gael, J.; and Andrzejewski, D. 2007. Improving Diversity in Ranking using Absorbing Random Walks. In *Proceedings of NAACL HLT 2007*. pp. 97-104. Rochester, NY.

Zhang, Y,; Callan, J.; and Minka, T. 2002. Novelty and redundancy detection in adaptive filtering. In *Proceedings of SIGIR-2002*. pp. 81-88. Tampere, Finland.

Zhang, Y.; Hildebrand, A. S.; and Vogel, S. 2006. Distributed Language Modeling for N-best List Re-ranking. In *Proceedings of EMNLP-2006*. Pp. 216-223. Sydney, Australia.

AUTHOR INDEX

AUTHOR INDEX

AUTHOR INDEX

AUTHOR INDEX

AUTHOR INDEX

Association for Computational Linguistics
209 N. Eighth Street
Stroudsburg, Pennsylvania 18360

CURRAN ASSOCIATES INC
proceedings.com

22nd International Conference on Computational Linguistics

(COLING 2008)

Manchester, United Kingdom
18-22 August 2008

Volume 2 of 2

ISBN: 978-1-62993-615-4

22nd International Conference on Computational Linguistics

(COLING 2008)

Manchester, United Kingdom
18-22 August 2008

Volume 2 of 2

ISBN: 978-1-62993-615-4

Printed from e-media with permission by:

Curran Associates, Inc.
57 Morehouse Lane
Red Hook, NY 12571

Some format issues inherent in the e-media version may also appear in this print version.

Copyright© (2008) by the Association for Computational Linguistics
All rights reserved.

Printed by Curran Associates, Inc. (2014)

For permission requests, please contact the Association for Computational Linguistics
at the address below.

Association for Computational Linguistics
209 N. Eighth Street
Stroudsburg, Pennsylvania 18360

Phone: 1-570-476-8006
Fax: 1-570-476-0860

acl@aclweb.org

Additional copies of this publication are available from:

Curran Associates, Inc.
57 Morehouse Lane
Red Hook, NY 12571 USA
Phone: 845-758-0400
Fax: 845-758-2634
Email: curran@proceedings.com
Web: www.proceedings.com

TABLE OF CONTENTS

VOLUME 1

PROCEEDINGS OF THE CONFERENCE

VOLUME 2

POSTERS

DEMONSTRATION PAPERS

Scientific Paper Summarization Using Citation Summary Networks

Vahed Qazvinian
School of Information
University of Michigan
Ann Arbor, MI
vahed@umich.edu

Dragomir R. Radev
Department of EECS and
School of Information
University of Michigan
Ann Arbor, MI
radev@umich.edu

Abstract

Quickly moving to a new area of research is painful for researchers due to the vast amount of scientific literature in each field of study. One possible way to overcome this problem is to summarize a scientific topic. In this paper, we propose a model of summarizing a single article, which can be further used to summarize an entire topic. Our model is based on analyzing others' viewpoint of the target article's contributions and the study of its citation summary network using a clustering approach.

1 Introduction

It is quite common for researchers to have to quickly move into a new area of research. For instance, someone trained in text generation may want to learn about parsing and someone who knows summarization well, may need to learn about question answering. In our work, we try to make this transition as painless as possible by automatically generating summaries of an entire research topic. This enables a researcher to find the chronological order and the progress in that particular field of study. An ideal such system will receive a topic of research, as the user query, and will return a summary of related work on that topic. In this paper, we take the first step toward building such a system.

Studies have shown that different citations to the same article often focus on different aspects of that article, while none alone may cover a full description of its entire contributions. Hence, the set of citation summaries, can be a good resource to understand the main contributions of a paper and how that paper affects others. The *citation summary* of an article (A), as defined in (Elkiss et al., 2008), is a the set of citing sentences pointing to that article. Thus, this source contains information about A from others' point of view. Part of a sample citation summary is as follows:

In the context of DPs, this edge based factorization method was proposed by **(Eisner, 1996)**.

Eisner (1996) *gave a generative model with a cubic parsing algorithm based on an edge factorization of trees.*

Eisner **(Eisner, 1996)** *proposed an $O(n^3)$ parsing algorithm for PDG.*

If the parse has to be projective, Eisner's bottom-up-span algorithm **(Eisner, 1996)** *can be used for the search.*

The problem of summarizing a whole scientific topic, in its simpler form, may reduce to summarizing one particular article. A citation summary can be a good resource to make a summary of a target paper. Then using each paper's summary and some knowledge of the citation network, we'll be able to generate a summary of an entire topic. Analyzing citation networks is an important component of this goal, and has been widely studied before (Newman, 2001).

Our main contribution in this paper is to use citation summaries and network analysis techniques to produce a summary of a single scientific article as a framework for future research on topic summarization. Given that the citation summary of any article usually has more than a few sentences, the main challenge of this task is to find a *subset* of these sentences that will lead to a better and shorter summary.

© 2008. Licensed under the *Creative Commons Attribution-Noncommercial-Share Alike 3.0 Unported* license (http://creativecommons.org/licenses/by-nc-sa/3.0/). Some rights reserved.

Cluster	Nodes	Edges
DP	167	323
PBMT	186	516
Summ	839	1425
QA	238	202
TE	56	44

Table 1: Clusters and their citation network size

1.1 Related Work

Although there has been work on analyzing citation and collaboration networks (Teufel et al., 2006; Newman, 2001) and scientific article summarization (Teufel and Moens, 2002), to the knowledge of the author there is no previous work that study the text of the citation summaries to produce a summary. (Bradshaw, 2003; Bradshaw, 2002) get benefit from citations to determine the content of articles and introduce "Reference Directed Indexing" to improve the results of a search engine.

In other work, (Nanba et al., 2004b; Nanba et al., 2004a) analyze citation sentences and automatically categorize citations into three groups using 160 pre-defined phrase-based rules. This categorization is then used to build a tool for survey generation. (Nanba and Okumura, 1999) also discuss the same citation categorization to support a system for writing a survey. (Nanba and Okumura, 1999; Nanba et al., 2004b) report that co-citation implies similarity by showing that the textual similarity of co-cited papers is proportional to the proximity of their citations in the citing article.

Previous work has shown the importance of the citation summaries in understanding what a paper says. The *citation summary* of an article A is the set of sentences in other articles which cite A. (Elkiss et al., 2008) performed a large-scale study on citation summaries and their importance. They conducted several experiments on a set of $2,497$ articles from the free PubMed Central (PMC) repository[1]. Results from this experiment confirmed that the "Self Cohesion" (Elkiss et al., 2008) of a citation summary of an article is consistently higher than the that of its abstract. (Elkiss et al., 2008) also conclude that citation summaries are more focused than abstracts, and that they contain additional information that does not appear in abstracts. (Kupiec et al., 1995) use the abstracts of scientific articles as a target summary, where they use 188 Engineering Information summaries that are mostly indicative in nature. Abstracts tend to summarize the documents topics well, however, they don't include much use of metadata. (Kan et al., 2002) use annotated bibliographies to cover certain aspects of summarization and suggest guidelines that summaries should also include metadata and critical document features as well as the prominent content-based features.

Siddharthan and Teufel describe a new task to decide the scientific attribution of an article (Siddharthan and Teufel, 2007) and show high human agreement as well as an improvement in the performance of Argumentative Zoning (Teufel, 2005). Argumentative Zoning is a rhetorical classification task, in which sentences are labeled as one of Own, Other, Background, Textual, Aim, Basis, Contrast according to their role in the author's argument. These all show the importance of citation summaries and the vast area for new work to analyze them to produce a summary for a given topic.

2 Data

The ACL Anthology is a collection of papers from the Computational Linguistics journal, and proceedings from ACL conferences and workshops and includes almost $11,000$ papers. To produce the **ACL A**nthology **N**etwork (AAN), (Joseph and Radev, 2007) manually performed some preprocessing tasks including parsing references and building the network metadata, the citation, and the author collaboration networks.

The full AAN includes all citation and collaboration data within the ACL papers, with the citation network consisting of $8,898$ nodes and $38,765$ directed edges.

2.1 Clusters

We built our corpus by extracting small clusters from the AAN data. Each cluster includes papers with a specific phrase in the title or content. We used a very simple approach to collect papers of a cluster, which are likely to be talking about the same topic. Each cluster consists of a set of articles, in which the topic phrase is matched within the title or the content of papers in AAN. In particular, the five clusters that we collected this way, are: **D**ependency **P**arsing (DP), **P**hrased **B**ased **M**achine **T**ranslation (PBMT), Text **Summ**arization (Summ), **Q**uestion **A**nswering (QA), and **T**extual **E**ntailment (TE). Table 1 shows the number of articles and citations in each cluster. For the evaluation purpose we

[1]http://www.pubmedcentral.gov

	ACL-ID	Title	Year	CS Size
DP	C96-1058	Three New Probabilistic Models For Dependency Parsing: An Exploration	1996	66
	P97-1003	Three Generative, Lexicalized Models For Statistical Parsing	1997	55
	P99-1065	A Statistical Parser For Czech	1999	54
	P05-1013	Pseudo-Projective Dependency Parsing	2005	40
	P05-1012	On-line Large-Margin Training Of Dependency Parsers	2005	71
PBMT	N03-1017	Statistical Phrase-Based Translation	2003	180
	W03-0301	An Evaluation Exercise For Word Alignment	2003	14
	J04-4002	The Alignment Template Approach To Statistical Machine Translation	2004	50
	N04-1033	Improvements In Phrase-Based Statistical Machine Translation	2004	24
	P05-1033	A Hierarchical Phrase-Based Model For Statistical Machine Translation	2005	65
Summ	A00-1043	Sentence Reduction For Automatic Text Summarization	2000	19
	A00-2024	Cut And Paste Based Text Summarization	2000	20
	C00-1072	The Automated Acquisition Of Topic Signatures For Text Summarization	2000	19
	W00-0403	Centroid-Based Summarization Of Multiple Documents: Sentence Extraction, ...	2000	31
	W03-0510	The Potential And Limitations Of Automatic Sentence Extraction For Summarization	2003	15
QA	A00-1023	A Question Answering System Supported By Information Extraction	2000	13
	W00-0603	A Rule-Based Question Answering System For Reading Comprehension Tests	2002	19
	P02-1006	Learning Surface Text Patterns For A Question Answering System	2002	74
	D03-1017	Towards Answering Opinion Questions: Separating Facts From Opinions ...	2003	42
	P03-1001	Offline Strategies For Online Question Answering: Answering Questions Before They Are Asked	2003	27
TE	D04-9907	Scaling Web-Based Acquisition Of Entailment Relations	2004	12
	H05-1047	A Semantic Approach To Recognizing Textual Entailment	2005	8
	H05-1079	Recognising Textual Entailment With Logical Inference	2005	9
	W05-1203	Measuring The Semantic Similarity Of Texts	2005	17
	P05-1014	The Distributional Inclusion Hypotheses And Lexical Entailment	2005	10

Table 2: Papers chosen from clusters for evaluation, with their publication year, and citation summary size

chose five articles from each cluster. Table 2 shows the title, year, and citation summary size for the 5 papers chosen from each cluster. The citation summary size of a paper is the size of the set of citation sentences that cite that paper.

3 Analysis

3.1 Fact Distribution

We started with an annotation task on 25 papers, listed in Table 2, and asked a number of annotators to read the citation summary of each paper and extract a list of the main contributions of that paper. Each item on the list is a *non-overlapping contribution* (***fact***) perceived by reading the citation summary. We asked the annotators to focus on the citation summary to do the task and not on their background on this topic.

As our next step we manually created the union of the shared and similar facts by different annotators to make a list of facts for each paper. This fact list made it possible to review all sentences in the citation summary to see which facts each sentence contained. There were also some unshared facts, facts that only appear in one annotator's result, which we ignored for this paper.

Table 3 shows the shared and unshared facts extracted by four annotators for P99-1065.

The manual annotation of P99-1065 shows that the fact "Czech DP" appears in 10 sentences out of all 54 sentences in the citation summary. This shows the importance of this fact, and that "Dependency Parsing of Czech" is one of the main contributions of this paper. Table 3 also shows the number of times each shared fact appears in P99-1065's citation summary sorted by occurrence.

	Fact	Occurrences
Shared	f_4: "Czech DP"	10
	f_1: "lexical rules"	6
	f_3: "POS/ tag classification"	6
	f_2: "constituency parsing"	5
	f_5: "Punctuation"	2
	f_6: "Reordering Technique"	2
	f_7: "Flat Rules"	2
Unshared	"Dependency conversion"	
	"80% UAS"	
	"97.0% F-measure"	
	"Generative model"	
	'Relabel coordinated phrases"	
	'Projective trees"	
	"Markovization"	

Table 3: Facts of P99-1065

After scanning through all sentences in the citation summary, we can come up with a ***fact distribution matrix*** for an article. The rows of this matrix represent sentences in the citation summary and the columns show facts. A 1 value in this matrix means that the sentence covers the fact. The matrix D shows the fact distribution of P99-1065. IDs in each row show the citing article's ACL ID, and the sentence number in the citation summary. These matrices, created using annotations, are particularly useful in the evaluation process.

$$
D = \left(\begin{array}{c|ccccccc}
 & f_1 & f_2 & f_3 & f_4 & f_5 & f_6 & f_7 \\
\hline
W06\text{-}2935{:}1 & 1 & 0 & 0 & 0 & 0 & 0 & 0 \\
W06\text{-}2935{:}2 & 0 & 0 & 0 & 0 & 0 & 0 & 0 \\
W06\text{-}2935{:}3 & 0 & 0 & 1 & 1 & 0 & 0 & 0 \\
W06\text{-}2935{:}4 & 0 & 0 & 0 & 0 & 0 & 0 & 1 \\
W06\text{-}2935{:}5 & 0 & 0 & 0 & 0 & 0 & 0 & 0 \\
W06\text{-}2935{:}6 & 0 & 0 & 0 & 0 & 1 & 0 & 0 \\
W05\text{-}1505{:}7 & 0 & 1 & 0 & 1 & 0 & 0 & 0 \\
W05\text{-}1505{:}8 & 0 & 0 & 0 & 0 & 0 & 1 & 0 \\
\vdots & \vdots & & & \vdots & & & \vdots \\
W05\text{-}1518{:}54 & 0 & 0 & 0 & 0 & 0 & 0 & 0
\end{array}\right)
$$

3.2 Similarity Measures

We want to build a network with citing sentences as nodes and similarities of two sentences as edge weights. We'd like this network to have a nice community structure, whereby each cluster corresponds to a fact. So, a similarity measure in which we are interested is the one which results in high values for pairs of sentences that cover the same facts. On the other hand, it should return a low value for pairs that do not share a common contribution of the target article.

The following shows two sample sentences from P99-1065 that cover the same fact and we want the chosen similarity measure to return a high value for them:

So, Collins et al (1999) proposed a tag classification for parsing the Czech treebank.

The Czech parser of Collins et al (1999) was run on a different data set... .

Conversely, we'd like the similarity of the two following sentences that cover no shared facts, to be quite low:

Collins (1999) explicitly added features to his parser to improve punctuation dependency parsing accuracy.

The trees are then transformed into Penn Treebank style constituencies- using the technique described in (Collins et al, 1999).

We used P99-1065 as the training sample, on which similarity metrics were trained, and left the others for the test. To evaluate a similarity measure for our purpose we use a simple approach. For each measure, we sorted the similarity values of all pairs of sentences in P99-1065's citation summary in a descending order. Then we simply counted the number of pairs that cover the same fact (out of 172 such fact sharing pairs) in the top 100, 200 and 300 highly similar ones out of total $2,862$ pairs. Table 4 shows the number of fact sharing pairs among the top highest similar pairs. Table 4 shows how cosine similarity that uses a tf-idf measure outperforms the others. We tried three different policies for computing IDF values to compute cosine similarity: a general IDF, an AAN-specific IDF where IDF values are calculated only using the documents of AAN, and finally DP-specific IDF in which we only used all-DP data set. Table 4 also shows the results for an asymmetric similarity measure, generation probability (Erkan, 2006) as well as two string edit distances: the longest common substring and the Levenshtein distance (Levenshtein, 1966).

Measure	Top 100	Top 200	Top 300
tf-idf (General)	34	66	74
tf-idf (AAN)	34	56	74
LCSS	26	37	54
tf	24	34	46
tf2gen	13	26	35
tf-idf (DP)	16	26	28
Levenshtein	2	9	16

Table 4: Different similarity measures and their performances in favoring fact-sharing sentences. Each column shows the number of fact-sharing pairs among top highly similar pairs.

4 Methodology

In this section we discuss our graph clustering method for article summarization, as well as other baseline methods used for comparisons.

4.1 Network-Based Clustering

The Citation Summary Network of an article A is a network in which each sentence in the citation summary of A is a node. This network is a *complete undirected weighted graph* where the weight of an edge between two nodes shows the *similarity* of the two corresponding sentences of those nodes. The similarity that we use, as described in section 3.2, is such that sentences with the same facts have high similarity values. In other words, strong edges in the citation summary network are likely to indicate a shared fact between two sentences.

A graph clustering method tries to cluster the nodes of a graph in a way that the average intra-cluster similarity is maximum and the average inter-cluster similarity is minimum. To find the communities in the citation summary network we use (Clauset et al., 2004), a hierarchical agglomeration algorithm which works by greedily optimizing the modularity in a linear running time for sparse graphs.

To evaluate how well the clustering method works, we calculated the *purity* for the clusters found of each paper. Purity (Manning et al., 2008) is a method in which each cluster is assigned to the class with the majority vote in the cluster, and then

	ACL-ID	#Facts $\|\mathbb{C}\|$	#Clusters $\|\Omega\|$	$Purity(\Omega, \mathbb{C})$
DP	C96-1058	4	4	0.636
	P97-1003	5	5	0.750
	P99-1065	7	7	0.724
	P05-1013	5	3	0.689
	P05-1012	7	5	0.500
PBMT	N03-1017	8	4	0.464
	W03-0301	3	3	0.777
	J04-4002	5	5	0.807
	N04-1033	5	4	0.615
	P05-1033	6	5	0.650
Summ	A00-1043	5	4	0.812
	A00-2024	5	2	0.333
	C00-1072	3	4	0.857
	W00-0403	6	4	0.682
	W03-0510	4	3	0.727
QA	A00-1023	3	2	0.833
	W00-0603	7	4	0.692
	P02-1006	7	5	0.590
	D03-1017	7	4	0.500
	P03-1001	6	4	0.500
TE	D04-9907	7	3	0.545
	H05-1047	4	3	0.833
	H05-1079	5	3	0.625
	W05-1203	3	3	0.583
	P05-1014	4	2	0.667

Table 5: Number of real facts, clusters and purity for each evaluated article

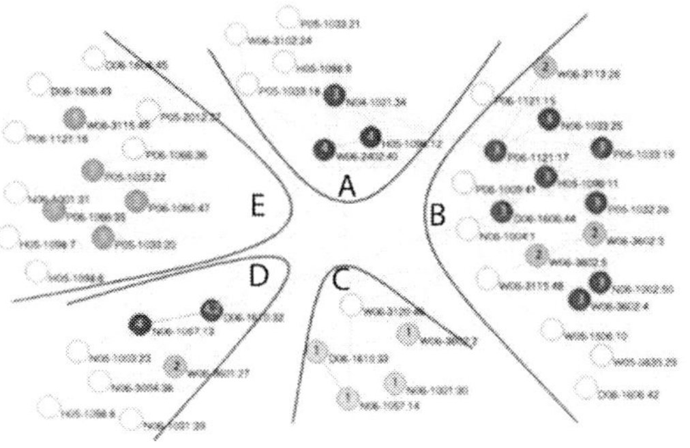

Figure 1: Each node is a sentence in the citation summary for paper J04-4002. Colors (numbers) represent facts and boundaries show the clustering result

the accuracy of this assignment is measured by dividing the number of correctly assigned documents by N. More formally:

$$\text{purity}(\Omega, \mathbb{C}) = \frac{1}{N} \sum_k \max_j |\omega_k \cap c_j|$$

where $\Omega = \{\omega_1, \omega_2, \ldots, \omega_K\}$ is the set of clusters and $\mathbb{C} = \{c_1, c_2, \ldots, c_J\}$ is the set of classes. ω_k is interpreted as the set of documents in ω_k and c_j as the set of documents in c_j. For each evaluated article, Table 5 shows the number of real facts ($|\mathbb{C}| = J$), the number of clusters ($|\Omega| = K$) and $purity(\Omega, \mathbb{C})$ for each evaluated article. Figure 1 shows the clustering result for J04-4002, in which each color (number) shows a real fact, while the boundaries and capital labels show the clustering result.

4.1.1 Sentence Extraction

Once the graph is clustered and communities are formed, to build a summary we extract sentences from the clusters. We tried these two different simple methods:

- *Cluster Round-Robin (C-RR)*
  We start with the largest cluster, and extract sentences in the order they appear in each cluster. So we extract first, the first sentences from each cluster, then the second ones, and so on, until we reach the summary length limit $|S|$. Previously, we mentioned that facts with higher weights appear in greater number of sentences, and clustering aims to cluster such fact-sharing sentences in the same communities. Thus, starting with the largest community is important to ensure that the system summary first covers the facts that have higher frequencies and therefore higher weights.

- *Cluster Lexrank (C-lexrank)*
  The second method we used was Lexrank (Erkan and Radev, 2004) inside each cluster. In other words, for each cluster Ω_i we made a lexical network of *the sentences in that cluster* (N_i) . Using Lexrank we can find the most central sentences in N_i as salient sentences of Ω_i to include in the main summary. We simply choose, for each cluster Ω_i, the most salient sentence of Ω_i, and if we have not reached the summary length limit, we do that for the second most salient sentences of each cluster, and so on. The way of ordering clusters is again by decreasing size.

Table 6 shows the two system summaries generated with C-RR and C-lexrank methods for P99-1065. The sentences in the table appear as they were extracted automatically from the text files of papers, containing sentence fragments and malformations occurring while doing the automatic segmentation.

4.2 Baseline Methods

We also conducted experiments with two baseline approaches. To produce the citation summary we used *Mead*'s (Radev et al., 2004) Random Summary and *Lexrank* (Erkan and Radev, 2004) on the entire citation summary network as baseline techniques. Lexrank is proved to work well in multi-document summarization (Erkan and Radev, 2004). It first builds a lexical network, in which

ID	Sentence
	C-RR
W05-1505:9	3 Constituency Parsing for Dependency Trees A pragmatic justification for using constituency- based parser in order to predict dependency struc- tures is that currently the best Czech dependency- tree parser is a constituency-based parser (Collins et al, 1999; Zeman, 2004).
W04-2407:27	However, since most previous studies instead use the mean attachment score per word (Eisner, 1996; Collins et al, 1999), we will give this measure as well.
J03-4003:33	3 We find lexical heads in Penn Treebank data using the rules described in Appendix A of Collins (1999).
H05-1066:51	Furthermore, we can also see that the MST parsers perform favorably compared to the more powerful lexicalized phrase-structure parsers, such as those presented by Collins et al (1999) and Zeman (2004) that use expensive O(n5) parsing al- gorithms.
E06-1011:21	5.2 Czech Results For the Czech data, we used the predefined train- ing, development and testing split of the Prague Dependency Treebank (Hajic et al, 2001), and the automatically generated POS tags supplied with the data, which we reduce to the POS tag set from Collins et al (1999).
	C-Lexrank
P05-1012:16	The Czech parser of Collins et al (1999) was run on a different data set and most other dependency parsers are evaluated using English.
W04-2407:26	More precisely, parsing accuracy is measured by the attachment score, which is a standard measure used in studies of dependency parsing (Eisner, 1996; Collins et al, 1999).
W05-1505:14	In an attempt to extend a constituency-based pars- ing model to train on dependency trees, Collins transforms the PDT dependency trees into con- stituency trees (Collins et al, 1999).
P06-1033:31	More specifi- cally for PDT, Collins et al (1999) relabel coordi- nated phrases after converting dependency struc- tures to phrase structures, and Zeman (2004) uses a kind of pattern matching, based on frequencies of the parts-of-speech of conjuncts and conjunc- tions.
P05-1012:17	In par- ticular, we used the method of Collins et al (1999) to simplify part-of-speech tags since the rich tags used by Czech would have led to a large but rarely seen set of POS features.

Table 6: System Summaries for P99-1065. (a) Using C-RR, (b) using C-Lexrank with length of 5 sentences

nodes are sentences and a weighted edge between two nodes shows the lexical similarity. Once this network is built, Lexrank performs a random walk to find the most central nodes in the graph and reports them as summary sentences.

5 Experimental Setup

5.1 Evaluation Method

Fact-based evaluation systems have been used in several past projects (Lin and Demner-Fushman, 2006; Marton and Radul, 2006), especially in the TREC question answering track. (Lin and Demner-Fushman, 2006) use stemmed unigram similarity of responses with nugget descriptions to produce the evaluation results, whereas (Marton and Radul, 2006) uses both human judgments and human descriptions to evaluate a response.

An ideal summary in our model is one that covers more facts and more important facts. Our definition for the properties of a "good" summary of a paper is one that is relatively short and consists of the main contributions of that paper. From this viewpoint, there are two criteria for our evaluation metric. First, summaries that contain more important facts are preferred over summaries that cover fewer relevant facts. Second, facts should not be equally weighted in this model, as some of them may show more important contributions of a paper, while others may not.

To evaluate our system, we use the pyramid evaluation method (Nenkova and Passonneau, 2004) at sentence level. Each fact in the citation summary of a paper is a *summarization content unit (SCU)* (Nenkova and Passonneau, 2004), and the fact distribution matrix, created by annotation, provides the information about the importance of each fact in the citation summary.

The score given by the pyramid method for a summary is a ratio of the sum of the weights of its facts to the sum of the weights of an optimal summary. This score ranges from 0 to 1, and high scores show the summary content contain more heavily weighted facts. We believe that if a fact appears in more sentences of the citation summary than another fact, it is more important, and thus should be assigned a higher weight. To weight the facts we build a pyramid, and each fact falls in a tier. Each tier shows the number of sentences a fact appears in. Thus, the number of tiers in the pyramid is equal to the citation summary size. If a fact appears in more sentences, it falls in a higher tier. So, if the fact f_i appears $|f_i|$ times in the citation summary it is assigned to the tier $T_{|f_i|}$.

The pyramid score formula that we use is computed as follows. Suppose the pyramid has n tiers, T_i, where tier T_n on top and T_1 on the bottom. The weight of the facts in tier T_i will be i (i.e. they appeared in i sentences). If $|T_i|$ denotes the number of facts in tier T_i, and D_i is the number of facts in the *summary* that appear in T_i, then the total fact weight for the summary is $D = \sum_{i=1}^{n} i \times D_i$. Additionally, the optimal pyramid score for a summary with X facts, is

$Max = \sum_{i=j+1}^{n} i \times |T_i| + j \times (X - \sum_{i=j+1}^{n} |T_i|)$ where $j = \max_i(\sum_{t=i}^{n} |T_t| \geq X)$. Subsequently, the pyramid score for a summary is calculated as $P = \frac{D}{Max}$.

5.2 Results and Discussion

Based on the described evaluation method we conducted a number of experiments to evaluate different summaries of a given length. In particular, we use a gold standard and a random summary to determine how good a system summary is. The gold standard is a summary of a given length that covers as many highly weighted facts as possible. To make a gold summary we start picking sentences that cover new and highly weighted facts, until the summary length limit is reached. On the other hand, in the random summary sentences are extracted from the citation summary in a random manner. We expect a good system summary to be closer to the gold than it is to the random one.

Table 7 shows the value of pyramid score P, for the experiments on the set of 25 papers. A P score of less than 1 for a gold shows that there are more facts than can be covered with a set of $|S|$ sentences.

This table suggests that C-lexrank has a higher average score, P, for the set of evaluated articles comparing C-RR and Lexrank.

As mentioned earlier in section 4.1.1, once the citation summary network is clustered in the C-RR method, the sentences from each cluster are chosen in a round robin fashion, which will not guarantee that a fact-bearing sentence is chosen.

This is because all sentences, whether they cover any facts or not, are assigned to some cluster anyway and such sentences might appear as the first sentence in a cluster. This will sometimes result in a low P score, for which P05-1012 is a good example.

	Article	Gold	Mead's Random	Lexrank	C-RR	C-lexrank
DP	C96-1058	1.00	0.27	0.73	0.73	0.73
	P97-1003	1.00	0.08	0.40	0.60	0.40
	P99-1065	0.94	0.30	0.54	0.82	0.67
	P05-1013	1.00	0.15	0.69	0.97	0.67
	P05-1012	0.95	0.14	0.57	0.26	0.62
PBMT	N03-1017	0.96	0.26	0.36	0.61	0.64
	W03-0301	1.00	0.60	1.00	1.00	1.00
	J04-4002	1.00	0.33	0.70	0.48	0.48
	N04-1033	1.00	0.38	0.38	0.31	0.85
	P05-1033	1.00	0.37	0.77	0.77	0.85
Summ	A00-1043	1.00	0.66	0.95	0.71	0.95
	A00-2024	1.00	0.26	0.86	0.73	0.60
	C00-1072	1.00	0.85	0.85	0.93	0.93
	W00-0403	1.00	0.55	0.81	0.41	0.70
	W03-0510	1.00	0.58	1.00	0.83	0.83
QA	A00-1023	1.00	0.57	0.86	0.86	0.86
	W00-0603	1.00	0.33	0.53	0.53	0.60
	P02-1006	1.00	0.49	0.92	0.49	0.87
	D03-1017	1.00	0.00	0.53	0.26	0.85
	P03-1001	1.00	0.12	0.29	0.59	0.59
TE	D04-9907	1.00	0.53	0.88	0.65	0.94
	H05-1047	1.00	0.83	0.66	0.83	1.00
	H05-1079	1.00	0.67	0.78	0.89	0.56
	W05-1203	1.00	0.50	0.71	1.00	0.71
	P05-1014	1.00	0.44	1.00	0.89	0.78
	Mean	**0.99**	**0.41**	**0.71**	**0.69**	**0.75**

Table 7: Evaluation Results ($|S| = 5$)

6 Conclusion and Future Work

In this work we use the citation summaries to understand the main contributions of articles. The citation summary size, in our experiments, ranges from a few sentences to a few hundred, of which we pick merely a few (5 in our experiments) most important ones.

As a method of summarizing a scientific paper, we propose a clustering approach where communities in the citation summary's lexical network are formed and sentences are extracted from separate clusters. Our experiments show how our clustering method outperforms one of the current state-of-art multi-document summarizing algorithms, Lexrank, on this particular problem.

A future improvement will be to use a reordering approach like Maximal Marginal Relevance (MMR) (Carbonell and Goldstein, 1998) to re-rank clustered documents within each cluster in order to reduce the redundancy in a final summary. Another possible approach is to assume the set of sentences in the citation summary as sentences talking about the same event, yet generated in different sources. Then one can apply the method inspired by (Barzilay et al., 1999) to identify common phrases across sentences and use language generation to form a more coherent summary. The ultimate goal, however, is to produce a topic summarizer system in which the query is a scientific topic and the output is a summary of all previous works in that topic, preferably sorted to preserve chronology and topicality.

7 Acknowledgments

The authors would like to thank Bonnie Dorr, Jimmy Lin, Saif Mohammad, Judith L. Klavans, Ben Shneiderman, and Aleks Aris from UMD, Bryan Gibson, Joshua Gerrish, Pradeep Muthukrishnan, Arzucan Özgür, Ahmed Hassan, and Thuy Vu from University of Michigan for annotations.

This paper is based upon work supported by the National Science Foundation grant "iOPENER: A Flexible Framework to Support Rapid Learning in Unfamiliar Research Domains", jointly awarded to U. of Michigan and U. of Maryland as IIS 0705832. Any opinions, findings, and conclusions or recommendations expressed in this paper are those of the authors and do not necessarily reflect the views of the National Science Foundation.

References

Barzilay, Regina, Kathleen R. McKeown, and Michael Elhadad. 1999. Information fusion in the context of multi-document summarization. In *ACL'99*, pages 550–557.

Bradshaw, Shannon. 2002. *Reference Directed Indexing: Indexing Scientific Literature in the Context of Its Use*. Ph.D. thesis, Northwestern University.

Bradshaw, Shannon. 2003. Reference directed indexing: Redeeming relevance for subject search in citation indexes. In *Proceedings of the 7th European Conference on Research and Advanced Technology for Digital Libraries*.

Carbonell, Jaime G. and Jade Goldstein. 1998. The use of MMR, diversity-based reranking for reordering documents and producing summaries. In *SIGIR'98*, pages 335–336.

Clauset, Aaron, Mark E. J. Newman, and Cristopher Moore. 2004. Finding community structure in very large networks. *Phys. Rev. E*, 70(6):066111, Dec.

Elkiss, Aaron, Siwei Shen, Anthony Fader, Güneş Erkan, David States, and Dragomir R. Radev. 2008. Blind men and elephants: What do citation summaries tell us about a research article? *Journal of the American Society for Information Science and Technology*, 59(1):51–62.

Erkan, Güneş and Dragomir R. Radev. 2004. Lexrank: Graph-based centrality as salience in text summarization. *Journal of Artificial Intelligence Research (JAIR)*.

Erkan, Güneş. 2006. Language model-based document clustering using random walks. In *Proceedings of the HLT-NAACL conference*, pages 479–486, New York City, USA, June. Association for Computational Linguistics.

Joseph, Mark T. and Dragomir R. Radev. 2007. Citation analysis, centrality, and the ACL Anthology. Technical Report CSE-TR-535-07, University of Michigan. Department of Electrical Engineering and Computer Science.

Kan, Min-Yen, Judith L. Klavans, and Kathleen R. McKeown. 2002. Using the Annotated Bibliography as a Resource for Indicative Summarization. In *Proceedings of LREC 2002*, Las Palmas, Spain.

Kupiec, Julian, Jan Pedersen, and Francine Chen. 1995. A trainable document summarizer. In *SIGIR '95*, pages 68–73, New York, NY, USA. ACM.

Levenshtein, Vladimir I. 1966. Binary Codes Capable of Correcting Deletions, Insertions and Reversals. *Soviet Physics Doklady*, 10:707.

Lin, Jimmy J. and Dina Demner-Fushman. 2006. Methods for automatically evaluating answers to complex questions. *Information Retrieval*, 9(5):565–587.

Manning, Christopher D., Prabhakar Raghavan, and Hinrich Schütze. 2008. *Introduction to Information Retrieval*. Cambridge University Press.

Marton, Gregory and Alexey Radul. 2006. Nuggeteer: Automatic nugget-based evaluation using descriptions and judgements. In *Proceedings of NAACL/HLT*.

Nanba, Hidetsugu and Manabu Okumura. 1999. Towards multi-paper summarization using reference information. In *IJCAI1999*, pages 926–931.

Nanba, Hidetsugu, Takeshi Abekawa, Manabu Okumura, and Suguru Saito. 2004a. Bilingual presri: Integration of multiple research paper databases. In *Proceedings of RIAO 2004*, pages 195–211, Avignon, France.

Nanba, Hidetsugu, Noriko Kando, and Manabu Okumura. 2004b. Classification of research papers using citation links and citation types: Towards automatic review article generation. In *Proceedings of the 11th SIG Classification Research Workshop*, pages 117–134, Chicago, USA.

Nenkova, Ani and Rebecca Passonneau. 2004. Evaluating content selection in summarization: The pyramid method. *Proceedings of the HLT-NAACL conference*.

Newman, Mark E. J. 2001. The structure of scientific collaboration networks. *PNAS*, 98(2):404–409.

Radev, Dragomir, Timothy Allison, Sasha Blair-Goldensohn, John Blitzer, Arda Çelebi, Stanko Dimitrov, Elliott Drabek, Ali Hakim, Wai Lam, Danyu Liu, Jahna Otterbacher, Hong Qi, Horacio Saggion, Simone Teufel, Michael Topper, Adam Winkel, and Zhu Zhang. 2004. MEAD - a platform for multidocument multilingual text summarization. In *LREC 2004*, Lisbon, Portugal, May.

Siddharthan, Advaith and Simone Teufel. 2007. Whose idea was this, and why does it matter? attributing scientific work to citations. In *Proceedings of NAACL/HLT-07*.

Teufel, Simone and Marc Moens. 2002. Summarizing scientific articles: experiments with relevance and rhetorical status. *Comput. Linguist.*, 28(4):409–445.

Teufel, Simone, Advaith Siddharthan, and Dan Tidhar. 2006. Automatic classification of citation function. In *Proceedings of the EMNLP*, Sydney, Australia, July.

Teufel, Simone. 2005. Argumentative Zoning for Improved Citation Indexing. *Computing Attitude and Affect in Text: Theory and Applications*, pages 159–170.

Exploiting Constituent Dependencies for Tree Kernel-based Semantic Relation Extraction

Longhua Qian Guodong Zhou Fang Kong Qiaoming Zhu Peide Qian
Jiangsu Provincial Key Lab for Computer Information Processing Technology
School of Computer Science and Technology, Soochow University
1 Shizi Street, Suzhou, China 215006
{qianlonghua,gdzhou,kongfang,qmzhu,pdqian}@suda.edu.cn

Abstract

This paper proposes a new approach to dynamically determine the tree span for tree kernel-based semantic relation extraction. It exploits constituent dependencies to keep the nodes and their head children along the path connecting the two entities, while removing the noisy information from the syntactic parse tree, eventually leading to a dynamic syntactic parse tree. This paper also explores entity features and their combined features in a unified parse and semantic tree, which integrates both structured syntactic parse information and entity-related semantic information. Evaluation on the ACE RDC 2004 corpus shows that our dynamic syntactic parse tree outperforms all previous tree spans, and the composite kernel combining this tree kernel with a linear state-of-the-art feature-based kernel, achieves the so far best performance.

1 Introduction

Information extraction is one of the key tasks in natural language processing. It attempts to identify relevant information from a large amount of natural language text documents. Of three subtasks defined by the ACE program[1], this paper focuses exclusively on Relation Detection and Characterization (RDC) task, which detects and classifies semantic relationships between predefined types of entities in the ACE corpus. For example, the sentence "*Microsoft Corp.* is based in *Redmond,* WA" conveys the relation "GPE-AFF.Based" between "*Microsoft Corp.*" [ORG] and "*Redmond*" [GPE]. Due to limited accuracy in state-of-the-art syntactic and semantic parsing, reliably extracting semantic relationships between named entities in natural language documents is still a difficult, unresolved problem.

In the literature, feature-based methods have dominated the research in semantic relation extraction. Featured-based methods achieve promising performance and competitive efficiency by transforming a relation example into a set of syntactic and semantic features, such as lexical knowledge, entity-related information, syntactic parse trees and deep semantic information. However, detailed research (Zhou et al., 2005) shows that it's difficult to extract new effective features to further improve the extraction accuracy. Therefore, researchers turn to kernel-based methods, which avoids the burden of feature engineering through computing the similarity of two discrete objects (e.g. parse trees) directly. From prior work (Zelenko et al., 2003; Culotta and Sorensen, 2004; Bunescu and Mooney, 2005) to current research (Zhang et al., 2006; Zhou et al., 2007), kernel methods have been showing more and more potential in relation extraction.

The key problem for kernel methods on relation extraction is how to represent and capture the structured syntactic information inherent in relation instances. While kernel methods using the dependency tree (Culotta and Sorensen, 2004) and the shortest dependency path (Bunescu and Mooney, 2005) suffer from low recall performance, convolution tree kernels (Zhang et al., 2006; Zhou et al., 2007) over syntactic parse trees achieve comparable or even better performance than feature-based methods.

However, there still exist two problems regarding currently widely used tree spans. Zhang et al. (2006) discover that the Shortest Path-

© 2008. Licensed under the *Creative Commons Attribution-Noncommercial-Share Alike 3.0 Unported* license (http://creativecommons.org/licenses/by-nc-sa/3.0/). Some rights reserved.

[1] http://www.ldc.upenn.edu/Projects/ACE/

enclosed Tree (SPT) achieves the best performance. Zhou et al. (2007) further extend it to Context-Sensitive Shortest Path-enclosed Tree (CS-SPT), which dynamically includes necessary predicate-linked path information. One problem with both SPT and CS-SPT is that they may still contain unnecessary information. The other problem is that a considerable number of useful context-sensitive information is also missing from SPT/CS-SPT, although CS-SPT includes some contextual information relating to predicate-linked path.

This paper proposes a new approach to dynamically determine the tree span for relation extraction by exploiting constituent dependencies to remove the noisy information, as well as keep the necessary information in the parse tree. Our motivation is to integrate dependency information, which has been proven very useful to relation extraction, with the structured syntactic information to construct a concise and effective tree span specifically targeted for relation extraction. Moreover, we also explore interesting combined entity features for relation extraction via a unified parse and semantic tree.

The other sections in this paper are organized as follows. Previous work is first reviewed in Section 2. Then, Section 3 proposes a dynamic syntactic parse tree while the entity-related semantic tree is described in Section 4. Evaluation on the ACE RDC corpus is given in Section 5. Finally, we conclude our work in Section 6.

2 Related Work

Due to space limitation, here we only review kernel-based methods used in relation extraction. For those interested in feature-based methods, please refer to Zhou et al. (2005) for more details.

Zelenko et al. (2003) described a kernel between shallow parse trees to extract semantic relations, where a relation instance is transformed into the least common sub-tree connecting the two entity nodes. The kernel matches the nodes of two corresponding sub-trees from roots to leaf nodes recursively layer by layer in a top-down manner. Their method shows successful results on two simple extraction tasks. Culotta and Sorensen (2004) proposed a slightly generalized version of this kernel between dependency trees, in which a successful match of two relation instances requires the nodes to be at the same layer and in the identical path starting from the roots to the current nodes. These strong constraints make their kernel yield high precision but very low recall on the ACE RDC 2003 corpus. Bunescu and Mooney (2005) develop a shortest path dependency tree kernel, which simply counts the number of common word classes at each node in the shortest paths between two entities in dependency trees. Similar to Culotta and Sorensen (2004), this method also suffers from high precision but low recall.

Zhang et al. (2006) describe a convolution tree kernel (CTK, Collins and Duffy, 2001) to investigate various structured information for relation extraction and find that the Shortest Path-enclosed Tree (SPT) achieves the F-measure of 67.7 on the 7 relation types of the ACE RDC 2004 corpus. One problem with SPT is that it loses the contextual information outside SPT, which is usually critical for relation extraction. Zhou et al. (2007) point out that both SPT and the convolution tree kernel are context-free. They expand SPT to CS-SPT by dynamically including necessary predicate-linked path information and extending the standard CTK to context-sensitive CTK, obtaining the F-measure of 73.2 on the 7 relation types of the ACE RDC 2004 corpus. However, the CS-SPT only recovers part of contextual information and may contain noisy information as much as SPT.

In order to fully utilize the advantages of feature-based methods and kernel-based methods, researchers turn to composite kernel methods. Zhao and Grishman (2005) define several feature-based composite kernels to capture diverse linguistic knowledge and achieve the F-measure of 70.4 on the 7 relation types in the ACE RDC 2004 corpus. Zhang et al. (2006) design a composite kernel consisting of an entity linear kernel and a standard CTK, obtaining the F-measure of 72.1 on the 7 relation types in the ACE RDC 2004 corpus. Zhou et al. (2007) describe a composite kernel to integrate a context-sensitive CTK and a state-of-the-art linear kernel. It achieves the so far best F-measure of 75.8 on the 7 relation types in the ACE RDC 2004 corpus.

In this paper, we will further study how to dynamically determine a concise and effective tree span for a relation instance by exploiting constituent dependencies inherent in the parse tree derivation. We also attempt to fully capture both the structured syntactic parse information and entity-related semantic information, especially combined entity features, via a unified parse and semantic tree. Finally, we validate the effectiveness of a composite kernel for relation extraction, which combines a tree kernel and a linear kernel.

3 Dynamic Syntactic Parse Tree

This section discusses how to generate dynamic syntactic parse tree by employing constituent dependencies to overcome the problems existing in currently used tree spans.

3.1 Constituent Dependencies in Parse Tree

Zhang et al. (2006) explore five kinds of tree spans and find that the Shortest Path-enclosed Tree (SPT) achieves the best performance. Zhou et al. (2007) further propose Context-Sensitive SPT (CS-SPT), which can dynamically determine the tree span by extending the necessary predicate-linked path information outside SPT. However, the key problem of how to represent the structured syntactic parse tree is still partially resolved. As we indicate as follows, current tree spans suffer from two problems:

(1) Both SPT and CS-SPT still contain unnecessary information. For example, in the sentence "...bought *one* of town's two meat-packing *plants*", the condensed information "*one* of *plants*" is sufficient to determine "DISC" relationship between the entities "*one*" [FAC] and "*plants*" [FAC], while SPT/CS-SPT include the redundant underlined part. Therefore more unnecessary information can be safely removed from SPT/CS-SPT.

(2) CS-SPT only captures part of context-sensitive information relating to predicate-linked structure (Zhou et al., 2007) and still loses much context-sensitive information. Let's take the same example sentence "...bought *one* of *town*'s two meat-packing plants", where indeed there is no relationship between the entities "*one*" [FAC] and "*town*" [GPE]. Nevertheless, the information contained in SPT/CS-SPT ("*one* of *town*") may easily lead to their relationship being misclassified as "DISC", which is beyond our expectation. Therefore the underlined part outside SPT/CS-SPT should be recovered so as to differentiate it from positive instances.

Since dependency plays a key role in many NLP problems such as syntactic parsing, semantic role labeling as well as semantic relation extraction, our motivation is to exploit dependency knowledge to distinguish the necessary evidence from the unnecessary information in the structured syntactic parse tree.

On one hand, lexical or word-word dependency indicates the relationship among words occurring in the same sentence, e.g. predicate-argument dependency means that arguments are dependent on their target predicates, modifier-head dependency means that modifiers are dependent on their head words. This dependency relationship offers a very condensed representation of the information needed to assess the relationship in the forms of the dependency tree (Culotta and Sorensen, 2004) or the shortest dependency path (Bunescu and Mooney, 2005) that includes both entities.

On the other hand, when the parse tree corresponding to the sentence is derived using derivation rules from the bottom to the top, the word-word dependencies extend upward, making a unique head child containing the head word for every non-terminal constituent. As indicated as follows, each CFG rule has the form:

$P \rightarrow L_n \ldots L_1 \boldsymbol{H} R_1 \ldots R_m$

Here, P is the parent node, $\boldsymbol{H}$ is the head child of the rule, $L_n \ldots L_1$ and $R_1 \ldots R_m$ are left and right modifiers of $\boldsymbol{H}$ respectively, and both n and m may be zero. In other words, the parent node P depends on the head child $\boldsymbol{H}$, this is what we call *constituent dependency*. Vice versa, we can also determine the head child of a constituent in terms of constituent dependency. Our hypothesis stipulates that the contribution of the parse tree to establishing a relationship is almost exclusively concentrated in the path connecting the two entities, as well as the head children of constituent nodes along this path.

3.2 Generation of Dynamic Syntactic Parse Tree

Starting from the Minimum Complete Tree (MCT, the complete sub-tree rooted by the nearest common ancestor of the two entities under consideration) as the representation of each relation instance, along the path connecting two entities, the head child of every node is found according to various constituent dependencies. Then the path nodes and their head children are kept while any other nodes are removed from the tree. Eventually we arrive at a tree called Dynamic Syntactic Parse Tree (DSPT), which is dynamically determined by constituent dependencies and only contains necessary information as expected.

There exist a considerable number of constituent dependencies in CFG as described by Collins (2003). However, since our task is to extract the relationship between two named entities, our focus is on how to condense Noun-Phrases (NPs) and other useful constituents for relation extraction. Therefore constituent dependencies can be classified according to constituent types of the CFG rules:

(1) **Modification within base-NPs**: base-NPs mean that they do not directly dominate an NP themselves, unless the dominated NP is a possessive NP. The noun phrase right above the entity headword, whose mention type is nominal or name, can be categorized into this type. In this case, the entity headword is also the headword of the noun phrase, thus all the constituents before the headword are dependent on the headword, and may be removed from the parse tree, while the headword and the constituents right after the headword remain unchanged. For example, in the sentence "...bought *one* of town's two meat-packing *plants*" as illustrated in Figure 1(a), the constituents before the headword "*plants*" can be removed from the parse tree. In this way the parse tree "*one* of *plants*" could capture the "DISC" relationship more concisely and precisely. Another interesting example is shown in Figure 1(b), where the base-NP of the second entity "*town*" is a possessive NP and there is no relationship between the entities "*one*" and "*town*" defined in the ACE corpus. For both SPT and CS-SPT, this example would be condensed to "*one* of *town*" and therefore easily misclassified as the "DISC" relationship between the two entities. In the contrast, our DSPT can avoid this problem by keeping the constituent "'s" and the headword "*plants*".

(2) **Modification to NPs**: except base-NPs, other modification to NPs can be classified into this type. Usually these NPs are recursive, meaning that they contain another NP as their child. The CFG rules corresponding to these modifications may have the following forms:

NP → ***NP*** *SBAR* [relative clause]

NP → ***NP*** *VP* [reduced relative]

NP → ***NP*** *PP* [PP attachment]

Here, the NPs in bold mean that the path connecting the two entities passes through them. For every right hand side, the NP in bold is modified by the constituent following them. That is, the latter is dependent on the former, and may be reduced to a single NP. In Figure 1(c) we show a sentence "*one* of about 500 *people* nominated for ...", where there exists a "DISC" relationship between the entities "*one*" and "*people*". Since the reduced relative "nominated for ..." modifies and is therefore dependent on the "*people*", they can be removed from the parse tree, that is, the right side ("NP VP") can be reduced to the left hand side, which is exactly a single NP.

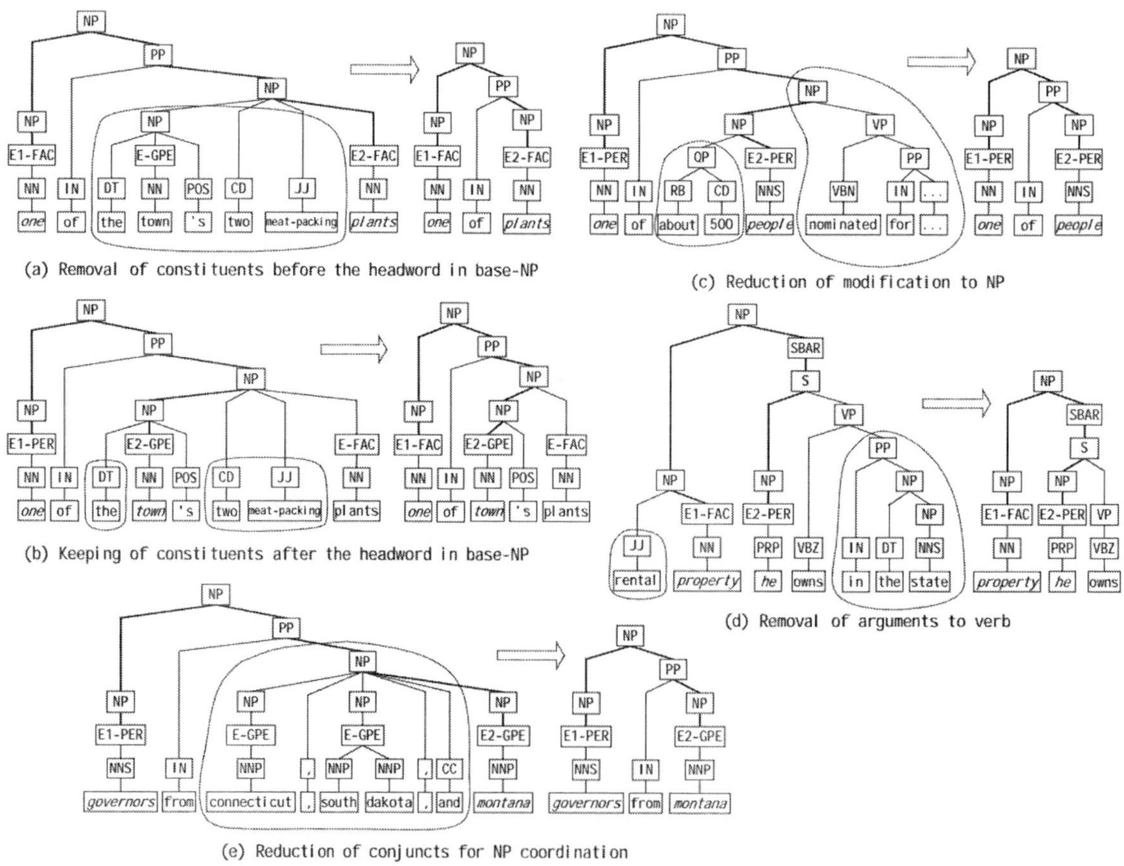

Figure 1. Removal and reduction of constituents using dependencies

(3) **Arguments/adjuncts to verbs**: this type includes the CFG rules in which the left side includes S, SBAR or VP. An argument represents the subject or object of a verb, while an adjunct indicates the location, date/time or way of the action corresponding to the verb. They depend on the verb and can be removed if they are not included in the path connecting the two entities. However, when the parent tag is S or SBAR, and its child VP is not included in the path, this VP should be recovered to indicate the predicate verb. Figure 1(d) shows a sentence "... maintain rental *property he* owns in the state", where the "ART.User-or-Owner" relation holds between the entities "*property*" and "*he*". While PP can be removed from the rule ("VP→ VBZ PP"), the VP should be kept in the rule ("S→ NP VP"). Consequently, the tree span looks more concise and precise for relation extraction.

(4) **Coordination conjunctions**: In coordination constructions, several peer conjuncts may be reduced into a single constituent. Although the first conjunct is always considered as the headword (Collins, 2003), actually all the conjuncts play an equal role in relation extraction. As illustrated in Figure 1(e), the NP coordination in the sentence ("*governors* from connecticut, south dakota, and *montana*") can be reduced to a single NP ("*governors* from *montana*") by keeping the conjunct in the path while removing the other conjuncts.

(5) **Modification to other constituents**: except for the above four types, other CFG rules fall into this type, such as modification to PP, ADVP and PRN etc. These cases are similar to arguments/adjuncts to verbs, but less frequent than them, so we will not detail this scenario.

In fact, SPT (Zhang et al., 2006) can be arrived at by carrying out part of the above removal operations using a single rule (i.e. all the constituents outside the linking path should be removed) and CS-CSPT (Zhou et al., 2007) further recovers part of necessary context-sensitive information outside SPT, this justifies that SPT performs well, while CS-SPT outperforms SPT.

4 Entity-related Semantic Tree

Entity semantic features, such as entity headword, entity type and subtype etc., impose a strong constraint on relation types in terms of relation definition by the ACE RDC task. Experiments by Zhang et al. (2006) show that linear kernel using only entity features contributes much when combined with the convolution parse tree kernel. Qian et al. (2007) further indicates that among these entity features, entity type, subtype, and mention type, as well as the base form of predicate verb, contribute most while the contribution of other features, such as entity class, headword and GPE role, can be ignored.

In order to effectively capture entity-related semantic features, and their combined features as well, especially bi-gram or tri-gram features, we build an Entity-related Semantic Tree (EST) in three ways as illustrated in Figure 2. In the example sentence "*they* 're *here*", which is excerpted from the ACE RDC 2004 corpus, there exists a relationship "Physical.Located" between the entities "*they*" [PER] and "*here*" [GPE.Population-Center]. The features are encoded as "TP", "ST", "MT" and "PVB", which denote type, subtype, mention-type of the two entities, and the base form of predicate verb if existing (nearest to the 2nd entity along the path connecting the two entities) respectively. For example, the tag "TP1" represents the type of the 1st entity, and the tag "ST2" represents the subtype of the 2nd entity. The three entity-related semantic tree setups are depicted as follows:

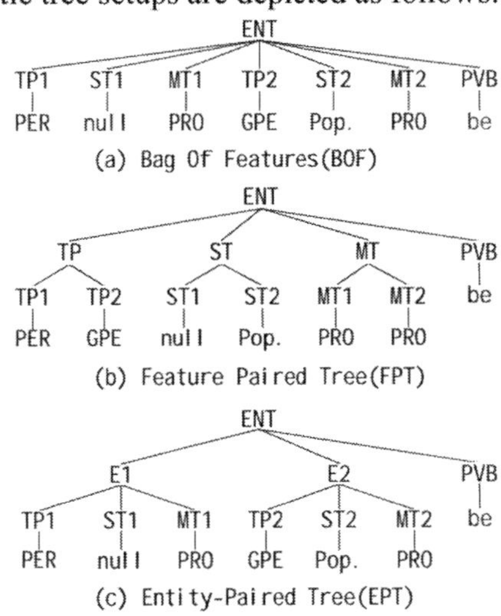

Figure 2. Different setups for entity-related semantic tree (EST)

(a) Bag of Features (BOF, e.g. Fig. 2(a)): all feature nodes uniformly hang under the root node, so the tree kernel simply counts the number of common features between two relation instances. This tree setup is similar to linear entity kernel explored by Zhang et al. (2006).

(b) Feature-Paired Tree (FPT, e.g. Fig. 2(b)): the features of two entities are grouped into different types according to their feature names, e.g. "TP1" and "TP2" are grouped to "TP". This tree setup is aimed to capture the additional similarity of the single feature combined from different entities, i.e., the first and the second entities.

(c) Entity-Paired Tree (EPT, e.g. Fig. 2(c)): all the features relating to an entity are grouped to nodes "E1" or "E2", thus this tree kernel can further explore the equivalence of combined entity features only relating to one of the entities between two relation instances.

In fact, the BOF only captures the individual entity features, while the FPT/EPT can additionally capture the bi-gram/tri-gram features respectively.

Rather than constructing a composite kernel, we incorporate the EST into the DSPT to produce a Unified Parse and Semantic Tree (UPST) to investigate the contribution of the EST to relation extraction. The entity features can be attached under the top node, the entity nodes, or directly combined with the entity nodes as in Figure 1. However, detailed evaluation (Qian et al., 2007) indicates that the UPST achieves the best performance when the feature nodes are attached under the top node. Hence, we also attach three kinds of entity-related semantic trees (i.e. BOF, FPT and EPT) under the top node of the DSPT right after its original children. Thereafter, we employ the standard CTK (Collins and Duffy, 2001) to compute the similarity between two UPSTs, since this CTK and its variations are successfully applied in syntactic parsing, semantic role labeling (Moschitti, 2004) and relation extraction (Zhang et al., 2006; Zhou et al., 2007) as well.

5 Experimentation

This section will evaluate the effectiveness of the DSPT and the contribution of entity-related semantic information through experiments.

5.1 Experimental Setting

For evaluation, we use the ACE RDC 2004 corpus as the benchmark data. This data set contains 451 documents and 5702 relation instances. It defines 7 entity types, 7 major relation types and 23 subtypes. For comparison with previous work, evaluation is done on 347 (nwire/bnews) documents and 4307 relation instances using 5-fold cross-validation. Here, the corpus is parsed using Charniak's parser (Charniak, 2001) and relation instances are generated by iterating over all pairs of entity mentions occurring in the same sentence with given "true" mentions and coreferential information. In our experimentations, SVM^{light} (Joachims, 1998) with the tree kernel function (Moschitti, 2004) [2] is selected as our classifier. For efficiency, we apply the *one vs. others* strategy, which builds K classifiers so as to separate one class from all others. For comparison purposes, the training parameters C (SVM) and λ (tree kernel) are also set to 2.4 and 0.4 respectively.

5.2 Experimental Results

Table 1 evaluates the contributions of different kinds of constituent dependencies to extraction performance on the 7 relation types of the ACE RDC 2004 corpus using the convolution parse tree kernel as depicted in Figure 1. The MCT with only entity-type information is first used as the baseline, and various constituent dependencies are then applied sequentially to dynamically reshaping the tree in two different modes:

--[M1] Respective: every constituent dependency is individually applied on MCT.

--[M2] Accumulative: every constituent dependency is incrementally applied on the previously derived tree span, which begins with the MCT and eventually gives rise to a Dynamic Syntactic Parse Tree (DSPT).

Dependency types	P(%)	R(%)	F
MCT (baseline)	75.1	53.8	62.7
Modification within base-NPs	76.5 (59.8)	59.8 (59.8)	67.1 (67.1)
Modification to NPs	77.0 (76.2)	63.2 (56.9)	69.4 (65.1)
Arguments/adjuncts to verb	77.1 (76.1)	63.9 (57.5)	69.9 (65.5)
Coordination conjunctions	77.3 (77.3)	65.2 (55.1)	70.8 (63.8)
Other modifications	**77.4** (75.0)	**65.4** (53.7)	**70.9** (62.6)

Table 1. Contribution of constituent dependencies in respective mode (inside parentheses) and accumulative mode (outside parentheses)

The table shows that the final DSPT achieves the best performance of 77.4%/65.4%/70.9 in precision/recall/F-measure respectively after applying all the dependencies, with the increase of F-measure by 8.2 units compared to the baseline MCT. This indicates that reshaping the tree by exploiting constituent dependencies may significantly improve extraction accuracy largely due to the increase in recall. It further suggests that constituent dependencies knowledge is very effec-

[2] http://ai-nlp.info.uniroma2.it/moschitti/

tive and can be fully utilized in tree kernel-based relation extraction. This table also shows that:

(1) Both modification within base-NPs and modification to NPs contribute much to performance improvement, acquiring the increase of F-measure by 4.4/2.4 units in mode M1 and 4.4/2.3 units in mode M2 respectively. This indicates the local characteristic of semantic relations, which can be effectively captured by NPs near the two involved entities in the DSPT.

(2) All the other three dependencies show minor contribution to performance enhancement, they improve the F-measure only by 2.8/0.9/-0.1 units in mode M1 and 0.5/0.9/0.1 units in mode M2. This may be due to the reason that these dependencies only remove the nodes far from the two entities.

We compare in Table 2 the performance of Unified Parse and Semantic Trees with different kinds of Entity Semantic Tree setups using standard convolution tree kernel, while the SPT and DSPT with only entity-type information are listed for reference. It shows that:

(1) All the three unified parse and semantic tree kernels significantly outperform the DSPT kernel, obtaining an average increase of ~4 units in F-measure. This means that they can effectively capture both the structured syntactic information and the entity-related semantic features.

(2) The Unified Parse and Semantic Tree with Feature-Paired Tree achieves the best performance of 80.1/70.7/75.1 in P/R/F respectively, with an increase of F-measure by 0.4/0.3 units over BOF and EPT respectively. This suggests that additional bi-gram entity features captured by FPT are more useful than tri-gram entity features captured by EPT.

Tree setups	P(%)	R(%)	F
SPT	76.3	59.8	67.1
DSPT	77.4	65.4	70.9
UPST (BOF)	80.4	69.7	74.7
UPST (FPT)	**80.1**	**70.7**	**75.1**
UPST (EPT)	79.9	70.2	74.8

Table 2. Performance of Unified Parse and Semantic Trees (UPSTs) on the 7 relation types of the ACE RDC 2004 corpus

In Table 3 we summarize the improvements of different tree setups over SPT. It shows that in a similar setting, our DSPT outperforms SPT by 3.8 units in F-measure, while CS-SPT outperforms SPT by 1.3 units in F-measure. This suggests that the DSPT performs best among these tree spans. It also shows that the Unified Parse and Semantic Tree with Feature-Paired Tree perform significantly better than the other two tree setups (i.e., CS-SPT and DSPT) by 6.7/4.2 units in F-measure respectively. This implies that the entity-related semantic information is very useful and contributes much when they are incorporated into the parse tree for relation extraction.

Tree setups	P(%)	R(%)	F
CS-SPT over SPT[3]	1.5	1.1	1.3
DSPT over SPT	1.1	5.6	3.8
UPST (FPT) over SPT	3.8	10.9	8.0

Table 3. Improvements of different tree setups over SPT on the ACE RDC 2004 corpus

Finally, Table 4 compares our system with other state-of-the-art kernel-based systems on the 7 relation types of the ACE RDC 2004 corpus. It shows that our UPST outperforms all previous tree setups using one single kernel, and even better than two previous composite kernels (Zhang et al., 2006; Zhao and Grishman, 2005). Furthermore, when the UPST (FPT) kernel is combined with a linear state-of-the-state feature-based kernel (Zhou et al., 2005) into a composite one via polynomial interpolation in a setting similar to Zhou et al. (2007) (i.e. polynomial degree d=2 and coefficient α=0.3), we get the so far best performance of 77.1 in F-measure for 7 relation types on the ACE RDC 2004 data set.

Systems	P(%)	R(%)	F
Ours: composite kernel	83.0	72.0	77.1
Zhou et al., (2007): composite kernel	82.2	70.2	75.8
Zhang et al., (2006): composite kernel	76.1	68.4	72.1
Zhao and Grishman, (2005):[4] composite kernel	69.2	70.5	70.4
Ours: CTK with UPST	80.1	70.7	75.1
Zhou et al., (2007): context-sensitive CTK with CS-SPT	81.1	66.7	73.2
Zhang et al., (2006): CTK with SPT	74.1	62.4	67.7

Table 4. Comparison of different systems on the ACE RDC 2004 corpus

[3] We arrive at these values by subtracting P/R/F (79.6/5.6/71.9) of Shortest-enclosed Path Tree from P/R/F (81.1/6.7/73.2) of Dynamic Context-Sensitive Shortest-enclosed Path Tree according to Table 2 (Zhou et al., 2007)

[4] There might be some typing errors for the performance reported in Zhao and Grishman (2005) since P, R and F do not match.

6 Conclusion

This paper further explores the potential of structured syntactic information for tree kernel-based relation extraction, and proposes a new approach to dynamically determine the tree span (DSPT) for relation instances by exploiting constituent dependencies. We also investigate different ways of how entity-related semantic features and their combined features can be effectively captured in a Unified Parse and Semantic Tree (UPST). Evaluation on the ACE RDC 2004 corpus shows that our DSPT is appropriate for structured representation of relation instances. We also find that, in addition to individual entity features, combined entity features (especially bi-gram) contribute much when they are combined with a DPST into a UPST. And the composite kernel, combining the UPST kernel and a linear state-of-the-art kernel, yields the so far best performance.

For the future work, we will focus on improving performance of complex structured parse trees, where the path connecting the two entities involved in a relationship is too long for current kernel methods to take effect. Our preliminary experiment of applying certain discourse theory exhibits certain positive results.

Acknowledgements

This research is supported by Project 60673041 under the National Natural Science Foundation of China, Project 2006AA01Z147 under the "863" National High-Tech Research and Development of China, and the National Research Foundation for the Doctoral Program of Higher Education of China under Grant No. 20060285008. We would also like to thank the excellent and insightful comments from the three anonymous reviewers.

References

Bunescu, Razvan C. and Raymond J. Mooney. 2005. A Shortest Path Dependency Kernel for Relation Extraction. In *Proceedings of the Human Language Technology Conference and Conference on Empirical Methods in Natural Language Processing (EMNLP-2005)*, pages 724-731. Vancover, B.C.

Charniak, Eugene. 2001. Intermediate-head Parsing for Language Models. In *Proceedings of the 39th Annual Meeting of the Association of Computational Linguistics (ACL-2001)*, pages 116-123.

Collins, Michael. 2003. Head-Driven Statistics Models for Natural Language Parsing. *Computational linguistics*, 29(4): 589-617.

Collins, Michael and Nigel Duffy. 2001. Convolution Kernels for Natural Language. In *Proceedings of Neural Information Processing Systems (NIPS-2001)*, pages 625-632. Cambridge, MA.

Culotta, Aron and Jeffrey Sorensen. 2004. Dependency tree kernels for relation extraction. In *Proceedings of the 42nd Annual Meeting of the Association of Computational Linguistics (ACL-2004)*, pages 423-439. Barcelona, Spain.

Joachims, Thorsten. 1998. Text Categorization with Support Vector Machine: learning with many relevant features. In *Proceedings of the 10th European Conference on Machine Learning (ECML-1998)*, pages 137-142. Chemnitz, Germany.

Moschitti, Alessandro. 2004. A Study on Convolution Kernels for Shallow Semantic Parsing. In *Proceedings of the 42nd Annual Meeting of the Association of Computational Linguistics (ACL-2004)*. Barcelona, Spain.

Qian, Longhua, Guodong Zhou, Qiaoming Zhu and Peide Qian. 2007. Relation Extraction using Convolution Tree Kernel Expanded with Entity Features. In *Proceedings of the 21st Pacific Asian Conference on Language, Information and Computation (PACLIC-21)*, pages 415-421. Seoul, Korea.

Zelenko, Dmitry, Chinatsu Aone and Anthony Richardella. 2003. Kernel Methods for Relation Extraction. *Journal of Machine Learning Research*, 3(2003): 1083-1106.

Zhang, Min, Jie Zhang, Jian Su and Guodong Zhou. 2006. A Composite Kernel to Extract Relations between Entities with both Flat and Structured Features. In *Proceedings of the 21st International Conference on Computational Linguistics and the 44th Annual Meeting of the Association of Computational Linguistics (COLING/ACL-2006)*, pages 825-832. Sydney, Australia.

Zhao, Shubin and Ralph Grishman. 2005. Extracting relations with integrated information using kernel methods. In *Proceedings of the 43rd Annual Meeting of the Association of Computational Linguistics (ACL-2005)*, pages 419-426. Ann Arbor, USA.

Zhou, Guodong, Jian Su, Jie Zhang and Min Zhang. 2005. Exploring various knowledge in relation extraction. In *Proceedings of the 43rd Annual Meeting of the Association of Computational Linguistics (ACL-2005)*, pages 427-434. Ann Arbor, USA.

Zhou, Guodong, Min Zhang, Donghong Ji and Qiaoming Zhu. 2007. Tree Kernel-based Relation Extraction with Context-Sensitive Structured Parse Tree Information. In *Proceedings of the 2007 Joint Conference on Empirical Methods in Natural Language Processing and Computational Natural Language Learning (EMNLP/CoNLL-2007)*, pages 728-736. Prague, Czech.

A Method for Automatic POS Guessing of Chinese Unknown Words

Likun Qiu
Department of Chinese Language and Literature, Peking University / No.5 Yiheyuan Road, Haidian District, Beijing, China 100871
NEC Laboratories, China
qiulk@pku.edu.cn

Changjian Hu, Kai Zhao
NEC Laboratories, China / 14F, Building.A, Innovation Plaza, No.1 Tsinghua Science Park, Zhongguancun East Road, Haidian District, Beijing, China 100084
{huchangjian, zhaokai}@research.nec.com.cn

Abstract

This paper proposes a method for automatic POS (part-of-speech) guessing of Chinese unknown words. It contains two models. The first model uses a machine-learning method to predict the POS of unknown words based on their internal component features. The credibility of the results of the first model is then measured. For low-credibility words, the second model is used to revise the first model's results based on the global context information of those words. The experiments show that the first model achieves 93.40% precision for all words and 86.60% for disyllabic words, which is a significant improvement over the best results reported in previous studies, which were 89% precision for all words and 74% for disyllabic words. Further, the second model improves the results by 0.80% precision for all words and 1.30% for disyllabic words.

1 Introduction

Since written Chinese does not use blank spaces to denote word boundaries, Chinese word segmentation becomes an essential task for natural language processing, as in many other Asian languages (Thai, Japanese, Tibetan, etc.). It is difficult to build a complete dictionary comprising all words, for new words are constantly being created. As such, unknown words may greatly influence the effectiveness of text processing. Studies on unknown words include detection, POS guessing, sense classification, etc. Current methods for automatic unknown word detection have been relatively successful and widely used in many systems, yet automatic POS guessing for unknown words still remains a challenge for natural language processing research.

The task of POS guessing is quite different from traditional POS tagging. Traditional POS tagging involves assigning a single POS tag to a word token, provided that it is known what POS tag this word can take on in principle. This task requires a lexicon that lists possible POS tags for all words. However, unknown words are not in the lexicon, so the task of POS guessing of unknown words involves the guessing of a correct POS for an unknown word from the whole POS set of the current language. Obviously, traditional methods of POS tagging cannot effectively solve the problem of POS guessing of unknown words.

In previous work, two types of features have been used for the task of POS guessing of unknown Chinese words. One type is contextual feature, including local contextual features and global contextual features, and the other is internal component feature. Previous work has mainly used context information to guess the POS tags of unknown Chinese words, while a few designs looked at internal component features. Although there have been some attempts to combine the two types of features together, no reasonable explanation of the relationship between the two types of features has been given.

It is well known that the properties of a structure always depend on its internal component structure. As such, it is natural for us to wonder whether models based on internal component features alone can perform the POS guessing task for unknown Chinese words with both high pre-

©2008. Licensed under the *Creative Commons Attribution-Noncommercial-Share Alike 3.0 Unported* license (http://creativecommons.org/licenses/by-nc-sa/3.0/). Some rights reserved.

cision and high recall. Here we present a model based on internal component features of unknown words using CRFs (conditional random fields). The results are very good, especially for multi-syllabic words (excluding disyllabic words).

While in the previous model the precision of POS guessing of disyllabic words is relatively high, there is still much room for further improvement. Considering that the usages of a word in real text can show the properties of a word, and that these features may be a useful complement to internal component features, we designed a scheme to effectively utilize the two types of features together. In this scheme, credibility scores for former guessing results are computed, and only those words with relatively lower credibility scores are revised by the model based on global context information. The model based on global context information simulates the behavior of linguists in judging the POS of a word. Though the recall of the latter model is low, it can revise some incorrect guessing results of the initial model.

According to Lu (2005), there are six main types of unknown Chinese words:

(1) Abbreviation (acronym): e.g., 中美 zhong-mei (*China-U.S*).
(2) Proper names (person's name, place name, company name): e.g., 王安石 Wang Anshi (person's name), 槟城 Penang (an island in Malaysia; place name), 华为 Huawei (company name).
(3) Derived words (words with affixes): e.g., 总经理 zong-jingli (*general manager*), 现代化 xiandai-hua (*modernize*).
(4) Compounds: e.g., 获允 huoyun (*obtain permission*), 泥沙 nisha (*mud*), 突变 tubian (*sudden change*)
(5) Numeric compounds: e.g., 四千日圆 siqian riyuan (*four thousand Japanese yen*), ２００３年 2003nian (*year 2003*)
(6) Reduplicated words: e.g., 应不应该 yingbuyinggai (*should or should not*), 出出进进 chuchujinjin (*go in and go out*)

Proper names and numeric compounds are all nouns, so they don't have the problem of POS guessing. We will focus on abbreviation, derived words, compounds, and reduplicated words.

The remainder of this paper is organized as follows: in Section 2, we introduce some previous work on POS guessing of unknown Chinese words. Sections 3, 4, and 5 describe our proposed method, which includes two models and an additional process linking the two models together. In detail, Section 3 considers POS guessing for unknown Chinese words as a sequence-labeling problem and proposes a model based on internal component features to solve this task. In Section 4, we compute a credibility score for each guessing result based on the sequence type of the words' internal component structure. This links the model in Section 3 and that of Section 5 together. Section 5 describes a model based on global context information to revise the guessing results of the initial model that have relatively lower credibility scores. Section 6 shows the experiments and results of our methods and a comparison with previous work. Section 7 presents our conclusions.

2 Previous Work

Considering the features used during POS guessing, we have classified previous studies on POS guessing of unknown words into three types.

The first type use only contextual features, including local context and global context. For example, Nakagawa and Matsumoto (2006) proposed a probabilistic model to guess the POS tags of unknown words by considering all the occurrences of unknown words with the same lexical form in a document. The parameters were estimated using Gibbs sampling. They also attempted to apply the model to semi-supervised learning, and conducted experiments on multiple corpora. The highest precision in the Chinese corpus of their experiments was 67.85%.

The second type use only internal component features, such as that of Chen and Bai (1997) and Wu and Jiang (2000). Chen and Bai (1997) examined all unknown nouns, verbs, and adjectives and reported 69.13% precision using Dice metrics to measure the affix-category association strength and an affix-dependent entropy weighting scheme for determining the weightings between prefix-category and suffix-category associations. This approach is effective in processing derived words such as 现代化 xiandai-hua (*modernize*), but performs poorly when encountering compounds such as 保值 baozhi (*inflation-proof*). Wu and Jiang (2000) calculated *P(Cat,Pos,Len)* for each character, where *Cat* is the POS of a word containing the character, *Pos* is the position of the character in that word, and *Len* is the length of that word. They then calculated the POS probabilities for each unknown word as the joint probabilities of *P(Cat,Pos,Len)* for its component characters. This approach was applied to unknown nouns, verbs, and adjectives of two to four characters in length. This approach exhibits lower recall for multi-syllabic words even if the training corpus is significantly large.

The third type attempt to combine internal component features and context information, such as that of Lu (2005) and Goh et al. (2006). Lu (2005) describes a hybrid model that combines a rule-based model with two statistical models for the task of POS guessing of unknown Chinese words. The rule-based model includes 35 manual rules concerning the type, length, and internal structure of unknown words, and the two statistical models utilize context information and the likelihood for a character to appear in a particular position of words of a particular length and POS category, one of which is Wu and Jiang's (2000) model. It achieves a precision of 89.00%, a significant improvement over the best result reported in previous studies, which was 69.00%. Goh et al. (2006) propose a method for guessing the part-of-speech tags of detected unknown words using contextual and internal component features with maximum entropy models. Both Lu (2005) and Goh et al. (2006) use only local context and not global context. As far as internal component features are concerned, Lu (2005) uses only the word category feature in his rule-based model while Goh et al. (2006) uses only the first character and last character features. From the above studies, we may find that methods based on internal component features are very promising, but this kind of features still needs much more attention. Moreover, none of them has proved that methods based on context information can improve the results of methods based on internal component features. They only attempted to utilize different types of features together and to give simultaneous results for both types of features.

Our method is among the third type of studies, but is different from the rest in the scheme of combining the two types of features together. In our method, internal component features play a more important role. We will prove that a model based on this type of features alone can perform very well. The other type of features acts as a useful supplement and can improve the results of some words in a certain degree. The two models are linked together by assigning a credibility score for each POS guessing result generated by the initial model. The results with a relatively lower credibility score are identified and put through reconsideration by a method based on global context information.

3 Model Based on Internal Component Features

In this model, we consider the task of POS guessing of unknown words as a problem of sequence labeling. The inspiration for this approach came from our observations of how humans understand a word. Usually an unknown word is regarded by human as a sequence of characters or morphemes that can be partitioned into several segments, where each segment is relatively coherent in meaning.

3.1 Conditional Random Fields

In contrast with other models for labeling sequences, such as HMM and MEMM, CRFs are good at avoiding the label bias problem. They condition on the entire observation sequence, thus avoiding the need for independent assumptions between observations and vastly expanding the set of features that can be incorporated into the model without violating its assumptions. One of the main advantages of a conditional model is its ability to explore a diverse range of features relevant to a specific task. As many studies have shown, CRFs are the best models for solving the sequence labeling problem (Lafferty et al., 2001; Vail et al., 2007). So we chose to use CRFs to solve the POS guessing problem.

3.2 The POS Guessing Model

While training, we use the words of a dictionary as training data. Those words will be considered as sentences and then segmented and assigned POS-tags by a standard word segmentation and POS tagging tool. By training with this data, we will obtain a POS guessing model for unknown words. While testing, we still consider an unknown word as a sentence and process it with the same tool.

In the dictionary, most words have one POS-tag while a few have more. The monosyllabic words were omitted from the training.

Feature Analysis

In our CRFs model, we employed three main types of features: the components of words, the lengths of those components, and the POS tags of those components.

Before the CRFs training, we analyzed the internal component structure of the dictionary words and assigned a proper POS-tag to each component. There are four analysis schemes that are different from each other in two aspects. The first aspect is the type of the component, which may be a character or immediate constituent (IC). Here, "immediate constituent" means constituents that directly form a word. For example, 科学技术部 kexuejishubu (*department of science and technology*) has the following constituents: 科 ke, 学 xue, 技 ji, 术 shu, 部 bu, 科学 kexue, and 技术 jishu, in which only 科学 kexue, 技术 jishu and 部 bu are the immediate constituents of 科学技术部 kexuejishubu. The second aspect is regarding the consideration of the POS-tag of the component. The four analysis schemes are listed in Table 1.

Component \ POS	With	Without
Character	Scheme 1	Scheme 2
Immediate Constituent	Scheme 3	Scheme 4

Table 1. Analysis Schemes

In Scheme 1 and Scheme 2, the tool segments a dictionary word until all components are characters, and in Scheme 1 only, each component is given a POS tag. In Scheme 3 and Scheme 4, the tool segments a dictionary word only once to get its immediate constituents, and in Scheme 3 only, each component is given a POS tag. For instance, 科学技术部 kexuejishubu (*department of science and technology*) will be segmented as "科/N 学/N 技/N 术/N 部/N" in Scheme 1 and "科学/N 技术/N 部/N" in Scheme 3.

Feature Template Selection

For each type of feature, we used the five templates in Figure 1. So in Schemes 1 and 3 there are 15 templates, and in Schemes 2 and 4 there are 10 templates.

For instance, when training, 科学技术部 will be transformed as 科学/N/N_B 技术/N/N_M 部/N/N_E in Scheme 3, in which N denotes that the POS of the word 科学技术部 is noun, while B, M and E denote the beginning, middle and end positions of the word.

U01:%x[-1,i]: the former component's *i*th feature
U02:%x[0,i]: the current component's *i*th feature
U03:%x[1,i]: the next component's *i*th feature
U04:%x[-1,i]/%x[0,i]: the former component's *i*th feature and the current component's *i*th feature
U05:%x[0,i]/%x[1,i]: the current component's *i*th feature and the next component's *i*th feature

Figure 1. List of Templates(i=1-3)

By using a dictionary with these feature templates for the training, we obtain a POS guessing model for unknown Chinese words. If an unknown word such as 用电 yongdian (*electricity used*) is tested, it would be analyzed as 用/V 电/N (*to use, electricity*) for the feature extraction and then it would be tagged as 用/V/N_B 电/N/N_E. That is, the word is assigned a POS of noun.

4 Credibility Computation

The initial model is based on the hypothesis that the syntactical properties of a word depend on its internal structure. But the internal structure of some words are ambiguous. For instance, both 用语 yongyu (*vocabulary* [literally, "used words"]) and 用劲 yongjing (*exert* [literally, "use strength"]) both have the sequence V1N1 (which is combined by a POS sequence of "VN" and a length sequence of "11"), yet the former one is a noun and the latter one is a verb.

There are some other sequences like V1N1. All the words (especially disyllabic words) fitting to these sequences bring difficulty for POS guessing model in Section 3. In this section, we attempt to identify those words by computing a credibility score for each type of sequence. The lower the score, less credible the result of the model.

In detail, Formula 1 is used to compute the credibility of a word that has a certain type of sequence, e.g., 用语 yongyu (*vocabulary* [literally, "used words"]) with the sequence "V1N1".

$$C_k = \frac{Count(S_k \mid P = P_j) - Count(S_k \mid P = P_{j+1})}{Count(S_k)} \qquad (1)$$

In Formula 1, C_k denotes the credibility score of words that have the *k*th type of sequence S_K. S_K denotes a sequence as $P_1L_1P_2L_2......P_nL_n$, in which n means the quantity of components in the sequence S_K; P_n *and* L_n mean the POS and length of the *n*th component of any word that has the sequence S_K, respectively; $Count(S_K)$ denotes the quantity of words in the dictionary that have the sequence S_K; and $Count(S_K|P{=}P_j)$ and $Count(S_K|P{=}P_{j+1})$ denote the quantity of words in the dictionary that have the sequence S_K and are tagged as POS P_j and P_{j+1}, respectively, in which P_j and P_{j+1} are the two POSs that make the value of $Count(S_K|P{=}P_j)$ a maximum of two. Some sequences with lower credibility scores are listed in Table 2.

For instance, the sequence type of the word 用电 yongdian (*electricity used*) is V1N1, so its credibility score is 0.65. If the threshold is 0.8, this word will be considered a low-credibility word and put through reconsideration by the following model.

Sequence	Credibility Score	Proportion
Vg1Ng1	0.7	0.50%
V1Ng1	0.67	1.90%
Vg1N1	0.67	0.55%
V1N1	0.65	2.99%
V1Vn2	0.57	0.04%
A1A1	0.55	0.22%
N1A1	0.48	0.15%
V1V2	0.44	0.05%
V1Vi2	0.25	0.08%

Table 2. Examples of Sequences with Low Credibility Scores

5 Model Based on Global Contextual Features

Words with relatively lower credibility scores (given in Section 4) will be revised by a model based on global context. In this paper, we implement a model of voting by syntactical templates, which derived from research results of linguists.

This process requires a relatively large corpus that can provide enough context instances for each under-processed word. It is difficult for us to find a corpus that can provide enough instances of most unknown words, because many of such instances have only been used for a relatively short time. In this paper, we use search engine as the source of corpus, i.e., throw a word to a search engine and pick out instances from the returned snippets.

Linguists have summarized systematic rules for judging the POS of a Chinese word based on its global distribution in real text (Guo, 2002). For example, generally a verb or adjective can be modified by the word "不" (*not*) while a noun cannot. Based on this knowledge, we designed a set of syntactical templates listed in Table 3. The templates indicate whether a word can be used in such ways.

For every word, we build phrases based on these templates (see Table 3 for instances of 喜欢 xihuan (*like*)) and send the phrases to a search engine as queries. For each query, the search engine returns some snippets, which are generally in sentence form. Then each word gets three scores through a voting process in which the sentences act as "voters." The three scores, Score(N), Score(V), and Score(A), denote the likelihood score for the word to be a noun, a verb or an adjective, respectively. Each voter votes by following the criteria given in Figure 2. In Figure 2, Value(N), Value(V), and Value(A) are constant values that are used to balance the three scores.

Templates	~	不+~	开始+~	进行+~	予以+~	仍+~	所+~	很+~	很不+~
Instance	喜欢	不喜欢	开始喜欢	进行喜欢*	予以喜欢*	仍喜欢	所喜欢	很喜欢	很不喜欢

Table 3. Syntactical Templates with Instances of "喜欢"[1]

If the unknown word follows a transitive verb and is at the end of a sentence or subsentence, Score(N)+=Value(N);
If the unknown word follows a quantitative word and is at the end of a sentence or subsentence, Score(N)+=Value(N);
If the unknown word follows the word "不", "仍" or "所", Score(V)+=Value(V);
If the unknown word follows the word "开始", "进行" or "予以" and is at the end of a sentence or subsentence, or there is a following word that is not a verb, Score(V)+=Value(N);
If the unknown word follows the word "不", "很" or "很不", Score(A)+=Value(A).

Figure 2. Criteria for Voting

For each instance, Score(N), Score(V), and Score(A) will be added to the scores Value(N), Value(V), and Value(A), respectively.

Although these templates are effective, there are some exceptions brought by morphology analysis errors or other reasons, so we use an outstanding method to filter the exceptions. We

[1] Here "*" means the structure is invalid.

compute an outstanding value with Formula 2 to judge whether the voting result is acceptable.

$$O = \frac{Max(Score(POS)) - Max'(Score(POS))}{Max(Score(POS))} \quad (2)$$

In Formula 2, O means the outstanding value of a voting result; $Max(Score(POS))$ means the maximum score among the three scores and $Max'(Score(POS))$ means the maximum score between the other scores. If O is larger than a threshold, we assume the voting result to be acceptable and adopt the result to revise the POS guessing result of the initial model.

For instance, Score(N), Score(V), and Score(A) of the word 用语 yongyu (*vocabulary* [literally, "used words"]) are 50, 5 and 3 respectively. So O(用语)=(50-5)/50=0.9.

6 Experiments and Results

6.1 Data Preparation

The model based on CRFs is trained on the Modern Chinese Grammar Information Dictionary (Yu, 1998) and tested on the Contemporary Chinese Corpus of Peking University (Yu et al., 2002). The corpus is segmented and POS-tagged. Both the dictionary and corpus were constructed by the Institute of Computational Linguistics, Peking University. The corpus was built using the content of all the news articles of the People's Daily newspaper published in China from January to June 1998. We selected all verbs, nouns and adjectives from the dictionary, excluding monosyllabic words, as training data. The nouns, verbs and adjectives in the corpus but not in the dictionary were considered to be unknown words and used as testing data. The distribution of word length of the training and testing data is presented in Table 4.

Word Length	Training	Testing
Disyllabic	40,103	11,108
Tri-syllabic	12,167	12,901
Four-character	1,180	1,055
Five-character	0	279
Total	53,450	25,343

Table 4. Distribution of Word Length in Training and Testing Data

We used ICTCLAS 1.0 (Zhang, 2002) to do word segmentation and POS tagging, because ICTCLAS is known as one of the best tools for those functions. "CRF++, Yet Another CRF" toolkit (Kudo, 2005) was used as the implementation of CRFs model and www.Baidu.com as the search engine for our model based on contextual features.

6.2 Results of the Proposed Method

The results for the four schemes of our method based on internal component features are listed in Table 5[2]. From these results we may see that Scheme 1 is the best and Scheme 3 the second best, which means POS-tag of internal components is very useful feature in the POS guessing work. The comparison between Scheme 1 and Scheme 3 indicates that character-based scheme is good for processing tri-syllabic words and five-character words while IC-based scheme is good for processing disyllabic words and four-character words. Considering that most tri-syllabic words and five-character words are derivative words, while disyllabic words and four-character words are compounds, the results show that the character-based scheme is good for processing derivative words while the IC-based scheme is good for processing compounds. All the following improvements will be based on Scheme 1.

We assign the threshold of credibility score as 0.8, and then there are 2,234 words with a credibility score lower than the threshold. These words are then put through the revision process. In the revision model, we set the values of Value(N), Value(V), Value(A) and the outstanding threshold as 4, 1, 1, and 0.5, respectively, based on experience. All above thresholds are experimentally determined. Finally, 1,357 out of the 2,234 words pass the outstanding examination. Among them, 462 results were different from the former results and 302 of those were correctly revised, which resulted in the precision of disyllabic words reaching 87.90% (see Table 6). Moreover, other 895 words, which have the same result in the two models, reaches the precision of 91.2%. That means the credibility will be very high when the two models generate the same result.

Although we believe that the former method may have equal effectiveness to most man-made rules, there are still several rules that must be incorporated in order to simplify our machine-learning method. Here we incorporated two reduplication rules to process two types of reduplicated unknown words, respectively. The form of the first kind of words is "V_1不V_2, such as 应不应该 yingbuyinggai (*should or should*

[2] Precision, recall, F-measure are the same.

not) and the form of the second kind of words is "$V_1V_1V_2V_2$," such as 出出进进 chuchujinjin (*go in and go out*). If a four-character word is associated with one of the two forms and the first character is a verb, we revise its POS as a verb tag.

The two reduplication rules correctly revised 68 four-character words, which increased the precision of four-character words to 97.10%, a significant improvement over the previous best result, which was 92.89% (see Table 6).

implement their model using the same data as our method. The results of Wu & Jiang's (2000) model are listed in Table 7. It shows that their model can guess the POS for disyllabic words with a relatively good F-measure (83.60%). However, the recall is not high for disyllabic (79.11%) and tri-syllabic (82.70%) words, and quite low for four-character (20.95%) and five-character (0%) words. Our model in Section 3 not only improves F-measure to 93.40%, but also improves recalls to 86.60%, 99.22%, 92.03% and 100% for multi-syllabic words in turn (Table 5, Scheme 1).

Word Length	Precision of Scheme 1	Precision of Scheme 2	Precision of Scheme 3	Precision of Scheme 4	Best Result
Disyllabic	86.60%	86.01	86.65%	85.21%	86.65%
Tri-syllabic	99.22%	99.17%	98.65%	97.48%	99.22%
Four-character	92.03%	91.47%	92.89%	89.76%	92.89%
Five-character	100.00%	98.20%	98.92%	98.92%	100.00%
Total	93.40%	93.08%	93.15%	91.80%	93.40%

Table 5. Results for Four Schemes of The Model Based on Internal Component Features

Lu (2005) proposed a hybrid model that achieved a precision of 89% for all words and 74% for disyllabic words. Compared with that method, the hybrid model in this paper improves the precision to 94.20% for all words and 87.90% for disyllabic words. Although the experiments were not taken on the same data, the figures reflect the difference of power between methods in a certain degree.

Word Length	Total number	Precision (Corresponding value of before)
Disyllabic	11,108	87.90% (86.60%)
Tri-syllabic	12,901	99.22% (99.22%)
Four-character	1,055	97.10% (92.89%)
Five-character	279	100% (100%)
Total	25,343	94.20% (93.40%)

Table 6. Results of Revision by Voting Model and Two Rules

Word Length	Total Number	Tagged Number	Precision	Recall	F-measure (Corresponding value of our method)
Disyllabic	11,108	10,408	84.43%	79.11%	81.68% (87.90%)
Tri-syllabic	12,901	11,091	96.20%	82.70%	88.94% (99.22%)
Four-character	1,055	225	98.22%	20.95%	34.53% (97.10%)
Five-character	279	0	0	0	0 (100%)
Total	25,343	21,724	90.58%	77.65%	83.60% (94.20%)

Table 7. Results of Wu & Jiang's (2000)

6.3 Comparison with Previous Work

Wu & Jiang's (2000)[3] method is the most analogous with our method, yet they did not directly report the results in their paper. In this paper, we

7 Conclusion and Future Work

The results of this experiment show that our model based on internal component features can achieve quite good results in POS guessing for unknown Chinese words, both in precision and recall. This proves that the internal component

[3] Lu (2005) implemented Wu & Jiang's (2000) model with a relatively small corpus as the training data. The precision of Wu & Jiang's method reported by the paper is 77.90% with a recall of 63.82%.

features of unknown words can be very useful in POS guessing. Moreover, the trained model based on internal component features is universal and robust. One evidence is that the model can identify POS correctly for most five-character words, even when there is no training data for that type of words.

Our results also show that the contextual features of unknown words can be an important complement to help improve POS guessing. Although models based on contextual features alone can't achieve the same precision and recall as models based on internal component features do, we may use contextual features as a complement in processing those words with ambiguous structure.

In contrast with Lu (2005), we don't use many manual rules. This does not mean that we believe those rules are useless in POS guessing. In fact, our initial model based on the CRFs model has learned the structure rules of Chinese words and can even give a credibility score for each rule. That is, most of the rules have been incorporated by the utilization of the CRFs model.

In the future, to improve the results, we attempt to manually revise the training data. Notice that the training data was formed by segmenting and tagging POS of each word in a dictionary using an existing tool like ICTCLAS. However, these tools usually generate quite a few errors on the words, because they are designed to handle sentence but not word. These errors were not revised in the experiment, which damaged the performance. Thus, by manually revising the training data, we hope to improve the results in a certain degree.

Although our experiments are mainly based on contemporary Chinese, we believe that this method will also be applicable to other Asian languages such as Japanese.

References

Andy Wu and Zixin Jiang. 2000. Statistically-enhanced New Word Identification in a Rule-based Chinese System. In *Proceedings of the 2nd Chinese Language Processing Workshop*, pages 46–51.

Chao-Jan Chen, Ming-Hong Bai, and Keh-Jiann Chen. 1997. Category Guessing for Chinese Unknown Words. In *Proceedings of the Natural Language Processing Pacific Rim Symposium*, pages 35–40.

Chooi-Ling Goh, Masayuki Asahara, and Yuji Matsumoto. 2006. Machine Learning-based Methods to Chinese Unknown Word Detection and POS Tag Guessing. In *Journal of Chinese Language and Computing* 16 (4):185-206

Douglas L. Vail, Manuela M. Veloso, and John D. Lafferty. 2007. Conditional Random Fields for Activity Recognition. In *Proceedings of 2007 International Joint Conference on Autonomous Agents and Multi-agent Systems*.

John Lafferty, Andrew McCallum, and Fernando Pereira. 2001. Conditional Random Fields: Probabilistic Models for Segmenting and Labeling Sequence Data. In *Proceedings of International Conference on Machine Learning*.

Kevin Zhang. ICTCLAS1.0. http://www.nlp.org.cn/project/project.php?proj_id=6.

Rui Guo. 2002. *Studies on Part-of-speech of Contemporary Chinese*. Commercial Press, Beijing, China.

Shiwen Yu. 1998. *Dictionary of Modern Chinese Grammar Information*. Tsinghua University Press. Beijing, China.

Shiwen Yu, Huiming Duan, Xuefeng Zhu, and Bing Sun. 2002. *The Basic Processing of Contemporary Chinese Corpus at Peking University*. Technical Report, Institute of Computational Linguistics, Peking University, Beijing, China.

T Nakagawa, Y Matsumoto. 2006. Guessing Parts-of-speech of Unknown Words Using Global Information. In *Proceedings of the 21st International Conference on Computational Linguistics and 44th Annual Meeting of Association for Computational Linguistics*, pages 705–712.

Taku Kudo. 2005. *CRF++: Yet Another CRF toolkit*. http://chasen.org/~taku/software/CRF++.

Xiaofei Lu. 2005. Hybrid Methods for POS Guessing of Chinese Unknown Words. In *Proceedings of the 43th Annual Meeting of Association for Computational Linguistics Student Research Workshop*, pages 1–6.

Almost Flat Functional Semantics for Speech Translation

Manny Rayner[1], **Pierrette Bouillon**[1], **Beth Ann Hockey**[2], **Yukie Nakao**[3]

[1] **University of Geneva, TIM/ISSCO**
40 bvd du Pont-d'Arve
CH-1211 Geneva 4, Switzerland
Emmanuel.Rayner@issco.unige.ch
Pierrette.Bouillon@issco.unige.ch

[2] **UCSC UARC, Mail Stop 19-26**
NASA Ames Research Center
Moffet Field, CA 94035
bahockey@ucsc.edu

[3] **University of Nantes, LINA**
2, rue de la Houssinière
BP 92208 44322 Nantes Cedex 03
yukie.nakao@univ-nantes.fr

Abstract

We introduce a novel semantic representation formalism, Almost Flat Functional semantics (AFF), which is designed as an intelligent compromise between linguistically motivated predicate/argument semantics and *ad hoc* engineering solutions based on flat feature/value lists; the central idea is to tag each semantic element with the functional marking which most closely surrounds it. We argue that AFF is well-suited for medium-vocabulary speech translation applications, and describe simple and general algorithms for parsing, generating and performing transfer using AFF representations. The formalism has been fully implemented within a medium-vocabulary interlingua-based Open Source speech translation system which translates between English, French, Japanese and Arabic.

1 Introduction

Many speech translation architectures require some way to represent the meaning of spoken utterances, but even a brief review of the literature reveals a serious divergence of opinion as to how this may best be done. At risk of oversimplifying a little, there are two competing heritages. On the one hand, there is the mainstream computational semantics approach, which ultimately goes back to philosophers like Montague, Russell and Frege and views predicate calculus as the paradigm representation language. On this view of things, a suitable way to represent meaning is to use complex structures, in which components and relationships are based on deep grammatical functions. Typical ways to realise this strategy are unscoped logical forms, neo-Davidsonian semantics, minimal recursion semantics, and similar formalisms. Thus a sentence like "I want a pepperoni pizza" might be represented as something like

```
want1(E, X, Y),
ref(X, pronoun(i)),
quant(Y, indef), pizza1(Y),
pepperoni1(Z), nn(Z, Y)
```

Approaches based in the linguistic tradition were dominant about 10 to 15 years ago, when they were used in major systems like Germany's Verbmobil (Wahlster, 2000) and SRI's Spoken Language Translator (Rayner et al., 2000). They are still reasonably popular today, as exemplified by major systems like PARC's XLE (Riezler et al., 2002).

The competing heritage has its roots in engineering approaches to spoken language systems, which historically have been intimately connected with Machine Learning. On this view of things, a typical semantic representation is a flat list of feature-value pairs, with the features representing semantic concepts: here, "I want a pepperoni pizza" would be represented as something like

```
[utterance_type=request,
 food=pizza, type=pepperoni]
```

It is interesting to see how little contact there has been between these two traditions. Writers on formal semantics usually treat *ad hoc* feature-value representations as not even worthy of serious discussion. Conversely, proponents of engineering/machine learning approaches often assume in practice that all semantic representations will be some version of a flat feature-value list; a good

©2008. Licensed under the *Creative Commons Attribution-Noncommercial-Share Alike 3.0 Unported* license (http://creativecommons.org/licenses/by-nc-sa/3.0/). Some rights reserved.

example of this tendency is Young's widely cited 2002 survey of machine learning approaches to spoken dialogue (Young, 2002).

Trying to be as neutral as possible, it is reasonable to argue that both approaches have important things to offer, and that it is worth trying to find some compromise between them. Other things being equal, flat feature-value representations have desirable formal properties: they are simple, and easy to manipulate and reason with. Their drawback is that they are an impoverished representation language, which can lose important information. This means that concepts may be impossible to represent, or, alternately viewed, that the representation format may conflate concepts which we would prefer to distinguish. In the other direction, hierarchical logic-based representations are highly expressive, but pose much more serious challenges in terms of formal manipulability. Although they are more easily capable of representing semantic distinctions, it is harder to use them to perform concrete reasoning operations. In translation systems, these abstract issues manifest themselves in a tradeoff between complexity of translation rules, and ambiguity of semantic representations. A flat semantic representation formalism means that translation rules are simple to write; however, it also means that the semantic representations they operate on are more likely to be ambiguous.

In this paper, we will explore the tradeoffs between the two competing positions outlined above in the context of a concrete Open Source system, the MedSLT medical speech translator. Previous versions of MedSLT have used a representation strategy intermediate between the "logic-based semantics" and the "flat semantics" approaches, though much closer to the "flat" end of the scale. We will discuss the strengths and weaknesses of the original MedSLT representation formalism, and then present a revised version, "Almost Flat Functional Semantics" (AFF). As the name suggests, AFF incorporates functional markings, characteristic of a logic-based semantics approach, into a representation formalism which still mainly consists of flat list structures. We will show how grammars using semantics written in AFF can be compiled into parsers and generators, and describe a simple formalism that can be used to specify rules for translating AFF expressions into AFF expressions. Finally, we will show how use of AFF in MedSLT has allowed us to address in a principled way most of the examples which are problematic for the original version of the system, while still retaining a simple and transparent framework for writing translation rules.

2 The MedSLT System

MedSLT (Bouillon et al., 2005) is a medium-vocabulary Open Source speech translation system for medical domains, implemented using the Open Source Regulus compiler (Rayner et al., 2006) and the Nuance recognition platform. Processing is primarily rule-based. Recognition uses a grammar-based language model, which produces a source-langage semantic representation. This is first translated by one set of rules into an interlingual form, and then by a second set into a target language representation. A target-language grammar, compiled into generation form, turns this into one or more possible surface strings, after which a set of generation preferences picks one out. Finally, the selected string is realised in spoken form. There is also some use of corpus-based statistical methods, both to tune the language model (Rayner et al., 2006, Section 11.5) and to drive a robust embedded help system (Chatzichrisafis et al., 2006).

The treatment of syntactic structure is a carefully thought-out compromise between linguistic and engineering traditions. All grammars used are extracted from general linguistically motivated resource grammars, using corpus-based methods driven by small sets of examples (Rayner et al., 2006, Chapter 9). This results in a simpler and flatter grammar specific to the domain, whose structure is similar to the *ad hoc* phrasal grammars typical of engineering approaches. The treatment of semantics is however less sophisticated, and basically represents a minimal approach in the engineering tradition. Each lexicon item contributes a set of zero or more feature-value pairs (in most cases exactly one pair). Most of the grammar rules simply concatenate the sets of pairs received from their daughters. A small number of rules, primarily those for subordinate clauses, create a nested substructure representing the embedded clause. Figure 1 shows an example representation.

It should be obvious from the example that the flat representation is potentially very ambiguous, since nearly all information about grammatical functions has been lost. The example also illustrates, however, why this is often unimportant in

```
[[utterance_type,sentence],
 [pronoun,vous],
 [path_proc,avoir],
 [voice,active],
 [tense,present],
 [cause,nausée], [sc,quand],
 [clause,
   [[pronoun,vous],
    [symptom,mal],
    [path_proc,avoir],
    [voice,active],
    [tense,present]]])]
```

Figure 1: Semantic representation produced by the current MedSLT system for the French sentence *Avez-vous des nausées quand vous avez mal?* ("Do you have nausea when you have the pain?")

practice. From a purely syntactic point of view, the fragment

```
[[pronoun,vous],
 [path_proc,avoir],
 [cause,nausée]]
```

could either represent *vous avez des nausées* ("you have nausea") or *des nausées vous ont* ("nausea has you"). Except, possibly, in certain kinds of literary contexts, the second realisation is so implausible that it can be discounted. It is thus reasonable to add sortal constraints to the lexical entries involved, which permit *des nausées* to occur in well-formed utterances as the object of *avoir*, but not as its subject. Thus the representation is in fact unambiguous, and will only generate one surface realisation.

With the moderate vocabularies used by MedSLT (for example, the current French module has a vocabulary of about 1 100 surface words), the vast majority of constructions can be rendered unambiguous using similar strategies. The result is that most translation rules are easy to write, since they have to do no more than map lists of feature-value pairs to lists of feature-value pairs. To take a typical example, the Japanese question *itami wa koutoubu desu ka* ("pain-TOPIC back-part-head is-Q") receives the representation

```
[[utterance_type,sentence],
 [symptom,itami],
 [body_part,koutoubu],
 [verb,desu], [tense,present]]
```

which we wish to map to the interlingua representation

```
[[utterance_type,ynq], [verb,be],
 [tense,present], [voice,active],
 [symptom,pain], [prep,in_loc],
 [part,back], [body_part,head]]
```

("is the pain in the back of the head"). In a more expressive semantic framework, the structural mismatches here would be non-trivial to resolve. In the flat MedSLT notation, we only need the following two list-to-list translation rules:

```
transfer_rule(
  [[body_part,koutoubu]],
  [[prep,in_loc], [part,back],
   [body_part,head]]).
```

(*koutoubu* → "in the back of the head") and

```
transfer_rule(
  [[verb, desu]],
  [[verb, be]]).
```

(*desu* → "is").

As usual, however, we pay a price for simplicity. In the terminology of Statistical Machine Translation, what we are essentially doing here is weakening the channel model, and relying on the strength of the target language model. This is a reasonable strategy partly because of the restricted nature of the domain, and partly because of the fact that the initial parsing stage makes it possible for us to work with bags of concepts rather than bags of words; clearly, bags of concepts are more expressive.

None the less, it is normal to expect the underspecified channel model to cause some problems, and this indeed proves to be the case. Although most semantic relationships in the domain are unambiguous even as bags of concepts ("back of the head" is possible; "head of the back" isn't), there are unpleasant counterexamples. For instance, {"visit", "doctor", "patient"} can be realised as either "patient visits doctor" or "doctor visits patient". Similarly, {"precede", "nausea", "headache"} can be either "nausea precedes headache" or "headache precedes nausea". Cases like these must be dealt with using *ad hoc* solutions based on domain pragmatics. In the current version of the system, "patient visits doctor" is forced by producing both surface realisations, and defining a generation preference. In the case of {"precede", "nausea", "headache"}, the problem is addressed by dividing symptoms into "primary" (the symptom the patient is being examined for, e.g. "headache") and "secondary" (other possibly

```
utterance:[sem=concat(Verb, [[tag, obj, Np]])] -->
    verb:[sem=Verb], np:[sem=Np].

np:[sem=concat(Adj, Noun)] -->
    spec:[], ?adj:[sem=Adj], noun:[sem=Noun].

np:[sem=concat(Np, PP)] -->
    np:[sem=Np], pp:[sem=PP].

pp:[sem=[[tag, Tag, Np]]] -->
    prep:[sem=Tag], np:[sem=Np].

verb:[sem=[[action, grasp]]] --> grasp.
noun:[sem=[[thing, block]]] --> block.
noun:[sem=[[loc, table]]] --> table.
adj:[sem=[[colour, red]]] --> red.
spec:[] --> the.
prep:[sem=on] --> on.
```

Figure 2: Toy grammar with nested predicate-argument semantics.

related symptoms, e.g. "nausea"). It is reasonable in practice to assume that the doctor will only be interested in secondary symptoms that may cause primary ones, and hence will precede them.

Although each language in the current version of MedSLT only contains a handful of similar cases, solutions like those outlined above are both inelegant and brittle. It would be desirable to find some more principled way to deal with them; we would, however, like to do this without sacrificing the appealing simplicity of the translation rule formalism. In the next section, we will show how it is possible to reconcile these two conflicting goals.

3 Almost Flat Functional Semantics

As we have seen, the problem with a simple bag-of-concepts representation is its ambiguity; what we would like to do is find some principled way to reduce that ambiguity, without greatly increasing the formalism's representational complexity. At this point, a linguistic intuition is helpful. The bag-of-concepts representation can reasonably be thought of as an artificial free word-order language. There are many natural free word-order languages; the reason why they are in general no more ambiguous than fixed word-order languages is that they use case-marking to convey functional information which constrains the space of possible interpretations. For speakers of European languages, the best-known example will probably be Classical Latin. For instance, when St. Jerome wrote *Amor ordinem nescit* ("love-NOM order-ACC not-know-PRES-3-SING"), the case-markings make it clear that he meant "Love does not know order" rather than "Order does not know love".

The comparison with free word-order languages suggests a natural extension of the original bag-of-concepts representation, where each element is associated with an additional functional tag which does the work that a case-marking would do in a natural free word-order language. It also suggests a simple construction which can be used to create an unordered linear representation that includes functional tags. We start by defining a standard nested predicate-argument semantics; we then flatten the representation of each clause S, marking each primitive semantic element with the immediately surrounding functional tag in S, or with a null marking if there is no such tag. The resulting semantic representations still represent each clause as an unordered list, but in contrast to the MedSLT bag-of-concepts representation now include functional information. We will call this style of representation *Almost Flat Functional* (AFF) semantics; the "almost" comes from the fact that there is still a minimal amount of nested structure, representing the distinction between main and embedded clauses.

Figures 2 and 3 give a concrete illustration of the

```
[[action, grasp],
 [tag, obj,
   [[colour, red],
    [thing, block],
    [tag, on,
      [[loc, table]]]]]]
```

```
[null=[action, grasp],
 obj=[colour, red],
 obj=[thing, block],
 on=[loc, table]]
```

Figure 3: Construction of AFF representation for "grasp the red block on the table". The AFF representation (right) is a flattened version of the original nested predicate-argument one (left).

AFF construction. Figure 2 presents a toy Regulus grammar, which allows a few sentences like "grasp the red block on the table" and assigns a nested functional semantics to them. The representations of most constituents are unordered lists. In the case of `utterance` and `np`, these are formed by concatenating the representations of their daughters. There are two examples of functional markings: the rule for `utterance` wraps an `[tag, obj ...]` around its `np` daughter, and the rule for `pp` wraps a tag around its `np` daughter, whose label is determined by the semantic value of the `p` daughter.

Figure 3 introduces the AFF construction itself. The left-hand side of the figure shows the nested predicate-argument representation of the sentence, in which elements of the form

```
[tag, Tag, Arg]
```

represent tags and their associated arguments. The right-hand side shows the derived AFF representation, where each element that is within the scope of a `[tag ...]` has been marked with the tag that would be immediately above it in the nested version. Thus the element `[loc, table]` is inside the scope of both the `obj` tag and the `on` tag; however, the AFF version assigns it the `on` tag, since this is the innermost one.

In the rest of this section, we will describe how we can parse surface strings into AFF representations, generate surface strings from AFF representations, and define translation rules which map AFF representations to AFF representations.

3.1 Analysis and generation

For both analysis and generation, the starting point is a grammar with a nested predicate-argument semantics like the one shown in the left half of Figure 3. Analysis is straightforward. We first use a standard parser-generator to compile the grammar into a parser; the nested predicate-argument representations it produces are then subjected to a post-processing phase, which flattens them in the way illustrated in the figure.

This simple approach is however not feasible for generation, since the flattening operation is highly non-deterministic in the reverse direction; finding all possible "unflattenings" and then attempting to generate from each one would in most cases be hopelessly inefficient. A better solution is to transform the original grammar into one with AFF semantics, where the current functional marking is specified as an extra features on relevant constituents, and percolated through the rules. In effect, the "unflattening" and generation operations can now proceed simultaneously, with each one constraining the other.

Figure 4 presents an example, showing the result of performing this transformation on the toy Regulus grammar from Figure 2. Here, the original `[tag, ...]` wrappers have been removed, and replaced by the new feature `tag`, which has been added to all constituents whose semantics is a list of items of the form `Tag=Value`. The value of the `tag` feature on each constituent where it is defined is the tag for the most closely enclosing `[tag, ...]` in the original grammar; these values are percolated down to the lexical rules, where they unify with the tags on the semantic fragment contributed by the rule. The transformation is straightforward to define in its general form, and the transformed grammars can be readily compiled into efficient generators by standard feature-grammar generator-compiler algorithms like Semantic Head-Driven Generation (Shieber et al., 1990). For the concrete experiments described later, we used a slightly extended version of the Open Source Regulus generator compiler.

3.2 Transfer

Our basic strategy for defining transfer between AFF expressions is to make it as close as possible to transfer on the original bag-of-concepts

```
utterance:[sem=concat(Verb, Np)] -->
    verb:[sem=Verb, tag=null], np:[sem=Np, tag=obj].

np:[sem=concat(Adj, Noun), tag=Tag] -->
    spec:[], ?adj:[sem=Adj, tag=Tag], noun:[sem=Noun, tag=Tag].

np:[sem=concat(Np, PP), tag=Tag] -->
    np:[sem=Np, tag=Tag], pp:[sem=PP, tag=Tag].

pp:[sem=Np] -->
    prep:[sem=Tag], np:[sem=Np, tag=Tag].

verb:[sem=[Tag=[action, grasp]], tag=Tag] --> grasp.
noun:[sem=[Tag=[thing, block]], tag=Tag] --> block.
noun:[sem=[Tag=[loc, table]], tag=Tag] --> table.
adj:[sem=[Tag=[colour, red]], tag=Tag] --> red.
spec:[] --> the.
prep:[sem=on] --> on.
```

Figure 4: Version of grammar from Figure 2 after transformation to AFF semantics.

representations, which is conditional mapping of lists to lists. Since AFF is an extension of bag-of-concepts, and bag-of-concepts is usually sufficiently unambiguous as it stands, we only want to add the functional markings in the cases where they are required. Most of our rules will thus still be `transfer_rules` like the ones shown in Section 2, except that they now map lists of function-marking-tagged items to lists of function-marking-tagged items; however, in accordance with the stated design principles, we allow tags to be omitted when desired, with the convention that an omitted tag denotes an uninstantiated tag value.

One of the underlying linguistic intuitions behind AFF is that there are correspondences between functional markings in different languages, with each given functional marking f_s in the source language typically mapping to a specific functional marking f_t in the target language. For this reason, it would be highly unnatural only to specify transformations of tag values using `transfer_rules`. We consequently introduce a second kind of rule, which we call a `tag_transfer_rule`; as the name suggests, this defines a direct mapping from tags to tags. Given the fact that functional tags have some claim to universality, it is reasonable to hope that many tags will map onto themselves. Thus a typical tag rule might map the English `subj` tag to the Arabic `subj` tag, which we write as

```
tag_transfer_rule(subj, subj).
```

Most tag transfer rules will be of the above simple form. However, there are always cases where languages diverge structurally, and here it will be necessary to make the tag transfer rule conditional on its surrounding context. For example, English constructions with the verb "last" ("Does the headache last more than ten minutes?") are realised differently in Arabic, using the transitive verb *tahus bi* ("feel"), thus here *hal tahus bi al soudaa li akthar min achr daqayq?* ("Do (you) feel the headache during more than ten minutes?"). Here, "headache" is marked as `subj` in English, but the correspoding Arabic word, *soudaa*, is the `obj` of *tahus bi*. We express the general fact that we wish to map `subj` to `obj` in the context of the verb "last" using the rule

```
tag_transfer_rule(subj, obj) :-
   context([state, last]).
```

We also require a normal `transfer_rule` which maps "last" to *tahus bi*. This also has to introduce an implicit second person subject, so the full rule is

```
transfer_rule(
  [[state, last]],
  [[state, tahus_bi],
   subj=[pronoun, anta]]).
```

(*anta* = "you"). Related sets of rules of this kind can be written more concisely with a small extension to the formalism, as follows:

```
transfer_rule(
  [[state, last]],
  [[state, tahus_bi],
   subj=[pronoun, anta]],
  [subj:obj]).
```

An important question we have so far postponed discussing is how to fill in unspecified tag values on the RHS of a `transfer_rule` application. At first, we believed that several possible strategies were feasible; rather to our surprise, examination of some examples convinced us that only one of these strategies actually made sense. The algorithm is as follows. We assume a `transfer_rule` R, whose LHS has successfully matched a set of tag/concept pairs, and consider the following cases:

1. R explicitly assigns values to all of the tags on its RHS. There is nothing more to do.

2. Not all of the tags on the RHS are assigned values by R. Apply `tag_transfer_rules` to all the matched tags on the LHS which were not originally assigned values by R, giving a set of tags $\{T_1 ... T_n\}$. There are now two subcases:

   (a) $n = 1$, i.e. only one transferred tag is produced. Set the values of all the uninstantiated tags on the transferred RHS to T_1.

   (b) $n > 1$, i.e. several different transferred tags are produced. Leave the values of the ininstantiated tags on the transferred RHS uninstantiated.

The least obvious part of this is (2a), which is easier to understand when we consider some more specific cases. The simplest and most common example is the case where R is a "lexical" `transfer_rule` which contains exactly one tag/concept pair on each side, each tag being left unspecified. We evidently need to apply a `tag_transfer` rule to the tag matched by the single pair on the LHS, to get the value of the tag attached to the transferred RHS.

To take a slightly more complex case, consider an English → Japanese rule which maps the expression "back of the head" to the single word *koutoubu*. We could write this as

```
transfer_rule(
  [[part, back],
   of=[body_part,head]],
  [[body_part, koutoubu]])
```

Here, it is clear that we want to translate the tag on the source-language pair that matches `[part, back]`, and assign it to the target-language element `[body_part, koutoubu]`. The translation of the tag `of` is irrelevant.

4 Using AFF in MedSLT

We have implemented and tested a version of AFF inside the Open Source MedSLT system, building AFF versions of the grammars for English, French Japanese, Arabic and the Interlingua. We also created AFF versions of the translation rules between the four surface languages and the Interlingua, in both directions. Coverage and performance of the two versions of the system on development data were essentially the same; the key differences were architectural in nature. We now briefly summarise these differences.

The basic tradeoff is between analysis and generation on one hand, and translation on the other. The more expressive AFF formalism implies that representations are less ambiguous, which means fewer problems in the analysis and generation components. The downside is that the translation rules become more complex. On the positive side, switching from bag-of-concepts to AFF allowed us to implement clean solutions to a substantial number of problems which were previously handled in an *ad hoc* manner. As previously noted, English constructions using verbs like "precede", "cause", "accompany", "visit" and "be in contact with" are in general ambiguous in the bag-of-words representation, and had to be solved by artificially constraining their arguments; AFF makes it possible to do this by simply differentiating between `subj` and `obj` tags. Similar considerations applied to constructions in the other two languages. For example, using bag-of-words, the Arabic frequency expressions *thalath marrat fi al ousbou* ("three times a week") and *marra kul thalathat assabii* ("once every three weeks") were previously represented in the same way, necessitating addition of a brittle generation preference. AFF once again allows the two expressions to be cleanly distinguished.

It was evident from the start that we would win on this kind of example; what was less clear was the price we would have to pay, in terms of increased complexity of the transfer rule set. Gratifyingly, the conservative nature of the extension meant that this price turned out to be quite low. We had originally wondered whether it would be necessary to write many conditional tag_transfer_rules, or add functional tags to a large proportion of the transfer_rules. In fact, out of the total of 4444 rules used by the eight language pairs together, only 39 (0.9%) were conditional tag_transfer_rules, and 524 (11.8%) were transfer_rules containing at least one functional tag. A further 120 rules (2.7%) were unconditional tag_transfer_rules. The remaining 3761 rules (84.6%) were transfer_rules which did not explicitly mention functional tags, and were thus essentially bag-of-concepts mapping rules. To summarise, less than a sixth of the rules were affected by moving to the new framework.

5 Summary and Conclusions

We have described Almost Flat Functional semantics, a formalism which adds functional markings to a flat atheoretical feature/value representation. The additional functional information in AFF is sufficient to resolve nearly all of the representational ambiguities which caused problems for the flat bag-of-concepts formalism. In terms of representational complexity, however, the AFF formalism appears to be only slightly less tractable than bag-of-concepts. It seems reasonable to us that, like bag-of-concepts, it could also support learnable surface-oriented parsing; this could be combined with statistical recognition to provide a robust back-up to grammar-based speech processing (Rayner et al., 2005), a claim that we hope to investigate empirically in the near future. It is much less clear that full logic-based representations could be used for such purposes.

What we find interesting here, from a general perspective, is that we were able to create a reduced, but still essentially clean, form of a mainstream linguistic treatment, and incorporate it into an *ad hoc* engineering framework in a way that only marginally affected that framework's performance characteristics. Without wishing to exaggerate the importance of our results, we think examples like AFF suggest that the gulf between these two types of approach is not, perhaps, as wide as is sometimes suggested.

References

Bouillon, P., M. Rayner, N. Chatzichrisafis, B.A. Hockey, M. Santaholma, M. Starlander, Y. Nakao, K. Kanzaki, and H. Isahara. 2005. A generic multilingual open source platform for limited-domain medical speech translation. In *Proceedings of the 10th Conference of the European Association for Machine Translation (EAMT)*, pages 50–58, Budapest, Hungary.

Chatzichrisafis, N., P. Bouillon, M. Rayner, M. Santaholma, M. Starlander, and B.A. Hockey. 2006. Evaluating task performance for a unidirectional controlled language medical speech translation system. In *Proceedings of the HLT-NAACL International Workshop on Medical Speech Translation*, pages 9–16, New York.

Rayner, M., D. Carter, P. Bouillon, V. Digalakis, and M. Wirén, editors. 2000. *The Spoken Language Translator*. Cambridge University Press.

Rayner, M., P. Bouillon, N. Chatzichrisafis, B.A. Hockey, M. Santaholma, M. Starlander, H. Isahara, K. Kanzaki, and Y. Nakao. 2005. A methodology for comparing grammar-based and robust approaches to speech understanding. In *Proceedings of the 9th International Conference on Spoken Language Processing (ICSLP)*, pages 1103–1107, Lisboa, Portugal.

Rayner, M., B.A. Hockey, and P. Bouillon. 2006. *Putting Linguistics into Speech Recognition: The Regulus Grammar Compiler*. CSLI Press, Chicago.

Riezler, S., T.H. King, R.M. Kaplan, R. Crouch, J.T. Maxwell, and M. Johnson. 2002. Parsing the wall street journal using a lexical-functional grammar and discriminative estimation techniques. In *Proceedings of the 40th Annual Meeting of the Association for Computational Linguistics (demo track)*, Philadelphia, PA.

Shieber, S., G. van Noord, F.C.N. Pereira, and R.C. Moore. 1990. Semantic-head-driven generation. *Computational Linguistics*, 16(1).

Wahlster, W., editor. 2000. *Verbmobil: Foundations of Speech-to-Speech Translation*. Springer.

Young, S. 2002. Talking to machines (statistically speaking). In *Proceedings of the 7th International Conference on Spoken Language Processing (ICSLP)*, pages 9–16, Denver, CO.

Unsupervised Induction of Labeled Parse Trees by Clustering with Syntactic Features

Roi Reichart
ICNC
Hebrew University of Jerusalem
roiri@cs.huji.ac.il

Ari Rappoport
Institute of computer science
Hebrew University of Jerusalem
arir@cs.huji.ac.il

Abstract

We present an algorithm for unsupervised induction of labeled parse trees. The algorithm has three stages: bracketing, initial labeling, and label clustering. Bracketing is done from raw text using an unsupervised incremental parser. Initial labeling is done using a merging model that aims at minimizing the grammar description length. Finally, labels are clustered to a desired number of labels using syntactic features extracted from the initially labeled trees. The algorithm obtains 59% labeled f-score on the WSJ10 corpus, as compared to 35% in previous work, and substantial error reduction over a random baseline. We report results for English, German and Chinese corpora, using two label mapping methods and two label set sizes.

1 Introduction

Unsupervised learning of grammar from text ('grammar induction') is of great theoretical and practical importance. It can shed light on language acquisition by humans and on the general structure of language, and it can potentially assist NLP applications that utilize parser output. The problem has attracted researchers for decades, and interest has greatly increased recently, in part due to the availability of huge corpora, computation power, and new learning algorithms (see Section 2).

A fundamental issue in this research direction is the representation of the resulting induced grammar. Most recent work (e.g., (Klein and Manning, 2004; Dennis, 2005; Bod, 2006a; Smith and Eisner, 2006; Seginer, 2007)) annotates text sentences using a hierarchical bracketing (constituents) or a dependency structure, and thus represents the induced grammar through its behavior in a parsing task. Solan et al. (2005) uses a graph representation, while (Nakamura, 2006) simply uses a grammar formalism such as PCFG. When the bracketing approach is taken, some algorithms label the resulting constituents, while most do not.

Each of these approaches can be justified or criticized; a detailed discussion of this issue is beyond the scope of this paper. The algorithm presented here belongs to the first group, annotating given sentences with labeled bracketing structures. The main theoretical justification for this approach is that many linguistic and psycho-linguistic theories posit some kind of a hierarchical labeled constituent (or constructional) structure, arguing that it has a measurable psychological (cognitive) reality (e.g., (Goldberg, 2006)). The main practical arguments in favor of this approach are that it enables a detailed and large-scale evaluation using annotated corpora, as is done in this paper, and that the output format is suitable for many applications.

When an algorithm generates labeled structures, the number of labels is an important issue. From a theoretical point of view, the algorithm should also discover the appropriate number of labels. However, for evaluation and application purposes it is useful to base the number of labels on a specific *target grammar*. In previous work, the number was set to be equal to that in the target grammar. This is a reasonable approach that we experiment with in this paper. In addition, to reduce the possible arbitrariness in this approach, we also experiment with the number of *prominent labels* in the target

©2008. Licensed under the *Creative Commons Attribution-Noncommercial-Share Alike 3.0 Unported* license (http://creativecommons.org/licenses/by-nc-sa/3.0/). Some rights reserved.

grammar, determined according to their coverage of corpus constituents.

Another issue relates to the nature of the input. In most cases (e.g., in the Klein, Smith, Dennis and Bod papers above), the input consists of part-of-speech (POS) sequences, derived from text corpora by manual or automatic POS tagging. In some cases (e.g., in the Seginer and Solan papers above) it can consist of plain text. Again, each approach has its pros and cons. The algorithm we present here requires POS tags for its labeling stages. Parts-of-speech are widely considered to have a psychological reality (at least in English, including when they are viewed as low-level constructions as in (Croft, 2001)), so this kind of input is reasonable for theoretical research. Moreover, as POS induction is of medium quality (Clark, 2003), using a manually POS tagged corpus enables us to measure the performance of other induction stages in a controlled manner. Since supervised POS tagging is of very high quality and very efficient computationally (Brants, 2000), this requirement does not seriously limit the practical applicability of a grammar induction algorithm.

Our labeled bracketings induction algorithm consists of three stages. We first induce unlabeled bracketing trees using the algorithm given in (Seginer, 2007)[1]. We then induce initial labels using a *Bayesian Model Merging (BMM)* labeling algorithm (Borensztajn and Zuidema, 2007), which aims at minimizing the description length of the input data and the induced grammar. Finally, the initial labels are clustered to a desired number of labels using syntactic features extracted from the initially labeled trees. Previous work on labeled brackets induction (Section 2) did not differentiate the unlabeled structure induction phase from the labeling phase, applying a single phase approach.

To evaluate labeled bracketings, we need a mapping between the label symbols of the induced and target grammars. Previous work used a 'greedy', many to one, mapping. We used both the greedy mapping and a label-to-label (LL) mapping, since greedy mapping is highly forgiving to structural problems in the induced labeling. We report results for two cases: one in which the number of labels in the induced and target grammars is the same, and one in which the former is the number of prominent labels in the target grammar. We discuss how this number can be defined and determined. We experimented with English (WSJ10, Brown10), German (NEGRA10) and Chinese (CTB10) corpora.

When comparing to previous work that used manually annotated corpora in its evaluation (Haghighi and Klein, 2006)[2], we obtained 59.5% labeled f-score on the WSJ10 setup vs. their 35.3% (Section 5). We also show substantial improvement over a random baseline, and that the clustering stage of our algorithm improves the results of the second merging stage.

Section 2 discusses previous work. In Section 3 we detail our algorithm. The experimental setup and results are presented in Sections 4 and 5.

2 Previous Work

Unsupervised parsing has attracted researchers for decades (see (Clark, 2001; Klein, 2005) for recent reviews). Many types of input, syntax formalisms, search procedures, and success criteria were used. Among the theoretical and practical motivations to this problem are the study of human language acquisition (in particular, an empirical study of the poverty of stimulus hypothesis), preprocessing for constructing large treebanks (Van Zaanen, 2001), and improving language models (Chen, 1995).

In recent years efforts have been made to evaluate the algorithms on manually annotated corpora such as the WSJ PennTreebank. Recently, works along this line have for the first time outperformed the right branching heuristic baseline for English. These include the constituent–context model (CCM) (Klein and Manning, 2002), its extension using a dependency model (Klein and Manning, 2004), (U)DOP based models (Bod, 2006a; Bod, 2006b; Bod, 2007), an exemplar–based approach (Dennis, 2005), guiding EM using contrastive estimation (Smith and Eisner, 2006), and the incremental parser of (Seginer, 2007). All of these use as input POS tag sequences, except of Seginer's algorithm, which uses plain text. All of these papers induce unlabeled bracketing or dependencies.

There are other algorithmic approaches to the problem (e.g., (Adriaans, 1992; Daelemans, 1995; Van Zaanen, 2001)). None of these had evaluated labeled bracketing on annotated corpora.

In this paper we focus on the induction of *labeled* bracketing. Bayesian Model Merging

[1]The algorithm uses raw (not POS tagged) sentences.

[2]Using, as they did, a greedy mapping with an equal number of labels in the induced and target grammars.

(BMM) (Stolcke, 1994; Stolcke and Omohundro, 1994) is a framework for inducing PCFG containing both a bracketing and a labeling. The characteristics of this framework (separating prior probability, data likelihood and heuristic search procedures) can also be found in the grammar induction models of (Wolf, 1982; Langley and Stromsten, 2000; Petasis et al., 2004; Solan et al., 2005). The BMM model used here (Borensztajn and Zuidema, 2007) combines features of (Petasis et al., 2004) and Stolcke's algorithm, applying the minimum description length (MDL) principle. We use it here only for initial labeling of existing bracketings. The MDL principle was also used in (Grunwald, 1994; de Marcken, 1995; Clark, 2001).

There are only two previous papers we are aware of that induce labeled bracketing and evaluate on corpora annotated with a similar representation (Haghighi and Klein, 2006; Borensztajn and Zuidema, 2007). We utilize and extend the latter's labeling algorithm. However, the evaluation done by the latter dealt only with labeling, using gold-standard (manually annotated) bracketings. Thus, we can directly compare our results only to (Haghighi and Klein, 2006), where two models (*PCFG × NONE* and *PCFG × CCM*) are fully unsupervised. These models use the inside-outside and EM algorithms to induce bracketing and labeling simultaneously, as opposed to our three step method[3].

3 Algorithm

Our model consists of three stages: bracketing, initial labeling, and label clustering.

3.1 Induction of Unlabeled Bracketing

In this step, we apply the algorithm of (Seginer, 2007) to induce bracketing from plain text[4]. We have chosen that algorithm because it is very fast (both learning and parsing) and its code is publicly available. We could have chosen any of the algorithms mentioned above producing a similar output format.

3.2 Initial Constituent Labeling

Our label clustering stage uses syntactic features. To obtain these, we need an initial labeling on the bracketings computed in the previous stage. To do that we modify the Bayesian Model Merging (BMM) algorithm of (Borensztajn and Zuidema, 2007), which induces context-free grammars (bracketing and labeling) from POS tags, combining features of the models of (Stolcke and Omohundro, 1994) and (Petasis et al., 2004).

The BMM algorithm (Borensztajn and Zuidema, 2007) uses an iterative heuristic greedy search for an optimal PCFG according to the Bayesian criterion of maximum posterior probability. Two operators define possible transitions between grammars: MERGE creates generalizations by replacing two existing non-terminals X_1 and X_2 that occur in the same contexts by a single new non-terminal Y; CHUNK concatenates repeating patterns by taking a sequence of two non-terminals X_1 and X_2 and creating a new non-terminal Y that expands to X_1X_2.

We have used the algorithm to deal only with labeling. It reads the initial rules of the grammar from all productions implicit in the bracketed corpus induced in the previous step. Every constituent (except of the start symbol) is given a unique label. Since only labeling is required, only MERGE operations are performed.

The objective function the algorithm tries to optimize at each step is the posterior probability calculated according to Bayes' Law:

$$M_{MAP} = argmax_M\ P(M|X) = argmax_M\ P(X|M) \cdot P(M) \quad (1)$$

where $P(X|M)$ is the likelihood of the data X given the grammar M and $P(M)$ is the prior probability of the grammar. This is equivalent to minimizing the function

$$-log(P(X|M)) - logP(m) := DDL + GDL := DL. \quad (2)$$

Using a Minimal Description Length (MDL) principle, BMM interprets this function as total description length (DL): The Grammar Description Length $GDL = -logP(M)$ is the space needed to encode the model, and the Data Description Length $DDL = -logP(X|M)$ is the space required to describe the data given the model. The rationale for MDL is to prefer smaller grammars that describe the data well. DDL and GDL are computed as in (Stolcke, 1994; Stolcke and Omohundro, 1994). In order to reduce the number of grammars considered at each step, which naively is quadratic in the number of non-terminals, a method based on (Petasis et al., 2004) for efficiently predicting DL gain is applied. The process

[3]Their other models, which were the core of their paper, are semi-supervised.

[4]http://www.seggu.net/ccl

is iterated until no additional merge operation improves the objective function. Full details are given in (Borensztajn and Zuidema, 2007).

3.3 Label Clustering

Label set size. BMM produces quite a large number of labels (4944 for WSJ10[5]). In the third step of our algorithm we reduce that number. We first discuss the issue of the number of labels in induced grammars, which is an important issue.

In many situations, it is reasonable to use a number T identical to the number of labels in a given target grammar, for example when that grammar is used for applications or evaluation. This is the approach in (Haghighi and Klein, 2006) for their unsupervised models[6], and we use it in part of our evaluation. However, it is also reasonable to argue that the granularity of syntactic categories (labels) in the gold standard annotation of the corpora we experiment with is somewhat arbitrary. For example, in the WSJ Penn Treebank noun phrases are annotated with the symbol NP, but there is no distinction between subject and object NPs. Incorporating such a distinction into the WSJ10 grammar would result in a 27 labels grammar instead of 26.

To examine this issue, consider Figure 1, which shows the amount of constituent coverage obtained by a certain number of labels in the four corpora we use (see Section 4). In all of them, about 95% of the constituents are covered by 23% – 37% of the labels, and the curve rises very sharply until that 95% value. Motivated by this observation, given a corpus annotated using a certain hierarchical labeled grammar, we refer to the set of P labels that cover at least 95% of the constituents in the corpus as the grammar's *prominent* labels.

The prominent labels are not only the most frequent in the corpus; each of them substantially contributes to constituent labeling, while the saliency of other labels is much smaller. It is thus reasonable to assume that by addressing only prominent labels, we address a level of granularity that is uniform and basic (to the annotation scheme used). As a result, by asking the induced grammar to produce P labels, we reduce arbitrariness and enable our testing to focus on our success in identifying the basic phenomena in the target grammar.

[5]For completeness, in Section 5 we provide results for this grammar using greedy mapping evaluation. LL mapping evaluation cannot be performed when the numbers of induced and target labels differ.

[6]Personal communication with the authors.

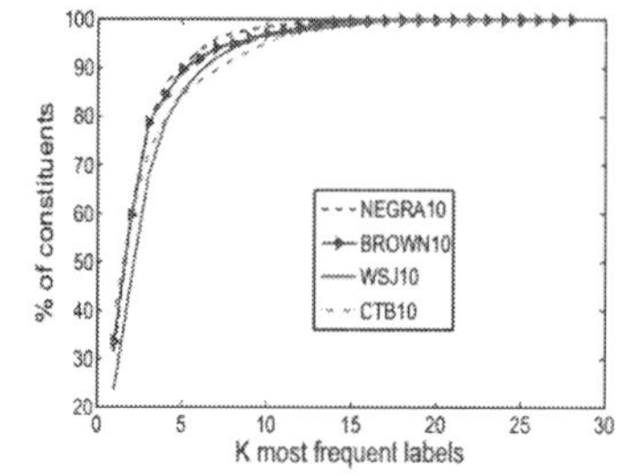

Figure 1: For each k, the fraction of constituents labeled with the k most frequent labels, for WSJ10 (solid), Brown10 (triangles), NEGRA10 (dashed) and CTB10 (dotted). In all corpora, more than 95% of the constituents are labeled using less than 10 *prominent* labels.

As a result, we generated two grammars for each corpus we experimented with, one having T labels and the other having P labels.

Clustering. we stop BMM when no improvement to its objective function is possible, and cluster the labels to conform to the size constraint. [7]

Denote the number of labels in the induced grammar with M, the set of D most frequent induced labels with A, and the set consisting of the other induced labels with B ($|B| = M - D$). If $M \ngtr D$, there is nothing to do since the constraint holds. Otherwise, we map each label in B to the label in A that exhibits the most similar syntactic behavior, as follows. We construct a feature vector representation of each of the labels, using $3M + |K|$ features, where K is the set of POS tags in the corpus. The first M features correspond to parent-child relationships between each of the induced labels and the represented label. The i-th feature ($i \in [1, M]$) is the number of times the i-th label is the parent of the represented label. Similarly, the next M features correspond to child-parent relationships, the next M features correspond to sibling relationships and the last $|K|$ features correspond to the number of times each POS tag is the leftmost POS tag in a constituent labeled by the represented label. Note that in order to compute the values of the first $3M$ features, we needed an initial labeling on the induced bracketings; this is the main reason for using the BMM stage.

For each label $b_i \in B$, we compute the cosine

[7]It is possible to force BMM to iterate until a desired number of induced labels (T or P) is achieved. However, the induced grammars are of very low quality (see Section 5).

metric between its vector b_i^v and that of every $a_j \in A$, mapping b_i to the label a_j with which it obtains the highest score:

$$Map(b_i) = argmax_j \frac{b_i^v \cdot a_j^v}{|b_i^v||a_j^v|} \quad (3)$$

The cosine metric grows when the same coordinates (features) in both vectors have higher values. As a result, vectors with high values of the same features (corresponding to similar syntactic behavior) get high scores.

4 Experimental Setup

We evaluated our algorithm on English, German and Chinese corpora: the WSJ Penn Treebank, containing economic English newspaper articles, the Brown corpus, containing various English genres, the Negra corpus (Brants, 1997) of German newspaper text, and version 5.0 of the Chinese Penn Treebank (Xue et al., 2002). In each corpus, we used the sentences of length at most 10[8], numbering 7422 (WSJ10), 9117 (Brown10), 7542 (NEGRA10) and 4626 (CTB10).

For each corpus the following T and P values were used: WSJ10: $26, 8$; Brown10: $28, 7$; NEGRA10: $22, 6$; CTB10: $24, 9$. Each number produces a different grammar.

For labeled f-score evaluation, the induced labels should be mapped to the target labels[9]. We evaluated with two different mapping schemes. For each pair (X_i, Y_j) of induced and target labels, let C_{X_i,Y_j} be the number of times they label a constituent having the same span in the same sentence. Following (Haghighi and Klein, 2006) we applied a greedy (many to one) mapping where the mapping is given by $Map(X_i) = argmax_{Y_j}\ C_{X_i,Y_j}$. This greedy mapping tends to map many induced labels to the same target label, and is therefore highly forgiving of large mismatches between the structures of the induced and target grammars. Hence, we also applied a label-to-label (LL) mapping, computed by reducing this problem to optimal assignment in a weighted complete bipartite graph, formally defined as follows. Given a weighted complete bipartite graph $G = (X \cup Y; X \times Y)$ where edge (X_i, Y_j) has weight w_{ij}, find a (one-to-one) matching M from X to Y having a maximal weight. In our case, X is the set of model symbols, Y is the set of T or P most frequent target symbols (depending on the desired label set size used), and $w_{ij} := C_{X_i,Y_j}$, computed as in greedy mapping (the number of times x_i and y_j share a constituent). To make the graph complete, we add zero weight edges between induced and target labels that do not share any constituent. The Kuhn-Munkres algorithm (Kuhn, 1955; Munkres, 1957) solves this problem, and we used it to perform the LL mapping (see also (Luo, 2005)).

We assessed the overall quality of our algorithm, the quality of its labeling stage and the quality of the syntactic clustering (SC) stage. For the overall quality of the induced grammar (both bracketing and labeling) we compare our results with (Haghighi and Klein, 2006), using their setup[10]. That setup was used for all numbers reported in this paper. Note that a random baseline would yield very poor results, so there is nothing to be gained from comparing to it.

We assessed the quality of the labeling (MDL and SC) stages alone, using only the correct bracketings produced by the first stage of the algorithm. We compare to a *random baseline* on these correct constituents that randomly selects (using a uniform distribution) a label for each constituent among the set of labels allowed to the algorithm.

To asses the quality of the third stage (SC) we compare the f-score performance of our three stages labeled trees induction algorithm (bracketing, MDL, SC) to an algorithm consisting of the first two stages only (bracketing and MDL) and the accuracy of the two stages labeling algorithm (MDL, SC) to an algorithm where the syntactic clustering stage is replaced by a simpler method (MDL, random clustering).

5 Results

We start with comparing our algorithm with (Haghighi and Klein, 2006), the only previous work that produces labeled bracketing and was tested on large manually annotated corpora. Their relevant models are PCFG $\times$ NONE and PCFG $\times$ CCM[11].

[8]Excluding punctuation and null elements, according to the scheme of (Klein, 2005).

[9]There are many possible methods for evaluating clustering quality (Rosenberg and Hirschberg, 2007). For our task, overall f-score is a very natural one. We will address other methods in future papers.

[10]Brackets covering a single word are not counted, multiple labels and the sentence level constituent are counted. Two sentence level constituents are usually used: one for the root symbol at the top (which was not counted), and one real symbol (in WSJ10 it is usually, but not always, S), which was counted. We had verified the setup with the authors.

[11]They focused on a different, semi-supervised, setting.

	This Paper	*PCFG × CCM*	*PCFG × NONE*
WSJ10	**59.5**	35.3	26.3

Table 1: F-scores of our algorithm and of the unsupervised models in (Haghighi and Klein, 2006) on WSJ10 (they did not test these models on the other corpora we experimented with).

The number of labels in their induced grammar equals the number of labels in the target grammar (26 for WSJ10), and they had used a greedy mapping. Table 1 shows that our algorithm achieves a superior f-score of 59.5% over their 35.3%. Haghighi and Klein (2006) did not experiment with the NEGRA10 and Brown10 corpora, and had used version 3.0 of CTB10 while we have used the substantially different version 5.0, so we can only compare our results on WSJ10.

Table 2 shows the labeled recall, precision and f-score of our algorithm on the various corpora and mappings we use. On Brown10, NEGRA10 and CTB10 (version 5.0) these are the first reported results for this task. For reference, the table also shows the unlabeled f-score results of Seginer's bracketing algorithm (our first stage)[12].

We can see that greedy mapping is indeed more forgiving than LL mapping, for both T labels and P labels. WSJ results are generally higher than for the other corpora, probably because WSJ bracketing results are higher than for the other corpora.

Comparing the left and right columns in each of the table sections reveals that for greedy mapping, mapping to a higher number of labels results in higher scores than mapping to a lower number. LL mapping behaves in exactly the opposite way. The explanation for this is that when we force the mapping to cover all of the target labels (as done by LL mapping for T labels), we move probability mass from the correct, heavy labels to smaller ones, thereby magnifying errors.

Table 4 addresses the quality of the whole labeling stage (MDL and SC) and of the SC stage. We report the quality of our labels (top line for each corpus in the table) the random baseline labels (third line) and the labels of an algorithm where MDL is performed and the syntactic clustering is replaced by a random clustering (RC) algorithm that, given a label L that is not one of the T or P most frequent labels, randomly selects one of the most frequent labels and adds L to its cluster (second line).[13] All three labeling algorithms used Seginer's bracketing and results are reported only for labels of correctly bracketed constituents. Reported are the algorithm and baselines accuracy (percentage of correctly labeled constituents after the mapping has been performed) and the error reduction of the algorithm over the baselines (bottom line). (MDL,SC) substantially outperforms both the random baseline, demonstrating the power of the whole labeling stage, and the (MDL,RC) algorithm, demonstrating the power of the SC stage.

	Greedy		LL	
	T	P	T	P
WSJ10				
MDL,SC	80	67	47	59
MDL,RC	67	61	37	42
Rand. Base.	30	30	5	14
Error Reduction	39%,71%	15%,53%	16%, 44%	29%, 52%
Brown10				
MDL,SC	73	61	48	60
MDL,RC	68	59	46	51
Rand. Base.	27	27	4	14
Error Reduction	16%,63%	5%, 47%	4%, 46%	18%, 53%
NEGRA10				
MDL,SC	79	72	65	72
MDL,RC	73	69	54	58
Rand. Base.	39	39	5	17
Error Reduction	22%,66%	10%,34%	24%,63%	33%,66%
CTB10				
MDL,SC	70	67	44	55
MDL,RC	36	32	40	45
Rand. Base.	29	29	5	12
Error Reduction	53%,58%	51%, 54%	7%,41%	18%,49%

Table 4: Pure labeling results (taking into account only the correct bracketings produced at stage 1), compared to the random and (MDL,RC) baselines. The left number in the Error Reduction lines slots compares (MDL,SC) to (MDL,RC) and the right number compares (MDL,SC) to random labeling. (MDL,SC) algorithm is substantially superior.

We compared our grammars to the grammars induced by the first two stages (bracketing and then MDL that stops when no DL improvement is possible) alone. Since the number of labels in these grammars is much larger than in the target grammar, only the evaluation with the greedy, many to one, mapping is performed. Using greedy mapping, the F-score of these grammars constitutes an upper bound on the F-score after the subsequent SC stage. For WSJ10 (4944 labels), NEGRA10 (5557 labels), CTB10 (2298 labels) and Brown10 (3314 labels) F-score values are 64.6, 49.9, 38.7 and 52.5 compared to F-score values of 59.5(50.2), 45.6(42), 36.4(34.7) and 49.4(41.3) after mapping all induced labels to the T (P) most frequent labels with SC (Table 2, 'greedy' section). The frac-

[12]The numbers slightly differ from those in Seginer's paper, since we use the (Haghighi and Klein, 2006) setup.

[13]Our algorithm's numbers can be deduced from Table 2. Results for all random baselines are averaged over 10 runs.

	Greedy Mapping						LL Mapping						Seginer (unlabeled)
	T labels			P labels			T labels			P labels			
Corpus	R	P	F	R	P	F	R	P	F	R	P	F	F
WSJ10	58	61	59.5	48.9	51.5	50.2	34.2	36.1	35.2	42.7	44.9	43.8	74.6
NEGRA10	54.2	39.3	45.6	50	36.2	42	44.7	32.4	37.6	49.5	35.9	41.7	58.1
CTB10	35.1	37.8	36.4	33.4	36	34.7	21.9	23.6	22.7	27.4	29.5	28.4	51.8
Brown10	47.6	51.3	49.4	39.9	43	41.3	31.3	33.7	32.4	38.9	41.9	40.3	67.8

Table 2: Labeled recall, precision and f-score of our algorithm, mapping model labels into target labels greedily (left) and using LL mapping (right). The number of induced labels was set to be the total number T of target labels or the number P of prominent labels in the target grammar (WSJ10: 26, 8; Brown10: 28, 7; NEGRA10: 22, 6; CTB10: 24, 9). Also shown are Seginer's unlabeled bracketing results (rightmost column), which constitute an upper bound on the quality of subsequent labeling steps.

	WSJ10						Brown10					
Label	T labels			P labels			T labels			P labels		
	R	P	F	R	P	F	R	P	F	R	P	F
S	77.1	77.6	77.3	75.4	67.9	71.5	72.3	60.9	66.1	69.3	63.2	66.1
NP	8.5	79.5	15.4	19.8	61.6	30	10.7	79.3	18.9	15.6	78	26
VP	20.4	67.6	31.3	64.2	36.7	46.7	9.8	72.5	17.3	14.1	59	22.8
PP	40.8	63.5	49.7	8	8.9	8.4	17.4	59.2	26.9	75.5	14.4	24.2

Table 3: Recall, Precision and F-score for constituents labeled with the 4 most frequent labels in the WSJ10 and Brown10 test sets. LL mapping is used for evaluation.

tion of constituents covered by the T (P) most frequent labels before mapping with SC is 0.42(0.29), 0.33(0.23), 0.58(0.45) and 0.66(0.42), emphasizing the effect of SC on the final result.

MDL finds the best merge at each iteration. Instead of stopping it when no DL gains are possible, we can keep merging after the deltas become worse than the total DL, stopping only when the desired number of labels (T or P) is achieved. We tried this version of a (bracketing and MDL) algorithm and obtained grammars of very low quality. This further demonstrates the importance of the SC stage.

Table 3 shows results for the four most frequent labels of WSJ10 and Brown10 .

6 Conclusion

Unsupervised grammar induction is a central research problem, possessing both theoretical and practical significance. There is great value in producing an output format consistent with and evaluated against formats used in large human annotated corpora. Most previous work of that kind produces unlabeled bracketing or dependencies. In this paper we presented an algorithm that induces labeled bracketing. The labeling stages of the algorithm use the MDL principle to induce an initial, relatively large, set of labels, which are then clustered using syntactic features. We discussed the issue of the desired number of labels, and introduced the concept of prominent labels, which allows us coverage of the basic and most salient level of a target grammar. Labels are clearly an important aspect of grammar induction. Future work will explore their significance for applications.

Evaluating induced labels is a complex issue. We applied greedy mapping as in previous work, and showed that our algorithm significantly outperforms it. In addition, we introduced LL mapping, which overcomes some of the shortcomings of greedy mapping. There are several other possible methods for evaluating labeled induced grammars, and we plan to explore them in future work. We evaluated on large human annotated corpora of different English domains and three languages, and showed that our labeling stages, and specifically the SC stage, outperform several baselines for all corpora and mapping methods.

Acknowledgments. We thank Gideon Borensztajn and Yoav Seginer for their help.

References

Pieter Adriaans, 1992. *Learning Language from a Categorical Perspective.* Ph.D. thesis, University of Amsterdam.

Rens Bod, 2006a. An All-Subtrees Approach to Unsupervised Parsing. *Proc. of the 44th Meeting of the ACL.*

Rens Bod, 2006b. Unsupervised Parsing with U-DOP. *Proc. of CoNLL X.*

Rens Bod, 2007. Is the End of Supervised Parsing in Sight? *Proc. of the 45th Meeting of the ACL.*

Gideon Borensztajn and Willem Zuidema, 2007. Bayesian Model Merging for Unsupervised Constituent Labeling and Grammar Induction. Technical Report, ILLC . http: //staff.science.uva.nl/~gideon/

Thorsten Brants, 1997. The NEGRA Export Format. *CLAUS Report, Saarland University.*

Thorsten Brants, 2000. TnT: A Statistical Part-Of-Speech Tagger. *Proc. of the 6th Applied Natural Language Processing Conference.*

Stanley F. Chen, 1995. Bayesian grammar induction for language modeling. *Proc. of the 33th Meeting of the ACL.*

Alexander Clark, 2001. *Unsupervised Language Acquisition: Theory and Practice.* Ph.D. thesis, University of Sussex.

Alexander Clark, 2003. Combining Distributional and Morphological Information for Part of Speech Induction. *Proc. of the 10th Meeting of the European Chapter of the ACL.*

Willliam A. Croft, 2001. *Radical Construction Grammar.* Cambridge University Press.

Carl G. de Marcken, 1995. *Unsupervised Language Acquisition.* Ph.D. thesis, MIT.

Walter Daelemans, 1995. Memory-based lexical acquisition and processing. *Lecture Notes In Artificial Intelligence*, 898:85–98.

Simon Dennis, 2005. An exemplar-based approach to unsupervised parsing. *Proceedings of the 27th Conference of the Cognitive Science Society.*

Adele E. Goldberg, 2006. *Constructions at Work.* Oxford University Press.

Peter Grunwald, 1994. A minimum description length approach to grammar inference. *Lecture Notes In Artificial Intelligence*, 1004 : 203-216.

Aria Haghighi and Dan Klein, 2006. Prototype-driven grammar induction. *Proc. of the 44th Meeting of the ACL.*

Jin–Dong Kim, Tomoko Ohta, Yuka Teteisi and Jun'ichi Tsujii, 2003. GENIA corpus – a semantically annotated corpus for bio-textmining. *Bioinformatics*, 19:i180–i182, Oxford University Press, 2003.

Dan Klein and Christopher Manning, 2002. A generative constituent-context model for improved grammar induction. *Proc. of the 40th Meeting of the ACL.*

Dan Klein and Christopher Manning, 2004. Corpus-based induction of syntactic structure: Models of dependency and constituency. *Proc. of the 42nd Meeting of the ACL.*

Dan Klein, 2005. *The unsupervised learning of natural language structure.* Ph.D. thesis, Stanford University.

Harold W. Kuhn, 1955. The Hungarian method for the assignment problem. *Naval Research Logistics Quarterly*, 2:83-97.

Pat Langley and Sean Stromsten, 2000. Learning context-free grammars with a simplicity bias. *Proc. of the 11th European Conference on Machine Learning.*

Xiaoqiang Luo, 2005. On coreference resolution performance metrics. *Proc. of the 2005 Conference on Empirical Methods in Natural Language Processing.*

James Munkres, 1957. Algorithms for the Assignment and Transportation Problems. *Journal of the SIAM*, 5(1):32–38.

Katsuhiko Nakamura, 2006. Incremental learning of context free grammars by bridging rule generation and search for semi-optimum rule sets. *Proc. of the 8th ICGI.*

Georgios Petasis, Georgios Paliouras and Vangelis Karkaletsis, 2004. E-grids: Computationally efficient grammatical inference from positive examples. *Grammars*, 7:69–110.

Andrew Rosenberg and Julia Hirschberg, 2007. Entropy-based external cluster evaluation measure. *Proc. of the 2007 Conference on Empirical Methods in Natural Language Processing.*

Yoav Seginer, 2007. Fast Unsupervised Incremental Parsing. *Proc. of the 45th Meeting of the ACL.*

Noah A. Smith and Jason Eisner, 2006. Annealing Structural Bias in Multilingual Weighted Grammar Induction . *Proc. of the 44th Meeting of the ACL.*

Zach Solan, David Horn, Eytan Ruppin, and Shimon Edelman, 2005. Unsupervised learning of natural languages. *Proceedings of the National Academy of Sciences*, 102 : 11629–11634.

Andreas Stolcke. 1994. *Bayesian Learning of Probabilistic Language Models.* Ph.D. thesis, University of of California at Berkeley.

Andreas Stolcke and Stephen M. Omohundro, 1994. Inducing probabilistic grammars by Bayesian model merging . *Proc. of the 2nd ICGI.*

Menno van Zaanen, 2001. *Bootstrapping Structure into Language: Alignment-Based Learning.* Ph.D. thesis, University of Leeds.

J. Gerard Wolff, 1982. Language acquisition, data compression and generalization. *Language and Communication*, 2(1): 57–89.

Nianwen Xue, Fu-Dong Chiou and Martha Palmer, 2002. Building a large–scale annotated Chinese corpus. *Proc. of the 40th Meeting of the ACL.*

Anomalies in the WordNet Verb Hierarchy

Tom Richens
Aston University
Aston Triangle
Birmingham B4 7ET, England
richentm@aston.ac.uk

Abstract

The WordNet verb hierarchy is tested, with a view to improving the performance of its applications, revealing topological anomalies and casting doubt on its semantic categories. Encoded troponyms frequently misrepresent other kinds of entailment. Approaches are proposed for correcting these anomalies including a new top ontology.

1 Introduction

WordNet is a lexical database widely used for NLP tasks. Any application of WordNet which measures *semantic distance* employs WordNet *relations* to do so.

As part of a wider project to build an improved and enriched lexical database using existing resources, in the hope of improving on the performance of WordNet, this study investigates the correctness of the hypernymy/troponymy relations between verbs.

The broader project would ideally model these hierarchical relations as trees but for the phenomenon of ***multiple inheritance,*** which is investigated here to see if it is semantically justified. Moreover it seems intuitively likely that anomalies will be concentrated where the relational structure is more complex.

1.1 Definitions

The only document found to specify the WordNet verbal relations is Fellbaum (1998), who defines *troponymy* (the verb equivalent of *hyponymy*) as a special case of *entailment*, where the entailing and entailed verb are *temporally co-extensive*, distinguishing it from *causation*, *temporal inclusion*, and *backward presupposition*, of which the last two are not encoded as distinct relations in WordNet, but are combined under the general heading of *entailment*. The expression *sister terms* is used to designate a pair of synsets which share a hypernym.

This study distinguishes between *transitive* causation (causing *another* to do something) and *reflexive* causation (causing *oneself* to do something). The term *quale* (plural: *qualia*) is borrowed from Pustejovsky (1991). As applied to verbs within the context of this study, the *formal* quale means what is physically done, while the *telic* quale means the purpose or intended result of the action.

1.2 Application of WordNet Relations

Banerjee & Pedersen (2003) have employed WordNet relations in an extension to the Lesk (1986) algorithm for word sense disambiguation. In order to establish the relatedness of two words, the glosses of their WordNet relatives are compared. Their results are noticeably inferior for verbs than for nouns. Moreover, while the most useful relations for disambiguating nouns were hyponymy and meronymy, in the case of verbs, the example sentences proved more useful than any relations. Their best results were obtained by using all relations between verbs indiscriminately. This finding reflects on the distinctions between kinds of verb relations and suggests that at least where verbs are concerned, the limited success achieved by algorithms relying on WordNet relations arises from the probability that when a relation is encoded, some relation exists, even though the *kind* of relation is not necessarily correct. This observation suggests that improvements to the WordNet relations may well be useful for improving on the performance

© 2008. Licensed under the *Creative Commons Attribution-Noncommercial-Share Alike 3.0 Unported* license (http://creativecommons.org/licenses/by-nc-sa/3.0/). Some rights reserved.

of WordNet as a tool for interlingual tasks and word sense disambiguation.

1.3 Validation of Wordnets

Smrž (2003) proposes a number of tests for validating wordnets. These involve checking for "cycles", "dangling uplinks" and "top-most synset not from the defined set" and critically examining "multi-parent relations". These tests have been applied in the development of BalkanNet (Various 2004). The present study looks for any of the listed faults or potential faults within WordNet 3.0. Without a defined set of *unique beginners*, it is impossible to distinguish a "dangling uplink" from "top-most synset not from the defined set". All verbs synsets without any hypernym will therefore be considered as *candidate unique beginners*.

1.4 Potential Hypernymy Faults

Liu et al. (2004) have found thousands of cases of *rings* within the hierarchies, which arise when a synset has two hypernyms within the same semantic category, which themselves have a common hypernym, along with *isolators*, trees isolated within their own category whose only hypernym lies in another category. Such deviations from a tree-structure, if not semantically justifiable, should be considered as faults.
The occurrence of a ring implies *multiple inheritance*, which is not necessarily a fault but merits investigation to ensure that it is justified. There are two other kinds of potential fault which should also be considered: another kind of ring is a *cycle*, which is formed where following the hypernymy relation in one direction leads back to where one started; a special case of an isolator occurs where a synset has no hypernym at all, which makes it a candidate unique beginner. Liu et al. (2004) dismiss this possibility as legitimate, without further consideration, on the grounds that this applies to the unique beginners of each semantic category. In fact, Fellbaum (1998) allows for more than one unique beginner per verb category. However cases where there is a large number of unique beginners in one category merit investigation.

1.5 Methodology

The present study has been conducted using a model of WordNet where synsets, word senses and relations are implemented as Java objects, constructed from the WordNet 3.0 Prolog files. Focussing mainly on verbs, three main aspects are investigated, *topological anomalies*, *anomalies relating to categories* and the *top ontology*.
An algorithm was developed to discover occurrences of each of the kinds of potential hypernymy fault identified above. To investigate topological anomalies, the algorithm recursively constructs an *upside-down tree* from each synset, using that synset as root with its most remote indirect *hypernyms* as the leaves. Where a *cycle* occurs, a stack error will result. A *ring* is identified wherever a synset is found more than once in the same upside-down tree. This approach is an extension of the methodology employed by Liu et al. (2004), in that it assumes no correlation between *semantic categories* and hypernymy so as to identify *rings* which straddle category boundaries. An examination of rings in the verb hierarchy leads onto a more general examination of dual inheritance among verbs (there are no verbs with more than 2 hypernyms).
An *isolator* occurs when the only hypernym is in a different semantic category to the synset under investigation. Examination of isolators reveals more anomalies in the verb hierarchy but also raises questions about the validity of the semantic categories.
A *candidate unique beginner* is identified whenever a synset has troponyms but no hypernym. The proliferation of unspecified unique beginners among verbs prompts a full review of the top ontology.
The full results which are analysed here are currently available at:
http://www.rockhouse.me.uk/Linguistics.

2 Topological Anomalies and Remedies

2.1 Cycle

The algorithm implementation generated a stack error when applied to a number of verbal synsets: in each case the same *cycle* was encountered, which is the only one in WordNet 3.0.

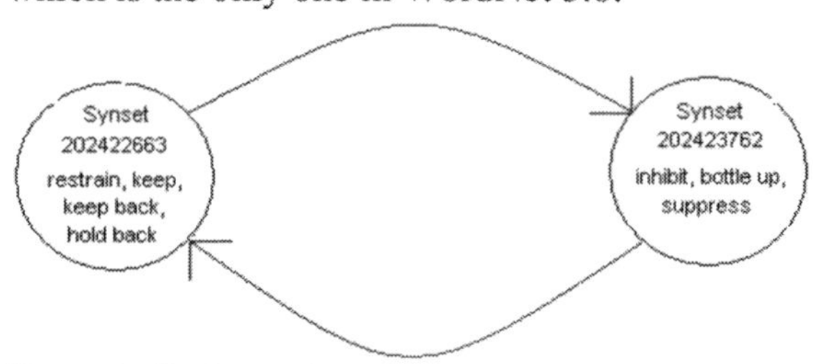

Figure 1. Cycle topology

The two synsets in fig. 1 appear to be synonymous. Merging them to remove the cycle would improve structural consistency.

2.2 Rings

Liu et al. (2004) define a ring as being formed where a synset "has at least 2 fathers in its own category", which have a common ancestor also within that category. Our algorithm uses a broader definition of ring as any instance of a synset having two hypernyms such that these hypernyms themselves have a common ancestor or one of them is the ancestor of the other (table 1).

Case with respect to semantic categories	**Verbs**	**Nouns**
Single category	5	1
Ancestry crosses categories but direct relations are in same category as headword	2	1984
Ancestry crosses categories and direct relations cross categories	1	379
TOTAL	**8**	**2364**
TOTAL using definition from Liu et al. (2004)	**7**	**1985**
Results of Liu et al. (2004) using WordNet 2.0	**17**	**1839**

Table 1. Rings in Wordnet

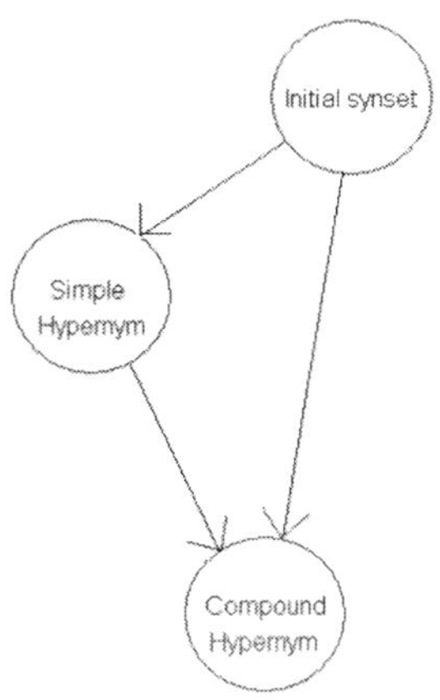

Figure 2. Asymmetric ring topology

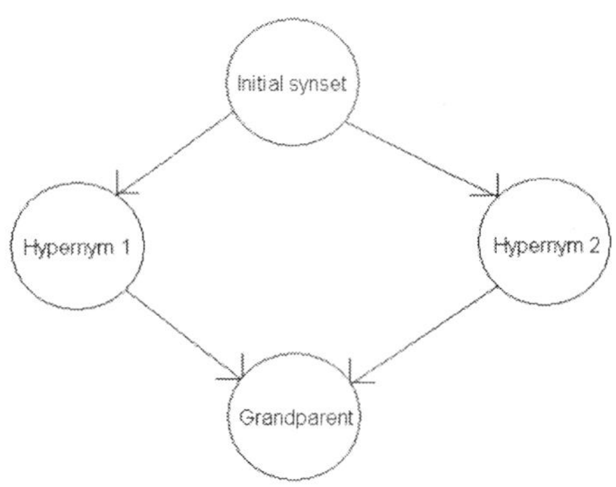

Figure 3. Symmetric ring topology

An analysis of the rings among nouns is outside the scope of this study. Out of the 8 rings in the verb hierarchies, 4 are asymmetric and 4 are symmetric.

In 3 out of 4 cases of the asymmetric topology (fig. 2), the link between the initial synset and the compound hypernym is redundant and can be removed. In the remaining case, "eat" (transitive) has the simple hypernym "eat" (intransitive) which simply fails to specify what is eaten. This can be considered as *synonymy* and so there is a case for merging these synsets. The compound hypernym "consume, ingest" would also seem to be a synonym, unless one relies on the gloss: "serve oneself to, or consume regularly", in which case it as ambiguous between *reflexive causation* and *iteration*, neither of which fits the definition of hypernymy.

The instances of symmetric topology (fig. 3) raise different issues. Liu et al. (2004) assert that a ring implies a paradox because they assume that two hyponyms of a single hypernym must have opposite properties in some dimension and therefore cannot have a common hyponym, as a hyponym must inherit all the properties of its hypernym. In fact there need not be any paradox as two hyponyms can modify two different properties of their hypernym (see Amaro et al., 2006, for a discussion with particular reference to *qualia* properties). The symmetric ring starting from the word "turn" in the sense "the leaves turn in Autumn" involves different properties: "turn, grow" is distinguished from "change" by specifying that the timescale is gradual, while "discolour" specifies which attribute is to change; "turn" in the above sense inherits both properties of gradual timescale and colour attribute.

In the remaining three cases of symmetric rings, the gloss for the initial synset contains the word "or", conveying an ambiguity. The two hypernyms in each case are in fact hypernyms or synonyms of the respective two meanings, and the grandparent is indeed a common ancestor. Splitting the ambiguous synsets to remove the ring would improve consistency.

We conclude that in 7 out of 8 instances, *rings* among verbs can be corrected and in the remaining case ("turn", above) the ring and the dual inheritance are justified. The question then arises as to why there should only be one case of a semantically justifiable ring. The answer to this question is sought through an investigation of the remaining 23 cases of dual inheritance among verbs, where there is no ring.

2.3 Dual inheritance

Table 2 shows the results of a review of the semantic relations encoded as hypernymy in a dual inheritance context. 3 hypernyms have an ambiguous troponym whose gloss contains the word "or", and 2 hypernyms are themselves ambiguous with glosses containing "or".

Correct: Telic quale	5
Correct: Formal quale	4
Otherwise correct hypernym	10
Hypernym of 1 sense of ambiguous troponym	3
No near relation	4
Synonym of other hypernym	2
Temporal inclusion	4
Backward presupposition	1
Ambiguous hypernym	2
Reflexive cause of sister term	1
Sister term	1
Reverse proper inclusion of 1 sense of ambiguous troponym	2
Intransitive form of transitive troponym	1
Synonym	1
Non-reflexive form of reflexive troponym	1
Transitive cause	1
Troponym	2
Literal sense of metaphor	1
TOTAL	**46**
% correct	**34.78%**

Table 2. Verb hypernyms involved in dual inheritance without rings

The cases of proper inclusion and backward presupposition should be encoded as entailments according to Fellbaum's (1998) specification and causes also should be encoded as such.

Word forms	Formal quale	Telic quale
date, date stamp	stamp	date
assemble, piece	join, bring together	make, create
execute, put to death	Kill	punish, penalize
Carve	Cut	shape, form
Sing	*Utter*	*interpret, render*

Table 3. Dual inheritance justified by *qualia*

Table 3 shows details of those 4 cases where dual inheritance can be justified in terms of inheritance of two different *qualia* (Amaro et al., 2006). The fifth example, in italics, is not as encoded in WordNet: "sing" (intransitive) is given as a hypernym of "sing" (transitive), which is otherwise synonymous, consistent with the encoding of "eat" mentioned above. The other hypernym, "interpret, render" is necessarily transitive. The hypernym of "sing" (intransitive) is given as "talk, speak", which is really a sister term whose common hypernym would be "utter" (Miller & Johnson-Laird, 1976), which represents the *formal quale*, while "interpret, render" represents the *telic quale*. So there is an *underlying* dual inheritance of different qualia properties.

The only cases of dual inheritance which can be considered legitimate are those where different but compatible properties are inherited. While this handful of examples has been identified, there are no doubt many more which could be discovered (Amaro et al., 2006). The encoding of these might well result in further justifiable rings.

3 Anomalies relating to Categories

3.1 Isolators

1593 examples were found of isolators among verbs and 2527 among nouns. These results approximate to those of Liu et al. (2004), who found 1551 verb isolators and 2654 noun isolators in WordNet 2.0. A review of the semantic relations was undertaken on a sample of 41 pairs of troponym and hypernym in different categories among verbs (table 4).

Correct hypernymy	26
Troponym is true troponym of *one meaning* of ambiguous hypernym	1
Hypernym is *cause* of troponym	2
Troponym is true troponym of *cause* of hypernym	2
Hypernym *temporally includes* troponym	1
Hypernym is *backward presupposition* of troponym	1
Synonymous	5
Metaphor	1
No near relation	2
TOTAL	**41**
% correct	**63%**

Table 4: Semantic relations among isolator samples

Again we find cases of causation and entailment encoded as hypernymy. In most cases the hypernymy relation is correct, while the synsets belong to different categories. This arises inevitably because the WordNet verb categories are, for the most part, not mutually exclusive. In only one sample were the categories found to be mutually exclusive (*change* and *stative*). 14 out of the 82 synsets were judged not to belong to the category to which they are assigned, while 17 synsets do belong to the other's category.

The majority of WordNet's verbal semantic categories represent overlapping *semantic fields*. It is not therefore surprising that the *isolator* phenomenon occurs and this does not necessarily imply an error. The only categories which could be considered not to overlap are *stative* with *change* and *creation,* and *weather* with most of the other semantic fields.

A more detailed examination was made of a sample of 76 cases of *isolator*, where the hypernym and troponym categories could be considered mutually exclusive. The incorrect examples in table 5 are typical of the kinds of errors we have already seen in the encoding of WordNet relations.

Valid relation	55
No near relation	5
Hypernym is *reflexive cause* of troponym	1
Indeterminate (ambiguous synset)	6
Syntactic alternation	2
Hypernym is *backward presupposition* of troponym	2
Hypernymy only because of misleading gloss	1
Sister terms	1
Hypernym is *reflexive* of troponym	1
Synonymous	1
Troponym is *transitive cause* of true troponym	1
TOTAL	**76**
% correct	**72%**

Table 5. Semantic relations among isolator samples involving mutually exclusive categories

Some 53 synsets (34.9%) were considered to be in the correct category. *Change* has been used indiscriminately to include both causative and inchoative alternations, while both *creation* and *stative* have been used for the causative alternations and *stative* has also been used for some of the inchoative alternations. By transferring all the inchoative alternations to *change*, and all the causative alternations to *creation*, some of the category mismatches disappear.

Some of the verbs in this dataset have generic meanings like *doing* and *happening,* which do not fit into any of the WordNet categories. Creating categories for these verbs might eliminate more anomalies.

3.2 Theoretical Basis of Categories

In theory, WordNet nouns and verbs are arranged as a set of hierarchies (Fellbaum 1998), each with an unique beginner, but multiple inheritance is not ruled out, particularly where the second hypernym of a synset is in a different semantic category. The semantic categories in WordNet are based, according to Fellbaum (1998) on a standard work on psycholinguistics (Miller & Johnson-Laird, 1976). The latter discusses in detail verbs of motion, possession, vision (*WordNet perception*) and communication, which are the basis for the corresponding WordNet categories. Other semantic fields mentioned are contact, bodily activity (*WN body*), thought (*WN cognition*) and affect (*WN emotion*). Miller & Johnson-Laird, (1976) acknowledge that these categories overlap, but WordNet does not allow a verb to belong to more than one category. No theoretical basis has been found for the remaining categories. *Competition* is subsumed by *social*, and *consumption* is subsumed by *body*. *Weather* would seem self-contained, but *change*, *creation* and *stative* are not semantic fields at all. *Stative* belongs to the *Aktionsart* categorisation of verbs distinguishing it from verbs of *activity*, *achievement* and *accomplishment*, which is orthogonal to the categorisation of verbs into semantic fields (Vendler, 1967, Moens & Steedman 1988, Amaro, 2006). Moreover, a verb can belong to more than one *Aktionsart* category, as these apply to verbs *in contexts*.

3.3 Suggested Revision of Categories

Among verbs, the level of arbitrariness and incorrectness of the WordNet categories seems greater than that of the relations. Whereas the theoretical basis for WordNet relations is consistent and the errors are failures to conform to the specification, in the case of categories, the theoretical basis is inconsistent, being, a compromise between more than one system of categorisation.

Many anomalies arise because WordNet only allows a verb to belong to one category. It is impossible to encode semantic categories correctly on the basis of one category per verb. At least two semantic fields need to be allowed, plus at least one orthogonal category. Miller & Johnson-Laird (1976) themselves point out that semantic components like *cause* and *intention* cross the boundaries between semantic fields as do operators like *happen*, *do*, *act*, *possible* and *permissible*.

4 Top Ontology

4.1 Candidate Unique Beginners

WordNet 3.0 has 559 verbs with no hypernym, spread over all categories. Of these, 225 have no troponyms either. A further 96 have a single troponym of which 80 have no further troponyms. This leaves 254 verbs which have no hypernym and more than 1 direct or indirect troponym, in contrast with the theoretical position that each verb category has at most a handful of unique beginners (Fellbaum, 1998). These 254 verbs will therefore be considered as *candidate* unique beginners.

More than one candidate was found in every category, the minimum being 5 for category 34 *consumption*. According to Fellbaum (1998), category 38 *motion* should have two unique beginners "expressing translational movement" and "movement without displacement" respectively. There are 17 other candidates in this category. Similarly category 40, *possession* should have 3 unique beginners, representing the basic concepts "give", "take" and "have", whereas there are 12 other candidates.

Again, according to Fellbaum (1998) "Communication verbs are headed by the verb *communicate* but immediately divide into two independent trees expressing verbal and nonverbal (gestural) communication". There are 7 senses of "communicate" in WordNet 3.0 all of which have hypernyms. Fellbaum (1998) identifies a further subdivision between spoken and written language, but the only reference to "write" among these 254 synsets occurs in category 36: *creation*. In fact category 32 *communication* has 18 candidates. There appears to be no connection between the theory and the practice here.

It is always possible to define a verb in terms of another verb with one or more arguments. This is a method of identifying hypernyms, which appears to have been used extensively, though inconsistently, in the construction of WordNet, using the glosses for semi-automatic hypernym generation. Full automation of such a technique would lead inevitably to the *cycle* scenario defined above. There have to be unique beginners in order to avoid this.

4.2 Deriving a New Top Ontology

On a dataset of this size, it is feasible to manually identify hypernyms for most of the synsets, though there is more than one possible solution in many cases. In some cases it is sufficient to provide a more generic verb or verbal phrase as hypernym, which already belongs to a hierarchy. In other cases a combination of a verb and one or more arguments (mostly involving an additional verb) is required in order to define the verb, in which case the syntactic main verb in the definition can be considered as the hypernym. Auxiliary verbs required by the definitions include one *modal* verb ("can") not included in WordNet.

The 254 synsets were manually annotated either with proposed hypernyms or with definitions in terms of verbs and arguments, without reference to semantic categories. In some cases auxiliaries act in conjunction with each other to form more complex definitions. The definitions are tentative, the objective being to demonstrate the possibility of generating a compact and consistent top ontology. However, there is scope for introducing more rigour by formalising the definitions along the lines of Jackendoff's (1983, 1990) lexical conceptual structures.

Table 6 shows the auxiliaries used in defining the candidate unique beginners. The first row represents verbs which can be defined as the passive of another verb, namely "hang" (*be supported from above*), "depend (on)" (*be caused by*) and "belong (to)" (*be had by*).

The next row but one represents transitive causation verbs e.g. "kill" (*cause to die*), "sensitize" (*cause to sense*), show (*cause to see*) etc. There is also negative causation, of which the most generic case is the verb "prevent". There are fewer, but a significant number of examples of reflexive causation, e.g. "look" (*cause self to see*) and more complex cases concerning possession: "give" (*cause to have + cause self to not have*), "take" (*cause to not have + cause self to have*).

There are a number of unique beginners which express starting or stopping e.g. "learn" (*start to know*), "get" (*start to have*), "become" (*start to be*) and "lose" (*stop having*).

Finally there are verbs which can be defined as the negation of other verbs: "displease" (*not please*), "reject" (*not accept*), "fail" (*not suc-*

ceed), "lack" (*not have*), "refrain" (*not do*). Although "NOT" is not a verb, "doesn't/don't" is a verb which is generally substituted for "NOT", except in the infinitive. On these grounds "NOT" is not out of place in this list.

Aux.	Syntax	n	Hyp.	Args.
Be	done	3	happen	
Can	do	1		
Cause	to do	43	make	
Cause	self to do	6	make	self
Feel	like doing	2		
Keep (repeat)	doing	6	do	again
Start	doing	11		
Stop	doing	8		
Tell (1)	(someone) to do	1	tell (2)	that you must
Try	to do	1	will	although NOT know whether can
NOT	do	22		
Additional verbs used to define above auxiliaries				
Tell (2)	*(someone) that*	*3*	*cause*	*know*
Must	*do*	*1*		
Will	*do*	*43*		

Table 6. Auxiliaries needed to define candidate unique beginners (Aux. = auxiliary; n = number of candidates defined; Hyp. = proposed hypernym; Args. = arguments)

In order to identify hypernyms from these definitions consistently, we take the auxiliaries, including "NOT", as the immediate hypernyms.

A second meaning of "tell" has been added to table 6 as this has not been subsumed. The hypernyms and arguments themselves introduce two more modal auxiliaries, "must" and "will" (in the Old English sense of volition).

The implementation of this approach to identifying hypernyms for candidate unique beginners, left 14 which could not be subsumed, (table 7). The two synonymous synsets in category 41 can be merged. Weather verbs of zero valency are subsumed by "happen".

Those auxiliaries used in the definitions which cannot be subsumed by a hypernym must be represented in the list of outstanding unique beginners. Of these, "feel", "start" and "stop" are already listed. The modals ("can", "must" and "will") and "NOT" need to be added to table 7 to complete a proposed new compact and consistent top ontology for verbs comprising 18 unique beginners.

There are relations between these concepts and the list could probably be further reduced. The modal verbs, together with "know" form a natural set of entailments for "do". The concept "do" compulsorily backwardly presupposes the combination of "can" and "will" ("able and willing"). "Will" may be underlain or superseded by "must". "Can" can mean either "is physically equipped to" or "knows how to" or both and corresponds to the operator *possible* in the schema of Miller & Johnson-Laird (1976) referred to above, while "must" means NOT(*permissible*(NOT to)) using the operator *permissible* from the same schema.

Synset ID	Word Forms	Cat.
200109660	change	30
200339934	happen, hap, go on	30
200594621	know, cognize, cognise	31
200628491	think, cogitate, cerebrate	31
201617192	make, create	36
201712704	perform, execute, do	36
201771535	feel, experience	37
201831531	move (*non-translational*)	38
201835496	travel, go, move (*translational*)	38
202106506	perceive, comprehend	39
202367363, 202419073	act, move	41
202603699	exist, be	42
202608347	begin, start	42
202609764	end, stop, finish, terminate	42
Addendum	***can***	***n/a***
Addendum	***must***	***n/a***
Addendum	***will***	***n/a***
Addendum	***NOT***	***n/a***

Table 7. New top ontology comprising outstanding unique beginners and modals

5 Conclusion

In the course of this study, one cycle has been found in WordNet and a number of "multi-parent relations" have been found to be unjustified. Over 500 instances have been found of "top-most synset not from the defined set" or "dangling uplinks" (Smrž, 2003). Many shortcomings have been found in the encoding of hypernymy between verbs, where the implementation frequently does not conform to the theory. In their present state, the encoded relations can only reliably serve to indicate that a relation exists between two verbs and not to elucidate what that relation is. One is left with the impression that many hypernyms have been encoded arbitrarily, whether manually or automatically, with little respect for distinctions between kinds of relation. The hierarchy could be improved by merging synonymous synsets and removing redundant relations and by adopting a consistent approach to causative/inchoative alternations. The only valid cases of dual inheritance are where different but compatible properties are inherited. Many more such relations could be encoded. The semantic categories are, for the most part, not mutually exclusive and lack a consistent theoretical basis. If semantic categories are required, then a verb needs to be allowed to belong to more than one. A new top ontology has been proposed which reduces the number of unique beginners from 254 to 18 with the aid of auxiliaries including modal verbs.

The issues identified can be addressed by building a new lexical database from the same sources, but there would be a very substantial overhead of applying manual corrections to the entire verb hierarchy or constructing an entirely new set of relations with a clear theoretical basis in a non-arbitrary manner, along the lines suggested by Guarino (1998). One possible alternative is to borrow the relational structure from another lexical database.

Acknowledgement

Thanks are due to Dr. S. H. S. Wong and Dr. C. Buckingham of Aston University for suggestions regarding the presentation of these findings.

References

Amaro, R. 2006. WordNet as a base lexicon model for computation of verbal predicates. *Proceedings of the Third Global WordNet Conference,* 22-26 January 2006, Jeju Island, Korea.

Amaro, R., Chaves, R. P., Marrafa, P. & Mendes S. 2006. Enriching Wordnets with new Relations and with Event and Argument Structures. *Seventh International Conference on Intelligent Text Processing and Computational Linguistics*, Mexico City, 2006, 28 - 40.

Banerjee, S. & Pedersen, P. 2003. Extended Gloss Overlaps as a Measure of Semantic Relatedness. *Proceedings of the Eighteenth International Joint Conference on Artificial Intelligence*, Acapulco, Mexico, August, 2003.

Fellbaum, C. 1998. A Semantic Network of English Verbs, Fellbaum, C. (ed.), *WordNet: An Electronic Lexical Database*, Cambridge, Massachusetts, MIT Press, 69-104.

Guarino, N., 1998. Some ontological principles for designing upper level lexical resources. In: *Proceedings of the First International Conference on Language Resources and Evaluation*, LREC 98.

Jackendoff, R., 1983, *Semantics & Cognition*, Cambridge, Massachusetts, MIT Press.

Jackendoff, R., 1990, *Semantic Structures, Current Studies in Linguistics Series*, Cambridge, Massachusetts, MIT Press.

Lesk, M., 1986. Automatic sense disambiguation using machine readable dictionaries: How to tell a pine cone from a ice cream cone. In *Proceedings of SIGDOC* '86,

Liu, Y., Jiangsheng Y., Zhengshan W. & Shiwen Y. 2004. Two Kinds of Hypernymy Faults in WordNet: the Cases of Ring and Isolator. *Proceedings of the Second Global WordNet Conference*. Brno, Czech Republic, 20-23 January 2004. 347-351.

Miller & Johnson-Laird. 1976. *Language & Perception*, Cambridge University Press, Chapter 7, 524-689.

Moens, M. & Steedman, M. 1998. Temporal Ontology and Temporal Reference, *Computational Linguistics*, 14 (2), June 1988, 15-28.

Pustejovsky, J., 1991. The Generative Lexicon, *Computational Linguistics*, 17, (4), 409-441

Smrž, P. 2004. Quality Control for Wordnet Development. *Proceedings of the Second Global WordNet Conference*. Brno, Czech Republic, 20-23 January 2004. 206-212.

Various, 2004. *Design and Development of a Multilingual Balkan Wordnet Balkanet, IST-2000-29388, WP8: Restructuring Improvement WordNets, Deliverable D8.1: Restructuring WordNets for the Balkan languages*, Project Report, European Commission

Vendler, Z., 1967, Verbs & Times, Vendler, Z. (ed.), *Linguistics in Philosophy*, Cornell University Press, Ithaca & London, 97-121,

Vossen, P. 2002. *EuroWordNet General Document*, Project Report.

Translating Queries into Snippets for Improved Query Expansion

Stefan Riezler and **Yi Liu** and **Alexander Vasserman**
Google Inc.
1600 Amphitheatre Parkway
Mountain View, CA 94043
{riezler,yliu,avasserm}@google.com

Abstract

User logs of search engines have recently been applied successfully to improve various aspects of web search quality. In this paper, we will apply pairs of user queries and snippets of clicked results to train a machine translation model to bridge the "lexical gap" between query and document space. We show that the combination of a query-to-snippet translation model with a large n-gram language model trained on queries achieves improved *contextual query expansion* compared to a system based on term correlations.

1 Introduction

In recent years, user logs of search engines have attracted considerable attention in research on query clustering, query suggestions, query expansion, or general web search. Besides the sheer size of these data sets, the main attraction of user logs lies in the possibility to capitalize on users' input, either in form of user-generated query reformulations, or in form of user clicks on presented search results. However noisy, sparse, incomplete, and volatile these data may be, recent research has presented impressive results that are based on simply taking the majority vote of user clicks as a signal for the relevance of results.

In this paper we will apply user logs to the problem of the "word mismatch" or "lexical chasm" (Berger et al., 2000) between user queries and documents. The standard solution to this problem, query expansion, attempts to overcome this mismatch in query and document vocabularies by adding terms with similar statistical properties to those in the original query. This will increase the chances of matching words in relevant documents and also decrease the ambiguity of the overall query that is inherent to natural language. A successful approach to this problem is local feedback, or pseudo-relevance feedback (Xu and Croft, 1996), where expansion terms are extracted from the top-most documents that were retrieved in an initial retrieval round. Because of irrelevant results in the initial retrieval, caused by ambiguous terms or retrieval errors, this technique may cause expansion by unrelated terms, leading to query drift. Furthermore, the requirement of two retrieval steps is computationally expensive.

Several approaches have been presented that deploy user query logs to remedy these problems. One set of approaches focuses on user reformulations of queries that differ only in one segment (Jones et al., 2006; Fonseca et al., 2005; Huang et al., 2003). Such segments are then identified as candidate expansion terms, and filtered by various signals such as cooccurrence in similar sessions or log-likelihood ratio of original and expansion phrases. Other approaches focus on the relation of queries and retrieval results, either by deploying the graph induced by queries and user clicks in calculating query similarity (Beeferman and Berger, 2000; Wen et al., 2002; Baeza-Yates and Tiberi, 2007), or by leveraging top results from past queries to provide greater context in finding related queries (Raghavan and Sever, 1995; Fitzpatrick and Dent, 1997; Sahami and Heilman, 2006). Cui et al. (2002) present an all together different way to deploy user clickthrough data by extracting expansion terms directly from clicked results. They claim significant improvements over

©2008. Licensed under the *Creative Commons Attribution-Noncommercial-Share Alike 3.0 Unported* license (http://creativecommons.org/licenses/by-nc-sa/3.0/). Some rights reserved.

the local feedback technique of Xu and Croft (1996).

Cui et al.'s (2002) work is the closest to ours. We follow their approach in extracting expansion terms directly from clicked results, however, with a focus on high precision of query expansion. While expansion from the domain of document terms has the advantage that expansion terms are guaranteed to be in the search domain, expansion precision may suffer from the noisy and indirect "approval" of retrieval results by user clicks. Thus expansion terms from the document domain are more likely to be generalizations, specifications, or otherwise related terms, than terms extracted from query substitutions that resemble synonyms more closely. Furthermore, if the model that learns to correlate document terms to query terms is required to ignore context in order to generalize, finding appropriate expansions for ambiguous query terms is difficult.

Our approach is to look at the "word mismatch" problem as a problem of translating from a source language of queries into a target language of documents, represented as snippets. Since both queries and snippets are arguably natural language, statistical machine translation technology (SMT) is readily applicable to this task. In previous work, this has been done successfully for question answering tasks (Riezler et al., 2007; Soricut and Brill, 2006; Echihabi and Marcu, 2003; Berger et al., 2000), but not for web search in general. Cui et al.'s (2002) model is to our knowledge the first to deploy query-document relations for direct extraction of expansion terms for general web retrieval. Our SMT approach has two main advantages over Cui et al.'s model: Firstly, Cui et al.'s model relates document terms to query terms by using simple term frequency counts in session data, without considering smoothing techniques. Our approach deploys a sophisticated machine learning approach to word alignment, including smoothing techniques, to map query phrases to snippet phrases. Secondly, Cui et al.'s model only indirectly uses context information to disambiguate expansion terms. This is done by calculating the relationship of an expansion term to the whole query by multiplying its contributions to all query terms. In our SMT approach, contextual disambiguation is done by deploying an n-gram language model trained on queries to decide about the appropriateness of an expansion term in the context of the rest of the query terms. As shown in an experimental evaluation, together the orthogonal information sources of a translation model and a language model provide significantly better contextual query expansion than Cui et al.'s (2002) correlation-based approach.

In the following, we recapitulate the essentials of Cui et al.'s (2002) model, and contrast it with our SMT-based query expansion system. Furthermore, we will present a detailed comparison of the two systems on a real-world query expansion task.

2 Query-Document Term Correlations

The query expansion model of Cui et al. (2002) is based on the principle that if queries containing one term often lead to the selection of documents containing another term, then a strong relationship between the two terms is assumed. Query terms and document terms are linked via clicked documents in user sessions. Formally, Cui et al. (2002) compute the following probability distribution of document words w^d given query words w^q from counts over clicked documents D:

$$P(w^d|w^q) = \sum_D P(w^d|D)P(D|w^q) \qquad (1)$$

The first term in the righthandside of equation 1 is a normalized *tfidf* weight of the the document term in the clicked document, and the second term is the relative cooccurrence of document and query term in sessions.

Since equation 1 calculates expansion probabilities for each term separately, Cui et al. (2002) introduce the following cohesion formula that respects the whole query Q by aggregating the expansion probabilities for each query term:

$$CoWeight_Q(w^d) = \ln(\prod_{w^q \in Q} P(w^d|w^q) + 1) \qquad (2)$$

In contrast to local feedback techniques (Xu and Croft, 1996), Cui et al.'s algorithm allows to precompute term correlations offline by collecting counts from query logs. This reliance on pure frequency counting is both a blessing and a curse: On the one hand it allows for efficient non-iterative estimation, on the other hand it makes the implicit assumption that data sparsity will be overcome by counting from huge datasets. The only attempt at smoothing that is made in this approach is a recurrence to words in query context, using equation 2, when equation 1 assigns zero probability to unseen pairs.

3 Query-Snippet Translation

The SMT system deployed in our approach is an implementation of the alignment template approach of Och and Ney (Och and Ney, 2004). The basic features of the model consist of a translation model and a language model which go back to the noisy channel formulation of machine translation in Brown et al. (1993). Their "fundamental equation of machine translation" defines the job of a translation system as finding the English string $\hat{\mathbf{e}}$ that is a translation of a foreign string $\mathbf{f}$ such that

$$\begin{aligned} \hat{\mathbf{e}} &= \arg\max_e P(\mathbf{e}|\mathbf{f}) \\ &= \arg\max_e P(\mathbf{f}|\mathbf{e})P(\mathbf{e}) \end{aligned} \tag{3}$$

Equation 3 allows for a separation of a language model $P(\mathbf{e})$, and a translation model $P(\mathbf{f}|\mathbf{e})$. Och and Ney (2004) reformulate equation 3 as a linear combination of feature functions $h_m(\mathbf{e}, \mathbf{f})$ and weights λ_m, including feature functions for translation models $h_i(\mathbf{e}, \mathbf{f}) = P(\mathbf{f}|\mathbf{e})$ and language models $h_j(\mathbf{e}) = P(\mathbf{e})$:

$$\hat{\mathbf{e}} = \arg\max_e \sum_{m=1}^{M} \lambda_m h_m(\mathbf{e}, \mathbf{f}) \tag{4}$$

The translation model used in our approach is based on the sequence of alignment models described in Och and Ney (2003). The relationship of translation model and alignment model for source language string $\mathbf{f} = f_1^J$ and target string $\mathbf{e} = e_1^I$ is via a hidden variable describing an alignment mapping from source position j to target position a_j:

$$P(f_1^J|e_1^I) = \sum_{a_1^J} P(f_1^J, a_1^J|e_1^I) \tag{5}$$

The alignment a_1^J contains so-called null-word alignments $a_j = 0$ that align source words to the empty word. The different alignment models described in Och and Ney (2003) each parameterize equation 5 differently so as to capture different properties of source and target mappings. All models are based on estimating parameters θ by maximizing the likelihood of training data consisting of sentence-aligned, but not word-aligned strings $\{(\mathbf{f}_s, \mathbf{e}_s) : s = 1, \ldots, S\}$. Since each sentence pair is linked by a hidden alignment variable $\mathbf{a} = a_1^J$, the optimal $\hat{\theta}$ is found using unlabeled-data log-likelihood estimation techniques such as the EM algorithm (Dempster et al., 1977):

$$\hat{\theta} = \arg\max_\theta \prod_{s=1}^{S} \sum_{\mathbf{a}} p_\theta(\mathbf{f}_s, \mathbf{a}|\mathbf{e}_s) \tag{6}$$

The final translation model is calculated from relative frequencies of phrases, i.e. consecutive sequences of words occurring in text. Phrases are extracted via various heuristics as larger blocks of aligned words from best word alignments, as described in Och and Ney (2004).

Language modeling in our approach deploys an n-gram language model that assigns the following probability to a string w_1^L of words (see Brants et al. (2007)):

$$P(w_1^L) = \prod_{i=1}^{L} P(w_i|w_1^{i-1}) \tag{7}$$

$$\approx \prod_{i=1}^{L} P(w_i|w_{i-n+1}^{i-1}) \tag{8}$$

Estimation of n-gram probabilities is done by counting relative frequencies of n-grams in a corpus of user queries. Remedies against sparse data problems are achieved by various smoothing techniques, as described in Brants et al. (2007).

For applications of the system to translate unseen queries, a standard dynamic-programming beam-search decoder (Och and Ney, 2004) that tightly integrates translation model and language model is used. Expansion terms are taken from those terms in the 5-best translations of the query that have not been seen in the original query string.

In our opinion, the advantages of using an alignment-based translation model to correlate document terms with query terms, instead of relying on a term frequency counts as in equation 1, are as follows. The formalization of translation models as involving a hidden alignment variable allows us to induce a probability distribution that assigns some probability of being translated into a target word to every source word. This is a crucial step towards solving the problem of the "lexical gap" described above. Furthermore, various additional smoothing techniques are employed in alignment to avoid overfitting and improved coping with rare words (see Och and Ney (2003)). Lastly, estimation of hidden-variable models can be based on the well-defined framework of statistical estimation via the EM algorithm.

Similar arguments hold for the language model: N-gram language modeling is a well-understood

	sentence pairs	source words	target words
tokens	3 billion	8 billion	25 billion
avg. length	-	2.6	8.3

Table 1: Statistics of query-snippet training data for translation model.

1-grams	2-grams	3-grams
9 million	1.5 billion	5 billion

Table 2: Statistics of unique query n-grams in language model.

	items w/ agreement	disagreements included
# items	102	125
mean item score	0.333	0.279
95% conf. int.	[0.216, 0.451]	[0.176, 0.381]

Table 3: Comparison of SMT-based expansion with correlation-based expansion on 7-point Likert-type scale.

problem, with a host of well-proven smoothing techniques to avoid data sparsity problems (see Brants et al. (2007).)

In combination, translation model and language model provide orthogonal sources of information to the overall translation quality. While the translation model induces a smooth probability distribution that relates source to target words, the language model deploys probabilities of target language strings to assess the adequacy of a target word as a *translation in context*. Reliance on ordering information of the words in the context of a source word is a huge advantage over the bag-of-words aggregation of context information in Cui et al's (2002) model. Furthermore, in the SMT model used in our approach, translation model and language model are efficiently integrated in a beam-search decoder.

In our application of SMT to query expansion, queries are considered as source language sentences and snippets of clicked result documents as target sentences. A parallel corpus of sentence-aligned data is created by pairing each query with each snippet of its clicked results. Further adjustments to system parameters were applied in order to adapt the training procedure to this special data set. For example, in order to account for the difference in sentence length between queries and snippets, we set the null-word probability to 0.9. This allows us to improve precision of alignment of noisy data by concentrating the alignment to a small number of key words. Furthermore, extraction of phrases in our approach is restricted to the intersection of alignments from both translation directions, thus favoring precision over recall also in phrase extraction. The only major adjustment of the language model to the special case of query-snippet translation is the fact that we train our n-gram model on queries taken from user logs, instead of on standard English text.

4 Experimental Evaluation

4.1 Data

The training data for the translation model and the correlation-based model consist of pairs of queries and snippets for clicked results taken from anonymized query logs. Using snippets instead of full documents makes iterative training feasible and also reduces noise considerably. This parallel corpus of query-snippet pairs is fed into a standard SMT training pipeline (modulo the adjustments to word and phrase alignment discussed above). The parallel corpus consists of 3 billion query-snippet pairs that are input to training of word and phrase alignment models. The resulting phrase translation table that builds the basis of the translation model consists 700 million query-snippet phrase translations. A collection of data statistics for the training data is shown in table 1.

The language model used in our experiment is a trigram language model trained on English queries in user logs. N-grams were cut off at a minimum frequency of 4. Data statistics for resulting unique n-grams are shown in table 2.

4.2 Experimental Comparison

Our experimental setup for query expansion deploys a real-world search engine, google.com, for a comparison of expansions from the SMT-based system and the correlation-based system. The experimental evaluation was done as direct comparison of search results for queries where both experimental systems suggested expansion terms. Since expansions from both experimental systems are done on top of the same underlying search engine, this allows us to abstract away from interactions with the underlying system. The queries used for evaluation were extracted randomly from 3+ word

query	SMT-based expansions	corr-based expansions	score
applying U.S. passport	passport - visa	applying - home	-1.0
configure debian to use dhcp	debian - linux configure - install	configure - configuring	-1.0
how many episodes of 30 rock?	episodes - season episodes - series	how many episodes - tv many episodes - wikipedia	-0.83
lampasas county sheriff department	department - office	department - home sheriff - office	-0.83
weakerthans cat virtue chords	chords - guitar chords - lyrics chords - tab	cat - tabs chords - tabs	-0.83
Henry VIII Menu Portland, Maine	menu - restaurant menu - restaurants	portland - six menu - england	1.3
ladybug birthday parties	parties - ideas parties - party	ladybug - kids	1.3
political cartoon calvin coolidge	cartoon - cartoons	political cartoon - encyclopedia	1.3
top ten dining, vancouver	dining - restaurants	dining vancouver - 10	1.3
international communication in veterinary medicine	communication - communications communication - skills	international communication - college	1.3

Table 4: SMT-based versus correlation-based expansions with mean item score.

queries in user logs in order to allow the systems to deploy context information for expansion.

In order to evaluate Cui et al.'s (2002) correlation-based system in this setup, we required the system to assign expansion terms to particular query terms. This could be achieved by using a linear interpolation of scores in equation 2 and equation 1. Equation 1 thus introduces a preference for a particular query term to the whole-query score calculated by equation 2. Our reimplementation uses unigram and bigram phrases in queries and expansions. Furthermore, we use *Okapi BM25* instead of *tfidf* in the calculation of equation 1 (see Robertson et al. (1998)).

Query expansion for the SMT-based system is done by extracting terms introduced in the 5-best list of query translations as expansion terms for the respective query terms.

The evaluation was performed by three independent raters. The raters were given task-specific rating guidelines, and were shown queries and 10-best search results from both systems, anonymized, and presented randomly on left or right sides. The raters' task was to evaluate the results on a 7-point Likert-type[1] scale, defined as:

-1.5: much worse

-1.0: worse

-0.5: slightly worse

0: about the same

0.5: slightly better

1.0: better

1.5: much better

Results on 125 queries where both systems suggested expansion terms are shown in table 3. For each query, rating scores are averaged over the scores assigned by three raters. The overall mean item score for a comparison of SMT-based expansion against correlation-based expansion was 0.333 for 102 items with rater agreement, and 0.279 for 125 items including rater disagreements. All result differences are statistically significant.

Examples for SMT-based and correlation-based expansions are given in table 4. The first five examples are losses for the SMT-based system. In the first example, *passport* is replaced by the related, but not synonymous term *visa* in the SMT-based expansion. The second example is a loss for SMT-based expansion because of a replacement of the specific term *debian* by the more general term *linux*. The correlation-based expansions *tv 30 rock* in the third example, *lampasas county sheriff home* in the fourth example, and *weakerthans tabs* in the fifth example directly hit the title of relevant web pages, while the SMT-based expansion terms do not improve retrieval results. However, even from these negative examples it becomes apparent that the SMT-based expansion terms are clearly related to the query terms, and for a majority cases this has a positive effect. Such examples are shown in

[1]Likert's (1932) original rating system is a 5-point scale using integer scores 1 through 5. Our system uses average scores over three raters for each item, and uses a 7-point instead of a 5-point scale. See Dawes (2008) on the comparability of 5-, 7-, or 10-point scales.

(herbs , herbs) (for , for) (chronic , chronic) (constipation , constipation)
(herbs , **herb**) (for , for) (chronic , chronic) (constipation , constipation)
(herbs , **remedies**) (for , for) (chronic , chronic) (constipation , constipation)
(herbs , **medicine**) (for , for) (chronic , chronic) (constipation , constipation)
(herbs , **supplements**) (for , for) (chronic , chronic) (constipation , constipation)
(herbs , herbs) (for , for) (mexican , mexican) (cooking , cooking)
(herbs , herbs) (for , for) (cooking , cooking) (mexican , mexican)
(herbs , herbs) (for , for) (mexican , mexican) (cooking , **food**)
(mexican , mexican) (herbs , herbs) (for , for) (cooking , cooking)
(herbs , **spices**) (for , for) (mexican , mexican) (cooking , cooking)

Table 5: Unique 5-best phrase-level translations of queries *herbs for chronic constipation* and *herbs for mexican cooking*.

query terms	n-best expansions		
herbs	**com**	treatment	encyclopedia
chronic	interpret	treating	**com**
constipation	**interpret**	**treating**	**com**
herbs for	medicinal	support	women
for chronic	com	gold	encyclopedia
chronic constipation	interpret	treating	
herbs	**cooks**	**recipes**	com
mexican	**recipes**	com	cooks
cooking	**cooks**	**recipes**	com
herbs for	medicinal	women	support
for mexican	**cooks**	com	allrecipes

Table 6: Correlation-based expansions for queries *herbs for chronic constipation* and *herbs for mexican cooking*.

the second set of expansions. SMT-based expansions such as *henry viii restaurant portland, maine*, or *ladybug birthday ideas*, or *top ten restaurants, vancouver* achieve a change in retrieval results that does not result in a query drift, but rather in improved retrieval results. In contrast, the terms introduced by the correlation-based system are either only vaguely related or noise.

5 Discussion

We attribute the experimental result of a significant preference for SMT-based expansions over correlation-based expansions to the fruitful combination of translation model and language model provided by the SMT system. The SMT approach can be viewed as a combined system that proposes candidate expansion via the translation model, and filters them by the language model. Thus we may find a certain amount of non-sensical expansion candidates at the phrase translation level. This can be seen from inspecting table 7 which shows the most probable phrase translations that are applicable to the queries *herbs for chronic constipation* and *herbs for mexican cooking*. The phrase table includes identity translations and closely related terms as most probable translations for nearly every phrase, however, it also clearly includes noisy and non-related terms. More importantly, an extraction of expansion terms from the phrase table alone would not allow to choose the appropriate term for the given query context. This can be attained by combining the phrase translations with a language model: As shown in table 5, the 5-best translations of the full queries attain a proper disambiguation of the senses of *herbs* by replacing the term by *remedies*, *medicine*, and *supplements* for the first query, and with *spices* for the second query. Expansion terms highlighted in bold face.

The fact that the most probable translation for the whole query mostly is the identity translation can be seen as a feature, not as a bug, of the SMT-based approach: By the option to prefer identity translations or word reorderings over translations of source words, the SMT model effectively can choose not to generate any expansion terms. This will happen if none of the candidate phrase translations fit with high enough probability into the context of the whole query, as assessed by the language model.

In contrast to the SMT model, the correlation-based model cannot fall back onto the ordering information of the language model, but aggregates information for the whole query from a bag-of-words of query terms. Table 6 shows the top three correlation-based expansion terms assigned to unigrams and bigrams in the queries *herbs for chronic constipation* and *herbs for mexican cooking*. Expansion terms are chosen by overall highest weight and shown in bold face. Relevant expansion terms such as *treatment* or *recipes* that would disambiguate the meaning of *herbs* are in fact proposed by the correlation-based model, however, the cohesion score also promotes terms such as *interpret* or *com* as best whole-query expansions, thus leading to query drift.

6 Conclusion

We presented an approach to *contextual query expansion* that deploys natural language technology in form of statistical machine translation. The key idea of our approach is to consider the problem of the "lexical gap" between queries and documents from a linguistic point of view, and attempt to bridge this gap by translating from the query language into the document language. Using search engine user logs, we could extract large amounts of parallel data of queries and snippets from clicked documents. These data were used to train an alignment-based translation model, and an n-gram based language model. The same data were used to train a reimplementation of Cui et al.'s (2002) term-correlation based query expansion system. An experimental comparison of the two systems showed a considerable preference for SMT-based expansions over correlation-based expansion. Our explanation for this result is the fruitful combination of the orthogonal information sources from translation model and language model. While in the SMT approach expansion candidates proposed by the translation model are effectively filtered by ordering information on the query context from the language model, the correlation-based approach resorts to an inferior bag-of-word aggregation of scores for the whole query. Furthermore, each component of the SMT model takes great care to avoid sparse data problems by various sophisticated smoothing techniques. In contrast, the correlation-based model relies on pure counts of term frequencies.

An interesting task for future work is to dissect the contributions of translation model and language model, for example, by combining a correlation-based system with a language model filter. The challenge here is a proper integration of n-gram lookup into correlation-based expansion.

References

Baeza-Yates, Ricardo and Alessandro Tiberi. 2007. Extracting semantic relations from query logs. In *Proceedings of the 13th ACM SIGKDD Conference on Knowledge Discovery and Data Mining (KDD'07)*, San Jose, CA.

Beeferman, Doug and Adam Berger. 2000. Agglomerative clustering of a search engine query log. In *Proceedings of the 6th ACM SIGKDD International Conference on Knowledge Discovery and Data Mining (KDD'00)*, Boston, MA.

Berger, Adam L., Rich Caruana, David Cohn, Dayne Freitag, and Vibhu Mittal. 2000. Bridging the lexical chasm: Statistical approaches to answer-finding. In *Proceedings of SIGIR'00*, Athens, Greece.

Brants, Thorsten, Ashok C. Popat, Peng Xu, Franz J. Och, and Jeffrey Dean. 2007. Large language models in machine translation. In *Proceedings of the Conference on Empirical Methods in Natural Language Processing (EMNLP'07)*, Prague, Czech Republic.

Brown, Peter F., Stephen A. Della Pietra, Vincent J. Della Pietra, and Robert L. Mercer. 1993. The mathematics of statistical machine translation: Parameter estimation. *Computational Linguistics*, 19(2):263–311.

Cui, Hang, Ji-Rong Wen, Jian-Yun Nie, and Wei-Ying Ma. 2002. Probabilistic query expansion using query logs. In *Proceedings of WWW 2002*, Honolulu, Hawaii.

Dawes, John. 2008. Do data characteristics change according to the number of scale points used? An experiment using 5-point, 7-point and 10-point scales. *International Journal of Market Research*, 50(1):61–77.

Dempster, A. P., N. M. Laird, and D. B. Rubin. 1977. Maximum Likelihood from Incomplete Data via the *EM* Algorithm. *Journal of the Royal Statistical Society*, 39(B):1–38.

Echihabi, Abdessamad and Daniel Marcu. 2003. A noisy-channel approach to question answering. In *Proceedings of the 41st Annual Meeting of the Association for Computational Linguistics (ACL'03)*, Sapporo, Japan.

Fitzpatrick, Larry and Mei Dent. 1997. Automatic feedback using past queries: Social searching? In *Proceedings of SIGIR'97*, Philadelphia, PA.

Fonseca, Bruno M., Paulo Golgher, Bruno Possas, Berthier Ribeiro-Neto, and Nivio Ziviani. 2005. Concept-based interactive query expansion. In *Proceedings of the 14th Conference on Information and Knowledge Management (CIKM'05)*, Bremen, Germany.

Huang, Chien-Kang, Lee-Feng Chien, and Yen-Jen Oyang. 2003. Relevant term suggestion in interactive web search based on contextual information in query session logs. *Journal of the American Society for Information Science and Technology*, 54(7):638–649.

Jones, Rosie, Benjamin Rey, Omid Madani, and Wiley Greiner. 2006. Generating query substitutions. In *Proceedings of the 15th International World Wide Web conference (WWW'06)*, Edinburgh, Scotland.

Likert, Rensis. 1932. A technique for the measurement of attitudes. *Archives of Psychology*, 140:5–55.

Och, Franz Josef and Hermann Ney. 2003. A systematic comparison of various statistical alignment models. *Computational Linguistics*, 29(1):19–51.

Och, Franz Josef and Hermann Ney. 2004. The alignment template approach to statistical machine translation. *Computational Linguistics*, 30(4):417–449.

Raghavan, Vijay V. and Hayri Sever. 1995. On the reuse of past optimal queries. In *Proceedings of SIGIR'95*, Seattle, WA.

Riezler, Stefan, Alexander Vasserman, Ioannis Tsochantaridis, Vibhu Mittal, and Yi Liu. 2007. Statistical machine translation for query expansion in answer retrieval. In *Proceedings of the 45th Annual Meeting of the Association for Computational Linguistics (ACL'07)*, Prague, Czech Republic.

Robertson, Stephen E., Steve Walker, and Micheline Hancock-Beaulieu. 1998. Okapi at TREC-7. In *Proceedings of the Seventh Text REtrieval Conference (TREC-7)*, Gaithersburg, MD.

Sahami, Mehran and Timothy D. Heilman. 2006. A web-based kernel function for measuring the similarity of short text snippets. In *Proceedings of the 15th International World Wide Web conference (WWW'06)*, Edinburgh, Scotland.

Soricut, Radu and Eric Brill. 2006. Automatic question answering using the web: Beyond the factoid. *Journal of Information Retrieval - Special Issue on Web Information Retrieval*, 9:191–206.

Wen, Ji-Rong, Jian-Yun Nie, and Hong-Jiang Zhang. 2002. Query clustering using user logs. *ACM Transactions on Information Systems*, 20(1):59–81.

Xu, Jinxi and W. Bruce Croft. 1996. Query expansion using local and global document analysis. In *Proceedings of SIGIR'96*, Zurich, Switzerland.

herbs	herbs herbal medicinal spices supplements remedies
herbs for	herbs for herbs herbs and with herbs
herbs for chronic	herbs for chronic and herbs for chronic herbs for
for	for
for chronic	for chronic chronic of chronic
for chronic constipation	for chronic constipation chronic constipation for constipation
chronic	chronic acute patients treatment
chronic constipation	chronic constipation of chronic constipation with chronic constipation
constipation	constipation bowel common symptoms
for mexican	for mexican mexican the mexican of mexican
for mexican cooking	mexican food mexican food and mexican glossary
mexican	mexican mexico the mexican
mexican cooking	mexican cooking mexican food mexican cooking
cooking	cooking culinary recipes cook food recipe

Table 7: Phrase translations applicable to source strings *herbs for chronic constipation* and *herbs for mexican cooking*.

Classifying chart cells for quadratic complexity context-free inference

Brian Roark and **Kristy Hollingshead**
Center for Spoken Language Understanding
Oregon Health & Science University, Beaverton, Oregon, 97006 USA
{roark,hollingk}@cslu.ogi.edu

Abstract

In this paper, we consider classifying word positions by whether or not they can either start or end multi-word constituents. This provides a mechanism for "closing" chart cells during context-free inference, which is demonstrated to improve efficiency and accuracy when used to constrain the well-known Charniak parser. Additionally, we present a method for "closing" a sufficient number of chart cells to ensure quadratic worst-case complexity of context-free inference. Empirical results show that this $O(n^2)$ bound can be achieved without impacting parsing accuracy.

1 Introduction

While there have been great advances in the statistical modeling of hierarchical syntactic structure in the past 15 years, exact inference with such models remains very costly, so that most rich syntactic modeling approaches involve heavy pruning, pipelining or both. Pipeline systems make use of simpler models with more efficient inference to reduce the search space of the full model. For example, the well-known Ratnaparkhi (1999) parser used a POS-tagger and a finite-state NP chunker as initial stages of a multi-stage Maximum Entropy parser. The Charniak (2000) parser uses a simple PCFG to prune the chart for a richer model; and Charniak and Johnson (2005) added a discriminatively trained reranker to the end of that pipeline.

Recent results making use of finite-state chunkers early in a syntactic parsing pipeline have shown both an efficiency (Glaysher and Moldovan, 2006) and an accuracy (Hollingshead and Roark, 2007) benefit to the use of such constraints in a parsing system. Glaysher and Moldovan (2006) demonstrated an efficiency gain by explicitly disallowing entries in chart cells that would result in constituents that cross chunk boundaries. Hollingshead and Roark (2007) demonstrated that high precision constraints on early stages of the Charniak and Johnson (2005) pipeline—in the form of base phrase constraints derived either from a chunker or from later stages of an earlier iteration of the same pipeline—achieved significant accuracy improvements, by moving the pipeline search away from unlikely areas of the search space. Both of these approaches (as with Ratnaparkhi earlier) achieve their improvements by ruling out parts of the search space for downstream processes, and the gain can either be realized in efficiency (same accuracy, less time) or accuracy (same time, greater accuracy). Parts of the search space are ruled out precisely when they are inconsistent with the generally reliable output of the chunker, i.e., the constraints are a by-product of chunking.

In this paper, we consider building classifiers that more directly address the problem of "closing" chart cells to entries, rather than extracting this information from taggers or chunkers built for a different purpose. We build two classifiers, which tag each word in the sequence with a binary class label. The first classifier decides if the word can *begin* a constituent of span greater than one word; the second classifier decides if the word can *end* a constituent of span greater than 1. Given a chart cell (i, j) with start word w_i and end word w_j, where $j>i$, that cell can be "closed" to entries if the first classifier decides that w_i cannot be the first word of a multi-word constituent or if the second classifier decides that w_j cannot be the last word in a multi-word constituent. In such a way, we can optimize classifiers specifically for the task of constraining chart parsers. Note that such classifier output would be relatively straightforward to incorporate into most existing context-free constituent parsers.

We demonstrate the baseline accuracies of such classifiers, and their impact when the constraints are placed on the Charniak and Johnson (2005) parsing pipeline. Various ways of using classifier output are investigated, including one method for guaranteeing quadratic complexity of the context-free parser. A proof of the quadratic complexity is included, along with a detailed performance evaluation when constraining the Charniak parser to be worst-case quadratic.

2 Background

Dynamic programming for context-free inference generally makes use of a chart structure, as shown in Fig. 1. Each cell in the chart represents a possible constituent spanning a substring, which is identified by the indices of the first and last words of the substring. Thus, the cell identified with

©2008. Licensed under the *Creative Commons Attribution-Noncommercial-Share Alike 3.0 Unported* license (http://creativecommons.org/licenses/by-nc-sa/3.0/). Some rights reserved.

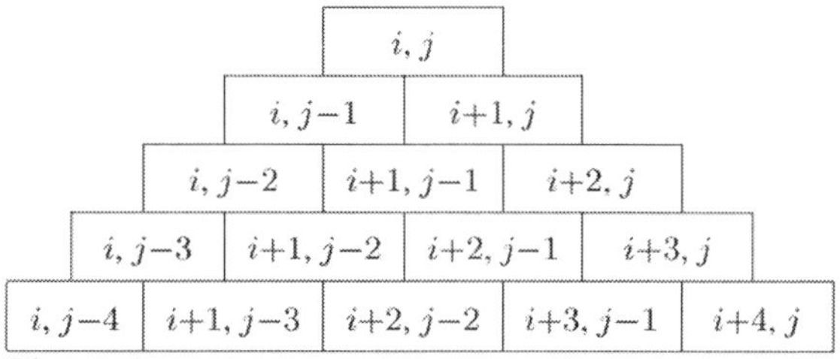

Figure 1: Fragment of a chart structure. Each cell is indexed with start and end word indices.

i, j will contain possible constituents spanning the substring $w_i \dots w_j$. Context-free inference has cubic complexity in the length of the string n, due to the $O(n^2)$ chart cells and $O(n)$ possible child configurations at each cell. For example, the CYK algorithm, which assumes a grammar in Chomsky Normal Form (hence exactly 2 non-terminal children for each constituent of span greater than 1), must consider the $O(n)$ possible midpoints for the two children of constituents at each cell.

In a parsing pipeline, some decisions about the hidden structure are made at an earlier stage. For example, base phrase chunking involves identifying a span as a base phrase of some category, often NP. A base phrase constituent has no children other than pre-terminal POS-tags, which all have a single terminal child, i.e., there is no internal structure in the base phrase involving non-POS non-terminals. This has a number of implications for the context-free parser. First, there is no need to build internal structure within the identified base phrase constituent. Second, constituents which cross brackets with the base phrase cannot be part of the final tree structure. This second constraint on possible trees can be thought of as a constraint on chart cells, as pointed out in Glaysher and Moldovan (2006): no multi-word spanning constituent can begin at a word falling within a base-phrase chunk, other than the first word of that chunk. Similarly, no multi-word spanning constituent can end at a word falling within a base-phrase chunk, other than the last word of that chunk. These constraints rule out many possible structures that the full context-free parser would have to otherwise consider.

These start and end constraints can be extracted from the output of the chunker, but the chunker is not trained to optimize the accuracy (or the precision) of these particular constraints, rather typically to optimize chunking accuracy. Further, these constraints can apply even for words which fall outside of typical chunks. For example, in English, verbs and prepositions tend to occur before their arguments, hence are often unlikely to end constituents, despite not being inside a typically defined base phrase. If we can build a classifier specifically for this task (determining whether a word can start or end a multi-word constituent), we can more directly optimize the classifier for use within a pipeline.

Strings in corpus	39832	
Word tokens in corpus	950028	
Tokens neither first nor last in string	870399	
Word tokens in S_1	439558	50.5%
Word tokens in E_1	646855	74.3%

Table 1: Statistics on word classes from sections 2-21 of the Penn Wall St. Journal Treebank

3 Starting and ending constituents

To better understand the particular task that we propose, and its likely utility, we first look at the distribution of classes and our ability to build simple classifiers to predict these classes. First, let us introduce notation. Given a string of n words $w_1 \dots w_n$, we will say that a word w_i $(1<i<n)$ is in the class $S_{>1}$ if there is a constituent spanning $w_i \dots w_j$ for some $j>i$; and $w_i \in S_1$ otherwise. Similarly, we will say that a word w_j $(1<j<n)$ is in the class $E_{>1}$ if there is a constituent spanning $w_i \dots w_j$ for some $i<j$; and $w_j \in E_1$ otherwise. These are two separate binary classification tasks.

Note that the first word w_1 and the last word w_n are unambiguous in terms of whether they start or end constituents of length greater than 1. The first word w_1 must start a constituent spanning the whole string, and the last word w_n must end that same constituent. The first word w_1 cannot end a constituent of length greater than 1; similarly, the last word w_n cannot start a constituent of length greater than 1. Hence our classifier evaluation omits those two word positions, leading to $n-2$ classifications for a string of length n.

Table 1 shows statistics from sections 2-21 of the Penn WSJ Treebank (Marcus et al., 1993). From the nearly 1 million words in approximately 40 thousand sentences, just over 870 thousand are neither the first nor the last word in the string, hence possible members of the sets S_1 or E_1, i.e., not beginning a multi-word constituent (S_1) or not ending a multi-word constituent (E_1). Of these, over half (50.5%) do not begin multi-word constituents, and nearly three quarters (74.3%) do not end multi-word constituents. This high latter percentage reflects English right-branching structure.

How well can we perform these binary classification tasks, using simple (linear complexity) classifiers? To investigate this question, we used sections 2-21 of the Penn WSJ Treebank as training data, section 00 as heldout, and section 24 as development. Word classes are straightforwardly extracted from the treebank trees, by measuring the span of constituents starting and ending at each word position. We trained log linear models with the perceptron algorithm (Collins, 2002) using fea-

Classification Task	Markov order		
	0	1	2
S_1 (no multi-word constituent start)	96.7	96.9	96.9
E_1 (no multi-word constituent end)	97.3	97.3	97.3

Table 2: Classification accuracy on development set for binary classes S_1 and E_1, for various Markov orders.

tures similar to those used for NP chunking in Sha and Pereira (2003), including surrounding POS-tags (provided by a separately trained log linear POS-tagger) and surrounding words, up to 2 before and 2 after the current word position.

Table 2 presents classification accuracy on the development set for both of these classification tasks. We trained models with Markov order 0 (each word classified independently), order 1 (features with class pairs) and order 2 (features with class triples). This did not change performance for the E_1 classification, but Markov order 1 was slightly (but significantly) better than order 0 for S_1 classification. Hence, from this point forward, all classification will be Markov order 1.

We can see from these results that simple classification approaches yield very high classification accuracy. The question now becomes, how can classifier output be used to constrain a context-free parser, and what is the impact on parser performance of using such a classifier in the pipeline.

4 Closing chart cells

Before moving on to an empirical investigation of constraining context-free parsers with the methods we propose, we first need to take a fairly detailed look at representations internal to these parsers. In particular, while we can rule out multi-word constituents with particular start and end positions, there may be intermediate or *incomplete* structures within the parser that should not be ruled out at these same start and end positions. Hence the notion of "closing" a chart cell is slightly more complicated than it may seem initially.

Consider the chart representation in Fig. 1. Suppose that w_i is in class S_1 and w_j is in class E_1, for $i<j$. We can "close" all cells (i,k) such that $i<k$ and all cells (l,j) such that $l<j$, based on the fact that multi-word constituents cannot begin with word w_i and cannot end with w_j. A closed cell will not take *complete* entries, and, depending on the constraint used to close the cell, will have restrictions on *incomplete* entries. To make this more explicit, let us precisely define complete and incomplete entries.

Context-free inference using dynamic programming over a chart structure builds longer-span constituents by combining smaller span constituents, guided by rules in a context-free grammar. A context-free grammar $G = (V, T, S^\dagger, P)$ consists of: a set of non-terminal symbols V, including a special start symbol $S^\dagger$; a set of terminal symbols T; and a set of rule productions P of the form $A \rightarrow \alpha$ for $A \in V$ and $\alpha \in (V \cup T)^*$, i.e., a single non-terminal on the left-hand side of the rule production, and a sequence of 0 or more terminals or non-terminals on the right-hand side of the rule. If we have a rule production $A \rightarrow B\ C$ in P, a completed B entry in chart cell (i,j) and a completed C entry in chart cell (j,k), then we can place a completed A entry in chart cell (i,k), typically with some indication that the A was built from the B and C entries. Such a chart cell entry is sometimes called an "edge".

The issue with incomplete edges arises when there are rule productions in P with more than two children on the right-hand side of the rule. Rather than trying to combine an arbitrarily large number of smaller cell entries, a more efficient approach, which exploits shared structure between rules, is to only perform pairwise combination, and store *incomplete* edges to represent combinations that require further combination to achieve a complete edge. This can either be performed in advance, e.g., by factoring a grammar to be in Chomsky Normal Form, as required by the CYK algorithm (Cocke and Schwartz, 1970; Younger, 1967; Kasami, 1965), resulting in "incomplete" non-terminals created by the factorization; or incomplete edges can be represented through so-called dotted rules, as with the Earley (1970) algorithm, in which factorization is essentially performed on the fly. For example, if we have a rule production $A \rightarrow B\ C\ D$ in P, a completed B entry in chart cell (i,j) and a completed C entry in chart cell (j,k), then we can place an *incomplete* edge $A \rightarrow B\ C \cdot D$ in chart cell (i,k). The dot signifies the division between what has already been combined (to the left of the dot), and what remains to be combined.[1] Then, if we have an incomplete edge $A \rightarrow B\ C \cdot D$ in chart cell (i,k) and a complete D in cell (k,l), we can place a completed A entry in chart cell (i,l).

If a chart cell (i,j) has been "closed" due to constraints limiting multi-word constituents with that span – either $w_i \in S_1$ or $w_j \in E_1$ (and $i<j$) – then it is clear that "complete" edges should not be entered in the cell, since these represent precisely the multi-word constituents that are being ruled out. How about incomplete edges? To the extent that an incomplete edge can be extended to a valid complete edge, it should be allowed. There are two cases. If $w_i \in S_1$, then under the assumption that incomplete edges are extended from left-to-right (see footnote 1), the incomplete edge should

[1]Without loss of generality, we will assume that edges are extended from left-to-right.

Parsing constraints	Parsing accuracy LR	LP	F	% of Cells Closed
None (baseline)	88.6	89.2	88.9	–
S_1 positions	87.6	89.1	88.3	44.6
E_1 positions	87.4	88.5	87.9	66.4
Both S_1 and E_1	86.5	88.6	87.4	80.3

Table 3: Charniak parsing accuracy on section 24 under various constraint conditions, using word labels extracted using Markov order 1 model.

be discarded, because any completed edges that could result from extending that incomplete edge would have the same start position, i.e., the chart cell would be (i, k) for some $k>i$, which is closed to the completed edge. However, if $w_i \notin S_1$, then $w_j \in E_1$. A complete edge achieved by extending the incomplete edge will end at w_k for $k>j$, and cell (i, k) may be open, hence the incomplete edge should be allowed in cell (i, j). See §6 for limitations on how such incomplete edges arise in closed cells, which has consequences for the worst-case complexity under certain conditions.

5 Constraining the Charniak parser

5.1 Parser overview and constraint methods

The Charniak (2000) parser is a multi-stage, agenda-driven, edge-based parser, that can be constrained by precluding edges from being placed on the agenda. Here we will briefly describe the overall architecture of that parser, and our method for constraining its search.

The first stage of the Charniak parser uses an agenda and a simple PCFG to build a sparse chart, which is used in later stages with the full model. We will focus on this first stage, since it is here that we will be constraining the parser. The edges on the agenda and in the chart are dotted rules, as described in §4. When edges are created, they are pushed onto the agenda. Edges that are popped from the agenda are placed in the chart, and then combined with other chart entries to create new edges that are pushed onto the agenda. When a complete edge spanning the whole string is placed in the chart, at least one full solution exists in the chart. After this happens, the parser continues adding edges to the chart and agenda until reaching some parameterized target number of additional edges in the chart, at which point the next stage of the pipeline receives the chart as input and any edges remaining on the agenda are discarded.

We constrain the first stage of the Charniak parser as follows. Using classifiers, a subset of word positions are assigned to class S_1, and a subset are assigned to class E_1. (Words can be assigned to both.) When an edge is created for cell (i, j), where $i < j$, it is not placed on the agenda if either of the following two conditions hold: 1) $w_i \in S_1$; or 2) the edge is complete and $w_j \in E_1$.

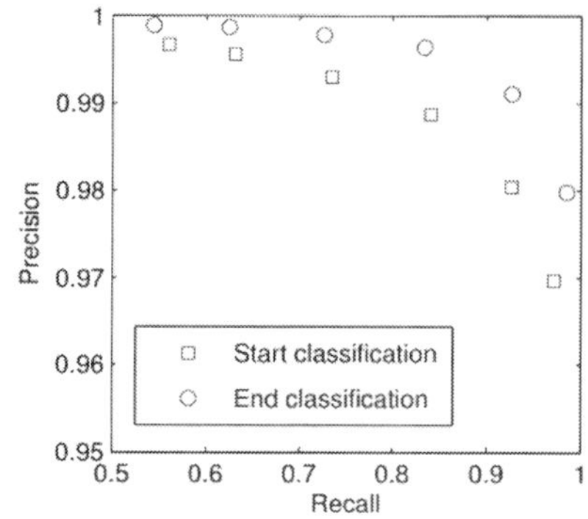

Figure 2: Precision/recall tradeoff of S_1 and E_1 tags on the development set.

Of course, the output of our classifier is not perfect, hence imposing these constraints will sometimes rule out the true parse, and parser accuracy may degrade. Furthermore, because of the agenda-based heuristic search, the efficiency of search may not be impacted as straightforwardly as one might expect for an exact inference algorithm. For these reasons, we have performed extensive empirical trials under a variety of conditions to try to clearly understand the best practices for using these sorts of constraints for this sort of parser.

5.2 Experimental trials

We begin by simply taking the output of the Markov order 1 taggers, whose accuracies are reported in Table 2, and using word positions labeled as S_1 or E_1 to "close" cells in the Charniak parser, as described above. Table 3 presents parser accuracy on the development set (section 24) under four conditions: the unconstrained baseline; using just S_1 words to close cells; using just E_1 word positions to close cells; and using both S_1 and E_1 positions to close cells. As can be seen from these results, all of these trials result in a decrease in accuracy from the baseline, with larger decreases associated with higher percentages of closed cells.

These results indicate that, despite the relatively high accuracy of classification, the precision of our classifier in producing the S_1 and E_1 tags is too low. To remedy this, we traded some recall for precision as follows. We used the forward-backward algorithm with our Markov order 1 tagging model to assign a conditional probability at each word position of the tags S_1 and E_1 given the string. At each word position w_i for $1<i<n$, we took the log likelihood ratio of tag S_1 as follows:

$$\text{LLR}(w_i \in S_1) \quad = \quad \log \frac{\text{P}(w_i \in S_1 \mid w_1 \dots w_n)}{\text{P}(w_i \notin S_1 \mid w_1 \dots w_n)} \qquad (1)$$

and the same for tag E_1. A default classification threshold is to label S_1 or E_1 if the above log likelihood is greater than zero, i.e., if the S_1 tag is more likely than not. To improve the precision, we can move this threshold to some greater value.

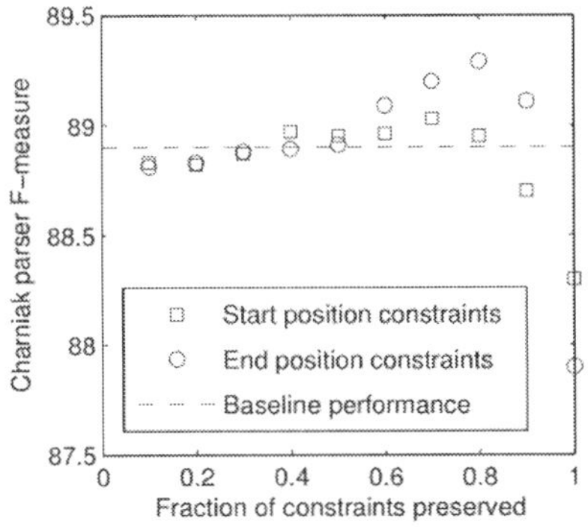

Figure 3: Charniak parser F-measure at various operating points of the fraction c of total constraints kept.

Each word position in a string was ranked with respect to these log likelihood ratios for each tag.[2] If the total number of words w_i with $\text{LLR}(w_i \in S_1) > 0$ is k, then we defined multiple operating points by setting the threshold such that ck words remained above threshold, for some constant c between 0 and 1. Fig. 2 shows the precision/recall tradeoff at these operating points for both S_1 and E_1 tags. Note that for both tags, we can achieve over 99% precision with recall above 70%, and for the E_1 tag (a more frequent class than S_1) that level of precision is achieved with recall greater than 90%.

Constraints were derived at each of these operating points and used within the Charniak parsing pipeline. Fig. 3 shows the F-measure parsing performance using either S_1 or E_1 constraints at various values of c for preserving ck of the original k constraints. As can be seen from that graph, with improved precision both types of constraints have operating points that achieve accuracy improvements over the baseline parser on the dev set under default parser settings.

This accuracy improvement is similar to results obtained in Hollingshead and Roark (2007), where base phrase constraints from a finite-state chunker were used to achieve improved parse accuracy. Their explanation for the accuracy improvement, which seems to apply in this case as well, is that the first stage of the Charniak parser is still passing the same number of edges in the chart to the second stage, but that the edges now come from more promising parts of the search space, i.e., the parser does a better job of exploring good parts of the search space. Hence the constraints seem to be doing what they should do, which is constrain the search without unduly excluding good solutions.

Note that these results are all achieved with the default parsing parameterizations, so that accuracy gains are achieved, but not necessarily efficiency gains. The Charniak parser allows for

[2]Perceptron weights were interpreted in the log domain and conditionally normalized appropriately.

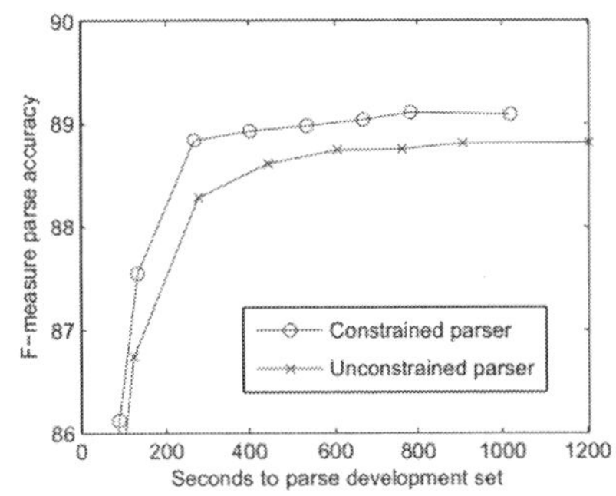

Figure 4: Speed/accuracy tradeoff for both the unconstrained Charniak parser and when constrained with high precision start/end constraints.

narrow search parameterizations, whereby fewer edges are added to the chart in the initial stage. Given the improved search using these constraints, high accuracy may be achieved at far narrower search parameterizations than the default setting of the parser. To look at potential efficiency gains to be had from these constraints, we chose the most constrained operating points for both start and end constraints that do not hurt accuracy relative to the baseline parser ($c = 0.7$ for S_1 and $c = 0.8$ for E_1) and used both kinds of constraints in the parser. We then ran the Charniak parser with varying search parameters, to observe performance when search is narrower than the default. Fig. 4 presents F-measure accuracy for both constrained and unconstrained parser configurations at various search parameterizations. The times for the constrained parser configurations include the approximately 20 seconds required for POS-tagging and word-boundary classification of the dev set.

These results demonstrate a sharper knee of the curve for the constrained runs, with parser accuracy that is above that achieved by the unconstrained parser under the default search parameterization, even after a nearly 5 times speedup.

5.3 Analysis of constraints on 1-best parses

There are two ways in which the constraints could be improving parser performance: by helping the parser to find higher probability parses that it was formerly losing because of search errors; or by not allowing the parser to select high probability parses that violate the constraints. To get a sense of whether the constraints on the parser are simply fixing search errors or are imposing constraints on the model itself, we examined the 1-best parses from both constrained and unconstrained scenarios. First, we calculated the geometric mean of the 1-best parse probabilities under both scenarios, which were (in logs) -207.99 for unconstrained and -208.09 for constrained. Thus, the constrained 1-best parses had very slightly less probability than the unconstrained parses, indicating that the constraints were not simply fixing search errors, but also eliminated some MAP parses.

To get a sense of how often search errors were corrected versus ruling out of MAP parses, we compared the constrained and unconstrained parses at each string, and tallied when the unconstrained parse probabilities were greater (or less) than the constrained parse probabilities, as well as when they were equal. At the default search parameterization (210), 84.8 percent of the strings had the same parses; in 9.2 percent of the cases the unconstrained parses had higher probability; and in 5.9 percent of the cases the constrained parses had higher probability. The narrower search parameterization at the knee of the curve in Fig. 4 had similar results: 84.6 percent were the same; in 8.6 percent of the cases the unconstrained probability was higher; and in 6.8 percent of the cases the constrained probability was higher. Hence, when the 1-best parse differs, the parse found via constraints has a higher probability in approximately 40 percent of the cases.

6 $O(n^2)$ complexity context-free parsing

Using sufficient S_1 and E_1 constraints of the sort we have been investigating, we can achieve worst-case quadratic (instead of cubic) complexity. A proof, based on the CYK algorithm, is given in Appendix A, but we can make the key points here. First, cubic complexity of context-free inference is due to $O(n^2)$ chart cells and $O(n)$ possible child configurations per cell. If we "close" all but $O(n)$ cells, the "open" cells will be processed with worst-case quadratic complexity ($O(n)$ cells with $O(n)$ possible child configurations per cell). If we can show that the remaining $O(n^2)$ "closed" cells each can be processed within constant time, then the overall complexity is quadratic. The proof in Appendix A shows that this is the case if closing a cell is such that: when a cell (i, j) is closed, then either all cells (i, k) for $k>i$ are closed or all cells (k, j) for $k<j$ are closed. These conditions are achieved when we select sets S_1 and E_1 and close cells accordingly.

Just as we were able to order word position log likelihood scores for classes S_1 and E_1 to improve precision in the previous section, here we will order them so that we can continue selecting positions until we have guaranteed less than some threshold of "open" cells. If the threshold is linear in the length of the string, we will be able to parse the string with worst-case quadratic complexity, as shown in Appendix A. We will set our threshold to kn for some constant k (in our experiments, k ranges from 2 to 10). Table 4 presents the percentage of cells closed, class (S_1 and E_1) precision and parser accuracy when the number of "open" cells is bounded to be less than the threshold. These results clearly demonstrate that such constraints can be placed on real context-free parsing problems without significant impact to accuracy–in fact, with small improvements.

Open cells	% cells closed	Class Prec	Parse accuracy LR	LP	F
all	–	–	88.6	89.2	88.9
$10n$	39.1	99.9	88.6	89.2	88.9
$8n$	50.4	99.9	88.6	89.2	88.9
$6n$	62.8	99.9	88.6	89.2	88.9
$4n$	75.7	99.8	88.8	89.4	89.1
$2n$	88.8	99.8	88.8	89.5	89.1

Table 4: Varying constant k for kn "open" cells, yielding $O(n^2)$ parsing complexity guarantees

We were quite surprised by these trials, fully expecting these limits to negatively impact accuracy. The likely explanation is that the existing Charniak search strategy itself is bounding processing in such a way that the additional constraints placed on the process do not interfere with standard processing. Note that our approach closes a higher percentage of cells in longer strings, which the Charniak pipeline already more severely prunes than shorter strings. Further, this approach appears to be relying very heavily on E_1 constraints, hence has very high precision of classification.

While the Charniak parser may not be the ideal framework within which to illustrate these worst-case complexity improvements, the lack of impairment to the parser provides strong evidence that other parsers could make use of the resulting charts to achieve significant efficiency gains.

7 Conclusion & Future Work

In this paper, we have presented a very simple approach to constraining context-free chart parsing pipelines that has several nice properties. First, it is based on a simple classification task that can achieve very high accuracy using very simple models. Second, the classifier output can be straightforwardly used to constrain any chart-based context-free parser. Finally, we have shown (in Appendix A) that "closing" sufficient cells with these techniques leads to quadratic worst-case complexity bounds. Our empirical results with the Charniak parser demonstrated that our classifiers were sufficiently accurate to allow for such bounds to be placed on the parser without hurting parsing accuracy.

Future work in this direction will involve trying different methods for defining effective operating points, such as more heavily constraining longer strings, in an attempt to further improve the search in the Charniak parser. We would also like to investigate performance when using other chart parsing strategies, such as when using cell pruning instead of an agenda.

CYK($w_1 \ldots w_n$, $G = (V, T, S^\dagger, P, \rho)$) ▷ PCFG G must be in CNF

1 **for** $t = 1$ to n **do** ▷ scan in words/POS-tags (span=1)

2 **for** $j = 1$ to $|V|$ **do**

3 $\alpha_j(t,t) \leftarrow \mathrm{P}(A_j \rightarrow w_t)$

4 **for** $s = 2$ to n **do** ▷ all spans > 1

5 **for** $t = 1$ to $n-s+1$ **do**

6 $e \leftarrow t+s-1$ ▷ end word position for this span

7 **for** $i = 1$ to $|V|$ **do**

8 $\zeta_i(t,e) \leftarrow \underset{t<m\leq e}{\operatorname{argmax}} \left(\underset{j,k}{\operatorname{argmax}}\ \mathrm{P}(A_i \rightarrow A_j\ A_k)\ \alpha_j(t, m-1)\ \alpha_k(m, e) \right)$

9 $\alpha_i(t,e) \leftarrow \max_{t<m\leq e} \left(\max_{j,k}\ \mathrm{P}(A_i \rightarrow A_j\ A_k)\ \alpha_j(t, m-1)\ \alpha_k(m, e) \right)$

Figure 5: Pseudocode of a basic CYK algorithm for PCFG in Chomsky Normal Form (CNF).

References

Charniak, E. and M. Johnson. 2005. Coarse-to-fine n-best parsing and MaxEnt discriminative reranking. In *Proceedings of the 43rd Annual Meeting of the Association for Computational Linguistics (ACL)*, pages 173–180.

Charniak, E. 2000. A maximum-entropy-inspired parser. In *Proceedings of the 1st Conference of the North American Chapter of the Association for Computational Linguistics*, pages 132–139.

Cocke, J. and J.T. Schwartz. 1970. Programming languages and their compilers: Preliminary notes. Technical report, Courant Institute of Mathematical Sciences, NYU.

Collins, M.J. 2002. Discriminative training methods for hidden Markov models: Theory and experiments with perceptron algorithms. In *Proceedings of the Conference on Empirical Methods in Natural Language Processing (EMNLP)*, pages 1–8.

Earley, J. 1970. An efficient context-free parsing algorithm. *Communications of the ACM*, 6(8):451–455.

Glaysher, E. and D. Moldovan. 2006. Speeding up full syntactic parsing by leveraging partial parsing decisions. In *Proceedings of the COLING/ACL 2006 Main Conference Poster Sessions*, pages 295–300.

Hollingshead, K. and B. Roark. 2007. Pipeline iteration. In *Proceedings of the 45th Annual Meeting of the Association for Computational Linguistics (ACL)*, pages 952–959.

Kasami, T. 1965. An efficient recognition and syntax analysis algorithm for context-free languages. Technical report, AFCRL-65-758, Air Force Cambridge Research Lab., Bedford, MA.

Marcus, M.P., M.A. Marcinkiewicz, and B. Santorini. 1993. Building a large annotated corpus of English: The Penn treebank. *Computational Linguistics*, 19:313–330.

Ratnaparkhi, A. 1999. Learning to parse natural language with maximum entropy models. *Machine Learning*, 34(1-3):151–175.

Sha, F. and F. Pereira. 2003. Shallow parsing with conditional random fields. In *Proceedings of HLT-NAACL*, pages 134–141.

Younger, D.H. 1967. Recognition and parsing of context-free languages in time n^3. *Information and Control*, 10(2):189–208.

Appendix A Proof of quadratic complexity parsing with constraints

For this proof, we will use the well-known CYK parsing algorithm, which makes use of grammars in Chomsky Normal Form (CNF). To achieve CNF, among other things, rules with more than 2 children on the right-hand side must be factored into multiple binary rules. To do this, composite non-terminals are created in the factorizations, which represent incomplete constituents, i.e., those edges that require further combination to be made complete.[3] For example, if we have a rule production $A \rightarrow B\ C\ D$ in the context-free grammar G, then a new composite non-terminal would be created, e.g., B-C, and two binary rules would replace the previous ternary rule: $A \rightarrow B\text{-}C\ D$ and $B\text{-}C \rightarrow B\ C$. The B-C non-terminal represents part of a rule expansion that needs to be combined with something else to produce a complete non-terminal from the original set of non-terminals. Let V' be the set of non-terminals that are created through factorization, which hence represent incomplete edges.

Fig. 5 shows pseudocode of a basic CYK algorithm for use with a probabilistic CFG in CNF, $G = (V, T, S^\dagger, P, \rho)$. The function ρ maps from rules in P to probabilities. Lines 1-3 of the algorithm in Fig. 5 initialize the span 1 cells. Lines 4-9 are where the cubic complexity comes in: $O(n)$ loops in line 4, each of which include $O(n)$ loops in line 5, each of which requires finding a maximum over $O(n)$ midpoints m in lines 8-9. For each non-terminal $A_i \in V$ at each cell (t, e), the algorithm stores a backpointer $\zeta_i(t, e)$ in line 8, for efficiently extracting the maximum likelihood solution at the end of inference; and maximum probabilities $\alpha_i(t, e)$ in line 9, for use in the dynamic program.

Given a set of word positions in the classes S_1 and E_1, as defined in the main part of this paper, we can designate all cells (i, j) in the chart where either $w_i \in S_1$ or $w_j \in E_1$ to be "closed". Chart cells that are not closed will be called "open". The total number of cells in the chart is $(n^2 + n)/2$, and if we set a threshold on the maximum number of open cells to be kn, the number of closed cells must be at least $(n^2+n)/2-kn$. Given an ordering of words (see §6 for one approach), we can add words to these sets one word at a time and close the

[3]As before, we assume that edges are extended from left-to-right, which requires a left-factorization of the grammar.

```
QUADCYK(w_1 ... w_n, G = (V, T, S†, P, ρ), V', S_1, E_1)    ▷ PCFG G must be in CNF
1  for t = 1 to n do                                        ▷ scan in words/POS-tags (span=1)
2      for j = 1 to |V| do
3          α_j(t,t) ← P(A_j → w_t)
4  for s = 2 to n do                                        ▷ all spans > 1
5      for t = 1 to n−s+1 do
6          e ← t+s−1                                        ▷ end word position for this span
7          if w_t ∈ S_1  CONTINUE                           ▷ start position t "closed"
8          else if w_e ∈ E_1                                ▷ end position e "closed"
9              for i = 1 to |V| do
10                 if A_i ∉ V'  CONTINUE    ▷ only "incomplete" factored non-terminals (V')
11                 ζ_i(t,e) ← argmax_{j,k} P(A_i → A_j A_k) α_j(t, e−1) α_k(e,e)
12                 α_i(t,e) ← max_{j,k} P(A_i → A_j A_k) α_j(t, e−1) α_k(e,e)
13         else                                             ▷ chart cell (t,e) "open"
14             for i = 1 to |V| do
15                 ζ_i(t,e) ← argmax_{t<m≤e} ( argmax_{j,k} P(A_i → A_j A_k) α_j(t, m−1) α_k(m,e) )
16                 α_i(t,e) ← max_{t<m≤e} ( max_{j,k} P(A_i → A_j A_k) α_j(t, m−1) α_k(m,e) )
```

Figure 6: Pseudocode of a modified CYK algorithm, with quadratic worst case complexity with $O(n)$ "open" cells. In addition to string and grammar, it requires specification of factored non-terminal set V' and position constraints (S_1, E_1).

related cells, until the requisite number of closures are achieved. Then the resulting sets of S_1 word positions and E_1 word positions can be provided to the parsing algorithm, in addition to the grammar G and the set of factored non-terminals V'.

Fig. 6 shows pseudocode of a modified CYK algorithm that takes into account S_1 and E_1 word classes. Lines 1-6 of the algorithm in Fig. 6 are identical to those in the algorithm in Fig. 5. At line 7, we have identified the chart cell being processed, which is (t, e). If $w_t \in S_1$ then the cell is completely closed, and there is nothing to do. Otherwise, if $w_e \in E_1$ (lines 8-12), then factored non-terminals from V' can be created in that cell by finding legal combinations of children categories. If neither of these conditions hold, then the cell is open (lines 13-16) and processing occurs as in the standard CYK algorithm (lines 14-16 of the algorithm in Fig. 6 are identical to lines 7-9 in Fig. 5).

If the number of "open" cells is less than kn for some constant k, then we can prove that the algorithm in Fig. 6 is $O(n^2)$ when given a left-factored grammar in CNF. A key part of the proof rests on two lemmas:

Lemma 1: *Let V' be the set of composite non-terminals created when left-factoring a CFG to be in CNF, as described earlier. Then, for any production $A_i \rightarrow A_j\ A_k$ in the grammar, $A_k \notin V'$.*

Proof: With left-factoring, any k-ary production $A \rightarrow A_1 \ldots A_{k-1} A_k$ results in new non-terminals that concatenate the first $k-1$ non-terminals on the right-hand side. These factored non-terminals are always the leftmost child in the new production, hence no second child in the resulting CNF grammar can be a factored non-terminal.□

Lemma 2: *For a cell (t, e) in the chart, if $w_e \in E_1$, then the only possible midpoint m for creating an entry in the cell is e.*

Proof: Placing an entry in cell (t, e) requires a rule $A_i \rightarrow A_j\ A_k$, an A_j entry in cell $(t, m-1)$ and an A_k entry in cell (m, e). Suppose there is an A_k entry in cell (m, e) for $m < e$. Recall that $w_e \in E_1$, hence the cell (m, e) is closed to non-terminals not in V'. By Lemma 1, $A_k \notin V'$, therefore the cell (m, e) is closed to A_k entries. This is a contradiction. Therefore, the lemma is proved.□

Theorem: *Let $\mathcal{O}$ be the set of cells (t, e) such that $w_t \notin S_1$ and $w_e \notin E_1$ ("open" cells). If $|\mathcal{O}| < kn$ for some constant k, where n is the length of the string, then the algorithm in Fig. 6 has worst case complexity $O(n^2)$.*

Proof: Lines 4 and 5 of the algorithm in Fig. 6 loop through $O(n^2)$ cells (t, e), for which there are three cases: $w_t \in S_1$ (line 7 of Fig. 6); $w_e \in E_1$ (lines 8-12); and $(t, e) \in \mathcal{O}$ (lines 13-16).

Case 1: $w_t \in S_1$. No further work to be done.

Case 2: $w_e \in E_1$. There is a constant amount of work to be done, for the reason that there is only one possible midpoint m for binary children combinations (namely e, as proved in Lemma 2), hence no need to perform the maximization over $O(n)$ midpoints.

Case 3: $(t, e) \in \mathcal{O}$. As with standard CYK processing, there are $O(n)$ possible midpoints m over which to maximize, hence $O(n)$ work required.

Only $O(n)$ cells fall in case 3, hence the total amount of work associated with the cells in $\mathcal{O}$ is $O(n^2)$. There are $O(n^2)$ cells associated with cases 1 and 2, each of which has a total amount of work bounded by a constant, hence the total amount of work associated with the cells not in $\mathcal{O}$ is also $O(n^2)$. Therefore the overall worst-case complexity of the algorithm under these conditions is $O(n^2)$. □

Shift-Reduce Dependency DAG Parsing

Kenji Sagae[†]
Institute for Creative Technologies
University of Southern California
13274 Fiji Way
Marina del Rey, CA 90292
sagae@ict.usc.edu

Jun'ichi Tsujii
Department of Computer Science
University of Tokyo
School of Computer Science
University of Manchester
National Center for Text Mining
tsujii@is.s.u-tokyo.ac.jp

Abstract

Most data-driven dependency parsing approaches assume that sentence structure is represented as trees. Although trees have several desirable properties from both computational and linguistic perspectives, the structure of linguistic phenomena that goes beyond shallow syntax often cannot be fully captured by tree representations. We present a parsing approach that is nearly as simple as current data-driven transition-based dependency parsing frameworks, but outputs directed acyclic graphs (DAGs). We demonstrate the benefits of DAG parsing in two experiments where its advantages over dependency tree parsing can be clearly observed: predicate-argument analysis of English and syntactic analysis of Danish with a representation that includes long-distance dependencies and anaphoric reference links.

1 Introduction

Natural language parsing with data-driven dependency-based frameworks has received an increasing amount of attention in recent years (McDonald et al., 2005; Buchholz and Marsi, 2006; Nivre et al., 2006). Dependency representations directly reflect word-to-word relationships in a dependency graph, where the words in a sentence are the nodes, and labeled edges correspond to head-dependent syntactic relations. In addition to being inherently lexicalized, dependency analyses can be generated efficiently and have been show to be useful in a variety of practical tasks, such as question answering (Wang et al., 2007), information extraction in biomedical text (Erkan et al., 2007; Saetre et al, 2007) and machine translation (Quirk and Corston-Oliver, 2006).

However, despite rapid progress in the development of parsers for several languages (Nivre et al., 2007) and algorithms for more linguistically adequate non-projective structures (McDonald et al., 2005; Nivre and Nilsson, 2006), most of the current data-driven dependency parsing approaches are limited to producing only dependency trees, where each word has exactly one head. Although trees have desirable properties from both computational and linguistic perspectives, the structure of linguistic phenomena that goes beyond shallow syntax often cannot be fully captured by tree representations. Well-known linguistically-motivated dependency-based syntactic frameworks, such as Hudson's Word Grammar (Hudson, 1984), recognize that to represent phenomena such as relative clauses, control relations and other long-distance dependencies, more general graphs are needed. Hudson (2005) illustrates his syntactic framework with the analysis shown in figure 1. In this example, the arcs above the sentence correspond to a typical dependency tree commonly used in dependency parsing. It is clear, however, that the entire dependency structure is not a tree, but a directed acyclic graph (DAG), where words may have one or more heads. The arcs below the sentence represent additional syntactic dependencies commonly ignored in current dependency parsing approaches that are limited to producing tree

[†] This work was conducted while the author was at the Computer Science Department of the University of Tokyo.

© 2008. Licensed under the *Creative Commons Attribution-Noncommercial-Share Alike 3.0 Unported* license (http://creativecommons.org/licenses/by-nc-sa/3.0). Some rights reserved.

structures. There are several other linguistic phenomena that cannot be represented naturally with dependency trees, but can easily be represented with dependency DAGs, including anaphoric reference and semantically motivated predicate-argument relations. Although there are parsing approaches (often referred to as *deep parsing* approaches) that compute DAG dependency structures, this is usually done through more complex lexicalized grammar formalisms (such as HPSG, CCG and LFG) and unification operations with tree-based parsing algorithms.

We introduce a new data-driven framework for dependency parsing that produces dependency DAGs directly from input strings, in a manner nearly as simple as other current transition-based dependency parsers (Nivre et al., 2007) produce dependency trees. By moving from tree structures to DAGs, it is possible to use dependency parsing techniques to address a wider range of linguistic phenomena beyond surface syntax. We show that this framework is effective and efficient in analysis of predicate-argument dependencies represented as DAGs, and in syntactic parsing using DAGs that include long-distance dependencies, gapping dependents and anaphoric reference information, in addition to surface syntactic dependents.

Our parsing framework, based on shift-reduce dependency parsing, is presented in section 2. Experiments and results are presented and discussed in section 3. We review related work in section 4, and conclude in section 5.

2 A shift-reduce parsing framework for dependency DAGs

One of the key assumptions in both graph-based (McDonald et al., 2005) and transition-based (Nivre, 2004; Nivre and Nilsson, 2006) approaches to data-driven dependency parsing is that the dependency structure produced by the parser is a tree, where each word has exactly one head (except for a single root word, which has no head in the sentence). This assumption, of course, has to be abandoned in dependency DAG parsing. McDonald et al. (2006) point out that, while exact inference is intractable if the tree constraints are abandoned in their graph-based parsing framework, it is possible to compute more general graphs (such as DAGs) using approximate inference, finding a tree first, and adding extra edges that increase the graph's overall score. Our approach, in contrast, extends shift-reduce (transition-based) approaches, finding a

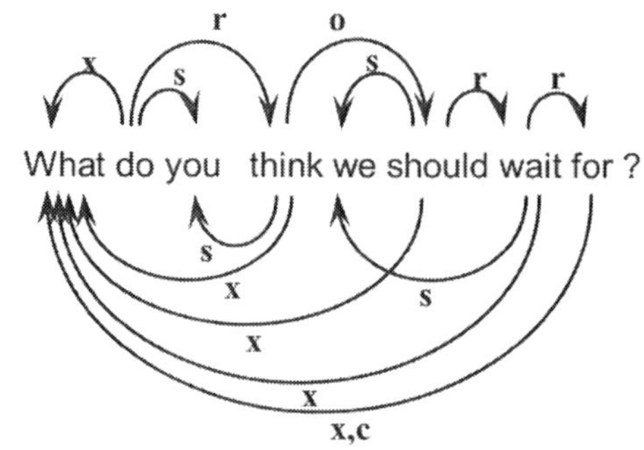

Figure 1: Word Grammar dependency graph (Hudson, 2005). Key for edge types: complement (c), object (o), sharer/xcomp (r), subject (s), and extractee (x).

DAG directly. Because data-driven shift-reduce dependency parsing is based on local decisions (informed by rich a rich feature set), the additional computational cost of computing DAGs instead of trees is small in practice, as we will show.

We first describe how the basic shift-reduce bottom-up dependency parsing algorithm described by Nivre (2004) can be modified to allow multiple heads per word. We then explore the same type of modification to Nivre's arc-eager algorithm, which is a variant of the basic shift-reduce algorithm where arcs can be created at the first opportunity. Like their tree counterparts, our algorithms for dependency DAGs produce only projective structures, assuming that projectivity for DAGs is defined in much the same way as for trees. Informally, we define a projective DAG to be a DAG where all arcs can be drawn above the sentence (written sequentially in its original order) in a way such that no arcs cross and there are no covered roots (although a *root* is not a concept associated with DAGs, we borrow the term from trees to denote words with no heads in the sentence). However, non-projectivity is predictably more wide-spread in DAG representations, since there are at least as many arcs as in a tree representation, and often more, including arcs that represent non-local relationships. We then discuss the application of pseudo-projective transformations (Nivre and Nilsson, 2005) and an additional arc-reversing transform to dependency DAGs. Using a shift-reduce algorithm that allows multiple heads per word and pseudo-projective transformations together forms a complete dependency DAG parsing framework.

2.1 Basic shift-reduce parsing with multiple heads

The basic bottom-up left-to-right dependency parsing algorithm described by Nivre (2004) keeps a list of tokens (initialized to contain the input string) and a stack (initialized to be empty), and allows three types of actions: (1) *shift*, which removes the next item from the input list and pushes it onto the top of the stack; (2) *left-reduce*, which pops the top two items from the stack, creates a left-arc between the words they represent in the sentence, and push the top item (which is now the head of the item previously below it) back onto the stack; and (3) *right-reduce*, which works in the same way as *left-reduce*, but creates a right-arc instead, and pushes back onto the stack the item that was below the top item on the stack (which is now the head of the item previously on top of the stack)[1]. New dependency edges (or arcs) are only created by reduce actions, which are constrained so that they can only be applied to create a head-dependent pair where the dependent has already found all of its own dependents (if any). This is necessary because once a word is assigned a head it is popped from the stack and never visited again, since each word has only one head. This constraint, responsible for the parser's bottom-up behavior, should be kept in mind, as it is relevant in the design of the multiple-head parsing algorithm below.

To allow words to have multiple heads, we first need to create two new parser actions that create dependency arcs without removing the dependent from further consideration for being a dependent of additional heads. The first new action is *left-attach*, which creates a left dependency arc attaching the top two items on the stack, making the top item the head of the item immediately below, as long as a right arc between the two items does not already exist. This action is similar to *left-reduce*, except that neither item is removed from the stack (no reduction occurs). The second new action, *right-attach*, includes one additional final step: first, it creates a right dependency arc between the top two items on the stack (as long as a left arc between the two items does not already exist), making the top item a dependent of the item immediately below;

[1] Like Nivre (2004), we consider the direction of the dependency arc to be from the head to the dependent.

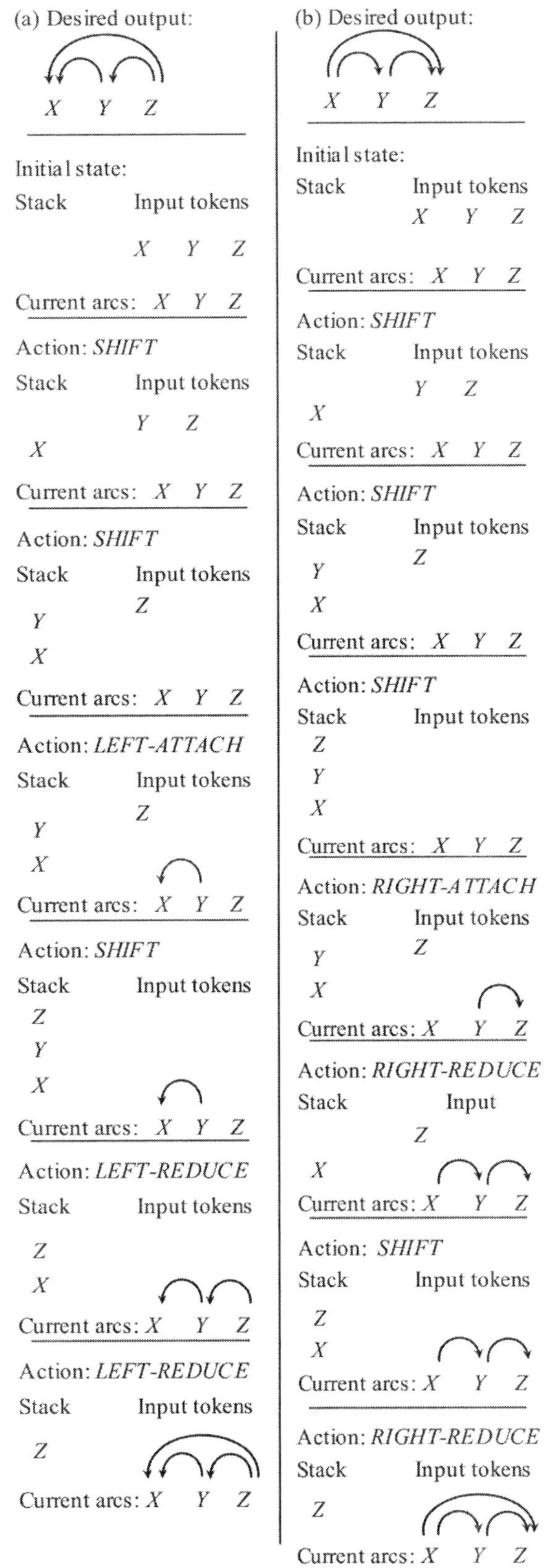

Figure 2: Example of how the basic algorithm builds dependencies with multiple heads.

and, as a second step, it pops the top item on the stack (newly made a dependent), and *places it back on the list of input words*. This second step is necessary because of the constraint that words can only be made dependents once all of its own dependents have been found. The behavior of the algorithm is illustrated in figure 2, where (a) shows an application of *left-attach*, and (b) shows an application of *right-attach*. In (b), we note that without placing the dependent in the *right-attach* action (*Z*) back on the input list, the dependency between *X* and *Y* could not be created. If we abandon the algorithm's bottom-up behavior, it is possible to modify the parser actions so that it is not necessary to place items back in the input list. This is discussed in section 2.2.

In summary, the algorithm has each of the three actions from the tree-based algorithm (*shift, right-reduce,* and *left-reduce*), and two additional actions that allow words to be dependents of more than one head (*right-attach* and *left-attach*). Although the algorithm as described so far builds unlabeled structures, the extension to labeled structures is straightforward: any action that results in a new arc being created must also choose a label for the arc. Another way to accomplish the same goal is to have a copy of each arc-producing action for each possible arc label. This is the same labeling extension as in the algorithm for trees. Finally, we note that the algorithm does not explicitly prevent multiple arcs (with the same direction) from being created between the same two words. In the unlabeled case, such a constraint can be easily placed on arc-producing actions. In the labeled case, however, it is useful to allow arcs with different labels to link the same two words[2].

2.2 Arc-eager shift-reduce parsing with multiple heads

Nivre's arc-eager algorithm was designed to build dependencies at the first opportunity, avoiding situations where items that form a chain of right arcs all have to be placed on the stack before any structure is built, as in figure 2(b) for example. This is done by creating dependencies not between the top two items on the stack, but between the single top item on the stack and the next word on the input list, resulting in a hybrid bottom-up/top-down strategy. A similar idea can result in an algorithm for dependencies that allow multiple heads per word, but in this case the resulting algorithm is not as similar to the arc-eager algorithm for trees as the algorithm in section 2.1 is to its tree-based counterpart.

The projective DAG arc-eager algorithm has four actions, each corresponding to one action of the tree-based algorithm, but only the shift action is the same as in the tree based algorithm. The four actions in the new algorithm are: (1) *shift*, which removes the next token from the input string and pushes it onto the top of the stack; (2) *reduce*, which pops the stack, removing only its top item, as long as that item has at least one head (unlike in the tree-based algorithm, however, the algorithm may not reduce immediately when an item that has a head is on the top of the stack); (3) *left-arc*, which creates a left dependency arc between the word on top of the stack and the next token in the input string, where the token in the input string is the head and the item on the stack is the dependent (the stack and input list are left untouched), as long as a right arc does not already exist between the two words; and (4) *right-arc*, which creates a right dependency arc between the word on top of the stack and the next token in the input list, where the item on the stack is the head and the token in the input list is the dependent (again, the stack and input list are left untouched), as long as a left arc does not already exist between the two words.

Like the algorithm in section 2.1, this algorithm can easily be extended to produce labeled structures, and it also allows multiple edges (with the same direction) between the same two words.

2.3 Graph transformations for DAGs

Although the algorithms presented in sections 2.1 and 2.2 can produce dependency structures where a word may have more than one head, they are of limited interest on their own, since they can only produce projective structures, and many of the interesting linguistic phenomena that can be represented with DAGs cannot be represented with projective DAGs. Fortunately, the pseudo-projective transformations (Nivre and Nilsson, 2006) used in tree-based dependency parsing can easily be applied to DAGs. These transformations consist of identifying specific non-projective arcs, and moving their heads up towards the root, making them projective. The process also involves creating markings on the labels of the edges involved, so that the transformations are (mostly) reversible. Because non-

[2] This means that the structures produced by the algorithm are technically not limited to projective DAGs, since they can also be projective labeled multi-digraphs.

projectivity is more common in linguistically interesting DAGs, however, the transform/detransform process may be more lossy than it is when applied to trees. This, of course, varies according to specific DAGs used for representing specific phenomena. For pseudo-transformations to work well, we must allow multiple differently labeled arcs between the same two words (which, as mentioned before, the algorithms do). Combining the algorithm in sections 2.1 or 2.2 with pseudo-projective parsing, we can use DAG training data and produce DAG output in the overall parsing framework.

An alternative to using pseudo-projective transformations is to develop an algorithm for DAG parsing based on the family of algorithms described by Covington (2001), in the same way the algorithms in sections 2.1 and 2.2 were developed based on the algorithms described by Nivre (2004). Although this may be straightforward, a potential drawback of such an approach is that the number of parse actions taken in a Covington-style algorithm is always quadratic on the length of the input sentence, resulting in parsers that are more costly to train and to run (Nivre, 2007). The algorithms presented here, however, behave identically to their linear runtime tree counterparts when they are trained with graphs that are limited to tree structures. Additional actions are necessary only when words with more than one head are encountered. For data sets where most words have only one head, the performance the algorithms described in sections 2.1 and 2.2 should be close to that of shift-reduce projective parsing for dependency trees. In data sets where most words have multiple heads (resulting in higher arc density), the use of a Covington-style algorithm may be advantageous, but this is left as an area of future investigation.

In addition to pseudo-projective transformations, an additional transformation that is useful in DAG parsing is *arc reversal*. This consists of simply reversing the direction of an edge, adding a special mark to its label to indicate that its direction has been reversed. Detransformation is trivial and can be done with perfect accuracy, since it can be accomplished by simply reversing the arcs marked as reversed. This transformation is useful in cases where structures are mostly in DAG form, but may sometimes contain cycles. Arc reversal can be used to change the direction of an arc in the cycle, making the previously cyclic structure a DAG, which can be handled in the framework presented here.

3 Experiments

To investigate the efficacy of our DAG parsing framework on natural language data annotated with dependency DAGs, we conducted two experiments. The first uses predicate-argument dependencies taken from the HPSG Treebank built by Miyao et al. (2004) from the WSJ portion of the Penn Treebank. These predicate-argument structures are, in general, dependency graphs that do contain cycles (although infrequently), and also contain a large number of words with multiple heads. Since the predicate-argument dependencies are annotated explicitly in the HPSG Treebank, extracting a corpus of gold-standard dependency graphs is trivial. The second experiment uses the Danish Dependency Treebank, developed by Kromann (2003). This treebank follows a dependency scheme that includes, in addition to standard grammatical relations commonly used in dependency parsing, long-distance dependencies, gapping dependents, and anaphoric reference links. As with the HPSG predicate argument data, a few structures in the data contain cycles, but most of the structures in the treebank are DAGs. In the experiments presented below, the algorithm described in section 2.1 was used. We believe the use of the arc-eager algorithm described in section 2.2 would produce similar results, but this is left as future work.

3.1 Learning component

The DAG parsing framework, as described so far, must decide when to apply each appropriate parser action. As with other data-driven dependency parsing approaches with shift-reduce algorithms, we use a classifier to make these decisions. Following the work of Sagae and Tsujii (2007), we use maximum entropy models for classification. During training, the DAGs are first projectivized with pseudo-projective transformations. They are then processed by the parsing algorithm, which records each action necessary to build the correct structure in the training data, along with their corresponding parser configurations (stack and input list contents). From each of these parser configurations, a set of features is extracted and used with the correct parsing action as a training example for the maximum entropy classifier. The specific features we used in both experiments are the same features described by Sagae and Tsujii, with the following two changes: (1) the addition of a feature that indicates whether an arc already exists between the top two items on the stack, or the top item on the stack and the next item on the input list, and if so, what type of arc (direction and label); and (2) we did not use lemmas, morphological information or coarse grained part-of-speech tags. For the complete list of features used, please see (Sagae and Tsujii, 2007).

During run-time, the classifier is used to determine the parser action according to the current parser configuration. Like Sagae and Tsujii, we use a beam search instead of running the algorithm in deterministic mode, although we also report deterministic parsing results.

3.2 Predicate-argument analysis

The predicate-argument dependencies extracted from the HPSG Treebank include information such as extraction, raising, control, and other long-distance dependencies. Unlike in structures from PropBank, predicate-argument information is provided for nearly all words in the data. Following previous experiments with Penn Treebank WSJ data, or data derived from it, we used sections 02-21 as training material, section 22 for development, and section 23 for testing. Only the predicate-argument dependencies were used, not the phrase structures or other information from the HPSG analyses. Part-of-speech tagging was done separately using a maximum entropy tagger (Tsuruoka and Tsujii, 2005) with accuracy of 97.1%.

Cycles were eliminated from the dependency structures using the arc reversal transform in the following way: for each cycle detected in the data, the shortest arc in the cycle was reversed until no cycles remained. We applied pseudo-projective transformation and detransformation to determine how much information is lost in this process. By detransforming the projective graphs generated from gold-standard dependencies, we obtain labeled precision of 98.1% and labeled recall of 97.7%, which is below the accuracy expected for detransformation of syntactic dependency trees, but still within a range we considered acceptable. This represents an upper-bound for the accuracy of the DAG parser (including the arc-reversal and pseudo-projective transformations, and the algorithm described in section 2.1).

Table 1 shows the results obtained with our DAG parsing framework in terms of labeled precision, recall and F-score (89.0, 88.5 and 88.7, respectively). For comparison, we also show previously published results obtained by Miyao and Tsujii (2005), and Sagae et al. (2007), which used the same data, but obtained the predicate-argument analyses using an HPSG parser. Our results are very competitive, at roughly the same level as the best previously published results on this data set, but obtained with significantly higher speed. The parser took less than four minutes to process the test set, and pseudo-projective and arc-reversal detransformation took less than one minute in standard hardware (a Linux workstation with a Pentium 4 processor and 4Gb of RAM). Sagae et al. (2007) reported that an HPSG parser took about 20 minutes to parse the same data. Our results were obtained with a beam width of 150 parser states. Running the parser with a beam width of 1 (a single parser state), emulating the deterministic search used by Nivre (2004), resulted in numerous parse failures (the end of the input string is reached, and no further dependency arcs are created) in the development set, and therefore very low dependency recall (90.1 precision and 36.2 recall on development data). Finally, in table 1 we also show results obtained with standard bottom-up shift-reduce dependency parsing for trees, using the parser described in (Sagae and Tsujii, 2007). To train the dependency tree parser, we transformed the DAG predicate-argument structures into trees by removing arcs. Arcs were selected for removal as follows: for each word that had more than one head, only the arc between the word and its closest head (in linear distance in the sentence) was kept. Although this strategy still produces dependency analyses with relatively high F-score (87.0), recall is far lower than when DAG parsing is used, and the tree parser has no mechanism for capturing some of the structures captured by the DAG parser.

Parser	Precision	Recall	F-score
DAG-beam	**89.0**	**88.5**	**88.7**
Tree only	89.8	84.3	87.0
Sagae et al.	88.5	88.0	88.2
Miyao & Tsujii	85.0	84.3	84.6

Table 1: Results from experiments with HPSG predicate-argument dependencies (*labeled* precision, recall and F-score). Our results are denoted by *DAG-beam* and *tree only*, and others are previously published results using the same data.

3.3 Danish Dependency Treebank experiments

Our experiments with the Danish Dependency Treebank followed the same setup as described for the HPSG predicate-argument structures. The accuracy of pseudo-projective transformation and detransformation was higher, at 99.4% precision and 98.8% recall. To divide the data into training, development and test sections, we followed the same procedure as McDonald et al. (2006), who used the same data, so our results could be compared directly (a small number of graphs that contained cycles was discarded, as done by McDonald et al.).

Our results are shown in table 2 (unlabeled precision and recall are used, for comparison with previous work, in addition to labeled precision and recall), along with the results obtained by McDonald et al., who used an approximate inference strategy in a graph-based dependency parsing framework, where a dependency tree is computed first, and arcs that improve on the overall graph score are added one by one. As in the previous section, we also include results obtained with tree-only parsing. Obtaining tree structures from the Danish Dependency Treebank is straightforward, since anaphoric reference and long-distance dependency arcs are marked as such explicitly and can be easily removed.

In addition to overall results, we also measured the parser's precision and recall on long-distance dependencies and anaphoric reference. On long-distance dependencies the parser had 83.2 precision and 82.0 recall. On anaphoric reference links the parser has 84.9 precision and 84.4 recall. Although these are below the parser's overall accuracy figures, they are encouraging results. Finally, unlike with the HPSG predicate-argument structures, using a beam width of 1 reduces precision and recall by only about 1.5.

Parser	Precision	Recall	F-score
DAG-beam	**87.3**	**87.1**	**87.2**
Tree only	87.5	82.7	85.0
McDonald et al.	86.2	84.9	85.6
DAG-labeled	82.7	82.2	82.4

Table 2: Results from experiments with the Danish Dependency Treebank. Precision, recall and F-score for the first three rows are for *unlabeled* dependencies. The last row, *DAG-labeled,* shows our results in *labeled* precision, recall and F-score (not directly comparable to other rows).

4 Related work

The work presented here builds on the dependency parsing work of Nivre (2004), as discussed in section 2, on the work of Nivre and Nilsson (2006) on pseudo-projective transformations, and on the work of Sagae and Tsujii (2007) in using a beam search in shift-reduce dependency parsing using maximum entropy classifiers. As mentioned before, McDonald et al. (2006) presented an approach to DAG parsing (that could also easily be applied to cyclic structures) using approximate inference in an edge-factored dependency model starting from dependency trees. In their model, the addition of extra arcs to the tree was learned with the parameters to build the initial tree itself, which shows the power and flexibility of approximate inference in graph-based dependency models.

Other parsing approaches that produce dependency graphs that are not limited to tree structures include those based on linguistically-motivated lexicalized grammar formalisms, such as HPSG, CCG and LFG. In particular, Clark et al. (2002) use a probabilistic model of dependency DAGs extracted from the CCGBank (Hockenmeier and Steedman, 2007) in a CCG parser that builds the CCG predicate-argument dependency structures following the CCG derivation, not directly through DAG parsing. Similarly, the HPSG parser of Miyao and Tsujii (2005) builds the HPSG predicate-argument dependency structure following unification operations during HPSG parsing. Sagae et al. (2007) use a dependency parsing combined with an HPSG parser to produce predicate-argument dependencies. However, the dependency parser is used only to produce a dependency tree backbone, which the HPSG parser then uses to produce the more general dependency graph. A similar strategy is used in the RASP parser (Briscoe et al., 2006), which builds a dependency graph through unification operations performed during a phrase structure tree parsing process.

5 Conclusion

We have presented a framework for dependency DAG parsing, using a novel algorithm for projective DAGs that extends existing shift-reduce algorithms for parsing with dependency trees, and pseudo-projective transformations applied to DAG structures.

We have demonstrated that the parsing approach is effective in analysis of predicate-argument structure in English using data from the HPSG Treebank (Miyao et al., 2004), and in parsing of Danish using a rich dependency representation (Kromann, 2003).

Acknowledgements

We thank Yusuke Miyao and Takuya Matsuzaki for insightful discussions. This work was partially supported by Grant-in-Aid for Specially Promoted Research (MEXT, Japan).

References

Briscoe, T., Carroll, J. and Watson, R. 2006. The second release of the RASP system. In *Proceedings of the COLING/ACL-06 Demo Session.*

Buchholz, Sabine and Erwin Marsi. 2006. CoNLL-X Shared Task on Multilingual Dependency Parsing. In *Proceedings of the 10th Conference on Computational Natural Language Learning (CoNLL-X) Shared Task session.*

Clark, Stephen, Julia Hockenmaier, and Mark Steedman. 2002. Building Deep Dependency Structures using a Wide-Coverage CCG Parser. In *Proceedings of the 40th Annual Meeting of the Association for Computational Linguistics (ACL).*

Covington, Michael A. 2001. A fundamental algorithm for dependency parsing. In *Proceedings of the Annual ACM Southeast Conference,* 95-102.

Erkan, Gunes, Arzucan Ozgur, and Dragomir R. Radev. 2007. Semisupervised classification for extracting protein interaction sentences using dependency parsing. In *Proceedings of CoNLL-EMNLP.*

Hudson, Richard. 1984. Word Grammar. Oxford: Blackwell.

Hudson, Richard. 2005. Word Grammar. In K. Brown (Ed.), *Encyclopedia of Language and Linguistics* (second ed., pp 633-642). Elsevier.

Hockenmaier, Julia and Mark Steedman. 2007. CCGbank: a corpus of CCG derivations and dependency structures extracted from the Penn Treebank. In *Computational Linguistics* 33(3), pp 355-396, MIT press.

Kromann, Matthias T. 2003. The Danish dependency treebank and the underlying linguistic theory. In *Proceedings of the Second Workshop on Treebanks and Linguistic Theories (TLT).*

McDonald, Ryan and Fernando Pereira. 2006. Online learning of approximate dependency parsing algorithms. In *Proceedings of the 11th Conference of the European Chapter of the Association for Computational Linguistics (EACL).*

McDonald, Ryan, Fernando Pereira, Kiril Ribarov and Jan Hajic. 2005. Non-projective Dependency Parsing using Spanning Tree Algorithms. In *Proceedings of the Human Language Technology Conference and Conference on Empirical Methods in Natural Language Processing (HLT-EMNLP).*

Miyao, Yusuke, Takashi Ninomiya, and Jun'ichi Tsujii. 2004. Corpus-oriented grammar development for acquiring a Head-driven Phrase Structure Grammar from the Penn Treebank. In *Proceedings of the International Joint Conference on Natural Language Processing (IJCNLP).*

Miyao Yusuke and Jun'ichi Tsujii. 2005. Probabilistic disambiguation models for wide-coverage HPSG parsing. In *Proceedings of the 43rd Annual Meeting on Association for Computational Linguistics.*

Nivre, Joakim. 2004. Incrementality in Deterministic Dependency Parsing. In *Incremental Parsing: Bringing Engineering and Cognition Together (Workshop at ACL-2004).*

Nivre, Joakim, Johan Hall, Sandra Kübler, Ryan McDonald, Jens Nilsson, Sebastian Riedel, Deniz Yuret. 2007. In *Proceedings of the CoNLL 2007 Shared Task in the Joint Conference on Empirical Methods in Natural Language Processing and Computational Natural Language Learning.*

Nivre, Joakim. and Jens Nilsson. 2005. Pseudo-Projective Dependency Parsing. In *Proceedings of the 43rd Annual Meeting of the Association for Computational Linguistics (ACL)*, pp. 99-106.

Nivre, Joakim. 2007. Incremental non-projective dependency parsing. In *Proceedings of Human Language Technologies: The Annual Conference of the North American Chapter of the Association for Computational Linguistics (NAACL-HLT'07).*

Saetre, R., Sagae, K., and Tsujii, J. 2007. Syntactic features for protein-protein interaction extraction. In *Proceedings of the International Symposium on Languages in Biology and Medicine (LBM short oral presentations).*

Sagae, Kenji., Yusuke Miyao Jun'ichi and Tsujii. 2007. HPSG Parsing with shallow dependency constraints. In *Proceedings of the 44th Meeting of the Association for Computational Linguistics.*

Sagae, K., Tsujii, J. 2007. Dependency parsing and domain adaptation with LR models and parser ensembles. In *Proceedings of the CoNLL 2007 Shared Task. in EMNLP-CoNLL.*

Tsuruoka, Yoshimasa and Tsujii, Jun'ichi. 2005. Bidirectional inference with the easiest-first strategy for tagging sequence data. In *Proceedings of the Human Language Technology Conference and Conference on Empirical Methods in Natural Language Processing (HLT-EMNLP)*, pp. 523-530.

Wang, Mengqiu, Noah A. Smith, and Teruko Mitamura. 2007. What is the Jeopardy Model? A Quasi-Synchronous Grammar for QA. In *Proceedings of the Joint Conference on Empirical Methods in Natural Language Processing and Computational Natural Language Learning (EMNLP-CoNLL).*

Event Frame Extraction Based on a Gene Regulation Corpus

Yutaka Sasaki [1] **Paul Thompson** [1] **Philip Cotter** [1] **John McNaught** [1, 2]
Sophia Ananiadou [1, 2]

[1] School of Computer Science, University of Manchester
[2] National Centre for Text Mining
MIB, 131 Princess Street, Manchester, M1 7DN, United Kingdom
Yutaka.Sasaki@manchester.ac.uk

Abstract

This paper describes the supervised acquisition of semantic event frames based on a corpus of biomedical abstracts, in which the biological process of *E. coli gene regulation* has been linguistically annotated by a group of biologists in the EC research project "BOOTStrep". Gene regulation is one of the rapidly advancing areas for which information extraction could boost research. Event frames are an essential linguistic resource for extraction of information from biological literature. This paper presents a specification for linguistic-level annotation of gene regulation events, followed by novel methods of automatic event frame extraction from text. The event frame extraction performance has been evaluated with 10-fold cross validation. The experimental results show that a precision of nearly 50% and a recall of around 20% are achieved. Since the goal of this paper is event frame extraction, rather than event instance extraction, the issue of low recall could be solved by applying the methods to a larger-scale corpus.

1 Introduction

This paper describes the automatic extraction of linguistic event frames based on a corpus of MEDLINE abstracts that has been annotated with *gene regulation* events by a group of domain experts. Annotation is centred on both verbs and nominalised verbs that describe relevant events. For each event, semantic arguments that occur within the same sentence are marked and labelled with *semantic roles* and *named entity (NE)* types.

The focus of the paper is the extraction of *event frames* on the basis of the annotated corpus using machine learning techniques. Event frames are linguistic specifications concerning the behaviour of verbs and nominalised verbs, in terms of the number and types of semantic arguments with which they typically co-occur in texts. Our eventual goal is to exploit such information to improve information extraction. *Event frame extraction is different to event instance extraction (or template filling).* Our event frames are destined for incorporation in the BOOTStrep *BioLexicon* to support identification of relevant event instances and discovery of event instance participants by NLP systems.

2 Background

There are several well-established, large-scale repositories of semantic frames for general language, e.g., VerbNet (Kipper-Schuler, 2005), PropBank (Palmer et al., 2005) and FrameNet (Rupenhoffer et al, 2006). These all aim to characterise verb behaviour in terms of the semantic arguments with which verbs occur but differ in how they represent semantic arguments and groupings of verbs.

In VerbNet, the semantic roles of arguments come from frame-independent roles, e.g. *Agent, Patient, Location* and *Instrument.*

In contrast, PropBank and FrameNet use a mixture of role types: some are common amongst a number of frames; others are specific to particular frames.

Whilst FrameNet and VerbNet differ in their treatment of semantic roles, they both specify

© 2008. Licensed under the *Creative Commons Attribution-Noncommercial-Share Alike 3.0 Unported* license (http://creativecommons.org/licenses/by-nc-sa/3.0/). Some rights reserved.

Table 1. Semantic Roles

Role Name	Description	Example (**bold** = semantic argument, *italics* = focussed verb)
AGENT	Drives/instigates event	**The narL gene product** *activates* the nitrate reductase operon
THEME	a) Affected by/results from event b) Focus of events describing states	**recA protein** was *induced* by UV radiation The **FNR protein** *resembles* CRP
MANNER	Method/way in which event is carried out	cpxA gene *increases* the levels of csgA transcription by **dephosphorylation** of CpxR
INSTRUMENT	Used to carry out event	EnvZ *functions* through **OmpR** to control NP porin gene expression in Escherichia coli K-12.
LOCATION	Where *complete* event takes place	Phosphorylation of OmpR *modulates* expression of the ompF and ompC genes in **Escherichia coli**
SOURCE	Start point of event	A transducing lambda phage was *isolated* from **a strain** harboring a glpD''lacZ fusion
DESTINATION	End point of event	Transcription of gntT is activated by *binding* of the cyclic AMP (cAMP)-cAMP receptor protein (CRP) complex to **a CRP binding site**
TEMPORAL	Situates event in time w.r.t another event	The Alp protease activity is *detected* in cells **after introduction** of plasmids carrying the alpA gene
CONDITION	Environmental conditions/changes in conditions	Strains carrying a mutation in the crp structural gene fail to *repress* ODC and ADC activities in response to **increased cAMP**
RATE	Change of level or rate	marR mutations *elevated* inaA expression by **10- to 20-fold** over that of the wild-type.
DESCRIPTIVE-AGENT	Provides descriptive information about the AGENT of the event	It is likely that HyfR *acts* as **a formate-dependent regulator** of the hyf operon
DESCRIPTIVE-THEME	Provides descriptive information about the AGENT of the event	The FNR protein *resembles* **CRP**.
PURPOSE	Purpose/reason for the event occurring	The fusion strains were *used* **to study** the regulation of the cysB gene by assaying the fused lacZ gene product

semantic frames that correspond to *groups* of verbs with similar behaviour. However, frames in PropBank correspond to individual verbs.

Biology-specific extensions have been attempted both for PropBank (Wattarujeekrit et al., 2004) and FrameNet (Dolbey et al., 2006). However, to our knowledge, there has been no such attempt at extending VerbNet into the biological domain.

In common with VerbNet, our work is focussed on producing event frames that use a set of *frame-independent* semantic roles. However, we adopt a smaller set of roles tailored to the domain. This use of frame-independent roles allows linguistic generalisations to be captured more easily (Cohen and Hunter, 2006). Also, the use of such roles is more suitable for direct exploitation by NLP systems (Zaphirain et al., 2008).

Unlike VerbNet, we aim to produce a set of frames that are *verb-specific* (rather than frames that apply to groups of verbs). Verb-specific frames are able to provide more detailed argument specifications—particularly important in the biomedical field, where phrases that identify information such as location, manner, timing and condition are essential for correct interpretation of events (Tsai et al, 2007).

3 Annotated corpus

To aid semantic event frame extraction, we need a corpus annotated with event-level information. Several already exist for biology. Some target extraction of PropBank-style frames (e.g. Chou et al. (2006), Kulick et al. (2004)). The corpus produced by Kim et al. (2008) uses frame-independent roles. However, only a few semantic argument types are annotated.

The target of our event frame extraction is a set of semantic frames which specify *all* potential arguments of gene regulation events. For this purpose, we had to produce our own annotated corpus, using a larger set of event-independent semantic roles than Kim et al. (2008). Our roles had to cover sufficiently wide scope to allow annotation and characterization of all instantiated arguments of relevant events within texts. To our knowledge, this makes our scheme unique within the biomedical field.

In contrast to many other comparable resources, annotated events are centred on both verbs *and* nominalised verbs, such as *transcription* and *control*. Nominalised verbs play an important and possibly dominant role in biological texts (Cohen and Hunter, 2006). Our own corpus confirms this, in that the nominalised verb *expression* is the most commonly annotated word on which gene regulation events are centred. By annotating events centred on nominalised verbs in a similar way to verbs, it becomes possible to extract separate event frames for nominalised verbs. This enables their potentially idiosyncratic behaviour to be accounted for.

Table 2. Description of NE super-classes

NE class	Definition
DNA	Entities chiefly composed of nucleic acids and their structural or positional references. This includes the physical structure of all DNA-based entities and the functional roles associated with regions thereof.
PROTEIN	Entities chiefly composed of amino acids and their positional references. This includes the physical structure and functional roles associated with each type.
EXPERIMENTAL	Both physical and methodological entities, either used, consumed or required for a reaction to take place.
ORGANISMS	Entities representing individuals or collections of living things and their component parts.
PROCESSES	A set of *event* classes used to label biological processes described in text.

Our annotated corpus consists of 677 MEDLINE abstracts on *E. Coli*. Within them, a total of 4770 gene regulation events have been annotated.

3.1 Semantic Roles

Based on the observations of Tsai et al (2007) regarding the most important types of information specified for biomedical events, together with detailed examination of a large number of relevant events within our corpus, in discussion with biologists, we defined a set of 13 frame-independent semantic roles that are suitable for the domain.

Certain roles within the set are domain-independent, and are based on those used in VerbNet, e.g. AGENT, THEME, and LOCATION. To these, we have added a number of domain-dependent roles, e.g. CONDITION and MANNER. The size of the role set attempts to balance the need for a sufficiently wide-ranging set of roles with the need for one that is as small and general as possible, to reduce the burden on annotators, whilst also helping to ensure consistency across extracted verb frames. The full set of semantic roles used is shown in Table 1.

3.2 Named Entity Categorisation

Although our semantic roles are rather general, the annotation scheme allows more detailed information about semantic arguments to be encoded in the corpus through the assignment of named entity (NE) tags. Unlike other corpus projects, we do not annotate *all* entities within each abstract, but just those entities that occur as semantic arguments of annotated gene regulation events.

Table 3. Most commonly annotated verbs and nominalised verbs

Word	Count	Type
expression	409	NV
encode	351	V
transcription	125	NV
bind	110	V
require	100	V
express	93	V
regulate	91	V
synthesis	90	NV
contain	80	V
induce	78	V

Our set of NE tags goes beyond the traditional view of NEs, in that labelling is extended to include *events* represented by nominalised verbs (e.g. *repression*). A total of 61 NE classes have been defined as being relevant to the gene regulation field, which are divided into four entity-specific super-classes (DNA, PROTEIN, EXPERIMENTAL and ORGANISMS) and one event-specific super-class (PROCESSES). The NEs within each of these classes are hierarchically-structured. Table 2 provides definitions of each of these five super-classes. The NEs correspond to classes in the Gene Regulation Ontology (Splendiani et al, 2007), which has been developed as part of the BOOTStrep project in which this work has been carried out. The Gene Regulation Ontology integrates parts of other established bio-ontologies, such as Gene Ontology (Ashburner et al., 2000) and Sequence Ontology (Eilbeck,2005).

3.3 Annotation process

Annotation was carried out over a period of three months by seven PhD students with experience in gene regulation and with native or near-native competence in English.

Prior to annotation, each abstract was automatically processed. Firstly, linguistic preprocessing (i.e. morphological analysis, POS tagging and syntactic chunking)[1] was carried out.

Secondly, all occurrences from a list of 700 biologically relevant verbs were automatically marked. Annotators then considered each marked verb within an abstract. If the verb denoted a gene regulation event, annotators then:

a. Identified all semantic arguments of the verb within the sentence
b. Assigned a semantic role to each identified argument

1 Each abstract to be annotated is first pre-processed with the GENIA tagger (Tsuruoka et al, 2005).

c. If appropriate, assigned named entity categories to (parts of) the semantic argument span
d. If the argument corresponded to a nominalised verb, repeated steps a–c to identify its own arguments.

Syntactic chunks were made visible to annotators. In conjunction with annotation guidelines, the chunks were used to help ensure consistency of annotated semantic arguments. For example, the guidelines state that semantic arguments should normally consist of complete (and preferably single) syntactic chunks. The annotation was performed using a customised version of WordFreak (Morton and LaCivita, 2003), a Java-based linguistic annotation tool.

3.4 Corpus statistics

The corpus is divided into 2 parts, i.e.

1) 597 abstracts, each annotated by a single annotator, containing a total of 3612 events,
2) 80 pairs of double-annotated documents, allowing checking of inter-annotator agreement and consistency, and containing 1158 distinct events.

In the corpus, 277 distinct verbs were annotated as denoting gene regulation events, of which 73 were annotated 10 times or more. In addition, annotation has identified 135 relevant nominalised verbs, of which 22 were annotated 10 times or more. The most commonly annotated verbs and nominalised verbs are shown in Table 3.

3.5 Inter-annotator agreement

Inter-annotator agreement statistics for the 80 pairs of duplicate-annotated abstracts are shown in Table 4.

The figures shown in Table 4 are direct agreement rates. Whilst the Kappa statistic is very familiar for calculating inter-annotator agreement, we follow Wilbur et al. (2006) and Pyysalo (2007) in choosing not to use it, because it is not appropriate or possible to calculate it for all of the above statistics. For instance:

1. For some tasks, like annotation of events and arguments spans, deciding how to calculate random agreement is not clear.
2. The Kappa statistic assumes that annotation categories are discrete and mutually exclusive. This is not the case for the NE categories, which are hierarchically structured.

Table 4. Inter-annotator agreement rates

AGREEMENT RATE	VALUE
Event identification	0.49
Argument identification (partial span match)	0.73
Semantic role assignment	0.78
NE identification (partial span match)	0.68
NE category assignment (exact)	0.62
NE category assignment (including parent)	0.65
NE category assignment (including ancestors)	0.73

Table 4 shows that, in terms of identifying events (i.e. determining which verbs denote gene regulation events), agreement between annotators is reached about half the time. The main reason for this relatively low figure is that reaching a consensus on the specific types of events to be annotated under the heading of "gene regulation" required a large amount of discussion. Thus, particularly towards the start of the annotation phase, annotators tended to either under- or over-annotate the events.

Greater amounts of consistency seem to be achievable for other sub-tasks of the annotation, with agreement rates for the identification and subsequent labelling of semantic arguments being achieved in around three quarters of cases.

Comparable, but slightly lower rates of agreement were achieved in the identification of NEs. In terms of assigning categories to them, the agreement rate for exact category matches is a little lower (62%). However, if we relax the matching conditions by exploiting the hierarchical structure of the NE categories (i.e. if we count as a match the cases where the category assigned by one annotator was the ancestor of the category assigned by the other annotator), then the agreement increases by around 11%.

The large number of NE categories (61), makes the decision of the most appropriate category rather complex; this was verified by the annotators themselves. Based on this, we will consider the use of a more coarse-grained scheme when carrying out further annotation of this type. However, in the current corpus, the hierarchical structuring of the NE categories means that it would be possible to use a smaller set of categories by mapping the specific categories to more general ones.

4 Corpus Format

For the purposes of event frame extraction, the annotations in the corpus were converted to an XML-style inline format consisting of three different types of element:

EVENT – surrounds text spans (i.e. verb phrases and nominalised verbs) on which events are centred.

SLOT – surrounds spans corresponding to semantic arguments (i.e. slots) of events. The head verb/nominalised verb of the event is also treated as a SLOT, with role type Verb. The eventid attribute links each slot with its respective event, whilst the Role attribute indicates the semantic role assigned to the slot.

NE – surrounds text spans annotated as named entities. The *cat* attribute stores the NE category assigned.

Where there are several annotations over some text span, elements are embedded inside each other. If more than one annotation begins at a particular offset, then the ordering of the embedding is fixed, so that SLOT elements are embedded inside EVENT elements, and that NE elements are embedded inside SLOT elements. An example of the annotation for the sentence "*TaqI restriction endonuclease has been subcloned downstream from an inducible phoA promoter*" is shown below:

```
<SLOT argid="4" eventid="5" Role="Theme">
<NE cat="ENZYME">TaqI restriction endonucle-
ase</NE></SLOT> <EVENT id="5">
has been <SLOT argid="6" eventid="5"
Role="Verb">subcloned </SLOT></EVENT>
<SLOT argid="8" eventid="5"
Role="Location">downstream from
<NE cat="PROMOTER">an inducible phoA pro-
moter</NE></SLOT>.
```

The EVENT created over the VP chunk *has been subcloned* has been annotated as having 2 semantic arguments (SLOTs), i.e. a THEME, *TaqI restriction endonuclease* and a LOCATION, i.e. *downstream from an inducible phoA promoter.* A 3rd SLOT element corresponds to the head verb in the VP chunk. Named entity tags have also been assigned to the THEME span and part of the LOCATION span.

5 Event Patterns and Event Frames

This section defines event patterns and event frames. Event patterns are syntactic patterns of sequences of surface words, NEs, and semantic roles, whilst event frames are the record-like data structures consisting of event slots and event slot values.

5.1 Event Patterns

Event patterns are fragments of event annotations in which semantic arguments are generalized to their semantic role and NE categories, if present.

An event pattern is extracted for each unique event id within an abstract. An event annotation span begins with the earliest SLOT span, and ends with the latest SLOT assigned to the event. An example event span is as follows:

```
<SLOT eventid="9" Role="Agent">
<NE cat="OPERON"> transfer operon</NE></SLOT>
<EVENT id="9"><SLOT eventid="9" Role="Verb">
expression </SLOT></EVENT></SLOT> of
<SLOT eventid="9" Role="Theme">
<NE cat="DNA_FRAGMENT"> F-like plasmids
</NE></SLOT>
```

For each event, each event span is generalized into an event pattern as follows:

- "Verb" role slots of the event are converted into a tuple consisting of the role type, part-of-speech and surface form, i.e., [Verb:*POS*:*verb*].
- Other semantic role slots and their NE slots for the event are generalized to tuples consisting of the role and NE super class, i.e., [*role*:*NE_super_class*].
- Other XML tags are removed.

The above example event span is thus generalized to the following event pattern:

```
[Agent:DNA] [Verb:NN:expression] of [Theme:DNA].
```

5.2 Event frames

Event frames are directly extracted from event patterns, and take the following general form:

```
event_frame_name(
     slot_name => slot_value,
     ...
     slot_name => slot_value).
```

where

- event_frame_name is the base form of the event verb or nominalized verb;
- slot_names are the names of the semantic roles within the event pattern;
- slot_values are NE categories, if present within the event pattern.

For example, the event frame corresponding to the event pattern shown in the previous section is as follows:

```
expression( Agent=>DNA,
            Theme=>DNA ).
```

6 Event Frame Extraction

Our event frame extraction is a fusion of sequential labelling based on Conditional Random Fields (CRF), and event pattern matching. Event frames are extracted in three steps. Firstly, a CRF-based Named Entity Recognizer (NER) assigns biological NEs to word sequences. Secondly, a CRF-based semantic role labeller determines the semantic roles of word sequences with NE labels. Thirdly, word sequences are compared with event patterns derived from the corpus. Only those event frames whose semantic roles, NEs, and verb POS satisfy event pattern conditions will be extracted.

6.1 Biological NER

Since it is costly and time-consuming to create a large-scale training corpus annotated by biologists, we need to concede to use coarse-grained biological NE categories. That is, the NER component is trained on the five NE super classes, i.e., *Protein, DNA, Experimental, Organisms,* and *Processes*.

The NER models are trained by CRFs (Lafferty et al., 2001) using the standard IOB2 labelling method. That is, the label ``B-*NE*" is given to the first token of the target *NE* sequence, "I-*NE*" to each remaining token in the target sequence, and ``O" to other tokens.

Features used are as follows:

- word feature
  - orthographic features:

the first letter and the last four letters of the word form, in which capital letters in a word are normalized to "A", lower case letters are normalized to "a", and digits are replaced by "0". For example, the word form "IL-2" is normalised to "AA-0".

  - postfix features: the last two and four letters
- POS feature

We applied first-order CRFs using the above features for the tokens within a window size of ±2 of the current token.

6.2 Semantic Role Labelling

First of all, each NE token sequence identified by B and I labels is merged into a single token with the NE category name. Then, the semantic role labelling models are trained by CRFs in a similar way to NER. That is, the label ``B-*Role*" is given to the first token of the target *Role* sequence, "I-*Role*" to each remaining token in the target sequence, and "O" to other tokens.

Features used here are as follows:

- word feature
- base form feature
- POS feature
- NE feature

The window size was ±2 of the current token.

6.3 Event pattern matching

When a new sentence is given, sequential labelling models decide NE and semantic role labels of tokenized input sentences. Then, the token sequences are converted into the following token sequences with POS, semantic role, and NE information (called *augmented token sequences*):

1. Each token sequence labelled by IOB semantic role labels is merged into a token labelled with the role.
2. Verbs and nominalized verbs are converted to `[Verb:`*POS*:*surface_form*`]`.
3. Tokens with semantic role label and NE super-class are converted into the form `[`*Role*:*NE_super_class*`]`.
4. Other tokens with O label are converted to surface tokens.

Then, event patterns are generalized:

5. Event patterns are modified so that elements corresponding to verbs and nominalized verbs will match any words with the same POS, e.g., `[Verb:`*POS*: `*]`.

Finally, each event pattern is applied to augmented token sequences one by one:

6. By matching the generalized event patterns with augmented token sequences, i.e. when verbs or nominalized verbs and the surrounding semantic roles and NEs satisfy the event pattern conditions, then successfully unified event patterns are extracted as new event patterns.
7. The newly obtained event patterns are converted into event frames in the same way as described in Section 5.2.

7 Experimental Results

The aim of this section is to evaluate semantic frame extraction performance, given a set of annotated training data.

The annotated corpus was randomly separated into 10 document groups and their event patterns

Table 5. 10-fold cross validation results

	Score	#TP	#FN	#FP
Recall	0.186	165	730	
Precision	0.490	165		172

Table 6. NE identification performance

NE Type	Recall	Precision	F
DNA	0.627	0.660	0.643
Protein	0.525	0.633	0.574
Experimental	0.224	0.512	0.312
Processes	0.125	0.337	0.182
Organisms	0.412	0.599	0.488

and event frames were segmented into 10 groups according to the document separation.

We conducted 10-fold cross validation based on the 10 document groups. Named entity recognizers and semantic role labellers were trained using 9 groups of annotated documents. Event frames were then extracted from the remaining group of documents. Micro-average precision and recall for the set of event frames extracted from *all* the folds were evaluated.

Table 5 shows the event frame extraction performance. #TP, #FN, and #FP indicate the number of true positives, false negatives, and false positives, respectively.

Named entity recognition performance was also evaluated (Table 6). Since the training data size is small, the performance is between approximately 20-60% F-measure. However, this will not cause a problem for the event frame extraction task. This is because, if a particular event frame occurs multiple times in a corpus, it is sufficient to extract only a single occurrence of the event description. So, whilst the NE and semantic role labelling may not be successful for all occurrences of the event frame, there is a good chance that at least one occurrence of the event will be realized in the text in such a way as to allow the labelling to be carried out successfully, thus allowing the extraction of an appropriate event frame.

8 Discussion

Linguistic-level event annotation of biological events is an inherently difficult task. This is supported by the fact that the inter-annotator agreement level for the identification of events was 0.49 (see Table 4). Therefore, in terms of event extraction performance, a precision of 49.0% on 10-fold cross validation is almost comparable to human experts. The low recall of 18.6% may not be an issue, as the recall is likely to improve with the size of the target corpus.

The precision may additionally be underestimated in the evaluation due to inconsistencies in the annotation. We found that the *average* precision of our event frame extraction over 10 folds is around 30%, despite the fact that the precision of *all* event frames extracted from 10 folds is almost 50% compared with the annotated event frames in the whole corpus. This happens because some events not annotated in a particular fold are annotated in the rest of corpus. From this insight, our conjecture is that the true precision against the whole corpus would be somewhat higher (potentially 70-80%) if we were using an annotated corpus 10 times larger for the evaluation.

The automatic NER performance was also comparable to human annotators.

There are several approaches to the generation of information extraction patterns (e.g. Soderland et al., 1995; Califf et al., 1997; Kim and Moldovan, 1995). Our event patterns are similar to information extraction rules used in conventional IE systems. However, the goal of this paper is not event *instance* extraction but event (or semantic) frame extraction. We also combined CRF-based NER and semantic role labelling tuned for gene regulation with event extraction from sentences so that the clues of gene regulation event frames could be assigned automatically to un-annotated text.

9 Conclusion

This paper has presented linguistic annotation of gene regulation events in MEDLINE abstracts, and automatic event frame extraction based on the annotated corpus. Semantic event frames are linguistic resources effective in bridging between domain knowledge and text in IE tasks.

Although biological event annotations carried out by domain experts is a challenging task, experimental results on event frame extraction demonstrate a precision of almost 50%, which is close to the inter-annotator agreement rate of human annotators.

The extracted event frames will be included in the BOOTStrep BioLexicon, which will be made available for research purposes.

Acknowledgement

This research is supported by EC IST project FP6-028099 (BOOTStrep), whose Manchester team is hosted by the JISC/BBSRC/EPSRC sponsored National Centre for Text Mining.

References

Califf, Mary E. and Raymond J. Mooney (1997). Relational Learning of Pattern-Match Rules for Information Extraction, *In Proceedings of the ACL-97 Workshop in Natural Language Learning*, pp 9–15.

Chou, Wen-Chi., Richard T.H. Tsai, Ying-Shan Su, Wei Ku, Ting-Yi Sung and Wen-Lian Hsu (2006). A Semi-Automatic Method for Annotating a Biomedical Proposition Bank. *In Proceedings of the Workshop on Frontiers in Linguistically Annotated Corpora 2006*, pp 5–12.

Cohen, K. Bretonnel and Laurence Hunter (2006). A critical review of PASBio's argument structures for biomedical verbs. *BMC Bioinformatics* 7 (Suppl. 3), S5.

Dolbey, Andrew, Michael Ellsworth and Jan Scheffczykx (2006). BioFrameNet: A Domain-Specific FrameNet Extension with Links to Biomedical Ontologies. In O. Bodenreider (Ed.), *In Proceedings of KR-MED*, pp 87–94.

Eilbeck, Karen, Suzanna .E Lewis., Christopher J. Mungall, Mark Yandell, Lincoln Stein, Richard Durbin and Michael Ashburner. (2005) The Sequence Ontology: A tool for the unification of genome annotations. *Genome Biology* 6:R44

Kim, Jin-Dong, Tomoko Ohta and Jun'ichi Tsujii (2008). Corpus annotation for mining biomedical events from literature. *BMC Bioinformatics* 9:10.

Kim, Jun-Tae and Dan I. Moldovan (1995). Acquisition of Linguistic Patterns for Knowledge-Based Information Extraction. *IEEE Transaction on Knowledge and Data Engineering (IEEE TKDE)*, 7(5), pp.713–724.

Kipper-Schuler, Karen (2005). VerbNet: A broad-coverage, comprehensive verb lexicon. *PhD Thesis. Computer and Information Science Dept., University of Pennsylvania*. Philadelphia, PA.

Kulick Seth, Ann Bies, Mark Liberman, Mark Mandel, Ryan McDonald, Martha Palmer, Andrew Schein, and Lyle Ungar (2004) Integrated Annotation for Biomedical Information Extraction. *In HLT-NAACL 2004 Workshop: BioLink 2004, Linking Biological Literature, Ontologies and Databases*, pp 61–68.

Lafferty John, Andrew McCallum and Fernando Pereira (2001). Conditional Random Fields: Probabilistic Models for Segmenting and Labelling Sequence Data. *In Proceedings of the Eighteenth International Conference on Machine Learning (ICML-2001)*, pp 282–289.

Morton, Thomas and Jeremy LaCivita (2003). WordFreak: an open tool for linguistic annotation. *In Proceedings of the 2003 Conference of the North American Chapter of the Association for Computational Linguistics on Human Language Technology*, pp 17–18.

Palmer Martha, Paul Kingsbury and Daniel Gildea (2005). The Proposition Bank: An Annotated Corpus of Semantic Roles. *Computational Linguistics*, 31(1), pp 71–106.

Pyysalo, Sampo, Filip Ginter, Juho Heimonen, Jari Björne, Jorma Boberg, Jouni Järvinen and Tapio Salakoski (2007). BioInfer: a corpus for information extraction in the biomedical domain". *BMC Bioinformatics* 8:50.

Ruppenhofer, Josef, Michael Ellsworth, Miriam R.L. Petruck, Christopher R. Johnson, and Jan Scheffczyk (2006). FrameNet II: Extended Theory and Practice. Available online at http://framenet.icsi.berkeley.edu/

Soderland, Steven, David Fisher, Jonathan Aseltine and Wendy Lenert (1995). CRYSTAL: Inducing a Conceptual Dictionary, *In Proceedings of The 13th International Joint Conference on Artificial Intelligence (IJCAI-95)*. pp.1314–1319.

The Gene Ontology Consortium. (2000). Gene Ontology: tool for the unification of biology. *Nature Genetetics* 25, pp 25–29.

Tsai Richard T.H, Wen-Chi Chou, Ying-San Su, Yu-Chun Lin, Chen-Lung Sung, Hong-Jie Dai, Irene T.H Yeh, Wei Ku, Ting-Yi Sung and Wen-Lian Hsu (2007). BIOSMILE: A semantic role labeling system for biomedical verbs using a maximum-entropy model with automatically generated template features, *BMC Bioinformatics* 8:325

Tsuruoka, Yoshimasa, Yuka Tateishi, Jin-Dong Kim, Tomoko Ohta, John McNaught, Sophia Ananiadou, and Jun'ichi Tsujii (2005). Developing a Robust Part-of-Speech Tagger for Biomedical Text, *In Advances in Informatics - 10th Panhellenic Conference on Informatics*, pp 382–392.

Wattarujeekrit, Tuangthong, Parantu K. Shah and Nigel Collier (2004). PASBio: predicate-argument structures for event extraction in molecular biology, *BMC Bioinformatics* 5:155.

Wilbur, W.John, Andrey Rzhetsky, and Hagit Shatkay (2006). New Directions in Biomedical Text Annotations: Definitions. Guidelines and Corpus Construction. *BMC Bioinformatics*. 7:356

Zapirain, Beñat, Eneko Agirre, Lluís Màrquez (2008). A Preliminary Study on the Robustness and Generalization of Role Sets for Semantic Role Labeling. In Alexander F. Gelbukh (Ed.), *Computational Linguistics and Intelligent Text Processing*, 9th International Conference, CICLing 2008.

A Fully-Lexicalized Probabilistic Model for Japanese Zero Anaphora Resolution

Ryohei Sasano*
Graduate School of Information Science and Technology, University of Tokyo
ryohei@nlp.kuee.kyoto-u.ac.jp

Daisuke Kawahara
National Institute of Information and Communication Technology
dk@nict.go.jp

Sadao Kurohashi
Graduate School of Infomatics, Kyoto University
kuro@i.kyoto-u.ac.jp

Abstract

This paper presents a probabilistic model for Japanese zero anaphora resolution. First, this model recognizes discourse entities and links all mentions to them. Zero pronouns are then detected by case structure analysis based on automatically constructed case frames. Their appropriate antecedents are selected from the entities with high salience scores, based on the case frames and several preferences on the relation between a zero pronoun and an antecedent. Case structure and zero anaphora relation are simultaneously determined based on probabilistic evaluation metrics.

1 Introduction

Anaphora resolution is one of the most important techniques in discourse analysis. In English, definite noun phrases such as *the company* and overt pronouns such as *he* are anaphors that refer to preceding entities (antecedents). On the other hand, in Japanese, anaphors are often omitted and these omissions are called *zero pronouns*. We focus on zero anaphora resolution of Japanese web corpus, in which anaphors are often omitted and zero anaphora resolution plays an important role in discourse analysis.

Zero anaphora resolution can be divided into two phases. The first phase is zero pronoun detection and the second phase is zero pronoun resolution. Zero pronoun resolution is similar to coreference resolution and pronoun resolution, which have been studied for many years (e.g. Soon et al. (2001); Mitkov (2002); Ng (2005)). Isozaki and Hirao (2003) and Iida et al. (2006) focused on zero pronoun resolution assuming perfect pre-detection of zero pronouns. However, we consider that zero pronoun detection and resolution have a tight relation and should not be handled independently. Our proposed model aims not only to resolve zero pronouns but to detect zero pronouns.

Zero pronouns are not expressed in a text and have to be detected prior to identifying their antecedents. Seki et al. (2002) proposed a probabilistic model for zero pronoun detection and resolution that uses hand-crafted case frames. In order to alleviate the sparseness of hand-crafted case frames, Kawahara and Kurohashi (2004) introduced wide-coverage case frames to zero pronoun detection that are automatically constructed from a large corpus. They use the case frames as selectional restriction for zero pronoun resolution, but do not utilize the frequency of each example of case slots. However, since the frequency is shown to be a good clue for syntactic and case structure analysis (Kawahara and Kurohashi, 2006), we consider the frequency also can benefit zero pronoun detection. Therefore we propose a probabilistic model for zero anaphora resolution that fully utilizes case frames. This model directly considers the frequency and estimates case assignments for overt case components and antecedents of zero pronoun simultaneously.

In addition, our model directly links each zero pronoun to an entity, while most existing models link it to a certain mention of an entity. In our model, mentions and zero pronouns are treated similarly and all of them are linked to corresponding entities. In this point, our model is similar to

©2008. Licensed under the *Creative Commons Attribution-Noncommercial-Share Alike 3.0 Unported* license (http://creativecommons.org/licenses/by-nc-sa/3.0/). Some rights reserved.

* Research Fellow of the Japan Society for the Promotion of Science (JSPS)

Table 1: Examples of Constructed Case Frames.

	case slot	examples	generalized examples with rate
tsumu (1) (load)	*ga* (subjective)	he, driver, friend, ···	[CT:PERSON]:0.45, [NE:PERSON]:0.08, ···
	wo (objective)	baggage, luggage, hay, ···	[CT:ARTIFACT]:0.31, ···
	ni (dative)	car, truck, vessel, seat, ···	[CT:VEHICLE]:0.32, ···
tsumu (2) (accumulate)	*ga* (subjective)	player, children, party, ···	[CT:PERSON]:0.40, [NE:PERSON]:0.12, ···
	wo (objective)	experience, knowledge, ···	[CT:ABSTRACT]:0.47, ···
⋮	⋮		⋮
hanbai (1) (sell)	*ga* (subjective)	company, Microsoft, firm, ···	[NE:ORGANIZATION]:0.16, [CT:ORGANIZATION]:0.13, ···
	wo (objective)	goods, product, ticket, ···	[CT:ARTIFACT]:0.40, [CT:FOOD]:0.07, ···
	ni (dative)	customer, company, user, ···	[CT:PERSON]:0.28, ···
	de (locative)	shop, bookstore, site ···	[CT:FACILITY]:0.40, [CT:LOCATION]:0.39, ···
⋮	⋮		⋮

the coreference model proposed by Luo (2007) and that proposed by Yang et al. (2008). Due to this characteristic, our model can utilize information beyond a mention and easily consider salience (the importance of an entity).

2 Construction of Case Frames

Case frames describe what kinds of cases each predicate has and what kinds of nouns can fill these case slots. We construct case frames from a large raw corpus by using the method proposed by Kawahara and Kurohashi (2002), and use them for case structure analysis and zero anaphora resolution. This section shows how to construct the case frames.

2.1 Basic Method

After a large corpus is parsed by a Japanese parser, case frames are constructed from modifier-head examples in the resulting parses. The problems of case frame construction are syntactic and semantic ambiguities. That is to say, the parsing results inevitably contain errors and predicate senses are intrinsically ambiguous. To cope with these problems, case frames are gradually constructed from reliable modifier-head examples.

First, modifier-head examples that have no syntactic ambiguity are extracted, and they are disambiguated by coupling a predicate and its closest case component. Such couples are explicitly expressed on the surface of text, and can be considered to play an important role in sentence meanings. For instance, examples are distinguished not by predicates (e.g., "*tsumu* (load/accumulate))", but by couples (e.g., "*nimotsu-wo tsumu* (load baggage)" and "*keiken-wo tsumu* (accumulate experience))". Modifier-head examples are aggregated in this way, and yield basic case frames.

Thereafter, the basic case frames are clustered to merge similar case frames. For example, since "*nimotsu-wo tsumu* (load baggage)" and "*busshi-wo tsumu* (load supplies)" are similar, they are clustered. The similarity is measured using a thesaurus (The National Language Institute for Japanese Language, 2004). Using this gradual procedure, we constructed case frames from approximately 1.6 billion sentences extracted from the web. In Table 1, some examples of the resulting case frames are shown.

2.2 Generalization of Examples

By using case frames that are automatically constructed from a large corpus, sparseness problem is alleviated to some extent, but still remains. For instance, there are thousands of named entities (NEs), which cannot be covered intrinsically. To deal with this sparseness problem, we generalize the examples of case slots. Kawahara and Kurohashi also give generalized examples such as "agent" but only a few types. We generalize case slot examples based on categories of common nouns and NE classes.

First, we use the categories that Japanese morphological analyzer JUMAN[1] adds to common nouns. In JUMAN, about twenty categories are defined and tagged to common nouns. For example, "*ringo* (apple)," "*inu* (dog)" and "*byoin* (hospital)" are tagged as "FOOD," "ANIMAL" and "FACILITY," respectively. For each category, we calculate the rate of categorized example among all case slot examples, and add it to the case slot as "[CT:FOOD]:0.07."

We also generalize NEs. We use a common standard NE definition for Japanese provided by IREX workshop (1999). IREX defined eight NE classes as shown in Table 2. We first recognize NEs in the source corpus by using an NE recognizer (Sasano and Kurohashi, 2008), and then construct case frames from the NE-recognized corpus.

[1] http://nlp.kuee.kyoto-u.ac.jp/nl-resource/juman.html

Table 2: Definition of NE in IREX.

NE class	Examples
ORGANIZATION	NHK Symphony Orchestra
PERSON	Kawasaki Kenjiro
LOCATION	Rome, Sinuiju
ARTIFACT	Nobel Prize
DATE	July 17, April this year
TIME	twelve o'clock noon
MONEY	sixty thousand dollars
PERCENT	20%, thirty percents

As well as categories, for each NE class, we calculate the NE rate among all case slot examples, and add it to the case slot as "[NE:PERSON]:0.12."

The generalized examples are also included in Table 1. This information is utilized to estimate the case assignment probability, which will be mentioned in Section 3.2.3.

3 Zero Anaphora Resolution Model

In this section, we propose a probabilistic model for Japanese zero anaphora resolution.

3.1 Overview

The outline of our model is as follows:

1. Parse an input text using the Japanese parser KNP[2] and recognize NEs.
2. Conduct coreference resolution and link each mention to an entity or create new entity.
3. For each sentence, from the end of the sentence, analyze each predicate by the following steps:
   (a) Select a case frame temporarily.
   (b) Consider all possible correspondence between each input case component and an case slot of the selected case frame.
   (c) Regard case slots that have no correspondence as zero pronoun candidates.
   (d) Consider all possible correspondence between each zero pronoun candidate and an existing entity.
   (e) For each possible case frame, estimate each correspondence probabilistically, and select the most likely case frame and correspondence.

In this paper, we concentrate on three case slots for zero anaphora resolution: "*ga* (subjective)," "*wo* (objective)" and "*ni* (dative)," which cover about 90% of zero anaphora.

[2]http://nlp.kuee.kyoto-u.ac.jp/nl-resource/knp.html

Morphological analysis, NE recognition, syntactic analysis and coreference resolution are conducted as pre-processes for zero anaphora resolution. Therefore, the model has already recognized existing entities before zero anaphora resolution.

For example, let us consider the following text:

(i) Toyota-*wa* 1997-*nen* hybrid car Prius-*wo* *hatsubai*(launch). 2000-*nen-karaha kaigai* (overseas)-*demo hanbai*(sell)-shiteiru.

(Toyota launched the hybrid car Prius in 1997. ϕ_1 started selling ϕ_2 overseas in 2000.)

Figure 1 shows the analysis process for this text. There are three mentions[3] in the first sentence, and the two mentions, *hybrid car* and *Prius*, appear in apposition. Thus, after the pre-processes, two entities, {Toyota} and {hybrid-car, Prius}, are created.

Then, case structure analysis for the predicate *hatsubai* (launch) is conducted. First, one of the case frames of *hatsubai* (launch) is temporarily selected and each input case component is assigned to an appropriate case slot. For instance, case component *Toyota* is assigned to *ga* case slot and *Prius* is assigned to *wo* case slot[4]. In this case, though there is a mention *hybrid-car* that is not a case component of *hatsubai* (launch) by itself, it refers to the same entity as *Prius* refers. Thus, there is no entity that is not linked to *hatsubai* (launch), and no further analysis is conducted.

Now, let us consider the second sentence. A mention *kaigai* (overseas) appears and a new entity {kaigai} is created. Then, case structure analysis for the predicate *hanbai* (sell) is conducted. There is only one overt case component *kaigai* (overseas), and it is assigned to a case slot of the selected case frame of *hanbai* (sell). For instance, the case frame *hanbai*(1) in Table 1 is selected and *kaigai* (overseas) is assigned to *de* (locative) case slot. In this case, the remaining case slots *ga*, *wo* and *ni* are considered as zero pronouns, and all possible correspondences between zero pronouns and remaining entities are considered. As a result of probabilistic estimation, the entity {Toyota} is assigned to *ga* case, the entity {hybrid-car, Prius} is assigned to *wo* case and no entity is assigned to *ni* case.

Now, we show how to estimate the correspondence probabilistically in the next subsection.

[3]In this paper, we do not consider time expressions, such as 1997, as mentions.

[4]Note that since there are some non case-making postpositions in Japanese, such as "*wa*" and "*mo*," several correspondences can be considered.

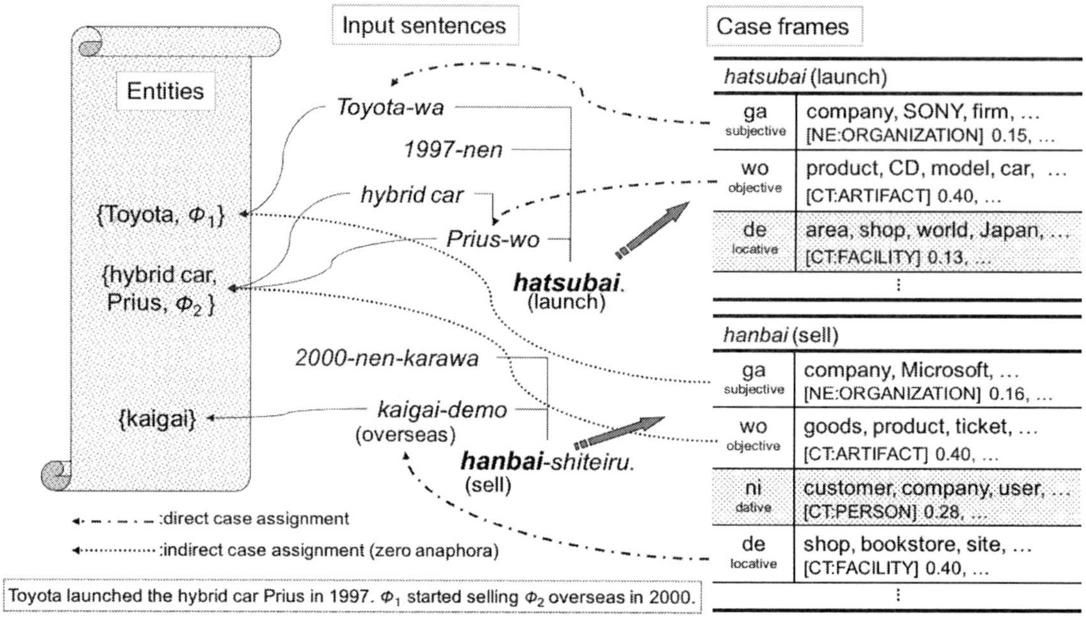

Figure 1: An Example of Case Assignment CA_k.

3.2 Probabilistic Model

The proposed model gives a probability to each possible case frame CF and case assignment CA when target predicate v, input case components ICC and existing entities ENT are given. It also outputs the case frame and case assignment that have the highest probability. That is to say, our model selects the case frame CF_{best} and the case assignment CA_{best} that maximize the probability $P(CF, CA|v, ICC, ENT)$:

$$(CF_{best}, CA_{best}) = \operatorname*{argmax}_{CF,CA} P(CF, CA|v, ICC, ENT) \quad (1)$$

Though case assignment CA usually represents correspondences between input case components and case slots, in our model it also represents correspondences between antecedents of zero pronouns and case slots. Hereafter, we call the former direct case assignment (DCA) and the latter indirect case assignment (ICA). Then, we transform $P(CF_l, CA_k|v, ICC, ENT)$ as follows:

$$\begin{aligned}
&P(CF_l, CA_k|v, ICC, ENT)\\
&= P(CF_l|v, ICC, ENT)\\
&\quad \times P(DCA_k|v, ICC, ENT, CF_l)\\
&\quad \times P(ICA_k|v, ICC, ENT, CF_l, DCA_k)\\
&\approx P(CF_l|v, ICC) \times P(DCA_k|ICC, CF_l)\\
&\quad \times P(ICA_k|ENT, CF_l, DCA_k) \quad (2)\\
&= P(CF_l|v) \times P(DCA_k, ICC|CF_l)/P(ICC|v)\\
&\quad \times P(ICA_k|ENT, CF_l, DCA_k) \quad (3)
\end{aligned}$$

$$\Bigg(\because P(CF_l|v, ICC) = \frac{P(CF_l, ICC|v)}{P(ICC|v)} = \frac{P(ICC|CF_l, v) \cdot P(CF_l|v)}{P(ICC|v)} = \frac{P(ICC|CF_l) \cdot P(CF_l|v)}{P(ICC|v)},$$

($\because CF_l$ contains the information about v.)

$$P(DCA_k|ICC, CF_l) = \frac{P(DCA_k, ICC|CF_l)}{P(ICC|CF_l)} \Bigg)$$

Equation (2) is derived because we assume that the case frame CF_l and direct case assignment DCA_k are independent of existing entities ENT, and indirect case assignment ICA_k is independent of input case components ICC.

Because $P(ICC|v)$ is constant, we can say that our model selects the case frame CF_{best} and the direct case assignment DCA_{best} and indirect case assignment ICA_{best} that maximize the probability $P(CF, DCA, ICA|v, ICC, ENT)$:

$$(CF_{best}, DCA_{best}, ICA_{best}) = \operatorname*{argmax}_{CF,DCA,ICA} \Big(P(CF|v) \times P(DCA, ICC|CF) \times P(ICA|ENT, CF, DCA)\Big) \quad (4)$$

The probability $P(CF_l|v)$, called *generative probability of a case frame*, is estimated from case structure analysis of a large raw corpus. The following subsections illustrate how to calculate $P(DCA_k, ICC|CF_l)$ and $P(ICA_k|ENT, CF_l, DCA_k)$.

3.2.1 Generative Probability of Direct Case Assignment

For estimation of *generative probability of direct case assignment* $P(DCA_k, ICC|CF_l)$, we follow Kawahara and Kurohashi's (2006) method. They decompose $P(DCA_k,\ ICC|CF_l)$ into the following product depending on whether a case slot s_j is filled with an input case component or vacant:

$$
\begin{aligned}
&P(DCA_k, ICC|CF_l) = \\
&\quad \prod_{s_j:A(s_j)=1} P(A(s_j)=1, n_j, c_j|CF_l, s_j) \\
&\quad \times \prod_{s_j:A(s_j)=0} P(A(s_j)=0|CF_l, s_j) \\
&= \prod_{s_j:A(s_j)=1} \Big\{P(A(s_j)=1|CF_l, s_j) \\
&\qquad \times P(n_j, c_j|CF_l, s_j, A(s_j)=1)\Big\} \\
&\quad \times \prod_{s_j:A(s_j)=0} P(A(s_j)=0|CF_l, s_j) \qquad (5)
\end{aligned}
$$

where the function $A(s_j)$ returns 1 if a case slot s_j is filled with an input case component; otherwise 0, n_j denotes the content part of the case component, and c_j denotes the surface case of the case component.

The probabilities $P(A(s_j) = 1|CF_l, s_j)$ and $P(A(s_j) = 0|CF_l, s_j)$ are called *generative probability of a case slot*, and estimated from case structure analysis of a large raw corpus as well as *generative probability of a case frame*.

The probability $P(n_j, c_j|CF_l, s_j, A(s_j) = 1)$ is called *generative probability of a case component* and estimated as follows:

$$
\begin{aligned}
&P(n_j, c_j|CF_l, s_j, A(s_j)=1) \\
&\approx P(n_j|CF_l, s_j, A(s_j)=1) \times P(c_j|s_j, A(s_j)=1) \quad (6)
\end{aligned}
$$

$P(n_j|CF_l, s_j, A(s_j) = 1)$ means the generative probability of a content part n_j from a case slot s_j in a case frame CF_l, and estimated by using the frequency of a case slot example in the automatically constructed case frames. $P(c_j|s_j, A(s_j) = 1)$ is approximated by $P(c_j|case\_type\_of(s_j), A(s_j)=1)$ and estimated from the web corpus in which the relationship between a surface case marker and a case slot is annotated by hand.

3.2.2 Probability of Indirect Case Assignment

To estimate *probability of indirect case assignment* $P(ICA_k|ENT, CF_l, DCA_k)$ we also decompose it into the following product depending on whether a case slot s_j is filled with an entity ent_j or vacant:

$$
\begin{aligned}
&P(ICA_k|ENT, CF_l, DCA_k) = \\
&\quad \prod_{s_j:A'(s_j)=1} P(A'(s_j)=1, ent_j|ENT, CF_l, s_j) \\
&\quad \times \prod_{s_j:A'(s_j)=0} P(A'(s_j)=0|ENT, CF_l, s_j) \qquad (7)
\end{aligned}
$$

where the function $A'(s_j)$ returns 1 if a case slot s_j is filled with an entity ent_j; otherwise 0. Note that we only consider case slots *ga*, *wo* and *ni* that is not filled with an input case component. We approximate $P(A'(s_j) = 1, ent_j|ENT, CF_l, s_j)$ and $P(A'(s_j) = 0|ENT, CF_l, s_j)$ as follows:

$$
\begin{aligned}
&P(A'(s_j)=1, ent_j|ENT, CF_l, s_j) \\
&\quad \approx P(A'(s_j)=1, ent_j|ent_j, CF_l, s_j) \\
&\quad = P(A'(s_j)=1|ent_j, CF_l, s_j) \qquad (8)
\end{aligned}
$$

$$
\begin{aligned}
&P(A'(s_j)=0|ENT, CF_l, s_j) \\
&\quad \approx P(A'(s_j)=0|case\_type\_of(s_j)) \quad (9)
\end{aligned}
$$

Equation (8) is derived because we assume $P(A'(s_j) = 1|CF_l, s_j)$ is independent of existing entities that are not assigned to s_j. Equation (9) is derived because we assume $P(A'(s_j) = 0)$ is independent of ENT and CF_l, and only depends on the case type of s_j, such as *ga*, *wo* and *ni*. $P(A'(s_j)=0|case\_type\_of(s_j))$ is the probability that a case slot has no correspondence after zero anaphora resolution and estimated from anaphoric relation tagged corpus.

Let us consider the probability $P(A'(s_j) = 1|ent_j, CF_l, s_j)$. We decompose ent_j into content part n_{j_m}, surface case c_{j_n} and location class l_{j_n}. Here, location classes denote the locational relations between zero pronouns and their antecedents. We defined twelve location classes as described in Table 3. In Table 3, V_z means a predicate that has a zero pronoun. Note that we also consider the

Table 3: Location Classes of Antecedents.

intra-sentence: case components of	
L_1 :	parent predicate of V_z
L_2 :	parent predicate of V_z" (parallel)
L_3 :	child predicate of V_z
L_4 :	child predicate of V_z (parallel)
L_5 :	parent predicate of parent noun phrase of V_z
L_6 :	parent predicate of parent predicate of V_z (parallel)
L_7 :	other noun phrases following V_z
L_8 :	other noun phrases preceding V_z
inter-sentence: noun phrases in	
L_9 :	1 sentence before
L_{10}:	2 sentences before
L_{11}:	3 sentences before
L_{12}:	more than 3 sentences before

locations of zero pronouns that are linked to the target entity as location class candidates. Now we roughly approximate $P(A'(s_j)=1|ent_j, CF_l, s_j)$ as follows:

$$
\begin{aligned}
&P(A' = 1|ent_j, CF_l, s_j)\\
&=P(A' = 1|n_{j_m}, c_{j_n}, l_{j_n}, CF_l, s_j)\\
&=\frac{P(n_{j_m}, c_{j_n}, l_{j_n}|CF_l, s_j, A'{=}1)\cdot P(A'{=}1|CF_l, s_j)}{P(n_{j_m}, c_{j_n}, l_{j_n}|CF_l, s_j)}\\
&\approx\frac{P(n_{j_m}|CF_l, s_j, A'{=}1)}{P(n_{j_m}|CF_l, s_j)}\cdot\frac{P(c_{j_n}|CF_l, s_j, A'{=}1)}{P(c_{j_n}|CF_l, s_j)}\\
&\quad\cdot\frac{P(l_{j_n}|CF_l, s_j, A'{=}1)}{P(l_{j_n}|CF_l, s_j)}\cdot P(A'{=}1|CF_l, s_j) \quad (10)\\
&\approx\frac{P(n_{j_m}|CF_l, s_j, A'{=}1)}{P(n_{j_m})}\\
&\quad\times\frac{P(c_{j_n}|case\_type\_of(s_j), A'{=}1)}{P(c_{j_n})}\\
&\quad\times P(A'{=}1|l_{j_n}, case\_type\_of(s_j)) \quad (11)
\end{aligned}
$$

$$
\Bigg(\because \frac{P(l_{j_n}|CF_l, s_j, A'{=}1)}{P(l_{j_n}|CF_l, s_j)}\cdot P(A'{=}1|CF_l, s_j) = \frac{P(A'{=}1, l_{j_n}|CF_l, s_j)}{P(l_{j_n}|CF_l, s_j)} = P(A'{=}1|CF_l, l_{j_n}, s_j)\Bigg)
$$

Note that because ent_j is often mentioned more than one time, there are several combinations of content part n_{j_m}, surface case c_{j_n} and location class l_{j_n} candidates. We select the pair of m and n with the highest probability.

Equation (10) is derived because we assume n_{j_m}, c_{j_n} and l_{j_n} are independent of each other. Equation (11) is derived because we approximate $P(A' = 1|CF_l, l_{j_n}, s_j)$ as $P(A' = 1|l_{j_n}, case\_type\_of(s_j))$, and assume $P(n_{j_m})$ and $P(c_{j_n})$ are independent of CF_l and s_j. Since these approximation is too rough, specifically, $P(n_{j_m})$ and $P(c_{j_n})$ tend to be somewhat smaller than $P(n_{j_m}|CF_l, s_j)$ and $P(c_{j_n}|CF_l, s_j)$ and equation (11) often becomes too large, we introduce a parameter $\alpha(\leq 1)$ and use the α-times value as $P(A' = 1|ent_j, CF_l, s_j)$.

The first term of equation (11) represents how likely an entity that contains n_{j_m} as a content part is considered to be an antecedent, the second term represents how likely an entity that contains c_{j_n} as a surface case is considered to be an antecedent, and the third term gives the probability that an entity that appears in location class l_{j_n} is an antecedent.

The probabilities $P(n_{j_m})$ and $P(c_{j_n})$ are estimated from a large raw corpus. The probabilities $P(c_{j_n}|case\_type\_of(s_j))$ and $P(A' = 1|l_{j_n}, case\_type\_of(s_j))$ are estimated from the web corpus in which the relationship between an antecedent of a zero pronoun and a case slot, and the relationship between its surface case marker and a case slot are annotated by hand. Then, let us consider the probability $P(n_{j_m}|CF_l, s_j, A'(s_j) = 1)$ in the next subsection.

3.2.3 Probability of Component Part of Zero Pronoun

$P(n_{j_m}|CF_l, s_j, A'{=}1)$ is similar to $P(n_j|CF_l, s_j, A{=}1)$ and can be estimated approximately from case frames using the frequencies of case slot examples. However, while $A'(s_j) = 1$ means s_j is not filled with input case component but filled with an entity as the result of zero anaphora resolution, case frames are constructed by extracting only the input case component. Therefore, the content part of a zero anaphora antecedent n_{j_m} is often not included in the case slot examples. To cope with this problem, we utilize generalized examples.

When one mention of an entity is tagged any category or recognized as an NE, we also use the category or the NE class as the content part of the entity. For examples, if an entity {Prius} is recognized as an artifact name and assigned to *wo* case of the case frame *hanbai*(1) in Table 1, the system also calculates:

$$\frac{P(NE{:}ARTIFACT|hanbai(1), wo, A'(wo){=}1)}{P(NE{:}ARTIFACT)}$$

besides:

$$\frac{P(Prius|hanbai(1), wo, A'(wo) = 1)}{P(Prius)}$$

and uses the higher value.

3.3 Salience Score

Previous works reported the usefulness of salience for anaphora resolution (Lappin and Leass, 1994; Mitkov et al., 2002). In order to consider salience of an entity, we introduce salience score, which is calculated by the following set of simple rules:

- $+2$: mentioned with topical marker "*wa*".
- $+1$: mentioned without topical marker "*wa*".
- $+0.5$: assigned to a zero pronoun.
- $\times 0.7$: beginning of each sentence.

For examples, we consider the salience score of the entity {Toyota} in (i) in Section 3.1. In the first sentence, since {Toyota} is mentioned with topical marker "*wa*", the salience score is 2. At the beginning of the second sentence it becomes 1.4,

Table 4: Data for Parameter Estimation.

probability	data
$P(n_j)$	raw corpus
$P(c_j)$	raw corpus
$P(c_j \mid case\_type\_of(s_j), A(s_j)=1)$	tagged corpus
$P(c_j \mid case\_type\_of(s_j), A'(s_j)=1)$	tagged corpus
$P(n_j \mid CF_l, s_j, A(s_j)=1)$	case frames
$P(n_j \mid CF_l, s_j, A'(s_j)=1)$	case frames
$P(CF_l \mid v_i)$	case structure analysis
$P(A(s_j)=\{0,1\} \mid CF_l, s_j)$	case structure analysis
$P(A'(s_j)=0 \mid case\_type\_of(s_j))$	tagged corpus
$P(A'(s_j)=1 \mid l_j, case\_type\_of(s_j))$	tagged corpus

Table 5: Experimental Results.

	R	P	F
Kawahara & Kurohashi	.230 (28/122)	.173 (28/162)	.197
Proposed ($\alpha = 1$)	**.426** (52/122)	.271 (52/192)	.331
($\alpha = 1/2$)	.410 (50/122)	.373 (50/134)	**.391**
($\alpha = 1/4$)	.295 (36/122)	**.419** (36/86)	.346

and after assigned to the zero pronoun of "*hanbai*" it becomes 1.9. Note that we use the salience score not as a probabilistic clue but as a filter to consider the target entity as a possible antecedent. When we use the salience score, we only consider the entities that have the salience score no less than 1.

4 Experiments

4.1 Setting

We created an anaphoric relation-tagged corpus consisting of 186 web documents (979 sentences). We selected 20 documents for test and used the other 166 documents for calculating several probabilities. Since the anaphoric relations in some web documents were not so clear and too difficult to recognize, we did not select such documents for test. In the 20 test documents, 122 zero anaphora relations were tagged between one of the mentions of the antecedent and the target predicate that had the zero pronoun.

Each parameter for proposed model was estimated using maximum likelihood from the data described in Table 4. The case frames were automatically constructed from web corpus comprising 1.6 billion sentences. The case structure analysis was conducted on 80 million sentences in the web corpus, and $P(n_j)$ and $P(c_j)$ were calculated from the same 80 million sentences.

In order to concentrate on zero anaphora resolution, we used the correct morphemes, named entities, syntactic structures and coreferential relations that were annotated by hand. Since correct coreferential relations were given, the number of created entities was same between the gold standard and the system output because zero anaphora resolution did not create new entities.

4.2 Experimental Results

We conducted experiments of zero anaphora resolution. As the parameter α introduced in Section 3.2.2., we tested 3 values 1, 1/2, and 1/4. For comparison, we also tested Kawahara and Kurohashi's (2004) model. The experimental results are shown in Table 5, in which recall R, precision P and F-measure F were calculated by:

$$R = \frac{\text{\# of correctly recognized zero anaphora}}{\text{\# of zero anaphora tagged in corpus}},$$

$$P = \frac{\text{\# of correctly recognized zero anaphora}}{\text{\# of system outputted zero anaphora}},$$

$$F = \frac{2}{1/R + 1/P}.$$

Kawahara and Kurohashi's model achieved almost 50% as F-measure against newspaper articles. However, as a result of our experiment against web documents, it achieved only about 20% as F-measure. This may be because anaphoric relations in web documents were not so clear as those in newspaper articles and more difficult to recognize. As to the parameter α, the larger α tended to output more zero anaphora, and the highest F-measure was achieved against $\alpha = 1/2$.

When using $\alpha = 1/2$, there were 72 (=122−50) zero pronouns that were tagged in the corpus and not resolved correctly. Only 12 of them were correctly detected and assigned to a wrong entity, that is, 60 of them were not even detected. Therefore, we can say our recall errors were mainly caused by the low recall of zero pronoun detection.

In order to confirm the effectiveness of generalized examples of case slots and salience score, we also conducted experiments under several conditions. We set $\alpha = 1/2$ in these experiments. The results are shown in Table 6, in which CT means generalized categories, NE means generalized NEs and SS means salience score.

Without using any generalized examples, the F-measure is less than Kawahara and Kurohashi's method, which use similarity to deal with sparseness of case slot examples, and we can confirm the effectiveness of the generalized examples. While generalized categories much improved the F-measure, generalized NEs contribute little. This may be because the NE rate is smaller than common noun rate, and so the effect is limited.

We also confirmed that the salience score filter improved F-measure. Moreover, by using salience score filter, the zero anaphora resolution becomes about ten times faster. This is because the system

Table 6: Experiments under Several Conditions.

CT	NE	SS	R	P	F
		√	.131 (16/122)	.205 (16/78)	.160
	√	√	.164 (20/122)	.247 (20/81)	.197
√		√	.402 (49/122)	.368 (49/133)	.384
√	√		.385 (47/122)	.196 (47/240)	.260
√	√	√	**.410** (50/122)	**.373** (50/134)	**.391**

can avoid checking entities with low salience as antecedent candidates.

4.3 Comparison with Previous Works

We compare our accuracies with (Seki et al., 2002). They achieved 48.9% in precision, 88.2% in recall, and 62.9% in F-measure for zero pronoun detection, and 54.0% accuracy for antecedent estimation on 30 newspaper articles, that is, they achieved about 34% in F-measure for whole zero pronoun resolution. It is difficult to directly compare their results with ours due to the difference of the corpus, but our method achieved 39% in F-measure and we can confirm that our model achieves reasonable performance considering the task difficulty.

5 Conclusion

In this paper, we proposed a probabilistic model for Japanese zero anaphora resolution. By using automatically constructed wide-coverage case frames that include generalized examples and introducing salience score filter, our model achieves reasonable performance against web corpus. As future work, we plan to conduct large-scale experiments and integrate this model to a fully-lexicalized probabilistic model for Japanese syntactic and case structure analysis (Kawahara and Kurohashi, 2006).

References

Iida, Ryu, Kentaro Inui, and Yuji Matsumoto. 2006. Exploiting syntactic patterns as clues in zero-anaphora resolution. In *Proceedings of COLING/ACL 2006*, pages 625–632.

IREX Committee, editor. 1999. *Proc. of the IREX Workshop*.

Isozaki, Hideki and Tsutomu Hirao. 2003. Japanese zero pronoun resolution based on ranking rules and machine learning. In *Proceedings of the Conference on Empirical Methods in Natural Language Processing (EMNLP)*, pages 184–191.

Kawahara, Daisuke and Sadao Kurohashi. 2002. Fertilization of Case Frame Dictionary for Robust Japanese Case Analysis. In *Proceedings of the 19th International Conference on Computational Linguistics*, pages 425–431.

Kawahara, Daisuke and Sadao Kurohashi. 2004. Zero pronoun resolution based on automatically constructed case frames and structural preference of antecedents. In *Proceedings of the 1st International Joint Conference on Natural Language Processing (IJCNLP-04)*, pages 334–341.

Kawahara, Daisuke and Sadao Kurohashi. 2006. A fully-lexicalized probabilistic model for japanese syntactic and case structure analysis. In *Proceedings of the Human Language Technology Conference of the NAACL, Main Conference*, pages 176–183.

Lappin, Shalom and Herbert J. Leass. 1994. An algorithm for pronominal anaphora resolution. *Computational Linguistics*, 20(4):535–562.

Luo, Xiaoqiang. 2007. Coreference or not: A twin model for coreference resolution. In *Human Language Technologies 2007: The Conference of the North American Chapter of the Association for Computational Linguistics; Proceedings of the Main Conference*, pages 73–80.

Mitkov, Ruslan, Richard Evans, and Constantin Orăsan. 2002. A new, fully automatic version of mitkov's knowledge-poor pronoun resolution method. In *Proceedings of the Third International Conference on Intelligent Text Processing and Computational Linguistics (CICLing-2002)*.

Ng, Vincent. 2005. Machine learning for coreference resolution: From local classification to global ranking. In *Proceedings of the 43rd Annual Meeting of the Asssociation for Computational Linguistics*, pages 157–164.

Sasano, Ryohei and Sadao Kurohashi. 2008. Japanese named entity recognition using structural natural language processing. In *Proceedings of the 3rd International Joint Conference on Natural Language Processing (IJCNLP-08)*, pages 607–612.

Seki, Kazuhiro, Atsushi Fujii, and Tetsuya Ishikawa. 2002. A probabilistic method for analyzing Japanese anaphora integrating zero pronoun detection and resolution. In *Proceedings of the 19th International Conference on Computational Linguistics*, pages 911–917.

Soon, Wee Meng, Hwee Tou Ng, and Daniel Chung Yong Lim. 2001. A machine learning approach to coreference resolution of noun phrases. *Computational Linguistics*, 27(4):521–544.

The National Language Institute for Japanese Language. 2004. *Bunruigoihyo*. Dainippon Tosho, (In Japanese).

Yang, Xiaofeng, Jian Su, Jun Lang, Ghew Lim Tan, Ting Liu, and Sheng Li. 2008. An entity-mention model for coreference resolution with inductive logic programming. In *Proceedings of ACL-08: HLT*, pages 843–851.

Estimation of Conditional Probabilities With Decision Trees and an Application to Fine-Grained POS Tagging

Helmut Schmid and Florian Laws
IMS, University of Stuttgart
{schmid,lawsfn}@ims.uni-stuttgart.de

Abstract

We present a HMM part-of-speech tagging method which is particularly suited for POS tagsets with a large number of fine-grained tags. It is based on three ideas: (1) splitting of the POS tags into attribute vectors and decomposition of the contextual POS probabilities of the HMM into a product of attribute probabilities, (2) estimation of the contextual probabilities with decision trees, and (3) use of high-order HMMs. In experiments on German and Czech data, our tagger outperformed state-of-the-art POS taggers.

1 Introduction

A Hidden-Markov-Model part-of-speech tagger (Brants, 2000, e.g.) computes the most probable POS tag sequence $\hat{t}_1^N = \hat{t}_1, ..., \hat{t}_N$ for a given word sequence w_1^N.

$$\hat{t}_1^N = \arg\max_{t_1^N} p(t_1^N, w_1^N)$$

The joint probability of the two sequences is defined as the product of context probabilities and lexical probabilities over all POS tags:

$$p(t_1^N, w_1^N) = \prod_{i=1}^{N} \underbrace{p(t_i|t_{i-k}^{i-1})}_{\text{context prob.}} \underbrace{p(w_i|t_i)}_{\text{lexical prob.}} \qquad (1)$$

HMM taggers are fast and were successfully applied to a wide range of languages and training corpora.

© 2008. Licensed under the *Creative Commons Attribution-Noncommercial-Share Alike 3.0 Unported* license (http://creativecommons.org/licenses/by-nc-sa/3.0/). Some rights reserved.

POS taggers are usually trained on corpora with between 50 and 150 different POS tags. Tagsets of this size contain little or no information about number, gender, case and similar morphosyntactic features. For languages with a rich morphology such as German or Czech, more fine-grained tagsets are often considered more appropriate. The additional information may also help to disambiguate the (base) part of speech. Without gender information, for instance, it is difficult for a tagger to correctly disambiguate the German sentence *Ist das Realität?* (Is that reality?). The word *das* is ambiguous between an article and a demonstrative. Because of the lack of gender agreement between *das* (neuter) and the noun *Realität* (feminine), the article reading must be wrong.

The German Tiger treebank (Brants et al., 2002) is an example of a corpus with a more fine-grained tagset (over 700 tags overall). Large tagsets aggravate sparse data problems. As an example, take the German sentence *Das zu versteuernde Einkommen sinkt* ("The to be taxed income decreases"; The taxable income decreases). This sentence should be tagged as shown in table 1.

Das	ART.Def.Nom.Sg.Neut
zu	PART.Zu
versteuernde	ADJA.Pos.Nom.Sg.Neut
Einkommen	N.Reg.Nom.Sg.Neut
sinkt	VFIN.Full.3.Sg.Pres.Ind
.	SYM.Pun.Sent

Table 1: Correct POS tags for the German sentence *Das zu versteuernde Einkommen sinkt.*

Unfortunately, the POS trigram consisting of the tags of the first three words does not occur in the Tiger corpus. (Neither does the pair consisting of the first two tags.) The unsmoothed context probability of the third POS tag is therefore 0. If the probability is smoothed with the backoff distribution $p(\bullet|PART.Zu)$, the most probable tag is ADJA.Pos.Acc.Sg.Fem rather than ADJA.Pos.Nom.Sg.Neut. Thus, the agreement between the article and the adjective is not checked anymore.

A closer inspection of the Tiger corpus reveals that it actually contains all the information needed to completely disambiguate each component of the POS tag ADJA.Pos.Nom.Sg.Neut:

- All words appearing after an article (ART) and the infinitive particle *zu* (PART.zu) are attributive adjectives (ADJA) (10 of 10 cases).
- All adjectives appearing after an article and a particle (PART) have the degree positive (Pos) (39 of 39 cases).
- All adjectives appearing after a nominative article and a particle have nominative case (11 of 11 cases).
- All adjectives appearing after a singular article and a particle are singular (32 of 32 cases).
- All adjectives appearing after a neuter article and a particle are neuter (4 of 4 cases).

By (1) decomposing the context probability of ADJA.Pos.Nom.Sg.Neut into a product of attribute probabilities

p(ADJA | 2:ART, 2:ART.Def, 2:ART.Nom, 2:ART.Sg, 2:ART.Neut, 1:PART, 1:PART.Zu)
∗ p(Pos| 2:ART, 2:ART.Def, 2:ART.Nom, 2:ART.Sg, 2:ART.Neut, 1:PART, 1:PART.Zu, 0:ADJA)
∗ p(Nom | 2:ART, 2:ART.Def, 2:ART.Nom, 2:ART.Sg, 2:ART.Neut, 1:PART, 1:PART.Zu, 0:ADJA, 0:ADJA.Pos)
∗ p(Sg | 2:ART, 2:ART.Def, 2:ART.Nom, 2:ART.Sg, 2:ART.Neut, 1:PART, 1:PART.Zu, 0:ADJA, 0:ADJA.Pos, 0:ADJA.Nom)
∗ p(Neut | 2:ART, 2:ART.Def, 2:ART.Nom, 2:ART.Sg, 2:ART.Neut, 1:PART, 1:PART.Zu, 0:ADJA, 0:ADJA.Pos, 0:ADJA.Nom, 0:ADJA.Sg)

and (2) selecting the relevant context attributes for the prediction of each attribute, we obtain the following expression for the context probability:

p(ADJA | ART, PART.Zu)
∗ p(Pos | 2:ART, 1:PART, 0:ADJA)
∗ p(Nom | 2:ART.Nom, 1:PART.Zu, 0:ADJA)
∗ p(Sg | 2:ART.Sg, 1:PART.Zu, 0:ADJA)
∗ p(Neut | 2:ART.Neut, 1:PART.Zu, 0:ADJA)

The conditional probability of each attribute is 1. Hence the context probability of the whole tag is also 1. Without having observed the given context, it is possible to deduce that the observed POS tag is the only possible tag in this context.

These considerations motivate an HMM tagging approach which decomposes the POS tags into a set of simple attributes, and uses decision trees to estimate the probability of each attribute. Decision trees are ideal for this task because the identification of relevant attribute combinations is at the heart of this method. The backoff smoothing methods of traditional n-gram POS taggers require an ordering of the reduced contexts which is not available, here. Discriminatively trained taggers, on the other hand, have difficulties to handle the huge number of features which are active at the same time if any possible combination of context attributes defines a separate feature.

2 Decision Trees

Decision trees (Breiman et al., 1984; Quinlan, 1993) are normally used as classifiers, i.e. they assign classes to objects which are represented as attribute vectors. The non-terminal nodes are labeled with attribute tests, the edges with the possible outcomes of a test, and the terminal nodes are labeled with classes. An object is classified by evaluating the test of the top node on the object, following the respective edge to a daughter node, evaluating the test of the daughter node, and so on until a terminal node is reached whose class is assigned to the object.

Decision Trees are turned into *probability estimation trees* by storing a probability for each possible class at the terminal nodes instead of a single result class. Figure 1 shows a probability estimation tree for the prediction of the probability of the nominative attribute of nouns.

2.1 Induction of Decision Trees

Decision trees are incrementally built by first selecting the test which splits the manually annotated training sample into the most homogeneous subsets with respect to the class. This test, which maximizes the information gain[1] wrt. the class, is

[1] The information gain measures how much the test decreases the uncertainty about the class. It is the difference between the entropy of the empirical distribution of the class variable in the training set and the weighted average entropy

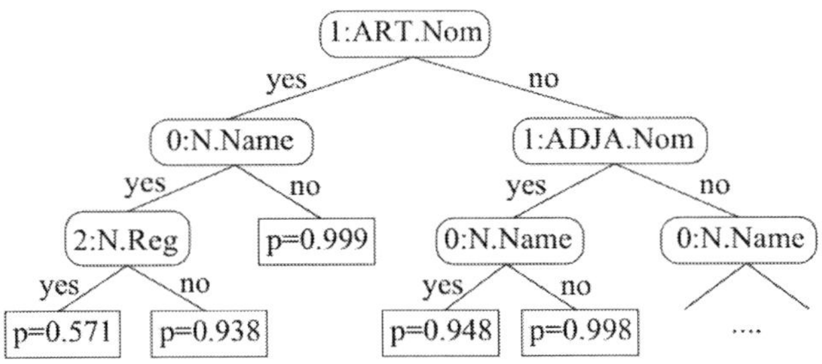

Figure 1: Probability estimation tree for the nominative case of nouns. The test *1:ART.Nom* checks if the preceding word is a nominative article.

assigned to the top node. The tree is recursively expanded by selecting the best test for each subset and so on, until all objects of the current subset belong to the same class. In a second step, the decision tree may be pruned in order to avoid overfitting to the training data.

Our tagger generates a predictor for each feature (such as base POS, number, gender etc.) Instead of using a single tree for the prediction of all possible values of a feature (such as *noun*, *article*, etc. for base POS), the tagger builds a separate decision tree for each value. The motivation was that a tree which predicts a single value (say *verb*) does not fragment the data with tests which are only relevant for the distinction of two other values (e.g. *article* and *possessive pronoun*).[2] Furthermore, we observed that such two-class decision trees require no optimization of the pruning threshold (see also section 2.2.)

The tree induction algorithm only considers binary tests, which check whether some particular attribute is present or not. The best test for each node is selected with the standard information gain criterion. The recursive tree building process terminates if the information gain is 0. The decision tree is pruned with the pruning criterion described below.

Since the tagger creates a separate tree for each attribute, the probabilities of a set of competing attributes such as *masculine*, *feminine*, and *neuter* will not exactly sum up to 1. To understand why, assume that there are three trees for the gender attributes. Two of them (say the trees for *masculine* and *feminine*) consist of a single terminal node which returns a probability of 0.3. The third tree for *neuter* has one non-terminal and two terminal nodes returning a probability of 0.3 and 0.5, respectively. The sum of probabilities is therefore either 0.9 or 1.1, but never exactly 1. This problem is solved by renormalizing the probabilities.

The probability of an attribute (such as "Nom") is always conditioned on the respective base POS (such as "N") (unless the predicted attribute is the base POS) in order to make sure that the probability of an attribute is 0 if it never appeared with the respective base POS. All context attributes other than the base POS are always used in combination with the base POS. A typical context attribute is "1:ART.Nom" which states that the preceding tag is an article with the attribute "Nom". "1:ART" is also a valid attribute specification, but "1:Nom" is not.

The tagger further restricts the set of possible test attributes by requiring that some attribute of the POS tag at position i-k (i=position of the predicted POS tag, $k \geq 1$) must have been used before an attribute of the POS tag at position i-(k+1) may be examined. This restriction improved the tagging accuracy for large contexts.

2.2 Pruning Criterion

The tagger applies[3] the critical-value pruning strategy proposed by (Mingers, 1989). A node is pruned if the information gain of the best test multiplied by the size of the data subsample is below a given threshold.

To illustrate the pruning, assume that D is the data of the current node with 50 positive and 25 negative elements, and that D_1 (with 20 positive and 20 negative elements) and D_2 (with 30 positive and 5 negative elements) are the two subsets induced by the best test. The entropy of D is $-2/3\ log_2 2/3 - 1/3\ log_2 1/3 = 0.92$, the entropy of D_1 is $-1/2\ log_2 1/2 - 1/2\ log_2 1/2 = 1$, and the entropy of D_2 is $-6/7\ log_2 6/7 - 1/7\ log_2 1/7 = 0.59$. The information gain is therefore $0.92 - (8/15 * 1 - 7/15 * 0.59) = 0.11$. The resulting score is $75 * 0.11 = 8.25$. Given a threshold of 6, the node is therefore not pruned.

We experimented with pre-pruning (where a node is always pruned if the gain is below the

in the two subsets. The weight of each subset is proportional to its size.

[2] We did not directly compare the two alternatives (two-valued vs. multi-valued tests), because the implementational effort required would have been too large.

[3] We also experimented with a pruning criterion based on binomial tests, which returned smaller trees with a slightly lower accuracy, although the difference in accuracy was never larger than 0.1% for any context size. Thus, the simpler pruning strategy presented here was chosen.

threshold) as well as post-pruning (where a node is only pruned if its sub-nodes are terminal nodes or pruned nodes). The performance of pre-pruning was slightly better and it was less dependent on the choice of the pruning threshold. A threshold of 6 consistently produced optimal or near optimal results for pre-pruning. Thus, pre-pruning with a threshold of 6 was used in the experiments.

3 Splitting of the POS Tags

The tagger treats dots in POS tag labels as attribute separators. The first attribute of a POS tag is the main category. The number of additional attributes is fixed for each main category. The additional attributes are category-specific. The *singular* attribute of a noun and an adjective POS tag are therefore two different attributes.[4]

Each position in the POS tags of a given category corresponds to a *feature*. The attributes occurring at a certain position constitute the value set of the feature.

4 Our Tagger

Our tagger is a HMM tagger which decomposes the context probabilities into a product of attribute probabilities. The probability of an attribute given the attributes of the preceding POS tags as well as the preceding attributes of the predicted POS tag is estimated with a decision tree as described before. The probabilities at the terminal nodes of the decision trees are smoothed with the parent node probabilities (which themselves were smoothed in the same way). The smoothing is implemented by adding the weighted class probabilities $p_p(c)$ of the parent node to the frequencies $f(c)$ before normalizing them to probabilities:

$$p(c) = \frac{f(c) + \alpha p_p(c)}{\alpha + \sum_c f(c)}$$

The weight α was fixed to 1 after a few experiments on development data. This smoothing strategy is closely related to Witten-Bell smoothing. The probabilities are normalized by dividing them by the total probability of all attribute values of the respective feature (see section 2.1).

The best tag sequence is computed with the Viterbi algorithm. The main differences of our tagger to a standard trigram tagger are that the order of the Markov model (the k in equation 1) is not fixed and that the context probability $p(t_i|t_{i-k}^{i-1})$ is internally computed as a product of attribute probabilities. In order to increase the speed, the tagger also applies a beam-search strategy which prunes all search paths whose probability is below the probability of the best path times a threshold. With a threshold of 10^{-3} or lower, the influence of pruning on the tagging accuracy was negligible.

4.1 Supplementary Lexicon

The tagger may use an external lexicon which supplies entries for additional words which are not found in the training corpus, and additional tags for words which did occur in the training data. If an external lexicon is provided, the lexical probabilities are smoothed as follows: The tagger computes the average tag probabilities of all words with the same set of possible POS tags. The Witten-Bell method is then applied to smooth the lexical probabilities with the average probabilities.

If the word w was observed with N different tags, and $f(w,t)$ is the joint frequency of w and POS tag t, and $p(t|[w])$ is the average probability of t among words with the same set of possible tags as w, then the smoothed probability of t given w is defined as follows:

$$p(t|w) = \frac{f(w,t) + Np(t|[w])}{f(w) + N}$$

The smoothed estimates of $p(tag|word)$ are divided by the prior probability $p(tag)$ of the tag and used instead of $p(word|tag)$.[5]

4.2 Unknown Words

The lexical probabilities of unknown words are obtained as follows: The unknown words are divided into four disjoint classes[6] with numeric expressions, words starting with an upper-case letter, words starting with a lower-case letter, and a fourth class for the other words. The tagger builds a suffix trie for each class of unknown words using the known word types from that class. The maximal length of the suffixes is 7.

The suffix tries are pruned until (i) all suffixes have a frequency of at least 5 and (ii) the information gain multiplied by the suffix frequency and di-

[4]This is the reason why the attribute tests in figure 1 used complex attributes such as *ART.Nom* rather than *Nom*.

[5]$p(word|tag)$ is equal to $p(tag|word)p(word)/p(tag)$ and $p(word)$ is a constant if the tokenization is unambiguous. Therefore dropping the factor $p(word)$ has no influence on the ranking of the different tag sequences.

[6]In earlier experiments, we had used a much larger number of word classes. Decreasing their number to 4 turned out to be better.

vided by the number of different POS tags is above a threshold of 1. More precisely, if T_α is the set of POS tags that occurred with suffix α, $|T|$ is the size of the set T, f_α is the frequency of suffix α, and $p_\alpha(t)$ is the probability of POS tag t among the words with suffix α, then the following condition must hold:

$$\frac{f_{a\alpha}}{|T_{a\alpha}|} \sum_{t \in T_{a\alpha}} p_{a\alpha}(t) \, log \frac{p_{a\alpha}(t)}{p_\alpha(t)} < 1$$

The POS probabilities are recursively smoothed with the POS probabilities of shorter suffixes using Witten-Bell smoothing.

5 Evaluation

Our tagger was first evaluated on data from the German Tiger treebank. The results were compared to those obtained with the TnT tagger (Brants, 2000) and the SVMTool (Giménez and Màrquez, 2004), which is based on support vector machines.[7] The training of the SVMTool took more than a day. Therefore it was not possible to optimize the parameters systematically. We took standard features from a 5 word window and M4-LRL training without optimization of the regularization parameter C.

In a second experiment, our tagger was also evaluated on the Czech Academic corpus 1.0 (Hladká et al., 2007) and compared to the TnT tagger.

5.1 Tiger Corpus

The German Tiger treebank (Brants et al., 2002) contains over 888,000 tokens. It is annotated with POS tags from the coarse-grained STTS tagset and with additional features encoding information about number, gender, case, person, degree, tense, and mood. After deleting problematic sentences (e.g. with an incomplete annotation) and automatically correcting some easily detectable errors, 885,707 tokens were left. The first 80% were used as training data, the first half of the rest as development data, and the last 10% as test data.

Some of the 54 STTS labels were mapped to new labels with dots, which reduced the number of main categories to 23. Examples are the nominal POS tags NN and NE which were mapped to N.Reg and N.Name. Some lexically decidable distinctions missing in the Tiger corpus have been automatically added. Examples are the distinction between definite and indefinite articles, and the distinction between hyphens, slashes, left and right parentheses, quotation marks, and other symbols which the Tiger treebank annotates with "$(".

A supplementary lexicon was created by analyzing a word list which included all words from the training, development, and test data with a German computational morphology. The analyses generated by the morphology were mapped to the Tiger tagset. Note that only the words, but not the POS tags from the test and development data were used, here. Therefore, it is always possible to create a supplementary lexicon for the corpus to be processed.

In case of the TnT tagger, the entries of the supplementary lexicon were added to the regular lexicon with a default frequency of 1 if the word/tag-pair was unknown, and with a frequency proportional to the prior probability of the tag if the word was unknown. This strategy returned the best results on the development data. In case of the SVM-Tool, we were not able to successfully integrate the supplementary lexicon.

5.1.1 Refined Tagset

Prepositions are not annotated with case in the Tiger treebank, although this information is important for the disambiguation of the case of the next noun phrase. In order to provide the tagger with some information about the case of prepositions, a second training corpus was created in which prepositions which always select the same case, such as *durch* (through), were annotated with this case (APPR.Acc). Prepositions which select genitive case, but also occur with dative case[8], were tagged with APPR.Gen. The more frequent ones of the remaining prepositions, such as *in* (in), were lexicalized (APPR.in). The refined tagset also distinguished between the auxiliaries *sein*, *haben*, and *werden*, and used lexicalized tags for the coordinating conjunctions *aber*, *doch*, *denn*, *wie*, *bis*, *noch*, and *als* whose distribution differs from the distribution of prototypical coordinating conjunctions such as *und* (and) or *oder* (or).

For evaluation purposes, the refined tags are mapped back to the original tags. This mapping is unambiguous.

[7] It was planned to include also the Stanford tagger (Toutanova et al., 2003) in this comparison, but it was not possible to train it on the Tiger data.

[8] In German, the genitive case of arguments is more and more replaced by the dative.

tagger	default	refined	ref.+lexicon
baseline	67.3	67.3	69.4
TnT	86.3	86.9	90.4
SVMTool	86.6	86.6	–
2 tags	87.0	87.9	91.5
10 tags	87.6	88.5	92.2

Table 2: Tagging accuracies on development data in percent. Results for 2 and for 10 preceding POS tags as context are reported for our tagger.

5.1.2 Results

Table 2 summarizes the results obtained with different taggers and tagsets on the development data. The accuracy of a baseline tagger which chooses the most probable tag[9] ignoring the context is 67.3% without and 69.4% with the supplementary lexicon.

The TnT tagger achieves 86.3% accuracy on the default tagset. A tag is considered correct if all attributes are correct. The tagset refinement increases the accuracy by about 0.6%, and the external lexicon by another 3.5%.

The SVMTool is slightly better than the TnT tagger on the default tagset, but shows little improvement from the tagset refinement. Apparently, the lexical features used by the SVMTool encode most of the information of the tagset refinement.

With a context of two preceding POS tags (similar to the trigram tagger TnT), our tagger outperforms TnT by 0.7% on the default tagset, by 1% on the refined tagset, and by 1.1% on the refined tagset plus the additional lexicon. A larger context of up to 10 preceding POS tags further increased the accuracy by 0.6, 0.6, and 0.7%, respectively.

	default	refined	ref.+lexicon
TnT STTS	97.28		
TnT Tiger	97.17	97.26	97.51
10 tags	97.39	97.57	97.97

Table 3: STTS accuracies of the TnT tagger trained on the STTS tagset, the TnT tagger trained on the Tiger tagset, and our tagger trained on the Tiger tagset.

These figures are considerably lower than e.g. the 96.7% accuracy reported in Brants (2000) for the Negra treebank which is annotated with STTS tags without agreement features. This is to be expected, however, because the STTS tagset is much smaller. Table 3 shows the results of an evaluation based on the plain STTS tagset. The first result was obtained with TnT trained on Tiger data which was mapped to STTS before. The second row contains the results for the TnT tagger when it is trained on the Tiger data and the output is mapped to STTS. The third row gives the corresponding figures for our tagger.

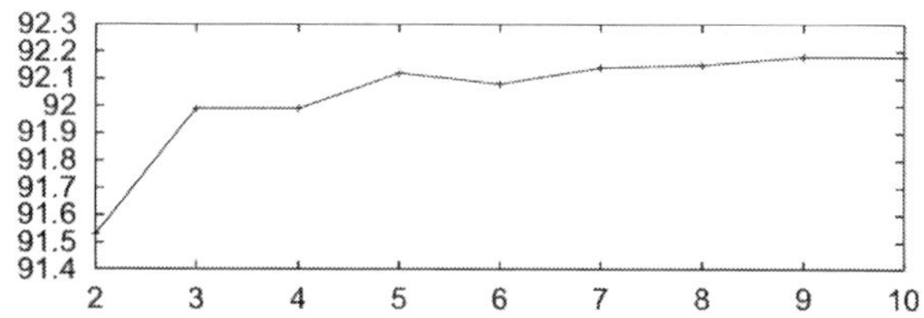

Figure 2: Tagging accuracy on development data depending on context size

Figure 2 shows that the tagging accuracy tends to increase with the context size. The best results are obtained with a context size of 10. What type of information is relevant across a distance of ten words? A good example is the decision tree for the attribute *first person* of finite verbs, which looks for a first person pronoun at positions -1 through -10 (relative to the position of the current word) in this order. Since German is a verb-final language, these tests clearly make sense.

Table 4 shows the performance on the test data. Our tagger was used with a context size of 10. The suffix length parameter of the TnT tagger was set to 6 without lexicon and to 3 with lexicon. These values were optimal on the development data. The accuracy of our tagger is lower than on the development data. This could be due to the higher rate of unknown words (10.0% vs. 7.7%). Relative to the TnT tagger, however, the accuracy is quite similar for test and development data. The differences between the two taggers are significant.[10]

tagger	default	refined	ref.+lexicon
TnT	83.45	84.11	89.14
our tagger	85.00	85.92	91.07

Table 4: Tagging accuracies on test data.

By far the most frequent tagging error was the confusion of nominative and accusative case. If

[9] Unknown words are tagged by choosing the most frequent tag of words with the same capitalization.

[10] 726 sentences were better tagged by TnT (i.e. with few errors), 1450 sentences were better tagged by our tagger. The resulting score of a binomial test is below 0.001.

this error is not counted, the tagging accuracy on the development data rises from 92.17% to 94.27%.

Our tagger is quite fast, although not as fast as the TnT tagger. With a context size of 3 (10), it annotates 7000 (2000) tokens per second on a computer with an Athlon X2 4600 CPU. The training with a context size of 10 took about 4 minutes.

5.2 Czech Academic Corpus

We also evaluated our tagger on the Czech Academic corpus (Hladká et al., 2007) which contains 652.131 tokens and about 1200 different POS tags. The data was divided into 80% training data, 10% development data and 10% test data.

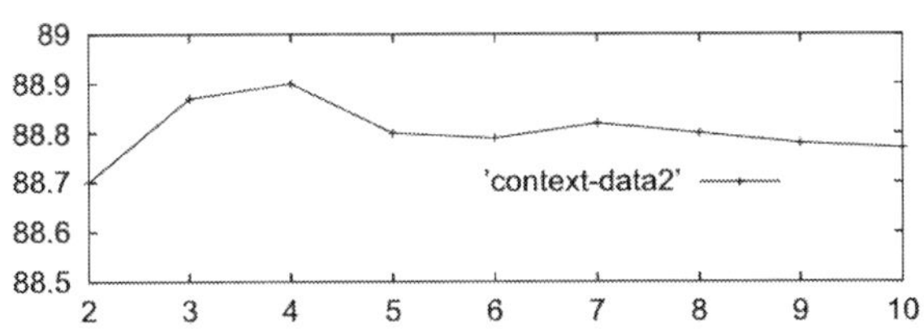

Figure 3: Accuracy on development data depending on context size

The best accuracy of our tagger on the development set was 88.9% obtained with a context of 4 preceding POS tags. The best accuracy of the TnT tagger was 88.2% with a maximal suffix length of 5. The corresponding figures for the test data are 89.53% for our tagger and 88.88% for the TnT tagger. The difference is significant.

6 Discussion

Our tagger combines two ideas, the decomposition of the probability of complex POS tags into a product of feature probabilities, and the estimation of the conditional probabilities with decision trees. A similar idea was previously presented in Kempe (1994), but apparently never applied again. The tagging accuracy reported by Kempe was below that of a traditional trigram tagger. Unlike him, we found that our tagging method out-performed state-of-the-art POS taggers on fine-grained POS tagging even if only a trigram context was used.

Schmid (1994) and Màrquez (1999) used decision trees for the estimation of contextual tag probabilities, but without a decomposition of the tag probability. Magerman (1994) applied probabilistic decision trees to parsing, but not with a generative model.

Provost & Domingos (2003) noted that well-known decision tree induction algorithms such as C4.5 (Quinlan, 1993) or CART (Breiman et al., 1984) fail to produce accurate probability estimates. They proposed to grow the decision trees to their maximal size without pruning, and to smooth the probability estimates with add-1 smoothing (also known as the Laplace correction). Ferri et al. (2003) describe a more complex backoff smoothing method. Contrary to them, we applied pruning and found that some pruning (threshold=6) gives better results than no pruning (threshold=0). Another difference is that we used N two-class trees with normalization to predict the probabilities of N classes. These two-class trees can be pruned with a fixed pruning threshold. Hence there is no need to put aside training data for parameter tuning.

An open question is whether the SVMTool (or other discriminatively trained taggers) could outperform the presented tagger if the same decomposition of POS tags and the same context size was used. We think that this might be the case if the SVM features are restricted to the set of relevant attribute combinations discovered by the decision tree, but we doubt that it is possible to train the SVMTool (or other discriminatively trained taggers) without such a restriction given the difficulties to train it with the standard context size.

Czech POS tagging has been extensively studied in the past (Hajič and Vidová-Hladká, 1998; Hajič et al., 2001; Votrubec, 2006). Spoustov et al. (2007) compared several POS taggers including an n-gram tagger and a discriminatively trained tagger (Morče), and evaluated them on the Prague Dependency Treebank (PDT 2.0). Morče's tagging accuracy was 95.12%, 0.3% better than the n-gram tagger. A hybrid system based on four different tagging methods reached an accuracy of 95.68%. Because of the different corpora used and the different amounts of lexical information available, a direct comparison to our results is difficult. Furthermore, our tagger uses no corpus-specific heuristics, whereas Morče e.g. is optimized for Czech POS tagging.

The German tagging results are, to the best of our knowledge, the first published results for fine-grained POS tagging with the Tiger tagset.

7 Summary

We presented a HMM POS tagger for fine-grained tagsets which splits the POS tags into attribute vectors and estimates the conditional probabilities of the attributes with decision trees. In experiments with German and Czech corpora, this method achieved a higher tagging accuracy than two state-of-the-art general-purpose POS taggers (TnT and SVMTool).

References

Brants, Sabine, Stefanie Dipper, Silvia Hansen, Wolfgang Lezius, and George Smith. 2002. The TIGER treebank. In *Proceedings of the Workshop on Treebanks and Linguistic Theories*, Sozopol.

Brants, Thorsten. 2000. TnT - a statistical part-of-speech tagger. In *Proceedings of the Sixth Applied Natural Language Processing Conference ANLP-2000*, Seattle, WA.

Breiman, L., J. H. Friedman, R. A. Olshen, and C. J. Stone. 1984. *Classification and Regression Trees*. Wadsworth and Brooks, Pacific Grove CA.

Ferri, C., P. Flach, and J. Hernández-Orallo. 2003. Improving the AUC of probabilistic estimators trees. In *Proceedings of 14th European Conference on Machine Learning (ECML'03)*, pages 121–132.

Giménez, Jesús and Lluís Màrquez. 2004. SVMTool: A general POS tagger generator based on support vector machines. In *Proceedings of the IV International Conference on Language Resources and Evaluation (LREC'04)*, pages 43–46, Lisbon, Portugal.

Hajič, Jan and Barbora Vidová-Hladká. 1998. Tagging inflective languages: Prediction of morphological categories for a rich, structured tagset. In *Proceedings of ACL-COLING'98*, Montreal, Canada.

Hajič, Jan, Pavel Krbec, Karel Oliva, Pavel Květoň, and Vladimír Petkevič. 2001. Serial combination of rules and statistics: A case study in czech tagging. In *Proceedings of the 39th Annual Meeting of the ACL*, Toulouse, France.

Hladká, Barbora Vidová, Jan Hajic, Jirí Hana, Jaroslava Hlavácová, Jirí Mírovský, and Jan Votrubec. 2007. *Czech Academic Corpus 1.0 Guide*. Karolinum Press, Prag, Czechia.

Kempe, André. 1994. Probabilistic tagging with feature structures. In *Proceedings of the 15th International Conference on Computational Linguistics (COLING 1994)*, pages 161–165, Kyoto, Japan.

Magerman, David M. 1994. *Natural Language Processing as Statistical Pattern Recognition*. Ph.D. thesis, Stanford University.

Màrquez, Lluís. 1999. *POS Tagging : A Machine Learning Approach based on Decision Trees*. Ph.D. thesis, Dep. LSI, Universitat Politecnica de Catalunya (UPC), Barcelona, Spain, July.

Mingers, John. 1989. An empirical comparison of pruning methods for decision tree induction. *Machine Learning*, 4:227–243.

Provost, Foster and Pedro Domingos. 2003. Tree induction for probability-based ranking. *Machine Learning*, 52(3):199–215.

Quinlan, J. Ross. 1993. *C4.5 : Programs for Machine Learning*. Morgan Kaufmann, San Mateo , CA.

Schmid, Helmut. 1994. Probabilistic part-of-speech tagging using decision trees. In *Proceedings of the International Conference on New Methods in Language Processing*, pages 44–49, Manchester, UK.

Spoustová, Drahomíra, Jan Hajič, Jan Votrubec, Pavel Krbec, and Pavel Květoň. 2007. The best of two worlds: Cooperation of statistical and rule-based taggers for czech. In *Proceedings of the Workshop on Balto-Slavonic Natural Language Processing*, pages 67–74, Prague, Czech Republic, June.

Toutanova, Kristina, Dan Klein, Christopher Manning, and Yoram Singer. 2003. Feature-rich part-of-speech tagging with a cyclic dependency network. In *Proceedings of HLT-NAACL 2003*, pages 252–259, Edmonton, Canada.

Votrubec, Jan. 2006. Morphological tagging based on averaged perceptron. In *Proceedings of the 15th Annual Conference of Doctoral Students (WDS)*, pages 191–195.

Toward a Psycholinguistically-Motivated Model of Language Processing

William Schuler
Computer Science and Engineering
University of Minnesota
schuler@cs.umn.edu

Samir AbdelRahman
Department of Computer Science
Cairo University
s.abdelrahman@fci-cu.edu.eg

Tim Miller
Computer Science and Engineering
University of Minnesota
tmill@cs.umn.edu

Lane Schwartz
Computer Science and Engineering
University of Minnesota
lschwar@cs.umn.edu

Abstract

Psycholinguistic studies suggest a model of human language processing that 1) performs incremental interpretation of spoken utterances or written text, 2) preserves ambiguity by maintaining competing analyses in parallel, and 3) operates within a severely constrained short-term memory store — possibly constrained to as few as four distinct elements. This paper describes a relatively simple model of language as a factored statistical time-series process that meets all three of the above desiderata; and presents corpus evidence that this model is sufficient to parse naturally occurring sentences using human-like bounds on memory.

1 Introduction

Psycholinguistic studies suggest a model of human language processing with three important properties. First, eye-tracking studies (Tanenhaus et al., 1995; Brown-Schmidt et al., 2002) suggest that humans analyze sentences incrementally, assembling and interpreting referential expressions even while they are still being pronounced. Second, humans appear to maintain competing analyses in parallel, with eye gaze showing significant attention to competitors (referents of words with similar prefixes to the correct word), even relatively long after the end of the word has been encountered, when attention to other distractor referents has fallen off (Dahan and Gaskell, 2007). Preserving ambiguity in a parallel, non-deterministic search like this may account for human robustness to missing, unknown, mispronounced, or misspelled words. Finally, studies of short-term memory capacity suggest human language processing operates within a severely constrained short-term memory store — possibly restricted to as few as four distinct elements (Miller, 1956; Cowan, 2001).

The first two observations may be taken to endorse existing probabilistic beam-search models which maintain multiple competing analyses, pruned by contextual preferences and dead ends (e.g. Roark, 2001). But the last observation on memory bounds imposes a restriction that until now has not been evaluated in a corpus study. Can a simple, useful human-like processing model be defined using these constraints? This paper describes a relatively simple model of language as a factored statistical time-series process that meets all three of the above desiderata; and presents corpus evidence that this model is sufficient to parse naturally occurring sentences using human-like bounds on memory.

The remainder of this paper is organized as follows: Section 2 describes some current approaches to incremental parsing; Section 3 describes a statistical framework for parsing using a bounded stack of explicit constituents; Section 4 describes an experiment to estimate the level of coverage of the Penn Treebank corpus that can be achieved with various stack memory limits, using a set of reversible tree transforms, and gives accuracy results of a bounded-memory model trained on this corpus.

2 Background

Much work on cognitive modeling in psycholinguistics is centered on modeling the *concepts* to which utterances refer. Coarsely, these concepts may correspond to activation patterns among neurons in specific regions of the brain. In some theories, a short-term memory store of several unrelated concepts may be retained by organizing the activation of these concepts into compatible patterns, only a few of which can be reliably main-

© 2008. Licensed under the *Creative Commons Attribution-Noncommercial-Share Alike 3.0 Unported* license (http://creativecommons.org/licenses/by-nc-sa/3.0/). Some rights reserved.

tained (Smolensky and Legendre, 2006). Activation is then theorized to spread through and among these groups of concepts in proportion to some learned probability that the concepts will be relevant (Anderson and Reder, 1999), with the most active concepts corresponding to the most likely linguistic analyses. Competition between rival activated groups of concepts (corresponding to incomplete linguistic analyses) has even been linked to reading delays (Hale, 2003).

This competition among mutually-exclusive variously-activated short term memory stores of concepts, essentially a weighted disjunction over conjunctions of concepts, can be modeled in language understanding as simple Viterbi decoding of a factored HMM-like time-series model (Schuler et al., in press). In this model, concepts (corresponding to vectors of individuals in a first-order world model) are introduced and composed (via set operations like intersection) in each hypothesized short-term memory store, using the elements of the memory store as a stack. These vectors of individuals can be considered a special case of vectors of concept elements proposed by Smolensky, with set intersection a special case of tensor product in the composition model. Referents in this kind of incremental model can be constrained by — but still distinguished from — higher-level referents while they are still being recognized.

It is often assumed that this semantic concept composition proceeds isomorphically with the composition of syntactic constituents (Frege, 1892). This parallel semantic and syntactic composition is considered likely to be performed in short-term memory because it has many of the characteristics of short-term memory processes, including nesting limits (Miller and Chomsky, 1963) and susceptibility to degradation due to interruption. Ericsson and Kintch (1995) propose a theory of long-term working memory that extends short-term memory, but only for inter-sentential references, which *do* seem to be retained across interruptions in reading. But while the relationship between competing probability distributions in such a model and experimental reading times has been evaluated (e.g. by Hale), the relationship between the syntactic demands on a short-term memory store and observations of human short-term memory limits is still largely untested. Several models have been proposed to perform syntactic analysis using a bounded memory store.

For example, Marcus (1980) proposed a deterministic parser with an explicit four-element working memory store in order to model human parsing limitations. But this model only stores *complete* constituents (whereas the model proposed in this paper stores *incompletely recognized* constituents, in keeping with the Tanenhaus et al. findings). As a result, the Marcus model relies on a suite of specialized memory operations to compose complete constituents out of complete constituents, which are not independently cognitively motivated.

Cascaded finite-state automata, as in FASTUS (Hobbs et al., 1996), also make use of a bounded stack, but stack levels in such systems are typically dedicated to particular syntactic operations: e.g. a word group level, a phrasal level, and a clausal level. As a result, some amount of constituent structure may overflow its dedicated level, and be sacrificed (for example, prepositional phrase attachment may be left underspecified).

Finite-state equivalent parsers (and thus, bounded-stack parsers) have asymptotically linear run time. Other parsers (Sagae and Lavie, 2005) have achieved linear runtime complexity with unbounded stacks in incremental parsing by using a greedy strategy, pursuing locally most probable shift or reduce operations, conditioned on multiple surrounding words. But without an explicit bounded stack it is difficult to connect these models to concepts in a psycholinguistic model.

Abney and Johnson (1991) explore left-corner parsing as a memory model, but again only in terms of (complete) syntactic constituents. The approach explored here is similar, but the transform is reversed to allow the recognizer to store recognized structure rather than structures being sought, and the transform is somewhat simplified to allow more structure to be introduced into syntactic constituents, primarily motivated by a need to keep track of disconnected semantic concepts rather than syntactic categories. Without this link to disconnected semantic concepts, the syntax model would be susceptible to criticism that the separate memory levels could be simply chunked together through repeated use (Miller, 1956).

Roark's (2001) top-down parser generates trees incrementally in a transformed representation related to that used in this paper, but requires distributions to be maintained over entire trees rather than stack configurations. This increases the beam width necessary to avoid parse failure. Moreover, although the system is conducting a beam search, the objects in this beam are growing, so the recognition complexity is not linear, and the connection to a bounded short-term memory store of unconnected concepts becomes somewhat complicated.

The model described in this paper is arguably simpler than many of the models described above in that it has no constituent-specific mechanisms, yet it is able to recognize the rich syntactic structures found in the Penn Treebank, and is still compatible with the psycholinguistic notion of a bounded short-term memory store of conceptual referents.

3 Bounded-Memory Parsing with a Time Series Model

This section describes a basic statistical framework — a factored time-series model — for recognizing hierarchic structures using a bounded store of memory elements, each with a finite number of states, at each time step. Unlike simple FSA compilation, this model maintains an explicit representation of active, incomplete phrase structure constituents on a bounded stack, so it can be readily extended with additional variables that depend on syntax (e.g. to track hypothesized entities or relations). These incomplete constituents are related to ordinary phrase structure annotations through a series of bidirectional tree transforms. These transforms:

1. binarize phrase structure trees into linguistically motivated head-modifier branches (described in Section 3.1);
2. transform right-branching sequences to left-branching sequences (described in Section 3.2); and
3. align transformed trees to an array of random variable values at each depth and time step of a probabilistic time-series model (described in Section 3.3).

Following these transforms, a model can be trained from example trees, then run as a parser on unseen sentences. The transforms can then be reversed to evaluate the output of the parser. This representation will ultimately be used to evaluate the coverage of a bounded-memory model on a large corpus of tree-annotated sentences, and to evaluate the accuracy of a basic (unsmoothed, unlexicalized) implementation of this model in Section 4.

It is important to note that these transformations are not postulated to be part of the human recognition process. In this model, sentences can be recognized and interpreted entirely in right-corner form. The transforms only serve to connect this process to familiar representations of phrase structure.

3.1 Binary branching structure

This paper will attempt to draw conclusions about the syntactic complexity of natural language, in terms of stack memory requirements in incremental (left-to-right) recognition. These requirements will be minimized by recognizing trees in a *right-corner* form, which accounts partially recognized phrases and clauses as *incomplete constituents*, lacking one instance of another constituent yet to come.

In particular, this study will use the trees in the Penn Treebank Wall Street Journal (WSJ) corpus (Marcus et al., 1994) as a data set. In order to obtain a linguistically plausible right-corner transform representation of incomplete constituents, the corpus is subjected to another, pre-process transform to introduce binary-branching nonterminal projections, and fold empty categories into nonterminal symbols in a manner similar to that proposed by Johnson (1998b) and Klein and Manning (2003). This binarization is done in such a way as to preserve linguistic intuitions of head projection, so that the depth requirements of right-corner transformed trees will be reasonable approximations to the working memory requirements of a human reader or listener.

3.2 Right-Corner Transform

Phrase structure trees are recognized in this framework in a *right-corner* form that can be mapped to and from ordinary phrase structure via reversible transform rules, similar to those described by Johnson (1998a). This transformed grammar constrains memory usage in left-to-right traversal to a bound consistent with the psycholinguistic results described above.

This right-corner transform is simply the left-right dual of a left-corner transform (Johnson, 1998a). It transforms all right branching sequences in a phrase structure tree into left branching sequences of symbols of the form A_1/A_2, denoting an incomplete instance of category A_1 lacking an instance of category A_2 to the right. These incomplete constituent categories have the same form

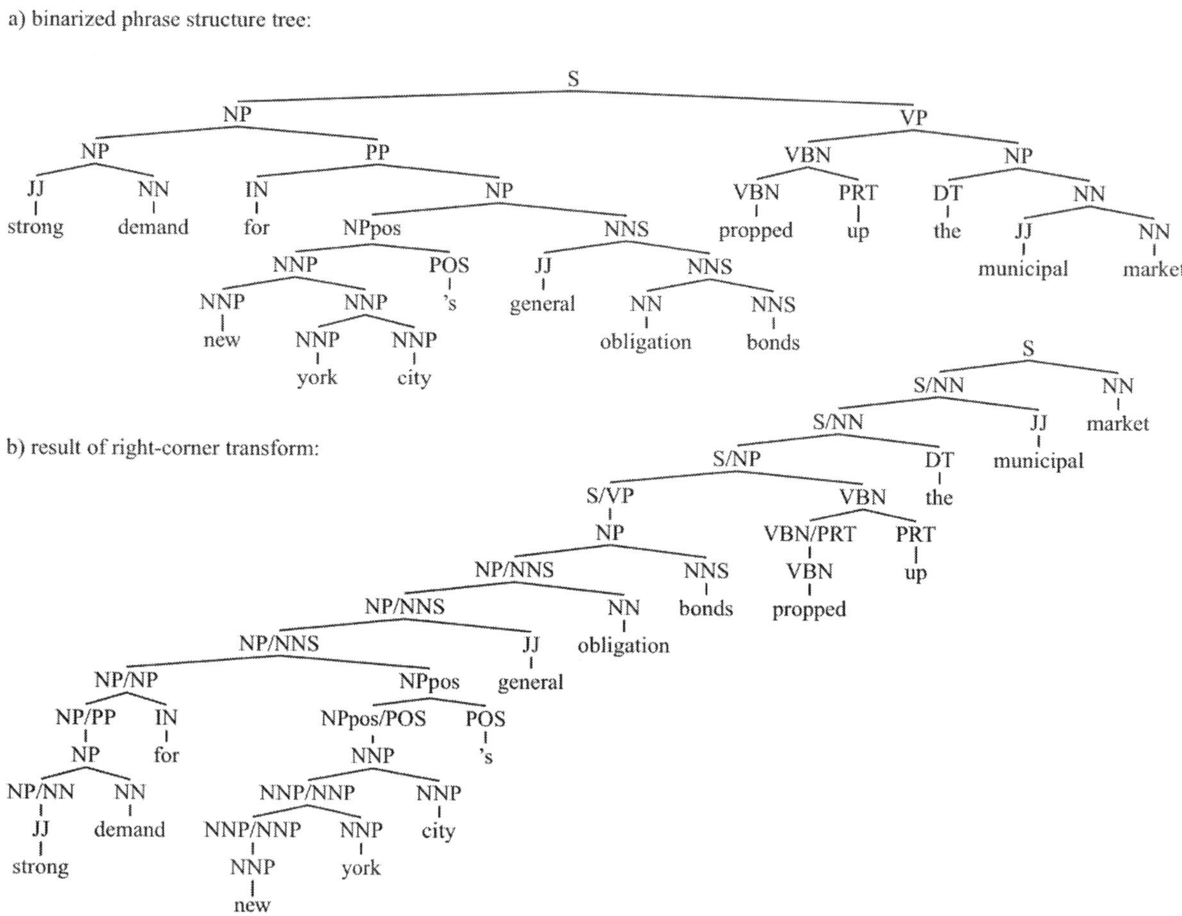

Figure 1: Trees resulting from a) a binarization of a sample phrase structure tree for the sentence *Strong demand for New York City's general obligations bonds propped up the municipal market,* and b) a right-corner transform of this binarized tree.

and much of the same meaning as non-constituent categories in a Combinatorial Categorial Grammar (Steedman, 2000).

Rewrite rules for the right-corner transform are shown below, first to flatten out right-branching structure:[1]

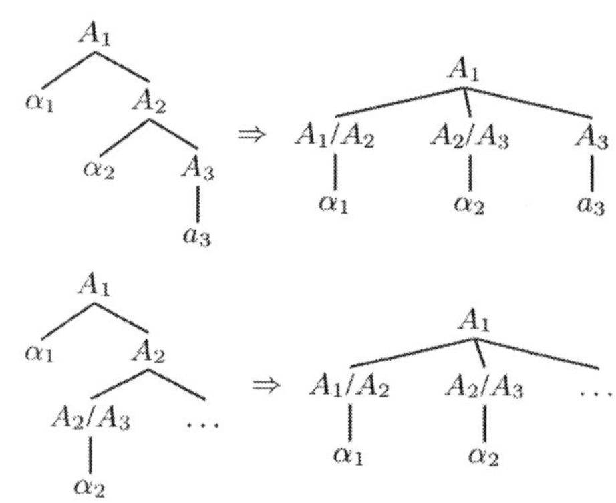

then to replace it with left-branching structure:

[1]The tree transforms presented in this paper will be defined in terms of *destructive rewrite rules* applied iteratively to each constituent of a source tree, from leaves to root, and from left to right among siblings, to derive a target tree. These rewrites are ordered; when multiple rewrite rules apply to the same constituent, the later rewrites are applied to the results of the earlier ones. For example, the rewrite:

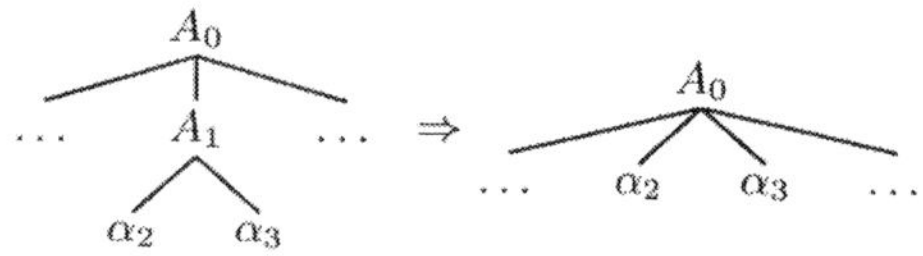

could be used to iteratively eliminate all binary-branching nonterminal nodes in a tree, except the root. In the notation used in this paper, Roman uppercase letters (A_i) are variables matching constituent labels, Roman lowercase letters (a_i) are variables matching terminal symbols, Greek lowercase letters (α_i) are variables matching entire subtree structure, Roman letters followed by colons, followed by Greek letters (A_i:α_i) are variables matching the label and structure, respectively, of the same subtree, and ellipses (...) are taken to match zero or more subtree structures, preserving the order of ellipses in cases where there are more than one (as in the rewrite shown above).

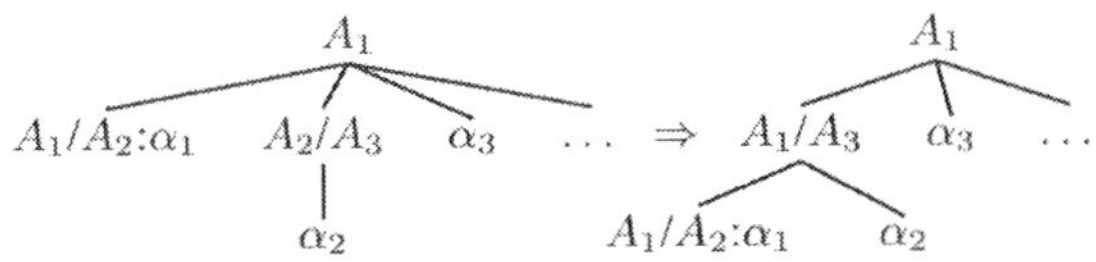

Here, the first two rewrite rules are applied iteratively (bottom-up on the tree) to flatten all right branching structure, using incomplete constituents to record the original nonterminal ordering. The third rule is then applied to generate left-branching structure, preserving this ordering. Note that the last rewrite above leaves a unary branch at the leftmost child of each flattened node. This preserves the nodes at which the original tree was not right-branching, so the original tree can be reconstructed when the right-corner transform concatenates multiple right-branching sequences into a single left-branching sequence.

An example of a right-corner transformed tree is shown in Figure 1(b). An important property of this transform is that it is reversible. Rewrite rules for reversing a right-corner transform are simply the converse of those shown above. The correctness of this can be demonstrated by dividing a tree into maximal sequences of right branches (that is, maximal sequences of adjacent right children). The first two 'flattening' rewrites of the right-corner transform, applied to any such sequence, will replace the right-branching nonterminal nodes with a flat sequence of nodes labeled with slash categories, which preserves the order of the nonterminal category symbols in the original nodes. Reversing this rewrite will therefore generate the original sequence of nonterminal nodes. The final rewrite similarly preserves the order of these nonterminal symbols while grouping them from the left to the right, so reversing this rewrite will reproduce the original version of the flattened tree.

3.3 Hierarchic Hidden Markov Models

Right-corner transformed phrase structure trees can then be mapped to random variable positions in a Hierarchic Hidden Markov Model (Murphy and Paskin, 2001), essentially a Hidden Markov Model (HMM) factored into some fixed number of stack levels at each time step.

HMMs characterize speech or text as a sequence of hidden states q_t (in this case, stacked-up syntactic categories) and observed states o_t (in this case, words) at corresponding time steps t. A most likely sequence of hidden states $\hat{q}_{1..T}$ can then be hypothesized given any sequence of observed states $o_{1..T}$, using Bayes' Law (Equation 2) and Markov independence assumptions (Equation 3) to define a full $\mathsf{P}(q_{1..T} \mid o_{1..T})$ probability as the product of a *Transition Model* (Θ_A) prior probability $\mathsf{P}(q_{1..T}) \stackrel{\text{def}}{=} \prod_t \mathsf{P}_{\Theta_A}(q_t \mid q_{t-1})$ and an *Observation Model* (Θ_B) likelihood probability $\mathsf{P}(o_{1..T} \mid q_{1..T}) \stackrel{\text{def}}{=} \prod_t \mathsf{P}_{\Theta_B}(o_t \mid q_t)$:

$$\hat{q}_{1..T} = \underset{q_{1..T}}{\text{argmax}}\, \mathsf{P}(q_{1..T} \mid o_{1..T}) \quad (1)$$

$$= \underset{q_{1..T}}{\text{argmax}}\, \mathsf{P}(q_{1..T}) \cdot \mathsf{P}(o_{1..T} \mid q_{1..T}) \quad (2)$$

$$\stackrel{\text{def}}{=} \underset{q_{1..T}}{\text{argmax}} \prod_{t=1}^{T} \mathsf{P}_{\Theta_A}(q_t \mid q_{t-1}) \cdot \mathsf{P}_{\Theta_B}(o_t \mid q_t) \quad (3)$$

Transition probabilities $\mathsf{P}_{\Theta_A}(q_t \mid q_{t-1})$ over complex hidden states q_t can be modeled using synchronized levels of stacked-up component HMMs in a Hierarchic Hidden Markov Model (HHMM) (Murphy and Paskin, 2001). HHMM transition probabilities are calculated in two phases: a *reduce* phase (resulting in an intermediate, marginalized state f_t), in which component HMMs may terminate; and a *shift* phase (resulting in a modeled state q_t), in which unterminated HMMs transition, and terminated HMMs are re-initialized from their parent HMMs. Variables over intermediate f_t and modeled q_t states are factored into sequences of depth-specific variables – one for each of D levels in the HMM hierarchy:

$$f_t = \langle f_t^1 \ldots f_t^D \rangle \quad (4)$$

$$q_t = \langle q_t^1 \ldots q_t^D \rangle \quad (5)$$

Transition probabilities are then calculated as a product of transition probabilities at each level, using level-specific *reduce* Θ_R and *shift* Θ_S models:

$$\mathsf{P}_{\Theta_A}(q_t | q_{t-1}) = \sum_{f_t} \mathsf{P}(f_t | q_{t-1}) \cdot \mathsf{P}(q_t | f_t\, q_{t-1}) \quad (6)$$

$$\stackrel{\text{def}}{=} \sum_{f_t^{1..D}} \prod_{d=1}^{D} \mathsf{P}_{\Theta_R}(f_t^d | f_t^{d+1} q_{t-1}^d q_{t-1}^{d-1}) \cdot \mathsf{P}_{\Theta_S}(q_t^d | f_t^{d+1} f_t^d\, q_{t-1}^d q_t^{d-1}) \quad (7)$$

with f_t^{D+1} and q_t^0 defined as constants. In Viterbi decoding, the sums are replaced with argmax operators. This decoding process preserves ambiguity by maintaining competing analyses of the entire memory store. A graphical representation of an HHMM with three levels is shown in Figure 3.

Shift and reduce probabilities can then be defined in terms of finitely recursive Finite State Automata (FSAs) with probability distributions over

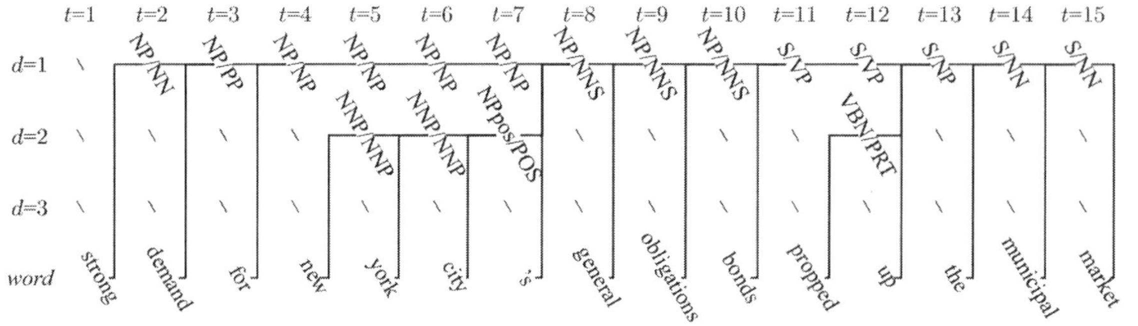

Figure 2: Sample tree from Figure 1 mapped to q_t^d variable positions of an HHMM at each stack depth d (vertical) and time step t (horizontal). This tree uses only two levels of stack memory. Values for final-state variables f_t^d are not shown. Note that some nonterminal labels have been omitted; labels for these nodes can be reconstructed from their children.

transition, recursive expansion, and final-state status of states at each hierarchy level. In simple HHMMs, each intermediate variable is a boolean variable over final-state status $f_t^d \in \{\mathbf{0}, \mathbf{1}\}$ and each modeled state variable is a syntactic, lexical, or phonetic state q_t^d. The intermediate variable f_t^d is true or false (equal to $\mathbf{1}$ or $\mathbf{0}$ respectively) according to $\Theta_{\text{F-Reduce}}$ if there is a transition at the level immediately below d, and false (equal to $\mathbf{0}$) with probability 1 otherwise:[2]

$$\mathsf{P}_{\Theta_\text{R}}(f_t^d \mid f_t^{d+1} q_{t-1}^d q_{t-1}^{d-1}) \stackrel{\text{def}}{=} \begin{cases} \text{if } f_t^{d+1}{=}\mathbf{0} : [f_t^d{=}\mathbf{0}] \\ \text{if } f_t^{d+1}{=}\mathbf{1} : \mathsf{P}_{\Theta_{\text{F-Reduce}}}(f_t^d \mid q_{t-1}^d, q_{t-1}^{d-1}) \end{cases} \quad (8)$$

where $f_t^{D+1} = \mathbf{1}$ and $q_t^0 = \mathbf{ROOT}$.

Shift probabilities over the modeled variable q_t^d at each level are defined using level-specific transition $\Theta_{\text{Q-Trans}}$ and expansion $\Theta_{\text{Q-Expand}}$ models:

$$\mathsf{P}_{\Theta_\text{S}}(q_t^d \mid f_t^{d+1} f_t^d\, q_{t-1}^d q_t^{d-1}) \stackrel{\text{def}}{=} \begin{cases} \text{if } f_t^{d+1}{=}\mathbf{0},\ f_t^d{=}\mathbf{0} : [q_t^d{=}q_{t-1}^d] \\ \text{if } f_t^{d+1}{=}\mathbf{1},\ f_t^d{=}\mathbf{0} : \mathsf{P}_{\Theta_{\text{Q-Trans}}}(q_t^d \mid q_{t-1}^d q_t^{d-1}) \\ \text{if } f_t^{d+1}{=}\mathbf{1},\ f_t^d{=}\mathbf{1} : \mathsf{P}_{\Theta_{\text{Q-Expand}}}(q_t^d \mid q_t^{d-1}) \end{cases} \quad (9)$$

where $f_t^{D+1} = \mathbf{1}$ and $q_t^0 = \mathbf{ROOT}$. This model is conditioned on final-state switching variables at and immediately below the current FSA level. If there is no final state immediately below the current level (the first case above), it deterministically copies the current FSA state forward to the next time step. If there is a final state immediately below the current level (the second case above), it transitions the FSA state at the current level, according to the distribution $\Theta_{\text{Q-Trans}}$. And if the state at the current level is final (the third case above), it re-initializes this state given the state at the level above, according to the distribution $\Theta_{\text{Q-Expand}}$. The overall effect is that higher-level FSAs are allowed to transition only when lower-level FSAs terminate. An HHMM therefore behaves like a probabilistic implementation of a pushdown automaton (or shift–reduce parser) with a finite stack, where the maximum stack depth is equal to the number of levels in the HHMM hierarchy.

[2]Here $[\cdot]$ is an indicator function: $[\phi] = 1$ if ϕ is true, 0 otherwise.

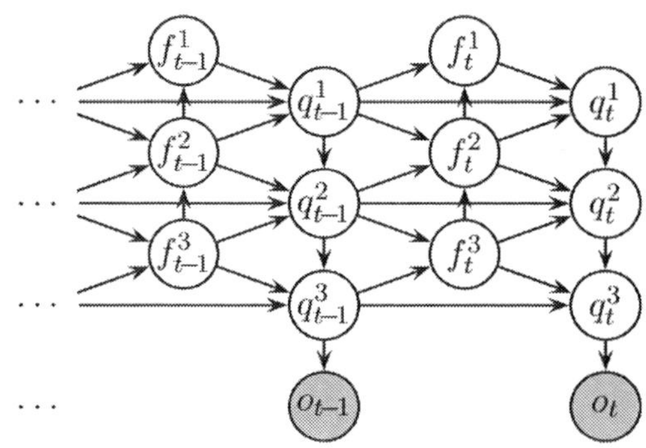

Figure 3: Graphical representation of a Hierarchic Hidden Markov Model. Circles denote random variables, and edges denote conditional dependencies. Shaded circles are observations.

Figure 2 shows the transformed tree from Figure 1 aligned to HHMM depth levels and time steps. Because it uses a bounded stack, recognition in this model is asymptotically linear (Murphy and Paskin, 2001).

This model recognizes right-corner transformed trees constrained to a stack depth corresponding to observed human short term memory limits. This

HHMM depth limit	sentences	coverage
no memory	127	0.32%
1 memory element	3,496	8.78%
2 memory elements	25,909	65.05%
3 memory elements	38,902	97.67%
4 memory elements	39,816	99.96%
5 memory elements	39,832	100.00%
TOTAL	39,832	100.00%

Table 1: Percent coverage of right-corner transformed treebank sections 2–21 with punctuation omitted, using HHMMs with depth limits D from zero to five.

is an attractive model of human language processing because the incomplete syntactic constituents it stores at each stack depth can be directly associated with (incomplete) semantic referents, e.g. by adding random variables over environment or discourse referents at each depth and time step. If these referents are calculated incrementally, recognition decisions can be informed by the values of these variables in an interactive model of language, following Tanenhaus et al. (1995). The corpus results described in the next section suggest that a large majority of naturally occurring sentences can be recognized using only three or four stack memory elements via this transform.

4 Empirical Results

In order to evaluate the coverage of this bounded-memory model, Sections 2–21 of the Penn Treebank WSJ corpus were transformed and mapped to HHMM variables as described in Section 3.3. In order to counter possible undesirable effects of an arbitrary branching analysis of punctuation, punctuation was removed. Coverage results on this corpus are shown in Table 1.

Experiments training on transformed trees from Sections 2–21 of the WSJ Treebank, evaluating reversed-transformed output sequences from Section 22 (development set) and Section 23 (test set), show an accuracy (F score) of 82.1% and 80.1% respectively.[3] Although they are lower than those for state-of-the-art parsers, these results suggest that the bounded-memory parser described here is doing a reasonably good job of modeling syntactic dependencies, and therefore may have some promise as a psycholinguistic model.

Although recognition in this system is linear, it essentially works top-down, so it has larger run-time constants than a bottom-up CKY-style parser. The experimental system described above runs at a rate of about 1 sentence per second on a 64-bit 2.6GHz dual core desktop with a beam width of 2000. In comparison, the Klein and Manning (2003) CKY-style parser runs at about 5 sentences per second on the same machine. On sentences longer than 40 words, the HHMM and CKY-style parsers are roughly equivalent, parsing at the rate of .21 sentences per second, versus .24 for the Klein and Manning CKY.

But since it is linear, the HHMM parser can be directly integrated with end-of-sentence detection (e.g. deciding whether '.' is a sentence delimiter based on whether the words preceding it can be reduced as a sentence), or with n-gram language models (if words are observations, this is simply an autoregressive HMM topology). The use of an explicit constituent structure in a time series model also allows integration with models of dynamic phenomena such as semantics and coreference which may depend on constituency. Finally, as a linear model, it can be directly applied to speech recognition (essentially replacing the hidden layer of a conventional word-based HMM language model).

5 Conclusion

This paper has described a basic incremental parsing model that achieves worst-case linear time complexity by enforcing fixed limits on a stack of explicit (albeit incomplete) constituents. Initial results show a use of only three to four levels of stack memory within this framework provides nearly complete coverage of the large Penn Treebank corpus.

Acknowledgments

The authors would like to thank the anonymous reviewers for their input. This research was supported by National Science Foundation CAREER/PECASE award 0447685. The views expressed are not necessarily endorsed by the sponsors.

[3]Using unsmoothed relative frequency estimates from the training set, a depth limit of $D = 3$, beam with of 2000, and no lexicalization.

References

Abney, Steven P. and Mark Johnson. 1991. Memory requirements and local ambiguities of parsing strategies. *J. Psycholinguistic Research*, 20(3):233–250.

Anderson, J.R. and L.M. Reder. 1999. The fan effect: New results and new theories. *Journal of Experimental Psychology: General*, 128(2):186–197.

Brown-Schmidt, Sarah, Ellen Campana, and Michael K. Tanenhaus. 2002. Reference resolution in the wild: Online circumscription of referential domains in a natural interactive problem-solving task. In *Proceedings of the 24th Annual Meeting of the Cognitive Science Society*, pages 148–153, Fairfax, VA, August.

Cowan, Nelson. 2001. The magical number 4 in short-term memory: A reconsideration of mental storage capacity. *Behavioral and Brain Sciences*, 24:87–185.

Dahan, Delphine and M. Gareth Gaskell. 2007. The temporal dynamics of ambiguity resolution: Evidence from spoken-word recognition. *Journal of Memory and Language*, 57(4):483–501.

Ericsson, K. Anders and Walter Kintsch. 1995. Long-term working memory. *Psychological Review*, 102:211–245.

Frege, Gottlob. 1892. Uber sinn und bedeutung. *Zeitschrift fur Philosophie und Philosophischekritik*, 100:25–50.

Hale, John. 2003. *Grammar, Uncertainty and Sentence Processing*. Ph.D. thesis, Cognitive Science, The Johns Hopkins University.

Hobbs, Jerry R., Douglas E. Appelt, John Bear, David Israel, Megumi Kameyama, Mark Stickel, and Mabry Tyson. 1996. Fastus: A cascaded finite-state transducer for extracting information from natural-language text. In *Finite State Devices for Natural Language Processing*, pages 383–406. MIT Press, Cambridge, MA.

Johnson, Mark. 1998a. Finite state approximation of constraint-based grammars using left-corner grammar transforms. In *Proceedings of COLING/ACL*, pages 619–623.

Johnson, Mark. 1998b. PCFG models of linguistic tree representation. *Computational Linguistics*, 24:613–632.

Klein, Dan and Christopher D. Manning. 2003. Accurate unlexicalized parsing. In *Proceedings of the 41st Annual Meeting of the Association for Computational Linguistics*, pages 423–430.

Marcus, Mitchell P., Beatrice Santorini, and Mary Ann Marcinkiewicz. 1994. Building a large annotated corpus of English: the Penn Treebank. *Computational Linguistics*, 19(2):313–330.

Marcus, Mitch. 1980. *A theory of syntactic recognition for natural language*. MIT Press.

Miller, George and Noam Chomsky. 1963. Finitary models of language users. In Luce, R., R. Bush, and E. Galanter, editors, *Handbook of Mathematical Psychology*, volume 2, pages 419–491. John Wiley.

Miller, George A. 1956. The magical number seven, plus or minus two: Some limits on our capacity for processing information. *Psychological Review*, 63:81–97.

Murphy, Kevin P. and Mark A. Paskin. 2001. Linear time inference in hierarchical HMMs. In *Proc. NIPS*, pages 833–840.

Roark, Brian. 2001. Probabilistic top-down parsing and language modeling. *Computational Linguistics*, 27(2):249–276.

Sagae, Kenji and Alon Lavie. 2005. A classifier-based parser with linear run-time complexity. In *Proceedings of the Ninth International Workshop on Parsing Technologies (IWPT'05)*.

Schuler, William, Stephen Wu, and Lane Schwartz. in press. A framework for fast incremental interpretation during speech decoding. *Computational Linguistics*.

Smolensky, Paul and Géraldine Legendre. 2006. *The Harmonic Mind: From Neural Computation to Optimality-Theoretic GrammarVolume I: Cognitive Architecture*. MIT Press.

Steedman, Mark. 2000. *The syntactic process*. MIT Press/Bradford Books, Cambridge, MA.

Tanenhaus, Michael K., Michael J. Spivey-Knowlton, Kathy M. Eberhard, and Julie E. Sedivy. 1995. Integration of visual and linguistic information in spoken language comprehension. *Science*, 268:1632–1634.

Metric Learning for Synonym Acquisition

Nobuyuki Shimizu
Information Technology Center
University of Tokyo
shimizu@r.dl.itc.u-tokyo.ac.jp

Masato Hagiwara
Graduate School of Information Science
Nagoya University
hagiwara@kl.i.is.nagoya-u.ac.jp

Yasuhiro Ogawa and **Katsuhiko Toyama**
Graduate School of Information Science
Nagoya University
{yasuhiro,toyama}@kl.i.is.nagoya-u.ac.jp

Hiroshi Nakagawa
Information Technology Center
University of Tokyo
n3@dl.itc.u-tokyo.ac.jp

Abstract

The distance or similarity metric plays an important role in many natural language processing (NLP) tasks. Previous studies have demonstrated the effectiveness of a number of metrics such as the Jaccard coefficient, especially in synonym acquisition. While the existing metrics perform quite well, to further improve performance, we propose the use of a supervised machine learning algorithm that fine-tunes them. Given the known instances of similar or dissimilar words, we estimated the parameters of the Mahalanobis distance. We compared a number of metrics in our experiments, and the results show that the proposed metric has a higher mean average precision than other metrics.

1 Introduction

Accurately estimating the semantic distance between words in context has applications for machine translation, information retrieval (IR), speech recognition, and text categorization (Budanitsky and Hirst, 2006), and it is becoming clear that a combination of corpus statistics can be used with a dictionary, thesaurus, or other knowledge source such as WordNet or Wikipedia, to increase the accuracy of semantic distance estimation (Mohammad and Hirst, 2006). Although compiling such resources is labor intensive and achieving wide coverage is difficult, these resources to some extent explicitly capture semantic structures of concepts and words. In contrast, corpus statistics achieve wide coverage, but the semantic structure of a concept is only implicitly represented in the context. Assuming that two words are semantically closer if they occur in similar contexts, statistics on the contexts of words can be gathered and compared for similarity, by using a metric such as the Jaccard coefficient.

Our proposal is to extend and fine-tune the latter approach with the training data obtained from the former. We apply metric learning to this task. Although still in their infancy, distance metric learning methods have undergone rapid development in the field of machine learning. In a setting similar to semi-supervised clustering, where known instances of similar or dissimilar objects are given, a metric such as the Mahalanobis distance can be learned from a few data points and tailored to fit a particular purpose. Although classification methods such as logistic regression now play important roles in natural language processing, the use of metric learning has yet to be explored.

Since popular current methods for synonym acquisition require no statistical learning, it seems that supervised machine learning should easily outperform them. Unfortunately, there are obstacles to overcome. Since metric learning algorithms usually learn the parameters of a Mahalanobis distance, the number of parameters is quadratic to the number of features. They learn how two features should interact to produce the final metric. While traditional metrics forgo examining of the interactions entirely, in applying metrics such as Jaccard coefficient, it is not uncommon nowadays to use more than 10,000 features, a number that a typical metric learner is incapable of processing. Thus we have two options: one is to find the most important features and model the interactions between

©2008. Licensed under the *Creative Commons Attribution-Noncommercial-Share Alike 3.0 Unported* license (http://creativecommons.org/licenses/by-nc-sa/3.0/). Some rights reserved.

them, and the other is simply to use a large number of features. We experimentally examined the two options and found that metric learning is useful in synonym acquisition, despite it utilizing fewer features than traditional methods.

The remainder of this paper is organized as follows: in section 2, we review prior work on synonym acquisition and metric learning. In section 3, we introduce the Mahalanobis distance metric and a learning algorithm based on this metric. In section 4 and 5, we explain the experimental settings and propose the use of normalization to make the Mahalanobis distances work in practice, and then in section 6, we discuss issues we encountered when applying this metric to synonym acquisition. We conclude in section 7.

2 Prior Work

As this paper is based on two different lines of research, we first review the work in synonym acquisition, and then review the work in generic metric learning. To the best of the authors' knowledge, none of the metric learning algorithms have been applied to automatic synonym acquisition.

Synonym relation is important lexical knowledge for many natural language processing tasks including automatic thesaurus construction (Croach and Yang, 1992; Grefenstette, 1994) and IR (Jing and Croft, 1994). Various methods (Hindle, 1990; Lin, 1998) of automatically acquiring synonyms have been proposed. They are usually based on the distributional hypothesis (Harris, 1985), which states that semantically similar words share similar contexts, and they can be roughly viewed as the combinations of two steps: context extraction and similarity calculation. The former extracts useful features from the contexts of words, such as surrounding words or dependency structure. The latter calculates how semantically similar two given words are based on similarity or distance metrics.

Many studies (Lee, 1999; Curran and Moens, 2002; Weeds et al., 2004) have investigated similarity calculation, and a variety of distance/similarity measures have already been compared and discussed. Weeds et al.'s work is especially useful because it investigated the characteristics of metrics based on a few criteria such as the relative frequency of acquired synonyms and clarified the correlation between word frequency, distributional generality, and semantic generality. However, all of the existing research conducted only a posteriori comparison, and as Weeds et al. pointed out, there is no one best measure for all applications. Therefore, the metrics must be tailored to applications, even to corpora and other settings.

We next review the prior work in generic metric learning. Most previous metric learning methods learn the parameters of the Mahalanobis distance. Although the algorithms proposed in earlier work (Xing et al., 2002; Weinberger et al., 2005; Globerson and Roweis, 2005) were shown to yield excellent classification performance, these algorithms all have worse than cubic computational complexity in the dimensionality of the data. Because of the high dimensionality of our objects, we opted for information-theoretic metric learning proposed by (Davis et al., 2007). This algorithm only uses an operation quadratic in the dimensionality of the data.

Other work on learning Mahalanobis metrics includes online metric learning (Shalev-Shwartz et al., 2004), locally-adaptive discriminative methods (Hastie and Tibshirani, 1996), and learning from relative comparisons (Schutz and Joahims, 2003). Non-Mahalanobis-based metric learning methods have also been proposed, though they seem to suffer from suboptimal performance, non-convexity, or computational complexity. Examples include neighborhood component analysis (Goldberger et al., 2004).

3 Metric Learning

3.1 Problem Formulation

To set the context for metric learning, we first describe the objects whose distances from one another we would like to know. As noted above regarding the distributional hypothesis, our object is the context of a target word. To represent the context, we use a sparse vector in R^d. Each dimension of an input vector represents a feature of the context, and its value corresponds to the strength of the association. The vectors of two target words represent their contexts as points in multidimensional feature-space. A suitable metric (for example, Euclidean) defines the distance between the two points, thereby estimating the semantic distance between the target words.

Given points $x_i, x_j \in R^d$, the (squared) Mahalanobis distance between them is parameterized by a positive definite matrix A as follows $d_A(x_i, x_j) = (x_i - x_j)^\top A(x_i - x_j)$. The Mahalanobis distance is a straightforward extension of the standard Euclidean distance. If we let A be the identity matrix, the Mahalanobis distance reduces to the Euclidean distance. Our objective is to obtain the positive definite matrix A that parameterizes the Mahalanobis distance, so that the distance between the vectors of two synonymous words is small, and the distance between the vectors of two dissimilar words is large. Stated more formally, the Mahalanobis distance between two similar points must be smaller than a given upper bound, i.e., $d_A(x_i, x_j) \leq u$ for a relatively small value of u. Similarly, two points are dissimilar if $d_A(x_i, x_j) \geq l$ for sufficiently large l.

As we discuss below, we were able to use the Euclidean distance to acquire synonyms quite well. Therefore, we would like the positive definite matrix A of the Mahalanobis distance to be close to the identity matrix I. This keeps the Mahalanobis distance similar to the Euclidean distance, which would help to prevent overfitting the data. To optimize the matrix, we follow the information theoretic metric learning approach described in (Davis et al., 2007). We summarize the problem formulation advocated by this approach in this section and the learning algorithm in the next section.

To define the closeness between A and I, we use a simple bijection (up to a scaling function) from the set of Mahalanobis distances to the set of equal mean multivariate Gaussian distributions. Without loss of generalization, let the equal mean be μ. Then given a Mahalanobis distance parameterized by A, the corresponding Gaussian is $p(x; A) = \frac{1}{Z}\exp(-\frac{1}{2}d_A(x, \mu))$ where Z is the normalizing factor. This enables us to measure the distance between two Mahalanobis distances with the Kullback-Leibler (KL) divergence of two Gaussians:

$$KL(p(x; I)||p(x; A)) = \int p(x, I) \log\left(\frac{p(x; I)}{p(x; A)}\right) dx.$$

Given pairs of similar points S and pairs of dissimilar points D, the optimization problem is:

$$\begin{array}{lll} \min_A & KL(p(x; I)||p(x; A)) & \\ \text{subject to} & d_A(x_i, x_j) \leq u & (i, j) \in S \\ & d_A(x_i, x_j) \geq l & (i, j) \in D \end{array}$$

3.2 Learning Algorithm

(Davis and Dhillon, 2006) has shown that the KL divergence between two multivariate Gaussians can be expressed as the convex combination of a Mahalanobis distance between mean vectors and the LogDet divergence between the covariance matrices. The LogDet divergence equals

$$D_{ld}(A, A_0) = tr(AA_0^{-1}) - \log\det(AA_0^{-1}) - n$$

for n by n matrices A, A_0. If we assume the means of the Gaussians to be the same, we have

$$KL(p(x; A_0||p(x, A)) = \frac{1}{2}D_{ld}(A, A_0)$$

The optimization problem can be restated as

$$\begin{array}{lll} \min_{A \succeq 0} & D_{ld}(A, I) & \\ \text{s.t.} & tr(A(x_i - x_j)(x_i - x_j)^\top) \leq u & (i, j) \in S \\ & tr(A(x_i - x_j)(x_i - x_j)^\top) \geq l & (i, j) \in D \end{array}$$

We then incorporate slack variables into the formulation to guarantee the existence of a feasible solution for A. The optimization problem becomes:

$$\begin{array}{lll} \min_{A \succeq 0} & D_{ld}(A, I) + \gamma D_{ld}(diag(\xi), diag(\xi_0)) & \\ \text{s.t.} & tr(A(x_i - x_j)(x_i - x_j)^\top) \leq \xi_{c(i,j)} & (i, j) \in S \\ & tr(A(x_i - x_j)(x_i - x_j)^\top) \geq \xi_{c(i,j)} & (i, j) \in D \end{array}$$

where $c(i, j)$ is the index of the (i, j)-th constraint and ξ is a vector of slack variables whose components are initialized to u for similarity constraints and l for dissimilarity constraints. The tradeoff between satisfying the constraints and minimizing $D_{ld}(A, I)$ is controlled by the parameter γ. To solve this optimization problem, the algorithm shown in Algorithm 3.1 repeatedly projects the current solution onto a single constraint.

This completes the summary of (Davis et al., 2007).

4 Experimental Settings

In this section, we describe the experimental settings including the preprocessing of data and features, creation of the query word sets, and settings of the cross validation.

4.1 Features

We used a dependency structure as the context for words because it is the most widely used and one of the best performing contextual information in the past studies (Ruge, 1997; Lin, 1998). As the extraction of an accurate and comprehensive dependency structure is in itself a complicated task, the sophisticated parser RASP Toolkit 2 (Briscoe et al., 2006) was utilized to extract this kind of word relation.

Let $N(w, c)$ be the raw cooccurrence count of word w and context c, the grammatical relation

Algorithm
3.1: INFORMATION THEORETIC METRIC LEARNING

Input :
X(d by n matrix), I(identity matrix)
S(set of similar pairs), D(set of dissimilar pairs)
γ(slack parameter), c(constraint index function)
u, l(distance thresholds)
Output :
A(Mahalanobis matrix)

$A := I$
$\lambda_{ij} := 0$
$\xi_{c(i,j)} := u$ for $(i,j) \in S$; otherwise, $\xi_{c(i,j)} := l$
repeat
  Pick a constraint $(i,j) \in S$ or $(i,j) \in D$
  $p := (x_i - x_j)^\top A(x_i - x_j)$
  $\delta := 1$ if $(i,j) \in S, -1$ otherwise.
  $\alpha := \min(\lambda_{ij}, \frac{\delta}{2}(\frac{1}{p} - \frac{\gamma}{\xi_{c(i,j)}}))$
  $\beta := \delta\alpha/(1 - \delta\alpha\xi_{c(i,j)})$
  $\xi_{c(i,j)} := \gamma\xi_{c(i,j)}/(\gamma + \delta\alpha\xi_{c(i,j)})$
  $\lambda_{ij} := \lambda_{ij} - \alpha$
  $A := A + \beta A(x_i - x_j)(x_i - x_j)^\top A$
until convergence
return (A)

in which w occurs. These raw counts were obtained from New York Times articles (July 1994) extracted from English Gigaword [1]. The section consists of 7,593 documents and approx. 5 million words. As discussed below, we limited the vocabulary to the nouns in the Longman Defining Vocabulary (LDV) [2]. The features were constructed by weighting them using pointwise mutual information: $\text{wgt}(w,c) = \text{PMI}(w,c) = \log \frac{P(w,c)}{P(w)P(c)}$.

Co-occurrence data constructed this way can yield more than 10,000 context types, rendering metric learning impractical. As the applications of feature selection reduce the performance of the baseline metrics, we tested them in two different settings: with and without feature selection. To mitigate this problem, we applied a feature selection technique to reduce the feature dimensionality. We selected features using two approaches. The first approach is a simple frequency cutoff, applied as a pre-processing to filter out words and contexts with low frequency and to reduce computational cost. Specifically, all words w such that $\sum_c N(w,c) < \theta_f$ and contexts c such that $\sum_w N(w,c) < \theta_f$, with $\theta_f = 5$, are removed from the co-occurrence data.

The second approach is feature selection by context importance (Hagiwara et al., 2008). First, the *context importance* score for each context type is calculated, and then the least important context types are eliminated, until a desired numbers of them remains. To measure the *context importance* score, we used the number of unique words the context co-occurs with: $df(c) = |\{w|N(w,c) > 0\}|$. We adopted this context selection criterion on the assumption that the contexts shared by many words should be informative, and the synonym acquisition performance based on normal distributional similarity calculation retains its original level of performance until up to almost 90% of context types are eliminated (Hagiwara et al., 2008). In our experiment, we selected features rather aggressively, finally using only 10% of the original contexts. These feature reduction operations reduced the dimensionality to a figure as small as 1,281, while keeping the performance loss at a minimum.

4.2 Similarity and Distance Functions

We compared seven similarity/distance functions in our experiments: cosine similarity, Euclidean distance, Manhattan distance, Jaccard coefficient, vector-based Jaccard coefficient (Jaccardv), Jensen-Shannon Divergence (JS) and skew divergence (SD99). We first define some notations. Let $C(w)$ be the set of context types that co-occur with word w, i.e., $C(w) = \{c|N(w,c) > 0\}$, and $\mathbf{w}_i$ be the feature vector corresponding to word w, i.e., $\mathbf{w}_i = [\text{wgt}(w_i, c_1) \ ... \ \text{wgt}(w_i, c_M)]^\top$. The first three, the cosine, Euclidean and Manhattan distance, are vector-based metrics.

cosine similarity

$$\frac{\mathbf{w}_1 \cdot \mathbf{w}_2}{||\mathbf{w}_1|| \cdot ||\mathbf{w}_2||}$$

Euclidean distance

$$\sqrt{\sum_{c \in C(w_1) \cup C(w_2)} (\text{wgt}(w_1, c) - \text{wgt}(w_2, c))^2}$$

Manhattan distance

$$\sum_{c \in C(w_1) \cup C(w_2)} |\text{wgt}(w_1, c) - \text{wgt}(w_2, c)|$$

Jaccard coefficient

$$\frac{\sum_{c \in C(w_1) \cap C(w_2)} \min(\text{wgt}(w_1, c), \text{wgt}(w_2, c))}{\sum_{c \in C(w_1) \cup C(w_2)} \max(\text{wgt}(w_1, c), \text{wgt}(w_2, c))},$$

[1] http://www.ldc.upenn.edu/Catalog/CatalogEntry.jsp?catalogId=LDC2003T05

[2] http://www.cs.utexas.edu/users/kbarker/working_notes/ldoce-vocab.html

vector-based Jaccard coefficient (Jaccardv)

$$\frac{\mathbf{w}_i \cdot \mathbf{w}_j}{||\mathbf{w}_i|| + ||\mathbf{w}_j|| - \mathbf{w}_i \cdot \mathbf{w}_j}.$$

Jensen-Shannon divergence (JS)

$$\frac{1}{2}\{KL(p_1||m) + KL(p_2||m)\},\ m = p_1 + p_2.$$

JS and SD99 are based on the KL divergence, so the vectors must be normalized to form a probability distribution. For notational convenience, we let p_i be the probability distribution representation of feature vector $\mathbf{w}_i$, i.e., $p_i(c) = N(\mathbf{w}_i, c)/N(\mathbf{w}_i)$. While the KL divergence suffers from the so-called zero-frequency problem, a symmetric version of the KL divergence called the Jensen-Shannon divergence naturally avoids it.

skew divergence (SD99)

$$KL(p_1||\alpha p_2 + (1-\alpha)p_1).$$

As proposed by (Lee, 2001), the skew divergence also avoids the zero-frequency problem by mixing the original distribution with the target distribution. Parameter α is set to 0.99.

4.3 Query Word Set and Cross Validation

To formalize the experiments, we must prepare a set of query words for which synonyms are known in advance. We chose the Longman Defining Vocabulary (LDV) as the candidate set of query words. For each word in the LDV, we consulted three existing thesauri: Roget's Thesaurus (Roget, 1995), Collins COBUILD Thesaurus (Collins, 2002), and WordNet (Fellbaum, 1998). Each LDV word was looked up as a noun to obtain the union of synonyms. After removing words marked "idiom", "informal" or "slang" and phrases comprised of two or more words, this union was used as the reference set of query words. LDV words for which no noun synonyms were found in any of the reference thesauri were omitted. From the remaining 771 LDV words, there were 231 words that had five or more synonyms in the combined thesaurus. We selected these 231 words to be the query words and distributed them into five partitions so as to conduct five-fold cross validation. Four partitions were used in training, and the remaining partition was used in testing. For each fold, we created the training set from four partitions as follows; for each query word in the partitions, we randomly selected five synonymous words and added the pairs of query words and synonymous words to S, the set of similar pairs. Similarly, five pairs of query words and dissimilar words were randomly added to D, the set of dissimilar pairs. The training set for each fold consisted of S and D. Since a learner trained on an imbalanced dataset may not learn to discriminate enough between classes, we sampled dissimilar pairs to create an evenly distributed training dataset.

To make the evaluation realistic, we used a different method to create the test set: we paired each query word with each of the 771 remaining words to form the test set. Thus, in each fold, the training set had an equal number of positive and negative pairs, while in the test set, negative pairs outnumbered the positive pairs. While this is not a typical setting for cross validation, it renders the evaluation more realistic since an automatic synonym acquisition system in operation must be able to pick a few synonyms from a large number of dissimilar words.

The meta-parameters of the metric learning model were simply set $u = 1$, $l = 2$ and $\gamma = 1$. Each training set consisted of 1,850 pairs, and the test set consisted of 34,684 pairs. Since we conducted five-fold cross validation, the reported performance in this paper is actually a summary over different folds.

4.4 Evaluation Measures

We used an evaluation program for KDD Cup 2004 (Caruana et al., 2004) called Perf to measure the effectiveness of the metrics in acquiring synonyms. To use the program, we used the following formula to convert each distance metric to a similarity metric. $s(x_i, x_j) = 1/(1 + \exp(d(x_i, x_j)))$. Below, we summarize the three measures we used: Mean Average Precision, TOP1, and Average Rank of Last Synonym.

Mean Average Precision (APR)

Perf implements a definition of average precision sometimes called "expected precision". Perf calculates the precision at every recall where it is defined. For each of these recall values, Perf finds the threshold that produces the maximum precision, and takes the average over all of the recall values greater than 0. Average precision is measured on each query, and then the mean of each query's average precision is used as the final metric. A mean average precision of 1.0 indicates perfect prediction. The lowest possible mean average precision is 0.0.

Average Rank of Last Synonym (RKL)

As in other evaluation measures, synonym candidates are sorted by predicted similarity, and this metric measures how far down the sorted cases we must go to find the last true synonym. A rank of 1 indicates that the last synonym is placed in the top position. Given a query word, the highest obtainable rank is N if there are N synonyms in the corpus. The lower this measure is the better. Average ranks near 771 indicate poor performance.

TOP1

In each query, synonym candidates are sorted by predicted similarity. If the word that ranks at the top (highest similarity to the query word) is a true synonym of the query word, Perf scores a 1 for that query, and 0 otherwise. If there are ties, Perf scores 0 unless all of the tied cases are synonyms. TOP1 score ranges from 1.0 to 0.0. To achieve 1.0, perfect TOP1 prediction, a similarity metric must place a true synonym at the top of the sorted list in every query. In the next section, we report the mean of each query's TOP1.

5 Results

The evaluations of the metrics are listed in Table 1. The figure on the left side of $\rightarrow$ represents the performance with 1,281 features, and that on the right side with 12,812 features. Of all the metrics in Table 1, only the Mahalanobis L2 is trained with the previously presented metric learning algorithm. Thus, the values for the Mahalanobis L2 are produced by the five-fold cross validation, while the rest are given by the straight application of the metrics discussed in Section 4.2 to the same dataset. Strictly speaking, this is not a fair comparison, since we ought to compare a supervised learning with a supervised learning. However, our baseline is not the simple Euclidean distance; it is the Jaccard coefficient and cosine similarity, a handcrafted, best performing metric for synonym acquisition, with 10 times as many features.

The computational resources required to obtain the Mahalanobis L2 results were as follows: in the training phase, each fold of cross validation took about 80 iterations (less than one week) to converge on a Xeon 5160 3.0GHz. The time required to use the learned distance was a few hours at most.

At first, we were unable to perform competitively with the Euclidean distance. As seen in Table 1, the TOP1 measure of the Euclidean distance is only 1.732%. This indicates that the likelihood of finding the first item on the ranked list to be a true synonym is 1.732%. The vector-based Jaccard coefficient performs much better than the Euclidean distance, placing a true synonym at the top of the list 30.736% of the time.

Table 2 shows the Top 10 Words for Query "branch". The results for the Euclidean distance rank "hut" and other dissimilar words highly. This is because the norm of such vectors is small, and in a high dimensional space, the sparse vectors near the origin are relatively close to many other sparse vectors. To overcome this problem, we normalized the input vectors by the L2 norm $x' = x/||x||$ This normalization enables the Euclidean distance to perform very much like the cosine similarity, since the Euclidean distance between points on a sphere acts like the angle between the vectors. Surprisingly, normalization by L2 did not affect other metrics all that much; while the performances of some metrics improved slightly, the L2 normalization lowered that of the Jaccardv metric.

Once we learned the normalization trick, the learned Mahalanobis distance consistently outperformed all other metrics, including the ones with 10 times more features, in all three evaluation measures, achieving an APR of 18.66%, RKL of 545.09 and TOP1 of 45.455%.

6 Discussion

Examining the learned Mahalanobis matrix revealed interesting features. The matrix essentially shows the covariance between features. While it was not as heavily weighted as the diagonal elements, we found that its positive non-diagonal elements were quite interesting. They indicate that some of the useful features for finding synonyms are correlated and somewhat interchangeable. The example includes a pair of features, (dobj begin *) and (dobj end *). It was a pleasant surprise to see that one implies the other. Among the diagonal elements of the matrix, one of the heaviest features was being the direct object of "by". This indicates that being the object of the preposition "by" is a good indicator that two words are similar. A closer inspection of the NYT corpus showed that this preposition overwhelmingly takes a person or organization as its object, indicating that words with this feature belong to the same class of a person or organization. Similarly, the class

Metric	APR	RKL	TOP1
Cosine	0.1184 → 0.1324	580.27 → 579.00	0.2987 → 0.3160
Euclidean	0.0229 → 0.0173	662.74 → 695.71	0.0173 → 0.0000
Euclidean L2	0.1182 → 0.1324	580.30 → 578.99	0.2943 → 0.3160
Jaccard	0.1120 → 0.1264	580.76 → 579.51	0.2684 → 0.2943
Jaccard L2	0.1113 → 0.1324	580.29 → 570.88	0.2640 → 0.2987
Jaccardv	0.1189 → 0.1318	580.50 → 580.19	0.3073 → 0.3030
Jaccardv L2	0.1184 → 0.1254	580.27 → 570.00	0.2987 → 0.3160
JS	0.0199 → 0.0170	681.97 → 700.53	0.0129 → 0.0000
JS L2	0.0229 → 0.0173	679.21 → 699.00	0.0303 → 0.0086
Manhattan	0.0181 → 0.0168	687.73 → 701.47	0.0043 → 0.0000
Manhattan L2	0.0185 → 0.0170	686.56 → 701.11	0.0043 → 0.0086
SD99	0.0324 → 0.1039	640.71 → 588.16	0.0173 → 0.2640
SD99 L2	0.0334 → 0.1117	633.32 → 586.78	0.0216 → 0.2900
Mahalanobis L2	**0.1866**	**545.09**	**0.4545**

Table 1: Evaluation of Various Metrics, as Number of Features Increase from 1,281 to 12,812

	Cosine	Euclidean	Euclidean L2	Jaccard	Jaccardv	Mahalanobis L2
1	(*) office	hut	(*) office	(*) office	(*) office	(*) division
2	area	wild	area	border	area	group
3	(*) division	polish	(*) division	area	(*) division	(*) office
4	border	thirst	border	plant	border	line
5	group	hollow	group	(*) division	group	period
6	organization	shout	organization	mouth	organization	organization
7	store	fold	store	store	store	(*) department
8	mouth	dear	mouth	circle	mouth	charge
9	plant	hate	plant	stop	plant	world
10	home	wake	home	track	home	body

(*) = a true synonym

Table 2: Top 10 Words for Query "branch"

of words that "to" and "within", take as an objects were clear from the corpus: "to" takes a person or place, "within" takes duration of time [3]. Other heavy features includes being the object of "write" or "about". While not obvious, we postulate that having these words as a part of the context indicates that a word is an event of some type.

7 Conclusion

We applied metric learning to automatic synonym acquisition for the first time, and our experiments showed that the learned metric significantly outperforms existing similarity metrics. This outcome indicates that while we must resort to feature selection to apply metric learning, the performance gain from the supervised learning is enough to offset the disadvantage and justify its usage in some applications. This leads us to think that a combination of the learned metric with unsupervised metrics with even more features may produces the best results. We also discussed interesting features found in the learned Mahalanobis matrix. Since metric learning is known to boost clustering performance in a semi-supervised clustering setting, we believe these automatically identified features would be helpful in assigning a target word to a word class.

[3] Interestingly, we note that not all prepositions were as heavy: "beyond" and "without" were relatively light among the diagonal elements. In the NYT corpus, the class of words they take was not as clear as, for example, "by".

References

T. Briscoe, J. Carroll and R. Watson. 2006. The Second Release of the RASP System. *Proc. of the COLING/ACL 2006 Interactive Presentation Sessions*, 77–80.

T. Briscoe, J. Carroll, J. Graham and A. Copestake, 2002. Relational evaluation schemes. *Proc. of the Beyond PARSEVAL Workshop at the Third International Conference on Language Resources and Evaluation*, 4–8.

A. Budanitsky and G. Hirst. 2006. Evaluating WordNet-based measures of semantic distance. *Computational Linguistics*, 32(1):13–47.

R. Caruana, T. Jachims and L. Backstrom. 2004. KDD-Cup 2004: results and analysis *ACM SIGKDD Explorations Newslatter*, 6(2):95–108.

C. J. Croach and B. Yang. 1992. Experiments in automatic statistical thesaurus construction. *the 15th*

Annual International ACM SIGIR Conference on Research and Development in Information Retrieval, 77–88.

J. R. Curran and M. Moens. 2002. Improvements in automatic thesaurus extraction. In Workshop on Unsupervised Lexical Acquisition. *Proc. of the ACL SIGLEX*, 231–238.

J. V. Davis and I. S. Dhillon. 2006. Differential Entropic Clustering of Multivariate Gaussians. *Advances in Neural Information Processing Systems (NIPS)*.

J. V. Davis, B. Kulis, P. Jain, S. Sra and I. S. Dhillon. 2007. Information Theoretic Metric Learning. *Proc. of the International Conference on Machine Learning (ICML)*.

A. Globerson and S. Roweis. 2005. Metric Learning by Collapsing Classes. *Advances in Neural Information Processing Systems (NIPS)*.

J. Goldberger, S. Roweis, G. Hinton and R. Salakhutdinov. 2004. Neighbourhood Component Analysis. *Advances in Neural Information Processing Systems (NIPS)*.

G. Grefenstette. 1994. Explorations in Automatic Thesuarus Discovery. Kluwer Academic Publisher.

M. Hagiwara, Y. Ogawa, and K. Toyama. 2008. Context Feature Selection for Distributional Similarity. *Proc. of IJCNLP-08*, 553–560.

Z. Harris. 1985. Distributional Structure. Jerrold J. Katz (ed.) *The Philosophy of Linguistics*. Oxford University Press. 26–47.

T. Hastie and R. Tibshirani. 1996. Discriminant adaptive nearest neighbor classification. *Pattern Analysis and Machine Intelligence, 18*, 607–616.

D. Hindle. 1990. Noun classification from predicate-argument structures. *Proc. of the ACL*, 268–275.

J. J. Jiang and D. W. Conrath. 1997. Semantic similarity based on corpus statistics and lexical taxonomy. *Proceedings of International Conference on Research on Computational Linguistics (ROCLING X)*, Taiwan.

Y. Jing and B. Croft. 1994. An Association Thesaurus for Information Retrieval. *Proc. of Recherche d'Informations Assistée par Ordinateur (RIAO)*, 146–160.

D. Lin. 1998. Automatic retrieval and clustering of similar words. *Proc. of COLING/ACL 1998*, 786–774.

L. Lee. 1999. Measures of distributional similarity. *Proc. of the ACL*, 23–32

L. Lee. 2001. On the Effectiveness of the Skew Divergence for Statistical Language Analysis. *Artificial Intelligence and Statistics 2001*, 65–72.

S. Mohammad and G. Hirst. 2006. Distributional measures of concept-distance: A task-oriented evaluation. *Proceedings of the Conference on Empirical Methods in Natural Language Processing (EMNLP)*, Sydney, Australia.

P. Resnik. 1995. Using information content to evaluate semantic similarity. *Proceedings of the 14th International Joint Conference on Artificial Intelligence (IJCAI-95)*, 448–453, Montreal, Canada.

G. Ruge. 1997. Automatic detection of thesaurus relations for information retrieval applications. *Foundations of Computer Science: Potential - Theory - Cognition*, LNCS, Volume 1337, 499–506, Springer Verlag, Berlin, Germany.

S. Shalev-Shwartz, Y. Singer and A. Y. Ng. 2004. Online and Batch Learning of Pseudo-Metrics. *Proc. of the International Conference on Machine Learning (ICML)*.

M. Schutz and T. Joachims. 2003. Learning a Distance Metric from Relative Comparisons. *Advances in Neural Information Processing Systems (NIPS)*..

J. Weeds, D. Weir and D. McCarthy. 2004. Characterising Measures of Lexical Distributional Similarity. *Proc. of COLING 2004*, 1015–1021.

K. Q. Weinberger, J. Blitzer and L. K. Saul. 2005. Distance Metric Learning for Large Margin Nearest Neighbor Classification. *Advances in Neural Information Processing Systems (NIPS)*.

E. P. Xing, A. Y. Ng, M. Jordan and S. Russell 2002. Distance metric learning with application to clustering with sideinformation. *Advances in Neural Information Processing Systems (NIPS)*.

Y. Yang and J. O. Pedersen. 1997. A Comparative Study on Feature Selection in Text Categorization. *Proc. of the International Conference on Machine Learning (ICML)*, 412–420.

Discourse Level Opinion Interpretation *

Swapna Somasundaran
Dept. of Computer Science
University of Pittsburgh
Pittsburgh, PA 15260
swapna@cs.pitt.edu

Janyce Wiebe
Dept. of Computer Science
University of Pittsburgh
Pittsburgh, PA 15260
wiebe@cs.pitt.edu

Josef Ruppenhofer
Intelligent Systems Program
University of Pittsburgh
Pittsburgh, PA 15260
josefr@cs.pitt.edu

Abstract

This work proposes *opinion frames* as a representation of discourse-level associations which arise from related opinion topics. We illustrate how *opinion frames* help gather more information and also assist disambiguation. Finally we present the results of our experiments to detect these associations.

1 Introduction

Opinions have been investigated at the phrase, sentence, and document levels. However, little work has been carried out regarding interpreting opinions at the level of the discourse.

Consider the following excerpt from a dialog about designing a remote control for a television (the opinion *targets* – what the opinions are about — are shown in *italics*).

(1) D :: And I thought **not too** *edgy* and *like a box*, **more** kind of *hand-held* **not** as *computery*, yeah, **more** *organic shape* I think. Simple designs, like the last one we just saw, **not too** *many buttons*.

Speaker *D* expresses an opinion in favor of a design that is simple and organic in shape, and against an alternative design which is not. Several individual opinions are expressed in this passage. The first is a negative opinion about the design being too edgy and box-like, the next is a positive opinion toward a hand-held design, followed by a negative opinion toward a computery shape, and so on. While recognizing individual expressions of opinions and their properties is important, discourse interpretation is needed as well. It is by understanding the passage as a discourse that we see *edgy*, *like a box*, *computery*, and *many buttons* as descriptions of the type of design *D* does not prefer, and *hand-held*, *organic shape*, and *simple designs* as descriptions of the type he does. These descriptions are not in general synonyms/antonyms of one another; for example, there are hand-held "computery" devices and simple designs that are edgy. The unison/opposition among the descriptions is due to how they are used in the discourse.

This paper focuses on such relations between the targets of opinions in discourse. Specifically, in this work, we propose a scheme of *opinion frames*, which consist of two opinions that are related by virtue of having united or opposed targets. We argue that recognizing opinion frames will provide more opinion information for NLP applications than recognizing individual opinions alone. Further, if there is uncertainty about any one of the components, we believe opinion frames are an effective representation incorporating discourse information to make an overall coherent interpretation (Hobbs et al., 1993). Finally, we also report the first results of experiments in recognizing the presence of these opinion frames.

We introduce our data in Section 2, present *opinion frames* in Section 3 and illustrate their utility in Section 4. Our experiments are in Section 5, related work is discussed in Section 6, and conclusions are in Section 7.

2 Data

The data used in this work is the AMI meeting corpus (Carletta et al., 2005) which contains multi-modal recordings of group meetings. Each meeting has rich transcription and seg-

This research was supported in part by the Department of Homeland Security under grant N000140710152.

© 2008. Licensed under the *Creative Commons Attribution-Noncommercial-Share Alike 3.0 Unported* license (http://creativecommons.org/licenses/by-nc-sa/3.0/). Some rights reserved.

ment (turn/utterance) information for each speaker. Each utterance consists of one or more sentences. We also use some of the accompanying manual annotations (like adjacency pairs) as features in our machine learning experiments.

3 Opinion Frames

In this section, we lay out definitions relating to opinion frames, illustrate with examples how these are manifested in our data, and consider them in the context of discourse relations.

3.1 Definitions

The components of opinion frames are individual opinions and the relationships between their targets. Following (Wilson and Wiebe, 2005; Somasundaran et al., 2007), we address two types of opinions, *sentiment* and *arguing*.

Sentiment includes positive and negative evaluations, emotions, and judgments. **Arguing** includes arguing *for* or *against* something, and arguing *that* something should or should not be done.

Opinions have a **polarity** that can be *positive* or *negative*. [1] The **target** of an opinion is the entity or proposition that the opinion is about. We establish relations between targets, in the process relating their respective opinions. We address two types of relations, *same* and *alternative*.

The **same** relation holds between targets that refer to the same entity, property, or proposition. Observing the relations marked by annotators, we found that *same* covers not only identity, but also part-whole, synonymy, generalization, specialization, entity-attribute, instantiation, cause-effect, epithets and implicit background topic, i.e., relations that have been studied by many researchers in the context of anaphora and co-reference (e.g. (Clark, 1975; Vieira and Poesio, 2000; Mueller and Strube, 2001)). Actually, *same* relations holding between entities often involve co-reference (where co-reference is broadly conceived to include relations such as part-whole listed above). However, there are no morphosyntactic constraints on what targets may be. Thus, *same* relations may also hold between adjective phrases, verb phrases, and clauses. An instance of this is Example 1, where the *same* target relation holds between the adjectives *edgy* and *computery*.

[1] Polarity can also be *neutral* or *both* (Wilson and Wiebe, 2005), but these values are not significant for our opinion frames.

SPSPsame, SNSNsame, APAPsame, ANANsame, SPAPsame, APSPsame, SNANsame, ANSNsame, SPSNalt, SNSPalt, APANalt, ANAPalt, SPANalt, SNAPalt, APSNalt, ANSPalt
SPSNsame, SNSPsame, APANsame, ANAPsame, SPANsame, APSNsame, SNAPsame, ANSPsame, SPSPalt, SNSNalt, APAPalt, ANANalt, SPAPalt, SNANalt, APSPalt, ANSNalt

Table 1: Opinion Frames

The **alternative** relation holds between targets that are related by virtue of being opposing (mutually exclusive) options in the context of the discourse. For example, in the domain of TV remote controls, the set of all shapes are alternatives to one another, since a remote control may have only one shape at a time. In such scenarios, a positive opinion regarding one choice may imply a negative opinion toward competing choices, and vice versa. Objects appear as alternatives via world and domain knowledge (for example, shapes of a remote); the context of the discourse (for example, Hillary Clinton and Barak Obama are alternatives in discussions of the primaries, but not in discussions of the general election); and the way the objects are juxtaposed while expressing opinions (for instance *hand-held* and *computery* in Example 1).

While *same* and *alternative* are not the only possible relations between targets, they commonly occur in task-oriented dialogs such as those in the data we use.

Now that we have all the ingredients, we can define opinion frames. An **opinion frame** is defined as a structure composed of two opinions and their respective targets connected via their target relations. With four opinion type/polarity pairs (*SN,SP,AN,AP*), for each of two opinion slots, and two possible target relations, we have 4 * 4 * 2 = 32 types of frame, listed in Table 1.

3.2 Examples

We will now illustrate how the frames are applied with the following meeting snippets from the AMI meeting corpus. In our examples, the lexical anchors revealing the opinion type (as the words are interpreted in context) are indicated in **bold face**. The text span capturing the target of the opinion (as interpreted in context) is indicated in *italics*. To make it easier to understand the opinion frames, we separately list each opinion, followed by the major relation between the targets and, in parentheses, the relevant subtype of the major relation.

In the passage below, the speaker *D* expresses

his preferences about the material for the TV remote.

(2) D:: ... this kind of rubbery material, *it's* a **bit more bouncy**, like you said they get chucked around a lot. A **bit more durable** and *that* [2] can also be **ergonomic** and *it* kind of feels **a bit different from all the other remote controls**.

Opinion Span - target Span	Type
O1 **bit more bouncy** - *it's* [t1]	SP
O2 **bit more durable** - ellipsis [t2]	SP
O3 **ergonomic** - *that* [t3]	SP
O4 **a bit different from all the other remote** - *it* [t4]	SP

Target - target	Rel
t1 - t2	same (ellipsis)
t3 - t4	same (identity)
t1 - t3	same (identity)

The speaker's positive sentiment regarding the rubbery material is apparent from the text spans **bit more bouncy** (Sentiment Positive or SP), **bit more durable** (SP), **ergonomic** (SP) and **a bit different from all the other remote controls** (SP). As shown, the targets of these opinions (*it's* [t1], *that* [t3], and *it* [t4]) are related by the *same* relation. The ellipsis occurs with **bit more durable**. Target [t2] represents the (implicit) target of that opinion, and [t2] has a *same* relation to [t1], the target of the **bit more bouncy** opinion. The opinion frames occurring throughout this passage are all *SPSPsame* denoting that both the opinion components are sentiments with positive polarity with a *same* relation between their targets. One frame occurs between O1 and O2, another between O3 and O4, and so on.

Example 2 illustrates relatively simple *same* relations between targets. Now let us consider the more involved passage below, in which a meeting participant analyzes two leading remotes on the market.

(3) D:: These are two **leading** *remote controls* at the moment. You know *they*'re **grey**, *this one*'s got **loads of buttons**, it's **hard to tell** from here what *they* actually do, and *they* **don't look very exciting at all**.

Opinion Span - target Span	Rel
O1 **leading** - *remote controls* [t1]	SP
O2 **grey** - *they* [t2]	SN
O3 **loads of buttons** - *this one* [t3]	SN
O4 **hard to tell** - *they* [t4]	SN
O5 **don't look very exciting at all** - *they* [t5]	SN

Target - target	Rel
t1 - t2	same (identity)
t2 - t3	same (t3 subset of t2)
t3 - t4	same (t4 partof t3)
t5 - t1	same (identity)

[2]Note that the "that" refers to the property of being durable; however, as our annotation scheme is not hierarchical, we connect it to the entity the opinion is about – in this case the rubbery material.

Target [t2] is the set of two leading remotes; [t3], which is in a *same* relation with [t2], is one of those remotes. Target [t4], which is also in a *same* relation with [t3], is a part of that remote, namely its buttons. Thus, opinion O3 is directly about one of the remotes, and indirectly about the set of both remotes. Similarly, O4 is directly about the buttons of one of the remotes, and indirectly about that remote itself. The assessments at different levels accrue toward the analysis of the main topic under consideration.

Moving on to *alternative* (*alt*) relations, consider the passage below, where the speaker is arguing for the curved shape.

(4) C:: . . . shapes **should be** *curved*, so round shapes. **Nothing** *square-like*.

:

C:: . . . So we **shouldn't have too** *square corners* and that kind of thing.

B:: Yeah okay. **Not *the old box look***.

Opinion Span - target Span	Rel
O1 **should be** - *curved* [t1]	AP
O2 **Nothing** - *square-like* [t2]	AN
O3 **shouldn't have** - *square corners* [t3]	AN
O4 **too** - *square corners* [t3]	SN
O5 **Not** - *the old box look* [t4]	AN
O6 **the old box look** - *the old box look* [t4]	SN

Target - target	Rel
t1 -t2	alternatives
t2 - t3	same (specification)
t3 - t4	same (epithet)

Opinion O1 argues for a curved shape, O2 argues against a square shape, and O3 argues against square corners. Note that *square corners* is also the target of a negative sentiment, O4, expressed here by **too**. Opinion O5 argues against the old box look. In addition, the wording **old box look** implies a negative sentiment – O6 (we list the target span as "old box look," which refers to the look of having square corners).

There is an *alt* relation between [t1] and [t2]. Thus, we have an opinion frame of type *APANalt* between O1 and O2. From this frame, we are able to understand that a positive opinion is expressed toward something and a negative opinion is expressed toward its alternative.

3.3 Link Transitivity

When individual targets are linked, they form a chain-like structure. Due to this, a connecting path may exist between targets that were not directly linked by the human annotators. This path can be traversed to create links between new pairs of targets, which in turn results in new opinion frame relations.

Let us illustrate this idea with Example 4. The frames with direct relations are *O1O2 APANalt*. By following the *alt* link from [t1] to [t2] and the *same* link from [t2] to [t3], we have an *alt* link between [t1] and [t3], and the additional frames *O1O3 APANalt* and *O1O4 APSNalt*. Repeating this process would finally link speaker *C's* opinion O1 with *B's* opinion O6 via a *APSNalt* frame.

Simple recipes such as this can be used by applications such as QA to gather more information from the discourse.

3.4 Frame Types

In our corpus, we found that the 32 frames of Table 1 can be categorized into two functional types: *reinforcing frames* and *non-reinforcing frames*.

The set of frames that occur in scenarios where the speaker intends to fortify or *reinforce* his opinion/stance are called ***reinforcing frames***. These are the ones in the top row of the Table 1. Note that these frames cover all opinion types, polarities and target relations. It is the particular combination of these frame components that bring about the reinforcement of the opinion in the discourse.

On the other hand, the frames at the bottom row of the table are ***non-reinforcing***. In our corpus, these frames occur when a speaker is ambivalent or weighing pros and cons.

Example 2 is characterized by opinion frames in which the opinions reinforce one another – that is, individual positive sentiments (SP) occurring throughout the passage fortify the positive regard for the rubbery material via the *same* target relations and the resulting *SPSPsame* frames.

Interestingly, interplays among different opinion types may show the same type of reinforcement. For instance, Example 4 is characterized by mixtures of opinion types, polarities, and target relations. However, the opinions are still unified in the intention to argue for a particular type of shape.

3.5 Discourse Relations and Opinion Frames

Opinion-frame recognition and discourse interpretation go hand in hand; together, they provide richer overall interpretations. For example, consider the opinion frames and the Penn Discourse Treebank relations (Prasad et al., 2007) for Example 2. PDTB would see a *list* or *conjunction* relation between the clauses containing opinions **bit more durable** (O2) and **ergonomic** (O3), as well as between the clauses containing opinions **ergonomic** (O3) and **a bit different from all the other remote controls** (O4). All of our opinion frames for this passage are of type *SPSPsame*, a reinforcing frame type. This passage illustrates the case in which discourse relations nicely correspond to opinion frames. The opinion frames flesh out the discourse relations: we have lists specifically of positive sentiments toward related objects.

However, opinion-frame and discourse-relation schemes are not redundant. Consider the following three passages.

(e1) **Non-reinforcing opinion frame (SNSPsame); Contrast discourse relation**
D:: . . . I draw for you this *schema* that can be maybe **too technical** for you but is **very important** for me . . . .

(e2) **Reinforcing opinion frame (SNAPalt); Contrast discourse relation**
D:: **not too** *edgy* and like *a box*, **more** kind of *hand-held*

(e3) **Reinforcing opinion frame (SPSPsame); no discourse relation**
. . . they **want** something that's *easier to use* straight away, *more intuitive* perhaps.

In both e1 and e2, the discourse relation between the two opinions is *contrast* ("too technical" is contrasted with "very important", and "not too edgy and like a box" is contrasted with "more kind of hand-held"). However, the opinion frame in e1 is *SNSPsame*, which is a non-reinforcing frame, while the opinion frame in e2 is *SNAPalt*, which is a reinforcing frame. In e3, the opinion frame holds between targets within a subordinated clause (*easier to use* and *more intuitive* are two desired targets); most discourse theories don't predict any discourse relation in this situation.

Generally speaking, we find that there are not definitive mappings between opinion frames and the relations of popular discourse theories. For example, Hobbs' (Hobbs et al., 1993) *contrast* covers at least four of our frames (*SPSPalt*, *APAPalt*, *APANsame*, *SPSNsame*), while, for instance, our *SPSPsame* frame can map to both the *elaboration* and *explanation* relations.

4 Benefits of Discourse Opinion Frames

This section argues for two motivations for opinion frames: they may unearth additional information over and above the individual opinions stated in the text, and they may contribute toward arriving

	Positive	Negative
Counting only individual opinions		
Accepted Items	120	20
Rejected Items	9	12
individual + opinions via Reinforcing Opinion frames		
Accepted Items	252	63
Rejected Items	22	26

Table 2: Opinion Polarity Distribution for Accepted/Rejected Items

at a coherent interpretation (Hobbs et al., 1993) of the opinions in the discourse.

4.1 Gathering More Information

Frame relations provide a mechanism to relate opinions expressed in non-local contexts - the opinion may occur elsewhere in the discourse, but will become relevant to a given target due to a relation between its target and the given target. For instance, in Example 3, there is one direct evaluation of the leading remotes (O1) and two evaluations via identity (O2, O5). Following frames constructed via t2-t3 and t3-t4, we get two more opinions (O3 and O4) for the leading remotes.

Furthermore, opinions regarding something not lexically or even anaphorically related can become relevant, providing more opinion information. This is particularly interesting when *alt* relations are involved, as opinions towards one alternative imply opinions of opposite polarity toward the competing options. For instance in Example 4, if we consider only the explicitly stated opinions, there is only one (positive) opinion, O1, about the curved shape. However, the speaker expresses several other opinions which reinforce his positivity toward the curved shape. Thus, by using the frame information, it is possible to gather more opinions regarding curved shapes for TV remotes.

As a simple proof of concept, we counted the number of positive and negative opinions towards the items that were accepted or rejected in the meetings (information about accepted and rejected items is obtained from the manual abstractive summaries provided by the AMI corpus). Counts are obtained, over opinions manually annotated in the data, for two conditions: with and without frame information. The items in our meeting data are mainly options for the new TV remote, which include attributes and features like different shapes, materials, designs, and functionalities. We observed that for the accepted items, the number of positive opinions is higher and, for rejected items, the number of negative opinions is higher. The top section of Table 2 shows a contingency table of counts of positive/negative opinions for accepted/rejected items for 5 AMI meetings.

Then we counted the number of reinforcing opinions that were expressed regarding these items. This meant also counting additional opinions that were related via reinforcing frames. The bottom section of Table 2 shows the counts when the reinforcing frames are considered. Compared to the counts of only individual opinions, we see that the numbers in each cell have increased, while maintaining the same pattern of distribution.

Thus, in effect we have procured more instances of opinions for the items. We believe this added information would help applications like meeting summarizers and QA systems to make more informed decisions.

4.2 Interdependent Interpretation

We believe that our opinion frames, anaphoric relations and discourse relations can symbiotically help disambiguate each other in the discourse. In particular, suppose that some aspect of an individual opinion, such as polarity, is unclear. If the discourse suggests certain opinion frames, this may in turn resolve the underlying ambiguity.

Revisiting Example 2 from above, we see that out of context, the polarities of **bouncy** and **different from other remotes** are unclear (bounciness and being different may be negative attributes for another type of object). However, the polarities of two of the opinions are clear (**durable** and **ergonomic**). There is evidence in this passage of discourse continuity and *same* relations such as the pronouns, the lack of contrastive cue phrases, and so on. This evidence suggests that the speaker expresses similar opinions throughout the passage, making the opinion frame *SPSPsame* more likely throughout. Recognizing the frames would resolve the polarity ambiguities of **bouncy** and **different**.

In the following example (5), the positive sentiment (SP) towards the *this* and the positive arguing (AP) for the *it* are clear. These two individual opinions can be related by a *same*/*alt* target relation, be unrelated, or have some other relation not covered by our scheme (in which case we would not have a relation between them). There is evidence in the discourse that makes one interpretation more likely than others. The "so" indicates that the two clauses are highly likely to be related by a *cause* discourse relation (PDTB). This information confirms a discourse continuity, as well as makes a reinforcing scenario likely, which makes the reinforcing frame *SPAPsame* highly probable. This increase in likelihood will in turn help a coreference system to increase its confidence that the "that" and the "it" co-refer.

(5) B :: ... and *this* will **definitely enhance our market sales, so we should** take *it* into consideration also.

Opinion Span - target Span	Rel
O1 **definitely enhance our market sales** - *this* [t1]	SP
O2 **so we should** - *it* [t2]	AP

Target - target	Rel
t1 -t2	same (identity)

5 Experiments

There has been much work on recognizing individual aspects of opinions like extracting individual opinions from phrases or sentences and recognizing opinion type and polarity. Accordingly, in our machine learning experiments we assume oracle opinion and polarity information. Our experiments thus focus on the new question: "Given two opinion sentences, determine if they participate in *any* frame relation." Here, an opinion sentence is a sentence containing one or more sentiment or arguing expression. In this work, we consider frame detection only between sentence pairs belonging to the same speaker.

5.1 Annotation of Gold Standard

Creating gold-standard opinion-frame data is accomplished by annotating frame components and then building the frames from those underlying annotations.

We began with annotations created by Somasundaran et al. (2007), namely four meetings of the AMI meeting corpus annotated for *sentiment* and *arguing* opinions (text anchor and type). Following that annotation scheme, we annotated an additional meeting. This gave us a corpus of 4436 sentences or 2942 segments (utterances). We added attributes to the existing opinion annotations, namely *polarity* and *target-id*. The *target-id* attribute links the opinion to its local target span. Relations between targets were then annotated. When a newly annotated target is similar (or opposed) to a set of targets already participating in *same* relations, then the *same* (or *alt*) link is made only to one of them - the one that seems most natural. This is often the one that is physically closest.

Content Word overlap between the sentence pair
Focus space overlap between the sentence pair
Anaphoric indicator in the second sentence
Time difference between the sentence pair
Number of intervening sentences
Existence of adjacency pair between the sentence pair
Bag of words for each sentence

Table 3: Features for Opinion Frame detection

Link transitivity is then used to connect targets that are not explicitly linked by the annotators.

All annotations were performed by two of the co-authors of this paper by consensus labeling. The details of our annotation scheme and inter-annotator agreement studies are presented in (Somasundaran et al., 2008).

Once the individual frame components are annotated, conceptually, a frame exists for a pair of opinions if their polarities are either *positive* or *negative* and their targets are in a *same* or *alt* relation. For our experiments, if a path exists between two targets, then their opinions are considered to be participating in an opinion-frame relation.

The experimental data consists of pairs of opinion sentences and the gold-standard information whether there exists a frame between them. We approximate continuous discourse by only pairing sentences that are not more than 10 sentences apart. We also filter out sentences that are less than two words in length in order to handle data skewness. This filters out very small sentences (e.g., "Cool.") which rarely participate in frames. The experiments were performed on a total of 2539 sentence pairs, of which 551 are positive instances.

5.2 Features

The factor that determines if two opinions are related is primarily the target relations between them. Instead of first finding the target span for each opinion sentence and then inferring if they should be related, we directly try to encode target relation information in our features. By this approach, even in the absence of explicit target-span information, we are able to determine if the opinion sentence pairs are related.

We explored a number of features to incorporate this. The set that give the best performance are listed in Table 3. The *content word overlap* feature captures the degree of topic overlap between the sentence pair, and looks for target relations via identity. The *focus space overlap* feature is motivated by our observation that partici-

	Acc.	Prec.	Recall	F-measure
False	78.3%	-	0%	-
Distribution	66%	21.7%	21.7%	21.4%
Random	50.0%	21.5%	49.4%	29.8 %
True	21.7%	21.6%	100%	35.5 %
System	67.6%	36.8%	64.9%	46%

Table 4: Automatic Detection of Opinion Frames

pants refer to an established discourse topic without explicitly referring to it. Thus, we construct a focus space for each sentence containing recently used NP chunks. The feature is the percent overlap between the focus spaces of the two opinion sentences. The *anaphoric indicator feature* checks for the presence of pronouns such as *it* and *that* in the second sentence to account for target relations via anaphora. The *time difference* between the sentences and the *number of intervening sentences* are useful features to capture the idea that topics shift with time. The *existence of an adjacency pair* [3] between the sentences can clue the system that the opinions in the sentences are related too. Finally, standard *bag of words* features are included for each sentence.

5.3 Results

We performed 5-fold cross validation experiments, using the standard SVMperf package (Joachims, 2005), an implementation of SVMs designed for optimizing multivariate performance measures. We found that, on our skewed data, optimizing on F-measure obtains the best results.

Our system is compared to four baselines in Table 4. The majority class baseline which always guesses false (*False*) has good accuracy but zero recall. The baseline that always guesses true (*True*) has 100% recall and the best f-measure among the baselines, but poor accuracy. We also constructed a baseline that guesses true/false over the test set based on the distribution in the training data (*Distribution*). This baseline is smarter than the other baselines, as it does not indiscriminately guess any one of the class. The last baseline *Random* guesses true 50% of the time.

The bottom row of Table 4 shows the performance of our system (*System*). The skewness of the data affects the baselines as well as our system. Our system beats the best baseline f-measure by over 10 percentage points, and the best baseline precision by 14 percentage points. Comparing it to the baseline which has comparable accuracy, namely *Distribution*, we see that our system improves in f-measure by 24 percentage points.

Our results are encouraging - even using simple features to capture target relations achieves considerable improvement over the baselines. However, there is much room for improvement. Using more detailed target and discourse information promises to further improve system performance. These are avenues for future work.

6 Related work

Evidence from the surrounding context has been used previously to determine if the current sentence should be subjective/objective (Riloff et al., 2003; Pang and Lee, 2004) and adjacency pair information has been used to predict congressional votes (Thomas et al., 2006). However, these methods do not explicitly model the relations between opinions. An application of the idea of alternative targets can be seen in Kim and Hovy's (2007) work on election prediction. They assume that if a speaker expresses support for one party, all mentions of the competing parties have negative polarity, thus creating automatically labeled training data.

In the field of product review mining, sentiments and features (*aspects*) have been mined (Popescu and Etzioni, 2005), where the aspects correspond to our definition of targets. However, the aspects themselves are not related to each other in any fashion.

Polanyi and Zaenen (2006), in their discussion on contextual valence shifters, have also observed the phenomena described in this work - namely that a central topic may be divided into subtopics in order to perform evaluations, and that discourse structure can influence the overall interpretation of valence. Snyder and Barzilay (2007) combine an agreement model based on contrastive RST relations with a local aspect model to make a more informed overall decision for sentiment classification. In our scheme, their aspects would be related as *same* and their high contrast relations would correspond to the non-reinforcing frames *SPSNsame*, *SNSPsame*. Additionally, our frame relations would link the sentiments across non-adjacent clauses, and make connections via *alt* target relations.

With regard to meetings, the most closely related work includes the dialog-related annotation

[3] Adjacency Pairs are manual dialog annotations available in the AMI corpus.

schemes for various available corpora of conversation (e.g., Carletta et al. (2005) for AMI). As shown by Somasundaran et al. (2007), dialog structure information and opinions are in fact complementary. We believe that, like the discourse relations, the dialog information will additionally help in arriving at an overall coherent interpretation.

7 Conclusions

In this paper, we described the idea of *opinion frames* as a representation capturing discourse level relations that arise from related opinion targets and which are common in task-oriented dialogs. We introduced the *alternative* relations that hold between targets by virtue of being opposing in the discourse context. We discussed how our opinion-frame scheme and discourse relations go hand in hand to provide a richer overall interpretation. We also illustrated that such discourse level opinion associations have useful benefits, namely they help gather more opinion information and help interdependent interpretation. Finally, we showed via our machine learning experiments that the presence of opinion frames can be automatically detected.

References

Carletta, J., S. Ashby, S. Bourban, M. Flynn, M. Guillemot, T. Hain, J. Kadlec, V. Karaiskos, W. Kraaij, M. Kronenthal, G. Lathoud, M. Lincoln, A. Lisowska, I. McCowan, W. Post, D. Reidsma, and P. Wellner. 2005. The AMI Meetings Corpus. In *Proceedings of Measuring Behavior Symposium on "Annotating and measuring Meeting Behavior"*.

Clark, H. H. 1975. Bridging. *Theoretical issues in natural language processing . New York: ACM.*

Hobbs, J., M. Stickel, D. Appelt, and P. Martin. 1993. Interpretation as abduction. *AI*, 63.

Joachims, T. 2005. A support vector method for multivariate performance measures. In *ICML 2005*.

Kim, Soo-Min and Eduard Hovy. 2007. Crystal: Analyzing predictive opinions on the web. In *EMNLP-CoNLL 2007*.

Mueller, C. and M. Strube. 2001. Annotating anaphoric and bridging relations with mmax. In *2nd SIGdial Workshop on Discourse and Dialogue*.

Pang, B. and L. Lee. 2004. A sentimental education: Sentiment analysis using subjectivity summarization based on minimum cuts. In *ACl 2004*.

Polanyi, L. and A. Zaenen, 2006. *Contextual Valence Shifters*, chapter 1. Computing Attitude and Affect in Text: Theory and Applications. Springer.

Popescu, A.-M. and O. Etzioni. 2005. Extracting product features and opinions from reviews. In *HLT-EMNLP 2005*.

Prasad, R., E. Miltsakaki, N. Dinesh, A. Lee, A. Joshi, L. Robaldo, and B. Webber, 2007. *PDTB 2.0 Annotation Manual*.

Riloff, E., J. Wiebe, and T. Wilson. 2003. Learning subjective nouns using extraction pattern bootstrapping. In *CoNLL 2003*.

Snyder, B. and R. Barzilay. 2007. Multiple aspect ranking using the good grief algorithm. In *HLT 2007: NAACL*.

Somasundaran, S., J. Ruppenhofer, and J. Wiebe. 2007. Detecting arguing and sentiment in meetings. In *SIGdial Workshop on Discourse and Dialogue 2007*.

Somasundaran, S, J Ruppenhofer, and J Wiebe. 2008. Discourse level opinion relations: An annotation study. In *SIGdial Workshop on Discourse and Dialogue*. ACL.

Thomas, M., B. Pang, and L. Lee. 2006. Get out the vote: Determining support or opposition from congressional floor-debate transcripts. In *EMNLP 2006*.

Vieira, R. and M. Poesio. 2000. An empirically based system for processing definite descriptions. *Comput. Linguist.*, 26(4).

Wilson, T. and J. Wiebe. 2005. Annotating attributions and private states. In *Proceedings of ACL Workshop on Frontiers in Corpus Annotation II: Pie in the Sky*.

Acquiring Sense Tagged Examples using Relevance Feedback

Mark Stevenson, Yikun Guo and **Robert Gaizauskas**
Department of Computer Science
University of Sheffield
Regent Court, 211 Portobello
Sheffield, S1 4DP
United Kingdom
inital.surname@dcs.shef.ac.uk

Abstract

Supervised approaches to Word Sense Disambiguation (WSD) have been shown to outperform other approaches but are hampered by reliance on labeled training examples (the *data acquisition bottleneck*). This paper presents a novel approach to the automatic acquisition of labeled examples for WSD which makes use of the Information Retrieval technique of relevance feedback. This semi-supervised method generates additional labeled examples based on existing annotated data. Our approach is applied to a set of ambiguous terms from biomedical journal articles and found to significantly improve the performance of a state-of-the-art WSD system.

1 Introduction

The resolution of lexical ambiguities has long been considered an important part of the process of understanding natural language. Supervised approaches to Word Sense Disambiguation (WSD) have been shown to perform better than unsupervised ones (Agirre and Edmonds, 2007) but require examples of ambiguous words used in context annotated with the appropriate sense (labeled examples). However these often prove difficult to obtain since manual sense annotation of text is a complex and time consuming process. In fact, Ng (1997) estimated that 16 person years of manual effort would be required to create enough labeled examples to train a wide-coverage WSD system. This limitation is commonly referred to as the *data acquisition bottleneck*. It is particularly acute in specific domains, such as biomedicine, where terms may have technical usages which only domain experts are likely to be aware of. For example, possible meanings of the term "ganglion" in UMLS (Humphreys et al., 1998) include 'neural structure' or 'benign mucinous tumour', although only the first meaning is listed in WordNet. These domain-specific semantic distinctions make manual sense annotation all the more difficult.

One approach to the data acquisition bottleneck is to generate labeled training examples automatically. Others, such as Leacock et al. (1998) and Agirre and Martínez (2004b), used information from WordNet to construct queries which were used to retrieve training examples. This paper presents a novel approach to this problem. Relevance feedback, a technique used in Information Retrieval (IR) to improve search results, is adapted to identify further examples for each sense of ambiguous terms. These examples are then used to train a semi-supervised WSD system either by combining them with existing annotated data or using them alone. The approach is applied to a set of ambiguous terms in biomedical texts, a domain for which existing resources containing labeled examples, such as the NLM-WSD data set (Weeber et al., 2001), are limited.

The next section outlines previous techniques which have been used to avoid the data acquisition bottleneck. Section 3 describes our approach based on relevance feedback. The WSD system we use is described in Section 4. Section 5 describes experiments carried out to determine the usefulness of the automatically retrieved examples. The final section summarises conclusions which can be drawn from this work and outlines future work.

© 2008. Licensed under the *Creative Commons Attribution-Noncommercial-Share Alike 3.0 Unported* license (http://creativecommons.org/licenses/by-nc-sa/3.0/). Some rights reserved.

2 Previous Approaches

A variety of approaches to the data acquisition bottleneck have been proposed. One is to use unsupervised algorithms, which do not require labeled training data. Examples include Lesk (1986) who disambiguated ambiguous words by examining their dictionary definitions and selecting the sense whose definition overlapped most with definitions of words in the ambiguous word's context. Leroy and Rindflesch (2005) presented an unsupervised approach to WSD in the biomedical domain using information derived from UMLS (Humphreys et al., 1998).

However, results from SemEval (Agirre et al., 2007) and its predecessors have shown that supervised approaches to WSD generally outperform unsupervised ones. It has also been shown that results obtained from supervised methods improve with access to additional labeled data for training (Ng, 1997). Consequently various techniques for automatically generating training data have been developed.

One approach makes use of the fact that different senses of ambiguous words often have different translations (e.g. Ng et al. (2003)). Parallel text is used as training data with the alternative translations serving as sense labels. However, disadvantages of this approach are that the alternative translations do not always correspond to the sense distinctions in the original language and parallel text is not always available.

Another approach, developed by Leacock et al. (1998) and extended by Agirre and Martínez (2004b), is to examine a lexical resource, WordNet in both cases, to identify unambiguous terms which are closely related to each of the senses of an ambiguous term. These "monosemous relatives" are used to as query terms for a search engine and the examples returned used as additional training data.

In the biomedical domain, Humphrey et al. (2006) use journal descriptors to train models based on the terms which are likely to co-occur with each sense. Liu et al. (2002) used information in UMLS to disambiguate automatically retrieved examples which were then used as labeled training data. The meanings of 35 ambiguous abbreviations were identified by examining the closeness of concepts in the same abstract in UMLS. Widdows et al. (2003) employ a similar approach, although their method also makes use of parallel corpora when available.

All of these approaches rely on the existence of an external resource (e.g. parallel text or a domain ontology). In this paper we present a novel approach, inspired by the relevance feedback technique used in IR, which automatically identifes additional training examples using existing labeled data.

3 Generating Examples using Relevance Feedback

The aim of relevance feedback is to generate improved search queries based on manual analysis of a set of retrieved documents which has been shown to improve search precision (Salton, 1971; Robertson and Spark Jones, 1976). Variations of relevance feedback have been developed for a range of IR models including Vector Space and probabilistic models. The formulation of relevance feedback for the Vector Space Model is most pertinent to our approach.

Given a collection of documents, C, containing a set of terms, C_{terms}, a basic premise of the Vector Space Model is that documents and queries can be represented by vectors whose dimensions represent the C_{terms}. Relevance feedback assumes that a retrieval system returns a set of documents, D, for some query, q. It is also assumed that a user has examined D and identified some of the documents as relevant to q and others as not relevant. Relevant documents are denoted by D_{+q} and the irrelevant as D_{-q}, where $D_{+q} \subseteq D$, $D_{-q} \subseteq D$ and $D_{+q} \cap D_{-q} = \emptyset$. This information is used to create a modified query, q_m, which should be more accurate than q. A standard approach to constructing q_m was described by Rocchio (1971):

$$q_m = \alpha q + \frac{\beta}{|D_{+q}|} \sum_{\forall d \in D_{+q}} d - \frac{\gamma}{|D_{-q}|} \sum_{\forall d \in D_{-q}} d \quad (1)$$

where the parameters α, β and γ are set for particular applications. Rocchio (1971) set α to 1.

Our scenario is similar to the relevance feedback problem since the sense tagged examples provide information about the documents in which a particular meaning of an ambiguous term is likely to be found. By identifying the features which distinguish the documents containing one sense from the others we can create queries which can then be used to retrieve further examples of the ambiguous words used in the same sense. However, unlike

$$score(t,s) = idf(t) \times \left(\frac{\alpha}{|D_{+s}|} \sum_{\forall d \in D_{+s}} count(t,d) - \frac{\beta}{|D_{-s}|} \sum_{\forall d \in D_{-s}} count(t,d) \right) \quad (2)$$

the relevance feedback scenario there is no original query to modify. Consequently we start with a query containing just the ambiguous term and use relevance feedback to generate queries which aim to retrieve documents where that term is being used in a particular sense.

The remainder of this section describes how this approach is applied in more detail.

3.1 Corpus Analysis

The first stage of our process is to analyse the labeled examples and identify good search terms. For each sense of an ambiguous term, s, the labeled examples are divided into two sets: those annotated with the sense in question and the remainder (annotated with another sense). In relevance feedback terminology the documents annotated with the sense in question are considered to be relevant and the remainder irrelevant. These examples are denoted by D_{+s} and D_{-s} respectively.

At its core relevance feedback, as outlined above, aims to discover how accurately each term in the collection discriminates between relevant and irrelevant documents. This approach was used to inspire a technique for identifying terms which are likely to indicate the sense in which an ambiguous word is being used. We compute a single score for each term, reflecting its indicativeness of that sense, using the formula in equation 2, where $count(t,d)$ is the number of times term t occurs in document d and $idf(t)$ is the inverse document frequency term weighting function commonly used in IR. We compute idf as follows:

$$idf(t) = log\frac{|C|}{df(t)} \quad (3)$$

where D is the set of all annotated examples (i.e. $D = D_{+s} \cap D_{-s}$) and $df(t)$ the number of documents in C which contain t.[1]

In our experiments the α and β parameters in equation 2 are set to 1. Documents are lemmatised and stopwords removed before computing relevance scores.

[1] Our computation of $idf(t)$ is based on only information from the labeled examples, i.e. we assume $C = D_{+s} \cap D_{-s}$. Alternatively idf could be computed over a larger corpus of labeled and unlabeled examples.

Table 1 shows the ten terms with the highest relevance score for two senses of the term "culture" in UMLS: 'laboratory culture' ("In peripheral blood mononuclear cell *culture* streptococcal erythrogenic toxins are able to stimulate tryptophan degradation in humans") and 'anthropological culture' ("The aim of this paper is to describe the origins, initial steps and strategy, current progress and main accomplishments of introducing a quality management *culture* within the healthcare system in Poland.").

'anthropological culture'		'laboratory culture'	
cultural	26.17	suggest	6.32
recommendation	14.82	protein	6.13
force	14.80	presence	5.86
ethnic	14.79	demonstrate	5.86
practice	14.76	analysis	5.78
man	14.76	gene	5.58
problem	13.04	compare	5.47
assessment	12.94	level	5.36
experience	11.60	response	5.35
consider	11.58	data	5.35

Table 1: Relevant terms for two senses of 'culture'

3.2 Query Generation

Unlike the traditional formulation of relevance feedback there is no initial query. To create a query designed to retrieve examples of each sense we simply combine the ambiguous term and the n terms with the highest relevance scores. We found that using the three highest ranked terms provided good results. So, for example, the queries generated for the two senses of culture shown in Table 1 would be "`culture cultural recommendation force`" and "`culture suggest protein presence`".

3.3 Example Collection

The next stage is to collect a set of examples using the generated queries. We use the Entrez retrieval system (`http://www.ncbi.nlm.nih.gov/sites/gquery`) which provides an online interface for carrying out boolean queries over the PubMed database of biomedical journal abstracts.

Agirre and Martínez (2004b) showed that it is important to preserve the bias of the original corpus when automatically retrieving examples and consequently the number retrieved for each sense is kept in proportion to the original corpus. For example, if our existing labeled examples contain 75 usages of 'culture' in the 'laboratoy culture' sense and 25 meaning 'anthropological culture' we would ensure that 75% of the examples returned would refer to the first sense and 25% to the second.

Unsurprisingly, we found that the most useful abstracts for a particular sense are the ones which contain more of the relevant terms identified using the process in Section 3.1. However, if too many terms are included Entrez may not return any abstracts. To ensure that a sufficient number of abstracts are returned we implemented a process of query relaxation which begins by querying Entrez with the most specific query for set of terms. If that query matches enough abstracts these are retrieved and the search for labeled examples for the relevant sense considered complete. However, if that query does not match enough abstracts it is relaxed and Entrez queried again. This process is repeated until enough examples can be retrieved for a particular sense.

The process of relaxing queries is carried out as follows. Assume we have an ambiguous term, a, and a set of terms T identified using the process in Section 3.1. The first, most specific query, is formed from the conjunction of all terms in $a \cup T$, i.e. "a and t_1 AND t_2 AND ... $t_{|T|}$". This is referred to as the level $|T|$ query. If this query does not return enough abstracts the more relaxed level $|T| - 1$ query is formed. This query returns documents which include the ambiguous word and all but one of the terms in T: "a AND ((t_1 AND t_2 AND ... AND t_{n-1}) OR (t_1 AND t_2 AND ... t_{n-2} AND t_n) OR ... OR (t_2 AND t_3 ... AND t_n))". Similarly, level $|T| - 2$ queries return documents containing the ambiguous term and all but two of the terms in T. Level 1 queries, the most relaxed, return documents containing the ambiguous term and one of the terms in T. We do not use just the ambiguous term as the query since this does not contain any information which could discriminate between the possible meanings. Figure 1 shows the queries which are formed for the ambiguous term "culture" and the three most salient terms identified for the 'anthropological culture' sense. The "matches" column lists the number of PubMed abstracts the query matches. It can be seen that there are no matches for the level 3 query and 83 for the more relaxed level 2 query. For this sense, abstracts returned by the level 2 query would be used if 83 or fewer examples were required, otherwise abstracts returned by the level 1 query would be used.

Note that the queries submitted to Entrez are restricted so the terms only match against the title and abstract of the PubMed articles. This avoids spurious matches against other parts of the records including metadata and authors' names.

4 WSD System

The basis of our WSD system was developed by Agirre and Martínez (2004a) and participated in the Senseval-3 challenge (Mihalcea et al., 2004) with a performance which was close to the best system for the English and Basque lexical sample tasks. The system has been adapted to the biomedical domain (Stevenson et al., 2008) and has the best reported results over the NLM-WSD corpus (Weeber et al., 2001), a standard data set for evaluation of WSD algorithms in this domain.

The system uses a wide range of features which are commonly employed for WSD:

Local collocations: A total of 41 features which extensively describe the context of the ambiguous word and fall into two main types: (1) bigrams and trigrams containing the ambiguous word constructed from lemmas, word forms or PoS tags, and (2) preceding/following lemma/word-form of the content words (adjective, adverb, noun and verb) in the same sentence with the target word.

Syntactic Dependencies: This feature models longer-distance dependencies of the ambiguous words than can be represented by the local collocations. Five relations are extracted: object, subject, noun-modifier, preposition and sibling. These are identified using heuristic patterns and regular expressions applied to PoS tag sequences around the ambiguous word (Agirre and Martínez, 2004a).

Salient bigrams: Salient bigrams within the abstract with high log-likelihood scores, as described by Pedersen (2001).

Unigrams: Lemmas of all content words (nouns, verbs, adjectives, adverbs) in the target word's sentence and, as a separate feature, lemmas of all content words within a 4-word window around the target word, excluding those in a list of corpus-specific stopwords (e.g. "ABSTRACT", "CONCLUSION"). In addition, the lemmas of any

Level	Matches	Query
3	0	`culture AND (cultural AND recommendation AND force)`
2	83	`culture AND ((cultural AND recommendation) OR (cultural AND force) OR (recommendation AND force))`
1	6,358	`culture AND (cultural OR recommendation OR force)`

Figure 1: Examples of various query levels

unigrams which appear at least twice in the entire corpus which are found in the abstract are also included as features. This feature was not used by Agirre and Martínez (2004a), but Joshi et al. (2005) found them to be useful for this task.

Features are combined using the **Vector Space Model**, a memory-based learning algorithm (see Agirre and Martínez (2004a)). Each occurrence of an ambiguous word is represented as a binary vector in which each position indicates the occurrence/absence of a feature. A single centroid vector is generated for each sense during training. These centroids are compared with the vectors that represent new examples using the cosine metric to compute similarity. The sense assigned to a new example is that of the closest centroid.

5 Experiments

5.1 Setup

The NLM-WSD corpus Weeber et al. (2001) was used for evaluation. It contains 100 examples of 50 ambiguous terms which occur frequently in MEDLINE. Each example consists of the abstract from a biomedical journal article which contains an instance of the ambiguous terms which has been manually annotated with a UMLS concept.

The 50 ambiguous terms which form the NLM-WSD data set represent a range of challenges for WSD systems. Various researchers (Liu et al., 2004; Leroy and Rindflesch, 2005; Joshi et al., 2005; McInnes et al., 2007) chose to exclude some of the terms (generally those with highly skewed sense distributions or low inter-annotator agreement) and evaluated their systems against a subset of the terms. The number of terms in these subsets range between 9 and 28. The Most Frequent Sense (MFS) heuristic has become a standard baseline in WSD (McCarthy et al., 2004) and is simply the accuracy which would be obtained by assigning the most common meaning of a term to all of its instances in a corpus. The MFS for the whole NLM-WSD corpus is 78% and ranges between 69.9% and 54.9% for the various subsets. We report results across the NLM-WSD corpus and four subsets from the literature for completeness.

The approach described in Section 3 was applied to the NLM-WSD data set. 10-fold cross validation is used for all experiments. Consequently 10 instances of each ambiguous term were held back for testing during each fold and additional examples generated by examining the 90 remaining instances. Three sets of labeled examples were generated for each fold, containing 90, 180 and 270 examples for each ambiguous term. The NLM-WSD corpus represents the only reliably labeled data to which we have access and is used to evaluate all approaches (that is, systems trained on combinations of the NLM-WSD corpus and/or the automatically generated examples).

5.2 Results

Various WSD systems were created. The "basic" system was trained using only the NLM-WSD data set and was used as a benchmark. Three systems, "+90", "+180" and "+270" were trained using the combination of the NLM-WSD data set and, respectively, the 90, 180 and 270 automatically retrieved examples for each term. A further three systems, "90", "180" and "270" were trained using only the automatically retrieved examples.

The performance of our system is shown in Table 2. The part of the table labeled "Subsets properties" lists the number of terms in each subset of the NLM-WSD corpus and the relevant MFS baseline.

Adding the first 90 automatically retrieved examples ("+90" column) significantly improves performance of our system from 87.2%, over all words, to 88.5% (Wilcoxon Signed Ranks Test, $p < 0.01$). Improvements are observed over all subsets of the NLM-WSD corpus. Although the improvements may seem modest they should be understood in the context of the WSD system we are using which has exceeded previously reported performance figures and therefore represents a high baseline.

Table 2 also shows that adding more automatically retrieved examples ("+180" and "+270" columns) causes a drop in performance and re-

Subset	Subset Properties		basic	Combined			New only		
	Terms	MFS		+90	+180	+270	90	180	270
All words	50	78.0	87.2	**88.5**	87.0	86.1	85.6	84.5	82.7
Joshi et. al.	28	66.9	82.3	**83.8**	81.6	80.9	79.8	78.0	76.3
Liu et. al.	22	69.9	77.8	**79.6**	76.9	76.1	74.9	72.0	70.9
Leroy	15	55.3	84.3	**85.9**	84.4	83.6	81.2	80.0	78.0
McInnes et. al.	9	54.9	79.6	**81.8**	80.4	79.4	75.2	73.0	71.4

Table 2: Performance of system using a variety of combinations of training examples

sults using these examples are worse than using the NLM-WSD corpus alone. The query relaxation process, outlined in Section 3.3, uses less discriminating queries when more examples are required and it is likely that this is leading to noise in the training examples.

The rightmost portion of Table 2 shows performance when the system is trained using only the automatically generated examples which is consistently worse than using the NLM-WSD corpus alone. Performance also decreases as more examples are added. However, results obtained using only the automatically generated training examples are consistently better than the relevant baseline.

Table 3 shows the performance of the system trained on the NLM-WSD data set compared against training using only the 90 automatically generated examples for each ambiguous term in the NLM-WSD corpus. It can be seen that there is a wide variation between the performance of the additional examples compared with the original corpus. For 11 terms training using the additional examples alone is more effective than using the NLM-WSD corpus. However, there are several words for which the performance using the automatically acquired examples is considerably worse than using the NLM-WSD corpus.

Information about the performance of a system trained using only the 90 automatically acquired examples can be used to boost WSD performance further. In this scenario, which we refer to as *example filtering*, the system has a choice whether to make use of the additional training data or not. For each word, performance of the WSD system trained using only the 90 automatically acquired examples is compared against the one trained on the NLM-WSD data set (i.e. results shown in Table 3). If the performance is as good, or better, then the additional examples are used, otherwise only examples in the NLM-WSD corpus are used as training data. Since the annotated examples in the NLM-WSD corpus have already been examined to generate the additional examples, example filtering does not require any more labeled data.

Results obtained when example filtering is used are shown in Table 4. The columns "+90(f)", "+180(f)" and "+270(f)" show performance when the relevant set of examples is filtered. (Note that all three sets of examples are filtered against the performance of the first 90 examples, i.e. results shown in Table 3.) This table shows that example filtering improves performance when the WSD system is trained using the automatically retrieved examples. Performance using the first 90 filtered examples ("+90(f)" column) is 89%, over all words, compared with 88.5% when filtering is not used. While performance decreases as larger sets of examples are used, results using each of the three sets of filtered examples is signifcantly better than the basic system (Wilcoxon Signed Ranks Test, $p < 0.01$ for "+90(f)" and "+180(f)", $p < 0.05$ for "+270(f)").

6 Conclusion and Future Work

This paper has presented a novel approach to the data acquisition bottleneck for WSD. Our technique is inspired by the relevance feedback technique from IR. This is a semi-supervised approach which generates labeled examples using available sense annotated data and, unlike previously published approaches, does not rely on external resources such as parallel text or an ontology. Evaluation was carried out on a WSD task from the biomedical domain for which the number of labeled examples available for each ambiguous term is limited. The automatically acquired examples improve the performance of a WSD system which has already been shown to exceed previously published results.

The approach presented in this paper could be extended in several ways. Our experiments focus

	basic	+90(f)	+180(f)	+270(f)
All words	87.2	89.0	88.2	87.9
Joshi et. al.	82.3	84.6	83.5	83.3
Liu et. al.	84.3	86.6	85.7	85.5
Leroy	77.8	80.3	79.1	78.5
McInnes et. al.	79.6	82.4	81.6	80.8

Table 4: Performance using example filtering

on the biomedical domain. The relevance feedback approach could be applied to other lexical ambiguities found in biomedical texts, such as abbreviations with multiple expansions (e.g. Liu et al. (2002)), or to WSD of general text, possibly using the SemEval data for evaluation.

Future work will explore alternative methods for generating query terms including other types of relevance feedback and lexical association measures (e.g. Chi-squared and mutual information). Experiments described here rely on a boolean IR engine (Entrez). It is possible that an IR system which takes term weights into account could lead to the retrieval of more useful MEDLINE abstracts. Finally, it would be interesting to explore the relation between query relaxation and the usefulness of the retrieved abstracts.

Acknowledgments

The authors are grateful to David Martinez for the use of his WSD system for these experiments and to feedback provided by three anonymous reviewers. This work was funded by the UK Engineering and Physical Sciences Research Council, grant number EP/E004350/1.

References

E. Agirre and P. Edmonds, editors. 2007. *Word Sense Disambiguation: Algorithms and Applications*. Text, Speech and Language Technology. Springer.

E. Agirre and D. Martínez. 2004a. The Basque Country University system: English and Basque tasks. In Rada Mihalcea and Phil Edmonds, editors, *Senseval-3: Third International Workshop on the Evaluation of Systems for the Semantic Analysis of Text*, pages 44–48, Barcelona, Spain, July.

E. Agirre and D. Martínez. 2004b. Unsupervised WSD based on automatically retrieved examples: The importance of bias. In *Proceedings of the Conference on Empirical Methods in Natural Language Processing (EMNLP-04)*, Barcelona, Spain.

E. Agirre, L. Marquez, and R. Wicentowski, editors. 2007. *SemEval 2007: Proceedings of the 4th International Workshop on Semantic Evaluations*, Prague, Czech Republic.

S. Humphrey, W. Rogers, H. Kilicoglu, D. Demner-Fushman, and T. Rindflesch. 2006. Word Sense Disambiguation by selecting the best semantic type based on Journal Descriptor Indexing: Preliminary experiment. *Journal of the American Society for Information Science and Technology*, 57(5):96–113.

L. Humphreys, D. Lindberg, H. Schoolman, and G. Barnett. 1998. The Unified Medical Language System: An Informatics Research Collaboration. *Journal of the American Medical Informatics Association*, 1(5):1–11.

M. Joshi, T. Pedersen, and R. Maclin. 2005. A Comparative Study of Support Vector Machines Applied to the Word Sense Disambiguation Problem for the Medical Domain. In *Proceedings of the Second Indian Conference on Artificial Intelligence (IICAI-05)*, pages 3449–3468, Pune, India.

C. Leacock, M. Chodorow, and G. Miller. 1998. Using corpus statistics and WordNet relations for sense identification. *Computational Linguistics*, 24(1):147–165.

G. Leroy and T. Rindflesch. 2005. Effects of Information and Machine Learning algorithms on Word Sense Disambiguation with small datasets. *International Journal of Medical Informatics*, 74(7-8):573–585.

M. Lesk. 1986. Automatic sense disambiguation using machine readable dictionaries: how to tell a pine cone from an ice cream cone. In *Proceedings of ACM SIGDOC Conference*, pages 24–26, Toronto, Canada.

H. Liu, S. Johnson, and C. Friedman. 2002. Automatic Resolution of Ambiguous Terms Based on Machine Learning and Conceptual Relations in the UMLS. *Journal of the American Medical Informatics Association*, 9(6):621–636.

H. Liu, V. Teller, and C. Friedman. 2004. A Multi-aspect Comparison Study of Supervised Word Sense Disambiguation. *Journal of the American Medical Informatics Association*, 11(4):320–331.

word	basic	90	Δ
adjustment	71	70	-1
association	100	100	0
blood_pressure	48	50	2
cold	88	86	-2
condition	89	90	1
culture	96	91	-5
degree	96	86	-10
depression	88	85	-3
determination	87	82	-5
discharge	95	92	-3
energy	98	99	1
evaluation	76	75	-1
extraction	85	82	-3
failure	66	71	5
fat	85	83	-2
fit	87	85	-2
fluid	100	100	0
frequency	95	94	-1
ganglion	97	95	-2
glucose	91	92	1
growth	70	67	-3
immunosuppression	79	79	0
implantation	90	88	-2
inhibition	98	98	0
japanese	73	75	2
lead	91	90	-1
man	87	82	-5
mole	95	84	-11
mosaic	87	83	-4
nutrition	53	43	-10
pathology	85	85	0
pressure	94	96	2
radiation	84	82	-2
reduction	89	90	1
repair	87	86	-1
resistance	98	97	-1
scale	86	79	-7
secretion	99	99	0
sensitivity	93	91	-2
sex	87	84	-3
single	99	99	0
strains	92	92	0
support	86	89	3
surgery	97	98	1
transient	99	99	0
transport	93	93	0
ultrasound	87	85	-2
variation	94	89	-5
weight	77	77	0
white	73	74	1
Average	87.2	85.6	-1.58

Table 3: Comparison of performance using original training data and 90 automatically generated examples

D. McCarthy, R. Koeling, J. Weeds, and J. Carroll. 2004. Finding Predominant Senses in Untagged Text. In *Proceedings of the 42nd Annual Meeting of the Association for Computational Lingusitics (ACL-2004)*, pages 280–287, Barcelona, Spain.

B. McInnes, T. Pedersen, and J. Carlis. 2007. Using UMLS Concept Unique Identifiers (CUIs) for Word Sense Disambiguation in the Biomedical Domain. In *Proceedings of the Annual Symposium of the American Medical Informatics Association*, pages 533–537, Chicago, IL.

R. Mihalcea, T. Chklovski, and A. Kilgarriff. 2004. The Senseval-3 English lexical sample task. In *Proceedings of Senseval-3: The Third International Workshop on the Evaluation of Systems for the Semantic Analysis of Text*, Barcelona, Spain.

H. Ng, B. Wang, and S. Chan. 2003. Exploiting Parallel Texts for Word Sense Disambiguation: an Empirical Study. In *Proceedings of the 41st Annual Meeting of the Association for Computational Linguistics (ACL-03)*, pages 455–462, Sapporo, Japan.

H. Ng. 1997. Getting serious about Word Sense Disambiguation. In *Proceedings of the SIGLEX Workshop "Tagging Text with Lexical Semantics: What, why and how?"*, pages 1–7, Washington, DC.

T. Pedersen. 2001. A Decision Tree of Bigrams is an Accurate Predictor of Word Sense. In *Proceedings of the Second Meeting of the North American Chapter of the Association for Computational Linguistics (NAACL-01)*, pages 79–86, Pittsburgh, PA., June.

S. Robertson and K. Spark Jones. 1976. Relevance weighting of search terms. *Journal of the American Society for Information Science and Technology*, 27(3):129–146.

J. Rocchio. 1971. Relevance feedback in Information Retrieval. In G. Salton, editor, *The SMART Retrieval System – Experiments in Automatic Document Processing*. Prentice Hall, Englewood Cliffs, NJ.

G. Salton. 1971. *The SMART Retrieval System – Experiments in Automatic Document Processing*. Prentice Hall Inc., Englewood Cliffs, NJ.

M. Stevenson, Y. Guo, R. Gaizauskas, and D. Martinez. 2008. Knowledge Sources for Word Sense Disambiguation of Biomedical Text. In *Proceedings of the Workshop on Current Trends in Biomedical Natural Language Processing at ACL 2008*, pages 80–87.

M. Weeber, J. Mork, and A. Aronson. 2001. Developing a Test Collection for Biomedical Word Sense Disambiguation. In *Proceedings of AMAI Symposium*, pages 746–50, Washington, DC.

D. Widdows, S. Peters, S. Cederberg, C. Chan, D. Steffen, and P. Buitelaar. 2003. Unsupervised Monolingual and Bilingual Word-sense Disambiguation of Medical Documents using UMLS. In *Workshop on "Natural Langauge Processing in Biomedicine" at ACL 2003*, pages 9–16, Sapporo, Japan.

Topic Identification for Fine-Grained Opinion Analysis

Veselin Stoyanov and **Claire Cardie**
Department of Computer Science
Cornell University
{stoyanov,cardie}@cs.cornell.edu

Abstract

Within the area of general-purpose fine-grained subjectivity analysis, *opinion topic identification* has, to date, received little attention due to both the difficulty of the task and the lack of appropriately annotated resources. In this paper, we provide an operational definition of *opinion topic* and present an algorithm for opinion topic identification that, following our new definition, treats the task as a problem in topic coreference resolution. We develop a methodology for the manual annotation of opinion topics and use it to annotate topic information for a portion of an existing general-purpose opinion corpus. In experiments using the corpus, our topic identification approach statistically significantly outperforms several non-trivial baselines according to three evaluation measures.

1 Introduction

Subjectivity analysis is concerned with extracting information about attitudes, beliefs, emotions, opinions, evaluations, sentiment and other private states expressed in texts. In contrast to the problem of identifying subjectivity or sentiment at the document level (e.g. Pang et al. (2002), Turney (2002)), we are interested in *fine-grained subjectivity analysis*, which is concerned with subjectivity at the phrase or clause level. We expect fine-grained subjectivity analysis to be useful for question-answering, summarization, information extraction and search engine support for queries of the form "How/what does entity X feel/think about topic Y?", for which document-level opinion analysis methods can be problematic.

Fine-grained subjectivity analyses typically identify SUBJECTIVE EXPRESSIONS in context, characterize their POLARITY (e.g. positive, neutral or negative) and INTENSITY (e.g. weak, medium, strong, extreme), and identify the associated SOURCE, or OPINION HOLDER, as well as the TOPIC, or TARGET, of the opinion. While substantial progress has been made in automating some of these tasks, opinion topic identification has received by far the least attention due to both the difficulty of the task and the lack of appropriately annotated resources.[1]

This paper addresses the problem of topic identification for fine-grained opinion analysis of general text.[2] We begin by providing a new, operational definition of *opinion topic* in which the topic of an opinion depends on the context in which its associated opinion expression occurs. We also present a novel method for general-purpose opinion topic identification that, following our new definition, treats the problem as an exercise in topic coreference resolution. We evaluate the approach using the existing MPQA corpus (Wiebe et al., 2005), which we extend with manual annotations that encode topic information (and refer to hereafter as the $\text{MPQA}_{\text{TOPIC}}$ corpus).

Inter-annotator agreement results for the manual annotations are reasonably strong across a number of metrics and the results of experiments that evaluate our topic identification method in the context of fine-grained opinion analysis are promising:

© 2008. Licensed under the *Creative Commons Attribution-Noncommercial-Share Alike 3.0 Unported* license (http://creativecommons.org/licenses/by-nc-sa/3.0/). Some rights reserved.

[1] Section 3 on related work provides additional discussion.

[2] The identification of products and their components and attributes from product reviews is a related, but quite different task from that addressed here. Section 3 briefly discusses, and provides references, to the most relevant research in that area.

using either automatically or manually identified topic spans, we achieve topic coreference scores that statistically significantly outperform two topic segmentation baselines across three coreference resolution evaluation measures (B^3, α and CEAF). For the B^3 metric, for example, the best baseline achieves a topic coreference score on the MPQA$_{\text{TOPIC}}$ corpus of 0.55 while our topic coreference algorithm scores 0.57 and 0.71 using automatically, and manually, identified topic spans, respectively.

In the remainder of the paper, we define opinion topics (Section 2), present related work (Section 3), and motivate and describe the key idea of topic coreference that underlies our methodology for both the manual and automatic annotation of opinion topics (Section 4). Creation of the MPQA$_{\text{TOPIC}}$ corpus is described in Section 5 and our topic identification algorithm, in Section 6. The evaluation methodology and results are presented in Sections 7 and 8, respectively.

2 Definitions and Examples

Consider the following opinion sentences:

(1)[OH John] adores [TARGET+TOPIC SPAN Marseille] and visits it often.

(2)[OH Al] thinks that [TARGET SPAN [TOPIC SPAN? the government] should [TOPIC SPAN? tax gas] more in order to [TOPIC SPAN? curb [TOPIC SPAN? CO_2 emissions]]].

A fine-grained subjectivity analysis should identify: the OPINION EXPRESSION[3] as "adores" in Example 1 and "thinks" in Example 2; the POLARITY as positive in Example 1 and neutral in Example 2; the INTENSITY as medium and low, respectively; and the OPINION HOLDER (OH) as "John" and "Al", respectively. To be able to discuss the opinion TOPIC in each example, we begin with three definitions:

– **Topic.** The TOPIC of a fine-grained opinion is the real-world object, event or abstract entity that is the subject of the opinion as intended by the opinion holder.

– **Topic span.** The TOPIC SPAN associated with an OPINION EXPRESSION is the closest, minimal span of text that mentions the topic.

– **Target span.** In contrast, we use TARGET SPAN to denote the span of text that covers the syntactic surface form comprising the contents of the opinion.

In Example 1, for instance, "Marseille" is both the TOPIC SPAN and the TARGET SPAN associated with the city of Marseille, which is the TOPIC of the opinion. In Example 2, the TARGET SPAN consists of the text that comprises the complement of the subjective verb "thinks". Example 2 illustrates why opinion topic identification is difficult: within the single target span of the opinion, there are multiple potential topics, each identified with its own topic span. Without more context, however, it is impossible to know which phrase indicates the intended topic. If followed by sentence 3, however,

(3) Although he doesn't like government-imposed taxes, he thinks that a fuel tax is the only effective solution.

the topic of Al's opinion in 2 is much clearer — it is likely to be fuel tax, denoted via the TOPIC SPAN "tax gas" or "tax".

3 Related Work

As previously mentioned, there has been much recent progress in extracting fine-grained subjectivity information from general text. Previous efforts have focused on the extraction of opinion expressions in context (e.g. Bethard et al. (2004), Breck et al. (2007)), the assignment of polarity to these expressions (e.g. Wilson et al. (2005), Kim and Hovy (2006)), source extraction (e.g. Bethard et al. (2004), Choi et al. (2005)), and identification of the source-expresses-opinion relation (e.g. Choi et al. (2006)), i.e. linking sources to the opinions that they express.

Not surprisingly, progress has been driven by the creation of language resources. In this regard, Wiebe et al.'s (2005) opinion annotation scheme for *subjective expressions* was used to create the MPQA corpus, which consists of 535 documents manually annotated for phrase-level expressions of opinions, their sources, polarities, and intensities. Although other opinion corpora exist (e.g. Bethard et al. (2004), Voorhees and Buckland (2003), the product review corpora of Liu[4]), we are not aware of any corpus that rivals the scale and depth of the MPQA corpus.

In the related area of opinion extraction from product reviews, several research efforts have focused on the extraction of the topic of the opinion (e.g. Kobayashi et al. (2004), Yi et al. (2003),

[3]For simplicity, we will use the term *opinion* throughout the paper to cover all types of private states expressed in subjective language.

[4]http://www.cs.uic.edu/ liub/FBS/sentiment-analysis.html

Popescu and Etzioni (2005), Hu and Liu (2004)). For this specialized text genre, it has been sufficient to limit the notion of topic to mentions of product names and components and their attributes. Thus, topic extraction has been effectively substituted with a lexicon look-up and techniques have focused on how to learn or acquire an appropriate lexicon for the task. While the techniques have been very successful for this genre of text, they have not been applied outside the product reviews domain. Further, there are analyses (Wiebe et al., 2005) and experiments (Wilson et al., 2005) that indicate that lexicon-lookup approaches to subjectivity analysis will have limited success on general texts.

Outside the product review domain, there has been little effort devoted to opinion topic annotation. The MPQA corpus, for example, was originally intended to include topic annotations, but the task was abandoned after confirming that it was very difficult (Wiebe, 2005; Wilson, 2005), although target span annotation is currently underway. While useful, target spans alone will be insufficient for many applications: they neither contain information indicating which opinions are about the same topic, nor provide a concise textual representation of the topics.

Due to the lack of appropriately annotated corpora, the problem of opinion topic extraction has been largely unexplored in NLP. A notable exception is the work of Kim and Hovy (2006). They propose a model that extracts opinion topics for subjective expressions signaled by verbs and adjectives. Their model relies on semantic frames and extracts as the topic the syntactic constituent at a specific argument position for the given verb or adjective. In other words, Kim and Hovy extract what we refer to as the target spans, and do so for a subset of the opinion-bearing words in the text. Although on many occasions target spans coincide with opinion topics (as in Example 1), we have observed that on many other occasions this is not the case (as in Example 2). Furthermore, hampered by the lack of resources with manually annotated targets, Kim and Hovy could provide only a limited evaluation.

As we have defined it, opinion topic identification bears some resemblance to topic segmentation, the goal of which is to partition a text into a linear sequence of topically coherent segments. Existing methods for topic segmentation typically assume that fragments of text (e.g. sentences or sequences of words of a fixed length) with similar lexical distribution are about the same topic; the goal of these methods is to find the boundaries where the lexical distribution changes (e.g. Choi (2000), Malioutov and Barzilay (2006)). Opinion topic identification differs from topic segmentation in that opinion topics are not necessarily spatially coherent — there may be two opinions in the same sentence on different topics, as well as opinions that are on the same topic separated by opinions that do not share that topic. Nevertheless, we will compare our topic identification approach to a state-of-the-art topic segmentation algorithm (Choi, 2000) in the evaluation.

Other work has successfully adopted the use of clustering to discover entity relations by identifying entities that appear in the same sentence and clustering the intervening context (e.g. Hasegawa et al. (2004), Rosenfeld and Feldman (2007)). This work, however, considers named entities and heads of proper noun phrases rather than topic spans, and the relations learned are those commonly held between NPs (e.g. senator-of-state, city-of-state, chairman-of-organization) rather than a more general coreference relation.

4 A Coreference Approach to Topic Identification

Given our initial definition of opinion topics (Section 2), the next task is to determine which computational approaches might be employed for automatic opinion topic identification. We begin this exercise by considering some of the problematic characteristics of opinion topics.

Multiple potential topics. As noted earlier via Example 2, a serious problem in opinion topic identification is the mention of multiple potential topics within the target span of the opinion. Although an issue for all opinions, this problem is typically more pronounced in opinions that do not carry sentiment (as in Example 2). Our current definition of opinion topic requires the NLP system (or a human annotator) to decide which of the entities described in the target span, if any, refers to the intended topic. This decision can be aided by the following change to our definition of opinion topic, which introduces the idea of a context-dependent information focus: *the* TOPIC *of an opinion is the real-world entity that is the subject of the opinion as intended by the opinion holder* **based**

on the discourse context.

With this modified definition in hand, and given Example 3 as the succeeding context for Example 2, we argue that the intended subject, and hence the TOPIC, of Al's opinion in 2 can be quickly identified as the FUEL TAX, which is denoted by the TOPIC SPANS "tax gas" in 2 and "fuel tax" in 3.

Opinion topics not always explicitly mentioned. In stark contrast to the above, on many occasions the topic is not mentioned explicitly at all within the target span, as in the following example:

(5)[$_{OH}$ John] identified the violation of Palestinian human rights as one of the main factors. TOPIC: ISRAELI-PALESTINIAN CONFLICT

We have further observed that the opinion topic is often not mentioned within the same paragraph and, on a few occasions, not even within the same document as the opinion expression.

4.1 Our Solution: Topic Coreference

With the above examples and problems in mind, we hypothesize that the notion of *topic coreference* will facilitate both the manual and automatic identification of opinion topics: **We say that two opinions are topic-coreferent if they share the same opinion topic.** In particular, we conjecture that judging whether or not two opinions are topic-coreferent is easier than specifying the topic of each opinion (due to the problems described above).

5 Constructing the MPQA$_{TOPIC}$ Corpus

Relying on the notion of topic coreference, we next introduce a new methodology for the manual annotation of opinion topics in text:

1. The annotator begins with a corpus of documents that has been annotated w.r.t. OPINION EXPRESSIONS. With each opinion expression, the corpus provides POLARITY and OPINION HOLDER information. (We use the aforementioned MPQA corpus.)

2. The annotator maintains a list of the opinion expressions that remain to be annotated (initially, all opinion expressions in the document) as well as a list of the current groupings (i.e. clusters) of opinion expressions that have been identified as topic-coreferent (initially this list is empty).

3. For each opinion expression, in turn, the annotator decides whether the opinion is on the same topic as the opinions in one of the existing clusters or should start a new cluster, and inserts the opinion in the appropriate cluster.

4. The annotator labels each cluster with a string that describes the opinion topic that covers all opinions in the cluster.

5. The annotator marks the TOPIC SPAN of each opinion. (This can be done at any point in the process.)

The manual annotation procedure is described in a set of instructions available at http://www.cs.cornell.edu/~ves. In addition, we created a GUI that facilitates the annotation procedure. With the help of these resources, one person annotated opinion topics for a randomly selected set of 150 of the 535 documents in the MPQA corpus. In addition, 20 of the 150 documents were selected at random and annotated by a second annotator for the purposes of an inter-annotator agreement study, the results of which are presented in Section 8.1. The MPQA$_{TOPIC}$ and the procedure by which it was created are described in more detail in (Stoyanov and Cardie, 2008).

6 The Topic Coreference Algorithm

As mentioned in Section 4, our computational approach to opinion topic identification is based on topic coreference: For each document (1) find the clusters of coreferent opinions, and (2) label the clusters with the name of the topic. In this paper we focus only on the first task, topic coreference resolution — the most critical step for topic identification. We conjecture that the second step can be performed through frequency analysis of the terms in each of the clusters and leave it for future work.

Topic coreference resolution resembles another well-known problem in NLP — noun phrase (NP) coreference resolution. Therefore, we adapt a standard machine learning-based approach to NP coreference resolution (Soon et al., 2001; Ng and Cardie, 2002) for our purposes. Our adaptation has three steps: (i) identify the topic spans; (ii) perform pairwise classification of the associated opinions as to whether or not they are topic-coreferent; and, (iii) cluster the opinions according to the results of (ii). Each step is discussed in more detail below.

6.1 Identifying Topic Spans

Decisions about topic coreference should depend on the text spans that express the topic. Ideally, we would be able to recover the topic span of each opinion and use its content for the topic coreference decision. However, the topic span depends on the topic itself, so it is unrealistic that topic spans can be recovered with simple methods. Nevertheless, in this initial work, we investigate two simple methods for automatic topic span identification and compare them to two manual approaches:

- **Sentence.** Assume that the topic span is the whole sentence containing the opinion.
- **Automatic.** A rule-based method for identifying the topic span (developed using MPQA documents that are not part of $\text{MPQA}_{\text{TOPIC}}$). Rules depend on the syntactic constituent type of the opinion expression and rely on syntactic parsing and grammatical role labeling.
- **Manual.** Use the topic span marked by the human annotator. We included this method to provide an upper bound on performance of the topic span extractor.
- **Modified Manual.** Meant to be a more realistic use of the manual topic span annotations, this method returns the manually identified topic span only when it is within the sentence of the opinion expression. When this span is outside the sentence boundary, this method returns the opinion sentence.

Of the 4976 opinions annotated across the 150 documents of $\text{MPQA}_{\text{TOPIC}}$, the topic spans associated with 4293 were within the same sentence as the opinion; 3653 were within the span extracted by our topic span extractor. Additionally, the topic spans of 173 opinions were outside of the paragraph containing the opinion.

6.2 Pairwise Topic Coreference Classification

The heart of our method is a pairwise topic coreference classifier. Given a pair of opinions (and their associated polarity and opinion holder information), the goal of the classifier is to determine whether the opinions are topic-coreferent. We use the manually annotated data to automatically learn the pairwise classifier. Given a training document, we construct a training example for every pair of opinions in the document (each pair is represented as a feature vector). The pair is labeled as a positive example if the two opinions belong to the same topic cluster, and a negative example otherwise.

Pairwise coreference classification relies critically on the expressiveness of the features used to describe the opinion pair. We use three categories of features: positional, lexico-semantic and opinion-based features.

Positional features These features are intended to exploit the fact that opinions that are close to each other are more likely to be on the same topic. We use six positional features:

- **Same Sentence/Paragraph**[5] True if the two opinions are in the same sentence/paragraph.
- **Consecutive Sentences/Paragraphs** True if the two opinions are in consecutive sentences/paragraphs.
- **Number of Sentences/Paragraphs** The number of sentences/paragraphs that separate the two opinions.

TOPIC SPAN-**based lexico-semantic features** The features in this group rely on the topic spans and are recomputed w.r.t. each of the four topic span methods. The intuition behind this group of features is that topic-coreferent opinions are likely to exhibit lexical and semantic similarity within the topic span.

- **tf.idf** The cosine similarity of the tf.idf weighted vectors of the terms contained in the two spans.
- **Word overlap** True if the two topic spans contain any contain words in common.
- **NP coref** True if the two spans contain NPs that are determined to be coreferent by a simple rule-based coreference system.
- **NE overlap** True if the two topic spans contain named entities that can be considered aliases of each other.

Opinion features The features in this group depend on the attributes of the opinion. In the current work, we obtain these features directly from the manual annotations of the $\text{MPQA}_{\text{TOPIC}}$ corpus, but they might also be obtained from automatically identified opinion information using the methods referenced in Section 3.

- **Source Match** True if the two opinions have the same opinion holder.
- **Polarity Match** True if the two opinions have the same polarity.

[5]We use sentence/paragraph to describe two features – one based on the sentence and one on the paragraph.

- **Source-Polarity Match** False if the two opinions have the same opinion holder but conflicting polarities (since it is unlikely that a source will have two opinions with conflicting polarities on the same topic).

We employ three classifiers for pairwise coreference classification – an averaged perceptron (Freund and Schapire, 1998), SVM^{light} (Joachims, 1998) and a rule-learner – RIPPER (Cohen, 1995). However, we report results only for the averaged perceptron, which exhibited the best performance.

6.3 Clustering

Pairwise classification provides an estimate of the likelihood that two opinions are topic-coreferent. To form the topic clusters, we follow the pairwise classification with a clustering step. We selected a simple clustering algorithm – single-link clustering, which has shown good performance for NP coreference. Given a threshold, single-link clustering proceeds by assigning pairs of opinions with a topic-coreference score above the threshold to the same topic cluster and then performs transitive closure of the clusters.[6]

7 Evaluation Methodology

For training and evaluation we use the 150-document $\text{MPQA}_{\text{TOPIC}}$ corpus. All machine learning methods were tested via 10-fold cross validation. In each round of cross validation, we use eight of the data partitions for training and one for parameter estimation (we varied the threshold for the clustering algorithm), and test on the remaining partition. We report results for the three evaluation measures of Section 7 using the four topic span extraction methods introduced in Section 6. The threshold is tuned separately for each evaluation measure. As noted earlier, all runs obtain opinion information from the $\text{MPQA}_{\text{TOPIC}}$ corpus (i.e. this work does not incorporate automatic opinion extraction).

7.1 Topic Coreference Baselines

We compare our topic coreference system to four baselines. The first two are the "default" baselines:

- **one topic** – assigns all opinions to the same cluster.
- **one opinion per cluster** – assigns each opinion to its own cluster.

The other two baselines attempt to perform topic segmentation (discussed in Section 3) and assign all opinions within the same segment to the same opinion topic:

- **same paragraph** – simple topic segmentation by splitting documents into segments at paragraph boundaries.
- **Choi 2000** – Choi's (2000) state-of-the-art approach to finding segment boundaries. We use the freely available C99 software described in Choi (2000), varying a parameter that allows us to control the average number of sentences per segment and reporting the best result on the test data.

7.2 Evaluation Metrics

Because there is disagreement among researchers w.r.t. the proper evaluation measure for NP coreference resolution, we use three generally accepted metrics[7] to evaluate our topic coreference system.

B-CUBED. B-CUBED (B^3) is a commonly used NP coreference metric (Bagga and Baldwin, 1998). It calculates precision and recall for each item (in our case, each opinion) based on the number of correctly identified coreference links, and then computes the average of the item scores in each document. Precision/recall for an item i is computed as the proportion of items in the intersection of the response (system-generated) and key (gold standard) clusters containing i divided by the number of items in the response/key cluster.

CEAF. As a representative of another group of coreference measures that rely on mapping response clusters to key clusters, we selected Luo's (2005) CEAF score (short for Constrained Entity-Alignment F-Measure). Similar to the ACE (2005) score, CEAF operates by computing an optimal mapping of response clusters to key clusters and assessing the goodness of the match of each of the mapped clusters.

Krippendorff's α. Finally, we use Passonneau's (2004) generalization of Krippendorff's (1980) α — a standard metric employed for inter-annotator

[6]Experiments using best-first and last-first clustering approaches provided similar or worse results.

[7]The MUC scoring algorithm (Vilain et al., 1995) was omitted because it led to an unjustifiably high MUC F-score (.920) for the ONE TOPIC baseline.

	B^3	α	CEAF
All opinions	.6424	.5476	.6904
Sentiment opinions	.7180	.7285	.7967
Strong opinions	.7374	.7669	.8217

Table 1: Inter-annotator agreement results.

reliability studies. Krippendorff's α is based on a probabilistic interpretation of the agreement of coders as compared to agreement by chance. While Passonneau's innovation makes it possible to apply Krippendorff's α to coreference clusters, the probabilistic interpretation of the statistic is unfortunately lost.

8 Results

8.1 Inter-annotator Agreement

As mentioned previously, out of the 150 annotated documents, 20 were annotated by two annotators for the purpose of studying the agreement between coders. Inter-annotator agreement results are shown in Table 1. We compute agreement for three subsets of opinions: all available opinions, only the sentiment-bearing opinions and the subset of sentiment-bearing opinions judged to have polarity of medium or higher.

The results support our conjecture that topics of sentiment-bearing opinions are much easier to identify: inter-annotator agreement for opinions with non-neutral polarity (SENTIMENT OPINIONS) improves by a large margin for all measures. As in other work in subjectivity annotation, we find that strong sentiment-bearing opinions are easier to annotate than sentiment-bearing opinions in general.

Generally, the α score aims to probabilistically capture the agreement of annotation data and separate it from chance agreement. It is generally accepted that an α score of .667 indicates reliable agreement. The score that we observed for the overall agreement was an α of .547, which is below the generally accepted level, while α for the two subsets of sentiment-bearing opinions is above .72. However, as discussed above, due to the way that it is adapted to the problem of coreference resolution, the α score loses its probabilistic interpretation. For example, the α score requires that a pairwise distance function between clusters is specified. We used one sensible choice for such a function (we measured the distance between clusters A and B as $dist(A, B) = (2 * |A \cap B|)/(|A| + |B|)$),

	B^3	α	CEAF
One topic	.3739	-.1017	.2976
One opinion per cluster	.2941	.2238	.2741
Same paragraph	.5542	.3123	.5090
Choi	.5399	.3734	.5370
Sentence	.5749	.4032	.5393
Rule-based	.5730	.4056	.5420
Modified manual	.6416	.5134	.6124
Manual	.7097	.6585	.6184

Table 2: Results for the topic coreference algorithms.

but other sensible choices for the distance lead to much higher scores. Furthermore, we observed that the behavior of the α score can be rather erratic — small changes in one of the clusterings can lead to big differences in the score.

Perhaps a better indicator of the reliability of the coreference annotation is a comparison with the baselines, shown in the top half of Table 2. All baselines score significantly lower than the inter-annotator agreement scores. With one exception, the inter-annotator agreement scores are also higher than those for the learning-based approach (results shown in the lower half of Table 2), as would typically be expected. The exception is the classifier that uses the manual topic spans, but as we argued earlier these spans carry significant information about the decision of the annotator.

8.2 Baselines

Results for the four baselines are shown in the first four rows of Table 2. As expected, the two baselines performing topic segmentation show substantially better scores than the two "default" baselines.

8.3 Learning methods

Results for the learning-based approaches are shown in the bottom half of Table 2. First, we see that each of the learning-based methods outperforms the baselines. This is the case even when sentences are employed as a coarse substitute for the true topic span. A Wilcoxon Signed-Rank test shows that differences from the baselines for the learning-based runs are statistically significant for the B^3 and α measures ($p < 0.01$); for CEAF, using sentences as topic spans for the learning algorithm outperforms the SAME PARAGRAPH baseline ($p < 0.05$), but the results are inconclusive when compared with the system of CHOI.

In addition, relying on manual topic span information (MANUAL and MODIFIED MANUAL) allows the learning-based approach to perform significantly better than the two runs that use automatically identified spans ($p < 0.01$, for all three measures). The improvement in the scores hints at the importance of improving automatic topic span extraction, which will be a focus of our future work.

9 Conclusions

We presented a new, operational definition of opinion topics in the context of fine-grained subjectivity analysis. Based on this definition, we introduced an approach to opinion topic identification that relies on the identification of topic-coreferent opinions. We further employed the opinion topic definition for the manual annotation of opinion topics to create the $\text{MPQA}_{\text{TOPIC}}$ corpus. Inter-annotator agreement results show that opinion topic annotation can be performed reliably. Finally, we proposed an automatic approach for identifying topic-coreferent opinions, which significantly outperforms all baselines across three coreference evaluation metrics.

Acknowledgments The authors of this paper would like to thank Janyce Wiebe and Theresa Wilson for many insightful discussions. This work was supported in part by National Science Foundation Grants BCS- 0624277 and IIS-0535099 and by DHS Grant N0014-07-1-0152.

References

ACE. 2005. The NIST ACE evaluation website. http://www.nist.gov/speech/tests/ace/.

Bagga, A. and B. Baldwin. 1998. Algorithms for scoring coreference chains. In *In Proceedings of MUC7*.

Bethard, S., H. Yu, A. Thornton, V. Hativassiloglou, and D. Jurafsky. 2004. Automatic extraction of opinion propositions and their holders. In *2004 AAAI Spring Symposium on Exploring Attitude and Affect in Text*.

Breck, E., Y. Choi, and C. Cardie. 2007. Identifying expressions of opinion in context. In *Proceedings of IJCAI*.

Choi, Y., C. Cardie, E. Riloff, and S. Patwardhan. 2005. Identifying sources of opinions with conditional random fields and extraction patterns. In *Proceedings of EMNLP*.

Choi, Y., E. Breck, and C. Cardie. 2006. Joint extraction of entities and relations for opinion recognition. In *Proceedings of EMNLP*.

Choi, F. 2000. Advances in domain independent linear text segmentation. *Proceedings of NAACL*.

Cohen, W. 1995. Fast effective rule induction. In *Proceedings of ICML*.

Freund, Y. and R. Schapire. 1998. Large margin classification using the perceptron algorithm. In *Proceedings of Computational Learing Theory*.

Hasegawa, T., S. Sekine, and R. Grishman. 2004. Discovering relations among named entities from large corpora. In *Proceedings of ACL*.

Hu, M. and B. Liu. 2004. Mining opinion features in customer reviews. In *AAAI*.

Joachims, T. 1998. Making large-scale support vector machine learning practical. In B. Schölkopf, C. Burges, A. Smola, editor, *Advances in Kernel Methods: Support Vector Machines*. MIT Press, Cambridge, MA.

Kim, S. and E. Hovy. 2006. Extracting opinions, opinion holders, and topics expressed in online news media text. In *Proceedings of ACL/COLING Workshop on Sentiment and Subjectivity in Text*.

Kobayashi, N., K. Inui, Y. Matsumoto, K. Tateishi, and T. Fukushima. 2004. Collecting evaluative expressions for opinion extraction. In *Proceedings of IJCNLP*.

Krippendorff, K. 1980. *Content Analysis: An Introduction to Its Methodology*. Sage Publications, Beverly Hills, CA.

Luo, X. 2005. On coreference resolution performance metrics. In *Proceedings of EMNLP*.

Malioutov, I. and R. Barzilay. 2006. Minimum cut model for spoken lecture segmentation. In *Proceedings of ACL/COLING*.

Ng, V. and C. Cardie. 2002. Improving machine learning approaches to coreference resolution. In *In Proceedings of ACL*.

Pang, B., L. Lee, and S. Vaithyanathan. 2002. Thumbs up? Sentiment classification using machine learning techniques. In *Proceedings of EMNLP*.

Passonneau, R. 2004. Computing reliability for coreference annotation. In *Proceedings of LREC*.

Popescu, A. and O. Etzioni. 2005. Extracting product features and opinions from reviews. In *Proceedings of HLT/EMNLP*.

Rosenfeld, B. and R. Feldman. 2007. Clustering for unsupervised relation identification. In *Proceedings of CIKM*.

Soon, W., H. Ng, and D. Lim. 2001. A machine learning approach to coreference resolution of noun phrases. *Computational Linguistics*, 27(4).

Stoyanov, V. and C. Cardie. 2008. Annotating topics of opinions. In *Proceedings of LREC*.

Turney, P. 2002. Thumbs up or thumbs down? Semantic orientation applied to unsupervised classification of reviews. In *Proceedings of ACL*.

Vilain, M., J. Burger, J. Aberdeen, D. Connolly, and L. Hirschman. 1995. A model-theoretic coreference scoring scheme. In *Proceedings of the MUC6*.

Voorhees, E. and L. Buckland. 2003. Overview of the TREC 2003 Question Answering Track. In *Proceedings of TREC 12*.

Wiebe, J., T. Wilson, and C. Cardie. 2005. Annotating expressions of opinions and emotions in language. *Language Resources and Evaluation*, 1(2).

Wiebe, J. 2005. Personal communication.

Wilson, T., J. Wiebe, and P. Hoffmann. 2005. Recognizing contextual polarity in phrase-level sentiment analysis. In *Proceedings of HLT/EMNLP*.

Wilson, T. 2005. Personal communication.

Yi, J., T. Nasukawa, R. Bunescu, and W. Niblack. 2003. Sentiment analyzer: Extracting sentiments about a given topic using natural language processing techniques. In *Proceedings of ICDM*.

From Words to Senses: A Case Study of Subjectivity Recognition

Fangzhong Su
School of Computing
University of Leeds, UK
fzsu@comp.leeds.ac.uk

Katja Markert
School of Computing
University of Leeds, UK
markert@comp.leeds.ac.uk

Abstract

We determine the subjectivity of word senses. To avoid costly annotation, we evaluate how useful existing resources established in opinion mining are for this task. We show that results achieved with existing resources that are *not* tailored towards word sense subjectivity classification can rival results achieved with supervision on a manually annotated training set. However, results with different resources vary substantially and are dependent on the different definitions of subjectivity used in the establishment of the resources.

1 Introduction

In recent years, subjectivity analysis and opinion mining have attracted considerable attention in the NLP community. Unlike traditional information extraction and document classification tasks which usually focus on extracting facts or categorizing documents into topics (e.g., "sports", "politics", "medicine"), subjectivity analysis focuses on determining whether a language unit (such as a word, sentence or document) expresses a *private state, opinion or attitude* and, if so, what *polarity* is expressed, i.e. a positive or negative attitude.

Inspired by Esuli and Sebastiani (2006) and Wiebe and Mihalcea (2006), we explore the automatic detection of the subjectivity of *word senses*, in contrast to the more frequently explored task of determining the subjectivity of *words* (see Section 2). This is motivated by many words being *subjectivity-ambiguous*, i.e. having both subjective and objective senses, such as the word *positive* with its two example senses given below.[1]

(1) positive, electropositive—having a positive electric charge;"protons are positive" (*objective*)

(2) plus, positive—involving advantage or good; "a plus (or positive) factor" (*subjective*)

Subjectivity labels for senses add an additional layer of annotation to electronic lexica and allow to group many fine-grained senses into higher-level classes based on subjectivity/objectivity. This can increase the lexica's usability. As an example, Wiebe and Mihalcea (2006) prove that subjectivity information for WordNet senses can improve word sense disambiguation tasks for subjectivity-ambiguous words (such as *positive*). In addition, Andreevskaia and Bergler (2006) show that the performance of automatic annotation of subjectivity at the *word* level can be hurt by the presence of subjectivity-ambiguous words in the training sets they use. Moreover, the prevalence of different word senses in different domains also means that a subjective or an objective sense of a word might be dominant in different domains; thus, in a science text *positive* is likely not to have a subjective reading. The annotation of words as subjective and objective or positive and negative independent of sense or domain does not capture such distinctions.

In this paper, we validate whether word sense subjectivity labeling can be achieved with existing resources for subjectivity analysis at the word and sentence level *without creating a dedicated, manually annotated training set of WordNet senses labeled for subjectivity*.[2] We show that such an ap-

© 2008. Licensed under the *Creative Commons Attribution-Noncommercial-Share Alike 3.0 Unported* license (http://creativecommons.org/licenses/by-nc-sa/3.0/). Some rights reserved.

[1] All examples in this paper are from WordNet 2.0.

[2] We use a subset of WordNet senses that are manually annotated for subjectivity as test set (see Section 3).

proach — even using a simple rule-based unsupervised algorithm — can compete with a standard supervised approach and also compares well to prior research on word sense subjectivity labeling. However, success depends to a large degree on the definition of subjectivity used in the establishment of the prior resources.

The remainder of this paper is organized as follows. Section 2 discusses previous work. Section 3 introduces our human annotation scheme for word sense subjectivity and also shows that subjectivity-ambiguous words are frequent. Section 4 describes our proposed classification algorithms in detail. Section 5 presents the experimental results and evaluation, followed by conclusions and future work in Section 6.

2 Related Work

There has been extensive research in opinion mining at the document level, for example on product and movie reviews (Pang et al., 2002; Pang and Lee, 2004; Dave et al., 2003; Popescu and Etzioni, 2005). Several other approaches focus on the subjectivity classification of sentences (Kim and Hovy, 2005; Kudo and Matsumoto, 2004; Riloff and Wiebe, 2003). They often build on the presence of subjective words in the sentence to be classified.

Closer to our work is the large body of work on the automatic, context-independent classification of words according to their polarity, i.e as positive or negative (Hatzivassiloglou and McKeown, 1997; Turney and Littman, 2003; Kim and Hovy, 2004; Takamura et al., 2005). They use either co-occurrence patterns in corpora or dictionary-based methods. Many papers assume that subjectivity recognition, i.e. separating subjective from objective words, has already been achieved prior to polarity recognition and test against word lists containing subjective words only (Hatzivassiloglou and McKeown, 1997; Takamura et al., 2005). However, Kim and Hovy (2004) and Andreevskaia and Bergler (2006) also address the classification into subjective/objective words and show this to be a potentially harder task than polarity classification with lower human agreement and automatic performance.

There are only two prior approaches addressing *word sense* subjectivity or polarity classification. Esuli and Sebastiani (2006) determine the polarity of word senses in WordNet, distinguishing among positive, negative and objective. They expand a small, manually determined seed set of strongly positive/negative WordNet senses by following WordNet relations and use the resulting larger training set for supervised classification. The resulting labeled WordNet gives three scores for each sense, representing the positive, negative and objective score respectively. However, there is no evaluation as to the accuracy of their approach. They then extend their work (Esuli and Sebastiani, 2007) by applying the Page Rank algorithm to ranking the WordNet senses in terms of how strongly a sense possesses a given semantic property (e.g., positive or negative).

Wiebe and Mihalcea (2006) label word senses in WordNet as subjective or objective. They use a method relying on distributional similarity as well as an independent, large manually annotated opinion corpus (MPQA) (Wiebe et al., 2005) for determining subjectivity. One of the disadvantages of their algorithm is that it is restricted to senses that have distributionally similar words in the MPQA corpus, excluding 23.2% of their test data from automatic classification.

3 Human Annotation of Word Sense Subjectivity and Polarity

In contrast to other researchers (Hatzivassiloglou and McKeown, 1997; Takamura et al., 2005), we do not see polarity as a category that is dependent on prior subjectivity assignment and therefore applicable to subjective senses only. We follow Wiebe and Mihalcea (2006) in that we see subjective expressions as private states "that are not open to objective observation or verification". This includes direct references to emotions, beliefs and judgements (such as *anger, criticise*) as well as expressions that let a private state be inferred, for example by referring to a doctor as a *quack*. In contrast, polarity refers to positive or negative associations of a word or sense. Whereas there *is* a dependency in that most subjective senses have a relatively clear polarity, polarity can be attached to objective words/senses as well. For example, *tuberculosis* is not subjective — it does not describe a private state, is objectively verifiable and would not cause a sentence containing it to carry an opinion, but it does carry negative associations for the vast majority of people.

We therefore annotate subjectivity of word senses similarly to Wiebe and Mihalcea (2006), distinguishing between *subjective (S)*, *objective (O)* or *both (B)*. *Both* is used if a literal and metaphoric sense of a word are collapsed into one WordNet synset or if a WordNet synset contains both opinionated and objective expressions (such as *bastard* and *illegitimate child* in Ex. 3 below).

We expand their annotation scheme by also annotating polarity, using the labels positive (*P*), negative (*N*) and varied (*V*). The latter is used when a sense's polarity varies strongly with the context, such as Example 8 below, where we would expect *uncompromising* to be a judgement but this judgement will be positive or negative depending on what a person is uncompromising about. To avoid prevalence of personalised associations, annotators were told to only annotate polarity for subjective senses, as well as objective senses that carry a strong association likely to be shared by most people at least in Western culture (such as the negative polarity for words referring to diseases and crime). Other objective senses would receive the label *O:NoPol*.

Therefore, we have 7 sub categories in total: *O:NoPol*, *O:P*, *O:N*, *S:P*, *S:N*, *S:V*, and *B*. The notation before and after the colon represents the subjectivity and polarity label respectively. We list some annotated examples below.

(3) bastard, by-blow, love child, illegitimate child, illegitimate, whoreson— the illegitimate offspring of unmarried parents (*B*)

(4) atrophy—undergo atrophy; "Muscles that are not used will atrophy" (*O:N*)

(5) guard, safety, safety device—a device designed to prevent injury (*O:P*)

(6) nasty, awful—offensive or even (of persons) malicious;"in a nasty mood";"a nasty accident"; "a nasty shock" (*S:N*)

(7) happy—enjoying or showing or marked by joy or pleasure or good fortune; "a happy smile";"spent many happy days on the beach"; "a happy marriage" (*S:P*)

(8) uncompromising, inflexible—not making concessions; "took an uncompromising stance in the peace talks" (*S:V*)

As far as we are aware, this is the first annotation scheme for both subjectivity and polarity of word senses. We believe both are relevant for opinion extraction: subjectivity for finding and analysing directly expressed opinions, and polarity for either classifying these further or extracting objective words that, however, serve to "colour" a text or present bias rather than explicitly stated opinions. Su and Markert (2008) describe the annotation scheme and agreement study in full.

3.1 Agreement Study

We used the Micro-WNOp corpus containing 1105 WordNet synsets to test our annotation scheme.[3] The Micro-WNOp corpus is representative of the part-of-speech distribution in WordNet.

Two annotators (both near-native English speakers) independently annotated 606 synsets of the Micro-WNOp corpus for subjectivity and polarity. One annotator is the second author of this paper whereas the other is not a linguist. The overall agreement using all 7 categories is 84.6%, with a kappa of 0.77, showing high reliability for a difficult pragmatic task. This at first seems at odds with the notion of sentiment as a fuzzy category as expressed in (Andreevskaia and Bergler, 2006) but we believe is due to three factors:

- The annotation of senses instead of words splits most subjectivity-ambiguous words into several senses, removing one source of annotation difficulty.
- The annotation of senses in a dictionary provided the annotators with sense descriptions in form of Wordnet glosses as well as related senses, providing more information than a pure word annotation task.
- The split of subjectivity and polarity annotation made the task clearer and the annotation of only very strong connotations for objective word senses "de-individualized" the task.

As in this paper we are only interested in subjectivity recognition, we collapse *S:V*, *S:P*, and *S:N* into a single label *S* and *O:NoPol*, *O:P*, and *O:N* into a single label *O*. Label *B* remains unchanged. For this three-way annotation overall percentage agreement is 90.1%, with a kappa of 0.79.

3.2 Gold Standard

After cases with disagreement were negotiated between the two annotators, a gold standard annotation was agreed upon. Our test set consists of this agreed set as well as the remainder of the Micro-WNOp corpus annotated by one of the annotators alone after agreement was established. This set is available for research purposes at `http://www.comp.leeds.ac.uk/markert/data`.

[3]The corpus has originally been annotated by the providers (Esuli and Sebastiani, 2007) with scores for positive, negative and objective/no polarity, thus a mixture of subjectivity and polarity annotation. We re-annotated the corpus with our annotation scheme.

How many words are subjectivity-ambiguous? As the number of senses increases with word frequency, we expect rare words to be less likely to be subjectivity-ambiguous than frequent words. The Micro-WNOp corpus contains relatively frequent words so we will get an overestimation of subjective-ambiguous word types from this corpus, though not necessarily of word tokens. It includes 298 different words with all their synsets in WordNet 2.0. Of all words, 97 (32.5%) are subjectivity-ambiguous, a substantial number.

4 Algorithms

In this section, we present experiments using five different resources as training sets or clue sets for this task. The first is the Micro-WNOp corpus with our own dedicated word sense subjectivity annotation which is used in a standard supervised approach as training and test set via 10-fold cross-validation. This technique presupposes a manual annotation effort tailored directly to our task to provide training data. As it is costly to create such training sets, we investigate whether existing resources such as two different subjective sentence lists (Section 4.2) and two different subjective word lists (Section 4.3) can be adapted to provide training data or clue sets although they do not provide *any* information about word senses. All resources are used to create training data for supervised approaches; the subjective word lists are also used in a simple rule-based unsupervised approach.

All algorithms were tested on the Micro-WNOp corpus by comparing to the human gold standard annotation. However, we excluded all senses with the label *both* from Micro-WNOp for testing the automatic algorithms, resulting in a final 1061 senses, with 703 objective and 358 subjective senses. We also compare all algorithms to a baseline of always assigning the most frequent category (objective) to each sense, which results in an overall accuracy of 66.3%.

4.1 Standard Supervised Approach: 10-fold Cross-validation (CV) on Micro-WNOp

We use 10-fold cross validation for training and testing on the annotated synsets in the Micro-WNOp corpus. We applied a Naive Bayes classifier, [4] using the following three types of features:

Lexical Features: These are unigrams in the glosses. We use a bag-of-words approach and filter out stop words.

As glosses are usually quite short, using a bag-of-word feature representation will result in high-dimensional and sparse feature vectors, which often deteriorate classification performance. In order to address this problem to some degree, we also explored other features which are available as training and test instances are WordNet synsets.

Part-of-Speech (POS) Features: each sense gets its POS as a feature (adjective, noun, verb or adverb).

Relation Features: WordNet relations are good indicators for determining subjectivity as many of them are *subjectivity-preserving*. For example, if sense A is subjective, then its antonym sense B is likely to be subjective. We employ 8 relations here—antonym, similar-to, derived-from, attribute, also-see, direct-hyponym, direct-hypernym, and extended-antonym. Each relation R leads to 2 features that describe for a sense A how many links of that type it has to synsets in the subjective or the objective training set respectively.

Finally, we represent the feature weights through a TF*IDF measure.

Considering the size of WordNet (115,424 synsets in WordNet 2.0), the labeled Micro-WNOp corpus is small. Therefore, the question arises whether it is possible to adapt other data sources that provide subjectivity information to our task.

4.2 Sentence Collections: Movie and MPQA

It is reasonable to cast word sense subjectivity classification as a sentence classification task, with the glosses that WordNet provides for each sense as the sentences to be classified. Then we can in theory feed any collection of annotated subjective and objective sentences as training data into our classifier while the annotated Micro-WNOp corpus is used as test data. We experimented with two different available data sets to test this assumption.

Movie-domain Subjectivity Data Set (Movie): Pang and Lee (2004) used a collection of labeled subjective and objective sentences in their work on review classification.[5] The data set contains 5000 subjective sentences, extracted from movie reviews collected from the Rotten Tomatoes web

[4] We also experimented with KNN, Maximum Entropy, Rocchio and SVM algorithms and overall Naive Bayes performed best.

[5] Available at http://www.cs.cornell.edu/People/pabo/movie-review-data/

site.[6] The 5000 objective sentences were collected from movie plot summaries from the Internet Movie Database (IMDB). The assumption is that all the snippets from the Rotten Tomatoes pages are subjective (as they come from a review site), while all the sentences from IMDB are objective (as they focus on movie plot descriptions).

The **MPQA Corpus** contains news articles manually annotated at the phrase level for opinions, their polarity and their strength. The corpus (Version 1.2) contains 11,112 sentences. We convert it into a corpus of subjective and objective sentences following exactly the approach in (Riloff et al., 2003; Riloff and Wiebe, 2003) and obtain 6127 subjective and 4985 objective sentences respectively. Basically any sentence that contains at least one strong subjective annotation at the phrase level is seen as a subjective sentence.

We again use a Naive Bayes algorithm with lexical unigram features. Note that part-of-speech and relation features are not applicable here as the training set consists of corpus sentences, not WordNet synsets.

4.3 Word Lists: General Inquirer and Subjectivity List

Several word lists annotated for subjectivity or polarity such as the General Inquirer (GI) [7]or the subjectivity clues list (SL) collated by Janyce Wiebe and her colleagues[8] are available.

The **General Inquirer (GI)** was developed by Philip Stone and colleagues in the 1960s. It concentrates on word polarity. Here we make the simple assumption that both positive and negative words in the GI list are subjective clues whereas all other words are objective.

The **Subjectivity Lexicon (SL)** centers on subjectivity so that it is ideally suited for our task. It provides fine-grained information for each clue, such as part-of-speech, subjectivity strength (strong/weak), and prior polarity (positive, negative, or neutral). For example, *object(verb)* is a subjective clue whereas *object(noun)* is objective. Regarding strength, the adjective *evil* is marked as strong subjective whereas the adjective *exposed* is marked as a weak subjective clue.

Both lexica *do not* include any information about word senses and therefore cannot be used directly for subjectivity assignment at the sense level. For example, at least one sense of any subjectivity-ambiguous word will be labeled incorrectly if we just adopt a word-based label. In addition, these lists are far from complete: compared to the over 100,000 synsets in WordNet, GI contains 11,788 words marked for polarity (1915 positive, 2291 negative and 7582 no-polarity words) and the SL list contains about 8,000 subjective words.

Still, it is a reasonable assumption that any gloss that contains several subjective words indicates a subjective sense overall. This intuition is strengthened by the characteristics of glosses. They normally are short and concise without a complex syntactic structure, thus the occurrence of subjective words in such a short string is likely to indicate a subjective sense overall. This contrasts, for example, with sentences in newspapers where one clause might express an opinion, whereas other parts of the sentence are objective.

Therefore, for the **rule-based unsupervised algorithm** we lemmatized and POS-tagged the glosses in the Micro-WNOp test set. Then we compute a subjectivity score S for each synset by summing up the weight values of all subjectivity clues in its gloss. If S is equal or higher than an agreed threshold T, then the synset is classified as subjective, otherwise as objective. For the GI lexicon, all subjectivity clues have the same weight 1, whereas for the SL list we assign a weight value 2 to strongly subjective clues and 1 to weakly subjective clues. We experimented with several thresholds T and report here the results for the best thresholds, which were 2 for SL and 4 for the GI word list. The corresponding methods are called Rule-SL and Rule-GI.

This approach does not allow us to easily integrate relational WordNet features. It might also suffer from the incompleteness of the lexica and the fact that it has to make decisions for borderline cases (at the value of the threshold set). We therefore explored instead to **generate larger, more reliable training data consisting of WordNet synsets** from the word lists. To achieve this, we assign a subjectivity score S as above to *all* WordNet synsets (excluding synsets in the test set). If S is higher or equal to a threshold T_1 it is added to the subjective training set, if it is lower or equal to T_2 it is added to the objective training set. This allows us to choose quite clear thresholds so that borderline cases with a score between T_1 and T_2 are not in the training set. It also allows to use part-

[6] http://www.rottentomatoes.com/
[7] http://www.wjh.harvard.edu/~inquirer/
[8] http://www.cs.pitt.edu/mpqa/

of-speech and relational features as the training set then consists of WordNet synsets. In this way, we can automatically generate (potentially noisy) training data of WordNet senses marked for subjectivity without annotating any WordNet senses manually for subjectivity.

We experimented with several different threshold sets but we found that they actually have a minimal impact on the final results. We report here the best results for a threshold T_1 of 4 and T_2 of 2 for the SL lexicon and of 3 and 1 respectively for the GI word list.

5 Experiments and Evaluation

We measure the classification performance with overall accuracy as well as precision, recall and balanced F-score for both categories (objective and subjective). All results are summarised in Table 1. Results are compared to the baseline of majority classification using a McNemar test at the significance level of 5%.

5.1 Experimental Results

Table 1 shows that SL* performs best among all the methodologies. All CV, Rule-SL and SL methods significantly beat the baseline. In addition, if we compare the results of methods with and without additional parts-of-speech and WordNet relation features, we see a small but consistent improvement when we use additional features. It is also worthwhile to expand the rule-based unsupervised method into a method for generating training data and use additional features as SL* significantly outperforms Rule-SL.

5.2 Discussion

Word Lists. Surprisingly, using SL greatly outperforms GI, regardless of whether we use the supervised or unsupervised method or whether we use lexical features only or the other features as well.[9] There are several reasons for this. First, the GI lexicon is annotated for polarity, not subjectivity. More specifically, words that we see as objective but with a strong positive or negative association (such as words for crimes) and words that we see as subjective are annotated with the same polarity label in the GI lexicon. Therefore, the GI definition of subjectivity does not match ours. Also, the GI lexicon does not operate with a clearly expressed polarity definition, leading to conflicting annotations and casting doubt on its widespread use in the opinion mining community as a gold standard (Turney and Littman, 2003; Takamura et al., 2005; Andreevskaia and Bergler, 2006). For example, *amelioration* is seen as non-polar in GI but *improvement* is annotated with positive polarity. Second, in contrast to SL, GI does not consider different parts-of-speech of a word and subjectivity strength (strong/weak subjectivity). Third, GI contains many fewer subjective clues than SL.

Sentence Data. When using the Movie dataset and MPQA corpus as training data, the results are not satisfactory. We first checked the purity of these two datasets to see whether they are too noisy. For this purpose, we used a naive Bayes algorithm with unigram features and conducted a 10-fold cross validation experiment on recognizing subjective/objective sentences within the Movie dataset and MPQA independently. Interestingly, the accuracy for the Movie dataset and MPQA corpus achieved 91% and 76% respectively. Considering that they are balanced datasets with a most frequent category baseline of about 50%, this accuracy is high, especially for the Movie dataset.

However, again the subjectivity definition in the Movie corpus does not seem to match ours. Recall that we see a word sense or a sentence as subjective if it expresses a private state (i.e., emotion, opinion, sentiment, etc.), and objective otherwise. Inspecting the movie data set, we found that indeed the sentences included in its subjective set would mostly be seen as subjective in our sense as well as they contain opinions *about* the movie such as *it desperately wants to be a wacky , screwball comedy , but the most screwy thing here is how so many talented people were convinced to waste their time*. It is also true that the sentences (plot descriptions) in its "objective" data set relatively rarely contain opinions *about the movie*. However, they still contain other opinionated content like opinions and emotions of the characters in the movie such as the obsession of a character with John Lennon in *the beatles fan is a drama about Albert, a psychotic prisoner who is a devoted fan of John Lennon and the beatles*. Since the data set's definition of subjective sentences is closer to ours than the one for objective sentences, we conducted a one-class learning approach (Li and Liu, 2003) using Movie's subjective sentences as

[9] This pattern is repeated for all threshold combinations, which are not reported here.

Table 1: Results

Method	Subjective			Objective			Accuracy
	Precision	Recall	F-score	Precision	Recall	F-score	
Baseline	N/A	0	N/A	66.3%	**100%**	79.7%	66.3%
CV	65.2%	52.8%	58.3%	78.1%	85.6%	81.7%	74.6%†
CV*	**69.5%**	55.3%	61.6%	79.4%	87.6%	**83.3%**	76.7%†
Movie	43.8%	60.1%	50.6%	74.9%	60.7%	67.1%	60.5%
MPQA	44.5%	**78.5%**	56.8%	82.1%	50.1%	62.2%	59.7%
GI	50.4%	39.4%	44.2%	72.2%	80.2%	76.0%	66.4%
GI*	54.5%	33.5%	41.5%	71.7%	85.8%	78.1%	68.1%
SL	64.3%	62.8%	63.6%	81.3%	82.2%	81.8%	75.7%†
SL*	66.2%	64.5%	**65.3%**	82.2%	83.2%	82.7%	**76.9%**†
Rule-GI	38.5%	5.6%	9.8%	66.5%	95.4%	78.4%	65.1%
Rule-SL	59.7%	70.4%	64.6%	**83.4%**	75.8%	79.4%	74.0%†

[1] CV, GI and SL correspond to methods using lexical features only.

[2] CV*, GI* and SL* correspond to methods using a feature combination of lexical, part-of-speech, and WordNet relations.

[3] † indicates results significantly better than the baseline.

the only training data. The algorithm [10] combines Expectation Maximization and Naive Bayes algorithms, and we used randomly extracted 50,000 unlabeled synsets in WordNet as the necessary unlabeled data. This approach achieves an accuracy of 69.4% on Micro-WNOp, which is significantly better than the baseline.

The subjectivity definition in the MPQA corpus is quite close to ours. However, our mapping from its phrase annotation to sentence annotation might be too coarse-grained as many sentences in the corpus span several clauses containing both opinions and factual description. We assume that this is possibly also the reason why its purity is lower than in the Movie dataset. We therefore experimented again with a one-class learning approach using just the *subjective phrases* in MPQA as training data. The accuracy does improve to 67.6% but is still not significantly higher than the baseline.

5.3 Comparison to Prior Approaches

Esuli and Sebastiani (2006) make their labeled WordNet *SentiWordNet 1.0* publically available.[11] Recall that they actually use polarity classification: however, as there is a dependency between polarity and subjectivity classification for subjective senses, we map their polarity scores to our subjectivity labels as follows. If the sum of positive and negative scores of a sense in SentiWordNet is more than or equal to 0.5, then it is subjective and otherwise objective.[12] Using this mapping, it achieves an accuracy of 75.3% on the Micro-WNOp corpus, compared to our gold standard. Therefore our methods CV* and SL* perform slightly better than theirs, although the improvement is not significant.

The task definition in Wiebe and Mihalcea (2006) is much more similar to ours but they use different annotated test data, which is not publically available, so an exact comparison is not possible. Both data sets, however, seem to include relatively frequent words. One disadvantage of their method is that it is not applicable to all WordNet senses as it is dependent on distributionally similar words being available in the MPQA. Thus, 23% of their test data is excluded from evaluation, whereas our methods can be used on any WordNet sense. They measure precision and recall for subjective senses in a precision/recall curve: Precision is about 48/9% at a recall of 60% for subjective senses whereas our best SL* method has a precision of 66% at about the same recall. Although this suggests better performance of our method, it is not possible to draw final conclusions from this comparison due to the data set differences.

[10] Available at http://www.cs.uic.edu/~liub/LPU/.

[11] Available at `http://sentiwordnet.isti.cnr.it/`

[12] We experimented with slightly different mappings but this mapping gave SentiWordNet the best possible result. There is a relatively large number of cases with a 0.5/0.5 split in SentiWordNet, making it hard to decide between subjective and objective senses.

6 Conclusion and Future Work

We proposed different ways of extracting training data and clue sets for word sense subjectivity labeling from existing opinion mining resources. The effectiveness of the resulting algorithms depends greatly on the generated training data, more specifically on the different definitions of subjectivity used in resource creation. However, we were able to show that at least one of these methods (based on the SL word list) resulted in a classifier that performed on a par with a supervised classifier that used dedicated training data developed for this task (CV). Thus, it is possible to avoid any manual annotation for the subjectivity classification of word senses.

Our future work will explore new methodologies in feature representation by importing more background information (e.g., syntactic information). Furthermore, our current method of integrating the rich relation information in WordNet (using them as standard features) does not use joint classification of several senses. Instead, we think it will be more promising to use the relations to construct graphs for semi-supervised graph-based learning of word sense subjectivity. In addition, we will also explore whether the derived sense labels improve applications such as sentence classification and clustering WordNet senses.

References

Andreevskaia, Alina and Sabine Bergler. 2006. Mining WordNet for Fuzzy Sentiment: Sentiment Tag Extraction from WordNet Glosses. *Proceedings of EACL'06.*

Dave, Kushal, Steve Lawrence, and David Pennock. 2003. Mining the Peanut Gallery: Opinion Extraction and Semantic Classification of Product Reviews. *Proceedings of WWW'03.*

Esuli, Andrea and Fabrizio Sebastiani. 2006. SentiWordNet: A Publicly Available Lexical Resource for Opinion Mining. *Proceedings of LREC'06.*

Esuli, Andrea and Fabrizio Sebastiani. 2007. PageRanking WordNet Synsets: An application to Opinion Mining. *Proceedings of ACL'07.*

Hatzivassiloglou, Vasileios and Kathleen McKeown. 1997. Predicting the Semantic Orientation of Adjectives. *Proceedings of ACL'97.*

Kim, Soo-Min and Eduard Hovy. 2004. Determining the Sentiment of Opinions. *Proceedings of COLING'04.*

Kim, Soo-Min and Eduard Hovy. 2005. Automatic Detection of Opinion Bearing Words and Sentences. *Proceedings of ICJNLP'05.*

Kudo, Taku and Yuji Matsumoto. 2004. A Boosting Algorithm for Classification of Semi-structured Text. *Proceedings of EMNLP'04.*

Li, Xiaoli and Bing Liu. 2003. Learning to classify text using positive and unlabeled data. *Proceedings of IJCAI'03.*

Pang, Bo and Lillian Lee. 2004. A Sentiment Education: Sentiment Analysis Using Subjectivity summarization Based on Minimum Cuts. *Proceedings of ACL'04.*

Pang, Bo, Lillian Lee, and Shivakumar Vaithyanathan. 2002. Thumbs up? Sentiment Classification using Machine Learning Techniques. *Proceedings of EMNLP'02.*

Popescu, Ana-Maria and Oren Etzioni. 2003. Extracting Product Fatures and Opinions from Reviews *Proceedings of EMNLP'05.*

Riloff, Ellen, Janyce Wiebe, and Theresa Wilson. 2003. Learning Subjective Nouns using Extraction Pattern Bootstrapping. *Proceedings of CoNLL'03*

Riloff, Ellen and Janyce Wiebe. 2003. Learning Extraction Patterns for Subjective Expressions. *Proceedings of EMNLP'03.*

Su, Fangzhong and Katja Markert. 2008. Eliciting Subjectivity and Polarity Judgements on Word Senses. *Proceedings of Coling'08 workshop of Human Judgements in Computational Linguistics.*

Takamura, Hiroya, Takashi Inui, and Manabu Okumura. 2005. Extracting Semantic Orientations of Words using Spin Model. *Proceedings of ACL'05.*

Turney, Peter and Michael Littman. 2003. Measuring Praise and Criticism: Inference of Semantic Orientation from Association. *ACM Transaction on Information Systems.*

Wiebe, Janyce and Rada Micalcea. 2006. Word Sense and Subjectivity. *Proceedings of ACL'06.*

Wiebe, Janyce, Theresa Wilson, and Claire Cardie. 2005. Annotating Expressions of Opinions and Emotions in Language. *Language Resources and Evaluation.*

Prediction of Maximal Projection for Semantic Role Labeling

Weiwei Sun*, **Zhifang Sui**
Institute of Computational Linguistics
Peking University
Beijing, 100871, China
{ws, szf}@pku.edu.cn

Haifeng Wang
Toshiba (China) R&D Center
501, Tower W2, Oriental Plaza
Beijing, 100738, China
wanghaifeng@rdc.toshiba.com.cn

Abstract

In Semantic Role Labeling (SRL), arguments are usually limited in a syntax subtree. It is reasonable to label arguments locally in such a sub-tree rather than a whole tree. To identify active region of arguments, this paper models Maximal Projection (MP), which is a concept in D-structure from the projection principle of the Principle and Parameters theory. This paper makes a new definition of MP in S-structure and proposes two methods to predict it: the anchor group approach and the single anchor approach. The anchor group approach achieves an accuracy of 87.75% and the single anchor approach achieves 83.63%. Experimental results also indicate that the prediction of MP improves semantic role labeling.

1 Introduction

Semantic Role Labeling (SRL) has gained the interest of many researchers in the last few years. SRL consists of recognizing arguments involved by predicates of a given sentence and labeling their semantic types. As a well defined task of shallow semantic parsing, SRL has a variety of applications in many kinds of NLP tasks.

A variety of approaches has been proposed for the different characteristics of SRL. More recent approaches have involved calibrating features (Gildea and Jurafsky, 2002; Xue and Palmer, 2004; Pradhan et al., 2005), analyzing the complex input – syntax trees (Moschitti, 2004; Liu and Sarkar, 2007), exploiting the complicated output – the predicate-structure (Toutanova et al., 2005), as well as capturing paradigmatic relations between predicates (Gordon and Swanson, 2007).

In prior SRL methods, role candidates are extracted from a whole syntax tree. Though several pruning algorithms have been raised (Xue and Palmer, 2004), the policies are all in global style. In this paper, a statistical analysis of Penn PropBank indicates that arguments are limited in a local syntax sub-tree rather than a whole one. Prior SRL methods do not take such locality into account and seek roles in a wider area. The neglect of locality of arguments may cause labeling errors such as constituents outside active region of arguments may be falsely recognized as roles.

This paper uses insights from generative linguistics to guide the solution of locality of arguments. In particular, Maximal Projection (MP) which dominates[1] active region of arguments according to the projection principle of principle and parameters. Two methods, the anchor group approach and the single anchor approach, are proposed to find the active sub-tree which is rooted by MP and covers all roles. The solutions put forward in this paper borrow ideas from NP-movement principle in generative linguistics and are in statistical flavor. The anchor group approach achieves an accuracy of 87.75%, and the single anchor approach achieves 83.63%. Though the accuracy is lower, the single anchor approach fits SRL better.

*This work was partial completed while this author was at Toshiba (China) R&D Center.

© 2008. Licensed under the *Creative Commons Attribution-Noncommercial-Share Alike 3.0 Unported* license (http://creativecommons.org/licenses/by-nc-sa/3.0/). Some rights reserved.

[1]Dominate is an concept in X-bar theory are modeled. Assuming α and β are two nodes in a syntax tree: α dominates β means α is ancestor of β.

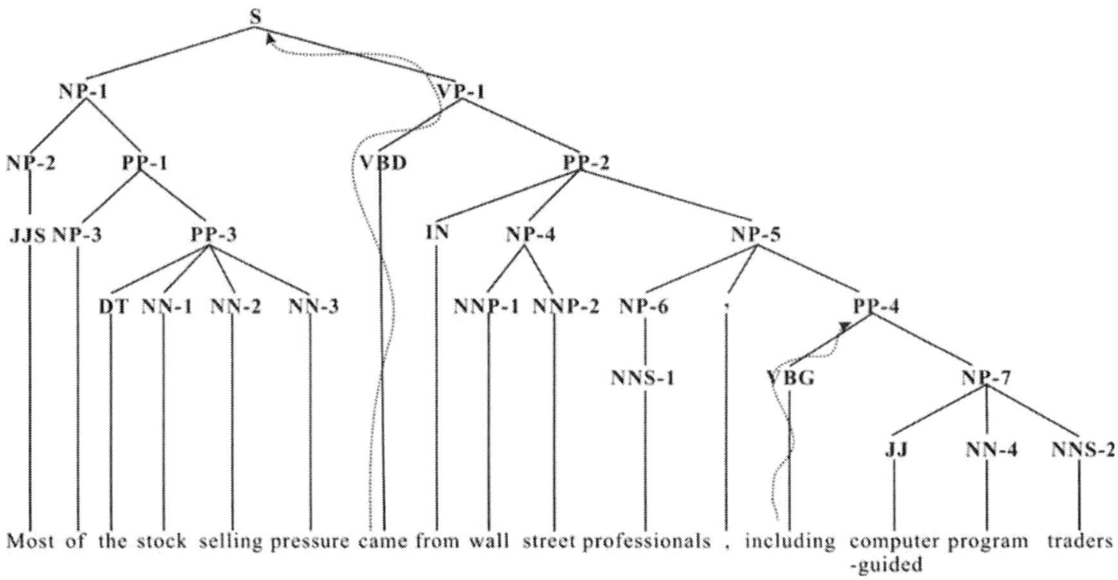

Figure 1: A sentence from WSJ test corpus of CoNLL-2005 shared task

2 Maximal Projection and Its Government of Arguments

2.1 Maximal Projection

Principle and parameters theory is a framework of generative grammar. X-bar theory, as a module of principle and parameters, restricts context-free phrase structure rules as follows:

1. a phrase always contains a head of the same type, i.e. NPs Ns, VPs Vs, PPs Ps, etc.
2. XP(X") → specifier X'
3. X'→X complement(s)

These structural properties are conventionally represented as shown in figure 2.

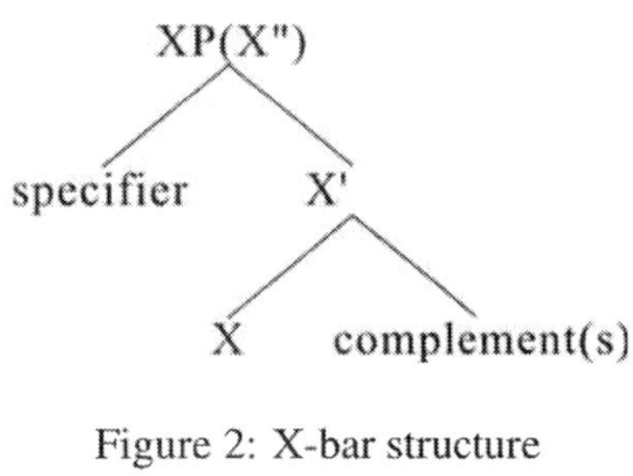

Figure 2: X-bar structure

X is the head of the phrase XP. X' and XP(X") are called projections of X. The head is also called the zero projection. X-bar structure is integrated with the properties of lexical items via the **Projection Principle** of principle and parameters. This principle is summed up as the properties of lexical information project onto the syntax of the sentence. For instance:

- Sue likes Picasso
- *Sue likes

The subcategorization frame of the lexical item *like* [_,NP] ensures that the verb is followed by an NP and the second sentence is of ungrammatical form.

Maximal Projection (MP) is the constituent which is projected to the highest level of an X-bar structure from lexical entities and is therefore the top node XP of the X-bar structure.

Take figure 1 for instance, *S* is the MP of the predicate *come*. Though the syntax tree is not in D-structure (deep structure), the S-structure (surface structure) headed by *come* is similar to its genuine D-structure. In a latter part of this section, a specific definition of MP in S-structure will be given for application.

2.2 MP Limits Active Region of Arguments

MP holds all lexical properties of heads. In particular, the MP of a predicate holds predicate structure information and the constituents out of its domain cannot occupy argument positions. θ-theory and government are two modules of principle and parameters. They both suggest that the possible positions of semantic roles are in the sub-tree rooted by MP.

Concerning assignment of semantic roles to constituents, θ-theory suggests that semantic roles are assigned by predicates to their sisters (Chomsky, 1986). Furthermore, in a X-bar theory, complements are assigned semantic roles by the predicate and specifiers get roles from the V'. In both situations the process of roles assignment is in sisterhood condition and limited in the sub-structure which is dominated by the MP. Only constituents under MP can get semantic roles. **The Case Assignment Principle** also points out: Case is assigned under government (Chomsky, 1981). Take figure 1 for instance, only *NP-1* and *PP-2* can get semantic roles of the head *come*.

From generative linguists' point, MP limits subtree of arguments. Therefore, finding the MP is equivalent to finding the active region of predicate structure.

2.3 Definition of MP in S-structure

Though a clear enough definition of MP in D-structure has been previously illustrated, it is still necessary to define a specific one in S-structure for application, especially for automatic parsing which are not exactly correct. This paper defines **MP in S-structure** (hereinafter denote MP for short) as following: for every predicate p in the syntax tree T, there exists one and only one MP mp s.t.

1. mp dominates all arguments of p;
2. all descendent nodes of mp don't satisfy the former condition.

Due to its different characteristics from arguments, adjunct-like arguments are excluded from the set of arguments in generative grammar and many other linguistic theories. For this reason, this paper does not take them into account.

For gold syntax tree, there exists a one-to-one mapping between arguments and nodes of syntax trees, whereas automatic syntactic parsing contains no such mapping. This paper do not take arguments which cannot get corresponding constituents into account to reduce the influence of automatic parsing error.

Take the sentence of figure 1 to illustrate our definition of MP: *S* is MP of *come* since *NP-1* and *PP-2* are arguments of it. There is no node mapping to the argument *Wall Street professionals* in the parsing tree. Instead of covering argument's fragments, we simply take it PP-4 as MP.

2.4 Using MP Information in SRL

The boundaries of a predicate structure are two word positions of the sentence. It is difficult to model these two words. On the contrary, MP, as one ancestor of predicate, has a clear-cut meaning and is ideal for modeling. In this paper, the policy to predict MP rather than two word positions is carried out to deal with locality of arguments.

Automatic prediction of MP can be viewed as a preprocessing especially a pruning preprocessing for SRL. Given a sentence and its parsing, SRL systems can take seeking the active sub-tree rooted by MP as the first step. Then SRL systems can work on the shrunk syntax tree, and follow-up labeling processes can be in a various form. Most of previous SRL methods still work without special processing. Take figure 1 for example: when labeling *include*, as the MP is *PP-4*, just *NP-7* will be extracted as argument candidate.

3 Analysis of Locality of Arguments

Principle and parameters suggests that MP bounds arguments. Additionally, a statistical analysis shows that possible positions of arguments are limited in a narrow region of syntax tree. An opposite experiment also shows that MP information is useful for SRL.

3.1 Data and Baseline System

In this paper, CoNLL-2005 SRL shared task data (Carreras and Màrquez, 2005) is used as corpus. The data consists of the Wall Street Journal (WSJ) part of the Penn TreeBank with information on predicate argument structures extracted from the PropBank corpus. In addition, the test set of the shared task includes three sections of the Brown corpus. Statistical analysis is based on section 02-21 of WSJ. Experiments are conducted on WSJ and Brown corpus. As defined by the shared task, section 02-21 of PropBank are used for training models while section 23 and Brown corpus are used for test. In terms of syntax information, we use Charniak parser for POS tagging and full parsing.

A majority of prior SRL approaches formulate the SRL propblem as a multi-class classification propblem. Generally speaking, these SRL approaches use a two-stage architecture: i) argument identification; ii) argument classification, to solve the task as a derivation of Gildea and Jurafsky's pioneer work (Gildea and Jurafsky, 2002). UIUC

	Precision	Recall	$F_{\beta=1}$
Arg0	86.28%	87.01%	86.64
Arg1	79.37%	75.06%	77.15
Arg2	69.48%	62.97%	66.07
Arg3	69.01%	56.65%	62.22
Arg4	72.64%	75.49%	74.04

Table 1: SRL performance of UIUC SRLer

	Precision	Recall	$F_{\beta=1}$
Arg0	91.84%	89.98%	90.90
Arg1	81.73%	75.93%	78.72
Arg2	69.86%	63.06%	66.29
Arg3	71.13%	58.38%	64.13
Arg4	73.08%	74.51%	73.79

Table 2: SRL performance of UIUC SRLer using information of gold MP

Semantic Role Labeler [2] (UIUC SRLer) is a state-of-the-art SRL system that based on the champion system of CoNLL-2005 shared task (Carreras and Màrquez, 2005). It is utilized as a baseline system in this paper. The system participated in CoNLL-2005 is based on several syntactic parsing results. However, experiments of this paper just use the best parsing result from Charniak parser. Parameters for training SRL models are the same as described in (Koomen, 2005).

3.2 Active Region of Arguments

According to a statistical analysis, the average depth from a target predicate to the root of a syntax tree is 5.03, and the average depth from a predicate to MP is just 3.12. This means about 40% of ancestors of a predicate do not dominate arguments directly. In addition, the quantity of leaves in syntax tree is another measure to analyze the domain. On average, a syntax tree covers 28.51 leaves, and MP dominates only 18.19. Roughly speaking, only about 60% of words are valid for semantic roles. Statistics of corpora leads to the following conclusion: arguments which are assigned semantic roles are in a local region of a whole syntax tree.

3.3 Typical Errors Caused by Neglect of Locality of Arguments

The neglect of the locality of arguments in prior SRL methods shows that it may cause errors. Some constituents outside active region of arguments may be falsely labeled as roles especially for those being arguments of other predicates. A statistical analysis shows 20.62% of falsely labeled arguments are constituents out of MP domain in labeling results of UIUC SRLer. Take figure 1 for instance, UIUC SRLer makes a mistake when labeling *NP-1* which is Arg1 of the predicate *come* for the target *include*; it labels Arg0 to *NP*. In fact, the active region of *include* is the sub-tree rooted by *PP-4*. Since *NP-1* is an argument of another predicate, some static properties of *NP-1* make it confusing as an argument.

3.4 SRL under Gold MP

If MP has been found before labeling semantic roles, the set of role candidates will be shrunk, and the capability to identify semantic roles may be improved. An opposite experiment verifies this idea. In the first experiment, UIUC SRLer is retrained as a baseline. For comparison, during the second experiment, syntax sub-trees dominated by gold MP are used as syntactic information. Both training and test data are preprocessed with gold MP information. That is to say we use pruned data for training, and test is conducted on pruned syntax sub-trees.

Table 1 and 2 show that except for Arg4, all arguments get improved labeling performance, especially Arg0. Since arguments except for Arg0 are realized as objects on the heel of predicate in most case, the information of MP is not so useful for them as Arg0. The experiment suggests that high performance prediction of MP can improve SRL.

4 Prediction of MP

Conforming to government and θ-theory, MP is not too difficult to predict in D-structure. Unfortunately, sentences being looked at are in their surface form and region of arguments has been expanded. Simple rules alone are not adequate for finding MP owing to a variety of movement between D-structure and S-structure. This paper designs two data driven algorithms based on movement principles for prediction of MP.

4.1 NP-movement and Prediction of MP

4.1.1 NP-movement in Principle and Parameters

The relationship between D-structure and S-structure is movement: S-structure equals D-

[2] http://l2r.cs.uiuc.edu/ cogcomp/srl-demo.php

structure plus movement. NP-movement principle in principle and parameters indicates that noun phrases only move from A-positions (argument position) which have been assigned roles to A-positions which have not, leaving an NP-trace. On account of θ-theory and government, A-positions are nodes m-commanded [3] by predicates in D-structure. In NP-movement, arguments move to positions which are C-commanded [4] by target predicate and m-commanded by other predicates. Broadly speaking, A-positions are C-commanded by predicates after NP-movement. The key of the well-known pruning algorithm raised in (Xue and Palmer, 2004) is extracting sisters of ancestors as role candidates. Those candidate nodes are all C-commanders of a predicate. NP-movement can give an explanation why the algorithm works.

4.1.2 Definition of Argument Anchor

To capture the characteristics of A-positions, we make definition of A-anchor as following. For every predicate p in the syntax tree $\mathcal{T}$, denote $\mathcal{A}$ the set of C-commanders of p:

- a **left-A-anchor** satisfies:
  1. left-A-anchor belongs to $\mathcal{A}$;
  2. left-A-anchor is a noun phrase (including NNS, NNP, etc.) or simple declarative clause (S);
  3. left-A-anchor is on the left hand of p.
- a **right-A-anchor** satisfies:
  1. right-A-anchor belongs to $\mathcal{A}$;
  2. right-A-anchor is a noun phrase (including NNS, NNP, etc.);
  3. right-A-anchor is on the right hand of p.

Take figure 1 for example, *NP-1*, *NP-4* and *NP-6* are left-A-anchors of *include*, and no right-A-anchor. There is a close link between A-position and the A-anchor that we defined, since A-anchors occupy A-positions.

4.1.3 Anchor Model for Prediction of MP

Parents of A-anchors and first branching ancestor of the predicate can cover 96.25% of MP and the number of those ancestors is 2.78 times of the number of MP. The number of all ancestors is 6.65 times. The data suggests that taking only these kinds of ancestors as MP candidates can shrink the candidate set with a relatively small loss.

4.2 Anchor Group Approach

MP is one ancestor of a predicate. An natural approach to predict MP is searching the set of all ancestors. This idea encounters the difficulty that there are too many ancestors. In order to reduce the noise brought by non-anchors' parents, the anchor group approach prunes away useless ancestors which are neither parents of A-anchors nor first branching node upon predicate from MP candidate set. Then the algorithm scores all candidates and chooses the MP in argmax flavor. Formally, we denote the set of MP candidates $\mathcal{C}$ and the score function $S(.)$.

$$\hat{mp} = \arg\max_{c \in \mathcal{C}} S(mp|c)$$

Probability function is chosen as score function in this paper. In estimating of the probability $P(MP|\mathcal{C})$, log-linear model is used. This model is often called maximum entropy model in research of NLP. Let the set $\{1,\text{-}1\}$ denotes whether a constituent is MP and $\Phi(c, \{-1, 1\}) \in \mathbb{R}^s$ denotes a feature map from a constituent and the possible class to the vector space $\mathbb{R}^s$. Formally, the model of our system is defined as:

$$\hat{mp} = \arg\max_{c \in \mathcal{C}} \frac{e^{<\Phi(c,1),\omega>}}{e^{<\Phi(c,1),\omega>} + e^{<\Phi(c,0),\omega>}}$$

The algorithm is also described in pseudo code as following.

Ancestor Algorithm:
1: collect parents of anchors and the first branching ancestor, denote them set $\mathcal{C}$
2: for every $c \in \mathcal{C}$
3: calculate $P(mp\|c)$
4: return $\hat{c}$ that gets the maximal $P(mp\|c)$

4.2.1 Features

We use some features to represent various aspects of the syntactic structure as well as lexical information. The features are listed as follows:

Path The path features are similar to the path feature which is designed by (Gildea and Jurafsky, 2002).A path is a sequential collection of phrase tags. There are two kinds of path features here: one is from target predicate through to the candidate; the other is from the candidate to the root of the syntax tree. For *include* in the sentence of figure 1, the first kind of path of *PP-2* is *VBG+PP+NP+PP* and the second is *PP+VP+S*.

[3]M-command is an concept in X-bar syntax. Assuming α and β are two nodes in a syntax tree: α m-commands β means α C-commands β and the MP of α dominates β

[4]C-command is an concept in X-bar theory. Assuming α and β are two nodes in a syntax tree: α C-commands β means every parent of α is ancestor of β.

C-commander Thread As well as path features, C-commander threads are other features which reflect aspects of the syntactic structures. C-commander thread features are sequential containers of constituents which C-command the target predicate. We design three kinds of C-commander threads: 1) down thread collects C-commanders from the anchor to the target predicate; 2) up thread collects C-commanders from the anchor to the left/right most C-commander; 3) full thread collects all C-commanders in the left/right direction from the target predicate. Direction is dependent on the type of the anchor - left or right anchor.

Considering the grammatical characteristics of phrase, we make an equivalence between such phrase types:

- JJ, JJR, JJS, ADJP
- NN, NNP, NNS, NNPS, NAC, NX, NP

Besides the equivalent constituents, we discard these types of phrases:

- MD, RB, RBS, RBR, ADVP

For *include* in figure 1, the up thread of *NP-4* is *VBG+,+NP+NP*; the down thread is *NP+IN+VBD+NP*; the full thread is *VBG+,+NP+NP+IN+VBD+NP*.

The phrase type of candidate is an important feature for prediction

Candidate of MP. We also select the rank number of the current candidate and the number of all candidates as features. For the former example, the two features for *PP-2* are *2* and *3*, since NP-4 is the second left-A-anchor and there are three A-anchors of *include*.

Anchor Features of anchor include the head word of the anchor, the boundary words and their POS, and the number of the words in the anchor. Those features are clues of judgment of whether the anchor's position is an A-position.

Forward predicate For the former example, the forward predicate of *NP-4* is *come*. The features include the predicate itself, the Levin class and the SCF of the predicate.

predicate Features of predicate include lemma, Levin class, POS and SCF of the predicate.

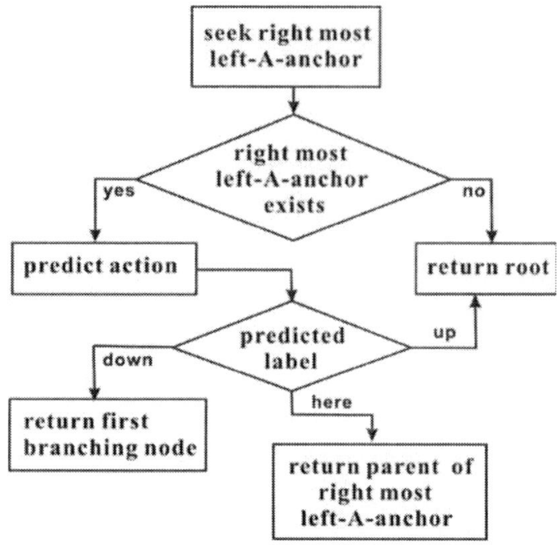

Figure 3: Flow diagram of the single anchor approach

Formal Subject An anchor may be formal subject. Take *It is easy to say the specialist is not doing his job* for example, the formal subject will be recognized as anchor of *do*. We use a heuristic rule to extract this feature: if the first NP C-commander of the anchor is "it" and the left word of predicate is "to", the value of this feature is 1; otherwise 0.

The Maximal Length of C-commanders Constituent which consists of many words may be a barrier between the predicate and an A-position. For the former example, if the target predicate is *include*, this feature of *NP-1* is *2*, since the largest constituent *NP-4* is made up of two words.

4.3 Single Anchor Approach

Among all A-anchors, the right most left-A-anchor such as *NP-6* of *include* in figure 1 is the most important one for MP prediction. The parent of this kind of left-A-anchor is the MP of the predicate, obtaining a high probability of 84.59%. The single anchor approach is designed based on right most left-A-anchor. The key of this approach is an action prediction that when right most left-A-anchor is found, the algorithm predicts next action to return which node of syntax tree as MP. There is a label set of three types for learning – *here*, *up*, *down*. After action is predicted, several simple rules are executed as post process of this prediction: i) if there is no left-A-anchor, return the root of the whole syntax tree as MP; ii)if the predicted label is *here*, return the parent of right most left-A-anchor; iii) if the predicted label is *down*, return

	Prediction Accuracy	
Corpus	Action	MP
WSJ	–	87.75%
Brown	–	88.84%

Table 3: Accuracy of the anchor group approach

	Prediction Accuracy	
Corpus	Action	MP
WSJ	88.45%	83.63%
Brown	90.10%	85.70%

Table 4: Accuracy of the single anchor approach

	Precision	Recall	$F_{\beta=1}$
Arg0	86.23%	87.90%	87.06
Arg1	80.21%	74.79%	77.41
Arg2	70.09%	62.70%	66.19
Arg3	71.74%	57.23%	63.67
Arg4	74.76%	75.49%	75.12

Table 5: SRL performance of UIUC SRLer using information of predicted MP; the anchor group approach; WSJ test corpus

	Precision	Recall	$F_{\beta=1}$
Arg0	87.03%	87.59%	87.31
Arg1	80.24%	74.77%	77.41
Arg2	70.35%	63.06%	66.51
Arg3	71.43%	57.80%	63.90
Arg4	73.33%	75.49%	74.40

Table 6: SRL performance of UIUC SRLer using information of predicted MP; the single anchor approach; WSJ test corpus

the first branching node upon the predicate; iv) if the predicted label is *up*, return the root. The action prediction also uses maximum entropy model. Figure 3 is the flow diagram of the single anchor approach. Features for this approach are similar to the former method. Features of the verb which is between the anchor and the predicate are added, including the verb itself and the Levin class of that verb.

5 Experiments and Results

Experiment data and toolkit have been illustrated in section 3. Maxent[5], a maximum entropy modeling toolkit, is used as a classifier in the experiments of MP prediction.

5.1 Experiments of Prediction of MP

The results are reported for both the anchor group approach and the single anchor approach. Table 3 summaries the accuracy results of MP prediction for the anchor group approach; table 4 summaries results of both action prediction and MP prediction for the single anchor approach. Both the anchor group approach and the single anchor approach have better prediction performance in Brown test set, though the models are trained on WSJ corpus. These results illustrate that anchor approaches which are based on suitable linguistic theories have robust performance and overcome limitations of training corpus.

5.2 Experiments of SRL Using MP Prediction

Like the experiments in the end of section 3, we perform similar experiments under predicted MP. Both training and test corpus make use of predicted MP information. It is an empirical tactic that predicted information of maximal projection, instead of gold information, is chosen for a training set. Experiments suggest predicted information is better. Table 5 is SRL performance using the anchor group approach to predict MP; Table 6 is SRL performance using the single anchor approach.

Compared with table 1 on page 4, table 5 and table 6 both indicate the predicted MP can help to label semantic roles. However, there is an interesting phenomenon. Even though the anchor group approach achieves a higher performance of MP, the single anchor approach is more helpful to SRL. 18.56% of falsely labeled arguments are out of MP domain using the single anchor approach to predict MP, compared to 20.62% of the baseline system.

In order to test robustness of the contribution of MP prediction to SRL, another opposite experiment is performed using the test set from Brown corpus. Table 7 is the SRL performance of UIUC SRLer on Brown test set. Table 8 is the corresponding performance using MP information predicted by the single anchor approach. Comparison between table 7 and table 8 indicates the approach of MP prediction proposed in this paper adapts to other genres of corpora.

Capability of labeling Arg0 gets significant improvement. Subject selection rule, a part of the-

[5] http://homepages.inf.ed.ac.uk/s0450736/maxent_toolkit.html

	Precision	Recall	$F_{\beta=1}$
Arg0	82.88%	85.51%	84.17
Arg1	66.30%	63.17%	64.70
Arg2	50.00%	45.58%	47.69
Arg3	0.00%	0.00%	0.00
Arg4	60.00%	20.00%	30.00

Table 7: SRL performance of UIUC SRLer; Brown test corpus

	Precision	Recall	$F_{\beta=1}$
Arg0	83.85%	86.22%	85.02
Arg1	66.67%	63.02%	64.79
Arg2	50.38%	44.90%	47.48
Arg3	0.00%	0.00%	0.00
Arg4	60.00%	20.00%	30.00

Table 8: SRL performance of UIUC SRLer using information of predicted MP; the single anchor approach; Brown test corpus

matic hierarchy theory, states that the argument that the highest role (i.e. proto-agent, Arg0 in PropBank) is the subject. This means that Arg0 is usually realized as a constituent preceding a predicate and has a long distance from the predicate. As a solution of finding active region of arguments, MP prediction is helpful to shrink the searching range of arguments preceding the predicate. From this point, we give a rough explanation why experiment results for Arg0 are better.

6 Conclusion

Inspired by the locality phenomenon that arguments are usually limited in a syntax sub-tree, this paper proposed to label semantic roles locally in the active region arguments dominated by maximal projection, which is a concept in D-structure from the projection principle of the principle and parameters theory. Statistical analysis showed that MP information was helpful to avoid errors in SRL, such as falsely recognizing constituents outside active region as arguments. To adapt the projection concept to label semantic roles, this paper defined MP in S-structure and proposed two methods to predict MP, namely the anchor group approach and the single anchor approach. Both approaches were based on NP-movement principle of principle and parameters. Experimental results indicated that our MP prediction methods improved SRL.

Acknowlegements

The work is supported by the National Natural Science Foundation of China under Grants No. 60503071, 863 the National High Technology Research and Development Program of China under Grants No.2006AA01Z144, 973 Natural Basic Research Program of China under Grants No.2004CB318102.

References

Carreras, Xavier and Lluís Màrquez. 2005. Introduction to the CoNLL-2005 shared task: semantic role labeling. In *Proceedings of Conference on Natural Language Learning*.

Chomsky, Noam. 1981. *Lectures on Government and Binding*. Foris Publications, Dordrecht.

Chomsky, Noam. 1986. *Barriers*. MIT Press, Barriers.

Gildea, Daniel and Daniel Jurafsky. 2002. Automatic Labeling of Semantic Roles. *Computional Linguistics*, 28(3):245–288.

Gordon, Andrew and Reid Swanson. 2007. Generalizing Semantic Role Annotations Across Syntactically Similar Verbs. In *Proceedings of Conference on Association for Computational Linguistics*.

Koomen, Peter, Vasina Punyakanok, Dan Roth and Wen-tau Yih. 2005. Generalized Inference with Multiple Semantic Role Labeling Systems. In *Proceedings of Conference on Natural Language Learning*.

Liu, Yudong and Anoop Sarkar. 2004. Experimental Evaluation of LTAG-Based Features for Semantic Role Labeling. In *Proceedings of Joint Conference on Empirical Methods in Natural Language Processing and Computational Natural Language Learning*.

Mocshitti, Alessandro. 2004. A Study on Convolution Kernels for Shallow Semantic Parsing. In *Proceedings of Conference on Association for Computational Linguistics*.

Pradhan, Sameer, Kadri Hacioglu, Valerie Krugler, Wayne Ward, James Martin and Daniel Jurafsky. 2005. Support Vector Learning for Semantic Argument Classification. In *Proceedings of Conference on Association for Computational Linguistics*.

Toutanova, Kristina, Aria Haghighi and Christopher Manning. 2005. Joint Learning Improves Semantic Role Labeling. In *Proceedings of Conference on Association for Computational Linguistics*.

Xue, Nianwen and Martha Palmer. 2004. Calibrating Features for Semantic Role Labeling. In *Proceedings of Empirical Methods in Natural Language Processing*.

Modeling Latent-Dynamic in Shallow Parsing: A Latent Conditional Model with Improved Inference

Xu Sun† **Louis-Philippe Morency**‡ **Daisuke Okanohara**† **Jun'ichi Tsujii**†§
†Department of Computer Science, The University of Tokyo, Hongo 7-3-1, Tokyo, Japan
‡USC Institute for Creative Technologies, 13274 Fiji Way, Marina del Rey, USA
§School of Computer Science, The University of Manchester, 131 Princess St, Manchester, UK
†{sunxu, hillbig, tsujii}@is.s.u-tokyo.ac.jp ‡morency@ict.usc.edu

Abstract

Shallow parsing is one of many NLP tasks that can be reduced to a sequence labeling problem. In this paper we show that the *latent-dynamics* (i.e., hidden substructure of shallow phrases) constitutes a problem in shallow parsing, and we show that modeling this intermediate structure is useful. By analyzing the automatically learned hidden states, we show how the latent conditional model explicitly learn latent-dynamics. We propose in this paper the Best Label Path (BLP) inference algorithm, which is able to produce the most probable label sequence on latent conditional models. It outperforms two existing inference algorithms. With the BLP inference, the LDCRF model significantly outperforms CRF models on word features, and achieves comparable performance of the most successful shallow parsers on the CoNLL data when further using part-of-speech features.

1 Introduction

Shallow parsing identifies the non-recursive cores of various phrase types in text. The paradigmatic shallow parsing problem is noun phrase chunking, in which the non-recursive cores of noun phrases, called base NPs, are identified. As the representative problem in shallow parsing, noun phrase chunking has received much attention, with the development of standard evaluation datasets and with extensive comparisons among methods (McDonald 2005; Sha & Pereira 2003; Kudo & Matsumoto 2001).

Syntactic contexts often have a complex underlying structure. Chunk labels are usually far too general to fully encapsulate the syntactic behavior of word sequences. In practice, and given the limited data, the relationship between specific words and their syntactic contexts may be best modeled at a level finer than chunk tags but coarser than lexical identities. For example, in the noun phrase (NP) chunking task, suppose that there are two lexical sequences, "*He is her –*" and "*He gave her –* ". The observed sequences, "*He is her*" and "*He gave her*", would both be conventionally labeled by '`BOB`', where `B` signifies the '*beginning NP*', and `O` the '*outside NP*'. However, this labeling may be too general to encapsulate their respective syntactic dynamics. In actuality, they have different latent-structures, crucial in labeling the next word. For "*He is her –*", the NP started by 'her' is still incomplete, so the label for – is likely to be `I`, which conveys the continuation of the phrase, e.g., "*[He] is [her brother]*". In contrast, for "*He gave her –*", the phrase started by '*her*' is normally self-complete, and makes the next label more likely to be `B`, e.g., "*[He] gave [her] [flowers]*".

In other words, latent-dynamics is an intermediate representation between input features and labels, and explicitly modeling this can simplify the problem. In particular, in many real-world cases, when the part-of-speech tags are not available, the modeling on latent-dynamics would be particularly important.

In this paper, we model latent-dynamics in shallow parsing by extending the Latent-Dynamic Conditional Random Fields (LDCRFs) (Morency et al. 2007), which offer advantages over previ-

©2008. Licensed under the *Creative Commons Attribution-Noncommercial-Share Alike 3.0 Unported* license (http://creativecommons.org/licenses/by-nc-sa/3.0/). Some rights reserved.

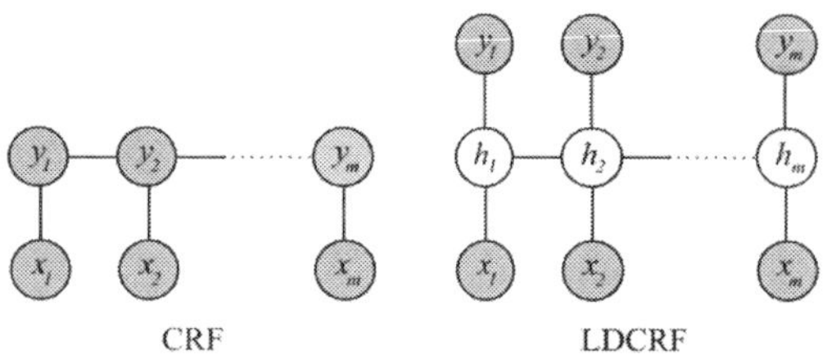

Figure 1: Comparison between CRF and LDCRF. In these graphical models, x represents the observation sequence, y represents labels and h represents hidden states assigned to labels. Note that only gray circles are observed variables. Also, only the links with the current observation are shown, but for both models, long range dependencies are possible.

ous learning methods by explicitly modeling hidden state variables (see Figure 1). We expect LDCRFs to be particularly useful in those cases without POS tags, though this paper is not limited to this.

The inference technique is one of the most important components for a structured classification model. In conventional models like CRFs, the optimal label path can be directly searched by using dynamic programming. However, for latent conditional models like LDCRFs, the inference is kind of tricky, because of hidden state variables. In this paper, we propose an exact inference algorithm, the Best Label Path inference, to efficiently produce the optimal label sequence on LDCRFs.

The following section describes the related work. We then review LDCRFs, and propose the BLP inference. We further present a statistical interpretation on learned hidden states. Finally, we show that LDCRF-BLP is particularly effective when pure word features are used, and when POS tags are added, as existing systems did, it achieves comparable results to the best reported systems.

2 Related Work

There is a wide range of related work on shallow parsing. Shallow parsing is frequently reduced to sequence labeling problems, and a large part of previous work uses machine learning approaches. Some approaches rely on k-order generative probabilistic models of paired input sequences and label sequences, such as HMMs (Freitag & McCallum 2000; Kupiec 1992) or multilevel Markov models (Bikel et al. 1999). The generative model provides well-understood training and inference but requires stringent conditional independence assumptions.

To accommodate multiple overlapping features on observations, some other approaches view the sequence labeling problem as a sequence of classification problems, including support vector machines (SVMs) (Kudo & Matsumoto 2001) and a variety of other classifiers (Punyakanok & Roth 2001; Abney et al. 1999; Ratnaparkhi 1996). Since these classifiers cannot trade off decisions at different positions against each other (Lafferty et al. 2001), the best classifier based shallow parsers are forced to resort to heuristic combinations of multiple classifiers.

A significant amount of recent work has shown the power of CRFs for sequence labeling tasks. CRFs use an exponential distribution to model the entire sequence, allowing for non-local dependencies between states and observations (Lafferty et al. 2001). Lafferty et al. (2001) showed that CRFs outperform classification models as well as HMMs on synthetic data and on POS tagging tasks. As for the task of shallow parsing, CRFs also outperform many other state-of-the-art models (Sha & Pereira 2003; McDonald et al. 2005).

When the data has distinct sub-structures, models that exploit hidden state variables are advantageous in learning (Matsuzaki et al. 2005; Petrov et al. 2007). Sutton et al. (2004) presented an extension to CRF called dynamic conditional random field (DCRF) model. As stated by the authors, training a DCRF model with unobserved nodes (hidden variables) makes their approach difficult to optimize. In the vision community, the LDCRF model was recently proposed by Morency et al. (2007), and shown to outperform CRFs, SVMs, and HMMs for visual sequence labeling.

In this paper, we introduce the concept of latent-dynamics for shallow parsing, showing how hidden states automatically learned by the model present similar characteristics. We will also propose an improved inference technique, the BLP, for producing the most probable label sequence in LDCRFs.

3 Latent-Dynamic Conditional Random Fields

The task is to learn a mapping between a sequence of observations $\mathbf{x} = x_1, x_2, \ldots, x_m$ and a sequence of labels $\mathbf{y} = y_1, y_2, \ldots, y_m$. Each y_j is a class label for the j'th token of a word sequence and is a member of a set $\mathbf{Y}$ of possible class labels. For each sequence, the model also assumes a vector of hidden state variables $\mathbf{h} = \{h_1, h_2, \ldots, h_m\}$, which are not observable in the training examples.

Given the above definitions, we define a latent conditional model as follows:

$$P(\mathbf{y}|\mathbf{x}, \mathbf{\Theta}) = \sum_h P(\mathbf{y}|\mathbf{h}, \mathbf{x}, \mathbf{\Theta}) P(\mathbf{h}|\mathbf{x}, \mathbf{\Theta}), \quad (1)$$

where $\mathbf{\Theta}$ are the parameters of the model. The LDCRF model can seem as a natural extension of the CRF model, and the CRF model can seem as a special case of LDCRFs employing one hidden state for each label.

To keep training and inference efficient, we restrict the model to have disjointed sets of hidden states associated with each class label. Each h_j is a member of a set $\mathbf{H}_{y_j}$ of possible hidden states for the class label y_j. We define $\mathbf{H}$, the set of all possible hidden states to be the union of all $\mathbf{H}_{y_j}$ sets. Since sequences which have any $\mathbf{h}_j \notin \mathbf{H}_{y_j}$ will by definition have $P(\mathbf{y}|\mathbf{x}, \mathbf{\Theta}) = 0$, we can express our model as:

$$P(\mathbf{y}|\mathbf{x}, \mathbf{\Theta}) = \sum_{\mathbf{h} \in \mathbf{H}_{\mathbf{y}_1} \times \ldots \times \mathbf{H}_{\mathbf{y}_m}} P(\mathbf{h}|\mathbf{x}, \mathbf{\Theta}), \quad (2)$$

where $P(\mathbf{h}|\mathbf{x}, \mathbf{\Theta})$ is defined using the usual conditional random field formulation: $P(\mathbf{h}|\mathbf{x}, \mathbf{\Theta}) = \exp \mathbf{\Theta} \cdot \mathbf{f}(\mathbf{h}|\mathbf{x}) / \sum_{\forall \mathbf{h}} \exp \mathbf{\Theta} \cdot \mathbf{f}(\mathbf{h}|\mathbf{x})$, in which $\mathbf{f}(\mathbf{h}|\mathbf{x})$ is the feature vector. Given a training set consisting of n labeled sequences $(\mathbf{x}_i, \mathbf{y}_i)$ for $i = 1 \ldots n$, training is performed by optimizing the objective function to learn the parameter $\mathbf{\Theta}^*$:

$$L(\mathbf{\Theta}) = \sum_{i=1}^{n} \log P(\mathbf{y}_i|\mathbf{x}_i, \mathbf{\Theta}) - R(\mathbf{\Theta}). \quad (3)$$

The first term of this equation is the conditional log-likelihood of the training data. The second term is the regularizer.

4 BLP Inference on Latent Conditional Models

For testing, given a new test sequence x, we want to estimate the most probable label sequence (Best Label Path), $\mathbf{y}^*$, that maximizes our conditional model:

$$\mathbf{y}^* = \text{argmax}_{\mathbf{y}} P(\mathbf{y}|\mathbf{x}, \mathbf{\Theta}^*). \quad (4)$$

In the CRF model, $\mathbf{y}^*$ can be simply searched by using the Viterbi algorithm. However, for latent conditional models like LDCRF, the Best Label Path $\mathbf{y}^*$ cannot directly be produced by the Viterbi algorithm because of the incorporation of hidden states.

In this paper, we propose an exact inference algorithm, the Best Label Path inference (BLP), for producing the most probable label sequence $\mathbf{y}^*$ on LDCRF. In the BLP schema, top-n hidden paths $\mathbf{HP}_n = \{\mathbf{h}_1, \mathbf{h}_2 \ldots \mathbf{h}_n\}$ over hidden states are efficiently produced by using A^* search (Hart et al., 1968), and the corresponding probabilities of hidden paths $P(\mathbf{h}_i|\mathbf{x}, \mathbf{\Theta})$ are gained. Thereafter, based on $\mathbf{HP}_n$, the estimated probabilities of various label paths, $\overline{P}(\mathbf{y}|\mathbf{x}, \mathbf{\Theta})$, can be computed by summing the probabilities of hidden paths, $P(\mathbf{h}|\mathbf{x}, \mathbf{\Theta})$, concerning the association between hidden states and each class label:

$$\overline{P}(\mathbf{y}|\mathbf{x}, \mathbf{\Theta}) = \sum_{\mathbf{h}:\, \mathbf{h} \in \mathbf{H}_{\mathbf{y}_1} \times \ldots \times \mathbf{H}_{\mathbf{y}_m} \wedge \mathbf{h} \in \mathbf{HP}_n} P(\mathbf{h}|\mathbf{x}, \mathbf{\Theta}). \quad (5)$$

By using the A^* search, $\mathbf{HP}_n$ can be extended incrementally in an efficient manner, until the algorithm finds that the Best Label Path is ready, and then the search stops and ends the BLP inference with success. The algorithm judges that y^* is ready when the following condition is achieved:

$$\overline{P}(\mathbf{y}_1|\mathbf{x}, \mathbf{\Theta}) \geq \overline{P}(\mathbf{y}_2|\mathbf{x}, \mathbf{\Theta}) + \sum_{\mathbf{h} \notin \mathbf{H}_{\mathbf{y}_1} \times \ldots \times \mathbf{H}_{\mathbf{y}_m}} P(\mathbf{h}|\mathbf{x}, \mathbf{\Theta}), \quad (6)$$

where $\mathbf{y}_1$ is the most probable label sequence, and $\mathbf{y}_2$ is the second ranked label sequence estimated by using $\mathbf{HP}_n$. It would be straightforward to prove that $\mathbf{y}^* = \mathbf{y}_1$, and further search is unnecessary, because in this case, the unknown probability mass can not change the optimal label path. The unknown probability mass can be computed by using

$$\sum_{\mathbf{h} \notin \mathbf{H}_{\mathbf{y}_1} \times \ldots \times \mathbf{H}_{\mathbf{y}_m}} P(\mathbf{h}|\mathbf{x}, \mathbf{\Theta}) = 1 - \sum_{\mathbf{h} \in \mathbf{H}_{\mathbf{y}_1} \times \ldots \times \mathbf{H}_{\mathbf{y}_m}} P(\mathbf{h}|\mathbf{x}, \mathbf{\Theta}). \quad (7)$$

The top-n hidden paths of $\mathbf{HP}_n$ produced by the A^*-search are exact, and the BLP inference is exact. To guarantee $\mathbf{HP}_n$ is exact in our BLP inference, an admissible heuristic function should be used in A^* search (Hart et al., 1968). We use a backward Viterbi algorithm (Viterbi, 1967) to compute the heuristic function of the forward A^* search:

$$\text{Heu}_i(\mathbf{h}_j) = \max_{\mathbf{h}'_i = \mathbf{h}_j \wedge \mathbf{h}'_i \in \mathbf{HP}_i^{|\mathbf{h}|}} P'(\mathbf{h}'|\mathbf{x}, \mathbf{\Theta}^*), \quad (8)$$

where $\mathbf{h}_i' = \mathbf{h}_j$ represents a partial hidden path started from the hidden state $\mathbf{h}_j$, and $\mathbf{HP}_i^{|\mathbf{h}|}$ represents all possible partial hidden paths from the position i to the ending position $|\mathbf{h}|$. $\text{Heu}_i(\mathbf{h}_j)$ is an admissible heuristic function for the A^* search over hidden paths, therefore $\mathbf{HP}_n$ is exact and BLP inference is exact.

The BLP inference is efficient when the probability distribution among the hidden paths is intensive. By combining the forward A^* with the backward Viterbi algorithm, the time complexity of producing $\mathbf{HP}_n$ is roughly a linear complexity concerning its size. In practice, on the CoNLL test data containing 2,012 sentences, the BLP inference finished in five minutes when using the feature set based on both word and POS information (see Table 3). The memory consumption is also relatively small, because it is an online style algorithm and it is not necessary to preserve $\mathbf{HP}_n$.

In this paper, to make a comparison, we also study the Best Hidden Path inference (BHP):

$$\mathbf{y}_{BHP} = \text{argmax}_{\mathbf{y}} P(\mathbf{h}_{\mathbf{y}}|\mathbf{x}, \mathbf{\Theta}^*), \qquad (9)$$

where $\mathbf{h}_{\mathbf{y}} \in \mathbf{H}_{\mathbf{y}_1} \times \ldots \times \mathbf{H}_{\mathbf{y}_m}$. In other words, the Best Hidden Path is the label sequence that is directly projected from the most probable hidden path $\mathbf{h}^*$.

In (Morency et al. 2007), $\mathbf{y}^*$ is estimated by using the Best Point-wise Marginal Path (BMP). To estimate the label $\mathbf{y}_j$ of token j, the marginal probabilities $P(\mathbf{h}_j = a|\mathbf{x}, \mathbf{\Theta})$ are computed for possible hidden states $a \in \mathbf{H}$. Then, the marginal probabilities are summed and the optimal label is estimated by using the marginal probabilities.

The BLP produces y^* while the BHP and the BMP perform an estimation on y^*. We will make an experimental comparison in Section 6.

5 Analyzing Latent-Dynamics

The chunks in shallow parsing are represented with the three labels shown in Table 1, and shallow parsing is treated as a sequence labeling task with those three labels. A challenge for most shallow parsing approaches is to determine the concepts learned by the model. In this section, we show how we can analyze the latent-dynamics.

5.1 Analyzing Latent-Dynamics

In this section, we show how to analyze the characteristics of the hidden states. Our goal is to find the words characterizing a specific hidden state, and then look at the selected words with their associated POS tags to determine if the LDCRF model has learned meaningful latent-dynamics.

B	words beginning a chunk
I	words continuing a chunk
O	words being outside a chunk

Table 1: Shallow parsing labels.

In the experiments reported in this section, we did not use the features on POS tags in order to isolate the model's capability of learning latent dynamics. In other words, the model could simply learn the dynamics of POS tags as the latent dynamics if the model is given the information about POS tags. The features used in the experiments are listed on the left side (Word Features) in Table 3.

The main idea is to look at the marginal probabilities $P(\mathbf{h}_j = a|\mathbf{x}, \mathbf{\Theta})$ for each word j, and select the hidden state a^* with the highest probability. By counting how often a specific word selected a as the optimal hidden state, i.e., $\delta(w, a)$, we can create statistics about the relationship between hidden states and words. We define relative frequency as the number of times a specific word selected a hidden state while normalized by the global frequency of this word:

$$\text{RltFreq}(w, h_j) = \frac{\text{Freq}(\ \delta(w, h_j)\ )}{\text{Freq}(w)}. \qquad (10)$$

5.2 Learned Latent-Dynamics from CoNLL

In this subsection, we show the latent-dynamics learned automatically from the CoNLL dataset. The details of these experiments are presented in the following section.

The most frequent three words corresponding to the individual hidden states of the labels, B and O, are shown in Table 2. As shown, the automatically learned hidden states demonstrate prominent characteristics. The extrinsic label B, which begins a noun phrase, is automatically split into 4 subcategories: wh-determiners (*WDT*, such as "*that*") together with wh-pronouns (*WP*, such as "*who*"), the determiners (*DT*, such as "*any, an, a*"), the personal pronouns (*PRP*, such as "*they, we, he*"), and the singular proper nouns (*NNP*, such as "*Nasdaq, Florida*") together with the plural nouns (*NNS*, such as "*cities*"). The results of B1 suggests that the wh-determiners represented by "*that*", and the wh-pronouns represented by "*who*", perform simi-

Labels	HidStat	Words	POS	RltFreq
B	B1	*That*	*WDT*	0.85
		who	*WP*	0.49
		Who	*WP*	0.33
	B2	*any*	*DT*	1.00
		an	*DT*	1.00
		a	*DT*	0.98
	B3	*They*	*PRP*	1.00
		we	*PRP*	1.00
		he	*PRP*	1.00
	B4	*Nasdaq*	*NNP*	1.00
		Florida	*NNP*	0.99
		cities	*NNS*	0.99
O	O1	*But*	*CC*	0.88
		by	*IN*	0.73
		or	*IN*	0.67
	O2	4.6	*CD*	1.00
		1	*CD*	1.00
		11	*CD*	0.62
	O3	*were*	*VBD*	0.94
		rose	*VBD*	0.93
		have	*VBP*	0.92
	O4	*been*	*VBN*	0.97
		be	*VB*	0.94
		to	*TO*	0.92

Table 2: Latent-dynamics learned automatically by the LDCRF model. This table shows the top three words and their gold-standard POS tags for each hidden states.

lar roles in modeling the dynamics in shallow parsing. Further, the singular proper nouns and the plural nouns are grouped together, suggesting that they may perform similar roles. Moreover, we can notice that B2 and B3 are highly consistent.

The label O is automatically split into the coordinating conjunctions (*CC*) together with the prepositions (*IN*) indexed by O1, the cardinal numbers (*CD*) indexed by O2, the past tense verbs (*VBD*) together with the personal verbs (*VBP*) indexed by O3, and another sub-category, O4. From the results we can find that gold-standard POS tags may not be adequate in modeling latent-dynamics in shallow parsing, as we can notice that three hidden states out of four (O1, O3 and O4) contains relating but different gold-standard POS tags.

6 Experiments

Following previous studies on shallow parsing, our experiments are performed on the CoNLL 2000 data set (Sang & Buchholz 2000; Ramshow & Marcus 1995). The training set consists of 8,936 sentences, and the test set consists of 2,012 sentences. The standard evaluation metrics for this task are precision p (the fraction of output chunks matching the reference chunks), recall r (the fraction of reference chunks returned), and the F-measure given by $F = 2pr/(p + r)$.

Word Features:
$\{w_{i-2}, w_{i-1}, w_i, w_{i+1}, w_{i+2}, w_{i-1}w_i, w_iw_{i+1}\}$
$\times\{h_i, h_{i-1}h_i, h_{i-2}h_{i-1}h_i\}$
POS Features:
$\{t_{i-1}, t_i, t_{i+1}, t_{i-2}t_{i-1}, t_{i-1}t_i, t_it_{i+1}, t_{i+1}t_{i+2},$
$t_{i-2}t_{i-1}t_i, t_{i-1}t_it_{i+1}, t_it_{i+1}t_{i+2}\}$
$\times\{h_i, h_{i-1}h_i, h_{i-2}h_{i-1}h_i\}$

Table 3: Feature templates used in the experiments. w_i is the current word; t_i is current POS tag; and h_i is the current hidden state (for the case of latent models) or the current label (for the case of conventional models).

6.1 LDCRF for Shallow Parsing

We implemented LDCRFs in C++, and optimized the system to cope with large scale problems, in which the feature dimension is beyond millions. We employ similar predicate sets defined in Sha & Pereira (2003). We follow them in using predicates that depend on words as well as POS tags in the neighborhood of a given position, taking into account only those 417,835 features which occur at least once in the training data. The features are listed in Table 3.

As for numerical optimization (Malouf 2002; Wallach 2002), we performed gradient decent with the Limited-Memory BFGS (L-BFGS) optimization technique (Nocedal & Wright 1999). L-BFGS is a second-order Quasi-Newton method that numerically estimates the curvature from previous gradients and updates. With no requirement on specialized Hessian approximation, L-BFGS can handle large-scale problems in an efficient manner. We implemented an L-BFGS optimizer in C++ by modifying the OWLQN package (Andrew & Gao 2007) developed by Galen Andrew. In our experiments, storing 10 pairs of previous gradients for the approximation of the function's inverse Hessian worked well, making the amount of the extra memory required modest. Using more previous gradients will probably decrease the number of iterations required to reach convergence, but would increase memory requirements significantly. To make a comparison, we also employed the Conjugate-Gradient (CG) optimization algorithm. For details of CG, see Shewchuk (1994).

Since the objective function of the LDCRF model is non-convex, it is suggested to use the random initialization of parameters for the training. To reduce overfitting, we employed an L_2 Gaussian weight prior (Chen & Rosenfeld 1999). During training and validation, we varied the number of hidden states per label (from 2 to 6 states per label), and also varied the L_2-regularization term (with values 10^k, k from -3 to 3). Our experiments suggested that using 4 or 5 hidden states per label for the shallow parser is a viable compromise between accuracy and efficiency.

7 Results and Discussion

7.1 Performance on Word Features

As discussed in Section 4, it is preferred to not use the features on POS tags in order to isolate the model's capability of learning latent dynamics. In this sub-section, we use pure word features with their counts above 10 in the training data to perform experimental comparisons among different inference algorithms on LDCRFs, including BLP, BHP, and existing BMP.

Since the CRF model is one of the successful models in sequential labeling tasks (Lafferty et al. 2001; Sha & Pereira 2003; McDonald et al. 2005), in this section, we also compare LDCRFs with CRFs. We tried to make experimental results more comparable between LDCRF and CRF models, and have therefore employed the same features set, optimizer and fine-tuning strategy between LDCRF and CRF models.

The experimental results are shown in Table 4. In the table, Acc. signifies 'label accuracy', which is useful for the significance test in the following sub-section. As shown, LDCRF-BLP outperforms LDCRF-BHP and LDCRF-BMP, suggesting that BLP inference [1] is superior. The superiority of BLP is statistically significant, which will be shown in next sub-section. On the other side, all the LDCRF models outperform the CRF model. In particular, the gap between LDCRF-BLP and CRF is 1.53 percent.

[1] In practice, for efficiency, we approximated the BLP on a few sentences by limiting the number of search steps.

Models: WF	Acc.	Pre.	Rec.	F_1
LDCRF-BLP	97.01	90.33	88.91	**89.61**
LDCRF-BHP	96.52	90.26	88.21	89.22
LDCRF-BMP	97.26	89.83	89.06	89.44
CRF	96.11	88.12	88.03	88.08

Table 4: Experimental comparisons among different inference algorithms on LDCRFs, and the performance of CRFs using the same feature set on pure word features. The BLP inference outperforms the BHP and BMP inference. LDCRFs outperform CRFs.

Models	F_1 Gap	Acc. Gap	Sig.
BLP vs. BHP	0.39	0.49	1e-10
BLP vs. CRF	1.53	0.90	5e-13

Table 5: The significance tests. LDCRF-BLP is significantly more accurate than LDCRF-BHP and CRFs.

7.2 Labeling Accuracy and Significance Test

As shown in Table 4, the accuracy rate for individual labeling decisions is over-optimistic as a measure for shallow parsing. Nevertheless, since testing the significance of shallow parsers' F-measures is tricky, individual labeling accuracy provides a more convenient basis for statistical significance tests (Sha & Pereira 2003). One such test is the McNemar test on paired observations (Gillick & Cox 1989). As shown in Table 5, for the LDCRF model, the BLP inference schema is statistically more accurate than the BHP inference schema. Also, Evaluations show that the McNemar's value on labeling disagreement between the LDCRF-BLP and CRF models is 5e-13, suggesting that LDCRF-BLP is significantly more accurate than CRFs.

On the other hand, the accuracy rate of BMP inference is a special case. Since the BMP inference is essentially an accuracy-first inference schema, the accuracy rate and the F-measure have a different relation in BMP. As we can see, the individual labeling accuracy achieved by the LDCRF-BMP model is as high as 97.26%, but its F-measure is still lower than LDCRF-BLP.

7.3 Convergence Speed

It would be interesting to compare the convergence speed between the objective loss function of LDCRFs and CRFs. We apply the L-BFGS optimiza-

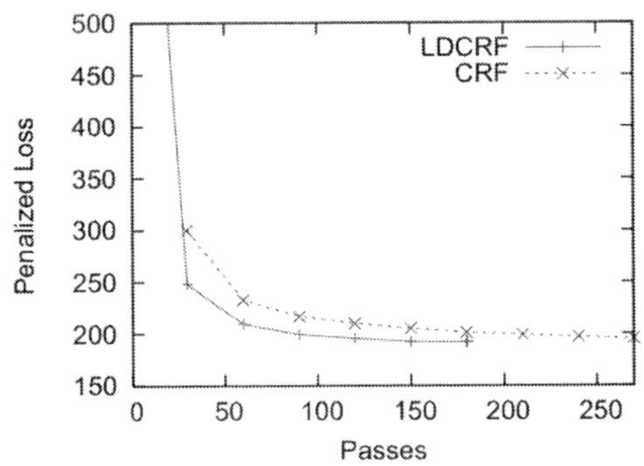

Figure 2: The value of the penalized loss based on the number of iterations: LDCRFs vs. CRFs.

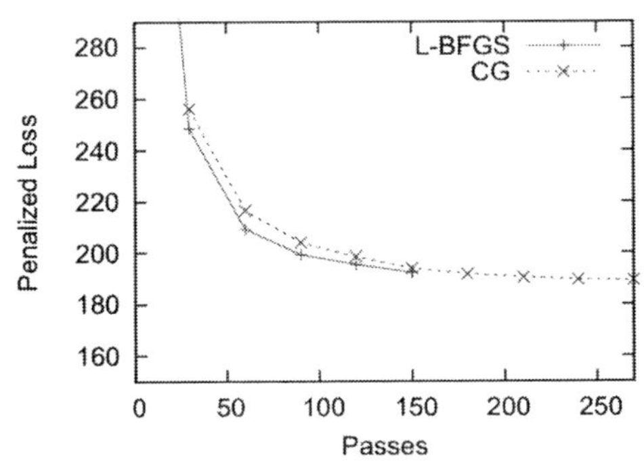

Figure 3: Training the LDCRF model: L-BFGS vs. CG.

tion algorithm to optimize the loss function of LDCRF and CRF models, making a comparison between them. We find that the iterations required for the convergence of LDCRFs is less than for CRFs (see Figure 2). Normally, the LDCRF model arrives at the plateau of convergence in 120-150 iterations, while CRFs require 210-240 iterations. When we replace the L-BFGS optimizer by the CG optimization algorithm, we observed as well that LDCRF converges faster on iteration numbers than CRF does.

On the contrary, however, the time cost of the LDCRF model in each iteration is higher than the CRF model, because of the incorporation of hidden states. The time cost of the LDCRF model in each iteration is roughly a quadratic increase concerning the increase of the number of hidden states. Therefore, though the LDCRF model requires less passes for the convergence, it is practically slower than the CRF model. Improving the scalability of the LDCRF model would be a interesting topic in the future.

Furthermore, we make a comparison between the L-BFGS and the CG optimizer for LDCRFs. We observe that the L-BFGS optimizer is slightly faster than CG on LDCRFs (see Figure 3), which echoes the comparison between the L-BFGS and the CG optimizing technique on the CRF model (Sha & Pereira 2003).

Models: WF+POS	Pre.	Rec.	F_1
LDCRF-BLP	94.65	94.03	**94.34**
CRF (Vishwanathan et al. 06)	*N/A*	*N/A*	93.6
CRF (McDonald et al. 05)	94.57	94.00	94.29
Voted perceptron (Collins 02)	*N/A*	*N/A*	93.53
Generalized Winnow (Zhang et al. 02)	93.80	93.99	93.89
SVM combination (Kudo & Matsumoto 01)	94.15	94.29	94.22
Memo. classifier (Sang 00)	93.63	92.89	93.26

Table 6: Performance of the LDCRF-BLP model, and the comparison with CRFs and other successful approaches. In this table, all the systems have employed POS features.

7.4 Comparisons to Other Systems with POS Features

Performance of the LDCRF-BLP model and some of the best results reported previously are summarized in Table 6. Our LDCRF model achieved comparable performance to those best reported systems in terms of the F-measure.

McDonald et al. (2005) achieved an F-measure of 94.29% by using a CRF model. By employing a multi-model combination approach, Kudo & Matsumoto (2001) also achieved a good performance. They use a combination of 8 kernel SVMs with a heuristic voting strategy. An advantage of LDCRFs over max-margin based approaches is that LDCRFs can output N-best label sequences and their probabilities using efficient marginalization operations, which can be used for other components in an information extraction system.

8 Conclusions and Future Work

In this paper, we have shown that automatic modeling on "latent-dynamics" can be useful in shallow parsing. By analyzing the automatically learned hidden states, we showed how LDCRFs can naturally learn latent-dynamics in shallow parsing.

We proposed an improved inference algorithm, the BLP, for LDCRFs. We performed experiments using the CoNLL data, and showed how the BLP inference outperforms existing inference engines. When further employing POS features as other systems did, the performance of the LDCRF-BLP model is comparable to those best reported results. The LDCRF model demonstrates a significant advantage over other models on pure word features in this paper. We expect it to be particularly useful in the real-world tasks without rich features.

The latent conditional model handles latent-dynamics naturally, and can be easily extended to other labeling tasks. Also, the BLP inference algorithm can be extended to other latent conditional models for producing optimal label sequences. As a future work, we plan to further speed up the BLP algorithm.

Acknowledgments

Many thanks to Yoshimasa Tsuruoka for helpful discussions on the experiments and paper-writing. This research was partially supported by Grant-in-Aid for Specially Promoted Research 18002007 (MEXT, Japan). The work at the USC Institute for Creative Technology was sponsored by the U.S. Army Research, Development, and Engineering Command (RDECOM), and the content does not necessarily reflect the position or the policy of the Government, and no official endorsement should be inferred.

References

Abney, S. 1991. Parsing by chunks. In R. Berwick, S. Abney, and C. Tenny, editors, Principle-based Parsing. *Kluwer Academic Publishers.*

Abney, S.; Schapire, R. E. and Singer, Y. 1999. Boosting applied to tagging and PP attachment. In Proc. *EMNLP/VLC-99.*

Andrew, G. and Gao, J. 2007. Scalable training of L1-regularized log-linear models. In Proc. *ICML-07.*

Bikel, D. M.; Schwartz, R. L. and Weischedel, R. M. 1999. An algorithm that learns what's in a name. *Machine Learning,* 34: 211-231.

Chen, S. F. and Rosenfeld, R. 1999. A Gaussian prior for smooth-ing maximum entropy models. *Technical Report CMU-CS-99-108,* CMU.

Collins, M. 2002. Discriminative training methods for hidden Markov models: Theory and experiments with perceptron algorithms. In Proc. *EMNLP-02.*

Freitag, D. and McCallum, A. 2000. Information extraction with HMM structures learned by stochastic optimization. In Proc. *AAAI-00.*

Gillick, L. and Cox, S. 1989. Some statistical issues in the comparison of speech recognition algorithms. In *International Conference on Acoustics Speech and Signal Processing,* v1, pages 532-535.

Hart, P.E.; Nilsson, N.J.; and Raphael, B. 1968. A formal basis for the heuristic determination of minimum cost path. IEEE Trans. On *System Science and Cybernetics,* SSC-4(2): 100-107.

Kudo, T. and Matsumoto, Y. 2001. Chunking with support vector machines. In Proc. *NAACL-01.*

Kupiec, J. 1992. Robust part-of-speech tagging using a hidden Markov model. *Computer Speech and Language.* 6:225-242.

Lafferty, J.; McCallum, A. and Pereira, F. 2001. Conditional random fields: Probabilistic models for segmenting and labeling sequence data. In Proc. *ICML-01,* pages 282-289.

Malouf, R. 2002. A comparison of algorithms for maximum entropy parameter estimation. In Proc. *CoNLL-02.*

Matsuzaki, T.; Miyao Y. and Tsujii, J. 2005. Probabilistic CFG with Latent Annotations. In Proc. *ACL-05.*

McDonald, R.; Crammer, K. and Pereira, F. 2005. Flexible Text Segmentation with Structured Multilabel Classification. In Proc. *HLT/EMNLP-05,* pages 987- 994.

Morency, L.P.; Quattoni, A. and Darrell, T. 2007. Latent-Dynamic Discriminative Models for Continuous Gesture Recognition. In Proc. *CVPR-07,* pages 1- 8.

Nocedal, J. and Wright, S. J. 1999. Numerical Optimization. *Springer.*

Petrov, S.; Pauls, A.; and Klein, D. 2007. Discriminative log-linear grammars with latent variables. In Proc. *NIPS-07.*

Punyakanok, V. and Roth, D. 2001. The use of classifiers in sequential inference. In Proc. *NIPS-01,* pages 995-1001. MIT Press.

Ramshaw, L. A. and Marcus, M. P. 1995. Text chunking using transformation-based learning. In Proc. Third Workshop on Very Large Corpora. In Proc. *ACL-95.*

Ratnaparkhi, A. 1996. A maximum entropy model for part-of-speech tagging. In Proc. *EMNLP-96.*

Sang, E.F.T.K. 2000. Noun Phrase Representation by System Combination. In Proc. *ANLP/NAACL-00.*

Sang, E.F.T.K and Buchholz, S. 2000. Introduction to the CoNLL-2000 shared task: Chunking. In Proc. *CoNLL-00,* pages 127-132.

Sha, F. and Pereira, F. 2003. Shallow Parsing with Conditional Random Fields. In Proc. *HLT/NAACL-03.*

Shewchuk, J. R. 1994. An introduction to the conjugate gradient method without the agonizing pain. http://www.2.cs.cmu.edu/jrs/jrspapers.html/#cg.

Sutton, C.; Rohanimanesh, K. and McCallum, A. 2004. Dynamic conditional random fields: Factorized probabilistic models for labeling and segmenting sequence data. In Proc. *ICML-04.*

Viterbi, A.J. 1967. Error bounds for convolutional codes and an asymptotically optimum decoding algorithm. *IEEE Transactions on Information Theory.* 13(2):260-269.

Vishwanathan, S.; Schraudolph, N. N.; Schmidt, M.W. and Murphy, K. 2006. Accelerated training of conditional random fields with stochastic meta-descent. In Proc. *ICML-06.*

Wallach, H. 2002. Efficient training of conditional random fields. In *Proc. 6th Annual CLUK Research Colloquium.*

Zhang, T.; Damerau, F. and Johnson, D. 2002. Text chunking based on a generalization of winnow. *Journal of Machine Learning Research,* 2:615-637.

Learning Entailment Rules for Unary Templates

Idan Szpektor
Department of Computer Science
Bar-Ilan University
Ramat Gan, Israel
szpekti@macs.biu.ac.il

Ido Dagan
Department of Computer Science
Bar-Ilan University
Ramat Gan, Israel
dagan@macs.biu.ac.il

Abstract

Most work on unsupervised entailment rule acquisition focused on rules between templates with two variables, ignoring *unary rules* - entailment rules between templates with a single variable. In this paper we investigate two approaches for unsupervised learning of such rules and compare the proposed methods with a binary rule learning method. The results show that the learned unary rule-sets outperform the binary rule-set. In addition, a novel directional similarity measure for learning entailment, termed *Balanced-Inclusion*, is the best performing measure.

1 Introduction

In many NLP applications, such as Question Answering (QA) and Information Extraction (IE), it is crucial to recognize whether a specific target meaning is inferred from a text. For example, a QA system has to deduce that "*SCO sued IBM*" is inferred from "*SCO won a lawsuit against IBM*" to answer "*Whom did SCO sue?*". This type of reasoning has been identified as a core semantic inference paradigm by the generic *Textual Entailment* framework (Giampiccolo et al., 2007).

An important type of knowledge needed for such inference is *entailment rules*. An entailment rule specifies a directional inference relation between two *templates*, text patterns with variables, such as 'X win lawsuit against $Y \rightarrow X$ sue Y'. Applying this rule by matching 'X win lawsuit against Y' in the above text allows a QA system to infer 'X sue Y' and identify "*IBM*", Y's instantiation, as the answer for the above question. Entailment rules capture linguistic and world-knowledge inferences and are used as an important building block within different applications, e.g. (Romano et al., 2006).

One reason for the limited performance of generic semantic inference systems is the lack of broad-scale knowledge-bases of entailment rules (in analog to lexical resources such as WordNet). Supervised learning of broad coverage rule-sets is an arduous task. This sparked intensive research on unsupervised acquisition of entailment rules (and similarly paraphrases) e.g. (Lin and Pantel, 2001; Szpektor et al., 2004; Sekine, 2005).

Most unsupervised entailment rule acquisition methods learn *binary rules*, rules between templates with two variables, ignoring *unary rules*, rules between *unary templates* (templates with only one variable). However, a predicate quite often appears in the text with just a single variable (e.g. intransitive verbs or passives), where inference requires unary rules, e.g. 'X take a nap $\rightarrow X$ sleep' (further motivations in Section 3.1).

In this paper we focus on unsupervised learning of unary entailment rules. Two learning approaches are proposed. In our main approach, rules are learned by measuring how similar the variable instantiations of two templates in a corpus are. In addition to adapting state-of-the-art similarity measures for unary rule learning, we propose a new measure, termed *Balanced-Inclusion*, which balances the notion of directionality in entailment with the common notion of symmetric semantic similarity. In a second approach, unary rules are derived from binary rules learned by state-of-the-art binary rule learning methods.

We tested the various unsupervised unary rule

©2008. Licensed under the *Creative Commons Attribution-Noncommercial-Share Alike 3.0 Unported* license (http://creativecommons.org/licenses/by-nc-sa/3.0/). Some rights reserved.

learning methods, as well as a binary rule learning method, on a test set derived from a standard IE benchmark. This provides the first comparison between the performance of unary and binary rule-sets. Several results rise from our evaluation: (a) while most work on unsupervised learning ignored unary rules, all tested unary methods outperformed the binary method; (b) it is better to learn unary rules directly than to derive them from a binary rule-base; (c) our proposed Balanced-Inclusion measure outperformed all other tested methods in terms of F1 measure. Moreover, only Balanced-Inclusion improved F1 score over a baseline inference that does not use entailment rules at all .

2 Background

This section reviews relevant distributional similarity measures, both symmetric and directional, which were applied for either lexical similarity or unsupervised entailment rule learning.

Distributional similarity measures follow the Distributional Hypothesis, which states that words that occur in the same contexts tend to have similar meanings (Harris, 1954). Various measures were proposed in the literature for assessing such similarity between two words, u and v. Given a word q, its set of features F_q and feature weights $w_q(f)$ for $f \in F_q$, a common symmetric similarity measure is Lin similarity (Lin, 1998a):

$$Lin(u,v) = \frac{\sum_{f \in F_u \cap F_v} [w_u(f) + w_v(f)]}{\sum_{f \in F_u} w_u(f) + \sum_{f \in F_v} w_v(f)}$$

where the weight of each feature is the pointwise mutual information (pmi) between the word and the feature: $w_q(f) = log[\frac{Pr(f|q)}{Pr(f)}]$.

Weeds and Weir (2003) proposed to measure the symmetric similarity between two words by averaging two directional (asymmetric) scores: the coverage of each word's features by the other. The coverage of u by v is measured by:

$$Cover(u,v) = \frac{\sum_{f \in F_u \cap F_v} w_u(f)}{\sum_{f \in F_u} w_u(f)}$$

The average can be arithmetic or harmonic:
$WeedsA(u,v) = \frac{1}{2}[Cover(u,v) + Cover(v,u)]$

$$WeedsH(u,v) = \frac{2 \cdot Cover(u,v) \cdot Cover(v,u)}{Cover(u,v) + Cover(v,u)}$$

Weeds et al. also used pmi for feature weights.

Binary rule learning algorithms adopted such lexical similarity approaches for learning rules between templates, where the features of each template are its variable instantiations in a corpus, such as $\{X$='*SCO*', Y='*IBM*'$\}$ for the example in Section 1. Some works focused on learning rules from *comparable corpora*, containing comparable documents such as different news articles from the same date on the same topic (Barzilay and Lee, 2003; Ibrahim et al., 2003). Such corpora are highly informative for identifying variations of the same meaning, since, typically, when variable instantiations are shared across comparable documents the same predicates are described. However, it is hard to collect broad-scale comparable corpora, as the majority of texts are non-comparable.

A complementary approach is learning from the abundant regular, non-comparable, corpora. Yet, in such corpora it is harder to recognize variations of the same predicate. The DIRT algorithm (Lin and Pantel, 2001) learns non-directional binary rules for templates that are paths in a dependency parse-tree between two noun variables X and Y. The similarity between two templates t and t' is the geometric average:

$$DIRT(t,t') = \sqrt{Lin_x(t,t') \cdot Lin_y(t,t')}$$

where Lin_x is the Lin similarity between X's instantiations of t and X's instantiations of t' in a corpus (equivalently for Lin_y). Some works take the combination of the two variable instantiations in each template occurrence as a single complex feature, e.g. $\{X$-Y='*SCO-IBM*'$\}$, and compare between these complex features of t and t' (Ravichandran and Hovy, 2002; Szpektor et al., 2004; Sekine, 2005).

Directional Measures Most rule learning methods apply a symmetric similarity measure between two templates, viewing them as paraphrasing each other. However, entailment is in general a directional relation. For example, 'X acquire $Y \rightarrow X$ own Y' and 'countersuit against $X \rightarrow$ lawsuit against X'.

(Weeds and Weir, 2003) propose a directional measure for learning hyponymy between two words, 'l $\rightarrow$ r', by giving more weight to the coverage of the features of l by r (with $\alpha > \frac{1}{2}$):

$$WeedsD(l,r) = \alpha Cover(l,r) + (1-\alpha) Cover(r,l)$$

When α=1, this measure degenerates into $Cover(l,r)$, termed $Precision(l,r)$. With

$Precision(l, r)$ we obtain a "soft" version of the inclusion hypothesis presented in (Geffet and Dagan, 2005), which expects l to entail r if the "important" features of l appear also in r.

Similarly, the LEDIR algorithm (Bhagat et al., 2007) identifies the entailment direction between two binary templates, l and r, which participate in a relation learned by (the symmetric) DIRT, by measuring the proportion of instantiations of l that are covered by the instantiations of r.

As far as we know, only (Shinyama et al., 2002) and (Pekar, 2006) learn rules between unary templates. However, (Shinyama et al., 2002) relies on comparable corpora for identifying paraphrases and simply takes any two templates from comparable sentences that share a named entity instantiation to be paraphrases. Such approach is not feasible for non-comparable corpora where statistical measurement is required. (Pekar, 2006) learns rules only between templates related by local discourse (information from different documents is ignored). In addition, their template structure is limited to only verbs and their direct syntactic arguments, which may yield incorrect rules, e.g. for light verbs (see Section 5.2). To overcome this limitation, we use a more expressive template structure.

3 Learning Unary Entailment Rules

3.1 Motivations

Most unsupervised rule learning algorithms focused on learning binary entailment rules. However, using binary rules for inference is not enough. First, a predicate that can have multiple arguments may still occur with only one of its arguments. For example, in "*The acquisition of TCA was successful*", '*TCA*' is the only argument of '*acquisition*'. Second, some predicate expressions are unary by nature. For example, modifiers, such as 'the elected X', or intransitive verbs. In addition, it appears more tractable to learn all variations for each argument of a predicate separately than to learn them for combinations of argument pairs.

For these reasons, it seems that unary rule learning should be addressed in addition to binary rule learning. We are further motivated by the fact that some (mostly supervised) works in IE found learning unary templates useful for recognizing relevant named entities (Riloff, 1996; Sudo et al., 2003; Shinyama and Sekine, 2006), though they did not attempt to learn generic knowledge bases of entailment rules.

This paper investigates acquisition of unary entailment rules from regular non-comparable corpora. We first describe the structure of unary templates and then explore two conceivable approaches for learning unary rules. The first approach directly assesses the relation between two given templates based on the similarity of their instantiations in the corpus. The second approach, which was also mentioned in (Iftene and Balahur-Dobrescu, 2007), derives unary rules from learned binary rules.

3.2 Unary Template Structure

To learn unary rules we first need to define their structure. In this paper we work at the syntactic representation level. Texts are represented by dependency parse trees (using the Minipar parser (Lin, 1998b)) and templates by parse sub-trees.

Given a dependency parse tree, any sub-tree can be a candidate template, setting some of its nodes as variables (Sudo et al., 2003). However, the number of possible templates is exponential in the size of the sentence. In the binary rule learning literature, the main solution for exhaustively learning all rules between any pair of templates in a given corpus is to restrict the structure of templates. Typically, a template is restricted to be a path in a parse tree between two variable nodes (Lin and Pantel, 2001; Ibrahim et al., 2003).

Following this approach, we chose the structure of unary templates to be paths as well, where one end of the path is the template's variable. However, paths with one variable have more expressive power than paths between two variables, since the combination of two unary paths may generate a binary template that is not a path. For example, the combination of 'X call indictable' and 'call Y indictable' is the template 'X call Y indictable', which is not a path between X and Y.

For every noun node v in a parsed sentence, we generate templates with v as a variable as follows:

1. Traverse the path from v towards the root of the parse tree. Whenever a candidate predicate is encountered (any noun, adjective or verb) the path from that node to v is taken as a template. We stop when the first verb or clause boundary (e.g. a relative clause) is encountered, which typically represent the syntactic boundary of a specific predicate.

2. To enable templates with control verbs and light verbs, e.g. 'X help preventing', 'X make noise', whenever a verb is encountered we generate templates that are paths between v and the verb's modifiers, either objects, prepositional complements or infinite or gerund verb forms (paths ending at stop words, e.g. pronouns, are not generated).

3. To capture noun modifiers that act as predicates, e.g. 'the losing X', we extract template paths between v and each of its modifiers, nouns or adjectives, that are derived from a verb. We use the Catvar database to identify verb derivations (Habash and Dorr, 2003).

As an example for the procedure, the templates extracted from the sentence "*The losing party played it safe*" with '*party*' as the variable are: 'losing X', 'X play' and 'X play safe'.

3.3 Direct Learning of Unary Rules

We applied the lexical similarity measures presented in Section 2 for unary rule learning. Each argument instantiation of template t in the corpus is taken as a feature f, and the pmi between t and f is used for the feature's weight. We first adapted DIRT for unary templates (*unary-DIRT*, applying Lin-similarity to the single feature vector), as well as its output filtering by LEDIR. The various Weeds measures were also applied[1]: symmetric arithmetic average, symmetric harmonic average, weighted arithmetic average and Precision.

After initial analysis, we found that given a right hand side template r, symmetric measures such as Lin (in DIRT) generally tend to prefer (score higher) relations $\langle l, r \rangle$ in which l and r are related but do not necessarily participate in an entailment or equivalence relation, e.g. the wrong rule 'kill X $\leftrightarrow$ injure X'.

On the other hand, directional measures such as Weeds Precision tend to prefer directional rules in which the entailing template is infrequent. If an infrequent template has common instantiations with another template, the coverage of its features is typically high, whether or not an entailment relation exists between the two templates. This behavior generates high-score incorrect rules.

Based on this analysis, we propose a new measure that balances the two behaviors, termed *Balanced-Inclusion* (*BInc*). BInc identifies entailing templates based on a directional measure but penalizes infrequent templates using a symmetric measure:

$$BInc(l,r) = \sqrt{Lin(l,r) \cdot Precision(l,r)}$$

3.4 Deriving Unary Rules From Binary Rules

An alternative way to learn unary rules is to first learn binary entailment rules and then derive unary rules from them. We derive unary rules from a given binary rule-base in two steps. First, for each binary rule, we generate all possible unary rules that are part of that rule (each unary template is extracted following the same procedure described in Section 3.2). For example, from 'X find solution to $Y \rightarrow X$ solve Y' we generate the unary rules 'X find $\rightarrow X$ solve', 'X find solution $\rightarrow X$ solve', 'solution to $Y \rightarrow$ solve Y' and 'find solution to $Y \rightarrow$ solve Y'. The score of each generated rule is set to be the score of the original binary rule.

The same unary rule can be derived from different binary rules. For example, 'hire $Y \rightarrow$ employ Y' is derived both from 'X hire $Y \rightarrow X$ employ Y' and 'hire Y for $Z \rightarrow$ employ Y for Z', having a different score from each original binary rule. The second step of the algorithm aggregates the different scores yielded for each derived rule to produce the final rule score. Three aggregation functions were tested: sum (*Derived-Sum*), average (*Derived-Avg*) and maximum (*Derived-Max*).

4 Experimental Setup

We want to evaluate learned unary and binary rule bases by their utility for NLP applications through assessing the validity of inferences that are performed in practice using the rule base.

To perform such experiments, we need a test-set of *seed templates*, which correspond to a set of target predicates, and a corpus annotated with all argument mentions of each predicate. The evaluation assesses the correctness of all argument extractions, which are obtained by matching in the corpus either the seed templates or templates that entail them according to the rule-base (the latter corresponds to *rule-application*).

Following (Szpektor et al., 2008), we found the ACE 2005 event training set[2] useful for this purpose. This standard IE dataset includes 33 types of event predicates such as *Injure, Sue* and *Divorce*.

[1] We applied the best performing parameter values presented in (Bhagat et al., 2007) and (Weeds and Weir, 2003).

[2] http://projects.ldc.upenn.edu/ace/

All event mentions are annotated in the corpus, including the instantiated arguments of the predicate. ACE guidelines specify for each event its possible arguments, each associated with a semantic role. For instance, some of the *Injure* event arguments are *Agent*, *Victim* and *Time*.

To utilize the ACE dataset for evaluating entailment rule applications, we manually represented each ACE event predicate by unary seed templates. For example, the seed templates for *Injure* are 'A injure', 'injure V' and 'injure in T'. We mapped each event role annotation to the corresponding seed template variable, e.g. '*Agent*' to A and '*Victim*' to V in the above example. Templates are matched using a syntactic matcher that handles simple morpho-syntactic phenomena, as in (Szpektor and Dagan, 2007). A rule application is considered correct if the matched argument is annotated by the corresponding ACE role.

For testing binary rule-bases, we automatically generated binary seed templates from any two unary seeds that share the same predicate. For example, for *Injure* the binary seeds 'A injure V', 'A injure in T' and 'injure V in T' were automatically generated from the above unary seeds.

We performed two adaptations to the ACE dataset to fit it better to our evaluation needs. First, our evaluation aims at assessing the correctness of inferring a specific target semantic meaning, which is denoted by a specific predicate, using rules. Thus, four events that correspond ambiguously to multiple distinct predicates were ignored. For instance, the *Transfer-Money* event refers to both *donating* and *lending* money, and thus annotations of this event cannot be mapped to a specific seed template. We also omitted 3 events with less than 10 mentions, and were left with 26 events (6380 argument mentions).

Additionally, we regard all entailing mentions under the textual entailment definition as correct. However, event mentions are annotated as correct in ACE only if they explicitly describe the target event. For instance, a Divorce mention does entail a preceding marriage event but it does not explicitly describe it, and thus it is not annotated as a *Marry* event. To better utilize the ACE dataset, we considered for a target event the annotations of other events that entail it as being correct as well. We note that each argument was considered separately. For example, we marked a mention of a divorced person as entailing the marriage of that person, but did not consider the place and time of the divorce act to be those of the marriage .

5 Results and Analysis

We implemented the unary rule learning algorithms described in Section 3 and the binary DIRT algorithm (Lin and Pantel, 2001). We executed each method over the Reuters RCV1 corpus[3], learning for each template r in the corpus the top 100 rules in which r is entailed by another template l, '$l \rightarrow r$'. All rules were learned in canonical form (Szpektor and Dagan, 2007). The rule-base learned by binary DIRT was taken as the input for deriving unary rules from binary rules.

The performance of each acquired rule-base was measured for each ACE event. We measured the percentage of correct argument mentions extracted out of all correct argument mentions annotated for the event (recall) and out of all argument mentions extracted for the event (precision). We also measured F1, their harmonic average, and report macro average *Recall*, *Precision* and *F1* over the 26 event types.

No threshold setting mechanism is suggested in the literature for the scores of the different algorithms, especially since rules for different right hand side templates have different score ranges. Thus, we follow common evaluation practice (Lin and Pantel, 2001; Geffet and Dagan, 2005) and test each learned rule-set by taking the top K rules for each seed template, where K ranges from 0 to 100. When K=0, no rules are used and mentions are extracted only by direct matching of seed templates.

Our rule application setting provides a rather simplistic IE system (for example, no named entity recognition or approximate template matching). It is thus useful for comparing different rule-bases, though the absolute extraction figures do not reflect the full potential of the rules. In Secion 5.2 we analyze the full-system's errors to isolate the rules' contribution to overall system performance.

5.1 Results

In this section we focus on the best performing variations of each algorithm type: binary DIRT, unary DIRT, unary Weeds Harmonic, BInc and *Derived-Avg*. We omitted the results of methods that were clearly inferior to others: (a) $WeedsA$, $WeedsD$ and $Weeds\text{-}Precision$ did not increase

[3]http://about.reuters.com/researchandstandards/corpus/

Recall over not using rules because rules with infrequent templates scored highest and arithmetic averaging could not balance well these high scores; (b) out of the methods for deriving unary rules from binary rule-bases, *Derived-Avg* performed best; (c) filtering with (the directional) LEDIR did not improve the performance of unary DIRT.

Figure 1 presents Recall, Precision and F1 of the methods for different cutoff points. First, we observe that even when matching only the seed templates (K=0), unary seeds outperform the binary seeds in terms of both Precision and Recall. This surprising behavior is consistent through all rule cutoff points: all unary learning algorithms perform better than binary DIRT in all parameters. The inferior behavior of binary DIRT is analyzed in Section 5.2.

The graphs show that symmetric unary approaches substantially increase recall, but dramatically decrease precision already at the top 10 rules. As a result, F1 only decreases for these methods. Lin similarity (DIRT) and Weeds-Harmonic show similar behaviors. They consistently outperform *Derived-Avg*. One reason for this is that incorrect unary rules may be derived even from correct binary rules. For example, from 'X gain seat on $Y \rightarrow$ elect X to Y' the incorrect unary rule 'X gain $\rightarrow$ elect X' is also generated. This problem is less frequent when unary rules are directly scored based on their corpus statistics.

The directional measure of BInc yields a more accurate rule-base, as can be seen by the much slower precision reduction rate compared to the other algorithms. As a result, it is the only algorithm that improves over the F1 baseline of K=0, with the best cutoff point at K=20. BInc's recall increases moderately compared to other unary learning approaches, but it is still substantially better than not using rules (a relative recall increase of 50% already at K=10). We found that many of the correct mentions missed by BInc but identified by other methods are due to occasional extractions of incorrect frequent rules, such as partial templates (see Section 5.2). This is reflected in the very low precision of the other methods. On the other hand, some correct rules were only learned by BInc, e.g. 'countersuit against $X \rightarrow X$ sue' and 'X take wife $\rightarrow X$ marry'.

When only one argument is annotated for a specific event mention (28% of ACE predicate mentions, which account for 15% of all annotated arguments), binary rules either miss that mention, or extract both the correct argument and another incorrect one. To neutralize this bias, we also tested the various methods only on event mentions annotated with two or more arguments and obtained similar results to those presented for all mentions. This further emphasizes the general advantage of using unary rules over binary rules.

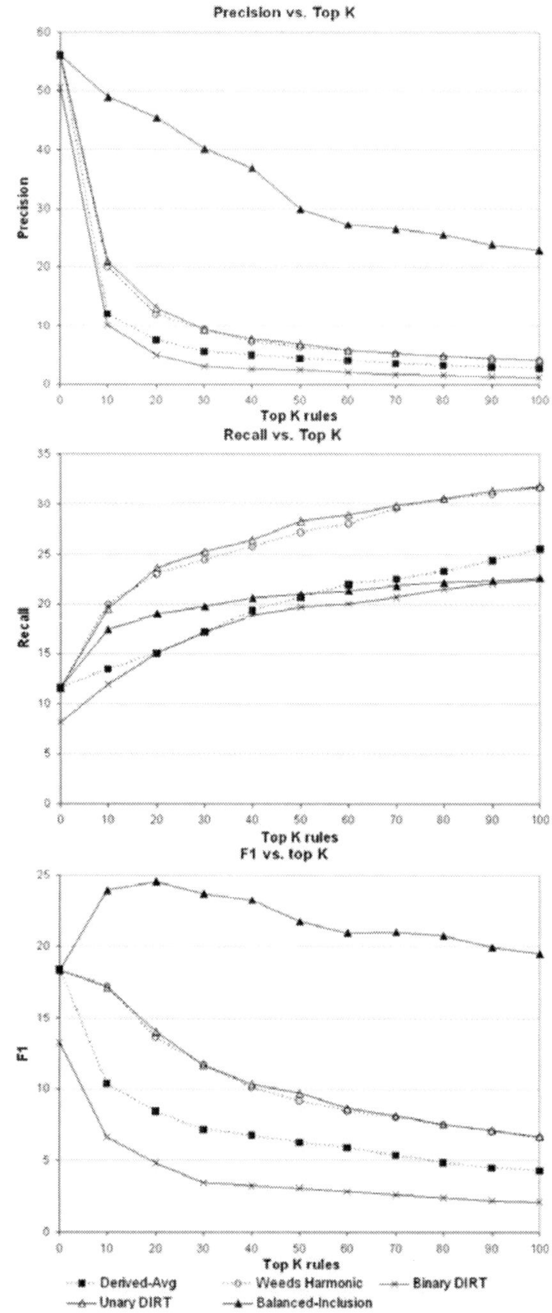

Figure 1: Average Precision, Recall and F1 at different top K rule cutoff points.

5.2 Analysis

Binary-DIRT We analyzed incorrect rules both for binary-DIRT and BInc by randomly sampling, for each algorithm, 200 rules that extracted incorrect mentions. We manually classified each rule '$l \rightarrow r$' as either: (a) *Correct* - the rule is valid in some contexts of the event but extracted some incorrect mentions; (b) *Partial Template* - l is only a part of a correct template that entails r. For example, learning 'X decide $\rightarrow$ X meet' instead of 'X decide to meet $\rightarrow$ X meet'; (e) *Incorrect* - other incorrect rules, e.g. 'charge X $\rightarrow$ convict X'.

Table 1 summarizes the analysis and demonstrates two problems of binary-DIRT. First, relative to BInc, it tends to learn incorrect rules for high frequency templates, and therefore extracted many more incorrect mentions for the same number of incorrect rules. Second, a large percentage of incorrect mentions extracted are due to partial templates at the rule left-hand-side. Such rules are leaned because many binary templates have a more complex structure than paths between arguments. As explained in Section 3.2 the unary template structure we use is more expressive, enabling to learn the correct rules. For example, BInc learned 'take Y into custody $\rightarrow$ arrest Y' while binary-DIRT learned 'X take Y $\rightarrow$ X arrest Y'.

System Level Analysis We manually analyzed the reasons for false positives (incorrect extractions) and false negatives (missed extractions) of BInc, at its best performing cutoff point (K=20), by sampling 200 extractions of each type.

From the false positives analysis (Table 2) we see that 39% of the errors are due to incorrect rules. The main reasons for learning such rules are those discussed in Section 3.3: (a) related templates that are not entailing; (b) infrequent templates. All learning methods suffer from these issues. As was shown by our results, BInc provides a first step towards reducing these problems. Yet, these issues require further research.

Apart from incorrectly learned rules, incorrect template matching (e.g. due to parse errors) and context mismatch contribute together 46% of the errors. Context mismatches occur when the entailing template is matched in inappropriate contexts. For example, 'slam X $\rightarrow$ attack X' should not be applied when X is a ball, only when it is a person. The rule-set net effect on system precision is better estimated by removing these errors and fixing the annotation errors, which yields 72% precision.

	Binary DIRT		Balanced Inclusion	
Correct	16	(70)	38	(91)
Partial Template	27	(2665)	6	(81)
Incorrect	157	(2584)	156	(787)
Total	200	(5319)	200	(959)

Table 1: Rule type distribution of a sample of 200 rules that extracted *incorrect* mentions. The corresponding numbers of incorrect mentions extracted by the sampled rules is shown in parentheses.

Reason	% mentions
Incorrect Rule learned	39.0
Context mismatch	27.0
Match error	19.0
Annotation problem	15.0

Table 2: Distribution of reasons for false positives (incorrect argument extractions) by BInc at K=20.

Reason	% mentions
Rule not learned	61.5
Match error	25.0
Discourse analysis needed	12.0
Argument is predicative	1.5

Table 3: Distribution of reasons for false negatives (missed argument mentions) by BInc at K=20.

Table 3 presents the analysis of false negatives. First, we note that 12% of the arguments cannot be extracted by rules alone, due to necessary discourse analysis. Thus, a recall upper bound for entailment rules is 88%. Many missed extractions are due to rules that were not learned (61.5%). However, 25% of the mentions were missed because of incorrect syntactic matching of correctly learned rules. By assuming correct matches in these cases we isolate the recall of the rule-set (along with the seeds), which yields 39% recall.

6 Conclusions

We presented two approaches for unsupervised acquisition of unary entailment rules from regular (non-comparable) corpora. In the first approach, rules are directly learned based on distributional similarity measures. The second approach derives unary rules from a given rule-base of binary rules. Under the first approach we proposed a novel directional measure for scoring entailment rules, termed Balanced-Inclusion.

We tested the different approaches utilizing a standard IE test-set and compared them to binary rule learning. Our results suggest the advantage of learning unary rules: (a) unary rule-bases perform better than binary rules; (b) it is better to directly learn unary rules than to derive them from binary rule-bases. In addition, the Balanced-Inclusion measure outperformed all other tested methods.

In future work, we plan to explore additional unary template structures and similarity scores, and to improve rule application utilizing context matching methods such as (Szpektor et al., 2008).

Acknowledgements

This work was partially supported by ISF grant 1095/05, the IST Programme of the European Community under the PASCAL Network of Excellence IST-2002-506778 and the NEGEV project (www.negev-initiative.org).

References

Barzilay, Regina and Lillian Lee. 2003. Learning to paraphrase: An unsupervised approach using multiple-sequence alignment. In *Proceedings of HLT-NAACL*.

Bhagat, Rahul, Patrick Pantel, and Eduard Hovy. 2007. Ledir: An unsupervised algorithm for learning directionality of inference rules. In *Proceedings of EMNLP*.

Geffet, Maayan and Ido Dagan. 2005. The distributional inclusion hypotheses and lexical entailment. In *Proceedings of ACL*.

Giampiccolo, Danilo, Bernardo Magnini, Ido Dagan, and Bill Dolan. 2007. The third pascal recognizing textual entailment challenge. In *Proceedings of WTEP*.

Habash, Nizar and Bonnie Dorr. 2003. A categorial variation database for english. In *Proceedings of NACL*.

Harris, Z. 1954. Distributional structure. *Word*, 10(23):146–162.

Ibrahim, Ali, Boris Katz, and Jimmy Lin. 2003. Extracting structural paraphrases from aligned monolingual corpora. In *Proceedings of IWP*.

Iftene, Adrian and Alexandra Balahur-Dobrescu. 2007. Hypothesis transformation and semantic variability rules used in recognizing textual entailment. In *Proceedings of WTEP*.

Lin, Dekang and Patrick Pantel. 2001. Discovery of inference rules for question answering. In *Natural Language Engineering*, volume 7(4), pages 343–360.

Lin, Dekang. 1998a. Automatic retrieval and clustering of similar words. In *Proceedings of COLING-ACL*.

Lin, Dekang. 1998b. Dependency-based evaluation of minipar. In *Proceedings of the Workshop on Evaluation of Parsing Systems at LREC*.

Pekar, Viktor. 2006. Acquisition of verb entailment from text. In *Proceedings of NAACL*.

Ravichandran, Deepak and Eduard Hovy. 2002. Learning surface text patterns for a question answering system. In *Proceedings of ACL*.

Riloff, Ellen. 1996. Automatically generating extraction patterns from untagged text. In *AAAI/IAAI, Vol. 2*, pages 1044–1049.

Romano, Lorenza, Milen Kouylekov, Idan Szpektor, Ido Dagan, and Alberto Lavelli. 2006. Investigating a generic paraphrase-based approach for relation extraction. In *Proceedings of EACL*.

Sekine, Satoshi. 2005. Automatic paraphrase discovery based on context and keywords between ne pairs. In *Proceedings of IWP*.

Shinyama, Yusuke and Satoshi Sekine. 2006. Preemptive information extraction using unrestricted relation discovery. In *Proceedings of HLT-NAACL*.

Shinyama, Yusuke, Satoshi Sekine, Sudo Kiyoshi, and Ralph Grishman. 2002. Automatic paraphrase acquisition from news articles. In *Proceedings of HLT*.

Sudo, Kiyoshi, Satoshi Sekine, and Ralph Grishman. 2003. An improved extraction pattern representation model for automatic ie pattern acquisition. In *Proceedings of ACL*.

Szpektor, Idan and Ido Dagan. 2007. Learning canonical forms of entailment rules. In *Proceedings of RANLP*.

Szpektor, Idan, Hristo Tanev, Ido Dagan, and Bonaventura Coppola. 2004. Scaling web-based acquisition of entailment relations. In *Proceedings of EMNLP*.

Szpektor, Idan, Ido Dagan, Roy Bar Haim, and Jacob Goldberger. 2008. Contextual preferences. In *Proceedings of ACL*.

Weeds, Julie and David Weir. 2003. A general framework for distributional similarity. In *Proceedings of EMNLP*.

Experiments with Reasoning for Temporal Relations between Events

Marta Tatu and **Munirathnam Srikanth**
Lymba Corporation
Richardson, Texas, United States
marta,srikanth@lymba.com

Abstract

Few attempts have been made to investigate the utility of temporal reasoning within machine learning frameworks for temporal relation classification between events in news articles. This paper presents three settings where temporal reasoning aids machine learned classifiers of temporal relations: (1) expansion of the dataset used for learning; (2) detection of inconsistencies among the automatically identified relations; and (3) selection among multiple temporal relations. Feature engineering is another effort in our work to improve classification accuracy.

1 Introduction

In recent years, there has been a growing interest in temporal information extraction, as more and more operational natural language processing (NLP) systems demand dealing with time-related issues in natural language texts. Machine learning-based temporal relation identification has been explored by only a few researchers, including Boguraev and Ando (2005), Mani et al. (2006), Chambers et al. (2007), and the TempEval 2007 participants (Verhagen et al., 2007).

For a given ordered pair of elements (x_1, x_2), where x_1 and x_2 are events or times, temporal relation resolution is the task of automatic identification of the relation $r_i \in TempRel$ that temporally links x_1 and x_2. For example, given the statement *Mr. Antar was charged*$_{e_{137}}$ *last month*$_{t_{237}}$ *in a civil suit*$_{e_{138}}$ *filed*$_{e_{140}}$ *in federal court in Newark by the Securities and Exchange Commission* (wsj_0778[1]) and the pairs (e_{137}, t_{137}), (e_{137}, e_{138}), and (e_{138}, e_{140}), the task is to automatically label the given pairs with the *is_included*, *is_included*, and *simultaneous* relations, respectively. We note that the granularity of the temporal relations ($TempRel$) varies from TimeML's 14 relations to TempEval's three coarse-grain relations.

While machine learning approaches attempt to improve classification accuracy through feature engineering, Mani et al. (2006) introduced a temporal reasoning component to greatly expand the training data. By computing the temporal closure of the training data relations, they increased the training set by a factor of 10. They reported encouraging accuracy of classification on event-event and event-time relations. According to their experiments, the event-event relation accuracy goes from 62.5% to 94.95% and the event-time relation accuracy ranges from 73.68% to 90.16%. Recently, extensions of Mani et al. (2006)'s research is briefly described in (Mani et al., 2007). This technical report addresses two problems found in (Mani et al., 2006): (1) feature vector duplication caused by the data normalization process (once fixed, the accuracy drops to 76.56% and 83.23%) and (2) a somewhat unrealistic evaluation scheme (we describe Mani et al. (2007)'s results in Section 4.1).

TempEval 2007 is the first standard evaluation arena that consists of three temporal relation classification tasks (Verhagen et al., 2007). The participants reported F-measure scores ranging from 42% to 55% for event-event relations, and 73% to 80% for event-time relations.

Because of their different experimental settings,

© Lymba Corporation 2008. Licensed under the *Creative Commons Attribution-Noncommercial-Share Alike 3.0 Unported* license (http://creativecommons.org/licenses/by-nc-sa/3.0/). Some rights reserved.

[1] All examples shown here are taken from TimeBank 1.2.

the results reported in (Mani et al., 2007) cannot be directly compared with those of TempEval 2007 participants. Among others, the three major differences are:

1. significantly different training and testing data. Although the datasets used TimeBank 1.2 (Pustejovsky et al., 2003), Mani et al. (2007) added the AQUAINT Corpus (www.timeml.org) to their experimental data;

2. different sets of temporal relations. Mani et al. (2006; 2007) target six normalized relations (*before*, *immediately before* (*ibefore*), *includes*, *ends*, *begins* and *simultaneous*). In TempEval 2007, a set of three coarse-grain temporal relations was used (*before*, *after*, and *overlap*).

3. different relation scope. In (Mani et al., 2006; Mani et al., 2007), event-event temporal relations are discourse-wide, i.e. *any* pair of events can be temporally linked. For TempEval 2007, the event-event relations are restricted to events within two consecutive sentences.

These two modeling frameworks for solving the problem of temporal relation classification produce highly dissimilar results. With this in mind, we are interested in two issues in this paper: (1) *How might temporal reasoning assist in temporal relation identification?* (2) *What other features might be used to improve the performance of classification?* As a byproduct of our exploration to these two questions, we hope to find some insights on why the same problem explored under different environment produces highly divergent results.

In this paper, we investigate several interactions between temporal reasoning and a machine learning approach for temporal ordering of events in natural language texts. We continue by describing the data used for our experiments. In Section 3, we briefly describe the set of features we currently use to build Support Vector Machine (SVM) (Chang and Lin, 2001) and Maximum Entropy (ME) models for temporal relation resolution. The three interactions we envision between temporal reasoning and the learned models are presented in Section 4. In conclusion, we present a discussion of our experimental results and future research directions.

2 Data Preparation and Analysis

2.1 TimeBank 1.2

In this paper, we use the TimeBank 1.2 data (Pustejovsky et al., 2003). This is the first attempt to create a corpus with human annotated temporal relations. It contains 183 news documents collected from several news agencies.

2.2 Data normalization

Similar to (Mani et al., 2006; Mani et al., 2007), we use a normalized version of the 14 temporal relations annotated in TimeBank where the inverse relations are removed and *simultaneous* and *identity* are collapsed as well as *during* and *is_included*. The distribution of the normalized event-event temporal relations annotated in the data we used for training our temporal resolution models is shown in Table 2.

2.3 Experimental data

For the experiments described in this paper, we used a random 80-20 percent split of the TimeBank data to train and test the learned classifiers (36 randomly selected documents for testing and the remaining 147 for training the models) and 5-fold-cross-validation of the training data for parameter tuning. We note that our experimental setup is closer to the one used in (Mani et al., 2006; Mani et al., 2007). Noting that we do not use the AQUAINT Corpus in our experiments, our results can be compared with theirs, but not with the TempEval system performances.

3 Feature Engineering

As reported by participants in TempEval 2007 (Verhagen et al., 2007), (Boguraev and Ando, 2005), (Chambers et al., 2007), and (Mani et al., 2007), most of the features used for learning are syntactic attributes extracted for single event terms. In our work, we have experimented with *semantic* features and attributes which take the *event's linguistic context* into consideration (Min et al., 2007). Our experiments show that only few features are critical and impact the classifier's accuracy (Table 1). These include the basic features available in TimeBank, e.g. *event-class*, *tense*, *aspect*, *polarity*, *modality*, *stem*, and *part of speech* of event terms (*Baseline* row in Table 1). Additional features that we explored include:

Feature set	Accuracy (%)
Baseline	46.3
Baseline with sameActor	+0.4
Baseline with eventCoref	+0.2
Baseline with oneSent	+4.0
Baseline with relToDocDate	+0.2
Baseline with tensebigram	+0.8
Baseline with tensetrigram	+0.6
Baseline with all	57.4

Table 1: New features impact

1. *sameActor*. This binary feature indicates whether the two events share the same semantic role AGENT. The motivation behind this feature is that two event terms, especially, verbs, which have the same agent, have a closer semantic relationship and, accordingly, are temporally related.

2. *eventCoref*. This binary attribute captures the event co-reference information. If two events co-refer, even though they have different surface forms, they must take place simultaneously. For instance, the *offer* and *deal* events, mentioned in the following sentences, refer to the same *transaction* and, therefore, must be linked by a *simultaneous* relation.

   a) Sony Corp. completed its tender ***offer*** *for Columbia Pictures Entertainment Inc., with Columbia shareholders tendering 99.3% of all common shares outstanding by the Tuesday deadline.*

   b) Sony Columbia Acquisition Corp., formed for the Columbia ***deal****, will formally take ownership of the movie studio later this month, a spokesman said.*

3. *oneSent*. This binary feature is true if the two events are part of the same sentence. Chambers et al.(2007) introduced this feature in their experiments, and our analysis shows that this attribute has a relatively larger contribution to the overall performance. The intuition behind this feature is that the closer two events get, the closer their temporal relationship is.

4. *relToDocDate*. This feature encodes the temporal relation between each event and the Document Date. This was one of the subtasks of TempEval 2007 and we used this relationship as a feature. Our motivation is that we might be able to infer the relationship between two events e_1 and e_2 from the temporal relations they have with the Document Date. For example, if $before(e_1, DocDate)$ and $after(e_2, DocDate)$ are true, then $before(e_1, e_2)$. There may be two reasons for the low impact of this feature: (1) an accurate computation of the temporal relation between an event and the Document Date is not easy, as demonstrated in TempEval 2007 and (2) if two events have the same relation with the Document Date, there is no way to determine the event-event relation.

5. *tenseBigram* and *tenseTrigram*. Going beyond using the *tense* attribute for single event terms, we extract bigrams and trigrams with the tense values of the current event and immediately preceding and following events. This feature is intended to reflect the tense shifts of sequential events as part of a larger context of the current event.

All these features have a positive impact on the performance of the learned classifiers (Table 1). Further improvement is desired and we use temporal reasoning in three different settings in an attempt to obtain more accurate temporal relations.

4 Temporal Reasoning

Following our feature set improvements for machine learned models of temporal relations, we turned to *temporal reasoning* and explored different ways in which it can aid the resolution of temporal relations. We experimented with three different interactions between our temporal reasoning and temporal relation resolution modules.

Our natural language reasoning engine (Tatu and Moldovan, 2005; Tatu and Moldovan, 2007) makes use of (1) a first-order logical representation of the input document which captures the concepts mentioned in the text, their attributes including named entity class values, event class or normalized values (for times) and the syntactic as well as the semantic dependencies between concepts[2]; (2) a rich set of axioms which encode the knowledge needed to derive meaningful information from a document; (3) a logic prover which operates in a proof by contradiction manner (a hypothesis H is entailed by a text T assumed to be true, denoted by $T \vdash H$, if and only if $(T \wedge \neg H) \vdash \bot$, where $\bot$ is *false*). Given the logical transformation of a text T, the prover uses the knowledge encoded in the

[2]These dependencies include the temporal relations identified either by human annotators or by the models presented in Section 3.

axioms (Bk) to derive new information ($T^{\star}$) about T^3 and scores the best mapping of the hypothesis H to $T^{\star}$.

For the temporal relation resolution experiments presented in this paper, we are interested in deriving additional temporal information from an input document without checking the entailment between this document and a hypothesis. Therefore, for the following tasks, the text T is a TimeBank 1.2 document and the set of axioms Bk used by the prover contains 94 temporal axioms which link each temporal relation with its inverse ($R^{-1}(x, y) \leftrightarrow R(y, x)$, for example $before(x, y) \rightarrow after(y, x)$) and define the temporal relation resulting from the combination of two relations ($R_1(x, y) \wedge R_2(y, z) \rightarrow R_3(x, z)$, for example, $before(x, y) \wedge before(y, z) \rightarrow before(x, z)$). These axioms were derived from Allen's interval algebra (Allen, 1983).

We note that the prover computes and uses temporal relations between any two temporal expressions mentioned in an input TimeBank document[4] (e.g. *now* [19891101] and *last year* [1988] are linked by a *before* temporal relation in *wsj_0324*).

Within this reasoning setup, the information derived by the prover ($T^{\star}$) will include the **temporal closure** of the input text's relations. We note that the temporal closure includes event-event, event-time and time-time temporal relations. We also note that the temporal axioms are considered 100% accurate (if the temporal relations given as input are correct, then the temporal relations derived using the axioms are also correct).

4.1 Training data expansion

Our first effort to create more accurate temporal relation resolution classifiers given our temporal reasoning engine is to *augment* the gold training data with new relations from the temporal closure of the relations identified by human annotators. Therefore, given the 3,527 temporal relations annotated in the TimeBank data used to train our initial temporal resolution models, we derived 12,270 new relations (an increase of 3.47 times). We show in Table 2 statistics of the normalized event-event relations for both the original and the closed training data. We note that the temporal inconsistencies identified in the original training data (by the

Relation	Original data		Closed (*) data	
	Freq.	%	Freq.	%
ibefore	51	2.06	137	1.59
begins	52	2.10	119	1.38
ends	61	2.47	125	1.45
includes	434	17.59	1,161	13.47
before	885	35.88	3,165	36.73
simultaneous	983	39.86	3,909	45.36
Total	2,466	100.00	8,616	100.00

Table 2: Normalized training data (event-event relations)

procedure described in Section 4.2) were resolved manually by one of the authors of this paper.

We built SVM and ME models from the total of 8,616 normalized temporal relations using the set of 15 features described in Section 3. Table 3 shows the performance of the learned models on the test data (original data as well as closed test data). Unlike (Mani et al., 2006), the accuracy of

Training data	Accuracy for event-event relations		
	Original test (845)	Closed test (4,189)	Train
	ME models		
Original (2,466)	50.4	46.1	83.3
Closed (8,616)	47.0	41.0	76.1
	SVM models		
Original (2,466)	56.9	45.8	74.2
Closed (8,616)	52.4	52.0	77.5

Table 3: Event-event temporal resolution

the learned classifiers drops when they are trained on the closed training dataset. By analyzing the results from Table 3, one cannot help but notice the high accuracy on the data used for training and the significant difference between the performance on the training and testing datasets. This may suggest that (1) the machine learners *overfit* the models on the training data and they are not able to generalize and resolve the relations in the test data[5] or (2) the two datasets are very different (in terms of feature values) and the data split happened to create a training data which is not (fully) characteristic to the problem we are trying to solve (the two datasets have different distributions). Therefore, we measured the accuracy of ME models for event-event relation resolution using 5-fold-cross-validation of the entire TimeBank data (Table 4). For these experiments, each TimeBank document (with all its temporal relations) was used as part

[3] $T^{\star}$ contains **all** the information the prover can derive from T given the axioms Bk.

[4] We restricted the time-time relations to only *before, simultaneous*, and *after*.

[5] The accuracy of the SVM models is lower on the training data when compared with the ME models while their performance on the test dataset is better.

	Test data 1/5 of the data	**Train data** remaining 4/5s
5-fold-cross split at the *document* level		
Original (3,311)	57.4	89.5
Closed (11,530)	58.2	85.5
5-fold-cross split at the *relation* level		
Original (3,311)	58.3	90.0
Closed (11,530)	73.4	85.3

Table 4: Average ME accuracy for event-event relations using 5-fold-cross-validation on the entire TimeBank data

of either the training or the testing dataset. Our results for the random 5-fold-cross split of the data *at the document level* are similar to the ones obtained for the models learned on the pre-established training data (top two rows in Table 4). Thus, our initial split of the data was not an 'unfortunate' division. The same significant difference between the performance on the unseen data and the training set can be seen. This suggests that some overfitting occurs. Features, such as the event term *stem*, with a large number of possible values mislead the machine learning algorithms and the models they create are not able to correctly classify event pairs with unseen values for these high-valued features. For instance, *showdown* is part of a single TimeBank document (*AP900816-0139*) and the models learned using other documents will misclassify *showdown*'s temporal relations. We note that, by expanding the training data using its temporal closure, *no* new events are added to the training set, only new temporal relations between the *same* set of events are added. Long-term solutions include (1) the expansion of the annotated data or (2) the reduction in the number of values for certain features (for example, by generalizing the event term stem to its WordNet hypernym). In an attempt to homogenize the feature values for the training and the testing datasets, we split the set of normalized event-event temporal relations annotated in TimeBank into training and testing *without* considering the document boundaries. The performance of the learned classifiers increases by 1% when trained on unclosed data and by more than 15% when the closed data is used (Table 4).

In their most recent technical paper, Mani et al. (2007) revise their evaluation method and report performance values for classifiers learned by partitioning the data at the document level (accuracy drops from 59.68% to 51.14% when closed training data is used). These results are consistent with our findings. In the near future, we shall experiment with the second solution we propose above.

4.2 Testing data validation

Given that almost half of the temporal relations automatically identified for the testing data are incorrect when compared to the gold annotation, we decided, as our second experiment, to use temporal reasoning to find *temporal inconsistencies* and replace some of the relations contributing to the inconsistency by the immediate lower confidence relation returned by the learned classifiers. For this purpose, we use an additional set of 77 temporal axioms which encode the *irreflexivity* of temporal relations ($\neg R(x,x)$, for example, $\neg before(x,x)$) and their *empty intersections* ($R_1(x,y) \rightarrow \neg R_2(x,y)$ when $R_1 \neq R_2$, for example $before(x,y) \rightarrow \neg simultaneous(x,y)$).

Our process of testing data validation is iterative. Once a temporal inconsistency is identified in the test data, it is resolved and the procedure which computes the temporal closure is re-started. A temporal inconsistency in a TimeBank document (T) is detected every time $\perp \in T^\star$. The automatically identified temporal relations (part of the text T) which contributed to the derivation of $\perp$ become candidates for the resolution of the inconsistency[6]. These candidates are sorted based on the confidence assigned by the machine learning algorithm[7] and the lowest confidence relation is replaced either by the temporal relation found by the prover which directly contradicted the automatically identified relation[8] (Figure 1(a)) or, for the cases where such a relation does not exist, by the immediate lower confidence relation identified by the learned models (Figure 1(b)).

If, for example, for the statement *The US is bolstering its military presence in the gulf, as President Clinton discussed*$_{e_1}$ *the Iraq crisis with the one ally who has backed*$_{e_2}$ *his threat*$_{e_3}$ *of force, British prime minister Tony Blair*, the ME classifier built in Section 3 identifies the temporal relations $before(e_2, e_1)$ (confidence: 0.53), $before(e_3, e_2)$ (0.47) and $includes(e_3, e_1)$ (0.42), the prover identifies the temporal inconsistency

[6]The temporal closure axioms are accurate and do not 'introduce' incorrect temporal relations.

[7]For all experiments which exploit the confidence assigned by the machine learning algorithm, we use the learned ME models (SVM models do not provide a confidence for their decision).

[8]The confidence of a relation derived by the prover is the average of the its 'parent's confidence values.

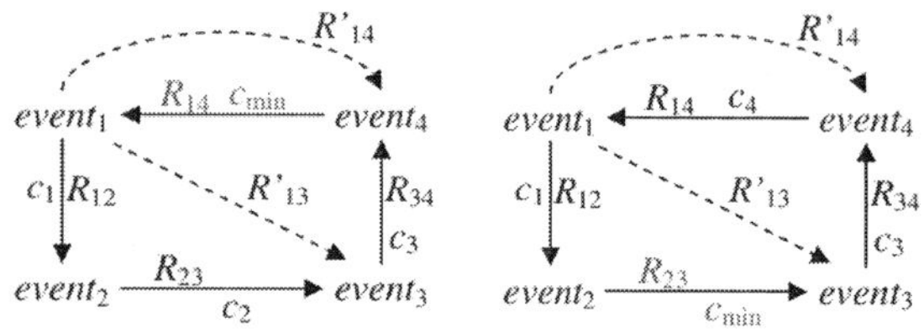

(a) R_{14} replaced by R'_{14}

(b) R_{23} replaced by the next best relation identified for $(event_2, event_3)$

Figure 1: Temporal inconsistency resolution

generated by these three relations and replaces the lowest confidence relation ($includes(e_3, e_1)$) with the relation it derives from the closure of the other two relations ($before(e_3, e_1)$, confidence: 0.50).

We note that, during the inconsistency checking process, all types of temporal relations are used (event-event, event-time and time-time). For this inconsistency resolution process, we make the assumption that only *one* of the temporal relations which generated the inconsistency is incorrect and should be replaced.

For the testing dataset described in Section 2.3, the validation algorithm found inconsistencies in only 25% of the test documents. This is not very encouraging, given that the accuracy of the temporal relations identified in the other 75% of the documents is 50.4%. The documents marked as inconsistent include, on average, 3.66 temporal inconsistencies (with a maximum of 8 in a single document). For each pair of events, we considered only the top three temporal relations (in terms of confidence) identified by the learned classifiers. When the third relation identified for a given pair of events had to be removed by the inconsistency resolution algorithm, no other temporal relation was added to replace it. Table 5 shows the impact of the validation step on the unclosed test data.

	Precision	Recall	F-measure
Baseline	50.4	50.4	50.4
With test validation	50.1	49.7	49.9

Table 5: Performance change after the testing data validation step. The baseline is the ME model learned on the original (unclosed) training data.

Our error analysis shows that, for each discovered temporal inconsistency, more than one incorrect relation lead to an inconsistent temporal closure. Frequently enough, replacing the lowest confidence relation does not resolve the inconsistency and the temporal relations used to replace it are, in turn, replaced in the next iterations (the confidence of the replacing relation is lower than the confidence of the replaced relation). The ME classifier's numerous errors and the low applicability of this process make its contribution to the overall temporal relation resolution process negative. Our future work will focus on (1) experimenting with less erroneous data for which our one-incorrect-relation-per-inconsistency assumption holds ((perhaps) the models learned from closed training data using a data split at the relation level) and (2) testing the existence of a consistent temporal closure in the absence of the lowest confidence relation. If none of the six temporal relations that we use to label an event-event relation can replace the lowest confidence relation and lead to a consistent temporal closure, then our candidate incorrect relation is among the other higher confidence relations. We also note that we rely heavily on the confidences automatically assigned by the ME classifiers.

Mani et al. (2007) briefly describe a Greedy method for ensuring global consistency of automatically labeled testing data. No evaluation results are reported. As far as we can tell, Mani at el. (2007) use this algorithm to decide whether or not to assign the top 1 relation automatically identified by ME classifiers to a given pair of events. No attempts are made to replace this relation. Our validation algorithm uses lower confidence relations found by the learned models for the same pair of events to replace the lowest confidence relation that leads to a temporal inconsistency.

4.3 Temporal relation alignment

In the previous section, we used temporal reasoning to replace certain relations automatically identified by the learned temporal relation resolution models with the next best relation (in terms of the confidence) found for the same pair of events. For our third experiment, we use the *top* n relations automatically identified for a single pair of events. Across a document, these relationships can be grouped to form different temporal orderings of the events mentioned in the document. For instance, for four pairs of events, 81 different temporal settings can be created using the top 3 temporal relations. Figure 2 shows two of these 81 facets ($\{R_{12}, R'_{23}, R'_{34}, R_{41}\}$ and $\{R"_{12}, R_{23}, R"_{34}, R"_{41}\}$) for events $e_1, \ldots, e_4$.

For these event temporal orderings, we pro-

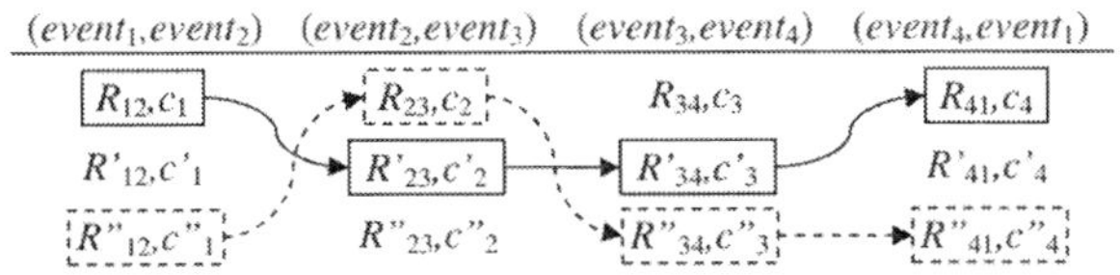

Figure 2: Two possible relation alignments

pose to use our temporal reasoning module to derive, score, and rank their temporal closures. We make the assumption that the correct document-level event ordering, the document's temporal cohesion can be identified by measuring the closure of the document's temporal relations and that orderings that use incorrect relations do not generate good closures. Thus, the relations that generate the best temporal closure will be considered final and will be used to label the test document's event-event and event-time pairs.

For the example shown in Figure 2, 81 different temporal closures are generated depending on the set of relations used to derive them from. In order to find the final four temporal relations between events $e_1, \ldots, e_4$, we score and order the derived temporal closures. The best closure decides, for each pair of events, which relation among the top 3 should be selected as final.

Our first step is to identify the best value for n. Table 6 shows the *maximum* gain in performance when multiple relations are considered for the same pair of events (an instance is considered correct if the gold annotation is among the top n relations returned by the system).

Top n relations	Accuracy (%)
1	57.40
2	80.66
3	94.49
4	97.38
5	99.12
6	100.00

Table 6: Top n oracle performance using 5-fold-cross-validation on the TimeBank data

Because there is substantial improvement in the top 3 relation set, we use for our experiments the first three relations identified by the ME classifiers. But, if we consider the top 3 relations for each pair of events in a document, we end up with 3^N possible alignments, where N is the number of event-event and event-time pairs[9] and the scoring

[9]For each time-time pair, there is a single temporal relation with confidence equal to 1.

	Accuracy
Baseline - top 1	50.4
Oracle (upper bound) - top 3	92.4
With test alignment	47.5

Table 7: Test dataset performance change after the testing data alignment step. The top 1 and top 3 baselines were generated using the ME model learned on the original (unclosed) training data.

and ranking of all 3^N temporal closures becomes hardly possible. Therefore, we use a more *Greedy* approach. Iteratively, we score and rank temporal closures derived from a small set of top 3 relations between N' event-event pairs ($N' < N$) and any final temporal relations. The best closure is used to decide on N' temporal relations which will be added to the best partial alignment and will be used to compute all the following temporal closures.

Secondly, we must identify the temporal closure scoring function. For our experiments, this function takes into account the size of the temporal closure ($|T^\star|$) as well as the confidence values of the relations identified by the ME classifiers in the test set (not derived by the temporal closure algorithm) (only $\{c_{12}, c'_{23}, c'_{34}, c_{41}\}$ and $\{c"_{12}, c_{23}, c"_{34}, c"_{41}\}$ for the example shown in Figure 2). The correlation between these parameters and the scoring function is not straightforward. A preference for the confidence values favors closures which use only the top relations (in terms of confidence). However, weighing the size of the temporal closure leads to a result dominated by relations that close very well[10], such as *simultaneous* or *before* (which are also very frequent in the dataset). In the settings which produced the results shown in Table 7, we used the $score_1$ function: for $T = \{(R_1, c_1), \ldots, (R_k, c_k)\}$,

$$score_1(T^\star) = \lg(|T^\star|) \times \sum_{i=1}^{k} c_i.$$

The temporal relation accuracy drops by 3% after the relation selection among the top 3 best temporal relations for the testing documents. Posibile explanation: $score_1$ does not promote the close-to-gold temporal closures. The difinition of a good scoring function is not an easy process. Machine learning approaches might give us better coeficients for the parameters we consider. Alternativelly, our main assumption might prove incorrect:

[10]When present, these relations will quickly generate many others in the temporal closure.

temporal closure is not a good indicator of a document's event ordering. The information conveyed by a document need not disclose a rich total ordering of its events.

5 Conclusion

In this paper, we briefly described our feature engineering efforts for temporal relation resolution and we analyzed three methods that exploit temporal reasoning and, more specifically, the closure of temporal relations, for the purpose of improving the performance of machine learned classifiers of temporal relations between events in text.

Based on our experiments, we find that feature engineering helps improve the classification problem, when compared with several baseline performances. However, given our current NLP capabilities, it is clear that we are faced with the performance bottleneck problem (accuracy below 60%). Any attempt to derive more advanced features demands more sophisticated methodologies of modeling temporal expressions, events and their relationships as well as advanced discourse understanding capabilities. For instance, the temporal duration or the start/end time points of events are highly useful for learning temporal relations. But, this introduces an even more challenging problem.

In terms of the utility of temporal reasoning in classifying temporal relation, the idea of using temporal reasoning to boost training data is certainly sound. But in order for the boosted training data to really take effect, more advanced features need to be investigated. Certainly, the process of dividing the data into training and testing has its impact on the system's performance and we are faced with the data sparseness problem. Temporal inconsistencies in our automatically labeled test dataset occurred in just a few test documents and the resolution process did not impact the system's performance. Improvements are needed in the process of selection of the to-be-replaced relations. Temporal data alignment largely depends on the function used to score the temporal closures and we plan to analyze the temporal closure of the training data and to explore other scoring functions.

References

Allen, J. F. 1983. Maintaining Knowledge about Temporal Intervals. *Communications of the ACM*, 26(11):832–843.

Boguraev, B. and R. K. Ando. 2005. TimeML-Compliant Text Analysis for Temporal Reasoning. In *Proceedings of Nineteenth International Joint Conference on Artificial Intelligence (IJCAI-05)*, pages 997–1003, Edinburgh, Scotland, August.

Chambers, N., S. Wang, and D. Jurafsky. 2007. Classifying Temporal Relations Between Events. In *Proceedings of the ACL 2007 Demo and Poster Sessions*, pages 173–176, Prague, Czech Republic, June.

Chang, C. and C. Lin, 2001. *LIBSVM: a library for support vector machines*. Software available at www.csie.ntu.edu.tw/~cjlin/libsvm.

Mani, I., M. Verhagen, B. Wellner, C. Min Lee, and J. Pustejovsky. 2006. Machine Learning of Temporal Relations. In *Proceedings of the 21st International Conference on Computational Linguistics and 44th Annual Meeting of the ACL*, pages 753–760, Sydney, Australia, July.

Mani, I., B. Wellner, M. Verhagen, and J. Pustejovsky. 2007. Three Approaches to Learning TLINKs in TimeML. Technical Report CS-07-268, Computer Science Department, Brandeis University, Waltham, USA.

Min, Congmin, Munirathnam Srikanth, and Abraham Fowler. 2007. LCC-TE: A Hybrid Approach to Temporal Relation Identification in News Text. In *Proceedings of the Fourth International Workshop on Semantic Evaluations (SemEval-2007)*, pages 219–222, Prague, Czech Republic, June.

Pustejovsky, J., P. Hanks, R. Sauri, A. See, R. Gaizauskas, A. Setzer, D. Radev, B. Sundheim, D. Day, L. Ferro, and M. Lazo. 2003. The TIMEBANK Corpus. In *Proceedings of Corpus Linguistics*, pages 647–656, Lancaster University (UK), March.

Tatu, Marta and Dan Moldovan. 2005. A Semantic Approach to Recognizing Textual Entailment. In *Proceedings of the HTL-EMNLP 2005*, pages 371–378, Vancouver, BC Canada, October.

Tatu, Marta and Dan Moldovan. 2007. COGEX at RTE3. In *Proceedings of the ACL-PASCAL Workshop on Textual Entailment and Paraphrasing*, pages 22–27, Prague, Czech Republic, June.

Verhagen, M., R. Gaizauskas, F. Schilder, M. Hepple, G. Katz, and J. Pustejovsky. 2007. SemEval-2007 Task 15: TempEval Temporal Relation Identification. In *Proceedings of the Fourth International Workshop on Semantic Evaluations (SemEval-2007)*, pages 75–80, Prague, Czech Republic, June.

The Ups and Downs of Preposition Error Detection in ESL Writing

Joel R. Tetreault
Educational Testing Service
660 Rosedale Road
Princeton, NJ, USA
JTetreault@ets.org

Martin Chodorow
Hunter College of CUNY
695 Park Avenue
New York, NY, USA
martin.chodorow@hunter.cuny.edu

Abstract

In this paper we describe a methodology for detecting preposition errors in the writing of non-native English speakers. Our system performs at 84% precision and close to 19% recall on a large set of student essays. In addition, we address the problem of annotation and evaluation in this domain by showing how current approaches of using only one rater can skew system evaluation. We present a sampling approach to circumvent some of the issues that complicate evaluation of error detection systems.

1 Introduction

The long-term goal of our work is to develop a system which detects errors in grammar and usage so that appropriate feedback can be given to non-native English writers, a large and growing segment of the world's population. Estimates are that in China alone as many as 300 million people are currently studying English as a second language (ESL). Usage errors involving prepositions are among the most common types seen in the writing of non-native English speakers. For example, (Izumi et al., 2003) reported error rates for English prepositions that were as high as 10% in a Japanese learner corpus. Errors can involve incorrect selection ("we arrived *to* the station"), extraneous use ("he went *to* outside"), and omission ("we are fond *null* beer"). What is responsible for making preposition usage so difficult for non-native speakers?

© 2008. Licensed under the *Creative Commons Attribution-Noncommercial-Share Alike 3.0 Unported* license (http://creativecommons.org/licenses/by-nc-sa/3.0/). Some rights reserved.

At least part of the difficulty seems to be due to the great variety of linguistic functions that prepositions serve. When a preposition marks the argument of a predicate, such as a verb, an adjective, or a noun, preposition selection is constrained by the argument role that it marks, the noun which fills that role, and the particular predicate. Many English verbs also display alternations (Levin, 1993) in which an argument is sometimes marked by a preposition and sometimes not (e.g., "They loaded the wagon with hay" / "They loaded hay on the wagon"). When prepositions introduce adjuncts, such as those of time or manner, selection is constrained by the object of the preposition ("at length", "in time", "with haste"). Finally, the selection of a preposition for a given context also depends upon the intended meaning of the writer ("we sat at the beach", "on the beach", "near the beach", "by the beach").

With so many sources of variation in English preposition usage, we wondered if the task of selecting a preposition for a given context might prove challenging even for native speakers. To investigate this possibility, we randomly selected 200 sentences from Microsoft's Encarta Encyclopedia, and, in each sentence, we replaced a randomly selected preposition with a blank line. We then asked two native English speakers to perform a cloze task by filling in the blank with the best preposition, given the context provided by the rest of the sentence. Our results showed only about 75% agreement between the two raters, and between each of our raters and Encarta.

The presence of so much variability in preposition function and usage makes the task of the learner a daunting one. It also poses special challenges for developing and evaluating an NLP error detection system. This paper addresses both the development and evaluation of such a system.

First, we describe a machine learning system that detects preposition errors in essays of ESL writers. To date there have been relatively few attempts to address preposition error detection, though the sister task of detecting determiner errors has been the focus of more research. Our system performs comparably with other leading systems. We extend our previous work (Chodorow et al., 2007) by experimenting with combination features, as well as features derived from the Google N-Gram corpus and Comlex (Grishman et al., 1994).

Second, we discuss drawbacks in current methods of annotating ESL data and evaluating error detection systems, which are not limited to preposition errors. While the need for annotation by multiple raters has been well established in NLP tasks (Carletta, 1996), most previous work in error detection has surprisingly relied on only one rater to either create an annotated corpus of learner errors, or to check the system's output. Some grammatical errors, such as number disagreement between subject and verb, no doubt show very high reliability, but others, such as usage errors involving prepositions or determiners are likely to be much less reliable. Our results show that relying on one rater for system evaluation can be problematic, and we provide a sampling approach which can facilitate using multiple raters for this task.

In the next section, we describe a system that automatically detects errors involving incorrect preposition selection ("We arrived *to* the station") and extraneous preposition usage ("He went *to* outside"). In sections 3 and 4, we discuss the problem of relying on only one rater for exhaustive annotation and show how multiple raters can be used more efficiently with a sampling approach. Finally, in section 5 we present an analysis of common preposition errors that non-native speakers make.

2 System

2.1 Model

We have used a Maximum Entropy (ME) classifier (Ratnaparkhi, 1998) to build a model of correct preposition usage for 34 common English prepositions. The classifier was trained on 7 million preposition contexts extracted from parts of the MetaMetrics Lexile corpus that contain textbooks and other materials for high school students. Each context was represented by 25 features consisting of the words and part-of-speech (POS) tags found in a local window of +/- two positions around the preposition, plus the head verb of the preceding verb phrase (PV), the head noun of the preceding noun phrase (PN), and the head noun of the following noun phrase (FH), among others. In analyzing the contexts, we used only tagging and heuristic phrase-chunking, rather than parsing, so as to avoid problems that a parser might encounter with ill-formed non-native text [1]. In test mode, the classifier was given the context in which a preposition occurred, and it returned a probability for each of the 34 prepositions.

2.2 Other Components

While the ME classifier constitutes the core of the system, it is only one of several processing components that refines or blocks the system's output. Since the goal of an error detection system is to provide diagnostic feedback to a student, typically a system's output is heavily constrained so that it minimizes false positives (i.e., the system tries to avoid saying a writer's preposition is used incorrectly when it is actually right), and thus does not mislead the writer.

Pre-Processing Filter: A pre-processing program skips over preposition contexts that contain spelling errors. Classifier performance is poor in such cases because the classifier was trained on well-edited text, i.e., without misspelled words. In the context of a diagnostic feedback and assessment tool for writers, a spell checker would first highlight the spelling errors and ask the writer to correct them before the system analyzed the prepositions.

Post-Processing Filter: After the ME classifier has output a probability for each of the 34 prepositions but before the system has made its final decision, a series of rule-based post-processing filters block what would otherwise be false positives that occur in specific contexts. The first filter prevents the classifier from marking as an error a case where the classifier's most probable preposition is an antonym of what the writer wrote, such as "with/without" and "from/to". In these cases, resolution is dependent on the intent of the writer and thus is outside the scope of information cap-

[1] For an example of a common ungrammatical sentence from our corpus, consider: "In consion, for some reasons, museums, particuraly known travel place, get on many people."

tured by the current feature set. Another problem for the classifier involves differentiating between certain adjuncts and arguments. For example, in the sentence "They described a part *for a kid*", the system's top choices were *of* and *to*. The benefactive adjunct introduced by *for* is difficult for the classifier to learn, perhaps because it so freely occurs in many locations within a sentence. A post-processing filter prevents the system from marking as an error a prepositional phrase that begins with *for* and has an object headed by a human noun (a WordNet hyponym of *person* or *group*).

Extraneous Use Filter: To cover extraneous use errors, we developed two rule-based filters: 1) Plural Quantifier Constructions, to handle cases such as "some *of* people" and 2) Repeated Prepositions, where the writer accidentally repeated the same preposition two or more times, such as "can find friends *with with*". We found that extraneous use errors usually constituted up to 18% of all preposition errors, and our extraneous use filters handle a quarter of that 18%.

Thresholding: The final step for the preposition error detection system is a set of thresholds that allows the system to skip cases that are likely to result in false positives. One of these is where the top-ranked preposition and the writer's preposition differ by less than a pre-specified amount. This was also meant to avoid flagging cases where the system's preposition has a score only slightly higher than the writer's preposition score, such as: "My sister usually gets home around 3:00" (writer: around = 0.49, system: by = 0.51). In these cases, the system's and the writer's prepositions both fit the context, and it would be inappropriate to claim the writer's preposition was used incorrectly. Another system threshold requires that the probability of the writer's preposition be lower than a pre-specified value in order for it to be flagged as an error. The thresholds were set so as to strongly favor precision over recall due to the high number of false positives that may arise if there is no thresholding. This is a tactic also used for determiner selection in (Nagata et al., 2006) and (Han et al., 2006). Both thresholds were empirically set on a development corpus.

2.3 Combination Features

ME is an attractive choice of machine learning algorithm for a problem as complex as preposition error detection, in no small part because of the availability of ME implementations that can handle many millions of training events and features. However, one disadvantage of ME is that it does not automatically model the interactions among features as some other approaches do, such as support vector machines (Jurafsky and Martin, 2008). To overcome this, we have experimented with augmenting our original feature set with "combination features" which represent richer contextual structure in the form of syntactic patterns.

Table 1 (first column) illustrates the four combination features used for the example context "take our place in the line". The p denotes a preposition, so N-p-N denotes a syntactic context where the preposition is preceded and followed by a noun phrase. We use the preceding noun phrase (PN) and following head (FH) from the original feature set for the N-p-N feature. Column 3 shows one instantiation of combination features: Combo:word. For the N-p-N feature, the corresponding Combo:word instantiation is "place-line" since "place" is the PN and "line" is the FH. We also experimented with using combinations of POS tags (Combo:tag) and word+tag combinations (Combo:word+tag). So for the example, the Combo:tag N-p-N feature would be "NN-NN", and the Combo:word+tag N-p-N feature would be place_NN+line_NN (see the fourth column of Table 1). The intuition with the Combo:tag features is that the Combo:word features have the potential to be sparse, and these capture more general patterns of usage.

We also experimented with other features such as augmenting the model with verb-preposition preferences derived from Comlex (Grishman et al., 1994), and querying the Google Terabyte N-gram corpus with the same patterns used in the combination features. The Comlex-based features did not improve the model, and though the Google N-gram corpus represents much more information than our 7 million event model, its inclusion improved performance only marginally.

2.4 Evaluation

In our initial evaluation of the system we collected a corpus of 8,269 preposition contexts, error-annotated by two raters using the scheme described in Section 3 to serve as a gold standard. In this study, we focus on two of the three types of preposition errors: using the incorrect preposition and using an extraneous preposition. We compared

Class	Components	Combo:word Features	Combo:tag Features
p-N	FH	line	NN
N-*p*-N	PN-FH	place-line	NN-NN
V-*p*-N	PV-PN	take-line	VB-NN
V-N-*p*-N	PV-PN-FH	take-place-line	VB-NN-NN

Table 1: Feature Examples for *take our place in the line*

different models: the baseline model of 25 features and baseline with combination features added. The precision and recall for the top performing models are shown in Table 2. These results do not include the extraneous use filter; this filter generally increased precision by as much as 2% and recall by as much as 5%.

Evaluation Metrics In the tasks of determiner and preposition selection in well-formed, native texts (such as (Knight and Chander, 1994), (Minnen et al., 2000), (Turner and Charniak, 2007) and (Gamon et al., 2008)), the evaluation metric most commonly used is *accuracy*. In these tasks, one compares the system's output on a determiner or preposition to the gold standard of what the writer originally wrote. However, in the tasks of determiner and preposition error detection, *precision* and *recall* are better metrics to use because one is only concerned with a subset of the prepositions (or determiners), those used incorrectly, as opposed to all of them in the selection task. In essence, accuracy has the problem of distorting system performance.

Results The baseline system (described in (Chodorow et al., 2007)) performed at 79.8% precision and 11.7% recall. Next we tested the different combination models: word, tag, word+tag, and all three. Surprisingly, three of the four combination models: tag, word+tag, all, did not improve performance of the system when added to the model, but using just the +Combo:word features improved recall by 1%. We use the +Combo:word model to test our sampling approach in section 4.

As a final test, we tuned our training corpus of 7 million events by removing any contexts with unknown or misspelled words, and then retrained the model. This "purge" resulted in a removal of nearly 200,000 training events. With this new training corpus, the +Combo:tag feature showed the biggest improvement over the baseline, with an improvement in both precision (+2.3%) and recall (+2.4%) to 82.1% and 14.1% respectively (last line of Table 2. While this improvement may seem small, it is in part due to the difficulty of the problem, but also the high baseline system score that was established in our prior work (Chodorow et al., 2007).

It should be noted that with the inclusion of the extraneous use filter, performance of the +Combo:tag rose to 84% precision and close to 19% recall.

Model	Precision	Recall
Baseline	79.8%	11.7%
+Combo:word	79.8%	12.8%
+Combo:tag (with purge)	82.1%	14.1%

Table 2: Best System Results on Incorrect Selection Task

2.5 Related Work

Currently there are only a handful of approaches that tackle the problem of preposition error detection in English learner texts. (Gamon et al., 2008) used a language model and decision trees to detect preposition and determiner errors in the CLEC corpus of learner essays. Their system performs at 79% precision (which is on par with our system), however recall figures are not presented thus making comparison difficult. In addition, their evaluation differs from ours in that they also include errors of omission, and their work focuses on the top twelve most frequent prepositions, while ours has greater coverage with the top 34. (Izumi et al., 2003) and (Izumi et al., 2004) used an ME approach to classify different grammatical errors in transcripts of Japanese interviews. They do not present performance of prepositions specifically, but overall performance for the 13 error types they target reached 25% precision and 7% recall. (Eeg-Olofsson and Knuttson, 2003) created a rule-based approach to detecting preposition errors in Swedish language learners (unlike the approaches presented here, which focus on English language learners), and their system performed at 25% accuracy. (Lee and Seneff, 2006) used a language model to tackle the novel problem of preposition selection in a dialogue corpus. While their performance results are quite high, 88% precision and

78% recall, it should be noted that their evaluation was on a small corpus with a highly constrained domain, and focused on a limited number of prepositions, thus making direct comparison with our approach difficult.

Although our recall figures may seem low, especially when compared to other NLP tasks such as parsing and anaphora resolution, this is really a reflection of how difficult the task is. For example, in the problem of preposition selection in native text, a baseline using the most frequent preposition (*of*) results in precision and recall of 26%. In addition, the cloze tests presented earlier indicate that even in well-formed text, agreement between native speakers on preposition selection is only 75%. In texts written by non-native speakers, rater disagreement increases, as will be shown in the next section.

3 Experiments with Multiple Raters

While developing an error detection system for prepositions is certainly challenging, given the results from our work and others, evaluation also poses a major challenge. To date, single human annotation has typically been the gold standard for grammatical error detection, such as in the work of (Izumi et al., 2004), (Han et al., 2006), (Nagata et al., 2006), (Eeg-Olofsson and Knuttson, 2003)[2]. Another method for evaluation is verification ((Gamon et al., 2008), where a human rater checks over a system's output. The drawbacks of this approach are: 1. every time the system is changed, a rater is needed to re-check the output, and 2. it is very hard to estimate recall. What these two evaluation methods have in common is that they side-step the issue of annotator reliability.

In this section, we show how relying on only one rater can be problematic for difficult error detection tasks, and in section 4, we propose a method ("the sampling approach") for efficiently evaluating a system that does not require the amount of effort needed in the standard approach to annotation.

3.1 Annotation

To create a gold-standard corpus of error annotations for system evaluation, and also to determine whether multiple raters are better than one, we trained two native English speakers with prior NLP annotation experience to annotate preposition errors in ESL text. The training was very extensive: both raters were trained on 2000 preposition contexts and the annotation manual was iteratively refined as necessary. To summarize the procedure, the two raters were shown sentences randomly selected from student essays with each preposition highlighted in the sentence. They marked each context ($\pm$2-word window around the preposition, plus the commanding verb) for grammar and spelling errors, and then judged whether the writer used an incorrect preposition, a correct preposition, or an extraneous preposition. Finally, the raters suggested prepositions that would best fit the context, even if there were no error (some contexts can license multiple prepositions).

3.2 Reliability

Each rater judged approximately 18,000 prepositions contexts, with 18 sets of 100 contexts judged by both raters for purposes of computing kappa. Despite the rigorous training regimen, kappa ranged from 0.411 to 0.786, with an overall combined value of 0.630. Of the prepositions that Rater 1 judged to be errors, Rater 2 judged 30.2% to be acceptable. Conversely, of the prepositions Rater 2 judged to be erroneous, Rater 1 found 38.1% acceptable. The kappa of 0.630 shows the difficulty of this task and also shows how two highly trained raters can produce very different judgments. Details on our annotation and human judgment experiments can be found in (Tetreault and Chodorow, 2008).

Variability in raters' judgments translates to variability of system evaluation. For instance, in our previous work (Chodorow et al., 2007), we found that when our system's output was compared to judgments of two different raters, there was a 10% difference in precision and a 5% difference in recall. These differences are problematic when evaluating a system, as they highlight the potential to substantially over- or under-estimate performance.

4 Sampling Approach

The results from the previous section motivate the need for a more refined evaluation. They suggest that for certain error annotation tasks, such as preposition usage, it may not be appropriate to use only one rater and that if one uses multiple raters

[2](Eeg-Olofsson and Knuttson, 2003) had a small evaluation on 40 preposition contexts and it is unclear whether multiple annotators were used.

for error annotation, there is the possibility of creating an adjudicated set, or at least calculating the variability of the system's performance. However, annotation with multiple raters has its own disadvantages as it is much more expensive and time-consuming. Even using one rater to produce a sizeable evaluation corpus of preposition errors is extremely costly. For example, if we assume that 500 prepositions can be annotated in 4 hours using our annotation scheme, and that the base rate for preposition errors is 10%, then it would take at least 80 hours for a rater to find and mark 1000 errors. In this section, we propose a more efficient annotation approach to circumvent this problem.

4.1 Methodology

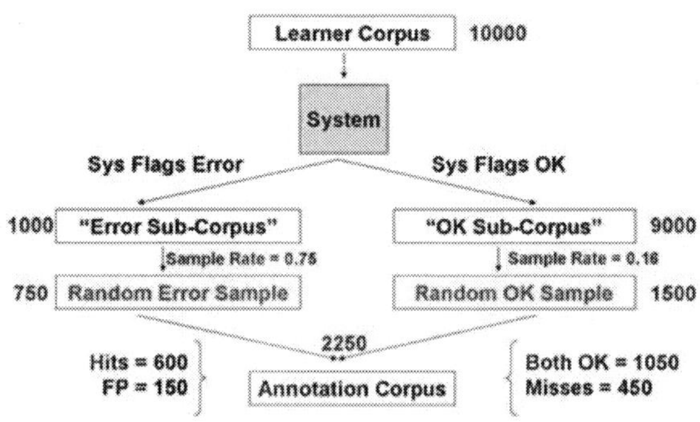

Figure 1: Sampling Approach Example

The sampling procedure outlined here is inspired by the one described in (Chodorow and Leacock, 2000) for the task of evaluating the usage of nouns, verbs and adjectives. The central idea is to skew the annotation corpus so that it contains a greater proportion of errors.

Here are the steps in the procedure:

1. Process a test corpus of sentences so that each preposition in the corpus is labeled "OK" or "Error" by the system.

2. Divide the processed corpus into two sub-corpora, one consisting of the system's "OK" prepositions and the other of the system's "Error" prepositions. For the hypothetical data in Figure 1, the "OK" sub-corpus contains 90% of the prepositions, and the "Error" sub-corpus contains the remaining 10%.

3. Randomly sample cases from each sub-corpus and combine the samples into an annotation set that is given to a "blind" human rater. We generally use a higher sampling rate for the "Error" sub-corpus because we want to "enrich" the annotation set with a larger proportion of errors than is found in the test corpus as a whole. In Figure 1, 75% of the "Error" sub-corpus is sampled while only 16% of the "OK" sub-corpus is sampled.

4. For each case that the human rater judges to be an error, check to see which sub-corpus it came from. If it came from the "OK" sub-corpus, then the case is a Miss (an error that the system failed to detect). If it came from the "Error" sub-corpus, then the case is a Hit (an error that the system detected). If the rater judges a case to be a correct usage and it came from the "Error" sub-corpus, then it is a False Positive (FP).

5. Calculate the proportions of Hits and FPs in the sample from the "Error" sub-corpus. For the hypothetical data in Figure 1, these values are 600/750 = 0.80 for Hits, and 150/750 = 0.20 for FPs. Calculate the proportion of Misses in the sample from the "OK" sub-corpus. For the hypothetical data, this is 450/1500 = 0.30 for Misses.

6. The values computed in step 5 are conditional proportions based on the sub-corpora. To calculate the overall proportions in the test corpus, it is necessary to multiply each value by the relative size of its sub-corpus. This is shown in Table 3, where the proportion of Hits in the "Error" sub-corpus (0.80) is multiplied by the relative size of the "Error" sub-corpus (0.10) to produce an overall Hit rate (0.08). Overall rates for FPs and Misses are calculated in a similar manner.

7. Using the values from step 6, calculate Precision (Hits/(Hits + FP)) and Recall (Hits/(Hits + Misses)). These are shown in the last two rows of Table 3.

	Estimated Overall Rates Sample Proportion * Sub-Corpus Proportion
Hits	0.80 * 0.10 = **0.08**
FP	0.20 * 0.10 = **0.02**
Misses	0.30 * 0.90 = **0.27**
Precision	0.08/(0.08 + 0.02) = **0.80**
Recall	0.08/(0.08 + 0.27) = **0.23**

Table 3: Sampling Calculations (Hypothetical)

This method is similar in spirit to *active learning* ((Dagan and Engelson, 1995) and (Engelson and Dagan, 1996)), which has been used to iteratively build up an annotated corpus, but it differs from active learning applications in that there are no iterative loops between the system and the human annotator(s). In addition, while our methodology is used for *evaluating* a system, active learning is commonly used for *training* a system.

4.2 Application

Next, we tested whether our proposed sampling approach provides good estimates of a system's performance. For this task, we used the +Combo:word model to separate a large corpus of student essays into the "Error" and "OK" sub-corpora. The original corpus totaled over 22,000 prepositions which would normally take several weeks for two raters to double annotate and then adjudicate. After the two sub-corpora were proportionally sampled, this resulted in an annotation set of 752 preposition contexts (requiring roughly 6 hours for annotation), which is substantially more manageable than the full corpus. We had both raters work together to make judgments for each preposition.

It is important to note that while these are not the exact same essays used in the previous evaluation of 8,269 preposition contexts, they come from the same pool of student essays and were on the same topics. Given these strong similarities, we feel that one can compare scores between the two approaches. The precision and recall scores for both approaches are shown in Table 4 and are extremely similar, thus suggesting that the sampling approach can be used as an alternative to exhaustive annotation.

	Precision	Recall
Standard Approach	80%	12%
Sampling Approach	79%	14%

Table 4: Sampling Results

It is important with the sampling approach to use appropriate sample sizes when drawing from the sub-corpora, because the accuracy of the estimates of hits and misses will depend upon the proportion of errors in each sub-corpus as well as on the sample sizes. The OK sub-corpus is expected to have even fewer errors than the overall base rate, so it is especially important to have a relatively large sample from this sub-corpus. The comparison study described above used an OK sub-corpus sample that was twice as large as the Error sub-corpus sample (about 500 contexts vs. 250 contexts).

In short, the sampling approach is intended to alleviate the burden on annotators when faced with the task of having to rate several thousand errors of a particular type in order to produce a sizeable error corpus. On the other hand, one advantage that exhaustive annotation has over the sampling method is that it makes possible the comparison of multiple systems. With the sampling approach, one would have to resample and annotate for each system, thus multiplying the work needed.

5 Analysis of Learner Errors

One aspect of automatic error detection that usually is under-reported is an analysis of the errors that learners typically make. The obvious benefit of this analysis is that it can focus development of the system.

From our annotated set of preposition errors, we found that the most common prepositions that learners used incorrectly were *in* (21.4%), *to* (20.8%) and *of* (16.6%). The top ten prepositions accounted for 93.8% of all preposition errors in our learner corpus.

Next, we ranked the common preposition "confusions", the common mistakes made for each preposition. The top ten most common confusions are listed in Table 5, where *null* refers to cases where no preposition is licensed (the writer used an extraneous preposition). The most common offenses were actually extraneous errors (see Table 5): using *to* and *of* when no preposition was licensed accounted for 16.8% of all errors.

It is interesting to note that the most common usage errors by learners overwhelmingly involved the ten most frequently occurring prepositions in native text. This suggests that our effort to handle the 34 most frequently occurring prepositions may be overextended and that a system that is specifically trained and refined on the top ten prepositions may provide better diagnostic feedback to a learner.

6 Conclusions

This paper has two contributions to the field of error detection in non-native writing. First, we discussed a system that detects preposition errors with high precison (up to 84%) and is competitive

Writer's Prep.	Rater's Prep.	Frequency
to	*null*	9.5%
of	*null*	7.3%
in	at	7.1%
to	for	4.6%
in	*null*	3.2%
of	for	3.1%
in	on	3.1%
of	in	2.9%
at	in	2.7%
for	to	2.5%

Table 5: Common Preposition Confusions

with other leading methods. We used an ME approach augmented with combination features and a series of thresholds. This system is currently incorporated in the *Criterion* writing evaluation service. Second, we showed that the standard approach to evaluating NLP error detection systems (comparing a system's output with a gold-standard annotation) can greatly skew system results when the annotation is done by only one rater. However, one reason why a single rater is commonly used is that building a corpus of learner errors can be extremely costly and time consuming. To address this efficiency issue, we presented a sampling approach that produces results comparable to exhaustive annotation. This makes using multiple raters possible since less time is required to assess the system's performance. While the work presented here has focused on prepositions, the arguments against using only one rater, and for using a sampling approach generalize to other error types, such as determiners and collocations.

Acknowledgements We would first like to thank our two annotators Sarah Ohls and Waverly VanWinkle for their hours of hard work. We would also like to acknowledge the three anonymous reviewers and Derrick Higgins for their helpful comments and feedback.

References

Carletta, J. 1996. Assessing agreement on classification tasks: The kappa statistic. *Computational Linguistics*, pages 249–254.

Chodorow, M. and C. Leacock. 2000. An unsupervised method for detecting grammatical errors. In *NAACL*.

Chodorow, M., J. Tetreault, and N-R. Han. 2007. Detection of grammatical errors involving prepositions. In *Proceedings of the Fourth ACL-SIGSEM Workshop on Prepositions*.

Dagan, I. and S. Engelson. 1995. Committee-based sampling for training probabilistic classifiers. In *Proceedings of ICML*, pages 150–157.

Eeg-Olofsson, J. and O. Knuttson. 2003. Automatic grammar checking for second language learners - the use of prepositions. In *Nodalida*.

Engelson, S. and I. Dagan. 1996. Minimizing manual annotation cost in supervised training from corpora. In *Proceedings of ACL*, pages 319–326.

Gamon, M., J. Gao, C. Brockett, A. Klementiev, W. B. Dolan, D. Belenko, and L. Vanderwende. 2008. Using contextual speller techniques and language modeling for esl error correction. In *IJCNLP*.

Grishman, R., C. Macleod, and A. Meyers. 1994. Comlex syntax: Building a computational lexicon. In *COLING*.

Han, N-R., M. Chodorow, and C. Leacock. 2006. Detecting errors in english article usage by non-native speakers. *Natural Language Engineering*, 12:115–129.

Izumi, E., K. Uchimoto, T. Saiga, T. Supnithi, and H. Isahara. 2003. Automatic error detection in the Japanese leaners' English spoken data. In *ACL*.

Izumi, E., K. Uchimoto, and H. Isahara. 2004. The overview of the sst speech corpus of Japanese learner English and evaluation through the experiment on automatic detection of learners' errors. In *LREC*.

Jurafsky, D. and J. Martin. 2008. *Speech and Language Processing (2nd Edition)*. Prentice Hall. To Appear.

Knight, K. and I. Chander. 1994. Automated postediting of documents. In *Conference on Artificial Intelligence*.

Lee, J. and S. Seneff. 2006. Automatic grammar correction for second-language learners. In *Interspeech*.

Levin, B. 1993. *English verb classes and alternations: a preliminary investigation*. Univ. of Chicago Press.

Minnen, G., F. Bond, and A. Copestake. 2000. Memory-based learning for article generation. In *CoNLL*.

Nagata, R., A. Kawai, K. Morihiro, and N. Isu. 2006. A feedback-augmented method for detecting errors in the writing of learners of English. In *Proceedings of the ACL/COLING*.

Ratnaparkhi, A. 1998. *Maximum Entropy Models for natural language ambiguity resolution*. Ph.D. thesis, University of Pennsylvania.

Tetreault, J. and M. Chodorow. 2008. Native Judgments of non-native usage: Experiments in preposition error detection. In *COLING Workshop on Human Judgments in Computational Linguistics*.

Turner, J. and E. Charniak. 2007. Language modeling for determiner selection. In *HLT/NAACL*.

A Framework for Identifying Textual Redundancy

Kapil Thadani and **Kathleen McKeown**
Department of Computer Science,
Columbia University,
New York, NY USA
{kapil,kathy}@cs.columbia.edu

Abstract

The task of identifying redundant information in documents that are generated from multiple sources provides a significant challenge for summarization and QA systems. Traditional clustering techniques detect redundancy at the sentential level and do not guarantee the preservation of all information within the document. We discuss an algorithm that generates a novel graph-based representation for a document and then utilizes a set cover approximation algorithm to remove redundant text from it. Our experiments show that this approach offers a significant performance advantage over clustering when evaluated over an annotated dataset.

1 Introduction

This paper approaches the problem of identifying and reducing redundant information in documents that are generated from multiple sources. This task is closely related to many well-studied problems in the field of natural language processing such as summarization and paraphrase recognition. Systems that utilize data from multiple sources, such as question-answering and extractive summarization systems that operate on news data, usually include a component to remove redundant information from appearing in their generated output.

However, practical attempts at reducing redundancy in the output of these types of systems usually involve clustering the sentences of the generated output, picking a representative sentence from each cluster and discarding the rest. Although this strategy would remove some redundant information, clustering approaches tuned for coarse matches could also remove non-redundant information whereas clustering approaches tuned for near-exact matches could end up removing very little repeated information. This is simply a consequence of the fact that information can, and usually does, exist at the sub-sentential level and that clusters of sentences don't necessarily correspond to clusters of *information*.

In this paper, we discuss a framework for building a novel graph-based representation to detect redundancy within documents. We identify redundancy at the sub-sentential level through pairwise alignment between the sentences of a document and use this to build a bipartite graph which enables us to keep track of redundant information across all sentences. Common information between pairs of sentences, detected with the alignment algorithm, can be extrapolated to document-wide units of information using the graph structure. Individual sentences that are encompassed by the information in the rest of the document can then be identified and removed efficiently by using a well-known greedy algorithm adapted for this representation.

2 Related Work

The challenge of minimizing redundant information is commonly faced by IR engines and extractive summarization systems when generating their responses. A well-known diversity-based reranking technique for these types of systems is MMR (Carbonell and Goldstein, 1998), which attempts to reduce redundancy by preferring sentences that differ from the sentences already selected for the summary. However, this approach does not attempt to identify sub-sentential redundancy.

Alternative approaches to identifying redundancy use clustering at the sentence level (Lin and Hovy, 2001) to remove sentences that are largely repetitive; however, as noted earlier, this is not well-suited to the redundancy task. The use of sen-

©2008. Licensed under the *Creative Commons Attribution-Noncommercial-Share Alike 3.0 Unported* license (http://creativecommons.org/licenses/by-nc-sa/3.0/). Some rights reserved.

tence simplification in conjunction with clustering (Siddharthan et al., 2004) could help alleviate this problem by effectively clustering smaller units, but this issue cannot be avoided unless sentences are simplified to atomic elements of information.

Other research has introduced the notion of identifying concepts in the input text (Filatova and Hatzivassiloglou, 2004), using a *set cover* algorithm to attempt to include as many concepts as possible. However, this approach uses *tf-idf* to approximate concepts and thus doesn't explicitly identify redundant text. Our work draws on this approach but extends it to identify all detectable redundancies within a document set.

Another approach does identify small sub-sentential units of information within text called "Basic Elements" and uses these for evaluating summarizations (Hovy et al., 2006). Our approach, in contrast, does not make assumptions about the size or structure of redundant information since this is uncovered through alignments.

We thus require the use of an alignment algorithm to extract the common information between two pieces of text. This is related to the well-studied problem of identifying paraphrases (Barzilay and Lee, 2003; Pang et al., 2003) and the more general variant of recognizing textual entailment, which explores whether information expressed in a hypothesis can be inferred from a given premise. Entailment problems have also been approached with a wide variety of techniques, one of which is dependency tree alignment (Marsi et al., 2006), which we utilize as well to align segments of text while respecting syntax. However, our definition of redundancy does not extend to include unidirectional entailment, and the alignment process is simply required to identify equivalent information.

3 Levels of Information

In describing the redundancy task, we deal with multiple levels of semantic abstraction from the basic lexical form. This section describes the terminology used in this paper and the graph-based representation that is central to our approach.

3.1 Terminology

The following terms are used throughout this paper to refer to different aspects of a document.

Snippet: This is any span of text in the document and is a lexical realization of information. While a snippet generally refers to a single sentence within a document, it can apply to multiple sentences or phrases within sentences. Since redundancy will be reduced by removing whole snippets, a snippet can be defined as the smallest unit of text that can be dropped from a document for the purpose of reducing redundancy.

To illustrate the levels of information that we consider, consider the following set of short sentences as snippets. Although this is a synthesized example to simplify presentation, sentences with this type of overlapping information occur frequently in the question-answering scenario over news in which our approach has been used.

$\mathbf{x}_1$: Whittington is an attorney.
$\mathbf{x}_2$: Cheney shot Whittington, a lawyer.
$\mathbf{x}_3$: Whittington, an attorney, was shot in Texas.
$\mathbf{x}_4$: Whittington was shot by Cheney while hunting quail.
$\mathbf{x}_5$: This happened during a quail hunt in Texas.

We can see that all the information in $\mathbf{x}_1$ is contained in both $\mathbf{x}_2$ and $\mathbf{x}_3$. While no other snippet is completely subsumed by any single snippet, they can be made redundant given combinations of other snippets; for example, $\mathbf{x}_4$ is redundant given $\mathbf{x}_2$, $\mathbf{x}_3$ and $\mathbf{x}_5$. In order to identify these combinations, we need to identify the elements of information within each snippet.

Concept: This refers to a basic unit of information within a document. Concepts may be facts, opinions or details. These are not necessarily *sememes*, which are atomic units of meaning, but simply units of information that are seen as atomic within the document. We further restrict the definition of a concept to a unit of information seen in *more than one snippet*, since we are only interested in concepts which help in identifying redundancy.

Formally, a document can be defined as a set of S snippets $\mathbf{X} = \{\mathbf{x}_1, \ldots, \mathbf{x}_S\}$, which is a literal representation of the document. However, it can also be defined in terms of its *information content*. We use $\mathbf{Z} = \{\mathbf{z}^1, \ldots, \mathbf{z}^C\}$ to represent the set of C concepts that cover all information appearing more than once in the document. In the example above, we can identify five non-overlapping concepts:

$\mathbf{z}^{\mathrm{A}}$: Whittington was shot
$\mathbf{z}^{\mathrm{B}}$: Whittington is an attorney
$\mathbf{z}^{\mathrm{C}}$: The shooting occurred in Texas
$\mathbf{z}^{\mathrm{D}}$: It happened during a hunt for quail
$\mathbf{z}^{\mathrm{E}}$: Cheney was the shooter

We use subscripts for snippet indices and superscripts for concept indices throughout this paper.

Nugget: This is a textual representation of a concept in a snippet and therefore expresses some information which is also expressed elsewhere in the document. Different nuggets for a given concept may have unique lexico-syntactic realizations, as long as they all embody the same semantics. With regard to the notation used above, nuggets can be represented by an $S \times C$ matrix $\mathbf{Y}$ where each $\mathbf{y}_s^c$ denotes the fragment of text (if any) from the snippet $\mathbf{x}_s$ that represents concept $\mathbf{z}^c$.

Since a concept itself has no unique textual realization, it can be simply represented by the combination of all its nuggets. For instance, in the example shown above, concept $\mathbf{z}^{\mathrm{D}}$ is seen in both $\mathbf{x}_4$ and $\mathbf{x}_5$ in the form of two nuggets $\mathbf{y}_4^{\mathrm{D}}$ ("... while hunting quail") and $\mathbf{y}_5^{\mathrm{D}}$ ("... during a quail hunt"), which are paraphrases. The degree to which we can consider this and other types of lexical or syntactic differences between nuggets that have the same semantic identity depends on the alignment algorithm used.

Intersection: This is the common information between two snippets that can be obtained through their alignment. For example, the intersection from the alignment between $\mathbf{x}_2$ and $\mathbf{x}_4$ consists of two fragments of text that express that Cheney shot Whittington (an active-voiced fragment from $\mathbf{x}_2$ and a passive-voiced fragment from $\mathbf{x}_4$).

In general, aligning $\mathbf{x}_i$ and $\mathbf{x}_j$ produces an intersection $\mathbf{v}_{i,j}$ which is simply a pair of aligned text fragments covering the set of concepts that $\mathbf{x}_i$ and $\mathbf{x}_j$ have in common. However, these undivided segments of text may actually contain multiple nuggets from a document-wide perspective. We assume that intersections can be *decomposed* into smaller intersections through further alignments with snippets or other intersections; this process is explained in Subsection 4.3.

3.2 Concept graph representation

Figure 1 illustrates the example introduced in Subsection 3.1 as a network with intersections represented as edges between snippets. This is the type of graph that would be built using pairwise alignments between all snippets. Note that although some intersections such as $\mathbf{v}_{1,2}$ (between $\mathbf{x}_1$ and $\mathbf{x}_2$) and $\mathbf{v}_{3,5}$ express concepts directly, other intersections such as $\mathbf{v}_{2,3}$ and $\mathbf{v}_{2,4}$ are undivided combinations of concepts. Since we cannot directly identify concepts and their nuggets, this graph is not immediately useful for reducing redundancy.

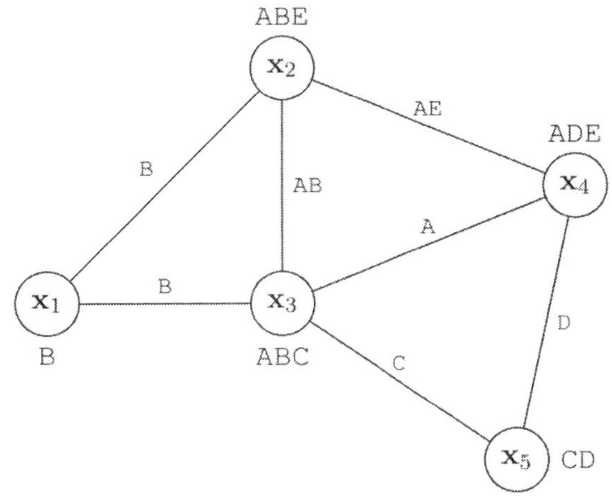

Figure 1: Graph representing pairwise alignments between the example snippets from Section 3. For clarity, alphabetic labels like A represent concepts $\mathbf{z}^{\mathrm{A}}$. Node labels show concepts within snippets and edge labels indicate concepts seen in intersections.

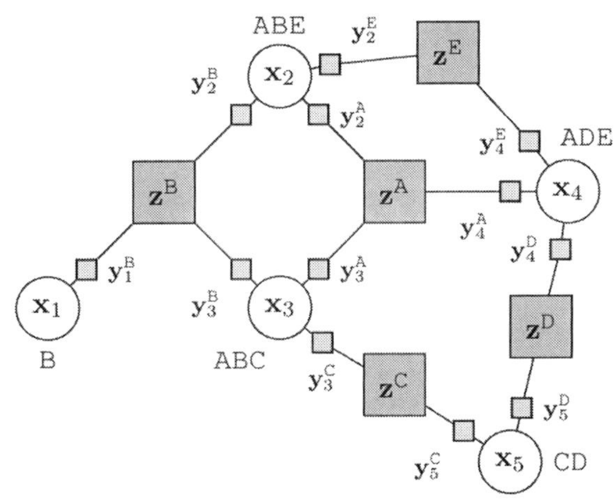

Figure 2: Structure of the equivalent concept graph for the example document illustrated in Figure 1. Circular nodes $\mathbf{x}_s$ represent snippets, large squares $\mathbf{z}^c$ represent concepts and small squares $\mathbf{y}_s^c$ depict nuggets for each concept within a snippet.

Now, since the matrix $\mathbf{Y}$ describes the interaction of concepts with snippets, it can be viewed as an incidence matrix that defines a bipartite graph between snippets and concepts with nuggets representing the edges. In this *concept graph* representation, each snippet can connect to any number of other snippets via a shared concept. Since concepts serve to connect multiple snippets together, the concept graph can also be seen as a hypergraph, which is a generalization of a graph in which each edge may connect together multiple vertices.

Figure 2 illustrates the structure of the equivalent concept graph for the previous example. This is simply the bipartite graph with the two types of nodes, namely snippets and concepts, represented using different symbols. For clarity, nuggets are also depicted as nodes in the graph, thereby reducing edges to simple links indicating membership. This representation identifies the redundancy between snippets in terms of non-overlapping concepts and is therefore more useful than the graph from Figure 1 for reducing redundancy.

4 Constructing the Concept Graph

We now describe how a concept graph can be constructed from a document by using dependency tree alignment and leveraging the existing structure of the graph during construction.

4.1 Alignment of snippets

In order to obtain the concept graph representation, the common information between each pair of snippets in the document must first be discovered by aligning all pairs of snippets with each other. We make use of dependency parsing and alignment of dependency parse trees to obtain intersections between each pair of snippets, where each intersection may be a discontiguous span of text corresponding to an aligned subtree within each snippet. In our experiments, dependency parsing is accomplished with Minipar (Lin, 1998) and alignment is done using a bottom-up tree alignment algorithm (Barzilay and McKeown, 2005) modified to account for the shallow semantic role labels produced by the parser. The alignment implementation is not the focus of this work, however, and the framework described here could by applied using any alignment technique between segments of text in potentially any language.

As seen in Figure 1, the intersections that can be extracted solely by pairwise comparisons are not unique and may contain multiple concepts. A truly information-preserving approach requires the explicit identification of concepts as in the concept graph from Figure 2, but efficiently converting the former into the latter poses a non-trivial challenge.

4.2 Extraction of irreducible concepts

Our approach attempts to obtain a set of *irreducible concepts* such that each concept in this set cannot wholly or partially contain any other concept in the set (thereby conforming to the definition of a concept in Subsection 3.1).

We attempt to build the concept graph and maintain irreducible concepts alongside each of the $S(S-1)/2$ pairwise alignment steps. Every intersection found by aligning a pair of snippets is assumed to represent some concept that these snippets share; it is then compared with existing concepts and is decomposed into smaller intersections if it overlaps partially with any one of them. This implies a worst-case of C comparisons at each pairwise alignment step ($2C$ if both fragments of an intersection are compared separately). However, this can be made more efficient by exploiting the structure of the graph. A new intersection only has to be compared with concepts which might be affected by it and only affects the other snippets containing these concepts. We can show that this leads to an algorithm that requires fewer than C comparisons, and additionally, that these comparisons can be performed efficiently.

Consider the definition of alignment along the lines of a mathematical relation. We require snippet alignment to be an *equivalence relation* and it therefore must have the following properties.

Symmetry: If an intersection $\mathbf{v}_{i,j}$ contains a concept $\mathbf{z}'$, then $\mathbf{v}_{j,i}$ will also contain $\mathbf{z}'$. This property allows only $S(S-1)/2$ alignments to suffice instead of the full $S(S-1)$. Therefore, without loss of generality, we can specify that all alignments between $\mathbf{x}_i$ and $\mathbf{x}_j$ should have $i < j$.

Transitivity: If intersections $\mathbf{v}_{i,j}$ and $\mathbf{v}_{j,k}$ both contain some concept $\mathbf{z}'$, then $\mathbf{v}_{i,k}$ will also contain $\mathbf{z}'$. This property leads to an interesting consequence. Assuming we perform alignments in order (initially aligning $\mathbf{x}_1$ and $\mathbf{x}_2$ and iterating for j within each i), we observe that $\mathbf{x}_i$ has been aligned with snippets $\{\mathbf{x}_1, \ldots, \mathbf{x}_{j-1}\}$ and, for any $i > 1$, snippets $\{\mathbf{x}_1, \ldots, \mathbf{x}_{i-1}\}$ were aligned with all snippets $\{\mathbf{x}_1, \ldots, \mathbf{x}_S\}$. Since $i < j$, this implies that $\mathbf{x}_i$ was directly aligned with snippets $\{\mathbf{x}_1, \ldots, \mathbf{x}_{i-1}\}$ which in turn were each aligned with all S snippets. Therefore, due to the property of transitivity, all concepts contained in a new intersection $\mathbf{v}_{i,j}$ that *also* exist in the partly-constructed graph would already be directly associated with $\mathbf{x}_i$. Note that this does not hold for $\mathbf{x}_j$ as well, since $\mathbf{x}_j$ has not been aligned with $\{\mathbf{x}_{i+1}, \ldots, \mathbf{x}_{j-1}\}$; therefore, it may not have encountered all relevant concepts.

This implies that for any i and j, all concepts that might be affected by a new intersection $\mathbf{v}_{i,j}$

have already been uncovered in $\mathbf{x}_i$ and thus $\mathbf{v}_{i,j}$ only needs to be compared to these concepts.

4.3 Comparisons after alignment

For every new intersection $\mathbf{v}_{i,j}$ produced by an alignment between $\mathbf{x}_i$ and $\mathbf{x}_j$, the algorithm compares it (specifically, the fragment from $\mathbf{x}_i$) with each existing nugget $\mathbf{y}_i^k$ for each concept $\mathbf{z}^k$ already seen in $\mathbf{x}_i$. Checking for the following cases ensures that the graph structure contains only irreducible concepts for all the alignments seen:

1. If $\mathbf{v}_{i,j}$ doesn't overlap with any current nugget from $\mathbf{x}_i$, it becomes a new concept that links to $\mathbf{x}_i$ and $\mathbf{x}_j$. In our example, the first intersection $\mathbf{v}_{1,2}$ contains "Whittington ... an attorney" from $\mathbf{x}_1$ and "... Whittington, a lawyer" from $\mathbf{x}_2$; this becomes a new concept $\mathbf{z}^{\text{B}}$ since $\mathbf{x}_1$ has no other nuggets.
2. If $\mathbf{v}_{i,j}$ overlaps completely with a nugget $\mathbf{y}_i^k$, then $\mathbf{x}_j$ must also be linked to concept $\mathbf{z}^k$. For example, $\mathbf{x}_1$'s fragment in the second intersection $\mathbf{v}_{1,3}$ is also "Whittington ... an attorney", so $\mathbf{x}_3$ must also link to $\mathbf{z}^{\text{B}}$.
3. If $\mathbf{v}_{i,j}$ subsumes $\mathbf{y}_i^k$, it is split up and the non-overlapping portion is rechecked against existing nuggets recursively. For example, $\mathbf{x}_2$'s fragment in the intersection $\mathbf{v}_{2,3}$ is "... shot Whittington, a lawyer", part of which overlaps with $\mathbf{y}_2^B$, so this intersection is divided up and the part representing "... shot Whittington ..." becomes a new concept $\mathbf{z}^A$.
4. If, on the other hand, $\mathbf{y}_i^k$ subsumes $\mathbf{v}_{i,j}$, the concept $\mathbf{z}^k$ is itself split up along with all nuggets that it links to, utilizing the present structure of the graph.

When comparing intersections, we can restrict the decomposition of nuggets to prevent the creation of overly-granular concepts. For instance, we can filter out intersections containing only isolated named-entities or syntactic artifacts like determiners since they contain no information by themselves. We can also prevent verbs and their arguments from being split apart using information from a snippet's dependency parse, if available.

4.4 Efficiency of the algorithm

Instead of C additional comparisons in the worst case after each pairwise snippet alignment, we need no more comparisons in the worst case than the maximum number of concepts that can exist in a single snippet. Since this value grows no faster than C as S increases, this is a significant improvement. Other factors, such as the overhead required to split up concepts, remain unchanged.

Furthermore, since all the additional comparisons are carried out between nuggets of the *same* snippet, we don't need to perform any further alignment among nuggets or concepts. Alignments are expensive; each is $O(n_1 n_2)$ where n_1 and n_2 are the number of words in the two segments of text being aligned (if dependency tree alignment is used) along with an overhead for checking word similarity. However, since we now only need to compare text from the same snippet, the comparison can be performed in linear time by simply comparing spans of word indices, thereby also eliminating the overhead for comparing words.

5 Decreasing redundancy

The concept graph can now be applied to the task of reducing redundancy in the document by dropping snippets which contain no information that is not already present in the rest of the document.

5.1 Reduction to set cover

Every snippet $\mathbf{x}_s$ in a document can be represented as a set of concepts $\{\mathbf{z}^c : \mathbf{y}_s^c \in \mathbf{Y}\}$. Since concepts are defined as information that is seen in more than one snippet as per the definition in Subsection 3.1, representing snippets as sets of concepts will overlook any unique information present in a snippet. Without loss of generality, we can add any such unique information in the form of an *artificial concept* for each snippet to $\mathbf{Z}$ so that snippets can be completely represented as sets of concepts from $\mathbf{Z}$. Note that the union of snippets $\bigcup_{s=1}^{S} \mathbf{x}_s$ equals $\mathbf{Z}$.

Reducing redundancy in the document while preserving all information requires us to identify the *most* snippets whose entire informational content is covered by the rest of the snippets in the document, thereby targeting them for removal. Since we express informational content in concepts, this problem reduces to the task of finding the smallest group of snippets that together cover all the concepts in the document, i.e. we need to find the *smallest* subset $\mathbf{X}' \subseteq \mathbf{X}$ such that, if $\mathbf{X}'$ contains R snippets $\mathbf{x}'_r$, the union of these snippets $\bigcup_{r=1}^{R} \mathbf{x}'_r$ also equals $\mathbf{Z}$. Therefore, every concept in a snippet from $\mathbf{X} - \mathbf{X}'$ also exists in at least one snippet from $\mathbf{X}'$ and no concept from $\mathbf{Z}$ is lost.

This formulation of the problem is the classic

set cover problem, which seeks to find the smallest possible group of subsets of a universe that covers all the other subsets. A more general variant of this problem is *weighted set cover* in which the subsets have weights to be maximized or costs to be minimized. While this problem is known to be NP-hard, there exists a straightforward local maximization approach (Hochbaum, 1997) which runs in polynomial time and is proven to give solutions within a known bound of the optimal solution. This greedy approximation algorithm can be adapted to our representation.

5.2 Selecting non-redundant snippets

The algorithm selects a snippet $\mathbf{x}_r$ to the subset $\mathbf{X}'$ such that *information content* of $\mathbf{X} \cup \mathbf{x}_r$ is maximized. In general, this implies that the snippet with the highest degree over uncovered concepts must be selected at each iteration. Other measures such as snippet length, fluency, or rank in an ordered list can be included in a weight measure in order to break ties and introduce a preference for shorter, more fluent, or higher-ranked snippets.

Consider the example from Section 3. The candidates for selection are $\mathbf{x}_2$, $\mathbf{x}_3$ and $\mathbf{x}_4$ since they contain the most *uncovered* concepts. If $\mathbf{x}_2$ is selected, its concepts $\mathbf{z}^A$, $\mathbf{z}^B$ and $\mathbf{z}^E$ are *covered.* At this stage, $\mathbf{x}_5$ contains two uncovered concepts while $\mathbf{x}_3$ and $\mathbf{x}_4$ contain just one each. Thus, $\mathbf{x}_5$ is selected next and its concepts $\mathbf{z}^C$ and $\mathbf{z}^D$ are covered. Since no uncovered concepts remain, all snippets which haven't been selected are redundant. This solution, which is shown in Figure 3, selects the following text to cover all the snippets:

$\mathbf{x}_2$: Cheney shot Whittington, a lawyer.

$\mathbf{x}_5$: This happened during a quail hunt in Texas.

Other solutions are also possible depending on the factors involved in choosing the snippet to be selected at each iteration. For example, the algorithm might choose to select $\mathbf{x}_3$ first instead of $\mathbf{x}_2$, thereby yielding the following solution:

$\mathbf{x}_3$: Whittington, an attorney, was shot in Texas.

$\mathbf{x}_4$: Whittington was shot by Cheney while hunting quail.

6 Experiments

To evaluate the effectiveness of this framework empirically, we ran experiments over documents containing annotations corresponding to concepts within the document. We also defined a metric

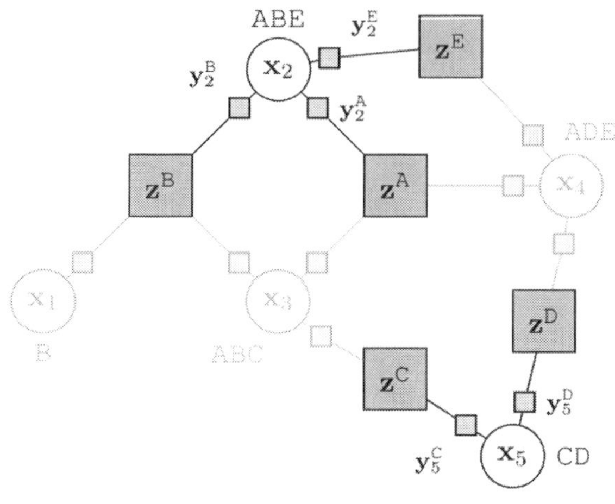

Figure 3: Pruned version of the concept graph example shown in Figure 2, illustrating the outcome of removing redundant snippets.

for comparing any concept graph over a document to a gold-standard concept graph. This was used to compare the concept graphs created by our approach to perturbed versions of the gold-standard graphs and graphs created by clustering.

6.1 Dataset

Due to the scarcity of available annotated datasets suitable for evaluating redundancy, we utilized the pyramid dataset from DUC 2005 (Nenkova et al., 2007) which was created from 20 articles for the purpose of summarization evaluation. Each pyramid document is a hierarchical representation of 7 summaries of the orginal news article. These summaries have been annotated to identify the individual *semantic content units* or SCUs where each SCU represents a certain fact, observation or piece of information in the summary. A sentence fragment representing an occurrence of an SCU in a summary is a *contributor* to the SCU.

The pyramid construction for a group of summaries of the same article mirrors the concept graph representation described in Subsection 3.2. SCUs with more than two contributors are similar in definition to concepts while their contributors fill the role of nuggets. Using this analogy, each dataset consists of a combination of the seven summaries in a single pyramid document; the 20 pyramid documents therefore yield 20 datasets.

6.2 Evaluation metrics

The evaluation task requires us to compare the concept graph generated by our algorithm to the ideal

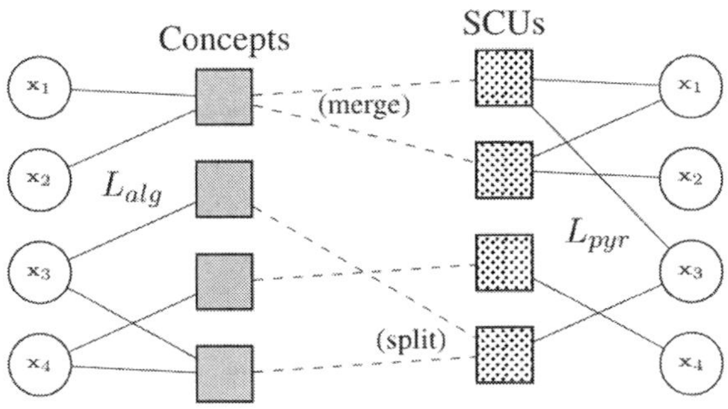

Figure 4: The bipartite graph on the left shows snippets $\mathbf{x}_s$ linked to concepts produced automatically; the one on the right shows the same snippets linked to SCUs from annotated data. Dashed lines indicate mappings between concepts and SCUs.

concept graph extracted from the pyramid document annotations. Standard metrics do not apply easily to the problem of comparing bipartite graphs, so we define a novel metric modeled on the well-known IR measures of precision, recall and F-measure. Figure 4 illustrates the elements involved in the evaluation task.

We define the metrics of precision, recall and F-measure over the *links* between snippets and concepts. Assuming we have a mapping between generated concepts and gold-standard SCUs, we can judge whether each link is correct. Let each single link between a snippet and a concept have an associated weight of 1 by default and let L indicate a set of such links. We use L_{alg} and L_{pyr} to distinguish between the sets of links generated by the algorithm and retrieved from the annotations respectively. Precision and recall are defined as follows while F-measure retains its traditional definition as their harmonic mean.

$$\text{Precision} = \frac{\text{Sum of weights in } L_{alg} \cap L_{pyr}}{\text{Sum of weights in } L_{alg}}$$

$$\text{Recall} = \frac{\text{Sum of weights in } L_{alg} \cap L_{pyr}}{\text{Sum of weights in } L_{pyr}}$$

To determine a mapping between concepts and SCUs, we identify every concept and SCU pair, say $\mathbf{z}^c$ and $\mathbf{z}^s$, which has one or more snippets in common and, for each snippet $\mathbf{x}_i$ that they have in common, we find the longest common subsequence between their nuggets $\mathbf{y}_i^c$ and $\mathbf{y}_i^s$ to obtain the following score which ranges from 0 to 1.

$$\text{LCS score} = \frac{length(\text{LCS})}{\min\left(length(\mathbf{y}_i^c), length(\mathbf{y}_i^s)\right)}$$

Measure	Random	Clustering	Concepts
Precision	0.0510	0.2961	**0.4496**
Recall	0.0515	0.1162	**0.3266**
F_1 score	0.0512	0.1669	**0.3783**

Table 1: Summary of the evaluation metrics averaged over all 20 pyramid documents when $m = 0.5$

This score is compared with a user-defined mapping threshold m to determine if the concept and SCU are sufficiently similar. In order to avoid biasing the metric by permitting multiple mappings per concept, we adjust for *merges* or $1 : N$ mappings by cloning the concept and creating N $1:1$ mappings in its place. We then adjust for *splits* or $N : 1$ mappings by dividing the weight of each of the links connected to a participating concept by N. Due to this normalization, the metrics are observed to be stable over variations in m.

6.3 Baselines

We compare the performance of the algorithm against two baselines. The first approach involves a random concept assignment scheme to build artificial concept graphs using the distributional properties of the gold-standard concept graphs. The number of concepts C and the number of snippets that each concept links to is determined by sampling from distributions over these properties derived from the statistics of the actual SCU graph for that document. For evaluation, these artificial concepts are randomly mapped to SCUs using m to control the likelihood of mapping. The best scores from 100 evaluation runs were considered.

The second baseline used for comparison is a clustering algorithm, since clustering is the most common approach to dealing with redundancy. For this purpose, we use a recursive spectral partitioning algorithm, a variant of spectral clustering (Shi and Malik, 2000) which obtains an average V-measure (Rosenberg and Hirschberg, 2007) of 0.93 when clustering just pyramid contributors labeled by their SCUs. The algorithm requires a parameter that controls the homogeneity of each cluster; we run it over the entire range of settings of this parameter. We consider the clustering that *maximizes* F-measure in order to avoid any uncertainty regarding optimal parameter selection and to implicitly compare our algorithm against an entire hierarchy of possible clusterings.

6.4 Results

Table 1 shows the F_1 scores over evaluation runs using the random concept assignment, clustering and concept graph techniques. These results are obtained at a mapping threshold of $m = 0.5$, which implies that we consider a mapping between a concept and an SCU if their nuggets over common sentences share more than 50% of their words on average. The results do not vary significantly at different settings of m.

We observe that the concepts extracted by our graph-based approach perform significantly better than the best-performing clustering configuration. Despite a fairly limited alignment approach that doesn't use synonyms or semantic analysis, the concept graph outperforms the baselines by nearly an order of magnitude on each document. This validates our initial hypothesis that clustering approaches are not suitable for tackling the redundancy problem at the sub-sentential level.

7 Conclusions and Future Work

We have described a graph-based algorithm for identifying redundancy at the sub-snippet level and shown that it outperforms clustering methods that are traditionally applied to the redundancy task.

Though the algorithm identifies redundancy at the sub-snippet level, redundancy can be decreased by dropping only entirely redundant snippets. We hope to be able to overcome this limitation by extending this information-preserving approach to the synthesis of new non-redundant snippets which minimize redundant content in the document.

In addition, this work currently assumes that redundancy is bidirectional; however, we intend to also address the case of unidirectional redundancy by considering entailment recognition approaches.

Acknowledgements

We are grateful to Andrew Rosenberg, David Elson, Mayank Lahiri and the anonymous reviewers for their useful feedback. This material is based upon work supported by the Defense Advanced Research Projects Agency under Contract No. HR0011-06-C-0023.

References

Barzilay, Regina and Lillian Lee. 2003. Learning to paraphrase: an unsupervised approach using multiple-sequence alignment. In *Proceedings of HLT-NAACL*, pages 16–23.

Barzilay, Regina and Kathleen R. McKeown. 2005. Sentence fusion for multidocument news summarization. *Computational Linguistics*, 31(3):297–328.

Carbonell, Jaime G. and Jade Goldstein. 1998. The use of MMR, diversity-based reranking for reordering documents and producing summaries. In *Proceedings of ACM-SIGIR*, pages 335–336.

Filatova, Elena and Vasileios Hatzivassiloglou. 2004. A formal model for information selection in multi-sentence text extraction. In *Proceedings of COLING*, page 397.

Hochbaum, Dorit S. 1997. Approximating covering and packing problems: set cover, vertex cover, independent set, and related problems. In *Approximation algorithms for NP-hard problems*, pages 94–143. PWS Publishing Co., Boston, MA, USA.

Hovy, Eduard, Chin-Yew Lin, Liang Zhou, and Junichi Fukumoto. 2006. Automated summarization evaluation with basic elements. In *Proceedings of LREC*.

Lin, Chin-Yew and Eduard Hovy. 2001. From single to multi-document summarization: a prototype system and its evaluation. In *Proceedings of ACL*, pages 457–464.

Lin, Dekang. 1998. Dependency-based evaluation of MINIPAR. In *Proceedings of the Workshop on the Evaluation of Parsing Systems, LREC*.

Marsi, Erwin, Emiel Krahmer, Wauter Bosma, and Mariet Theune. 2006. Normalized alignment of dependency trees for detecting textual entailment. In *Second PASCAL Recognising Textual Entailment Challenge*, pages 56–61.

Nenkova, Ani, Rebecca Passonneau, and Kathleen McKeown. 2007. The pyramid method: Incorporating human content selection variation in summarization evaluation. *ACM Transactions on Speech and Language Processing*, 4(2):4.

Pang, Bo, Kevin Knight, and Daniel Marcu. 2003. Syntax-based alignment of multiple translations: extracting paraphrases and generating new sentences. In *Proceedings of HLT-NAACL*, pages 102–109.

Rosenberg, Andrew and Julia Hirschberg. 2007. V-measure: A conditional entropy-based external cluster evaluation measure. In *Proceedings of EMNLP*, pages 410–420.

Shi, Jianbo and Jitendra Malik. 2000. Normalized cuts and image segmentation. *IEEE Transactions on Pattern Analysis and Machine Intelligence*, 22(8):888–905.

Siddharthan, Advaith, Ani Nenkova, and Kathleen McKeown. 2004. Syntactic simplification for improving content selection in multi-document summarization. In *Proceedings of COLING*, page 896.

Emotion Classification Using Massive Examples Extracted from the Web

Ryoko TOKUHISA[†‡] **Kentaro INUI**[‡] **Yuji MATSUMOTO**[‡]
[†]Toyota Central R&D Labs., INC.
Nagakute Aichi JAPAN
tokuhisa@mosk.tytlabs.co.jp
[‡]Nara Institute of Science and Technology
Ikoma Nara JAPAN
{ryoko-t,inui,matsu}@is.naist.jp

Abstract

In this paper, we propose a data-oriented method for inferring the emotion of a speaker conversing with a dialog system from the semantic content of an utterance. We first fully automatically obtain a huge collection of emotion-provoking event instances from the Web. With Japanese chosen as a target language, about 1.3 million emotion provoking event instances are extracted using an emotion lexicon and lexical patterns. We then decompose the emotion classification task into two sub-steps: sentiment polarity classification (coarse-grained emotion classification), and emotion classification (fine-grained emotion classification). For each subtask, the collection of emotion-proviking event instances is used as labelled examples to train a classifier. The results of our experiments indicate that our method significantly outperforms the baseline method. We also find that compared with the single-step model, which applies the emotion classifier directly to inputs, our two-step model significantly reduces sentiment polarity errors, which are considered fatal errors in real dialog applications.

1 Introduction

Previous research into human-computer interaction has mostly focused on task-oriented dialogs, where the goal is considered to be to achieve a given task as precisely and efficiently as possible by exchanging information required for the task through dialog (Allen et al., 1994, etc.). More recent research (Foster, 2007; Tokuhisa and Terashima, 2006, etc.), on the other hand, has been providing evidence for the importance of the affective or emotional aspect in a wider range of dialogic contexts, which has been largely neglected in the context of task-oriented dialogs.

A dialog system may be expected to serve, for example, as an *active listening* [1] partner of an elderly user living alone who sometimes wishes to have a chat. In such a context, the dialog system is expected to understand the user's emotions and sympathize with the user. For example, given an utterance *I traveled far to get to the shop, but it was closed* from the user, if the system could infer the user's emotion behind it, it would know that it would be appropriate to say *That's too bad* or *That's really disappointing*. It can be easily imagined that such affective behaviors of a dialog system would be beneficial not only for active listening but also for a wide variety of dialog purposes including even task-oriented dialogs.

To be capable of generating sympathetic responses, a dialog system needs a computational model that can infer the user's emotion behind his/her utterence. There have been a range of studies for building a model for classifying a user's emotions based on acoustic-prosodic features and facial expressions (Pantic and Rothkrantz, 2004, etc.). Such methods are, however, severely limited in that they tend to work well only when the user expresses his/her emotions by "exaggerated"

©2008. Licensed under the *Creative Commons Attribution-Noncommercial-Share Alike 3.0 Unported* license (http://creativecommons.org/licenses/by-nc-sa/3.0/). Some rights reserved.

[1] Active listening is a specific communication skill, based on the work of psychologist Carl Rogers, which involves giving free and undivided attention to the speaker (Robertson, 2005).

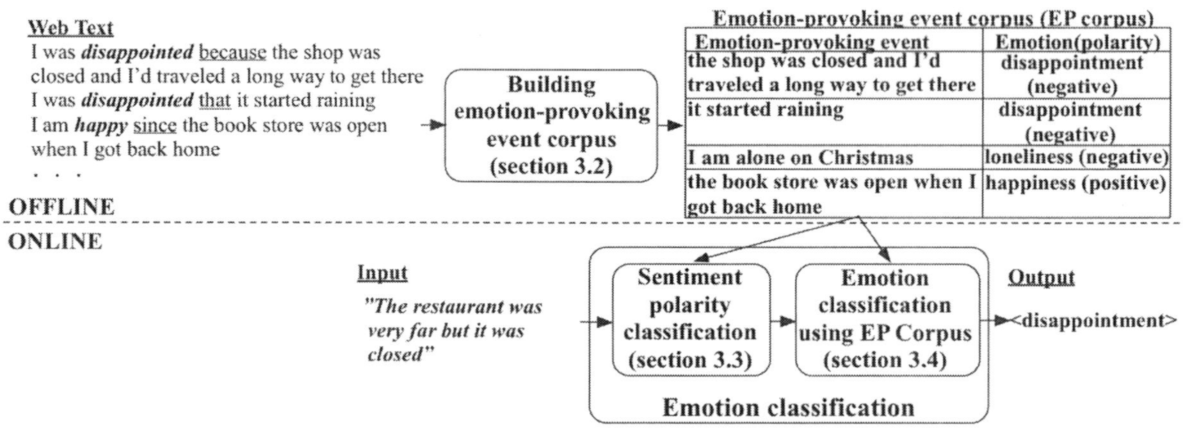

Figure 1: Overview of our approach to emotion classification

prosodic or facial expressions. Furthermore, what is required in generating sympathetic responses is the identification of the user's emotion in a finer grain-size. For example, in contrast to the above example of *disappointing*, one may expect the response to *My pet parrot died yesterday* should be *That's really sad*, wheras the response to *I may have forgotten to lock my house* should be *You're worried about that.*

In this paper, we address the above issue of emotion classification in the context of human-computer dialog, and demonstrate that massive examples of emotion-provoking events can be extracted from the Web with a reasonable accuracy and those examples can be used to build a semantic content-based model for fine-grained emotion classification.

2 Related Work

Recently, several studies have reported about dialog systems that are capable of classifying emotions in a human-computer dialog (Batliner et al., 2004; Ang et al., 2002; Litman and Forbes-Riley, 2004; Rotaru et al., 2005). ITSPOKE is a tutoring dialog system, that can recognize the user's emotion using acoustic-prosodic features and lexical features. However, the emotion classes are limited to *Uncertain* and *Non-Uncertain* because the purpose of ITSPOKE is to recognize the user's problem or discomfort in a tutoring dialog. Our goal, on the other hand, is to classify the user's emotions into more fine-grained emotion classes.

In a more general research context, while quite a few studies have been presented about opinion mining and sentiment analysis (Liu, 2006), research into fine-grained emotion classification has emerged only recently. There are two approaches commonly used in emotion classification: a rule-based approach and a statistical approach. Masum et al. (2007) and Chaumartin (2007) propose a rule-based approach to emotion classification. Chaumartin has developed a linguistic rule-based system, which classifies the emotions engendered by news headlines using the WordNet, SentiWordNet, and WordNet-Affect lexical resources. The system detects the sentiment polarity for each word in a news headline based on linguistic resources, and then attempts emotion classification by using rules based on its knowledge of sentence structures. The recall of this system is low, however, because of the limited coverage of the lexical resources. Regarding the statistical approach, Kozareva et al. (2007) apply the theory of (Hatzivassiloglou and McKeown, 1997) and (Turney, 2002) to emotion classification and propose a method based on the co-occurrence distribution over content words and six emotion words (e.g. joy, fear). For example, *birthday* appears more often with *joy*, while *war* appears more often with *fear*. However, the accuracy achieved by their method is not practical in applications assumed in this paper. As we demonstrate in Section 4, our method significantly outperforms Kozareva's method.

3 Emotion Classification

3.1 The basic idea

We consider the task of emotion classification as a classification problem where a given input sentence (a user's utterance) is to be classified either into such 10 emotion classes as given later in Table 1 or as ⟨neutral⟩ if no emotion is involved in the input. Since it is a classification problem, the task should be approached straightforwardly in a vari-

Table 1: Distribution of the emotion expressions and examples

Sentiment Polarity	10 Emotion Classes	Emotion lexicon (349 Japanese emotion words)	
		Total	Examples
Positive	happiness	90	嬉しい (happy), 狂喜 (joyful), 喜ぶ (glad), 歓ぶ (glad)
	pleasantness	7	楽しい (pleasant), 楽しむ (enjoy), 楽しめる (can enjoy)
	relief	5	安心 (relief), ほっと (relief)
Negative	fear	22	恐い (fear), 怖い (fear), 恐ろしい (frightening)
	sadness	21	悲しい (sad), 哀しい (sad), 悲しむ (feel sad)
	disappointment	15	がっかり (lose heart), がっくり (drop *one's* head)
	unpleasantness	109	嫌 (disgust), 嫌がる (dislike), 嫌い (dislike)
	loneliness	15	寂しい (lonely), 淋しい (lonely), わびしい (lonely)
	anxiety	17	不安 (anxiety), 心配 (anxiety), 気がかり (worry)
	anger	48	腹立たしい (angry), 腹立つ (get angry), 立腹 (angry)

ety of machine learning-based methods if a sufficient number of labelled examples were available. Our basic idea is to learn what emotion is typically provoked in what situation, from massive examples that can be collected from the Web. The development of this approach and its subsequent implementation has forced us to consider the following two issues.

First, we have to consider the quantity and accuracy of emotion-provoking examples to be collected. The process we use to collect emotion-provoking examples is illustrated in the upper half of Figure 1. For example, from the sentence *I was disappointed because the shop was closed and I'd I traveled a long way to get there*, pulled from the Web, we learn that the clause *the shop was closed and I'd traveled a long way to get there* is an example of an event that provokes ⟨disappointment⟩. In this paper, we refer to such an example as an *emotion-provoking event* and a collection of event-provoking events as an *emotion-provoking event corpus (an EP corpus)*. Details are described in Section 3.2.

Second, assuming that an EP corpus can be obtained, the next issue is how to use it for our emotion classification task. We propose a method whereby an input utterance (sentence) is classified in two steps, sentiment polarity classification followed by fine-grained emotion classification as shown in the lower half of Figure 1. Details are given in Sections 3.3 and 3.4.

3.2 Building an EP corpus

We used ten emotions *happiness, pleasantness, relief, fear, sadness, disappointment, unpleasantness, loneliness, anxiety, anger* in our emotion classification experiment. First, we built a hand-crafted lexicon of emotion words classified into the ten emotions. From the Japanese Evaluation Expression Dictionary created by Kobayashi et al. (2005), we identified 349 emotion words based on the definition of emotion words proposed by Teramura (1982). The distribution is shown in Table 1 with major examples.

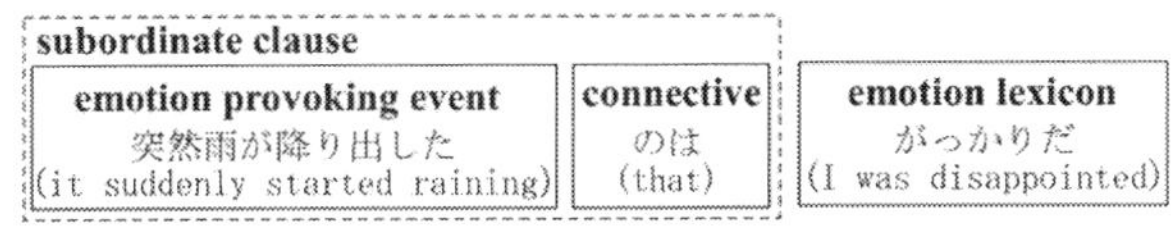

Figure 2: An example of a lexico-syntactic pattern

Table 2: Number of emotion-provoking events

10 Emotions	EP event	10 Emotions	EP event
happiness	387,275	disappoint-ment	106,284
pleasantness	209,682	unpleasantness	396,002
relief	46,228	loneliness	26,493
fear	49,516	anxiety	45,018
sadness	31,369	anger	8,478

We then went on to find sentences in the Web corpus that possibly contain emotion-provoking events. A subordinate clause was extracted as an emotion-provoking event instance if (a) it was subordinated to a matrix clause headed by an emotion word and (b) the relation between the subordinate and matrix clauses is marked by one of the following eight connectives: ので, から, ため, て, のは, のが, ことは, ことが. An example is given in Figure 2. In the sentence "突然雨が降り出したのはがっかりだ *(I was disappointed that it suddenly started raining)*", the subordinate clause "突然雨が降り出した *(it suddenly started raining)*" modifies "がっかりだ *(I was disappointed)*" with the connective "のは *(that)*". In this case, therefore, the event mention "突然雨が降り出した *(it suddenly started raining)*" is learned as an event instance that provokes⟨disappointment⟩.

Applying the emotion lexicon and the lexical patterns to the Japanese Web corpus (Kawahara and Kurohashi, 2006), which contains 500 million sentences, we were able to collect about 1.3 million events as causes of emotion. The distribution is shown in Table 2.

Tables 3 and 4 show the results of our evalua-

Table 4: Examples from in the EP corpus

EP-Corpus			Result of evaluation	
Emotion-provoking Event	Emotion word	10 Emotions (P/N)	Polarity	Emotion
花持ちが悪い (A flower died quickly)	残念だ (diappointed)	⟨disappointment(N)⟩	Correct	Correct
敵が多い (There are a lot of enemies)	飽きる (lose interest)	⟨unpleasantness(N)⟩	Correct	Context-dep.
ちんげん菜が多い (There is a lot of Chinese cabbage)	嬉しい (happy)	⟨happiness(P)⟩	Context-dep.	Context-dep.
ジュースが飲みたい (I would like to drink orange juice)	大変だ (terrible)	⟨unpleasantness(N)⟩	Error	Error

Table 3: Correctness of samples from the EP corpus

	Polarity	Emotion
Correct	1140 (57.0%)	988 (49.4%)
Context-dep.	678 (33.9%)	489 (24.5%)
Error	182 (9.1%)	523 (26.2%)

tion for the resultant EP corpus. One annotator, who was not the developer of the EP corpus, evaluated 2000 randomly chosen events. The "Polarity" column in Table 3 shows the results of evaluating whether the sentiment polarity of each event is correctly labelled, whereas the"Emotion" column shows the correctness at the level of the 10 emotion classes. The correctness of each example was evaluated as exemplified in Table 4. *Correct* indicates a correct example, *Contex-dep.* indicates a context-dependent example, and *Error* is an error example. For example, in the case of *There are a lot of enemies* in Table 4, the "Polarity" is *Correct* because it represents a negative emotion. However, its emotion class⟨unpleasantness⟩ is judged *Context-dep.*

As Table 3 shows, the Sentiment Polarity is correct in 57.0% of cases and partially correct (Correct + Context-dep.) in 90.9% of cases. On the other hand, the Emotion is correct in only 49.4% of cases and partially correct in 73.9% of cases. These figures may not seem very impressive. As far as its impact on the emotion classification accuracy is concerned, however, the use of our EP corpus, which requires no supervision, makes remarkable improvements upon Kozareva et al. (2007)'s unsupervised method as we show later.

3.3 Sentiment Polarity Classification

Given the large collection of emotion-labelled examples, it may seem straightforward to develop a trainable model for emotion classification. Before moving on to emotion classification, however, it should be noted that a user's input utterance may not involve any emotion. For example, if the user gives an utterance *I have a lunch at the school cafeteria every day*, it is not appropriate for the system to make any sympathetic response. In such a case, the user's input should be classified as ⟨neutral⟩.

The classification between *emotion-involved* and *neutral* is not necessarily a simple problem, however, because we have not found yet any practical method for collecting training examples of the class⟨neutral⟩. We cannot rely on the analogy to the pattern-based method we have adopted to collect emotion-provoking events — there seems no reliable lexico-syntactic pattern for extracting neutral examples. Alternatively, if the majority of the sentences on the Web were neutral, one would simply use a set of randomly sampled sentences as labelled data for ⟨neutral⟩. This strategy, however, does not work because neutral sentences are not the majority in real Web texts. As an attempt, we collected 1000 sentences randomly from the Web and investigated their distribution of sentiment polarity. The results, shown in Table 5, revealed that the ratio of neutral events was unexpectedly low. These results indicate the difficulty of collecting neutral events from Web documents.

Taking this problem into account, we adopt a two-step approach, where we first classify a given input into three sentiment polarity classes, either positive, negative or neutral, and then classify only those judged positive or negative into our 10 fine-grained emotion classes. In the first step, i.e. sentiment polarity classification, we use only the positive and negative examples stored in the EP corpus and assume sentence to be neutral if the output of the classification model is near the decision boundary. There are additional advantages in this approach. First, it is generally known that performing fine-grained classification after coarse classification often provides good results particularly when the number of the classes is large. Second, in the context of dialog, a misunderstanding the user's emotion at the sentiment polarity level would be a disaster. Imagine that the system says *You must be happy* when the user in fact feels sad. As we show in Section 4.2, such fatal errors can be reduced by taking the two-step approach.

Table 5: Distribution of the Sentiment polarity of sentences randomly sampled from the Web

Sentiment Polarity	Number	Ratio
positive	650	65.0%
negative	153	15.3%
neutral	117	11.7%
Context-dep.	80	8.0%

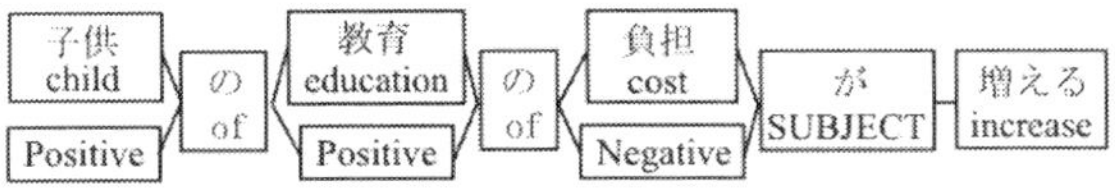

Figure 3: An example of a word-polarity lattice

Various methods have already been proposed for sentiment polarity classification, ranging from the use of co-occurrence with typical positive and negative words (Turney, 2002) to bag of words (Pang et al., 2002) and dependency structure (Kudo and Matsumoto, 2004). Our sentiment polarity classification model is trained with SVMs (Vapnik, 1995), and the features are {1-gram, 2-gram, 3-gram} of words and the sentiment polarity of the words themselves. Figure 3 illustrates how the sentence "子供の教育の負担が増える *(The cost of educating my child increases)*" is encoded to a feature vector. Here we assume the sentiment polarity of the "子供 *(child)*" and "教育 *(education)*" are positive, while the "負担 *(cost)*" is negative. These polarity values are represented in parallel with the corresponding words, as shown in Figure 3. By expanding {1-gram, 2-gram, 3-gram} in this lattice representation, the following list of features are extracted: 子供 *(child), Positive,* 子供 *(child)*-の *(of), Positive*-の *(of),* 子供 *(child)*-の *(of)*-教育 *(education), etc.*. The polarity value of each word is defined in our sentiment polarity dictionary, which includes 1880 positive words and 2490 negative words. To create this dictionary, one annotator identified positive and negative words from the 50 thousand most frequent words sampled from the Web. Table 6 shows some examples.

3.4 Emotion Classification

For fine-grained emotion classification, we propose a k-nearest-neighbor approach (kNN) using the EP corpus.

Given an input utterance, the kNN model retrieves k-most similar labelled examples from the EP corpus. Given the input *The restaurant was very far but it was closed* as Figure 1, for example, the kNN model finds similar labelled examples, say, labelled example {the shop was closed and I'd traveled far to get there} in the EP corpus.

Table 6: Examples of positive and negative words

P	子供 (child), 夏休み (summer vacation), 役立つ (useful), 成功する (succeed)
N	負担 (cost), 難しい (difficult), 難しい (difficult), 失敗する (failure)

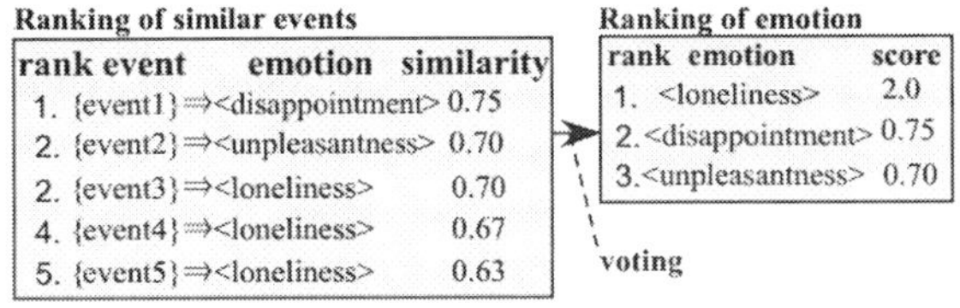

Figure 4: Emotion Classification by kNN (k=5)

For the similarity measure, we use cosine similarity between bag-of-words vectors; $sim(I, EP) = \frac{I \cdot EP}{|I||EP|}$ for input sentence I and an emotion-provoking event EPin the EP corpus. The score of each class is given by the sum of its similarity scores.

An example is presented in Figure 4. The emotion of the most similar event is ⟨disappointment⟩, that of the second-most similar event is ⟨unpleasantness⟩ tied with ⟨loneliness⟩. After calculating the sum for each emotion, the system outputs ⟨loneliness⟩ as the emotion for the input I because the score for ⟨loneliness⟩ is the highest.

4 Experiments

4.1 Sentiment polarity classification

We conducted experiments on sentiment polarity classification using the following two test sets:

TestSet1: The first test set was a set of utterances which 6 subject speakers produced interacting with our prototype dialog system. This data include 31 positive utterances, 34 negative utterances, and 25 neutral utterances.

TestSet2: For the second test set, we used the 1140 samples that were judged *Correct* with respect to sentiment polarity in Table 3. 491 samples (43.1%) were positive and 649 (56.9%) were negative. We then added 501 neutral sentences newly sampled from the Web. These samples are disjoint from the EP corpus used for training classifiers.

For each test set, we tested our sentiment polarity classifier in both the two-class (positive/negative) setting, where only positive or negative test samples were used, and the three-class (positive/negative/neutral) setting. The performance was evaluated in F-measure.

Table 7: F-values of sentiment polarity classification (positive/negative)

	TestSet1		TestSet2	
	Pos	Neg	Pos	Neg
Word	0.839	0.853	0.794	0.842
Word + Polarity	0.833	0.857	0.793	0.841

Table 8: F-values of sentiment polarity classification (positive/negative/neutral)

	TestSet1		TestSet2	
	Pos	Neg	Pos	Neg
Word	0.743	0.758	0.610	0.742
Word + Polarity	0.758	0.769	0.610	0.742

Table 7 shows the results for the two-class setting, whereas Table 8 shows the results for the three-class. "Word" denotes the model trained with only word n-gram features, whereas "Word+Polarity" denotes the model trained with n-gram features extracted from a word-polarity lattice (see Figure 3).

The results shown in Table 7 indicate that both the "Word" and "Word+Polarity" models are capable of separating positive samples from negative ones at a high level of accuracy. This is an important finding, given the degree of the correctness of our EP corpus. As we have shown in Table 3, only 57% of samples in our EP corpus are "exactly" correct in terms of sentiment polarity. The figures in Table 7 indicate that context-dependent samples are also useful for training a classifier. Table 7 also indicates that no significant difference is found between the "Word" and "Word+Polarity" models. In fact, we also examined another model which used dependency-structure information as well; however, no significant gain was achieved. From these results, we speculate that, as far as the two-class sentiment polarity problem is concerned, word n-gram features might be sufficient if a very large set of labelled data are available.

On the other hand, Table 8 indicates that the three-class problem is much harder than the two-class problem. Specifically, positive sentences tend to be classified as neutral. This method has to be improved in future models.

4.2 Emotion classification

For fine-grained emotion classification, we used the following three test sets:

TestSet1 (2p, best): Two annotators were asked to annotate each positive or negative sentence in TestSet1 with one of the 10 emotion classess. The annotators chose only one emotion class even if they thought several emotions would fit a sentence. Some examples are shown in Table 9. The inter-annotator agreement is κ=0.76 in the kappa statistic (Cohen, 1960). For sentences annotated with two different labels (i.e. in the cases where the two annotators disagreed with), both labels were considered correct in the experiments — a model's answer was considered correct if it was identical with either of the two labels.

TestSet1 (1p, acceptable): One of the above two annotators was asked to annotate each positive or negative sentence in TestSet1 with all the emotions involved in it. The number of emotions for a positive sentence was 1.48 on average, and 2.47 for negative sentences. Table 10 lists some examples. In the experiments, a model's answer was considered correct if it was identical with one of the labelled classes.

TestSet2: For TestSet2, we used the results of our judgments on the correctness for estimating the quality of the EP corpus described in Section 3.2.

In the experiments, the following two models were compared:

Baseline: The baseline model simulates the method proposed by (Kozareva et al., 2007). Given an input sentence, their model first estimates the pointwise mutual information (PMI) between each content word cw_j included in the sentence and emotion expression $e \in \{anger, disgust, fear, joy, sudness, surprise\}$ by $PMI(e, cw) = \log \frac{hits(e,cw)}{hits(e)hits(cw)}$, where $hits(x)$ is a hit count of word(s) x on a Web search engine. The model then calculates the score of each emotion class E_i by summing the PMI scores between each content word cw_j in the input and emotion expression e_i corresponding to that emotion class: $score(E_i) = \sum_j PMI(e_i, cw_j)$. Finally, the model chooses the best scored emotion class as an output. For our experiments, we selected the following 10 emotion expressions:

嬉しい (happy), 楽しい (pleased), 安心 (relieved), 恐い (affraid), 悲しい (sad), 残念 (disappointed), 嫌 (hate), 寂しい (lonely), 不安 (anxious), 腹立たしい (angry)

For hit counts, we used the Google search engine.

Table 9: Examples of TestSet1 (2p, best)

	Annotator A	Annotator B
クリスマスにプレゼントをもらった (I got a Christmas present)	⟨happiness⟩	⟨happiness⟩
友達の家に遊びに行く (I'm going to go to my friend's house)	⟨pleasantness⟩	⟨pleasantness⟩
花見に行ったら突然雨が降り出した (It rained suddenly when I went to see the cherry blossoms)	⟨sadness⟩	⟨sadness⟩
渋滞でほとんど動かない (My car can't move because of the traffic jam)	⟨unpleasantness⟩	⟨anger⟩

Table 10: Examples of TestSet1 (1p, acceptable)

	Annotator A
クリスマスにプレゼントをもらった (I got a Christmas present)	⟨happiness⟩
友達の家に遊びに行く (I'm going to go to my friend's house)	⟨pleasantness⟩, ⟨happiness⟩
花見に行ったら突然雨が降り出した (It rained suddenly when I went to see the cherry blossoms)	⟨anger⟩, ⟨sad⟩, ⟨unpleasantness⟩, ⟨disappointment⟩
渋滞でほとんど動かない (My car can't move because of the traffic jam)	⟨unpleasantness⟩, ⟨anger⟩

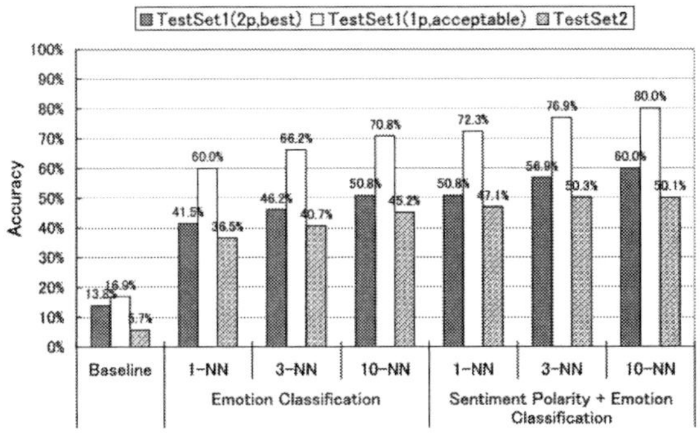

Figure 5: Results of emotion classification

k-NN: We tested the 1-NN, 3-NN and 10-NN models. In each model, we examined a single-step emotion classification and two-step emotion classification. In the former method, the kNN model retrieves k-most similar examples from the all of the EP corpus. In the latter method, when the sentiment polarity of the input utterance has obtained by the sentiment polarity classifier, the kNN model retrieves similar examples from only the examples whose sentiment polarity are the same as the input utterance in the EP corpus.

The results are shown in Figure 5. "Emotion Classification" denotes the single-step models, whereas "Sentiment Polarity + Emotion Classification" denotes the two-step models.

An important observation from Figure 5 is that our models remarkably outperformed the baseline. Apparently, an important motivation behind Kozareva et al. (2007)'s method is that it does not require any manual supervion. However, our models, which rely on emotion-provoking event instances, are also totally unsupervised — no supervision is required to collect emotion-provoking event instances. Given this commonality between the two methods, the superiority of our method in accuracy can be considered as a crucial advantage.

Regarding the issue of single-step vs. two-step, Figure 5 indicates that the two-step models tended to outperform the single-step models for all the test set. A paired t-test for TestSet2, however, did not reach significance [2]. So we next examined this issue in further detail.

As argued in Section 3.3, in the context of human-computer dialog, a misunderstanding of the user's emotion at the level of sentiment polarity would lead to a serious problem, which we call a *fatal error*. On the other hand, misclassifying a case of⟨happiness⟩ as, for example,⟨pleasantness⟩ may well be tolerable. Table 11 shows the ratio of fatal errors for each model. For TestSet2, the single-step 10-NN model made fatal errors in 30% of cases, while the two-step 10-NN model in only 17%. This improvement is statistically significant ($p<0.01$).

5 Conclusion

In this paper, we have addressed the issue of emotion classification assuming its potential applications to be human-computer dialog system including active-listening dialog. We first automatically collected a huge collection, as many as 1.3M, of emotion-provoking event instances from the Web. We then decomposed the emotion classification task into two sub-steps: sentiment polarity classification and emotion classification. In sentiment polarity classification, we used the EP-corpus as training data. The results of the polarity classification experiment showed that word n-gram features alone are more or less sufficient to classify positive and negative sentences when a very large amount of training data is available. In the emotion classification experiments, on the other hand,

[2]The data size of TestSet1 was not sufficient for statistical significance test

Table 11: Fatal error rate in emotion classification experiments

	Baseline	Emotion Classification			Sentiment Polarity
		1-NN	3-NN	10-NN	+ Emotion Classification
TestSet1	49.2%	29.2%	26.2%	24.6%	15.4%
TestSet2	41.5%	37.6%	32.8%	30.0%	17.0%

we adopted the k-nearest-neighbor (kNN) method. The results of the experiments showed that our method significantly outperformed the baseline method. The results also showed that our two-step emotion classification was effective for fine-grained emotion classification. Specifically, fatal errors were significantly reduced with sentiment polarity classification before fine-grained emotion classification.

For future work, we first need to examine other machine learning methods to see their advantages and disadvantages in our task. We also need an extensive improvement in identifying neutral sentences. Finally, we are planning to apply our model to the active-listening dialog system that our group has been developing and investigate its effects on the user's behavior.

References

Allen, James F., Lenhart K. Schubert, George Ferguson, Peter Heeman, Chung Hee Hwang, Tsuneaki Kato, Marc Light, Nathaniel G. Martin, Bradford W. Miller, Massimo Poesio, and David R. Traum. 1994. The TRAINS Project: A case study in building a conversational planning agent. *Journal of Experimental and Theoretical AI (JETAI)*.

Ang, Jeremy, Rajdip Dhillon, Ashley Krupski, Elizabeth Shriberg, and Andreas Stolcke. 2002. Prosody-Based Automatic Detection Of Annoyance And Frustration In Human-Computer Dialog. *Spoken Language Processing*, pages 2037–2040.

Batliner, A., K. Fischer, R. Huber, J. Spilker, and E. Noth. 2004. How to find trouble in communication. *Speech Communication*, 40(1-2):117–143.

Chaumartin, Francois-Regis. 2007. A knowledge-based system for headline sentiment tagging. *In Proceedings of the 4th International Workshop on Semantic Evaluations*.

Cohen, Jacob. 1960. A coefficient of agreement for nominal scales. *Educational and Psychological Measurement 20*, pages 37–46.

Foster, Mary Ellen. 2007. Enhancing Human-Computer Interaction with Embodied Conversational Agents. *Lecture Notes in Computer Science*, 4555:828–837.

Hatzivassiloglou, Vasileios and Kathleen R. McKeown. 1997. Predicting the semantic orientation of adjectives. *Proceedings of the 35th Annual Meeting of the Association for Computational Linguistics*.

Kawahara, Daisuke and Sadao Kurohashi. 2006. Case Frame Compilation from the Web using High-Performance Computing. *In Proceedings of the 5th International Conference on Language Resources and Evaluation*.

Kobayashi, Nozomi, Ryu Iida, Kentaro Inui, and Yuji Matsumoto. 2005. Collecting Evaluative Expressions for Opinion Extraction. *Lecture Notes in Artificial Intelligence*, 3248.

Kozareva, Zornitsa, Borja Navarro, Sonia Vazquez, and Andres Nibtoyo. 2007. UA-ZBSA: A Headline Emotion Classification through Web Information. *In Proceedings of the 4th International Workshop on Semantic Evaluations*.

Kudo, Taku and Yuji Matsumoto. 2004. A Boosting Algorithm for Classification of Semi-Structured Text. *In Proceedings of the EMNLP*.

Litman, Diane J. and Kate Forbes-Riley. 2004. Predicting Student Emotions in Computer-Human Tutoring Dialogues. *Proceedings of the 42nd Annual Meeting of the Association for Computational Linguistics*.

Liu, Bing. 2006. Web Data Mining. *Springer*, pages 411–440.

Masum, Shaikh Mostafa Al, Helmut Prendinger, and Mitsuru Ishizuka. 2007. Emotion Sensitive News Agent: An Approach Towards User Centric Emotion Sensing from the News. *In Proceedings of the IEEE/WIC/ACM International Conference on Web Intelligence*.

Pang, Bo, Lillian Lee, and Shivakumar Vaithyanathan. 2002. Thumbs up? sentiment classification using machine learning techniques. *Proceedings of the Conference on Empirical Methods in Natural Language Processing*, pages 76–86.

Pantic, Maja and Leon J. M. Rothkrantz. 2004. Facial Action Recognition for Facial Expression Analysis From Static Face Images. *IEEE Transactions on SMC-B*, 34(3):1449–1461.

Robertson, Kathryn. 2005. Active listening: more than just paying attention. *Aust Fam Physician*, 34(12):1053–1055.

Rotaru, Mihai, Diane J. Litman, and Katherine Forbes-Riley. 2005. Interactions between Speech Recognition Problems and User Emotions. *Proceedings 9th European Conference on Speech Communication and Technology*.

Teramura, Hideo. 1982. Japanese Syntax and Meaning. *Kurosio Publishers (in Japanese)*.

Tokuhisa, Ryoko and Ryuta Terashima. 2006. Relationship between Utterance and "Enthusiasm" in Non-Task-Orieinted Conversational Dialogue. *In Proceedings of the 7th SIGdial Workshop on Discourse and Dialogue*.

Turney, P.D. 2002. Thumbs up? thumbs down? semantic orientation applied to unsupervised classification of reviews. *Proceedings of the 40th Annual Meeting of the Association for Computational Linguistics*, pages 417–424.

Vapnik, Vladimir N. 1995. The Nature of Statistical Learning Theory. *Springer*.

Relational-Realizational Parsing

Reut Tsarfaty and Khalil Sima'an
Institute for Logic, Language and Computation, University of Amsterdam
Plantage Muidergracht 24, 1018TV, Amsterdam, The Netherlands
{rtsarfat,simaan}@science.uva.nl

Abstract

State-of-the-art statistical parsing models applied to free word-order languages tend to underperform compared to, e.g., parsing English. Constituency-based models often fail to capture generalizations that cannot be stated in structural terms, and dependency-based models employ a 'single-head' assumption that often breaks in the face of multiple exponence. In this paper we suggest that the position of a constituent is a *form* manifestation of its grammatical *function*, one among various possible means of realization. We develop the *Relational-Realizational* approach to parsing in which we untangle the *projection* of grammatical functions and their means of *realization* to allow for phrase-structure variability and morphological-syntactic interaction. We empirically demonstrate the application of our approach to parsing Modern Hebrew, obtaining 7% error reduction from previously reported results.

1 Introduction

Many broad-coverage statistical parsers to date are constituency-based with a Probabilistic Context-Free Grammar (PCFG) or a Stochastic Tree Substitution Grammar (STSG) at their backbone. The majority of such models belong to a *Head-Driven* paradigm, in which a head constituent is generated first, providing a positional anchor for subsequent (e.g., Markovian) sisters' generation.

© 2008. Licensed under the *Creative Commons Attribution-Noncommercial-Share Alike 3.0 Unported* license (http://creativecommons.org/licenses/by-nc-sa/3.0/). Some rights reserved.

Constituency-based models, lexicalized and unlexicalized alike, demonstrate state-of-the-art performance for parsing English (Charniak, 1997; Collins, 2003; Klein and Manning, 2003; Bod, 2003), yet a direct application of such models to parsing less configurational languages often fails to yield comparable results. The parameters of such parsers capture generalizations that are easily stated in structural terms (e.g., subjects linearly precede predicates, VPs dominate objects, etc.) which may not be adequate for parsing languages with less configurational character.

A different vein of research explores data-driven dependency-based parsing methods (e.g., (McDonald et al., 2005)) which seem to be intuitively more adequate for the task. It turns out, however, that even such models fail to provide the desired remedy. Recent reports by (Nivre, 2007) delineated a class of richly-inflected languages with relatively free word-order (including Greek, Basque, and Modern Standard Arabic) for which the parsers performed poorly, regardless of the parsing method used. The need for parsing methods that can effectively cope with such phenomena doesn't seem to have been eliminated by dependency parsing — perhaps quite the contrary.

The essential argument we promote here is that in order to deal with the kind of variation that is empirically observed cross-linguistically an alternative view of the generation process is required. Our *Relational-Realizational* parsing proposal, strongly inspired by Relational Grammar (Perlmutter, 1982), takes grammatical relations such as 'Subject' and 'Predicate' as central, primitive notions of the syntactic representation, and retains a distinction between the projection of such relations and the means by which they are realized. The grammar we develop here, formally represented as a PCFG, articulates two alternating generation phases: a *Relational* phase, in which a clause-level category projects a monostratal Relational Network (RN) representation for the clause, and a *Realizational* phase, in which the projected relations are realized in a certain surface configuration. Paradigmatic morphosyntactic representations are constructed for all non-terminal nodes, allowing for morphosyntactic interaction at various levels of the syntactic parse tree.

We illustrate the application of our theoretical reconstruction to the representation of clause-level categories in Modern Hebrew (MH) and their interaction with a handful of morphological features. The treebank grammar resulting from our application yields 13% error reduction relative to a treebank PCFG which uses the same information in the form of state-splits, and our best result shows a 7% error reduction over the best parsing results for MH so far. Through a quantitative and qualitative analysis we illustrate the advantages of the *Relational-Realizational* approach and its potential promise for parsing other "exotic" languages.

2 Background

Recent decades have seen a surge of interest in statistical models using a body of annotated text for learning the distributions of grammatically meaningful structures, in order to assign the most likely ones to unseen sentences. Probabilistic Context Free Grammars (PCFGs) have become popular in the articulation of such models, and unlexicalized treebank grammars (or representational variations thereof) were shown to perform reasonably well on English benchmark corpora (Johnson, 1998; Klein and Manning, 2003).

A major leap in the performance of PCFG-based statistical parsers has been introduced by the move towards a *Head-Driven* paradigm (Collins, 2003; Charniak, 1997), in which syntactic categories are enriched with head information percolated up the tree. The head-driven generation process allows one to model the relation between the information content of a constituent and the information content of its head-marked sister. At the same time, such models introduce a bias with respect to the positioning of a non-head constituent relative to its head-marked sister. The vast improvement in parsing results came about not without modeling costs, e.g., additional ad-hoc modifications for capturing complex structures such as conjunction.

An inherent difficulty with the application of constituency-based parsing models is the implicit assumption that the relation between the position of a constituent and its grammatical function is fully predictable. For languages with relatively free word-order, this assumption often breaks down. Distinguishing, e.g., "left" and "right" distributions for constituents of the same 'sort' implicitly takes the position of a constituent to be a primitive syntactic notion, and their grammatical function to be a secondary, derived one. Theoretical accounts show that this may be insufficient (Perlmutter, 1982). A subsequent difficulty with the head-driven paradigm, also shared by dependency-based parsing methods, is the stipulation that all grammatically relevant properties of a phrase are recovered from a single head. In fact, it is typologically established that grammatically meaningful properties of a constituent may jointly emerge from different surface forms dominated by it (*co-heads* or *multiple exponence* (Zwicky, 1993; Blevins, 2008)).[1]

The task we undertake here is to suggest a statistical generative parsing method which is linguistically plausible as well as technologically viable for parsing languages with relatively free word-order and variable means of realization. In what follows we remain within the computationally efficient framework of PCFGs, and propose a variation that draws on insights from syntactic and morphological theories that have been explored cross-linguistically.

3 Approach

3.1 Relational Grammars (RGs)

Relational Grammars (RGs) were introduced in the early 80's when attempts to find a universal definition for notions such as a 'Subject' in terms of various "behavioral properties" seemed to have failed (Perlmutter, 1982). The unsuccessful attempts to recover an adequate definition of grammatical functions in structural terms led to a revival of a view in which grammatical relations such as 'Subject' and 'Object' are primitive notions by

[1] We refrain here from referring to the increasingly popular approach of discriminative parsing, firstly, because we are interested in a generative parsing model that assigns a probability distribution to all sentence-structure pairs in the language, essentially allowing it to be used as a language model (e.g., in SR or SMT applications). Secondly, so far the features that have been explored in these frameworks are mainly those easily stated in structural terms, with not much effort towards modeling morphosyntactic interactions systematically.

which syntactic structures are defined (Postal and Perlmutter, 1977). This view proved useful for descriptive purposes, influencing the design of formalisms such as Arc-Pair grammars (Postal, 1982) and LFG (Bresnan, 1979).

The two main primitive elements used in RGs are (a) a set of nodes representing linguistic elements (which we refer to using upper case letters), and (b) a set of names of grammatical relations (which we refer to as $gr_1...gr_n$). RGs represent the fact that a linguistic element bears a certain relation to another element using a structure called an 'Arc', represented as $[gr_i(A, B)]$. Arcs are represented as arrows, with A the head of the Arc and B its tail, and a Relational Network (RN) is defined to be a set of Arcs that share a single head.[2]

Now, a few theoretical observations are due. Firstly, the essential difference between RGs and dependency-based grammars is that RNs take the linguistic element at the head of a network to be a clause-level category, not a particular surface form. The corresponding tails are then the various nominals bearing the different grammatical relations to the clause (including a 'Predicate', a 'Subject', an 'Object', etc.). In addition, RNs abstract away from elements such as auxiliary verbs and particles which do not have their own arc representation. RGs also differ from phrase-structure grammars in that their RNs are unordered. Therefore, linear precedence need not play a role in stating generalizations. RGs differ from both constituency- and dependency-based formalisms in that they do not weigh heavily the 'single-head' assumption – RNs may delineate a whole chunk as bearing a certain grammatical relation to the clause.

The set-theoretic notion of RNs in RGs abstracts away from surface phenomena crucial for generating phrase-structure trees. Thus, we next turn to modeling how grammatical relations are realized.

3.2 Form, Function and Separation

Morphological phenomena such as suprasegmentation, interdigitation, reduplication, subtractive morphology, templatic morphology, and methathesis demonstrate that it is sometimes impossible to find a direct correspondence between a certain part of a word (a 'morpheme') and the function it has in altering the word's meaning (Anderson, 1992). Attempts to model such morphological phenomena brought forward the hypothesis that 'form' and 'function' need not stand in one-to-one correspondence, and that one is not necessarily immediately predicted by the other. This hypothesis is known as the "Separation Hypothesis" (Beard, 1988). The problem of modeling certain surface phenomena then boils down to modeling form and function correlations, bearing in mind that these may be quite complex.

Bringing this general notion of separation into the syntactic derivation, we propose to view the position of a constituent in a phrase as its *form* and the articulated grammatical relation as its *function*. The task of learning the position of different constituents realizing the grammatical relations in an RN is now delegated to a statistical component. A set of parameters which we refer to as "configuration" determines the syntactic *position* in which each of the grammatical relations is to be realized.

3.3 Morphosyntactic Representations

In order to connect the abstract RN representation with the constituents that syntactic parse trees are "made of" we propose to view the internal nodes of a tree as *Morphosyntactic Paradigms*. Our morphosyntactic representation for constituents, loosely inspired by (Anderson, 1992), is a structured representation of morphological and syntactic properties for an internal node in the parse tree. In our model, the morphological features associated with a syntactic constituent are percolated from its dominated surface forms, and we allow the specification of head (PoS tag) information and structural features such as vertical markovization. Given the grammatical relation an element bears to a clause, it is statistically feasible to learn the morphosyntactic paradigm by which it is realized.

4 The Model

4.1 The Generative Model

Let $S_p \rightarrow \langle S_{c_1}\text{-}gr_1 \ldots S_{c_n}\text{-}gr_n \rangle$ be a context-free rule where S_p is the morphosyntactic representation of a parent constituent, $gr_1...gr_n$ are the grammatical relations forming its RN, and $\langle S_{c_1} \ldots S_{c_n} \rangle$ are ordered morphosyntactic representations of the child constituents bearing the respective relations to the parent. Our grammar then conceptualizes the generation of such a rule in three phases:

[2] RGs also define the notion of a stratum, a single level of syntactic representation, and for the current discussion we assume a monostratal representation. We do not claim that our framework is capable of dealing with the full range of phenomena multistratal RNs were shown to account for, yet there is nothing in our proposal that excludes extending the representation into a multistratal framework that does so.

- **Projection:**
  $S_p \rightarrow \{gr_i\}_{i=1}^n @S_p$
- **Configuration:**
  $\{gr_i\}_{i=1}^n @S_p \rightarrow \langle gr_1 @S_p \ldots gr_n @S_p\rangle$
- **Realization:**
  $\{gr_i @S_p \rightarrow S_{c_i}\}_{i=1}^n$

In the projection stage we generate the set of grammatical relations in the RN of a constituent. In the configuration stage we order these grammatical relations, and in realization we generate the morphosyntactic representation of each child constituent given the relation to its parent. Figure (1) shows the application of this process to two clauses bearing identical RNs that are in turn realized in different possible configurations.

This three-step process does not generate functional elements (such as auxiliary verbs and special-purpose particles) that are outside of constituents' RNs. We thus let the configuration stage place obligatory or optional "realizational slots" between the ordered elements (marked $gr_i : gr_j$), signalling periphrastic adpositions and/or modification. Note that modification may introduce more than one constituent, to be generated in realization.

- **Projection:**
  $S_p \rightarrow \{gr_i\}_{i=1}^n @S_p$
- **Configuration:**
  $\{gr_i\}_{i=1}^n @S_p \rightarrow$
  $\langle gr_0 : gr_1 @S_p \; gr_1 @S_p \ldots gr_n : gr_{n+1} @S_p\rangle$
- **Realization:**
  $\{gr_i @S_p \rightarrow S_{c_i}\}_{i=1}^n$
  $\{gr_i : gr_{i+1} @S_p \rightarrow \langle S_{c_{i_1}} \ldots S_{c_{i_{m_i}}}\rangle\}_{i=0}^n$

In figure (2), the configuration stage reserves a slot for an obligatory punctuation mark at the end of an affirmative sentence. It further reserves a slot for an optional adverbial modifier at a position commonly employed in MH for interjections.

In the current framework, grammatical relations may be realized in a certain surface position via configuration, or using explicit morphological marking per grammatical relation independently of linear context. Figure (3) demonstrates how the realization phase models the correlation between grammatical relations and morphological information percolated from dominated surface forms. In particular, our model can capture the interaction between marked features, e.g., the 'exclusive or' relation between definiteness and accusativity in marking direct objects in MH (Danon, 2001).

Finally, a conjunction structure in our model is simply an RN representation of multiple morphosyntactically equivalent conjuncts, as illustrated in figure (4). This modeling choice avoids the need to stipulate a single head for such structures (cf. head-driven processes) and allows the different conjuncts to share a realization distribution — essentially implying homogeneity in the assignment of heads and morphosyntactic features across conjuncts.

4.2 The Probabilistic Model

Our probablistic model is a PCFG, where CFG rules capture the three stages of generation. Every time we apply our projection-configuration-realization cycle we replace the rule probability with the probabilities of the three stages, multiplied ($n + \sum_{i=0}^n m_i$ daugthers , gr_0=gr_{n+1}=null).

$$
\begin{aligned}
&P(\langle S_{c_{i_1}}, .., S_{c_{i_{m_i}}} S_{c_i}\text{-}gr_i, S_{c_{i+1_1}}, .., S_{c_{i+1_{m_{i+1}}}}\rangle_{i=0}^n | S_p) = \\
&\quad P(\{gr_i\}_{i=1}^n | S_p) \times \\
&\quad P(\langle gr_0 : gr_1, g_1, \ldots\rangle | \{gr_i\}_{i=1}^n, S_p) \times \\
&\quad \textstyle\prod_{i=1}^n P(S_{c_i} | gr_i, S_p) \times \\
&\quad P(\langle S_{c_{0_1}}, ..., S_{c_{0_{m_0}}}\rangle | gr_0 : gr_1, S_p) \times \\
&\quad \textstyle\prod_{i=1}^n P(\langle S_{c_{i_1}}, ..., S_{c_{i_{m_i}}}\rangle | gr_i : gr_{i+1}, S_p)
\end{aligned}
$$

The multiplication implements the independence assumption between form and function underlying the Separation Hypothesis, and the conditioning we articulate captures one possible way to model a systematic many-to-many correspondence.

4.3 The Grammar

We use a probabilistic treebank grammar in which the different parameters and their probability distributions are read off and estimated from the treebank trees. Clause-level (or clause-like) constituents such as S, SQ, FRAG, FRAGQ, internally complex VPs and a small number NPs can head RNs. For the rest we use flat CFG rules. We use a limited set of grammatical relations, namely, 'Predicate', 'Subject', 'Object' and 'Complement' — making the distinction between a nominal complement and a verbal (infinitival) one. Our linguistic elements are morphosyntactic representations of labeled non-terminal constituents, where the morphosyntactic representations of constituents incorporate morphological information percolated from surface forms and syntactic information about the constituent's environment.

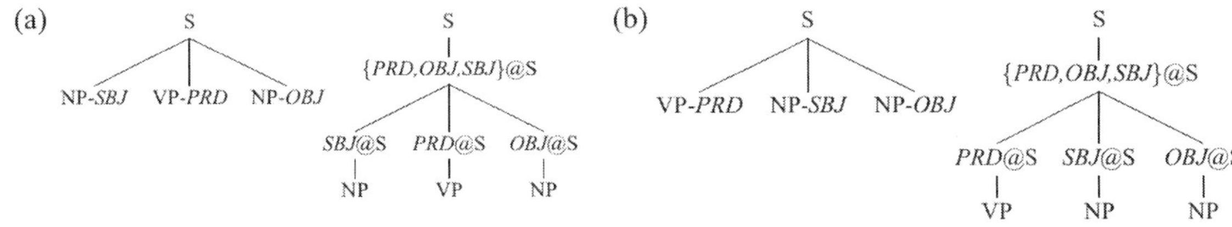

Figure 1: **Generating Canonical and Non-Canonical Configurations:** The CF depictions of the S level constituents at the LHS of (a) and (b) are distinct, whereas the *RR*-CFG representations at the RHS of (a) and (b) share the **projection** of GRs and differs in their **configuration** — while (a) generates an SVO order, (b) generates a so-called Verb-Initial (VI) construction.

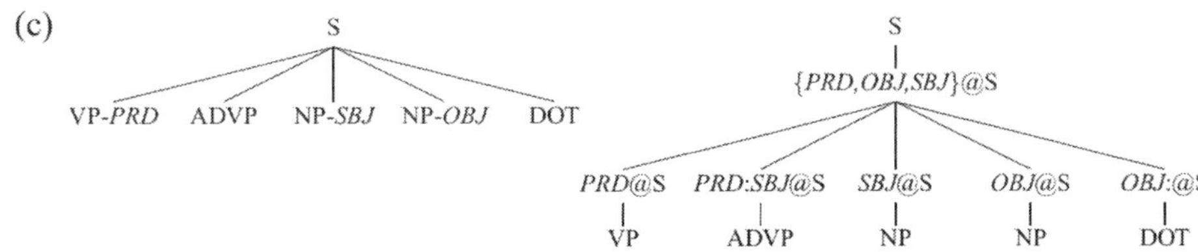

Figure 2: **Generating Adjunction and Periphrastic Configurations:** The CF depiction of S at the LHS of (c) generates complements, adjuncts, and punctuation in one go, whereas the RR-CFG representation at the RHS generates first the projection of core grammatical elements and then the configuration of a modified affirmative sentence in which they are realized. (Similarly, realising a question configuration using inversion in, e.g., English, naturally follows).

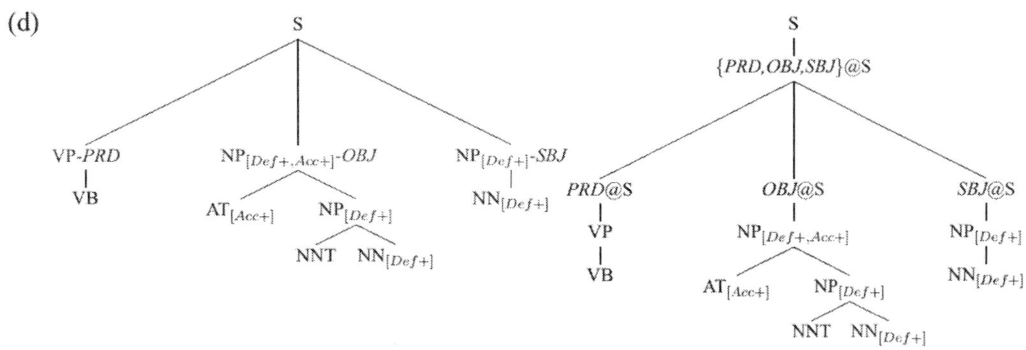

Figure 3: **Realizing Grammatical Relations with bounded and unbounded Morphemes:** The CF depiction of the S level constituent at the LHS of (d) shows a strong dependence between the position of syntactic constituents and the morphologically realized features percolated from lower surface forms. In the *RR*-CFG representation at the RHS the feature distribution among sub constituents is dependent on grammatical relations, independently of their positioning. The realization stage generates a morphosyntactic paradigm in one go, allowing to capture meaningful collocations and idiosyncrasies, e.g., the Xor relation of the *Acc+* and *def+* features when marking direct objects in MH (Danon, 2001).

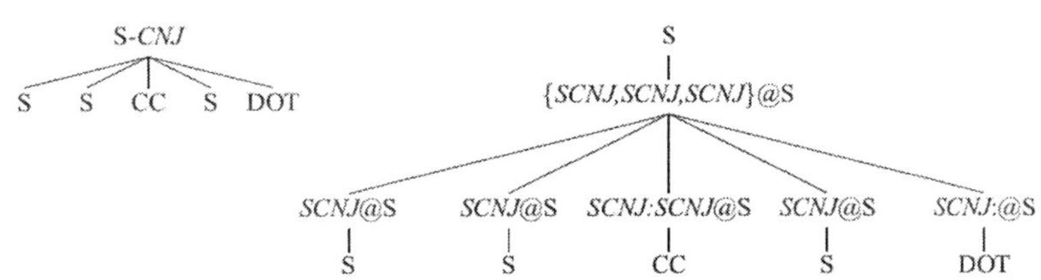

Figure 4: **Generating a Conjunction Structure:** The conjunction structure in the LHS of (e) is generated by the *RR*-CFG on the RHS in three stages. First, a relational network of finite number of conjuncts is generated, then a configuration for the conjuncts and conjunction markers (in MH, a CC before the last conjunct) is proposed, and finally the different conjuncts are generated conditioned on the same grammatical relation and the same parent. (Note that the possibility of different means for realizing conjunction, e.g., using morphemes, punctuation or multiple adpositions, falls out naturally from this setup.)

5 Experiments

Data The data we use is taken from the Modern Hebrew Treebank (MHTB) (Sima'an et al., 2001) which consists of 6501 sentences from the newspaper 'haaretz' annotated with phrase-structure trees and decorated with various morphological and functional features. We use version 2.0 of the treebank[3] which we processed and head-annotated as in (Tsarfaty and Sima'an, 2007). We experimented with sentences 1–500 (development set) and sentences 501–6001 (training set), and used sentences 6001-6501 (test set) for confirming our best result.

Models Our *Plain* models use the coarse-level MHTB category-labels enriched with various morphological features. Our morphological representation **Base** varies with respect to the use of the percolated features definiteness **Def** and accusativity **Acc**. Constituents' morphosyntactic representations enriched with their head PoS tag are referred to as *Head* and grand-parent encodings as *Parent*. For each combination of morphological and syntactic features we experimented with a state-split PCFG and with our *RR*-PCFG implementation.

Procedure We read off our models' parameters from the decorated phrase-structure trees in the MHTB, and use relative frequency estimation to instantiate their probability distributions. We smooth lexical rules using a PoS-tags distribution we learn for rare-words, where the 'rare' threshold is set to 1. We then use BitPar, a general purpose chart parser,[4] to find the most likely structures, and we extract the corresponding coarse-grained tree-skeletons for the purpose of evaluation.[5] We use PARSEVAL measures to quantitatively evaluate our models and perform a qualitative analysis of the resulting parse trees.

Results Table 1 shows the average F-Measure value for all sentences of length ≤40 in our development set with/without punctuation. The naïve baseline implementation for our experiments, the **Base***Plain* PCFG, performs at the level of 67.61/68.67 (comparable to the baseline reported in (Tsarfaty and Sima'an, 2007)). For all models in the *Plain* column the simple PCFG outperforms the *RR*-variety. Yet, the contribution of percolated morphological features is higher with the *RR*-PCFG than with the simple PCFG.

Morphology	*Syntax*	*Plain*	*Head*	*Parent*	*ParentHead*
Base	(PCFG)	67.61/68.77	71.01/72.48	73.56/73.79	73.44/73.61
	(*RR*-PCFG)	65.86/66.86	71.84/72.76	74.06/74.28	75.13/75.29
BaseDef	(PCFG)	67.68/68.86	71.17/72.47	74.13/74.39	72.54/72.79
	(*RR*-PCFG)	66.65/67.86	73.09/74.13	74.59/74.59	76.05/76.34
BaseDefAcc	(PCFG)	68.11/69.30	71.50/72.75	74.16/ 74.41	72.77/73.01
	(*RR*-PCFG)	67.13/68.01	73.63/74.69	74.65/74.79	**76.15/ 76.43**

Table 1: **Parsing Results for Sentences of Length** $<$ 40 **in the Development Set:** Averaged F-Measure With/Without Punctuation. **Base** refers to coarse syntactic categories, **Def** indicates percolating definiteness values, **Acc** indicated percolating accusativity marking. The underlined results replicate previously reported results in similar settings.

Moving to the *Head* column, we see that all *RR*-models already outperform their enriched PCFG counterparts. Again, morphological information contributes more to the *RR*-variety. The best result for this column, achieved by the **BaseDefAcc***Head* *RR*-model (63.73/64.69), outperforms its PCFG counterpart as well as all two-dimensional models reported by (Tsarfaty and Sima'an, 2007). In the *Parent* column), our *RR*-variety continues to outperform the PCFG albeit in an insignificant rate. (Both results are at the same level as the best model of (Tsarfaty and Sima'an, 2007).)

Finally, for all models in the *ParentHead* column the *RR*-models outperform their PCFG counterparts to a significant degree. Similarly to the *Head* column, the more morphological information is added, the greater the improvement is. Our best *RR*-model, **BaseDefAcc***ParentHead*, scores almost 10pt (25% error reduction) more than the *Plain* PCFG, it is about 3.5pt better (13% error reduction) than a state-split PCFG using the same information, and almost 2pt (7% error reduction) more than the best results reported for MH so far.

We confirmed the results of our best model on our test set, for which our baseline (**Base***Plain*) obtained 69.63/70.31. The enriched PCFG of **DaseDefAcc***HeadParent* yields 73.66/73.86 whereas the *RR*-PCFG yields 75.83/75.89. The overall performance for PCFGs is higher on this set, yet the *RR*-model shows a notable improvement (about 9% error reduction).

6 Analysis and Discussion

The trends in our quantitative analysis suggest that the *RR*-models are more powerful in exploiting different sorts of information encoded in parse

[3] `http://www.mila.cs.technion.ac.il/english/resources/corpora/treebank/ver2.0/index.html`

[4] `:http://www.ims.uni-stuttgart.de/tcl/SOFTWARE/BitPar.html`

[5] Our setup is comparable to English, which means that our surface forms are segmented per PoS tag without specifying their respective PoS tags and morphological features.

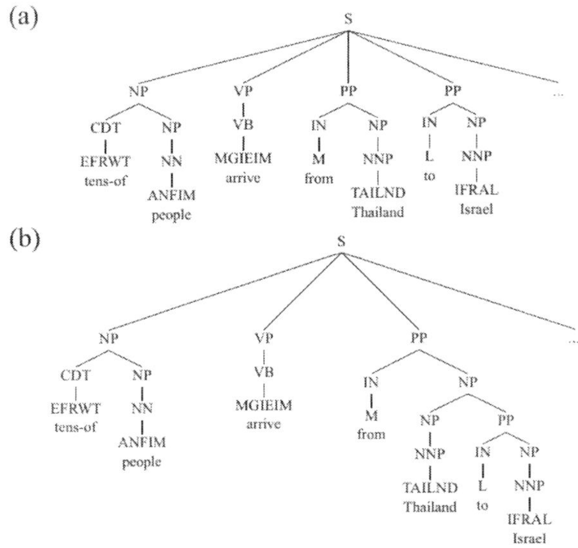

Figure 5: **Qualitative Analysis of Sentence (Fragment) #1:** (a) is the gold tree fragment, correctly predicted by our best *RR*-PCFG model. (b) is the tree fragment predicted by the PCFG corresponding to previously reported results.

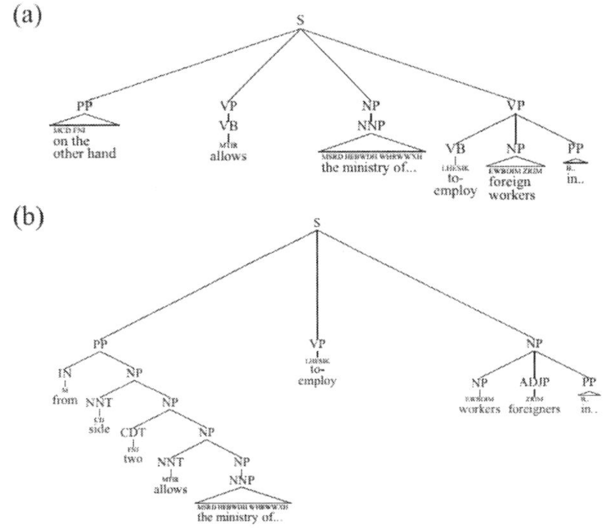

Figure 6: **Qualitative Analysis of Sentence (Fragment) #4:** (a) is the gold tree fragment, correctly predicted by our best *RR*-PCFG model. (b) is the tree fragment predicted by the PCFG corresponding to previously reported results.

trees, be it morphological information coming from dominated surface forms or functional information on top of syntactic categories.

We have shown that head information, which has very little contribution to parsing accuracy as a mere state-split, turns out to have crucial effects within the *RR*-models. For state-splits based PCFGs, adding head information brings about a category fragmentation and decreasing performance. The separation between form and function we articulate in the *RR*-approach allows us to capture generalizations concerning the distribution of syntactic constituents under heads based on their grammatical function, and use fine-grained features to predict their morphosyntactic behaviour.

We have further shown that morphological information contributes a substantial improvement when adopting the *RR*-approach, which is inline with the linguistic insight that there is a correlation between morphological marking on top of surface forms and the grammatical function their dominating constituents realize. Morphological information is particularly useful in the presence of heads. Taken together, head and percolated features implement a rather complete conceptualization of multiple exponence.

To wrap up the discussion, we leave numbers aside and concentrate on the *kind* of structures predicted by our best model in comparison to the ones suggested by previously reported unlexicalized PCFGs ((Tsarfaty and Sima'an, 2007), underlined in our table). Due to lack of space we only discuss errors found within the first 10 parsed sentence, yet we note that the qualitative trend we describe here persists throughout our development set. Figures (5) and (6) show a gold tree (a fragment of sentence #1) correctly predicted by our best *RR*-model (a) in comparison with the one predicted by the respective PCFG (b). The tree fragment in figure (5) shows that the *RR*-grammar bracketed and attached correctly all the constituents that bear grammatical relations to the S clause (5a). The corresponding PCFG conflated the "to" and "from" phrases to a rather meaningless prepositional phrase (5b). For (a fragment of) sentence #4 in our set (figure 6) the *RR*-model recovered all grammatically meaningful constituents under the S clause and under the internal VP (6a). Notably, the PCFG in (6b) recovered *none* of them. Both grammars make attachment mistakes internal to complex NPs, but the *RR*-model is better at identifying higher level constituents that correlate with meaningful grammatical functions.

Our qualitative analysis suggests that our model is even more powerful than our quantitative analysis indicates, yet we leave the discussion of better ways to quantify this for future research.

A Note on Related Work Studies on parsing MH to date concentrate mostly on spelling out the integration of a PCFG parser with a morphological disambiguation component (e.g., (Tsarfaty, 2006; Goldberg and Tsarfaty, 2008)). On a setup identical to ours (gold segmentation, no PoS) the latter obtained 70pt. (Tsarfaty and Sima'an,

2007) examined the contribution of horizontal and vertical conditioning to an unlexicalized MH parser and concluded that head-driven Markovization performs below the level of vertical conditioning enriched with percolated features. We do not know of existing dependency-parsers applied to parsing MH or mildly-context-sensitive broad-coverage parsers applied to parsing a Semitic language.[6] To the best of our knowledge, this is the first fully generative probabilistic framework that models explicitly morpho-syntactic interaction to enhance parsing for non-configrational languages.

7 Conclusion

Projection and *Realization* are two sides of the same coin. *Projection* determines *which* grammatical relations appear in the syntactic representation, and *Realization* determines *how* such relations are realized. We suggest that the *Relational-Realizational* (*RR*) approach is adequate for parsing languages characteristically different from English, and we illustrate it with an application to parsing MH. We show that our approach to modeling the interaction between syntactic categories and a handful of percolated features already yields a notable improvement in parsing accuracy and substantially improves the quality of suggested parses. Incorporating additional functional and morphological information, we expect, will help bridging the gap in performance between Hebrew and configurational languages such as English.

Acknowledgements We thank Remko Scha, Jelle Zuidema, Yoav Goldberg, and three anonymous reviewers for comments on earlier drafts. The first author wishes to thank Jim Blevins, Julia Hockenmeir, Mark Johnson, Kevin Knight, Chris Manning, Joakim Nivre and Gerald Penn for stimulating discussion. Errors are our own. The work of the first author is funded by the Dutch Science Foundation (NWO), grant number 017.001.271.

References

Anderson, S. R. 1992. *A-Morphus Morphology*. Cambridge University Press.

Beard, R. 1988. The Separation of Derivation and Affixation: Toward a Lexeme-Morpheme Base Morphology. *Quarderni di semantica*, pages 277–287.

Blevins, J. P. 2008. Periphrasis as Syntactic Exponence. In Ackerman, F., J.P. Blevins, and G.S. Stump, editors, *Patterns in Paradigms*. CSLI.

Bod, R. 2003. An Efficient Implementation of a New Dop Model. In *Proceedings of EACL*.

Bresnan, Joan. 1979. *A Theory of Grammatical Representation*. Duplicated Lecture Notes. Department of Linguistics and Philosophy, MIT.

Charniak, E. 1997. Statistical Parsing with a Context-Free Grammar and Word Statistics. In *AAAI/IAAI*.

Collins, M. 2003. Head-Driven Statistical Models for Natural Language Parsing. *Comp. Linguistics*.

Danon, G. 2001. Syntactic Definiteness in the Grammar of Modern Hebrew. *Linguistics*, 6(39).

Goldberg, Y. and R. Tsarfaty. 2008. A Single Generative Framework for Joint Morphological Segmentation and Syntactic Parsing. In *Proceedings of ACL*.

Johnson, M. 1998. PCFG Models of Linguistic Tree Representations. *Computational Linguistics*, 24(4).

Klein, D. and C. Manning. 2003. Accurate Unlexicalized Parsing. In *Proceedings of ACL*.

McDonald, R., F. Pereira, K. Ribarov, and J. Hajič. 2005. Non-Projective Dependency Parsing using Spanning Tree Algorithms. In *Proceedings of HLT*.

Nivre, J. 2007. Data-driven Dependency Parsing Across Languages and Domains; Perspectives from the CoNLL-2007 Shared Task. In *Proceedings of IWPT*.

Perlmutter, D. M. 1982. Syntactic Representation, Syntactic levels, and the Notion of Subject. In Jacobson, Pauline and Geoffrey Pullum, editors, *The Nature of Syntactic Representation*. Springer.

Postal, P. M. and D. M. Perlmutter. 1977. Toward a Universal Characterization of Passivization. In *BLS3*.

Postal, P. M. 1982. Some Arc-Pair Grammar Decriptions. In Jacobson, P. and G. K. Pullum, editors, *The Nature of Syntactic Representation*. Dordrecht.

Sima'an, K., A. Itai, Y. Winter, A. Altman, and N. Nativ. 2001. Building a Tree-Bank for Modern Hebrew Text. In *Traitement Automatique des Langues*.

Tsarfaty, R. and K. Sima'an. 2007. Three-Dimensional Parametrization for Parsing Morphologically Rich Languages. In *Proceedings of IWPT*.

Tsarfaty, R. 2006. Integrated Morphological and Syntactic Disambiguation for Modern Hebrew. In *Proceeding of ACL-SRW*.

Zwicky, A. M. 1993. Heads, Bases, and Functors. In Corbett, G.G., N. Fraser, and S. McGlashan, editors, *Heads in Grammatical Theory*. Cambridge.

[6] Parsing MSA has been explored with a treebank three times as large as ours using a head-driven lexicalized parser obtaining around 78% accuracy (`http://papers.ldc.upenn.edu/`). The input setup assumes gold segmentation as well as PoS tags information and some diacritization.

Training Conditional Random Fields Using Incomplete Annotations

Yuta Tsuboi, Hisashi Kashima
Tokyo Research Laboratory,
IBM Research, IBM Japan, Ltd
Yamato, Kanagawa 242-8502, Japan
{yutat,hkashima}@jp.ibm.com

Shinsuke Mori
Academic Center for Computing and
Media Studies, Kyoto University
Sakyo-ku, Kyoto 606-8501, Japan
forest@i.kyoto-u.ac.jp

Hiroki Oda
Shinagawa, Tokyo, Japan
oda@fw.ipsj.or.jp

Yuji Matsumoto
Graduate School of Information Science,
Nara Institute of Science and Technology
Takayama, Ikoma, Nara 630-0101, Japan
matsu@is.naist.jp

Abstract

We address corpus building situations, where complete annotations to the whole corpus is time consuming and unrealistic. Thus, annotation is done only on crucial part of sentences, or contains unresolved label ambiguities. We propose a parameter estimation method for Conditional Random Fields (CRFs), which enables us to use such incomplete annotations. We show promising results of our method as applied to two types of NLP tasks: a domain adaptation task of a Japanese word segmentation using partial annotations, and a part-of-speech tagging task using ambiguous tags in the Penn treebank corpus.

1 Introduction

Annotated linguistic corpora are essential for building statistical NLP systems. Most of the corpora that are well-known in NLP communities are completely-annotated in general. However it is quite common that the available annotations are partial or ambiguous in practical applications. For example, in domain adaptation situations, it is time-consuming to annotate all of the elements in a sentence. Rather, it is efficient to annotate certain parts of sentences which include domain-specific expressions. In Section 2.1, as an example of such efficient annotation, we will describe the effectiveness of partial annotations in the domain adaptation task for Japanese word segmentation (JWS). In addition, if the annotators are domain experts rather than linguists, they are unlikely to be confident about the annotation policies and may prefer to be allowed to defer some linguistically complex decisions. For many NLP tasks, it is sometimes difficult to decide which label is appropriate in a particular context. In Section 2.2, we show that such ambiguous annotations exist even in a widely used corpus, the Penn treebank (PTB) corpus.

This motivated us to seek to incorporate such incomplete annotations into a state of the art machine learning technique. One of the recent advances in statistical NLP is Conditional Random Fields (CRFs) (Lafferty et al., 2001) that evaluate the global consistency of the complete structures for both parameter estimation and structure inference, instead of optimizing the local configurations independently. This feature is suited to many NLP tasks that include correlations between elements in the output structure, such as the interrelation of part-of-speech (POS) tags in a sentence. However, conventional CRF algorithms require fully annotated sentences. To incorporate incomplete annotations into CRFs, we extend the structured output problem in Section 3. We focus on partial annotations or ambiguous annotations in this paper. We also propose a parameter estimation method for CRFs using incompletely annotated corpora in Section 4. The proposed method marginalizes out the unknown labels so as to optimize the likelihood of a set of possible label structures which are consistent with given incomplete annotations.

We conducted two types of experiments and observed promising results in both of them. One was a domain adaptation task for JWS to assess the proposed method for partially annotated data. The other was a POS tagging task using ambiguous annotations that are contained in the PTB corpus. We summarize related work in Section 6, and conclude

© 2008. Licensed under the *Creative Commons Attribution-Noncommercial-Share Alike 3.0 Unported* license (http://creativecommons.org/licenses/by-nc-sa/3.0/). Some rights reserved.

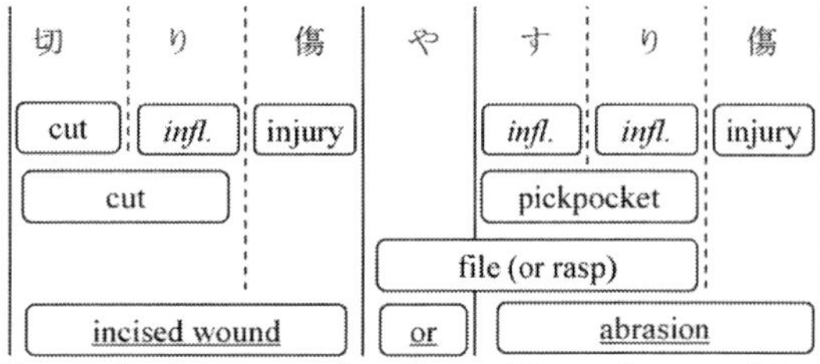

Figure 1: An example of word boundary ambiguities: *infl.* stands for an inflectional suffix of a verb.

in Section 7.

2 Incomplete Annotations

2.1 Partial Annotations

In this section, we describe an example of an efficient annotation which assigns partial word boundaries for the JWS task.

It is not trivial to detect word boundaries for non-segmented languages such as Japanese or Chinese. For example, the correct segmentation of the Japanese phrase "切り傷やすり傷" (incised wound or abrasion) is shown by the lowest boxes segmented by the solid lines in Figure 1. However, there are several overlapping segmentation candidates, which are shown by the other boxes, and possible segmentation by the dashed lines. Thus, the decisions on the word segmentation require considering the context, so simple dictionary lookup approach is not appropriate. Therefore statistical methods have been successfully used for JWS tasks. Previous work (Kudo et al., 2004) showed CRFs outperform generative Markov models and discriminative history-based methods in JWS. In practice, a statistical word segment analyzer tends to perform worse for text from different domains, so that additional annotations for each target domain are required. A major cause of errors is the occurrence of unknown words. For example, if "すり傷" (abrasion) is an unknown word, the system may accept the word sequence of "切り傷やすり傷" as "切り傷" (incised wound), "やすり" (file), and "傷" (injury) by mistake.

On one hand, lists of new terms in the target domain are often available in the forms of technical term dictionaries, product name lists, or other sources. To utilize those domain word lists, Mori (2006) proposed a KWIC (KeyWord In Context) style annotation user interface (UI) with which a user can delimit a word in a context with a single user action. In Figure 2, an annotator marks the occurrences of "すり傷", a word in the domain word

	感染、角膜のこ	すり傷	、角膜潰瘍、
○	皮膚に切り傷や	すり傷	を負った場合
○	泥まみれの深い	すり傷	や、皮下深く

Figure 2: An example of KWIC style annotation: marked lines are identified as a correct segmentation.

list, if they are used as a real word in their context. The "すり傷" in the first row is a part of another word "こすり傷" (scratch), and the annotator marks the last two rows as correctly segmented examples. This UI simplifies annotation operations for segmentation to yes/no decisions, and this simplification can also be effective for the reduction of the annotation effort for other NLP tasks. For example, the annotation operations for unlabeled dependency parsing can be simplified into a series of yes/no decisions as to whether or not given two words have syntactic dependency. Compared with sentence-wise annotation, the partial annotation is not only effective in terms of control operations, but also reduces annotation errors because it does not require annotating the word boundaries that an annotator is unsure of. This feature is crucial for annotations made by domain experts who are not linguists. [1] We believe partial annotation is effective in creating corpora for many other structured annotations in the context of the domain adaptations.

2.2 Ambiguous Annotations

Ambiguous annotations in this paper refer to a set of candidate labels annotated for a part of a structured instance. For example, the following sentence from the PTB corpus includes an ambiguous annotation for the POS tag of "pending":

That/DT suit/NN is/VBZ pending/VBG|JJ ./. ,

where words are paired with their part-of-speech tag by a forward slash ("/").[2] Uncertainty concerning the proper POS tag of "pending" is represented by the disjunctive POS tag ("VBG and JJ") as indicated by a vertical bar.

The existence of the ambiguous annotations is due to the task definition itself, the procedure man-

[1]The boundary policies of some words are different even among linguists. In addition, the boundary agreement is even lower in Chinese (Luo, 2003).

[2]These POS tags used here are DT:determiner, NN:common noun, VBZ:present tense 3rd person singular verb, VBG:gerund or present participle verb, JJ:adjective, NNS:plural noun, RBR:comparative adverb, IN:preposition or subordinating conjunction, and RB:adverb.

frequency	word	POS tags
15	data	NN|NNS
10	more	JJR|RBR
7	pending	JJ|VBG
4	than	IN|RB

Table 1: Words in the PTB with ambiguous POSs.

ual for the annotators, or the inadequate knowledge of the annotators. Ideally, the annotations should be disambiguated by a skilled annotator for the training data. However, even the PTB corpus, whose annotation procedure is relatively well-defined, includes more than 100 sentences containing POS ambiguities such as those listed in Table 1. Although the number of ambiguous annotations is not considerably large in PTB corpus, corpora could include more ambiguous annotations when we try to build wider coverage corpora. Also, ambiguous annotations are more common in the tasks that deal with semantics, such as information extraction tasks so that learning algorithms must deal with ambiguous annotations.

3 Problem Definition

In this section, we give a formal definition of the supervised structured output problem that uses partial annotations or ambiguous annotations in the training phase. Note that we assume the input and output structures are sequences for the purpose of explanation, though the following discussion is applicable to other structures, such as trees.

Let $\boldsymbol{x}{=}(x_1, x_2, \cdots, x_T)$ be a sequence of observed variables $x_t \in X$ and $\boldsymbol{y}{=}(y_1, y_2, \cdots, y_T)$ be a sequence of label variables $y_t \in Y$. Then the supervised structured output problem can be defined as learning a map $\boldsymbol{X} \rightarrow \boldsymbol{Y}$. In the Japanese word segmentation task, $\boldsymbol{x}$ can represent a given sequence of character boundaries and $\boldsymbol{y}$ is a sequence of the corresponding labels, which specify whether the current position is a word boundary.[3] In the POS tagging task, $\boldsymbol{x}$ represents a word sequence and $\boldsymbol{y}$ is a corresponding POS tag sequence. An incomplete annotation, then, is defined as a sequence of subset of the label set instead of a sequence of labels. Let $\boldsymbol{L}{=}(L_1, L_2, \cdots, L_T)$ be a sequence of label subsets for an observed sequence $\boldsymbol{x}$, where $L_t \in 2^Y - \{\emptyset\}$. The partial annotation at position s is where L_s is a singleton and the rest $L_{t \neq s}$ is $\boldsymbol{Y}$. For example, if a sentence with 6 character boundaries (7 characters) is partially annotated using the KWIC UI described in Section 2.1, a word annotation where its boundary begins with $t = 2$ and ends with $t = 5$ will be represented as:

$$\boldsymbol{L} = (\{\bigcirc, \times\}, \underbrace{\{\bigcirc\}, \{\times\}, \{\times\}, \{\bigcirc\}}_{\text{partial annotation}}, \{\bigcirc, \times\}),$$

where $\bigcirc$ and $\times$ denote the word boundary label and the non-word boundary label, respectively. The ambiguous annotation is represented as a set which contains candidate labels. The example sentence including the ambiguous POS tag in Section 2.2 can be represented as:

$$\boldsymbol{L} = (\{\mathrm{DT}\}, \{\mathrm{NN}\}, \{\mathrm{VBZ}\}, \underbrace{\{\mathrm{VBG}, \mathrm{JJ}\}}_{\text{ambiguous annotation}}, \{.\}).$$

Note that, if all the elements of a given sequence are annotated, it is the special case such that the size of all elements is one, i.e. $|L_t| = 1$ for all $t = 1, \cdots, T$. The goal in this paper is training a statistical model from partially or ambiguously annotated data, $D = \{(\boldsymbol{x}^{(n)}, \boldsymbol{L}^{(n)})\}_{n=1}^{N}$.

4 Marginalized Likelihood for CRFs

In this section, we propose a parameter estimation procedure for the CRFs (Lafferty et al., 2001) incorporating partial or ambiguous annotations. Let $\boldsymbol{\Phi}(\boldsymbol{x}, \boldsymbol{y}) : \boldsymbol{X} \times \boldsymbol{Y} \rightarrow \Re^d$ denote a map from a pair of an observed sequence $\boldsymbol{x}$ and a label sequence $\boldsymbol{y}$ to an arbitrary feature vector of d dimensions, and $\boldsymbol{\theta} \in \Re^d$ denotes the vector of the model parameters. CRFs model the conditional probability of a label sequence $\boldsymbol{y}$ given an observed sequence $\boldsymbol{x}$ as:

$$P_{\boldsymbol{\theta}}(\boldsymbol{y}|\boldsymbol{x}) = \frac{e^{\boldsymbol{\theta} \cdot \boldsymbol{\Phi}(\boldsymbol{x}, \boldsymbol{y})}}{Z_{\boldsymbol{\theta}, \boldsymbol{x}, \boldsymbol{Y}}}, \qquad (1)$$

where $\cdot$ denotes the inner product of the vectors, and the denominator is the normalization term that guarantees the model to be a probability:

$$Z_{\boldsymbol{\theta}, \boldsymbol{x}, \boldsymbol{S}} = \sum_{\boldsymbol{y} \in \boldsymbol{S}} e^{\boldsymbol{\theta} \cdot \boldsymbol{\Phi}(\boldsymbol{x}, \boldsymbol{y})}.$$

Then once $\boldsymbol{\theta}$ has been estimated, the label sequence can be predicted by $\hat{\boldsymbol{y}} = \mathrm{argmax}_{\boldsymbol{y} \in \boldsymbol{Y}} P_{\boldsymbol{\theta}}(\boldsymbol{y}|\boldsymbol{x})$. Since the original CRF learning algorithm requires a completely labeled sequence $\boldsymbol{y}$, the incompletely annotated data $(\boldsymbol{x}, \boldsymbol{L})$ is not directly applicable to it.

[3] Peng et al. (2004) defined the word segmentation problem as labeling each character as whether or not the previous character boundary of the current character is a word boundary. However, we employ our problem formulation since it is redundant to assign the first character of a sentence as the word boundary in their formulation.

Let $\boldsymbol{Y_L}$ denote all of the possible label sequence consistent with $\boldsymbol{L}$. We propose to use the conditional probability of the subset $\boldsymbol{Y_L}$ given $\boldsymbol{x}$:

$$P_{\boldsymbol{\theta}}(\boldsymbol{Y_L}|\boldsymbol{x}) = \sum_{\boldsymbol{y} \in \boldsymbol{Y_L}} P_{\boldsymbol{\theta}}(\boldsymbol{y}|\boldsymbol{x}), \tag{2}$$

which marginalizes the unknown $\boldsymbol{y}$s out. Then the maximum likelihood estimator for this model can be obtained by maximizing the log likelihood function:

$$\begin{aligned}\mathrm{LL}(\boldsymbol{\theta}) &= \sum_{n=1}^{N} \ln P_{\boldsymbol{\theta}}(\boldsymbol{Y}_{\boldsymbol{L}^{(n)}}|\boldsymbol{x}^{(n)}) \qquad (3)\\ &= \sum_{n=1}^{N}\left(\ln Z_{\boldsymbol{\theta},\boldsymbol{x}^{(n)},\boldsymbol{Y}_{\boldsymbol{L}^{(n)}}} - \ln Z_{\boldsymbol{\theta},\boldsymbol{x}^{(n)},\boldsymbol{Y}}\right).\end{aligned}$$

This modeling naturally embraces label ambiguities in the incomplete annotation.[4]

Unfortunately, equation (3) is not a concave function[5] so that there are local maxima in the objective function. Although this non-concavity prevents efficient global maximization of equation (3), it still allows us to incorporate incomplete annotations using gradient ascent iterations (Sha and Pereira, 2003). Gradient ascent methods require the partial derivative of equation (3):

$$\begin{aligned}\frac{\partial\,\mathrm{LL}(\boldsymbol{\theta})}{\partial\boldsymbol{\theta}} = &\sum_{n=1}^{N}\Bigg(\sum_{\boldsymbol{y}\in\boldsymbol{Y}_{\boldsymbol{L}^{(n)}}} P_{\boldsymbol{\theta}}(\boldsymbol{y}|\boldsymbol{Y}_{\boldsymbol{L}^{(n)}},\boldsymbol{x}^{(n)})\boldsymbol{\Phi}(\boldsymbol{x}^{(n)},\boldsymbol{y})\\ &- \sum_{\boldsymbol{y}\in\boldsymbol{Y}} P_{\boldsymbol{\theta}}(\boldsymbol{y}|\boldsymbol{x}^{(n)})\boldsymbol{\Phi}(\boldsymbol{x}^{(n)},\boldsymbol{y})\Bigg), \qquad (4)\end{aligned}$$

where

$$P_{\boldsymbol{\theta}}(\boldsymbol{y}|\boldsymbol{Y_L},\boldsymbol{x}) = \frac{e^{\boldsymbol{\theta}\cdot\boldsymbol{\Phi}(\boldsymbol{x},\boldsymbol{y})}}{Z_{\boldsymbol{\theta},\boldsymbol{x},\boldsymbol{Y_L}}} \tag{5}$$

is a conditional probability that is normalized over $\boldsymbol{Y_L}$.

Equations (3) and (4) include the summations of all of the label sequences in $\boldsymbol{Y}$ or $\boldsymbol{Y_L}$. It is not practical to enumerate and evaluate all of the label configurations explicitly, since the number of all of the possible label sequences is exponential on the number of positions t with $|L_t| > 1$. However, under the Markov assumption, a modification of the *Forward-Backward algorithm* guarantees polynomial time computation for the equations (3) and (4). We explain this algorithm in Appendix A.

[4]It is common to introduce a prior distribution over the parameters to avoid over-fitting in CRF learning. In the experiments in Section 5, we used a Gaussian prior with the mean 0 and the variance σ^2 so that $-\frac{||\boldsymbol{\theta}||^2}{2\sigma^2}$ is added to equation (3).

[5]Since its second order derivative can be positive.

	domain	#sentences	#words
(A)	conversation	11,700	145,925
(B)	conversation	1,300	16,348
(C)	medical manual	1,000	29,216

Table 2: Data statistics.

Types	Template
Characters	$c_{-1}, c_{+1},$
Character types	$c_{-2}c_{-1}, c_{-1}c_{+1}, c_{+1}c_{+2},$
Term in dic.	$c_{-2}c_{-1}c_{+1}, c_{-1}c_{+1}c_{+2}$
Term in dic. starts at	c_{-1}, c_{+1}
Term in dic. ends at	

Table 3: Feature templates: Each subscript stands for the relative distance from a character boundary.

5 Experiments

We conducted two types of experiments, assessing the proposed method in 1) a Japanese word segmentation task using partial annotations and 2) a POS tagging task using ambiguous annotations.

5.1 Japanese Word Segmentation Task

In this section, we show the results of domain adaptation experiments for the JWS task to assess the proposed method. We assume that only partial annotations are available for the target domain. In this experiment, the corpus for the source domain is composed of example sentences in a dictionary of daily conversation (Keene et al., 1992). The text data for the target domain is composed of sentences in a medical reference manual (Beers, 2004) . The sentences of all of the source domain corpora (A), (B) and a part of the target domain text (C) were manually segmented into words (see Table 2).

The performance measure in the experiments is the standard F measure score, $F = 2RP/(R+P)$ where

$$R = \frac{\text{\# of correct words}}{\text{\# of words in test data}} \times 100$$
$$P = \frac{\text{\# of correct words}}{\text{\# of words in system output}} \times 100.$$

In this experiment, the performance was evaluated using 2-fold cross-validation that averages the results over two partitions of the data (C) into the

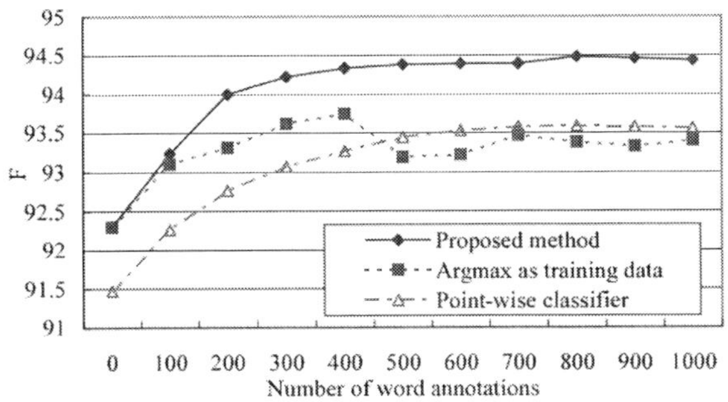

Figure 3: Average performances varying the number of word annotations over 2 trials.

data for annotation and training (C1) versus the data for testing (C2).

We implemented first order Markov CRFs. As the features for the observed variables, we use the characters and character type n-gram (n=1, 2, 3) around the current character boundary. The character types are categorized into *Hiragana*, *Katakana*, *Kanji*, English alphabet, Arabic numerals, and symbols. We also used lexical features consulting a dictionary: one is to check if any of the above defined character n-grams appear in a dictionary (Peng et al., 2004), and the other is to check if there are any words in the dictionary that start or end at the current character boundary. We used the *unidic*[6] (281K distinct words) as the general purpose dictionary, and the *Japanese Standard Disease Code Master* (JSDCM)[7] (23K distinct words) as the medical domain dictionary. The templates for the features we used are summarized in Table 3. To reduce the number of parameters, we selected only frequent features in the source domain data (A) or in about $50K$ of the unsegmented sentences of the target domain.[8] The total number of distinct features was about $300K$.

A CRF that was trained using only the source domain corpus (A), CRF^{S}, achieved F=96.84 in the source domain validation data (B). However, it showed the need for the domain adaptation that this CRF^{S} suffered severe performance degradation (F=92.3) on the target domain data. This experiment was designed for the case in which a user selects the occurrences of words in the word list using the KWIC interface described in Section 2.1. We employed JSDCM as a word list in which 224 distinct terms appeared on average over 2 test sets (C1). The number of word annotations varied from 100 to 1000 in this experiment. We prioritized the occurrences of each word in the list using a selective sampling technique. We used label entropy (Anderson et al., 2006), $H(\boldsymbol{y}_t^s) = \sum_{\boldsymbol{y}_t^s \in \boldsymbol{Y}_t^s} P_{\tilde{\boldsymbol{\theta}}}(\boldsymbol{y}_t^s|\boldsymbol{x}) \ln P_{\tilde{\boldsymbol{\theta}}}(\boldsymbol{y}_t^s|\boldsymbol{x})$, as importance metric of each word occurrence, where $\tilde{\boldsymbol{\theta}}$ is the model parameter of CRF^{S}, and $\boldsymbol{y}_t^s = (y_t, y_{t+1}, \cdots, y_s) \in \boldsymbol{Y}_t^s$ is a subsequence starting at t and ending at s in $\boldsymbol{y}$. Intuitively, this metric represents the prediction confidence of CRF^{S}.[9] As training data, we mixed the complete annotations (A) and these partial annotations on data (C1) because that performance was better than using only the partial annotations.

We used *conjugate gradient* method to find the local maximum value with the initial value being set to be the parameter vector of CRF^{S}. Since the amount of annotated data for the target domain was limited, the hyper-parameter σ was selected using the corpus (B).

For the comparison with the proposed method, the CRFs were trained using the most probable label sequences consistent with $\boldsymbol{L}$ (denoted as *argmax*). The most probable label sequences were predicted by the CRF^{S}. Also, we used a *point-wise classifier*, which independently learns/classifies each character boundary and just ignores the unannotated positions in the learning phase. As the point-wise classifier, we implemented a maximum entropy classifier which uses the same features and optimizer as CRFs.

Figure 3 shows the performance comparisons varying the number of word annotations. The combination of both the proposed method and the selective sampling method showed that a small number of word annotations effectively improved the word segmentation performance. In addition, the proposed method significantly outperformed *argmax* and *point-wise classifier* based on the *Wilcoxon signed rank test* at the significance level of 5%. This result suggests that the proposed method maintains CRFs' advantage over the *point-wise classifier* and properly incorporates partial annotations.

5.2 Part-of-speech Tagging Task

In this section, we show the results of the POS tagging experiments to assess the proposed method using ambiguous annotations.

[6]Ver. 1.3.5; http://www.tokuteicorpus.jp/dist/

[7]Ver. 2.63; http://www2.medis.or.jp/stdcd/byomei/

[8]The data (B) and (C), which were used for validation and test, were excluded from this feature selection process.

[9]We selected word occurrences in a batch mode since each training of the CRFs takes too much time for interactive use.

	Ex.1	Ex.2
ambiguous sentences (training)	118	
unique sentences (training)	1,480	2,960
unique sentences (test)	11,840	

Table 4: Training and test data for POS tagging.

As mentioned in Section 2.2, there are words which have two or more candidate POS tags in the PTB corpus (Marcus et al., 1993). In this experiment, we used 118 sentences in which some words (82 distinct words) are annotated with ambiguous POS tags, and these sentences are called the *POS ambiguous sentences*. On the other hand, we call sentences in which the POS tags of these terms are uniquely annotated as the *POS unique sentences*.

The goal of this experiment is to effectively improve the tagging performance using both these POS ambiguous sentences and the POS unique sentences as the training data. We assume that the amount of training data is not sufficient to ignore the POS ambiguous sentences, or that the POS ambiguous sentences make up a substantial portion of the total training data. Therefore we used a small part ($1/10$ or $1/5$) of the POS unique sentences for training the CRFs and evaluated their performance using other ($4/5$) POS unique sentences. We conducted two experiments in which different numbers of unique sentences were used in the training phases, and these settings are summarized in Table 4.

The feature sets for each word are the case-insensitive spelling, the orthographic features of the current word, and the sentence's last word. The orthographic features are whether a spelling begins with a number or an upper case letter; whether it begins with an upper case letter and contains a period ("."); whether it is all upper case letters or all lower case letters; whether it contains a punctuation mark or a hyphen; and the last one, two, and three letters of the word. Also, the sentence's last word corresponds to a punctuation mark (e.g. ".", "?", "!"). We employed only features that appeared more than once. The total number of resulting distinct features was about $14K$. Although some symbols are treated as distinct tags in the PTB tag definitions, we aggregated these symbols into a symbol tag (SYM) since it is easy to restore original symbol tags from the SYM tag. Then, the number of the resulting tags was 36.

For the comparison with the proposed method (*mrg*), we used three heuristic rules that disambiguated the annotated candidate POS tags in the POS ambiguous sentences. These rules selected a POS tag 1) at *random*, 2) as the *first* one in the description order[10], 3) as the most *frequent* tag in the corpus. In addition, we evaluated the case when the POS ambiguous sentences are 4) *discarded* from the training data.

For evaluation, we employed the Precision (P) and Average Precision for Ambiguous words (APA):

$$\text{P} = \frac{\text{\# of correctly tagged word}}{\text{\# of all word occurrences}} \times 100,$$

$$\text{APA} = \frac{1}{|\boldsymbol{A}|} \sum_{w \in \boldsymbol{A}} \frac{\text{\# of the correctly tagged } w}{\text{\# of all occurrences of } w} \times 100,$$

where $\boldsymbol{A}$ is a word set and is composed of the word for which at least one of its occurrences is ambiguously annotated. Here, we employed APA to evaluate each ambiguous words equally, and $|\boldsymbol{A}|$ was 82 in this experiment. Again, we used the *conjugate gradient* method to find the local maximum value with the initial value being set to be the parameters obtained in the CRF learning for the *discarded* setting.

Table 5 shows the average performance of POS tagging over 5 different POS unique data. Since the POS ambiguous sentences are only a fraction of all of the training data, the overall performance (P) was slightly improved by the proposed method. However, according to the performance for ambiguously annotated words (APA), the proposed method outperformed other heuristics for POS disambiguation. The P and APA scores between the proposed method and the comparable methods are significantly different based on the *Wilcoxon signed rank test* at the 5% significance level. Although the performance improvement in this POS tagging task was moderate, we believe the proposed method will be more effective to the NLP tasks whose corpus has a considerable number of ambiguous annotations.

6 Related Work

Pereira and Schabes (1992) proposed a grammar acquisition method for partially bracketed corpus. Their work can be considered a generative model for the tree structure output problem using partial annotations. Our discriminative model can be extended to such parsing tasks.

[10] Although the order in which the candidate tags appear has not been standardized in the PTB corpus, we assume that annotators might order the candidate tags with their confidence.

		mrg	random	first	frequent	discarded
Ex.1	P	**94.39**	94.27	94.26	94.27	94.19
	APA	**73.10**	71.58	72.65	71.68	71.91
Ex.2	P	**95.08**	94.98	94.97	94.97	94.98
	APA	**76.70**	74.27	75.28	74.32	75.16

Table 5: The average POS tagging performance over 5 trials.

Our model is interpreted as one of the CRFs with hidden variables (Quattoni et al., 2004). There are previous work which handles hidden variables in discriminative parsers (Clark and Curran, 2006; Petrov and Klein, 2008). In their methods, the objective functions are also formulated as same as equation (3).

For interactive annotation, Culotta et al. (2006) proposed corrective feedback that effectively reduces user operations utilizing partial annotations. Although they assume that the users correct entire label structures so that the CRFs are trained as usual, our proposed method extends their system when the users cannot annotate all of the labels in a sentence.

7 Conclusions and Future Work

We are proposing a parameter estimation method for CRFs incorporating partial or ambiguous annotations of structured data. The empirical results suggest that the proposed method reduces the domain adaptation costs, and improves the prediction performance for the linguistic phenomena that are sometimes difficult for people to label.

The proposed method is applicable to other structured output tasks in NLP, such as syntactic parsing, information extraction, and so on. However, there are some NLP tasks, such as the word alignment task (Taskar et al., 2005), in which it is not possible to efficiently calculate the sum score of all of the possible label configurations. Recently, Verbeek and Triggs (2008) independently proposed a parameter estimation method for CRFs using partially labeled images. Although the objective function in their formulation is equivalent to equation (3), they used *Loopy Belief Propagation* to approximate the sum score for their application (scene segmentation). Their results imply these approximation methods can be used for such applications that cannot use dynamic programming techniques.

Acknowledgments

We would like to thank the anonymous reviewers for their comments. We also thank Noah Smith, Ryu Iida, Masayuki Asahara, and the members of the T-PRIMAL group for many helpful discussions.

References

Anderson, Brigham, Sajid Siddiqi, and Andrew Moore. 2006. Sequence selection for active learning. Technical Report CMU-IR-TR-06-16, Carnegie Mellon University.

Beers, Mark H. 2004. *The Merck Manual of Medical Information (in Japanese)*. Nikkei Business Publications, Inc, Home edition.

Clark, Stephen and James R. Curran. 2006. Partial training for a lexicalized-grammar parser. In *Proceedings of the Annual Meeting of the North American Association for Computational Linguistics*, pages 144–151.

Culotta, Aron, Trausti Kristjansson, Andrew McCallum, and Paul Viola. 2006. Corrective feedback and persistent learning for information extraction. *Artificial Intelligence Journal*, 170:1101–1122.

Keene, Donald, Hiroyoshi Hatori, Haruko Yamada, and Shouko Irabu, editors. 1992. *Japanese-English Sentence Equivalents (in Japanese)*. Asahi Press, Electronic book edition.

Kudo, Taku, Kaoru Yamamoto, and Yuji Matsumoto. 2004. Applying conditional random fields to Japanese morphological analysis. In *Proceedings of Empirical Methods in Natural Language Processing*.

Lafferty, John, Andrew McCallum, and Fernando Pereira. 2001. Conditional random fields: Probabilistic models for segmenting and labeling sequence data. In *Proceedings of the 18th International Conference on Machine Learning*.

Luo, Xiaoquan. 2003. A maximum entropy chinese character-based parser. In *Proceedings of the Conference on Empirical Methods in Natural Language Processing*, pages 192–199.

Marcus, Mitchell P., Mary Ann Marcinkiewicz, and Beatrice Santorini. 1993. Building a large annotated corpus of English: The Penn treebank. *Computational Linguistics*, 19(2).

Mori, Shinsuke. 2006. Language model adaptation with a word list and a raw corpus. In *Proceedings of the 9th International Conference on Spoken Language Processing*.

Peng, Fuchun, Fangfang Feng, and Andrew McCallum. 2004. Chinese segmentation and new word detection using conditional random fields. In *Proceedings of the International Conference on Computational Linguistics*.

Pereira, Fernando C. N. and Yves Schabes. 1992. Inside-outside reestimation from partially bracketed corpora. In *Proceedings of Annual Meeting Association of Computational Linguistics*, pages 128–135.

Petrov, Slav and Dan Klein. 2008. Discriminative log-linear grammars with latent variables. In *Advances in Neural Information Processing Systems*, pages 1153–1160, Cambridge, MA. MIT Press.

Quattoni, Ariadna, Michael Collins, and Trevor Darrell. 2004. Conditional random fields for object recognition. In *Advances in Neural Information Processing Systems*.

Sha, Fei and Fernando Pereira. 2003. Shallow parsing with conditional random fields. In *Proceedings of Human Language Technology-NAACL*, Edmonton, Canada.

Taskar, Ben, Simon Lacoste-Julien, and Dan Klein. 2005. A discriminative matching approach to word alignment. In *Proceedings of the Conference on Empirical Methods in Natural Language Processing*.

Verbeek, Jakob and Bill Triggs. 2008. Scene segmentation with CRFs learned from partially labeled images. In *Advances in Neural Information Processing Systems*, pages 1553–1560, Cambridge, MA. MIT Press.

Appendix A Computation of Objective and Derivative functions

Here we explain the effective computation procedure for equation (3) and (4) using dynamic programming techniques.

Under the first-order Markov assumption[11], two types of features are usually used: one is pairs of an observed variable and a label variable (denoted as $\boldsymbol{f}(x_t, y_t) : X \times Y$), the other is pairs of two label variables (denoted as $\boldsymbol{g}(y_{t-1}, y_t) : Y \times Y$) at time t. Then the feature vector can be decomposed as $\boldsymbol{\Phi}(\boldsymbol{x}, \boldsymbol{y}) = \sum_{t=1}^{T+1} \boldsymbol{\phi}(x_t, y_{t-1}, y_t)$ where $\boldsymbol{\phi}(x_t, y_{t-1}, y_t) = \boldsymbol{f}(x_t, y_t) + \boldsymbol{g}(y_{t-1}, y_t)$. In addition, let S and E be special label variables to encode the beginning and ending of a sequence, respectively. We define $\boldsymbol{\phi}(x_t, y_{t-1}, y_t)$ to be $\boldsymbol{\phi}(x_t, S, y_t)$ at the head $t = 1$ and $\boldsymbol{g}(y_{t-1}, E)$ at the tail where $t = T + 1$. The technique of the effective calculation of the normalization value is the precomputation of the $\alpha_{\boldsymbol{\theta},\boldsymbol{x},\boldsymbol{L}}[t, j]$, and$\beta_{\boldsymbol{\theta},\boldsymbol{x},\boldsymbol{L}}[t, j]$ matrices with given $\boldsymbol{\theta}, \boldsymbol{x}$, and $\boldsymbol{L}$. The matrices α and β are defined as follows, and should be calculated in the order of $t = 1, \cdots, T$, and $t = T+1, \cdots, 1$, respectively

$$\alpha_{\boldsymbol{\theta},\boldsymbol{x},\boldsymbol{L}}[t, j] = \begin{cases} 0 & \text{if } j \notin L_t \\ \boldsymbol{\theta} \cdot \boldsymbol{\phi}(x_t, S, j) & \text{else if } t = 1 \\ \ln \sum_{i \in L_{t-1}} e^{\alpha[t-1,i] + \boldsymbol{\theta} \cdot \boldsymbol{\phi}(x_t, i, j)} & \text{else} \end{cases}$$

$$\beta_{\boldsymbol{\theta},\boldsymbol{x},\boldsymbol{L}}[t, j] = \begin{cases} 0 & \text{if } j \notin L_t \\ \boldsymbol{\theta} \cdot \boldsymbol{g}(j, E) & \text{else if } t = T+1 \\ \ln \sum_{k \in L_{t+1}} e^{\boldsymbol{\theta} \cdot \boldsymbol{\phi}(x_t, j, k) + \beta[t+1,k]} & \text{else} \end{cases}$$

Note that $\boldsymbol{L} = (Y, \cdots, Y)$ is used to calculate all the entries in $\boldsymbol{Y}$. In the rest of this section, we omit the subscripts $\boldsymbol{\theta}, \boldsymbol{x}$, and $\boldsymbol{L}$ of α, β, Z unless misunderstandings could occur. The time complexity of the $\alpha[t, j]$ or $\beta[t, j]$ computation is $O(T|Y|^2)$.

Finally, equations (3) and (4) are efficiently calculated using α, β. The logarithm of Z in equation (3) is calculated as:

$$\ln Z_{\boldsymbol{\theta}, \boldsymbol{Y_L}} = \ln \sum_{j \in L_T} e^{\alpha_{\boldsymbol{\theta},\boldsymbol{L}}[T,j] + \boldsymbol{\theta} \cdot \boldsymbol{g}(j,E)}.$$

Similarly, the first and second terms of equation (4) can be computed as:

$$\sum_{\boldsymbol{y} \in \boldsymbol{Y_L}} P_{\boldsymbol{\theta},\boldsymbol{L}}(\boldsymbol{y}|\boldsymbol{x}) \boldsymbol{\Phi}(\boldsymbol{x}, \boldsymbol{y}) = \sum_{i \in L_T} \varepsilon_{\boldsymbol{L}}(T, i, E) \boldsymbol{g}(i, E)$$
$$+ \sum_{t=1}^{T} \sum_{j \in L_t} \left(\gamma_{\boldsymbol{L}}(t, j) \boldsymbol{f}(x_t, j) + \sum_{i \in L_{t-1}} \varepsilon_{\boldsymbol{L}}(t, i, j) \boldsymbol{g}(i, j) \right)$$

where $\boldsymbol{\theta}, \boldsymbol{x}$ are omitted in this equation, and $\gamma_{\boldsymbol{\theta},\boldsymbol{x},\boldsymbol{L}}$ and $\varepsilon_{\boldsymbol{\theta},\boldsymbol{x},\boldsymbol{L}}$ are the marginal probabilities:

$$\gamma_{\boldsymbol{\theta},\boldsymbol{x},\boldsymbol{L}}(t, j) = P_{\boldsymbol{\theta},\boldsymbol{L}}(y_t = j | \boldsymbol{x}) = e^{\alpha[t,j] + \beta[t,j] - \ln Z_{\boldsymbol{Y_L}}}, \text{ and}$$

$$\varepsilon_{\boldsymbol{\theta},\boldsymbol{x},\boldsymbol{L}}(t, i, j) = P_{\boldsymbol{\theta},\boldsymbol{L}}(y_{t-1} = i, y_t = j | \boldsymbol{x}) = e^{\alpha[t-1,i] + \boldsymbol{\theta} \cdot \boldsymbol{\phi}(x_t, i, j) + \beta[t,j] - \ln Z_{\boldsymbol{Y_L}}}.$$

Note that $\boldsymbol{Y_L}$ is replaced with $\boldsymbol{Y}$ and $\boldsymbol{L} = (Y, \cdots, Y)$ to compute the second term.

[11]Note that, although the rest of the explanation based on the first-order Markov models for purposes of illustration, the following arguments are easily extended to the higher order Markov CRFs and semi-Markov CRFs.

A Uniform Approach to Analogies, Synonyms, Antonyms, and Associations

Peter D. Turney
National Research Council of Canada
Institute for Information Technology
M50 Montreal Road
Ottawa, Ontario, Canada
K1A 0R6
peter.turney@nrc-cnrc.gc.ca

Abstract

Recognizing analogies, synonyms, antonyms, and associations appear to be four distinct tasks, requiring distinct NLP algorithms. In the past, the four tasks have been treated independently, using a wide variety of algorithms. These four semantic classes, however, are a tiny sample of the full range of semantic phenomena, and we cannot afford to create ad hoc algorithms for each semantic phenomenon; we need to seek a unified approach. We propose to subsume a broad range of phenomena under analogies. To limit the scope of this paper, we restrict our attention to the subsumption of synonyms, antonyms, and associations. We introduce a supervised corpus-based machine learning algorithm for classifying analogous word pairs, and we show that it can solve multiple-choice SAT analogy questions, TOEFL synonym questions, ESL synonym-antonym questions, and similar-associated-both questions from cognitive psychology.

1 Introduction

A pair of words (petrify:stone) is *analogous* to another pair (vaporize:gas) when the semantic relations between the words in the first pair are highly similar to the relations in the second pair. Two words (levied and imposed) are *synonymous* in a context (levied a tax) when they can be interchanged (imposed a tax), they are are *antonymous* when they have opposite meanings (black and white), and they are *associated* when they tend to co-occur (doctor and hospital).

On the surface, it appears that these are four distinct semantic classes, requiring distinct NLP algorithms, but we propose a uniform approach to all four. We subsume synonyms, antonyms, and associations under analogies. In essence, we say that X and Y are antonyms when the pair $X{:}Y$ is analogous to the pair black:white, X and Y are synonyms when they are analogous to the pair levied:imposed, and X and Y are associated when they are analogous to the pair doctor:hospital.

There is past work on recognizing analogies (Reitman, 1965), synonyms (Landauer and Dumais, 1997), antonyms (Lin et al., 2003), and associations (Lesk, 1969), but each of these four tasks has been examined separately, in isolation from the others. As far as we know, the algorithm proposed here is the first attempt to deal with all four tasks using a uniform approach. We believe that it is important to seek NLP algorithms that can handle a broad range of semantic phenomena, because developing a specialized algorithm for each phenomenon is a very inefficient research strategy.

It might seem that a lexicon, such as WordNet (Fellbaum, 1998), contains all the information we need to handle these four tasks. However, we prefer to take a corpus-based approach to semantics. Veale (2004) used WordNet to answer 374 multiple-choice SAT analogy questions, achieving an accuracy of 43%, but the best corpus-based approach attains an accuracy of 56% (Turney, 2006). Another reason to prefer a corpus-based approach to a lexicon-based approach is that the former requires less human labour, and thus it is easier to extend to other languages.

In Section 2, we describe our algorithm for recognizing analogies. We use a standard supervised

© 2008, National Research Council of Canada (NRC). Licensed to the Coling 2008 Organizing Committee for publication in Coling 2008 and for re-publishing in any form or medium.

machine learning approach, with feature vectors based on the frequencies of patterns in a large corpus. We use a support vector machine (SVM) to learn how to classify the feature vectors (Platt, 1998; Witten and Frank, 1999).

Section 3 presents four sets of experiments. We apply our algorithm for recognizing analogies to multiple-choice analogy questions from the SAT college entrance test, multiple-choice synonym questions from the TOEFL (test of English as a foreign language), ESL (English as a second language) practice questions for distinguishing synonyms and antonyms, and a set of word pairs that are labeled *similar*, *associated*, and *both*, developed for experiments in cognitive psychology.

We discuss the results of the experiments in Section 4. The accuracy of the algorithm is competitive with other systems, but the strength of the algorithm is that it is able to handle all four tasks, with no tuning of the learning parameters to the particular task. It performs well, although it is competing against specialized algorithms, developed for single tasks.

Related work is examined in Section 5 and limitations and future work are considered in Section 6. We conclude in Section 7.

2 Classifying Analogous Word Pairs

An analogy, $A{:}B{::}C{:}D$, asserts that A is to B as C is to D; for example, traffic:street::water:riverbed asserts that traffic is to street as water is to riverbed; that is, the semantic relations between traffic and street are highly similar to the semantic relations between water and riverbed. We may view the task of recognizing word analogies as a problem of classifying word pairs (see Table 1).

Word pair	Class label
carpenter:wood	artisan:material
mason:stone	artisan:material
potter:clay	artisan:material
glassblower:glass	artisan:material
traffic:street	entity:carrier
water:riverbed	entity:carrier
packets:network	entity:carrier
gossip:grapevine	entity:carrier

Table 1: Examples of how the task of recognizing word analogies may be viewed as a problem of classifying word pairs.

We approach this as a standard classification problem for supervised machine learning. The algorithm takes as input a training set of word pairs with class labels and a testing set of word pairs without labels. Each word pair is represented as a vector in a feature space and a supervised learning algorithm is used to classify the feature vectors. The elements in the feature vectors are based on the frequencies of automatically defined patterns in a large corpus. The output of the algorithm is an assignment of labels to the word pairs in the testing set. For some of the experiments, we select a unique label for each word pair; for other experiments, we assign probabilities to each possible label for each word pair.

For a given word pair, such as mason:stone, the first step is to generate morphological variations, such as masons:stones. In the following experiments, we use *morpha* (morphological analyzer) and *morphg* (morphological generator) for morphological processing (Minnen et al., 2001).[1]

The second step is to search in a large corpus for all phrases of the following form:
"[0 to 1 words] X [0 to 3 words] Y [0 to 1 words]"
In this template, $X{:}Y$ consists of morphological variations of the given word pair, in either order; for example, mason:stone, stone:mason, masons:stones, and so on. A typical phrase for mason:stone would be "the mason cut the stone with". We then normalize all of the phrases that are found, by using *morpha* to remove suffixes.

The template we use here is similar to Turney (2006), but we have added extra context words before the X and after the Y. Our morphological processing also differs from Turney (2006). In the following experiments, we search in a corpus of 5×10^{10} words (about 280 GB of plain text), consisting of web pages gathered by a web crawler.[2] To retrieve phrases from the corpus, we use Wumpus (Büttcher and Clarke, 2005), an efficient search engine for passage retrieval from large corpora.[3]

The next step is to generate patterns from all of the phrases that were found for all of the input word pairs (from both the training and testing sets). To generate patterns from a phrase, we replace the given word pairs with variables, X and Y, and we replace the remaining words with a wild card symbol (an asterisk) or leave them as they are.

[1] http://www.informatics.susx.ac.uk/research/groups/nlp/carroll/morph.html.

[2] The corpus was collected by Charles Clarke, University of Waterloo. We can provide copies on request.

[3] http://www.wumpus-search.org/.

For example, the phrase "the mason cut the stone with" yields the patterns "the X cut * Y with", "* X * the Y *", and so on. If a phrase contains n words, then it yields $2^{(n-2)}$ patterns.

Each pattern corresponds to a feature in the feature vectors that we will generate. Since a typical input set of word pairs yields millions of patterns, we need to use feature selection, to reduce the number of patterns to a manageable quantity. For each pattern, we count the number of input word pairs that generated the pattern. For example, "* X cut * Y *" is generated by both mason:stone and carpenter:wood. We then sort the patterns in descending order of the number of word pairs that generated them. If there are N input word pairs (and thus N feature vectors, including both the training and testing sets), then we select the top kN patterns and drop the remainder. In the following experiments, k is set to 20. The algorithm is not sensitive to the precise value of k.

The reasoning behind the feature selection algorithm is that shared patterns make more useful features than rare patterns. The number of features (kN) depends on the number of word pairs (N), because, if we have more feature vectors, then we need more features to distinguish them. Turney (2006) also selects patterns based on the number of pairs that generate them, but the number of selected patterns is a constant (8000), independent of the number of input word pairs.

The next step is to generate feature vectors, one vector for each input word pair. Each of the N feature vectors has kN elements, one element for each selected pattern. The value of an element in a vector is given by the logarithm of the frequency in the corpus of the corresponding pattern for the given word pair. For example, suppose the given pair is mason:stone and the pattern is "* X cut * Y *". We look at the normalized phrases that we collected for mason:stone and we count how many match this pattern. If f phrases match the pattern, then the value of this element in the feature vector is $\log(f+1)$ (we add 1 because $\log(0)$ is undefined). Each feature vector is then normalized to unit length. The normalization ensures that features in vectors for high-frequency word pairs (traffic:street) are comparable to features in vectors for low-frequency word pairs (water:riverbed).

Now that we have a feature vector for each input word pair, we can apply a standard supervised learning algorithm. In the following experiments, we use a sequential minimal optimization (SMO) support vector machine (SVM) with a radial basis function (RBF) kernel (Platt, 1998), as implemented in Weka (Waikato Environment for Knowledge Analysis) (Witten and Frank, 1999).[4] The algorithm generates probability estimates for each class by fitting logistic regression models to the outputs of the SVM. We disable the normalization option in Weka, since the vectors are already normalized to unit length. We chose the SMO RBF algorithm because it is fast, robust, and it easily handles large numbers of features.

For convenience, we will refer to the above algorithm as PairClass. In the following experiments, PairClass is applied to each of the four problems with no adjustments or tuning to the specific problems. Some work is required to fit each problem into the general framework of PairClass (supervised classification of word pairs) but the core algorithm is the same in each case.

3 Experiments

This section presents four sets of experiments, with analogies, synonyms, antonyms, and associations. We explain how each task is treated as a problem of classifying analogous word pairs, we give the experimental results, and we discuss past work on each of the four tasks.

3.1 SAT Analogies

In this section, we apply PairClass to the task of recognizing analogies. To evaluate the performance, we use a set of 374 multiple-choice questions from the SAT college entrance exam. Table 2 shows a typical question. The target pair is called the *stem*. The task is to select the choice pair that is most analogous to the stem pair.

Stem:		mason:stone
Choices:	(a)	teacher:chalk
	(b)	carpenter:wood
	(c)	soldier:gun
	(d)	photograph:camera
	(e)	book:word
Solution:	(b)	carpenter:wood

Table 2: An example of a question from the 374 SAT analogy questions.

The problem of recognizing word analogies was first attempted with a system called Argus (Reit-

[4] http://www.cs.waikato.ac.nz/ml/weka/.

man, 1965), using a small hand-built semantic network with a spreading activation algorithm. Turney et al. (2003) used a combination of 13 independent modules. Veale (2004) used a spreading activation algorithm with WordNet (in effect, treating WordNet as a semantic network). Turney (2006) used a corpus-based algorithm.

We may view Table 2 as a binary classification problem, in which mason:stone and carpenter:wood are positive examples and the remaining word pairs are negative examples. The difficulty is that the labels of the choice pairs must be hidden from the learning algorithm. That is, the training set consists of one positive example (the stem pair) and the testing set consists of five unlabeled examples (the five choice pairs). To make this task more tractable, we randomly choose a stem pair from one of the 373 other SAT analogy questions, and we assume that this new stem pair is a negative example, as shown in Table 3.

Word pair	Train or test	Class label
mason:stone	train	positive
tutor:pupil	train	negative
teacher:chalk	test	hidden
carpenter:wood	test	hidden
soldier:gun	test	hidden
photograph:camera	test	hidden
book:word	test	hidden

Table 3: How to fit a SAT analogy question into the framework of supervised pair classification.

To answer the SAT question, we use PairClass to estimate the probability that each testing example is positive, and we guess the testing example with the highest probability. Learning from a training set with only one positive example and one negative example is difficult, since the learned model can be highly unstable. To increase the stability, we repeat the learning process 10 times, using a different randomly chosen negative training example each time. For each testing word pair, the 10 probability estimates are averaged together. This is a form of bagging (Breiman, 1996).

PairClass attains an accuracy of 52.1%. For comparison, the ACL Wiki lists 12 previously published results with the 374 SAT analogy questions.[5] Only 2 of the 12 algorithms have higher accuracy. The best previous result is an accuracy of 56.1% (Turney, 2006). Random guessing would yield an accuracy of 20%. The average senior high school student achieves 57% correct (Turney, 2006).

[5]For more information, see *SAT Analogy Questions (State of the art)* at http://aclweb.org/aclwiki/.

3.2 TOEFL Synonyms

Now we apply PairClass to the task of recognizing synonyms, using a set of 80 multiple-choice synonym questions from the TOEFL (test of English as a foreign language). A sample question is shown in Table 4. The task is to select the choice word that is most similar in meaning to the stem word.

Stem:		levied
Choices:	(a)	imposed
	(b)	believed
	(c)	requested
	(d)	correlated
Solution:	(a)	imposed

Table 4: An example of a question from the 80 TOEFL questions.

Synonymy can be viewed as a high degree of semantic similarity. The most common way to measure semantic similarity is to measure the distance between words in WordNet (Resnik, 1995; Jiang and Conrath, 1997; Hirst and St-Onge, 1998). Corpus-based measures of word similarity are also common (Lesk, 1969; Landauer and Dumais, 1997; Turney, 2001).

We may view Table 4 as a binary classification problem, in which the pair levied:imposed is a positive example of the class *synonymous* and the other possible pairings are negative examples, as shown in Table 5.

Word pair	Class label
levied:imposed	positive
levied:believed	negative
levied:requested	negative
levied:correlated	negative

Table 5: How to fit a TOEFL question into the framework of supervised pair classification.

The 80 TOEFL questions yield 320 (80×4) word pairs, 80 labeled positive and 240 labeled negative. We apply PairClass to the word pairs using ten-fold cross-validation. In each random fold, 90% of the pairs are used for training and 10% are used for testing. For each fold, the model that is learned from the training set is used to assign probabilities to the pairs in the testing set. With ten separate folds, the ten non-overlapping testing sets cover the whole dataset. Our guess for each TOEFL question is the choice with the highest probability of being positive, when paired with the corresponding stem.

PairClass attains an accuracy of 76.2%. For comparison, the ACL Wiki lists 15 previously published results with the 80 TOEFL synonym questions.[6] Of the 15 algorithms, 8 have higher accuracy and 7 have lower. The best previous result is an accuracy of 97.5% (Turney et al., 2003), obtained using a hybrid of four different algorithms. Random guessing would yield an accuracy of 25%. The average foreign applicant to a US university achieves 64.5% correct (Landauer and Dumais, 1997).

3.3 Synonyms and Antonyms

The task of classifying word pairs as either synonyms or antonyms readily fits into the framework of supervised classification of word pairs. Table 6 shows some examples from a set of 136 ESL (English as a second language) practice questions that we collected from various ESL websites.

Word pair	Class label
galling:irksome	synonyms
yield:bend	synonyms
naive:callow	synonyms
advise:suggest	synonyms
dissimilarity:resemblance	antonyms
commend:denounce	antonyms
expose:camouflage	antonyms
unveil:veil	antonyms

Table 6: Examples of synonyms and antonyms from 136 ESL practice questions.

Lin et al. (2003) distinguish synonyms from antonyms using two patterns, "from X to Y" and "either X or Y". When X and Y are antonyms, they occasionally appear in a large corpus in one of these two patterns, but it is very rare for synonyms to appear in these patterns. Our approach is similar to Lin et al. (2003), but we do not rely on hand-coded patterns; instead, PairClass patterns are generated automatically.

Using ten-fold cross-validation, PairClass attains an accuracy of 75.0%. Always guessing the majority class would result in an accuracy of 65.4%. The average human score is unknown and there are no previous results for comparison.

3.4 Similar, Associated, and Both

A common criticism of corpus-based measures of word similarity (as opposed to lexicon-based measures) is that they are merely detecting associations (co-occurrences), rather than actual semantic similarity (Lund et al., 1995). To address this criticism, Lund et al. (1995) evaluated their algorithm for measuring word similarity with word pairs that were labeled *similar*, *associated*, or *both*. These labeled pairs were originally created for cognitive psychology experiments with human subjects (Chiarello et al., 1990). Table 7 shows some examples from this collection of 144 word pairs (48 pairs in each of the three classes).

Word pair	Class label
table:bed	similar
music:art	similar
hair:fur	similar
house:cabin	similar
cradle:baby	associated
mug:beer	associated
camel:hump	associated
cheese:mouse	associated
ale:beer	both
uncle:aunt	both
pepper:salt	both
frown:smile	both

Table 7: Examples of word pairs labeled *similar*, *associated*, or *both*.

Lund et al. (1995) did not measure the accuracy of their algorithm on this three-class classification problem. Instead, following standard practice in cognitive psychology, they showed that their algorithm's similarity scores for the 144 word pairs were correlated with the response times of human subjects in priming tests. In a typical priming test, a human subject reads a *priming* word (*cradle*) and is then asked to complete a partial word (complete *bab* as *baby*). The time required to perform the task is taken to indicate the strength of the cognitive link between the two words (*cradle* and *baby*).

Using ten-fold cross-validation, PairClass attains an accuracy of 77.1% on the 144 word pairs. Since the three classes are of equal size, guessing the majority class and random guessing both yield an accuracy of 33.3%. The average human score is unknown and there are no previous results for comparison.

[6]For more information, see *TOEFL Synonym Questions (State of the art)* at http://aclweb.org/aclwiki/.

4 Discussion

The four experiments are summarized in Tables 8 and 9. For the first two experiments, where there are previous results, PairClass is not the best, but it performs competitively. For the second two experiments, PairClass performs significantly above the baselines. However, the strength of this approach is not its performance on any one task, but the range of tasks it can handle.

As far as we know, this is the first time a standard supervised learning algorithm has been applied to any of these four problems. The advantage of being able to cast these problems in the framework of standard supervised learning problems is that we can now exploit the huge literature on supervised learning. Past work on these problems has required implicitly coding our knowledge of the nature of the task into the structure of the algorithm. For example, the structure of the algorithm for latent semantic analysis (LSA) implicitly contains a theory of synonymy (Landauer and Dumais, 1997). The problem with this approach is that it can be very difficult to work out how to modify the algorithm if it does not behave the way we want. On the other hand, with a supervised learning algorithm, we can put our knowledge into the labeling of the feature vectors, instead of putting it directly into the algorithm. This makes it easier to guide the system to the desired behaviour.

With our approach to the SAT analogy questions, we are blurring the line between supervised and unsupervised learning, since the training set for a given SAT question consists of a single real positive example (and a single "virtual" or "simulated" negative example). In effect, a single example (mason:stone) becomes a *sui generis*; it constitutes a class of its own. It may be possible to apply the machinery of supervised learning to other problems that apparently call for unsupervised learning (for example, clustering or measuring similarity), by using this *sui generis* device.

5 Related Work

One of the first papers using supervised machine learning to classify word pairs was Rosario and Hearst's (2001) paper on classifying noun-modifier pairs in the medical domain. For example, the noun-modifier expression *brain biopsy* was classified as *Procedure*. Rosario and Hearst (2001) constructed feature vectors for each noun-modifier pair using MeSH (Medical Subject Headings) and UMLS (Unified Medical Language System) as lexical resources. They then trained a neural network to distinguish 13 classes of semantic relations, such as *Cause*, *Location*, *Measure*, and *Instrument*. Nastase and Szpakowicz (2003) explored a similar approach to classifying general-domain noun-modifier pairs, using WordNet and Roget's Thesaurus as lexical resources.

Turney and Littman (2005) used corpus-based features for classifying noun-modifier pairs. Their features were based on 128 hand-coded patterns. They used a nearest-neighbour learning algorithm to classify general-domain noun-modifier pairs into 30 different classes of semantic relations. Turney (2006) later addressed the same problem using 8000 automatically generated patterns.

One of the tasks in SemEval 2007 was the classification of semantic relations between nominals (Girju et al., 2007). The problem is to classify semantic relations between nouns and noun compounds in the context of a sentence. The task attracted 14 teams who created 15 systems, all of which used supervised machine learning with features that were lexicon-based, corpus-based, or both.

PairClass is most similar to the algorithm of Turney (2006), but it differs in the following ways:

- PairClass does not use a lexicon to find synonyms for the input word pairs. One of our goals in this paper is to show that a pure corpus-based algorithm can handle synonyms without a lexicon. This considerably simplifies the algorithm.
- PairClass uses a support vector machine (SVM) instead of a nearest neighbour (NN) learning algorithm.
- PairClass does not use the singular value decomposition (SVD) to smooth the feature vectors. It has been our experience that SVD is not necessary with SVMs.
- PairClass generates probability estimates, whereas Turney (2006) uses a cosine measure of similarity. Probability estimates can be readily used in further downstream processing, but cosines are less useful.
- The automatically generated patterns in PairClass are slightly more general than the patterns of Turney (2006).
- The morphological processing in PairClass (Minnen et al., 2001) is more sophisticated than in Turney (2006).

Experiment	Number of vectors		Number of features		Number of classes
SAT Analogies	2,244	(374×6)	44,880	$(2,244 \times 20)$	374
TOEFL Synonyms	320	(80×4)	6,400	(320×20)	2
Synonyms and Antonyms	136		2,720	(136×20)	2
Similar, Associated, and Both	144		2,880	(144×20)	3

Table 8: Summary of the four tasks. See Section 3 for explanations.

Experiment	Accuracy	Best previous	Human	Baseline	Rank
SAT Analogies	52.1%	56.1%	57.0%	20.0%	2 higher out of 12
TOEFL Synonyms	76.2%	97.5%	64.5%	25.0%	8 higher out of 15
Synonyms and Antonyms	75.0%	none	unknown	65.4%	none
Similar, Associated, and Both	77.1%	none	unknown	33.3%	none

Table 9: Summary of experimental results. See Section 3 for explanations.

However, we believe that the main contribution of this paper is not PairClass itself, but the extension of supervised word pair classification beyond the classification of noun-modifier pairs and semantic relations between nominals, to analogies, synonyms, antonyms, and associations. As far as we know, this has not been done before.

6 Limitations and Future Work

The main limitation of PairClass is the need for a large corpus. Phrases that contain a pair of words tend to be more rare than phrases that contain either of the members of the pair, thus a large corpus is needed to ensure that sufficient numbers of phrases are found for each input word pair. The size of the corpus has a cost in terms of disk space and processing time. In the future, as hardware improves, this will become less of an issue, but there may be ways to improve the algorithm, so that a smaller corpus is sufficient.

Another area for future work is to apply PairClass to more tasks. WordNet includes more than a dozen semantic relations (e.g., synonyms, hyponyms, hypernyms, meronyms, holonyms, and antonyms). PairClass should be applicable to all of these relations. Other potential applications include any task that involves semantic relations, such as word sense disambiguation, information retrieval, information extraction, and metaphor interpretation.

7 Conclusion

In this paper, we have described a uniform approach to analogies, synonyms, antonyms, and associations, in which all of these phenomena are subsumed by analogies. We view the problem of recognizing analogies as the classification of semantic relations between words.

We believe that most of our lexical knowledge is relational, not attributional. That is, meaning is largely about relations among words, rather than properties of individual words, considered in isolation. For example, consider the knowledge encoded in WordNet: much of the knowledge in WordNet is embedded in the graph structure that connects words.

Analogies of the form $A{:}B{::}C{:}D$ are called *proportional analogies*. These types of lower-level analogies may be contrasted with higher-level analogies, such as the analogy between the solar system and Rutherford's model of the atom (Falkenhainer et al., 1989), which are sometimes called *conceptual analogies*. We believe that the difference between these two types is largely a matter of complexity. A higher-level analogy is composed of many lower-level analogies. Progress with algorithms for processing lower-level analogies will eventually contribute to algorithms for higher-level analogies.

The idea of subsuming a broad range of semantic phenomena under analogies has been suggested by many researchers. Minsky (1986) wrote, "How do we ever understand anything? Almost always, I think, by using one or another kind of analogy." Hofstadter (2007) claimed, "all meaning comes from analogies." In NLP, analogical algorithms have been applied to machine translation (Lepage and Denoual, 2005), morphology (Lepage, 1998), and semantic relations (Turney and Littman, 2005). Analogy provides a framework that has the potential to unify the field of semantics. This paper is a small step towards that goal.

Acknowledgements

Thanks to Joel Martin and the anonymous reviewers of Coling 2008 for their helpful comments.

References

Breiman, Leo. 1996. Bagging predictors. *Machine Learning*, 24(2):123–140.

Büttcher, Stefan and Charles Clarke. 2005. Efficiency vs. effectiveness in terabyte-scale information retrieval. In *Proceedings of the 14th Text REtrieval Conference (TREC 2005)*, Gaithersburg, MD.

Chiarello, Christine, Curt Burgess, Lorie Richards, and Alma Pollock. 1990. Semantic and associative priming in the cerebral hemispheres: Some words do, some words don't ... sometimes, some places. *Brain and Language*, 38:75–104.

Falkenhainer, Brian, Kenneth D. Forbus, and Dedre Gentner. 1989. The structure-mapping engine: Algorithm and examples. *Artificial Intelligence*, 41(1):1–63.

Fellbaum, Christiane, editor. 1998. *WordNet: An Electronic Lexical Database*. MIT Press.

Girju, Roxana, Preslav Nakov, Vivi Nastase, Stan Szpakowicz, Peter Turney, and Deniz Yuret. 2007. Semeval-2007 task 04: Classification of semantic relations between nominals. In *SemEval 2007*, pages 13–18, Prague, Czech Republic.

Hirst, Graeme and David St-Onge. 1998. Lexical chains as representations of context for the detection and correction of malapropisms. In Fellbaum, Christiane, editor, *WordNet: An Electronic Lexical Database*, pages 305–332. MIT Press.

Hofstadter, Douglas. 2007. *I Am a Srange Loop*. Basic Books.

Jiang, Jay J. and David W. Conrath. 1997. Semantic similarity based on corpus statistics and lexical taxonomy. In *ROCLING X*, pages 19–33, Tapei, Taiwan.

Landauer, Thomas K. and Susan T. Dumais. 1997. A solution to Plato's problem: The latent semantic analysis theory of the acquisition, induction, and representation of knowledge. *Psychological Review*, 104(2):211–240.

Lepage, Yves and Etienne Denoual. 2005. Purest ever example-based machine translation: Detailed presentation and assessment. *Machine Translation*, 19(3):251–282.

Lepage, Yves. 1998. Solving analogies on words: An algorithm. In *Proceedings of the 36th Annual Conference of the Association for Computational Linguistics*, pages 728–735.

Lesk, Michael E. 1969. Word-word associations in document retrieval systems. *American Documentation*, 20(1):27–38.

Lin, Dekang, Shaojun Zhao, Lijuan Qin, and Ming Zhou. 2003. Identifying synonyms among distributionally similar words. In *IJCAI-03*, pages 1492–1493.

Lund, Kevin, Curt Burgess, and Ruth Ann Atchley. 1995. Semantic and associative priming in high-dimensional semantic space. In *Proceedings of the 17th Annual Conference of the Cognitive Science Society*, pages 660–665.

Minnen, Guido, John Carroll, and Darren Pearce. 2001. Applied morphological processing of English. *Natural Language Engineering*, 7(3):207–223.

Minsky, Marvin. 1986. *The Society of Mind*. Simon & Schuster, New York, NY.

Nastase, Vivi and Stan Szpakowicz. 2003. Exploring noun-modifier semantic relations. In *Fifth International Workshop on Computational Semantics (IWCS-5)*, pages 285–301, Tilburg, The Netherlands.

Platt, John C. 1998. Fast training of support vector machines using sequential minimal optimization. In *Advances in Kernel Methods: Support Vector Learning*, pages 185–208. MIT Press Cambridge, MA, USA.

Reitman, Walter R. 1965. *Cognition and Thought: An Information Processing Approach*. John Wiley and Sons, New York, NY.

Resnik, Philip. 1995. Using information content to evaluate semantic similarity in a taxonomy. In *IJCAI-95*, pages 448–453, San Mateo, CA. Morgan Kaufmann.

Rosario, Barbara and Marti Hearst. 2001. Classifying the semantic relations in noun-compounds via a domain-specific lexical hierarchy. In *EMNLP-01*, pages 82–90.

Turney, Peter D. and Michael L. Littman. 2005. Corpus-based learning of analogies and semantic relations. *Machine Learning*, 60(1–3):251–278.

Turney, Peter D., Michael L. Littman, Jeffrey Bigham, and Victor Shnayder. 2003. Combining independent modules to solve multiple-choice synonym and analogy problems. In *RANLP-03*, pages 482–489, Borovets, Bulgaria.

Turney, Peter D. 2001. Mining the Web for synonyms: PMI-IR versus LSA on TOEFL. In *Proceedings of the Twelfth European Conference on Machine Learning*, pages 491–502, Berlin. Springer.

Turney, Peter D. 2006. Similarity of semantic relations. *Computational Linguistics*, 32(3):379–416.

Veale, Tony. 2004. WordNet sits the SAT: A knowledge-based approach to lexical analogy. In *Proceedings of the 16th European Conference on Artificial Intelligence (ECAI 2004)*, pages 606–612, Valencia, Spain.

Witten, Ian H. and Eibe Frank. 1999. *Data Mining: Practical Machine Learning Tools and Techniques with Java Implementations*. Morgan Kaufmann, San Francisco.

Tighter Integration of Rule-based and Statistical MT in Serial System Combination

Nicola Ueffing[1], Jens Stephan[2], Evgeny Matusov[3], Loïc Dugast[2], George Foster[1], Roland Kuhn[1], Jean Senellart[2], and Jin Yang[2]
[1]Institute for Information Technology
National Research Council of Canada (NRC)
Gatineau, Québec, Canada

[2]SYSTRAN SA
Paris, France

[3]RWTH Aachen University
Aachen, Germany

Abstract

Recent papers have described machine translation (MT) based on an *automatic post-editing* or *serial combination* strategy whereby the input language is first translated into the target language by a rule-based MT (RBMT) system, then the target language output is automatically post-edited by a phrase-based statistical machine translation (SMT) system. This approach has been shown to improve MT quality over RBMT or SMT alone. In this previous work, there was a very loose coupling between the two systems: the SMT system only had access to the final 1-best translations from RBMT. Furthermore, the previous work involved European language pairs and relatively small training corpora. In this paper, we describe a more tightly integrated serial combination for the Chinese-to-English MT task. We will present experimental evaluation results on the 2008 NIST constrained data track where a significant gain in terms of both automatic and subjective metrics is achieved through the tighter coupling of the two systems.

© 2008, National Research Council of Canada (NRC). Licensed to the COLING 2008 Organizing Committee for publication in COLING 2008 and for re-publishing in any form or medium.

1 Introduction

MT systems tend to make the same errors over and over again. A recent paper (Simard *et al.*, 2007a) proposed that a phrase-based SMT sys tem be trained on the *manually* post-edited output of an RBMT system to become an *automatic* post-editor for the output of that system. Thus, the SMT system learns how to "translate" the output of the RBMT system to another version of these same translations that will more closely resemble translations produced by qualified humans. In the above-cited paper, this serial combination approach was shown to produce large improvements in translation performance for the English-French language pair (both directions) compared not only to the RBMT system but also compared to the SMT system trained to translate directly from the source language. However, these experiments were carried out in an unusual context, where a large corpus of manually corrected RBMT output was available.

Simard *et al.* (2007b) examines the impact of an automatic post-editor trained on more commonly available data. The source-language part of a bilingual parallel corpus is input to an RBMT system, thus creating a corpus where each manually produced target-language sentence is aligned with an *independently* generated automatic translation of the same source sentence. Training an automatic post-editor on this kind of corpus is quite different from training one on a corpus containing corrected MT output: a manually post-edited translation will have similar word choices and word order to the original translation, while two independently generated translations of the same text may differ radically.

The experiments in (Simard *et al.* 2007b) are carried out on English-French data (both directions) from the 2007 Workshop on Statistical Machine Translation[1]. SMT post-editing significantly improves the BLEU scores of the RBMT system for both translation directions and for both domains tested, the News Commentary domain (50K training sentence pairs) and the Europarl domain (1.3M training sentence pairs). In terms of BLEU score, the hybrid system and the pure SMT system are essentially tied in the Europarl domain (for both language directions), while in the News Commentary domain, the hybrid system outperforms the pure SMT system by about 3 BLEU points for English-to-French and by about 1.5 points for French-to-English.

These results suggest that if one has little training data, serial RBMT-SMT combination is the best strategy, while with more training data, serial combination or the use of a pure SMT system yields equivalent results. However, the BLEU score may underestimate the advantages of serial system combination. **Table 1** shows some data from the 2007 Workshop on SMT (Callison-Burch *et al.* 2007) involving an RBMT system from the company Systran (Yang *et al.* 2003), and the SMT system PORTAGE from National Research Council Canada (Ueffing *et al.* 2007). The BLEU score is shown in italics along with human rankings of system output (for Europarl). Although the BLEU scores of the pure SMT system and the hybrid system are nearly identical, human evaluators ranked the hybrid system first of eight English-to-French systems and second of seven French-to-English systems, as compared to inferior rankings for SMT or RBMT alone: the serial combination makes a more favorable impression on human evaluators than BLEU would predict.

System	En→Fr: *(BLEU)* **Rank/8**	Fr→En: (BLEU) **Rank/7**
RBMT (Systran)	*(23.3)* 6	*(21.1)* **6**
SMT (PORTAGE)	*(29.4)* **5**	*(31.2)* **5**
RBMT→SMT	*(30.1)* **1**	*(31.3)* **2**

Table 1: BLEU score and human rankings for En→Fr and Fr→En (SMT 2007 Europarl data)

Dugast *et al.* (2007) describes similar experiments for the other four language pairs in the WMT 2007 evaluation: the Systran RBMT system is serially combined with the Moses SMT system. This paper also presents a qualitative analysis of the changes made by the SMT post-editor on the RBMT output.

The experiments described above involve European language pairs and relatively small amounts of training data. We decided to carry out serial combination experiments on the Chinese-to-English translation task, for which large amounts of training data are available. As explained above, the serial combination is built by first having the RBMT system translate all Chinese training data into English. The SMT component is then trained on sentence pairs where each RBMT English output is aligned with the English reference sentence for the original Chinese sentence. Thus, the SMT system is capable of "translating" RBMT output into even better English.

The Chinese-English experiments were carried out in the context of both the GALE project and the 2008 NIST Chinese-to-English MT evaluation. The integration of the two components of the serial combination was deepened by having the RBMT component break its output into chunks, with some of these chunks being annotated with a confidence level; chunks with low confidence are more likely to be changed by the SMT component.

2 Description of RBMT System

The RBMT system in these experiments is the Systran Chinese-English system. This system is described extensively in (Yang *et al.* 2003). In particular, it uses a rule-based word-boundary module and a bilingual lexicon with about 1.2M entries, containing words, expressions and rules. This system is specifically geared to translation in the domain of science and technology. Recent evolution of this system has focused on developing structured markup making it possible to monitor rule application and to interact with the rule engine (Attnäs *et al* 2005).

3 Description of SMT System

The SMT system in these experiments is the PORTAGE system from the National Research Council of Canada (Ueffing *et al.* 2007). PORTAGE is a standard phrase-based system that carries out beam search decoding using a loglinear model. Major features in this

[1] http://www.statmt.org/wmt07/

loglinear model include phrase tables derived from symmetrized IBM2 and HMM word alignments (with a phrase length limit of seven words), and a static 4-gram language model (LM) trained on the Gigaword corpus using the SRILM toolkit (Stolcke 2002). An important feature is an adapted 4-gram LM derived from the parallel corpus using the technique of (Foster and Kuhn 2007); it is a linear mixture of N-gram models trained on parallel subcorpora (Hong Kong Hansard, FBIS, UN, *etc.*). Other features are word count and phrase-displacement distortion. Parameter tuning of this loglinear combination is performed using Och's max-BLEU algorithm (Och 2003) with a closest-match brevity penalty. Decoding uses the cube-pruning algorithm of (Huang and Chiang 2007) with a seven-word distortion limit.

4 Annotating RBMT Output

The output of the RBMT system is broken into annotated "chunks"; some of these chunks have confidence values assigned to them. The annotations come from several steps of the RBMT translation process. Currently, the following five types of chunk are annotated:

- Named entities, dates, numbers, *etc.* (one chunk type) – a confidence value is assigned based partly on how well the hypothesized entity matches source-language entity patterns and partly on the extent to which the entity matches entries in the bilingual lexicon (*e.g.*, a hypothesized compound proper name is assigned a higher confidence if it is made up of individual proper names).
- Unknown words or unlikely sequence of short words (two different chunk types) – unknown words identify words that are not in the lexicon or that have no meaning. For Chinese, unknown words are rare since any expression can be decomposed into single characters, each of which is almost always a possible word. However, a sequence of single-character words is unlikely in Chinese and such a sequence is also detected and annotated.
- 'Strong' rules output – two different chunk types identifying *e.g.*, rules based on a long distance syntactic relationship, or a long multiword expression. These chunks are very reliable.

This information is passed on to the SMT system in two different ways. In both methods, each chunk output by the RBMT consists of a translation into the target language and a probability for this translation. The SMT decoder hypothesizes both the translation provided in the RBMT output and translations provided by the phrase tables. The translation yielding the highest overall sentence score will be the one chosen. The two different ways of using the markup are:

1. The information in the chunk is inserted into the phrase table with the given probability, which replaces any other probability for that phrase pair.
2. As in **1**, but in addition, each chunk type is defined as a decoder feature outputting a confidence value. The weight assigned to this feature is

RBMT output	<rule><entity type="HUMANS" confidence="1"><expression type="1">US Secretary of State Powell</expression></entity></rule> the other day the visit which carried on to <entity type="GPE" confidence="1">Russia</entity> is still a public opinion widely attention focal point.
Input to baseline SMT:	us secretary of state powell the other day the visit which carried on to russia is still a public opinion widely attention focal point .
Output of baseline:	us secretary of state colin powell said the other day visit to russia is still a wide public opinion focus .
Input to SMT (markup strategy 1B):	<rule target="us secretary of state powell" prob="1">us secretary of state powell</rule> the other day the visit which carried on to <rule target="russia" prob="1">russia</rule> is still a public opinion widely attention focal point .
Output from SMT (markup strategy 1B):	us secretary of state powell 's visit to russia is still a public opinion generally focus of attention .
Reference:	u.s. secretary of state powell 's recent visit to russia remains a focus of widespread public opinion .

Table 2: Example sentence from the test set showing annotated RBMT output and its use in SMT.

found by the optimization algorithm (see Sec.3).

Orthogonal to these two approaches, we must decide whether to use

A. all five types of chunks

B. or only those chunks that have confidence values associated with them.

In strategy B, each chunk's confidence value is used directly; in strategy A, missing confidence values are assigned manually.

5 Experiments

5.1 GALE system combination

Recent work has focused on computation of a consensus translation from the outputs of multiple MT systems (Matusov *et al.* 2006, Rosti *et al.* 2007). This approach to system combination was applied to Chinese-English data available within the DARPA-sponsored GALE project by researchers at RWTH. One of the systems in the RWTH system combination is itself a combination: our hybrid RBMT→SMT (Systran→PORTAGE) system. This version of the hybrid system had loosely coupled components (confidence information isn't output by the RBMT). The other systems in this "parallel" combination were all pure SMT systems. In earlier experiments, an attempt had been made to include the RBMT system (Systran) by itself, but it always received a negligible weight in the parallel system combination.

Although the RBMT→SMT hybrid system is not the best among the systems combined, as measured either by BLEU score or TER score, it is always assigned a heavy weight by the system combination algorithm (usually the heaviest weight). Since the heavy weights assigned to the RBMT→SMT system could be dismissed as an artifact, experiments were also done (using 554 newswire sentences as test data) in which one system at a time was dropped from the five-way system combination. The results are shown in **Table 3** for case-sensitive BLEU and TER (high BLEU and low TER are desirable). Note that in addition to RBMT→SMT we also trained a "direct" Chinese-English system using the same SMT software (PORTAGE). When RBMT→SMT is dropped, the system combination performs worse by 0.9 BLEU and 2.6 TER. This performance drop is worse than that caused by dropping any other single system. One may infer that despite its unremarkable BLEU and TER scores taken in isolation, the RBMT→SMT serial combination provides information that complements that of the other systems (which were all SMT systems).

Description	BLEU	TER
All (system comb).	**17.0**	**65.4**
drop PORTAGE	17.0	64.9
drop system 1	17.2	65.0
drop system 2	17.2	65.6
drop system 3	16.6	65.4
drop Systran→PORTAGE	**16.1**	**68.0**

Table 3: "drop-one" in GALE system combination.

5.2 Markup experiments

We experimentally evaluated the methods for using markup proposed in Section 4 above on the so-called constrained data track for Chinese-English of the 2008 NIST MT evaluation. The evaluation was carried out on the test sets from 2004 and 2008. **Table 2** shows an example sentence from the test set. The first row presents the RBMT output in which different chunks are annotated as described in Section 4. This annotation can be nested as the first chunk shows. In this example, both chunks are assigned confidence 1. Note that other chunks in the RBMT output have lower confidence, and many of them are not annotated with confidence at all.

The RBMT system has recognized that "US Secretary of State Powell" is a human with confidence 1, and also a multiword expression. This markup in the RBMT output is stripped off before being input to the baseline SMT system. The example also shows the input to the SMT system under markup strategy 1B described in Section 4, and the output from that strategy. Finally, a reference translation is shown. Note that the baseline system inserted two spurious words, "colin" and "said" into the translation. By contrast, when markup strategy 1B was applied, the SMT system decided to retain the expression "us secretary of state powell" passed to it in the RBMT output (and this had the side-effect of removing the spurious word "said" and generating a better translation for the rest of the sentence).

Table 4 presents the results of the four different ways of using the markup of the RBMT output described in Section 4, along with baseline results without markup. The results show that the hybrid system is improved through the use of markup. There is no clear preference for one of the two approaches to using the markup (phrase table insertion only *vs.* decoder feature). However, it is clear that using only the chunks with assigned confidence performs better than the use of all chunk types. This might be due to the fact that the chunks with assigned confidence include many named entities which are particularly hard to translate for MT systems. Thus, having confidence values expressing the reliability of the translations improves the hybrid system significantly.

Description	NIST04	NIST08
Baseline (no markup)	34.0	25.0
Phrase table insertion of markup (approach 1, p.3)		
All markup (A)	34.6	24.7
Only markup with confidence (B)	**35.0**	25.8
Markup as decoder feature (approach 2, p.3)		
All markup (A)	34.4	25.3
Only markup with confidence (B)	34.6	**26.0**

Table 4 Translation quality in terms of BLEU score on NIST data

In addition to the automatic evaluation, we had an English native speaker manually assess the translations of the first 100 sentences of the 2004 test set for the baseline and "strategy 1B" output. Outputs were shuffled for each sentence to get reliable blind evaluation of the two systems. Fluency and adequacy were judged on a scale of 0-5 (0=worst, 5=best). The results are shown in **Table 5**, and they support the outcome of the automatic evaluation: the hybrid system which uses the markup is significantly preferred to the one which does not use the markup. The evaluation scores for fluency and adequacy increase by 10% and 13% relative, respectively. The table also shows which of the two translations receives a higher evaluation score, and this clearly indicates the superiority of the system with markup: in a third of all cases, this system was judged better than the baseline serial combination system.

	Fluency	Adequacy
Baseline (no markup)	1.9	2.2
Strategy 1B	2.1 (+10%)	2.5 (+13%)
Comparison no markup vs. strategy 1B: 1B worse/equal/better	10/58/32	6/64/30

Table 5 NIST04 – Qualitative human evaluation

5.3 Participation in NIST MT 2008

Both the pure statistical system PORTAGE and the serial combination Systran→PORTAGE (with markup strategy 1B) participated in the 2008 NIST Chinese-English MT evaluation. Both systems were trained on data from the constrained data track (thus, to create the Systran→PORTAGE system all the Chinese constrained-track training data was translated by Systran, and the English output aligned with the English references was then used to train PORTAGE). Both systems placed roughly in the middle of competing systems according to BLEU score, with PORTAGE obtaining a score of 24.58 and Systran→PORTAGE obtaining a score of 25.23. (Internal tests of Systran alone on the same data give 18.21). However, Systran→PORTAGE excelled according to an important human evaluation metric. In cases where human evaluators had ranked a translated sentence sufficiently highly, they were asked an additional question as to whether the translation captured all the needed information. Systran→PORTAGE obtained the highest number of "yes" answers (35.82% of all sentences) among all 14 Chinese-English systems evaluated.

6 Discussion and Future Work

In this paper, we built on earlier work showing the advantages of coupling RBMT and SMT in a serial combination RBMT→SMT where the SMT system "translates" output from the RBMT system into the target language. The conclusions to be drawn about the performance of our serial system combination Systran→PORTAGE depend on whether one consults automatic metrics like BLEU or scores assigned by human evaluators. According to BLEU, Systran→PORTAGE is typically superior to Systran alone and roughly tied with PORTAGE (if enough data are available to train the latter). According to human evaluators, however, Systran→PORTAGE is clearly superior to either of its "parents". This can be seen from the results in (Callison-Burch *et al.* 2007) and from the fact that Systran→PORTAGE placed first among all systems according to the "additional qualitative question" metric in the NIST 2008 Chinese-English MT evaluation (PORTAGE alone did not do well according to this metric; Systran alone was not evaluated, but has a BLEU score low enough to ensure it would have done poorly). Another result of this paper (in Section 5.1) is that the hybrid system appears to contribute information complementary to that provided by pure SMT systems, as judged by its important contribution to a "parallel combination" system.

Why does Systran→PORTAGE yield superior translations to those produced by either Systran or PORTAGE on its own? We have not yet conducted a thorough study to answer this question. However, our perception is that Systran's syntactic rules preserve structure and allow long-distance movement of constituents. On the other hand, this system has a weak model of the target language (English), yielding disfluencies. Post-editing by PORTAGE preserves syntactically motivated rearrangements while correcting disfluencies in the output and making more appropriate lexical choices. Although we have not systematiccally studied this behaviour, we have observed it in several examples, such as the one shown in **Table 6**.

Description	**Sentence**
Chinese	欧盟 官员 现在 最 担心 的 是 即将 从 非洲 飞回 的 候鸟。
Systran	What the EU officials most were worried now is soon the migratory bird which flies back from Africa.
PORTAGE	EU officials are most concerned about is coming from Africa flew back to the migratory birds.
Systran→ PORTAGE	The EU officials are most worried about the migratory birds that fly back from Africa.

Table 6: three translations of a Chinese sentence

The main purpose of the current paper is to show that tighter integration of the two systems further improves the hybrid system, both in terms of automatic and human evaluation. This was achieved by having the RBMT system (Systran) mark up its output in such a way that the SMT system (PORTAGE) could distinguish between more and less reliable chunks in the output.

The integration of the two systems could be further deepened, *e.g.*, by passing on more complex annotation between the two systems, or by exploring the fact that source and target language for the SMT system are the same. This provides an interesting alternative to training data gigantism: rather than using ever more data, we make better use of existing data.

Moreover, the two combined MT paradigms can benefit from each other. For instance, the RBMT confidence estimation could be data-driven, and the SMT post-editing could be constrained by basic linguistic rules.

Acknowledgement

This material is partly based upon work supported by the Defense Advanced Research Projects Agency (DARPA) under Contract No. HR0011-06-C-0023. Any opinions, findings and conclusions or recommendations expressed in this material are those of the authors and do not necessarily reflect the views of the Defense Advanced Research Projects Agency (DARPA).

References

M. Attnäs, P. Senellart and J. Senellart. Integration of SYSTRAN MT Systems in an Open Workflow. *Proc. MT Summit X*, 2005.

C. Callison-Burch, C. Fordyce, P. Koehn, C. Monz, and J. Schroeder. (Meta-) Evaluation of Machine Translation. *Proc. 2nd ACL Workshop on Statistical Machine Translation*, pp. 136-158, June 2007.

L. Dugast, J. Senellart and P. Koehn. Statistical Post-Editing on SYSTRAN's Rule-Based Translation System. *Proc. 2nd ACL Workshop on Statistical Machine Translation*, pp. 220-223, June 2007.

G. Foster and R. Kuhn. Mixture-Model Adaptation for SMT. *Proc. 2nd ACL Workshop on Statistical Machine Translation*, pp. 128-135, June 2007.

L. Huang and D. Chiang. Forest Rescoring: Faster Decoding with Integrated Language Models. *Proc. ACL 2007*, pp. 144-151, June 2007.

E. Matusov, N. Ueffing and H. Ney. Computing Consensus Translation from Multiple Machine Translation Systems Using Enhanced Hypotheses Alignment. *Proc.EACL 2006*, pp. 33-40, April 2006.

F. Och. Minimum Error Rate Training for Statistical Machine Translation. *Proc. ACL 2003*, July 2003.

A.-V. Rosti, S. Matsoukas, and R. Schwartz. Improved Word-Level System Combination for Machine Translation. *Proc. ACL 2007*, June 2007.

M. Simard, C. Goutte, and P. Isabelle. Statistical Phrase-based Post-Editing. *Proc. HLT-NAACL*, pp. 508-515, April 2007a.

M. Simard, N. Ueffing, P. Isabelle and R. Kuhn. Rule-Based Translation with Statistical Phrase-based Post-editing. *Proc. 2nd ACL Workshop on Statistical Machine Translation*, pp. 203-206, June 2007b.

A. Stolcke. SRILM - An Extensible Language Modeling Toolkit. *Proc. ICSLP*, pp. 901-904, Septermber 2002.

N. Ueffing, M. Simard, S. Larkin, and J. H. Johnson. NRC's PORTAGE System for WMT 2007. *Proc. 2nd ACL Workshop on Statistical Machine Translation*, pp. 185-188, June 2007.

J. Yang, J. Senellart and R. Zajac. SYSTRAN's Chinese Word Segmentation. *Proc. Second SIGHAN Workshop on Chinese Language Processing*, July 2003.

This page is intentionally blank.

Class-Driven Attribute Extraction

Benjamin Van Durme, **Ting Qian** and **Lenhart Schubert**
Department of Computer Science
University of Rochester
Rochester, NY 14627, USA

Abstract

We report on the large-scale acquisition of class attributes with and without the use of lists of representative instances, as well as the discovery of *unary* attributes, such as typically expressed in English through prenominal adjectival modification. Our method employs a system based on compositional language processing, as applied to the British National Corpus. Experimental results suggest that document-based, open class attribute extraction can produce results of comparable quality as those obtained using web query logs, indicating the utility of exploiting explicit occurrences of class labels in text.

1 Introduction

Recent work on the task of acquiring attributes for concept classes has focused on the use of precompiled lists of class representative instances, where attributes recognized as applying to multiple instances of the same class are inferred as being likely to apply to most, or all, members of that class. For example, the class *US President* might be represented as a list containing the entries *Bill Clinton*, *George Bush*, *Jimmy Carter*, etc. Phrases such as *Bill Clinton's chief of staff* ..., or search queries such as *chief of staff bush*, provide evidence that the class *US President* has as an attribute *chief of staff*.

Usually the focus of such systems has been on *binary* attributes, such as the example *chief of staff*, while less attention has been paid to *unary* class attributes such as *illegal* for the class *Drug*, or *warm-blooded* for the class *Animal*.[1] These attributes are most typically expressed in English through prenominal adjectival modification, with the nominal serving as a class designator. When attribute extraction is based entirely on instances and not the class labels themselves, this form of modification goes undiscovered.

In what follows we explore both the impact of gazetteers in attribute extraction as well as the acquisition and filtering of unary class attributes, through a process based on logical form generation from syntactic parses derived from the British National Corpus.

2 Extraction Framework

Extraction was performed using a modified version of the KNEXT system, a knowledge acquisition framework constructed for large scale generation of abstracted logical forms through compositional linguistic analysis. The following provides an overview of KNEXT and its target knowledge representation, Episodic Logic.

2.1 Episodic Logic

Automatically acquiring general world knowledge from text is not a task that provides an immediate solution to any real world problem.[2] Rather, the motivation for acquiring large stores of background knowledge is to enable research within other areas of artificial intelligence, e.g., the construction of systems that can engage in dialogues about everyday topics in unrestricted English, use

©2008. Licensed under the *Creative Commons Attribution-Noncommercial-Share Alike 3.0 Unported* license (http://creativecommons.org/licenses/by-nc-sa/3.0/). Some rights reserved.

[1] Almuhareb and Poesio (2004) treat unary attributes as values of binary attributes; e.g., *illegal* might be the value of a *legality* attribute. But for many unary attributes, this is a stretch.

[2] Unless one regularly needs reminding of facts such as, A WOMAN MAY BOIL A GOAT.

```
(Some e0:
    [e0 at-about Now0]
    [(Many.det x :
        [x ((attr athletic.a) (plur youngster.n))]
        [x want.v
            (Ka
              (become.v
                (plur
                  ((attr professional.a) athlete.n))))])
    ** e0])
```

Figure 1: Example EL formula; square brackets indicate a sentential infix syntax of form [*subject pred object* ...], *Ka* reifies action predicates, and *attr* "raises" adjectival predicates to predicate modifiers; *e0* is the situation characterized by the sentence.

common sense in answering questions or solving problems, pursue intrinsic goals independently, and show awareness of their own characteristics, biography, and cognitive capacities and limitations. An important challenge in the pursuit of these long-range goals is the design and implementation of a knowledge representation that is as expressively rich as natural language and facilitates language understanding and commonsense reasoning.

Episodic Logic (EL) (Schubert and Hwang, 2000), is a superset of FOL augmented with certain semantic features common to all human languages: generalized quantification, intensionality, uncertainty, modification and reification of predicates and propositions, and event characterization by sentences. An implementation of EL exists as the EPILOG system (Schaeffer et al., 1993), which supports both forward and backward inference, along with various specialized routines for dealing with, e.g., color, time, class subsumption, etc. EPILOG is under current development as a platform for studying a notion of explicit self-awareness as defined by Schubert (2005).

As an indication of EL's NL-like syntax, figure 1 contains the output of EPILOG's parser/logical-form generator for the sentence, *Many athletic youngsters want to become professional athletes.*

2.2 KNEXT

If "deep" language understanding and commonsense reasoning involve items as complex and structured as seen in figure 1, then automated knowledge acquisition cannot simply be a matter of accumulating rough associations between word strings, along the lines "(Youngster) (want become) (professional athlete)". Rather, acquired knowledge needs to conform with a systematic, highly expressive KR syntax such as EL.

The KNEXT project is aimed at extracting such structured knowledge from text. One of the major obstacles is that the bulk of commonsense knowledge on which people rely is not explicitly written down – precisely because it is *common*. Even it were written down, most of it could not be reliably interpreted, because reliable interpretation of language is itself dependent on commonsense knowledge (among other things).

In view of these difficulties, KNEXT has initially focused on attempting to abstract world knowledge "factoids" from texts, based on the logical forms derived from parsed sentences. The idea is that nominal pre- and post-modifiers, along with subject-verb-object relations, captured in logical forms similar to that in figure 1, give a glimpse of the common properties and relationships in the world – even if the source sentences describe invented situations. For example, the following were extracted by KNEXT, then automatically verbalized back into English for ease of readability:

- SOME_NUMBER_OF YOUNGSTERS MAY WANT TO BECOME ATHLETES.
- YOUNGSTERS CAN BE ATHLETIC.
- ATHLETES CAN BE PROFESSIONAL.

2.3 Attribute Extraction via KNEXT

In order to study the contribution of lists of instances (i.e., generalized *gazetteers*) to the task of attribute extraction, the version of KNEXT as presented by Schubert (2002) was modified to provide output of a form similar to that of the extraction work of Paşca and Van Durme (2007).

KNEXT's abstracted, propositional output was automatically verbalized into English, with any resultant statements of the form, *A(N) X MAY HAVE A(N) Y*, taken to suggest that the class *X* has as an attribute the property *Y*.

KNEXT was designed from the beginning to make use of gazetteers if available, where a phrase such as *Bill Clinton vetoed the bill* supports the (verbalized) proposition *A PRESIDENT MAY VETO A BILL.* just as would *The president vetoed the bill.* We instrumented the system to record which propositions did or did not require gazetteers in their construction, allowing for a numerical breakdown of the respective contributions of known instances of a class, versus the class label itself.

Paşca and Van Durme (2007) described the results of an informal survey asking participants to enumerate what they felt to be important attributes for a small set of example classes. Some of these resultant attributes were not of the form targeted by the authors' system. For example, *nonprofit* was given as an important potential attribute for the class *Company*, as well as *legal* for the class *Drug*. These attributes correspond to *unary* predicates as compared to the targeted *binary* predicates underlying such attributes as *cost(X, Y)* for the class *Drug*.

We extracted such unary attributes by focusing on verbalizations of the form, *A(N) X CAN BE Y* as in *AN ANIMAL CAN BE WARM-BLOODED*.

3 Experimental Setting

3.1 Corpus Processing

Initial reports on the use of KNEXT were focused on the processing of manually created parse trees, on a corpus of limited size (the Brown corpus of Kucera and Francis (1967)). Since that time the system has been modified into a fully automatic extraction system, making use of syntactic parse trees generated by parsers trained on the Penn Treebank.

For our studies here, the parser employed was that of Collins (1997) applied to the sentences of the British National Corpus (BNC Consortium, 2001). Our choice of the BNC was motivated by its breadth of genre, its substantial size (100 million words) and its familiarity (and accessibility) to the community.

3.2 Gazetteers

KNEXT's gazetteers were used as-is, and were defined based on a variety of sources: miscellaneous publicly available lists, as well as manual enumeration. The classes covered can be seen in the Results section in table 2, where the minimum, maximum and mean size were 2, 249, and 41, respectively.

3.3 Filtering out Non-predicative Adjectives

Beyond the pre-existing KNEXT framework, additional processing was introduced for the extraction of unary attributes in order to filter out vacuous or unsupported propositions derived from non-compositional phrases.

This filtering was performed through the creation of three lists: a whitelist of accepted predicative adjectives; a graylist containing such adjectives that are meaningful as unary predicates only when applied to plural nouns; and a blacklist derived from Wikipedia topic titles, representing lexicalized, non-compositional phrases.

Whitelist The creation of the whitelist began with calculating part-of-speech (POS) tagged bigram counts using the Brown corpus. The advantage of using a POS-tagged bigram model lies in the saliency of phrase structures, which enabled frequency calculations for both attributive and predicative uses of a given adjective. Attributive counts were based on instances when an adjective appears in the pre-nominal position and modifies another noun. Predicative counts were derived by summing over occurrences of a given adjective after all possible copulas. These counts were used to compute a p/a ratio - the quotient of predicative count over attributive count - for each word classified by WordNet (Fellbaum, 1998) as a having an adjectival use. After manual inspection, two cut-off points were chosen at ratios of .06 and 0, as seen in table 1.

Words not appearing in the Brown corpus (i.e. having 0 count for both uses), were sampled and inspected, with the decision made to place the majority within the whitelist, excluding just those with suffixes including -al, -c, -an, -st, -ion, -th, -o, -ese, -er, -on, -i, -x, -v, and -ing.

This process resulted in a combined whitelist of 14,249 (usually) predicative adjectives.

p/a ratio (r)	Cut-off decision
$r \geq .06$	keep the adjective*
$0 < r < .06$	remove the adjective*
otherwise	keep the adjective*

Table 1: Cut-off decision given the p/a ratio of an adjective. **Note: except for hand-selected cases.*

Graylist We manually constructed a short list (currently 33 words) containing adjectives that are generally inappropriate as whitelist entries, but could be acceptable when applied to plurals. For example, the verbalized proposition *OBJECTS CAN BE SIMILAR* was deemed acceptable, while a statement such as *AN OBJECT CAN BE SIMILAR* is erroneous because of a missing argument.

Blacklist From an exhaustive set of Wikipedia topic titles was derived a blacklist consisting of entries that had to satisfy four criteria: 1) no more than three words in length; 2) has no closed-class words, such as prepositions or adverbs; 3) must begin with an adjective and end with a noun (determined by WordNet); and 4) does not contain any numerical characters or miscellaneous symbols that are usually not meaningful in English. Therefore, each title in the resultant list is literally a short noun phrase with adjectives as premodifiers. It was observed that in these encyclopedia titles, the role of adjectives is predominantly to restrict the scope of the object that is being named (e.g. CRIMINAL LAW), rather than to describe its attributions or features (e.g. DARK EYES). More often than not, only cases similar to the second example can be safely verbalized as *X CAN BE Y* from a noun phrase *Y X*, with Y being the pre-nominal adjective.

We further refined this list by examining trigram frequencies as reported in the web-derived n-gram collection of Brants and Franz (2006). For each title of the form *(Adj N)* ..., we gathered trigram frequencies for adverbial modifications such as *(very Adj N)* ..., and *(truly Adj N)* .... Intuitively, high relative frequency of such modification with respect to the non-modified bigram supports removal of the given title from the blacklist.

Trigram counts were collected using the modifiers: *absolutely*, *almost*, *entirely*, *highly*, *nearly*, *perfectly*, *truly* and *very*. These counts were summed for a given title then divided by the aforementioned bigram score. Upon sampled inspection, all three-word titles were kept on the blacklist, along with any two-word title with a resultant ratio less than 0.028. For example, the titles *Hardy Fish*, *Young Galaxy*, and *Sad Book* were removed, while *Common Cause*, *Bouncy Ball*, and *Heavy Oil* were retained.

4 Results

From the parsed BNC, 6,205,877 propositions were extracted, giving an average of 1.396 propositions per input sentence.[3] These results were then used to explore the necessity of gazetteers, and the potential for extracting unary attributes. Quality judgements were performed using a 5 point scale as seen in figure 2.

[3]These approximately six million verbalized propositions, along with their underlying logical form and respective source sentence(s), may be browsed interactively through an online browser available at: http://www.cs.rochester.edu/u/vandurme/epik

THE STATEMENT ABOVE IS A REASONABLY CLEAR, ENTIRELY PLAUSIBLE GENERAL CLAIM AND SEEMS NEITHER TOO SPECIFIC NOR TOO GENERAL OR VAGUE TO BE USEFUL:
1. I agree.
2. I lean towards agreement.
3. I'm not sure.
4. I lean towards disagreement.
5. I disagree.

Figure 2: Instructions for scaled judging.

4.1 Necessity of Gazetteers

From the total set of extracted propositions, 638,809 could be verbalized as statements of the form *X MAY HAVE Y*. There were 71,531 unique classes (*X*) for which at least a single candidate attribute (*Y*) was extracted, with 9,743 of those having at least a single such attribute that was supported by a minimum of two distinct sentences.

Table 2 gives the number of attributes extracted for the given classes when using only gazetteers, when using only the given names as class labels, and when using both together. While instance-based extraction generated more unique attributes, there were still a significant number of results derived based exclusively on class labels. Further, as can be seen for cases such as *Artist*, class-driven extraction provided a large number of attribute candidates not observed when relying only on gazetteers (701 total candidate attributes were gathered based on the union of 441 and 303 candidates respectively extracted with, and without a gazetteer for *Artist*).

We note that this volume measure is potentially biased against class-driven extraction, as no effort was made to pick an optimal label for a given gazetteer, (the original hand-specified class labels were retained). For example, one might expect the label *Drink* to generate more, yet still appropriate, propositions than *Beverage*, *Actor* and/or *Actress* as compared to *Show Biz Star*, or the semantically similar *Book* versus *Literary Work*. This is suggested by the entries in the table based on using supertypes of the given class, as well as in figure 3, which favorably compares top attributes discovered for select classes against those reported elsewhere in the literature.

Table 3 gives the assessed quality for the top ten attributes extracted for five of the classes in table 2. As can be seen, class-driven extraction can produce attributes of quality assessed at par with attributes extracted using only gazetteers.

BasicFood	**Religion**
K (*Food*): quality, part, taste, value, portion..	K: basis, influence, name, truths, symbols, principles, strength, practice, origin, adherent, god, defence..
D: species, pounds, cup, kinds, lbs, bowl..	D: teachings, practice, beliefs, religion spread, principles, emergence, doctrines..
Q: nutritional value, health benefits, glycemic index, varieties, nutrition facts, calories..	Q: basic beliefs, teachings, holy book, practices, rise, branches, spread, sects..

HeavenlyBody	**Painter**
K_G (*Planet*): surface, orbit, bars, history, atmosphere..	K_G (*Artist*) : works, life, career, painting, impression, drawings, paintings, studio, exhibition..
K (*Planet*): surface, history, future, orbit, mass, field..	K (*Artist*): works, impression, career, life, studio..
K (*Star*): surface, mass, field, regions..	K (*Painter*) : works, life, wife, eye..
D: observations, spectrum, planet, spectra, conjunction, transit, temple, surface..	Q': paintings, works, portrait, death, style, artwork, bibliography, bio, autobiography, childhood..
Q: atmosphere, surface, gravity, diameter, mass, rotation, revolution, moons, radius..	

Figure 3: Qualitative comparison of top extracted attributes; K_G is KNEXT using gazetteers, K (*class*) is KNEXT for a class label similar to the heading, D and Q are document- and query-based results as reported in (Paşca et al., 2007), Q' is query-based results reported in (Paşca and Van Durme, 2007).

The noticeable drop in quality for the class *Planet* when only using gazetteers (3.2 mean judged acceptability) highlights the recurring problem of word sense ambiguity in extraction. The names of Roman deities, such as Mars or Mercury, are used to refer to a number of conceptually distinct items, such as planets within our solar system. Two of the attributes judged as poor quality for this class were *bars* and *customers*, respectively derived from the noun phrases: (NP (NNP Mars) (NNS bars)), and (NP (NNP Mercury) (NNS customers)). Note that in both cases the underlying extraction is correctly performed; the error comes from abstracting to the wrong class. These NPs may arguably support the verbalized propositions, e.g.: A CANDY-COMPANY MAY HAVE BARS, and A CAR-COMPANY MAY HAVE CUSTOMERS.

These examples point to additional areas for improvement beyond sense disambiguation: non-compositional phrase filtering for all NPs, rather than just in the cases of adjectival modification (*Mars bar* is a Wikipedia topic); and relative discounting of patterns used in the extraction process[4]. This later technique is commonly used in specialized extraction systems, such as constructed by Snow et al. (2005) who fit a logistic regression model for hypernym (X is-a Y) classification based on WordNet, and Girju et al. (2003) who trained a classifier to look specifically for part-whole relations.

[4]For example, (NP (NNP X) (NNS Y)) may be more semantically ambiguous than, e.g., the possessive construction (NP (NP (NNP X) (POS 's)) (NP (NNS Y))).

4.2 Unary Attributes

Table 4 shows how filtering non-compositional phrases from CAN BE propositions affects extraction volume. Table 5 shows the difference between such post-filtered propositions and those that were deleted. As our filter lists were not built fully automatically, evaluation was performed exclusively by an author with negligible direct involvement in the lists' creation (so-as to minimize judgement bias).

As examples, the top ten unary attributes for select classes are given in table 6, which the authors believe to be high quality on average, with some bad entries present. Attributes such as *pre-raphaelite* for *Painter* are considered obscure, while those such as *favourite* for *Animal* are considered unlikely to be useful as a unary predicate.

The importance of class-driven extraction can be seen in results such as those given for the class *Apple*. Even if it were the case that gazetteer-based extraction could deliver perfect results for those classes whose instances occasionally appear explicitly in text, there are a number of classes for which such instances are entirely lacking. For example, there are many instances of the class *Company* which have been individually named and appear in text with some frequency, e.g., Microsoft, Walmart, or Boeing. However, despite the many real-world instantiations of the class *Apple*, this does not translate into a list of individually named members in text.[5] If our goal is to acquire attributes for as many classes as possible, our results

[5]Instances of *Apple* are referred to directly as such; "an apple."

Class	Both	Gaz.	Class Lbl.
Continent	777	698	96
Country	7,285	5,993	1,696
US State	1,289	1,286	609*
US City	2,216	2,120	813*
World City	4,780	4,747	813*
Beverage	53	53	0
Tycoon	19	10	10
TV Network	71	71	0
Artist	706	441	303
Medicine	29	2	27
Weekday	1,234	1,232	2
Month	2,282	1,875	474
Dictator	533	509	28
Conqueror	103	84	19
Philosopher	672	649	37
Conductor	118	74	45
Singer	220	179	49
Band	349	58	303
King	811	208	664
Queen	541	17	532
Religious Leader	127	127	0
Adventurer	32	27	5
Planet	289	163	141
Criminal/Outlaw	30	30	6/4*
Service Agency	85	83	2
Architect	72	67	63
Show Biz Star	82	82	0
Film Maker	42	33	9
Composer	722	651	98
Humanitarian	5	5	0
Pope	235	123	113
River	402	168	253
Company	3,968	1,553	2,941
Deity	1,037	1,027	19
Scientist	798	750	60
Religious Holiday	594	593	65*
Civic Holiday	3	3	65*
Military Commander	71	71	26*
Intl Political Entity	673	673	0
Sports Celebrity	45	45	0
Activist Organization	63	63	0
Martial Art	3	3	0
Government Agency	295	294	2
Criminal Organization	0	0	0
US President	596	596	1,421*
Political Leader	568	568	170*
Supreme Court Justice	0	0	18*
Emperor	436	211	259
Fictitious Character	227	227	180*
Literary Work	9	9	0
Engineer/Inventor	10	10	73/13*
Famous Lawyer	0	0	72*
Writer	1,116	957	236
TOTAL	35,723	29,518	8,506

Table 2: Extraction volume with and without using gazetteers. **Note: When results are zero after gaz. omission, values are reported for super-types, such as* Holiday *for the sub-type* Civic Holiday, *or* City *for* US City. *A/B scores reported for each class used separately, e.g.,* Engineer/Inventor.

Class	Both	Gazetteer	Class Label
King	1.2	1.9	1.3
Composer	1.5	1.5	2.1
River	1.9	1.9	1.5
Continent	1.5	1.9	2.0
Planet	1.9	**3.2**	1.6

Table 3: Average judged acceptability for the top ten attributes extracted for the given classes when using/not-using gazetteer information.

Collection	**Size**	% of	
		Original	CAN BE
Original total	6,204,184	100	-
Filtered total	5,382,282	87	-
Original CAN BE	2,895,325	46	100
Filtered CAN BE	2,073,417	33	72
Whitelist	812,146	15	28
Blacklist	19,786	1<	1

Table 4: Impact of filtering on volume. For example, those propositions removed because of the whitelist comprised 15% of the total propositions extracted, or 28% of those specifically verbalized as *X CAN BE Y*.

indicate the benefits of exploiting the explicit appearance of class labels in text.

5 Related Work

Paşca and Van Durme (2007) presented an approach to attribute extraction based on the use of search engine query logs, a previously unexplored source of data within information extraction. Results confirmed the intuition that a significant number of high quality, characteristic attributes for many classes may be derived based on the relative frequency with which anonymous users request particular pieces of information for known instances of a concept class. Paşca et al. (2007) compared the quality of shallow attribute extraction techniques as applied to documents versus search engine query logs, concluding that such methods are more applicable to query logs than to documents. We note that while search queries do seem ideally suited for extracting class attributes, existing large-scale collections of query logs are proprietary and thus unavailable to the general research community. At least until such a resource becomes available, it is of interest to the community that (qualitatively) similar extraction results may be achieved exclusively using publicly available document collections.

Alternative approaches to harvesting large-scale knowledge repositories based on logical forms include that reported by Suchanek et al. (2007). The authors used non-linguistic information avail-

	1	10	100	1,000
Filtered	3.18	3.60	2.74	2.76
Blacklist	3.88	4.00	4.08	4.06
Whitelist	3.78	3.76	3.74	3.80

Table 5: Mean evaluated acceptability for 50 unary attributes randomly sampled from each of the given levels of support (attribute occurred once, less than 10 times, less than 100 times, ...). Filtered refers to the final "clean" results, Blacklist and Whitelist refer to propositions deleted due to the given list.

Painter	famous, romantic, distinguished, celebrated, well-known, pre-raphaelite, flemish, dutch, abstract
Animal	dead, trapped, dangerous, unfortunate, intact, hungry, wounded, tropical, sick, favourite
Drug	dangerous, powerful, addictive, safe, illegal, experimental, effective, prescribed, harmful, hallucinatory
Apple	red, juicy, fresh, bad, substantive, stuffed, shiny, ripe, green, baked
Earthquake	disastrous, violent, underwater, prolonged, powerful, popular, monstrous, fatal, famous, epic

Table 6: Top ten unary attributes for select classes, gathered exclusively without the use of gazetteers.

able via Wikipedia to populate a KB based on a variant of the logic underlying the Web Ontology Language (OWL). Results were limited to 14 predefined relation types, such as *diedInYear* and *politicianOf*, with membership of instances within particular concept classes inferred based on Wikipedia's category pages. Authors report 5 million so-called *ontological* facts being extracted.

Almuhareb and Poesio (2004) performed attribute extraction on webtext using simple extraction patterns (e.g., "the * of the C [is|was]", and "[a|an|the] * C [is|was]", which respectively match *The color of the rose was red* and *A red rose was* ...), and showed that such attributes could improve concept clustering. Subsequently they tested an alternative approach to the same problem using a dependency parser, extracting syntactic relations such as (ncmod, rose, red) and (ncsubj, grow, rose) (Almuhareb and Poesio,). They concluded that syntactic information is relatively expensive to derive, and serves primarily to alleviate data sparsity problems (by capturing dependencies between potentially widely separated words) that may no longer be an issue given the scale of the Web. We take a different view, first because attribute extraction is an offline task for which a 60% overhead cost (reported by the authors) is not a major issue, but more importantly because we regard approaches that process language compositionally as ultimately necessary for deeper meaning representation and language understanding.

Following intuitions similar to those laid out by Schubert (2002), Banko et al. (2007) presented TextRunner, the latest in a series of ever more sophisticated general information extraction systems (Cafarella et al., 2005; Etzioni et al., 2004). The authors constructed a non-parser based extractor for open domain text designed to efficiently process web-sized datasets. Results are in the form of bracketed text sequences that hint at a sentence's underlying semantics. For example, *(Bletchley Park) was location of (Station X)*.

Cimiano et al. (2005) performed a limited form of class-driven extraction in order to induce class hierarchies via the methods of Formal Concept Analysis (FCA). For example, a *car* is both *driveable* and *rentable* based on its occurrence in object position of the relevant verbs. A *bike* shares these properties with *car*, as well as having the property *rideable*, leading to these classes being near in the resultant automatically constructed taxonomy. Experiments were performed on limited domains for which pre-existing ontologies existed for measuring performance (*tourism* and *finance*).

Lin (1999) gave a corpus-based method for finding various types of non-compositional phrases, including the sort discussed in this paper. Identification was based on mutual information statistics conditioned on a given syntactic context (such as our targeted prenominal adjectival modification). If the mutual information of, e.g., *white house*, shows strong differences from that for constructions with similar components, e.g., *red house*, and *white barn*, then the given phrase was determined to be non-compositional. The use of this method to supplement that explored here is a matter of current investigation. Early results confirm our intuition regarding the correlation between such automatically discovered non-compositional phrases and Wikipedia topic titles, where high scoring phrases not already in our list tend to suggest miss-

Yes	cooking pot, magic flute, runny nose, skimmed milk, acquired dyslexia, charged particles, earned income
No	causal connectives, golden oldies, ruling junta, graduated pension, unsung heroes, viral rna

Table 7: Example high-scoring phrases as ranked by Lin's metric when applied to KNEXT logical forms, along with whether there is, at the time of this writing, an associated Wikipedia entry.

A CAR MAY HAVE A ...
back, boot, side, driver, front, roof, seat, end, interior, owner, door, control, value, bonnet, wheel, window, engine, headlights..
A CAR CAN BE ...
black, parked, red, white, armoured, nice, hired, bloody, open, beautiful, wrecked, unmarked, secondhand, powerful, brand-new, out-of use, damaged, heavy, dark, competitive, broken-down..
A CAR MAY BE ... IN SOME WAY
parked, stolen, driven, damaged, serviced, stopped, lost, clamped, overturned, locked, involved in an accident, found, turned, transported..

Table 8: Top attributes extracted for the class *Car*, where MAY BE relational properties (akin to those used by Cimiano et al. (2005)) are similarly acquired via verbalization of abstracted logical forms.

ing entries in the encyclopedia (see table 7). The ability to perform such "missing topic discovery" should be of interest to those within the emerging community of Wikipedia-focused AI researchers.

6 Conclusion

We have shown that an open knowledge extraction system can effectively yield class attributes, even when named instances of the class are unavailable or scarce (as a final example see table 8). We studied the quantitative contributions of instances (as given in KNEXT gazetteers) and explicitly occurring class nominals to the discovery of attributes, and found both to be important. We paid particular attention to the acquisition of *unary* class attributes, for which access to class labels is of particular importance because of their typical manner of expression in text.

Acknowledgements The authors are grateful to Daniel Gildea for contributing a parsed version of the BNC. This work was supported by NSF grants IIS-0328849 and IIS-0535105.

References

Almuhareb, Abdulrahman and Massimo Poesio. Finding concept attributes in the web using a parser. In *Proceedings Corpus Linguistics Conference*.

Almuhareb, Abdulrahman and Massimo Poesio. 2004. Attribute-based and value-based clustering: an evaluation. In *Proceedings of EMNLP*.

Banko, Michele, Michael J Cafarella, Stephen Soderland, Matt Broadhead, and Oren Etzioni. 2007. Open Information Extraction from the Web. In *Proceedings of IJCAI*.

BNC Consortium. 2001. The British National Corpus, version 2 (BNC World). Distributed by Oxford University Computing Services.

Brants, Thorsten and Alex Franz. 2006. Web 1T 5-gram Version 1. Distributed by the Linguistic Data Consortium.

Cafarella, Michael J., Doug Downey, Stephen Soderland, and Oren Etzioni. 2005. KnowItNow: Fast, Scalable Information Extraction from the Web. In *Proceedings of HLT-EMNLP*.

Cimiano, Philipp, Andreas Hotho, and Steffen Stabb. 2005. Learning concept hierarchies from text corpora using formal concept analysis. *Journal of Artificial Inteligence Research*.

Collins, Michael. 1997. Three generative, lexicalised models for statistical parsing. In *Proceedings of ACL*.

Etzioni, Oren, Michael Cafarella, Doug Downey, Stanley Kok, AnaMaria Popescu, Tal Shaked, Stephen Soderland, Daniel S. Weld, and Alexander Yates. 2004. Web-scale Information Extraction in KnowItAll. In *Proceedings of WWW*.

Fellbaum, Christiane. 1998. *WordNet: An Electronic Lexical Database*. MIT Press.

Girju, R., A. Badulescu, and D. Moldovan. 2003. Learning semantic constraints for the automatic discovery of part-whole relations. In *Proceedings of HLT-NAACL*.

Kucera, H. and W. N. Francis. 1967. *Computational Analysis of Present-Day American English*. Brown University Press, Providence, RI.

Lin, Dekang. 1999. Automatic identification of non-compositional phrases. In *Proceedings of ACL*.

Paşca, Marius and Benjamin Van Durme. 2007. What you seek is what you get: Extraction of class attributes from query logs. In *Proceedings of IJCAI*.

Paşca, Marius, Benjamin Van Durme, and Nikesh Garera. 2007. The role of documents vs. queries in extracting class attributes from text. In *Proceedings of CIKM*.

Schaeffer, S.A., C.H. Hwang, J. de Haan, and L.K. Schubert. 1993. EPILOG, the computational system for episodic logic: User's guide. Technical report, Dept. of Computing Science, Univ. of Alberta, August.

Schubert, Lenhart K. and Chung Hee Hwang. 2000. Episodic logic meets little red riding hood: A comprehensive, natural representation for language understanding. In Iwanska, L. and S.C. Shapiro, editors, *Natural Language Processing and Knowledge Representation: Language for Knowledge and Knowledge for Language*. MIT/AAAI Press.

Schubert, Lenhart K. 2002. Can we derive general world knowledge from texts? In *Proceedings of HLT*.

Schubert, Lenhart K. 2005. Some Knowledge Representation and Reasoning Requirements for Self-awareness. In *Proc. AAAI Spring Symposium on Metacognition in Computation*.

Snow, Rion, Daniel Jurafsky, and Andrew Y. Ng. 2005. Learning syntactic patterns for automatic hypernym discovery. In *Proceedings of NIPS 17*.

Suchanek, Fabian M., Gjergji Kasneci, and Gerhard Weikum. 2007. YAGO: A core of semantic knowledge unifying WordNet and Wikipedia. In *Proceedings of WWW*.

Using Three Way Data for Word Sense Discrimination

Tim Van de Cruys
Humanities Computing
University of Groningen
t.van.de.cruys@rug.nl

Abstract

In this paper, an extension of a dimensionality reduction algorithm called NON-NEGATIVE MATRIX FACTORIZATION is presented that combines both 'bag of words' data and syntactic data, in order to find semantic dimensions according to which both words and syntactic relations can be classified. The use of three way data allows one to determine which dimension(s) are responsible for a certain sense of a word, and adapt the corresponding feature vector accordingly, 'subtracting' one sense to discover another one. The intuition in this is that the syntactic features of the syntax-based approach can be disambiguated by the semantic dimensions found by the bag of words approach. The novel approach is embedded into clustering algorithms, to make it fully automatic. The approach is carried out for Dutch, and evaluated against EuroWordNet.

1 Introduction

Automatically acquiring semantics from text is a subject that has gathered a lot of attention for quite some time now. As Manning and Schütze (Manning and Schütze, 2000) point out, most work on acquiring semantic properties of words has focused on *semantic similarity*. 'Automatically acquiring a relative measure of how similar a word is to known words [...] is much easier than determining what the actual meaning is.' (Manning and Schütze, 2000, §8.5)

© 2008. Licensed under the *Creative Commons Attribution-Noncommercial-Share Alike 3.0 Unported* license (http://creativecommons.org/licenses/by-nc-sa/3.0/). Some rights reserved.

Most work on semantic similarity relies on the distributional hypothesis (Harris, 1985). This hypothesis states that words that occur in similar contexts tend to be similar. With regard to the context used, two basic approaches exist. One approach makes use of 'bag of words' co-occurrence data; in this approach, a certain window around a word is used for gathering co-occurrence information. The window may either be a fixed number of words, or the paragraph or document that a word appears in. Thus, words are considered similar if they appear in similar windows (documents). One of the dominant methods using this method is LATENT SEMANTIC ANALYSIS (LSA).

The second approach uses a more fine grained distributional model, focusing on the syntactic relations that words appear with. Typically, a large text corpus is parsed, and dependency triples are extracted.[1] Words are considered similar if they appear with similar syntactic relations. Note that the former approach does not need any kind of linguistic annotation, whereas for the latter, some form of syntactic annotation is needed.

The results yielded by both approaches are typically quite different in nature: the former approach typically puts its finger on a broad, thematic kind of similarity, while the latter approach typically grasps a tighter, synonym-like similarity. Example (1) shows the difference between both approaches; for each approach, the top ten most similar nouns to the Dutch noun *muziek* 'music' are given. In (a), the window-based approach is used, while (b) uses the syntax-based approach. (a) shows indeed more thematic similarity, whereas (b) shows tighter similarity.

[1] e.g. dependency relations that qualify *apple* might be 'object of *eat*' and 'adjective *red*'. This gives us dependency triples like $< apple, obj, eat >$.

(1) a. **muziek** 'music': *gitaar* 'guitar', *jazz* 'jazz', *cd* 'cd', *rock* 'rock', *bas* 'bass', *song* 'song', *muzikant* 'musician', *musicus* 'musician', *drum* 'drum', *slagwerker* 'drummer'
b. **muziek** 'music': *dans* 'dance', *kunst* 'art', *klank* 'sound', *liedje* 'song', *geluid* 'sound', *poëzie* 'poetry', *literatuur* 'literature', *popmuziek* 'pop music', *lied* 'song', *melodie* 'melody'

Especially the syntax-based method has been adopted by many researchers, in order to find semantically similar words. There is, however, one important problem with this kind of approach: the method is not able to cope with ambiguous words. Take the examples:

(2) een oneven nummer
a odd number
an odd number

(3) een steengoed nummer
a great number
'a great song'

The word *nummer* does not have the same meaning in these examples. In example (2), *nummer* is used in the sense of 'designator of quantity'. In example (3), it is used in the sense of 'musical performance'. Accordingly, we would like the word *nummer* to be disambiguated into two senses, the first sense being similar to words like *getal* 'number', *cijfer* 'digit' and the second to words like *liedje* 'song', *song* 'song'.

While it is relatively easy for a human language user to distinguish between the two senses, this is a difficult task for a computer. Even worse: the results get blurred because the attributes of both senses (in this example *oneven* and *steengoed*) are grouped together into one sense. This is the main drawback of the syntax-based method. On the other hand, methods that capture semantic dimensions are known to be useful in disambiguating different senses of a word. Particularly, PROBABILISTIC LATENT SEMANTIC ANALYSIS (PLSA) is known to simultaneously encode various senses of words according to latent semantic dimensions (Hofmann, 1999). In this paper, we want to explore an approach that tries to remedy the shortcomings of the former, syntax-based approach with the benefits of the latter. The intuition in this is that the syntactic features of the syntax-based approach can be disambiguated by the 'latent semantic dimensions' found by the window-based approach.

2 Previous Work

2.1 Distributional Similarity

There have been numerous approaches for computing the similarity between words from distributional data. We mention some of the most important ones.

With regard to the first approach – using a context window – we already mentioned LSA (Landauer and Dumais, 1997). In LSA, a term-document matrix is created, containing the frequency of each word in a specific document. This matrix is then decomposed into three other matrices with a mathematical technique called SINGULAR VALUE DECOMPOSITION. The most important dimensions that come out of the SVD allegedly represent 'latent semantic dimensions', according to which nouns and documents can be presented more efficiently.

LSA has been criticized for not being the most appropriate data reduction method for textual applications. The SVD underlying the method assumes normally-distributed data, whereas textual count data (such as the term-document matrix) can be more appropriately modeled by other distributional models such as Poisson (Manning and Schütze, 2000, §15.4.3). Successive methods such as PROBABILISTIC LATENT SEMANTIC ANALYSIS (PLSA) (Hofmann, 1999), try to remedy this shortcoming by imposing a proper latent variable model, according to which the values can be estimated. The method we adopt in our research – NON-NEGATIVE MATRIX FACTORIZATION – is similar to PLSA, and adequately remedies this problem as well.

The second approach – using syntactic relations – has been adopted by many researchers, in order to acquire semantically similar words. One of the most important is Lin's (1998). For Dutch, the approach has been applied by Van der Plas & Bouma (2005).

2.2 Discriminating senses

Schütze (1998) uses a disambiguation algorithm – called context-group discrimination – based on the clustering of the context of ambiguous words. The clustering is based on second-order co-occurrence: the contexts of the ambiguous word are similar if the words they in turn co-occur with are similar.

Pantel and Lin (2002) present a clustering algorithm – coined CLUSTERING BY COMMITTEE (CBC) – that automatically discovers word senses from text. The key idea is to first discover a set of tight, unambiguous clusters, to which possibly ambiguous words can be assigned. Once a word has been assigned to a cluster, the features associated with that particular cluster are stripped off the word's vector. This way, less frequent senses of the word can be discovered.

The former approach uses a window-based method; the latter uses syntactic data. But none of the algorithms developed so far have combined both sources in order to discriminate among different senses of a word.

3 Methodology

3.1 Non-negative Matrix Factorization

3.1.1 Theory

Non-negative matrix factorization (NMF) (Lee and Seung, 2000) is a group of algorithms in which a matrix V is factorized into two other matrices, W and H.

$$V_{n \times m} \approx W_{n \times r} H_{r \times m} \tag{1}$$

Typically r is much smaller than n, m so that both instances and features are expressed in terms of a few components.

Non-negative matrix factorization enforces the constraint that all three matrices must be non-negative, so all elements must be greater than or equal to zero. The factorization turns out to be particularly useful when one wants to find additive properties.

Formally, the non-negative matrix factorization is carried out by minimizing an objective function. Two kinds of objective function exist: one that minimizes the Euclidean distance, and one that minimizes the Kullback-Leibler divergence. In this framework, we will adopt the latter, as – from our experience – entropy-based measures tend to work well for natural language. Thus, we want to find the matrices W and H for which the Kullback-Leibler divergence between V and WH (the multiplication of W and H) is the smallest.

Practically, the factorization is carried out through the iterative application of update rules. Matrices W and H are randomly initialized, and the rules in 2 and 3 are iteratively applied – alternating between them. In each iteration, each vector is adequately normalized, so that all dimension values sum to 1.

$$H_{a\mu} \leftarrow H_{a\mu} \frac{\sum_i W_{ia} \frac{V_{i\mu}}{(WH)_{i\mu}}}{\sum_k W_{ka}} \tag{2}$$

$$W_{ia} \leftarrow W_{ia} \frac{\sum_\mu H_{a\mu} \frac{V_{i\mu}}{(WH)_{i\mu}}}{\sum_v H_{av}} \tag{3}$$

3.1.2 Example

We can now straightforwardly apply NMF to create semantic word models. NMF is applied to a frequency matrix, containing bag of words co-occurrence data. The additive property of NMF ensures that semantic dimensions emerge, according to which the various words can be classified. Two sample dimensions are shown in example (4). For each dimension, the words with the largest value on that dimension are given. Dimension (a) can be qualified as a 'transport' dimension, and dimension (b) as a 'cooking' dimension.

(4) a. *bus* 'bus', *taxi* 'taxi', *trein* 'train', *halte* 'stop', *reiziger* 'traveler', *perron* 'platform', *tram* 'tram', *station* 'station', *chauffeur* 'driver', *passagier* 'passenger'

b. *bouillon* 'broth', *slagroom* 'cream', *ui* 'onion', *eierdooier* 'egg yolk', *laurierblad* 'bay leaf', *zout* 'salt', *deciliter* 'decilitre', *boter* 'butter', *bleekselderij* 'celery', *saus* 'sauce'

3.2 Extending Non-negative Matrix Factorization

We now propose an extension of NMF that combines both the bag of words approach and the syntactic approach. The algorithm finds again latent semantic dimensions, according to which nouns, contexts and syntactic relations are classified.

Since we are interested in the classification of nouns according to both 'bag-of-words' context and syntactic context, we first construct three matrices that capture the co-occurrence frequency information for each mode. The first matrix contains co-occurrence frequencies of nouns cross-classified by dependency relations, the second matrix contains co-occurrence frequencies of nouns cross-classified by words that appear in the noun's context window, and the third matrix contains co-occurrence frequencies of dependency relations cross-classified by co-occurring context words.

We then apply NMF to the three matrices, but we interleave the separate factorizations: the results of the former factorization are used to initialize the factorization of the next matrix. This implies that we need to initialize only three matrices at random; the other three are initialized by calculations of the previous step. The process is represented graphically in figure 1.

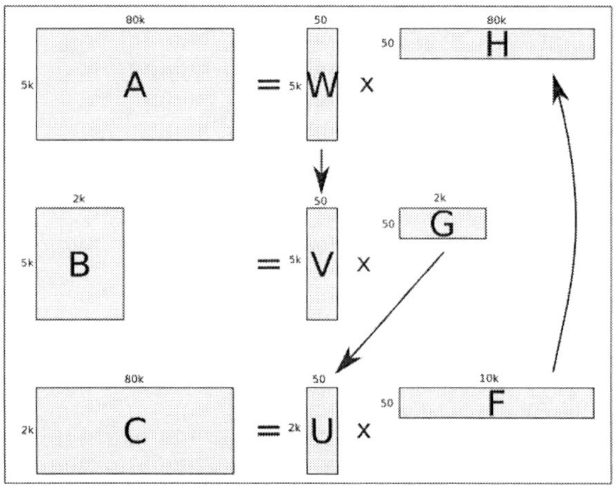

Figure 1: A graphical representation of the extended NMF

In the example in figure 1, matrix H is initialized at random, and the update of matrix W is calculated. The result of update W is then used to initialize matrix V, and the update of matrix G is calculated. This matrix is used again to initialize matrix U, and the update of matrix F is calculated. This matrix can be used to initialize matrix H, and the process is repeated until convergence.

In (5), an example is given of the kind of semantic dimensions found. This dimension may be coined the 'transport' dimension, as is shown by the top 10 nouns (a), context words (b) and syntactic relations (c).

(5) a. *auto* 'car', *wagen* 'car', *tram* 'tram', *motor* 'motorbike', *bus* 'bus', *metro* 'subway', *automobilist* 'driver', *trein* 'trein', *stuur* 'steering wheel', *chauffeur* 'driver'

b. *auto* 'car', *trein* 'train', *motor* 'motorbike', *bus* 'bus', *rij* 'drive', *chauffeur* 'driver', *fiets* 'bike', *reiziger* 'reiziger', *passagier* 'passenger', *vervoer* 'transport'

c. viertraps$_{adj}$ 'four pedal', verplaats_met$_{obj}$ 'move with', toeter$_{adj}$ 'honk', tank_in_houd$_{obj}$ [parsing error], tank$_{subj}$ 'refuel', tank$_{obj}$ 'refuel', rij_voorbij$_{subj}$ 'pass by', rij_voorbij$_{adj}$ 'pass by', rij_af$_{subj}$ 'drive off', peperduur$_{adj}$ 'very expensive'

3.3 Sense Subtraction

Next, we want to use the factorization that has been created in the former step for word sense discrimination. The intuition is that we 'switch off' one dimension of an ambiguous word, to reveal possible other senses of the word. From matrix H, we know the importance of each syntactic relation given a dimension. With this knowledge, we can 'subtract' the syntactic relations that are responsible for a certain dimension from the original noun vector:

$$\overrightarrow{v}_{new} = \overrightarrow{v}_{orig}(\overrightarrow{1} - \overrightarrow{h}_{dim}) \qquad (4)$$

Equation 4 multiplies each feature (syntactic relation) of the original noun vector ($\overrightarrow{v}_{orig}$) with a scaling factor, according to the load of the feature on the subtracted dimension ($\overrightarrow{h}_{dim}$ – the vector of matrix H containing the dimension we want to subtract). $\overrightarrow{1}$ is a vector of ones, the size of $\overrightarrow{h}_{dim}$.

3.4 A Clustering Framework

The last step is to determine which dimension(s) are responsible for a certain sense of the word. In order to do so, we embed our method in a clustering approach. First, a specific word is assigned to its predominant sense (i.e. the most similar cluster). Next, the dominant semantic dimension(s) for this cluster are subtracted from the word vector (equation 4), and the resulting vector is fed to the clustering algorithm again, to see if other word senses emerge. The dominant semantic dimension(s) can be identified by 'folding in' the cluster centroid into our factorization (so we get a vector $\overrightarrow{w}$ of dimension size r), and applying a threshold to the result (in our experiments a threshold of $\delta = .05$ — so dimensions responsible for $> 5\%$ of the centroid are subtracted).

We used two kinds of clustering algorithms to determine our initial centroids. The first algorithm is a standard K-means algorithm. The second one is the CBC algorithm by Pantel and Lin (2002). The initial vectors to be clustered are adapted with pointwise mutual information (Church and Hanks, 1990).

3.4.1 K-means

First, a standard K-means algorithm is applied to the nouns we want to cluster. This yields a hard clustering, in which each noun is assigned to exactly one (dominant) cluster. In the second step, we try to determine for each noun whether it can be assigned to other, less dominant clusters. First, the salient dimension(s) of the centroid to which the noun is assigned are determined. We compute the centroid of the cluster by averaging the frequencies of all cluster elements except for the target element we want to reassign, and adapt the centroid with pointwise mutual information. After subtracting the salient dimensions from the noun vector, we check whether the vector is reassigned to another cluster centroid (i.e. whether it is more similar to a different centroid). If this is the case, (another instance of) the noun is assigned to the cluster, and we repeat the second step. If there is no reassignment, we continue with the next word. The target element is removed from the centroid to make sure that we only subtract the dimensions associated with the sense of the cluster.

Note that K-means requires to set the number of clusters beforehand, so k is a parameter to be set.

3.4.2 CBC

The second clustering algorithm operates in a similar vein, but instead of using simple K-means, we use Pantel and Lin's CBC algorithm to find the initial centroids (coined COMMITTEES).

In order to find committees, the top k nouns for each noun in the database are clustered with average-link clustering. The clusters are scored and sorted in such a way that preference is given to tight, representative clusters. If the committees do not cover all elements sufficiently, the algorithm recursively tries to find more committees. An elaborate description of the algorithm can be found in (Pantel and Lin, 2002).

In the second step, we start assigning elements to committees. Once an element is assigned, the salient dimensions are subtracted from the noun vector in the same way as in 3.4.1 (only do we not have to remove any target word from the centroid; committees are supposed to represent tight, unambiguous clusters).

CBC attempts to find the number of committees automatically from the data, so k does not have to be set.

4 Examples

4.1 Sense Subtraction

In what follows, we will talk about semantic dimensions as, e.g., the 'music' dimension or the 'city' dimension. In the vast majority of the cases, the dimensions are indeed as clear-cut as the transport dimension shown above, so that the dimensions can be rightfully labeled this way.

Two examples are given of how the semantic dimensions that have been found can be used for word sense discrimination. We will consider two ambiguous nouns: *pop*, which can mean 'pop music' as well as 'doll', and *Barcelona*, which can designate either the Spanish city or the Spanish football club.

First, we look up the top dimensions for each noun. Next, we successively subtract the dimensions dealing with a particular sense of the noun, as described in 3.3. This gives us three vectors for each noun: the original vector, and two vectors with one of the dimensions eliminated. For each of these vectors, the top ten similar nouns are given, in order to compare the changes brought about.

(6) a. *pop, rock, jazz, meubilair* 'furniture', *popmuziek* 'pop music', *heks* 'witch', *speelgoed* 'toy', *kast* 'cupboard', *servies* '[tea] service', *vraagteken* 'question mark'

b. *pop, meubilair* 'furniture', *speelgoed* 'toy', *kast* 'cupboard', *servies* '[tea] service', *heks* 'witch', *vraagteken* 'question mark' *sieraad* 'jewel', *sculptuur* 'sculpture', *schoen* 'shoe'

c. *pop, rock, jazz, popmuziek* 'pop music', *heks* 'witch', *danseres* 'dancer', *servies* '[tea] service', *kopje* 'cup', *house* 'house music', *aap* 'monkey'

Example (6) shows the top similar words for the three vectors of *pop*. In (a), the most similar words to the original vector are shown. In (b), the top dimension (the 'music dimension') has been subtracted from (a), and in (c), the second highest dimension (a 'domestic items' dimension) has been subtracted from (a).

The differences between the three vectors are clear: in vector (a), both senses are mixed together, with 'pop music' and 'doll' items interleaved. In (b), no more music items are present. Only items related to the doll sense are among the top similar words. In (c), the music sense emerges much more clearly, with *rock, jazz* and *popmuziek* being the most similar, and a new music term (*house*) showing up among the top ten.

Admittedly, in vector (c), not all items related to the 'doll' sense are filtered out. We believe this is due to the fact that this sense cannot be adequately filtered out by one dimension (in this case, a dimension of 'domestic items' alone), whereas it is much easier to filter out the 'music' sense with only one 'music' dimension. We will try to remedy this in our clustering framework, in which it is possible to subtract multiple dimensions related to one sense.

A second example, the ambiguous proper name *Barcelona*, is given in (7).

(7) a. *Barcelona, Arsenal, Inter, Juventus, Vitesse, Milaan* 'Milan', *Madrid, Parijs* 'Paris', *Wenen* 'Vienna', *München* 'Munich'

b. *Barcelona, Milaan* 'Milan', *München* 'Munich', *Wenen* 'Vienna', *Madrid, Parijs* 'Paris', *Bonn, Praag* 'Prague', *Berlijn* 'Berlin', *Londen* 'London'

c. *Barcelona, Arsenal, Inter, Juventus, Vitesse, Parma, Anderlecht, PSV, Feyenoord, Ajax*

In (a), the two senses of *Barcelona* are clearly mixed up, showing cities as well as football clubs among the most similar nouns. In (b), where the 'football dimension' has been subtracted, only cities show up. In (c), where the 'city dimension' has been subtracted, only football clubs remain.

4.2 Clustering Output

In (8), an example of our clustering algorithm with initial K-means clusters is given.

(8) a. *werk* 'work' *beeld* 'image' *foto* 'photo' *schilderij* 'painting' *tekening* 'drawing' *doek* 'canvas' *installatie* 'installation' *afbeelding* 'picture' *sculptuur* 'sculpture' *prent* 'picture' *illustratie* 'illustration' *handschrift* 'manuscript' *grafiek* 'print' *aquarel* 'aquarelle' *maquette* 'scale-model' *collage* 'collage' *ets* 'etching'

b. *werk* 'work' *boek* 'book' *titel* 'title' *roman* 'novel' *boekje* 'booklet' *debuut* 'debut' *biografie* 'biography' *bundel* 'collection' *toneelstuk* 'play' *bestseller* 'bestseller' *kinderboek* 'child book' *autobiografie* 'autobiography' *novelle* 'short story'

c. *werk* 'work' *voorziening* 'service' *arbeid* 'labour' *opvoeding* 'education' *kinderopvang* 'child care' *scholing* 'education' *huisvesting* 'housing' *faciliteit* 'facility' *accommodatie* 'acommodation' *arbeidsomstandigheid* 'working condition'

The example shows three different clusters to which the noun *werk* 'work' is assigned. In (a), *werk* refers to a work of art. In (b), it refers to a written work. In (c), the 'labour' sense of *werk* emerges.

5 Evaluation

5.1 Methodology

The clustering results are evaluated according to Dutch EuroWordNet (Vossen and others, 1999). Precision and recall are calculated by comparing the results to EuroWordNet synsets. The precision is the number of clusters found that correspond to an actual sense of the word. Recall is the number of word senses in EuroWordNet that are found by the algorithm. Our evaluation method is largely the same as the one used by Pantel and Lin (2002).

Both precision and recall are based on wordnet similarity. A number of similarity measures have been developed to calculate semantic similarity in a hierarchical wordnet. Among these measures, the most important are Wu & Palmer's (Wu and Palmer, 1994), Resnik's (Resnik, 1995) and Lin's (Lin, 1998). In this evaluation, Wu & Palmer's (1994) measure will be adopted. The similarity is calculated according to the formula in (5), in which N_1 and N_2 are the number of *is-a* links from A and B to their most specific common superclass C; N_3 is the number of *is-a* links from C to the root of the taxonomy.

$$sim_{Wu\&Palmer}(A,B) = \frac{2N_3}{N_1 + N_2 + 2N_3} \quad (5)$$

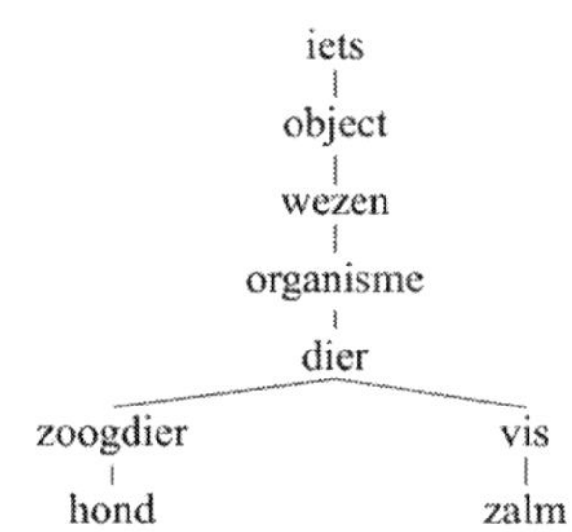

Figure 2: Extract from the Dutch EuroWordNet Hierarchy

For example, the most common superclass of *hond* 'dog' en *zalm* 'salmon' is *dier* 'animal' (as can be seen on the extract from Dutch EuroWordNet in figure 2). Consequently, $N_1 = 2$, $N_2 = 2$, $N_3 = 4$ and $sim_{WP}(hond, zalm) = 0.67$.

To calculate precision, we apply the same methodology as Pantel and Lin (2002).[2] Let $S(w)$ be the set of EuroWordNet senses. $sim_W(s,u)$, the similarity between a synset s and a word u is then defined as the maximum similarity between s and a sense of u:

$$sim_W(s,u) = \max_{t \epsilon S(u)} sim(s,t) \quad (6)$$

Let c_k be the top k-members of a cluster c, where these are the k most similar members to the centroid of c. $simC(c,s)$, the similarity between s and c, is then defined as the average similarity between s and the top-k members of c:

$$sim_C(s,c) = \frac{\sum_{u \epsilon c_k} simW(s,u)}{k} \quad (7)$$

[2]Note, however, that our similarity measure is different. Where Pantel and Lin use Lin's (1998) measure, we use Wu and Palmer's (1994) measure.

An assigment of a word w to a cluster c can now be classified as correct if

$$\max_{s \in S(w)} simC(s,c) > \theta \quad (8)$$

and the EuroWordNet sense of w that corresponds to c is

$$\arg\max_{s \in S(w)} simC(s,c) \quad (9)$$

When multiple clusters correspond to the same EuroWordNet sense, only one of them is counted as correct.

Precision of a word w is the percentage of correct clusters to which it is assigned. Recall of a word w is the percentage of senses from EuroWordnet that have a corresponding cluster.[3] Precision and recall of a clustering algorithm is the average precision and recall of all test words.

5.2 Experimental Design

We have applied the interleaved NMF presented in section 3.2 to Dutch, using the TWENTE NIEUWS CORPUS (Ordelman, 2002), containing > 500M words of Dutch newspaper text. The corpus is consistently divided into paragraphs, which have been used as the context window for the bag-of-words mode. The corpus has been parsed by the Dutch dependency parser Alpino (van Noord, 2006), and dependency triples have been extracted. Next, the three matrices needed for our method have been constructed: one containing nouns by dependency relations (5K × 80K), one containing nouns by context words (5K × 2K) and one containing dependency relations by context words (80K × 2K). We did 200 iterations of the algorithm, factorizing the matrices into 50 dimensions. The NMF algorithm has been implemented in Matlab.

For the evaluation, we use all the words that appear in our original clustering input as well as in EuroWordNet. This yields a test set of 3683 words.

5.3 Results

Table 1 shows precision and recall figures for four different algorithms, according to two similarity thresholds θ (equation 8). kmeans$_{nmf}$ describes the results of our algorithm with K-means clusters, as described in section 3.4.1. CBC describes the results of our algorithm with the CBC committees, as described in section 3.4.2. For comparison, we have also included the results of a standard K-means clustering (kmeans$_{orig}$, $k = 600$), and the original CBC algorithm (CBC$_{orig}$) as described by Pantel and Lin (2002).

		threshold θ	
		.40 (%)	.60 (%)
kmeans$_{nmf}$	prec.	78.97	55.16
	rec.	63.90	44.77
CBC$_{nmf}$	prec.	82.70	54.87
	rec.	60.27	40.51
kmeans$_{orig}$	prec.	86.13	58.97
	rec.	60.23	41.80
CBC$_{orig}$	prec.	44.94	29.74
	rec.	69.61	48.00

Table 1: Precision and recall for four different algorithms according to two similarity thresholds

The results show the same tendency across all similarity thresholds: kmeans$_{nmf}$ has a high precision, but lower recall compared to CBC$_{orig}$. Still the recall is higher compared to standard K-means, which indicates that the algorithm is able to find multiple senses of nouns, with high precision. The results of CBC$_{nmf}$ are similar to the results of kmeans$_{orig}$, indicating that few words are reassigned to multiple clusters when using CBC committees with our method.

Obviously, kmeans$_{orig}$ scores best with regard to precision, but worse with regard to recall. CBC$_{orig}$ finds most senses (highest recall), but precision is considerably worse.

The fact that recall is already quite high with standard K-means clustering indicates that the evaluation is skewed towards nouns with only one sense, possibly due to a lack of coverage in EuroWordNet. In future work, we specifically want to evaluate the discrimination of ambiguous words. Also, we want to make use of the new Cornetto Database[4], a successor of EuroWordNet for Dutch which is currently under development.

Still, the evaluation shows that our method provides a genuine way of finding multiple senses of words, while retaining high precision. Especially the method using a simple K-means clustering per-

[3]Our notion of recall is slightly different from the one used by Pantel and Lin, as they use 'the number of senses in which w was used in the corpus' as gold standard. This information, as they acknowledge, is difficult to get at, so we prefer to use the sense information in EuroWordNet.

[4]`http://www.let.vu.nl/onderzoek/projectsites/cornetto/index.html`

forms particularly well. The three way data allows the algorithm to put its finger on the particular sense of a centroid, and adapt the feature vector of a possibly ambiguous noun accordingly.

6 Conclusion & Future Work

In this paper, an extension of NMF has been presented that combines both bag of words data and syntactic data in order to find latent semantic dimensions according to which both words and syntactic relations can be classified. The use of three way data allows one to determine which dimension(s) are responsible for a certain sense of a word, and adapt the corresponding feature vector accordingly, 'subtracting' one sense to discover another one. When embedded in a clustering framework, the method provides a fully automatic way to discriminate the various senses of words. The evaluation against EuroWordNet shows that the algorithm is genuinely able to disambiguate the features of a given word, and accordingly its word senses.

We conclude with some issues for future work. First of all, we would like to test the method that has been explored in this paper with other evaluation frameworks. We already mentioned the focus on ambiguous nouns, and the use of the new Cornetto database for Dutch. Next, we would like to work out a proper probabilistic framework for the 'subtraction' of dimensions. At this moment, the subtraction (using a cut-off) is somewhat ad hoc. A probabilistic modeling of this intuition might lead to an improvement.

And finally, we would like to use the results of our method to learn selectional preferences. Our method is able to discriminate the syntactic features that are linked to a particular word sense. If we can use the results to improve a parser's performance, this will also provide an external evaluation of the algorithm.

References

Church, Kenneth Ward and Patrick Hanks. 1990. Word association norms, mutual information & lexicography. *Computational Linguistics*, 16(1):22–29.

Harris, Z. 1985. Distributional structure. In Katz, Jerrold J., editor, *The Philosophy of Linguistics*, pages 26–47. Oxford University Press.

Hofmann, Thomas. 1999. Probabilistic latent semantic analysis. In *Proc. of Uncertainty in Artificial Intelligence, UAI'99*, Stockholm.

Landauer, Thomas and Se Dumais. 1997. A solution to Plato's problem: The Latent Semantic Analysis theory of the acquisition, induction, and representation of knowledge. *Psychology Review*, 104:211–240.

Lee, Daniel D. and H. Sebastian Seung. 2000. Algorithms for non-negative matrix factorization. In *NIPS*, pages 556–562.

Lin, D. 1998. Automatic retrieval and clustering of similar words. In *Proceedings of COLING/ACL 98*, Montreal, Canada.

Manning, Christopher and Hinrich Schütze. 2000. *Foundations of Statistical Natural Language Processing*. MIT Press, Cambridge, Massachussets.

Ordelman, R.J.F. 2002. Twente Nieuws Corpus (TwNC), August. Parlevink Language Techonology Group. University of Twente.

Pantel, Patrick and Dekang Lin. 2002. Discovering word senses from text. In *Proceedings of the eighth ACM SIGKDD international conference on Knowledge discovery and data mining*, pages 613–619, New York, NY, USA. ACM Special Interest Group on Knowledge Discovery in Data, ACM Press.

Resnik, Philip. 1995. Using information content to evaluate semantic similarity in a taxonomy. In *IJCAI*, pages 448–453.

Schütze, Hinrich. 1998. Automatic word sense discrimination. *Computational Linguistics*, 24(1):97–123.

van der Plas, Lonneke and Gosse Bouma. 2005. Syntactic contexts for finding semantically similar words. In van der Wouden, Ton et al., editors, *Computational Linguistics in the Netherlands 2004. Selected Papers from the Fifteenth CLIN Meeting*, pages 173–184, Utrecht. LOT.

van Noord, Gertjan. 2006. At Last Parsing Is Now Operational. In Mertens, Piet, Cedrick Fairon, Anne Dister, and Patrick Watrin, editors, *TALN06. Verbum Ex Machina. Actes de la 13e conference sur le traitement automatique des langues naturelles*, pages 20–42, Leuven.

Vossen, Piek et al. 1999. The Dutch Wordnet, July. University of Amsterdam.

Wu, Zhibiao and Martha Palmer. 1994. Verb semantics and lexical selection. In *32nd. Annual Meeting of the Association for Computational Linguistics*, pages 133–138, New Mexico State University, Las Cruces, New Mexico.

Source Language Markers in EUROPARL Translations

Hans van Halteren
Radboud University Nijmegen
Department of Linguistics / CLST
P.O. Box 9103, NL-6500HD Nijmegen
The Netherlands
hvh@let.ru.nl

Abstract

This paper shows that it is very often possible to identify the source language of medium-length speeches in the EUROPARL corpus on the basis of frequency counts of word n-grams (87.2%-96.7% accuracy depending on classification method). The paper also examines in detail which positive markers are most powerful and identifies a number of linguistic aspects as well as culture- and domain-related ones.

1 Introduction

The EUROPARL Corpus (Koehn, 2005) is one of the most important resources for translation research. It is used extensively, mostly but certainly not exclusively in statistical machine translation. In much of that research, the relation between a source language SL and target language TL is investigated on the basis of aligned sentences of SL and TL without considering whether SL is indeed the actual source language. In this paper we question the lack of attention for the true SL, because we expect significant differences between texts written originally in TL, texts translated from SL to TL and texts translated from another language into TL, even if all three types have been produced by native speakers of TL.[2] At least with respect to the differences between original and translated texts, our expectations are supported by the literature (for an overview, see e.g. Baroni and Bernardini, 2006).

We embarked on a data-driven investigation, using several text classification techniques to determine if the differences are salient enough to distinguish between different source languages for various texts and target languages. In this paper, we first describe the data and methods we used (Sections 2 and 3). Then we present the classification results (Section 4), after which we give a description of some types of markers we were able to identify (Section 5). Finally, in Section 6, we present our conclusions and plans for future research.

2 Experimental Data

The experimental data was taken from the EUROPARL Corpus, but had to be preprocessed to some degree to be suitable for our experiments. First of all, the annotation of the corpus includes a LANGUAGE attribute, indicating the original language of the text. However, it is often absent in one or more versions of the text. If we examine the speeches of at least 100 words in the whole corpus, we find that 11% of them lack the attribute in all available versions and for 5% the attribute has different values in different versions. We linked the attribute across the various versions and excluded all speeches showing inconsistent values.

We decided to focus on the six most common languages in the corpus: English (EN), German (DE), French (FR), Dutch (NL), Spanish (ES) and Italian (IT). For each of these languages as a source language, we aimed for 1000 speeches (henceforth: *texts*) which were present as original and as translations into each of the other five languages. Furthermore, we decided to focus on the medium range as for length, avoiding very short and very long texts, as these were likely to

© 2008. Licensed under the *Creative Commons Attribution-Noncommercial-Share Alike 3.0 Unported* license (http://creativecommons.org/licenses/by-nc-sa/3.0/). Some rights reserved.

[2] In principle, the EU translation service always lets translators translate into their mother tongue. Given that we will here be working only with major EU languages, it is unlikely that the principle was violated for our selected texts.

be different in nature.[3] Our aim of 1000 texts from each source language led us to settle on texts between 380 and 2500 words.

Finally, as we wanted the classification systems to focus on language use rather than contents, we transformed the tokens in the texts, separately for each target language. Only tokens that occurred in at least 10% of the texts remained intact. Other tokens were mapped to a marker <X>.

3 Methods

We classified all texts in our experimental set with several text classification methods (see Sections 3.1 to 3.3), using 10-fold cross-validation, each time with 80% of the texts used to train models for each source language, 10% of the texts used to tune parameters and to base thresholds on and 10% of the texts to test classification accuracy. For all methods, the same train/ tune/test splits were used and some dozens of promising parameter settings were tried, after which the best one for each specific run was selected on the basis of tune set results.

Each method was provided with the same text features, viz. n-gram counts. From each selected text (in its mapped version), we extracted counts for all uni-, bi- and trigrams of tokens occurring in at least 10% of the texts (i.e. those not transformed to `<X>`) and allowing `<X>` markers to intervene between any two tokens in the n-gram. For example, the sequence `"I join with Roy Perry in"` would give rise to the n-gram `<3>_I_<X>_with_<X>_<X>_in`, with the `<3>` indicating that there are three real tokens in the n-gram, and possibly any number of intervening `<X>` markers.

3.1 Marker-Based Classification

Our first classification method attempts to classify texts on the basis of individual markers which are by themselves a strong indication that the text originated in a certain source language. All n-grams which occurred more often in the training data with a specific source language SL than with all other source languages taken together were deemed to be *markers* for SL.

When classifying test data, each marker for an SL observed in the test text leads to an increase of the score for that SL for that text. The exact calculation of the increase depends on some parameter settings. It always involves both the marker's precision (how often its presence indeed coincides with the specific SL) and its recall (how many of the specific SL texts contain the marker), but with a weighting favouring precision over recall by a factor of 10 to 100. Precision and recall can be based on either raw or smoothed counts. The calculation may also involve the frequency of the marker in the test text. In this way, the frequency of a marker is not taken into account for determining whether it is a marker and what value it is given, but may be taken into account when classifying test texts.

3.2 Linguistic Profiling

The second classification system was Linguistic Profiling, which was previously shown to be useful for language verification (van Halteren and Oostdijk, 2004), a task which is similar to the current task. Roughly speaking, it classifies on the basis of noticeable over- and underuse of specific n-grams. As the marker-based classification only used overuse and the necessary degree of overuse is lower for Linguistic Profiling, the latter pays attention to many more features and should be able to attain a better classification rate. However, if we want to determine which features are most powerful, interpreting the workings of Linguistic Profiling will be more difficult than for the marker-based approach.

All n-gram counts were normalized to counts per 1000 words. Furthermore, in order to reduce the number of counts, so that the system could cope with the resulting vectors, we included only n-grams which occurred in at least 10 texts. This led to vectors with about 90,000 counts for each target language.

3.3 Support Vector Methods

Finally, we employed Support Vector Machines, viz. LIBSVM (Chang and Lin, 2001). We offered the same vectors we used for Linguistic Profiling to both standard Support Vector Classification (SVC; RBF kernel, various settings for C and γ) and Support Vector Regression (ν-SVR; RBF kernel, various settings for C, γ and ν).

The Support Vector methods use all available information rather than focusing on over- and underuse. They should therefore attain the best classification results. However, extracting information about salient features from the results will be virtually impossible.

[3] E.g., short texts tend to be interruptions and statements such as the opening of the session, where long texts include presentations of written reports.

	MB	LP	SVC	SVR
SL vs TL: TL	84.1	91.5	92.6	95.2
SL vs TL: SL	75.3	88.4	87.6	91.6
Combination	87.2	94.7	90.1	96.9
SL vs SL: SL	74.2	85.8	85.4	89.7
Combination	81.1	91.8	85.4	94.3

Table 1: Average accuracies for two-way SL vs SL choices for various classification methods. The top part represents cases where one of the SL is the TL, the bottom where neither SL is TL.

3.4 Score Comparability

For all methods except SVC, the ranges of test text scores vary greatly as train sets and parameter settings are changed. As we wanted to combine scores from classifications based on models for various SL, however, we needed the scores to be comparable. In order to make them so, we compared the score for each test text with the scores for all tune texts.[4] All lower scoring positive examples provided a increase of the final (comparable) score and all higher scoring negative examples a decrease. For fine tuning, the relative position of the test text's score between the next higher and next lower scoring tune texts was also taken into consideration.[5]

4 Classification Results

We first used our classification techniques to choose between every possible pair of source languages for each text (Section 4.1). Then we combined the various two-way decisions into a single six-way decision (Section 4.2).

4.1 Two-Way Decisions

For each choice between two possible source languages, there are two classification models (one for each of the SL) that can make the choice individually, but we can also combine the two opinions by choosing the SL whose classification model claims the text with a higher score.[6]

The quality of these decisions, for those cases where the actual SL is present in the pair, is shown in Table 1. We distinguish two types of choices. The top of the table shows the results for the cases in which one of the two SL is the target language, with SL equal to TL indicating that the text is an original TL text rather than a translation. For the cases represented in the table, i.e. cases where one of the two SL is the actual one, the task measured here is in fact translation recognition. As the table shows, the accuracy for this task is higher when modeling original TL text than when modeling translations, meaning that it is easier to spot (violations against) regularities in the target language than it is to spot regularities in the translations from a specific source language. Combining the two models yields even better classification, except for SVC, where combination cannot be used properly because SVC only produces scores of 1 and -1. The bottom of the table shows the results for the cases in which both SL are different from the target language. Here the choices appear to be more difficult on average, but the classification quality is still impressive.

	MB	LP	SVC	SVR
ES	64.7	82.9	81.1	87.4
DE	62.0	81.6	80.8	87.5
EN	60.4	80.6	79.3	86.8
FR	58.7	77.0	77.7	85.7
NL	58.4	76.7	75.2	83.1
IT	52.8	73.6	60.7	81.5
ALL TL	87.2	90.6	91.5	96.7

Table 2: Average accuracies for six-way SL choices for various classification methods. The rows with a TL indication represent the results when the text is only available in that TL. The bottom row shows the combined result, using all six versions of the text.

4.2 Six-Way Decisions

Once we had classification scores for the choice between all fifteen possible pairs of source languages (actually the combination scores), we could use these to choose a single SL from among the set of six possible SL. For the current paper, we did this by simply adding all classification scores in favour of each specific SL and then choosing the SL with the highest total. The addition can either be done over all two-way choices referring to a specific target language, or over all choices for all six possible target languages.

The quality of these decisions is shown in Table 2. For the individual target languages, the

[4] We deliberately chose a non-parametric technique here. However, preliminary additional experiments show that a parametric alternative may actually provide slightly better results.

[5] This technique did not work for SVC, as SVC only scores a text with 1 or -1. However, for SVC the technique was also not needed as the scores were already comparable. We did add a very small random number to each score to resolve ties where necessary.

[6] Remember that we made all classification scores comparable.

	EN	DE	FR	NL	ES	IT
EN	980	1	12	2	1	4
DE	16	961	6	9	3	5
FR	15	3	969	2	7	4
NL	16	10	12	956	4	2
ES	14	5	13	2	960	6
IT	8	2	9	0	8	973

Table 3: Confusion table for SVR classification of each of the 6000 selected speeches on the basis of all six language versions of each speech. Rows are actual languages; columns are languages assigned by the classifier.

accuracies are not all that high, but this was to be expected. Interestingly, the relative difficulty of the choice for the various TL is largely independent of the classification method used, with texts in Spanish being most easily classifiable and texts in Italian least easily. The relative performance of the classification methods is again as expected, except that SVC is slightly behind Linguistic Profiling for the individual languages.

For the best performing classification method, Support Vector Regression, we also show the confusion table for SL assignment (Table 3). In general, there are more confusions within the Germanic and Romance language families than between them. However, English seems to take an intermediate position between the two families. On the other hand, the English model appears to be somewhat greedier than the others, which confuses the analysis. Also, given that the LANGUAGE attribute does not seem to be assigned perfectly, it would be advisable to examine the misassigned texts, so as to check if they are indeed misassigned or merely mislabeled.

5 A Look at Source Language Markers

Now we have shown that word n-grams provide a solid basis for source language identification, we proceed to an examination of the n-grams that are the most useful in this identification. Unfortunately, as stated above, Linguistic Profiling and the Support Vector methods are not very amenable to extracting information about the most salient features. Therefore, for now, we will have to fall back on the marker-based classification where it is trivial to identify the source language markers which characterize their source languages most strongly. Admittedly, the marker-based classification had the lowest performance in the classification task, but still it is good enough for an examination to make sense.

	Occurring only once; With SL	Occurring more often; Only with SL	Occurring also with non-SL
DE	137256	6691	9459
FR	122386	4916	7102
NL	120071	5594	7653
ES	119899	5740	8495
IT	129251	5900	8538

Table 4: Numbers of source language markers for various source languages SL in translation to English.

To optimize understandability for all readers, we focus on English as the target language in this examination. We distinguish between two kinds of marker strength. Obviously, there is the strength in the SL classification described above. For a marker to be strong in this sense, it has to occur more often with the source language in question than with all other source languages taken together (Section 5.1). If, however, we envision an application where we know that a specific SL is being translated to a specific TL and we want to give feedback to the translator that the translation contains strong influences from the SL, then strength can also be taken to be the degree to which the marker occurs more in texts translated from SL than in original TL texts (Section 5.2). For both kinds of marker strength, we can identify specific types of markers, related either to linguistic or culture- and domain-related aspects of texts and their translations (Section 5.3)

5.1 Statistics for SL vs All Others

We took all n-grams from the English versions of the texts in our experimental data and counted the number of texts they were contained in for each of the six source languages. We then calculated their strength for each source language SL by dividing the observed number of SL texts, plus one, by the number of non-SL texts, again plus one. The classification described in Section 3.1 in principle used all markers with strength greater than one.

If the full set of texts were used as training material, we would find the numbers of markers as shown in Table 4. The majority of n-grams occurs only once (Column 2) and necessarily with a single specific SL so that they can be taken to be markers. Note, however, that these markers did not play a role in the classification in the ten-fold cross-validation, since they were always either only in the training set, only in the tune set or only in the test set. The third column represents n-grams which also occur only with

SL	n-gram	texts
DE	<3>_is_,_though	10
	<2>_Commission_here <3>_,_again_and <3>_are_right_<X>_you <3>_If_,_though <3>_me_say_this <3>_the_Commission_here <3>_the_<X>_Council_Presidency	7
	<3>_._What_that <2>_What_that <3>_reason_we_must <3>_must_at_last <2>_more_able <3>_go_without_saying <3>_not_,_though <2>_need_<X>_- <2>_taken_here <3>_believe_that_here <3>_is_needed_here <3>_gentlemen_,_<X>_<X>_is	6
FR	<3>_common_to_the <3>_quality_of_her	6
	<3>_with_no_regard <3>_no_regard_for <2>_no_regard <3>_conditions_of_<X>_of <2>_into_<X>_this <2>_on_<X>_services <2>_particular_about <2>_various_policies <3>_all_those_, <3>_of_cooperation_is <3>_the_United_<X>_<X>_Commissioner <3>_,_<X>_society_,	5
NL	<3>_like_to_<X>_off	23
	<3>_to_<X>_off_with	16
	<3>_On_a_final	14
	<2>_Commissioner_whether <3>_the_Commissioner_whether	10
	<3>_and_such_like <2>_such_like	8
	<3>_past_<X>_of_years <3>_,_it_<X>_as <3>_are_in_order <3>_too_<X>_for_words <3>_to_<X>_off_by	7
ES	<3>_going_to_support	11
	<3>_amendments_presented_by <3>_end_here_, <3>_Community_system_for <3>_the_people_responsible	8
	<3>_citizens_._And <3>_going_to_debate	7
	<3>_the_Community_<X>_sector <2>_Community_<X>_sector <2>_than_<X>_<X>_<X>_million <3>_million_<X>_year_. <3>_President_,_without <3>_Let_us_see <3>_adopt_measures_to <3>_move_<X>_with_the <3>_And_the_Commission <3>_people_responsible_for	6
IT	<3>_least_in_that	9
	<2>_task_before <3>_or_,_<X>_still	7
	<3>_change_the_current <3>_is_the_Europe <3>_feel_that_Parliament <3>_task_before_us <3>_of_my_Commission <2>_with_<X>_<X>_' <3>_the_<X>_available_. <2>_:_<X>_which <3>_security_and_peace	6

Table 5: Strongest n-grams occurring only with a specific SL

one specific SL. These markers are in principle the most useful because of their precision. However, their number of occurrences turns out to be generally very low, with a maximum of 23 and a mean of 2.1, so that their recall is low to very low. Finally, there are the n-grams which do occur with various source languages, but most often with one specific SL. They are represented by the last column.

Probably more insightful than the general statistics are the actual markers themselves, here represented by the strongest ones for each source language, still with English as the target language.

SL	n-gram	SL texts	other source language texts
DE	<3>_means_is_that	11	1 IT
	<2>_framework_conditions	22	2 EN, 1 FR
	<3>_in_future_be	14	1 EN, 1 IT
	<3>_,_that_being	13	2 NL
	<2>_action_here	8	1 FR
	<3>_So_let_me	8	1 FR
	<3>_to_at_last	8	1 FR
FR	<3>_why_I_shall	8	1 NL
	<2>_certain_number	25	1 DE, 2 IT, 2 NL
	<3>_certain_number_of	25	1 DE, 2 IT, 2 NL
	<3>_a_certain_number	24	1 DE, 2 IT, 2 NL
	<3>_thank_our_rapporteur	7	1 NL
	<3>_We_now_know	6	1 NL
	<3>_provide_itself_with	6	1 ES
NL	<3>_._<X>_to_say	61	4 EN, 2 DE, 1 FR
	<3>_that_is_concerned	10	1 DE
	<3>_we_as_Parliament	9	1 IT
	<3>_group_,_it	9	1 ES
	<3>_is_every_reason	9	1 ES
	<3>_deal_of_support	8	1 DE
	<3>_think_that_that	12	1 ES, 1 FR
ES	<3>_._<X>_this_context	9	1 IT
	<3>_I_<X>_this_to	9	1 EN
	<2>_people_responsible	8	1 NL
	<3>_going_to_deal	8	1 NL
	<3>_President_,_<X>_allow	8	1 IT
	<3>_legislation_in_force	8	1 FR
	<3>_report_,_since	8	1 FR
IT	<2>_the_now	10	1 FR
	<3>_other_,_there	10	1 DE
	<3>_the_individual_States	10	1 DE
	<3>_,_<X>_<X>_,_ladies	10	1 DE
	<2>_my_Commission	8	1 FR
	<3>_due_regard_for	12	1 EN, 1 NL
	<2>_quite_aware	16	3 FR

Table 6: Strongest n-grams occurring also with other languages

guage. The lists we find are always headed by n-grams which occur only with a specific SL (Table 5). Then follow the n-grams which can also be found with other languages. We show the strongest ones of this type separately as Table 6.

As already stated above, most of the stronger markers occur in only few SL texts. The big exception seems to be Dutch, which has several markers (notably <3>_._<X>_to_say with competing languages and <3>_like_to_<X>_off exclusively) which show up quite often. Only <2>_framework_conditions for German and the certain_number cluster for French occur over 20 times too, but they are not exclusive. We also see various clusters, where longer strings are represented by several n-grams, such as "a certain number of" and "with no regard for" for

token	EN	DE	FR	NL	ES	IT
<1>_ladies	11	574	362	197	273	378
<1>_gentlemen	14	584	383	205	304	388
<1>_And	69	154	160	164	307	128
<1>_above	58	151	119	115	145	198
<1>_guarantee	53	97	110	87	164	151
<1>_favour	75	157	197	173	164	122
<1>_everyone	55	144	141	126	57	93
<1>_namely	54	158	94	184	54	60
<1>_opinion	140	164	244	272	250	311
<1>_mention	65	109	120	86	127	121
<1>_although	95	122	110	116	233	219
<1>_therefore	296	396	488	477	580	525
<1>_regard	174	212	292	254	408	286
<1>_shall	108	178	240	144	166	169
<1>_though	80	215	131	116	82	117
<1>_everything	69	152	126	98	97	98
<1>_various	107	168	188	154	186	175
<1>_hand	103	160	183	178	145	171
<1>_freedom	72	118	119	88	105	157
<1>_Office	73	158	110	77	142	102

Table 7: Strongest individual tokens marking translations into English

French and "the people responsible for" for Spanish.

5.2 Markers for Translation vs Original

If we want to call a translator's attention to a translation which deviates from the general language use in the target language, the marker identifying the deviation need not be exclusive to a single source language. Such markers are much more common than source language specific markers. They also include large numbers of single tokens (i.e. unigrams; Table 7), something we did not find in Section 5.1.

Most remarkable are the top two, `ladies` and `gentlemen`. Apparently, speakers from all over Europe address the whole house when opening their speech, but those speaking English only address the President (i.e. the chairperson). The rest are mostly words providing discourse functions, either by themselves, such as `therefore` and `though`, or in larger combinations, such as `hand` in "on the one hand" and `opinion` in "in my opinion". There are only a few words with actual content, such as `guarantee`, `freedom` and `Office`, although the latter may also well be part of a parliament term.

As for the longer n-grams, we will not present the full list of strongest markers, but instead a filtered selection (Table 8). The reason for this is that there is quite a lot of repetition in the full list. The strongest eleven, and fifteen more of the strongest fifty, are (parts of) combinations of vocatives, such as "Commissioner, ladies and gentlemen", which we already addressed above. As vocative use in the European Parliament could well be a separate study in itself, and is probably not something we need to bother translators with, we leave out all vocatives.

token	EN	DE	ES	FR	IT	NL
<3>_of_the_Group	0	27	41	19	16	34
<2>_end_by	0	2	42	18	25	7
<3>_,_by_means	0	13	40	21	11	8
<3>_s_<X>_(_<X>_<X>_)	0	35	13	8	11	21
<3>_)_and_European	0	29	14	8	11	21
<3>_,_for_we	0	25	0	7	26	20
<3>_at_last_,	0	9	3	5	53	5
<3>_countries_,_which	0	13	16	24	10	9
<2>_we_therefore	0	10	19	8	22	10
<3>_the_Europe_of	0	5	12	18	30	3
<3>_order_to_guarantee	0	9	26	14	6	11
<3>_and_above_all	1	35	29	26	28	13
<3>_out_that_,	0	11	22	12	12	8
<2>_therefore_believe	1	13	67	21	19	8
<3>_think_that_this	1	14	22	29	15	46
<3>_think_that_,	0	9	15	14	10	11
<3>_like_to_<X>_this	0	5	15	4	7	27
<3>_of_third_countries	0	4	17	15	12	9
<2>_here_too	0	27	1	4	8	15
<3>_of_all_like	0	4	12	14	2	22
<3>_,_though_,	3	128	4	17	14	53
<3>_too_,_we	0	21	0	6	11	15
<3>_I_shall_not	0	3	10	21	7	12
<3>_State_or_Government	0	15	5	10	16	6

Table 8: Selection from the strongest n-grams marking translations into English

5.3 Types of Markers

The markers shown in the previous sections are of a rather varied nature. Some of them have linguistic explanations, but there are also quite a few which are more culture- and domain-related.

The best example in the latter category is the already mentioned use of vocatives. Although there are clear links to at least one source language, English, this is not something that is caused by translation. Another example of seemingly typical parliamentary behaviour are the phrases "like to finish off" and "On a final note", responsible for the three strongest Dutch markers in Table 5. The Dutch (or Flemish) parliamentarians announce in some way that they are nearing the end of their speech. However, if we examine the original Dutch text, we observe a much more varied phrasing. We find the literal counterpart ("ik wil afsluiten"), but also "ter afsluiting" ("to close") and "dan nog iets" ("then another thing"). Apparently, one or more of the Dutch to English translators have developed their own favourite phrases to cover this general situation.

Another domain-specific type of marker can be found in content words (here mostly compounds) referring to parliamentary matters. Here we turn to German for some examples. In Table

5 we find <3>_the_<X>_Council_Presidency. One might think that only Germans are interested in who runs the council at any given time, but in fact this is an idiosyncratic alternative translation as "Council Presidency" is generally just called Presidency. Another example is <2>_framework_conditions in Table 6, with 22 German SL occurrences, 2 English and 1 French. When examining the source text, we find Rahmenbedingungen, elsewhere translated (probably better) as "basic conditions". From these examples it would seem that some work may still be needed on harmonizing terminology.[7] A lack of (knowledge of) central terms leads in one case to a translation with some unfortunate connotations and in another case to an acceptable but deviant translation. In both cases the use of a single term would most certainly also improve information retrieval on the parliament proceedings.

Related to the domain, but much more culture specific is the variation in the way the speakers organize their argumentation. The example of speakers of Dutch announcing the last part of their speech has already been mentioned. Another thing speakers of Dutch seem to do is that they exaggerate their viewpoint, both positively and negatively. The positive exaggeration is visible in the word natuurlijk (naturally, obviously, ...), which is found in almost a third (326) of the originally Dutch speeches. One of the translations chosen for this word is "needless to say", thus giving rise to the extremely strong marker for Dutch in Table 6. The negative exaggeration is present in cases where a situation is called insane: waanzinnig, "te gek voor woorden" ("too crazy for words") or "te gek om los te lopen" ("too crazy to walk around freely"). A possible translation template here is "too crazy/absurd/ridiculous for words", explaining another marker for Dutch in Table 5. A further obviously discourse-related marker is therefore. As Table 7 shows, it is found from 30% (DE) to 100% (ES) more in translations than in original English text. This may mean that speakers of the other languages place more causal relations in their arguments, but it can also be that therefore just happens to be a favourite translation option among the translators. Again, this could be a research topic by itself and a thorough investigation is beyond the scope of this paper.

[7] Since EUROPARL only contains speeches some years in the past, the situation may well have been remedied in the meantime.

Obviously, each source language has some words or phrases in its vocabulary which make themselves felt in the translations. Apart from the ones already mentioned, the strongest example here is the French marker "a certain number of". The original turns out to be "un certain nombre", elsewhere more English-like translated as "some of".

There must also be instances of influences from languages' syntax, but these are much harder to find. It is possible that the overuse of shall, especially for French, is linked to verbs which are morphologically marked for future tense. Also the overuse of And at the beginning of sentences may be linked to splitting source language long sentences into two English sentences or merely to more extensive use of a coordinating connective in the other languages. For both these words, there are also far too many occurrences to examine at this time.

6 Comparison to Other Work

The most similar investigation we are aware of is that by Baroni and Bernardini (2006). They worked on a corpus of Italian geopolitical journal articles and used SVMs to distinguish translated and original Italian text on the basis of mostly n-gram features representing both types of text. They did not attempt to identify the source language. Their task corresponds to the translation recognition task presented in the top half of Table 1 and their method is comparable to the combination of the two models for original texts and translations. They report an accuracy of 86.7%. If we examine the texts with TL equal to Italian, we find combination scores of 85.4% (MB), 86.0% (SVC), 93.2% (LP) and 96.3% (SVR). Although their work is different in the choice of domain (geopolitical journal articles) and they do not distinguish translated texts as to source language, the results for SVM classifiers are comparable.

They also mention that in earlier research (Baroni and Bernardini, 2003), they found that *"bigrams most characteristic of translated text are sequences of function words"*, for both the Italian corpus already mentioned and a corpus of EU reports written in and translated into English. The 2003 paper itself, however, reports that *"a more thorough investigation of the EU data ... failed to reveal systematic differences between translated and original documents"*. We must therefore conclude that their observation must refer to the Italian texts. Still, our tables do show quite a few function word bigrams, but of course we have contributed to any such predominance by blanking out most content words.

Borin and Prütz (2001) examined translations from Swedish into English, using news articles. They examine over- and underuse of POS n-grams. They manage to explain some of their observations, but not the overuse in the translations of adverbs, infinitives, pronouns and sentence-initial prepositions. We have not examined POS classes, but only specific words. However, we do see various adverbs in prominent positions, especially in Table 7, which indeed shows overuse. The sentence-initial prepositions might also be partly explained by (often lexicalized) adverbial prepositional phrases.

7 Conclusions

We have shown that classification on the basis of word n-grams markers is able to identify the source language of medium-length European Parliament speeches. Depending on the classification method used, the actual source language can be identified for 87.2% to 96.7% of the texts when all six target language versions of the text can be accessed. If only a single version is available, classification is considerably worse and only Support Vector Regression consistently shows relatively high scores, with accuracies of 81.5% for the Italian rendering to 87.4% for the Spanish one.

We also examined the strongest markers. We found that they are rather varied in nature and represent a wide range of information sources. Vocabulary, discourse structure and probably syntax of the source language all contribute. Contrasts between source and target languages can be seen to have an influence too, both purely linguistically and through the behaviour of the translators. But also the behaviour patterns of the parliamentarians of the various countries have a clear influence. Some of these influences are harmless or even attractive. Others should be followed up on, e.g. it would be good to attempt a harmonization of terminology throughout the various translation services, so that information retrieval on the parliamentary proceedings can be improved.

As for further research, it is vital to first investigate how exactly the European Parliament proceedings have been translated in the past, are being translated in the present and will be translated in the future. It may well be that some of the effects we are finding are limited to individual translators, or caused by their use of (machine) translation tools. Once it is clear that we are measuring what we think we are measuring, namely general trends in speaker and translator behaviour, we need to automate the retrieval of target language and source language phrases (maybe using statistical machine translation methodology), and possibly also to address semantically related clusters. Only then can we really investigate if observations like *"Dutch speakers exaggerate more often"* are valid or are just false impressions from looking at the data through too small a window.

Once all this is in place, we will have the means for a whole range of activities, e.g. to study parliamentary behaviour, to study the translation process, to determine if source language should be taken more into account in EUROPARL translation models and potentially even to give useful advise to the EU translation services.

References

Marco Baroni and Silvia Bernardini. 2003. A Preliminary Analysis of Collocational Differences in Monolingual Comparable Corpora. *Proc. Corpus Linguistics 2003, Lancaster, UK.*

Marco Baroni and Silvia Bernardini.2006. A New Approach to the Study of Translationese: Machine-Learning the Difference between Original and Translated Text. *Literary and Linguistic Computing*, 21(3): 259-274.

Lars Borin and Klas Prütz. 2001. Through a glass darkly: Part of speech distribution in original and translated text. *Computational linguistics in the Netherlands 2000.* Edited by Walter Daelemans, Khalil Sima'an, Jorn Veenstra, Jakub Zavrel. Amsterdam: Rodopi. 2001. 30-44

Chih-Chung Chang and Chih-Jen Lin, LIBSVM: a library for support vector machines, 2001. Available at http://www.csie.ntu.edu.tw/~cjlin/libsvm

Hans van Halteren and Nelleke Oostdijk. 2004. Linguistic Profiling of Texts for the Purpose of Language Verification. *COLING 2004, Geneva*: 966-972.

Philipp Koehn. 2005. Europarl: A Parallel Corpus for Statistical Machine Translation. *MT Summit X, Phuket, Thailand*: 79-86.

A Fluid Knowledge Representation for Understanding and Generating Creative Metaphors

Tony Veale
School of Computer Science
University College Dublin
Ireland
tony.veale@ucd.ie

Yanfen Hao
School of Computer Science
University College Dublin
Ireland
yanfen.hao@ucd.ie

Abstract

Creative metaphor is a phenomenon that stretches and bends the conventions of semantic description, often to humorous and poetic extremes. The computational modeling of metaphor thus requires a knowledge representation that is just as stretchable and semantically accommodating. We present here a flexible knowledge representation for metaphor interpretation and generation, called *Talking Points*, and describe how talking points can be acquired on a large scale from WordNet (Fellbaum, 1998) and from the web. We show how talking points can be fluidly connected to form a slipnet, and demonstrate that talking points provide an especially concise representation for concepts in general.

1 Introduction

Metaphor serves two important roles in language. The first of these is to make the unfamiliar and the strange seem more familiar and understandable (Indurkhya, 1992). For instance, one might describe a burqa (a full body covering for Muslim women) as a suit of armor, as a shield against prying eyes or, depending on one's communication goal, as a wearable cage. The other role of metaphor is most often associated with the poetic and fanciful use of language, but is no less important: to make the familiar and mundane seem strange and unfamiliar. In this latter guise, metaphor allows us to view a commonplace idea from a new and revealing category perspective (Camac and Glucksberg, 1984). For instance, one might describe makeup as "the Western burqa", to communicate not just the idea that each involves a covering of the female form, but that each reflects a society-imposed expectation on the public presentation of women. Each of these roles is a manifestation of the same underlying mechanism for combining concepts, for understanding how they interact (Black, 1962) and for determining how they are connected (Fauconnier and Turner, 1998), even if those connections are tenuous, hidden or not always obvious (Collins and Loftus, 1975). For example, consider the connections needed to make and understand the above metaphors:

Burqa $\Rightarrow$
$\equiv$ *for concealing a Muslim woman*
$\approx$ *for protecting a Muslim woman*
$\approx$ *protecting a woman*
$\approx$ *for protecting a person*
Armor $\Leftarrow$

Make-up $\Rightarrow$
$\equiv$ *typically worn by women*
$\approx$ *expected to be worn by women*
$\approx$ *must be worn by women*
$\approx$ *must be worn by Muslim women*
Burqa $\Leftarrow$

In each case we see how metaphor draws out and highlights, in a modified or exaggerated form, an existing aspect of each target concept. In other words, metaphor does not indiscriminately transplant arbitrary aspects of a source concept onto a target, but accommodates a selective graft of the most salient aspects of this source concept onto those aspects of the target that can

© 2008. Licensed under the *Creative Commons Attribution-Noncommercial-Share Alike 3.0 Unported* license (http://creativecommons.org/licenses/by-nc-sa/3.0/). Some rights reserved.

be highlighted by the comparison (Ortony, 1979). This connection between concepts requires a flexible knowledge representation, one that allows the connections between non-identical source and target aspects to be recognized, reconciled and even compressed (Fauconnier and Turner, 1998). This fluid representation (Hofstadter *et al.*, 1995) defines the search space in which the processes of metaphor generation and metaphor understanding are cognitively situated (Veale and O'Donoghue, 2000): for generation, fluid connectivity allows a system to search outwards from a given target to find those potential source concepts that offer a new yet appropriate perspective; for understanding purposes, connectivity allows an agent to focus on those key aspects of a source concept that are most apt for a target because they can be linked to that target.

In this paper we describe the construction of a fluid knowledge representation for creative metaphor processing, one that is acquired automatically from WordNet (Fellbaum, 1998) and from the texts of the web. In section 2 we summarize related work in the field of metaphor as it pertains to flexible knowledge representation. In section 3 we describe two complementary means of acquiring the basic elements of this representation, from WordNet and from the web, before describing how these elements can be placed into a fluid network of connections - what Hofstadter (ibid) calls a *slipnet* - in section 4. We then present in section 5 some empirical evaluation of the acquired representation on an objective test of term categorization, before concluding with some consideration of future work in section 6.

2 Related Work

Since metaphor can be viewed as a stretching of linguistic conventions to cover new conceptual ground, the interpretation of metaphor crucially hinges on a systems ability to recognize these conventions and accommodate the exceptional meaning conveyed by each figurative expression. Indeed, most computational approaches embody a sense of what it means to be literal, and accommodate metaphoric meanings within this conventional scheme through a form of relaxation, mapping or translation. Wilks (1978) advocates that the typically *hard* constraints that define a literal semantics should instead be modeled as *soft* preferences that can accommodate the violations that arise in metaphoric utterances, while Fass (1991) builds on this view to show how these violations can be repaired to thus capture the literal intent behind each metaphor. This repair process in turn relies on the availability of a concept taxonomy through which metaphoric uses can be mapped onto their literal counterparts; a car that "drinks gasoline" would thus be understood as a car that "consumes gasoline". Way (1991) emphasizes the importance of this taxonomy by positing a central role for a dynamic type hierarchy (DTH) in metaphor, one that can create new and complex taxonyms on the fly. For instance, Way's DTH would understand the "make-up as Western burqa" metaphor via a dynamically created taxonym like *things-women-are-expected-to-wear-in-public*, though Way offers no algorithmic basis for the workings of such a remarkable taxonomy. Another family of computational approaches combines explicit knowledge about certain metaphors with knowledge about the domains connected by these metaphors. Martin's (1990) *Midas* system encodes schematic knowledge about conventionalized metaphors such as "to kill a process" and "to open a program", and uses this knowledge to fit novel variations of these metaphors into the most appropriate schemas. Barnden and Lee (2002) focus on the role of inference in a metaphorically-structured domain, and describe a system called *ATTMeta* that contains sufficient knowledge about e.g., conventional metaphors of mind to reason about the mental states implied by these metaphors. Each of these approaches sees metaphor interpretation as a process of fitting what is said to what can meaningfully be represented and reasoned about. This fitting process is most explicitly modelled by Hofstadter *et al.* (1995), who focus on the slippage processes that are required to understand analogies in abstract domains that e.g., involve the mapping of letter sequences or the mirroring of actions in a highly stylized tabletop environment. Though simplified and toy-like, these are non-deterministic problem domains that are nonetheless shaped by a wide range of pragmatic pressures. Hofstadter and Mitchell (1994) model these pressures using a *slipnet*, a probabilistic network in which concepts are linked to others into which they can slip or be substituted with. In this view, deeply embedded concepts that are further removed from direct observation are less likely to engage in slippage than more superficial concepts.

To take a linguistic example, word choice in natural language generation is more susceptible to slippage (as influenced by synonym availability) than the concepts underlying the meaning of a sentence.

Slippage can be seen as a lossy form of conceptual re-representation: the greater the slippage, the more dramatic the re-representation and the greater the potential for loss of accuracy. For instance, a recent magazine cover proclaims the governor of California, Arnold Schwarzenegger, as "president of 12% of the United States". This conceptualization can be viewed as an intermediate stage in a slippage path from Governor to President as follows:

Governor of California ⇒

≈ *governor of 12% of the United States*

≈ *leader of 12% of the United States*

≈ *president of 12% of the United States*

≈ *president of 100% of the United States*

President of the U.S. ⇐

This labeling is creative enough to grace a magazine cover because it involves an ambitious level of re-conceptualization, at least from a computational perspective. The pivotal insight comes from *California = 12% of the United States*, an ad-hoc synonym that one is unlikely to find in a dictionary or general-purpose resource like WordNet. While ultimately aiming for this kind of creative transformation, our goal in this paper is more modest: to build a slippage network of concepts that are connected via their most salient features, one that combines the principled flexibility of a Hofstadter-style slipnet with the comprehensive scale of a resource like WordNet.

3 Acquiring Conceptual *Talking Points*

We refer to the knowledge elements connected by this slipnet as conceptual *talking points*. We first describe the form of these talking points and how they are acquired, before describing in section 4 how slippage operates between these talking points. We discuss two complementary kinds of talking point here: objective descriptions, extracted from WordNet glosses, and informal, stereotypical descriptions, harvested from the text of the web via a search engine like Google.

3.1 Objective Talking Points

Objective talking points are aspects of conceptual description that contribute to the consensus definitional view of a concept. Though WordNet does not provide explicit semantic criteria for the definition of each lexical concept, many of these criteria can be gleaned from a shallow parse of the pithy dictionary gloss it associates with each (e.g., see Ahlswede and Evans, 1988). Thus, whenever the head phrase of a concept's gloss has the form "ADJ$^+$ NOUN" where NOUN can denote a hypernym of the concept, we can associate the talking point *is_ADJ:NOUN* with that concept. For example, the gloss of {Hamas} is "a militant Islamic fundamentalist political movement that ...", which yields the talking points *is_militant:movement*, *is_islamic:movement*, *is_fundamentalist:movement* and *is_political:movement* for Hamas. When a WordNet concept has a hypernym of the form {ADJ_NOUN}, where NOUN can denote a hypernym of this concept, we likewise associate the talking point *is_ADJ:NOUN* with that concept. For example, {Taliban, Taleban} has {religious_movement} as a hypernym, which yields *is_religious:movement* as a talking point for Taliban.

Objective talking points can also be gleaned from the subject-verb-object structure of a WordNet gloss. For instance, the gloss for synset {conductor, music_director} is "the person who leads a musical group", which yields the talking point *leads:musical_group*. The hypernym of this concept, {musician}, has the gloss "*artist who composes or conducts music* ...", which yields the talking points *composes:music* and *conducts:music* that are then inherited by {conductor, ...} and other sub-types of musician in WordNet. A shallow parse will generally not lead to a complete understanding of a concept, but will typically produce some interesting talking points of the *predicate:object* variety that can be used to relate a concept to others that are analogically or metaphorically similar. Using WordNet's noun and verb taxonomies, we can identify the following slippage paths between talking points:

composes:music → *composes:speech* → *writes:speech* → *writes:oration* → *writes:sermon* → *writes:law* → *writes:philosophy* → *writes:theorem* → *writes:plan* → ...

In all, we extract talking points of the form *is_adj:noun* for over 40,000 WordNet concepts, and talking points of the form *verb:noun* for over 50,000 concepts. However, the real power of talking points emerges when they are connected to form a slipnet, as we discuss in section 4.

3.2 Stereotypical Talking Points

The talking points we harvest from the web do not have the authoritative, definitional character we find in hand-crafted resources like WordNet, but they do reflect how people typically speak of (and, perhaps, actually think of) the world. Veale and Hao (2007) argue that similes present the clearest window into the stereotypical talking points that underpin everyday conversations, and collect from the web instances of the pattern "*as ADJ as a* *" for thousands of WordNet adjectives. Though the simile frame is somewhat leaky in English, and prone to subversion by irony, Veale and Hao construct a comprehensive database of more than 12,000 highly stereotypical adjective:noun associations, such as *precise:surgeon*, *straight:arrow*, *balanced:pyramid* and *sharp:knife*. We use their data here, as the basis of an additional web harvesting process to gather stereotypical talking points of the form *has_ADJ:facet*. For every stereotypical association ADJ:NOUN in their database, we send the query "*the ADJ * of a|an|the NOUN*" to Google and collect noun values for the wildcard * from the first 200 hits returned for each query.

This pattern allows us to determine the conceptual attributes that are implicit in each stereotypical *adjective:noun* pairing. For instance, "the delicate hands of a surgeon" and "the inspiring voice of a preacher" reveal that *hand* is a salient attribute of surgeons while *voice* is a salient attribute of preachers. The frequency with which we find these attributes on the web also allows us to build a textured representation for each concept. So while these expanded web patterns also reveal that surgeons have a thorough *eye* and steady *nerves*, "the hands of a surgeon" are mentioned far more frequently and are thus far more salient to our understanding of surgeons. To avoid noise, the set of allowable attribute nouns, such as *hands*, *soul*, *heart*, *voice*, etc., is limited to the nouns in WordNet that denote a kind of trait, body part, quality, activity, ability or faculty. This allows us to acquire meaningful talking points like *has_magical:skill* for Wizard, *has_brave:spirit* for Lion and *has_enduring:beauty* for Diamond, while avoiding dubious or misleading talking points like *has_proud:owner* for Peacock that lack either representational value or insight. In all, this process acquires 18,794 stereotypical talking points for 2032 different WordNet noun senses, for an average of 9 facet:feature pairs per sense. Specific senses are identified automatically, by exploiting WordNet's network of hypernymy and synonymy relations to connect talking points that describe variations of the same concept.

4 Building a Slipnet of Talking Points

To construct a slipnet in the style of Hofstadter and Mitchell (1994), but on the scale of WordNet, we need to connect those talking points that express similar but different meanings, and to quantify the difference between these meanings. Issues of scale mean that we need only connect talking points that are close in meaning, since greater slippage can be achieved by following longer paths through the slipnet. This slippage can be based on semantic *or* pragmatic criteria. Thus, the talking points *has_sacred:authority* (for Pope) and *has_sacred:power* (for God) are semantically similar since the potency sense of "authority" is a specialization of the control sense of "power" in WordNet. Likewise, *writes:speech* and *composes:speech* are similar because "compose" and "write" are synonymous in the context of literary creation, and it is this particular linkage that supports a slippage pathway from *composes:music* to *writes:poetry*. In contrast, *is_political:movement* (for Hamas) and *is_religious:movement* (for Taliban) are pragmatically similar since movements that are religious often have a political agenda also. We can use WordNet to construct the semantic links of the slipnet, but pragmatic links like these require not just word senses but a sense of the world, of a kind we can distil from the text of the web.

Two talking points *is_*ADJ_1*:*OBJ_1 and *is_*ADJ_2*:*OBJ_2 should be connected in the slipnet if: OBJ_1 and OBJ_2 are semantically close (i.e., synonymous, or semantic siblings in WordNet); and ADJ_1 and ADJ_2 are synonymous, or ADJ_1 frequently implies ADJ_2 or ADJ_2 frequently implies ADJ_1. These implications are recognized and quantified using another web trawling process, in which the query "*as * and * as*" is used to harvest pairs of adjectives that are seen to mutually reinforce each other in web comparisons. This search reveals that "religious" reinforces "superstitious" (5 times), "moral" (4), "political" (3), "conservative" (3), "intolerant" (2) and "irrational" (1). These slippage connections link *is_religious:movement* to *is_political:movement* (pragmatic) to *is_political:campaign* (semantic) to *is_military:campaign* (pragmatic), thereby connecting Taliban (*is_religious:movement*) to Crusade (*is_military:campaign*).

4.1 The Slipnet in Action

Slippage is a phenomenon best explained with an example, so consider again the task of creating metaphors for the concept Pope. We have already seen that slippage among talking points allows Pope to be linked to the concept God via Pope → *has_sacred:authority* → *has_sacred:power* ← God. Pope can also be linked to Rabbi via the path Pope → *has_sacred:words* → *has_wise:words* ← Rabbi and to Judge by extending this pathway: Pope → *has_sacred:words* → *has_wise:words* → *has_solemn:words* ← Judge. Black (1962) saw metaphor as an interaction between concepts, in which the interpretation of a particular source concept depends crucially on how it is able to interact with a specific target concept. This concept-sensitive interplay is clearly on display here. The Pope can be metaphorically viewed as a warrior not by considering what it means for a generic person to be a warrior, but by considering how the concept Pope actually interacts with the concept Warrior, e.g., Pope → *has_infallible:voice* → *has_powerful:voice* ← Warrior.

Consider the potential for slippage between objective talking points from WordNet:

Pope ⇒
≡ *leads:Roman_Catholic_Church*
≈ *leads:congregation*
≈ *leads:flock*
≈ *leads:mob*
≈ *leads:organized_crime*
Don (Crime Father) ⇐

Pope ⇒
≡ *leads:Roman_Catholic_Church*
≈ *leads:congregation*
≈ *leads:political_movement*
≈ *leads:gang*
≈ *leads:military_force*
Warlord (Military Leader) ⇐

One can typically terminate a slippage path at any point, to produce different metaphors with varying semantic similarity to the starting concept. Thus, at *leads:flock* one can reach Shepherd, and from leads:political_movement, one can reach Civil_rights_leader.

A lexicon alone, like WordNet, is generally insufficient for metaphor processing, but such a resource can still reveal useful lexical resonances that may enrich an interpretation. In the example above, we see a resonance between the Pope, which WordNet also lexicalizes as "holy father", and a mafia Don, which WordNet also lexicalizes as "father". Indeed, since WordNet conceptualizes Roman_Catholic_Church as a specialization of Organized_religion, the metaphor establishes a parallelism between crime and religion as organized activities.

5 Empirical Evaluation

To understand whether talking points are sufficiently descriptive of the concepts they are acquired for, we replicate here the clustering experiments of Almuhareb and Poesio (2004, 2005) which are designed to measure the effectiveness of web-acquired conceptual descriptions. Since Almuhareb and Poesio use WordNet as a semantic gold-standard, we consider here the effectiveness of stereotypical talking points alone; it would be circular to consider objective talking points, since these are extracted from WordNet.

Almuhareb and Poesio describe two different clustering experiments. In the first, they choose 214 English nouns from 13 of WordNet's upper-level semantic categories, and proceed to harvest property values for these concepts from the web using the pattern "*a|an|the * C is|was*". This pattern yields a combined total of 51,045 values for all 214 nouns; these values are primarily adjectives, such as *hot*, *black*, etc., but noun-modifiers of C are also allowed, such as *fruit* for cake. They also harvest 8934 attribute nouns, such as *temperature* and *color*, using the query pattern "*the * of the C is|was*". These values and attributes are then used as the basis of a clustering algorithm to partition the 214 nouns back into their original 13 categories. Comparing these clusters with the original WordNet-based groupings, Almuhareb and Poesio report a cluster accuracy of 71.96% using just values like *hot* (all 51,045), an accuracy of 64.02% using just attributes like *temperature* (all 8934), and

Table 1: Experiment 1, accuracy for 214 nouns

Approach	*Values only*	*Attr's only*	*All (V + A)*
Almu. + Poesio	71.96% (51045 vals)	64.02% (8934 attr)	85.51% (59979 v+a)
Talking Points	70.2% (2209 vals)	78.7% (4974 attr)	90.2% (7183 v+a)

Table 2: Experiment 2, accuracy for 402 nouns

Approach	*Values only*	*Attr's only*	*All (V + A)*
Almu. + Poesio (no filtering)	56.7% (94989 vals)	65.7% (24178 attr)	67.7% (119167 v+a)
Almu. + Poesio (with filtering)	62.7% (51345 vals)	70.9% (12345 attr)	66.4% (63690 v+a)
Talking Points	64.3% (5547 vals)	54.7% (3952 attr)	69.85% (9499 v+a)

an accuracy of 85.5% using both together (59979 features).

In a second, larger experiment, Almuhareb and Poesio select 402 nouns from 21 different semantic classes in WordNet, and proceed to harvest 94,989 property values (again mostly adjectives) and 24,178 attribute nouns from the web using the same retrieval patterns. They then applied the *repeated bisections clustering* algorithm to this larger data set, and report an initial cluster purity measure of 56.7% using only property values like *hot*, 65.7% using only attributes like *temperature*, and 67.7% using both together. Suspecting that noisy features contribute to the perceived drop in performance, those authors then applied a variety of noise filters to reduce the value set to just 51,345 values and the attribute set to just 12,345 attributes, for a size reduction of about 50% in each case. This in turn leads to an improved cluster purity measure of 62.7% using property values only and 70.9% using attributes only. Surprisingly, filtering actually appears to reduce the clustering performance of both data-sets used together, to 66.4%.

We replicate here both of these experiments using the same data-sets of 214 and 402 nouns respectively. For fairness, we collect *raw* descriptions for each of these nouns directly from the web, and use no filtering (manual or otherwise) to remove poor or ill-formed descriptions. We thus use the pattern "*as * as a|an|the C*" to collect 2209 raw adjectival values for the 214 nouns of experiment 1, and 5547 raw adjectival values for the 402 nouns of experiment 2. We then use the pattern "*the ADJ * of a|an|the C*" to collect 4974 attributes for the 214 nouns of experiment 1, and 3952 for the 402 nouns of experiment 2; in each case, ADJ is bound to the raw adjectival values that were acquired using "*as * as a|an|the C*". A comparison of clustering results is given in Tables 1 and 2. These tables illustrate that clustering is most effective when it is performed on the basis of both values *and* attributes (yielding the highest scores, 90.2% and 69.85%, in each experiment respectively). These results thus support the combination of conceptual attributes with specific adjectival values into integrated talking points which reflect how people actually talk about the concepts concerned.

6 Conclusions

Metaphor is a knowledge-hungry phenomenon, so any computational treatment of metaphor will only be as good as the knowledge representation that supports it. Moreover, from a computational perspective, any theory of metaphor – cognitive, linguistic, or otherwise – is only as good as the algorithmic and representational insights that it provides, and the scale of the implementation that it ultimately allows us to realize. In this paper we have given computational form to some of the key insights in the metaphor literature, from the interaction theory of Black (1962) to the salience imbalance theory of Ortony (1979) to the theory of conceptual blending of Fauconnier and Turner (1998). We also employ a key insight from the work of Hofstadter and his fluid analogies group (1995), that robust reasoning on a conceptual level requires a degree of slippage that must be supported by the underlying knowledge representation.

Our knowledge base of talking points is derived from two complementary information sources: the objective definitions contained in WordNet (Fellbaum, 1998) and the stereotypical comparisons that pepper the texts of the web. These sources yield a knowledge-base that is neither small nor hand-crafted. While the knowledge-base needs to grow by at least an order of magnitude, slippage means that non-identical talking points can be treated as equivalent for purposes of robust processing, which in turn extends the *halo* of talking points that surrounds each concept in the knowledge-base (Hofstadter *et al.*, 1995). The experiments of section 5 also indicate that, in a pinch, new talking points for a previously under-represented concept can be acquired dynamically from the web with reasonable accuracy. As it currently stands, the talking points approach to metaphor is robust enough and scalable enough to generate simple but imaginative metaphors on demand for a wide range of user inputs.

But what does it mean to state, at a knowledge-representation level, that *lions* and *knights* both have a *brave heart*, that *wolves* and *tyrants* both have a *cruel* face, or that eagles and warriors have a *fierce expression*? Stereotypical talking points such as these can be poetic or metaphorical, and may express a viewpoint that is overly simplistic, subjective or even technically inaccurate. Nonetheless, our experiments suggest that the linguistic insights we acquire from non-literal descriptions strongly reflect our ontological intuitions about concepts and are more than mere linguistic decorations. Most significantly, we see from these experiments that stereotypical talking points yield an especially concise representation, since with no filtering of any kind, this approach achieves comparable clustering results with feature sets that are many times smaller than those used in previous work. We anticipate therefore that stereotypical descriptions will be a key growth area for the development of the talking points knowledge-base.

The Pope examples of section 4.1. exemplify the competence of the system as it is currently implemented, while the Burqa and Governor/President examples of sections 1 and 2 mark out our future directions. The Burqa examples demonstrate the need for a more complex representation of talking points that can accommodate nested propositions, while the Governor example demonstrates the need for more radical and ad-hoc slippage patterns in creative metaphors. Rather than add special rules to handle such individual cases (which are creative *because* of their one-off disposal nature), our ambition is to develop a general corpus-grounded mechanism for explaining *all* metaphor-related slippage. We remain a considerable distance from this goal, yet believe it is best attained using the kind of robust and scalable approach described here.

References

Almuhareb, A. and M. Poesio. 2004. Attribute-Based and Value-Based Clustering: An Evaluation In *proceedings of EMNLP*, the Conference on Empirical Methods on Natural Language Processing. Barcelona.

Almuhareb, A. and M. Poesio. 2005. Concept Learning and Categorization from the Web. In *proceedings of the annual meeting of the Cognitive Science society*. Italy.

Ahlswede, T. and M. Evans. 1998. Parsing vs. Text Processing in the analysis of dictionary definitions. In *proceedings of the 26th Annual Meeting of the Association for Computational Linguistics*, 217–224.

Barnden, J. A. and M. G. Lee. 2002. An Artificial Intelligence Approach to Metaphor Understanding. *Theoria et Historia Scientiarum*, 6(1):399–412.

Black, M. 1962. *Models and Metaphor: studies in language and philosophy*. Ithaca, NY: Cornell University Press.

Camac, K. and S. Glucksberg. 1984. Metaphors do not use associations between concepts, they are used to create them. *Journal of Psycholinguistic Research*,13(6).

Collins, A. and E. F. Loftus. 1975. A Spreading-Activation Theory of Semantic Processing. *Psychological Review* 82, 407–428.

Fauconnier, G. and M. Turner. 1998. Conceptual Integration Networks. *Cognitive Science*, 22(2):133–187.

Fellbaum, C. (ed.). 1998. *WordNet: An electronic lexical database*. The MIT Press. 1985 *A comprehensive grammar of the English*.

Hofstadter, D. R. and M. Mitchell. 1994. The Copycat Project: A model of mental fluidity and analogy-making. *In Holyoak, K.J. & Barnden, J. A. (Eds.) Advances in Connectionist and Neural Computation Theory*, Vol. 2. Norwood, NJ: Ablex.

Hofstadter, D. R. and the Fluid Analogy Research Group. 1995. *Fluid Concepts and Creative Analogies: Computer Models of the Fundamental Mechanisms of Thought*. NY: Basic Books.

Fass, D. 1991. Met*: a method for discriminating metonymy and metaphor by computer. *Computational Linguistics*, 17(1):49–90.

Indurkhya, B. 1992. *Metaphor and Cognition: Studies in Cognitive Systems*. Kluwer Academic Publishers, Dordrecht: The Netherlands.

Martin, J. H. 1990. *A Computational Model of Metaphor Interpretation*. NY: Academic Press.

Ortony, A. 1979. Beyond literal similarity. *Psychological Review*, 86, 161–180.

Veale, T. and Y. Hao. 2007. Making WordNet Functional and Context-Sensitive. In *proceedings of the 45th Annual Meeting of the Association for Computational Linguistics*. Czech Republic.

Veale, T. and O'Donoghue. 2000. Computation and Blending. *Cognitive Linguistics*, 11(3–4), special issue on Conceptual Blending.

Way, E. C. 1991. Knowledge Representation and Metaphor. *Studies in Cognitive systems*. Holland: Kluwer.

Wilks, Y. 1978. Making Preferences More Active, *Studies in Cognitive systems. Artificial Intelligence* 11(3), 197–223.

Using Syntactic Information for Improving *Why*-Question Answering

Suzan Verberne, Lou Boves, Nelleke Oostdijk and Peter-Arno Coppen
Department of Linguistics
Radboud University Nijmegen
s.verberne@let.ru.nl

Abstract

In this paper, we extend an existing paragraph retrieval approach to *why*-question answering. The starting-point is a system that retrieves a relevant answer for 73% of the test questions. However, in 41% of these cases, the highest ranked relevant answer is not ranked in the top-10. We aim to improve the ranking by adding a re-ranking module. For re-ranking we consider 31 features pertaining to the syntactic structure of the question and the candidate answer. We find a significant improvement over the baseline for both success@10 and MRR@150. The most important features for re-ranking are the baseline score, the presence of cue words, the question's main verb, and the relation between question focus and document title.

1 Introduction

Recently, some research has been directed at problems involved in *why*-question answering (*why*-QA). About 5% of all questions asked to QA systems are *why*-questions (Hovy et al., 2002). They need a different approach from factoid questions, since their answers cannot be stated in a single phrase. Instead, a passage retrieval approach seems more suitable. In (Verberne et al., 2008), we proposed an approach to *why*-QA that is based on paragraph retrieval. We reported mediocre performance and suggested that adding linguistic information may improve ranking power.

In the present paper, we implement a similar paragraph retrieval approach and extend it by adding a re-ranking module based on structural linguistic information. Our aim is to find out whether syntactic knowledge is relevant for discovering relations between question and answer, and if so, which type of information is the most beneficial.

In the following sections, we first discuss related work (section 2). In sections 3 and 4, we introduce the data that we used for development purposes and the baseline retrieval and ranking method that we implemented. In section 5, we present our re-ranking method and the results obtained, followed by a discussion in section 6, and directions for further research in section 7.

2 Related work

A substantial amount of work has been done in improving QA by adding syntactic information (Tiedemann, 2005; Quarteroni et al., 2007; Higashinaka and Isozaki, 2008). All these studies show that syntactic information gives a small but significant improvement on top of the traditional bag-of-words (BOW) approaches.

The work of (Higashinaka and Isozaki, 2008) focuses on the problem of ranking candidate answer paragraphs for Japanese *why*-questions. They find a success@10 score of 70.3% with an MRR of 0.328. They conclude that their system for Japanese is the best-performing fully implemented *why*-QA system. In (Tiedemann, 2005), passage retrieval for Dutch factoid QA is enriched with syntactic information from dependency structures. The baseline approach, using only the BOW, resulted in an MRR of 0.342. With the addition of syntactic structure, MRR improved to 0.406.

The work by (Quarteroni et al., 2007) considers the problem of answering definition questions.

© Suzan Verberne, 2008. Licensed under the *Creative Commons Attribution-Noncommercial-Share Alike 3.0 Unported* license (http://creativecommons.org/licenses/by-nc-sa/3.0/). Some rights reserved.

They use predicate-argument structures (PAS) for improved answer ranking. Their results show that PAS make a very small contribution compared to BOW only (F-scores 70.7% vs. 69.3%).

The contribution of this paper is twofold: (1) we consider the relatively new problem of *why*-QA for English and (2) we not only improve a simple passage retrieval approach by adding syntactic information but we also perform extensive feature selection in order to find out which syntactic features contribute to answer ranking and to what extent.

3 Data

As data for developing and testing our system for *why*-QA, we use the Webclopedia question set by (Hovy et al., 2002). This set contains questions that were asked to the online QA system *answers.com*. 805 of these questions are *why*-questions. As answer corpus, we use the off-line Wikipedia XML corpus, which consists of 659,388 articles (Denoyer and Gallinari, 2006). We manually inspect a sample of 400 of the Webclopedia *why*-questions. Of these, 93 have an answer in the Wikipedia corpus. Manual extraction of one relevant answer for each of these questions results in a set of 93 *why*-questions and their reference answer. We also save the title of the Wikipedia article in which each of the answers is embedded, in order to be able to evaluate document retrieval together with answer retrieval.

4 Paragraph retrieval for *why*-QA

4.1 Baseline method

We index the Wikipedia XML corpus using the Wumpus Search Engine (Buttcher, 2007). In Wumpus, queries can be formulated in the GCL format, which is especially geared to retrieving XML items. Since we consider paragraphs as retrieval units, we let the engine retrieve text fragments marked with *¡p¿* as candidate answers.

We implement a baseline method for question analysis in which first stop words are removed[1]. Also, any punctuation is removed from the question. What remains is a set of question content words. Next, we automatically create a query for each question that retrieves paragraphs containing (a subset of) these question terms. For ranking the paragraphs retrieved, we use the QAP algorithm created by MultiText, which has been implemented in Wumpus. QAP is a passage scoring algorithm specifically developed for QA tasks (Buttcher et al., 2004). For each question, we retrieve and rank the top 150 of highest scoring answer candidates.

4.2 Evaluation method

For evaluation of the results, we perform manual assessment of all answers retrieved, starting at the highest-ranked answer and ending as soon as we encounter a relevant answer[2]. Then we count the proportion of questions that have at least one relevant answer in the top n of the results for $n = 10$ and $n = 150$, giving us success@10 and success@150. For the highest ranked relevant answer per question, we determine the reciprocal rank (RR). If there is no relevant answer retrieved by the system at $n = 150$, the RR is 0. Over all questions, we calculate the Mean RR (MRR@150).

We also measure the performance of our system for document retrieval: the proportion of questions for which at least one of the answers in the top 10 comes from the reference document (success@10 for document retrieval) and the MRR@150 for the highest position of the reference document[3].

4.3 Results and discussion

Table 1: Baseline results for the *why* passage retrieval system for answer retrieval and document retrieval in terms of success@10, success@150 and MRR@150

	S@10	S@150	MRR@150
Answer retrieval	43.0%	73.1%	0.260
Document retrieval	61.8%	82.2%	0.365

There are two possible directions for improving our system: (1) by improving retrieval and (2) by improving ranking. Since success@150 is 73.1%, for 68 of the 93 questions in our set at least one relevant answer is retrieved in the top 150. For the other 25 questions, the reference answer was not included in the long list of 150 results.

In the present paper we focus on improving answer *ranking*. The results show that for 30.1% of

[1]To this end the stop word list is used that can be found at *http://marlodge.supanet.com/museum/ funcword.html*. We use all categories except the numbers and the word *why*

[2]We don't need to assess the tail since we are only interested in the highest-ranked relevant answer for calculating MRR

[3]Note that we consider as relevant all documents in which a relevant answer is embedded. So the relevant document with the highest rank is either the reference document or the document in which the relevant answer with the highest rank is embedded.

the questions[4], a relevant answer is retrieved but is not placed in the top 10 by the ranking algorithm. For these 28 questions in our set, re-ranking may be an option. Since re-ranking will not improve the results for the questions for which there is no relevant answer in the top-150, the maximum success@10 that we can achieve by re-ranking is 73.1% for answer paragraphs and 82.8% for documents.

5 Answer re-ranking

Before we can decide on our re-ranking approach, we take a closer look at the ranking method that is applied in the baseline system. The QAP algorithm includes the following variables: (1) term overlap between query and passage, (2) passage length and (3) total corpus frequency for each term (Buttcher et al., 2004). Let us consider three example questions from our collection to see the strengths and weaknesses of these variables.

1. Why do people sneeze?
2. Why do women live longer than men on average?
3. Why are mountain tops cold?

In (1), the corpus frequencies of the question terms *people* and *sneeze* ensure that the relatively unique term *sneeze* is weighted heavier for ranking than the very common noun *people*. This matches the goal of the query, which is finding an explanation for sneezing. However, in (2), the frequency variables used by QAP do not reflect the importance of the terms. Thus, *women*, *live*, *longer* and *average* are considered to be of equal importance, while obviously the latter term is only peripheral to the goal of the query. This cannot be derived from its corpus frequency, but may be inferred from its syntactic function in the question: an adverbial on sentence level. In (3), *mountain* and *tops* are interpreted as two distinct terms by the baseline system, whereas the interpretation of *mountain tops* as compound item is more appropriate.

Examples 2 and 3 above show that a question-answer pair may contain more information than is represented by the frequency variables implemented in the QAP algorithm. Our aim is to find out which features from a question-answer pair constitute the information that discloses a relation between the question and its answer. Moreover, we aim at weighting these features in such a way that we can optimize ranking performance.

[4] 73.1% – 43.0%

5.1 Features for re-ranking

As explained above, baseline ranking is based on term overlap. The features that we propose for re-ranking are also based on term overlap, but instead of considering all question content words indiscriminately in one overlap function, we select a subset of question terms for each of the re-ranking features. By defining different subsets based on syntactic functions and categories, we can investigate which syntactic features of the question, and which parts of the answer are most important for re-ranking.

The following subsections list the syntactic features that we consider. Each feature consists of two item sets: a set of question items and a set of answer items. The value that is assigned to a feature is a function of the intersection between these two sets. For a set of question items Q and a set of answer items A, the proportion P of their intersection is:

$$P = \frac{|Q \in A| + |A \in Q|}{|Q| + |A|} \quad (1)$$

Our approach to composing the set of features is described in subsections 5.1.1 to 5.1.4 below. We label the features using the letter f followed by a number so that we can back-reference to them.

5.1.1 The syntactic structure of the question

Example 2 in the previous section shows that some syntactic functions in the question may be more important than other functions. Since we do not know as yet which syntactic functions are the most important, we include both heads (f1) and modifiers (f2) as item sets. We also include the four main syntactic constituents for *why*-questions: subject (f4), main verb (f6), nominal predicate (f8) and direct object (f10) to be matched against the answer terms. For these features, we add a variant where as answer items only words/phrases with the same syntactic function are included (f5, f7, f9, f11).

Example 3 in the previous section exemplifies the potential relevance of noun phrases (f3).

5.1.2 The semantic structure of the question

The features f12 to f15 come from earlier data analyses that we performed. We saw that often there is a link between a specific part of the question and the title of the document in which the reference answer is found. For example, the answer to the question "Why did B.B. King name his guitar Lucille?" is in the Wikipedia article with the title *B.B. King*. The answer document and the question apparently share the same topic (*B.B. King*). In analogy to linguistically motivated approaches to factoid QA (Ferret et al., 2002) we introduce the term *question focus* for this topic.

The focus is often the syntactic subject of the question. From our data, we found the following two exceptions to this general rule: (1) If the subject is semantically poor, the question focus is the (verbal or nominal) predicate: "Why do people sneeze?", and (2) in case of etymology questions (which cover about 10% of *why*-questions), the focus is the subject complement of the passive sentence: "Why are chicken wings called Buffalo Wings?" In all other cases, the question focus is the grammatical subject: 'Why do cats sleep so much?'

We include a feature (f13) for matching words from the question focus to words from the document title. We also add a feature (f12) for the relation between all question words and words from the document title, and a feature (f14) for the relation between question focus words and all answer words.

5.1.3 Synonyms

For each of the features f1 to f15, we add an alternative feature (f16 to f30) covering the set of all WordNet synonyms for all items in the original feature. Note that the original words are no longer included for these features; we only include the terms from their synonym sets. For synonyms, we apply a variant of equation 1 in which $|Q \in A|$ is interpreted as the number of question items that have at least one synonym in the set of answer items and $|A \in Q|$ as the number of answer items that occur in at least one of the synonym sets of the question items.

5.1.4 Cue words

Finally, we add a closed set of cue words that often occur in answers to *why*-questions[5] (f31).

5.2 Extracting feature values from the data

For the majority of features we need the syntactic structure of the input question, and for some of the features also of the answer. We experimented with two different parsers for these tasks: a development version of the Pelican parser[6] and the EP4IR dependency parser (Koster, 2003).

Given a question-answer pair and the parse trees of both question and answer, we extract values from each parser's output for all features in section 5.1 by means of a Perl script.

Our script has access to the following external components: A stop word list (see section 4.1), a fixed set of cue words, the CELEX Lemma lexicon (Burnage et al., 1990), all WordNet synonym sets, and a list of pronouns and semantically poor nouns[7].

Given one question-answer pair, the feature extraction script performs the following actions. Based on the question's parse tree, it extracts the subject, main verb, direct object (if present) and nominal predicate (if present) from the question. The script decides on question focus using the rules suggested in section 5.1.2. For the answer, it extracts the document title. From the parse trees created for the answer paragraph, it extracts all subjects, all verbs, all direct objects, and all nominal predicates.

For each feature, the script composes the required sets of question items and answer items. All items are lowercased and punctuation is removed. In multi-word items, spaces are replaced by underscores before stop words are removed from the question and the answer. Then the script calculates the proportion of the intersection of the two sets for each feature following equation 1[8].

Whether or not to lemmatize the items before matching them is open to debate. In the literature, there is some discussion on the benefit of lemmatization for information extraction (Bilotti et al., 2004). Lemmatization can be problematic in the case of proper names (which are not always recognizable by capitalization) and noun phrases that are fixed expressions such as *sailors of old*. Noun phrases are involved not only in the NP feature (f3), but also in our features involving subject, direct object, nominal predicate and question focus. Therefore, we decided only to lemmatize verbs (for features f6 and f7) in the current version of our system.

For each question-answer pair in our data set, we extract all feature values using our script. We

[5]These cue words come from earlier work that we did on the analysis of *why*-answers: *because, since, therefore, why, in order to, reason, reasons, due to, cause, caused, causing, called, named*

[6]The Pelican parser is a constituency parser that is currently being developed at Nijmegen University. See also *http://lands.let.ru.nl/projects/pelican/*

[7]These are the nouns *humans* and *people*

[8]A multi-word term is counted as one item

use three different settings for feature extraction: (1) feature extraction from gold standard constituency parse trees of the questions in accordance with the descriptive model of the Pelican parser[9]; (2) feature extraction from the constituency parse trees of the questions generated by Pelican[10]; and (3) feature extraction from automatically generated dependency parse trees from EP4IR.

Our training and testing method using the extracted feature values is explained in the next section.

5.3 Re-ranking method

As the starting point for re-ranking we run the baseline system on the complete set of 93 questions and retrieve 150 candidate answers per question, ranked by the QAP algorithm. As described in section 5.2, we use two different parsers. Of these, Pelican has a more detailed descriptive model and gives better accuracy (see section 6.3 on parser evaluation) but EP4IR is at present more robust for parsing long sentences and large amounts of text. Therefore, we parse all answers (93 times 150 paragraphs) with EP4IR only. The questions are parsed by both Pelican and EP4IR.

As presented in section 5.1, we have 31 re-ranking features. To these, we add the score that was assigned by QAP, which makes 32 features in total. We aim to weight the feature values in such a way that their contribution to the overall system performance is optimal. We set each feature weight as an integer between 0 and 10, which makes the number of possible weighting configurations 11^{32}. In order to choose the optimal configuration from this huge set of possible configurations, we use a genetic algorithm[11] (Goldberg and Holland, 1988). The variable that we optimize during training is MRR. We tune the feature weights over 100 generations of 1000 individuals. For evaluation, we apply cross valuation on five question folds: in five turns, we train the feature weights on four of the five folds and evaluate them on the fifth.

We use the feature values that come from the gold standard parse trees for training the feature weights, because the benefit of a syntactic item type can only be proved if the extraction of that item from the data is correct. At the testing stage, we re-rank the 93 questions using all three feature extraction settings: feature values extracted from gold standard parse trees, feature values extracted with Pelican and feature values extracted with EP4IR. We again regard the distribution of questions over the five folds: we re-rank the questions in fold five according to the weights found by training on folds one to four.

5.4 Results from re-ranking

Table 2 on the next page shows the results for the three feature extraction settings.

Using the Wilcoxon Signed-Rank Test we find that all three re-ranking conditions give significantly better results than the baseline ($Z = -1.91$, $P = 0.0281$ for paired reciprocal ranks). The differences between the three re-ranking conditions are, however, not significant[12].

5.5 Which features made the improvement?

If we plot the weights that were chosen for the features in the five folds, we see that for some features very different weights were chosen in the different folds. Apparently, for these features, the weight values do not generalize over the five folds. In order to only use reliable features, we only consider features that get similar weights over all five folds: their weight values have a standard deviation < 2 and an average weight > 0. We find that of the 32 features, 21 are reliable according to this definition. Five of these features make a substantial contribution to the re-ranking score (table 3). Behind each feature is its reference number from section 5.1 and its average weight on a scale of 0 to 10.

Moreover, there are three other features that to a limited extent contribute to the overall score (table 4).

Thirteen other reliable features get a weight < 1.5 assigned during training and thereby slightly contribute to the re-ranking score.

[9] Pelican aims at producing all possible parse trees for a given sentence. A linguist can then decide on the correct parse tree given the context. We created the gold standard for each question by manually selecting the correct parse tree from the parse trees generated by the parser.

[10] For this setting, we run the Pelican parser with the option of only giving one parse (the most likely according to Pelican) per question. As opposed to the gold standard setting, we do not perform manual selection of the correct parse.

[11] We chose to work with a genetic algorithm because we are mainly interested in feature selection and ranking. We are currently experimenting with Support Vector Machines (SVM) to see whether the results obtained from using the genetic algorithm are good enough for reliable feature selection.

[12] The slightly lower success and MRR scores for re-ranking with gold standard parse trees compared to Pelican parse trees can be explained by the absence of the gold standard for one question in our set.

Table 2: Re-ranking results for three different parser settings in terms of success@10, success@150 and MRR@150.

	Answer/paragraph retrieval			Document retrieval		
Version	S@10	S@150	MRR	S@10	S@150	MRR
Baseline	43.0%	73.1%	0.260	61.8%	82.8%	0.365
Re-ranking w/ gold standard parse trees	54.4%	73.1%	0.370	63.1%	82.8%	0.516
Re-ranking w/ Pelican parse trees	54.8%	73.1%	0.380	64.5%	82.8%	0.518
Re-ranking w/ EP4IR parse trees	53.8%	73.1%	0.349	63.4%	82.8%	0.493

Table 3: Features that substantially contribute to the re-ranking score, with their average weight

Question focus synonyms to doctitle (f28)	9.2
Question verb synonyms to answer verbs (f22)	9
Cue words (f31)	9
QAP	8.8
Question focus to doctitle (f13)	7.8

Table 4: Features that to a limited extent contribute to the re-ranking score, with their average weight

Question subject to answer subjects (f5)	2.2
Question nominal predicate synonyms (f23)	1.8
Question object synonyms to answer objects (f26)	1.8

6 Discussion

Our re-ranking method scores significantly better than the baseline, with use of a small subset of the 32 features. It reaches a success@10 score of 54.8% with an MRR@150 of 0.380 for answer retrieval. This compares to the MRR of 0.328 that Higashinaka and Isozaki found for *why*-QA and the MRR of 0.406 that Tiedemann reaches for syntactically enhanced factoid-QA (see section 2), showing that our method performs reasonable well. However, the MRR of 0.380 also shows that a substantial part of the problem of *why*-QA is still to be solved.

6.1 Error analysis

For analysis of our results, we counted for how many questions the ranking was improved, and for how many the ranking deteriorated. First of all, ranking remained equal for 35 questions (37.6%). 25 of these are the questions for which no relevant answer was retrieved by the baseline system at $n = 150$ (26.9% of questions). For these questions the ranking obviously remained equal (RR is 0) after re-ranking. For the other 10 questions for which ranking did not change, RR was 1 and remained 1. Apparently, re-ranking does not affect excellent rankings.

For two third (69%) of the remaining questions, ranking improved and for one third (31%), it deteriorated. There are eleven questions for which the reference answer was ranked in the top 10 by the baseline system but it drops out of the top 10 by re-ranking. On the other hand, there are 22 questions for which the reference answer enters the top 10 by re-ranking the answers, leading to an overall improvement in success@10.

If we take a look at the eleven questions for which the reference answer drops out of the top 10 by re-ranking, we see that these are all cases where there is no lexical overlap between the question focus and the document title. The importance of features 13 and 28 in the re-ranking weights works against the reference answer for these questions. Here are three examples (question focus as detected by the feature extraction script is underlined):

1. Why do neutral atoms have the same number of protons as electrons? (answer in 'Oxidation number')
2. Why do flies walk on food? (answer in 'Insect Habitat')
3. Why is Wisconsin called the Badger State? (answer in 'Wisconsin')

In example 1, the reference answer is outranked by answer paragraphs from documents with one of the words *neutral* and *atoms* in its title. In example 2, there is actually a semantic relation between the question focus (*flies*) and the document title (*insect*); however, this relation is not synonymy but hyperonymy and therefore not included in our re-ranking features. One could dispute the definition of question focus for etymology questions (example 3), but there are simply more cases where the subject complement of the question leads to document title than cases where its subject (such as *Winsconsin*) does.

6.2 Feature selection analysis

We think that the outcome of the feature selection (section 5.5) is very interesting. We are not surprised that the original score assigned by QAP is still important in the re-ranking module: the frequency variables apparently do provide useful information on the relevance of a candidate answer.

We also see that the presence of cue words (f31) gives useful information in re-ranking answer paragraphs. In fact, incorporating the presence of cue words is a first step towards recognizing that a paragraph is potentially an answer to a *why*-question. We feel that identifying a paragraph as a potential answer is the most salient problem of *why*-QA, since answers cannot be recognized by simple semantic-syntactic units such as named entities as is the case for factoid QA. The current results show that surface patterns (the literal presence of items from a fixed set of cue words) are a first step in the direction of answer selection.

More interesting than the baseline score and cue words are the high average weights assigned to the features f13 and f28. These two features refer to the relation between question focus and document title. As explained in section 5.1.2, we already had the intuition that there is some relation between the question focus of a *why*-question and the document title. The high weights that are assigned to the question focus features show that our procedure for extracting question focus is reliable. The importance of question focus for *why*-QA is especially interesting because it is a question feature that is specific to *why*-questions and does not similarly apply to factoids or other question types. Moreover, the link from the question focus to the document title shows that Wikipedia as an answer source can provide QA systems with more information than a collection of plain texts without document structure does.

From the other features discussed in section 5.5, we learn that all four main question constituents contribute to the re-ranking score, but that synonyms of the main verb make the highest contribution (f22). Subject (f5), object (f26) and nominal predicate (f23) make a lower contribution. We suspect that this may be due to our decision to only lemmatize verbs, and not nouns (see section 5.2). It could be that since lemmatization leads to more matches, a feature can make a higher contribution if its items are lemmatized.

6.3 The quality of the syntactic descriptions

We already concluded in the previous section that our feature extraction module is very well capable of extracting the question focus, since f13 and f28 get assigned high weights by training. However, in the training stage, we used gold standard parse trees. In this section we evaluate the two automatic syntactic parsers Pelican and EP4IR, in order to be able to come up with fruitful suggestions for improving our system in the future.

As a measure for parser evaluation, we consider constituent extraction: how well do both parsers perform in identifying and delimiting the four main constituents from a *why*-question: subject, main verb, direct object and nominal predicate? As the gold standard for this experiment we use manually verified constituents that were extracted from the gold standard parse trees. We adapt our feature extraction script so that it prints each of the four constituents per question. Then we calculate the recall score for each parser for each constituent type.

Recall is the number of correctly identified constituents of a specific type divided by the total number of constituents of this type in the goldstandard parse tree. This total number is not exactly 93 for all constituent types: only 34 questions have a direct object in their main clause and 31 questions have a nominal predicate. The results of this exercise are in Table 5.

Table 5: Recall for constituent extraction (in %)

	subjs	verbs	objs	preds	all
Pelican	79.6	94.6	64.7	71.0	82.1
EP4IR	63.4	64.5	44.1	48.4	59.4

We find that over all constituent types, Pelican reaches significantly better recall scores than EP4IR ($Z = 5.57$; $P < 0.0001$ using the Wilcoxon Signed-Rank Test).

Although Pelican gives much better results on constituent extraction than EP4IR, the results on the re-ranking task do not differ significantly. The most plausible explanation for this is that the high accuracy of the Pelican parses is undone by the poor syntactic analysis on the answer side, which is in all settings performed by EP4IR.

7 Future directions

In section 4.3, we mentioned two directions for improving our pipeline system: improving retrieval and improving ranking. Recently we have been working on optimizing the retrieval module of our pipeline system by investigating the influence of different retrieval modules and passage segmentation strategies on the retrieval performance. This work has resulted in a better passage retrieval module in terms of success@150. Details on these experiments are in (Khalid and Verberne, 2008).

Moreover, we have been collecting a larger data collection in order to do make feature selection for our re-ranking experiments more reliable and less depending on specific cases in our dataset. This work has resulted in a total set of 188 *why*-question answer pairs. We are currently using this data collection for further research into improving our pipeline system.

In the near future, we aim to investigate what type of information is needed for further improving our system for *why*-QA. With the addition of syntactic information our system reaches an MRR score of 0.380. This compares to the MRR scores reached by other syntactically enhanced QA systems (see section 2). However, an MRR of 0.380 also shows that a substantial part of the problem of *why*-QA is still to be solved. We are currently investigating what type information is needed for further system improvement.

Finally, we also plan experiments with a number of dependency parsers to be used instead of EP4IR for the syntactic analysis of the answer paragraphs. Current experiments with Charniak (Charniak, 2000) show better constituent extraction than with EP4IR. It is still to be seen whether this also influences the overall performance of our system.

8 Conclusion

We added a re-ranking step to an existing paragraph retrieval method for *why*-QA. For re-ranking, we took the score assigned to a question answer pair by the ranking algorithm QAP in the baseline system, and weighted it with a number of syntactic features. We experimented with 31 features and trained the feature weights on a set of 93 *why*-questions with 150 answers provided by the baseline system for each question. Feature values for training the weights for the 31 features were extracted from gold standard parse trees for each question answer pair.

We evaluated the feature weights on automatically parsed questions and answers, in five folds. We found a significant improvement over the baseline for both success@10 and MRR@150. The most important features were the baseline score, the presence of cue words, the question's main verb, and the relation between question focus and document title.

We think that, although syntactic information gives a significant improvement over baseline passage ranking, more improvement is still to be gained from other types of information. Investigating the type of information needed is part of our future directions.

References

Bilotti, M.W., B. Katz, and J. Lin. 2004. What works better for question answering: Stemming or morphological query expansion. *Proc. IR4QA at SIGIR 2004*.

Burnage, G., R.H. Baayen, R. Piepenbrock, and H. van Rijn. 1990. *CELEX: A Guide for Users*.

Buttcher, S., C.L.A. Clarke, and G.V. Cormack. 2004. Domain-Specific Synonym Expansion and Validation for Biomedical Information Retrieval.

Buttcher, S. 2007. The Wumpus Search Engine. http://www.wumpus-search.org/.

Charniak, E. 2000. A maximum-entropy-inspired parser. *ACM International Conference Proceeding Series*, 4:132–139.

Denoyer, L. and P. Gallinari. 2006. The Wikipedia XML corpus. *ACM SIGIR Forum*, 40(1):64–69.

Ferret, O., B. Grau, M. Hurault-Plantet, G. Illouz, L. Monceaux, I. Robba, and A. Vilnat. 2002. Finding an answer based on the recognition of the question focus. *Proc. of TREC 2001*, pages 500–250.

Goldberg, D.E. and J.H. Holland. 1988. Genetic Algorithms and Machine Learning. *Machine Learning*, 3(2):95–99.

Higashinaka, R. and H. Isozaki. 2008. Corpus-based Question Answering for why-Questions. In *Proc. of IJCNLP, vol.1*, pages 418–425.

Hovy, E.H., U. Hermjakob, and D. Ravichandran. 2002. A Question/Answer Typology with Surface Text Patterns. In *Proc. of HLT 2002*.

Khalid, M. and S. Verberne. 2008. Passage Retrieval for Question Answering using Sliding Windows. In *Proc. of IR4QA at COLING 2008*.

Koster, CHA. 2003. Head-modifier frames for everyone. *Proc. of SIGIR 2003*, page 466.

Quarteroni, S., A. Moschitti, S. Manandhar, and R. Basili. 2007. Advanced Structural Representations for Question Classification and Answer Re-ranking. In *Proc. of ECIR 2007*, volume 4425, pages 234–245.

Tiedemann, J. 2005. Improving passage retrieval in question answering using NLP. In *Proc. of EPIA 2005*.

Verberne, S., L. Boves, N. Oostdijk, and P.A. Coppen. 2008. Evaluating paragraph retrieval for *why*-QA. In *Proc. of ECIR 2008*.

Coreference Systems based on Kernels Methods

Yannick Versley
SFB 441
University of Tübingen
versley@sfs.uni-tuebingen.de

Alessandro Moschitti
DISI
University of Trento
moschitti@disi.unitn.it

Massimo Poesio
DISI
University of Trento
massimo.poesio@unitn.it

Xiaofeng Yang
Data Mining Department
Institute for Infocomm Research
xiaofengy@i2r.a-star.edu.sg

Abstract

Various types of structural information - e.g., about the type of constructions in which binding constraints apply, or about the structure of names - play a central role in coreference resolution, often in combination with lexical information (as in expletive detection). Kernel functions appear to be a promising candidate to capture structure-sensitive similarities and complex feature combinations, but care is required to ensure they are exploited in the best possible fashion. In this paper we propose kernel functions for three subtasks of coreference resolution - binding constraint detection, expletive identification, and aliasing - together with an architecture to integrate them within the standard framework for coreference resolution.

1 Introduction

Information about coreference relations–i.e., which noun phrases are mentions of the same entity–has been shown to be beneficial in a great number of NLP tasks, including information extraction (McCarthy and Lehnert 1995), text planning (Barzilay and Lapata 2005) and summarization (Steinberger et al. 2007). However, the performance of coreference resolvers on unrestricted text is still quite low. One reason for this is that coreference resolution requires a great deal of information, ranging from string matching to syntactic constraints to semantic knowledge to discourse salience information to full common sense reasoning (Sidner 1979; Hobbs 1978, 1979; Grosz et al. 1995; Vieira and Poesio 2000; Mitkov 2002). Much of this information won't be available to robust coreference resolvers until better methods are found to represent and encode common sense knowledge; but part of the problem is also the need for better methods to encode information that is in part structural, in part lexical. Enforcing binding constraints –e.g., ruling out *Peter* as antecedent of *him* in (1a) requires recognizing that the anaphor occurs in a particular type of construction (Chomsky 1981; Lappin and Leass 1994; Yang et al. 2006) whose exact definition however has not yet been agreed upon by linguists (indeed, it may only be definable in a graded sense (Sturt 2003; Yang et al. 2006)), witness examples like (1b). Parallelism effects are a good example of structural information inducing preferences rather than constraints. Recognizing that *It* in examples such as (1c,d) are expletives requires a combination of structural information and lexical information (Lappin and Leass 1994; Evans 2001). But some sort of structure also underlies our interpretation of other types of coreference: e.g., knowledge about the structure of names certainly plays a role in recognizing that *BJ Habibie* is a possible antecedent for *Mr. Habibie*.

(1) a. John thinks that Peter hates *him*.
b. John hopes that Jane is speaking only to *himself*.
c. *It*'s lonely here.
d. *It* had been raining all day.

The need to capture such information suggests a role for kernel methods (Vapnik 1995) in coreference resolution. Kernel functions make it possible to capture the similarity between structures

© 2008. Licensed under the *Creative Commons Attribution-Noncommercial-Share Alike 3.0 Unported* license (http://creativecommons.org/licenses/by-nc-sa/3.0/). Some rights reserved.

without explicitly enumerating all the substructures, and have therefore been shown to be a viable approach to feature engineering for natural language processing for any task in which structural information plays a role, e.g. (Collins and Duffy 2002; Zelenko et al. 2003; Giuglea and Moschitti 2006; Zanzotto and Moschitti 2006; Moschitti et al. 2007). Indeed, they have already been used in NLP to encode the type of structural information that plays a role in binding constraints (Yang et al. 2006); however, the methods used in this previous work do not make it possible to exploit the full power of kernel functions. In this work, we extend the use of kernel functions for coreference by designing and testing kernels for three subtasks of the coreference task:

- Binding constraints
- Expletive detection
- Aliasing

and developing distinct classifiers for each of these tasks. We show that our developed kernels produce high accuracy for both distinct classifiers for these subtasks as well as for the complete coreference system.

In the remainder: Section 2, briefly describes the basic kernel functions that we used; Section 3 illustrates our new kernels for expletive, binding and name alias detection along with a coreference context kernel; Section 4 reports the experiments on individual classifiers on expletives, binding and names whereas Section 5 shows the results on the complete coreference task; Finally, Section 6 derives the conclusions.

2 Kernel for Structured Data

We used three kernel functions in this work: the String Kernel (SK) proposed in Shawe-Taylor and Cristianini (2004) to evaluate the number of subsequences between two sequences, the Syntactic Tree Kernel (STK; see Collins and Duffy 2002) which computes the number of syntactic tree fragments and the Partial Tree Kernel (PTK; see Moschitti 2006) which provides a more general representation of trees in terms of tree fragments. We discuss each in turn.

2.1 String Kernels (SK)

The string kernels that we consider count the number of substrings shared by two sequences containing gaps, i.e. some of the characters of the original string are skipped. Gaps penalize the weight associated with the matched substrings. More in detail, (a) longer subsequences receive lower weights. (b) Valid substrings are sequences of the original string with some characters omitted, i.e. gaps. (c) Gaps are accounted by weighting functions and (d) symbols of a string can also be whole words, i.e. the word sequence kernel Cancedda et al. (2003).

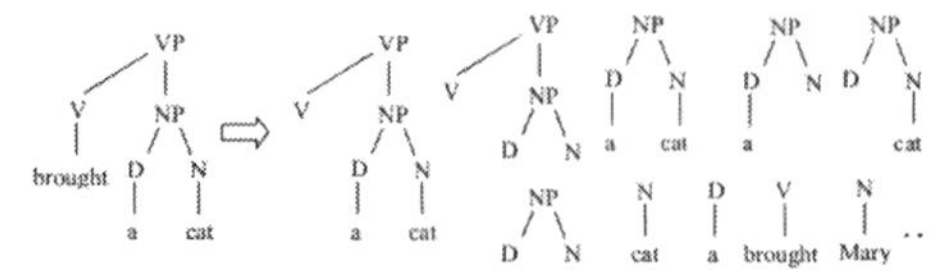

Figure 1: A tree with some of its STFs .

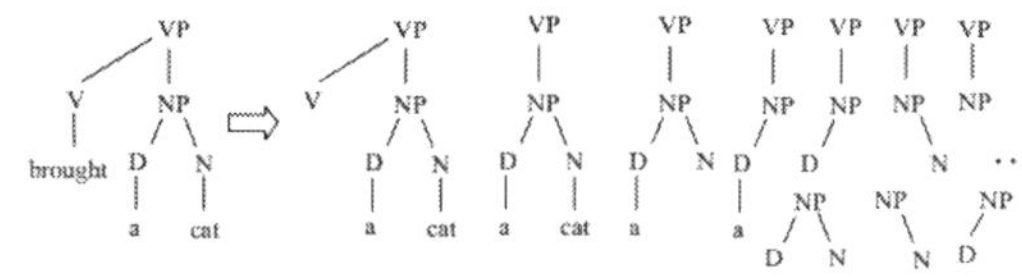

Figure 2: A tree with some of its PTFs.

2.2 Tree Kernels

The main idea underlying tree kernels is to compute the number of common tree fragments between two trees without explicitly considering the whole fragment space. The type of fragments characterize different kernel functions. We consider syntactic tree fragments (STFs) and partial tree fragments (PTFs)

2.2.1 Syntactic Tree Kernels (STK)

An STF is a connected subset of the nodes and edges of the original tree, with the constraint that any node must have all or none of its children. This is equivalent to stating that the production rules contained in the STF cannot be partial. For example, Figure 1 shows a tree with its PTFs: *[VP [V NP]]* is an STF, *[VP [V]]* or *[VP [NP]]* are not STFs.

2.2.2 Partial Tree Kernel (PTK)

If we relax the production rule constraint over the STFs, we obtain a more general substructure type, i.e. PTF, generated by the application of partial production rules, e.g. Figure 2 shows that *[VP [NP[D]]]* is indeed a valid fragment. Note that PTK can be seen as a STK applied to all possible child sequences of the tree nodes, i.e. a string kernel combined with a STK.

2.3 Kernel Engineering

The Kernels of previous section are basic functions that can be applied to feature vectors, strings and trees. In order to make them effective for a specific task, e.g. for coreference resolution: (a) we can combine them with additive or multiplicative operators and (b) we can design specific data objects (vectors, sequences and tree structures) for the target tasks.

It is worth noting that a basic kernel applied to an innovative view of a structure yields a new kernel (e.g. Moschitti and Bejan (2004); Moschitti et al. (2006)), as we show below:

Let $K(t_1, t_2) = \phi(t_1) \cdot \phi(t_2)$ be a basic kernel, where t_1 and t_2 are two trees. If we map t_1 and t_2 into two new structures s_1 and s_2 with a mapping $\phi_M(\cdot)$, we obtain: $K(s_1, s_2) = \phi(s_1) \cdot \phi(s_2) = \phi(\phi_M(t_1)) \cdot \phi(\phi_M(t_2)) = \phi'(t_1) \cdot \phi'(t_2) = K'(t_1, t_2)$, which is a noticeably different kernel induced by the mapping $\phi' = \phi \circ \phi_M$.

3 Kernels for Coreference Resolution

In this paper we follow the standard learning approach to coreference developed by Soon et al. (2001) and also used the few variants in Ng and Cardie (2002). In this framework, training and testing instances consist of a pair (anaphor, antecedent). During training, a positive instance is created for each anaphor encountered by pairing the anaphor with its closest antecedent; each of the non-coreferential mentions between anaphor and antecedent is used to produce a negative instance. During resolution, every mention to be resolved is paired with each preceding antecedent candidate to form a testing instance. This instance is presented to the classifier which then returns a class label with a confidence value indicating the likelihood that the candidate is the antecedent.

The nearest candidate with a positive classification will be selected as the antecedent of the possible anaphor. The crucial point is that in this approach, the classifier is trained to identify positive and negative instances of the resolution process. In previous work on using kernel functions for coreference (Yang et al. 2006), structural information in the form of tree features was included in the instances. This approach is appropriate for identifying contexts in which the binding constraints apply, but not, for instance, to recognize expletives. In this work we adopted therefore a more general approach, in which separate classifiers are used to recognize each relevant configuration, and their output is then used as an input to the coreference classifier. In this section we discuss the types of structures and kernel functions we used for three different kinds of classifiers: expletive, binding and alias classifiers. We then present the results of these classifiers, and finally the results with the coreference resolver as a whole.

3.1 Expletive Kernels

In written text, about a third of the occurrences of the pronoun *it* are not coreferent to a previous mention, but either refer to a general discourse topic (*it's a shame*) or do not refer at all, as in the case of extraposed subjects (*it is thought that* ...) or weather verbs (*it's raining*). It is desirable to minimize the impact that these non-anaphoric pronouns have on the accuracy of a anaphora resolution: Lappin and Leass (1994), for example, use several heuristics to filter out expletive pronouns, including a check for patterns including modal adjectives (it is good/necessary/... that ...), and cognitive verbs (it is thought/believed/... that ...).

Newer approaches to the problem use machine-learning on hand-annotated examples: Evans (2001) compares a shallow approach based on surrounding lemmas, part-of-speech tags, and the presence of certain elements such as modal adjectives and cognitive verbs, trained on 3171 examples from Susanne and the BNC to a reimplementation of a pattern-based approach due to Paice and Husk (1987) and finds that the shallower machine-learning approach compares favorably to it. Boyd et al. (2005) use an approach that combines some of Evans' shallow features with hand-crafted patterns in a memory based learning approach and find that the more informative features are beneficial for the system's performance (88% accuracy against 71% for their reimplementation using Evans' shallow features).

Evans' study also mentions that incorporating the expletive classifier as a filter for a pronoun resolver gives a gain between 2.86% (for manually determined weights) and 1% (for automatically optimized weights).

Tree kernels are a good fit for expletive classification since they can naturally represent the lexical and structural context around a word. Our final classifier uses the combination of an unmodified tree (UT) (where the embedding clause or verb phrase of the pronoun is used as a tree), and a tree that only preserves the most salient structural features (ST).

The reduced representation prunes all nodes that

would not be seen as indicative in a pattern approach, essentially keeping verb argument structure and important lexical items, such as the governing verb and, in the case of copula constructions, the predicate. For example, the phrase

```
(S (NP (PRP It))
   (VP (VBZ has)
      (NP (NP (DT no) (NN bearing))
      (PP (IN on)
          (NP (NP (PRP$ our)
                  (NN work)
                  (NN force))
              (NP (NN today)))))
   (. .))
```

would be reduced to the ST:

```
(S-I (NP-I (PRP-I It))
      (VP (VBX have)
          (NP))
      (.))
```

or, in a similar fashion,

```
(S (NP (PRP it))
   (VP (VBZ 's)
      (NP (NP (NN time))
          (PP (IN for)
              (NP (PRP$ their)
                  (JJ biannual)
                  (NN powwow))))))
```

would just be represented as the ST:

```
(S-I (NP-I (PRP-I it))
     (VP (BE VBZ)
         (NP-PRD (NN time))))
```

3.2 Binding Kernels

The resolution of pronominal anaphora heavily relies on the syntactic information and relationships between the anaphor and the antecedent candidates, including binding and other constraints, but also context-induced preferences in sub-clauses.

Some researchers (Lappin and Leass 1994; Kennedy and Boguraev 1996) use manually designed rules to take into account the grammatical role of the antecedent candidates as well as the governing relations between the candidate and the pronoun, while others use features determined over the parse tree in a machine-learning approach (Aone and Bennett 1995; Yang et al. 2004; Luo and Zitouni 2005). However, such a solution has limitations, since the syntactic features have to be selected and defined manually, and it is still partly an open question which syntactic properties should be considered in anaphora resolution.

We follow (Yang et al. 2006; Iida et al. 2006) in using a tree kernel to represent structural information using the subtree that covers a pronoun and its antecedent candidate. Given a sentence like "The man in the room saw him.", we represent the syntactic relation between "*The man*" and "*him*", by the shortest node path connecting the pronoun and the candidate, along with the first-level of the node children in the path.

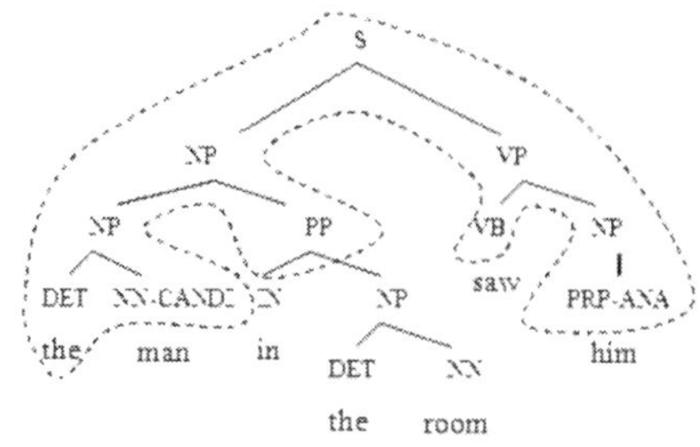

Figure 3: The structure for binding detection for the instance inst("the man", "him") in the sentence 'the man in the room saw him"

Figure 3 graphically shows such tree highlighted with dash lines. More in detail we operate the following tree transformation:
(a) To distinguish from other words, we explicitly mark up in the structured feature the pronoun and the antecedent candidate under consideration, by appending a string tag "ANA" and "CANDI" in their respective nodes, i.e. "NN-CANDI" for "man" and "PRP-ANA" for "him".
(b) To reduce the data sparseness, the leaf nodes representing the words are not incorporated in the feature, except that the word is the word node of the "DET" type (this is to indicate the lexical properties of an expression, e.g., whether it is a definite, indefinite or bare NP).
(c) If the pronoun and the candidate are not in the same sentence, we do not include the nodes denoting the sentences (i.e., "S" nodes) before the candidate or after the pronoun.

The above tree structures will be jointly used with the basic STK which extracts tree fragments able to characterize the following information: (a) the candidate is post-modified by a preposition phrase, (the node "PP" for "in the room" is included), (b) the candidate is a definite noun phrase (the article word "the" is included), (c) the candidate is in a subject position (NP-S-VP structure), (d) the anaphor is an object of a verb (the node "VB" for "saw" is included) and (e) the candidate is c-commanding the anaphor (the parent of the NP node for "the main in the room" is dominating the anaphor ("him"), which are important for reference determination in the pronoun resolution.

3.3 Encoding Context via Word Sequence Kernel

The previous structures aim at describing the interaction between one referential and one referent; if such interaction is observed on another mention pair, an automatic algorithm can establish if they corefer or not. This kind of information is the most useful to characterize the target problem, however, the context in which such interaction takes place is also very important. Indeed, natural language proposes many exceptions to linguistic rules and these can only be detect by looking at the context. To be able to represent context words or phrases, we use context word windows around the mentions and the subsequence kernel function (see section 2.1) to extract many features from it.

For example, in the context of *"and so **Bill Gates** says that"*, a string kernel would extract features including: *Bill_Gates_says_that*, *says_that*, *Gates*, *Gates_says_that*, *Bill_says_that*, *so_Gates_says_that*, *and_so_that* and so on.

Name	Alias
BJ Habibie	Mr. Habibie
Federal Express	Fedex
Ju Rong Zhi	Ju

Table 1: Examples of coreferent named entities (aliases) taken from the MUC 6 corpus.

3.4 Kernels for Alias Resolution

Most methods currently employed by coreference resolution (CR) systems for identifying coreferent named entities, i.e. aliases, are fairly simplistic in nature, relying on simple surface features such as the edit distance between two strings representing names. We investigate the potential of using the structure contained within names. This can be very useful to solve complex cases like those shown in Table 1, taken from the MUC 6 corpus (Chinchor and Sundheim 2003). For this purpose, we add syntactic information to the feature set by tagging the parts of a name (e.g. *first name*, *last name*, etc.) as illustrated in Figure 4.

To automatically extract such structure we used the High Accuracy Parsing of Name Internal Structure (HAPNIS) script[1]. HAPNIS takes a name as input and returns a tagged name like what is shown in Figure 4. It uses a series of heuristics in making its classifications based on information such as the

[1]The script is freely available at http://www.cs.utah.edu/ hal/HAPNIS/.

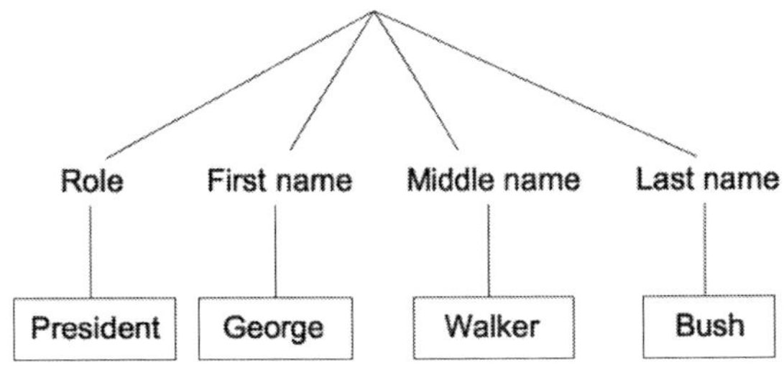

Figure 4: A proper name labeled with syntactic information.

serial positions of tokens in a name, the total number of tokens, the presence of meaningful punctuation such as periods and dashes, as well as a library of common first names which can be arbitrarily extended to any size. The tag set consists of the following: *surname*, *forename*, *middle*, *link*, *role*, and *suffix*[2].

Once the structure for a name has been derived, we can apply tree kernels to represent it in the learning algorithms thus avoiding the manual feature design. Such structures are not based on any particular grammar, therefore, any tree subpart may be relevant. In this case the most suitable kernel is PTK, which extracts any tree subpart. It is worth to note that the name tree structure can be improved by inserting a separate node for each name character and exploiting the string matching approximation carried out by PTK. For example, *Microsoft Inc.* will have a large match with *Microsoft Incorporated* whereas the standard string matching would be null.

4 Experiments with Coreference Subtask Classifiers

In these experiments we test the kernels devised for expletive (see Section 3.1), binding (see Section 3.2) and alias detection (see Section 3.4), to study the level of accuracy reachable by our kernel-based classifiers. The baseline framework is constituted by SVMs along with a polynomial kernel over the Soon et al.'s features.

4.1 Experiments on Expletive Classification

We used the BBN Pronoun corpus[3] as a source of examples, with the training set consisting of sections 00-19, yielding more than 5800 instances of

[2]Daumé reports a 99.1% accuracy rate on his test data set. We therefore concluded that it was sufficient for our purposes.

[3]Ralph Weischedel and Ada Brunstein (2005): BBN Pronoun Coreference and Entity Type Corpus, LDC2005T33

it, with the testing set consisting of sections 20 and 21, using the corresponding parses from the Penn Treebank for the parse trees. Additionally, we report on the performance of the classifier learnt on only the first 1000 instances to verify that our approach also works for small datasets. The results in Table 2 show that full tree (UT) achieves good results whereas the salient tree (ST) leads to a better ability to generalize, and the combination approach outperforms both individual trees.

	BBN large			BBN small		
	Prec	Recl	Acc	Prec	Recl	Acc
UT	83.87	61.54	84.35	78.76	52.66	80.85
ST	78.08	67.46	83.98	77.61	61.54	82.50
UT+ST	81.12	68.64	85.27	80.74	64.50	84.16

Table 2: Results for kernel-based expletive detection (using STK)

Note that the accuracy we get by training on 1000 examples (84% accuracy; see the *small* column in Table 2) is better than Boyd's replication of Evans (76% accuracy) or their decision tree classifier (81% accuracy) even though Boyd et al.'s dataset is three times bigger. On the other hand, Boyd et al's full system, which uses substantial hand-crafted knowledge, gets a still better result (88% accuracy), which is also higher than the accuracy of our classifier even when trained on the full 5800 instances.

	MUC-6		
	Prec	Recl	F
Soon et al.	51.25	55.51	53.29
STK	71.93	55.41	62.59

Table 3: Binding classifier: coreference classification on same-sentence pronouns

4.2 Experiments with the Binding Classifier

To assess the effect of the binding classifier on same-sentence pronoun links, we extracted 1398 mention pairs from the MUC-6 training data where both mentions were in the same sentence and at least one item of the pair included a pronoun, using the first 1000 for training and the remaining 398 examples for testing. The results (see Table 3) show that the syntactic tree kernel (STK) considerably improves the precision of classification of the Soon et al.'s features.

4.3 Experiments on Alias Classification

For our preliminary experiments, we extracted only pairs in the MUC 6 testing set in which both mentions were proper names, as determined by the coreference resolver's named entity recognizer. This set of proper names contained about 37,000 pairs of proper names of which about 600 were positive instances. About 5,500 pairs were randomly selected as test instances and the rest were used for training.

In the first experiment, we trained a decision tree classifier to detect if two names are aliases. For this task, we used either the string kernel score over the sequence of characters or the edit distance. The results in Table 4 show that the string kernel score performs better by 21.6 percentage points in F-measure.

In the second experiments we used SVMs trained with the string kernel over the name-character sequences and with PTK, which takes into account the structure of names. The results in Table 5 show that the structure improves alias detection by almost 5 absolute percent points. This suggests that an effective coreference system should embed PTK and name structures in the coreference pair representation.

	Recall	Precision	F-measure
String kernel	49.5%	60.8%	54.6%
Edit distance	23.9%	53.1%	33.0%

Table 4: Decision-tree based classification of name aliases using string kernels and edit distance.

	Recall	Precision	F-measure
String kernel	58.4%	67.5%	62.6%
PTK	64.8%	70.0%	67.3%

Table 5: SVM-based classification of name aliases using string kernels and tree-based feature.

5 Experiments on Coreference Systems

In this section we evaluate the contribution in the whole coreference task of the expletive classifier and the binding kernel. The predictions of the former are used as a feature of our basic coreference system whereas the latter is used directly in the coreference classifier by adding it to the polynomial kernel of the basic system.

Our basic system is based on the standard learning approach to coreference developed by Soon et al. (2001). It uses the features from Soon et al's work, including lexical properties, morphologic type, distance, salience, parallelism, grammatical role and so on. The main difference with

Soon et al. (2001) is the use of SVMs along with a polynomial kernel.

	MUC-6		
	Prec	Recl	F
plain	65.2	66.9	66.0
plain+expletive	66.1	66.9	66.5
upper limit	70.0	66.9	68.4

Table 6: Expletive classification: influence on pronoun resolution

5.1 Influence of Expletive classification

To see how useful a classifier for expletives can be, we conducted experiments using the expletive classifier learned on the BBN pronoun corpus on the MUC-6 corpus. Preliminary experiments indicated that perfect detection of expletives (i.e. using gold standard annotation) could raise the precision of pronoun resolution from 65.2% to 70.0%, yielding a 2.4% improvement in the F-score for pronoun resolution alone, or 0.6% improvement in the overall coreference F-score (see Table 6).

For a more realistic assessment, we used the classifier learned on the BBN pronoun corpus examples as an additional feature to gauge the improvement that could be achieved using it. While the gain in precision is small even in comparison to the achievable error reduction, we need to keep in mind that our baseline is in fact a well-tuned system.

	MUC-6			ACE02-BNews		
	R	P	F	R	P	F
PK	64.3	63.1	63.7	58.9	68.1	63.1
PK+TK	65.2	80.1	71.9	65.6	69.7	67.6

Table 7: Results of the pronoun resolution

5.2 Binding and Context Kernels

In these experiments, we compared our coreference system based on Polynomial Kernel (PK) against its combinations with Syntactic Tree Kernels (STK) over the binding structures (Sec. 3.2) and Word Sequence Kernel (WSK) on context windows (Sec. 3.3). We experimented with both the only pronoun and the complete coreference resolution tasks on the standard MUC-6 and ACE03-BNews data sets.

On the validation set, the best kernel combination between PK and STK was $STK(T1,T2) \cdot PK(\vec{x}_1,\vec{x}_2)+PK(\vec{x}_1,\vec{x}_2)$. Then an improvement arises when simply summing WSK.

Table 7 lists the results for the pronoun resolution. We used PK on the Soon et al.'s features as the baseline. On MUC-6, the system achieves a recall of 64.3% and precision 63.1% and an overall F-measure of 63.7%. On ACE02-BNews, the recall is lower 58.9% but the precision is higher, i.e. 68.1%, for a resulting F-measure of 63.1%. In contrast, adding the binding kernel (PK+STK) leads to a significant improvement in 17% precision for MUC-6 with a small gain (1%) in recall, whereas on the ACE data set, it also helps to increase the recall by 7%. Overall, we can see an increase in F-measure of around 8% for MUC and 4.5% for ACE02-BNews. These results suggest that the structured feature is very effective for pronoun resolution.

	MUC-6			ACE02-BNews		
	R	P	F	R	P	F
PK	61.5	67.2	64.2	54.8	66.1	59.9
PK+STK	63.4	67.5	65.4	56.6	66.0	60.9
PK+STK+WSK	64.4	67.8	66.0	57.1	65.4	61.0

Table 8: Results of the coreference resolution

Table 8 lists the results on the coreference resolution. We note that adding the structured feature to the polynomial kernel, i.e. using the model PK+STK, improves the recall of 1.9% for MUC-6 and 1.8% for ACE-02-BNews and keeps invariant the precision. Compared to pronoun resolution, the improvement of the overall F-measure is smaller (about 1%). This occurs since the resolution of non-pronouns case does not require a massive use of syntactic knowledge as in the pronoun resolution problem. WSK further improves the system's F1 suggesting that adding structured features of different types helps in solving the coreferece task.

6 Conclusions

We presented four examples of using kernel-based methods to take advantage of a structured representation for learning problems that arise in coreference systems, presenting high-accuracy classifiers for expletive detection, binding constraints and same-sentence pronoun resolution, and name alias matching. We have shown the accuracy of the individual classifiers for the above tasks and the impact of expletives and binding classifiers/kernels in the complete coreference resolution system. The improvement over the individual and complete tasks suggests that kernel methods are a promising research direction to achieve state-of-the-art coreference resolution systems.

Future work is devoted on making the use of kernels for coreference more efficient since the size of the ACE-2 corpora prevented us to directly use the combination of all kernels that we designed. In this paper, we have also studied a solution which relates to factoring out decisions into separate classifiers and using the decisions as binary features. However, this solution shows some loss in terms of accuracy. We are currently investigating methods that allow us to combine the accuracy and flexibility of the integrated approach with the speed of the separate classifier approach.

Acknowledgements Y. Versley was funded by the Deutsche Forschungsgemeinschaft as part of SFB (Collaborative Research Centre) 441. A. Moschitti has been partly supported by the FP6 IST LUNA project (contract No. 33549). Part of the work reported in this paper was done at the Johns Hopkins Summer Workshop in 2007, funded by NSF and DARPA. We are especially grateful for Alan Jern's implementation help for name structure identification.

References

Aone, C. and Bennett, S. W. (1995). Evaluating automated and manual acquisition of anaphora resolution strategies. In *Proc. ACL 1995*, pages 122–129.

Barzilay, R. and Lapata, M. (2005). Modelling local coherence: An entity-based approach. In *Proc. of ACL*, Ann Arbor, MI.

Boyd, A., Gegg-Harrison, W., and Byron, D. (2005). Identifying non-referential it: a machine learning approach incorporating linguistically motivated features. In *Proc. ACL WS on Feature Engineering for Machine Learning in Natural Language Processing*.

Cancedda, N., Gaussier, E., Goutte, C., and Renders, J. M. (2003). Word sequence kernels. *JMLR*, 3:1059–1082.

Chinchor, N. and Sundheim, B. (2003). Muc 6 corpus. *Message Understanding Conference (MUC) 6*.

Chomsky, N. (1981). *Lectures on government and binding*. Foris, Dordrecht, The Netherlands.

Collins, M. and Duffy, N. (2002). New ranking algorithms for parsing and tagging: kernels over discrete structures and the voted perceptron. In *Proc. ACL 2002*, pages 263–270.

Evans, R. (2001). Applying machine learning toward an automatic classification of it. *Literary and Linguistic Computing*, 16(1):45–57.

Giuglea, A.-M. and Moschitti, A. (2006). Semantic role labeling via framenet, verbnet and propbank. In *Proceedings of Coling-ACL*, Sydney, Australia.

Grosz, B., Joshi, A., and Weinstein, S. (1995). Centering: a framework for modeling the local coherence of discourse. *CL*, 21(2):203–225.

Hobbs, J. (1978). Resolving pronoun references. *Lingua*, 44:339–352.

Hobbs, J. (1979). Resolving pronoun references. *Coherence and Coreference*, 3(1):67–90.

Iida, R., Inui, K., and Matsumoto, Y. (2006). Exploiting syntactic patterns as clues in zero-anaphora resolution. In *Proc. Coling/ACL 2006*, pages 625–632.

Kennedy, C. and Boguraev, B. (1996). Anaphora for everyone: pronominal anaphora resolution without a parser. In *Proc. Coling 1996*.

Lappin, S. and Leass, H. (1994). An algorithm for pronominal anaphora resolution. *CL*, 20(4):525–561.

Luo, X. and Zitouni, I. (2005). Multi-lingual coreference resolution with syntactic features. In *Proc. HLT/EMNLP 05*.

McCarthy, J. and Lehnert, W. (1995). Using decision trees for coreference resolution. In *Proc. IJCAI 1995*.

Mitkov, R. (2002). *Anaphora resolution*. Longman.

Moschitti, A. (2006). Efficient convolution kernels for dependency and constituent syntactic trees. *Proc. ECML 2006*.

Moschitti, A. and Bejan, C. A. (2004). A semantic kernel for predicate argument classification. In *CoNLL-2004*, USA.

Moschitti, A., Pighin, D., and Basili, R. (2006). Semantic Role Labeling via Tree Kernel Joint Inference. In *Proceedings of CoNLL-X*.

Moschitti, A., Quarteroni, S., Basili, R., and Manandhar, S. (2007). Exploiting syntactic and shallow semantic kernels for question answer classification. In *Proceedings ACL*, Prague, Czech Republic.

Ng, V. and Cardie, C. (2002). Improving machine learning approaches to coreference resolution. In *Proc. ACL 2002*.

Paice, C. D. and Husk, G. D. (1987). Towards an automatic recognition of anaphoric features in english text: The impersonal pronoun 'it'. *Computer Speech and Language*, 2:109–132.

Shawe-Taylor, J. and Cristianini, N. (2004). *Kernel Methods for Pattern Analysis*. Cambridge University Press.

Sidner, C. (1979). Toward a computational theory of definite anaphora comprehension in english. Technical report AI-TR-537, MIT, Cambridge, MA.

Soon, W., Ng, H., and Lim, D. (2001). A machine learning approach to coreference resolution of noun phrases. *CL*, 27(4):521–544.

Steinberger, J., Poesio, M., Kabadjov, M., and Jezek, K. (2007). Two uses of anaphora resolution in summarization. *Information Processing and Management*, 43:1663–1680. Special issue on Summarization.

Sturt, P. (2003). The time-course of the application of binding constraints in reference resolution. *Journal of Memory and Language*.

Vapnik, V. (1995). *The Nature of Statistical Learning Theory*. Springer.

Vieira, R. and Poesio, M. (2000). An empirically based system for processing definite descriptions. *CL*, 27(4):539–592.

Yang, X., Su, J., and Tan, C. (2006). Kernel-based pronoun resolution with structured syntactic knowledge. In *Proc. COLING-ACL 06*.

Yang, X., Su, J., Zhou, G., and Tan, C. (2004). Improving pronoun resolution by incorporating coreferential information of candidates. In *Proc. ACL 2004*.

Zanzotto, F. M. and Moschitti, A. (2006). Automatic learning of textual entailments with cross-pair similarities. In *Proceedings of Coling-ACL*, Sydney, Australia.

Zelenko, D., Aone, C., and Richardella, A. (2003). Kernel methods for relation extraction. *JMLR*, 3(6):1083 – 1106.

CollabRank: Towards a Collaborative Approach to Single-Document Keyphrase Extraction

Xiaojun Wan and Jianguo Xiao
Institute of Computer Science and Technology
Peking University, Beijing 100871, China
{wanxiaojun,xiaojianguo}@icst.pku.edu.cn

Abstract

Previous methods usually conduct the keyphrase extraction task for single documents separately without interactions for each document, under the assumption that the documents are considered independent of each other. This paper proposes a novel approach named CollabRank to collaborative single-document keyphrase extraction by making use of mutual influences of multiple documents within a cluster context. CollabRank is implemented by first employing the clustering algorithm to obtain appropriate document clusters, and then using the graph-based ranking algorithm for collaborative single-document keyphrase extraction within each cluster. Experimental results demonstrate the encouraging performance of the proposed approach. Different clustering algorithms have been investigated and we find that the system performance relies positively on the quality of document clusters.

1 Introduction

A keyphrase is defined as a meaningful and significant expression consisting of one or more words in a document. Appropriate keyphrases can be considered as a highly condensed summary for a document, and they can be used as a label for the document to supplement or replace the title or summary, thus facilitating users' fast browsing and reading. Moreover, document keyphrases have been successfully used in the following IR and NLP tasks: document indexing (Gutwin et al., 1999), document classification (Krulwich and Burkey, 1996), document clustering (Zhang et al., 2004; Hammouda et al., 2005) and document summarization (Berger and Mittal, 2000; Buyukkokten et al., 2001).

Keyphrases are usually manually assigned by authors, especially for journal or conference articles. However, the vast majority of documents (e.g. news articles, magazine articles) do not have keyphrases, therefore it is beneficial to automatically extract a few keyphrases from a given document to deliver the main content of the document. Here, keyphrases are selected from within the body of the input document, without a predefined list (i.e. controlled vocabulary). Most previous work focuses on keyphrase extraction for journal or conference articles, while this paper focus on keyphrase extraction for news articles because news article is one of the most popular document genres on the web and most news articles have no author-assigned keyphrases.

Very often, keyphrases of all single documents in a document set are required to be extracted. However, all previous methods extract keyphrases for a specified document based only on the information contained in that document, such as the phrase's TFIDF, position and other syntactic information in the document. One common assumption of existing methods is that the documents are independent of each other. Hence the keyphrase extraction task is conducted separately without interactions for each document. However, the multiple documents within an appropriate cluster context usually have mutual influences and contain useful clues which can help to extract keyphrases from each other. For example, two documents about the same topic "earthquake" would share a few common phrases, e.g. "earthquake", "victim", and they can provide additional knowledge for each other to better evaluate and extract salient keyphrases from each other. The idea is borrowed from human's perception that a user would better understand a topic expressed in a document if the user reads more documents about the same topic.

© 2008. Licensed under the *Creative Commons Attribution-Noncommercial-Share Alike 3.0 Unported* license (http://creativecommons.org/licenses/by-nc-sa/3.0/). Some rights reserved.

Based on the above assumption, we propose a novel framework for collaborative single-document keyphrase extraction by making use of the additional information from multiple documents within an appropriate cluster context. The collaborative framework for keyphrase extraction consists of the step of obtaining the cluster context and the step of collaborative keyphrase extraction in each cluster. In this study, the cluster context is obtained by applying the clustering algorithm on the document set, and we have investigated how the cluster context influences the keyphrase extraction performance by employing different clustering algorithms. The graph-based ranking algorithm is employed for collaborative keyphrase extraction for each document in a specified cluster. Instead of making only use of the word relationships in a single document, the algorithm can incorporate the "voting" or "recommendations" between words in all the documents of the cluster, thus making use of the global information existing in the cluster context. The above implementation of the collaborative framework is denoted as CollabRank in this paper.

Experiments have been performed on a dataset consisting of 308 news articles with human-annotated keyphrases, and the results demonstrate the good effectiveness of the CollabRank approach. We also find that the extraction performance is positively correlated with the quality of cluster context, and existing clustering algorithms can yield appropriate cluster context for collaborative keyphrase extraction.

The rest of this paper is organized as follows: Section 2 introduces the related work. The proposed CollabRank is described in detail in Section 3. Empirical evaluation is demonstrated in Section 4 and lastly we conclude this paper in Section 5.

2 Related Work

The methods for keyphrase (or keyword) extraction can be roughly categorized into either unsupervised or supervised.

Unsupervised methods usually involve assigning a saliency score to each candidate phrases by considering various features. Krulwich and Burkey (1996) use heuristics based on syntactic clues to extract keyphrases from a document. Barker and Cornacchia (2000) propose a simple system for choosing noun phrases from a document as keyphrases. Muñoz (1996) uses an unsupervised learning algorithm to discover two-word keyphrases. The algorithm is based on Adaptive Resonance Theory (ART) neural networks. Steier and Belew (1993) use the mutual information statistics to discover two-word keyphrases. Tomokiyo and Hurst (2003) use pointwise KL-divergence between multiple language models for scoring both phraseness and informativeness of phrases. More recently, Mihalcea and Tarau (2004) propose the TextRank model to rank keywords based on the co-occurrence links between words. Such algorithms make use of "voting" or "recommendations" between words to extract keyphrases.

Supervised machine learning algorithms have been proposed to classify a candidate phrase into either keyphrase or not. GenEx (Turney, 2000) and Kea (Frank et al., 1999; Witten et al., 1999) are two typical systems, and the most important features for classifying a candidate phrase are the frequency and location of the phrase in the document. More linguistic knowledge has been explored by Hulth (2003). Statistical associations between keyphrases have been used to enhance the coherence of the extracted keyphrases (Turney, 2003). Song et al. (2003) present an information gain-based keyphrase extraction system called KPSpotter. Medelyan and Witten (2006) propose KEA++ that enhances automatic keyphrase extraction by using semantic information on terms and phrases gleaned from a domain-specific thesaurus. Nguyen and Kan (2007) focus on keyphrase extraction in scientific publications by using new features that capture salient morphological phenomena found in scientific keyphrases.

The tasks of keyphrase extraction and document summarization are similar and thus they have been conducted in a uniform framework. Zha (2002) proposes a method for simultaneous keyphrase extraction and text summarization by using the heterogeneous sentence-to-word relationships. Wan et al. (2007a) propose an iterative reinforcement approach to simultaneous keyphrase extraction and text summarization. Other related works include web page keyword extraction (Kelleher and Luz, 2005; Zhang et al., 2005; Chen et al., 2005), advertising keywords finding (Yih et al., 2006).

To the best of our knowledge, all previous work conducts the task of keyphrase extraction for each single document independently, without making use of the collaborative knowledge in multiple documents. We focus on unsupervised methods in this study.

3 The Proposed CollabRank Approach

3.1 Framework Description

Given a document set for keyphrase extraction of each single document, CollabRank first employs the clustering algorithm to group the documents into a few clusters. The documents within each cluster are expected to be topic-related and each cluster can be considered as a context for any document in the cluster. Given a document cluster, CollabRank makes use of the global word relationships in the cluster to evaluate and rank candidate phrases for each single document in the cluster based on the graph-based ranking algorithm. Figure 1 gives the framework of the proposed approach.

1. **Document Clustering**: *Group the documents in the document set D into a few clusters using the clustering algorithm;*

2. **Collaborative Keyphrase Extraction**: *For each cluster C, perform the following steps respectively to extract keyphrases for single documents in the cluster in a batch mode:*

1) **Cluster-level Word Evaluation**: *Build a global affinity graph G based on all candidate words restricted by syntactic filters in the documents of the given cluster C, and employ the graph-ranking based algorithm to compute the cluster-level saliency score for each word.*

2) **Document-level Keyphase Extraction**: *For any single document d in the cluster, evaluate the candidate phrases in the document based on the scores of the words contained in the phrases, and finally choose a few phrases with highest scores as the keyphrases of the document.*

Figure 1. The Framework of CollabRank

In the first step of the above framework, different clustering algorithms will yield different clusters. The documents in a high-quality cluster are usually deemed to be highly topic-related (i.e. appropriate cluster context), while the documents in a low-quality cluster are usually not topic-related (i.e. inappropriate cluster context). The quality of a cluster will influence the reliability of the contextual information for evaluating the words in the cluster. A number of clustering algorithms will be investigated in the experiments, including the agglomerative algorithm (both average-link and complete-link), the divisive algorithm, and the kmeans algorithm (Jain et al., 1999), whose details will be described in the evalution section.

In the second step of the above framework, substep 1) aims to evaluate all candidate words in the cluster based on the graph-based ranking algorithm. The global affinity graph aims to reflect the cluster-level co-occurrence relationships between all candidate words in the documents of the given cluster. The saliency scores of the words are computed based on the global affinity graph to indicate how much information about the main topic the words reflect. Substep 2) aims to evaluate candidate phrases of each single document based on the cluster-level word scores, and then choose a few salient phrases as keyphrases of the document. Substep 1) is performed on all documents in the cluster in order to evaluate the words from a global perspective, while substep 2) is performed on each single document in order to extract keyphrases from a local perspective. A keyphrase of a document is expected to include highly salient words. We can see that the keyphrase extraction tasks are conducted in a batch mode for each cluster. The substeps of 1) and 2) will be described in next sections respectively. If substep 1) is performed on each single document without considering the cluster context, the approach is degenerated into the simple TextRank model (Mihalcea and Tarau, 2004), which is denoted as SingleRank in this paper.

It is noteworthy that in addition to the graph-based ranking algorithm, other keyphrase extraction methods can also be integrated in the proposed collaborative framework to exploit the collaborative knowledge in the cluster context.

3.2 Cluster-Level Word Evaluation

Like the PageRank algorithm (Page et al., 1998), the graph-based ranking algorithm employed in this study is essentially a way of deciding the importance of a vertex within a graph based on global information recursively drawn from the entire graph. The basic idea is that of "voting" or "recommendation" between the vertices. A link between two vertices is considered as a vote cast from one vertex to the other vertex. The score associated with a vertex is determined by the votes that are cast for it, and the score of the vertices casting these votes.

Formally, given a specified cluster C, let $G=(V, E)$ be an undirected graph to reflect the relationships between words in the cluster. V is the set of vertices and each vertex is a candidate word[2] in the cluster. Because not all words in the documents are good indicators of keyphrases, the words added to the graph are restricted with syntactic filters, i.e., only the words with a certain part of speech are added. As in Mihalcea and Tarau (2004), the documents are tagged by a

[2] The original words are used without stemming.

POS tagger, and only the nouns and adjectives are added into the vertex set[3]. E is the set of edges, which is a subset of $V\times V$. Each edge e_{ij} in E is associated with an affinity weight $aff(v_i,v_j)$ between words v_i and v_j. The weight is computed based on the co-occurrence relation between the two words, controlled by the distance between word occurrences. The co-occurrence relation can express cohesion relationships between words. Two vertices are connected if the corresponding words co-occur at least once within a window of maximum k words, where k can be set anywhere from 2 to 20 words. The affinity weight $aff(v_i,v_j)$ is simply set to be the count of the controlled co-occurrences between the words v_i and v_j in the whole cluster as follows:

$$aff(v_i,v_j)=\sum_{d\in C} count_d(v_i,v_j) \quad (1)$$

where $count_d(v_i,v_j)$ is the count of the controlled co-occurrences between words v_i and v_j in document d.

The graph is built based on the whole cluster and it is called *Global Affinity Graph*. The biggest difference between CollabRank and SingleRank is that SingleRank builds a local graph based on each single document.

We use an affinity matrix M to describe G with each entry corresponding to the weight of an edge in the graph. $M=(M_{i,j})_{|V|\times|V|}$ is defined as follows:

$$M_{i,j}=\begin{cases} aff(v_i,v_j), & \text{if } v_i \text{ links with } v_j \text{ and } i\neq j; \\ 0, & \text{otherwise} \end{cases} \quad (2)$$

Then M is normalized to $\widetilde{M}$ as follows to make the sum of each row equal to 1:

$$\widetilde{M}_{i,j}=\begin{cases} M_{i,j}\Big/\sum_{j=1}^{|V|} M_{i,j}, & \text{if } \sum_{j=1}^{|V|} M_{i,j}\neq 0 \\ 0, & \text{otherwise} \end{cases} \quad (3)$$

Based on the global affinity graph G, the cluster-level saliency score $WordScore_{clus}(v_i)$ for word v_i can be deduced from those of all other words linked with it and it can be formulated in a recursive form as in the PageRank algorithm:

$$WordScore_{clus}(v_i)=\mu\cdot\sum_{all\, j\neq i} WordScore_{clus}(v_j)\cdot\widetilde{M}_{j,i}+\frac{(1-\mu)}{|V|} \quad (4)$$

And the matrix form is:

$$\vec{\lambda}=\mu\widetilde{M}^T\vec{\lambda}+\frac{(1-\mu)}{|V|}\vec{e} \quad (5)$$

where $\vec{\lambda}=[WordScore_{clus}(v_i)]_{|V|\times 1}$ is the vector of word saliency scores. $\vec{e}$ is a vector with all elements equaling to 1. μ is the damping factor usually set to 0.85, as in the PageRank algorithm.

The above process can be considered as a Markov chain by taking the words as the states and the corresponding transition matrix is given by $\mu\widetilde{M}^T+\frac{(1-\mu)}{|V|}\vec{e}\vec{e}^T$. The stationary probability distribution of each state is obtained by the principal eigenvector of the transition matrix.

For implementation, the initial scores of the words are set to 1 and the iteration algorithm in Equation (4) is adopted to compute the new scores of the words. Usually the convergence of the iteration algorithm is achieved when the difference between the scores computed at two successive iterations for any words falls below a given threshold (0.0001 in this study).

For SingleRank, the saliency score $WordScore_{doc}(v_i)$ for word v_i is computed in the same iterative way based on the local graph for the single document.

3.3 Document-Level Keyphrase Extraction

After the scores of all candidate words in the cluster have been computed, candidate phrases are selected and evaluated for each single document in the cluster. The candidate words (i.e. nouns and adjectives) of a specified document d in the cluster, which is a subset of V, are marked in the document text, and sequences of adjacent candidate words are collapsed into a multi-word phrase. The phrases ending with an adjective are not allowed, and only the phrases ending with a noun are collected as the candidate phrases for the document. For instance, in the following sentence: "*Mad/JJ cow/NN disease/NN has/VBZ killed/VBN 10,000/CD cattle/NNS*", the candidate phrases are "*Mad cow disease*" and "*cattle*". The score of a candidate phrase p_i is computed by summing the cluster-level saliency scores of the words contained in the phrase.

$$PhraseScore(p_i)=\sum_{v_j\in p_i} WordScore_{clus}(v_j) \quad (6)$$

All the candidate phrases in the document are ranked in decreasing order of the phrase scores and the top n phrases are selected as the keyphrases of the document. n ranges from 1 to 20 in this study. Similarly for SingleRank, the phrase score is computed based on the document-level saliency scores of the words.

[3] The corresponding POS tags of the candidate words include "JJ", "NN", "NNS", "NNP", "NNPS". We used the Stanford log-linear POS tagger (Toutanova and Manning, 2000) in this study.

4 Empirical Evaluation

4.1 Data Set

To our knowledge, there is no gold standard news dataset with assigned keyphrases for evaluation. So we manually annotated the DUC2001 dataset (Over, 2001) and used the annotated dataset for evaluation in this study. The dataset was originally used for document summarization. It consisted of 309 news articles collected from TREC-9, in which two articles were duplicate (i.e. d05a\FBIS-41815 and d05a\FBIS-41815~). The average length of the documents was 740 words. Two graduate students were employed to manually label the keyphrases for each document. At most 10 keyphrases could be assigned to each document. The annotation process lasted two weeks. The Kappa statistic for measuring inter-agreement among annotators was 0.70. And the annotation conflicts between the two subjects were solved by discussion. Finally, 2488 keyphrases were labeled for the dataset. The average keyphrase number per document was 8.08 and the average word number per keyphrase was 2.09.

The articles have been grouped into 30 clusters manually by NIST annotators for multi-document summarization, and the documents within each cluster were topic-related or relevant. The manually labeled clusters were considered as the ground truth clusters or gold clusters. In order to investigate existing clustering algorithms, the documents in the clusters were mixed together to form the whole document set for automatic clustering.

4.2 Document Clustering Algorithm

In the experiments, several popular clustering algorithms and random clustering algorithms are explored to produce cluster contexts. Note that we have already known the number (i.e. 30) of the clusters for the dataset beforehand and thus we simply use it as input for the following clustering algorithms[4].

Gold Standard Clustering: It is a pseudo clustering algorithm by manually grouping the documents. We use the ground truth clusters as the upperbound of the following automatic clustering algorithms.

Kmeans Clustering: It is a partition based clustering algorithm. The algorithm randomly selects 30 documents as the initial centroids of the 30 clusters and then iteratively assigns all documents to the closest cluster, and recomputes the centroid of each cluster, until the centroids do not change. The similarity between a document and a cluster centroid is computed using the standard Cosine measure.

Agglomerative (AverageLink) Clustering: It is a bottom-up hierarchical clustering algorithm and starts with the points as individual clusters and, at each step, merges the most similar or closest pair of clusters, until the number of the clusters reduces to the desired number 30. The similarity between two clusters is computed using the AverageLink method, which computes the average of the Cosine similarity values between any pair of documents belonging to the two clusters respectively as follows:

$$sim(c_1,c_2)=\frac{\sum_{i=1}^{m}\sum_{j=1}^{n} sim(d_i,d_j)}{|c_1|\times|c_2|} \quad (7)$$

where d_i, d_j are two documents in cluster c_1 and cluster c_2 respectively, and $|c_1|$ and $|c_2|$ are respectively the numbers of documents in clusters c_1 and c_2.

Agglomerative (CompleteLink) Clustering: It differs from the above agglomerative (AverageLink) clustering algorithm only in that the similarity between two clusters is computed using the CompleteLink method, which computes the minimum of the Cosine similarity values between any pair of documents belonging to the two clusters respectively as follows:

$$sim(c_1,c_2)=\min_{d_i\in c_1, d_j\in c_2}\{sim(d_i,d_j)\} \quad (8)$$

Divisive Clustering: It is a top-down hierarchical clustering algorithm and starts with one, all-inclusive cluster and, at each step, splits the largest cluster (i.e. the cluster with most documents) into two small clusters using the Kmeans algorithm until the number of clusters increases to the desired number 30.

Random Clustering: It produces 30 clusters by randomly assigning each document into one of the k clusters. Three different randomization processes are performed and we denote them as Random1, Random2 and Random3, respectively.

CollabRank relies on the clustering algorithm for document clustering, and the combination of CollabRank and any clustering algorithm will be investigated.

4.3 Evaluation Metric

For evaluation of document clustering results, we adopt the widely used F-Measure to measure the

[4] How to obtain the number of desired clusters is not the focus of this study.

performance of the clustering algorithm (i.e. the quality of the clusters) by comparing the produced clusters with the gold clusters (classes) (Jain et al., 1999).

For evaluation of keyphrase extraction results, the automatic extracted keyphrases are compared with the manually labeled keyphrases. The words are converted to their corresponding basic forms using word stemming before comparison. The precision $p=count_{correct}/count_{system}$, recall $r=count_{correct}/count_{human}$, F-measure ($F=2pr/(p+r)$) are used as evaluation metrics, where $count_{correct}$ is the total number of correct keyphrases extracted by the system, and $count_{system}$ is the total number of automatic extracted keyphrases, and $count_{human}$ is the total number of human-labeled keyphrases.

4.4 Evaluation Results

First of all, we show the document clustering results in Table 1. The gold standard clustering result is the upperbound of all automatic clustering results. Seen from the table, all the four popular clustering algorithms (i.e. CompleteLink, AverageLink, KMeans and Divisive) perform much better than the three random clustering algorithms (i.e. Random1, Random2 and Random3). Different clustering results lead to different document relationships and a high-quality cluster produced by popular algorithms is deemed to build an appropriate cluster context for collaborative keyphrase extraction.

Clustering Algorithm	F-Measure
Gold	1.000
CompleteLink	0.907
AverageLink	0.877
Divisive	0.924
Kmeans	0.866
Random1	0.187
Random2	0.189
Random3	0.183

Table 1. Clustering Results

Now we show the results for keyphrase extraction. In the experiments, the keyphrase number is typically set to 10 and the co-occurrence window size is also simply set to 10. Table 2 gives the comparison results of baseline methods and the proposed CollabRank methods with different clustering algorithms. The TFIDF baseline computes the word scores for each single document based on the word's TFIDF value. The SingleRank baseline computes the word scores for each single document based on the graph-based ranking algorithm. The two baselines do not make use of the cluster context.

Seen from Table 2, the CollabRank methods with the gold standard clustering algorithm or popular clustering algorithms (i.e. Kmeans, CompleteLink, AverageLink and Divisive) perform much better than the baseline methods over all three metrics. The results demonstrate the good effectiveness of the proposed collaborative framework. We can also see that the performance is positively correlated with the clustering results. The CollabRank method with the best performing gold standard clustering results achieves the best performance. While the methods with low-quality clustering results (i.e. the three random clustering results) do not perform well, even much worse than the baseline SingleRank method. This is because that the documents in a low-quality cluster are not truly topic-related, and the mutual influences between the documents are not reliable for evaluating words from a global perspective.

System	Precision	Recall	F-measure
TFIDF	0.232	0.281	0.254
SingleRank	0.247	0.303	0.272
CollabRank (Gold)	**0.283**	**0.348**	**0.312**
CollabRank (Kmeans)	0.276	0.339	0.304
CollabRank (CompleteLink)	0.281	0.345	0.310
CollabRank (AverageLink)	0.277	0.340	0.306
CollabRank (Divisive)	0.274	0.337	0.302
CollabRank (Random1)	0.210	0.258	0.232
CollabRank (Random2)	0.216	0.265	0.238
CollabRank (Random3)	0.209	0.257	0.231

Table 2. Keyphrase Extraction Results

In order to investigate how the co-occurrence window size k and the keyphrase number n influence the performance, we first vary k from 2 to 20 when n is fixed as 10 and the results are shown in Figures 2-4 over three metrics respectively. The results demonstrate that all the methods are not significantly affected by the window size. We then vary n from 1 to 20 when k is fixed as 10 and the results are shown in Figures 5-7. The results demonstrate that the precision values decrease with the increase of n, and the recall values increases with the increase of n, while the F-measure values first increase and then tend to decrease with the increase of n.

We can also see from Figures 2-7 that the CollabRank methods with high-quality clustering results always perform better than the baseline

SingleRank method under different window sizes and different keyphrase numbers, and they always lead to poor performance with low-quality clustering results. This further proves that an appropriate cluster context is very important for the CollabRank method. Fortunately, existing clustering algorithms can obtain the desired cluster context.

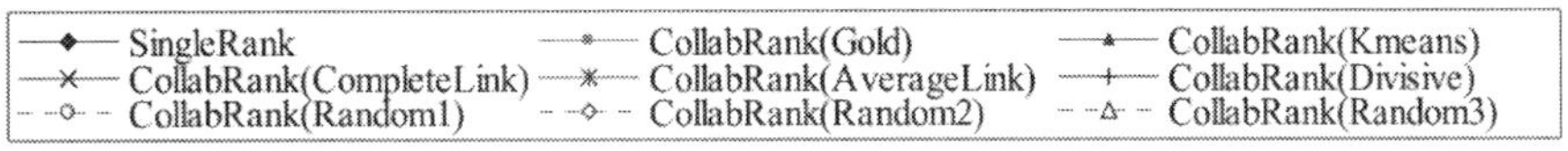

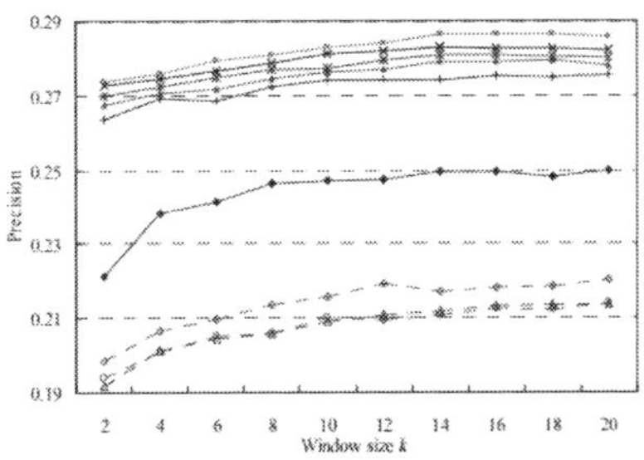

Figure 2. Precision vs. Window Size k

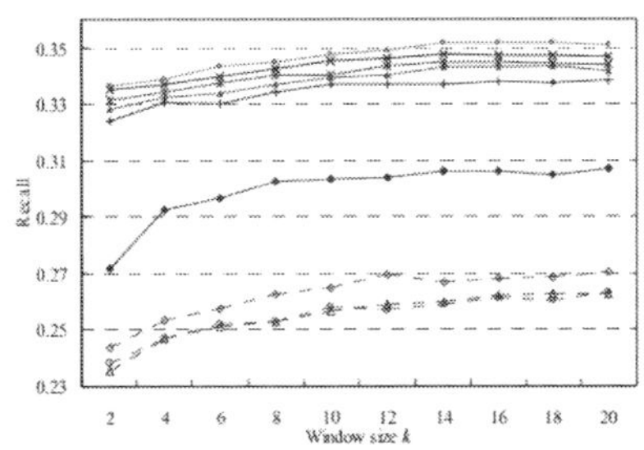

Figure 3. Recall vs. Window Size k

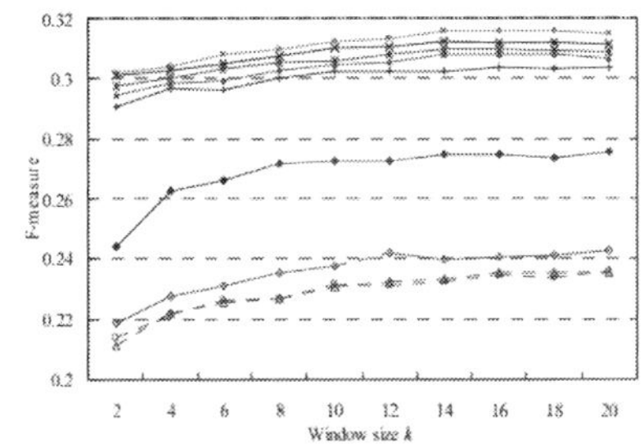

Figure 4. F-measure vs. Window Size k

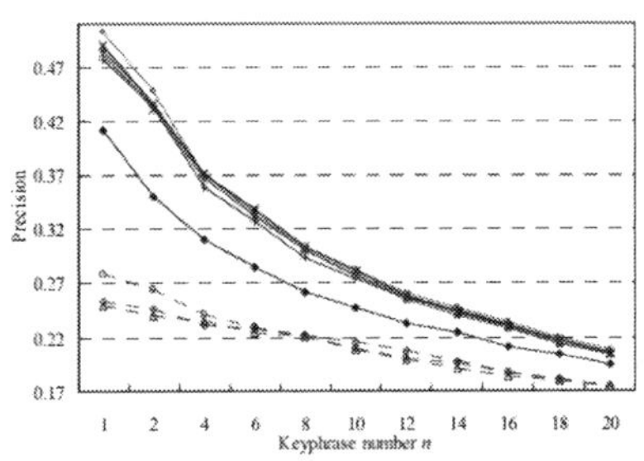

Figure 5. Precision vs. Keyphrase Number n

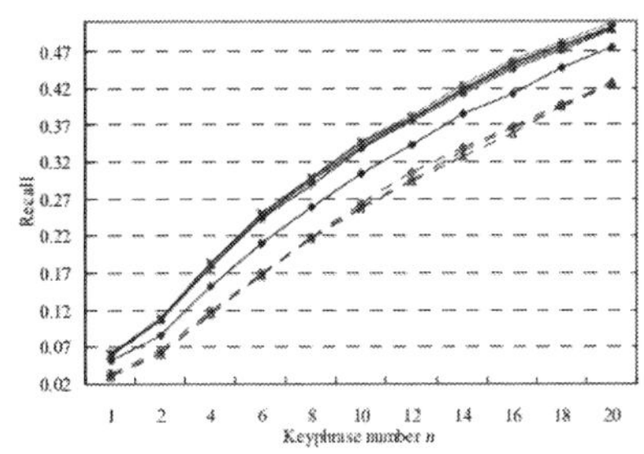

Figure 6. Recall vs. Keyphrase Number n

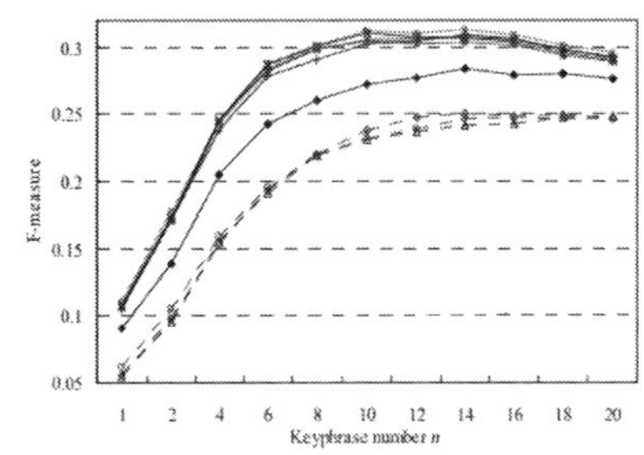

Figure 7. F-measure vs. Keyphrase Number n

The proposed CollabRank method makes only use of the global information based on the global graph for the cluster. In order to investigate the relative contributions from the whole cluster and the single document to the final performance, we experiment with the method named RankFusion which makes both of the cluster-level global information and the document-level local information. The overall word score $WordScore_{fusion}(v_i)$ for word v_i in a document in RankFusion is a linear combination of the global word score and the local word score as follows:

$$WordScore_{fusion}(v_i) = \lambda \cdot WordScore_{clus}(v_i) + (1-\lambda) \cdot WordScore_{doc}(v_i) \quad (9)$$

where $\lambda \in [0,1]$ is the fusion weight. Then the phrase score is computed based on the fusion scores of the words. The RankFusion method is the same with CollabRank if λ=1 and it is the same with SingleRank if λ=0.

Figure 8 shows the F-measure curves for the RankFusion methods with different high-quality clustering algorithms under different fusion weights. We can see that when $\lambda \in (0.5,1)$, the RankFusion methods with high-quality clusters can outperform both the corresponding SingleRank and the corresponding CollabRank. However, the performance improvements of RankFusion over CollabRank are not significant. We can conclude that the cluster-level global information plays the key role for evaluating the true saliency of the words.

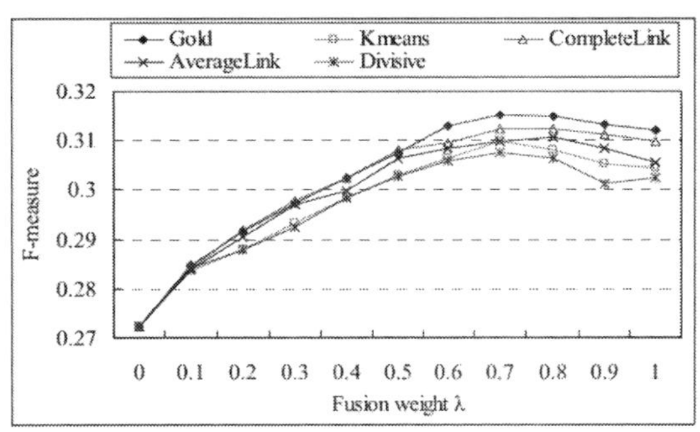

Figure 8. RankFusion Results (F-measure) vs. Fusion Weight λ

5 Conclusion and Future Work

In this paper, we propose a novel approach named CollabRank for collaborative single-document keyphrase extraction, which makes use of the mutual influences between documents in appropriate cluster context to better evaluate the saliency of words and phrases. Experimental results demonstrate the good effectiveness of CollabRank. We also find that the clustering algorithm is important for obtaining the appropriate cluster context and the low-quality clustering results will deteriorate the extraction performance. It is encouraging that most existing popular clustering algorithms can meet the demands of the proposed approach.

The proposed collaborative framework has more implementations than the implementation based on the graph-based ranking algorithm in this study. In future work, we will explore other keyphrase extraction methods in the proposed collaborative framework to validate the robustness of the framework.

Acknowledgements

This work was supported by the National Science Foundation of China (No.60703064), the Research Fund for the Doctoral Program of Higher Education of China (No.20070001059) and the National High Technology Research and Development Program of China (No.2008AA01Z421).

References

A. Berger and V. Mittal. 2000. OCELOT: A system for summarizing Web Pages. In *Proceedings of SIGIR2000.*

K. Barker and N. Cornacchia. 2000. Using nounphrase heads to extract document keyphrases. In *Canadian Conference on AI.*

O. Buyukkokten, H. Garcia-Molina, and A. Paepcke. 2001. Seeing the whole in parts: text summarization for web browsing on handheld devices. In *Proceedings of WWW2001.*

M. Chen, J.-T. Sun, H.-J. Zeng and K.-Y. Lam. 2005. A practical system for keyphrase extraction for web pages. In *Proceedings of CIKM2005.*

E. Frank, G. W. Paynter, I. H. Witten, C. Gutwin, and C. G. Nevill-Manning. 1999. Domain-specific keyphrase extraction. *Proceedings of IJCAI-99*, pp. 668-673.

C. Gutwin, G. W. Paynter, I. H. Witten, C. G. Nevill-Manning and E. Frank. 1999. Improving browsing in digital libraries with keyphrase indexes. *Journal of Decision Support Systems*, 27, 81-104.

K. M. Hammouda, D. N. Matute and M. S. Kamel. 2005. CorePhrase: keyphrase extraction for document clustering. In *Proceedings of MLDM2005.*

A. Hulth. 2003. Improved automatic keyword extraction given more linguistic knowledge. In *Proceedings of EMNLP2003*, Japan, August.

A. K. Jain, M. N. Murty and P. J. Flynn. 1999. Data clustering: a review. *ACM Computing Surveys*, 31(3):264-323.

D. Kelleher and S. Luz. 2005. Automatic hypertext keyphrase detection. In *Proceedings of IJCAI2005.*

B. Krulwich and C. Burkey. 1996. Learning user information interests through the extraction of semantically significant phrases. In *AAAI 1996 Spring Symposium on Machine Learning in Information Access.*

O. Medelyan and I. H. Witten. 2006. Thesaurus based automatic keyphrase indexing. In *Proceedings of JCDL2006.*

R. Mihalcea and P. Tarau. 2004. TextRank: Bringing order into texts. In *Proceedings of EMNLP2004.*

A. Muñoz. 1996. Compound key word generation from document databases using a hierarchical clustering ART model. *Intelligent Data Analysis,* 1(1).

T. D. Nguyen and M.-Y. Kan. 2007. Keyphrase extraction in scientific publications. In *Proceedings of ICADL2007.*

P. Over. 2001. Introduction to DUC-2001: an intrinsic evaluation of generic news text summarization systems. In *Proceedings of DUC2001.*

L. Page, S. Brin, R. Motwani, and T. Winograd. 1998. The pagerank citation ranking: Bringing order to the web. *Technical report*, Stanford Digital Libraries.

M. Song, I.-Y. Song and X. Hu. 2003. KPSpotter: a flexible information gain-based keyphrase extraction system. In *Proceedings of WIDM2003.*

A. M. Steier and R. K. Belew. 1993. Exporting phrases: A statistical analysis of topical language. In *Proceedings of Second Symposium on Document Analysis and Information Retrieval*, pp. 179-190.

T. Tomokiyo and M. Hurst. 2003. A language model approach to keyphrase extraction. In: *Proceedings of ACL Workshop on Multiword Expressions.*

K. Toutanova and C. D. Manning. 2000. Enriching the knowledge sources used in a maximum entropy Part-of-Speech tagger. In *Proceedings of EMNLP/VLC-2000.*

P. D. Turney. 2000. Learning algorithms for keyphrase extraction. *Information Retrieval*, 2:303-336.

P. D. Turney. 2003. Coherent keyphrase extraction via web mining. In *Proc. of IJCAI-03*, pages 434–439.

X. Wan, J. Yang and J. Xiao. 2007a. Towards an iterative reinforcement approach for simultaneous document summarization and keyword extraction. In *Proceedings of ACL2007.*

I. H. Witten, G. W. Paynter, E. Frank, C. Gutwin, and C. G. Nevill-Manning. 1999. KEA: Practical automatic keyphrase extraction. *Proceedings of Digital Libraries 99 (DL'99),* pp. 254-256.

W.-T. Yih, J. Goodman and V. R. Carvalho. 2006. Finding advertising keywords on web pages. In *Proceedings of WWW2006.*

H. Y. Zha. 2002. Generic summarization and keyphrase extraction using mutual reinforcement principle and sentence clustering. In *Proceedings of SIGIR2002*, pp. 113-120.

Y. Zhang, N. Zincir-Heywood, and E. Milios. 2004. Term-Based Clustering and Summarization of Web Page Collections. In *Proceedings of the Seventeenth Conference of the Canadian Society for Computational Studies of Intelligence.*

Y. Zhang, N. Zincir-Heywood and E. Milios. 2005. Narrative text classification for automatic key phrase extraction in web document corpora. In *Proceedings of WIDM2005.*

Investigating the Portability of Corpus-Derived Cue Phrases for Dialogue Act Classification

Nick Webb and **Ting Liu**
ILS Institute
University at Albany, SUNY
Albany, NY, USA
{nwebb|tl7612}@albany.edu

Abstract

We present recent work in the area of Cross-Domain Dialogue Act tagging. Our experiments investigate the use of a simple dialogue act classifier based on purely intra-utterance features - principally involving word n-gram cue phrases. We apply automatically extracted cues from one corpus to a new annotated data set, to determine the portability and generality of the cues we learn. We show that our automatically acquired cues are general enough to serve as a cross-domain classification mechanism.

1 Introduction

A number of researchers (Hirschberg and Litman, 1993; Grosz and Sidner, 1986) speak of *cue* or *key phrases* in utterances that can serve as useful indicators of discourse structure. We have previously investigated the use of such cue phrases to predict dialogue acts or DAs (functional tags which represent the communicative intentions behind each user utterance) (Webb et al., 2005a). We developed an approach, in common with the work of Samuel et al. (1999), where word n-grams that might serve as cue phrases are automatically detected in a corpus and we have previously reported the results of experiments evaluating this approach on the SWITCHBOARD corpus, where our results rival the best reported over that data (Stolcke et al., 2000), although our method adopts a significantly less complex algorithm.

©2008. Licensed under the *Creative Commons Attribution-Noncommercial-Share Alike 3.0 Unported* license (http://creativecommons.org/licenses/by-nc-sa/3.0/). Some rights reserved.

An interesting by-product of our approach is the ranked list of cue phrases derived from the source corpus. Visual inspection of these cues reveals that, as one might expect, there is a high degree of correlation between phrases such as *"can you"* and the DA <yes/no question>, *"where is"* and *"who is"* with the DA <wh-question> and *"right"* or *"ok"* with DA <agree/accept>. These cues appear to be of a general nature, unrelated to the source domain or application. Therefore, despite being automatically acquired from one domain specific corpus, these cues should be equally applicable to new corpora, from a different domain and it is this hypothesis we test. This paper presents our work on dialogue act classification using cues automatically extracted from a corpus from one domain, and applying these cues directly as a classifier over a new corpus from a different domain.

The material is presented as follows: Previous work with dialogue act modelling is outlined in Section 2. An overview of the corpora used for the experiments we report can be seen in Section 3. A brief overview of our classification method is given in Section 4. Our experiments evaluating the cue-based dialogue act classifier tagging new, out-of-domain data are given in Section 5. Finally we end with some discussion and an outline of intended further work.

2 Related Work

Dialogue Acts (DAs) (Bunt, 1994), also known as speech acts or dialogue moves, represent the functional performance of a speaker's utterance, such as a greeting *"Hello there"*, asking a question like *"How is your mother?"* or making a request *"Can you move your foot?"*.

There are two broad categories of computational model used to interpret these acts. The first, in-

Corpus	*Availability*	*Utterance count*	*Dialogue count*	*Word count*	*Distinct words*	*Dialogue type*
SWITCHBOARD	public	223606	1155	1431725	21715	Conversational
AMITIÉS GE	restricted	30206	1000	228165	7841	Task-oriented

Figure 1: Summary data for the dialogue corpora

cluding the work of Cohen and Perrault (1979) relies on processing belief logics, centring on the impact each utterance has on the hearer - what the hearer believes the speaker intended to communicate. These models can be very accurate, but often are complex, and require significant world-knowledge to create.

The second model type is cue-based, and centres on the notion of repeated, predictive cues - subsections of language which are strong indicators of specific DAs. In this second category, much of the work is cast as a probabilistic classification task, solved by training approaches on labelled examples of dialogue acts. As an example of these probabilistic methods, Stolcke et al. (2000) apply a HMM method to the SWITCHBOARD corpus, one that exploits both the order of words *within* utterances and the order of dialogue acts *over* utterances. They use a single split of the data for their experiments, with 198k utterances for training and 4k utterances for testing, achieving a DA tagging accuracy of 71.0% on word transcripts. Another learning approach by Samuel et al. (1998) uses transformation-based learning over a number of utterance features, including utterance length, speaker turn and the dialogue act tags of adjacent utterances. They achieved an average score of 75.12% tagging accuracy over the VERBMOBIL corpus. A significant aspect of this work is the automatic identification of word sequences that might serve as useful dialogue act cues (Samuel et al., 1999). A number of statistical criteria are applied to identify potentially useful word n-grams that are then supplied to the transformation-based learning method as 'features'.

What has been less explored is the portability or adaptability of these models to new corpora and new domains. Prasad and Walker (2002) look at applying models generated from a Human-Computer corpus to a Human-Human corpus in the same domain, that of travel planning, and score a very low 36.72% accuracy using their model. The work of Tur et al. (2006) is closer to the work reported here - they apply models derived from the SWITCHBOARD corpus to the ICSI-MRDA corpus (Shriberg et al., 2004) using boosting, applied to a high level of representation (comprising only 5 DA categories, one of which they exclude), where they achieve 57.37% tagging accuracy. This seems to indicate that cross-domain application of models is possible, although the level of accuracy as presently reported is low.

3 Experimental Corpora

Our work as described here applies to two corpora - the DA-tagged portion of the SWITCHBOARD corpus (Jurafsky et al., 1998), and the AMITIÉS GE corpus (Hardy et al., 2002; Hardy et al., 2003), created as part of the AMITIÉS European 5th Framework program project (Hardy et al., 2005). A summary of the two corpora can be seen in Figure 1.

3.1 Switchboard

The annotated portion of the SWITCHBOARD corpus comprises 1155 annotated conversations between two human participants, where the dialogues are of an unstructured, non-directed character. Participants do not know each other, and are provided only with a set of topics which they may wish to discuss. The SWITCHBOARD corpus is annotated using an elaboration of the DAMSL tag set. In 1998 the Discourse Resource Initiative finalised a task-independent set of DAs, called DAMSL (Dialogue Act Markup in Several Layers), for use across different domains. DAMSL has been used to mark-up several dialogue corpora, such as TRAINS (Core and Allen, 1997), and the SWITCHBOARD corpus (Jurafsky et al., 1998).

The annotation over the SWITCHBOARD corpus involves 50 major classes, together with a number of diacritic marks, which combine to generate 220 distinct labels. Jurafsky et al. (1998) propose a clustering of these 220 tags into 42 larger classes and it is this clustered set that was used both in our experiments and those of Stolcke et al. (2000). In measuring the agreement between annotators in labelling this data, Jurafsky et al. (1998) report an average pair-wise kappa of .80 (Carletta et al.,

<Turn Id="utt3" Speaker="A" DA-Type="Open-question"> **what do you think was different ten years ago from now?**</Turn>

<Turn Id="utt4" Speaker="B" DA-Type="Statement-opinion"> **Well I would say as far as social changes go I think families were more together.**</Turn>

<Turn Id="utt5" Speaker="B" DA-Type="Statement-opinion"> **They did more things together**</Turn>

<Turn Id="utt6" Speaker="A" DA-Type="Acknowledge"> **Uh-huh**</Turn>

Figure 2: Excerpt of dialogue from the SWITCHBOARD corpus

1997). An excerpt of dialogue from the SWITCHBOARD corpus can be seen in Figure 2.

3.2 AMITIÉS

The AMITIÉS project (Hardy et al., 2005) collected 1000 English human-human dialogues from European GE call centres. These calls are of an information seeking or transactional type, in which customers interact with their financial accounts by phone to check balances, make payments and report lost credit cards. The resulting data has been sanitised, to replace identifying features such as names, addresses and account numbers with generic information (*"John Doe", "1 The Street"*) and the corpus is annotated with DAs using XDML, combining slight variant of the 42-class DAMSL (Hardy et al., 2002) with domain specific semantic information such as account numbers and credit card details (Hardy et al., 2003).

The most frequent tag in the AMITIÉS corpus is *Influence-on-listener="Information-request"*, which occurs 20% of the time. For this corpus, the average pair-wise kappa score of .59 was significantly lower than the SWITCHBOARD corpus. For the major categories (questions, answers), average pair-wise kappa scores were around .70. Again, according to the work of Carletta et al. (1997), a minimum kappa score of 0.67 is required to draw tentative conclusions. An excerpt of dialogue from the AMITIÉS corpus can be seen in Figure 3.

4 DA Classification

In this section we briefly describe our approach to DA classification, based solely on intra-utterance features. A key aspect of the approach is the selection of the word n-grams to use as cue phrases. Samuel et al. (1999) investigate a series of different statistical criteria for use in automatically selecting cue phrases, but we use a criterion of *predictivity*, described below, which is one that Samuel et al. (1999) do not consider.

4.1 Cue Phrase Selection

For our experiments, the word n-grams used as potential cue phrases during classification are computed from the training data. All word n-grams of length 1–4 within the data are considered as candidates. The phrases chosen as cue phrases are selected principally using a criterion of *predictivity*, which is the extent to which the presence of a certain n-gram in an utterance is predictive of it having a certain dialogue act category. For an n-gram n and dialogue act d, this corresponds to the conditional probability: $P(d \mid n)$, a value that can be straightforwardly computed. For each n-gram, we are interested in its *maximal* predictivity, i.e. the highest predictivity value found for it with any DA category. This set of n-grams is then reduced by applying thresholds of predictivity and occurrence, i.e. eliminating any n-gram whose maximal predictivity is below some minimum requirement, or whose maximal number of occurrences in any category falls below some threshold value. This thresholding removes some low frequency, high predictivity n-grams that skew classification performance. The n-grams that remain are identified as our cue phrases. The threshold values that are used in all experiments were arrived at empirically, using a validation set to automatically set the threshold levels independently of the test data, as described in Webb et al. (2005b).

4.2 Using Cue Phrases in Classification

To classify an utterance, we identify all the word n-grams it contains, and determine which of these has the highest predictivity of some dialogue act category (i.e. is performing as some cue). If multiple cue phrases share the same maximal predictivity, but predict different categories, we select the

```
<Turn Id="2.1" Speaker="Operator" Info-level="Communication-mgt"
Conventional="Opening">good morning customer services sam speaking</Turn>

<Turn Id="3.1" Speaker="Customer" Info-level="Communication-mgt"
Conventional="Opening">erm good morning</Turn>

<Turn Id="3.2" Speaker="Customer" Info-level="Task"
Forward-function="Explanation">erm I was away for about two months and i came back
and my card i don't know whether i have lost it or it is stolen</Turn>

<Turn Id="4.1" Speaker="Operator" Understanding="Backchannel"
Response-to="T3.2">right okay</Turn>

<Turn Id="4.2" Speaker="Operator" Info-level="Task"
Influence-on-listener="Info-request-explicit">can you confirm your name
for me please</Turn>
```

Figure 3: Excerpt of dialogue from the AMITIÉS GE corpus

DA for the phrase with the highest frequency. If the combination of predicitivity and occurrence count is insufficient to determine a single DA, then a random choice is made amongst the remaining candidate DAs. If no cue phrases are present, then a default tag is assigned, corresponding to the most frequent tag within the training corpus.

Our best reported figures on the 202k utterance SWITCHBOARD corpus are a cross-validated score of 69.09%, with a single high score of 71.29%, which compares very favourably with the (not cross-validated) 71% reported in Stolcke et al. (2000) for the same corpus. We also presented information that shows that adding a sequence model of DA progressions - an n-gram model of DAs - results in no significant increase in performance (Webb et al., 2005a). This is surprising considering that Stolcke et al. (2000) report their best figures when *combining* a HMM model of the words inside utterances with a tri-gram model of the Dialogue Act sequence, as in the work of Reithinger and Klesen (1997). When Stolcke et al. (2000) add the sequence model to the HMM language model, it adds around 20% points to the final accuracy score over the SWITCHBOARD data.

However, our observation is confirmed by both Serafin and Eugenio (2004) and Ries (March 1999). On the basis of this result, we hypothesise that our cues are highly predictive of dialogue structure, and that much dialogue processing may take place at a very shallow level.

5 Cross-Domain Classification

The central purpose of this paper is to examine the use of automatically extracted cues to tag data *other* than the corpus from which they are derived. The hypothesis we wish to test is that these cues are sufficiently general to work as a classification device on a corpus from a different domain, even containing interactions of a different conversational style. Specifically, SWITCHBOARD is an open domain spoken human-human conversational corpus and we have shown state-of-the-art tagging performance over this data using our cue-based model. We now wish to see how well these same cues perform over the AMITIÉS GE corpus of spoken *t*ask-based dialogues. The dialogues in the AMITIÉS GE corpus are far more goal directed, and contain domain specific cues not found in the general conversational SWITCHBOARD corpus.

The ability to apply cues extracted from one corpus to new data is an interesting challenge. It could confirm work which indicates the prominence of such word cues in language (Hirschberg and Litman, 1993). A tag mechanism that can operate across domains presents a range of benefits - for example it can be used to annotate or partially annotate new data collections.

5.1 DA Mapping

Cross-corpus classification would be simplified if both corpora were annotated with identical DA taxonomies. In actuality, the SWITCHBOARD corpus and the AMITIÉS GE corpus are annotated with *variants* of the DAMSL DA annotation scheme. In the SWITCHBOARD corpus, the hierarchical nature of the DAMSL schema has been flattened and clustered, to produce 42 major classes. In the AMITIÉS GE corpus, the dialogue level schema has been left largely untouched from the DAMSL original. In order to be able to compare automatic classification performance across the two corpora, a mapping is required between the 42-class schema of SWITCHBOARD and the DAMSL-like XDML schema of the AMITIÉS GE corpus. In their work, Jurafsky et al. (1998) include such a mapping between SWITCHBOARD and DAMSL that covers approximately 80% of the labels in the SWITCHBOARD corpus. We have adapted this slightly to cover minor differences between the XDML used in the AMITIÉS GE corpus and the original DAMSL, although this leaves us with two issues that we need to address.

First there are differences in granularity on both sides. Importantly, in many instances we may identify the most salient role of the utterance, but miss modification information which may make little interpretative difference. For example, markup in the AMITIÉS GE corpus makes the distinction between <Forward-function="Assert"> and <Forward-function="Reassert">, whereas markup in the SWITCHBOARD corpus ignores such a distinction, and annotates both as type <Forward-function="Assert"> - although the SWITCHBOARD corpus captures the difference between assertions that are opinions, and those that are not, whereas the original DAMSL does not capture this distinction. To address this mismatch we create a set of super classes by relating the annotations of SWITCHBOARD-DAMSL and the AMITIÉS GE-XDML corpora at the most salient level, according to the mapping contained in Jurafsky et al. (1998). Whilst the majority of tags have a one-to-one correlation, there are elements of both the Forward-Looking Function (see Figure 4) and Backward-Looking Function (Figure 5) that require mapping in both directions.

Secondly, there are a number of AMITIÉS GE tags that we know a-priori we have little or no chance to recognise. For example, the AMITIÉS GE corpus is meticulously annotated to include that certain utterances are perceived as answers to prior utterances. Our approach to DA tagging is purely *intra*-utterance, taking no account of the wider discourse structure, so will not recognise these distinctions. Although such a model of discourse structure should be trivial, based for example on an adjacency pair approach, this will be evaluated further in future work.

5.2 Evaluation Criteria

These issues require that we create two evaluation criteria for our subsequent experiments - **strict** and **lenient**. With strict evaluation, we are required to match *all* elements of the AMITIÉS GE corpus annotation - despite knowing in advance that this is not possible for a range of utterances. We use our strict evaluation criteria to establish a lower bound of performance for our classifier. Our lenient approach is a back-off model, where we require that we correctly identify the most critical part of the multi-part annotation - those that are identified as the most salient.

We'll use the dialogue excerpt shown in Figure 3 as an example of how these two scoring mechanisms work. The first utterance (2.1) is marked as <Info-level="Communication-mgt" Conventional="Opening">. This has a one-to-one correlation with the SWITCHBOARD-DAMSL tag <conventional-opening>. In the case of this example, and in all instances in the AMITIÉS GE corpus, utterances are marked as <Info-level="Task">, *unless* they are from a small set of exceptions, including openings, closings or backchannels, that are annotated as <Info-level="Communication-mgt">. Once an utterance is tagged as one of these exceptions, we know to change the <Info-level> assignment accordingly.

There will be no difference between our strict and lenient evaluation models for the interpretation of this utterance. The same is true for the second (3.1) utterance annotation, which has a direct correlation with SWITCHBOARD-DAMSL annotations. However, the fourth utterance (4.1) includes a <Response-to="T3.2"> annotation that we will not be able to identify using our intra-utterance model. This utterance will be judged correct using the lenient model, and incorrect using the strict metric.

The third utterance (3.2) is marked as <Forward-function="Explanation">. Using the Forward-function map shown in Figure 4, we see that this maps to the super class <Forward-function="Assert">, that in turn maps to the SWITCHBOARD-DAMSL tags <statement-non-opinion> and <statement-opinion>. This means that any utterance identified by the presence of a cue phrase as either <statement-non-opinion> or <statement-opinion> will in fact be tagged as <Info-level="Task" Forward-function="Assert">. Whilst this annotation

$$\left.\begin{array}{l} Forward-function = \text{“}Assert\text{”} \\ Forward-function = \text{“}Reassert\text{”} \\ Forward-function = \text{“}Explanation\text{”} \\ Forward-function = \text{“}Rexplanation\text{”} \\ Forward-function = \text{“}Expression\text{”} \end{array}\right\} Forward-function = \text{“}Assert\text{”} \left\{\begin{array}{l} statement-non-opinion \\ statement-opinion \end{array}\right.$$

Figure 4: Partial Forward-Looking Function mapping table (XDML } SUPERCLASS { SWITCHBOARD-DAMSL)

$$\left.\begin{array}{l} Inf-on-list = \text{“}Info-req-explicit\text{”} \\ Inf-on-list = \text{“}Info-req-implicit\text{”} \\ Inf-on-list = \text{“}Conf-req-implicit\text{”} \\ Inf-on-list = \text{“}Conf-req-explicit\text{”} \end{array}\right\} \begin{array}{c} Influence-on-listener = \\ \text{“}Information-request\text{”} \end{array} \left\{\begin{array}{l} yes-no-question \\ wh-questions \\ open-questions \\ or-clause \\ declarative-question \\ tag-question \end{array}\right.$$

Figure 5: Partial Backward-Looking Function mapping table (XDML } SUPERCLASS { SWITCHBOARD-DAMSL)

captures the salient behaviour of the utterance, it is not an exact match to the original AMITIÉS GE corpus annotation and correspondingly when scoring the lenient model will score this as correct, whereas the exact model will not.

The same is true with the fifth utterance (4.2), annotated in this case as <Influence-on-listener="Info-request-explicit">. A classifier trained over the SWITCHBOARD corpus would identify this (through the mapping see in Figure 5) as <Influence-on-listener="Information-request">, which would be scored as correct using the lenient measure, and incorrect using the exact.

5.3 Classification Experiments

The results of our experiments are summarised in Figure 6. First, to establish our baseline tagging performance, we take the classification algorithm outlined earlier in Section 4, and apply it to the SWITCHBOARD corpus for both training and testing, replicating the work reported in Webb et al. (2005a). In this case, 198,000 utterances are used for training, and a separate 4,000 utterances are used for testing. We achieve a cross-validated score of 69.6%, where the most frequent tag in SWITCHBOARD, <statement-non-opinion>, occurs 36% of the time. This is a confirmation of the work reported in Webb et al. (2005a), and demonstrates that this simple model works exceptionally well for this task.

For the first of the new experiments to test our hypothesis, we substitute the AMITIÉS GE corpus for the SWITCHBOARD corpus in both steps - training and testing - which will give us an upper bound of performance of this particular classification algorithm over this data. In this experiment, we used 10% of the corpus for testing - giving us a total of 27,000 utterances for training and 3,000 utterances for testing. For all experiments where AMITIÉS GE data is used as a test corpus, both strict and lenient scoring will be used. Strict scoring sets a lower bound for this exercise, and should be greater than chance, which corresponds to the distribution of the most frequent DA tag in each corpus. For strict scoring, where we are required to match all the elements of the AMITIÉS GE XDML tag, we score 65.9% accuracy in this experiment. For lenient, where we must match only the most salient features, we score 70.8% accuracy. Whilst there is no direct comparison to other work on this corpus, Hardy et al. (2005) show partial results for DA classification on this task, looking only at a few major classes, and achieve a score of 86%. However, this includes only the 5 most frequent DA categories, and considers utterances shorter than a certain number of words.

Finally, we attempt cross-domain classification: First, we train our classifier using SWITCHBOARD data, and test using AMITIÉS GE data. We recorded a strict evaluation score of 39.8% tagging accuracy. Using the lenient score, we achieve around 55.7% accuracy. This can be considered a very good result, given the lower bound score of 20% - that is the count of the most frequent tag.

Training corpus	*Training utterances*	*Testing corpus*	*Test utterances*	*Common tag (%)*	*Lenient score*	*Strict score*
SWITCHBOARD	198,000	SWITCHBOARD	4,000	36%	n/a	69%
AMITIÉS GE	27,000	AMITIÉS GE	3,000	20%	70.8%	65.9%
SWITCHBOARD	198,000	AMITIÉS GE	30,000	20%	55.7%	39.8%
AMITIÉS GE	27,000	SWITCHBOARD	198,000	36%	48.3%	40%
SWITCHBOARD	27,000	AMITIÉS GE	3,000	20%	53.2%	38%

Figure 6: Experimental Results

Then we apply the classification in reverse - we train on AMITIÉS GE data, and test on the SWITCHBOARD corpus, using all available data in both cases. Using the strict evaluation metric, we achieve a score of 40.0%, and a lenient score of 48.3%. This compares to a baseline of 36%, so is not a drastic improvement over our lower bound. Some inspection of the data informed us that the AMITIÉS GE data did not include many <backchannel> utterances, so subsequently most of these instances in the SWITCHBOARD corpus were missed by our classifier. By changing the default tag to be <backchannel>, rather than the most frequent tag for the training corpus, we achieve a performance gain to 47.7% with strict scoring, and 56.0% with the lenient metric.

For the last experiment, we also wanted to study the effect of limiting the training data on cross-domain classification, by reducing the SWITCHBOARD data to match that of the AMITIÉS GE training set - that is, to use only 27,000 utterances of the SWITCHBOARD corpus as training data to extract cues, which are then applied both to itself (for reference), and to the AMITIÉS GE corpus. On a related note, part of the work conducted in Webb et al. (2005a) studied the impact of different size training models when classifying SWITCHBOARD data, using models of 4k, 50k and 202k utterances. Whilst substantial improvement was seen when moving from 4k utterances to 50k utterances, the subsequent increase from 50k to 202k utterances had a negligible impact on classification accuracy. With the reduced SWITCHBOARD training set, we score 53.2% with the lenient metric, and 38% with strict, indicating that the reduction is size of the training data has some effect on classification accuracy.

6 Discussion, Future Work

We have shown that the cues extracted from the SWITCHBOARD corpus can be used to successfully classify utterances in the AMITIÉS GE corpus. We achieve almost 80% of the upper baseline performance over the AMITIÉS GE corpus, when judged using our lenient scoring mechanism - scoring 55.7% using the cross-domain cues, compared to the 70.8% when using in-domain cues. When using the strict measure we still achieve around 60% of the upper bound performance, both results being a substantial improvement over the baseline measure of 20%, corresponding to the most frequent tag in the AMITIÉS GE corpus. This is a significant result, which confirms the idea that cues can be sufficiently general across domains to be used in classification.

However, whilst the experiment using SWITCHBOARD corpus derived cues to classify AMITIÉS GE data works well, the same is not true in reverse. There are two possible explanations for this result. It could be related to the size of data available for training, although our experiments in this area seem to suggest otherwise and so we believe that the composition of the training data is a more crucial element. Although the DA distribution in the SWITCHBOARD corpus is uneven, there is sufficient data for the major classes to be effective on new data that also contains these classes. Although the AMITIÉS GE contains a lot of questions and statements, there is very little of the other significant categories, such as <backchannels>, a key DA in the SWITCHBOARD corpus and conversational speech in general. Correspondingly, the cues derived from the AMITIÉS GE data perform well on a selection of utterances in the SWITCHBOARD corpus, but very poorly on others. We want to perform an in-depth error analysis to see if the errors we obtain in classification accuracy are consistent. We can also compare our list of automatically derived cues phrases, particularly those that overlap between the two corpora, to those reported in prior literature. It might be interesting to see if more complex models, derived using state-of-the art machine learning approaches, could demonstrate similar portability - i.e is it the simplicity of our model that allows for the observed robust portability?

Finally, we wish to combine SWITCHBOARD and AMITIÉS corpora in the cue learning phase, to see how this effects classification, and apply the results to a range of other corpora, including the ICSI-MRDA corpus (Shriberg et al., 2004).

References

Bunt, Harry. 1994. Context and dialogue control. *THINK*, 3:19–31.

Carletta, J. C., A. Isard, S. Isard, J. Kowtko, G. Doherty-Sneddon, and A. Anderson. 1997. The Reliability of a Dialogue Structure Coding Scheme. *Computational Linguistics*, 23:13–31.

Cohen, P. R. and C. R. Perrault. 1979. Elements of a plan based theory of speech acts. *Cognitive Science*, 3.

Core, Mark G. and James Allen. 1997. Coding dialogs with the DAMSL annotation scheme. In *AAAI Fall Symposium on Communicative Action in Humans and Machines*, MIT, Cambridge, MA.

Grosz, Barbara and Candace Sidner. 1986. Attention, Intentions, and the Structure of Discourse. *Computational Linguistics*, 19(3).

Hardy, Hilda, Kirk Baker, Laurence Devillers, Lori Lamel, Sophie Rosset, Tomek Strzalkowski, Cristian Ursu, and Nick Webb. 2002. Multi-layered dialogue annotation for automated multilingual customer service. In *Proceedings of the ISLE workshop on Dialogue Tagging for Multimodal Human Computer Interaction, Edinburgh.*

Hardy, H., K. Baker, H. Bonneau-Maynard, L. Devillers, S. Rosset, and T. Strzalkowski. 2003. Semantic and dialogic annotation for automated multilingual customer service. In *Eurospeech, Geneva, Switzerland.*

Hardy, H., A. Biermann, R. Bryce Inouye, A. McKenzie, T. Strzalkowski, C. Ursu, N. Webb, and M. Wu. 2005. The AMITIES System: Data-Driven Techniques for Automated Dialogue. *Speech Communication*, 48:354–373.

Hirschberg, Julia and Diane Litman. 1993. Empirical Studies on the Disambiguation of Cue Phrases. *Computational Linguistics*, 19(3):501–530.

Jurafsky, Daniel, Rebecca Bates, Noah Coccaro, Rachel Martin, Marie Meteer, Klaus Ries, Elizabeth Shriberg, Andreas Stolcke, Paul Taylor, and Carol Van Ess-Dykema. 1998. Switchboad discourse language modeling project final report. Research Note 30, Center for Language and Speech Processing, Johns Hopkins University, Baltimore.

Prasad, Rashmi and Marilyn Walker. 2002. Training a Dialogue Act Tagger for Humna-Human and Human-Computer Travel Dialogues. In *Proceedings of the 3rd SIGdial workshop on Discourse and Dialogue*, Philadelphia, Pennsylvania.

Reithinger, Norbert and Martin Klesen. 1997. Dialogue act classification using language models. In *Proceedings of EuroSpeech-97.*

Ries, Klaus. March, 1999. Hmm and neural network based speech act classification. In *Proceddings of the IEEE Conference on Acoustics, Speech and Signal Processing, volume 1, pages 497–500*, Phoenix, AZ.

Samuel, Ken, Sandra Carberry, and K. Vijay-Shanker. 1998. Dialogue act tagging with transformation-based learning. In *Proceedings of the 36th Annual Meeting of the Association for Computational Linguistics and 17th International Conference on Computational Linguistics*, Montreal.

Samuel, Ken, Sandra Carberry, and K. Vijay-Shanker. 1999. Automatically selecting useful phrases for dialogue act tagging. In *Proceedings of the Fourth Conference of the Pacific Association for Computational Linguistics, Waterloo, Ontario, Canada.*

Serafin, Riccardo and Barbara Di Eugenio. 2004. FLSA: Extending Latent Semantic Analysis with features for dialogue act classification. In *Proceedings of the 42nd Annual Meeting on Association for Computational Linguistics*, Barcelona, Spain.

Shriberg, E., R. Dhillon, S. Bhagat, J. Ang, and H. Carvey. 2004. The ICSI meeting recorder dialog act (MRDA) corpus. In *Special Interest Group on Discourse and Dialogue (SIGdial)*, Boston, USA.

Stolcke, A., K. Ries, N. Coccaro, E. Shriberg, R. Bates, D. Jurafsky, P. Taylor, R. Martin, C. Van Ess-Dykema, and M. Meteer. 2000. Dialogue act modeling for automatic tagging and recognition of conversational speech. In *Computational Linguistics 26(3), 339–373.*

Tur, Gokhan, Umit Guz, and Dilek Hakkani-Tur. 2006. Model Adaptation for Dialogue Act Tagging. In *IEEE Spoken Language Technology Workshop.*

Webb, Nick, Mark Hepple, and Yorick Wilks. 2005a. Dialogue Act Classification Based on Intra-Utterance Features. In *Proceedings of the AAAI Workshop on Spoken Language Understanding.*

Webb, Nick, Mark Hepple, and Yorick Wilks. 2005b. Empirical determination of thresholds for optimal dialogue act classification. In *Proceedings of the Ninth Workshop on the Semantics and Pragmatics of Dialogue.*

Extractive Summarization Using Supervised and Semi-supervised Learning

Kam-Fai Wong[*], **Mingli Wu**[*†]
[*]Department of Systems Engineering and Engineering Management
The Chinese University of Hong Kong
New Territories, Hong Kong
{kfwong,mlwu}@se.cuhk.edu.hk

Wenjie Li[†]
[†]Department of Computing
The Hong Kong Polytechnic University
Kowloon, Hong Kong
cswjli@comp.polyu.edu.hk

Abstract

It is difficult to identify sentence importance from a single point of view. In this paper, we propose a learning-based approach to combine various sentence features. They are categorized as surface, content, relevance and event features. Surface features are related to extrinsic aspects of a sentence. Content features measure a sentence based on content-conveying words. Event features represent sentences by events they contained. Relevance features evaluate a sentence from its relatedness with other sentences. Experiments show that the combined features improved summarization performance significantly. Although the evaluation results are encouraging, supervised learning approach requires much labeled data. Therefore we investigate co-training by combining labeled and unlabeled data. Experiments show that this semi-supervised learning approach achieves comparable performance to its supervised counterpart and saves about half of the labeling time cost.

1 Introduction

[1] Automatic text summarization involves condensing a document or a document set to produce a human comprehensible summary. Two kinds of summarization approaches were suggested in the past, i.e., extractive (Radev et al., 2004; Li et al., 2006) and abstractive summarization (Dejong, 1978). The abstractive approaches typically need to "understand" and then paraphrase the salient concepts across documents. Due to the limitations in natural language processing technology, abstractive approaches are restricted to specific domains. In contrast, extractive approaches commonly select sentences that contain the most significant concepts in the documents. These approaches tend to be more practical.

Recently various effective sentence features have been proposed for extractive summarization, such as signature word, event and sentence relevance. Although encouraging results have been reported, most of these features are investigated individually. We argue that it is ineffective to identify sentence importance from a single point of view. Each sentence feature has its unique contribution, and combing them would be advantageous. Therefore we investigate combined sentence features for extractive summarization. To determine weights of different features, we employ a supervised learning framework to identify how likely a sentence is important. Some researchers explored learning based summarization, but the new emerging features are not concerned, such as event features (Li et. al, 2006).

We investigate the effectiveness of different sentence features with supervised learning to decide which sentences are important for summarization. After feature vectors of sentences are examined, a supervised learning classifier is then employed. Particularly, considering the length of final summaries is fixed, candidate sentences are re-ranked. Finally, the top sentences are extracted to compile the final summaries. Experiments show that combined features improve summarization performance significantly.

Our supervised learning approach generates promising results based on combined features. However, it requires much labeled data. As this procedure is time consuming and costly, we investigate semi-supervised learning to combine labeled data and unlabeled data. A semi-

© 2008. Licensed under the *Creative Commons Attribution-Noncommercial-Share Alike 3.0 Unported* license (http://creativecommons.org/licenses/by-nc-sa/3.0/). Some rights reserved.

supervised learning classifier is used instead of a supervised one in our extractive summarization framework. Two classifiers are co-trained iteratively to exploit unlabeled data. In each iteration step, the unlabeled training examples with top classifying confidence are included in the labeled training set, and the two classifiers are trained on the new training data. Experiments show that the performance of our semi-supervised learning approach is comparable to its supervised learning counterpart and it can reduce the labeling time cost by 50%.

The remainder of this paper is organized as follows. Section 2 gives related work and Section 3 describes our learning-based extractive summarization framework. Section 4 outlines the various sentence features and Section 5 describes supervised/semi-supervised learning approaches. Section 6 presents experiments and results. Finally, Section 7 concludes the paper.

2 Related Work

Traditionally, features for summarization were studied separately. Radev et al. (2004) reported that position and length are useful surface features. They observed that sentences located at the document head most likely contained important information. Recently, content features were also well studied, including centroid (Radev et al., 2004), signature terms (Lin and Hovy, 2000) and high frequency words (Nenkova e t al., 2006). Radev et al. (2004) defined centroid words as those whose average *tf*idf* score were higher than a threshold. Lin and Hovy (2000) identified signature terms that were strongly associated with documents based on statistics measures. Nenkova et al. (2006) later reported that high frequency words were crucial in reflecting the focus of the document.

Bag of words is somewhat loose and omits structural information. Document structure is another possible feature for summarization. Barzilay and Elhadad (1997) constructed lexical chains and extracted strong chains in summaries. Marcu (1997) parsed documents as rhetorical trees and identified important sentences based on the trees. However, only moderate results were reported. On the other hand, Dejong (1978) represented documents using predefined templates. The procedure to create and fill the templates was time consuming and it was hard to adapt the method to different domains.

Recently, semi-structure events (Filatovia and Hatzivassiloglou, 2004; Li et al., 2006; Wu, 2006) have been investigated by many researchers as they balanced document representation with words and structures. They defined events as verbs (or action nouns) plus the associated named entities. For instance, given the sentence "Yasser Arafat on Tuesday accused the United States of threatening to kill PLO officials", they first identified "accused", "threatening" and "kill" as event terms; and "Yasser Arafat", "United States", "PLO" and "Tuesday" as event elements. Encouraging results based on events were reported for news stories.

From another point of view, sentences in a document are somehow connected. Sentence relevance has been used as an alternative means to identify important sentences. Erkan and Radev (2004) and Yoshioka (2004) evaluate the relevance (similarity) between any two sentences first. Then a web analysis approach, PageRank, was used to select important sentences from a sentence map built on relevance. Promising results were reported. However, the combination of these features is not well studied. Wu et al. (2007) conducted preliminary research on this problem, but event features were not considered.

Normally labeling procedure in supervised learning is very time consuming. Blum and Mitchell (1998) proposed co-training approach to exploit labeled and unlabeled data. Promising results were reported from their experiments on web page classification. A number of successful studies emerged thereafter for other natural language processing tasks, such as text classification (Denis and Gilleron, 2003), noun phrase chunking (Pierce and Cardie, 2001), parsing (Sarkar, 2001) and reference or relation resolution (Muller et al., 2001; Li et al., 2004). To our knowledge, there is little research in the application of co-training techniques to extractive summarization.

3 The Framework for Extractive Summarization

Extractive summarization can be regarded as a classification problem. Given the features of a sentence, a machine-learning based classification model will judge how likely the sentence is important. The classification model can be supervised or semi-supervised learning. Supervised approaches normally perform better, but require more labeled training data. SVMs perform well in many classification problems. Thus we employ it for supervised learning. For semi-supervised learning, we co-trained a probabilistic

SVM and a Naïve Bayesian classifier to exploit unlabeled data.

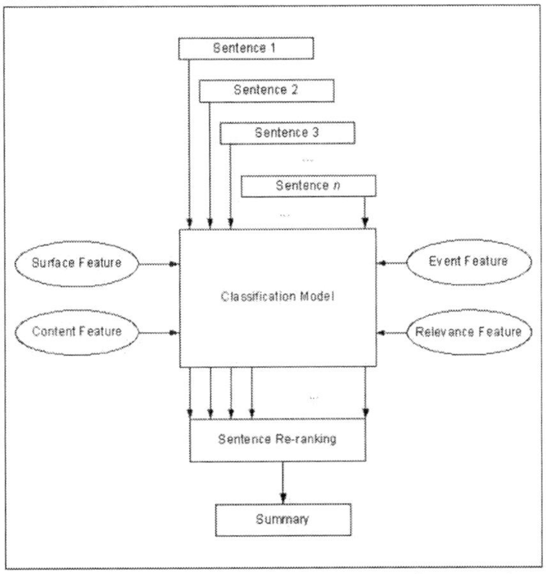

Figure 1. Learning-based Extractive Summarization Framework

The automatic summarization procedure is shown in Figure 1. First, each input sentence is examined by going through the pre-specified feature functions. The classification model will then predict the importance of each sentence according to its feature values. A re-ranking algorithm is then used to revise the order. Finally, the top sentences are included in the summaries until the length limitation is reached. The re-ranking algorithm is crucial, as more important content are expected to be contained in the final summary with fixed length. Important sentences above a threshold are regarded as candidates. The one with less words and located at the beginning part of a document is ranked first. The re-ranking algorithm is described as follows.

$Rank_i = RankPos_i + RankLength_i$

where $RankPos_i$ is the rank of sentence i according to its position in a document (i.e. the sentence no.) and $RankLength_i$ is rank of sentence i according to its length.

4 Sentence Features for Extractive Summarization

This section provides a detailed description on the four types of sentence features, i.e., surface, content, event and relevance features, which will be examined systematically.

4.1 Surface Features

Surface features are based on structure of documents or sentences, including sentence position in the document, the number of words in the sentence, and the number of quoted words in the sentence (see Table 1).

Name	Description
Position	1/sentence no.
Doc_First	Whether it is the first sentence of a document
Para_First	Whether it is the first sentence of a paragraph
Length	The number of words in a sentence
Quote	The number of quoted words in a sentence

Table 1. Types of surface features

The intuition with respect to the importance of a sentence stems from the following observations: (1) the first sentence in a document or a paragraph is important; (2) the sentences in the earlier parts of a document is more important than sentences in later parts; (3) a sentence is important if the number of words (except stop words) in it is within a certain range; (4) a sentence containing too many quoted words is unimportant.

4.2 Content Features

We integrate three well-known sentence features based on content-bearing words i.e., centroid words, signature terms, and high frequency words. Both unigram and bigram representations have been investigated. Table 2 summarizes the six content features we studied.

Name	Description
Centroid_Uni	The sum of the weights of centroid uni-gram
Centroid_Bi	The sum of the weights of centroid bi-grams
SigTerm_Uni	The number of signature uni-grams
SigTerm_Bi	The number of signature bi-grams
FreqWord_Uni	The sum of the weights of frequent uni-grams
FreqWord_Bi	The sum of the weights of frequent bi-grams

Table 2. Types of content features

4.3 Event Features

An event is comprised of an event term and associated event elements. In this study, we choose verbs (such as "elect and incorporate") and action nouns (such as "election and incorporation") as event terms that can characterize actions. They relate to "did what". One or more associated named entities are considered as event elements. Four types of named entities are currently under consideration. The GATE system (Cunningham et al., 2002) is used to tag named entities, which are categorized as <Person>, <Organization>, <Location> and <Date>. They convey the information about "who", "whom", "when" and "where". A verb or an action noun is deemed an event term only when it appears at least once between two named entities.

Event summarization approaches based on instances or concepts are investigated. An occurrence of an event term (or event element) in a document is considered as an instance, while the collection of the same event terms (or event elements) is considered as a concept. Given a document set, instances of event terms and event elements are identified first. An event map is then built based on event instances or concepts (Wu , 2006; Li et al., 2006). PageRank algorithm is used to assign weight to each node (an instance or concept) in the event map. The final weight of a sentence is the sum of weights of event instances contained in the sentence.

4.4 Relevance Features

Relevance features are incorporated to exploit inter-sentence relationships. It is assumed that: (1) sentences related to important sentences are important; (2) sentences related to many other sentences are important. The first sentence in a document or a paragraph is important, and other sentences in a document are compared with the leading ones. Two types of sentence relevance, FirstRel_Doc and FirstRel_Para (see Table 3), are measured by comparing pairs of sentences using word-based cosine similarity.

Another way to exploit sentence relevance is to build a sentence map. Every two sentences are regarded relevant if their similarity is above a threshold. Every two relevant sentences are connected with a unidirectional link. Based on this map, PageRank algorithm is applied to evaluate the importance of a sentence. These relevance features are shown in Table 3.

Name	Description
FirstRel_Doc	Similarity with the first sentence in the document
FirstRel_Para	Similarity with the first sentence in the paragraph
PageRankRel	PageRank value of the sentence based on the sentence map

Table 3. Types of relevance features

5 Supervised/Semi-supervised Learning Approaches

To incorporate features described in Section 4, we investigate supervised and semi-supervised learning approaches. Probabilistic Support Vector Machine (PSVM) is employed as supervised learning (Wu et al., 2004), while the co-training of PSVM and Naïve Bayesian Classifier (NBC) is used for semi-supervised learning. The two learning-based classification approaches, PSVM and NBC, are described in following sections.

5.1 Probabilistic Support Vector Machine (PSVM)

For a set of training examples (x_i , y_i), $i = 1,..., l$, where x_i is an instance and y_i the corresponding label, basic SVM requires the solution of the following optimization problem.

$$\min_{w,b,\xi} \frac{1}{2} w^T w + C \sum_{i=1}^{l} \xi_i$$

$$\text{subject to} \quad \begin{array}{l} y_i(w^T \phi(x_i) + b) \geq 1 - \xi_i, \\ \xi_i \geq 0 \end{array}$$

Here the SVM classifier is expected to find a hyper-plane to separate testing examples as positive and negative. Wu et al. (2004) extend the basic SVM to a probabilistic version. Its goal is to estimate

$$p_i = p(y = i \mid x), i = 1,...k .$$

First the pairwise (one-against-one) probabilities $r_{ij} \approx p(y = i \mid y = i \text{ or } j, x)$ is estimated using

$$r_{ij} \approx \frac{1}{1 + e^{Af + B}}$$

where A and B are estimated by minimizing the negative log-likelihood function using training data and their decision values f. Then p_i is obtained by solving the following optimization problem

$$\min_{p} \frac{1}{2} \sum_{i=1}^{k} \sum_{j:j \neq i} (r_{ji} p_i - r_{ij} p_j)^2$$

$$\text{subject to} \quad \begin{array}{l} y_i(w^T \phi(x_i) + b) \geq 1 - \xi_i, \\ \xi_i \geq 0 \end{array}$$

The problem can be reformulated as

$$\min_{P} \frac{1}{2} P^T Q P$$

where $Q_{ij} = \begin{cases} \sum_{s:s\neq i} r_{si}^2 & \text{if } i = j \\ -r_{ji}r_{ij} & \text{if } i \neq j \end{cases}$

The problem is convex and the optimality conditions a scalar b such that

$$\begin{bmatrix} Q & e \\ e^T & 0 \end{bmatrix} \begin{bmatrix} \mathrm{P} \\ \mathrm{b} \end{bmatrix} = \begin{bmatrix} \mathrm{z} \\ 1 \end{bmatrix}$$

where e is the vector of all 1s and z is the vector of all 0s, and b is the Lagrangian multiplier of the equality constraint $\sum_{i=1}^{k} p_i = 1$.

5.2 Naïve Bayesian Classier (NBC)

Naïve Bayesian Classier assumes features are independent. It learns prior probability and conditional probability of each feature, and predicts the class label by highest posterior probability. Given a feature vector (F_1, F_2, F_3,…, F_n), the classifier need to decide the label c:

$$c = \arg\max_c P(c \mid F_1, F_2, F_3, \ldots F_n)$$

By applying Bayesian rule, we have

$$P(c \mid F_1, F_2, F_3, \ldots, F_n) = \frac{P(c)P(F_1, F_2, F_3, \ldots, F_n \mid c)}{P(F_1, F_2, F_3, \ldots, F_n)}$$

Since the denominator does not depend on c and the values of F_i are given, therefore the denominator is a constant and we are only interested in the numerator. As features are assumed independent,

$$P(c \mid F_1, F_2, F_3, \ldots F_n) = P(c)P(F_1, F_2, F_3, \ldots F_n \mid c)$$
$$\approx P(c)\prod_{i=1}^{n} P(F_i \mid c)$$

where $P(F_i \mid c)$ is estimated with MLE from training data with Laplace Smoothing.

5.3 Co-Training (COT)

Supervised learning approaches require much labeled data and the labeling procedure is very time-consuming. Literature (Blum and Mitchell, 1998; Collins, 1999) has suggested that unlabeled data can be exploited together with labeled data by co-training two classifiers. (Blum and Mitchell, 1998) trained two classifiers of same type on different features, and (Li et al., 2004) trained two classifiers of different types. In this paper, as the number of involved features is not too many, we train two different classifiers, PSVM and NBC, on the same feature spaces. The co-training algorithm is described as follows.

Given:
  L is the set of labeled training examples
  U is the set of unlabeled training examples
Loop: until the unlabeled data is exhausted
  Train the first classifier C_1 (PSVM) on L
  Train the second classifier C_2 (NBC) on L
  For each classifier C_i
    C_i labels examples from U
    C_i chooses p positive and n negative examples E from U. These examples have top classifying confidence.
    C_i removes examples E from U
    C_i adds examples E with the corresponding labels to L
End
Output: label the test examples by the optimal classifier which is evaluated on training data according to the classification performance.

6 Experiments

DUC 2001[2] has been used in our experiments. It contains 30 clusters of relevant documents and 308 documents in total. Each cluster deals with a specific topic (e.g. a hurricane) and comes with model summaries created by NIST assessors. 50, 100, 200 and 400 word summaries are provided. Twenty-five of the thirty document clusters are used as training data and the remaining five are used as testing. The training/testing configuration is same in experiments of supervised learning and semi-supervised learning, while the difference is that some sentences in training data are not tagged for semi-supervised learning.

An automatic evaluation package, i.e., ROUGE (Lin and Hovy, 2003) is employed to evaluate the summarization performance. It compares machine-generated summaries with model summaries based on the overlap. Precision and recall measures are used to evaluate the classification performance. For comparison, we evaluate our approaches on DUC 2004 data set also. It contains 50 clusters of documents. Only 665-character summaries are given by assessors for each cluster.

6.1 Experiments on Supervised Learning Approach

We use LibSVM[3] as our classification model for SVM classifiers normally perform better. Types of features presented in previous section are evaluated individually first. Precision measures

[2] http://duc.nist.gov/
[3] http://www.csie.ntu.edu.tw/~cjlin/libsvm/

the percentage of true important sentences among all important sentences labeled by the classifier. Recall measures the percentage of true important sentences labeled by the classifier among all true important sentences.

Table 4 shows the precisions and recalls of different feature groups under the PSVM classifier. Table 5 records the ROUGE evaluation results – ROUGE-1, ROUGE-2 and ROUGE-L. They evaluate the overlap between machine-generated summaries and model summaries based on unigram, bigram and long distance respectively. The summary length is limited to 200 words here.

Feature	Precision	Recall
Sur	0.488	0.146
Con	0.407	0.167
Rel	0.488	0.146
Event	0.344	0.146
Sur+Con	0.575	0.160
Sur+Rel	0.488	0.146
Con+Rel	0.588	0.139
Sur+Event	0.600	0.125
Con+Event	0.384	0.194
Rel+Event	0.543	0.132
Sur+Con+Event	0.595	0.153
Sur+Rel+Event	0.553	0.146
Con+Rel+Event	0.581	0.125
Sur+Con+Rel	**0.595**	**0.174**
Sur+Con+Rel+Event	0.579	0.153

Table 4. Classification performance based on different feature groups

Feature	Rouge-1	Rouge-2	Rouge-L
Sur	0.373	0.103	0.356
Con	0.352	0.074	0.334
Rel	0.373	0.103	0.356
Event	0.344	0.064	0.325
Sur+Con	0.380	0.109	0.363
Sur+Rel	0.373	0.103	0.356
Con+Rel	0.375	0.103	0.358
Sur+Event	0.348	0.091	0.332
Con+Event	0.344	0.071	0.330
Rel+Event	0.349	0.089	0.356
Sur+Con+Event	0.379	0.106	0.363
Sur+Rel+Event	0.371	0.101	0.353
Sur+Con+Rel	**0.396**	**0.116**	**0.358**
Sur+Con+Rel+Event	0.375	0.106	0.359

Table 5. ROUGE evaluation results for different feature groups

From Table 4, we can see the most useful feature groups are "surface" and "relevance", i.e. the external characteristics of a sentence in the document and the relationships of a sentence with other sentences in a cluster. The evaluation scores from surface features and relevance features are the same. We found that the reason is that the dominating feature in each feature group is about whether a sentence is the first sentence in a document. The influence of event features is not very positive. Based on our analysis the reason is that not all clusters contain enough event terms/elements to build a good event map.

From Table 5, it can be seen that the combination of multiple features or multiple feature groups outperforms individual feature or feature groups. When surface, content and relevance features are employed, the best performance is achieved, i.e., ROUGE-1 and ROUGE-2 score are 0.396 and 0.116 respectively. In our preliminary experiments, we find ROUGE-1 score of a model summary is 0.422 (without stemming and filtering stop words). Therefore summaries generated by our supervised learning approach received comparable performance with model summaries when evaluated by ROUGE. Although ROUGE is not perfect at this time, it is automatic and good complement to subjective evaluations.

We also find that the Rouge scores are similar for variations on the feature set. Sentences from original documents are selected to build the final summaries. Normally, only four to six sentences are contained in one 200-word summary in our experiments, i.e., few sentences will be kept in a summary. As variations of the feature set only induce little change of the order of most important sentences, the ROUGE scores change little.

6.2 Experiments on Semi-supervised Learning Approach

Supervised learning approaches normally achieve good performance but require manually labeled data. Recent literature (Blum and Mitchell, 1998; Collins, 199) has suggested that co-training techniques reduce the amount of labeled data. They trained two homogeneous classifiers based on different feature spaces. However this method is unsuitable for our application as the number of required features in our case is not too many. Therefore we develop a co-training approach to train different classifiers based on same feature space. PSVM and NBC are applied to the combination of surface, content and relevance features.

The capability of different learning approaches to identify important sentences is shown in Figure 2. The "x" axis shows the number of labeled sentences employed. The remained training sentences in DUC 2001 are employed as unlabeled training data. The y axis shows f-measures of important sentences identified from the test set. The size of the training seed set is investigated. For each size, three different seed sets which are chose randomly are used. The average evaluation scores are used as the final performance. This procedure avoids the variance of the final evaluation results. The ROUGE evaluation results of these supervised learning approaches and semi-supervised learning approaches are shown in Table 6 (2000 labeled sentences). It can be seen that the ROUGE performance of co-trained classifiers is better than that of individual classifiers.

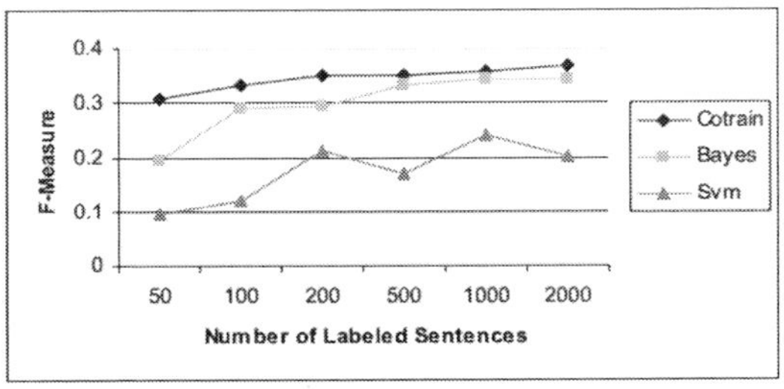

Figure 2. Performance of supervised learning and semi-supervised learning approaches

Learning Approaches	Rouge-1	Rouge-2	Rouge-L
PSVM	0.358	0.082	0.323
NBC	0.353	0.061	0.317
COT	**0.366**	**0.090**	**0.329**

Table 6. ROUGE evaluation results of supervised learning and semi-supervised learning

6.3 Experiments on Summary Length

In DUC 2001 dataset, 50, 100, 200 and 400-word summaries are provided to evaluate summaries with different length. Our supervised approach, which generates the best performance in previous experiments, is employed. The ROUGE scores of evaluations on different summary length are shown in Table 7. Our summaries consist of extracted sentences. It can be seen that these summaries achieve lower ROUGE scores when the length of summary is reduced. The reason is that when people try to write a more concise summary, condensed contents are included in the summaries, which may not use the original contents directly. Therefore the word-overlapping test tool in ROUGE generates lower scores.

We then tested the same classifier and same features on DUC 2004. The length of summaries is only 665 characters (about 100 words). ROUGE-1 and ROUGE-2 are 0.329 and 0.073 respectively. It confirms that the performance of our approach is sensitive to the length of the summary.

Sum_length	Rouge-1	Rouge-2	Rouge-L
50	0.241	0.036	0.205
100	0.309	0.085	0.277
200	0.396	0.116	0.358
400	**0.423**	**0.118**	**0.402**

Table 7. ROUGE evaluation results for different summary length

7 Conclusions and Future Work

We explore surface, content, event, relevance features and their combinations for extractive summarization with supervised learning approach. Experiments show that the combination of surface, content and relevance features perform best. The highest ROUGE-1, ROUGE-2 scores are 0.396 and 0.116 respectively. The Rouge-1 score of manually generated summaries is 0.422. This shows the ROUGE performance of our supervised learning approach is comparable to that of manually generated summaries. The ROUGE-1 scores of extractive summarization based on centroid, signature word, high frequency word and event individually are 0.319, 0.356, 0.371 and 0.374 respectively. It can be seen that our summarization approach based on combination of features improves the performance obviously.

Although the results of supervised learning approach are encouraging, it required much labeled data. To reduce labeling cost, we apply co-training to combine labeled and unlabeled data. Experiments show that compare with supervised learning, semi-supervised learning approach saves half of the labeling cost and maintains comparable performance (0.366 vs 0.396). We also find that our extractive summarization is sensitive to length of the summary. When the length is extended, the ROUGE scores of same summarization method are improved. In the future, we plan to investigate sentence compression to improve performance of our summarization approaches on short summaries.

Acknowledgement

The research described in this paper is partially supported by Research Grants Council of Hong Kong (RGC: PolyU5217/07E), CUHK Strategic Grant Scheme (No: 4410001) and Direct Grant Scheme (No: 2050417).

References

Regina Barzilay, and Michael Elhadad. 1997. Using lexical chains for text summarization. In *Proceedings of the 35th Annual Meeting of the Association for Computational Linguistics Workshop on Intelligent Scalable Text Summarization*, pages 10-17.

Avrim Blum and Tom Mitchell. 1998. Combining labeled and unlabeled data with co-training. In *Proceedings of the 11th Annual Conference on Computational Learning Theory*, pages 92-100.

Hamish Cunningham, Diana Maynard, Kalina Bontcheva, Valentin Tablan. 2002. GATE: a framework and graphical development environment for robust NLP tools and applications. In *Proceedings of the 40th Annual Meeting of the Association for computational Linguistics.*

Francois Denis and Remi Gilleron. 2003. Text classification and co-training from positive and unlabeled examples. In *Proceedings of the 20th International Conference on Machine Learning Workshop: the Continuum from Labeled Data to Unlabeled Data in Machine Learning and Data Mining.*

Gunes Erkan and Dragomir R. Radev. 2004. LexPageRank: prestige in multi-document text summarization. In *Proceedings of the 2004 Conference on Empirical Methods in Natural Language Processing*, pages 365-371.

Elena Filatova and Vasileios Hatzivassiloglou. Event-based extractive summarization. 2004. In *Proceedings of the 42nd Annual Meeting of the Association for Computational Linguistics Workshop*, pages 104-111.

Gerald Francis DeJong. 1978. Fast skimming of news stories: the FRUMP system. Ph.D. thesis, Yale University.

Wenjie Li, Guihong Cao, Kam-Fai Wong and Chunfa Yuan. 2004. Applying machine learning to Chinese temporal relation resolution. In *Proceedings of the 42nd Annual Meeting of the Association for Computational Linguistics*, pages 583-589.

Wenjie Li, Wei Xu, Mingli Wu, Chunfa Yuan, Qin Lu. 2006. Extractive summarization using inter- and intra- event relevance. In *proceedings of Proceedings of the 21st International Conference on Computational Linguistics and 44th Annual Meeting of the Association for Computational Linguistics*, pages 369-376.

Chin-Yew Lin; Eduard Hovy. 2000. The automated acquisition of topic signatures for text summarization. In *Proceedings of the 18th International Conference on Computational Linguistics*, pages 495-501.

Chin-Yew Lin and Eduard Hovy. 2003. Automatic evaluation of summaries using n-gram co-occurrence statistics. In *Proceedings of the 2003 Human Language Technology Conference of the North American Chapter of the Association for Computational Linguistics*, Edmonton, Canada.

Daniel Marcu. 1997. The rhetorical parsing of natural language texts. In *Proceedings of the 35th Annual Meeting of the Association for computational Linguistics*, pages 96-103.

Christoph Muller, Stefan Rapp and Michael Strube. 2001. Applying co-training to reference resolution. In *Proceedings of the 40th Annual Meeting on Association for Computational Linguistics.*

Ani Nenkova, Lucy Vanderwende and Kathleen McKeown. 2006. A compositional context sensitive multi-document summarizer: exploring the factors that influence summarization. In *Proceedings of the 29th Annual International ACM SIGIR Conference on Research and Development in Information Retrieval.*

David Pierce and Claire Cardie. 2001. Limitations of co-training for natural language learning from large datasets. In *Proceedings of the 2001 Conference on Empirical Methods in Natural Language Processing*, pages 1-9.

Dragomir R. Radev, Timothy Allison, et al. 2004. MEAD - a platform for multidocument multilingual text summarization. In *Proceedings of 4th International Conference on Language Resources and Evaluation.*

Anoop Sarkar. 2001. Applying co-training methods to statistical parsing. In *Proceedings of 2nd Meeting of the North American Chapter of the Association for Computational Linguistics on Language Technologies.*

Mingli Wu. 2006. Investigations on event-based summarization. In *proceedings of the 21st International Conference on Computational Linguistics and 44th Annual Meeting of the Association for Computational Linguistics Student Research Workshop*, pages 37-42.

Mingli Wu, Wenjie Li, Furu Wei, Qin Lu and Kam-Fai Wong. 2007. Exploiting surface, content and relevance features for learning-based extractive summarization. In *Proceedings of 2007 IEEE International Conference on Natural Language Processing and Knowledge Engineering.*

Ting-Fan Wu, Chih-Jen Lin and Ruby C. Weng. 2004. Probability estimates for multi-class classification by pairwise coupling. *Journal of Machine Learning Research*, 5:975-1005.

Masaharu Yoshioka and Makoto Haraguchi. 2004. Multiple news articles summarization based on event reference information. In *Working Notes of the Fourth NTCIR Workshop Meeting*, National Institute of Informatics.

Domain Adaptation for Statistical Machine Translation with Domain Dictionary and Monolingual Corpora

Hua Wu, Haifeng Wang
Toshiba (China) R&D Center
Beijing, 100738, China
wuhua@rdc.toshiba.com.cn
wanghaifeng@rdc.toshiba.com.cn

Chengqing Zong
NLPR, Institute of Automation
Chinese Academy of Sciences
Beijing 100080, China
cqzong@nlpr.ia.ac.cn

Abstract

Statistical machine translation systems are usually trained on large amounts of bilingual text and monolingual text. In this paper, we propose a method to perform domain adaptation for statistical machine translation, where in-domain bilingual corpora do not exist. This method first uses out-of-domain corpora to train a baseline system and then uses in-domain translation dictionaries and in-domain monolingual corpora to improve the in-domain performance. We propose an algorithm to combine these different resources in a unified framework. Experimental results indicate that our method achieves absolute improvements of 8.16 and 3.36 BLEU scores on Chinese to English translation and English to French translation respectively, as compared with the baselines using only out-of-domain corpora.

1 Introduction

In statistical machine translation (SMT), the translation process is modeled to obtain the translation $\mathbf{e}_{best}$ of the source sentence $\mathbf{f}$ by maximizing the following posterior probability (Brown et al., 1993).

$$\begin{aligned}\mathbf{e}_{best} &= \arg\max_{\mathbf{e}} p(\mathbf{e} \mid \mathbf{f}) \\ &= \arg\max_{\mathbf{e}} p(\mathbf{f} \mid \mathbf{e}) p_{LM}(\mathbf{e})\end{aligned} \quad (1)$$

State-of-the-art SMT systems are trained on large collections of bilingual corpora for the translation model $p(\mathbf{f} \mid \mathbf{e})$ and monolingual target language corpora for the language model (LM) $p_{LM}(\mathbf{e})$. The trained SMT systems are suitable for translating texts in the same domain as the training corpus. However, for some specific domains, it is difficult to obtain a bilingual corpus. In this case, the performance of SMT systems will be degraded.

Generally, it is easier to obtain in-domain monolingual corpora in either source or target language. Moreover, in some specific domains, although in-domain bilingual corpora do not exist, in-domain translation dictionaries, which usually contain domain-specific terms and their translations, are available. And even if such dictionaries are not available, it is easier to compile one than to build a bilingual corpus. Thus, in this paper, we address the problem of domain-specific SMT, where only domain-specific dictionaries and/or monolingual corpora exist. In a specific domain, there are two kinds of words: common words, which also frequently occur in out-of-domain corpora, and domain-specific words, which only occur in the specific domain. Thus, we can combine the out-of-domain bilingual corpus, the in-domain translation dictionary, and monolingual corpora for in-domain translation.

If an in-domain translation dictionary is available, we combine it with the out-of-domain translation model to improve translation quality. If an in-domain target language corpus (TLC) is available, we use it to build an in-domain language model, which can be combined with the out-of-domain language model to further improve translation quality. Moreover, if an in-domain source language corpus (SLC) is available, we automatically translate it and obtain a synthetic in-domain bilingual corpus. By adding this synthetic bilingual corpus to the training data, we rebuild the translation model to improve

©2008. Licensed under the *Creative Commons Attribution-Noncommercial-Share Alike 3.0 Unported* license (http://creativecommons.org/licenses/by-nc-sa/3.0/). Some rights reserved.

translation quality. We can repeatedly translate the in-domain source language corpus with the improved model until no more improvement can be made. This is similar to transductive learning described in (Ueffing et al., 2007).

We perform domain adaptation experiments on two tasks: one is the Chinese to English translation, using the test set released by the International Workshop on Spoken Language Translation 2006 (IWSLT 2006), and the other is the English to French translation, using the data released by the Second Workshop on Statistical Machine Translation (WMT 2007) (Callison-Burch et al., 2007).

Experimental results indicate that our method achieves absolute improvements of 8.16 and 3.36 BLEU scores on Chinese to English translation and English to French translation respectively, as compared with the baselines only using the out-of-domain corpora. The results on both translation tasks also show that the translation quality achieved by our methods is comparable to that of the method using both in-domain and out-of-domain bilingual corpora. Moreover, even if in-domain and out-of-domain bilingual corpora are available, adding an in-domain dictionary also helps to improve the translation quality.

The remainder of the paper is organized as follows. In section 2, we describe the related work. Section 3 briefly introduces the baseline MT system used in our experiments. Section 4 describes our domain adaptation method of using in-domain dictionary and monolingual corpora. And then we present the experimental results in sections 5. In the last section, we conclude this paper.

2 Related Work

Translation model and language model adaptation are usually used in domain adaptation for SMT. Language model adaptation has been widely used in speech recognition (Bacchiani and Roark, 2003). In recent years, language model adaptation has also been studied for SMT (Bulyko et al., 2007). They explored discriminative estimation of language model weights by directly optimizing machine translation performances such as BLEU score (Papineni et al., 2002). Their experiments indicated about 0.4 BLEU score improvement.

A shared task is organized as part of the Second Workshop on Statistical Machine Translation. A part of this shared task focused on domain adaptation for machine translation among European languages. Several studies investigated mixture model adaptation for both translation model and language model in SMT (Civera and Juan, 2007; Foster and Kuhn, 2007). Koehn and Schroeder (2007) investigated different adaptation methods for SMT. Their experiments indicate an absolute improvement of more than 1 BLEU score.

To enlarge the in-domain bilingual corpus, Munteanu and Marcu (2005) automatically extracted in-domain bilingual sentence pairs from comparable corpora. Adding the extracted bilingual corpus to the training data improved the performance of the MT system. In addition, Ueffing et al. (2007) explored transductive learning for SMT, where source language corpora are used to train the models. They repeatedly translated source sentences from the development set and test set. Then the generated translations are used to improve the performance of the SMT system. This kind of transductive learning can be seen as a means to adapt the SMT system to a new type of texts.

In this paper, we use an in-domain translation dictionary and/or in-domain monolingual corpora (in both source language and target language) to improve the performance of a SMT system trained on the out-of-domain corpora. Thus, our method uses these resources, instead of an in-domain bilingual corpus, to adapt a baseline system trained on the out-of-domain corpora to in-domain texts.

3 Baseline MT System

The phrase-based SMT system used in our experiments is Moses (Koehn et al., 2007). In Moses, phrase translation probabilities, reordering probabilities, and language model probabilities are combined in the log-linear model to obtain the best translation $\mathbf{e}_{best}$ of the source sentence $\mathbf{f}$:

$$\begin{aligned} \mathbf{e}_{best} &= \arg\max_{\mathbf{e}} p(\mathbf{e} \mid \mathbf{f}) \\ &\approx \arg\max_{\mathbf{e}} \sum_{m=1}^{M} \lambda_m h_m(\mathbf{e}, \mathbf{f}) \end{aligned} \tag{2}$$

The weights are set by a discriminative training method using a held-out data set as described in (Och, 2003). The models or features which are employed by the decoder are (a) one or several phrases tables, (b) one or more language models trained with SRILM toolkit (Stolcke, 2002), (c) distance-based and lexicalized distortion models, (d) word penalty, (e) phrase penalty.

Input Out-of-domain training data L_O

In-domain translation dictionary D_I

In-domain target language corpus T_I (optional)

In-domain source language corpus S_I (optional)

Begin Assign translation probabilities to D_I

If T_I is available

Training step: $\pi = \textbf{Estimate}(L_O, D_I, T_I)$, where π represents the general model.

Else

Training step: $\pi = \textbf{Estimate}(L_O, D_I)$

End if

If S_I is available

$\pi^{(0)} = \pi,\ i = 0$

Repeat

$i = i + 1$

Labeling step: Translate S_I with $\pi^{(i-1)}$ to get a synthetic bilingual corpus L_I

Training step: $\pi^{(i)} = \textbf{Re-estimate}(L_O, D_I, L_I)$

Until no more improvement can be achieved

$\pi = \pi^{(i)}$

End if

End

Output Model π for in-domain translation

Figure 1.The domain adaptation algorithm

4 The Framework

4.1 The Algorithm

The detailed information about the algorithm is shown in Figure 1. In our algorithm, a phrase table and a language model are first constructed based on the out-of-domain corpus L_O. Then probabilities are automatically assigned to the entries in the in-domain translation dictionary D_I, from which another phrase table is constructed. At last, the two phrase tables are combined. This is the procedure of the training step $\pi = \textbf{Estimate}(L_O, D_I)$.

If an in-domain target language corpus is available, we train an in-domain LM, which is combined with the out-of-domain LM. The built phrase tables and LMs are integrated in the log-linear model as described in section 3. This is the procedure of $\pi = \textbf{Estimate}(L_O, D_I, T_I)$.

Moreover, if an in-domain source language corpus is available, we use the built log-linear model to translate the in-domain source texts and obtain a synthetic bilingual corpus. And then we add the synthetic bilingual corpus into the training data to improve the current log-linear model ($\pi^{(i)} = \textbf{Re-estimate}(L_O, D_I, L_I)$). With the improved model, we repeatedly translate the in-domain source texts until no more improvement on a development set can be achieved.

4.2 Dictionary Probabilities

In general, there is no translation probability in a manually-made translation dictionary. In order to construct a phrase table, we have to assign probabilities to the entries in the dictionary.

Uniform Translation Probability: Since we have no parallel corpus to estimate the translation probabilities, we simply assign uniform probabilities to the entries in the dictionary. With this method, if a source word has n translations, then we assign $1/n$ to each translation of this phrase for all the four scores of the phrase pair.

Constant Translation Probability: For each entry in the dictionary, we assign a fixed score. In this case, the sum of the translation probability is not necessarily equal to 1.

Corpus Translation Probability: If an in-domain monolingual source corpus exists, we translate it with the method as described in Figure 1, and then estimate the translation probabilities for the entries in the dictionary. And for the entries whose translation probabilities are not estimated, we assign average probabilities that are calculated from the entries that have obtained probabilities.

4.3 Combining Phrase Tables

In the algorithm, there are two kinds of phrase tables. We need to combine them to translate the in-domain texts.

Mixture Model: The most commonly-used method is linear interpolation.

$$p(\mathsf{e} \mid \mathsf{f}) = \lambda p_I(\mathsf{e} \mid \mathsf{f}) + (1-\lambda) p_o(\mathsf{e} \mid \mathsf{f}) \quad (3)$$

Where $p_I(\mathsf{e} \mid \mathsf{f})$ and $p_o(\mathsf{e} \mid \mathsf{f})$ are the in-domain and out-of-domain translation probabilities. λ is the interpolation weight.

Discriminative Model: An alternative is to combine the two tables in the log-linear model. During translation with Moses, for each phrase in the sentence, the decoder obtains all of its translations in both phrase tables, and then uses them for translation expansion.

4.4 Combining Language Models

If an in-domain target language corpus exists, we use it to construct an in-domain language model, which is combined with the out-of-domain language model. In this paper, we investigate two combination methods: linear interpolation and log-linear interpolation.

5 Experiments

5.1 Setting

We ran experiments on two different tasks: one is the Chinese to English translation in IWSLT 2006 evaluation, and the other is the English to French domain adaptation translation in the WMT 2007 shared task.

For the Chinese to English translation task, we use the Chinese-English bilingual corpus provided by the Chinese Linguistic Data Consortium (CLDC)[2] as the out-of-domain corpus. It contains 156,840 sentence pairs, with about 3 million English words and about 5 million Chinese characters. In addition, we use the Basic Traveling Expression Corpus (BTEC) released by IWSLT 2006 (Paul, 2006) to construct an in-domain phrase table, as a comparison with that one constructed with the in-domain dictionary.

Corpora	Sentences	OOV
CLDC	156,840	89 (6.31%)
BTEC	39,953	179 (12.69%)
IWSLT06-dev4	489	NA
IWSLT06-test	500	NA

Table 1. Chinese-English corpora

Dictionaries	Entries	OOV
LDC	82,090	228 (16.16%)
in-domain	32,821	121 (8.57%)

Table 2. Chinese-English dictionaries

Corpora	Sentences	OOV
Europarl	949,410	412 (5.90%)
NC	43,060	599 (8.58%)
WMT07 dev	1,057	NA
WMT07 test	2,007	NA

Table 3. English-French corpora

Its source part and target part are separately used as the in-domain monolingual corpora in our experiments. The target parts of both CLDC and BTEC are used for language model construction (see Table 1). From the IWSLT 2006 evaluation, we choose the devset4 as our development data. Evaluation was performed on IWSLT 2006 test set. The references for the test set contain lowercase words and punctuations. The detailed information is shown in Table 1.

We use two kinds of manually-made dictionaries for comparison: one is the LDC Chinese-English Translation Lexicon Version 3.0 (LDC2002L27), and the other is the in-domain spoken language dictionary made by ourselves, which contains in-domain Chinese words and their English translations. The dictionary is manually constructed. Some entries of the dictionary are collected from phrase books. Some of them are collected from the general-domain dictionaries. And then, the entries are filtered and modified by a Chinese native speaker specialized in English. The detailed information is shown in Table 2. If a source word has two translations, it is counted as two entries. The OOV rates of the test set uncovered by the LDC dictionary and the in-domain dictionary are 16.16% and 8.57%, respectively.

For the English to French translation task, the out-of-domain corpus is the Europarl corpus distributed for the shared task of WMT 2007 (Callison-Burch et al., 2007)[3]. We filter the sentence pairs whose lengths are above 40 words. For the

[2] http://www.chineseldc.org/EN/index.htm. The catalog number is CLDC-LAC-2003-004. It is a balanced corpus containing sentence pairs in multiple domains.

[3] http://www.statmt.org/wmt07/shared-task.html

in-domain corpus, we use the News Commentary (NC) corpus distributed in WMT 2007. We also use the same development set and test set in the domain adaptation shared task (see Table 3). We manually built an in-domain English-French dictionary according to the in-domain bilingual corpus, which includes 26,821 entries. It contains in-domain English words and their French translations. The OOV rate of the test set uncovered by this dictionary is 22.34%.

5.2 Evaluation Measures

To perform phrase-based SMT, we use the Moses decoder and its support training scripts. We run the decoder with its default settings and then use Moses' implementation of minimum error rate training (Och, 2003) to tune the feature weights on the development set. Translation quality was evaluated using BLEU score (Papineni et al., 2002).

5.3 Results on Chinese-English Translation

Translation Dictionary

With the out-of-domain bilingual corpus, we train an out-of-domain phrase table. With the in-domain translation dictionary, we construct in-domain phrase tables by assigning different translation probabilities with two different methods: uniform and constant. For the constant translation probability, we set the score using the development set. In our experiments, we set it to 1. We use the target part of the out-of-domain corpus to train a language model[4].

With two phrase tables, we combine them in a linear or log-linear method as described in section 4.3. In our experimental results, log-linear translation models outperform the linear models (16.38 vs. 15.12), where the entries of the dictionary are assigned with the constant translation probabilities. Thus, we will use log-linear models for phrase table combination in the following experiments.

Another method to combine the out-of-domain corpus and the translation dictionary is to add the in-domain dictionary into the training corpus. In this case, only one phrase table is trained.

Table 4 describes the results using the out-of-domain corpus and the in-domain dictionary. The baseline method only uses the out-of-domain corpus to train a phrase table. Then we use both the out-of-domain corpus and the in-domain dictionary. The results indicate that adding an in-domain dictionary significantly improves the translation quality by 2.79 BLEU score[5]. The methods using the dictionary as a phrase table outperform the method adding it to the training corpus. And the method using constant translation probabilities significantly outperforms that using the uniform translation probabilities.

Methods	Resources Used	BLEU(%)
baseline	out-of-domain corpus	13.59
baseline + dictionary	+dictionary as corpus	15.52
	+uniform prob.	16.00
	+constant prob.	16.38
	+corpus prob.	16.72

Table 4. Translation results of using out-of-domain corpus and in-domain dictionary

For comparison, we also assign corpus probabilities to the entries in the dictionary by translating the source part of the BTEC corpus with the method described in Section 4.2. This also improves the translation quality.

In-Domain Monolingual Corpora

We use the target part of the BTEC corpus to train an in-domain LM. We combine it with the out-of-domain LM in two methods: linear interpolation and log-linear interpolation. The experimental results indicate that linear interpolation outperforms log-linear interpolation (17.16 vs. 16.20). Thus, we will use linear interpolation for LMs in all of the following experiments.

Table 5 describes the results of using the interpolated language model. As compared with the results in Table 4, it can be seen that adding the in-domain language model greatly improves the translation quality. It achieves an absolute improvement of 3.57 BLEU score as compared with the baseline model. If the in-domain translation dictionary is used, the translation quality is further improved by 4 BLEU score.

If the in-domain source language data is available, we translate it and obtain a synthetic bilingual corpus. Then we perform transductive learning as described in Figure 1. The difference between our method and that in (Ueffing et al., 2007) is that we translate a larger in-domain source corpus, and we use 1-best translation

[4] We also used LDC English Gigaword to train a large language model. However, this language model did not improve the translation quality.

[5] We use the method described in (Koehn and Monz, 2006) for significance test. In this paper, significant improvement means method A outperforms method B on a significance level of no less than 95%.

Methods	Models	Resources used	BLEU(%)
baseline	Model 1	out-of-domain corpus	13.59
baseline + TLC	Model 2	+ in-domain TLC	17.16
baseline + TLC + dictionary	Model 3	+ in-domain TLC + dictionary (uniform prob.)	20.83
	Model 4	+ in-domain TLC + dictionary (constant prob.)	21.16
transductive learning	Model 5	+ in-domain SLC	15.98
	Model 6	+ in-domain SLC and TLC	18.19
	Model 7	+ in-domain SLC and TLC + dictionary (corpus prob.)	21.75

Table 5. Translation results of using in-domain resources

Dictionary types		Entries	OOV	BLEU(%)
general domain	LDC	82,090	228 (16.16%)	19.11
in-domain	manual	32,821	121 (8.57%)	21.16
	extracted	11,765	330 (23.39%)	19.88
combined	LDC + manual	106,572	45 (3.19%)	21.34
	LDC + extracted	95,660	202 (14.31%)	20.49

Table 6. Comparison of different dictionaries

result with full re-training. The results indicate that transductive learning improves translation quality in all cases. For example, Model 5 achieves an absolute improvement of 2.39 BLEU score over Model 1, and Model 6 achieves 1.03 BLEU score improvement over Model 2. Model 7 uses the in-domain dictionary with corpus translation probabilities, which are obtained from the phrase table trained with the synthetic bilingual corpus. The results indicate that Model 7 outperforms Model 4, with a significant improvement of 0.59 BLEU score.

The results also indicate that when only the in-domain monolingual corpus is used, the translation quality is improved by 4.6 BLEU score (Model 6 vs. Model 1). By adding the in-domain dictionary, the translation quality is further improved, achieving an absolute improvement of 8.16 BLEU score (Model 7 vs. Model 1).

Comparison of Different Dictionaries

We compare the effects of different dictionaries with concern to the translation quality. Besides the manually-made in-domain dictionary, we use other two dictionaries: the LDC dictionary and an automatically built dictionary, which is extracted from the BTEC corpus. This extracted dictionary only contains Chinese words and their translations. The extraction method is as follows:

- Build a phrase table with the in-domain bilingual corpus.
- Filter those phrase pairs whose values are below a threshold as described in (Wu and Wang, 2007).
- From the filtered phrase table, extract the Chinese words and their translations.
- Assign constant translation probabilities to the entries of the extracted dictionary.

Table 6 shows the translation results. All of the methods use the out-of-domain corpus, the in-domain target language corpus, and the corresponding translation dictionaries with constant translation probabilities. The results indicate that using the general-domain dictionary also improves translation quality, achieving an improvement of about 2 BLEU score as compared with Model 2 in Table 5. It can also be seen that the in-domain dictionaries significantly outperform the LDC dictionary although the extracted dictionary has a higher OOV rate than the LDC dictionary. Further analysis shows that the LDC dictionary does not contain the in-domain translations of some words. Results also indicate that combining the two kinds of dictionaries helps to slightly improve translation quality since the OOV rates are reduced.

Comparison with In-domain Bilingual Corpus

The aim of this section is to investigate whether the in-domain dictionary helps to improve translation quality when an in-domain bilingual corpus is available. And we will also compare the translation results with those of the methods only using in-domain dictionaries and monolingual corpora.

To train the in-domain translation model, we use the BTEC corpus. The translation results are

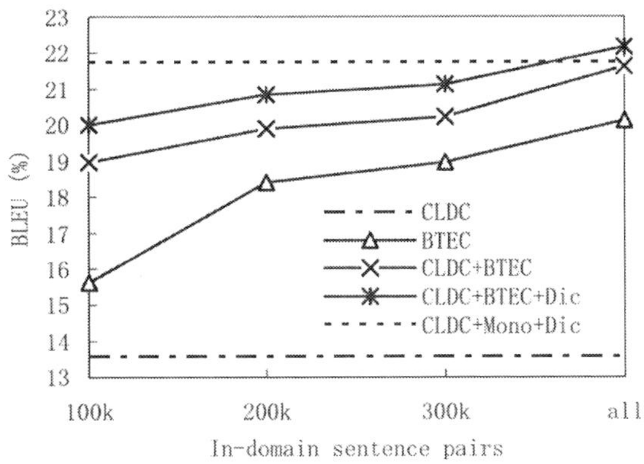

Figure 2. Comparison of different methods using different resources.

shown in Figure 2. CLDC and BTEC represent the methods that only use the out-of-domain and the in-domain corpus, respectively. The method "CLDC+BTEC" uses linear interpolation of the phrase tables and LMs trained with CLDC and BTEC. "Dic" means using the in-domain dictionary, and "Mono" means using in-domain source and target language corpora.

From the results, it can be seen that (a) even if an in-domain bilingual corpus exists, the in-domain dictionary also helps to improve the translation quality, as "CLDC+BTEC+Dic" achieves an improvement of about 1 BLEU score in comparison with "CLDC+BTEC"; (b) the method "CLDC+Mono+Dic", which uses both the in-domain monolingual corpora and the in-domain dictionary, achieves high translation quality. It achieves slightly higher translation quality than "CLDC+BTEC" that uses the in-domain bilingual corpus (21.75 vs. 21.62) and achieves slightly lower translation quality than "CLDC+BTEC+Dic" (21.75 vs. 22.05). But the differences are not significant. This indicates that our method using an in-domain dictionary and in-domain monolingual corpora is effective for domain adaptation.

5.4 Results on English-French Translation

We perform the same experiments for English to French translation. Table 7 describes the domain adaptation results. "Interpolated LM" means that we use the target part of the NC corpus to train an in-domain LM, and then linearly interpolate it with the out-of-domain LM trained with the Europarl corpus. The results indicate that using an in-domain target corpus significantly improves the translation quality, achieving an improvement of 2.19 BLEU score (from 25.44 to 27.63).

Methods	Out-of-domain LM	Interpolated LM
Europarl	25.44	27.63
Europarl+Dic	26.24	28.22
transductive learning	-	28.80
Europarl+NC	-	29.19
Europarl+NC+Dic	-	29.41

Table 7. Translation results of using in-domain dictionary and monolingual corpora

Using the in-domain translation dictionary improves translation quality in all cases, even when the in-domain bilingual corpus is used (from 29.19 to 29.41).

We also perform transductive learning with the source part of the NC corpus. The model used to translate the corpus is that one created by "Europarl+Dic" in Table 7. The results indicate that transductive learning significantly improves translation quality, achieving an absolute improvement of 0.58 BLEU score (from 28.22 to 28.80).

In summary, using an in-domain dictionary and in-domain monolingual corpora improves the translation quality by 3.36 BLEU score (from 25.44 to 28.80). Although the translation quality is slightly lower than that method of using both in-domain and out-of-domain bilingual corpora, the difference is not statistically significant.

6 Conclusion

This paper proposed a domain adaptation approach for statistical machine translation. This approach first used an out-of-domain corpus to build a baseline system, and then used an in-domain translation dictionary and in-domain monolingual corpora to adapt it to the in-domain texts. The contribution of this paper lies in the following points:

- We proposed a method to integrate a domain-specific translation dictionary into a phrase-based SMT system for domain adaptation.
- We investigated the way of using in-domain monolingual corpora in either source or target language, together with the in-domain translation dictionary, to improve the translation quality of a baseline system.

We performed experiments on both Chinese to English and English to French translation. Experimental results on Chinese to English translation indicate that all of the in-domain resources are useful to improve in-domain translation quality, with an overall improvement of 8.16 BLEU score as compared with the baseline trained with out-of-domain corpora. Results on English to French translation also show that using in-domain translation dictionaries and in-domain monolingual corpora is effective for domain adaptation, achieving an absolute improvement of 3.36 BLEU score. And the results on both translation tasks indicate that the translation quality achieved by our methods is comparable with that of the method using both in-domain and out-of-domain bilingual corpora. Moreover, even if in-domain and out-of-domain bilingual corpora are available, adding an in-domain dictionary also helps to improve the translation quality.

In the future work, we will investigate to assign translation probabilities to the dictionaries using comparable in-domain corpora and examine its effect on the MT performance. And we will also examine the effect of an in-domain dictionary on transductive learning in more details.

References

Bacchiani, Michiel and Brian Roark. 2003. Unsupervised Language Model Adaptation. In *Proc. of the 28th International Conference on Acoustics, Speech, and Signal Processing (ICASSP-2003)*, pages 224-227.

Brown, Peter F., Stephen A. Della Pietra, Vincent J. Della Pietra, and Robert L. Mercer. 1993. The Mathematics of Statistical Machine Translation: Parameter Estimation. *Computational Linguistics*, 19(2): 263-311.

Bulyko, Ivan, Spyros Matsoukas, Richard Schwartz, Long Nguyen, and John Makhoul. 2007. Language Model Adaptation in Machine Translation from Speech. In *Proc. of the 32nd International Conference on Acoustics, Speech, and Signal Processing (ICASSP-2007)*, pages 117-120.

Callison-Burch, Chris, Cameron Fordyce, Philipp Koehn, Christof Monz, and Josh Schroeder. 2007. (Meta-) Evaluation of Machine Translation. In *Proc. of the Second Workshop on Statistical Machine Translation*, pages 136-158.

Civera, Jorge and Alfons Juan. 2007. Domain Adaptation in Statistical Machine Translation with Mixture Modelling. In *Proc. of the Second Workshop on Statistical Machine Translation*, pages 177-180.

Foster, George and Roland Kuhn. 2007. Mixture-Model Adaptation for SMT. In *Proc. of the Second Workshop on Statistical Machine Translation*, pages 128-135.

Koehn, Philipp and Christof Monz. 2006. Manual and Automatic Evaluation of Machine Translation between European Languages. In *Proc. of the HLT-NAACL 2006 Workshop on Statistical Machine Translation*, pages 102-121.

Koehn, Philipp, Hieu Hoang, Alexanda Birch, Chris Callison-Burch, Marcello Federico, Nicola Bertoldi, Brooke Cowan, Wade Shen, Christine Moran, Richard Zens, Chris Dyer, Ondrej Bojar, Alexandra Constantin, and Evan Herbst. 2007. Moses: Open Source Toolkit for Statistical Machine Translation. In *Proc. of the 45th Annual Meeting of the Association for Computational Linguistics (ACL-2007), demonstration session*, pages 177-180.

Koehn, Philipp and Josh Schroeder. 2007. Experiments in Domain Adaptation for Statistical Machine Translation. In *Proc. of the Second Workshop on Statistical Machine Translation*, pages 224-227.

Munteanu, Dragos Stefan, and Daniel Marcu. 2005. Improving Machine Translation Performance by Exploiting Non-Parallel Corpora. *Computational Linguistics*, 31(4): 477-504.

Och, Franz Josef. 2003. Minimum Error Rate Training in Statistical Machine Translation. In *Proc. of the 41st Annual Meeting of the Association for Computational Linguistics (ACL-2003)*, pages 160-167.

Papineni, Kishore, Salim Roukos, Todd Ward, and Wei-Jing Zhu. 2002. BLEU: a Method for Automatic Evaluation of Machine Translation. In *Proc. of the 40th Annual Meeting of the Association of Computational Linguistics (ACL-2002)*, pages 311-318.

Paul, Michael. 2006. Overview of the IWSLT 2006 Evaluation Campaign. In *Proc. of the International Workshop on Spoken Language Translation (IWSLT-2006)*, pages 1-15.

Stolcke, Andrea. 2002. SRILM -- an Extensible Language Modeling Toolkit. In *Proc. of International Conference on Spoken Language Processing (ICSLP-2002)*, pages 901-904.

Ueffing, Nicola, Gholamreza Haffari, and Anoop Sarkar. 2007. Transductive Learning for Statistical Machine Translation. In *Proc. of 45th Annual Meeting of the Association of Computational Linguistics (ACL-2007)*, pages 25-32.

Wu, Hua and Haifeng Wang. 2007. Comparative Study of Word Alignment Heuristics and Phrase-Based SMT. In *Proc. of Machine Translation Summit XI*, pages 507-514.

Exploiting Graph Structure for Accelerating the Calculation of Shortest Paths in Wordnets

Holger Wunsch
Collaborative Research Center 441 "Linguistic Data Structures"
University of Tübingen, Germany
wunsch@sfs.uni-tuebingen.de

Abstract

This paper presents an approach for substantially reducing the time needed to calculate the shortest paths between all concepts in a wordnet. The algorithm exploits the unique "star-like" topology of wordnets to cut down on time-expensive calculations performed by algorithms to solve the all-pairs shortest path problem in general graphs. The algorithm was applied to two wordnets of two different languages: Princeton WordNet (Fellbaum, 1998) for English, and GermaNet (Kunze and Lemnitzer, 2002), the German language wordnet. For both wordnets, the time needed for finding all shortest paths was brought down from several days to a matter of minutes.

1 Introduction

Significant effort has been devoted in linguistic research to the problem of determining the semantic distance[1] between two concepts. Many of the approaches that were developed to provide a solution for the task use wordnets as their basic knowledge resource. Budanitsky and Hirst (2006) present an extensive number of approaches for determining lexical semantic relatedness based on the Princeton WordNet (Fellbaum, 1998). A large number of these solutions have in common that at some point in the calculation, the length of the shortest path that connects the two concepts in question has to be taken into account. The length of the shortest path between two concepts is thus a vital piece of information in virtually any approach for determining their semantic distance.

From a computer science perspective, a wordnet is a directed graph. The nodes in the graph correspond to the concepts that are stored in the wordnet. Two nodes are connected by an edge if there exists a semantic relation between the two concepts that correspond to the nodes. The edges are directed, reflecting the directedness of semantic relations in wordnets, such as the relation of hypernymy. The problem of finding the shortest path between two nodes in a graph has been well studied in computer science. Sedgewick (1990) presents two algorithms:

- *Dijkstra's algorithm* finds the shortest path between two concepts in quadratic time, and is extensible to find the shortest paths between all concepts in cubic time.
- The *Floyd-Warshall algorithm*, which is very easy to implement, solves the all-pairs shortest path problem in cubic time as well. The Floyd-Warshall algorithm served as the baseline algorithm for this paper.

Both algorithms operate on general directed graphs. The structure of a directed graph is sketched in figure 1. Given two nodes, there exist multiple different paths that connect the two nodes. In figure 1, in order to get from L to D, one could take the path L–G–E–D, but also L–G–C–A–F–E–D, and several other paths. An algorithm that looks for the shortest path must deal with this situation and basically be able to consider all alternatives.

Computing of the length of all shortest paths with the Floyd-Warshall algorithm takes about 120

©2008. Licensed under the *Creative Commons Attribution-Noncommercial-Share Alike 3.0 Unported* license (http://creativecommons.org/licenses/by-nc-sa/3.0/). Some rights reserved.

[1] see Budanitsky and Hirst (2006) for a critical discussion of the term "semantic distance".

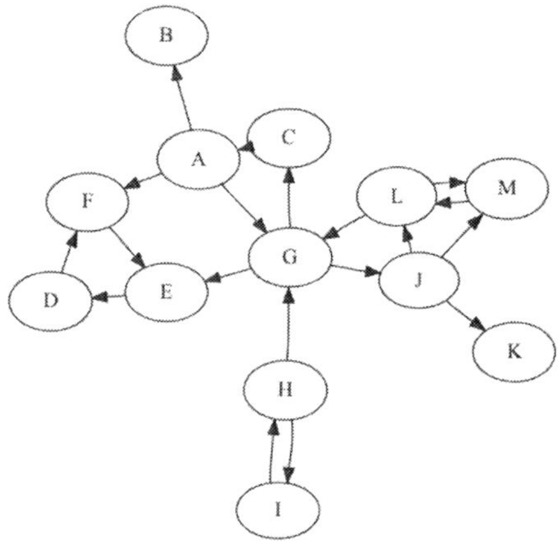

Figure 1: Schematic structure of a general graph. Example taken from Sedgewick (1990).

hours for GermaNet, using a compiler-optimized C implementation on a machine equipped with two AMD Opteron processors. GermaNet, which contains 53,312 synsets[2] in its current release 5, is of moderate size, compared to the Princeton WordNet, which contains more than twice as many synsets. The execution time of 120 hours is acceptable if the wordnet does not change, and the shortest paths are calculated once and then kept for later use. However, when the task involves the modification of the wordnet itself and the repeated recalculation of all shortest paths, this is unacceptable. In such cases the execution time will most likely prohibit research involving such techniques.

It has been shown that there is no faster way for solving the all-pairs shortest paths problem in general graphs. However, the structure of wordnets is somewhat different to that of a general directed graph. It can best be described to be similar to that of a star, as depicted in figure 2. In the middle, there is a unique top node that dominates all other nodes[3]. In the center area around the top node, the synsets represent general concepts. Closer to the fringe, the synsets become more and more specific. A typical configuration in this region would be a biological taxonomy of animals, or specific kinds of vehicles. The number of such specialized synsets in the outer regions of the wordnet outweighs the number of core concepts by several orders of magnitude. In other words, the majority of synsets in a wordnet is part of tree structures that are arranged around a relatively small core graph.

In the remainder of this paper, we will present an approach to solving the all-pairs shortest paths problem in wordnets that is superior in execution time by consistently exploiting this specific structure of wordnets.

2 Finding Paths In a Wordnet

We implemented the Floyd-Warshall algorithm as our baseline. The Floyd-Warshall algorithm uses a dynamic programming approach. The basic idea is to find all shortest paths by first computing and storing the paths lengths between nodes that are close to each other, and then moving on to longer paths by combining the results of the shorter paths. The Floyd-Warshall algorithm uses a matrix that contains for each pair of nodes the length of the shortest path that connects the two nodes. The matrix is initialized by setting the length of the shortest path between any two adjacent nodes to 1[4]. All other fields are set to ∞ (which indicates that no path has been found (yet)). Then the algorithm checks for any pair of nodes x and y whether there exists a node z such that the path from x to y that runs along z is shorter than the path between x and y that has been found so far.

Floyd-Warshall Algorithm

N: set of nodes
p: matrix that contains the lengths of the shortest path between any node x and $y \in N$.

Initialization Step
for all $x, y \in N$ **do**
  if $neighbors(x, y)$ **then**
    $p_{xy} := 1$
  else
    $p_{xy} := \infty$
  end if
end for

[2] A *synset* is a set of words that are synonymous. Throughout this paper, we will use the term *synset* synonymously to *nodes in a graph*, since the relevant relations (which are represented by edges in the graph) hold between synsets.

[3] In most wordnets such as Princeton WordNet or GermaNet, there is usually no unique top node. Instead, there is a set of most general concepts, called *unique beginners*. In the example in figure 2, the unique beginners would be the synsets s1, s3, s11, s15, and s23. The algorithm presented here requires the wordnet to be a connected graph, therefore we stipulate an explicit artificial top node.

[4] The Floyd-Warshall algorithm can also be used to calculate shortest paths in weighted graphs in which case the matrix would be initialized with the weights of the edges between adjacent nodes. We will focus on unweighted graphs in this paper.

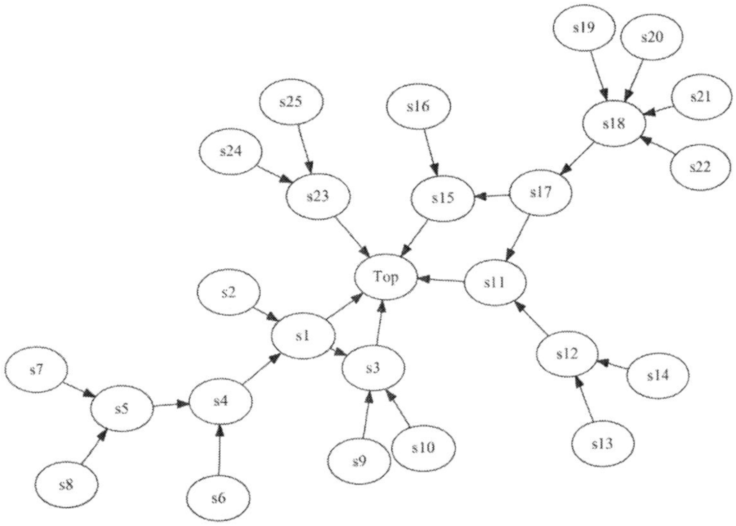

Figure 2: Schematic star-like structure of a wordnet.

Shortest Path Calculation
for all $z \in N$ **do**
  for all $x, y \in N$ **do**
    $p_{xy} := min(p_{xy}, p_{xz} + p_{zy})$
  end for
end for

Since the *shortest* of all possible paths must be found, the Floyd-Warshall algorithm has to check for *any* node z if the path x–z–y is the shortest. Returning to the example in figure 2, the shortest path between x = s1 and y = s16 is s1–Top–s15–s16. The Floyd-Warshall algorithm also considers the other possible paths, such as s1–**s3**–Top–s15–s16 or s1–Top–**s11**–**s17**–s15–s16, which are eventually discarded because they turn out to be not the shortest connection.

Now consider a path such as the one illustrated in figure 3, which is the shortest undirected path between the synsets s8 and s20[5]. In order to find this shortest path, the Floyd-Warshall algorithm would check *all possible combinations* of nodes x–z–y in order to find a potential shorter alternative. To the human reader it is obvious that this is an unnecessary amount of work: there is only one path that leads from s8 to s1, because the part of the wordnet rooted in s4 is in fact a *tree*, and paths connecting two nodes in trees are always unique. The same is true for the structure rooted in s18. Moreover, there is a unique link from s4 to s1, and from s18 to s17. The synsets s1 and s17 are part of the core structure of the wordnet with higher density. Here, between s1 and s17 there do exist more than one paths which must all be considered by the path finding algorithm.

The complexity of the Floyd-Warshall algorithm results from the necessity of considering all possible paths through a general graph in order to find the shortest one. Wordnets are graphs – but, as explained above, they have a very special structure: There is a core graph consisting of a limited number of synsets, but the majority of all synsets is arranged in tree structures that are attached to the core graph, which gives wordnets the star-like structure described earlier.

This structure, which is specific to wordnets, can be exploited such that expensive calculations are only performed where necessary – in the core graph of the wordnet – while specialized cheaper calculations are used in the outer parts.

3 Structure-Adapted Shortest Path Search

The observations about the structure of wordnets and the nature of general algorithms to find all shortest paths lead to the conclusion that an algorithm that is adapted to the specific structure of wordnets should be superior over general algorithms with respect to execution time. In this section, we will present such a structure-adapted approach. It operates in two stages: In the first stage,

[5] Since the edges in the graph correspond to the hypernymy relations in the wordnet, they all point towards the top node. In order to get from s8 to s20, one must first follow the path up to the top node along the hypernymy axis, and then down to s20 in the opposite direction. Therefore, paths are undirected.

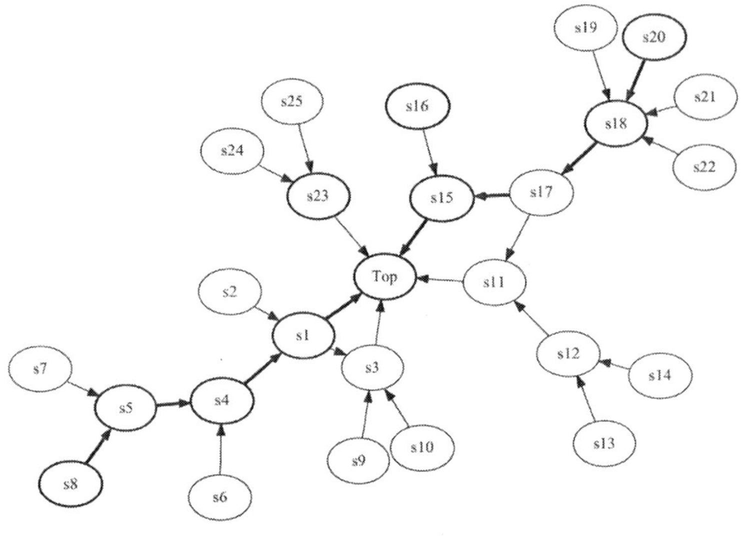

Figure 3: A path through the wordnet.

all nodes in the wordnet are classified whether they are part of the core graph or a peripheral tree structure. The second stage is the shortest path search proper, which uses the information about the structure of the wordnet that was acquired in the first stage.

3.1 Stage 1: Node classification

In the first stage, the algorithm determines whether a node belongs to the graph proper which constitutes the core network, or to a tree structure in the periphery. The algorithm classifies nodes in four classes, which are illustrated in figure 4.

1. **Inner nodes**: Inner nodes belong to the graph in the center of the network. A node is an inner node if it has more than one parent node, or if one of its children is an inner node. In figure 4, inner nodes have a white background.

2. **Root nodes**: A root node, as suggested by its name, is the root node of a tree. Root nodes have a unique parent node, which must be an inner node. In figure 4, root nodes have a dark gray background, and thick borders.

3. **Tree nodes**: Tree nodes are part of a tree, i.e. they have one unique parent node. This parent node must either be a root node, or a tree node as well. In figure 4, tree nodes have a dark gray background (and thin borders).

4. **Leaf nodes**: Leaf nodes have a unique parent node, which must be an inner node. They do not have any child nodes. As such, leaf nodes are actually a special case of a root node. But for performance reasons, they will be handled separately from root nodes. In figure 4, leaf nodes have a light gray background.

Two remarks are in order. The tree structures referred to in this classification rely on a well defined parent-child relation. The hypernymy relation, which is the only relation between synsets we consider in this paper, is a directed relation that satisfies this property: if synset x is a hypernym of synset y, then x is a parent node of y.

The difference between the terms *tree node* and *leaf node* may seem a little arbitrary – considering for example s8, which is a tree node, and s9, which is a leaf node. Both nodes do not have child nodes. However, from a performance perspective, it is advantageous to treat leaf nodes and tree nodes differently in the algorithm, which is why two different nodes types are assumed.

3.2 Stage 2: Shortest Path Search

The second stage is the actual pathfinding step. The underlying basic idea is to *split* the calculation: Consider the sample path in figure 3 between synsets s8 and s20. This path runs through three regions of the wordnet. The synsets in the first part of the path, s8-s5-s4 all belong to the tree that is rooted in synset s4. Then the path enters the core

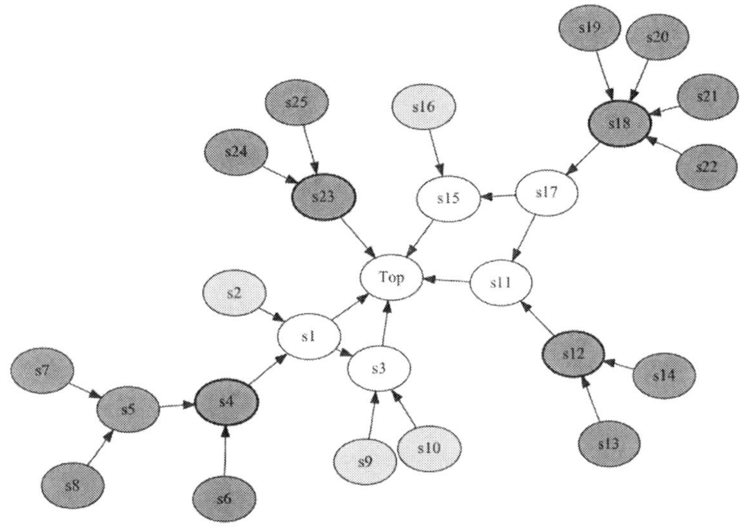

Figure 4: Node classes. White: inner nodes; dark gray: tree nodes; dark gray with thick border: root nodes; light gray: leaf nodes.

graph and runs along s1-Top-s15-s17[6]. The third part of the path is s18-s20. Again, the corresponding synsets are members of a tree whose root is s18.

The important point is that for any part of a path that runs though a tree, this is the *only possible* path through the tree. A general algorithm for finding the shortest path out of a set of multiple possible paths is not necessary here. This way, it is possible to restrict the application of general but time-expensive algorithms to the area of the wordnet where this is needed – the core of the network, while elsewhere it is sufficient to just determine the length of a path through a tree, a task which can be solved very efficiently.

Returning to our example, the algorithm splits the calculation of the shortest path between s8 and s20 as follows: Both s8 and s20 are part of a tree, as determined in step 1. The root of the tree that s8 is a member of is s4. The length of the path between s2 and s4 is 2. s4's parent node is s1. Root nodes have a unique parent node by definition. Therefore we know that only s1 can be the next node on the path, and its distance is 1, since s4 and s1 are neighbors. So, the length of the path up to s1 is 3. In the same fashion, the length of the other part of the path that is located in a tree, the path between s20 and s17, can be computed. The length of this part is 2. Now there remains the part between node s1 and s17. This part of the path runs through the core graph. Here, a general algorithm for finding shortest paths, such as the Floyd-Warshall algorithm, must be used to compute the path's length. The length of the shortest possible path within this region turns out to be 3. Now the lengths of all parts of the path have been determined – and the total length of the shortest path is just the sum of the three parts, which is 8.

[6]there are actually two possible paths of the same length (8) – the other possible path would be the one that runs along synset s11.

4 Implementation

This section will present pseudo-code for the two stages of structure-adapted shortest path search.

4.1 Stage 1: Node classification

Stage 1 explores a wordnet and classifies every node whether it is an inner node, or a root, tree, or leaf node. The procedure starts out by classifying as leaf nodes all nodes that are childless and that have one unique parent node. Note however that the definition of a leaf node requires that its parent node be an inner node. This constraint can not be checked at this point, since information about inner nodes is not yet available. Therefore the check is postponed until later.

Next, any node that has more than one parent node is classified as an inner node. The transitive closure of all of this node's parent nodes is classified as inner nodes as well.

The remaining nodes that have not been classified so far are either root or tree nodes. A node is a root node if its parent node is an inner node, otherwise it is a tree node.

The last step is to check the constraint on leaf nodes which has been postponed. As stated in the definition, leaf nodes are childless and have an inner node as parent. Nodes with no children whose parent node is either a root node or a tree node are *not* leaf nodes, but rather tree nodes. Thus, each potential leaf node is visited to ensure that its parent node is in fact an inner node in which case the classification as a leaf node remains unchanged. Otherwise, the node is reclassified as tree node.

The pseudocode of the node classification algorithm is listed below.

Node Classification Algorithm[7]

```
N: set of nodes
Node classes: inner, leaf, root, tree, undefined
Classify leaf nodes
for all n ∈ N do
  if |children(n)| = 0 ∧ |parents(n)| = 1 then
    assign_class(n, leaf)
  end if
end for
Classify inner nodes
for all n ∈ N do
  if |parents(n)| > 1 then
    if class(n) ≠ inner then
      assign_class(n, inner)
      {All parent nodes of inner nodes are inner nodes as well}
      for all m ∈ parents*(n) do
        assign_class(m, inner)
      end for
    end if
  end if
end for
Classify root and tree nodes
for all n ∈ N do
  if class(n) = undefined then
    if class(parents(n)[0]) = inner then
      assign_class(n, root)
    else
      assign_class(n, tree)
    end if
  end if
end for
Reclassify leaf nodes as tree nodes if they are children of tree nodes
for all n ∈ N do
  if class(n) = leaf then
    if class(parents(n)[0]) = root ∨ class(parents(n)[0]) = leaf then
      assign_class(n, tree)
    end if
  end if
end for
```

[7]**Notes on the notation:** $parents(n)$ and $children(n)$ are functions that return a list of all parent or child nodes of the node n. $parents(n)[0]$ returns the first node in the list of parent nodes of n. $parents^*(n)$ is the transitive closure of all parent nodes of n. $|parents(n)|$ is the number of parent nodes of n.

4.2 Stage 2: Finding Shortest Paths

The actual calculation of shortest paths takes place in stage 2. In order to calculate the shortest paths between two nodes x and y, two main cases are considered.

4.2.1 x and y do not belong to the same tree

x and y do not belong to the same tree if the root nodes of the trees that x and y are members of are different: $root(x) \neq root(y)$.

The path from x to y is then split into three parts:

- l_{xi_x}: the length of the subpath from x to the first inner node i_x on the path.
- l_{yi_y}: the length of the subpath from y to the first inner node i_y on the path.
- $l_{i_xi_y}$: the length of the subpath from i_x to i_y, which runs through the core.

The following cases are considered by the algorithm:

1. **x is an inner node**: $i_x = x$, and $l_{xi_x} = 0$.
2. **x is a tree node**: l_{xi_x} is the length of the path from x to the root node of the tree r_x, plus 1 to get from r_x to i_x: $l_{xi_x} := l_{xr_x} + 1$.
3. **x is a leaf node or a root node**: l_{xi_x} is 1.
4. **y is an inner node**: $i_y = y$, and $l_{yi_y} = 0$.
5. **y is a tree node**: l_{yi_y} is the length of the path from y to the root node of the tree r_y, plus 1 to get from r_y to i_y: $l_{yi_y} := l_{yr_y} + 1$.
6. **y is a leaf node or a root node**: l_{yi_y} is 1.

The length of the path $l_{i_x i_y}$ (the path running through the core graph) is calculated using the Floyd-Warshall algorithm, that is $l_{i_x i_y} = p_{i_x i_y}$ (see the description of the Floyd-Warshall algorithm above).

The total length of the shortest path is then $l_{xy} := l_{xi_x} + l_{i_x i_y} + l_{yi_y}$.

4.2.2 x and y belong to the same tree

This is a special case that is treated differently from all other cases. Let z be the lowest node in the tree that dominates both x and y (where z may be equal to x or y). Then $l_{xy} = l_{xz} + l_{yz}$.

Shortest Paths Algorithm

Input:
Two nodes $x, y \in N$.
Path matrix p for nodes in the core graph as calculated by Floyd-Warshall

Output:
The length of the shortest path between x and y, l_{xy}.
if $((class(x) = root \vee class(x) = tree) \wedge (class(y) = root \vee class(y) = tree)) \wedge root(x) = root(y)$ **then**
  First case: x and y belong to the same tree
  Let $z \in S$ be the lowest common subsumer of x and y.
  $l_{xy} := l_{xz} + l_{yz}$
  return l_{xy}
else
  Second case: x and y do not belong to the same tree
  $i_x := x$;
  $i_y := y$;
  if $class(x) = tree$ **then**
    $r_x := root(x)$
    $l_{xi_x} := l_{xr_x} + 1$
  else if $class(x) = root \vee class(x) = leaf$ **then**
    $l_{xi_x} := 1$
  else
    $l_{xi_x} := 0$
  end if
  if $class(y) = tree$ **then**
    $r_y := root(y)$
    $l_{yi_y} := l_{yr_y} + 1$
  else if $class(y) = root \vee class(y) = leaf$ **then**
    $l_{yi_y} := 1$
  else
    $l_{yi_y} := 0$
  end if
  $l_{xy} := l_{xi_x} + l_{i_x i_y} + l_{yi_y}$
end if

5 Experiments and Results

5.1 The Data

In order to assess the performance of structure adapted path search, we experimented with two different wordnets. For English, we looked at Princeton WordNet (Fellbaum, 1998) in its current release 3, which contains 117,659 synsets. Only 4,250 of these synsets belong to the core network. The remaining 113,410 nodes are members of peripheral tree structures, which amounts to 96 % of all nodes.

Furthermore, we applied the approach to GermaNet (Kunze and Lemnitzer, 2002) for German. The architecture of GermaNet is modelled after Princeton WordNet and is largely compatible. GermaNet, in its current release 5.0, contains 53,312 synsets. Out of these, 8,728 synsets are members of the core of the network (i.e. the part of the network that is a graph proper). The remaining 44,273 synsets are part of peripheral tree structures (or leaf nodes). Hence, 83% of the synsets in GermaNet are part of substructures that do not require a general algorithm for calculating shortest paths.

The topology of GermaNet is thus slightly different than that of WordNet. The fact that more nodes belong to the core graph indicates that GermaNet's density with respect to the hypernymy relation is higher than the density of WordNet on the level of the more abstract concepts.

5.2 Application of the Algorithm

We conducted our experiments on a machine equipped with two AMD Opteron 250 processors running at 2.4 GHz and 8 GB of main memory.

For the path-finding stage, we implemented two C programs. Both operate on the same input. Both programs were compiled using gcc's `-O3` option for maximum optimization.

The first program only used the Floyd-Warshall algorithm – the node classes were effectively ignored. For WordNet, the estimated processing time was at least 35 days. This value was computed by interpolating the time that had passed to process 15,000 synsets. At this point, the tests were aborted. Since Floyd-Warshall becomes

Princeton WordNet	
Synsets	117,659
Inner nodes	4,250
Root nodes	7,174
Tree nodes	56,532
Leaf nodes	49,704
Node classification time	ca. 1 second
Floyd-Warshall path search	> 35 days
Structure-adapted path search	9 minutes
GermaNet	
Synsets	53,312
Inner nodes	8,728
Root nodes	4,641
Tree nodes	18,949
Leaf nodes	20,683
Node classification time	1.2 seconds
Floyd-Warshall path search	120 hours
Structure-adapted path search	40 minutes

Table 1: Structure-adapted path search – Summary of results

slower the more nodes have been processed, this value is likely to be even higher. GermaNet contains only half of the synsets, and the Floyd-Warshall algorithm completed in 120 hours[8]. The result, a matrix of 53,312×53,312 elements, containing the lengths of the shortest paths between all nodes, was written to a binary file whose size was roughly 3 GB.

In the second program, we implemented the structure-adapted shortest path search approach. For calculating shortest paths in the core graph area of the network, we used the same implementation of the Floyd-Warshall algorithm as in the first program. With the same input data and the same machine, we were able to bring the execution time down to 40 minutes for GermaNet, and only 9 minutes for WordNet. This includes creating the output file, which had the same binary format as the one generated by the first program. The difference in processing time between WordNet and GermaNet stems from the smaller core graph in WordNet, which allows for even more nodes to be excluded from the time consuming Floyd-Warshall calculation. The results of the experiments are summarized in table 1.

[8]The complexity of the Floyd-Warshall algorithm is cubic, therefore twice as many synsets result in a processing effort that is eight times higher.

6 Discussion

The experiments show that with a thorough pre-analysis of the structure of a wordnet and consistent usage of this additional information, the time it takes to calculate all shortest paths can be reduced dramatically. This is because most nodes in a wordnet are part of substructures that are proper trees and not general graphs. In trees, it is possible to calculate the length of a path very much more efficiently than in an arbitrarily-structured graph.

We successfully applied structure-adapted path search to two wordnets, the Princeton WordNet and GermaNet. Since the algorithm does not rely on concrete properties of a specific wordnet, it can easily be applied to wordnets for other languages.

The benefits of structure adaptation diminish with increasing density of the network as more and more nodes become part of the core graph. In this case, the execution time will approach that of the Floyd-Warshall algorithm. It is also obvious that the approach does not generalize to arbitrary graphs. As long as the structure of graphs is similar to the star-like structure of wordnets, we expect the approach to be beneficial in applications involving such graphs as well.

References

Budanitsky, A. and Hirst, G. (2006). Evaluating WordNet-based Measures of Lexical Semantic Relatedness. In *Computational Linguistics*, volume 32. Association for Computational Linguistics.

Fellbaum, C. (1998). *WordNet: An Electronic Lexical Database*. MIT Press, Cambridge, MA.

Kunze, C. and Lemnitzer, L. (2002). GermaNet – Representation, Visualization, Application. In *Proceedings of LREC*, pages 1485–1491.

Sedgewick, R. (1990). *Algorithms in C*. Addison Wesley.

Linguistically Annotated BTG for Statistical Machine Translation

Deyi Xiong, Min Zhang, Aiti Aw and Haizhou Li
Human Language Technology
Institute for Infocomm Research
21 Heng Mui Keng Terrace, Singapore 119613
{dyxiong, mzhang, aaiti}@i2r.a-star.edu.sg

Abstract

Bracketing Transduction Grammar (BTG) is a natural choice for effective integration of desired linguistic knowledge into statistical machine translation (SMT). In this paper, we propose a Linguistically Annotated BTG (LABTG) for SMT. It conveys linguistic knowledge of source-side syntax structures to BTG hierarchical structures through linguistic annotation. From the linguistically annotated data, we learn annotated BTG rules and train linguistically motivated phrase translation model and reordering model. We also present an annotation algorithm that captures syntactic information for BTG nodes. The experiments show that the LABTG approach significantly outperforms a baseline BTG-based system and a state-of-the-art phrase-based system on the NIST MT-05 Chinese-to-English translation task. Moreover, we empirically demonstrate that the proposed method achieves better translation selection and phrase reordering.

1 Introduction

Formal grammar used in statistical machine translation (SMT), such as Bracketing Transduction Grammar (BTG) proposed by (Wu, 1997) and the synchronous CFG presented by (Chiang, 2005), provides a natural platform for integrating linguistic knowledge into SMT because hierarchical structures produced by the formal grammar resemble linguistic structures.[1] Chiang (2005) attempts to integrate linguistic information into his formally syntax-based system by adding a constituent feature. Unfortunately, the linguistic feature does not show significant improvement on the test set. In this paper, we further this effort by integrating linguistic knowledge into BTG.

We want to augment BTG's formal structures with linguistic structures since they are both hierarchical. In particular, our goal is to learn a more linguistically meaningful BTG from real-world bitexts by projecting linguistic structures onto BTG formal structures. In doing so, we hope to (1) maintain the strength of phrase-based approach since phrases are still used on BTG leaf nodes; (2) obtain a tight integration of linguistic knowledge in the translation model; (3) and finally avoid inducing a complicated linguistic synchronous grammar with expensive computation. The challenge, of course, is that BTG hierarchical structures are not always aligned with the linguistic structures in the syntactic parse trees of source or target language.

Along this line, we propose a novel approach: Linguistically Annotated BTG (LABTG) for SMT. The LABTG annotates BTG rules with *linguistic elements* that are learned from syntactic parse trees on the source side through an annotation algorithm, which is capable of labelling both syntactic and non-syntactic phrases. The linguistic elements extracted from parse trees capture both internal lexical content and external context of phrases. With these linguistic annotations, we expect the LABTG to address two traditional issues of standard phrase-based SMT (Koehn et al., 2003) in a more effective manner. They are (1) phrase translation: translating phrases according to their contexts; (2) phrase reordering: incorporating richer linguistic features for better reordering.

The proposed LABTG displays two unique characteristics when compared with BTG-based SMT (Wu, 1996; Xiong et al., 2006). The first is that two linguistically-informed sub-models are introduced for better phrase translation and reordering: annotated phrase translation model and

©2008. Licensed under the *Creative Commons Attribution-Noncommercial-Share Alike 3.0 Unported* license (http://creativecommons.org/licenses/by-nc-sa/3.0/). Some rights reserved.

[1] We inherit the definitions of *formal* and *linguistic* from (Chiang, 2005) which makes a distinction between formally syntax-based SMT and linguistically syntax-based SMT.

annotated reordering model. The second is that our proposed annotation algorithm and scheme are capable of conveying linguistic knowledge from source-side syntax structures to BTG structures. We describe the LABTG model and the annotation algorithm in Section 4. To better explain the LABTG model, we establish a unified framework of BTG-based SMT in Section 3. We conduct a series of experiments to study the effect of the LABTG in Section 5.

2 Related Work

There have been various efforts to integrate linguistic knowledge into SMT systems, either from the target side (Marcu et al., 2006; Hassan et al., 2007; Zollmann and Venugopal, 2006), the source side (Quirk et al., 2005; Liu et al., 2006; Huang et al., 2006) or both sides (Eisner, 2003; Ding et al., 2005; Koehn and Hoang, 2007), just to name a few. LABTG can be considered as, but not limited to, a new attempt that enriches translation model with source-side linguistic annotations.

(Huang and Knight, 2006) and (Hassan et al., 2007) introduce relabeling and supertagging on the target side, respectively. The former re-annotates syntactified phrases to learn grammatical distinctions while the latter supertags standard plain phrases, both applied on the target side. The difference between their work and LABTG is significant because we annotate standard plain phrases using linguistic elements on the source side. Compared with the target side annotation which improves fluency and grammaticality of translation output, linguistic annotation on the source side helps to improve translation adequacy.

Recently, some researchers have extended and created several variations of BTG/ITG. Zhang et al. (2005) propose lexicalized ITG for better word alignment. Xiong et al. (2006) demonstrate that their MEBTG, a BTG variation with MaxEnt-based reordering model, can improve phrase reordering significantly. Similarly, Setiawan et al. (2007) use an enhanced BTG variation with function words for reordering. LABTG differs from these BTG variations in that the latter does not use any external linguistic knowledge.

Zhang et al. (2007) describe a phrase reordering model based on BTG-style rules which integrates source-side syntactic knowledge. Our annotated reordering model of LABTG differs from their work in two key aspects. Firstly, we allow any phrase reorderings while they only reorder syntactic phrases. In their model, only syntactic phrases can use linguistic knowledge from parse trees for reordering while non-syntactic phrases are combined monotonously with a constant reordering score since no syntactic knowledge can be used at all. Our proposed LABTG successfully overcomes this limitation by supporting linguistic annotation on both syntactic and non-syntactic phrases. Moreover, we show that excluding non-syntactic phrase from reordering does hurt the performance. Secondly, we use richer linguistic knowledge in reordering, including head words and syntactic labels of context nodes, when compared with their model. Our experiments show that these additional information can improve reordering.

3 BTG Based SMT

We establish a unified framework for BTG-based SMT in this section. There are two kinds of rules in BTG, lexical rules (denoted as r^l) and merging rules (denoted as r^m):

$$r^l : A \rightarrow x/y$$

and

$$r^m : A \rightarrow [A_l, A_r] | \langle A_l, A_r \rangle$$

Lexical rules translate source phrase x into target phrase y and generate a leaf node A in BTG tree. Merging rules combine left and right neighboring phrases A_l and A_r into a larger phrase A in an order $o \in \{straight, inverted\}$.

We define a BTG derivation D as a sequence of independent applications of lexical and merging rules ($D = \langle r^l_{1..n_l}, r^m_{1..n_m} \rangle$). Given a source sentence, the decoding task of BTG-based SMT is to find a best derivation, which yields the best translation.

Similar to (Xiong et al., 2006), we can assign a probability to each rule using a log-linear model with different features and corresponding λ weights, then multiply them to obtain $P(D)$. For convenience of notation and keeping in line with the common understanding of standard phrase-based model, here we re-organize these features into translation model (P_T), reordering model (P_R) and target language model (P_L) as follows

$$P(D) = P_T(r^l_{1..n_l}) \cdot P_R(r^m_{1..n_m})^{\lambda_R} \cdot P_L(e)^{\lambda_L} \cdot exp(|e|)^{\lambda_w} \quad (1)$$

where $exp(|e|)$ is the word penalty.

The translation model is defined as:

$$P_T(r^l_{1..n_l}) = \prod_{i=1}^{n_l} P(r^l_i)$$

$$P(r^l) = p(x|y)^{\lambda_1} \cdot p(y|x)^{\lambda_2} \cdot p_{lex}(x|y)^{\lambda_3} \cdot p_{lex}(y|x)^{\lambda_4} \cdot exp(1)^{\lambda_5} \quad (2)$$

where $p(\cdot)$ represent the phrase translation probabilities in both directions, $p_{lex}(\cdot)$ denote the lexical translation probabilities in both directions, and $exp(1)$ is the phrase penalty.

Similarly, the reordering model is defined on the merging rules as follows

$$P_R(r^m_{1..n_m}) = \prod_{i=1}^{n_m} P(r^m_i) \quad (3)$$

In the original BTG model (Wu, 1996), $P(r^m)$ was actually a prior probability which can be set based on the order preference of the language pairs. In MEBTG (Xiong et al., 2006), however, the probability is calculated more sophisticatedly using a MaxEnt-based classification model with boundary words as its features.

4 Linguistically Annotated BTG Based SMT

We extend the original BTG into the linguistically annotated BTG by adding linguistic annotations from source-side parse trees to both BTG lexical rules and merging rules. Before we elaborate how the LABTG extends the baseline, we introduce annotated BTG rules.

In the LABTG, both lexical rules and merging rules are annotated with linguistic elements as follows

$$ar^l : A^a \rightarrow x\#a/y$$

and

$$ar^m : A^a \rightarrow [A^{a_l}_l, A^{a_r}_r] | \langle A^{a_l}_l, A^{a_r}_r \rangle$$

The annotation a comprises three linguistic elements from source-side syntactic parse tree: (1) head word hw, (2) the part-of-speech (POS) tag ht of head word and (3) syntactic label sl. In annotated lexical rules, the three elements are combined together and then attached to x as an annotation unit. In annotated merging rules, each node involved in merging is annotated with these three elements individually.

There are various ways to learn the annotated rules from training data. The straight-forward way is to first generate the best BTG tree for each sentence pair using the way of (Wu, 1997), then annotate each BTG node with linguistic elements by projecting source-side syntax tree to BTG tree, and finally extract rules from these annotated BTG trees. This way restricts learning space to only the best BTG trees[2], and leads to the loss of many useful annotated rules.

Therefore, we use an alternative way to extract the annotated rules as illustrated below. Firstly, we run GIZA++ (Och and Ney, 2000) on the training corpus in both directions and then apply the "grow-diag-final" refinement rule (Koehn et al., 2003) to obtain many-to-many word alignments. Secondly, we extract bilingual phrases from the word-aligned corpus, then annotate their source sides with linguistic elements to obtain the annotated lexical rules.[3] Finally, we learn reordering examples (Xiong et al., 2006), annotate their two neighboring sub-phrases and whole phrases, and then generalize them in the annotated merging rules. Although this alternative way may also miss reorderings due to word alignment errors, it is still more flexible and robust than the straight-forward one, and can learn more annotated BTG rules without constructing BTG trees explicitly.

4.1 LABTG Annotation Algorithm

During the process of rule learning and decoding, we need to annotate bilingual phrases or BTG nodes generated by the decoder given a source sentence together with its parse tree. Since both phrases and BTG nodes can be projected to a span on the source sentence, we run our annotation algorithm on source-side spans and then assign annotation results to the corresponding phrases or nodes. If the span is exactly covered by a single subtree in the source-side parse tree, it is called **syntactic span**, otherwise **non-syntactic span**. One of the challenges in this annotation algorithm is that BTG nodes (or phrases) are not always covering syntactic span, in other words, are not always aligned to constituent nodes in the source-side tree. To solve this problem, we use heuristic rules to generate pseudo head word and **composite label** which consists of syntactic labels of three relevant constituents for the non-syntactic span.

The annotation algorithm is shown in Fig. 1. For a syntactic span, the annotation is trivial. Annotation elements directly come from the subtree that exactly covers the span. For a non-syntactic

[2]Producing BTG forest for each sentence pair is very time-consuming.

[3]This makes the number of extracted annotated lexical rules proportional to that of bilingual phrases.

```
1: Annotator (span s = ⟨i, j⟩, source-side parse tree t)
2: if s is a syntactic span then
3:    Find the subtree c in t which exactly covers s
4:    s.a := {c.hw, c.ht, c.sl}
5: else
6:    Find the smallest subtree c* subsuming s in t
7:    if c*.hw ∈ s then
8:       s.a.hw := c*.hw and s.a.ht := c*.ht
9:    else
10:      Find the word w ∈ s which is nearest to c*.hw
11:      s.a.hw := w and s.a.ht := w.t /*w.t is the POS
         tag of w*/
12:   end if
13:   Find the left context node ln of s in c*
14:   Find the right context node rn of s in c*
15:   s.a.sl := ln.sl-c*.sl-rn.sl
16: end if
```

Figure 1: The LABTG Annotation Algorithm.

span, the process is much complicated. Firstly, we need to locate the smallest subtree c^* subsuming the span (line 6). Secondly, we try to identify the head word/tag of the span (line 7-12) by using c^*'s head word hw directly if it is within the span. Otherwise, the word within the span which is nearest to hw will be assigned as the head word of the span. Finally, we determine the composite label of the span (line 13-15), which is formulated as L-C-R. L/R refers to the syntactic label of the left/right **context node** of s which is a sub-node of c^*. There are different ways to define the context node of a span in the source-side parse tree. It can be the closest neighboring node or the boundary node which is the highest leftmost/rightmost sub-node of c^* not overlapping the span. If there is no such context node (the span s is exactly aligned to the left/right boundary of c^*), L/R will be set to NULL. C is the label of c^*. L, R and C together define the external syntactic context of s.

Fig. 2 shows a syntactic parse tree for a Chinese sentence, with head word annotated for each internal node.[4] Some sample annotations are given in Table 1. We also show different composite labels for non-syntactic spans with different definitions of their context nodes. sl_1 is obtained when the boundary node is defined as the context node while sl_2 is obtained when the closest neighboring node is defined as the context node.

4.2 LABTG Model

To better model annotated rules, the LABTG contributes two significant modifications to formula (1). First is the annotated phrase translation model with source side linguistically enhanced to replace the standard phrase translation model, and second is the additional MaxEnt-based reordering model that uses linguistic annotations as features. The LABTG model is formulated as follows

$$P(D) = P_{T_a}(ar^l_{1..n_l}) \cdot P_{R_b}(r^m_{1..n_m})^{\lambda_{R_b}} \cdot P_{R_a}(ar^m_{1..n_m})^{\lambda_{R_a}} \cdot P_L(e)^{\lambda_L} \cdot exp(|e|)^{\lambda_w} \quad (4)$$

Here P_{T_a} is the annotated phrase translation model, P_{R_b} is the reordering model from MEBTG using boundary words as features and P_{R_a} is the annotated reordering model using linguistic annotations of nodes as features.

Annotated Phrase Translation Model The annotated phrase translation model P_{T_a} is similar to formula (2) except that phrase translation probabilities on both directions are $p(x\#a|y)$ and $p(y|x\#a)$ respectively, instead of $p(x|y)$ and $p(y|x)$. By introducing annotations into the translation model, we integrate linguistic knowledge into the statistical selection of target equivalents.

Annotated Reordering Model The annotated reordering model P_{R_a} is a MaxEnt-based classification model which uses linguistic elements of each annotated node as its features. The model can be formulated as

$$P_{R_a}(ar^m) = p_\theta(o|A^a, A_l^{a_l}, A_r^{a_r})$$

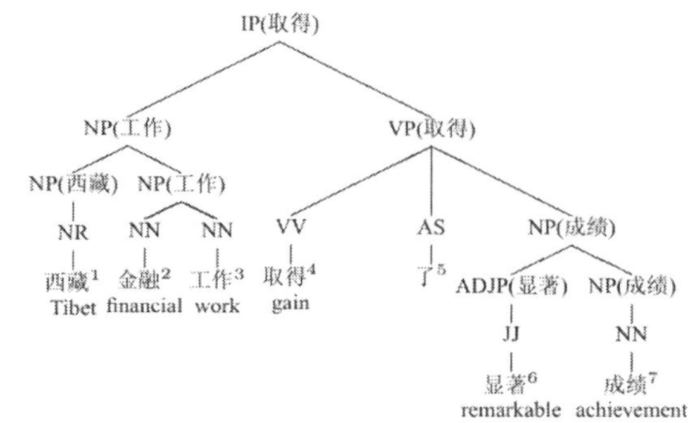

Figure 2: A syntactic parse tree with head word annotated for each internal node. The superscripts of leaf nodes denote their surface positions from left to right.

$span$	hw	ht	sl_1 (boundary node)	sl_2 (neighboring node)
⟨1, 2⟩	金融	NN	NULL-NP-NN	NULL-NP-NN
⟨2, 3⟩	工作	NN	NP	NP
⟨2, 4⟩	取得	VV	NP-IP-NP	NP-IP-AS
⟨3, 4⟩	取得	VV	NP-IP-NP	NN-IP-AS

Table 1: Annotation samples according to the tree shown in Fig. 2. hw/ht represents head word/tag, respectively. sl means the syntactic label.

[4]In this paper, we use phrase labels from the Penn Chinese Treebank (Xue et al., 2005).

$$= \frac{exp(\sum_i \theta_i h_i(o, A^a, A_l^{a_l}, A_r^{a_r}))}{\sum_o exp(\sum_i \theta_i h_i(o, A^a, A_l^{a_l}, A_r^{a_r}))}$$

where the functions $h_i \in \{0, 1\}$ are reordering features and θ_i are weights of these features.

Each merging rule involves 3 nodes $(A^a, A_l^{a_l}, A_r^{a_r})$ and each node has 3 linguistic elements (hw, ht, sl). Therefore, the model has 9 features in total. Taking the left node $A_l^{a_l}$ as an example, the model could use its head word w as feature as follows

$$h_i(o, A^a, A_l^{a_l}, A_r^{a_r}) = \begin{cases} 1, & A_l^{a_l}.hw = w, o = straight \\ 0, & otherwise \end{cases}$$

4.3 Training

To train the annotated translation model, firstly we extract all annotated lexical rules from source-side parsed, word-aligned training data. Then we estimate the annotated phrase translation probabilities $p(x\#a|y)$ and $p(y|x\#a)$ using relative counts from all collected annotated lexical rules. For example, $p(y|x\#a)$ can be calculated as follows

$$p(y|x\#a) = \frac{count(x\#a, y)}{\sum_y count(x\#a, y)}$$

One might think that linguistic annotations would cause serious data sparseness problem and the probabilities should be smoothed. However, according to our statistics (described in the next section), the differences in annotations for the same source phrase x are not so diverse. So we take a direct backoff strategy to map unseen annotated lexical rules to their un-annotated versions on the fly during decoding, which is detailed in the next subsection.

To train the annotated reordering model, we generate all annotated reordering examples, then obtain features using linguistic elements of these examples, and finally estimate feature weights based on the maximum entropy principle.

4.4 Decoding

A CKY-style decoder with beam search is developed, similar to (Xiong et al., 2006). Each input source sentence is firstly parsed to obtain its syntactic tree. Then the CKY-style decoder tries to generate the best annotated BTG tree using the trained annotated lexical and merging rules. We store all annotated lexical rules and their probabilities in a standard phrase table Ω, where source phrases are augmented with annotations. During the application of annotated lexical rules, we label each source phrase x with linguistic annotation a through the annotation algorithm given the source-side parse tree, and retrieve $x\#a$ from Ω. In the case of unseen combination $x\#a$, we map it to x and lookup x in the phrase table so that we can use the un-annotated lexical rule $A \rightarrow x/y$. We set $p(y|x) = max_{a'} p(y|x\#a')$ and $p(x|y) = max_{a'} p(x\#a'|y)$ where $(x, a', y) \in \Omega$. When two neighboring nodes are merged in a specific order, the two reordering models, P_{R_b} and P_{R_a}, will evaluate this merging independently with individual scores. The former uses boundary words as features while the latter uses the linguistic elements as features, annotated on the BTG nodes through the annotation algorithm according to the source-side parse tree.

5 Experiments and Analysis

In this section we conducted a number of experiments to demonstrate the competitiveness of the proposed LABTG based SMT when compared with two baseline systems: Moses (Koehn et al., 2007), a state-of-the-art phrase-based system and MEBTG (Xiong et al., 2006), a BTG based system. We also investigated the impact of different annotation schemes on the LABTG model and studied the effect of annotated phrase translation model and annotated reordering model on translation selection and phrase reordering respectively. All experiments were carried out on the Chinese-to-English translation task of the NIST MT-05 with case-sensitive BLEU scores reported.

The systems were trained on the FBIS corpus. We removed 15,250 sentences, for which the Chinese parser (Xiong et al., 2005) failed to produce syntactic parse trees. The parser was trained on the Penn Chinese Treebank with a F1 score of 79.4%. From the remaining FBIS corpus (224, 165 sentence pairs), we obtained 4.55M standard bilingual phrases (including 2.75M source phrases) for the baseline systems and 4.65M annotated lexical rules (including 3.13M annotated source phrases augmented with linguistic annotations) for the LABTG system using the algorithm mentioned above. These statistics reveal that there are 1.14 (3.13M/2.75M) annotations per source phrase, which means our annotation algorithm does not increase the number of extracted rules exponentially.

We extracted 2.8M reordering examples, from

System	BLEU
Moses	0.2386
MEBTG	0.2498
LABTG	0.2667

Table 2: LABTG vs. Moses and MEBTG.

which we generated 114.8K reordering features for the reordering model P_{R_b} (shared by both MEBTG and LABTG systems) using the right boundary words of phrases and 85K features for the annotated reordering model P_{R_a} (only included in the LABTG system) using linguistic annotations. We ran the MaxEnt toolkit (Zhang, 2004) to tune reordering feature weights with iteration number being set to 100 and Gaussian prior to 1 to avoid overfitting.

We built our four-gram language model using Xinhua section of the English Gigaword corpus (181.1M words) with the SRILM toolkit (Stolcke, 2002). For the efficiency of minimum-error-rate training (Och, 2003), we built our development set (580 sentences) using sentences not exceeding 50 characters from the NIST MT-02 evaluation test data.

5.1 LABTG vs. phrase-based SMT and BTG-based SMT

We compared the LABTG system with two baseline systems. The results are given in Table 2. The LABTG outperforms Moses and MEBTG by 2.81 and 1.69 absolute BLEU points, respectively. These significant improvements indicate that BTG formal structures can be successfully extended with linguistic knowledge extracted from syntactic structures without losing the strength of phrase-based method.

5.2 The Effect of Different Annotation Schemes

A great amount of linguistic knowledge is conveyed through the syntactic label sl. To obtain this label, we tag syntactic BTG node with single label C from its corresponding constituent in the source-side parse tree while annotate non-syntactic BTG node with composite label formulated as L-C-R. We conducted experiments to study the effect of different annotation schemes on the LABTG model by comparing three different annotation schemes for non-syntactic BTG node: (1) using single label C from its corresponding smallest subtree c^* (C), (2) constructing composite label using neighboring node as context node (N-C-N), and (3) constructing composite label using boundary node as context node (B-C-B). The results are shown in Table 3.

Annotation scheme	BLEU
C	0.2626
N-C-N	0.2591
B-C-B	0.2667
Annotating syntactic nodes with composite label	0.2464

Table 3: Comparison of different annotation schemes.

On the one hand, linguistic annotation provides additional information for LABTG, transferring knowledge from source-side linguistic structures to BTG formal structures. On the other hand, however, it is also a constraint on LABTG, guiding the annotated translation model and reordering model to the selection of target alternatives and reordering patterns, respectively. A tight constraint always means that annotations are too specific, although they incorporate rich knowledge. Too specific annotations are more sensitive to parse errors, and easier to make the model lose correct translations or use wrong reordering patterns. That is the reason why the annotation scheme "N-C-N" and "Annotating syntactic nodes with composite label" [5] both hurt the performance. Conversely, a loose constraint means that annotations are too generic and have less knowledge incorporated. The annotation scheme "C" is such a scheme with loose constraint and less knowledge.

Therefore, an ideal annotation scheme should not be too specific or too generic. The annotation scheme "B-C-B" achieves a reasonable balance between knowledge incorporation and constraint, which obtains the best performance. Therefore we choose boundary node as context node for label annotation of non-syntactic BTG nodes in experiments described later.

5.3 The Effect of Annotated Translation Model

To investigate the effect of the annotated translation model on translation selection, we compared the standard phrase translation model P_T used in MEBTG with the annotated phrase translation

[5] In this annotation scheme, we produce composite label L-C-R for both syntactic and non-syntactic BTG nodes. For syntactic node, sibling node is used as context node while for non-syntactic node, boundary node is used as context node.

Translation model	BLEU
P_T	0.2498
P_{T_a}	0.2581
P_{T_a} (-NULL)	0.2548

Table 4: The effect of annotated translation model.

Reordering Configuration	BLEU
P_{R_b}	0.2498
$P_{R_b} + P_{R_a}$ (SL)	0.2588
$P_{R_b} + P_{R_a}$ (+BNL)	0.2627
$P_{R_b} + P_{R_a}$ (+BNL+HWT)	0.2652
$P_{R_b} + P_{R_a}$ (SL+BNL+HWT): only allowed syntactic phrase reordering	0.2512

Table 5: The effect of annotated reordering model.

model P_{T_a}. The experiment results are shown in Table 4. The significant improvement in the BLEU score indicates that the annotated translation model helps to select better translation options.

Our study on translation output shows that annotating phrases with source-side linguistic elements can provide at least two kinds of information for translation model to improve the adequacy: category and context. The category knowledge of a phrase can be used to select its appropriate translation related to its category. For example, Chinese phrase "值" can be translated into "value" if it is a verb or "at/on" if it is a proposition. However, the baseline BTG-based system always selects the proposition translation even if it is a verb because the language model probability for proposition translation is higher than that of verb translation. This wrong translation of content words is similar to the incorrect omission reported in (Och et al., 2003), which both hurt translation adequacy. The annotated translation model can avoid wrong translation by filtering out phrase candidates with unmatched categories.

The context information (provided by context node) is also quite useful for translation selection. Even the "NULL" context, which we used in label annotation to indicate that a phrase is located at the boundary of a constituent, provides some information, such as, transitive or intransitive attribute of a verb phrase. The last row of Tabel 4 shows that if we remove "NULL" in label annotation, the performance is degraded. (Huang and Knight, 2006) also reported similar result by using sisterhood annotation on the target side.

5.4 The Effect of Annotated Reordering Model

To investigate the effect of the annotated reordering model, we integrate P_{R_a} with various settings in MEBTG while keeping its original phrase translation model P_T and reordering model P_{R_b} unchanged. We augment P_{R_a}'s feature pool incrementally: firstly using only single labels [6](SL) as features (132 features in total), then constructing composite labels for non-syntactic phrases (+BNL) (6.7K features), and finally introducing head words into the feature pool (+BNL+HWT) (85K features). This series of experiments demonstrate the impact and degree of contribution made by each feature for reordering. We also conducted experiments to investigate the effect of restricting reordering to syntactic phrases using the best reordering feature set (SL+BNL+HWT) for P_{R_a}. The experimental results are presented in Table 2, from which we have the following observations:

(1) Source-side syntactic labels (SL) capture reordering patterns between source structures and their target counterparts. Even when the baseline feature set SL with only 132 features is used for P_{R_a}, the BLEU score improves from 0.2498 to 0.2588. This is because most of the frequent reordering patterns between Chinese and English have been captured using syntactic labels. For example, the pre-verbal modifier PP in Chinese is translated into post-verbal counterpart in English. This reordering can be described by a rule with an inverted order: $VP \rightarrow \langle PP, VP \rangle$, and captured by our syntactic reordering features.

(2) Context information, provided by labels of context nodes (BNL) and head word/tag pairs (HWT), also improves phrase reordering. Producing composite labels for non-syntactic BTG nodes (+BNL) and integrating head word/tag pairs into P_{R_a} as reordering features (+BNL+HWT) are both effective, indicating that context information complements syntactic label for capturing reordering patterns.

(3) Restricting phrase reordering to syntactic phrases is harmful. The BLEU score plummets from 0.2652 to 0.2512.

6 Conclusions

In this paper, we have presented a Linguistically Annotated BTG based approach to effectively integrate linguistic knowledge into SMT by merging

[6]For non-syntactic node, we only use the single label C, without constructing composite label L-C-R.

source-side linguistic structures with BTG hierarchical structures. The LABTG brings BTG-based SMT towards linguistically syntax-based SMT and narrows the linguistic gap between them. Our experimental results show that the LABTG significantly outperforms the state-of-the-art phrase-based SMT and the baseline BTG-based SMT. The proposed method also offers better translation selection and phrase reordering by introducing the annotated phrase translation model and the annotated reordering model with linguistic annotations.

We conclude that (1) source-side syntactic information can improve translation adequacy; (2) linguistic annotations of BTG nodes well capture reordering patterns between source structures and their target counterparts; (3) integration of linguistic knowledge into SMT should be carefully conducted so that the incorporated knowledge could not have negative constraints on the model[7].

References

David Chiang. 2005. A hierarchical phrase-based model for statistical machine translation. In *Proceedings of ACL 2005*.

Yuan Ding and Martha Palmer. 2005. Machine Translation Using Probabilistic Synchronous Dependency Insertion Grammars. In *Proceedings of ACL 2005*.

Jason Eisner. 2003. Learning non-isomorphic tree mappings for machine translation. In *Proceedings of ACL 2003*.

Hany Hassan, Khalil Sima'an and Andy Way. 2007. Supertagged Phrase-based Statistical Machine Translation. In *Proceedings of ACL 2007*.

Bryant Huang, Kevi Knight. 2006. Relabeling Syntax Trees to Improve Syntax-Based Machine Translation Quality. In *Proceedings of NAACL-HLT 2006*.

Liang Huang, Kevi Knight and Aravind Joshi. 2006. Statistical Syntax-directed Translation with Extended Domain of Locality. In *Proceedings of AMTA 2006*.

Philipp Koehn, Franz Joseph Och, and Daniel Marcu. 2003. Statistical Phrase-Based Translation. In *Proceedings of HLT/NAACL*.

Philipp Koehn, Hieu Hoang. 2007. Factored Translation Models. In *Proceedings of EMNLP 2007*.

Philipp Koehn, Hieu Hoang, Alexandra Birch, Chris Callison-Burch, Marcello Federico, Nicola Bertoldi, Brooke Cowan, Wade Shen, Christine Moran, Richard Zens, Chris Dyer, Ondrej Bojar, Alexandra Constantin, Evan Herbst. 2007. Moses: Open Source Toolkit for Statistical Machine Translation. ACL 2007, demonstration session, Prague, Czech Republic, June 2007.

[7]For example, the annotation scheme "N-C-N" incorporates rich syntactic knowledge, but also tightens the constraint on the model, which therefore loses robustness.

Yang Liu, Qun Liu, Shouxun Lin. 2006. Tree-to-String Alignment Template for Statistical Machine Translation. In *Proceedings of ACL-COLING 2006*.

Daniel Marcu, Wei Wang, Abdessamad Echihabi, and Kevin Knight. 2006. SPMT: Statistical Machine Translation with Syntactified Target Language Phraases. In *Proceedings of EMNLP*.

Franz Josef Och and Hermann Ney. 2000. Improved statistical alignment models. In *Proceedings of ACL 2000*.

Franz Josef Och. 2003. Minimum Error Rate Training in Statistical Machine Translation. In *Proceedings of ACL 2003*.

Franz Josef Och, Daniel Gildea, Sanjeev Khudanpur, Anoop Sarkar, Kenji Yamada, Alex Fraser, Shankar Kumar, Libin Shen, David Smith, Katherine Eng, Viren Jain, Zhen Jin, Dragomir Radev. 2003. Final Report of Johns Hopkins 2003 Summer Workshop on Syntax for Statistical Machine Translation.

Chris Quirk, Arul Menezes and Colin Cherry. 2005. Dependency Treelet Translation: Syntactically Informed Phrasal SMT. In *Proceedings of ACL 2005*.

Hendra Setiawan, Min-Yen Kan and Haizhou Li. 2007. Ordering Phrases with Function Words. In *Proceedings of ACL 2007*.

Andreas Stolcke. 2002. SRILM - an extensible language modeling toolkit. In *Proceedings of International Conference on Spoken Language Processing*, volume 2, pages 901-904.

Dekai Wu. 1996. A Polynomial-Time Algorithm for Statistical Machine Translation. In *Proceedings of ACL 1996*.

Dekai Wu. 1997. Stochastic Inversion Transduction Grammars and Bilingual Parsing of Parallel Corpora. *Computational Linguistics*, 23(3):377-403.

Deyi Xiong, Shuanglong Li, Qun Liu, Shouxun Lin, Yueliang Qian. 2005. Parsing the Penn Chinese Treebank with Semantic Knowledge. In *Proceedings of IJCNLP*, Jeju Island, Korea.

Deyi Xiong, Qun Liu and Shouxun Lin. 2006. Maximum Entropy Based Phrase Reordering Model for Statistical Machine Translation. In *Proceedings of ACL-COLING 2006*.

Nianwen Xue, Fei Xia, Fu-Dong Chiou, and Martha Palmer. 2005. The Penn Chinese TreeBank: Phrase Structure Annotation of a Large Corpus. *Natural Language Engineering*, 11(2):207-238.

Dongdong Zhang, Mu Li, Chi-Ho Li and Ming Zhou. 2007. Phrase Reordering Model Integrating Syntactic Knowledge for SMT. In *Proceedings of EMNLP-CoNLL 2007*.

Hao Zhang and Daniel Gildea. 2005. Stochastic Lexicalized Inversion Transduction Grammar for Alignment. In *Proceedings of ACL 2005*.

Le Zhang. 2004. Maximum Entropy Modeling Tooklkit for Python and C++. Available at http://homepages.inf.ed.ac.uk/s0450736 /maxent_toolkit.html.

Andreas Zollmann and Ashish Venugopal. 2006. Syntax Augmented Machine Translation via Chart Parsing. In NAACL 2006 - Workshop on statistical machine translation, New York. June 4-9.

Bayesian Semi-Supervised Chinese Word Segmentation for Statistical Machine Translation

Jia Xu[†], **Jianfeng Gao**[*], **Kristina Toutanova**[*], **Hermann Ney**[†]

Computer Science 6[†]
RWTH Aachen University
D-52056 Aachen, Germany
{xujia,ney}@cs.rwth-aachen.de

Microsoft Corporation[*]
One Microsoft Way
Redmond, WA 98052, USA
{jfgao,kristout}@microsoft.com

Abstract

Words in Chinese text are not naturally separated by delimiters, which poses a challenge to standard machine translation (MT) systems. In MT, the widely used approach is to apply a Chinese word segmenter trained from manually annotated data, using a fixed lexicon. Such word segmentation is not necessarily optimal for translation. We propose a Bayesian semi-supervised Chinese word segmentation model which uses both monolingual and bilingual information to derive a segmentation suitable for MT. Experiments show that our method improves a state-of-the-art MT system in a small and a large data environment.

1 Introduction

Chinese sentences are written in the form of a sequence of Chinese characters, and words are not separated by white spaces. This is different from most European languages and poses difficulty in many natural language processing tasks, such as machine translation.

It is difficult to define "correct" Chinese word segmentation (CWS) and various definitions have been proposed. In this work, we explore the idea that the best segmentation depends on the task, and concentrate on developing a CWS method for MT, which leads to better translation performance.

The common solution in Chinese-to-English translation has been to segment the Chinese text using an off-the-shelf CWS method, and to apply a standard translation model given the fixed segmentation. The most widely applied method for MT is unigram segmentation, such as segmentation using the LDC (LDC, 2003) tool, which requires a manual lexicon containing a list of Chinese words and their frequencies. The lexicon and frequencies are obtained using manually annotated data. This method is sub-optimal for MT. For example, 纸(paper) and 牌(card) can be two words or composed into one word 纸牌(cards). Since 纸牌does not exist in the manual lexicon, it cannot be generated by this method.

In addition to unigram segmentation, other methods have been proposed. For example, (Gao et al., 2005) described an adaptive CWS system, and (Andrew, 2006) employed a conditional random field model for sequence segmentation. However, these methods are not specifically developed for the MT application, and significant improvements in translation performance need to be shown.

In (Xu et al., 2004) and (Xu et al., 2005), word segmentations are integrated into MT systems during model training and translation. We refine the method in training using a Bayesian semi-supervised CWS approach motivated by (Goldwater et al., 2006). We describe a generative model which consists of a word model and two alignment models, representing the monolingual and bilingual information, respectively. In our methods, we first segment Chinese text using a unigram segmenter, and then learn new word types and word distributions, which are suitable for MT.

Our experiments on both large (NIST) and small (IWSLT) data tracks of Chinese-to-English translation show that our method improves the performance of a state-of-the-art machine translation system.

2 Review of the Baseline System

2.1 Word segmentation

In statistical machine translation, we are given a Chinese sentence in characters $c_1^K = c_1 \dots c_K$ which is to be translated into an English sentence $e_1^I = e_1 \dots e_I$. In order to obtain a more adequate mapping between Chinese and English words, c_1^K is usually segmented into words $f_1^J = f_1 \dots f_J$ in preprocessing.

In our baseline system, we apply the commonly

© 2008. Licensed under the *Creative Commons Attribution-Noncommercial-Share Alike 3.0 Unported* license (http://creativecommons.org/licenses/by-nc-sa/3.0/). Some rights reserved.

used **unigram model** to generate the segmentation. Given a manually compiled lexicon containing words and their relative frequencies $P_s(f'_j)$, the best segmentation f_1^J is the one that maximizes the joint probability of all words in the sentence, with the assumption that words are independent of each other[1]:

$$\begin{aligned} f_1^J &= \operatorname*{argmax}_{f'^{J'}_1} Pr(f'^{J'}_1 | c_1^K) \\ &\approx \operatorname*{argmax}_{f'^{J'}_1} \prod_{j=1}^{J'} P_s(f'_j), \end{aligned}$$

where the maximization is taken over Chinese word sequences whose character sequence is c_1^K.

2.2 Translation system

Once we have segmented the Chinese sentences into words, we train standard alignment models in both directions with GIZA++ (Och and Ney, 2002) using models of IBM-1 (Brown et al., 1993), HMM (Vogel et al., 1996) and IBM-4 (Brown et al., 1993).

Our MT system uses a phrase-based decoder and the log-linear model described in (Zens and Ney, 2004). Features in the log-linear model include translation models in two directions, a language model, a distortion model and a sentence length penalty. The feature weights are tuned on the development set using a downhill simplex algorithm (Press et al., 2002). The language model is a statistical ngram model estimated using modified Kneser-Ney smoothing.

3 Unigram Dirichlet Process Model for CWS

The simplest version of our model is based on a unigram Dirichlet Process (DP) model, using only monolingual information. Different from a standard unigram model for CWS, our model can introduce new Chinese word types and learn word distributions automatically from unlabeled data.

According to this model, a corpus of Chinese words $f_1, \ldots f_m, \ldots, f_M$ is generated via:

$$G|\alpha, P_0 \sim DP(\alpha, P_0)$$

$$f_m|G \sim G$$

where G is a distribution over words drawn from a Dirichlet Process prior with base measure P_0 and concentration parameter α.

We never explicitly estimate G but instead integrate over its possible values and perform Bayesian inference. It is easy to compute the probability of a Chinese word given a set of already generated words, while integrating over G. This is done by casting Chinese word generation as a Chinese restaurant process (CRP) (Aldous, 1985), i.e. a restaurant with an infinite number of tables (approximately corresponding to Chinese word types), each table with infinite number of seats (approximately corresponding to Chinese word frequencies).

The Dirichlet Process model can be viewed intuitively as a cache model (Goldwater et al., 2006). Each word f_j in the corpus is either retrieved from a cache or generated anew given the previously observed words f_{-j}:

$$P(f_j|f_{-j}) = \frac{N(f_j) + \alpha P_0(f_j)}{N + \alpha}, \qquad (1)$$

where $N(f_j)$ is the number of Chinese words f_j in the previous context. N is the total number of Chinese words, P_0 is the base probability over words, and α influences the probability of introducing a new word at each step and controls the size of the lexicon. The probability of generating a word from the cache increases as more instances of that word are seen.

For the base distribution P_0, which governs the generation of new words, we use the following distribution (called the **spelling model**):

$$\begin{aligned} P_0(f) &= P(L)P_0(f|L) \\ &= \frac{\lambda^L}{L!} e^{-\lambda} u^L \qquad (2) \end{aligned}$$

where $\frac{1}{u}$ is the number of characters in the document, i.e. character vocabulary size, and L is the number of Chinese characters of word f. We note that this is a Poisson distribution on word length and a unigram distribution on characters given the length. We used $\lambda = 2$ and $\alpha = 0.3$ in our experiments.

4 CWS Model for MT

As a solution to the problems with the conventional approach to CWS mentioned in Section 1, we propose a generative model for CWS in Section 4.1, and then extend the model to a more general but deficient model, similar to a maximum entropy model in which most features are derived from the submodels of the generative model.

4.1 Generative Model

The generative model assume that a corpus of parallel sentences $(c_1{}^K, e_1{}^I)$ is generated along with a hidden sequence of Chinese words $f_1{}^J$ and a hidden word alignment $b_1{}^I$ for every sentence. The alignment indicates the aligned Chinese word f_{b_i} for each English word e_i, where f_0 indicates a special *null* word as in the IBM models.

[1] The notational convention will be as follows: we use the symbol $Pr(\cdot)$ to denote general probability distributions with (nearly) no specific assumptions. In contrast, for model-based probability distributions, we use the generic symbol $P(\cdot)$.

Without assuming any special form for the probability of a sentence pair along with hidden variables, we can factor it into a monolingual Chinese sentence probability and a bilingual translation probability as follows:

$$\begin{aligned} & Pr({c_1}^K, {e_1}^I, {f_1}^J, {b_1}^I) \\ & = Pr(c_1^K, f_1^J) Pr(e_1^I, b_1^I | f_1^J) \\ & = Pr(f_1^J) \delta({f_1}^J, {c_1}^K) Pr(e_1^I, b_1^I | f_1^J), \end{aligned}$$

where $\delta(f_1^J, c_1^K)$ is 1 if the characters of the sequence of words ${f_1}^J$ are ${c_1}^K$, and to 0 otherwise. We can drop the conditioning on ${c_1}^K$ in $Pr(e_1^I, b_1^I | f_1^J)$, because the characters are deterministic given the words.

The joint probability of the observations $({c_1}^K, e_1^I)$ can be obtained by summing over all possible values of the hidden variables f_1^J and b_1^I.

In Sections 4.1.1 and 4.1.2, we will describe the modeling assumptions behind the monolingual Chinese sentence model and the translation model, respectively.

4.1.1 Monolingual Chinese sentence model

We use the Dirichlet Process unigram word model introduced in section 3. In this model, the parameters of a distribution over words G are first drawn from the Dirichlet prior $DP(\alpha, P_0)$. Words are then independently generated according to G. The probability of a sequence of Chinese words in a sentence is thus:

$$Pr(f_1^J) \approx \prod_{j=1}^{J} P(f_j | G) \qquad (3)$$

4.1.2 Translation model

We employ the Dirichlet Process inverse IBM model 1 to generate English words and alignment given the Chinese words. In this model, for every Chinese word f (including the *null* word), a distribution over English words G_f is first drawn from a Dirichlet Process prior $DP(\alpha, P_0(e))$, where $P_0(e)$ we used the empirical distribution over English words in the parallel data. Then, given these parameters, the probability of an English sentence and alignment given a Chinese sentence (sequence of words) is given by:

$$P(e_1^I, b_1^I | f_1^J, G_f) = \prod_{i=1}^{I} \frac{1}{J+1} P(e_i | G_{f_{b_i}})$$

This is the same model form as inverse IBM model 1, except we have placed Dirichlet Process priors on the Chinese-word specific distributions over English words. [2]

[2] f_{b_i} is the Chinese word aligned to e_i and $G_{f_{b_i}}$ is the distribution over English words conditioned on the word f_{b_i}. Similarly, e_{a_j} is the English word aligned to f_j in the other direction and $G_{e_{a_j}}$ is the distribution over Chinese words conditioned on e_{a_j}.

In practice, we observed that using a word-alignment model in one direction is not sufficient. We then added a factor to our model which includes word alignment in the other direction , i.e. a Dirichlet Process IBM model 1. We ignore the detailed description here, because the calculation is the same as that of the inverse IBM model 1. According to this model, for every English word e (including the *null* word), a distribution over Chinese words G_e is first drawn from a Dirichlet Process prior $DP(\alpha, P_0(f))$. Here, for the base distribution $P_0(f)$ we used the same spelling model as for the monolingual unigram Dirichlet Process prior. The probability of a sequence of Chinese words f_1^J and a word alignment a_1^J given a sequence of English words e_1^I is then:

$$P(f_1^J, a_1^J | e_1^I, G_e) = \prod_{j=1}^{J} \frac{1}{I+1} P(f_j | G_{e_{a_j}})$$

4.2 Final Model

We put the monolingual model and the translation models in both directions together into a single model, where each of the component models is weighted by a scaling factor. This is similar to a maximum entropy model. We fit the weights of the sub-models on a development set by maximizing the BLEU score of the final translation.

$$\begin{aligned} & P(c_1^K, e_1^I, f_1^J, a_1^J, b_1^I) \qquad (4) \\ & \approx \frac{1}{Z} P(f_1^J)^{\lambda_1} \cdot P(e_1^I, b_1^I | f_1^J)^{\lambda_2} \\ & \cdot P(f_1^J, a_1^J | e_1^I)^{\lambda_3}, \end{aligned}$$

where Z is the normalization factor.

In practice we do not re-normalize the probabilities and our model is thus deficient because it does not sum to 1 over valid observations. However, we found the model work very good in our experiments. Similar deficient models have been used very successfully before, for example, in the IBM models 3–6 and in the unsupervised grammar induction model of (Klein and Manning, 2002).

5 Gibbs Sampling Training

It is generally impossible to find the most likely segmentation according to our Bayesian model using exact inference, because the hidden variables do not allow exact computation of the integrals. Nonetheless, it is possible to define algorithms using Markov chain Monte Carlo (MCMC) that produce a stream of samples from the posterior distribution of the hidden variables given the observations. We applied the Gibbs sampler (Geman and Geman, 1984) — one of the simplest MCMC methods, in which transitions between states of the

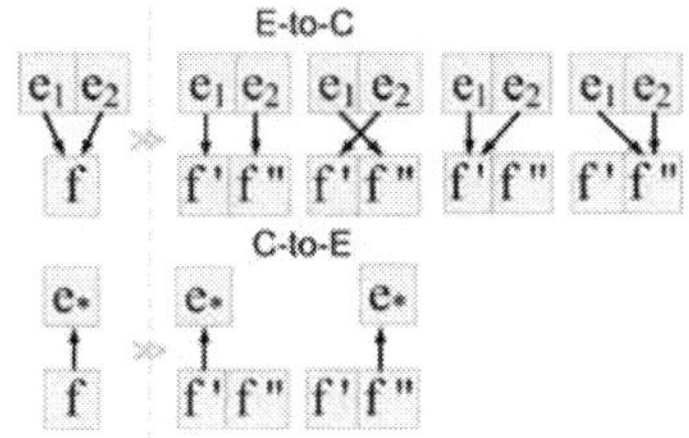

Figure 1: Case I, transition from a no-boundary to a boundary state, f to $f'f''$.

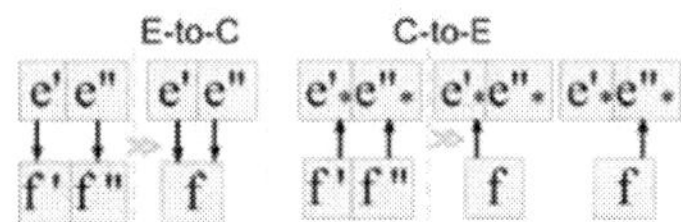

Figure 2: Case II, transition from a boundary to a no-boundary state, $f'f''$ to f.

Markov chain result from sampling each component of the state conditioned on the current value of all other variables.

In our problem, the observations are $D = (d_1, ..d_n, .., d_N)$, where $d_n{=}(c_1^K, e_1^I)$ indicates a bilingual sentence pair, the hidden variables are the word segmentations f_1^J and the alignments in two directions a_1^J and b_1^I.

To perform Gibbs sampling, we start with an initial word segmentation and initial word alignments, and iteratively re-sample the word-segmentation and alignments according to our model of Equation 4.

Note that for efficiency, we only allow limited modifications to the initial word alignments. Thus we only use models derived from IBM-1 (instead of IBM-4) for comparing different word segmentations. On the other hand, re-sampling the segmentation causes re-linking alignment points to parts or groups of the original words.

Hence, we organize our sampling process around possible word boundaries. For each character c_k in each sentence, we consider two alternative segmentations: $c_k{}^+$ indicates the segmentation where there is a boundary after c_k and $c_k{}^-$ indicates the segmentation where there is no boundary after c_k, keeping all other boundaries fixed. Let f denote the single word spanning character c_k when there is no boundary after it, and f',f'' denote the two adjacent words resulting if there is a boundary: f' includes c_k and f'' starts just to the right, with character c_{k+1}. The introduction of f' and f'' leads to M new possible alignments in the E-to-C direction $b_{k1}^+, \ldots, b_{kM}^+$, such as in Figure 1. Together with the boundary vs no-boundary state at each character position, we re-sample a set of alignment links between English words and any of the Chinese words f,f', and f'', keeping all other word alignments in the sentence pair fixed. (See Figures 1 and 2.)

Table 1: General Algorithm of GS for CWS.

Input: D with an initial segmentation and alignments
Output: D with sampled segmentation and alignments
for $n = 1$ to $\hat{N}$
  for $k = 1$ to K that $c_k \in d_n$
    Create M+1 candidates, $cba_{k,m}^+$ and cba_k^-, where
      $cba_{k,m}^+$: there is a word boundary after c_k
      cba_k^-: there is no word boundary after c_k
    Compute probabilities
      $P(cba_{k,m}^+ | dh_{nk}{}^-)$
      $P(cba_k^- | dh_{nk}{}^-)$
    Sample boundary and relevant alignments
    Update counts

Thus at each step in the Gibbs sampler, we consider a set of alternatives for the boundary after c_k and relevant alignment links, keeping all other hidden variables fixed. At each step, we need to compute the probability of each of the alternatives, given the fixed values of the other hidden variables.

We introduce some notation to make the presentation easier. For every position k in sentence pair n, we denote by $dh_{nk}{}^-$ the observations and hidden variables for all sentences other than sentence n, and the observations and hidden variables inside sentence n, not involving character position c_k. The fixed variables inside the sentence are the words not neighboring position k, and the alignments in both directions to these words.

In the process of sampling, we consider a set of alternatives: segmentation $c_k{}^+$ along with the product space of relevant alignments in both directions $b_{k1}^+, \ldots, b_{kM}^+$, and a_k^+, and segmentation c_k^- along with relevant alignments $b_k{}^-$ and a_k^-. For brevity, we denote these alternatives by $cba_{k,m}{}^+$ and $cba_k{}^-$.

We describe how we derive the set of alternatives in section 5.2 and how we compute their probabilities in section 5.1.

Table 1 shows schematically one iteration of Gibbs sampling through the whole training corpus of parallel sentences, where $\hat{N}$ is the number of parallel sentences.

5.1 Computing probabilities of alternatives

For the Gibbs sampling algorithm in Table 1, we need to compute the probability of each alternative segmentation/alignments, given the fixed values of the rest of the data $dh_{nk}{}^-$. The probability of the hidden variables in the alternatives is proportional to the joint probability of the hidden variables and observations, and thus it is sufficient to compute the probability of the latter. We compute these probabilities using the Chinese restaurant process sampling scheme for the Dirichlet Process, thus integrating over all of the possible values of the distributions G, G_f and G_e.

Let cba_k denote an alternative hypothesis including boundary or no boundary at position k, and relevant alignments to English words in both directions of the one or two Chinese words resulting from the segmentation at k. The probability of this configuration given by our model is:

$$P(cba_k|dh_{nk}^-) \propto P_m(cba_k|dh_{nk}^-)^{\lambda_1} \cdot P_{ef}(cba_k|dh_{nk}^-)^{\lambda_2} \cdot P_{fe}(cba_k|dh_{nk}^-)^{\lambda_3}, \quad (5)$$

where $P_m(cba_k|dh_{nk}^-)$ is the monolingual word probability, and $P_{fe}(cba_k|dh_{nk}^-)$ and $P_{ef}(cba_k|dh_{nk}^-)$ are the translation probabilities in the two directions.

We now describe the computations of each of the component probabilities.

5.1.1 Word model probability

The word model probability $P_m(cab_k|dh_{nk}^-)$ in Equation 5 is derived from Equations 3 and 1:

There are two cases, depending on whether the hypothesis specifies that there is a boundary after character c_k, in which case we need the probabilities of the two resulting words f', and f'', or there is no boundary, in which case we need the probability of the single word f. (See the initial states in Figures 1 and 2, respectively.)

Let N denote the total number of word tokens in the rest of the corpus dh_{nk}^-, and $N(f)$ denote the number of instances of word f in dh_{nk}^-. The probabilities in the two cases are

$$P_m(c_k^+|dh_{nk}^-) \propto \frac{N(f') + \alpha P_0(f')}{N + \alpha} \cdot \frac{N(f'') + \alpha P_0(f'')}{N + \alpha}$$

$$P_m(c_k^-|dh_{nk}^-) \propto \frac{N(f) + \alpha P_0(f)}{N + \alpha}$$

Here $P_0(f)$ is computed using Equation 2.

5.1.2 Translation model probability

The translation model probabilities depend on whether or not there is a segmentation boundary at c_k and which English words are aligned to the relevant Chinese words.

In the first case, assume that there is a word boundary in cab_k, and that English words $\{e'\}$ are aligned to f' and words $\{e''\}$ are aligned to f'' in the E-to-C direction according to the alignment b_k, and that f' is aligned to e_*' and f'' is aligned to e_*'' in the C-to-E direction according to the alignment a_k (see the initial state in Figure 1). Here we overloaded notations and use b_k and a_k to indicate the alignments of the relevant Chinese words at position k to any English words. Let I denote the total number of English words in the sentence, and $J+1$ denote the number of Chinese words according to this segmentation. We also denote the total number of English words aligned to either f' or f'' in the E-to-C direction by P.

The translation model probability in the E-to-C direction is thus:

$$P_{ef}(c_k^+, b_k, a_k|dh_{nk}^-) \propto \left(\frac{1}{(J+2)}\right)^P \prod_{e'} P(e'|f', dh_{nk}^-) \prod_{e''} P(e''|f'', dh_{nk}^-)$$

Here we compute $P(e|f, dh_{nk}^-)$ as:

$$P(e|f, dh_{nk}^-) = \frac{N(e, f) + \alpha P_0(e)}{N(f) + \alpha},$$

where the counts are computed over the fixed assignments dh_{nk}^-.

The translation probability in the other direction is similarly computed as:

$$P_{fe}(c_k^+, b_k, a_k|dh_{nk}^-) \propto \left(\frac{1}{I+1}\right)^2 P(f'|e_*, dh_{nk}^-)P(f''|e_*, dh_{nk}^-)$$

And $P(f|e, dh_{nk}^-)$ is computed as:

$$P(f|e, dh_{nk}^-) = \frac{N(f, e) + \alpha P_0(f)}{N(e) + \alpha},$$

where the counts are computed over the fixed assignments dh_{nk}^-.

In the second case, if the hypothesis in evaluation does not have a word boundary at position k, the total number of Chinese words would be one less, i.e. J instead of $J+1$ in the equations above, and there would be a single set of English words aligned to the word f in the E-to-C direction, and a single word e_* aligned to f in the C-to-E direction (see the initial state in Figure 2. The probability of this hypothesis is computed analogously.

5.2 Determining the set of alternative hypotheses

As mentioned earlier, we consider alternative alignments which deviate minimally from the current alignments, and which satisfy the constraints of the IBM model 1 in both directions. In order to describe the set of alternatives, we consider two cases, depending on whether there is a boundary at the current character before sampling at position k.

Case 1. There was no boundary at c_k in the previous state (see Figure 1).

If there is no boundary at c_k, there is a single word f spanning that position. We denote by $\{e\}$ the set of English words aligned to f at that state in the E-to-C direction and by e_* the English word aligned to f in the C-to-E direction. Since every state we consider satisfies the IBM one-to-many constraints, there is exactly one English word aligned to f in the C-to-E direction and the words $\{e\}$ have no other words aligned to them in the E-to-C direction.

In this case, we consider as hypothesis cba_k^- the same segmentation and alignment as in the previous state. (see Table 1 for an overview of the alternative hypotheses.)

We consider M different hypotheses which include a boundary at k in this case, where M depends on the number of words $\{e\}$ aligned to f in the previous state. Because we are breaking the word f into two words f' and f'' by placing a boundary at c_k, we need to re-align the words $\{e\}$ to either f' or f''. Additionally we need to align f' and f'' to English words in the C-to-E direction. The number of different hypotheses is equal to 2^P where $P = |\{e\}|$. These alternatives arise by considering that each of the words in $\{e\}$ needs to align to either f' or f'', and there are 2^P combinations of these alignments. For example, if $\{e\} = \{e_1, e_2\}$, after splitting the word f there are four possible alignments, illustrated in Figure 1: I. (f', e_1) and (f'', e_2), II. (f', e_2) and (f'', e_1), III. (f', e_1) and (f', e_2), IV. (f'', e_1) and (f'', e_2). For the alignment a_k in the C-to-E direction, we consider only one option, in which both resulting words f' and f'' align to e_*. These alternatives form $cba_{k,m}^+$ in Table 1.

Case 2. There was a boundary at c_k in the previous state (see Figure 2).

In this case, for the hypotheses c_k^+ we consider only one alternative, which is exactly the same as the assignment of segmentation and alignments in the previous state. Thus we have $M = 1$ in Table 1.

Let f' and f'' denote the two words at position k in the previous state, $\{e'\}$ and $\{e''\}$ denote the sets of English words aligned to them in the E-to-C direction, respectively, and $e_*{}'$ and $e_*{}''$ denote the English words aligned to f' and f'' in the C-to-E direction.

We consider only one hypothesis cba_k^- where there is no boundary at c_k. In this hypothesis, there is a single word $f = f'f''$ spanning position k, and all words $\{e'\} \cup \{e''\}$ align to f in the E-to-C direction. For the C-to-E direction we consider the "better" of the alignments (f, e_*') and (f, e_*'') where the better alignment is defined as the one having higher probability according to the C-to-E word translation probabilities.

Table 2: Complete Algorithm of Gibbs Sampler for CWS including Alignment Models.

Input: D, F_0
Output: A_T, F_T
for $t = 1$ to T
Run GIZA++ on (D, F_{t-1}) to obtain A_t
Run GS on (D, F_{t-1}, A_t) to obtain F_t

5.3 Complete segmentation algorithm

So far, we have described how we re-sample word segmentation and alignments according to our model, starting from an initial segmentation and alignments from GIZA++. Putting these pieces together, the algorithm is summarized in Table 1.

We found that we can further improve performance by repeatedly aligning the corpus using GIZA++, after deriving a new segmentation using our model. The complete algorithm which includes this step is shown in Table 2, where F_t indicates the word segmentation at iteration t and A_t denotes the GIZA++ corpus alignment in both directions. The GS re-segmentation step is done according to the algorithm in Table 1.

Using this algorithm, we obtain a new segmentation of the Chinese data and train the translation models using this segmentation as in the baseline MT system. To segment the test data for translation, we use a unigram model, trained with maximum likelihood estimation off of the final segmentation of the training corpus F_T.

6 Translation Experiments

We performed experiments using our models for CWS on a large and a small data track. We evaluated performance by measuring WER (word error rate), PER (position-independent word error rate), BLEU (Papineni et al., 2002) and TER (translation error rate) (Snover et al., 2006) using multiple references.

6.1 Translation Task: Large Track NIST

We first report the experiments using our monolingual unigram Dirichlet Process model for word segmentation on the NIST machine translation task (NIST, 2005). Because of the computational requirements, we only employed the monolingual word model for this large data track, i.e. the feature weights were $\lambda_1 = 1, \lambda_2 = 0, \lambda_3 = 0$. Therefore, no alignment information needs to be maintained in this case.

The bilingual training corpus is a superset of corpora in the news domain collected from different sources.

We took LDC (LDC, 2003) as a baseline CWS method (Base). As shown in Table 3, the training corpus in each language contains more than two million sentences. There are 56 million Chinese

Table 3: Statistics of corpora in task NIST.

Data	Sents.	Words[K]		Voc.[K]	
		Cn.	En.	Cn.	En.
Chars	2M	56M	49.5M	65.4	211
Base		39.2M		95.7	
GS		40.5M		95.4	
02	878	23.1	28.0	2.04	4.34
03	919	24.6	29.2	2.21	4.91
04	1788	49.8	60.7	2.61	6.71
05	1082	30.8	34.2	2.30	5.39

Table 4: Translation performance [% BLEU] with the baseline(LDC) and GS method on NIST.

MT-eval	LDC(Base)	GS
2005	32.85	33.26
2002	34.32	34.36
2003	33.41	33.75
2004	33.74	34.06

characters. The LDC and GS word segmentation methods generated 39.2 and 40.5 million running words, respectively.

The scaling factors of the translation models described in Section 2.2 were optimized on the development corpus, MT-eval 05 with 1082 sentences. The resulting systems were evaluated on the test corpora MT-eval 02-04. For convenience, we only list the statistics of the first English reference.

Starting from the baseline LDC output as initial word segmentation, we performed Gibbs sampling (GS) of word segmentations using 30 iterations over the Chinese training corpus.

Since BLEU is the official NIST measure of translation performance, we show the translation results measured in BLEU score only. As shown in Table 4, on the development data MT-eval 05, the BLEU score was improved by 0.4% absolute or more than 1% relative using GS. Similarly, the absolute BLEU scores are also improved on all other test sets, in the range of 0.04% to 0.4%.

We can see that even a monolingual semi-supervised word segmentation method can outperform a supervised one in MT, probably because the training/test corpora contain many unknown words and words have different frequencies in our MT data from they do in the manually labeled CWS data.

6.2 Translation Task: Small Track IWSLT

We evaluate our full model, using both monolingual and bilingual information, on the IWSLT data.

As shown in Table 5, the Chinese training corpus was segmented using the unigram segmenter (Base) described in Section 2.1 and our GS method. Since the unigram segmenter performs better in our experiments, we took it as the baseline and the method for initialization in later experiments. We see that the vocabulary size of the Chinese training corpus was reduced more significantly by GS than by the baseline method, even

Table 5: Statistics of corpora in task IWSLT.

Test	Sents.	Words[K]		Voc.	
		Cn.	En.	Cn.	En.
Chars	42.9K	520	420	2780	9930
Base		394		8800	
GS		398		6230	
Dev2	500	3.74	3.82	1004	821
Dev3	506	4.01	3.90	980	820
Eval	489	3.39	3.72	904	810

Table 6: Translation performance with different CWS methods on IWSLT[%].

Test	Method	WER	PER	BLEU	TER
Dev2	Unigram (Base)	38.2	31.2	55.4	37.0
	GS	36.8	30.0	56.6	35.5
Dev3	Unigram (Base)	33.5	27.5	60.4	32.1
	GS	32.3	26.6	61.0	31.4
Eval	Characters	49.3	41.8	35.4	47.5
	LDC	46.2	40.0	39.2	45.0
	ICT	45.9	40.4	40.1	44.9
	Unigram (Base)	46.8	40.2	41.6	45.6
	9-gram	46.9	40.4	40.1	45.4
	GS	45.9	40.0	41.6	44.8

though they resulted in a similar number of running words. This shows that the distribution of Chinese words is more concentrated when using GS.

The parameter optimizations were performed on the Dev2 data with 500 sentences, and evaluations were done both on Dev3 and on Eval data, i.e. the evaluation corpus of (IWSLT, 2007).

The model weights λ of GS from Section 5.1.2 were optimized using the Powell (Press et al., 2002) algorithm with respect to the BLEU score. We obtained $\lambda_1 = 1.4$, $\lambda_2 = 1$ and $\lambda_3 = 0.8$ as optimal values and $T = 4$ as the optimal number of iterations of re-alignment with GIZA++.

For a fair comparison, we evaluated on various CWS methods including translation on characters , LDC (LDC, 2003), ICT (Zhang et al., 2003), unigram, 9-gram and GS. Improvements using GS can be seen in Table 6. Under all test sets and evaluation criteria, GS outperforms the baseline method. The absolute WER decreases with 1.2% on Dev3 and with 1.1% on Eval data over baseline.

We compared the translation outputs using GS with the baseline method. On the Eval data, 196 sentences are different out of 489 lines, where 64 sentences from GS are better, 33 sentences are worse, and the rests have similar translation qualities. Table 7 shows two examples from the Eval corpus. We list segmentations produced by the baseline and GS methods, as well as the translations corresponding to these segmentations. The GS method generates better translation results than the baseline method in these cases.

Table 7: Segmentation and translation outputs with baseline and GS methods.

a)	Baseline	有 近路 吗 ?
		do you have a ?
	GS	有 近 路 吗 ?
		do you have a shorter way ?
	REF	is there a shorter route ?
b)	Baseline	请 告诉 我 总 金额。
		please show me the in .
	GS	请 告诉 我 总 金 额 。
		please show me the total price .
	REF	can you tell me the total amount ?

7 Conclusion and future work

We showed that it is possible to learn Chinese word boundaries such that the translation performance of Chinese-to-English MT systems is improved.

We presented a Bayesian generative model for parallel Chinese-English sentences which uses word segmentation and alignment as hidden variables, and incorporates both monolingual and bilingual information to derive a segmentation suitable for MT.

Starting with an initial word segmentation, our method learns both new Chinese words and distributions for these words. In a large and a small data environment, our method outperformed the standard Chinese word segmentation approach in terms of the Chinese to English translation quality. In future work, we plan to enrich our monolingual and bilingual models to better represent the true distribution of the data.

8 Acknowledgments

Jia Xu conducted this research during her internship at Microsoft Research. This material is also partly based upon work supported by the Defense Advanced Research Projects Agency (DARPA) under Contract No. HR0011-06-C-0023.

References

Aldous, D. 1985. Exchangeability and related topics. In *École d'été de probabilités de Saint-Flour, XIII-1983*, pages 1–198, Springer, Berlin.

Andrew, G. 2006. A hybrid markov/semi-markov conditional random field for sequence segmentation. In *Proceedings of EMNLP*, Sydney, July.

Brown, P. F., S. A. Della Pietra, V. J. Della Pietra, and R. L. Mercer. 1993. The mathematics of statistical machine translation: Parameter estimation. *Computational Linguistics*, 19(2):263–311, June.

Gao, J., M. Li, A. Wu, and C. Huang. 2005. Chinese word segmentation and named entity recognition: A pragmatic approach. *Computational Linguistics*, 31(4).

Goldwater, S., T. L. Griffiths, and M. Johnson. 2006. Contextual dependencies in unsupervised word segmentation. In *Proceedings of Coling/ACL*, Sydney, July.

IWSLT. 2007. International workshop on spoken language translation home page. http://www.slt.atr.jp/IWSLT2007.

Klein, D. and C. D. Manning. 2002. A generative constituent-context model for improved grammar induction. In *Proceedings of ACL*, pages 128–135.

LDC. 2003. Linguistic data consortium Chinese resource home page. http://www.ldc.upenn.edu/Projects/Chinese.

NIST. 2005. Machine translation home page. http://www.nist.gov/speech/tests/mt/index.htm.

Och, F. J. and H. Ney. 2002. Discriminative training and maximum entropy models for statistical machine translation. In *Proceedings of ACL*, pages 295–302, Philadelphia, PA, July.

Papineni, K. A., S. Roukos, T. W., and W. J. Zhu. 2002. Bleu: a method for automatic evaluation of machine translation. In *Proceedings of ACL*, pages 311–318, Philadelphia, July.

Press, W. H., S. A. Teukolsky, W. T. Vetterling, and B. P. Flannery. 2002. *Numerical Recipes in C++*. Cambridge University Press, Cambridge, UK.

Snover, M., B. Dorr, R. Schwartz, L. Micciulla, and J. Makhoul. 2006. A study of translation edit rate with targeted human annotation. In *Proceedings of AMTA*, pages 223–231, Cambridge, MA, August.

Vogel, S., H. Ney, and C. Tillmann. 1996. HMM-based word alignment in statistical translation. In *Proceedings of COLING*.

Xu, J., R. Zens, and H. Ney. 2004. Do we need Chinese word segmentation for statistical machine translation? In *Proceedings of the SIGHAN Workshop on Chinese Language Learning*, pages 122–128, Barcelona, Spain, July.

Xu, J., E. Matusov, R. Zens, and H. Ney. 2005. Integrated Chinese word segmentation in statistical machine translation. In *Proceedings of IWSLT*, pages 141–147, Pittsburgh, PA, October.

Zens, R. and H. Ney. 2004. Improvements in phrase-based statistical machine translation. In *Proceedings of HLT/NAACL*, Boston, MA, May.

Zhang, H., H. Yu, D. Xiong, and Q. Liu. 2003. HHMM-based Chinese lexical analyzer ICTCLAS. In *Proceedings of the Second SIGHAN Workshop on Chinese Language Learning*, pages 184–187, July.

Switching to Real-Time Tasks in Multi-Tasking Dialogue

Fan Yang and **Peter A. Heeman**
Center for Spoken Language Understanding
OGI School of Science & Engineering
Oregon Health & Science University
fly,heeman@cslu.ogi.edu

Andrew Kun
Electrical and Computer Engineering
University of New Hampshire
andrew.kun@unh.edu

Abstract

In this paper we describe an empirical study of human-human multi-tasking dialogues (MTD), where people perform multiple verbal tasks overlapped in time. We examined how conversants switch from the ongoing task to a real-time task. We found that 1) conversants use discourse markers and prosodic cues to signal task switching, similar to how they signal topic shifts in single-tasking speech; 2) conversants strive to switch tasks at a less disruptive place; and 3) where they cannot, they exert additional effort (even higher pitch) to signal the task switching. Our machine learning experiment also shows that task switching can be reliably recognized using discourse context and normalized pitch. These findings will provide guidelines for building future speech interfaces to support multi-tasking dialogue.

1 Introduction

Existing speech interfaces have mostly been used to perform a single task. However, we envision that next-generation speech interfaces will be able to work with the user on multiple tasks at the same time, which is especially useful for real-time tasks. For instance, a driver in a car might use a speech interface to catch up on emails, while occasionally checking upcoming traffic conditions, and receiving navigation instructions.

Several speech interfaces that allow multi-tasking dialogues have been built (Lemon et al., 2002; Kun et al., 2004). However, these interfaces freely switch between different tasks without much signaling. Thus the user might be confused about which task the interface is talking about. Multi-tasking dialogues, even in the best circumstances, will be difficult for users, as users need to remember the details of each task and be aware of task switching.

In order to build a speech interface that supports multi-tasking dialogue, there needs to be a set of conventions for the user and the interface to follow in switching between tasks. To design such a set, we propose to start with conventions that are actually used in human-human conversations, which are natural for users to follow and probably efficient in problem-solving. Multi-tasking dialogues, where multiple independent topics overlap with each other in time, regularly arise in human-human conversation: for example, a driver and a navigator in a car might be talking about their summer plans, while occasionally interjecting road directions or conversation about what music to listen to.

In order to better understand the human conventions on task switching, we have collected the MTD corpus (Heeman et al., 2005), which consists of a set of human-human dialogues where pairs of conversants have multiple overlapping verbal tasks to perform: an ongoing task that takes a long time to finish, and a real-time task that can be done in a couple of turns but has a time constraint. This paper is focused on how conversants switch from the ongoing task to a waiting real-time task.

Previous research suggested the correlation between task switching and certain discourse context; for example, conversants try to avoid task switching in the middle of an adjacency pair (Shyrokov et al., 2007). In a preliminary study (Heeman et al., 2005), we examined the timing when conversants switched from the ongoing task to a real-time task using some pilot data, and found that

© 2008. Licensed under the *Creative Commons Attribution-Noncommercial-Share Alike 3.0 Unported* license (http://creativecommons.org/licenses/by-nc-sa/3.0/). Some rights reserved.

conversants did not always switch to a real-time task as soon as it arose, but instead waited for different amounts of time depending on its time constraint. In this study, we hypothesize that conversants strive to switch at an opportune place in the ongoing task, and we examine the discourse context where task switching occurs for evidence to support this hypothesis.

We are also interested in the cues that conversants use to signal task switching. Although there is a substantial body of research on how people signal topic shifts in single-tasking speech (monologue and dialogue), such as using discourse markers and prosodic cues (see Section 2.2), little research work has been done in investigating task switching in multi-tasking dialogues. In this study, we examine discourse markers and prosodic cues for their correlations with task switching. We also examine combining these cues to recognize task switching with machine learning techniques.

In Section 2, we review related literature. In Section 3, we describe the MTD corpus. In Section 4, we examine the discourse contexts in which task switching occurs. In Section 5, we examine the use of discourse markers and prosody associated with task switching. In Section 6, we examine automatic recognizing task switching with machine learning techniques. We conclude the paper in Section 7.

2 Related Research

In this section, we first describe two existing speech interfaces that allow multi-tasking dialogues. These speech interfaces, however, freely switch between tasks as soon as a new task arises, and without much signaling. We then review literature on how people signal topic shifts in single-tasking speech, which sheds light on our research of signaling task switching in multi-tasking dialogues.

2.1 Speech Interfaces for MTD

Kun et al. (2004) developed a system called Project54, which allows a user to interact with multiple devices in a police cruiser using speech. The architecture of Project54 allows for handling multiple tasks overlapped in time. For example, when pulling over a vehicle, an officer can first issue a spoken command to turn on the lights and siren, then issue spoken commands to initiate a data query, go back to interacting with the lights and siren (perhaps to change the pattern after the vehicle has been pulled over), and finally receive the spoken results of the data query. While the current implementation of Project54 assumes that the officer initiates the task switching (e.g. the one about lights and the one about data query), the system can initiate task switching too. However, Project54 does not provide infrastructure for signaling to the officer a system-initiated switch. Any such signaling would have to be hand-coded by developers.

Lemon et al. (2002) also explored multi-tasking in a dialogue system. They built a multi-tasking dialogue system for a human operator to direct a robotic helicopter on executing multiple tasks, such as searching for a car and flying to a tower. The system keeps an ordered set of active dialogue tasks, and interprets the user utterance in terms of the most active task for which the utterance makes sense. Conversely, during the system's turn of speaking, it can produce an utterance for any of the dialogue tasks. Thus the system does not take into account the user's cost of task switching. The system switches to a new task as soon as it arises, instead of at an opportune place to minimize the user's effort. Moreover, the system does not signal when it switches between tasks. As with the approach of Kun et al. (2004) to multiple devices, it is unclear whether an actual user will be able to understand such conversations. The user might become confused about which task the system is on.

2.2 Signaling Topic Shifts in STP

Although speech interfaces have not used cues to signal task switching, researchers have found various cues that people naturally use in single-tasking speech to signal topic shifts. These cues are a good starting point from which to study how people signal task switching in multi-tasking dialogue.

Signaling topic shifts in single-tasking speech is about signaling the boundary of related discourse segments that contribute to the achievement of a task. Two types of cues have been identified for signaling topic shifts. The first type is discourse markers (Moser and Moore, 1995; Schiffrin, 1987; Grosz and Sidner, 1986; Passonneau and Litman, 1997; Bangerter and Clark, 2003). Discourse markers can be used to signal the start of a new discourse segment and its relation to other discourse segments. For example, "now" might signal moving on to the next topic, while "well" might signal a negative or unexpected response.

The second type of cue is prosody. In read speech, Grosz and Hirschberg (1992) studied broadcast news and found that pause length is the most important factor that indicates a new discourse segment. Ayers (1992) found that pitch range appears to correlate more closely with hierarchical topic structure in read speech than in spontaneous speech. In spontaneous monologue, Butterworth (1972) found that the beginning of a discourse segment exhibited slower speaking rate; Swerts (1995), and Passonneau and Litman (1997) found that pause length correlates with discourse segment boundaries; Hirschberg and Nakatani (1996) found that the beginning of a discourse segment correlates with higher pitch. In human-human dialogue, similar behavior was observed: the pitch value tends to be higher for starting a new discourse segment (Nakajima and Allen, 1993). In human-computer dialogue, Swerts and Ostendorf (1995) found that the first utterance of a discourse segment correlates with slower speaking rate and longer preceding pause. Clearly, prosody is used to signal topic shifts in single-tasking speech.

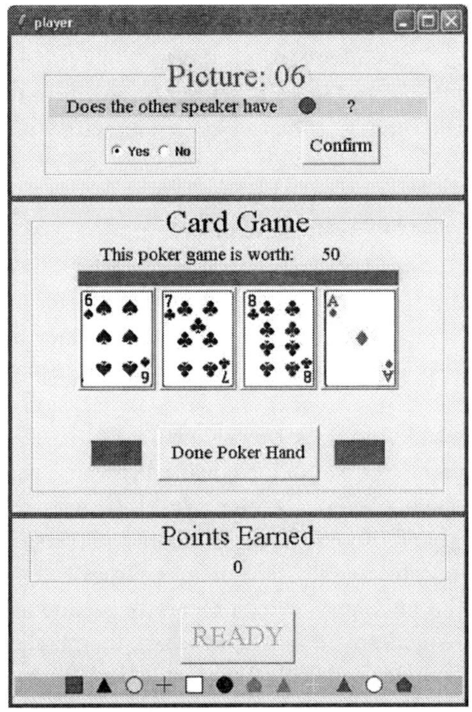

Figure 1: The game display for players

3 The MTD Corpus

In order to fully understand multi-tasking human-human dialogue, we collected the MTD corpus, in which pairs of subjects perform overlapping verbal tasks. Details of the corpus collection can be found in (Heeman et al., 2005).

3.1 Design of Tasks

Conversants work on two types of tasks via conversation: an on-going task that takes a long time to finish and a real-time task that just takes a couple turns to complete but has a time constraint.

In the ongoing task, a pair of players work together to form as many poker hands as possible, where a poker hand consists of a full house, flush, straight, or four of a kind. Each player has three cards in hand, which the other cannot see (players are separated so that they cannot see each other.) Players take turns drawing an extra card and then discarding one, until they find a poker hand, for which they earn 50 points; they then start over to form another poker hand. To discourage players from simply rifling through the cards to look for a specific card without talking, one point is deducted for each picked-up card, and 10 points for a missed poker hand or incorrect poker hand. To complete this game, players converse to share card information, explore and establish strategies based on the combined cards in their hands (Toh et al., 2006).

The poker game is played on computers. The game display, which each player sees, is shown in Figure 1. The player with four cards can click on a card to discard it. The card disappears from the screen, and an extra card is automatically dealt to the other player. The player with four cards clicks the "Done Poker Hand" button to start a new game once they find a poker hand.

From time to time, the computer generates a prompt for one player to find out whether the other has a certain picture on the bottom of the display. The picture game has a time constraint of 10, 25 or 40 seconds, which is (pseudo) randomly determined. The players get 5 points for the picture game if the correct answer is given in time. The overall goal of the players is to earn as many points as possible from the two games.

To alert the player to the picture game, two solid bars flash above and below the player's cards. Thus the player will know that there is a waiting picture game without taking the attention away from the poker game. The color of the flashing bars depends on how much time is remaining: green for 26-40 seconds, yellow for 11-25 seconds and red for 0-10 seconds. The player can see the exact amount of time in the heading for the picture game. In Figure 1, the player needs to find out whether the other has a blue circle, with 6 seconds left.

3.2 Corpus Annotations

We transcribed and annotated ten MTD dialogues totaling about 150 minutes of conversation. The dialogues were by five pairs of players, all native American-English speakers. Each pair participated in two sessions and each session lasted about 15 minutes. During each session, 9 picture games (3 for each time constraint) were prompted for each player. Of the total 180 picture game prompted, 8 were never started by players[1]. Thus the corpus contains 172 picture games.

The ongoing task can naturally be divided into individual poker games, in which the players successfully complete a poker hand. Each poker game can be further divided into a sequence of card segments, in which players discuss which card to discard, or a poker hand is found. In total, there are 105 game segments and 690 card segments in the corpus. As well, we grouped the utterances involved in each picture game into segments. Figure 2 shows an excerpt from an MTD dialogue with these annotations. Here b7 is a game segment in which players got a poker hand of flush; and b8, b10, b11, b12 and b14, inside of b7, are card segments. Also embedded in b7 are b9 and b13, each of which is an segment for a picture game. As can be seen, players switched from the ongoing poker-playing to a picture game. After the picture game was completed, the conversation on the poker-playing resumed.

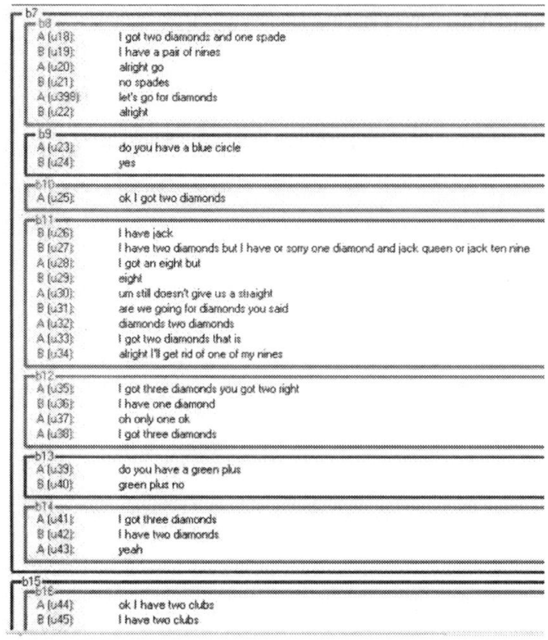

Figure 2: An excerpt of an MTD dialogue

4 Where to Switch

In a preliminary study (Heeman et al., 2005), we found that players did not always switch to a real-time task as soon as it arose, but instead waited for different amounts of time depending on the time constraint of the real-time task. We thus hypothesize that players strive to switch at an opportune place in the ongoing task (poker-playing). There are three types of places where a player could suspend the poker playing and switch to a waiting picture game: (G) immediately after completing a poker game (at the end of a game), (C) immediately after discarding a card (at the end of a card), and (E) embedded inside a card segment, where players are deciding which card to discard. In this section, we examine where task switching occurs.

4.1 Time Constraint and Place of Switching

We first examine the place of switching under different time constraints. As shown in Table 1, for the time constraint of 10s, 75% of the task switching was embedded inside a card segment, 23% at the end of a card, and 2% at the end of a game; for the time constraints of 25s and 40s[2], 46% embedded inside a card segment, 33% at the end of a card, and 21% at the end of a game. The difference in the places of switching between the time constraint of 10s and 25s/40s is statistically significant ($\chi^2(2) = 15.92$, $p < 0.001$). The time constraint of 10s requires players to start a picture game very quickly in order to complete it in time. On the other hand, when given 25s or 40s, players are in a less hurry to switch. Compared with 10s, when players had 25s or 40s, the percentage of switching embedded inside a card segment decreases by 29%, while at the end of a card increases by 10%, and at the end of a game increases by 19%. These results suggest that when given more time, players try to switch at the end of a game or a card.

[1]Although in the post-experiment survey all players reported that they never ignored a picture game on purpose

[2]We combined the time constraints of 25s and 40s because 25s seemed to be sufficient for most players.

Table 1: Time constraint and place of switching

	E	C	G	Total
10s	42 (75%)	13 (23%)	1 (2%)	56 (100%)
25/40s	54 (46%)	38 (33%)	24 (21%)	116 (100%)

Table 2: Waiting time and place of switching

	E	C	G	Total
$\leq 3s$	47 (69%)	18 (27%)	3 (4%)	68 (100%)
$> 3s$	49 (47%)	33 (32%)	22 (21%)	104 (100%)

4.2 Waiting Time and Place of Switching

We next examine the place of task switching from the perspective of waiting time. Waiting time refers to the time interval between when a picture game is prompted to a player and when the player actually starts the picture game. Our question is: if players wait at least a certain amount of time, where would they switch tasks? We arbitrary choose a time amount of 3 seconds. We assume that when the waiting time is shorter than 3s, the player starts the picture game as soon as he or she notices it without significant waiting; in other words, based on human reaction time, if players are going to respond to it right away, they should be able to do so within 3s. The results are shown in Table 2. When the waiting time is shorter than 3s, 69% of the task switching is embedded inside a card segment, 27% at the end of a card, and only 4% at the end of a game; when longer than 3s, 47% is embedded inside a card segment, 32% at the end of a card, and 21% at the end of a game. The difference in the places of switching is statistically different ($\chi^2(2) = 11.88$, $p = 0.003$). When the waiting time is longer than 3s, the percentage of switching inside a card decreases by 22%, while switching at the end of a card increases by 5%, and at the end of a game increases by 17%. These results suggest that players wait for the end of a game or a card to switch to a picture game.

4.3 Discussion

We examined the discourse context of task switching, and found that 1) when given more time, players intend to switch to a picture game at the end of a (poker) game or a card; and (2) if players wait, they are waiting for the end of a (poker) game or a card to switch to a picture game. These results suggest that players strive to switch to a picture game at the end of a (poker) game or a card.

In fact, we also observed that after a picture game that is at the end of a game, players smoothly start a new poker game as if nothing had happened; after a picture game that is at the end of a card, players might sometimes remind each other what cards they have in hands; while after a picture game that is in the middle of a card segment, players might even repeat or clarify the previous utterances that were said before the interruption. It is thus reasonable to assume that switching embedded inside a card segment is the most disruptive, followed by at the end of a card, and at the end of a game is the least. Our experiment results hence suggest that players strive to switch to a real-time task at a less disruptive place in the ongoing task. This is consistent with Clark and Wilkes-Gibbs (1986), that conversants try to minimize collaborative effort.

5 How to Switch

In Section 2.2, we discussed how people use certain cues, such as discourse markers and prosody, to signal topic shifts in single-tasking speech. This suggests that people might also signal task switching in multi-tasking dialogues. In this section, we examine how players signal that they are switching from the ongoing task to a real-time task with discourse markers and prosody.

5.1 Task Switching and Discourse Markers

Close examination of the MTD corpus found that "oh" was the most frequently used discourse marker when switching to a picture game. Another discourse marker, "wait" (including "wait a minute"), was often used together with "oh" in the way of "oh wait". Thus we examined the use of "oh" and "wait" in switching to a picture game.

Players used the discourse markers "oh" or "wait" 14.5% (25/172) of the time in switching to a picture game. In poker playing, 5.7% (238/4192) of utterances contain the words "oh" or "wait", and only 4.6% (32/690) of card segments are initiated with the two discourse markers (i.e. the first utterance of a card segment has "oh" or "wait" at the very beginning). Players have a statistically higher percentage of using "oh" or "wait" at task switching than in poker playing ($\chi^2(1) = 22.89$, $p < 0.001$) or to initiate a card segment ($\chi^2(1) = 21.84$, $p < 0.001$).

5.2 Task Switching and Prosody

To understand the prosodic cues in initiating a topic, traditionally researchers compared the prosody of the first utterance in each segment with other utterances (e.g. (Nakajima and Allen, 1993; Hirschberg and Nakatani, 1996)). This approach encounters two problems here. First, the words in an utterance might affect the prosody. For example, the duration and energy of "bat" are usually larger than "bit". Thus a large amount of data are required to balance out these differences. Second, in the MTD corpus, players typically switch to a picture game by using a yes-no question, such as "do you have a blue circle", while most forward utterances (c.f. Core and Allen 1997) in the ongoing task are statements or proposals. As questions have very different prosody than statements or proposals, a direct comparison is further biased.

Examination of the MTD corpus found that 86% (148/172) of the picture games were initiated by "do you have ..." with optional discourse markers at the beginning. While in the poker game, players used "do you have ..." 108 times to ask whether the other had certain cards, such as "do you have a queen?" This observation inspired us to compare the prosody of the phrase "do you have" in switching to a picture game and during poker-playing.[3] This avoids comparing prosody of different words or of different types of utterances.

We measure pitch, energy (local root mean squared measurement), and duration of each case of "do you have". We aggregate on each player and calculate the average values. The results are shown in Table 3. The second and third columns show the average pitch of the phrase "do you have" for task-switching (SWT) and poker-playing (PKR) respectively. When switching to a picture game, players' average pitch is statistically higher than poker-playing ($t(9) = 4.15, p = 0.001$). In fact, for each of the ten players, the average pitch of "do you have" in switching to a picture game is higher than in poker-playing. These results show a strong correlation between task switching and higher pitch.

We next examine the correlation between energy and task switching. The fourth and fifth columns in Table 3 show the average energy of the phrase "do you have" for task switching and poker-playing respectively. We do not find a statistically significant difference ($t(9) = 0.80, p = 0.44$). We also examine the duration of "do you have". The sixth and seventh columns in Table 3 show the results. We do not find a statistically significant difference either ($t(9) = 1.03, p = 0.33$). These results do not support that energy or duration (i.e. speaking rate) is correlated to task switching.

[3]Note that most cases of "do you have" in poker-playing are not at the beginning of a card segment. It would have also been interesting to compare the prosody of "do you have" of initiating a picture game and of initiating a card segment. However, we do not have enough data for the latter.

Table 3: Average prosodic values for each player

Player	pitch (Hz)		energy		duration (s)	
	SWT	PKR	SWT	PKR	SWT	PKR
4A	136	123	383	266	0.28	0.38
4B	178	156	466	506	0.32	0.30
5A	164	152	357	367	0.37	0.25
5B	214	182	231	153	0.36	0.28
6A	144	126	414	370	0.32	0.21
6B	122	117	564	496	0.25	0.23
8A	238	199	973	1061	0.36	0.21
8B	150	143	246	180	0.33	0.35
9A	109	102	538	465	0.44	0.59
9B	125	122	702	814	0.33	0.24

Table 4: Pitch (Hz) and place of switching

Player	E	C & G	PKR
4A	137	131	123
4B	180	173	156
5A	167	161	152
5B	219	206	182
6A	146	143	126
6B	124	121	117
8A	245	233	199
8B	152	140	143
9A	110	108	102
9B	130	117	122

5.3 Intensity of Signal

To better understand how pitch is used in signaling task switching, we next examine whether it correlates with place of switching, i.e., switching at the end of a game, at the end of a card, or embedded inside a card segment. Because there are relatively less data for switching at the end of a game (see Table 1 and 2), we combine switching at the end of a game and at the end of a card (C & G) as a category.

Table 4 shows the average pitch of "do you have" when switching to a picture game embedded inside a card segment, at the end of a card or game segment, and during poker-playing. The difference between these three conditions is statistically significant ($F(2,9) = 15.61, p < 0.001$). Switching embedded inside a card segment has a statistically higher pitch than switching at the end of a card or game segment ($t(9) = 5.54, p < 0.001$), which in turn has a statistically higher pitch than during poker-playing ($t(9) = 2.91, p = 0.01$).

5.4 Discussion

Consistent with previous research on topic shifts in single-tasking speech, our experiments show that switching to a real-time task correlates with the use of certain discourse markers and prosodic variations. It is not surprising that "oh" and "wait" correlate with task switching. Task switching involves a sudden change of the conversation topic, and previous research found that conversants use "oh" to mark a change of state in orientation or awareness (Heritage, 1984). "Wait" is used to mark a discontinuity in the ongoing topic, which is also required by task switching. Thus people may use these discourse markers to signal switching to a real-time task. In terms of prosodic variations, we find that task switching correlates with higher pitch. This suggests that pitch is used to signal switching to a real-time task.

Our experiments have also shown that pitch correlates to place of switching. As discussed in Section 4.3, task switching embedded inside a card segment is the most disruptive, switching at the end of a card is less, and at the end of a game is the least. Our results show that switching embedded in a card segment has a higher pitch than switching at the end of a card or a game, which in turn has a higher pitch than non-switching (poker-playing). This suggests that the degree of disruptiveness corresponds to the value of pitch: the more disruptive place to switch, the higher is the pitch.

From our results we speculate that pitch is used to divert the hearer from the ongoing task, signaling an unexpected event (c.f. (Sussman et al., 2003)). When task switching is more disruptive, the speaker uses higher pitch; probably because the hearer has a stronger expectation of the next utterance to be in the context of poker-playing. The use of higher pitch servers as a cue that the hearer should suspend the ongoing context and interpret the utterance in a new context. According to the theory of *least collaborative effort*, the effort of raising the pitch by the speaker is probably to reduce the effort of recognizing and processing the task switching by the hearer (Clark and Wilkes-Gibbs, 1986).

6 Machine Learning Experiment

In the previous sections, we showed the correlation of various cues with task switching. In this section, we conduct a machine learning experiment to determine whether we can reliably recognize task switching using these cues. For the reasons given in Section 5.2, we limit our experiment to the 256 cases of "do you have", 148 for task switching and 108 for poker playing. We train a decision tree classifier (C4.5) to discriminate task switching from poker playing. We use 5-fold cross validation to evaluate the performance. We use decision tree learning because its output is interpretable and we have found its performance comparable to other discriminative classifiers for this task.

The feature set includes 1) discourse context: whether the utterance before "do you have" is the end of a poker game, the end of a card segment, or in the middle of a card segment[4]; 2) cue word: whether the "do you have" follows the cue word "oh" or "wait"; and 3) normalized pitch: the pitch of "do you have" divided by the average pitch of the speaker during the dialogue.

The decision tree learning obtains an accuracy of 83% in identifying whether a "do you have" initiates a task switching or belongs to poker playing; and the recall, precision, and F measure for task switching are 90%, 82%, and 86% respectively. As a baseline, if we blindly assume that all cases of "do you have" are for task switching, we have an accuracy of 58%. Thus decision tree learning with the three features has 43% relative error reduction over the baseline.

To examine the structure of the decision tree, we build a single tree from all 256 cases of "do you have". We find that the decision tree first examines the normalized pitch; if it is greater than 1.085, it is a task-switch. Otherwise, if the discourse context is at the end of a game, then it is for task switching; if the discourse context is embedded in a card segment, it is for poker playing; if the discourse context is at the end of a card: if normalized pitch is higher than 0.975 then it is for task switching, otherwise for poker playing. Interestingly, the feature of cue word is not used in the tree.

The performance and structure of the learned tree suggest that discourse context and normalized pitch are useful features for discriminating task switching.

7 Conclusion

In this paper we have described an empirical study of human-human multi-tasking dialogues, where people perform multiple verbal tasks overlapped

[4]Card and game segments can be determined fairly accurately from the mouse clicks even without the speech.

in time. We first examined the place of task switching, i.e. where players suspend the ongoing task and switch to a real-time task. Our analysis showed that people strive to switch at a less disruptive place. We then examined the cues to signal task switching. We found that task switching correlates with certain discourse markers and prosodic variations. More interestingly, the more disruptive the switching is, the higher is the pitch. We thus speculate that pitch is used by the speaker to help the listener be aware of task switching and understand the utterance. Finally, our machine learning experiment showed that discourse context and pitch are useful features to reliably identify task switching.

Acknowledgement

This work was funded by the National Science Foundation under IIS-0326496.

References

Ayers, Gayle M. 1992. Discourse functions of pitch range in spontaneous and read speech. Presented at the Linguistic Society of America Annual Meeting.

Bangerter, Adrian and Herbert H. Clark. 2003. Navigating joint projects with dialogue. *Cognitive Science*, 27:195–229.

Butterworth, Brian. 1972. Hesitation and semantic planning in speech. *Journal of Psycholinguistic Research*, 4:75–87.

Clark, Herbert H. and Deanna Wilkes-Gibbs. 1986. Referring as a collaborative process. *Cognitive Science*, 22:1–39.

Core, Mark G. and James F. Allen. 1997. Coding dialogues with the DAMSL annotation scheme. In *Working Notes: AAAI Fall Symposium on Communicative Action in Humans and Machines*, pages 28–35, Cambridge.

Grosz, Barbara J. and Julia Hirschberg. 1992. Some intonational characteristics of discourse structure. In *Proceedings of 2nd ICSLP*, pages 429–432.

Grosz, Barbara J. and Candace L. Sidner. 1986. Attention, intentions, and the structure of discourse. *Computational Linguistics*, 12(3):175–204.

Heeman, Peter A., Fan Yang, Andrew L. Kun, and Alexander Shyrokov. 2005. Conventions in human-human multithreaded dialogues: A preliminary study. In *Proceedings of IUI (short paper session)*, pages 293–295, San Diego CA.

Heritage, John. 1984. A change-of-state token and aspects of its sequential placement. In Atldnson, J. M. and J. Heritage, editors, *Structures of social action: Studies in conversation analysis*, chapter 13, pages 299–345. Cambridge University Press.

Hirschberg, Julia and Christine H. Nakatani. 1996. A prosodic analysis of discourse segments in direction-giving monologues. In *Proceedings of 34th ACL*, pages 286–293.

Kun, Andrew L., W. Thomas Miller, and William H. Lenharth. 2004. Computers in police cruisers. *IEEE Pervasive Computing*, 3(4):34–41, October-December.

Lemon, Oliver, Alexander Gruenstein, Alexis Battle, and Stanley Peters. 2002. Multi-tasking and collaborative activities in dialogue systems. In *Proceedings of 3rd SIGdial*, Philadelphia PA.

Moser, Megan and Johanna D. Moore. 1995. Investigating cue selection and placement in tutorial discourse. In *Proceedings of 33rd ACL*, pages 130–135.

Nakajima, Shin'ya and James F. Allen. 1993. A study on prosody and discourse structure in cooperative dialogues. Technical report, Rochester, NY, USA. technical report.

Passonneau, Rebecca J. and Diane J. Litman. 1997. Discourse segmentation by human and automated means. *Computational Linguistics*, 23(1):103–139.

Schiffrin, Deborah. 1987. *Discourse Markers*. Cambridge University Press.

Shyrokov, Alexander, Andrew Kun, and Peter Heeman. 2007. Experiments modeling of human-human multi-threaded dialogues in the presence of a manual-visual task. In *Proceedings of 8th SIGdial*, pages 190–193.

Sussman, E., I. Winkler, and E. Schrgöer. 2003. Top-down control over involuntary attention switching in the auditory modality. *Psychonomic Bulletin & Review*, 10(3):630–637.

Swerts, Marc and Mari Ostendorf. 1995. Discourse prosody in human-machine interactions. In *Proceedings of ESCA workshop on spoken dialogue systems: theories and applications*, pages 205–208, Visgo Denmark.

Swerts, Marc. 1995. Combining statistical and phonetic analyses of spontaneous discourse segmentation. In *Proceedings of the 12th ICPhS*, volume 4, pages 208–211.

Toh, Siew Leng, Fan Yang, and Peter A. Heeman. 2006. An annotation scheme for agreement analysis. In *Proceedings of 9th ICSLP*, pages 201–204, Pittsburgh PA.

Chinese Term Extraction Using Minimal Resources

Yuhang Yang
School of Computer Science and Technology, Harbin Institute of Technology, Harbin 150001, China
1983yang@gmail.com

Qin Lu
Department of Computing, The Hong Kong Polytechnic University, Hong Kong, China
csluqin@comp.polyu.edu.hk

Tiejun Zhao
School of Computer Science and Technology, Harbin Institute of Technology, Harbin 150001, China
tjzhao@mtlab.hit.edu.cn

Abstract

This paper presents a new approach for term extraction using minimal resources. A term candidate extraction algorithm is proposed to identify features of the relatively stable and domain independent term delimiters rather than that of the terms. For term verification, a link analysis based method is proposed to calculate the relevance between term candidates and the sentences in the domain specific corpus from which the candidates are extracted. The proposed approach requires no prior domain knowledge, no general corpora, no full segmentation and minimal adaptation for new domains. Consequently, the method can be used in any domain corpus and it is especially useful for resource-limited domains. Evaluations conducted on two different domains for Chinese term extraction show quite significant improvements over existing techniques and also verify the efficiency and relative domain independent nature of the approach. Experiments on new term extraction also indicate that the approach is quite effective for identifying new terms in a domain making it useful for domain knowledge update.

1 Introduction

Terms are the lexical units to represent the most fundamental knowledge of a domain. Term extraction is an essential task in domain knowledge acquisition which can be used for lexicon update, domain ontology construction, etc. Term extraction involves two steps. The first step extracts candidates by unithood calculation to qualify a string as a valid term. The second step verifies them through termhood measures (Kageura and Umino, 1996) to validate their domain specificity.

Existing techniques extract term candidates mainly by two kinds of statistic based measures including *internal association* (e.g. Schone and Jurafsky, 2001) and *context dependency* (e.g. Sornlertlamvanich et al., 2000). These techniques are also used in Chinese term candidate extraction (e.g. Luo and Sun, 2003; Ji and Lu, 2007). Domain dependent features of domain terms are used in a weighted manner to identify term boundaries. However, these algorithms always face the dilemma that fewer features are not enough to identify terms from non-terms whereas more features lead to more conflicts among selected features in a specific instance.

Most term verification techniques use features on the difference in distribution of a term occurred within a domain and across domains, such as *TF-IDF* (Salton and McGill, 1983; Frank, 1999) and *Inter-Domain Entropy* (Chang, 2005). Limited distribution information on term candidates in different documents are far from enough to distinguish terms from non-terms. Other researches attempted to use more direct information. The therm verification algorithm, *TV_ConSem,* proposed in (Ji and Lu, 2007) for Chinese calculate the percentage of context words in a domain lexicon using both frequency information and semantic information. However, this technique requires a large domain lexicon and relies heavily on both the size and the quality of the lexicon. Some supervised learning

© 2008. Licensed under the *Creative Commons Attribution-Noncommercial-Share Alike 3.0 Unported* license (http://creativecommons.org/licenses/by-nc-sa/3.0/). Some rights reserved.

approaches have been applied to protein/gene name recognition (Zhou et al., 2005) and Chinese new word identification (Li et al., 2004) using *SVM* classifiers (Vapnik, 1995) which also require large domain corpora and annotations, and intensive training is needed for a new domain.

Current term extraction techniques (e.g. Frank et al., 1999; Chang, 2005; Ji and Lu, 2007) suffer from three major problems. The first problem is that these algorithms cannot identify certain kinds of terms such as the ones that have less statistical significance. The second problem is their dependency on full segmentation for Chinese text which is particularly vulnerable to handle domain specific data (Huang et al., 2007). The third problem is their dependency on some a priori domain knowledge such as a domain lexicon making it difficult to be applied to a new domain.

In this work, the proposed algorithm extracts candidates by identifying the relatively stable and domain independent term boundary markers instead of looking for features associated with the term candidate themselves. Furthermore, a novel algorithm for term verification is proposed using link analysis to calculate the relevance between term candidates and the sentences in domain specific corpus to validate their domain specificity.

The rest of the paper is organized as follows. Section 2 describes the proposed algorithms. Section 3 explains the experiments and the performance evaluation. Section 4 is the conclusion.

2 Methodology

2.1 Delimiters Based Term Candidate Extraction

Generally speaking, sentences are constituted by substantives and functional words. Domain specific terms (*terms* for short) are more likely to be domain substantives. Words immediate before and after these terms, called *predecessors* and *successors* of the terms, are likely to be either functional words or other general substantives connecting terms. These predecessors and successors can be considered as markers of terms, and are referred to as *term delimiters* in this paper. In contrast to terms, delimiters are relatively stable and domain independent. Thus, they can be extracted more easily. Instead of looking for features associated with terms as in other works, this paper looks for features associated with term delimiters. That is, term delimiters are identified first. Words between delimiters are then taken as term candidates.

The proposed delimiter identification based algorithm, referred to as *TCE_DI* (Term Candidate Extraction – Delimiter Identification), extracts term candidates from a domain corpus by using a delimiter list, referred to as the *DList*. Given a *DList*, the algorithm *TCE_DI* itself is straight forward. For a given character string *CS* ($CS = C_1C_2...C_n$) shown in Figure 1, where C_i is a Chinese character. Suppose there are two delimiters $D_1 = C_{i1}...C_{il}$ and $D_2 = C_{j1}...C_{jm}$ in *CS* where $D_1 \in DList$ and $D_2 \in DList$. The string *CS* is then segmented to five substrings: $C_1...C_{ib}$, $C_{i1}...C_{il}$, $C_{ia}...C_{jb}$, $C_{j1}...C_{jm}$, and $C_{ja}...C_n$. Since $C_{i1}...C_{il}$ and $C_{j1}...C_{jm}$ are delimiters, $C_1...C_{ib}$, $C_{ia}...C_{jb}$, and $C_{ja}...C_n$ are regarded as term candidates as labeled by TC_1, TC_2 and TC_3 in Figure 1, respectively. If there is no delimiter contained in *CS*, the whole string $C_1C_2...C_n$ is regarded as one term candidate.

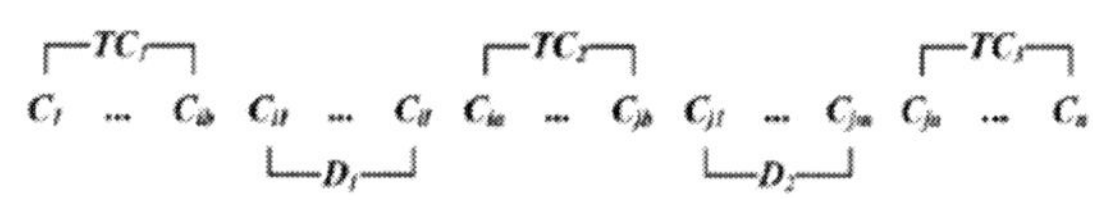

Figure 1. Paradigm of Term Candidate Extraction

DList can be obtained either from a delimiter training corpus or from a given stop word list. Given a delimiter training corpus, $Corpus_{Training}$, normally a domain specific corpus, and a domain lexicon *Lexicon*, *DList* can be obtained based on the following algorithm, referred to as *DList_Ext* (*DelimiterList Extraction Algorithm*).

Step 1: For each term T_i in *Lexicon*, mark T_i in $Corpus_{Training}$ as a non-divisible lexical unit.

Step 2: Segment remaining text in $Corpus_{Training}$.

Step 3: Extracts predecessors and successors of all T_i as delimiter candidates.

Step 4: Remove delimiter candidates that are contained in a T_i in *Lexicon*.

Step 5: Rank delimiter candidates by frequency and the top N_{DI} number of items are considered delimiters.

The *DList_Ext* algorithm basically use known terms in a domain specific *Lexicon* to find the delimiters. It can be shown in the experiments later that *Lexicon* does not need to be comprehensive. Even if a small training corpus, $Corpus_{Training}$, is not available in a language without sufficient domain specific NLP resources, a stop-word list produced by experts or from a general corpus can serve as *DList* directly without using the *DList_Ext* algorithm.

2.2 Link Analysis Based Term Verification

In a domain corpus, some sentences are *domain relevant sentences* which contain more domain specific information whereas others are *general sentences* which contain less domain information. A domain specific term is more likely to be contained in domain relevant sentences, which means that domain relevant sentences and domain specific terms have a mutually reinforcing relationship. A novel algorithm, referred to as *TV_LinkA* (Term Verification – Link Analysis) based the Hyperlink-Induced Topic Search (*HITS*) algorithm (Kleinberg, 1997) originally proposed for information retrieval, is proposed using link analysis to calculate the relevance between term candidates and the sentences in domain specific corpora for term verification.

In *TV_LinkA*, a node p can either be a sentence or a term candidate. If a term candidate $Term_C$ is contained in a sentence *Sen* of the corpus $Corpus_{Extract}$ where the candidates were extracted, there is a directional link from *Sen* to $Term_C$. This way, a graph for the candidates and the sentences in $Corpus_{Extract}$ can be constructed and the links between them indicate their relationships. A good *hub* in $Corpus_{Extract}$ is a sentence that contains many good authorities; a good *authority* is a term candidate that is contained in many good hubs. Each node p is associated with a non-negative authority weight $w(p)^A$ and a non-negative hub weight $w(p)^H$. Link analysis in *TV_LinkA* makes use of the relationship between hubs and authorities via an iterative process to maintain and update authority/hub weights for each node of the graph.

Let V^A denote the authority vector $(w(p_1)^A, w(p_2)^A, \ldots, w(p_n)^A)$ and V^H denote the hub vector $(w(p_1)^H, w(p_2)^H, \ldots, w(p_n)^H)$, where n is the sum of the total number of sentences and the total number of term candidates. Given weights V^A and V^H with a directional link $p \to q$, the I operation(an in-pointer to a node) and the O operation(an out-pointer to a node) update $w(q)^A$ and $w(p)^H$ as follows.

$$I \text{ operation: } w(q)^A = \sum_{p \to q \in E} w(p)^H \quad (1)$$

$$O \text{ operation: } w(p)^H = \sum_{p \to q \in E} w(q)^A \quad (2)$$

Let k be the iteration termination parameter and z be the vector (1, 1, 1,…, 1) , and V^A and V^H are initialized to $V_0^A = V_0^H = z$. Hubs and authorities can then be calculated as follows.

For i = 1, 2,…, k

Apply the I operation to (V_{i-1}^A , V_{i-1}^H), obtaining new $V_i'^A$.

Apply the O operation to ($V_i'^A$, V_{i-1}^H), obtaining new $V_i'^H$.

Normalize $V_i'^A$ by dividing the normalization factor $\sqrt{\sum (w'(p)^A)^2}$ to obtain V_i^A.

Normalize $V_i'^H$ by dividing the normalization factor $\sqrt{\sum (w'(p)^H)^2}$ to obtain V_i^H.

End

Return (V_k^A , V_k^H)

In $Corpus_{Extract}$, term candidates with high authority in a few documents are likely to be domain specific terms whereas candidates with high authority in many documents are more likely to be commonly used general words. Based on this observation, the termhood of each candidate term $Term_C$, denoted as $Termhood_C$, is calculated according to formula (3) defined below.

$$Termhood_C = (\sum_j w(C)_j^A)\log(\frac{|D|}{DF_C}) \quad (3)$$

where $w(C)_j^A$ is the authority of $Term_C$ in a document D_j of $Corpus_{Extract}$, $|D|$ is the total number of documents in $Corpus_{Extract}$ and DF_C is the total number of documents in which $Term_C$ occurs. $Term_C$s are then ranked according to their termhood values $Termhood_C$, and the top ranked N_{TCList} candidates are considered terms. N_{TCList} is an algorithm parameter to be determined experimentally.

3 Performance Evaluation

3.1 Data Preparation

To evaluate the performance of the proposed algorithms for Chinese, experiments are conducted on four corpora of two different domains as listed in Table 1. $Corpus_{IT\_Small}$ and $Corpus_{IT\_Large}$ are two sets of non-overlapping academic papers in the IT domain and $Corpus_{IT\_Small}$ is identical to the corpus used in *TV_ConSem(Ji and Lu, 2007)*. $Corpus_{Legal\_Small}$ is a complete set of official Chinese criminal law articles. $Corpus_{Legal\_Large}$ includes the complete set of official Chinese constitutional law articles and Economics/Finance law articles (http://www.law-lib.com/). Three domain lexicons used in the experiments are detailed in Table 2. $Lexicon_{IT}$ is obtained according to the term extraction algorithm (Ji and Lu, 2007) with manual verification. $Lexicon_{Legal}$ is extracted from $Corpus_{Legal\_Small}$ by manual verification too. Because legal text covers a lot of different areas such finance, science, advertisement, etc., the actually legal specific terms are relatively small in size. $Lexicon_{PKU}$ contains a total of 144K manually verified IT terms supplied by the Institute of Computational Linguistics, Peking University. $Lexicon_{PKU}$, is used as the standard term set for evaluation on the IT domain. $Corpus_{IT\_Small}$ and $Lexicon_{IT}$ are used to obtain the delimiter list of IT domain, $DList_{IT}$. $Corpus_{Legal\_Small}$ and $Lexicon_{Legal}$ are used to obtain the delimiter list of legal domain, $DList_{Legal}$. $Corpus_{IT\_Large}$ and $Corpus_{Legal\_Large}$ are used as open test data to evaluate the proposed algorithms in IT domain and legal domain, respectively.

Corpus	Domain	Size	Text type
$Corpus_{IT\_Small}$	IT	77K	Academic papers
$Corpus_{IT\_Large}$	IT	6.64M	Academic papers
$Corpus_{Legal\_Small}$	Legal	344K	Law article
$Corpus_{Legal\_Large}$	Legal	1.04M	Law article

Table 1. Different Corpora Used for Experiments

Lexicon	Domain	Size	Source
$Lexicon_{IT}$	IT	3,337	$Corpus_{IT\_Small}$
$Lexicon_{Legal}$	Legal	394	$Corpus_{Legal\_Small}$
$Lexicon_{PKU}$	IT	144K	PKU

Table 2. Different Lexicons Used for Experiments

To verify that the approach works with a simple stop word list without delimiter extraction, a stop word list, $DList_{SW}$, is also used as reference by taking the 494 general purpose stop words downloaded from a Chinese NLP resource website (www.nlp.org.cn) without any modification.

The performance of the algorithm in the IT domain is evaluated by precision according to the follow formula:

$$precision_{TE} = \frac{N_{Lexicon} + N_{New}}{N_{TCList}} \quad (4)$$

where N_{TCList} is the number of term candidates in term candidate list *TCList* extracted by an evaluated algorithm, $N_{Lexicon}$ denotes the number of term candidates in *TCList* contained in $Lexicon_{PKU}$, N_{New} denotes the number of extracted term candidates that are not in $Lexicon_{PKU}$, yet are considered correct. Thus, N_{New} is the number of newly discovered terms with respect to $Lexicon_{PKU}$. The verification of all the new terms is carried out manually by two experts independently. A new term is considered correct if both experts marked them as correct terms. As there is no reasonably large standard legal term list available, the evaluation of the legal domain in terms of precision is conducted manually. No evaluation on new term extraction is conducted.

To evaluate the ability of the algorithms in identify new terms in the IT domain, another measurement is applied to the IT corpus against $Lexicon_{PKU}$ based on the following formula:

$$R_{NTE} = \frac{N_{New}}{N_{TCList}} \quad (5)$$

where *TCList* and N_{New} are the same as given in formula (4). A higher R_{NTE} indicates that more extracted terms are outside of $Lexicon_{PKU}$ and are thus considered new terms. This is similar to the measurements of out of vocabulary (OOV) in Chinese segmentation. A higher R_{NTE} indicates the algorithm can be useful for domain knowledge update including lexicon expansion.

3.2 Evaluation on Term Extraction

For comparison, a statistical based term candidate extraction algorithm, *TCE_SEF&CV* with the best performance in (Ji and Lu, 2007) using both internal association and external strength, is used as the reference algorithm for the evaluation of *TCE_DI*. A statistics based term verification algorithm, *TV_ConSem* (Ji and Lu, 2007) using semantic information within a context window is used for the evaluation of *TV_LinkA*. $Lexicon_{PKU}$ is also used in *TV_ConSem*. Two popular methods integrated without division of candidate extraction and verification steps are used for comparison. The first one is based on *TF-IDF* (Salton and McGill, 1983; Frank et al., 1999). The second one is a supervised learning approach based on a *SVM* classifier, SVM^{light} (Joachims, 1999). The features used by SVM^{light} are shown in Table 3. Two training sets are constructed for the *SVM* classifier. The first one includes 3,337 positive examples ($Lexicon_{IT}$) and 5,950 negative examples extracted from $Corpus_{IT\_Small}$. The second one includes 394 positive examples

(*$Lexicon_{Legal}$*) and 28,051 negative examples extracted from *$Corpus_{Legal\_Small}$*.

No.	Feature Explanation
1	Percentage of the Chinese characters occurred in *$Lexicon_{Domain}$*
2	Frequency in the domain corpus
3	Frequency in the general corpus
4	Part of speech
5	The length of Chinese characters in the candidate
6	The length of non-Chinese characters in the candidate
7	Contextual evidence

Table 3. Features Used in the SVM Classifier

Figure 2 shows the performance of the proposed *TCE_DI* and *TV_LinkA* for term extraction compared to the reference algorithms for IT domain using *$Corpus_{IT\_Large}$*. *TCE_DI_{IT}* and *TCE_DI_{legal}* indicate *TCE_DI* using extracted delimiter lists *$DList_{IT}$* and *$DList_{Legal}$* with N_{DI} = 500, respectively. *TCE_DI_{SW}* simply uses the stop word list *$DList_{SW}$*.

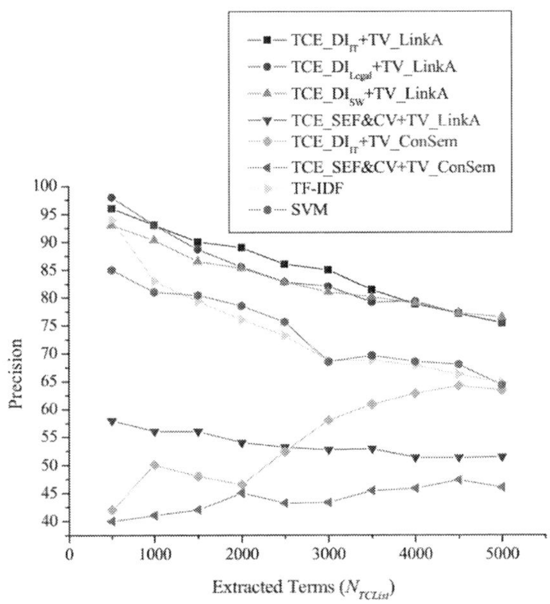

Figure 2 Performance of Different Algorithms on IT Domain

As shown in Figure 2, term extraction based on *TCE_DI_{IT}* combined with *TV_LinkA* gives the best performance. It achieves 75.4% precision when the number of extracted terms N_{TCList} reaches 5,000. The performance is 9.6% and 29.4% higher in precision compared to *TF-IDF* and *TCE_SEF&CV* combined with *TV_ConSem*, respectively. These translate to improvements of precision of over 14.8% and 63.9%, respectively.

When applying the same *TV_LinkA* algorithm for term verification, *TCE_DI* using different delimiter lists provide 24% better performance on average compared to the *TCE_SEF&CV* algorithm which translates to improvement of over 47%. The result from using delimiters of legal domain (*$DList_{Legal}$*) to data in IT domain (as shown in *TCE_DI_{legal}*) is better on average than using a simple general stop word list. It should be noted, however, that *TCE_DI_{SW}* still performs much better than the reference algorithms, which means that delimiter based term candidate extraction algorithm can improve performance even without any domain specific training. When applying the same *TCE_DI_{IT}* algorithm in term candidate extraction, *TV_LinkA* provides 10% higher performance compared to the *TV_ConSem* algorithm which translates to improvement of over 15.3%. It is important to point out that *TV_LinkA* using only the stop word list without any domain specific knowledge performs better than *TV_ConSem* using a large domain lexicon. In other words, delimiter based extraction with link analysis use much less resources and still improve performance of *TV_ConSem*.

The performance of *TCE_DI_{IT}* or *TCE_SEF&CV* combined with *TV_ConSem* have an upward trend when more terms are extracted which seems to be against intuition. The principle of the *TV_ConSem* algorithm is that a candidate is considered a valid term if a majority of its context words already appear in the domain lexicon. General words are more likely to be ranked on top because they are commonly used which explains the low performance of *TV_ConSem* in the lower range of N_{TCList}. When N_{TCList} increases, more domain terms are included. Thus, there is an upward trend in precision. But, the upward trend reverts at around 4,500 because the measurement in percentage is too low to distinguish valid terms from non-term candidates.

It is also interesting to point out that the simple *TF-IDF* algorithm which was rarely used in Chinese term extraction performs as well as the *SVM* classifier. The main reason is that the test corpus consists of academic papers. So, many terms are consistent and repeated a lot of times in different documents which accords with the idea of *TF-IDF*. Thus, *TF-IDF* performs relatively well because of the high-quality domain corpus. However, *TF-IDF*, as a statistics based algorithm suffers from similar problem as others based on statistics. Thus it does not perform as well as the proposed *TCE_DI* and *TV_LinkA* algorithms.

Figure 3 shows that the proposed algorithms achieve similar performance on the legal domain. TCE_DI_{Legal} combined with *TV_LinkA* perform the best. The result from using IT domain delimiters ($DList_{IT}$) in legal domain as shown in TCE_DI_{IT} is better on average than using the general purpose stop list. This further proves that extracted delimiter list even from a different domain can be more effective than a general stop word list. When applying the same *TV_LinkA* algorithm for term verification, *TCE_DI* using different delimiter lists are better than all the reference algorithms. Without large lexicon in Chinese legal domain, the *TV_ConSem* algorithm does not even work. *TV_LinkA* using no prior domain knowledge for term verification still achieves similar improvement compared to that of the IT domain where a comprehensive domain lexicon is available.

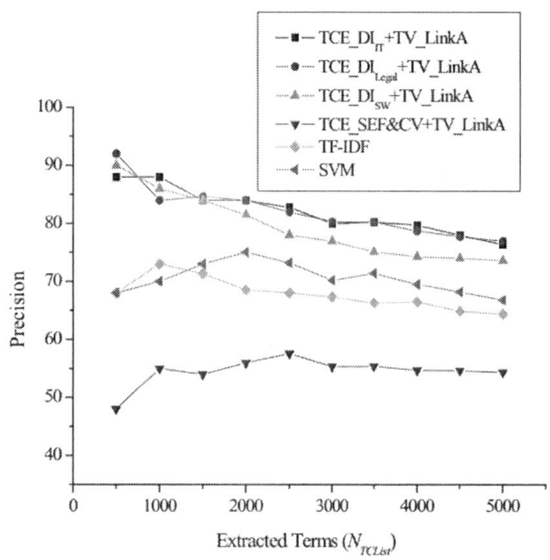

Figure 3. Performance of Different Algorithms on Legal Domain

There are three main reasons for the performance improvements of the proposed *TCE_DI* and *TV_LinkA* algorithms. Firstly, the delimiters which are mainly functional words (e. g. "在"(at/in), "或"(or)) and general substantive (e.g. "是"(be), "采用"(adopt)) can be extracted easily and are effective term boundary markers since they are quite domain independent and stable. Secondly, the granularity of domain specific terms extracted the proposed algorithm is much larger than words obtained by word segmentation. This keeps many noisy strings out of the term candidate set. Thus, the proposed delimiter based algorithm performs much better over segmentation based statistical methods. Thirdly, the proposed approach is not as sensitive to term frequency as other statistical based approaches because term candidates are identified without regards to the frequencies of the candidates. In the *TV_LinkA* algorithm, terms are verified by calculating the relevance between candidates and the sentences instead of the distributions of terms in different types of documents. Terms having low frequencies can be identified as long as they are in domain relevant sentences whereas in the previous approaches including *TF-IDF*, terms with less statistical significance are weeded out. For example, a long IT term "层次化存储系统" (Hierarchical storage system) with a low frequency of 6 is extracted using the proposed approach. It cannot be identified by *TF-IDF* since the statistical information is not significant. This term cannot be extracted by the segmentation based algorithms either because general segmentor split long terms into pieces making them difficult to be reunited using term extraction techniques.

It is interesting to know that the proposed approach not only achieves the best performance for both domains, it also achieves second best when using extracted delimiters from a different domain. The results confirm that delimiters are quite stable across domains and the relevance between candidates and sentences are efficient for distinguishing terms from non-terms in different domains. In fact, the proposed approach can be applied to different domains with minimal training or no training if resources are limited.

3.3 Evaluation on New Term Extraction

As $Lexicon_{PKU}$ is the only ready-to-use domain lexicon, the evaluation on new term extraction is conducted on $Corpus_{IT\_Large}$ only. Figure 4 shows the evaluation of the proposed algorithms compared to the reference algorithms in terms of R_{NTE}, the ratio of new terms among all identified terms.

It can be seen that the proposed algorithms TCE_DI_{IT} combined with *TV_LinkA* is basically the top performer throughout the range. It can identify 4% (with respect to *TCE_SEF&CV +TV_ConSem*) to 27% (with respect to *TF-IDF*) more new terms when N_{TCList} reaches 5,000 which translate to improvements of over 9% to 170%, respectively. The second best performer is TCE_DI_{legal} combined with *TV_LinkA* using delimiters of legal domain. In fact, it only underperforms in the lower range of N_{TCList}

compared to *TCE_DI*$_{IT}$. When N_{TCList} reaches 5,000, their performance is basically the same. However, the *TCE_DI*$_{SW}$ algorithm using stop words performs much worse than using extracted delimiter lists as shown for *TCE_DI*$_{IT}$ and *TCE_DI*$_{legal}$. In the *TCE_DI* algorithm, character strings are split by delimiters and the remained parts are taken as term candidates. Generally speaking, if a new term contains a delimiter or a stop word as its component, it cannot be identified correctly. Consequently, if a new term contains a stop word as its component, it cannot be extracted correctly using *TCE_DI*$_{SW}$. However, new terms are less likely to contain delimiters because the delimiter extraction algorithm *DList_Ext* would not consider a component as a delimiter if it is contained in a term in *Lexicon*$_{Domain}$. Consequently, *TCE_DI*$_{SW}$ is less adaptive to domain specific data compared to *TCE_DI*$_{IT}$ and *TCE_DI*$_{legal}$. That is also why *TCE_DI*$_{SW}$ picks up new terms much more slowly.

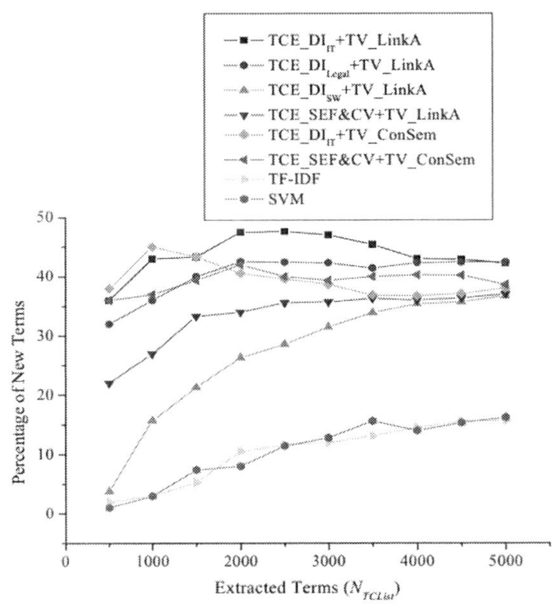

Figure 4. Performance of Different Algorithms for New Term Extraction

It is interesting to know that *TCE_DI*$_{IT}$ combined with *TV_ConSem* identifies more new terms in the low range of N_{TCList}. In the *TV_ConSem* algorithm, the major information used for term verification is the percentage of the context words appear in the domain lexicon. As discussed earlier in Section 3.2, *TV_ConSem* ranks commonly used general words higher than others which leads to the low precision of *TV_ConSem* for term extraction. A new term faces a similar scenario because more of its context words occur in the domain lexicon than that of other terms. Thus, new terms are actually ranked higher than other terms in *TV_ConSem* which explains its higher ability to identify new terms in the low range of N_{TCList}. However, its performance drops in the high range of N_{TCList} because the influence of context words diminishes in terms of percentage in the domain lexicon to distinguish terms from non-terms. Figure 4 also shows that *TF-IDF* and *SVM* perform the worst in new term extraction compared to other algorithms. *TF-IDF* has relatively low ability to identify new terms since new terms are not widely used and they do not repeat a lot of times in many documents. As *SVM* is sensitive to training data, it is naturally not adaptive to new terms.

All current Chinese term extraction algorithms rely on segmentation with comprehensive lexical knowledge and yet Chinese segmentation algorithms have the OOV (out of vocabulary) problem. This makes Chinese term extraction particularly vulnerable to new term extraction. The proposed approach, on the other hand, is based on delimiters which is more stable, domain independent, and OOV independent. Figure 4 shows that *TCE_DI* and *TV_LinkA* using minimal training from different domains can extract much more new terms than previous techniques. In fact, the proposed approach can serve as a much better tool to identify new domain terms and can be quite effective for domain lexicon expansion.

4 Conclusion

In conclusion, this paper presents a robust term extraction approach using minimal resources. It includes a delimiter based algorithm for term candidate extraction and a link analysis based algorithm for term verification. The proposed approach is not sensitive to term frequency as the previous works. It requires no prior domain knowledge, no general corpora, no full segmentation, and minimal adaptation for new domains.

Experiments for term extraction are conducted on IT domain and legal domain, respectively. Evaluations indicate that the proposed approach has a number of advantages. Firstly, the proposed approach can improve precision of term extraction quite significantly. Secondly, the fact that the proposed approach achieves the best performance on two different domains verifies its domain independent nature. The proposed approach using delimiters extracted from a different domain also achieves the second best performance which indicates that the delimiters are quite stable and domain independent. The proposed approach still performs much better than the reference algorithms when using a general purpose stop word list, which means that the proposed approach can improve performance well even as a completely unsupervised approach without any training. Consequently, the results demonstrate that the proposed approach can be applied to different domains easily even without training. Thirdly, the proposed approach is particularly good for identifying new terms so that it can serve as an effective tool for domain lexicon expansion.

Acknowledgements

This work was done while the first author was working at the Hong Kong Polytechnic University supported by CERG Grant B-Q941 and Central Research Grant: G-U297.

References

Chang Jing-Shin. 2005. Domain Specific Word Extraction from Hierarchical Web Documents: A First Step toward Building Lexicon Trees from Web Corpora. In *Proceedings of the Fourth SIGHAN Workshop on Chinese Language Learning*: 64-71.

Chien LF. 1999. Pat-tree-based adaptive keyphrase extraction for intelligent Chinese information retrieval. *Information Processing and Management*, vol.35: 501-521.

Eibe Frank, Gordon. W. Paynter, Ian H. Witten, Carl Gutwin, and Craig G. Nevill-Manning. 1999. Domain-specific Keyphrase Extraction. In *Proceedings of 16th International Joint Conference on Artificial Intelligence IJCAI-99*: 668-673.

Feng Haodi, Kang Chen, Xiaotie Deng , and Weimin Zheng, 2004. Accessor variety criteria for Chinese word extraction. *Computational Linguistics*, 30(1):75-93.

Hiroshi Nakagawa, and Tatsunori Mori. 2002. A simple but powerful automatic term extraction method. In *COMPUTERM-2002 Proceedings of the 2nd International Workshop on Computational Term*: 29-35. Taiwan, August 2002.

Hisamitsu T., and Y. Niwa. 2002. A measure of term representativeness based on the number of co-occurring salient words. In *Proceedings of the 19th COLING, 2002*.

Huang Chu-Ren, Petr ˇSimon, Shu-Kai Hsieh, and Laurent Pr´evot. 2007. Rethinking Chinese Word Segmentation: Tokenization, Character Classification, or Wordbreak Identification. In *Proceedings of the ACL 2007 Demo and Poster Sessions*: 69–72. Joachims T. 2000. Estimating the Generalization Performance of a SVM Efficiently. In *Proceedings of the International Conference on Machine Learning*, Morgan Kaufman, 2000.

Kageura K., and B. Umino. 1996. Methods of automatic term recognition: a review. *Term* 3(2):259-289.

Kleinberg J. 1997. Authoritative sources in a hyperlinked environment. In *Proceedings of the 9th ACM-SIAM Symposium on Discrete Algorithms*: 668-677. New Orleans, America, January 1997.

Ji Luning, and Qin Lu. 2007. Chinese Term Extraction Using Window-Based Contextual Information. In *Proceedings of CICLing 2007, LNCS 4394*: 62 – 74.

Li Hongqiao, Chang-Ning Huang, Jianfeng Gao, and Xiaozhong Fan. The Use of SVM for Chinese New Word Identification. In *Proceedings of the 1st International Joint Conference on Natural Language Processing (IJCNL P2004)*: 723-732. Hainan Island, China, March 2004.

Luo Shengfen, and Maosong Sun. 2003. Two-Character Chinese Word Extraction Based on Hybrid of Internal and Contextual Measures. In *Proceedings of the Second SIGHAN Workshop on Chinese Language Processing*: 24-30.

McDonald, David D. 1993. Internal and External Evidence in the Identification and Semantic Categorization of Proper Names. In Proceedings of the Workshop on Acquisition of Lexical Knowledge from Text, pages 32--43, Columbus, OH, June. Special Interest Group on the Lexicon of the Association for Computational Linguistics.

Nasreen AbdulJaleel and Yan Qu. 2005. Domain Term Extraction and Structuring via Link Analysis. In *Proceedings of the AAAI '05 Workshop on Link Analysis*: 39-46.

Salton, G., and McGill, M.J. (1983). *Introduction to Modern Information Retrieval*. McGraw-Hill.

Schone, P. and Jurafsky D. 2001. Is Knowledge-free Induction of Multiword Unit Dictionary Headwords a solved problem? In *Proceedings of EMNLP2001*.

Sornlertlamvanich V., Potipiti T., and Charoenporn T. 2000. Automatic Corpus-based Thai Word Extraction with the C4.5 Learning Algorithm. In *Proceedings of COLING 2000*.

Vladimir N. Vapnik. 1995. *The Nature of Statistical Learning Theory*. Springer, 1995.

Zhou GD, Shen D, Zhang J, Su J, and Tan SH. 2005. Recognition of Protein/Gene Names from Text using an Ensemble of Classifiers. *BMC Bioinformatics* 2005, 6(Suppl 1):S7.

Measuring and Predicting Orthographic Associations: Modelling the Similarity of Japanese Kanji

Lars Yencken and **Timothy Baldwin**
{lljy,tim}@csse.unimelb.edu.au
NICTA Research Lab
University of Melbourne

Abstract

As human beings, our mental processes for recognising linguistic symbols generate perceptual neighbourhoods around such symbols where confusion errors occur. Such neighbourhoods also provide us with conscious mental associations between symbols. This paper formalises orthographic models for similarity of Japanese kanji, and provides a proof-of-concept dictionary extension leveraging the mental associations provided by orthographic proximity.

1 Introduction

Electronic dictionary interfaces have evolved from mere digitised forms of their paper ancestors. They now enhance accessibility by addressing the separate needs of language consumers and language producers, of learners from non-speakers to native speakers, and by targeting the specific difficulties presented by individual languages.

For languages with logographic orthographies, such as Japanese and Chinese, accessibility remains poor due to the difficulties in looking up an unknown character in the dictionary. The traditional method of character lookup in these languages involves identifying the primary component (or "radical"), counting its strokes, looking it up in the index, counting the remainder of strokes in the original character, then finding the character in a sub-index. This presents several opportunities for error, but fortunately improvements have been made, as we discuss in Section 2.

We are interested in the perceptual process of identifying characters, in particular the behaviour of perception within dense visual neighbourhoods. Within the dictionary accessibility space, we are motivated by the potential to correct confusion errors, but also to leverage the mental associations provided by visual proximity to allow advanced learners to find unknown characters faster. As proof-of-concept, we propose a method for looking up unknown words with unfamiliar characters, based on similarity with known characters.

In essence, our method is based on the user plausibly "mistyping" the word based on closely-matching kanji they are familiar with (and hence can readily access via a standard input method editor), from which we predict the correct kanji combination based on kanji similarity and word frequency. For example, given the input 補左, the system could suggest the word 補佐 [hosa] "help" based on similarity between the high-frequency 左 and the graphically-similar but low-frequency 佐.

The proposed method is combined with the FOKS lookup strategy proposed by Bilac (2002) for looking up unknown words via plausibly incorrect *readings*.

The contributions of this paper are the proposal of a range of character similarity models for logographic scripts, a novel evaluation method for logographic character confusability, and the incorporation of kanji similarity into a word-level lookup model.

The remainder of this paper is structured as follows. Firstly, we review related lookup systems (Section 2), and go on to discuss how we measure and model kanji similarity, including an evaluation of the methods (Section 3). We then focus on the conversion of similarity models into confusion models, and their integration into a search interface (Section 4). Examining both our models and the interface itself, we discuss our findings (Section 5) before finally concluding (Section 6).

2 A review of related systems

2.1 Associative lookup systems

Associative lookup systems are based on the premise that characters and words form a highly

© 2008. Licensed under the *Creative Commons Attribution-Noncommercial-Share Alike 3.0 Unported* license (http://creativecommons.org/licenses/by-nc-sa/3.0/). Some rights reserved.

connected lexical network. They focus on finding and making accessible the mental links provided by proximity within this network. In contrast, systems which correct for confusion model plausible errors in order to recover from them. Examples of associative systems are as follows:

	Semantic (for producers)	**Orthographic** (for consumers)
Monolingual	Visual WordNet	*this paper*
Bilingual	standard bilingual dictionaries	Pinyomi dictionary interface

Ferret and Zock (2006) introduce the distinction between language producers as encoders of semantic information, and language consumers as decoders of orthographic (or phonetic) information. We first consider systems to aid production of language.

Systems for production give form and sound to known semantics. The most common such systems are bilingual dictionaries which associate words in one language with their near-synonyms in a second language. Even within a monolingual context, the problem of selecting the right word can be difficult, whether the difficulty is one of limited knowledge or simply one of access, as in the case of the tip-of-the-tongue problem. Work in this area (Zock, 2002; Zock and Bilac, 2004) has more recently focused on extending WordNet with syntagmatic relationships (Ferret and Zock, 2006). Access could take the form of the Visual WordNet Project.[1]

For language consumers, the challenge is to find the meaning or sound of a word with known form. For logographic languages, where characters are entered phonetically[2] using an input method editor, computer input of an unknown word with known form remains difficult, since the reading is unknown.

In a bilingual context, the Pinyomi Chinese-Japanese dictionary interface overcomes this obstacle by allowing Japanese speakers to look up a Chinese word via the Japanese-equivalent characters based on orthographic associations between similar characters (Yencken et al., 2007).

Our proposed extension to the FOKS dictionary is functionally similar to Pinyomi, but in a monolingual Japanese context. In our case, a Japanese word containing unknown characters is found by querying with known characters that are visually similar. Unlike Pinyomi, which uses an ideogram transliteration table to determine associations, we use direct models of character similarity to determine associations.

2.2 Kanji lookup systems

We next provide a brief review of five kanji lookup systems in order to situate our proposed interface appropriately.

The SKIP (System of Kanji Indexing by Patterns) system of lookup provides an indexing scheme based on a kanji's overall shape rather than its primary radical (Halpern, 1999). For example, 明 [aka] "bright" has skip code 1-4-4, with the first number indicating it is horizontally split into two parts, and the second and third numbers representing the respective stroke counts of the two parts.

The Kansuke dictionary simplifies the method of counting strokes, to form a three-number code representing the horizontal, vertical and other strokes that make up a character (Tanaka-Ishii and Godon, 2006). Characters can also be looked up from their components. For our earlier example 明 consists of 日 with code 3-2-0 and 月 with code 3-1-1.

The Kanjiru dictionary (Winstead, 2006) attempts to interactively assemble a character by shape and stroke via mouse movements, providing the user with structural ways of building up components until the desired character is found.

Finally, hand-writing interfaces attempt to circumvent the computer input problem altogether, but still suffer from several issues: the awkwardness of mouse input for drawing characters; sensitivity to both stroke order and connectivity of components; and the difference in hand-writing styles between learners and native speakers.

These lookup methods contrast with our proposed similarity-based search in several ways.

Firstly, our method combines word- and character-level information directly, yet provides the means to lookup words with unknown characters without the use of wildcards. The downside to this is that the user needs to use kanji in the search query, limiting potential users to intermediate and advanced learners with some knowledge of kanji.

Secondly, we are able to cater to both intentional similarity-based searches, and unintentional input errors, increasing the accessibility of the base dictionary. This approach shares much with the FOKS dictionary interface (Bilac, 2002), which provides

[1] `http://kylescholz.com/projects/wordnet/`

[2] A notable exception is the Wubizixing lookup method for Chinese.

error-correcting lookup for reading-based dictionary queries. Suppose, for example, a user wishes to look up the word 山車 "festival float", but is unsure of its pronunciation. FOKS allows them to guess the pronunciation based on readings they know for each character in other contexts. In this case, they might combine 山 [yama] "mountain" and 車 [kuruma] "car" and guess the word reading as [yamakuruma]. The correct reading [dashi] cannot be guessed from the word's parts, but our educated guess would lead the user to the word and provide access to both the correct reading and meaning.

This approach is complementary to our proposed method. Suppose, analogously, that the user wishes to look up the word 訪問 but is unfamiliar with the first kanji. A query for 方問 would trigger an inference based on the similarity between 訪 and 方, and provide the desired word in the results, allowing the user to determine both its pronunciation [hōmoN] and its meaning "visit".

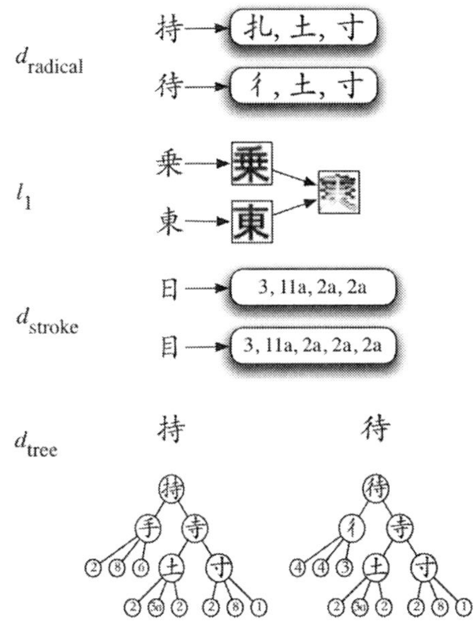

Figure 1: A summary of our kanji distance metrics

3 Modelling similarity

3.1 Metric space models

There has been little work on methods for measuring or predicting the similarity between two kanji. While there have been many psycholinguistic studies on various specific aspects of perception of Chinese and Japanese logographic characters, few touch directly on orthographic confusion. For a brief discussion, see Yencken and Baldwin (2006).

Broadly, current literature suggests that kanji recognition may be hierarchical, building radicals from strokes, and whole characters from radicals. Each point of recognition and combination suggests a potential site for misrecognition or confusion with an orthographic or semantic neighbour.

The most directly relevant study involved two experiments by Yeh and Li (2002). In a sorting task, subjects tended to categorise characters by their structure, rather than their shared components. In a subsequent search task, presence of shared structure between target and distractors was the dominant factor in subjects' response times.

We previously proposed two naive kanji similarity measures: a cosine similarity metric operating on boolean radical vectors, and the l_1 norm (Manhattan distance) between rendered images of kanji (Yencken and Baldwin, 2006). Evaluating on a set of human similarity judgements, we determined that the cosine similarity method outperformed the l_1 norm, although it had lower precision for high-similarity pairs.

3.1.1 Bag of radicals with shape

When learners of Japanese study a new character, they do not study its strokes in isolation, but instead build on prior knowledge of its component radicals. For example, 明 [aka] "bright" could be analysed as being made up of the 日 [sun] "hi" and 月 [moon] "tsuki" radicals.

Radicals are useful in several ways. The number of radicals in any kanji is much smaller than the number of strokes for any kanji, making such kanji easier to chunk and recall in memory. Furthermore, radicals can provide cues to the meaning and pronunciation of characters which contain them.[3]

The original metric used in Yencken and Baldwin (2006) simply calculates the cosine similarity between radical vectors. This ignores the position of radicals, which is known to be important in similarity judgements, and also the number of times each radical occurs within a kanji. Hence, 木, 林 and 森 are all considered identical (radical = 木), as are 日 and 晶 (radical = 日). The metric is cal-

[3]For example, kanji containing the radical 月, such as 胸 [mune] "chest" and 腕 [ude] "arm", are reliably body parts. Kanji containing the radical 同, as in 銅 [dō] "copper" and 胴 [dō] "body", often have the Chinese or *on* reading [dō] amongst their valid pronunciations.

culated by:

$$d_{\text{radical}}(x,y) = 1 - \frac{r_x \cdot r_y}{|r_x||r_y|} \quad (1)$$

To address radical multiplicity, and the findings of Yeh and Li's study, we set the above metric to unit distance whenever the two characters differ in their basic shape. To approximate shape, we use the first part of each kanji's 3-part SKIP code, which can take values *horizontal*, *vertical*, *containment* or *other*. SKIP codes for each kanji are provided in Kanjidic,[4] and radical membership in the Radkfile.[5]

This change allows the metric to distinguish between examples with repeated components. The altered metric aims to capture the visual and semantic salience of radicals in kanji perception, and to also take into account some basic shape similarity.

3.1.2 Distance of rendered images

In contrast to the previous approach, we can consider kanji as arbitrary symbols rendered in print or on screen, and then attempt to measure their similarity. The simplest way to do this is to simply render each kanji to an image of fixed size, and to then use some distance metric over images.

A common and simple distance metric is the l_1 norm, which simply sums the difference in luminance between pixels of the two images for some alignment. Fortunately, all kanji are intended to occupy an identically sized block, so alignment is via a grid, constant across all kanji. Considering $p_x(i,j)$ to be the luminance of the pixel at position (i,j) of rendered kanji x, we evaluate the l_1 norm as follows:

$$l_1(x,y) = \sum_{i,j} |p_x(i,j) - p_y(i,j)| \quad (2)$$

This calculation depends on the image representation chosen, and could differ slightly across fonts, image sizes and rasterisation methods. We used the MS Gothic font, rendering to 80x80 images, with anti-aliasing.

This metric is aimed at capturing the general overlap of strokes between the two characters, along with the overlap of whitespace, which gives useful structure information. This metric is known to be noisy for low-to-medium similarity pairs, but is very useful in distinguishing near neighbours.

[4] http://www.csse.monash.edu.au/~jwb/kanjidic.html

[5] http://www.csse.monash.edu.au/~jwb/kradinf.html

3.1.3 Stroke edit distance

A third possibility is to reduce kanji to the very strokes used to write them. Two features of the orthography make this possible: (1) kanji are not arbitrary symbols, but configurations of strokes chosen from within a finite and limited set; and (2) each kanji has a precise stroke order which is consistent for reused kanji components, such that if two or more arbitrary components were combined to form a new pseudo-character, native speakers would largely agree on the stroke order.

To define a metric based on strokes, we need both a source of stroke data and a comparison method. For stroke data, we look to a hierarchical data set for Japanese kanji created by Apel and Quint (2004). Each kanji is specified by its strokes, grouped into common stroke groups (components), and broken down in a hierarchical manner into relative positions within the kanji (for example: left and right, top and bottom). The strokes themselves are based on a taxonomy of some 26 stroke types (46 including sub-variants).

For any given kanji, we can flatten its hierarchy to generate an ordered sequence of strokes: a signature for that character. The natural distance metric across such sequences is the string edit distance. This forms our d_{stroke} metric.

Much useful information is preserved within stroke signatures. Since radicals are written in sequence, they form contiguous blocks in the signature. The edit distance will thus align shared radicals when their position is similar enough. Since components are usually drawn in a left-to-right, top-to-bottom order, the order of components in a signature also reflects their position as part of the larger character. Finally, it provides a smooth blending from stroke similarity to radical similarity, and can recognise the similarity between pairs like 日 [hi] "sun" and 目 [me] "eye".

3.1.4 Tree edit distance

In our previous approach, we discarded much of the hierarchical information available, relying on stroke order to approximate it. We can instead use the full data, and calculate the ordered *tree edit distance* between kanji XML representations. Tree edit distance is defined as the length of the shortest sequence of *inserts*, *deletions* and *relabellings* required to convert one tree into another (Bille, 2005). Though a cost function between labels can be specified, we gave inserts/deletions and relabellings unit cost.

Figure 1 provides an overview of the structure of each kanji's representation. Actual trees also contain phonetic elements, radicals, and stroke groups whose strokes are spread across several non-contiguous blocks. Another motivation for including tree edit distance is to determine if this additional information is useful in determining kanji similarity.

3.2 Evaluation

We evaluate our distance metrics over three data sets.

The first data set is the human similarity judgements from Yencken and Baldwin (2006). This data set is overly broad in that it weights the ability to distinguish low and medium similarity pairs equally with distinguishing medium and high similarity pairs. It is clear that for most applications, determining the high similarity pairs with high precision is most important. Nevertheless, this data set is useful for comparing our metrics with those proposed in previous research.

In order to better measure performance on high-similarity pairs, which we expect to form the basis of incorrect kanji inputs, we need a set of human-selected confusion data. The second data set is drawn from the White Rabbit JLPT Level 3[6] kanji flashcards. Each flashcard contains either one or two highly-similar neighbours which might be confused with a given kanji. We use this set to determine our likely performance in a search task.

Our third data set is based on human confusability judgements for kanji pairings.

3.2.1 Similarity experiment data

The first data consists of human similarity judgements to pairs of kanji, scored on a 5 point scale (Yencken and Baldwin, 2006). The experiment had 179 participants, covering a broad range of Japanese proficiency. The key participant groupings are: (1) non-speakers of Chinese, Japanese or Korean (Non-CJK); (2) Japanese second-language learners (JSL); and (3) Japanese first-language speakers (JFL). Figure 2 gives the rank correlation ρ between each metric and a rater, averaged over all raters in each proficiency group.

For each metric, the mean rank correlation increased with the participants' knowledge of

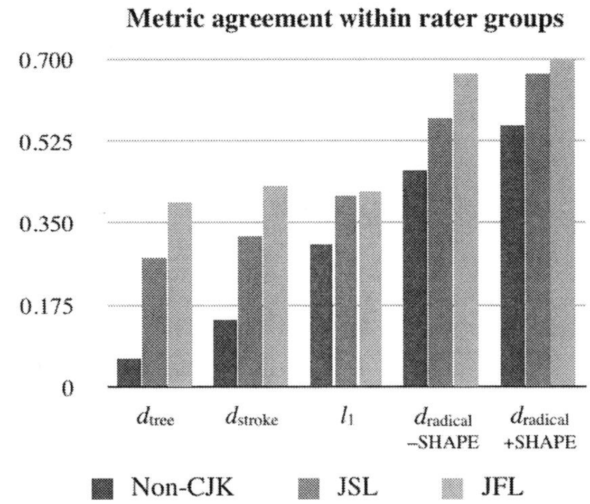

Figure 2: Mean value of Spearman's rank correlation ρ over rater groups for each metric ($d_{\text{radical}}(-\text{SHAPE})$ is the original metric, and $d_{\text{radical}}(+\text{SHAPE})$ is our augmented version)

Japanese (from Non-CJK to JSL to JFL), indicating that the raters made more motivated and consistent similarity judgements. The d_{radical} (+SHAPE) metric dominates the other metrics, including the original d_{radical} (−SHAPE), at all levels of knowledge. This confirms the salience of radicals and the tendency for individuals to classify kanji by their broad shape, as suggested by Yeh and Li (2002). l_1, d_{stroke} and d_{tree} perform poorly in comparison. Interestingly, these three metrics have large performance differences for non-speakers, but not for native-speakers.

Despite overall poor performance from our new metrics, we were able to improve on the original d_{radical} (−SHAPE). We now evaluate over the flashcard data set for comparison.

3.2.2 Flashcard data set

The flashcard data differs greatly from the previous experimental data, as it consists of only human-selected high-similarity pairs. Accordingly, we took two approaches to evaluation.

Firstly, for each high-similarity pair (a *pivot* kanji and its distractor), we randomly select a third kanji from the jōyō character set[7] and combine it with the pivot to form a second pair which is highly likely to be low similarity. We then compare how well each metric can classify the two pairs by imposing the correct ordering on them, in the form of classification accuracy. The results of this evaluation are shown in Table 1. We include a theoretical random baseline of 0.500, since any decision has a

[6]Japanese Language Proficiency Test: the standard government test for foreigners learning Japanese.

[7]The "common use" government kanji set, containing 1945 characters.

Metric	Accuracy
d_{tree}	0.979
d_{stroke}	0.968
l_1	0.957
d_{radical}	0.648
random baseline	0.500

Table 1: Accuracy at detecting which of two pairs (flashcard vs. random) has high similarity

Metric	*MAP*	*p@1*	*p@5*	*p@10*
d_{stroke}	0.594	0.313	0.151	0.100
d_{tree}	0.560	0.313	0.149	0.094
l_1	0.503	0.257	0.139	0.089
d_{radical}	0.356	0.197	0.087	0.063

Table 2: The mean average precision (MAP), and precision at $N \in \{1, 5, 10\}$ over the flashcard data

50% a priori chance of being successful.

The performance of d_{radical} – close to our random baseline, despite performing best in the previous task – is suggestive of the different characteristics of this task. In particular, a metric which orders well across the broad spectrum of similarity pairs may not be well suited to identifying high-similarity pairs, and vice-versa.

The other three metrics have accuracy above 0.95 on this task, indicating the ease with which they can identify high-similarity pairs. However, this does not guarantee that the neighbourhoods they generate will be free from noise, since the real-world prevalence of highly similar characters is likely to be very low.

To better determine what dictionary search results might be like, we consider each flashcard kanji as a query, and its high-similarity distractors as relevant documents (and implicitly all remaining kanji as irrelevant documents, i.e. dissimilar characters). We can then calculate the Mean Average Precision (MAP, i.e. the mean area under the precision–recall curve for a query set) and the precision at N neighbours, for varied N. The results of this approach are presented in Table 2.

The precision statistics confirm the ranking of metrics found in the earlier classification task. The d_{stroke} metric outperforms l_1 by a greater margin in the MAP statistic and precision at $N = 1$, but narrows again for greater N. This suggests that it is more reliable in the upper similarity ranking.

3.2.3 Distractor pool experiment

The flashcard data provides good examples of high-similarity pairs, but suffers from several problems. Firstly, the constraints of the flashcard format limit the number of high-similarity neighbours that can be presented on each flashcard to at most two; in some cases we might expect more. Secondly, the methodology behind the selection of these high-similarity neighbours is unclear.

For these reasons, we conducted an experiment to attempt to replicate the flashcard data. 100 kanji were randomly chosen from the JLPT 3 set (hereafter *pivots*). For each pivot kanji, we generated a pool of possible high-similarity neighbours in the following way. Firstly, we seeded the pool with the neighbours from the flashcard data set. We then added the highest similarity neighbour as given by each of our similarity metrics. Since these could overlap, we iteratively continued adding an additional neighbour from all of our metrics until our pool contained at least four neighbours.

Native or native-like speakers of Japanese were solicited as participants. After a dry run, each participant was presented with a series of pivot kanji. For each pivot kanji, they were asked to select from its pool of neighbours which (if any) might be confused for that kanji based on their graphical similarity. The order of pivots was randomised for each rater, as was the order of neighbours for each pivot. Kanji were provided as images using MS Gothic font for visual consistency across browsers.

Three participants completed the experiment, selecting 1.32 neighbours per pivot on average, less than 1.86 per pivot provided by the flashcard data. Inter-rater agreement was quite low, with a mean κ of 0.34 across rater pairings, suggesting that participants found the task difficult. This is unsurprising, since as native speakers the participants are experts at discriminating between characters, and are unlikely to make the same mistakes as learners. Comparing their judgements to the flashcard data set yields a mean κ of 0.37.

Ideally, this data generates a frequency distribution over potential neighbours based on the number of times they were rated as similar. However, since the number of participants was small, we simply combined the neighbours with high-similarity judgements for each pivot, yielding an average of 2.45 neighbours per pivot. Re-evaluating our metrics on this data gives the figures in Table 3.

Metric	*MAP*	*p@1*	*p@5*	*p@10*
d_{stroke}	1.046	0.530	0.228	0.146
d_{tree}	1.028	0.540	0.228	0.136
l_1	0.855	0.480	0.200	0.117
d_{radical}	0.548	0.270	0.122	0.095

Table 3: The mean average precision (MAP), and precision at $N \in \{1, 5, 10\}$ over the distractor data

Compared to the flashcard data set, the ordering and relative performance of metrics is similar, with d_{stroke} marginally improving on d_{tree}, but both significantly outperforming l_1 and d_{radical}. The near-doubling of high similarity neighbours from 1.32 to 2.45 is reflected by a corresponding increase in MAP and precision@N scores, though the effect is somewhat reduced as N increases.

4 From similarity to search

Having examined several character distance metrics, and evaluated them over our three data sets, we now consider their application to dictionary word search.

4.1 Overall model

Our broad probability model for looking up words based on similar kanji is identical to the FOKS model for search based on readings, save that we substitute readings for kanji in our query. A unigram approximation leads us to Equation 3 below, where $q = q_0 \ldots q_n$ is the query given by the user, $w = w_0 \ldots w_n$ is the desired word, and each q_i and w_i is a kanji character:

$$\begin{aligned} \Pr(w|q) &\propto \Pr(w)\Pr(q|w) \\ &= \Pr(w)\prod_i \Pr(q_i|w, q_0 \ldots q_{i-1}) \\ &\approx \Pr(w)\prod_i \Pr(q_i|w_i) \end{aligned} \quad (3)$$

The final line of Equation 3 requires two models to be supplied. The first, $\Pr(w)$, is the probability that a word will be looked up. Here we approximate using corpus frequency over the Nikkei newspaper data, acknowledging that a newspaper corpus is skewed differently to learner data. The second model is our confusion model $\Pr(q_i|w_i)$, interpreted either as the probability of confusing kanji w_i with kanji q_i, or of the user intentionally selecting q_i to query for w_i. It is this model that we now focus on.

4.2 Confusion model

Although we can construct a confusion model using our distance metric alone, it is clear that frequency effects will occur. For example, the likelihood of confusion is increased if the target w_i is rare and unknown, but q_i is a highly-similar high-frequency neighbour; certainly this is a typical use case for intentional similarity-based querying. We thus propose a generic confusion model based a similarity measure between kanji:

$$\Pr(q_i|w_i) \approx \frac{\Pr(q_i)s(q_i, w_i)}{\sum_j \Pr(q_{i,j})s(q_{i,j}, w_i)} \quad (4)$$

The confusion model uses a similarity function $s(q_i, w_i)$ and a kanji frequency model $\Pr(q_i)$ to determine the relative probability of confusing w_i with q_i amongst other candidates. We convert the desired distance metric d into s according to $s(x,y) = 1 - d(x,y)$ if the range of d is $[0,1]$, or $s(x,y) = \frac{1}{1+d(x,y)}$ if the range of d is $[0,\infty)$.

To maximise the accessibility of this form of search, we must find the appropriate trade-off between providing sufficient candidates and limiting the noise. We use a thresholding method borrowed from Clark and Curran (2004), where our threshold is set as a proportion of the first candidate's score. For example, using 0.9 as our threshold, if the first candidate has a similarity score of 0.7 with the target kanji, we would then accept any neighbours with a similarity greater than 0.63. Using the d_{stroke} metric with a ratio of 0.9, there are on average 2.65 neighbours for each kanji in the jōyō character set.

4.3 Evaluating search

Search by similar grapheme has an advantage to search by word reading: reading results are naturally ambiguous due to homophony in Japanese, and attempts to perform error correction may interfere with exact matches in the results ranking. Grapheme-based search may have only one exact match, so additional secondary candidates are not in direct competition with existing search practices.

We can estimate the accessibility improvement given by this form of search as follows. Let us assume that learners study kanji in frequency order. For each kanji learned, one or more high-similarity neighbours also become accessible. Taking all pairings of kanji within the JIS X 0208-1990 character set, using the d_{stroke} metric with a cutoff ratio of 0.9, and assuming full precision on the neighbour graph this generates, we get the accessibility curve found in Figure 3. Our baseline is a single kanji accessible for each kanji learned.

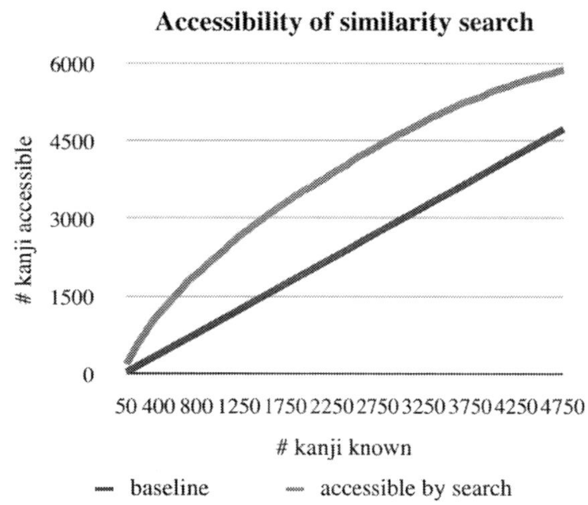

Figure 3: The accessibility improvement of kanji similarity search

Our actual precision makes the proportion of usable neighbours smaller; we will thus need to expose the user to a larger set of candidates to get this level of improvement. Improvements in precision and recall are still needed to reduce noise.

5 Discussion and future work

A current difficulty in evaluating this form of search is the lack of available query data to objectively evaluate the search before deployment. This restricts evaluation to longer-term post-hoc analysis based on query logs. Such logs will also provide additional real-world similarity and confusion data to improve our metrics.

This form of search is directly extensible to Chinese, and is limited only by the availability of character data. Indeed, preliminary similarity models for Chinese already exist (Liu and Lin, 2008). Our similarity modelling may also suggest approaches for more general symbol systems that lack adequate indexing schemes, for example heraldry.

There is much potential in the adaption of dictionaries as drill tutors in the context of language learning (Zock and Quint, 2004). The models presented in this paper could provide dynamic kanji drills, to aid early learners to distinguish similar kanji and provide challenge more advanced learners.

6 Conclusion

We have proposed a method of searching the dictionary for Japanese words containing unknown kanji, based on their visual similarity to familiar kanji. In order to achieve this, we have considered several metrics over characters, improved on existing baselines and evaluated further over a flashcard set. Of these metrics, the edit distance taken over stroke descriptions performed the best for high-similarity cases, and was used to construct similarity-based search at the word level.

References

[Apel and Quint2004] Apel, Ulrich and Julien Quint. 2004. Building a graphetic dictionary for Japanese kanji – character look up based on brush strokes or stroke groups, and the display of kanji as path data. In *Proc. COLING 2004*, Geneva, Switzerland.

[Bilac2002] Bilac, Slaven. 2002. Intelligent dictionary interface for learners of Japanese. Master's thesis, Tokyo Institute of Technology.

[Bille2005] Bille, Philip. 2005. A survey on tree edit distance and related problems. *Theoretical Computer Science*, 337(1-3):217–239.

[Clark and Curran2004] Clark, Stephen and James R. Curran. 2004. The importance of supertagging for wide-coverage CCG parsing. In *Proc. COLING 2004*, page 282–288, Geneva, Switzerland.

[Ferret and Zock2006] Ferret, Olivier and Michael Zock. 2006. Enhancing electronic dictionaries with an index based on associations. In *Proc. COLING/ACL 2006*, pages 281–288, Sydney, Australia.

[Halpern1999] Halpern, Jack, editor. 1999. *The Kodansha Kanji Learner's Dictionary*. Kodansha International, Tokyo.

[Liu and Lin2008] Liu, Chao-Lin and Jen-Hsiang Lin. 2008. Using structural information for identifying similar Chinese characters. In *Proc. ACL 2008: HLT, Short Papers (Companion Volume)*, pages 93–96, Columbus, Ohio.

[Tanaka-Ishii and Godon2006] Tanaka-Ishii, Kumiko and Julian Godon. 2006. Kansuke: A kanji look-up system based on a few stroke prototype. In *Proc. ICCPOL 2006*, Singapore.

[Winstead2006] Winstead, Chris. 2006. Electronic kanji dictionary based on "Dasher". *Proc. IEEE SMCals 2006* , pages 144–148, Logan, USA.

[Yeh and Li2002] Yeh, Su-Ling and Jing-Ling Li. 2002. Role of structure and component in judgements of visual similarity of Chinese characters. *Journal of Experimental Psychology: Human Perception and Performance*, 28(4):933–947.

[Yencken and Baldwin2006] Yencken, Lars and Timothy Baldwin. 2006. Modelling the orthographic neighbourhood for Japanese kanji. In *Proc. ICCPOL 2006*, Singapore.

[Yencken et al.2007] Yencken, Lars, Zhihui Jin, and Kumiko Tanaka-Ishii. 2007. Pinyomi - dictionary lookup via orthographic associations. In *Proc. PACLING 2007*, Melbourne, Australia.

[Zock and Bilac2004] Zock, Michael and Slaven Bilac. 2004. Word lookup on the basis of associations: from an idea to a roadmap. In *Proc. COLING 2004*, pages 89–95, Geneva, Switzerland.

[Zock and Quint2004] Zock, Michael and Julien Quint. 2004. Why have them work for peanuts, when it is so easy to provide reward? Motivations for converting a dictionary into a drill tutor. In *Proc. PAPILLON 2004*, Grenoble, France.

[Zock2002] Zock, Michael. 2002. Sorry, what was your name again, or how to overcome the tip-of-the tongue problem with the help of a computer? In *Proc. COLING 2002*, pages 1–6, Taipei, Taiwan.

Chinese Dependency Parsing with Large Scale Automatically Constructed Case Structures

Kun Yu
Graduate School of Informatics,
Kyoto University, Japan
kunyu@nlp.kuee.kyoto-u.ac.jp

Daisuke Kawahara
National Institute of Information and Communications Technology, Japan
dk@nict.go.jp

Sadao Kurohashi
Graduate School of Informatics,
Kyoto University, Japan
kuro@i.kyoto-u.ac.jp

Abstract

This paper proposes an approach using large scale case structures, which are automatically constructed from both a small tagged corpus and a large raw corpus, to improve Chinese dependency parsing. The case structure proposed in this paper has two characteristics: (1) it relaxes the predicate of a case structure to be all types of words which behaves as a head; (2) it is not categorized by semantic roles but marked by the neighboring modifiers attached to a head. Experimental results based on Penn Chinese Treebank show the proposed approach achieved 87.26% on unlabeled attachment score, which significantly outperformed the baseline parser without using case structures.

1 Introduction

Case structures (i.e. predicate-argument structures) represent what arguments can be attached to a predicate, which are very useful to recognize the meaning of natural language text. Researchers have applied case structures to Japanese syntactic analysis and improved parsing accuracy successfully (Kawahara and Kurohashi, 2006(a); Abekawa and Okumura, 2006). However, few works focused on using case structures in Chinese parsing. Wu (2003) proposed an approach to learn the relations between verbs and nouns and applied these relations to a Chinese parser. Han et al. (2004) presented a method to acquire the sub-categorization of Chinese verbs and used them in a PCFG parser.

Normally, case structures are categorized by semantic roles for verbs. For example, Kawahara and Kurohashi (2006(b)) constructed Japanese case structures which were marked by post positions. Wu (2003) classified the Chinese verb-noun relations as 'verb-object' and 'modifier-head'. In this paper, we propose a new type of Chinese case structure, which is different from those presented in previous work (Wu, 2003; Han et al., 2004; Kawahara and Kurohashi, 2006(a); Abekawa and Okumura, 2006) in two aspects:

(1) It relaxes the predicate of a case structure to be all types of words which behaves as a head;

(2) It is not categorized by semantic roles but marked by the neighboring modifiers attached to a head. The sibling modification information remembers the parsing history of a head node, which is useful to correct the parsing error such as a verb 看 (see) is modified by two nouns 电影 (film) and 简介 (introduction) as objects (see Figure 1).

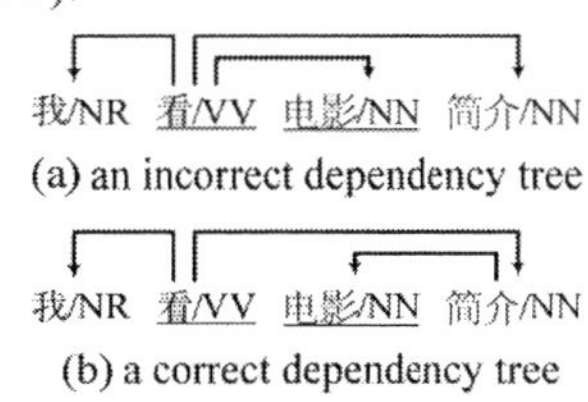

Figure 1. Dependency trees of an example sentence (I see the introduction of a film).

We automatically construct large scale case structures from both a small tagged corpus and a large raw corpus. Then, we apply the large scale case structures to a Chinese dependency parser to improve parsing accuracy.

The Chinese dependency parser using case structures is evaluated by Penn Chinese Treebank 5.1 (Xue et al., 2002). Results show that the

© 2008. Licensed under the *Creative Commons Attribution-Noncommercial-Share Alike 3.0 Unported* license (http://creativecommons.org/licenses/by-nc-sa/3.0/). Some rights reserved.

automatically constructed case structures helped increase parsing accuracy by 2.13% significantly.

The rest of this paper is organized as follows: Section 2 describes the proposed Chinese case structure and the construction method in detail; Section 3 describes a Chinese dependency parser using constructed case structures; Section 4 lists the experimental results with a discussion in section 5; Related work is introduced in Section 6; Finally, Section 7 gives a brief conclusion and the direction of future work.

2 Chinese Case Structure and its Construction

2.1 A New Type of Chinese Case Structure

We propose a new type of Chinese case structure in this paper, which is represented as the combination of a case pattern and a case element (see Figure 2). Case element remembers the bi-lexical dependency relation between all types of head-modifier pairs, which is also recognized in previous work (Wu, 2003; Han et al., 2004; Kawahara and Kurohashi, 2006(a); Abekawa and Okumura, 2006). Case pattern keeps the pos-tag sequence of all the modifiers attached to a head to remember the parsing history of a head node.

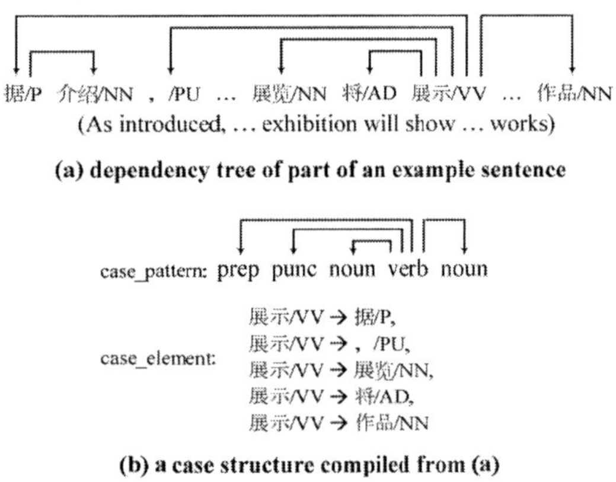

Figure 2. An example of constructed case structure.

2.2 Construction Corpus

We use 9,684 sentences from Penn Chinese Treebank 5.1 as the tagged corpus, and 7,338,028 sentences written in simplified Chinese from Chinese Gigaword (Graff et al., 2005) as the raw corpus for Chinese case structure construction.

Before constructing case structures from the raw corpus, we need to get the syntactic analysis of it. First, we do word segmentation and pos-tagging for the sentences in Chinese Gigaword by a Chinese morphological analyzer (Nakagawa and Uchimoto, 2007). Then a Chinese deterministic syntactic analyzer (Yu et al., 2007) is used to parse the whole corpus.

To guarantee the accuracy of constructed case structures, we only use the sentences with less than k words from Chinese Gigaword. It is based on the assumption that parsing short sentences is more accurate than parsing long sentences. The performance of the deterministic parser used for analyzing Chinese Gigaword (see Figure 3) shows smaller k ensures better parsing quality but suffers from lower sentence coverage. Referring to Figure 2, we set k as 30.

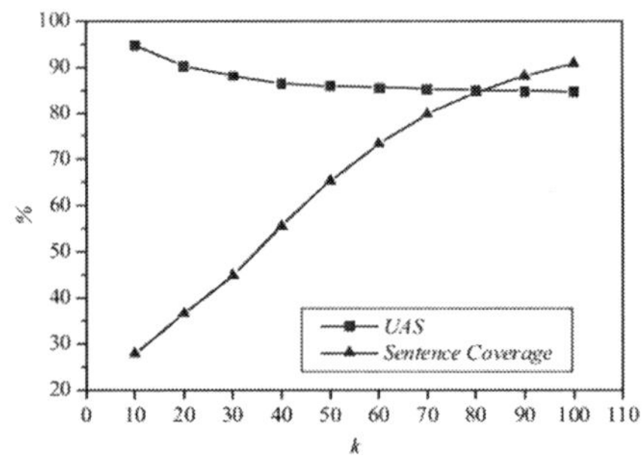

Figure 3. Performance of the deterministic parser with different k on 1,800 sentences[2].

2.3 Case Pattern Construction

A case pattern consists of a sequence of pos-tags indicating the order of all the modifiers attached to a head (see Figure 1), which can be represented as following.

$$cp_i =< [pos_m, pos_{m-1}, ..., pos_1]_l, [pos_1, ..., pos_{n-1}, pos_n]_r >$$

Here, $[pos_m, pos_{m-1}, ..., pos_1]_l$ means the pos-tag sequence of the modifiers attached to a head from the left side, and $[pos_1, ..., pos_{n-1}, pos_n]_r$ means the pos-tag sequence of the modifiers attached to a head from the right side.

We use the 33 pos-tags defined in Penn Chinese Treebank (Xue et al., 2002) to describe a case pattern, and make following modifications:

- group common noun, proper noun and pronoun together and mark them as '*noun*';
- group predicative adjective and all the other verbs together and mark them as '*verb*';
- only regard comma, pause, colon and semi-colon as punctuations and mark them as '*punc*', and neglect other punctuations.

[2] *UAS* means unlabeled attachment score (Buchholz and Marsi, 2006). The sentences used for this evaluation are from Penn Chinese Treebank with gold word segmentation and pos-tag.

- group cardinal number and ordinal number together and mark them as '*num*';
- keep the original definition for other pos-tags but label them by new tags, such as labeling 'P' as 'prep' and labeling 'AD' as 'adv'.

The task of case pattern construction is to extract cp_i for each head from both the tagged corpus and the raw corpus. As we will introduce later, the Chinese dependency parser using case structures applies CKY algorithm for decoding. Thus the following substrings of cp_i are also extracted for each head as horizontal Markovization during case pattern construction.

$$< [pos_k, pos_{k-1}, ..., pos_1]_l, [pos_1, ..., pos_{j-1}, pos_j]_r > \quad \forall k \in [1, m], j \in [1, n]$$

$$< [pos_k, pos_{k-1}, ..., pos_1]_l >, \forall k \in [1, m]$$

$$< [pos_1, ..., pos_{j-1}, pos_j]_r >, \forall j \in [1, n]$$

2.4 Case Element Construction

As introduced in Section 2.1, a case element keeps the lexical preference between a head and its modifier. Therefore, the task of case element construction is to extract head-modifier pairs from both the tagged corpus and the raw corpus.

Although only the sentences with less than k (k=30) words from Chinese Gigaword are used as raw corpus to guarantee the accuracy, there still exist some dependency relations with low accuracy in these short sentences because of the non-perfect parsing quality. Therefore, we apply a head-modifier (HM) classifier to the parsed sentences from Chinese Gigaword to further extract head-modifier pairs with high quality. This HM classifier is based on SVM classification. Table 1 lists the features used in this classifier.

Feature	Description
Pos_{head}/ Pos_{mod}	Pos-tag pair of head and modifier
Distance	Distance between head and modifier
HasComma	If there exists comma between head and modifier, set as 1; otherwise as 0
HasColon	If there exists colon between head and modifier, set as 1; otherwise as 0
HasSemi	If there exists semi-colon between head and modifier, set as 1; otherwise as 0

Table 1. Features for HM classifier.

The HM classifier is trained on 3500 sentences from Penn Chinese Treebank with gold-standard word segmentation and pos-tag. All the sentences are parsed by the same Chinese deterministic parser used for Chinese Gigaword analysis. The correct dependency relations created by the parser are looked as positive examples and the left dependency relations are used as negative examples. TinySVM[3] is selected as the SVM toolkit. A polynomial kernel is used and degree is set as 2. Tested on 346 sentences, which are from Penn Chinese Treebank and parsed by the same deterministic parser with gold standard word segmentation and pos-tag, this HM classifier achieved 96.77% on precision and 46.35% on recall.

3 A Chinese Dependency Parser Using Case Structures

3.1 Parsing Model

We develop a lexicalized Chinese dependency parser to use constructed case structures. This parser gives a probability $P(T|S)$ to each possible dependency tree T of an input sentence $S=w_1,w_2,\ldots,w_n$ (w_i is a node representing a word with its pos-tag), and outputs the dependency tree T^* that maximizes $P(T|S)$ (see equation 1). CKY algorithm is used to decode the dependency tree from bottom to up.

$$T^* = \arg\max_T P(T \mid S) \tag{1}$$

To use case structures, $P(T|S)$ is divided into two parts (see equation 2): the probability of a sentence S generating a root node w_{ROOT}, and the product of the probabilities of a node w_i generating a case structure CS_i.

$$P(T \mid S) = P(w_{ROOT} \mid S) \times \prod_{i=1}^{m} P(CS_i \mid w_i) \tag{2}$$

As introduced in Section 2, a case structure CS_i is composed of a case pattern cp_i and a case element cm_i. Thus

$$\begin{aligned} P(CS_i \mid w_i) &= P(cp_i, cm_i \mid w_i) \\ &= P(cp_i \mid w_i) \times P(cm_i \mid w_i, cp_i) \end{aligned} \tag{3}$$

A case element cm_i consists of a set of dependencies $\{D_j\}$, in which each D_j is a tuple $<w_j, dis_j, comma_j>$. Here w_j means a modifier node, dis_j means the distance between w_j and its head, and $comma_j$ means the number of commas between w_j and its head. Assuming any D_j and D_k are independent of each other when they belong to the same case element, $P(cm_i|w_i,cp_i)$ can be written as

$$\begin{aligned} P(cm_i \mid w_i, cp_i) &= \prod_j P(D_j \mid w_i, cp_i) \\ &= \prod_j P(w_j, dis_j, comma_j \mid w_i, cp_i) \end{aligned} \tag{4}$$

[3] http://chasen.org/~taku/software/TinySVM/

Finally, $P(w_j,dis_j,comma_j \mid w_i,cp_i)$ is divided as

$$P(w_j,dis_j,comma_j \mid w_i,cp_i) \\ = P(w_j \mid w_i,cp_i) \times P(dis_j,comma_j \mid w_i,w_j,cp_i) \quad (5)$$

Maximum likelihood estimation is used to estimate $P(w_{ROOT}|S)$ on training data set with the smoothing method used in (Collins, 1996). The estimation of $P(cp_i|w_i)$, $P(w_j|w_i,cp_i)$, and $P(dis_j, comma_j |w_i,w_j,cp_i)$ will be introduced in the following subsections.

3.2 Estimating $P(cp_i|w_i)$ by Case Patterns

Three steps are used to estimate $P(cp_i|w_i)$ by maximum likelihood estimation using the constructed case patterns:

- Estimate $P(cp_i|w_i)$ only by the case patterns from the tagged corpus and represent it as $\hat{P}_{tagged}(cp_i \mid w_i)$;
- Estimate $P(cp_i|w_i)$ only by the case patterns from the raw corpus and represent it as $\hat{P}_{raw}(cp_i \mid w_i)$;
- Estimate $P(cp_i|w_i)$ by equation 6, in which $\lambda_{pattern}$ is calculated by equation 7 to set proper ratio for the probabilities estimated by the case patterns from different corpora.

$$\hat{P}(cp_i \mid w_i) \\ = \lambda_{pattern} \times \hat{P}_{tagged}(cp_i \mid w_i) + (1-\lambda_{pattern}) \times \hat{P}_{raw}(cp_i \mid w_i) \quad (6)$$

$$\lambda_{pattern} = \frac{\delta_{tagged} + \eta_{tagged} + \delta_{raw} + \eta_{raw}}{\delta_{tagged} + \eta_{tagged} + \delta_{raw} + \eta_{raw} + 1} \quad (7)$$

In equation 7, δ_{tagged} and δ_{raw} mean the occurrence of a lexicalized node w_i=<lex_i, pos_i> generating cp_i in the tagged or raw corpus, η_{tagged} and η_{raw} mean the occurrence of a back-off node w_i=<pos_i> generating cp_i in the tagged or raw corpus. To overcome the data sparseness problem, we not only apply the smoothing method used in (Collins, 1996) for a lexicalized head to back off it to its part-of-speech, but also assign a very small value to $P(cp_i|w_i)$ when there is no cp_i modifying w_i in the constructed case patterns.

3.3 Estimating $P(w_j|w_i,cp_i)$ and $P(dis_j, comma_j |w_i,w_j,cp_i)$ by Case Elements

To estimate $P(w_j|w_i,cp_i)$ and $P(dis_j, comma_j |w_i,w_j,cp_i)$ by maximum likelihood estimation, we also use three steps:

- Estimate the two probabilities only by the case elements from the tagged corpus and represent them as $\hat{P}_{tagged}(w_j \mid w_i,cp_i)$ and $\hat{P}_{tagged}(dis_j,comma_j \mid w_i,w_j,cp_i)$;
- Estimate the two probabilities only by the case elements from the raw corpus, and represent them as $\hat{P}_{raw}(w_j \mid w_i,cp_i)$ and $\hat{P}_{raw}(dis_j,comma_j \mid w_i,w_j,cp_i)$;
- Estimate $P(w_j|w_i,cp_i)$ and $P(dis_j, comma_j |w_i,w_j,cp_i)$ by equation 8 and equation 9.

$$\hat{P}(w_j \mid w_i,cp_i) \\ = \lambda_{element} \times \hat{P}_{tagged}(w_j \mid w_i,cp_i) + \\ (1-\lambda_{element}) \times \hat{P}_{raw}(w_j \mid w_i,cp_i) \quad (8)$$

$$\hat{P}(dis_j,comma_j \mid w_i,w_j,cp_i) \\ = \lambda_{element} \times \hat{P}_{tagged}(dis_j,comma_j \mid w_i,w_j,cp_i) + \\ (1-\lambda_{element}) \times \hat{P}_{raw}(dis_j,comma_j \mid w_i,w_j,cp_i) \quad (9)$$

The smoothing method used in (Collins, 1996) is applied during estimation.

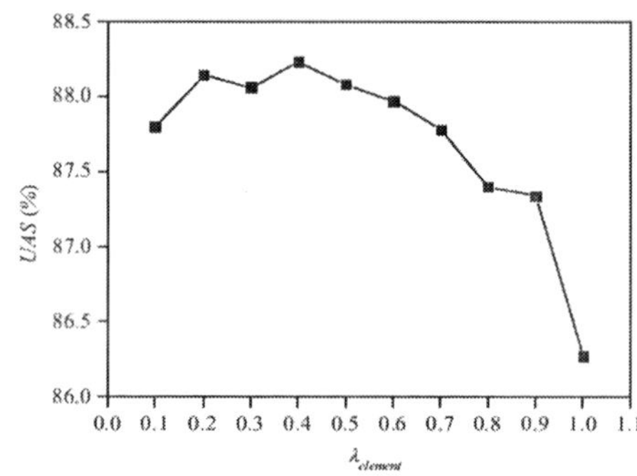

Figure 4. Parsing accuracy with different $\lambda_{element}$ on development data set.

In order to set proper ratio for the probabilities estimated by the case elements from different corpora, we use a parameter $\lambda_{element}$ in equation 8 and 9. The appropriate setting ($\lambda_{element}$ =0.4) is learned by a development data set (see Figure 4).

4 Evaluation Results

4.1 Experimental Setting

We use Penn Chinese Treebank 5.1 as data set to evaluate the proposed approach. 9,684 sentences from Section 001-270 and 400-931, which are also used for constructing case structures, are used as training data. 346 sentences from Section 271-300 are used as testing data. 334 sentences from Section 301-325 are used as development data. Penn2Malt[4] is used to transfer the phrase structure of Penn Chinese Treebank to dependency structure. Gold-standard word segmentation and pos-tag are applied in all the experiments.

[4] http://w3.msi.vxu.se/~nivre/research/Penn2Malt.html

Unlabeled attachment score (*UAS*) (Buchholz and Marsi, 2006) is used as evaluation metric. Because of the difficulty of assigning correct head to Chinese punctuation, we calculate *UAS* only on the dependency relations in which the modifier is not punctuation.

4.2 Results

Three parsers were evaluated in this experiment:

- '*baseline*': a parser not using case structures, where $P(T|S)$ is calculated by equation 11 and $P(w_j|w_i)$ and $P(dis_j,\ comma_j\ |w_i,w_j)$ are estimated by training data set only.

$$\begin{aligned} &P(T \mid S) \\ &= P(w_{ROOT} \mid S) \times \prod_{i,j \in [1,n], i \neq j} P(w_j, dis_j, comma_j \mid w_i) \\ &= P(w_{ROOT} \mid S) \times \prod_{i,j \in [1,n], i \neq j} (P(w_j \mid w_i) \times P(dis_j, comma_j \mid w_i, w_j)) \end{aligned} \quad (11)$$

- '*w/ case elem*': a parser only using case element, which also calculates $P(T|S)$ by equation 11 but estimates $P(w_j|w_i)$ and $P(dis_j,\ comma_j\ |w_i,w_j)$ by constructed case elements.
- '*proposed*': the parser introduced in Section 3, which uses both case elements and case patterns.

The evaluation results on testing data set (see Table 2) shows the *proposed* parser achieved 87.26% on *UAS*, which was 2.13% higher than that of the *baseline* parser. This improvement is regarded as statistically significant (McNemar's test: $p<0.0005$). Besides, Table 2 shows only using case elements increased parsing accuracy by 1.30%. It means both case elements and case patterns gave help to parsing accuracy, and case elements contributed more in the proposed approach.

Parsing model	*baseline*	*w/ case elem*	*proposed*
UAS (%)	85.13	86.43 (+1.30)	**87.26 (+2.13)**

Table 2. Parsing accuracy of different parsing models.

Figure 5 and Figure 6 show the dependency trees of two example sentences created by both the *baseline* parser and the *proposed* parser. In Figure 5, *the baseline* parser incorrectly assigned 签订/NN (signing) as the head of 合作/NN (cooperation). However, after using the case element 项目/NN (project) → 合作/NN, the correct head of 合作/NN was found by the *proposed* parser. Figure 6 shows the *baseline* parser recognized 开幕/VV (opening) as the head of 据/P (as) incorrectly. But in the *proposed* parser, the probability of 开幕/VV generating the case pattern '$[prep,\ punc,\ prep]_l$' was much lower than that of 开幕/VV generating the case pattern '$[prep]_l$'. Therefore, the proposed parser rejected the incorrect dependency that 据/P modified 开幕/VV and got the correct head of 据/P as 展示/VV (show) successfully.

5 Discussion

5.1 Influence of the Number of Case Structures on Parsing Accuracy

During case structure construction, we only used the sentences with less than k (k=30) words from Chinese Gigaword as the raw corpus. Enlarging k will introduce more sentences from Chinese Gigaword and increase the number of case structures. Table 4 lists the number of case structures and parsing accuracy of the *proposed* parser on testing data set with different k[5]. It shows enlarging the number of case structures is a possible way to increase parsing accuracy. But simply setting larger k did not help parsing, because it decreased the parsing accuracy of Chinese Gigaword and consequently decreased the accuracy of constructed case structures. Using good parse selection (Reichart and Rappoport, 2007; Yates et al., 2006) on the syntactic analysis of Chinese Gigaword is a probable way to construct more case structures without decreasing their accuracy. We will consider about it in the future.

k	10	20	30	40
# of Case Element (M)	0.66	1.14	1.81	2.75
# of Case Pattern (M)	0.57	1.55	3.91	8.48
UAS (%)	85.16	86.42	87.26	87.07

Table 4. Case structure number and parsing accuracy with different k.

5.2 Influence of the Case Structure Construction Corpus on Parsing Accuracy

We also evaluated the *proposed* parser on testing data set using case structures constructed from different corpora.

Results (see Table 5) show that parsing accuracy was improved greatly only when using case structures constructed from both the two corpora. The case structures constructed from either of a

[5] Considering about the time expense of case structure construction, we only did test for $k \leq 40$.

single corpus only gave a little help to parsing. It is because among all the case structures used during testing (see Table 6), 19.57% case elements were constructed from the tagged corpus only and 54.18% case patterns were constructed from the raw corpus only. The incorrect head-modifier pairs extracted from Chinese Gigaword is a possible reason for the fact that some case elements only existing in the tagged corpus. Enhancing good parse selection on Chinese Gigaword could improve the quality of extracted head-modifier pairs and solve this problem. In addition, the strict definition of case pattern is a probable reason that makes more than half of the case patterns only exist in the raw corpus and 18.18% case patterns exist in neither of the two corpora. We will modify the representation of case pattern to make it more flexible to the number of modifiers to resolve this issue in the future.

Corpus	Tagged	Raw	Tagged+Raw
UAS (%)	85.25	85.90	87.26

Table 5. Parsing accuracy with case structures constructed from different corpora.

Corpus	Tagged	Raw	Tagged+Raw	None
% of case element	19.57	8.95	68.07	3.41
% of case pattern	0.03	54.18	27.61	18.18

Table 6. Ratio of case structures constructed from different corpora.

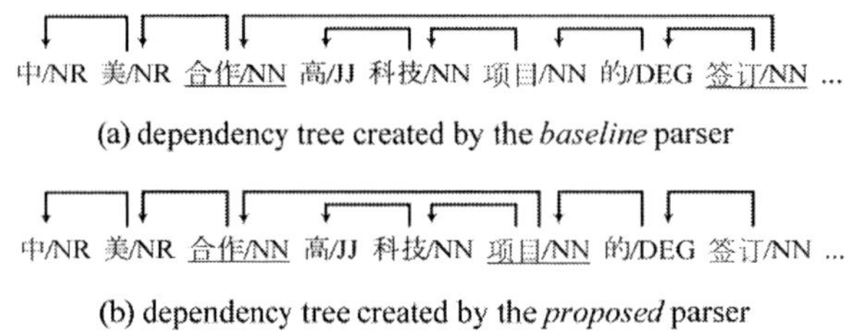

Figure 5. Dependency trees of an example sentence (The signing of China-US cooperation high tech project ...).

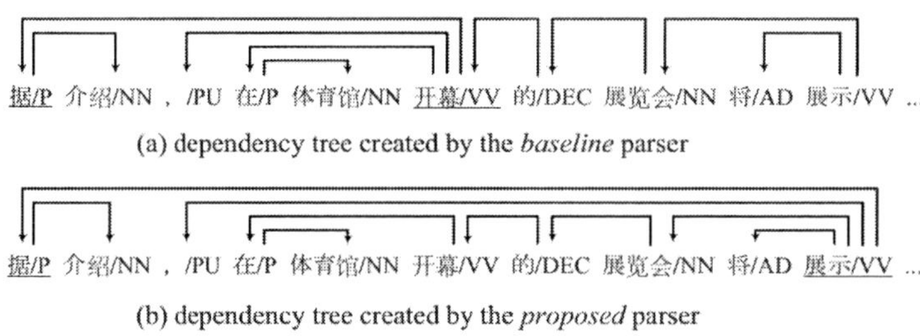

Figure 6. Dependency trees of an example sentence (As introduced, the exhibition opening in the stadium will show...).

5.3 Parsing Performance with Real Pos-tag

Gold standard word segmentation and pos-tag are applied in previous experiments. However, parsing accuracy will be affected by the incorrect word segmentation and pos-tag in the real applications. Currently, the best performance of Chinese word segmentation has achieved 99.20% on F-score, but the best accuracy of Chinese pos-tagging was 96.89% (Jin and Chen, 2008). Therefore, we think pos-tagging is more crucial for applying parser in real task compared with word segmentation. Considering about this, we evaluated the parsing models introduced in Section 4 with real pos-tag in this experiment.

Parsing model	*baseline*	*proposed*
UAS (%)	80.91	**82.90 (+1.99)**

Table 7. Parsing accuracy of different parsing models with real pos-tag.

An HMM-based pos-tagger is used to get pos-tag for testing sentences with gold word segmentation. The pos-tagger was trained on the same training data set described in Section 4.1 and achieved 93.70% F-score on testing data set. Results (see Table 7) show that even if with real pos-tags, the *proposed* parser still outperformed the *baseline* parser significantly. However, the results in Table 7 indicate that incorrect pos-tag affected the parsing accuracy of the *proposed* parser greatly. Some researchers integrated pos-tagging into parsing and kept n-best pos-tags to reduce the effect of pos-tagging errors on parsing accuracy (Cao et al., 2007). We will also consider about this in our future work.

6 Related Work

To our current knowledge, there were few works about using case structures in Chinese parsing, except for the work of Wu (2003) and Han et al. (2004). Compared with them, our proposed approach presents a new type of case structures for all kinds of head-modifier pairs, which not only recognizes bi-lexical dependency but also remembers the parsing history of a head node.

Parsing history has been used to improve parsing accuracy by many researchers (Yamada and Matsumoto, 2003; McDonald and Pereira, 2006). Yamada and Matsumoto (2003) showed that keeping a small amount of parsing history was useful to improve parsing performance in a shift-reduce parser. McDonald and Pereira (2006) expanded their first-order spanning tree model to be second-order by factoring the score of the tree into the sum of adjacent edge pair scores. In our proposed approach, the case patterns remember the neighboring modifiers for a head node like McDonald and Pereira's work. But it keeps all the parsing histories of a head, which is different from only keeping adjacent two modifiers in (McDonald and Pereira, 2006). Besides, to use the parsing histories in CKY decoding, our approach applies horizontal Markovization during case pattern construction. In general, the success of using case patterns in Chinese parsing in his paper proves again that keeping parsing history is crucial to improve parsing performance, no matter in which way and to which parsing model it is applied.

There were also some works that handled lexical preference for Chinese parsing in other ways. For example, Cheng et al. (2006) and Hall et al. (2007) applied shift-reduce deterministic parsing to Chinese. Sagae and Tsujii (2007) generalized the standard deterministic framework to probabilistic parsing by using a best-first search strategy. In these works, lexical preferences were introduced as features for predicting parsing action. Besides, Bikel and Chiang (2000) applied two lexicalized parsing models developed for English to Penn Chinese Treebank. Wang et al. (2005) proposed a completely lexicalized bottom-up generative parsing model to parse Chinese, in which a word-similarity-based smoothing was introduced to replace part-of-speech smoothing.

7 Conclusion and Future Work

This paper proposes an approach to use large scale case structures, which are automatically constructed from both a small tagged corpus and the syntactic analysis of a large raw corpus, to improve Chinese dependency parsing. The proposed case structures not only recognize the lexical preference between all types of head-modifier pairs, but also keep the parsing history of a head word. Experimental results show the proposed approach improved parsing accuracy significantly. Besides, although we only apply the proposed approach to Chinese dependency parsing currently, the same idea could be adapted to other languages easily because it doesn't use any language specific knowledge.

There are several future works under consideration, such as modifying the representation of case patterns to make it more robust, enhancing good parse selection on the analysis of raw corpus, and integrating pos-tagging into parsing model.

References

T.Abekawa and M.Okumura. 2006. Japanese Dependency Parsing Using Co-occurrence Information and a Combination of Case Elements. In *Proceedings of the joint conference of the International Committee on Computational Linguistics and the Association for Computational Linguistics 2006*. pp. 833-840.

D.Bikel. 2004. Intricacies of Collins' Parsing Model. *Computational Linguistics*, 30(4): 479-511.

D.Bikel and D.Chiang. 2000. Two Statistical Parsing Models Applied to the Chinese Treebank. In *Proceedings of the 2nd Chinese Language Processing Workshop*. pp. 1-6.

S.Buchholz and E.Marsi. 2006. CoNLL-X Shared Task on Multilingual Dependency Parsing. In *Proceedings of the 10th Conference on Computational Natural Language Learning*.

H.Cao et al.. 2007. Empirical Study on Parsing Chinese Based on Collins' Model. In *Proceedings of the 10th Conference of the Pacific Association for Computational Linguisitcs*. pp. 113-119.

Y.Cheng, M.Asahara and Y.Matsumoto. 2006. Multilingual Dependency Parsing at NAIST. In *Proceedings of the 10th Conference on Computational Natural Language Learning*. pp. 191-195.

M.Collins. 1996. A New Statistical Parser Based on Bigram Lexical Dependencies. In *Proceedings of the 34th Annual Meeting of the Association for Computational Linguistics*. pp. 184-191.

M.Collins. 1999. Head-Driven Statistical Models for Natural Language Parsing. *Ph.D Thesis*. University of Pennsylvania.

D.Graff et al.. 2005. Chinese Gigaword Second Edition. *Linguistic Data Consortium*, Philadelphia.

J.Hall et al. 2007. Single Malt or Blended? A Study in Multilingual Parser Optimization. In *Proceedings of the shared task at the Conference on Computational Natural Language Learning 2007*. pp. 933-939.

X.Han et al.. 2004. Subcategorization Acquisition and Evaluation for Chinese Verbs. In *Proceedings of the 20th International Conference on Computational Linguistics*.

G.Jin and X.Chen. 2008. The Fourth International Chinese Language Processing Bakeoff: Chinese Word Segmentation, Named Entity Recognition and Chinese Pos Tagging. In *Proceedings of the 6th SIGHAN Workshop on Chinese Language Processing*.

D.Kawahara and S.Kurohashi. 2006 (a). A Fully-lexicalized Probabilistic Model for Japanese Syntactic and Case frame Analysis. In *Proceedings of the Human Language Technology conference - North American chapter of the Association for Computational Linguistics annual meeting 2006*. pp. 176-183.

D.Kawahara and S.Kurohashi. 2006 (b). Case Frame Compilation from the Web Using High-performance Computing. In *Proceedings of the 5th International Conference on Language Resources and Evaluation*.

T.Kudo and Y.Matsumoto. 2002. Japanese Dependency Analysis Using Cascaded Chunking. In *Proceedings of the Conference on Natural Language Learning*. pp. 29-35.

R.McDonald and F.Pereira. 2006. Online Learning of Approximate Dependency Parsing Algorithm. In *Proceedings of the 11th Conference of the European Chapter of the Association for Computational Linguistics*.

R.McDonald and J.Nivre. 2007. Characterizing the Errors of Data-driven Dependency Parsing Models. In *Proceedings of the Conference on Empirical Methods in Natural Language Processing Conference on Computational Natural Language Learning 2007*.

T.Nakagawa and K.Uchimoto. 2007. A Hybrid Approach to Word Segmentation and POS Tagging. In *Proceedings of the 45th Annual Meeting of the Association for Computational Linguistics*. pp. 217-220.

R.Reichart and A.Rappoport. 2007. An Ensemble Method for Selection of High Quality Parses. In *Proceedings of the 45th Annual Meeting of the Association for Computational Linguistics*. pp. 408-415.

K.Sagae and J.Tsujii. 2007. Dependency Parsing and Domain Adaptation with LR Models and Parser Ensembles. In *Proceedings of the shared task at the Conference on Computational Natural Language Learning 2007*. pp. 1044-1050.

Q.Wang, D.Schuurmans, and D.Lin. 2005. Strictly Lexical Dependency Parsing. In *Proceedings of the 9th International Workshop on Parsing Technologies*. pp. 152-159.

A.Wu. 2003. Learning Verb-Noun Relations to Improve Parsing. In *Proceedings of the 2nd SIGHAN Workshop on Chinese Language Processing*. pp. 119-124.

N.Xue, F.Chiou and M.Palmer. 2002. Building a Large-Scale Annotated Chinese Corpus. In *Proceedings of the 18th International Conference on Computational Linguistics*.

N.Xue and M.Palmer. 2003. Annotating the Propositions in the Penn Chinese Treebank. In *Proceedings of the 2nd SIGHAN Workshop on Chinese Language Processing*.

N.Xue and M.Palmer. 2005. Automatic Semantic Rule Labeling for Chinese Verbs. In *Proceedings of the 19th International Joint Conference on Artificial Intelligence*.

H.Yamada and Y.Matsumoto. 2003. Statistical Dependency Analysis with Support Vector Machines. In *Proceedings of the 7th International Workshop on Parsing Technologies*.

A.Yates, S.Schoenmackers, and O.Etzioni. 2006. Detecting Parser Errors Using Web-based Semantic Filters. In *Proceedings of the 2006 Conference on Empirical Methods in Natural Language Processing*. pp. 27-34.

J.You and K.Chen. 2004. Automatic Semantic Role Assignment for a Tree Structure. In *Proceedings of the 3rd SIGHAN Workshop on Chinese Language Processing*.

K.Yu, S.Kurohashi, and H.Liu. 2007. A Three-step Deterministic Parser for Chinese Dependency Parsing. In *Proceedings of the Human Language Technologies: the Annual Conference of the North American Chapter of the Association for Computational Linguistics 2007*. pp. 201-204.

OntoNotes: Corpus Cleanup of Mistaken Agreement Using Word Sense Disambiguation

Liang-Chih Yu and **Chung-Hsien Wu**
Dept. of Computer Science and Information Engineering
National Cheng Kung University
Tainan, Taiwan, R.O.C.
{lcyu,chwu}@csie.ncku.edu.tw

Eduard Hovy
Information Sciences Institute
University of Southern California
Marina del Rey, CA 90292, USA
hovy@isi.edu

Abstract

Annotated corpora are only useful if their annotations are consistent. Most large-scale annotation efforts take special measures to reconcile inter-annotator disagreement. To date, however, no-one has investigated how to automatically determine exemplars in which the annotators agree but are wrong. In this paper, we use OntoNotes, a large-scale corpus of semantic annotations, including word senses, predicate-argument structure, ontology linking, and coreference. To determine the mistaken agreements in word sense annotation, we employ word sense disambiguation (WSD) to select a set of suspicious candidates for human evaluation. Experiments are conducted from three aspects (*precision*, *cost-effectiveness ratio*, and *entropy*) to examine the performance of WSD. The experimental results show that WSD is most effective on identifying erroneous annotations for highly-ambiguous words, while a baseline is better for other cases. The two methods can be combined to improve the cleanup process. This procedure allows us to find approximately 2% remaining erroneous agreements in the OntoNotes corpus. A similar procedure can be easily defined to check other annotated corpora.

1 Introduction

Word sense annotated corpora are useful resources for many natural language applications. Various machine learning algorithms can then be trained on these corpora to improve the applications' effectiveness. Lately, many such corpora have been developed in different languages, including SemCor (Miller et al., 1993), LDC-DSO (Ng and Lee, 1996), Hinoki (Kasahara et al., 2004), and the sense annotated corpora with the help of Web users (Chklovski and Mihalcea, 2002). The SENSEVAL[1] (Kilgarriff and Palmer, 2000; Kilgarriff, 2001; Mihalcea and Edmonds, 2004) and SemEval-2007[2] evaluations have also created large amounts of sense tagged data for word sense disambiguation (WSD) competitions.

The OntoNotes (Pradhan et al., 2007a; Hovy et al., 2006) project has created a multilingual corpus of large-scale semantic annotations, including word senses, predicate-argument structure, ontology linking, and coreference[3]. In word sense creation, sense creators generate sense definitions by grouping fine-grained sense distinctions obtained from WordNet and dictionaries into more coarse-grained senses. There are two reasons for this grouping instead of using WordNet senses directly. First, people have trouble distinguishing many of the WordNet-level distinctions in real text, and make inconsistent choices; thus the use of coarse-grained senses can improve inter-annotator agreement (ITA) (Palmer et al., 2004; 2006). Second, improved ITA enables machines to more accurately learn to perform sense tagging automatically. Sense grouping in OntoNotes has been calibrated to ensure that ITA averages at least 90%. Table 1 shows the OntoNotes sense

© 2008. Licensed under the Creative Commons Attribution-Noncommercial-Share Alike 3.0 Un-ported license (http://creativecommons.org/licenses/by-nc-sa/3.0/). Some rights reserved.

[1] http://www.senseval.org
[2] http://nlp.cs.swarthmore.edu/semeval
[3] Year 1 of the OntoNotes corpus has been released by Linguistic Data Consortium (LDC) (http://www.ldc.upenn.edu) in early 2007. The Year 2 corpus will be released in early 2008.

Sense Tag	Sense Definition	WordNet sense
arm.01	The forelimb of an animal	WN.1
arm.02	A weapon	WN.2
arm.03	A subdivision or branch of an organization	WN.3
arm.04	A projection, a narrow extension of a structure	WN.4 WN.5

Table 1. OntoNotes sense tags and definitions. The WordNet version is 2.1.

Example sentence:	
The 45-year-old Mr. Kuehn, who has a background in crisis **management**, succeeds Alan D. Rubendall, 45.	
management.01:	*Overseeing or directing. Refers to the act of managing something.* He was given overall management of the program. I'm a specialist in risk management. The economy crashed because of poor management.
management.02:	*The people in charge. The ones actually doing the managing.* Management wants to start downsizing. John was promoted to Management. I spoke to their management, and they're ready to make a deal.

Table 2. Example sentence for the target word *management* along with its sense definitions.

tags and definitions for the word *arm* (noun sense). The OntoNotes sense tags have been used for many applications, including the SemEval-2007 evaluation (Pradhan et al., 2007b), sense merging (Snow et al., 2007), sense pool verification (Yu et al., 2007), and class imbalance problems (Zhu and Hovy, 2007).

In creating OntoNotes, each word sense annotation involves two annotators and an adjudicator. First, all sentences containing the target word along with its sense distinctions are presented independently to two annotators for sense annotation. If the two annotators agree on the same sense for the target word in a given sentence, then their selection is stored in the corpus. Otherwise, this sentence is double-checked by the adjudicator for the final decision. The major problem of the above annotation scheme is that only the instances where the two annotators disagreed are double-checked, while those showing agreement are stored directly without any adjudication. Therefore, if the annotators happen to agree but are both wrong, then the corpus becomes polluted by the erroneous annotations. Table 2 shows an actual occurrence of an erroneous instance (sentence) for the target word *management*. In this example sentence, the actual sense of the target word is *management.01*, but both of our annotators made a decision of *management.02*. (Note that there is no difficulty in making this decision; the joint error might have occurred due to annotator fatigue, habituation after a long sequence of *management.02* decisions, etc.)

Although most annotations in OntoNotes are correct, there is still a small (but unknown) fraction of erroneous annotations in the corpus. Therefore, some cleanup procedure is necessary to produce a high-quality corpus. However, it is impractical for human experts to evaluate the whole corpus for cleanup. Given that we are focusing on word senses, this study proposes the use of WSD to facilitate the corpus cleanup process. WSD has shown promising accuracy in recent SENSEVAL and SemEval-2007 evaluations.

The rest of this work is organized as follows. Section 2 describes the corpus cleanup procedure. Section 3 presents the features for WSD. Section 4 summarizes the experimental results. Conclusions are drawn in Section 5.

2 Corpus Cleanup Procedure

Figure 1 shows the cleanup procedure (dashed lines) for the OntoNotes corpus. As mentioned earlier, each word along with its sentence instances is annotated by two annotators. The anno-

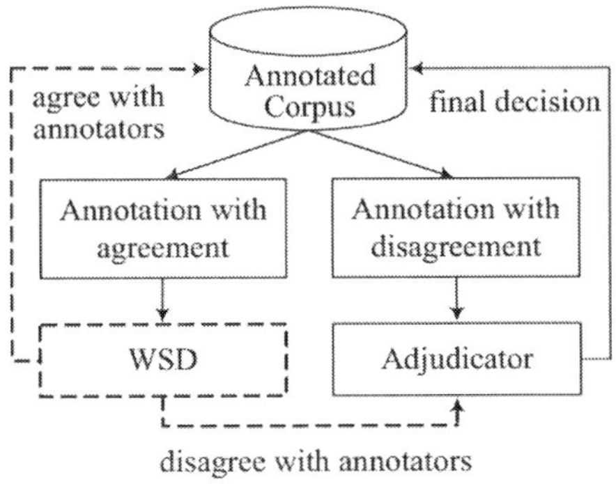

Figure 1. Corpus cleanup procedure.

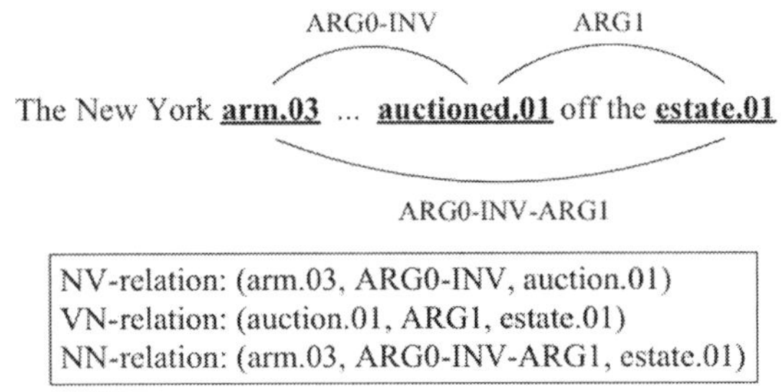

Figure 2. Example of predicate-argument structure. The label "-INV" denotes an inverse direction (i.e., from a noun to a verb).

tated corpus can thus be divided into two parts according to the annotation results. The first part includes the annotation with disagreement among the two annotators, which is then double-checked by the adjudicator. The final decisions made by the adjudicator are stored into the corpus. Since this part is double-checked by the adjudicator, it will not be evaluated by the cleanup procedure.

The second part of the corpus is the focus of the cleanup procedure. The WSD system evaluates each instance in the second part. If the output of the WSD system disagrees with the two annotators, the instance is considered to be a suspicious candidate, otherwise it is considered to be clean and stored into the corpus. The set of suspicious candidates is collected and subsequently evaluated by the adjudicator to identify erroneous annotations.

3 Word Sense Disambiguation

This study takes a supervised learning approach to build a WSD system from the OntoNotes corpus. The feature set used herein is similar to several state-of-the-art WSD systems (Lee and Ng., 2002; Ando, 2006; Tratz et al., 2007; Cai et al., 2007; Agirre and Lopez de Lacalle, 2007; Specia et al., 2007), which is further integrated into a Naïve Bayes classifier (Lee and Ng., 2002; Mihalcea, 2007). In addition, a new feature, predicate-argument structure, provided by the OntoNotes corpus is also integrated. The feature set includes:

Part-of-Speech (POS) tags: This feature includes the POS tags in the positions (P_{-3}, P_{-2}, P_{-1}, P_0, P_1, P_2, P_3), relative to the POS tag of the target word.

Local Collocations: This feature includes single words and multi-word n-grams. The single words include (W_{-3}, W_{-2}, W_{-1}, W_0, W_1, W_2, W_3), relative to the target word W_0. Similarly, the multi-word n-grams include ($W_{-2,-1}$, $W_{-1,1}$, $W_{1,2}$, $W_{-3,-2,-1}$, $W_{-2,-1,1}$, $W_{-1,1,2}$, $W_{1,2,3}$).

Bag-of-Words: This feature can be considered as a global feature, consisting of 5 words prior to and after the target word, without regard to position.

Predicate-Argument Structure: The predicate-argument structure captures the semantic relations between the predicates and their arguments within a sentence, as shown in Figure 2. These relations can be either *direct* or *indirect*. A direct relation is used to model a verb-noun (VN) or noun-verb (NV) relation, whereas an indirect relation is used to model a noun-noun (NN) relation. Additionally, an NN-relation can be built from the combination of an NV-relation and VN-relation. For instance, in Figure 2, the NN-relation (R3) can be built by combining the NV-relation (R1) the VN-relation (R2). Therefore, the two features, R1 and R3, can be used to disambiguate the noun *arm*[4].

4 Experimental Results

4.1 Experiment setup

The experiment data used herein was the 35 nouns from the SemEval-2007 English Lexical Sample Task (Pradhan et al., 2007b). All sentences containing the 35 nouns were selected from the OntoNotes corpus, resulting in a set of 16,329 sentences. This data set was randomly split into training and test sets using different proportions (1:9 to 9:1, 10% increments). The WSD systems (described in Section 3) were then

[4] Our WSD system does not include the sense identifier (except for the target word) for word-level training and testing.

	Baseline (MFS)	WSD								
		0.1	0.2	0.3	0.4	0.5	0.6	0.7	0.8	0.9
Accuracy	0.696	0.751	0.798	0.809	0.819	0.822	0.824	0.831	0.836	0.832

Table 3. Accuracy of the baseline and WSD systems with different training portions.

	Baseline (MFS)	WSD								
		0.1	0.2	0.3	0.4	0.5	0.6	0.7	0.8	0.9
Prec	0.090 (17/188)	0.113 (20/177)	0.112 (16/143)	0.113 (17/150)	0.124 (16/129)	0.123 (15/122)	0.127 (16/126)	**0.142** (17/120)	0.130 (14/108)	0.125 (14/112)

Table 4. Cleanup precision of the baseline and WSD systems with different training portions.

built from the different portions of the training set, called WSD_1 to WSD_9, respectively, and applied to their corresponding test sets. In each test set, the instances with disagreement among the annotators were excluded, since they have already been double-checked by the adjudicator. A baseline system was also implemented using the principle of *most frequent sense* (MFS), where each word sense distribution was retrieved from the OntoNotes corpus. Table 3 shows the accuracy of the baseline and WSD systems.

The output of WSD may agree or disagree with the annotators. The instances with disagreement were selected from each WSD system as suspicious candidates. This experiment randomly selected at most 20 suspicious instances for each noun to form a suspicious set of 687 instances. An adjudicator who is a linguistic expert then evaluated the suspicious set, and agreed in 42 instances with the WSD systems, indicating about 6% (42/687) truly erroneous annotations. This corresponds to 2.6% (42/16329) erroneous annotations in the corpus as a whole, which we verified by an independent random spot check.

In the following sections, we examine the performance of WSD from three aspects: precision, cost-effectiveness ratio, and entropy, and finally summarize a general cleanup procedure for other sense annotated corpora.

4.2 Cleanup precision analysis

The cleanup precision for a single WSD system can be defined as the number of erroneous instances identified by the WSD system, divided by the number of suspicious candidates selected by the WSD system. An erroneous instance refers to an instance where the annotators agree with each other but disagree with the adjudicator. Table 4 lists the cleanup precision of the baseline and WSD systems. The experimental results show that WSD_7 (trained on 70% training data) identified 17 erroneous instances, out of 120 selected suspicious candidates, thus yielding the highest precision of 0.142. Another observation is that the upper bound of WSD_7 was 0.35 (42/120) under the assumption that it identified all erroneous instances. This low precision discourages the use of WSD to automatically correct erroneous annotations.

4.3 Cleanup cost-effectiveness analysis

The cleanup procedure used herein is a semi-automatic process; that is, WSD is applied in the first stage to select suspicious candidates for human evaluation in the later stage. Obviously, we would like to minimize the number of candidates the adjudicator has to examine. Thus we define a metric, the cost-effectiveness (CE) ratio, to measure the performance of WSD. The *cost* rate is defined as the number of suspicious instances selected by a single WSD system, divided by the total number of suspicious instances in the suspicious set. The *effectiveness* rate is defined as the number of erroneous instances identified by a single WSD system, divided by the total number of erroneous instances in the suspicious set. In this experiment, the baseline value of the cost-effectiveness ratio is 1, which means that human expert needs to evaluate all 687 instances in the suspicious set to identify 42 erroneous instances. Figure 3 illustrates the CE ratio of the WSD systems. The most cost-effective WSD system was WSD_7. The CE ratios of the baseline and WSD_7 are listed in Table 5. The experimental results indicate that 17.5% of suspicious instances were required to be evaluated to identify about 40% erroneous annotations when using WSD_7.

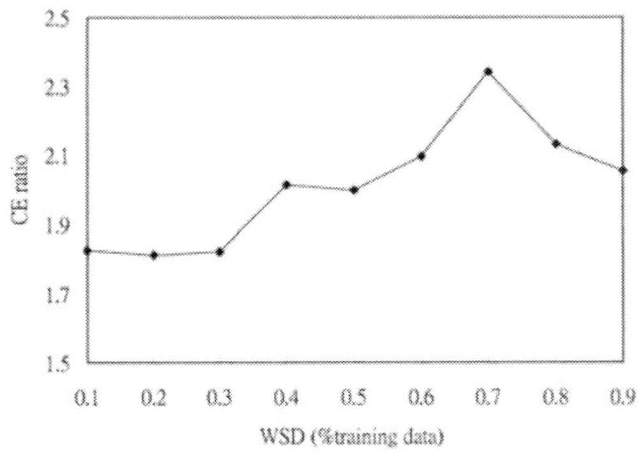

Figure 3. CE ratio of WSD systems with different training portions.

	Cost	Effect	CE Ratio
Baseline (MFS)	0.274 (188/687)	0.405 (17/42)	1.48
WSD_7	0.175 (120/687)	0.405 (17/42)	2.31

Table 5. CE ratio of the baseline and WSD_7.

4.4 Entropy analysis

So far, the experimental results show that the best WSD system can help human experts identify about 40% erroneous annotations, but it still missed the other 60%. To improve performance, we conducted experiments to analyze the effect of word entropy with respect to WSD performance on identifying erroneous annotations.

For the SemEval 35 nouns used in this experiment, some words are very ambiguous and some words are not. This property of ambiguity may affect the performance of WSD systems on identifying erroneous annotation. To this end, this experiment used *entropy* to measure the ambiguity of words (Melamed, 1997). The entropy of word can be computed by the word sense distribution, defined as

$$H(W) = -\sum_{ws_i \in W} P(ws_i)\log_2 P(ws_i), \qquad (1)$$

where $H(W)$ denotes the entropy of a word W, and ws_i denotes a word sense. A high entropy value indicates a high ambiguity level. For instance, the noun *defense* has 7 senses (see Table 7) in the OntoNotes corpus, occurring with the distribution {.14, .18, .19, .08, .04, .28, .09}, thus yielding a relative high entropy value (2.599). Conversely, the entropy of the noun *rate* is low (0.388), since it has only two senses with very skewed distribution {.92, .08}.

Consider the two groups of the SemEval nouns: the nouns for which at least one (Group 1) or none (Group 2) of their erroneous instances can be identified by the machine. The average entropy of these two groups of nouns was computed, as shown in Table 6. An independent *t-test* was then used to determine whether or not the difference of the average entropy among these two groups was statistically significant. The experimental results show that WSD_7 was more effective on identifying erroneous annotations occurring in highly-ambiguous words ($p<0.05$), while the baseline system has no such tendency ($p=0.368$).

Table 7 shows the detail analysis of WSD performance on different words. As indicated, WSD_7 identified the erroneous instances (7/7) occurring in the two top-ranked highly-ambiguous nouns, i.e., *defense* and *position*, but missed all those (0/12) occurring in the two most unambiguous words, i.e., *move* and *rate*. The major reason is that the sense distribution of unambiguous words is often skew, thus WSD systems built from such imbalanced data tend to suffer from the over-fitting problem; that is, tend to over-fit the predominant sense class and ignore small sense classes (Zhu and Hovy, 2007). Fortunately, the over-fitting problem can be greatly reduced when the entropy of words exceeds a certain threshold (e.g., the dashed line in Table 7), since the word sense has become more evenly distributed.

4.5 Combination of WSD and MFS

Another observation from Table 7 is that WSD_7 identified more erroneous instances when the word entropy exceeded the cut-point, since the over-fitting problem was reduced. Conversely, MFS identified more ones when the word entropy is below the cut-point. This finding encourages the use of a combination of WSD_7 and MFS for corpus cleanup; that is, different strategies can be used with different entropy intervals. For this experiment data, MFS and WSD_7 can be applied below and above the cut-point, respectively, to select the suspicious instances for human evaluation. As illustrated in Figure 4, when the entropy of words increased, the accumulated effectiveness rates of both WSD_7 and MFS increased accordingly, since more erroneous instances were identified. Additionally, the difference of the accumulated effect rate of MFS

	Group 1	Group 2	Difference	p-value
Baseline (MFS)	1.226	1.040	0.186	0.368
WSD_7	1.401	0.932	0.469*	0.013

*$p<0.05$

Table 6. Average entropy of two groups of nouns for the baseline and WSD_7.

Noun	#sense	Major Sense	Entropy	#err. instances	WSD_7	MFS	WSD_7+ MFS
defense	7	0.28	2.599	5	5	4	5
position	7	0.30	2.264	2	2	2	2
base	6	0.35	2.023	1	1	0	1
system	6	0.54	1.525	2	1	0	1
chance	4	0.49	1.361	1	1	1	1
order	8	0.72	1.348	4	1	0	1
part	5	0.70	1.288	1	1	1	1
power	3	0.51	1.233	3	1	3	3
area	3	0.72	1.008	2	1	2	2
management	2	0.62	0.959	2	1	0	0
condition	3	0.71	0.906	1	0	1	1
job	3	0.78	0.888	1	0	0	0
state	4	0.83	0.822	1	0	0	0
hour	4	0.85	0.652	1	1	1	1
value	3	0.90	0.571	2	1	1	1
plant	3	0.88	0.556	1	0	0	0
move	4	0.93	0.447	6	0	0	0
rate	2	0.92	0.388	6	0	1	1
Total	—	—	—	42	17	17	21

Nouns without erroneous instances: *authority, bill, capital, carrier, development, drug, effect, exchange, future, network, people, point, policy, president, share, source, space*

Table 7. Entropy of words versus WSD performance. The dashed line denotes a cut-point for the combination of the baseline and WSD_7.

and WSD_7 increased gradually from the beginning until the cut-point, since MFS identified more erroneous instances than WSD_7 did in this stage. When the entropy exceeded the cut-point, WSD_7 was more effective and thus its effectiveness rate kept increasing, while that of MFS increased slowly, thus their difference was decreased with the rise of the entropy. For the combination of MFS and WSD_7, its effectiveness rate before the cut-point was the same as that of MFS, since MFS was used in this stage to select the suspicious set. When WSD was used after the cut-point, the effectiveness rate of the combination system increased continuously, and finally reached 0.5 (21/42).

Based on the above experimental results, the most cost-effective way for corpus cleanup is to use the combination method and begin with the most ambiguous words, since the WSD system in the combination method is more effective on identifying erroneous instances occurring in highly-ambiguous words and these words are also more important for many applications. Figure 5 shows the curve of the CE ratios of the combination method by starting with the most ambiguous word. The results indicate that the CE ratio of the combination method decreased gradually after more words with lower entropy were involved in the cleanup procedure. Additionally, the CE ratio of the combination method was improved by using MFS after the cut-point and finally reached 2.50, indicating that 50% (21/42) erroneous instances can be identified by double-checking 20% (137/687) of the suspicious set. This CE ratio was better than 2.31 and 1.48, reached by WSD_7 and MFS respectively.

The proposed cleanup procedure can be applied to other sense annotated corpora by the following steps:

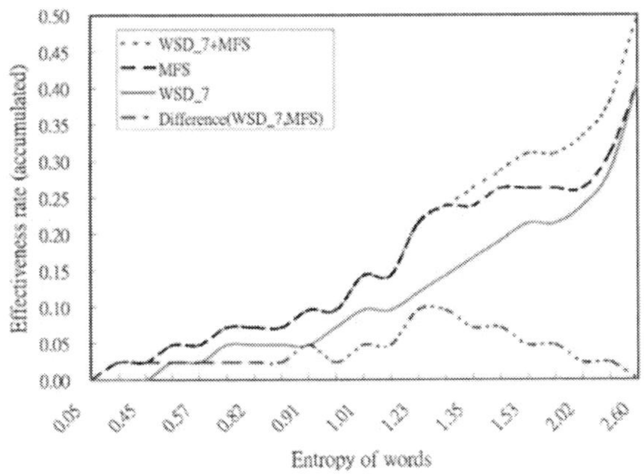

Figure 4. Effectiveness rate against word entropy.

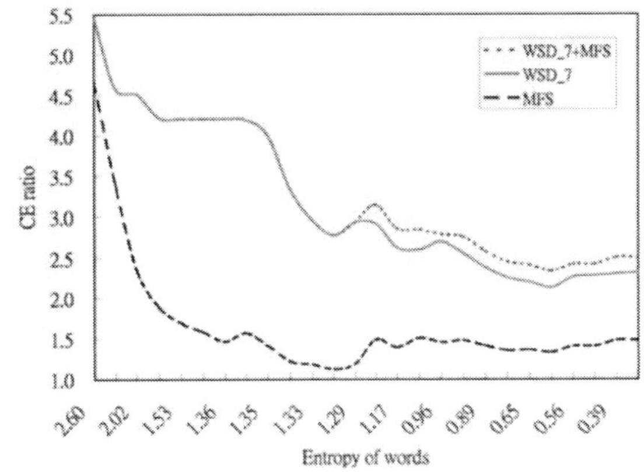

Figure 5. CE ratio against word entropy.

- Build the baseline (MFS) and WSD systems from the corpus.
- Create a suspicious set from the WSD systems.
- Calculate the entropy for each word in terms of it sense distribution in the corpus.
- Choose a cut-point value. Select a small portion of words with entropy within a certain interval (e.g., 1.0 ~ 1.5 in Table 7) for human evaluation to decide an appropriate cut-point value. The cut-point value should not be too low or too high, since WSD systems may suffer from the over-fitting problem if it is too low, and the performance would be dominated by the baseline system if it is too high.
- Combine the baseline and best single WSD system through the cut-point.
- Start the cleanup procedure in the descending order of word entropy until the CE ratio is below a predefined threshold.

5 Conclusion

This study has presented a cleanup procedure to identify incorrect sense annotation in a corpus. The cleanup procedure incorporates WSD systems to select a set of suspicious instances for human evaluation. The experiments are conducted from three aspects: precision, cost-effectiveness ratio, and entropy, to examine the performance of WSD. The experimental results show that the WSD systems are more effective on highly-ambiguous words. Additionally, the most cost-effective cleanup strategy is to use the combination method and begin with the most ambiguous words. The incorrect sense annotations found in this study can be used for SemEval-2007 to improve the accuracy of WSD evaluation.

The absence of related work on (semi-) automatically determining cases of erroneous agreement among annotators in a corpus is rather surprising. Variants of the method described here, replacing WSD for whatever procedure is appropriate for the phenomenon annotated in the corpus (sentiment recognition for a sentiment corpus, etc.), are easy to implement and may produce useful results for corpora in current use. Future work will focus on devising an algorithm to perform the cleanup procedure iteratively on the whole corpus.

References

E. Agirre and O. Lopez de Lacalle. 2007. UBC-ALM: Combining k-NN with SVD for WSD. In *Proc. of the 4th International Workshop on Semantic Evaluations (SemEval-2007) at ACL-07*, pages 342-345.

R.K. Ando. 2006. Applying Alternating Structure Optimization to Word Sense Disambiguation. In *Proc. of CoNLL*, pages 77-84.

J.F. Cai, W.S. Lee, and Y.W. Teh. 2007. Improving Word Sense Disambiguation Using Topic Features. In *Proc. of EMNLP-CoNLL*, pages 1015-1023.

T. Chklovski and R. Mihalcea. 2002. Building a Sense Tagged Corpus with Open Mind Word Expert. In *Proc. of the Workshop on Word Sense Disambiguation: Recent Successes and Future Directions at ACL-02*, pages 116-122.

C. Fellbaum. 1998. *WordNet: An Electronic Lexical Database*. Cambridge, MA: MIT Press.

E.H. Hovy, M. Marcus, M. Palmer, L. Ramshaw, and R. Weischedel. 2006. OntoNotes: The 90% Solution. In *Proc. of HLT/NAACL-06*, pages 57-60.

K. Kasahara, H. Sato, F. Bond, T. Tanaka, S. Fujita, T. Kanasugi, and S. Amano. 2004. Construction of a apanese Semantic Lexicon: Lexeed. In *IPSG SIG: 2004-NLC-159*, Tokyo, pages 75-82.

A. Kilgarriff. 2001. English Lexical Sample Task Description. In *Proc. of the SENSEVAL-2 Workshop*, pages 17-20.

A. Kilgarriff and M. Palmer, editors. 2000. SENSEVAL: Evaluating Word Sense Disambiguation Programs, *Computer and the Humanities*, 34(1-2):1-13.

Y.K. Lee and H.T. Ng. 2002. An Empirical Evaluation of Knowledge Sources and Learning Algorithms for Word Sense Disambiguation. In *Proc. of EMNLP*, pages 41-48.

I.D. Melamed. 1997. Measuring Semantic Entropy. In *Proc. of ACL-SIGLEX Workshop*, pages 41-46.

R. Mihalcea. 2007. Using Wikipedia for Automatic-Word Sense Disambiguation. In *Proc. of NAACL/HLT-07*, pages 196-203.

R. Mihalcea and P. Edmonds, editors. 2004. In *Proc. of SENSEVAL-3*.

G. Miller, C. Leacock, R. Tengi, and R. Bunker. 1993. A Semantic Concordance. In *Proc. of the 3rd DARPA Workshop on Human Language Technology*, pages 303–308.

H.T. Ng and H.B. Lee. 1996. Integrating Multiple Knowledge Sources to Disambiguate Word Sense: An Exemplar-based Approach. In *Proc. of the 34th Meeting of the Association for Computational Linguistics (ACL-96)*, pages 40-47.

M. Palmer, O. Babko-Malaya, and H.T. Dang. 2004. Different Sense Granularities for Different Applications. In *Proc. of the 2nd International Workshop on Scalable Natural Language Understanding at HLT/NAACL-04*.

M. Palmer, H.T. Dang, and C. Fellbaum. 2006. Making Fine-grained and Coarse-grained Sense Distinctions, Both Manually and Automatically. *Journal of Natural Language Engineering*, 13:137–163.

S. Pradhan, E.H. Hovy, M. Marcus, M. Palmer, L. Ramshaw, and R. Weischedel. 2007a. OntoNotes: A Unified Relational Semantic Representation. In *Proc. of the First IEEE International Conference on Semantic Computing (ICSC-07)*, pages 517-524.

S. Pradhan, E. Loper, D. Dligach, and M. Palmer. 2007b. SemEval-2007 Task 17: English Lexical Sample, SRL and All Words. In *Proc. of the 4th International Workshop on Semantic Evaluations (SemEval-2007) at ACL-07*, pages 87-92.

R. Snow, S. Prakash, D. Jurafsky, and A.Y. Ng. 2007. Learning to Merge Word Senses. In *Proc. of EMNLP-CoNLL*, pages 1005-1014.

L. Specia, M. Stevenson, and M. das Gracas V. Nunes. 2007. Learning Expressive Models for Word Sense Disambiguation. In *Proc. of the 45th Annual Meeting of the Association of Computational Linguistics (ACL-07)*, pages 41–48.

S. Tratz, A. Sanfilippo, M. Gregory, A. Chappell, C. Posse, and P. Whitney. 2007. PNNL: A Supervised Maximum Entropy Approach to Word Sense Disambiguation. In *Proc. of the 4th International Workshop on Semantic Evaluations (SemEval-2007) at ACL-07*, pages 264-267.

L.C. Yu, C.H. Wu, A. Philpot, and E.H. Hovy. 2007. OntoNotes: Sense Pool Verification Using Google N-gram and Statistical Tests. In *Proc. of the OntoLex Workshop at the 6th International Semantic Web Conference (ISWC 2007)*.

J. Zhu and E.H. Hovy. 2007. Active Learning for Word Sense Disambiguation with Methods for Addressing the Class Imbalance Problem, In *Proc. of EMNLP-CoNLL*, pages 783-790.

An Integrated Probabilistic and Logic Approach to Encyclopedia Relation Extraction with Multiple Features *

Xiaofeng YU   Wai LAM

Information Systems Laboratory
Department of Systems Engineering & Engineering Management
The Chinese University of Hong Kong
Shatin, N.T., Hong Kong
{xfyu,wlam}@se.cuhk.edu.hk

Abstract

We propose a new integrated approach based on Markov logic networks (MLNs), an effective combination of probabilistic graphical models and first-order logic for statistical relational learning, to extracting relations between entities in encyclopedic articles from Wikipedia. The MLNs model entity relations in a unified undirected graph collectively using multiple features, including contextual, morphological, syntactic, semantic as well as Wikipedia characteristic features which can capture the essential characteristics of relation extraction task. This model makes simultaneous statistical judgments about the relations for a set of related entities. More importantly, implicit relations can also be identified easily. Our experimental results showed that, this integrated probabilistic and logic model significantly outperforms the current state-of-the-art probabilistic model, Conditional Random Fields (CRFs), for relation extraction from encyclopedic articles.

1 Introduction

Relation extraction is a growing area of research that discovers various predefined semantic relations (e.g., visited, associate, and executive) between entity pairs in text. As a subtask in Information Extraction (IE), this problem has generated much interest and has been formulated as part of Message Understanding Conferences (MUC) and Automatic Content Extraction (ACE) Evaluation.

Reliably extracting relations between entities in natural-language documents is still a difficult, unsolved problem. A large number of engineered systems were developed for identifying relations of interest. Recent approaches to this problem include statistical parsing (Miller *et al.*, 2000), logistic regression (Kambhatla, 2004), feature-based methods (Zhou *et al.*, 2005; Toru *et al.*, 2007), and kernel methods (Zelenko *et al.*, 2003; Culotta and Sorensen, 2004; Bunescu and Mooney, 2005, 2006).

In text, this usually amounts to examining pairs of entities in a document and determining whether a relation exists between them. In general, the above approaches to relation extraction suffer from the following three difficulties: (1) enumerating all pairs of entities, even when restricted to pairs within a sentence, results in a low density of positive relation examples, (2) these approaches assume that relations only exist within document, and classify them independently without considering dependencies between entities. However, this assumption does not hold in practice, and ignoring dependencies between entities may lead to reduced performance, and (3) implicit relations can hardly be discovered in these models since they generally exist in cross document and they are only implied by the text. And these are the sorts of relations on which current extraction models perform most poorly.

In this paper we propose a new integrated approach based on Markov logic networks (MLNs) to extracting relations between entities in English encyclopedic articles from Wikipedia. We predict only relations between the *principal entity* and each mentioned *secondary entity* in Wikipedia articles. By anchoring one argument of relations to be the principal entity, we alleviate the difficulty of enumerating all pairs of entities in a document. This approach can incorporate rich dependencies between entities by modeling entity relations in a coherent undirected graph in a *collective* manner, and make simultaneous statistical judgments about the relations for a set of related entities. It can also exploit relational *autocorrelation*, a widely observed characteristic of relational data

The work described in this paper is substantially supported by grants from the Research Grant Council of the Hong Kong Special Administrative Region, China (Project Nos: CUHK4193/04E and CUHK4128/07) and the Direct Grant of the Faculty of Engineering, CUHK (Project Codes: 2050363 and 2050391). This work is also affiliated with the Microsoft-CUHK Joint Laboratory for Human-centric Computing and Interface Technologies.

© 2008. Licensed under the *Creative Commons Attribution-Noncommercial-Share Alike 3.0 Unported* license (http://creativecommons.org/licenses/by-nc-sa/3.0/). Some rights reserved.

in which the value of a variable for one instance is highly correlated with the value of the same variable on another instance. We show how a variety of well-engineered features can be easily and concisely formulated as first-order logic and incorporated into MLNs, and we show how implicit relations can be easily discovered in this modeling. We apply Gibbs sampling, a widely used Markov chain Monte Carlo (MCMC) algorithm, to perform collective inference in MLNs. Experimental results showed that this model yields substantially better results on encyclopedia relation extraction over the current state-of-the-art probabilistic relation extraction model, such as Conditional Random Fields (CRFs).

2 Wikipedia

Wikipedia[1] is the world's largest free online encyclopedia, representing the outcome of a continuous collaborative effort of a large number of volunteer contributors. Virtually any Internet user can create or edit a Wikipedia webpage, and this "freedom of contribution" has a positive impact on both the quantity (fast-growing number of articles) and the quality (potential mistakes are quickly corrected within the collaborative environment) of this online resource. Currently Wikipedia has approximately 9.25 million articles in more than 200 languages.

We investigate the task of discovering semantic relations between entity pairs from Wikipedia's English encyclopedic articles. The basic entry in Wikipedia is an *article*, which mainly defines and describes an entity (also known as *principal entity*) or an event, and consists of a hypertext document with hyperlinks to other pages within or outside Wikipedia. This document mentions some other entities as *secondary entities* related to the *principal entity* (Culotta *et al.*, 2006). All the entities are hyper-linked within the text, and the topic of an article usually defines the principal entity. Moreover, Wikipedia has the category hierarchy structure which is used to classify articles according to their content. All these characteristics make Wikipedia an appropriate resource for the task of relation extraction. In this paper, we predict only relations between the principal entity and each mentioned secondary entity.

An illustrative example of Wikipedia article is shown in Figure 2, where the principal entity *Albert Einstein* is boxed and in italic font, and secondary entities are in italic font. Our goal is to predict what relation, if any, each secondary entity has to the principal entity. For example, there is a *job_title* relation between *theoretical physicist* and *Albert Einstein* and a *father* relation between *Hermann Einstein* and *Albert Einstein*, but no relation between *salesman* and *Albert Einstein*.

[1] http://www.wikipedia.org/

> *Albert Einstein*
>
> Albert Einstein (*March 14, 1879 - April 18, 1955*) was a *theoretical physicist*. He was born in *Germany*. His father was *Hermann Einstein*, a *salesman* and *engineer*, and his mother was *Pauline Einstein*. In 1880, the family moved to *Munich*. Albert attended a *Catholic elementary school* and finally he was enrolled in the mathematics program at *ETH Zurich*. Einstein received the *Nobel Prize in Physics* for his services to Theoretical Physics in 1921.

Figure 1: An example of Wikipedia article for relation extraction. The principal entity is boxed and in italic font, and secondary entities are in italic font.

3 Relation Extraction as Sequence Labeling: A Baseline Approach

Note that our goal is to extract relations between the principal entity and each mentioned secondary entity in Wikipedia's English encyclopedic articles. This formulation allows us to view relation extraction as a sequence labeling task such as part-of-speech tagging. Motivated by this observation, we therefore apply Conditional Random Fields (CRFs) (Lafferty *et al.*, 2001), a probabilistic graphical model that has been successfully employed on sequence labeling tasks with state-of-the-art performance. By using the CRF model, each secondary entity's label is its relation to the principal entity, and we can capture the dependency between adjacent labels. For example, in the dataset it is common to see phrases such as "*Albert Einstein* (*1879 - 1955*) was born in *Germany*" for which the labels *birth_year*, *death_year*, and *birth_place* occur consecutively. Sequence models are specifically designed to handle these kinds of dependencies. The modeling flexibility of CRFs permits the feature functions to be complex, arbitrary, nonindependent, and overlapping features of the input without requiring additional assumptions, allowing the multiple features described in Section 5 to be directly exploited. To avoid overfitting, we penalized the log-likelihood by the commonly used zero-mean Gaussian prior over the parameters. This gives us a competitive baseline CRF model for relation extraction.

4 Markov Logic Networks for Collective Relation Extraction

Markov logic networks (MLNs) conduct *statistical relational learning* (SRL) by incorporating the expressiveness of first-order logic into the flexibility of probabilistic graphical models under a single coherent framework (Richardson and Domingos, 2006). An MLN consists of a set of weighted formulae and provides a way of softening first-order logic by making situations, in which not all formulae are satisfied, less likely but not impossible. More formally, the probability distribution of a particular truth assignment x to X specified by the ground Markov network $M_{L,C}$[2] is given by

$$P(X = x) = \frac{1}{Z}\exp\left(\sum w_i n_i(x)\right) = \frac{1}{Z}\prod \phi_i\left(x_{\{i\}}\right)^{n_i(x)} \quad (1)$$

where X is the set of all propositions describing a world x (i.e. all gliterals formed by grounding the predicates with the constants in the domain), $\mathcal{F}$ is the set of all clauses in the MLN, w_i is the weight associated with clause $F_i \in \mathcal{F}$, $n_i(x)$ is the number of true groundings of F_i in x, $x_{\{i\}}$ is the true value of the atoms appearing in F_i, Z is the normalizing partition function, ϕ_i is a real-valued potential function and $\phi_i\left(x_{\{i\}}\right) = e^{w_i}$.

MLNs model the relation extraction task in a *collective* manner and take into account the relation types of related entities. Note that this is different from other relation extraction methods that predict relations independently without considering the relationship between entities. Attributes can be represented in MLNs as predicates of the form $A(x, v)$, where A is an attribute, x is an entity, and v is the value of A in x. The relation is a designated attribute C, representable by $C(x, v)$, where v is x's relation. The relations of different entities depend on each other. Classification is now simply the problem of inferring the truth value of $C(x, v)$ for all x and v of interest given all known $A(x, v)$. In this collective modeling, the Markov blanket of $C(x_i, v)$ includes other $C(x_j, v)$, even after conditioning on the known $A(x, v)$. Relations between entities are represented by predicates of the form $R(x_i, x_j)$.

[2]The graphical structure of $M_{L,C}$ is that: there is an edge between two nodes of $M_{L,C}$ iff the corresponding ground atoms appear together in at least one grounding of one first-order formula.

4.1 Weight Learning

Given a relational database and a set of first-order logic, the weight of each clause can in principle be learned very efficiently by maximizing the pseudo-log-likelihood of this database on the closed world assumption using the limited-memory BFGS algorithm (Liu and Nocedal, 1989). These weights reflect how often the clauses are actually observed in the training data.

To estimate the weights, we maximize the logarithm of the conditional likelihood of the training data

$$\sum_{(x_h, x_o)\in T} \log\Big(p(X_h = x_h | X_o = x_o)\Big) \quad (2)$$

where X_h is a list of possible variables and x_h are the corresponding values in the observation. X_h contains all variables referring to possible ground atoms of entity relations. X_o is the set of variables corresponding to all possible instantiations of the predicates. T is the set of training observations (x_h, x_o). For relation extraction, Equation 2 can be rewritten as

$$p(X_h = x_h | X_o = x_o) = \prod_{Entity\_pairs(p,q)} p\Big(X_{e(p,q)} = x_{e(p,q)} | X_{g(p,q)} = x_{g(p,q)}\Big) \quad (3)$$

where $X_{e(p,q)}$ corresponds to the ground atoms, and $X_{g(p,q)}$ is a list of all variables corresponding to predicates.

With Equation 3, the conditional likelihood in Equation 2 simplifies to

$$\sum_{(x_h, x_o)\in T} \sum_{Entity\_pairs(p,q)} \log\Big(p\big(x_{e(p,q)} | x_{g(p,q)}\big)\Big). \quad (4)$$

where $p(x|y)$ is the abbreviation for $p(X = x|Y = y)$. To calculate the conditional likelihood, we have

$$p\big(x_{e(p,q)} | x_{g(p,q)}\big) = \frac{p\big(x_{e(p,q)}, x_{g(p,q)}\big)}{p\big(1, x_g(p,q)\big) + p\big(0, x_g(p,q)\big)} \quad (5)$$

During MLN weight learning, each first-order formula is converted to Conjunctive Normal Form (CNF). The probabilities of all formulae collectively determine all weights, if we view them as empirical probabilities and learn the maximum likelihood weights. Conversely, the weights in a learned MLN can be viewed as collectively encoding the empirical formula probabilities.

4.2 Inference

In order to perform inference over a given MLN, one needs to ground it into its corresponding Markov network (Pearl, 1988). A large number of efficient inference techniques are applicable and the most widely used approximate solution to probabilistic inference in MLNs is Markov chain Monte Carlo (MCMC) (Gilks *et al.*, 1996). One such algorithm to perform collective inference is called Gibbs sampling. Gibbs sampling starts by assigning a truth value to each query gliteral (a ground literal, i.e. one that contains only ground terms). It then proceeds in rounds to re-sample a value for gliteral X, given the truth values of its Markov blanket MB_X (i.e. the nodes with which it participates in ground clauses).

5 Feature Set

We describe the features used in our model. These features have been shown to be very effective for relation extraction.

Contextual features: Bag-of-words consisting of 4 words to the left and right of the target entity.

Part-of-Speech: Part-of-speech tags are obtained using the Stanford POS Tagger[3], which used rich knowledge sources and features in a log-linear model. POS tags with a window size of 4 around the target entity are used.

Morphological features: Such as whether the entity is capitalized or contains digits or punctuation, whether the entity ends in some suffixes such as *-eer* and *-ician*, etc.

Syntactic features: Syntactic information can lead to significant improvements in extraction accuracy (e.g., Culotta and Sorensen (2004), Bunescu and Mooney (2005)). The POS-tagged corpus is submitted to the Stanford Lexicalized Dependency Parser[4] which generates a dependency parse tree for each sentence and assigns word positions to each word. This parser can also output grammatical relations (typed dependency). The grammatical relations are of the form $relation(rel_i, w_i, w_j)$, where rel_i is one of the fixed set of relations assigned by the parser, and w_i and w_j are two words. The dependency paths, which contain the relevant terms describing the relations between the entity pairs, can be easily extracted. We design a set of first-order formulae that captures some of the most important syntactic phenomena for relation extraction.

Table 1: Representative relation types and corresponding keywords.

Relation	Keywords
job_title	secretary, writer, novelist, captain, cartoonist, actor, actress, physicist, mathematician, singer, naturalist, architect, musician, physician, professor, journalist, banker, businessman, producer, philosopher, worker
visited	from, to, in, at, near, along, visited
associate	work for, along with, together with, perform with, work with, colleague, struck with
member_of	member of, serve in, serve at, serve with, select to, campaign for, election to, involve in, captain with, play for, fellow of, enter
opus	sitcom, picture, film, teleplay, novel, essay, comedy, autobiography, show, movie, plot, drama, painting, book, cartoon, song, music
education	university, academy, school, college, institute
executive	lead, head, leader, president, chairman, committee, executive, officer, mayor, prince, chair, governor
birth_place	born in, born at, birth
death_place	bury in, died in, died at, pass away, inter
nationality	American, English, Irish, French, Italian, Australian, Canadian, Jewish, Russian
award	award, medal, fellowship, prize, pennant, scholarship
participant	during, through

Entity features: Important entities are hyperlinked within the text, but they are not classified by type. Entity type is very helpful for relation extraction. For instance, the relation between a *person* and a *location* should be *visited*, *birth_place*, *death_place*, etc., but cannot be *executive*, *founder*, etc. We identify named entities (person, location and organization) by applying the Stanford Named Entity Recognizer[5], a CRF based sequence labeling model coupled with well-engineered features including additional distributional similarity features. The model is trained on data from CoNLL, MUC-6, MUC-7, and ACE, making it fairly robust in practice. Types of other entities (e.g., date, year, and month) can be well classified by rule-based approach due to their relatively fixed forms.

Keyword features: Some keywords provide crucial clues for relationships between entity pairs. Consider the following sentence:

Bill Gates is the founder of the *Microsoft* Corporation.

If *Bill Gates* is the principal entity and *Microsoft* is the secondary entity, the keyword *founder* implies that there is a *founder* relation between them. Similarly, the *executive* relation may be implied by

[3]http://nlp.stanford.edu/software/tagger.shtml

[4]http://nlp.stanford.edu/software/lex-parser.shtml

[5]http://nlp.stanford.edu/software/CRF-NER.shtml

keywords *lead, head, leader, president, chairman, executive officer, director,* and *administrator.* Moreover, it is particularly interesting that some entities indicate their relation types to corresponding principal entities. Entities containing keywords such as *secretary, writer, novelist* or *actor* show a *job_title* relation to their principal entities. We exploit tf-idf approach to co-occurrence (collocation) analysis for keyword extraction. Tf-idf is used to measure the relevance of words with a window size of 8 to each relation between entity pairs. And then we rank the relevance scores with respect to each relation and choose keywords with scores higher than the user-defined threshold.

Semantic features: Due to data sparseness, tf-idf model might be unsatisfactory to extract sufficient keywords. We employ WordNet (Fellbaum, 1998), an online lexical database, to extend and enrich each keyword candidate to its synonyms (synsets). For example, the keyword *university* for relation *education* is extended to the set {*university, academy, college, institute*}. Table 1 shows some representative relation types and keywords using tf-idf method and semantic extension.

Wikipedia characteristic features: Relations only exist between principal entities and secondary entities. There is no relation between any two principal entities p, q or two secondary entities x, y.

6 First-Order Logic Representation

All the features described in Section 5 can be easily and concisely represented by first-order formulae, which are used during the MLN learning. First-order formulae are recursively constructed from atomic formulae using logical connectives and quantifiers. Atomic formulae are constructed using constants, variables, functions, and predicates. We give a couple of examples here.

For **contextual features**, it is common to see two secondary entities x and y occur consecutively, accompanied by conjunctions such as "and" or punctuation such as ",", then probably the two entities may have the same relation to the principal entity p. This can be written in first-order logic form as `occur_conse(x,y)` ⇒ `same_relation(x,y)`. For **morphological features**, suffixes such as *-eer* and *-ician* may probably show a *job_title* relation to the principal entity p. We therefore can easily write down the logic `person(p)` ∧ `job_suffix(x)` ⇒ `job_title(x,p)` to capture this information.

Entity features can be represented using some first-order formulae such as:
`person(p)` ∧ `location(x)` ⇒ `visited(x,p)` ∨ `birth_place(x,p)` ∨ `death_place(x,p)`
`person(p)` ∧ `location(x)` ⇒ `!executive(x,p)` ∧ `!founder(x,p)`. The formula `founder_key(x,p)` ⇒ `founder_relation(x,p)` can be used for **keyword features**. And **Wikipedia characteristic features** can be well and easily expressed by the logic `principal(p)` ∧ `principal(q)` ⇒ `no_relation(p,q)` and `secondary(x)` ∧ `secondary(y)` ⇒ `no_relation(x,y)`.

It is worth noticing that some features can be combined in first-order logic formulation. For example, `person(p)` ∧ `organization(x)` ∧ `founder_key(x,p)` ⇒ `founder_relation(x,p)` means if there is a *founder* keyword between a person and an organization, probably there is a *founder* relation between them.

7 Implicit Relation Extraction

Implicit relations are those that do not have direct contextual evidence. Implicit relations generally exist in different paragraphs, or even across documents. They require additional knowledge to be detected. Notably, these are the sorts of relations that are likely to have significant impact on performance. A system that can accurately discover knowledge that is implied by the text will effectively provide access to the implications of a corpus. Unfortunately, extracting implicit relations is challenging even for current state-of-the-art relation extraction models.

We show that MLNs can enable this technology. By employing the first-order logic formalism, the implicit relations can be easily discovered from text. Since these formulae will not always hold, we would like to handle them probabilistically by estimating the confidence of each formula. One

Table 2: Examples of first-order logic for implicit relation extraction.

`wife(x,y)` ⇒ `husband(y,x)`
`father(x,y)` ⇒ `son(y,x)` ∨ `daughter(y,x)`
`brother(x,y)` ⇒ `brother(y,x)` ∨ `sister(y,x)`
`husband(x,y)` ∧ `daughter(z,x)` ⇒ `mother(y,z)`
`father(x,y)` ∧ `father(y,z)` ⇒ `grandfather(x,z)`
`founder(x,y)` ∧ `superior(x,z)` ⇒ `employer(z,y)`
`associate(x,y)` ∧ `member_of(x,z)` ⇒ `member_of(y,z)`
`executive(x,y)` ∧ `member_of(z,y)` ⇒ `superior(x,z)`

of the benefits of the MLN probabilistic extraction model is that confidence estimates can be straightforwardly obtained.

Consider the following 2 sentences in Wikipedia articles:

1. On November 4, 1842 *Abraham Lincoln* married *Mary Todd*.

2. *Abraham Lincoln* had a son named *Robert Todd Lincoln* and he was born in Springfield, Illinois on 1 August 1843.

State-of-the-art extraction models may be able to detect the *wife* relation between *Mary Todd* and *Abraham Lincoln*, and the *son* relation between *Robert Todd Lincoln* and *Abraham Lincoln* successfully from local contextual clues. However, in the descriptive article of *Robert Todd Lincoln* in Wikipedia, *Robert Todd Lincoln* becomes the principal entity, and the *mother* relation between *Mary Todd* and *Robert Todd Lincoln* is only implied by the text and it is an implicit relation. First-order formalism allows the representation of deep and relational knowledge. Using the logic `wife(x,y)` $\wedge$ `son(z,y)` $\Rightarrow$ `mother(x,z)`, the relational knowledge in the above example can be easily captured to infer the implicit relation. These formulae are generally simple, and capture important knowledge for implicit relation extraction. Examples of first-order logic to infer implicit relations are listed in Table 2.

8 Experiments

8.1 Data

We use the same dataset as in (Culotta *et al.*, 2006) to conduct our experiments. This dataset consists of 1127 paragraphs from 441 pages from the online encyclopedia Wikipedia with 4701 relation instances and 53 relation types labeled. Table 3 shows the relation types and corresponding frequencies of this dataset.

This dataset was split into training and testing sets (70%-30% split), attempting to separate the entities into connected components. There are still occasional paths connecting entities in the training set to those in the testing set, and we believe this methodology reflects a typical real-world scenario.

8.2 Results and Discussion

We design 38 first-order logic formulae (15 formulae are used for implicit relation extraction) to construct the structure of MLNs. Using the features described in Section 5, we train MLNs using a Gaussian prior with zero mean and unit variance on each weight to penalize the pseudo-likelihood, and with the weights initialized at the mode of the prior (zero). The features specify a ground Markov network (e.g., ground atoms) containing one feature for each possible grounding of a first-order formula. Inference is performed for answering the query predicates, given the evidence predicates and other relations that can be deterministically derived. We apply Gibbs sampling to predict relations of entity pairs simultaneously.

Table 3: Statistics of relation types and corresponding frequencies.

Relation	Frequency	Relation	Frequency
job_title	379	daughter	35
visited	368	husband	33
birth_place	340	religion	32
associate	326	influence	31
birth_year	287	underling	27
member_of	283	sister	20
birth_day	283	grandfather	20
opus	267	ancestor	19
death_year	210	grandson	18
death_day	199	inventor	15
education	185	cousin	13
nationality	148	descendant	11
executive	127	role	10
employer	111	nephew	9
death_place	93	uncle	6
award	86	supported_person	6
father	84	granddaughter	6
participant	81	owns	4
brother	71	great_grandson	4
son	68	aunt	4
associate_competition	58	supported_idea	3
wife	57	great_grandfather	3
superior	54	gpe_competition	3
mother	50	brother_in_law	2
political_affiliation	44	grandmother	1
friend	43	discovered	1
founder	43	Overall	4701

Table 4 presents the performance of our relation extraction system based on MLNs compared to CRFs for different types of relations. We use the same set of features for both MLNs and CRFs. For MLNs, all the features are represented using first-order logic. It shows that the MLN system performing collective relation prediction and integrating implicit relation extraction yields substantially better results, leading to an improvement of up to 1.84% on the overall F-measure over the current state-of-the-art CRF model. The improvement is statistically significant ($p < 0.05$ with a 95% confidence interval) according to McNemar's paired tests.

As shown in Table 4, the performance varies greatly from different relation types. Both of the two systems perform quite well on 4 relations: *death_day*, *death_year*, *birth_day*, and *birth_year*.

Table 4: Comparative relation extraction performance. Both CRFs and MLNs are tested on the same set of features in Section 5.

	CRFs			MLNs		
Relation	Precision	Recall	$F_{\beta=1}$	Precision	Recall	$F_{\beta=1}$
death_day	100.00%	94.74%	97.30	98.85%	96.00%	**97.40**
death_year	98.21%	94.83%	96.49	98.14%	95.18%	**96.64**
birth_year	95.12%	95.12%	95.12	94.59%	95.68%	**95.13**
birth_day	93.90%	95.06%	94.48	93.20%	95.80%	94.48
nationality	88.37%	95.00%	**91.57**	88.10%	95.02%	91.43
birth_place	86.81%	92.94%	89.77	87.78%	93.32%	**90.47**
job_title	87.07%	91.82%	89.38	87.63%	91.55%	**89.55**
death_place	89.47%	80.95%	85.00	91.66%	82.99%	**87.11**
education	72.41%	89.36%	80.00	75.11%	90.22%	**81.97**
father	70.97%	88.00%	78.57	71.88%	89.82%	**79.85**
wife	72.22%	81.25%	76.47	72.30%	81.75%	**76.74**
award	94.12%	61.54%	**74.42**	80.88%	66.49%	72.98
mother	81.82%	64.29%	72.00	80.89%	69.33%	**74.67**
political_affiliation	100.00%	53.33%	**69.57**	85.66%	57.12%	68.54
husband	66.67%	60.00%	63.16	67.39%	62.48%	**64.84**
visited	66.29%	55.14%	60.20	66.70%	55.83%	**60.78**
daughter	66.67%	54.55%	60.00	63.67%	59.00%	**61.25**
founder	81.82%	47.37%	60.00	77.39%	52.63%	**62.65**
member_of	59.32%	49.30%	53.85	60.91%	51.66%	**55.90**
executive	64.00%	44.44%	52.46	60.20%	48.48%	**53.71**
superior	66.67%	42.11%	**51.61**	60.55%	44.23%	51.12
brother	50.00%	46.67%	48.28	48.80%	48.57%	**48.68**
opus	68.00%	33.33%	44.74	50.55%	44.75%	**47.47**
son	50.00%	39.13%	43.90	49.30%	41.55%	**45.09**
associate	42.28%	45.22%	43.70	40.77%	47.89%	**44.04**
participant	41.67%	23.81%	**30.30**	31.98%	26.05%	28.71
employer	46.67%	21.21%	29.17	47.78%	27.33%	**34.77**
associate_competition	23.08%	20.00%	21.43	24.38%	20.42%	**22.22**
religion	100.00%	8.33%	**15.38**	15.55%	10.23%	12.34
friend	0	0	0	50.38%	42.33%	**46.01**
sister	0	0	0	34.66%	20.55%	**25.80**
grandfather	0	0	0	23.74%	16.56%	**19.51**
grandson	0	0	0	20.01%	13.39%	**16.04**
cousin	0	0	0	22.00%	7.13%	**10.77**
other types	0	0	0	0	0	0
Overall	73.57%	64.20%	68.57	74.70%	66.58%	**70.41**

Since these relations can be easily identified using the distinct contextual evidence. However, some relations (e.g., *role*, *owns*, etc.) can hardly be extracted. One possible reason is the lack of training data (these relations occur rarely in the dataset). Among all the 53 relation types in the dataset, MLNs successfully extract 34 relations, while CRFs can only detect 29. For all the 34 relations listed in Table 4, MLNs outperform CRFs on 27 types of them. It is particularly interesting that MLNs can successfully predict relations *friend*, *sister*, *grandfather*, *grandson*, and *cousin*, whereas CRFs cannot. CRFs perform relation extraction sequentially without considering connections between entities. This may lead to the label inconsistency problem. For example, CRF sometimes fails to label the *father* relation between *George H. W. Bush* and *George W. Bush*. Implicit relations can hardly be investigated in this sequence labeling model. These disadvantages limit the ability of CRFs for relation extraction to a large extent.

9 Related Work

Only a few research work has attempted relation extraction from Wikipedia. Culotta *et al.* (2006) proposed a probabilistic model based on CRFs to integrate extraction and data mining tasks performed on biographical Wikipedia articles. Relation extraction was treated as a sequence labeling problem and relational patterns were discovered to boost the performance. However, this model extracts relations without considering dependencies between entities, and the best reported F-measure is 67.91, which is significantly (by 2.5%) lower than our MLN system when evaluated on the same training and testing sets. Nguyen *et al.* (2007b,a) proposed a subtree mining approach to extracting relations from Wikipedia by incorporating information from the Wikipedia structure and by the analysis of Wikipedia text. In this approach, a syntactic tree that reflects the relation between a given entity pair was built, and a tree-mining algorithm was used to identify the basic elements of syntactic structure of sentences for relations. This approach mainly relies on syntactic structures to extract relations. Syntactic structures are important for relation extraction, but insufficient to extract relations accurately. The obtained F-measure was only 37.76, which shows that there is a large room for improving. To the best of our knowledge, our approach is the first attempt at using MLNs for relation extraction from Wikipedia which achieves state-of-the-art performance.

We mention some other related work. Bunescu and Mooney (2007) presented an approach to extract relations from the Web using minimal supervision. Rosenfeld and Feldman (2007) presented a method for improving semi-supervised relation extraction from the Web using corpus statistics on entities. Our work is different from these research work. We investigate supervised relation extraction from Wikipedia based on probabilistic and logic integrated graphical models.

10 Conclusion

We summarize the contribution of this paper. First, we propose a new integrated model based on MLNs, which provide a natural and systematic way by modeling entity relations in a coherent undirected graph collectively and integrating implicit relation extraction easily, to extract relations in encyclopedic articles from Wikipedia. Second, we design multiple features which can be concisely formulated by first-order logic and exploit the collective inference algorithm (Gibbs sampling) to predict relations between entity pairs simultaneously. Third, our system achieved significantly better results compared to the current state-of-the-art probabilistic model for relation extraction from encyclopedic articles.

Having established this relation extraction model, our next step will be to evaluate it on larger datasets, where we expect collective relation extraction and implicit relation discovery to be even more interesting.

References

Razvan C. Bunescu and Raymond J. Mooney. A shortest path dependency kernel for relation extraction. In *Proceedings of HLT-EMNLP 2005*, pages 724–731, Vancouver, British Columbia, Canada, 2005.

Razvan C. Bunescu and Raymond J. Mooney. Subsequence kernels for relation extraction. In Y. Weiss, B. Schölkopf, and J. Platt, editors, *Advances in Neural Information Processing Systems 18*, pages 171–178. MIT Press, Cambridge, MA, 2006.

Razvan C. Bunescu and Raymond J. Mooney. Learning to extract relations from the Web using minimal supervision. In *Proceedings of ACL-07*, pages 576–583, Prague, Czech Republic, June 2007.

Aron Culotta and Jeffrey Sorensen. Dependency tree kernels for relation extraction. In *Proceedings of ACL-04*, Barcelona, Spain, 2004.

Aron Culotta, Andrew McCallum, and Jonathan Betz. Integrating probabilistic extraction models and data mining to discover relations and patterns in text. In *Proceedings of HLT-NAACL 2006*, pages 296–303, New York, 2006.

Christiane Fellbaum, editor. *WordNet: An Electronic Lexical Database*. The MIT Press, 1998.

W.R. Gilks, S. Richardson, and D.J. Spiegelhalter. *Markov chain Monte Carlo in practice*. Chapman and Hall, London, UK, 1996.

Nanda Kambhatla. Combining lexical, syntactic, and semantic features with maximum entropy models for extracting relations. In *Proceedings of ACL-04*, Barcelona, Spain, 2004.

John Lafferty, Andrew McCallum, and Fernando Pereira. Conditional random fields: Probabilistic models for segmenting and labeling sequence data. In *Proceedings of ICML-01*, pages 282–289. Morgan Kaufmann, San Francisco, CA, 2001.

Dong C. Liu and Jorge Nocedal. On the limited memory BFGS method for large scale optimization. *Mathematical Programming*, 45:503–528, 1989.

Scott Miller, Heidi Fox, Lance Ramshaw, and Ralph Weischedel. A novel use of statistical parsing to extract information from text. In *Proceedings of NAACL-2000*, pages 226–233, Seattle, Washington, 2000.

Dat P. T. Nguyen, Yutaka Matsuo, and Mitsuru Ishizuka. Relation extraction from Wikipedia using subtree mining. In *Proceedings of AAAI-07*, pages 1414–1420, Vancouver, British Columbia, Canada, 2007.

Dat P. T. Nguyen, Yutaka Matsuo, and Mitsuru Ishizuka. Subtree mining for relation extraction from Wikipedia. In *Proceedings of HLT-NAACL 2007*, pages 125–128, Rochester, New York, 2007.

Judea Pearl. *Probabilistic reasoning in intelligent systems: Networks of plausible inference*. Morgan Kaufmann Publishers Inc., San Francisco, CA, 1988.

Matthew Richardson and Pedro Domingos. Markov logic networks. *Machine Learning*, 62(1-2):107–136, 2006.

Benjamin Rosenfeld and Ronen Feldman. Using corpus statistics on entities to improve semi-supervised relation extraction from the Web. In *Proceedings of ACL-07*, pages 600–607, Prague, Czech Republic, June 2007.

Hirano Toru, Matsuo Yoshihiro, and Kikui Genichiro. Detecting semantic relations between named entities in text using contextual features. In *Proceedings of ACL-07*, pages 157–160, Prague, Czech Republic, June 2007.

Dmitry Zelenko, Chinatsu Aone, and Anthony Richardella. Kernel methods for relation extraction. *Journal of Machine Learning Research*, 3:1083–1106, 2003.

Guodong Zhou, Jian Su, Jie Zhang, and Min Zhang. Exploring various knowledge in relation extraction. In *Proceedings of ACL-05*, pages 427–434, Ann Arbor, Michigan, 2005.

Automatic Seed Word Selection for Unsupervised Sentiment Classification of Chinese Text

Taras Zagibalov John Carroll
University of Sussex
Department of Informatics
Brighton BN1 9QH, UK
{T.Zagibalov,J.A.Carroll}@sussex.ac.uk

Abstract

We describe and evaluate a new method of automatic seed word selection for unsupervised sentiment classification of product reviews in Chinese. The whole method is unsupervised and does not require any annotated training data; it only requires information about commonly occurring negations and adverbials. Unsupervised techniques are promising for this task since they avoid problems of domain-dependency typically associated with supervised methods. The results obtained are close to those of supervised classifiers and sometimes better, up to an F_1 of 92%.

1 Introduction

Automatic classification of document sentiment (and more generally extraction of opinion from text) has recently attracted a lot of interest. One of the main reasons for this is the importance of such information to companies, other organizations, and individuals. Applications include marketing research tools that help a company see market or media reaction towards their brands, products or services, or search engines that help potential purchasers make an informed choice of a product they want to buy. Sentiment classification research has drawn on and contributed to research in text classification, unsupervised machine learning, and cross-domain adaptation.

This paper presents a new, automatic approach to automatic seed word selection as part of sentiment classification of product reviews written in Chinese, which addresses the problem of domain-dependency of sentiment classification that has been observed in previous work. It may also facilitate building sentiment classification systems in other languages since the approach assumes a very small amount of linguistic knowledge: the only language-specific information required is a basic description of the most frequent negated adverbial constructions in the language.

The paper is structured as follows. Section 2 surveys related work in sentiment classification, unsupervised machine learning and Chinese language processing. Section 3 motivates our approach, which is described in detail in Section 4. The data used for experiments and baselines, as well as the results of experiments are covered in Section 5. Section 6 discusses the lessons learned and proposes directions for future work.

2 Related Work

2.1 Sentiment Classification

Most work on sentiment classification has used approaches based on supervised machine learning. For example, Pang *et al.* (2002) collected movie reviews that had been annotated with respect to sentiment by the authors of the reviews, and used this data to train supervised classifiers. A number of studies have investigated the impact on classification accuracy of different factors, including choice of feature set, machine learning algorithm, and pre-selection of the segments of text to be classified. For example, Dave *et al.* (2003) experiment with the use of linguistic, statistical and n-gram features and measures for feature selection and weighting. Pang and Lee (2004) use a graph-based technique to identify and analyze only subjective parts of texts. Yu and Hatzivassiloglou (2003) use semantically-oriented words for identification of polarity at the sentence level. Most of this work assumes binary classification (positive and negative), some-

© 2008. Licensed under the *Creative Commons Attribution-Noncommercial-Share Alike 3.0 Unported* license (http://creativecommons.org/licenses/by-nc-sa/3.0/). Some rights reserved.

times with the addition of a neutral class (in terms of polarity, representing lack of sentiment).

While supervised systems generally achieve reasonably high accuracy, they do so only on test data that is similar to the training data. To move to another domain one would have to collect annotated data in the new domain and retrain the classifier. Engström (2004) reports decreased accuracy in cross-domain classification since sentiment in different domains is often expressed in different ways. However, it is impossible in practice to have annotated data for all possible domains of interest. Aue and Gamon (2005) attempt to solve the problem of the absence of large amounts of labeled data by customizing sentiment classifiers to new domains using training data from other domains. Blitzer *et al.* (2007) investigate domain adaptation for sentiment classifiers using structural correspondence learning. Read (2005) also observed significant differences between the accuracy of classification of reviews in the same domain but published in different time periods.

Recently, there has been a shift of interest towards more fine-grained approaches to processing of sentiment, in which opinion is extracted at the sentence level, sometimes including information about different features of a product that are commented on and/or the opinion holder (Hu and Liu, 2004; Ku *et al.*, 2006). But even in such approaches, McDonald *et al.* (2007) note that information about the overall sentiment orientation of a document facilitates more accurate extraction of more specific information from the text.

2.2 Unsupervised Approach

One way of tackling the problem of domain dependency could be to use an approach that does not rely on annotated data. Turney (2002) describes a method of sentiment classification using two human-selected seed words (the words *poor* and *excellent*) in conjunction with a very large text corpus; the semantic orientation of phrases is computed as their association with the seed words (as measured by pointwise mutual information). The sentiment of a document is calculated as the average semantic orientation of all such phrases.

Yarowsky (1995) describes a 'semi-unsupervised' approach to the problem of sense disambiguation of words, also using a set of initial seeds, in this case a few high quality sense annotations. These annotations are used to start an iterative process of learning information about the contexts in which senses of words appear, in each iteration labeling senses of previously unlabeled word tokens using information from the previous iteration.

2.3 Chinese Language Processing

A major issue in processing Chinese text is the fact that words are not delimited in the written language. In many cases, NLP researchers working with Chinese use an initial segmentation module that is intended to break a text into words. Although this can facilitate the use of subsequent computational techniques, there is no a clear definition of what a 'word' is in the modern Chinese language, so the use of such segmenters is of dubious theoretical status; indeed, good results have been reported from systems which do not assume such pre-processing (Foo and Li, 2004; Xu *et al.*, 2004).

2.4 Seed Word Selection

We are not aware of any sentiment analysis system that uses unsupervised seed word selection. However, Pang *et al.* (2002) showed that it is difficult to get good coverage of a target domain from manually selected words, and even simple corpus frequency counts may produce a better list of features for supervised classification: human-created lists resulted in 64% accuracy on a movie review corpus, while a list of frequent words scored 69%. Pang *et al.* also observed that some words without any significant emotional orientation were quite good features: for example, the word “still” turned out to be a good indicator of positive reviews as it was often used in sentences such as “Still, though, it was worth seeing".

3 Our Approach

Our main goal is to overcome the problem of domain-dependency in sentiment classification. Unsupervised approaches seem promising in this regard, since they do not require annotated training data, just access to sufficient raw text in each domain. We base our approach on a previously described, 'almost-unsupervised' system that starts with only a single, human-selected seed 好 (*good*) and uses an iterative method to extract a training sub-corpus (Zagibalov & Carroll, 2008). The approach does not use a word segmentation module; in this paper we use the term 'lexical item' to denote any sequence of Chinese characters that is treated by the system as a unit, whatever it is linguistically — a morpheme, a word or a phrase.

Our initial aim was to investigate ways of improving the classifier by automatically finding a better seed, because Zagibalov & Carroll indicate that in different domains they could, by manual trial and error, find a seed other than 好 (*good*) which produced better results.

To find such a seed automatically, we make two assumptions:

1. Attitude is often expressed through the negation of vocabulary items with the opposite meaning; for example in Chinese it is more common to say *not good* than *bad* (Tan, 2002). Zagibalov & Carroll's system uses this observation to find negative lexical items while nevertheless starting only from a positive seed. This leads us to believe that it is possible to find candidate seeds themselves by looking for sequences of characters which are used with negation.
2. The polarity of a candidate seed needs to be determined. To do this we assume we can use the lexical item 好 (*good*) as a gold standard for positive lexical items and compare the pattern of contexts a candidate seed occurs in to the pattern exhibited by the gold standard.

Looking at product review corpora, we observed that *good* is always more often used without negation in positive texts, while in negative texts it is more often used with negation (e.g. *not good*). Also, *good* occurs more often in positive texts than negative, and more frequently without negation than with it. We use the latter observation as the basis for identifying seed lexical items, finding those which occur with negation but more frequently occur without it.

As well as detecting negation[1] we also use adverbials[2] to avoid hypothesizing non-contentful seeds: the characters following the sequence of a negation and an adverbial are in general contentful units, as opposed to parts of words, function words, etc. In what follows we refer to such constructions as negated adverbial constructions.

4 Method

We use a similar sentiment classifier and iterative retraining technique to the almost-unsupervised system of Zagibalov & Carroll (2008), summarized below in Sections 4.2 and 4.3. The main new contributions of this paper are techniques for automatically finding the seeds from raw text in a particular domain (Section 4.1), and for detecting when the process should stop (Section 4.4). This new system therefore differs from that of Zagibalov & Carroll (2008) in being completely unsupervised and not depending on arbitrary iteration limits. (The evaluation also differs since we focus in this paper on the effects of domain on sentiment classification accuracy).

4.1 Seed Lexical Item Identification

The first step is to identify suitable positive seeds for the given corpus. The intuition behind the way this is done is outlined above in Section 3. The algorithm is as follows:

1. find all sequences of characters between non-character symbols (i.e. punctuation marks, digits and so on) that contain negation and an adverbial, split the sequence at the negation, and store the character sequence that follows the negated adverbial construction;
2. count the number of occurrences of each distinct sequence that follows a negated adverbial construction (X);
3. count the number of occurrences of each distinct sequence without the construction (Y);
4. find all sequences with $Y - X > 0$.

4.2 Sentiment Classification

This approach to Chinese language processing does not use pre-segmentation (in the sense discussed in Section 2.3) or grammatical analysis: the basic unit of processing is the 'lexical item', each of which is a sequence of one or more Chinese characters excluding punctuation marks (so a lexical item may actually form part of a word, a whole word or a sequence of words), and 'zones', each of which is a sequence of characters delimited by punctuation marks.

Each zone is classified as either positive or negative based whether positive or negative vocabulary items predominate. As there are two parts of the vocabulary (positive and negative), we correspondingly calculate two scores (S_i,

[1]We use only six frequently occurring negations: 不 (*bu*), 不会 (*buhui*), 没有 (*meiyou*), 摆脱 (*baituo*), 免去 (*mianqu*), and 避免 (*bimian*). We are trying to be as language-independent as possible so we take a simplistic approach to detecting negation.

[2]We use five frequently occurring adverbials: 很 (*hen*), 非常 (*feichang*), 太 (*tai*), 最 (*zui*), and 比较 (*bijiao*). Similarly to negation, we deliberately take a simplistic approach.

where i is either *positive* or *negative*) using Equation (1), where L_d is the length in characters of a matching lexical item (raised to the power of two to increase the significance of longer items which capture more context), L_{phrase} is the length of the current zone in characters, S_d is the current sentiment score of the matching lexical item (initially 1.0), and N_d is a negation check coefficient.

$$S_i = \frac{L_d^2}{L_{phrase}} S_d N_d \quad (1)$$

The negation check is a regular expression which determines if the lexical item is preceded by a negation within its enclosing zone. If a negation is found then N_d is set to −1.

The sentiment score of a zone is the sum of sentiment of all the items found in it.

To determine the sentiment orientation of the whole document, the classifier computes the difference between the number of positive and negative zones. If the result is greater than zero the document is classified as positive, and vice versa.

4.3 Iterative Retraining

Iterative retraining is used to enlarge the initial seed vocabulary into a comprehensive vocabulary list of sentiment-bearing lexical items. In each iteration, the current version of the classifier is run on the input corpus to classify each document, resulting in a training subcorpus of positive and a negative documents. The subcorpus is used to adjust the scores of existing positive and negative vocabulary items and to find new items to be included in the vocabulary.

Each lexical item that occurs at least twice in the corpus is a candidate for inclusion in the vocabulary list. After candidate items are found, the system calculates their relative frequencies in both the positive and negative parts of the current training subcorpus. The system also checks for negation while counting occurrences: if a lexical item is preceded by a negation, its count is reduced by one.

For all candidate items we compare their relative frequencies in the positive and negative documents in the subcorpus using Equation (2).

$$difference = \frac{|F_p - F_n|}{(F_p + F_n)/2} \quad (2)$$

If $difference < 1$, then the frequencies are similar and the item does not have enough distinguishing power, so it is not included in the vocabulary. Otherwise the sentiment score of the item is (re-)calculated – according to Equation (3) for positive items, and analogously for negative items.

$$F_p - F_n \quad (3)$$

Finally, the adjusted vocabulary list with the new scores is ready for the next iteration[3].

4.4 Iteration Control

To maximize the number of productive iterations while avoiding unnecessary processing and arbitrary iteration limits, iterative retraining is stopped when there is no change to the classification of any document over the previous two iterations.

5 Experiments

5.1 Data

As our approach is unsupervised, we do not use an annotated training corpus, but run our iterative procedure on the raw data extracted from an annotated test corpus, and evaluate the final accuracy of the system with respect to the annotations in that corpus.

Our test corpus is derived from product reviews harvested from the website IT168[4]. All the reviews were tagged by their authors as either positive or negative overall. Most reviews consist of two or three distinct parts: positive opinions, negative opinions, and comments ('other') – although some reviews have only one part. We removed duplicate reviews automatically using approximate matching, giving a corpus of 29531 reviews of which 23122 are positive (78%) and 6409 are negative (22%). The total number of different products in the corpus is 10631, the number of product categories is 255, and most of the reviewed products are either software products or consumer electronics. Unfortunately, it appears that some users misuse the sentiment

[3]An alternative approach might be to use point-wise mutual information instead of relative frequencies of newly found features in a subcorpus produced in the previous iteration. However, in preliminary experiments, SO-PMI did not produce good corpora from the first iteration. Also, it is not clear how to manage subsequent iterations since PMI would have to be calculated between thousands of new vocabulary items and every newly found sequence of characters, which would be computationally intractable.

[4]http://product.it168.com

tagging facility on the website so quite a lot of reviews have incorrect tags. However, the parts of the reviews are much more reliably identified as being positive or negative so we used these as the items of the test corpus. In the experiments described below we use 10 subcorpora containing a total of 7982 reviews, distributed between product types as shown in Table 1.

Corpus/product type	*Reviews*
Monitors	683
Mobile phones	2317
Digital cameras	1705
MP3 players	779
Computer parts (CD-drives, motherboards)	308
Video cameras and lenses	361
Networking (routers, network cards)	350
Office equipment (copiers, multifunction devices, scanners)	611
Printers (laser, inkjet)	569
Computer peripherals (mice, keyboards, speakers)	457

Table 1. Product types and sizes of the test corpora.

We constructed five of the corpora by combining smaller ones of 100–250 reviews each (as indicated in parentheses in Table 1) in order to have reasonable amounts of data.

Each corpus has equal numbers of positive and negative reviews so we can derive upper bounds from the corpora (Section 5.2) by applying supervised classifiers. We balance the corpora since (at least on this data) these classifiers perform less well with skewed class distributions[5].

5.2 Baseline and Upper Bound

Since the corpora are balanced with respect to sentiment orientation the naïve (unsupervised) baseline is 50%. We also produced an upper bound using Naive Bayes multinomial (NBm) and Support Vector Machine (SVM)[6] classifiers with the NTU Sentiment Dictionary (Ku *et al.*, 2006) vocabulary items as the feature set. The dictionary contains 2809 items in the 'positive' part and 8273 items in the 'negative'. We ran both classifiers in 10-fold stratified cross-validation mode, resulting in the accuracies shown in Table 2. The macroaveraged accuracies across all 10 corpora are 82.78% (NBm) and 80.89% (SVM).

Corpus	*Nbm (%)*	*SVM (%)*
Monitors	86.21	83.87
Mobile phones	86.52	84.49
Digital cameras	82.27	82.04
MP3 players	82.64	79.43
Computer parts	81.10	79.47
Video cameras and lenses	83.05	84.16
Networking	77.65	75.35
Office equipment	82.13	80.00
Printers	81.33	79.57
Computer peripherals	84.86	80.48

Table 2. Upper bound accuracies.

We also tried adding the negations and adverbials specified in Section 3 to the feature set, and this resulted in slightly improved accuracies, of 83.90% (Nbm) and 82.49% (SVM).

An alternative approach would have been to automatically segment the reviews and then derive a feature set of a manageable size by setting a threshold on word frequencies; however the extra processing means that this is a less valid upper bound.

Another possible comparison could be with a version of Turney's (2002) sentiment classification method applied to Chinese. However, the results would not be comparable since Turney's method would require the additional use of very large text corpus and the manual selection of positive and negative seed words.

5.3 Experiment 1

To be able to compare to the accuracy of the almost-unsupervised approach of Zagibalov & Carroll (2008), we ran our system using the seed 好 (*good*) for each corpus. The results are shown in Table 3. We compute precision, recall and F_1 measure rather than just accuracy, since our classifier can omit some reviews whereas the supervised classifiers attempt to classify all reviews. The macroaveraged F_1 measure is 80.55, which beats the naïve baseline by over 30 percentage points, and approaches the two upper bounds.

[5]We have made this corpus publicly available at http://www.informatics.sussex.ac.uk/users/tz21/coling08.zip

[6]We used WEKA 3.4.11 (http://www.cs.waikato.ac.nz/~ml/weka)

Corpus	*Iter*	*P*	*R*	F_1
Monitors	12	86.62	86.24	86.43
Mobile phones	11	90.15	89.68	89.91
Digital cameras	13	81.33	80.23	80.78
MP3 players	13	86.10	85.10	85.60
Computer parts	10	69.10	67.53	68.31
Video cameras and lenses	10	82.81	81.44	82.12
Networking	11	69.28	68.29	68.78
Office equipment	12	81.83	80.36	81.09
Printers	12	81.04	79.61	80.32
Computer peripherals	10	82.20	81.84	82.02
Macroaverage		81.05	80.03	**80.54**

Table 3. Results with the single, manually chosen seed 好 (*good*) for each corpus.

5.4 Experiment 2

We then ran our full system, including the seed identifier. Appendix A shows that for most of the corpora the algorithm found different (highly domain-salient) seeds. Table 4 shows the results achieved.

Corpus	*Iter*	*P*	*R*	F_1
Monitors	11	85.57	85.07	85.32
Mobile phones	10	92.63	92.19	92.41
Digital cameras	13	84.92	83.58	84.24
MP3 players	13	88.69	87.55	88.11
Computer parts	12	77.78	77.27	77.52
Video cameras and lenses	11	83.62	81.99	82.8
Networking	13	72.83	72.00	72.41
Office equipment	10	82.42	81.34	81.88
Printers	12	81.04	79.61	80.32
Computer peripherals	10	82.24	82.06	82.15
Macroaverage		83.17	82.27	**82.72**

Table 4. Results with the seeds automatically identified for each corpus.

Across all 10 subcorpora, the improvement using automatically identified seed words compared with just using the seed *good* is significant (paired t-test, $P<0.0001$), and the F_1 measure lies between the two upper bounds.

6 Conclusions and Future Work

The unsupervised approach to seed words selection for sentiment classification presented in this paper produces results which in most cases are close to the results of supervised classifiers and to the previous almost-unsupervised approach: eight out of ten results showed improvement over the human selected seed word and three results outperformed the supervised approach, while three other results were less than 1% inferior to the supervised ones.

How does it happen that the chosen seed is usually (in our dataset – always) positive? We think that this happens due to the socially accepted norm of behaviour: as a rule one needs to be friendly to communicate with others. This in turn defines linguistic means of expressing ideas – they will be at least slightly positive overall. The higher prevalence of positive reviews has been observed previously: for example, in our corpus before we balanced it almost 80% of reviews were positive; Pang *et al.* (2002) constructed their move review corpus from an original dataset of 1301 positive and 752 negative reviews (63% positive). Ghose *et al.* (2007) quote typical examples of highly positive language used in the online marketplace. We can make a preliminary conclusion that a relatively high frequency of positive words is determined by the usage of language that reflects the social behaviour of people.

In future work we intend to explore these issues of positivity of language use. We will also apply our approach to other genres containing some quantity of evaluative language (for example newspaper articles), and see if it works equally well for languages other than Chinese. It is also likely we can use a smaller set of negation words and adverbials to produce the seed lists.

Acknowledgements

The first author is supported by the Ford Foundation International Fellowships Program.

References

Aue, Anthony, and Michael Gamon. 2005. Customizing Sentiment Classifiers to New Domains: a Case Study. In *Proceedings of the International Conference RANLP-2005 Recent Advances in Natural Language Processing*.

Blitzer, John, Mark Dredze, and Fernando Pereira. 2007. Biographies, Bollywood, Boom-boxes and Blenders: Domain Adaptation for Sentiment Classification. In *Proceedings of the 45th Annual Meeting of the Association of Computational Linguistics*. 440–447.

Dave, Kushal, Steve Lawrence, and David M. Pennock. 2003. Mining the Peanut Gallery: Opinion Extraction and Semantic Classification of Product Reviews. In *Proceedings of the Twelfth International World Wide Web Conference*. 519–528.

Engström, Charlotte. 2004. *Topic Dependence in Sentiment Classification*. Unpublished MPhil Dissertation. University of Cambridge.

Foo, Schubert, and Hui Li. 2004. Chinese Word Segmentation and Its Effects on Information Retrieval. *Information Processing and Management*, 40(1). 161–190.

Ghose, Anindya, Panagiotis Ipeirotis, and Arun Sundararajan. 2007. Opinion Mining using Econometrics: A Case Study on Reputation Systems. In *Proceedings of the 45th Annual Meeting of the Association of Computational Linguistics*. 416–423.

Hu, Minqing, and Bing Liu. 2004. Mining and Summarizing Customer Reviews. In *Proceedings of the 10th ACM SIGKDD International Conference on Knowledge Discovery and Data Mining*. 168–177.

Ku, Lun-Wei, Yu-Ting Liang, and Hsin-Hsi Chen. 2006. Opinion Extraction, Summarization and Tracking in News and Blog Corpora. In *Proceedings of the AAAI-2006 Spring Symposium on Computational Approaches to Analyzing Weblogs*. AAAI Technical Report.

McDonald, Ryan, Kerry Hannan, Tyler Neylon, Mike Wells, and Jeff Reynar. 2007. Structured Models for Fine-to-Coarse Sentiment Analysis. In *Proceedings of the 45th Annual Meeting of the Association of Computational Linguistics*. 432–439.

Pang, Bo, and Lillian Lee. 2004. A Sentimental Education: Sentiment Analysis Using Subjectivity Summarization Based on Minimum Cuts. In *Proceedings of the 42nd Annual Meeting of the Association for Computational Linguistics*. 271–278.

Pang, Bo, Lillian Lee, and Shivakumar Vaithyanathan. 2002. Thumbs up? Sentiment Classification using Machine Learning Techniques. In *Proceedings of the 2002 Conference on Empirical Methods in Natural Language Processing*. 79–86.

Read, Jonathon. 2005. Using Emoticons to Reduce Dependency in Machine Learning Techniques for Sentiment Classification. In *Proceedings of the ACL Student Research Workshop at ACL-05*. 43–48.

Tan, Aoshuang. 2002. Problemy skrytoj grammatiki. Sintaksis, semantika i pragmatika jazyka izolirujuščego stroja na primere kitajskogo jazyka [Problems of a hidden grammar. Syntax, semantics and pragmatics of a language of the isolating type, taking the Chinese language as an example]. *Jazyki Slavjanskoj Kultury*.

Turney, Peter D. 2002. Thumbs Up or Thumbs Down? Semantic Orientation Applied to Unsupervised Classification of Reviews. In *Proceedings of the 40th Annual Meeting of the Association for Computational Linguistics*. 417–424.

Xu, Jia, Richard Zens, and Hermann Ney. 2004. Do We Need Chinese Word Segmentation for Statistical Machine Translation? In *Proceedings of the Third SIGHAN Workshop on Chinese Language Learning*. 122–128.

Yarowsky, David. 1995. Unsupervised Word Sense Disambiguation Rivaling Supervised Methods. In *Proceedings of the 33rd Annual Meeting of the Association for Computational Linguistics*. 189–196.

Yu, Hong, and Vasileios Hatzivassiloglou. 2003. Towards Answering Opinion Questions: Separating Facts from Opinions and Identifying the Polarity of Opinion Sentences. In *Proceedings of the 2003 Conference on Empirical Methods in Natural Language Processing*. 129–136.

Zagibalov, Taras, and John Carroll. 2008. Unsupervised Classification of Sentiment and Objectivity in Chinese Text. In *Proceedings of the Third International Joint Conference on Natural Language Processing*. 304–311.

Appendix A. Seeds Automatically Identified for each Corpus.

Corpus	*Seed*	*Corpus*	*Seed*
Monitors	好 (*good*) 便 (*convenient; cheap*) 清晰 (*clear*) 直 (*straight*) 方便 (*comfortable*) 满 (*fill, fulfill*) 锐利 (*sharp*) 舒服 (*comfortable*) 爽 (*cool*)	Video cameras and lenses	清晰 (*clear* – of sound or image) 方便 (*comfortable*) 实用 (*practical*) 理想 (*perfect*) 爽 (*cool*)
Mobile phones	好 (*good*) 支持 (*support*) 便 (*convenient; cheap*) 方便 (*comfortable*) 清晰 (*clear* –of sound or image) 足 (*sufficient*) 好用 (*easy to use*) 舒服 (*comfortable*) 人性化 (*user friendly*) 流畅 (*smooth and easy*) 清楚 (*distinct*) 爽 (*cool*) 好了 (has become *better*) 耐用 (*durable*) 方便的 (*comfortable*) 满意的 (*satisfied*) 适应 (*fit, suit*) 方便了 (has become *comfortable*) 适用 (*applicable*) 顺手 (*handy*) 科学 (*science, scientific*)	Digital cameras	好 (*good*) 便 (*convenient; cheap*) 方便 (*comfortable*) 清晰 (*clear*–of sound or image) 专业 (*special*) 爽 (*cool*) 满意 (*satisfied*) 耐用 (*durable*) 舒服 (*comfortable*) 理想 (*perfect*) 真实 (*straight*) 稳定 (*stable*) 方便了 (has become *comfortable*) 客气 (*polite*) 详细 (*detailed*)
Networking	稳定 (*stable*)	Printers	好 (*good*)
MP3 players	好 (*good*) 便 (*convenient; cheap*) 方便 (*comfortable*) 实用 (*practical*) 灵敏 (*sensitive*) 舒服 (*comfortable*) 爽 (*cool*) 方便了 (has become *comfortable*)	Computer peripherals	好 (*good*) 便 (*convenient;cheap*) 方便 (*comfortable*) 准 (*precise*) 舒服 (*comfortable*) 习惯 (*habitual*) 流畅 (*smooth and easy*) 稳定 (*stable*)
Computer parts	好 (*good*) 稳定 (*stable*)	Office equipment	好 (*good*) 方便 (*comfortable*) 稳定 (*stable*) 实用 (*practical*)

Extracting Synchronous Grammar Rules From Word-Level Alignments in Linear Time

Hao Zhang and **Daniel Gildea**
Computer Science Department
University of Rochester
Rochester, NY 14627, USA

David Chiang
Information Sciences Institute
University of Southern California
Marina del Rey, CA 90292, USA

Abstract

We generalize Uno and Yagiura's algorithm for finding all common intervals of two permutations to the setting of two sequences with many-to-many alignment links across the two sides. We show how to maximally decompose a word-aligned sentence pair in linear time, which can be used to generate all possible phrase pairs or a Synchronous Context-Free Grammar (SCFG) with the simplest rules possible. We also use the algorithm to precisely analyze the maximum SCFG rule length needed to cover hand-aligned data from various language pairs.

1 Introduction

Many recent syntax-based statistical machine translation systems fall into the general formalism of Synchronous Context-Free Grammars (SCFG), where the grammar rules are found by first aligning parallel text at the word level. From word-level alignments, such systems extract the grammar rules consistent either with the alignments and parse trees for one of languages (Galley et al., 2004), or with the the word-level alignments alone without reference to external syntactic analysis (Chiang, 2005), which is the scenario we address here.

In this paper, we derive an optimal, linear-time algorithm for the problem of decomposing an arbitrary word-level alignment into SCFG rules such that each rule has at least one aligned word and is *minimal* in the sense that it cannot be further decomposed into smaller rules. Extracting minimal rules is of interest both because rules with fewer words are more likely to generalize to new data, and because rules with lower *rank* (the number of nonterminals on the right-hand side) can be parsed more efficiently.

This algorithm extends previous work on factoring permutations to the general case of factoring many-to-many alignments. Given two permutations of n, a *common interval* is a set of numbers that are consecutive in both. The breakthrough algorithm of Uno and Yagiura (2000) computes all K common intervals of two length n permutations in $O(n+K)$ time. This is achieved by designing data structures to index possible boundaries of common intervals as the computation proceeds, so that not all possible pairs of beginning and end points need to be considered. Landau et al. (2005) and Bui-Xuan et al. (2005) show that all common intervals can be encoded in $O(n)$ space, and adapt Uno and Yagiura's algorithm to produce this compact representation in $O(n)$ time. Zhang and Gildea (2007) use similar techniques to factorize Synchronous Context Free Grammars in linear time.

These previous algorithms assume that the input is a permutation, but in machine translation it is common to work with word-level alignments that are many-to-many; in general any set of pairs of words, one from each language, is a valid alignment for a given bilingual sentence pair. In this paper, we consider a generalized concept of common intervals given such an alignment: a common interval is a pair of phrases such that no word pair in the alignment links a word inside the phrase to a word outside the phrase. Extraction of such phrases is a common feature of state-of-the-art phrase-based and syntax-based machine translation systems (Och and Ney, 2004a; Chiang, 2005). We generalize Uno and Yagiura's algorithm to this setting, and demonstrate a linear time algorithm for a pair of aligned sequences. The output is a tree representation of possible phrases, which directly provides a set of minimal synchronous grammar

© 2008. Licensed under the *Creative Commons Attribution-Noncommercial-Share Alike 3.0 Unported* license (http://creativecommons.org/licenses/by-nc-sa/3.0/). Some rights reserved.

rules for an SCFG-based machine translation system. For phrase-based machine translation, one can also read all phrase pairs consistent with the original alignment off of the tree in time linear in the number of such phrases.

2 Alignments and Phrase Pairs

Let $[x, y]$ denote the sequence of integers between x and y inclusive, and $[x, y)$ the integers between x and $y-1$ inclusive. An *aligned sequence pair* or simply an *alignment* is a tuple (E, F, A), where $E = e_1 \cdots e_n$ and $F = f_1 \cdots f_m$ are strings, and A is a set of links (x, y), where $1 \leq x \leq n$ and $1 \leq y \leq m$, connecting E and F. For most of this paper, since we are not concerned with the identity of the symbols in E and F, we will assume for simplicity that $e_i = i$ and $f_j = j$, so that $E = [1, n]$ and $F = [1, m]$.

In the context of statistical machine translation (Brown et al., 1993), we may interpret E as an English sentence, F its translation in French, and A a representation of how the words correspond to each other in the two sentences. A pair of substrings $[s, t] \subset E$ and $[u, v] \subset F$ is a *phrase pair* (Och and Ney, 2004b) if and only if the subset of links emitted from $[s, t]$ in E is equal to the subset of links emitted from $[u, v]$ in F, and both are nonempty.

Figure 1a shows an example of a many-to-many alignment, where $E = [1, 6]$, $F = [1, 7]$, and $A = \{(1,6), (2,5), (2,7), (3,4), (4,1), (4,3), (5,2), (6,1), (6,3)\}$. The eight phrase pairs in this alignment are:

$$([1,1],\ [6,6]),\ ([1,2],\ [5,7]),$$
$$([3,3],\ [4,4]),\ ([1,3],\ [4,7]),$$
$$([5,5],\ [2,2]),\ ([4,6],\ [1,3]),$$
$$([3,6],\ [1,4]),\ ([1,6],\ [1,7]).$$

In Figure 1b, we show the *alignment matrix* representation of the given alignment. By default, the columns correspond to the tokens in E, the rows correspond to the tokens in F, and the black cells in the matrix are the alignment links in A. Using the matrix representation, the phrase pairs can be viewed as submatrices as shown with the black-lined boundary boxes. Visually, a submatrix represents a phrase pair when it contains at least one alignment link and there are no alignment links directly above, below, or to the right or left of it.

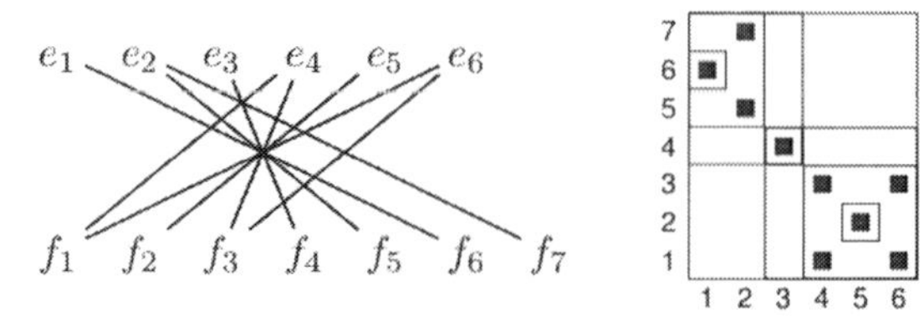

Figure 1: An example of (a) a many-to-many alignment and (b) the same alignment as a matrix, with its phrase pairs marked.

2.1 Number of Phrase Pairs

In this section, we refine our definition of phrase pairs with the concept of *tightness* and give an asymptotic upper bound on the total number of such phrase pairs as the two sequences' lengths grow. In the original definition, the permissive many-to-many constraint allows for unaligned tokens in both sequences E and F. If there is an unaligned token adjacent to a phrase pair, then there is also a phrase pair that includes the unaligned token. We say that a phrase pair $([s, t], [u, v])$ is *tight* if none of e_s, e_t, f_u and f_v is unaligned. By focusing on tight phrase pairs, we eliminate the non-tight ones that share the same set of alignment links with their tight counterpart.

Given $[s, t]$ in E, let l be the first member of F that any position in $[s, t]$ links to, and let u be the last. According to the definition of tight phrase pair, $[l, u]$ is the only candidate phrase in F to pair up with $[s, t]$ in E. So, the total number of tight phrase pairs is upper-bounded by the total number of intervals in each sequence, which is $O(n^2)$.

If we do not enforce the tightness constraint, the total number of phrase pairs can grow much faster. For example, if a sentence contains only a single alignment link between the midpoint of F and the midpoint of E, then there will be $O(n^2m^2)$ possible phrase pairs, but only a single tight phrase pair. From now on, term *phrase pair* always refers to a tight phrase pair.

2.2 Hierarchical Decomposition of Phrase Pairs

In this section, we show how to encode all the tight phrase pairs of an alignment in a tree of size $O(n)$.

Lemma 2.1. *When two phrase pairs overlap, the intersection, the differences, and the union of the two are also phrase pairs.*

The following picture graphically represents the two possible overlapping structures of two phrase

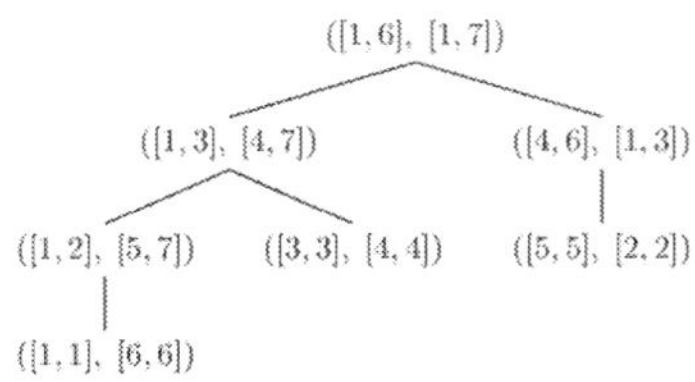

Figure 2: The normalized decomposition tree of the alignment in Figure 1.

pairs: $([s, t], [u, v])$ and $([s', t'], [u', v'])$.

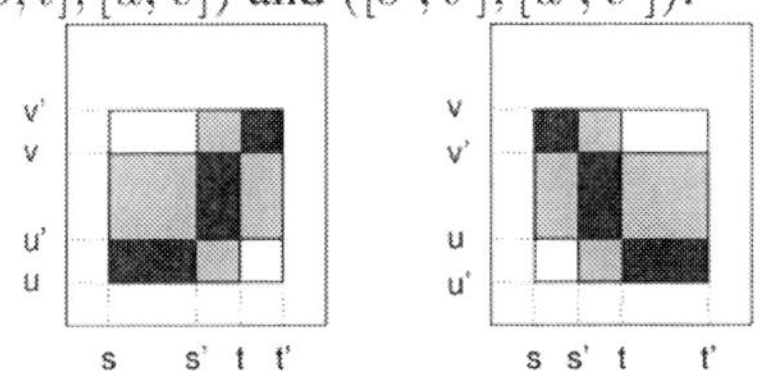

Let AB and BC be two overlapping English phrases, with B being their overlap. There are six possible phrases, A, B, C, AB, BC, and ABC, but if we omit BC, the remainder are nested and can be represented compactly by $((AB)C)$, from which BC can easily be recovered. If we systematically apply this to the whole sentence, we obtain a hierarchical representation of all the phrase pairs, which we call the *normalized decomposition tree*. The normalized decomposition tree for the example is shown in Figure 2.

Bui-Xuan et al. (2005) show that the family of common intervals is *weakly partitive*, i.e. closed under intersection, difference and union. This allows the family to be represented as a hierarchical decomposition. The normalized decomposition focuses on the *right strong intervals*, those that do not overlap with any others on the right. Lemma 2.1 shows that the family of phrase pairs is also a weakly partitive family and can be hierarchically decomposed after normalization. A minor difference is we prefer *left strong intervals* since our algorithms scan F from left to right. Another difference is that we binarize a linearly-arranged sequence of non-overlapping phrase pairs instead of grouping them together.

In the following sections, we show how to produce the normalized hierarchical analysis of a given alignment.

3 Shift-Reduce Algorithm

In this section, we present an $O(n^2+m+|A|)$ algorithm that is similar in spirit to a shift-reduce algorithm for parsing context-free languages. This algorithm is not optimal, but its left-to-right bottom-up control will form the basis for the improved algorithm in the next section.

First, we can efficiently test whether a span $[x, y]$ is a phrase as follows. Define a pair of functions $l(x, y)$ and $u(x, y)$ that record the minimum and maximum, respectively, of the positions on the French side that are linked to the positions $[x, y]$:

$$l(x, y) = \min\{j \mid (i, j) \in A, i \in [x, y]\}$$
$$u(x, y) = \max\{j \mid (i, j) \in A, i \in [x, y]\}$$

Note that $l(\cdot, y)$ is monotone increasing and $u(\cdot, y)$ is monotone decreasing. Define a *step* of $l(\cdot, y)$ (or $u(\cdot, y)$) to be a maximal interval over which $l(\cdot, y)$ (resp., $u(\cdot, y)$) is constant. We can compute $u(x, y)$ in constant time from its value on smaller spans:

$$u(x, y) = \max\{u(x, z), u(z + 1, y)\}$$

and similarly for $l(x, y)$.

We define the following functions to count the number of links emitted from prefixes of F and E:

$$F_c(j) = |\{(i', j') \in A \mid j' \leq j\}|$$
$$E_c(i) = |\{(i', j') \in A \mid i' \leq i\}|$$

Then the difference $F_c(u) - F_c(l - 1)$ counts the total number of links to positions in $[l, u]$, and $E_c(y) - E_c(x - 1)$ counts the total number of links to positions in $[x, y]$. E_c and F_c can be precomputed in $O(n + m + |A|)$ time.

Finally, let

$$f(x, y) = F_c(u(x, y)) - F_c(l(x, y) - 1) - (E_c(y) - E_c(x - 1))$$

Note that f is non-negative, but not monotonic in general. Figure 4 provides a visualization of u, l, and f for the example alignment from Section 2. This gives us our phrase-pair test:

Lemma 3.1. *$[x, y]$ and $[l(x, y), u(x, y)]$ are a phrase pair if and only if $f(x, y) = 0$.*

This test is used in the following shift-reduce-style algorithm:

$X \leftarrow \{1\}$
for $y \in [2, n]$ from left to right **do**
  append y to X
  for $x \in X$ from right to left **do**
    compute $u(x, y)$ from $u(x + 1, y)$
    compute $l(x, y)$ from $l(x + 1, y)$
    if $f(x, y) = 0$ **then**
      $[x, y]$ is a phrase

remove $[x+1, y]$ from X
end if
end for
end for

In the worst case, at each iteration we traverse the entire stack X without a successful reduction, indicating that the worst case time complexity is $O(n^2)$.

4 A Linear Algorithm

In this section, we modify the shift-reduce algorithm into a linear-time algorithm that avoids unnecessary reduction attempts. It is a generalization of Uno and Yagiura's algorithm.

4.1 Motivation

The reason that our previous algorithm is quadratic is that for each y, we try every possible combination with the values in X. Uno and Yagiura (2000) point out that in the case of permutations, it is not necessary to examine all spans, because it is possible to delete elements from X so that $f(\cdot, y)$ is monotone decreasing on X. This means that all the $x \in X$ such that $f(x, y) = 0$ can always be conveniently found at the end of X. That this can be done safely is guaranteed by the following:

Lemma 4.1. *If $x_1 < x_2 < y$ and $f(x_1, y) < f(x_2, y)$, then for all $y' \geq y$, $f(x_2, y') > 0$ (i.e., $[x_2, y']$ is not a phrase).*

Let us say that x_2 *violates monotonicity* if x_1 is the predecessor of x_2 in X and $f(x_1, y) < f(x_2, y)$. Then by Lemma 4.1, we can safely remove x_2 from X.

Furthermore, Uno and Yagiura (2000) show that we can enforce monotonicity at all times in such a way that the whole algorithm runs in linear time. This is made possible with a shortcut based on the following:

Lemma 4.2. *If $x_1 < x_2 < y$ and $u(x_1, y-1) > u(x_2, y-1)$ but $u(x_1, y) = u(x_2, y)$, then for all $y' \geq y$, $f(x_2, y') > 0$ (i.e., $[x_2, y']$ is not a phrase). The same holds* mutatis mutandis *for l.*

Let us say that y *updates* a step $[x', y']$ of u (or l) if $u(x', y) > u(x', y-1)$ (resp., $l(x', y) < l(x', y-1)$). By Lemma 4.2, if $[x_1, y_1]$ and $[x_2, y_2]$ are different steps of $u(\cdot, y-1)$ (resp., $l(\cdot, y-1)$) and y updates both of them, then we can remove from X all x' such that $x_2 \leq x' < y$.

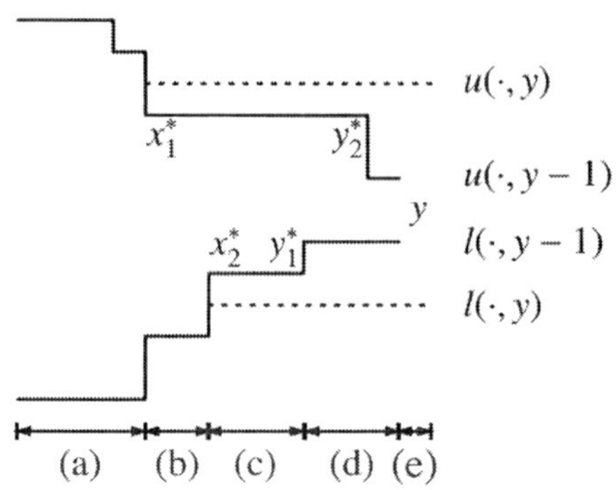

Figure 3: Illustration of step (3) of the algorithm. The letters indicate substeps of (3).

4.2 Generalized algorithm

These results generalize to the many-to-many alignment case, although we must introduce a few nuances. The new algorithm proceeds as follows:

Initialize $X = \{1\}$. For $y \in [2, n]$ from left to right:

1. Append y to X.
2. Update u and l:
   (a) Traverse the steps of $u(\cdot, y-1)$ from right to left and compute $u(\cdot, y)$ until we have found the leftmost step $[x^*, y^*]$ of $u(\cdot, y-1)$ that gets updated by y.
   (b) Do the same for l.

   We have computed two values for x^*; let x_1^* be the smaller and x_2^* be the larger. Similarly, let y_1^* be the smaller y^*.
3. Enforce monotonicity of $f(\cdot, y)$ (see Figure 3):
   (a) The positions left of the smaller x^* always satisfy monotonicity, so do nothing.
   (b) For $x \in [x_1^*, x_2^*) \cap X$ while x violates monotonicity, remove x from X.
   (c) For $x \in [x_2^*, y_1^*] \cap X$ while x violates monotonicity, remove x from X.
   (d) The steps right of y_1^* may or may not violate monotonicity, but we use the stronger Lemma 4.2 to delete all of them (excluding y).[1]

[1] In the special case where $[x^*, y^*]$ is updated by y to the

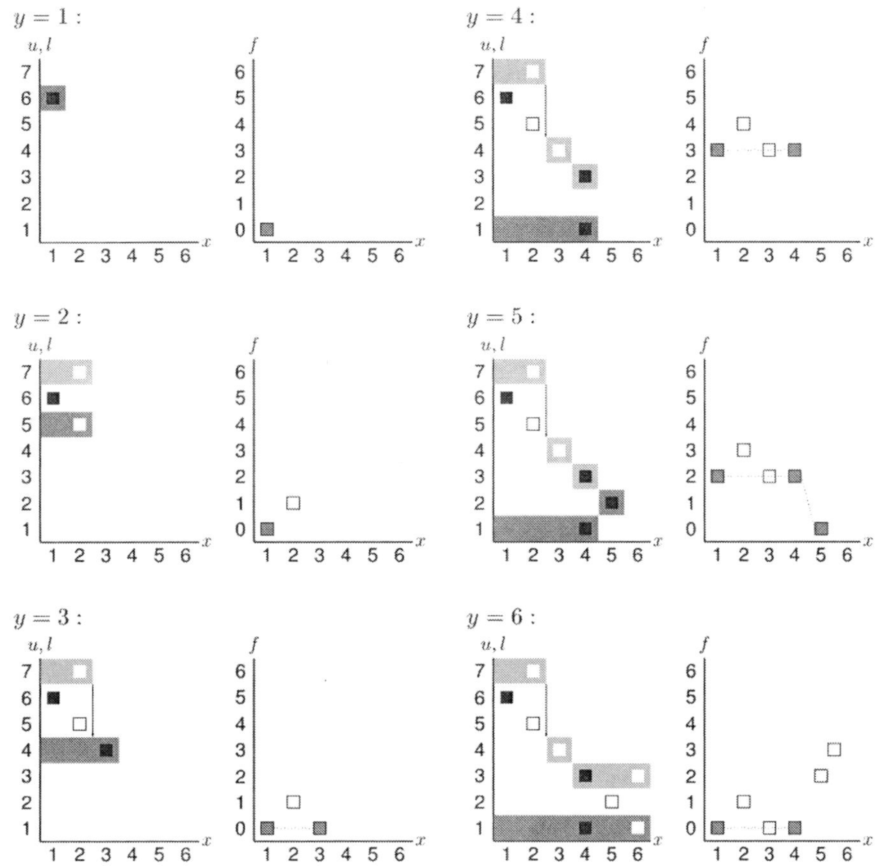

Figure 4: The evolution of $u(x, y)$, $l(x, y)$, and $f(x, y)$ as y goes from 1 to 6 for the example alignment. Each pair of diagrams shows the state of affairs between steps (3) and (4) of the algorithm. Light grey boxes are the steps of u, and darker grey boxes are the steps of l. We use solid boxes to plot the values of remaining x's on the list but also show the other values in empty boxes for completeness.

(e) Finally, if y violates monotonicity, remove it from X.

4. For $x \in X$ from right to left until $f(x, y) > 0$, output $[x, y]$ and remove x's successor in X.[2]

An example of the algorithm's execution is shown in Figure 4. The evolution of $u(x, y)$, $l(x, y)$, and $f(x, y)$ is displayed for increasing y (from 1 to 6). We point out the interesting steps. When $y = 2$, position 2 is eliminated due to step (3e) of our algorithm to ensure monotonicity of f at the right end, and $[1, 2]$ is reduced. When $y = 3$, two reductions are made: one on $[3, 3]$ and the other on $[1, 3]$. Because of leftmost normalization, position 3 is deleted. When $y = 6$, we have $x_1^* = x_2^* = y_1^* = 5$, so that position 5 is deleted by step (3c) and position 6 is deleted by step (3e).

4.3 Correctness

We have already argued in Section 4.1 that the deletion of elements from X does not alter the output of the algorithm. It remains to show that step (3) guarantees monotonicity:

Claim 4.3. *For all y, at the end of step (3), $f(\cdot, y)$ is monotone decreasing.*

Proof. By induction on y. For $y = 1$, the claim is trivially true. For $y > 1$, we want to show that for x_1, x_2 adjacent in X such that $x_1 < x_2$, $f(x_1, y) \geq f(x_2, y)$. We consider the five regions of X covered by step (3) (cf. Figure 3), and then

same value as the step to its left, we can use Lemma 4.2 to delete $[x^*, y^*]$ and y as well, bypassing steps (3b),(3c), and (3e).

[2]If there are any such x, they must lie to the left of x_1^*. Therefore a further optimization would be to perform step (4) before step (3), starting with the predecessor of x_1^*. If a reduction is made, we can jump to step (3e).

the boundaries between them.

Region (a): $x_1, x_2 \in [1, x_1^*]$. Since $u(x_i, y) = u(x_i, y-1)$ and $l(x_i, y) = l(x_i, y-1)$, we have:

$$f(x_i, y) - f(x_i, y-1) = 0 - (E_c(y) - E_c(y-1))$$

i.e., in this region, f shifts down uniformly from iteration $y-1$ to iteration y. Hence, if $f(\cdot, y-1)$ was monotonic, then $f(\cdot, y)$ is also monotonic within this region.
Region (b): $x_1, x_2 \in [x_1^*, x_2^*)$. Since $u(x_1, y-1) = u(x_2, y-1)$ and $u(x_1, y) = u(x_2, y)$ and similarly for l, we have:

$$f(x_1, y) - f(x_1, y-1) = f(x_2, y) - f(x_2, y-1)$$

i.e., in this region, f shifts up or down uniformly.[3] Hence, if $f(\cdot, y-1)$ was monotonic, then $f(\cdot, y)$ is also monotonic within this region.
Region (c): $x_1, x_2 \in [x_2^*, y_1^*]$. Same as Case 2.
Region (d) and (e): Vacuous (these regions have at most one element).

The remaining values of x_1, x_2 are those that straddle the boundaries between regions. But step (3) of the algorithm deals with each of these boundaries explicitly, deleting elements until $f(x_1) \geq f(x_2)$. Thus $f(\cdot, y)$ is monotonic everywhere. □

4.4 Implementation and running time

X should be implemented in a way that allows linear-time traversal and constant-time deletion; also, u and l must be implemented in a way that allows linear-time traversal of their steps. Doubly-linked lists are appropriate for all three functions.
Claim 4.4. *The above algorithm runs in* $O(n + m + |A|)$ *time.*

We can see that the algorithm runs in linear time if we observe that whenever we traverse a part of X, we delete it, except for a constant amount of work per iteration (that is, per value of y): the steps traversed in (2) are all deleted in (3d) except four (two for u and two for l); the positions traversed in (3b), (3c), and (4) are all deleted except one.

4.5 SCFG Rule extraction

The algorithm of the previous section outputs the normalized decomposition tree depicted in Figure 2. From this tree, it is straightforward to obtain a set of maximally-decomposed SCFG rules. As an example, the tree of Figure 2 produces the rules shown in Figure 5.

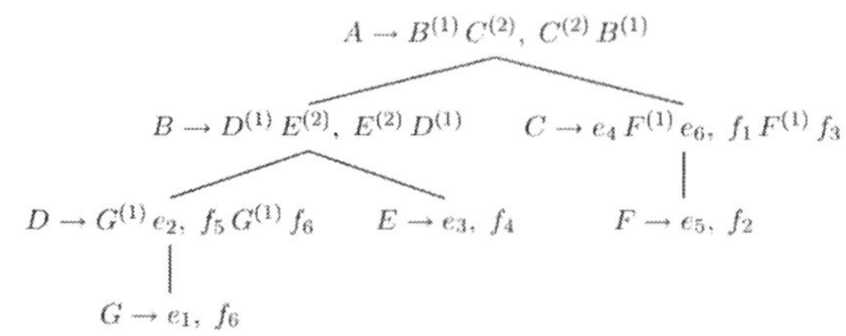

Figure 5: Each node from the normalized decomposition tree of Figure 2 is converted into an SCFG rule.

We adopt the SCFG notation of Satta and Peserico (2005). Each rule has a right-hand side sequence for both languages, separated by a comma. Superscript indices in the right-hand side of grammar rules such as:

$$A \rightarrow B^{(1)}\, C^{(2)},\; C^{(2)}\, B^{(1)}$$

indicate that the nonterminals with the same index are linked across the two languages, and will eventually be rewritten by the same rule application. The example above inverts the order of B and C when translating from the source language to the target language.

The SCFG rule extraction proceeds as follows. Assign a nonterminal label to each node in the tree. Then for each node (S, T) in the tree top-down, where S and T are sequences of positions,

1. For each child (S', T'), S' and T' must be subsequences of S and T, respectively. Replace their occurrences in S and T with a pair of coindexed nonterminals X', where X' is the nonterminal assigned to the child.

2. For each remaining position i in S, replace i with e_i.

3. For each remaining position j in T, replace j with f_j.

4. Output the rule $X \rightarrow S,\ T$, where X is the nonterminal assigned to the parent.

As an example, consider the node $([4, 6], [1, 3])$ in Figure 2. After step 1, it becomes

$$(4\, F^{(1)}\, 6, 1\, F^{(1)}\, 3)$$

and after steps 2 and 3, it becomes

$$(e_4\, F^{(1)}\, e_6, f_1\, F^{(1)}\, f_3)$$

[3]It can be shown further that in this region, f shifts up or is unchanged. Therefore any reductions in step (4) must be in region (a).

	0	1	2	3	4	5	6
Hindi/English	52.8	53.5	99.9		99.9	100.0	
Chinese/English	51.0	52.4	99.7	99.8	100.0	100.0	100.0
French/English	52.1	53.5	99.9	100.0	100.0	100.0	
Romanian/English	50.8	52.6	99.9	99.9	100.0		100.0
Spanish/English	50.7	51.8	99.9	100.0	100.0	100.0	

Table 1: Cumulative percentages of rule tokens by number of nonterminals in right-hand side. A blank indicates that no rules were found with that number of nonterminals.

Finally, step 4 outputs

$$C \rightarrow e_4\, F^{(1)}\, e_6,\ f_1\, F^{(1)}\, f_3$$

A few choices are available to the user depending on the application intended for the SCFG extraction. The above algorithm starts by assigning a nonterminal to each node in the decomposition tree; one could assign a unique nonterminal to each node, so that the resulting grammar produces exactly the set of sentences given as input. But for machine translation, one may wish to use a single nonterminal, such that the extracted rules can recombine freely, as in Chiang (2005).

Unaligned words in either language (an empty row or column in the alignment matrix, not present in our example) will be attached as high as possible in our tree. However, other ways of handling unaligned words are possible given the decomposition tree. One can produce all SCFG rules consistent with the alignment by, for each unaligned word, looping through possible attachment points in the decomposition tree. In this case, the number of SCFG rules produced may be exponential in the size of the original input sentence; however, even in this case, the decomposition tree enables a rule extraction algorithm that is linear in the output length (the number of SCFG rules).

4.6 Phrase extraction

We briefly discuss the process of extracting all phrase pairs consistent with the original alignment from the normalized decomposition tree. First of all, every node in the tree gives a valid phrase pair. Then, in the case of overlapping phrase pairs such as the example in Section 2.1, the decomposition tree will contain a left-branching chain of binary nodes all performing the same permutation. While traversing the tree, whenever we identify such a chain, let $\eta_1, \ldots, \eta_k$ be the sequence of all the children of the nodes in the chain. Then, each of the subsequences $\{\eta_i, \ldots, \eta_j \mid 1 < i < j \leq k\}$ yields a valid phrase pair. In our example, the root of the tree of Figure 2 and its left child form such a chain, with three children; the subsequence $\{([3,3],[4,4]),([4,6],[1,3])\}$ yields the phrase $([3,6],[1,4])$. In the case of unaligned words, we can also consider all combinations of their attachments, as discussed for SCFG rule extraction.

5 Experiments on Analyzing Word Alignments

One application of our factorization algorithm is analyzing human-annotated word alignments. Wellington et al. (2006) argue for the necessity of discontinuous spans (i.e., for a formalism beyond Synchronous CFG) in order for synchronous parsing to cover human-annotated word alignment data under the constraint that rules have a rank of no more than two. In a related study, Zhang and Gildea (2007) analyze the rank of the Synchronous CFG derivation trees needed to parse the same data. The number of discontinuous spans and the rank determine the complexity of dynamic programming algorithms for synchronous parsing (alignment) or machine translation decoding.

Both studies make simplifying assumptions on the alignment data to avoid dealing with many-to-many word links. Here, we apply our alignment factorization algorithm directly to the alignments to produce a normalized decomposition tree for each alignment and collect statistics on the branching factors of the trees.

We use the same alignment data for the five language pairs Chinese-English, Romanian-English, Hindi-English, Spanish-English, and French-English as Wellington et al. (2006). Table 1 reports the number of rules extracted by the rank, or number of nonterminals on the right-hand side. Almost all rules are binary, implying both that binary synchronous grammars are adequate for MT, and that our algorithm can find such grammars. Table 2 gives similar statistics for the number of *terminals* in each rule. The phrases we extract are short enough that they are likely to generalize to new sentences. The apparent difficulty of

	0	1	2	3	4	5	6	7	8	9	≥10	max
Hindi/English	39.6	92.2	97.7	99.5	99.7	99.9	99.9	100.0				7
Chinese/English	39.8	87.2	96.2	99.0	99.7	99.9	100.0	100.0	100.0	100.0	100.0	12
French/English	44.5	89.0	93.4	95.8	97.5	98.4	99.0	99.3	99.6	99.8	100.0	18
Romanian/English	42.9	89.8	96.9	98.9	99.5	99.8	99.9	100.0		100.0		9
Spanish/English	47.5	91.8	97.7	99.4	99.9	99.9	100.0	100.0		100.0		9

Table 2: Cumulative percentages of rule tokens by number of terminals in right-hand side. A blank indicates that no rules were found with that number of terminals.

the French-English pair is due to the large number of "possible" alignments in this dataset.

6 Conclusion

By extending the algorithm of Uno and Yagiura (2000) from one-to-one mappings to many-to-many mappings, we have shown how to construct a hierarchical representation of all the phrase pairs in a given aligned sentence pair in linear time, which yields a set of minimal SCFG rules. We have also illustrated how to apply the algorithm as an analytical tool for aligned bilingual data.

Acknowledgments Thanks to Bob Moore for suggesting the extension to phrase extraction at SSST 2007. This work was supported in part by NSF grants IIS-0546554 and ITR-0428020, and DARPA grant HR0011-06-C-0022 under BBN Technologies subcontract 9500008412.

References

Brown, Peter F., Stephen A. Della Pietra, Vincent J. Della Pietra, and Robert L. Mercer. 1993. The mathematics of statistical machine translation: Parameter estimation. *Computational Linguistics*, 19(2):263–311.

Bui-Xuan, Binh Minh, Michel Habib, and Christophe Paul. 2005. Revisiting T. Uno and M. Yagiura's algorithm. In *The 16th Annual International Symposium on Algorithms and Computation (ISAAC '05)*, pages 146–155.

Chiang, David. 2005. A hierarchical phrase-based model for statistical machine translation. In *Proceedings of ACL 2005*, pages 263–270.

Galley, Michel, Mark Hopkins, Kevin Knight, and Daniel Marcu. 2004. What's in a translation rule? In *Proceedings of NAACL 2004*.

Landau, Gad M., Laxmi Parida, and Oren Weimann. 2005. Gene proximity analysis across whole genomes via PQ trees. *Journal of Computational Biology*, 12(10):1289–1306.

Och, Franz Josef and Hermann Ney. 2004a. The alignment template approach to statistical machine translation. *Computational Linguistics*, 30(4).

Och, Franz Josef and Hermann Ney. 2004b. The alignment template approach to statistical machine translation. *Computational Linguistics*, 30:417–449.

Satta, Giorgio and Enoch Peserico. 2005. Some computational complexity results for synchronous context-free grammars. In *Proceedings of EMNLP 2005*, pages 803–810, Vancouver, Canada, October.

Uno, Takeaki and Mutsunori Yagiura. 2000. Fast algorithms to enumerate all common intervals of two permutations. *Algorithmica*, 26(2):290–309.

Wellington, Benjamin, Sonjia Waxmonsky, and I. Dan Melamed. 2006. Empirical lower bounds on the complexity of translational equivalence. In *Proceedings of COLING-ACL 2006*.

Zhang, Hao and Daniel Gildea. 2007. Factorization of synchronous context-free grammars in linear time. In *Proceedings of the NAACL Workshop on Syntax and Structure in Statistical Translation (SSST)*.

Sentence Type Based Reordering Model for Statistical Machine Translation

Jiajun Zhang, Chengqing Zong, Shoushan Li
National Laboratory of Pattern Recognition
Institute of Automation, Chinese Academy of Sciences, Beijing 100190, China
{jjzhang, cqzong, sshanli}@nlpr.ia.ac.cn

Abstract

Many reordering approaches have been proposed for the statistical machine translation (SMT) system. However, the information about the type of source sentence is ignored in the previous works. In this paper, we propose a group of novel reordering models based on the source sentence type for Chinese-to-English translation. In our approach, an SVM-based classifier is employed to classify the given Chinese sentences into three types: special interrogative sentences, other interrogative sentences, and non-question sentences. The different reordering models are developed oriented to the different sentence types. Our experiments show that the novel reordering models have obtained an improvement of more than 2.65% in BLEU for a phrase-based spoken language translation system.

1 Introduction

The phrase-based translation approach has been the popular and widely used strategy to the statistical machine translation (SMT) since Och, *et al.* (2002) proposed the log-linear model. However, reordering is always a key issue in the decoding process. A number of models have been developed to deal with the problem of reordering. The existing reordering approaches could be divided into two categories: one is integrated into the decoder and the other is employed as a preprocessing module.

© 2008. Licensed under the *Creative Commons Attribution-Noncommercial-Share Alike 3.0 Unported* license (http://creativecommons.org/licenses/by-nc-sa/3.0/). Some rights reserved.

Many reordering methods belong to the former category. Distortion model was first employed by Koehn *et al.* (2003); a lexicalized reordering model was proposed by Och *et al.* (2004) and Koehn *et al.* (2005); and the formal syntax-based reordering models were proposed by Chiang (2005) and Xiong *et al.* (2006). It is worthy to note that little syntactic knowledge is used in the models mentioned above.

Compared to the reordering models that are integrated into the decoder, the reordering at the source side can utilize more syntactic knowledge, with the goal of adjusting the source language sentence to make its word order closer to that of the target language. The most notable models are given by Xia and McCord (2004), Collins *et al.* (2005), Li *et al.* (2007) and Wang *et al.* (2007). Xia and McCord (2004) parsed the source and target sides of the training data and then automatically extracted the rewriting patterns. The rewriting patterns are employed on the input source sentence to make the word order more accordant to target language. Collins *et al.* (2005) described an approach to reorder German in German-to-English translation. The method concentrates on the German clauses and six types of transforming rules are applied to the parsed source sentence. However, all the rules are manually built. Li *et al.* (2007) used a parser to get the syntactic tree of the source language sentence. In this method, a maximum entropy model is developed to determine how probable the children of a node are to be reordered. Obviously, there is also disadvantage in this method because the parsing tree is obtained by a full parser and contains too many nodes that are not involved in desired reorderings. Wang *et al.* (2007) discussed three categories which are considered to be the most prominent candidates for reordering in Chinese-to-English translation, including verb phrases (VPs), noun phrases (NPs), and localizer phrases (LCPs). The method deals with some special modifiers of VPs and NPs because they have the property that some specific modifiers appear before VPs or NPs in Chinese but occur after VPs or NPs in its English translation. We observe that all the transformation rules in this method are hard crafted. Furthermore, there are some other related works, such as Costa-jussa and Fonollosa's work (2006) and Zhang *et al.*'s work (2007). Costa-jussa and Fonollosa (2006) considered the source reordering as a translation task which translates the source sentence into reordered source sentence. A chunk-level reordering model was first proposed by Zhang *et al.* (2007).

However, all the existing models make no distinction between the different types of the source sentence. Intuitively, we have different reordering information in different sentence type. Taking Chinese special interrogative sentence as an example, there is a fixed phrase that usually occurs at the end of Chinese sentence but appears at the beginning part of its English translation. See the following Chinese to English translation:

Chinese: 你 想 要 什么样 的 座位 ?
English: What kind of seats do you like ?

Obviously, the Chinese question phrase "什么样 的 座位 (What kind of seats)" should be put at the beginning of its English translation. However, many phrase-based systems fail to do this.

In this paper, we are interested in investigating the value of Chinese sentence types in reordering for Chinese-to-English spoken language translation. Due to the syntactic difference between Chinese and English, different sentence type provides different reordering information. A phrase-ahead model is developed to exploit and utilize the reordering information of special interrogative sentences. A phrase-back model is employed to catch and make use of the reordering information of other sentence types. However, the sentence type should be first identified by an SVM-based classifier before reordering the source sentence. The method overall is used as a preprocessing module for translation. We will introduce our method in detail later.

The remainder of this paper is organized as follows: Section 2 introduces our motivations; Section 3 gives the details on the implementation of our approach; the experiments are shown in Section 4; and the final concluding remarks are given in Section 5.

2 Our Motivations

In this section, before we analyze the Chinese-to-English spoken language translation corpus, some definitions are given first.

2.1 Definitions

- Special interrogative sentence / other interrogative sentence / non-question sentence

Chinese sentence can be divided into question sentence and non-question sentence. If a Chinese question sentence is translated into the English sentence of wh-questions, the sentence is named as a Chinese special interrogative sentence; otherwise, it is called the Chinese other interrogative sentence. Figure 1-3 show some examples for the three sentence types respectively.

- SQP / TP / SP

In Chinese special interrogative sentence, the question phrase is always moved ahead while it is translated into English. Correspondingly, the question phrase is named as the special question phrase (SQP). For example, the question phrase "什么样 的 座位 (What kind of seats)" in the example mentioned above is an SQP.

A few quantifier phrases (QPs) like "多 次 (many times)", "很多 年 (many years)" in Chinese and some LCPs like "事故 发生 后 (after the accident happened)", "会议 结束 前 (before the meeting ends)" together with some NPs like temporal phrases are named temporal phrase (TP) in our model. Some LCPs like "宾馆 前 (at the front of the hotel)", "桌子 旁 (near the table)" and a few NPs like spatial phrases are called spatial phrase (SP) in our model. As PPs[1], TPs and SPs are the most prominent candidates for reordering in Chinese other interrogative sentences and non-question sentences, they will be handled in the phrase-back reordering model.

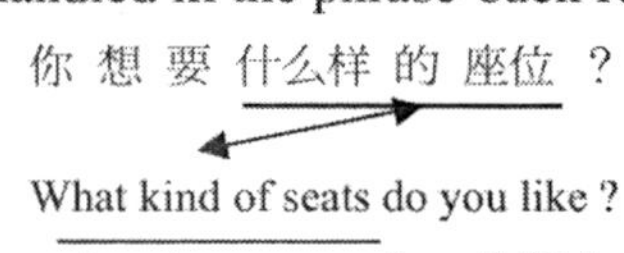

Figure 1. An example of Chinese special interrogative sentence with its English translation.

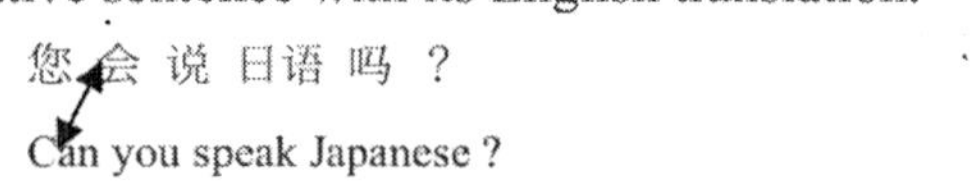

Figure 2. An example of Chinese other interrogative sentence with its English translation.

[1] PPs here mean prepositional phrases

Figure 3. An example of Chinese non-question sentence with its English translation.

2.2 Analysis of Corpus and Our Motivations

In order to have an overview of the distribution of the Chinese sentence types, we have made a survey based on our training set for translation, which contains about 277k Chinese and English sentence pairs. We found that about 17.2% of the sentences are special interrogative sentences, about 25.5% of sentences are other interrogative sentences and the remainders are all non-question sentences.

Each sentence type has its own reordering strategy, as demonstrated in Figures 1-3. There is a settled phrase (SQP) in Chinese special interrogative sentence which usually appears at the end but will be translated first in English, just as Figure 1 illustrates. For other interrogative sentences, some specific Chinese words like "会、能、可以" will just be translated into "Can" or "Do" and come first in English. At present, this information is not used in our approach. Figure 2 gives an example. For non-questions, the reordering candidates usually need to be moved back during translation. An example is shown in Figure 3.

According to the analysis above, it is meaningful to develop reordering models based on the source sentence types.

2.3 Framework

As we mentioned above, our framework is illustrated as follows:

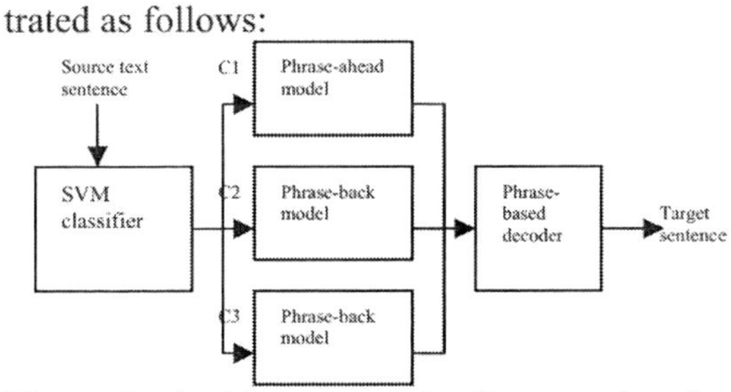

Figure 4. Architecture of the framework, where C1 means the special interrogative sentence, C2 is other interrogative sentence and C3 is non-question sentence.

Conventional preprocessing approaches divide the translation into two phases:

$$S \rightarrow S' \rightarrow T \quad (1)$$

Reordering is first done in the source side which changes the source sentence S into reordered one S', and then a standard phrase-based translation engine is used to translate the reordered source sentence S' into target language sentence T.

In our method, to utilize the information of sentence types, a new approach is proposed to improve the translation performance by developing a hybrid model as follows:

$$S \rightarrow S^c \rightarrow S' \rightarrow T \quad (2)$$

Before the source sentence is reordered, an SVM-based classifier is first employed to determine its sentence type S^c, then, different reordering model is used to reorder the source sentence with the specific sentence type S^c. After getting the reordered source sentence S', we use our phrase-based SMT to obtain the optimal target language sentence.

The contribution of this paper is embodied in the first two steps of our method.

In the first step, an SVM classifier is used to identify the type of source sentence[2].

In the second step, two reordering models are built according to the different sentence types. A phrase-ahead reordering model is developed for the special interrogative sentences which uses shallow parsing technology to recognize the most prominent candidates for reordering (special question phrase) and extracts reordering templates from bilingual corpus. For other sentence types, we build a phrase-back reordering model which uses shallow parsing technology to identify the phrases that are almost always moved back during translation and applies maximum entropy algorithm to determine whether we should reorder them.

3 Models and Algorithms

In this section, we first introduce the sentence type classifier model, and then we describe in detail the two reordering models, phrase-ahead reordering model and phrase-back reordering model.

3.1 Sentence Type Identification

Many models are used for classification such as Naïve Bayes, decision tree and maximum entropy. In our approach, we use an SVM-based classifier to classify the sentence types. SVM

[2] There are three sentence types: special interrogative sentence, other interrogative sentence and non-question sentence, which are defined in sub-section 2.1.

has been shown to be highly effective at traditional text categorization. For our problem, we regard a sentence as a text. The decision boundary in SVM is a hyperplane, represented by vector $\vec{w}$, which separates the two classes, leaving the largest margin between the vectors of the two classes (Vapnik, 1998). The search of margin corresponds to a constrained optimization problem. Suppose $c_j \in \{1,-1\}$ (positive and negative) be the correct class of sentence s_j, the solution can be formalized as:

$$\vec{w} := \sum_j \alpha_j c_j \vec{s}_j \quad \alpha_j \geq 0 \tag{3}$$

Where the $\vec{s}_j$ is feature vector of our sentence s_j. We get α_j s through solving a dual optimization problem. Identifying the type of a sentence is just to determine which side of $\vec{w}$'s hyperplane it will fall in.

Feature selection is an important issue. We directly use all the words occurring in the sentence as features.

Some readers may argue that the features to distinguish the sentence types are very obvious in Chinese. For example, "?" can easily separate the interrogative sentences from non-question sentences. In this case, a simple classifier like decision tree will work. It is true when the punctuation always appears in the sentence. However, sometimes there is no punctuation in the spoken language text. Under this situation, the decision tree will lose the most powerful features, but the performance of SVM is not affected by the punctuations. The experimental results verifying this will be given in Section4.

3.2 Phrase-ahead Reordering Model

As we mentioned above, about 17.2% of the spoken language sentences are special interrogative sentences. Furthermore, we note that each Chinese special interrogative sentence has one or more special question phrases (SQP) that we defined in section 2.1. Due to the difference between Chinese and English word order, the SQP needs to be moved ahead[3] when it is translated into English.

Let S be a Chinese special interrogative sentence, our first problem is to recognize the *SQPs* in S. If we have known the *SQP*, namely S becomes S^0 *SQP* S^1 (S^0 is the left part of the sentence before *SQP*, and S^1 is the right part of the sentence after *SQP*), our second problem is to find the correct position in S^0 where *SQP* will be moved to.

For the first problem, because each syntactic component is possible a SQP, for example, "什么样 的 座位" in Figure 1 is NP, "在 哪里 (Where)" in Chinese sentence "我 在 哪里 能 买 到 票 ? (Where can I buy the ticket?)" is PP (also a VP modifier), "怎么 走 (How to go)" in "去 海滨 怎么 走 ? (How to go to the beach?)" is VP, it is very difficult to find the SQP by syntax. In our model, we first find out all the key words, which we list below, in the special interrogative sentences through mutual information. Then, we define the syntactic component containing the key word as an SQP. Instead of full syntactic parser, we utilize a CRF toolkit named FlexCrfs[4] to train, test and predict the SQPs chunking.

什么	What
哪 (哪里 / 哪儿…)	Where
多 (多大 / 多长…)	How much/many/old…
怎 (怎样/怎么办 …)	What about/How
谁 (谁的 / 是谁…)	Who/whose/whom
几 (几点 / 几个…)	How many/old When…
为什么	Why
何(何时 / 何地…)	When/where

Table 1. The special key words set

For the second problem, we note that there are only three positions where the SQP will be moved to: (1) the beginning of the sentence; (2) just after the rightmost punctuation (",", ";" or ":") before the SQP; (3) or after a regular phrase such as "请问 (May I ask)" and "告诉 我 (Please tell me)". Therefore, we can learn the reordering templates from bilingual corpus[5]. The simple algorithm is illustrated in Figure 5, and some reordering templates are shown in Table 2.

On the whole, When we reorder the special interrogative sentence, we first identify the SQP, then we find out whether there are punctuations ("," , ";" or ":") before SQP; if any, we keep the rightmost punctuation index, otherwise we keep the index 0 (beginning of sentence). In the third

[3] There is a specific situation that the SQP don't have to be moved. In this case, we suppose it needs to be moved, but the distance is 0.

[4] See http://flexCRF.sourceforge.net

[5] The bilingual corpus is the corpus combined by the training corpus for chunking *SQPs* and its corresponding English translation.

step, if we find that a reordering template like some one given in Table 2 can match the sentence, we just apply the template, otherwise we just move the SQP after the index that we kept before (0 or punctuation index).

```
Input: special interrogative sentence pair (s, t) in which SQP is labeled and their alignment M is given
R={}
Find the rightmost punctuation index c_punc_index before SQP and English index e_punc_index aligned to c_punc_index
Find the smallest index e_smallest_index of English which align to the SQP
Get the Chinese phrase C_Phrase which aligns to [e_punc_index+1, e_smallest_index-1]
if C_Phrase is NONE then
    Continue ;
end if
if C_Phrase in R then
    Count(C_Phrase)++;
else
    Insert C_Phrase into R;
    Count(C_Phrase)=1;
end if
remove C_Phrase if Count(C_Phrase)<N
output R
```

Figure 5. Reordering template extraction algorithm. The empirical value N is 10 in our experiment.

X1 请问 *X2 SQP*	*X1* 请问 *SQP X2*
X1 告诉 我 *X2 SQP*	*X1* 告诉 我 *SQP X2*
X1 我 想 知道 *X2 SQP*	*X1* 我 想 知道 *SQP X2*
X1 然而 *X2 SQP*	*X1* 然而 *SQP X2*
......	......

Table 2. Some reordering templates

3.3 Phrase-back Reordering Model

In this paper, we employ the phrase-back reordering model for Chinese other interrogative sentences and non-question sentences.

Inspired by the work of Wang *et al.* (2007), we only consider the most prominent candidates for reordering. The VP modifiers like PP, TP, and SP which we defined in sub-section 2.1 are typically in pre-verb position in Chinese but almost always appear after the verb in its corresponding English translation. Wang *et al.* (2007) concentrate on VP, NP, then determine whether their modifiers should be moved back. Instead, our interests are focused on the modifiers: PP, TP and SP; namely, we consider the modifiers PP, TP and SP as triggers, and the first VP occurring after triggers will be the candidate position where the triggers may be moved to.

Changing the focus gives us the ability to handle a specific situation that there is no VP after the triggers for recognition error or other reasons. As the example in Figure 6, there is no VP after PP ("在 这里") because the phrase "签名" next to PP is wrongly recognized to be a NP. To deal with the case, we will further define a fake verb phrase (FVP): the phrase after PP (TP or SP) until the punctuation (",", ";" or "."). The phrase "签名 (sign your name)" in Figure 6 is an FVP. Here, FVP is given the same function with VP, thus it makes our model suitable for more situations.

请 在 这里 签名 。

Figure 6. An example of FVP. In our model the whole sentence is recognized as a VP, "在 这里 (here)" is a PP, and "签名 (sign your name)" is identified as a NP.

Unlike hard reordering rules of Wang *et al.* (2007), we develop a probabilistic reordering model to alleviate the impact of the errors caused by the parser when recognizing PPs, TPs, SPs and VPs. We believe that no reordering is better than bad reordering. The rule forms and the probabilistic model will be given as follows:

- The form of phrase-back reordering rules:

$$A: A_1XA_2 \Rightarrow \begin{cases} A_1XA_2 & straight \\ XA_2A_1 & inverted \end{cases}$$

Where, $A_1 \in \{PP, TP, SP\}$ $A_2 \in \{VP, FVP\}$ $X \in \{phrases\ between\ A_1\ and\ A_2\}$

- We use the Maximum Entropy Model which is implemented by Zhang[6]. The model is trained from bilingual spoken language corpus to determine whether A_1 should be moved after A_2. The features that we investigated include the leftmost, rightmost, and their POSs of A_1 and A_2. It leads to the following formula:

$$P(O \mid A) = \frac{\exp(\sum_i \lambda_i h_i(O, A))}{\sum_O \exp(\sum_i \lambda_i h_i(O, A))} \quad (4)$$

Where, $O \in \{straignt, inverted\}$, $h_i(O, A)$ is a feature, and λ_i is the weight of the feature.

When applying the rules, we first identify pairs like (A_1XA_2) in the sentence, and then from beginning to end of the sentence, we move A_1 behind A_2 if $P(inverted \mid A) > P(straight \mid A)$. After all the pairs are processed, we will get the reordered source result.

[6]http://homepages.inf.ed.ac.uk/s0450736/maxent_toolkit.html

4 Experiments

We have conducted several experiments to evaluate the models. In this section, we first introduce the corpora, and then we discuss the performance of the SVM-based classifier, chunking and reordering models respectively.

4.1 Corpora

We perform our experiments on Chinese-to-English speech translation task. The statistics of the corpus is given in Table 3 where CE_train means the Chinese-to-English training data released by IWSLT 2007; CE_sent_filtered means the bilingual sentence pairs filtered from the open resources of the bilingual sentences on the website; CE_dict_filtered means the bilingual dictionary filtered from the open resources of the bilingual dictionaries on the website; CE_dev123 denotes the bilingual sentence pairs obtained by the combination of the development data IWSLT07_CE_devset1, IWSLT07_CE_devset2 and IWSLT07_CE_devset3 which are released by the IWSLT 2007; CE_dev4 and CE_dev5 are the remainder of development data released by IWSLT 2007; CE_test means the final test set released by IWSLT 2007.

We combine the data from the top four rows as our training set. We use CE_dev4 as our development set. CE_dev5 and CE_test are our two test data. The test data released by IWSLT 2007 is based on the clean text with punctuation information, so we add the punctuation information on the Chinese sentences of CE_dev4 and CE_dev5 by our SVM sentence type classifier to form the final development set. The detailed statistics are given in Table 4.

4.2 Classification Result

To evaluate the performance of SVM-based classifier on classifying the sentence types, we first use a simple decision tree to divide the Chinese sentences of our training data for translation into three sentence types. Then we clean them by hand in order to remove the errors. At last, 10k sentences for each sentence type are randomly selected as the experiment data. For each sentence type, 80% of the data are used as training data, 20% as test data. Table 5 gives the classification results.

Punctuation in Table 5 means the punctuation which occurs at the end of the sentence such as "。" and "？". We can see from the table that SVM classifier performs very well even if we remove the punctuations at the end of every sentence. Therefore, almost no errors will be passed to the reordering stage.

Data	Chinese	English
CE_train	39,953	39,953
CE_sent_filtered	188,282	188,282
CE_dict_filtered	31,132	31,132
CE_dev123	24,192	24,192
CE_dev4	489	3,423
CE_dev5	500	3,500
CE_test	489	2,934

Table 3. Statistics of training data, development data and test data

		Chinese	English
Train set	sentences	276,633	
	words	1,665,073	1,198,984
Dev set CE_dev4	sentences	489	489*7
	words	6241	47609
Test set CE_dev5	sentences	500	500*7
	words	6596	52567
Test set CE_test	sentences	489	489*6
	words	3166	22574

Table 4. Detailed statistics of training data on development set

	Accuracy (%)
With punctuation	99.80
Without punctuation	98.00

Table 5. The accuracy of SVM classifier

4.3 Chunking Results

In our experiment, except that VPs are obtained by a syntactic parser (Klein and Manning, 2003), SQPs, PPs, TPs, SPs are all chunked by the FlexCrfs.

The chunking data used for training and test in Table 6 are annotated by ourselves. Every chunk is annotated according to the definition that we define in sub-section 2.1. The raw training and test data are all extracted from our training set for translation. TPs, SPs are annotated together; SQPs, PPs are annotated respectively. The statistics of the training and test data are shown in Table 6. Table 7 gives the chunking results.

The precision, recall and F-Measure are metrics for the chunking results. F-Measure follows the criteria of CoNLL-2000[7].

$$F-Measure = \frac{2*(precision*recall)}{precision+recall}$$

[7] See http://www.cnts.ua.ac.be/conll2000/chunking/

Because the SQPs have the regularity that each one contains a key word listed in Table 1, the result of SQPs chunking is quite good. Moreover, the chunking of PPs, TPs and SPs also performs well.

		Train	Test
SQP	sentences	10,000	500
	chunks	10030	501
PP	sentences	10,000	500
	chunks	10106	512
SP and TP	sentences	11,000	500
	chunks	10342	523

Table 6. Statistics of train and test data

	Precision (%)	Recall (%)	F-Measure (%)
SQP	95.52	95.52	95.52
PP	94.65	93.31	93.98
SP and TP	93.92	92.68	93.25

Table 7. Chunking results on test set

4.4 Translation Results

For the translation experiments, BLEU-4 and NIST are used as the evaluation metric. The baseline SMT uses the standard phrase-based decoder that applies the log-linear model (Och and Ney, 2002).

In the preprocessing module, all the Chinese words are segmented by the free software toolkit ICTCLAS3.0[8], and the POS tags are obtained by using the Stanford parser with its POS parsing function. For the decoder, the phrase table is obtained as described in (Koehn *et al.*, 2005), and our 4-gram language model is trained by the open SRILM[9] toolkit. It should be noted that we use monotone decoding in translation.

We have done three groups of experiments for translation. The first one is to test the effect of phrase-ahead reordering model, the result of which is shown in Table 8. Compared to the baseline system, phrase-ahead reordering model improves the results of the two test sets by 0.41% and 1.87% in BLEU respectively. The difference in the performance gains can be attributed to the fact that there are 100 Chinese special interrogative sentences in Test 2, while only 30 are found in Test 1. Accordingly, the reordering candidates of Test 1 are much fewer than that of Test 2. Thus, we can conclude that the more special interrogative sentences the better performance of the translation. Furthermore, the results show that the reordering on special interrogative sentences is a good try.

The second experiment is conducted to test the effect of phrase-back reordering model. Table 8 gives the results. For the two test sets, the model brings an improvement to the baseline by 2.24% and 0.93% in BLEU respectively. However, the difference between them is still very big. We think there are two reasons: firstly, there are much more special interrogative sentences in Test 2 than in Test 1, so the sentences of other sentence types in Test 2 are much fewer than that in Test 1. Thus, fewer candidates are found in Test 2 than in Test 1. Secondly, the average sentence length of Test 2 (6.5 words) is much shorter than that of Test 1 (13.2 words). We know that if the sentence is very short, the PP, TP, and SP will seldom occur. Naturally, only 89 candidates are found in Test 2 but 366 in Test 1. Regardless of the difference, the phrase-back reordering model indeed improves the translation quality significantly.

The last experiment merges the two reordering model together. The results in Table 8 show that the overall reordering model has done very well in both test sets: it improves the two test sets by 2.65% and 2.78% in BLEU score respectively. It demonstrates that every reordering model has a positive effect on translation. Therefore, our reordering model based on the sentence type is quite successful.

5 Conclusions and Future Work

In this paper, we have investigated the effect of the Chinese sentence types on reordering problem for Chinese-to-English statistical machine translation. We have succeeded in applying a phrase-ahead reordering model to process the special interrogative sentences and a phrase-back reordering model to deal with other sentence types. Experiments show that our reordering model obtains a significant improvement in BLEU score on the IWSLT-07 task.

With the encouraging experimental results, we believe that we can mine more reordering information from the Chinese sentence types. In this paper, we only apply a phrase-back model to reorder Chinese other interrogative sentences. In the next step, we will try to develop a special reordering model for this sentence type. Furthermore, we plan to integrate the phrase-back model into phrase-ahead model for special interrogative sentences and investigate the value of this integration.

[8] See http://www.nlp.org.cn

[9] See http://www.speech.sri.com/projects/srilm

		BLEU (%)	NIST	Sentences	Candidates
Test 1 CE_dev5	Baseline	32.16	6.4844	500	
	Phrase-ahead reordering	32.57	6.5579	30	31
	Phrase-back reordering	34.40	6.6857	470	366
	Phrase-ahead+phrase-back	34.81	6.7584	500	397
Test 2 CE_test	Baseline	34.04	5.8340	489	
	Phrase-ahead reordering	35.91	6.0693	100	97
	Phrase-back reordering	34.97	5.9172	389	89
	Phrase-ahead+phrase-back	36.82	6.1535	489	186

Table 8. Statistics of translation results

Notes: candidates here mean how many candidate reordering phrases are recognized for each model. Sentences mean the number of sentences belonging to the specific sentence type, i.e. for phrase-ahead reordering in Test 1, 31 special question phrases (SQP) are recognized in 30 Chinese special interrogative sentences.

Acknowledgments

The research work described in this paper has been partially supported by the Natural Science Foundation of China under Grant No. 60575043 and 60736014, the National High-Tech Research and Development Program (863 Program) of China under Grant No. 2006AA01Z194 and 2006AA010108, the National Key Technologies R&D Program of China under Grant No. 2006BAH03B02, and Nokia (China) Co. Ltd as well.

References

Cao Wang, Michael Collins and Philipp Koehn. 2007. Chinese syntactic reordering for statistical machine translation. *In Proceedings of joint Conference on Empirical Methods in Natural Language Processing and Computational Natural Language Learning, 2007.*

Chi-Ho Li, Dongdong Zhang, Mu Li, Ming Zhou Minghui Li and Yi Guan. 2007. A probabilistic approach to syntax-based reordering for statistical machine translation. *In Proceedings of 45th Meeting of the Association for Computational Linguistics .*

Dan Klein and Christopher D. manning. 2003. Accurate unlexicalized parsing. *In Proceedings of 41st Meeting of the Association for Computational Linguistics.*

David Chiang. 2005. A hierarchical phrase-based model for statistical machine translation. *In Proceedings of 43rd Meeting of Association for Computational Linguistics.*

Deyi Xiong, Qun Liu and Shouxun Lin. 2006. maximum entropy based phrase reordering model for statistical machine translation. *In Proceedings of the joint conference of the International Committee on Computational Linguistics and the Association for Computational Linguistics 2006.*

Fei Xia and Michael McCord. 2004. Improving a Statistical MT system with automatically learned rewrite patterns. *In Proceedings of 20th International Conference on Computational Linguistics.*

Franz Josef Och and Hermann Ney. 2002. Discriminative training and maximum entropy models for statistical machine translation. *In Proceedings of 40th Meeting of Association for Computational Linguistics.*

Franz Josef Och and Hermann Ney. 2004. The alignment template approach to statistical machine translation. *Computational Linguistics, 30:417-449*

Marta R. Costa-jussa and Jose A.R. Fonollosa. 2006. Statistical machine reordering. *In proceedings of Conference on Empirical Methods in Natural Language Processing 2006.*

Michael Collins, Philipp Koehn, and Ivona Kucerova. 2005. Clause restructuring for statistical machine translation. *In proceedings of 43rd Meeting of the Association for Computational Linguistics.*

Philipp Koehn, Franz J. Och. and Daniel Marcu. 2003. Statistical Phrase-based Translation. *In proceedings of HLT-NAACL 2003.*

Philipp Koehn, Amittai Axelrod, Alexandra Birch Mayne, Chris Callison-Burch, Miles Osborne and David Talbot. 2005. Edinburgn System Description for the 2005 IWSLT Speech Translation Evaluation. *In International Workshp on Spoken Language Translation.*

Yuqi Zhang, Richard Zens and Hermann Ney. 2007. Chunk-level reordering of source language sentence with automatically learned rules for statistical machine translation. *In Proceedings of SSST, NAACL-HLT 2007/AMTA Workshop on Syntax and Structure in Statistical Translation.*

Vladimir Naumovich Vapnik. 1998. Statistical Learning Theory. John Wiley and Sons, Inc.

Grammar Comparison Study for Translational Equivalence Modeling and Statistical Machine Translation

Min Zhang[1], Hongfei Jiang[2], Haizhou Li[1], Aiti Aw[1] and Sheng Li[2]
[1]Institute for Infocomm Research, Singapore
[2]Harbin Institute of Technology, China
{mzhang, hli, aaiti}@i2r.a-star.edu.sg
{hfjiang, lisheng}@mtlab.hit.edu.cn

Abstract

This paper presents a general platform, namely synchronous tree sequence substitution grammar (STSSG), for the grammar comparison study in Translational Equivalence Modeling (TEM) and Statistical Machine Translation (SMT). Under the STSSG platform, we compare the expressive abilities of various grammars through synchronous parsing and a real translation platform on a variety of Chinese-English bilingual corpora. Experimental results show that the STSSG is able to better explain the data in parallel corpora than other grammars. Our study further finds that the complexity of structure divergence is much higher than suggested in literature, which imposes a big challenge to syntactic transformation-based SMT.

1 Introduction

Translational equivalence is a mathematical relation that holds between linguistic expressions with the same meaning (Wellington et al., 2006). The common explicit representations of this relation are word alignments, phrase alignments and structure alignments between bilingual sentences. Translational Equivalence Modeling (TEM) is a process to describe and build these alignments using mathematical models. Thus, the study of TEM is highly relevant to Statistical Machine Translation (SMT).

Grammar is the most important infrastructure for TEM and SMT since translation models' expressive and generative abilities are mainly determined by the grammar. Many grammars, such as finite-state grammars (FSG), bracket/inversion transduction grammars (BTG/ITG) (Wu, 1997), context-free grammar (CFG), tree substitution grammar (TSG) (Comon et al., 2007) and their synchronous versions, have been explored in SMT. Based on these grammars, a great number of SMT models have been recently proposed, including string-to-string model (Synchronous FSG) (Brown et al., 1993; Koehn et al., 2003), tree-to-string model (TSG-string) (Huang et al., 2006; Liu et al., 2006; Liu et al., 2007), string-to-tree model (string-CFG/TSG) (Yamada and Knight, 2001; Galley et al., 2006; Marcu et al., 2006), tree-to-tree model (Synchronous CFG/TSG, Data-Oriented Translation) (Chiang, 2005; Cowan et al., 2006; Eisner, 2003; Ding and Palmer, 2005; Zhang et al., 2007; Bod, 2007; Quirk wt al., 2005; Poutsma, 2000; Hearne and Way, 2003) and so on.

Although many achievements have been obtained by these advances, it is still unclear which of these important pursuits is able to best explain human translation data, as each has its advantages and disadvantages. Therefore, it has great meaning in both theory and practice to do comparison studies among these grammars and SMT models to see which of them are capable of better describing parallel translation data. This is a fundamental issue worth exploring in multilingual information processing. However, little effort in previous work has been put in this point. To address this issue, in this paper we define a general platform, namely synchronous tree sequence substitution grammar (STSSG), for the comparison studies. The STSSG can be seen as a generalization of Synchronous TSG (STSG) by replacing elementary tree (a single subtree used in STSG) with contiguous tree sequence as the basic translation unit. As a result, most of previous grammars used in SMT can be interpreted as the reduced versions of the STSSG. Under the STSSG platform, we compare the expressive

© 2008. Licensed under the *Creative Commons Attribution-Noncommercial-Share Alike 3.0 Unported* license (http://creativecommons.org/licenses/by-nc-sa/3.0/). Some rights reserved.

abilities of various grammars and translation models through linguistically-based synchronous parsing and a real translation platform. By synchronous parsing, we aim to study which grammar can well explain translation data (i.e. translational equivalence alignment) while by the real translation platform, we expect to investigate which model can achieve better translation performance. In addition, we also measure the impact of various factors in this study, including the genera of corpora (newspaper domain via spoken domain), the accuracy of word alignments and syntax parsing (automatically vs. manually).

We report our experimental settings, experimental results and our findings in detail in the rest of the paper, which is organized as follows: Section 2 reviews previous work. Section 3 elaborates the general framework while Section 4 reports the experimental results. Finally, we conclude our work in Section 5.

2 Previous Work

There are only a few of previous work related to the study of translation grammar comparison.

Fox (2002) is the first to look at how well proposed translation models fit actual translation data empirically. She examined the issue of phrasal cohesion between English and French and discovered that while there is less cohesion than one might desire, there is still a large amount of regularity in the constructions where breakdowns occur. This suggests that reordering words by phrasal movement is a reasonable strategy (Fox, 2002). She has also examined the differences in cohesion between Treebank-style parse trees, trees with flattened verb phrases, and dependency structures. Their experimental results indicate that the highest degree of cohesion is present in dependency structures.

Motivated by the same problem raised by Fox (2002), Galley et al. (2004) study what rule can better explain human translation data. They first propose a theory that gives formal semantics to word-level alignments defined over parallel corpora, and then use the theory to introduce a linear algorithm that is used to derive from word-aligned, parallel corpora the minimal set of syntactically motivated transformation rules to explain human translation data. Their basic idea is to create transformation rules that condition on larger fragments of tree structure. Their experimental results suggest that their proposed rules provide a good, realistic indicator of the complexities inherent in translation than SCFG.

Wellington et al. (2006) describes their study of the patterns of translational equivalence exhibited by a variety of bilingual/monolingual bitexts. They empirically measure the lower bounds on alignment failure rates with and without gaps under the constraints of word alignment alone or with one or both side parse trees. Their study finds surprisingly many examples of translational equivalence that could not be analyzed using binary-branching structures without discontinuities. Thus, they claim that the complexity of these patterns in every bitext is higher than suggested in the literature. In addition, they suggest that the low coverage rates without gaps under the constraints of independently generated monolingual parse trees might be the main reason why "syntactic" constraints have not yet increased the accuracy of SMT systems. However, they find that simply allowing a single gap in bilingual phrases or other types of constituent can improve coverage dramatically.

DeNeefe et al. (2007) compares the strengths and weaknesses of a syntax-based MT model with a phrase-based MT model from the viewpoints of translational equivalence extraction methods and coverage. They find that there are surprising differences in phrasal coverage – neither is merely a superset of the other. They also investigate the reason why some phrase pairs are not learned by the syntax-based model. They further propose several solutions and evaluate on the syntax-based extraction techniques in light of phrase pairs captured and translation accuracy. Finally, significant performance improvement is reported using their solutions.

Different from previous work discussed above, this paper mainly focuses on the expressive ability comparison studies among different grammars and models through synchronous parsing and a real SMT platform. Fox (2002), Galley et al (2004) and Wellington et al. (2006) examine TEM only. DeNeefe et al. (2007) only compares the strengths and weaknesses of a syntax-based MT model with a phrase-based MT model.

3 The General Platform: the STSSG

In this section, we first define the STSSG platform in Subsection 3.1, and then explain why it is a general framework that can cover most of previous syntax-based translation grammars and models in Subsection 3.2. In Subsection 3.3 and 3.4, we discuss the STSSG-based SMT and synchronous parsing, which are used to compare different grammars and translation models.

3.1 Definition of the STSSG

The STSSG is an extension of the STSG by using tree sequences (rather than elementary trees) as the basic translation unit. A STSSG is a septet $G = < \Sigma_s, \Sigma_t, N_s, N_t, S_s, S_t, P >$, where:

- Σ_s and Σ_t are source and target terminal alphabets (POSs or lexical words), respectively, and
- N_s and N_t are source and target non-terminal alphabets (linguistic phrase tag, i.e. NP/VP…), respectively, and
- $S_s \in N_s$ and $S_t \in N_t$ are the source and target start symbols (roots of source and target parse trees), and
- P is a production rule set.

A grammar rule r_i in the STSSG is an aligned tree sequence pair, $< \xi_s, \xi_t, \tilde{A} >$, where ξ_s and ξ_t are tree sequences of source side and target sides, respectively, and $\tilde{A}$ is the alignments between leaf nodes of two tree sequences. Here, the key concept of "tree sequence" refers to an ordered subtree sequence covering a consecutive tree fragment in a complete parse tree. The leaf nodes of a subtree in a tree sequence can be either non-terminal symbols or terminal symbols. Fig. 2 shows two STSSG rules extracted from the aligned tree pair shown in Fig. 1, where r_1 is also a STSG rule.

In the STSSG, a translational equivalence is modeled as a tree sequence pair while MT is viewed as a tree sequence substitution process. From the definition of "tree sequence", we can see that a subtree in a tree sequence is a so-called elementary tree used in TSG. This suggests that SCFG and STSG are only a subset of STSSG and SCFG is a subset of STSG. The next subsection discusses how to configure the STSSG to implement the other two simplified grammars. This is the reason why we call the STSSG a general framework for synchronous grammar-based translation modeling.

It is worth noting that, from rule rewriting viewpoint, STSSG can be thought of as a restricted version of synchronous multi-component TAGs (Schuler et al., 2000) although TAG is more powerful than TSG due to the additional operation "adjunctions". The synchronous multi-component TAG can also rewrite several non-terminals in one step of derivation. The difference between them is that the rewriting sites (i.e. the substitution nodes) must be contiguous in STSSG. In addition, STSSG is also related to tree automata (Comon et al., 2007). However, the discussion on the theoretical relation and comparison between them is out of the scope of the paper. In this paper, we focus on the comparison study of SMT grammars using the STSSG platform.

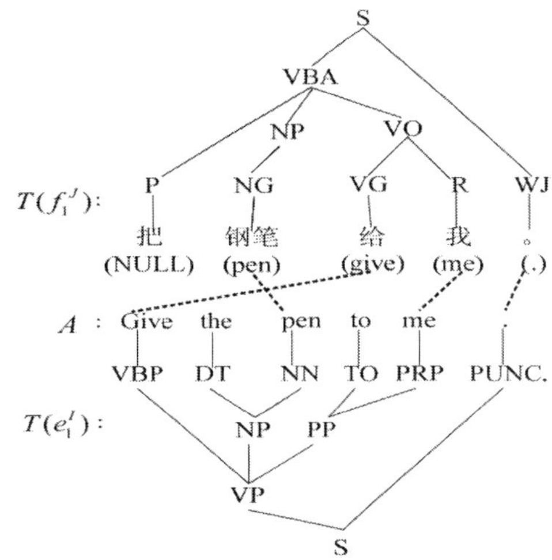

Figure 1. A word-aligned parse tree pairs of a Chinese sentence and its English translation

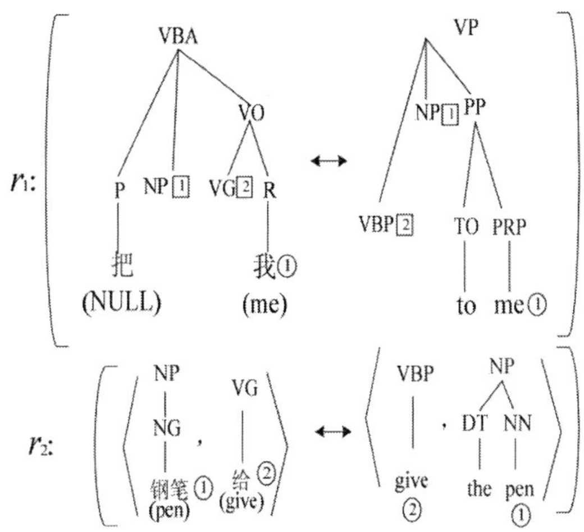

Figure 2. Two examples of translation rules

3.2 Rule Extraction and Grammar Configuration

All the STSSG mapping rules are extracted from bi-parsed trees. Our rule extraction algorithm is an extension of that presented at (Chiang, 2005; Liu et al., 2006; Zhang et al., 2007). We modify their tree-to-tree/string rule extraction algorithms to extract tree-sequence-to-tree-sequence rules. Our rules[2] are extracted in two steps:

[2] We classify the rules into two categories: *initial rules*, whose leaf nodes must be terminals, and *ab-*

1) Extracting *initial rules* from bi-parsed trees. This is rather straightforward. We first generate all fully lexicalized source and target tree sequences (whose leaf nodes must be lexical words) using a DP algorithm and then iterate over all generated source and target sequence pairs. If their word alignments are all within the scope of the current tree sequence pair, then the current tree sequence pair is an *initial rule*.

2) Extracting *abstract rules* from the extracted *initial rules*. The idea behind is that we generate an *abstract rule* from a "big" *initial rule* by removing one or more "small" *initial rules* from the "big" one, where the "small" ones must be a sub-graph of the "big" one. Please refer to (Chiang, 2005; Liu et al., 2006; Zhang et al., 2007) for the implementation details.

As indicated before (Chiang, 2005; Zhang et al., 2007), the above scheme generates a very large number of rules, which not only makes the system too complicated but also introduces too many undesirable ambiguities. To control the overall model complexity, we introduce the following parameters:

1) The maximal numbers of trees in the source and target tree sequences: α_s and α_t.

2) The maximal tree heights in the source and target tree sequences: β_s and β_t.

3) The maximal numbers of non-terminal leaf nodes in the source and target tree sequences: γ_s and γ_t.

Now let us see how to implement other models in relation to STSSG based the STSSG through configuring the above parameters.

1) STSG-based tree-to-tree model (Zhang et al., 2007; Bod, 2007) when $\alpha_s = \alpha_t = 1$.

2) SCFG-based tree-to-tree model when $\alpha_s = \alpha_t = 1$ and $\beta_s = \beta_t = 2$.

3) Phrase-based translation model only (no reordering model) when $\gamma_s = \gamma_t = 0$ and $\beta_s = \beta_t = 1$.

4) TSG-CFG-based tree-to-string model (Liu et al., 2006) when $\alpha_s = \alpha_t = 1$, $\beta_t = 2$ and ignore phrase tags in target side.

5) CFG-TSG-based string-to-tree model (Galley et al., 2006) when $\alpha_s = \alpha_t = 1$ and $\beta_s = 2$.

6) TSSG-CFG-based tree-sequence-to-string model (Liu et al., 2007) when $\beta_t = 2$ and ignore phrase tags in target side.

stract rule that having at least one non-terminal leaf node.

From the above definitions, we can see that all of previous related models/grammars can be can be interpreted as the reduced versions of the STSSG. This is the reason why we use the STSSG as a general platform for our model and grammar comparison studies.

3.3 Model Training and Decoder for SMT

We use the tree sequence mapping rules to model the translation process. Given the source parse tree $T(f_1^J)$, there are multiple derivations[3] that could lead to the same target tree $T(e_1^I)$, the mapping probability $Pr(T(e_1^I) \mid T(f_1^J))$ is obtained by summing over the probabilities of all derivations. The probability of each derivation θ is given by the product of the probabilities of all the rules $p(r_i)$ used in the derivation (here we assume that a rule is applied *independently* in a derivation).

$$\begin{aligned} Pr(e_1^I \mid f_1^J) &= Pr(T(e_1^I) \mid T(f_1^J)) \\ &= \sum_{\theta} \prod_{r_i \in \theta} p(r_i) \end{aligned} \quad (1)$$

The model is implemented under log-linear framework. We use seven basic features that are analogous to the commonly used features in phrase-based systems (Koehn, 2004): 1) bidirectional rule mapping probabilities; 2) bidirectional lexical translation probabilities; 3) the target language model; 4) the number of rules used and 5) the number of target words. Besides, we define two new features: 1) the number of lexical words in a rule to control the model's preference for lexicalized rules over un-lexicalized rules and 2) the average tree height in a rule to balance the usage of hierarchical rules and more flat rules. The overall training process is similar to the process in the phrase-based system (koehn et al., 2007): word alignment, rule extraction, feature extraction and probability calculation and feature weight tuning.

Given $T(f_1^J)$, the decoder is to find the best derivation θ that generates $< T(f_1^J), T(e_1^I) >$.

$$\begin{aligned} \hat{e} &= \arg\max_{e_1^I} Pr(T(e_1^I) \mid T(f_1^J)) \\ &\approx \arg\max_{e_1^I, \theta} \prod_{r_i \in \theta} p(r_i) \end{aligned} \quad (2)$$

By default, same as other SMT decoder, here we use Viterbi derivation in Eq (2) instead of the

[3] A derivation is a sequence of tree sequence rules that maps a source parse tree to its target one.

summing probabilities in Eq (3). This is to make the decoder speed not too slow. The decoder is a standard span-based chart parser together with a function for mapping the source derivations to the target ones. To speed up the decoder, we utilize several thresholds to limit the search beams for each span, such as the number of rules used and the number of hypotheses generated.

3.4 Synchronous Parsing

A synchronous parser is an algorithm that can infer the syntactic structure of each component text in a multitext and simultaneously infer the correspondence relation between these structures. When a parser's input can have fewer dimensions than the parser's grammar, we call it a translator. When a parser's grammar can have fewer dimensions than the parser's input, we call it a synchronizer (Melamed, 2004). Therefore, synchronous parsing and MT are closed to each other. In this paper, we use synchronous parsing to compare the ability of different grammars in translational equivalence modeling.

Given a bilingual sentence pair f_1^J and e_1^I, the synchronous parser is to find a derivation θ that generates $< T(f_1^J), T(e_1^I) >$. Our synchronous parser is similar to the synchronous CKY parser presented at (Melamed, 2004). The difference is that we implement it based on our STSSG decoder. Therefore, in nature the parser is a standard synchronous chart parser but constrained by the rules of the STSSG grammar. In our implementation, we simply use our decoder to simulate the bilingual parser: 1) for each sentence pair, we extract one model; 2) we use the model and the decoder to translate the source sentence of the given sentence pair; 3) if the target sentence is successfully generated by the decoder, then we say the symphonious parsing is successful. Please note that the synchronous parsing is considered as successful once the last words in the source and target sentences are covered by the decoder even if there is no a complete target parse tree generated (it may be a tree sequence). This is because our study only concerns whether all translational equivalences are linked together by the synchronous parser correctly.

4 Experiments

4.1 Experimental Settings

Synchronous parsing settings: Our experiments of synchronous parsing are carried on three Chinese-to-English bilingual corpora: the FBIS corpus, the IWSLT 2007 training set and the HIT Corpus. The FBIS data is a collection of translated newswire documents published by major news agencies from three representative locations: Beijing, Taipei and Hongkong. The IWSLT data is a multilingual speech corpus on travel domain while the HIT corpus consists of example sentences of a Chinese-English dictionary. The first two corpora are sentence-aligned while the HIT corpus is a manually bi-parsed corpus with manually annotated word alignments. We use the three corpora to study whether the models' expressive abilities are domain dependent and how the performance of word alignment and parsing affect the ability of translation models. We selected 2000 sentence pairs from each individual corpus for the comparison study of translational equivalence modeling. Table 1 gives descriptive statistics of the tree data set.

	Chinese	English
FBIS	48,331	59,788
IWSLT	17,667	18,427
HIT	18,215	20,266

Table 1. # of words of experimental data for synchronous parsing (there are 2k sentence pairs in each individual corpus)

In the synchronous parsing experiments, we compared three synchronous grammars: SCFG, STSG and STSSG using the STSSG platform. We use the same settings except the following parameters (please refer to Subsection 3.2 for their definitions): $\alpha_s = \alpha_t = 1$, $\beta_s = \beta_t = 2$ for SCFG ; $\alpha_s = \alpha_t = 1$ and $\beta_s = \beta_t = 6$ for STSG; $\alpha_s = \alpha_t = 4$ and $\beta_s = \beta_t = 6$ for STSSG. We iterate over each sentence pair in the three corpora with the following process:

1) to used Stanford parser (Klein and Manning, 2003) to parse bilingual sentences separately, this means that our study is based on the Penn Treebank style grammar.

2) to extract SCFG, STSG and STSSG rules form each sentence pair, respectively;

3) to do synchronous parsing using the exacted rules.

Finally, we can calculate the successful rate of the synchronous parsing on each corpus.

SMT evaluation settings: For the SMT experiments, we trained the translation model on the FBIS corpus (7.2M (Chinese)+9.2M(English) words) and trained a 4-gram language model on the Xinhua portion of the English Gigaword corpus (181M words) using the SRILM Toolkits (Stolcke, 2002) with modified Kneser-Ney smoothing (Chen and Goodman, 1998). We used these sentences with less than 50 characters from the NIST MT-2002 test set as our development set and the NIST MT-2005 test set as our test set. We used the Stanford parser (Klein and Manning, 2003) to parse bilingual sentences on the training set and Chinese sentences on the development and test sets. The evaluation metric is case-sensitive BLEU-4 (Papineni et al., 2002). We used GIZA++ and the heuristics "grow-diag-final" to generate m-to-n word alignments. For the MER training, we modified Koehn's MER trainer (Koehn, 2004) for our STSSG-based system. For significance test, we used Zhang et al's implementation (Zhang et al, 2004). We compared four SMT systems: Moses (Koehn et al., 2007), SCFG-based, STSG-based and STSSG-based tree-to-tree translation models. For Moses, we used its default settings. For the others, we implemented them on the STSSG platform by adopting the same settings as used in the synchronous parsing. We optimized the decoding parameters on the development sets empirically.

4.2 Experimental Results

	SCFG	STSG	STSSG
FBIS	7 (0.35%)	143 (7.15%)	388 (19.4%)
IWSLT	171 (8.6%)	1179 (58.9%)	1708 (85.4%)
HIT	65 (3.23%)	1133 (56.6%)	1532 (76.6%)

Table 2. Successful rates (numbers inside bracket) of synchronous parsing over 2,000 sentence pairs, where the integers outside bracket are the numbers of successfully-parsed sentence pairs

Table 2 reports the experimental results of synchronous parsing. It shows that:

1) As an extension of STSG/SCFG, STSSG outperforms STSG and SCFG consistently in the three data sets. The significant difference suggests that the STSSG is much more effective in modeling translational equivalences and structure divergences. The reason is simply because the STSSG uses tree sequences as the basic translation unit so that it can model non-syntactic phrase equivalence with structure information and handle structure reordering in a large span.

2) STSG shows much better performance than SCFG. It is mainly due to that STSG allow multiple level tree nodes operation and reordering in a larger span than SCFG. It reconfirms that only allowing sibling nodes reordering as done in SCFG may be inadequate for translational equivalence modeling (Galley et al., 2004)[4].

3) All the three models on the FBIS corpus show much lower performance than that on the other two corpora. The main reason, as shown in Table 1, is that the sentences in the FBIS corpus are much longer than that in the other corpus, so their syntactic structures are significantly more complicated than the other two. In addition, although tree sequences are utilized, STSSG show much lower performance in the FBIS corpus. This implies that the complexity of structure divergence between two languages is higher than suggested in literature (Fox, 2002; Galley et al., 2004). Therefore, structure divergence is still a big challenge to translational equivalence modeling when using syntactic structure mapping.

4) The HIT corpus does not show better performance than the IWSLT corpus although the HIT corpus is manually annotated with parse trees and word alignments. In order to study whether high performance word alignment and parsing results can help synchronous parsing, we do several cross validations and report the experimental results in Table 3.

	Gold Word Alignment	Automatic Word Alignment
Gold Parse	3.2/56.6/76.6	2.9/57.7/80.9
Automatic Parse	3.2/55.6/76.0	2.9/54.2/78.8

Table 3. Successful rates (SCFG/STSG/STSSG)(%) with regards to different word alignments and parse trees on the HIT corpus

Table 3 compares the performance of synchronous parsing on the HIT corpus when using gold and automatic parser and word alignment. It is surprised that gold word alignments and parse trees do not help and even decrease the performance slightly. Our analysis further finds that

[4] This claim is mainly hold for linguistically-informed SCFG since formal SCFG and BTG already showed much better performance in the formally syntax-based translation framework (Chiang, 2005). This is because the formal syntax is learned from phrase translational equivalences directly without relying on any linguistic theory (Chiang, 2005). Thus, it may not suffer from the issues of non-isomorphic structure alignment and non-syntactic phrase usage heavily (Wellington et al., 2006).

more than 90% sentence pairs out of all the sentence pairs that can be successfully bi-parsed are in common in the four experiments. This suggests that the STSSG/STSG (SCFG achieves too much lower performance) and our rule extraction algorithm are robust in dealing with the errors introduced by the word alignment and parsing programs. If a parser, for example, makes a systematic error, we expect to learn a rule that can nevertheless be systematically used to model correct translational equivalence. Our error analysis on the three corpora shows that most of the failures of synchronous parsing are due to the structure divergence (i.e. the nature of non-isomorphic structure mapping) and the long distance dependence in the syntactic structures.

	SCFG	Moses	STSG	STSSG
BLEU(%)	22.72	23.86	24.71	26.07

Table 3. Performance comparison of different grammars on FBIS corpus

Table 3 compares different grammars in terms of translation performance. It shows that:

1) The same as synchronous parsing, the STSSG-based model statistically significantly outperforms ($p < 0.01$) previous phrase-based and linguistically syntax-based methods. This empirically verifies the effect of the tree-sequence-based grammar for statistical machine translation.

2) Both STSSG and STSG outperform Moses significantly and STSSG clearly outperforms STSG, which suggest that:

- The linguistically motivated structure features are still useful for SMT, which can be captured by the two syntax-based grammars through tree node operations.
- STSSG is much more effective in utilizing linguistic structures than STSG since it uses tree sequence as the basic translation unit. This enables STSSG not only to handle structure reorderings by tree node operations in a larger span, but also to capture non-syntactic phrases with syntactic information, and hence giving the grammar more expressive power.

3) The linguistic-based SCFG shows much lower performance. This is largely because SCFG only allows sibling nodes reordering and fails to utilize both non-syntactic phrases and those syntactic phrases that cannot be covered by a single CFG rule. It thereby suggests that SCFG is less effective in modelling parse tree structure transfer.

The above two experimental results show that STSSG achieves significant improvements over the other two grammars in terms of synchronous parsing's successful rate and translation Bleu score.

5 Conclusions

Grammar is the fundamental infrastructure in translational equivalence modeling and statistical machine translation since grammar formalizes what kind of rule to be learned from a parallel text. In this paper, we first present a general platform STSSG and demonstrate that a number of synchronous grammars and SMT models can be easily implemented based on the platform. We then compare the expressive abilities of different grammars on the platform using synchronous parsing and statistical machine translation. Our experimental results show that STSSG can better explain the data in parallel corpora than the other two synchronous grammars. We further finds that, although syntactic structure features are helpful in modeling translational equivalence, the complexity of structure divergence is much higher than suggested in literature, which imposes a big challenge to syntactic transformation-based SMT. This may explain why traditional syntactic constraints in SMT do not yield much performance improvement over robust phrase-substitution models.

The fundamental assumption underlying much recent work on syntax-based modeling, which is considered to be one of next technology breakthroughs in SMT, is that translational equivalence can be well modeled by structural transformation. However, as discussed in prior arts (Galley et al., 2004) and this paper, linguistically-informed SCFG is an inadequate model for parallel corpora due to its nature that only allowing child-node reorderings. Although STSG shows much better performance than SCFG, its two major limitations are that it only allows structure distortion operated on a single sub-tree and cannot model non-syntactic phrases. STSSG extends STSG by using tree sequence as the basic translation unit. This gives the grammar much more expressive power.

There are many open issues in the syntactic transformation-based SMT due to the divergence nature between bilingual structure mappings. We find that structural divergences are more serious than suggested in the literature (Fox, 2002; Gallery et al., 2004) or what we expected when sentences are longer. We will continue to investigate whether and how parallel corpora can be well modeled by syntactic structure mappings.

References

Rens Bod. 2007. *Unsupervised Syntax-Based Machine Translation: The Contribution of Discontinuous Phrases.* MT-Summmit-07. 51-56.

Peter F. Brown, S. A. Della Pietra, V. J. Della Pietra, and R. L. Mercer. 1993. *The mathematics of machine translation: Parameter estimation*. Computational Linguistics, 19(2):263–311.

S. F. Chen and J. Goodman. 1998. *An empirical study of smoothing techniques for language modeling*. Technical Report TR-10-98, Harvard University Center for Research in Computing Technology.

David Chiang. 2005. *A hierarchical phrase-based model for SMT*. ACL-05. 263-270.

H. Comon, M. Dauchet, R. Gilleron, F. Jacquemard, D. Lugiez, S. Tison, and M. Tommasi. 2007. Tree automata techniques and applications. Available at: http://tata.gforge.inria.fr/.

Brooke Cowan, Ivona Kucerova and Michael Collins. 2006. *A discriminative model for tree-to-tree translation*. EMNLP-06. 232-241.

S. DeNeefe, K. Knight, W. Wang and D. Marcu. 2007. *What Can Syntax-based MT Learn from Phrase-based MT?* EMNLP-CoNLL-07. 755-763

Yuan Ding and Martha Palmer. 2005. *Machine translation using probabilistic synchronous dependency insertion grammars*. ACL-05. 541-548.

Bonnie J. Dorr (1994). *Machine Translation Divergences: A formal description and proposed solution*. Computational Linguistics, 20(4): 597-633

Jason Eisner. 2003. *Learning non-isomorphic tree mappings for MT*. ACL-03 (companion volume).

Heidi J. Fox. 2002. *Phrasal Cohesion and Statistical Machine Translation*. EMNLP-2002. 304-311

Michel Galley, J. Graehl, K. Knight, D. Marcu, S. DeNeefe, W. Wang and I. Thayer. 2006. *Scalable Inference and Training of Context-Rich Syntactic Translation Models.* COLING-ACL-06. 961-968

M. Galley, M. Hopkins, K. Knight and D. Marcu. 2004. *What's in a translation rule?* HLT-NAACL.

Liang Huang, Kevin Knight and Aravind Joshi. 2006. *Statistical Syntax-Directed Translation with Extended Domain of Locality*. AMTA-06 (poster).

Mary Hearne and Andy Way. 2003. *Seeing the wood for the trees: data-oriented translation.* MT Summit IX, 165-172.

Dan Klein and Christopher D. Manning. 2003. *Accurate Unlexicalized Parsing*. ACL-03. 423-430.

Philipp Koehn, F. J. Och and D. Marcu. 2003. *Statistical phrase-based translation.* HLT-NAACL-03. 127-133.

Philipp Koehn. 2004. *Pharaoh: a beam search decoder for phrase-based statistical machine translation models.* AMTA-04, 115-124.

Philipp Koehn, H. Hoang, A. Birch, C. Callison-Burch, M. Federico, N. Bertoldi, B. Cowan, W. Shen, C. Moran, R. Zens, C. Dyer, O. Bojar, A. Constantin and E. Herbst. 2007. *Moses: Open Source Toolkit for Statistical Machine Translation.* ACL-07 (poster) 77-180.

Yang Liu, Qun Liu and Shouxun Lin. 2006. *Tree-to-String Alignment Template for Statistical Machine Translation*. COLING-ACL-06. 609-616.

Yang Liu, Yun Huang, Qun Liu and Shouxun Lin. 2007. *Forest-to-String Statistical Translation Rules*. ACL-07. 704-711.

Daniel Marcu, W. Wang, A. Echihabi and K. Knight. 2006. *SPMT: Statistical Machine Translation with Syntactified Target Language Phrases*. EMNLP-06. 44-52.

I. Dan Melamed. 2004. *Statistical machine translation by parsing*. ACL-04. 653-660.

K. Papineni, Salim Roukos, ToddWard and Wei-Jing Zhu. 2002. *BLEU: a method for automatic evaluation of machine translation*. ACL-02. 311-318.

Arjen Poutsma. 2000. *Data-oriented translation. COLING-2000*. 635-641

Chris Quirk, Arul Menezes and Colin Cherry. 2005. *Dependency treelet translation: Syntactically informed phrasal SMT*. ACL-05. 271-279.

William Schuler, David Chiang and Mark Dras. 2000. *Multi-Component TAG and Notions of Formal Power*. ACL-2000. 448-455

Andreas Stolcke. 2002. *SRILM - an extensible language modeling toolkit*. ICSLP-02. 901-904.

Benjamin Wellington, Sonjia Waxmonsky and I. Dan Melamed. 2006. *Empirical Lower Bounds on the Complexity of Translational Equivalence*. COLING-ACL-06. 977-984.

Dekai Wu. 1997. *Stochastic inversion transduction grammars and bilingual parsing of parallel corpora*. Computational Linguistics, 23(3):377-403.

K. Yamada and Kevin Knight. 2001. *A syntax-based statistical translation model*. ACL-01. 523-530.

M. Zhang, H. Jiang, A. Aw, J. Sun, S. Li and C. Tan. 2007. *A Tree-to-Tree Alignment-based Model for SMT*. MT-Summit-07. 535-542.

Y. Zhang, S. Vogel and A. Waibel. 2004. Interpreting BLEU/NIST scores: How much improvement do we need to have a better system? LREC-04.

Automatic Generation of Parallel Treebanks

Ventsislav Zhechev
NCLT, School of Computing
Dublin City University
Dublin, Ireland
vzhechev@computing.dcu.ie

Andy Way
NCLT, School of Computing
Dublin City University
Dublin, Ireland
away@computing.dcu.ie

Abstract

The need for syntactically annotated data for use in natural language processing has increased dramatically in recent years. This is true especially for parallel treebanks, of which very few exist. The ones that exist are mainly hand-crafted and too small for reliable use in data-oriented applications. In this paper we introduce a novel platform for fast and robust automatic generation of parallel treebanks. The software we have developed based on this platform has been shown to handle large data sets. We also present evaluation results demonstrating the quality of the derived treebanks and discuss some possible modifications and improvements that can lead to even better results. We expect the presented platform to help boost research in the field of data-oriented machine translation and lead to advancements in other fields where parallel treebanks can be employed.

1 Introduction

In recent years much effort has been made to make use of syntactic information in statistical machine translation (MT) systems (Hearne and Way, 2006, Nesson et al., 2006). This has led to increased interest in the development of parallel treebanks as the source for such syntactic data. They consist of a parallel corpus, both sides of which have been parsed and aligned at the sub-tree level.

So far parallel treebanks have been created manually or semi-automatically. This has proven to be a laborious and time-consuming task that is prone to errors and inconsistencies (Samuelsson and Volk, 2007). Because of this, only a few parallel treebanks exist and none are of sufficient size for productive use in any statistical MT application.

In this paper we present a novel platform for the automatic generation of parallel treebanks from parallel corpora and discuss several methods for the evaluation of the results. We discuss algorithms both for cases in which monolingual parsers exist for both languages and for cases in which such parsers are not available. The parallel treebanks created with the methods described in this paper can be used by different statistical MT applications and for translation studies.

We start in section 2 by introducing the techniques for automatic generation of parallel treebanks. The evaluation methods and results are introduced in section 3 and in section 4 we give suggestions for possible improvements to the generation technology and to the evaluation algorithms. Finally, in section 5 we present existing parallel treebanks and conclude in section 6.

2 Automatic Generation of Parallel Treebanks

In this section we introduce a method for the automatic generation of parallel treebanks from parallel corpora. The only tool that is required besides the software presented in this paper is a word alignment tool. Such tools exist and some are freely available (eg. GIZA++ (Och and Ney, 2003)). If monolingual phrase-structure parsers[1] or at least POS taggers exist for both languages, their use for pre-processing the data is highly recommended.

In all cases, a word alignment tool is used to first obtain word-alignment probabilities for the

© 2008. Licensed under the Creative Commons Attribution-Noncommercial-Share Alike 3.0 Unported license (http://creativecommons.org/licenses/by-nc-sa/3.0/). Some rights reserved.

[1] Henceforth, we will use 'parser' to mean 'monolingual phrase-structure parser', unless stated otherwise.

parallel corpus in question for both language directions. We will start with the description of the case in which parsers are available for both languages, as this is the core of the system. The parsers are used to parse both sides of the parallel corpus. The resulting parsed data and word-alignment probability tables are then used as the input to a sub-tree alignment algorithm that introduces links between nodes in corresponding trees according to their translational equivalence scores. The output of the sub-tree aligner is the desired parallel treebank.

If there is no parser available for at least one of the languages, the parallel corpus — together with the word-alignment tables — is fed directly to a modified version of the sub-tree aligner. In this modification of the alignment algorithm, all possible binary phrase-structure trees are hypothesised for each sentence in a sentence pair. Afterwards — during the induction of alignments — only those tree nodes are left intact that take part in the alignments or are necessary for the production of connected trees. Thus, the output is again a parallel treebank with unambiguous phrase-structure trees for each language side.

In the present version of our software, if a parser or a POS tagger exists only for one of the languages in the parallel corpus you want to work with, they cannot be made use of. With the tree-to-tree and string-to-string modules in place, it is a minor task to add a tree-to-string and string-to-tree modules that will allow for the maximum utilisation of any available resources. We plan to start the development and evaluation of these new modules shortly.

We will now look at the currently available alignment algorithms in greater detail, starting with the tree-to-tree alignment and then moving on to the string-to-string case.

2.1 Tree-to-Tree Alignment

First, the tree-to-tree aligner has to follow certain principles to fit in the framework described above:

- Independence with respect to language pair, constituent-labelling scheme and POS tag set. Any language-dependence would require human input to adjust the aligner to a new language pair.
- Preservation of the original tree structures. We regard these structures as accurate encodings of the languages, and any change to them might distort the encoded information.
- Dependence on a minimal number of external resources, so that the aligner can be used even for languages with few available resources.
- The word-level alignments should be guided by links higher up the trees, where more context information is available.

These principles guarantee the usability of the algorithm for any language pair in many different contexts. Additionally, there are a few well-formedness criteria that have to be followed to enforce feasible alignments:

- A node in a tree may only be linked once.
- Descendants / ancestors of a source linked node may only be linked to descendants / ancestors of its target linked counterpart.

Links produced according to these criteria encode enough information to allow the inference of complex translational patterns from a parallel treebank, including some idiosyncratic translational divergences, as discussed in (Hearne et al., 2007). In what follows, a hypothesised alignment is regarded as incompatible with the existing alignments if it violates any of these criteria.

The sub-tree aligner operates on a per sentence-pair basis and each sentence-pair is processed in two stages. First, for each possible hypothetical link between two nodes, a translational equivalence score is calculated. Only the links for which a nonzero score is calculated are stored for further processing. Unary productions from the original trees, if available, are collapsed to single nodes, preserving all labels. Thus the aligner will consider a single node — instead of several nodes — for the same lexical span. This does not reduce the power of the aligner, as the translational equivalence scores are based on the surface strings and not on the tree structures.

During the second stage, the optimal combination of links is selected from among the available nonzero links. The selection can be performed using either a greedy search, or a full search for the best combination.

Translational Equivalence

Given a tree pair $\langle S, T\rangle$ and a hypothesis $\langle s, t\rangle$, we first compute the strings in (1), where $\langle s_i \ldots s_{ix}\rangle$ and $\langle t_j \ldots t_{jy}\rangle$ denote the terminal sequences dominated by s and t respectively, and $\langle S_1 \ldots S_m\rangle$ and $\langle T_1 \ldots T_n\rangle$ denote the terminal sequences dominated by S and T. Here, *inside* are the strings that represent the spans of the nodes being linked and *outside* are the strings that lay outside the spans of those nodes.

inside *outside*

$$(1)\quad s_l = \langle s_i \ldots s_{ix} \rangle \qquad \bar{s}_l = \langle S_1 \ldots s_{i-1} s_{ix+1} \ldots S_m \rangle$$

$$t_l = \langle t_j \ldots t_{jy} \rangle \qquad \bar{t}_l = \langle T_1 \ldots t_{j-1} t_{jy+1} \ldots T_n \rangle$$

$$(2)\quad \gamma(\langle s, t \rangle) = \alpha(s_l | t_l) \cdot \alpha(t_l | s_l) \cdot \alpha(\bar{s}_l | \bar{t}_l) \cdot \alpha(\bar{t}_l | \bar{s}_l)$$

$$(3)\quad \alpha(x|y) = \prod_i^{|x|} \sum_j^{|y|} P(x_i|y_j) \Big/ |y|$$

The score for the given hypothesis $\langle s, t \rangle$ is computed using (2) and (3). According to the formula in (3), the word-alignment probabilities are used to get an average vote by the source tokens for each target token. Then the product of the votes for the target words gives the alignment probability for the two strings. The final translational equivalence score is the product of the alignment probabilities for the inside and outside strings in both language directions as in (2).

Greedy-Search Algorithm

The greedy-search algorithm is very simple. The set of nonzero-scoring links is processed iteratively by linking the highest-scoring hypothesis at each iteration and discarding all hypotheses that are incompatible with it until the set is empty.

Problems arise when there happen to be several hypotheses that share the same highest score. There are two distinct cases that can be observed here: these top-scoring hypotheses may or may not represent incompatible links. If all such hypotheses are compatible, they are all linked at the same time and all remaining unprocessed hypotheses that are incompatible with any of those links are discarded. In case even one among the top-scoring hypotheses is incompatible with the others, these hypotheses are skipped and processed at a later stage.

The sub-tree aligner can be built to use one of two possible skipping strategies, which we will call *skip1* and *skip2*. According to the *skip1* strategy, hypotheses are simply skipped until a score is reached, for which only one hypothesis exists. This hypothesis is then linked and the selection algorithm continues as usual.

The *skip2* strategy is more complex, in that we also keep track of which nodes take part in the skipped hypotheses. Then, when a candidate for linking is found, it is only linked if it does not include any of these nodes. The motivation behind this strategy is that a situation may occur in which a low-scoring hypothesis for a given constituent is selected in the same iteration as higher-scoring hypotheses for the same constituent were skipped, thereby preventing one of the competing higher-scoring hypotheses from being selected and resulting in an undesired link.

Regardless of whether *skip1* or *skip2* is used, sometimes a situation occurs in which the only hypotheses remaining unprocessed are equally likely candidates for linking according to the selection strategy. In such ambiguous cases our decision is not to link anything, rather than make a decision that might be wrong.

During initial testing of the aligner we found that often lexical links would get higher scores than the non-lexical links,[2] which sometimes resulted in poor lexical links preventing the selection of bona fide non-lexical ones. To address this issue, an extension to the selection algorithm was developed, which we call *span1*. When enabled, this extension results in the set of nonzero hypotheses being split in two subsets: one containing all hypotheses for lexical links, and one containing the hypotheses for non-lexical links. Links are then first selected from the second subset, and only when it is exhausted does the selection continue with the lexical one. This division does not affect the discarding of incompatible links after linking; incompatible links are discarded in whichever set they are found.

Full-Search Algorithm

This is a backtracking recursive algorithm that enumerates all possible combinations of non-crossing links. All maximal combinations[3] found during the search are stored for further processing. After the search is complete, the probability mass of each combination is calculated by summing the translational equivalence scores for all the links in the combination. The maximal combination of non-crossing links that has the highest probability mass is selected as the best alignment for the sentence pair.

Often, there are several distinct maximal combinations that share the highest probability mass; for longer sentences this number can rise to several hundred. The disambiguation strategy that we currently employ is to take the largest common subset of all maximal combinations. Another strategy would be to output all possible combinations and mark them as relating to the same sentence pair, thus leaving the disambiguation to the application that uses the resulting parallel treebank.

---

[2] *lexical* are such links, for which at least one of the linked nodes spans over only one word. All other links are *non-lexical*.

[3] A maximal combination of non-crossing links is a combination of links for which any newly added link would be incompatible with at least one of the links already in the combination.

2.2 String-to-String Alignment

The string-to-string aligner can accept as its input plain or POS-tagged data. For a pair of sentences, all possible binary trees are first constructed for each sentence. All nodes in these trees have the same label (X) and are then used as available link targets. In the case of POS-tagged data, the pre-terminal nodes receive the POS tags as labels. Here it is obvious that the number of links will be much higher than for the sub-tree alignment case, so the string-to-string aligner will operate much more slowly.

After all link-hypothesis scores have been calculated, the string-to-string aligner continues with the selection of links in the same manner as the sub-tree aligner, with one extension; after a link has been selected — besides all incompatible links — all binary trees that do not include the linked nodes are discarded with any nonzero hypotheses attached to them. In this way, only those binary trees that are compatible with the selected links remain after the linking process.

In an additional step for the string-to-string aligner, all non-linked nodes (except for the root nodes) are discarded, thus allowing for the construction of unambiguous n-ary trees for the source and target sentences. If necessary, non-linked nodes are left intact to provide supporting structure in the trees.

3 Evaluation and Results

The quality of a parallel treebank depends directly on the quality of the sub-tree alignments that it contains. Because of this, we use the evaluation results mainly as a metric for the improvements in the sub-tree aligner during development. Of course, the evaluation presented in this section also presents an insight into the usability of the parallel treebanks produced using our method.

For the evaluation of the aligner, a battery of intrinsic and extrinsic tests was developed. As a reference for the tests, a hand-crafted parallel treebank was used (HomeCentre (Hearne and Way, 2006)). This treebank consists of 810 English–French sentence pairs. As discussed in section 5, we are not aware of an existing parallel treebank besides the HomeCentre that can be used directly for cross evaluation and comparison to versions automatically generated using the sub-tree aligner.

The word-alignment probabilities required by our system were obtained by running the Moses decoder[4] (Koehn et al., 2007) on the plain sentences from the HomeCentre in both language directions.

We will first describe the intrinsic testing and then go into the details of the extrinsic evaluation.

3.1 Intrinsic Evaluation

The intrinsic evaluation is performed by comparing the links induced by the automatic aligner to the manually annotated links in the HomeCentre treebank. This evaluation can only be performed for the result of the tree-to-tree alignment, as the string-to-string alignment produces different trees. The metrics used for the comparison are precision and recall for all alignments and lexical and non-lexical alignments alone. The results of the evaluation are shown in Table 1.[5]

	all links		lexical links		non-lexical links	
Configurations	precision	recall	precision	recall	precision	recall
skip1	*61,29%*	*77,46%*	*51,06%*	*79,99%*	**80,75%**	*75,69%*
skip2	61,54%	77,50%	51,29%	80,03%	**80,75%**	75,70%
skip1_span1	61,56%	78,44%	51,53%	80,51%	*78,67%*	**77,22%**
skip2_span1	**61,79%**	**78,49%**	**51,76%**	**80,60%**	78,73%	**77,22%**

Table 1. Intrinsic evaluation results

Looking first to the *all links* column, it is immediately apparent that recall is significantly higher than precision for all configurations. In fact, all aligner variations consistently induce on average two more links than exist in the manual version. Considering the *lexical links* and *non-lexical links* columns, apparently the bulk of the automatically induced links that do not occur in the manual annotation are at the lexical level, as attested by the low precision at the lexical level and balanced precision and recall at the non-lexical level.

If the manual alignments in the HomeCentre are regarded as a gold standard, it would seem that fewer lexical links should be produced, while the quality of the non-lexical links needs improvement. We will try to judge whether this is really the case using the extrinsic evaluation techniques described below.

3.2 Extrinsic Evaluation

For extrinsic evaluation, we trained and tested a DOT system (Hearne and Way, 2006) using the manually aligned HomeCentre treebank and evaluated the output translations to acquire baseline scores. We then trained the system on the automatically generated treebank and repeated

[4] We found that using the Moses word-alignment probabilities yielded better results than those output directly by GIZA++.

[5] Throughout the paper we use **boldface** to highlight the best results and *italics* for the worst.

the same tests, such that the only difference across runs are the alignments.

For testing, we used the six English–French training / test splits for the HomeCentre used in (Hearne and Way, 2006). Each test set contains 80 test sentences and each training set contains 730 tree pairs. We evaluated the translation output using three automatic evaluation metrics: BLEU (Papineni et al., 2002), NIST (Doddington, 2002) and METEOR (Banerjee and Lavie, 2005). We averaged the results over the six splits. We also measured test-data coverage of the translation system, i.e. the percentage of test sentences for which full trees were generated during translation.

We performed this evaluation using both the tree-to-tree algorithm and the string-to-string algorithm, employing greedy-search selection. For the latter case we extracted POS-tagged sentences from the HomeCentre and used them as input for the aligner. The results for the tree-to-tree case are presented in Table 2 and for the string-to-string case in Table 3.

Configurations	BLEU	NIST	METEOR	Coverage
manual	*0,5222*	6,8931	*71,8531%*	*68,5417%*
skip1	0,5236	*6,8412*	72,2485%	**72,0833%**
skip2	0,5233	6,8617	72,2847%	71,8750%
skip1_span1	0,5296	6,8570	**72,9833%**	**72,0833%**
skip2_span1	**0,5334**	**6,9210**	72,9736%	71,8750%

Table 2. Tree-to-tree extrinsic evaluation

Let us first look at the results from the tree-to-tree aligner. Overall, the scores obtained when using the manual alignments are very competitive with those derived using the manually aligned data. In fact, NIST is the only metric for which the performance is below the baseline. An important observation is that the coverage of the translation system is up to 3.5% higher when using the automatic alignments. Another observation is that *skip2* leads to better performance on the NIST metric over *skip1*, but the results from the other metrics are not so conclusive. The use of *span1* leads to better translation scores. These results seem to point at the *skip1_span1* and *skip2_span1* configurations as the best-suited for further development.

Unexpectedly, the results of the extrinsic evaluation do not strictly follow the trends found in the intrinsic evaluation. Further analysis of the data revealed that direct comparison of the manual and automatic alignments is not appropriate, especially regarding the lexical alignments. The manual alignments were produced with the aim of maximising precision, but the coverage-based automatic alignments lead to higher translation scores. This is the result of having many fewer manual word-alignments than automatic ones, as the low precision scores in the intrinsic evaluation show. From this we conclude that the improvement of the automatic aligner should not be aimed at better matching the manual alignments, but rather at improving the quality of the translations produced using the automatic alignments.

Configurations	BLEU	NIST	METEOR	Coverage
manual	**0,5222**	**6,8931**	*71,8531%*	*68,5417%*
skip1	0,4939	6,6321	72,5192%	**92,5000%**
skip2	0,4886	6,5777	72,8241%	92,2917%
skip1_span1	*0,4661*	*6,3090*	73,1017%	92,2917%
skip2_span1	0,4683	6,3353	**73,2828%**	92,2917%

Table 3. String-to-string extrinsic evaluation

If we now look at the evaluation of the string-to-string aligner, we see quite peculiar results. There is more than 20% increase in coverage compared to the tree-to-tree aligner, but the only other metric that sees improvement — albeit modest — is METEOR. It is also the only metric that follows the trends observed in the tree-to-tree evaluation results. Not only are the results for the BLEU and NIST metrics lower, but they also seem to follow reversed trends. It is unclear what the reason for such an outcome is, and further investigation — including on other data sets — is needed. Still, as far as the METEOR metric is concerned, the use of the string-to-string algorithm for the generation of parallel treebanks seems to be warranted.

The results obtained from the intrinsic and extrinsic evaluations show that the methods described in this paper produce high quality parallel treebanks. Using the automatically generated treebanks, a DOT system produces results with similar translation quality and better coverage compared to its performance using manually aligned data. This makes our methods a good alternative to the manual construction of parallel treebanks.

3.3 Using the Full-Search Algorithm as an Evaluation Metric

The full-search selection algorithm is combinatorial in nature and for sentence pairs with more than 100 nonzero link hypotheses its time requirements become prohibitive. Still, this algorithm can be used in its current form for development purposes.

It is reasonable to ask whether the greedy-search algorithm produces the best set of alignments for a given sentence pair. It could be that it picks a local maximum differing greatly from the absolute maximal set of alignments, thus producing either low quality links or a small number of links.

The full-search selection algorithm can be used to test the performance of the greedy search, as it by definition produces the best available set of alignments. We decided to use the rate of coincidence between the alignments induced using both selection algorithms as a metric for the quality of the links derived using the greedy search: the higher the number of cases in which the greedy-search algorithm matches the result of the full-search algorithm, the better the quality of the greedy search.

We ran this coincidence evaluation for all four configurations of the aligner. The results are presented in Table 4. It should be noted that 30 sentence pairs from the HomeCentre could not be handled by the full-search algorithm within a reasonable timeframe and were skipped.

	all links		lexical links		non-lexical links	
Configurations	precision	recall	precision	recall	precision	recall
skip1	98,71%	99,18%	98,36%	99,14%	**99,57%**	*99,21%*
skip2	**99,23%**	**99,21%**	**99,06%**	**99,17%**	**99,57%**	**99,23%**
skip1_span1	*95,78%*	*97,00%*	*95,92%*	*96,33%*	*95,19%*	*99,21%*
skip2_span1	96,27%	97,09%	96,58%	96,44%	95,25%	*99,21%*

Table 4. Evaluation against full-search results

The outcome of this test seems to be unexpected and a little disconcerting in view of the results obtained from the extrinsic evaluation. It does not seem reasonable that the configurations including *span1* should obtain scores that are relatively much worse than the scores for the other configurations, when we saw them perform better at the extrinsic evaluation tests.

The reason for this discrepancy might not be obvious, but it is fairly simple and lies in the nature of the *span1* extension. As discussed in section 2.1, *span1* introduces a separation in the induction of lexical and non-lexical links. The full-search algorithm, however, derives the maximal link set from a common pool of all nonzero alignment hypotheses. This suggests that an extension to the full-search algorithm similar to *span1* should be developed to allow for the evaluation of configurations using this feature.

Nevertheless, this evaluation shows some very important results. Besides the fact that configurations using *skip2* perform slightly better than those using *skip1*, we see that the greedy search comes very close to the best maximal link set. Our tests show that in over 95% of the cases the greedy search finds the best maximal link set available for the particular sentence pair.

The results are very encouraging and show that the fast greedy-search algorithm produces the desired results and there is no need to use the prohibitively slow full-search algorithm, except for comparison purposes.

4 A Review of Possible Enhancements

Here, we discuss possible avenues for the improvement of the quality of the parallel treebanks produced using the methods presented in this paper.

As already stated in section 3, the quality of a parallel treebank is to be judged by the quality of the induced sub-tree alignments. Thus, all effort should be directed at producing better alignments. There are two possible ways to address this: one option is to work on improving the alignment algorithm, and the other option is to improve the scoring mechanism used by the aligner.

Improvements to the alignment algorithm can be evaluated against the full-search selection algorithm. The evaluation results from section 3.3 suggest, however, that the margin for improvement here is very small. Thus, we do not expect any improvements here to bring serious boosts in overall performance. Nevertheless, we plan to investigate one possible modification to the greedy search.

It can be argued that each newly induced link in a sentence pair should affect the decisions regarding which links to select further in the alignment process for this sentence pair. This can be simulated to a certain extent by the introduction of a simple re-scoring module to the aligner. Each time a new link has been selected, this module will be used to recalculate the scores of the remaining links, considering the restrictions on the possible word-level alignments introduced by this link, e.g. that words within the spans of the nodes being linked cannot be aligned to words outside those spans.

The effects of changes to the scoring mechanism used can only be evaluated using extrinsic methods, as such changes also influence the operation of the full-search selection. On this front, we plan to investigate a maximum-entropy-based scoring mechanism. We expect such a mechanism to better encode mathematically the dependence of the translational equivalence scores on the word-alignment probabilities.

Besides the improvements to the sub-tree aligner, we plan to extend the whole generation framework with two additional modules: for string-to-tree and tree-to-string alignment. This would allow for better utilisation of all available resources for the derivation of a parallel treebank from a parallel corpus.

We also plan to perform large-scale extrinsic evaluation experiments. Though the evaluation results presented in section 3 are very promising, they were performed on a very small set of data. (John Tinsley (p.c.) reports successfully deriving a parallel treebank with over 700 000 sentence-pairs using our software.) Further experiments on larger data sets — from different languages, as well as from different domains — should help better understand the real qualities of the methods presented here.

5 Existing Parallel Treebanks

In this section we look at several attempts at the creation of parallel treebanks besides the HomeCentre treebank presented earlier.

Closest to the material presented in this paper comes the parallel treebank presented in (Samuelsson and Volk, 2006). This manually created treebank aligns three languages — German, English and Swedish — consisting of over 1000 sentences from each language. The main difference compared to our method is that they allow many-to-many lexical alignments and one-to-many non-lexical alignments. The authors also allow unary productions in the trees, which, as stated in section 2.1, does not provide any additional useful information. Another difference is that they deepen the original German and Swedish trees before alignment, rather than preserve their original form.

A further attempt to align phrase-structure trees is presented in (Uibo et al., 2005). The authors develop a rule-based method for aligning Estonian and German sentences. The parallel treebank consist of over 500 sentences, but in the version presented only NPs are aligned.

In (Han et al., 2002) the authors claim to have built a Korean–English parallel treebank with over 5000 phrase-structure tree pairs, but at the time of writing we were unable to find details about this treebank.

Although the Prague Czech–English Dependency Treebank (PCEDT (Čmejrek et al., 2004)) can be used as a parallel treebank, it is not such per se. The authors do not use phrase-structure trees. Instead, tectogrammatical dependency structures are used (Hajičová, 2000). Either a word alignment tool like GIZA++ or a probabilistic electronic dictionary (supplied with the treebank) can be used to automatically align the dependency structures. The presented version contains over 21000 sentence pairs that can be aligned. Because of its nature, this treebank can only be used by MT systems that employ tectogrammatical dependency structures.

We are also aware of the existence of the LinES (Ahrenberg, 2007), CroCo (Hansen-Schirra et al., 2006) and FuSe (Cyrus, 2006) parallel corpora. Although it seems possible to use them as parallel treebanks, they have been designed to serve as resources for the study of translational phenomena and it does not appear that they can be used effectively for other natural language processing tasks.

An attempt to develop an automatic tree-to-tree aligner is described in (Groves et al., 2004). The authors present a promising rule-based system. Further testing, however, has shown that the rules are only applicable to a particular treebank and language pair. This means that the set of rules has to be adjusted for each particular case.

Thus, the methods presented in this paper are the only available ones that can be used to produce a sufficiently large parallel treebank appropriate for use by state-of-the-art statistical MT applications (eg. DOT (Hearne and Way, 2006)).[6]

6 Conclusions

We have presented a novel platform for the fast and robust automatic generation of parallel treebanks. The algorithms described are completely language-pair-independent and require a minimal number of resources; besides a parallel corpus, a word alignment tool is the only extra software required. If available, POS taggers or monolingual phrase-structure parsers can be used to preprocess the data. Certain extensions to the current software are planned that will assure the optimal use of any available resources.

A series of evaluations have shown promising results. The quality of the automatically generated parallel treebanks is very high, even improving on a manually created treebank on certain metrics. We plan to carry out extensive large-scale testing on a range of language pairs, which we expect to corroborate the results reported in this paper. The planned improvements to the algorithms discussed in section 4 are expected to further increase the quality of the generated parallel treebanks.

Currently existing treebanks are small and require extensive human resources to be created and extended, which has limited their use for data-oriented tasks. The platform presented in this paper provides a means to circumvent these problems by allowing for the fast automatic generation of very large parallel treebanks with very little human effort, thus overcoming this hurdle for research in tree-based machine translation.

[6] An alternative methodology is described in (Lavie et al., to appear), but this work was not available at the time of writing.

Acknowledgements

We would like to thank Khalil Sima'an, Mary Hearne and John Tinsley for many insightful discussions. This work was generously supported by Science Foundation Ireland (grant no. 05/RF/CMS064) and the Irish Centre for High-End Computing (http://www.ichec.ie).

References

Ahrenberg, Lars. 2007. LinES: An English-Swedish Parallel Treebank. In *Proceedings of the 16th Nordic Conference of Computational Linguistics (NODALIDA '07)*, pp. 270–274. Tartu, Estonia.

Banerjee, Satanjeev and Alon Lavie. 2005. METEOR: An Automatic Metric for MT Evaluation with Improved Correlation with Human Judgements. In *Proceedings of the Workshop on Intrinsic and Extrinsic Evaluation Measures for MT and/or Summarization at the 43rd Annual Meeting of the Association for Computational Linguistics (ACL '05)*, pp. 65–72. Ann Arbor, MI.

Čmejrek, Martin, Jan Cuřín, Jiří Havelka, Jan Hajič and Vladislav Kuboň. 2004. Prague Czech-English Dependency Treebank: Syntactically Annotated Resources for Machine Translation. In *Proceedings of the 4th International Conference on Language Resources and Evaluation (LREC '04)*. Lisbon, Portugal.

Cyrus, Lea. 2006. Building a resource for studying translation shifts. In *Proceedings of the 5th Conference of Language Resources and Evaluation (LREC '06)*, pp. 1240–1245. Genoa, Italy.

Doddington, George. 2002. Automatic Evaluation of Machine Translation Quality Using N-Gram Co-Occurrence Statistics. In *Proceedings of the ARPA Workshop on Human Language Technology*, pp. 128–132. San-Diego, CA.

Groves, Declan, Mary Hearne and Andy Way. 2004. Robust Sub-Sentential Alignment of Phrase-Structure Trees. In *Proceedings of the 20th International Conference on Computational Linguistics (CoLing '04)*, pp. 1072–1078. Geneva, Switzerland: COLING.

Hajičová, Eva. 2000. Dependency-Based Underlying-Structure Tagging of a Very Large Czech Corpus. *TAL (Special Issue Grammaires de Dépendance / Dependency Grammars)*, 41 (1): 47–66.

Han, Chung-hye, Na-Rare Han, Eon-Suk Ko and Martha Palmer. 2002. Development and Evaluation of a Korean Treebank and its Application to NLP. In *Proceedings of the 3rd International Conference on Language Resources and Evaluation (LREC '02)*, pp. 1635–1642. Las Palmas, Canary Islands, Spain.

Hansen-Schirra, Silvia, Stella Neumann and Mihaela Vela. 2006. Multi-dimensional Annotation and Alignment in an English-German Translation Corpus. In *Proceedings of the workshop on Multi-dimensional Markup in Natural Language Processing (NLPXML '06)*, pp. 35–42. Trento, Italy.

Hearne, Mary and Andy Way. 2006. Disambiguation Strategies for Data-Oriented Translation. In *Proceedings of the 11th Conference of the European Association for Machine Translation (EAMT '06)*, pp. 59–68. Oslo, Norway.

Hearne, Mary, John Tinsley, Ventsislav Zhechev and Andy Way. 2007. Capturing Translational Divergences with a Statistical Tree-to-Tree Aligner. In *Proceedings of the 11th International Conference on Theoretical and Methodological Issues in Machine Translation (TMI '07)*, pp. 85–94. Skövde, Sweden: Skövde University Studies in Informatics.

Koehn, Philipp, Hieu Hoang, Alexandra Birch, Chris Callison-Burch, Marcello Federico, Nicola Bertoldi, Brooke Cowan, Wade Shen, Christine Moran, Richard Zens, Chris Dyer, Ondřej Bojar, Alexandra Constantin and Evan Herbst. 2007. Moses: Open Source Toolkit for Statistical Machine Translation. In *Proceedings of the Demo and Poster Sessions of the 45th Annual Meeting of the Association for Computational Linguistics (ACL '07)*, pp. 177–180. Prague, Czech Republic.

Lavie, Alon, Alok Parlikar and Vamshi Ambati. to appear. Syntax-driven Learning of Sub-sentential Translation Equivalents and Translation Rules from Parsed Parallel Corpora. In *Proceedings of the 2nd Workshop on Syntax and Structure in Statistical Translation (SSST '08)*. Columbus, OH.

Nesson, Rebecca, Stuart M. Shieber and Alexander Rush. 2006. Induction of Probabilistic Synchronous Tree-Insertion Grammars for Machine Translation. In *Proceedings of the 7th Conference of the Association for Machine Translation in the Americas (AMTA '06)*, pp. 128–137. Boston, MA.

Och, Franz Josef and Hermann Ney. 2003. A Systematic Comparison of Various Statistical Alignment Models. *Computational Linguistics*, 29 (1): 19–51.

Papineni, Kishore, Salim Roukos, Todd Ward and Wei-Jing Zhu. 2002. BLEU: A Method for Automatic Evaluation of Machine Translation. In *Proceedings of the 40th Annual Meeting of the Association of Computational Linguistics (ACL '02)*, pp. 311–318. Philadelphia, PA.

Samuelsson, Yvonne and Martin Volk. 2006. Phrase Alignment in Parallel Treebanks. In *Proceedings of the 5th Workshop on Treebanks and Linguistic Theories (TLT '06)*, pp. 91–102. Prague, Czech Republic.

Samuelsson, Yvonne and Martin Volk. 2007. Alignment Tools for Parallel Treebanks. In *Proceedings of the GLDV Frühjahrstaggung*. Tübingen, Germany.

Uibo, Heli, Krista Liin and Martin Volk. 2005. Phrase alignment of Estonian-German parallel treebanks. Paper presented at *Workshop 'Exploiting parallel corpora in up to 20 languages'*, Arona, Italy.

A Hybrid Generative/Discriminative Framework to Train a Semantic Parser from an Un-annotated Corpus

Deyu Zhou and Yulan He
Information Research Centre
The University of Reading
Reading, RG6 6BX, UK
d.zhou@rdg.ac.uk, y.he@rdg.ac.uk

Abstract

We propose a hybrid generative/discriminative framework for semantic parsing which combines the hidden vector state (HVS) model and the hidden Markov support vector machines (HM-SVMs). The HVS model is an extension of the basic discrete Markov model in which context is encoded as a stack-oriented state vector. The HM-SVMs combine the advantages of the hidden Markov models and the support vector machines. By employing a modified K-means clustering method, a small set of most representative sentences can be automatically selected from an un-annotated corpus. These sentences together with their abstract annotations are used to train an HVS model which could be subsequently applied on the whole corpus to generate semantic parsing results. The most confident semantic parsing results are selected to generate a fully-annotated corpus which is used to train the HM-SVMs. The proposed framework has been tested on the DARPA Communicator Data. Experimental results show that an improvement over the baseline HVS parser has been observed using the hybrid framework. When compared with the HM-SVMs trained from the fully-annotated corpus, the hybrid framework gave a comparable performance with only a small set of lightly annotated sentences.

© 2008. Licensed under the *Creative Commons Attribution-Noncommercial-Share Alike 3.0 Unported* license (http://creativecommons.org/licenses/by-nc-sa/3.0/). Some rights reserved.

1 Introduction

Semantic parsing maps the natural language sentences to complete formal meaning representations. Traditionally, research in the field of semantic parsing can be divided into two categories: rule-based approaches and statistical approaches. Based on hand-crafted semantic grammar rules, rule-based approaches fill slots in semantic frames using word pattern and semantic tokens (Dowding et al., 1994; Ward and Issar, 1994). Such rule-based approaches are typically domain-specific and often fragile. Statistical approaches are generally based on stochastic models. They can be further categorized into three types: generative approaches, discriminative approaches and a hybrid of the two. Generative approaches learn the joint probability model, $P(W, C)$, of input sentence W and its semantic tag sequence C, compute $P(C|W)$ using the Bayes rule, and then take the most probable tag sequence C. The hidden Morkov model (HMM), being a generative model, has been predominantly used in statistical semantic parsing. It models sequential dependencies by treating a semantic parse sequence as a Markov chain, which leads to an efficient dynamic programming formulation for inference and learning. The hidden vector state (HVS) model (He and Young, 2005) is a discrete HMM model in which each HMM state represents the state of a push-down automaton with a finite stack size. State transitions are factored into separate stack pop and push operations constrained to give a tractable search space. The result is a model which is complex enough to capture hierarchical structure but which can be trained automatically from only lightly annotated data. Discriminative approaches directly model posterior probability $P(C|W)$ and learn mappings from W to C. One representative example is support vector machines (SVMs) (Vapnik, 1995). More recently, the hidden Markov support vector machines (HM-SVMs) (Altun et al., 2003) have been proposed which combine the flexibility of kernel methods with the idea of HMMs to predict a label sequence given an input sequence. However, HM-SVMs require full annotated corpora for training which are difficult to obtain in practical applications. On the other hand, the HVS model can be easily trained from only lightly annotated corpora. It is thus interesting to explore the feasibility to combine the advantages of the HVS model and the HM-SVMs.

We propose a hybrid generative/discriminative framework here where a modified K-means clustering method is first applied to select a small set of the most representative sentences automatically from an un-annotated corpus. These sentences together with their abstract annotations are used to train an HVS model which could be subsequently applied on the whole corpus to generate semantic parsing results. The most confident semantic parsing results are selected to generate a fully-annotated corpus which is used to train the HM-SVMs. Experimental results show that an improvement over the baseline HVS parser has been achieved using the hybrid framework. When compared with the HM-SVMs trained from the fully-annotated corpus, the hybrid framework gave a comparable performance with only a small set of lighted annotated sentences.

The rest of this paper is organized as follows. Section 2 reviews other proposed hybrid generative/discriminative frameworks in recent years. Section 3 briefly describes the HVS model and the HM-SVMs followed by the presentation of the proposed hybrid framework. In Section 4, experimental setup and results are discussed. Finally, Section 5 concludes the paper.

2 Related Work

Combination of generative and discriminative models for data classification has recently attracted much interests in the machine learning community. It has been shown theoretically and experimentally in (Jaakkola and Haussler, 1998; Ng and Jordan, 2002; Bouchard and Triggs, 2004) that the hybrid model combines the complementary powers of the both models. The first extensive study on hybrid models were discussed in (Jaakkola and Haussler, 1998) where discriminative features were extracted using generative models and were later used in discriminative models. More recently, the HM-SVMs (Altun et al., 2003) have been proposed which incorporate kernel methods into HMMs to predict a label sequence given an input sequence.

There have also been several studies on exploring the hybrid generative/discriminative frameworks which combine the generative and discriminative models in a pipelined way. One example is the hybrid framework proposed in (Abou-Moustafa et al., 2004) for sequential data classification. The framework employs HMMs to map the variable length sequential data into a fixed size P-dimensional vector that can be classified using any discriminative model. Experiments were conducted on the NIST database for handwritten digits and results showed a better recognition rate than that of standard HMMs. Another example is the hybrid generative/discriminative approach proposed in (Holub et al., 2008) for detecting and classifying object categories in the machine version domain. In this approach, "Fisher Kernels" were used to retain most of the desirable properties of generative methods and a discriminative setting was used to increase the classification performance. Experimental results showed significant performance improvement over the generative counterpart.

3 Methodologies

This section first introduces the hidden vector state (HVS) model and the hidden Markov support vector machines (HM-SVMs) followed by the presentation of the proposed hybrid generative/discriminative framework.

3.1 Hidden Vector State Model

Given a model and an observed word sequence $W = (w_1 \cdots w_T)$, semantic parsing can be viewed as a pattern recognition problem and the most likely semantic representation can be found through statistical decoding. If assuming that the hidden data take the form of a semantic parse tree C then the model should be a push-down automata which can generate the pair $\langle W, C \rangle$ through some canonical sequence of moves $D = (d_1 \cdots d_T)$. That is,

$$P(W, C) = \prod_{t=1}^{T} P(d_t | d_{t-1} \cdots d_1) \quad (1)$$

For the general case of an unconstrained hierarchical model, D will consist of three types of probabilistic move:

1. popping semantic category labels off the stack;
2. pushing one or more non-terminal semantic category label onto the stack;
3. generating the next word.

When considering a constrained form of automata where the stack is finite depth and $\langle W, C\rangle$ is built by repeatedly popping 0 to n labels off the stack, pushing exactly one new label onto the stack and then generating the next word, it defines the Hidden Vector State (HVS) model in which conventional grammar rules are replaced by three probability tables.

Given a word sequence W, concept vector sequence C and a sequence of stack pop operations N, the joint probability of $P(W, C, N)$ can be decomposed as

$$P(W, C, N) = \prod_{t=1}^{T} P(n_t|\mathbf{c}_{t-1})P(c_t[1]|c_t[2 \cdots D_t]) P(w_t|\mathbf{c}_t) \quad (2)$$

where $\mathbf{c}_t$, the vector state at word position t, is a vector of D_t semantic concept labels (tags), i.e. $\mathbf{c}_t = [c_t[1], c_t[2], ..c_t[D_t]]$ where $c_t[1]$ is the preterminal concept label and $c_t[D_t]$ is the root concept label, n_t is the vector stack shift operation at word position t and take values in the range $0, \ldots, D_{t-1}$ and $c_t[1] = c_{w_t}$ is the new preterminal semantic tag assigned to word w_t at word position t.

3.2 Hidden Markov Support Vector Machines

To learn a function that assigns to a sequence of words $W = (w_1 \cdots w_T), w_i \in \mathbf{W}, i = 1, \ldots T$ a sequence of semantic tags $C = \mathbf{c}_1\mathbf{c}_2 \ldots \mathbf{c}_T, \mathbf{c}_i \in \mathbf{C}, i = 1, \ldots T$, a common approach is to determine a discriminant function $F : \mathcal{W} \times \mathcal{C} \rightarrow \mathbb{R}$ that assigns a score to every input $W \in \mathcal{W} := \mathbf{W}^*$ and every semantic tag sequence $\mathbf{C} \in \mathcal{C} := \mathbf{C}^*$, where $\mathbf{W}^*$ denotes the Kleene closure of $\mathbf{W}$. In order to obtain a prediction $f(W) \in \mathcal{C}$, the function is maximized with respect to $f(W) = \underset{C \in \mathcal{C}}{\text{argmax}} F(W, C)$.

In particular, the function $F(W, C)$ is assumed to be linear in some combined feature representation of W and C in HM-SVMs (Altun et al., 2003), $F(W, C) := \langle w, \Phi(W, C)\rangle$. Given a set of training data $(W_i, C_i), i = 1, \ldots N$, the parameters w are adjusted so that the true semantic tag sequence C_i scores higher than all other tag sequences $C \in \mathcal{C}_i := \mathcal{C} \backslash C_i$ with a large margin. To achieve the goal, the following optimization problem is solved instead.

$$\min_{\xi_i \in \mathbb{R}, w \in \mathcal{F}} \quad Cons \sum_i \xi_i + \frac{1}{2}\|w\|^2 \quad (3)$$
$$\text{s.t.} \quad \langle w, \Phi(W, C_i)\rangle - \langle w, \Phi(W, C)\rangle \geq 1 - \xi_i,$$
$$\forall i = 1, \ldots N \text{ and } C \in \mathcal{C} \backslash C_i$$

where ξ_i is non-negative slack variables allowing one to increase the global margin by paying a local penalty on some outlying examples, and $Cons$ dictates the desired trade off between margin size and outliers. To solve the equation 3, the dual of the equation is solved instead. The solution w^* can be written as

$$w^* = \sum_{i=1}^{N} \sum_{C \in \mathcal{C}} \alpha_i(C)\Phi(W_i, C), \quad (4)$$

where $\alpha_i(C)$ is the Lagrange multiplier of the constraint associated with example i and C_i.

3.3 A Hybrid Generative/Discriminative Framework for Semantic Parsing

The framework of combining the HVS model and the HM-SVMs is illustrated in Figure 1. It consists of three main stages, *Representative Sentences Selection*, *Fully Annotated Corpus Generation*, and *HM-SVM Training and Testing*. Each of them is discussed in details below.

- *Representative Sentences Selection*. Given an un-annotated corpus, the modified K-means clustering algorithm is first employed to select the most representative sentences for annotation. This is to avoid annotating the whole corpus and hopefully the model trained from the subset of the original corpus would still give a similar performance when compared with the model trained from the full corpus. The modified K-means clustering algorithm is described in Figure 3.3.

  Initially, k different sentences are randomly selected as the initial centroids. Then, each sentence s_i in the training data is assigned to one of the k clusters based on the similarity measurement which will be discussed later.

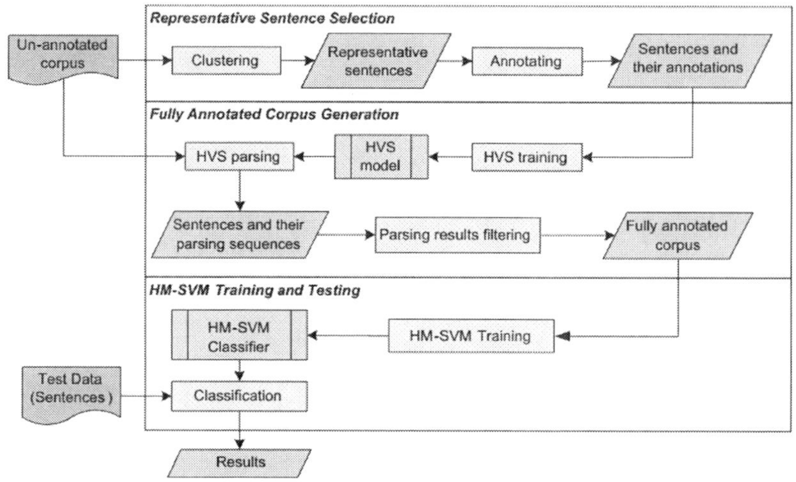

Figure 1: The hybrid generative/discriminative framework for semantic parsing.

After that, the centroids of the k clusters are recalculated. The above process repeats until there are no further changes in the centroids.

The similarity between two sentences is calculated based on sequence alignment. Suppose $\mathbf{a} = a_1 a_2 \cdots a_n$ and $\mathbf{b} = b_1 b_2 \cdots b_m$ are the two word sequences of length of n and m, $Sim(i,j)$ is defined as the score of the optimal alignment between the initial segment from a_1 to a_i of $\mathbf{a}$ and the initial segment from b_1 to b_j of $\mathbf{b}$, where $Sim(i,j)$ is recursively calculated as follows:

$$\begin{aligned} Sim(i,0) &= 0, i = 1,2,...n \\ Sim(0,j) &= 0, j = 1,2,...m \\ Sim(i,j) &= \max \begin{cases} 0, \\ Sim(i-1,j-1) + s(a_i,b_j), \\ Sim(i-1,j) + s(a_i,'-'), \\ Sim(i,j-1) + s('-',b_j) \end{cases} \end{aligned}$$

Here $s(a_i,b_j)$ is the score of aligning a_i with b_j and is defined as:

$$s(a_i,b_j) = \log\left[\frac{p(a_i,b_j)}{p(a_i) \times p(b_j)}\right] \quad (5)$$

where, $p(a_i)$ denotes the occurrence probability of the word a_i and $p(a_i,b_j)$ denotes the probability that a_i and b_j appear at the same position in two aligned sequences.

To ensure that content words containing key information are weighted more heavily than the less relevant words such as function words, a score matrix can then be built and dynamic programming is used to find the largest score between two sequences. The distance between the two sentences is defined as the negation of the similarity between them.

After generating k clusters, the centroid in each of the clusters is selected as the representative sentence for annotation. This results in an exactly k sentences being selected. There are however two ways to construct the annotated corpus depending on the neighborhood threshold value d. When $d = 1$, the annotated corpus only contains k sentences. When $d < 1$, both the centroid and some of its nearest neighboring sentences in each cluster will receive the same abstract annotation. Thus, the annotated corpus will contain more than k sentences. It has to be noted that in both cases, only k sentences (centroids) need to be annotated.

- *Fully Annotated Corpus Generation.* An HVS model is trained from the annotated corpus constructed in the previous stage which is then applied to the original un-annotated corpus to generate a semantic tag sequence for each sentence. The generated semantic tag sequences essentially define the explicit word/tag alignments which could serve as the full annotation required by HM-SVMs training. However, the HVS model does not guarantee to parse the sentences with 100% accuracy. Based on a user-defined parse probabil-

Input: A set of sentences $S = \{s_i, i = 1, \dots, N\}$, a distance threshold α, a neighborhood threshold d
Output: A set of representative sentences $R = \{r_j, j = 1, \dots, M\}$, and a set of the centroids of the generated clusters $Cent$

Algorithm:

1. For each $s_i \in S$, set $Flag_i = 1$. Initialize R and $Cent$ to be empty sets.
2. Select sentences from S with $Flag$ equal to 1 , then reconstruct $\hat{S} = \{s_j | Flag_j = 1, j = 1, \dots, \hat{N}\}$, $\hat{N}$ is the number of sentences with $Flag$ equal to 1 in S.
3. Randomly select k different sentences c_k from $\hat{S}$, the default value of k is 1000. Construct k clusters $C = \{c_l\}, l = 1, \dots, k$. Set NumOfFlag = $\|\hat{S}\|$
4. Loop for each sentences $s_i \in \hat{S}$
   Loop for each cluster c_l
      Calculate the distance between s_i and the centroid of c_l. $Dist_{il}$ = Distance(s_i, c_l).
      If $Dist_{il} < \alpha$, then $c_l = c_l \bigcup s_i$, set $Flag_i = 0$, ExitLoop.
   EndLoop
   If $Flag_i \neq 0$, then find the cluster $l' = \underset{l}{\operatorname{argmin}}\{Dist_{il}, l = 1, \dots, k\}$, $c_{l'} = c_{l'} \bigcup s_i$
   EndLoop
   If $\|\{s_i | s_i \in \hat{S}, Flag_i = 1\}\|$ <NumOfFlag, then set NumOfFlag = $\|\{s_i | s_i \in \hat{S}, Flag_i = 1\}\|$, go to Step 4.
   $Cent = Cent \bigcup Cent_l, l = 1, \dots, k, \|c_l\| \neq 0$.
5. If NumOfFlag > 0 then Go to step 2.
   Else
      $R = R \bigcup Cent$.
      Construct $\|Cent\|$ clusters $\hat{C} = \{c_l\}, l = 1, \dots, \|Cent\|$.
      Loop for each sentences $s_i \in S$
         Find the cluster $l' = \underset{l}{\operatorname{argmin}}\{Dist_{il}, l = 1, \dots, \|Cent\|\}$, $c'_l = c'_l \bigcup s_i$
         If $Dist_{il'} < d$, then $R = R \bigcup s_i$
      EndLoop
   EndIf

Figure 2: A modified K-means clustering method.

ity threshold, the most confident parse results are selected for the construction of the fully annotated corpus.

- *HM-SVMs Training and Testing*. Given the fully annotated corpus generated in the previous stage, the HM-SVMs can then be trained which could later be used to derive the semantic tag sequences for the test data.

4 Experiment

Experiments have been conducted on the DARPA Communicator data (CUData, 2004) which are available to the public as open source download. The data contain utterance transcriptions and the semantic parse results from the rule-based Phoenix parser[1]. The DARPA Communicator data were collected in 461 days. From these, 46 days were randomly selected for use as test set data and the remainder were used for training. After cleaning up the data, the training set consist of 12702 utterances while the test set contains 1178 utterances.

[1]http://communicator.colorado.edu/phoenix

The abstract annotation used for training and the reference annotation needed for testing were derived by hand correcting the Phoenix parse results. For example, for the sentence "Show me flights from Boston to New York", the abstract annotation would be
`FLIGHT(FROMLOC(CITY) TOLOC(CITY))`.
Such an annotation need only list a set of valid semantic concepts and the dominance relationships between them without considering the actual realized concept sequence or attempting to identify explicit word/concept pairs. Thus, it avoids the need for expensive tree-bank style annotations.

To evaluate the performance of the model, a reference frame structure was derived for every test set sentence consisting of slot/value pairs. An example of a reference frame is:

Show me flights from Boston to New York.	
Frame:	FLIGHT
Slots:	FROMLOC.CITY = Boston
	TOLOC.CITY = New York

Performance was then measured in terms of F -measure on slot/value pairs, which combines

Table 1: Feature templates used in HM-SVMs. w_i is the current word, and $w_1, \ldots, w_n$ is the entire sentence.

Current word	w_i
Previous word	w_{i-1}
Word two back	w_{i-2}
Next word	w_{i+1}
Word two ahead	w_{i+2}
Bigram features	w_{i-2}, w_{i-1} w_{i-1}, w_i w_i, w_{i+1} w_{i+1}, w_{i+2}

Table 2: The number of representative sentences vs the different settings of α and d.

d \ α	0.5	0.6	0.7	0.8	0.9
1	350	663	1068	1743	2763
0.6	6878	7596	9810	9640	11872

the precision (P) and recall (R) values with equal weight and is defined as $F = (P + R)/2PR$.

In all the subsequent experiments, the open source SVM^{hmm}(Tsochantaridis et al., 2005) [2] has been used to train and test the HM-SVMs. The features used in the HM-SVMs are listed in Table 1.

4.1 Comparison between HVS and HM-SVMs

In the modified K-means clustering algorithm described in Figure 3.3, the number of representative sentences depends on both the distance threshold α and the neighborhood threshold d. Table 2 shows the number of representative sentences obtained by varying α and d.

First, a set of experiments were conducted to compare the performance of the HVS model with the HM-SVMs only without incorporating the hybrid framework. Based on the different values of d and α, we constructed different sets of the annotated corpus. For example, when $\alpha = 0.5$, there are 350 clusters generated from a total of 12702 sentences in the un-annotated corpus. The centroid from each of the cluster is then selected for annotation. These 350 sentences were annotated with abstract annotation for the HVS model training. And they were also fully annotated by providing word-level annotations for HM-SVMs training.

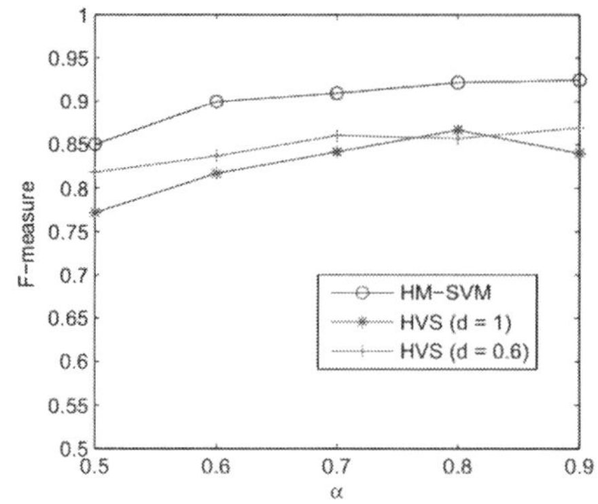

Figure 3: Comparisons of the performance of HVS and HM-SVMs on different α.

Since only abstract annotations need to be provided for the HVS model training, it is possible to automatically enlarge the annotated corpus by including some of the neighboring sentences if the same annotation of the centroid can be assigned to them. This is controlled by varying the neighborhood threshold d. If $d = 1$, then the annotated corpus only contains 350 sentences with their abstract annotations. If varying d to 0.6, then for each cluster, some of the neighboring sentences also receive the same abstract annotation as that of the centroid, thus the annotated corpus is enlarged to contain 6878 sentences.

The performance comparison of the HVS and the HM-SVMs is shown in Figure 3. It can be observed that in general, HM-SVMs outperforms HVS. This is not surprising as HM-SVMs was trained from the fully annotated corpus. The HVS model based on $d = 0.6$ achieved better performance over the one based on $d = 1$ since the enlarged annotated corpus was used for training. The best performance given by HM-SVMs is 92.5% of F-measure when $\alpha = 0.9$ and 2793 annotated sentences were used for training, while the HVS model gave an F-measure of 86.9%.

Though HM-SVMs outperforms HVS by 5.5%, it should be noted that the time consumed for preparing the fully annotated corpus for HM-SVMs is far more than the time spent for abstract annotation for HVS as shown in Figure 4. When $\alpha = 0.5$, annotating 350 sentences with the explicit word/semantic tag mappings took about 17.5 hours while abstract annotation only took about 3 hours. When $\alpha = 0.9$, the time spent on fully annotating 2763 sentences is almost six times that of abstract annotation.

[2]http://www.cs.cornell.edu/People/tj/svm_light/svm_hmm.html

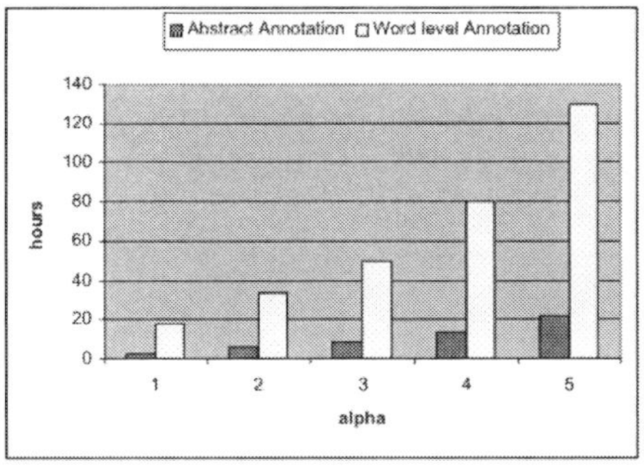

Figure 4: Comparison of time Consuming in preparing training data for the HVS model and the HM-SVMs.

4.2 Comparison between HVS and the Hybrid Framework with Clustering

Figure 5 shows the performance comparison between the HVS model and the hybrid framework by varying α. It can be observed that when the size of the annotated corpus is small, the HVS model outperforms the hybrid framework. However, with increased number of annotated sentences, the hybrid framework achieves the better performance. For both the HVS model and the hybrid framework, improved performance is observed by training the model/framework from the augmented annotated corpus with the neighboring sentences automatically added in (cf. Figure 5(a) and (b)). We notice from Figure 5(a) that when the number of annotated sentences increases from 1743 to 2763, the performances of both the HVS model and the hybrid framework decrease. By analyzing the clustering results generated from the modified K-means algorithm, we found that some of the clusters formed actually contain those rare sentences and they represent the outliers of the original training set. This therefore leads to the decreased performance of the HVS model and the hybrid framework.

With only 2763 annotated sentences, the hybrid framework trained under $d = 0.6$ achieves 88.5% in F-measure which results in a relative error reduction of 12% when compared with the HVS model where the F-measure value of 87.0% was obtained.

4.3 Comparison between HVS and the Hybrid Framework without Clustering

Experiments have also been conducted to compare the performance of the HVS model and the hybrid framework without employing the modified K-means clustering algorithm to automatically select the most representative sentences for annotation. That is, the whole corpus of 12702 sentences were provided with abstract annotations. Both the HVS model and the hybrid framework were trained from the training set which was formed by randomly selecting the annotated sentences from the original corpus. Figure 6 illustrates the performance of the HVS model and the hybrid framework versus the varying sizes of the training data. Here 10-fold cross validation was performed and the F-measure value at each point of the curve in Figure 6 was calculated by averaging the performance of the 10 experiments each time with different training set of the same size.

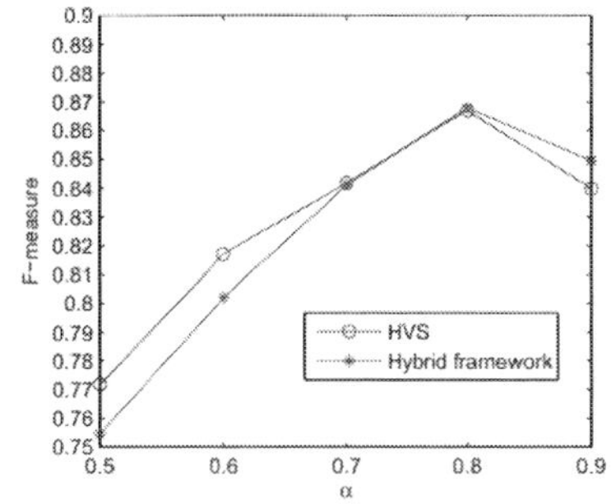

(a) $d = 1$.

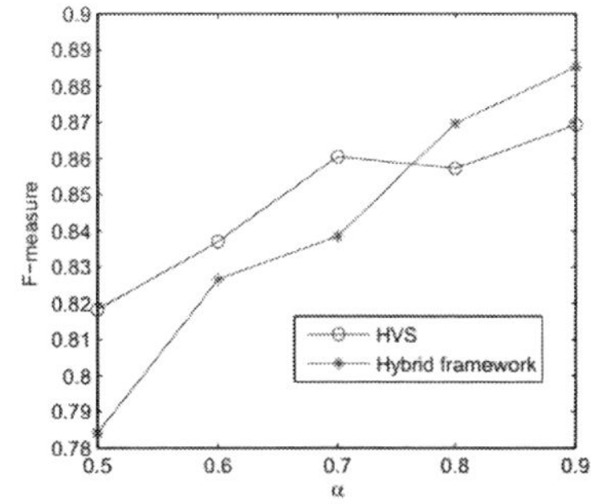

(b) $d = 0.6$.

Figure 5: Comparison of the performance of the HVS model and the hybrid framework

It can be observed that the performance of both the HVS model and the proposed hybrid framework increases with the increased size of the training data. The hybrid framework outperforms the HVS model when the size of the training data is beyond 6000. The improvement is more substantial by incorporating more training data.

The best performance achieved by the HVS model and the proposed hybrid framework is listed

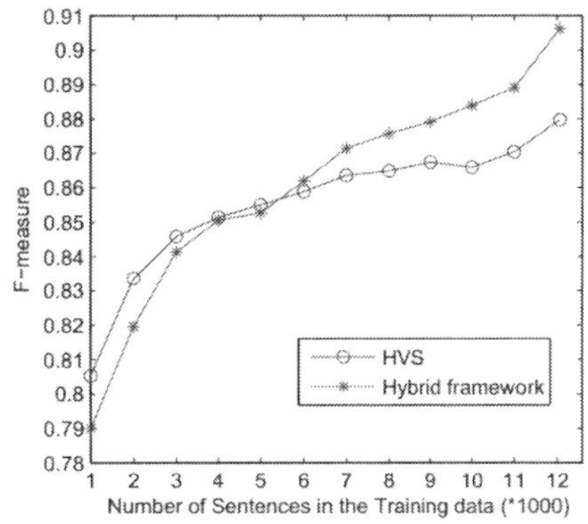

Figure 6: Performance of the HVS model and the hybrid framework vs the size of the training data.

in Table 3. It can be observed that the hybrid framework gives the relative error reduction of 22% when compared with the performance of the HVS model where only 87.97% was achieved.

Table 3: Performance comparison between HVS and the hybrid framework.

Measurement	HVS	Hybrid Framework
Recall	87.81%	90.99 %
Precision	88.13%	90.25%
F-measure	87.97%	90.62%

It should also be noted that the best performance of 87.97% in F-measure was obtained when the HVS model was trained on the whole annotated corpus of 12702 sentences. By employing the clustering method to select the most representative sentences, the hybrid framework trained with less than one fourth of the original training data (2763 annotated sentences) achieves 88.53% in F-measure, which is better than that of the HVS model.

5 Conclusions

This paper presented a hybrid framework by combining the HVS model and the HM-SVMs for semantic parsing. Experimental results show that 22% relative error reduction in F-measure was obtained using the hybrid framework on the DARPA Communicator Data when compared with the performance of the HVS model. Furthermore, employing the modified K-means clustering algorithm to automatically select the most representative sentences for annotation greatly reduces the human effort for annotation. With only 2763 annotated sentences, the hybrid framework gives the better performance compared with the HVS model trained on the full 12702 annotated sentences. Also, the hybrid framework gives the comparable performance with that of the HM-SVMs but without the use of the expensive word-level annotations.

References

Abou-Moustafa, K.T., C.Y. Suen, and M. Cheriet. 2004. A generative-discriminative hybrid for sequential data classification. In *Acoustics, Speech, and Signal Processing, 2004 (ICASSP '04)*, volume 5, pages 805–808.

Altun, Y., I. Tsochantaridis, and T. Hofmann. 2003. Hidden markov support vector machines. In *International Conference in Machine Learning*, pages 3–10.

Bouchard, Guillaume and Bill Triggs. 2004. The tradeoff between generative and discriminative classifiers. In *Proc. of COMPSTAT 2004*, pages 721–728.

CUData. 2004. Darpa communicator travel data. university of colorado at boulder. Avaiable from http://communicator.colorado.edu/phoenix.

Dowding, J., R. Moore, F. Andry, and D. Moran. 1994. Interleaving syntax and semantics in an efficient bottom-up parser. In *Proc. of the 32th Annual Meeting of the Association for Computational Linguistics*, pages 110–116, Las Cruces, New Mexico, USA.

He, Yulan and Steve Young. 2005. Semantic processing using the hidden vector state model. *Computer Speech and Language*, 19(1):85–106.

Holub, Alex D., Max Welling, and Pietro Peronal. 2008. Hybrid generative-discriminative visual categorization. *International Journal of Computer Vision*, 77:239–258.

Jaakkola, T. and D. Haussler. 1998. Exploiting generative models in discriminative classifiers. In *Proc. of Advances in Neural Information Processing 11*.

Ng, A. and M. Jordan. 2002. On generative vs. discriminative classifiers: A comparison of logistic regression and naive bayes. In *Proc. of Advances in Neural Information Processing 15*, pages 841–848.

Tsochantaridis, Ioannis, Thorsten Joachims, Thomas Hofmann, and Yasemin Altun. 2005. Large margin methods for structured and interdependent output variables. *J. Mach. Learn. Res.*, 6:1453–1484.

Vapnik, Vladimir N. 1995. *The nature of statistical learning theory*. Springer-Verlag New York, Inc., New York, NY, USA.

Ward, W. and S. Issar. 1994. Recent improvements in the cmu spoken language understanding system. In *Proc. of the workshop on Human Language Technology*, pages 213–216, Plainsboro, New Jerey, USA.

Diagnostic Evaluation of Machine Translation Systems Using Automatically Constructed Linguistic Check-Points

Ming Zhou[1], Bo Wang[2], Shujie Liu[2], Mu Li[1], Dongdong Zhang[1], Tiejun Zhao[2]

[1]Microsoft Research Asia
Beijing, China
{mingzhou,muli,dozhang}
@microsoft.com

[2]Harbin Institute of Technology
Harbin, China
{bowang,Shujieliu,tjzhao}
@mtlab.hit.edu.cn

Abstract

We present a diagnostic evaluation platform which provides multi-factored evaluation based on automatically constructed check-points. A check-point is a linguistically motivated unit (e.g. an ambiguous word, a noun phrase, a verb~obj collocation, a prepositional phrase etc.), which are pre-defined in a linguistic taxonomy. We present a method that automatically extracts check-points from parallel sentences. By means of check-points, our method can monitor a MT system in translating important linguistic phenomena to provide diagnostic evaluation. The effectiveness of our approach for diagnostic evaluation is verified through experiments on various types of MT systems.

1 Introduction

Automatic MT evaluation is a crucial issue for MT system developers. The state-of-the-art methods for automatic MT evaluation are using an n-gram based metric represented by BLEU (Papineni et al., 2002) and its variants. Ever since its invention, the BLEU score has been a widely accepted benchmark for MT system evaluation. Nevertheless, the research community has been aware of the deficiencies of the BLEU metric (Callison-Burch et al., 2006). For instance, BLEU fails to sufficiently capture the vitality of natural languages: all grams of a sentence are treated equally ignoring their linguistic significance; only consecutive grams are considered ignoring the skipped grams of certain linguistic relations; candidate translation gets acknowledged only if it uses exactly the same lexicon as the reference ignoring the variation in lexical choice. Furthermore, BLEU is useful for optimizing and improving statistical MT systems but it has shown to be ineffective in comparing systems with different architectures (e.g., rule-based vs. phrase-based) (Callison-Burch et al., 2006).

Another common deficiency of the state-of-the-art evaluation approaches is that they cannot clearly inform MT developers on the detailed strengths and flaws of an MT system, and therefore there is no way for us to understand the capability of certain modules of an MT system, and the capability of translating certain kinds of language phenomena. For the purpose of system development, MT developers need a diagnostic evaluation approach to provide the feedback on the translation ability of an MT system with regard to various important linguistic phenomena.

We propose a novel diagnostic evaluation approach. Instead of assigning a general score to an MT system we evaluate the capability of the system in handling various important linguistic test cases called **Check-Points**. A check-point is a linguistically motivated unit, (e.g. an ambiguous word, a noun phrase, a verb~obj collocation, a prepositional phrase etc.) which are pre-defined in a linguistic taxonomy for diagnostic evaluation. The reference of a check-point is its corresponding part in the target sentence. The evaluation is performed by matching the candidate translation corresponding to the references of the check-points. The extraction of the check-points is an automatic process using word aligner and parsers. We control the noise of the word aligner and parsers within tolerable scope by selecting

© 2008. Licensed under the *Creative Commons Attribution-Noncommercial-Share Alike 3.0 Unported* license (http://creativecommons.org/licenses/by-nc-sa/3.0/). Some rights reserved.

reliable subset of the check-points and weighting the references with confidence.

The check-points of various kinds extracted in this way have shown to be effective in performing diagnostic evaluation of MT systems. In addition, scores of check-points are also approved to be useful to improve the ranking of MT systems as additional features at sentence level and document level.

The rest of the paper is structured in the following way: Section 2 gives the overview of the process of the diagnostic evaluation. Section 3 introduces the design of check-point taxonomy. Section 4 explains the details of construction of check-point database and the methods of reducing the noise of aligner and parsers. Section 5 explains the matching approach. In Section 6, we introduce the experiments on different MT systems to demonstrate the capability of the diagnostic evaluation. In Section 7, we show that the check-points can be used to improve the current ranking methods of MT systems. Section 8 compares our approach with related evaluation approaches. We conclude this work in Section 9.

2 Overview of Diagnostic Evaluation

In our implementation, we first build a check-point database encoded in XML by associating a test sentence with qualified check-points it contains. This process can be described as following steps:

- Collect a large amount of parallel sentences from the web or book collections.
- Parse the sentences of source language and target language.
- Perform the word alignments between each sentence pair.
- For each category of check-points, extract the check-points from the parsed sentence pairs.
- Determine the references of each check-point in source language based on the word alignment.

With the extracted check-point database, the diagnostic evaluation of an MT system is performed with the following steps:

- The test sentences are selected from the database based on the selected categories of check-points to be evaluated.
- For each check-point, we calculate the number of matched n-grams of the references against the translated sentence of the MT system. The credit of the MT system in translating this check-point is obtained after necessary normalization.
- The credit of a category can be obtained by summing up the credits of all check-points of this category. Then the credit of an MT system can be obtained by summing up the credits of all categories.
- Finally, scores of system, category groups (e.g. Words), single category (e.g. Noun), and detail information of n-gram matching of each check-point are all provided to the developers to diagnose the MT system.

3 Linguistic Check-Point Taxonomy

The taxonomy of automatic diagnostic evaluation should be widely accepted so that the diagnostic results can be explained and shared with each other. We will also need to remove the sophisticated categories that are out of the capability of current NLP tools to recognize.

In light of this consideration, for Chinese-English machine translation, we adopted the manual taxonomy introduced by (Lv, 2000; Liu, 2002) and removed items that are beyond the capability of our parsers. The taxonomy includes typical check-pints at word, phrase and sentence levels. Some examples of the representative check-points at different levels are provided below:

- Word level check-points:
  a. Preposition word e.g., 于(in), 在(at)
  b. Ambiguous word e.g., 打(play)
  c. New word[1] e.g., 朋克(Punk)
- Phrase level check-points:
  a. Collocation. e.g., 油炸-食品(fired – food)
  b. Repetitive word combination. e.g., 看看 (have a look)
  c. Subjective-predicate phrase e.g., 他*说, (he*said)
- Sentence level check-points:
  a. "BA" sentence[2]: 他把(BA)书拿走了. (He took away the book.)
  b. "BEI" sentence[3]: 花瓶被(BEI)打碎了. (The vase was broken.)

[1] New words are the terms extracted from web which can be a name entity or popular words emerging recently.
[2] In a "BA" sentence, the object which normally follows the verb occurs preverbally, marked by word "BA".
[3] "BEI" sentence is a kind of passive voice in Chinese marked by word "BEI".

Our implementation of Chinese-English check-point taxonomy contains 22 categories and English-Chinese check-point taxonomy contains 20 categories. Table 1 and 2 show the two taxonomies. In practice, any tag in parsers (e.g. NP) can be easily added as new category.

Word level		
Ambiguous word	New word	Idiom
Noun	Verb	Adjective
Pronoun	Adverb	Preposition
Quantifier	Repetitive word	Collocation
Phrase level		
Subject-predicate phrase	Predicate-object phrase	Preposition-object phrase
Measure phrase	Location phrase	
Sentence level		
BA sentence	BEI sentence	SHI sentence
YOU sentence	Compound sentence	

Table 1: Chinese check-point taxonomy

Word level		
Noun	Verb (with Tense)	Modal verb
Adjective	Adverb	Pronoun
Preposition	Ambiguous word	Plurality
Possessive	Comparative & Superlative degree	
Phrase level		
Noun phrase	Verb phrase	Adjective phrase
Adverb phrase	Preposition phrase	
Sentence level		
Attribute clause	Adverbial clause	Noun clause
Hyperbaton		

Table 2: English check-point taxonomy

4 Construction of Check-Point Database

Given a bilingual corpus with word alignment, the construction of check-point database consists of following two steps. First, the information of pos-tag, dependency structure and constituent structure can be identified with parsers. Then check-points of different categories are identified. Check-points of word-level categories such as Chinese idiom and English ambiguous words are extracted with human-made dictionaries, and the check-points of New-Word are extracted with a new word list mined from the web. A set of human-made rules are employed to extract certain categories involving sentence types such as compound sentence.

Second, for a check-point, with the word alignment information, the corresponding target language portion is identified as the reference of this check-point. The following example illustrates the process of extracting check-points from a parallel sentence pair.

- A Chinese-English sentence pair:
  他们反对建立储备金.
  They opposed the building of reserve funds.
- Word segmentation and pos-tagging:
  他们/R 反对/V 建立/V 储备金/N . /P
- Parsing result (e.g. a dependency result):
  (SUB, 1/反对, 0/他们) (OBJ, 1/反对, 2/建立) (OBJ, 2/建立, 3/储备金)
- Word alignment:
  (1; 1); (2; 2); (3; 4); (4; 6,7);
- The check-points in table 3 are extracted:

Category	Check-point	Reference
New word	储备金	*reserve funds*
Ambiguous word	建立	*building*
Predicate – object phrase	建立储备金	*the building of reserve funds*
Subject-predicate phrase	他们反对	*They opposed*

Table 3: Example of check-point extraction

To extract the categories of check-points of different schema of syntactic analysis such as constitute structure and dependency structure, three parsers including a Chinese skeleton parser (a kind of dependency parser) (Zhou, 2000), Stanford statistical parser and Berkeley statistical parser (Klein 2003) are used to parse the Chinese and English sentences. As explained in next section, these multiple parsers are also used to select high confident check-points. To get word alignment, an existing tool GIZA++ (Och 2003) is used.

4.1 Reducing the Noise of the Parser

The reliability of the check-points mainly depends on the accuracy of the parsers. We can achieve high quality word level check-points with the state-of-the-art POS tagger (94% precision) and dictionaries of various purposes. For sentence level categories, the parser tags and manually compiled rules can also achieve 95% accuracy. For some kinds of categories at phrase level which parsers cannot produce high accuracy, we only select the check-points which can be identified by multiple parsers, that is, adopt the intersection of the parsers results. Table 4 shows the improvement brought by this approach. Column 1 and 2 shows the precision of 6 major types of phrases in Stanford and Berkeley parser. Column 3 shows the precision of intersection and column 4 shows the reduction of the number of check-points when adopting the intersection results. The test corpus is a part of

Penn Chinese Treebank which is not contained in the training corpus of two statistical parsers. (Klein 2003).

	Stf%	Brk%	Inter%	Tpts redu%
NP	87.37	86.03	95.83	17.06
VP	87.34	82.87	95.23	19.68
PP	90.60	88.56	96.00	11.50
QP	98.12	92.90	99.21	6.31
ADJP	91.95	90.87	96.41	10.20
ADVP	95.21	94.25	92.64	3.92

Table 4: Precision of parsers and their intersection (Stf is Stanford, Brk is Berkelry)

4.2 Alleviating the Impact of Alignment Noise

Except for sentence level check-points whose references are the whole sentences and New Word, Idiom check-points whose references are extracted from dictionary, the quality of the references are impacted by the alignment accuracy. To alleviate the noise of aligner we use the lexical dictionary to check the reliability of references. Suppose c is a check-point, for each reference $c.r$ of c we calculate the dictionary matching degree $DM(c.r)$ with the source side $c.s$ of c:

$$DM(c.r) = Max(0.1, \frac{CoCnt(c.r, Dic(c.s))}{WordCnt(c.r)}) \quad (1)$$

Where $Dic(x)$ is a word bag contains all words in the dictionary translations of each source word in x. $CoCnt(x, y)$ is the count of the common words in x and y. $WordCnt(x)$ is the count of words in x. Specially, if $c.r$ is not obtained based on alignment $DM(c.r)$ will be 1. Because the limitation of dictionary, a zero DM score not always means the reference is completely wrong, so we force the DM score to be not less than a minimum value (e.g. 0.1). DM score will further be used in evaluation in section 5.

To better understand the reliability of the references and explore whether increasing the number of check-points could also alleviate the impact of noise, we built two check-point databases from a human-aligned corpus (with 60,000 sentence pairs) and an automatically aligned corpus (using GIZA++) respectively and tested 10 different SMT systems[4] with them. The Spearman correlation is calculated between two ranked lists of the 10 evaluation results against the two databases. A higher correlation score means that the impact of the mistakes in word alignment is weaker. The experiment is repeated on 6 subsets of the database with the size from 500 sentences to 16K sentences to check the impact of the corpus size.

At system level, high correlations are found at different corpus sizes. At category level, correlations are found to be low for some categories at small size and become higher at larger corpus size. The results indicate that the impact of the alignment quality can be ignored if the corpus size is at large scale. As the check-points can be extracted fully automatically, increasing the size of check-point database will not bring extra cost and efforts. Empirically, the proper scale is set to be 2000 or more sentences according to the Table 6.

	500	1K	2K	4K	8K	16K
Ambiguous word	0.98	0.98	0.98	0.98	0.96	0.98
Noun	0.93	0.99	0.99	0.89	0.8	0.86
Verb	0.97	0.97	0.99	0.99	0.95	0.92
Adjective	0.16	0.19	0.57	0.75	0.77	0.97
Pronoun	0.96	1	0.93	0.99	0.97	0.99
Adverb	0.38	0.77	0.8	0.96	0.72	0.84
Preposition	0.56	0.86	0.9	0.9	0.97	0.96
Quantifier	1	0.46	0.46	0.98	0.85	0.96
Repetitive Word	0.99	0.99	0.97	0.89	0.73	0.95
Collocation	0.42	0.77	0.77	0.77	0.73	0.88
Subject-predicate phrase	0.06	0.8	0.95	1	0.96	0.84
Predicate-object phrase	0.84	0.96	0.78	0.7	0.78	0.88
Preposition-object phrase	0.51	0.5	0.93	0.95	0.87	0.99
Measure phrase	0.91	0.67	0.95	0.95	0.87	0.97
Location phrase	0.62	0.54	0.55	0.55	0.85	0.89
SYSTEM	0.95	0.95	0.98	0.99	0.97	0.98

Table 6: Impact of word alignment at different sizes of test corpus.

5 Matching Check-Points for Evaluation

Evaluation can be carried out at multiple options: for certain linguistic category, a group of categories or entire taxonomy. For instance, in Chinese-English translation task, if a MT developer would like to know the ability to translate idiom, then a number of parallel sentences containing idiom check-points are selected from the database. Then the system translation sentences are matched to the references of the check-points of idioms.

[4] These systems are derived from an in-house phrase based SMT engine with different parameter sets.

To calculate the credit at different occasions of matching, similar to BLEU, we split each reference of a check-point into a set of n-grams and sum up the gains over all grams as the credit of this check-point. Especially, if the check-point is not consecutive we use a special token (e.g. "*") to represent a component which can be wildcard matched by any word sequence. We use the following examples to demonstrate the splitting and matching of grams.

- Consecutive check-point:
  Check- point: 在打鼓
  Reference: playing a drum
  Candidate translation: He is playing a drum.
  Matched n-grams: playing; a; drum; playing a; a drum; playing a drum

- Not consecutive check-point:
  Check- point: 他们*打
  Reference: They*playing
  Candidate translation: They are playing cop per drum.
  Matched n-grams: They; playing; They * playing

Additionally, to match word inflections, 3 different options of matching granularity are defined as follows.

- Normal: matching with exact form.
- Lower-case: matching with lowercase.
- Stem: matching with the stem of the word.

For a check-point c and references set R of c, we select the r^* in R which matches the translation best based on formula (2).

$$r^* = \arg\max_{r \in R}\left(DM(r) \bullet \frac{\sum_{n-gram \in r} Match(n-gram)}{\sum_{n-gram' \in r} Count(n-gram')}\right) \quad (2)$$

When we calculate the recall of a set of check-points C (C can be a single check-point, a category or a category group), r^* of each check-point c in C are merged into one reference set R^* and the recall of C is obtained using formula (3) on R^*.

$$\mathrm{Re}(C) = \frac{\sum_{r \in R^*} (DM(r) \bullet \sum_{n-gram \in r} Match(n-gram))}{\sum_{r' \in R^*} (DM(r') \bullet \sum_{n-gram' \in r'} Count(n-gram'))} \quad (3)$$

A penalty is also introduced to punish the redundancy of candidate sentences, where *length(T)* is the average length of all translation sentences and *length(R)* is the average length of all reference sentences.

$$Penalty = \begin{cases} \frac{length(R)}{length(T)} & if\ length(T) > length(R) \\ 1 & Otherwise \end{cases} \quad (4)$$

Then, the final score of C will be:

$$Score\ (C) = \mathrm{Re}\,(C) \bullet Penalty \quad (5)$$

6 Experiments on MT System Diagnoses

In this section, to demonstrate the ability of our approach in the diagnoses of MT systems, we apply diagnostic evaluation to 3 statistical MT (SMT) systems and a rule-based MT (RMT) system respectively. We compare two SMT systems to understand the strength and shortcoming of each of them, and also compare a SMT system with the RMT system. The test corpus is NIST05 test data with 54852 check-points.

First SMT system (system A) is an implementation of classical phrase based SMT. The second SMT system (system B) shares the same decoder with system A and introduces a preprocess to reorder the long phrases in source sentences according to the syntax structure before decoding (Chiho Li et al., 2007). The third SMT system (system C) is a popular internet service and the RMT system (system D) is a popular commercial system.

In the first experiment, we diagnose the system A and B and compare the results as shown in table 7. When evaluated using BLEU, system B achieved a 0.005 points increase on top of system A which is not a very significant difference. The diagnostic results in table 7 provide much richer information. The results indicate that two systems perform similar at the word level categories while at all phrase level categories, system B performs better. This result reflects the benefit from the reordering of complex phrases in system B. Paired t-statistic score for each pair of category scores is also calculated by repeating the evaluation on a random copy of the test set with replacement (Koehn 2004). An absolute score beyond 2.17 of paired t-statistic means the difference of the samples is statistically significant (above 95%). Table 8 and 9 show an instance of the check-point and its evaluation in this experiment.

	System A	System B	T score
WORDs			
Idiom	0.1933	0.2370	13.38
Adjective	0.5836	0.5577	-17.43
Pronoun	0.7566	0.7344	-13.49
Adverb	0.5365	0.5433	7.11
Preposition	0.6529	0.6456	-6.21
Repetitive word	0.3363	0.3958	9.86
PHRASEs			
Subject-predicate	0.5117	0.5206	7.36
Predicate-object	0.4041	0.4180	15.52
Predicate-complement	0.4409	0.5125	9.51
Measure phrase	0.5030	0.5092	3.56
Location phrase	0.5245	0.5338	2.83
GROUPs			
WORDs	0.4839	0.4855	2.03
PHRASEs	0.4744	0.4964	13.97
SYSTEM (Linguistic)	0.4263	0.4370	16.50
SYSTEM (BLEU)	0.3564	0.3614	7.91

Table 7: Diagnose of SMT systems

Source Sentence	不过泰国总理戴克辛誓言将继续在其国内进行搜寻.
Category	Preposition_Object_Phrase
Check-Point	在 其 国内
Reference 1	in this country $DM = 0.5$
Reference 2	in his country $DM = 0.5$
System A Translation	but the prime minister of thailand Dex-in vowed to continue in domestic the search.
System B Translation	but the prime minister of thailand Dex-in vowed to continue the search in his country.

Table 8: An instance of the check-point.

	System A	System B
Ref 1: Match/Total	1/6	2/6
Ref 2: Match/Total	1/6	6/6
Score	0.17	1

Table 9: N-gram matching rate and scores.

Type	Normal	Lower	Stem
Ambiguous word	0.49/0.42	0.50/0.42	0.53/0.46
New word	0.13/0.13	0.37/0.32	0.42/0.35
Idiom	0.43/0.66	0.46/0.67	0.51/0.71
Pronoun	0.60/0.68	0.69/0.75	0.66/0.75
Preposition	0.38/0.42	0.42/0.45	0.43/0.46
Collocation	0.66/0.54	0.66/0.55	0.70/0.56
Subject-predicate phrase	0.46/0.30	0.51/0.36	0.58/0.42
Predicate-object phrase	0.37/0.25	0.37/0.26	0.47/0.29
Compound sentence	0.22/0.16	0.23/0.16	0.23/0.17

Table 10: Diagnose of SMT and RMT.

In the second experiment, we diagnose system C and D and compare the results. The BLEU score of system C is 0.3005 and system D is 0.2606. Table 10 shows the diagnostic results on categories with significant differences. Scores calculated with 3 matching options described in section 5 are given ("Lower" means Lowercase. The scores are listed in the form "SMT score/RMT score"). The diagnostic results indicate that system C performs better on most categories than system D, but system D performs better on categories like idiom, pronoun and preposition. This result reveals a key difference between two types of MT systems: the SMT works well on the open categories that can be handled by context, while the RMT works well on closed categories which are easily translated by linguistic rules.

As the results of two experiments demonstrate, the diagnostic evaluation provides rich information of the capability of translating various important linguistic categories beyond a single system score. It successfully distinguishes the specific difference between the MT systems whose system level performance is similar. It can also diagnose the MT system with different architectures. Diagnostic evaluation tells the developers about the direction to improve the system. Along with the scores of categories, the diagnostic evaluation provides the system translation and references at every check-point so that the developers can trace and understand about how the MT system works on every single instance.

7 Experiments on Ranking MT Systems

Offering a general evaluation at system level is the major goal of state-of-the-art evaluation methods including widely accepted n-gram metrics. The absence of linguistic knowledge in BLEU motivated many work to integrate linguistic features into evaluation metric. In (Yang 2007), the evaluation of SMT systems is alternately formulated as a ranking problem. Different linguistic features are combined with BLEU such as matching rate of dependency relations of translation candidates against the reference sentences. The experiments demonstrate that the dependency matching rate feature can increase the ranking accuracy in some cases. Compared to dependency structure, the linguistic categories in our approach showcase more extensive features. It would be interesting to see whether the linguistic categories can be used to further improve the ranking of SMT systems.

In experiments, we use the scores of linguistic categories, dependency matching rate, scores of BLEU and other popular metrics as ranking features of MT systems and trained by Ranking SVM of SVMlight (Joachims, 1998). We performed the ranking experiments on ACL 2005 workshop data, ranking 7 MT translations with three-fold cross-validation both on sentence level and document level. The Spearman score is used to calculate the correlation with human assessments. Table 11 and 12 show the results of the different feature sets on sentence level and document level respectively.

As shown in experiment results linguistic categories (LC), when used alone, are better related with human assessments than BLEU and GTM. When combined with the baseline metrics (BLEU & NIST), LC scores further improve the correlation score, better than dependence matching rate (DP). LC scores are obtained by matching the exact form of the words as METEOR(exact) does. NIST+LC combination score is better than METEOR(exact) at sentence and document level, and also better than METEOR(exact&syn) (syn means wn_synonymy module in METEOR) at document level. This results indicate the ability of linguistic features in improving the performance of ranking task.

	Mean Correlation
BLEU 4	0.245
NIST 5	0.307
GTM (e=2)	0.251
METEOR(exact)	0.306
METEOR(exact&syn)	0.327
DP	0.246
LC	0.263
BLEU+DP	0.270
BLEU+ LC	0.288
BLEU+ DP +LC	0.307
NIST+ LC	0.322
NIST+ DP +LC	0.333

Table11: Sentence level ranking (DP means dependency and LC means linguistic categories)

	Mean Correlation
BLEU 4	0.305
NIST 5	0.373
GTM (e=2)	0.327
METEOR(exact)	0.363
METEOR(exact&syn)	0.394
DP	0.323
LC	0.369
BLEU+DP	0.325
BLEU+ LC	0.387
BLEU+ DP +LC	0.332
NIST+ LC	0.409
NIST+ DP +LC	0.359

Table 12: Document level ranking

8 Comparison with Related Work

This work is inspired by (Yu, 1993) with many extensions. (Yu, 1993) proposed MTE evaluation system based on check-points for English-Chinese machine translation systems with human craft linguistic taxonomy including 3,200 pairs of sentences containing 6 classes of check-points. Their check-points were manually constructed by human experts, therefore it will be costly to build new test corpus while the check-points in our approach are constructed automatically. Another limitation of their work is that only binary score is used for credits while we use n-gram matching rate which provides a broader coverage of different levels of matching.

There are many recent work motivated by n-gram based approach. (Callison-Burch et al., 2006) criticized the inadequate accuracy of evaluation at the sentence level. (Lin and Och, 2004) used longest common subsequence and skip-bigram statistics. (Banerjee and Lavie, 2005) calculated the scores by matching the unigrams on the surface forms, stemmed forms and senses. (Liu et al., 2005) used syntactic features and unlabeled head-modifier dependencies to evaluate MT quality, outperforming BLEU on sentence level correlations with human judgment. (Gimenez and Marquez, 2007) showed that linguistic features at more abstract levels such as dependency relation may provide more reliable system rankings. (Yang et al., 2007) formulates MT evaluation as a ranking problems leading to greater correlation with human assessment at the sentence level.

There are many differences between these n-gram based methods and our approach. In n-gram approach, a sentence is viewed as a collection of n-grams with different length without differentiating the specific linguistic phenomena. In our approach, a sentence is viewed as a collection of check-points with different types and depth, conforming to a clear linguistic taxonomy. Furthermore, in n-gram approach, only one general score at the system level is provided which make it not suitable for system diagnoses, while in our approach we can give scores of linguistic categories and provide much richer information to help developers to find the concrete strength and flaws of the system, in addition to the general score. The n-gram based metric is not very effective when comparing the systems with different architectures or systems with similar general score, while our approach is more effective in both cases by digging into the multiple linguistic levels and disclosing the latent differences of the systems.

9 Conclusion and Future Work

This paper presents an automatically diagnostic evaluation methods on MT based on linguistic check-points automatically constructed. In contrast with the metrics which only give a general score, our evaluation system can give developers feedback about the faults and strength of an MT system regarding specific linguistic category or category group. Different with the existing work based on check-points, our work presents an approach to automatically generate the check-point database. We show that although there is some noise brought from word alignment and parsing, we can effectively alleviate the problem by refining the parser results, weighting the reference with confidence score and providing large quantity of check-points.

The experiments demonstrate that this method can uncover the specific difference between MT systems with similar architectures and different architectures. It is also demonstrated that the linguistic check-points can be used as new features to improve the ranking task of MT systems.

Although we present the diagnostic evaluation method with Chinese-English language pair, our approach can be applied to other language pair if syntax parser and word aligner are available.

The taxonomy used in current proposal is based on the human-made linguistic system. An interesting problem to be explored in the future is whether the taxonomy could be constructed automatically from the parsing results.

References

Statanjeev Banerjee, Alon Lavie. 2005. *METEOR: An Automatic Metric for MT Evaluation with Improved Correlation with Human Judgements*. In Proceedings of the ACL Workshop on Intrinsic and Extrinsic Evaluation Measures for Machine Translation and/or Summarization 2005.

Chris Callison-Burch, Miles Osborne, Philipp Koehn. 2006. *Re-evaluating the Role of Bleu in Machine Translation Research*. In Proceedings of the European Chapter of the ACL 2006.

Martin Chodorow, Claudia Leacock. 2000. *An unsupervised method for detecting grammatical errors,* In 1st Meeting of the North America Chapter of the ACL, pp.140–147, 2000.

Thorsten Joachims. 1998. *Making Large-scale Support Vector Machine Learning Practical*, In B. Scholkopf, C. Burges, A. Smola. Advances in Kernel Methods: Support VectorMachines, MIT Press, Cambridge, MA, December.

Jesus Gimenez and Llis Marquez. 2007. *Linguistic features for automatic evaluation of heterogeneous MT systems*, Workshop of statistical machine translation in conjunction with 45th ACL, 2007.

Dan Klein, Christopher Manning. 2003. *Accurate Unlexicalized Parsing*, Proceedings of the 41th Meeting of the ACL, pp. 423-430.

Philipp Koehn. 2004. *Statistical Significance Tests for Machine Translation Evaluation*. In Proc. of the EMNLP, Barcelona, Spain.

Chiho Li, Minghui Li, Dongdong Zhang, Mu Li, Ming Zhou, Yi Guan. 2007. *A Probabilistic Approach to Syntax-based Reor-dering for SMT*. In Proceedings of the 45th ACL, 2007.

Chin-Yew Lin and Franz Josef Och. 2004. *Automatic evaluation of machine translation quality using longest common subsequence and skip-bigram statistics*. In Proceedings of the 42th ACL 2004.

Ding Liu, Daniel Gildea. 2005. *Syntactic Features for Evaluation of Machine Translation*, ACL Workshop on Intrinsic and Extrinsic Evaluation Measures for Machine Translation and/or Summarization.

Shuxin Liu. 2002. *Linguistics of Contemporary Chinese Language (in Chinese)*, Advanced Education Publisher.

Jiping Lv. 2000. *Foundation of Mandarin Grammar (in Chinese)*, Shangwu Publisher.

Franz Josef Och, Hermann Ney. 2003. *A Systematic Comparison of Various Statistical Alignment Models*, Computational Linguistics, volume 29, number 1, pp. 19-51 March 2003.

Kishore Papieni, Salim Roukos, Todd Ward, Wei-Jing Zhu. 2002. *BLEU: a method for automatic evaluation of machine translation*, In Proceedings of the ACL 2002.

Shiwen Yu. 1993. *Automatic evaluation of output quality for machine translation systems*, In Proceedings of the evaluators' forum, April 21-24, 1991, Les Rasses, Vaud, 1993.

Yang Ye, Ming Zhou, Chinyew Lin. 2007. *Sentence level machine translation evaluation as a ranking problem: one step aside from BLEU*, In Workshop of statistical machine translation, in conjunction with 45th ACL, 2007.

Ming Zhou. 2000, *A Block-Based Robust Dependency Parser for Unrestricted Chinese Text*. Proceedings of Second Chinese Language Processing Workshop, 2000, held in conjunction with ACL, 2000.

Multi-Criteria-based Strategy to Stop Active Learning for Data Annotation

Jingbo Zhu Huizhen Wang
Natural Language Processing Laboratory
Northeastern University
Shenyang, Liaoning, P.R.China 110004
zhujingbo@mail.neu.edu.cn
wanghuizhen@mail.neu.edu.cn

Eduard Hovy
University of Southern California
Information Sciences Institute
4676 Admiralty Way
Marina del Rey, CA 90292-6695
hovy@isi.edu

Abstract

In this paper, we address the issue of deciding when to stop active learning for building a labeled training corpus. Firstly, this paper presents a new stopping criterion, classification-change, which considers the potential ability of each unlabeled example on changing decision boundaries. Secondly, a multi-criteria-based combination strategy is proposed to solve the problem of predefining an appropriate threshold for each confidence-based stopping criterion, such as max-confidence, min-error, and overall-uncertainty. Finally, we examine the effectiveness of these stopping criteria on uncertainty sampling and heterogeneous uncertainty sampling for active learning. Experimental results show that these stopping criteria work well on evaluation data sets, and the combination strategies outperform individual criteria.

1 Introduction

Creating a large labeled training corpus is very expensive and time-consuming in some real-world applications. For example, it is a crucial issue for automated word sense disambiguation task, because validations of sense definitions and sense-tagged data annotation have to be done by human experts, e.g. OntoNotes project (Hovy *et al.*, 2006).

Active learning aims to minimize the amount of human labeling effort by automatically selecting the most informative unlabeled example for human annotation. In recent years active learning has been widely studied in natural language processing (NLP) applications, such as word sense disambiguation (WSD) (Chen *et al.*, 2006; Zhu and Hovy, 2007), text classification (TC) (Lewis and Gale, 1994; McCallum and Nigam, 1998a), named entity recognition (Shen *et al.*, 2004), chunking (Ngai and Yarowsky, 2000), and statistical parsing (Tang *et al.*, 2002).

However, deciding when to stop active learning is still an unsolved problem and seldom mentioned issue in previous studies. Actually it is a very important practical issue in real-world applications, because it obviously makes no sense to continue the active learning procedure until the whole unlabeled corpus has been labeled. The active learning process can be ended when the current classifier reaches the maximum effectiveness. In principle, how to learn a stopping criterion is a problem of estimation of classifier (i.e. learner) effectiveness during active learning (Lewis and Gale, 1994).

In this paper, we address the issue of a stopping criterion for pool-based active learning with uncertainty sampling (Lewis and Gale, 1994), and propose a multi-criteria-based approach to determining when to stop active learning process. Firstly, this paper makes a comprehensive analysis on some confidence-based stopping criteria (Zhu and Hovy, 2007), including max-confidence, min-error and overall-uncertainty, then proposes a new stopping criterion, *classification-change*, which considers the potential ability of each unlabeled example on changing decision boundaries. Secondly, a combination strategy is proposed to solve the problem of predefining an appropriate threshold for each confidence-based stopping criterion in a specific task.

In uncertainty sampling scheme, the most uncertain unlabeled example is considered as the most informative case selected by active learner at each learning cycle. However, an uncertain example for one classifier may be not an uncer-

© 2008. Licensed under the *Creative Commons Attribution-Noncommercial-Share Alike 3.0 Unported* license (http://creativecommons.org/licenses/by-nc-sa/3.0/). Some rights reserved.

tain example for other classifiers. When using active learning for real-world applications such as WSD, it is possible that a classifier of one type selects samples for training a classifier of another type, called the heterogeneous approach (Lewis and Catlett, 1994). For example, the final trained classifier for WSD is often different from the classifier used in active learning for constructing the training corpus.

To date, no one has studied the stopping criterion issue for the heterogeneous approach. In this paper, we examine the effectiveness of each stopping criterion on both traditional uncertainty sampling and heterogeneous uncertainty sampling for active learning. Experimental results of active learning for WSD and TC tasks show that these proposed stopping criteria work well on evaluation data sets, and the combination strategies outperform individual criteria.

2 Active Learning Process

In this paper, we are interested in *uncertainty sampling* for pool-based active learning (Lewis and Gale, 1994), in which an unlabeled example x with maximum uncertainty is selected to augment the training data at each learning cycle. The maximum uncertainty implies that the current classifier has the least confidence on its classification of this unlabeled example.

Actually active learning is a two-stage process in which a small number of labeled samples and a large number of unlabeled examples are first collected in the initialization stage, and a closed-loop stage of query and retraining is adopted.

Procedure: Active Learning Process

Input: initial small training set L, and pool of unlabeled data set U

Use L to train the initial classifier C

Repeat

1. Use the current classifier C to label all unlabeled examples in U
2. Use uncertainty sampling technique to select m most informative unlabeled examples, and ask oracle H for labeling
3. Augment L with these m new examples, and remove them from U
4. Use L to retrain the current classifier C

Until the predefined stopping criterion SC is met.

Figure 1. Active learning with uncertainty sampling technique

3 Stopping Criteria for Active Learning

In this section, we mainly address the problem of general stopping criteria for active leanring, and study how to define a reasonable and appropriate stopping criterion SC shown in Fig. 1.

3.1 Effectiveness Estimation and Confidence Estimation

To examine whether the classifier has reached the maximum effectiveness during active learning procedure, it seems an appealing solution when repeated learning cycles show no significant performance improvement. However, this is often not feasible. To investigate the impact of performance change on defining a stopping criterion for active learning, we first give an example of active learning for WSD shown in Fig. 2.

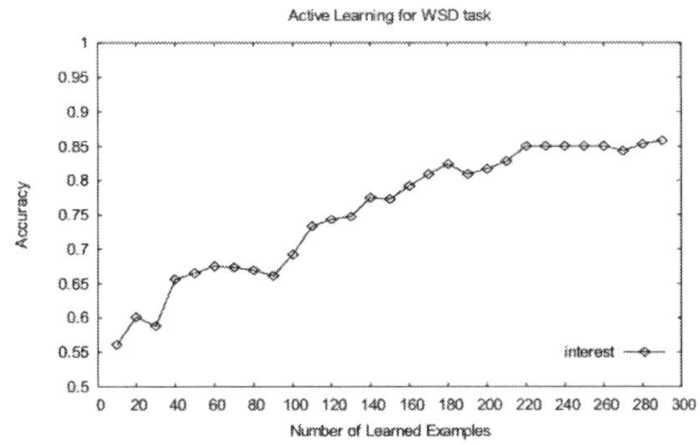

Figure 2. An example of active learning for WSD on word "*interest*".

Fig. 2 shows that the accuracy performance generally increases, but apparently degrades at iterations 30, 90 and 190, and does not change anymore during iterations 220-260 in the active learning process. Actually the first time of the highest performance of 91.5% is achieved at 900 which is not shown in Fig. 2. Although the accuracy performance curve shows an increasing trend, it is not monotonically increasing. It is not easy to automatically determine the point of no significant performance improvement on the validation set, because points such as 30 or 90 would mislead a final judgment.

Besides, there is a problem of performance estimation of the current classifier during active learning process, because a separate validation set should be prepared in advance, a procedure that causes additional (high) cost since it is often done manually. Besides, how many samples are required for the pregiven separate validation set is an open question. Too few samples may not be adequate for a reasonable estimate and may result in an incorrect result. Too many samples would increase the building cost.

To define a stopping criterion for active learning, Zhu and hovy (2007) considered the estimation of the classifier's effectiveness as the second task of confidence estimation of the classifier on its classification of all remaining unlabeled data. In the following section, we first introduce two confidence-based criteria, max-confidence and min-error, proposed by Zhu and Hovy (2007).

3.2 Max-Confidence

In uncertainty sampling scheme, if the uncertainty value of the most informative unlabeled example is sufficiently small, we can assume that the current classifier has sufficient confidence on its classification of the remaining unlabeled data. So the active learning process can be ended. Based on such assumption, Zhu and Hovy (2007) proposed *max-confidence* criterion based on the uncertainty estimation of the most informative unlabeled example. Its strategy is to consider whether the uncertainty value of the most informative unlabeled example is less than a very small predefined threshold.

3.3 Min-Error

As shown in Fig. 1, in uncertainty sampling scheme, the current classifier has the least confidence on its classification of these top-m selected unlabeled examples. If the current classifier can correctly classify these most informative examples, we can assume that the current classifier have sufficient confidence on its classification of the remaining unlabeled data. Based on such assumption, Zhu and Hovy (2007) proposed *min-error* criterion based on feedback from the oracle. Its strategy is to consider whether the current classifier can correctly predict the labels on these selected unlabeled examples, or the accuracy performance of the current classifier on these most informative examples is larger than a predefined threshold.

3.4 Overall-Uncertainty

The motivation behind the *overall-uncertainty* method is similar to that of the max-confidence method. However, the max-confidence method only considers the most informative example at each learning cycle. The overall-uncertainty method considers the overall uncertainty on all unlabeled examples. If the overall uncertainty of all unlabeled examples becomes very small, we can assume that the current classifier has sufficient confidence on its classification of the remaining unlabeled data. Based on such assumption, we propose overall-uncertainty method which is to consider whether the average uncertainty value of all remaining unlabeled examples is less than a very small predefined threshold.

3.5 Classification-Change

There is another problem of estimating classifier performance during active learning process. Cross-validation on the training set is almost impractical during the active learning procedure, because the alternative of requiring a held-out validation set for active learning is counterproductive. Hence we should look for a self-contained method.

Actually the motivation behind uncertainty sampling is to find some unlabeled examples near decision boundaries, and use them to clarify the position of decision boundaries. The current classifier considers such unlabeled examples near decision boundaries as the most informative examples in uncertainty sampling scheme for active learning. In other words, we assume that an unlabeled example with maximum uncertainty has the highest chance to change the decision boundaries.

Based on the above analysis, we think the active learning process can stop if there is no unlabeled example that can potentially change the decision boundaries. However, in practice, it is almost impossible to exactly recognize which unlabeled example can truly change the decision boundaries in the next learning cycle, because the true label of each unlabeled example is unknown.

To solve this problem, we make an assumption that labeling an unlabeled example may shift the decision boundaries if this example was previously "outside" and is now "inside". In other words, if an unlabeled example is automatically assigned to two different labels during two recent learning cycles[2], we think that the labeling of this unlabeled example has a good chance to change the decision boundaries.

Based on such assumption, we propose a new approach based on classification change of each unlabeled example during two recent consecutive learning cycles ("previous" and "current"), called the *classification-change* method. Its strategy is to stop the active learning process by considering whether no classification change happens to the remaining unlabeled examples during two recent consecutive learning cycles. If true, we assume that the current classifier has sufficient confidence on its classification of the remaining unla-

[2] For example, an unlabeled example x was classified into class A at i^{th} iteration, and class B at $i+1^{th}$ iteration.

beled data, because all unlabeled examples near decision boundaries have been exhausted, and no further labeling will affect active learner.

4 Combination Strategy

As for the above three confidence-based stopping criteria such as max-confidence, min-error and overall-uncertainty, how to automatically determine an appropriate threshold in a specific task is a crucial problem. We think that different appropriate thresholds are needed for various active learning applications.

To solve this problem, in this section we propose a general combination strategy by considering the best of both classification-change and a confidence-based criterion, in which the predefined threshold of the confidence-based stopping criterion can be automatically updated during active learning.

The motivation behind the general combination strategy is to check whether the active learning becomes stable (i.e. check whether the classification-change method is met) when the current confidence-based stopping criterion is satisfied. If not, we think there are some remaining unlabeled examples that can potentially shift the decision boundaries, even if they are considered as certain cases from the current classifier's viewpoints. In this case, the threshold of the current confidence-based stopping criterion should be automatically revised to keep continuing the active learning process. The general combination strategy can be summarized as follows.

Procedure: General combination strategy
Given:
- stopping criterion 1: max-confidence or min-error or overall-uncertainty
- Stopping criterion 2: classification-change
- The predefined threshold for stopping criterion 1 is initially set to β

Steps(during active learning process):
1. First check whether stopping criterion 1 is satisfied. If yes, go to 2;
2. Then check whether stopping criterion 2 is satisfied. If yes, goto 4), otherwise goto 3;
3. Automatically update the current threshold to be a new smaller value for max-confidence and overall-uncertainty, or to be a new larger value for min-error, and then goto 1.
4. Stop active learning process.

Figure 3. General combination strategy

- **Strategy 1**: This strategy combines the max-confidence and classification-change methods simultaneously.
- **Strategy 2**: This strategy combines the min-error and classification-change methods simultaneously.
- **Strategy 3**: This strategy combines the overall-uncertainty and classification-change methods simultaneously.

5 Evaluation

5.1 Experimental Settings

In the following sections, we evaluate the effectiveness of seven stopping criteria for active learning for WSD and TC tasks, including *max-confidence (MC)*, *min-error (ME)*, *overall-uncertainty (OU)*, *classification-change (CC)*, *strategy 1 (CC-MC)*, *strategy 2 (CC-ME)*, and *strategy 3 (CC-OU)*. Following previous studies (Zhu and Hovy, 2007), the predefined thresholds[3] used for MC, ME and OU are set to 0.01, 0.9 and 0.01, respectively.

To evaluate the effectiveness of each stopping criterion, we first construct two types of *baseline* methods called "*All*" and "*First*" methods. "All" method is defined as when all unlabeled examples in the pool are learned. "First" method is defined as when the current classifier reaches the same performance of the "All" method at the first time during the active learning process.

A better stopping criterion can not only achieve almost the same performance given by the "All" baseline method (i.e. *accuracy performance*), but also learn almost the same number of unlabeled examples by the "First" baseline method (i.e. *percentage performance*).

In uncertainty sampling scheme, the well-known entropy-based uncertainty measurement (Chen *et al.*, 2006; Schein and Ungar, 2007) is used in our active learning study as follows:

$$UM(x) = -\sum_{y \in Y} P(y \mid x) \log P(y \mid x) \qquad (1)$$

where $P(y|x)$ is the *a posteriori* probability. We denote the output class $y \in Y = \{y_1, y_2, ..., y_k\}$. *UM* is the uncertainty measurement function based on the entropy estimation of the classifier's posterior distribution.

We utilize maximum entropy (MaxEnt) model (Berger *et al.*, 1996) to design the basic classifier used in active learning for WSD and TC tasks. The advantage of the MaxEnt model is the ability to freely incorporate features from diverse sources into a single, well-grounded statistical

[3] In the following experiments, these thresholds are also used as initial values of β for individual criteria in the general combination strategy shown in Fig. 3.

model. A publicly available MaxEnt toolkit[4] was used in our experiments. To build the MaxEnt-based classifier for WSD, three knowledge sources are used to capture contextual information: *unordered single words in topical context, POS of neighboring words with position information, and local collocations*, which are the same as the knowledge sources used in (Lee and Ng, 2002). In the design of text classifier, the maximum entropy model is also utilized, and no feature selection technique is used.

In the following active learning comparison experiments, the algorithm starts with a randomly chosen initial training set of 10 labeled examples, and makes 10 queries after each learning iteration. A 10 by 10-fold cross-validation was performed. All results reported are the average of 10 trials in each active learning process. In the following comparison experiments, the performance reported on Ontonotes data set is the macro-average on ten nouns, and the performance on TWA data set is the macro-average on six words.

5.2 Data Sets

Six publicly available natural data sets have been used in the following active learning comparison experiments. Three data sets are used for TC tasks: *WebKB*, *Comp2a* and *Comp2b*. The other three data sets are used for WSD tasks: *OntoNotes*, *Interest* and *TWA*.

The WebKB dataset was widely used in TC research. Following previous studies (McCallum and Nigam, 1998b), we use the four most populous categories: *student, faculty, course* and *project*, altogether containing 4199 web pages. In the preprocessing step, we only remove those words that occur merely once without using stemming. The resulting vocabulary has 23803 words.

The Comp2a data set consists of *comp.os.ms-windows.misc* and *comp.sys.ibm.pc.hardware* subset of NewsGroups. The Comp2b data set consists of *comp.graphics* and *comp.windows.x* categories from NewsGroups. Both two data sets have been previously used in active learning for TC (Roy and McCallum, 2001; Schein and Ungar, 2007).

The OntoNotes project (Hovy *et al.*, 2006) uses the WSJ part of the Penn Treebank. The senses of noun words occurring in OntoNotes are linked to the Omega ontology. Ontonotes has been used previously in active learning for WSD tasks (Zhu and Hovy, 2007). In the following comparison experiments, we focus on 10 most frequent nouns[5] previously used in (Zhu and Hovy, 2007): *rate, president, people, part, point, director, revenue, bill, future*, and *order*.

The Interest data set developed by Bruce and Wiebe (1994) has been previously used for WSD (Ng and Lee, 1996). This data set consists of 2369 sentences of the noun "interest" with its correct sense manually labeled. The noun "*interest*" has six different senses in this data set. TWA developed by Mihalcea and Yang on 2003, is sense tagged data for six words with two-way ambiguities, previously used in WSD research. These six words are *bass, crane, motion, palm, plant* and *tank*. All instances were drawn from the British National Corpus.

5.3 Stopping Criteria for Uncertainty Sampling

In order to evaluate the effectiveness of our stopping criteria, we first apply them to uncertainty sampling for active learning for WSD and TC tasks. Table 1 shows that "First" method generally achieves higher performance than that of the "All" method. We can see from the "*Average*" row that stopping criteria MC, ME, CC-MC, CC-ME and CC-OU achieve close average accuracy performance to the "All" method whereas OU and CC achieve lower average accuracy performance. OU method achieves the lowest average accuracy performance. CC-ME achieves the highest average accuracy of 89.6%, followed by CC-MC.

Compared to the "First" method, CC-OU achieves the best average percentage performance of 37.03% (i.e. the closest one to the "First" method), followed by ME method. On six evaluation data sets, Table 1 shows that CC-ME method achieves 4 out of 6 highest accuracy performances, followed by CC-MC and MC methods. And CC-ME method also achieves 3 out of 6 best percentage performance, followed by CC, CC-OU and ME methods.

Among these four individual stopping criteria, ME outperforms MC, OU and CC. However, ME method can only be applied to batch-based selection because ME criterion is based on the feedback from Oracle. Too few informative candidates may not be adequate for obtaining a reasonable feedback for ME criterion.

[4]See http://homepages.inf.ed.ac.uk/s0450736/maxent_toolkit.html

[5] See http://www.nlplab.com/ontonotes-10-nouns.rar

Data set	All	First	MC	ME	OU	CC	CC-MC	CC-ME	CC-OU
WebKB	0.910	0.911	0.910	0.910	0.837	0.912	0.912	**0.913**	0.912
	100%	31.50%	27.11%	29.11%	8.42%	**31.53%**	32.37%	33.02%	**31.53%**
Comp2a	0.880	0.884	0.877	0.879	0.868	0.876	0.879	**0.880**	0.876
	100%	35.12%	31.35%	31.28%	23.29%	27.35%	32.36%	**36.80%**	27.35%
Comp2b	0.900	0.901	0.887	0.888	0.880	0.879	0.891	**0.893**	0.882
	100%	41.66%	37.52%	36.76%	28.36%	30.80%	37.95%	**40.03%**	31.81%
Ontonotes	0.939	0.942	0.929	0.934	0.928	0.936	**0.940**	0.939	0.939
	100%	22.81%	30.19%	**22.14%**	21.81%	18.96%	34.77%	25.60%	24.75%
Interest	0.908	0.910	**0.910**	0.906	0.906	0.901	**0.910**	0.906	0.906
	100%	29.83%	37.54%	28.25%	28.51%	25.55%	37.54%	**28.67%**	28.62%
TWA	0.846	0.858	0.843	0.844	0.837	0.820	0.841	**0.845**	0.838
	100%	59.67%	80.34%	72.71%	70.47%	**61.54%**	86.99%	80.15%	78.12%
Average	0.897	0.901	0.892	0.893	0.876	0.887	0.895	**0.896**	0.892
	100%	37.43%	40.67%	36.71%	30.14%	32.62%	43.66%	40.71%	**37.03%**

Table 1. Effectiveness of seven stopping criteria for uncertainty sampling for active learning. For each data set, Table 1 shows the accuracy of the classifier and percentage of learned instances over all unlabeled data when each stopping criterion is met. The boldface numbers indicate the best corresponding performances.

Data set	All	MC	ME	OU	CC	CC-MC	CC-ME	CC-OU
WebKB	0.858	0.808	0.818	0.601	0.820	0.820	**0.824**	0.820
	100%	27.11%	29.11%	8.42%	31.53%	32.37%	33.02%	31.53%
Comp2a	0.894	0.838	0.839	0.825	0.837	0.838	**0.846**	0.837
	100%	31.35%	31.28%	23.29%	27.35%	32.36%	36.80%	27.35%
Comp2b	0.922	**0.884**	0.882	0.878	0.874	0.885	0.883	0.879
	100%	37.52%	36.76%	28.36%	30.80%	37.95%	40.03%	31.81%
Ontonotes	0.925	0.923	0.924	0.921	0.921	**0.932**	0.927	0.929
	100%	30.19%	22.14%	21.81%	18.96%	34.77%	25.60%	24.75%
Interest	0.899	**0.906**	0.890	0.890	0.885	**0.906**	0.891	0.890
	100%	37.54%	28.25%	28.51%	25.55%	37.54%	28.67%	28.62%
TWA	0.812	0.784	0.793	0.765	0.775	0.799	**0.810**	0.794
	100%	80.34%	72.71%	70.47%	61.54%	86.99%	80.15%	78.12%
Average	0.885	0.857	0.857	0.813	0.852	**0.863**	**0.863**	0.858
	100%	40.67%	36.71%	30.14%	32.62%	43.66%	40.71%	37.03%

Table 2. Effectiveness of seven stopping criteria for heterogeneous uncertainty sampling for active learning. Table 2 shows the accuracy of the classifier and percentage of learned instances over all unlabeled data when each stopping criterion is met. The boldface numbers indicate the best corresponding performances.

Interestingly, our proposed CC method acheves the best macro-average percentage performance on the TWA data set, however, other criteria work poorly, compared to the "First" method. Actually the sense distribution of each noun in TWA set is very skewed. From WSD experimental results on TWA, we found that only few learned instances can train the MaxEnt-based classifier with the highest accuracy performance.

In Table 1, the boldface numbers indicate the best performances. Three combination strategies achieve 12 out of 16 best performances[6]. We think the general combination strategy outperform individual stopping criteria for uncertainty sampling for active learning, because four individual stopping criteria only totally achieve 4 out of 16 best performances.

5.4 Stopping Criteria for Heterogeneous Uncertainty Sampling

In the following comparison experiments on heterogeneous uncertainty sampling, a MaxEnt-based classifier is used to select the most informative examples for training an another type of classifier based on multinomial naïve Bayes (NB) model (McCallum and Nigam, 1998b).

[6] CC and CC-OU methods achieve the same best percentage performance of 31.53% on WebKB data set. MC and CC-MC methods achieve the same highest accuracy performance of 91% on Interest data set.

Table 2 shows that the NB-based classifier trained on all data (i.e. "All method") achieves only 1.2% lower average accuracy performance than that of MaxEnt-based classifier. However, we can see from Table 2 that accuracy performances of each stopping criterion for heterogeneous uncertainty sampling are apparently lower than that for uncertainty sampling shown in Table 1. The main reason is that an uncertain example for one classifier (i.e. MaxEnt) may not be an uncertain example for other classifiers (i.e. NB). This comparison experiments aim to analyze the accuracy effectiveness of stopping criteria for heterogeneous uncertainty sampling, compared to that for uncertainty sampling shown in Table 1. Therefore we do not provide the results of the "First" method for heterogeneous uncertainty sampling. The "*Average*" row shows that CC-MC and CC-ME achieve the highest average accuracy performance of 86.3%, followed by CC-OU. On six data sets, CC-ME achieves 3 out of 6 highest accuracy performances.

Interestingly, these stopping criteria work very well on the Ontonotes and Interest data sets. Three combination strategies achieve higher accuracy performance than the "All" method on Ontonotes. However, the accuracy performances of these seven stopping criteria for heterogeneous uncertainty sampling on WebKB, Comp2a, Comp2b, and TWA degrade, compared to the "All" method.

The general combination strategy achieves 7 out of 9 boldface accuracy performances[7]. And only MC method achieves other 2 boldface accuracy performances. Experimental results show that the general combination strategy outperforms individual stopping criteria in overall for heterogeneous uncertainty sampling.

6 Related Work

Zhu and Hovy (2007) proposed a confidence-based framework to predict the upper bound and the lower bound for a stopping criterion in active learning. Actually this framework is a very coarse solution that simply uses *max-confidence* method to predict the upper bound, and uses *min-error* method to predict the lower bound. Zhu *et. al.* (2008) proposed a minimum expected error strategy to learn a stopping criterion through estimation of the classifier's expected error on future unlabeled examples. However, both two studies did not give an answer to the problem of how to define an appropriate threshold for the stopping criterion in a specific task.

Vlachos (2008) also studied a stopping criterion of active learning based on the estimate of the classifier's confidence, in which a separate and large dataset is prepared in advance to estimate the classifier's confidence. However, there is a risk to be misleading because how many examples are required for this pregiven separate dataset is an open question in real-world applications, and it can not guarantee that the classifier shows a rise-peak-drop confidence pattern during active learning process.

Schohn and Cohn (2000) proposed a stopping criterion for active learning with support vector machines based on an assumption that the data used is linearly separable. However, in most real-world cases this assumption seems to be unreasonable and difficult to satisfy. And their stopping criterion cannot be applied for active learning with other type of classifier such as NB, MaxEnt models.

7 Discussion

We believe that a classifier's performance change is a good signal of stopping the active learning process. It is worth studying further how to combine the factor of performance change with our proposed stopping criteria.

Among these stopping criteria, ME, CC, CC-ME can be used directly for committee-based sampling (Engelson and Dagan, 1999) for active learning. However, to use MC, OU, CC-MC and CC-OU for committee-based sampling, we should adopt a new uncertainty measurement such as *vote entropy* to measure the uncertainty of each unlabled example in the pool.

In the above active learning comparison experiments, the confidence estimation for each confidence-based stopping criterion is done within the unlabeled pool *U*. We think that for these confidence-based stopping criteria except SA method, confidence estimation on a large-scale outside unlabeled data set is worth studying in the future work.

8 Conclusion and Future Work

In this paper, we address the stopping criterion issue of active learning, and propose a new stopping criterion, classification-change, which considers the potential ability of each unlabeled ex-

[7] MC and CC-MC methods achieve the same highest accuracy performance of 90.6% on Interest data set. CC-MC and CC-CA methods achieve the same highest average accuracy performance of 86.3%.

ample on changing decision boundaries. To solve the problem of predefining an appropriate threshold for each confidence-based stopping criterion, a multi-criteria-based general combination strategy is proposed. Experimental results on uncertainty sampling and heterogeneous uncertainty sampling show that these stopping criteria work well on evaluation data sets, and combination strategies can achieve better performance than individual criteria. Some interesting future work is to investigate further how to combine the best of these criteria, and how to consider performance change to define an appropriate stopping criterion for active learning.

Acknowledgments

This work was supported in part by the National 863 High-tech Project (2006AA01Z154) and the Program for New Century Excellent Talents in University (NCET-05-0287).

References

Berger Adam L., Vincent J. Della Pietra, Stephen A. Della Pietra. 1996. *A maximum entropy approach to natural language processing*. Computational Linguistics 22(1):39–71.

Bruce Rebecca and Janyce Wiebe. 1994. *Word sense disambiguation using decomposable models*. Proceedings of the 32nd annual meeting on Association for Computational Linguistics, pp. 139-146.

Chen Jinying, Andrew Schein, Lyle Ungar and Martha Palmer. 2006. *An empirical study of the behavior of active learning for word sense disambiguation*. Proceedings of the main conference on Human Language Technology Conference of the North American Chapter of the Association of Computational Linguistics, pp. 120-127

Engelson S. Argamon and I. Dagan. 1999. *Committee-based sample selection for probabilistic classifiers*. Journal of Artificial Intelligence Research (11):335-360.

Hovy Eduard, Mitchell Marcus, Martha Palmer, Lance Ramshaw and Ralph Weischedel. 2006. *Ontonotes: The 90% Solution*. In Proceedings of the Human Language Technology Conference of the NAACL, pp. 57-60.

Lee Yoong Keok and Hwee Tou Ng. 2002. *An empirical evaluation of knowledge sources and learning algorithm for word sense disambiguation*. In Proceedings of the ACL conference on Empirical methods in natural language processing, pp. 41-48

Lewis David D. and Jason Catlett. 1994. *Heterogeneous uncertainty sampling for supervised learning*. In Proceedings of 11th International Conference on Machine Learning, pp. 148-156

Lewis David D. and William A. Gale. 1994. *A sequential algorithm for training text classifiers*. In Proceedings of the 17th annual international ACM SIGIR conference on Research and development in information retrieval, pp. 3-12

McCallum Andrew and Kamal Nigam. 1998a. *Employing EM in pool-based active learning for text classification*. In Proceedings of the 15th International Conference on Machine Learning, pp.350-358

McCallum Andrew and Kamal Nigam. 1998b. *A comparison of event models for naïve bayes text classification*. In AAAI-98 workshop on learning for text categorization.

Ng Hwee Tou and Hian Beng Lee. 1996. *Integrating multiple knowledge sources to disambiguate word sense: an exemplar-based approach*. In Proceedings of the 34th Annual Meeting of the Association for Computational Linguistics, pp.40-47

Ngai Grace and David Yarowsky. 2000. *Rule writing or annotation: cost-efficient resource usage for based noun phrase chunking*. In Proceedings of the 38th Annual Meeting of the Association for Computational Linguistics, pp. 117-125

Roy Nicholas and Andrew McCallum. 2001. *Toward optimal active learning through sampling estimation of error reduction*. In Proceedings of the Eighteenth International Conference on Machine Learning, pp. 441-448

Schein Andrew I. and Lyle H. Ungar. 2007. *Active learning for logistic regression: an evaluation*. Machine Learning 68(3): 235-265

Schohn Greg and David Cohn. 2000. *Less is more: Active learning with support vector machines*. In Proceedings of the Seventeenth International Conference on Machine Learning, pp. 839-846

Shen Dan, Jie Zhang, Jian Su, Guodong Zhou and Chew-Lim Tan. 2004. *Multi-criteria-based active learning for named entity recognition*. In Proceedings of the 42nd Annual Meeting on Association for Computational Linguistics.

Tang Min, Xiaoqiang Luo and Salim Roukos. 2002. *Active learning for statistical natural language parsing*. In Proceedings of the 40th Annual Meeting on Association for Computational Linguistics, pp. 120-127

Vlachos Andreas. 2008. *A stopping criterion for active learning*. Computer Speech and Language. 22(3): 295-312

Zhu Jingbo and Eduard Hovy. 2007. *Active learning for word sense disambiguation with methods for addressing the class imbalance problem*. In Proceedings of the 2007 Joint Conference on Empirical Methods in Natural Language Processing and Computational Natural Language Learning, pp. 783-790

Zhu Jingbo, Huizhen Wang and Eduard Hovy. 2008. *Learning a stopping criterion for active learning for word sense disambiguation and text classification*. In Proceedings of the Third International Joint Conference on Natural Language Processing, pp. 366-372

Active Learning with Sampling by Uncertainty and Density for Word Sense Disambiguation and Text Classification

Jingbo Zhu Huizhen Wang Tianshun Yao
Natural Language Processing Laboratory
Northeastern University
Shenyang, Liaoning, P.R.China 110004
zhujingbo@mail.neu.edu.cn
wanghuizhen@mail.neu.edu.cn

Benjamin K Tsou
Language Information Sciences
Research Centre
City University of Hong Kong
HK, P.R.China
rlbtsou@cityu.edu.hk

Abstract

This paper addresses two issues of active learning. Firstly, to solve a problem of uncertainty sampling that it often fails by selecting outliers, this paper presents a new selective sampling technique, sampling by uncertainty and density (SUD), in which a k-Nearest-Neighbor-based density measure is adopted to determine whether an unlabeled example is an outlier. Secondly, a technique of sampling by clustering (SBC) is applied to build a representative initial training data set for active learning. Finally, we implement a new algorithm of active learning with SUD and SBC techniques. The experimental results from three real-world data sets show that our method outperforms competing methods, particularly at the early stages of active learning.

1 Introduction

Creating a large labeled training corpus is expensive and time-consuming in some real-world applications (e.g. word sense annotation), and is often a bottleneck to build a supervised classifier for a new application or domain. Our study aims to minimize the amount of human labeling efforts required for a supervised classifier (e.g. for automated word sense disambiguation) to achieve a satisfactory performance by using *active learning*.

Among the techniques to solve the knowledge bottleneck problem, active learning is a widely used framework in which the learner has the ability to automatically select the most informative unlabeled examples for human annotation. The ability of the active learner can be referred to as *selective sampling*. *Uncertainty sampling* (Lewis and Gale, 1994) is a popular selective sampling technique, and has been widely studied in natural language processing (NLP) applications such as word sense disambiguation (WSD) (Chen *et al.*, 2006; Chan and Ng, 2007), text classification (TC) (Lewis and Gale, 1994; Zhu *et al.*, 2008), statistical syntactic parsing (Tang *et al.*, 2002), and named entity recognition (Shen *et al.*, 2004).

Actually the motivation behind uncertainty sampling is to find some unlabeled examples near decision boundaries, and use them to clarify the position of decision boundaries. However, uncertainly sampling often fails by selecting outliers (Roy and McCallum, 2001; Tang *et al.*, 2002). These selected outliers (i.e. unlabeled examples) have high uncertainty, but can not provide much help to the learner. To solve the outlier problem, we proposed in this paper a new method, *sampling by uncertainty and density* (SUD), in which a *K-Nearest-Neighbor-based density* (KNN-density) measure is used to determine whether an unlabeled example is an outlier, and a combination strategy based on KNN-density measure and uncertainty measure is designed to select the most informative unlabeled examples for human annotation at each learning iteration.

The second effort we made is to study how to build a representative initial training data set for active learning. We think building a more representative initial training data set is very helpful for active learning. In previous studies on active learning, the initial training data set is generally generated at random, based on an assumption that random sampling will be likely to build the initial training set with same prior data distribution as that of whole corpus. However, this situation seldom occurs in real-world applications due to the small size of initial training set used. In

© 2008. Licensed under the *Creative Commons Attribution-Noncommercial-Share Alike 3.0 Unported* license (http://creativecommons.org/licenses/by-nc-sa/3.0/). Some rights reserved.

this paper, we utilize an approach, *sampling by clustering* (SBC), to selecting the most representative examples to form initial training data set for active learning. To do it, the whole unlabeled corpus should be first clustered into predefined number of clusters (i.e. the predefined size of the initial training data set). The example closest to the centroid of each cluster will be selected to augment initial training data set, which is considered as the most representative case.

Finally, we describe an implementation of active learning with SUD and SBC techniques. Experimental results of active learning for WSD and TC tasks show that our proposed method outperforms competing methods, particularly at the early stages of active learning process. It is noteworthy that these proposed techniques are easy to implement, and can be easily applied to several learners, such as Maximum Entropy (ME), naïve Bayes (NB) and Support Vector Machines (SVMs).

2 Active Learning Process

In this work, we are interested in *uncertainty sampling* (Lewis and Gale, 1994) for pool-based active learning, in which an unlabeled example x with maximum uncertainty is selected for human annotation at each learning cycle. The maximum uncertainty implies that the current classifier (i.e. the learner) has the least confidence on its classification of this unlabeled example.

Actually active learning is a two-stage process in which a small number of labeled samples and a large number of unlabeled examples are first collected in the initialization stage, and a closed-loop stage of query and retraining is adopted.

Procedure: Active Learning Process
Input: initial small training set L, and pool of unlabeled data set U
Use L to train the initial classifier C
Repeat
1. Use the current classifier C to label all unlabeled examples in U
2. Use uncertainty sampling technique to select m[2] most informative unlabeled examples, and ask oracle H for labeling
3. Augment L with these m new examples, and remove them from U
4. Use L to retrain the current classifier C

Until the predefined stopping criterion SC is met.

Figure 1. Active learning with uncertainty sampling technique

[2] A batch-based sample selection labels the top-m most informative unlabeled examples at each learning cycle to decrease the number times the learner is retrained.

3 Uncertainty Measures

In real-world applications, only limited size of training sample set can be provided to train a supervised classifier. Due to manual efforts involved, such brings up a considerable issue: what is the best subset of examples to annotate. In the uncertainty sampling scheme, the unlabeled example with maximum uncertainty is viewed as the most informative case. The key point of uncertainty sampling is how to measure the uncertainty of an unlabeled example x.

3.1 Entropy Measure

The well-known *entropy* is a popular uncertainty measurement widely used in previous studies on active learning (Tang *et al.,* 2002; Chen *et al.* 2006; Zhu and Hovy, 2007):

$$H(x) = -\sum_{y \in Y} P(y \mid x) \log P(y \mid x) \quad (1)$$

where $P(y|x)$ is the *a posteriori* probability. We denote the output class $y \in Y=\{y_1, y_2, ..., y_k\}$. H is the uncertainty measurement function based on the entropy estimation of the classifier's posterior distribution.

In the following comparison experiments, the uncertainty sampling based on entropy criterion is considered as the baseline method, also called traditional uncertainty sampling.

3.2 Density*Entropy Measure

To analyze the outlier problem of traditional uncertainty sampling, we first give an example to explain our motivation.

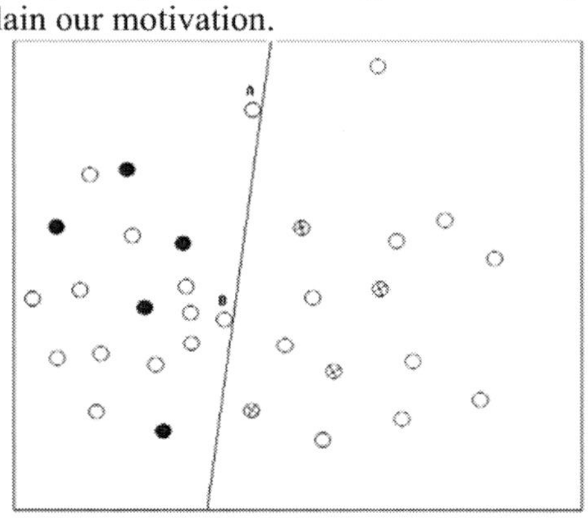

Figure 2. An example of two points A and B with maximum uncertainty at the ith learning iteration

As mentioned in Section 1, the motivation behind uncertainty sampling is to find some unlabeled examples near decision boundaries, and assume that these examples have the maximum uncertainty. Fig. 2 shows two unlabeled examples A and B with maximum uncertainty at the ith

learning cycle. Roughly speaking, there are three unlabeled examples near or similar to *B*, but, none for *A*. We think example B has higher representativeness than example A, and A is likely to be an outlier. We think adding B to the training set will help the learner more than A.

The motivation of our study is that we prefer not only the most informative example in terms of uncertainty measure, but also the most representative example in terms of density measure. The density measure can be evaluated based on how many examples there are similar or near to it. An example with high density degree is less likely to be an outlier.

In most real-world applications, because the scale of unlabeled corpus would be very large, Tang *et al.* (2002) and Shen *et al.* (2004) evaluated the density of an example within a cluster. Unlike their work[3], we adopt a new approach, called *K-Nearest-Neighbor-based density* (KNN-density) measure, to evaluating the density of an unlabeled example x. Given a set of K (i.e. =20 used in our experiments) most similar examples $S(x)=\{s_1, s_2, ..., s_K\}$ of the example x, the KNN-density DS(.) of example x is defined as:

$$DS(x) = \frac{\sum_{s_i \in S(x)} \cos(x, s_i)}{K} \quad (2)$$

As discussed above, we prefer to select examples with maximum uncertainty and highest density for human annotation. We think getting their labels can help the learner greatly. To do it, we proposed a new method, *sampling by uncertainty and density* (SUD), in which entropy-based uncertainty measure and KNN-density measure are considered simultaneously.

In SUD scheme, a new uncertainty measure, called *density*entropy* measure[4], is defined as:

$$DSH(x) = DS(x) \times H(x) \quad (3)$$

4 Initial Training Set Generation

As shown in Fig. 1, only a small number of training samples are provided at the beginning of active learning process. In previous studies on active learning, the initial training set is generally generated by random sampling from the whole unlabeled corpus. However, random sampling technique can not guarantee selecting a most representative subset, because the size of initial training set is generally too small (e.g. 10). We think selecting some representative examples to form initial training set can help the active learner.

In this section we utilize an approach, *sampling by clustering* (SBC), to selecting the most representative examples to form initial training data set. In the SBC scheme, the whole unlabeled corpus has been first clustered into a predefined number of clusters (i.e. the predefined size of the initial training set). The example closest to the centroid of each cluster will be selected to augment initial training set, which is viewed as the most representative case.

We use the K-means clustering algorithm (Duda and Hart, 1973) to cluster examples in the whole unlabeled corpus. In the following K-means clustering algorithm, the traditional cosine measure is adopted to estimate the similarity between two examples, that is

$$\cos(w_i, w_j) = \frac{w_i \bullet w_j}{\|w_i\| \cdot \|w_j\|} \quad (4)$$

where w_i and w_j are the feature vectors of the examples *i* and *j*.

To summarize the SBC-based initial training set generation algorithm, let $U=\{U_1, U_2, ..., U_N\}$ be the set of unlabeled examples to be clustered, and k be the predefined size of initial training data set. In other words, SBC technique selects k most representative unlabeled examples from U to generate the initial training data set. The SBC-based initial training set generation procedure is summarized as follows:

SBC-based Initial Training Set Generation
Input: U, k
Phrase 1: Cluster the corpus U into k clusters Ψ_j(j=1,…,k) by using K-means clustering algorithm as follows:

1. Initialization. Randomly choosing k examples as the *centroid* ϕ_j(j=1,…,k) for initial clusters Ψ_j(j=1,…,k), respectively.
2. Re-partition $\{U_1, U_2, ..., U_N\}$ into k clusters Ψ_j(j=1,…,k), where $\Psi_j = \{U_i : \cos(U_i, \phi_j) \geq \cos(U_i, \phi_t), t \neq j\}$.
3. Re-estimate the *centroid* ϕ_j for each clusters Ψ_j, that is: $\phi_j = \frac{\sum_{U_i \in \Psi_j} U_i}{m}$, where m is the size of Ψ_j.
4. Repeat Step 2 and Step 3 until the algorithm converges.

[3] We also tried their cluster-based density measure, but performance was essentially degraded.

[4] We also tried other ways like λ *$DS(x)$+(1- λ) $H(x)$ measure used in previous studies, but it seems to be random. Actually it is very difficult to determine an appropriate λ value for a specific task.

Phrase 2: Select the example u_j closest to the centroid ϕ_j for each cluster Ψ_j to augment initial training data set Ω, where

$$\Omega = \{u_j : \cos(u_j, \phi_j) \geq \cos(U_i, \phi_j), u_j \neq U_i, j \in [1, k]\}$$

Return Ω;

The computation complexity of the K-means clustering algorithm is *O(NdkT)*, where *d* is the number of features and *T* is the number of iterations. In practice, we can define the stopping criterion (i.e. shown in Step 4) of K-means clustering algorithm that relative change of the total distortion is smaller than a threshold.

5 Active Learning with SUD and SBC

Procedure: Active Learning with SUD and SBC
Input: Pool of unlabeled data set *U*; *k* is the predefined size of initial training data set
Initialization.

- Evaluate the density of each unlabeled example in terms of *KNN-density* measure;
- Use *SBC* technique to generate the small initial training data set of size *k*.

Use *L* to train the initial classifier *C*
Repeat

1. Use the current classifier *C* to label all unlabeled examples in *U*
2. Use uncertainty sampling technique in terms of *density*entropy* measure to select *m* most informative unlabeled examples, and ask oracle *H* for labeling, namely SUD scheme.
3. Augment *L* with these *m* new examples, and remove them from *U*
4. Use *L* to retrain the current classifier *C*

Until the predefined stopping criterion *SC* is met.

Figure 3. Active learning with SUD and SBC

Fig. 3 shows the algorithm of active learning with SUD and SBC techniques. Actually there are some variations. For example, if the initial training data set is generated by SBC, and entropy-based uncertainty measure is used, it is active learning with SBC. Similarly, if the initial training data set is generated at random, and the density*entropy uncertainty measure is used, it is active learning with SUD. If both SBC and SUD techniques are not used, we call it (traditional) uncertainty sampling as baseline method.

6 Evaluation

In the following comparison experiments, we evaluate the effectiveness of various active learning methods for WSD and TC tasks on three publicly available real-world data sets.

6.1 Deficiency Measure

To compare various active learning methods, *deficiency* is a statistic developed to compare performance of active learning methods globally across the learning curve, which has been used in previous studies (Schein and Unga, 2007). The deficiency measure can be defined as:

$$Def_n(AL, REF) = \frac{\sum_{t=1}^{n}(acc_n(REF) - acc_t(AL))}{\sum_{t=1}^{n}(acc_n(REF) - acc_t(REF))} \quad (5)$$

where acc_t is the average accuracy at t^{th} learning iteration. REF is the baseline active learning method, and AL is the active learning variant of the learning algorithm of REF, e.g. active learning with SUD and SBC. *n* refers to the evaluation stopping points (i.e. the number of learned examples). Smaller deficiency value (i.e. <1.0) indicates AL method is better than REF method. Conversely, a larger value (i.e. >1.0) indicates a negative result.

In the following comparison experiments, we evaluate the effectiveness of six active learning methods, including *random sampling (random), uncertainty sampling (uncertainty), SUD, random sampling with SBC (random+SBC), uncertainty sampling with SBC (uncertainty+SBC),* and *SUD with SBC (SUD+SBC).* "+SBC" indicates initial training data set generated by SBC technique. Otherwise, initial training set is generated at random. To evaluate deficiency of each method, the REF method (i.e. the baseline method) defined in Equation (5) refers to (traditional) uncertainty sampling.

6.2 Experimental Settings

We utilize a maximum entropy (ME) model (Berger *et al.*, 1996) to design the basic classifier for WSD and TC tasks. The advantage of the ME model is the ability to freely incorporate features from diverse sources into a single, well-grounded statistical model. A publicly available ME toolkit[5] was used in our experiments. To build the ME-based classifier for WSD, three knowledge sources are used to capture contextual information: *unordered single words in topical context, POS of neighboring words with position information*, and *local collocations*, which are the same as the knowledge sources used in (Lee and Ng, 2002). In the design of text classifier, the maximum entropy model is also utilized, and no feature selection technique is used.

[5]See http://homepages.inf.ed.ac.uk/s0450736/maxent_toolkit.html

In the following comparison experiments, the algorithm starts with a initial training set of 10 labeled examples, and make 10 queries after each learning iteration. A 10 by 10-fold cross-validation was performed. All results reported are the average of 10 trials in each active learning process.

6.3 Data Sets

Three publicly available natural data sets have been used in the following active learning comparison experiments. *Interest* data set is used for WSD tasks. *Comp2* and *WebKB* data sets are used for TC tasks.

The Interest data set developed by Bruce and Wiebe (1994) has been previously used for WSD (Ng and Lee, 1996). This data set consists of 2369 sentences of the noun "*interest*" with its correct sense manually labeled. The noun "interest" has six different senses in this data set.

The Comp2 data set consists of *comp.graphics* and *comp.windows.x* categories from NewsGroups, which has been previously used in active learning for TC (Roy and McCallum, 2001; Schein and Ungar, 2007).

The WebKB dataset was widely used in TC research. Following previous studies (McCallum and Nigam, 1998), we use the four most populous categories: *student, faculty, course* and *project*, altogether containing 4199 web pages. In the preprocessing step, we remove those words that occur merely once without using stemming. The resulting vocabulary has 23803 words.

Data sets	Interest	Comp2	WebKB
Accuracy	0.908	0.90	0.91

Table 1. Average accuracy of supervised learning on each data set when all examples have been learned.

6.4 Active Learning for WSD Task

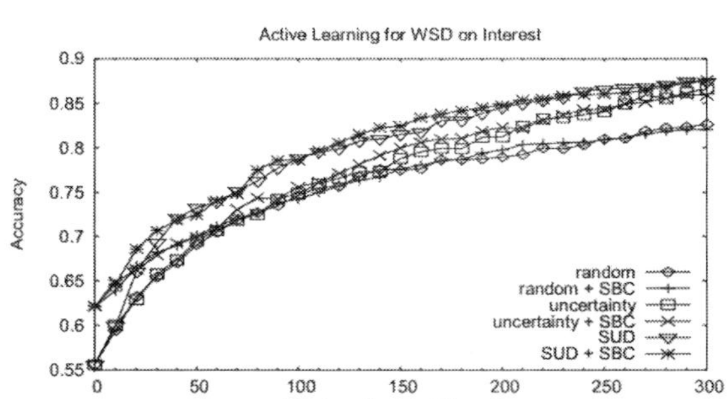

Figure 4. Active learning curve for WSD on Interest data set

Random	Random+SBC	Uncertainty
1.926	1.886	NA
Uncertainty+SBC	SUD	SUD+SBC
0.947	0.811	**0.758**

Table 2. Average *deficiency* achieved by various active learning methods on Interest data set. The stopping point is 300.

Fig. 4 depicts performance curves of various active learning methods for WSD task on Interest data set. Among these six methods, random sampling method shows the worst performance. SUD method constantly outperforms uncertainty sampling. As discussed above, SUD method prefers not only the most uncertainty examples, but also the most representative examples. In the SUD scheme, the factor of KNN-density can effectively avoid selecting the outliers that often cause uncertainty sampling to fail.

It is noteworthy that using SBC to generate initial training data set can improve random (-0.04 deficiency), uncertainty (-0.053 deficiency) and SUD (-0.053 deficiency) methods, respectively. If the initial training data set is generated at random, the initial accuracy is only 55.6%. Interestingly, SBC achieves 62.2% initial accuracy, and makes 6.6% accuracy performance improvement. However, SBC only makes performance improvement for each method at the early stages of active learning. After 50 unlabeled examples have been learned, it seems that SBC has very little contribution to random, uncertainty and SUD methods. Table 2 shows that the best method is SUD with SBC (0.758 deficiency), followed by SUD method.

6.5 Active Learning for TC Tasks

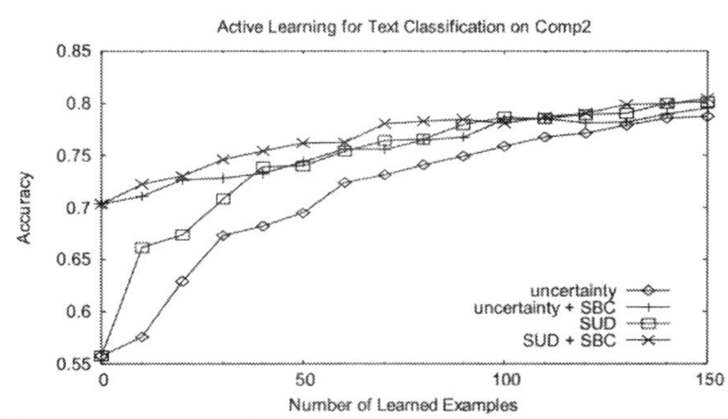

Figure 5. Active learning curve for text classification on Comp2 data set

Uncertainty	Uncertainty+SBC	SUD	SUD+SBC
NA	0.409	0.588	**0.257**

Table 3. Average *deficiency* achieved by various active learning methods on Comp2 data set. The stopping point is 150.

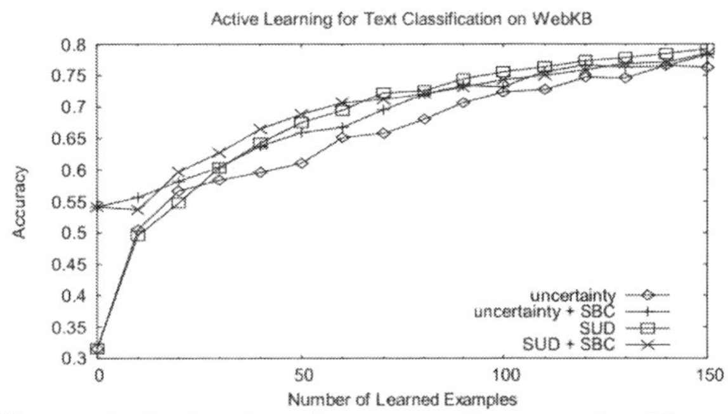

Figure 6. Active learning curve for text classification on WebKB data set

Uncertainty	Uncertainty+SBC	SUD	SUD+SBC
NA	0.669	0.748	**0.595**

Table 4. Average *deficiency* achieved by various active learning methods on WebKB data set. The stopping point is 150.

Fig. 5 and 6 show the effectiveness of various active learning methods for text classification tasks. Since random sampling performs poorly as shown in Fig. 4, it is not further shown in Fig. 5 and 6. We only compare uncertainty sampling and our proposed methods for both text classification tasks.

Similarly, SUD method constantly outperforms uncertainty sampling on two data sets. SBC greatly improves uncertainty sampling (i.e. 0.591 and 0.331 deficiencies degraded) and SUD method (i.e. 0.331 and 0.153 deficiencies degraded), respectively. Interestingly, unlike WSD task shown in Fig. 4, Table 3 and 4 show that uncertainty sampling with SBC outperforms our SUD method for text classification on both data sets. The reason is that SBC makes about 15% initial accuracy improvement on Comp2 data set, and about 23% initial accuracy improvement on WebKB data set. Such improvements indicate that selecting high representative initial training set is very necessary and helpful for active learning. Table 3 and 4 show that the best active learning method for TC task is SUD with SBC, following by uncertainty sampling with SBC method. It is noteworthy that on WebKB uncertainty sampling with SBC (0.669 deficiency) achieves only slight better performance than SUD method (0.748 deficiency) as shown in Table 4, simply because SBC only introduce good performance improvement at the early stages. Actually on WebKB SUD method achieves slight better performance than uncertainty sampling with SBC after about 50 unlabeled examples have been learned.

7 Related Work

In recent years active learning has been widely studied in various natural language processing (NLP) tasks, such as word sense disambiguation (Chen *et al.,* 2006; Zhu and Hovy, 2007), text classification (TC) (Lewis and Gale, 1994; McCallum and Nigam, 1998), named entity recognition (NER) (Shen *et al.,* 2004), chunking (Ngai and Yarowsky, 2000), information extraction (IE) (Thompson *et al.,* 1999), and statistical parsing (Tang *et al.,* 2002).

In addition to uncertainty sampling, there is another popular selective sampling scheme, *Query-by-committee* (Engelson and Dagan, 1999), which generates a committee of classifiers (always more than two classifiers) and selects the next unlabeled example by the principle of maximal disagreement among these classifiers. A method similar to committee-based sampling is *co-testing* proposed by Muslea *et al.* (2000), which trains two learners individually on two compatible and uncorrelated views that should be able to reach the same classification accuracy. In practice, however, these conditions of view selection are difficult to meet in real-world applications. Cohn *et al.* (1996) and Roy and McCallum (2001) proposed a method that directly optimizes expected future error on future test examples. However, the computational complexity of their methods is very high.

There are some similar previous studies (Tang *et al.,* 2002; Shen *et al.,* 2004) in which the representativeness criterion in active learning is considered. Unlike our sampling by uncertainty and density technique, Tang *et al.* (2002) adopted a sampling scheme of *most uncertain per cluster* for NLP parsing, in which the learner selects the sentence with the highest uncertain score from each cluster, and use the density to weight the selected examples while we use density information to select the most informative examples. Actually the scheme of most uncertain per cluster still can not solve the outlier problem faced by uncertainty sampling technique. Shen *et al.* (2004) proposed an approach to selecting examples based on informativeness, representativeness and diversity criteria. In their work, the density of an example is evaluated within a cluster, and multiple criteria have been linearly combined with some coefficients. However, it is difficult to automatically determine sufficient coefficients in real-world applications. Perhaps there are different appropriate coefficients for various applications.

8 Discussion

For batch mode active learning, we found sometimes there is a redundancy problem that some selected examples are identical or similar. Such situation would reduce the representativeness of selected examples. To solve this problem, we tried the sampling scheme of "most uncertain per cluster" (Tang *et al.*, 2002) to select the most informative examples. We think selecting examples from each cluster can alleviate the redundancy problem. However, this sampling scheme works poorly for WSD and TC on the three data sets, compared to traditional uncertainty sampling. From the clustering results, we found these resulting clusters are very imbalanced. It makes sense that more informative examples are contained in a bigger cluster. In this work, we only use SUD technique to select the most informative examples for active learning. We plan to study how combining SBC and SUD techniques can enhance the selection of the most informative examples in the future work.

Furthermore, we think that a misclassified unlabeled example may convey more information than a correctly classified unlabeled example which is closer to the decision boundary. But there is a difficulty that the true label of each unlabeled example is unknown. To use misclassification information to select the most informative examples, we should study how to automatically determine whether an unlabeled example has been misclassified. For example, we can make an assumption that an unlabeled example may be misclassified if this example was previously "outside" and is now "inside". We will study this issue in the future work.

Actually these proposed techniques can be easily applied for committee-based sampling for active learning. However, to do so, we should adopt a new uncertainty measurement such as *vote entropy* to measure the uncertaity of each unlabled example in committee-based sampling scheme.

9 Conclusion and Future Work

In this paper, we have addressed two issues of active learning, involving the outlier problem of traditional uncertainty sampling, and initial training data set generation. To solve the outlier problem of traditional uncertainly sampling, we proposed a new method of sampling by uncertainty and density (SUD) in which KNN-density measure and uncertainty measure are combined together to select the most informative unlabeled example for human annotation at each learning cycle. We employ a method of sampling by clustering (SBC) to generate a representative initial training data set. Experimental results on three evaluation data sets show that our combined SUD with SBC method achieved the best performance compared to other competing methods, particularly at the early stages of active learning process. In future work, we will focus on the redundancy problem faced by batch mode active learning, and how to make use of misclassified information to select the most useful examples for human annotation.

Acknowledgments

This work was supported in part by the National 863 High-tech Project (2006AA01Z154) and the Program for New Century Excellent Talents in University (NCET-05-0287).

References

Berger Adam L., Vincent J. Della Pietra, Stephen A. Della Pietra. 1996. *A maximum entropy approach to natural language processing*. Computational Linguistics 22(1):39–71.

Bruce Rebecca and Janyce Wiebe. 1994. *Word sense disambiguation using decomposable models*. Proceedings of the 32nd annual meeting on Association for Computational Linguistics, pp. 139-146.

Chan Yee Seng and Hwee Tou Ng. 2007. *Domain adaptation with active learning for word sense disambiguation*. Proceedings of the 45th annual meeting on Association for Computational Linguistics, pp. 49-56

Chen Jinying, Andrew Schein, Lyle Ungar and Martha Palmer. 2006. *An empirical study of the behavior of active learning for word sense disambiguation*. Proceedings of the main conference on Human Language Technology Conference of the North American Chapter of the Association of Computational Linguistics, pp. 120-127

Cohn David A., Zoubin Ghahramani and Michael I. Jordan. 1996. *Active learning with statistical models*. Journal of Artificial Intelligence Research, 4, 129–145.

Duda Richard O. and Peter E. Hart. 1973. *Pattern classification and scene analysis*. New York: Wiley.

Engelson S. Argamon and I. Dagan. 1999. *Committee-based sample selection for probabilistic classifiers*. Journal of Artificial Intelligence Research (11):335-360.

Lee Yoong Keok and Hwee Tou Ng. 2002. *An empirical evaluation of knowledge sources and learning algorithm for word sense disambiguation*. In Proceedings of the ACL-02 conference on Empirical methods in natural language processing, pp. 41-48

Lewis David D. and William A. Gale. 1994. *A sequential algorithm for training text classifiers*. In Proceedings of the 17th annual international ACM SIGIR conference on Research and development in information retrieval, pp. 3-12

McCallum Andrew and Kamal Nigam. 1998. *A comparison of event models for naïve bayes text classification*. In AAAI-98 workshop on learning for text categorization.

Muslea Ion, Steven Minton and Craig A. Knoblock. 2000. *Selective sampling with redundant views*. In Proceedings of the Seventeenth National Conference on Artificial Intelligence and Twelfth Conference on Innovative Applications of Artificial Intelligence, pp. 621-626.

Ng Hwee Tou and Hian Beng Lee. 1996. *Integrating multiple knowledge sources to disambiguate word sense: an exemplar-based approach*. In Proceedings of the Thirty-Fourth Annual Meeting of the Association for Computational Linguistics, pp. 40-47

Ngai Grace and David Yarowsky. 2000. *Rule writing or annotation: cost-efficient resource usage for based noun phrase chunking*. In Proceedings of the 38th Annual Meeting of the Association for Computational Linguistics, pp. 117-125

Roy Nicholas and Andrew McCallum. 2001. *Toward optimal active learning through sampling estimation of error reduction*. In Proceedings of the Eighteenth International Conference on Machine Learning, pp. 441-448

Schein Andrew I. and Lyle H. Ungar. 2007. *Active learning for logistic regression: an evaluation*. Machine Learning 68(3): 235-265

Schohn Greg and David Cohn. 2000. *Less is more: Active learning with support vector machines*. In Proceedings of the Seventeenth International Conference on Machine Learning, pp. 839-846

Shen Dan, Jie Zhang, Jian Su, Guodong Zhou and Chew-Lim Tan. 2004. *Multi-criteria-based active learning for named entity recognition*. In Proceedings of the 42nd Annual Meeting on Association for Computational Linguistics.

Tang Min, Xiaoqiang Luo and Salim Roukos. 2002. *Active learning for statistical natural language parsing*. In Proceedings of the 40th Annual Meeting on Association for Computational Linguistics, pp. 120-127

Thompson Cynthia A., Mary Elaine Califf and Raymond J. Mooney. 1999. *Active learning for natural language parsing and information extraction*. In Proceedings of the Sixteenth International Conference on Machine Learning, pp. 406-414

Zhu Jingbo and Eduard Hovy. 2007. *Active learning for word sense disambiguation with methods for addressing the class imbalance problem*. In Proceedings of the 2007 Joint Conference on Empirical Methods in Natural Language Processing and Computational Natural Language Learning, pp. 783-790

Zhu Jingbo, Huizhen Wang and Eduard Hovy. 2008. *Learning a stopping criterion for active learning for word sense disambiguation and text classification*. In Proceedings of the Third International Joint Conference on Natural Language Processing, pp. 366-372

A Systematic Comparison of Phrase-Based, Hierarchical and Syntax-Augmented Statistical MT

Andreas Zollmann* and **Ashish Venugopal*** and **Franz Och** and **Jay Ponte**
Google Inc.
1600 Amphitheatre Parkway
Mountain View, CA 94303, USA
{zollmann,ashishv}@cs.cmu.edu {och,ponte}@google.com

Abstract

Probabilistic synchronous context-free grammar (PSCFG) translation models define weighted transduction rules that represent translation and reordering operations via nonterminal symbols. In this work, we investigate the source of the improvements in translation quality reported when using two PSCFG translation models (hierarchical and syntax-augmented), when extending a state-of-the-art phrase-based baseline that serves as the lexical support for both PSCFG models. We isolate the impact on translation quality for several important design decisions in each model. We perform this comparison on three NIST language translation tasks; Chinese-to-English, Arabic-to-English and Urdu-to-English, each representing unique challenges.

1 Introduction

Probabilistic synchronous context-free grammar (PSCFG) models define weighted transduction rules that are automatically learned from parallel training data. As in monolingual parsing, such rules make use of nonterminal categories to generalize beyond the lexical level. In the example below, the French (source language) words "ne" and "pas" are translated into the English (target language) word "not", performing reordering in the context of a nonterminal of type "VB" (verb).

$$\text{VP} \rightarrow \text{ne VB pas, do not VB} : w_1$$

$$\text{VB} \rightarrow \text{veux, want} : w_2 .$$

As with probabilistic context-free grammars, each rule has a left-hand-side nonterminal (VP and VB in the two rules above), which constrains the rule's usage in further composition, and is assigned a weight w, estimating the quality of the rule based on some underlying statistical model. Translation with a PSCFG is thus a process of composing such rules to parse the source language while synchronously generating target language output. PSCFG approaches such as Chiang (2005) and Zollmann and Venugopal (2006) typically begin with a phrase-based model as the foundation for the PSCFG rules described above. Starting with bilingual phrase pairs extracted from automatically aligned parallel text (Och and Ney, 2004; Koehn et al., 2003), these PSCFG approaches augment each contiguous (in source and target words) phrase pair with a left-hand-side symbol (like the VP in the example above), and perform a generalization procedure to form rules that include nonterminal symbols. We can thus view PSCFG methods as an attempt to generalize beyond the purely lexical knowledge represented in phrase based models, allowing reordering decisions to be explicitly encoded in each rule. It is important to note that while phrase-based models cannot explicitly represent context sensitive reordering effects like those in the example above, in practice, phrase based models often have the potential to generate the same target translation output by translating source phrases out of order, and allowing empty translations for some source words. Apart from one or more language models scoring these reordering alternatives, state-of-the-art phrase-based systems are also equipped with a lexicalized distortion model accounting for reordering behavior more directly. While previous work demonstrates impres-

*Work done during internships at Google Inc.

© 2008. Licensed under the *Creative Commons Attribution-Noncommercial-Share Alike 3.0 Unported* license (http://creativecommons.org/licenses/by-nc-sa/3.0/). Some rights reserved.

sive improvements of PSCFG over phrase-based approaches for large Chinese-to-English data scenarios (Chiang, 2005; Chiang, 2007; Marcu et al., 2006; DeNeefe et al., 2007), these phrase-based baseline systems were constrained to distortion limits of four (Chiang, 2005) and seven (Chiang, 2007; Marcu et al., 2006; DeNeefe et al., 2007), respectively, while the PSCFG systems were able to operate within an implicit reordering window of 10 and higher.

In this work, we evaluate the impact of the extensions suggested by the PSCFG methods above, looking to answer the following questions. Do the relative improvements of PSCFG methods persist when the phrase- based approach is allowed comparable long-distance reordering, and when the n-gram language model is strong enough to effectively select from these reordered alternatives? Do these improvements persist across language pairs that exhibit significantly different reodering effects and how does resource availablility effect relative performance? In order to answer these questions we extend our PSCFG decoder to efficiently handle the high order LMs typically applied in state-of-the-art phrase based translation systems. We evaluate the phrase-based system for a range of reordering limits, up to those matching the PSCFG approaches, isolating the impact of the nonterminal based approach to reordering. Results are presented in multiple language pairs and data size scenarios, highlighting the limited impact of the PSCFG model in certain conditions.

2 Summary of approaches

Given a source language sentence $\mathbf{f}$, statistical machine translation defines the translation task as selecting the most likely target translation $\mathbf{e}$ under a model $P(\mathbf{e}|\mathbf{f})$, i.e.:

$$\hat{\mathbf{e}}(\mathbf{f}) = \arg\max_{\mathbf{e}} P(\mathbf{e}|\mathbf{f}) = \arg\max_{\mathbf{e}} \sum_{i=1}^{m} h_i(\mathbf{e}, \mathbf{f})\lambda_i$$

where the $\arg\max$ operation denotes a search through a structured space of translation ouputs in the target language, $h_i(\mathbf{e}, \mathbf{f})$ are bilingual features of $\mathbf{e}$ and $\mathbf{f}$ and monolingual features of $\mathbf{e}$, and weights λ_i are trained discriminitively to maximize translation quality (based on automatic metrics) on held out data (Och, 2003).

Both phrase-based and PSCFG approaches make independence assumptions to structure this search space and thus most features $h_i(\mathbf{e}, \mathbf{f})$ are designed to be local to each phrase pair or rule. A notable exception is the n-gram language model (LM), which evaluates the likelihood of the sequential target words output. Phrase-based systems also typically allow source segments to be translated out of order, and include distortion models to evaluate such operations. These features suggest the efficient dynamic programming algorithms for phrase-based systems described in Koehn et al. (2004).

We now discuss the translation models compared in this work.

2.1 Phrase Based MT

Phrase-based methods identify contiguous bilingual phrase pairs based on automatically generated word alignments (Och et al., 1999). Phrase pairs are extracted up to a fixed maximum length, since very long phrases rarely have a tangible impact during translation (Koehn et al., 2003). During decoding, extracted phrase pairs are reordered to generate fluent target output. Reordered translation output is evaluated under a distortion model and corroborated by one or more n-gram language models. These models do not have an explicit representation of how to reorder phrases. To avoid search space explosion, most systems place a limit on the distance that source segments can be moved within the source sentence. This limit, along with the phrase length limit (where local reorderings are implicit in the phrase), determine the scope of reordering represented in a phrase-based system. All experiments in this work limit phrase pairs to have source and target length of at most 12, and either source length or target length of at most 6 (higher limits did not result in additional improvements). In our experiments phrases are extracted by the method described in Och and Ney (2004) and reordering during decoding with the lexicalized distortion model from Zens and Ney (2006). The reordering limit for the phrase based system (for each language pair) is increased until no additional improvements result.

2.2 Hierarchical MT

Building upon the success of phrase-based methods, Chiang (2005) presents a PSCFG model of translation that uses the bilingual phrase pairs of phrase-based MT as starting point to learn hierarchical rules. For each training sentence pair's set of extracted phrase pairs, the set of induced PSCFG rules can be generated as follows: First, each phrase pair is assigned a generic X-nonterminal as left-hand-side, making it an *initial rule*. We can now recursively generalize each already obtained rule (initial or including nonterminals)

$$N \rightarrow f_1 \dots f_m / e_1 \dots e_n$$

for which there is an *initial* rule

$$M \rightarrow f_i \dots f_u / e_j \dots e_v$$

where $1 \leq i < u \leq m$ and $1 \leq j < v \leq n$, to obtain a new rule

$$N \rightarrow f_1^{i-1} X_k f_{u+1}^m / e_1^{j-1} X_k e_{v+1}^n$$

where e.g. f_1^{i-1} is short-hand for $f_1 \dots f_{i-1}$, and where k is an index for the nonterminal X that indicates the one-to-one correspondence between the new X tokens on the two sides (it is not in the space of word indices like i, j, u, v, m, n). The recursive form of this generalization operation allows the generation of rules with multiple nonterminal symbols.

Performing translation with PSCFG grammars amounts to straight-forward generalizations of chart parsing algorithms for PCFG grammars. Adaptations to the algorithms in the presence of n-gram LMs are discussed in (Chiang, 2007; Venugopal et al., 2007; Huang and Chiang, 2007).

Extracting hierarchical rules in this fashion can generate a large number of rules and could introduce significant challenges for search. Chiang (2005) places restrictions on the extracted rules which we adhere to as well. We disallow rules with more than two nonterminal pairs, rules with adjacent source-side nonterminals, and limit each rule's source side length (i.e., number of source terminals and nonterminals) to 6. We extract rules from initial phrases of maximal length 12 (exactly matching the phrase based system).[1] Higher length limits or allowing more than two nonterminals per rule do not yield further improvements for systems presented here.

During decoding, we allow application of all rules of the grammar for chart items spanning up to 15 source words (for sentences up to length 20), or 12 source words (for longer sentences), respectively. When that limit is reached, only a special glue rule allowing monotonic concatenation of hypotheses is allowed. (The same holds for the Syntax Augmented system.)

[1] Chiang (2005) uses source length limit 5 and initial phrase length limit 10.

2.3 Syntax Augmented MT

Syntax Augmented MT (SAMT) (Zollmann and Venugopal, 2006) extends Chiang (2005) to include nonterminal symbols from target language phrase structure parse trees. Each target sentence in the training corpus is parsed with a stochastic parser—we use Charniak (2000))—to produce constituent labels for target spans. Phrases (extracted from a particular sentence pair) are assigned left-hand-side nonterminal symbols based on the target side parse tree constituent spans. Phrases whose target side corresponds to a constituent span are assigned that constituent's label as their left-hand-side nonterminal. If the target span of the phrase does not match a constituent in the parse tree, heuristics are used to assign categories that correspond to partial rewriting of the tree. These heuristics first consider concatenation operations, forming categories such as "NP+V", and then resort to CCG (Steedman, 1999) style "slash" categories such as "NP/NN." or "DT\NP". In the spirit of isolating the additional benefit of syntactic categories, the SAMT system used here also generates a purely hierarchical (single generic nonterminal symbol) variant for each syntax-augmented rule. This allows the decoder to choose between translation derivations that use syntactic labels and those that do not. Additional features introduced in SAMT rules are: a relative frequency estimated probability of the rule given its left-hand-side nonterminal, and a binary feature for the the purely hierachial variants.

3 Large N-Gram LMs for PSCFG decoding

Brants et al. (2007) demonstrate the value of large high-order LMs within a phrase-based system. Recent results with PSCFG based methods have typically relied on significantly smaller LMs, as a result of runtime complexity within the decoder. In this work, we started with the publicly available PSCFG decoder described in Venugopal et al. (2007) and extended it to efficiently use distributed higher-order LMs under the Cube-Pruning decoding method from Chiang (2007). These extensions allow us to verify that the benefits of PSCFG models persist in the presence of large, powerful n-gram LMs.

3.1 Asynchronous N-Gram LMs

As described in Brants et al. (2007), using large distributed LMs requires the decoder to perform asynchronous LM requests. Scoring n-grams under this distributed LM involves queuing a set of n-gram probability requests, then distributing these requests in batches to dedicated LM servers, and waiting for the resulting probabilities, before accessing them to score chart items. In order to reduce the number of such roundtrip requests in the chart parsing decoding algorithm used for PSCFGs, we batch all n-gram requests for each cell.

This single batched request per cell paradigm requires some adaptation of the Cube-Pruning algorithm. Cube-Pruning is an early pruning technique used to limit the generation of low quality chart items during decoding. The algorithm calls for the generation of N-Best chart items at each cell (across all rules spanning that cell). The n-gram LM is used to score each generated item, driving the N-Best search algorithm of Huang and Chiang (2005) toward items that score well from a translation model *and* language model perspective. In order to accomodate batched asynchronous LM requests, we queue n-gram requests for the top N*K chart items *without the n-gram LM* where K=100. We then generate the top N chart items *with the n-gram LM* once these probabilties are available. Chart items attempted to be generated during Cube-Pruning that would require LM probabilities of n-grams *not* in the queued set are discarded. While discarding these items could lead to search errors, in practice they tend to be poorly performing items that do not affect final translation quality.

3.2 PSCFG Minimal-State Recombination

To effectively compare PSCFG approaches to state-of-the-art phrase-based systems, we must be able to use high order n-gram LMs during PSCFG decoding, but as shown in Chiang (2007), the number of chart items generated during decoding grows exponentially in the the order of the n-gram LM. Maintaining full $n-1$ word left and right histories for each chart item (required to correctly select the arg max derivation when considering a n-gram LM features) is prohibitive for $n > 3$.

We note however, that the full $n - 1$ left and right word histories are unneccesary to safely compare two competing chart items. Rather, given the sparsity of high order n-gram LMs, we only need to consider those histories that can actually be found in the n-gram LM. This allows significantly more chart items to be recombined during decoding, without additional search error. The n-gram LM implementation described in Brants et al. (2007) indicates when a particular n-gram is not found in the model, and returns a shortened n-gram or ("state") that represents this shortened condition. We use this state to identify the left and right chart item histories, thus reducing the number of equivalence classes per cell.

Following Venugopal et al. (2007), we also calculate an estimate for the quality of each chart item's left state based on the words represented within the state (since we cannot know the target words that might precede this item in the final translation). This estimate is only used during Cube-Pruning to limit the number of chart items generated.

The extensions above allows us to experiment with the same order of n-gram LMs used in state-of-the-art phrase based systems. While experiments in this work include up to 5-gram models, we have succesfully run these PSCFG systems with higher order n-gram LM models as well.

4 Experiments

4.1 Chinese-English and Arabic-English

We report experiments on three data configurations. The first configuration (Full) uses all the data (both bilingual and monolingual) data available for the NIST 2008 large track translation task. The parallel training data comprises of 9.1M sentence pairs (223M Arabic words, 236M English words) for Arabic-English and 15.4M sentence pairs (295M Chinese Words, 336M English words) for Chinese-English. This configuration (for both Chinese-English and Arabic-English) includes three 5-gram LMs trained on the target side of the parallel data (549M tokens, 448M 1..5-grams), the LDC Gigaword corpus (3.7B tokens, 2.9B 1..5-grams) and the Web 1T 5-Gram Corpus (1T tokens, 3.8B 1..5-grams). The second configuration (TargetLM) uses a single language model trained only on the target side of the parallel training text to compare approaches with a relatively weaker n-gram LM. The third configuration is a simulation of a low data scenario (10%TM), where only 10% of the bilingual training data is used, with the language model from the TargetLM configuration. Translation quality is automatically evaluated by the IBM-BLEU metric (Papineni et al., 2002) (case-sensitive, using length of the closest reference translation) on the following publicly

Ch.-En. System \ %BLEU	Dev (MT04)	MT02	MT03	MT05	MT06	MT08	TstAvg
FULL							
Phraseb. reo=4	37.5	38.0	38.9	36.5	32.2	26.2	**34.4**
Phraseb. reo=7	40.2	40.3	41.1	38.5	34.6	27.7	**36.5**
Phraseb. reo=12	41.3*	41.0	41.8	39.4	35.2	27.9	**37.0**
Hier.	41.6*	40.9	42.5	40.3	36.5	28.7	**37.8**
SAMT	41.9*	41.0	43.0	40.6	36.5	29.2	**38.1**
TARGET-LM							
Phraseb. reo=4	35.9*	36.0	36.0	33.5	30.2	24.6	**32.1**
Phraseb. reo=7	38.3*	38.3	38.6	35.8	31.8	25.8	**34.1**
Phraseb. reo=12	39.0*	38.7	38.9	36.4	33.1	25.9	**34.6**
Hier.	38.1*	37.8	38.3	36.0	33.5	26.5	**34.4**
SAMT	39.9*	39.8	40.1	36.6	34.0	26.9	**35.5**
TARGET-LM, 10%TM							
Phraseb. reo=12	36.4*	35.8	35.3	33.5	29.9	22.9	**31.5**
Hier.	36.4*	36.5	36.3	33.8	31.5	23.9	**32.4**
SAMT	36.5*	36.1	35.8	33.7	31.2	23.8	**32.1**
Ar.-En. System \ %BLEU	Dev (MT04)	MT02	MT03	MT05	MT06	MT08	TstAvg
FULL							
Phraseb. reo=4	51.7	64.3	54.5	57.8	45.9	44.2	**53.3**
Phraseb. reo=7	51.7*	64.5	54.3	58.2	45.9	44.0	**53.4**
Phraseb. reo=9	51.7	64.3	54.4	58.3	45.9	44.0	**53.4**
Hier.	52.0*	64.4	53.5	57.5	45.5	44.1	**53.0**
SAMT	52.5*	63.9	54.2	57.5	45.5	44.9	**53.2**
TARGET-LM							
Phraseb. reo=4	49.3	61.3	51.4	53.0	42.6	40.2	**49.7**
Phraseb. reo=7	49.6*	61.5	51.9	53.2	42.8	40.1	**49.9**
Phraseb. reo=9	49.6	61.5	52.0	53.4	42.8	40.1	**50.0**
Hier.	49.1*	60.5	51.0	53.5	42.0	40.0	**49.4**
SAMT	48.3*	59.5	50.0	51.9	41.0	39.1	**48.3**
TARGET-LM, 10%TM							
Phraseb. reo=7	47.7*	59.4	50.1	51.5	40.5	37.6	**47.8**
Hier.	46.7*	58.2	48.8	50.6	39.5	37.4	**46.9**
SAMT	45.9*	57.6	48.7	50.7	40.0	37.3	**46.9**

Table 1: Results (% case-sensitive IBM-BLEU) for Ch-En and Ar-En NIST-large. Dev. scores with * indicate that the parameters of the decoder were MER-tuned for this configuration and also used in the corresponding non-marked configurations.

available NIST test corpora: MT02, MT03, MT05, MT06, MT08. We used the NIST MT04 corpus as development set to train the model parameters λ. All of the systems were evaluated based on the argmax decision rule. For the purposes of stable comparison across multiple test sets, we additionally report a TstAvg score which is the average of all test set scores.[2]

Table 1 shows results comparing phrase-based, hierarchical and SAMT systems on the Chinese-English and Arabic-English large-track NIST 2008 tasks. Our primary goal in Table 1 is to evaluate the relative impact of the PSCFG methods above the phrase-based approach, and to verify that these improvements persist with the use of of large n-gram LMs. We also show the impact of larger reordering capability under the phrase-based approach, providing a fair comparison to the PSCFG approaches.

[2]We prefer this over taking the average over the aggregate test data to avoid artificially generous BLEU scores due to length penalty effects resulting from e.g. being too brief in a hard test set but compensating this by over-generating in an easy test set.

Chinese-to-English configurations: We see consistent improvements moving from phrase-based models to PSCFG models. This trend holds in both LM configurations (Full and TargetLM) as well as the 10%TM case, with the exception of the hierarchical system for TargetLM, which performs slightly worse than the maximum-reordering phrase-based system.

We vary the reordering limit "reo" for the phrase-based Full and TargetLM configurations and see that Chinese-to-English translation requires significant reordering to generate fluent translations, as shown by the TstAvg difference between phrase-based reordering limited to 4 words (34.4) and 12 words (37.0). Increasing the reordering limit beyond 12 did not yield further improvement. Relative improvements over the most capable phrase-based model demonstrate that PSCFG models are able to model reordering effects more effectively than our phrase-based approach, even in the presence of strong n-gram LMs (to aid the distortion models) and comparable reordering constraints.

Our results with hierarchical rules are consistent with those reported in Chiang (2007), where the hierarchical system uses a reordering limit of 10 (implicit in the maximum length of the initial phrase pairs used for the construction of the rules, and the decoder's maximum source span length, above which only the glue rule is applied) and is compared to a phrase-based system with a reordering limit of 7.

Arabic-to-English configurations: Neither the hierarchical nor the SAMT system show consistent improvements over the phrase-based baseline, outperforming the baseline on some test sets, but underperforming on others. We believe this is due to the lack of sufficient reordering phenomena between the two languages, as evident by the minimal TstAvg improvement the phrase-based system can achieve when increasing the reordering limit from 4 words (53.3) to 9 words (53.4).

N-Gram LMs: The impact of using additional language models in configuration Full instead of only a target-side LM (configuration TargetLM) is clear; the phrase-based system improves the TstAvg score from 34.6 to 37.0 for Chinese-English and from 50.0 to 53.4 for Arabic-English. Interestingly, the hierarchical system and SAMT benefit from the additional LMs to the same extent, and retain their relative improvement compared to the phrase-based system for Chinese-English.

Expressiveness: In order to evaluate how much of the improvement is due to the relatively weaker expressiveness of the phrase-based model, we tried to regenerate translations produced by the hierarchical system with the phrase-based decoder by limiting the phrases applied during decoding to those matching the desired translation ('forced translation'). By forcing the phrase-based system to follow decoding hypotheses consistent with a specific target output, we can determine whether the phrase-based system could possibly generate this output. We used the Chinese-to-English NIST MT06 test (1664 sentences) set for this experiment. Out of the hierarchical system's translations, 1466 (88%) were generable by the phrase-based system. The relevant part of a sentence for which the hierarchical translation was not phrase-based generable is shown in Figure 1. The reason for the failure to generate the translation is rather unspectacular: While the hierarchical system is able to delete the Chinese word meaning 'already' using the rule spanning [27-28], which it learned by generalizing a training phrase pair in which 'already' was not explicitly represented in the target side, the phrase-based system has to account for this Chinese word either directly or in a phrase combining the previous word (Chinese for 'epidemic') or following word (Chinese for 'outbreak').

Out of the generable forced translations, 1221 (83%) had a higher cost than the phrase-based system's preferred output; in other words, the fact that the phrase-based system does not prefer these forced translations is mainly inherent in the model rather than due to search errors.

These results indicate that a phrase-based system with sufficiently powerful reordering features and LM might be able to narrow the gap to a hierarchical system.

System \ %BLEU	Dev	MT08
Phr.b. reo=4	12.8	**18.1**
Phr.b. reo=7	14.2	**19.9**
Phr.b. reo=10	14.8*	**20.2**
Phr.b. reo=12	15.0	**20.1**
Hier.	16.0*	**22.1**
SAMT	16.1*	**22.6**

Table 2: Translation quality (% case-sensitive IBM-BLEU) for Urdu-English NIST-large. We mark dev. scores with * to indicate that the parameters of the corresponding decoder were MER-tuned for this configuration.

4.2 Urdu-English

Table 2 shows results comparing phrase-based, hierarchical and SAMT system on the Urdu-English large-track NIST 2008 task. Systems were trained on the bilingual data provided by the NIST competition (207K sentence pairs; 2.2M Urdu words / 2.1M English words) and used a n-gram LM estimated from the English side of the parallel data (4M 1..5-grams). We see clear improvements moving from phrase-based to hierarchy, and additional improvements from hierarchy to syntax. As with Chinese-to-English, longer-distance reordering plays an important role when translating from Urdu to English (the phrase-based system is able to improve the test score from 18.1 to 20.2), and PSCFGs seem to be able to take this reordering better into account than the phrasal distance-based and lexical-reordering models.

4.3 Are all rules important?

One might assume that only a few hierarchical rules, expressing reordering phenomena based on common words such as prepositions, are sufficient to obtain the desired gain in translation quality

```
Source:        ... 怀疑 (suspect) 疫情 (epidemic) 已经 (already) 爆发 (outbreak) 的 ('s) 消息 (news) .
Reference:     ... news ... about suspicions of breakouts of the epidemic.
Phasebased:    ... the epidemic has already broke the news of doubts.
Hierarchical system:
        ( [26-32: @X -> @X 的 @X . / the @X^2 of the @X^1 .]   the
            ( [31-31: @X -> 消息 / news]   news
            ) of the
            ( [26-29: @X -> 怀疑 @X / suspected @X^1]   suspected
                ( [27-29: @X -> @X 爆发 / outbreak of the @X^1]   outbreak of the
                    ( [27-28: @X -> @X 已经 / @X^1]
                        ( [27-27: @X -> 疫情 / epidemic]   epidemic
                        )
                    )
                )
            ) .
        )
```

Figure 1: Example from NIST MT06 for which the hierarchical system's first best hypothesis was not generable by the phrase-based system. The hierarchical system's decoding parse tree contains the translation in its leaves in infix order (shaded). Each non-leaf node denotes an applied PSCFG rule of the form: [Spanned-source-positions:Left-hand-side->source/target]

Ch.-En. System \ %BLEU	Dev (MT04)	MT02	MT03	MT05	MT06	MT08	TstAvg
Phraseb.	41.3*	41.0	41.8	39.4	35.2	27.9	**37.0**
Hier. default (mincount=3)	41.6*	40.9	42.5	40.3	36.5	28.7	**37.8**
Hier. mincount=4	41.4	41.0	42.5	40.4	36.1	28.4	**37.7**
Hier. mincount=8	41.0	41.0	42.0	40.5	35.7	27.8	**37.4**
Hier. mincount=16	40.7	40.3	41.5	40.0	35.2	27.8	**37.0**
Hier. mincount=32	40.4	40.0	41.5	39.5	34.8	27.5	**36.6**
Hier. mincount=64	39.8	40.0	40.9	39.1	34.6	27.3	**36.4**
Hier. mincount=128	39.4	39.8	40.3	38.7	34.0	26.6	**35.9**
Hier. 1NT	40.1*	39.8	41.1	39.1	35.1	28.1	**36.6**
Urdu-En. System \ %BLEU	Dev	MT08					
Phraseb.	15.0*	**20.1**					
Hier. default (mincount=2)	16.0*	**22.1**					
Hier. mincount=4	15.7	**22.0**					
Hier. mincount=8	15.4	**21.5**					
Hier. mincount=16	15.1	**21.3**					
Hier. mincount=32	14.9	**20.7**					
Hier. mincount=64	14.6	**20.1**					
Hier. mincount=128	14.4	**19.6**					
Hier. 1NT	15.3*	**20.8**					

Table 3: Translation quality (% case-sensitive IBM-BLEU) for Chinese-English and Urdu-English NIST-large when restricting the hierarchical rules. We mark dev. scores with * to indicate that the parameters of the corresponding decoder were MER-tuned for this configuration.

over a phrase-based system. Limiting the number of rules used could reduce search errors caused by spurious ambiguity during decoding. Potentially, hierarchical rules based on rare phrases may not be needed, as these phrase pairs can be substituted into the nonterminal spots of more general and more frequently encountered hierarchical rules.

As Table 3 shows, this is not the case. In these experiments for Hier., we retained all non-hierarchical rules (i.e., phrase pairs) but removed hierarchical rules below a threshold 'mincount'. Increasing mincount to 16 (Chinese-English) or 64 (Urdu-English), respectively, already deteriorates performance to the level of the phrase-based system, demonstrating that the highly parameterized reordering model implicit in using more rules does result in benefits. This immediate reduction in translation quality when removing rare rules can be explained by the following effect. Unlike in a phrase-based system, where any phrase can potentially be reordered, rules in the PSCFG must compose to generate sub-translations that can be reordered. Removing rare rules, even those that are highly lexicalized and do not perform any reordering (but still include nonterminal symbols), increases the likelihood that the glue rule is applied simply concatenating span translations without reordering.

Removing hierarchical rules occurring at most twice (Chinese-English) or once (Urdu-English), respectively, did not impact performance, and led to a significant decrease in rule table size and decoding speed.

We also investigate the relative impact of the

rules with two nonterminals, over using rules with a single nonterminal. Using two nonterminals allows more lexically specific reordering patterns at the cost of decoding runtime. Configuration "Hier. 1NT" represents a hierarchical system in which only rules with at most one nonterminal pair are extracted instead of two as in Configuration "Hier. default". The resulting test set score drop is more than one BLEU point for both Chinese-to-English and Urdu-to-English.

5 Conclusion

In this work we investigated the value of PSCFG approaches built upon state-of-the-art phrase-based systems. Our experiments show that PSCFG approaches can yield substantial benefits for language pairs that are sufficiently non-monotonic. Suprisingly, the gap (or non-gap) between phrase-based and PSCFG performance for a given language pair seems to be consistent across small and large data scenarios, and for weak and strong language models alike. In sufficiently non-monotonic languages, the relative improvements of phrase-based systems persist when compared against a state-of-the art phrase-based system that is capable of equally long reordering operations modeled by a lexicalized distortion model and a strong n-gram language model. We hope that this work addresses several of the important questions that the research community has regarding the impact and value of these PSCFG approaches.

Acknowledgments

We thank Richard Zens and the anonymous reviewers for their useful comments and suggestions.

References

Brants, Thorsten, Ashok C. Popat, Peng Xu, Franz J. Och, and Jeffrey Dean. 2007. Large language models in machine translation. In *Proc. of EMNLP-CoNLL*.

Charniak, Eugene. 2000. A maximum entropy-inspired parser. In *Proc. of HLT/NAACL*.

Chiang, David. 2005. A hierarchical phrase-based model for statistical machine translation. In *Proc. of ACL*.

Chiang, David. 2007. Hierarchical phrase based translation. *Computational Linguistics*, 33(2):201–228.

DeNeefe, Steve, Kevin Knight, Wei Wang, and Daniel Marcu. 2007. What can syntax-based MT learn from phrase-based MT? In *Proc. of EMNLP-CoNLL*.

Huang, Liang and David Chiang. 2005. Better k-best parsing. In *Proc. of IWPT*.

Huang, Liang and David Chiang. 2007. Forest rescoring: Faster decoding with integrated language models. In *Proc. of ACL*.

Koehn, Philipp, Franz Josef Och, and Daniel Marcu. 2003. Statistical phrase-based translation. In *Proc. of HLT/NAACL*.

Koehn, Philipp, Franz Josef Och, and Daniel Marcu. 2004. Pharaoh: A beam search decoder for phrase-base statistical machine translation models. In *Proc. of AMTA*.

Marcu, Daniel, Wei Wang, Abdessamad Echihabi, and Kevin Knight. 2006. SPMT: Statistical Machine Translation with Syntactified Target Language Phrases. In *Proc. of EMNLP*.

Och, Franz and Hermann Ney. 2004. The alignment template approach to statistical machine translation. *Computational Linguistics*, 30(4):417–449.

Och, Franz Josef, Christoph Tillmann, and Hermann Ney. 1999. Improved alignment models for statistical machine translation. In *Proc. of EMNLP*.

Och, Franz Josef. 2003. Minimum error rate training in statistical machine translation. In *Proc. of ACL*.

Papineni, Kishore, Salim Roukos, Todd Ward, and Wei-Jing Zhu. 2002. Bleu: a method for automatic evaluation of machine translation. In *Proc. of ACL*.

Steedman, Mark. 1999. Alternative quantifier scope in CCG. In *Proc. of ACL*.

Venugopal, Ashish, Andreas Zollmann, and Vogel Stephan. 2007. An efficient two-pass approach to synchronous-CFG driven statistical MT. In *Proc. of HLT/NAACL*.

Zens, Richard and Hermann Ney. 2006. Discriminative reordering models for statistical machine translation. In *Proc. of the Workshop on Statistical Machine Translation, HLT/NAACL*.

Zollmann, Andreas and Ashish Venugopal. 2006. Syntax augmented machine translation via chart parsing. In *Proc. of the Workshop on Statistical Machine Translation, HLT/NAACL*.

Choosing the Right Translation: A Syntactically Informed Classification Approach

Simon Zwarts
Centre for Language Technology
Macquarie University
Sydney, Australia
szwarts@ics.mq.edu.au

Mark Dras
Centre for Language Technology
Macquarie University
Sydney, Australia
madras@ics.mq.edu.au

Abstract

One style of Multi-Engine Machine Translation architecture involves choosing the best of a set of outputs from different systems. Choosing the best translation from an arbitrary set, even in the presence of human references, is a difficult problem; it may prove better to look at mechanisms for making such choices in more restricted contexts.

In this paper we take a classification-based approach to choosing between candidates from syntactically informed translations. The idea is that using multiple parsers as part of a classifier could help detect syntactic problems in this context that lead to bad translations; these problems could be detected on either the source side—perhaps sentences with difficult or incorrect parses could lead to bad translations—or on the target side—perhaps the output quality could be measured in a more syntactically informed way, looking for syntactic abnormalities.

We show that there is no evidence that the source side information is useful. However, a target-side classifier, when used to identify particularly bad translation candidates, can lead to significant improvements in BLEU score. Improvements are even greater when combined with existing language and alignment model approaches.

© 2008. Licensed under the *Creative Commons Attribution-Noncommercial-Share Alike 3.0 Unported* license (http://creativecommons.org/licenses/by-nc-sa/3.0/). Some rights reserved.

1 Introduction

It is fairly safe to say that whenever there are multiple approaches to solving a problem in Artificial Intelligence, the idea of trying to find a better solution by combining those approaches has been proposed: blackboard architectures, ensemble methods for machine learning, and so on.

In Machine Translation (MT), there is a long tradition of combining multiple machine translations, as through a Multi-Engine MT (MEMT) architecture; the origins of this are generally credited to Frederking and Nirenburg (1994). One way of dividing up such systems is into those that take the whole output from multiple systems and judge between them to select the best candidate, and those that combine elements of the outputs to construct a best candidate.

Deciding between whole sentence level outputs looks like a classical classification problem. Of course, deciding between MT outputs in the general case is a problem that currently has no good solution, and is unlikely to in the near future: BLEU (and similar metrics) require one or more reference texts to distinguish between candidate outputs with the level of accuracy that they achieve, and even then they are open to substantial criticism (Callison-Burch et al., 2006). However, there are reasons to think that there is some promise in considering this as a classification problem. Corston-Oliver et al. (2001) build a classifier to distinguish between human and machine translations with an 80% accuracy. Several other later systems have some success in distinguishing between MT outputs using language models, alignment models, and voting schemes. In addition, while the problem of deciding between arbitrary MT outputs is difficult, it may be feasible in specific cases. The classifier constructed by Corston-Oliver et al. (2001) takes advantage of characteristic mistakes found in the output of the particular MT system used.

In general, we are interested in MT where syntax is involved. The first part of the main idea of this paper is that there are two ways in which problematic translations might be detected. One is on the source side: perhaps sentences with difficult or incorrect parses could lead to bad use of syntax and hence bad translations, and this could be detected by a classifier. The other is that on the target side, perhaps the output quality could be measured in a more syntactically informed way, looking for syntactic abnormalities.

As to the particular system, in this paper we look at a specific type of MT, the output of systems that use syntactic reordering as preprocessing (Collins et al., 2005; Wang et al., 2007; Zwarts and Dras, 2007). In these systems, the source language is reordered to mirror the syntax of the target language in certain respects, leading to an improvement in the aggregate quality of the output over the baseline, although it is not always the case that each individual sentence in the reordered version is better. This could then be framed as an MEMT, where the reordered candidate is considered the default one, backing off to the baseline where the reordered one is worse, based on the decision of a classifier. Given the 'unnatural' order of the preprocessed source side, there is reason to expect that bad or unsuccessful reordered translations might be detectable.

The second part of the main idea of the paper is that a classifier could use a combination of multiple parsers, as in Mutton et al. (2007), to indicate problems. In that work, designed to assess fluency of output of generation systems, metrics were developed from various parsers—log probability of most likely parse, number of tree fragments, and so on—that correlated with human judgements, and that could be combined in a classifier to produce a better evaluation metric. We take such an approach as a starting point for developing classifiers to indicate problematic source and target sides within a reordering MT system.

In Section 2 we review some related work. In Section 3 we investigate the potential gain in correctly choosing the better translation candidate in our context. In Section 4 we build a classifier using an approximation to fairly standard language and alignment model features, mostly for use as a comparator, while Sections 5 and 6 present our models based on source and target language sides respectively. Section 7 concludes.

2 Related work

In this section we briefly review some relevant work on deciding between translation candidates in 'sentence-level' MEMT.

Most common is the use of language models, or voting which may be based on some kind of alignment, or a combination. Callison-Burch and Flournoy (2001) use a trigram language model (LM) on MT outputs to decide the best candidate, looking at nine systems across four language directions and domains, and treating them as black boxes; evaluation is by human judges and on a fairly small data set. Akiba et al. (2002) score MT outputs by a combination of a standard LM and an alignment model (here IBM 4), and then use statistical tests to determine rankings of MT system outputs. Eisele (2005) uses a heuristic voting scheme based on n-gram overlap of the different outputs, and adds an LM to make decisions; the LM reportedly achieves further improvement. Rosti et al. (2007) look at sentence-level combinations (as well as word- and phrase-level), using reranking of n-best lists and confidence scores derived from generalised linear models with probabilistic features from n-best lists. Huang and Papineni (2007) propose a hierarchical model for word, phrase and sentence level combination; they use LMs and interestingly find that incorporating rudimentary linguistic information like Part-of-Speech is helpful. Riezler and Maxwell (2006) combine transfer-based and statistical MT; they back off to the SMT translation when the grammar is inadequate, analysing the grammar to determine this.

Other work, like ours, uses a classifier. The goal of Corston-Oliver et al. (2001) is slightly different, in that it aims to distinguish human translations from MT output. The classifier uses syntactic features derived from a manual error analysis, taking advantage of characteristics specific to their MT system and parser. Nomoto (2003) uses a LM and an IBM-based alignment model, and then constructs separate SVMs for regression based on these, each with a single feature (i.e. the LM value or the alignment model value); the SVM is thus not strictly used as a classifier, but as a regression tool. Nomoto (2004) extends this by deciding on the best LM through a voting scheme. Other related work not in an MEMT context that uses parsers to distinguish better from worse translations are on syntax-based language models (Charniak et al., 2003) and on syntactically informed reranking (Och et al., 2003). Both use only single parsers and work only with candidate translations generated inside an SMT system (either all candidates or n-best).

3 Potential Gain

The type of system we focus on in this paper operates in two stages. First, syntactically based reordering takes place to make the source sentence more similar in structure to the syntax of the target language. This is then passed to a Phrase-based SMT (PSMT) component (Pharaoh (Koehn, 2004) in the cited work). For German to English (Collins et al., 2005) and Dutch to English (Zwarts and Dras, 2007) this reordering involves moving some long-distance dependencies closer together, such as clause-final participles and verb-second auxiliaries. This improves translation quality by compensating for the weakness in PSMT of long-distance word reordering: Collins et al. (2005) report a 1.6 BLEU percentage point improvement, Zwarts and Dras (2007) a 1.0 BLEU percentage point improvement.

However, individual sentences translated from the original non-reordered source sentences are sometimes better than their reordered equivalent; examples are given in both Collins et al. (2005) and Zwarts and Dras (2007). (We refer to these in the rest of the paper as non-reordered translations and reordered translations respectively.) For there to be a point to constructing an MEMT-style system where the reordered translation is the default translation and the non-reordered translation the fallback, it is necessary for the non-reordered version to be better a reasonable proportion of the time, allowing scope for a BLEU improvement across the system.

To determine if this is the case, we construct an approximate oracle to choose the better of each pair of reordered and non-reordered translation sentences. While BLEU is a reasonable choice for evaluating the quality of the overall composite set of translation sentences, it is not suitable for sentence-level decisions. However, in line with Nomoto (2003)'s motivation for developing m-precision as an alternative to BLEU, we make the following observation.

The BLEU score (ignoring brevity) is an harmonic mean between the different n-gram components:

$$exp(\sum_{n=1}^{N} \log p_n)$$

Here p_n is the precision for the different n-gram overlap counts of a candidate sentence with a gold standard sentence. If we want to globally optimise this score for an optimal BLEU document score, we need to pick for each sentence the n-gram counts that contribute most to the overall score. For example, if we have to pick between sentence A and sentence B, where A has 2 unigram counts and 1 bigram count, and B has 2 unigram counts only, A is clearly preferred; however, for sentences C and D, where C has 4 unigram counts and D has 2 unigram counts and 1 bigram count, we do not know which eventually will lead to the global maximum BLEU.

However we observe that because it is an harmonic mean, small values are weighted exponentially heavier, due to the log operator. Our heuristic to achieve the highest score is to have the most extreme possible small values. Since we know that an n-gram is always less frequent than an $(n-1)$-gram we concentrate on the higher n-grams first. The decision process between sentences is therefore to choose the candidate with higher n-gram counts for the maximum value of n, then $n-1$-gram counts, and so on down to unigrams.

Here we will work with the Dutch–English data used by Zwarts and Dras (2007). We use the portions of the Europarl corpus (Koehn, 2003) that were used for training in that work; and BLEU with 1 reference with n-grams up to length 4. We then use our heuristic to select between the reordered and non-reordered

Not-BLEU comparable	
Identical	179,327
Undecidable	119,725
Total	299,052
BLEU comparable	
Non-Reordered better	128,585
Reordered better	163,172
Total	291,757
Overall Total	590,809

Table 1: Comparing translation quality

Learner	Baseline	Accuracy
English → Dutch		
SVM - Polynomial	56.0%	56.6%
SVM - Polynomial	50.0%	51.2%
Maximum Entropy	50.0%	51.0%
Dutch → English		
SVM - Polynomial	50.0%	51.4%

Table 2: Results for internal language decider

translation candidates of Zwarts and Dras (2007) for the language direction Dutch to English. Selecting the reordered translation as default and backing off leads to a 1.1 BLEU percentage point improvement over the 1.0 already mentioned. Results for English to Dutch are similar.

In Table 1 we see the breakdown of the entire corpus we work with. Some sentences are identical, and some are different but with no indication by our heuristic as to which of the two is better. In the cases where we do have an indication we see a sizeable 44% of the non-reordered translations are better.

4 Internal Indicators

Before looking at our syntax-related approaches, it would be useful to have a comparison based on the approaches of previous work. As noted in Section 2, these generally use language models and alignment models, as usual to estimate fluency and fidelity of candidate translations.

Because our two candidate solutions are both ultimately produced by Pharaoh (Koehn, 2004), our quick-and-dirty solution can use Pharaoh's own final translation probabilities, which capture language and alignment model information. We build a classifier

Learner	Baseline	Accuracy
English → Dutch		
SVM - Polynomial	50.0%	50.1%
SVM - Radial	50.0%	49.7%
Maximum Entropy	50.0%	50.2%

Table 3: Results for Source language decider

that attempts to distinguish the better of a pair of reordered and non-reordered translations. Denoting the non-reordered translation T_n, and the reordered T_r, we take as features $\log(P(T_n))$, $\log(P(T_r))$, and $\log(P(T_n))$-$\log(P(T_r))$. In addition, because the sentences do not always have equal length and we do not want to penalise longer sentences, we also have three features describing the perplexity: $e^{\log(P(T_n))/\text{length}(T_n)}$, $e^{\log(P(T_r))/\text{length}(T_r)}$, and the difference between these two. Here *length* is the function returning the length of a sentence in tokens. Our training data we get by partitioning the sentences according to whether reordering is beneficial as measured by our heuristic from Section 3. As machine learners we used SVM-light[1] (Joachims, 1998) and the MaxEnt decider from the Stanford Classifier[2] (Manning and Klein, 2003).

Table 2 shows the results the classifier produces on this data set. While the accuracy rates for the classifiers are all statistically significantly different (at a 95% confidence level) from the baseline (using a standard test of proportions), the results are not promising.

5 Source Language Indicators

5.1 All Data

The finding that almost half of the reordered translations degrade the actual translation quality raises the question of why. Our initial hypothesis is that because we use more linguistic tools, this is likely to introduce new errors. We hypothesise that one of the problems of reordering is either the parser getting it wrong, or the rules getting it wrong because of parse complexity. Our idea for estimating the wrongness of a parse, or the complexity of a parse that might lead to incorrect reordering rule application, is to use 'side-effect' informa-

[1] `http://svmlight.joachims.org`

[2] `http://nlp.stanford.edu/software/classifier.shtml`

Top	Correct	Accuracy
10	5	50%
50	23	46%
100	48	48%
200	100	50%
500	240	48%
1000	490	49%

Table 4: Accuracy range for Source Side Extreme Predictions

tion from multiple parsers, in a modification of an idea taken from Mutton et al. (2007).[3] For example, the parser of Collins (1999), in addition to the actual parse, gives a probability for the most likely parse; if this most likely parse is not at all likely, this may be because the parser is having difficulty. The Link Parser (Grinberg et al., 1995) produces dependency-style parses, and gives an unlinked fragment count where a complete parse cannot be made; this unlinked fragment count may be indicative of parse difficulty. For this part, we therefore look only at translations with English as source side and Dutch as target, in order to be able to use multiple parsers on the source side sentences.

Again, we construct a machine learner to predict which is the better of the reordered and non-reordered translations. Our training data is as in Section 4.

As a feature set we use: character and token length of the sentence, probability values as supplied by the Collins parser, and the unlinked fragment count as supplied by the Link Parser. We used machine learners as in Section 4. Both the SVM and the features are similar to Mutton et al. (2007).

The results are calculated on 39k examples, split 30k training, 9k testing. Table 3 shows the results for different learning techniques with different settings. The accuracy scores show selection no different from random: none of the differences are statistically significant. With such poor results, we do not bother to calculate the BLEU effect of using the classifier as a decider here.

[3]Similar work is that of Albrecht and Hwa (2007); however this requires human references unavailable here.

Learner	Baseline	Accuracy
Dutch → English		
SVM - Polynomial	50.0%	52.3%
Maximum Entropy	50.0%	52.9%

Table 5: Results for target language decider

5.2 Thresholding

Because our MEMT uses the non-reordered translations as a back-off, even if the classifier is not accurate over the whole set of sentences, it could still be useful to identify the poorest reordered translations and back off only in those cases. SVM-light gives prediction scores as part of its classification; data points that are firmly within the positive (negative) classification spaces are higher positive (negative) values, while border-line cases have a value very close to 0. Here we interpret these as an estimate of the magnitude of the difference in quality between reordered and non-reordered translations. We calculated the accuracy over the n most extreme predictions for different values of n. The results in Table 4 show that the 'extreme range' does not have a higher accuracy either.

6 Target Language Indicators

6.1 All Data

We now consider our second approach, trying to classify syntactic abnormality of the translations. Inspecting the sentences by hand, we found that there are some sentences with markedly poor grammaticality, even by the standards of MT output. Examples of often reoccurring problems include verb positioning (often still sentence-final), positioning of modals in the sentence, etc. Most are in the realm of problems the reordering rules actually try to target.

Here we use the multiple-parser approach in a way more like that of Mutton et al. (2007), as an estimate of the fluency of the sentence with a focus on syntactic characteristics. As in Section 5, we construct a classifier using multiple parser outputs to distinguish the better of a pair of reordered and non-reordered translations. Similarly, we use as features the most likely parse probability of the Collins parser (Collins, 1999) and unlinked fragment count

Learner	Baseline	Accuracy
SVM - Complete	50.0%	52.3%
SVM - LargeDiff	50.0%	52.9%
SVM - HugeDiff	50.0%	51.2%

Table 6: Varying BLEU training data

from the Link parser (Grinberg et al., 1995). We combine these with the sentences lengths in both character count and token count of the two candidate sentences.

Our translation direction in this section, Dutch to English, is the opposite of Section 5, for the same reason that we want to use multiple parsers on the target side. The reordering on the Dutch language is done on the results of the Alpino (Bouma et al., 2000) parser. The rules for reordering are found in Zwarts and Dras (2006). Our training data is again as in Section 4.

Table 5 shows the accuracy, calculated on a 38k examples, split 30k training, 8k testing. The accuracy again is close to baseline performance, although it is clearly better than our LM and alignment classifier of Section 4. Here all the improvements are statistically significant on a 95% confidence level. This is surprising as Mutton et al. (2007) on a somewhat similar task was much more successful. Their performance is expressed as a correlation with human judgement rather than accuracy, but compared to our performance where the improvement in accuracy is only a couple of times the standard error, their approach performed much better. A possible explanation could be that the data we work on has much subtler differences than their work. We know both translations are ultimately generated from the same input, which makes our both candidates very close.

6.2 Varying Training Data

In particular in (Mutton et al., 2007) the training data used human sentences as positive exemplars and very simple bigram-generated sentences as negative ones, so that there was a big difference in quality between them. So perhaps there are too many borderline cases in the training data here.

Therefore we retrained the classifier of Section 6.1, selecting only those sentence pairs where the difference was more distinct. For the LargeDiff set the difference was at least 4 or more unigrams or 3 or more bigrams; for the HugeDiff set the difference was at least 6 or more unigrams or 5 or more bigrams.

Table 6 shows the results; all accuracy scores are better than the baseline with 95% confidence. For LargeDiff, there is an improvement over using the complete data set. Surprisingly, for the HugeDiff training data the gain is not only gone, but this decider performs statistically significantly worse than using all the data.

We therefore conclude that the nature of mistakes made when using reordering as a preprocessing step is of a very subtle kind. Very big mistakes are made as part of translation process completely independent of reordering, while the improvement due to reordering is only where subtly a small set of words, compared to the reference, has been changed for the better. The training size however is only reduced to three quarters of the complete training size. It is therefore very unlikely this sudden drop in performance is due to data sparsity.

Top	Correct	Accuracy
10	9	90%
20	19	95%
50	40	80%
100	79	79%
200	145	72.5%
500	300	66.6%
1000	538	53.8%

Table 7: Accuracy of Prediction in the extreme range

6.3 Thresholding

As in Section 5.2, we look at the cases where our SVM gives a higher prediction score that indicates a greater difference in quality of the non-reordered translation over the reordered one. Here we use as training data the LargeDiff set from Section 6.2.

Results are in Table 7, which unlike the thresholded results of Section 5.2 are quite promising. There is a clear pattern here, with very high accuracy scores in the top range, slowly dropping to around overall performance

System	BLEU
Baseline	0.208
Reordered	0.221
SVM-pick	0.238

Table 8: BLEU results for the different selections

Features	Accuracy
SVM - all	52.3%
SVM - length only	49.8%
SVM - length and Link	50.5%
SVM - length and Collins	50.1%

Table 9: Contribution of Parsers

Learner	Baseline	Accuracy
Dutch → English		
SVM Polynomial	50.0%	60.5%

Table 10: Combining internal features with target side features

Top	Reordering		Non-reordered	
10	9	90%	10	100%
20	18	90%	18	90%
50	33	66%	43	86%
100	61	61%	77	77%
200	114	57%	148	74%
500	289	58%	383	76%
1000	564	56%	748	75%

Table 11: Accuracy of the Combined model

after 1000 samples. This 1000 mark is out of 3461 negative samples in the test set range, roughly marking the first third mark before accuracy scores have reached average performance.

Predictions with an extreme score on the other side of the scale hardly show an improvement. Because this subset of sentences shows a higher accuracy, it is worthwhile to calculate BLEU scores over the sentences in the test set belonging to the top 500 SVM-predictions positive (reordered translation is better) and the 500 SVM predictions negative (non-reordered is better). Table 8 shows the improvement of BLEU scores.[4]

The first interesting thing which can be seen in the table is that this subset of sentences already has higher improvement than is seen in the whole data set simply by choosing the reordered only, because the SVM is already used to pick the most discriminating sentences. We note that on this subset of sentences our technique of picking the right sentence actually scores an improvement equal to the use of reordering by itself.

6.4 Parser Contribution

In Table 9 we show the effects of individual parsers, taking as the starting point the SVM of Table 5. Clearly, combining parsers leads to a much better decider.

6.5 Combining Models

As the results of classifying translation outputs using features derived from multiple parsers are promising, we next look at whether it is useful to combine this information with the language and alignment model information from Section 4. Remarkably, as can be seen in Table 10, the combination of these two features has a much greater effect that the two features sets individually. Comparing these scores against 80% accuracy achieved in distinguish MT output from human output in the work of Corston-Oliver et al. (2001), this 60% on a dataset with much more subtle differences is quite promising.

Furthermore Table 11 shows the accuracy ranking of the SVM for the combining model for the extreme SVM-predictions, similar to Tables 4 and 7. The last column of Table 11 matches previous tables, but now we also show an improvement in correct prediction for the reordered cases.

7 Conclusion

In this paper we have looked at a restricted MEMT scenario, where we choose between a syntactic-reordering-as-preprocessing translation candidate, in the style of (Collins et al., 2005), and a baseline PSMT candidate. We have shown that using a classifier built around outputs of multiple parsers, to decide

[4]Baseline here is the same baseline from Zwarts and Dras (2007), which is the parser read-off of the tree.

whether to back off to the baseline candidate, can be successful in selecting the right candidate. There is no indication that classifying information on the source side—looking to see whether sentences with difficult or incorrect parses could lead to bad reorderings and hence bad translations—is useful; however, applying such a classifier to the target side—looking to see whether the output quality could be measured in a syntactically informed way, looking for syntactic abnormalities—is successful in detecting particularly bad translation candidates, and leads to an improvement in BLEU score over the reordered translations equal to the improvement gained by the reordering approach over the baseline. Multiple parsers clearly improve the results over single parsers. The target-side classifier can also be usefully combined with language and alignment model features, improving its accuracy substantially; continuing with such an approach looks like a promising direction. As a further step, the results are sufficiently positive to extend to other sorts of syntactically informed SMT.

References

Akiba, Yasuhrio, Taro Watanabe, and Eiichiro Sumita. 2002. Using Language and Translation Models to Select the Best among Outputs from Multiple MT systems. In *Proc. of Coling*, pages 8–14.

Albrecht, Joshua S. and Rebecca Hwa. 2007. Regression for Sentence-Level MT Evaluation. In *Proc. of ACL*, pages 296–303.

Bouma, Gosse, Gertjan van Noord, and Robert Malouf. 2000. Alpino: Wide Coverage Computational Analysis of Dutch. In *Computational Linguistics in the Netherlands (CLIN)*.

Callison-Burch, Chris and Raymond S. Flournoy. 2001. A Program for Automatically Selecting the Best Output from Multiple Machine Translation Engines. In *Proc. MT Summit*, pages 63–66.

Callison-Burch, Chris, Miles Osborne, and Philipp Koehn. 2006. Re-evaluating the Role of Bleu in Machine Translation Research. In *Proc. of EACL*, pages 249–256.

Charniak, Eugene, Kevin Knight, and Kenju Yamada. 2003. Syntax-based Language Models for Statistical Machine Translation. In *Proc. of MT Summit*, pages 40–46.

Collins, Michael, Philipp Koehn, and Ivona Kucerova. 2005. Clause restructuring for statistical machine translation. In *Proc. of ACL*, pages 531–540, Ann Arbor, Michigan, June.

Collins, Michael. 1999. *Head-Driven Statistical Models for Natural Language Parsing*. Ph.D. thesis, University of Pennsylvania.

Corston-Oliver, Simon, Michael Gamon, and Chris Brockett. 2001. A machine learning approach to the automatic evaluation of machine translation. In *Proc. of ACL*, pages 148–155.

Eisele, Andreas. 2005. First steps towards multi-engine machine translation. In *Proc. of the ACL Workshop on Building and Using Parallel Texts*, pages 155–158.

Frederking, Robert and Sergei Nirenburg. 1994. Three Heads are Better than One. In *Proc. of the ACL Conference on Applied Natural Language Processing*, pages 95 – 100.

Grinberg, Dennis, John Lafferty, and Daniel Sleator. 1995. A robust parsing algorithm for link grammars. In *Proc. of the International Workshop on Parsing Technologies*.

Huang, Fei and Kishore Papineni. 2007. Hierarchical System Combination for Machine Translation. In *Proc. of EMNLP*, pages 277–286.

Joachims, T. 1998. Making large-scale support vector machine learning practical. In B. Schölkopf, C. Burges, A. Smola, editor, *Advances in Kernel Methods: Support Vector Machines*. MIT Press, Cambridge, MA.

Koehn, Philipp. 2003. Europarl: A Multilingual Corpus for Evaluation of Machine Translation Philipp Koehn, Draft, Unpublished.

Koehn, Philipp. 2004. Pharaoh: a Beam Search Decoder for Phrase-Based Statistical Machine Translation Models. In *Proc. of AMTA*, pages 115–124.

Manning, Christopher and Dan Klein. 2003. Optimization, Maxent Models, and Conditional Estimation without Magic. *Tutorial at HLT-NAACL 2003 and ACL 2003*.

Mutton, Andrew, Mark Dras, Stephan Wan, and Robert Dale. 2007. Gleu: Automatic evaluation of sentence-level fluency. In *Proc of ACL*, pages 344–351.

Nomoto, Tadashi. 2003. Predictive Models of Performance in Multi-Engine Machine Translation. In *Proc. of MT Summit*, pages 269–276.

Nomoto, Tadashi. 2004. Multi-Engine Machine Translation with Voted Language Model. In *Proc. of ACL*, pages 494–501.

Och, Franz Josef, Daniel Gildea, Sanjeev Khundanpur, Anoop Sarkar, Kenju Yamada, Alex Fraser, Shankar Kumar, Libin Shen, David Smith, Katherine Eng, Viren Jainand Zhen Jin, and Dragomir Radev. 2003. Final report of Johns Hopkins 2003 summer workshop on syntax for statistial machine translation.

Riezler, Stefan and John Maxwell, III. 2006. Grammatical machine translation. In *Proc of NAACL*, pages 248–255.

Rosti, Antti-Veikko, Necip Fazil Ayan, Bing Xiang, Spyros Matsoukas, Richard Schwartz, and B Bonnie J. Dorr. 2007. Combining Outputs from Multiple Machine Translation Systems" in Human Language. In *Proc. of NAACL*, pages 228–235.

Wang, Chao, Michael Collins, and Philipp Koehn. 2007. Chinese Syntactic Reordering for Statistical Machine Translation. In *Proc of EMNLP*, pages 737–745.

Zwarts, Simon and Mark Dras. 2006. This Phrase-Based SMT System is Out of Order: Generalised Word Reordering in Machine Translation. In *Proc. of the Australasian Language Technology Workshop*, pages 149–156.

Zwarts, Simon and Mark Dras. 2007. Syntax-Based Word Reordering in Phrase-Based Statistical Machine Translation: Why Does it Work? In *Proc. of MT Summit*, pages 559–566.

Metaphor in Textual Entailment

Rodrigo Agerri
School of Computer Science, University of Birmimgham
B15 2TT Birmingham, UK
r.agerri@cs.bham.ac.uk

Abstract

Metaphor understanding in Computational Linguistics has largely been focused on the development of stand-alone prototypes for which only small-scale evaluations are carried out. This has made difficult the inclusion of metaphor in the development of natural language processing applications. However, dealing with metaphor properly is ultimately crucial for any automated language technology that is to be truly human-friendly or able to properly appreciate utterances by humans. This paper proposes to bring metaphor into the Recognizing Textual Entailment task. By doing so, the coverage of textual entailment systems would be broadened and metaphor research would benefit from the textual entailment evaluation framework.

1 Introduction

Using metaphorical language is common in most forms of everyday language, from ordinary conversation, "having ideas in the back of the mind", through newspaper articles, "global oil prices clung near their highest levels", to scientific articles, "the variable N goes from 1 to 100". Metaphor is important in part because it is an economical and directly appealing way of talking about many sorts of subject matter in human life, such as time, money, relationships, emotions, politics, etc. Most importantly, metaphor can have major effects on what can be properly inferred from an utterance or passage.

©2008. Licensed under the *Creative Commons Attribution-Noncommercial-Share Alike 3.0 Unported* license (http://creativecommons.org/licenses/by-nc-sa/3.0/). Some rights reserved.

Most of the development of natural language processing (NLP) applications has been focused on specific tasks such as Information Retrieval (IR) and Question Answering (QA), largely ignoring the question of figurative use of language. Moreover, considering the inherent difficulty in evaluating deep approaches to language in a large-scale manner, up to date there is not a common evaluation framework, corpora or other resources for metaphor processing. It certainly has not helped that most of the computational developments on metaphor processing have largely been stand-alone systems that are not empirically evaluated on a large scale (Fass, 1997; Falkenhainer et al., 1989; Hobbs, 1992; Martin, 1990; Barnden et al., 2003).

This paper proposes to address this by adapting the Recognizing Textual Entailment (RTE) framework for metaphor interpretation. RTE aims to be an abstract and generic task that captures *major semantic inference* needs across applications (Dagan et al., 2007). RTE is considered central for the development of intelligent yet robust natural language processing systems because most of the semantic inference needed in natural language applications such as QA and IE can be characterized as problems in RTE (Dagan et al., 2007). Intuitively, textual entailment consists of determining whether a hypothesis can be inferred from a given text. The textual entailment operational definition is a directional relation between two text fragments, *Text* T and *Hypothesis* H such that T entails H if humans reading T and considering H will infer that H follows from T. An illustration can be given by example 1560 of the RTE-1 dataset (which involves a metaphor in the use of 'incubate'):

T: The technological triumph known as GPS was incubated in the mind of Ivan Getting.

H: Ivan Getting invented the GPS.

As in other NLP applications, figurative language has merely been noted as problem in the RTE field. However, we believe that RTE provides a general evaluation framework for semantic processing which can be adapted for the computational testing and evaluation of theories that aim to explain the semantic inferences involved in metaphor resolution. Furthermore, including metaphor in the RTE task may improve the performance and scope of textual entailment systems, which in turn may allow to bring metaphor into the development of NLP systems.

2 The Role of Metaphor in Textual Inference

Metaphorical use of language crucially affects the inferences that can be drawn from a text. Including metaphor in textual entailment would amount to establish whether a hypothesis H can be inferred from a text T, where (at least) T contains a metaphorical expression whose processing is relevant to judge the entailment.

2.1 Re-formulating the problem

It is usual to assume a view of metaphor understanding as involving some notion of properties and relations of events that are transferred from a source domain into a target domain. In this view, a (declarative) metaphorical text conveys information about some target domain by means of a number of correspondences between entities in the source and the target domains. Lakoff and associates argue that source to target correspondences are part of more general schemes called "conceptual metaphors" (Lakoff, 2004) which we call "metaphorical views". For the GPS T-H pair in the previous section, a metaphorical view such as MIND AS PHYSICAL SPACE would capture the correspondence between *mind* in the source to *special container or incubator* in the target.

Most of the computational approaches to metaphor processing have focused on the development of reasoning systems which take a metaphorical expression as input and perform some reasoning to prove the correct output – previously given by the researcher. The difficulties in scaling-up and the lack of empirical evaluation have been the main chronic problems of metaphor understanding systems. Furthermore, a task consisting of providing an interpretation of a text such as T above – the GPS being incubated in the mind of Ivan Getting – is very complex because it needs to consider and resolve what the "correct interpretation" is from the number of possible interpretations that can be conveyed by (the use of) 'incubating'. Conversely, the task becomes easier if the task faced is to judge whether H follows from T; in the GPS example above, H sets up the context to interpret the metaphorical expression in T, which in turn would help to correctly judge that the GPS was invented by Ivan Getting ('incubate' can be used instead of 'develop', 'invent', etc.). Thus, a slightly modified H would presumably lead to connotations of the metaphorical use of 'incubate' previously not considered:

T: The technological triumph known as GPS was incubated in the mind of Ivan Getting.

H': Ivan Getting accidentally invented the GPS.

A reasonable judgment is that H is not entailed by T, since an incubation process in this particular example would seem to indicate a careful nurturing of ideas that were brought slowly into life and so on, within Ivan Getting's mind. The modified H brings extra connotations of the metaphorical use of 'incubate' that are crucial to establish the negative entailment judgment.

2.2 Metaphor in RTE Challenges

Even though annotators aimed to filter out metaphorical uses of language from the RTE datasets (Zaenen et al., 2005), some metaphorical texts have eluded the annotators' selection policies (Bos and Markert, 2006). Our study of RTE datasets looking for pairs in which resolving a metaphorical expression was relevant for the entailment judgment uncovered few and mostly conventional metaphors. We have focused on 10 pairs in RTE-1 and 9 in RTE-2. Some of them are listed here:

T1: Lyon is actually the gastronomic capital of France.

H1: Lyon is the capital of France.

T2: The upper house of the Russian parliament has approved a controversial bill to tighten state control over non-governmental organisations (NGOs).

H2: Russian parliament closes NGOs.

T3: Convinced that pro-American officials are in the ascendancy in Tokyo, they talk about turning Japan into "the Britain of the Far East."

H3: Britain is located in the Far East.

T4: Stocks rallied for a second session Thursday, boosted by falling oil prices and ongoing relief that the presidential election has passed without incident.

H4: The falling oil prices had a positive impact on stocks.

An evaluation of the systems' accuracy for the pairs involving metaphor was performed to test if there was any significant difference with respect to the overall accuracy results reported in the official RTE challenges. The RTE-1 results are not publicly available, so the study is restricted to the 7 runs which were made available – including 4 of the best 5 systems. Table 1 shows the official overall accuracy results and the results of the evaluation over the 10 pairs involving metaphor:

Author (Group)	Overall	Metaphor
Bayer (MITRE)	0.586	0.4
Herrera (UNED)	0.566	0.2
	0.558	0.2
Bos (Rome/Leeds)	0.563	0.2
	0.555	0.1
Newman (Dublin)	0.563	0.1
	0.565	0.6

Table 1: RTE-1 Accuracy Comparison.

Although the sample of metaphor pairs is fairly small, table 1 shows that there is a trend for the accuracy to be significantly lower when metaphor is involved than for the overall results (which agrees with Bos and Markert's (2006) diagnostic).

RTE-2 results are publicly available and for this study 8 runs of the best scoring systems (only those which also submitted the average precision results are considered) and 2 with lower accuracy were chosen. Table 2 confirms the trend suggested by table 1, namely, that the accuracy score is lower when the judgement depends on processing metaphorical uses of language. How significant are these results? For the RTE-1 pairs, a Fisher's test of independence establishes that for 5 out of the 7 runs the difference in performance is statistically significant at the 0.05 level. The same results were obtained for 7 of the 10 RTE-2 runs compared in table 2.

Author (Group)	Overall	Metaphor
Hickl (LCC)	0.7538	0.4444
Tatu (LCC)	0.7375	0.5555
Zanzotto (Milan/Rome)	0.6388	0.2222
Adams (Dallas)	0.6262	0.3333
Bos (Rome/Leeds)	0.6162	0.1111
Kouylekov (Trento)	0.6050	0.1111
Vanderwende (Stanford)	0.6025	0.1111
Herrera (UNED)	0.5975	0.1111
Clarke (Sussex)	0.5275	0.1111
Newman (Dublin)	0.5250	0.4444

Table 2: RTE-2 Accuracy Comparison.

3 Discussion

Although only few pairs containing fairly conventional metaphors were uncovered from the RTE datasets, the results obtained confirm the hypothesis that the ability to process metaphor would broaden the coverage of textual entailment systems, thereby improving their overall performance. It should also be considered that achieving statistical significance is harder when the overall results are not that high, as shown by the fact that we get statistical significance for Hickl's system and not for Newman's and Adam's.

Moreover, it is envisaged that the relatively good performance of some of the systems (e.g, Hickl and Tatu) is due to the relative lack of open-ended metaphors in the pairs used for the analysis. This also shows that shallow techniques can be fruitful for processing conventional metaphor. However, open-ended metaphors may pose more complex problems. For example, a fairly deep analysis may presumably be needed to extract the metaphorical connotations conveyed by 'incubate' (about the source to target transfer of *carefully growing and nurturing*) to correctly judged the lack of entailment for the modified hypothesis 'Ivan Getting accidentally invented the GPS'. This is also true for metaphors about "deepest recesses of the mind" (in RTE-1 dataset), etc. This type of open-ended metaphors have been subjected to a in-depth analysis (both formal and computational) within the ATT-Meta system and approach for metaphor interpretation (Agerri et al., 2007; Barnden et al., 2003). Adapting it for textual entailment may facilitate the processing of open-ended metaphor in a textual entailment task.

Metaphor understanding systems have not aimed to be empirically evaluated on a large-scale, but have chosen to focus instead on the in-depth analysis of small number of examples. As a consequence, there are not common resources such as corpora or shared task evaluation exercises for metaphor resolution. In order to make use of the RTE evaluation framework to promote empirically-based research on metaphor understanding, the first task would aim to build datasets that for the first time would allow researchers to train and (empirically) evaluate their systems. An obvious strategy would be to follow RTE guidelines with the additional requirement that at least T should contain a metaphorical expression relevant to judge the entailment.

The RTE evaluation framework has the advantage that it is theory neutral, namely, it does not depend on any semantic formalism and works on open domain data. However, the RTE evaluation framework has the disadvantage of being a "black-box" type of evaluation. It makes very difficult to isolate the semantic task from the task of retrieving the necessary background knowledge (Zaenen et al., 2005; Bos, 2008). Furthermore, it is not designed to measure performance on specific semantic phenomena, and it is therefore difficult to know why a system is working correctly or incorrectly. For example, all but one of the RTE-1 runs studied incorrectly judged the T1-H1 pair to be true (about 'gastronomic capital'). It is difficult to be certain that this was solely due to a lack of ability to deal with metaphor instead of a problem about noun modifiers. However, there is not currently a suitable alternative to RTE semantic evaluation as trying to isolate the semantic task (e.g., metaphor) from background knowledge usually results in using artificial examples. On the bright side, the RTE framework will allow metaphor research to grapple more extensively than before with the interactions between metaphor and other language phenomena.

4 Concluding Remarks

The aim of this paper is two fold: Firstly, it provides evidence showing that the ability of processing metaphor may improve the performance of textual inference systems. Secondly, it argues that RTE may provide a much needed general semantic framework for common evaluations and computational testing of theories that aim to explain open-ended usages of metaphor in everyday text. The ATT-Meta approach and system to metaphor interpretation may be adapted for this particular task (Barnden et al., 2003). Including metaphor processing in textual entailment systems can also promote the inclusion of metaphor resolution in NLP applications such as Question Answering, Document Summarization or Information Retrieval.

Acknowledgments

Thanks to the RTE-1 participants that made available their results. Special thanks to John Barnden and Alan Wallington for their comments and suggestions.

References

Agerri, R., J.A. Barnden, M.G. Lee, and A.M. Wallington. 2007. Metaphor, inference and domain independent mappings. In *Proceedings of Research Advances in Natural Language Processing (RANLP 2007)*, pages 17–24, Borovets, Bulgaria.

Barnden, J., S. Glasbey, M. Lee, and A. Wallington. 2003. Domain-transcending mappings in a system for metaphorical reasoning. In *Companion Proceedings of the 10th Conference on the European Chapter of the Association for Computational Linguistics (EACL-03)*, pages 57–61.

Bos, J. and K. Markert. 2006. Recognizing textual entailment with robust logical inference. In Quiñonero-Candela, J., I. Dagan, B. Magnini, and F. d'Alché Buc, editors, *MLCW 2005*, volume 3944 of *LNAI*, pages 404–426. Springer-Verlag.

Bos, J. 2008. Lets not argue about semantics. In *Proceedings of the Sixth International Language Resources and Evaluation (LREC'08)*, Marrakech, Morocco.

Dagan, I., O. Glickman, and B. Magnini. 2007. The PASCAL Recognising Textual Entailment challenge. In Quiñonero-Candela, J., I. Dagan, B. Magnini, and F. d'Alché Buc, editors, *MLCW 2005*, volume 3944 of *LNAI*, pages 177–190. Springer-Verlag.

Falkenhainer, B., K.D. Forbus, and D. Gentner. 1989. The structure-mapping engine: algorithm and examples. *Artificial Intelligence*, 41(1):1–63.

Fass, D. 1997. *Processing metaphor and metonymy*. Ablex, Greenwich, Connecticut.

Hobbs, J.R. 1992. Metaphor and abduction. In Ortony, A., J. Slack, and O. Stock, editors, *Communication from an Artificial Intelligence Perspective*, pages 35–58. Springer-Verlag, Berlin.

Lakoff, G. 2004. Conceptual metaphor home page. http://cogsci.berkeley.edu/lakoff/MetaphorHome.html.

Martin, J.H. 1990. *A computational model of metaphor interpretation*. Academic Press, New York.

Zaenen, A., L. Karttunen, and R. Crouch. 2005. Local textual inference: Can it be defined or circumscribed? In *Proceedings of the ACL 05 Workshop on Empirical Modelling of Semantic Equivalence and Entailment*, pages 31–36.

Distilling Opinion in Discourse: A Preliminary Study

Nicholas Asher and Farah Benamara
IRIT-CNRS Toulouse,
France
{asher, benamara}@irit.fr

Yvette Yannick Mathieu
LLF-CNRS Paris,
France
yannick.mathieu@linguist.jussieu.fr

Abstract

In this paper, we describe a preliminary study for a discourse based opinion categorization and propose a new annotation schema for a deep contextual opinion analysis using discourse relations.

1 Introduction

Computational approaches to sentiment analysis eschew a general theory of emotions and focus on extracting the affective content of a text from the detection of expressions of sentiment. These expressions are assigned scalar values, representing a positive, a negative or neutral sentiment towards some topic. Using information retrieval, text mining and computational linguistic techniques together with a set of dedicated linguistic resources, one can calculate opinions exploiting the detected "bag of sentiment words". Recently, new methods aim to assign fine-grained affect labels based on various psychological theories–e.g., the MPQA project (Wiebe et al., 2005) based on literary theory and linguistics and work by (Read et al., 2007) based on the Appraisal framework (Martin and White, 2005).

We think there is still room for improvement in this field. To get an accurate appraisal of opinion in texts, NLP systems have to go beyond positive/negative classification and to identify a wide range of opinion expressions, as well as how they are discursively related in the text. In this paper, we describe a preliminary study for a discourse based opinion categorization. We propose a new annotation schema for a fine-grained contextual opinion analysis using discourse relations. This analysis is based on a lexical semantic analysis of a wide class of expressions coupled together with an analysis of how clauses involving these expressions are related to each other within a discourse. The aim of this paper is to establish the feasibility and stability of our annotation scheme at the subsentential level and propose a way to use this scheme to calculate the overall opinion expressed in a text on a given topic.

© 2008. Licensed under the *Creative Commons Attribution-Noncommercial-Share Alike 3.0 Unported* license (http://creativecommons.org/licenses/by-nc-sa/3.0/). Some rights reserved.

2 A lexical semantic analysis of opinion expressions

We categorize opinion expressions using a typology of four top-level categories (see table 1): REPORTING expressions, which provide an evaluation of the degree of commitment of both the holder and the subject of the reporting verb, JUDGMENT expressions, which express normative evaluations of objects and actions, ADVISE expressions, which express an opinion on a course of action for the reader, and SENTIMENT expressions, which express feelings (for a more detailed description of our categories see (Asher et al, 2008)).

Our approach to categorize opinions uses the lexical semantic research of (Wierzbicka, 1987), (Levin, 1993) and (Mathieu, 2004). From these classifications, we selected opinion verb classes and verbs which take opinion expressions within their scope and which reflect the holder's commitment on the opinion expressed. We removed some verb classes, modified others and merged related classes into new ones. Subjective verbs were split into these new categories which were then extended by adding nouns and adjectives.

Our classification is the same for French and English. It differs from psychologically based classifications like Martin's Appraisal system : in ours

Groups	SubGroups	Examples
Reporting	a) Inform	*inform, notify, explain*
	b) Assert	*assert, claim, insist*
	c) Tell	*say, announce, report*
	d) Remark	*comment, observe, remark*
	e) Think	*think, reckon, consider*
	f) Guess	*presume, suspect, wonder*
Judgment	g) Blame	*blame, criticize, condemn*
	h) Praise	*praise, agree, approve*
	i) Appreciation	*good, shameful, brilliant*
Advise	j) Recommend	*advise, argue for*
	k) Suggest	*suggest, propose*
	l) Hope	*wish, hope*
Sentiment	m) Anger/CalmDown	*irritation, anger*
	n) Astonishment	*astound, daze, impress*
	o) Love, fascinate	*fascinate, captivate*
	p) Hate, disappoint	*demoralize, disgust*
	q) Fear	*fear, frighten, alarm*
	r) Offense	*hurt, chock*
	s) Sadness/Joy	*happy, sad*
	t) Bore/entertain	*bore, distraction*
	u) Touch	*disarm, move, touch*

Table 1: Top-Level opinion categories.

the contents of the JUDGMENT and SENTIMENT categories are quite different, and more detailed for SENTIMENT descriptions with 14 sub-classes. Ours is also broader: the REPORTING and the ADVISE categories do not appear as such in the Appraisal system. In addition, we choose not to build our discourse based opinion categorization on the top of MPQA (Wiebe et al, 2005) for two reasons. First, we suggest a more detailed analysis of private states by defining additional sets of opinion classes such as HOPES and RECOMMENDATIONS. We think that refined categories are needed to build a more nuanced appraisal of opinion expressions in discourse. Second, text anchors which correspond to opinion in MPQA are not well defined since each annotator is free to identify expression boundaries. This is problematic if we want to integrate rhetorical structure into opinion identification task. MPQA often groups discourse indicators (but, because, etc.) with opinion expressions leading to no guarantee that the text anchors will correspond to a well formed discourse unit.

3 Towards a Discursive Representation of Opinion Expressions

Rhetorical structure is an important element in understanding opinions conveyed by a text. The following simple examples drawn from our French corpus show that discourse relations affect the strength of a given sentiment. S1 : *[I agree with you]$_a$ even if I was shocked* and S2 : *Buy the DVD, [you will not regret it]$_b$*. Opinions in S1 and S2 are positive but the contrast introduced by *even* in S_1 decreases the strength of the opinion expressed in (a) whereas the explanation provided by (b) in S2 increases the strength of the recommendation.

Using the discourse theory SDRT (Asher and Lascarides, 2003) as our formal framework, our four opinion categories are used to label opinion expressions within a discourse segment. For example, there are three opinion segments in the sentence S3: *[[It's poignant]$_d$, [sad]$_e$]$_g$ and at the same time [horrible]$_f$*

We use five types of rhetorical relations: CONTRAST, CORRECTION, SUPPORT, RESULT and CONTINUATION (For a more detailed description see (Asher et al, 2008)). Within a discourse segment, negations were treated as reversing the polarities of the opinion expressions within their scope. Conditionals are hard to interpret because they affect the opinion expressed within the consequent of a conditional in different ways. For example, conditionals,expressions of ADVISE can block the advice or reverse it. Thus *if you want to waste you money, buy this movie* will be annotated as a recommendation not to buy it. On the other hand, conditionals can also strengthen the recommendation as in *if you want to have good time, go and see this movie*. We have left the treatment of conditionals as well as disjunctions for future work.

3.1 Shallow Semantic Representation

In order to represent and evaluate the overall opinion of a document, we characterize discourse segments using a shallow semantic representation using a feature structure (FS) as described in (Asher et al, 2008). Figure 1 shows the discursive representation of the review movie S4: *[This film is amazing.]$_a$. [[One leaves not completely convinced] $_{b.1}$, but [one is overcome]$_{b.2}$]. [[It's poignant]$_{c.1}$, [sad]$_{c.2}$] and at the same time [horrible]$_{c.3}$].[Buy it]$_d$. [You won't regret it]$_e$.*

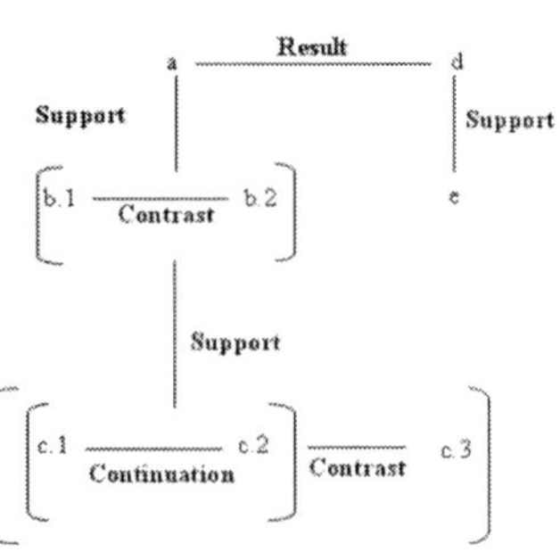

Figure 1: Discursive representation of S4.

Once we have constructed the discursive representation of a text, we have to combine the different FS in order to get a general representation that goes beyond standard positive/negative representation of opinion texts. In this section, we first explain the combination process of FS. We then show how an opinion text can be summarized using a graphical representation.

The combination of low-level FS is performed in two steps: (1) combine the structures related by coordinating relations (such as CONTRAST and CONTINUATION). In figure 1, this allows to build from the segments b.1 and b.2 a new FS ; (2) combine the strutures related via subordinating relations (such as SUPPORT and RESULT) in a bottom up way. In figure 1, the FS of the segment a is combined with the structure deduced from step 1. During this process, a set of dedicated rules is used. The procedure is formalized as follows. Let a, b be two segments related by the rhetorical relation R such as: $R(a,\ b)$. Let S_a, S_b be the FS associated respectively to a and b i.e $S_a : [category : [group_a : subgroup_a], modality : [polarity : p_a, strength : s_a] \cdots]$ and $S_b : [category : [group_b : subgroup_b], modality : [polarity : p_b, strength : s_b] \cdots]$ and let $S : [category : [group], modality : [polarity : p, strength : s] \cdots]$ be the FS deduced from the combination of S_a and S_b. Some of our rules are:

CONTINUATIONS strengthen the polarity of the common opinion. One of the rule used is: if $(group_a = group_b)$ and $(subgroup_a \neq subgroup_b))$ $then$ if $((p_a = neutral)$ and $(p_b \neq neutral))$ $then$ $group = group_a$ and $p = p_b$ and $s = max(s_a,\ s_b)$, as in *moving and sad news*.

For CONTRAST, let OW_i be the set of opinion words that belongs to a segment S_i. We have for $OW_a = \emptyset$ and $OW_b \neq \emptyset$: $group = group_b, p = p_b$ and $s = s_b + 1$, as in *I don't know a lot on Edith Piaf's life but I was enthraled by this movie*.

Finally, an opinion text is represented by a graph $G = (\aleph, \Re)$ such as:

– $\aleph = H \cup T$ is the set of nodes where : $H = \{ho_i / ho_i\ is\ an\ opinion\ holder\}$ and $T = \{to_i : value/to_i\ is\ a\ topic\ and\ value\ is\ a\ FS\}$, such as : $value = [Polarity : p, Strength : s, Advice : a]$, where: $p = \{positive,\ negative,\ neutral\}$ and $s,\ a = \{0,\ 1,\ 2\}$.

– $\Re = \Re_H \cup \Re_T \cup \Re_{H-T}$ where: $\Re_H = \{(h_i,\ h_j)/h_i,\ h_j \in H\}$ means that two topics are related via an ELABORATION relation. This holds generally between a topic and a subtopic, such as a movie and a scenario ; $\Re_T = \{(t_i,\ t_j,\ type)/t_i,\ t_j \in T\ and\ type = support/contrast\}$ means that two holders are related via a CONTRAST (holders h_i and h_j have a contrasted opinion on the same topic) or a SUPPORT relation (holders share the same point of view) ; and $\Re_{H-T} = \{(h_i,\ t_j,\ type)/h_i \in H\ and\ t_j \in T\ and\ type = attribution/commitment\}$ means that an opinion towards a topic t_j is attributed or committed to a holder h_i. For example, in *John said that the film was horrible*, the opinion is only attributed to John because verbs from the TELL group do not convey anything about the author view. However, in *John infomed the commitee that the situation was horrible*, the writer takes the information to be established. The figure 2 below shows the general representation of the movie review S4.

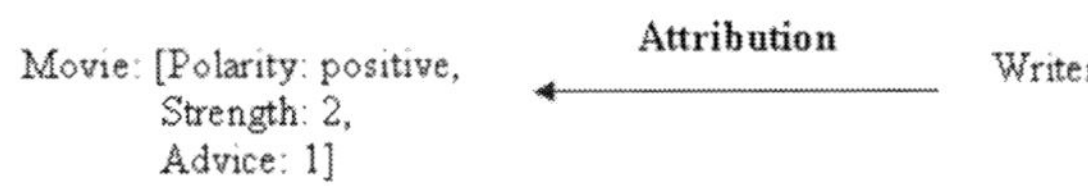

Figure 2: General representation of S4.

4 Annotating Opinion Segments: Experiments and Preliminary Results

We have analyzed the distribution of our categories in three different types of digital corpora, each with a distinctive style and audience : movie reviews, Letters to the Editor and news reports in English and in French. We randomly selected 150 articles for French corpora (around 50 articles for each genre). Two native French speakers annotated respectively around 546 and 589 segments. To check the cross linguistic feasability of generalisations made about the French data, we also annotated opinion categories for English. We have annotated around 30 articles from movie reviews and letters. For news reports, the annotation in English was considerably helped by using texts from the MUC 6 corpus (186 articles), which were annotated independently with discourse structure by three annotators in the University of Texas's DISCOR project (NSF grant, IIS-0535154); the annotation for our opinion expressions involved a collapsing of structures proposed in DISCOR.

The annotation methodology is described in (Asher et al, 2008). For each corpus, annotators first begin to annotate elementary discourse segments, define its shallow representation and finally, connect the identified segments using the set of rhetorical relations we have identified. A segment is annotated only if *it explicitly* contains an opinion word that belong to our lexicon or if it bears a rhetorical relation to an opinion segment.

The average distribution of opinion expressions in our corpus across our categories for each language is shown in table 2. The annotation of movie reviews was very easy. The opinion expressions are mainly adjectives and nouns. We found an average of 5 segments per review. Opinion words in Letters to the Editor are adjectives and nouns but also verbs. We found an average of 4 segments per letter. Finally, opinions in news documents involve principally reported speech. As we only annotated segments that clearly expressed opinions or were related via one of our rhetorical relations to a segment expressing an opinion, our annotations typically only covered a fraction of the whole document. This corpus was the hardest to annotate and generally contained lots of embedded structure introduced by REPORTING type verbs.

To compute the inter-annotator agreements (IAA) we did not take into account the opinion holder and the topic as well as the polarity and the strength because we chose to focus, at a first step, only on agreements on opinion categorization, segment idendification and rhetorical structure detection. We computed the agreements only on the French corpus. The French annotators performed a two step annotation where an intermediate analysis of agreement and disagreement between the two annotators was carried out. This analysis allowed each annotator to understand the reason of some annotation choices. Using the Kappa measure, the IAA on opinion categorization is 95% for movie reviews, 86% for Letters to the Editors and 73% for news documents.

Annotators had good agreement concerning what the basic segments were (82%), which shows that the discourse approach in sentiment analysis is easier compared to the lexical task where annotators have low agreements on the identification of opinion tokens. The principal sources of disagreement in the annotation process came from annotators putting opinion expressions in different categories (mainly between PRAISE/BLAME group and APPRECIATION group, such as *shame*) and the choice of rhetorical relations. Nevertheless, by using explicit discourse connectors, we were able to get relatively high agreement on the choice of rhetorical relations. We also remained quite unsure how to distinguish between the reporting of neutral opinions and the reporting of facts. The main extension of this work are to (1) deepen our opinion typology, specifically to include modals and moods like the subjunctive, and to (2) provide a deep semantic representation that associates for each category of opinion a lambda term involving the proferred content and a lambda term for the presuppositional content of the expression, if it has one. In terms of automatization, we plan to exploit a syntactic parser to get the argument structure of verbs and then a discourse segmenter like that developed in the DISCOR project, followed by the detection of discourse relations using cue words.

Groups	Movie (%)		Letters (%)		News (%)	
	French	English	French	English	French	English
Reporting	2.67	2.12	14.80	13.34	43.91	42.85
a	0	0	0.71	1.33	4.02	4.76
b	0.53	0	0	4	5.83	0
c	0	0	1.79	0	4.51	35.71
d	0.88	0	2.17	0	11.82	0
e	1.33	0	10.12	6.67	5.89	1.34
f	0	2.12	0	1.34	11.77	0
Judgment	60.53	40.52	52.50	73.34	39.23	33.34
g	0.54	0	6.32	26.66	13.69	16.67
h	2.45	2.12	7.54	20	1.81	4.76
i	54.49	38.29	33.48	26.87	23.72	11.90
Advise	6.92	10.63	10.05	13.34	7.27	9.52
j	6.26	8.51	0.70	5.33	1.37	0
k	0.66	2.12	3.94	1.33	3.61	0
l	0	0	5.38	6.67	2.28	9.52
Sentiment	27.30	34.04	33.08	2.67	11.35	16.67
m	0.54	0	3.23	0	0,90	0
n	2.23	6.38	3.96	2.66	0,90	7.14
o	7.38	4.25	3.74	0	1,87	9.52
p	4.97	2.12	5.03	0	2,72	0
q	2.23	0	5.03	0	1,86	0
r	0.89	0	7.17	0	2,28	0
s	3.79	4.25	2.87	0	0.88	0
t	1.33	14.9	0	0	0	0
u	4.46	2.12	2.15	2.12	0	0

Table 2: Average distribution of our categories.

References

Asher N. and Benamara F. and Mathieu Y.Y. 2008. *Categorizing Opinions in Discourse*. ECAI08.

Asher N. and Lascarides A. 2003. *Logics of Conversation*. Cambridge University Press.

Levin B. 1993. *English Verb Classes and Alterna-tions: A Preliminary Investigation*. University of Chicago Press

Martin J.R and White P.R.R. 2005. *Language of Evaluation: Appraisal in English*. Palgrave Macmillan.

Mathieu Y. Y. 2004. *A Computational Semantic Lexicon of French Verbs of Emotion*. In Shanahan, G., Qu, Y., Wiebe, J. (eds.): Computing Attitude and Affect in Text. Dordrecht.

Read J., Hope D. and Carroll J. 2007. *Annotating Expressions of Appraisal in English*. The Linguistic Annotation Workshop, ACL 2007.

Wiebe J., Wilson T. and Cardie C. 2005. *Annotating Expressions of Opinions and Emotions in Language*. Language Resources and Evaluation 1(2).

Wierzbicka A. 1987. *Speech Act Verbs*. Sydney: Academic Press.

Towards Incremental End-of-Utterance Detection in Dialogue Systems

Michaela Atterer, Timo Baumann, David Schlangen
Institute of Linguistics
University of Potsdam, Germany
{atterer,timo,das}@ling..uni-potsdam.de

Abstract

We define the task of *incremental* or *0-lag utterance segmentation*, that is, the task of segmenting an ongoing speech recognition stream into utterance units, and present first results. We use a combination of hidden event language model, features from an incremental parser, and acoustic / prosodic features to train classifiers on real-world conversational data (from the Switchboard corpus). The best classifiers reach an F-score of around 56%, improving over baseline and related work.

1 Introduction

Unlike written language, speech—and hence, automatic speech transcription—does not come segmented into units. Current spoken dialogue systems simply wait for the speaker to turn silent to segment their input. This necessarily reduces their responsiveness, as further processing can only even commence a certain duration after the turn has ended (Ward et al., 2005). Moreover, given the typically simple domains, such work mostly does not deal with the problem of segmenting the turn into utterances, i.e. does not distinguish between *utterance* and *turn* segmentation. However, as our corpus shows (see below), multi-utterance turns are the norm in natural dialogues. The work that does treat intra-turn utterance segmentation does so in an offline context, namely the post-processing of automatic transcripts of recorded speech such as meeting protocols (Fung et al., 2007), and relies heavily on right-context pause information.

In this paper, we define the task of *incremental* or *0-lag utterance segmentation*, that is, the task of segmenting an ongoing speech recognition stream into utterance units using only left-context information.[1] This work is done in the context of developing an incremental dialogue system architecture (as proposed among others by (Aist et al., 2007)), where, ideally, a considerable part of the analysis has already been done while the speaker still speaks. The incremental parser and other components of such a system need to be reset at turn-internal utterance-boundaries with as little delay as possible. Hence it is of vital importance to predict the end-of-utterance while the last word of a sentence is processed (or even earlier). We investigate typical features an incremental system can access, such as partial parse trees and parser internal information. These experiments are a first important step towards online endpointing in an incremental system.

2 Data

We used section 2 of the Switchboard corpus (Godfrey et al., 1992) for our experiments. Section 3 was used for training the language models and the parser that we used. Some of the Switchboard dialogues are of a very low quality. We excluded those where transcription notes indicated high rate of problems due to static noise, echo from the other speaker or background noise. As our parser became very slow for long sentences, we excluded sentences that were longer than 25 words from the

©2008. Licensed under the *Creative Commons Attribution-Noncommercial-Share Alike 3.0 Unported* license (http://creativecommons.org/licenses/by-nc-sa/3.0/). Some rights reserved.

[1] 0-lag here refers to the time where feature extraction starts. As the modules on which feature extraction is based require processing time themselves, a complete absence of prediction delay is of course not possible.

analysis (4% of the sentences). We also excluded back-channel utterances (typically one-word turns) from the corpus.

Of the remaining corpus we only used the first 100,000 instances to reduce the computational load for training the classifiers. 80 % of those were used as a training corpus, and 20 % as a test corpus. For follow-up experiments that investigated turn-initial or turn-internal utterance boundaries only (see below), we used the relevant subsets of the first 200,000 instances.

3 Feature Extraction

Our features comprise prosodic features, and syntactic features.

Prosodic features are *pitch*, *logarithmized signal energy* and derived features, extracted from the audio every 10 ms. In order to track changes over time, we derive features by windowing over past values of pitch, energy, and energy in voiced regions only, with window sizes ranging from 50 ms to 5000 ms. We calculate the arithmetic *mean* and the *range* of the values, the *mean difference* between values within the window and the *relative position* of the minimum and maximum. We also perform a linear regression and use its *slope*, the *MSE* of the regression and the *error* of the regression for the last value in the window.

As classification was done word-wise (final vs. non-final word), each word was attributed the prosodic features of the last corresponding 10-ms-frame.

For the extraction of **syntactic features** we used both n-gram models and a parser. The parser was a modified version of Amit Dubey's `sleepy` parser,[2] which can produce syntactic structure incrementally online. The n-gram model was a hidden event model as typically used in the sentence unit detection literature (see e.g. (Fung et al., 2007)). For the time being, all features based on word identities are computed on gold standard transcriptions. We trained n-gram models both based on words and on words plus POS-information that was incrementally obtained from the parser.[3] We calculated the log-probability of trigrams with the last token in the n-gram being a place-holder for end-of-utterance (i.e. the probability of (*I,would,end-of-utterance*) or (*Thank,you,end-of-utterance*). We also calculated log probabilities for trigrams such as (*I, end-of-utterance - 1,end-of-utterance*). Thirdly, the log probability was also computed for a string consisting of 4 word/POS-pairs followed by an end marker.

Further syntactic features can be roughly divided into two classes: *parser-based features*, which are related to internal states of the parser, and *structure-based features* which refer to properties of the syntactic tree. The former try to capture the expectation of there being more incomplete edges towards the beginning of a sentence than towards the end. We also might expect a relative decrease in the overall number of edges towards the end of a sentence. Therefore we track a selection of numbers referring to the various kinds of edges stored in the chart. Moreover, we utilize some of the parser's information about the best intermediate edge, and use the category after the dot of this edge as an estimate for the most probable category to come next. Furthermore, we use the forward probability of the best tree as a rounded log probability.

The structure-based features are simple features such as the part-of-speech category of the current word and the number of the word in the current utterance, and more complex features that try to (roughly) approximate semantic notions of completeness by counting the number of verbs or number of nominal phrases encountered, as we would usually expect a sentence to be incomplete if we haven't heard a verb or nominal phrase yet. For example, in sentences of the structure *(NP) (VP (V NP))* or *(NP) (VP (V NP (N PP)))*, humans would typically be aware that the last phrase has probably been reached during the last noun phrase or prepositional phrase (cf. (Grosjean, 1983)). However, the length and internal structure of these phrases can vary a great deal. We try to capture some of this variation by features referring to the last non-terminal seen, the second-to-last non-terminal seen and the number of words seen since the last non-terminal. A number of features (the *count features*) are simple features that record the number of words since the turn or utterance started and the time elapsed since the utterance started. They are also subsumed under syntactic features.

We also used dialogue act features like the previous dialogue act, and the previous dialogue act of the last speaker. Those currently come from

[2] `http://homepages.inf.ed.ac.uk/adubey/software/`

[3] The models were trained using the SRILM-tools (Stolcke, 2002) for $n = 3$ using Chen and Goodman's modified Kneser-Ney discounting (Chen and Goodman, 1998).

the gold standard. We assume that in a dialogue system the system would at least have information about its own dialogue acts.

4 Experimental Settings

We tested a number of classifiers as implemented in the Weka toolkit (Witten and Frank, 2005), and found that the JRip-classifier, an implementation of the RIPPER-algorithm (Cohen, 1995), performed best. A number of attribute selection algorithms also did not result in a significant change of performance. Therefore, we only report the plain results by JRip. We also tested the impact each of our information sources had on the results. The aim was to find out how important parser, part-of-speech information and pitch and energy features are, respectively.

As turn-internal utterance-ends might be more difficult to detect than those that coincide with turn-ends, we repeat the experiment with turn-internal utterances only. Deleting turn-final utterances from our initial 200,000-instance corpus resulted in 128,686 remaining word instances, 80 % of which were used for training. For a third experiment, where we look at turn-initial utterances, we use again a subset of those 200,000 word-instances.

For clarity, we simply use precision/recall for evaluation; see (Liu and Shriberg, 2007) for a discussion of other metrics. As a baseline we assume non-existent utterance segmentation, which results in a recall of 0 and a precision of 100 %.

5 Results

	Precision	Recall	F
baseline	100	0	0
all features	73.8	45.0	55.9
all syntactic features	74.8	44.0	55.4
word/POS n-gram features	73.4	45.8	56.4
word n-gram features	66.9	34.7	45.7
only count features	59.3	7.7	13.6
prosodic features only	49.5	8.3	14.2
pitch features	100	0	0
energy features	48.2	7.4	12.8

Table 1: Results for end-of-utterance classification for all utterances.

Tables 1 and 2 show the results for the experimental settings described above. Dialogue act features were included in the syntactic features, but JRip did not use them in its rules eventually. Table 1 shows that the overall F-score is best when n-grams with POS information are used. Adding a parser, however, increases precision. Prosody features in general do not seem to have much of an influence on end-of-utterance prediction in our data, with energy features contributing more than pitch features. Table 2 indicates, as expected, that

	Precision	Recall	F
baseline	100	0	0
all features	71.2	40.3	51.4
all syntactic features	72.7	38.2	50.0
word/POS n-gram features	70.5	41.1	51.9
word n-gram features	70.9	26.4	38.5
only count features	60.4	1.0	2.0
prosodic features only	41.7	1.7	3.3
pitch features	100	0	0
energy features	31.6	1.2	2.3

Table 2: Results for end-of-utterance classification for utterances which are not turn-final.

the end of an utterance is harder to predict when it is not turn-final. Performance drops compared to the results shown in Table 1. Note that some of the performance drop must be attributed to the use of a different data set. However, the performance drop is much more dramatic for the experiments where only prosody is used than for those where syntax is used. We speculate that the count features also loose their impact because one-word utterances like 'Okay' are usually turn-initial.

The results shown in Tables 1 and 2 can be regarded as an upper bound for a dialogue system, because our experiments so far work with gold standard sentence boundaries for creating syntactic features (e.g., for resetting our parser). Strictly speaking, they are only realistic for turn-initial utterances. For the remaining 14,737 of our 26,401 utterances, we therefore report a lower bound, where we use only features that do not have knowledge about the beginning of the sentence (Table 3). No count and parser-based features were used for this experiment, only n-gram (word-based without POS information) and pitch features. The Table also shows the results for the 11,664 turn-initial utterances, where we use all features.[4] We then derive the overall performance from the fractions of initial and non-initial utterances.

Future work aims at putting together a system where the parser is restarted using predictions based on its own output.

[4]Note that turn-initial utterances can at the same time be turn-final.

	Precision	Recall	F
non-initial	65.0	28.6	39.7
initial	74.5	55.1	63.3
overall	70.4	40.3	51.3

Table 3: Results for end-of-utterance classification for utterances which are not turn-initial (reduced feature set), and utterances that are turn-initial (full feature set) and the derived overall performance.

6 Related Work

(Fuentes et al., 2007) report F-measures of 84% using prosodic features only, but they use left–right-windows for feature calculation, where our processing is truly incremental and more suitable for real-time usage in a dialogue system. Moreover, they only seem to use one-utterance turns, which makes the task easier when prosodic features are used. In our dialogue corpus (Switchboard, section 2), however, each turn contains on average 2.5 utterances, and turn-internal utterances also need to be recognized. (Fung et al., 2007) reach an F-score of 75.3% , but report that the best feature was pause-duration—a feature we don't use because we want to find out how well we can predict the end of a sentence before a pause makes this clear. Similarly, (Ferrer et al., 2002) rely largely on pause features. (Schlangen, 2006) investigates incremental prediction of end-of-utterance and end-of-turn for various pause-lengths, and achieves an F-score of 35.5% for pause length 0, on which we can improve here.

7 Discussion and Conclusion

We investigated *0-lag end-of-utterance detection* for incremental dialogue systems. In our setup, we aim to recognise the end of an utterance as soon as possible, while the potentially last word is processed, without the help of information about subsequent silence. We investigate a number of features an incremental system would be able to access, such as information from an incremental parser. We find that remaining (non-pause) prosodic information is not as helpful as in non-incremental studies, especially for non-turn-final utterances. Syntactic information, on the other hand, increases performance. Future work aims at more sophisticated prosodic modelling and at testing the impact of using real or simulated speech recognition output. We also intend to implement end-of-utterance prediction in the context of a real incremental system we are building.

8 Acknowledgement

This work was funded by DFG ENP SCHL845/3-1.

References

Aist, Gregory, James Allen, Ellen Campana, Carlos Gomez-Gallo, Scott Stoness, Mary Swift, and Michael Tanenhaus. 2007. Incremental understanding in human-computer dialogue and experimental evidence for advantages over non-incremental methods. In *Proc. of the 2007 Workshop on the Semantics and Pragmatics of Dialogue (DECALOG)*.

Chen, S.F. and J. Goodman. 1998. An empirical study of smoothing techniques for language modeling. Technical report, Center for Research in Computing Technology (Harvard University).

Cohen, William W. 1995. Fast effective rule induction. In *Machine Learning: Proceedings of the Twelfth International Conference*.

Ferrer, L., E. Shriberg, and A. Stolcke. 2002. Is the speaker done yet? Faster and more accurate end-of-utterance detection using prosody in human-computer dialog. In *Proc. Intl. Conf. on Spoken Language Processing*, Denver.

Fuentes, Olac, David Vera, and Thamar Solorio. 2007. A filter-based approach to detect end-of-utterances from prosody in dialog systems. In *Proc. Human Language Technologies 2007*, Rochester, New York.

Fung, J., D. Hakkani-Tur, M. Magimai-Doss, E. Shriberg, S. Cuendet, and N. Mirghafori. 2007. Prosodic features and feature selection for multi-lingual sentence segmentation. In *Proc. Interspeech*, pages 2585–2588, Antwerp.

Godfrey, John J., E. C. Holliman, and J. McDaniel. 1992. SWITCHBOARD: Telephone speech corpus for research and development. In *Proc. of ICASSP-1992*, pages 517–520, San Francisco, USA, March.

Grosjean, François. 1983. How long is the sentence? Prediction and prosody in the on-line processing of language. *Linguistics*, 21:501–529.

Liu, Y. and E. Shriberg. 2007. Comparing evaluation metrics for sentence boundary detection. In *Proc. IEEE ICASSP*, Honolulu,USA.

Schlangen, David. 2006. From reaction to prediction: Experiments with computational models of turn-taking. In *Proc. Interspeech 2006, Panel on Prosody of Dialogue Ac ts and Turn-Taking*, Pittsburgh, USA.

Stolcke, Andreas. 2002. SRILM – an extensible language modeling toolkit. In *Proc. ICSLP 2002*.

Ward, Nigel G., Anais G. Rivera, Karen Ward, and David G. Novick. 2005. Root causes of lost time and user stress in a simple dialog system. In *Proc. of Interspeech*, El Paso, USA.

Witten, Ian H. and Eibe Frank. 2005. *Data Mining: Practical Machine Learning Tools and Techniques*. Morgan Kaufmann.

The power of negative thinking: Exploiting label disagreement in the min-cut classification framework

Mohit Bansal
Dept. of Computer Science & Engineering
Indian Institute of Technology Kanpur
mbansal47@gmail.com

Claire Cardie and **Lillian Lee**
Dept. of Computer Science
Cornell University
{cardie,llee}@cs.cornell.edu

Abstract

Treating classification as seeking *minimum cuts* in the appropriate graph has proven effective in a number of applications. The power of this approach lies in its ability to incorporate label-agreement preferences among pairs of instances in a provably tractable way. Label *disagreement* preferences are another potentially rich source of information, but prior NLP work within the minimum-cut paradigm has not explicitly incorporated it. Here, we report on work in progress that examines several novel heuristics for incorporating such information. Our results, produced within the context of a politically-oriented sentiment-classification task, demonstrate that these heuristics allow for the addition of label-disagreement information in a way that improves classification accuracy while preserving the efficiency guarantees of the minimum-cut framework.

1 Introduction

Classification algorithms based on formulating the classification task as one of finding *minimum s-t cuts in edge-weighted graphs* — henceforth *minimum cuts* or *min cuts* — have been successfully employed in vision, computational biology, and natural language processing. Within NLP, applications include sentiment-analysis problems (Pang and Lee, 2004; Agarwal and Bhattacharyya, 2005; Thomas et al., 2006) and content selection for text generation (Barzilay and Lapata, 2005).

©2008. Licensed under the *Creative Commons Attribution-Noncommercial-Share Alike 3.0 Unported* license (http://creativecommons.org/licenses/by-nc-sa/3.0/). Some rights reserved.

As a classification framework, the minimum-cut approach is quite attractive. First, it provides a principled, yet flexible mechanism for allowing problem-specific relational information — including several types of both hard and soft constraints — to influence a collection of classification decisions. Second, in many important cases, such as when all the edge weights are non-negative, finding a minimum cut can be done in a provably efficient manner.

To date, however, researchers have restricted the semantics of the constraints mentioned above to encode pair-wise "agreement" information only. There is a computational reason for this restriction: "agreement" and "disagreement" information are arguably most naturally expressed via positive and negative edge weights, respectively; but in general, the inclusion of even a relatively small number of negative edge weights makes finding a minimum cut NP-hard (McCormick et al., 2003).

To avoid this computational issue, we propose several heuristics that encode disagreement information with non-negative edge weights. We instantiate our approach on a sentiment-polarity classification task — determining whether individual conversational turns in U.S. Congressional floor debates support or oppose some given legislation. Our preliminary results demonstrate promising improvements over the prior work of Thomas et al. (2006), who considered only the use of agreement information in this domain.

2 Method

2.1 Min-cut classification framework

Binary classification problems are usually approached by considering each classification decision in isolation. More formally, let $X_{test} =$

$\{x_1, x_2, \ldots, x_n\}$ be the test instances, drawn from some universe X, and let $C = \{c_1, c_2\}$ be the two possible classes. Then, the usual approach can often be framed as labeling each x_i according to some *individual*-preference function $\text{Ind}: X \times C \rightarrow \Re$, such as the signed distance to the dividing hyperplane according to an SVM or the posterior class probability assigned by a Naive Bayes classifier.

But when it is difficult to accurately classify a particular x_i in isolation, there is a key insight that can help: knowing that x_i has the same label as an easily-categorized x_j makes labeling x_i easy. Thus, suppose we also have an association-preference function $\text{Assoc}: X \times X \rightarrow \Re$ expressing a reward for placing two items in the same class; an example might be the output of an agreement classifier or a similarity function. Then, we can search for a classification function $c(x_i|X_{test})$ — note that all of X_{test} can affect an instance's label — that minimizes the total "pining" of the test items for the class they were not assigned to due to either their individual *or* associational preferences:

$$\sum_i \text{Ind}(x_i, \bar{c}(x_i|X_{test})) + \alpha \times \sum_{i,j: c(x_i|X_{test}) = \bar{c}(x_j|X_{test})} \text{Assoc}(x_i, x_j),$$

where $\bar{c}(x_i|X_{test})$ is the class "opposite" to $c(x_i|X_{test})$, and the free parameter α regulates the emphasis on agreement information. Solutions to the above minimization problem correspond to *minimum s-t cuts* in a certain graph, and *if* both Ind and Assoc are non-negative functions, then, surprisingly, minimum cuts can be found in polynomial time; see Kleinberg and Tardos (2006, Section 7.10) for details. But, as mentioned above, allowing negative values makes finding a solution intractable in the general case.

2.2 Prior work discards some negative values

The starting point for our work is Thomas et al. (2006) (henceforth TPL). The reason for this choice is that TPL used minimum-cut-based classification wherein signed distances to dividing SVM hyperplanes were employed to define $\text{Ind}(x, c)$ and $\text{Assoc}(x, x')$. It was natural to use SVMs, since association was determined by classification rather than similarity — specifically, categorizing references by one congressperson to another as reflecting agreement or not — but as a result, negative association-preferences (e.g., negative distance to a hyperplane) had to be accounted for.

We formalize TPL's approach at a high level as follows. Let $\text{Ind}': X \times C \rightarrow \Re$ and $\text{Assoc}': X \times X \rightarrow \Re$ be *initial* individual- and association-preference functions, such as the signed distances mentioned above. TPL create two *non-negative conversion* functions $f: \Re \rightarrow [0, 1]$ and $g: \Re \rightarrow [0, 1]$, and then define

$$\begin{aligned} \text{Ind}(x_i, c) &:= f(\text{Ind}'(x_i, c)) \\ \text{Assoc}(x_i, x_j) &:= g(\text{Assoc}'(x_i, x_j)) \end{aligned}$$

so that an optimal classification can be found in polynomial time, as discussed above. We omit the exact definitions of f and g in order to focus on what is important here: roughly speaking, f and g normalize values and handle outliers[1], with the following crucial exception. While negative initial individual preferences for one class can be translated into positive individual preferences for the other, there is no such mechanism for negative values of Assoc'; so TPL resort to defining g to be 0 for negative arguments. They thus *discard* potentially key information regarding the strength of label *disagreement* preferences.

2.3 Encoding negative associations

Instead of discarding the potentially crucial label-disagreement information represented by negative Assoc' values, we propose heuristics that seek to incorporate this valuable information, but that keep Ind and Assoc non-negative (by piggy-backing off of TPL's pre-existing conversion-function strategy[2]) to preserve the min-cut-classification efficiency guarantees.

We illustrate our heuristics with a running example. Consider a simplified setting with only two instances x_1 and x_2; $f(z) = z$; $g(z) = 0$ if $z < 0$, 1 otherwise; and Ind' values (numbers labeling left or right arrows in the diagrams below, e.g., $\text{Ind}'(x_1, c_1) = .7$) and Assoc' value (the -2 labeling the up-and-down arrow) as depicted here:

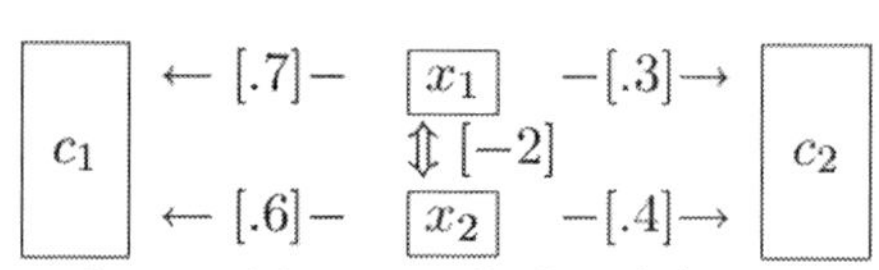

Then, the resulting TPL Ind and Assoc values are

[1] Thus, strictly speaking, f and g also depend on Ind', Assoc', and X_{test}, but we suppress this dependence for notational compactness.

[2] Our approach also applies to definitions of f and g different from TPL's.

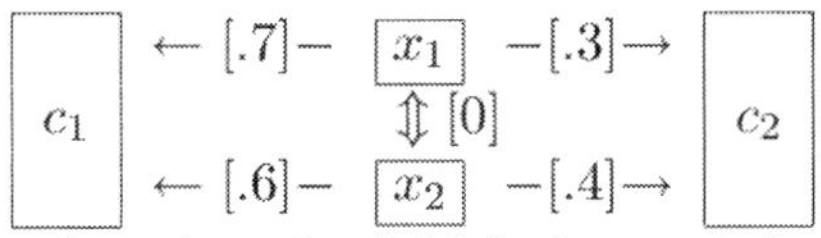

Note that since the initial -2 association value is ignored, $c(x_1|X_{test}) = c(x_2|X_{test}) = c_1$ appears to be a good classification according to TPL.

The *Scale all up* heuristic Rather than discard disagreement information, a simple strategy is to just scale up all initial association preferences by a sufficiently large positive constant N:

$$\begin{aligned} \mathrm{Ind}(x_i, c) &:= f(\mathrm{Ind}'(x_i, c)) \\ \mathrm{Assoc}(x_i, x_j) &:= g(\mathrm{Assoc}'(x_i, x_j) + N) \end{aligned}$$

For $N = 3$ in our example, we get

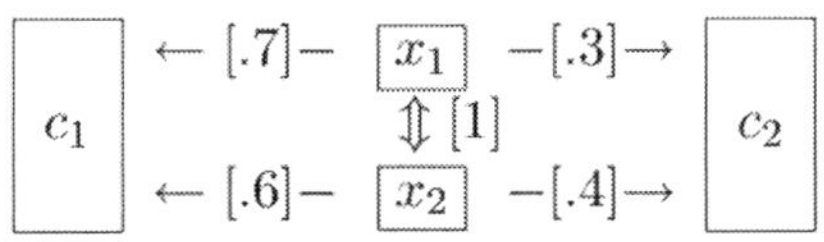

This heuristic ensures that the more negative the Assoc' value, the lower the cost of separating the relevant item pair (whereas TPL don't distinguish between negative Assoc' values). The heuristic below tries to be more proactive, *forcing* such pairs to receive different labels.

The *SetTo* heuristic We proceed through $x_1, x_2, \ldots$ in order. Each time we encounter an x_i where $\mathrm{Assoc}'(x_i, x_j) < 0$ for some $j > i$, we try to force x_i and x_j into different classes by altering the four relevant individual-preferences affecting this pair of instances, namely, $f(\mathrm{Ind}'(x_i, c_1))$, $f(\mathrm{Ind}'(x_i, c_2))$, $f(\mathrm{Ind}'(x_j, c_1))$, and $f(\mathrm{Ind}'(x_j, c_2))$. Assume without loss of generality that the largest of these values is the first one. If we respect that preference to put x_i in c_1, then according to the association-preference information, it follows that we should put x_j in c_2. We can instantiate this chain of reasoning by setting

$\mathrm{Ind}(x_i, c_1) := \max(\beta, f(\mathrm{Ind}'(x_i, c_1)))$
$\mathrm{Ind}(x_i, c_2) := \min(1 - \beta, f(\mathrm{Ind}'(x_i, c_2)))$
$\mathrm{Ind}(x_j, c_1) := \min(1 - \beta, f(\mathrm{Ind}'(x_j, c_1)))$
$\mathrm{Ind}(x_j, c_2) := \max(\beta, f(\mathrm{Ind}'(x_j, c_2)))$

for some constant $\beta \in (.5, 1]$, and making no change to TPL's definition of Assoc. For $\beta = .8$ in our example, we get

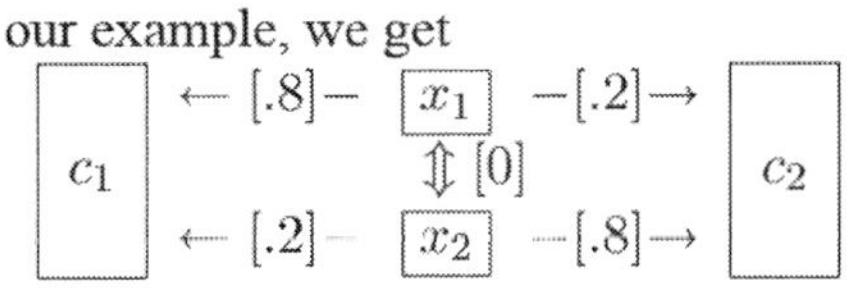

Note that as we proceed through $x_1, x_2, \ldots$ in order, some earlier changes may be undone.

The *IncBy* heuristic A more conservative version of the above heuristic is to increment and decrement the individual-preference values so that they are somewhat preserved, rather than completely replace them with fixed constants:

$\mathrm{Ind}(x_i, c_1) := \min(1, f(\mathrm{Ind}'(x_i, c_1)) + \beta)$
$\mathrm{Ind}(x_i, c_2) := \max(0, f(\mathrm{Ind}'(x_i, c_2)) - \beta)$
$\mathrm{Ind}(x_j, c_1) := \max(0, f(\mathrm{Ind}'(x_j, c_1)) - \beta)$
$\mathrm{Ind}(x_j, c_2) := \min(1, f(\mathrm{Ind}'(x_j, c_2)) + \beta)$

For $\beta = .1$, our example becomes

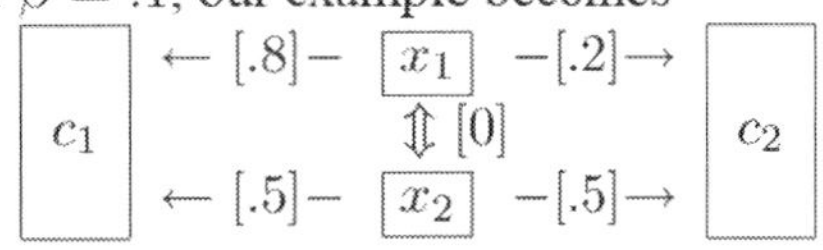

3 Evaluation

For evaluation, we adopt the sentiment-classification problem tackled by TPL: classifying *speech segments* (individual conversational turns) in a U.S. Congressional floor debate as to whether they support or oppose the legislation under discussion. TPL describe many reasons why this is an important problem. For our purposes, this task is also very convenient because all of TPL's computed raw and converted Ind' and Assoc' data are publicly available at www.cs.cornell.edu/home/llee/data/convote.html. Thus, we used their calculated values to implement our algorithms as well as to reproduce their original results.[3]

One issue of note is that TPL actually inferred association preferences between *speakers*, not speech segments. We do the same when applying *SetTo* or *IncBy* to a pair $\{x_i, x_j\}$ by considering the *average* of $f(\mathrm{Ind}'(x_k, c_1))$ over *all* x_k uttered by the speaker of x_i, instead of just $f(\mathrm{Ind}'(x_i, c_1))$. The other three relevant individual values are treated similarly. We also make appropriate modifications (according to *SetTo* and *IncBy*) to the individual preferences of all such x_k simultaneously, not just x_i, and similarly for x_j.

A related issue is that TPL assume that all speech segments by the same speaker should have the same label. To make experimental comparisons meaningful, we follow TPL in considering two different instantiations of this assumption. In *segment-based classification*, $\mathrm{Assoc}(x_i, x_j)$ is set to an arbitrarily high positive constant if the same speaker uttered both x_i and x_j. In *speaker-based classification*, $\mathrm{Ind}'(x_i, c)$ is produced by running

[3]For brevity, we omit TPL's "high-threshold" variants.

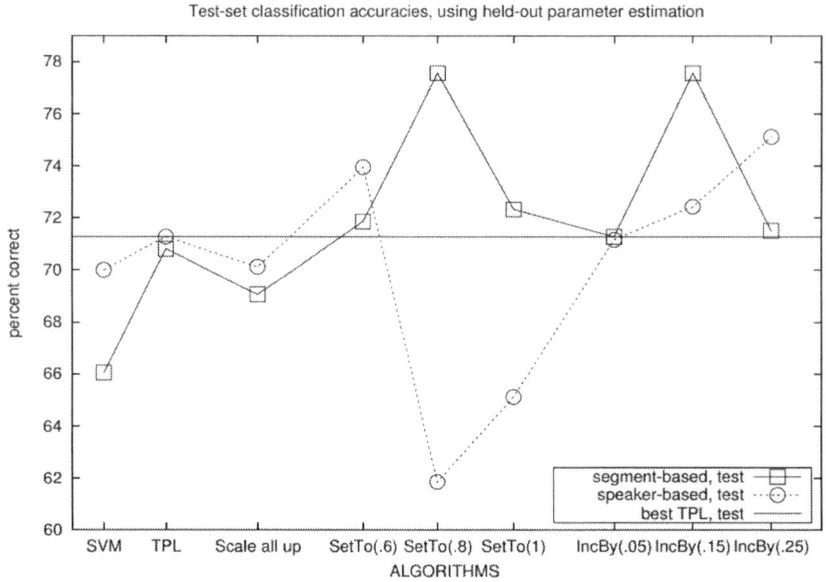

Figure 1: Experimental results. "SVM": classification using only individual-preference information. Values of β are indicated in parentheses next to the relevant algorithm names.

an SVM on the concatenation of all speeches uttered by x_i's speaker.

Space limits preclude inclusion of further details; please see TPL for more information.

3.1 Results and future plans

The association-emphasis parameter α was trained on held-out data, with ties broken in favor of the largest α in order to emphasize association information. We used Andrew Goldberg's HIPR code (http://avglab.com/andrew/soft.html) to compute minimum cuts. The resultant test-set classification accuracies are presented in Figure 1.

We see that *Scale all up* performs worse than TPL, but the more proactive heuristics (*SetTo*, *IncBy*) almost always outperform TPL on segment-based classification, sometimes substantially so, and outperform TPL on speaker-based classification for half of the variations. We therefore conclude that label disagreement information is indeed valuable; and that incorporating label disagreement information on top of the (positive) label agreement information that TPL leveraged can be achieved using simple heuristics; and that good performance enhancements result without any concomitant significant loss of efficiency.

These results are preliminary, and the divergence in behaviors between different heuristics in different settings requires investigation. Additional future work includes investigating more sophisticated (but often therefore less tractable) formalisms for joint classification; and looking at whether approximation algorithms for finding minimum cuts in graphs with negative edge capacities can be effective.

Acknowledgments We thank Jon Kleinberg and the reviewers for helpful comments. Portions of this work were done while the first author was visiting Cornell University. This paper is based upon work supported in part by the National Science Foundation under grant nos. IIS-0329064, BCS-0624277, and IIS-0535099, a Cornell University Provost's Award for Distinguished Scholarship, a Yahoo! Research Alliance gift, an Alfred P. Sloan Research Fellowship, and by DHS grant N0014-07-1-0152. Any opinions, findings, and conclusions or recommendations expressed are those of the authors and do not necessarily reflect the views or official policies, either expressed or implied, of any sponsoring institutions, the U.S. government, or any other entity.

References

A. Agarwal, P. Bhattacharyya. 2005. Sentiment analysis: A new approach for effective use of linguistic knowledge and exploiting similarities in a set of documents to be classified. *ICON*.

R. Barzilay, M. Lapata. 2005. Collective content selection for concept-to-text generation. *HLT/EMNLP*, pp. 331–338.

J. Kleinberg, É. Tardos. 2006. *Algorithm Design*. Addison Wesley.

S. T. McCormick, M. R. Rao, G. Rinaldi. 2003. Easy and difficult objective functions for max cut. *Mathematical Programming*, Series B(94):459–466.

B. Pang, L. Lee. 2004. A sentimental education: Sentiment analysis using subjectivity summarization based on minimum cuts. *ACL*, pp. 271–278.

M. Thomas, B. Pang, L. Lee. 2006. Get out the vote: Determining support or opposition from Congressional floor-debate transcripts. *EMNLP*, pp. 327–335.

Phrasal Segmentation Models for Statistical Machine Translation

Graeme Blackwood, Adrià de Gispert, William Byrne
Machine Intelligence Laboratory
Department of Engineering, Cambridge University
Trumpington Street, Cambridge, CB2 1PZ, U.K.
{gwb24|ad465|wjb31}@cam.ac.uk

Abstract

Phrasal segmentation models define a mapping from the words of a sentence to sequences of translatable phrases. We discuss the estimation of these models from large quantities of monolingual training text and describe their realization as weighted finite state transducers for incorporation into phrase-based statistical machine translation systems. Results are reported on the NIST Arabic-English translation tasks showing significant complementary gains in BLEU score with large 5-gram and 6-gram language models.

1 Introduction

In phrase-based statistical machine translation (Koehn et al., 2003) phrases extracted from word-aligned parallel data are the fundamental unit of translation. Each phrase is a sequence of contiguous translatable words and there is no explicit model of syntax or structure.

Our focus is the process by which a string of words is segmented as a sequence of such phrases. Ideally, the segmentation process captures two aspects of natural language. Firstly, segmentations should reflect the underlying grammatical sentence structure. Secondly, common sequences of words should be grouped as phrases in order to preserve context and respect collocations. Although these aspects of translation are not evaluated explicitly, phrases have been found very useful in translation. They have the advantage that, within phrases, words appear as they were found in fluent text. However, reordering of phrases in translation can lead to disfluencies. By defining a distribution over possible segmentations, we hope to address such disfluencies. A strength of our approach is that it exploits abundantly available monolingual corpora that are usually only used for training word language models.

Most prior work on phrase-based statistical language models concerns the problem of identifying useful phrasal units. In (Ries et al., 1996) an iterative algorithm selectively merges pairs of words as phrases with the goal of minimising perplexity. Several criteria including word pair frequencies, unigram and bigram log likelihoods, and a correlation coefficient related to mutual information are compared in (Kuo and Reichl, 1999). The main difference between these approaches and the work described here is that we already have a definition of the phrases of interest (i.e. the phrases of the phrase table extracted from parallel text) and we focus instead on estimating a distribution over the set of possible alternative segmentations of the sentence.

2 Phrasal Segmentation Models

Under the generative model of phrase-based statistical machine translation, a source sentence s_1^I generates sequences $u_1^K = u_1, \ldots, u_K$ of source language phrases that are to be translated. Sentences cannot be segmented into phrases arbitrarily: the space of possible segmentations is constrained by the contents of the phrase table which consists of phrases found with translations in the parallel text. We start initially with a distribution in which segmentations assume the following dependencies:

$$P(u_1^K, K|s_1^I) = P(u_1^K|K, s_1^I)P(K|I). \quad (1)$$

The distribution over the number of phrases K is chosen to be uniform, i.e. $P(K|I) = 1/I$, $K \in \{1, 2, \ldots, I\}$, and all segmentations are considered equally likely. The probability of a particular segmentation is therefore

$$P(u_1^K|K, s_1^I) = \begin{cases} C(K, s_1^I) & \text{if } u_1^K = s_1^I \\ 0 & \text{otherwise} \end{cases} \quad (2)$$

©2008. Licensed under the *Creative Commons Attribution-Noncommercial-Share Alike 3.0 Unported* license (http://creativecommons.org/licenses/by-nc-sa/3.0/). Some rights reserved.

where $C(K, s_1^I)$ is chosen to ensure normalisation and the phrases $u_1, \ldots, u_K$ are found in the phrase table. This simple model of segmentation has been found useful in practice (Kumar et al., 2006).

Our goal is to improve upon the uniform segmentation of equation (2) by estimating the phrasal segmentation model parameters from naturally occuring phrase sequences in a large monolingual training corpus. An order-n phrasal segmentation model assigns a probability to a phrase sequence u_1^K according to

$$P(u_1^K|K, s_1^I) = \prod_{k=1}^{K} P(u_k|u_1^{k-1}, K, s_1^I) \approx$$
$$\begin{cases} C(K, s_1^I) \prod_{k=1}^{K} P(u_k|u_{k-n+1}^{k-1}) & \text{if } u_1^K = s_1^I \\ 0 & \text{otherwise} \end{cases} \quad (3)$$

where the approximation is due to the Markov assumption that only the most recent $n-1$ phrases are useful when predicting the next phrase. Again, each u_k must be a phrase with a known translation. For a fixed sentence s_1^I, the normalisation term $C(K, s_1^I)$ can be calculated. In translation, however, calculating this quantity becomes harder since the s_1^I are not fixed. We therefore ignore the normalisation and use the unnormalised likelihoods as scores.

2.1 Parameter Estimation

We focus on first-order phrasal segmentation models. Although we have experimented with higher-order models we have not yet found them to yield improved translation.

Let $f(u_{k-1}, u_k)$ be the frequency of occurrence of a string of words w_i^j in a very large training corpus that can be split at position x such that $i < x \leq j$ and the substrings w_i^{x-1} and w_x^j match precisely the words of two phrases u_{k-1} and u_k in the phrase table. The maximum likelihood probability estimate for phrase bigrams is then their relative frequency:

$$\hat{P}(u_k|u_{k-1}) = \frac{f(u_{k-1}, u_k)}{f(u_{k-1})}. \quad (4)$$

These maximum likelihood estimates are discounted and smoothed with context-dependent backoff such that

$$P(u_k|u_{k-1}) =$$
$$\begin{cases} \delta(u_{k-1}, u_k)\hat{P}(u_k|u_{k-1}) & \text{if } f(u_{k-1}, u_k) > 0 \\ \alpha(u_{k-1})P(u_k) & \text{otherwise} \end{cases} \quad (5)$$

where $\delta(u_{k-1}, u_k)$ discounts the maximum likelihood estimates and the context-specific backoff weights $\alpha(u_{k-1})$ are chosen to ensure normalisation.

3 The Transducer Translation Model

The Transducer Translation Model (TTM) (Kumar and Byrne, 2005; Kumar et al., 2006) is a generative model of translation that applies a series of transformations specified by conditional probability distributions and encoded as Weighted Finite State Transducers (Mohri et al., 2002).

The generation of a target language sentence t_1^J starts with the generation of a source language sentence s_1^I by the source language model $P_G(s_1^I)$. Next, the source language sentence is segmented according to the uniform phrasal segmentation model distribution $P_W(u_1^K, K|s_1^I)$ of equation (2). The phrase translation and reordering model $P_\Phi(v_1^R|u_1^K)$ generates the reordered sequence of target language phrases v_1^R. Finally, the reordered target language phrases are transformed to word sequences t_1^J under the target segmentation model $P_\Omega(t_1^J|v_1^R)$. These component distributions together form a joint distribution over the source and target language sentences and their possible intermediate phrase sequences as $P(t_1^J, v_1^R, u_1^K, s_1^I)$.

In translation under the generative model, we start with the target sentence t_1^J in the foreign language and search for the best source sentence $\hat{s}_1^I$. Encoding each distribution as a WFST leads to a model of translation as a series of compositions

$$L = G \circ W \circ \Phi \circ \Omega \circ T \quad (6)$$

in which T is an acceptor for the target language sentence and L is the word lattice of translations obtained during decoding. The most likely translation $\hat{s}_1^I$ is the path in L with least cost.

The above approach generates a word lattice L under the unweighted phrasal segmentation model of equation (2). In the initial experiments reported here, we apply the weighted phrasal segmentation model via lattice rescoring. We take the word lattice L and compose it with the unweighted transducer W to obtain a lattice of phrases $L \circ W$; this lattice contains phrase sequences and translation scores consistent with the initial translation. We also extract the complete list of phrases relevant to each translation.

We then wish to apply the phrasal segmentation model distribution of equation (3) to this phrase lattice. The conditional probabilities and backoff structure defined in equation (5) can be encoded as a weighted finite state acceptor (Allauzen et al., 2003). In this acceptor, Ψ, states encode histories and arcs define the bigram and backed-off unigram phrase probabilities. We note that the raw counts of equation (4) are collected prior to translation and the first-order probabilities are estimated only for phrases found in the lattice.

The phrasal segmentation model is composed with the phrase lattice and projected on the input to obtain the rescored word lattice $L' = (L \circ W) \circ \Psi$. The most likely translation after applying the phrasal segmentation model is found as the path in L' with least cost. Apart from likelihood pruning when generating the original word lattice, the model scores are included correctly in translation search.

4 System Development

We describe experiments on the NIST Arabic-English machine translation task and apply phrasal segmentation models in lattice rescoring.

The development set *mt02-05-tune* is formed from the odd numbered sentences of the NIST MT02–MT05 evaluation sets; the even numbered sentences form the validation set *mt02-05-test*. Test performance is evaluated using the NIST subsets from the MT06 evaluation: *mt06-nist-nw* for newswire data and *mt06-nist-ng* for newsgroup data. Results are also reported for the MT08 evaluation. Each set contains four references and BLEU scores are computed for lower-case translations.

The uniformly segmented TTM baseline system is trained using all of the available Arabic-English data for the NIST MT08 evaluation[1]. In first-pass translation, decoding proceeds with a 4-gram language model estimated over the parallel text and a 965 million word subset of monolingual data from the English Gigaword Third Edition. Minimum error training (Och, 2003) under BLEU optimises the decoder feature weights using the development set *mt02-05-tune*. In the second pass, 5-gram and 6-gram zero-cutoff stupid-backoff (Brants et al., 2007) language models estimated using 4.7 billion words of English newswire text are used to generate lattices for phrasal segmentation model rescoring. The phrasal segmentation model parameters

[1]http://www.nist.gov/speech/tests/mt/2008/

	mt02-05-tune	mt02-05-test
TTM+MET	48.9	48.6
+6g	51.9	51.7
+6g+PSM	52.7	52.7

Table 2: BLEU scores for phrasal segmentation model rescoring of 6-gram rescored lattices.

are trained using a 1.8 billion word subset of the same monolingual training data used to build the second-pass word language model. A phrasal segmentation model scale factor and phrase insertion penalty are tuned using the development set.

5 Results and Analysis

First-pass TTM translation lattices generated with a uniform segmentation obtain baseline BLEU scores of 48.9 for *mt02-05-tune* and 48.6 for *mt02-05-test*. In our experiments we demonstrate that phrasal segmentation models continue to improve translation even for second-pass lattices rescored with very large zero-cutoff higher-order language models. Table 1 shows phrasal segmentation model rescoring of 5-gram lattices. The phrasal segmentation models consistently improve the BLEU score: +1.1 for both the development and validation sets, and +1.4 and +0.4 for the in-domain newswire and out-of-domain newsgroup test sets. Rescoring MT08 gives gains of +0.9 on *mt08-nist-nw* and +0.3 on *mt08-nist-ng*.

For a limited quantity of training data it is not always possible to improve translation quality simply by increasing the order of the language model. Comparing tables 1 and 2 shows that the gains in moving from a 5-gram to a 6-gram are small. Even setting aside the practical difficulty of estimating and applying such higher-order language models, it is doubtful that further gains could be had simply by increasing the order. That the phrasal segmentation models continue to improve upon the 6-gram lattice scores suggests they capture more than just a longer context and that they are complementary to word-based language models.

The role of the phrase insertion penalty is to encourage longer phrases in translation. Table 3 shows the effect of tuning this parameter. The upper part of the table shows the BLEU score, brevity penalty and individual n-gram precisions. The lower part shows the total number of words in the output, the number of words translated as a phrase of the specified length, and the average number of words per phrase. When the insertion

	mt02-05-tune	mt02-05-test	mt06-nist-nw	mt06-nist-ng	mt08-nist-nw	mt08-nist-ng
TTM+MET	48.9	48.6	46.1	35.2	48.4	33.7
+5g	51.5	51.5	48.4	36.7	49.1	36.4
+5g+PSM	52.6	52.6	49.8	37.1	50.0	36.7

Table 1: BLEU scores for phrasal segmentation model rescoring of 5-gram rescored lattices.

PIP	-4.0	-2.0	0.0	2.0	4.0
BLEU	48.6	50.1	51.1	49.9	48.7
BP	0.000	0.000	0.000	-0.034	-0.072
1g	82.0	83.7	84.9	85.7	86.2
2g	57.3	58.9	59.9	60.5	61.1
3g	40.8	42.2	43.1	43.6	44.2
4g	29.1	30.3	31.1	31.5	32.0
words	70550	66964	63505	60847	58676
1	58840	46936	25040	15439	11744
2	7606	12388	18890	19978	18886
3	2691	4890	11532	13920	14295
4	860	1820	5016	6940	8008
5	240	450	1820	2860	3500
6+	313	480	1207	1710	2243
w/p	1.10	1.21	1.58	1.86	2.02

Table 3: Effect of phrase insertion penalty (PIP) on BLEU score, brevity penalty (BP), individual n-gram precisions, phrase length distribution, and average words per phrase (w/p) for *mt02-05-tune*.

penalty is too low, single word phrases dominate the output and any benefits from longer context or phrase-internal fluency are lost. As the phrase insertion penalty increases, there are large gains in precision at each order and many longer phrases appear in the output. At the optimal phrase insertion penalty, the average phrase length is 1.58 words and over 60% of the translation output is generated from multi-word phrases.

6 Discussion

We have defined a simple model of the phrasal segmentation process for phrase-based SMT and estimated the model parameters from naturally occurring phrase sequence examples in a large training corpus. Applying first-order models to the NIST Arabic-English machine translation task, we have demonstrated complementary improved translation quality through exploitation of the same abundantly available monolingual data used for training regular word-based language models.

Comparing the in-domain newswire and out-of-domain newsgroup test set performance shows the importance of choosing appropriate data for training the phrasal segmentation model parameters. When in-domain data is of limited availability, count mixing or other adaptation strategies may lead to improved performance.

Acknowledgements

This work was supported in part under the GALE program of the Defense Advanced Research Projects Agency, Contract No. HR0011-06-C-0022.

References

Allauzen, Cyril, Mehryar Mohri, and Brian Roark. 2003. Generalized algorithms for constructing statistical language models. In *Proceedings of the 41st Meeting of the Association for Computational Linguistics*, pages 557–564.

Brants, Thorsten, Ashok C. Popat, Peng Xu, Franz J. Och, and Jeffrey Dean. 2007. Large language models in machine translation. In *Proceedings of the 2007 Joint Conference on EMNLP and CoNLL*, pages 858–867.

Koehn, Philipp, Franz Josef Och, and Daniel Marcu. 2003. Statistical phrase-based translation. In *Proceedings of the 2003 Conference for Computational Linguistics on Human Language Technology*, pages 48–54, Morristown, NJ, USA.

Kumar, Shankar and William Byrne. 2005. Local phrase reordering models for statistical machine translation. In *Proceedings of the conference on HLT and EMNLP*, pages 161–168.

Kumar, Shankar, Yonggang Deng, and William Byrne. 2006. A weighted finite state transducer translation template model for statistical machine translation. *Natural Language Engineering*, 12(1):35–75.

Kuo, Hong-Kwang Jeff and Wolfgang Reichl. 1999. Phrase-based language models for speech recognition. In *Sixth European Conference on Speech Communication and Technology*, pages 1595–1598.

Mohri, Mehryar, Fernando Pereira, and Michael Riley. 2002. Weighted finite-state transducers in speech recognition. In *Computer Speech and Language*, volume 16, pages 69–88.

Och, Franz Josef. 2003. Minimum error rate training in statistical machine translation. In *Proceedings of the 41st Meeting of the Association for Computational Linguistics*, pages 160–167, Morristown, NJ, USA.

Ries, Klaus, Finn Dag Bu, and Alex Waibel. 1996. Class phrase models for language modeling. In *Proceedings of the 4th International Conference on Spoken Language Processing*.

A Scalable MMR Approach to Sentence Scoring for Multi-Document Update Summarization

Florian Boudin [♮] and **Marc El-Bèze** [♮]
[♮] Laboratoire Informatique d'Avignon
339 chemin des Meinajaries, BP1228,
84911 Avignon Cedex 9, France.
florian.boudin@univ-avignon.fr
marc.elbeze@univ-avignon.fr

Juan-Manuel Torres-Moreno [♮,♭]
[♭] École Polytechnique de Montréal
CP 6079 Succ. Centre Ville H3C 3A7
Montréal (Québec), Canada.
juan-manuel.torres@univ-avignon.fr

Abstract

We present SMMR, a scalable sentence scoring method for query-oriented update summarization. Sentences are scored thanks to a criterion combining query relevance and dissimilarity with already read documents (history). As the amount of data in history increases, non-redundancy is prioritized over query-relevance. We show that SMMR achieves promising results on the DUC 2007 update corpus.

1 Introduction

Extensive experiments on query-oriented multi-document summarization have been carried out over the past few years. Most of the strategies to produce summaries are based on an extraction method, which identifies salient textual segments, most often sentences, in documents. Sentences containing the most salient concepts are selected, ordered and assembled according to their relevance to produce summaries (also called extracts) (Mani and Maybury, 1999).

Recently emerged from the Document Understanding Conference (DUC) 2007[1], update summarization attempts to enhance summarization when more information about knowledge acquired by the user is available. It asks the following question: has the user already read documents on the topic? In the case of a positive answer, producing an extract focusing on only new facts is of interest. In this way, an important issue is introduced: redundancy with previously read documents (history) has to be removed from the extract.

A natural way to go about update summarization would be extracting temporal tags (dates, elapsed times, temporal expressions...) (Mani and Wilson, 2000) or to automatically construct the timeline from documents (Swan and Allan, 2000). These temporal marks could be used to focus extracts on the most recently written facts. However, most recently written facts are not necessarily new facts. Machine Reading (MR) was used by (Hickl et al., 2007) to construct knowledge representations from clusters of documents. Sentences containing "new" information (i.e. that could not be inferred by any previously considered document) are selected to generate summary. However, this highly efficient approach (best system in DUC 2007 update) requires large linguistic resources. (Witte et al., 2007) propose a rule-based system based on fuzzy coreference cluster graphs. Again, this approach requires to manually write the sentence ranking scheme. Several strategies remaining on post-processing redundancy removal techniques have been suggested. Extracts constructed from history were used by (Boudin and Torres-Moreno, 2007) to minimize history's redundancy. (Lin et al., 2007) have proposed a modified Maximal Marginal Relevance (MMR) (Carbonell and Goldstein, 1998) re-ranker during sentence selection, constructing the summary by incrementally re-ranking sentences.

In this paper, we propose a scalable sentence scoring method for update summarization derived from MMR. Motivated by the need for relevant novelty, candidate sentences are selected according to a combined criterion of query relevance and dissimilarity with previously read sentences. The rest of the paper is organized as follows. Section 2

© 2008. Licensed under the *Creative Commons Attribution-Noncommercial-Share Alike 3.0 Unported* license (http://creativecommons.org/licenses/by-nc-sa/3.0/). Some rights reserved.

[1]Document Understanding Conferences are conducted since 2000 by the National Institute of Standards and Technology (NIST), http://www-nlpir.nist.gov

introduces our proposed sentence scoring method and Section 3 presents experiments and evaluates our approach.

2 Method

The underlying idea of our method is that as the number of sentences in the history increases, the likelihood to have redundant information within candidate sentences also increases. We propose a scalable sentence scoring method derived from MMR that, as the size of the history increases, gives more importance to non-redundancy that to query relevance. We define H to represent the previously read documents (history), Q to represent the query and s the candidate sentence. The following subsections formally define the similarity measures and the scalable MMR scoring method.

2.1 A query-oriented multi-document summarizer

We have first started by implementing a simple summarizer for which the task is to produce query-focused summaries from clusters of documents. Each document is pre-processed: documents are segmented into sentences, sentences are filtered (words which do not carry meaning are removed such as functional words or common words) and normalized using a lemmas database (i.e. inflected forms "go", "goes", "went", "gone"... are replaced by "go"). An N-dimensional term-space Γ, where N is the number of different terms found in the cluster, is constructed. Sentences are represented in Γ by vectors in which each component is the term frequency within the sentence. Sentence scoring can be seen as a passage retrieval task in Information Retrieval (IR). Each sentence s is scored by computing a combination of two similarity measures between the sentence and the query. The first measure is the well known cosine angle (Salton et al., 1975) between the sentence and the query vectorial representations in Γ (denoted respectively $\vec{s}$ and $\vec{Q}$). The second similarity measure is based on the Jaro-Winkler distance (Winkler, 1999). The original Jaro-Winkler measure, denoted JW, uses the number of matching characters and transpositions to compute a similarity score between two terms, giving more favourable ratings to terms that match from the beginning. We have extended this measure to calculate the similarity between the sentence s and the query Q:

$$\mathrm{JW}_e(s,Q) = \frac{1}{|Q|} \cdot \sum_{q \in Q} \max_{m \in S'} \mathrm{JW}(q,m) \quad (1)$$

where S' is the term set of s in which the terms m that already have maximized $\mathrm{JW}(q,m)$ are removed. The use of JW_e smooths normalization and misspelling errors. Each sentence s is scored using the linear combination:

$$Sim_1(s,Q) = \alpha \cdot cosine(\vec{s},\vec{Q}) + (1-\alpha) \cdot \mathrm{JW}_e(s,Q) \quad (2)$$

where $\alpha = 0.7$, optimally tuned on the past DUCs data (2005 and 2006). The system produces a list of ranked sentences from which the summary is constructed by arranging the high scored sentences until the desired size is reached.

2.2 A scalable MMR approach

MMR re-ranking algorithm has been successfully used in query-oriented summarization (Ye et al., 2005). It strives to reduce redundancy while maintaining query relevance in selected sentences. The summary is constructed incrementally from a list of ranked sentences, at each iteration the sentence which maximizes MMR is chosen:

$$\mathrm{MMR} = \arg\max_{s \in S} \left[\lambda \cdot Sim_1(s,Q) - (1-\lambda) \cdot \max_{s_j \in E} Sim_2(s,s_j) \right] \quad (3)$$

where S is the set of candidates sentences and E is the set of selected sentences. λ represents an interpolation coefficient between sentence's relevance and non-redundancy. $Sim_2(s,s_j)$ is a normalized Longest Common Substring (LCS) measure between sentences s and s_j. Detecting sentence rehearsals, LCS is well adapted for redundancy removal.

We propose an interpretation of MMR to tackle the update summarization issue. Since Sim_1 and Sim_2 are ranged in $[0,1]$, they can be seen as probabilities even though they are not. Just as rewriting (3) as (NR stands for Novelty Relevance):

$$\mathrm{NR} = \arg\max_{s \in S} \left[\lambda \cdot Sim_1(s,Q) + (1-\lambda) \cdot (1 - \max_{s_h \in H} Sim_2(s,s_h)) \right] \quad (4)$$

We can understand that (4) equates to an OR combination. But as we are looking for a more intuitive AND and since the similarities are independent, we have to use the product combination. The scoring method defined in (2) is modified into a double maximization criterion in which the best ranked sentence will be the most relevant to the query AND the most different to the sentences in H.

$$\text{SMMR}(s) = Sim_1(s, Q) \cdot \left(1 - \max_{s_h \in H} Sim_2(s, s_h)\right)^{f(H)} \quad (5)$$

Decreasing λ in (3) with the length of the summary was suggested by (Murray et al., 2005) and successfully used in the DUC 2005 by (Hachey et al., 2005), thereby emphasizing the relevance at the outset but increasingly prioritizing redundancy removal as the process continues. Similarly, we propose to follow this assumption in SMMR using a function denoted f that as the amount of data in history increases, prioritize non-redundancy ($f(H) \to 0$).

3 Experiments

The method described in the previous section has been implemented and evaluated by using the DUC 2007 update corpus[2]. The following subsections present details of the different experiments we have conducted.

3.1 The DUC 2007 update corpus

We used for our experiments the DUC 2007 update competition data set. The corpus is composed of 10 topics, with 25 documents per topic. The update task goal was to produce short (~100 words) multi-document update summaries of newswire articles under the assumption that the user has already read a set of earlier articles. The purpose of each update summary will be to inform the reader of new information about a particular topic. Given a DUC topic and its 3 document clusters: A (10 documents), B (8 documents) and C (7 documents), the task is to create from the documents three brief, fluent summaries that contribute to satisfying the information need expressed in the topic statement.

1. A summary of documents in cluster A.
2. An update summary of documents in B, under the assumption that the reader has already read documents in A.
3. An update summary of documents in C, under the assumption that the reader has already read documents in A and B.

Within a topic, the document clusters must be processed in chronological order. Our system generates a summary for each cluster by arranging the high ranked sentences until the limit of 100 words is reached.

3.2 Evaluation

Most existing automated evaluation methods work by comparing the generated summaries to one or more reference summaries (ideally, produced by humans). To evaluate the quality of our generated summaries, we choose to use the ROUGE[3] (Lin, 2004) evaluation toolkit, that has been found to be highly correlated with human judgments. ROUGE-N is a n-gram recall measure calculated between a candidate summary and a set of reference summaries. In our experiments ROUGE-1, ROUGE-2 and ROUGE-SU4 will be computed.

3.3 Results

Table 1 reports the results obtained on the DUC 2007 update data set for different sentence scoring methods. $cosine + \text{JW}_e$ stands for the scoring method defined in (2) and NR improves it with sentence re-ranking defined in equation (4). SMMR is the combined adaptation we have proposed in (5). The function $f(H)$ used in SMMR is the simple rational function $\frac{1}{H}$, where H increases with the number of previous clusters ($f(H) = 1$ for cluster A, $\frac{1}{2}$ for cluster B and $\frac{1}{3}$ for cluster C). This function allows to simply test the assumption that non-redundancy have to be favoured as the size of history grows. Baseline results are obtained on summaries generated by taking the leading sentences of the most recent documents of the cluster, up to 100 words (official baseline of DUC). The table also lists the three top performing systems at DUC 2007 and the lowest scored human reference.

As we can see from these results, SMMR outperforms the other sentence scoring methods. By ways of comparison our system would have been ranked second at the DUC 2007 update competition. Moreover, no post-processing was applied to the selected sentences leaving an important margin of progress. Another interesting result is the high performance of the non-update specific method ($cosine + \text{JW}_e$) that could be due to the small size

[2]More information about the DUC 2007 corpus is available at http://duc.nist.gov/.

[3]ROUGE is available at http://haydn.isi.edu/ROUGE/.

of the corpus (little redundancy between clusters).

	ROUGE-1	ROUGE-2	ROUGE-SU4
Baseline	0.26232	0.04543	0.08247
3rd system	0.35715	0.09622	0.13245
2nd system	0.36965	0.09851	0.13509
$cosine + \text{JW}_e$	0.35905	0.10161	0.13701
NR	0.36207	0.10042	0.13781
SMMR	**0.36323**	**0.10223**	**0.13886**
1st system	0.37032	0.11189	0.14306
Worst human	0.40497	0.10511	0.14779

Table 1: ROUGE average recall scores computed on the DUC 2007 update corpus.

4 Discussion and Future Work

In this paper we have described SMMR, a scalable sentence scoring method based on MMR that achieves very promising results. An important aspect of our sentence scoring method is that it does not requires re-ranking nor linguistic knowledge, which makes it a simple and fast approach to the issue of update summarization. It was pointed out at the DUC 2007 workshop that Question Answering and query-oriented summarization have been converging on a common task. The value added by summarization lies in the linguistic quality. Approaches mixing IR techniques are well suited for query-oriented summarization but they require intensive work for making the summary fluent and coherent. Among the others, this is a point that we think is worthy of further investigation.

Acknowledgments

This work was supported by the *Agence Nationale de la Recherche*, France, project RPM2.

References

Boudin, F. and J.M. Torres-Moreno. 2007. A Cosine Maximization-Minimization approach for User-Oriented Multi-Document Update Summarization. In *Recent Advances in Natural Language Processing (RANLP)*, pages 81–87.

Carbonell, J. and J. Goldstein. 1998. The use of MMR, diversity-based reranking for reordering documents and producing summaries. In *21st annual international ACM SIGIR conference on Research and development in information retrieval*, pages 335–336. ACM Press New York, NY, USA.

Hachey, B., G. Murray, and D. Reitter. 2005. The Embra System at DUC 2005: Query-oriented Multi-document Summarization with a Very Large Latent Semantic Space. In *Document Understanding Conference (DUC)*.

Hickl, A., K. Roberts, and F. Lacatusu. 2007. LCC's GISTexter at DUC 2007: Machine Reading for Update Summarization. In *Document Understanding Conference (DUC)*.

Lin, Z., T.S. Chua, M.Y. Kan, W.S. Lee, L. Qiu, and S. Ye. 2007. NUS at DUC 2007: Using Evolutionary Models of Text. In *Document Understanding Conference (DUC)*.

Lin, C.Y. 2004. Rouge: A Package for Automatic Evaluation of Summaries. In *Workshop on Text Summarization Branches Out*, pages 25–26.

Mani, I. and M.T. Maybury. 1999. *Advances in Automatic Text Summarization*. MIT Press.

Mani, I. and G. Wilson. 2000. Robust temporal processing of news. In *38th Annual Meeting on Association for Computational Linguistics*, pages 69–76. Association for Computational Linguistics Morristown, NJ, USA.

Murray, G., S. Renals, and J. Carletta. 2005. Extractive Summarization of Meeting Recordings. In *Ninth European Conference on Speech Communication and Technology*. ISCA.

Salton, G., A. Wong, and C. S. Yang. 1975. A vector space model for automatic indexing. *Communications of the ACM*, 18(11):613–620.

Swan, R. and J. Allan. 2000. Automatic generation of overview timelines. In *23rd annual international ACM SIGIR conference on Research and development in information retrieval*, pages 49–56.

Winkler, W. E. 1999. The state of record linkage and current research problems. In *Survey Methods Section*, pages 73–79.

Witte, R., R. Krestel, and S. Bergler. 2007. Generating Update Summaries for DUC 2007. In *Document Understanding Conference (DUC)*.

Ye, S., L. Qiu, T.S. Chua, and M.Y. Kan. 2005. NUS at DUC 2005: Understanding documents via concept links. In *Document Understanding Conference (DUC)*.

Hindi Compound Verbs and their Automatic Extraction

Debasri Chakrabarti
Humanities and Social Sciences Department
IIT Bombay
debasri@iitb.ac.in

Hemang Mandalia
Computer Science and Engineering Department
IIT Bombay
hemang.rm@gmail.com

Ritwik Priya
Computer Science and Engineering Department
IIT Bombay
ritwik@cse.iitb.ac.in

Vaijayanthi Sarma
Humanities and Social Sciences Department
IIT Bombay
vsarma@iitb.ac.in

Pushpak Bhattacharyya
Computer Science and Engineering Department
IIT Bombay
pb@cse.iitb.ac.in

Abstract

We analyse Hindi complex predicates and propose linguistic tests for their detection. This analysis enables us to identify a category of V+V complex predicates called *lexical compound verbs* (*LCpdVs*) which need to be stored in the dictionary. Based on the linguistic analysis, a simple automatic method has been devised for extracting *LCpdVs* from corpora. We achieve an accuracy of around 98% in this task. The *LCpdVs* thus extracted may be used to automatically augment lexical resources like wordnets, an otherwise time consuming and labour-intensive process

1 Introduction

Complex predicates (CPs) abound in South Asian languages [Butt, 1995; Hook, 1974] primarily as either, noun+verb combinations (*conjunct verbs*) or verb+verb (V+V) combinations (*compound verbs*). This paper discusses the latter.

Of the many V+V sequences in Hindi, only a subset constitutes true CPs. Thus, we first need diagnostic tests to differentiate between CP and non-CP V+V sequences. Of the CPs thus isolated, we need to distinguish between those CPs that are formed in the syntax (derivationally) and those that are formed in the lexicon (*LCpdVs)* in order to include only the latter in lexical knowledge bases. Further, automatic extraction of *LCpdVs* from electronic corpora and their inclusion in lexical knowledge bases is a desirable goal for languages like Hindi, which liberally use CPs.

This paper discusses Hindi Verb+Verb (V+V) CPs and their automatic extraction from a corpus.

1.1 Related work

Alsina (1996) discusses the general theory of complex predicates. Early work on conjunct and compound verbs in Hindi appears in Burton-Page (1957) and Arora (1979). Our work on diagnostic tests for CPs, as reported here, has been inspired by Butt (1993, 1995 for Urdu) and Paul (2004, for Bengali). The analysis of lexical derivation of *LCpdVs* derives from the work on compound verbs by Abbi (1991, 1992) and Gopalkrishnan and Abbi (1992).

This work is motivated primarily by the need to automatically augment lexical networks such as the Princeton Wordnet (Miller *et. al.,* 1990) and the Hindi Wordnet (Narayan *et. al.*, 2002). Pasca (2005) and Snow et. al. (2006) report work on such augmentations by processing web documents.

To the best of our knowledge ours is the first attempt at automatic extraction of *LCpdVs* from Hindi corpora.

© 2008. Licensed under the *Creative Commons Attribution-Noncommercial-Share Alike 3.0 Unported* license (http://creativecommons.org/licenses/by-nc-sa/3.0/). Some rights reserved.

1.2 Organization of the paper

Section 2 discusses CPs in Hindi and the ways to distinguish them from other, similar looking, constructions. Section 3 discusses the automatic extraction of CPs from corpora. Section 4 concludes the paper.

2 V+V Complex Predicates in Hindi

We have identified five different types of V+V sequences in Hindi. These are:

1. V1 stem+V2: *maar Daalnaa* (kill-put) 'kill'.
2. V1 inf-e+lagnaa: *rone lagnaa* (cry-feel) 'start crying'.
3. V1 inf+paRnaa: *bolnaa paRaa* (say-lie) 'say'.
4. V1 inf-e+V2: *likhne ko/ke lie kahaa* 'asked to write'.
5. V1–kar+V2: ***lekar gayaa* 'took and went'.**

2.1 Identification of CPs]

Following Butt (1993) and Paul (2004), we use the following diagnostic tests to identify CPs in Hindi:

1. Scope of adverbs
2. Scope of negation
3. Nominalization
4. Passivization
5. Causativization
6. Movement

(see Appendix A for an example of these tests)

The tests above have been exhaustively applied to varied data. The results of these tests show that some V+V sequences function as single semantic units and others do not. They also show that the **V1stem+V2**, **V1inf-e+lagnaa** and **V1inf+paRnaa** sequences show similar properties and the **V1 inf-e+V2** stem and the **V1–kar+V2** behave similarly. We call these Group 1 and Group 2 respectively.

Group 1 sequences are true CPs in Hindi. The V+V sequences are simple predicates (monoclausal) with one subject. Group 2 constructions are not CPs. They show clausal embedding and each verb behaves as if it were an independent syntactic entity. In the next section we summarize the semantic properties of CPs (Group 1).

2.2 Semantic Properties of V2 in Group 1

After identifying the CPs from among different V+V sequences, the next step was to determine how they are formed. To accomplish this we examined the semantic properties of the second verbs (V2) in Group 1:

(1) V1inf+paRnaa:
Examples include *karnaa paRaa* 'do-lie (had to do)', *bolnaa paRaa* 'say-lie (had to say)' etc. The second verb is always *paRnaa* 'to lie (lay)'. It appears in its stem form and bears all the inflections. As V2, *paRnaa* has the meaning of *compulsion/force*. *paRnaa* 'lie' as a V2 can be combined with any V1 irrespective of the latter's semantic properties. Since there are no syntactic or semantic restrictions on the selection of V1, this construction should be treated in the syntax as a combination of a V1 and a modal auxiliary.

(2) V1 inf-e+lagnaa:
Examples include *karne lagaa* 'do-feel (start to do)', *bolne lagaa* 'say-feel (start to say)' etc. The V2 in this sequence is always *lagnaa* 'feel' in the bare form and carries all the inflections. The core meaning of *lagnaa* 'feel' is lost when it is combined with a V1. As a V2 it always has the meaning of *beginning, happening of an event*. *lagnaa* 'feel' as a V2 can be combined with any V1 irrespective of the latter's semantic properties. Thus, this is also an instance of a modal auxiliary and should be derived in the syntax.

(3) V1stem+V2
In the formation of V1 stem+V2, the V2 may be any one of ten verbs, as shown in Figure 1.

1. **Daalnaa *'put'***
2. **lenaa *'take'***
3. **denaa *'give'***
4. **uThnaa *'wake'***
5. **jaanaa *'go'***
6. **paRnaa *'lie'***
7. **baiThnaa *'sit'***
8. **maarnaa *'kill'***
9. **dhamaknaa *'throb'***
10. **girnaa *'fall'***

Figure 1: The 10 vector verbs

All these V2s also occur as main verbs. As V2, the core meaning of these verbs is lost (bleached), but they acquire some new semantic properties which are otherwise not seen (Abbi, 1991, 1992; Gopalkrishnan and Abbi, 1992). The semantic properties of V2s include *finality, definiteness, negative value, manner of the action, attitude of the speaker etc.*

The combination of V1 and V2 is subject to the semantic compatibility between the two verbs.

The argument structure of the CP is determined by V1 as is the case-marking on the internal arguments, but the case-marking on the external argument (subject) is determined by both verbs.

From this analysis we conclude that V+V CPs are formed both lexically and syntactically in Hindi. Detailed investigation shows us that the V2 in the **V1inf-e+lagnaa** and the **V1inf+paRnaa constructions** is a type of modal auxiliary and its semantic features are predictable and unvarying. We propose to deal with these verbs in the syntax and call these verbs *syntactic compound verbs* (*SCpdVs*). The V2 choice in the V1stem+V2 is not predictable and the CPs function as a single complex of syntactic and semantic features. We call these verbs *lexical compound verbs* (***LCpdVs***) and we propose to include them in the lexical knowledge base. In the next section we provide a heuristic for automatic extraction of *LCpdVs* for storage in the lexicon.

2.3 The Extraction Process

By scanning the corpus, V1stem+V2 sequences were found given the heuristic H^* specified in Figure 2.

(Heuristic H*)
If a verb V1 is in the stem form and is followed by a verb V2 from a pre-stored list of verbs that can form the second component of the CP (section 2.2, Figure 3), i.e., the 'vector', then this verb along with the V2 is taken to be an instance of an LCpdV.

Figure 2: Main heuristic for identifying *LCpdVs*

Ten native speakers of Hindi were consulted. They were asked to construct sentences with the extracted sequences. If they were able to do so, that sequence was registered as a true *LCpdV*.

The precision of the heuristic is calculated as the ratio of the *actual LCpdVs* arrived at through manual validation to the total number of *anticipated LCpdVs* identified by the heuristic.

The results of these calculations are shown in Table 1, with a precision rate of 70% for the BBC corpus and 79% for the CIIL one.

Corpus	Total detections	POS ambiguities	Passive forms	*LCpdVs* (manually detected)	Precision
BBC	40	8	4	28	0.7 (28/40)
CIIL	174	32	7	135	0.79 (135/174)

Table 1: Precision of *LCpdV* extraction

The loss in precision was caused by (i) part of speech ambiguity, (ii) passivisation and (iii) idiomatic usages. For lack of space, we do not discuss this here.

When measures were taken to remedy these errors, we reached an accuracy of close to 98% (see table 2).

	BBC	CIIL
Confirmed *LCpdVs* (A)	423	953
Not *LCpdVs* (B)	13	12
Different POS (C)	65	179
Possible *LCpdVs* but contexts insufficient (D)	44	36
Minimum Precision (A/(A+B+D))	0.88 (423/480)	0.95 (953/1001)
Maximum Precision ((A+B)/(A+B+D))	0.97 (467/480)	0.99 (989/1001)
Total V1stem+V2 constructions in the corpus	10,145	36,115

Table 2: Final results of LCpdV extraction

A partial list of *LCpdVs* extracted from a test run on the CIIL corpus is presented in Table 3.

baandh denaa 'tie'	Kar lenaa 'do'	Bhar denaa 'fill'	le jaanaa 'take'	Banaa denaa 'make'
jaan lenaa 'know'	kaaT denaa 'cut'	Kar denaa 'do'	Badal jaanaa 'change'	Bhuul jaanaa 'forget'
jalaa denaa 'burn'	Gir jaanaa 'fall'	Samajh lenaa 'understand'	Samjhaa denaa 'make understand'	Khod lenaa 'dig'
lauTaa denaa 'return'	Rah jaanaa 'stay'	Le lenaa 'take'	De denaa 'give'	ghusaa denaa 'enter'

Table 3: Examples of LCpdV extraction

3 Conclusions and Future Work

In this paper, we have presented a study of Hindi compound verbs, proposed diagnostic tests for their detection and given automatic methods for their extraction from a corpus. Native speakers verify that the accuracy of our method is close to 98% on representative corpora.

Future work will consist in inserting the extracted *LCpdVs* into lexical resources such as the Hindi wordnet[2] at the right places with the right links.

References

Abbi, Anvita. 1991. *Semantics of explicator compound verbs*. In South Asian Languages, Language Sciences, 13:2, 161-180

.Abbi, Anvita. 1992. *The explicator compound verb: some definitional issues and criteria for identification*. Indian Linguistics, 53, 27-46.

Alsina, Alex. 1996. *Complex Predicates:Structure and Theory*. CSLI Publications,Stanford, CA.

Arora, H. 1979. *Aspects of Compound Verbs in Hindi*. M.Litt. dissertation, Delhi University.

Burton-Page, J. 1957. *Compound and conjunct verbs in Hindi*. BSOAS 19 469-78.

Butt, M. 1993. *Conscious choice and some light verbs in Urdu*. In M. K. Verma ed. (1993) Complex Predicates in South Asian Languages. Manohar Publishers and Distributors, New Delhi.

Butt, M. 1995. *The Structure of Complex Predicates in Urdu*. Doctoral Dissertation, Stanford University.

Cruys Time De and B. V. Moiron. 2007. *Semantics-based multiword expression extraction*. ACL-2007 Workshop on Multiword Expressions.

Gopalkrishnan, D. and Abbi, A. 1992. *The explicator compound verb: some definitional issues and criteria for identification*. Indian Linguistics, 53, 27-46.

Miller,G., R. Beckwith, C. Fellbaum,, D. Gross, and K. Miller, *Five Papers on WordNet*. CSL Report 43, Cognitive Science Laboratory, Princeton University, Princeton, 1990.

http://www.cogsci.princeton.edu/~wn

Narayan, D., D. Chakrabarty, P. Pande, and P. Bhattacharyya. 2002. *An experience in building the Indo WordNet - a WordNet for Hindi*, International Conference on Global WordNet (GWC 02), Mysore, India, January.

Pasca, Marius, 2005. *finding instance names and alternative glosses on the web: WordNet reloaded*. Proceedings of CICLing, Mexico City.

Snow, Rion, Dan Jurafsky, and Andrew Y. Ng. 2006. *Semantic taxonomy induction from heterogenous evidence*. Proceedings of COLING/ACL, Sydney.

[2] Developed by the wordnet team at IIT Bombay, www.cfilt.iitb.ac.in/webhwn

Appendix A. Example of a diagnostic Test for *LCpdVs:* scope of adverbs

Verb Type	Example	Comment	CP?
V1 stem+ V2	us-ne jaldii jaldii khaa li-aa'(S)he ate quickly.'	Scope over the whole sequence	Yes
V1inf-e+ lag-naa	vah jaldii se khaan-e lag-aa 'He started eating immediately.'	Scope over the whole sequence	Yes
V1 inf+ paRnaa	mujhe yah kaam jaldii karnaa paR-aa 'I had to do the work quickly.'	Scope over the whole sequence	Yes
V1inf-e+V2	us-ne mujhe khat jaldii se likhn-e kah-aa 'He asked me to write the letter quickly.'	Either over V1 or V2 depends upon the syntactic position of the adverb	No
V1–kar+ V2	vah jaldii se nahaa-kar aa-yeg-aa 'He will take bath quickly and come.'	Either over V1 or V2 depends upon the syntactic position of the adverb	No

Detecting Erroneous Uses of Complex Postpositions in an Agglutinative Language

Arantza Díaz de Ilarraza **Koldo Gojenola** **Maite Oronoz**

IXA NLP group. University of the Basque Country

jipdisaa@si.ehu.es koldo.gojenola@ehu.es maite.oronoz@ehu.es

Abstract

This work presents the development of a system that detects incorrect uses of complex postpositions in Basque, an agglutinative language. Error detection in complex postpositions is interesting because: 1) the context of detection is limited to a few words; 2) it implies the interaction of multiple levels of linguistic processing (morphology, syntax and semantics). So, the system must deal with problems ranging from tokenization and ambiguity to syntactic agreement and examination of local contexts. The evaluation was performed in order to test both incorrect uses of postpositions and also false alarms.

1 Structure of complex postpositions

Basque postpositions play a role similar to English prepositions, with the difference that they appear at the end of noun phrases or postpositional phrases. They are defined as "forms that represent grammatical relations among phrases appearing in a sentence" (Euskaltzaindia, 1994). There are two main types of postpositions in Basque: (1) a suffix appended to a lemma and, (2) a suffix followed by a lemma (main element) that can also be inflected.

(1) *etxe-**tik***
house-(from the)
from the house

(2) *etxe-**aren gain-etik***
house-(of the) top-(from the)
from the top of the house

The last type of elements has been termed as *complex postposition*. We will use this term to name the whole sequence of two words involved, and not just to refer to the second element. Complex postpositions can be described as:

(3) $lemma_1$ + ($suffix_1$ + $lemma_2$ + $suffix_2$)

In these constructions, the second lemma is fixed for each postposition, while the first lemma allows for much more variation, ranging from every noun to some specific semantic classes. The above description (3) is intended to stress (with parentheses) the fact that the combination of both suffixes with the second lemma acts as a complex case-suffix that is "appended" to the first lemma. Both suffixes present different combinations of number and case, which can agree in several ways, depending on the lemma, case or contextual factors. Table 1 shows the different variants of two complex postpositions, derived from the lemmas *bitarte* and *aurre*. For example, the lemma *bitarte* is polysemous ("means, by means of, instrument, while (temporal), between"). Multiple factors affect the correctness of a postposition, including morphological and syntactic constraints. We also discovered a number of relevant contextual factors, which are not explicitly accounted for in standard grammars.

2 The corpus

The detection of erroneous uses of complex postpositions needs first a corpus that can serve for both development and evaluation of the system. To obtain such a corpus is a labor-intensive task, to which it must be added the examination and markup of incorrect examples. The use of a big "correct" corpus will allow us to test our system *negatively*, thoroughly testing the system's behavior in respect to false alarms. We used an automatic system for detecting complex postpositions in order to get development and test data. There are two text types: Newspaper corpora (henceforth NC, 8,207,919 word-forms) that is subject to an edition process and style guides, and Learner corpora (LC, 994,658 word-forms), which come from texts written by learners of Basque and University students. These texts are more "susceptible" of containing errors.

© 2008. Licensed under the *Creative Commons Attribution-Noncommercial-Share Alike 3.0 Unported* license (http://creativecommons.org/licenses/by-nc-sa/3.0/). Some rights reserved.

lemma$_2$	suffix$_1$	suffix$_2$	Examples
bitarte (noun)	*-en* (genitive)	*-z* (instrumental)	*etxearen bitartez* (by means of the house)
	-ra (alative)	*-n* (inessive, sg.)	*etxera bitartean* (while going to the house)
	-a (absolutive, sg.)	*-n* (inessive, sg.)	*ordubata bitartean* (around one o´clock)
	-ϕ (no case)	*-n* (inessive, sg.)	*meza bitartean* (while attending mass)
	-en (genitive)	*-n* (inessive, sg.)	*mendeen bitartean* (between those centuries)
	-ϕ (no case)	*-ϕ/ko* (no case/genitive)	*Lau hektarea bitarte* (in a range of four hectares)
	-ak (absolutive, pl.)	*-ϕ/ko* (no case/genitive)	*seiak bitarte* (around six o'clock)
	-ra (alative)	*-ϕ/ko* (no case/genitive)	*etxera bitarte* (in the way home)
aurre (noun)	*-ϕ/-en* (no case/genitive)	*-n/-ra/-tik/-ko* (inessive/ alative/ ablative/ genitive)	*eliza aurrean* (in front of the church)
	-tik (ablative)	*-ra* (alative)	*hemendik aurrera* (from here onwards)

Table 1. Complex postpositions for *bitarte* and *aurre*.

We decided to study those types of postpositions that appear most frequently in texts, those containing the following lemmas as their second element: *arte*, *aurre*, *bitarte*, *buruz*, and *zehar*[2]. We selected these postpositions given that they are well documented in grammar books, with detailed descriptions of their correct and incorrect uses (e.g. see Table 1 for *bitarte*), and also that they are very frequent in both types of texts.

Each kind of syntactic error occurs with very low frequency and, therefore, big corpora are needed for evaluation and testing[3]. Even if such corpora are available, to obtain naturally occurring test data, hundreds of texts should be manually examined and marked. As a result, we decided to only manually mark errors in Learners' Corpora (LC), because NC, an order of magnitude bigger than LC, is presumed to contain less errors. This implies that we will be able to measure precision[4] in both corpora, while recall[5] will only be evaluated in LC. Table 2 shows the number of sentences used for development (60% of each corpus) and test (40%). We treated LC and NC separately, as they presumably differ in the number of errors.

3 Linguistic Processing Tools

The corpus was automatically analyzed by means of several linguistic processors: a morphosyntactic analyzer (Aduriz et al., 2000), EUSTAGGER, the lemmatizer/tagger for Basque, and the Constraint Grammar parser (CG, Tapanainen, 1996) for morphological disambiguation.

Added to these, we also used other resources:

- Grammar books which describe errors in postpositions (Zubiri & Zubiri, 1995).
- Place names. Two of the selected postpositions (*arte*, *aurre*) are used in expressions that denote temporal and spatial coordinates, but their variants impose different restrictions and agreement (case, number). In order to recognize common nouns that refer to a spatial context, we made use of a new lexical resource: electronic versions of dictionaries (Sarasola, 2007; Elhuyar, 2000). 168 and 242 words were automatically acquired from each dictionary. To this, we added proper names corresponding to places.
- Animate/inanimate distinction. Regarding postpositions formed with *aurre*, Zubiri et al. (1995) point out that "typically the previous word takes the genitive case, although it can also be used without a case mark with inanimate nouns". For this reason, we used a dictionary enriched with semantic features, such as animate/inanimate, time or instrument. We selected 1,642 animate words. We also added person names and pronouns.

4 Rule design

The system will assign an error-tag to those word-forms that show the presence of an incorrect use of a postposition. We use the CG formalism (Tapanainen, 1996) for this task. CG allows

	NC		LC	
	Dev	**Test**	**Dev**	**Test**
arte	7769	5179	1209	806
aurre	8129	5420	1157	771
bitarte	3846	2564	772	514
buruz	5435	3623	560	373
zehar	1500	1000	186	126
Total	26679	17786	3884	2590
Errors			60	29

Table 2. Number of sentences in development and test sets, including the errors in LC.

[2] As each lemma has several meanings depending on each variant, we will not give their translation equivalence.

[3] We made an estimate of more than 1% of elements in general corpora being complex postpositions.

[4] Number of errors correctly identified by the system / total number of elements identified as erroneous.

[5] Number of errors correctly identified by the system / total number of real errors.

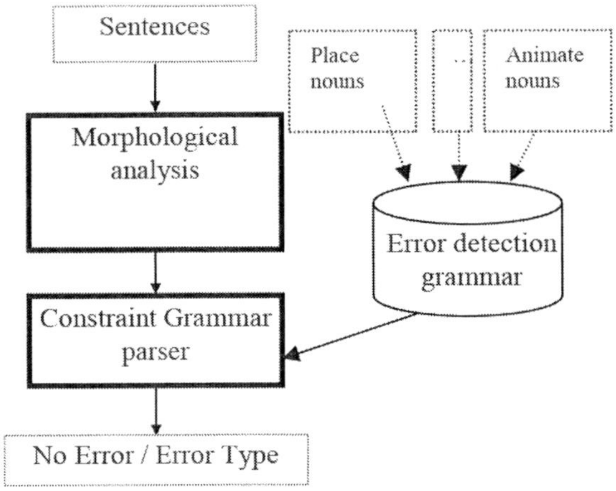

Figure 1. General architecture.

the definition of complex contextual rules in order to detect error patterns by means of mapping rules and a notation akin to regular expressions.

Fig. 1 shows a general overview of the system. Syntactic constraints are encoded by means of CG rules using morphosyntactic categories (part of speech, case, number, ...). Semantic restrictions are enforced by lists of words belonging to a semantic group. All of the five postpositions have clear requirements about the combinations of case and number in the surrounding context.

Overall, the CG grammar contains 30 rules for the set of 5 postpositions. We found that although the study of authoritative grammatical descriptions was exhaustive, the grammarians' descriptions of correct and incorrect uses refer mainly to morphology and syntax. Nevertheless, we discovered empirically that most of the rules needed to be extended with several classes of semantic restrictions. Among others, distinctions were needed for animate nouns, place names, or several classes of time expressions, depending on each different variant of each postposition.

5 Evaluation

The rules were applied both to the (presumably) correct newspapers texts (NC) and to the learners' texts (LC). The actual errors in LC were marked in advance but not in NC, which means that recall can only be evaluated in LC. Table 3 shows the main results including all the selected five postpositions. The LC corpus contains 60 and 29 error instances in development and test corpus, respectively. If we concentrate on precision, Table 4 shows the overall precision results for the total of errors detected in the test corpora. When we consider the whole set of postpositions precision is 50.5%, giving 42 false alarms out of 85 detected elements. We performed an analysis of false alarms which showed several causes:

	NC		LC	
	Dev	**Test**	**Dev**	**Test**
Sentences	26679	17786	3884	2590
Errors	-	-	60	29
Undetected	-	-	10	10
Detected	30	24	50	19
False alarms	45	33	2	9
Recall	-	-	83%	65%
Precision	40%	42%	96%	67%

Table 3. Evaluation results.

Postpositions	**Precision**
arte, aurre, bitarte, buruz, zehar	**50.5%** (43/85)
aurre, bitarte, buruz, zehar	**70.4%** (31/44)
bitarte, buruz, zehar	**78.3%** (29/37)

Table 4. Precision for the test sets (NC + LC).

- Morphological ambiguity (43% of alarms).
- Semantic ambiguity (28%). We included sets of context words to identify the correct senses, but it still causes many false alarms.
- Syntactic ambiguity (22%). The false alarms are mostly concerned with coordination.
- Tokenization errors (7%).

As most of the false alarms came from postpositions formed with *arte*, the most ambiguous one, we counted the errors when dealing only with the other four postpositions, giving a better precision (70.4%, second row in Table 4), although detecting less true errors. If the system only deals with three postpositions (third row in Table 4), then precision reaches 78.3%. Johannessen et al. (2002) note that the acceptable number of false alarms in a grammar checker should not exceed 30%, that is, at least 70% of all alarms had to report true errors. Our experiments show that our system performs within that limit, albeit restricting its application to the most "profitable" postpositions. Although the number of rules varies widely (from 15 rules for *arte* to 2 rules in the case of *zehar*) their effectiveness greatly depends on the complexity and ambiguity of the contextual factors. For that reason, *arte* presents the worst precision results even when it contains by far the biggest set of detection rules. On the other hand, *zehar*, with 2 rules, presents the best precision, due to its limited ambiguity. So, to deal with the full set postpositions (several works estimate more than 150), it will be more profitable to make a preliminary study on ambiguities and variants for each postposition.

6 Related work

Kukich (1992) surveys the state of the art in syntactic error detection. She estimates that a proportion of all the errors varying between 25% and over 50% are valid words. Atwell and Elliott

(1987) concluded that 55% of them are local syntactic errors (detectable by an examination of the local syntactic context), 18% are due to global syntactic errors (which need a full parse of the sentence), and 27% are semantic errors. Regarding their treatment, there have been proposals ranging from error patterns (Kukich 1992; Golding and Schabes 1996), in the form of hand-coded rules or automatically learned ones, to systems that integrate syntactic analysis.

(Chodorow et al., 2007) present a system for detecting errors in English prepositions using machine learning. Although both English prepositions and Basque postpositions have in some part relation with semantic features, Basque postpositions are, in our opinion, qualitatively more complex, as they are distributed across two words, and they also show different kinds of syntactic agreement in case and number, together with a high number of variants. This is the main reason why we chose a knowledge-based method.

7 Conclusions

We have presented a system for the detection of errors in complex postpositions in Basque. Although at first glance it could seem that postpositions imply the examination of two consecutive words, a posterior analysis showed that they offer rich and varied contexts of application, requiring the inspection of several context words, albeit not enough to need a full syntactic or semantic analysis of sentences. The system uses a varied set of linguistic resources, ranging from morphological analysis to specialized lexical resources. As the detection of these errors implies a detailed and expert linguistic knowledge, the system uses a purely knowledge-based approach.

A considerable effort has been invested in the compilation of a corpus that provides a testbed for the system, which should be representative enough as to predict the behaviour of the system in an environment of a grammar checker. For that reason, we have tried to put a real emphasis on avoiding false alarms, that is, treating also lots of correct instances. The results show that good precision can be obtained. Regarding recall, our experiments do not allow to make an estimation, as the NC test corpora is too big to perform a detailed examination. However, the LC corpora can give us an upper bound of 65% (see Table 3).

This work also shows that the use of purely morphosyntactic information is not enough for the detection of errors in postpositions. For that reason we were forced to also include several types of semantic features into the system. On the other hand, the process of automatic error detection has also helped us to explore new sets of semantic distinctions. So, the process of error detection has helped us to organize concepts into sets of semantically related elements, and can serve to make explicit types of knowledge that can be used to enrich other linguistic resources.

We can conclude saying that descriptive linguistics could benefit from error diagnosis and detection, as this could help to deeply understand the linguistic descriptions of postpositions, which are done at the moment mainly by means of morphosyntactic information, insufficient to give an account of the involved phenomena.

Acknowledgements

This research is supported by the University of the Basque Country (GIU05/52) and the Basque Government (ANHITZ project, IE06-185).

References

Aduriz I., Agirre E., Aldezabal I., Alegria I., Arregi X., Arriola J., Artola X., Gojenola K., Sarasola K. 2000. A Word-grammar based morphological analyzer for agglutinative languages. *COLING-00.*

Atwell E., Elliott S. (1987) Dealing with Ill-Formed English Text. *In The Computational Analysis of English: a Corpus-Based Approach*. Longman.

Chodorow M., Tetreault J. and Han N. 2007. Detection of Grammatical Errors Involving Prepositions. *4th ACL-SIGSEM Workshop on Prepositions.*

Díaz de Ilarraza A., Gojenola K., Oronoz M. 2008. Detecting Erroneous Uses of Complex Postpositions in an Agglutinative Language. Internal report (extended version). (https://ixa.si.ehu.es/Ixa/Argitalpenak)

Elhuyar. 2000. *Modern Basque Dictionary*. Elkar.

Euskaltzaindia. 1994. *Basque Grammar: First Steps* (in Basque). Euskaltzaindia.

Golding A. and Schabes. Y. (1996) Combining trigram-based and feature-based methods for context-sensitive spelling correction. *ACL 1996*.

Johannessen J.B., Hagen K., and Lane P. 2002. The performance of a grammar checker with deviant language input. *Proceedings of* COLING, Taiwan.

Kukich K. 1992. Techniques for automatically correcting words in text. *ACM Computing Surveys*.

Tapanainen P. 1996. *The Constraint Grammar parser CG-2*. Publications of the Univ. of Helsinki, 27.

Sarasola, Ibon. 2007. *Basque Dictionary* (in Basque). Donostia : Elkar, L.G. ISBN 978-84-9783-258-8.

Zubiri I. and Zubiri E. 1995. E. *Euskal Gramatika Osoa* (in Basque). Didaktiker, Bilbo.

Underspecified Modelling of Complex Discourse Constraints

Markus Egg
egg@let.rug.nl
University of Groningen

Michaela Regneri
regneri@coli.uni-sb.de
Saarland University

Abstract

We introduce a new type of discourse constraints for the interaction of discourse relations with the configuration of discourse segments. We examine corpus-extracted examples as soft constraints. We show how to use Regular Tree Gramamrs to process such constraints, and how the representation of some constraints depends on the expressive power of this formalism.

1 Introduction

Discourse structures cannot always be described completely, either because they are ambiguous (Stede, 2004), or because a discourse parser fails to analyse them completely. In either case, *underspecification formalisms* (UFs) can be used to represent partial information on discourse structure. UFs are used in semantics to model structural ambiguity without disjunctive enumeration of the readings (van Deemter and Peters, 1996).

Underspecified descriptions of discourse must handle two kinds of incomplete information, on the *configuration* of discourse segments (how they combine into larger units), and on the discourse *relations* that bring about this configuration: Our corpus studies on the RST Discourse Treebank (Carlson et al., 2002) showed *interdependencies* between relations and configuration, a phenomenon first noted by (Corston-Oliver, 1998). These interdependencies can be formulated as constraints that contribute to the disambiguation of underspecified descriptions of discourse structure.

E.g., in discourse segments constituted by the relation *Condition*, the premiss tends to be a discourse atom (or at least, maximally short).[1] Similarly, there is evidence for an interdependency constraint for the relation *Purpose(1)* [2]. In most cases, *Purpose(1)* has a discourse atom as its nucleus.

The corpus evaluation furthermore shows that those patterns never occur exclusively but only as tendencies. Realised as *soft* constraints, such tendencies can help to sort the set of readings according to the established preferences, which allows to focus on the best reading or the n-best readings. This is of high value for an UF-based approach to discourse structure, which must cope with extremely high numbers of readings. To model interdependency constraints, we will use Regular Tree Grammars (RTGs) (Comon et al., 2007). RTGs can straightforwardly be extended to *weighted* Regular Tree Grammars (wRTGs), which can represent both soft and hard constraints.

Apart from our corpus-extracted examples, we also consider a hard interdependency constraint similar to the Right Frontier Constraint. We show that we can integrate this attachment constraint with our formalism, and how its representation depends on the expressiveness of RTGs.

2 Underspecified Discourse Structure

We describe (partial) information on discourse structure by expressions of a suitable UF, here, dominance graphs (Althaus et al., 2003). Consider e.g. Fig. 1(a), the dominance graph for (1):

(1) [C_1 I try to read a novel] [C_2 if I feel bored] [C_3 because the TV programs disappoint me] [C_4 but I can't concentrate on anything.]

© 2008. Licensed under the *Creative Commons Attribution-Noncommercial-Share Alike 3.0 Unported* license (http://creativecommons.org/licenses/by-nc-sa/3.0/). Some rights reserved.

[1] Following Rhetorical Structure Theory (Mann and Thompson, 1988), most discourse relations have a central nucleus argument, and a peripheral satellite argument. For *Condition*, the premiss is the satellite, the nucleus, the conclusion.

[2] '(n)' as part of a relation name indicates that the nucleus is its n-th argument; relations with names without such an affix are multinuclear, i.e., link two segments of equal prominence. We sometimes omit the numbers where the position of the nucleus is clear from the context.

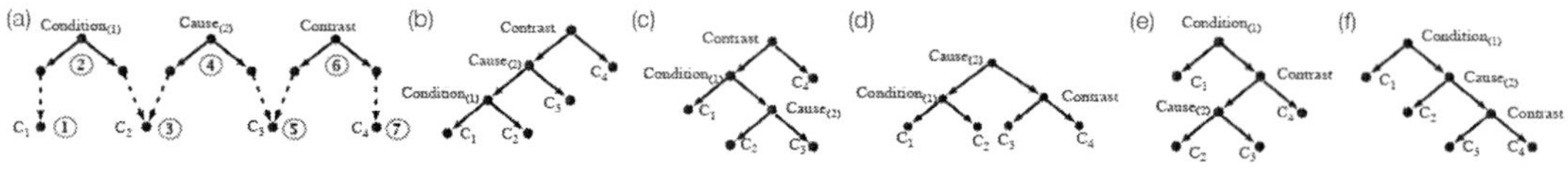

Figure 1: An underspecified discourse structure and its five configurations

$\{1\text{-}7\} \rightarrow$ *Condition*$(\{1\},\{3\text{-}7\})$ [1]	$\{1\text{-}7\} \rightarrow$ *Cause*$(\{1\text{-}3\},\{5\text{-}7\})$ [1]	$\{3\text{-}7\} \rightarrow$ *Contrast*$(\{3\text{-}5\},\{7\})$ [1]
$\{3\text{-}5\} \rightarrow$ *Cause*$(\{3\},\{5\})$ [1]	$\{1\text{-}7\} \rightarrow$ *Contrast*$(\{1\text{-}5\},\{7\})$ [1]	$\{1\text{-}5\} \rightarrow$ *Cause*$(\{1\text{-}3\},\{5\})$ [1]
$\{5\text{-}7\} \rightarrow$ *Contrast*$(\{5\},\{7\})$ [1]	$\{1\text{-}5\} \rightarrow$ *Condition*$(\{1\},\{3\text{-}5\})$ [3]	$\{1\text{-}3\} \rightarrow$ *Condition*$(\{1\},\{3\})$ [9]
$\{3\text{-}7\} \rightarrow$ *Cause*$(\{3\},\{5\text{-}7\})$ [1]	$\{1\} \rightarrow C_1$ [1] $\{3\} \rightarrow C_2$ [1]	$\{5\} \rightarrow C_3$ [1] $\{7\} \rightarrow C_4$ [1]

Figure 2: A wRTG modelling the interdependency constraint for Fig. 1

Such constraints describe a set of discourse structures (formalised as binary tree structures). Their key ingredient are (reflexive, transitive and antisymmetric) *dominance relations*, which are indicated by dotted lines. Dominance of X_1 over X_2 means that X_2 is part of the structure below (and including) X_1, but there might be additional material intervening between X_1 and X_2.

Fig. 1(a) states that C_1 is linked to a part of the following discourse (including at least C_2) by *Condition*, *Cause(2)* connects two discourse segments (comprising at least C_2 and C_3, respectively), and *Contrast* links a discourse segment to its left (including at least C_3) to C_4.

This constraint describes (is compatible with) exactly the five tree structures in Fig. 1(b-f), if described tree structures may only comprise material that is already introduced in the constraint. They model the potential discourse structures for (1) (see Webber (2004)). Dominance graphs like Fig. 1a. are *pure chains*. Pure chains describe all binary trees with the same leaf language, here the discourse segments, in their textual order. Pure chains define a left-to-right order, in that not only the leaves always form the same sequence, but also the inner nodes: If a labelled node X is further to the left in the chain than another node Y, in every described tree, X will either be Y's left child, or Y will be X's right child, or there will be a fragment F of which X is a successor on the left and Y is a right successor. Henceforth we will refer to fragments with their index in the chain (indicated by encircled numbers in Fig. 1a).

3 Representing Soft Interdependencies

The interdependency constraint for *Condition(1)* is that its satellite tends to be *maximally short*, i.e., mostly consists of only one discourse atom, and in most remaining cases, of two atoms. Thus, (b) and (d) are preferred among the configurations in Fig. 1, (c) is less preferred, and (e) and (f) are the least preferred. *Regular Tree Grammars* (RTGs) as UF (Koller et al., 2008) can express such complex constraints straightforwardly, and provide a convenient framework to process them. They allow to extract a best configuration with standard algorithms very efficiently.

Koller et al. (2008) show how to generate an RTG describing the same set of trees as a dominance graph. Similar to a context free grammar, an RTG uses production rules with terminal symbols and nonterminal symbols (NTs), whereby the left-hand side (LHS) is always a nonterminal and the right-hand side (RHS) contains at least one terminal symbol. One NT is the start symbol. A tree is accepted by the grammar if the grammar contains a derivation for it. An example for an RTG is given in Fig. 2, which describes the same trees as the dominance graph in Fig. 1a. The start symbol is $\{1\text{-}7\}$. To derive e.g. the tree in Fig. 1d, we first select the rule $\{1\text{-}7\} \rightarrow$ *Cause*$(\{1\text{-}3\},\{5\text{-}7\})$ that determines *Condition* as root for the whole tree. The left child of *Condition* is then derived from $\{1\text{-}7\}$, and the right child from $\{5\text{-}7\}$ respectively. To emphasize the association with the dominance graph, we mark nonterminals as the subgraphs they represent, e.g., $\{1\text{-}7\}$ denotes the whole graph. The terminal in the RHS of a grammar rule determines the root of the LHS subgraph.

Koller et al. (2008) also use *weighted* RTGs (wRTGs, an extension of RTG with weights) to express soft dominance constraints (which, unlike hard constraints, do not restrict but rather rank the set of configurations). We use wRTGs to model the soft interdependency constraints. The grammar in Fig. 2 is also a wRTG that assigns a weight to each derived tree: Its weight is the product over all weights of all rules used for the derivation. Weights appear in squared brackets after the rules.

The (merely expository) weights in our example encode the preference of *Condition* for a maximally short right child: There are three grammar rules that establish *Condition* as the root of a subgraph (shaded in Fig. 2), which are distinguished by the size of the right child of the root (one ($\{3\}$), three ($\{3\text{-}5\}$) or five ($\{3\text{-}7\}$) nodes). The shorter the right child, the higher the weight associated with the rule. (1 is a neutral weight by definition.) The grammar thus assigns different weights to the trees in Fig. 1; (b) and (d) get the maximum weight of 9, (b), a medium weight of 3, and (e) and (f), the lowest weight of 1.

4 Expressive Power of RTGs

As Koller et al. (2008) show, the expressive power of RTGs is superior to other common underspecification formalism. We show an important application of the increased expressiveness with Ex. 2, where a. can be continued by b. but not by c:

(2) a. [C_1 Max and Mary are falling apart.] [C_2 They no longer meet for lunch.] [C_3 And, last night, Max went to the pub] [C_4 but Mary visited her parents.]
b. [C_{5a} She complained bitterly about his behaviour.]
c. [C_{5b} He left after his fifth pint of lager.]

Segment C_{5a} continues the preceding clause about Mary's visit with additional information about the visit, it thus attaches directly to C_4. To find a coherent integration of C_{5b}, we would have to connect it to C_3, as it provides more details about Max' night at the pub. However, in the given constellation of C_3 and C_4, that form a *Contrast* together, C_3 is not available any longer for attachment of further discourse units. (This constraint is reminiscent of the *Right Frontier Constraint*, as it is used by Asher and Lascarides (2003). However, it is unclear how the Right Frontier Constraint in its exact definition can carry over to binary trees.)

The given attachment constraint is not expressible with dominance graphs: it excludes the configurations of its dominance graph (Fig. 3) in which *Contrast* shows up as a direct left child, e.g., (3b/e/f) as opposed to (3c/d). For instance, the excluded structure emerges in (3e/f) by choosing *Cause* as root of the the subgraph 5-9 (i.e., including the *Contrast*- and *Sequence*-fragments). For convenience, we will talk about this constraint as the "left child constraint" (LCC).

$$S \rightarrow Contrast(S,S) \qquad L \rightarrow Evid(S,S)$$
$$S \rightarrow Sequ(L,S) \qquad L \rightarrow List(S,S)$$
$$S \rightarrow L$$
$$L \rightarrow C_1 \quad L \rightarrow C_2 \quad L \rightarrow C_3 \quad L \rightarrow C_4 \quad L \rightarrow C_5$$

Figure 5: A filter RTG corresponding to Ex. 2

This additional constraint, however, can be expressed by an RTG like Fig. 4. We explicitly distinguish between subgraphs (referred to with numbers) and their associated NTs here. Crucially, some subgraphs can be processed in different derivations here, e.g., $\{5\text{-}9\}$ (as right child of *List*, irrespective of the relative scope of *Evidence* and *List*), or $\{3\text{-}7\}$ (in the expansions of both $\{EvLiCo\}$ and $\{LiCoSe\}$, like in (3c) as opposed to (3d)). Sometimes this derivation history is irrelevant, like in the case of $\{5\text{-}9\}$ (here, only *Contrast* may be chosen as root anyway), but there are cases where it matters: If $\{3\text{-}7\}$ is the left child of *Sequence*, as in (3b/d), the choice of *Contrast* as its root is excluded, since this would make *Contrast* the left child of *Sequence*, as in (3b). In contrast, $\{3\text{-}7\}$ as the right child of *Evidence*, like in (3c), allows both *Contrast* and *List* as root, because *Contrast* emerges as a right child in either case. Thus, the two occurrences of $\{3\text{-}7\}$ are distinguished in terms of different NTs in the grammar, and only in the NT for the latter occurrence is there more than one further expansion rule.

Regular tree languages are closed under intersection. Thus, one can derive a grammar like Fig. 4 by intersecting a completely underspecified RTG (here, the one derived from Fig. 3a) with a suitable *filter grammar*, e.g., Fig. 4. The filter grammar produces an infinite language, containing the fragments of Fig. 3a and excluding any derivation in which *Sequence* is the direct parent of *Contrast*. This is guaranteed by introducing the nonterminal L (the left child NT for *Sequence*), for which there is no derivation with *Contrast* as its root.

For an arbitrary pure chain with n fragments, the filter grammar generating the LCC is constructed as follows: S is the start symbol. For every fragment i s.t. $0 < i < n$, there is a derivation rule with S as its LHS and i in its RHS, thus either $S \rightarrow i$, for singleton fragments, or $S \rightarrow i(A, S)$, for binary fragments. If i is binary, we must determine A: If there is at least one fragment $f < i$ s.t. the LCC is assumed for f, we create a new NT L_i; every derivation rule with i on its RHS follows the pattern $X \rightarrow i(L_i, S)$ (thus $A = L_i$ in particular). If there is no LCC fragment to the left

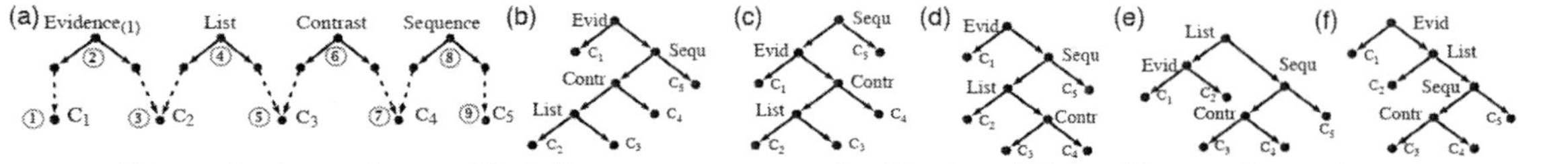

Figure 3: An underspecified discourse structure for Ex. 2 and five of its configurations

$\{EvLiCoSe\}$	$\rightarrow$	$Evid(\{C_1\}, \{LiCoSe\})$	$\{EvLiCo\}$	$\rightarrow$	$List(\{Ev\}, \{Co\})$	$\{Ev\}$	$\rightarrow$	$Evid(\{C_1\}, \{C_2\})$
$\{EvLiCoSe\}$	$\rightarrow$	$List(\{Ev\}, \{CoSe\})$	$\{CoSe\}$	$\rightarrow$	$Cont(\{C_3\}, \{Se\})$	$\{Li\}$	$\rightarrow$	$List(\{C_2\}, \{C_3\})$
$\{EvLiCoSe\}$	$\rightarrow$	$Cont(\{EvLi\}, \{Se\})$	$\{EvLi\}$	$\rightarrow$	$Evid(\{C_1\}, \{Li\})$	$\{Co\}$	$\rightarrow$	$Cont(\{C_3\}, \{C_4\})$
$\{EvLiCoSe\}$	$\rightarrow$	$Sequ(\{EvLiCo\}, \{C_5\})$	$\{EvLi\}$	$\rightarrow$	$List(\{Ev\}, \{C_3\})$	$\{Se\}$	$\rightarrow$	$Sequ(\{C_4\}, \{C_5\})$
$\{LiCoSe\}$	$\rightarrow$	$Sequ(\{LiCo\}_L, \{C_5\})$	$\{LiCo\}_L$	$\rightarrow$	$List(\{C_2\}, \{Co\})$			
$\{LiCoSe\}$	$\rightarrow$	$List(\{C_2\}, \{CoSe\})$	$\{LiCo\}_S$	$\rightarrow$	$Cont(\{Li\}, \{C_4\})$	$\{C_1\} \rightarrow C_1$		$\{C_2\} \rightarrow C_2$
$\{LiCoSe\}$	$\rightarrow$	$Cont(\{Li\}, \{Se\})$	$\{LiCo\}_S$	$\rightarrow$	$Li(\{Li\}, \{C_4\})$		$\{C_3\} \rightarrow C_3$	
$\{EvLiCo\}$	$\rightarrow$	$Evid(\{C_1\}, \{LiCo\}_S)$				$\{C_4\} \rightarrow C_4$		$\{C_5\} \rightarrow C_5$

Figure 4: A RTG integrating the attachment constraint for *Contrast* from Ex. 2 into Fig. 3

of i, $A = S$. If a new NT L_i was created, we need to create its RHSs: For every fragment h s.t. $0 < h < i$ and there is no LCC for h, there is a rewrite rule directly deriving h from L_i. If h is a singleton fragment, the rule is $L_i \rightarrow h$. Otherwise the rule is $L_i \rightarrow h(A', S)$, whereby $A' = S$, if there is no L_h, or $A' = L_h$ if there is some LCC fragment on the left of h.[3]

The grammar in Fig. 4 can be generated with that scheme; it has been reduced afterwards in that a general rule $S \rightarrow L$ substitutes for all rules of the form $S \rightarrow NT$ for which there is a corresponding rule $L \rightarrow NT$ (e.g., $S \rightarrow Evid(S, S)$).

5 Conclusion

Interdependency constraints that arise from the interaction of discourse relations and their surrounding structures are introduced as a new technique for disambiguating discourse structure. We integrate those constraints in underspecified discourse structures by exploiting the expressive power of Regular Tree Grammars as UF. As the corpus analysis yields in many cases only soft interdependency constraints, we use the weighted extension of RTGs, which allows to sort the readings of an underspecified representation and to identify preferred discourse structures. We then showed that the representation of some discourse constraints depend on the expressive power of RTGs. For notes on implementation and tractability of our approach, see Regneri et al. (2008).

[3]To model this as a preference rather than as a hard constraint, no rules for the L-NTs are omitted, but rather weighted low. An intersection with a preference-neutral wRTG would rank the configurations violating the constraint low, and all others with neutral weights.

References

Althaus, Ernst, Denys Duchier, Alexander Koller, Kurt Mehlhorn, Joachim Niehren, and Sven Thiel. 2003. An efficient graph algorithm for dominance constraints. *Journal of Algorithms*, 48:194–219.

Asher, Nicholas and Alex Lascarides. 2003. *Logics of Conversation*. Cambridge UP, Cambridge.

Carlson, Lynn, Daniel Marcu, and Mary Ellen Okurowski. 2002. RST Discourse Treebank. LDC.

Comon, H., M. Dauchet, R. Gilleron, C. Löding, F. Jacquemard, D. Lugiez, S. Tison, and M. Tommasi. 2007. Tree Automata Techniques and Applications. Available on: `http://www.grappa.univ-lille3.fr/tata`. Release 12-10-2007.

Corston-Oliver, Simon H. 1998. *Computing Representations of Discourse Structure*. Ph.D. thesis, Dept. of Linguistics, University of California, Santa Barbara.

van Deemter, Kees and Stanley Peters, editors. 1996. *Semantic ambiguity and underspecification*. CSLI, Stanford.

Koller, Alexander, Michaela Regneri, and Stefan Thater. 2008. Regular tree grammars as a formalism for scope underspecification. In *Proceedings of the ACL 08*.

Mann, William C. and Sandra A. Thompson. 1988. Rhetorical Structure Theory: Toward a functional theory of text organization. *Text*, 8:243–281.

Regneri, Michaela, Markus Egg, and Alexander Koller. 2008. Efficient Processing of Underspecified Discourse Representations. In *Proceedings of the ACL 08 (Short Papers)*.

Stede, Manfred. 2004. The Potsdam Commentary Corpus. In Webber, Bonnie and Donna K. Byron, editors, *ACL 2004 Workshop on Discourse Annotation*.

Webber, Bonnie. 2004. D-LTAG: extending lexicalized TAG to discourse. *Cognitive Science*, 28:751–779.

The Impact of Reference Quality on Automatic MT Evaluation

Olivier Hamon[1,2] **and Djamel Mostefa**[1]
(1) Evaluation and Language Resources Distribution Agency (ELDA)
55-57 rue Brillat-Savarin, 75013 Paris, France
(2) LIPN (UMR 7030) – Université Paris 13 & CNRS
99 av. J.-B. Clément, 93430 Villetaneuse, France
{hamon,mostefa}@elda.org

Abstract

Language resource quality is crucial in NLP. Many of the resources used are derived from data created by human beings out of an NLP context, especially regarding MT and reference translations. Indeed, automatic evaluations need high-quality data that allow the comparison of both automatic and human translations. The validation of these resources is widely recommended before being used. This paper describes the impact of using different-quality references on evaluation. Surprisingly enough, similar scores are obtained in many cases regardless of the quality. Thus, the limitations of the automatic metrics used within MT are also discussed in this regard.

1 Introduction

Language resources (LRs) are essential components in research and development of NLP systems. However, the production of most LRs is done by human beings and is therefore subject to errors or imperfections. The creation of LRs requires a quality assurance procedure that helps control their quality and make sure that they comply with the specifications.

The importance of validation criteria is even higher when it comes to evaluation, as reference LRs are used to measure system performance and, thus, quality. An evaluation must be done in a suitable qualitative framework and data used should be as good-quality as possible. Bearing that in mind, validation standards have been defined (Van den Heuvel et al., 2003) and resources should follow the specifications as close as possible for that purpose.

The problem also applies to reference translations in MT. Most of the automatic metrics used compare human reference translations to the output obtained from MT systems. Generally, more than one reference is used to get multiple translation possibilities (Papineni et al., 2001), but the evaluation of sentences depends highly on the human reference(s) translation(s) used. However, only a few studies have gone deeper into a definition of quality and have tried to detail how to evaluate it (Van den Heuvel & Sanders, 2006). N-gram metrics give scores that strongly depend on the reference and, thus, we wonder how much scores computed with a poor reference translation diverge from the ones computed with a high quality reference translation. This paper focuses on two issues: 1) how to validate the quality of a human translation; 2) study of the impact of the quality of reference translations on MT evaluations. The final objective behind this work is to find out to what an extent a validation is useful within the evaluation protocol. The building of reference translations is very time and money consuming, but the cost of validation should not be underestimated either (Fersøe et al., 2006).

2 Context

In our experiments, we used the material from the TC-STAR [1] second evaluation campaign (Mostefa et al., 2006) and the third one (Mostefa et al., 2007). For both campaigns, three language directions were used: English-to-Spanish (EnEs), Spanish-to-English (EsEn) and Chinese-to-English (ZhEn). Data came from European Parliament Plenary Sessions (EPPS) for EnES and

© 2008. Licensed under the *Creative Commons Attribution-Noncommercial-Share Alike 3.0 Unported* license (http://creativecommons.org/licenses/by-nc-sa/3.0/). Some rights reserved.

[1] http://www.tc-star.org

EsEn, Spanish Parliament Sessions (Cortes) for EsEn, and Voice of America (VoA) for ZhEn. Three kinds of input were considered: automatic transcriptions from Automatic Speech Recognition (ASR) systems, manual transcriptions (Verbatim) and Final Text Editions (FTE) provided by the European Parliament. This represents 14 sets consisting of source documents, reference translations translated twice by two different agencies, and translations obtained from MT systems. Each set contains around 25,000 words. Therefore, we had an overall set of 28 reference translations on the evaluations, directions and inputs from both years. During the campaigns, MT systems have been evaluated with automatic metrics such as BLEU (Papineni et al., 2001).

3 Validation

3.1 Guidelines

The quality of reference translations is considered in two ways. First, translation guidelines are given to the translators. Then, translated files are sent to a validation agency in order to check their quality according to the defined criteria.

Guidelines were produced within the TC-STAR project. They were discussed internally but also with the Linguistic Data Consortium (LDC) who has had the experience of producing many reference translations.

Translation agencies are informed about the quality control and extra attention is paid to the recommendations given for translation quality: meaning and style should remain as close to the original source documents as possible; no additional annotations should be added to the translation; capitalization has to be carefully respected; the translation of neologisms and unknown words should take into account the speaker's intention; date format should also follow the established conventions, etc.

3.2 Criteria and Procedure

For each reference translation of the three language directions, the Speech Processing EXpertise centre (SPEX)[2] validated 600 words from contiguous segments randomly selected. Translations were checked by professional translators, who classified errors into categories. Points are given to references, according to the penalty scheme presented in Table 1.

[2] http://www.spex.nl

Error category	**Penalty points**	
	Year 2	**Year 3**
Syntactical	4	3
Deviation from guidelines	3	-
Lexical	2	3
Poor usage	1	1
Capitalization	-	1
Punctuation / spelling (max.10)	0.5	0.5

Table 1. Translation errors penalties.

In order to be considered valid, a reference translation must have less than 40 penalty points. A non-valid reference translation is sent back to the translation agency/ies to be proofread and improved with the help of an errors report.

3.3 Typical Errors

Most errors are lexical ones, followed by poor usage of the language. Syntactic and spelling category errors are considerably fewer. In terms on input type, the number of lexical, spelling and syntactic errors is higher for FTE than Verbatim. On the other hand, the number of errors for usage and deviation from guidelines (including global translation quality) is higher for Verbatim.

Likewise, general errors are more frequent for English-to-Spanish than for Spanish-to-English. Chinese-to-English produces many more errors, in particular lexical ones. Syntactic errors could be wrong placement of adjective, wrong choice of person for pronouns, wrong use of verb tense or use of adjective as noun. Deviations from guidelines do not offer a wide variety: word/part of sentence omission, proper nouns mistranslation or translation quality/odd sentence problems. Thus, they have been regrouped under the others for the 3rd year evaluation. Lexical errors show the widest variety, probably due to the specificity of the vocabulary: mistranslation of acronyms, wrong word order, missing plural, literal translation, bad terminology or approximation, wrong preposition or translation inconsistencies. Other errors are wrong punctuation or spelling errors.

All these errors will lower the quality of the reference translations, which would imply a biased evaluation. The aim of the validation is then to reduce, as much as possible, the impact of mistranslation in order to improve *a priori* the assessment of the automatic translations.

4 Results

The following format is adopted for each set: "Year/Data-Input_Direction", e.g. "3/EPPS-FTE _EsEn" refers to the third-year set on Spanish-to-English using the FTE input on EPPS data.

4.1 Results of the Validation

On the overall 14 sets, 10 sets have been translated again and revalidated at least once (for either one or the two reference translations). Table 2 gives the scores of validation for each of these sets together with the Word Error Rate with its respective validated reference. The left-hand side number gives the result for the first reference and the right-hand side one gives the result for the second reference. The different lines for each set give results for the different types of reference (from intermediate to final), thus showing the evolution of their validation.

Set	Validation score		WER / final reference	
	Ref 1	Ref 2	Ref 1	Ref 2
3/EPPS-FTE_EsEn	59.5 18 **18**	104.5 73.5 **38**	12.5 -	8.2 1.3
3/Cortes-FTE_EsEn	43.5 34 **34**	120.5 70.5 **35**	6.2 -	5.1 1.2
3/Cortes-Verb_EsEn	54 **26.5**	67 **22.5**	0.5	0.3
3/VoA-Verb_ZhEn	130 53.5 **27**	129 37 **37**	24.2 6.3	15.3 -
2/EPPS-FTE_EnEs	23 **23**	31 **23.5**	-	0.9
2/EPPS-FTE_EsEn	18.5 **18.5**	33 **17**	-	2.6
2/EPPS-Verb_EnEs	59.5 **11.5**	17 **17**	0.7	-
2/Cortes-FTE_EsEn	42 **6**	61.5 9	0.2	5.3
2/Cortes-Verb_EsEn	69 **18.5**	54 **0**	20.7	4.7
2/VoA-Verb_ZhEn	84 **39.5**	38 **38**	17.0	-

Table 2. Validation scores of reference translations and WER between intermediate (upper line) and final references (bottom line) for the first reference (Ref 1) and the second one (Ref 2).

The mean score for the reference translations before any correction takes place is around 71, while after correction this is around 23. Thus, final translations are not perfect but their quality is sufficient to serve as reference. However, a maximum of 130 is obtained from the translation for Chinese-to-English, which seems to be more difficult than the other directions. WER was also computed between the non-validated translations and their corresponding validated versions. As it can be observed, are not necessarily very high and many WER values are below 1%.

4.2 Intermediate vs. Final Reference

When comparing the differences between the validation scores and WER for each translation, no correlation is found. The correlation coefficient between the score differences and the WER is around 58%. For instance, a score difference of 36 between non-validated and validated references corresponds to a WER of 0.2, while another difference of 26.5 corresponds to a WER of 6.3. There is no direct correlation between the quality of the references and the WER scores. Thus, *a priori*, the quality of reference translations has no impact on the WER, which could be extended to the scoring of MT systems. Indeed, if WER does not reflect in a precise manner the quality increase of a human translation, how can it be useful/reliable for scoring MT systems?

Figure 1 presents the correlation between these score differences and WER. It shows that quality is not necessarily well correlated with WER. The explanation is twofold: firstly, the improvement of a human translation does not necessarily imply many changes; secondly, WER does not reflect the quality of a translation accurately, as it does not seem to focus on essential language issues.

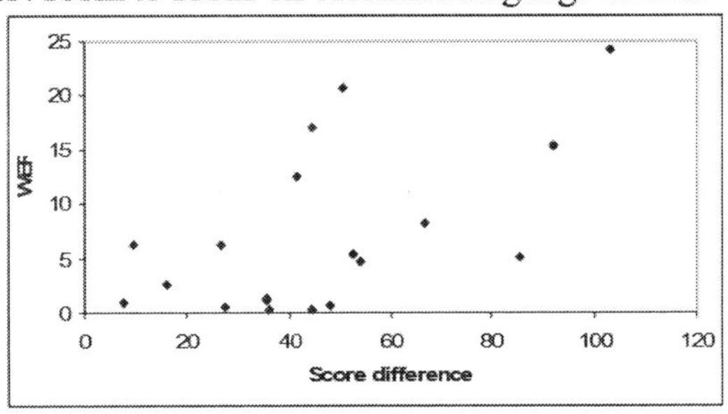

Figure 1. Correlation of score difference and WER between non-validated and validated references.

4.3 BLEU Results of MT Systems

BLEU scores have been computed for MT system output, using each set and each reference (whether validated or not). Then, either scores are quite identical or scores are slightly divergent. With the aim of studying this in detail, we assembled together the mean difference BLEU scores and the WER (against the final reference) for all the intermediate reference translations, as shown in Table 3.

The correlation coefficient between the absolute value of the mean difference score and mean of the WER is around 80%. Thus, the changes made into the references seem to have an impact on BLEU scores. However, given that quality is not correlated with WER, the absolute variation of the BLEU scores cannot be interpreted as a difference in MT system quality. It rather shows that comparing systems is the only plausible thing with BLEU, instead of evaluating systems in an absolute way.

Set	Mean diff. BLEU score	WER / final reference
3/EPPS-FTE_EsEn	1.18 -0.08	12.5 / 8.2 - / 1.3
3/Cortes-FTE_EsEn	0.67 0.035	6.2 / 5.1 - / 1.2
3/Cortes-Verb_EsEn	0.021	0.5 / 0.3
3/VoA-Verb_ZhEn	-1.71 0.001	24.2 / 15.3 6.3 / -
2/EPPS-FTE_EnEs	0.02	- / 0.9
2/EPPS-FTE_EsEn	0.24	- / 2.6
2/EPPS-Verb_EnEs	-0.05	0.7 / -
2/Cortes-FTE_EsEn	1.152	0.2 / 5.3
2/Cortes-Verb_EsEn	-2.21	20.7 / 4.7
2/VoA-Verb_ZhEn	0.08	17.0 / -

Table 3. Mean difference BLEU scores for each reference translation and WER between intermediate and final references.

4.4 Correlations of systems' evaluations

Correlations for BLEU scores were computed between 2 different-quality references. This allowed us to obtain 2 correlation coefficients for 2 non-validated references. For the correlation on scores, all coefficients are over 99%, so that even if scores increase or decrease, the distance between systems does not change. This is confirmed by the correlation on ranks, since the coefficients are between 96% and 100%. Thus, better reference translations could hardly distinguish MT systems in an easier way during evaluation.

5 Discussion and Conclusions

This work has used the BLEU metric to score MT system output and has demonstrated that the quality of reference translations does not have a clear impact on WER, also using n-grams. Even when using lower-quality translations, scores remain similar from one reference to another and important modifications of the human translation do not affect strongly the scores of the MT systems. This behaviour concerns all the languages tested, and remains the same regardless of the input or language used. However, we should not forget that the context of this experiment concerns actual automatic metrics. When reference translations have been modified, the impact on scores is not that clear, and even worse, this impact could be argued, to a certain extent, when the aim is to compare systems. Indeed, we also observed changes into scores when references were modified. Moreover, the quality of MT systems should not be ignored: if the overall quality of a system output is low, changes in reference translation will certainly have a lower impact on their scores.

Over the modification of the scores, the validation of the reference translation leads up to the validation criteria (although they are rigorously defined they are sometimes not very easy to apply by the validation team), the consistencies between agencies and translators (differences between reference translations show how the human translation quality may vary according to the translator) and some errors made by agencies (could be argued and validation can be difficult depending on the context, input, etc). Those points have to be carefully checked during a validation procedure and scores given by automatic metrics should be studied in agreement with the variation of the quality and validation.

Acknowledgements

This work was supported by the TC-STAR project (grant number IST-506738). We would like to thank SPEX, especially Henk Van den Heuvel and Eric Sanders, for the validation work. Our thanks also to Victoria Arranz for her help.

References

Fersøe H., Van den Heuvel H., Olsen S. 2006. *Validation of third party Spoken and Written Language Resources Methods for performing Quick Quality Checks.* Proceedings of Workshop "Quality assurance and quality measurement for language and speech resources", LREC 2006, Genoa, Italy.

Mostefa D., Garcia M-N., Hamon O. and Moreau N. 2006. *Evaluation report, Technology and Corpora for Speech to Speech Translation (TC-STAR) project.* Deliverable D16.

Mostefa D., Hamon O., Moreau N. and Choukri K. 2007. *Evaluation report, Technology and Corpora for Speech to Speech Translation (TC-STAR) project.* Deliverable D30.

Papineni K, Roukos S, Ward T, and Wei-Jing Z. 2001. *BLEU: A Method for Automatic Evaluation of Machine Translation.* IBM Research Division, Thomas J. Watson Research Center.

Van den Heuvel H., Choukri K., Höge H., Maegaard B., Odijk J., Mapelli V. 2003. *Quality Control of Language Resources at ELRA.* Proceedings of Eurospeech, Geneva, Switzerland, pp. 1541-1544.

Word Sense Disambiguation for All Words using Tree-Structured Conditional Random Fields

Jun Hatori* **Yusuke Miyao*** **Jun'ichi Tsujii*†‡**

*Graduate School of Interdisciplinary Information Studies, University of Tokyo

*Graduate School of Information Science and Technology, University of Tokyo

†National Centre for Text Mining / 131 Princess Street, Manchester, M1 7DN, UK

‡School of Computer Science, University of Manchester

{hatori,yusuke,tsujii}@is.s.u-tokyo.ac.jp

Abstract

We propose a supervised word sense disambiguation (WSD) method using tree-structured conditional random fields (TCRFs). By applying TCRFs to a sentence described as a dependency tree structure, we conduct WSD as a labeling problem on tree structures. To incorporate dependencies between word senses, we introduce a set of features on tree edges, in combination with coarse-grained tagsets, and show that these contribute to an improvement in WSD accuracy. We also show that the tree-structured model outperforms the linear-chain model. Experiments on the SENSEVAL-3 data set show that our TCRF model performs comparably with state-of-the-art WSD systems.

1 Introduction

Word sense disambiguation (WSD) is one of the fundamental underlying problems in computational linguistics. The task of WSD is to determine the appropriate sense for each polysemous word within a given text.

Traditionally, there are two task settings for WSD: the *lexical sample task*, in which only one targeted word is disambiguated given its context, and the *all-words task*, in which all content words within a text are disambiguated. Whilst most of the WSD research so far has been toward the lexical sample task, the all-words task has received relatively less attention, suffering from a serious knowledge bottleneck problem. Since it is considered to be a necessary step toward practical applications, there is an urgent need to improve the performance of WSD systems that can handle the all-words task.

In this paper, we propose a novel approach for the all-words task based on *tree-structured conditional random fields* (TCRFs). Our TCRF model incorporates the inter-word sense dependencies, in combination with WORDNET hierarchical information and a coarse-grained tagset, namely supersenses, by which we can alleviate the data sparseness problem.

2 Background

2.1 Inter-word sense dependencies

Since the all-words task requires us to disambiguate all content words, it seems reasonable to assume that we could perform better WSD by considering the sense dependencies among words, and optimizing word senses over the whole sentence. Specifically, we base our model on the assumption that there are strong sense dependencies between a head word and its dependents in a dependency tree; therefore, we employ the dependency tree structures for modeling the sense dependencies.

There have been a few WSD systems that incorporate the inter-word sense dependencies (e.g. Mihalcea and Faruque (2004)). However, to the extent of our knowledge, their effectiveness has not explicitly examined thus far for supervised WSD.

2.2 WORDNET information

Supersense A *supersense* corresponds to the lexicographers' file ID in WORDNET, with which each noun or verb synset is associated. Since

© Jun Hatori, Yusuke Miyao, and Jun'ichi Tsujii, 2008. Licensed under the *Creative Commons Attribution-Noncommercial-Share Alike 3.0 Unported* license (http://creativecommons.org/licenses/by-nc-sa/3.0/). Some rights reserved.

they are originally introduced for ease of lexicographers' work, their classification is fairly general, but not too abstract, and is hence expected to act as good coarse-grained semantic categories. The numbers of the supersenses are 26 and 15 for nouns and verbs. The effectiveness of the use of supersenses and other coarse-grained tagsets for WSD has been recently shown by several researchers (e.g. Kohomban and Lee (2005), Ciaramita and Altun (2006), and Mihalcea et al. (2007)).

Sense number A *sense number* is the number of a sense of a word in WORDNET. Since senses of a word are ordered according to frequency, the sense number can act as a powerful feature for WSD, which offers a preference for frequent senses, and especially as a back-off feature, which enables our model to output the first sense when no other feature is available for that word.

2.3 Tree-structured CRFs

Conditional Random Fields (CRFs) are graph-based probabilistic discriminative models proposed by Lafferty et al. (2001).

Tree-structured CRFs (TCRFs) are different from widely used linear-chain CRFs, in that the probabilistic variables are organized in a tree structure rather than in a linear sequence. Therefore, we can consider them more appropriate for modeling the semantics of sentences, which cannot be represented by linear structures.

Although TCRFs have not yet been applied to WSD, they have already been applied to some NLP tasks, such as semantic annotation (Tang et al., 2006), proving to be useful in modeling the semantic structure of a text.

Formulation In CRFs, the conditional probability of a label set $\mathbf{y}$ for an observation sequence $\mathbf{x}$ is calculated by

$$p(\mathbf{y}|\mathbf{x}) = \frac{1}{Z(\mathbf{x})} \exp\Big[\sum_{e \in E, j} \lambda_j f_j(e, \mathbf{x}, \mathbf{y}) + \sum_{v \in V, k} \mu_k g_k(v, \mathbf{x}, \mathbf{y})\Big] \quad (1)$$

where E and V are the sets of edges and vertices, f_j and g_k are the feature vectors for an edge and a vertex, λ_j and μ_k are the weight vectors for them, and $Z(\mathbf{x})$ is the normalization function. For a detailed description of TCRFs, see Tang et al. (2006).

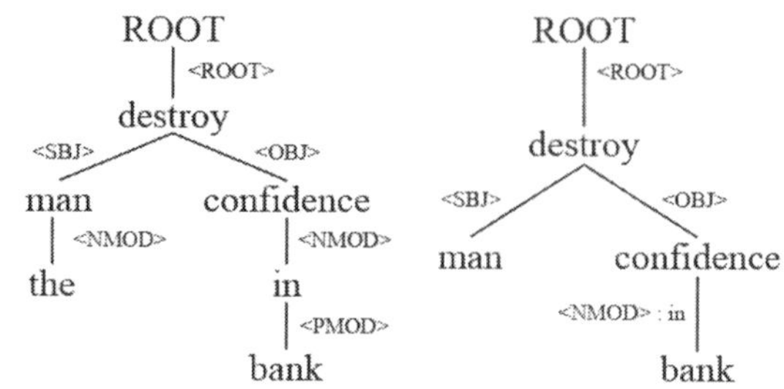

Figure 1: An example sentence described as a dependency tree structure.

3 WSD Model using Tree-structured CRFs

3.1 Overview

Let us consider the following sentence.

(i) *The man destroys confidence in banks.*

In the beginning, we parse a given sentence by using a dependency parser. The left-hand side of Figure 1 shows the dependency tree for Sentence (i) in the CoNLL-X dependency format.

Next, we convert the outputted tree into a tree of content words, as illustrated in the right-hand side of Figure 1, since our WSD task does not focus on the disambiguation of function words.

Finally, we conduct WSD as a labeling task on tree structures, by maximizing the probability of a tree of word senses, given scores for vertex and edge features.

3.2 Sense Labels

Using the information in WORDNET, we define four sense labels for a word: a *sense* $s_1(v)$, a *synset* $s_2(v)$, a *topmost synset* $s_3(v)$, and a *supersense* $s_4(v)$. A topmost synset $s_3(v)$ is the superordinate synset at the topmost level in the WORDNET hierarchy, and note that a supersense $s_4(v)$ is only available for nouns and verbs. We incorporate all these labels together into the vertex and edge features described in the following sections.

3.3 Vertex features

Most of the vertex features we use are those used by Lee and Ng (2002). All these features are combined with each of the four sense labels $s_n(v)$, and incorporated as g_k in Equation (1).

- Word form, lemma, and part of speech.
- Word forms, lemmas, and parts of speech of the head and dependents in a dependency tree.

	#sentences	#words
Development	470	5,178
Brown-1	10,712	100,804
Brown-2	8,956	85,481
SENSEVAL-3	300	2,081

Table 1: Statistics of the corpora.

- Bag-of-words within 60-words window.
- Parts-of-speech of neighboring six words.
- Local n-gram within neighboring six words.

Additionally, we include as a vertex feature the sense number, introduced in Section 2.2.

3.4 Edge features

For each edge, all possible sense bigrams (i.e. $s_1(v)$-$s_1(v')$,$s_1(v)$-$s_2(v')$,$\cdots$,$s_4(v)$-$s_4(v')$), and the combination of sense bigrams with dependency relation labels (e.g. 'SUB,' 'NMOD') and/or removed function words in between (e.g. 'of,' 'in') are defined as edge features, which correspond to f_j in Equation (1).

4 Experiment

4.1 Experimental settings

In the experiment, we use as our main evaluation data set the *Brown-1* and *Brown-2* sections of SEMCOR. The last files in the five largest categories in Brown-1 are used for development, and the rest of Brown-1 and all files in Brown-2 are alternately used for training and testing. We also use the SENSEVAL-3 English all-words data (Snyder and Palmer, 2004) for testing, in order to compare the performance of our model with other systems. The statistics of the data sets are shown in Table 1.

All sentences are parsed by the Sagae's dependency parser (Sagae and Tsujii, 2007), and the TCRF model is trained using Amis (Miyao and Tsujii, 2002). During the development phase, we tune the parameter of L_2 regularization for CRFs. Note that, in all experiments, we try all content words annotated with WORDNET synsets; therefore, the recalls are always equal to the precisions.

4.2 Results

First, we trained and evaluated our models on SEMCOR. Table 2 shows the overall performance of our models. BASELINE model is the first sense baseline. NO-EDGE model uses only the vertex features, while each of the Sn-EDGE models makes use of the edge features associated with a sense label s_n, where $n \in \{1, 2, 3, 4\}$. The ALL-EDGE model incorporates all possible combinations of sense labels. The only difference in the ALL-EDGE' model is that it omits features associated with dependency relation labels, so that we can compare the performance with the ALL-EDGE'(Linear) model, which is based on the linear-chain model.

System	Recall
PNNL (Tratz et al., 2007)	67.0%
Simil-Prime (Kohomban and Lee, 2005)	66.1%
ALL-EDGE	65.5%
GAMBL (Decadt et al., 2004)	65.2%
SENSELEARNER (Mihalcea et al.,2004)	64.6%
BASELINE	62.2%

Table 3: The comparison of the performance of WSD systems evaluated on the SENSEVAL-3 English all-words test set.

In the experiment, all models with one or more edge features outperformed both the NO-EDGE and BASELINE model. The ALL-EDGE model achieved 75.78% and 77.49% recalls for the two data sets, with 0.41% and 0.43% improvements over the NO-EDGE model. By the stratified shuffling test (Cohen, 1995), these differences are shown to be statistically significant[1], with the exception of S3-EDGE model. Also, the tree-structured model ALL-EDGE' is shown to outperform the linear-chain model ALL-EDGE'(Linear) by 0.13% for both data sets ($p = 0.013, 0.006$).

Finally, we trained our models on the Brown-1 and Brown-2 sections, and evaluated them on the SENSEVAL-3 English all-words task data. Table 3 shows the comparison of our model with the state-of-the-art WSD systems. Considering the difference in the amount of training data, we can conclude that the performance of our TCRF model is comparable to state-of-the-art WSD systems, for all systems in Table 3 other than Simil-Prime (Kohomban and Lee, 2005)[2] utilizes other sense-annotated data, such as the SENSEVAL data sets and example sentences in WORDNET.

[1]Although some of the improvements seem marginal, they are still statistically significant. This is probably because sense bigram features are rarely active, given the size of the training corpus, and most of the system outputs are the first senses. Indeed, 91.3% of the outputs of ALL-EDGE model are the first senses, for example.

[2]Kohomban and Lee (2005) used almost the same training data as our system, but they utilize the instance weighting technique and the combination of several classifiers, which our system does not.

Training set	Brown-1				Brown-2			
Testing set	Brown-2				Brown-1			
Model	Recall	Offset		#correct	Recall	Offset		#correct
ALL-EDGE'	75.77%	0.40%	$\gg$	64766/85481	77.45%	0.39%	$\gg$	78077/100804
ALL-EDGE' (Linear)	75.64%	0.27%	$\gg$	64662/85481	77.32%	0.26%	$\gg$	77944/100804
ALL-EDGE	75.78%	0.41%	$\gg$	64779/85481	77.49%	0.43%	$\gg$	78114/100804
S4-EDGE	75.46%	0.09%	$\gg$	64507/85481	77.15%	0.09%	$\gg$	77769/100804
S3-EDGE	75.40%	0.03%	$\sim$	64452/85481	77.13%	0.07%	$\gg$	77750/100804
S2-EDGE	75.45%	0.08%	$\gg$	64494/85481	77.12%	0.06%	$\gg$	77738/100804
S1-EDGE	75.44%	0.07%	$\gg$	64491/85481	77.10%	0.04%	$>$	77724/100804
NO-EDGE	75.37%	0.00%		64427/85481	77.06%	0.00%		77677/100804
BASELINE	74.36%			63567/85481	75.91%			76524/100804

Table 2: The performance of our system trained and evaluated on SEMCOR. The statistical significance of the improvement over NO-EDGE model is shown in the 'Offset' fields, where '$\gg$,' '$>$,' and '$\sim$' denote $p < 0.01$, $p < 0.05$, and $p \geq 0.05$, respectively.

5 Conclusion

In this paper, we proposed a novel approach for the all-words WSD based on TCRFs. Our proposals are twofold: one is to apply tree-structured CRFs to dependency trees, and the other is to use bigrams of fine- and coarse-grained senses as edge features.

In our experiment, the sense dependency features are shown to improve the WSD accuracy. Since the combination with coarse-grained tagsets are also proved to be effective, they can be used to alleviate the data sparseness problem. Moreover, we explicitly proved that the tree-structured model outperforms the linear-chain model, indicating that dependency trees are more appropriate for representing semantic dependencies.

Although our model is based on a simple framework, its performance is comparable to state-of-the-art WSD systems. Since we can use additionally other sense-annotated resources and sophisticated machine learning techniques, our model still has a great potential for improvement.

References

Ciaramita, M. and Y. Altun. 2006. Broad-coverage sense disambiguation and information extraction with a supersense sequence tagger. In *Proc. of the Conf. on Empirical Methods in Natural Language Processing (EMNLP)*.

Cohen, P. R. 1995. *Empirical methods for artificial intelligence*. MIT Press.

Decadt, B., V. Hoste, W. Daelemans, and A. V. den Bosch. 2004. GAMBL, genetic algorithm optimization of memory-based WSD. In *Senseval-3: Third Int'l Workshop on the Evaluation of Systems for the Semantic Analysis of Text*.

Kohomban, U. S. and W. S. Lee. 2005. Learning semantic classes for word sense disambiguation. In *Proc. of the 43rd Annual Meeting on Association for Computational Linguistics (ACL)*.

Lafferty, J., A. McCallum, and F. Pereira. 2001. Conditional random fields: Probabilistic models for segmenting and labeling sequence data. In *Proc. of 18th Int'l Conf. on Machine Learning (ICML)*.

Lee, Y. K. and H. T. Ng. 2002. An empirical evaluation of knowledge sources and learning algorithms for word sense disambiguation. In *Proc. of the Conf. on Empirical Methods in Natural Language Processing (EMNLP)*.

Mihalcea, R. and E. Faruque. 2004. SenseLearner: Minimally supervised word sense disambiguation for all words in open text. In *Proc. of ACL/SIGLEX Senseval-3*, Barcelona, Spain, July.

Mihalcea, R., A. Csomai, and M. Ciaramita. 2007. UNT-Yahoo: SuperSenseLearner: Combining SenseLearner with SuperSense and other coarse semantic features. In *Proc. of the 4th Int'l Workshop on the Semantic Evaluations (SemEval-2007)*.

Miyao, Y. and J. Tsujii. 2002. Maximum entropy estimation for feature forests. In *Proc. of Human Language Technology Conf. (HLT 2002)*.

Sagae, K. and J. Tsujii. 2007. Dependency parsing and domain adaptation with LR models and parser ensembles. In *Proc. of the CoNLL Shared Task Session of EMNLP-CoNLL 2007*.

Snyder, B. and M. Palmer. 2004. The english all-words task. In *Senseval-3: Third Int'l Workshop on the Evaluation of Systems for the Semantic Analysis of Text*.

Tang, J., M. Hong, J. Li, and B. Liang. 2006. Tree-structured conditional random fields for semantic annotation. In *Proc. of the 5th Int'l Semantic Web Conf.*

Tratz, S., A. Sanfilippo, M. Gregory, A. Chappell, C. Posse, and P. Whitney. 2007. PNNL: A supervised maximum entropy approach to word sense disambiguation. In *Proc. of the 4th Int'l Workshop on Semantic Evaluations (SemEval-2007)*.

ILP-based Conceptual Analysis for Chinese NPs

Paul D. Ji
Center for Language and Philology
Oxford University
Paul_dji@yahoo.com.uk

Stephen Pulman
Computing Laboratory
Oxford University
sgp@clg.ox.ac.uk

ABSTRACT

In this paper, we explore a conceptual resource for Chinese nominal phrases, which allows multi-dependency and distinction between dependency and the corresponding exact relation. We also provide an ILP-based method to learn mapping rules from training data, and use the rules to analyze new nominal phrases.

1 Introduction

Nominal phrases have long been a concern in linguistic research and language processing (e.g., Copestake and Briscoe, 2005; Giegerich, 2004). Generally, nominal phrases can be classified into two categories according to whether they contain attributive clauses or not. We focus on nominal phrases without attributive clauses.

Closely related with nominal phrases, nominal compounds or base NPs have also attracted a great attention in language processing. Generally, nominal compounds refer to nominal phrases consisting of a series of nouns, while base NPs refer to non-recursive nominal phrases. However, such compounds or base NPs usually co-occur with other non-nominal words in running texts, and it is impossible to separate them during analysis. Furthermore, there exist syntactic makers for attributive clauses, e.g., 'which' or 'who' in English and ' (of)' in Chinese, nominal phrases without attributive clauses tend to be a better linguistic category for theoretical and practical investigation.

To analyze NPs, we need first to determine what kinds of information are to be recognized. In this work, we focus on conceptual relatedness between words. For example, in *linguistics and law books*, *linguistic* and *law* are both conceptually related with *books*, although *linguistics* doesn't have a superficial syntactic relation with *books*. Then, we need to fulfill two sub-tasks. One is about representation, i.e., what schemes are to be used. The other is about analysis, i.e., how to derive the formal representation.

Regarding representation scheme, one possible strategy would be using syntactic structures, as are usually used in analysis for sentences. However, syntactic components for NPs, unlike those for sentences (e.g., V, VP, A, AP, and S, etc.), are difficult to differentiate, and rules governing nominal phrases are especially difficult to determine. As an example, consider (bank loan interest), which is a nominal compound consisting of three serial nouns. For such a NP, if a rule with binary combination is used, it would produce two structures for the unambiguous NP. If a rule with triple combination is used, as in Chinese Treebank (Xue et al., 2005), it would be difficult to disclose the lexical relation between (bank) and (loan).

Another possible representation strategy would be using dependency structures (Mel'cuk, 1988). Under this strategy, a NP could be represented as a dependency tree, which captures various lexical *control* or *dependency* in the phrase. However, traditional framework only focuses on syntactic dependency, while conceptual relatedness may exist without syntactic relations. For example, for *(economic development and law construction in Shanghai)*, in traditional dependency analysis, (Shanghai) would depend on the conjunction word (and), since conjunction words are usually regarded as *heads* in coordinate structures. Although the relatedness may go downward from the head, it would be difficult to derive the relatedness between (Shanghai) and (economic) or (law), since the two words are even not heads of the conjuncts (eco-

© 2008. Licensed under the *Creative Commons Attribution-Noncommercial-Share Alike 3.0 Unported* license (http://creativecommons.org/licenses/by-nc-sa/3.0/). Some rights reserved.

nomic development) and (law development).

As to analysis of NPs, there have been a lot of work on statistical techniques for lexical dependency parsing of sentences (Collins and Roark, 2004; McDonald et al., 2005), and these techniques potentially can be used for analysis of NPs if appropriate resources for NPs are available. However, these techniques are all meant to building a dependency tree, while the conceptual relatedness in NPs may form a graph, with multi-dependency allowed. Additionally, these methods generally suffer from the difficulty of local estimation from limited contexts and the structural information is difficult to be exploited (Califf and Mooney, 2003).

Recently, relational learning methods in general and inductive logic programming (ILP) in particular have attracted a great of attention due to their capability of going beyond finite feature vectors and exploiting unbounded structural information from data (Califf and Mooney, 2003; Page et al., 2003; Srinivasan et al., 2003).

In this work, we try to extend syntactic dependency to conceptual dependency to capture the embedded lexical relatedness, and use ILP to analyze nominal phrases, making use of the structural information provided by the resources based on conceptual dependency.

2 Conceptual dependency

In comparison with syntactic dependency, conceptual dependency may allow a word to be dependent on multiple words at the same time. For example, in (Economic development and law construction in Shanghai), (Shanghai) conceptually relates with both (economic) and (law), while in (activity of blood donation for university student volunteers), (university student) relates on both (volunteer) and (blood donation).

In addition, syntactic dependency doesn't exactly specify what kind of relatedness held between words, although the words denoting the relatedness may occur within NPs. For example, 1) is an ambiguous compound with two possible interpretations listed in 2).

1) (student discussion)

2) i) discussion by students

ii) discussion about students

However, the dependency trees corresponding with the two interpretations remain the same: (student) depends on (discussion) in both cases. In fact, their difference lies in the exact semantic relations held between the words: (student) is *agent* and *patient* of (discussion) in 2i) and 2ii) respectively. This suggests that only syntactic dependency is not enough to reflect conceptual difference.

Notice that in (2), the relations between the two words (student) and (discussion) are denoted by two proper nouns, *agent* and *patient*, which may never co-occur with them in running texts. However, in some cases, some word co-occurring with two conceptually related words do denote the relatedness exactly. Consider (car in read color), where (color) relates with both (car) and (red). In the conceptual view, (color) can be seen as a feature of (car), and (red) can be seen as a kind of value for the feature, as was also adopted in dealing with adjectives in WordNet (Fellbaum, 1988). In this setting, (red) directly depends on (car), and (color) represents the relation between them.

In building the resource for Chinese NPs, the conceptual relatedness is based on semantic reference, while the dependency is based on syntactic or potential syntactic relations. The feature words we adopt are mostly listed in a medium class, coded as *Dn*, in a Chinese thesaurus, Tongyici Cilin (henceafter Cilin, Mei et al., 1982). Function words (e.g., (from)), Part words (e.g., (leg)) and Number words (e.g., (count)) are also regarded as feature words.

3 ILP-based Analysis

Fig. 1 gives the overall structure of the analysis procedure.

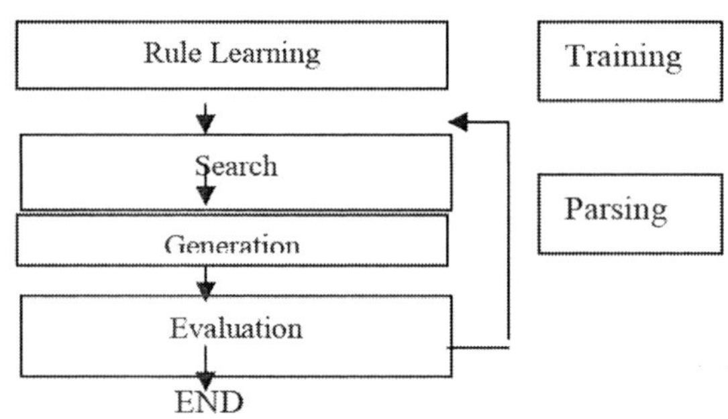

Fig. 1 Overall structure of analysis procedure

The analysis consists of two phases, training and parsing. During the training phase, rules are learned for mapping from conceptual dependency graphs to word strings based on training examples. During the parsing phase, there are three steps. Search is to find candidate dependency graphs, Generation is to generate word strings from candidate dependency graphs using the learned rules, and Evaluation is to compare the generated word strings with the original NPs.

3.1 Training: learning rules

For each training sample, we have a nominal phrase and its corresponding conceptual dependency graph. To learn the rules mapping from dependency graphs to word strings, we need to tag the words with their sense labels, which denote the synsets in the thesaurus (Mei et al., 1982). For the sense tagging, we used the same method as in (Yarowsky, 1992) and used the minor categories in the thesaurus as the synsets.

Generally, a rule consists of two parts, Gr and Sr. Gr is a dependency sub-graph and Sr is a sense label string. Intuitively, conceptual configuration in Gr is represented by the label string of Sr.

To capture more structural information, we need to find the maximal sub-graph in the training data, whose corresponding labels form a continuous substring in the training data. But the problem is NP hard, and we thus use heuristics to find am optimally maximal sub-graphs. However, the search has a bias to larger sub-graphs, and to avoid the bias, we set the coverage of a sub-graph as the penalty. Here, the coverage of the sub-graph refers to the percentage of the nodes in the sub-graphs among all the nodes in the training data. The overall algorithm is:

i) to find the most common edge in the training data, whose corresponding label strings are continuous;
ii) to add another edge to the sub-graph, if the label strings corresponding with the new sub-graph are still continuous until the coverage of the sub-graph doesn't increase.

After finding such a sub-graph, we merge all the nodes into one, and merge the sense label strings into one, and repeat the process until all the nodes in the training data are covered The result of the learning is a set of rules, and each rule specifies a sub-graph and a label string.

For example, w got a rule which includes the sub-graph in Fig. 2 and sense label string in 3).

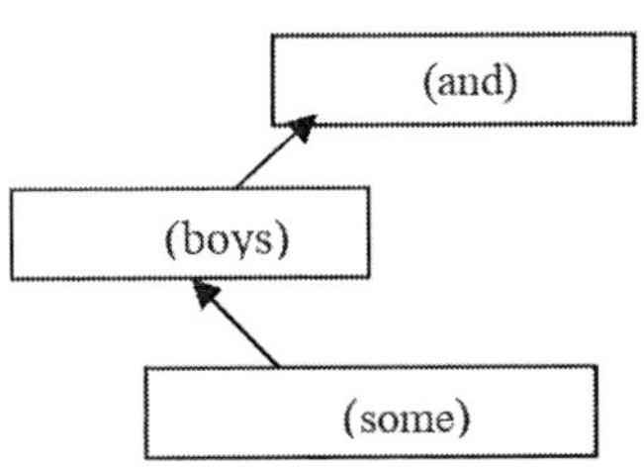

Fig. 2. Sub-graph in a rule.

3) SL( )SL( )SL( )

For rule generalization, we don't try to compress the rule set, and simply use the sense hierarchy in the thesaurus, including the minor, medium and major classes.

3.2 Parsing

After training phase, we get a set of learned rules. During parsing, the task is to find a conceptual dependency graph for a new input data, which would generate the NP using the learned rules.

The optimal parsing can be implemented in a greedy manner. First, one dependency with two words is selected. Then, another word is added if the resulted conceptual dependency graph generates a word string which *best* matches the input nominal phrase. This process can be repeated until the graph includes all the words in the data.

To compare the generated word string with the original input, we use *edit distance* between them, which is based on the times of *operations* (including *adjacent move*, *deletion*, *insertion*) needed to convert one word string to another.

4 Experiments and Evaluation

There are 10,000 nominal phrases annotated in the resource, and they were selected from 1,221 articles form the corpora of China daily, 1992. Table 1 gives the statistics of the resource.

num	'de' structure	Nominal compound	Dependency with feature	Multi-dependency
10K	4,234	5,766	1,235	976

Table 1. Statistics of NP resource

Here, 'de' structure refer to the phrase with word ' ' (of). Nominal compounds refer to the nominal phrases with no occurrence of ' '(of). Dependency with features refers to those tagged with features, which also occur in the same NPs. Multi-dependency refers to the number of mono-dependencies occurring in the multi-dependency.

We randomly selected 10% of the training data as closed test data, and the other 90% or less as training data. To evaluate the performance of the dependency analysis, we used *F*-scores as evaluation measure as usual. Fig. 4 shows the results for overall dependency, multi-dependency and dependency with features. The results are averaged over 10 random runs.

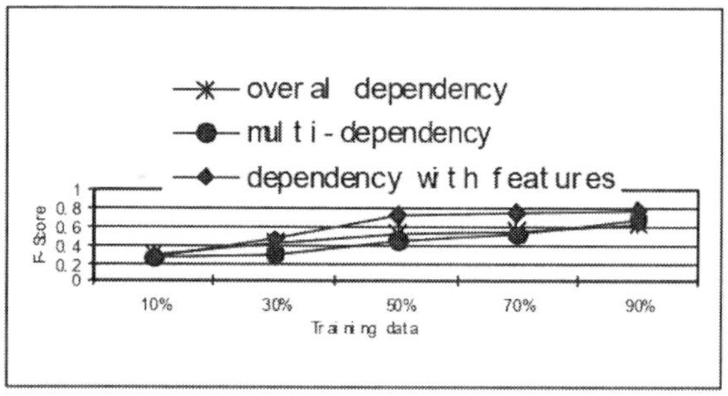

Fig. 3 Performance with varying training data

Fig. 3 demonstrates that with more training data, the performance generally improved. The performance for dependency with features seemed better than that for overall dependency or multi-dependency. To check the reason, we found that we treated the Amount words in Number-Amount structures as features, and these words are generally easier to be identified, since they tend to be unambiguous. Once they were recognized as Amount words, the relevant dependency would be correctly identified.

For an open test, we selected another 1,000 nominal phrases from the same corpus, but from different time period (1994). Such phrases were annotated with the same standard as those training data. Fig. 4 shows the results with varying training data.

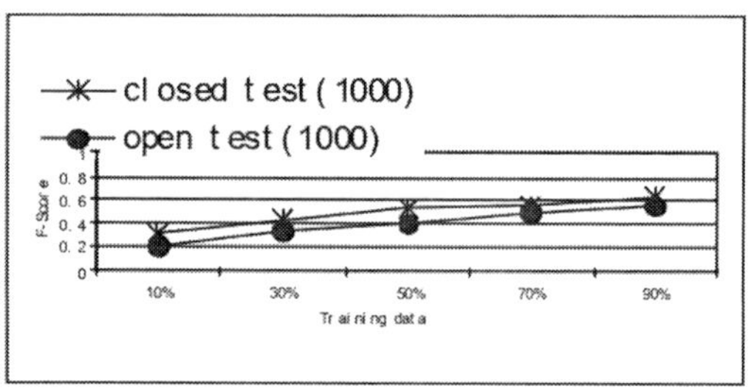

Fig. 4 Comparison: Closed test and open test

Fig. 4 shows that the open test performance is generally worse than that of the closed test. Notice that although the test data was selected from the same resource, but with a different period, which may account for the different performance.

5 Conclusion

In this paper, we described a resource for lexical conceptual dependency of Chinese nominal phrases. Compared with other ones, it allows multi-dependency and distinguishes dependency and relation, which exactly denotes what kinds of dependency held. We also provided an ILP-based analysis method, in which some rules mapping from conceptual dependency to word strings are learned from the training data, and then the rules are used to find the conceptual dependency graph for a new data. Compared with other search strategies, this method makes use of the structural information and allows construction of a dependency graph, not just a dependency tree.

References

Califf, M.R. and Mooney, R.J. 2003. Bottom-Up Relational Learning of Pattern Matching Rules for Information Extraction, JMLR: 4:177-210.

Collins M. and Roark, B. 2004. Incremental parsing with the perceptron algorithm. In *Proc. of the 42rd Annual Meeting of the ACL.*

Copestake, A. and Briscoe, T. 2005. Noun compounds revisited. In John I. Tait, editor, *Charting a New Course: Natural Language Processing and Information Retrieval*. Springer, Berlin, 2005.

Fellbaum, editor. 1998. WordNet: An Electronic Lexical Database. The MIT Press.

Giegerich, H.J. Compound or phrase? English noun-plus-noun constructions and the stress criterion. *English Language and Linguistics*, 8(1):1-24, 2004.

McDonald, R., Pereira, F., Ribarov, K. and Haji˘c, J. 2005. Non-projective dependency parsing using spanning tree algorithms. In *Proc. of HLT/EMNLP.*

Mei, J., Zhu, Y., Gao, Y., and Yin, H. 1982. Tongyici Cilin. Shanghai Dictionary Press.

Mel'cuk, I., 1988. Dependency Syntax: Theory and Practice. Albany. State Univ. of New York Press.

Page, D. Srinivasan A. 2003. ILP: A Short Look Back and a Longer Look Forward. Journal of Machine Learning Research 4: 415-430

Srinivasan, A. Ross D. K., Michael B. 2003. An Empirical Study of the Use of Relevance Information in Inductive Logic Programming. Journal of Machine Learning Research 4: 369-383.

Xue, N.W., Xia, F., Chiou, F.D.and Palmer, M. The Penn Chinese TreeBank: Phrase Structure Annotation of a Large Corpus. Natural Language Engineering, 11(2): 207-238.

Yarowsky, D. 1982. Word-Sense Disambiguation Using Statistical Models of Roget's Categories Trained on Large Corpora. In *Proceedings, COLING-92.* pp. 454-460, 1992.

Scaling up Analogical Learning

Philippe Langlais
Université de Montréal / Dept. I.R.O.
C.P. 6128, Québec, H3C3J7, Canada
felipe@iro.umontreal.ca

François Yvon
Univ. Paris Sud 11 & LIMSI-CNRS
F-91401 Orsay, France
yvon@limsi.fr

Abstract

Recent years have witnessed a growing interest in analogical learning for NLP applications. If the principle of analogical learning is quite simple, it does involve complex steps that seriously limit its applicability, the most computationally demanding one being the identification of analogies in the input space. In this study, we investigate different strategies for efficiently solving this problem and study their scalability.

1 Introduction

Analogical learning (Pirrelli and Yvon, 1999) belongs to the family of lazy learning techniques (Aha, 1997). It allows to map forms belonging to an *input* space $\mathcal{I}$ into forms of an *output* space $\mathcal{O}$, thanks to a set of known observations, $\mathcal{L} = \{(i, o) : i \in \mathcal{I}, o \in \mathcal{O}\}$. $I(u)$ and $O(u)$ respectively denote the projection of an observation u into the input space and output space: if $u \equiv (i, o)$, then $I(u) \equiv i$ and $O(u) \equiv o$. For an incomplete observation $u \equiv (i, ?)$, the inference of $O(u)$ involves the following steps:

1. building $\mathcal{E}_{\mathcal{I}}(u)$ the set of analogical triplets of $I(u)$, that is $\mathcal{E}_{\mathcal{I}}(u) = \{(s, v, w) \in \mathcal{L}^3 : [I(s) : I(v) = I(w) : I(u)]\}$
2. building the set of solutions to the target equations formed by projecting source triplets: $\mathcal{E}_{\mathcal{O}}(u) = \{t \in \mathcal{O} : [O(s) : O(v) = O(w) : t] , \forall (s, v, w) \in \mathcal{E}_{\mathcal{I}}(u)\}$
3. selecting candidates among $\mathcal{E}_{\mathcal{O}}(u)$.

©2008. Licensed under the *Creative Commons Attribution-Noncommercial-Share Alike 3.0 Unported* license (http://creativecommons.org/licenses/by-nc-sa/3.0/). Some rights reserved.

where $[x : y = z : t]$ denotes an *analogical proportion*, that is a relation between these four items, meaning that "x is to y as z is to t", in a sense to be specified. See (Lepage, 1998) or (Stroppa and Yvon, 2005) for possible interpretations.

Analogical learning has recently regained some interest in the NLP community. Lepage and Denoual (2005) proposed a machine translation system entirely based on the concept of *formal analogy*, that is, analogy on forms. Stroppa and Yvon (2005) applied analogical learning to several morphological tasks also involving analogies on words. Langlais and Patry (2007) applied it to the task of translating unknown words in several European languages, an idea investigated as well by Denoual (2007) for a Japanese to English translation task.

If the principle of analogical learning is quite simple, it does involve complex steps that seriously limit its applicability. As a matter of fact, we are only aware of studies where analogical learning is applied to restricted tasks, either because they arbitrarily concentrate on words (Stroppa and Yvon, 2005; Langlais and Patry, 2007; Denoual, 2007) or because they focus on limited data (Lepage and Denoual, 2005; Denoual, 2007).

In this study, we investigate different strategies for making step 1 of analogical learning tractable. We propose a data-structure and algorithms that allow to control the balance between speed and recall. For very high-dimensional input spaces (hundreds of thousand of elements), we propose a heuristic which reduces computation time with a limited impact on recall.

2 Identifying input analogical relations

2.1 Existing approaches

A brute-force approach for identifying the input triplets that define an analogy with the incomplete observation $u = (t, ?)$ consists in enumerating triplets in the input space and checking for an analogical relation with the unknown form t:

$$\mathcal{E}_{\mathcal{I}}(u) = \{ \langle x, y, z \rangle \ : \ \langle x, y, z \rangle \in \mathcal{I}^3, \ [x : y = z : t] \ \}$$

This amounts to check $o(|\mathcal{I}|^3)$ analogies, which is manageable for toy problems only.

Langlais and Patry (2007) deal with an input space in the order of tens of thousand forms (the typical size of a vocabulary) using following strategy for $\mathcal{E}_{\mathcal{I}}(u)$. It consists in solving analogical equations $[y : x = t : ?]$ for some pairs $\langle x, y \rangle$ belonging to the neighborhood[1] of $I(u)$, denoted $\mathcal{N}(t)$. Those solutions that belong to the input space are the z-forms retained.

$$\mathcal{E}_{\mathcal{I}}(u) = \{ \langle x, y, z \rangle \ : \ \langle x, y \rangle \in \mathcal{N}(t)^2, \ [y : x = t : z] \ \}$$

This strategy (hereafter named LP) directly follows from a symmetrical property of an analogy ($[x : y = z : t] \Leftrightarrow [y : x = t : z]$), and reduces the search procedure to the resolution of a number of analogical equations which is quadratic with the number of pairs $\langle x, y \rangle$ sampled.

2.2 Exhaustive tree-count search

The strategy we propose here exploits a property on character counts that an analogical relation must fulfill (Lepage, 1998):

$$[x : y = z : t] \Rightarrow |x|_c + |t|_c = |y|_c + |z|_c \quad \forall c \in \mathcal{A}$$

where $\mathcal{A}$ is the alphabet on which the forms are built, and $|x|_c$ stands for the number of occurrences of character c in x. In the sequel, we denote $\mathcal{C}(\langle x, t \rangle) = \{\langle y, z \rangle \in \mathcal{I}^2 \ : \ |x|_c + |t|_c = |y|_c + |z|_c \quad \forall c \in \mathcal{A}\}$ the set of pairs that satisfy the count property with respect to $\langle x, t \rangle$.

The strategy we propose consists in first selecting an x-form in the input space. This enforces a set of necessary constraints on the counts of characters that any two forms y and z must satisfy for $[x : y = z : t]$ to be true. By considering all forms x in turn,[2] we collect a set of candidate triplets for t. A verification of those that define with t a analogy must then be carried out. Formally, we built:

$$\mathcal{E}_{\mathcal{I}}(u) = \{ \langle x, y, z \rangle \ : \ x \in \mathcal{I}, \ \langle y, z \rangle \in \mathcal{C}(\langle x, t \rangle), \ [x : y = z : t] \ \}$$

[1] The authors proposed to sample x and y among the closest forms in terms of edit-distance to $I(u)$.

[2] Anagram forms do not have to be considered separately.

This strategy will only work if (i) the number of quadruplets to check is much smaller than the number of triplets we can form in the input space (which happens to be the case in practice), and if (ii) we can efficiently identify the pairs $\langle y, z \rangle$ that satisfy a set of constraints on character counts. To this end, we propose to organize the input space thanks to a data structure called a *tree-count* (see Section 3), which is easy to built and supports efficient runtime retrieval.

2.3 Sampled tree-count search

As shown in (Langlais and Yvon, 2008), using tree-count to constraint the search allows to *exhaustively* solve step 1 for reasonably large input spaces. Computing analogies in very large input space (hundreds of thousand forms) however remains computationally demanding, as the retrieval algorithm must be carried out $o(\mathcal{I})$ times. In this case, we propose to sample the x-forms:

$$\mathcal{E}_{\mathcal{I}}(u) = \{ \langle x, y, z \rangle \ : \ x \in \mathcal{N}(t), \ \langle y, z \rangle \in \mathcal{C}(\langle x, t \rangle), \ [x : y = t : z] \ \}$$

There is unfortunately no obvious way of selecting a good subset $\mathcal{N}(t)$ of input forms, as analogies does not necessarily entail the similarity of "diagonal" forms, as illustrated by the analogy [*une pomme verte* : *des pommes vertes* = *une voiture rouge* : *des voitures rouges*], which involves singular/plural commutations in French nominal groups. In this situation, randomly selecting a subset of the input space seems to be a reasonable strategy (hereafter RAND).

For some analogies however, the first and last forms share some sequences of characters. This is obvious in [*dream* : *dreamer* = *dreams* : *dreamers*], but can be more subtle, as in our first example [***This** guy **drinks** too much* : *This boat sinks* = *These guys drank too much* : ***These** boats **sank***] where the diagonal terms share some n-grams reminiscent of the number (***This***/***These***) and tense (***drink***/***drank***) commutations involved.

We thus propose a sampling strategy (hereafter EV) which selects x-forms that share with t some sequences of characters. To this end, input forms are represented in a vector space whose dimensions are frequent character n-grams, retaining the k-most frequent n-grams, where $n \in [\mathtt{min}; \mathtt{max}]$. A form is thus encoded as a binary vector of dimension k, in which ith coefficient indicates whether the form contains an occurrence of the ith n-gram.[3] At runtime, we select the N forms that are the closest to a given form t, according to a distance[4]. Figure 1 illustrates some forms selected by this process. For comparison purposes, we also tested a sampling strategy which consists in selecting the x-forms that are closest to the source form t, according to the usual edit-distance (hereafter ED).

establish a report – order to establish a – has tabled this report – is about the report – basis of the report – other problem is that – problem that arises – problem is that those

Figure 1: The 8 nearest neighbors of *to establish a report* in a vector space computed from an input space of over a million phrases.

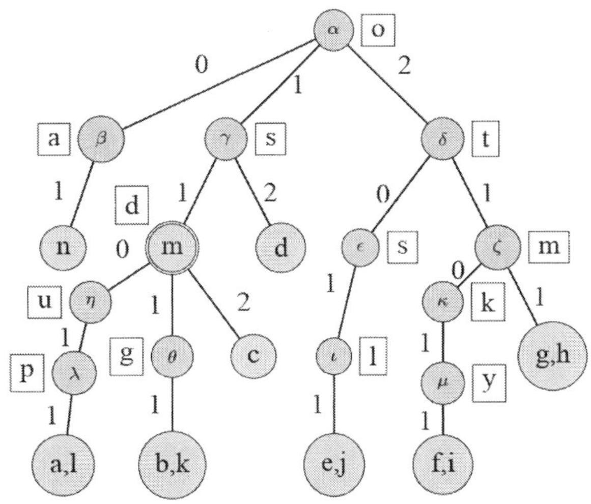

Figure 2: The tree-count encoding the set: {*soup*(a), *gods*(b), *odds*(c), *sos*(d), *solo*(e), *tokyo*(f), *moot*(g), *moto*(h), *kyoto*(i), *oslo*(j), *dogs*(k), *opus*(l), *os*(m), *a*(n)}. The character labeling a node is represented in a box; the counts of each character labels each vertice. Roman letters in nodes represent pointers to input forms; greek symbols label internal nodes.

3 The tree-count data-structure

A tree-count is a tree which encodes a set of forms. Nodes are labeled by an alphabetical symbol and contain a (possibly empty) set of pointers to forms. A vertice from a node n labeled c to a node m is weighted by the count of c in the forms encoded by m, that is, the set of forms that can be reached from this node and its descendants. Thus, a path in a tree-count represents a set of constraints on the counts of the characters encountered along this path. This structure allows for instance the identification of anagrams in a set of forms: it suffices to search the tree-count for nodes that contain more than one pointer to forms in the vocabulary.

An example of a tree-count is provided in Figure 2 for a small set of forms. The node double circled in this figure is labeled by the character d and encodes the 6 input forms that contain 1 occurrence of 'o' and 1 occurrence of 's'. One form is *os*, referenced by the pointer m, the other five forms are found by descending the tree from this node; among which *gods* and *dogs*, two anagrams encoded by the leave which set of pointers is b, k.

3.1 Construction time

The construction of a tree-count from a set of forms only needs an arbitrary order on the characters of the alphabet. This is the order in which we will encounter them while descending the tree. The lack of space prevents us to report the construction algorithm (see (Langlais and Yvon, 2008)), but it is important to note that it only involves a simple traversal of the input forms and is therefore time efficient. Also worth mentioning, our construction procedure only stores necessary nodes. This means that when enumerating characters in order, we only store zero-count nodes as required. As a result, the depth of a tree-count is typically much lower than the size of the alphabet.

[3]Typical values are min=max=3 and k=20 000.

[4]We used the Manhattan distance in this study.

3.2 Retrieval time

The retrieval of $C(\langle x, t\rangle)$ can be performed by traversing the tree-count while maintaining a *frontier*, that is, the set of pairs of nodes in the tree-count that satisfy the constraints on counts encountered so far. Imagine, for instance, that we are looking for the pairs of forms that contain exactly 3 occurrences of characters o, 2 of characters s and 1 character l, and no other character. Starting from the root node labelled by o, there is only one pair of nodes that satisfy the constraint on o: the frontier is therefore $\{(\gamma, \delta)\}$. The constraint on s leads to the frontier $\{(d, \iota)\}$ (since the count of t must be null). Finally, descending this node yields the frontier $\{(m, (e, j))\}$, which identifies the pairs (os, $solo$) and (os, $oslo$) to be the only ones satisfying the initial set of constraints.

The complexity of retrieval is mainly dominated by the size of the frontier built while traversing a tree-count. In practice, because of the sparsity of the space we manipulate in NLP applications, retrieval is also a fast operation.

4 Checking for an analogy

Stroppa (2005) provides a dynamic programming algorithm for checking that a quadruplet is an analogy, whose complexity is $o(|x| \times |y| \times |z| \times |t|)$.[5] Depending on the application, a large number of calls to this algorithm must be performed during step 1 of analogical learning. The following property helps cutting down the computations:

$$[x : y = z : t] \Rightarrow$$
$$(x[1] \in \{y[1], z[1]\}) \;\vee\; (t[1] \in \{y[1], z[1]\})$$
$$(x[\$] \in \{y[\$], z[\$]\}) \;\vee\; (t[\$] \in \{y[\$], z[\$]\})$$

where $\bullet[\$]$ denotes the last character of $\bullet$. A simple and efficient trick consists in calling the analogy checking routine only for those triplets that pass this test.

5 Discussion

We investigated the aforementioned search strategies by translating 1 000 new words (resp. phrases) thanks to a translation table populated with pairs of words (resp. pairs of phrases). We studied the scalability of each strategy by varying the size of the transfer table (small, medium, large). Precise figures can be found in (Langlais and Yvon, 2008); we summarize here the main outcomes.

On the *word*-task, we compared the tree-count search strategy to the LP one. On the largest wordset (84 000 input words), the former (exact) strategy could find an average of 34 597 input analogies for 964 test-words at an average response time of 1.2 seconds per word, while with the latter strategy, an average of 56 analogies could be identified for 890 test-words, in an average of 6.3 seconds.

On the *sequence*-task, where input spaces are much larger, we compared the various sampling strategies presented in Section 2.3. We set N, the number of sampled input forms, to 10^3 for all sampling strategies. On the medium size dataset (293 000 input phrases), both ED and RAND perform badly compared to EV. With the two former filtering strategies, we could at best identify 17 input analogies for 38% of the test-phrases (at an average response time of 9 seconds), while with EV, an average 46 analogies could be identified for 75% of the test-phrases (in 3 seconds on average).

Finally, we checked that the approach we proposed scales to very large datasets (several millions of input phrases), which to the best of our knowledge is simply out of the reach of existing approaches. This opens up interesting prospects for analogical learning, such as enriching a phrase-based table of the kind being used in statistical machine translation.

[5] In this study, we used the definition of a formal analogy provided by Stroppa and Yvon (2005). Lepage (1998) proposes a less general definition, which is faster to check.

Acknowledgment

This study has been accomplished while the first author was visiting Télécom ParisTech.

References

Aha, David A. 1997. Editorial. *Artificial Intelligence Review*, 11(1-5):7–10. Special Issue on Lazy Learning.

Denoual, Etienne. 2007. Analogical translation of unknown words in a statistical machine translation framework. In *Machine Translation Summit, XI*, Copenhagen, Sept. 10-14.

Langlais, Philippe and Alexandre Patry. 2007. Translating unknown words by analogical learning. In *EMNLP-CoNLL*, pages 877–886, Prague, Czech Republic, June.

Langlais, Philippe and François Yvon. 2008. Scaling up analogies. Technical report, Télécom ParisTech, France.

Lepage, Yves and Étienne Denoual. 2005. Purest ever example-based machine translation: Detailed presentation and assessment. *Machine Translation*, 29:251–282.

Lepage, Yves. 1998. Solving analogies on words: an algorithm. In *COLING-ACL*, pages 728–734, Montreal, Canada.

Pirrelli, Vitto and François Yvon. 1999. The hidden dimension: a paradigmatic view of data-driven NLP. *Journal of Experimental & Theroretical Artifical Intelligence*, 11:391–408.

Stroppa, Nicolas and François Yvon. 2005. An analogical learner for morphological analysis. In *9th Conf. on Computational Natural Language Learning (CoNLL)*, pages 120–127, Ann Arbor, MI, June.

Stroppa, Nicolas. 2005. *Définitions et caractérisations de modèles à base d'analogies pour l'apprentissage automatique des langues naturelles*. Ph.D. thesis, ENST, Paris, France, Nov.

Multilingual alignments by monolingual string differences

Adrien Lardilleux and **Yves Lepage**
GREYC, University of Caen Basse-Normandie,
BP 5186, Caen Cedex, France
Firstname.Lastname@info.unicaen.fr

Abstract

We propose a method to obtain subsentential alignments from several languages simultaneously. The method handles several languages at once, and avoids the complexity explosion due to the usual pair-by-pair processing. It can be used for different units (characters, morphemes, words, chunks). An evaluation of word alignments with a trilingual machine translation corpus has been conducted. A comparison of the results with those obtained by state of the art alignment software is reported.

1 Introduction

Several tools are available nowadays for alignment of pairs of languages. Among them, the bilingual word aligner GIZA++ (Och and Ney, 2003) can perform high quality alignments based on words statistics and is considered the most efficient tool. Three main criticisms may be addressed to this kind of tool.

Firstly, as denoted by Moore (2005), one needs to tune numerous parameters in order to optimize the results for a particular alignment task, which can be very time consuming. This is all the more important when multilingual alignment is concerned, since every language pair will require its own set of parameter values.

Secondly, the best methods available nowadays can only work on language pairs, which results in a complexity explosion when multilingual alignments are needed. Simard (1999) showed how to adapt a bilingual method to align more than two versions of a text at the sentence level, but languages have to be processed by pairs to identify which ones are the most similar.

Thirdly, these approaches are also designed to align specific units of texts (almost always words). The same method cannot be applied indifferently on different units. Languages which do not separate words by spaces require to be first segmented into words, while a character-based approach could be a worthy alternative.

To deal with all these issues, we propose a method which is primarily intended to align many languages simultaneously from sentence-aligned parallel corpora, whatever the segmentation unit.

2 Alignment by string differences

2.1 String differences

In order to introduce the operation we use, let us start with a well-known similar technique, the Longest Common Subsequence (LCS) (Hirschberg, 1975). Given two strings A and B, it is always possible to find their longest subsequence. Such a subsequence is a sequence of non necessarily contiguous characters.

For instance, assume we have the following short English sentences (space characters are marked by an underscore and have the same status as any other character):

$$A = \text{I\_would\_like\_a\_donut,\_please.}$$
$$B = \text{Regular\_size,\_please.}$$

In this case, the LCS for A and B would be:[1]

$$\text{LCS}(A, B) = \text{ul\_ie,\_please.}$$

which is 14 characters long. It is then possible to form their string difference:

[1]For purpose of simplicity, we do not mention that the LCS operation, as well as the difference operation, may deliver a plurality of strings.

© 2008. Licensed under the *Creative Commons Attribution-Noncommercial-Share Alike 3.0 Unported* license (http://creativecommons.org/licenses/by-nc-sa/3.0/). Some rights reserved.

$$A \ominus B = \text{I␣wodlk␣a␣donut}$$
$$B \ominus A = \text{Regarsz}$$

where we define $A \ominus B = A - LCS(A, B)$.

Because several isolated characters are discarded, this results in a malformed string that is of limited interest. To avoid misinformed strings, we rather resort to Longest Common Substrings (LCSubstr), that are contiguous.

On the previous example, the LCSubstr is:

$$\text{LCSubstr}(A, B) = \text{,␣please.}$$

which is 9 characters long and by far more meaningful. By removing this substring from A and B, we obtain:[2]

$$A \ominus B = \text{I␣would␣like␣a␣donut}$$
$$B \ominus A = \text{Regular␣size}$$

2.2 A monolingual operation for multilingual alignment

String differences are monolingual. They serve as a starting point to compute alignments. It suffices to apply them in parallel on the source text and all aligned target texts.

Let us consider anew the previous English sentences and their translations into Japanese ($\widehat{A}$ stands for "A's translation"):

$$\widehat{A} = \text{ドーナツを下さい。}$$
/dônatu wo kudasai./

$$\widehat{B} = \text{普通サイズを下さい。}$$
/hutuu saizu wo kudasai./

$$\text{LCSubstr}(\widehat{A}, \widehat{B}) = \text{を下さい。}$$
$$\widehat{A} \ominus \widehat{B} = \text{ドーナツ}$$
$$\widehat{B} \ominus \widehat{A} = \text{普通サイズ}$$

By performing simultaneously the difference between A and B and between $\widehat{A}$ and $\widehat{B}$, their aligned translations, we obtain:

$$\text{,␣please.} \leftrightarrow \text{を下さい。}$$
$$\text{I␣would␣like␣a␣donut} \leftrightarrow \text{ドーナツ}$$
$$\text{Regular␣size} \leftrightarrow \text{普通サイズ}$$

The method assumes that the three strings computed in the source language are translations of their corresponding strings in the target language That is:

$$\widehat{\text{LCSubstr}(A, B)} = \text{LCSubstr}(\widehat{A}, \widehat{B})$$
$$\widehat{A \ominus B} = \widehat{A} \ominus \widehat{B}$$
$$\widehat{B \ominus A} = \widehat{B} \ominus \widehat{A}$$

[2] Idem. Experiments show that they are not as numerous as for LCS. For the sake of simplicity, we shall assume that LCSubstr's are unique.

2.3 Iterative application

Assume we want to extract the translation equivalent of "Chicago" in Japanese from the following pairs of sentences:

$$A_0 = \text{Is␣this␣a␣train␣for␣Chicago?}$$
$$\widehat{A_0} = \text{この列車はシカゴ行きですか。}$$
/kono ressya ha sikago yuki desu ka./

$$B = \text{Is␣this␣price␣correct?}$$
$$\widehat{B} = \text{この値段で正しいですか。}$$
/kono nedan de tadasii desu ka./

$$C = \text{What␣track␣does␣the␣train␣for␣Boston␣start␣from?}$$
$$\widehat{C} = \text{ボストン行きの列車は何番から出ますか。}$$
/bosuton yuki no ressya ha nani ban kara syutu masu ka./

A direct application of the method described above does not ensure that "Chicago" will correspond to a string difference. A way to solve the problem is to apply the method iteratively. String differences are applied on the sentence where "Chicago" appears (*i.e.*, A), in order to gradually cut it down to "Chicago" only. By applying the same process in parallel on all target sentences, strings are expected to reduce to the translation of "Chicago" as well. Also, we add the constraint that the string to be aligned must not be altered during the iterative process, *i.e.*, it should not be included in any LCSubstr.

Thus, starting with A_0 containing "Chicago", we perform at each step:

$$A_{n+1} = A_n \ominus S_n$$
$$\widehat{A_{n+1}} = \widehat{A_n} \ominus \widehat{S_n}$$

where S_n is the first sentence S in the list of all source sentences sorted by the length of $\text{LCSubstr}(A_n, S)$. In other words, amongst the available English sentences S, select the one that shares the longest substring with A_n, and remove this substring from A_n. The corresponding differences are applied in the target languages simultaneously.

Table 1 gives the details of an execution of the iterative process. On a large amount of data, the method may yield a plurality results; each of them may be obtained a certain number of times. We shall judge the quality of alignments based on these frequencies.

2.4 Best alignments selection

In practice, it is not possible to perform all the differences between sentences that would lead to the alignment of a particular string. This complexity explosion, where most of the LCSubstr's would be very short, would result in non reliable alignments.

n	A_n	S_n	LCSubstr(A_n, S_n)	$\widehat{A}_n$	LCSubstr($\widehat{A}_n, \widehat{S}_n$)
0	Is␣this␣a␣train␣for␣**Chicago**?	C	␣train␣for␣	この列車はシカゴ行きですか。	の列車は
1	Is␣this␣a**Chicago**?	B	Is␣this␣	こシカゴ行きですか。	ですか。
2	a**Chicago**?	B	?	こシカゴ行き	こ
3	a**Chicago**	C	a	シカゴ行き	行き
4	**Chicago**			シカゴ	

Table 1: Details of the steps necessary to extract one alignment for "Chicago" in Japanese. "Chicago" may not be modified during the iterative process and is not used to compute the LCSubstr's. The resulting alignment is $\widehat{A}_4$ = シカゴ */sikago/*, which is correct.

We cut down the complexity by examining only the c first longest LCSubstr's longer than a predefined threshold. The threshold was set to half of the longest LCSubstr. Different values of c were tested for in the experiments reported in Section 3.3. This parameter is used in the source language only.

Well-formedness of strings is also tested by checking the presence of all their n-sequences of characters in the initial data. This is performed in the target languages.

Eventually, each alignment is scored by its frequency divided by the number of sentences that were required to obtain it. The reason for doing so is that, in practice, the less sentences required, the longer and the safer the LCSubstr's used.

3 Evaluation

3.1 Data used

We used the English, Japanese and Arabic training parts of the IWSLT 2007 machine translation campaign corpus (Fordyce, 2007) to conduct our experiments. It is made of nearly 20,000 triples of aligned sentences from the BTEC corpus (Takezawa et al., 2002).

3.2 Result samples

As mentioned earlier, one advantage of our method is that it can align any string of text, providing the data is sufficient. Table 2 shows a sample of alignments obtained using English as the source language. The strings requested to be aligned can be anything, from one character (see the first lines of the table) to entire sentences (see last line). Most alignments, if not perfect, differ from the expected meaning by slight differences only, even in Arabic.

3.3 Comparison against GIZA++

We compared our system to the state of the art device, GIZA++, in the particular case of bilingual word alignments on two pairs of languages: English to Arabic and English to Japanese. Our system aligned the three languages simultaneously, using English words as input. For each target language, the target unit with the best score (see Section 2.4) was kept. Different values of c were tested.

GIZA++ was used to compute IBM model 4. The default set of parameter values, which typically produces good results, was used. For each source word, the most probable pair of words (source, target) was kept. Note that the output of IBM model 4 produces word to word alignments, while there is no guaranty that our system would output a single target word as the unit of processing is the character.

For an objective assessment, we resort to two bilingual dictionaries: English-Japanese, and English-Arabic.[3] As for English-Japanese, the best results were obtained for $c = 40$, and are as good as those of GIZA++ (628 alignments found in the reference dictionary vs. 629, see Table 3). As for English-Arabic, the best results were obtained for $c = 20$, but only 37% of GIZA++'s results could be achieved (63 alignments found in the reference dictionary vs. 170).

Those alignments output by the two systems that do not belong to the reference dictionaries are not necessarily erroneous, since we relied on exact matching. Specifically, for our method, one extra character only may be responsible for an alignment to be considered wrong.

[3] We used an English-Arabic dictionary from sdict (87,000 entries): `http://sdict.com` and the EDICT English-Japanese dictionary (115,000 entries): `http://www.csse.monash.edu.au/~jwb/j_edict.html`. The Arabic part of the English-Arabic dictionary being lemmatized, we had to preprocess the Arabic part of our corpus so that it be lemmatized too (Debili and Achour, 1998).

English	Arabic			Japanese		
.	.	/./	'.'	。	/./	'.'
?	؟	/?/	'?'	か。	/ka ./	'?'
Wh	أين	/ʾayn/	'where'	何	/nani/, /nan/	'what', 'wh…'
here	هنا	/hnā/	'here'	ここ	/koko/	'here'
I 'd like	أريد	/ʾaryd/	'I'd like'	下さい	/kudasai/	'please'
Thank you	شكرا	/škrā/	'thank you'	ありがとう	/arigatou/	'thank you'
Ice	آيس كريم	/ʾāys krym/	'ice cream'	氷を	/koori wo/	'ice'
I have to get	عليصلقبل ال ساعة /ʿlyṣlqbl āl sāʿh/ * *malformed string* *			入手しなければなりません /nyuusyu si nakerebanarimasen/ 'I have to get'		
At seven o'clock	في ال ساعة ال سابعة /fy āl sāʿh āl sābʿh/ 'at seven o'clock'			七時に /sitizi ni/ 'at seven o'clock'		

Table 2: A sample of alignments obtained using English as the source language. The Arabic and Japanese strings were generated in parallel by aligning the three languages at once. Parameter c was set to 20 in this experiment.

	GIZA++	Our system					
		$c = 1$	$c = 10$	$c = 20$	$c = 30$	$c = 40$	$c = 50$
English-Japanese	**629** / 4,268	369 / 1,569	573 / 2,629	603 / 3,038	598 / 3,165	**628** / 3,219	615 / 3,248
English-Arabic	**170** / 1,569	36 / 540	57 / 863	**63** / 982	57 / 1,017	51 / 1,025	51 / 1,029

Table 3: Comparison of our system against GIZA++. Each cell gives the number of alignments found in the reference dictionary over the number of alignments obtained.

4 Conclusion

We introduced a simple method to obtain subsentential alignments from several languages simultaneously. Its focus is on contexts rather than on units to be aligned. It avoids the complexity explosion due to the usual pair-by-pair processing by relying on the simultaneous application of a monolingual operation. The method comes close to GIZA++'s results in some word alignment task, while being by far much simpler.

References

Debili, Fathi and Hadhemi Achour. 1998. Voyellation automatique de l'arabe. In *Proceedings of the Workshop on Computational Approaches to Semitic Languages (COLING-ACL'98)*, pages 42–49, Montreal, Quebec, Canada, August.

Fordyce, Cameron Shaw. 2007. Overview of the IWSLT 2007 evaluation campaign. In *Proceedings of the 4th International Workshop on Spoken Language Translation (IWSLT 2007)*, pages 1–12, Trento, Italy, October.

Hirschberg, Dan. 1975. A linear space algorithm for computing maximal common subsequences. *Communications of the ACM*, 18:341–353, June.

Moore, Robert. 2005. A discriminative framework for bilingual word alignment. In *Proceedings of Human Language Technology Conference and Conference on Empirical Methods in Natural Language Processing*, pages 81–88, Vancouver, British Columbia, October.

Och, Franz Josef and Hermann Ney. 2003. A systematic comparison of various statistical alignment models. *Computational Linguistics*, 29:19–51, March.

Simard, Michel. 1999. Text-translation alignment: Three languages are better than two. In *Proceedings of the Joint SIGDAT Conference of Empirical Methods in Natural Language Processing and Very Large Corpora (EMNLP/VLC)*, College Park, Maryland, USA.

Takezawa, Toshiyuki, Eiichiro Sumita, Fumiaki Sugaya, Hirofumi Yamamoto, and Seiichi Yamamoto. 2002. Toward a broad-coverage bilingual corpus for speech translation of travel conversation in the real world. In *Proceedings of the third International Conference on Language Resources and Evaluation (LREC 2002)*, pages 147–152, Las Palmas de Gran Canaria, Spain.

Bayes Risk-based Dialogue Management for Document Retrieval System with Speech Interface

Teruhisa Misu [†] [‡]

Tatsuya Kawahara[†]

[†]School of Informatics,
Kyoto University
Sakyo-ku, Kyoto, Japan

[‡]National Institute of Information
and Communications Technology
Hikari-dai, Seika-cho, Soraku-gun,
Kyoto, Japan

Abstract

We propose an efficient dialogue management for an information navigation system based on a document knowledge base with a spoken dialogue interface. In order to perform robustly for fragmental speech input and erroneous output of an automatic speech recognition (ASR), the system should selectively use N-best hypotheses of ASR and contextual information. The system also has several choices in generating responses or confirmations. In this work, we formulate the optimization of the choices based on a unified criterion: Bayes risk, which is defined based on reward for correct information presentation and penalty for redundant turns. We have evaluated this strategy with a spoken dialogue system which also has question-answering capability. Effectiveness of the proposed framework was confirmed in the success rate of retrieval and the average number of turns.

1 Introduction

In the past years, a great number of spoken dialogue systems have been developed. Their typical task domains include airline information (ATIS & DARPA Communicator) and bus location tasks. Although the above systems can handle simple database retrieval or transactions with constrained dialogue flows, they are expected to handle more complex tasks. Meanwhile, more and more electronic text resources are recently being accumulated. Since most documents are indexed (e.g., via Web search engines), we are potentially capable of accessing these documents. Reflecting such a situation, in recent years, the target of spoken dialogue systems has been extended to retrieval of general documents (Chang et al., 2002).

There are quite a few choices for handling user utterances and generating responses in the spoken dialogue systems that require parameter tuning. Since a subtle change in these choices may affect the behavior the entire system, they are usually tuned by hand by an expert. It is also the case in speech-baed document retrieval systems. We can make use of N-best hypotheses to realize robust retrieval against errors in automatic speech recognition (ASR). Input queries are often vague or fragmented in speech interfaces, thus concatenation of contextual information is important to make meaningful retrieval. Such decisions tend to be optimized module by module, but they should be done in an integrated way. For example, we could make more appropriate retrieval by rescoring the N-best ASR hypotheses by the information retrieval scores. Even if the target document is identified, the system has several choices for generating responses. Confirmation is needed to eliminate any misunderstandings caused by ASR errors, but users easily become irritated with so many redundant confirmations. Although there are several works dealing with dialogue management in call routing systems (Levin and Pieraccini, 2006), they cannot handle the complex decision making processes in information guidance tasks.

Therefore, we address the extension of conventional optimization methods of dialogue management to be applicable to general document retrieval

© 2008. Teruhisa Misu and Tatsuya Kawahara, Licensed under the *Creative Commons Attribution-Noncommercial-Share Alike 3.0 Unported* license (http://creativecommons.org/licenses/by-nc-sa/3.0/). Some rights reserved.

tasks. In particular, we propose a dialogue management that optimizes the choices in response generation by minimizing Bayes risk. The Bayes risk is defined based on reward for correct information presentation and penalty for redundant turns as well as the score of document retrieval and answer extraction.

2 Task and Knowledge Base (KB)

As the target domain, we adopt a sightseeing guide for Kyoto city. The KBs of this system are Wikipedia documents concerning Kyoto and the official tourist information of Kyoto city (810 documents, 220K words in total).

"Dialogue Navigator for Kyoto City" is a document retrieval system with a spoken dialogue interface. The system can retrieve information from the above-mentioned document set. This system is also capable of handling user's specific question, such as "Who built this shrine?" using the QA technique.

3 Dialogue Management and Response Generation in Document Retrieval System

3.1 Choices in Generating Responses

We analyzed the dialogue sessions collected in the field trial of the "Dialogue Navigator for Kyoto City", and found that we could achieve a higher success rate by dealing with following issues.

1. **Use of N-best hypotheses of ASR**
   There have been many studies that have used the N-best hypotheses (or word graph) of ASR for making robust interpretations of user utterances in relational database query tasks (Raymond et al., 2003). We also improved retrieval by using all of the nouns in the 3-best hypotheses(Misu and Kawahara, 2007). However, the analysis also showed that some retrieval failures were caused by some extraneous nouns included in erroneous hypotheses, and a higher success rate could be achieved by selecting an optimal hypothesis.

2. **Incorporation of contextual information**
   In interactive query systems, users tend to make queries that include anaphoric expressions. In these cases, it is impossible to extract the correct answer using only the current query. For example, "When was it built?" makes no sense when used by itself. We deal with this problem by concatenating the contextual information or keywords from the user's previous utterances to generate a query. However, this may include inappropriate context when the user changes the topic.

3. **Choices in generating responses or confirmations**
   An indispensable part of the process to avoid presenting inappropriate documents is confirmation, especially when the score of retrieval is low. This decision is also affected by points 1 and 2 mentioned above. The presentation of the entire document may also be "safer" than presenting the specific answer to the user's question, when the score of answer extraction is low.

3.2 Generation of Response Candidates

The manners of response for a document d consist of the following three actions. One is the presentation ($Pres(d)$) of the document d, which is made by summarizing it. Second is making a confirmation ($Conf(d)$) for presenting the document d. The last is answering ($Ans(d)$) the user's specific question, which is generated by extracting one specific sentence from the document d.

For these response candidates, we define the Bayes risk based on the reward for success, the penalty for a failure, and the probability of success. Then, we select the candidate with the minimal Bayes risk. The system flow of these processes is summarized below.

1. Make search queries $W_i (i = 1, \ldots, 8)$ using the 1st, 2nd, and 3rd hypothesis of ASR, and all of them, with/without contextual information.
2. For each query W_i, retrieve from the KB and obtain a candidate document d_i and its likelihood $p(d_i)$.
3. For each document d_i, generate presentation $Pres(d_i)$, confirmation $Conf(d_i)$, and answering $Ans(d_i)$ response candidates.
4. Calculate the Bayes risk for 25 response candidates, which are the combination of 4 (N-best hypotheses) $\times$ 2 (use of contextual information) $\times$ 3 (choice in response generation) + 1 (rejection).
5. Select the optimal response candidate that has the minimal Bayes risk.

3.3 Definition of Bayes Risk for Candidate Response

For these response candidates, we define the Bayes risk based on the reward for success, the penalty for a failure, and the probability of success (approximated by the confidence measure). That is, a reward is given according to the manner of response (Rwd_{Ret} or Rwd_{QA}) when the system presents an appropriate response. On the other hand, a penalty is given based on extraneous time, which is approximated by the number of sentences before obtaining the appropriate information when the system presents an incorrect response. For example, the penalty for a confirmation is 2 {system's confirmation + user's approval}, and that of a rejection is 1 {system's rejection}. When the system presents incorrect information, the penalty for a failure $FailureRisk$ (FR) is calculated, which consists of the improper presentation, the user's correction, and the system's request for a rephrasal. Additional sentences for the completion of a task ($AddSent$) are also given as extraneous time before accessing the appropriate document when the user rephrases the query/question. The value of $AddSent$ is calculated as an expected number of risks assuming the probability of success by rephrasal was p[1].

The Bayes risk for the response candidates is formulated as follows using the likelihood of retrieval $p(d)$, likelihood of answer extraction $p_{QA}(d)$, and the reward pair (Rwd_{Ret} and Rwd_{QA}; $Rwd_{Ret} < Rwd_{QA}$) for successful presentations as well as the FR for inappropriate presentations.

- **Presentation of document** d (without confirmation)

$$Risk(Pres(d)) = -Rwd_{Ret} * p(d) + (FR + AddSent) * (1 - p(d))$$

- **Confirmation for presenting document** d

$$Risk(Conf(d)) = (-Rwd_{Ret} + 2) * p(d) + (2 + AddSent) * (1 - p(d))$$

- **Answering user's question using document** d

$$Risk(Ans(d)) = -Rwd_{QA} * p_{QA}(d) * p(d) + (FR + AddSent) * (1 - p_{QA}(d) * p(d))$$

- **Rejection**

$$Risk(Rej) = 1 + AddSent$$

[1]In the experiment, we use the success rate of the field trial presented in (Misu and Kawahara, 2007).

User utterance: When did the shogun order to build the temple?
(Previous query:) Tell me about the Silver Pavilion.
Response candidates:
* With context:
→ p(Silver Pavilion history) = 0.4
→ p_{QA}(Silver Pavilion history) = 0.2 : In 1485
- $Risk(Pres$(Silver Pavilion history)) = 6.4
- **Risk(Conf(Silver Pavilion history))= 4.8**
- $Risk(Ans$(Silver Pavilion history; In1485)) = 9.7
...
* Rejection
- $Risk(Rej)$ = 9.0
↓
Response: Conf (Silver Pavilion history)
"Do you want to know the history of the Silver Pavilion?"

Figure 1: Example of calculating Bayes risk

Figure 1 shows an example of calculating a Bayes risk (where $FR = 6$, $Rwd_{Ret} = 5$, $Rwd_{QA} = 40$). In this example, an appropriate document is retrieved by incorporating the previous user query. However, since the answer to the user's question does not exist in the knowledge base, the score of answer extraction is low. Therefore, the system chooses a confirmation before presenting the entire document.

4 Experimental Evaluation by Cross Validation

We have evaluated the proposed method using the user utterances collected in the "Dialogue Navigator for Kyoto City" field trial. We transcribed in-domain 1,416 utterances (1,084 queries and 332 questions) and labeled their correct documents/NEs by hand.

The evaluation measures we used were the success rate and the average number of sentences for information access. We regard a retrieval as successful if the system presents (or confirms) the appropriate document/NE for the query. The number of sentences for information access is used as an approximation of extraneous time before accessing the document/NE. That is, it is 1 {user utterance} if the system presents the requested document without a confirmation. If the system makes a confirmation before presentation, it is 3 {user utterance + system's confirmation + user's approval}, and that for presenting an incorrect document is 15 {user utterance + improper presentation (3 = # presented sentences) + user's correction + system's apology + request for rephrasing + additional sentences for task completion} ($FR = 6$ & $AddSent = 8$), which are determined based on the typical recovery pattern observed in the field trial.

We determined the value of the parameters by a 2-fold cross validation by splitting the test set into two (set-1 & set-2), that is, set-1 was used as a development set to estimate FR and Rwd for evaluating set-2, and vice versa. The parameters were tuned to minimize the total number of sentences for information access in the development set. We compared the proposed method with the following conventional methods. Note that method 1 is the baseline method and method 2 was adopted in the original "Dialogue Navigator for Kyoto City" and used in the field trial.

Method 1 (baseline)

- Make a search query using the 1st hypothesis of ASR.
- Incorporate the contextual information related to the current topic.
- Make a confirmation when the ASR confidence of the pre-defined topic word is low.
- Answer the question when the user query is judged a question.

Method 2 (original system)

- Make a search query using all nouns in the 1st-3rd hypotheses of ASR.
- The other conditions are the same as in method 1.

The comparisons to these conventional methods are shown in Table 1. The improvement compared with that in baseline method 1 is 6.4% in the response success rate and 0.78 of a sentence in the number of sentences for information access.

A breakdown of the selected response candidates by the proposed method is shown in Table 2. Many of the responses were generated using a single hypothesis from the N-best list of ASR. The result confirms that the correct hypothesis may not be the first one, and the proposed method selects the appropriate one by considering the likelihood of retrieval. Most of the confirmations were generated using the 1st hypothesis of ASR. The Answers to questions were often generated from the search queries with contextual information. This result suggests that when users used anaphoric expressions, the appropriate contextual information was incorporated into the question.

Table 1: Comparison with conventional methods

	Success rate	# sentences for presentation
Method 1 (baseline)	59.2%	5.49
Method 2	63.4%	4.98
Proposed method	65.6%	4.71

Table 2: Breakdown of selected candidates

	w/o context			with context		
	Pres	Conf	Ans	Pres	Conf	Ans
1st hyp.	233	134	65	2	151	2
2nd hyp.	140	43	28	2	2	6
3rd hyp.	209	50	46	1	6	5
merge all	75	11	3	18	0	91
rejection	111					

5 Conclusion

We have proposed a dialogue framework to generate an optimal response. Specifically, the choices in response generation are optimized as a minimization of the Bayes risk based on the reward for a correct information presentation and a penalty for redundant time. Experimental evaluations using real user utterances were used to demonstrate that the proposed method achieved a higher success rate for information access with a reduced number of sentences. Although we implemented only a simple confirmation using the likelihood of retrieval, the proposed method is expected to handle more complex dialogue management such as the confirmation considering the impact for the retrieval (Misu and Kawahara, 2006).

References

Chang, E., F. Seide, H. Meng, Z. Chen, Y. Shi, and Y. Li. 2002. A System for Spoken Query Information Retrieval on Mobile Devices. *IEEE Trans. on Speech and Audio Processing*, 10(8):531–541.

Levin, E. and R. Pieraccini. 2006. Value-based Optimal Decision for Dialog Systems. In *Proc. Spoken Laguage Technology Workshop (SLT)*, pages 198–201.

Misu, T. and T. Kawahara. 2006. Dialogue strategy to clarify user's queries for document retrieval system with speech interface. *Speech Communication*, 48(9):1137–1150.

Misu, T. and T. Kawahara. 2007. Speech-based interactive information guidance system using question-answering technique. In *Proc. ICASSP*.

Raymond, C., Y. Esteve, F. Bechet, R. De Mori, and G. Damnati. 2003. Belief Confirmation in Spoken Dialog Systems using Confidence Measures. In *Proc. Automatic Speech Recognition and Understanding Workshop (ASRU)*.

Exact Inference for Multi-label Classification using Sparse Graphical Models

Yusuke Miyao[†] **Jun'ichi Tsujii**[†‡*]
[†]Department of Computer Science, University of Tokyo, Japan
[‡]School of Computer Science, University of Manchester, UK
[*]National Center for Text Mining, UK
{yusuke,tsujii}@is.s.u-tokyo.ac.jp

Abstract

This paper describes a parameter estimation method for multi-label classification that does not rely on approximate inference. It is known that multi-label classification involving label correlation features is intractable, because the graphical model for this problem is a complete graph. Our solution is to exploit the sparsity of features, and express a model structure for each object by using a sparse graph. We can thereby apply the junction tree algorithm, allowing for efficient exact inference on sparse graphs. Experiments on three data sets for text categorization demonstrated that our method increases the accuracy for text categorization with a reasonable cost.

1 Introduction

This paper describes an exact inference method for multi-label classification (Schapire and Singer, 2000; Ghamrawi and McCallum, 2005), into which label correlation features are incorporated. In general, directly solving this problem is computationally intractable, because the graphical model for this problem is a complete graph. Nevertheless, an important characteristic of this problem, in particular for text categorization, is that only a limited number of features are *active*; i.e., non-zero, for a given object x. This sparsity of features is a desirable characteristic, because we can remove the edges of the graphical model when no corresponding features are active. We can therefore expect that a graphical model for each object is a sparse graph. When a graph is sparse, we can apply the junction tree algorithm (Cowell et al., 1999), allowing for efficient exact inference on sparse graphs.

© 2008. Licensed under the *Creative Commons Attribution-Noncommercial-Share Alike 3.0 Unported* license (http://creativecommons.org/licenses/by-nc-sa/3.0/). Some rights reserved.

Our method is evaluated on three data sets for text categorization; one is from clinical texts, and the others are from newswire articles. We observe the trade-off between accuracy and training cost, while changing the number of label correlation features to be included.

2 Multi-label Classification

Given a set of labels, $L = \{l_1, \ldots, l_{|L|}\}$, multi-label classification is the task of assigning a subset $y \subseteq L$ to a document x. In the framework of statistical machine learning, this problem can be formulated as a problem of maximizing a scoring function η:

$$\hat{y} = \operatorname*{argmax}_y \eta(x, y) = \operatorname*{argmax}_y \eta(\mathbf{f}(x, y)). \quad (1)$$

As is usually the case in statistical machine learning, we represent a probabilistic event, $\langle x, y\rangle$, with a feature vector, $\mathbf{f}(x,y) = \langle f_1(x,y), \ldots, f_{|\mathbf{f}|}(x,y)\rangle$. In text categorization, most effective features represent a frequency of a word w in a document; i.e.,

$$f_{l,w}(x,y) = \begin{cases} c_x(w) & \text{if } l \in y, \\ 0 & \text{otherwise,} \end{cases}$$

where $c_x(w)$ is a frequency of w in x.

The most popular method for multi-label classification is to create $|L|$ binary classifiers, each of which determines whether or not to assign a single label (Yang and Pedersen, 1997). However, since the decision for each label is independent of the decision for other labels, this method cannot be sensitive to *label correlations*, or the tendency of label cooccurrences.

A recent research effort has been devoted to the modeling of label correlations. While a number of approaches have been proposed for dealing with label correlations (see Tsoumakas and

Katakis (2007) for the comprehensive survey), the intuitively-appealing method is to incorporate features on two labels into the model (Ghamrawi and McCallum, 2005). The following *label correlation feature* indicates a cooccurrence of two labels and a word:

$$f_{l,l',w}(x,y) = \begin{cases} c_x(w) & \text{if } l, l' \in y, \\ 0 & \text{otherwise.} \end{cases}$$

3 A Method for Exact Inference

A critical difficulty encountered in the model with label correlation features is the computational cost for training and decoding. When features on every pair of labels are included in the model, its graphical model becomes a complete graph, which indicates that the exact inference for this model is NP-hard. However, not all edges are necessary in actual inference, because of the sparsity of features. That is, we can remove edges between l and l' when no corresponding features are active; i.e., $f_{l,l',w}(x,y) = 0$ for all w. In text categorization, when feature selection is performed, many edges can be removed because of this characteristic.

Therefore, our idea is to enjoy this sparsity of features. We construct a graphical model for each document, and put edges only when one or more features are active on the corresponding label pair. When a graph is sparse, we can apply a method for exact inference, such as the junction tree algorithm (Cowell et al., 1999). The junction tree algorithm is a generic algorithm for exact inference on any graphical model, and it allows for efficient inference on sparse graphs. The method converts a graph into a *junction tree*, which is a tree of cliques in the original graph. When we have a junction tree for each document, we can efficiently perform belief propagation in order to compute argmax in Equation (1), or the marginal probabilities of cliques and labels, necessary for the parameter estimation of machine learning classifiers, including perceptrons (Collins, 2002), and maximum entropy models (Berger et al., 1996). The computational complexity of the inference on junction trees is proportional to the exponential of *the tree width*, which is the maximum number of labels in a clique, minus one.

An essential idea of this method is that a graphical model is constructed for each document. Even when features are defined on all pairs of labels, active features for a specific document are limited. When combined with feature selection, this method greatly increases the sparsity of the resulting graphs, which is key to efficiency.

	# train	# test	# labels	card.
cmc2007	978	976	45	1.23
reuters10	6,490	2,545	10	1.10
reuters90	7,770	3,019	90	1.24

Table 1: Statistics of evaluation data sets

	κ	ν	c
cmc2007	1,000	10	0
reuters10	5,000	20	5
reuters90	5,000	80	5

Table 2: Parameters for evaluation data sets

A weakness of this method comes from the assumption of feature sparseness. We are forced to apply feature selection, which is considered effective in text categorization, but not necessarily for other tasks. The design of features is also restricted in order to ensure the sparsity of features.

4 Experiments

4.1 Experimental Settings

We evaluate our method for multi-label classification using three data sets for text categorization. Table 1 shows the statistics of these data. In this table, "card." denotes the average number of labels assigned to a document.

cmc2007 is a data set used in the Computational Medicine Center (CMC) Challenge 2007 (Pestian et al., 2007)[1]. This challenge aimed at the assignment of ICD-9-CM codes, such as *cough* and *pneumonia*, to clinical free texts. It should be noted that this data is controlled, so that both training and test sets include the exact same label combinations, and the number of combinations is 90. This indicates that this task can be solved as a classification of 90 classes. However, since this is an unrealistic situation for actual applications, we do not rely on this characteristic in this work.

reuters10 and reuters90 are taken from the Reuters-21578 collection,[2] which is a popular benchmark for text categorization. This text collection consists of newswire articles, and each document is assigned topic categories, such as *grain* and *ship*. We split the data into training and test sets, according to the so-called *ModApte* split.

[1] Available at http://www.computationalmedicine.org

[2] Available at http://www.daviddlewis.com/resources/testcollections/reuters21578/

cmc2007				
	BPM		ME	
γ	micro-F1	sub. acc.	micro-F1	sub. acc.
0	82.79	69.88	83.09	69.06
100	83.49	70.70	83.68	70.39
200	82.95	69.67	83.67	70.18
400	83.03	69.98	83.49	70.49
800	83.51	71.41	83.58	70.70
1600	83.10	70.49	83.56	71.00
3200	80.74	66.70	82.02	69.57
reuters10				
	BPM		ME	
γ	micro-F1	sub. acc.	micro-F1	sub. acc.
0	94.23	89.71	93.71	88.76
500	94.22	89.98	93.80	89.19
1000	94.43	90.37	94.07	89.55
2000	94.46	90.61	94.04	89.94
4000	94.12	90.26	94.12	89.98
8000	94.14	90.61	94.50	90.81
16000	93.92	90.29	94.30	90.88
reuters90				
	BPM		ME	
γ	micro-F1	sub. acc.	micro-F1	sub. acc.
0	84.07	77.91	86.83	79.50
500	84.96	78.27	86.89	79.66
1000	85.38	78.70	86.94	79.99
2000	85.73	79.79	86.55	79.93
4000	85.72	79.73	86.54	80.23
8000	85.90	80.19	86.77	80.39
16000	86.17	80.52	—	—

Table 3: Accuracy for cmc2007, reuters10, and reuters90

From this data, we create two data sets. The first set, reuters10, is a subset of the *ModApte* split, to which the 10 largest categories are assigned. The other, reuters90, consists of documents that are labeled by 90 categories, having at least one document in each of the training and test sets.

In the following experiments, we run two machine learning classifiers: Bayes Point Machines (BPM) (Herbrich et al., 2001), and the maximum entropy model (ME) (Berger et al., 1996). For BPM, we run 100 averaged perceptrons (Collins, 2002) with 10 iterations for each. For ME, the orthant-wise quasi-Newton method (Andrew and Gao, 2007) is applied, with the hyper parameter for l_1 regularization fixed to 1.0.

We use word unigram features that represent the frequency of a particular word in a target document. We also use features that indicate the *non-existence* of a word, which we found effective in preliminary experiments; feature $f_{l,\bar{w}}(x, y)$ is 1 if $l \in y$ and w is not included in the document x. Words are stemmed and number expressions are normalized to a unique symbol. Words are not used if they are included in the stopword list (322 words), or they occur fewer than a threshold, c, in training data. We set $c = 5$ for reuters10 and reuters90, following previous works (Ghamrawi and McCallum, 2005), while $c = 0$ for cmc2007, because the data is small.

These features are selected according to averaged mutual information (information gain), which is the most popular method in previous works (Yang and Pedersen, 1997; Ghamrawi and McCallum, 2005). For each label, features are sorted according to this score, and top-ranked features are included in the model. By preliminary experiments, we fixed parameters, κ for word unigram features and ν for non-existence features, for each data set, as shown in Table 2.

The same method is applied to the selection of label correlation features. In the following experiments, we observe the accuracy and training time by changing the threshold parameter γ for the selection of label correlation features.

cmc2007			
γ	max. width	avg. width	time (sec.)
0	0	0.00	90
100	2	1.17	132
200	3	1.51	145
400	3	1.71	165
800	4	2.11	200
1600	5	2.93	427
3200	4	3.99	2280
reuters10			
γ	max. width	avg. width	time (sec.)
0	0	0.00	787
500	2	1.72	1378
1000	3	2.00	1752
2000	4	2.16	2594
4000	6	2.90	7183
8000	6	4.22	21555
16000	6	5.67	116535
reuters90			
γ	max. width	avg. width	time (sec.)
0	0	0.00	26172
500	5	1.74	28067
1000	6	2.24	38510
2000	6	3.22	42479
4000	8	3.68	60029
8000	14	4.56	153268
16000	17	6.39	—

Table 4: Tree width and training time for cmc2007, reuters10, and reuters90

4.2 Results

Table 3[3] shows microaveraged F-scores (micro-F1) and subset accuracies (sub. acc.) (Ghamrawi and McCallum, 2005) while varying γ, the num-

[3] The experiment with $\gamma = 16000$ for ME was not performed due to its cost (estimated time is approx. two weeks).

ber of label correlation features. In all data sets and with all classifiers, the accuracy is increased by incorporating label correlation features. The results also demonstrate that the accuracy saturates, or even decreases, with large γ. This indicates that the feature selection is necessary not only for obtaining efficiency, but also for higher accuracy.

Table 4 shows tree widths, and the time for the training of the ME models. As shown, the graphical model is represented effectively with sparse graphs, even when the number of label correlation features is increased. With these results, we can conclude that our method can model label correlations with a tractable cost.

The accuracy for `cmc2007` is significantly better than the results reported in Patrick et al. (2007) (micro-F1=81.1) in a similar setting, in which only word unigram features are used. Our best result is approaching the results of Crammer et al. (2007) (micro-F1=84.6), which exploits various linguistically motivated features. Numerous results have been reported for `reuters10`, and most of them report the microaveraged F-score around 91 to 94, while our best result is comparable to the state-of-the-art accuracy. For `reuters90`, Ghamrawi and McCallum (2005) achieved an improvement in the microaveraged F-score from 86.34 to 87.01, which is comparable to our result.

5 Conclusion

This paper described a method for the exact inference for multi-label classification with label correlation features. Experimental results on text categorization with the CMC challenge data and the Reuters-21578 text collection demonstrated that our method improves the accuracy for text categorization with a tractable cost. The availability of exact inference enables us to apply various machine learning methods not yet investigated in this paper, including support vector machines.

From the perspective of machine learning research, feature selection methods should be reconsidered. While we used a feature selection method that is widely accepted in text categorization research, it has no direct connection with machine learning models. Since feature selection methods motivated by the optimization criteria of machine learning models have been proposed (Riezler and Vasserman, 2004), we expect that the integration of our proposal with those methods will open up a new framework for multi-label classification.

Acknowledgments

This work was partially supported by Grant-in-Aid for Specially Promoted Research (MEXT, Japan) and Grant-in-Aid for Young Scientists (MEXT, Japan).

References

Andrew, G. and J. Gao. 2007. Scalable training of l_1-regularized log-linear models. In *24th Annual International Conference on Machine Learning*.

Berger, A. L., S. A. Della Pietra, and V. J. Della Pietra. 1996. A maximum entropy approach to natural language processing. *Computational Linguistics*, 22(1):39–71.

Collins, M. 2002. Discriminative training methods for hidden markov models: Theory and experiments with perceptron algorithms. In *2002 Conference on Empirical Methods in Natural Language Processing*.

Cowell, R. G., A. P. Dawid, S. L. Lauritzen, and D. J. Spiegelhalter. 1999. *Probabilistic Networks and Expert Systems*. Springer-Verlag, New York.

Crammer, K., M. Dredze, K. Ganchev, and P. P. Talukdar. 2007. Automatic code assignment to medical text. In *BioNLP 2007*, pages 129–136.

Ghamrawi, N. and A. McCallum. 2005. Collective multi-label classification. In *ACM 14th Conference on Information and Knowledge Management*.

Herbrich, R., T. Graepel, and C. Campbell. 2001. Bayes point machines. *Journal of Machine Learning Research*, 1:245–279.

Patrick, J., Y. Zhang, and Y. Wang. 2007. Evaluating feature types for encoding clinical notes. In *10th Conference of the Pacific Association for Computational Linguistics*, pages 218–225.

Pestian, J. P., C. Brew, P. Matykiewicz, DJ Hovermale, N. Johnson, K. B. Cohen, and W. Duch. 2007. A shared task involving multi-label classification of clinical free text. In *BioNLP 2007*, pages 97–104.

Riezler, S. and A. Vasserman. 2004. Gradient feature testing and l_1 regularization for maximum entropy parsing. In *42nd Meeting of the Association for Computational Linguistics*.

Schapire, R. E. and Y. Singer. 2000. Boostexter: a boosting-based system for text categorization. *Machine Learning*, 39(2/3):135–168.

Tsoumakas, G. and I. Katakis. 2007. Multi-label classification: an overview. *Journal of Data Warehousing and Mining*, 3(3):1–13.

Yang, Y. and J. O. Pedersen. 1997. A comparative study on feature selection in text categorization. In *14th International Conference on Machine Learning*, pages 412–420.

Modelling Multilinguality in Ontologies

Elena Montiel-Ponsoda, Guadalupe Aguado de Cea, Asunción Gómez-Pérez
Ontology Engineering Group
Universidad Politécnica de Madrid
emontiel@delicias.dia.fi.upm.es,
{lupe,asun}@fi.upm.es

Wim Peters
Sheffield Natural Language Processing Group
University of Sheffield
w.peters@dcs.shef.ac.uk

Abstract

Multilinguality in ontologies has become an impending need for institutions worldwide with valuable linguistic resources in different natural languages. Since most ontologies are developed in one language, obtaining multilingual ontologies implies to *localize* or adapt them to a concrete language and culture community. As the adaptation of the ontology conceptualization demands considerable efforts, we propose to modify the ontology terminological layer, and provide a model called *Linguistic Information Repository* (LIR) that associated to the ontology meta-model allows terminological layer localization.

1 Introduction

Multilinguality in ontologies is nowadays demanded by institutions worldwide with a huge number of resources in different languages. One of these institutions is the FAO[1]. Within the NeOn project[2], the FAO is currently leading a case study on fishery stocks in order to improve the interoperability of its information systems. The FAO, as an international organization with five official languages -English, French, Spanish, Arabic and Chinese- deals with heterogeneous and multilingual linguistic resources with different granularity levels. This scenario is an illustrative example of the need for semantically organizing great amounts of multilingual data. When providing ontologies with multilingual data, one of the activities identified in the NeOn ontology network development process is the Ontology Localization Activity, that consists in *adapting an ontology to a concrete language and culture community*, as defined in (Suárez-Figueroa et al., 2007). In particular, our aim is to obtain multilingual ontologies by localizing its terminological layer (terms or labels that name ontology classes), rather than modifying its conceptualization. Thus, we propose to link ontologies with a linguistic model, called LIR, whose main feature is that it is holistic in the sense that it (1) provides a complete and complementary amount of linguistic data that allows localization of ontology concepts to a specific linguistic and cultural universe, and, (2) provides a unified access to aggregated multilingual data. The model we present in this paper is an enhanced version of the one introduced in (Peters et al., 2007).

2 Related work

The most widespread modality for introducing multilingual data in ontology meta-models consists in using some ontology properties (`rdfs:label` and `rdfs:comment`[3]) that define labels and descriptions in natural language of ontology classes. In this system, information is embedded in the ontology. In a similar way, the Simple Knowledge Organization System (SKOS[4]) data model for semantically structuring thesauri, taxonomies, etc., permits the labelling of ontology classes with multilingual strings, and even the establishment of some relations between labels (*preferred* label against the *alternative* one). In any case, however, both modelling modalities restrict the amount of linguistic data that can be included in the ontology, and assume full synonym relations among the multilingual labels associated to one and the same concept.

A further multilingual model is one adopted by the general purpose lexicon EuroWordNet[5]

© 2008. Licensed under the *Creative Commons Attribution-Noncommercial-Share Alike 3.0 Unported* license (http://creativecommons.org/licenses/by-nc-sa/3.0/). Some rights reserved.

[1] http://www.fao.org/

[2] http://www.neon-project.org/

[3] www.w3.org/TR/rdf-schema/

[4] http://www.w3.org/2004/02/skos/specs

[5] http://www.illc.uva.nl/EuroWordNet/

(EWN). EWN consists of monolingual ontologies, each one reflecting the linguistic and cultural specificities of a certain language, linked to each other through an interlingual set of common concepts that allows building equivalences among ontologies. Although concept equivalences among localized ontologies are reliable and reflect cultural differences, the quantity of linguistic information is also limited to labels and definitions attached to concepts.

Finally, we come to the upward trend in recent research for providing ontologies with linguistic data, which is the association of the ontology meta-model to a linguistic model keeping both separate. The model for representing and organizing the linguistic information can be a data base (as in GENOMA-KB[6] or OncoTerm[7]), or an ontology (as in the case of LingInfo (Buitelaar et al., 2006) or LexOnto (Cimiano et al. 2007)). The main advantage of this modeling modality is that it allows the inclusion of as much linguistic information as wished, as well as the possibility of establishing relations among linguistic elements. Thus, conceptual information is greatly enriched with linguistic data. Additionally, these systems are considered domain independent, and can be linked to any domain ontology.

The differentiating aspect among the mentioned systems is determined by the kind of linguistic classes that make up each model. Depending on the linguistic needs of the end user, some models will be more suitable than others. LingInfo or LexOnto can offer not only multilingual strings to classes and properties of the ontology, but also a deeper morphosyntactic decomposition of linguistic elements, in the case of LingInfo, or a greater focus on syntactic structures by means of *subcategorization frames*, in LexOnto. Our LIR model, however, is more in the line of GENOMA-KB or OncoTerm, in the sense that they follow localization or translational approaches. The main objective of the LIR is to localize a certain ontology category to the linguistic and cultural universe of a certain natural language and to capture translation specificities among languages. Morphosyntactic information is left in the background, although interoperability with ISO standards for representing that sort of information is foreseen. Contrary to GENOMA-KB or OncoTerm, the LIR is represented as an ontology and will be provided with the necessary infrastructure to access external resources for obtaining linguistic data and maintaining links to supplier resources (cf. 5).

2.1 Interoperability with existing standards

Lexical knowledge is expressed in various ways in terminological and linguistic resources. There is a wealth of proposals for enhancing the interoperability of lexical knowledge by encoding it following standard models. As the most important initiatives we take into account two ISO (International Organization for Standardization[8]) standards: The Terminological Markup Framework (TMF[9]) (and the associated TermBase eXchange format; TBX[10]), which captures the underlying structure and representation of computerized terminologies, and the Lexical Markup Framework (LMF) (Francopoulo et al., 2006), an abstract meta-model that provides a common, standardized framework for the construction of computational lexicons.

The LIR model adopts a number of data categories from these standards in order to guarantee interoperability with them. For instance, the notion of *lexical entry* or *lexeme*, in itself a well known central linguistic notion of a unit of form and meaning, has been taken from LMF, whereas the attribute *term type*, which covers representational aspects such as full forms versus abbreviations, has been taken from TMF.

3 Linguistic Information Repository

As shown in Figure 1, the linguistic information captured in the LIR is organized around the `LexicalEntry` class. A lexical entry is *a unit of form and meaning in a certain language* (Saloni et al., 1990). Therefore, it is associated to the classes `Language`, `Lexicalization` and `Sense`. A set of related lexicalizations or term variants shares the same meaning within the specific context of a certain cultural and linguistic universe. E.g., *Food and Agriculture Organization* and *FAO* would be two lexicalizations linked to the same sense. Thanks to the expressiveness of the `hasVariant` relation, it is possible to say that the one is acronym of the other.

The `Language` class at the `LexicalEntry` level allows launching searches in which just those lexical entries related to one natural language are shown to the user, thus displaying the ontology in the selected language.

[6] http://genoma.iula.upf.edu:8080/genoma

[7] http://www.ugr.es/~oncoterm/alpha-index.html

[8] www.iso.org

[9] http://www.loria.fr/projets/TMF/

[10] http://www.lisa.org/standards/tbx/

`Sense` is considered a *language-specific unit of intensional lexical semantic description* (*ibidem*), which comes to fruition through the `Definition` class expressed in natural language. Therefore, `Sense` is an empty class realized by means of the `Definition`. By keeping senses in the linguistic model independent from ontology concepts, we allow capturing cultural specificities that may slightly differ from the concept expressed in the ontology. `Definition` has a pointer to the linguistic resource it has been obtained from. In this way reliability and authority of definitions are guaranteed.

Then, `Lexicalization` is related to its `Source` or provenance, to a `Note` class and to a `UsageContext` class. The `Source` class aims again at being a pointer to the resource where the information has been extracted from. `Note` is here linked to `Lexicalization`, but it could be linked to any other class in the model. It allows the inclusion of supplemental information; e.g., usage specificities of a certain lexicalization within its language system. By linking `Note` to the `Sense` or `Definition` classes we could make explicit possible differences among senses in different languages. The `UsageContext` class provides information about the behaviour of a certain lexicalization within the language system it belongs to. Finally, lexical semantic equivalences are established among lexical entries within the same language (`hasSynonym` or `hasAntonym`), or across languages (`hasTranslation`). Note that we use the latter label to establish equivalences between lexicalizations in different languages, although it is assumed that words identified as translation equivalents are rarely identical in sense. As Hirst (2004) stated, *more usually they are merely cross-lingual near-synonyms*, but this approach is adopted for the practical reason of providing multilinguality.

The LIR is linked to the `OntologyElement` class of the OWL meta-model permitting in this way the association of multilingual information to any element of the ontology. Finally, it is left to say that the rationale underlying LIR is not to design a lexicon for different natural languages and then establish links to ontology concepts, but to associate multilingual linguistic knowledge to the conceptual knowledge represented by the ontology. What the LIR does is to associate *word senses* –as defined by Hirst (2004)- in different languages to ontology concepts, although word senses and concepts can not be said to overlap since they are tightly related to the particular vision of a language and its culture, whereas ontology concepts try to capture objects of the real world, and are defined and organized according to expert criteria agreed by consensus.

4 Application of the LIR in NeOn

The LIR has been developed within the NeOn project and is currently being implemented. In order to check its suitability, it was evaluated against the linguistic requirements of the use cases participating in this project (see Note 2): the Spanish pharmaceutical industry, and the Fisheries Stock system of the FAO. Both use cases are working in the development of ontologies for organizing the information they have in several languages. As a consequence, one of the requirements for the NeOn architecture was to support multilingual ontologies.

As already introduced, the LIR not only provides multilingual information to any ontology element, but it also enables unified access to aggregated multilingual data, previously scattered in heterogeneous resources. In that way, it integrates the necessary linguistic information from use case resources and offers a complete and complementary amount of linguistic data.

Regarding the FAO use case, the LIR was evaluated against the recent developed model for the AGROVOC thesaurus, the AGROVOC Concept Server (Liang et al., 2008). This is a concept-based multilingual repository, which, compared to a traditional Knowledge Organization System, allows the representation of more semantics such as specific relationships between concepts and relationships between multilingual lexicalizations. It serves as a pool of agricultural concepts and is a starting point in the development of domain ontologies. The adequacy of the LIR model was positively evaluated against the linguistic requirements of the Concept Server in terms of flexible association of language specific lexicalizations with agricultural domain concepts, and compatibility with TBX.

5 Conclusions and future research

In this contribution we have raised the impending need of international organizations dealing with multilingual information for representing multilinguality in ontologies. In order to obtain multilingual ontologies, we have proposed the association of the ontology meta-model to a linguistic

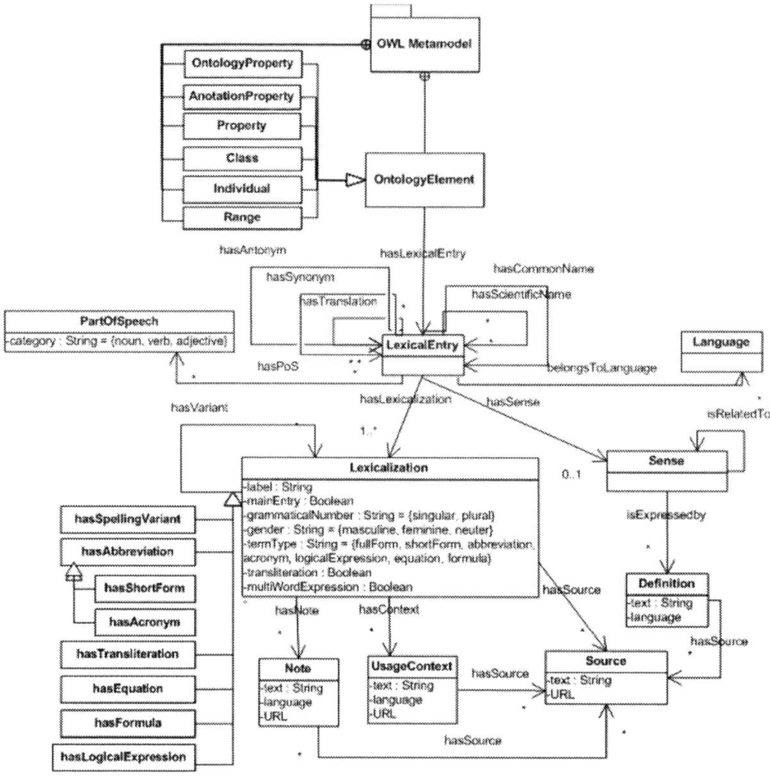

Figure 1. LIR model.

model, the LIR. The LIR has proven to be a holistic linguistic information repository with the following benefits:

- Provision of a complete and complementary set of linguistic elements in each language for localizing ontology elements
- Homogeneous access to linguistic information distributed in heterogeneous resources with different granularity
- Establishment of relations between linguistic elements, and solution to conceptualization mismatches among different cultures

Besides, within NeOn there is a current research regarding the integration of the LIR with the *LabelTranslator* tool (Espinoza et al., 2007), that allows: (1) quick access to external multilingual resources, (2) an automatic translation of the ontology terminological layer, (3) an automatic storage of the resulting multilingual information in the LIR, and (4) convenient editing possibilities for users in distributed environments.

Acknowlegements. This research was supported by the *NeOn* project (FP6-027595)

References

Buitelaar, P., M. Sintek, M. Kiesel. 2006. *A Multilingual/Multimedia Lexicon Model for Ontologies*. In Proc. of ESWC, Budva, Montenegro.

Cimiano, P., P. Haase, M. Herold, M. Mantel, P. Buitelaar. 2007. *LexOnto: A Model for Ontology Lexicons for Ontology-based NLP*. Proc. of OntoLex.

Espinoza, M., A. Gómez-Pérez, and E. Mena. 2008. *Enriching an Ontology with Multilingual Information*. Proc. of ESWC, Tenerife, Spain.

Francopoulo, G, M. George, N. Calzolari, M. Monachini, N. Bel, M. Pet, C. Soria. 2006. *Lexical Markup Framework (LMF)*. Proc. of LREC.

Hirst, G. 2004. Ontology and the Lexicon. In S. Staab, and R. Studer (eds.) *Handbook on Ontologies and Information Systems*. Springer, Berlin.

Liang, A.C., B. Lauser, M. Sini, J. Keizer, S. Katz. 2008. *From AGROVOC to the Agricultural Ontology Service/Concept Server. An OWL model for managing ontologies in the agricultural domain*. In Proc. of the "OWL: Experiences and Directions" Workshop, Mancherter, U.K.

Peters, W., E. Montiel-Ponsoda, G. Aguado de Cea. 2007.*Localizing Ontologies in OWL*.Proc. OntoLex

Saloni, Z., S. Szpakowicz, M. Swidzinski. 1990. The Design of a Universal Basic Dictionary of Contemporary Polish. *International Journal of Lexicography*, vol. 3 no1. Oxford University Press.

Suárez-Figueroa, M.C. (coord.) 2007. *NeOn Development Process and Ontology Life Cycle*. NeOn Project D5.3.1

Quantification and Implication in Semantic Calendar Expressions Represented with Finite-State Transducers

Jyrki Niemi and **Kimmo Koskenniemi**
Department of General Linguistics, University of Helsinki
PO Box 9, FI–00014 University of Helsinki, Finland
{jyrki.niemi, kimmo.koskenniemi}@helsinki.fi

Abstract

This paper elaborates a model for representing semantic calendar expressions (SCEs), which correspond to the intensional meanings of natural-language calendar phrases. The model uses finite-state transducers (FSTs) to mark denoted periods of time on a set of timelines represented as a finite-state automaton (FSA). We present a treatment of SCEs corresponding to quantified phrases (*any Monday*; *every May*) and an implication operation for requiring the denotation of one SCE to contain completely that of another.

1 Introduction

This paper elaborates the temporal representation model proposed in Niemi and Koskenniemi (2007) and developed in Niemi and Koskenniemi (2008). This *bracketing FST model* covers temporal information ranging from simple dates to such meanings as *6–8 pm on every Monday in April, except on Easter Monday*. The model represents *semantic calendar expressions* (SCEs) using finite-state transducers (FSTs) that bracket periods of time on timelines represented as a finite-state automaton (FSA). Motivations for a finite-state representation include an efficient treatment of periodicity and certain kinds of sparse sets of sets common in calendar information, as well as a well-known theory.

In this paper, we treat SCEs corresponding to quantified calendar phrases, such as *any Monday* and *every May*. We also present implication for representing such cases as a course with compulsory attendance, whose all class times should coincide with the free slots of time of a student.

© 2008. Licensed under the *Creative Commons Attribution-Noncommercial-Share Alike 3.0 Unported* license (http://creativecommons.org/licenses/by-nc-sa/3.0/). Some rights reserved.

2 Semantic Calendar Expressions (SCEs) and the Bracketing FST Model

We use the semi-formal SCEs as the basic representation. An SCE typically corresponds to the disambiguated intensional meaning of a natural-language calendar phrase. An SCE may denote either a specific period of time or a set of periods. An SCE is compiled to a sequence of *bracketing FSTs* through regular (relation) expressions.

Table 1 lists some implemented SCE constructs and the corresponding calendar phrases. Most constructs can be combined with each other.

Construct	SCE example; calendar phrase
calendar period	may; fri; calday *May; Friday; (calendar) day*
list (union)	union (mon, fri, sun) *Monday, Friday and Sunday*
common part (intersection)	intersect (aug, y2008) *August 2008*
interval	interval (may, jun) *May to June*
anchored	nth_following (3, mon, easter) *the third Monday after Easter*
quantified	any_n (1, mon) *any (single) Monday*

Table 1: Examples of SCE constructs and the corresponding calendar phrases

The bracketing FST model represents the denotations of an SCE as an acyclic *timeline FSA* defining a finite *timeline string* for each alternative denotation.[1] A *basic timeline FSA* defines a single timeline consisting of brackets and labels for calendar periods, with no denotations marked. The following is a (simplified) timeline for the year 2008 at month level (spaces separate symbols):

[1]Timeline FSAs are equivalent to the timeline FSTs of Niemi and Koskenniemi (2008).

[y y2008 [m Jan]m [m Feb]m ... [m Dec]m]y

To represent the denotation of an SCE *s*, a basic timeline FSA is composed with a bracketing FST (sequence) representing *s*. The result is a timeline FSA with the denotation marked with *marker brackets* {in ... }in. The following timeline corresponds to union (jan, mar) (*January and March*):

[y y2008 {i3 {i1 [m Jan]m }i1 }i3 [m Feb]m {i3 {i2 [m Mar]m }i2 }i3 [m Apr]m ... [m Dec]m]y

First, January is marked with i1 and March with i2. Then the bracketing FST for union marks each period i1 and i2 with i3, the denotation of the whole.

3 Representing Quantified SCEs

A natural-language calendar phrase may be unquantified, such as *Monday*, or it may contain different kinds of quantification, such as *all Mondays*, *any Monday*, *three Mondays* and *all Mondays in some May*.[2] We treat *any Monday*, *some Monday* and *one Monday* as meaning any single Monday, and we equate *all Mondays*, *each Monday* and *every Monday*. Numerical quantification can be generalized to intervals, possibly open-ended, such as *two to five Mondays* and *at most four Mondays*.

3.1 Collective Representation (*All*)

The meaning *all Mondays* is represented simply as the SCE mon, which is represented as a timeline FSA with each Monday marked on the same timeline, as illustrated in Fig. 1 (simplified).[3] We call this the *collective representation* of an SCE.

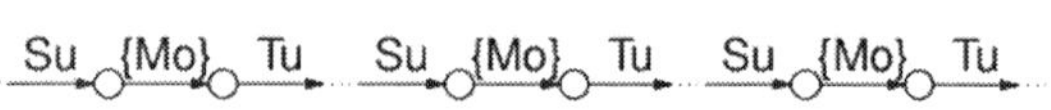

Figure 1: A timeline FSA for the SCE mon (*all Mondays*); "{Mo}" denotes a marked Monday

The denotation can be interpreted in several ways: as the union of all Mondays, as all the parts of a timeline that are part of a Monday, as the recurring "event" of Monday, or as a disconnected (non-convex) interval of all Mondays.

3.2 Distributive Representation (*Any*)

The meaning *any Monday* is represented as the SCE any_n (1, mon) and as a timeline FSA with each Monday marked on a separate, alternative timeline of its own, as illustrated in Fig. 2. We call this the *distributive representation* of an SCE.[4]

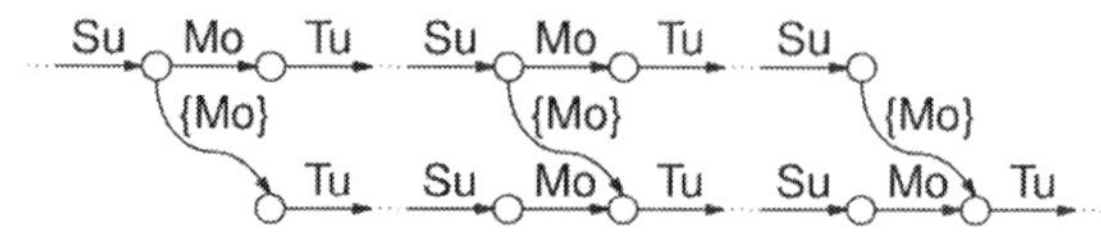

Figure 2: A timeline FSA representing the SCE any_n (1, mon) denoting any single Monday

For numerical quantification, we combine collective and distributive representation. For example, any_n (3, mon) (*three Mondays*) is represented as a timeline FSA defining a set of timelines, each with three Mondays marked, so that the set covers all possible combinations. A collective representation alone would not suffice: a single timeline with all periods of three Mondays marked would in effect represent all Mondays.

3.3 Collective Representation as Primary

In natural language, an unquantified calendar phrase, such as *Monday*, is typically underspecified and refers to the closest preceding or following Monday relevant in the context. In the bracketing FST model, however, we represent unquantified expressions collectively: the SCE mon represents both *Monday* and *all Mondays*.

A major practical reason for preferring the collective representation is that it is easy to construct a bracketing FST that splits a single timeline with each Monday marked to a set of alternative timelines, each with only one of the Mondays marked, whereas the converse operation is not possible. In effect, a bracketing FST can only refer to symbols on a single timeline at a time.

A single timeline with all Mondays marked can also be used as a basis for such an SCE as nth_following (3, mon, easter) (*the third Monday after Easter*). The bracketing FST corresponding to nth_following gets as its input a timeline with each Monday and each Easter marked. It then counts the third Monday after each Easter and marks it. This would be much more difficult with each Monday marked on a timeline of its own.

3.4 Combining Quantified SCEs

Multiple SCEs with quantification can be combined appropriately. For example, *all Mondays in*

[2] *All* could be regarded as universal quantification, and *any* resembles existential quantification, but because of some differences, we avoid using these logical terms.

[3] Each transition in the figures corresponds to a number of states and transitions between them in the actual timeline FSA, as the representation of each day consists of the calendar day brackets, symbols for the day of the week and the day of the month, and possibly finer granularities inside.

[4] We deviate from the common terminology that uses *collective* for *all Mondays* and *distributive* for *each Monday*.

any (single) May is represented by a timeline FSA defining a set of timelines, each with all Mondays of a single May marked, and *any (single) Monday in every May* by one with a single Monday marked in each May, covering all possible combinations.

Combinations of quantified SCEs can often be represented compositionally with intersection. For example, *all Mondays in every May* is represented as intersect (mon, may), *all Mondays in any May* as intersect (mon, any_n (1, may)) and *any Monday in any May* as intersect (any_n (1, mon), any_n (1, may)).

However, *any Monday in every May* cannot be represented simply with intersection, since intersecting a set of timelines, each with only one Monday marked, and a timeline with every May marked would result in timelines with one Monday marked in (at most) one May. For this case, we have defined the SCE operation n_within_each (*n, period, frame*), which marks *n periods* within each *frame*. *Any Monday in every May* is then represented as n_within_each (1, mon, may).

3.5 Other Uses of Distributive Representation

A distributive representation is obligatory for an SCE denoting possibly overlapping periods of time, although each alternative timeline may contain several non-overlapping periods.

For example, we represent n_consecutive (3, calday) (*three consecutive days*) as a set of timelines, each with one possible combination of non-overlapping periods of three consecutive days marked.[5] If each timeline had only a single period marked, it would complicate representing such an SCE as union (intersect (n_consecutive (3, calday), may), intersect (n_consecutive (3, calday), jun)) (*three consecutive days in May and in June*) so that the periods of consecutive days in May and June are marked on the same timeline. In contrast, a single timeline with all possible non-overlapping periods marked would not cover the periods overlapping with the marked ones.

A distributive representation is also used for SCEs containing a distributive union operation to represent a disjunctive meaning. For example, distr_union (union (mon, fri), union (tue, sun)) (*Monday and Friday or Tuesday and Sunday*) is represented as a timeline FSA defining two timelines, one with every Monday and Friday marked and the other with every Tuesday and Sunday.

3.6 Distributive Representation and *First*

Distributive representation requires special considerations in conjunction with some SCE operations, most notably nth_within (*n, period, frame*), which marks the *n*th *period* within each longer period *frame*. Although a *period* might be the *n*th marked one within a *frame* on one timeline, alternative timelines might contain earlier occurrences.

As an example, we consider nth_within (1, n_consecutive (3, workday), jun) (*the first period of three consecutive working days in June*).[6] For a June beginning on a Sunday, we have alternative timelines with the first period of three working days beginning on Monday, Tuesday and Wednesday, but we would like to mark only the one beginning on Monday. However, a bracketing FST cannot refer to the alternative timelines to test if any of them contains an earlier applicable period.

As a solution, we have such operations as n_consecutive insert an *alternative marker bracket* (denoted by [. . .] below) on each timeline into each position in which it adds a marker bracket ({. . .}) on another timeline. The following simplified alternative timelines illustrate the example above:

Su { Mo [Tu [We } Th] Fr] Sa
Su [Mo { Tu [We] Th } Fr] Sa
Su [Mo [Tu { We] Th] Fr } Sa

The operation nth_within seeks the first marked period in June with no opening alternative marker bracket between it and the beginning of June.

4 Implication: All or Nothing

In some applications, an SCE may denote a set of periods of times all of which should be contained in those denoted by another SCE, or if impossible, none of them should be. For example, all the class times of a course with compulsory attendance should coincide with the free slots of time in the calendar of a student wishing to attend the course. An intersection of the class times and the student's free slots of time would also contain partial results if he or she could attend only some of the classes.

[5] Since consecutive days are adjacent, they can be enclosed in marker brackets and treated as a single connected period, with several periods on a single timeline. In contrast, the multiple disconnected periods of *three consecutive Mondays* cannot be represented in a general way on the same timeline in the bracketing FST model, but only by having a different marker bracket index for each period of three Mondays.

[6] The SCE nth_within (1, n_consecutive (3, calday), jun) (*the first period of three consecutive (calendar) days in June*) denotes the same as first_n_within (3, calday, jun) (*the first three days in June*). A similar rephrasing would not be correct for working days, however.

To obtain the desired result, we use the operation impl (a, b) to mark all the periods a if and only if they all are fully contained in the periods b. If a point of time is in a, it must also be in b for a to be marked, so the operation can be regarded of as a kind of an implication $a \rightarrow b$. Above, we would compute impl (course, student_free).

A course with alternative instances would be represented with a timeline FSA defining an alternative timeline for each instance. The bracketing FST corresponding to the above implication would then mark the class times of each instance that is completely within the student's free slots of time.

5 Related Work

We briefly mention the approaches to quantification of some research related to the bracketing FST model in purpose or coverage. TEL (Endriss, 1998) represents universally quantified expressions like unquantified ones. TEL has numerical quantification and quantifier negation. TCNL (Han and Lavie, 2004) represents universal quantification as an enumeration. An unquantified expression denotes an underspecified time. Like TEL, TCNL has no explicit existential quantification. Ohlbach and Gabbay (1998) represent universal quantification with a parametrized modal operator "always within a period" and existential with "sometime within a period". Cukierman and Delgrande (1998) represent quantified expressions in a way resembling that of ours but unquantified expressions effectively as existentially quantified. TimeML (Saurí et al., 2006) represents quantification by quantifier and frequency attributes. OWL-Time (Pan and Hobbs, 2005) uses temporal aggregates for universal and numerical quantification.

6 Discussion and Further Work

In our view, SCEs corresponding to typical quantified calendar phrases can be represented in the bracketing FST model fairly naturally, although the naturalness of representing unquantified, underspecified phrases collectively can be disputed, and the representation of *any Monday in every May* is not compositional. Implication, in turn, would seem useful for representing a set of periods of time fully contained in another set of periods.

Although some types of calendar information are impossible to represent exactly or naturally with finite-state methods, we find the bracketing FST model a promising representation for many common types. However, to be usable in practice, the model needs further work in both coverage and efficiency. Moreover, applications would benefit from a component to parse a (restricted) natural-language calendar phrase to an SCE and another one to generate the former from the latter.

Acknowledgements

This paper represents independent work by the first author based on the suggestions of the second author and funded by the Graduate School of Language Technology in Finland. We thank the anonymous reviewers for their valuable comments.

References

Cukierman, Diana and James P. Delgrande. 1998. Expressing time intervals and repetition within a formalization of calendars. *Computational Intelligence*, 14(4):563–597.

Endriss, Ulrich. 1998. Semantik zeitlicher Ausdrücke in Terminvereinbarungsdialogen. Verbmobil Report 227, Technische Universität Berlin, Fachbereich Informatik, Berlin, August.

Han, Benjamin and Alon Lavie. 2004. A framework for resolution of time in natural language. *ACM Transactions on Asian Language Information Processing (TALIP)*, 3(1):11–32, March.

Niemi, Jyrki and Kimmo Koskenniemi. 2007. Representing calendar expressions with finite-state transducers that bracket periods of time on a hierarchical timeline. In Nivre, Joakim, Heiki-Jaan Kaalep, Kadri Muischnek, and Mare Koit, editors, *Proceedings of the 16th Nordic Conference of Computational Linguistics NODALIDA-2007*, pages 355–362, Tartu, Estonia. University of Tartu.

Niemi, Jyrki and Kimmo Koskenniemi. 2008. Representing and combining calendar information by using finite-state transducers. In *Proceedings of the Seventh International Workshop on Finite-State Methods and Natural Language Processing (FSMNLP) 2008*. To appear.

Ohlbach, Hans Jürgen and Dov Gabbay. 1998. Calendar logic. *Journal of Applied Non-classical Logics*, 8(4):291–324.

Pan, Feng and Jerry R. Hobbs. 2005. Temporal aggregates in OWL-Time. In *Proceedings of the 18th International Florida Artificial Intelligence Research Society Conference (FLAIRS-2005)*, pages 560–565, Clearwater Beach, Florida. AAAI Press.

Saurí, Roser, Jessica Littman, Bob Knippen, Robert Gaizauskas, Andrea Setzer, and James Pustejovsky. 2006. TimeML annotation guidelines, version 1.2.1. http://timeml.org/site/publications/timeMLdocs/annguide_1.2.1.pdf, January.

Using very simple statistics for review search: An exploration

Bo Pang
Yahoo! Research
bopang@yahoo-inc.com

Lillian Lee
Computer Science Department, Cornell University
llee@cs.cornell.edu

Abstract

We report on work in progress on using very simple statistics in an unsupervised fashion to re-rank search engine results when review-oriented queries are issued; the goal is to bring opinionated or subjective results to the top of the results list. We find that our proposed technique performs comparably to methods that rely on sophisticated pre-encoded linguistic knowledge, and that both substantially improve the initial results produced by the Yahoo! search engine.

1 Introduction

One important information need shared by many people is to find out about opinions and perspectives on a particular topic (Mishne and de Rijke, 2006; Pang and Lee, 2008). In fact, locating relevant subjective texts was a core task in the 2006 and 2007 TREC Blog tracks (Ounis et al., 2006; Ounis et al., 2008). Most participants considered a two-phase re-ranking approach, where first topic-based relevancy search was employed, and then some sort of filtering for subjectivity was applied; these filters were based on trained classifiers or subjectivity lexicons.

We propose an alternative approach to review search, one that is unsupervised and that does not rely on pre-existing dictionaries. Rather, it in essence simply re-ranks the top k topic-based search results by placing those that have the *least idiosyncratic* term distributions, with respect to the statistics of the top k results, at the head of the list. The fact that it is the least, not the most, rare terms with respect to the search results that are most indicative of subjectivity may at first seem rather counterintuitive; indeed, previous work has found rare terms to be important subjectivity cues (Wiebe et al., 2004). However, reviews within a given set of search results may tend to resemble each other because they tend to all discuss salient attributes of the topic in question.

© 2008. Licensed under the *Creative Commons Attribution-Noncommercial-Share Alike 3.0 Unported* license (http://creativecommons.org/licenses/by-nc-sa/3.0/). Some rights reserved.

2 Algorithm

Define a *search set* as the top n webpages returned in response to a review- or opinion-oriented query by a high-quality initial search engine, in our case, the top 20 returned by Yahoo!. As a question of both pragmatic and scientific value, we consider how much information can be gleaned simply from the items in the search set itself; in particular, we ask whether the subjective texts in the search set can be ranked above the objective ones solely from examination of the patterns of term occurrences across the search-set documents.

The idea we pursue is based in part on the assumption that the initial search engine is of relatively high quality, so that many of the search-set documents probably are, in fact, subjective. Therefore, re-ordering the top-ranked documents by how much they resemble the other search-set documents in aggregate may be a good way to identify the reviews. Indeed, perhaps the reviews will be similar to one another because they all tend to discuss salient features of the topic in question.

Suppose we have defined a *search-set rarity function* $\text{Rarity}_{ss}(t)$ (see Section 2.1 below) that varies inversely with the number of documents in the search set that contain the term t. Then, we define the *idiosyncrasy* score of a document d as the average search-set rarity of the most common terms it contains:

$$I(d,k) = \frac{1}{k} \sum_{t \in k\text{-commonest-terms}(d)} \text{Rarity}_{ss}(t), \tag{1}$$

where $k\text{-commonest-terms}(d)$ is the k commonest terms in the search set that also occur in d. For example, when we set k to be the size of the vocabulary of d, the idiosyncrasy score is the average search-set rarity of all the terms d contains. Then, to instantiate the similarity intuition outlined above, we simply rank by decreasing idiosyncrasy.

The reason we look at just the top most common terms is that the rarer terms might be noise. For example, terms that occur in just a few of the search-set documents might represent page- or site-specific information that is irrelevant to the query; but the presence of such terms does not necessarily indicate that the document in question is objective.

One potential problem with the approach outlined above is the presence of stopwords, since all documents, subjective or objective, can be expected to contain many of them. Therefore, stopword removal is indicated as an important preprocessing step. As it turns out, the commonly-used InQuery stopword list (Allan et al., 2000) contains terms like "less" that, while uninformative for topic-based information retrieval, may be important for subjectivity detection. Therefore, we used a 102-item list[1] based solely on frequencies in the British National Corpus.

2.1 Defining search-set rarity

There are various ways to define a search-set rarity function on terms. Inspired by the efficacy of the inverse document frequency (IDF) in information retrieval, we consider several definitions for $\text{Rarity}_{ss}(t)$. Let $n_{ss}(t)$ be the number of documents in the *search set* (not the entire corpus) that contain the term t. Due to space constraints, we only report results for:

$$\text{Rarity}_{ss}(t) \stackrel{def}{=} \frac{1}{n_{ss}(t)},$$

which is linearly increasing in $1/n_{ss}(t)$, (as befits a measure of "idiosyncrasy"). The other definitions we considered were logarithmic or polynomial in $1/n_{ss}(t)$, and performed similarly to the linear function.

2.2 Comparison algorithms

OpinionFinder is a state-of-the-art publicly available software package for sentiment analysis that can be applied to determining sentence-level subjectivity (Riloff and Wiebe, 2003; Wiebe and Riloff, 2005). It employs a number of pre-processing steps, including sentence splitting, part-of-speech tagging, stemming, and shallow parsing. Shallow parsing is needed to identify the extraction patterns that the sentence classifiers incorporate.

We used OpinionFinder's sentence-level output[2] to perform document-level subjectivity re-ranking as follows. The result of running OpinionFinder's sentence classifier is that each valid sentence[3] is annotated with one of three labels: "subj", "obj", or "unknown". First, discard the sentences labeled "unknown". Then, rank the documents by decreasing percentage of subjective sentences among those sentences that are left. In the case of ties, we use the ranking produced by the initial search engine.

We also considered a more lightweight way to incorporate linguistic knowledge: score each document according the percentage of adjectives within the set of tokens it contains. The motivation is previous work suggesting that the presence of adjectives is a strong indicator of the subjectivity of the enclosing sentence (Hatzivassiloglou and Wiebe, 2000; Wiebe et al., 2004).

[1] www.eecs.umich.edu/~qstout/586/bncfreq.html

[2] There are actually two versions. We used the accuracy-optimized version, as it outperformed the precision-optimized version.

[3] OpinionFinder will only process documents in which all strings identified as sentences by the system contain fewer than 1000 words. For the 31 documents in our dataset that failed this criterion, we set their score to 0.

	p@1	p@2	p@3	p@4	p@5	p@10	p@S	MAP
Search-engine baseline	.536	.543	.541	.554	.554	.528	.538	.612
OpinionFinder (accuracy version)	.754	.717	.729	.725	**.733**	**.675**	**.690**	**.768**
% of adjectives (type-based)	.710	.703	.696	.681	.678	.625	.633	.715
$idiosyncrasy(linear)$, $k = 50$	**.797**	**.783**	.739	.717	.696	.613	.640	.729
$idiosyncrasy(linear)$, $k = 100$	.754	**.783**	**.768**	<u>.739</u>	<u>.716</u>	<u>.630</u>	<u>.665</u>	<u>.743</u>
$idiosyncrasy(linear)$, $k = 200$	<u>.768</u>	<u>.761</u>	.744	**.746**	<u>.716</u>	.623	.653	.731
$idiosyncrasy(linear)$, $k = 300$	.754	<u>.761</u>	<u>.749</u>	.736	.704	.614	.641	.724

Table 1: Average search-set subjective-document precision results. "S": number of subjective documents. Bold and underlining: best and second-best performance per column, respectively.

3 Evaluation

Our focus is on the quality of the documents placed at the very top ranks, since users often look only at the first page or first half of the first page of results (Joachims et al., 2005). Hence, we report the precision of the top 1-5 and 10 documents, as well as precision at the number of subjective documents and mean average precision (MAP) for the subjective documents. All performance numbers are averages over the 69 search sets in our data, described next.

Data Here, we sketch the data acquisition and labeling process. In order to get real user queries targeted at reviews, we began with a randomly selected set of queries containing the word "review" or "reviews"[4] from the the query log available at `http://www.sigkdd.org/kdd2005/kddcup/KDDCUPData.zip`. We created a search set for each query by taking the top 20 webpages returned by the Yahoo! search engine and applying some postprocessing. Over a dozen volunteer annotators then labeled the documents as to whether they were subjective or objective according to a set of detailed instructions. The end result was over 1300 hand-labeled documents distributed across 69 search sets, varying widely with respect to query topic. Our dataset download site is `http://www.cs.cornell.edu/home/llee/data/search-subj.html`.

For almost every annotator, at least two of his or her search sets were labeled by another person as well, so that we could measure pair-wise agreement with respect to multiple queries. On average, there was agreement on 88.2% of the documents per search set, with the average Kappa coefficient (κ) being an acceptable 0.73, reflecting in part the difficulty of the judgment.[5] The lowest κ occurs on a search set with a 75% agreement rate.

Results A natural and key baseline is the ranking provided by the Yahoo! search engine, which is a high-quality, industrial-strength system. We consider this to be a crucial point of comparison. The results are shown in the top line in Table 1.

OpinionFinder clearly outperforms the initial search engine by a substantial margin, indicating that there are ample textual cues that can help achieve better subjectivity re-ranking.

The adjective-percentage baseline is also far superior to that of the search-engine baseline at all ranks, but does not quite match OpinionFinder. (Note that to achieve these results, we first discarded all terms contained in three or fewer of the search-set documents, since including such terms decreased performance.) Still, it is interesting to see that it appears that a good proportion of the improvements provided by OpinionFinder can be achieved using just adjective counts alone.

We now turn to subjectivity re-ranking based on term-distribution (idiosyncrasy) information. For

[4]Subsequent manual filtering discarded some non-opinion-oriented queries, such as "alternative medicine review volume5 numer1 pages 28 38 2000".

[5]One source of disagreement that stems from the specifics of our design is that we instructed annotators to mark "sales pitch" documents as non-reviews, on the premise that although such texts are subjective, they are not valuable to a user searching for unbiased reviews. (Note that this policy presumably makes the dataset more challenging for automated algorithms.) There are several cases where only one annotator identified this type of bias, which is not surprising since the authors of sales pitches may actively try to fool readers into believing the text to be unbiased.

consistency with the adjective-based method just described, we first discarded all terms contained in three or fewer of the search-set documents.

As shown in Table 1, the idiosyncrasy-based algorithm posts results that are overall strongly superior to those of the initial, high-quality search engine algorithm and also generally better than the adjective-percentage algorithm. Note that these phenomena hold for a range of values of k. The overall performance is also on par with OpinionFinder; for instance, according to the paired t-test, the only statistically significant performance difference (.05 level) between the accuracy-emphasizing version of OpinionFinder and the idiosyncrasy-based algorithm for $k = 100$ is for precision at 10. In some sense, this is a striking result: just looking at within-search-set frequencies yields performance comparable to that of a method that utilizes rich linguistic knowledge and external resources regarding subjectivity indicators.

Another interesting observation is that term-distribution information seems to be more effective for achieving high precision at the very top ranks (precision at 1, 2, 3, and 4), whereas in contrast, relatively deep NLP seems to be more effective at achieving high precision at the "lower" top ranks, as demonstrated by the results for precision at 5, 10, and the number of subjective documents, and for MAP. These results suggest that a combination of the two methods could produce even greater improvements.

4 Concluding remarks

We considered the task of document-level subjectivity re-ranking of search sets, a task modeling a scenario in which a search engine is queried to find reviews. We found that our proposed term-distributional, idiosyncrasy-based algorithm yielded the best precision for the very top ranks, whereas the more linguistically-oriented, knowledge-rich approach exemplified by OpinionFinder gave the best results for precision at lower ranks. It therefore seems that both types of information can be very valuable for the subjectivity re-ranking task, since they have somewhat complementary performance behaviors and both outperform the initial search engine and an adjective-based approach.

Our motivation that within a search set, reviews tend to resemble one another rather than differ is reminiscent of intuitions underlying the use of *pseudo relevance feedback (PF)* in IR (Ruthven and Lalmas, 2003, Section 3.5). Future work includes comparison against PF methods and investigation of ways to select the value of k.

Acknowledgments We thank Eli Barzilay, Rich Caruana, Thorsten Joachims, Jon Kleinberg, Ravi Kumar, and the reviewers for their very useful help. We are also very grateful to our annotators, Mohit Bansal, Eric Breck, Yejin Choi, Matt Connelly, Tom Finley, Effi Georgala, Asif-ul Haque, Kersing Huang, Evie Kleinberg, Art Munson, Ben Pu, Ari Rabkin, Benyah Shaparenko, Ves Stoyanov, and Yisong Yue. This paper is based upon work supported in part by the NSF under grant no. IIS-0329064, a Yahoo! Research Alliance gift, Google Anita Borg Memorial Scholarship funds, a Cornell Provost's Award for Distinguished Research, and an Alfred P. Sloan Research Fellowship. Any opinions, findings, and conclusions or recommendations expressed are those of the authors and do not necessarily reflect the views or official policies, either expressed or implied, of any sponsoring institutions, the U.S. government, or any other entity.

References

Allan, James, Margaret E. Connell, W. Bruce Croft, Fang-Fang Feng, David Fisher, and Xiaoyan Li. 2000. INQUERY and TREC-9. In *Proceedings of TREC*, pages 551–562. NIST Special Publication 500-249.

Hatzivassiloglou, Vasileios and Janyce Wiebe. 2000. Effects of adjective orientation and gradability on sentence subjectivity. In *Proceedings of COLING*.

Joachims, Thorsten, Laura Granka, Bing Pan, Helene Hembrooke, and Geri Gay. 2005. Accurately interpreting clickthrough data as implicit feedback. In *Proceedings of SIGIR*, pages 154–161.

Mishne, Gilad and Maarten de Rijke. 2006. A study of blog search. In *Proceedings of ECIR*.

Ounis, Iadh, Maarten de Rijke, Craig Macdonald, Gilad Mishne, and Ian Soboroff. 2006. Overview of the TREC-2006 Blog Track. In *Proceedings of TREC*.

Ounis, Iadh, Craig Macdonald, and Ian Soboroff. 2008. On the TREC Blog Track. In *Proceedings of ICWSM*.

Pang, Bo and Lillian Lee. 2008. *Opinion Mining and Sentiment Analysis*. Foundations and Trends in Information Retrieval series. Now publishers.

Riloff, Ellen and Janyce Wiebe. 2003. Learning extraction patterns for subjective expressions. In *Proceedings of EMNLP*.

Ruthven, Ian and Mounia Lalmas. 2003. A survey on the use of relevance feedback for information access systems. *Knowledge Engineering Review*, 18(2):95–145.

Wiebe, Janyce M. and Ellen Riloff. 2005. Creating subjective and objective sentence classifiers from unannotated texts. In *Proceedings of CICLing*, number 3406 in LNCS, pages 486–497.

Wiebe, Janyce M., Theresa Wilson, Rebecca Bruce, Matthew Bell, and Melanie Martin. 2004. Learning subjective language. *Computational Linguistics*, 30(3):277–308, September.

Generation under Space Constraints

Cécile Paris, Nathalie Colineau, Andrew Lampert
CSIRO – ICT Centre
Locked Bag 17
North Ryde, NSW 1670, Australia
FirstName.LastName@csiro.au

Joan Giralt Duran
Barcelona School of Informatics
Technical University of Catalonia
Barcelona, Spain
joangi@gmail.com

Abstract

Reasoning about how much to generate when space is limited is a challenge for generation systems. This paper presents two algorithms that exploit the discourse structure to decide which content to drop when there are space restrictions, in the context of producing documents from pre-authored text fragments. We analyse the effectiveness of both algorithms and show that the second is near optimal.

1 Introduction

Many organisations employ content management systems to store information, typically at the paragraph level. The use of such systems enables the application of NLG techniques without the cost of acquiring a knowledge base or forming text from first principles. But it brings its own challenge: how to produce a coherent and well structured text satisfying specific space requirements when a system has no control over the text at the sentence level?

The ability to reason about space constraints becomes more pressing as the amount of available information increases and delivery channels become more diverse in terms of space requirements (e.g., web browsers, email, PDAs).

We, as humans, address this problem by shortening our sentences or restricting the content we include. We achieve the former by manipulating vocabulary and syntax. This requires careful attention to the text at sentence level and often does not reclaim significant amount of space. We achieve the latter by dropping those pieces of content whose contribution to the communicative goal is most limited. This approach can reduce a text's length significantly but requires an understanding of the text's discourse structure.

© CSIRO 2008. Licensed under the *Creative Commons Attribution-Noncommercial-Share Alike 3.0 Unported* license (http://creativecommons.org/licenses/by-nc-sa/3.0/). Some rights reserved.

In our application domain, we answer people's information needs by retrieving content from a repository of pre-authored text fragments and delivering that content via a variety of media (e.g., web, paper, email), each with their own space constraints. In this paper, we show how we exploit the discourse structure to determine what should be realised to best fit some specific space. In particular, we present two algorithms that perform this reasoning and analyse their comparative performance.

2 Related Work

NLG systems have exploited the discourse structure for a number of tasks – e.g., to generate appropriate cue phrases (e.g., Scott and de Souza, 1990) or reason about layout (e.g., Bateman et al., 2001). Our system uses the discourse structure to reason about how much to realise to fit a specific space. It produces one discourse tree that is then realised for different delivery channels, each with its own space requirements.

Like other systems (e.g., Moore and Paris, 1993), our system specifies the RST relations (Mann and Thompson, 1988) that hold between text spans during discourse planning. It then exploits the RST principle of nuclearity to decide what to realise. The intuition is that nuclei are important while satellites can be dropped. This intuition has been exploited in some systems to produce summaries (e.g., Sparck-Jones, 1993; Marcu, 1998). Our purpose is different, however. We do not aim to produce a summary but a text that fits into some space requirements,

Figure 1. A brochure generated by our system

potentially only slightly shortening a text. Our task brings new challenges, e.g., filling the space optimally and producing a balanced text.

Our system exploits the notion that some relations are more important than others. O'Donnell (1997) used this principle to produce documents of variable length. In his approach, sentence fragments were manually marked up with RST and the text was manipulated at or below the sentence level. In our work, we cannot manipulate text at sentence level nor manually mark up the documents to be shortened.

3 Reasoning about Space Constraints

We focus on applications in which the generated text is delivered through several channels. One such application is SciFly, which produces tailored brochures about our organisation. Given a query from a user (topic(s) of interest), the system consults a staff directory and a repository of text fragments to gather relevant information. The fragments, written by our marketing team, are self contained and comprised of one or two paragraphs. SciFly integrates all the relevant information into a coherent whole (see Figure 1) using the meta-data describing each fragment's content. A text fragment can be used with different rhetorical relations in different brochures. The system produces a 2-page paper brochure, a web output, and a PDF version of the paper brochure is emailed to the user with a summary in the email body. All outputs are generated from the same discourse structure by our algorithm.

Our need to deliver the brochure via multiple channels led us to design algorithms that reason about the content to be expressed and the space available for each channel. The system follows a two-stage approach: during discourse planning, content and organisation are selected, and a discourse tree is built. The tree includes the top level communicative goal, intermediate goals and the rhetorical relations that exist between text spans, encoding both the purpose of each fragment and how they relate to each other. Then, at the presentation stage, the system reasons about this structure to decide what to realise when there is too much content for some channel.

We implemented and tested two algorithms for this reasoning. Both algorithms embody the principle of nuclearity and exploit the notion that some relations are more important than others. An importance value is assigned to relations based on their contribution to the communicative goal. Table 1 shows our assignments, which are based on judgments from our marketing staff.

To explain the algorithms, we represent the discourse tree using an abstract view, as shown in Figure 2. Each node is a communicative goal. White nodes indicate nuclei. Satellites are shaded in grey corresponding to the importance of the rhetorical relation linking them to the nucleus. The number inside each node is the approximate amount of content that node produces (in lines).

Shading	Discourse Relations	Importance
Black	Illustration, Background, Circumstance, Elaboration	Low Low-Medium
Dark Grey	Context, Motivation, Evidence, Summary , Justification,	Medium
Light Grey	Preparation, Enablement	Medium-High High

Table 1. Importance score for some relations[1]

Each node is the root of a subtree (empty if the node is a leaf) which generates some content. In both algorithms, the system computes for each node an *approximation* of the space required for that content in number of lines (an approximation as it depends on style, line-wrapping and other formatting attributes in the final output). This is computed bottom-up in an iterative manner by looking at the retrieved content at each node.

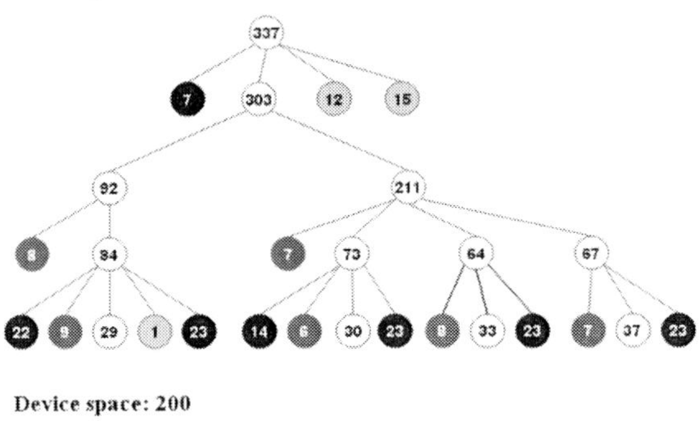

Figure 2. Discourse tree with space annotations

3.1 Simple Algorithm

The first algorithm is simple. It checks whether the top level node would result in too much content given the space requirements of the output channel (e.g., lines of content per page). If yes, the system traverses the tree, selects satellites with the lowest importance value and drops them with their sub-trees. The algorithm repeats this process until the total amount of content fits the required space. We deployed the SciFly system with this algorithm at a trade fair in 2005 and 2006 and measured the experience visitors had with the system. On average, people rated the system positively but noted that there was sometimes a lot of blank space in the brochures, when they felt that more information could have been included. This is because our simple algorithm drops many sub-trees at once, thus potentially deleting a lot of content in each step. This led us to our enhanced algorithm.

[1] In our system, we consider 5 levels of importance. We have merged levels here to avoid too many shades of grey.

3.2 Enhanced Algorithm

We redesigned the algorithm to take into account the depth of a node in addition to its rhetorical status. We assign each node a *weight,* computed by adding the weight of the node's parent and the *penalty score* of the rhetorical relation, which is (inversely) related to its importance score. Penalty scores range from 1 to 6, in increments of 1: A nucleus has a score of 1 to take the tree depth into account, high importance relations have a score of 2, and low importance relations have a score of 6. In a discourse tree, a child node is always *heavier* than its parent. The larger the weight, the less important the node is to the overall comunicative goal. The system orders the nodes by their weight, and the heaviest nodes are dropped first. Thus, nodes deeper in the tree and linked by discourse relations with lower importance get removed first. Nodes are dropped one by one, until the top level node has an amount of content that satisfies the space constraint. This provides finer control over the amount of realised content and avoids the limitation of the first algorithm.

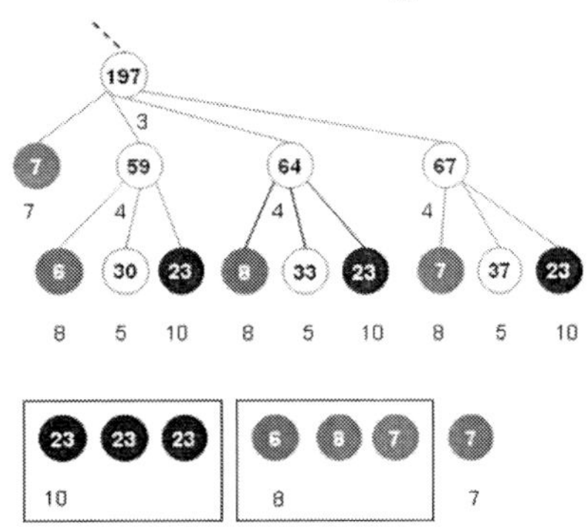

Figure 3. Ordered list of (satellite) cluster nodes

Sometimes, a discourse structure contains parallel sub-structures (e.g., bulletted points) that, if pruned unevenly, result in unbalanced text that seems odd. In such cases, the discourse structure typically contains several sub-trees with the same structure. In SciFly, such parallel structures occur when describing a list of projects. These are generated during discourse planning by a plan containing a *foreach* statement, e.g., *(foreach project in project-list (describe project))*. To address this situation, the system annotates all sub-structures issued from such a foreach statement. When constructing the ordered list of satellites, nodes at the same depth in the sub-structures are clustered together, as shown in Figure 3, taking into account their relationship to the nucleus. When dropping nodes, the whole cluster is deleted toegether, rather than node by node. So, in Figure 3, the whole cluster of weight 10 is dropped first, then the cluster of weight 8, etc. This prevents one sub-structure from being pruned more than its sibling structures and ensures the resulting brochure is balanced.

4 Evaluation

We evaluated the algorithms to assess their comparative effectiveness, based on a test set of 1507 automatically generated brochures about randomly selected topics. We observed that 82.5% of the brochures generated with the enhanced algorithm filled over 96% of the available space (leaving at most 8 lines of empty space), compared to 29% of brochures generated with the simple algorithm. In addition, 96.5% of the brochures generated with the new algorithm filled at least 90% of the space, compared with 44.5% of brochures with the simple algorithm.

We also found that 75% of brochures included more content using the enhanced algorithm (an average of 32 additional lines), but 12% of the brochures contained less content. We examined the latter in detail and found that, for these cases, the difference was on average 4 lines, and that the reduction was due to our treatment of parallel discourse structures, thus representing a desirable loss of content to create balanced brochures.

We also performed a user evaluation to verify that the improvement in space usage had not decreased users' satisfaction. We asked users to compare pairs of brochures (simple algorithm vs. enhanced algorithm), indicating their preference if any. Seventeen users participated in the evaluation and were presented with seven pairs of brochures. To control any order effect, the pairs were randomly presented from user to user, and, in each pair, each brochure was randomly assigned a left-right configuration. Participants mostly preferred the brochures from the enhanced algorithm, or found the brochures equivalent, thus showing that our more effective use of space had not decreased users' satisfaction.

Overall, our results show that our enhanced algorithm is close to optimal in terms of conveying a message appropriately while filling up the space and producing a coherent and balanced text.

5 Conclusions

Reasoning about how much to generate when space is limited presents an important challenge for generation systems. Most systems either control their generation process to avoid producing large amounts of text at the onset, or control the generation at the sentence level. In our application, we cannot resort to any of these approaches as we generate text reusing existing text fragments and need to produce one discourse tree with all the appropriate available content and then select what to realise to output on several delivery channels. To satisfy space constraints, we implemented and tested two algorithms that embody the notions of nuclearity and importance of information to decide which content to keep and which to withhold. Our approach produces documents that fill most of the available space while maintaining users' satisfaction.

Acknowledgements

We thank M. Raji for her work on the user experiment, the members of our group and K. Vander Linden for their input, and everyone who participated in our evaluation.

References

John Bateman, T. Kamps, K. K. Reichenberger, K. and J. Kleinz. 2001. Constructive text, diagram and layout generation for information presentation: the DArt_bio system. *Computational Linguistics*, 27 (3): 409–449.

William C. Mann and Sandra A. Thompson. 1988. Rhetorical Structure Theory: Toward a functional theory of text organisation. *Text* 8(3):243–281.

Daniel Marcu. 1998. To build text summaries of high quality, nuclearity is not sufficient. In *Working Notes of the AAAI-98 Spring Symposium on Intelligent Text Summarization,* Stanford, CA, 1–8.

Johanna D. Moore and Cécile L. Paris. 1993. Planning Text for Advisory Dialogues: Capturing Intentional and Rhetorical Information. *Computational Linguistics*, 19 (4):651–694, Cambridge, MA.

Donia R. Scott and Clarisse S. de Souza. 1990. Getting the message across in RST-based text generation. In Dale, Mellish & Zock (eds). *Current Research in NLG.* London: Academic Press. 119–128.

Mick O'Donnell (1997). Variable Length On-Line Document Generation. *Proceedings of EWNLG.* Gerhard-Mercator University, Duisburg, Germany.

Karen Spark Jones (1993). What might be in a summary? *Information Retrieval 93:* Von der Modellierung zur Anwendung. (Ed: Knorz, Krause and Womse-Hacker), Konstanz: Universitatsverlag Konstanz, 9–26.

A Language-Independent Approach to Keyphrase Extraction and Evaluation

Mari-Sanna Paukkeri, Ilari T. Nieminen, Matti Pöllä and Timo Honkela
Adaptive Informatics Research Centre, Helsinki University of Technology
first.last@tkk.fi

Abstract

We present *Likey*, a language-independent keyphrase extraction method based on statistical analysis and the use of a reference corpus. *Likey* has a very light-weight preprocessing phase and no parameters to be tuned. Thus, it is not restricted to any single language or language family. We test *Likey* having exactly the same configuration with 11 European languages. Furthermore, we present an automatic evaluation method based on Wikipedia intra-linking.

1 Introduction

Keyphrase generation is an approach to collect the main topics of a document into a list of phrases. The methods for automatic keyphrase generation can be divided into two groups: keyphrase assignment and keyphrase extraction (Frank et al., 1999). In keyphrase assignment, all potential keyphrases appear in a predefined vocabulary and the task is to classify documents to different keyphrase classes. In keyphrase extraction, keyphrases are supposed to be available in the processed documents themselves, and the aim is to extract these most meaningful words and phrases from the documents.

Most of the traditional methods for keyphrase extraction are highly dependent on the language used and the need for preprocessing is extensive, e.g. including part-of-speech tagging, stemming, and use of stop word lists and other language-dependent filters.

©2008. Licensed under the *Creative Commons Attribution-Noncommercial-Share Alike 3.0 Unported* license (http://creativecommons.org/licenses/by-nc-sa/3.0/). Some rights reserved.

1.1 Related Work

In the statistical keyphrase extraction, many variations for term frequency counts have been proposed in the literature including relative frequencies (Damerau, 1993), collection frequency (Hulth, 2003), term frequency–inverse document frequency (*tf.idf*) (Salton and Buckley, 1988), among others. Additional features to frequency that have been experimented are e.g. relative position of the first occurrence of the term (Frank et al., 1999), importance of the sentence in which the term occurs (HaCohen-Kerner, 2003), and widely studied part-of-speech tag patterns, e.g. Hulth (2003). Matsuo and Ishizuka (2004) present keyword extraction method using word co-occurrence statistical information. Most of the presented methods need a reference corpus or a training corpus to produce keyphrases. The reference corpus acts as a sample of general language, whereas the training corpus is used to tune the parameters of the system.

Statistical keyphrase extraction methods without reference corpora have also been proposed, e.g. (Matsuo and Ishizuka, 2004; Bracewell et al., 2005). The later study is carried out for bilingual corpus.

1.2 Reference Corpora

The reference corpus of natural language processing systems acts as a sample of general language. The corpus should be as large as possible to get sufficiently many examples of language use. In our study, we used the Europarl corpus that consists of transcriptions of European Parliament speeches in eleven European languages, including four Romance languages (Spanish, French, Italian and Portuguese), five Germanic languages

(Danish, German, English, Dutch and Swedish), Finnish and Greek (Koehn, 2005). The number of words in the corpora is between 23 million in Finnish and 38 million in French, while the number of word types differs from 98 thousand in English to 563 thousand in Finnish.

2 The *Likey* Method

We present a keyphrase extraction method *Likey* that is an extension of Damerau's method (Honkela et al., 2007). In Damerau's (1993) method, terms are ranked according to the likelihood ratio and the top m terms are used as index terms. Both single words and bigrams are considered to be terms. *Likey* produces keyphrases using relative ranks of n-gram frequencies. It is a simple language-independent method: The only language-specific component is a reference corpus in the corresponding language. *Likey* keyphrases may be single words as well as longer phrases.

The preprocessing phase of *Likey* consists of extraction of the main text body without captions of figures and tables, and removing special characters (except for some hyphens and commas). Numbers are replaced with <NUM> tags.

An integer rank value is assigned to each phrase according to its frequency of occurrence, where the most frequent phrase has rank value one and phrases with the same frequency are assigned the same rank. Rank values rank_a and rank_r are calculated from the text and the reference corpus, respectively, for each phrase. Rank order rank is calculated separately for each phrase length n. Thus we get ranks from unity to $\mathrm{max\_rank}$ for each n. This way n-gram frequencies for $n \geq 2$ are scaled to follow approximately the same distribution as 1-grams in the corpus. The ratio

$$\mathrm{ratio} = \frac{\mathrm{rank}_a}{\mathrm{rank}_r} \quad (1)$$

of ranks is used to compare the phrases.

In highly inflective languages, such as Finnish, and languages with frequent word concatenation, such as German, many of the phrases occurring in the analysed document do not occur in the reference corpus. Thus, their ratio value is related to the maximum rank value, according to Eq. 2,

$$\mathrm{ratio} = \frac{\mathrm{rank}_a}{\mathrm{max\_rank}_r + 1} \quad (2)$$

where $\mathrm{max\_rank}_r$ is the maximum rank in the reference corpus. The ratios are sorted in increasing order and the phrases with the lowest ratios are selected as the extracted keyphrases. Phrases occurring only once in the document cannot be selected as keyphrases.

3 Evaluation

The most straightforward way to evaluate the extracted keyphrases is to first decide which phrases are appropriate to the document and then calculate how many of the extracted keyphrases belong to the appropriate phrases set, e.g. by using precision and recall measures.

There are two widely used approaches for defining the appropriate phrases for a document. The first method is to use human evaluators for rating extracted keyphrases. The other approach is to analyse documents that have author-provided keyword lists. Each document has a list of keyphrases which are easy to accept to be correct. Anyway, automated keyphrase extraction methods are usually poor in predicting author-provided keyphrases since many of the provided phrases do not exist in the document at all but they are sort of superconcepts.

3.1 Multilingual Approach

In our framework, there are keyphrases in 11 languages to be evaluated. Due to many problems related to human evaluation in such a context, we needed a new way of evaluating the results of our language-independent keyphrase extraction method. We took our evaluation data from Wikipedia, a free multilingual online encyclopedia.[1] We present a novel way to use Wikipedia articles in evaluation of a multilingual keyphrase extraction method. Wikipedia corpus has lately been used as a resource for automatic keyword extraction for English (Mihalcea and Csomai, 2007) as well as to many other tasks.

We suppose that those articles which are linked from the article at hand and which link back to the article, are potential keyphrases of the article. For example, a Wikipedia article about some concept may link to its higher-level concept. Likewise, the higher-level concept may list all concepts including to the group.

3.2 Evaluation Data

Finding Wikipedia articles of adequate extent in all the languages is quite challenging, basically due

[1] http://wikipedia.org

to generally quite short articles in Greek, Finnish and Danish. We gathered 10 articles that have sufficient amount of content in each of the 11 Europarl languages. These 110 selected Wikipedia articles were collected in March 2008 and their English names are Beer, Cell (biology), Che Guevara, Leonardo da Vinci, Linux, Paul the Apostle, Sun, Thailand, Vietnam War, and Wolfgang Amadeus Mozart.

The average lengths of articles in Finnish, Dutch and Swedish are below 2 000 words, the lengths of articles in Portuguese, Greek and Danish are around 3 000 words and the rest are between 5 000 and 7 000 words. The normalised lengths would switch the order of the languages slightly.

Among the 67 links extracted from the English Wikipedia article *Cell* include phrases such as *adenosine triphosphate, amino acid, anabolism, archaea, bacteria, binary fission, cell division, cell envelope, cell membrane*, and *cell nucleus*. The extracted links serve as evaluation keyphrases for the article.

4 Results

In our study, we extracted keyphrases of length $n = 1 \ldots 4$ words. Longer phrases than four words did not occur in the keyphrase list in our preliminary tests. As a baseline, the state-of-the-art keyphrase extraction method *tf.idf* keyphrases were extracted from the same material. *Tf.idf* (Salton and Buckley, 1988) is another simple and non-parameterized language-independent method that can be used for keyphrase extraction. For *tf.idf* we split the Europarl reference corpora in 'documents' of 100 sentences and used the same preprocessing that for *Likey*. To remove uninteresting *tf.idf*-produced phrases like *of the cell*, a *Likey*-like post processing was tried, and it gave slightly better results. Thus the post processing is used for all the reported results of *tf.idf*.

Generally, *Likey* produces longer phrases than *tf.idf*. Each keyphrase list characterises the topic quite well, and most of the extracted keyphrases recur in every language. Both methods extracted a French word *re* that is frequently used in the article as an acronym for *réticulum endoplasmique*. The same word in Dutch is extracted by *tf.idf* in a form *endoplasmatisch reticulum er*.

We compared our *Likey* keyphrase extraction method to the baseline method *tf.idf* by calculating precision and recall measures according to the Wikipedia-based evaluation keyphrases for both methods. We extracted 60 keyphrases from each document for the first evaluation round and the number of keyphrases available in the evaluation keyphrase list for the document for the second evaluation round. Precision and recall values of both *Likey* and *tf.idf* evaluated with Wikipedia intra-links are comparatively low (Table 1) but one has to take into account the nature of the evaluation set with notably varying number of 'correct keyphrases'.

	60 keyphrases		*N* keyphrases	
Method	Prec.	Recall	Prec.	Recall
Likey	0.1475	0.2470	0.1795	0.1795
tf.idf	0.1225	0.2203	0.1375	0.1375
tf.idf + p	0.1343	0.2341	0.1622	0.1622

Table 1: Average precisions and recalls for *Likey*, *tf.idf* and *tf.idf* with post processing (p). *N* keyphrases refers to the amount of evaluation keyphrases available for each article.

The obtained precisions and recalls of the first evaluation differed significantly between languages. In Figure 1, the precision and recall of *Likey* and *tf.idf* with post processing for each language is given. Within the 11 European languages, English and German performed best according to the precision (*Likey:* 23.0% and 22.8%, respectively), but not that well according to the recall, where best performed Dutch and Greek (*Likey:* 33.4% and 31.8%, respectively).

5 Conclusions and Discussion

In this paper, we have introduced *Likey*, a statistical keyphrase extraction method that is able to analyse texts independently of the language in question. In the experiments, we have focused on European languages among which Greek and Finnish differ considerably from Romance and Germanic languages. Regardless of these differences, the method gave comparable results for each language.

The method enables independence from the language being analysed. It is possible to extract keyphrases from text in previously unknown language provided that a suitable reference corpus is available. The method includes only lightweight preprocessing, and no auxiliary language-dependent methods such as part-of-speech tagging are required. No particular param-

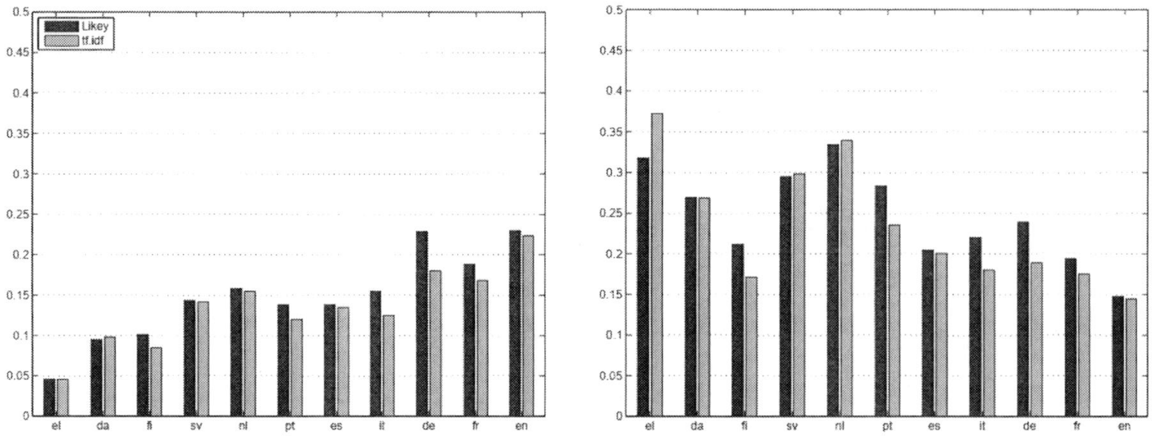

Figure 1: Average precisions (left-hand side) and recalls (right-hand side) of *Likey* and *tf.idf* with post processing for each language. The number of extracted keyphrases is 60.

eter tuning is needed either. A web-based demonstration of *Likey* is available at `http://cog.hut.fi/likeydemo/` as well as more detailed information on the method. The system highlights keyphrases of a document written in one of eleven languages.

Future research includes an extension of *Likey* in which unsupervised detection of morphologically motivated intra-word boundaries (Creutz, 2006) is used. This extension could also handle languages that have no white space between words. We also plan to apply the method within statistical machine translation. A methodological comparison of keyphrase-based dimension reduction and e.g. PCA will also be conducted.

Acknowledgements

This work was supported by the Academy of Finland through the Adaptive Informatics Research Centre that is a part of the Finnish Centre of Excellence Programme. We warmly thank Jaakko J. Väyrynen and Sami Hanhijärvi for their useful comments and ideas.

References

Bracewell, David B., Fuji Ren, and Shingo Kuriowa. 2005. Multilingual single document keyword extraction for information retrieval. In *Proceedings of NLP-KE'05*.

Creutz, Mathias. 2006. *Induction of the Morphology of Natural Language: Unsupervised Morpheme Segmentation with Application to Automatic Speech Recognition*. Ph.D. thesis, Helsinki University of Technology.

Damerau, Fred. 1993. Generating and evaluating domain-oriented multi-word terms from text. *Information Processing and Management*, 29(4):433–447.

Frank, Eibe, Gordon W. Paynter, Ian H. Witten, Carl Gutwin, and Craig G. Nevill-Manning. 1999. Domain-specific keyphrase extraction. In *Proceedings of IJCAI'99*, pages 668–673.

HaCohen-Kerner, Yaakov. 2003. Automatic extraction of keywords from abstracts. In Palade, V., R.J. Howlett, and L.C. Jain, editors, *KES 2003, LNAI 2773*, pages 843–849. Springer-Verlag.

Honkela, Timo, Matti Pöllä, Mari-Sanna Paukkeri, Ilari Nieminen, and Jaakko J. Väyrynen. 2007. Terminology extraction based on reference corpora. Technical Report E12, Helsinki University of Technology, Laboratory of Computer and Information Science, Espoo. Unpublished.

Hulth, Anette. 2003. Improved automatic keyword extraction given more linguistic knowledge. In *Proceedings of the Conference on Empirical Methods in Natural Language Processing*, pages 216–223.

Koehn, Philipp. 2005. Europarl: A parallel corpus for statistical machine translation. In *MT Summit 2005*.

Matsuo, Yutaka and Mitsuru Ishizuka. 2004. Keyword extraction from a single document using word co-occurrence statistical information. *Int'l Journal on Artificial Intelligence Tools*, 13(1):157–169.

Mihalcea, Rada and Andras Csomai. 2007. Wikify!: linking documents to encyclopedic knowledge. In *CIKM '07: Proceedings of the sixteenth ACM conference on Conference on information and knowledge management*, pages 233–242, New York, NY, USA. ACM.

Salton, G. and C. Buckley. 1988. Term weighting approaches in automatic text retrieval. *Information Processing and Management*, 24(5):513–523.

Easily Identifiable Discourse Relations

Emily Pitler, Mridhula Raghupathy, Hena Mehta, Ani Nenkova, Alan Lee, Aravind Joshi
University of Pennsylvania
3330 Walnut Street
Philadelphia, PA 19104

Abstract

We present a corpus study of local discourse relations based on the Penn Discourse Tree Bank, a large manually annotated corpus of explicitly or implicitly realized relations. We show that while there is a large degree of ambiguity in temporal explicit discourse connectives, overall connectives are mostly unambiguous and allow high-accuracy prediction of discourse relation type. We achieve 93.09% accuracy in classifying the explicit relations and 74.74% accuracy overall. In addition, we show that some pairs of relations occur together in text more often than expected by chance. This finding suggests that global sequence classification of the relations in text can lead to better results, especially for implicit relations.

1 Introduction

Discourse relations between textual units are considered key for the ability to properly interpret or produce discourse. Various theories of discourse have been developed (Moore and Wiemer-Hastings, 2003) and different relation taxonomies have been proposed (Hobbs, 1979; McKeown, 1985; Mann and Thompson, 1988; Knott and Sanders, 1998). Among the most cognitively salient relations are causal (contingency), contrast (comparison), and temporal.

Very often, the discourse relations are *explicit*, signaled directly by the use of appropriate discourse connectives:

© 2008. Licensed under the *Creative Commons Attribution-Noncommercial-Share Alike 3.0 Unported* license (http://creativecommons.org/licenses/by-nc-sa/3.0/). Some rights reserved.

(E1) He is very tired **because** he played tennis all morning.

(E2) He is not very strong, **but** he can run amazingly fast.

(E3) We had some tea in the afternoon and **later** went to a restaurant for a big dinner.

Discourse relations can also be *implicit*, inferred by the context of the utterance and general world knowledge.

(I1) I took my umbrella this morning. [**because**] The forecast was rain in the afternoon.

(I2) She is never late for meetings. [**but**] He always arrives 10 minutes late.

(I3) She woke up early. [**afterward**] She had breakfast and went for a walk in the park.

An additional complication for automatic classification of discourse relations is that even in the presence of an explicit discourse connective, the connective might be ambiguous between several senses. For example, *since* can be used to signal either a temporal or a contingency relation.

They have not spoken to each other **since** they argued last fall. (Temporal)

I assumed you were not coming **since** you never replied to the invitation. (Causal)

Several questions directly related to efforts in automatic recognition of discourse relations arise:

In a general text, what is the proportion of explicit versus implicit relations? Since implicit relations are presumably harder to recognize automatically, the larger their proportion, the more difficult the overall prediction of discourse relation will be.

How ambiguous are discourse connectives? The degree of ambiguity would give an upper bound on the accuracy with which explicit relations can be identified. The more ambiguous discourse connectives are, the more difficult it would be to automatically decide which discourse relation is expressed in a given sentence, even in the presence of a connective.

In a text, are adjacent discourse relations independent of each other or are certain sequences of relations more likely? In the latter case, a "discourse grammar" of text can be used and easy to identify relations such as unambiguous explicit relations can help determine the class of implicit relations that immediately follow or precede them.

In this study, we address the above questions using the largest existing corpus manually annotated with discourse relations—the Penn Discourse Tree Bank (Prasad et al., 2008).

2 The Penn Discourse Tree Bank

The Penn Discourse Treebank (PDTB) is a new resource (Prasad et al., 2008) of annotated discourse relations. The annotation covers the same 1 million word Wall Street Journal (WSJ) corpus used for the Penn Treebank (Marcus et al., 1994).

he PDTB is the first corpus to systematically identify and distinguish explicit and implicit discourse relations. By definition, an *explicit relation* is triggered by the presence of a discourse connective which occurs overtly in the text. The discourse connective can essentially be viewed as a discourse-level predicate which takes two clausal arguments. For example, sentence E1 above could be represented as BECAUSE("He is very tired", "he played tennis all morning"). The corpus recognizes 100 such explicit connectives and contains annotations for 19,458 explicit relations [1].

The PDTB also contains provisions for the annotation of *implicit discourse relations* between adjacent sentences which are inferred by the reader but are not overtly marked by a discourse connective. In this case, the annotator was asked to provide a connective that best captured the inferred relation. There are a total of 16,584 implicit relations annotated in the corpus. [2]

In addition to discourse relations and their arguments, the PDTB also provides the *senses* of each relation(Miltsakaki et al., 2008). The tagset of senses is organized hierarchically into three levels - class, type, and subtype. The top class level contains the four major semantic classes: Expansion, Comparison, Contingency and Temporal.

[1]The PDTB allows annotators to tag a relation with multiple senses. In this work we count both of the annotated senses. So even though there are only 18,459 explicit relations, there are 19,458 explicit senses.

[2]Again, because of multiple senses per relation, the 16,584 senses are part of 16,224 relations.

Class	Explicit (%)	Implicit (%)	Total
Comparison	5590 (69.05%)	2505 (30.95%)	8095
Contingency	3741 (46.75%)	4261 (53.25%)	8002
Temporal	3696 (79.55%)	950 (20.45%)	4646
Expansion	6431 (42.04%)	8868 (57.96%)	15299

Table 1: Discourse relation distribution in semantic and explicit/implicit classes in the PDTB

3 Distribution and ambiguity of connectives

Table 1 shows the distribution of discourse relations between the four main relation classes and their type of realization (implicit or explicit). Interestingly, temporal and comparison relations are predominantly explicit. About 80% and 70%, respectively, of their occurrences are marked by a discourse connective. The contingency relations are almost evenly distributed between explicit and implicit. The expansion relations, the overall largest class of discourse relations, is in most cases implicit and not marked by a discourse connective.

Given the figures in Table 1, we would expect that overall temporal and comparison relations will be more easily identified since they are overtly marked. Of course this would only be the case if discourse markers are mostly unambiguous.

Here we show all connectives that appear more than 50 times in the PDTB, their predominant sense (comparison, contingency, temporal or expansion), as well as the percentage of occurrences of the connective in its predominant sense. For example the connective *but* has *comparison* as its predominant sense and 97.19% of the 3,308 occurrences of this connective were comparisons.

Comparison *but* (3308; 97.19%), *while* (781; 66.07%), *however* (485; 99.59%), *although* (328; 99.70%), *though* (320; 100.00%), *still* (190; 98.42%), *yet* (101; 97.03%)

Expansion *and* (3000; 96.83%), *also* (1746; 99.94%), *for example* (196; 100.00%), *in addition* (165; 100.00%), *instead* (112; 97.32%), *indeed* (104; 95.19%), *moreover* (101; 100.00%), *for instance* (98, 100.00%), *or* (98; 96.94%), *unless* (95; 98.95%), *in fact* (82; 92.68%) *separately* (74; 100.00%)

Contingency *if* (1223; 95.99%), *because* (858, 100.00%), *so* (263; 100.00%), *since* (184; 52.17%), *thus* (112; 100.00%), *as a result* (78; 100.00%)

Temporal *when* (989; 80.18%), *as* (743; 70.26%), *after* (577; 99.65%), *then* (340; 93.24%), *before* (326; 100.00%), *meanwhile* (193; 48.70%), *until* (162; 87.04%), *later* (91; 98.90%), *once* (84; 95.24%)

The connectives that signal comparison and contingency are mostly unambiguous. Obvious exceptions are two of the connectives that are often used to signal temporal relations: *while* and *since*.

The predominant senses of these connectives are comparison (66.07%) and contingency (52.17%) respectively. Disambiguating these problematic connectives has already been addressed in previous work (Miltsakaki et al., 2005), but even the predominantly temporal connectives are rather ambiguous. For example less than 95% of the occurrances of *meanwhile, as, when, until,* and *then* are temporal relaions.

While some connectives such as "since" are ambiguous, most are not. The discourse connectives in the corpus appear in their predominant sense 93.43% (for comparsion), 94.72% (for contingency), 84.10% (for temporal), and 97.63% (for expansion) of the time. Temporal connectives are most ambiguous and connectives signaling expansion are least ambiguous.

4 Automatic classification

The analyses in the previous section show two very positive trends: many of the discourse relations are explicitly marked by the use of a discourse connective, especially comparison and temporal relations, and discourse connectives are overall mostly unambiguous. These facts would suggest that even based only on the connective, classification of discourse relations could be done well for all data (including both implicit and explicit examples) and particularly well for explicit examples alone. Indeed, Table 2 shows the performance of a decision tree classifier for discourse relations, on all data and on the explicit subset in the second and third column respectively.

We use the natural distribution of relation classes found in the Wall Street Journal texts, without downsampling to get balanced distribution of classes. There are four task settings, distinguishing each type of relation from all others. For example, comparison relations can be distinguished from all other relations in the corpus with overall accuracy of 91.28%, based only on the discourse connective (first line in Table 2). The recall for recognizing comparison relations is 0.66, directly reflecting the fact that 31% of all comparison relations are implicit (Table 1) and the connective feature did not help at all in those cases. Over explicit data only, the classification accuracy for comparison relation versus any other relation is 97.23%, and precision and recall is 0.95 and above.

As expected, the overall accuracy of identifying contingency and expansion relations is lower,

Task	All relations	Explicit relations only
Comparison	91.28% (76.54%)	97.23% (69.72%)
Contingency	84.44% (76.81%)	93.99% (79.73%)
Temporal	94.79% (86.54%)	95.4% (79.98%)
Expansion	77.51% (55.67%)	97.61% (65.16%)

Table 2: Decision tree classification accuracy using only the presence of connectives as binary features. The majority class is given in brackets.

Class	Precision	Recall
Temporal	0.841 [0.841]	0.729 [0.903]
Expansion	0.658 [0.973]	0.982 [0.957]
Contingency	0.948 [0.947]	0.369 [0.844]
Comparison	0.935 [0.935]	0.671 [0.971]

Table 3: Four-way classification. The first number is for all data, thesecond for explicit relations only.

84.44% and 77.51% on all data respectively, reflecting the fact that these relations are often implicit. But by themselves these accuracy numbers are actually reasonable, setting a rather high baseline for any more sophisticated method of classifying discourse relations. On explicit data only, the two-way classification accuracy for the four main types of relations is 94% and higher.

In four-way classification, disambiguating between the four main semantic types of discourse relations leads to 74.74% classification accuracy. The accuracy for four-way classification of explicit relations is 93.09%. The precision and recall for each class is shown in Table 4. The worst performance on the explicit portion of the data is the precision for temporal relations and the recall for contingency relations, both of which are 0.84.

5 N-gram discourse relation models

We have shown above that some relations, such as comparison, can be easily identified because they are often explicit and are expressed by an unambiguous connective. However, one must build a more subtle automatic classifier to find the implicit relations. We now look at the frequencies in which various relations are adjacent in the PDTB. Results from previous studies of discourse relations suggest that the *context* of a relation can be helpful in disambiguating the relation (Wellner et al., 2006). Here we identify specific dependencies that exist between sequences of relations.

We computed χ^2 statistics to test the independence of each pair of relations. The question is: do relations A and B occur adjacent to each other more than they would simply due to chance? The

First Relation	Second Relation	χ^2	p-value
E. Comparison	I. Contingency	20.1	.000007
E. Comparison	E. Comparison	17.4	.000030
E. Comparison	I. Expansion	9.91	.00161
I. Temporal	E. Temporal	9.42	.00214
I. Contingency	E. Contingency	9.29	.00230
I. Expansion	E. Expansion	6.34	.0118
E. Expansion	I. Expansion	5.50	.0191
I. Contingency	E. Comparison	4.95	.0260

Table 4: χ^2 results for pairs of relations

pairs of implicit and explicit relations which have significant associations with each other ($pval < 0.05$) are shown in Table 4. For example, explicit comparison and implicit contingency co-occur much more often than would be expected if they were independent. As explicit comparisons are generally fairly easy to identify, knowing that they tend to co-occur may be helpful when searching for implicit contingency relations in a text.

6 Conclusion

We have tried to summarize the difficulty of finding discourse relations using the Penn Discourse Treebank. We noted that explicit and implicit relations are approximately evenly distributed overall, making the task easier than many researchers have feared. We have found that some relations, such as temporal and comparison, are more likely to be explicit than implicit, making them relatively easier to find, while contingency and expansion are more often implicit. Among the discourse connectives, the majority are not very ambiguous between the different types of relations, with some notable exceptions such as *since* and *meanwhile*.

We have carried out a novel quantitative study of the patterns of dependencies between discourse relations. We found that while there does not appear to be a clear template for the sequence of relations, there are individual relation pairs that tend to co-occur. Specifically, we found that even though contingency relations are likely to be implicit and thus difficult to find, they are likely to be found near an explicit comparison. We plan to exploit these findings in future work, addressing discourse relation labeling in text as a sequence labeling problem and using the explicit cue words of surrounding relations as features for finding the "hidden" implicit relations.

7 Acknowledgments

This work was partially supported by an Integrative Graduate Education and Research Traineeship grant from National Science Foundation (NSF-IGERT 0504487) and by NSF Grant IIS -07-05671. We would like to thank Nikhil Dinesh for help with the PDTB, and Rashmi Prasad, Bonnie Webber and Eleni Miltsakaki for insightful discussions.

References

Hobbs, J. 1979. Coherence and coreference. *Cognitive Science*, 3:67–90.

Knott, A. and T. Sanders. 1998. The classification of coherence relations and their linguistic markers: An exploration of two languages. *Journal of Pragmatics*, 30(2):135–175.

Mann, W. and S. Thompson. 1988. Rhetorical structure theory: Toward a functional theory of text organization. *Text*, 8:243–281.

Marcus, M.P., B. Santorini, and M.A. Marcinkiewicz. 1994. Building a Large Annotated Corpus of English: The Penn Treebank. *Computational Linguistics*, 19(2):313–330.

McKeown, Kathleen R. 1985. *Text generation: using discourse strategies and focus constraints to generate natural language text.* Cambridge University Press, New York, NY, USA.

Miltsakaki, E., N. Dinesh, R. Prasad, A. Joshi, and B. Webber. 2005. Experiments on sense annotations and sense disambiguation of discourse connectives. In *Proceedings of the Fourth Workshop on Treebanks and Linguistic Theories (TLT2005).*

Miltsakaki, Eleni, Livio Robaldo, Alan Lee, and Aravind Joshi. 2008. Sense annotation in the penn discourse treebank. *Computational Linguistics and Intelligent Text Processing, Lecture Notes in Computer Science*, 4919:275–286.

Moore, J. and P. Wiemer-Hastings. 2003. Discourse in computational linguistics and artificial intelligence.

Prasad, R., N. Dinesh, A. Lee, E. Miltsakaki, L. Robaldo, A. Joshi, and B. Webber. 2008. The penn discourse treebank 2.0. In *Proceedings of the 6th International Conference on Language Resources and Evaluation (LREC).*

Wellner, B., J. Pustejovsky, C. Havasi, R. Sauri, and A. Rumshisky. 2006. Classification of discourse coherence relations: An exploratory study using multiple knowledge sources. In *Proceedings of the 7th SIGDIAL Workshop on Discourse and Dialogue.*

Rank Distance as a Stylistic Similarity

Marius Popescu
University of Bucharest
Department of Computer Science
Academiei 14, Bucharest, Romania
mpopescu@phobos.cs.unibuc.ro

Liviu P. Dinu
University of Bucharest
Department of Computer Science
Academiei 14, Bucharest, Romania
ldinu@funinf.cs.unibuc.ro

Abstract

In this paper we propose a new distance function (rank distance) designed to reflect stylistic similarity between texts. To assess the ability of this distance measure to capture stylistic similarity between texts, we tested it in two different machine learning settings: clustering and binary classification.

1 Introduction

Computational stylistics investigates texts from the standpoint of individual style (author identification) or functional style (genres, registers). Because in all computational stylistic studies / approaches, a process of comparison of two or more texts is involved, in a way or another, there was always a need for a distance function to measure similarity (more precisely dissimilarity) of texts from the stylistic point of view. Such distance measures were proposed and used for example in authorship identification (Labbé and Labbé, 2001; Burrows, 2002) or clustering texts by genre (Luyckx et al., 2006).

In this paper we propose a new distance measure designed to reflect stylistic similarity between texts. As style markers we used the function word frequencies. Function words are generally considered good indicators of style because their use is very unlikely to be under the conscious control of the author and because of their psychological and cognitive role (Chung and Pennebaker, 2007). Also function words prove to be very effective in many author attribution studies. The novelty of our approach resides in the way we use information given by the function word frequencies. Given a fixed set of function words (usually the most frequent ones), a ranking of these function words according to their frequencies is built for each text; the obtained ranked lists are subsequently used to compute the distance between two texts. To calculate the distance between two rankings we used *Rank distance* (Dinu, 2003), an ordinal distance tightly related to the so-called *Spearman's footrule* (Diaconis and Graham, 1977).

Usage of the ranking of function words in the calculation of the distance instead of the actual values of the frequencies may seem as a loss of information, but we consider that the process of ranking makes the distance measure more robust acting as a filter, eliminating the *noise* contained in the values of the frequencies. The fact that a specific function word has the rank 2 (is the second most frequent word) in one text and has the rank 4 (is the fourth most frequent word) in another text can be more relevant than the fact that the respective word appears 349 times in the first text and only 299 times in the second.

To assess the ability of this distance function to capture stylistic similarity between texts, we tested it in two different machine learning settings: clustering and binary classification.

Compared with other machine learning and statistical approaches, clustering was relatively rarely used in stylistic investigations. However, few researchers (Labbé and Labbé, 2001; Luyckx et al., 2006) have recently proved that clustering can be a useful tool in computational stylistic studies. Apart of this, clustering is a very good test bed for a distance measure behavior. We plugged our distance function into a standard hierarchical clustering algorithm and test it on a collection of 21 nine-

©2008. Licensed under the *Creative Commons Attribution-Noncommercial-Share Alike 3.0 Unported* license (http://creativecommons.org/licenses/by-nc-sa/3.0/). Some rights reserved.

teenth century English books (Koppel et al., 2007). The results are very encouraging. The family trees produced grouped together texts according to their author, genre, even gender.

Also a distance measure can be used to solve classification problems if it is coupled with proper learning algorithm. One of the simplest such algorithms is nearest neighbor classification algorithm. We chose nearest neighbor algorithm because its performance is entirely based on the appropriateness to the data of the distance function on which it relies. In this way the accuracy of the classification will reflect the adequacy of the distance measure to data and domain on which the method was applied. We used the new distance function in conjunction with nearest neighbor classification algorithm and tested it on the well known case of authorship of disputed Federalist papers. The method attributed all disputed papers to Madison, the result being consistent with that of Mosteller and Wallace.

To check if the usage of ranks of function words is better suited for capturing stylistic differences than the usage of actual frequencies of the function words, we repeated the above experiments on clustering and binary classification with the standard euclidean distance between the vectors of frequencies of the same function words that were used in computing the rank distance. The comparison is in favor of rank distance.

2 Rank Distance and Its Use as a Stylistic Distance Between Texts

Rank distance (Dinu, 2003) is an ordinal metric able to compare different rankings of a set of objects. It is tightly related to the Spearman's footrule (Diaconis and Graham, 1977), and it had already been successfully used in computational linguistics, in such problems as the similarity of Romance languages (Dinu and Dinu, 2005).

A ranking of a set of n objects can be represented as a permutation of the integers $1, 2, \ldots, n$, $\sigma \in S_n$. $\sigma(i)$ will represent the place (rank) of the object i in the ranking. The Rank distance in this case is simply the distance induced by L_1 norm:

$$D(\sigma_1, \sigma_2) = \sum_{i=1}^{n} |\sigma_1(i) - \sigma_2(i)| \qquad (1)$$

This is a distance between what is called full rankings. However, in real situations, the problem of *tying* arises, when two or more objects claim the same rank (are ranked equally). For example, two or more function words can have the same frequency in a text and any ordering of them would be arbitrary.

a	been	had	its	one	that	was
all	but	has	may	only	the	were
also	by	have	more	or	their	what
an	can	her	must	our	then	when
and	do	his	my	shall	there	which
any	down	if	no	should	things	who
are	even	in	not	so	this	will
as	every	into	now	some	to	with
at	for	is	of	such	up	would
be	from	it	on	than	upon	your

Table 1: Function words used in computing the distance

The Rank distance allocates to tied objects a number which is the average of the ranks the tied objects share. For instance, if two objects claim the rank 2, then they will share the ranks 2 and 3 and both will receive the rank number $(2+3)/2 = 2.5$. In general, if k objects will claim the same rank and the first x ranks are already used by other objects, then they will share the ranks $x+1, x+2, \ldots, x+k$ and all of them will receive as rank the number: $\frac{(x+1)+(x+2)+\ldots+(x+k)}{k} = x + \frac{k+1}{2}$. In this case, a ranking will be no longer a permutation ($\sigma(i)$ can be a non integer value), but the formula (1) will remain a distance (Dinu, 2003).

Rank distance can be used as a stylistic distance between texts in the following way:

First a set of function word must be fixed. The most frequent function words may be selected or other criteria may be used for selection. In all our experiments we used the set of 70 function words identified by Mosteller and Wallace (Mosteller and Wallace, 1964) as good candidates for author-attribution studies. The set is given in Table 1.

Once the set of function words is established, for each text a ranking of these function words is computed. The ranking is done according to the function word frequencies in the text. Rank 1 will be assigned to the most frequent function word, rank 2 will be assigned to the second most frequent function word, and so on. The ties are resolved as we discussed above. If some function words from the set don't appear in the text, they will share the last places (ranks) of the ranking.

The distance between two texts will be the Rank distance between the two rankings of the function words corresponding to the respective texts.

3 Clustering Experiments

One good way to test the virtues of a distance measure is to use it as a base for a hierarchical cluster-

Group	Author	Book
American Novelists	Hawthorne	Dr. Grimshawe's Secret
		House of Seven Gables
	Melville	Redburn
		Moby Dick
	Cooper	The Last of the Mohicans
		The Spy
		Water Witch
American Essayists	Thoreau	Walden
		A Week on Concord
	Emerson	Conduct Of Life
		English Traits
British Playwrights	Shaw	Pygmalion
		Misalliance
		Getting Married
	Wilde	An Ideal Husband
		Woman of No Importance
Bronte Sisters	Anne	Agnes Grey
		Tenant Of Wildfell Hall
	Charlotte	The Professor
		Jane Eyre
	Emily	Wuthering Heights

Table 2: The list of books used in the experiment

ing algorithm. The family trees (dendogram) thus obtained can reveal a lot about the distance measure behavior.

In our experiments we used an agglomerative hierarchical clustering algorithm (Duda et al., 2001) with average linkage.

In the first experiment we cluster a collection of 21 nineteenth century English books written by 10 different authors and spanning a variety of genres (Table 2). The books were used by Koppel et al. (Koppel et al., 2007) in their authorship verification experiments.

The resulted dendogram is shown in Figure 1. As can be seen, the family tree produced is a very good one, accurately reflecting the stylistic relations between books. The books were grouped in three big clusters (the first three branches of the tree) corresponding to the three genre: dramas (lower branch), essays (middle branch) and novels (upper branch). Inside each branch the works were first clustered according to their author. The only exceptions are the two essays of Emerson which instead of being first cluster together and after that merged in the cluster of essays, they were added one by one to this cluster. Apart of this, the family tree is perfect. Even more, in the cluster of novels one may distinguished two branches clearly separated that can correspond to the gender or nationality of the authors: female English (lower part) and male American (upper part).

For comparison, the dendogram in Figure 2 show the same books clustered with the same algorithm, but using the standard euclidean distance instead of the rank distance as measure of stylistic similarity. The same set of function words as in the case of rank distance was used. This time though, each text was represented as a vector of

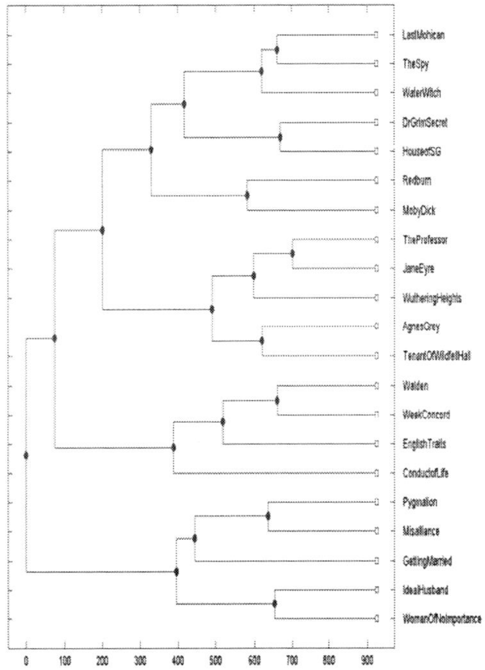

Figure 1: Dendogram of 21 nineteenth century English books (Rank Distance)

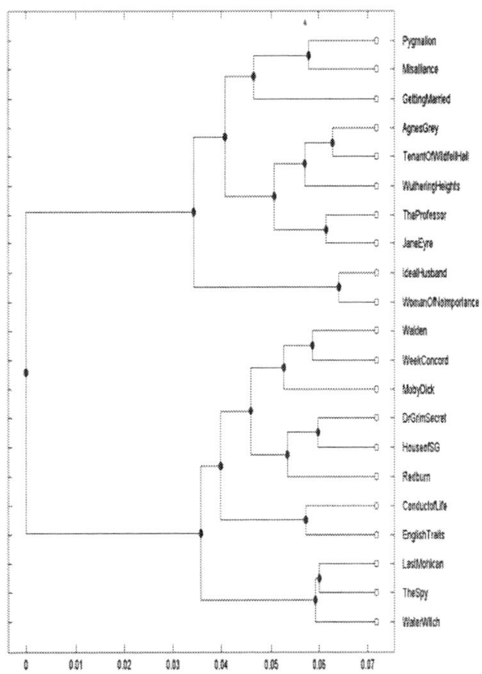

Figure 2: Dendogram of 21 nineteenth century English books (Euclidean Distance)

relative frequencies of these function words in the text. The relative frequency of a particular function word in a text is calculated as the number of appearances of the respective function word in the text divided by the length (in tokens) of the text. The distance between two texts is given by the euclidean distance between the corresponding vectors of relative frequencies of function words. In the family tree obtained using euclidean distance, most of the books are still grouped according to their author, but the distinct clusters corresponding to genre and gender disappeared and the novels of Melville were separated: one being clustered with the essays of Thoreau (Moby Dick) and the other with the novels of Hawthorne.

4 Binary Classification Experiments

When a distance measure is available, the most natural choice of a classification algorithm is the nearest neighbor algorithm (Duda et al., 2001).

We tested the nearest neighbor classification algorithm combined with both rank distance and euclidean distance on the case of the 12 disputed federalist papers (Mosteller and Wallace, 1964). In our experiments we followed the Mosteller and Wallace setting, treating the problem as a binary classification problem. Each one of the 12 disputed papers has to be classified as being written by Hamilton or Madison. For training are used the 51 papers written by Hamilton and the 14 papers written by Madison.

Tested on disputed papers, the nearest neighbor classification algorithm combined with rank distance attributed all the 12 papers to Madison. This matches the results obtained by Mosteller and Wallace and is in agreement with today accepted thesis that the disputed papers belong to Madison. When the nearest neighbor classification algorithm was combined with euclidean distance only 11 papers were attributed to Madison, the paper 56 was attributed to Hamilton.

5 Discussion

In this paper we have proposed a new distance measure based on the ranking of function words, designed to capture stylistic similarity between texts. We have tested it in two different machine learning settings: clustering and binary classification; we have compared its performance with that of standard euclidean distance on vectors of frequencies of the function words. Though testing on more data is needed, the initial experiments shown that the new distance measure is indeed a good indicator of stylistic similarity and better suited for capturing stylistic differences between texts than the standard euclidean distance.

In future work it would be useful to test this distance measure on other data sets and especially in other machine learning paradigms like one-class classification to solve authorship verification problems (Koppel et al., 2007).

Acknowledgments Research supported by MEdC-ANCS, PNII-Idei, project 228 and University of Bucharest.

References

Burrows, John. 2002. 'delta': a measure of stylistic difference and a guide to likely authorship. *Literary and Linguistic Computing*, 17(3):267–287.

Chung, Cindy K. and James W. Pennebaker. 2007. The psychological function of function words. In Fiedler, K., editor, *Social communication: Frontiers of social psychology*, pages 343–359. Psychology Press, New York.

Diaconis, P. and R.L. Graham. 1977. Spearman's footrule as a measure of disarray. *Journal of the Royal Statistical Society, Series B (Methodological)*, 39(2):262–268.

Dinu, Anca and Liviu Petrisor Dinu. 2005. On the syllabic similarities of romance languages. In *CICLing-2005*, pages 785–788.

Dinu, Liviu Petrisor. 2003. On the classification and aggregation of hierarchies with different constitutive elements. *Fundamenta Informaticae*, 55(1):39–50.

Duda, R. O., P. E. Hart, and D. G. Stork. 2001. *Pattern Classification (2nd ed.)*. Wiley-Interscience Publication.

Koppel, Moshe, Jonathan Schler, and Elisheva Bonchek-Dokow. 2007. Measuring differentiability: Unmasking pseudonymous authors. *Journal of Machine Learning Research*, 8:1261–1276.

Labbé, Cyril and Dominique Labbé. 2001. Intertextual distance and authorship attribution corneille and moliere. *Journal of Quantitative Linguistics*, 8(3):213–231.

Luyckx, Kim, Walter Daelemans, and Edward Vanhoutte. 2006. Stylogenetics: Clustering-based stylistic analysis of literary corpora. In *Proceedings of LREC-2006, the fifth International Language Resources and Evaluation Conference*, pages 30–35.

Mosteller, Frederick and David L. Wallace. 1964. *Inference and Disputed Authorship: The Federalist*. Addison-Wesley, Massachusetts.

Integrating Motion Predicate Classes with Spatial and Temporal Annotations

James Pustejovsky
Computer Science Department
Brandeis University
jamesp@cs.brandeis.edu

Jessica L. Moszkowicz
Computer Science Department
Brandeis University
jlittman@cs.brandeis.edu

Abstract

We propose a spatio-temporal markup for the annotation of motion predicates in text, informed by a lexical semantic classification of these verbs. We incorporate this classification within a spatial event structure, based on Generative Lexicon Theory. We discuss how the spatial event structure suggests changes to annotation systems designed solely for temporal or spatial phenomena, resulting in spatio-temporal annotation.

1 Introduction and Motivation

The recognition of spatial entities in natural language is an important component of understanding a text (Mani et al., 2008). However, simply identifying fixed geospatial regions and specific "facilities" is not enough to achieve a complete representation of all the spatial phenomena present. In fact, this leaves out one of the most crucial aspects of spatial information, motion. To capture motion, we must integrate temporal and spatial information with the lexical semantics of motion predicates and prepositions.

The goal of this research is to further the representational support for spatio-temporal reasoning from natural language text in the service of practical applications. To create such support, we propose to use lexical resources for motion predicates to integrate two existing annotation schemes, SpatialML and TimeML, creating a representation that captures, in a fine-grained manner, the movement of individuals through spatial and temporal indexes. This work is part of a larger effort to automate such annotation and reasoning over natural language documents using symbolic and machine learning methods.

In this paper, we investigate different resources and annotations for spatio-temporal information. In section 2, we describe some of the resources we employed for our investigation. Section 3 elaborates on the classes we focus on as we work towards developing a classification for the purpose of annotating motion predicates, which we discuss in section 4.

2 Previous Work on Motion Classifications in Language

There has been considerable research on the linguistic behavior of spatial predicates and prepositions in language (e.g., (Jackendoff, 1983), (Herskovits, 1986), (Boas, 2001), (Cappelle and Declerck, 2005)). Within qualitative spatial reasoning (QSR), work has recently started to focus on incorporating mereo-topological concepts into the calculus of relations between regions. The most successful of these is the Regional Connection Calculus, or RCC (Randell et al., 1992). RCC8 and other systems like it do an adequate job of representing static information about space, but they cannot help us deal with motion, since that task requires a temporal component. Galton ((Galton, 1993; Galton, 1997)) began work on a commonsense theory of motion, but this work did not focus on merging temporal and spatial phenomena. Muller (Muller, 1998), however, proposes just such a system with his qualitative theory of motion based on spatio-temporal primitives. The result of Muller's system is a set of six motion classes: *leave*, *hit*, *reach*, *external*, *internal*, and *cross*.

Asher and Sablayrolles offer their own account

© 2008. Licensed under the *Creative Commons Attribution-Noncommercial-Share Alike 3.0 Unported* license (http://creativecommons.org/licenses/by-nc-sa/3.0/). Some rights reserved.

of motion verbs and spatial prepositional phrases in French (Asher and Sablayrolles, 1995). They propose ten groups of motion verbs as follows: *s'approcher* (to approach), *arriver* (to arrive), *entrer* (to enter), *se poser* (to alight), *s'éloigner* (to distance oneself from), *partir* (to leave), *sortir* (to go out), *décoller* (to take off), *passer (par)* (to go through), *dévier* (to deviate). This verb classification is more fine-grained than Muller's.

While Muller, Asher, Sablayrolles, and Vieu among others have focused on the formal semantics of motion, other work has been done to represent motion in the FrameNet (Baker et al., 1998) and VerbNet (Kipper et al., 2006) projects. The Motion frame is a high level frame in the FrameNet hierarchy. It is defined as "Some entity (Theme) starts out in one place (Source) and ends up in some other place (Goal), having covered some space between the two (Path)."

To explore VerbNet's take on motion predicates, we mapped Asher and Sablayrolles' verbs to VerbNet classes. The mapping revealed that, while many of the motion predicates we care about have specific classes in VerbNet, it is not always clear what these classes have in common unless we look to FrameNet to find a higher level representation.

3 Classifying spatio-temporal predicates

Following (Muller, 1998), (Vieu, 1991), and (Asher and Sablayrolles, 1995), we assume spatial variables are incorporated into the representation of motion predicates in language. For this paper, we generally follow (Muller, 2002) by representing the individuals participating in spatial relations as spatio-temporal regions ($s{\cdot}i$). For modeling motion, however, we restrict our discussion to spatio-temporal regions occupied by physical matter denoted by the type $s \cdot i \cdot p$.

For this work, we performed several mappings between Muller, Asher and Sablayrolles, and FrameNet. The result of this mapping was a group of classes based largely on Muller's classifications with some very slight modifications detailed in the table below. The spatial event structures for each of these classes will describe their formal semantics (as in Figure 1 below).

In addition to these classes, we model the spatial semantics of prepositions, following (Asher and Sablayrolles, 1995), generally. Because of space limitations, we will not discuss the contritbution of prepositional semantics in this paper.

Move	run, fly, drive
Move_External	drive around, pass
Move_Internal	walk around the room
Leave	leave, desert
Reach	arrive, enter, reach
Detach	take off, disconnect, pull away
Hit	land, hit
Follow	follow, chase
Deviate	flee, run from
Stay	remain, stay

Table 1: Motion Classes

There is a complex interaction between a motion verb class and the interpretation of its arguments. For example, not all regions are occupied by the extent of physical matter (see above), but there are some objects which are properly both physical and spatial, such as the concept *building*. Notice the ambiguity inherent in the statement below, where both **Move_Internal** and **Move_External** are possible interpretations.

(1) The man walked around the building.

This is due to the semantic nature of *building* as both a physical object with extent, and also as a volume/aperture.

To model the mapping of objects to specific argument and event structures, we adopt the framework of Generative Lexicon Theory (GL). The notion of "polarity" in the (Muller, 1998) sense is quite similar to the semantic effect brought about by event headedness in (Pustejovsky, 1995). GL provides an explicitly typed argument structure, a typed subeventual structure, and a predicative body, which we will use to express RCC8 relations. For example, a representation of the Spatial Event Structure (SES) for the motion predicate *leave* is illustrated below in Figure 1. Note that the statement *Polarity=initial* is equivalent to saying *Head=left*. The relation BT is shorthand for boundary transition, which is composed of the following RCC8 relations: TPP, O, and EC.

Each motion class in Table 1 maps to a unique predicative body (qualia structure) in the spatial event structure for a verb. We demonstrate below how these representations are then embedded in the annotation of a text as RCC8 relations in a modified SpatialML/TimeML format, called Spatio-temporal Markup (STM).

The robustness of the mapping from the motion classes in Table 1 to FrameNet is currently being

$$
\begin{bmatrix}
\textbf{leave} & \\
\text{ARGSTR} = & \begin{bmatrix} \text{ARG1} = x\text{:}\ s \cdot i \cdot p \\ \text{ARG2} = y\text{:}\ s \cdot i \end{bmatrix} \\
\text{EVENTSTR} = & \begin{bmatrix} \text{E}_1 = \mathbf{e_1\text{:}process} \\ \text{E}_2 = \mathbf{e_2\text{:}state} \\ \text{RESTR} = <_{\propto} \\ \text{POLARITY} = \textbf{initial} \end{bmatrix} \\
\text{QUALIA} = & \begin{bmatrix} \text{AGENTIVE} = \mathbf{NTTP(e_1,x,y)} \\ \wedge\ \mathbf{BT(e_1,x,y)} \\ \text{FORMAL} = \mathbf{DC(e_2,x,y)} \end{bmatrix}
\end{bmatrix}
$$

Figure 1: Spatial Event Structure

tested and evaluated.

4 Spatio-temporal Annotation

Throughout the development of the classification described here, we have tried to focus on how the classification will impact the task of annotating spatio-temporal information in text. There are currently two distinct annotation schemes for spatial and temporal information. If we are to successfully capture motion phenomena in text, these annotations must be merged just as a topological base and a temporal calculus need to be combined to model motion predicates.

TimeML (Pustejovsky et al., 2003) is an annotation scheme for representing temporal information in text. The basic elements of a TimeML annotation are temporal expressions such as dates, times, and durations, and events that can be anchored or ordered to those expressions or with respect to each other.

For the annotation of spatial information, SpatialML (MITRE, 2007) is being developed. The focus of SpatialML is the markup of spatial locations that can be integrated with additional resources such as databases that provide information about a given domain (e.g. physical feature databases, gazetteers).

While SpatialML does a reasonable job of capturing locations in space, it cannot model moving objects such as people and cars, and in fact lacks a mechanism for capturing motion since predicates are not annotated. As we saw above, the motion event must be captured in addition to the locations involved in the motion. The development of our motion classification also reveals that the participants of the event are also needed, even if they are not spatial locations. For example, in *John flew to Boston*, *John* must be included in the motion annotation because he is a moving object.

We can enhance the spatio-temporal information from SpatialML and TimeML with lexical semantic information from a lexicon of motion predicates, resulting in annotation that is rich enough to be able to (1) infer motion of individuals invovled in specific events; and (2) to compose motions to create motion sequences (cf. (Pustejovsky and Verhagen, 2007)).

To create a spatio-temporal markup, TimeML and SpatialML must be enriched so that they can adequately capture the motion predicates we are discussing. TimeML will already annotate motion predicates as events, but to truly reveal the motion involved, additional attributes must be added to account for the beginning, middle, and end points of the event. The spatio-temporal annotation will require a new kind of spatial link to capture motion paths. Essentially, the motion path will combine the event information from TimeML with the spatial information from SpatialML. This motion path is at the core of a spatio-temporal markup or STM. The spatial event structure described in the previous section motivates the construction of the STM.

The concept of polarity or headedness will also motivate some aspects of the annotation. Depending on the polarity of the motion predicate or spatial prepositional phrase, the annotator will know to look for the source or goal of the event in the text and include that in the motion path.

The exact details of the resulting spatio-temporal markup are still under development. However, the following examples give an idea of how motion class information allow us to integrate spatial and temporal annotation.

(2) *John drove from Boston to NY on Thursday.*

```
<MOVER id=0>John</MOVER>
<EVENT id=1 tense=past start=t1 end=t2>drove</EVENT>
<SIGNAL id=2 type=spatial polarity=initial>from</SIGNAL>
<PLACE id=3>Boston</PLACE>
<SIGNAL id=4 type=spatial polarity=final>to</SIGNAL>
<PLACE id=5>New York</PLACE>
<SIGNAL id=6 type=temporal>on</SIGNAL>
<TIMEX3 id=7>Thursday</TIMEX3>
<TLINK eventID=1 timeID=7 relType=INCLUDES
   signalID=6 />
<MOTION eventID=1 moverID=0 source=3
   sourceTime=t1 sourceSignal=2 goal=5
   goalTime=t2 goalSignal=4 class=MOVE/>
```

(3) *John left Boston for New York.*

```
<MOVER id=0>John</MOVER>
<EVENT id=1 tense=past start=t1 end=t2
   polarity=intitial>left</EVENT>
<PLACE id=2>Boston</PLACE>
<SIGNAL id=3 type=spatial
   polarity=final>for</SIGNAL>
<PLACE id=4>New York</PLACE>
<MOTION eventID=1 moverID=0 source=2 sourceTime=t1
   goal=4 goalTime=t2 goalSignal=3 class=LEAVE/>
```

The `Motion` tag in the above examples tells us the class of the motion predicate. This provides a link to both the spatial event structure (as in Figure 1) and a spatio-temporal markup, which embeds the annotaton of a text as RCC8 relations in a modified SpatialML/TimeML format. The example in 4 shows the STM for *leave*:

$$(4)\quad \begin{bmatrix} \textbf{motion} \\ \text{TYPE} = \textbf{leave} \\ \text{EVENTID} = \textbf{e} \\ \text{MOVERID} = \textbf{x} \\ \text{SOURCE} = \mathbf{l_1} \\ \text{SOURCETIME} = \mathbf{t_1} \\ \text{GOAL} = \mathbf{l_2} \\ \text{GOALTIME} = \mathbf{t_2} \end{bmatrix} \Longrightarrow \begin{bmatrix} IN(t_1, x, l_1) \\ IN(t_2, x, l_2) \\ DC(t_2, x, l_1) \end{bmatrix}$$

This STM indicates what additional information is needed for the spatio-temporal annotation. In the case of example 3, three temporally anchored SpatialML `link` tags are indiated for each of the RCC8-like relations to the second part of the STM:

(5)
```
<LINK linkType=IN source=0 target=2 time=t1/>
<LINK linkType=DC source=0 target=2 time=t2/>
<LINK linkType=IN source=0 target=4 time=t2/>
```

These links that can be automatically generated at a later stage in the annotation set up the locations of moving objects at given times. The first link in example 5 reveals that the moving object *John* was in *Boston* at time *t1*, which is the start time of the motion given in the annotation.

5 Conclusion

In this paper, we investigate how an expressive classification for verbs of motion can be used to integrate spatial and temporal annotation information, in order to represent objects in motion, as expressed in text. We adopt a modified version of the classifications of verbs of motion in (Muller, 1998) and (Asher and Sablayrolles, 1995) and demonstrated how verb classes are mapped to RCC8+1 relations in a temporally anchored SpatialML. We are currently evaluating the reliability of the FrameNet encoding of motion predicates, and are developing algorithms for translating lexical structures to Spatio-temporal markup.

References

Asher, N. and P. Sablayrolles. 1995. A typology and discourse for motion verbs and spatial pps in french. *Journal of Semantics*, 12:163–209.

Baker, C., C. Fillmore, and J. Lowe. 1998. The berkeley framennet project. In *Proceedings of the COLING_ACL*, Montreal, Canada.

Boas, H. 2001. Frame semantics as a framework for describing polysemy and syntactic structures of english and german motion verbs in contrastive computational lexicography. Rayson, P., A. Wilson, T. McEnery, A. Hardie, and S. Khoja, eds., *Corpus linguistics 2001* , vol.13, Lancaster, UK.

Cappelle, B. and R. Declerck. 2005. Spatial and temporal boundedness in english motion events. *Journal of Pragmatics*, 37(6):889–917, June.

Galton, A. 1993. Towards an integrated logic of space, time, and motion. *IJCAI*.

Galton, A. 1997. Space, time, and movement. Stock, O., ed., *Spatial and temporal reasoning*. Kluwer.

Herskovits, A. 1986. *Language and Spatial Cognition: an Interdisci- plinary Study of the Prepositions in English*. Cambridge University Press.

Jackendoff, R. 1983. *Semantics and Cognition*. MIT.

Kipper, K., A. Korhonen, N. Ryant, and M. Palmer. 2006. Extensive classifications of english verbs. In *12th EURALEX*, Turin, Italy.

Mani, I., J. Hitzeman, and C. Clark. 2008. Annotating natural language geographic references. In *Workshop on Methodologies and Resources for Processing Spatial Language*. LREC'2008.

MITRE. 2007. Spatialml: Annotation scheme for marking spatial expressions in natural language. http://sourceforge.net/projects/spatialml/.

Muller, P.. 1998. A qualitative theory of motion based on spatio-temporal primitives. Cohn, A., L. Schubert, and S. Shapiro, eds., *KR'98: Principles of Knowledge Representation and Reasoning*, pages 131–141. Morgan Kaufmann.

Muller, P. 2002. Topological spatio-temporal reasoning and representation. *Computational Intelligence*, 18(3):420–450.

Pustejovsky, J. and M. Verhagen. 2007. Inferring spatio-temporal trajectories of entities from natural language documents. Tech. report, Brandeis U.

Pustejovsky, J., J. Castaño, R. Ingria, R. Saurí, R. Gaizauskas, A. Setzer, and G. Katz. 2003. Timeml: Robust specification of event and temporal expressions in text. In *IWCS-5, Fifth International Workshop on Computational Semantics*.

Pustejovsky, J. 1995. *The Generative Lexicon*. MIT.

Randell, D. A., Z. Cui, and A. G. Cohn. 1992. A spatial logic based on regions and connections. Kaufmann, M., ed., *3rd International Conference on Knowledge Representation and Reasoning*.

Vieu, L. 1991. *Sémantique des relations spatiales et inférences spatio-temporelles: une contribution à l'étude des structures formelles de l'espace en langage naturel*. Ph.D. thesis, Université Paul Sabatier.

On the weak generative capacity of weighted context-free grammars*

Anders Søgaard
University of Potsdam
soegaard@ling.uni-potsdam.de

Abstract

It is shown how weighted context-free grammars can be used to recognize languages beyond their weak generative capacity by a one-step constant time extension of standard recognition algorithms.

1 Introduction

Weighted context-free grammars (WCFGs) are used to disambiguate strings and thus filter out subsets of the tree languages of the underlying context-free grammars (CFGs). Weights can either be used as probabilities, i.e. higher weights are preferred, or as penalities, i.e. lower weights are preferred. The first convention, also followed by Smith and Johnson (2007), is followed here. The subsets of the tree languages that consist of the heaviest tree for each yield are called the Viterbi tree languages. String languages are the yields of tree languages, and Viterbi string languages are the yields of Viterbi tree languages.

Infante-Lopez and de Rijke (2006) show that the Viterbi tree languages strictly extend the tree languages.

The idea explored in this paper is simple. If trees must have particular weights for their yields to be recognized, weights can be used to encode non-local dependencies. Technically, the $\{r_1, \ldots, r_n\}$-language is defined as all the strings for which the heaviest, i.e. most probable, tree has weight $r_i \in \{r_1, \ldots, r_n\}$. It is shown that this class of languages includes common classes of context-sensitive languages. In other words, standard Viterbi-style recognition algorithms for WCFGs can be used to recognize these classes by a one-step look-up that checks if the weight of the heaviest tree is in $\{r_1, \ldots, r_n\}$. We say that $\{r_1, \ldots, r_n\}$-languages are $\{r_1, \ldots, r_n\}$-recognized.

Sect. 1.1 presents formal preliminaries and a Viterbi-style recognition algorithm for WCFGs. Note that for simplicity we restrict weights to be rational numbers.

Sect. 2 defines $\{r_1, \ldots, r_n\}$-languages and presents some examples of WCFGs that $\{r_1, \ldots, r_n\}$-recognize context-sensitive languages. Sect. 3 gives a rough characterization of the class of languages that can be $\{r_1, \ldots, r_n\}$-recognized by WCFGs.

Cortes and Mohri (2000) introduced a similar idea in the context of weighted finite-state automata (WFSAs) and showed that WFSAs can be used to $\{r_1, \ldots, r_n\}$-recognize context-free languages. Their results are extended in Sect. 4. It is shown that WFSAs can also be used to $\{r_1, \ldots, r_n\}$-recognize context-sensitive languages. It is shown, however, that the non-context-free languages that can be $\{r_1, \ldots, r_n\}$-recognized by WCFGs strictly extend the non-context-free languages that can be $\{r_1, \ldots, r_n\}$-recognized by WFSAs.

Sect. 5 discusses a more exact characterization of the weak generative capacity of WCFGs in this view. Coprime WCFGs (CWCFGs), i.e. a subclass of WCFGs where the weights can be partitioned into reciprocal coprimes, are introduced. It is conjectured that the infinite hierarchy of k-CWCFGs is non-collapsing, and the classes of languages that can be $\{r_1, \ldots, r_n\}$-recognized by k-CWCFGs are characterized in terms of an untraditional modifi-

* Thanks to Mark Hopkins, Daniel Quernheim and the anonymous reviewers for helpful comments.

© 2008. Licensed under the *Creative Commons Attribution-Noncommercial-Share Alike 3.0 Unported* license (http://creativecommons.org/licenses/by-nc-sa/3.0/). Some rights reserved.

cation of indexed grammars.

1.1 Preliminaries

A CFG is a 4-tuple $G = \langle N, T, P, S \rangle$ where N, T are finite and disjoint sets of nonterminal and terminal symbols, P a finite set of production rules of the form $A \rightarrow \phi$ where $A \in N$ and $\phi \in (N \cup T)^*$, and $S \in N$ is the start symbol. A WCFG is a 2-tuple $G' = \langle G, \pi \rangle$ where $G = \langle N, T, P, S \rangle$ is a CFG and $\pi : P \rightarrow \{\frac{m}{n} \mid m \in \mathbb{Z}^+, n \in \mathbb{Z}^+, m, n \neq 0\}$ a (total) weight function.

A left-most derivation $t(\omega)$ for some CFG $G = \langle N, T, P, S \rangle$ is a sequence of production rules $\langle p_1, \ldots, p_m \rangle$ with $1 \leq i \leq m : p_i \in P$ such that

$$S \stackrel{p_1}{\Longrightarrow} \phi_1 \ldots \phi_{m-1} \stackrel{p_m}{\Longrightarrow} \omega$$

ω is called the yield of $t(\omega)$. The tree language $T(G)$ is the set of all left-most derivations licensed by the production rules of G. The string language of G is the set of yields:

$$L(G) = \{\omega \mid t(\omega) \in T(G)\}$$

The accumulated weight of a derivation of a string ω $\pi(t(\omega))$ is the product of the weight of all the productions in $t(\omega)$. The Viterbi tree language of a WCFG then is:

$$V(G) = \{t(\omega) \mid t(\omega) \in \arg \max_{t'(\omega) \in T(G)} (\pi(t'(\omega)))\}$$

A simple Viterbi recognition algorithm for WCFGs is presented in Figure 1 for further reference.

2 Our extension

For a set of n many rational numbers $\{r_1, \ldots, r_n\}$, the language that is $\{r_1, \ldots, r_n\}$-recognized by the WCFG G, $L_{\{r_1,\ldots,r_n\}}(G)$, is defined:

$$L_{\{r_1,\ldots,r_n\}}(G) = \{\omega \mid t(\omega) \in V(G), \pi(t(\omega)) \in \{r_1, \ldots, r_n\}\}$$

Call the class of all languages that can be $\{r_1, \ldots, r_n\}$-recognized by a WCFG for all finite and non-empty sets of rational numbers $\{r_1, \ldots, r_n\}$ for *balanced* weighted context-free languages (BWCFLs). In all our examples $\{r_1, \ldots, r_n\}$ will be a singleton set.

Note that all there is needed to do to recognize the BWCFLs is to change line 7 of the Viterbi algorithm in Figure 1 to:

if $(S, r_i) \in t(0, n), r_i \in \{r_1, \ldots, r_n\}$ **then** ...

3 Bounds on weak generative capacity

The first result of this paper is the following:

Theorem 3.1. *The BWCFLs strictly extend the context-free languages.*

Proof. It is not difficult to see that any context-free language is a BWCFL. Simply construct a WCFG $G = \langle G', \pi \rangle$ for any CFG $G' = \langle N, T, P, S \rangle$ such that the weight associated with each production rule in P is $\frac{1}{1}$. It then holds that $L_{\{\frac{1}{1}\}}(G) = L(G')$.

The other direction is not very difficult either. It is shown that $\{a^n b^n c^n \mid n \geq 0\}$, which is non-context-free by the Bar-Hillel lemma, is a BWCFL. The language is, for instance, the set of strings $L_{\{\frac{1}{1}\}}(G)$ for the WCFG $G = \langle\langle \{S, S'\}, \{a, b, c\}, P, S \rangle, \pi \rangle$ where P is the following set of production rules, and π assigns the weights in the left column to the items in the right column:

$$\begin{array}{llll} \frac{1}{2}: & \text{S} & \rightarrow & \text{Sc} \\ \frac{2}{1}: & \text{S} & \rightarrow & \text{S'} \\ \frac{2}{1}: & \text{S'} & \rightarrow & \text{aS'b} \\ \frac{1}{2}: & \text{S'} & \rightarrow & \epsilon \end{array}$$

$L_{\{\frac{1}{1}\}} = \{a^n b^n c^n \mid n \geq 0\}$. Some example derivations are presented in Example 3.2. □

Example 3.2. Consider the only and thus heaviest tree for *abc*, resp. *ab*:

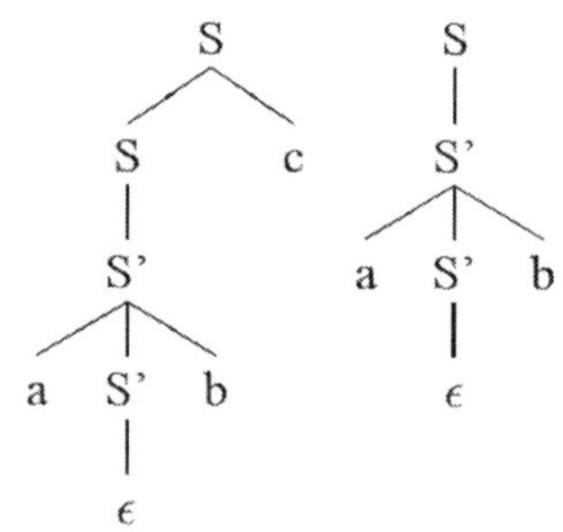

The weight of the left tree, whose yield is *abc*, is $\frac{1}{1}$. The weight of the left tree is $\frac{2}{1}$.

Consider also the $\{\frac{1}{1}\}$-language of $G = \langle\{S, D, T, T'\}, \{a, b, c, d\}, P, S \rangle$ with production rules P:

$$\begin{array}{llll} \frac{1}{1}: & \text{S} & \rightarrow & \text{TD} \\ \frac{1}{2}: & \text{D} & \rightarrow & \text{dD} \\ \frac{1}{1}: & \text{D} & \rightarrow & \epsilon \\ \frac{1}{1}: & \text{T} & \rightarrow & \text{aTc} \\ \frac{1}{1}: & \text{T} & \rightarrow & \text{T'} \\ \frac{2}{1}: & \text{T'} & \rightarrow & \text{bT'} \\ \frac{1}{1}: & \text{T'} & \rightarrow & \epsilon \end{array}$$

BUILD$(t, [w_1 \dots w_n])$

for $j \leftarrow 1$ **to** n
do $t(j-1, j) \leftarrow \{(A, \alpha) \mid A \rightarrow w_j \in P, \log(\pi(A \rightarrow w_j)) = \alpha\}$
  for $k \leftarrow (j-1)$ **to** 0
  do $t(k, j) \leftarrow \{(A, \alpha + \beta) \mid A \rightarrow B \in P, \log(\pi(A \rightarrow B)) = \alpha,$
    $(B, \beta) \in t(k, j)$, **if** $(A, \alpha') \in t(k, j)$ **then** $\alpha > \alpha'\}$
  for $i \leftarrow (j-2)$ **to** 0
  do $t(i, j) \leftarrow \{(A, \alpha + \beta + \kappa) \mid A \rightarrow BC \in P, \log(\pi(A \rightarrow BC)) = \alpha,$
    $\exists k.(B, \beta) \in t(i, k), (C, \kappa) \in t(k, j)$, **if** $(A, \alpha') \in t(i, j)$ **then** $\alpha > \alpha'\}$
if $(S, r_i) \in t(0, n)$ **then return** *success* **else** *failure*

Figure 1: A Viterbi recognition algorithm for WCFGs

It should be relatively easy to see that $L(G) = \{a^n b^m c^n d^m \mid n \geq 0\}$.

It is not difficult to see that the BWCFLs are a subset of the context-sensitive languages. This follows from the fact that the left-most derivations in the Viterbi tree languages of WCFGs are linear in the length of the input string; in other words, BWCFLs can be recognized in nondeterministic linear space and thus by a linear bounded automaton. Since any language that can be represented by a linear bounded automaton is context-sensitive, the BWCFLs must be a subset of the context-sensitive ones.

The set of BWCFLs is also a subset of the range concatenation languages (Boullier, 1998) by the observation made in the introduction that they can be recognized in polynomial (i.e. cubic) time by standard algorithms and a one-step inspection of the weight of the heaviest tree; and by the fact that the range concatenation languages are exactly the languages that can be recognized in polynomial time (Boullier, 1998).

4 Weighted finite-state automata

Cortes and Mohri (2000) showed, in similar work, that WFSAs can be used to recognize context-free, i.e. non-regular, languages.

Example 4.1. The weighted finite-state automaton $T = \langle\{q_0, q_1\}, \{a, b\}, \delta, q_0, \{q_1\}\rangle$ with the following δ-transitions $\{\frac{1}{1}\}$-recognizes the language $L_{\{\frac{1}{1}\}}(T) = \{a^n b^n \mid n \geq 0\}$:

$$\begin{array}{rlcl} \frac{1}{2}: & \delta(q_0, a) & = & q_0 \\ \frac{1}{1}: & \delta(q_0, \lambda) & = & q_1 \\ \frac{2}{1}: & \delta(q_1, b) & = & q_1 \end{array}$$

It is not difficult to see that the strings $ab, aabb, \dots$ have derivations with weights $\frac{1}{1}$, whereas the string aab, for example, only has a derivation with weight $\frac{1}{2}$. Since $\frac{1}{2} \notin \{\frac{1}{1}\}$, $aab \notin L_{\{\frac{1}{1}\}}(T)$.

Cortes and Mohri (2000) also formulated an extension of WFSAs over cross-products of semirings that recognized certain context-sensitive, i.e. non-context-free languages, but their results can be considerably extended. The automaton in Example 4.2, for example, even recognizes a language conjectured to be outside the linear indexed languages, namely the MIX language (Gazdar, 1988).

Example 4.2. The weighted finite-state automaton $T = \langle\{q_0, q_1, q_2, q_3\}, \{a, b, c\}, \delta, q_0, \{q_0\}\rangle$ with the following δ-transitions $\{\frac{1}{1}\}$-recognizes the MIX language:

$$\begin{array}{rlcl} \frac{1}{8}: & \delta(q_0, a) & = & q_1 \\ \frac{1}{8}: & \delta(q_1, a) & = & q_2 \\ \frac{1}{8}: & \delta(q_2, a) & = & q_3 \\ \frac{1}{125}: & \delta(q_0, b) & = & q_1 \\ \frac{1}{125}: & \delta(q_1, b) & = & q_2 \\ \frac{1}{125}: & \delta(q_2, b) & = & q_3 \\ \frac{1}{729}: & \delta(q_0, c) & = & q_1 \\ \frac{1}{729}: & \delta(q_1, c) & = & q_2 \\ \frac{1}{729}: & \delta(q_2, c) & = & q_3 \\ \frac{90^3}{1}: & \delta(q_3, \lambda) & = & q_0 \end{array}$$

This example is a bit more complicated. Note that $8 \times 125 \times 729 = 90^3$. The strings $cab, bcabac, \dots$ have derivations with weights $\frac{1}{1}$, since $\frac{90^3}{8 \times 125 \times 729} = \frac{1}{1}$, whereas the string $cababa$, for instance, has no derivations with weight $\frac{1}{1}$. The string $cababa$ has exactly one derivation whose weight is $\frac{90^3}{8^2 \times 125}$.

5 Coprime WCFGs

A 2-CWCFG is a WCFG over subsets of the rational numbers $\mathbb{C} = \{\frac{1}{n} \mid n \in \Sigma\} \cup \{\frac{n}{1} \mid n \in \Sigma\}$

	B. (2000)	WCFGs
$\{a_1^n \dots a_k^n \mid n \geq 0\}$	✓	✓
MIX	✓	✓
$\{a^n b^m c^n d^m \mid m, n \geq 0\}$	✓	✓
$\{wcw \mid w \in \{a, b\}^*\}$	✓	✓

Figure 2: Classes of languages $\{r_1, \dots, r_n\}$-recognized by WCFGs and recognized by the extension in Boullier (2000).

where Σ is an arbitrary set of coprimes ($\Sigma \subseteq \mathbb{N}^*$) such that there is a bijection from the production rules onto themselves such that if a production rule has weight $\frac{1}{1}$ it is projected onto itself, and otherwise, i.e. if it has weight $\frac{1}{m}$ with $m \neq 1$ it is projected onto a production rule with weight $\frac{m}{1}$. A k-CWCFG for $k \geq 1$ is now the extension of CWCFG where the sets of production rules the product of whose weights is 1, can be of size at most k, e.g. the WFSA in Example 4.2 is a 3-CWCFG.

The infinite hierarchy of k-CWCFGs seems to be non-collapsing. A k-CWCFG $\{r_1, \dots, r_n\}$-recognizes the language $\{a_1^n \dots a_{2k}^n \mid n \geq 0\}$, but not $\{a_1^n \dots a_{2k+1}^n \mid n \geq 0\}$. It has this property in common with k-multiple context-free grammars (Seki et al., 1991). 2-CWCFG can be shown to be weakly equivalent with the extension of linear indexed grammars (LIGs) (Gazdar, 1988) where the stack is a multiset or a bag that is globally accessible and not just along spines. The universal recognition problem for this extension of LIGs can be shown to be NP-complete by reduction of the vertex cover problem, similar to Søgaard et al. (2007). The generalization to k-CWCFG requires stacks of stacks, but is otherwise relatively straight-forward.

6 Conclusions

It was shown how weighted context-free grammars can be used to recognize languages beyond their weak generative capacity by a one-step constant time extension of standard recognition algorithms. The class of languages that can be recognized this way strictly extends the context-free languages, but is included in the cubic time recognizable ones.

Boullier (2000) defines what he calls a "cubic time extension of CFG" that recognizes generalizations of the copy language that are beyond WCFG. It remains to be seen if the set of BWCFLs is a strict subset of the set of languages that can be recognized by this formalism. They all recognize the classes of languages in Figure 2.

References

Boullier, Pierre. 1998. Proposal for a natural language processing syntactic backbone. Technical report, INRIA, Le Chesnay, France.

Boullier, Pierre. 2000. A cubic time extension of context-free grammars. *Grammars*, 3(2–3):111–131.

Cortes, Corinna and Mehryar Mohri. 2000. Context-free recognition with weighted automata. *Grammars*, 3(2–3):133–150.

Gazdar, Gerald. 1988. Applicability of indexed grammars to natural languages. In Reyle, Uwe and Christian Rohrer, editors, *Natural language parsing and linguistic theories*, pages 69–94. Reidel, Dordrecht, the Netherlands.

Infante-Lopez, Gabriel and Maarten de Rijke. 2006. A note on the expressive power of probabilistic context free grammars. *Journal of Logic, Language and Information*, 15(3):219–231.

Seki, Hiroyuki, Takashi Matsumura, Mamoru Fujii, and Tadao Kasami. 1991. On multiple context-free grammars. *Theoretical Computer Science*, 88(2):191–229.

Smith, Noah and Mark Johnson. 2007. Weighted and probabilistic context-free grammars are equally expressive. *Computational Linguistics*, 33(4):477–491.

Søgaard, Anders, Timm Lichte, and Wolfgang Maier. 2007. On the complexity of linguistically motivated extensions of tree-adjoining grammar. In *Proceedings of Recent Advances in Natural Language Processing 2007*, Borovets, Bulgaria.

Range concatenation grammars for translation

Anders Søgaard
University of Potsdam
soegaard@ling.uni-potsdam.de

Abstract

Positive and bottom-up non-erasing binary range concatenation grammars (Boullier, 1998) with at most binary predicates ((2,2)-BRCGs) is a $\mathcal{O}(|G|n^6)$ time strict extension of inversion transduction grammars (Wu, 1997) (ITGs). It is shown that (2,2)-BRCGs induce inside-out alignments (Wu, 1997) and cross-serial discontinuous translation units (CDTUs); both phenomena can be shown to occur frequently in many hand-aligned parallel corpora. A CYK-style parsing algorithm is introduced, and induction from aligment structures is briefly discussed.

Range concatenation grammars (RCG) (Boullier, 1998) mainly attracted attention in the formal language community, since they recognize exactly the polynomial time recognizable languages, but recently they have been argued to be useful for data-driven parsing too (Maier and Søgaard, 2008). Bertsch and Nederhof (2001) present the only work to our knowledge on using RCGs for translation. Both Bertsch and Nederhof (2001) and Maier and Søgaard (2008), however, only make use of so-called *simple* RCGs, known to be equivalent to linear context-free rewrite systems (LCFRSs) (Weir, 1988; Boullier, 1998). Our strict extension of ITGs, on the other hand, makes use of the ability to copy substrings in RCG derivations; one of the things that makes RCGs strictly more expressive than LCFRSs. Copying enables us to recognize the intersection of any two translations that we can recognize and induce the union of any two alignment structures that we can induce. Our extension of ITGs in fact introduces two things: (i) A clause may introduce any number of terminals. This enables us to induce multiword translation units. (ii) A clause may copy a substring, i.e. a clause can associate two or more nonterminals $A_1, \dots A_n$ with the same substring and thereby check if the substring is in the intersection of the languages of the subgrammars with start predicate names $A_1, \dots A_n$.

The first point is motivated by studies such as Zens and Ney (2003) and simply reflects that in order to induce multiword translation units in this kind of synchronous grammars, it is useful to be able to introduce multiple terminals simultaneously. The second point gives us a handle on context-sensitivity. It means that (2,2)-BRCGs can define translations such as $\{\langle a^n b^m c^n d^m, a^n b^m d^m c^n\rangle \mid m, n \geq 0\}$, i.e. a translation of cross-serial dependencies into nested ones; but it also means that (2,2)-BRCGs induce a larger class of alignment structures. In fact the set of alignment structures that can be induced is closed under union, i.e. any alignment structure can be induced. The last point is of practical interest. It is shown below that phenomena such as inside-out alignments and CDTUs, which cannot be induced by ITGs, but by (2,2)-BRCGs, occur frequently in many hand-aligned parallel corpora.

1 (2,2)-BRCGs and ITGs

(2,2)-BRCGs are *positive* RCGs (Boullier, 1998) with binary start predicate names, i.e. $\rho(S) = 2$. In RCG, predicates can be negated (for complementation), and the start predicate name is typically unary. The definition is changed only for aesthetic reasons; a positive RCG with a binary start predicate name S is turned into a positive RCG with a

© 2008. Licensed under the *Creative Commons Attribution-Noncommercial-Share Alike 3.0 Unported* license (http://creativecommons.org/licenses/by-nc-sa/3.0/). Some rights reserved.

unary start predicate name S' simply by adding a clause $S'(X_1X_2) \to S(X_1, X_2)$.

Definition 1.1 (Positive RCGs). A positive RCG is a 5-tuple $G = \langle N, T, V, P, S \rangle$. N is a finite set of predicate names with an arity function ρ: $N \to \mathbb{Z}^*$, T and V are finite sets of, resp., terminal and variables. P is a finite set of clauses of the form $\psi_0 \to \psi_1 \ldots \psi_m$, where and each of the $\psi_i, 0 \leq i \leq m$, is a predicate of the form $A(\alpha_1, \ldots, \alpha_{\rho(A)})$. Each $\alpha_j \in (T \cup V)^*$, $1 \leq j \leq \rho(A)$, is an argument. $S \in N$ is the start predicate name with $\rho(S) = 2$.

Note that the order of RHS predicates in a clause is of no importance. Three subclasses of RCGs are introduced for further reference: An RCG $G = \langle N, T, V, P, S \rangle$ is *simple* iff for all $c \in P$, it holds that no variable X occurs more than once in the LHS of c, and if X occurs in the LHS then it occurs exactly once in the RHS, and each argument in the RHS of c contains exactly one variable. An RCG $G = \langle N, T, V, P, S \rangle$ is a *k-RCG* iff for all $A \in N, \rho(A) \leq k$. Finally, an RCG $G = \langle N, T, V, P, S \rangle$ is said to be *bottom-up non-erasing* iff for all $c \in P$ all variables that occur in the RHS of c also occur in its LHS.

A positive RCG is a (2,2)-BRCG iff it is a 2-RCG, if an argument of the LHS predicate contains at most two variables, and if it is bottom-up non-erasing.

The language of a (2,2)-BRCG is based on the notion of *range*. For a string pair $\langle w_1 \ldots w_n, v_{n+2} \ldots v_{n+1+m} \rangle$ a range is a pair of indices $\langle i, j \rangle$ with $0 \leq i \leq j \leq n$ or $n < i \leq j \leq n + 1 + m$, i.e. a string span, which denotes a substring $w_{i+1} \ldots w_j$ in the source string or a substring $v_{i+1} \ldots v_j$ in the target string. Only consequtive ranges can be concatenated into new ranges. Terminals, variables and arguments in a clause are bound to ranges by a substitution mechanism. An *instantiated* clause is a clause in which variables and arguments are consistently replaced by ranges; its components are *instantiated predicates*. For example $A(\langle g \ldots h \rangle, \langle i \ldots j \rangle) \to B(\langle g \ldots h \rangle, \langle i+1 \ldots j-1 \rangle)$ is an instantiation of the clause $A(X_1, aY_1b) \to B(X_1, Y_1)$ if the target string is such that $v_{i+1} = a$ and $v_j = b$. A *derive* relation $\Longrightarrow$ is defined on strings of instantiated predicates. If an instantiated predicate is the LHS of some instantiated clause, it can be replaced by the RHS of that instantiated clause. The language of a (2,2)-BRCG $G = \langle N, T, V, P, S \rangle$ is the set $L(G) = \{\langle w_1 \ldots w_n, v_{n+2} \ldots v_{n+1+m} \rangle \mid S(\langle 0, n \rangle, \langle n+1, n+1+m \rangle) \stackrel{*}{\Longrightarrow} \epsilon\}$, i.e. an input string pair $\langle w_1 \ldots w_n, v_{n+2} \ldots v_{n+1+m} \rangle$ is recognized iff the empty string can be derived from $S(\langle 0, n \rangle, \langle n+1, n+1+m \rangle)$.

Theorem 1.2 ((Boullier, 2000)). *The recognition problem of bottom-up non-erasing k-RCG can be solved in time* $\mathcal{O}(|G|n^d)$ *where* $d = max_{c_j \in P}(k_j + v_j)$ *where* c_j *is the jth clause in P,* k_j *is the arity of its LHS predicate, and* v_j *is the number of different variables in that LHS predicate.*

It follows immediately that the recognition problem of (2,2)-BRCG can be solved in time $\mathcal{O}(|G|n^6)$, since k_j can be at most 2, and v_j can be at most 4.

Example 1.3. Consider the (2,2)-BRCG $G = \langle \{S_0, S_1, S_2\}, \{a, b, c, d, e, f, g, h\}, \{X_1, X_2, Y_1, Y_2\}, P, S_0 \rangle$ with P the following set of clauses:

$$\begin{array}{rcl}
S_0(X_1, Y_1) & \to & S_1(X_1, Y_1)S_2(X_1, Y_1) \\
S_1(X_1d, Y_1Y_2) & \to & A_0(X_1, Y_2)E(Y_1) \\
A_0(X_1c, Y_1h) & \to & A_1(X_1, Y_1) \\
A_1(aX_1, g) & \to & B(X_1) \\
S_2(aX_1, Y_1Y_2) & \to & T_0(X_1, Y_1)G(Y_2) \\
T_0(X_1d, Y_1f) & \to & T_1(X_1, Y_1) \\
T_1(bX_1, e) & \to & C(X_1)
\end{array}$$

$$\begin{array}{rcl|rcl}
B(b) & \to & \epsilon & C(c) & \to & \epsilon \\
E(ef) & \to & \epsilon & G(gh) & \to & \epsilon
\end{array}$$

which when words that are recognized simultaneously are aligned, induces the alignment:

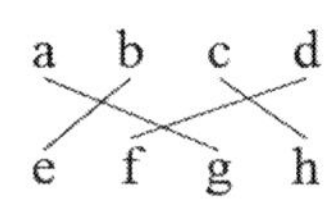

by inducing the alignments in the, resp., S_1 and S_2 derivations:

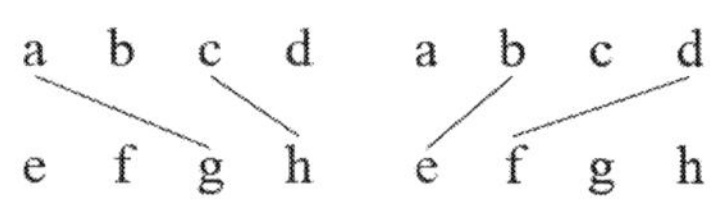

Example 1.4. Consider the (2,2)-BRCG $G = \langle \{S_s, S_0, S_0', S_1, S_1', A, B, C, D\}, \{a, b, c, d\}, \{X_1, X_2, Y_1, Y_2\}, P, S_s \rangle$ with P the following set of clauses:

$$\begin{array}{rcl}
S_s(X_1, Y_1) & \to & S_0(X_1, Y_1)S_0'(X_1, Y_1) \\
S_0(X_1X_2, Y_1) & \to & S_1(X_1, Y_1)D(X_2) \\
S_1(aX_1c, abY_1) & \to & S_1(X_1, Y_1) \\
S_1(X_1, Y_1Y_2) & \to & B(X_1)C(Y_1)D(Y_2)
\end{array}$$

$$\begin{array}{rcl}
S_0'(X_1X_2, Y_1) & \to & S_1'(X_2, Y_1)A(X_1) \\
S_1'(bX_1d, Y_1cd) & \to & S_1'(X_1, Y_1) \\
S_1'(X_1, Y_1Y_2) & \to & C(X_1)A(Y_1)B(Y_2)
\end{array}$$

$$\begin{array}{rcl|rcl}
A(aX_1) & \to & A(X_1) & A(\epsilon) & \to & \epsilon \\
B(bX_1) & \to & B(X_1) & B(\epsilon) & \to & \epsilon \\
C(cX_1) & \to & C(X_1) & C(\epsilon) & \to & \epsilon \\
D(dX_1) & \to & D(X_1) & D(\epsilon) & \to & \epsilon
\end{array}$$

Note that $L(G) = \{\langle a^n b^m c^n d^m, (ab)^n (cd)^m \rangle \mid m, n \geq 0\}$.

Since the component grammars in ITGs are context-free, Example 1.4 shows that there is at least one translation not recognizable by ITGs that is recognized by a (2,2)-BRCG; $\{a^n b^m c^n d^m \mid m, n \geq 0\}$ is known to be non-context-free. ITGs translate into simple (2,2)-BRCGs in the following way; see Wu (1997) for a definition of ITGs. The left column is ITG production rules; the right column their translations in simple (2,2)-BRCGs.

$A \rightarrow [BC]$	$A(X_1X_2, Y_1Y_2) \rightarrow B(X_1, Y_1)C(X_2, Y_2)$
$A \rightarrow \langle BC \rangle$	$A(X_1X_2, Y_1Y_2) \rightarrow B(X_1, Y_2)C(X_2, Y_1)$
$A \rightarrow e \mid f$	$A(e, f) \rightarrow \epsilon$
$A \rightarrow e \mid \epsilon$	$A(e, \epsilon) \rightarrow \epsilon$
$A \rightarrow \epsilon \mid f$	$A(\epsilon, f) \rightarrow \epsilon$

It follows immediately that

Theorem 1.5. *(2,2)-BRCGs are strictly more expressive than ITGs.*

2 Alignment capacity

Zens and Ney (2003) identify a class of alignment structures that cannot be induced by ITGs, but that can be induced by a number of similar synchronous grammar formalisms, e.g. synchronous tree substitution grammar (STSG) (Eisner, 2003).

Inside-out alignments (Wu, 1997), such as the one in Example 1.3, cannot be induced by *any* of these theories; in fact, there seems to be no useful synchronous grammar formalisms available that handle inside-out alignments, with the possible exceptions of synchronous tree-adjoining grammars (Shieber and Schabes, 1990), Bertsch and Nederhof (2001) and generalized multitext grammars (Melamed et al., 2004), which are all way more complex than ITG, STSG and (2,2)-BRCG. Nevertheless, Wellington et al. (2006) report that 5% of the sentence pairs in an aligned parallel Chinese–English corpus contained inside-out alignments. Example 1.3 shows that (2,2)-BRCGs induce inside-out alignments.

An even stronger motivation for using (2,2)-BRCG for translation is the existence of cross-serial DTUs (CDTUs). Informally, a CDTU is a DTU such that there is a part of another DTU in its gap. Here's a simple example:

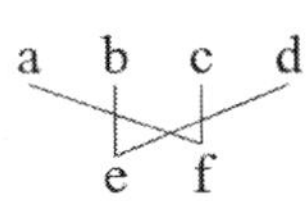

Neither ITGs nor STSGs can induce CDTUs; ITGs cannot induce DTUs with multiple gaps (MDTUs) either. Our experiments are summarized in Figure 1. Overall the results show that handling CDTUs is important for alignment error rates.

3 Parsing and induction from alignments

A CYK-style algorithm is presented for (2,2)-BRCG in Figure 2; it is assumed, w.l.o.g, that if the same variable occurs twice in the LHS of a clause, the clause is of the form $A_0(X_1, Y_1) \rightarrow A_1(X_1, Y_1)A_2(X_1, Y_1)$. It modifies the original CYK algorithm (Younger, 1967) in four ways: (i) It uses two charts; one for the source string (s) and one for the target string (t). (ii) Pairs of nonterminals and integers (A, ι), rather than just nonterminals, are stored in the cells of the chart (l. 2,4,6,7). Integers represent derivation steps at which nonterminals are inserted. (iii) Multiple terminals are allowed (l. 2,6,7). (iv) If a clause is copying, the same two cells in the chart are visited twice (l. 4). Note that the variable ι in insertion, e.g. in l. 4/1, is the *current* derivation step, but ι_i in look-up, e.g. in l. 4/2, is the derivation step in which the associated nonterminal was added to the chart.

The overall runtime of this algorithm is in $\mathcal{O}(|G|n^6)$, since it has, for branching clauses, six embedded loops that iterate over the string, i.e. the four **for** loops and the two $\exists$s in Figure 2.

The induction problem from alignments can be reduced to the induction problem for ITGs by simply unravelling the alignment structures. The simplest algorithm for doing this assumes that alignments are sequences of translation units, and considers each at a time. If a gap is found, the translation unit is a DTU and is moved to a new alignment structure. The complexity of the algorithm is quadratic in the length of the input sentences, i.e. linear in the size of the alignment structure, and for a sentence pair $\langle w_1 \dots w_n, v_1 \dots v_m \rangle$ the ITG induction algorithm has to consider at most $\frac{\min(n+m)}{2}$ aligment structures.

4 Conclusion

A new class of grammars for syntax-based machine translation was presented; while its recognition problem remains solvable in time $\mathcal{O}(|G|n^6)$, the grammars induce frequently occurring alignment configurations that cannot be induced by comparable classes of grammars in the literature. A parsing and an induction algorithm were presented.

	Sent.	TUs	DTUs	CDTUs	MDTUs	CDTUs/Sent.
English–French:	100	937	95	36	11	36%
English-Portuguese:	100	939	100	52	3	52%
English–Spanish:	100	950	90	26	7	26%
Portuguese–French:	100	915	77	19	3	19%
Portuguese–Spanish:	100	991	80	40	3	40%
Spanish–French:	100	975	74	24	8	24%

Figure 1: Statistics for six 100-sentence hand-aligned Europarl bitexts (Graca et al., 2008).

$\textsc{Build}(s, [w_1 \dots w_n]), (t, [v_1 \dots v_m])$

1 **for** $j \leftarrow 1$ **to** n, **for** $j' \leftarrow 1$ **to** m
2 **do** $s(i-1, j), t(i'-1, j') \leftarrow \{(A, \iota) \mid A(w_i \dots w_j, v_{i'} \dots v_{j'}) \rightarrow \epsilon \in P\}$
3 **for** $k \leftarrow (j-1)$ **to** 0, **for** $k' \leftarrow (j'-1)$ **to** 0
4 **do** $s(k, j), t(k', j') \leftarrow \{(A, \iota) \mid A(X_1, Y_1) \rightarrow B(X_1, Y_1)C(X_1, Y_1) \in P,$
$(B, \iota_1), (C, \iota_2) \in s(k, j), (B, \iota_1), (C, \iota_2) \in t(k', j')\}$
5 **for** $l \leftarrow (j-2)$ **to** 0, **for** $l' \leftarrow (j'-2)$ **to** 0
6 **do** $s(l, j), t(l', j') \leftarrow \{(A, \iota) \mid A(\phi_1 X_1 \phi_2 X_2 \phi_3, \psi_1 Y_1 \psi_2 Y_2 \psi_3) \rightarrow B(X_1, Y_1)C(X_2, Y_2) \in P,$
$\exists i.(B, \iota_1) \in s(l + |\phi_1|, i), (C, \iota_2) \in s(i + |\phi_2|, j - |\phi_3|), \phi_1 = w_{l+1} \dots w_{l+|\phi_1|},$
$\phi_2 = w_{i+1} \dots w_{i+|\phi_2|}, \phi_3 = w_{j-|\phi_3|} \dots w_j,$
$\exists i'.(B, \iota_1) \in t(l' + |\psi_1|, i'), (C, \iota_2) \in t(i' + |\psi_2|, j' - |\psi_3|), \psi_1 = v_{l'+1} \dots v_{l'+|\psi_1|},$
$\psi_2 = v_{i'+1} \dots v_{i'+|\psi_2|}, \psi_3 = v_{j'-|\psi_3|} \dots v_{j'}\}$
7 **do** $s(l, j), t(l', j') \leftarrow \{(A, \iota) \mid A(\phi_1 X_1 \phi_2 X_2 \phi_3, \psi_1 Y_1 \psi_2 Y_2 \psi_3) \rightarrow B(X_1, Y_1)C(X_2, Y_2) \in P,$
$\exists i.(B, \iota_1) \in s(l + |\phi_1|, i), (C, \iota_2) \in s(i + |\phi_2|, j - |\phi_3|), \phi_1 = w_{l+1} \dots w_{l+|\phi_1|},$
$\phi_2 = w_{i+1} \dots w_{i+|\phi_2|}, \phi_3 = w_{j-|\phi_3|} \dots w_j,$
$\exists i'.(C, \iota_2) \in t(l' + |\psi_1|, i'), (B, \iota_1) \in t(i' + |\psi_2|, j' - |\psi_3|), \psi_1 = v_{l'+1} \dots v_{l'+|\psi_1|},$
$\psi_2 = v_{i'+1} \dots v_{i'+|\psi_2|}, \psi_3 = v_{j'-|\psi_3|} \dots v_{j'}\}$
8 **if** $(S, \iota_1) \in s(0, n), (S, \iota_1) \in t(0, m)$ **then return** *success* **else** *failure*

Figure 2: CYK-style parsing algorithm for (2,2)-BRCG.

References

Bertsch, Eberhard and Mark-Jan Nederhof. 2001. On the complexity of some extensions of RCG parsing. In *Proceedings of the 7th International Workshop on Parsing Technologies*, pages 66–77, Beijing, China.

Boullier, Pierre. 1998. Proposal for a natural language processing syntactic backbone. Technical report, INRIA, Le Chesnay, France.

Boullier, Pierre. 2000. A cubic time extension of context-free grammars. *Grammars*, 3(2–3):111–131.

Eisner, Jason. 2003. Learning non-isomorphic tree mappings for machine translation. In *Proceedings of the 41st Annual Meeting of the Association for Computational Linguistics*, pages 205–208, Sapporo, Japan.

Graca, Joao, Joana Pardal, Luísa Coheur, and Diamantino Caseiro. 2008. Building a golden collection of parallel multi-language word alignments. In *Proceedings of the 6th International Conference on Language Resources and Evaluation*, Marrakech, Morocco.

Maier, Wolfgang and Anders Søgaard. 2008. Treebanks and mild context-sensitivity. In *Proceedings of the 13th Conference on Formal Grammar*, Hamburg, Germany.

Melamed, Dan, Giorgio Satta, and Benjamin Wellington. 2004. Generalized multitext grammars. In *Proceedings of the 42nd Annual Meeting of the Association for Computational Linguistics*, pages 661–668, Barcelona, Spain.

Shieber, Stuart and Yves Schabes. 1990. Synchronous tree-adjoining grammars. In *Proceedings of the 13th Conference on Computational Linguistics*, pages 253–258, Helsinki, Finland.

Weir, David. 1988. *Characterizing mildly context-sensitive grammar formalisms*. Ph.D. thesis, University of Pennsylvania, Philadelphia, Pennsylvania.

Wellington, Benjamin, Sonjia Waxmonsky, and Dan Melamed. 2006. Empirical lower bounds on the complexity of translational equivalence. In *Proceedings of the 44th Annual Conference of the Association for Computational Linguistics*, pages 977–984, Sydney, Australia.

Wu, Dekai. 1997. Stochastic inversion transduction grammars and bilingual parsing of parallel corpora. *Computational Linguistics*, 23(3):377–403.

Younger, Daniel. 1967. Recognition and parsing of context-free languages in time n^3. *Information and Control*, 10(2):189–208.

Zens, Richard and Hermann Ney. 2003. A comparative study on reordering constraints in statistical machine translation. In *Proceedings of the 41st Annual Meeting on Association for Computational Linguistics*, pages 144–151, Sapporo, Japan.

Comparative Evaluation of Arabic Language Morphological Analysers and Stemmers

Majdi Sawalha
School of Computing,
University of Leeds,
Leeds LS2 9JT, UK.
sawalha@comp.leeds.ac.uk

Eric Atwell
School of Computing,
University of Leeds,
Leeds LS2 9JT, UK.
eric@comp.leeds.ac.uk

Abstract

Arabic morphological analysers and stemming algorithms have become a popular area of research. Many computational linguists have designed and developed algorithms to solve the problem of morphology and stemming. Each researcher proposed his own gold standard, testing methodology and accuracy measurements to test and compute the accuracy of his algorithm. Therefore, we cannot make comparisons between these algorithms. In this paper we have accomplished two tasks. First, we proposed four different fair and precise accuracy measurements and two 1000-word gold standards taken from the Holy Qur'an and from the Corpus of Contemporary Arabic. Second, we combined the results from the morphological analysers and stemming algorithms by voting after running them on the sample documents. The evaluation of the algorithms shows that Arabic morphology is still a challenge.

1 Three Stemming Algorithms

We selected three stemming algorithms for which we had ready access to the implementation and/or results.

Shereen Khoja Stemmer : We obtained a Java version of Shereen Khoja's stemmer (Khoja,1999). Khoja's stemmer removes the longest suffix and the longest prefix. It then matches the remaining word with verbal and noun patterns, to extract the root. The stemmer makes use of several linguistic data files such as a list of all diacritic characters, punctuation characters, definite articles, and 168 stop words (Larkey & Connell 2001).

Tim Buckwalter Morphological analyzer: Tim Buckwalter developed a morphological analyzer for Arabic. Buckwalter compiled a single lexicon of all prefixes and a corresponding unified lexicon for suffixes instead of compiling numerous lexicons of prefixes and suffix morphemes. He included short vowels and diacritics in the lexicons[1].

Tri-literal Root Extraction Algorithm : Al-Shalabi, Kanaan and Al-Serhan developed a root extraction algorithm which does not use any dictionary. It depends on assigning weights for a word's letters multiplied by the letter's position, Consonants were assigned a weight of zero and different weights were assigned to the letters grouped in the word "سألتمونيها" where all affixes are formed by combinations of these letters. The algorithm selects the letters with the lowest weights as root letters (Al-Shalabi et al, 2003).

2 Our Approach: Reuse Others' Work

The reuse of existing components is an established principle in software engineering. We procured results from several candidate systems, and then developed a program to allow "voting" on the analysis of each word: for each word, examine the set of candidate analyses. Where all systems were in agreement, the common analysis is copied; but where contributing systems disagree on the analysis; take the "majority vote", the analysis given by most systems. If there is a tie, take the result produced by the system with the highest accuracy (Atwell & Roberts, 2007).

3 Experiments and Results

Experiments are done by executing the three stemming algorithms, discussed above, on a ran-

© 2008. Licensed under the *Creative Commons Attribution-Noncommercial-Share Alike 3.0 Unported* license (http://creativecommons.org/licenses/by-nc-sa/3.0/). Some rights reserved.

[1] Tim Buckwalter web site: http://www.qamus.org

domly selected chapter number 29 of the Qur'an **"Souraht Al-Ankaboot" "The Spider"** in English see figure 1; and a newspaper text taken from the Corpus of Contemporary Arabic developed at the University of Leeds, UK. We selected the test document from the politics, sports and economics section, taken from newspaper articles, see figure 2 (Al-Sulaiti & Atwell, 2006). Each test document contains about 1000 words. We manually extracted the roots of the test documents' words to compare results from different stemming systems. Roots extracted have been checked by Arabic Language scholars who are experts in the Arabic Language.

Table 1 shows a detailed analysis been done for the sample test documents, the Qur'an corpus as one unit, and a daily newspaper of contemporary Arabic test document, taken from Al-Rai daily newspaper published in Jordan. The analysis also shows that function words such as **"في" "fi" "in", "من" "min" "from", "على" "Ala" "on"** and **"الله" "Allah" "GOD"** are the most frequent words in any Arabic text. On the other hand, non functional words with high frequency such as **"الجامعات" "Al-Jami'at" "Universities"** and **"الكويت" "Al-Kuwait" "Kuwait"** gives a general idea about the main topic of the article.

Simple tokenization is applied for the text of the gold standard documents. This will ensure that test documents can be used to test any stemming algorithm smoothly and correctly.

4 Four Accuracy measurements

In order to fairly compare between different stemming algorithms we applied four different

الم أَحَسِبَ النَّاسُ أن يُتْرَكُوا أن يَقُولُوا آمَنَّا وَهُمْ لَا يُفْتَنُونَ
وَلَقَدْ فَتَنَّا الَّذِينَ مِن قَبْلِهِمْ فَلَيَعْلَمَنَّ اللَّهُ الَّذِينَ صَدَقُوا وَلَيَعْلَمَنَّ
الْكَاذِبِينَ أَمْ حَسِبَ الَّذِينَ يَعْمَلُونَ السَّيِّئَاتِ أن يَسْبِقُونَا سَاء مَا
يَحْكُمُونَ مَن كَانَ يَرْجُو لِقَاء اللَّهِ فَإِنَّ أَجَلَ اللَّهِ لَآتٍ وَهُوَ
السَّمِيعُ الْعَلِيمُ وَمَن جَاهَدَ فَإِنَّمَا يُجَاهِدُ لِنَفْسِهِ إِنَّ اللَّهَ لَغَنِيٌّ
عَنِ الْعَالَمِينَ وَالَّذِينَ آمَنُوا وَعَمِلُوا الصَّالِحَاتِ لَنُكَفِّرَنَّ عَنْهُمْ
سَيِّئَاتِهِمْ وَلَنَجْزِيَنَّهُمْ أَحْسَنَ الَّذِي كَانُوا يَعْمَلُونَ وَوَصَّيْنَا
الْإِنسَانَ بِوَالِدَيْهِ حُسْنًا وَإِن جَاهَدَاكَ لِتُشْرِكَ بِي مَا لَيْسَ لَكَ بِهِ
عِلْمٌ فَلَا تُطِعْهُمَا إِلَيَّ مَرْجِعُكُمْ فَأُنَبِّئُكُم بِمَا كُنتُمْ تَعْمَلُونَ وَالَّذِينَ
آمَنُوا وَعَمِلُوا الصَّالِحَاتِ لَنُدْخِلَنَّهُمْ فِي الصَّالِحِينَ

Figure 1: Sample from Gold Standard first document taken from Chapter 29 of the Qur'an.

ستبقى العولمة وإلى وقت ممتد مثيرة للأسئلة والأجوبة
وفي هذا المقال وقفة تأمل عميقة في بعض هذه الأسئلة
بدأت منذ فترة موجة جديدة من الكتابات تروج للعولمة
باعتبارها الشكل الجديد لحياة البشر في ظل القطب
الأمريكي وهناك نمط من هذه الكتابات يروج للنمط
الأمريكي متعدد الأعراق والثقافات بوصفه النمط الأمثل
للحياة في القرية الكونية الجديدة التي قاربت وسائل
الاتصالات والمواصلات ونظم المعلومات ووسائل الإعلام
بين أجزائه المختلفة ويبشر أصحاب هذه النظرة ببشر من
نوع جديد بشر كوزموبوليتان

Figure 2: Sample from Gold Standard document taken from the Corpus of Contemporary Arabic.

Table 1: Summary of detailed analysis.

	Qur'an Corpus		Gold Standard First Document Chapter 29 of the Qur'an		Gold Standard Second Document "Corpus of Contemporary Arabic"		Al-Rai daily Newspaper Test Document	
Total number of Tokens	77,789		987		1005		977	
Word Types	19,278		616		710		678	
Top 10 Tokens	Token	Freq.	Token	Freq.	Token	Freq.	Token	Freq.
1	فِي	1179	فِي	21	في	35	في	39
2	مِن	872	اللَّهِ	17	من	21	من	16
3	مَا	832	مِن	14	على	12	على	13
4	الَّذِينَ	808	اللَّهُ	12	التي	12	التي	10
5	عَلَى	652	وَمَا	12	الكويت	11	إلى	9
6	وَمَا	640	إِلَّا	12	أن	10	المبنى	8
7	إِنَّ	605	الَّذِينَ	11	هذه	10	الجامعات	8
8	اللَّهِ	464	مَا	8	إلى	8	أن	7
9	أَن	499	اللَّهَ	8	امام	8	السلام	7
10	قَالَ	416	كَانُوا	8	عن	7	جلالته	7

accuracy measurements. Each time we ran the experiment, a comparison of the results with the gold standard was performed.
The first experiment was done by comparing each root extracted using the three stemming algorithms with the roots of words in the gold standard.

Table 2: Tokens Accuracy of stemming algorithms after testing on Qur'an gold standard

Number of Tokens including Stop words (978 tokens)				
Stemming Algorithm		Errors	Fault Rate	Accuracy
Khoja stemmer		311	31.8%	68.2%
Tim Buckwalter morph. Analyzer		419	42.8%	57.16%
Tri-literal Root algorithm		394	40.3%	59.71%
Voting algorithm	Ex.1	434	44.4%	55.6%
	Ex.2	405	41.4%	58.6%
Number of Tokens excluding Stop words (554 tokens)				
Khoja stemmer		209	37.73%	62.27%
Tim Buckwalter morph. Analyzer		123	22.2%	77.8%
Tri-literal Root algorithm		279	50.36%	49.64%
Voting algorithm	Ex.1	266	48.0%	52.0%
	Ex.2	229	41.3%	58.7%

Table 3: Word type Accuracy of stemming algorithms after testing on Qur'an gold standard

Number of Word Types including Stop words (616 word types)				
Stemming Algorithm		Errors	Fault Rate	Accuracy
Khoja stemmer		224	36.36%	63.64%
Tim Buckwalter morph. Analyzer		267	43.34%	56.66%
Tri-literal Root algorithm		266	43.18%	56.82%
Voting algorithm	Ex.1	242	39.3%	60.7%
	Ex.2	219	35.6%	64.4%
Number of Word types excluding Stop words (451 word types)				
Khoja stemmer		155	34.37%	65.63%
Tim Buckwalter morph. Analyzer		251	55.65%	44.34%
Tri-literal Root algorithm		214	47.45%	52.55%
Voting algorithm	Ex.1	174	38.6%	61.4%
	Ex.2	151	33.5%	66.5%

The second experiment excludes from the words' list stop words. The third experiment compares all word-type roots to the gold standard's roots. Finally, word-type roots excluding the stop words are compared to the gold standard's roots. Tables 4-7 show the accuracy rates resulting from the four different accuracy measurements.

Table 4: Token Accuracy of stemming algorithms. Tested on newspaper gold standard

Number of Tokens including Stop words(1005 tokens)				
Stemming Algorithm		Errors	Fault Rate	Accuracy
Khoja stemmer		231	22.99%	77.01%
Tim Buckwalter morph. Analyzer		596	59.30%	40.70%
Tri-literal Root algorithm		234	23.28%	76.72%
Voting algorithm	Ex.1	303	30.15%	69.85%
	Ex.2	266	26.47%	73.53%
Number of Tokens excluding Stop words (766 tokens)				
Khoja stemmer		212	27.7%	72.3%
Tim Buckwalter morph. Analyzer		431	60.70%	39.30%
Tri-literal Root algorithm		253	35.63%	64.37%
Voting algorithm	Ex.1	303	39.56%	60.44%
	Ex.2	266	34.73%	65.27%

Table 5: Word type Accuracy of stemming algorithms. Tested on newspaper gold standard

Number of Word Types including Stop words (710 word types)				
Stemming Algorithm		Errors	Fault Rate	Accuracy
Khoja stemmer		232	32.68%	67.32%
Tim Buckwalter morph. Analyzer		431	60.70%	39.30%
Tri-literal Root algorithm		253	35.63%	64.37%
Voting algorithm	Ex.1	248	34.93%	65.07%
	Ex.2	215	30.28%	69.71%
Number of Word types excluding Stop words (640 word types)				
Khoja stemmer		184	28.75%	71.25%
Tim Buckwalter morph. Analyzer		423	66.09%	33.91%
Tri-literal Root algorithm		224	35.00%	65.00%
Voting algorithm	Ex.1	252	39.4%	60.6%
	Ex.2	195	30.5%	69.5%

Experiments are done for results generated from the three stemming algorithms after executing them on both gold standard documents.

The output analysis of the stemming algorithms is considered as input for the "voting" program. The program reads in these files, tokenizes them, and stores the words and the roots extracted by each stemming algorithm in temporary lists to be used by the voting procedures.

The temporary lists work as a bag of words that contains all the result analysis of the stemming algorithms. Khoja and the tri-literal stemming algorithms generate only one result analysis for each input word, while Tim Buckwalter morphological analyzer generates one or more result analysis. These roots are ranked in best-first order according to accuracy measurement done before. Khoja stemmer results are inserted to the list first then the results from tri-literal stemming algorithm and finally the results of Tim Buckwalter morphological analyzer.

After the construction of the lists of all words and their roots, a majority voting procedure is applied to it to select the most common root among the list. If the systems disagree on the analysis, the voting algorithm selects "Majority Vote" root as the root of the word. If there is a tie, where each stemming algorithm generates a different root analysis then the voting algorithm selects the root by two ways. Firstly, it simply selects the root randomly from the list using the `FreqDist()` Python function in experiment 1. Secondly, In experiment 2, the algorithm selects the root generated from the highest accuracy stemming algorithm which is simply placed in the first position of the list as the root of the word are inserted to the list using the best-first in terms of accuracy strategy.

After the voting algorithm, the selected root is compared to the gold standard. Tables 2-5 show the result of the voting algorithm which achieves promising accuracy results of slightly better than the best stemming algorithm in experiment 2 and a similar accuracy rates for the best stemming algorithms in experiment 1.

5 Conclusions

In this paper, we compared between three stemming algorithms; Shereen Khoja's stemmer, Tim Buckwalter's morphological analyzer and the Tri-literal root extraction algorithm.

Results of the stemming algorithms are compared with the gold standard using four different accuracy measurements. The four accuracy measurements show the same accuracy rank for the stemming algorithms: the Khoja stemmer achieves the highest accuracy then the tri-literal root extraction algorithm and finally the Buckwalter morphological analyzer.

The voting algorithm achieves about 62% average accuracy rate for Qur'an text and about 70% average accuracy for newspaper text. The results show that the stemming algorithms used in the experiments work better on newspaper text than Quran text, not unexpectedly as they were originally designed for stemming newspaper text.

All stemming algorithms involved in the experiments agreed and generate correct analysis for simple roots that do not require detailed analysis. So, more detailed analysis and enhancements are recommended as future work.

Most stemming algorithms are designed for information retrieval systems where accuracy of the stemmers is not important issue. On the other hand, accuracy is vital for natural language processing. The accuracy rates show that the best algorithm failed to achieve accuracy rate of more than 75%. This proves that more research is required. We can not rely on such stemming algorithms for doing further research as Part-of-Speech tagging and then Parsing because errors from the stemming algorithms will propagate to such systems.

Our experiments are limited to the three stemming algorithms. Other algorithms are not available freely on the web, and we have been unable so far to acquire them from the authors. We hope Arabic NLP researchers can cooperate further in open-source development of resources.

References

Al-Shalabi, R., Kanaan, G., & Al-Serhan, H. (2003, December). *New approach for extracting Arabic roots*. Paper presented at the International Arab Conference on Information Technology (ACIT'2003), Egypt.

Al-Sulaiti, Latifa; Atwell, Eric 2006. *The design of a corpus of contemporary Arabic*. International Journal of Corpus Linguistics, vol. 11, pp. 135-171. 2006.

Atwell, Eric and Roberts, Andy, 2007. *CHEAT: combinatory hybrid elementary analysis of text* in: Proceedings of Corpus Linguistics 2007.

Khoja, Shereen, 1999. Stemming Arabic Text. http://zeus.cs.pacificu.edu/shereen/research.htm

Larkey Leah. S. and Connell Margrate. E. 2001. *Arabic information retrieval at UMass*. In Proceedings of TREC 2001, Gaithersburg: NIST, 2001.

A Complete and Modestly Funny System for Generating and Performing Japanese Stand-Up Comedy

Jonas Sjöbergh
Hokkaido University
js@media.eng.hokudai.ac.jp

Kenji Araki
Hokkaido University
araki@media.eng.hokudai.ac.jp

Abstract

We present a complete system that generates Japanese stand-up comedy. Different modules generating different types of jokes are tied together into a performance where all jokes are connected in some way to the other jokes. The script is converted to speech and two robots perform the comedy routine. Evaluations show that the performances are perceived as funny by many, almost half the evaluation scores for the total impression were 4 or 5 (top score).

1 Introduction

When it comes to computer processing of humor two main areas exist, humor recognition and humor generation (Binsted et al., 2006). This paper falls under generation. We present a system that automatically creates short stand-up comedy like performances. Most generation systems only generate simple types of jokes, by themselves. There are few systems generating complete comic shows. Our system combines several different methods for generating quite simple jokes and then combines these into one short performance made for two performers. This is then automatically converted into speech audio, and presented by two small robots.

The performances generated are in Japanese, and similar to Japanese *manzai*, a form of stand up comedy. *Manzai* is generally performed by two comedians, one straight-man (*tsukkomi*) and one funny man (*boke*). *Boke* misunderstands or says stupid things, and *tsukkomi* has to berate or correct, for instance by exclaiming "Idiot!" and hitting *boke* on the head.

©2008. Licensed under the *Creative Commons Attribution-Noncommercial-Share Alike 3.0 Unported* license (http://creativecommons.org/licenses/by-nc-sa/3.0/). Some rights reserved.

2 System

Several components are combined to produce short comedy performances. We first give an overview of the system and then explanations of the components. Though the system only generates jokes in Japanese, for ease of understanding examples in English similar to the Japanese original jokes are used in the explanations.

2.1 Overall System

First a script for the performance is generated. It starts with an introduction like "Hi, we are two not very proficient joke robots, please listen to our performance.", simply selected from a short list. Next, one robot uses a proverb or saying in Japanese, along the lines of "Recently my life has felt like 'jack of all trades, master of none', you know." The other robot then makes a vulgar joke by modifying this, perhaps like "For me it has been more like 'jacking off all trades, masturbate none', I must say.". The way of berating your stupid partner common in Japanese comedy has been incorporated in the system. After the vulgar joke above, the first (*tsukkomi*) robot says a phrase from a list of fairly generic put-down phrases, like "What the hell are you saying?".

Then the *boke* robot tells a joke from a database of wordplay jokes, selected from those with one noun already in the script. So in the example above, perhaps: "Speaking of 'life' [mentioned before], 'shotgun wedding: a case of wife or death' comes to mind." Again followed by a put-down by the *tsukkomi* robot.

Next comes a simple punning riddle generator. A noun already used that also sounds like a rude word is selected and a riddle is created. The riddle jokes are quite weak, similar to: "'speaking' [used earlier] is 'speaking', but what is a naughty kind of speaking?", "What?", "Spanking the monkey!" ("speak" sounds like "spank" and "spanking the monkey" is a euphemism). Again followed by a put-down, "Idiot! Would you please stop.".

Finally, one more joke from the database and another put-down are used. The robots then close with "Thank you, the end." or similar. All the lines are then converted to speech using a text-to-speech tool. The audio files are then input into two small robots, that perform the routine.

2.2 Proverb Jokes

The proverb joke module has a list of almost 1,000 proverbs and sayings in Japanese. These were collected by simply downloading a few lists of Japanese proverbs. Since many of these are quite rare and thus people in general would not understand them or any joke based on them, rare proverbs are filtered out automatically. This is done by simply searching the web for the proverb verbatim. If it occurs more times than some threshold value (currently arbitrarily set to 50) it is considered common and can be used to make jokes, starting with a generic statement like "Recently my life has felt like <proverb>".

To make a joke, a proverb is twisted into a new variant by changing words to similar sounding dirty words instead. The dirty words are taken from a collection a few hundred dirty words in Japanese. These have been grouped into three categories, sex related, feces related, and insults. Words can belong to several or all of these groups (e.g. "asshole") and are then present in all groups.

A dirty variant of a proverb has to contain at least two new words, and these must be of the same type, and they must also sound reasonably similar to the words they replace. This is determined using a table of which sounds are how similar in Japanese, which is almost the same as the one used in (Takizawa et al., 1996). Since the same character in Japanese can have several different readings, we use a standard morphological analyzer for Japanese called ChaSen (Matsumoto et al., 1997) to get the pronunciation for the words. This leads to some problems, since the analyzer does not work all that well on proverbs (often using rare grammatical constructions, words, etc.), nor on dirty words (often missing from ChaSen's lexicons). If there are more than one way to change a proverb into a new variant, one is selected at random. The joke is then presented as described in the overview section, i.e. one robot saying the original proverb and the other saying the variant.

2.3 Riddle Jokes

There have been a few systems that generate word play riddles (Binsted, 1996; Binsted and Takizawa, 1998) and our module is not very innovative, it follows the same basic ideas. First, the script that has been created so far is run through the ChaSen morphological analyzer also used earlier. Nouns and their pronunciations are then checked against the collection of dirty words to see if there are any dirty words with similar pronunciation. A random noun sounding similar to a dirty word is then used.

The riddle is built with this noun and the corresponding dirty word using a simple pattern. The *boke* robot says :"A <noun> is a <noun>, but what kind of <noun> is <hint>?" followed by: "What?", and the answer: "<Dirty word>". The most difficult part is finding a hint that describes the dirty word in a good but not too obvious way without also being a good description of the original word. Hints are generated by searching the Internet for phrases like "a <dirty word> is <hint>." Things found in this way are then assumed to be reasonable descriptions of the dirty word (often not true, unfortunately), and are then checked to see if they are also often used for the original word. This is done by checking the co-occurrences of the hint and the original noun, and the hint and the dirty word, also using web frequencies. The log-likelihood ratios are then compared, and if the hint is more closely connected to the dirty word it is used. There is also a short stop list of hints that are very common but useless, such as Japanese particles similar to the word "exist".

Since the dirty words in our collection are not that common on the Internet, it happens that no usable hints are found at all. In such cases a simple hint meaning "naughty", "rude", or "dirty", is used for sex related words, insults, and feces related words respectively. It is also happens that no noun used in the script sounds similar to a dirty word. Currently, for such cases, the whole script is abandoned and the system starts over.

2.4 Database of Puns

We automatically collected a database of word play jokes in Japanese, using a few seed jokes. If for instance a seed joke occurred in an HTML list on the Internet, all other list items were taken as jokes too. The database consists of almost 2,200 jokes, mostly very weak word play jokes, though some are perceived as quite funny by many people. The jokes are often written using contractions (e.g. "dontcha"), dialectal pronunciation instead of standard orthography, strange punctuation or choice of alphabets etc. This causes problems for the morphological analyzer, leading to errors.

When a joke from the database is needed, all the nouns from the script up until this point are extracted as above. A joke from the database containing at least one of these is then selected and presented along the lines of "Speaking of <noun>, this reminds me of <joke with noun>".

2.5 Put-Downs and Come-Backs

We asked an amateur comedian to write a short list of generic put-down phrases, giving things like "Ha ha, very funny", "What the hell are you talking about?", "Idiot", "That is not what I meant", and similar. Put-downs are drawn at random from the list, excluding any phrase already used.

For database jokes, two other put-downs are also possible. There is a a simple web frequency check to see if the joke is old. Any joke occurring more than 20 times on the Internet is currently considered "Old!". Jokes that are not old can instead get the "Stupid foreigner!" put-down (quite common in Japanese comedy). This is used on jokes with words written either in English letters or katakana letters. Katakana is mainly used for foreign loan words in Japanese, but is also other things (similar perhaps to using upper case in English), which leads to some errors.

For some put-downs it is also possible for the *boke* robot to make a come-back. When possible this is also added to the script. For instance, when the *tsukkomi* robot says "Old!" it goes on to say for example: "By the way, how is the new apartment you moved into?", and the *boke* robot replies with the phrase used on him, "Old!".

2.6 Robots

The script is converted into audio for the robots using the AquesTalk[1] text-to-speech system, and the robots are given different synthetic voices. The text-to-speech conversion works fairly well, but sometimes the speech is hard to understand.

[1]http://www.a-quest.com/aquestal/

Figure 1: The robots used.

The two robots used in the performances are both Robovie-i robots, see Figure 1, one blue and one gold. The Robovie-i can move its legs and lean its body sideways. It has a small speaker attached, to produce the speech. This is the weakest link in the system so far, since the speaker is quite weak. The sound quality is not great, and the volume is low. This is also compounded by the text-to-speech system output sometimes being quite hard to understand to begin with, and also by the generated jokes sometimes being incomprehensible. The main merits of the Robovie-i are that it is easily programmable, cheap, and cute. The robots did not move very much. They walked a little bit forward and bowed during the introduction, then remained stationary, leaning their torsos a little to one side when speaking.

3 Evaluation

We generated two scripts and had the robots perform them for evaluators. Script 1 was shown first, then a short questionnaire for script 1 was filled out, then script 2 was performed and another questionnaire filled out. The impression of each whole performance was rated from 1 (not funny) to 5 (funny). Each individual joke was also rated.

Evaluators were found by going to a student cafeteria and offering chocolate for participating. Since the speech from the robot was a bit difficult to understand it was sometimes very difficult to hear some jokes when there was a lot of background noise. The evaluators where also given the script in written form after they had watched the performance and could thus read any parts they did not hear before evaluating the funniness. 33 evaluators took part in the evaluations. How funny the jokes are thought to be of course varies a lot from person to person. The highest and lowest means of an evaluator were 4.2 and 1.2 respectively. The results are shown in Tables 1 and 2.

Table 1 shows the overall impression of the scripts, 3.3 on a scale from 1 to 5. Joke genera-

	Script 1	Script 2	Both
Score	3.4 (0.9)	3.2 (1.0)	3.3 (1.0)
4 or 5	16 (48%)	14 (42%)	30 (45%)

Table 1: Mean (and standard deviation) evaluation scores and the number of 4s or 5s assigned, for the total impression of the two evaluated scripts.

tion systems tend to get fairly low scores, so we believe a score of over 3 is good. What meaning evaluators put into a 3 on a scale from 1 to 5 is hard to estimate, but many seemed to enjoy the performances. It was also not uncommon to laugh a lot during the performance and still rate everything as 1 or 2 so, for some, laughter does not equal funny. A score of 4 or more should reasonably indicate a funny joke. For the total impression of the performances, 30 scores (of 66) were either a 4 or a 5, so almost half of the evaluators though it was funny in this sense. We believe this is a good result, considering that individual tastes in humor vary a lot.

In Table 2 the scores of the individual jokes are shown. It seems that the proverb jokes are of about the same level as the human made jokes from the Internet. The riddle jokes lag a little behind, as does the come-back joke that was included.

While the system makes mistakes, joke generation seems rather robust to errors. Since the robots are supposed to say stupid things anyway, if they do so by mistake instead of on purpose it can still be funny. There were comments from evaluators about mistakes that they disliked too, though: "This put-down is inappropriate for that joke", "They should bow while saying thank you, not after.", "The dirty jokes are too direct, subtle is funnier".

The biggest problem was the robot speakers. This should be fairly easy to fix. The other problems stem mainly from the generated jokes not being overly funny, which seems harder to deal with.

4 Conclusions

We have implemented a complete system for automatically generating and performing short stand-up comedy routines in Japanese. Different modules generate different types of jokes then tied together so that the jokes used have something in common. This is then converted to speech and uploaded into two robots that perform the comedy.

In the evaluation, the performances were rated

	Score	4 or 5
Proverb 1	2.6 (1.2)	9 (27%)
Proverb 2	3.0 (1.0)	11 (33%)
Proverb Avg.	2.8 (1.1)	20 (30%)
Riddle 1	2.4 (1.1)	4 (12%)
Riddle 2	2.3 (1.1)	5 (15%)
Riddle Avg.	2.4 (1.1)	9 (13%)
Comeback	2.6 (1.1)	6 (18%)
Database 1a	3.6 (1.1)	19 (57%)
Database 1b	2.5 (1.2)	6 (18%)
Database 2a	3.1 (1.1)	13 (39%)
Database 2a	2.9 (1.1)	13 (39%)
Database Avg.	3.0 (1.2)	51 (38%)

Table 2: Mean (and standard deviation) evaluation scores and the number of 4s or 5s assigned to the different jokes.

as 3.3 on a scale from 1 (not funny) to 5 (funny) and many evaluators enjoyed the performances. Almost half of the evaluation scores assigned to the total impression of the system were 4 or 5. This seems quite promising, though there are still many things that can be improved in the system.

References

Binsted, Kim and Osamu Takizawa. 1998. BOKE: A Japanese punning riddle generator. *Journal of the Japanese Society for Artificial Intelligence*, 13(6):920–927.

Binsted, Kim, Benjamin Bergen, Seana Coulson, Anton Nijholt, Oliviero Stock, Carlo Strapparava, Graeme Ritchie, Ruli Manurung, Helen Pain, Annalu Waller, and Dave O'Mara. 2006. Computational humor. *IEEE Intelligent Systems*, 21(2):59–69.

Binsted, Kim. 1996. *Machine Humour: An Implemented Model of Puns*. Ph.D. thesis, University of Edinburgh, Edinburgh, United Kingdom.

Matsumoto, Y., A. Kitauchi, T. Yamashita, Y. Hirano, O. Imaichi, and T. Imamura. 1997. Japanese morphological analysis system ChaSen manual. Technical Report NAIST-IS-TR97007, NAIST.

Takizawa, Osamu, Masuzo Yanagida, Akira Ito, and Hitoshi Isahara. 1996. On computational processing of rhetorical expressions - puns, ironies and tautologies. In *International Workshop on Computational Humor*, pages 39–52, Enschede, The Netherlands.

On "redundancy" in selecting attributes for generating referring expressions

Philipp Spanger **Kurosawa Takehiro** **Tokunaga Takenobu**

Department of Computer Science
Tokyo Institute of Technology
Tokyo Meguro Ôokayama 2-12-1, 152-8550 Japan
{philipp, kurosawa, take}@cl.cs.titech.ac.jp

Abstract

We seek to develop an efficient algorithm selecting attributes that approximates human selection. In contrast to previous work we sought to combine the strengths of cognitive theories and simple learning algorithms. We then developed a new algorithm for attribute selection based on observations from a corpus, which outperformed a simple base algorithm by a significant margin. We then carried out a detailed comparison between our algorithm and Reiter & Dale's "Incremental Algorithm". In terms of achieving a *human-like* attribute selection, the overall performance of both algorithms is fundamentally equivalent, while differing in the handling of *redundancy* in selected attributes. We further investigated this phenomenon and draw some conclusions for further improvement of attribute-selection algorithms.

1 Introduction

Referring expressions are a key research area in human-agent communication. In the generation of referring expressions humans do not necessarily produce the most effective (i.e. minimal) expressions in a computational sense. Given evolutionary development of human linguistic capabilities, we can assume that human-produced expressions are generally optimal to identify a target for other human subjects. Thus the generation of human-like referring expressions is an important task as the generation of those expressions that are most easily understandable for humans.

The seminal work in this field is the "Incremental algorithm" (IA) (Dale and Reiter, 1995). Their work is based on an analysis of the overall cognitive tendencies of humans in the selection of attributes. In recent years, there have been a number of important extensions to this algorithm, dealing with very specific problems. This need for a systematic approach and unified evaluation of those vastly differing algorithms provided the motivation for the creation of the TUNA-corpus[1] that was developed at Aberdeen University as part of the TUNA project (van Deemter, 2007). Work has begun to use this corpus for evaluating different algorithms for attribute selection.

Our research is carried out within this general trend, seeking to take advantage of common resources (e.g. TUNA-corpus). A critical question is how to combine the generic human cognitive tendencies and the dependency of attribute selection on a specific distribution of attributes in a specific case. In this research we tackle this question in a corpus-based approach. Specifically, in a given environment, we seek to develop an efficient algorithm for selection of attributes that approximates human selection.

2 The corpus

We utilized a simplified version of the TUNA-corpus, which was also the basis for the GRE-challenge held as part of the UCNLG+MT workshop in 2007 (Belz and Gatt, 2007). The corpus consists of a collection of paired pictures of objects and human-produced referring expressions annotated with attribute sets. Figure 1 shows an image

© 2008. Licensed under the *Creative Commons Attribution-Noncommercial-Share Alike 3.0 Unported* license (http://creativecommons.org/licenses/by-nc-sa/3.0/). Some rights reserved.

[1] TUNA-corpus: www.csd.abdn.ac.uk/research/tuna

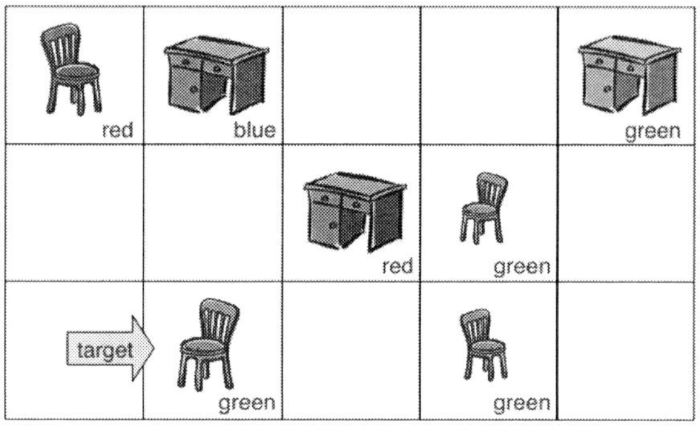

Figure 1: Image of a TUNA-corpus picture

of such a case[2]. This corpus provides information on the attribute-value pairs of the target and the distractors as well as of the referring expressions humans produced. Every item in our corpus consists of an input part ("case") and an output part ("description"). Each individual case consists of seven case entities: one target referent and six distractors. Every entity consists of a set of attribute-value pairs and all descriptions consist of a subset of the attribute-value pairs of the target referent in the same format as any entity. This corpus comprises two domains: a "Furniture" and a "Person" - domain. We note that within the corpus there were some cases that we judged as inappropriate for this study and thus excluded from the overall evaluation. This included cases where attribute-values were unspecified and/or inconsistent.

3 The base algorithm

We developed a base algorithm as a baseline for evaluation. We define "discriminative power" of a specific attribute as the number of entities in the case that have a different value from the target for this attribute.

We add attributes in descending order of discriminative power until the target can be identified uniquely. The generated attribute set is the output.

Every time an attribute is selected, we recalculate the discriminative power of the attributes of exclusively those distractors that could not be excluded by this stage.

4 Analysis of human-produced referring expressions

Our hypothesis is that in human generation of referring expressions, a combination of generic cognitive factors as well as case-dependent factors have to be dealt with. In order to account for the cognitive factor, we define a "selection probability" over a whole domain (i.e. independent from a specific case) and calculate the differences of this selection probability over the different attributes. We define the selection probability of a specific attribute a in a specific domain as equation (1).

$$SP(a) = \frac{C(a)}{\sum_{x \in X} C(x)} \tag{1}$$

where $C(x)$ denotes the number of occurrences of attribute x in the corpus.

We observe that in the Furniture-domain the attributes *colour* and *type* have extraordinarily high selection probabilities and in particular the attribute *type* is selected virtually unconditionally. We observe the same tendency of a very high selection probability for the attribute *type* in the Person-domain, even though all distractors as well as the target are of same type "person". Since the attribute *type* becomes the head of the noun phrase in the linguistic realisation of a referring expression, it is natural to mention the type. Overall, we can conclude that the different values for the selection probabilities reflect the cognitive load humans assign different attributes in a given domain.

4.1 Co-occurrence of attributes

We hypothesize that the selection of attributes is limited by co-occurence - dependencies between attributes.

In order to measure this degree of co-occurrence, we defined a "degree of dependency" between attributes as in equation (2). If the degree of dependency approaches 1, there is practically no dependency in the occurrence of attributes a and b. If this factor grows above 1, the two attributes easily occur jointly in the referring expression, on the other hand, the further it decreases below 1, the less likely are the two attributes to occur jointly. In the equation $\mathrm{P}(a, b)$ is the probability that the two attributes will be selected together, $\mathrm{P}(x)$ is the probability that the attribute x will be selected. $D(a, b)$ is the degree of dependency between attributes

$$D(a, b) = \frac{\mathrm{P}(a, b)}{\mathrm{P}(a) \times \mathrm{P}(b)} \tag{2}$$

We observed that in the Furniture-domain, size or orientation and dimension are less likely to oc-

[2]Actual pictures in the TUNA-corpus do neither show colour labels nor a target-marker.

cur together in a referring expression. Furthermore, in the Person - domain, *hairColour* and *hasHair* or *hasBeard* have a high degree of dependency, i.e. they likely occur together.

4.2 Redundancy of attributes

Even though in many referring expressions unique identification with few attributes is possible, humans show a tendency to add "redundant" attributes, i.e. that are in a strict sense not necessary for identification. By adding redundancy, humans add robustness to the expression as well as possibly reducing the cognitive load for humans in a specific context. Within the corpus, we counted the number of expressions containing redundancy. In the Furniture-domain there were 220 out of all 278 expressions and in the Person-domain there were 213 out of 230.

Table 1: Number of selected redundant attributes

Furniture (278 cases)		Person (230 cases)	
attribute	occurrences	attribute	occurrences
colour	110	*type*	201
orientation	15	*x-dimension*	4
size	10	*hasBeard*	42
type	210	*hasGlasses*	41
x-dimension	18	*hasHair*	32

This level of redundancy indicates that in order to produce human-like sets of attributes for the generation of referring expressions, it is not necessary to aim for a minimal set.

5 Our proposed algorithm for effective attribute selection

Based on our analysis of co-occurrence and redundancy of attributes, we centrally implemented the following improvements of the base algorithm.

Co-occurrence Based on the results from section 4.1, when a certain attribute is selected, we raise the selection probabilities of those attributes that have a tendency to co-occur with it, on the other hand we lower the selection probabilities of those attributes that have a tendency not to co-occur with this attribute.

Redundancy Based on the results in section 4.2, having selected the attributes to uniquely determine the target, we add the next candidate in the list of attributes as a redundant attribute .

Combination We combine both individual improvements. First of all, we add the type-attribute and then score the result based on the selection probability. With each selection of a specific attribute, we change the scores based on co-occurrence, and at the end we add a redundant attribute.

6 Evaluation of proposed algorithm

We measured the proximity of the sets of attributes by our system to the human-produced set of attributes. We utilize the Dice-coefficient (DC) – a measure of proximity for sets. For purposes of comparison, we implemented a version of the Incremental algorithm, where we calculated the order of selection of attributes according to the selection probabilities of attributes in the overall domain (Furniture or Person). It is of note that our algorithm (combination of all individual improvements) performs almost equivalent to the IA.

Table 2: Average DC for key improvements

	Furniture	Person
Base algorithm	0.305	0.314
Base+selection probability	0.784	0.669
Base+co-occurrence	0.254	0.314
Base+redundancy	0.401	0.341
Combination	0.811	0.703
Incremental algorithm	0.811	0.705

6.1 Comparison with Incremental Algorithm

We carried out a detailed analysis of the results of our algorithm and those of the IA. We found that the results of both algorithms in the Furniture - domain are exactly the same; however the results of the Person - domain show significant differences. Thus we concentrate on further analysis of the results in the Person - domain.

We divided all cases from the Person - domain into three sets; a set of cases where our algorithm performs better than the IA (sys-superior cases: 27 cases), a set of cases where the opposite is true (IA-superior cases: 24 cases) and a set of tie cases. We then compared the first two sets.

Investigating these sets, we observed that the key difference between these two algorithms lay in the treatment of redundancy. The IA often fails in the case where humans use fewer attributes and add only *type* as redundant attribute. On the other hand, our algorithm fails in the case where humans use more complex expressions, that is, more attributes including several redundant ones.

We investigated the redundant attributes which are selected by humans but not by the algorithms.

In the IA-superior cases, our system fails to select the *hasBeard* attribute compared with the IA in 20 out of 24 cases, while in the sys-superior cases both algorithms fail to select almost the same redundant attributes. We investigated for both algorithms, which attributes the algorithms wrongly select; i.e. which are not selected by humans. In the sys-superior cases, the IA wrongly selects attributes in all 27 cases, with 23 out of those including the wrongly-selected *hasBeard* attribute. In the IA-superior cases, the number of cases with wrongly selected attributes is much smaller (9 cases for each) and they are largely equiavalent.

Thus, our detailed analysis showed an overall opposite tendency in one attribute; *hasBeard*. While in sys-superior cases about 85% of the cases in which the IA output wrong attributes included *hasBeard*, in IA-superior cases our system failed to select exactly *hasBeard* at a largely equivalent rate (about 83%). At this moment, we do not have any reasonable explanation for this peculiarity of *hasBeard*, but suspect it might possibly be related to the characteristics of the corpus.

However, from the overall observation that our algorithm achieved an equivalent level of human-likeness to the IA while being weaker in cases of more complex redundancy, we conclude that further improvement in selecting redundant attributes is crucial to outperform the IA.

7 Concluding Remarks

Based on observations from the TUNA-corpus, we developed an algorithm for attribute-selection modeling human referring expressions. Our corpus-based algorithm sought to combine human generic tendencies of attribute selection in a certain domain with case-dependent variation of the salience of specific attributes. Our improved algorithm outperformed the base algorithm by a significant margin. However, we got qualitatively equivalent results to our implementation of the IA.

A detailed analysis of the characteristics of our algorithm in comparison to the IA pointed to the importance of the phenomenon of redundancy as possibly a central aspect that needs to be further investigated to achieve a qualitative improvement over the IA.

Our investigations into redundancy show that in those cases where our algorithm outperformed the IA, our algorithm almost exclusively added solely the *type*-attribute. In contrast in more complex cases of redundancy in referring expressions, the IA has shown to be superior. Since we achieved overall parity to the IA even though generally performing worse than the IA in cases of more complex redundancy, we can conclude that outside of this phenomenon our algorithm performs better than the IA in terms of human-likeness.

In previous research there has been some discussion on "redundancy" vs. "minimality" in referring expressions (e.g. (Viethen and Dale, 2006)). Through our research we have identified the phenomenon of redundancy as a critical topic for further research and for achieving further progress in the generation of human-like referring expressions.

Our algorithm includes some strong simplifications, e.g. our treatment of attributes did not take account of the fact that attribute-values are also of different type and did not explore what implications this has for the process of producing referring expressions; binary (*hasHair*), discrete (*hairColour*) or graded (*x-dim*). In future these factors should be integrated into attribute selection algorithms.

In future work, we will seek to provide a more detailed investigation of the phenomenon of redundancy, including its variation over different domains. Such an analysis should also contribute to further our understanding of the human cognitive process in the selection of attributes for the generation of referring expressions.

References

Belz, Anja and Albert Gatt. 2007. The attribute selection for GRE challenge: Overview and evaluation results. In *Proceedings of the MT Summit XI Workshop Using Corpora for Natural Language Generation: Language Generation and Machine Translation (UCNLG+MT)*, pages 75–83.

Dale, Robert. and Ehud Reiter. 1995. Computational interpretation of the gricean maxims in the generation of referring expressions. *Cognitive Science*, 19(2):233–263.

van Deemter, Kees. 2007. TUNA: Towards a unified algorithm for the generation of referring expressions - Final Report -. http://www.csd.abdn.ac.uk/research/tuna/pubs/TUNA-final-report.pdf.

Viethen, Jette and Robert Dale. 2006. Algorithms for generating referring expressions: Do they do what people do? In *Proceedings of the Fourth International Natural Language Generation Conference*, pages 63–70.

Construction of an Infrastructure for Providing Users with Suitable Language Resources

Hitomi Tohyama† **Shunsuke Kozawa**† **Kiyotaka Uchimoto**‡
Shigeki Matsubara† and **Hitoshi Isahara**‡
†Nagoya University, Furo-cho, Chikusa-ku, Nagoya, 464-8601, Japan
{hitomi,kozawa,matubara}@el.itc.nagoya-u.ac.jp
‡National Institute of Information and Communications Technology
3-5 Hikari-dai, Seika-cho, Soraku-gun, Kyoto, 619-0289, Japan
{uchimioto,isahara}@nict.go.jp

Abstract

Our research organization has been constructing a large scale database named SHACHI by collecting detailed meta information on language resources (LRs) in Asia and Western countries. The metadata database contains more than 2,000 compiled LRs such as corpora, dictionaries, thesauruses and lexicons, forming a large scale metadata of LRs archive. Its metadata, an extended version of OLAC metadata set conforming to Dublin Core, have been collected semi-automatically. This paper explains the design and the structure of the metadata database, as well as the realization of the catalogue search tool.

1 Introduction

The construction of LRs such as corpora, dictionaries, thesauruses, etc., has boomed for years throughout the world in its aim of encouraging research and development in the main media of spoken and written languages, and its importance has also been widely recognized. Of the organizations willing to store and distribute LRs, there exist some consortia fulfilling their function such as LDC[1], ELRA[2], CLARIN[3], and OLAC[4], in Western countries, and GSK[5] which does so mainly in Japan. However, those released LRs are scarcely connected with each other because of the difference between written and spoken language as well as the difference between languages such as Japanese, English, and Chinese (OLAC User Guide, 2008).

This situation makes it difficult for researchers and users to find LRs which are useful for their researches. In the meantime, by connecting systematically existing various LRs with Wrapper Program, the attempt to realize multilingual translation services has already begun (Ishida et al, 2008, Hayashi et al, 2008). Moreover, since language information tags given to those LRs and their data formats are multifarious, each LR is operated individually. As LR development generally entails enormous cost, it is highly desirable that the research efficiency be enhanced by systematically combining those existing LRs altogether and extending them, which will encourage an efficient development of unprecedented LRs.

Our research organization has been constructing a large scale metadata database named SHACHI[6] by collecting detailed meta information on LRs in Western and Asian countries. This research project aims to extensively collect metadata such as tag sets, formats, and usage information about researches on those LRs. and recorded contents of LRs existing at home and abroad and store them systematically. Meanwhile, we have already developed a search system of LRs by the use of meta information and are attempting the experiment of widely providing meta information on our stored

© 2008. Licensed under the *Creative Commons Attribution-Noncommercial-Share Alike 3.0 Unported* license (http://creativecommons.org/licenses/by-nc-sa/3.0/). Some rights reserved.

[1]LDC:Linguistic Data Consortium, http://www.ldc.upenn.edu/

[2]ELRA: European LRs Association

[3]CLARIN: Common Language Resources and Technologies Infrastructure, http://www.ilsp.gr/clarin_eng.html

[4]OLAC: Open Language Archives Community, http://www.language-archives.org/

[5]GSK: Gengo Shigen Kyokai; Language Resource Association, http://www.gsk.or.jp/

[6]SHACHI: Metadata Database of Language Resources-SHACHI, Shachi means "orca" in English.

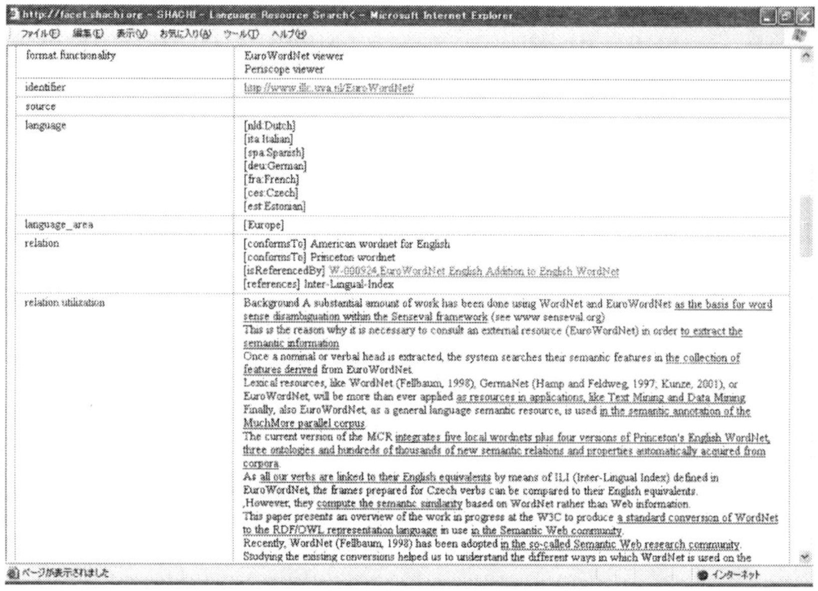

Figure 1: A sample page of SHACHI catalogue (ex. Euro WordNet)

LRs to those from researchers to common users. This metadata database has been now open to the public in the Web and allows every Internet user to access it for the search and read information of LRs at will.

2 Purpose of Metadata Database Construction

The purpose of the construction of the database is the following fivefold.

1. **To store language resource metadata:** SHACHI semi-manually collects detailed metadata of language resources and constructs their detailed catalogues. Figure 1 shows a sample page of a LR catalogue stored in SHACHI (ex. Euro WordNet). The catalogue provides more detailed meta information than other LR consortia do.

2. **To systematize language resource metadata:** Language resource ontology is tentatively constructed by classifying types of language resources (in this paper, it is called "ontology"). Figure 2 shows an example of its ontology. At the moment, it is under investigation what is the most useful and functional ontology for users by developing some ontologies such as human-made ontology, semi-automatically produced ontology, and automatically produced ontology.

3. **To make each language resource related to each other:** The detailed metadata enabled us to describe characteristics of each language resource and to expectably specify relationships among language resources. Figure 3 shows a part of the SHACHI search screen. It shows language resources found as a search result, the references to which these language resources conform as well as other language resources whose formats are common to theirs.

4. **To statistically investigate language resources:** By statistically analyzing the metadata, users are able to grasp what kinds of language resources exist in different part of the world and to understand current tendencies of language resources which have been available to the public.

5. **To promote the distribution of language resources:** Since this metadata database enables users to easily gain access to language resources in accordance with their needs, owing to fully equipped search functions, SHACHI will be able to support an effective use and an efficient development of language resources.

Some 2,000 resources of metadata have already been collected in the database so far and they will be enlarged by a further 3,000. To that end, it is

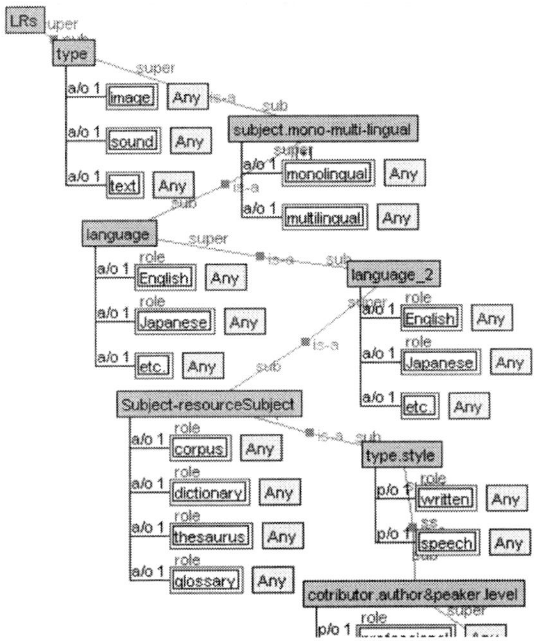

Figure 2: Automatically produced ontology

indispensable for us to work in cooperation with language resource consortia at home and abroad and to take the initiative in contributing to Asian language resources.

3 SHACHI Metadata Set

3.1 Policy for Collecting Metadata

The LRs which our metadata database stores should satisfy the following conditions:

- Those resources should be stored in a digital format.
- Those resources should be one of the following: corpus, dictionary, thesaurus, or lexicon. (Numeric data are not considered to be the subject of collection for SHACHI.)
- Those resources should be collected from English websites and its data must be open to the public.
- Those resources should be created by research institutions, researchers, or business organizations. (Developed tools such as facet search.)

LRs metadata database SHACHI covers meta information provided by LR consortia such as ELRA, LDC, and OLAC whose more detailed metadata are fed into the database by semi-automatic means of importing.

3.2 Extensions of Metadata Element

Since users sometimes search for LRs without a clear objective, it is necessary for language resource providers to construct language resource ontology. This database conforms to the OLAC metadata set which is based on 15 kinds of fundamental elements of Dublin Core[7] and constitutes an extended vision of OLAC with 19 newly added metadata elements which were judged to be indispensable for describing characteristics of LRs. SHACHI provides usage information about how and in which situation language resource researchers utilized each language resource, which is also important for users. The usage information about LRs is automatically retrieved from academic article databases (Kozawa et al, 2008). (See "Utilization" in Figure1).

3.3 Systematic Storage of LRs

Clear description of the relations among LRs can be applied to the efficient development of LRs and search tools for common users of database. Figure 2 shows ontology generated through automatic means, based on language resource metadata stored in SHACHI. We first surveyed the frequency of possible values of metadata element choicesand generated the ontology by hierarchicalizing meta elements of our meta categories. While ontology can be constructed in various ways from different standpoints, our ontology is particularly designed for users to enable to find them efficiently by following the hierarchical classes of our ontology.

4 Search Tools for Providing Users-Oriented Information

Figure 3 shows a screen image of a search result through SHACHI. This section discusses three search functions provided in SHACHI.

4.1 Three Types of Search Functions

For the purpose of facilitating users of this metadata database to find their intended language resource catalogues, SHACHI provides three search functions:

1. **Keyword search function:** This tool is suitable for users who have clear images to search

[7]Dublin Core Metadata Initiative, http://dublincore.org/

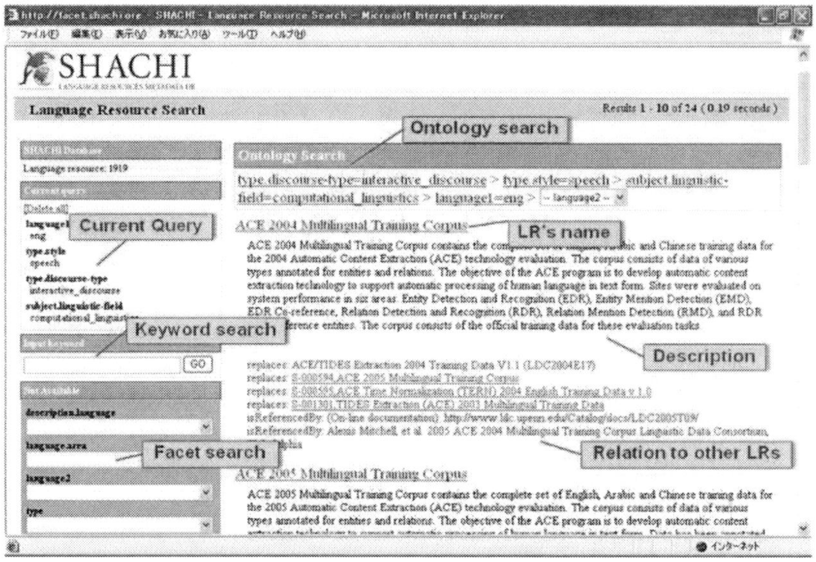

Figure 3: Catalogue search tool

for specified LRs and a technical knowledge of language processing. It allows them to input keywords as they want and to search all words stored in SHACHI metadata archive.

2. **Facet search function:** This tool is suitable for users who have a vague idea of what kind of LR they want. It is equipped with a choice of 15 kinds of metadata elements selected from the SHACHI metadata set. The users narrow down the target LRs one by one in order to find the intended one. For example, with one click on "age", three choices such as "Childrenfs utterance?", "Adultsf utterance?" and "Both are OK?" will be shown.

3. **Ontology search function:** This tool was developed by adopting the idea acquired by systematizing LRs registered in SHACHI. When using the ontology search function, users find the intended LRs by following the vertical relationship of the ontology. It was ascertained that ontology search function tool had the merit of enabling users to discover LRs that have not been ever found by keyword search and facet search functions.

5 Conclusion

In this paper, we reported on the design of SHACHI, a metadata database of LRs now being developed, the expansion and construction of metadata for it, and an actualization of a search function. At present, it contains approximately 2,000 pieces of meta information on LRs such as corpora, dictionaries and thesauruses. One of SHACHIfs characteristic features is that with a collection of tag sets, format samples, and usage information on LRs which is automatically retrieved from scholarly papers given to LRs. From now on the SHACHI project is intended to promote cooperation among other LRs consortia abroad as well as in Japan and to take the initiative in contributing to the development of LRs in Asia.

References

Ishida,T., Nadamoto, A., Murakami,Y., Inaba, R. et al. 2008. A Non-Profit Operation Model for the Language Grid, In proceedings of the 1st International Conference on Global Interoperability for language Resources, pp.114-121.

Kozawa, S., Tohyama, H., Uchimoto, K., Matsubara, S., and Isahara. H. 2008. Automatic Acquisition of Usage Infor-mation for Language Resources, In proceedings of the 6th edition of the Language Resources and Evaluation Conference.

OLAC (Open Language Archives Communi-ty), 2008. Searching of OLAC Metadata: User Guide, http:// www.language-archives.org/tools/search/searchDoc.html

Yoshihito Hayashi, Thierry Declerck, Paul Buitelaar, Monica Monachini. 2008. Ontologies for a Global Language Infrastructure, In proceedings of the 1st International Conference on Global Interoperability for language Resources, pp.105-112.

Experiments in Base-NP Chunking and Its Role in Dependency Parsing for Thai

Shisanu Tongchim, Virach Sornlertlamvanich
Thai Computational Linguistics Laboratory
NICT Asia Research Center
112 Paholyothin Road
Klong 1, Klong Luang
Pathumthani 12120, Thailand
{shisanu,virach}@tcllab.org

Hitoshi Isahara
NICT
3-5, Hikari-dai, Seika-cho
Soraku-gun, Kyoto, 619-0289, Japan
isahara@nict.go.jp

Abstract

This paper studies the role of base-NP information in dependency parsing for Thai. The baseline performance reveals that the base-NP chunking task for Thai is much more difficult than those of some languages (like English). The results show that the parsing performance can be improved (from 60.30% to 63.74%) with the use of base-NP chunk information, although the best chunker is still far from perfect ($F_{\beta=1} = 83.06\%$).

1 Introduction

Many NLP applications require syntactic information and tools for syntactic analysis. However, these linguistic resources are only available for some languages. In case of Thai, the research in developing tools for syntactic analysis and syntactically annotated corpora is still limited. Most research in the past has focused on morphological analysis (i.e. word segmentation, part-of-speech (POS) tagging). This can be viewed as a bottleneck for developing NLP applications that require a deeper understanding of the language.

We have an ongoing project in developing a syntactically annotated corpus. To accelerate the corpus annotation, some syntactic analysis tools can be applied in a preprocessing step before correcting the results by human annotators. In this paper, we use the first portion of completely annotated corpus to examine the dependency parsing and base-NP chunking. The findings will provide some guidelines in selecting a parser and a base-NP chunker for our corpus annotation workflow.

© 2008. Licensed under the *Creative Commons Attribution-Noncommercial-Share Alike 3.0 Unported* license (http://creativecommons.org/licenses/by-nc-sa/3.0/). Some rights reserved.

2 Dependency Parsing for Thai

The dependency structure for Thai is more flexible than some languages like Japanese (Sekine et al., 2000), Turkish (Eryigit and Oflazer, 2006), while it is close to Chinese (Cheng et al., 2005) and English (Nivre and Scholz, 2004). An example of a Thai sentence with dependency relations is outlined in Fig. 1. Note that the dependency links are drawn from the dependents to their heads. The dependency relations of Thai are bidirectional in nature and the root node can be found in arbitrary positions. Some languages (e.g. Japanese) have more constrained dependency structures, for example, the dependency relations are only from left to right and the root node is at the rightmost. Due to the lack of structural constraints and larger number of possible candidates, finding the correct dependency structure for Thai is more difficult.

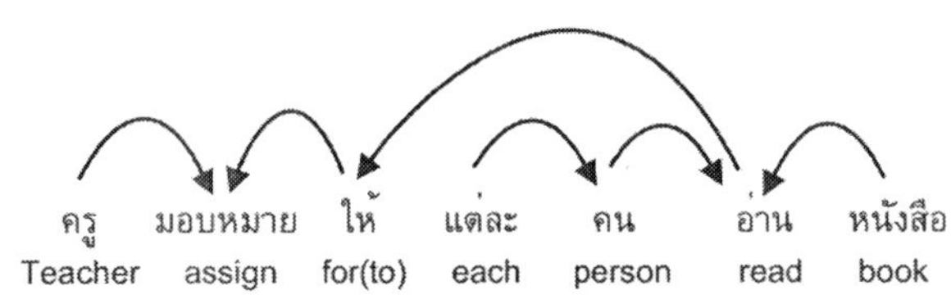

"The teacher assigns each person to read a book"

Figure 1: An example of a Thai sentence with dependency relations.

There are only few studies investigating the dependency parsing for Thai. To our knowledge, the first research regarding dependency analysis was done in (Aroonmanakun, 1989). However, this research is based on a very small corpus (50 sentences). The lack of syntactically annotated corpora may be a possible explanation why not much research has been done in this area. Some have been developed, but they are relatively small or not public, for example, a treebank of 400 sentences used in (Satayamas et al., 2005).

To overcome the shortage of corpora, we initiate the development of a syntactically annotated corpus. This corpus will be used as a fundamental linguistic resource for various projects. To improve the annotation workflow, we use the first portion of completely annotated corpus in experimenting with dependency parsing and base-NP chunking. The results will be used to improve the preprocessing step of annotation.

Two dependency parsers are included in our experiments. Both are data-driven.

- *Model 1* : The first model has been widely studied in parsing Japanese text. Some machine learning techniques are used to estimate the probability that word w_i modifies word w_j. Thus, the probability matrix of binary dependency relations can be derived from this estimation. Some search algorithms are then used to find the most probable dependency structure. In this study, we use support vector machines (SVMs) to estimate the probability values and use a beam search algorithm to find the most likely dependency structure.

  In parsing Japanese text, the root position is not an issue. For Thai, however, we have to identify the root position before finding the complete dependency relations. Thus, we incorporate an additional module to identify the root node of the sentence. This root finding module is also based on an SVM.

  The root finding module selects the word with highest probability of being the root node. The following features are used in the root model: 1. POS, 2. position, 3. number of verbs, 4. number of equivalent POS in front of this word, 5. number of equivalent POS after this word, 6. number of equivalent major POS in front of this word and 7. number of equivalent major POS after this word.

  For building the dependency model (e.g. relation between w_i and w_j), the following features are used: 1. POS of w_i and w_j, 2. dependency direction, 3. distance, 4. major category of w_i and w_j, 5. major POS of w_i and w_j and 6. positions of w_i and w_j.

  After identifying the root node and creating the probability matrix, the beam search (beam width=3) is performed.

- *Model 2* : For the second model, we adopt MaltParser 1.0.4 (Nivre et al., 2007) which is a shift-reduce parser. Machine learning algorithms are used to predict the sequence of actions for parsing. In this study, we use the default setting that utilizes an SVM for predicting parsing actions.

  Assuming that $\{i_0, i_1, i_2, i_4\}$ are the first four tokens in the remaining input and $\{s_0, s_1\}$ are the two topmost tokens on the stack, we use the default features including: 1. POS of $\{i_0, i_1, i_2, i_3, s_0, s_1\}$, 2. word form of $\{s_0, i_0, i_1, head(s_0)\}$, 3. dependency type of s_0 and its leftmost and rightmost dependent and the leftmost dependent of i_0.

Table 1: Performance of dependency parsing

	RA	DA	CSA
Model 1†	85.4%	76.0%	44.8%
Model 1‡	**86.2%**	**77.5%**	**47.9%**
Model 2†	89.31%	83.53%	60.30%
Model 2‡	**91.22%**	**86.03%**	**65.27%**

Note: † (without chunk), ‡ (with chunk)

To examine the role of base-NP chunk information in dependency parsing, we include chunk labels in the feature sets of both parsers. Base-NP chunks are represented by using the IOB2 format (Sang and Veenstra, 1999). In the first parsing model, the chunk label of the current word is added as a feature of the root model, while the chunk labels of both considered words are added in the dependency model. We also add a feature showing that both words reside in the same chunk or not to the dependency model. In the second model, we include chunk labels of $\{s_0, s_1, i_0, i_1, i_2, i_3\}$ as its feature set.

We use a section of completely annotated corpus consisting of 2616 sentences to experiment with dependency parsing. The sentence length ranges between 2 words to 20 words with an average of 5.68. These Thai sentences are part of our Thai-Japanese parallel corpus developed for the MT project. Since our MT project aims for the conversation domain, the source sentences are adopted mainly from dialogues and conversation books. A morphological analyzer is applied to these Thai sentences for word segmentation and POS tagging, and the results are revised manually by our annotators. The sentences are then assigned chunk labels with IOB2 representation and syntactic structure respectively.

The corpus is divided into 2355 sentences as the training set and 261 sentences as the test set. The experiment is done with gold-standard POS tags and chunk labels. Three performance metrics are used: 1. *Root accuracy (RA)*: a portion of sentences with correctly identified roots, 2. *Dependency accuracy (DA)*: a ratio of correct dependency relations to all dependency links and 3. *Complete sentence accuracy (CSA)*: a portion of sentences with correct roots and dependency patterns.

Table 1 shows the accuracy of two parsers with and without using chunk information. The results show that chunk information helps in improving the performance of both parsers, especially in the number of completely correct sentences. MaltParser (Model 2) which is a shift-reduce parser performs better in parsing Thai sentences. This conforms with previously published literature that shift-reduce parsers have been widely applied to languages with dependency structure close to Thai (e.g. English and Chinese), while variants of Model 1 are applied to languages with more constraints in dependency structure (like Japanese).

Although the parsing accuracy can be improved by chunk information, the results are based on gold-standard chunk labels. To examine the possibility for deriving chunk labels automatically, we implement and evaluate base-NP chunkers in the next section.

3 Base-NP Chunking

We implement a simplified version of Kudo's chunker (Kudo and Matsumoto, 2001). Kudo's chunker obtained very promising results on standard English chunking tasks (e.g. precision=94.2%, recall=94.3%, $F_{\beta=1} = 94.2\%$). We use forward parsing method and employ an SVM for identifying chunk labels. The original feature set of Kudo's chunker consists of: word form, POS and previous chunk labels. Specifically, the following features are used in identifying the chunk label of the word w_i: word form and POS of $\{w_{i-2}, w_{i-1}, w_i, w_{i+1}, w_{i+2}\}$, chunk labels of $\{w_{i-2}, w_{i-1}\}$. However, some preliminary results show that the original feature set does not work well with our problem. The obtained model suffers from overfitting and lack of generalization. Thus, we modify the feature set as: POS of $\{w_{i-2}, w_{i-1}, w_i, w_{i+1}\}$, chunk labels of $\{w_{i-2}, w_{i-1}\}$ and the current size of NP chunk in front of w_i. An SVM is trained to estimate the probability of the current word being each of three chunk labels (B, I, O). A beam search strategy is used to find the most probable chunk sequence.

In additional to the SVM-based chunkers, we also examine chunkers based on conditional random fields (CRFs). We use the implementation of CRF++ (Kudo, 2008). CRFs outperform several methods on this task (Sha and Pereira, 2003). Three CRF-based chunkers are included in the experiment: the first one uses word form and POS as its feature set, the second one includes word class (function word, content word) as an additional feature, the third one uses the previous three features and the major POS category.

We use the training set and test set from previous section to experiment with chunking. Table 2 shows the performance of all chunkers. A baseline algorithm selects the chunk label which is most frequently associated with POS of the current word. From the results, all chunkers outperform the baseline algorithm. The best performance can be obtained by one of CRF-based chunkers ($F_{\beta=1} = 83.06\%$). The inclusion of more features for CRF-based chunkers helps in improving the performance. In contrast, SVM-based chunkers tend to suffer from overfitting when adding more features. The results also confirm the findings of (Sha and Pereira, 2003) that CRF-based chunkers can beat any single model. However, the results are still lower than the results found in English experiments. A reason may be that Thai NPs are more ambiguous than English NPs. This is confirmed by a comparison between our baseline result ($F_{\beta=1}$=55.4%) and some baseline results of English base-NP chunking task (e.g. precision=81.9%, recall=78.2%, $F_{\beta=1}$=80.0% (Ramshaw and Marcus, 1995)). Since the baseline algorithms work exactly in the same way, the results imply that the Thai chunking task is more difficult.

We also examine the use of the best chunker as a preprocessing step of dependency parsing. Using the parser Model 2, the results are as follows: RA=90.84%, DA=84.99%, CSA=63.74%. Overall, the accuracy of using predicted chunk labels is

Table 2: Performance of base-NP chunking

	Pr.	R.	$F_{\beta=1}$
Baseline	48.5%	64.5%	55.4%
SVM+beam search			
beam width=1	70.1%	65.5%	67.7%
beam width=3	70.6%	66.6%	68.5%
beam width=5	69.6%	65.5%	67.5%
beam width=10	71.0%	66.9%	68.9%
beam width=20	71.0%	66.9%	68.9%
CRF			
word+POS	84.79%	78.52%	81.54%
word+POS+class	85.34%	79.93%	82.54%
word+POS+class+main POS	**86.04%**	**80.28%**	**83.06%**

lower than the use of gold-standard chunk labels, but still better than without any chunk information. Although the chunking accuracy is not high as in the reported results of English chunking tasks, the results show that the dependency parsing still benefits from the predicted chunk information.

4 Conclusions

The results from the chunking task show that the chunk identification for Thai is not trivial due to ambiguities in Thai NPs. The CRF-based chunkers (best:$F_{\beta=1} = 83.06\%$) are found to be more effective than the SVM-based chunkers (best:$F_{\beta=1} = 68.9\%$).

Using the predicted chunk labels from the best chunker in dependency parsing, the performance of the best dependency parser can be improved from CSA:60.30% to CSA:63.74%. This accuracy may further be improved if the performance of chunker can be increased (as is shown in parsing accuracy when using gold-standard chunk labels).

References

Aroonmanakun, Wirote. 1989. A dependency analysis of thai sentences for a computerized parsing system. Master thesis, Department of Linguistics, Chulalongkorn University.

Cheng, Yuchang, Masayuki Asahara, and Yuji Matsumoto. 2005. Chinese deterministic dependency analyzer: Examining effects of global features and root node finder. In *Proceedings of the Fourth SIGHAN Workshop on Chinese Language Processing*, pages 17–24.

Eryigit, Gülsen and Kemal Oflazer. 2006. Statistical dependency parsing for turkish. In *EACL*. The Association for Computer Linguistics.

Kudo, Taku and Yuji Matsumoto. 2001. Chunking with support vector machines. In *NAACL*.

Kudo, Taku. 2008. CRF++: Yet another CRF toolkit. http://crfpp.sourceforge.net/.

Nivre, Joakim and Mario Scholz. 2004. Deterministic dependency parsing of english text. In *Proceedings of Coling 2004*, pages 64–70, Geneva, Switzerland, Aug 23–Aug 27. COLING.

Nivre, Joakim, Johan Hall, Jens Nilsson, Atanas Chanev, Gülşen Eryiğit, Sandra Kübler, Stetoslav Marinov, and Erwin Marsi. 2007. Maltparser: A language-independent system for data-driven dependency parsing. *Natural Language Engineering Journal*, 13(2):99–135.

Ramshaw, Lance A. and Mitchell P. Marcus. 1995. Text chunking using transformation-based learning. In *Proceedings of the Third Workshop on Very Large Corpora*, pages 82–94.

Sang, Erik F. Tjong Kim and Jorn Veenstra. 1999. Representing text chunks. In *Proceedings of the ninth conference on European chapter of the Association for Computational Linguistics*, pages 173–179, Morristown, NJ, USA. Association for Computational Linguistics.

Satayamas, Vee, Chalatip Thumkanon, and Asanee Kawtrakul. 2005. Bootstrap cleaning and quality control for Thai tree bank construction. In *The 9th National Computer Science and Engineering Conference*, Bangkok, Thailand, Oct 27–Oct 28. (In Thai).

Sekine, Satoshi, Kiyotaka Uchimoto, and Hitoshi Isahara. 2000. Backward beam search algorithm for dependency analysis of japanese. In *COLING*, pages 754–760. Morgan Kaufmann.

Sha, Fei and Fernando C. N. Pereira. 2003. Shallow parsing with conditional random fields. In *HLT-NAACL*.

Building a Bilingual Lexicon Using Phrase-based Statistical Machine Translation via a Pivot Language

Takashi Tsunakawa[†] **Naoaki Okazaki**[†] **Jun'ichi Tsujii**[†‡]

[†]Department of Computer Science, Graduate School of Information Science and Technology, University of Tokyo 7-3-1, Hongo, Bunkyo-ku, Tokyo, 113-0033 Japan

[‡]School of Computer Science, University of Manchester / National Centre for Text Mining 131 Princess Street, Manchester, M1 7DN, UK

{tuna, okazaki, tsujii}@is.s.u-tokyo.ac.jp

Abstract

This paper proposes a novel method for building a bilingual lexicon through a pivot language by using phrase-based statistical machine translation (SMT). Given two bilingual lexicons between language pairs L_f–L_p and L_p–L_e, we assume these lexicons as parallel corpora. Then, we merge the extracted two phrase tables into one phrase table between L_f and L_e. Finally, we construct a phrase-based SMT system for translating the terms in the lexicon L_f–L_p into terms of L_e and, obtain a new lexicon L_f–L_e. In our experiments with Chinese-English and Japanese-English lexicons, our system could cover 72.8% of Chinese terms and drastically improve the utilization ratio.

1 Introduction

The bilingual lexicon is a crucial resource for multilingual applications in natural language processing including machine translation (Brown et al., 1990) and cross-lingual information retrieval (Nie et al., 1999). A number of bilingual lexicons have been constructed manually, despite their expensive compilation costs. However, it is unrealistic to build a bilingual lexicon for every language pair; thus, comprehensible bilingual lexicons are available only for a limited number of language pairs.

One of the solutions is to build a bilingual lexicon of the source language L_f and the target L_e through a pivot language L_p, when large bilingual lexicons L_f–L_p and L_p–L_e are available. Numerous researchers have explored the use of pivot languages (Tanaka and Umemura, 1994; Schafer and Yarowsky, 2002; Zhang et al., 2005). This approach is advantageous because we can obtain a bilingual lexicon between L_e and L_f, even if no bilingual lexicon exists between these languages.

Pivot-based methods for dictionary construction may produce incorrect translations when the word w_e is translated from a word w_f by a polysemous pivot word w_p[1]. Previous work addressed the polysemy problem in pivot-based methods (Tanaka and Umemura, 1994; Schafer and Yarowsky, 2002). Pivot-based methods also suffer from a mismatch problem, in which a pivot word w_p from a source word w_f does not exist in the bilingual lexicon L_p–L_e[2]. Moreover, a bilingual lexicon for technical terms is prone to include a number of pivot terms that are not included in another lexicon.

This paper proposes a method for building a bilingual lexicon through a pivot language by using phrase-based statistical machine translation (SMT) (Koehn et al., 2003). We build a translation model between L_f and L_e by assuming two lexicons L_f–L_p and L_p–L_e as parallel corpora, in order to increase the obtained lexicon size by handling multi-word expressions appropriately. The main advantage of this method is its ability to incorporate various translation models that associate languages L_f–L_e; for example, we can further improve the translation model by integrating a small bilingual lexicon L_f–L_e.

©2008. Licensed under the *Creative Commons Attribution-Noncommercial-Share Alike 3.0 Unported* license (http://creativecommons.org/licenses/by-nc-sa/3.0/). Some rights reserved.

[1]A Japanese term "土手": *dote*, embankment, may be associated with a Chinese term "银行," *yínháng*: banking institution, using the pivot word *bank* in English.

[2]It is impossible to associate two translation pairs ("地球温暖化 (*chikyū-ondanka*)," global warming), and (global heating, "全球变暖 (*quánqiú-biànnuǎn*)") because of the difference in English (pivot) terms.

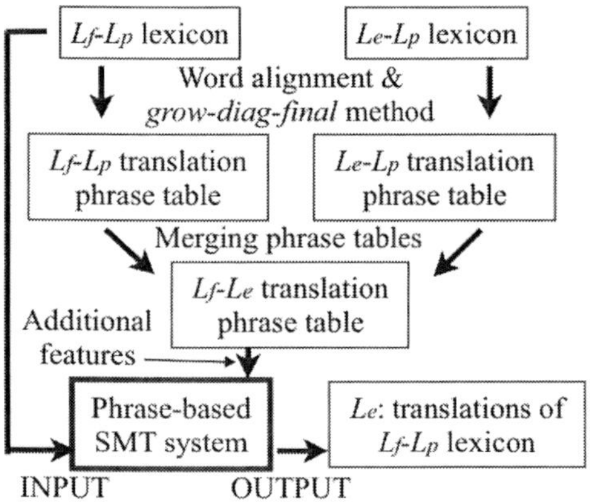

Figure 1: Framework of our approach

2 Merging two bilingual lexicons

We introduce phrase-based SMT for merging the lexicons, in order to improve both the merged lexicon size and its accuracy. Recently, several researchers proposed the use of the pivot language for phrase-based SMT (Utiyama and Isahara, 2007; Wu and Wang, 2007). We employ a similar approach for obtaining phrase translations with the translation probabilities by assuming the bilingual lexicons as parallel corpora. Figure 1 illustrates the framework of our approach.

Let us suppose that we have two bilingual lexicons L_f–L_p and L_p–L_e. We obtain word alignments of these lexicons by applying GIZA++ (Och and Ney, 2003), and *grow-diag-final* heuristics (Koehn et al., 2007). Let $\bar{w}_x$ be a phrase that represents a sequence of words in the language L_x. For phrase pairs $(\bar{w}_p, \bar{w}_f)$ and $(\bar{w}_e, \bar{w}_p)$, the translation probabilities $p(\bar{w}_p|\bar{w}_f)$ and $p(\bar{w}_e|\bar{w}_p)$ are computed using the maximum likelihood estimation from the co-occurrence frequencies, consistent with the word alignment in the bilingual lexicons. We calculate the direct translation probabilities between source and target phrases,

$$p(\bar{w}_e|\bar{w}_f) = \frac{\sum_{\bar{w}_p} p(\bar{w}_e|\bar{w}_p)p(\bar{w}_p|\bar{w}_f)}{\sum_{\bar{w}'_e}\sum_{\bar{w}_p} p(\bar{w}'_e|\bar{w}_p)p(\bar{w}_p|\bar{w}_f)}. \quad (1)$$

We employ the log-linear model of phrase-based SMT (Och and Ney, 2002) for translating the source term $\bar{w}_f$ in the lexicon L_f–L_p into the target language by finding a term $\hat{\bar{w}}_e$ that maximizes the translation probability,

$$\begin{aligned} \hat{\bar{w}}_e &= \text{argmax}_{\bar{w}_e} \Pr(\bar{w}_e|\bar{w}_f) \\ &= \text{argmax}_{\bar{w}_e} \sum_{m=1}^{M} \lambda_m h_m(\bar{w}_e, \bar{w}_f), \quad (2) \end{aligned}$$

where we have M feature functions $h_m(\bar{w}_e, \bar{w}_f)$ and model parameters λ_m.

In addition to the typical features for the SMT framework, we introduce two features: *character-based similarity*, and *additional bilingual lexicon*. We define a *character-based similarity* feature,

$$h_{\text{char\_sim}}(\bar{w}_e, \bar{w}_f) = 1 - \frac{\text{ED}(\bar{w}_e, \bar{w}_f)}{\max(\bar{w}_e, \bar{w}_f)}, \quad (3)$$

where $\text{ED}(x, y)$ represents a Levenshtein distance of characters between the two terms x and y[3]. We also define an *additional bilingual lexicon* feature,

$$h_{\text{add\_lex}}(\bar{w}_e, \bar{w}_f) = \sum_i \log p'(\bar{w}_e^{(i)}|\bar{w}_f^{(i)}), \quad (4)$$

where $\bar{w}_e^{(i)}$ and $\bar{w}_f^{(i)}$ represent an i-th translated phrase pair on the term pair $(\bar{w}_e, \bar{w}_f)$ during the decoding, and $p'(\bar{w}_e^{(i)}|\bar{w}_f^{(i)})$ represents the phrase translation probabilities derived from the additional lexicon. The probability $p'(\bar{w}_e^{(i)}|\bar{w}_f^{(i)})$ is calculated using the maximum likelihood estimation.

3 Experiment

3.1 Data

For building a Chinese-to-Japanese lexicon, we used the Japanese-English lexicon released by JST[4] (527,206 term pairs), and the Chinese-English lexicon compiled by Wanfang Data[5] (525,259 term pairs). Both cover a wide range of named entities and technical terms that may not be included in an ordinary dictionary. As an additional lexicon, we used the Japanese-English-Chinese trilingual lexicon[6] (596,967 term pairs) generated from EDR[7] Japanese-English lexicon.

We lower-cased and tokenized all terms by the following analyzers: JUMAN[8] for Japanese, the MEMM-based POS tagger[9] for English, and *cjma* (Nakagawa and Uchimoto, 2007) for Chinese.

3.2 The sizes and coverage of merged lexicons

Table 1 shows the distinct numbers of terms in the original and merged lexicons, and the *uti-*

[3] We regard the different shapes of Han characters between Chinese and Japanese as identical in our experiments.

[4] Japan Science and Technology Agency (JST) http://pr.jst.go.jp/others/tape.html

[5] http://www.wanfangdata.com/

[6] This data was manually compiled by NICT, Japan.

[7] http://www2.nict.go.jp/r/r312/EDR/index.html

[8] http://nlp.kuee.kyoto-u.ac.jp/nl-resource/juman.html

[9] http://www-tsujii.is.s.u-tokyo.ac.jp/~tsuruoka/postagger/

Lexicon	L_C size	L_E size	L_J size
L_C–L_E	375,990	429,807	-
L_E–L_J	-	418,044	465,563
L_E (distinct)	-	783,414	-
Additional lex.	94,928	-	90,605
Exact matching	98,537 (26.2%)	68,996	103,437 (22.2%)
Unique matching	4,875 (1.3%)	4,875	4,875 (1.0%)

Table 1: The statistics of lexicons

lization ratio[10] in the parentheses. For comparison, we prepared two baseline systems for building Chinese-Japanese lexicons. *Exact matching* connects source and target terms that share at least one common translation term in the pivot language. *Unique matching* is an extreme approach for avoiding negative effects of polysemous pivot terms: it connects source and target terms if source, pivot, and target terms appear only once in the corresponding lexicons.

Exact matching achieved 26.2% of the utilization ratio in Japanese-to-Chinese translation, and 22.2% in Chinese-to-Japanese translation. These figures imply that about 75% of the terms remained unused in building the Japanese-Chinese lexicon. With *unique matching*, as little as 1% of Japanese and Chinese terms could be used. In contrast, our method could cover 72.8% of Chinese terms by generating Japanese terms, which was a drastic improvement in the utilization ratio.

3.3 Generating Japanese translations of the Chinese-English lexicon

For evaluating the correctness of the merged lexicons, we assumed the lexicon generated by the *unique matching* as a development/test set. Development and test sets consist of about 2,400 term pairs, respectively. Next, we input Chinese terms in the development/test set into our system based on Moses (Koehn et al., 2007), and obtained the Japanese translations. We evaluated the performance by using BLEU, NIST, and accuracy measures. Table 2 shows the evaluation results on the test set. Our system could output correct translations for 68.5% of 500 input terms. The table also reports that additional features were effective in improving the performance.

We also conducted another experiment to generate Japanese translations for Chinese terms included in an external resource. We randomly extracted 500 Chinese-English term pairs from the Wanfang Data lexicon, for which the English term cannot be mapped by the JST lexicon, but can be mapped by another lexicon *Eijiro*[11]. Table 3 shows the results for these 500 terms. *Prec1* or *Prec10* are the precisions that the 1- or 10-best translations include the correct one, respectively. *MRR* (mean reciprocal rank) is $(1/500)\sum_i(1/r_i)$, where r_i is the highest rank of the correct translations for the i-th term.

[10] The number of terms in the original lexicon used for building the merged lexicon.

Features	BLEU	NIST	Acc.
Typical features	0.4519	7.4060	0.676
w/ *character similarity*	0.4670	7.4963	0.682
w/ *additional lexicon*	0.4800	7.5907	0.674
All	0.4952	7.7046	0.685

Table 2: Translation performance on the test set

Features/Models	Prec1	Prec10	MRR
Typical features	0.142	0.232	0.1719
w/ *character similarity*	0.136	0.224	0.1654
w/ *additional lexicon*	0.140	0.230	0.1704
All	0.140	0.230	0.1714
E-to-J translation	0.090	0.206	0.1256

Table 3: Evaluation results for the *Eijiro* dictionary

Since the input lexicons are Chinese-English term pairs, their Japanese translations can be generated directly from the English terms by applying an English-Chinese translation system. We compared our system to an English-Japanese phrase-based SMT system (*E-to-J translation*), constructed from the JST Japanese-English lexicon. Table 3 shows that our system outperformed the English-to-Japanese direct translation system.

Table 4 displays translation examples. The first example shows that our system could output a correct translation (denoted by [T]); and the E-to-J system failed to translate the source term ([F]), because it could not reorder the source English words and translate the word *pubis* correctly. In the second example, our system could reproduce Chinese characters "流体 (fluid)", but the E-to-J system output a semantically acceptable but awkward Japanese term. In the last example, the word segmentation of the source Chinese term was incorrect ("中间 腰(lumber) 淋巴(lymph) 结" is correct). Thus, our system received an invalid word "腰淋" and could not find a translation for the word.

[11] http://www.eijiro.jp/

English	**Chinese**	**Japanese (*Eijiro*)**	**Japanese (C-to-J)**	**Japanese (E-to-J)**
symphysis pubis	耻骨 联合	恥骨結合	恥 骨 結合 [T]	結合 恥 (symphysis shame) [F]
ideal fluid dynamics	理想 流体 动力学	理想流体力学	理想 流体 力学 [T]	理想 液 (fluid) 力学 [F]
intermediate lumbar lymph nodes	中间 腰淋 巴结	中間腰リンパ節	中 間 節 腰 淋 (intermediate node [lumbar-lymph]INVALID) [F]	中間 腰 リンパ 節 [T]

Table 4: Translation examples on *Eijiro* dictionary

4 Conclusion

This paper proposed a novel method for building a bilingual lexicon by using a pivot language. Given two bilingual lexicons L_f–L_p and L_p–L_e, we constructed a phrase-based SMT system from L_f–L_e by merging the lexicons into a phrase translation table L_f–L_e. The experimental results demonstrated that our method improves the utilization ratio of given lexicons drastically. We also showed that the pivot approach was more effective than the SMT system that translates from L_p to L_e directly.

The future direction would be to introduce other resources such as the parallel corpora and other pivot languages into the SMT system for improving the precision and the coverage of the obtained lexicon. We are also planning on evaluating a machine translation system that integrates our model.

Acknowledgments

This work was partially supported by Grant-in-Aid for Specially Promoted Research (MEXT, Japan) and Japanese/Chinese Machine Translation Project in Special Coordination Funds for Promoting Science and Technology (MEXT, Japan).

References

Brown, Peter F., John Cocke, Stephen A. Della Pietra, Vincent J. Della Pietra, Fredrick Jelinek, John D. Lafferty, Robert L. Mercer, and Paul S. Roossin. 1990. A statistical approach to machine translation. *Computational Linguistics*, 16(2):79–85.

Koehn, Philipp, Franz Josef Och, and Daniel Marcu. 2003. Statistical phrase-based translation. In *Proc. of the 2003 Conference of the North American Chapter of the Association for Computational Linguistics on Human Language Technology*, pages 48–54.

Koehn, Philipp, Hieu Hoang, Alexandra Birch, Chris Callison-Burch, Marcello Federico, Nicola Bertoldi, Brooke Cowan, Wade Shen, Christine Moran, Richard Zens, Chris Dyer, Ondrej Bojar, Alexandra Constantin, and Evan Herbst. 2007. Moses: Open source toolkit for statistical machine translation. In *Proc. of the 45th Annual Meeting of the Association for Computational Linguistics, demonstration session*, pages 177–180.

Nakagawa, Tetsuji and Kiyotaka Uchimoto. 2007. Hybrid approach to word segmentation and POS tagging. In *Companion Volume to the Proc. of the 45th Annual Meeting of the Association for Computational Linguistics*, pages 217–220.

Nie, Jian-Yun, Michel Simard, Pierre Isabelle, and Richard Durand. 1999. Cross-language information retrieval based on parallel texts and automatic mining of parallel texts from the Web. In *Proc. of the 22nd Annual International ACM SIGIR Conference on Research and Development in Information Retrieval*, pages 74–81.

Och, Franz Josef and Hermann Ney. 2002. Discriminative training and maximum entropy models for statistical machine translation. In *Proc. of the 40th Annual Meeting of the Association for Computational Linguistics*, pages 295–302.

Och, Franz Josef and Hermann Ney. 2003. A systematic comparison of various statistical alignment models. *Computational Linguistics*, 29(1):19–51.

Schafer, Charles and David Yarowsky. 2002. Inducing translation lexicons via diverse similarity measures and bridge languages. In *Proc. of the 6th Conference on Natural Language Learning*, volume 20, pages 1–7.

Tanaka, Kumiko and Kyoji Umemura. 1994. Construction of a bilingual dictionary intermediated by a third language. In *Proc. of the 15th International Conference on Computational Linguistics*, pages 297–303.

Utiyama, Masao and Hitoshi Isahara. 2007. A comparison of pivot methods for phrase-based statistical machine translation. In *Proc. of Human Language Technologies 2007: The Conference of the North American Chapter of the Association for Computational Linguistics*, pages 484–491.

Wu, Hua and Haifeng Wang. 2007. Pivot language approach for phrase-based statistical machine translation. In *Proc. of the 45th Annual Meeting of the Association for Computational Linguistics*, pages 856–863.

Zhang, Yujie, Qing Ma, and Hitoshi Isahara. 2005. Construction of a Japanese-Chinese bilingual dictionary using English as an intermediary. *International Journal of Computer Processing of Oriental Languages*, 18(1):23–39.

Explaining Similarity of Terms

Vishnu Vyas
USC Information Sciences Institute
Marina del Rey, CA
vishnu@isi.edu

Patrick Pantel
Yahoo! Inc.
Santa Clara, CA 95054
me@patrickpantel.com

Abstract

Computing the similarity between entities is a core component of many NLP tasks such as measuring the semantic similarity of terms for generating a distributional thesaurus. In this paper, we study the problem of explaining post-hoc why a set of terms are similar. Given a set of terms, our task is to generate a small set of explanations that best characterizes the similarity of those terms. Our contributions include: 1) an information-theoretic objective function for quantifying the utility of an explanation set; 2) a survey of psycholinguistics and philosophy for evidence of different sources of explanations such as descriptive properties and prototypes; 3) computational baseline models for automatically generating various types of explanations; and 4) a qualitative evaluation of our explanation generation engine.

1 Introduction

Computing similarity is at the core of many computer science tasks. Many have developed algorithms for computing the semantic similarity of words (Lee, 1999), of expressions to generate paraphrases (Lin and Pantel, 2001) and of documents (Salton and McGill, 1983). However, little investigation has been spent on automatically explaining why a particular set of elements are similar to one another.

Explaining similarity is an important part of various natural language applications such as question answering and building lexical ontologies such as WordNet (Fellbaum, 1998). Several questions must be addressed before one can begin to explore this topic. First, what constitutes a good explanation and what are the sources of these explanations? Second, how can we automatically generate these different types of explanations? Third, how do we empirically evaluate the quality of an explanation? In this paper, we propose a first analysis of these questions.

© 2008. Licensed under the *Creative Commons Attribution-Noncommercial-Share Alike 3.0 Unported* license (http://creativecommons.org/licenses/by-nc-sa/3.0/). Some rights reserved.

2 Related Work

The task of generating explanations has been studied in relation to Question Answering (Hirschman and Gaizauskas, 2001) and Knowledge Representation and Reasoning (Cohen et al., 1998). Within Question Answering, explanations have mostly been viewed from a deductive framework and have focused on proof trees and inference traces as sources of explanations (Moldovan and Rus, 2001). Summarization and text generation from proof trees have also been explored as explanations in QA systems (Barker et al., 2004). Lester (1997) proposed explanation design packages, a hybrid representation for discourse knowledge that generates multi-sentential explanations.

Detailed psycholinguistic studies into how people explain things suggests that people explain similarity using "feature complexes" (Fillenbaum, 1969), a bundle of features semantically related with a term. This suggests considering explanations of similarity as the shared features among a set of terms. Another competing idea from linguistic philosophy is the Prototype theory by Rosch (1975). It is argued that objects within a semantic category are represented by another, more commonly used or much simpler member of the same semantic category, called a prototype. And, within this view, explanations for similarity are prototypes from the same semantic category as the given terms. Deese (1966) investigated similarity in terms of stimulus-response word association experiments providing empirical evidence to consider other semantically similar words as explanations.

3 An Information Theoretic Framework for Explaining Similarity

In this section, we present an information-theoretic framework that defines a *good explanation* using the intuition that they are highly informative and reduce the uncertainty in the set of query terms. For example, consider the set of query terms {*Maybach, Maserati, Renault*}. One possible explanation of their similarity which is very informative is *they are all like a Ford* (i.e., a prototype explanation). Other possible explanations include *they can be driven using a steering wheel and they have wheels* (i.e., descriptive properties as explanations). Each of these explanations reduces the uncertainty regarding the semantics of the original set of terms. In information theory, the concept of reduction in uncertainty is related to information gain, and good explanation sets can be quantified in terms of information gain.

Formally, given a set of query terms Q, and a set of explanations E, we define the best explanation set as one which provides maximum information to the set Q, or in other words,

$$E = argmax_{E' \in \phi(\Xi)} I(Q; E') \tag{1}$$

where Ξ is the set of all explanations (discussed in detail in Section 4) and $\phi(X)$ represents the power set of X. The problem of choosing the best explanation set for a given query set is now reduced to a problem of optimization under I.

3.1 The Information Function

The information function I in Eq. (1) is a set function which defines the amount of information contributed by the set of explanations E' to the set of query words Q. There are many possible information functions, but we would like all of them to have some common properties.

Consistency

The information function should be consistent. For two sets, E and E', if $E \subseteq E'$ then $I(Q; E') \geq I(Q; E)$. In other words, given two explanation sets E and E', with E' containing extra explanations, not in E, the information function should assign larger values to E' with respect to Q than it assigns to E.

Explanation Set Cardinality

Another important requirement regarding I, is the size of the explanation sets. Any consistent information function would assign larger values to larger sets of explanations. This leads to a problem where the optimal solution is always the set of all explanations. We overcome this by fixing an upper bound for the size of explanation sets that are generated by the function I.

Redundancy and Joint Information

Many explanations in an explanation set might overlap semantically and the information function has to account for such overlaps. However, information functions which take such semantic overlap into account are computationally hard to optimize. One approach to this problem is to find approximate solutions using heuristic search techniques, however, relaxing this constraint lets us use common association measures such as mutual information (Cover and Thomas, 1991) as information functions.

3.2 Marginal Formulation of the Information Function

Another equivalent formulation of Eq. (1) is to use marginal information gains. This formulation also gives a simple greedy algorithm to the optimization problem when the size of explanation set is fixed. Let us define the marginal gain in information to the set Q, when the explanation e is added to the set of explanations E as:

$$IG_{Q;E}(e) = I(Q; E \cup \{e\}) - I(Q; E)$$

Then, the best set of explanations of size k can be recursively defined as

$$E_0 = \{\}$$

$$E_n = E_{n-1} \cup \{e\}$$

such that

$$e = argmax_{e' \in \Xi} IG_{Q;E_{n-1}}(e')$$

and

$$|E_n| \leq k$$

If our marginal information gain is independent of the set of explanations to which it is added, we can rank explanations by their marginal information gains as added to the empty set. Then, choosing the top k explanations gives us the k-best explanation set for the query.

4 Sources for Similarity Explanations

In Section 3, we presented a framework for quantifying a good explanation set. In this section we present two sources of explanations, using *descriptive properties* and using *prototypes*.

4.1 Explanations from Descriptive Properties

The concept of *essence* as discussed by early empiricists was the first study of using descriptive properties to explain the similarity of a set of terms. Descriptive properties are the shared essential attributes of a set of similar terms and one way of explaining the similarity of a set of terms is to generate descriptive properties.

Within our framework in Section 3, let the query set Q be a set of similar words, and let Ξ, the set of all explanations be the set of all properties that are shared by all the words within the query set. Using mutual information as our measure of association between properties and terms we can rewrite our information function I as:

$$I(Q;E) = \sum_{q \in Q} p(q) \sum_{e \in E} p(e \mid q) \log \frac{p(e \mid q)}{p(e)}$$

The marginal information gain for a single explanation e is:

$$IG_{Q;E}(e) = \sum_{q \in Q} p(q) \cdot p(e \mid q) \log \frac{p(e \mid q)}{p(e)}$$

Since the information gain is independent of the explanation set E, we can find the best set of size k by greedily choosing explanations until our explanation set reaches the desired size.

4.2 Explanations from Prototypes

As discussed in Section 2 given a set of query terms, people can represent their meaning using other common members from the same semantic category, called prototypes. Within the framework of Section 3, let Q be our set of query terms. To generate the set of all explanations Ξ, we use clusters in the CBC resource (Pantel and Lin, 2002) as an approximation to semantic categories and we collect all possible words that belong to that cluster which then becomes our candidate set.

Let C_q denote the cluster to which the query term q belongs to. Also let the set $C(Q)$ be the set of all clusters to which the query terms of Q belong to. Then

$$\Xi = \{w \mid C_w \in C(Q)\}$$

Now our information function can be written as:

$$I(Q;E) = \sum_{q \in Q} p(C_q) \sum_{e \in E} p(e \mid C_q) \log \frac{p(e \mid C_q)}{p(e)}$$

The marginal formulation of the above function is:

$$I_{Q;E}(e) = \sum_{q \in Q} p(C_q) \cdot p(e \mid C_q) \log \frac{p(e \mid C_q)}{p(e)}$$

We can find the optimal set of explanations of size k using a greedy algorithm as in Section 4.1.

5 Experimental Results

5.1 Experimental Setup

For each source of explanation discussed in Section 4, we estimated the model probabilities using corpus statistics extracted from the 1999 AP newswire collection (part of the TREC-2002 Aquaint collection).

In order to obtain a representative set of similar terms as queries to our systems, we randomly chose 100 concepts from the CBC collection (Pantel and Lin, 2002) consisting of 1628 clusters of nouns. For each of these concepts, we randomly chose a set of cluster instances (nouns), where the size of each set was randomly chosen to consist of two to five nouns.

Each of these samples forms a query. For each explanation source described in Section 4, we generated explanation sets for the random samples and in the next section we show a random selection of these system outputs.

5.2 Examples of Explanations using Descriptive Properties

For the algorithm discussed in Section 4.1, we derived our descriptive properties using the output of the dependency analysis generated by the Minipar (Lin, 1994) dependency parser. We use syntactic dependencies between words to model their semantic properties. The assumption here is that some grammatical relations, such as subject and object can yield semantic properties of terms. For example, from a phrase like "students eat many apples", we can infer the properties *can-be-eaten* for *apples* and *can-eat* for *students*. In this paper, we use a combination of corpus statistics and manual filters for grammatical relations to uncover candidate semantic properties.

Table 1: Explanations generated using descriptive properties.

Query Sets	Explanations
Palestinian-Israeli, India-Pakistan	talks(NN), conflict(NN), dialogue(NN), relation(NN), peace(NN).
TV, television-station	cable(NN), watch(obj), see(ON), channel(NN), local(ADJ-MOD)
Britney Spears, Janet Jackson	like(OBJ), concert(NN), video(NN), fan(NN), album(GEN)
Crisis, Uncertainty, Difficulty	face(OBJ), resolve(OBJ), overcome(OBJ), financial(ADJ-MOD), political(ADJ-MOD)

Intuitively, one would prefer adjectival modifiers and verbal propositions as good descriptive properties for explanations, and from the examples, we can see our algorithm generates such descriptive properties because of the high information contribution of such properties to the query set. However, our algorithm does not try to reduce the redundancy within the sets of explanations. We can see redundant explanations for examples in Table 1. The reason is that each explanation added to the set is independent of the ones already present in the set. In Pantel and Vyas (2008) we propose a joint information model to overcome this problem.

5.3 Explanations using Prototypes

The algorithm discussed in Section 4.2 uses words that share the semantic category with words within the query set as the set of candidate explanations.

We can approximate the notion of semantic categories using clusters of semantically similar words. For this we used the CBC collection (Pantel and Lin 2002) of nouns. Using these clusters as semantic categories, the candidate set of all explanations is the set of all the words that belong to the same cluster. Table 2 shows some system outputs.

Table 2: Explanations generated using prototypes.

Query Sets	Explanations
TV, television station	station, network, radio, channel, television
Budweiser, Coors Light	Anheuser-Busch, Heineken, Coors, San Miguel, Lion Nathan
atom, electron,photon	particle, molecule, proton, Ion, isotope
Temple University,Michigan State University	University of Texas, University of Massachusetts, University of North Carolina,University of Virginia, University of Minnesota

6 Conclusions and Future Work

Computing the similarity between entities forms the basis of many computer science algorithms. However, we have little understanding of what constitutes the underlying similarity. In this paper, we investigated the problem of explaining why a set of terms are similar. We proposed an information-theoretic objective function for quantifying the utility of an explanation set, by capturing the intuition that the best explanation will be the one that is highly informative to the original query terms. We also explored various sources of explanations such as descriptive properties and prototypes. We then proposed baseline algorithms to automatically generate these types of explanations and we presented a qualitative evaluation of the baselines.

However, many other explanation sources were not addressed. Hypernyms and other hierarchical relations among words also form good explanation sources; for example the similarity of the terms $\{Ford,\ Toyota\}$ can be explained using the term *car*, a hypernym. Also our current explanation types would fail for query sets consisting of related terms such as $\{bus,\ road\}$. More appropriate for these queries would be identifying the relation linking the terms or giving analogies such as $\{boat,\ water\}$. We are working on algorithms to generate these explanation types within our information-theoretic framework. We are also investigating application-level quantitative evaluation methodologies. Candidate applications include providing answer support by explaining the answers generated by a QA system and explaining why a document was returned in an IR system.

References

Barker, K., Chaw, S., Fan, J., Porter, B., Tecuci, D., Yeh, P. Z., Chaudhri, V., Israel, D., Mishra, S., Romero, P., and Clark, P. 2004. *A Question-Answering System for AP Chemistry: Assessing KR&R Technologies.* In Proceedings of the Ninth International Conference on the Principles of Knowledge Representation and Reasoning (KR 2004). Whistler, 488-497

Cohen, P., Schrag, R., Jones, E., Pease, A., Lin, A., Start, B., Gunning, D., and Burke, M. 1998. *The DARPA High Performance Knowledge Bases Project.* AI Magazine 19(4): 5-49.

Cover, T. M. and Thomas, J. A. 1991. *Elements of Information Theory.* Wiley Interscience, New York.

Deese, J. 1966. *The Structure of Associations in Language and Thought.* John Hopkins Press, Oxford, England.

Fellbaum, C. 1998. *WordNet: An electronic lexical database.* MIT Press.

Fillenbaum, S. 1969. *Words as feature complexes : false recognition of antonyms and synonyms* Journal of Exp.Psychology, 1969.

L Hirschman, R Gaizauskas - Natural Language Engineering 2001. *Natural language question answering: the view from here.* Natural Language Engineering.

Lee, Lillian. 1999. *Measures of Distributional Similarity.* In Proceedings of ACL-93. pp. 25-32. College Park, MD

Lester, J. C., and Porter, B. W. 1997. *Developing and Empirically Evaluating Robust Explanation Generators: The KNIGHT Experiments* Computational Linguistics, v.23(1) p.65-101.

Lin, D. and Pantel, P. 2001. *Discovery of Inference Rules for Question Answering.* Natural Language Engineering 7(4):343-360.

Lin, D. 1994. *Principar - an efficient, broad-coverage, principle-based parser.* In Proceedings of COLING-94. pp. 4248. Kyoto, Japan.

Moldovan, D. I., and Rus, V. 2001. *Logic Form Transformation of WordNet and its Applicability to Question Answering* Meeting of the Association for Computational Linguistics, p. 394-401.

Pantel, P. and Lin, D. 2002. *Discovering Word Senses from Text.* In Proceedings of SIGKDD-02. pp. 613619. Edmonton, Canada.

Pantel, P. and Vyas, V. 2008 *A Joint Information Model for n-best Ranking* In Procesedings of COLING-2008. Manchester, UK.

Rosch, E. 1975. *Cognitive representations of semantic categories.* Journal of Exp.Psychology: General, 104, 192-233.

Salton, G. and McGill, M. J. 1983. *Introduction to Modern Information Retrieval.* McGraw Hill.

Robust and Efficient Chinese Word Dependency Analysis with Linear Kernel Support Vector Machines

Yu-Chieh Wu
Dept. of Computer Science and Information Engineering
National Central University
Taoyuan, Taiwan
bcbb@db.csie.ncu.edu.tw

Jie-Chi Yang
Graduate Institute of Network Learning Technology
National Central University
Taoyuan, Taiwan
yang@cl.ncu.edu.tw

Yue-Shi Lee
Dept. of Computer Science and Information Engineering
Ming Chuan University
Taoyuan, Taiwan
{leeys}@mcu.edu.tw

Abstract

Data-driven learning based on shift reduce parsing algorithms has emerged dependency parsing and shown excellent performance to many Treebanks. In this paper, we investigate the extension of those methods while considerably improved the runtime and training time efficiency via L_2-SVMs. We also present several properties and constraints to enhance the parser completeness in runtime. We further integrate root-level and bottom-level syntactic information by using sequential taggers. The experimental results show the positive effect of the root-level and bottom-level features that improve our parser from 81.17% to 81.41% and 81.16% to 81.57% labeled attachment scores with modified Yamada's and Nivre's method, respectively on the Chinese Treebank. In comparison to well-known parsers, such as MaltParser (80.74%) and MSTParser (78.08%), our methods produce not only better accuracy, but also drastically reduced testing time in 0.07 and 0.11, respectively.

1 Introduction

With the late development of Chinese Treebank (Xue et al. 2005), parsing Chinese is still an ongoing research issue. The goal of dependency parsing is to find the head-modifier (labeled) relations in texts. Though some of the parsing algorithms are language independent and show state-of-the-art performance on multilingual dependency Treebanks (Nivre et al., 2007; Buchholz and Marsi, 2006), they are often too slow for online purpose. Therefore, to develop an efficient and effective dependency parser is indispensable.

Over the past few years, several research studies had addressed the use of shift-reduce and edge-factored-based approaches attend fairly accurate performance in Chinese (Cheng et al., 2005; Hall, 2005; Wang et al., 2006). The former (shift-reduce) is a linear time algorithm, while the latter involves n^3 for decoding where n is the length of sentence. Even the shift-reduce approaches seems to be very efficient, most studies (Hall et al., 2007; Nivre et al., 2006) yet employ nonlinear kernel methods such as polynomial kernel support vector machines (SVMs). Furthermore, there is no research work directly compare with the two methods with Chinese Treebank. Nevertheless, the empirical training and testing time comparisons of those methods has not been reported yet.

In this paper, we present an efficient and robust parser for Chinese based on linear classifiers and shift-reduce parsing algorithms. We propose several useful properties to enhance the completeness of the two well-known shift-reduce algorithms, namely Nivre's shift reduce (NSR) (Nivre, 2003) and Yamada's shift reduce (YSR) (Yamada and Matsumoto, 2003) algorithms. To enhance the performance, we add root and bottom (neighbor) information by adopting sequential taggers. We also perform experiments on the Chinese Treebank and compare with two of the state-of-the-art parsers.

2 Parsing Algorithms

At the beginning, we briefly review the selected two parsing algorithm as follows. The NSR makes use of four parse actions to incrementally construct the dependency graph. By following the same notations as (Nivre, 2003), NSR initializes with $(S, I, A) = (\phi, W, \phi)$ where S is the stack (represented as a list), I is the queue initiated with all words, and A is the set of directed and labeled edges for the dependency graph. The stack is a list of words whose parent or child has not been found entirely. NSR incrementally parses a pair of words (one is the top of the stack and the other is the first word of the queue) and uses four parse actions to construct the dependency graph. The four parse actions are: {*Left-Arc* (*LA*), *Right-Arc* (*RA*), *Shift*, *Reduce*}. Both *LA* and *RA* could be parameterized with a dependence rela-

© 2008. Licensed under the *Creative Commons Attribution-Noncommercial-Share Alike 3.0 Unported* license (http://creativecommons.org/licenses/by-nc-sa/3.0/). Some rights reserved.

tion type. By parsing a pair of words step-by-step, the parser terminates when the queue is empty.

Similar to NSR, YSR constructs the dependency graph by incrementally parse a pair of no_head words. The original YSR algorithm (Yamada and Matsumoto, 2003) makes use of three parse actions to parse a sentence left-to-right and involves n^2 parser transitions. Recently, Chang et al. (2006) showed that by adding an extra parse action *Wait-Left* and performing the "step-back" operation can accomplish parse in linear time. The step-back means that after an action determined, the parse pair moves back with except for *Shift* action. *Wait-Left* is mainly proposed to wait the next word until all its right children having attached to heads. In this paper, we employ such modification to form our basic YSR algorithm.

2.1 Useful Properties

We give more formal definitions of the dependency graph as follows.

Let $R = \{r_1, r_2, r_3, \ldots, r_N\}$ be the finite set of dependency arc labels with N types. A dependency graph $G=(W, A)$ where W is the string of words $W= w_1, w_2, w_3$, etc. and A is the set of directed labeled arcs (w_x, r, w_y) where $r \in R$, and $w_x, w_y \in W$. For a parse pair w_x and w_y in a sentence, we introduce the following notation:

1. $w_x \rightarrow w_y$: w_x is the head of w_y, and $w_x \leftarrow w_y$: w_y is the head of w_x.
2. $w_x < w_y$: word w_x is on the left hand side of word w_y in the sentence.
3. (w_x, r, w_y): denotes the word w_y is the head of w_x with relation r.

Definition 1: Valid dependency graph

A dependency graph G is well formed and valid iff the following conditions are true.

1. G is connected
2. G is acyclic (cycle free)
3. G is projective
4. For each node in G, there is only one parent except the root word
5. G is a single rooted graph

Definition 2: Parse pair

When the parsing algorithm considers a pair of word (w_x, w_y), we name the pair "parse pair".

Definition 1 gives the formal definition of a valid dependency graph. Condition 3 and condition 5 are not always true for all languages. For example, there are multiple roots in Arabic dependency Treebank, while the dependency graph is usually non-projective according to the linguistic characteristics. Fortunately the dependency graphs in Chinese are fully projective and single rooted and thus compatible with Definition 1.

However, we can not always assume the classifier is perfect. During run-time, the classifier might make incorrect decision which leads to incorrect parse graph and even constructs an incomplete and invalid parse graph. For example, for NSR it is usually retain more than two words that are not attached to their heads in the stack. To solve it, we propose the following properties to enhance the completeness of the original NSR/YSR parsers.

Definition 3: One word sentence

If there is only one unparsed word, then it must be the root.

Proposition 4: Constrained parsing I

For a parse pair (w_x, w_y), if the head of w_x is not found previously, then the parse action *Reduce* is invalid.

Proof. The parse action *Reduce* will remove w_x from the stack and leads to an unconnected and multiple roots dependency graph (violates definition 1).

Proposition 5: Unique pair parsing

If there are only two unparsed words in G, then the parse action of this pair of words is limited to be $\{LA, RA\}$.

Proof. Clearly if the parse action is *Reduce*, then it violates Proposition 4 (unconnected graph). Similarly when applying *Shift*, the state does not change, i.e., there are still two unparsed words. Nonetheless, by applying either *LA* or *RA*, the two isolated words will be linked and gives a connected graph.

Proposition 6: Constrained parsing II

For a parse pair (w_x, w_y), if the head of w_x is found, then the parse action *RA* is invalid.

Proof. Assume the head of w_x is w_m. If the parser predicts *RA*, then it regards w_y as the head of w_x. Therefore it violates Definition 1 (for each word there should be at most one head in the sentence). On the other hand, actions *Reduce* and *Shift* do not change the structure of G and is intuitively valid parsing actions. In the case of *LA*, by adding the edge from w_x to w_y, the dependency graph does not violate definition 1. Thus, *LA* is also a valid action.

Definition 3 is very common and intuitively seen in the case of one word parsing at the final stage. The Proposition 4 limits the parser actions that bring about a single-rooted dependency graph. Proposition 5 is particularly useful when there are only two unparsed words in the stack for the NSR. On the basis of the original NSR algorithm, the parse work is done when the input queue is empty. However, words will be shift and put onto the stack if their heads are not found currently. Finally if the queue is empty and these words are still retained in the stack, then it will produce multiple roots and lead to an unconnected graph. Proposition 6 is proposed to avoid the case of multiple heads in the sentence when there are two no-head words. To handle more than two words on the stack, the "step-back" operation is used.

Some of the above properties can also be applied to YSR with slightly modifications. We skip the details here owing to the space constraints.

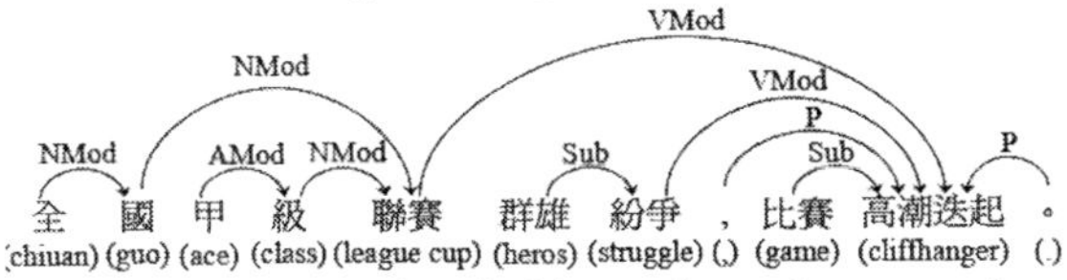

Figure 1: An example of Chinese dependency graph

3 Root and Neighbor Information

In general, the shift-reduce parsing algorithm incrementally parse a pair of words until the final parse graph has built. However, it is usually the case that when an error decision made at earlier stage, the real heads of the following words will be misattached. In particular the head is nearby the current pair of words. Similarly if the root word is misclassified as a child of other word, then the all nodes immediately modified by the root will attached to the wrong root.

One solution to improve this problem is to enhance the root and bottom (neighbor) information during parse. To obtain such information, we employ the sequential taggers to predict. That is one sequential tagger learns to determine whether the current word is the child of its left/right word or none of them while the other is to recognize the root word. For example, if the word is labeled as "leftMod", then it means its left word is the head of it and the relation tag is "Mod".

Finding root in Chinese is even simpler, since there is only one root word in the same sentence in Chinese Treebank. Here, we adopt the same technology to label the root by using sequential taggers. Such solution had also been applied to English Treebank where a polynomial kernel SVM was used (Isozaki et al., 2004). However, there are two differences to our method. First, we enable our root tagger to incorporate bottom-level features. More precisely, the two taggers are cascaded combined. Second, to enhance the top-level syntactic information, our root tagger does not only recognize the root word, but also the words which belong to the immediate child of it. We give the following property to prove that attaching all root children to the root still leads to a valid dependency graph.

Proposition 7: Cycle-free for root tagger

The dependency graph is a cycle-free graph by linking root child to the root words.

Proof. The minimum cycle length in a valid dependency graph is two (two edges for two words by linked each other). Assume there are *K* children for a root. By attaching all children to the root, it leads to the out-degree of each child is 1, while the in-degree of the root is *K*. According to the Definition 1, the root word does not have any parent (out-degree of the root is exactly zero) and will never attach to any word in the sentence (include its children).

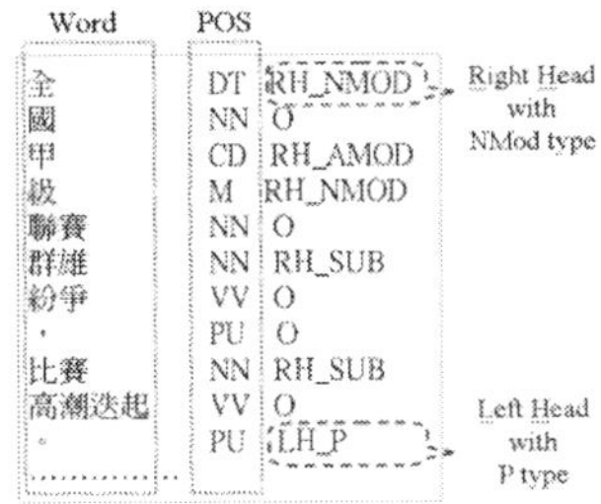

Figure 2: Attaching neighbor relations with sequental taggers

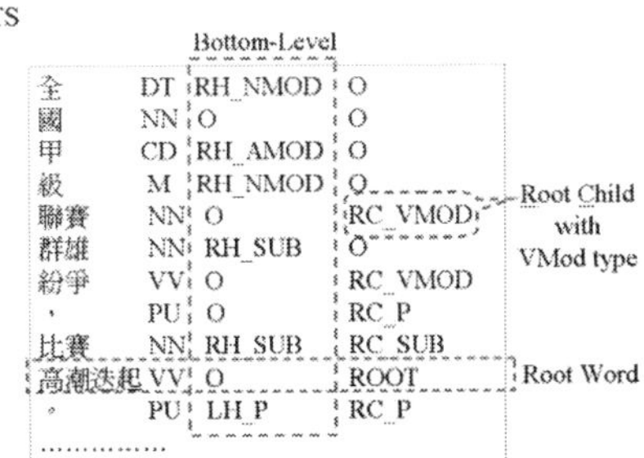

Figure 3: Attaching root words with sequential taggers

The sequential tagger used in this paper is CRF++ (Kudo et al., 2004). One advantage of conditional random fields (CRF) is that it is a structural learning method and can search optimal tag sequence with efficient Viterbi search algorithm.
Features used for the two taggers include word, part-of-speech tag, and prefix/suffix Chinese characters with context window = 3. Features that occurs less than twice in the training data is removed. Figure 1 shows an example of Chinese dependency graph. Figure 2 illustrates the sample of attaching neighbors with CRF++ by using the same sentence as in Figure 1. Figure 3 shows the example of identifying root and its children with CRF++.

Table 1: Feature set used for NSR and YSR

Feature type	Stack position	Queue position
Word	-1,0	0,+1,+2,+3
POS	-1,0	0,+1,+2,+3
BiWord	(-2,-1),(-1,0),(-2,0),(-1,+1)	(0,1),(1,2),(2,3),(0,2),(1,3)
BiPOS	(-2,-1),(-1,0),(-2,0),(-1,+1)	(0,1),(1,2),(2,3),(0,2),(1,3)
Neighbor (NSR)	-2,-1,0	0,+1,+2
Root (NSR)	-1,0	
Neighbor (YSR)	0	0
Root (YSR)	0	
History	-2,-1	
Child (Word)	0	0
Child (POS)	0	0

4 Experiments

We randomly select 90% of the Chinese Treebank 5.1 corpus for training and the remaining 10% is used for testing. Totally there are 0.45 million words in the training data and 50144 words for testing. By following (Hall et al., 2006), we use the same headword table to convert the CTB into dependency structure. The gold-tagged POS tags are used in the experiments. All experimental results are evaluated by LAS (label attachment score), UAS (unlabeled attachment score), and root accuracy.

4.1 Settings

In this paper, we employ the MSTParser (McDonald et al., 2006) and MaltParser (Nivre, 2003) for comparison. We adopt the best settings for MaltParser with SVM and MBL learners as reported by (Hall et al., 2006)[2]. For MSTParser, the Eisner's decoding algorithm is used.

The learner we used in this paper is L_2-SVM with linear kernel (Keerthi and DeCoste, 2005). The one-versus-all (OVA) strategy is applied to handle multiclass problems. Features that appear less than twice are removed from the feature set. Table 4 lists the feature set for the NSR and YSR.

4.2 Results

Table 2 summarizes overall experimental results. The final two rows list the entire training and testing time of the corresponding methods. From this table, we can see that our method (both NSR and YSR) achieve the best and second best parsing accuracy in terms of LAS, UAS, and root accuracy. For testing time efficiency, both our NSR and YSR also outperform the other methods. Meanwhile there is no significant difference between NSR and YSR from the aspect of run time efficiency view. In comparison to MaltParser, NSR yields 14 times faster in parsing speed.

Next, we analyze the effect of the two sequential taggers. The pure system performance of the neighbor tagger is 88.54 in $F_{(\beta)}$ rate, while the root tagger only achieves 61.67 $F_{(\beta)}$ score. The entire training time of the two taggers takes about 10 hours. Table 3 shows the compared results. It is clear that adding the two taggers leads better parsing accuracy than pure NSR and YSR. For example, it enhances the LAS score from 81.17 to 81.41 for NSR. Furthermore, the pure NSR and YSR still produce better parsing accuracy than MaltParser and MSTParser.

5 Conclusion

This paper presents an efficient and robust Chinese dependency parsing based on shift reduce parsing algorithms. We employ two sequential taggers to label the root and neighbor information as features. Experimental results show that our methods outperform two top-performed parsers, MaltParser and MSTParser in both accuracy and run-time efficiency. In the future, we will to investigate the effect of full parsing Chinese by applying shift-reduce-like approaches.

[2] http://w3.msi.vxu.se/~nivre/research/chiMaltSVM.html

Table 2: Parsing accuracy of each parsing algorithm

Evaluation Metrics	MaltParser (SVM)	MaltParser (MBT)	MST	this paper	
				NSR	YSR
LAS	80.74	73.53	78.08	81.41	**81.57**
UAS	81.98	75.40	79.53	82.60	**82.76**
LAC	91.28	86.26	89.21	92.26	**92.37**
Root	65.88	69.36	73.71	74.93	**77.61**
Sentence	33.12	25.67	24.07	32.85	**33.44**
TrainTime	6.74hr	**3.42min**	7.51hr	2.76hr	2.24hr
TestTime	15.92min	3.22min	10.15min	**1.12min**	1.15min

Table 3: Effective of the additional root and neighbor information

Improvement rate	NSR	YSR
LAS	81.17→81.41	81.16→81.57
UAS	82.33→82.60	82.37→82.76
LAC	92.07→92.26	92.15→92.37
Root_ Accuracy	74.14→74.93	76.24→77.61

References

Sabine Buchholz and Erwin Marsi. 2006. CoNLL-X Shared Task on Multilingual Dependency Parsing. In *Proc. of CoNLL*, pp. 149-164.

Ming-Wei Chang, Quang Do, and Dan Roth. 2006. Multilingual dependency parsing: a pipeline approach. *Recent Advances in Natural Language Processing*, pp. 195-204.

Yuchang Cheng, Masayuki Asahara, and Yuji Matsumoto. 2005. Chinese deterministic dependency analyzer: examining effects of global features and root node finder. In *Proc. of SIGHAN*, pp. 17-24.

Yuchang Cheng, Masayuki Asahara, and Yuji Matsumoto. 2006. Multilingual Dependency Parsing at NAIST. In Proc. of CoNLL, pp. 191-195.

Jason Eisner. 1996. Three New Probabilistic Models for Dependency Parsing: An Exploration. In *Proc. of COLING*, pp. 340-345.

Johan Hall, Joakim Nivre, and Jens Nilsson. 2006. Discriminative Classifiers for Deterministic Dependency Parsing. In *Proc. of COLING-ACL Main Conference Poster Sessions*, pp. 316-323.

Hideki Isozaki, Hideto Kazawa, and Tsutomu Hirao. 2004. A deterministic word dependency analyzer enhanced with preference learning. In *Proc. of COLING*, pp. 275-281.

Sathiya Keerthi and Dennis DeCoste. 2005. A modified finite Newton method for fast solution of large scale linear SVMs, JMLR, 6: 341-361.

Taku Kudo and Yuji Matsumoto. 2003. Fast methods for kernel-based text analysis. In Proc. of ACL, pp. 24-31.

Taku Kudo, Kaoru Yamamoto, and Yuji Matsumoto. 2004. Applying conditional random fields to Japanese morphological analysis, In *Proc. of EMNLP*, pp. 230-237.

Ryan McDonald, Kevin Lerman, and Fernando Pereira. 2006. Multilingual dependency analysis with a two-stage discriminative. In *Proc. of CoNLL*, pp. 216-220.

Joakim Nivre. 2003. An efficient algorithm for projective dependency parsing. In *Proc. of IWPT*, pp. 149-160.

Joakim Nivre, Johan Hall, Jens Nilsson, Gülsen Eryigit, and Svetoslav Marinov. 2006. Labeled pseudo-projective dependency parsing with support vector machines. In *Proc. of CoNLL*, pp. 221-226.

Joakim Nivre, Johan Hall, Sandra Kübler, Ryan McDonald, Jens Nilsson, Sebastian Riedel, and Deniz Yuret. 2007. The CoNLL 2007 shared task on dependency parsing. In *Proc. of EMNLP-CoNLL*, pp. 915-932.

Qin Iris Wang, Dekang Lin, and Dale Schuurmans. 2007. Simple training of dependency parsers via structured boosting. In *Proc. of IJCAI*, pp. 1756-1762.

Yu-Chieh Wu, Jie-Chi Yang, and Yue-Shi Lee. 2007. Multilingual deterministic dependency parsing framework using modified finite Newton method support vector machines. In *Proc. of EMNLP-CoNLL*, pp. 1175-1181.

Nianwen Xue, Fei Xia, Fu-Dong Chiou and Martha Palmer. 2005. The Penn Chinese Treebank: phrase structure annotation of a large corpus. Natural Language Engineering, 11(2):207-238.

Hiroyasu Yamada and Yuji Matsumoto. 2003. Statistical dependency analysis with support vector machines. In *Proc. of IWPT*, pp. 195-206.

Sentence Compression as a Step in Summarization or an Alternative Path in Text Shortening

Mehdi Yousfi-Monod
University of Montpellier 2, CNRS
LIRMM, 161 rue Ada
34392 Montpellier Cedex 5
yousfi@lirmm.fr

Violaine Prince
University of Montpellier 2, CNRS
LIRMM, 161 rue Ada
34392 Montpellier Cedex 5
prince@lirmm.fr

Abstract

The originality of this work leads in tackling text compression using an unsupervised method, based on a deep linguistic analysis, and without resorting on a learning corpus. This work presents a system for dependent tree pruning, while preserving the syntactic coherence and the main informational contents, and led to an operational software, named COLIN. Experiment results show that our compressions get honorable satisfaction levels, with a mean compression ratio of 38 %.

1 Introduction

Automatic summarization has become a crucial task for natural language processing (NLP) since information retrieval has been addressing it as one of the most usual user requirements in its panel of products. Most traditional approaches are considering the sentence as a minimal unit in the summarization process. Some more recent works get into the sentence in order to reduce the number of words by discarding incidental information. Some of these approaches rely on statistical models (Knight and Marcu, 2002; Lin and Hovy, 2002; Hovy et al., 2005), while some other works use rule-based linguistically-motivated heuristics (McKeown et al., 2002; Dorr et al., 2003; Gagnon and Sylva, 2005) to improve the determination of the importance of textual segments. Considering a deeper linguistic analysis could considerably improve the quality of reduced sentences, we decided to develop a sentence compression approach exclusively focused on linguistic heuristics. Our first work (Yousfi-Monod and Prince, 2005), slightly anterior to (Gagnon and Sylva, 2005), showed interesting results, and led to a deeper and more complete work fully detailed in (Yousfi-Monod, 2007). This paper sums up our approach.

©2008. Licensed under the *Creative Commons Attribution-Noncommercial-Share Alike 3.0 Unported* license (http://creativecommons.org/licenses/by-nc-sa/3.0/). Some rights reserved.

2 Theoretical framework

The main hypothesis of this work leans on the observation that incident sentence constituents are often not as important as principal constituents. For instance, let us consider the temporal adverbial in the following sentence: "Taiwan elected <u>on Saturday</u> its first president". While the subject 'Taiwan' and the verb 'elected' are principal constituents of the sentence, 'on Saturday' is incident and can be removed without causing neither an agrammaticality nor a weighty content lost. Two aspects of the constituent significance: *Grammaticality* and *content*, are dealt with in this section.

2.1 Grammaticality preservation thanks to the syntactic function

The principal/incident constituent principle can be found in constituent or dependency grammar representations. The approach embedded in COLIN is based on such grammars, while adapting them to the relevant proprieties for sentence compression. As we aim at preserving sentences grammaticality, our first goal is to get a syntactic tree based on the grammatical importance, where for each node, a daughter node is an incident constituent which may be removed under certain conditions. We opted for the X-bar theory (Chomsky, 1970), which represents a sentence through a tree of constituents, composed by *heads* and *governed constituents* (also dependents). While a head is grammatically mandatory, its dependents can often be removed, depending on some of their linguistic properties and/or those of their heads. Our goal is first to have a syntactic structure modeling based on constituents grammatical importance. Syntactic writing rules of the X-bar theory are focusing on sentence construction by placing specifiers, complements and adjuncts in the subtree of their constituent. While adjuncts are systematically removable, we have had to adopt a case-by-case study for specifiers and complements. For instance, in a noun phrase (NP), the article, if present, is a specifier, and it cannot be removed, while in an adjective phrase, the specifier is typically an adverb, which is removable. The removability of a complement depends on the subcategorisation properties of its head. On a clause scale, the dependents are not well defined in the X-bar theory and may include the subject and verbal groups, as, respectively, the specifier and the complement of the clause. Thus, the specifier (subject) cannot be removed. Our study has then consisted in a categorization of the X-bar's functional entities according to their removal property. We have decided (i) to consider mandatory specifiers as complements required by their head and (ii) to bring together optional specifiers and adjuncts in a different category: *Modifiers*[1].

We have defined two classes of functions: *Complements* (X-bar complements and mandatory specifiers) and *Modifiers* (X-bar adjuncts and optional specifiers). This syntactic function classification allows us to clearly define which sentence objects can be candidates for removal.

Nevertheless, the syntactic function information, although crucial, is not sufficient. One has to use other linguistic properties in order to refine the assessment of the constituent importance.

2.2 Important content preservation thanks to linguistic proprieties

Subcategorisation. For noun and clause heads, some of our complements have been identified as systematically mandatory in order to preserve the sentence coherence (subject, verbal group, articles...). Other heads (verb, adjective, adverb, preposition and pronoun) may admit optional or mandatory complements, depending on either the lexical head category or a particular head instance (a lexical entry). Indeed, prepositions are systematically requiring a complement[2], while other heads must be considered on a case-by-case basis. Once we get the subcategorisation information for a head, we are able to determine whether its complement(s) can be removed without causing an incoherence.

Other linguistic proprieties. We identified several other linguistic clues that may help assessing the importance of dependents. We do not detail our analysis here for space reasons, refer to (Yousfi-Monod, 2007) for the full description. These clues include lexical functions, fixed expressions, type of the article (definite or indefinite), parenthetical phrases, detached noun modifiers, the dependent constituent position in the sentence, negation and interrogation.

3 CoLIN's compressor: System architecture and implementation

3.1 Architecture

We assume we have a raw text as an input, which may be the output of an extract summarizer, and we have to produce a compressed version of it, by reducing as many sentences as we can, without deleting a single one.

Syntactic analysis. This step consists in using a syntactic analyzer to produce, from the source text, dependent trees according to our syntactic model (heads, complements, modifiers). In order to handle the important content assessment, the parser uses linguistic resources including subcategorisation information, lexical functions, and the other linguistic properties (section 2.2), and then enriches the trees with this information.

Pruning and linearization. The trees will be then pruned according to a set of compression rules defined from our theoretical analysis. Several set of rules can be defined according to (i) the desired importance conservation, (ii) the desired compression rate, (iii) the confidence in syntactic analysis results, (iv) the trust in the identified linguistic clues, (v) the textual genre of the source text. In order to get effective rules, we have first defined a relatively reliable kernel of rules. Then we have decided to define and test, during our evaluation

[1]We have chosen the term 'modifier' as its definitions in the literature fit quite well our needs.

[2]Accordingly to the X-bar structure as well as ours: The preposition is the head of the prepositional syntagm.

described in the next section, several rules configurations, taking into account each of the five points, in order to find the most effective ones. Rules tag each tree node (complements and modifiers) which will be removed, then trees are pruned and linearized to get back new sentences, compressed.

3.2 Implementation

The first step in our implementation was to select a parser satisfying our syntactic requirements as much as possible. SYGFRAN (described in (Yousfi-Monod, 2007)), is the one that has been chosen as: (i) It produces constituent trees very close to our model, (ii) it has a good syntactic coverage, (iii) it has a very good parsing complexity ($O(n.log(n))$, with n the size of the data in words), and (iv) its author and developer, Jacques Chauché, works in our research team at LIRMM[3], which considerably eases the adaptation of the syntactic model to ours. SYGFRAN consists in a set of grammar networks, each of them containing several set of transformational rules. COLIN and SYGFRAN's rules are implemented with the parser SYGMART, a tree transducers system (Chauché, 1984). COLIN's rules are split into several grammars including (i) a basic anaphora resolution, (ii) a tagging of candidate nodes[4], (iii) a pruning of tagged constituents and a linearization of leaves.

4 Evaluation, experimentation and results

This section sums up the validation process used for our approach. Our evaluation protocol is manual intrinsic, focuses on facilitating the evaluator' task and is inspired from (Knight and Marcu, 2002)'s one. For space reasons, we do not detail the protocol here, a full description of the protocol as well as the experimentation is available in (Yousfi-Monod, 2007).

Setting up. As our approach deeply relies on syntactic properties, which are not always properly detected by current parsers, we decided to manually improve the syntactic analysis of our evaluation corpus. Otherwise, the evaluation would have more reflected the users' satisfaction about parsing than their opinion about the quality of our importance criteria. In order to assess the genre influence, we selected three genres: Journalistic, narrative and scientific. We composed 5 texts per genres, each of them contained about 5 paragraphs, 16 sentences and 380 words, thus a total of 240 sentences. We decided to test the importance of different clause modifiers, i.e. adverbial phrases, according to their type. We considered the following types: Temporal, locative and other ones. So, while keeping the core rules for each rules configuration, we tested the removal of (i) all adverbials, (ii) temporal adverbials, (iii) locative adverbials, (iv) only other adverbials (keeping temporal and place ones).
We got 25 active users participating to the evaluation, who were mainly composed of PhD students and PhDs, working in NLP or computational linguistic domains, and being fluent in French. Some of them did a set of manual compressions, used to compare the quality with COLIN compressions in the scoring stage of the evaluation. 59 text compressions were done, corresponding to about 3,9 compressions per text. In the scoring stage, judges gave about 5,2 notations per compressed paragraph for manual and automatic compressions.

Results. Tables 1 and 2 present the results of respectively obtained average compression rates[5] and paragraph scorings[6], per genre. For COLIN's evaluation, we only display the rules configuration which has obtained the best results for the compression rate relatively to the paragraph scoring, i.e. the rules configuration (iv).

	Jour.	Narr.	Scien.	Mean
Manual	36 %	17 %	23 %	25 %
COLIN	38 %	35 %	41 %	38 %

Table 1: Average compression rates.

	Jour.	Jour.	Scien.	Mean
Manual	4,03	3,67	3,41	3,7
COLIN	3,7	3	3	3,23

Table 2: Average paragraph scorings.

The compression rate proposed by COLIN is quite better than the manual one for a quality scoring just below the latter. COLIN is obviously

[3]http://www.lirmm.fr

[4]We tag trees before pruning them as COLIN can work in a semi-automatic mode (not presented here) where a user can modify the tagging.

[5]A higher percentage means a shorter compressed text.

[6]Scores are between 1 and 5, a value of 1 means a completely unsatisfying compression, while a value of 5 means a very good compression for the judge.

far better in compression time, with about 5 seconds per document versus between 200 and 300 seconds for the manual compressions. CoLIN's compression–quality–time ratio is therefore really better than the manual compressions. Each genre obtained a good compression rate as well as a correct quality scoring, particularly for the journalistic one. Note that our results could have been improved if they weren't sensibly degraded because of an imperfect parsing, despite some focused improvements we did on it.

A performance comparison with similar approaches was an issue for our approach for at least two reasons: (i) As our parser is exclusively for French, we had to do comparisons with French tongue systems only. The system presented in (Gagnon and Sylva, 2005) is the only that matches this constraint. (ii) Our evaluation protocol drastically differs from traditional ones in several points: 1. Having a single human judge who compresses sentences produces compressions which are too much subjective to the latter, that's why each of our texts were compressed about 4 times by different humans. Evaluating compressions rise the same issue of subjectivity, so each of our compressions were evaluated about 5 times. 2. We consider assessing the quality of separated compressed sentences is harder and less relevant for evaluators than assessing full paragraphs as we did. 3. Text genre has an actual influence on NLP approaches, thus we took into account this factor in our evaluation, as described above, while the above cited system extracted random sentences in a single corpus. For all these reasons, we haven't been able to perform a comparison with the above cited system yet.

5 Conclusion

In this paper we have addressed the task of sentence compression based on a deep linguistic analysis. The system we developed, called CoLIN, theoretically relies on a constituents and dependencies sentence tree pruning, removing those branches which could be cut without jeopardizing the sentence construction, or tempering too strongly with the sentence meaning. A careful study of syntactic properties, lexical functions, verbs arguments has led us to design several different configurations in which the sentence compression quality could degrade if compression goes too far. The appreciation of a compression quality has been here demonstrated as a user satisfaction protocol. If CoLIN has been able to shorten texts by an average 38%, humans were not able to remove more than 25%. At the same time, the satisfaction mean score is 3.23 over 5, whereas the same users attribute to human compressors a satisfaction mean score of 3.7, really not so much more.

References

Chauché, Jacques. 1984. Un outil multidimensionnel de l'analyse du discours. In *Coling'84*, pages 11–15.

Chomsky, Noam. 1970. Remarks on nominalization. In *R. Jacobs and P. Rosenbaum (eds.) Reading in English Transformational Grammar*, pages 184–221, Waltham: Ginn.

Dorr, Bonnie, David Zajic, and Richard Schwartz. 2003. Hedge trimmer: A parse-and-trim approach to headline generation. In *In R. Radev & S. Teufel (Eds.), Proceedings of the HLT-NAACL 2003 Workshop on Text Summarization. Omnipress*, pages 1–8.

Gagnon, Michel and Lyne Da Sylva. 2005. Text summarization by sentence extraction and syntactic pruning. In *Computational Linguistics in the North East (CliNE'05)*, Université du Québec en Outaouais, Gatineau, 26 August.

Hovy, Eduard H., Chin-Yew Lin, and Liang Zhou. 2005. A be-based multi-document summarizer with sentence compression. In *the Multilingual Summarization Evaluation Workshop at the ACL 2005 conference*.

Knight, Kevin and Daniel Marcu. 2002. Summarization beyond sentence extraction: a probabilistic approach to sentence compression. *Artificial Intelligence archive*, 139(1):91–107, July.

Lin, Chin-Yew and Eduard H. Hovy. 2002. Automated multi-document summarization in neats. In *the DARPA Human Language Technology Conference*, pages 50–53.

McKeown, K., D. Evans, A. Nenkova, R. Barzilay, V. Hatzivassiloglou, B. Schiffman, S. Blair-Goldensohn, J. Klavans, and S. Sigelman. 2002. The columbia multi-document summarizer for duc 2002.

Yousfi-Monod, Mehdi and Violaine Prince. 2005. Automatic summarization based on sentence morpho-syntactic structure: narrative sentences compression. In *the 2nd International Workshop on Natural Language Understanding and Cognitive Science (NLUCS 2005)*, pages 161–167, Miami/USA, May.

Yousfi-Monod, Mehdi. 2007. *Compression automatique ou semi-automatique de textes par élagage des constituants effaçables : une approche interactive et indépendante des corpus*. Ph.D. thesis, University of Montpellier II, Montpellier, November.

Online-Monitoring of Security-Related Events

Martin Atkinson, Jakub Piskorski, Bruno Pouliquen
Ralf Steinberger, Hristo Tanev, Vanni Zavarella
Joint Research Centre of the European Commission
Institute for the Protection and Security of the Citizen
Via Fermi 2749, 21027 Ispra (VA), Italy
firstname.lastname@jrc.it

Abstract

This paper presents a fully operational real-time event extraction system which is capable of accurately and efficiently extracting violent and natural disaster events from vast amount of online news articles per day in different languages. Due to the requirement that the system must be multilingual and easily extendable, it is based on a shallow linguistic analysis. The event extraction results can be viewed on a publicly accessible website.

1 Introduction

Gathering information about violent and natural disaster events from online news is of paramount importance to better understand conflicts and to develop global monitoring systems for the automatic detection of precursors for threats in the fields of conflict and health. This paper reports on a fully operational live event extraction system to detect information on violent events and natural disasters in large multilingual collections of online news articles collected by the news aggregation system Europe Media Monitor (Best et al., 2005), http://press.jrc.it/overview.html.

Although a considerable amount of work on the automatic extraction of events has been reported, it still appears to be a lesser studied area in comparison to the somewhat easier tasks of named-entity and relation extraction. Two comprehensive examples of the current functionality and capabilities of event extraction technology dealing with the identification of disease outbreaks and conflict incidents are given in (Grishman et al., 2002) and (King and Lowe, 2003) respectively. The most recent trends and developments in this area are reported in (Ashish et al., 2006)

In order to be capable of processing vast amounts of textual data in real time (as in the case of EMM) we follow a linguistically lightweight approach and exploit clustered news at various processing stages (pattern learning, information fusion, geo-tagging, etc.). Consequently, only a tiny fraction of each text is analysed. In a nutshell, our system deploys simple 1 and 2-slot extraction patterns to identify event-relevant entities. These patterns are semi-automatically acquired in a bootstrapping manner by using clustered news data. Next, information about events scattered over different documents is integrated by applying voting heuristics. The results of the core event extraction system are integrated into a real-world global monitoring system. Although we mainly cover the security domain, the techniques deployed in our system can be applied to other domains, such as for instance tracking business-related events for risk assessment.

In the remaining part of this paper we give a brief overview of the real-time event extraction processing chain and describe the particularities of selected subcomponents. Finally, the online application is presented.

2 Real-time Event Extraction Process

The real-time event extraction processing chain is depicted in Figure 1. First, news articles are gathered by dedicated software for electronic media monitoring, namely the EMM system (Best et al., 2005). EMM receives an average of 50,000 news articles per day from about 1,500 news sources in

©2008. Licensed under the *Creative Commons Attribution-Noncommercial-Share Alike 3.0 Unported* license (http://creativecommons.org/licenses/by-nc-sa/3.0/). Some rights reserved.

over 40 languages, and regularly checks for updates of news. Secondly, the input data is grouped into news clusters ideally including documents on one topic or event. Then, clusters describing security-related events are selected using keyword-based heuristics. For each such cluster, the system tries to detect and extract only the main event by analysing all documents in the cluster.

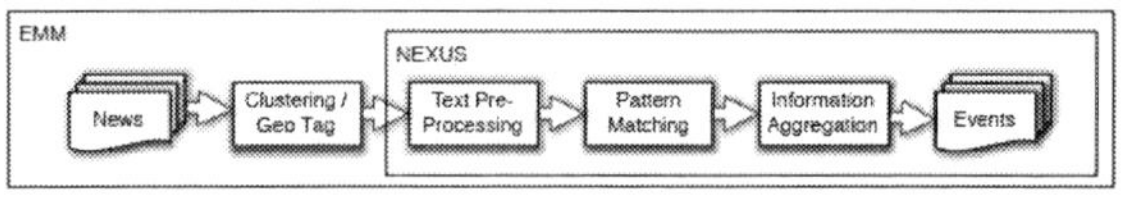

Figure 1: Real-time processing chain.

Next, each cluster is processed by our core event extraction engine. For each detected violent event, it produces a frame, whose main slots are: date and location, number of killed, injured or kidnapped people, actors, type of event, weapons used, etc. In an initial step, each document in the cluster is linguistically pre-processed in order to produce a more abstract representation of the texts. This encompasses: fine-grained tokenisation, sentence splitting, matching of known named entities, labelling of key terms and phrases like action words (e.g. *kill*, *shoot*) and person groups.

Once texts are grouped into clusters and linguistically pre-processed, the pattern engine applies a cascade of extraction grammars (consisting of 1 and 2-slot extraction patterns) on each document within a cluster. For creating extraction patterns, we apply a blend of machine learning and knowledge-based techniques. The extraction patterns are matched against the first sentence and the title of each article from the cluster. By processing only the top sentence and the title, the system is more likely to capture facts about the most important event in the cluster. Even if we fail to detect a single piece of information in one document in a cluster, the same information is likely to be found in another document of the cluster, where it may be expressed in a different way.

Finally, since information about events is scattered over different articles, the last step consists of cross-document cluster-level information fusion, i.e., we aggregate and validate information extracted locally from each single article in the same cluster. For this purpose, simple voting-like heuristics are deployed.

Every ten minutes, EMM clusters the articles found during the last four hours. The event extraction engine analyses each of these clusters. The event information is thus always up-to-date. The output of the event extraction engine constitutes the input for a global monitoring system.

3 Geo-tagging Clusters

Challenges for geo-tagging clusters are that place names can be homographic with person names and with other place names. We solve the former ambiguity by first identifying person names found in our automatically populated database of known people and organisations. For the latter ambiguity, we adopted a cluster-centric approach by weighting all place names found in a cluster and by selecting the one with the highest score. For each cluster, we thus first establish all possible candidate locations by looking up in the texts all place, province, region and country names found in a multilingual gazetteer (including name variants). The weights of the locations are then based on the place name significance (e.g., a capital city scores higher than a village) and on the place name hierarchy (i.e. if the province or region to which the place belongs are also mentioned in the text, it scores higher).

4 Pattern Acquisition

For pattern acquisition, we deploy a weakly supervised bootstrapping algorithm (Tanev and Oezden-Wennerberg, 2008) similar in spirit to the one described in (Yangarber, 2003), which involves some manual validation. Contrary to other approaches, the learning phase exploits the knowledge to which cluster the news items belong. Intuitively, this guarantees better precision of the learned patterns. In particular, for each event-specific semantic role (e.g. *killed*), a separate cycle of learning iterations is executed (usually up to three) in order to learn 1-slot extraction patterns. Each cluster includes articles from different sources about the same news story. Therefore, we assume that each entity appears in the same semantic role (actor, victim, injured) in the context of one cluster. An automatic procedure for syntactic expansion complements the learning. This procedure accepts a manually provided list of words which have identical (or similar) syntactic usage patterns (e.g. *killed*, *assassinated*, *murdered*, etc.). It then generates new patterns from the old ones by substituting for each other the words in the list. After 1-slot patterns are acquired, some of them are used to manually create 2-slot patterns like `X shot Y`.

5 Pattern matching engine

In order to guarantee that massive amounts of textual data can be processed in real time, we have developed ExPRESS (Piskorski, 2007), an efficient extraction pattern engine, which is capable of matching thousands of patterns against MB-sized texts within seconds. The pattern specification language is a blend of two previously introduced IE-oriented grammar formalisms, namely JAPE used in GATE (Cunningham et al., 2000) and XTDL, used in SPROUT (Drożdżyński et al., 2004).

A single pattern is a regular expression over flat feature structures (FS), i.e., non-recursive typed feature structures without structure sharing, where features are string-valued and – unlike in XTDL types – are not organised in a hierarchy. Each such regular expression is associated with a list of FSs which constitute the output specification. Like in XTDL, we deploy variables and functional operators for forming slot values and for establishing contact with the 'outer world'. Further, we adapted JAPEs feature of associating patterns with multiple actions, i.e., producing multiple annotations (possibly nested). An empirical comparison of the run-time behaviour of the new formalism against the other 2 revealed that significant speed-ups can be achieved (at least 30 times faster). ExPRESS comes with a pool of highly efficient core linguistic processing resources (Piskorski, 2008).

6 Information Aggregation

Once single pieces of information are extracted by the pattern engine, they are merged into event descriptions by applying an information aggregation algorithm. This algorithm assumes that each cluster reports at most one main event of interest. It takes as input the text entities extracted from one news cluster with their semantic roles and considers the sentences from which these entities are extracted. If one and the same entity has two roles assigned, a preference is given to the role assigned by the most reliable group of patterns (e.g., 2-slot patterns are more reliable). Another ambiguity which has to be resolved arises from the contradictory information which news sources give about the number of victims. We use an ad-hoc heuristic for computing the most probable estimation for these numbers, i.e., firstly the largest group of numbers which are close to each other is selected and secondly the number closest to the average in that group is chosen. After this estimation is computed, the system discards from each news cluster all the articles whose reported victim numbers significantly differ from the estimated numbers for the whole cluster. Additionally, some victim arithmetic is applied, i.e., a small taxonomy of person classes is used to sum victim numbers (e.g., *gunmen* and *terrorists* belong to the same class of *NonGovernmentalArmedGroup*).

7 Event Classification

After the single pieces of information are assembled into the event description, an event classification is performed. Some of the most used event classes are *Terrorist Attack*, *Bombing*, *Shooting*, *Air Attack*, etc. The classification algorithm uses a blend of keyword matching and domain specific rules. As an example, consider the following domain-specific rule: if the event description includes named entities, which are assigned the semantic role *kidnapped*, as well as entities which are assigned the semantic role *released*, then the type of the event is *Hostage Release*, rather than *Kidnapping*. If the event refers to kidnapped people and at the same time the news articles contain words like *video* or *videotape*, then the event type is *Hostage Video Release*. The second rule has a higher priority, therefore it impedes the *Hostage Release* rule to fire erroneously, when the release of a hostage video is reported.

8 Monitoring Events

The core event extraction engine for English is fully operational since December 2007. There are two online applications running on top of it which allow monitoring events. The first one is a dedicated webpage using the Google Maps JavaScript API (see Figure 2). It is publicly accessible at: `http://press.jrc.it/geo?type=event&format=html&language=en` and provides an instant overview of what is occurring where in the world. A small problem with this application is that it overlays and hides events that are close to each other.

The second application shows the same events using the Google Earth client application. The geo-located data is transmitted via the Keyhole Markup Language (KML) format[1] supported directly by Google Earth.[2] The application is re-

[1] http://code.google.com/apis/kml/documentation/

[2] In order to run it, start Google Earth with KML: http://press.jrc.it/geo?type=event&format=kml&language=en

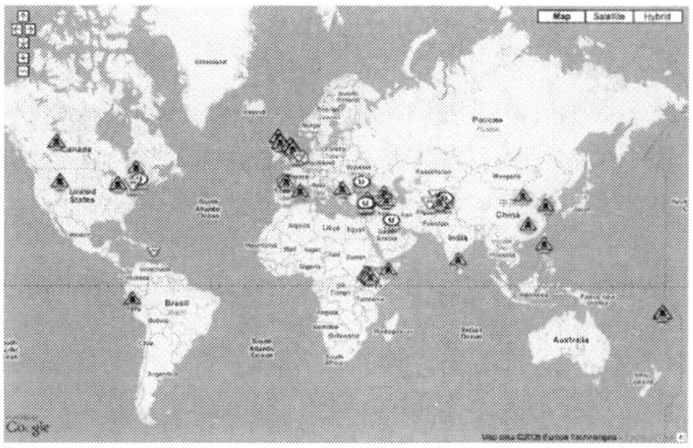

Figure 2: Event visualisation with Google Maps

Figure 3: Key to event type icons and magnitude indicators

stricted to displaying at most half the globe, but it allows expanding overlaid events.

Since it is important for stakeholders to be quickly and efficiently informed about the type and gravity of the event, various icons are used to represent the type or group of events visually (see Figure 3). We use general forms of icons for violent events and specific forms of icons for natural and man-made disasters. For violent events, the general form represents the major consequence of the event, except for kidnappings, where specific icons are used. Independently of the type of event, all icons are sized according to the damage caused, i.e. it is dependent on the number of victims involved in the event. Also, to highlight the events with a more significant damage, a border is drawn around the icon to indicate that a threshold of people involved has been passed.

The online demo is available for English, Italian and French. We are currently working on adapting the event extraction engine to other languages, including Russian, Spanish, Polish, German and Arabic. A more thorough description of the system can be found in (Tanev et al., 2008; Piskorski et al., 2008).

References

Ashish, N., D. Appelt, D. Freitag, and D. Zelenko. 2006. *Proceedings of the workshop on Event Extraction and Synthesis, held in conjunction with the AAAI 2006 conference*. Menlo Park, California, USA.

Best, C., E. van der Goot, K. Blackler, T. Garcia, and D. Horby. 2005. Europe Media Monitor. Technical Report EUR 22173 EN, European Commission.

Cunningham, H., D. Maynard, and V. Tablan. 2000. JAPE: a Java Annotation Patterns Engine (Second Edition). Technical Report, CS–00–10, University of Sheffield, Department of Computer Science.

Drożdżyński, W., H.-U. Krieger, J. Piskorski, U. Schäfer, and F. Xu. 2004. Shallow Processing with Unification and Typed Feature Structures — Foundations and Applications. *Künstliche Intelligenz*, 2004(1):17–23.

Grishman, R., S. Huttunen, and R. Yangarber. 2002. Real-time Event Extraction for Infectious Disease Outbreaks. Proceedings of the Human Language Technology Conference (HLT) 2002.

King, G. and W. Lowe. 2003. An Automated Information Extraction Tool for International Conflict Data with Performance as Good as Human Coders: A Rare Events Evaluation Design. *International Organization*, 57:617–642.

Piskorski, J., H. Tanev, M. Atkinson, and E. Van der Goot. 2008. Cluster-centric Approach to News Event Extraction. In *Proceedings of MISSI 2008*, Wroclaw, Poland.

Piskorski, J. 2007. ExPRESS Extraction Pattern Recognition Engine and Specification Suite. In *Proceedings of the International Workshop Finite-State Methods and Natural language Processing 2007 (FSMNLP'2007)*, Potsdam, Germany.

Piskorski, J. 2008. CORLEONE – Core Linguistic Entity Online Extraction. Technical report 23393 EN, Joint Research Centre of the European Commission, Ispra, Italy.

Tanev, H. and P. Oezden-Wennerberg. 2008. Learning to Populate an Ontology of Violent Events (in print). In Fogelman-Soulie, F. and Perrotta, D. and Piskorski, J. and Steinberger, R., editor, *NATO Security through Science Series: Information and Communication Security*. IOS Press.

Tanev, H., J. Piskorski, and M. Atkinson. 2008. Real-Time News Event Extraction for Global Crisis Monitoring. In *Proceedings of the* 13th *International Conference on Applications of Natural Language to Information Systems (NLDB 2008, Lecture Notes in Computer Science Vol. 5039)*, pages 207–218. Springer-Verlag Berlin Heidelberg.

Yangarber, R. 2003. Counter-Training in Discovery of Semantic Patterns. In *Proceedings of the* 41st *Annual Meeting of the ACL*.

A Grammar Checking System for Punjabi

Mandeep Singh Gill
Department of Computer Science
Punjabi University
Patiala – 147002, India
msgill_in@yahoo.com

Gurpreet Singh Lehal
Department of Computer Science
Punjabi University
Patiala – 147002, India
gslehal@yahoo.com

Abstract

This article provides description about the grammar checking system developed for detecting various grammatical errors in Punjabi texts. This system utilizes a full-form lexicon for morphological analysis, and applies rule-based approaches for part-of-speech tagging and phrase chunking. The system follows a novel approach of performing agreement checks at phrase and clause levels using the grammatical information exhibited by POS tags in the form of feature value pairs. The system can detect and suggest rectifications for a number of grammatical errors, resulting from the lack of agreement, order of words in various phrases etc., in literary style Punjabi texts. To the best of our knowledge, this grammar checking system is the first such system reported for Indian languages.

1 Introduction

Grammar checking is one of the most widely used tools within natural language engineering applications. Most of the word processing systems available in the market incorporate spelling, grammar, and style-checking systems for English and other widely used languages. Naber (2003) discussed one such rule-based grammar checking system for English. However, when it comes to the smaller languages, specifically the Indian languages, most of such advanced tools have been lacking. Although, spell checking has been addressed for most of the Indian languages, still grammar and style checking systems are lacking. In this article, a grammar checking system for Punjabi has been provided. Punjabi is a member of the Modern Indo-Aryan family of languages.

There is an n-gram based grammar checking system for Bangla (Alam et al., 2006). However, the authors admit that its accuracy is very low and there is no description about whether the system provides any suggestions to correct errors or not. However, the system that we discuss here for Punjabi detects errors and suggests corrections as well. While doing so, it provides enough information for the user to understand the error reason and the suggestions provided, if any.

2 Purpose

The purpose of the system is to find various grammatical mistakes in the formal texts written in Punjabi language. While detecting grammatical mistakes, the focus is on keeping the false alarms to minimum. For every detected error, system provides enough information for the user to understand why the error is being marked. It also provides suggestions, if possible, to rectify those errors.

3 Potential Applications

This system as a whole and its subsystems will find numerous applications in natural language processing of Punjabi. Following are some of the application areas of this system as a whole or its subsystems:

- It can be used with various information processing systems for Punjabi, where the input needs to be corrected grammatically before processing.

© 2008. Licensed under the *Creative Commons Attribution-Noncommercial-Share Alike 3.0 Unported* license (http://creativecommons.org/licenses/by-nc-sa/3.0/). Some rights reserved.

- Parts of this system like morphological analyzer, morphological generator, part-of-speech tagger, phrase chunker etc., will find use in almost every natural language processing application like machine translation, text to speech synthesis, and search engines etc., for Punjabi.
- This system as a whole can be used as a post editor for a number of applications for Punjabi like machine translation, optical character recognition etc., where the output needs to be corrected grammatically before providing the end results.
- Second language learners of Punjabi can use this system as a writing aid to learn grammatical categories operating in Punjabi sentences, and thus improve their writings by learning from their mistakes.
- In the word processing field, this system can be used for checking essays, formal reports, and letters written in Punjabi.

4 System Design & Implementation

The design of this grammar checking is provided below in figure 1. A sketchy idea of this proposed design is provided below in terms of how the input text is processed to find potential grammatical errors.

For grammar checking, the input text is first given to a preprocessor, which breaks the input text into sentences and then into words. It also performs filtering, i.e. marks any phrases, fixed expressions etc. in the text. Then the tokenized text is passed on to a morphological analyzer, which uses a full form lexicon to assign each word its all possible part-of-speech (POS) information (i.e. POS tags). Then the text along with the POS tags moves on to a POS tagger, which attempts to disambiguate the information using hand-written disambiguation rules. Then this POS tagged text is passed on to a phrase chunker, which builds phrases using hand-written phrase chunking rules targeted at the POS tag information. Phrase chunker also marks clause boundaries and headwords in noun phrases and clauses. Then in the last stage, syntax/agreement checks are performed based on the grammatical information (exhibited by POS tags) at the phrase level and then at the clause level, using the marked headwords. Any discrepancy found is reported to the user along with the suggested corrections and detailed error information.

All the sub activities of this grammar checking system are fully automated and have been designed exclusively from scratch as part of this work. No such sub system was available for Punjabi for our use. All the sub activities have been implemented in Microsoft Visual C# 2005 and the databases are in XML format with Punjabi text in Unicode.

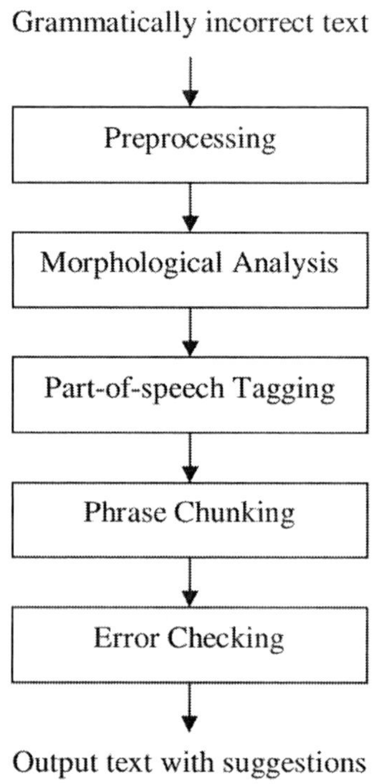

Figure 1. Punjabi Grammar Checking System Design

For the purpose of morphological analysis, we have divided the Punjabi words into 22 word classes depending on the grammatical information required for the words of these word classes. The information that is in the database depends upon the word class, like for noun and inflected adjective, it is gender, number, and case. As mentioned earlier, all the word forms of the commonly used Punjabi words are kept in the lexicon along with their root and other grammatical information.

For part-of-speech tagging, we have devised a tag set keeping into mind all the grammatical categories that can be helpful for agreement checking. The tag set is very user friendly and while choosing tag names existing tag sets for English and other such languages were taken into consideration, like NNMSD – masculine, singular, and direct case noun, PNPMPOF –

masculine, plural, oblique case, and first person personal pronoun. The approach followed for part-of-speech tagging is rule-based, as there is no tagged corpus for Punjabi available at present. The part-of-speech tagging rules take into account the potential grammatical agreement errors.

For phrase chunking, again a rule-based approach was selected. The tag set that is being used for phrase chunking includes tags like NPD – noun phrase in direct case, NPNE – noun phrase followed by ਨੇ *ne* etc. The rules for phrase chunking take into account the potential errors in the text, like lack of agreement in words of a potential phrase.

In the last phase i.e. error checking, there are manually designed error detection rules to detect potential errors in the text and provide corrections to resolve those errors. For example, rule to check modifier and noun agreement, will go through all the noun phrases in a sentence to check if the modifiers of those sentences agree with their respective headwords (noun/pronoun) in terms of gender, number, and case or not. For this matching, the grammatical information from the tags of modifiers and headwords is used. In simple terms, it will compare the grammatical information (gender, number, and case) of modifier with the headword (noun/pronoun) and displays an error message if some grammatical information fails to match. To resolve this error, the error checking module will use morphological generator to generate the correct form (based on headword's gender, number, and case) for that modifier from its root word.

For example, consider the grammatically incorrect sentence ਸੋਹਣੇ ਲੜਕਾ ਜਾਂਦਾ ਹੈ *sohne larka janda hai* 'handsome boy goes'. In this sentence, in the noun phrase ਸੋਹਣੇ ਲੜਕਾ *sohne larka* 'handsome boy', the modifier ਸੋਹਣੇ *sohne* 'handsome' (root word – ਸੋਹਣਾ *sohna* 'handsome'), with masculine gender, plural number, and direct case, is not in accordance with the gender, number, and case of its headword ਲੜਕਾ *larka* 'boy'. It should be in singular number instead of plural. The grammar checking module will detect this as an error as 'number' for modifier and headword is not same, then it will use morphological generator to generate the 'singular number form' from its root word, which is same as root form i.e. ਸੋਹਣਾ *sohna* 'handsome' (masculine gender, singular number, and direct case). So, the input sentence will be corrected as ਸੋਹਣਾ ਲੜਕਾ ਜਾਂਦਾ ਹੈ *sohna larka janda hai* 'handsome boy goes'.

5 Sample Input and Output

This section provides some sample Punjabi sentences that were given as input to the Punjabi grammar checking system along with the output generated by this system. **Input/Output** specify the input Punjabi sentence and the output produced by this grammar checking system respectively.

Sentence 1

This sentence shows the grammatical errors related to 'Modifier and noun agreement' and 'Order of the modifiers of a noun in noun phrase'. In this sentence noun is ਲੜਕਾ *larka* 'boy' and its modifiers are ਸੋਹਣੀ ਇੱਕ ਭੱਜੀ ਜਾਂਦਾ *sohni ek bhajji janda* 'handsome one running'.

Input: ਸੋਹਣੀ ਇੱਕ ਭੱਜੀ ਜਾਂਦਾ ਲੜਕਾ ਆਇਆ
Input1: sohni ek bhajji janda larka aaeya
Input2: Handsome one running boy came

Output: ਇੱਕ ਭੱਜਿਆ ਜਾਂਦਾ ਸੋਹਣਾ ਲੜਕਾ ਆਇਆ
Output1: ek bhajjia janda sohna larka aaeya
Output2: One running handsome boy came

Sentence 2

This sentence covers the grammatical error related to 'Subject and verb agreement'. Subject is ਬਾਰਸ਼ *barish* 'rain' and verb phrase is ਹੋ ਰਿਹਾ ਹਨ *ho riha han* 'is raining'.

Input: ਬਾਹਰ ਬਾਰਸ਼ ਹੋ ਰਿਹਾ ਹਨ
Input1: bahr barish ho riha han
Input2: It is raining outside

Output: ਬਾਹਰ ਬਾਰਸ਼ ਹੋ ਰਹੀ ਹੈ
Output1: bahr barish ho rahi hai
Output2: It is raining outside

6 Testing & Evaluation

The evaluation results for our morphological analyzer shows that it provides correct analysis for 87.64% words. This evaluation was performed on a corpus of 8 million Punjabi words. The part-of-speech tagger reports an accuracy of 80.29% when applied on a randomly selected corpus of 25,000 words. This accuracy improves to 88.86% if we exclude unknown words from evaluation results, the reason being the absence of an unknown word guesser in our part-of-speech tagger. The phrase chunker reports average precision of 81.18%, recall of 85.07%, and F-measure of 83.07%. These results include evaluation performed on 100 sentences for noun, adjective, and verb phrases. On randomly selected 1,000 sentences, this grammar checking system reports precision of 76.79%, recall of 87.08%, and F-measure of 81.61%.

The grammatical errors covered by this system includes – modifier and noun agreement, subject/object and verb agreement, order of modifiers in a noun phrase, order of words in a verb phrase, use of contractions etc. In its present state, the system may generate some false alarms for complex and compound sentences. We will work to reduce these false alarms in the future.

Comparison with existing systems

Our system covers a different class of errors and results for grammar checking systems for English, Swedish etc. are reported for different error sets, with only some errors covered being common. Some of the systems that are to some extent close to our system in terms of errors covered are provided here for comparison. A grammar checker for German (Schmidt-Wigger, 1998) using pattern matching rules reports 81% precision and 57%. A system for Korean (Young-Soog, 1998) reports 99.05% precision and 95.98% recall. Another system for German (Fliedner, 2002) reports precision and recall of 67% for only noun phrase agreement. A grammar checker for Bangla (Alam et al., 2006) reports accuracy of 53.7% using manual POS tagging and 38% for automated POS tagging. When compared with these systems, 76.79% precision and 87.08% recall of our grammar checker seams reasonably good.

7 Conclusions

This article presented design and implementation details of the grammar checking system for Punjabi. This grammar checking system is capable of detecting various grammatical errors in formal Punjabi texts. To the best of our knowledge, this is the first such system for Punjabi and other Indian languages. We hope that this research work will attempt to narrow down the gap that exists between Punjabi and other natural languages in the natural language processing field. We are confident that this research work will motivate future researchers in developing various advanced resources for Punjabi. This article presented a novel approach for performing grammar checking using phrase and clause level information coupled with grammatical information (POS information) in the form of feature values. This approach can be applied for languages that lack advanced resources like full parser, and pattern-matching approaches are not competent enough to detect different agreement errors.

The web-based version of this grammar checking is available for free use along with three other resources for the Punjabi language – morphological analyzer, part-of-speech tagger, and phrase chunker. Morphological analyzer is also available as free download for non-commercial use.

References

Alam, Md. Jahangir, Naushad UzZaman, and Mumit Khan. 2006. N-gram based Statistical Grammar Checker for Bangla and English. In *Proc. of ninth International Conference on Computer and Information Technology (ICCIT 2006)*, Dhaka, Bangladesh.

Chander, Duni. 1964. *Punjabi Bhasha da Viakaran (Punjabi)*. Punjab University Publication Bureau, Chandigarh, India.

Fliedner, Gerhard. 2002. A System for Checking NP Agreements in German Texts. In *Proceedings of the ACL Student Research Workshop*, pages 12-17, Philadelphia, US.

Gill, Harjeet S. and Henry A. Gleason, Jr. 1986. *A Reference Grammar of Punjabi*. Publication Bureau, Punjabi University, Patiala, India.

Naber, Daniel. 2003. *A Rule-Based Style and Grammar Checker*. Diplomarbeit Technische Fakultät, Universität Bielefeld, Germany.

Puar, Joginder S. 1990. *The Punjabi verb form and function*. Publication Bureau, Punjabi University, Patiala, India.

Schmidt-Wigger, Anje. 1998. Grammar and Style Checking for German. In *Proceedings of the Second International Workshop on Control Language Applications (CLAW-1998)*, pages 76-86, Pittsburgh, PA.

Young-Soog, Chae. 1998. Improvement of Korean Proofreading System Using Corpus and Collocation Rules. In *Proceedings of the 12th Pacific Asia Conference on Language, Information and Computation*, pages 328-333, National University of Singapore, Singapore.

A Toolchain for Grammarians

Bruno Guillaume
LORIA
INRIA Nancy Grand-Est
Bruno.Guillaume@loria.fr

Joseph Le Roux
LORIA
Nancy Université
Joseph.Leroux@loria.fr

Jonathan Marchand
LORIA
Nancy Université
Jonathan.Marchand@loria.fr

Guy Perrier
LORIA
Nancy Université
Guy.Perrier@loria.fr

Karën Fort
LORIA
INRIA Nancy Grand-Est
Karen.Fort@loria.fr

Jennifer Planul
LORIA
Nancy Université
Jennifer.Planul@loria.fr

Abstract

We present a chain of tools used by grammarians and computer scientists to develop grammatical and lexical resources from linguistic knowledge, for various natural languages. The developed resources are intended to be used in Natural Language Processing (NLP) systems.

1 Introduction

We put ourselves from the point of view of researchers who aim at developing formal grammars and lexicons for NLP systems, starting from linguistic knowledge. Grammars have to represent all common linguistic phenomena and lexicons have to include the most frequent words with their most frequent uses. As everyone knows, building such resources is a very complex and time consuming task.

When one wants to formalize linguistic knowledge, a crucial question arises: which mathematical framework to choose? Currently, there is no agreement on the choice of a formalism in the scientific community. Each of the most popular formalisms has its own advantages and drawbacks. A good formalism must have three properties, hard to conciliate: it must be sufficiently expressive to represent linguistic generalizations, easily readable by linguists and computationally tractable. Guided by those principles, we advocate a recent formalism, Interaction Grammars (IGs) (Perrier, 2003), the goal of which is to synthesize two key ideas, expressed in two kinds of formalisms up to now: using the resource sensitivity of natural languages as a principle of syntactic composition, which is a characteristic feature of Categorial Grammars (CG) (Retoré, 2000), and viewing grammars as constraint systems, which is a feature of unification grammars such as LFG (Bresnan, 2001) or HPSG (Pollard and Sag, 1994).

Researchers who develop large lexicons and grammars from linguistic knowledge are confronted to the contradiction between the necessity to choose a specific grammatical framework and the cost of developing resources for this framework. One of the most advanced systems devoted to such a task is LKB (Copestake, 2001). LKB allows grammars and lexicons to be developed for different languages, but only inside the HPSG framework, or at most a typed feature structure framework. Therefore, all produced resources are hardly re-usable for other frameworks. Our goal is to design a toolchain that is as much as possible re-usable for other frameworks than IG.

Our toolchain follows the following architecture (see Figure 1):

- First, for building grammars, we use XMG (Section 3.1) which translates the *source grammar* into an *object grammar*.
- IGs that we have developed with XMG are all lexicalized. Therefore, the object grammar has to be anchored in a lexicon (Section 3.2) in order to produce the *anchored grammar*.
- Then, when analyzing a sentence, we start with a lexical disambiguation module (Section 3.3).
- The resulting lexical selections, presented in the compact form of an *automaton*, are finally sent to the LEOPAR parser (Section 3.4).

© 2008. Licensed under the *Creative Commons Attribution-Noncommercial-Share Alike 3.0 Unported* license (http://creativecommons.org/licenses/by-nc-sa/3.0/). Some rights reserved.

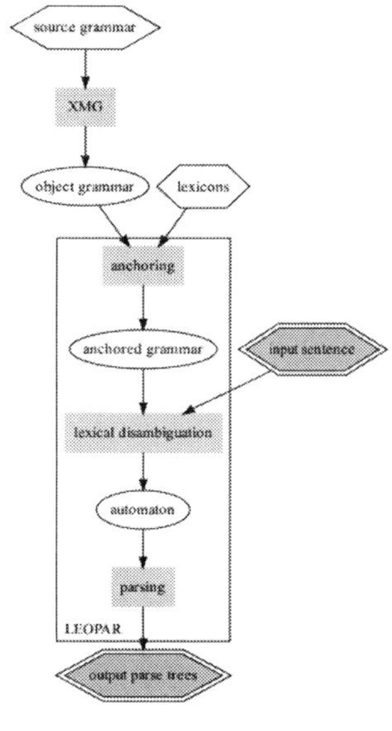

Figure 1: Toolchain architecture

2 Interaction Grammars

IGs (Perrier, 2003) are a grammatical formalism based on the notion of polarity. Polarities express the resource sensitivity of natural languages by modeling the distinction between saturated and unsaturated syntactic structures. Syntactic composition is represented as a chemical reaction guided by the saturation of polarities. In a more precise way, syntactic structures are underspecified trees equipped with polarities expressing their saturation state. They are superposed under the control of polarities in order to saturate them. In CG, Tree Adjoining Grammars (TAGs) and Dependency Grammars, syntactic composition can also be viewed as a mechanism for saturating polarities, but this mechanism is less expressive because node merging is localized at specific places (root nodes, substitution nodes, foot nodes, adjunction nodes ...). In IGs, tree superposition is a more flexible way of realizing syntactic composition. Therefore, it can express sophisticated constraints on the environment in which a polarity has to be saturated. From this angle, IGs are related to Unification Grammars, such as HPSG, because tree superposition is a kind of unification, but with an important difference: polarities play an essential role in the control of unification.

3 Description of the Toolchain

3.1 The XMG Grammar Compiler

The first piece of software in our toolchain is XMG[1] (Duchier et al., 2004), a tool used to develop grammars. XMG addresses the issue of designing wide-coverage grammars: it is based on a distinction between *source grammar*, written by a human, and *object grammar*, used in NLP systems. XMG provides a high level language for writing source grammars and a compiler which translates those grammars into operational object grammars.

XMG is particularly adapted to develop lexicalized grammars. In those grammars, parsing a sentence amounts to combining syntactical items attached to words. In order to have an accurate language model, it may be necessary to attach a huge number of syntactical items to some words (verbs and coordination words, in particular) that describe the various usages of those words. In this context, a grammar is a collection of items representing syntactical behaviors. Those items, although different from each other, often share substructures (for instance, almost all verbs have a substructure for subject verb agreement). That is to say, if a linguist wants to change the way subject-verb agreement is modeled, (s)he would have to modify all the items containing that substructure. This is why designing and maintaining strongly lexicalized grammars is a difficult task.

The idea behind the so-called metagrammatical approach is to write only substructures (called fragments) and then add rules that describe the combinations (expressed with conjunctions, disjunctions and unifications) of those fragments to obtain complete items.

Fragments may contain syntactic, morpho-syntactic and semantic pieces of information. An object grammar is a set of structures containing syntactic and semantic information, that can be anchored using morpho-syntactic information stored in the *interface* of the structure (see Section 3.2).

During development and debugging stages, portions of the grammar can be evaluated independently. The grammar can be split into various modules that can be shared amongst grammars. Finally, graphical tools let the users explore the inheritance hierarchy and the partial structures before complete evaluation.

[1] XMG is freely available under the CeCILL license at `http://sourcesup.cru.fr/xmg`

XMG is also used to develop TAGs (Crabbé, 2005) and it can be easily extended to other grammatical frameworks based on tree representations.

3.2 Anchoring the Object Grammar with a Lexicon

The tool described in the previous section builds the set of elementary trees of the grammar. The toolchain includes a generic anchoring mechanism which allows to use formalism independent linguistic data for the lexicon part.

Each structure produced by XMG comes with an interface (a two-level feature structure) which describes morphological and syntactical constraints used to select words from the lexicon. Dually, in the lexicon, each inflected form of the natural language is described by a set of two-level feature structures that contain morphological and syntactical information.

If the interface of an unanchored tree unifies with some feature structure associated with w in the lexicon, then an anchored tree is produced for the word w.

The toolchain also contains a modularized lexicon manager which aims at easing the integration of external and formalism independent resources. The lexicon manager provides several levels of linguistic description to factorize redundant data. It also contains a flexible compilation mechanism to improve anchoring efficiency and to ease lexicon debugging.

3.3 Lexical Disambiguation

Neutralization of polarities is the key mechanism in the parsing process as it is used to control syntactic composition. This principle can also be used to filter lexical selections. For a input sentence, a *lexical selection* is a choice of an elementary tree from the anchored grammar for each word of the sentence.

Indeed, the number of possible lexical selections may present an exponential complexity in the length of the sentence. A way of filtering them consists in abstracting some information from the initial formalism F to a new formalism F_{abs}. Then, parsing in F_{abs} allows to eliminate wrong lexical selections at a minimal cost (Boullier, 2003). (Bonfante et al., 2004) shows that polarities allow original methods of abstraction.

Following this idea, the lexical disambiguation module checks the global neutrality of every lexical selection for each polarized feature: a set of trees bearing negative and positive polarities can only be reduced to a neutral tree if the sum of the negative polarities for each feature equals the sum of its positive polarities.

Counting the sum of positive and negative features can be done in a compact way by using an automaton. This automaton structure allows to share all paths that have the same global polarity balance (Bonfante et al., 2004).

3.4 The LEOPAR Parser

The next piece of software in our toolchain is a parser based on the IGs formalism[2]. In addition to a command line interface, the parser provides an intuitive graphical user interface. Parsing can be highly customized in both modes. Besides, the processed data can be viewed at each stage of the analysis via the interface so one can easily check the behavior of the grammar and the lexicons in the parsing process.

The parsing can also be done manually: one first chooses a lexical selection of the sentence given by the lexer and then proceeds to the analysis by neutralizing nodes from the selection. This way, the syntactic composition can be controlled by the user.

4 Results

Our toolchain has been used first to produce a large coverage French IG. Most of the usual syntactical constructions of French are covered. Some non trivial constructions covered by the grammar are, for instance: coordination, negation (in French, negation is expressed with two words with complex placement rules), long distance dependencies (with island constraints). The object grammar contains 2,074 syntactic structures which are produced by 455 classes in the source grammar.

The French grammar has been tested on the French TSNLP (Test Suite for the Natural Language Processing) (Lehmann et al., 1996); this test suite contains around 1,300 grammatical sentences and 1,600 ungrammatical ones. The fact that our grammar is based on linguistic knowledge ensures a good coverage and greatly limits overgeneration: 88% of the grammatical sentences are correctly parsed and 85% of the ungrammatical sentences are rejected by our grammar.

[2] LEOPAR is freely available under the CeCILL license at `http://www.loria.fr/equipes/calligramme/leopar`

A few months ago, we started to build an English IG. The modularity of the toolchain was an advantage to build this grammar by abstracting the initial grammar and then specifying the abstract kernel for English. The English TSNLP has been used to test the new grammar: 85% of the grammatical sentences are correctly parsed and 84% of the ungrammatical sentences are rejected. It is worth noting that those scores are obtained with a grammar that is still being developed .

5 Future work

The toolchain we have presented here aims at producing grammars and lexicons with large coverage from linguistic knowledge. This justifies the choice of discarding statistical methods in the first stage of the toolchain development: in the two steps of lexical disambiguation and parsing, we want to keep all possible solutions without discarding even the less probable ones. Now, in a next future, we have the ambition of using the toolchain for parsing large raw corpora in different languages.

For French, we have a large grammar and a large lexicon, which are essential for such a task. The introduction of statistics in the two modules of lexical disambiguation and parsing will contribute to computational efficiency. Moreover, we have to enrich our parsing strategies with robustness. We also ambition to integrate semantics into grammars and lexicons.

Our experience with English is a first step to take multi-linguality into account. The crucial point is to make our grammars evolve towards an even more multi-lingual architecture with an abstract kernel, common to different languages, and different specifications of this kernel for different languages, thus following the approach of the Grammatical Framework (Ranta, 2004).

Finally, to make the toolchain evolve towards multi-formalism, it is first necessary to extend XMG for more genericity; there is no fundamental obstacle to this task. Many widespread formalisms can then benefit from our original methods of lexical disambiguation and parsing, based on polarities. (Kahane, 2006) presents the polarization of several formalisms and (Kow, 2007) shows that this way is promising.

References

Bonfante, G., B. Guillaume, and G. Perrier. 2004. Polarization and abstraction of grammatical formalisms as methods for lexical disambiguation. In *CoLing'2004, 2004*, pages 303–309, Geneva, Switzerland.

Boullier, P. 2003. Supertagging: A non-statistical parsing-based approach. In *IWPT 03*, pages 55–65, Nancy, France.

Bresnan, J. 2001. *Lexical-Functional Syntax*. Blackwell Publishers, Oxford.

Copestake, A. 2001. *Implementing Typed Feature Structure Grammars*. CSLI Publications.

Crabbé, B. 2005. *Représentation informatique de grammaires fortement lexicalisées : application à la grammaire d'arbres adjoints*. Phd thesis, Université Nancy 2.

Duchier, D., J. Le Roux, and Y. Parmentier. 2004. The metagrammar compiler : A NLP Application with a Multi-paradigm Architecture. In *Second International Mozart/Oz Conference - MOZ 2004, Charleroi, Belgium*.

Kahane, S. 2006. Polarized unification grammars. In *21st International Conference on Computational Linguistics and 44th Annual Meeting of the Association for Computational Linguistics*, pages 137–144, Sydney, Australia.

Kow, E. 2007. *Surface realisation: ambiguity and determinism*. Phd thesis, Université Nancy 2.

Lehmann, S., S. Oepen, S. Regnier-Pros, K. Netter, V. Lux, J. Klein, K. Falkedal, F. Fouvry, D. Estival, E. Dauphin, H. Compagnion, J. Baur, L. Balkan, and D. Arnold. 1996. TSNLP — Test Suites for Natural Language Processing. In *CoLing 1996, Kopenhagen*.

Perrier, G. 2003. *Les grammaires d'interaction*. Habilitation thesis, Université Nancy 2.

Pollard, C.J. and I.A. Sag. 1994. *Head-Driven Phrase Structure Grammar*. University of Chicago Press.

Ranta, A. 2004. Grammatical Framework: A Type-Theoretical Grammar Formalism. *Journal of Functional Programming*, 14(2):145–189.

Retoré, C. 2000. The Logic of Categorial Grammars. ESSLI'2000, Birmingham.

A Punjabi To Hindi Machine Translation System

Gurpreet Singh Josan
Lecturer, Yadvindra College of Engineering, Talwandi Sabo Bathinda.
josangurpreet@rediffmail.com

Gurpreet Singh Lehal
Professor, Dept. of Comp. Sci., Punjabi University Patiala.
gslehal@gmail.com

Abstract

Punjabi and Hindi are two closely related languages as both originated from the same origin and having lot of syntactic and semantic similarities. These similarities make direct translation methodology an obvious choice for Punjabi-Hindi language pair. The purposed system for Punjabi to Hindi translation has been implemented with various research techniques based on Direct MT architecture and language corpus. The output is evaluated by already prescribed methods in order to get the suitability of the system for the Punjabi Hindi language pair.

1. Introduction

The Direct MT system is based upon exploitation of syntactic similarities between more or less related natural languages. Although its deficiencies soon became apparent, it remains popular in certain situations due to its usefulness, robustness and relative simplicity. One of such situation is machine translation of closely related languages. The general opinion is that it is easier to create an MT system for a pair of related languages (Hajic et.al. 2000). In the last decade, some of the systems utilizing this approach for translating between similar languages have confirmed this concept. In this paper, our attempt to use the same concept for language pair of Punjabi-Hindi is described.

Punjabi and Hindi both are classified as Indo-Iranian languages. Although they are in the same family, but still they have lot of differences in order to make them not mutually intelligible. Punjabi and Hindi are not mutually intelligible in written form. As far as spoken form is concerned, Punjabi and Hindi are mutually intelligible to certain degree. This relation is further asymmetric with the speakers of Punjabi more able to understand Hindi but reverse is not true.

1.1 Punjabi Language

Punjabi is the official language of the Indian state of Punjab and also one of the official languages of Delhi. It is used in government, education, commerce, art, mass media and in every day communication. A good deal of Sikh religious literature is written in Punjabi language. According to SIL Ethnologue, Punjabi is the language of about 57 million people and ranked 20th among the total languages of the world. It is written in Gurmukhy, Shahmukhy and roman scripts.

1.2 Hindi Language

Hindi on the other hand has been one of the two official languages of all of India. Hindi is a language of about 577 million peoples all over the world and is ranked as 5th most widely spoken language by SIL Ethnologue.

2. The Need

India being a large and multilingual society, and in the interest of the regional languages, the government of India has allowed to use regional languages as the official language of respective region and adopt bilingual form (Hindi/English) as the official language of Union Government. Most of the state governments work in their respective regional languages whereas the union government's official documents and reports are in bilingual form (Hindi/English). In order to have a proper communication there is a need to translate these reports and documents in the respective regional languages and vice versa. Some other applications of Punjabi to Hindi MT system are Text Translation, Website Translation, Message Translation (Email), Cross Language Information Retrieval and Web Service.

© 2008. Licensed under the *Creative Commons Attribution-Noncommercial-Share Alike 3.0 Unported* license (http://creativecommons.org/licenses/by-nc-sa/3.0/). Some rights reserved.

Existing system: Keeping in view the importance of MT system among Indian languages, an MT system called "Anusaarka" has been developed at IIIT Hyderabad covering all the major Indian languages. It is a language accessor and produces an image of source language in target language. Output will have to be post-edited by a person, to make it grammatically correct, stylistically proper, etc. Moreover, some amount of training will be needed on the part of the reader to read and understand the output. Our system is more practical in nature than Anusaarka and it produce more grammatical and stylistic output. No training is needed on the part of reader.

3. System description

To start with, a direct translation system is created on windows platform, in which words from source language are chosen, their equivalents in target language are found out from the lexicon and are replaced to get target language. The source text is passed through various pre processing phase and out put is also passed through a post processing phase.

3.1 Lexical Resources

In this research work, we have developed and used various resources as follow:

Root word Lexicon: It is a bilingual dictionary that contains Punjabi language word, its lexical category like whether it is noun, verb or adjective etc and corresponding Hindi word. It also contains the gender information in case of nouns and type information (i.e. transitive or intransitive) in case of verb. This dictionary contains about 33000 entries covering almost all the root words of Punjabi language.

inflectional form lexicon: It contains all the inflectional forms, root word and corresponding Hindi word. Ambiguous words has the entry "amb" in the Hindi word field. It contains about 90,000 entries.

Ambiguous word lexicon: It contains about 1000 entries covering all the ambiguous words with their most frequent meaning.

Bigram Table: Used for resolving ambiguity, this table contains Punjabi bigrams along with Hindi meaning. Bigrams are created from a corpus of 7 million words.

Trigram Table: Same as Bigram, but contain Punjabi trigrams used for resolving ambiguity. Created from 7 million words corpus.

3.2 System Architecture

The system architecture, as shown in figure 3.1, has the following stages through which the source text is passed.

Text normalization

There are number of ASCII based fonts to represent Punjabi text and each font has variations in assigning ASCII code to Punjabi Alphabets. This cause a problem while scanning a text. Therefore, the first step is to normalize the source text by converting it into Unicode format. It gives us three fold advantages; first it will reduce the text scanning complexity. Secondly it also helps in internationalizing the system as if the output is in Unicode format then it can be used in various applications in various ways. Thirdly, it eases the transliteration task.

Tokenization

The system is designed to do sentence level translation in order to have a track about the context of a word. Once the whole text is scanned, next step is to break up the data into sentences. Individual words or tokens are extracted out from the sentence and processed to find out its equivalent in the target language. Tokens are separated by using break characters like space, comma, question mark etc.

Translation Engine

The translation engine is responsible for translation of each token obtained from the previous step. It uses various lexical resources for finding the match of a given token in target language. It involves different modules like Named Entity Recognition, Repetitive construct handler, Word Mapping, Ambiguity Resolution, and Transliteration.

The token obtained in the previous stage is passed through following stages:

1. The token is checked for proper names of persons as they need to be transliterated.
2. If token is not a proper name then it is checked for repetitive units like ਘਰੋਂ ਘਰ{gharōṁ ghar}(home to home) by comparing the word and its root with next or previous words and their roots. A limited morph analysis is required for this step. The repetitive construct handling involves two stages. First, detection of repetitive construct and second, handling of such construct.
Detection: For detection of repetitive construct, we check the next and previous word. If the next and previous words are same or the roots of next and previous words are same as that of current word, then we

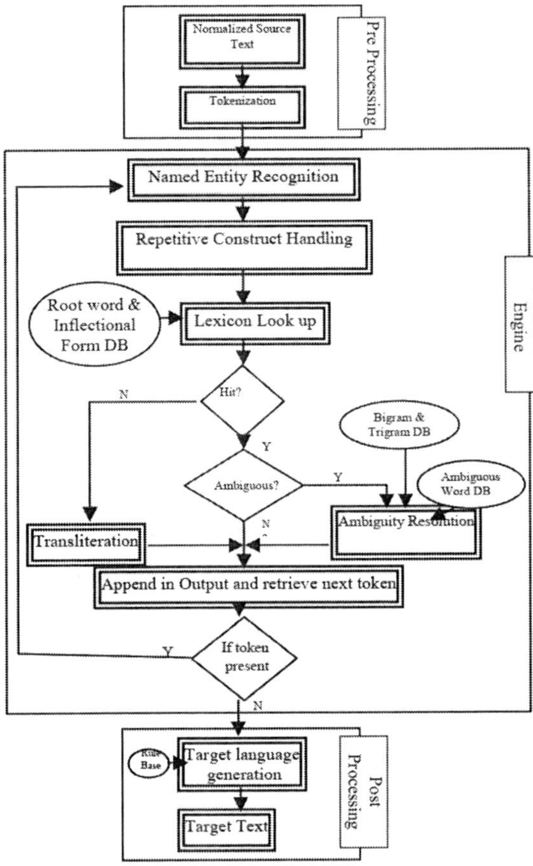

Figure 3.1 System Architecture

mark it as a repetitive construct. The root of the words will be obtained from the database discussed earlier.

Handling: If repetitive construct is found then the next step is to get the lexical information of the token. This information is again obtained from the database. The lexical information of token is used to trigger the handling process. If the token is noun then the token is replaced by its root and then passed to the next step. E.g. in case of ਘਰੋਂ ਘਰ{gharōṁ ghar}(home to home) we check the token ਘਰੋਂ and its root i.e. ਘਰ with the next token which in this case is again ਘਰ. Thus, system marks it as repetitive constructs. Then the lexical category of ਘਰ is checked from the database which comes out to be noun. So we replace the ਘਰੋਂ with its root ਘਰ and pass the replaced token to the next step.

3. Then the token is looked into the database for a match. The Database contains various types of tables. First of all token is checked in the root database and inflectional form database. It gives two types of output if match occurs. Either the corresponding Hindi word is produced or "amb" is appeared which shows that word is ambiguous.
4. For the ambiguous words, we call "resolver" module that resolve the ambiguity with the help of n-gram language modeling. The system uses trigram table in the first place, which contains the two words in the vicinity of an ambiguous word and corresponding meaning for that particular context. If it fails to resolve the ambiguity then bigram table is searched. Bigram table is similar to trigram table except it contains only one word in the vicinity of ambiguous words. If both trigram and bigram fails to resolve then module will use most frequently used meaning.
5. If token is not matched in inflectional form database, then word may be a foreign word i.e. word of other language like English. Such words and all those tokens, for which no entry is found in database, are transliterated. Transliteration is performed in three stages as follow:
   a. Direct Mapping
   b. Rule Based Improvement
   c. Soundex technique Based improvement.
6. The system uses Direct mapping approach at first stage and then applies some rules to make the spellings of output similar to target language. In the third stage soundex technique is used to deal with the special cases like occurrence of half characters and other symbols not present in Punjabi.
7. All these steps are repeated for all the sentences in the source text.

Target Language Generation

After converting all source text to target text, there are some discrepancies as discussed previously and need to be solved. For removing these discrepancies a rule base is used. This database gives the rules to make the text grammatically correct.

4. Implementation

The system is implemented in ASP.net at front end and MSAccess at back end. A class is created whose object will accept a string in Punjabi language and returns its corresponding Hindi string. Based on this class, various online applications are created. A web site is created with interface that enables a user to write his input sentence in Punjabi and system will produce the output in Hindi. Another application enables the user to translate a webpage in Punjabi to Hindi on the fly. The user has to mention the URL of webpage to be translated. In another application, an online interface for cross language information retrieval system has been created whereby a user can enter his key word in Punjabi. These keywords are translated in Hindi and result is posted to Google search engine. The user is presented with the results returned by Google from Hindi web pages. Another interface enables the users to write E-mail in Punjabi. This message is translated to Hindi and send to the target email address. The receiver get the mail in Hindi. For the developers who want to use this Punjabi To Hindi MT module, a web service is also created.

5. Results

5.1 Subjective test analysis

The overall rating grade for Intelligibility of the translated text came out to be 2.76 on a 3 point scale. About 94% sentences are intelligible.
The overall rating grade for fidelity of the translated text came out to be 2.72 on 3 point scale. Similarly, the accuracy percentage for the system is found out to be 90.67%. The accuracy score is comparable with other similar systems (Hajic J. et.al. 2000; Hric J. et.al. 2000; Homola et.al. 2005) as shown in table 5.1.

MT SYSTEM	Accuracy
RUSLAN	40% correct 40% with minor errors. 20% with major error.
CESILKO (Czech-to-Slovak)	90%
Czech-to-Polish	71.4%
Czech-to-Lithuanian	87.6%
Our System	90.67%

Table 5.1 Comparative analysis of %age accuracy

5.2 Error Analysis

Word Error rate, which is the percentage of erroneous words from all words, is found out to be 2.34%. It is comparably lower than that of the general systems like Salt, Incyta, Internostrum, where it ranges from 3.0 to 4.9 (Tomas J. et.al., 2003). The Sentence Error rate is found out to be 24.26%.

6. Conclusion

The accuracy of the translation achieved by our system justifies the hypothesis that the simple word-for-word translation along with statistical and rule based approach provides a high accuracy and simple solution for language pair of Punjabi and Hindi especially when the objective is just to have a rough idea on the subject matter.

References

Altintas K., Cicekli I., "A Machine Translation System Between a Pair of Closely Related Languages", In Proceedings of ISCIS 2002, October 2002, Orlando, Florida.

Anusaarka-overcoming the language barrier in India, http://www.iiit.net/ltrc/Publications/anuvad.html

Bemova A., Oliva K. Panevova J.," Some Problems of Machine translation between closely related languages", In Proceedings of the 12th conference on Computational linguistics - Volume 1, Budapest, Hungry, 1988 pp 46 - 48

HAJIC J, HRIC J, KUBON V., "CESILKO– an MT system for closely related languages", In *ACL2000, Tutorial Abstracts and Demonstration Notes*, pp. 7-8. ACL, Washington.

Hajic J., "Ruslan-An MT System between closely related languages", In *Proceedings of the 3rd Conference of The European Chapter of the Association for Computational Linguistics*, Copenhagen, Denmark, 1987, pp.113-117.

HRIC J, HAJIC J, KUBON V., "Machine Translation of Very Close Languages", proceedings of the 6th Applied Natural Language Processing Conference, April 29--May 4, 2000, Seattle, Washington, USA. pp 7-12.

Homola P., Kubon V., "A Machine Translationn System into a Minority Language", In Proceddings of the Workshop on *Modern Approaches in Translation Technologies 2005* - Borovets, Bulgaria, pp 31-35.

Marote R. C, Guillen E., Alenda A.G., Savall M.I.G., Bellver A.I., Buendia S.M., Rozas S.O., Pina H.P., Anton P.M.P., Forcada M.L., "The Spanish-Catalan machine translation system interNOSTRM", In proceedings of MT Summit VIII, 18-22 Sept. 2001, Santiago de Compostela, Galicia, Spain.

Scannell K.P.,"Machine Translation for Closely Related language Pair", Proceedings of the Workshop on Strategies for developing machine translation for minority languages at LREC 2006, Genoa, Italy, May 2006, pp103-107.

Slype V., 1979. "Critical Methods for Evaluating the Quality of Machine Translation," Prepared for the European Commission Directorate General Scientific and Technical Information and Information Management. Report BR-19142. Bureau Marcel van Dijk.

"Build Your Own" Spoken Dialogue Systems: Automatically Generating ISU Dialogue Systems from Business User Resources

Oliver Lemon, Xingkun Liu, and **Helen Hastie**
School of Informatics
University of Edinburgh
Informatics Forum
10 Crichton Street
Edinburgh, EH8 9AB
{olemon,xliu4,hhastie}@inf.ed.ac.uk

Abstract

Building effective spoken dialogue systems (SDS) is currently a complex task requiring expert knowledge. Our tools give control of SDS application development to non-experts, who need only use a Graphical User Interface or GUI to develop state-of-the-art "Information State Update" (ISU) dialogue systems. Behind the GUI is a set of Advanced Dialogue Tools (ADT) that generate complete SDS based on Business User Resources. These resources include a database and a Process Model that captures the structure of an application, for example, banking or restaurant information. Also generated are speech recognition Language Models and grammars for robust interpretation of spontaneous speech. We will demonstrate how our simple GUI allows developers to easily and quickly create and modify SDS without the need for expensive speech application service providers. This demonstration shows the interface, the ADT components, and discusses some of the research issues involved. We also show an example application built with the tools: a tourist information system running on an ultra-mobile PC.

1 Introduction

As automated call centres are becoming more and more commonplace, new challenges are emerging such as having to rely on expensive service providers to build systems, the inability to quickly and easily modify live systems, and the time and cost needed to create new SDS applications. This paper describes a solution to these problems using our Advanced Dialogue Tools (ADT). This prototype system allows developers to take already established business user resources such as Business Process Models (BPM) and databases, and use them to automatically generate spoken dialogue systems. Simple customisations can then be made through the easy-to-use ADT interface or GUI, which is example-driven. This radically new way of creating spoken dialogue systems will put control into the hands of the business user who is familiar with customer needs and business goals, thus improving usability and making spoken dialogue systems more widely and rapidly available.

Currently, VoiceXML is widely used for such tasks. However, VoiceXML applications are difficult to build and maintain, because developers must anticipate and represent every possible dialogue path in the finite-state VoiceXML model. ADT will generate VoiceXML dynamically, but the easy-to-use interface allows developers to select, deploy, and monitor different advanced dialogue strategies without needing to code VoiceXML directly. We apply the "Information State Update" (ISU) approach (Lemon, 2004) that enables more robust, flexible and natural conversations than VoiceXML. ISU uses a more concise and maintainable representation of dialogue flow, based on rules operating over dialogue contexts, which can generalise to unforeseen states.

2 The ADT Architecture

Figure 1 shows the ADT architecture whereby the main algorithm takes business user resources and databases as input and uses these to automatically

©2008. Licensed under the *Creative Commons Attribution-Noncommercial-Share Alike 3.0 Unported* license (http://creativecommons.org/licenses/by-nc-sa/3.0/). Some rights reserved.

generate the spoken dialogue system. Figure 2 shows part of one such resource, namely a BPM for hotel bookings. First the caller will hear an introduction, then they will be asked what price range they want, and then whether they want a hotel in the centre of town or not. Advantages of using BPMs include the fact that graphical interfaces and authoring environments are widely available for them, for example: Eclipse, IBM Websphere-Process Server, BEA WeblogicWorkshop etc.. In addition, Business User Resources can contain a lot of additional information as well as call flows including context, multi-media, and multiple customer interactions.

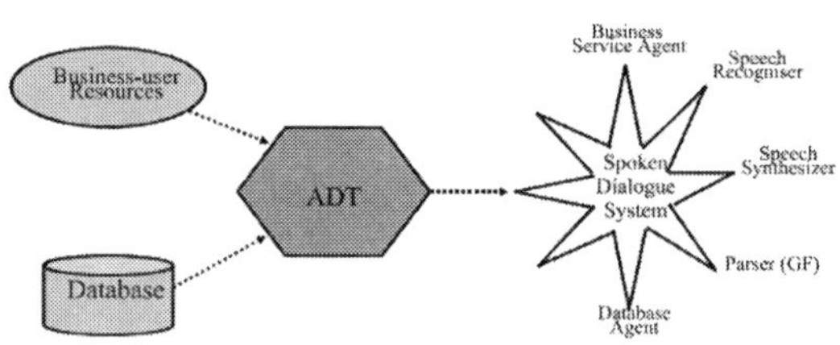

Figure 1: The ADT Architecture

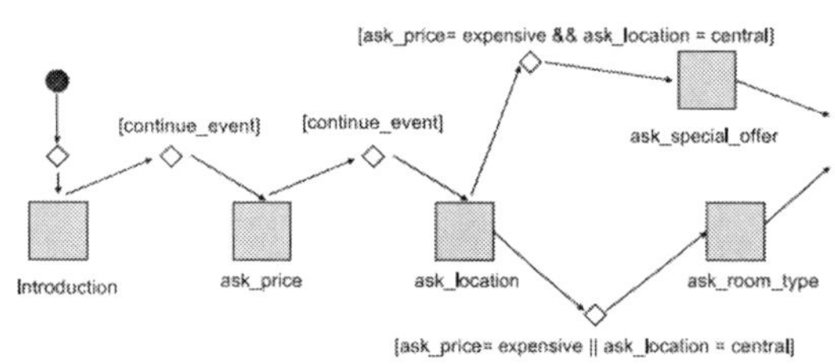

Figure 2: Part of an example Business Process Model for searching for Hotels

The resulting spoken dialogue system deploys the following main modules:

- Speech Recogniser module, e.g. ATK/HTK (Young, 2007; Young, 1995) or Nuance (Nuance, 2002)
- Spoken Language Understanding module, e.g. Grammatical Framework (GF) parser (Ranta, 2004)
- BPM and Database modules
- Speech synthesiser e.g. Festival (Taylor et al., 1998) or Cereproc (Aylett and Pidcock, 2007)

2.1 Generic Dialogue Modelling

Sophisticated research systems have been developed only for specific applications and cannot be easily transferred to another, even very similar task or domain. The problem of components being domain specific is especially prevalent in the core area of dialogue management. For example MIT's Pegasus and Mercury systems (Seneff, 2002) have dialogue managers (DM) that use approximately 350 domain-specific hand-coded rules each. The sheer amount of labour required to construct systems prevents them from being more widely and rapidly deployed. Our solution uses BPMs and related authoring tools to specify *domain-specific* dialogue interactions which are combined with a *domain-general* dialogue manager. Specifically, the DM consults the BPM to determine what task-based steps to take next, such as asking for a cinema name. General aspects of dialogue, such as confirmation and clarification strategies, are handled by the domain-general DM. Values for constraints on transitions and branching in the BPM, for example "present insurance option if the user is business-class", are compiled into domain-specific parts of the DM's update rules. XML format is used for BPMs, and they are compiled into finite state machines consulted by the spoken dialogue system through the BPM module. The domain-general DM was mostly abstracted from the TALK system (Lemon et al., 2006).

2.2 Compiling Grammars for Business User Resources and Databases

For Spoken Language Understanding, ADT currently uses Grammatical Framework (GF) (Ranta, 2004) which is a language for writing multilingual grammars, on top of which various applications such as machine translation and human-machine interaction have been built. A GF grammar not only defines syntactic well-formedness, but also semantic content.

Using ADT, system developers do not have to write a single line of GF grammar code. The system compiles all database entries and their properties into the appropriate "slot-filling" parts of the GF grammar for each specific BPM.

For example, a generated GF rule is:

```
Bpm_generalTypeRule_4:
town_info_hotels_name->Utt=>{ s = np.s}
```

This rule was generated because "name" is a database field for the subtask `hotels` in the "town_info" BPM. It specifies that all hotel names are valid utterances.

A core GF grammar has been developed to cover basic information-seeking interactions. This is combined with a domain-specific grammar which is automatically generated from the BPM, database and the example utterances provided by the developer in the GUI. Finally, GF is a robust parser – it skips all disfluencies and unknown words to produce an interpretation of the user input if one exists.

2.3 Speech Recognition and Text To Speech

The grammars for Spoken Language Understanding generated by ADT are also compiled to grammar-based language models (LM) for speech recognition. ADT is plug-and-play and adheres to industry standards such as GSML, GrXML. This allows for greater flexibility since the application developer is not tied to one recogniser or TTS engine. For this demonstration, the speech recogniser is ATK (Young, 2007; Young, 1995) and the speech synthesiser is Cereproc (Aylett and Pidcock, 2007). Future work will involve automatically generating context sensitive language models (Lemon and Gruenstein, 2004).

2.4 ADT GUI

As mentioned above, the prototype ADT GUI can be used to define system prompts and add likely user responses to the grammar. Figure 3 shows the developer associating "spotter" phrases with subtasks in the BPM. Here the developer is associating the phrases "hotels, hotel, stay, room, night, sleep" and "rooms" with the hotels task. This means that, for example, if the user says "I need a place to stay", the hotel-booking BPM will be triggered. Note that multi-word phrases may also be defined. The defined spotters are automatically compiled into the GF grammar for parsing and speech recognition. By default all the lexical entries for answer-types for the subtasks will already be present as

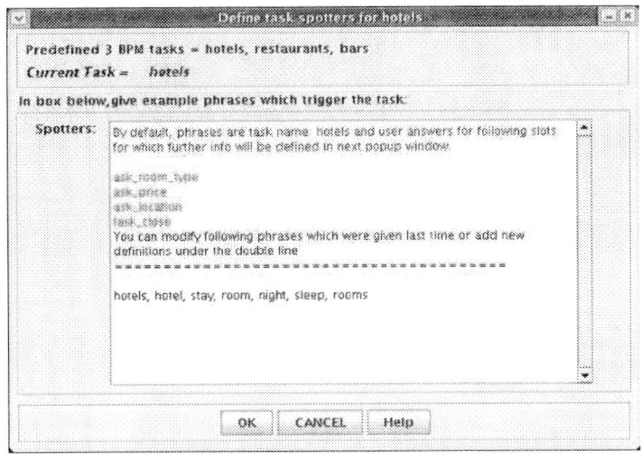

Figure 3: Example: using the ADT GUI to define "spotter" phrases for different BPM subtasks

spotter phrases. ADT also checks for possible ambiguities, for example whether "pizza" is a spotter for both cuisine_type for a restaurant task and food_type for a shopping task, and it uses clarification sub-dialogues to resolve them at runtime.

Figure 4 shows the developer's overview of the subtasks of a BPM, in this case hotel information. The developer can navigate this representation and edit it to define prompts and manipulate the associated databases.

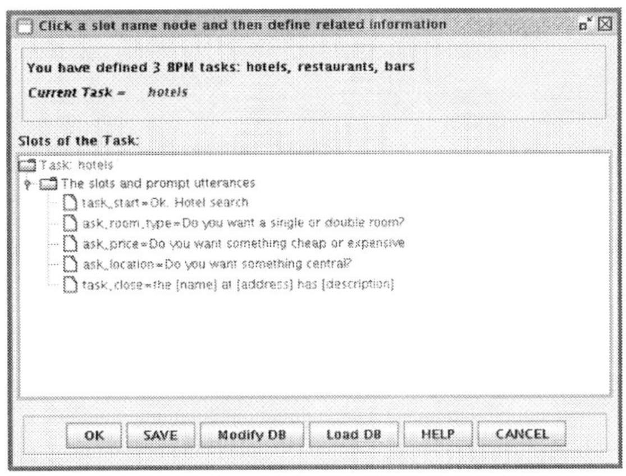

Figure 4: Sub-dialogue structure generated from the Hotel booking BPM

Figure 5 shows the developer specifying the required linguistic information to automate the ask_price subtask of the hotels BPM. Here the developer specifies the system prompt for the information "Do you want something cheap or expensive?"; a phrase for implicit confirmation of provided values "a [X] hotel", where [X] is the semantics of the speech recognition hypothesis for the user input; and a clarifying phrase for this subtask

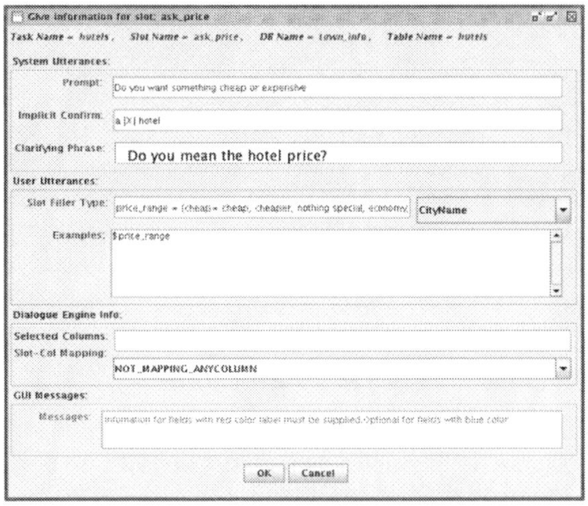

Figure 5: Example: using ADT to define prompts, answer sets, and database mappings for the ask_price subtask of the BPM in Figure 4

"Do you mean the hotel price?" for use when disambiguating between two or more tasks. The developer also specifies here the answer type that will resolve the system prompt. There are many predefined answer-types extracted from the databases associated with the BPM, and the developer can select and/or edit these. Optionally, they can give additional example phrases that users might say to answer the prompt, and these are automatically added to the GF grammar.

2.5 Usability

Several demonstration systems have been built using ADT with an average development time of under an hour. However, our planned evaluation will test the ability of novice users, with some knowledge of BPMs and databases, to iteratively develop their own ISU dialogue systems.

3 Summary

This paper describes the Advanced Dialogue Tools for creating Information State Update based dialogue systems automatically from Business User Resources such as BPMs and databases. The tools include automatic generation of grammars for robust interpretation of spontaneous speech, and uses the application databases and BPMs to generate lexical entries and grammar rules for speech recognition language modelling. We also demonstrate an easy-to-use prototype interface that allows the user to easily and quickly modify aspects of the dialogue, thus eliminating the need for third party service providers. This paper describes ADT, its main components, and some of the research issues involved in its development.

4 Acknowledgement

This project is funded by a Scottish Enterprise Proof of Concept Grant (project number 8-ELM-004).

References

Aylett, Matthew P. and Christopher J. Pidcock. 2007. The cerevoice characterful speech synthesiser sdk. In *AISB*, pages 174–8.

Lemon, Oliver and Alexander Gruenstein. 2004. Multithreaded context for robust conversational interfaces: context-sensitive speech recognition and interpretation of corrective fragments. *ACM Transactions on Computer-Human Interaction (ACM TOCHI)*, 11(3):241–267.

Lemon, Oliver, Kallirroi Georgila, James Henderson, and Matthew Stuttle. 2006. An ISU dialogue system exhibiting reinforcement learning of dialogue policies: generic slot-filling in the TALK in-car system. In *Proceedings of EACL*, pages 119–122.

Lemon, Oliver. 2004. Context-sensitive speech recognition in Information-State Update dialogue systems: results for the grammar switching approach. In *Proceedings of the 8th Workshop on the Semantics and Pragmatics of Dialogue, CATALOG'04*, pages 49–55.

Nuance, 2002. http://www.nuance.com. As of 1 Feb 2002.

Ranta, A. 2004. Grammatical framework. a type-theoretical grammar formalism. *Journal of Functional Programming*, 14(2):145–189.

Seneff, Stephanie. 2002. Response Planning and Generation in the Mercury Flight Reservation System. *Computer Speech and Language*, 16.

Taylor, P., A. Black, and R. Caley. 1998. The architecture of the the Festival speech synthesis system. In *Third International Workshop on Speech Synthesis, Sydney, Australia*.

Young, Steve. 1995. Large vocabulary continuous speech recognition: A review. In *Proceedings of the IEEE Workshop on Automatic Speech Recognition and Understanding*, pages 3–28.

Young, Steve. 2007. ATK: An Application Toolkit for HTK, Version 1.6. Technical report, Cambridge University Engineering Department.

Multilingual Mobile-Phone Translation Services for World Travelers

Michael Paul, Hideo Okuma, Hirofumi Yamamoto, Eiichiro Sumita, Shigeki Matsuda, Tohru Shimizu, Satoshi Nakamura
† NICT Spoken Language Communication Group
‡ ATR Spoken Language Communication Research Labs
Hikaridai 2-2-2, Keihanna Science City, 619-0288 Kyoto, Japan
Michael.Paul@nict.go.jp

Abstract

This demonstration introduces two new multilingual translation services for mobile phones. The first translation service provides state-of-the-art text-to-text translations of Japanese as well as English conversational spoken language in the travel domain into 17 languages using statistical machine translation technologies trained automatically from a large-scale multilingual corpus. The second demonstration is a speech translation service between Japanese and English for real environments. It is based on distributed speech recognition with noise suppression. Flexible interfaces between internal and external speech translation resources ease the portability of the system to other languages and enable real-time location-free communication world-wide.

1 Introduction

Spoken language translation technologies attempt to bridge the language barriers between people with different native languages who each want to engage in conversation by using their mother-tongue. The importance of these technologies is increasing due to increases in the number of opportunities for cross-language communication in face-to-face conversation, especially in the domain of tourism.

We demonstrate two multilingual translation services for mobile phones that are built on corpus-based speech recognition and translation technologies. These services enable smooth and location-free communication in real environments covering the major languages of most nations (see Figure 1).

©NICT/ATR, 2008. Licensed under the *Creative Commons Attribution-Noncommercial-Share Alike 3.0 Unported* license (http://creativecommons.org/licenses/by-nc-sa/3.0/). Some rights reserved.

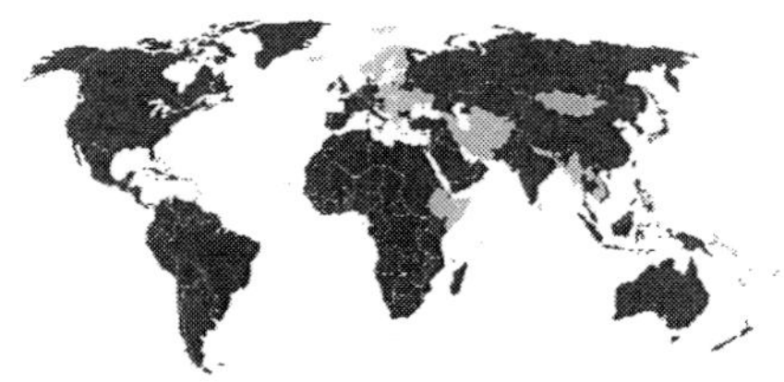

Figure 1: Global Language Coverage

The first multilingual translation service described in this paper is a text-to-text translation service that enables users to translate Japanese and English conversational spoken language sentences in the travel domain into 17 other languages. The system's core components consist of a multilingual, sentence-aligned spoken language corpus covering 18 of the major world languages and state-of-the-art statistical machine translation (SMT) engines that are trained automatically from this corpus covering 306 (=18x17) translation directions. A graphical user-interface (GUI) allows 24x7 world-wide access to the translation service (see Section 2).

The second multilingual translation service is an extension of the text-based translation service that additionally provides speech recognition capabilities. This is the first commercial speech translation service in the world. The system is based on distributed speech recognition and operates as follows: (1) front-end processing (noise suppression, feature extraction, and feature parameter compression) is carried out on the mobile phone, (2) back-end processing (recognition, translation) is done on a server and (3) translation results are sent back and displayed on the mobile phone (see Section 3).

2 Multilingual Text Translation Service (MTTS)

The multilingual text translation service for mobile phones can be accessed via 'http://atr-langue.jp/smlt' or by using the QR code in Figure 2 that also illustrates the graphical user interface of

Figure 2: QR Code and GUI of MTTS

the translation service. Two different modes are distinguished: (1) the *multilingual mode* where the input is translated into all 17 languages simultaneously and the translation results are displayed side-by-side and (2) the *bilingual mode* where a single language out of 17 languages can be selected as the target language of the Japanese or English input text translation. The *bilingual mode* also features *back-translation* functionality, i.e., a reverse translation of the generated translation output into the source language, that enables immediate feedback on the quality of the translation output. In order to solve font problems of mobile phones, the translated sentences are rendered on the server side and an image is sent and displayed in the mobile phone.

2.1 Multilingual Travel Conversation Corpus

The translation engines used for the translation service are trained on the *Basic Travel Expressions Corpus* (ATR-BTEC) which is a collection of sentences that travel experts consider useful for people going abroad and cover a large variety of topics in travel situations like *shopping* or *stay* (Kikui et al., 2006). The multilingual corpus consists of 160K sentences for each of the 18 languages, aligned at the sentence-level. The characteristics of all ATR-BTEC corpus languages are summarized in Table 1. These languages differ largely in *word order* (SVO, SOV), *segmentation unit* (phrase, word, none), and *morphology* (poor, medium, rich). Concerning word segmentation, the corpora were preprocessed using simple tokenization tools for all European languages and language-specific word-segmentation tools for languages like Chinese, Japanese, Korean, or Thai that do not use white-space to separate word/phrase tokens. All data sets were lower-cased and punctuation marks were removed.

Table 1: Language Characteristics

Language		Order	Segments	Morphology
Arabic	(ar)	SVO	phrase	rich
Danish	(da)	SVO	words	medium
German	(de)	SVO	words	medium
English	**(en)**	**SVO**	**words**	**poor**
Spanish	(es)	SVO	words	medium
French	(fr)	SVO	words	medium
Indonesian	(id)	SVO	words	rich
Italian	(it)	SVO	words	medium
Japanese	**(ja)**	**SOV**	**none**	**poor**
Korean	(ko)	SOV	phrase	poor
Malay	(ms)	SVO	words	rich
Dutch	(nl)	SVO	words	medium
Portuguese	(pt)	SVO	words	medium
Brazilian Portuguese	(pt-b)	SVO	words	medium
Russian	(ru)	SVO	words	rich
Thai	(th)	SVO	none	none
Vietnamese	(vi)	SVO	phrase	none
Chinese	(zh)	SVO	none	none

2.2 Statistical Machine Translation Engines

Phrase-based statistical machine translation approaches continue to dominate the field of machine translation. The translation service makes use of state-of-the-art phrase-based SMT systems within the framework of feature-based exponential models containing the following features:

- Phrase translation probability
- Inverse phrase translation probability
- Lexical weighting probability
- Inverse lexical weighting probability
- Phrase penalty
- Language model probability
- Simple distance-based distortion model
- Word penalty

Table 2: Language Model Perplexity

Language	Entropy	Total Entropy	Eval Data Words	Eval Data Vocab
ar	5.73	21,663	3,780	1,067
da	5.66	17,411	3,077	884
de	5.58	16,698	2,995	910
en	**4.53**	**14,370**	**3,169**	**807**
es	5.35	15,622	2,919	943
fr	4.77	16,793	3,521	929
id	6.09	18,145	2,977	908
it	5.52	16,078	2,914	956
ja	**4.03**	**15,080**	**3,745**	**929**
ko	4.21	15,011	3,567	943
ms	6.43	19,144	2,977	909
nl	5.66	17,609	3,110	909
pt-b	5.73	16,981	2,962	932
pt	5.54	16,064	2,900	946
ru	6.20	16,040	2,587	1,143
th	5.12	20,230	3,953	738
vi	4.84	19,531	4,034	792
zh	5.11	14,748	2,887	944

Table 3: Automatic Evaluation Results

	BLEU (%)				METEOR (%)			
	en-*	*-en	ja-*	*-ja	en-*	*-en	ja-*	*-ja
ar	18.21	51.01	13.03	46.09	40.90	69.01	37.52	58.02
da	59.70	70.90	45.94	55.34	75.08	82.56	64.41	65.83
de	56.48	69.25	41.99	59.20	74.01	81.48	63.69	69.61
en	–	–	61.56	68.53	–	–	78.19	75.39
es	65.22	73.82	51.77	63.24	78.15	85.28	68.30	72.17
fr	64.69	71.04	52.36	63.16	79.28	83.05	71.14	72.82
id	48.35	59.69	40.59	57.24	66.82	75.83	62.33	69.00
it	56.80	70.43	43.45	60.77	72.41	82.96	62.35	70.70
ja	68.53	61.56	–	–	75.39	78.19	–	–
ko	37.00	58.82	69.96	85.10	57.89	75.92	83.25	89.73
ms	40.99	57.63	36.13	55.84	61.08	74.75	58.73	67.33
nl	57.46	72.85	41.43	59.70	75.88	84.52	63.42	72.19
pt-b	59.99	69.41	46.50	58.07	72.77	80.70	64.68	69.14
pt	62.81	70.25	48.24	59.20	75.65	83.32	67.38	68.32
ru	44.46	61.23	36.08	55.13	66.41	73.75	60.59	64.55
th	46.49	51.35	43.75	50.85	62.47	73.12	60.25	62.91
vi	55.18	57.42	50.86	55.07	71.04	73.98	68.67	70.81
zh	53.08	59.33	51.68	69.43	69.85	74.68	65.88	77.62

The basic framework within which all the MT systems were constructed is shown in Figure 3.

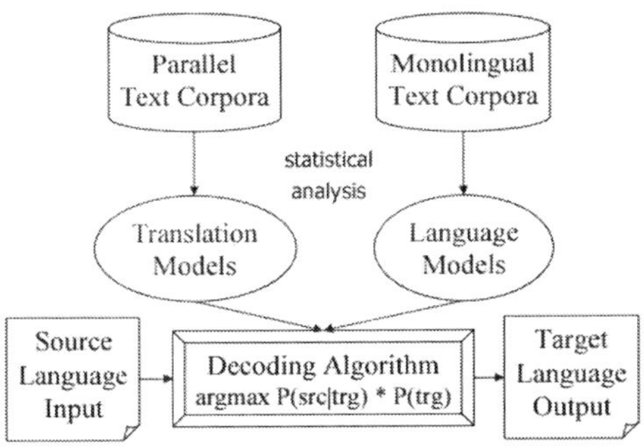

Figure 3: SMT Framework

Translation examples from the respective bilingual text corpus are aligned in order to extract phrasal equivalences and to calculate the bilingual feature probabilities. Monolingual features like the *language model probability* are trained on monolingual text corpora of the target language whereby standard word alignment and language modeling tools were used. For decoding, the *CleopATRa* decoder (Finch et al., 2007), a multi-stack phrase-based SMT decoder is used.

2.3 Evaluation

In order to get an idea of how difficult the translation tasks are, we trained standard 5gram language models on 160K sentence pairs and evaluated the *entropy* and *total entropy*, i.e., the *entropy* multiplied by *word counts*, of each language on an evaluation data set of 510 sentences each. Table 2 shows that the total entropy of European languages like Danish, German, English, Spanish, etc. does not differ much. Moreover, languages with phrasal segments and/or rich morphology like Arabic, Malay, Russian or Vietnamese have a high total entropy and thus can be expected to be more difficult to translate. This is confirmed by the translation experiments in which the evaluation data sets were translated using the servers translation engines and the translation quality was evaluated using the standard automatic evaluation metrics BLEU (Papineni et al., 2002) and METEOR (Banerjee and Lavie, 2005) where scores range between 0 (worst) and 1 (best). Besides Korean (single references only), all languages were evaluated using 16 reference translations. The evaluation results in Table 3 show that closely related language pairs like Japanese-Korean or Portuguese-Brazilian can be translated very accurately, whereas translations into languages with high total entropy are of lower quality.

3 Multilingual Speech Translation Service (MSTS)

The speech translation service[1] can be accessed via 'http://www.atr-trek.co.jp/contents_html' or using the QR code in Figure 4 that also illustrates the graphical user interface of the translation service. After connecting to the top page, the translation service is activated by selecting the "Translation" option. In order to achieve robust speech recogni-

[1]The speech translation service for Japanese⇔English on Docomo 905i mobile phones started November 2007.

Figure 4: QR Code and GUI of MSTS

tion, the service features a push-to-talk functionality, i.e., the user (1) presses the key to start the service (2) speaks freely into the integrated microphone of the mobile phone, and (3) presses the key again after the speech input is finished. Fast and accurate front-end and back-end processing algorithms enable high-speed speech translation of the input. Both, the speech recognition results as well as the translation results are sent back to and displayed on the mobile phone.

3.1 Multilingual Speech Corpus

Similar to the statistical machine translation approach introduced in Section 2.2, the speech recognition components are based on large-sized multilingual speech corpora. For Japanese, speech recordings of 4000 speakers were collected resulting on a total of 200 hours of speech. For English, almost the same amount of speech data were collected from 500 speakers in North America (300 speakers), the UK (100 speakers), and Australia (100 speakers).

3.2 Distributed Speech Recognition

The speech interface is based on *distributed speech recognition* (DSR) that is integrated as a client-server architecture compatible with the ETSI ES 202 050 standards. The usage of *Speech Translation Markup Language* (STML) enables flexible connections between internal and external speech translation resources like speech recognition and translation servers via a network. Figure 5 illustrates the architecture of the utilized DSR system. The front-end processing includes noise suppression, feature extraction and feature parameter compression and is carried out on the mobile phone. The data stream is then sent via internet to the application service provider (ASP) for back-end processing, i.e. speech recognition and statistical machine translation. The recognition and translation results are sent back to the mobile phone for display to the user.

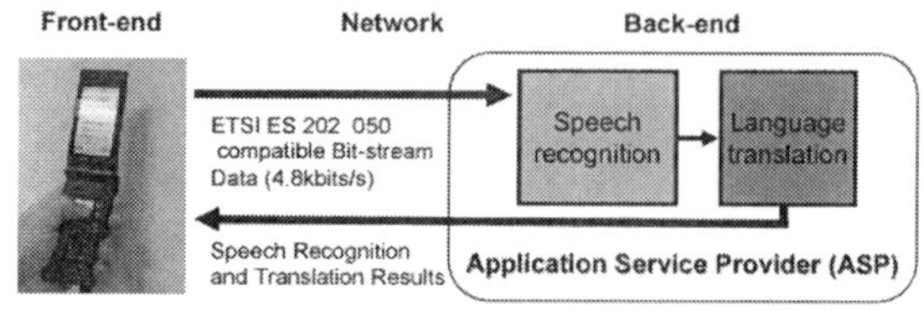

Figure 5: MSTS Architecture

4 Conclusion

This paper introduced the first commercial speech translation service in the world. State-of-the-art spoken language translation technologies (distributed speech recognition with noise suppression, multilingual statistical machine translation) are implemented into a flexible client-server architecture that covers the major languages of most countries and enables users to communicate in real environments all over the world using their own mobile phones.

5 Acknowledgments

This work is partly supported by the Grant-in-Aid for Scientific Research (C) and the Special Coordination Funds for Promoting Science and Technology of the Ministry of Education, Culture, Sports, Science and Technology, Japan.

References

Banerjee, S. and A. Lavie. 2005. METEOR: An automatic metric for MT evaluation with improved correlation with human judgments. In *Proceedings of the ACL Workshop on Intrinsic and Extrinsic Evaluation Measures for Machine Translation and/or Summarization*, pages 65–72, Ann Arbor, Michigan.

Finch, A., E. Denoual, H. Okuma, M. Paul, H. Yamamoto, K. Yasuda, R. Zhang, and E. Sumita. 2007. The NICT/ATR Speech Translation System for IWSLT 2007. In *Proc. of the IWSLT*, pages 103–110, Trento, Italy.

Kikui, G., S. Yamamoto, T. Takezawa, and E. Sumita. 2006. Comparative study on corpora for speech translation. *IEEE Transactions on Audio, Speech and Language Processing*, 14(5):1674–1682.

Papineni, K., S. Roukos, T. Ward, and W. Zhu. 2002. BLEU: a method for automatic evaluation of machine translation. In *Proc. of the 40th ACL*, pages 311–318, Philadelphia, USA.

Multilingual Assistant for Medical Diagnosing and Drug Prescription Based on Category Ranking

Fernando Ruiz-Rico
University of Alicante
frr@alu.ua.es

Jose-Luis Vicedo
University of Alicante
vicedo@dlsi.ua.es

María-Consuelo Rubio-Sánchez
University of Alicante
mcrs7@alu.ua.es

Abstract

This paper presents a real-world application for assisting medical diagnosis and drug prescription, which relies on the exclusive use of machine learning techniques. We have automatically processed an extensive biomedical literature to train a categorization algorithm in order to provide it with the capability of matching symptoms to MeSH descriptors. To interact with the classifier, we have developed a multilingual web interface so that professionals in medicine can easily get some help in their decisions about diagnoses (lookfordiagnosis.com) and prescriptions (lookfortherapy.com). We also demonstrate the effectiveness of this approach with a test set containing several hundreds of real clinical histories.

1 Introduction

Text categorization consists of automatically assigning documents to pre-defined classes. It has been extensively applied to many fields and in particular, some efforts have been focused on MEDLINE abstracts classification (Ibushi and Tsujii, 1999). However, as far as we are concerned, it has never been used to assist multilingual medical diagnosing and drug prescription by using the textual information provided by biomedical literature together with patient histories.

Every year, thousands of documents are added to the *National Library of Medicine* and the *National Institutes of Health* databases[1]. Most of them have been manually indexed by assigning each document to one or several entries in a controlled vocabulary called MeSH[2] (Medical Subject Headings). The MeSH tree is a hierarchical structure of medical terms which are used to define the main subjects that a medical article or report is about. Due to the wide use of this terminology, we can find translations into several languages such as Portuguese and Spanish (i.e. DeCS[3] - Health Science Descriptors). This paper focuses on both the diseases sub-tree (from C01 to C23) and drugs subtree (from D01 to D20). The first one defines on its own more than 4,000 pathological states, and also offers the chance to search for documented case reports related to each of them. The drugs sub-tree provides the capability of arranging around 8,000 active principles, which can be directly matched to commercial drugs.

Our proposal tries to estimate a ranked list of diagnoses and possible prescriptions from a patient history. To tackle this problem, we have selected an existing categorization algorithm, and we have trained it using the textual information provided by lots of previously reported cases and laboratory findings. This way, a detailed symptomatic description is sufficient to obtain a list of possible diseases and prescriptions, along with an estimation of probabilities and bibliography.

We have not used binary decisions from binary categorization methods, since they might leave some interesting MeSH entries out, which should probably be taken into consideration. Instead, we have chosen a category ranking algorithm to obtain an ordered list of all possible diagnoses and pre-

©2008. Licensed under the *Creative Commons Attribution-Noncommercial-Share Alike 3.0 Unported* license (http://creativecommons.org/licenses/by-nc-sa/3.0/). Some rights reserved.

[1] http://www.pubmed.gov
[2] http://www.nlm.nih.gov/mesh
[3] http://decs.bvs.br/I/homepagei.htm

scriptions so that the user can finally decide which of them better suits the clinical history.

In this paper, first of all, we will explain the way we have developed our experiments, including a full description of the sources and methods used to get both training and test data. Secondly, we will provide an example of a patient history and both the expected and provided diagnoses. We will also show the suggested drugs recommended by the algorithm for a common disease. And we will finish by showing and commenting several evaluation results on.

2 Procedures

2.1 Medical Diagnosis

We have extracted the training data from the *PubMed* database[1] by selecting every case reports on diseases written in English including abstract and related to human beings. These documents were extracted by using the "diseases category[MAJR]" query, where [MAJR] stands for "MeSH Major Topic", asking the system for retrieving only documents whose subject is mainly a disease. The query provided us with 483,726 documents[4] leading us to 4,024 classes with at least one training sample each.

With respect to the test set, we have used 400 medical histories from the School of Medicine of the University of Pittsburgh (Department of Pathology[5]). Although, so far the web page contains more than 500 histories[4], not all of them are suitable for our purposes. There are some which do not provide a concrete diagnosis but only a discussion about the case, and some others do not have a direct matching to the MeSH tree. We have used from each document both the title and all the clinical history, including radiological findings, gross and microscopic descriptions, etc. To get the expected output, we extracted the top level MeSH diseases categories corresponding to the diagnoses given on the titles of the "final diagnosis" files (dx.html).

As the ranking algorithm, we have chosen the Sum of Weights (SOW) approach (Ruiz-Rico et al., 2006), that is more suitable than the rest for its efficiency, accuracy and incremental training capacity. Since medical databases are frequently updated and they also grow continuously, we have preferred using a fast and unattended approach that lets us perform updates easily with no substantial performance degradation after incrementing the number of categories or training samples. The restrictive complexity of other classifiers such as SVM could derivate to an intractable problem, as stated by (Ruch, 2005).

To evaluate how worth our suggestion is, we have measured accuracy through three common ranking performance measures (Ruiz-Rico et al., 2006): Precision at recall = 0 ($P_{r=0}$), mean average precision (*AvgP*) and Precision/Recall break even point (*BEP*). Sometimes, only one diagnosis is valid for a particular patient. In these cases, $P_{r=0}$ let us quantify the mistaken answers, since it indicates the proportion of correct topics given at the top ranked position. To know about the quality of the full ranking list, we use the AvgP, since it goes down the arranged list averaging precision until all possible answers are covered. BEP is the value where precision equals recall, that is, when we consider the maximum number of relevant topics as a threshold. To follow the same procedure as (Joachims, 1998), the performance evaluation has been computed over the top diseases level.

2.2 Drug Prescription

Multilingual drug prescription can be achieved through the international active principles, which are the constituents of drugs on which the characteristic therapeutic action of the substance largely depends. The appropriate nomenclature for the active principles can be found translated to several languages from MeSH, and can lead to the final commercial medicaments in most of the countries around the world.

To train the algorithm for this new purpose, we have launched the following query to the *PubMed* database:

("Plant Families and Groups"[majr] OR "Inorganic Chemicals"[majr] OR "Organic Chemicals"[majr] OR "Heterocyclic Compounds"[majr] OR "Polycyclic Compounds"[majr] OR "Macromolecular Substances"[majr] OR "Hormones, Hormone Substitutes, and Hormone Antagonists"[majr] OR "Enzymes and Coenzymes"[majr] OR "Carbohydrates" OR "Lipids"[majr] OR "Amino Acids, Peptides, and Proteins"[majr] OR "Nucleic Acids, Nucleotides, and Nucleosides"[majr] OR "Complex Mixtures"[majr]) AND "therapeutic use"[sh] NOT ("adverse effects"[sh] OR "contraindications"[sh] OR "poisoning"[sh] OR "radiation effects"[sh] OR "toxicity"[sh])

After filtering only articles written in English which have abstract, a total amount of 540,235[4] training documents are left.

[4]Data obtained on February 14th 2007

[5]http://path.upmc.edu/cases

Order	Diseases	Probability	Expand
1	Nervous System Diseases	100	+
2	Neoplasms	93	+
3	Pathological Conditions, Signs and Symptoms	61	+
4	Congenital, Hereditary, and Neonatal Diseases and Abnormalities	25	+
5	Endocrine System Diseases	23	+
...	...	...	...

Figure 1: Example of the first level of a hierarchical diagnosis

2.3 Multilingual Environment

Since all training data is written in English, every symptom provided to the algorithm must also be written in English. For this purpose, an automatic translation tool is used for input data in other languages than English. We also promote the translation by using the MeSH vocabulary, which has been delivered by human experts, and provides a reliable correspondence of thousands of non phrases in many language pairs. Although the automatic translation method is not accurate enough for natural speaking, it may be capable of giving quite good results for independent noun phrases (Ruiz-Rico et al., 2006), which are the pieces of information the ranking algorithm uses.

2.4 Availability and Requirements

No special hardware nor software is necessary to interact with the assistant. Just an Internet connection and a standard browser are enough to access on-line through the following sites: *www.lookfordiagnosis.com* and *www.lookfortherapy.com*.

By using a web interface and by presenting results in text format, we allow users to access from many types of portable devices (laptops, PDA's, etc.). Moreover, they will always have available the latest version, with no need of installing specific applications nor software updates.

3 A Couple of Examples

3.1 Medical Diagnosis

One of the 400 histories included in the test set looks as follows:

Case 177 – Headaches, Lethargy and a Sellar/Suprasellar Mass

A 16 year old female presented with two months of progressively worsening headaches, lethargy and visual disturbances. Her past medical history included developmental delay, shunted hydrocephalus, and tethered cord release ...

The final diagnosis expected for this clinical history is: "Rathke's Cleft Cyst", which is a syn-

Nervous System Diseases
Nervous System Neoplasms
Central Nervous System Neoplasms

Order	Diseases	Probability	Expand
1	Brain Neoplasms	100	+
2	Central Nervous System Cysts	44	+
3	Meningeal Neoplasms	13	+
4	Spinal Cord Neoplasms	3	+

Order	Diseases	Probability
1	Craniopharyngioma	100
2	Cysts	63
3	Pituitary Neoplasms	59
4	Central Nervous System Cysts	48
5	Headache	46
6	Xanthomatosis	44
...	...	...

Figure 2: Output example after manual expansion of high ranked topics (up) and by selecting the flat diagnosis mode (down)

rheumatoid arthritis

Order	Active principles	Rating	Drugs	Expand
1	Gold	100	+	
2	Gold Sodium Thiomalate	72	+	
3	Immunoglobulin G	62	+	->
4	Antibodies, Monoclonal	47	+	
5	Hydroxychloroquine	46	+	
6	Aurothioglucose	45	+	->
7	Isoxazoles	43	+	->
8	Auranofin	36	+	
9	Indomethacin	28	+	->
10	Biological Products	23	+	->
11	Antibodies	19	+	->
12	Glucocorticoids	18	+	
13	Immunoconjugates	18	+	->

Myocrisin

Prescription only

Main Use	Active Ingredient	Manufacturer
Rheumatoid arthritis	Sodium Aurothiomalate.	JHC

How does it work?

Sodium aurothiomalate is an injectable form of the precious metal gold. It is often simply called "Gold".

Whilst it is not known exactly how this medicine works it is thought to damp down some elements of the body's immune response, which is indirectly responsible for the swelling, pain and inflammation of the disease.

Sodium aurothiomalate belongs to a mixed group of medicines called "disease-modifying anti-rheumatic drugs" (DMARDs). Unlike simple painkillers, sodium aurothiomalate actually slows progression of the underlying disease. It does, however, produce more serious side effects.

It is used in the treatment active, progressive rheumatoid arthritis and progressive juvenile chronic arthritis.

What is it used for?

- Inflammatory disease of the joints (rheumatoid arthritis)

Figure 3: Example of the drug prescription suggestions for *rheumatoid arthritis* (up) and the final medicament (down) found through the *drugs* link provided by the assistant.

onym of the preferred term "Central Nervous System Cysts". Translating this into one or several of the 23 top MeSH diseases categories we are led to the following entries: "Neoplasms", "Nervous System Diseases" and "Congenital, Hereditary, and Neonatal Diseases and Abnormalities".

In hierarchical mode, our approach provides automatically a first categorization level with expanding possibilities as shown in figure 1. We provide navigation capabilities to allow the user to go down the tree by selecting different branches, depending on the given probabilities and his/her own criteria. Moreover, a flat diagnosis mode can be activated to directly obtain a ranked list of all diseases, as shown on the lower part of figure 2.

After an individual evaluation of this case, we have obtained the following values: $P_{r=0} = 1$, $AvgP = 0.92$, and $BEP = 0.67$, since the right topics in figure 1 are given at positions 1, 2 and 4.

3.2 Drug Prescription

As an example for drug prescription, figure 3 shows the suggestions that the ranking algorithm provides for *rheumatoid arthritis*, where the user obtains a ranked list of active principles. Finally, we reach the name of one of the possible medicaments containing the selected active principle, along with particular recommendations from pharmacists (secondary effects, etc).

4 Results

Last row in table 1 shows the performance measures calculated for each medical history and its diagnosis, averaged afterwards across all the 400 decisions. $P_{r=0}$ indicates that we get 69% of the histories correctly diagnosed with the top ranked MeSH entry. AvgP value means that the rest of the list also contains quite valid topics, since it reaches a value of 73%.

First row in table 1 provides a comparison between SVM (Joachims, 1998) and sum of weights (Ruiz-Rico et al., 2006) algorithms using the well known OHSUMED evaluation benchmark. Even using a training and test set containing different document types, BEP indicates that the performance is not far away from that achieved in text classification tasks, meaning that category ranking can also be effectively applied to our scenario.

Regarding drug prescription tests, we are still working under the evaluation process, colaborating with companies such as *CMPMedica*, which is in charge of many sites containing drug compendiums (vademecum.es, vidal.fr, cddata.co.uk, etc.). We have already performed preliminary tests by using the symptoms and diseases in the MeSH tree as the input data, and an arranged list of active principles as the output data. We have reached an *AvgP* around 0.9.

Table 1: Averaged performance for both text categorization and diagnosis

Corpus	Algor.	$P_{r=0}$	AvgP	BEP
OHSUMED	SVM	-	-	0.66
	SOW	-	-	0.71
Case reports and patient histories	SOW	0.69	0.73	0.62

5 Conclusions and Further Work

We believe that category ranking algorithms may help in multilingual medical diagnosing and drug prescription from clinical histories. Although the output of the categorization process should not be directly taken as a medical advice, the accuracy achieved could be good enough to assist human experts. However, due to the large amount of new articles continuously added to biomedical literature, it becomes quite difficult for a practitioner to keep up to date. Further works are focused on providing bibliographic references for each suggestion of the classifier. We pretend to select from the PubMed database those entries most related to the pathological states entered by the user.

References

Ibushi, Katsutoshi, Collier-Nigel and Jun'ichi Tsujii. 1999. Classification of medline abstracts. *Genome Informatics, volume 10*, pages 290–291.

Joachims, Thorsten. 1998. Text categorization with support vector machines: learning with many relevant features. In *Proceedings of ECML-98, 10th European Conference on Machine Learning*, pages 137–142.

Ruch, Patrick. 2005. Automatic assignment of biomedical categories: toward a generic approach. *Bioinformatics, volume 22 no. 6 2006*, pages 658–664.

Ruiz-Rico, Fernando, Jose Luis Vicedo, and María-Consuelo Rubio-Sánchez. 2006. Newpar: an automatic feature selection and weighting schema for category ranking. In *Proceedings ofDocEng-06, 6th ACM symposium on Document engineering*, pages 128–137.

Entailment-based Question Answering for Structured Data

Bogdan Sacaleanu♣, Constantin Orasan♦, Christian Spurk♣, Shiyan Ou♦, Oscar Ferrandez♥, Milen Kouylekov♠ and Matteo Negri♠
♣LT-Lab, DFKI GmbH / Saarbrücken, Germany
♦RIILP, University of Wolverhampton / Wolverhampton, UK
♠Fondazione Bruno Kessler (FBK) / Trento, Italy
♥University of Alicante / Alicante, Spain

Abstract

This paper describes a Question Answering system which retrieves answers from structured data regarding cinemas and movies. The system represents the first prototype of a multilingual and multi-modal QA system for the domain of tourism. Based on specially designed domain ontology and using Textual Entailment as a means for semantic inference, the system can be used in both monolingual and cross-language settings with slight adjustments for new input languages.

1 Introduction

Question Answering over structured data has been traditionally addressed through a deep analysis of the question in order to reconstruct a logical form, which is then translated in the query language of the target data (Androutsopoulos et al, 1995, Popescu et al, 2003). This approach implies a complex mapping between linguistic objects (e.g. lexical items, syntactic structures) and against data objects (e.g. concepts and relations in a knowledge base). Unfortunately, such a mapping requires extensive manual work, which in many cases represents a bottleneck preventing the realization of large scale and portable natural language interfaces to structured data.

This paper presents the first prototype of a question answering system which can answer questions in several languages about movies and cinema using a multilingual ontology and textual entailment. The remainder of the paper is structured as follows: Section 2 presents the concept of entailment-based question answering; Section 3 describes our prototype which implements this concept; A brief evaluation is presented in Section 4, followed by conclusions in Section 5.

© 2008. Licensed under the *Creative Commons Attribution-Noncommercial-Share Alike 3.0 Unported* license (http://creativecommons.org/licenses/by-nc-sa/3.0/). Some rights reserved.

2 Entailment-based QA

Recently Textual Entailment (TE) has been proposed as a unifying framework for applied semantics (Dagan and Glickman, 2004), where the need for an explicit representation of a mapping between linguistic objects and data objects can be, at least partially, bypassed through the definition of semantic inferences at a textual level. In this framework, a text (T) is said to entail a hypothesis (H) if the meaning of H can be derived from the meaning of T.

On the basis of the TE framework, the QA problem can be recast as an entailment problem, where the text (*T*) is the question (or its affirmative version) and the hypothesis (*H*) is a relational answer pattern, which is associated to instructions for retrieving the answer to the input question. In this framework, given a question *Q* and a set of relational answer patterns *P*, a QA system needs to select those patterns in *P* that are entailed by *Q*. Instructions associated to answer patterns may be viewed as high precision procedures for answer extraction, which are dependent on the specific source which is asked for. In case of QA over structured data, instructions could be queries to a database; whilst in case of QA on the Web, an instruction could be the URL of a Web page containing the answer to a question or some form of IR query to a search engine.

Therefore, the underlying idea of an entailment-based QA system is to match the user's request to a set of predefined question patterns in order to get some kind of analysis for the request.

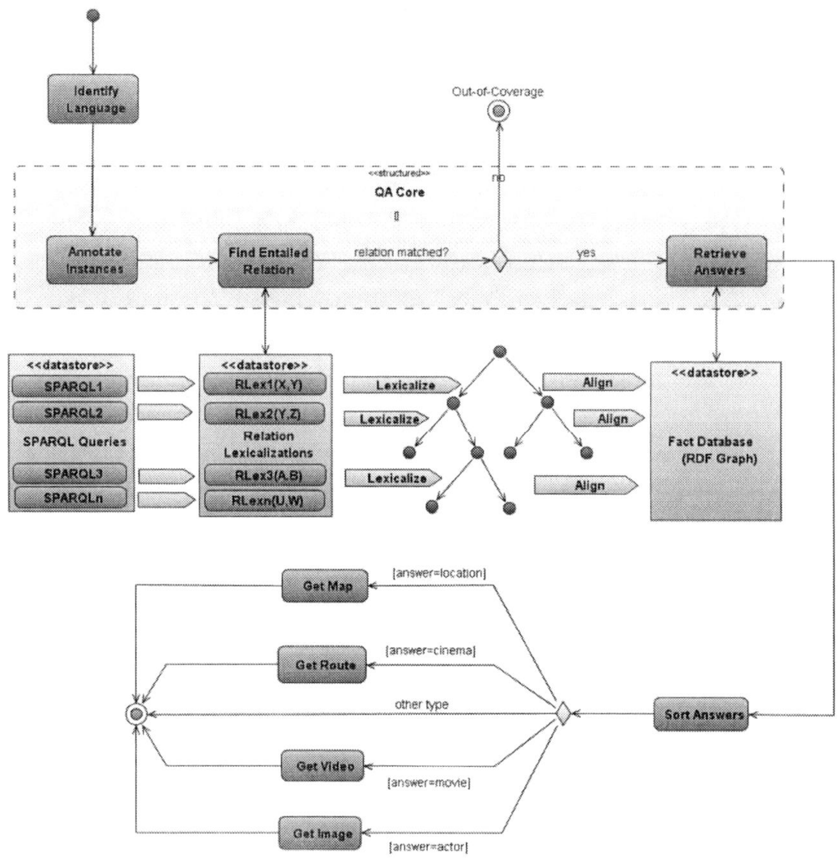

Figure 1. System Architecture

As an example consider the question "*Where can I watch the movie 'Dreamgirls' next Saturday?*" and the predefined question patterns:

- Which movies are currently running in `[CINEMA]?` → EAT = `[MOVIE]`
- Where can I watch the movie `[MOVIE]` on `[WEEKDAY]?` → EAT = `[CINEMA]`
- Where can I see `[MOVIE]?` → EAT = `[CINEMA]`

In the example, each of the patterns contains placeholders for relevant named entities and has an *expected answer type* (EAT) associated with it. The entailment-based QA system should return that pattern (2) is entailed by the question and as a result the retrieval instructions associated to it will be used to answer the question.

3 Description of system

Our question answering system implements the concept of entailment-based question answering described in the previous section. The overall structure of our system is presented in Figure 1.

Given a question asked by a user of the system in a known location, the QA planner forwards it to the *Instance Annotator* in order to find any concepts that might be related to the targeted domain (i.e. cinema, city, movie). The result is then analyzed by the *Relation Matcher*, which on the basis of entailment can either select the most appropriate interpretation of the question and implicitly its associated procedure of answering the question, or decide that the user request is **out-of-coverage** if no such interpretation is available.

The cross-linguality of our system and, to a certain extent, the interaction between its components is ensured by a domain ontology which is used for all four languages involved in the project: English, German, Italian and Spanish, and its modules (Ou et al., 2008). Concepts from the ontology are used to annotate the user questions as well as data from which the answer is extracted. In the current stage of the project, the answers are contained in databases obtained from content provides or built from structured web pages. As a result, the information in the database tables was annotated with concepts from the ontology and then converted into an RDF graph to

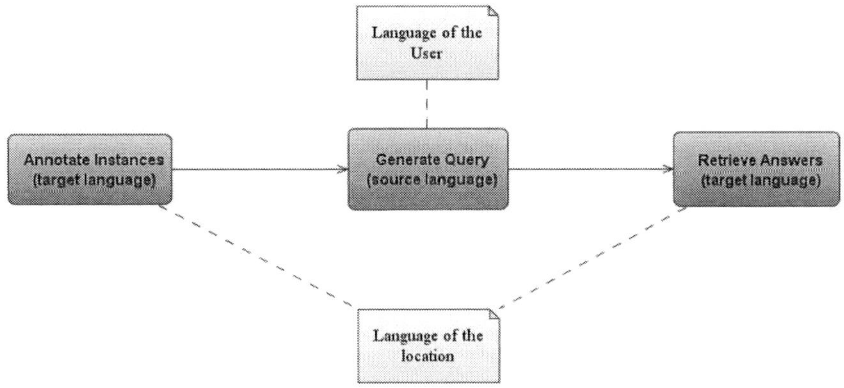

Figure 2. Cross-language Setting

facilitate retrieval using SPARQL query language (Prud'hommeaux and Seaborne, 2006). Question patterns corresponding to one or several ontological relations were produced after questions for users were collected and used in the entailment module. The question patterns used by the system are very similar to those presented in the previous section and contain placeholders for the actual entities that are expected to appear in a question.

The SPARQL query associated with a pattern selected for a user question is used to retrieve the answers from the knowledge base and prepare for presentation. Given that our system is not limited to returning only textual information, further processing can be applied to the retrieved data. For example, for proximity questions the list of answers consists of cinema names and their GPS-coordinates, which are used by the *Answer Sorting* component to reorder the list of answers on the basis of their distance to the user's location.

Besides presenting the possible answers to a given question, the system can offer additional information based on the answer's type:

- a map for answers that are location names,
- a route description for answers that are cinema names,
- a video-trailer for answers that are movie names and
- an image for answers that are person names.

Due to the fact that a common semantics is shared by all four languages by way of a domain ontology, the system can be used not only in a monolingual setting, but also in a cross-language setting. This corresponds to a user-scenario where a tourist asks for information in their own language in a foreign location (i.e. English speaker in Italy). The only difference between monolingual and cross-language scenarios is that in the cross-language setting, the *QA Core* subsystem (Figure 1) selects a *Find Entailed Relation* component according to the user input's language. This is due to the entailment algorithms that tend to use language specific resources in order to attain high accuracy results of matching the user request with one of the lexicalized relations (patterns). It is only the entailment component that has to be provided in order to adapt the system to new input languages, once the lexicalized relations have been translated either manual or automatically.

Both the *Instance Annotator* and the *Answer Retriever* are language independent, but location dependent (Figure 2). The *Answer Retriever* depends on the location since it is querying data found at that place (i.e. Italy), while the *Instance Annotator* looks up instances of the data in the user's question (i.e. annotates an English question). They are language independent since they are working with data abstractions like SPARQL queries (*Answer Retriever*) or work at character level and do not consider language specific aspects, like words, in their look-up process (*Instance Annotator*).

The current version of the system[1] is designed according to the SOA (Service Oriented Architecture) and is implemented as point-to-point integrated web services. Any of the system's components can be substituted by alternative implementations with no need for further changes as long as the functionality remains the same.

[1] http://attila.dfki.uni-sb.de:8282/ QallMe_Prototype_WEB_Update/faces/Page6.jsp

4 Evaluation

A preliminary evaluation of the first prototype was carried out on randomly selected questions from a benchmark specifically designed for the project. This benchmark was developed to contain questions about various aspects from the domain of tourism and for this reason we filtered out questions not relevant to cinema or movies. The evaluation of the system did not assess whether it can extract the correct answer. Instead, it measured to what extent the system can select the right SPARQL pattern. The explanation for this can be found in the fact that once a correct question pattern is selected, the extraction of the answer requires only retrieval of the answer from the database. Moreover, it should be pointed out that the main purpose of this preliminary evaluation was to test the interaction between components and indicate potential problems, and it was less about their performances.

Table 1 summarises the results of the evaluation. The number of questions used in the evaluation is different from one language to another. This can be explained by the fact that for each language a number of questions (in general 500) was randomly selected from the benchmark and only the ones which referred to cinema or movies were selected. The column *Questions* indicates the number of questions assessed. The *Correct* column indicates for how many questions a correct SPARQL was generated. The *Wrong* column corresponds to the number of questions where a wrong or incomplete SPARQL was generated. This number also includes cases where no SPARQL was generated due to lack of corresponding answer pattern.

	Questions	Correct	Wrong
English	167	74 (44.31%)	93 (55.68%)
German	214	120 (56.04%)	94 (43.92%)
Spanish	58	50 (86.20%)	8 (13.79%)
Italian	99	46 (46.46%)	53 (53.53%)

Table 1: Evaluation results

As can be seen, the results are very different from one language to another. This can be explained by the fact that different entailment engines are used for each language. In addition, even though the benchmark was built using a common set of guidelines, the complexity of questions varies from one language to another. For this reason, for some questions it is more difficult to find the correct pattern than for others.

Analysis of the results revealed that one of the easiest ways to improve the performance of the system is to increase the number of patterns. Currently the average number of patterns per language is 42. Improvement of the entailment engines is another direction which needs to be pursued. Most of the partners involved in the project have more powerful entailment engines than those integrated in the prototype which were ranked highly in RTE competitions. Unfortunately, many of these engines cannot be used directly in our system due to their slow speed. Our system is supposed to give users results in real time which imposes some constraints on the amount of processing that can be done.

5 Conclusions

This paper presented the first prototype of an entailment-based QA system, which can answer questions about movies and cinema. The use of a domain ontology ensures that the system is cross-language and can be extended to new languages with slight adjustments at the entailment engine. The system is implemented as a set of web services and along a Service Oriented Architecture.

6 Acknowledgements

This work is supported by the EU-funded project QALL-ME (FP6 IST-033860).

References

Androutsopoulos, I. and G.D. Ritchie and P. Thanisch. 1995. *Natural Language Interfaces to Databases -- An Introduction*, Journal of Natural Language Engineering, vol.1, no.1, Cambridge University Press.

Popescu Ana-Marie, Oren Etzioni, and Henry Kautz. 2003. *Towards a theory of natural language interfaces to databases*. In Proceedings of the conference on Intelligent User Interfaces.

Dagan Ido and Oren Glickman. 2004. *Probabilistic textual entailment: Generic applied modeling of language variability*. In PASCAL Workshop on Learning Methods for Text Understanding and Mining, Grenoble.

Ou Shiyan, Viktor Pekar, Constantin Orasan, Christian Spurk, Matteo Negri. 2008. *Development and alignment of a domain-specific ontology for question answering*. In Proceedings of the 6th Edition of the Language Resources and Evaluation Conference (LREC-08).

Prud'hommeaux Eric, Andy Seaborne (eds.). 2006. *SPARQL Query Language for RDF*. RDF Data Access Working Group.

Shahmukhi to Gurmukhi Transliteration System

Tejinder Singh Saini
ACTDPL, Punjabi University,
Patiala 147 002, India
tej@pbi.ac.in

Gurpreet Singh Lehal
DCS, Punjabi University,
Patiala 147 002, India
gslehal@yahoo.com

Virinder S Kalra
Sociology, SOSS
University of Manchester
kalra@manchester.uk

Abstract

The existence of two scripts for Punjabi language has created a script barrier between the Punjabi literature written in India and Pakistan. This research has developed a new system for the first time of its kind for Shahmukhi text without diacritical marks. The purposed system for Shahmukhi to Gurmukhi transliteration has been implemented with various research techniques based on language corpus. The corpus analysis of both scripts is performed for generating statistical data of different types like character and word frequencies and bi-gram frequencies. This statistical analysis is used in different phases of transliteration. Potentially, all members of the substantial Punjabi community will benefit vastly from this transliteration system.

1 Introduction

One of the great challenges before Information Technology is to overcome language barriers across the whole humanity so that everyone can communicate with everyone else on the planet in real time. South Asia is one of those unique parts of the world where a single language is written in different scripts. This is the case, for example, with Punjabi language, spoken by tens of millions of people, but written in Indian East Punjab (20 million) in Gurmukhi script (a Left to Right script based on Devanagari) and in Pakistani West Punjab (80 million), written in Shahmukhi script (a Right to Left script based on Arabic), and by growing number of Punjabis (2 million) in the EU and the US in the Roman script. Whilst in speech Punjabi spoken in the Eastern and the Western parts is mutually comprehensible, in the written form it is not so. The existence of two scripts for Punjabi has created a script barrier between the Punjabi literature written in India and Pakistan. More than 60 per cent of Punjabi literature of medieval period (500-1450 AD) is available in Shahmukhi script only, while most of the modern Punjabi writings are in Gurmukhi. Potentially, all members of the substantial Punjabi community will benefit vastly from this transliteration system.

© 2008. Licensed under the *Creative Commons Attribution-Noncommercial-Share Alike 3.0 Unported* license (http://creativecommons.org/licenses/by-nc-sa/3.0/). Some rights reserved.

1.1 Gurmukhi Script

The Gurmukhi script, derived from the Sharada script and standardised by Guru Angad Dev in the 16th century, was designed to write the Punjabi language. The meaning of "Gurmukhi" is literally "from the mouth of the Guru". The Gurmukhi script has forty one letters, including thirty eight consonants and three basic vowel sign bearers. There are five nasal consonants (ਙ, ਞ, ਣ, ਨ, ਮ) and two additional nasalization signs, bindi ◌ਂ [ɲ] and tippi ◌ੰ [ɲ]. In addition to this, there are nine dependent vowel signs (◌ੁ[ʊ], ◌ੂ [u], ◌ੋ[o], ◌ਾ[ɘ], ਿ◌[ɪ], ◌ੀ[i], ◌ੇ[e], ◌ੈ[æ], ◌ੌ[ɔ]) used to create ten independent vowels with three bearer characters: Ura ੳ[ʊ], Aira ਅ [ə] and Iri ੲ[ɪ].

1.2 Shahmukhi Script

The meaning of "Shahmukhi" is literally "from the King's mouth". Shahmukhi is a local variant of the Urdu script used to record the Punjabi language. It is based on right to left Nastalique style of the Persian and Arabic script. It has thirty seven simple consonants, eleven frequently used aspirated consonants, four long vowels and three short vowel symbols (Malik 2006).

2 Comparison with the Existing System

In actual practice, Shahmukhi script is written without short vowels and other diacritical marks. The PMT system discussed by Malik A. (2006) claims 98% accuracy only when the input text

Input text (right to left)
اس گل وچ جدوں اسیں بہتے پنجابیاں نوں ویکھدے ہاں تاں پرنسپل تیجا سنگھ دے لیکھ وچ بیانیاں گئیاں کوڑیاں سچائیاں ہور وی شدت نال محسوس ہندیاں ہین۔ اسیں دیس نوں پیار کرن دا دعویٰ کردے ہاں پر اپنے صوبے نوں وساری بیٹھے ہاں۔ اس دا سبھ توں وڈا ثبوت ایہہ ہے کہ بھارت دے لگ بھگ بہتے صوبے اپنے اپنے ستھاپنا دوس بڑے اتشاہ تے جذبے نال مناؤندے ہین۔ اپنی زبان، اپنے سبھیاچار، اپنے پچھوکڑ تے اپنے ورثے تے مان کردے ہین۔ اپنی قومی پچھان تے مان کردے ہین۔ پر ساڈا بابا آدم ہی نرالا ہے۔ سرکاراں توں لے کے عام لوکاں تک پنجابی صوبے دے بنن دن بارے پوری طرحاں اویسلے ہی رہندے ہین۔
Output-A of PMT system (left to right)
ਅਸ ਗਲ ਵਚ ਜਦੋਂ ***ਅਸੇਂ ਬਹਤੇ ਪਨਜਾਬੇਆਂ ਨੋਂ*** ਵੇਖਦੇ ਹਾਂ ਤਾਂ ***ਪਰਨਸਪਲ*** ਤੇਜਾ ***ਸਨਘ*** ਦੇ ਲੇਖ ***ਵਚ ਬੇਅਨੇਆਂ*** ਗਈਆਂ ***ਕੋੜੇਆਂ*** ਸਚਾਈਆਂ ਹੋਰ ਵੀ ***ਸ਼ਦਤ*** ਨਾਲ ***ਮਹਸੋਸ ਹਨਦੇਆਂ ਹੇਨ।*** ***ਅਸੇਂ*** ਦੇਸ ***ਨੋਂ ਪੇਆਰ*** ਕਰਨ ਦਾ ਦਾਵਾ ਕਰਦੇ ਹਾਂ ਪਰ ***ਅਪਨੇ ਸੋਬੇ ਨੋਂ*** ਵਸਾਰੀ ***ਬੇਠੇ*** ਹਾਂ। ***ਅਸ*** ਦਾ ਸਭ ਤੋਂ ***ਵਡਾ ਸਬੋਤ ਇਹਾ ਹੇ ਕਹ*** ਭਾਰਤ ਦੇ ਲਗ ਭਗ ***ਬਹਤੇ ਸੋਬੇ ਅਪਨੇ ਅਪਨੇ*** ਸਥਾਪਨਾ ***ਦੋਸ*** ਬੜੇ ***ਅਤਸ਼ਾਹ*** ਤੇ ਜਜ਼ਬੇ ਨਾਲ ***ਮਨਾਈਵਨਦੇ ਹੇਨ।*** ***ਅਪਨੀ*** ਜ਼ਬਾਨ, ***ਅਪਨੇ ਸਭੇਅਚਾਰ, ਅਪਨੇ ਪਛੋਕੜ*** ਤੇ ***ਅਪਨੇ ਵਰਸੇ*** ਤੇ ***ਮਾਨ*** ਕਰਦੇ ***ਹੇਨ।*** ***ਅਪਨੀ ਕੋਮੀ ਪਛਾਨ*** ਤੇ ***ਮਾਨ*** ਕਰਦੇ ***ਹੇਨ।*** ਪਰ ਸਾਡਾ ਬਾਬਾ ਆਦਮ ਹੀ ***ਨਰਾਲਾ ਹੇ।*** ਸਰਕਾਰਾਂ ਤੋਂ ***ਲੇ*** ਕੇ ਆਮ ਲੋਕਾਂ ***ਤਕ ਪਨਜਾਬੀ ਸੋਬੇ*** ਦੇ ***ਬਨਨ ਦਨ*** ਬਾਰੇ ***ਪੋਰੀ ਤਰਹਾਂ ਉ੦ਸਲੇ*** ਹੀ ***ਰਹਨਦੇ ਹੇਨ।***
Output-B of proposed system (left to right)
ਇਸ ਗੱਲ ਵਿਚ ਜਦੋਂ ਅਸੀਂ ਬਹੁਤੇ ਪੰਜਾਬੀਆਂ ਨੂੰ ਵੇਖਦੇ ਹਾਂ ਤਾਂ ਪ੍ਰਿੰਸੀਪਲ ਤੇਜਾ ਸਿੰਘ ਦੇ ਲੇਖ ਵਿਚ ਬਿਆਨੀਆਂ ਗਈਆਂ ਕੌੜੀਆਂ ਸਚਾਈਆਂ ਹੋਰ ਵੀ ਸ਼ਿੱਦਤ ਨਾਲ ਮਹਿਸੂਸ ਹੁੰਦੀਆਂ ਹੈਨ। ਅਸੀਂ ਦੇਸ ਨੂੰ ਪਿਆਰ ਕਰਨ ਦਾ ਦਾਵਾ ਕਰਦੇ ਹਾਂ ਪਰ ਆਪਣੇ ਸੂਬੇ ਨੂੰ ***ਵਸਾਰੀ*** ਬੈਠੇ ਹਾਂ। ਇਸ ਦਾ ਸਭ ਤੋਂ ਵੱਡਾ ਸਬੂਤ ਇਹ ਹੈ ਕਿ ਭਾਰਤ ਦੇ ਲਗ ਭਗ ਬਹੁਤੇ ਸੂਬੇ ਆਪਣੇ ਆਪਣੇ ਸਥਾਪਨਾ ***ਦੋਸ*** ਬੜੇ ਉਤਸ਼ਾਹ ਤੇ ਜਜ਼ਬੇ ਨਾਲ ਮਨਾਉਂਦੇ ਹੈਨ। ਆਪਣੀ ਜ਼ਬਾਨ, ਆਪਣੇ ਸਭਿਆਚਾਰ, ਆਪਣੇ ਪਿਛੋਕੜ ਤੇ ਆਪਣੇ ਵਿਰਸੇ ਤੇ ਮਾਣ ਕਰਦੇ ਹੈਨ। ਆਪਣੀ ਕੌਮੀ ਪਛਾਣ ਤੇ ਮਾਣ ਕਰਦੇ ਹੈਨ। ਪਰ ਸਾਡਾ ਬਾਬਾ ਆਦਮ ਹੀ ਨਿਰਾਲਾ ਹੈ। ਸਰਕਾਰਾਂ ਤੋਂ ਲੈ ਕੇ ਆਮ ਲੋਕਾਂ ਤੱਕ ਪੰਜਾਬੀ ਸੂਬੇ ਦੇ ਬਣਨ ਦਿਨ ਬਾਰੇ ਪੂਰੀ ਤਰ੍ਹਾਂ ਅਵੇਸਲੇ ਹੀ ਰਹਿੰਦੇ ਹੈਨ।

Table 1. I/O of PMT and Proposed Systems

Output Type	Transliteration Tokens			Accuracy %
	Total	Wrong	Right	
A	116	64	52	44.8275
B	116	02	114	98.2758

Table 2. Comparison of Output-A & B

has all necessary diacritical marks for removing ambiguities. But this process of putting missing diacritical marks is not practically possible due to many reasons like large input size, manual intervention, person having knowledge of both the scripts and so on. We have manually evaluated PMT system against the following Shahmukhi input published on a web site and the output text is shown as output-A in Table 1.The output of proposed system on the same input is shown as output-B. The wrong transliteration of Gurmukhi tokens is shown in bold and italic and the comparison of both outputs is shown in Table 2.Clearly, our system is more practical in nature than PMT and we got good transliteration with different inputs having missing diacritical marks.

3 The Complexity

The Shahmukhi script has many complexities by its nature and the major two of them are:

3.1 Recognition of Shahmukhi Text without Diacritical Marks

Shahmukhi script is usually written without short vowels and other diacritical marks, often leading to potential ambiguity. Arabic orthography does not provide full vocalization of the text, and the reader is expected to infer short vowels from the context of the sentence. In the written Shahmukhi script it is not mandatory to put short vowels below or above the Shahmukhi character to clear its sound. These special signs are called "Aerab" in Urdu. It is a big challenge in the process of machine transliteration to recognize the right word from the written text.

3.2 Multiple Mappings

It is observed that there is multiple possible mapping in Gurmukhi script corresponding to a single character in the Shahmukhi script as shown in Table 3.

Name	Shahmukhi Character	Gurmukhi Mapping
Vav	و [v]	ਵ [v], ੋ [o], ੌ [ɔ], ੁ [ʊ], ੂ [u], ਓ [o]
Yeh	ی[j]	ਯ [j], ਿ [ɪ], ੇ [e], ੈ[æ], ੀ[i], ਈ [i]

Table 3. Multiple Mapping into Gurmukhi Script

4 Transliteration System

The transliteration system as shown in figure 1 is virtually divided into two phases. The first phase performs pre-processing on the input Shahmukhi token by performing dictionary lookup. If the dictionary lookup fails then the token will go for rule based transliteration and ultimately this phase will generate best possible Gurmukhi token(s). The second phase performs the task of post-processing. Unicode Alignment component performs context analysis of input Gurmukhi token(s). All Forms generator (AFG) component will perform critical task of handling missing diacritical marks. This component will suggest similar possible forms of a Gurmukhi token which is not most frequent one. The queue manager of post-processing phase is designed to work on bi-gram language model. This will select the best possible unigram for final output by consulting bi-gram weights of the current token with its neighboring tokens

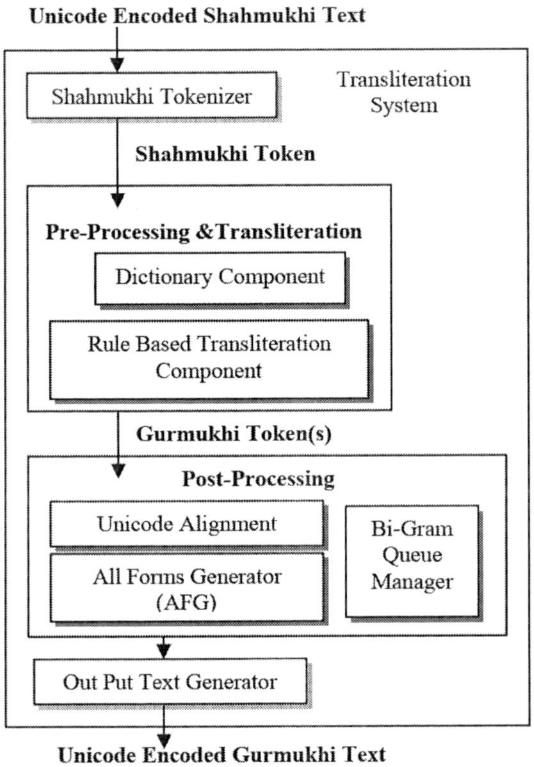

Figure 1. System Overview

5 Lexical Resources Used

Shahmukhi Corpus: 3.3 million words.
Gurmukhi Corpus: 7 million words.
Shahmukhi-Gurmukhi Dictionary
Unigram and Bi-gram Table
All Forms Generator (AFG)

6 Example

Here we show the internal working of the system through an example. Suppose we observe a Shahmukhi string as shown in figure 2. First, we pass this through the pre-processing and transliteration phase where the input string has been tokenized into eleven Shahmukhi tokens. Every input token has been searched in the dictionary for their existence. This status result is shown in table 4 where the tokens 1st, 2nd, 4th, 5th, 6th, 7th, 8th, 10th and 11th are found in dictionary and their intermediate Weighted Gurmukhi Forms (WGF) have been generated. These tokens directly jump to bi-gram queue manager for bi-gram analysis in post-processing phase.

Input 11 Shahmukhi tokens (Right to Left)

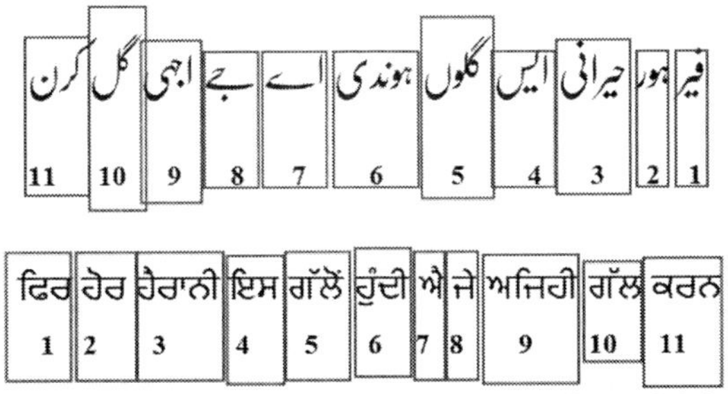

Transliterated 11 Gurmukhi tokens (Left to Right)

Figure 2. Shahmukhi Gurmukhi Tokens

Token	Shahmukhi Token	Found in Dictionary	WGF token{weight}
1	فیر	Yes	ਫੇਰ{4513}; ਫਿਰ{8714}
2	ہور	Yes	ਹੋਰ{14054}; ਹੌਰ{18}
3	حیرانی	No	ਹੇਰਾਨੀ{524}
4	ایس	Yes	ਇਸ{59998}; ਏਸ{1186}
5	گلوں	Yes	ਗੱਲੋਂ{107}
6	ہوندی	Yes	ਹੁੰਦੀ{7699}
7	اے	Yes	ਏ{7927}; ਐ{3600}
8	جے	Yes	ਜੈ{295}; ਜੇ{9791}
9	اجی	No	ਅਜਹੀ{4}
10	گل	Yes	ਗੱਲ{447};ਗਲ{47};ਗਿੱਲ{9} ਗੁਲ{5};ਗੁੱਲ{5}
11	کرن	Yes	ਕਰਨ{21582};ਕਰਣ{174}; ਕਿਰਨ{159}

Table 4. Pre-Processing Transliteration Status

On the other hand, the input tokens 3rd and 9th are not found in dictionary. Therefore, in this phase they will pass through transliteration component and then in post-processing phase they will pass through Unicode formatting. After that they will test for Most Frequent (MF) check by comparing their weights with a predefined threshold value[2]

[2] Threshold value is minimum probability of occurrence among most frequent tokens in target script corpus.

(100 in this case). As shown in table 5 the WGF of 3rd token ਹੇਰਾਨੀ{524} is most frequent one and will move to bi-gram queue whereas the WGF of 9th token ਅਜਹੀ{4} is not a most frequent token and will reach at bi-gram queue manager only after passing through all forms generator (AFG).

Token	MF	AFG Status	Bi-gram Found	Output
1	-	-	hold ਫੇਰ;ਫਿਰ	-
2	-	-	ਫੇਰ-ਹੇਰ,12; ਫਿਰ-ਹੇਰ, 20;	ਫਿਰ
3	Yes	-	hold ਹੇਰ	ਹੇਰ
4	-	-	ਹੇਰਾਨੀ-ਇਸ,10;	ਹੇਰਾਨੀ
5	-	-	hold ਇਸ	ਇਸ
6	-	-	ਇਸ-ਗੱਲੇਂ,45;	ਗੱਲੇਂ
7	-	-	ਹੁੰਦੀ-ਏ,86; ਹੁੰਦੀ-ਐ,125;	ਹੁੰਦੀ
8	-	-	hold ਐ	ਐ
9	No	ਅਜੇਹੀ{310} ਅਜਿਹੀ{1486} ਅਜਹੀ{4}	ਐ-ਜੇ,22; ਜੇ-ਅਜਿਹੀ,13;	ਜੇ
18	Yes	-	hold ਅਜਿਹੀ	ਅਜਿਹੀ
11	-	-	ਅਜਿਹੀ-ਗੱਲ,38; ਗੱਲ-ਕਰਨ,179; ਗਲ-ਕਰਨ,18;	ਗੱਲ
	EOS	-	hold ਕਰਨ	ਕਰਨ

Table 5. Post-Processing Status and output

Here, we see that the AFG has generated two additional forms ਅਜੇਹੀ{310} ਅਜਿਹੀ{1486} (table 5) for this token. These new forms are having additional diacritical marks of short vowels those are missing in the original form. Clearly, AFG has supplied the best possible forms. Next, we show how bi-gram manager will work on WGF tokens to generate final Gurmukhi token. In this model the next token will decide the selection of its previous one. Consider the case of second WFG token ਹੇਰ{14054} having bi-gram combinations with previous one as ਫੇਰ-ਹੇਰ with weight 12 and ਫਿਰ-ਹੇਰ with weight 20. Clearly, the token ਫਿਰ will produce as output not ਫੇਰ because ਫਿਰ-ਹੇਰ combination has higher weight than ਫੇਰ-ਹੇਰ. Similarly, this table shows found bi-gram weights and correspondingly decided Gurmukhi token as output.

7 Results and Discussion

The transliteration system was tested on a small set of poetry, article and story. The results are tabulated in Table 6.

As we can observe an average transliteration accuracy of 91.37% has been obtained. We got good transliteration with different inputs. The main source of error is the existence of vowel-consonant mapping between the two scripts. The Shahmukhi vowel characters Vav(و) and Yeh(ی) have mapping into Gurmukhi consonants Vava(ਵ) and Ya(ਯ) respectively. This kind of vowel-consonant mapping can not be resolved fully with dependency rules but can be minimized by refining the dictionary and phonetic code generation rules of AFG component. In other cases, system makes errors showing deficiency in handling those tokens which are not belonging to common vocabulary domain.

Type	Transliterated Tokens	Accuracy %
Poetry	3,301	90.63769
Article	584	92.60274
Story	3,981	90.88043
Total	**7,866**	**91.37362**

Table 6. Transliteration Results

8 References

Arbabi, Mansur, Scott M. Fischthal, Vincent C. Cheng and Elizabeth Bar. 1994. Algorithms for Arabic name transliteration. IBM Journal of research and Development, pp 183-193.

Haizhou Li, Min Zhang and Jian Su. 2004. A Joint Source-Channel Model for Machine Transliteration. Proceedings of the 42nd Annual Meeting of the Association for Computational Linguistics, pp 159-166.

Malik, M. G. Abbas. 2006. Punjabi Machine Transliteration. Proceedings of the 21st International Conference on Computational Linguistics and 44th Annual Meeting of the ACL, pp 1137-1144.

Y. Gal, 2002. An HMM Approach to Vowel Restoration in Arabic and Hebrew. Proceedings of ACL Workshop on Computational Approaches to Semitic Languages, pp 27-33.

Youngim Jung, Donghun Lee, Aesun Yoon, Hyuk Chul Kwon. 2004. Transliteration System for Arabic-Numeral Expressions using Decision Tree for Intelligent Korean TTS, volume 1. 30th Annual Conference of IEEE, pp 657-662.

A Linguistic Knowledge Discovery Tool: Very Large Ngram Database Search with Arbitrary Wildcards

Satoshi Sekine

New York University

715 Broadway, 7th floor, New York, NY 10003

sekine@cs.nyu.edu

Abstract

In this paper, we will describe a search tool for a huge set of ngrams. The tool supports queries with an arbitrary number of wildcards. It takes a fraction of a second for a search, and can provide the fillers of the wildcards. The system runs on a single Linux PC with reasonable size memory (less than 4GB) and disk space (less than 400GB). This system can be a very useful tool for linguistic knowledge discovery and other NLP tasks.

1 Introduction

Currently, NLP research is shifting towards semantic analysis. In order to understand what a sentence means, we require substantial background knowledge which must be gathered in advance. Building such knowledge is not an easy task. This is the so-called "knowledge bottleneck" problem, which was one of the major reasons for the failure of much AI research in the 1980's. However, now, the circumstances have quite changed. We have an almost unlimited amount of text and machine power has drastically improved. Using these fortunate assets, research on knowledge discovery in NLP is booming. The work by (Hearst 92) (Collins and Singer 99) (Brin 99) (Hasegawa et al. 04) are only a few examples of this research direction. Notice that most of these methods use local context. For example, a lexico-syntactic pattern, like "NP such as NP" can extract hyponym relationships (Hearst 92), and contexts between two named entities can indicate a relationship between those names (Hasegawa et al. 04).

© 2008. Licensed under the *Creative Commons Attribution-Noncommercial-Share Alike 3.0 Unported* license (http://creativecommons.org/licenses/by-nc-sa/3.0/). Some rights reserved.

It is quite natural to believe that the larger the corpus, the larger and the more reliable the discovered knowledge can be. However, it leads to problems in terms of speed and machine power. In order to solve these problems, some people use commercial search engines (Chklovski and Pantel 04). However, using such search engines has serious problems: 1) Only a limited number of results available, 2) Only a limited number of accesses permitted, 3) Mysterious ranking function, 4) Unstable results over a long time period, 5) Slow, as it is over the internet. Another idea to overcome this difficulty is to create one's own (maybe smaller) search engine (Cafarella and Etzioni 05) (Shinzato et al. 08). Although creating one's own search engine has advantages (one of which is the freedom to design the form of the query; such as POS and dependency), it is a huge, expensive task; not everybody can afford to make a search engine. More seriously, not everybody can use it as he/she may want.

In this paper, we will propose an alternative solution which should enable researchers with modest resources to conduct research using huge corpora for knowledge discovery. It is an ngram search tool with the following requirements.

Requirements

1. It searches for ngrams which include an arbitrary number of wildcards, such as "* such as * and", "Mr. * said", "from * to * by *" or "* attack by * * on *".
2. It returns the fillers of the wildcards as well as ngram frequencies
3. It produces the results in a fraction of a second (for most reasonable queries)
4. It runs on a single PC
5. It needs only a reasonable amount of memory (4GB) for processing
6. It needs only a reasonable amount of disk space (400GB) for indexing 10^8-10^9 ngrams

2 Algorithm Overview

There are two reasonable choices for the search algorithm. One is "inverted indexing" (used by *"lucene"* and others) and the other is "trie". We used trie. Using inverted indexing, it is easy to create an index at the cost of runtime speed. We prefer an algorithm which requires more complicated indexing in order to achieve the speed in searching. Trie is an indexing tree structure in which each node represents a symbol (in our case, words) and each link represents the sequence of the symbols (in our case n-gram). Searching can be done by traversing the tree, which is usually done in time constant in the size of the corpus. However, it is important to mention that the trie structure is order sensitive. For example, if the query includes wildcards, such as "*Mr. * * said yesterday*", searching the trie is not an optimal solution.

One naive solution is to create a search system (or a trie) for each possible combination of wildcards. For example, for the query pattern *"Mr. * * said yesterday"*, we should prepare a search system for modified ngrams which have the first, fourth and fifth words of the original ngrams as the first three words. For ngrams of length N, the number of possible combinations of literals and wildcards is 2^N. In theory, if we make that many search systems, we can solve the problem. However, the number of search systems is too large considering the number of ngrams we aim to handle (Table 1). Although we applied two implementation techniques to reduce the size of index (which will be described in the next section), it is still likely that we could not satisfy requirement #6.

We solved the problem by using a single search system for different kinds of search patterns, reducing the number of needed search systems significantly. It can be observed that a pattern with wildcards at suffix positions can be searched using the same trie used for patterns without those wildcards. Also, we don't always need to start the trie by indexing the first word. If we build an alternative trie which starts by indexing the second word, we can cover more patterns with fewer tries. For example, using the trie constructed to search for 5-grams "DEABC" (We will call this a "trie pattern": each letter represents a literal, with A representing the first token in the original ngram), four "search patterns" (i.e. ngram pattern used in the queries), "AB*DE", "A**DE", "***DE" and "***D*", can be searched efficiently.

We found that the minimum number of trie patterns needed to cover all possible search patterns of length N is ${}_{N/2}C_{N}$. We have constructed minimal sets of patterns for all N up to 9. Once the system receives a query with one or more wildcards, it finds the trie pattern which covers the search pattern of the query.

3 Implementation

We also implemented two ideas to reduce the size of the index. One is related to a common technique to reduce the size of trie nodes by deleting the index of unique suffixes. In addition, we don't store the remaining data within the trie. We just store the ngram ID at the node in order to further reduce the size of the index. Because there are many search systems, storing the ngram data in a single master database saves a lot of space. When the user wants to see the words of an ngram which was identified by the search, the system retrieves the ngram from the master database using the ngram ID. The benefit of this technique is quite large (more than 50% reduction of index size in 9gram), as many ngrams have long unique suffixes.

The other idea is based on the fact that once the ngram data is provided, no update will be requested (i.e. insertion or replacement procedure in the trie is not necessary). We can eliminate the pointers to the parents and the siblings for each node, which contributes to about 30% additional reduction in the index size.

Because the tries are very large, we divide them into segments (128 segments for 9-grams and 118 for 5-grams), so that an individual trie index segment is small enough to fit in a memory of modest size (requirement #5). Each segment contains a lexicographically contiguous sequence of ngrams. Furthermore, we use *"mmap"* to get the index into memory from the disk, so that only the portions of the trie segment that are actually used will be loaded.

System Flow

We will briefly describe the system flow

1) First, all the words in the input query are looked up in the dictionary. If there are out of vocabulary words, then there is no ngram which matches the query. If all words are known, find the appropriate trie pattern for the input query based on the locations of wildcards.

2) Then the appropriate segment(s) of the trie data is found for the search query. It was done

by searching the table of segment index sorted in lexicographic order.

3) Now, the search in the trie is performed. Note that there are 16,128 tries for 9 -gram (128 segments for 126 trie patterns). If the search ends with an internal node, there is more than one matched ngram. If the search ends with a terminal node, just one ngram matches. If the trie ends before the end of query, you have to retrieve the ngram from the master database and match the retrieved ngram against the query.

4) Once one or several ngram IDs are identified as matched ngram(s), the system will output the information. There are three output modes. a) Only instance and type frequency are printed. b) Only ngram IDs are printed. These two types can be achieved quickly without consulting the ngram master database. c) Ngram instances are printed using the ngram master database.

4 Experiments and Evaluation

4.1 Ngram data

We implemented this using two ngram data sets.

Google 1T Web 5gram

This is a part of the ngram data provided by Google through LDC (Web 1T). The data was generated from approximately 1 trillion word tokens of publicly accessible Web pages.

9-grams from 82 years of newspaper

For knowledge discovery purposes, 5-grams are generally unsatisfactory. A 5-gram can only cover 2 words of context on each side of a single word term. So we extracted 9-grams from a number of newspaper corpora available to us. Including NANTC: LATWP(94-97), NYT, REUFF, REUTE, WSJ (94-96), BBN GigaWord corpus (news archive only): BBC(99-06), People Daily, Taipei Times, The Hindu (00-06), Arab News, Gulf News, India Times (01-06), AQUAINT corpus: APW, NYT (98-00), Xinhua (96-00), CSR corpus: WSJ (87-94).

These corpora are cleaned up by several methods, because some of them have article duplications/minor variants and some of them contain many non-sentences. We use a simple method to reduce such noise, which is to "uniq" all the sentences for each year of each newspaper and count each distinct sentence only once. This is not a perfect solution, but it reduces a lot of noise to an amount almost unnoticeable for the ngram search result. The statistics of the data are shown in Table 1.

Corpus	Google 1T	82 yrs. News
Original Text	1 T words	1.8 G words
Ngram	5-gram	9-gram
Threshold	40	2
#of ngrams	1,176,470,663	119,456,373
# of patterns	10	126
# of nodes	1.4G x 10	160M x 126
Index size	277GB	322GB

Table 1 Statistics of the data

4.2 Example

Obviously, the tool is useful for knowledge discovery tasks for hyponym relations, binary relations, name extraction, relations between names and so on. It is also useful to extract more specific relations, such as "what kind of attack occurred by whom on what/when" by searching for "* *attack on* * * *by* * **". Figure 1 shows a snapshot of the tool's output on this query.

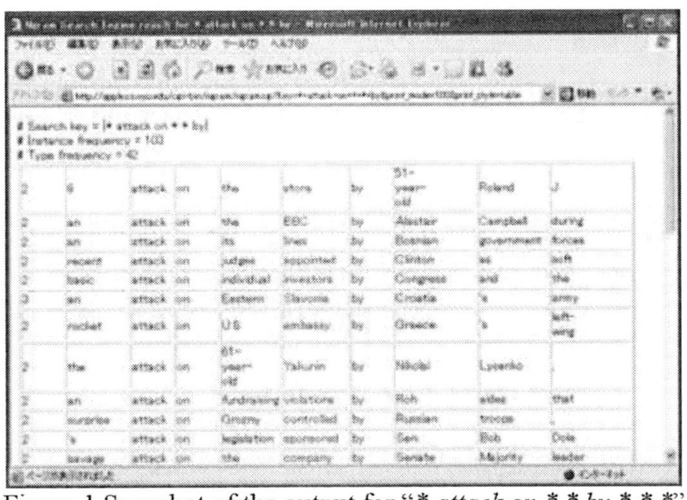

Figure 1 Snapshot of the output for "* *attack on* * * *by* * * *"

Importantly, because of the speed, we can modify the query in an interactive manner. The speed is helpful for batch processing, too, when we need to search millions of patterns.

4.3 Evaluation

The speed evaluation was conducted using 9grams. We randomly selected 1017 9grams from the original data to form a test set, and also created another test set in which 1 to 3 words are randomly replaced by wildcards in those 9grams. We measure the average time to find the ngrams. In the case of a query with wildcards, we checked if the original ngram is found among all returned ngrams to verify the accuracy of the tool. The system runs in three output modes (we use a file output rather than *stdout*). Producing Ngram output takes a long time if the number of ngrams is very large, so we limited the number of ngrams to be printed to 100. In the experiment, the number of returned ngrams ranged from 1 to 100 with an average of 1.26. The result is shown in Table 2 and the times are given in milliseconds.

Print mode	Freq.	IDs	Ngram
Original	19	19	20
With wildcards	19	19	29

Table 2 Speed of search (Newspaper 9gram)

5 Related Work and Discussion

One of the most related works is the CMU-Cambridge Statistical LM toolkit (CMU-Cambridge). It's a tool to search ngrams in Speech fields. However, it does not handle wildcards, which is important for knowledge discovery purposes. There are several ngram tools in the field of genome sequence analysis (MUMmer) (REPuter). However, the size of the alphabets are quite different (handful of genome bases vs. about 1.08 million words), and their main purpose is to discover similarity or repetition. These systems are not directly useful for linguistic knowledge discovery purposes. As a document retrieval tool, there is a public domain search engine, such as *"lucene"* (Lucene). However, its primary purpose is document retrieval and the inverted index algorithm can't handle well very frequent terms. Searching is relatively slow.

It should be noted that creating the index is a huge task. It took about 2 months using five 4GB-memory machines. However, it took only about one week with 64GB-memory machine.

As for the future direction, we are improving the tool to show the original sentences from which the ngram was extracted. We have some evidence that a longer context is needed for the knowledge discovery purpose.

This tool is merely a tool, but we believe it's a very powerful tool for linguistic knowledge discovery among other related objectives. The next step we would like to take is to apply this tool to find linguistic knowledge for NLP applications.

Acknowledgements

This research was supported in part by the National Science Foundation under Grant IIS-00325657. This paper does not necessarily reflect the position of the U.S. Government. We would like to thank our colleagues at New York University, who provided useful suggestions and discussions, including Prof. Grishman.

References

CMU-Cambridge Statistical LM toolkit homepage: http://www.speech.cs.cmu.edu/SLM/toolkit_documentation.html

Lucene homepage: http://lucene.apache.org/

MUMmer hompage: http://mummer.sourceforge.net/

REPuter homepage: http://bibiserv.techfak.uni-bielefeld.de/reputer/

Web 1T 5-gram. by Google. LDC Catalog No.: LDC2006T13

M. J. Cafarella and O. Etzioni. "A Search Engine for Natural Language Applications". 2005. In Proc. of World Wide Web Conference.

S. Brin. "Extracting Patterns and Relations from the World Wide Web". 1998. In Proc. of Workshop on Web and DataBase-98.

T. Chklovski and P. Pantel. "VerbOcean: Mining the Web for Fine-Grained Semantic Verb Relations". 2004. In Proc. of EMNLP-04. pp. 33-40.

M. Collins and Y. Singer. "Unsupervised Models for Named Entity Classification". 1998. In Proc. of EMNLP-99.

M. Hearst. "Automatic Acquisition of Hyponyms from Large Text Corpora". 1992. In Proc. of COLING-92.

T. Hasegawa, S. Sekine and R. Grishman "Discovering Relations among Named Entities from Large Corpora". 2004. In Proc. of ACL-04.

K. Shinzato, T. Shibata, D. Kawahara, C. Hashimoto and S. Kurohashi. "TSUBAKI: An Open Search Engine Infrastructure for Developing New Information Access Methodology", 2008. In Proc. of the 3rd IJCNLP-08.

Semantic visualization and meaning computation

Fabienne Venant
Loria
Campus Scientifique
BP 239
54506 Vandoeuvre-les-Nancy
fabienne.venant@loria.fr

Abstract

We present here VISUSYN, a prototype we developed in order to study meaning construction. This software implements the model of dynamic construction of meaning proposed by Victorri and Fuchs (1996). It allows a semantic visualization that can be used to compute the meaning of a lexical unit in a given context

1 Introduction

Meaning construction – how words take meaning in a sentence or in a text –i s an important issue for computational linguistics. The major problem we have to deal with is that each word can have a lot of different meanings, depending on context. This phenomenon – called polysemy – is constitutive of language, and is the basis of its richness. However it is quite difficult to formalize. In most models of language, polysemy is considered as a kind of artefact. In these models, polysemy amounts to very little: a choice in a list of pre-existing meanings. However the omnipresence of polysemy always leads this kind of computation to combinatorial explosions. To avoid this problem, we want to give a central place in meaning construction to polysemy: that is why we define our model within the framework of continuous mathematics. This model was first proposed by Victorri and Fuchs (1996). It is deeply rooted in *Gestalttheorie* (Guillaume, 1979). Each linguistic unit is associated with a semantic space, where its different meanings are organized according to semantic proximity. The other units of the utterance define a potential function, which allows us to determinate the region of the semantic space corresponding to the meaning of the unit studied within the utterance.

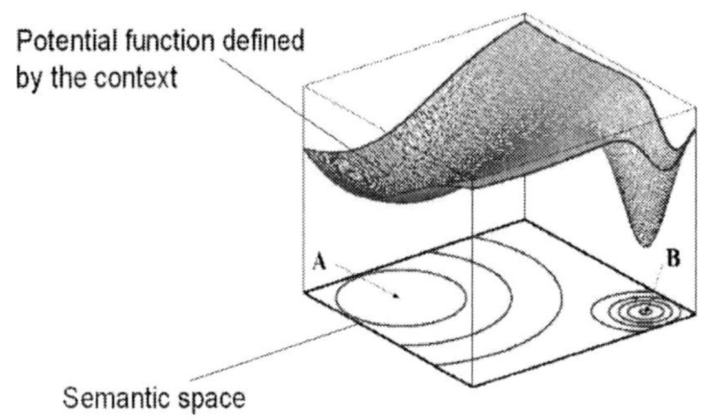

Figure 1: Model

We present here VISUSYN, the software we developed in order to implement this model. VISUSYN is still a work in progress. The working version was developed in Matlab. A Java version will be developed as soon as possible.

2 Presentation of VISUSYN

VISUSYN makes two kinds of operations, corresponding to the two componants of the model: it constructs semantics spaces and then computes meaning functions defined on these semantic spaces.

The algorithm for building semantic spaces relies on the analysis of a graph of synonyms. The aim of the exploration is to reveal the structure of the lexicon modelled by the graph so an automatic system can reach the information it contains. VISUSYN can construct local spaces, representing the semantic of a given unit, as well as global spaces, representing a lexical paradigm in its whole (for French adjectives, or adverbs for instance). Local

©2008. Licensed under the *Creative Commons Attribution-Noncommercial-Share Alike 3.0 Unported* license (http://creativecommons.org/licenses/by-nc-sa/3.0/). Some rights reserved.

spaces are used to compute meaning of the unit under study when accompanied by a given word in a sentence. To compute the corresponding potential function, VISUSYN uses cooccurence data from large scale corpora.

3 Small-world graphs

It has been discovered recently that most lexical graphs belong to the class of small-world graphs. This term denotes graphs where most nodes are neighbors of one another, but every node can be reached from other by a small number of hops or steps. Small-world networks were defined by Watts and Strogatz (1998). They noted that graphs could be classified according to their clustering coefficient (C) and their characteristic path length (L). Additionally, a third property can be associated with small-world networks even though it is not required for that classification. Specifically, if a small-world network has a degree-distribution which can be fitted with a power law distribution, it is taken as a sign that the network is small-world. These networks are known as scale-free networks. Ravasz and Barabási (2003) showed that a high clustering coefficient with scale free topology determines an original combination of modularity and hierarchical organization. It is not a simply pyramidal organization. The structure is made of groups of nodes, with small clusters at the bottom and very large groups at the top. Moreover, groups of nodes may overlap at any level. This self-similar nesting of different groups or module into each other forces a strict fine structure on real networks (Ravasz and Barabási, 2003).

4 Building semantic spaces

The algorithm will be here illustraded on the French adjective lexicon. The graph under study, called Synadj, is a graph of synonymy with 3,699 vertices and 22,568 links. We verified the small-word structure of this graph (C, L and degree distribution). This small-world structure led us to use the cliques[1] of the graph as a tool for building the semantic space. A clique in a graph is a maximal set of pairwise adjacent vertices, or – in other words – an induced subgraph which is a maximal complete graph. In the present case, a clique is made of adjectives which are all synonyms in a one to one relationship. By virtue of the definition, small-world networks will inevitably have high representation of cliques, and subgraphs that are a few edges shy of being cliques, i.e. small-world networks will have sub-networks that are characterized by the presence of connections between almost any two nodes within them. This follows from the requirement of a high cluster coefficient. We can consider as a first approximation that the cliques define very precise meanings that can be considered as the intersection of the meanings of all the units belonging to the clique. We thus define the semantic space as the euclidian space generated by the vertices of the graph (the adjectives, here). Each clique of the graph is associated with a point of this space, which coordinates depend on wich vertices belong to the clique. VISUSYN uses the chi-square distance to compute the distances between the cliques. Then a principal component analysis is applied to reduce the dimensionality of the space. In order to build a local semantic space (for example associated with a given word), we select a sub-graph, made only by the word under study and all its synonyms. The local space only contains the cliques of this subgraph[2]. Figure 2 shows a visualization of the semantic space associated with the French adjective *sec* (*dry, severe, brusque...*). It accounts for the six main meanings we can find in a dictionary.

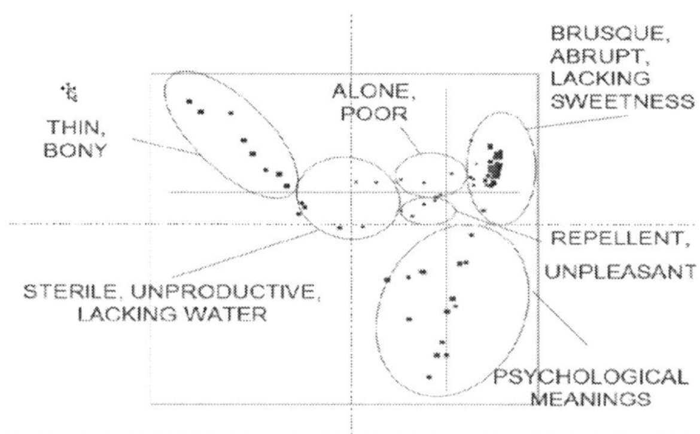

Figure 2: Local space associated with the French adjectives *sec*

The global semantic space is generated by all the vertices of Synadj. It contains all the 11,900 cliques of Synadj. Figure 3 shows a part of the global space of French adjectives. The

[1]Following the idea first proposed by Ploux and Victorri (1998)

[2]Ploux and Victorri (1998) first proposed the algorithm and built the lexical data. Local semantic spaces can be consulted at http://elsap1.unicaen.fr/dicosyn.html or http://dico.isc.cnrs.fr/fr/index.html.

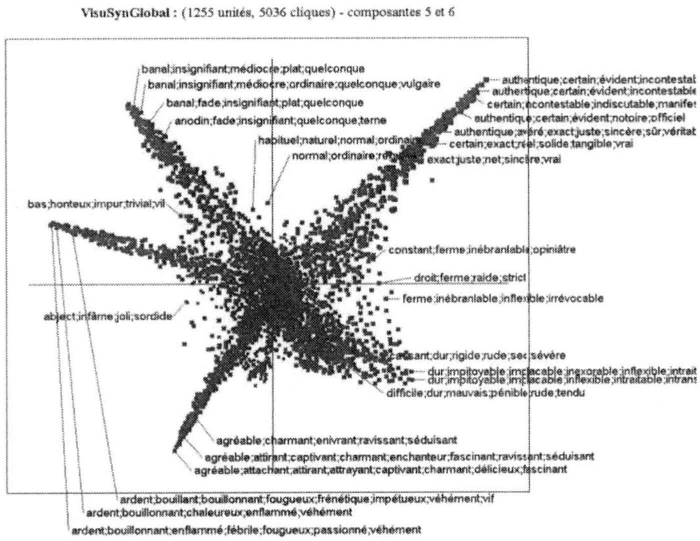

Figure 3: Global semantic space: French adjectives (2D)

very centre of the space only contains intensive meanings like *authentique; certain; evident; incontestable (authentic; certain; evident; incontestable)* or *agréable; charmant; enivrant; ravissant; séduisant (agreeable; delightful; exciting; attractive).* These meanings are very general meanings and can apply to any nouns.

There are now many semantic branches more or less long growing out from the central core. These branches are very dense near the centre and then go in all the directions becoming sparser and sparser. They are homogenous from a semantic viewpoint. Each branch only contains one sort of adjectival meaning: relational, qualificative, or intensive. VISUSYN had also been used to explore other global lexicons, like French verbs (Figure 4 – (Gaume et al., 2006)) or French adverbs ending in -ment (more or less corresponding to english adverbs ending in -ly).

5 Meaning Computation

Let's go on with French adjectives. An attributive adjective is always linked to a noun. It is this noun which mostly constrains the meaning of this adjective, even if other units like the article can play a role.

We show here how Visynsyn can be used to automatically find which synonyms match better the meaning of an adjective (here the French adjective *sec*) when used with a given noun. In order to do this, VISUSYN associates a characteristic function with each synonym. To compute the value of the function in a given point, it evaluates wether the synonym belongs to the corresponding clique or not. The basins of this function represent the meaning zones of the semantic space in which the synonymy between the word and the given synonym is relevant.

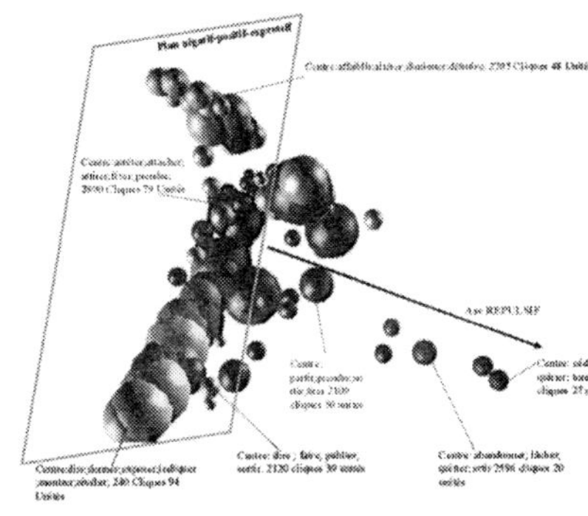

Figure 4: Global semantic space: French verbs (3D)

To compute the meaning of *sec* when used with a given noun, VISUSYN associates a potential function with the noun. The value of this function in each point depends on the frequencies of cooccurrence of the noun with the adjectives of the corresponding clique. The basins of the function determine the zone of the semantic space corresponding to the meaning of *sec* when used with the associated noun. Figure 6 shows the potential function associated with *fleur* (*flower*). In this case the noun *fleur* forces *sec* to take a precise meaning in the zone 'lack of water'.

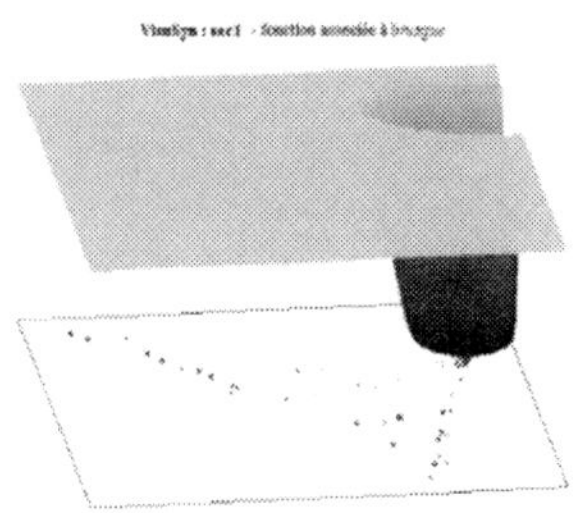

Figure 5: Characteristic function associated with the adjective *brusque*

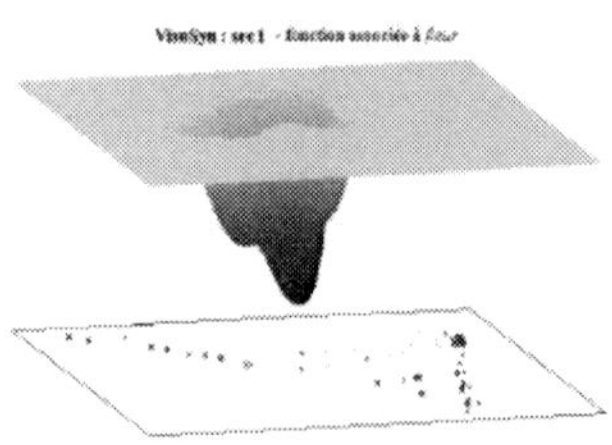

Figure 6: Potential function associated with *fleur* (*flower*)

The method of disambiguation consists in comparing the function of a synonym to the function of the noun under focus. The more the functions overlap, the more you can replace *sec* with its synonym without changing the meaning of the syntagm. This method has been used to compute the overlap rate for 20 nouns among the most frequently used with *sec* in a large corpus (Frantext, http://atilf.atilf.fr/frantext.htm). The results automatically processed were compared with the human answers on the same task. The rate of success is 79% (Venant, 2006).

This works for a fined grained disambiguation. VISUSYN can also deal with a more macrocopic partition of the semanctic space. Figure 2 shows a division of the semantic space of *sec* in 6 zones. VISUSYN can decide automatically which of these six zones correspond to the meaning of *sec* , when used with a given noun. The method is similar to the previous: It now associates each zone (and not only each synonym) with a characteristic function. This function is computed according to the cliques belonging to the zone. For each noun, VISUSYN compares its potential function with that of each zone. It thus computes an affinity rate between each noun and each zone. This method gives better results than the previous

6 Conclusion

Although VISUSYN is still a prototype, it seems very promising. Our basic result is that the kind of visualization presented here displays the structure of lexical graphs. It also constitutes an original tools to explore the structure of small-world graphs. As the algorithm is independent of the nature of the relation modelized by the graph, it could be used to explore other small-world graphs

It offers interesting possibilities of using semantic informations in computational linguistics, especially in the domain of automatic disambiguation. (We also evaluated its results on verbs and noun). From a more theoretical point of view, it accounts for the validity of the underlying model. Of course this model has some limits and the work is still in progress. We have to develop the system. However, this work shows how continuous mathematics can be relevant for semantic modelization and encourages us in the challenge of using continuity for corpus linguistics.

References

Gaume, Bruno, Fabienne Venant, and Bernard Victorri. 2006. Hierarchy in lexical organisation of natural languages. *Hierarchy in Natural and social Sciences Denise Pumain (ed)*, pages 121–142.

Guillaume, Gustave. 1979. *La psychologie de la forme*. Flammarion.

Ploux, Sabine and Victorri Bernard. 1998. Construction déspaces sémantiques á láide de dictionnaires de synonymes. *Traitement automatique des langues*, 39:161–182.

Ravasz, Erzsébet and Albert László Barabási. 2003. Hierarchical organization in complex networks. *Physical Review*, E 67:026112.

Venant, Fabienne. 2006. A geometric approach to graph exploration. In *Fourth Workshop in Information and Human Language Technology (TIL'2006)*.

Victorri, Bernard and Catherine Fuchs. 1996. *La polysémie, construction dynamique du sens*. Hermès.

Watts, Duncan .J. and Steven H. Strogatz. 1998. Collective dynamics of small-world networks. *Nature*, 393:440–442.

Temporal Processing with the TARSQI Toolkit

Marc Verhagen
Brandeis University
Computer Science Dept.
Waltham, MA 02454-9110
marc@cs.brandeis.edu

James Pustejovsky
Brandeis University
Computer Science Dept.
Waltham, MA 02454-9110
jamesp@cs.brandeis.edu

Abstract

We present the TARSQI Toolkit (TTK), a modular system for automatic temporal and event annotation of natural language texts. TTK identifies temporal expressions and events in natural language texts, and parses the document to order events and to anchor them to temporal expressions.

1 Introduction

A keyword-based search is not sufficient to answer temporally loaded questions like *"did Brazil win the soccer world championship in 1970?"* since a boolean keyword search cannot distinguish between those documents where the event *win* is actually anchored to the year 1970 versus those that are not. The TARSQI Project (Temporal Awareness and Reasoning Systems for Question Interpretation) focused on enhancing natural language question answering systems so that temporally-based questions about the events and entities in news articles can be addressed. To explicitly mark the needed temporal relations the project delivered a series of tools for extracting time expressions, events, subordination relations and temporal relations (Verhagen et al., 2005; Mani et al., 2006; Saurí et al., 2005; Saurí et al., 2006a). But although those tools performed reasonably well, they were not integrated in a principled way.

This paper describes the TARSQI Toolkit (TTK), which takes the TARSQI components and integrates them into a temporal parsing framework. The toolkit is different from the system described in (Verhagen et al., 2005) in several major aspects:

1. the components were integrated in a toolkit which, amongst others, split the parsing of properties typical for a particular document type from the temporal parsing of the text

2. a component was added that takes the results from the various components that generate temporal relations and merges them into a consistent temporal graph

3. a new way of visualizing the results was used

In addition, some components were updated and test suites with unit tests and regression tests were added. In this paper, we focus on the merging of temporal links and the visualization of temporal relations.

There has been a fair amount of recent research on extraction of temporal relations, including (Chambers et al., 2007; Lapata and Lascarides, 2006; Bramsen et al., 2006; Bethard and Martin, 2007; Min et al., 2007; Puşcaşu, 2007). However, we are not aware of approaches that integrate temporal relations from various sources in one consistent whole.

All TTK components use the TimeML annotation language (Pustejovsky et al., 2003; Pustejovsky et al., 2005). TimeML is an annotation scheme for markup of events, times, and their temporal relations in news articles. The TimeML scheme flags tensed verbs, adjectives, and nominals with EVENT tags with various attributes, including the class of event, tense, grammatical aspect, polarity (negative or positive), and any modal operators which govern the event being tagged. Time expressions are flagged with TIMEX3 tags, an extension of the ACE 2004 TIMEX2 annotation scheme (tern.mitre.org).

© 2008. Licensed under the *Creative Commons Attribution-Noncommercial-Share Alike 3.0 Unported* license (http://creativecommons.org/licenses/by-nc-sa/3.0/). Some rights reserved.

Subordination relations between events, as for example between reporting events and the embedded event reported on, are annotated with the SLINK tag. For temporal relations, TimeML defines a TLINK tag that links tagged events to other events and/or times.

In section 2, we will give a short overview of the toolkit. In section 3, we focus on the component that merges TLINKs, and in section 4 we will dwell on the visualization of temporal relations.

2 Overview of the toolkit

The overall architecture of TTK is illustrated in figure 1 below. Input text is first processed by the *DocumentModel*, which takes care of document-level properties like encoding and meta tags. The DocumentModel hands clean text to the other components which are allowed to be more generic.

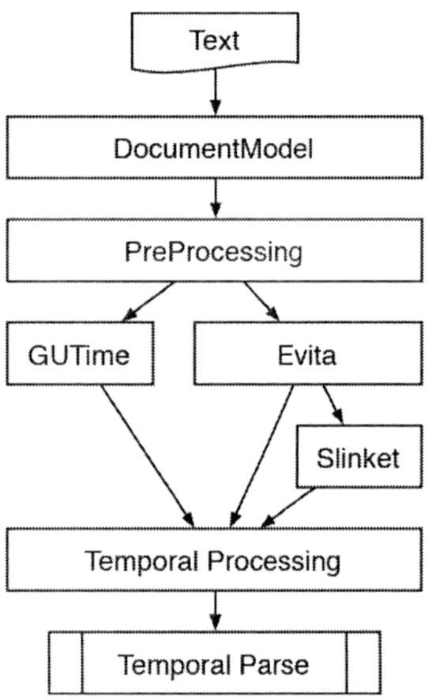

Figure 1: TTK Architecture

The preprocessor uses standard approaches to tokenization, part-of-speech tagging and chunking. GUTime is a temporal expression tagger that recognizes the extents and normalized values of time expressions. Evita is a domain-independent event recognition tool that performs two main tasks: robust event identification and analysis of grammatical features such as tense and aspect.

Slinket is an application developed to automatically introduce SLINKs, which in TimeML specify subordinating relations between pairs of events, and classify them into factive, counterfactive, evidential, negative evidential, and modal, based on the modal force of the subordinating event (Saurí et al., 2006b). SLINKs are introduced by a well-delimited subgroup of verbal and nominal predicates (such as *regret*, *say*, *promise* and *attempt*), and in most cases clearly signaled by a subordination context. Slinket thus relies on a combination of lexical and syntactic knowledge.

The temporal processing stage includes three modules that generate TLINKs: Blinker, S2T and the TLink Classifier.

Blinker is a rule-based component that applies to certain configurations of events and timexes. It contains rule sets for the following cases: (i) event and timex in the same noun phrase, (ii) events and the document creation time, (iii) events with their syntactically subordinated events, (iv) events in conjunctions, (v) two main events in consecutive sentences, and (vi) timexes with other timexes. Each of these rule sets has a different flavor. For example, the rules in (vi) simply calculate differences in the normalized ISO value of the timex tag while the rules in (v) refer to the tense and aspect values of the two events. Blinker is a re-implementation and extension of GutenLink (Verhagen et al., 2005).

S2T takes the output of Slinket and uses about a dozen syntactic rules to map SLINKs onto TLINKs. For example, one S2T rule encodes that in SLINKs with reporting verbs where both events are in past tense, the reporting event occurred after the event reported on.

The TLink Classifier is a MaxEnt classifier that identifies temporal relations between identified events in text. The classifier accepts its input for each pair of events under consideration as a set of features. It is trained on the TimeBank corpus (see www.timeml.org).

Of the three TLINK generating components, S2T derives a relatively small number of TLINKs, but Blinker and the classifier are quite prolific. In many cases the TLINKs derived by Blinker and the classifier are inconsistent with each other. The system in (Verhagen et al., 2005) used a simple voting mechanism that favors TLINKs from components that exhibit higher precision. In addition, if confidence measures are available then these can be used by the voting mechanism. However, this approach does not factor in consistency of temporal relations: choosing the TLINKs with the highest probability may result in TLINKs that are inconsistent. For example, say we have two TLINKs: BEFORE(x,y) and BEFORE(y,z). And say we have two competing TLINKs, derived by Blinker and the classifier respectively: BEFORE(x,z) and BEFORE(z,x). If the second of these two has a higher confidence, then we will end up with an inconsistent annotation. In the following section we describe how in TTK this problem is avoided.

3 Link Merger

The link merger, together with the three TLINK-generating components, is part of the temporal processing module of TTK, as shown in the diagram in figure 2 below.

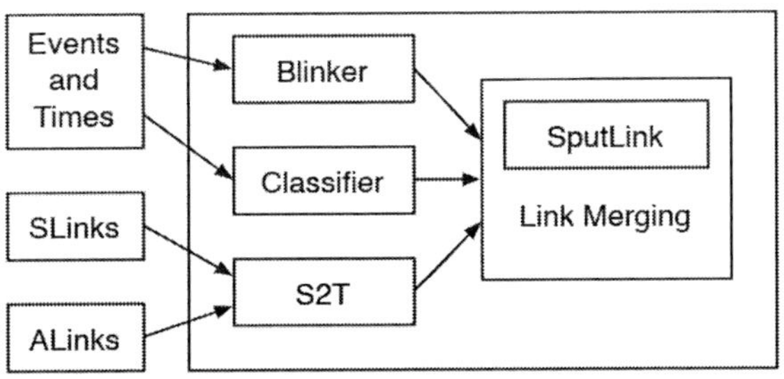

Figure 2: TTK Temporal Processing

The link merging component uses a greedy algorithm to merge TLinks into a consistent whole. First all links are ordered on their confidence score. Currently these scores are either global or local. Global confidence scores are derived from the observed precision of the component that generated the links. For example, links generated by S2T are considered high precision and are always deemed more reliable than links generated by the classifier. Links generated by the classifier come with a confidence score assigned by the classifier and these scores are used to order all classifier links.

Merging proceeds by first creating a graph that contains all events and time expressions as nodes, but that has no constraints expressed on the edges. Those constraints are added by the temporal links. Links are ordered on confidence score and are added one by one. Each time a link is added a constraint propagation component named Sputlink, based on Allen's interval algebra (Allen, 1983; Verhagen, 2005), is applied. If a link cannot be added because it is inconsistent with the constraint already on the edge, then the link is skipped. The result is a consistent annotation where high precision links are prefered over lower precision links.

4 Visualization

Providing a good visualization of a temporal graph can be tricky. A table of temporal relations is only useful for relations inside sentences. Full graphs, like the ones generated by GraphViz (http://www.graphviz.org/), do not make it that much easier for the reader to quickly obtain a picture of the temporal structure of the document. Timelines can be misleading because so many events in a document cannot be ordered with respect to a time stamp.

TTK uses a visualization scheme named TBox (Verhagen, 2007). It uses left-to-right arrows, box inclusion and stacking to encode temporal precedence, inclusion, and simultaneity respectively (see figure 3).

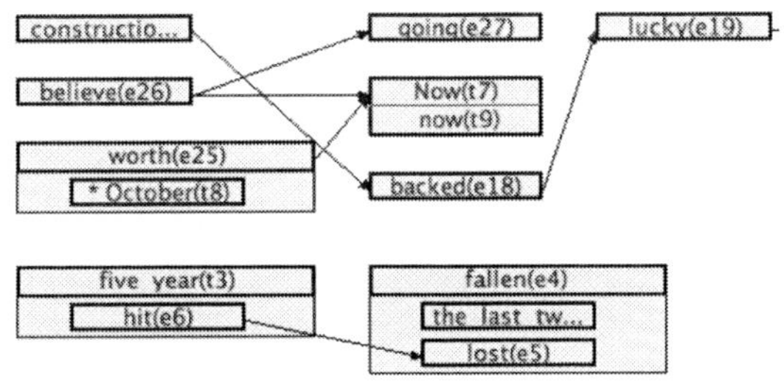

Figure 3: The TBox Representation

This visualization makes it easier to convey the temporal content of a document since temporal relations are strictly and unambiguously mapped to specific ways of drawing them. And vice versa, a particular way of positioning two events always indicates the same temporal relation. Note that vertical positioning does not imply any temporal relation.

5 Conclusion and Future Work

We have described TTK, a toolkit that integrates several components that generate tags to mark up events and time expressions, as well as non-consuming tags that encode relations between events and times. TTK includes a module that combines potentially conflicting temporal relations into a consistent temporal graph of a document, which can be succinctly displayed using the TBox representation.

In current work, we are exploring how to split up the task of temporal relation extraction into more subtasks and write specialized components, both rule-based and machine learning based, to extract temporal relations for that task. The link merging would then have many more input streams, each with their own reported reliability.

The TARSQI Toolkit can be downloaded from http://timeml.org/site/tarsqi/toolkit/.

Acknowledgments

The work reported in the paper was carried out in the context of the AQUAINT program and was funded under ARDA/DoD/IARPA grant NBCHC040027.

References

Allen, James. 1983. Maintaining Knowledge about Temporal Intervals. *Communications of the ACM*, 26(11):832–843.

Bethard, Steven and James H. Martin. 2007. CU-TMP: Temporal relation classification using syntactic and semantic features. In *Proceedings of the Fourth International Workshop on Semantic Evaluations (SemEval-2007)*, pages 129–132, Prague, Czech Republic, June. Association for Computational Linguistics.

Bramsen, Philip, Pawan Deshpande, Yoong Keok Leeand, and Regina Barzilay. 2006. Finding temporal order in discharge summaries. In *Proceedings of EMNLP*.

Chambers, Nathanael, Shan Wang, and Dan Jurafsky. 2007. Classifying temporal relations between events. In *Proceedings of the 45th Annual Meeting of the Association for Computational Linguistics Companion Volume Proceedings of the Demo and Poster Sessions*, pages 173–176, Prague, Czech Republic, June. Association for Computational Linguistics.

Lapata, Mirella and Alex Lascarides. 2006. Learning sentence-internal temporal relations. *Journal of Artificial Intelligence Research*, 27:85–117.

Mani, Inderjeet, Ben Wellner, Marc Verhagen, Chong Min Lee, and James Pustejovsky. 2006. Machine learning of temporal relations. In *Proceedings of the 44th Annual Meeting of the Association for Computational Linguistics*, Sydney. ACL.

Min, Congmin, Munirathnam Srikanth, and Abraham Fowler. 2007. LCC-TE: A hybrid approach to temporal relation identification in news text. In *Proceedings of the Fourth International Workshop on Semantic Evaluations (SemEval-2007)*, pages 219–222, Prague, Czech Republic, June. Association for Computational Linguistics.

Puşcaşu, Georgiana. 2007. WVALI: Temporal relation identification by syntactico-semantic analysis. In *Proceedings of the Fourth International Workshop on Semantic Evaluations (SemEval-2007)*, pages 484–487, Prague, Czech Republic, June. Association for Computational Linguistics.

Pustejovsky, James, José Castaño, Robert Ingria, Roser Saurí, Robert Gaizauskas, Andrea Setzer, and Graham Katz. 2003. TimeML: Robust Specification of Event and Temporal Expressions in Text. In *IWCS-5 Fifth International Workshop on Computational Semantics*.

Pustejovsky, James, Robert Knippen, Jessica Littman, and Roser Saurí. 2005. Temporal and event information in natural language text. *Language Resources and Evaluation*, 39:123–164, May.

Saurí, Roser, Robert Knippen, Marc Verhagen, and James Pustejovsky. 2005. Evita: A robust event recognizer for qa systems. In *Proceedings of the HLT/EMNLP 2005*, pages 700–707.

Saurí, Roser, Marc Verhagen, and James Pustejovsky. 2006a. Annotating and recognizing event modality in text. In *Proceedings of of the 19th International FLAIRS Conference, FLAIRS 2006*, Melbourne Beach, Florida, USA.

Saurí, Roser, Marc Verhagen, and James Pustejovsky. 2006b. SlinkET: A partial modal parser for events. In *Proceedings of LREC 2006*, Genoa, Italy.

Verhagen, Marc, Inderjeet Mani, Roser Sauri, Jessica Littman, Robert Knippen, Seok Bae Jang, Anna Rumshisky, John Phillips, and James Pustejovsky. 2005. Automating temporal annotation with TARSQI. In *Proceedings of the 43th Annual Meeting of the Association for Computational Linguistics*, Ann Arbor, USA. Demo session.

Verhagen, Marc. 2005. Temporal closure in an annotation environment. *Language Resources and Evaluation*, 39:211–241, May.

Verhagen, Marc. 2007. Drawing TimeML relations with TBox. In Katz, Graham, James Pustejovsky, and Frank Schilder, editors, *Annotating, Extracting and Reasoning about Time and Events*, volume 4795 of *Lecture Notes in Computer Science*, pages 7–28. Springer.

AUTHOR INDEX

AUTHOR INDEX

AUTHOR INDEX

AUTHOR INDEX

AUTHOR INDEX

Association for Computational Linguistics
209 N. Eighth Street
Stroudsburg, Pennsylvania 18360

CURRAN ASSOCIATES INC
proceedings.com